Part II / Teil II

A-Z   Reversed Edition

International Encyclopedia of Abbreviations and Acronyms in Science and Technology

Series B: Ecology, Environment, Geosciences

Compiled by Michael Peschke

Internationale Enzyklopädie der Abkürzungen und Akronyme in Wissenschaft und Technik

Reihe B: Ökologie, Umwelt, Geowissenschaften

Bearbeitet von Michael Peschke

A-Z   Reversed Edition

K · G · Saur München 2007

Bibliographic information published by the Deutsche Nationalbibliothek

The Deutsche Nationalbibliothek lists this publication in the Deutsche Nationalbibliografie; detailed bibliographic data are available in the Internet at http://dnb.d-nb.de.

Gedruckt auf säurefreiem Papier
Printed on permanent paper
The paper used in this publication meets the minimum requirements of
American National Standard – Permanence of Paper
for Publications and Documents in Libraries and Archives
ANSI/NISO Z39.48-1992 (R1997)

Datenerfassung und Satz / Computer-controlled keyboarding,
data preparation and automatic data processing by
Michael Peschke, Berlin

Druck und Binden/Printed and bound by
Strauss GmbH, Mörlenbach

978-3-598-23511-5 (Set)
978-3-598-23513-9 (Part II)

Contents / Inhalt

Series B / Serie B (Reversed Edition)

A - Z

Preface

Abbreviations, Acronyms, and Initials in all their various forms confront us today more than ever. We encounter them in all areas of daily life, both at home and at work: they are often the basis of documentation and communication and frequently themselves contain the central information in a given context. Decoding them is, however, often difficult, sometimes even impossible because adequate reference sources are either not available or not readily accessible.

As the use and the invention of abbreviations is increasing world-wide, no one reference work can hope to answer all queries concerning them correctly. The present volume of *Abbreviations and Acronyms in Science and Technology* lists more than 68,000 entries in each of 2 volumes. It continues the *International Encyclopedia of Abbreviations in Science and Technology* with its over 1 million entries in 17 volumes and 6 yearbooks. This extensive continuance now is opened up for individual science and society areas and is updated. The series B of the continuation and expansion of the reason work grasps abbreviations from the areas ecology, environment and geosciences as well as from adjoining areas.

Where the use of punctuation within the abbreviation is erratic, the most commonly-used form has been given preference. Further information of this nature can be found in the "Notes for the User".

Notes for the User

1. The abbreviations are presented in alphabetical order from a to z. Ä, æ, ç, ä, ö, ü are arranged lexically. Symbols and (diacritic) signs such as . - () [] ´` ^° & + are of no importance in regard to the alphabetical order.
1. 1. Alphanumeric sequences are listed in the alphabetical place of the respective letter(s).
1.2. Roman numerals are arranged in their value as literal character. Arabs numerals in alphanumeric sequences are arranged in their value as number. Abbreviations beginning with a number are arranged after the character z.
2. Styles of type are used as follows:
2.1. boldface for the abbreviation
2.2. italics for the language code
2.3. plain for the remaining text
3. Within each entry (beginning with the abbreviation pro-

truding to the left), the meanings are likewise listed a) in alphabetical order of the label indicating the language in which the abbreviation is used, b) in alphabetical order.
3.1. Each abbreviation is followed by the label indicating the area or sphere in which the abbreviation is used and/or the pertinent language.
3.2. The sign of equality (=) normally separates explanatory remarks (usually abbreviated) from each other as well as from the remaining text. In connection with the grammalogue of a language the colon (:) refers to a different expression in another language of the respective meaning.
3.3. Any additional explanations are enclosed in parentheses ().
3.4. Brackets [] are components of abbreviations as well as of meanings. However, parentheses are also used for marking a word that can be substituted for the preceding word, and for marking that part of a word, which, if omitted, will result in a different meaning or spelling.

Language Codes

A	Afrikaans	ko	Korean
a	Danish	kr	Croatian
al	Albanian	l	Latin
b	Bulgarian	le	Latvian
c	Czech	li	Lithanian
ch	Chinese	ma	Malayan
d	German	N	Norwegian
e	English	n	Dutch
eo	Esperanto	P	Polish
es	Estonian	p	Portuguese
F	Finnish	ph	Philippine
f	French	R	Russian
g	Greek	r	Swedish
H	Hungarian	ru	Romanian
h	Hebrew	S	Slowenian
ha	Haitian	s	Spanish (too:
i	Italian		Catalan, a.o.)
id	Indian	se	Serbian
ir	Irish	sk	Slovakian
in	Indonesian	U	Ukrainian
is	Icelandic	z	Turkish
j	Japanese		

Berlin, November 2007

Michael Peschke

Vorwort

Abkürzungen, Akronyme und Initialen in ihren mannigfachen Erscheinungsformen begegnen uns heute überall und mehr denn je. Sie treten in allen Bereichen des täglichen und beruflichen Lebens auf; sie sind oft Grundlage von Dokumentation und Kommunikation und vielfach die entscheidenden Informationsträger. Ihre Bedeutung zu entschlüsseln, ist gleichwohl oft schwierig, manchmal unmöglich, weil geeignete Hilfsmittel fehlen oder diese nur schwer greifbar sind.

Weil der Gebrauch und die Erfindung von Abkürzungen und Abbreviaturen in der ganzen Welt ständig zunehmen, vermag niemand allein auf diesem Gebiet alle Fragen zutreffend zu beantworten. Der vorliegende Band der *Abkürzungen und Akronyme in Wissenschaft und Technik* verzeichnet in 2 Bänden jeweils ca. 68.000 Einträge mit Entsprechungen. Es setzt die 17-bändige *Internationale Enzyklopädie der Abkürzungen und Akronyme in Wissenschaft und Technik* sowie 6 Jahrbücher mit ihren über 1 Million Einträgen fort. Dieser umfangreiche Bestand wird jetzt für einzelne Wissenschaftsgebiete und Gesellschaftsbereiche erschlossen und aktualisiert. Die Reihe B der Fortsetzung und Erweiterung des Grundwerkes enthält Abkürzungen aus den Bereichen Ökologie, Umwelt und Geowissenschaften sowie aus angrenzenden Gebieten.

Abkürzungen, die teils mit, teils ohne Punkt geschrieben werden, sind nach der jeweils überwiegenden Verwendung verzeichnet. Im übrigen geben die "Hinweise für den Benutzer" alle Erläuterungen über die Anlage der Einträge wie des gesamten Werkes.

Hinweise für den Benutzer

1. Die Abkürzungen werden in der alphabetischen Reihenfolge a...z gebracht. Ä, æ, ç, ä, ö, ü werden lexikalisch eingereiht. Zeichen wie . - ( ) [ ] ´` ^ ° & + sind für die alphabetische Reihe ohne Bedeutung.
1. 1. Alphanumerische Folgen stehen an der von dem (den) Buchstaben bestimmten alphabetischen Stelle.
1.2. Römische Zahlzeichen werden nach ihrem Buchstabenwert eingereiht. Arabische Zahlzeichen innerhalb alphanumerischer Folgen werden nach ihrem Zahlenwert geordnet.
2. Die Schriftarten werden wie folgt verwendet:
2.1. halbfett für die Abkürzung
2.2. kursiv für das Sprachkürzel
2.3. Grundschrift für den übrigen Text

3. Innerhalb einer (mit einer links herausgerückten Abkürzung beginnenden) Wortstelle sind die Bedeutungen a) nach ihrem Bedeutungsbereich (Sortierung Sprache), b) in ihrer alphabetischen Reihenfolge aufgeführt.
3.1. Der Abkürzung folgt die Angabe der Sprache.
3.2. Das Gleichheitszeichen (=) trennt im allgemeinen abgekürzte erläuternde Hinweise voneinander und vom übrigen Text. Der Doppelpunkt (:) in Verbindung mit einem Sprachkürzel verweist auf anderssprachige Bezeichnungen der entsprechenden Bedeutung.
3.3. Sonstige Erläuterungen stehen in runden Klammern ().
3.4. Eckige Klammern [] schließen Bestandteile von Abkürzungen und von Bedeutungen ein. Bei den Bedeutungen werden diese Klammern mitunter auch dazu benutzt, ein Wort zu kennzeichnen, das an die Stelle des vorangehenden gesetzt werden kann, bzw. Wortteile zu markieren, die, läßt man sie weg, eine andere Bedeutung oder eine andere Schreibung ergeben.

Sprachenkürzel

A	afrikaans	ko	koreanisch
a	dänisch	kr	kroatisch
al	albanisch	l	lateinisch
b	bulgarisch	le	lettisch
c	tschechisch	li	litauisch
ch	chinesisch	ma	malaiisch
d	deutsch	N	norwegisch
e	englisch	n	holländisch
eo	Esperanto	P	polnisch
es	estnisch	p	portugiesisch
F	finnisch	ph	philippinisch
f	französisch	R	russisch
g	griechisch	r	schwedisch
H	ungarisch	ru	rumänisch
h	hebräisch	S	slowenisch
ha	haitianisch	s	spanisch
i	italienisch		(auch: katala
id	indisch		nisch u.a.)
ir	irisch	se	serbisch
in	indonesisch	sk	slowakisch
is	isländisch	U	ukrainisch
j	japanisch	z	türkisch

Berlin, November 2007

Michael Peschke

VIII

Reversed Edition

A - Z

A

A climatology and persistence model   *e:* **SHIFOR**

A collaborative, on-line, biological information system for the insects and terrestrial arthropods of the south-central United States and adjacent Mexico   *e:* **TIARA**

A Consortium for the Application of Climate Impact Assessments   *e:* **ACACIA**

A coupled global ocean-atmosphere model   *e:* **ECHAM-1/LSG**

a device-independent color space   *e:* **CIELAB**

A EUREKA Environmental Project   *e:* **EUROENVIRON**

A high altitude remote sensing aircraft   *e:* **U-2**

A hydrostatic model that employs the eta vertical coordinate   *e:* **Eta model**

A Knowledge-Based Approach to Quality Control to Provide a Unified Quality Environment   *e:* **UNIQUE**

A Marina project regarding the Baltic sea   *e:* **Marina Balt**

A meteor found in the Allen Hills region of Antarctica   *e:* **ALH84001**

A Navigator of Natural Language Organized Data   *e:* **ANNOD**

A One-in-a-Million Change of Death from an Environmental Hazard[s]   *e:* **MICROMORT**

A Soviet ocean radar satellite   *e:* **OKEAN**

A subset of the hydrocarbons   *e:* **carbohydrate**

[A] theoretical uraniumencased atomic or hydrogen bomb, the shell of which would be transformed into deadly radioactive dust upon detonation   *e:* **U (Bomb)**

A weather service work station at PROFS   *e:* **DARE-1**

Aargauischer Bund für Naturschutz   *d:* **ABN**

Abastumanskaya Astrofzicheskaya Observatoriya   *R:* **AAO**

Abbot Biological and Chemical Data   *e:* **ABCD**

Abbreviated New Animal Drug Application   *e:* **ANADA**

ABEA Better Environment   *e:* **ABFC**

Aberdeen   *e:* **Aber.**

Aberdeen Airways Ltd.   *e:* **AAW**

Aberdeen and North of Scotland Library and Information Cooperative Service   *e:* **ANSLICS**

Aberdeen Association of Civil Engineers   *e:* **A.A.C.E.**

Aberdeen Fishing Vessel Owners Association   *e:* **AFVOA**

Aberdeen Ground/Materiel Testing Directorate   *e:* **APG/MT**

Aberdeen Marine Laboratory   *e:* **AML**

Aberdeen Medico-Chirurgical Society   *e:* **AMCS**

Aberdeen Philosophical Society   *e:* **A.P.S.**

Aberdeen Press and Journal   *e:* **APJ**

Aberdeen Proving Ground   *e:* **APG**

Aberdeen Proving Ground - Ballistic[s] Research Laboratory   *e:* **APGBRL**

Aberdeen Proving Ground - Human Engineering Laboratory   *e:* **APG/HEL**

Aberdeen Proving Ground/Ordnance Bomb Disposal Center   *e:* **APG/OBDC**

Aberdeen Proving Ground - Ordnance Testing Command   *e:* **APG-OTC**

Aberdeen Proving Ground/Ordnance Training Command   *e:* **APC./OTC**

Aberdeen Public Library, Aberdeen   *e:* **WaA**

Aberdeen Pulsed Reactor Facility   *e:* **APR**, *e:* **APRF**

Aberdeen Research and Development Center   *e:* **ARDC**

Aberdeen Steam Packet Line   *e:* **A.S.P.L.**

Aberdeen University Library   *e:* **AUL**

Aberdeen University Press   *e:* **AUP**

Aberdeen University Review   *e:* **AUR**

Abfallbeseitigung, Wasser- und Luftreinhaltung, Lärmbekämpfung   *d:* **AWALU**

Abfrageoperation   *d:* **AO**

abgeordnet   *d:* **abg.**

Abgeordnetengesetz   *d:* **AbgG**

Abgeordnetenhaus   *d:* **Abg.-H.**, *d:* **Abghs.**, *d:* **A.-H.**

Abgeordnetenkonvent   *d:* **AC**

Abgeordneter   *d:* **Abg.**

Abhand-lungen des Naturwissenschaftlichen Vereins zu Bremen   *d:* **Abh. Nat.wiss. Ver. Bremen**

Abhandlung. Naturhistorische Gesellschaft Nürnberg   *d:* **ANGNDT**

Abhandlungen. Akademie der Wissenschaften und der Literatur, Mainz. Mathematisch-Naturwissenschaftliche Klasse   *d:* **Abh. Akad. Wiss. Lit. Mainz Math.-Nat.wiss. Kl.**

Abhandlungen aus dem Westfälischen Museum für Naturkunde   *d:* **Abh. Westfäl. Mus. Nat.kd.**

Abhandlungen der Naturforschenden Gesellschaft in Zürich   *d:* **Abh. Nat.forsch. Ges. Zür.**

Abnormally Polarized Waves   *e:* **APW**

Aborgines' (or Aboriginal) Protection Society   *e:* **APS**

Aboriginal Government, Resources, Economy and Environment   *e:* **AGREE**

Aborigines Protection Society   *e:* **Aps**

Abort/Hold/Orbit   *e:* **A/H/O**

Abort To Orbit   *e:* **ATO**

Above Main Sea Level   *e:* **AMSL**

Above Mean Sea Level   *e:* **AMSL**

Above Sea Level   *e:* **ASL**

Above Water   *e:* **a.w.**

Above Water Torpedo Tube   *e:* **AWTT**

Above Water Warfare   *e:* **AWW**

Abrasive Water Jet   *e:* **AWJ**

Abraumförderbrücke   *d:* **AFB**

Abridged Index Medicus   *e:* **ABIM**, *e:* **AbrIMed**, *e:* **Abr Index Med**, *e:* **AIM**

Abridged Index Medicus via the Teletypewriter Exchange Network   *e:* **AIM-TWX**

Abrupt Climate Change   *e:* **ACC**

Abrupt Space Charge Edge   *e:* **ASCE**

absolute Atmosphäre[n]   *d:* **at abs**

absolute atmosphere   *e:* **ata**

Absolute Space Time   *e:* **AST**

Abstract Distributed Data Environment   *e:* **ADDE**

Abstracts of North American Geology   *e:* **ANAG**

Abteilung Datenverarbeitung und Instrumentierung   *d:* **ADI**

Abteilung für medizinische Verstärkung   *d:* **AmV**

Abteilung für Transfusionsmedizin   *e:* **AfTM**

Abteilung Umweltschutz   *d:* **U**

Abteilung Wetterberatung der Bundeswehr   *d:* **AbtWeBBw**

Abwasser   *d:* **Abw**, *d:* **AW**

Abwasserabgaben-Gesetz   *d:* **AbwAG**

Abwasserbehandlungsanlage   *d:* **ABA**

Abwassereinleitungsbedingungen   *d:* **AEB**

Abwasserherkunftsverordnung   *d:* **AbwHerkV**

Abwasserlabor   *d:* **AWL**

Abwasserreinigungsanlage   *d:* **ARA**

Abwassertechnische Vereinigung e.V.   *d:* **ATV**

Abwasserverband Saar   *d:* **AV Saar**

Academia Colombiana de Ciencias Exactas Físicas y Naturales   *s:* **ACCEFN**

Academia de Geografía e Historia de Guatemala   *s:* **AGHG**

Academia de Stiinte Medicale   *ru:* **A.S.M.**

Academia Nacional de Ciencias Exactas, Físicas y Naturales   *s:* **ANCEFN**

Academia Nacional de Geografía   *s:* **ANG**

Academia Nacional de Medicina   *p:* **ANM**

Academia Nacional de Medicina de México   *s:* **ANMM**

Academic Emergency Medicine   *e:* **Acad Emerg Med**, *e:* **AEM**

Academic Health Services Complexes   *e:* **AHSC**

Academic Medicine   *e:* **Acad Med**

Academie Nacional de Historia y Geografía   *s:* **ANHG**

Academy for Health Services Marketing   *e:* **AHSM**

Academy for Healthcare Management   *e:* **AHM**

Academy for International Health Studies   *e:* **AIHS**

Academy for the Development of a Democratic Environment   *e:* **AZAD**

Academy of Air Traffic Control Medicine   *e:* **AATCM**

Academy of Behavioral Medicine Research   *e:* **ABMR**

Academy of Dental Sleep Medicine   *e:* **ADSM**

Academy of Health Care Consultants   *e:* **AHCC**

Academy of Health Information Professionals   *e:* **AHIP**

Academy of Health Sciences   *e:* **AHS**

Academy of Medical Royal Colleges   *e:* **AMRC**

Academy of Medical Royal Colleges Information Group   *e:* **ACIG**

Academy of Medical Sciences   *e:* **A.S.M.**

Academy of Medical-Surgical Nursing   *e:* **AMSN**

Academy of Medicine   *e:* **Acad Med**, *e:* **A.O.M.**

Academy of Medicine of New Jersey, Bloomfield   *e:* **NjBlM**

Academy of Medicine, Toronto   *e:* **AMT**

Academy of Natural Sciences   *e:* **ANS**

Academy of Natural Sciences, Journal   *e:* **Acad of Nat Sci Jour**

Academy of Natural Sciences of Philadelphia e: **ANSP**

Academy of Natural Sciences of Philadelphia, Philadelphia, PA e: **PPAN**

Academy of Natural Sciences of Philadelphia Proceedings e: **Acad Natur Sci Phila Proc**

Academy of Ortho-Molecular Medicine e: **AOM**

Academy of Parapsychology and Medicine e: **APM**

Academy of Physical Medicine e: **APM**

Academy of Psychosomatic Medicine e: **APM**

Academy of Religion and Mental Health e: **ARMH**

Academy of Underwater Arts and Sciences e: **AUAS**

Academy on Architecture for Health e: **AAH**

Acadêmia Chilena de Ciéncias Naturales s: **ACCN**, s: **ACHCN**

Académie Royale des Beaux-Arts, École supérieure des arts décoratifs et École supérieure f: **ARABE**

Académie Suisse des Sciences Médicales f: **ASSM**

Accademia Ambrosiana Medici Umanisti e Scrittori i: **A.A.M.U.S.**

Accademia di medicina di Roma i: **A.m.Roma**

Accademia di Medicina di Torino i: **A.m.Tor.**

Accademia Internazionale Medica i: **AIM**

Accademia Italiana di Medicina Omeopatica i: **AIMO**

Accademia Italiana di Medicina Omeopatica Hahnemanniana i: **AIMOH**

Accademia Medica Internazionale i: **A.M.I.**

Accademia Medica Lombarda i: **A.M.L.**

Accademia Svizzera delle Scienze Mediche i: **ASSM**

Accelerated Climatic Simulator e: **ACS**

Accelerated Computing Environment e: **ACE**

Accelerated Environmental Test e: **AET**

Accelerated Environmental Test Mockup e: **AETM**

Acceptable Biological Catch e: **ABC**

Acceptable Biological Removal e: **ABR**

Acceptable Environmental Range Test e: **AERT**

Access Protection and Priority Control Mechanism e: **APPCM**

Access to Information for Medicine e: **AIM**

Access to Remote Catalogues by Implementing SR Target Functions e: **ARCA**

Accident and Health e: **A and H**, e: **A & H**

Accidental Earth e: **AE**

Accidental Launch Protection System e: **ALPS**

Acclimatization Experiences Institute e: **AEI**

Accord Dangereuse Routier e: **ADR**

Accord partiel ouvert en matière de prévention, de protection et d'organisation des secours contre les risques naturels et technologiques majeurs f: **PP-ORMNT**

Accountable Health Plan e: **AHP**

Accreditation Association for Ambulatory Health Care e: **AAAHC**

Accreditation Council for Continuing Medical Education e: **ACCME**

Accreditation Council for Graduate Medical Education e: **ACGME**

Accreditation Council for Gynecologic Endoscopy e: **ACGE**

Accreditation Manual for Ambulatory Health Care e: **AMAHC**

Accreditation Manual for Managed Behavioral Health Care e: **AMMBHC**

Accrediting Bureau of Health Education Schools e: **ABHES**

Accrediting Bureau of Medical Laboratory Schools e: **ABMLS**

Accrediting Commission on Education for Health Services Administration e: **ACEHSA**

Accurate and Reliable Prototype Earth Sensor Head e: **ARPESH**, e: **ARPESH**

acetaldehyde dehydrogenase e: **ahd**

Acetohydroxamic Acid e: **AHA**

acetohydroxy acid synthase e: **ahas**

Acetone/Water e: **AC/W**

Acid Cholesteryl Ester Hydrolase e: **ACEH**

Acid Deposition and Atmospheric Research Division e: **ADARD**

Acid Open Hearth e: **AOH**

Acidified Boiling Water e: **ABW**

Acoustic Environment[al] Support Detachment e: **AESD**

acoustic intercept receiver/multimode hydrophone e: **air/mmh**

Acoustic Meteorological and Oceanographic Survey e: **AMOS**

Acoustic Noise Environment e: **ANE**, e: **ANF**

Acoustic Thermography of Ocean Climate e: **ATOC**

Acoustic Thermometry of Ocean Climates e: **ATOC**

Acoustic Travel Time Ocean Current Monitor e: **ATTOM**

Acoustic Underwater Range Determination e: **ACURAD**

Acoustic Variable Density e: **AVD**

Acoustic Velocity e: **AV**

Acoustically Navigated Geological Underwater Survey e: **ANGUS**

Acoustically-Navigated Geophysical Underwater Survey e: **ANGUS**

Acquisition Orbit Determination Program e: **AODP**

Acryl Hydrocarbon Hydroxylase e: **AHH**

Acta Academiae Agriculturae ac Technicae Olstenensis. Geodaesia et Ruris Regulatio l: **Acta Acad. Agric. Tech. Olst., Geod. Ruris Regul.**

Acta Academiae Agriculturae ac Technicae Olstenensis. Protectio Aquarum et Piscatoria l: **Acta Acad. Agric. Tech. Olst., Protect. Aquar. Piscat.**

Acta Bio-medica De L Ateneo Parmense l: **Acta Biomed Ateneo Parmense**

Acta Biologica Cracoviensia. Serie Botanique l: **Acta Biol. Cracov., Bot.**

Acta Biologica Cracoviensia. Serie Zoologique l: **Acta Biol. Cracov., Zool.**

Acta Biologica et Medica Societas Scientiarum Gedanensis l: **Acta Biol. Med. Soc. Sci. Gedanensis**

Acta Biologica Hungarica l: **Acta Biol Hung**

Acta Biologica Jugoslavica. Serija B. Mikrobiologija l: **Acta Biol. Jugosl.,. B**

Acta Biologica Jugoslavica. Serija E. Ichthyologia l: **Acta Biol. Jugosl., E**

Acta Biologica Montana l: **Acta Biol. Mont.**

Acta Biologica Paranaense l: **Acta Biol. Paran.**

Acta Biologica Venezuelica l: **Acta Biol. Venez.**

Acta Ecologica Sinica l: **Acta Ecol. Sin.**

Acta Geneticae Medicae et Gemellologiae l: **Acta Genet Med Gemellol**

Acta Geneticae Medicae et Gemellologiae. Istituto Gregorio Mendel. Roma. i: **IGM/AGMG.**

Acta Geographica Lodziensia e: **SAGLBQ**

Acta Geologica Leopoldensia l: **Acta Geol. Leopold.**

Acta Geologica Lilloana l: **Acta Geol. Lillo.**

Acta Geologica Polonica l: **Acta Geol. Pol.**

Acta Geologica Sinica l: **TCHPAX**

Acta Geologica Taiwanica e: **SRTUAW**

Acta Geophysica Sinica l: **Acta Geophys. Sin.**

Acta Hydrobiologica l: **Acta Hydrobiol.**

Acta Hydrobiologica Lituanica l: **Acta Hydrobiol. Litu.**

Acta Hydrobiologica Sinica l: **Acta Hydrobiol. Sin.**

Acta Hydrochimica et Hydrobiologica l: **Acta Hydrochim. Hydrobiol.**

Acta Hydrophysica l: **Acta Hydrophys.**

Acta Medica Austriaca l: **Acta Med Austriaca**

Acta Medica Croatica l: **Acta Med Croatica**

Acta Medica Okayama l: **Acta Med Okayama**

Acta Medica Portuguesa l: **Acta Med Port**

Acta Medica Scandinavica e: **AMS**

Acta Medicinae Legalis et Socialis l: **Acta Med Leg Soc**

Acta Meteorologica Sinica l: **Acta Meteorol. Sin.**

Acta Microbiologica Bulgarica l: **Acta Microbiol Bulg**

Acta Microbiologica et Immunologica Hungarica l: **Acta Microbiol Immunol Hung**

Acta Microbiologica Hungarica l: **Acta Microbiol. Hung.**

Acta Microbiologica Polonica l: **Acta Microbiol Pol**

Acta Musei Macedonici Scientiarum Naturalium l: **Acta Mus. Maced. Sci. Nat.**

Acta Musei Nationalis Pragae. Series B. Historia Naturalis l: **SNMPAM**

Acta Neurobiologiae Experimentalis l: **Acta Neurobiol Exp**

Acta Obstetricia et Gynecologica Scandinavica l: **Acta Obstet Gynecol Scand**

Acta Oceanographica Taiwanica l: **Acta Oceanogr. Taiwan.**

Acta Oceanologica Sinica l: **Acta Oceanol. Sin.**

Acta Oecologica l: **Acta Oecol.**

Acta Oecologica. International Journal of Ecology *l:* **Acta Oecol. Int. J. Ecol.**

Acta Pathologica, Microbiologica et Immunologica Scandinavica *l:* **APMIS**

Acta Phytogeographica Suecica *l:* **Acta Phytogeogr. Suec.**

Acta Phytomedica *l:* **Acta Phytomed.**

Acta Rerum Naturalium. Musei Nationalis Slovaci Bratislava *l:* **ZSNMAS**

Acta Scientiarum Naturalium. Academiae Scientiarum Bohemoslovacae *c:* **PPUCA4**

Acta Scientiarum Naturalium Universitatis Sunyatseni *l:* **Acta Sci. Nat. Univ. Sunyatseni**

Acta Universitatis Carolinae. Medica *l:* **Acta Univ Carol [Med]**

Acta Universitatis Carolinae. Medica. Monographia *l:* **Acta Univ Carol Med Monogr**

Acta Universitatis Palackianae Olomucensis Facultatis Medicae *l:* **Acta Univ Palacki Olomuc Fac Med**

Actas. Congreso Geologico Argentino *s:* **Actas Cong Geol Argent**

Actas. Congreso Internacional de Historia de la Medicina *e:* **Actas Int Congr Hist Med**

Actas Jomadas Geologicas Argentinas *e:* **Actas Jornadas Geol Argent**

Actes de la Société Helvétique des Sciences Naturelles *f:* **Actes Soc. Helv. Sci. Nat.**

Action Catholique de la Jeunesse Luxembourgeoise *f:* **ACJL**

Action Catholique des Femmes Luxembourgeoises *f:* **ACFL**

Action Committee for European Aerospace *e:* **ACEA**

Action for the Victims of Medical Accidents *e:* **AVMA**

Action Health 2000-International Voluntary Health Association *e:* **AH 2000**

Action in International Medicine *e:* **AIM**

Action Médicale et Sociale à Domicile *f:* **AMSD**

Action on Smoking and Health *e:* **ASH**

Active Control Evaluation for Spacecraft *e:* **ACES**

Active Control of Space Structures *e:* **ACOSS**

Active Living Environment Program *e:* **ALEP**

Active Remote Sensing Cloud Layer *e:* **ARSCL**

Active Therrnal Protection for Avionics Crew and Heat-Exchange *e:* **APACHE**

Active Tracer High Resolution Atmospheric Model *e:* **ATHAM**

Active Work Space *e:* **AWS**

Activists for Protecive Animal Legislation *e:* **A-PAL**

Actors and Others for Animals *e:* **AOA**

Actualidad Medicas *s:* **Actual Med**

Actualidades Biologicas *e:* **Actual Biol**

Actualite Medicale *f:* **Actual Med**

Actualites Biologiques [Paris] *e:* **Actual Biol [Paris]**

Actualites Medico-Chirurgicales [Marseille] *f:* **Actual Med [Mars]**

Actualités de l'environnement et du développement *f:* **SOLAGRAL**

Acuerdo Parcial Abierto sobre Prevención, Protección y Socorro en caso de Catástrofes Naturales y Tecnológicas Importantes [Consejo de Europa] *s:* **PP-ORMNT**

Acute Physiology and Chronic Health Evaluation *e:* **APACHE**

Acylcholine Acyl-Hydrolase *e:* **ACAH**

Ad Hoc Collective Protection *e:* **AHCP**

Ad Hoc Group for Medical Research Funding *e:* **AHGMRF**

Ad Hoc Open-Ended Inter-Sessional Working Group on Article 8[j] and Related Provisions of the Convention on Biological Diversity *e:* **WG8j**

Ad hoc Task Team to Study the Implications, for the Commission, of the United Nations Convention on the Law of the Sea and the New Ocean Regime *e:* **LOSI**

Ad hoc Technical Expert Group on Biological Diversity and Climate Change *e:* **TEGCC**

Ad Manus Medici *l:* **AD MAN MED**

Ada Integrated Environment *e:* **AIE**

ADA Programming [and] Support Environment[s] *e:* **APSE**

Ada Runtime Environment Working Group *e:* **ARTEWG**

Adaptable Hydrologic Data Acquisition System *e:* **AHDAS**

Adaptation Controlled Environment System *e:* **ACES**

Adaptation of Numerical Hydrodynamic Tools for Integration into Ship Design Systems *e:* **ADONIS**

Adaptierter Schwimmbecken-Tank-Reaktor, Austria *d:* **ASTRA**

Adaptive Control Geometrical *e:* **ACG**

Adaptive Decision-Maker in an Information Retrieval Environment *e:* **ADMIRE**

Adaptive Environmental Assessment and Management *e:* **AEAM**

Addis Abeba Water and Sewerage Authority *e:* **AAWSA**

Additional Personal Injury Protection *e:* **APIP**

Address Space *e:* **AS**

Address Space Control Block *e:* **ASCB**

Address Space Control Task *e:* **ASCT**

Address Space Identification (or Identifier) *e:* **ASID**

Address Space Identifier *e:* **ASSI**

Address Space Register *e:* **ASR**

Addressable Remote Multiplexer Unit *e:* **ARMU**

Adelaide Medical Students' Society *e:* **AMSS**

Aden and Protectorate of South Arabia *e:* **A&PSA**

Adeninylhydroxypropanoic Acid *e:* **AHPA**

Adequate Program for Education in Georgia *e:* **APEG**

Adirondack Watershed Data Base *e:* **AWDB**

Adjacent Arctic Ocean *e:* **AAO**

adjustieren *e:* **adj.**

Administración Meteorológica China *s:* **CMA**

Administración Nacional Oceánica y Atmosférica *s:* **NOAA**

Administración Principal de Geodesia y Cartografía *s:* **GUGK**

Administratie Milieu-, Natuur-, Land- en Waterbeheer van het Vlaamse Gewest *n:* **AMINAL**

Administration de météorologie et de protection de l'environnement *f:* **MEPA**

Administration Forestière *f:* **AF**

Administrative Medical Officer *e:* **AMO**

Administrative Medicine *e:* **ADM**

Administrative Protective Order *e:* **APO**

Administrative Unit/Medical Inspection Room *e:* **AU/MIR**

Administrators in Medicine *e:* **AIM**

Admiral of the Ocean Sea *e:* **A of OS**, *e:* **AOTOS**

Admiralty Compass Observatory [Laboratory] *e:* **ACO**

Admiralty Underwater Weapons Establishment *e:* **AUWE**

admittiert *d:* **adm.**

Adriatic Sea *e:* **Adriatic**, *e:* **Adr S**

Adult Day Health Care *e:* **ADHC**

Advance Base Sea Dock *e:* **ABSD**

advance space vehicle engineering operation *e:* **asveo**

Advanced Aerospace Flight Experiment *e:* **AAFE**

Advanced Aerospace Flight Experiment/Radiometer-Scatterometer *e:* **AAFE/RADSCAT**

Advanced Aerospace Vehicle *e:* **AAV**

Advanced Airborne Remote Instrumentation *e:* **AARI**

Advanced Aircrew Vision Protection *e:* **AAVP**

Advanced Animal Breeder *e:* **Adv Anim Breed**

Advanced Architectures in Intelligent Medical Instrumentation *e:* **A2IMI-ITDC-139**

Advanced Atmosphere Sounder and Imaging Radiometer *e:* **AASIR**

Advanced Atmospheric Burst Location *e:* **AABL**

Advanced Atmospheric Sounder and Imaging Radiometer *e:* **AAIR**

Advanced Atmospheric Sounding & Imaging Radiometer *e:* **AASIR**

Advanced Ballistic-type Lodistic Spacecraft System *e:* **ABLSS**

Advanced Biomedical Capsule *e:* **ABC**

Advanced Boiling Water Reactor *e:* **ABWR**

Advanced Cartographic Environment *e:* **ACE**

Advanced Civilian Earth Remote Sensing System *e:* **ACERSS**

Advanced Climate Model *e:* **ACM**

Advanced Computer Environmental Systems Support Inc. *e:* **ACESS**

Advanced Computer for Medical Research *e:* **ACME**, *e:* **ACMER**, *e:* **ACMR**

Advanced Computer Training In a Versatile Environment *e:* **ACTIVE**

Advanced Computing Environments *e:* **ACE**

Advanced Cosmic-ray Composition Experiment for the Space Station *e:* **ACCESS**

Advanced Depot of Medical Stores *e:* **A.D.M.S.**

Advanced Development Environment *e:* **ADE**

Advanced Distributed Environment for Production Technology e: **ADEPT**

Advanced Double Pass Reverse Osmosis Water Purification Unit e: **ADROWPU**

Advanced Dungeons & Dragons e: **AD&D**

Advanced Earth Observation (or Observing) Satellite (or System) e: **ADEOS**

Advanced Earth Observing satellite e: **ADEO**

Advanced Earth Observing Satellite 2 e: **ADEOS 2**

Advanced Earth Resources Observation[al] Satellite (or System) e: **AEROS**

Advanced Earth Resources Satellite e: **AERS**

Advanced Earth Satellite Weapon System e: **AEWS**

Advanced Electrochemical Depolarized Concentrator Module e: **AEDCM**

Advanced Engine Aerospace e: **AEA**

Advanced Environmental Acoustic Support e: **AEAS**

Advanced Environmental ASW Support e: **AEAS**

Advanced Environmental Control System e: **AECS**

Advanced Environmental Control Technology Research Center e: **AECTRC**

Advanced Environmental Research and Technology e: **AERT**

Advanced Environmental Research Group e: **AERG**

Advanced Environmental Research Incorporated e: **AERI**

Advanced Extravehicular Protective System e: **AEPS**

Advanced Fighter Crew Protection System e: **APS**

Advanced Geometry Blade e: **AGB**

Advanced Geosynchronous Observation Environment Satellite e: **AGOES**

Advanced Geosynchronous Platform e: **AGP**

Advanced Global Atmospheric Gases Experiment e: **AGAGE**

Advanced Informatics in Medicine [in Europe] e: **AIM**

Advanced Infrared Radiometer Sounder (Atmospheric Infrared Sounder)/Microwave Humidity Sounder e: **AIRS/MHS**

Advanced Intelligence Center, Pacific Ocean Area e: **AICPOA**

Advanced Land Observation Satellite e: **ALOS**

Advanced Light Water Reactor e: **ALWR**

Advanced Liquid Hydrogen e: **ALH**

Advanced Logistics Spacecraft e: **ALS**

Advanced Lunar Orbital Rendezvous e: **ALOR**

Advanced Maneuvering Orbit-to-Orbit Shuttle e: **AMOOS**

Advanced Manned Space Simulator e: **AMSS**

Advanced Manned Spacecraft e: **AMS**

Advanced Medical Technology Association e: **AdvaMed**

Advanced Meteorological Ground Station e: **AMGS**

Advanced Meteorological Image and Graphics Analysis System e: **AMIGAS**

Advanced Meteorological Processing System e: **AMPS**

Advanced Meteorological Satellite e: **AMS**

Advanced Meteorological Sounding System e: **AMSS**

Advanced Meteorological System e: **AMS**

Advanced Meteorological & Temperature Sounder e: **AMTS**

Advanced Meteorological Temperature Sounding Study e: **AMTS**

Advanced Military Spaceflight Technology e: **AMST**

Advanced Military Spacelift Capability e: **AMSC**

Advanced Millimeter Wave Atmospheric Sounder e: **AMAS**

Advanced Multiple Environment Simulator e: **AMES**

Advanced Ocean Drilling Program e: **AODP**

Advanced Ocean Engineering Laboratory e: **AOEL**

Advanced Orbit/Ephemeris Subsystem e: **AOES**

Advanced Orbital Launch Operations e: **AOLO**

Advanced Orbiting Astronautical Observatory e: **AOAO**

Advanced Orbiting Geophysical Observatory e: **AOGO**

Advanced Orbiting Solar Observatory e: **AOSO**

Advanced Orbiting System e: **AOS**

Advanced Organization Saint Hill for Australia New Zealand and Oceania e: **AOSHANZO**

Advanced Passive Light Water Reactor e: **APLWR**

Advanced Planetary Spacecraft System e: **APSS**

Advanced Polar Orbiting Satellite e: **APOS**

Advanced Polaris Guidance Information e: **APOGI**

Advanced Polarization Diversity Autotrack Receiver e: **APDAR**

Advanced Portable Coronary Observation Radio e: **APCOR**

Advanced Pressurized-Water Reactor e: **APWR**

Advanced Radio Interferometry between Space and Earth e: **ARISE**

Advanced Reconnaissance Electrically Propelled Spacecraft e: **AREPS**

Advanced Remote Display Station (or System) e: **ARDS**

Advanced Remote Imaging Systems e: **ARIS**

Advanced Remote Minehunting System e: **ARMS**

Advanced Remotely Operated Underwater Vehicle e: **ARDROV**

Advanced Remotely Piloted Vehicle e: **ARPV**

Advanced Research and Global Observation Satellite e: **ARGOS**

Advanced Research and Global Observation Satellite/Extreme Ultraviolet Imaging Photometer e: **ARGOS/EUVIP**

Advanced Research and Global Observation Satellite/ Unconventional Stellar Aspect e: **ARGOS/USA**

Advanced Research Environmental Test Satellite e: **ARENTS**

Advanced Research Geophysical Observatory e: **ARGO**

Advanced Research Testbed for Medical Informatics e: **ARTEMIS**

Advanced SAGE (Semi-Automatic Ground Environment) Tracking Study e: **ASTS**

Advanced Satellite (or Space) Technology for EHF Communications e: **ASTEC**

Advanced Sea-Based Deterrer e: **ASBD**

Advanced Sea-Based Deterrent Program e: **ASBD Program**

Advanced Sea Ice Zone e: **ASIZ**

Advanced Sea-Launched Cruise Missile e: **ASLCM**

Advanced Sea Mine e: **ASM**

Advanced Secondary [Wastewater] Treatment e: **AST**

Advanced Self-Protection Integrated Suite e: **ASPIS**

Advanced Self-Protective Jammer e: **ASPJ**

Advanced Server Environment e: **ASE**

Advanced Solar Observatory e: **ASO**

Advanced Space Computer e: **ASC**

Advanced Space Computing Module e: **ASCM**

Advanced Space Engine e: **ASE**

Advanced Space Ground Link [Sub]system e: **ASGLS**

Advanced Space Station e: **ASS**

Advanced Space Structures Technology Research Experiment e: **ASTREX**

Advanced Space Technology Division e: **ASTD**

Advanced Space Technology Program e: **ASTP**

Advanced Space Vehicle Engineering Operation e: **ASVEO**

Advanced Spaceborne Computer Module e: **ASCM**

Advanced Spaceborne Thermal Emission and Radiometer e: **ASTER**

Advanced Spaceborne Thermal Emission and Reflection (or Reflectance) e: **ASTER**

Advanced Spacecraft Truck (or Trainer, or Transport) Reusable Orbiter e: **ASTRO**

Advanced Stokes Polarimeter e: **ASP**

Advanced Study Institute on Underwater Acoustics and Signal Processing e: **ASI**

Advanced Synchronous Meteorological Satellite e: **ASMES**, e: **ASMS**

Advanced Tactical Aircraft Protection System e: **ATAPS**

Advanced Technology for Large Area Space Structures e: **ATLASS**

Advanced Technology Spacecraft e: **ATS**

Advanced Telecom and Multimedia Design Technology Environments e: **ATAME-KIT107**

Advanced Teleoperation for Earthwork Equipment Navigation e: **ATHENA**

Advanced Television Infrared Observation Satellite e: **TIROS-N**

Advanced Traffic Observation and Management Information Collection System e: **ATOMICS**

Advanced Treatment [water] e: **AT**

Advanced Underwater Acoustic Modeling Project e: **AUAMP**

Advanced Underwater Missile e: **AUM**

advanced underwater weapon[s] e: **auw**

© K · G · Saur, München

Advanced Wastewater Treatment e: **AWT**

Advanced Weather Analysis and Prediction System e: **AWAPS**

Advanced Weather Information Processing System e: **AWIPS**

Advanced Weather Interactive Processing System for the 90's e: **AWIPS-90**

Advanced Weather Interactive Processing System[s] e: **AWIPS**

Advanced Wild Weasel e: **AWW**

Advanced Workstation Environment e: **AWE**

Advances in Anatomy, Embryology and Cell Biology e: **Adv Anat Embryol Cell Biol**

Advances in Animal Physiology and Animal Nutrition e: **Adv Anim Physiol Anim Nutr**

Advances in Applied Microbiology e: **Adv Appl Microb**, e: **Adv Appl Microbiol**

Advances in Atmospheric Sciences e: **Adv. Atmos. Sci.**

Advances in Behavioral Biology e: **Adv Behav Biol**

Advances in Biological and Medical Physics e: **Adv Biol Med Phys**

Advances in Biological Psychiatry e: **Adv Biol Psychiatry**

Advances in Biology of the Skin e: **Adv Biol Skin**

Advances in Biomedical Engineering e: **Adv Biomed Eng**

Advances in Biomedical Engineering and Medical Physics e: **Adv Biomed Eng Med Phys**

Advances in Cell and Molecular Biology e: **Adv Cell Moi Biol**

Advances in Cell Biology e: **Adv Cell Biol**

Advances in Cellular Neurobiology e: **Adv Cell Neurobiol**

Advances in Ecological Research e: **Adv. Ecol. Res.**

Advances in Environmental Science and Technology e: **Adv. Environ. Sci. Technol.**

Advances in Experimental Medicine and Biology e: **Adv Exp Med Biol**

Advances in Geophysics e: **Advances Geophys**, e: **Advan Geophys**, e: **Adv. Geophys.**, e: **Adv. Geophys.**

Advances in ihe Biology of Disease e: **Adv Biol Dis**

Advances in Internal Medicine e: **Advances Int Med**, e: **Adv Intern Med**

Advances in Marine Biology e: **Adv. Mar. Biol.**

Advances in Obstetrics and Gynecology e: **Adv. Obstet. Gynecol.**, e: **AOGYA**

Advances in Oral Biology e: **AOR[B]**

Advances in Organic Geochemistry e: **Adv. Org. Geochem.**

Advances in Psychosomatic Medicin e: **Adv Psychosom Med**

Advances in Radiation Biology e: **Adv. Radiat. Biol.**

Advances in Space Biology and Medicine e: **Adv Space Biol Med**

Advances in Space Research e: **Adv. Space Res.**

Advances in Space Science and Technology e: **Adv. Space Sci. Technol.**

Advances in Veterinary Science and Comparative Medicine e: **Adv Vet Sci Comp Med**

Advances in Water Resources e: **Adv. Water Resour.**

Advancing Frontiers of Plant Sciences e: **Advan Front Plant Sd**

Advent Orbital Test and Operation Plan e: **AOTOP**

Adventist Health Network of North America e: **AHN**

Adverse Weather Aerial Delivery System e: **Awads**

Adverse-Weather/All Weather Precision Guided Weapon e: **AW-PGW**

Adverse Weather Precision Guided Munition e: **AWPGM**

Advisory Agricultural Meteorologist e: **AAM**

Advisory Board on the Built Environment e: **ABBE**

Advisory Board on the Law of the Sea e: **ABLOS**

Advisory Body of Experts on the Law of the Sea e: **ABE-LOS**

Advisory Commission on Conferences in Ocean Shipping e: **ACCOS**

Advisory Committee for Atmospheric Sciences e: **ACAS**

Advisory Committee for Biology and Medicine e: **ACBM**

Advisory Committee for Operational Hydrology e: **ACOH**

Advisory Committee for the United States Meat Animal Research Center e: **USMARC**

Advisory Committee for the World Climate Applications and Data Programmes e: **ACCAD**

Advisory Committee on Animal Import Priorities e: **ACAIP**

Advisory Committee on Business and the Environment e: **ACBE**

Advisory Committee on Chemicals in the Environment e: **ACCE**

Advisory Committee on Climate Applications and Data e: **ACCAD**, e: **ACCI**

Advisory Committee on Conservation of Biological Diversity e: **ACCBD**

Advisory Committee on Environmental Employment Opportunities e: **ACCEEO**

Advisory Committee on Environmental Resources e: **ACER**

Advisory Committee on Health Research e: **ACHR**

Advisory Committee on International Oceanographic Affairs e: **ACIOA**

Advisory Committee on Medical Establishment e: **ACME**

Advisory Committee on Medical Training e: **ACMT**

Advisory Committee on Oceanic Meteorological Research e: **ACOMR**

Advisory Committee on Oil Pollution of the Sea e: **ACOPS**

Advisory Committee on Polar Programs e: **ACPP**

Advisory Committee on Protection of the Sea e: **ACOPS**

Advisory Committee on Radiological Protection e: **ACRP**

Advisory Committee on Releases into the Environment e: **ACRE**

Advisory Committee on the Biological Effects of Ionizing Radiations e: **BEIR**

Advisory Committee on the Environment e: **ACE**

Advisory Committee on the Marine Environment e: **ACME**

Advisory Committee on Weather Control e: **ACWC**

Advisory Committee to the Canada Centre for Inland Waters d: **ACCC**

Advisory Council for the International Geophysical Year e: **ACIGY**

Advisory Council on Medical Education e: **ACME**

Advisory Federal Committee on Radiological Protection e: **SSK**

Advisory Group for Ocean Engineering e: **AGOE**

Advisory Group for [on] Aeronautical (or Aerospace) Research and Development e: **AGARD**

Advisory Group on Medical and Dental Education, Training and Staffing e: **AGMETS**

Advisory Group on Ocean Research e: **AGOR**

Advisory Panel for Oceanography e: **APO**

Advisory Panel on Environmental Change e: **APEC**

Advisory Services. Sea Grant Program. Southern California University e: **Advis. Serv. Sea Grant Program South. Calif. Univ.**

Aegaean Sea e: **G & C**

Aegean Sea e: **Aegean**, e: **Aeg S**

Aequitron Medical, Inc. e: **AQTN**

Aerated Waters Trade Board e: **A.W.T.B.**

Aerial Cartographic and Geodetic Squadron e: **ACGS**, e: **ACGSq**

Aerial Locations of Hazardous Atmospheres e: **ALOHA**

Aerial Observation Post e: **AOP**

Aerially Deployed Ice Thickness Transponder e: **ADITT**

Aero Geo Astro Corp. e: **A.G.A.**, e: **AGAC**

Aero-Medical Acceleration Laboratory e: **AMAL**

Aero-Medical Association e: **AeMA**, e: **AMA**

Aero-Medical Association of the United States of America e: **AMAUS**

Aero Medical Equipment Laboratory e: **AMEL**

Aero-Medical Evacuation e: **AME**

Aero Medical Examiner e: **AME**

Aero Medical Services e: **AMS**

Aero-Space Environment Simulation System e: **ASESS**

Aero-Space Institute e: **ASI**

Aero Spacelines e: **AP**

Aeroassisted Orbital Transfer Vehicle e: **AOTV**

Aerobiology and Evaluation Laboratory e: **AEL**

aeromedical e: **aeromed**

Aeromedical Airlift Group e: **AAG**, e: **AAGp**

Aeromedical Airlift Squadron e: **AAS**, e: **AASq**

Aeromedical Airlift Wing *e:* **AAW,** *e:* **AAWg**

Aeromedical Association of France *e:* **AAMF**

Aeromedical Education Division *e:* **AED**

Aeromedical Environmental Health Laboratory *e:* **AEHL**

Aeromedical Evacuation *e:* **AE,** *e:* **AIREVAC,** *e:* **AMDLEVAC**

Aeromedical Evacuation and Hospitalization Model *e:* **AEHM**

Aeromedical Evacuation Control Center *e:* **AECC**

Aeromedical Evacuation Control Element *e:* **AECE**

Aeromedical Evacuation Control Officer *e:* **AECO**

Aeromedical Evacuation Crew Member[s] *e:* **AECM**

Aeromedical Evacuation Flight *e:* **AEF**

Aeromedical Evacuation Group *e:* **AEG,** *e:* **AEGp**

Aeromedical Evacuation Liaison Officer *e:* **AELO**

Aeromedical Evacuation Liaison Team *e:* **AELT**

Aeromedical Evacuation Operations Office[rs] *e:* **AEOO**

Aeromedical Evacuation Squadron *e:* **AES,** *e:* **AESq**

Aeromedical Evacuation Support Team *e:* **AEST**

Aeromedical Evacuation System *e:* **AEROMED,** *e:* **AES,** *e:* **AMES**

Aeromedical Evacuation Technician *e:* **AET**

Aeromedical Evacuation Unit *e:* **AEU**

Aeromedical Field Laboratory *e:* **AFB,** *e:* **AFL**

Aeromedical Laboratory *e:* **AML**

Aeromedical Liaison Office[r] *e:* **AMLO**

Aeromedical Monitor Console *e:* **AMC**

Aeromedical Research Laboratory *e:* **ARL**

Aeromedical Research Unit *e:* **ARU**

Aeromedical Staging Facility *e:* **ASF**

Aeromedical Staging Flight *e:* **ASF**

Aeromedical Staging Unit *e:* **ASU**

Aeronautical Meteorology Programme *e:* **AeMP**

Aeronautical Satellite Earth Terminal *e:* **ASET**

Aeronautical weather report *e:* **AERO**

Aeronautics and Space *e:* **AEROSPACE**

Aeronautics and Space Engineering Board [National Academy of Engineering] *e:* **ASEB**

Aeronautics and Space Historical Center *e:* **ASHC**

aeronautics + space *e:* **aerospace**

Aeronautics Upper Atmosphere Impact Program *e:* **AUAIP**

Aeronomy and Space Data Center *e:* **ASDC**

Aeronomy Satellite - Neutral Atmosphere Temperature Experiment *e:* **AEROS-NATE**

Aerophysics and Aerospace Engineering Research Report *e:* **AAERR**

Aeroplane (or Aerospace) & Armament Experimental Establishment *e:* **A&AEE**

Aerosol Climatic Effects *e:* **ACE**

Aerosol Lidar Experiment in Space *e:* **ALEX S**

Aerospace *e:* **A,** *e:* **AERO,** *e:* **Aerosp**

Aerospace Ancillary Equipment *e:* **AAE**

Aerospace and Electronic *e:* **A and E,** *e:* **A & E**

Aerospace [and] Electronic Systems *e:* **AES**

Aerospace and Electronic[s] Systems Society *e:* **AESS**

Aerospace and Environmental Medicine Information System *e:* **AEMIS**

Aerospace and Equipment *e:* **A and E**

Aerospace and Equipmnent *e:* **A & E**

Aerospace and Navigational Electronics *e:* **ANE**

Aerospace Applications Studies Committee *e:* **AASC**

Aerospace Audio-Visual Service *e:* **AAVS**

Aerospace Auxiliary Equipment *e:* **AABA,** *e:* **AAE**

Aerospace Bearing Support Inc. *e:* **ABS**

Aerospace Business Environment Simulator *e:* **abes**

Aerospace Cartographic and Geodetic Service *e:* **ACGS**

Aerospace Catalog Automated Microfilm, Inc. *e:* **ASCAM**

Aerospace Center *e:* **AC**

Aerospace Command and Control System *e:* **ACCS**

Aerospace Communication and Controls Division *e:* **ACCD**

aerospace communication[s] *e:* **aerospacecom**

Aerospace Communications Complex *e:* **AIRCOM**

Aerospace Communications Wing *e:* **ACOMMW**

Aerospace Computer Automatic Program[me] Evaluator *e:* **ACAPE**

Aerospace Computer Program[me] *e:* **ACP**

Aerospace Computer Program[me] Model *e:* **ACPM**

Aerospace Contract Engineers *e:* **ACE**

Aerospace Control Environment *e:* **ACE**

Aerospace Control Squadron *e:* **ACONS**

Aerospace Corporation *e:* **AC**

Aerospace Crew Equipment Development *e:* **ACED**

Aerospace Data Acquisition System *e:* **ADAS**

Aerospace Data Adapter Programmable Tester *e:* **ADAPT**

Aerospace Data Systems *e:* **ADS**

Aerospace Defense Command *e:* **ADC,** *e:* **ADCOM**

Aerospace Defense Command Intelligence Center *e:* **ADIC**

Aerospace Defense Command Region *e:* **ADCOMR**

Aerospace & Defense Sales Inc. *e:* **ADSI**

Aerospace Defense Software Engineering Environment *e:* **ASD/SEE**

Aerospace Defense Systems Officer *e:* **ADSO**

Aerospace Department Chairmens Association *e:* **ADCA**

Aerospace Design Hugo Marom Ltd. *e:* **ADHM**

Aerospace Digital Development *e:* **ADD**

Aerospace Draftsman's Education and Proficiency Training *e:* **ADEPT**

Aerospace Education *e:* **AE**

Aerospace Education Association *e:* **AEA**

Aerospace Education Foundation *e:* **AEF**

Aerospace Education Workshop Project *e:* **AEWP**

Aerospace Education[al] Instructor *e:* **AEI**

Aerospace Electrical Division *e:* **AED**

Aerospace Electrical Society *e:* **AES**

Aerospace Electronics Laboratory *e:* **AEL**

Aerospace Energy Conversion Committee *e:* **AECC**

Aerospace Engine Life Committee *e:* **AELC**

Aerospace Engineering *e:* **Aero Eng,** *e:* **Aerosp Eng**

Aerospace Engineering and Engineering Mechanics *e:* **AEEM**

Aerospace Engineering Facility *e:* **AEF**

Aerospace Engineering Process Institute *e:* **AEPI**

Aerospace Engineering Test Establishment *e:* **AETE**

Aerospace Environment *e:* **AE**

Aerospace Environmental Support Unit *e:* **AESU**

Aerospace Facilities Engineer *e:* **AFE**

Aerospace Facts and Figures *e:* **Aero F & F**

Aerospace Flight Test Radio Coordinating Council *e:* **AFTRCC**

Aerospace Flight Vehicle *e:* **AFV**

Aerospace Ground Equipment Department *e:* **AGED**

Aerospace Ground Equipment Installation *e:* **AGEI**

Aerospace Ground Equipment out of Commission for Parts *e:* **AGEOCP**

Aerospace Ground Equipment Recommendation (or Requirements) Data *e:* **AGERD**

Aerospace Ground Equipment/Support Equipment *e:* **AGE/SE**

Aerospace Ground-Support Equipment *e:* **AGE**

Aerospace Ground Support Equipment *e:* **AGSE**

Aerospace Ground Unit *e:* **AGU**

Aerospace Group *e:* **AG**

Aerospace Guidance and Meteorology Center *e:* **AGMC**

Aerospace High School *e:* **AHS**

Aerospace Human Factors Association *e:* **ASHA**

Aerospace Industrial Life Sciences Association *e:* **AILSA**

Aerospace Industrial Modernization *e:* **AIM**

Aerospace Industrial (or Industry) Association *e:* **AIA**

Aerospace Industries Association of America *e:* **AIA/NAS**

Aerospace Industries Association of America, Inc. *e:* **AIAA**

Aerospace Industries Association of Canada *e:* **ORAE**

Aerospace Industry Standards Committee *e:* **AISC**

Aerospace Industry Technology Program *e:* **AITP**

Aerospace Information Digest *e:* **AID**

Aerospace Information Division *e:* **AID**

Aerospace Information Report *e:* **AIR**

Aerospace Installation Diagnostic Equipment *e:* **AIDE,** *e:* **AJDE**

Aerospace Instrumentation Committee *e:* **ASIC**

Aerospace Instrumentation Laboratory e: **AIL**

Aerospace Instrumentation Range Station e: **AESIR**

Aerospace Intelligence e: **AI**

Aerospace Intelligence Data System e: **AIDS**

Aerospace Intelligence File e: **AIF**

Aerospace Intelligence Squadron e: **AEROIS**

Aerospace Internal Data Report e: **AIDR**

Aerospace Maintenance and Operational Status e: **AMOS**

Aerospace Maintenance and Regeneration Center e: **AMARC**

Aerospace Maintenance Cell e: **AMC**

Aerospace Maintenance Manpower Information System e: **AMMIS**

Aerospace Management Liaison Section e: **AMLS**

Aerospace Manufacturers' Council e: **AMC**

Aerospace, Maritime and Military Systems e: **AMMS**

Aerospace Material Document e: **AMD**

Aerospace Material Specification e: **AMS**

Aerospace Materials Information e: **AMI**

Aerospace Materials Information Center e: **AMIC**

Aerospace Medical Association e: **AMA**, e: **ASMA**

Aerospace Medical Association of the Philippines e: **AMAP**

Aerospace Medical Command e: **AMC**

Aerospace Medical Division e: **AMD**

Aerospace Medical Laboratory [Clinical] e: **AMLC**

Aerospace Medical Operations Office e: **AMOO**

Aerospace Medical Panel e: **AMP**, e: **ASMP**

Aerospace Medical Research e: **AMR**

Aerospace Medical Research Laboratory e: **AMRL**

Aerospace Medicine e: **Aerosp. Med.**, e: **Aerosp Med**, e: **AM**

Aerospace Medicine and Biology e: **AMB**

Aerospace Medicine Consultation Service e: **ACS**

Aerospace Nuclear Safety Information Center e: **ANSIC**

Aerospace Observation Platform d: **AOP**

Aerospace (or Air) Defense Command Post e: **ADCP**

Aerospace (or Air) Defense Communications Office e: **ADCO**

Aerospace (or Air) Defense Division e: **ADD**

Aerospace Photographic Reconnaissance Equipment e: **APRE**

Aerospace Physiologists Society e: **ASPS**

Aerospace Physiology Officer e: **APO**

Aerospace Plane e: **ASP**

Aerospace Primus Club e: **APC**

Aerospace Products Division, SED Systems Ltd., Saskatoon, Saskatchewan e: **SSSEDA**

Aerospace Program[me]-Oriented Language e: **APOL**

Aerospace Radioisotope Power Information Center e: **ARPIC**

Aerospace Recommened Practice e: **ARP**

Aerospace Reconnaissance Technical Wing e: **ARTW**

Aerospace Reference Project e: **ARP**

Aerospace Rescue and Recovery e: **ARR**

Aerospace Rescue and Recovery Center e: **ARRC**

Aerospace Rescue and Recovery Group e: **ARRG[p]**

Aerospace Rescue and Recovery Service e: **ARRS**

Aerospace Rescue and Recovery Squadron e: **ARRS**, e: **ARRSq**

Aerospace Rescue and Recovery Training Center e: **ARRTC**

Aerospace Rescue and Recovery Wing e: **ARRW[g]**

Aerospace Research Applications Center e: **ARAC**

Aerospace Research Associates Inc. e: **ARA**

Aerospace Research Association e: **ARA**

Aerospace Research Laboratory e: **ARL**

Aerospace Research Pilot School e: **ARPS**

Aerospace Research Pilot School--Edwards Air Force Base e: **ARPS-E**

aerospace research satellite e: **ars**

Aerospace Research Satellite Program e: **ARSP**

Aerospace Research Support Program e: **ARSP**

Aerospace Research Vehicle e: **ARV**

Aerospace Resource Information Network e: **ARIN**

Aerospace Safety Advisory Panel e: **ASAP**

Aerospace Safety Research and Data Institute e: **ASRDI**

Aerospace Security Force e: **ASF**

Aerospace Services Division e: **ASD**

Aerospace Spin-Off Laboratory e: **AEROSOL**

Aerospace Standard[s] e: **AS**

Aerospace Static Converter e: **ASC**

Aerospace Static Inverter e: **ASI**

Aerospace Structural Material e: **ASM**

Aerospace Structures Information and Analysis Center e: **ASIAC**

Aerospace Structures Test Facility e: **ASTF**

Aerospace Studies e: **AS**

Aerospace Studies Institute e: **ASI**

Aerospace Support Equipment e: **ASE**

Aerospace Support Group e: **AEROSG**

Aerospace Support Squadron e: **AEROSS**, e: **AEROSSq**

aerospace surveillance and control e: **as & c**

Aerospace Surveillance and Control Squadron e: **ASCS**

Aerospace Surveillance and Warning e: **ASSAW**

Aerospace Surveillance and Warning System e: **ASWS**

Aerospace Surveillance System e: **ASS**

Aerospace System Test and Evaluation Complex e: **ASTEC**

Aerospace Systems Center e: **ASC**

Aerospace Systems Division e: **ASD**

Aerospace Systems Safety Society e: **ASSS**

Aerospace Systems Security Program e: **ASSP**

Aerospace Systems Test Environment e: **ASTE**

Aerospace Systems Test Reactor e: **ASTR**

Aerospace Technical Council e: **ATC**

Aerospace Technical Intelligence Center e: **ATIC**

Aerospace Technologies of Australia e: **ATA**

Aerospace Technologies of Australia Pty Ltd e: **ASTA**

Aerospace Technology e: **Aerosp Technol**, e: **AST**

Aerospace Technology Division e: **ATD**

Aerospace Test Equipment e: **ATE**

Aerospace Test Group e: **ASTG**

Aerospace Test Wing e: **ASTWg**, e: **ATW**

Aerospace Traffic Control Center e: **ATCC**

Aerospace Vehicle e: **ASV**, e: **AV**

Aerospace Vehicle Distribution Office[r] e: **AVDO**

Aerospace Vehicle Electronics e: **AVE**

Aerospace Vehicle Equipment e: **AVE**

Aerospace Vehicle Inventory Status and Utilization Reporting System e: **AVISURS**

Aerospace Vehicle Simulation e: **AVS**

Aerospatiale observation helicopter built in Brazil by Embraer e: **SA-341**

Aerothermodynamic-Aerotheromelastic Structural Systems Environmental Test e: **Asset**

Aerothermodynamic Elastic Structural System Environmental Tests e: **ASSET**

Aerotriangulation [by Observation of] Indepenent Models e: **AIM**

AES Regina Weather Oftice, Environment Canada Saskatchewan e: **SREAE**

AEW/Ground Environment Integration System e: **AEGIS**

Affiliate of the Royal Society of Health e: **Affil RSH**

Affinely Connected Space e: **ACS**

Affordable Signature Control e: **ASC**

Afghan Geodesy and Cartography Head Office e: **AGCHO**

Afghan Geodesy and Cartography Office e: **ACGO**, e: **AGCO**

AFGL Interactive Meteorological System e: **AIMS**

Africa, India Ocean Region Air Navigation e: **AFI-RAN**

African Association for Biological Nitrogen Fixation e: **AABNF**

African Association of Remote Sensing of the Environment e: **AARSE**

African Centre for/of Meteorological Applications for Development e: **ACMAD**

African Council for the Training and Promotion of Health Sciences Teachers and Specialists e: **ACHSTS**

African Council on Remote Sensing e: **ACRS**

African Environmental Research and Consulting Group e: **AERGC**

African-Eurasian Migratory Waterbird Agreement e: **AEWA**

African Index Medicus e: **AIM**

African India Ocean Region e: **AFI**

African Irrigated Rice Observational Nursery e: **AIRON**

African Journal of Ecology e: **Afr. J. Ecol.**

African Journal of Medicine and Medical Sciences e: **Afr J Med Med Sci**

African Journal of Reproductive Health *e:*
AJRH

African Medical and Research [and
Education] Foundation *e:* **AMREF**

African Medical and Research Foundation
e: **AM & RF**

African Ministerial (or Ministers)
Conference on the Environment *e:*
AMCEN

African Network for the Development and
Ecological Agriculture *e:* **ANDEA**

African Network for [the] Prevention and
Protection against Child Abuse and
Neglect *e:* **ANPPCAN**

African Networks for Health Research &
Development *e:* **AFRO-NETS**

African NGOs [Nongovernment
Organizations] Environment Network *e:*
ANEN

African Organization for Cartography and
Remote Sensing *e:* **AOCARS**

African Regional Network for Microbiology
e: **ARNM**

African Remote Sensing Council *e:* **ARSC**

African Technical Regional Environment
Group *e:* **ATREG**

African Upland Rice Observational Nursery
e: **AURON**

African Wild Dog Conservation Fund *e:*
AWDCF

African Wildlife Foundation *e:* **AWF**

African Wildlife Leadership Foundation *e:*
AWLF

African Wildlife Resource *e:* **AWR**

African Youth for Environment *e:* **AYE**

After-Hyperpolarization *e:* **AH**

Against Medical Advice *e:* **AMA**

AGARD [Advisory Group for Aerospace
Research and Development] Advisory *e:*
AGARDA

AGARD [Advisory Group for Aerospace
Research and Development] Advisory
Report *e:* **AGARD Ady Rep**

AGARD [Advisory Group for Aerospace
Research and Development] Anual
Meeting *e:* **AGARD Annu Meet**

AGARD [Advisory Group for Aerospace
Research and Development] Conference
Proccedings *e:* **AGARDCP**

AGARD [Advisory Group for Aerospace
Research and Development] Conference
Proceedings *e:* **AGARD Conf Proc**

AGARD [Advisory Group for Aerospace
Research and Development] Lecture
Serials *e:* **AGARD Lect Ser**

AGARD [Advisory Group for Aerospace
Research and Development] Manual *e:*
AGARD Man

AGARD [Advisory Group for Aerospace
Research and Development] Report *e:*
AGARD Rep

AGARD [Advisory Group for Aerospace
Research and Development] Specification
e: **AGARD Specif**

Agassiz National Wildlife Refuge *e:*
ANWR

Aged and Community Care Division.
Australian Department of Health & Aged
Care *e:* **ACC**

Aged Intact Animal *e:* **AI**

Agena Class Lunar Orbiter *e:* **ACLO**

Agence de l'Environnement et de la Maîtrise
de l'Énergie *f:* **ADEME**

Agence de Presse Médicale *f:* **APM**

Agence des Etats-Unis pour la protection de
lenvironnement *f:* **EPA**

Agence d'études de Géologie appliquée à
l'Étranger *f:* **AGE**

Agence Européene de Promotion et de
realisations-Tiers-Monde *f:* **AGEP-
Tiers-Monde**

Agence européenne de l'environnement *f:*
AEE

Agence Française Intermédicale *f:* **AFIM**

Agence Générale de Publicité Routiére *f:*
AGPR

Agence nationale de protection de
l'environnement *f:* **NEPA**

Agence Nationale d'Information,
d'Accréditation et d'Évaluation Médicale
f: **ANIADEM**

Agence Nationale pour le Déement de
l'Évaluation Médicale *f:* **ANDEM**

Agence pour la Protection de la Sécurité des
Informations de la Santé *f:* **APSIS**

Agency for Health Care Administration *e:*
AHCA

Agency for Health Care Policy and
Research *e:* **AHCPR**

Agency for Healthcare Research and
Quality *e:* **AHRQ**

Agency of Natural Resources and Energy
e: **ANRE**

Agenda for Leadership in Programs for
Healthcare Accreditation *e:* **ALPHA**

Agenda of Science for Environment and
Development into the 21st Century *e:*
ASCEND

Agent Building Environment *e:* **ABE**

Agente Meteorológico de Puerto *s:* **PMO**

Agents Indépendents, Courtiers et
Concessionnaires du commerce et de
l'industrie *f:* **AICC**

Agents of Biological Origin *e:* **ABO**

Agenzia Spaziale Italiana *i:* **ASI**

Agfa Publishing Systems Environment *e:*
APSE

Agicultural Climate Service System *e:*
AGRICLIMSS

Aging Health Policy Center *e:* **AHPC**

AGOR [Auxiliary General Occanographic
Research] Oceanographic Digital Data
System *e:* **AGODDS**

Agrar- und Hydrotechnik GmbH *d:* **AHT**

Agrarmeteorologische Datenbank
Rheinland-Pfalz *e:* **AGMEDA**

Agrarmeteorologische[s]
Meßnetzstation[en] *e:* **AMM**

Agrecol Development Information *e:*
AGRECOL

Agreement on the Conservation of
Cetaceans of the Black Sea,
Mediterranean Sea and Contiguous
Atlantic Area *e:* **ACCOBAMS**

Agri-residue used for animal feed *e:* **AF**

AGRICOLA-Gesellschaft zur Förderung der
Geschichte der Naturwissenschaften und
der Technik e.V. *d:* **AGRICOLA**

Agricultura Biológica y Tecnología
Apropiada para el Trópico *s:* **ABITAT**

Agricultural and Biological Chemistry
[Tokyo] *e:* **Agric [&] Biol Chem**

Agricultural and Forest Meteorology *e:*
Agric For Meteorol

Agricultural Biological Literature
Evaluation *e:* **ABLE**

Agricultural Biological Literature
Exploitation *e:* **ABLE**

Agricultural Climatological Office *e:*
ACO

Agricultural, Ecological and Geographical
Information System *e:* **AEGIS**

Agricultural Environmental Quality
Institute *e:* **AEQI**

Agricultural Meteorology *e:* **Agric Met**

Agricultural Meteorology Programme *e:*
AgMP

Agricultural Protection Board *e:* **APB**

Agricultural Research Council [Great
Britain]. Radiobiological Laboratory *e:*
Agric Res Counc [GB] Radiobiol Lab

Agricultural Research Council [Great
Britain]. Radiobiological Laboratory.
ARCRL *e:* **Agric Res Counc [GB]
Radiobiol Lab ARCRL**

Agricultural Research Council
Radiobiological Laboratory *e:* **ARCRL**

Agricultural Research Department, Ministry
of Agriculture, Nature Conservation and
Fisheries *e:* **DLO**

Agricultural Space Informatics Network
Experiment *e:* **AGRISPINE**

Agricultural Water Management *e:* **Agric.
Water Manage.**

Agriculturally Sustainable System[s] and
Environmental Transformation *e:*
ASSET

Agriculture and Animal Husbandry *e:*
Agric Anim Hub

Agriculture and Environment *e:* **Agric
Env**

Agriculture and Resources Inventory
Survey through Aerospace Remote
Sensing *e:* **AgRISTARS**

Agriculture and Resources Inventory
Surveys Through Aerospace Remote
Sensing *e:* **AGRISTARS**

Agriculture and Water Project *e:* **AGWAT**

Agriculture, Ecosystems and Environment
e: **Agric Ecosyst & Environ**

Agriculture, Hydrology and Meteorology
e: **AGRHYMET**

Agrimensura Geológica de los Estados
Unidos *s:* **USGS**

Agrimex Gesellschaft zur Verwertung von
Tieraufzuchtpatenten GmbH *d:* **Agrimex**

Agro-Environmental Monitoring System *e:*
AEMS

agrobiological *e:* **agro**

agrobiologic[al][ly] *e:* **agrobio**

Agrobiologist *e:* **Agro.**

agrobiologist *e:* **agrobio**

agrobiology *e:* **ag**, *e:* **agbio**, *e:* **agro**, *e:*
agrobio

Agroecological Zone *e:* **AEZ**

agrogeology *e:* **agrogeol**

Agronmeteorology and Operational
Hydrology and their Applications *e:*
AGRHYMET

Agronomy, Plant Physiology and
Agroecology Division *e:* **APPA**

Agrupación de Mujeres Tierra Viva *s:*
AMTV

Agrupamento Científico de Estudios de
Geologia, Lisboa *p:* **ACEG**

Agrupamento Cientifico de Formacognósia
para o Estudo das Plantas Medicinais do
Ultramar *p:* **ACFPM**

Agrupamento Científico de Preparação de Geógrafos para o Ultramar Português p: **ACPG**

Agua Intermedia Circumpolar s: **CPIW**

Agusta Aerospace Services e: **AAS**

AHFC's Enhanced Weatherization Program e: **WX+**

AHFC's Low-Income Weatherization Program e: **WX**

AIBS [American Institute of Biological Sciences] Bulletin e: **AIBS Bull**

AIC [Asian Information Centre] for Geotechnical Engineering e: **AGE**

Aid for/of International Medicine e: **AIM**

Aide au Développement Économico-Écologique de l'East de l'Afrique et de l'Ocean Indien f: **ECO-DEV**

Aide au Tiers-Monde f: **ATM**

Aide et Protection à l'Enfance Malheureuse et Inadaptée f: **APEMI**

Aide Médicale Internationale f: **AMI**

Aide Routière Automobile f: **ARA**

AIDS Medical Foundation e: **AMF**

Aids to Identification in Difficult Groups of Animals and Plants e: **AIDGAP**

AIM project on methods and architectures for logic engineering in medicine e: **LEMMA**

Air and Earth Shock e: **AES**

air at atmosphere pressure e: **aap.**

Air, Atmospheric Chemistry and Air Pollution. Seminar e: **Air Atmos Chem Air Pollut Semin**

Air Call Medical Services e: **ACMS**

Air Cleaner Cold Weather Modulator e: **ACCWM**

Air Combat Environment Test and Evaluation Facility e: **ACETEF**

Air Communications and Weather e: **ACAW**, e: **AC & W**

Air Conditioned Microclimate System e: **ACMS**

Air Containment Atmosphere Dilution e: **ACAD**

Air Coordinating Committee Meteorological Subcommittee e: **ACC/MET**

Air Corporations Joint Medical Services e: **ACJMS**

Air Corps Medical Forces e: **ACMF**

Air-Cure Environmental e: **AIRE**

Air Defence All-weather e: **ADX**

Air Defence Ground Environment e: **ADGE**

Air Defense Electronic Environment e: **ADEE**

Air Deployable Ice Beacon e: **ADIB**

Air Droppable, Expendable Ocean Sensor e: **ADEOS**

Air-Espace Techniques e: **Air-Espace Tech**

Air Force Aerospace Fuel Petroleum Supply Office e: **AFAFPSO**

Air Force Aerospace Fuels Field Office e: **AFAFFO**

Air Force Aerospace Materials Information Center e: **AFAMIC**

Air Force Aerospace Medical Research Laboratory e: **AFAMRL**

Air Force Aerospace Rescue and Recovery Service e: **AARS**

Air Force and Space Digest e: **AF/SD**

Air Force Association-Space Education Foundation e: **AFA-SEF**

Air Force Center for Environmental Excellence e: **AFCEE**

Air Force Combat Climatology Center e: **AFCCC**

Air Force Environmental Rocket-Sounding System e: **AFERSS**

Air Force Environmental Technical Applications Center e: **AFETAC**

Air Force European Office of Aerospace Research e: **AFEOAR**

Air Force Geographic Information Handling System e: **AFGIHS**

Air Force Geophysical Laboratory e: **AFGL**

Air Force Geophysics Laboratory e: **AFGL**

Air Force Global Weather Center e: **AWGWC**

Air Force Global Weather Center (or Central) e: **AFGWC**

Air Force Global Weather Information System e: **AFGWIS**

Air Force Global Weather Reconnaissance Program e: **AFGWRP**

Air Force Health Professions Scholarship Program e: **AFHPSP**

Air Force Medical Center e: **AFMC**

Air Force Medical Information and Control System e: **AFMEDICS**

Air Force Medical Logistics Office e: **AFMLO**

Air Force Medical Management Engineering Team e: **AFMEDMET**

Air Force Medical Materiel Field Office e: **AFMMFO**

Air Force Medical Materiel Letter e: **AFMML**

Air Force Medical Operations Agency e: **AFMOA**

Air Force Medical Publications Agency e: **AFMPA**

Air Force Medical Service e: **AFMS**

Air Force Medical Service Center e: **AFMSC**

Air Force Medical Services Information System Plan e: **AFMSISP**

Air Force Medical Specialist Corps e: **AFMSC**

Air Force Medical Support Agency e: **AFMSA**

Air Force Meteorological Center e: **AFMeTC**

Air Force Meteorological Satellite Program e: **AFMSP**

Air Force-Military Interdepartmental Purchase Requests e: **AF-MIPR**

Air Force Occupational and Environmental Health Laboratory e: **AFOEHL**

Air Force Occupational Safety and Health e: **AFOSH**

Air Force Office for [of] Aerospace Research e: **AFOAR**

Air Force Office of Aerospace Industry Modernization e: **AIM**

Air Force Office of Aerospace Sciences e: **AFOAS**

Air Force Office of Medical Support e: **AFOMS**

Air Force Polaris Material Office e: **AFPMO**

Air Force School of Aviation Medicine e: **AFSAM**

Air Force Space and Missile Organization e: **AFSMO**

Air Force Space and Missile Systems Organization e: **AFSAMSO**

Air Force Space Command e: **AFSPACECOM**, e: **AFSPC**, e: **SPACECMD**

Air Force Space Division e: **AFSD**

Air Force Space Forecast Center e: **AFSFC**

Air Force Space Plan e: **AFSP**

Air Force Space Program e: **AFSP**

Air Force Space Systems Division e: **AFSSD**

Air Force Space Technology Center e: **AFSTC**

Air Force Space Technology Satellite e: **AFSTS**

Air Force Space Test Center e: **AFSTC**

Air Force Spacecraft Control Facility e: **AFSCF**

Air Force Surveys in Geophysics e: **AFSIC**

Air Force Systems Command Space Systems Division e: **AFSC/SSD**

Air Force Weather Agency e: **AFWA**

Air Force Weather Observing and Forecasting System e: **AFWOFS**

Air Force Weather Wing e: **AFWW**

Air/Land/Sea e: **ALS**

Air, Land, Sea Application centre e: **ALSA**

Air Ministry's Meteorological Office e: **AMMO**

Air-Natural, Air-Natural Cooling e: **ANAN Cooling**

Air Natural (Cooling) e: **AN**

Air, Noise and Radiation Health Research Division e: **ANRHRD**

Air Observation Plane e: **AOP**

Air Observation Post e: **AOP**

Air-Ocean Environmental Specialist e: **AOES**

Air Ocean Exchange Experiment e: **AEROCE**

Air (or Aerospace) Crew Equipment Laboratory, Philadelphia e: **ACEL**

Air Pollution Meteorologist e: **APM**

Air quality, urban environment, noise, transport and energy e: **DG XI-D3**

Air Raid Protection e: **ARP**

Air Resources Atmospheric Turbulence and Diffusion Laboratory e: **ARATDL**

air, sea, and land defense e: **triad**

Air-Sea Convective Intraseasonal Interaction e: **ASCII**

Air Sea Experiment e: **ASE**

Air Sea Fluxes e: **ASF**

Air-Sea-Ice Interaction e: **ASII**

Air-Sea Interaction e: **ASI**

Air-Sea Interaction, Cloud and Precipitation Experiment over the Baltic Sea e: **ASCAP**

Air-Sea Rescue e: **ASR**

Air-Sea Rescue Craft e: **ASRC**

air-sea rescue service e: **a-s rs**

Air-Sea Rescue Squadron e: **VH**

Air/Sea Warfare Development Unit e: **A.S.W.D.U.**

Air-Space Cable e: **as cable**

Air Space Management e: **ASM**

Air-Space Multiple-Twin *e:* **ASMT**

Air-Space Multiple-Twin Cable *e:* **ASMT Cable**

Air Space Paper Core *e:* **ASPC**

Air Space Paper Core Cable *e:* **ASPC cable**

Air Space Transportation *e:* **ASTRA**

Air Space Travel Research Organization *e:* **ASTRO**

Air-Spaced *e:* **as**

Air-Space[d] Cable *e:* **ASC**

Air Surgeon *e:* **TAS**

Air-to-Underwater Missile *e:* **AUM**

air-to- underwater missile *e:* **aum**

Air-to-Underwater Missile-Nuclear *e:* **AUM-N**

Air-to-Water *e:* **aw**

Air Traffic Control Assigned Airspace *e:* **ATCAA**

Air Transport Association Meteorological Committee *e:* **ATAMC**

Air Transportable Earth Station *e:* **ATES**

Air Water Interface *e:* **AWI**

Air/Water Pollution Report *e:* **A/WPR**

Air/Water Ratio *e:* **AWR**

Air Weather Group *e:* **AWG**

Air Weather Network *e:* **AIRWEANET**

Air Weather Officer *e:* **AWO**

Air Weather Service *e:* **AWEASVC**, *e:* **AWS**

Air Weather Service Management Information System *e:* **AWSMIS**

Air Weather Service Manual *e:* **AWSM**

Air Weather Service Master Station Catalog *e:* **AWSMSC**

Air Weather Service, Technical Library, Scott AFB, IL *e:* **SCA**

Air Weather Service Training Guide *e:* **AWSTG**

Air Weather Wing *e:* **Air Wea Wg**

Airborne Atmospheric Uranium Sensor *e:* **AAUS**

Airborne Chromatograph for Atmospheric Trace Species *e:* **ACATS**

Airborne Countermeasures Environment and Radar Target Simulation (or Simulator) *e:* **ACEARTS**

Airborne Dual-channel Variable Input Severe Environmental Recorder (or Reproducer) *e:* **ADVISER**

Airborne Environmental Reporting System *e:* **AERS**

Airborne Equipment for Remote Imaging of the Environment *e:* **AERIE**

Airborne Infrared Observatory *e:* **AIO**

Airborne Ionospheric Observatory *e:* **AIO**

Airborne Laser Extended Atmospheric Characterization Experiment *e:* **ABLE ACE**

Airborne Laser Polarization Sensor *e:* **ALPS**

Airborne Lidar Agent Remote Monitor *e:* **ALARM**

Airborne LIDAR [Light Detection and Ranging] Oceanographic Probing Experiment *e:* **ALOPE**

Airborne Lidar Observations and Hawaiian Airglow *e:* **ALOHA**

Airborne Light Observation System *e:* **ALOS**

Airborne Night Observation Device *e:* **ANOD**

Air[borne] Observation Post *e:* **AOP**

Airborne Ocean Colour Imager *e:* **AOCI**

Airborne Oceanographic Lidar *e:* **AOL**

Airborne Polar Experiment[s] *e:* **APE**

Airborne Radar Orbital Determination *e:* **AROD**

Airborne Radar Orbital Determination System *e:* **ARODS**

Airborne Range (or Ranging) and Orbit Determination *e:* **AROD**

Airborne Ranging and Orbit Determination System *e:* **AROD System**

Airborne Remote Control Officer *e:* **ARCO**

Airborne Remote Mapping *e:* **ARM**

Airborne Remotely Operated Device *e:* **AROD**

Airborne Science Spacelab Experiments- Simulation System *e:* **ASSESS**

Airborne Sea Swell Recorder *e:* **ASSR**

Airborne Self-Protection Jammer *e:* **ASPJ**

Airborne Self-Protective [Jamming] System *e:* **ASPI**

Airborne Weather and Reconnaissance System *e:* **AWARS**

Airborne Weather Radar *e:* **WX**

Airborne Weather Radar System *e:* **AWRS**

Airborne Weather Reconnaissance System *e:* **AWRS**

Aircraft Cabin Water Spray System *e:* **ACWAS**

Aircraft De-Ice and Inhibitor *e:* **ADI**

Aircraft Earth Station *e:* **AES**

Aircraft Electronic[s] Warfare Self- Protection System *e:* **AEWSPS**

Aircraft Emergency Procedures over Water *e:* **AEPW**

Aircraft Environmental Support Office *e:* **AESO**

Aircraft Meteorological *e:* **AC/M**

Aircraft Meteorological Data Relay *e:* **AMDAR**

Aircraft Paint Stripping Wastewater *e:* **APSW**

Aircraft Produced Ice Particles *e:* **APIP**

Aircraft Self-Protection *e:* **ASP**

Aircraft Weather Report *e:* **AIRE**

Aircraft weather report *e:* **AIREP**

Aircrew Eye/Respiratory Protection *e:* **AERP**

Aircrew Microclimate Conditioning System *e:* **AMCS**

Aircrew Respiratory Protection *e:* **ARP**

Aire a tierra *s:* **A/G**

Airfields Environment Federation *e:* **AEF**

Airline[s] Medical Directors Association *e:* **AMDA**

Airman's Meteorological Information *e:* **AIRMET**

Airplane Observation *e:* **APOB**

Airport and Airspace Simulation Model *e:* **SIMMOD**

Airspace *e:* **AS**, *e:* **ASPA**

Airspace and Traffic Management Center (or Centre) *e:* **ATMC**

Airspace Control Authority *e:* **ACA**

Airspace Control Center *e:* **ACC**

Airspace Control Element *e:* **ACE**

Airspace Control & Operations Training simulator *e:* **ASCOT**

Airspace Control Order *e:* **ACO**

Airspace Control Plan *e:* **ACP**

Airspace Coordination Area *e:* **ACA**

Airspace Coordination Element *e:* **ACE**

Airspace Coordination Order *e:* **ACO**

Airspace Eurocontrol Project Class *e:* **U**

Airspace Eurocontrol Project Class K *e:* **K**

Airspace Eurocontrol project Class N *e:* **N**

Airspace ICAO Class A *e:* **A**

Airspace ICAO Class B *e:* **B**

Airspace ICAO Class C *e:* **C**

Airspace ICAO Class D *e:* **D**

Airspace ICAO Class E *e:* **E**

Airspace ICAO Class F *e:* **F**

Airspace ICAO Class G *e:* **G**

Airspace Management Cell *e:* **AMC**

Airspace Management Center *e:* **AMC**

Airspace Management Element *e:* **AAME**, *e:* **AME**

Airspace Management Systems *e:* **AMS**

Airspace Navigation Team *e:* **ANT**

Airspace Organistion & Management *e:* **ASO&M**

Airspace Reservation Coordination Office *e:* **ARCO**

Airspace Subcommittee *e:* **ASP**

Airspace Surveillance Display & Control System *e:* **ASDCS**

Airways Environmental Radar Information System *e:* **AERIS**

Airways Weather Office *e:* **AWO**

AIT Project to Support Research in an Open Environment *e:* **AIT-PRO**

Aiur Sea Rescue *e:* **A.S.R.**

Akademie der Medizinischen Wissenschaften *d:* **AdMW**

Akademie des Sanitäts- und Gesundheitswesen der Bundeswehr *d:* **SanAkBw**

Akademie des Sanitäts- und Gesundheitswesens der Bundeswehr *d:* **SanAkBw**

Akademie für Ethik in der Medizin e.V. *d:* **AEM**

Akademie für öffentliches Gesundheitswesen *d:* **AföG**

Akademie für Raumforschung und Landesplanung *d:* **AfRL**

Akademie für Raumforschung und Landesplanung, Hannover *d:* **ARL**

Akkadica. Périodique bimestriel de la Fondation assyriologique Georges Dossin *f:* **Akkadica**

Akkreditierung und Zertifizierung von Mittel- und Osteuropäischen Staaten *d:* **AMOS**

Akkreditierungsstelle der Länder für Meß- und Prüfstellen zum Vollzug des Gefahrstoffrechts *d:* **AKMP**

Akkreditierungsstelle Hannover *d:* **AKS Hannover**

Aktiengesellschaft für elektromedizinische Apparate *d:* **Agema**

Aktiengesellschaft für Gas-, Wasser- und Elektrizitätsanlagen *d:* **Agwea**

Aktion für ein freiheitliches Gesundheitswesen *d:* **AFREG**

Aktion gesünder essen *d:* **AGE**

Aktion Umwelt Mülheim/Ruhr *d:* **AUM**

Aktionsgemeinschaft Bessere Umwelt e.V. *d:* **A.B.U.**

Aktionsgemeinschaft Gesunde Umwelt *d:* **AGU**

Aktionsgemeinschaft Natur- und Umweltschutz Baden-Württemberg *d:* **ANU**

Aktionsgemeinschaft Schweizer Tierversuchsgegner d: **STG**

Aktionsgemeinschaft Umweltschutz d: **AGU**

Aktionskreis Umwelt- und Tierschutz d: **AKUT**

Aktionsorientierte Datenverarbeitung d: **AOD**

aktionsorientierte Datenverarbeitung d: **AODV**

Aktionszentrum Umweltschutz Berlin d: **AZU**

akute intermittierende Porphyrie d: **AIP**

akzeptiert d: **akz.**

AL Environmental Protection Division e: **AL/EPD**

AL Health Protection Division e: **AL/HPD**

AL Office of Environment, Safety and Health e: **AL/OESH**

Alabama, Arkansas, Florida, Georgia, Louisiana, Mississippi, North Carolina, South Carolina, Tennessee and Virginia e: **Southeast Sun Belt**

Alabama Department of Public Health e: **ADPH**

Alabama Environmental Quality Association e: **AEQA**

Alabama Geological Survey e: **Ala Geol Surv**

Alabama Journal of Medical Sciences e: **Ala.J.Med. Sci.**

Alabama Medicine e: **Ala Med**

Alabama Space and Rocket Center e: **ASRC**

Alabama Veterinary Medical Association e: **AVMA**

ALARA Protective Measure e: **APM**

Alarm & Power Remote-Control Unit e: **APCU**

Alaska Cooperative Wildlife Research Unit e: **ACWR**

Alaska Defense Frontier e: **ADF**

Alaska Department of Environmental Conservation e: **DEC**

Alaska Department of Natural Resources e: **ADNR**

[Alaska] Department of Natural Resources e: **DNR**

Alaska Hydrography Digitizing System e: **AHDS**

Alaska Medicine e: **Alaska Med**

Alaska Mental Health Trust Authority e: **AMHTA**

Alaska Meteor Burst Communications System e: **AMBCS**

Alaska National Wildlife Refuge e: **ANWR**

Alaska Native Health Service e: **ANHS**

Alaska Native Medical Center e: **ANMC**

Alaska Natural Gas Transportation Act e: **ANGTA**

Alaska Natural Gas Transportation System e: **ANGTS**

Alaska Sea Grant Report. Alaska Sea Grant Program, University of Alaska e: **Alsk. Sea Grant Rep. Alsk. Sea Grant Program, Univ. Alsk.**

Alaska State Medical Association e: **ASMA**

Alaska Territorial Medical Association e: **ATMA**

Alaskan Arctic National Wildlife Refuge e: **AANWR**

Alaskan Health Sciences Information Center e: **AHSIC**

Alaskan Meteorological Data System e: **ALMEDS**

Alaskan Sea Frontier e: **AL SEA FRON**, e: **ASF**

Alaskans Concerned for Neglected Environments e: **ACNE**

Albany Medical Center e: **AMC**

Albany Medical College e: **AMC**

Albany Medical College, Albany e: **NAlA**

Albany Medical College, Schaffer Library of Health Sciences, Albany e: **VXL**

Albany Naval Air Station [Georgia] e: **KNAB**

Albert Einstein College of Medicine e: **AECM**

Albert Einstein Medical Center e: **AEMC**

Albert Einstein Medical Center, Northern Division, Philadelphia, PA e: **PPAEM**

Albert Einstein School of Medicine e: **AESM**

Alberta Association of General Surgeons e: **AAGS**

Alberta Association of Medical Radiation Technologists e: **AAMRT**

Alberta Environment Library e: **AEL**

Alberta Environment, Peace River, Alberta e: **APREN**

Alberta Environmental Centre, Vegreville e: **AECV**

Alberta Environmental Network e: **AEN**

Alberta Geological Survey e: **AGS**

Alberta Heritage Foundation for Medical Research e: **AHFMR**

Alberta Information Retrieval for Health, Physical Education, and Recreation e: **AIRHPER**

Alberta Provincial Museum. Natural History. Occasional Paper [Canada] e: **APMNHOP**

Alberta Section of Rural Medicine e: **ASRM**

Albury-Wodonga Environment Centre e: **AWEC**

Alcatel Espace Systems e: **ATES**

Alchemical Medicine Research and Teaching Association e: **AMR'TA**

ALCOA [Aluminium Company of America] Picture-phone Remote Information System e: **APRIS**

Alcohol and Public Health Research Unit e: **APHRU**

Alcohol Dehydrogenase e: **AD**, e: **ADH**, e: **ADHase**

al[cohol] dehy[drogenated]-dehydrogenated [oxidized] alcohol e: **aldehyde**

Alcohol 5%, Dextrose 5%, in Water e: **A5D5W**

Alcohol, Drug Abuse, and Mental Health e: **ADA/MH**

Alcohol, Drug Abuse and Mental Health Administration e: **ADAMHA**

Alcohol Health and Research World e: **AHRW**

Alcoholus dehydrogenatus l: **Aldehyd**

Aldehyddehydrogenase d: **ALDH**

aldehyde dehydrogenase e: **aldh**

Alderbourne Valleay Environmental Protection Society e: **AVEPS**

ALE [Atmospheric Lifetime Experiment]/Global Atmospheric Gases Experiment e: **ALE/GAGE**

Aleutian Islands National Wildlife Refuge e: **AINWR**

Alexandria Digital Earth Prototype e: **ADEPT**

Alfred-Wegener-Institut für Polar- und Meeresforschung, Bremerhaven d: **AWI**

Alfred-Wegener-Institut für Polarforschung d: **AWIP**

Alfred-Wegener Institute for Polar and Marine Research e: **AWI**

Algemeen Comité voor het Georganiseerd Overleg van het Overheidspersoneel n: **ACOP**

Algemeen Hoofdkwartier n: **AHK**

Algemene Aannemersvereniging voor Waterbouwkundige Werken n: **AAW**

Algemene Nederlandse Bond van Gepensioneerden n: **ANBG**

Algemene Nederlandse Watersportbond n: **ANWB**

Algonquin Radio Observatory e: **ARO**

Algorithmic Remote Manipulation e: **ARM**

Aliança dos Naturais do Zombo p: **ALIAZO**

Alimentos para Animales, SA s: **ALIANSA**

Alive and Healthy e: **A and H**, e: **A & H**

Alkaline Earth Precipitate e: **AEP**

Alkaline Earth Zeolite e: **AEZ**

Alkoholdehydrogenase d: **ADH**

All Critical Atmosphere Turbulence Program e: **ALLCAT Program**

All Digital Video Imaging System for Atmospheric Research e: **ADVISAR**

All India Institute of Hygiene and Public Health e: **AIIHPH**

All-India Institute of Medical Sciences e: **AIIMS**

All India Institute of Mental Health e: **AIIMH**

All India Institute of Physical Medicine and Rehabilitation e: **AIIPMR**

All Propulsive Orbited Transfer Vehicle e: **APOTV**

All-Purpose Rocket for Collecting Atmospheric Soundings e: **APRCAS**

All-Purpose Rocket for [the] Collection of Atmospheric Soundings e: **ARCAS**

All-Russian Institute of Hydrometeorological Information-World Data Center e: **VNIIGMI-MCD**

All-Russian Research Institute of Hydrometeorological Information-World Data Center e: **RIHMI-WDC**

All-Russian Research Institute of Ocean Geology e: **VNIIO**

All-Russian Scientific Institute for Methods and Techniques of Geological Prospecting e: **VITR**

All-Russian Scientific Research Institute of Marine Fisheries and Oceanography e: **VNIRO**

All-Terrain All Climate e: **ATAC**

All Union Scientific Institute on Hydrometeorological Information-World Data Center, State Committee on Hydrometeorology e: **MTsD**

All Water e: **a/w**

All Weather e: **AW**

All Weather Aerial Delivery System e: **Awads**

All-Weather Airborne Reconnaissance System e: **AWARS**

All-Weather Aircraft e: **AWX**

All-Weather Aircraft (Fighter) e: **AWX(F)**

All-Weather Aircraft (Intruder) e: **AWX(I)**

All-Weather Attack e: **AWA**

All-Weather Attack Squadron e: **AWATKRON**

All Weather Carrier Landing System e: **ACLS**

All-Weather Carrier Landing System e: **AWCLS**

All-Weather Electronics e: **AWE**

All-Weather Fighter e: **AWF**

All-Weather Fighter Squadron e: **AWFS**

All Weather Flare e: **AWF**

All-Weather Ground Surveillance Radar e: **AGSR**

All Weather Interceptor e: **AWI**

All-Weather Interceptor e: **AWX**

All Weather Landing e: **AWL**

All-weather Landing System e: **ALS**

All-Weather Landing System e: **AWLS**

All-Weather Operations e: **AWO**

All-Weather Operations Division e: **AWOD**

All-Weather Operations Panel e: **AWOP**

All-Weather Reconnaissance System e: **AWRS**

All-Weather Stand-off Aircraft Control System e: **AWSACS**

All-Weather Stand-off Attack System e: **AWSAS**

All-Weather Tactical Bombing System e: **AWTBS**

All-Weather Tactical Strike System e: **AWTSS**

All-Weather Topographic Mapping System e: **AWTMS**

All-Weather Training Unit e: **ALL Wea Tra U**

All-Weather Training Unit, Atlantic Fleet e: **AllWeaTraULant**

All-Weather Training Unit, Pacific Fleet e: **AllWeaTraUPac**

all-weather wood foundation[s] e: **awwf**

All Weather Yaw Damper Computer e: **AWYDC**

Alladin Smartcard Environment e: **ASE**

Allagash River and Allagash Wilderness Waterway, Maine e: **Allagash**

Allan Hancock Monographs in Marine Biology e: **Allan Hancock Monogr. Mar. Biol.**

Allantic Geoscience Association e: **AGS**

Allergy Relief Medicine e: **A.R.M.**

Allgemeine Bedingungen für die Neuwertversicherung Wohngebäuden gegen Feuer-, Leitungswasser- und Sturmschäden d: **VGB**

Allgemeine Forst Zeitschrift für Waldwirtschaft und Umweltvorsorge d: **Allg. Forst Z. Waldwirtsch. Umweltvorsorge**

Allgemeine Gesellschaft für die Fahrenden auf See und auf Binnengewässern d: **AMVV**

Allgemeine Gesellschaft für Natur, Integration und Menschwerdung e.V. d: **AGNIM**

Allgemeine Tierarzneimittel-Fabrik Rostock GmbH d: **Atarost**

Allgemeine Versicherungsbedingungen für Tierlebensversicherung d: **AVBTL**

Allgemeines Hochschul-Orientierungs- und Informationssystem d: **AHOI**

Alliance for Alternative Health Care e: **AAHC**

Alliance for Alternatives in Healthcare e: **AAH**

Alliance for Balanced Environmental Solutions e: **ABES**

Alliance for Engineering in Medicine and Biology e: **AEMB**

Alliance for Environmental Education e: **AEE**, e: **AEF**

Alliance Médicale Internationale f: **AMI**

Alliance of Medical Internet Professionals e: **AMIP**

Alliance Touristique de l'Océan Indien f: **ATOI**

Allied and Alternative Medicine e: **AMED**

Allied Command Europe Air Defence Ground Environment e: **AADGE**

Allied Geographic Section e: **AGS**

Allied Health Professionals e: **AHP**

Allied Health Professions Admissions Test e: **AHPAT**

Allied Home Health Association e: **AHHA**

Allied Hydrographic Publication e: **AHP**

Allied Maritime Air Commander-in-Chief Channel [and Southern North Sea] e: **CINCMAIRCHAN**

Allied Medical Publication e: **AMEDP**

Allied Meteorological Office e: **AMO**

Allied Signal Aerospace Company e: **ASAC**

Allied-Signal Aerospace Service Corp. e: **ASASCO**

Allied Weather Publication e: **AWP**

Allmählichkeits- und Abwasserschäden d: **AAS**

allotetrahydrocortisol e: **athe**

Allowable Biological Catch e: **ABC**

alloy-steel protective plating e: **aspp**

Allwetterschutzgehäuse d: **ASG**

alpha hydroxy acid e: **aha**

Alpha Hydroxybutyrat-Dehydrogenase d: **AHBDH**, e: **AHBDH**

Alpha-Hydroxybutyric Dehydrogenase e: **AHBD**

Alpine and Mediterranean Hydrology component of FRIENDS e: **AMHY**

Alternate Bipolar e: **ABP**

alternate geologies e: **ag**

Alternate Geology Test Facility e: **AGTF**

Alternate Molecular Orbital e: **AMO**

Alternate Space Defense Operations Center e: **ASPADOC**

Alternate Space Inversion e: **ASI**

Alternate Transoceanic Abort Landing e: **ATAL**

Alternative Environmental Futures e: **AEF**

Alternat[iv]e Fluorocarbon[s] Environmental Acceptability (or Acceptance) Study e: **AFEAS**

Alternative Health Care e: **AHC**

Alternative Health Care Systems Inc. e: **AHCS**

Alternative Health Plans e: **AHP**

Alternative Liste für Demokratie und Umweltschutz d: **AL**, d: **ALDU**

Alternative Space Defence Centre e: **ASDC**

Alternativer Förderkreis Umweltschutz d: **AFU**

Alternatives. Perspectives on Society and Environment [Canada] e: **APSE**

Alternatives to Laboratory Animals e: **ATLA**

Aluminium Dihydroxyaminoacetate e: **ADA**

Aluminum Biogeochemistry in Soils e: **ALBIOS**

Aluminum hydroxide e: **Al hydrox**

Amateur Radio Observation Service e: **AROS**

Amazon Biogeochemistry and Atmospheric Chemistry Experiment e: **AMBIACE**

Amazon Deep-sea Fan e: **ADSF**

Amazon Environmental Research Institute [Brazil] e: **IPAM**

Ambient Environmental Quality e: **AEQ**

Ambient sea Noise Directionality Estimator s: **ANODE**

Ambient Sea Noise Indication e: **ASNI**

ambient temperature and pressure-saturated with water vapor e: **atps**

Ambient Water Quality e: **AWQ**

Ambient Water Quality Criteria e: **ANQC**, e: **AWQC**

Ambtenaar Gemeentelijke Civiele Verdediging n: **AGCV**

Ambulante medizinische Betreuung d: **AMB**

Ambulatory Health Care Information System e: **AHCIS**

Ambulatory Medical Care e: **AMC**

AmeDAS [Automated Meteorological Data Acquisition System] e: **AMD**

Amelioration Tactique Hydrodynamique Silence Transmission Ecoute f: **AMETHYSTE**

American Academic Environments, Inc. e: **AAE**

American Academy for Cerebral Palsy and Developmental Medicine e: **AACPDM**

American Academy of Behavioral Medicine e: **AABM**

American Academy of Compensation Medicine e: **AACM**, e: **AALIM**

American Academy of Dental Medicine e: **AADM**

American Academy of Emergency Medicine e: **AAEM**

American Academy of Environmental Engineers e: **AAEE**

American Academy of Environmental Medicine e: **AAEM**

American Academy of Health Administration e: **AAHA**

American Academy of Health Behavior e: **AAHB**

American Academy of Health & Fitness Professionals e: **AAHFP**

American Academy of Healthcare Attorneys e: **AAHA**

American Academy of Homeopathic Medicine e: **AAHM**

American Academy of Hospice and Palliative Medicine e: **AAHPM**

American Academy of Insurance Medicine e: **AAIM**

American Academy of Legal and Industrial Medicine e: **AALIM**

American Academy of Male Sexual Health e: **AAMSH**

American Academy of Medical Acupuncture *e:* **AAMA**

American Academy of Medical Administrators *e:* **AAMA**

American Academy of Medical Directors *e:* **AAMD**

American Academy of Microbiology *e:* **AAM**

American Academy of Occupational Medicine *e:* **AAOM**

American Academy of Oral Medicine *e:* **AAOM**

American Academy of Orthopaedic Surgeons (or Surgery) *e:* **AAOS**

American Academy of Pain Medicine *e:* **AAPM**

American Academy of Physical Medicine and Rehabilitation *e:* **AAPMR**

American Academy of Podiatric Sports Medicine *e:* **AAPSM**

American Academy of Spinal Surgeons *e:* **AASS**

American Academy of Tropical Medicine *e:* **AATM**

American Academy of Underwater Sciences *e:* **AUS**

American Accreditation Health Care Commission *e:* **URAC**

American Accreditation Healthcare Commission *e:* **AAHC**

American Aerospace Controls Inc. *e:* **AAC**

American Aerospace Industries Inc. *e:* **AAI**

American Alliance for Health, Physical Education, Recreation and Dance *e:* **AAHPERD**

American Animal Health Pharmaceutical Association *e:* **AAHPhA**

American Animal Hospital Association *e:* **AAHA**

American Animal Therapy Association *e:* **AATA**

American Association for Accreditation of Laboratory Animal Care *e:* **AAALAC**

American Association for Automotive Medicine *e:* **A.A.A.M.**

American Association for Comprehensive Health Planning *e:* **AACHP**

American Association for Health Education *e:* **AAHE**

American Association for Health, Physical Education and Recreation *e:* **AAHPER**

American Association for Maternal and Child Health *e:* **AAMCH**

American Association for Maternal and Infant Health *e:* **AAMIH**

American Association for Medical Systems [and] Informatics *e:* **AAMSI**

American Association for Medical Systems Informatics *e:* **AAMSI**

American Association for Medical Transcription *e:* **AAMT**

American Association for/of Acupuncture and Oriental Medicine *e:* **AAAOM**

American Association for/of Geodetic Surveying *e:* **AAGS**

American Association for/of Laboratory Animal Science *e:* **AALAS**

American Association for the History of Medicine *e:* **AAHM**

American Association for Vital Records and Public Health Statistics *e:* **AAVRPHS**

American Association for World Health *e:* **AAWH**

American Association of Acupuncture and Bio-Energetic Medicine *e:* **AAABEM**

American Association of Certified Allied Health Personnel in Ophthalmology *e:* **AACAHPO**

American Association of Clinic Physicians and Surgeons *e:* **AACPS**

American Association of Colleges of Osteopathic Medicine *e:* **AACOM**

American Association of Colleges of Osteopathic Medicine Applications Service *e:* **AACOMAS**

American Association of Colleges of Podiatric Medicine *e:* **AACPM**

American Association of Colleges of Podiatric Medicine Application Service *e:* **AACPMAS**

American Association of Community Mental Health Center Psychiatrists *e:* **AACMHP**

American Association of Electrodiagnostic Medicine *e:* **AAEM**

American Association of Foreign Medical Graduates *e:* **AAFMG**

American Association of Genito-Urinary Surgeons *e:* **AAGUS**

American Association of Geographers (or Association of American Geographers) *e:* **AAG**

American Association of Gynecologic[al] Laparoscopists *e:* **AAGL**

American Association of Health Data Systems *e:* **AAHDS**

American Association of Health Plans *e:* **AAHP**

American Association of Healthcare Administrative Management *e:* **AAHAM**

American Association of Healthcare Consultants *e:* **AAHC**

American Association of Hip and Knee Surgeons *e:* **AAHKS**

American Association of Industrial Physicians and Surgeons *e:* **AAIPS**

American Association of Integrated Healthcare Delivery Systems *e:* **AAIHDS**

American Association of Medical Assistants *e:* **AAMA**

American Association of Medical Clinics *e:* **AAMC**

American Association of Medical Colleges *e:* **AAMC**

American Association of Medical Dosimetrists *e:* **AAMD**

American Association of Medical Milk Commissioners (or Commissions) *e:* **AAMMC**

American Association of Medical Record Librarians *e:* **AAMRL**

American Association of Medical Review Officers *e:* **AAMRO**

American Association of Medical Social Workers *e:* **AAMSW**

American Association of Medical Society Executives *e:* **AAMSE**

American Association of Medical Writers *e:* **AAMW**

American Association of Medico-Legal Consultants *e:* **AAMC**

American Association of Medico-Physical Research *e:* **AAMPR**

American Association of Mental Health Professionals in Corrections *e:* **AAMHPC**

American Association of Microbiology *e:* **AAM**

American Association of Naturopathic Physicians *e:* **AANP**

American Association of Neurological Surgeons (or Surgery) *e:* **AANS**

American Association of Obstetricians and Gynecologists *e:* **AAOG**

American Association of Obstetricians, Gynecologists and Abdominal Surgeons *e:* **AAOGAS**

American Association of Occupational Health Nurses *e:* **AAOHN**

American Association of Oral and Maxillofacial Surgeons *e:* **AAOMS**

American Association of Oral and Plastic Surgeons *e:* **AAOPS**

American Association of Oral Biologists *e:* **AAOB**

American Association of Oriental Medicine *e:* **AAOM**

American Association of Orthomolecular Medicine *e:* **AAOM**

American Association of Orthop[a]edic Medicine *e:* **AAOM**

American Association of Orthopaedic Surgeons *e:* **AAOS**

American Association of Orthopedic Medicine *e:* **AAOrthMed**

American Association of Osteopathic Medical Examiners *e:* **AAOME**

American Association of Petroleum Geologists *e:* **AAPG**

American Association of Petroleum Geologists Bulletin *e:* **Am. Assoc. Pet. Geol. Bull.**, *e:* **Amer. Assoc. Pet. Geol. Bull.**

American Association of Physicists in Medicine *e:* **AAPM**

American Association of Plastic Surgeons *e:* **AAPS**

American Association of Podiatric Physicians and Surgeons *e:* **AAPPS**

American Association of Pro Life Obstetricians and Gynecologists *e:* **AAPLOG**

American Association of Public Health Dentists (or Dentistry) *e:* **AAPHD**

American Association of Public Health Physicians *e:* **AAPHP**

American Association of Public Health Veterinarians *e:* **AAPHV**

American Association of Railway Surgeons *e:* **AARS**

American Association of State Climatologists *e:* **AASC**

American Association of State Geologists *e:* **AASG**

American Association of Surgeon's Assistants *e:* **AASA**

American Association of University Professors of Urban Affairs and Environmental Sciences *e:* **AAUP-UAES**

American Association of Wildlife Veterinarians *e:* **AAWV**

American Biological Safety Association *e:* **ABSA**

American Biological Society *e:* **ABS**

American Biology Teacher *e:* **Am. Biol. Teach.**

American Board for Occupational Health Nurses *e:* **ABOHN**

American Board of Abdominal Surgeons *e:* **ABAS**

American Board of Bloodless Medicine and Surgery *e:* **ABBMS**

American Board of Dental Medicine and Surgery *e:* **ABDMS**

American Board of Dental Public Health *e:* **ABDPH**

American Board of Environmental Medicine *e:* **ABEM**

American Board of Health Physics *e:* **ABHP**

American Board of Homeopathic Medicine *e:* **ABHM**

American Board of Independent Medical Examiners *e:* **ABIME**

American Board of Industrial Medicine and Surgery *e:* **ABIMS**

American Board of Internal Medicine *e:* **ABIM**

American Board of Managed Care Medicine *e:* **ABMCM**

American Board of Medical Genetics *e:* **ABMG**

American Board of Medical-Legal Analysis in Medicine and Surgery *e:* **ABMLAMS**

American Board of Medical Management *e:* **ABMM**

American Board of Medical Microbiology *e:* **ABMM**

American Board of Medical Physics *d:* **ABMP**

American Board of Medical Psychotherapists *e:* **ABMP**

American Board of Medical Specialities *e:* **AMS**

American Board of Medical Specialties *e:* **ABMS**

American Board of Medical Toxicology *e:* **ABMT**

American Board of Neurological and Orthopaedic Medicine and Surgery *e:* **ABNOMS**

American Board of Nuclear Medicine *e:* **ABNM**

American Board of Obstetrics and Gynecology *e:* **ABOG**

American Board of Physical Medicine and Rehabilitation *e:* **ABPMR**

American Board of Preventive Medicine *e:* **ABPM**

American Board of Ringside Medicine and Surgery *e:* **ABRMS**

American Board of Science in Nuclear Medicine *e:* **ABSNM**

American Board of Thoracic Neurological Orthopaedic Medicine and Surgery *e:* **ABTNOMS**

American Board of Tropical Medicine *e:* **ABTM**

American Board of Urologic Allied Health Professionals *e:* **ABUAHP**

American Bottled Water Association *e:* **ABWA**

American Bureau for Medical Advancement (or Aid) to China *e:* **ABMAC**

American Canine Sports Medicine Association *e:* **ACSMA**

American Center for Chinese Medical Sciences *e:* **ACCMS**

American Child Health Association *e:* **ACHA**

American Chinese Medical Society *e:* **ACMS**

American Clean Water Association *e:* **ACWA**

American Clinical and Climatological Association *e:* **ACCA**

American College for [of] Advancement in Medicine *e:* **ACAM**

American College Health Association *e:* **ACHA**

American College of Animal Laboratory Medicine *e:* **ACALM**

American College of Ecology *e:* **ACE**

American College of Foot Surgeons *e:* **ACFS**

American College of General Practitioners in Osteopathic Medicine and Surgery *e:* **ACGP[OMS]**

American College of Health Care Administrators *e:* **ACHCA**

American College of Healthcare Executives *e:* **ACHE**

American College of Laboratory Animal Medicine *e:* **ACLAM**

American College of Legal Medicine *e:* **ACLM**

American College of Managed Care Medicine *e:* **ACMCM**

American College of Medical Genetics *e:* **ACMG**

American College of Medical Genetics Foundation *e:* **ACMGF**

American College of Medical Group Administrators *e:* **ACMGA**

American College of Medical Informatics *e:* **ACMI**

American College of Medical Physics (or Physicists) *d:* **ACMP**

American College of Medical Practice Executives *e:* **ACMPE**

American College of Medical Quality *e:* **ACMQ**

American College of Medical Technologists *e:* **ACMT**

American College of Medicine *e:* **ACM**

American College of Mental Health Administration *e:* **ACMHA**

American College of Nuclear Medicine *e:* **ACNM**

American College of Obstetricians and Gynecologists *e:* **ACOG**

American College of Obstetrics and Gynecology *e:* **ACOG**

American College of Occupational and Environmental Medicine *e:* **ACOEM**

American College of Oral and Maxillofacial Surgeons *e:* **ACOMS**

American College of Osteopathic Obstetricians and Gynecologists *e:* **ACOOG**

American College of Osteopathic Surgeons *e:* **ACOS**

American College of Prehospital Medicine *e:* **ACPM**

American College of Sports Medicine *e:* **ACSM**

American College of Surgeons *e:* **ACS**

American College of Surgeons Committee on Trauma *e:* **ACSCOT**

American College of Toxicology *e:* **ACT**

American College of Veterinary Internal Medicine *e:* **ACVIM**

American College of Veterinary Microbiologists *e:* **ACVM**

American College of Veterinary Preventive Medicine *e:* **ACVPM**

American College of Veterinary Surgeons *e:* **ACVS**

American Commission for Protection and Salvage of Artistic and Historical Monuments in War Areas *e:* **ACPSAHMWA**

American Committee for International Wild Life Protection *e:* **ACIWLP**

American Committee for Protection of Foreign Born *e:* **ACPFB**

American Committee on Laboratory Animal Diseases *e:* **ACLAD**

American Congress for/on Preventive Medicine *e:* **ACPM**

American Congress of Physical Medicine and Rehabilitation *e:* **ACPMR**

American Congress of Rehabilitation Medicine *e:* **ACRM**

American Coordinated Medical Society *e:* **ACMS**

American Correctional Health Services Association *e:* **ACHSA**

American Council for Health Care Reform *e:* **ACHCR**

American Council for Healthful Living *e:* **ACHL**

American Council of Certified Podiatric Physicians and Surgeons *e:* **ACCPPS**

American Council on Science and Health *e:* **ACSH**

American Council on the Environment *e:* **ACE**

American Crop Protection Association *e:* **ACPA**

American Dental Association Health Foundation *e:* **ADAHF**

American Digestive Health Foundation *e:* **ADHF**

American Electromedics Corporation *e:* **AECO**

American Environmental Health Foundation *e:* **AEHF**

American Environmental Manufacturers Association *e:* **AEMA**

American Environments Company Inc. *e:* **AE**

American Federation for/of Medical Research *e:* **AFMR**

American Fisheries Protection Act *e:* **AFPA**

American Foot Health Foundation *e:* **AFHF**

American Forces Radio and Television-Bentwaters *e:* **AFRT-B**

American Foreign Service Protective Association *e:* **AFSPO**

American Foundation for Health *e:* **AFH**

American Foundation for Health Care Research and Development *e:* **AFAHCRD**

American Foundation for Tropical Medicine *e:* **AFTM**

American Fund for Alternatives to Animal Research *e:* **AFAAR**

American Fund for Dental Health *e:* **AFDH**

American Geographical and Statistical Society e: **A.G.S.S.**

American Geographical Institute e: **AGI**

American Geographical Society e: **AGS**, e: **Amer.G.S.**

American Geographical Society Bulletin e: **Am Geog Soc Bull**

American Geographical Society, New York e: **NNA**

American Geographical Union e: **AGU**

American Geological Institute e: **AGI**, e: **Am Geol**

American Geological Research Institute e: **AGRI**

American Geophysical Society e: **Amer.G.S.**

American Geophysical Union e: **AGU**, e: **Am Geophysical**

American Guild of Animal Artists e: **AGAA**

American Gynecological and Obstetrical Society e: **AGOS**

American Gynecological Society e: **AGS**

American Health e: **AH**

American Health and Beauty Aids Institute e: **AHBAI**

American Health and Temperance Society e: **AHTS**

American Health Assistance Foundation e: **AHAF**

American Health Association e: **AHA**

American Health Care Advisory Association e: **AHCAA**

American Health Care Association e: **AHCA**

American Health Consultants e: **AHC**

American Health Decisions e: **AHD**

American Health Foundation e: **AHF**

American Health Industries Institute e: **AHII**, e: **AMI**

American Health Information Management Association e: **AHIMA**

American Health Planning Association e: **AHPA**

American Health Professionals e: **AHP**

American Health Quality Association e: **AHQA**

American Health Services Corp. e: **AHTS**

American Health[care] Institute e: **AHI**

American Healthcare Management e: **AHLTMG**

American Healthcare Management, Incorporated e: **QAHI**

American Healthcare Radiology Administrators e: **AHRA**

American Holistic Health Sciences Association e: **AHHSA**

American Holistic Medical Association e: **AHMA**

American Holistic Medical Foundation e: **AHMF**

American Holistic Medical Institute e: **AHMI**

American Holistic Veterinary Medical Association e: **AHVMA**

American Horse Protection Association e: **AHPA**

American Indian and Alaska Native Mental Health Research e: **Am Indian Alsk Native Ment Health Res**

American Indian and Alaska Native Mental Health Research. Monograph Series e:

Am Indian Alsk Native Ment Health Res Monogr Ser

American Indian Environmental Council e: **AIEC**

American Indian Lands Environmental Support Project e: **AILESP**

American Indian Medical Clinic e: **AIMC**

American Industrial Health Conference (or Council) e: **AIHC**

American Institute for Medical and Biological Engineering e: **AIMBE**

American Institute for Research and Education in Naturopathy e: **AIREN**

American Institute for the Medical Research of Trauma e: **AIMRT**

American Institute of Biological (or Biology) Society e: **AIBS**

American Institute of Biological Sciences e: **AIBS**

American Institute of Biomedical Climatology e: **AIBC**

American Institute of Crop Ecology e: **AICE**

American Institute of Fishery Research Biologists e: **AIFRB**

American Institute of Hydrology e: **AIH**

American Institute of Medical Climatology e: **AIMC**

American Institute of Oral Biology e: **AIOB**

American Institute of Professional Geologists e: **AIFG**, e: **AIPG**

American Institute of Ultrasound in Medicine e: **AIUM**

American International Health Alliance e: **AIHA**

American International Institute for the Protection of Childhood e: **AIIPC**

American Journal of Chinese Medicine e: **AJCM**, e: **Am J Chin Med**

American Journal of Chiropractic Medicine e: **AJCM**

American Journal of Emergency Medicine e: **AJEM**, e: **Am J Emerg Med**

American Journal of Ethics & Medicine e: **AJEM**

American Journal of Forensic Medicine and Pathology e: **Am J Forensic Med Pathol**

American Journal of Health Behavior e: **AJHB**

American Journal of Health Communications e: **AJHC**

American Journal of Health Education e: **AJHE**

American Journal of Health Promotion e: **AJHP**

American Journal of Health-system Pharmacy e: **AJHP**

American Journal of Health-System Pharmacy e: **Am J Health Syst Pharm**

American Journal of Industrial Medicine e: **AJIM**, e: **Am J Ind Med**

American Journal of Integrated Healthcare e: **AJIH**

American Journal of Law and Medicine e: **AJLM**, e: **Am J Law Med**, e: **Am. J. L.&Med.**

American Journal of Maternal/Child Health Nursing e: **MCN**

American Journal of Medical Genetics e: **AJMG**, e: **Am J Med Genet**

American Journal of Medical Quality e: **AJMQ**, e: **Am J Med Qual**

American Journal of Medical Technology e: **AJMT**, e: **Amer. J. Med. Technol.**

American Journal of Medicine e: **AJM**, e: **Amer. J. Med.**, e: **Am J Med**

American Journal of Obstetrics and Gynecology e: **AJOG**, e: **Amer. J. Obstet. Gynecol.**, e: **Am J Obstet Gynecol**

American Journal of Pharmacy and Sciences Supporting Public Health e: **Amer. J. Pharm.**

American Journal of Pharmacy and the Sciences Supporting Public Health e: **APSHDH..**

American Journal of Physical Medicine e: **Amer. J. Phys. Med.**

American Journal of Physical Medicine and Rehabilitation e: **Am J Phys Med Rehabil**

American Journal of Preventive Medicine e: **AJPM**, e: **Am J Prev Med**

American Journal of Public Health e: **AJPH**, e: **Am J Pub Health**, e: **Am J Public Health**

American Journal of Public Health and the Nation's Health e: **Amer. J. Public Health**

American Journal of Reproductive Immunology and Microbiology e: **AJRIM**

American Journal of Respiratory and Critical Care Medicine e: **AJRCCM**, e: **Am J Respir Crit Care Med**

American Journal of Respiratory Cell and Molecular Biology e: **AJRCMB**, e: **Am J Respir Cell Mol Biol**

American Journal of Roentgenology, Radium Therapie and Nuclear Medicine e: **Amer. J. Roentgenol. Radium Th**

American Journal of Sports Medicine e: **AJSM**, e: **Am J Sports Med**

American Journal of the Medical Science e: **Amer. J. Med. Sci.**

American Journal of the Medical Sciences e: **AJMS**, e: **Am J Med Sci**

American Journal of Tropical Medicine and Hygiene e: **Amer. J. Trop. Med. Hyg.**, e: **Am J Trop Med Hyg**

American Journal of Tropical Medicine & Hygiene e: **AJTMH**

American Labor Health Association e: **ALHA**

American Medical Acceleration Laboratory e: **AMAL**

American Medical Accreditation Program e: **AMAP**

American Medical Association e: **AMA**

American Medical Association/California Medical Association e: **AMA/CMA**

American Medical Association Committee on Insurance and Prepayment Plans e: **AMA-CIPP**

American Medical Association-Drug Evaluation[s] e: **AMA-DE**

American Medical Association Education and Research Foundation e: **AMA-ERF**

American Medical Association Enterprise Information Base e: **AMA EIB**

American Medical Association Women's Auxiliary e: **AMAWA**

American Medical Assurance Company *e:* **AMACO**

American Medical Center *e:* **AMC**

American Medical Center at Denver *e:* **AMCD**

American Medical Center for Burma *e:* **AMCB**

American Medical College Application Service *e:* **AMCAS**

American Medical College Association *e:* **AMCA**

American Medical Computer Center *e:* **AMCC**

American Medical Curling Association *e:* **AMCA**

American Medical Directors Association *e:* **AMDA**

American Medical Education Foundation *e:* **AMEF**

American Medical Electroencephalographic Association *e:* **AMEEGA**

American Medical Fly Fishing Association *e:* **AMFFA**

American Medical Group Association *e:* **AMGA**

American Medical Informatics Association *e:* **AMIA**

American Medical International, Inc. *e:* **AMI**

American Medical Joggers Association *e:* **AMJA**

American Medical Mission to Russia *e:* **A.M.M.R.**

American Medical News *e:* **AMNews**

American Medical Optics *e:* **AMO**

American Medical Peer Review Organization *e:* **AMPRO**

American Medical Political Action Committee *e:* **AMPAC**

American Medical Publishers Association *e:* **AMPA**

American Medical Qualification *e:* **AMQ**

American Medical Record[s] Association *e:* **AMRA**

American Medical Relief for Italy *e:* **AMRI**

American Medical Sailing and Yachting Association *e:* **AMSYA**

American Medical Society for Sports Medicine *e:* **AMSSM**

American Medical Society on Alcoholism *e:* **AMSA**

American Medical Society on Alcoholism and other Drug Dependencies *e:* **AMSAODD**

American Medical Specialty Organization *e:* **AMSO**

American Medical Student Association *e:* **AMSA**

American Medical Support Flight Team *e:* **AMSFT**

American Medical Technologist[s] *e:* **AMT**

American Medical Tennis Association *e:* **AMTA**

American Medical Women's Association *e:* **AMWA**

American Medico-Legal Society *e:* **AMLS**

American Medicorp, Inc. *e:* **Medicorp**

American Mental Health Alliance *e:* **AMHA**

American Mental Health Counselors Association *e:* **AMHCA**

American Mental Health Foundation *e:* **AMHF**

American Metal Climax, Inc. *e:* **AMAX**, *e:* **AMM**, *e:* **AMX**

American Meteor Association *e:* **AMA**

American Meteor Society *e:* **AMS**

American Meteorite Laboratory *e:* **AML**, *e:* **Am Meteorite**

American Meteorological Society *e:* **AmeS**, *e:* **AMS**

American Midland Naturalist *e:* **Amer. Midland Nat.**, *e:* **Am Midl Nat**, *e:* **Am. Midl. Nat.**

American Museum of Natural History *e:* **AMNH**

American Museum of Natural History, New York *e:* **NNM**

American National Council for Health Education of the Public *e:* **ANCHEP**

American Natural Gas Co. *e:* **ANG**

American Natural Hygiene Society *e:* **ANHS**

American Natural Resources Co. *e:* **ANR**

American Naturalist *e:* **Amer. Nat.**, *e:* **Am Nat**, *e:* **Am Natural**

American Naturalized Citizen Welfare Association *e:* **ANCWA**

American Nature Association *e:* **ANA**

American Nature Study Society *e:* **ANSS**

American Naturopathic Association *e:* **ANA**

American Naturopathic Medical Association *e:* **ANMA**

American Occupational Health Conference *e:* **AOHC**

American Occupational Medical Association *e:* **AOMA**

American Oceanographic and Meteorological Laboratory *e:* **AOML**

American Ocean[ograph]ic Organization *e:* **AOO**

American Oceanology Association *e:* **AOA**

American Orthopaedic Society for Sports Medicine *e:* **AOSSM**

American Osteopathic Academy of Sports Medicine *e:* **AOASM**

American Osteopathic College of Physical Medicine and Rehabilitation *e:* **AOCPMR**

American Osteopathic College of Preventive Medicine *e:* **AOCPM**

American Osteopathic College of Rehabilitation Medicine *e:* **AOCRM**

American Paramedical Institute *e:* **API**

American Petroleum Institute. Medical Research Publications *e:* **API Med Res Publ**

American Pheasant and Waterfowl Society *e:* **APW**, *e:* **AP&WS**

American Physicians Association of Computer Medicine *e:* **APACM**

American Physicians Fellowship for the Israel Medical Association *e:* **APF**

American Pigeon Racing Association *e:* **APRA**

American Podiatric Medical Association Auxiliary *e:* **APMAA**

American Podiatric Medical [Students] Association *e:* **APMA**

American Podiatric Medical Writers Association *e:* **APMWA**

American Polar Society *e:* **APS**

American Polarity Therapy Association *e:* **APTA**

American Pre-Veterinary Medical Association *e:* **APVMA**

American Preventive Medical Association *e:* **APMA**

American Protective Association *e:* **APA**

American Protective League *e:* **APL**

American Public Health Association *e:* **Am Public Health**, *e:* **APHA**

American Public Health Association. Public Health Education. Section Newsletter *e:* **APHA**

American Public Water Works Association *e:* **APWWA**

American Racing Pigeon Union *e:* **ARPU**

American Regional Interprofessional Advisory Committee of World Federation for Mental Health *e:* **IPAC**

American Registry of Diagnostic Medical Sonographers *e:* **ARDMS**

American Registry of Medical Assistants *e:* **ARMA**

American Registry of Professional Animal Scientists *e:* **ARPAS**

American Rheumatic Arthritis Medical Information System *e:* **ARAMIS**

American Rheumatism Association Medical Information System *e:* **ARAMIS**

American School Health Association *e:* **ASHA**

American Self-Protection Association *e:* **ASP**

American Shoulder and Elbow Surgeons *e:* **ASES**

American Social Health Association *e:* **ASHA**

American Society for Aerospace Education *e:* **AEA**, *e:* **ASAE**

American Society for Biochemistry and Molecular Biology *e:* **ASBC**, *e:* **ASBMB**

American Society for Circumpolar Health *e:* **ASCH**

American Society for Ecological (or Environmental) Education *e:* **ASEE**

American Society for Health Care Marketing and Public Relations *e:* **ASHCMPR**

American Society for Healthcare Central Service Personel *e:* **ASHCSP**

American Society for Healthcare Education and Training *e:* **ASHET**

American Society for Healthcare Engineering *e:* **ASHE**

American Society for Healthcare Environmental Services *e:* **ASHES**

American Society for Healthcare Human Resources Administration *e:* **ASHHRA**

American Society for Healthcare Risk Management *e:* **ASHRM**

American Society for Laser Medicine and Surgery *e:* **ASLMS**

American Society for Medical Technology *e:* **ASMT**

American Society for Oceanography *e:* **ASO**

American Society for/of Cell Biology *e:* **ASCB**

American Society for/of Microbiology *e:* **ASM**

American Society for/of Photobiology *e:* **ASP**

American Society for/of Photogrammetry and Remote Sensing e: **ASP**

American Society for/of Reproductive Medicine e: **ASRM**

American Society for Photogrammetry and Remote Sensing e: **ASPRS**

American Society for the Prevention of Cruelty to Animals e: **ASPCA**

American Society of Addiction Medicine e: **ASAM**

American Society of Allied Health Professions e: **ASAHP**

American Society of Animal Production e: **ASAP**

American Society of Animal Science e: **ASAS**

American Society of Anthropometric Medicine and Nutrition e: **ASAMN**

American Society of Biological Chemists e: **ASBC**

American Society of Chinese Medicine e: **ASCM**

American Society of Civil Engineers. Environmental Engineering Division. Journal e: **Am Soc Civ Eng Environ Eng Div J**

American Society of Civil Engineers. Waterway, Port, Coastal and Ocean Division e: **Am Soc Civ E J Waterway Port Div**

American Society of Colon and Rectal Surgeons e: **ASCRS**

American Society of Contemporary Medicine and Surgery e: **ASCMS**

American Society of Dental Surgeons e: **ASDS**

American Society of General Surgeons e: **ASGS**

American Society of Geolinguistics e: **ASG**

American Society of Health Care Risk Managers e: **ASHCRM**

American Society of Health-System Pharmacists e: **ASHP**

American Society of Internal Medicine e: **ASIM**

American Society of Laboratory Animal Practitioners e: **ASLAP**

American Society of Law and Medicine e: **ASLM**

American Society of Law, Medicine and Ethics e: **ASLME**

American Society of Limnology and Oceanography e: **ASLO**

American Society of Maxillofacial Surgeons e: **ASMS**

American Society of Medical Technologists e: **ASMT**

American Society of Naturalists e: **ASN**

American Society of Oral Surgeons e: **ASOS**

American Society of Paramedics e: **ASPM**

American Society of Pediatric Neurosurgeons e: **ASPN**

American Society of Plant Biologists e: **ASPB**

American Society of Plastic and Reconstructive Surgeons e: **ASPRS**

American Society of Plastic Surgeons e: **ASPS**

American Society of Polar Philatelists e: **ASPP**

American Society of Professional Biologists e: **ASPB**

American Society of Psychosomatic Dentistry and Medicine e: **ASPDM**

American Society of Psychosomatic Dentistry and Medicine. Journal e: **JPDMB**

American Society of Temporomandibular Joint Surgeons e: **ASTMJS**

American Society of Transplant Surgeons e: **ASTS**

American Society of Tropical Medicine e: **A.S.T.M.**

American Society of Tropical Medicine and Hygiene e: **ASTMH**

American-Soviet Medical Society e: **ASMS**

American Space Foundation e: **ASF**

American Sports Medicine Institute e: **ASMI**

American Student Health Association e: **ASHA**

American Surgeon e: **Amer. Surg.**, e: **Am Surg**

American Telemedicine Association e: **ATA.**

American Underground-Space Association e: **AUA**

American Veterinary Medical Association e: **AVMA**

American Veterinary Medical Association. Journal e: **Am Vet Med Assn J**

American Veterinary Medical Association. Proceedings e: **Am Vet Med Assn Proc**

American Veterinary Medical Association. Scientific Proccedings of the Annual Meeting e: **Am Vet Med Assoc Sci Proc Annu Meet**

American Veterinary Medical Foundation e: **AVMF**

American Veterinary Society for Computer Medicine e: **AVSCM**

American Veterinary Society of Animal Behavior e: **AVSAB**

American Water Color Society e: **AWCS**

American Water Resources Association e: **AWRA**

American Water Resources Association. Proceedings Series e: **Am Water Resour Assoc Proc Ser**

American Water Resources Association. Symposium. Proceedings e: **Am Water Resour Assoc Symp Proc**

American Water Resources Association. Technical Publication Series. TPS85-1 e: **Am Water Resour Assoc Tech Publ Ser TPS-85-1**

American Water Ski Association e: **AWSA**

American Water Works Association e: **JAWWAS**

American Water Works Association. Annual Conference. Prowedings e: **Am Water Works Assoc Annu Conf Proc**

American Water Works Association. Disinfection Seminar. Proceedings e: **Am Water Works Assoc Disinfed Semin Proc**

American Water Works Association. Jounal. Southeastern Section e: **Am Water Works Assoc Jour Southeastern Sec**

American Water Works Association. Journal e: **Am Water Works Assn J**, e: **Am Water Works Assoc J**

American Water Works Association. Ontario Section. Proceedings Annual Conference e: **Am Water Works Assoc Ont Sect Proc Annu Conf**

American Water Works Association Research Foundation e: **AWWARF**

American Water Works Association. Technology Conference Proceedings e: **Am Water Works Asoc Technol Conf Proc**

American Water Works Co. e: **AWK**

American Water Works Utility Council e: **AWWUC**

American Waterfowl Association e: **AWA**

American Watershed Council e: **AWC**

American Waterways Operators e: **AWO**

American Waterways Operators Incorporated e: **AWOI**

American Waterworks Association e: **AWWA**

American Weather Service e: **AWS**

American Whitewater Affiliation e: **AWA**, e: **AWWA**

American Wildlife Foundation e: **AWF**

American Wire Weavers Protective Association e: **AWWPA**

American Women's Medical Association e: **AWMA**

Americans for Medical Progress e: **AMP**

Americans for the Environment e: **AFE**

America's Interhemisphere Geobiosphere Organization e: **AMIGO**

AMETS [Artillery Meteorological System] Instrumentation Vehicle e: **AIV**

amilprilose hydrocholoride e: **amilpri**

Amino Polycyclic Aromatic Hydrocarbon e: **APAH**

Amitiés Italo-Luxembourgeoises f: **AIL**

Ammonium Dehydrogen[e] Phosphate e: **ADP**

Ammonium Dihydrogen Arsenate e: **ADA**

ammonium hydroxide e: **ammonia water**

Ammonium hydroxide/hydrogen Peroxide Mixture e: **APM**

Ammoniumhydroxid d: **E 527**

Ammunition Stores Management and Remote Set Fuzing e: **SM/RSF**

Ammunition, Toxic Material Open Space e: **ATMOS**

Amold's Geological Series e: **AGS**

Amorphous, Hydrogenated Carbon e: **AHC**

Amphibious Forces-North West African Waters e: **PHIBNAW**

Amphibious Observation Regiment e: **AORegt**

amputiert d: **amp.**

Amputierter d: **Amp.**

Amsterdamse Geografische Studenten Vereniging voor Sociografie n: **AGSV**

Amsterdamse Glazenwassers Ontspanningsvereniging n: **AGO**

Amsterdamse Stichting Onderwateronderzoek n: **ASO**

Amsterdamse vereniging tot bevordering der Tandheelkundig verzorging van Ziekenfondsverzekerden n: **ATZ**

Amt für Gewässerschutz d: **AGS**

Amt für Landwirtschaft und Tierzucht d: **AfLuT**

Amt für Umweltschutz d: **DOE**

Amt für Umweltschutz und Stadtverwaltung Dresden d: **AfUS**

Amt für Volksgesundheit d: **AVG**

Amt für Wasserwirtschaft d: **AfW**, d: **AW**, d: **Awa**

Ämter für Land- und Wasserwirtschaft d: **ÄLW**

Amtliche Materialprüfanstalt für Steine und Erden d: **AMPA**

Amtliche Materialprüfungsanstalt Steine und Erden d: **AMSE**

An EUREKA project on operational modelling of regional seas and coastal waters e: **OPMODD**

An Implantable Telemetric Unit for Biomedical Research e: **ITUBR-INCO-DC95-917**

an integrated energy-economic-environmental model e: **MERG**

An Intersociety Liaison Committee on the Environment e: **AISLE**

An NOAA research program on hydrothermal activity in the oceans e: **VENTS**

An nual Report. Institute of Food Microbiology. Chiba University e: **Annu Rep Inst Food Microbiol Chiba Univ**

Anaesthesiologie und Intensivmedizin d: **ANIMD2**

Anaesthesiology and Intensive Care Medicine e: **Anaesthesiol Intensive Care Med**, e: **ANIMD2**

Anais de Faculdade de Medicina Veterinaria, Lisbon p: **An. Fac. Med. Vet., Lisb.**

Anais do Instituto de Higiene e Medicina Tropical, Lisbon p: **An. Inst. Hig. Med. Trop., Lisb.**

Analecta Sacri Ordinis Cisterdensis e: **An O Cist**

Analele Universitatii Bucurestii. Biologie ru: **An. Univ. Bucur., Biol.**

Anales de Biologia p: **An. Biol.**

Anales de la Real Academia Nacional de Medicina f: **An R Acad Nac Med [Madr]**

Anales de Medicina Interna s: **An Med Interna**

Anales del Instituto de Biologia, Universidad Nacional Autonoma de Mexico. Serie Botanica s: **An. Inst. Biol., Univ. Nac. Auton. Mex., Bot.**

Anales del Instituto de Biologia, Universidad Nacional Autonoma de Mexico. Serie Zoologia s: **An. Inst. Biol., Univ. Nac. Auton. Mex., Zool.**

Anales del Museo de Historia Natural de Valparaiso s: **An. Mus. Hist. Nat. Valpso**

Analog Protection System e: **APS**

Analog[ue] Remote Unit e: **ARU**

Analog[ue]-to-Digital Data-Reduction System for Oceanographic Research e: **ADDRESOR**

Analysis and Application of Rare Earth Materials. NATO [North Atlantic Treaty Organization] Advanced Study Institute e: **Anal Appl Rare Earth Mater NATO Adv Study Inst**

Analysis and Programming for Space Systems e: **APSS**

Analysis of Dendroecological Variability and Natural Climates in Eurasia: the Last 10,000 Years e: **ADVANCE-10K**

Analysis of Rapid and Recent Climate Change [Project] e: **ARRCC**

Analysis of Recent Climate Change e: **ARCC**

Analytic Geometry Interpretive Language e: **AGIL[E]**

Analytic Orbit Deterrnination Program e: **ANODE**

Analytical Aspects of Environmental Chemistry e: **Anal Aspects Environ Chem**

ANARE [Australian National Antarctic Research Expeditions] Scientific Reports. Series B-IV. Medical Science e: **ANARE Sci Rep Ser B-IV Med Sci**

ANARE Mapping and Geographic Information Committee e: **ANAREMAGIC**

Anästhesie, Intensivtfierapie, Notfallmedizin d: **Anästh Intensivther Notfallmed**

Anästhesie, Intensivtherapie, Notfallmedizin d: **Anästh Intensivther Notfallmed**

Anasthesiologie, Intensivmedizin, Notfallmedizin, Schmerztherapie d: **Anasthesiol Intensivmed Notfallmed Schmerzther**

Anästhesiologie und Intensivmedizin d: **Anästhesiol Intensivmed**

Anästhesiologische und Intensivmedizinische Praxis d: **Anästbesiol Intensivmed Prax**, d: **Anästhesiol Intensivmed Prax**

Andhra Pradesh Ground Water Department. District Series e: **Andhra Pradesh Ground Water Dep Dist Ser**

Andhra Pradesh Ground Water Department. Research Series e: **Andhra Pradesh Ground Water Dep Res Ser**

Andrew Development Environment Workbench e: **ADEW**

Andrew User Environment e: **AUE**

Andrew W. Breidenbach Environmental Research e: **AWBERC**

Anechoic Water Tank e: **AWT**

Angell on Tide Waters e: **Ang Tide Waters**, e: **AngTW**

Angell on Water Courses e: **Ang Wat**, e: **Ang Water Courses**

Angestelltenverband Deutscher Milchkontroll- und Tierzuchtangestellten d: **ADM**

Angio-Medical Corp. e: **ANME**

Anglian Water Authority e: **AWA**

Anglo-Australian Observatory e: **AAO**

Anglo-Brazilian Amazonian Climate Observational Study e: **ABRACOS**

Anglo-French Variable Geometry e: **AFVG**

Anglo-French Variable Geometry Aircraft e: **AFVG Aircraft**

Anglo-French Variable Geometry Fighter e: **AFVG Fighter**

Anglo-German Medical Review e: **Ang"er Med Rev**, e: **Anglo-Ger. Med.Rev.**

Anglo-German variable-geometry aircraft e: **AGvga**

Angular Magnetic-hydrodynamic Integrating Accelerometer e: **AMIA**

Angus Wildlife Review e: **Angus Wildl Rev**

Anhydroenneaheptitol d: **AEH**

Anhydroglucic e: **AHG**

Anhydroglucochloral d: **AGC**

Anhydroglucose e: **AHG**

Anhydroglucose Unit[s] e: **AGU**

Anhydrous e: **ANH**, e: **ANHY**, e: **ANHYD**

Anhydrous Hydrazine e: **AH**

Anhydrous Hydrofluoric Acid e: **AHF**

Anhydrous Hydrogen Flouride e: **AHF**

Aniline Hydrogen Phthalate e: **AHP**

Animal e: **A**, e: **ANI**, e: **anl**

animal e: **anim**

Animal Acupuncture Academy e: **AAA**

Animal Air Transportation Association e: **AATA**

Animal Ambassadors International e: **AAI**

Animal and Dairy Science Research Institute e: **ADSRI**

Animal and Plant Control Commission e: **APCC**

Animal and Plant Health Inspection Service e: **APHIS**

Animal-Assisted Activities e: **AAA**

Animal-Assisted Therapy [Teams] e: **AAT**

Animal-Assisted-Therapy Team[s] e: **AATT**

Animal Behavior Abstracts e: **Anim Behav Abstr**

Animal Behavior Monographs e: **ANBMAW**

Animal Behaviour e: **AnB**, e: **ANBEA**, e: **Anim Behav**

Animal Behaviour. Monographs e: **Anim Behav Monogr**

Animal Behavio[u]r Society e: **ABS**

Animal Birth Control e: **ABC**

Animal Blood Groups and Biochemical Genetics e: **Anim Blood Groups Biochem Genet**

Animal Blood Groups and Biochemical Genetics [Supplement] e: **Anim Blood Groups Biochem Genet [Suppl]**

Animal Breeding e: **Anim Breed**

Animal Breeding Abstracts e: **Anim Breed Abstr**

Animal Breeding and Feeding e: **Anim Breed Feed**

Animal Breeding and Genetics Research Organization e: **ABGRO**

Animal Breeding and Research Institute e: **AB & RI**

Animal Breeding Research Organisation (or Organization) e: **ABRO**

Animal By-Products Order e: **ABPO**

Animal Care Panel e: **ACP**

Animal Control Operations e: **ACO**

animal damage control e: **adc**

Animal de Compagnie f: **Anim Compagnie**

Animal Defence Society e: **ADS**

Animal Disease and Parasite e: **ADP**

Animal Disease and Parasite Research e: **ADP Research**

Animal Disease and Parasite Research Division e: **A.D.P.**

Animal Disease Eradication e: **ADE**

Animal Disease Occurrence e: **ADO**

Animal Diseases Pathogenesis and Control Trust Fund e: **ADPC**

Animal Diseases Research Association e: **ADRA**

Animal Diseases Research Institute, Agriculture Canada Ottawa, Ontario e: **OOAGA**

Animal Drug Research Center *e:* **ADRC**
Animal Educational League *e:* **AEL**
Animal Emergency Information System *e:*
  ANEMIS
Animal Enclosure Module *e:* **AEM**
Animal Ethics Committee *e:* **AEC**
Animal Experimentation Ethics Committee
  e: **AEEC**
Animal-Facilitated Therapy *e:* **AFT**
Animal Feed and Tissue Residue Research
  Center *e:* **AFTRRC**
Animal Feed Science and Technology *e:*
  Anim Feed S
Animal Feed Science and Technology
  [Netherlands] *e:* **Anim Feed Sci
  Technol**
Animal Feeding Operations *e:* **AFO**
Animal Feeding Stuffs *e:* **AFS**
Animal Genetic Resources *e:* **AGR**, *e:*
  AnGR
Animal Genetic Resources for Food and
  Agriculture *e:* **AnGRFA**
Animal Genetics *e:* **Anim Genet**
Animal Genetics and Breeding Unit *e:*
  AGBU
Animal Guild of America *e:* **AGA**
Animal Health *e:* **ANHEA4**, *e:* **Anim
  Health**, *e:* **Anim Hlth**
Animal Health and Industries Training
  Institute *e:* **AHITI**
Animal Health Board *e:* **AHB**
Animal Health Committee *e:* **AHC**
Animal Health Distributors Association *e:*
  AHDA
Animal Health Divisional Office *e:* **AHDO**
Animal Health/Emerging Animal Disease
  e: **AHEAD**
Animal Health Information Specialists *e:*
  AHIS
Animal Health Institute *e:* **AHI**
Animal Health Insurance *e:* **AHI**
Animal Health Laboratories *e:* **AHL**
Animal Health Office *e:* **AHO**
Animal Health Research Center *e:* **AHRC**
Animal Health Technician *e:* **AHT**
Animal Health Trust *e:* **AHT**
Animal Health Yearbook *e:* **Anim Hlth Yb**
Animal Husbandry *e:* **AH**
Animal Husbandry and Dairy Research
  Institute *e:* **AHDRI**
Animal Husbandry Division *e:* **AHD**
Animal Husbandry Research Division
  [Department of Agriculture] *e:* **AH**
Animal Improvement Programs Laboratory
  e: **AIPL**
Animal Industries Advisory Group *e:*
  AIAG
Animal Industries Division *e:* **AID**
Animal Industries Research Committee *e:*
  AIRC
Animal Industry Foundation *e:* **AIF**
Animal Industry Research Institute *e:*
  AIRI
Animal Inspection and Quarantine *e:* **AI
  and Q**, *e:* **AI & Q**
Animal Inspection and Quarantine Division
  e: **AIQ**
Animal Learning and Behavior *e:* **Anim.
  Learn. Behav.**
Animal Legal Defense Fund *e:* **ALDF**
Animal Liberation Front *e:* **ALF**
Animal life of a place or time *e:* **Fauna**
Animal Medical Center *e:* **AMC**

Animal Nutrition Research Council *e:*
  ANRC, *e:* **ANRD**
Animal Parasitic Systems *e:* **APS**
Animal Pathology Laboratory, Food
  Production and Inspection Branch,
  Agriculture Canada , Saskatoon,
  Saskatchewan *e:* **SSAGA**
Animal Pest Control *e:* **APC**
Animal Pests Disease Eradication and
  Control *e:* **APDEC**
Animal Pharm World Animal Health News
  e: **APH**
Animal population ratio living in cool
  climate region *e:* **A%C**
Animal population ratio living in temperate
  climate region *e:* **B%T**
Animal population ratio living in warm
  climate region *e:* **C&W**
Animal Procurement Office[r] *e:* **APO**
Animal Production *e:* **Animal Prod**, *e:*
  Anim. Prod.
Animal Production and Health Commission
  for Asia and the Pacific *e:* **APHCA**
Animal Production Committee *e:* **APC**
Animal Productivity and Health Information
  Network *e:* **APHIN**
Animal Protection Institute of America *e:*
  API, *e:* **APIA**
animal protein factor *e:* **apf**
Animal Rescue League *e:* **A.R.L.**
Animal Research and Development *e:*
  Anim. Res. Dev.
Animal Research Facility *e:* **ARF**
Animal Research Institute *e:* **ARI**
Animal Research Institute, Agriculture
  Canada Ottawa, Ontario *e:* **OOAGAR**
Animal Research Review Panel *e:* **ARRP**
Animal Resources Centre *e:* **ARC**
Animal Rights Coalition *e:* **ARC**
Animal Rights International *e:* **ARI**
Animal Rights Law Reporter *e:* **AninW
  Rights L Rep**
Animal Rights Resource Site *e:* **ARRS**
Animal Service International *e:* **ASI**
Animal Technicians' Association *e:*
  A.T.A.
Animal Transport *e:* **APA**
Animal Transport Company *e:* **A.T.C.**
Animal Tub Sized *e:* **ATS**
Animal Tumor Research Facility *e:* **ATRF**
Animal Unit Month[s] *e:* **AUM**
Animal Vegetable and Mineral *e:* **AVM**
Animal Virus Information System *e:* **AVIS**
Animal Virus Research Institute *e:*
  A.V.R.I.
Animal Watch Australia *e:* **AWA**
Animal Welfare Advisory Committee *e:*
  AWAC
Animal Welfare Advisory Council *e:*
  AWAC
Animal Welfare Information Center *e:*
  AWIC
Animal Welfare Institute *e:* **AWI**
Animal Welfare League *e:* **AWL**
Animals Defender and Anti-Vivisectionist
  e: **Anti-Viv**
Animals without Frontiers-International *e:*
  AWF-International
Animated Biological Laboratories *e:* **ABL**
Animated Dissection of Anatomy for
  Medicine *e:* **ADAM**
Anisotropic Spin-Orbit *e:* **ASO**

Anlagen zum Herstellen, Behandeln und
  Verwenden wassergefährdender Stoffe
  e: **HBV-Anlagen**
Anlagen zum Lagern, Abfüllen und
  Umschlagen wassergefährdender Stoffe
  d: **LAU-Anlagen**
Annalen der Meteorologie *d:* **Ann.
  Meteorol.**
Annalen der Meteorologie. Neue Folge *d:*
  Ann. Meteorol. N.F.
Annalen der Natur- und Kulturphilosophie
  e: **Ann Natur Kulturphil**
Annalen der Naturphilosophie *e:* **Ann
  Naturphil**, *e:* **Ann N Ph**
Annalen der Schweizerischen
  meteorologischen Anstalt *d:* **Ann.
  Schweiz. meteorol. Anst.**
Annalen dcs Naturhistorischen Museums in
  Wien *d:* **Ann. Nat.hist. Mus. Wien**, *e:*
  ANMWAF, *e:* **Annin Naturh Mus Wien**,
  e: **Ann Naturhist Mus Wien**
Annalen des Naturhistorischen Museums in
  Wien. Serie A. Mineralogie und
  Petrographie, Geologie und
  Palaeontologie, Antrhopologie und
  Prähistorie *d:* **Ann. Nat.hist. Mus.
  Wien, A**
Annalen des Naturhistorischen Museums in
  Wien. Serie B. Botanik und Zoologie *d:*
  Ann. Nat.hist. Mus. Wien, B, *e:* **Ann
  Naturhist Mus Wien Ser B Bot Zool**
Annalen des Naturhistorischen Museums in
  Wien. Serie C. Jahresberichte *d:* **Ann.
  Nat.hist. Mus. Wien, C**
Annales Academiae Medicae Stetinensis *l:*
  Ann Acad Med Stetin
Annales Biologiques *f:* **Ann. Biol.**
Annales Chirurgiae et Gynaecologiae *l:*
  Ann Chir Gynaecol
Annales de Biologie Clinique *f:* **Ann Biol
  Clin**
Annales de Geographie *f:* **Ann. Geogr.**
Annales de Geophysique *f:* **Ann Geophys**
Annales de la Société des Sciences
  Naturelles de la Charente-Maritime *f:*
  Ann. Soc. Sci. Nat. Charente-Marit.
Annales de la Station Biologique de Besse-
  en-Chandesse *f:* **Ann. Stn. Biol. Besse-
  en-Chandesse**
Annales de l'Institut Oceanographique *f:*
  Ann. Inst. Oceanogr.
Annales de l'Institut Oceanographique,
  Paris. Nouvelle Serie *f:* **Ann. Inst.
  Oceanogr., Paris, Nouv. Ser.**
Annales de l'Observatoire National
  d'Athenes *f:* **Ann. Obs. Nat. Athenes**
Annales des Sciences Naturelles. B.
  Zoologie *f:* **Ann. Sci. Nat., B**
Annales des Sciences Naturelles. 12ème
  Serie. Zoologie et Biologie Animale *f:*
  Ann. Sci. Nat., 12
Annales Geologiques des Pays Helleniques
  f: **Ann. Geol. Pays Hell.**
Annales Geophysicae. Atmospheres,
  Hydrospheres and Space Sciences *e:*
  **Ann. Geophys. Atmos. Hydrosph. Space
  Sci.**
Annales Historico-Naturales Musei
  Nationalis Hungarici *l:* **Ann. Hist.-Nat.
  Mus. Natl. Hung.**
Annales Hydrographiques. 5ème serie *f:*
  Ann. Hydrogr., 5

Annales Instituti Biologici [Tihany] *i:*
Ann. Inst. Biol. [Tihany]

Annales Medicinae Militaris Fenniae *l:*
SOAIAG

Annales Medico-Psychologiques *f:* **Ann**
Med Psychol

Annales Scientifiques de l'Universite de
Besancon. 4ème serie. Geologie *f:* **Ann.**
Sci. Univ. Besancon., 4

Annales Universitatis Mariae Curie-
Sklodowska. Sectio D, Medicina *l:* **Ann**
Univ Mariae Curie Sklodowska [Med]

Annali di Geofisica *i:* **Ann. Geofis.**

Annali di Museo Civico di Storia Naturale
di Genova *i:* **Ann. Mus. Civ. Stor. Nat.**
Genova

Annali di Museo Civico di Storia Naturale
di Giacomo Doria *i:* **Ann. Mus. Civ.**
Stor. Nat. Giacomo Doria

Annali Italiani di Medicina Interna *i:* **Ann**
Ital Med Int

Annalis. Historico-Naturales Musei
Nationalis Hungarici *e:* **Annalis Hist-**
Nat Mus Natn Hung

Annals. Academy of Medicine [Singapore]
e: **Ann Acad Med [Singapore]**

Annals and Magazine of Natural History *e:*
An Mag N H, *e:* **Annals and Mag Nat**
History, *e:* **Ann and Mag Nat Hist,** *e:*
Ann Mag Nat Hist, *e:* **Ann Mag Natur**
Hist

Annals. Association of American
Geographers *e:* **Ann As Am G,** *e:* **Ann**
Ass Amer Geogr, *e:* **Ann Assoc Am**
Geog

Annals. Australian College of Dental
Surgeons *e:* **Ann Aust Coll Dent Surg**

Annals. ICRP [International Commission on
Radiolological Protection] *e:* **ANICD6**

Annals. Indian Academy of Medical
Sciences *e:* **AIADAX**

Annals. Lyceum of Natural History [New
York] *e:* **Ann Lyceum Nat Hist [NY]**

Annals. Medical Section. Polish Academy
of Sciences *e:* **Ann Med Sect Pol Acad**
Sci

Annals. National Academy of Medical
Sciences *e:* **Ann Natl Acad Med Sci**

Annals. National Academy of Medical
Sciences [India] *e:* **ANAIDI**

Annals of Air and Space Law *e:* **Annals**
Air and Space, *e:* **Annals Air and Space**
L

Annals of American Geographers *e:* **AAG**

Annals of Applied Biology *e:* **Ann Ap**
Biol, *e:* **Ann Appl Biol,** *e:* **Arm App Biol**

Annals of Applied Biology. Supplement *e:*
Arm Appl Biol Suppl

Annals of Behavioral Medicine *e:* **Ann**
Behav Med

Annals of Biochemistry and Experimental
Medicine [Calcutta and NewDelhi] *e:*
Ann Biochem Exp Med

Annals of Biology *e:* **Ann. Biol.**

Annals of Biomedical Engineering *e:*
ABME, *e:* **Ann Biomed Eng**

Annals of Emergency Medicine *e:* **Ann**
Emerg Med

Annals of Health Law *e:* **Annals Health L.**

Annals of Human Biology *e:* **AHUBBJ,** *e:*
Ann Hum Biol

Annals of Internal Medicine *e:* **AIM,** *e:*
Ann. Intern. Med.

Annals of Kentucky Natural History *e:*
Annals KY Nat History

Annals of Life Insurance Medicine *e:* **Ann**
lafe Ins Med

Annals of Medical History *e:* **Ann Med**
Hist

Annals of Medicine *e:* **Ann Med**

Annals of Medicine [Hagerstown,
Maryland] *e:* **Ann Med [Hagerstown**
Maryland]

Annals of Nuclear Medicine *e:* **Ann Nucl**
Med

Annals of Physical Medicine *e:* **Ann Phys**
Med, *e:* **APMDA6**

Annals of Science. Kanazawa University.
Part 2. Biology-Geology *e:* **Ann Sci**
Kanazawa Univ Part 2 Bio Geol, *e:*
KDSRA2

Annals of the Association of American
Geographers *e:* **AAAG**

Annals of the Royal College of Surgeons of
England *e:* **Ann R Coll Surg Engl**

Annals of Tropical Medicine and
Parasitology *e:* **Ann. Trop. Med.**
Parasitol.

Annals of Western Medicine and Surgery.
Los Angeles County Medical Association
e: **Ann Western Med Surg**

Annals. Research Institute of Epidemiology
and Microbiology *e:* **TNEMBJ**

Annals. Warsaw Agricultural University.
SGGW-AR [Szkola Glowna
Gospodarstwa Wiejskiego-Akademia
Rolnicza]. Animal Science *e:* **Arm**
Warsaw Agric Univ SGGW-AR Anim
Sci

Annals. Zimbabwe Geological Survey *e:*
Ann Zimbabwe Geol Surv

Annee Biologique *e:* **ANBLAT,** *f:* **Annee**
Biol.

Annexe de l'École d'Enseignement
Technique de l'Armée de Terre *f:*
A.E.E.T.A.T.

Annie Interactive Development
Environment *e:* **AIDE**

Anno Geofisico Internazionale *i:* **AGI**

Annotated Bibliography. Animal/Human
Series. Commonwealth Bureau of Animal
Health *e:* **Annot Bibliogr Anirn/Hum**
Ser Commonw Bur Anim Health

Annotated Bibliography of Economic
Geology *e:* **Annot Bibliogr Econ Geol**

Annotated Bibliography of Econornic
Geology *e:* **Annot Bibliography of**
Econ Geology

Annotated Bibliography of Medical
Mycology *e:* **Annot Bibliogr Med Myc**

Annuaire de l'Institut Meteorologique et
Climatologique. Universite de
Thessaloniki *f:* **Annu. Inst. Meteorol.**
Climatol. Univ. Thessalon.

Annual Conference on Engineering in
Medicine and Biology *e:* **ACEMB**

Annual Natural Forest Cleared *e:* **ANFC**

Annual of Animal Psychology *e:* **Ann**
Anim Ps

Annual Progress Report Geological
Survey.Western Australia *e:* **Ann Prog**
Rep Geol Surv West Austr

Annual Progress Report. SEATO [Southeast
Asia Treaty Organization] Medical
Research Laboratories *e:* **APRSCA**

Annual Report and Accounts. Anglian
Water *e:* **Annu. Rep. Acc. Anglian**
Water

Annual Report and Accounts. Irish Sea
Fisheries Board *e:* **Annu. Rep. Acc. Ir.**
Sea Fish. Board

Annual Report and Accounts. Sea Fish
Industry Authority *e:* **Annu. Rep. Acc.**
Sea Fish Ind. Auth.

Annual Report and Accounts. South West
Water Authority *e:* **Annu. Rep. Acc.**
South West Water Auth.

Annual Report and Accounts. Thames
Water Authority *e:* **Annu. Rep. Acc.**
Thames Water Auth.

Annual Report and Accounts. Yorkshire
Water Authority *e:* **Annu. Rep. Acc.**
Yorks. Water Auth.

Annual Report. Bermuda Biological Station
for Research *e:* **Annu. Rep. Bermud.**
Biol. Stn. Res.

Annual Report. Canada Water Act *e:*
Annu. Rep. Can. Water Act

Annual Report. Department of Environment
Affairs. S. Africa *e:* **Annu. Rep. Dep.**
Environ. Aff., S. Afr.

Annual Report. Department of Fisheries and
Oceans *e:* **Annu. Rep. Dep. Fish.**
Oceans

Annual Report. Department of
Oceanography, University of British
Columbia *e:* **Annu. Rep. Dep.**
Oceanogr. , Univ. B. C.

Annual Report. Durban Natural History
Museum *e:* **Annu. Rep. Durb. Nat.**
Hist. Mus.

Annual Report. Environment Canada *e:*
Annu. Rep. Environ. Can.

Annual Report. Environmental Pollution
Research Center. Fukui Prefecture *e:*
Annu Rep Environ Pollut Res Cent
Fukui Prefect

Annual Report. Environmental Pollution
Research Center of Ibaraki-Ken *e:* **Annu**
Rep Environ Pollut Res Cent Ibaraki-
Ken

Annual Report. Environmental Research
Laboratories, National Oceanic and
Atmospheric Administration *e:* **Annu.**
Rep. ERL/NOAA

Annual Report. Faculty of Education.
Gunma University. Art, Technology,
Health and Physical Education and
Science of Human Living Series *e:*
GDKKD2

Annual Report. Fish Health Unit, Faculty of
Veterinary Medicine, University of Prince
Edward Island *e:* **Annu. Rep. Fish**
Health Unit, Fac. Vet. Med., Univ.
P.E.I.

Annual Report. Fisheries Development Act.
Department of Fisheries and Oceans *e:*
Annu. Rep. Fish. Dev. Act Dep. Fish.
Oceans

Annual Report. Fisheries Improvement
Loans Act. Department of Fisheries and
Oceans [Canada] *e:* **Annu. Rep. Fish.**
Improv. Loans Act Dep. Fish. Oceans
[Can.]

Annual Report. Freshwater Biological
Association *e:* **Annu. Rep. Freshw.**
Biol. Ass.

Annual Report. Freshwater Fisheries Centre, Christchurch *e:* **Annu. Rep. Freshw. Fish. Cent., Christch.**

Annual Report. Geolecal Survey. Federation of Nigeria *e:* **Annu Rep Geol Surv Fed Niger**

Annual Report. Geological Survey and Mines Department [Swaziland] *e:* **Annu Rep Geol Surv Mines Dep [Swaziland]**

Annual Report. Geological Survey Department [Cyprus] *e:* **Annu Rep Geol Surv Dep [Cyprus]**

Annual Report. Geological Survey Department [Malawi] *e:* **Annu Rep Geol Surv Dep [Malawi]**

Annual Report. Geological Survey Division [Nigeria] *e:* **Annu Rep Geol Surv Div [Niger]**

Annual Report. Geological Survey of Malaysia] *e:* **Annu Rep Geol Surv Malays**

Annual Report. Geological Survey of Malaysia *e:* **Annu Rep Geol Surv Malaysia**

Annual Report. Geological Survey. Westem Australia *e:* **Annu Rep Geol Surv West Aust**

Annual Report. Geophysical Commission [Norway] *e:* **Annu Rep Geophys Comm [Norw]**

Annual Report. Institute of Landscape Ecology *e:* **Annu. Rep. Inst. Landsc. Ecol.**

Annual Report. Institute of Oceanographic Sciences *e:* **Annu. Rep. Inst. Oceanogr. Sci.**

Annual Report. Iowa Cooperative Fish and Wildlife Research Unit *e:* **Annu. Rep. Iowa Coop. Fish Wildl. Res. Unit**

Annual Report. Laboratory of Public Health. Hiroshirna Prefecture *e:* **Annu Rep Lab Public Health Hiroshima Prefect**

Annual Report. Marine Biological Association of the United Kingdom *e:* **Annu. Rep. Mar. Biol. Assoc. U.K.**

Annual Report. Natinal Oceanic and Atmospheric Administration, Environmental Reserach Laboratories, Pacific Marine Environmental Research Laboratory *e:* **Annu. Rep. NOAA/ERL/PMEL**

Annual Report. National Center for Atmospheric Research *e:* **Annu. Rep. Natl. Cent. Atmos. Res.**

Annual Report. National Institute for Freshwater Fisheries Research *e:* **Annu. Rep. Natl. Inst. Freshw. Fish. Res.**

Annual Report. National Oceanic and Atmospheric Administration, Enrivonmental Research Laboratories, Great Lakes Environmental Research Laboratory *e:* **Annu. Rep. NOAA/ERL/GLEL**

Annual Report. National Oceanographic Data Center *e:* **Annu. Rep. NODC**

Annual Report. Natural Products Research Institute. Seoul National University *e:* **STSODQ**

Annual Report. Netherlands Institute for Sea Research *e:* **Annu Rep Neth Inst Sea Res**

Annual Report. Netherlands Institute for the Law of the Sea *e:* **Annu. Rep. Neth. Inst. Law Sea**

Annual Report. Nigerian Institute for Oceanography and Marine Research [Lagos] *e:* **Annu Rep Nigerian Inst Oceanogr Mar Res [Lagos]**

Annual Report. North West Water Authority *e:* **Annu. Rep. North West Water Auth.**

Annual Report. Nothumbrian Water *e:* **Annu. Rep. Northumbr. Water**

Annual Report. Oceanic Institute, Honolulu *e:* **Annu. Rep. Ocean. Inst., Honolulu**

Annual Report of Chicago Natural History Museum *e:* **Annu. Rep. Chicago Nat. Hist. Mus.**

Annual Report of Natural Science and Home Economics. Kinjo Gakuin College *e:* **Annu Rep Natur Sci Home Econ Kinio Gakuin Coll**

Annual Report of Oceanographic Observations. National Fisheries Research and Development Agency *e:* **Annu. Rep. Oceanogr. Obs. Natl. Fish. Res. Dev. Agency**

Annual Report of the Director Department of Plant Biology *e:* **Annu. Rep. Dir. Dep. Plant Biol.**

Annual Report of the National Institute of Oceanography *e:* **Annu. Rep. Natl. Inst. Oceanogr.**

Annual Report on Geophysical Research in Norway *e:* **Annu Rep Geophys Res Norw**

Annual Report. Sado Marine Biological Station. Niigata University *e:* **SRJKAK**

Annual Report. Scottish Marine Biological Association *e:* **Annu. Rep. Scott. Mar. Biol. Ass.**

Annual Report. Scripps Institution of Oceanography *e:* **Annu. Rep. Scripps Inst. Oceanogr.**

Annual Report. Sea Fisheries Institute, Gdynia *e:* **Annu. Rep. Sea Fish. Inst., Gdynia**

Annual Report. Sir Alister Hardy Foundation for Ocean Science *e:* **Annu. Rep. Sir Alister Hardy Found. Ocean Sci.**

Annual Report. Southern California Coastal Water Research Project *e:* **Annu. Rep. South. Calif. Coast. Water Res. Proj.**

Annual Report. University Marine Biological Station, Millport *e:* **Annu. Rep. Univ. Mar. Biol. Stn., Millport**

Annual Reports in Medicinal Chemistry *e:* **Annu Rep Med Chem**

Annual Reports. Natural Products Research Institute. Seoul National University *e:* **Annu Rep Nat Prod Res Inst Seoul Natl Univ**

Annual Research Reviews. Proteins of Animal Cell Plasma Membranes *e:* **Annu Res Rev Proteins Anim Cell Plasma Membr**

Annual Review. Freshwater Fisheries Laboratory of Pitlochry *e:* **Annu. Rev. Freshw. Fish. Lab. Pitlochry**

Annual Review. Marine Laboratory, Aberdeen *e:* **Annu. Rev. Mar. Lab., Aberd.**

Annual Review of Cell Biology *e:* **Annu Rev Cell Biol**

Annual Review of Earth and Planetary Science Letters *e:* **Annu. Rev. Earth Planet. Sci. Lett.**

Annual Review of Earth and Planetary Sciences *e:* **Annu Rev Earth Planet Sci**

Annual Review of Energy and the Environment *e:* **Annu. Rev. Energy Environ.**

Annual Review of Medicine *e:* **Annu. Rev. Med.**

Annual Review of Microbiology *e:* **Annu. Rev. Microbiol.**

Annual Review of Ocean Affairs: Law and Policy, Main Documents *e:* **Annu. Rev. Ocean Aff. Law Policy Main Docs.**

Annual Review of Plant Physiology and Plant Molecular Biology *e:* **Annu. Rev. Plant Physiol. Plant Mol. Biol.**

Annual Review of Public Health *e:* **Annu Rev Public Health**

Annual Site Environmental Report *e:* **ASER**

Annual Summary of Fish Harvesting Activities, Western Canadian Freshwater Fisheries *e:* **Annu. Summ. Fish Harvest. Act. ,West. Can. Freshw. Fish.**

Annual Symposium. Eastern Pennsylvania Branch, American Society for Microbiology. Proceedings *e:* **Annu Symp East PA Branch Am Soc Microbiol Proc**

Annual to Decadal Variability in Climate in Europe *e:* **ADVICE**

Annual UMR-DNR [University of Missouri, Rolla-Department of Natural Resources] Conference on Energy. Proceedings *e:* **Annu UMR-DNR Conf Energy Proc**

Année Géophysique Internationale *f:* **AGI**

Année internationale de l'espace *f:* **ISY**

Año Geofísico Internacional *s:* **AGI**

Año Polar Internacional *s:* **API**

Anomalistic Observational Phenomena *e:* **AOP**

Antarctic and other Ocean Environment *e:* **ASOE**

Antarctic and Southern Ocean Environment *e:* **ASOE**

Antarctic benthic DEEP-sea biodiversity *e:* **ANDEEP**

Antarctic Bottom Water *e:* **ABW**

Antarctic Bottom Water [science] *e:* **AABW**

Antarctic Circumpolar Current *e:* **ACC**

Antarctic Circumpolar Current Levels from Altimetry and Island Measurement *e:* **ACCLAIM**

Antarctic Circumpolar Wave *e:* **ACW**

Antarctic Environmental Data Centre *e:* **AEDC**

Antarctic Environmental Implications of Mineral Exploration and Exploitation *e:* **AEIMEE**

Antarctic Environmental Officers Network *e:* **AEON**

Antarctic Geodesy Symposium *e:* **AGS**

Antarctic Geophysical Observatory Network *e:* **AGONET**

Antarctic Ice Drifting Buoy Programme *e:* **AIDBP**

Antarctic Ice Margin Evolution *e:* **ANTIME**

Antarctic Ice Thickness Measurement Programme *e:* **AnITMP**

Antarctic Ice Thickness Monitoring Project *e:* **AnITMP**

Antarctic Intermediate Water *e:* **AAIW**

Antarctic Marine Ecosystem Research at the Ice-edge Zone *e:* **AMERIEZ**

Antarctic Meteorite Bibliography *e:* **AMB**

Antarctic Observation Team *e:* **AOT**

Antarctic Ocean *e:* **Antarc O**

Antarctic Pack Ice Seals Programme *e:* **APIS**

Antarctic Protected Area *e:* **APA**

Antarctic Reception Imagery for Environmental Studies *e:* **ARIES**

Antarctic Remote Sensing Aerial Photography and Mapping Information System *e:* **ARAMIS**

Antarctic Sea Ice Processes, Ecosystems and Climate *e:* **ASPECT**

Antarctic Sea Ice Thickness Project /WCRP/ *e:* **ASITP**

Antarctic Specially Protected Area *e:* **ASPA**

Antarctic Submillimeter Telescope and Remote Observatory *e:* **ASTRO**

Antarctic Water Mass *e:* **AAWM**

Antarctic Wilderness Park *e:* **AWP**

Antarctic[a] and Southern Ocean[s] Coalition *e:* **ASOC**

Anteil der nach unten reflektierten Strahlung *d:* **DRC**

Anthrahydroquinone *e:* **AHQ**

Anthropogenic Climate Change *e:* **ACC**, *e:* **CLIVAR-ACC**

Anthropogenic Hydrocarbons *e:* **AHC**

Anthropogeography *e:* **anthro**

Anthropological Papers. American Museum of Natural History *e:* **APAM**, *e:* **APAMNH**

Anti-Aircraft Observation Post *e:* **AAOP**

Anti-Aitcraft Artillery Remote-Controlled Aerial Target *e:* **AAARCAT**

Anti-Bonding Molecular Orbital *e:* **ABMO**

Anti-ice/De-ice System *e:* **ADS**

Anti-Slavery and Aborigines Protection Society *e:* **A.S.A.P.S.**

Anti-Slavery Society for the Protection of Human Rights *e:* **A.S.S.**, *e:* **ASSPHR**

Anti-Submarine Warfare Environmental Prediction Service[s] *e:* **ASWEPS**

Anti-Submarine Warfare Environmental Prediction System *e:* **ASWEPS**

Anti-trust and Consumer Protection Division *e:* **ACPD**

Antiaircraft Artillery Remote Control *e:* **AAARC**

Antiaircraft Artillery Remote Control Repair Foreman *e:* **AAARC Rep Fman**

Antiaircraft Artillery Remote Control Repair Helper *e:* **AAARC Rep Hlpr**

Antiaircraft Artillery Remote Control Repair Inspector *e:* **AAARC Rep Insp**

Antiaircraft Artillery Remote Control Repairman *e:* **AAARC Repm**

Antiaircraft Artillery Remote-Controlled Aerial Target Detachment *e:* **AAARCAT Det**, *e:* **AARCAT Det**

Antibiotic Medicine and Clinical Therapy *e:* **AM & CT**

anticlimactic[al][ly] *e:* **anticli**

anticlimax *e:* **anticli**

antigenpräsentierende Zelle *d:* **APZ**

Antimissile Missile and Space Defense Office *e:* **AMMSDO**

Antioquia Medica *e:* **ANMDAQ**

Antisubmarine Warfare/Underwater Warfare *e:* **ASW/UW**

Antiunderwater Warfare *e:* **AUW**

Anuario Estadistico de Pesca. Secretaria de Medio Ambiente Recursos Naturales y Pesca *s:* **Anu. Estad. Pesca Secr. Medio Ambient. Recur. Nat. Pesca**

Anuarul. Comitetului de Stat Geologiei. Republica Romania *ru:* **Anu Com Stat Geol Repub Soc Rom**

Anuarul. Institutului de Patologie si Igiena Animala [Bucurcsti] *ru:* **APIGAT**

Anuarul. Institutului de Patologie si Igiena Animala *ru:* **Anu Inst Patol Ig Anim**

Anuarul. Institutului Geologie [Romania] *ru:* **Anu Inst Geol [Rom]**

Anuário Geográfico do Estado do Rio de Janeiro. Conselho Nacional de Geografía, Instituto Brasileiro de Geografía e Estadística. Rio *p:* **IBGE/A.**

anverdelse *a:* **anv**

Anwendungs- und bedienungsorientiertes Computersystem *d:* **ABC**

Anzeiger für Schädlingskunde, Pflanzenschutz, Umweltschutz *d:* **Anz. Schädl.kd. Pflanzenschutz Umweltschutz**

Aomori Journal of Medicine *e:* **AOPA Med**

Aperture Card Remote Imaging System *e:* **ACRIS**

Aplicaciones Geológicas de la Teledetección *s:* **GARS**

Aplicación de las computadoras a la climatología *s:* **CLICOM**

Apollo Bioenvironmental Information System *e:* **ABIS**

Apollo Earth-Orbiting Station *e:* **AES**

Apollo Environmental Control System *e:* **AECS**

Apollo Lunar Orbit *e:* **ALO**

Apollo Lunar Orbital Science *e:* **ALOS**

Apollo Lunar Polar Orbiter *e:* **ALPO**

Apollo Orbital Research Laboratory *e:* **AORL**

Apollo Orbiting Laboratory Module *e:* **AOLM**

Apollo Simulated Remote Site *e:* **ASRS**

Apollo Space Program *e:* **ASP**

Apollo Spacecraft Development Test Plan *e:* **ASDTP**

Apollo Spacecraft Hardware Utilization Request *e:* **ASHUR**

Apollo Spacecraft Parts and Materials Information Service[s] *e:* **ASPMIS**

Apollo Space[craft] Program (or Project) Office *e:* **ASPO**

Apollo Spacecraft Project *e:* **ASP**

Apostleship of the Sea *e:* **AOS**

Appalachian Center for Occupational Safety and Health *e:* **ACOSH**

Appalachian Environmental Laboratory *e:* **AEL**

Appalachian Geological Society *e:* **AGS**

Appalachian Geological Society. Bulletin *e:* **Appalachian Geol Soc Bull**

Appalachian Laboratory for Occupational Safety and Health *e:* **ALOSH**

Appareil Normal de Protection *f:* **ANP**

Apparent Polar Wander *e:* **APW**

Apparent Polar Wander Path *e:* **APWP**

Apple Media Tool Programming Environment *e:* **AMTPE**

Appleton-Century-Crofts Medical *e:* **ACCM P-H**

Application de l'informatique à la climatologie *f:* **CLICOM**

Application Development Environment *e:* **ADE**

Application Environment Profile *e:* **AEP**

Application Environment Services *e:* **AES**

Application Environment Standard *e:* **AES**

Application of Isotope Techniques in Hydrology and Hydraulics *e:* **Appl Isot Tech Hydrol Hydraul**

Application of Remote Manipulators in Space *e:* **ARMS**

Application of Remote Manipulators in Space Robot *e:* **ARMS Robot**

Application of Space Techniques Relating to Aviation *e:* **ASTRA**

Application of Space Techniques Relating to Aviation Panel *e:* **ASTRAP**

Application Operating Environment *e:* **AOE**

Application Remote Database *e:* **ARD**

Application Specific Depository of Object Oriented Environment *e:* **ADOORE-CP94-764**

Application Support Environment *e:* **ASE**

Applications and Research Involving Space Techniques for the Observation of the Earth's fields from Low-Earth-orbit Spacecraft *e:* **ARISTOTELES**

Applications and Research Involving Space Technologies Observing Earth's Field from Low Orbiting Satellite *e:* **ARISTOTLES**

Applications Environment System *e:* **AES**

Applications Execution Environment *e:* **AXE**

Applications of Commercial Oxygen to Water and Wastewater Systems *e:* **Appl Commer Oxygen Water Wastewater Syst**

Applications of Hamlet Tools to Embedded Medical Instruments Design *e:* **AHMED-CP96-144**

Applications of Meteorology Programme *e:* **AMP**

Applications Program Environment *e:* **API**

Applied and Environmental Microbiology *e:* **AEM**, *e:* **App Environ Microbiol**, *e:* **Appl Environ Microbiol**

Applied and Environmentat Microbiology *e:* **Appl Envir Microbiol**

Applied Animal Behaviour Science *e:* **Appl Anim Behav Sci**

Applied Animal Ethology *e:* **Appl Anim Ethol**, *e:* **Appl Anim Ethology**

Applied Biochemistry and Microbiology *e:* **Appl Biochem Micr**, *e:* **Appl Biochem Microbiol**

Applied Biochemistry and Microbiology [English Translation of Prikladnaya Biokhimiya i Mikrobiologiya] *e:* **Appl Biochem Microbiol [Engl Transl Prikl Biokhim Mikrobiol]**

Applied Biological Science *e:* **Appl. Biol. Sci.**

Applied Biology/Chemistry *e:* **ABC**

Applied Climate Research Unit *e:* **ACRU**

Applied Ecology Abstracts *e:* **Appl. Ecol. Abstr.**

Applied Geochemistry e: **Appl. Geochem.**

Applied Geography and Development e: **Appl. Geogr. Dev.**

Applied Geomechanics e: **App Geomech**

Applied Health Physics Ind. e: **AHP**

Applied Meteorology Unit e: **AMU**

Applied Microbiology e: **AM**, e: **APMBAY**, e: **ApMicrobiol**, e: **Appl Microbiol**, e: **App Microbiol**

Applied Microbiology and Biotechnology e: **Appl Microbiol Biotechnol**

Applied Microbiology, Inc. e: **APLY**

Applied Ocean Research e: **Appl Ocean Res**

Applied Plant Ecology Research Unit e: **APERU**

Applied Radiology and Nuclear Medicine e: **Appl Radiol Nud Med**

Applied Rangeland Ecology Program e: **AREP**

Applied Remote Sensing Program e: **ARSP**

Applied Research for Child Health e: **ARCH**

Applied Soil Ecology e: **Appl. Soil Ecol.**

Applied Space Technology-Regional Advancement e: **ASTRA**

Applied Water e: **AW**

Appreciation of Capital, Protection, Income e: **API**

appretieren d: **appr.**

appretiert d: **appr.**

Approaches to the Cell Biology of Neurons e: **Approaches Cell Biol Neurons**

Approbationsordnung für Tierärzte d: **TAppO**

Appropriate Health Resources and Technologies Action Group e: **AHRTAG**

Appropriate Technology for Health Information System e: **ATHIS**

Aquatic Biological Laboratory e: **ABL**

Aquatic Biology Abstracts e: **Ab**

Aquatic Ecosystem Health and Management Society e: **AEHMS**

Aquatic Environment Monitoring Report. Directorate of Fisheries Research e: **Aquat. Environ. Monit. Rep. Dir. Fish. Res.**

Aquatic Environment Protection. Analytical methods. Directorate of Fisheries Research e: **Aquat. Environ. Prot. Anal. Methods Dir. Fish. Res.**

Aquatic Environmental Protection e: **AEP**

Aquatic Geochemistry e: **Aquat. Geochem.**

Aquatic Microbial Ecology e: **Aquat. Microb. Ecol.**

Aquatic Microbiological Ecology. Procceding e: **Aquat Microbiol Ecol Proc**

Aquatic Sciences and Fisheries Abstracts. Part I. Biological Sciences and Living Resources e: **Aquat Sci Fish Abst Part I**

Aquatic Sciences and Fisheries Abstracts. Part II. Ocean Technology, Policy, and Non-Living Resources e: **Aquat Sci Fish Abst Part II**

Aquatic Sciences and Fisheries Abstracts. Pt. 3. Aquatic Pollution and Environmental Quality e: **Aquat. Sci. Fish. Abstr., 3**

Aqueous Water-Soluble Chelator e: **AWSC**

Arab Center (or Centre) for Medical Research e: **ACMR**

Arab Centre for Medical Literature e: **ACML**

Arab Company for Drug Industries and Medical Appliances e: **ACDIMA**

Arab Medical Information Network e: **AMIN**

Arab Organization for Space Communications e: **AOSC**

Arab Union for/of Pharmaceutical Manufacturers and Medical Appliance Manufacturers e: **AUPAM**

Aracytidine\Hydroxyurea e: **ara-C-HU**

Arafura Sea between Australia and New Guinea e: **Arafura**

Aral Sea e: **Aral**

Aransas National Wildlife Refuge near Rockport, Texas e: **Aransas**

Araucariana. Serie Geociencias s: **Araucariana Ser Geocienc**

Arbeiten. Biologischen Reichsanstalt für Land- und Forstwirtschaft [Berlin] d: **Arb Biol Reichanst Land Forstw [Berlin]**

Arbeitgeberverband Gas, Wasser, Elektrizität d: **GWE**

Arbeitgeberverband von Gas-, Wasser- und Elektrizitätsunternehmungen d: **AGWE**

Arbeitsgemeinschaft beruflicher und ehrenamtlicher Naturschutz e.V. d: **ABN**

Arbeitsgemeinschaft Betriebsfunk der Straßenunterhaltungs-, Pannenhilfs- und Wasserregulierungsdienste d: **ABS**

Arbeitsgemeinschaft der Akkreditierungsstellen für Umweltanalytik d: **ARGE-Umwelt**

Arbeitsgemeinschaft der leitenden Medizinalbeamten der Länder d: **AGLMB**

Arbeitsgemeinschaft der Sozialdemokraten im Gesundheitswesen d: **ASG**

Arbeitsgemeinschaft der Verbände der Gas- und Wasserwerke d: **AGW**

Arbeitsgemeinschaft der Volksgesundheitsbewegung e.V. d: **ADV**

Arbeitsgemeinschaft der Wasserwerke im Wesereinzugsgebiet d: **AWW**

Arbeitsgemeinschaft der Wasserwirtschaftsverbände e.V. d: **AWWV**

Arbeitsgemeinschaft der Wissenschaftlichen Medizinischen Fachgesellschaften d: **ZÖWMF**

Arbeitsgemeinschaft Deutscher Beauftrager für Naturschutz und Landschaftspflege d: **ADBNL**

Arbeitsgemeinschaft Deutscher Tierschutz d: **ADT**

Arbeitsgemeinschaft Deutscher Tierzüchter d: **ADT**

Arbeitsgemeinschaft für Berufs- und Umweltdermatologie e.V. in der Deutschen Dermatologischen Gesellschaft d: **ABD**

Arbeitsgemeinschaft für die geordnete und kontrollierte Ablagerung von industriellen und gewerblichen Abfällen d: **AfIA**

Arbeitsgemeinschaft für Forstschutz und Naturkunde d: **Arfo**

Arbeitsgemeinschaft für internistische Intensivmedizin d: **AIM**

Arbeitsgemeinschaft für medizinische Ethik und Gesellschaftsbildung e.V. d: **AMEG**

Arbeitsgemeinschaft für naturnahen Obst- Gemüse- und Feldfruchtanbau e: **ANOG**

Arbeitsgemeinschaft für Ornithologie und Naturschutz d: **AGON**

Arbeitsgemeinschaft für physikalische Weltraumforschung d: **APW**

Arbeitsgemeinschaft für Regionale Struktur- und Umweltforschung d: **ARSU**

Arbeitsgemeinschaft für soziale und medizinische Entwicklungshilfe e.V. d: **ASME**

Arbeitsgemeinschaft für sparsamen und umweltfreundlichen Energieverbrauch e.V. d: **ASUE**

Arbeitsgemeinschaft für theoretische und klinische Leistungsmedizin der Hochschullehrer Österreichs d: **ATKL**

Arbeitsgemeinschaft für Umweltfragen e.V. d: **AGU**

Arbeitsgemeinschaft für Wasser- und Lufttechnik d: **AWL**

Arbeitsgemeinschaft für Weltraumforschung d: **AfW**

Arbeitsgemeinschaft für Wirkstoffe in der Tierernährung e.V. d: **AWT**

Arbeitsgemeinschaft für Zucht und Prüfung deutscher Pferde d: **ADP**

Arbeitsgemeinschaft Hamburger Jugendverbände für Natur- und Umweltschutz d: **AGJNU**

Arbeitsgemeinschaft Kritische Tiermedizin d: **AGKT**

Arbeitsgemeinschaft Limnologie und Gewässerschutz d: **ALG**

Arbeitsgemeinschaft Luftfahrt- und Raumfahrttechnik d: **ALRT**

Arbeitsgemeinschaft medizinischer Laboratoriumsdiagnostik d: **AML**

Arbeitsgemeinschaft Rheinwasserwerke e.V. d: **ARW**

Arbeitsgemeinschaft Spacelab-Nutzung d: **ASN**

Arbeitsgemeinschaft Spina bifida und Hydrocephalus e.V. d: **ASbH**

Arbeitsgemeinschaft Strahlen- und Umweltschutz d: **ASTRUM**

Arbeitsgemeinschaft Umweltplanung Niederelbe d: **AUN**

Arbeitsgemeinschaft Umweltschutz d: **AGUS**

Arbeitsgemeinschaft Wasser d: **AWA**

Arbeitsgemeinschaft Wasserwerke Bodensee-Rhein d: **AWBR**

Arbeitsgemeinschaft wissenschaftlich- medizinischer Fachgesellschaften d: **AWMF**

Arbeitsgruppe Boden, Wasser, Luft des VSTV [Verband der schweizerischen Textilveredlungsindustrie] d: **BWL Textil**

Arbeitsgruppe für Luft- und Raumfahrt d: **ALR**

Arbeitsgruppe "Gesundes Bauen - Gesundes Wohnen" d: **AGBW**

Arbeitsgruppe Leben und Umwelt d: **ALU**

Arbeitsgruppe Umwelt, Gesellschaft, Energie d: **AUGE**

Arbeitsgruppe Umwelt-Statistik d: **ARGUS**

Arbeitsgruppe Umweltfragen in der Lehrerausbildung d: **AGUL**

Arbeitsgruppen für Strukturelle Molekularbiologie der MPG am DESY d: **ASMB**

Arbeitskreis Deutscher Klein- und Pelztierzüchter d: **ADKPZ**

Arbeitskreis für gesundes Leben d: **AKGL**

Arbeitskreis für medizinische Entwicklung d: **AKME**

Arbeitskreis [für] Umweltschutz d: **AKU**

Arbeitskreis für Wildbiologie und Jagdwissenschaft d: **AKW**

Arbeitskreis Geographische Informationssysteme d: **AKGIS**

Arbeitskreis Ingenieure und Naturwissenschaftler in der Industrie d: **AIN**

Arbeitskreis Orientierungs- und Bildungshilfe [gegen Analphabetismus] d: **AOB**

Arbeitskreis Umwelt d: **AkU**

Arbeitskreis Umwelt Dortmund d: **AKU-DO**

Arbeitskreis Umweltschutz d: **AU**

Arbeitskreis Wildbiologie und Jagdwissenschaft d: **AKWJ**

Arbeitsmedizin e: **ARB**

Arbeitsschutz und Arbeitsmedizin d: **A & A**

Arbeitswissenschaftliche Projektierung d: **AWP**

Arcansas National Wildlife Refuge e: **ANWR**

ARCAS (All-Purpose Rocket for Collecting Atmospheric Soundings) Piggyback Emulsi e: **APEX**

Archaeologia Geographica l: **ArchGeogr**

Archaeological Research, Environment Canada Ottawa, Ontario e: **OOEAB**

Archaeological Resources Protection Act e: **ARPA**

Archäologie und Naturwissenschaften d: **A Natur Wiss**

Architectural Space Laboratory, Zürich e: **ASL**

Archiv der Freunde der Naturgeschichte in Mecklenburg d: **Arch. Freunde Naturgesch. Mecklenbg.**

Archiv für Hydrobiologie d: **Arch. Hydrobiol.**

Archiv für Hydrobiologie. Supplementband. Algological Studies d: **Arch. Hydrobiol. Suppl. Algol. Stud.**

Archiv für Hydrobiologie. Supplementband. Arbeiten aus dem Limnologischen Institut der Universität Konstanz d: **Arch. Hydrobiol. Suppl. Arb. Limnol. Inst. Univ. Konstanz**

Archiv für Hydrobiologie. Supplementband. Large Rivers d: **Arch. Hydrobiol. Suppl. Large Rivers**

Archiv für Hydrobiologie. Supplementband. Monographische Beiträge d: **Arch. Hydrobiol. Suppl. Monogr. Beitr.**

Archiv für Hydrobiologie. Supplementband. Untersuchungen des Elbe-Aestuars d: **Arch. Hydrobiol. Suppl. Unters. Elbe-Aestuars**

Archiv für Meteorologie, Geophysik und Bioklimatologie, Serie A d: **Arch. Meteorol. Geophys. Biokl**

Archiv für Meteorologie, Geophysik und Bioklimatologie, Serie B d: **Arch. Meteorol. Geophys. Biokl**, d: **Arch. Meteorol. Geophys. Bioklimatol., Ser. B**

Archiv für Mikrobiologie d: **Arch. Mikrobiol.**

Archiv für Naturschutz und Landschaftsforschung d: **Arch. Nat.schutz Landsch.forsch.**

Archiv für Tierernährung d: **Arch Tierernahr**

Archival Climatic History Survey e: **ARCHISS**

Archives. Centre de Recherches Oceanographique, Dakar-Thiaroye f: **Arch. Cent. Rech. Oceanogr., Dakar-Thiaroye**

Archives des Freres des Ecoles Chretiennes f: **QLFECA**

Archives Geologiques du Vietnam f: **VNAGA2**

Archives Italiennes de Biologie f: **Arch Ital Biol**

Archives of Environmental Contamination and Toxicology e: **AECTC**, e: **Arch Environ Contam Toxicol**

Archives of Environmental Health e: **AEH**, e: **Arch. Environ Health**

Archives of Family Medicine e: **Arch Fam Med**

Archives of Gynecology snd Obstetrics e: **Arch Gynecol Obstet**

Archives of Internal Medicine e: **Arch. Intern. Med.**

Archives of Medical Research e: **Arch Med Res**

Archives of Microbiology e: **Arch Microbiol**

Archives of Natural History e: **ANHIDJ**

Archives of Oral Biology e: **Arch. Oral Biol.**

Archives of Pathology and Laboratory Medicine e: **APLMAS**, e: **Arch Pathol Lab Med**

Archives of Pediatrics and Adolescent Medicine e: **Arch Pediatr Adolesc Med**

Archives of Physical Medicine and Rehabilitation e: **Arch Phys Med Rehabil**

Archives of Physics, Medicine and Rehabilitation e: **APMHAI**

Archives of Podiatric Medicine and Foot Surgery e: **APMSDK**

Archives Portupises des Sciences Biologigues f: **APSBAU**

Archives. Sciences de la Mer. Biologie Marine. Centre de Noumea, ORSTOM f: **Arch. Sci. Mer Biol. Mar. Cent. Noumea, ORSTOM**

Archives. Sciences de la Mer. Oceanographie Physique. Centre de Noumea, ORSTOM f: **Arch. Sci. Mer Oceanogr. Phys. Cent. Noumea, ORSTOM**

Archiving, Validation and Investigation in Satellite Oceanography (France) e: **AVISO**

Archivio di Oceanografia e Limnologia i: **Arch. Oceanogr. Limnol.**

Archivists and Librarians in the History of the Health Sciences e: **ALHHS**

Archivo Iberoamericano de Historia de la Medicina. Consejo Superior de Investigaciones Científicas, Instituto s: **IAV/AIHM.**

Archivo, Validación e Interpretación de Datos de Satélites Oceanográficos s: **AVISO**

Archivos de Biologia y Medicina Experimental s: **Arch. Biol. Med. Exp.**

ARCS Meteorological Instruments e: **SMET**

Arctic Aeromedical Laboratory e: **AAML**

Arctic Aeromedical (or Aerospace) Laboratory e: **AAL**

Arctic/Atlantic/Atmospheric Boundary Layer Experiment e: **ABLE-2B**

Arctic Atmospheric Radiation and Cloud Station e: **A-ARCS**

Arctic Beaufort Sea Oilspill Research Body e: **ABSORB**

Arctic Biological Station, Fisheries and Oceans Canada Ste-Anne-De-Bellevue, Quebec e: **QMFR**

Arctic Climate Systems Study e: **ACSYS**

Arctic Environment Information and Data Center e: **AEIDC**

Arctic Environment[al] Data Directory e: **AEDD**

Arctic Environmental Data Directory Working Group e: **AEDDWG**

Arctic Environmental Data System e: **AEDS**

Arctic Environmental Database for Europe and Asia e: **AEDEA**

Arctic Environmental Engineering Laboratory e: **AEEL**

Arctic Environmental Field Station e: **AEFS**

Arctic Environmental Information [and] Data Center (or Centre) e: **AEIDC**

Arctic Environment[al] Protection Strategy e: **AEPS**

Arctic Environmental Research Laboratory e: **AERL**

Arctic Environmental System in Global Change and its Impact to East Asia e: **AESEA**

Arctic Geographic Information System e: **AGIS**

Arctic Health Research Laboratory e: **AHRL**

Arctic Health Services Research Center e: **AHSRC**

Arctic Ice Deformation Joint Experiment e: **AIDJEX**

Arctic Ice Monitoring System e: **AIMS**

Arctic Ice-Ocean-Atmosphere Interactions e: **ARICE**

Arctic Ice Thickness Monitoring Project e: **AITMP**

Arctic Ice Thickness Project e: **AITP**

Arctic International Wildlife Range Society e: **AIWRS**

Arctic Long-Term Environmental Research Transects [program] e: **ALERT**

Arctic Marine Engineering Geological Expedition e: **AMEGE**

Arctic Marine Engineering Geological Expeditions e: **AMIGE**

Arctic Medical Research e: **Arctic Med Res**

Arctic Meteorology Photographic Probe e:
AMPP
Arctic Military Environmental Cooperation
e: **AMEC**
Arctic National Wildlife Refuge e: **ANWR**
Arctic National Wildlife Reserve e:
ANWR
Arctic Natural Sciences Program e: **ANSP**
Arctic Natural Wildlife Refuge in Alaska
e: **ANWR**
Arctic Ocean e: **Arc O**
Arctic Ocean and Region e: **r**
Arctic Ocean Buoy e: **AOB**
Arctic Ocean Buoy Program e: **AOBP**
Arctic Ocean Climate Station e: **AOCS**
Arctic Ocean Climate Station Network e:
AOCSN
Arctic Ocean Environment Simulator e:
AOES
Arctic Ocean Grand Challenge e: **AOGC**
Arctic Ocean Radiative Fluxes e: **AORF**
Arctic Ocean Science[s] Board e: **AOSB**
Arctic Ocean System in the Global
Environment e: **AOSGE**
Arctic Ocean Variability Project e: **AOVP**
Arctic Regional Climate simulation e:
ARCsym
Arctic Regional Climate System Model e:
ARCSYM
Arctic Remote Autonomous Measurement
Platform e: **ARAMP**
Arctic Research Laboratory Ice Station e:
ARLIS
Arctic Terrestrial Environmental Research
Programs e: **ATERP**
Arctic Wildlife Refuge e: **AWR**
Area Airspace Management Authority e:
AAMA
Area Health Authority e: **AHA**
Area Health Authority (Teaching) e:
AHA(T)
Area Health Education Center e: **AHEC**
Area Health Education Officer e: **AHEO**
Area Medical Officer e: **AMO**
Area Meteorological Coordinator e: **AMC**
Área OceÁnica de Control s: **OCA**
Area of equatorial plane of Earth e: **F**
Area Protect Feature e: **APF**
Area[s] of Critical Environmental Concern
e: **ACEC**
Arecibo Initiative with Dynamics of the
Atmosphere e: **AIDA**
Arecibo Ionospheric Observatory e: **AIO**
Argonne Boiling Water Reactor e:
ARBOR
Argonne National Laboratory. Energy and
Environmental Systems Division. Report
ANL/CNSV e: **ANLSD**
Arhitektonsko-Gradevinarsko-Geodetski
fakultet se: **AGG**
Arianespace SA, Paris f: **AE**
Arid Climate, Adaptation and Cultural
Innovation in Africa e: **ACACIA**
Arid Land Ecology Project e: **ALE**
Project
Arid Land[s] Ecology e: **ALE**
Arid Lands Environment Centre e: **ALEC**
Arizona Bureau of Geology and Mineral
Technology e: **ABGMT**
Arizona Department of Water Resources e:
ADWR
Arizona Geographic Information Council
e: **AGIC**

Arizona Highway Department -
Environment Planning Division e:
AZHD-EPD
Arizona Photopolarimeter Telescope e:
APT
Arizona Regional Ecological Test Site e:
ARETS
Arizona State Medical Association e:
ASMA
Arizona Water Information System e:
AWIS
Arkansas Department of Health e: **ADH**
Arkansas Department of Pollution Control
and Ecology e: **ADPCE**
Arkansas Geological Commission e: **AGC**
Arkansas National Wildlife Refuge e:
ANWR
Arkansas Veterinary Medical Association
e: **AVMA**
ARM-FIRE Water Vapor Experiment e:
AFWEX
ARM Ocean Working Group e: **AWOG**
Armed Forces Central Medical Registry e:
AFCMR
Armed Forces Health Professions
[Professional] Scholarship Program e:
AFHPSP
Armed Forces Medical Aid Association e:
AFMAA
Armed Forces Medical Intelligence Center
e: **AFMIC**
Armed Forces Medical Library e: **AFML**
Armed Forces Medical Procurement Agency
e: **AFMPA**
Armed Forces Medical Publication Agency
e: **AFMPA**
Armed Forces Medical Services e: **AFMS**
Armed Forces Radiobiological (or
Radiobiology) Research Institute e:
AFRRI
Armed Forces Radiobiology Research
Institute e: **AFRADBIORSCHINST**
Armed Forces Research Institute of Medical
Sciences e: **AFRIMS**
Armed Services Biomedical Research,
Evaluation & Management committee e:
ASBREM
Armed Services Medical Material
Coordination Committee e: **ASMMCC**
Armed Services Medical Procurement
Agency e: **ASMPA**
Armed Services Medical Regulating Office
e: **ASMRO**
Armed Services Medical Regulatory
Organization Reporting System e:
ASRMO
Armee-Pferdelazarett d: **A.Pf.Laz.**, d:
Arm.Pf.Laz.
Armee-Pferdepark d: **A.Pf.Park.**, d:
Arm.Pf.P.
Armeehauptquartier d: **AHQ**
Armeewetterwarte d: **Awewa.**
Armor Protection Program e: **APP**
Armored Combat Earthmover e: **ACE**
Armour Remote Target System e: **ARETS**
Armo[u]red Observation Post e: **AOP**
Arms Control Observation Satellite e:
ACOS
Armstrong Areospace Medical Research
Laboratory e: **AAMRL**
Army Aerobiology and Evaluation
Laboratory e: **ARMY AEL**

Army Aeromedical Research Laboratory e:
AARL
Army Air Force Weather Service Bulletin
e: **AAFWSB**
Army Air Force Weather Service Manual
e: **AAFWSM**
Army Air Forces, Pacific Ocean Areas e:
AAFPOA
Army Air Forces Weather Service e:
AAFWS
Army Airspace Command and Control e:
AýCý
Army and Navy Medical Procurement
Office e: **ANMPO**
Army Aviation Medical Officer's Badge e:
AR Av MO Bad
Army Biological Laboratory e: **ABL**
Army Biological Warfare Research Center
e: **ABWRC**
Army Chemical Corps Medical Laboratories
e: **ACCML**
Army Engineer Geodesy, Intelligence and
Mapping Research and Development
Agency e: **AEGIMRDA**
Army Engineer[s] Waterway[s] Experiment
Station e: **AEWES**
Army Environmental Center e: **AEC**
Army Environmental Health Agency e:
AEHA
Army Environment[al] Health Laboratory
e: **AEHL**
Army Environmental Hygiene Agency e:
AEHA
Army Health Nurse e: **AHN**
Army Integrated Meteorological Systems
e: **AIMS**
Army Map Service-Geographical Section-
General Staff e: **AMS-GSGS**
Army Medical Advisory Board e: **AMAB**
Army Medical Biochemical Research
Laboratory e: **AMBRL**
Army Medical Bioengineering Research and
Development Laboratory e: **AMBRDL**
Army Medical Biomechanical Research
Laboratory e: **AMBRL**
Army Medical Center (or Centre) e: **AMC**
Army Medical Corps e: **A.M.C.**
Army Medical Department e: **AMD**, e:
AMED, e: **AMEDD**
Army Medical Department Property
Accounting System e: **AMEDDPAS**
Army Medical Equipment Depot e: **AMED**
Army Medical Laboratory e: **A Med Lab**
Army Medical Library e: **AML**
Army Medical Material Maintenance
Center, Europe e: **AMMCE**
Army Medical Materiel Agency e: **AMMA**
Army Medical Nutrition Laboratory e:
AMNL
Army Medical Officer e: **AMO**
Army Medical Publication[s] e: **AMedP**
Army Medical Regulating Office e:
AMRO
Army Medical Research and Nutrition
Laboratory e: **AMRNL**
Army Medical Research Institute of
Infectious Diseases e: **AMRIID**
Army Medical Research Laboratory e:
AMRL
Army Medical Service e: **AMEDS**
Army Medical Service Graduate School e:
AMSGS, e: **ANISGS**

Army Medical Service Research and
  Development Command e: **AMSRDC**
Army Medical Service School e: **AMSS**
Army Medical Service[s] e: **AMS**
Army Medical Specialist Corps e: **AMCS**
Army Medical Specialist[s] Corps e:
  AMSC
Army Medical Staff e: **AMS**
Army Medical Supply Control Officer e:
  AMSCO
Army Medical Supply Support Activity e:
  AMSSA
Army Medical Unit e: **AMU**
Army Medical Working Party e: **AMWP**
Army, Navy, NASA, Air Force Geodetic
  Satellite e: **ANNA**
Army Nuclear, Biological and Chemical
  Information System e: **ANBACIS**
Army Observation Plane e: **AOP**
Army Observation Post e: **AOP**
Army of the United States Medical Corps
  e: **A.U.S.M.C.**
Army Pigeon Service e: **APS**
Army Polar Research and Development
  Center e: **APRDC**
Army Reactor Systems Health and Safety
  Review Committee e: **ARCHS**
Army Research Institute of Environmental
  Medicine e: **ARIEM**
Army Snow, Ice, and Permafrost Research
  Establishment e: **ASIPR**
Army Snow, Ice and Permafrost Research
  Establishment e: **ASIPRE**
Army Space Command e: **ARSPACE**
Army Space Council e: **ASC**
Army Space Office e: **ASO**
Army Space Program Office e: **ASPO**
Army Space Study Group e: **ASSG**
Army Space Working Group e: **ASWG**
Army Surgeon General e: **ASG**
Army Surgeon General's Office e: **ASGO**
Army Waterways Experiment[al] Station
  e: **AWES**
Army Weather Service e: **AWS**
Army's Electronic Environmental Test
  Facility e: **AEETF**
Arnerican Protestant Health Association e:
  APHA
Aromatic Hydrocarbon Hydroxylase e:
  AHH
Aromatics Hydrogenation e: **AHY**, e:
  AHYD
Aromatische Kohlenwasserstoffe d: **AKW**
Aroostook Health Information and Resource
  Consortium e: **AHIRC**
ARPA [Advanced Research Projects
  Agency] Environmental Test Satellite e:
  ARENTS
ARPA [Advanced Research Projects
  Agency]-Lincoln Coherent Observable
  Radar e: **ALCOR**
ARPA [Advanced Research Projects
  Agency] Midcourse Observatory Site e:
  AMOS
Arquipelago. Ciencias Biologicas e
  Marinhas s: **Arquipel. Cienc. Biol.
  Mar.**
Arrea[s] of Outstanding Natural Beauty e:
  AONB
arretieren d: **arret.**
arretiert d: **arret.**
Arretierung d: **Arret.**
Arrival First Sea Pilot Station e: **AFSPS**

Arrowhead National Wildlife Refuge e:
  ANWR
Arsenic Atmosphere Czochralski e: **AAC**
Arteriosclerosis, Thrombosis, and Vascular
  Biology e: **Arterioscler Thromb Vasc
  Biol**
Arteriosclerosis, Thrombosis and Vascular
  Biology e: **ATVB**
Arteriosclerosis, Thrombosis and Vascular
  Biology: Journal of the American Heart
  Association e: **ATVB**
Arthritis Health Professions Association e:
  AHPA
Arthropod-Borne Animal Diseases Research
  Laboratory e: **ABADRL**
[Arthur Holley] Compton Gamma Ray
  Observatory e: **CGRO**
Artic Lidar Observatory for Middle
  Atmospheric Research e: **ALOMAR**
Artificial Earth Pulse e: **AEP**
Artificial Earth Research and Orbiting
  Satellite e: **AEROS**
Artificial Earth Satellite e: **AES**
Artificial Earth Satellite Observation
  Program e: **AESOP**
Artificial Intelligence in Medicine e: **AIM**,
  e: **Artif Intell Med**
Artificial Intelligence Research in
  Environmental Science e: **AIRES**
Artificial Life Interactive Video
  Environment e: **ALIVE**
Artificial Pond Water e: **APW**
Artificial Pond Water with additional
  Saccharose e: **APWS**
Artificial Satellite Time and Radio Orbit e:
  ASTRO
Artificial Seawater e: **ASW**
Artillery Ballistic Meteorological System
  e: **ABMS**
Artillery Communication Aural Protection
  System e: **ACAPS**
Artillery Meteorological e: **ARTYMEY**
Artillery Meteorological System e:
  AMETS, e: **AMS**
Artillery Observation e: **AO**
Artillery Observation Post e: **AOP**
Artillery Observation Vehicle e: **AOV**, e:
  VOA
Artisans Order of Mutual Protection e:
  AOMP
Aryl Hydrocarbon Hydroxylase e: **AHM**
Arylhydroxamicacyltransferase e: **AHAT**
Ärztliche Wirtschafts-GmbH, Medizinische
  Groß-Drogenhandlung d: **Aewige**
ASAE: The society for engineering in
  agricultural, food, and biological systems
  e: **ASAE**
Asamblea Oceanográfica Mixta f: **JOA**
Asean Consumer Protection Agency e:
  ACPA
Asean Council for Higher Education in
  Environment e: **ACHEE**
ASEAN Experts Group on the Environment
  e: **AEGE**
ASEAN Federation for Psychatric and
  Mental Health e: **AFPMH**
ASEAN Regional Specialized
  Meteorological Centre e: **ARSMC**
ASEAN Senior Environment Officers e:
  ASOEM
ASEAN Senior Officials on the
  Environment e: **ASOE[N]**

ASEAN Specialized Meteorological Centre
  e: **ASMC**
ASEAN Subregion Environment Program
  e: **ASEP**
ASEAN Training Centre for Primary Health
  Care Development e: **ATC/PHC**
Ashmolean Natural History Society of
  Oxfordshire e: **A.N.H.S.O.**
Ashmore and Cartier Islands e: **u-ac**
Ashmore/Cartier Reef e: **ACR**
Asia and Oceania Society for Comparative
  Endocrinology e: **AOSCE**
Asia and Oceania Workshop e: **AOW**
Asia and Oceania Workshop (OSI) e:
  AOW
Asia and Pacific Plant Protection
  Commission e: **APPPC**
Asia Oceanian Congress of Perinatology e:
  AOCP
Asia Oceanic WorkShop e: **AOWS**
Asia Pacific Association for Medical
  Informatics e: **APAMI**
Asia-Pacific Journal of Public Health e:
  Asia Pac J Public Health
Asia-Pacific People's Environrnent Network
  e: **APPEN**
Asia-Pacific Youth Environmental
  Federation e: **APYEF**
Asian American Health Initiative e: **AAHI**
Asian American Medical Student Group e:
  AAMSG
Asian-Americans in Public Health e:
  AAPH
Asian and Oceania Thyroid Association e:
  AOTA
Asian and Pacific Information Network on
  Medicinal and Aromatic Plants e:
  APINMAP
Asian Association for Biology Education
  e: **AABE**
Asian Association of Occupational Health
  e: **AAOH**
Asian Association of Pediatric Surgeons e:
  AAPS
Asian Association on Remote Sensing e:
  AARS
Asian-Austral[as]ian Association of Animal
  Production Societies e: **AAAP**
Asian-Australasian Society of Neurological
  Surgeons e: **AASNS**
Asian Community Health Action Network
  e: **ACHAN**
Asian Community Mental Health Services
  e: **ACMHS**
Asian Conference on Remote Sensing e:
  ACRS
Asian Dust Input to the Oceanic System e:
  ADIOS
Asian Environmental Society e: **AES**
Asian Federation of Catholic Medical
  Associations e: **AFCMA**
Asian Federation of Obstetrics and
  Gynaecology e: **AFOG**
Asian Federation of Societies for
  Ultrasound in Medicine and Biology e:
  AFSUMB
Asian Forum of Environmental Journalists
  e: **AFEJ**
Asian Geotechnical Engineering
  Information Center e: **AGE**
Asian Health Institute e: **AHI**
Asian Health Services e: **AHS**

Asian Journal of Modern Medicine *e:*
AJMM
Asian Marine Biology *e:* **Asian Mar. Biol.**
Asian Medical Students Association *e:*
AMSA
Asian Natural Environmental Science
Centre (Japan) *e:* **ANESC**
Asian Network for/of Biological Sciences
e: **ANBS**
Asian-Oceanian Computing Industry
Organization *e:* **ASOCIO**
Asian Oceanic Computing Industry
Organization *e:* **ASCIO**
Asian Oceanic Postal Union *e:* **AOPU**
Asian Office of Aerospace Research and
Development *e:* **AOARD**
Asian-Pacific Global Environmental
Research Network *e:* **APGERN**
Asian & Pacific Islander American Health
Forum *e:* **APIAHF**
Asian Pacific Medical Student Association
e: **APAMSA**
Asian Pacific Society on Biomedical
Research on Alcoholism *e:* **APSBRA**
Asian Regional Coordinating Committee on
Hydrology *e:* **ARCCOH**
Asian Regional Medical Student
Association *e:* **ARMSA**
Asian Regional Remote Sensing Training
Centre *e:* **ARRSTC**
Asian Symposium on Medicinal Plants,
Spices and other Natural Products *e:*
ASOMPS
Asociacion Argentina de los Medicos por el
Medio Ambiente *s:* **AAMMA**
Asociacion Medica Mundial *s:* **AMM**
Asociació de Médicos Veterinarions de El
Salvador *d:* **AMVES**
Asociación Argentina de Ciencias Naturales
"Physis" *s:* **AACNP**
Asociación Argentina de Geofisicos y
Geodestas *s:* **AAGG**
Asociación Argentina de Informática
Médica *s:* **AAIM**
Asociación Argentina de Producción
Animal *s:* **AAPA**
Asociación Canadiense de Meteorología y
Oceanografía *s:* **SCMO,** *s:* **SCMO**
Asociación Canaria para Defensa de la
Naturaleza *s:* **ASCAN**
Asociación Centroamericana de Facultades
de Medicina *s:* **ACAFAM**
Asociación Centroamericana de Historia
Natural *s:* **ACAHN**
Asociación Chilena Microbiología *s:*
ACHM
Asociación China de Investigación y
Desarrollo de los Recursos Minerales
Oceánicos *s:* **COMRA**
Asociación Colombiana de Fabricantes de
Alimentos para Animales *s:* **ACOFAL**
Asociación Colombiana de Facultades de
Medicina *s:* **ASCOFAME**
Asociación Colombiana de Geófraos *s:*
ACOGE
Asociación de Egresados de la Escuela
Inter-americana de Bibliotecología *s:*
ASEIBA
Asociación de Egresados de la Escuela
Interamericana de Bibliotecología de la
Universidad de Antioquia *s:* **ASEIBI**
Asociación de Estudiantes de Medicina *s:*
AEM

Asociación de Facultades de Medicina *s:*
ACAFAM
Asociación de Geografos de Geografos del
Uruguay *s:* **AGU**
Asociación de Ingenieros y Geólogos de
Yacimientos Petrolíferos Fiscales
Bolivianos *s:* **AIGYPFB**
Asociación de Médicos Veterinarios
Zootecnistas *s:* **AMVZ**
Asociación de Servicios Geológicos
Africanos *s:* **ASGA**
Asociación Ecologica Eterna Primavera *s:*
ASEEPRI
Asociación Guatemalteca de Servicios
Medicos *s:* **AGSM**
Asociación Internacional de Ecología *s:*
INTECOL
Asociación Internacional de Geodesia *s:*
AIG
Asociación Internacional de
Geomagnetismo y Aeronomía *s:* **AIGA**
Asociación Internacional de Hidrogeólogos
s: **AIH**
Asociación Internacional de Ingeniería
Geológica *s:* **IAEG**
Asociación Internacional de las Sociedas de
Microbiología *s:* **AISM**
Asociación Internacional de Meteorología y
Ciencias Atmosféricas *s:* **AIMCA**
Asociación Internacional de Meteorología y
Física Atmosférica *s:* **AIMFA**
Asociación Internacional de Oceanografía
Biológica *s:* **AIOB**
Asociación Internacional de Sismología y
de Física del Interior de la Tierra *s:*
IASPEI
Asociación Internacional de Vulcanología y
Química del Interior de la Tierra *s:*
IAVCEI
Asociación Internacional para la Ecología
de Paisajes *s:* **IALE**
Asociación Internacional para la Prevención
y la Atenuación de los Riesgos Naturales
s: **NHS**
Asociación Internacional para las Ciencias
Físicas del Océano *s:* **AICFO**
Asociación Internacional Veterinaria de
Producción Animal *s:* **AJVPA**
Asociación Latinoamericana de Editores en
Geociencias *s:* **ALEGEO**
Asociación Latinoamericana de Escuelas de
Bibliothecología y Ciencias de la
Información *s:* **ALEBCI**
Asociación Latinoamericana de
Microbiología *s:* **ALM**
Asociación Latinoamericana de Redactores
de Revistas Biológicas *s:* **ALERB**
Asociación Latinoamericana de Sociedades
de Biología y Medicina Nuclear *s:*
ALASBIMN
Asociación Lationoamericana de
Producción Animal *s:* **ALPA**
Asociación Medica Mexicana *s:* **AMM**
Asociación Mediterránea de Biología *s:*
AMBMO
Asociación Meteorológica Estadounidense
s: **AMS**
Asociación Mexicana de Geólogeos
Petroleros *s:* **AMGP**
Asociación Mexicana de Microbiología *s:*
AMM
Asociación Mexicana de Producción
Animal *s:* **AMPA**

Asociación Monegasca para la Protección
de la Naturaleza *s:* **AMPN**
Asociación Mundial para la Historia de la
Medicina Veterinaria *s:* **AMHMV**
Asociación Mundial para la Producción
Animal *s:* **AMPA**
Asociación Mundial Veterinaria de
Pequeños Animales *s:* **AMVPA**
Asociación Médica Argentina *s:* **AMA**
Asociación Médica de Estudios *s:* **AME**
Asociación Médica Dominicana *s:* **AMD**
Asociación Médico Latino-Americano de
Rehabilitacíon *s:* **AMLAR**
Asociación Nacional Campesina Pro-Tierra
s: **ANC**
Asociación Nacional de Médicos
Veterenarios Zootecnistas *s:* **ASMEVEZ**
Asociación Nacional para la Conservactón
de la Naturaleza *s:* **ANCON**
Asociación para la Defensa de la Naturaleza
s: **ADENA**
Asociación para la Promoción Protección y
Desarollo de la Naturaleza *s:* **APDENA**
Asociación Permanente de Cultura
Ecologica *s:* **APCE**
Asociación Venezolana de Facultades de
Medicina *s:* **AVEFAM**
Asociación Venezolana de Geología, Minas
y Petróleo *s:* **AVGMP**
Asociation for the Introduction of New
Biological Nomenclature *e:* **AINBN**
Asocio por la Enkondukode Nova Biologia
Nomenklaturo *eo:* **AINBN**
Aspects du cycle hydrologique se rapportant
à la biosphère *f:* **BAHC**
asphaltieren *d:* **asph.**
asphaltiert *d:* **asph.**
Asscciate of the Institute of Health Service
Administrators *e:* **AHA**
Asseciation for Health Services Research
e: **AMR**
Assembly Concept for Construction of
Erectable Space Structures *e:* **ACCESS**
Assemblée de l'Ecole *f:* **AE**
Assemblée des Présidents des Chambres des
Métiers de France *f:* **A.P.C.M.F.**
Assemblée Permanente des Présidents des
Chambres des Métiers *f:* **APCM**
Assessment and Coordination Branch,
Environmental Protection Service,
Environment Canada Yellowknife,
Northwest Territories *e:* **NWYEEP**
Assessment Biological and Chemical *e:*
ABC
Assessment of Effectiveness of Geologic
Isolation System[s] *e:* **AEGIS**
Assessment of Environmental Effects *e:*
AEE
Assessment of Sea Bases Air Platform
Project *e:* **ASBAPP**
Asset Protection Trust *e:* **APT**
Assigned Protection Factor *e:* **APF**
Assistance Médicale Intérim *f:* **AMI**
Assistant Chief Medical Director *e:*
ACMD
Assistant Chief Surgeon *e:* **Asst CS**
Assistant Director-General of Medical
Services *e:* **ADGMS**
Assistant Director of Army Health *e:*
ADAH
Assistant Director of Medical Services *e:*
ADMS

Assistant Director of Meteorological Office [Civil Aviation] e: **A.D.M.O.[C.A.]**

Assistant Director of Sea Transport e: **AD of ST**, e: **ADST**

Assistant Director of the Meteorological Office e: **ADMO**

Assistant House Surgeon e: **AHS**

Assistant Manager for Safety, Environment and Security e: **AMS**

Assistant Manager for Safety, Environment, and Security e: **AMSES**

Assistant Medical Officer e: **AMO**

Assistant Polaris Systems Officer e: **APSO**

Assistant Private Secretary to the First Sea Lord e: **APSFSL**

Assistant Secretary for Environment, Safety and Health e: **ASESH**

[Assistant Secretary for] Environment, Safety and Health e: **EH**

Assistant Secretary for Health e: **ASH**

Assistant Secretary for Policy, Safety and Environment e: **ASPE**

Assistant Secretary for Policy, Safety, and Environment e: **PE-1**

Assistant Secretary for the Environment e: **ASEV**

Assistant Secretary of Defense, Health Affairs e: **ASD [HA]**

Assistant Secretary of Defense [Health and Environment] e: **ASD[H&E]**

Assistant Secretary of Defense [Health and Medical] e: **ASD[H&M]**

Assistant Staff Meteorologist e: **ASM**

Assistant Surgeon e: **as**, e: **Asst. Surg.**

Assistant Surgeon General e: **ASG**

Assistant to the Surgeon General e: **A Surg G**

Assisted Health Insurance Plan e: **AHIP**

assistieren d: **ass.**

assistiert d: **ass.**

Assoc. of Ice Monitoring Contractors of Canada e: **AIMCC**

Associação dos Geografos Brasileiros p: **AGB**

Associação Gaucha de Proteção ao Ambiente Natural p: **AGAPAN**

Associação Medica do Rio Grande do Sul p: **AMRIGS**

Associação Médica Brasileira p: **AMB**

Associação Protectora dos Diabéticos de Portugal p: **A.P.D.P.**

Associate Administrator for Manned Space Flight e: **AA/MSF**

Associate Administrator for Space Flight e: **AASF**

Associate Committee of Geodesy and Geophysics e: **ACGG**

Associate Committee on Aviation Medical Research e: **ACAMR**

Associate Committee on Geotechnical Research e: **ACGR**

Associate Director for Energy and Environment e: **ADEE**

Associate Fellow of the Institute of the Aerospace Sciences e: **AFIAS**

Associate in Medical Technology e: **A.M.T.**

Associate in Science in Medical Secretarial e: **ASMS**

Associate in Wildlife Technology e: **AWT**

Associate Learning from Relative Environmental Data e: **ALFRED**

Associate Member of the Institution of Public Health Engineers e: **AMIPHE**

Associate Member of the Institution of Water Engineers e: **AMIWE**

Associate of Public Health Association e: **APHA**

Associate of the Association of Public Health Inspectors e: **AAPHI**

Associate of the Australian College of Health Service Administrators e: **AACHSA**

Associate [of the] Faculty of Occupational Medicine e: **AFOM**

Associate of the Faculty of Pharmaceutical Medicine e: **AFPM**

Associate of the Institute of Animal Technicians e: **AIAT**

Associate of the Institute of Medical Laboratory Sciences e: **AIMLS**

Associate of the Institution of Public Health Engineers e: **AIPHE**

Associate of the Institution of Water Engineers e: **AIWE**

Associate of the Royal College of Surgeons e: **ARCS**

Associate of the Royal College of Veterinary Surgeons e: **ARCVS**

Associate of the Royal Institute of Public Health and Hygiene e: **ARIPHH**

Associate of the Royal Society for the Promotion of Health e: **ARSH**

Associate of the Royal Society for the Promotion of the Health e: **ARSPH**

Associate of the Royal Society of Painters and Water Colours e: **A.R.W.S.**

Associated Biomedic Systems Inc. e: **ABS**

Associated Geographers of America e: **AGA**

Associated Health Foundation e: **AHF**

Associated Health Services e: **AHS**

Associated Medical Care Plans e: **AMCP**

Associated Water and Air Resources Engineers, Inc. e: **AWARE**

Association Africaine de Microbiologie et d'Hygiène Alimentaire f: **AAMHA**

Association Amicale des anciens élèves de l'École Centrale des arts et manufactures f: **AAEC**

Association Amicale des Anciens Élèves de l'École Nationale Agronomique d'Alger f: **AAAEENAA**

Association Amicale des Anciens Élèves de l'École Nationale du Génie Rural et des Ingénieurs du Génie Rural f: **E.N.G.R.**

Association Amicale des Ingénieurs Horticoles et des élèves de l'École nationale d'horticulture de Versailles f: **AAIH**

Association Architectes Sans Frontières f: **AASF**

Association Aéromédicale de France f: **AAMF**

Association Belge des Matières Plastiques f: **ABMP**

Association Belgo-Luxembourgeoise des Gaz de Pétrole Liquefiés f: **ABLGPL**

Association Canadienne de l'Industrie du Médicament f: **ACIM**

Association Canadienne de Protection Médicale f: **ACPM**

Association Canadienne des Géographes f: **ACG**

Association Canadienne des Techniciens en Radiation Medicale e: **ACTRM**, f: **ACTRM**

Association Canadienne des Technologues en Radiation Médicale f: **ACTRM**

Association Canadienne des Écoles de Bibliothécaires f: **ACEB**

Association Canadienne des Écoles de Traduction f: **A.C.E.T.**

Association Canadienne des Écoles Universitaires de Nursing f: **ACÉUN**

Association canadienne d'hydrographie f: **CHA**

Association Canadienne et Therapie Animale e: **ACTA**, f: **ACTA**

Association Catholique Internationale de Œuvres de Protection de la Jeune Fille f: **ACIOPJF**

Association Catholique Internationale d'Études Médico-Psychologiques f: **ACIEMP**

Association centrale des Moniteurs d'Autoécoles f: **AMA**

Association chypriote pour la protection du milieu marin f: **CYMEPA**

Association Confédérale pour la Formation Médicale f: **ACFM**

Association de Bretagne pour l'Information Médicale des Établissements de Santé f: **ABIMES**

Association de Déménageurs Internationaux Routiers f: **ADIR**

Association de Formation aux métiers de la Viande f: **AFORVIA**

Association de Géographes Français f: **AGF**

Association de Géologistes Arabes f: **AGA**

Association de Géoscientifiques pour le Développement International f: **AGID**

Association de la Presse Europe-Tiers Monde f: **APETM**

Association de l'Industrie Laitière de la CEE f: **ASSILEC**

Association de l'École Nationale Supérieure des Bibliothèques f: **AENSB**

Association de Maurice pour la protection et la sauvegarde de la mer f: **MMCS**

Association de Prevention des Accidents dans l'Industrielle Forestiere f: **APAW**

Association de Prévention et d'Études des Maladies Gynécologiques et Obstétricales f: **APEMGO**

Association de Prévoyance Interentreprise Arts et Métiers f: **APIAM**

Association de Recherche Géographique et Cartographique f: **AREG**

Association de Recherche sur la Pollutions, l'Environnement, les Nuisances et Transports f: **ARPENT**

Association de Recherches Médicales Européennes f: **ARME**

Association de Recherches Universitaires Géographiques et Cartographiques f: **AUREG**

Association de Topographes, Géomètres et Techniciens d'études f: **ATGT**

Association des Agents de Maîtrise de l'Institut Géographique Nationale f: **AAMIGN**

Association des Agréés de Protection Incendie f: **AGREPI**

Association des anciens elèves de l'Institut agricole d'Algerie et de l'École nationale d'agriculture d'Alger *f:* **AAEIAA**

Association des anciens Elèves de l'École de l'Air *f:* **A.E.A.**

Association des anciens élèves de l'École de l'Air dans le Civil *f:* **AEAC**

Association des anciens élèves de l'École Militaire de l'Air *f:* **AEMA**

Association des anciens élèves de l'École Navale *f:* **A.E.N.**

Association des anciens élèves de l'École Supérieure de Technologie Électrique *f:* **AESTE**

Association des Anciens Élèves des Écoles des Frères Chrétiennes *f:* **ASSANEF**

Association des Consommateurs Tiers Monde *f:* **ACTM**

Association des Diplômés de l'École de Bibliothécaires-Documentalistes *f:* **DEBD**

Association des Ecoles Internationales *f:* **AEI**

Association des Ecoles Paroissiales *f:* **A.E.P.**

Association des Enseignants des Écoles de Bloc Opératoire *f:* **AEEIBO**

Association des Entrepreneurs Luxembourgeois de Lignes d'Autobus *f:* **AELLA**

Association des Fabricants d'Instruments Chirugicaux et Appareillage Médical *f:* **AFICAM**

Association des Fabricants Européens de Butylated Hydroxytoluene *f:* **EBHA**

Association des Facultés de Médicine d'Amérique Centrale *f:* **ACAFAM**

Association des Functions publiques artiellement ou Entièrement de Langue Française *f:* **AFOPELF**

Association des Gynecologues d'Essey-Les-Nancy *f:* **A.g.E.**

Association des Géophysiciens en Exploration et Recherches en Afrique de l'Ouest *f:* **AGERA**

Association des Géophysiciens, Océanographes et Archéologues *f:* **AGOA**

Association des Ingénieurs de l'École Nationale Supérieure Agronomique de Nancy *f:* **AIENSAN**

Association des Ingénieurs-Géographes *f:* **AIG**

Association des Ingénieurs sortis des Écoles Spéciales annexés à l'Université de Grand *f:* **AIESG**

Association des Inspecteurs et Directeurs d'École Primaire de la Suisse romande et du Tessin *f:* **AIDEP**

Association des Institutions Écologiques du Pacifique Sud *f:* **ASPEI**

Association des Jeunes Naturalistes Française *f:* **AJNF**

Association des Journalistes et écrivains pour la Nature et l'Ecologie *f:* **JNE**

Association des Journalistes et Écrivains pour la Protection de la Nature *f:* **AJEPN**

Association des Journalistes Professionnels de l'Aéronautique et de l'Espace *f:* **AJPAE**

Association des Maîtres du Cycle d'Orientation Fribourgeois *f:* **AMCOF**

Association des Microbiologistes de Langue Française *f:* **AMILAF**, *f:* **AMLF**

Association des Médicins anciens étudiants de l'Université Libre de Bruxelles *f:* **AMUB**

Association des ONG francophones et germanophones pour la cooperation avec le Tiers Monde *f:* **Association des ONG**

Association des Parents et Amis Gestionnaires d'Établissements Sociaux et Médicaux Sociaux *f:* **APAGESMS**

Association des Pharmaciens Directeurs de Laboratoires d'Analyses biologiques *f:* **APDILA**

Association des Physiciens et Ingénieurs Biomédicaux du Québec *f:* **APIBQ**

Association des Producteurs de Sorbitol de la CEE *f:* **ASPEC**

Association des Professeurs d'Histoire et de Géographie de l'Enseignement Public *f:* **A.P.H.G.**

Association des Psychologues del' Ocean Indien *f:* **A Psy OI**

Association des Secteurs des Métiers pour la participation à la gestion des Intérêts Publics *f:* **ASMIP**

Association des Services Geologiques Africains *f:* **ASGA**

Association des Sociétés Scientifiques Médicales Belges *f:* **ASSMB**

Association des Soldats du Service Militaire Obligatoire Luxembourgeois *f:* **ASSMOL**

Association des Techniciens d'Information Médicale d'Ile de France *f:* **ATIMIF**

Association des Transporteurs Routiers Internationaux en Hongrie *f:* **ATRIH**

Association des Universités Partiellement ou Entièrement de Langue Française *f:* **AUPELF**

Association des Universités Partiellement ou Entièrement de Langue Française-Universités des Réseaux d'Expression Française *f:* **AUPELF-UREF**

Association des Usagers de l'Hôpital et des Soins Médicaux *f:* **AUHSM**

Association des Utilisateurs de Dossiers Informatisés en Périnatalogie, Obstétrique et Gynécologie *f:* **AUDIPOG**

Association du Négoce des Gains Oléagineuses, Huiles, et Graisses Animales et Végétales et Leurs Derives de la CEE *e:* **ANGO**

Association Départemental de Protection Civile *f:* **ADPC**

Association Européenne de Medecine Thermale et Climatique *f:* **AEMTC**

Association Européenne des Institutions de recherche et de formation en matière de Développement *f:* **AEID**

Association Européenne des Reserves Naturelles Libres *f:* **EUREL**

Association Européenne des Véhicules Électriques Routiers *f:* **AVERE**

Association Européenne des École s et Collèges d'Optométrie *f:* **AESCO**

Association Européenne Océanique *f:* **EUROCEAN**

Association Européenne pour le Développement de l'Information et la Connaissance de l'Environmental *f:* **EUDICE**

Association faîtière des enseignantes et enseignants suisses *f:* **ECH**

Association Financiére Internationale de l'Océan Indien *f:* **AFIOI**

Association for Biology Laboratory Education *e:* **ABLE**

Association for Biomedical Research *e:* **ABR**

Association for Computing Machinery-Special Interest Group on Biomedical Computing *e:* **ACM-SIGBIO**

Association for Computing Machinery-Special Interest Group on Computers and the Public Health *e:* **ACM-SIGCAPH**

Association for Computing Machinery-Special Interest Group on Measurement and Environment *e:* **ACM-SIGME**

Association for Electronic Health Care Transactions *e:* **AFEHCT**

Association for Environmental Archaeology *e:* **AEA**

Association for Environmental Education *e:* **AEE**

Association for Equine Sports Medicine *e:* **AESM**

Association for Faculty in the Medical Humanities *e:* **AFMH**

Association for Geographic Information *e:* **AGI**

Association for Health Information and Libraries in Africa *e:* **AHILA**

Association for Health Records *e:* **AHR**

Association for Health Services Research *e:* **AHSR**

Association for Healthcare Quality *e:* **AHQ**

Association for Healthcare Resource & Materials Management *e:* **AHRMM**

Association for Holistic Health *e:* **AHH**

Association for Hospital Medical Education *e:* **AHME**

Association for Hospital Medical Education. Journal *e:* **AHME J**

Association for Infant Mental Health *e:* **A.I.M.H.**

Association for Infant Mental Health [United Kingdom] *e:* **A.I.M.H.[UK]**

Association for Informatics in Medicine, Singapore *e:* **AIMS**

Association for Integrative Medicine *e:* **AIM**

Association for International Medical Study *e:* **AIMS**

Association for Medical Deans in Europe *e:* **AMDF**

Association for Medical Education in Europe *e:* **AMEE**

Association for Medical Education in the Western Pacific *e:* **AMEWP**

Association for Medical Physics Technology *e:* **AMPT**

Association for [of] Computing Machinery Geographic Information Systems *e:* **ACMGIS**

Association for/of Geoscientists for International Development *e:* **AGID**

Association for/of International Health Researches *e:* **AIHR**

Association for [of] Maternal and Child Health Programs *e:* **AMCHP**

Association for/of Medical Deans in Europe *e:* **AMDE**

Association for/of Medical Education and
Research in Substance Abuse e:
AMERSA

Association for/of Medical Schools in
Africa e: **AMSA**

Association for/of Schools of Public Health
in the European Region e: **ASPHER**

Association for/of Tropical Biology e:
ATB

Association for Psychoanalytic and
Psychosomatic Medicine e: **APPM**

Association for Psychoanalytic Medicine
e: **APM**

Association for Quality in Healthcare e:
AQH

Association for Research and
Environmental Aid Ltd. e: **AREA**

Association for Retarded Citizens/Georgia
e: **ARC/Georgia**

Association for Rural Mental Health e:
ARMH

Association for Social Anthropology in
Oceania asap analog system assembly
pack e: **ASAO**

Association for Software Protection e:
ASP

Association for Spina Bifida and
Hydrocephalus e: **ASBAH**

Association for the Accreditation of Human
Research Protection Programs e:
AAHRPP

Association for [the] Advancement of
Automotive Medicine e: **AAAM**

Association for the Advancement of Health
Care Managers e: **AAHCM**

Association for [the] Advancement of
Health Education e: **AAHE**

Association for the Advancement of
Medical Education e: **AAME**

Association for the Advancement of
Medical Instrumentation e: **AAMI**

Association for the Advancement of Private
Health e: **AAPH**

Association for [the] Behavioral Sciences
and Medical Education e: **ABSAME**

Association for the Care of Children's
Health e: **ACCH**

Association for the Ice Cream Industries of
the EEC e: **EUROGLACES**

Association for the Improvement of
Geometrical Teaching e: **A.I.G.T.**

Association for the Promotion of Space
Activities in Europe e: **C**

Association for the Protection of Fur-
Bearing Animals e: **APFBA**

Association for the Protection of Native
Races e: **APNR**

Association for the Protection of Patients
and Staff e: **APPS**

Association for the Protection of Rural
Scotland e: **APRS**

Association for the Protection of the
Adirondacks e: **APA**

Association for the Protection of Wildlife
e: **PROFAUNA**

Association for the Study of Animal
Behavio[u]r e: **ASAB**

Association for the Study of Animal
Behaviour e: **Assn Study Anim Behav**

Association for the Study of Literature and
the Environment e: **ASLE**

Association for the Study of Man
Environment Relations e: **ASMER**

Association for the Study of Medical
Education e: **ASME**

Association for the Study of Snow and Ice
e: **ASSI**

Association for Women Geoscientists e:
AWG

Association for Worksite Health Promotion
e: **AWHP**

Association Forestière Québeçoise f: **AFQ**

Association Française d'Agriculture
Biologique f: **AFAB**

Association Française d'Echange pour
l'Environnement et le Développement f:
AFEED

Association Française des Ingénieurs et
Techniciens de l'Aéronautique et de
l'Espace f: **AFITAE**

Association française des Responsables et
Archivistes de Dossiers médicaux f:
ARAD

Association Française des Techniciens de
l'Alimentation Animale f: **A.F.T.A.A.**

Association Française des Transporteurs
Routiers Internationaux f: **AFTRI**

Association Française du Personnel
Paramédical en Électroradiologie f:
AFPPE

Association Française du World Wildlife
Fund f: **AFWWF**

Association Française d'Études
Industrielles, Agricoles, Géographiques et
Sociales f: **AFEIAGS**

Association Française Laitière f: **AFL**

Association Française pour la Diffusion du
Livre Scientifique, Technique et Médical
f: **SODEX-PORT**

Association Française pour la Défense de
l'Environnement contre les pollutions et
nuisances f: **AFDE**

Association Française pour la Protection de
l'Environnement Rural et l'Amílioration
de l'Élevage f: **AFPERAE**

Association Française pour la Protection
des Eaux f: **AFPE**

Association Française pour l'Information
Médicale et Chirurgicale f: **AFIMEC**

Association Française pour l'École
Paysanne f: **AFEP**

Association Francaise pour l'Étude du Tiers
Monde f: **AFETIMON**

Association Fribourgeoise du Corps
enseignant des Écoles Primaires et
Enfantines f: **AFCEPE**

Association Genevoise de Écoles Privées
f: **AGEP**

Association Geologique Carpatho-
Balkanique e: **AGCB**

Association Geologique du Canada f:
AGC

Association Générale de l'Industrie du
Médicament f: **AGIM**

Association Générale des Industries,
Métiers, Négoces et Professions f:
A.G.I.M.N.P.

Association Générale des Médicins de
Belgique f: **A.G.M.B.**

Association Générale des Étudiants en
Médicine de Paris f: **AGEM**

Association Générale des Étudiants en
médicine de Paris f: **A.G.E.M.P.**

Association générale des étudiants
luxembourgeois f: **ASSOS**

Association Hellénique de Protection de
l'Environnement Marin f: **HELMEPA**

Association international pour la Promotion
et la Protection des Investissements privés
en territoire étrangers f: **APPPI**

Association Internationale de Géochimie et
de Cosmochimie f: **AIGC**

Association Internationale de Géodésie f:
AIG

Association Internationale de Géodésie et
de Géophysique f: **AIGG**

Association Internationale de Géologie de
l'Ingénieur f: **AIGI**

Association Internationale de
Géomagnétisme et d'Aéronomie f: **AIGA**

Association Internationale de Medicine et
de Biologie de l'Environnement f:
AIMBE

Association Internationale de Médecine et
de Biologie de l'Environnement f:
AIMBE

Association Internationale de Météorologie
f: **AIM**

Association Internationale de Météorologie
et de Physique de l'Atmosphère f:
AIMPA

Association Internationale de Météorologie
et de Sciences de l'Atmosphère f:
AIMSA

Association Internationale de Reeducation
en Uro-Gynécologie f: **AIRUG**

Association Internationale de
Standardisation Biologique f: **AISB**

Association Internationale des
Anthropobiologistes f: **AIAB**

Association Internationale des Courtiers
Aériens f: **AICA**

Association Internationale des
Hydrogéologes f: **AIH**

Association Internationale des Maires et
responsables des capitales et Métropoles
partiellement ou entiérement
Francophones f: **AIMF**

Association Internationale des Musées
Médicaux f: **AIMM**

Association Internationale des Métiers et
Enseignements d'Art f: **AIMEA**

Association internationale des sciences
hydrologiques f: **AISH**

Association Internationale des Sciences
Physiques de l'Océan f: **AISPO**

Association Internationale des Sociétés de
Microbiologie f: **AISM**

Association Internationale des
Sélectionneurs pour la protection des
obtentions végétales f: **ASSINSEL**

Association Internationale des Techniciens
Biologistes de langue française f:
ASSITEB

Association Internationale des Écoles de
Service Social f: **AIESS**

Association Internationale des Écoles des
Sciences de l'Information f: **AIESI**

Association Internationale des Écoles et
Instituts d'Administration f: **AIEIA**

Association Internationale des Écoles ou
instituts Supérieurs d'Éducation Physique
et sportive f: **AIESEP**

Association Internationale des Écoles
Privées Européennes f: **AIEPE**

Association Internationale d'Hydrologie
Scientifique f: **AIHS**

Association Internationale d'Océanographie Biologique f: **AIOB**

Association Internationale d'Océanographie Physique f: **AIOP**

Association Internationale d'Écologie f: **INTECOL**

Association Internationale d'Études Médicales, Psychologiques et Religieuses f: **AIEMPR**

Association internationale d'études pour la Promotion et la Protection des Investissements privés enterritoires étrangers f: **APPI**

Association internationale d'études pour la Protection des Investissements f: **ADPI**

Association Internationale Olympique pour la Recherche Medico-Sportive f: **AIORMS**

Association internationale pour la protection contre les radiations f: **IRPA**

Association Internationale pour la Protection de la Propriété Industrielle f: **AIPPI**, f: **IVfgR**

Association internationale pour la protection des especes en peril f: **AVIORNIS**

Association Internationale pour la Recherche Médicale et les Échanges Culturels f: **AIRMEC**

Association Internationale pour le Développement des Sciences médicales et médico-sociales f: **AIDEMES**

Association Internationale pour le Développement et l'Environnement f: **AIDE**

Association Internationale pour le Recherche Médicale dans l'Quest Africain f: **AIRMOA**

Association internationale pour l'utilisation des langues regionales a l'ecole f: **SCOLARE**

Association internationale pour l'écologie des paysages f: **IALE**

Association Internationale Vétérinaire de Production Animale f: **AIVPA**

Association Interprofessionnelle des Centres Médicaux et Sociaux de la Région Parisienne f: **A.C.M.S.**

Association Interprofessionnelle pour la Protection de la Santé f: **AIPS**

Association Juridique pour la Protection du Droit d'Auteur f: **AJPDA**

Association Laitiére Ferme-Usine f: **ALFU**

Association Laitiére Française pour le développement de la production et des industries du lait f: **ALF**

Association Latinoaméricaine des Matiéres Refractaires f: **ALAFAR**

Association Latinoaméricaine des Sociétés de Biologie et Médecine Nucléaires f: **ALASBIMN**

Association Latinoaméricaine des Écoles de Service Social f: **ALEASS**

Association Liégeoise-Verviétoise pour Travaux Spéciaux f: **Alvets**

Association Luxembourgeoise Contre le Bruit f: **ALCB**

Association Luxembourgeoise de Journalistes Professionnels f: **ALJP**

Association Luxembourgeoise des Ingénieurs et Industriels f: **ALII**

Association Luxembourgeoise des Juristes Européens f: **ALJE**

Association Luxembourgeoise des Kinésithérapeutes Diplomés f: **A.L.K.D.**

Association Luxembourgeoise des Pilotes de Ligne f: **ALPL**

Association Luxembourgeoise Des Éditeurs de Jounaux f: **ALEJ**

Association Luxembourgeoise pour l'Alimentation et l'Hygiène Rationnelles f: **ALPAR**

Association luxembourgeoise pour le Développement de l'Épargne et la Défense des Intérêts de valeurs mobilière f: **DEDID**

Association Luxembourgeoise pour l'Utilisation Pacifique de l'energie Atomique f: **ALUPA**

Association Marocaine des Écoles Supérieures de Commerce f: **AMESCO**

Association Medicale Mondiale f: **AMM**

Association Medicale pour la Prevention de la Guerre Nucleaire f: **AMPGN**

Association Medico-Sociale protestante de langue française f: **AMS**

Association Medico-Sociale Protestante de langue française f: **AMSP**

Association Mondialc des Veterinaires Microbiologistes, Immunologistes et Specialistes des Maladies Infectieuses f: **AMVMI**

Association Mondiale des Vétérinaires Microbiologistes, Immunologistes et Spécialistes des Maladies Infectieuses f: **A.M.V.M.I.**

Association Mondiale d'Histoire de la Médicine Vétérinaire f: **AMHMV**

Association mondiale pour l'École Instrument de Paix f: **EIP**

Association Monégasque pour la Protection de la Nature f: **AMPN**

Association Médical pour la Recherche et Unité Syndicale f: **AMRUS**

Association Médicale Canadienne f: **AMC**

Association Médicale d'Israel f: **AMI**

Association Médicale d'Études et de Recherches Scientifiques f: **AMERS**

Association Médicale Franco-Américaine f: **AMFA**

Association Médicale Franco-Libanaise f: **AMFL**

Association Médicale Inter-Entreprise f: **AMIE**

Association Médicale Internationale pour l'Étude des conditions de Vie et de la santé f: **AMIEV**

Association Médicale Latino-Américaine de Réhabilitation f: **ALMAR**

Association Médicale pour l'Enseignement Post-Universitaire f: **AMEPU**

Association Nationale des Cadres Infirmiers et Médico-techniques f: **ANCIM**

Association Nationale des Contrôleurs Routiers f: **ANCR**

Association Nationale des entreprises Albanaises des Transports Routiers f: **ANALTIR**

Association Nationale des Infirmerès Luxembourgeois[es] f: **ANIL**

Association Nationale des Journalistes d'Information Médicale f: **ANJIM**

Association Nationale des Manipulateurs et Techniciens Diplomés en Électro-Radiologie Médicale f: **ANMTDERM**

Association Nationale des Services d'Ambulances Correspondants du Secours Routier Français f: **ANSACSRF**

Association Nationale des Techniciens et Techniciennes Diplômés en Électroradiologie Médicale f: **ANTTDERM**

Association Nationale des Équipes et Centres d'Action Médico-Sociale Précoce f: **ANECAMSP**

Association Nationale pour la Défence des Arbres et Éspaces Verts f: **ANDAEV**

Association nationale pour la Formation et le perfectionnement professionnelle dans les métiers de l'Édition f: **ASFORED**

Association Nationale pour la Protection contre l'Incendie f: **ANPI**

Association nationale pour la Protection des Animaux Sauvages et du patrimoine naturel f: **ASPAS**

Association Nationale pour la Protection des Eaux f: **ANPE**

Association of Academic Health Centers e: **AAHC**, e: **AHC**

Association of Academic Health Sciences Libraries e: **AAHSL**

Association of Academic Health Sciences Library Directors e: **AAHSLD**

Association of Accredited Medical Laboratory Schools e: **AAMLS**

Association of African Geological Surveys e: **AAGS**

Association of Air Medical Services e: **AAMS**

Association of Ambulatory Behavior Healthcare e: **AABH**

Association of American Boards of Examiners in Veterinary Medicine e: **AABEVM**

Association of American Medical Book Publishers e: **AAMBP**

Association of American Medical Colleges e: **AAMC**

Association of American Physicians and Surgeons e: **AAPS**

Association of American State Boards of Examiners in Veterinary Medicine e: **AASBEVM**

Association of American Veterinary Medical Colleges e: **AAVMC**

Association of American Weather Observers e: **AAWO**

Association of Applied Biologists e: **AAB**

Association of Applied Insect Ecologists e: **AAIE**

Association of Asian Pacific Community Health Organizations e: **AAPCHO**

Association of Australian Aerospace Industries e: **AAAI**

Association of Aviation and Space Museums e: **AASM**

Association of Behavioral Healthcare Management e: **ABHM**

Association of Biological Collections Appraisers e: **ABCA**

Association of Biomedical Communication[s] Directors e: **ABCD**

Association of British Climatologists e: **ABC**

Association of British Geodesists e: **ABG**

Association of British Healthcare Industries e: **ABHI**

Association of British Oceanic (or Oceanological) Industries *e:* **ABOI**

Association of British Tree Surgeons and Arborists *e:* **ABTSA**

Association of British Wild Animal Keepers *e:* **ABWAK**

Association of Canadian Faculties of Environmental Studies *e:* **ACFES**

Association of Canadian Medical Colleges *e:* **ACMC**

Association of Central American Departments of Medicine *e:* **ACAFAM**

Association of Chief Administrators of Health Authorities *e:* **ACAHA**

Association of Community Health Councils *e:* **ACHlC**

Association of Community Health Councils for England and Wales *e:* **ACHCEW**

Association of Community Health Nursing Educators *e:* **ACHNE**

Association of Consumer Health Information Specialists *e:* **ACHIS**

Association of County Public Health Officers *e:* **AssCPHO's**

Association of Earth Science Editors *e:* **AESE**

Association of Editors in the South-East Asia, Australasia and Oceania *e:* **EDITEAST**

Association of Employers of Waterside Labour *e:* **AEWL**

Association of Engineering Firms Practicing in the Geosciences *e:* **ASFE**

Association of Engineering Geologists *e:* **AEG**

Association of Environmental and Outdoor Education *e:* **AEOE**

Association of Environmental and Resource[s] Economists *e:* **AERE**

Association of Environmental Engineering Professors *e:* **AEEP**

Association of Environmental Laboratories *e:* **AEL**

Association of Environmental Scientists and Administrators *e:* **AESA**

Association of European Aerospace Industries *e:* **AECMA**

Association of European Geological Societies *e:* **AEGS**, *e:* **AFGS**

Association of European Manufacturers of Storage Gas-Waterheaters *e:* **ACCUGAZ**

Association of Exploration Geochemists *e:* **AEG**

Association of Forest Service Employees for Environmental Ethics *e:* **AFSEEE**

Association of Former Secretaries of Health *e:* **AFSH**

Association of Former Secretaries of the Department of Health, Education and Welfare *e:* **AFSHEW**

Association of Geology Teachers *e:* **AGT**

Association of Ground Water Scientists and Engineers *e:* **AGWSE**

Association of Health and Pleasure Resorts *e:* **A.H.P.R.**

Association of Health Care Information and Medical Records Officers *e:* **AMRO**

Association of Health Centre and Practicec Administrators *e:* **AHCPA**

Association of Health Facility Licensure and Certification Directors *e:* **AHFLCD**

Association of Health Service Personnel Managers *e:* **AHSPM**

Association of Health Service Treasurers *e:* **AHST**

Association of Healthcare Human Resource Management *e:* **AHHRM**

Association of High Medicare Hospitals *e:* **AHMH**

Association of Hospital Directors of Medical Education *e:* **AHDME**

Association of Independent Medical Equipment Suppliers *e:* **AIMES**

Association of Industrial Medical Officers *e:* **AIMO**

Association of Institute for Research and Development in the Indian Ocean *e:* **ARDOI**

Association of Interns and Medical Students *e:* **AIMES**

Association of Interpretive Naturalists *e:* **AIN**

Association of Japanese Geographers *e:* **AJG**

Association of Librarians in the History of the Health Sciences *e:* **ALHHS**

Association of Life Insurance Medical Directors *e:* **ALIMD**

Association of Life Insurance Medical Directors of America *e:* **ALIMDA**

Association of Management in Public Health *e:* **AMPH**

Association of Manipulative Medicine *e:* **AMM**

Association of Manufacturers of Animal-Derived Food Enzymes *e:* **AMAFE**

Association of Manufacturers of Medicinal Preparations *e:* **AMMP**

Association of Marine Undewaters of the United States *e:* **AMUUS**

Association of Medical Advertising Agencies *e:* **AMAA**

Association of Medical Advisers in the Pharmaceutical Industry *e:* **AMAPI**

Association of Medical Doctors for Asia *e:* **AMDA**

Association of Medical Expenses Insurers *e:* **AMEI**

Association of Medical Group Psychoanalysts *e:* **AMGP**

Association of Medical Illustrators *e:* **AMI**

Association of Medical Record Consultants *e:* **AMRC**

Association of Medical Record Officers *e:* **AMRO**

Association of Medical Rehabilitation Directors and Coordinators *e:* **AMRDC**

Association of Medical Research Charities *e:* **AMRC**

Association of Medical School Pediatric Department Chairmen *e:* **AMSPDC**

Association of Medical Schools in the Middle East *e:* **AMSME**

Association of Medical Secretaries, Practice Administrators and Receptionists *e:* **AMSPAR**

Association of Medical Superintendents of Mental Hospitals *e:* **AMSMH**

Association of Mental Health Administrators *e:* **AMHA**

Association of Mental Health Clergy *e:* **AMHC**

Association of Mental Health Librarians *e:* **AMHL**

Association of Metropolitan Water Agencies *e:* **AMWA**

Association of Military Dental Surgeons *e:* **AMDS**

Association of Military Surgeons *e:* **AMS**

Association of Military Surgeons of the United States *e:* **AMSUS**

Association of Minority Health Professions Schools *e:* **AMHPS**

Association of National Health Service Corps Scholarship Recipients *e:* **ANHSCSR**

Association of National Health Service Officers *e:* **ANHSO**

Association of National Health Service Supplies Officers *e:* **ANHSSO**

Association of Natural Rubber Producing Countries *e:* **ANRPC**

Association of North Dakota Geographers *e:* **ANDG**

Association of Occupational & Environmental Clinics *e:* **AOEC**

Association of Occupational Health Professionals *e:* **AOHP**

Association of Occupational Therapists in Mental Health *e:* **AOTMH**

Association of Ontario Health Centres *e:* **AOHC**

Association of Osteopathic Directors and Medical Educators *e:* **AODME**

Association of Pacific Coast Geographers *e:* **APCG**

Association of Physical Oceanographers *e:* **APO**

Association of Physical Oceanography *e:* **APO**

Association of Physician Assistants in Obstetrics and Gynecology *e:* **APAOG**

Association of Police Surgeons of Great Britain *e:* **APSGB**

Association of Polish Geomorphologists *e:* **APG**

Association of Private Weather Related Companies *e:* **APWRC**

Association of Professional Engineers, Geologists and Geophysicists of Alberta *e:* **APEGGA**

Association of Professional Geological Scientists *e:* **APGS**

Association of Professors of Gynecology and Obstetrics *e:* **APGO**

Association of Professors of Human or Medical Genetics *e:* **APHMG**

Association of Professors of Medicine *e:* **APM**

Association of Program Directors in Internal Medicine *e:* **APDIM**

Association of Public Health *e:* **APH**

Association of Public Health Inspectors *e:* **APHI**

Association of Reproductive Health Professionals *e:* **ARHP**

Association of Researchers in Medical (or Medicine) Science[s] *e:* **ARMS**

Association of School Natural History Societies *e:* **ASNHS**

Association of Schools of Allied Health Professions *e:* **ASAHP**

Association of Schools of Public Health *e:* **ASPH**

Association of Scientists and Engineers of the Naval Sea Systems Command *e:* **ASE**

Association of Scottish Local Health Councils *e:* **ASLHC**

Association of Sea Grant Program Institutes *e:* **ASGPI**

Association of Societies for Occupational Safety and Health *e:* **ASOSH**

Association of Sorbitol Producers within the European Community *e:* **ASPEC**

Association of South Pacific Environmental Institutions *e:* **ASPEI**

Association of South Polar Research *e:* **ASPR**

Association of Southeastern Biologists *e:* **ASB**

Association of Space Explorers *e:* **ASE**

Association of Sports Medicine of the Balkans *e:* **ASMB**

Association of State and Interstate Water Pollution Control Administrators *e:* **ASIWCPA**, *e:* **ASIWPCA**

Association of State and Public Health Laboratory Directors *e:* **ASTPHLD**

Association of State and Territorial Directors of Health Promotion and Public Health Education *e:* **ASTDHPPHE**

Association of State and Territorial Directors of Local Health Services *e:* **ASTDLHS**

Association of State and Territorial Directors of Public Health Nursing *e:* **ASTDPHN**

Association of State and Territorial Health Officers (or Officials) *e:* **ASTHO**

Association of State and Territorial Public Health Nutrition Directors *e:* **ASTPHND**

Association of State Drinking Water Administrators *e:* **ASDWA**

Association of State Public Health Veterinarians *e:* **ASPHV**

Association of Surgeons and Physicians of Malta *e:* **ASPM**

Association of Surgeons in Training *e:* **ASIT**

Association of Surgeons of Great Britain and Ireland *e:* **AS**, *e:* **ASGBI**

Association of Teachers of Maternal and Child Health *e:* **ATMCH**

Association of Teachers of Preventive Medicine *e:* **ATPM**

Association of Telemedicine Service Providers *e:* **ATSP**

Association of [the] Directors of Medical Student Education in Psychiatry *e:* **ADMSEP**

Association of the Health Occupations Teacher Educators *e:* **AHOTE**

Association of Trust Medical Directors *e:* **ATMD**

Association of Underwater Contractors *e:* **AUC**

Association of United States Members of the International Institute of Space Law *e:* **AUSMIISL**

Association of University Programs in Health Administration *e:* **AUPHA**

Association of University Radiation Protection Officers *e:* **AURPO**

Association of Veterinarians for Animal Rights *e:* **AVAR**

Association of Water Officers *e:* **AWO**

Association of Water Transportation Accounting Officers *e:* **AWTAO**

Association of Women's Health, Obstetric and Neonatal Nurses *e:* **AWHONN**

Association Petroliere pour la Conservation de l'Environnement Canadien *e:* **APCEC**

Association Peugeot-Renault *f:* **APR**

Association Pilot des Achats Médicaux *f:* **APAM**

Association pour Favoriser la Diffusion des Appareils et Produits de Détection, de Protection et de Décontamination *f:* **PROSEC**

Association pour la Cooperation des Eglises, l'environnement et le Développement de l'Afrique Centrale *f:* **ACEDAC**

Association pour la Cooperation des Eglises, l'Environnement et le Développement de l'Afrique Centrale *f:* **ACEEDAC**

Association pour la Formation Continue des personnels des coopératives Laitiéres *f:* **AFCIL**

Association pour la Formation dans l'Industrie Routiére *f:* **AFIR**

Association pour la Gérance des Écoles d'Apprentissage Maritime *f:* **A.G.E.A.M.**

Association pour la Promotion de l'Information Médicale sur Internet *f:* **APIMI**

Association pour la Protection de l'Enfance au Laos *f:* **APPEL**

Association pour la Protection des Automobilistes *f:* **APA**

Association pour la Protection des Interets des Consommateurs *e:* **APIC**

Association pour la Protection des Salmonidés *f:* **APPS**

Association pour la Protection Familiale des Travailleurs Immigrés *f:* **APFTI**

Association pour la Protection Industrielle et la Recherche Scientifique *f:* **APIRS**

Association pour la Prévention de la Pollution Atmosphérique *f:* **APPA**

Association pour la Rationalisation et la Mécanisation de l'Exploitation Forestière *f:* **ARMEF**

Association pour la Recherche Biologique et des Applications Médicales *f:* **ARBAM**

Association pour la Recherche et la Confrontation de l'Environnement, Aménagement et Urbanisme *f:* **ARCEAU**

Association pour la Vigilance en matière d'Implants Orthopédiques *f:* **AVIO**

Association pour le Développement de la Recherche sur la Biologie Médicale *f:* **ADRBM**

Association pour le Développement de l'Enseignement Médical par l'Audiovisuel *f:* **ADEMA**

Association pour le Développement de l'Information Médicale et Économique en Hospitalisation Privée *f:* **ADIMEHP**

Association pour le Développement des Industries utilisatrices de Caoutchouc et de matières Plastiques dans la région Rhône *f:* **ADICAP**

Association pour le Développement des Relations Écoles-Professions *f:* **ADRE[P]P**

Association pour le développement des Sciences et Techniques de l'Environnement *f:* **ASTE**

Association pour le Développement des Techniques de Transport, d'Environnement et de Circulation *f:* **ATEC**

Association pour le Développement des Études sur l'Environnement et l'Atmosphère *f:* **ADEEA**

Association pour le Développement et l'Enseignement de la Réanimation Médicale *f:* **ADERM**

Association pour le Développement et l'Étude des Techniques des Arts et Métiers *f:* **ADETAM**

Association pour l'Enseignement Médical en Europe *f:* **AEME**

Association pour l'Information Technique des Cadres Géomètres de la Région des Alpes *f:* **AITCGRA**

Association pour l'Introduction de la Nomenclature Biologique Nouvelle *f:* **AINBN**

Association pour l'Éducation Sexuelle à l'École *f:* **APESE**

Association Professionnelle de Géographes *f:* **APG**

Association Professionnelle des exploitants de Service Réguliers routiers *f:* **APSR**

Association professionnelle des Fabricants de Compléments pour l'Alimentation Animale *f:* **AFCA**

Association Professionnelle des Transporteurs publics routiers de voyageurs de la Région parisienne *f:* **APTR**

Association Professionnelle Internationale des Medicins *e:* **APIM**

Association Professionnelle Régionale des Affréteurs Routiers *f:* **APRAR**

Association Romande pour la Protection de l'Air *f:* **ARPA**

Association Roumaine pour Transports Routiers Internationaux *f:* **ROMTRANS**

Association Routière des Assurances *f:* **ARA**

Association Régionale de Protection des Animaux *f:* **ARPA**

Association Scientifique et Technique pour l'Exploration des Oceans *f:* **ASTEO**

Association scientifique méditerranéenne de protection de l'environnement *f:* **MSAEP**

Association Scientifique pour la Culture et le Développement de l'Hydroponique *f:* **ASCDH**

Association Sportive et Artistique de l'École d'Application des Transmissions *f:* **ASAEAT**

Association Suisse des géologues et ingénieurs du Pétrole *f:* **ASP**

Association Suisse des Maîtres-Cordonniers et Bottiers-Orthopédistes *f:* **ASMCBO**

Association Suisse des Maîtres Ferblantiers et Appareilleurs *f:* **ASMFA**

Association suisse des Professeurs des Écoles Techniques Supérieures *f:* **ETS-Prof.**

Association suisse des Professeurs d'Éducation Physique aux École s secondaires supérieures *f:* **APEP**

Association Suisse des Techniciens-
Géomètres f: **ASTG**

Association Suisse des Écoles de Musique
f: **ASEM**

Association Suisse d'Économie Forestière
f: **ASEF**

Association Suisse d'Éducation Physique à
l'École f: **ASEP**

Association Technique de l'Industrie
Papetière f: **ATIP**

Association Technique pour la
Vulgarisation Forestière f: **ATVF**

Association Technique pour l'Utilisation du
Laitier des hauts-fourneaux f: **ATUL**

Association Universitaire pour
l'Environnement f: **AUE**

Association Vaudoise des Écoles Privées f:
AVDEP

Association Vaudoise d'Établissements
Médico-Sociaux f: **AVDEMS**

Associazione Campana degli Insegnanti di
Scienze Naturali i: **ACISN**

Associazione Commercianti Importatori
Macchine de Cantiere ed Affini i:
CANTIERMACCHINE

Associazione degli Industriali delle
Conserve Animali i: **AICA**

Associazione dei Biologi delle Facoltà di
Farmacia i: **AbF**

Associazione dei Geografi Italiani i:
A.GE.I.

Associazione di Medicina Sociale i: **AMS**

Associazione Europea di Medicina Interna
i: **AEMIE**

Associazione Geofisica Italiana i: **AGI**

Associazione Internazionale delle Società di
Microbiologia i: **AISM**

Associazione Italiana de Medicina
Aeronautica e Spaziale i: **AIMAS**

Associazione Italiana degli Insegnanti di
Geografia i: **AIIG**

Associazione Italiana dei Commercianti e
degli Utilizzatori de Amidi, Fecole e
Prodotti Derivati i: **COMAMIDI**

Associazione Italiana di Ingegneria Medica
e Biologica i: **A.I.I.M.B.**

Associazione Italiana di Microbiologia
Applicata i: **SIMA**

Associazione Italiana di Oncologia Medica
i: **A.I.O.M.**

Associazione Italiana di Radiobiologia
Medica i: **AIRBM**

Associazione Italiana di Radiologia e
Medicina Nucleare i: **A.I.R.M.N.**

Associazione Italiana di Urologia
Ginecologicae del Pavimento Pelvico i:
AIUG

Associazione Italiana Lattiero-Casearia i:
ASSOLATTE

Associazione Medica Italiana i: **AMI**

Associazione Medica Italiana di Paraplegia
i: **A.M.I.P.**

Associazione Medica Italiana per lo Studio
della Ipnosi i: **A.M.I.S.I.**

Associazione Medici Cattolici Italiana i:
A.M.C.I.

Associazione Medici Dentisti Italiani i:
AMDI, i: **AMIDI**

Associazione Medici Geriatri Italiani i:
AMGI

Associazione Micologica ed Ecologica
Romana i: **A.M.E.R.**

Associazione Naturista Italiana i: **AN-ITA**

Associazione Nazionale Aziende
Distributrici Specialità-Medicinali e
Prodotti Chimico-Farmaceutici i:
ANADISME

Associazione Nazionale dei Granatieri i:
A.N.G.

Associazione Nazionale Grassi Animali i:
ASSOGRASSI

Associazione Professionale Italiana Medici
Oculisti i: **APIMO**

Associazione Scientifica di Produzione
Animale i: **ASPA**

Associazione Stampa Medica Italiana i:
ASMI

Associazione Svizzera dei Medici Assistenti
e Capiclinica i: **ASMAC**

Associometrics Remote Terminal Inquiry
Control System e: **ARTIC System**

Assurance des Machines et Chantiers f:
AMC

Assurance Medical Society e: **AMS**

Assured Mission Support Space
Architecture e: **AMSSA**

Astarte: Journal of Arctic Biology e:
Astarte: J. Arctic Biol.

Aston Dark Space e: **ADS**

astrobiological e: **astrobio**

astrobiologist e: **astrobio**

astrobiology e: **astrobio**

Astrobiology e: **ASTROBIOL**

Astrogeodetic World Datum e: **AWD**

Astrogeological e: **astrog.**

astrogeologist e: **astrog**

astrogeology e: **astrog**

astrogeology of celestial bodies e:
astrogeo

Astrogeophysical Transmission Network
e: **ATN**

Astromedicine e: **ASTROMED**

Astronautics and Space e: **ASTROSPACE**

Astronomical and Space Techniques for
Research on the Atmosphere e: **ASTRA**

Astronomical, Atmospheric, Earth and
Ocean Sciences e: **AAEO**

Astronomical, Earth and Ocean Sciences
e: **AEOS**

Astronomical Observatory e: **AO**

Astronomical Observatory of Cordoba e:
MAS

Astronomical Observatory Satellite e:
AOS

Astronomical Radio Interferometric Earth
Surveying e: **ARIES**

astronomical roentgen observatory e: **asro**

Astronomical Space Telescope Research
Assembly e: **Astra**

Astronomy, Space and Radio Division e:
ASRD

Astronomy with a Neutrino Telescope and
Abyss environmental Research e:
ANTARES

Astrophysical Observatory e: **APO**, e:
Astlo Obsv, e: **Astro. Obsv.**

Astrophysical Observatory, Potsdam e:
AOP

Astrophysical, Planetary and Atmospheric
Sciences e: **APAS**

ASW Environmental Aquatic Support e:
AEAS

ASWEPS [Anti-Submarine Warfare
Environmental Prediction Warfare]
Submarine Ocean e: **ASODDS**

Asynchronous Bipolar Pulse Length
Modulation e: **ABPLM**

Asynchronous Remote Takeover e: **ART**

Asynchronous Remote Takeover Server e:
ARTS

Asynchronous Remote Takeover Terminal
e: **ARTT**

at-sea calibration procedure e: **ascap**

Atelier Permanent d'Initiation à
l'Environnement Urbain f: **APIEU**

Atelier sur les données relatives au système
océan/climat f: **OCDW**

Atelier Technique des Espaces Naturels f:
ATEN

Atelier-École Professionnel f: **A.E.P.**

Ateliers de Mécanique et Décolletage de
Précision f: **AMDEP**

Ateliers et Chantiers de la Manche f: **ACM**

Ateliers et chantiers de la Manche de
Dieppe f: **A.C.M.**

Ateliers et Chantiers de la Manche de
Dieppe f: **A.C.M. Dieppe**

Ateliers et Chantiers de l'Afrique
Équatoriale f: **ACAE**

Ateliers et Chantiers de Mali f: **ACM**

Ateliers et Chantiers de Seine Maritime f:
ACSM

Ateliers et Chantiers Navals de La
Rochelle-Pallice f: **ACRP**

Ateneo de Historia de la Medicina s: **AHM**

Athmospheric Temperature e: **TO**

Atlantic Aerospace Rescue and Recovery
Center e: **AARC**, e: **AARRC**

Atlantic Circulation and Climate
Experiment e: **ACCE**

Atlantic Climate Change Programme e:
ACCP

Atlantic Database for Exchange Processes
at the Deep Sea Floor e: **ADEPD**

Atlantic Deeper Waterways Association e:
ADWA

Atlantic Environmental Group e: **AEG**

Atlantic Fleet Polaris Material Office e:
AFPMO

Atlantic Geology e: **Atl. Geol.**

Atlantic Geoscience Centre e: **AGC**

Atlantic Intracoastal Waterway e: **AIW**

Atlantic Marine Oceanographic Laboratory
e: **AMOL**

Atlantic Meteorology Experiment e:
AMEX

Atlantic [Ocean] e: **ATL**

Atlantic Ocean e: **Atl O**, e: **L**

Atlantic Ocean Area e: **AOA**

Atlantic Ocean Recovery Area e: **AORA**

Atlantic Ocean Region e: **AOR**

Atlantic Ocean Ship e: **AOS**

Atlantic Oceanographic and Meteorological
Laboratories (or Laboratory) e: **AOML**

Atlantic Oceanographic Group e: **AOG**

Atlantic Oceanographic Laboratories (or
Laboratory) e: **AOL**

Atlantic Oceanography Laboratories e:
AOL

Atlantic-Pacific Interoceanic Canal Study
Commission e: **APICSC**

Atlantic-Pacific Interoceanic-Canal Study
Commission e: **APISC**

Atlantic Region\Atmospheric Environment
Service, Environment Canada Halifax,
Nova Scova e: **NSHW**

Atlantic Richfield Co., Geoscience Library,
Dallas e: **TxDaAR-G**

Atlantic Sea Run Salmon Commission *e:* **ASRSC**

Atlantic Underwater (or Undersea) Test Evaluation Center *e:* **AUTEC**

Atlantic Waterfowl Council *e:* **AWC**

Atlas Biomedical Literature System *e:* **ABLS**

Atlas Geológicos/Geofísicos Internacionales de los Océanos Atlántico y Pacífico *s:* **GAPA**

Atmosféricos *s:* **XS**

Atmosphäre *d:* **Atm.**

Atmosphäre, technische *d:* **attech**

Atmosphäre[n] absolut *d:* **ata**

Atmosphäre[n] Überdruck *d:* **atü**

Atmosphäre[n] Unterdruck *d:* **atu**

atmosphärisch *d:* **atm.**

atmosphärische Abbremsanalyse *d:* **AAA**

Atmosphere *e:* **A**, *e:* **AT**, *e:* **ATMOS**

atmosphere absolute *e:* **atm. abs.**

Atmosphere and Land Surface Processes *e:* **ALSP**

Atmosphere and Space *e:* **AS**

Atmosphere Boundary Layer Facility *e:* **ABLF**

Atmosphere Climate Study *e:* **ACS**

Atmosphere Control System *e:* **ACS**

Atmosphere Ecosystem Gas Interchange Study *e:* **AEGIS**

Atmosphere Exchange System *e:* **AES**

Atmosphere Explorer *e:* **AE**

Atmosphere Explorer B *e:* **AE-B**

Atmosphere Explorer E *e:* **AE-E**

Atmosphere General Circuiation Experiment *e:* **AGCE**

Atmosphere, Ionosphere and Magnetosphere *e:* **AIM**

Atmosphere Launched Boost Intercept System *e:* **ALBIS**

Atmosphere Model Working Group *e:* **AMWG**

Atmosphere, Normal *e:* **an**

Atmosphere Normale Internationale *f:* **ANI**

Atmosphere-Ocean *e:* **AO**, *e:* **Atmos.-Ocean**

Atmosphere/Ocean Chemistry Experiment *e:* **AEROCE**

Atmosphere-Ocean General Circulation Model *e:* **AOGCM**

Atmosphere-Ocean System *e:* **Atmos.-Ocean Syst.**

Atmosphere (or Atmospheric) Radiation and Cloud Station *e:* **ARCS**

Atmosphere par Lidar Sur Saliout *f:* **ALISSA**

Atmosphere Particulate Radioactivity Detector *e:* **APRD**

Atmosphere Radiation Monitor *e:* **ARM**

Atmosphere Reactants Supply System *e:* **ARSS**

Atmosphere Revitalization Section *e:* **ARS**

Atmosphere Revitalization System *e:* **ARS**

Atmosphere Sensing and Maintenance System *e:* **ASMS**

Atmosphere Spectroscopy Applications *e:* **ASA**

Atmosphere Storage and Control Section *e:* **ASCS**

Atmosphere Storage and Control [Sub]system *e:* **ASCS**

Atmosphere-Surface Turbulent Exchange Research *e:* **ASTER**

atmosphere [technical] *e:* **at.**

atmosphere[s] *e:* **at.**

Atmosphere[s] *e:* **ATM**

Atmospheres Absolute *e:* **ATA**

atmospheres absolute *e:* **atm ab**

Atmospheres absolute over Sea level *e:* **ATS**

Atmospheric *e:* **ATMOS**

Atmospheric Analysis and Prediction *e:* **AAP**

Atmospheric [and] Environmental Research, Inc. *e:* **AER**

Atmospheric and Meteorological Ocean Remote Sensing Assembly *e:* **AMORSA**

Atmospheric and Meteorological Remote Sensing Assembly *e:* **AMRSA**

Atmospheric and Ocean Sciences Program *e:* **AOSP**

Atmospheric and Oceanic (or Oceanographic) Information Proeessing System *e:* **AOIPS**

Atmospheric and Oceanic Physics *e:* **Atmos. Oceanic Phys.**, *e:* **Atmos. Oceanic Phys.**

Atmospheric and Oceanographic Image Processing System *e:* **AOIPS**

Atmospheric and Oceanographic Satellite *e:* **ATMOS**

Atmospheric and Space Physics *e:* **AP**

Atmospheric and Space Plasma Physics *e:* **ASPP**

Atmospheric Angular Momentum *e:* **AAM**

Atmospheric Applications *e:* **AA**

Atmospheric Attack Indications System *e:* **AAIS**

Atmospheric Boundary Layer *e:* **ABL**

Atmospheric Boundary Layer Experiment *e:* **ABLE**

Atmospheric Burst Locator *e:* **ABL**

Atmospheric Camp *e:* **ATM**

Atmospheric Center of Data Working Group *e:* **ACDWG**

atmospheric changes *e:* **atm. chgs.**

Atmospheric Chemical Transformations *e:* **ACT**

Atmospheric Chemical-Transport *e:* **ACT**

Atmospheric Chemical Transport Model *e:* **ACTM**

Atmospheric Chemistry and Environmental Education in Global Change *e:* **ACEED**

Atmospheric Chemistry Division *e:* **ACD**

Atmospheric Chemistry Education in Global Change *e:* **ACE**

Atmospheric Chemistry Model *e:* **ACHEM**

Atmospheric Chemistry of Aerosols *e:* **ACA**

Atmospheric Chemistry of Transient Species *e:* **ACTS**

Atmospheric Chemistry Program *e:* **ACP**

Atmospheric Circulation in Relation to Oscillations of Sea-Ice and Salinity *e:* **ACROSS**

Atmospheric Collection Equipment *e:* **ACE**

Atmospheric Compensation (or Composition Satellite *e:* **ATCOS**

Atmospheric constituent model *e:* **AFGL**

Atmospheric Contamination Potential *e:* **ACP**

Atmospheric Control Experimentation *e:* **ACE**

Atmospheric Corrosion-rate Monitor[s] *e:* **ACM**

Atmospheric Corrosion Resistant *e:* **ACR**

Atmospheric Data Acquisition System *e:* **ADAS**

Atmospheric Defense Initiative *e:* **ADI**

Atmospheric Devices Laboratory *e:* **ADL**

Atmospheric Diffusion Measuring System *e:* **ADMS**

Atmospheric Diffusion of Beryllium Program *e:* **ADOBE**

Atmospheric Dispersion of Beryllium Program *e:* **ADOBE Program**

Atmospheric Dispersion of Radionuclides *e:* **AIRDOS-EPA**

Atmospheric Diving Suit *e:* **ADS**

Atmospheric Diving System *e:* **ADS**

Atmospheric Dump Valves *e:* **ADV**

Atmospheric dynamics and fluxes in the Mediterranean Sea *e:* **DYFAMED**

Atmospheric Dynamics Program *e:* **ADP**

Atmospheric Effect Correction System *e:* **AECS**

Atmospheric Effects of Stratospheric Aircraft *e:* **AESA**

Atmospheric Electric Detection System *e:* **AEDS**

Atmospheric Electrical Hazards Protection *e:* **AHEP**

Atmospheric Electricity Hazard *e:* **AEH**

Atmospheric Electricity Hazards Protection *e:* **AEHP**

Atmospheric Electromagnetic Pulse *e:* **AEMP**

Atmospheric Emissions Photo[metric] Imaging [experiment] *e:* **AEPI**

Atmospheric Emitted Radiance Instrument *e:* **AEEI**, *e:* **AERI**

Atmospheric Emitted Radiance Interferometer *e:* **AERI**

Atmospheric Emitted Radiance Interferometer-extended resolution *e:* **AERI-X**

Atmospheric Entry *e:* **AE**

Atmospheric Environment *e:* **Atmos. Environ.**

Atmospheric Environment Service, Environment Canada Dorval, Quebec *e:* **QMEA**

Atmospheric Environment Service, Environment Canada Ville St-Laurent, Quebec *e:* **QVSLEA**

Atmospheric Environment[al] Service *e:* **AES**

Atmospheric Exchange System *e:* **AES**

Atmospheric Experiment on Orographic flows, Leewaves, Upslope Snowstorms, severe downslope wind storms *e:* **AEOLUS**

atmospheric experimental branch *e:* **SGG**

Atmospheric Explorer Mission *e:* **AEM**

Atmospheric Explorer Satellite *e:* **AE**

Atmospheric Fleet Support *e:* **AERO**

Atmospheric Flight *e:* **AF**

Atmospheric Flight Test *e:* **AFT**

Atmospheric Fluid Bed Combustion *e:* **AFB Combustion**

Atmospheric Fluid[ized] Bed *e:* **AFB**

Atmospheric Fluidized Bed Coal *e:* **AFBC**

Atmospheric Fluidized-Bed Combustion (or Combustor) *e:* **AFBC**

Atmospheric Forcings for the Mid-Atlantic Bight *e:* **AFMAB**

Atmospheric Gas Measurements Section *e:* **AGM**

Atmospheric Gas Oil *e:* **AGO**

Atmospheric General Circulation Model *e:* **ACCM**

Atmospheric General Circulation Model[s] *e:* **AGCM**

Atmospheric Global Climate Model *e:* **AGCM**

atmospheric head [symbol] *e:* **h**

Atmospheric Infrared-Advanced Microwave Sounding Unit *e:* **AIRS-AMSU**

Atmospheric Infrared Attenuation Coefficient *e:* **AIRAC**

Atmospheric Infrared Sounder *e:* **AIRS**

Atmospheric Integrated Research Monitoring Network *e:* **AIRMON**

Atmospheric Interceptor Technology *e:* **AIT**

Atmospheric Kinetics Project *e:* **AKP**

Atmospheric Laboratory for Applications and Science *e:* **ATLAS**

Atmospheric Laboratory for Applications Science *e:* **ALAS**

Atmospheric Laser Doppler Instrument *e:* **ALADIN**

Atmospheric Layer and Density Distribution of Ions and Neutrons [Rocket] *e:* **ALADDIN [Rocket]**

Atmospheric Lidar *e:* **ATLID**

Atmospheric LIDAR Experiment in Space *e:* **ALEXIS**

Atmospheric Lifetime Experiment/ Global Atmospheric Gases Experiment *e:* **AGAGE**

Atmospheric Lifetime[s] Experiment *e:* **ALE**

Atmospheric Light Detection and Ranging Facility *e:* **LIDAR**

Atmospheric Lyman Alpha Emissions (or Experiment) *e:* **ALAE**

Atmospheric, Magnetospheric and Plasma Studies *e:* **AMPS**

Atmospheric Magnetospheric Plasma in Space *e:* **AMPS**

Atmospheric Magnetospheric Plasma System *e:* **AMPS**

Atmospheric Mass Balance of Industrially Emitted and Natural Sulfur *e:* **AMBIENS**

Atmospheric Measurement System *e:* **AMS**

Atmospheric Mesoscale Campaigns *e:* **AMC**

Atmospheric Meteorological Probe *e:* **AMP**

Atmospheric Model Intercomparison Project *e:* **AMIP**

Atmospheric Model Intercomparison Project, phase I *e:* **AMIP I**

Atmospheric Model Intercomparison Project, phase II *e:* **AMIP II**

Atmospheric Moisture Intercomparison Study *e:* **ATMIS-II**

Atmospheric Monitor System *e:* **AMS**

Atmospheric Nutrient Input to Coastal Areas *e:* **ANICA**

Atmospheric Observation Panel for Climate *e:* **AOPC**

Atmospheric Odd Nitrogen species project *e:* **AON**

Atmospheric Particle Monitor *e:* **APM**

Atmospheric Passivation Module *e:* **APM**

Atmospheric Physical and Chemical (or Chemistry) Monitor *e:* **APACM**

Atmospheric Physics and Chemistry Laboratory *e:* **APCL**

Atmospheric Pollution Sensor *e:* **APS**

Atmospheric Pressure *e:* **AP**

atmospheric pressure *e:* **atm. pr.,** *e:* **atm press**

Atmospheric Pressure and Composition Control *e:* **APCC**

Atmospheric Pressure at Aerodrome Elevation *e:* **QFE**

Atmospheric Pressure Chemical Ionization *e:* **APCI**

Atmospheric Pressure Chemical Vapor Deposition *e:* **APCVD**

Atmospheric Pressure Converted to Mean Sea Level Elevation *e:* **QFF**

Atmospheric Pressure Ion Evaporation *e:* **APIE**

Atmospheric Pressure Ionization *e:* **API**

Atmospheric Pressure Ionization Mass Spectroscopy *e:* **APIMS**

Atmospheric Pressure Plasma Sprayed *e:* **APPS**

Atmospheric Pressure Supply [Sub]system *e:* **APSS**

Atmospheric Protection System *e:* **APS**

Atmospheric Quality and Modification *e:* **AQM**

Atmospheric Quality Division *e:* **AQD**

Atmospheric Radiation Analysis *e:* **ARA**

Atmospheric Radiation Measurement-Clouds and Radiation Testband *e:* **ARM-CART**

Atmospheric Radiation Measurement [program] *e:* **ARM**

Atmospheric Radiation Measurement Satellite *e:* **ARMSAT**

Atmospheric Radiation Monitoring *e:* **ARM**

Atmospheric Radiation Working Group *e:* **ARWG**

Atmospheric Radiative Heating *e:* **ARH**

Atmospheric Radio Noise *e:* **ARN**

Atmospheric Radio Wave *e:* **ARW**

Atmospheric Release Advisory Capability [program] *e:* **ARAC**

Atmospheric Research *e:* **Atmos. Res.**

Atmospheric Research and Environment Programme *e:* **AREP**

Atmospheric Research and Exposure Assessment Laboratory *e:* **AREAL**

Atmospheric Research and Remote Sensing Plane *e:* **ARAT**

Atmospheric Research Information Exchange Study *e:* **ARIES**

Atmospheric Research Program *e:* **ARP**

Atmospheric Research Program Staff *e:* **ARPS**

atmospheric research satellite carrying experiments from Italy Germany and the United States *e:* **San Marco D**

Atmospheric Revitalization *e:* **AR**

Atmospheric Revitalization Pressure Control System *e:* **ARPCS**

Atmospheric Science Facility *e:* **ASF**

Atmospheric Sciences Center *e:* **ASC**

Atmospheric Sciences Department *e:* **ASD**

Atmospheric Science[s] Laboratory *e:* **ASL**

Atmospheric Sciences Laboratory *e:* **SL**

Atmospheric Sciences Modeling Division *e:* **ASMD**

Atmospheric Sciences Research Center *e:* **ASRC**

Atmospheric Science[s] Research Laboratory *e:* **ASRL**

Atmospheric Simulations Over Complex Terrain *e:* **ASCOT**

Atmospheric Sound-Focusing Gain *e:* **ASFG**

Atmospheric Sound Refraction *e:* **ASR**

Atmospheric Sounding, Central Evaluation and Test Support *e:* **ASCENT**

Atmospheric Sounding Projectile *e:* **ASP**

Atmospheric Stablization Framework *e:* **ASF**

Atmospheric Studies in Complex Terrain *e:* **ASCOT**

Atmospheric Surface Layer *e:* **ASL**

Atmospheric Surveillance Technology *e:* **AST**

Atmospheric Tactical Missile *e:* **ATM**

Atmospheric Tactical Warning Connectivity *e:* **ATWC**

Atmospheric Technology Division *e:* **ATD**

Atmospheric Trace Molecules Observed by Spectroscopy *e:* **ATMOS**

Atmospheric Transmission Factor *e:* **ATF**

Atmospheric Transmission Measurement Equipment *e:* **ATME**

Atmospheric Transport and Dispersion *e:* **ATAD**

Atmospheric Transport Model *e:* **ATM**

Atmospheric Transport Model Evaluation Study *e:* **ATMES**

Atmospheric Turbulence and Diffusion Division *e:* **ATDD**

Atmospheric Turbulence and Diffusion Laboratory *e:* **ATDL**

Atmospheric Utility Signatures-Predictions and Experiments *e:* **AUSPEX**

Atmospheric Variability Experiment *e:* **AVE**

Atmospheric Vehicle Detection *e:* **AVD**

Atmospheric Vertical Profiling System *e:* **AVAPS**

Atmospheric Wind Velocity *e:* **AWV**

Atmospheric Winds Aloft *e:* **AWA**

Atmospheric[al] *e:* **atm**

atmospheric[al][ly] *e:* **atmos**

Atmospheric[s] *e:* **ATM**

Atmospherics *e:* **Sferics,** *e:* **Xs**

atomare, biologische und chemische Waffen *d:* **ABC-Waffen**

Atomedic Research Center *e:* **ARC**

Atomenergiegegner Bürgerinitiative für umweltfreundliche Energiepolitik *d:* **AEG**

Atomic and Space Development Authority *e:* **ASDA**

Atomic, Biological and Chemical Defense *e:* **ABCD**

Atomic, Biological, and Chemical Washdown *e:* **ABC Washdown**

Atomic, Biological, Chemical *e:* **ABC**

Atomic, Biological, Chemical and Damage [Control] *e:* **ABCD**

Atomic, Biological, Chemical, and Damage Control *e:* **ABCD Control**

Atomic, Biological, Chemical, and Radiological *e:* **ABCR**

Atomic, Biological, Chemical Warfare *e:* **ABCW**

Atomic Defense and Space Group *e:* **ADSG**

Atomic Energy Commission-National Aeronautics and Space Administration *e:* **AEC-NASA**

atomic hydrogen weld *e:* **at/w**

Atomic Hydrogen Welding *e:* **AHW**

Atomic Industrial [Health] Forum, Inc. *e:* **AIF**

Atomic Orbital *e:* **AO**

Atomic Reactor in Space *e:* **ARIS**

Atomic Spin Orbital *e:* **ASO**

Atomorbitale *d:* **AO**

Attack Geometry Display *e:* **AGD**

Atti de la Societa Italiana di Scienze Naturali *i:* **Atti Soc. Ital. Sci. Nat.**

Atti del Museo Civico di Storia Naturale-Trieste *i:* **Atti Mus. Civ. Stor. Nat., Trieste**

Atti della Societa Peloritana di Scienze Fisiche Matematiche e Naturali *i:* **Atti Soc. Pelorit. Sci. Fis. Mat. Nat.**

Atti dell'Accademia Nazionale dei Lincei. Classe di Scienze Fisiche, Matematiche e Naturali. Memorie. Sezione 3 *i:* **Atti Accad. Naz. Lincei Cl. Sci. Fis. Mat. Nat. Mem., 3**

Attitude and Orbit Control *e:* **AOC**

Attitude and Orbit Control System *e:* **AOCS**

Attitude and Orbital Control Subsystem *e:* **AOCS**

Atwater Kent Museum, Philadelphia, PA *e:* **PPAK**

Atwater Library Montreal, Quebec *e:* **QMMI**

Audiovisual Conference of Medical and Allied Sciences *e:* **ACMAS**

Audubon National Wildlife Refuge *e:* **ANWR**

Audubon Naturalist Society of the Central Atlantic States *e:* **ANS**

Audubon Shrine and Wildlife Sanctuary *e:* **ASWS**

Aufbereitunggssystem, kernspeicherorientiert *d:* **ASKO**

Aufbereitungssystem, festplattenspeicherorientiert *d:* **ASFO**

Aufbereitungssystem, magnetbandorientiert *d:* **ASMO**

Aufbereitungssystem, plattenspeicherorientiert *d:* **ASPO**

Aufbereitungssystem, trommelorientiert *d:* **ASTO**

Augusta Area Committee for Health Information Resources *e:* **AACHIR**

Auroral Atmospheric Radiance Code *e:* **AARC**

Auroral Hydrogen Line *e:* **AHL**

Auroral Hydrogen Line Emission *e:* **AHLE**

Auroral Imaging Observatory *e:* **AIO,** *e:* **AURIO**

Auroral Imaging Remote Sensor *e:* **AIRS**

Ausbildungsgerät Unterwasserwaffen *d:* **AGUW**

Ausgabekonvertierung - tetradische *d:* **AUKO-T**

Ausschuß für biologische Sicherheit *d:* **ABS**

Ausschuß Lebensmittelchemie der Arbeitsgemeinschaft der für das Gesundheitswesen zuständigen Landesminister *d:* **ALAG**

Ausstellung für Gesundheitspflege, soziale Fürsorge und Leibesübungen *d:* **Gesolei**

Australasian Bulletin of Medical Physics and Biophysics *e:* **Australas. Bull. Med. Phy. Bio**

Australasian College for Advancement in Medicine *e:* **ACAM**

Australasian College for [of] Emergency Medicine *e:* **ACEM**

Australasian College of Nutritional & Environmental Medicine *e:* **ACNEM**

Australasian College of Physical Scientists and Engineers in Medicine *e:* **ACPESM,** *e:* **ACPSEM**

Australasian Faculty of Public Health Medicine *e:* **AFPHM**

Australasian Federation for Medical and Veterinary Mycology *e:* **AFMVM**

Australasian Medical Writers Association *e:* **AMWA**

Australasian Physical and Engineering Sciences in Medicine *e:* **Australas Phys Eng Sci Med**

Australasian Physical & Engineering Sciences in Medicine *e:* **APESM**

Australasian Society for HIV Medicine *e:* **ASHM**

Australasian Society for Ultrasound in Medicine *e:* **ASUM**

Australasian Society of Oral Medicine and Toxicology *e:* **ASOMAT**

Australasian Wildlife Management Society *e:* **AWMS**

Australia. Commonwealth Scientific and Industrial Organisation. Division of Fisheries and Oceanography. Fisheries Synopsis *e:* **AOFSA9**

Australia. Commonwealth Scientific and Industrial Research Organisation. Division of Meteorological Physics. Technical Paper *e:* **AOMPAZ**

Australia/France Joint Working Group on the Environment *e:* **AFJWG**

Australia New Zealand and Oceania *e:* **ANZO**

Australia-New Zealand-United Kingdom Intergovernmental Agreement On Climate Change *e:* **ANZUK**

Australia.Commonwealth Scientific and Industrial Research Organisation. Groundwater Research. Technical Paper *e:* **GRTPEP**

Australian Aerial Medical Services *e:* **AAMS**

Australian Agricultural Health and Quarantine Service *e:* **AAHQS**

Australian Alternative Health Directory *e:* **AAHD**

Australian and New Zealand Association for Medical Education *e:* **ANZAME**

Australian and New Zealand Council for the Care of Animals in Research and Teaching (or Training) *e:* **ANZCCART**

Australian and New Zealand Environment Council *e:* **ANZEC**

Australian and New Zealand Environment[al] and Conservation Council *e:* **ANZECC**

Australian and New Zealand Environmental Report *e:* **ANV**

Australian and New Zealand Federation of Animal Societies *e:* **ANZFAS**

Australian and New Zealand Journal of Medicine *e:* **Aust. N.Z.J. Med.**

Australian and New Zealand Journal of Obstetrics and Gynaecology *e:* **Aust. N.Z.J. Obstet. Gynaecol.**

Australian and New Zealand Society for Epidemiology and Research in Community Health *e:* **ANZSERCH**

Australian and New Zealand Society of Nuclear Medicine *e:* **ANZSNM**

Australian and New Zealand Society of Occupational Medicine *e:* **ANZSOM**

Australian and New Zealand Society of Oral Surgeons *e:* **ANZSOS**

Australian Animal Health Council *e:* **AAHC**

Australian Animal Health Laboratory *e:* **AAHL**

Australian Animal Resources Network *e:* **AARNET**

Australian Antarctic Marine Biological Ecosystem Research *e:* **AAMBER**

Australian Army Medical Corps *e:* **AAMC**

Australian Army Medical Women's Service *e:* **AAMWS**

Australian Association for Environmental Education *e:* **AAEE**

Australian Association of Animal Breeding and Genetics *e:* **AAABG**

Australian Association of Infant Mental Health *e:* **AAIMHI**

Australian Association of Surgeons *e:* **AAS**

Australian Association of Veterinary Conservation Biologists *e:* **AAVCB**

Australian Biogeographic Information System *e:* **ABIS**

Australian Biological and Environmental Survey *e:* **ABES**

Australian Biological Resources Study *e:* **ABRS**

Australian Biological Resources Study Advisory Committee (or Council) *e:* **ABRSAC**

Australian Bureau of Animal Health *e:* **ABAH**

Australian Bureau of Meteorology *e:* **ABOM,** *e:* **BOM**

Australian Cancer Fund for Medical Research *e:* **ACFMR**

Australian Capital Territory Electricity and Water *e:* **ACTEW**

Australian Catholic Health Care Association *e:* **ACHCA**

Australian Centre for Catchment Hydrology *e:* **ACCH**

Australian Centre for Environmental Law *e:* **ACEL**

Australian Centre for Remote Sensing *e:* **ACRES**

Australian Centre for Water Quality Research *e:* **ACWQR**

Australian College of Dental Surgeons *e:* **ACDS**

Australian College of Health Service Executives *e:* **ACHSE**

Australian College of Herbal Medicine *e:* **ACoHM**

Australian College of Obstetricians and Gynaecologists *e:* **A.C.O.G.**

Australian College of Occupational Medicine *e:* **ACOM**

Australian College of Rural and Remote Medicine e: **ACRRM**

Australian Committee for Earth Resources Satellites e: **ACERTS**

Australian Committee for the International Union for the Conservation of Nature and Natural Resources e: **ACIUCN**

Australian Committee for the World Climate Research Programme e: **ACWCRP**

Australian Community Health Association e: **ACHA**

Australian Companion Animal Health Foundation e: **ACAHF**

Australian Congress of Mental Health Nurses e: **ACMHN**

Australian Council for Care of Animals in Research and Teaching e: **ACCART**

Australian Council for Health, Physical Education, and Recreation e: **ACHPER**

Australian Council on Healthcare Standards e: **ACHS**

Australian Data Archive for Meteorology e: **ADAM**

Australian Department of Health & Aged Care e: **ACC**

Australian Department of Health and Family Services e: **HFS**

Australian Drug and Medical Information Group e: **ADMIG**

Australian Earth Science[s] Information Systems [Advisory Committee (or Council)] e: **AESIS**

Australian Environment[al] Council e: **AEC**

Australian Environmental Geographic Information System e: **AEGIS**

Australian Environment[al] Management Export Corporation Ltd e: **AUSTEMEX**

Australian Environmental On-line Service e: **AEOS**

Australian Environmental Statistics Project e: **AESOP**

Australian Federation for Medical and Biological Engineering e: **AFMBE**

Australian Federation for the Welfare of Animals e: **AFWA**

Australian Federation of Medical Women e: **AFMW**

Australian Fire Protection Association e: **AFPA**

Australian Fish Health Reference Laboratory e: **AFHRL**

Australian Fresh Water Fishermen's Assembly e: **AFWFA**

Australian Frontier Incorporated e: **AFI**

Australian Geodetic Datum e: **AGD**

Australian Geographic e: **Aust. Geogr.**

Australian Geographic Data Base e: **AGDB**

Australian Geographic[al] Society e: **AGS**

Australian Geographical Studies e: **AGS**

Australian Geography Teachers Association e: **AGTA**

Australian Geological Survey Organisation (or Organization) e: **AGSO**

Australian Geomechanics Journal e: **Aust. Geomech. J.**

Australian Geomechanics Society e: **AGS**

Australian Global Ocean Observing System e: **AGOOS**

Australian Health Education Advisory Digest e: **AHEAD**

Australian Health Industry Development Forum e: **AHIDF**

Australian Health Informatics Association e: **AHIA**

Australian Health Information and Research Service e: **AHIRS**

Australian Health Insurance Association e: **AHIA**

Australian Health Insurance Program e: **AHIP**

Australian Health Ministers Conference e: **AHMC**, e: **ARMC**

Australian Health Outcomes Clearing House e: **AHOCH**

Australian Health Services Financial Management Association e: **AHSFMA**

Australian Healthcare Association e: **AHA**

Australian Historical Geography e: **AHG**

Australian Industrial Safety, Health, and Welfare Cases e: **AISHWC**

Australian Institute of Biology e: **AIB**

Australian Institute of Environmental Health e: **AIEH**

Australian Institute of Geoscientists e: **AIG**

Australian Institute of Health e: **AIH**

Australian Institute of Health and Welfare e: **AIHW**

Australian Institute of Health Surveyors e: **AIHS**

Australian Institute of Medical and Biological Illustrators e: **AIMBI**

Australian Institute of Medical Laboratory Technology e: **AIMLT**

Australian Institute of Medical Scientists e: **AIMS**

Australian Institute of Medical Technologists e: **AIMT**

Australian Integrative Medicine Association e: **AIMA**

Australian International Gravitational Observatory e: **AIGO**

Australian Journal for Health, Physical Education and Recreation e: **AJHPER**

Australian Journal of Biological Sciences e: **Aust. J. Biol. Sci.**

Australian Journal of Earth Sciences e: **Aust. J. Earth Sci.**

Australian Journal of Ecology e: **AJ Ecol**, e: **Aust. J. Ecol.**

Australian Journal of Experimental Agriculture and Animal Husbandry e: **Aust. J. Exp. Agric. Anim. Hus**

Australian Journal of Experimental Biology and Medical Science e: **Aust. J. Exp. Biol. Med. Sci.**

Australian Journal of Marine and Freshwater Research e: **Aust. J. Mar. Freshw. Res.**

Australian Journal of Medical Technology e: **Aust. J. Med. Technol.**

Australian Journal of Mental Health Nursing e: **AJMHN**

Australian Journal of Public Health e: **Aust J Public Health**

Australian Journal of Science and Medicine in Sport e: **Aust J Sci Med Sport**

Australian Liaison Committee on Remote Sensing by Satellite e: **ALCORSS**

Australian Marine Environment Protection Association e: **AUSMEPA**

Australian Medical Acupuncture College e: **AMAC**

Australian Medical Acupuncture Society e: **A.M.A.S.**

Australian Medical Association e: **AMA**

Australian Medical Index e: **AMI**

Australian Medical Informatics Association e: **AMIA**

Australian Medical Service[s] e: **AMS**

Australian Medical Students Association e: **AMSA**

Australian Medical Workforce Advisory Committee e: **AMWAC**

Australian Medical Writers Association e: **AMWA**

Australian Meteorological and Oceanographic Society e: **AMOS**

Australian Meteorological Association e: **AMA**

Australian Meteorological Magazine e: **AMM**

Australian Military Medical Association e: **AMMA**

Australian Minerals and Energy Environmental Foundation e: **AMEEF**

Australian Modular Optical Remote Sensor e: **AMORS**

Australian National Animal Disease Information System e: **ANADIS**

Australian National Animal Health Laboratory e: **ANAHL**

Australian National Association for Mental Health. Newsletter e: **Newsl Aust Natn Ass Ment Hlth**

Australian National Committee, International Geosphere Biosphere Program e: **ANCIGBP**

Australian National Geoscience Information Service e: **ANGIS**

Australian National Parks and Wildlife Service e: **ANPWS**

Australian National Radio Astronomy Observatory e: **ANRAO**, e: **ANROA**

Australian National Wildlife Collection e: **ANWC**

Australian Nature Conservation Agency e: **ANCA**

Australian NGO Environment Network e: **ANEN**

Australian Numerical Meteorology Research Center e: **ANMRC**

Australian Occupational Health & Safety Commission e: **AOHSC**

Australian People for Health, Education and Development Abroad e: **APHEDA**

Australian Photogrammetric and Remote Sensing Society e: **APRSS**

Australian Postgraduate Federation in Medicine e: **APFM**

Australian Radiation Protection and Nuclear Safety Agency e: **ARPANSA**

Australian Radiation Protection Society e: **ARPS**

Australian Remote Sensing Conference e: **ARSC**

Australian Resources and Environment Assessment e: **AREA**

Australian Rural Health Research Institute e: **ARHRI**

Australian Salaried Medical Officers Federation e: **ASMOF**

Australian Small Animal Veterinary Association e: **ASAVA**

Australian Society for Fish Biology e: **ASFB**

Australian Society for Geriatric Medicine *e:* **ASGM**

Australian Society for Laboratory Animal Science *e:* **ASLAS**

Australian Society for Medical Research *e:* **ASMR**

Australian Society for Microbiology *e:* **A.S.M.**

Australian Society for/of Animal Production *e:* **ASAP**

Australian Society for Reproductive Biology *e:* **ASRB**

Australian Society of Orthopaedic Surgeons *e:* **ASOS**

Australian Society of Plastic Surgeons *e:* **ASPS**

Australian Space Board *e:* **ASB**

Australian Space Office *e:* **ASO**

Australian Sports Medicine Federation *e:* **ASMF**

Australian Standard Geographical Classification *e:* **ASGC**

Australian Transcultural Mental Health Network *e:* **ATMHN**

Australian Underwater Federation *e:* **AUF**

Australian Water and Wastewater Association *e:* **AuWWA**, *e:* **AWWA**

Australian Water Quality Centre *e:* **AWQC**

Australian Water Research Advisory Council *e:* **AWRAC**

Australian Water Resources Council *e:* **AWRC**

Australian Water Resources Council Standing Committee *e:* **AWRCSC**

Australian Women's Health Network *e:* **AWHN**

Australia's Long-term Ecological Research & Monitoring Program *e:* **ALTERM**

Austrian Society for Aerospace Medicine *e:* **ASM**

Austrian Solar and Space Agency *e:* **ASSA**

Austrian Space Agency *e:* **ASA**

Auswertungsstelle für Strahlendosimeter bei der Gesellschaft für Strahlen- und Umweltforschung mbH *d:* **ASGSU**

Authentic Reproduction of an Independent Earth Satellite *e:* **ARIES**

Authority for Removal of Accepted Spacecraft Installations *e:* **AFROASI**

Authority Health and Safety Branch *e:* **AHSB**

Authority Health and Safety Division, Warrington, Lancashire *e:* **AHSD**

Authorized Medical Allowance List *e:* **AMAL**

Authorized Protective Connecting Module *e:* **APCM**

Auto-Dialled Remote Message Players *e:* **ADRMPS**

Auto Remote STUIII *e:* **ARSTU**

Automated Aeromedical Evacuation System *e:* **AAES**

Automated Audio Remote Test System *e:* **AARTS**

Automated Biological and Chemical Data *e:* **ABCD**

Automated Biological and Chemical Data System *e:* **ABCD System**

Automated Biological Laboratory *e:* **ABL**

Automated Biology Library *e:* **ABL**

Automated Budget Interactive Data Environment System *e:* **ABIDES**

Automated Classification of Medical Entities *e:* **ACME**

Automated Cloud Observation System *e:* **ACOS**

Automated Debugging Environment *e:* **ADE**

Automated Digital Weather Communications Program[me] *e:* **ADWCP**

Automated Environmental Control System *e:* **AECS**

Automated Environmental Prediction *e:* **AEP**

Automated Environmental Prediction System *e:* **AEPS**

Automated Geographic Information System *e:* **AGIS**

Automated Geomagnetic Airborne Survey System *e:* **AGASS**

Automated Health Research Information System *e:* **AHRIS**

Automated Ice Information System for Arctic *e:* **AIISA**

Automated Medical Examination System *e:* **AMES**

Automated Medical History *e:* **AMH**

Automated Medical Payment *e:* **AMP**

Automated Meteorological Data Acquisition System *e:* **AmeDAS**, *e:* **AMEDA System**

Automated Meteorological Observing System *e:* **AMOS**

Automated Meteorological Station *e:* **AMS**

Automated Meteorological Terminal Information Service *e:* **AMATIS**

Automated Military Medical Outpatient System *e:* **AMOS**

Automated Multi-phase Health Testing *e:* **AMHT**

Automated Multi-phase Health Testing and Services *e:* **AMHTS**

Automated (or Automatic) Digital Weather Switch *e:* **ADWS**

Automated (or Automatic) Geophysical Observatory *e:* **AGO**

Automated (or Automatic) Weather Station *e:* **AWS**

Automated Processing of Medical English *e:* **APME**

Automated Production Control Environment *e:* **APCE**

Automated Program to Project AIT [Advanced Individual Training] Training Spaces *e:* **APPATS**

Automated Remote Network Evaluation *e:* **ARNE**

Automated Remote Tracking System *e:* **ARTS**

Automated Remote Workstation *e:* **ARWS**

Automated Responsive Environment *e:* **ARE**

Automated Seismological Observation System *e:* **ASOS**

Automated Space Management *e:* **ASM**

Automated Surface Observation System *e:* **ASOS**, *e:* **ASOS`**

Automated Terminal Weather Dissemination Display System *e:* **ATWDDS**

Automated Weather Acquisition and Retrieval Data System *e:* **AWARDS**

Automated Weather Distribution System *e:* **AWDS**

Automated Weather Information Processing System *e:* **AIPS**

Automated Weather Information Systems *e:* **AWIS**

Automated Weather Network Coordinating System *e:* **AWNCS**

Automated Weather Network (USAF) *e:* **AWN**

Automated Weather Observing Station *e:* **AWOS**

Automated Weather Observing System *e:* **AWOS**

Automatic Audio Remote Test Set *e:* **AARTS**

Automatic Aviation Weather Service *e:* **AAWS**

Automatic Chemical Biological Warning System *e:* **ACBWS**

Automatic Climate Control *e:* **ACC**

Automatic Climate Station *e:* **ACS**

Automatic Climatological Recording Equipment *e:* **ACRE**

Automatic Combustion Control and Feedwater Control *e:* **ACC/FWC**

Automatic Direction Finder, Remote-control[led] *e:* **ADFR**

Automatic Environment Monitoring *e:* **AEM**

Automatic Flight Weather Advisory *e:* **AFWA**

Automatic Ground Environment Computer *e:* **AGEC**

Automatic Hydrologic Observing System *e:* **AHOS**

Automatic Hydrologic Radio Reporting Network *e:* **AHRRN**

Automatic Interface Management in Medicine *e:* **AIM**

Automatic Meteorological Correction *e:* **AUTOMET Correction**

Automatic Meteorological Data Acquisition and Processing System *e:* **AMDAPS**

Automatic Meteorological Data and Reporting *e:* **AMDAR**

Automatic Meteorological Observation (or Observing) Station *e:* **AMOS**

Automatic Meteorological Observation System *e:* **AMOS**

Automatic Meteorological Oceanographic Buoy *e:* **AMOB**

Automatic Meteorological Sensors System *e:* **AMSS**

Automatic Meteorological System *e:* **AMS**

Automatic Orbiting Operations System *e:* **AOOSY**

Automatic Polarity Indication *e:* **AUTOPOL Indication**, *e:* **AUTPOL Indication**

Automatic Power Protection *e:* **APP**

Automatic Protection Switch[ing] *e:* **APS**

Automatic Radio Meteorological Station *e:* **ARMS**

Automatic Recovery of Remotely piloted Aircraft *e:* **AURORA**

Automatic Remote Control *e:* **ARC**

Automatic Remote Control Unit *e:* **ARC Unit**

Automatic Remote Data Terminal *e:* **ARDT**

Automatic Remote Geomagnetic Observatory System *e:* **ARGOS**

Automatic-Remote-Meter *e:* **Armeter**

Automatic Remote Tracking Stations *e:*
ARTS

Automatic Signature Verification System
e: **ASVS**

Automatic Storm Observation Service *e:*
ASOS

Automatic Train Protection *e:* **ATP**

Automatic Trains, Protection, Operation
and Supervision *e:* **AUTOPOS**

Automatic Transportation, Protection,
Operation, and Supervision *e:*
AUTOPOS

Automatic, Unified Orbiting Station[s] *e:*
AUOS

Automatic Unmanned Weather Station *e:*
AUWS

Automatic Voice Link Observation *e:*
AVOLO

automatic water check *e:* **autmwtr ck**

Automatic Water Monitoring Station[s] *e:*
AWMS

Automatic Weapons Effects Signature
Simulator *e:* **AWESS**

Automatic Weather Broadcast Equipment
e: **AWBE**

Automatic Weather Data Acquisition and
Archiving System *e:* **AWDAAS**

Automatically Programmed Remote
Indication Logged (or Logging) *e:*
APRIL

Automation and Remote Control *e:*
Automat. Remote Contr.

Automation of Field Observations and
Services *e:* **AFOS**

Automatische Fernschreib-
Speichervermittlung beim Deutschen
Wetterdienst *d:* **AFSD**

Automatische Flugwetteransage *d:* **AFWA**

Automatische universelle Orbitalstation *d:*
AUOS

Automatische Wetterstation *e:* **AWSt**

Automatischer implantierbarer Defibrillator
d: **AID**

automatischer Überdeckungsrepeater *d:*
AÜR

Automatisches Biologisches Laboratorium
d: **ABL**

Automatisiertes Reproduktions-, Copier-
und Sortiersystem *d:* **ARCS**

automatisiertes System der Projektierung
d: **AS Proj.**

automatisiertes System der Projektierung
und Organisation des Bauwesens *d:*
ASPOB

Automatisierung der technologischen
Projektierung *d:* **AUTOPROJEKT**

automatic voice link observation *e:* **avolo**

Automedica Corp. *e:* **AM**

Automized Medical Anamnesis Dialog[ue]
Assistant *e:* **AMANDA**

Automized Medical Anamnesis Dialog[ue]
Assistant Computer *e:* **AMANDA**
Computer

Automobile, Aerospace, and Agricultural
Implement Workers of America *e:*
AAAIWA

Automobile-Club Luxembourgeois *f:*
A.C.L.

Automobile Protection Association *e:*
APA

Automotive Occupant Protection
Association *e:* **AOPA**

Automotive Pigeon Loft *e:* **APL**

Autonomous Machine Environmental
Surveillance System *e:* **AMESS**

Autonomous Space Processor for Orbital
Debris *e:* **ASPOD**

Autonomous Underwater Vehicle *e:* **AUV**

Autorización de Certificación Geopolítica
s: **GCA**

AUTOVON Remote Reprogrammable
Conference Arranger *e:* **ARPCA**

Auxiliary Area Environmental Control
System *e:* **AAECS**

Auxiliary Aviation Weather Facility *e:*
AAWF

Auxiliary Component Cooling Water
System *e:* **ACCWS**

Auxiliary Essential Raw Cooling Water *e:*
AERCW

Auxiliary Feedwater *e:* **AF**, *e:* **AFW**

Auxiliary Feedwater Actuating System *e:*
AFAS, *e:* **AFWAS**

Auxiliary Feedwater Control *e:* **AFWC**

Auxiliary Feedwater Storage Tank *e:*
AFST

Auxiliary Feedwater System *e:* **AFS**, *e:*
AFWS

Auxiliary Fresh Water *e:* **AFW**

Auxiliary General Oceanographic Research
e: **AGOR**

Auxiliary General Oceanographic Research
Vessel *e:* **AGOR Vessel**

Auxiliary Geographical Ship *e:* **AGS**

Auxiliary Ocean Tug *e:* **ATA**

Auxiliary Spacecraft Power *e:* **ASP**

Auxiliary to the National Medical
Association *e:* **ANMA**

Available Space List *e:* **ASL**, *e:* **AVSL**

Avances en Produccion Animal *e:*
APANDD

Aviación Ligera des Ejército de Tierra *s:*
ALET

Aviation Automated Weather-Observation
System *e:* **AV-AWOS**

Aviation Medical *e:* **AVM**

Aviation Medical Acceleration Laboratory
e: **AMAL**

Aviation Medical Examiner[s] *e:* **AME**

Aviation Medical Officer *e:* **AMO**

Aviation Medical (or Medicine) Society of
Australia and New Zealand *e:* **AMSANZ**

Aviation Medical Report[s] *e:* **AMR**

Aviation Medicine *e:* **AM**, *e:* **AVNMED**

Aviation Medicine Technician *e:* **AVT**

aviation observation *e:* **aviob**

Aviation (or Space) Writers Association *e:*
AWA

Aviation Sans Frontieres *f:* **ASF**

Aviation School of Medicine *e:* **ASM**

Aviation Space and Environmental
Medicine *e:* **Aviat Space Environ Med**

Aviation, Space & Environmental Medicine
e: **AS&EM**

Aviation/Space Writers' Association *e:*
A/SWA

Aviation Weather and Notice to Airmen
System *e:* **AWANAS**

Aviation Weather Center *e:* **AWC**

Aviation Weather Development Laboratory
e: **AWDL**

Aviation Weather Development Program
e: **AWDP**

Aviation Weather Facility *e:* **AWF**

Aviation Weather Forecasting Task Force
e: **AWFTF**

Aviation Weather Network *e:* **AWN**

Aviation Weather Processor *e:* **AWP**

Aviation Weather Products Generator *e:*
AWPG

Aviation Weather Program *e:* **AWP**

Aviation Weather Reporting Station *e:*
AWRS

Aviation Weather Service *e:* **AWS**

Aviation Week and Space Technology *e:*
Aviat. Week Space Technol., *e:*
AW&ST

Aviation Week and Space Technology
magazine *e:* **AWST**

Aviation Week & Space Technology *e:*
AW & ST

Aviator's Protective Helmet *e:* **APH**

Avion a Geometrie Variable *f:* **AGV**

Avion de recherche atmosphérique et de
télédétection *f:* **ARAT**

Avionic Observation of Intruder Danger *e:*
AVOID

Avionic Observation of Intruder Danger
System[s] *e:* **AVOIDS**

Avión de Investigación Atmosférica y de
Teledetección *s:* **ARAT**

AVL Gesellschaft für medizinische
Meßtechnik mbH *d:* **AVL**

AWIS Meteorological Applications *e:*
AMA

Axial Seamount Hydrothermal Emissions
Study *e:* **ASHES**

Axiolabiolingual *d:* **ALAL**

Ayrshire Archaeological and Natural
History Society *e:* **A.A.N.H.S.**

Azotierung *d:* **Azotier.**

Aéroclub des Grandes Écoles *f:* **AGE**

B

Baccalaureus Medicinae *l:* **BM**

Bachelor Noncommissioned Officers'
Quartiers *e:* **BNCOQ**

Bachelor of Ayurvedic Medicine and
Surgery *e:* **B.A.M.S.**

Bachelor of Biological Chemistry *e:* **B Bi**
Ch, *e:* **B Bi Chem**

Bachelor of Biological Engineering *e:* **B**
Bi E, *e:* **B Bi Eng**

Bachelor of Biological Physics *e:* **B Bi**
Phy

Bachelor of Biological Sciences *e:* **B Bi Sc**

Bachelor of Geological Engineering *e:*
B.G.E., *e:* **B Ge E**, *e:* **B Ge Eng**

Bachelor of Indian Medicine *e:* **BIM**, *e:*
B.I.M.

Bachelor of Medical Biology *e:*
B.Med.Biol.

Bachelor of Medical Engineering *e:* **BME**

Bachelor of Medical Science *e:* **B Med Sc**,
e: **BMedSci**, *e:* **B.M.S.**

Bachelor of Medical Technology *e:*
B.M.T.

Bachelor of Medicine *e:* **BM**, *e:* **B Med**, *e:*
M.B.

Bachelor of Medicine/Bachelor of Surgery
e: **BMBCh**, *e:* **BMBS**

Bachelor of Microbiology *e:* **B Mic**

Bachelor of Natural Science *e:* **B.N.S.**

Bachelor of Physical and Health Education
e: **B.P.H.E.**

Bachelor of Physical Biology *e:* **BPB**

Bachelor of Public Health *e:* **BPH**

Bachelor of Public Health Education *e:*
BPH Ed
Bachelor of Public Health Engineering *e:*
BPHE, *e:* **BPH Eng**
Bachelor of Public Health Nursing *e:*
BPHN
Bachelor of Science (Animal Husbandry)
e: **BSc (AH)**
Bachelor of Science in Agriculture and
Animal Husbandry *e:* **B.Sc.Ag. & A.H.**
Bachelor of Science in Basic Medical
Science *e:* **BS in Med S**
Bachelor of Science in Basic Medical
Sciences *e:* **BS in BMS**
Bachelor of Science in Biology *e:* **BS Biol**
Bachelor of Science in Business-Medical
Records *e:* **BS Bus-MR**
Bachelor of Science in Engineering in
Geodesy and Surveying *e:* **BSE (Geod
& Surv)**
Bachelor of Science in Geodesy and
Surveying *e:* **BS in Geod & Surv**
Bachelor of Science in Geography *e:*
B.S.Geog., *e:* **BS Ggr**
Bachelor of Science in Geological
Engineering *e:* **BS Gl E**
Bachelor of Science In Geological
Engineering *e:* **BS Geol E**
Bachelor of Science in Geological
Engineering *e:* **BS Geol Eng,** *e:* **BS Gl
E,** *e:* **BS in Ge E,** *e:* **BS in Geol E**
Bachelor of Science in Geology *e:* **BS
Geol,** *e:* **BS Gl**
Bachelor of Science in Geology and Physics
e: **BSGP**
Bachelor of Science in Geophysical
Engineering *e:* **BS in Gph E**
Bachelor of Science in Geophysics *e:* **BS
Gph**
Bachelor of Science in Health and Physical
Education *e:* **BS Health and Phy Ed,** *e:*
BS in H & PE
Bachelor of Science in Health Education *e:*
BSHE, *e:* **BS Health Ed,** *e:* **BSHEd,** *e:*
BS in H Ed
Bachelor of Science in Liberal Arts and
Medicine *e:* **BSLA and Med**
Bachelor of Science in Medical Record
Library Science *e:* **BS in MRL Sc**
Bachelor of Science in Medical Records *e:*
BS in Med Rec, *e:* **B.S.Med.Rec.**
Bachelor of Science in Medical Records
Librarianship *e:* **BS in Med Rec Lib,** *e:*
BS Med Rec Lib
Bachelor of Science in Medical Science *e:*
BS Med Sc
Bachelor of Science in Medical Secretarial
Science *e:* **BS in Med Sc**
Bachelor of Science in Medical Technology
e: **B Sc in Med Techn,** *e:* **BS in MdT,** *e:*
BS in Med Tech, *e:* **BS in MT,** *e:* **BS
Mech Techn,** *e:* **BS Med T,** *e:* **BS Med
Tech,** *e:* **BS MT**
Bachelor of Science in Medicine *e:* **B Sc in
Med,** *e:* **BScMed,** *e:* **BS in Med,** *e:* **BSM,**
e: **BS Med**
Bachelor of Science in Meteorology *e:* **BS
in Met,** *e:* **BS Met**
Bachelor of Science in Natural-Gas
Engineering *e:* **BS in Nat G Engin**
Bachelor of Science in Natural History *e:*
BS in Nat Hist, *e:* **BS Nat Hist**

Bachelor of Science in Natural Science *e:*
BS in NS, *e:* **BS in N Sc**
Bachelor of Science in Oceanography *e:*
BS in Ocean
Bachelor of Science in Professional
Geology *e:* **BS in Pr Ge**
Bachelor of Science in Professional
Meteorology *e:* **BS in Pr Met**
Bachelor of Science in Public Health *e:*
BSPH
Bachelor of Science in Public Health and
Preventative Medicine *e:* **BS in PHN,** *e:*
BS in PHPM
Bachelor of Science in Public Health
Nursing *e:* **BSPHN**
Bachelor of Science in Range Animal
Husbandry *e:* **BS in RAH**
Bachelor of Science (Medical Laboratory
Science) *e:* **BSc (MLS)**
Bachelor of Science [Medicine] *e:*
BSc[Med]
Bachelor of Science ín Agricultural Biology
e: **B.Sc.Agr.Bio.**
Bachelor of Suddha Ayurvedic Medicine
e: **B.S.A.M.**
Bachelor of Urani Medicine and Surgery *e:*
B.U.M.S.
Bachelor of Veterinary Medicine *e:*
B.Vet.Med., *e:* **BVM,** *e:* **Vet MB**
Bachelor of Veterinary Medicine and
Surgery *e:* **BVMS**
Bachelor of Veterinary Science and Animal
Husbandry *e:* **B.V.Sc. & A.H.**
Bachelor of Vetinary Medicine *e:* **BVM**
back-water valve *e:* **bwv**
Background Atmospheric Pollution
Monitoring *e:* **BAPMoN**
Backup Aerospace-vehicle Inventory *e:*
BAI
Bacteriological (or Biological) & Chemical
weapons *e:* **B&C**
Bacteriological (or Biological) & Toxic
Weapons Convention *e:* **BWC**
Bacteriology & Applied Microbiology *e:*
BAM
Bad Weather Watch *e:* **BWW**
Baden-Württemberg: Gesetz über den
öffentlichen Gesundheitsdienst *d:*
ÖGDG
Badlands Natural History Society *e:*
BNHA
Bag of Water *e:* **BOW**
Bahamas Environment, Science and
Technology Commission *e:* **BEST**
BAHC [Biospheric Aspects of the
Hydrological Cycle] Scientific Steering
Committee *e:* **BAHC-SSC**
Baikal International Centre for Ecological
Research *e:* **BICER**
Baillieres Clinical Obstetrics and
Gynaecology *e:* **Baillieres Clin Obstet
Gynaecol**
Baker Street and Waterloo Railway *e:*
B.S.W.R.
Baksan Neutrino Observatory *e:* **Baksan**
Balance de Radiación de la Tierra *s:* **ERB**
Balance of Space to Space Control
Agencies *e:* **BALSPACON**
Balance[d] Biological Communities *e:*
BBC
Balanced Groundwater Scenario *e:* **BGS**
Balanced Job Execution on Remote
Network *e:* **BJOERN**

Balcke-Rapid-Stufenverfahren [der Wasser-
enthärtung] *d:* **Barastu-Verfahren**
Balkan Environment Research and
Development Institute *e:* **BERDI**
Ball Aerospace Systems Division *e:* **BASD**
Ball Corp. Aerospace [Systems] Group *e:*
BASG
Ball Space Systems Division *e:* **BSSD**
Ballastable Earthmoving Sectionalized
Tractor *e:* **BEST**
Ballistic Environmental Characteristics and
Measurement Program *e:* **BECAMP**
Ballistic/Laser Armour Protective Posture
e: **BLAPP**
Ballistic & Laser Protection Spectacles *e:*
BLPS
Ballistic Recovery of Orbiting Man *e:*
BROOM
Ballistic Trajectory calculators allowing for
Meteorological conditions *e:* **BALMET**
Ballistischer Wetterzug *d:* **BalWeZg**
Balloon Atmospheric Propagation
Experiment *e:* **BAPE**
Balloon-Borne Polar Nephelometer *e:*
BBPN
Balloon-borne Polar Nephelometer *e:* **BPN**
Balloon Observations of Millimetric
Extragalactic Radiation and Geophysics
e: **BOOMERANG**
Baltic Air-Sea Ice Study *e:* **BASIS**
Baltic and North Sea Radiotelephone
Conference *e:* **BNRC**
Baltic and North Sea Telecommunication
Meeting *e:* **BNTM**
Baltic Marine Biologists *e:* **BMB**
Baltic Open Sea Experiment *e:* **BOSEX**
Baltic Sea *e:* **Bsea**
Baltic Sea Experiment *e:* **BALTEX**
Baltic Sea Hydrographic Commission *e:*
BSHC
Baltic Sea Position Reporting System *e:*
BAREP
Baltic Sea Protected Area *e:* **BSPA**
Baltic sea region on-Line Environmental
information Resources for Internet Access
e: **BALLERINA**
Baltic Sea Salmon Standing Committee *e:*
BSSC, *e:* **BSSSC**
Baltic Sea Seismic Programme *e:* **BABEL**
Baltic Sea System Study *e:* **BASYS**
Baltic Sea Vertical Mixing and Advection
Experiment *e:* **BAVAMEX**
Bandipur Wildlife Sanctuary *e:* **BWS**
Bandsortierprogramm *d:* **BASO**
Banff Park Natural History Museum *e:*
BPNHM
Bangladesh Medical Research Council
Bulletin *e:* **Bangladesh Med Res Counc
Bull**
Bangladesh Water Development Board *e:*
BWDB
Bankstown General Practice Division,
Health Service *e:* **BGPDHS**
Banque de Données Automatisée sur les
Médicaments *f:* **BIAM**
Banting Research Centre Library,
Department of National Health and
Welfare Ottawa, Ontario *e:* **OONHBR**
Baptist Hospital, Medical Library,
Nashville *e:* **TNBH**
Barbados Oceanographic and
Meteorological Analysis Program(or
Project) *e:* **BOMAP**

Barbados Oceanographic and Meteorological Experiment *e:* **BOMEX**

Barber Blue Sea *e:* **BBS**

Barding Sands Underwater Test Range *e:* **BARSTUR**

Bardsey Bird and Field Observatory, Ispley, near Redditch, Worcestershire *e:* **BBFO**

Bardsey Observatory Report *e:* **RBOBDY**

Barents Sea *e:* **Barents**

Barents Sea Impact Study *e:* **BASIS**

Barimetric & Manifold Atmosphere Pressure *e:* **BMAP**

Barisan Kemerdeka'an Rakyat *ma:* **BAKER**

Barking Sands Tactical Underwater Range *e:* **BARSTUR**

Barking Sands Underwater Range Expansion *e:* **BSURE**

Barometric Atmosphere Pressure *e:* **BAP**

barrels of basic sediment and water *e:* **bbs & w**

Barrels of Load Salt Water *e:* **BLSW**

Barrels of Load Salt Water per Day *e:* **BLSWD**

barrels of oil and water *e:* **bo & w**

Barrel[s] of Salt Water *e:* **BSW**

Barrel[s] of Salt Water per Day *e:* **BSWD**

Barrel[s] of Water per Day *e:* **BWD**

barrels of water per day *e:* **bwpd**

Barrel[s] of Water per Hour *e:* **BWH**

barrels of water per hour *e:* **bwph**

Barrel[s] of Water per Minute *e:* **BWM**

Barrel[s] Water per Day *e:* **BWPD**

Barren Grounds Nature Reserve *e:* **BGNR**

Barrier Waterproof *e:* **BWP**

Barriered Landscape Water Renovation System *e:* **BLWRS**

Barrow Environmental Observatory *e:* **BEO**

Barrow Observatory *e:* **BRW**

Barton & Guestier *e:* **B&G**

Base Air Defense Ground Environment System *e:* **BADGES**

Base Air (or Area) Defense Ground Environment *e:* **BADGE**

Base de Datos Marinos Climatológicos y Oceánicos Conexos *s:* **MCODB**

Base de données de climatologie maritime et de données océaniques connexes *f:* **MCODB**

Base Depot of Medical Stores *e:* **BDMS**

Base Environmental Engineering Technician *e:* **BEET**

base for/of natural logarithms *e:* **e**

Base Medical Equipment Depot *e:* **BMED**

Base Medical Supply Office *e:* **BMSO**

Base Océanologique de la Méditerranée *f:* **BOM**

Base Opérationnelle de la Force Océanique Stratégique *f:* **BOFOST**

Base-École *f:* **B.E.**

Base-École de Parachutistes d'Outre-Mer *f:* **BEPOM**

Base-École de Télécommunications *f:* **B.E.T.**

Base-École des Troupes Aéroportées *f:* **B.E.T.A.**

Baseboard Hot Water *e:* **BBHW**

Basic & Applied Geosciences Division *e:* **G**

Basic Dungeons & Dragons *e:* **BD&D**

Basic Earthquake Education *e:* **BEE**

Basic ECM Environment Simulator *e:* **BEES**

Basic Environmental Compliance and Monitoring Program *e:* **BECAMP**

Basic Hydrological Network Assessment Project *e:* **BNAP**

Basic Linear Algebra for Distributed Environments *e:* **BLADE**

Basic Medical Insurance Plan *e:* **BMIP**

Basic Meteorological Services *e:* **BMS**

Basic Open Hearth *e:* **BOH**

Basic Operational Sea Training *e:* **BOST**

Basic Overall Polarity *e:* **BOP**

Basic Overall Polarity Test *e:* **BOP Test**

Basic Remote Module *e:* **BRM**

Basic Remote User's Content Editor *e:* **BRUCE**

basic sediment and water *e:* **bs & w**

Basic Synoptic Network of World Weather Watch *e:* **BSN**

Basic Underwater Demoliton/SEAL [Sea, Air and Land Capability] Training Department *e:* **BUD[/]S**

Basic Weather Network *e:* **BWN**

Basin Planning Report. New York State Water Resources Commission. Series ENB *e:* **NWRBBE**

Basin-wide Extended Climate Study *e:* **BECS**

Basler Beiträge zur Geographie *d:* **Basl. Beitr. Geogr.**

Basutoland Socio-Medical Services *e:* **BASOMED**

Bataan Ocean Petroleum Depot *e:* **BOPD**

Bataillon Médical *f:* **B.M.**

Bataillons-Medizinalpunkt *d:* **BMP**

Bataillonsstabsquartier *d:* **Btl.St.Q.**

Bathyscaphe Oceanographic Program *e:* **BOP**

battaglione pontieri *i:* **btg.pt.**

Battalion Medical Officer *e:* **Bn MO**

Batterie des Mortiers Lourds *f:* **B.M.L.**

Battery and Earth Loop *e:* **BEL**

Battery Observation Post *e:* **BOP**

Battery Power Feed, Overvoltage Protection, Ringing, Supervision (or Signalling) *e:* **BORSCHT**

Battlefiedl Environment *e:* **BE**

Battlefield Electromagnetic Environments Office *e:* **BEEO**

Battlefield Environment Directorate *e:* **BED**

Battlefield Inoculation Remote Initiation System *e:* **BIRIS**

Battlefield Meteorological System *e:* **BMETS**

Battlefield Weather Observation & Forecast System *e:* **BWOFS**

Battleship Observation Squadron *e:* **VO**

Baubiologisches Zentrum BBZ Rhein-Main GmbH *d:* **BBZ**

Baugrund- und Bodenaufschluß-, Wasser und Grundbaugesellschaft mbH *d:* **BWG**

baumorientiertes interaktives Entwurfswerkzeug *d:* **BOIE**

Bay Area Digital Geo-Resource *e:* **BADGER**

Bay Medical Center, Bay City *e:* **MiBayM**

Bayerische Akademie der Wissenschaften. Mathematisch-Naturwissenschaftliche Abte *d:* **Bayer Akad Wiss Math-Naturw Ab**

Bayerische Großwasserkraftwerke *d:* **B.G.W.W.**

Bayerische Landesanstalt für Tierseuchenbekämpfung Schleißheim *d:* **L.T.Schl.**

Bayerische Landesanstalt für Tierzucht *d:* **BLT**

Bayerische Vereinigung von Fachhändlern des sanitären Installations-, Gas- und Wasserleitungsbedarfs *d:* **SANIFA**

Bayerische Wasserkraftwerke AG *d:* **BAWAG**

Bayerischer Klimaforschungsverbund *e:* **BayFORKLIM**

Bayerischer Wasserwirtschaftsverband e.V. *d:* **BWWV**

Bayerisches Klimaforschungsprogramm *d:* **BayFORKLIM**

Bayerisches Staatsministerium für Landesentwicklung und Umweltfragen *d:* **BStMLU**, *d:* **StMLU**

Bayerisches Wassergesetz *d:* **BayWG**

Bayfield Laboratory, Ocean Science and Surveys, Fisheries and Oceans Canada Burlington, Ontario *e:* **OBUFBL**

Baylor College of Medicine *e:* **BCM**

B.C. Health Information Management Professionals Society *e:* **BCHIMPS**

Beach Protection Authority *e:* **BPA**

Beacon Observation Laser Team *e:* **BOLT**

Bechuanaland Protectorate Federal Party *e:* **BPFP**

Bedford Institute of Oceanography *e:* **BIO**, *e:* **NSDB**

Beech Aerospace Services Inc. *e:* **BASI**

Beef Hearth Infusion Broth *e:* **BHIB**

Befehlshaber der Baltischen Gewässer *d:* **B.B.G.**

Begin Standard Radar Refuel Orbit *e:* **BSRRO**

Behavior Observation Program *e:* **BOP**

Behavioral and Social Aspects of Health *e:* **BASAH**

Behavioral Medicine *e:* **Behav Med**

Behavioural Ecology *e:* **Behav. Ecol.**

Behavioural Ecology and Sociobiology *e:* **Behav. Ecol. Sociobiol.**

Beiheft zu den Annalen der Schweizerischen meteorologischen Anstalt *d:* **Beih. Ann. Schweiz. meteorol. Anst.**

Beiheft zum Jahrbuch der Schweizerischen naturforschenden Gesellschaft *d:* **Beih. Jahrb. Schweiz. nat.forsch. Ges.**

Beirat für Lagerung und Transport wassergefährdender Stoffe *d:* **LTwS**

Beiträge zum Naturschutz in der Schweiz *d:* **Beitr. Nat.schutz Schweiz**

Beiträge zur Biologie der Pflanzen *d:* **Beitr. Biol. Pflanz.**

Beiträge zur geobotanischen Landesaufnahme der Schweiz *d:* **Beitr. geobot. Landesaufn. Schweiz**

Beiträge zur Geologie der Schweiz: Hydrologie *d:* **Beitr. Geol. Schweiz: Hydrol.**

Beiträge zur Gerichtlichen Medizin *d:* **Beitr Gerichtl Med**

Beiträge zur Hydrologie der Schweiz *d:* **Beitr. Hydrol. Schweiz**

Beiträge zur Infusionstherapie und Transfusionsmedizin *d:* **Beitr Infusionsther Transfusionsmed**

Beiträge zur Jagd- und Wildforschung *d:*
Beitr. Jagd-Wildforsch.
Beiträge zur naturkundlichen Forschung in
Südwestdeutschland *d:* **Beitr. nat.kdl.
Forsch. Südwestdtschl.**
Beiträge zur Physik der Atmosphäre *d:*
Beitr. Phys. Atmos.
Belastungsorientierte Auftragsfreigabe *d:*
BOA
Belfast Natural History and Philosophical
Society *e:* **BNHPS**
Belgian Inst. For Space Aeronomy *e:*
BISA
Belgian Society of Medicine and Surgery of
the Foot *e:* **SBMCP**
Belgisch Studie- en Documentatie-Centrum
voor Water *n:* **BSDCW**
Belgische Vereniging voor Medische
Informatica *N:* **M.I.M.**
Bell Aerospace Co. *e:* **LNBA**
Bell Aerospace Corporation *e:* **BAC**
Bellmetica Gesellschaft für Institute der
Kosmetik, Gesundheits- und
Schönheitspflege mbH *d:* **Bellmetica**
below sea level *e:* **bsl**
Below Sea-Level Flying Club *e:*
B.S.L.F.C.
Below Water *e:* **BW**
Belt Weather Kit *e:* **BWK**
Beltsville Space Center *e:* **BSC**
bemannter Raumflug *d:* **BR**
Bendigo & District Environment Council
e: **BDEC**
Bendix Interactive Geographic Information
System *e:* **BIGIS**
Benevolent and Protective Order of Elks *e:*
BPOE
Benevolent Protective Order-Wolves of the
World *e:* **BPO-WOW**
Benguela Environment Fisheries Interaction
& Training *e:* **BENEFIT**
Benton-Franklin District Health Department
e: **BFHD**
benutzerorientiert *d:* **BONT**
Beobachtermission der Vereinten Nationen
in Georgien *d:* **UNOMIG**
Bephenium Hydroxynaphthoate *e:* **BHN**
bephenium hydroynaphthoate *e:* **bhn**
Beratergremium für umweltrelevante
Altstoffe der GDCh *d:* **BUA**
Beratungszentrum Energiesparende und
Baubiologische Produkte *d:* **BEB**
Bergische Energie- und Wasser-GmbH *d:*
BEW
Bergische Gas- und Wasserversorgung
GmbH *d:* **BGW**
Bergische Licht-, Kraft- und Wasser-Werke
GmbH *d:* **BELKAW**
Bergische Licht-, Kraft- und Wasserwerke
GmbH *d:* **Belkaw**
Berichte der Akademie für Naturschutz und
Landschaftspflege *d:* **Ber. Akad.
Nat.schutz Landsch.pfl.**
Berichte der Botanisch-Zoologischen
Gesellschaft Liechtenstein-Sargans-
Werdenberg *d:* **Ber. Bot.-Zool. Ges.
Liecht.-Sargans-Werdenberg**
Berichte der Physikalisch-Medizinischen
Gesellschaft zu Würzburg *d:* **Ber. Phys.-
Med. Ges. Würzburg**
Berichte der Sankt Gallischen
Naturwissenschaftlichen Gesellschaft *d:*
Ber. St. Gallen Nat.wiss. Ges.

Berichte der Schwyzerischen
Naturforschenden Gesellschaft *d:* **Ber.
Schwyzerische Nat.forsch. Ges.**
Berichte der Versuchsanstalt für Wasserbau,
Hydrologie und Glaziologie an der
Eidgenössischen Technischen Hochschule
Zürich *d:* **Ber. Vers.anst. Wasserbau
Hydrol. Glaziol. Eidgenöss. Tech.
Hochsch. Zür.**
Berichte der zentralen Erfassungs- und
Bewertungsstelle für Umweltchemikalien
des Bundesgesundheitsamtes *d:* **ZEBS-
Berichte**
Berichte des Deutschen Wetterdienstes *d:*
Ber. Dtsch. Wetterd.
Berichte des Geobotanischen Institutes der
Eidgenössischen Technischen
Hochschule, Stiftung Rübel *d:* **Ber.
Geobot. Inst. Eidgenöss. Tech.
Hochsch., Stift. Rübel**
Berichte des Instituts für Sozialmedizin und
Epidemiologie *d:* **SOZEP-Berichte**
Berichte des Instituts für Veterinärmedizin
d: **VETMED-Berichte**
Berichte des Instituts für Wasser-, Boden-
und Lufthygiene *d:* **WABOLU-Berichte**
Bering Sea Expedition *e:* **BESEX**
Bering Sea Experiment *e:* **BEMEX,** *e:*
BESEX
Bering Sea FOCI *e:* **BS FOCI**
Bering Sea Impact Study *e:* **BESIS**
Bering Sea Patrol *e:* **BERSEAPAT,** *e:*
BSP
Berliner Betrieb für Zentrale
Gesundheitliche Aufgaben *d:* **BBGes**
Berliner Entwässerungswerke *d:* **BEW**
Berliner Forschungsverbund Public Health
d: **BFPH**
Berliner Städtische Wasserwerke *d:*
BStWW
Berliner und Münchener Tierärztliche
Wochenschrift *d:* **Berlin. München.
TierÄrztl. Wo**
Berliner Wasserwart- und
Hausinstandsetzungs-GmbH *d:* **Bewaga**
Berliner Wasserwerke *d:* **BWW**
Bermuda Biological Station *e:* **BBS**
Bermuda Biological Station for Research,
Inc. *e:* **BBSR**
Bernard Price Institute [of Geophysical
Research, Johannesburg] *e:* **BPI**
Bernhard-Nocht-Institut für Tropenmedizin,
Hamburg *e:* **BNI**
Berufliches Rehabilitierungsgesetz *d:*
BerRehaG
Berufsgenossenschaft für Gesundheitsdienst
und Wohlfahrtspflege *d:* **BGW**
Berufsgenossenschaftlicher
Arbeitsmedizinischer Dienst e.V. *d:*
BAD
Berufsverband der Praktischen Ärzte und
Ärzte für Allgemeinmedizin Deutschlands
e.V. *d:* **BPA**
Berufsverband freiberuflich tätiger
Tierärzte Österreichs *d:* **BFÖ**
Berwickshire Naturalists' Club *e:* **BNC**
Beschwerdeabteilung *d:* **BA**
Beschwerdedienst *d:* **BD**
Beschwerdeführer *d:* **BeschwF,** *d:* **Bf**
Beschwerdegegner *d:* **Bg**
Beschwerdesenat *d:* **BS**
Best Estimate of Orbital Parameters *e:*
BEOP

Best Practical Environmental Option *e:*
BPEO
Best Practical Wastewater Treatment
Technology *e:* **BPWTT**
Beth Israel Medical Center, New York *e:*
VVI
Bethany Medical Center, Kansas City *e:*
KKcBM
Bethlehem Natural Science Association *e:*
BNSA
Betriebserde *d:* **BE**
Betriebswasserspiegel *d:* **B.W.Sp.**
Bevelvoerder [van dienst] *n:* **BD**
Bevitron Orbit Code *e:* **BOC**
Bewässerung *d:* **Bew.,** *d:* **BewÄsser.**
Bewässerungsanlage *d:* **Bew.-Anl.**
Bexar County Medical Library Association,
San Antonio *e:* **TxSaBM**
Bezirks-Tier[zucht]inspektion *d:* **BTI**
Bezirksinspektion Gesundheitsschutz in den
Betrieben *d:* **BIG**
Bezirksstelle[n] für Naturschutz und
Landschaftspflege *d:* **BNL**
Bezirkstierklinik *d:* **BTK**
BI [Bürgerinitiative] Umweltschutz
Rendsburg *d:* **BUR**
Bi-Phase-Space *e:* **Bi-è-S,** *e:* **Bi-Phase-S**
Bible and Medical Missionary Fellowship
e: **BMMF**
Bibliographia Scientiae Naturalis Helvetica
l: **Bibliogr. Sci. Nat. Helv.**
Bibliography and Index of Geology
Exclusive of North America *e:* **BIGENA**
Bibliography of Medical Reviews *e:* **BMR**
Bibliography of Medical Translations *e:*
BMT
Bibliography of the Computer in
Environmental Design *e:* **BCED**
Bibliomed Medizinische
Verlagsgesellschaft mbH, Melsungen *d:*
Bibliomed
Biblioteca Nacional de Medicina *s:*
BINAME
Biblioteca Regional de Medicina *s:*
BIREME
Bibliotheca Medica Canadiana *e:* **BMC,** *l:*
BMC
Bibliotheque des Freres des Ecoles
Chretiennes, Quebec *f:* **QQBL**
Bibliothèque des Écoles Françaises
d'Athènes et de Rome *f:* **BEFAR**
Bibliotheque Medicale, Hopital Charles
Lemoyne, Greenfield Park, Quebec *f:*
QMHCL
Bibliotheque Medicale, Hopital du Haut-
Richelieu, St.-Jean-Sur-Richelieu,
Quebec *f:* **QSTJH**
Bibliotheque Medicale Hopital General La
Salle, Quebec *f:* **QLSHG**
Bibliotheque Medicale, Hotel-Dieu de
Roberval, Quebec *f:* **QRHD**
Bibliotheque Municipale, Pott-Cartier,
Quebec *f:* **QPCM**
Bidirectional Polarization Distribution
Function *e:* **BPDF**
Big Bear Solar Observatory *e:* **BBSO**
Big, Juicy, Gorgeous *e:* **BJG**
Big Lake National Wildlife Refuge *e:*
BLNWR
Bilan Radiatif de l'Atmosphere par Micro-
Accélérometrie Spatiale *f:* **BIRAMIS**
Bilateral Observation *e:* **Bi Obsn**

Bilderberg Continuum Atmosphere *e:*
BCA

Bildungsstätte Umwelt und Gesellschaft
e.V. *d:* **BUG**

Bilgenentwässerungsverband *d:* **BEV**

Bill of Health *e:* **BH**, *e:* **BoH**

Billingsgate Fish Workers' Protection
Society *e:* **B.F.W.P.S.**

Binary Electromagnetic Signal Signature
e: **BESS**

Binary Universal Form for [the]
Representation [of meteorological data]
e: **BUFR**

Bingham Oceanographic Collection *e:*
BOC

Bingham Oceanography Collection *e:*
BOC

Binnenmarkt-Tierseuchenschutzverordnung
d: **BmTierSSchV**

Binnenschiffahrt und Wasserstraßen *d:*
BW

Binnenwasserstraßenverkehrsordnung *d:*
BWVO

Bio-Environmental Health Center *e:*
BEHC

Bio-Geochemical Cycle (or Cycling) *e:*
BGC

Bio-geographic Information System *e:* **BIS**

Bio-Medical Data Package *e:* **BMDP**

Bio-Medical Electronics *e:* **BME**

Bio-Medical Engineering *e:* **Bio-Med
Eng.,** *e:* **BME**

Bio-medical Instrumentation Development
Unit *e:* **BIDU**

Bio-medical Materials and Engineering *e:*
Biomed Mater Eng

Bioastronautic[al] Orbital (or Orbiting)
Space System *e:* **BOSS**

Bioastronautics Orbital Space Program *e:*
BOSP

Biochemical and Molecular Medicine *e:*
Biochem Mol Med

Biochemical Medicine *e:* **Biochem. Med.**

Biochemistry and Cell Biology *e:*
Biochem Cell Biol

Biochemistry and Molecular Biology
International *e:* **BAMBI,** *e:* **Biochem
Mol Biol Int**

Bioclimatic Prediction and Modelling
System *e:* **BIOCLIM**

Biodegradation of Environmental
Chemicals Modeled with Aquatic,
Relative-Rate Coefficients *e:*
BENCHMARC

Biodiversity and Biological Collections
Web Server *e:* **BBCWS**

Biodiversity Mapping for Protection and
Sustainable Use of Natural Resources *e:*
BIOMAPS

Bioenvironmental Engineering *e:* **BEE**

Bioenvironmental Engineering Services *e:*
BES

bioenvironmentalist *e:* **bioenv**

bioenvironment[al][y] *e:* **bioenv**

BIOFA - Naturfarben GmbH *d:* **BIOFA**

Biogeochemical Global Climate [models]
e: **BGC**

Biogeochemical Ocean Flux[es] Study *e:*
BOFS

Biogeochemie und Verteilung von
Schwebstoffen in der Nordsee und ihr
Bezug zur Fischereibiologie *d:* **TOSCH**

Biogeochemistry Working Group *e:*
BGCWG

Biogeoclimatic *e:* **BGC**

Biogeoclimatic Ecosystem Classification
e: **BEC**

biogeographer *e:* **biogeog**

biogeographic[al] *e:* **biogeog**

biogeography *e:* **biogeog**

Biographical Inventory for Medicine *e:*
BIM

Biologe *d:* **Biol.**

Biologia Gallo-hellenica *l:* **Biol. Gallo-
hellenica**

biologic false reactor *e:* **bfr**

Biological *e:* **B**

Biologic[al] *e:* **BIO**

Biological *e:* **Biol.**

Biological Abstract on Tape *e:* **BAT**

Biological Abstracts *e:* **BA,** *e:* **Biol Abstr**

Biological Abstracts Previews *e:* **BAP**

Biological Abstracts/Reports, Reviews,
Meetings *e:* **BA/RRM**

Biological Abstracts Subjects in Context
e: **BASIC**

Biological Activated Carbon *e:* **BAC**

Biological Agent Detection System *e:*
BADS

Biological Agricultural Reactor of the
Netherlands *e:* **BARN**

Biological Analysis Detection
Instrumentation and Control *e:* **BADIC**

Biological and Chemical Research Institute
e: **BCRI**

Biological and Chemical Warfare Division
e: **BCWD**

Biological and Chemical Weapons *e:*
BCW

Biological and Climatic (or Climatological)
Effects Research *e:* **BACER**

Biological and Conservation Data *e:* **BCD**

Biological and Environmental Research *e:*
BER

Biological and Pharmaceutical Bulletin *e:*
Biol Pharm Bull

Biological and Social Sciences *e:* **BSS**

Biological Anthropological Section *e:*
BIO

Biological Aspects of the Hydrological
Cycle *e:* **BAHC**

Biological Assessment *e:* **BA**

Biological Assessment Laboratory *e:* **BAL**

Biological [Attack] Report *e:* **BIOREP**

Biological Bulletin *e:* **Biol. Bull.**

Biological & Chemical Weapon Disposal
e: **BCWD**

Biological Chemistry Hoppe-Seyler *e:*
Biol Chem Hoppe Seyler

Biological Component of the Air Pollution
Studies *e:* **BCAPS**

Biological Computer Laboratory *e:* **BCL**

Biological Conservation *e:* **BC,** *e:* **Biol.
Conserv.**

Biological control *e:* **Biocon**

Biological Control Acts *e:* **BCA**

Biological Control Products *e:* **BCP**

Biological Cybernetics *e:* **Biol Cybern**

Biological Damage Indicator *e:* **BDI**

Biological Data System *e:* **BIOS**

Biological Defense *e:* **BIODEF**

biological defense *e:* **biodef**

Biological Defense *e:* **BIOLDEF**

Biological Detection System *e:* **BDS**

Biological Diversity Advisory Committee
e: **BDAC,** *e:* **BIDAC**

Biological Effects of Atomic Radiation *e:*
BEAR

biological effects of ionizing radiation *e:*
beir

Biological Electronics *e:* **BIONICS**

Biological Engineering *e:* **BE**

biological engineer[ing] *e:* **bioeng**

Biological Engineering Society *e:* **BES**

Biological environment Monitor *e:* **BEM**

Biological & Environmental Research
Program *e:* **BERP**

Biological Equivalent Weight *e:* **BEW**

Biological Experiment Scientific Satellite
e: **BESS**

Biological Exposure Index *e:* **BEI**

Biological False Positive *e:* **BFP**

Biological False Positive Reaction *e:* **BFP
Reaction**

biological false-positive [reactions] *e:* **bfp**

Biological Farmers Association *e:* **BFA**

Biological graphite steel temperature *e:*
BGST

Biological Half Life *e:* **BHL**

biological hazard potential *e:* **bbp**

Biological Hazard Potential *e:* **BHP**

Biological Imaging and Observational
Mission to Earth *e:* **BIOME**

Biological Information-Processing
Organization *e:* **BIO**

Biological Information Service *e:* **BIS**

Biological Institute of Tropical America *e:*
BIOTA

Biological-Instrumentation *e:* **BIO-INSTR**

Biological Investigation[s] of Marine
Antarctic Systems and Stocks *e:*
BIOMASS

Biological Investigation[s] of Space *e:*
BIOS

Biological Investigations of Terrestrial
Antarctic Systems *e:* **BIOTAS**

Biological Isolation Garment *e:* **BIG**

biological isolation garment *e:* **big.,** *e:*
bigs

Biological Journal of the Linnean Society
e: **Biol. J. Linn. Soc.**

Biological Laboratories *e:* **BioLab**

Biological Laboratory *e:* **BL**

Biological Laboratory, Brunswick, Georgia
e: **BLBG**

biological mass source of ethanol and
methanol from crops and trees *e:* **biomass**

Biological Material Oxidizer *e:* **BMO**

Biological Medical *e:* **BIOMED**

Biological Medicine *e:* **BIOMED**

Biological Modelling *e:* **BIOMOD**

Biological Monitoring and Abatement
Program *e:* **BMAP**

Biological Nitrogen Fixation *e:* **BNF**

Biological Oceanography *e:* **Biol.
Oceanogr.**

Biological Operation[s] *e:* **BIOLOP**

Biological Opinion *e:* **BO**

Biological Orbiting Space Station *e:*
BOSS

Biological Origin *e:* **BO**

Biological Oxygen Demand *e:* **BOD**

Biological Oxygen Demand after five days
e: **BOD5**

Biological Pack *e:* **BIOPACK**

Biological Photographers Association e:
   BPA
Biological Photographic Association Inc.
   e: **BPA**
Biological Psychiatry e: **Biol Psychiatry**
Biological Psychology e: **Biol Psychol**
Biological Radio Communications e: **BRC**
Biological Recording in Scotland
   Committee e: **BRISC**
Biological Records Centre e: **BRC**
Biological Report e: **BIOLREPT**
Biological Research e: **Biol Res**
Biological Research Center e: **BRC**
Biological Research Institute e: **BRI**
Biological Research Institute of America
   e: **BRIA**
Biological Research Module e: **BRM**
Biological Research Reactor ANL e:
   JANUS
Biological Resource Division e: **BRD**, e:
   BRS
Biological Resources Development [Team]
   e: **BIORED**
Biological Response Modifi[er|cation] e:
   BRM
Biological Review e: **Biol. Rev.**
Biological Reviews of the Cambridge
   Philosophical Society e: **Biol Rev Camb
   Philos Soc**
biological satellite e: **bios**
Biological Sciences Center e: **BSC**
Biological Sciences Communication Project
   e: **BSCP**
Biological Sciences Curriculum Study e:
   BSCS
Biological Sciences Division e: **BSD**
Biological Sequence/Structure
   Computational Facility e: **BS/SCF**
Biological Serial Record Center e: **BSRC**
Biological Services Program e: **BSP**
Biological Signals e: **Biol Signals**
Biological, Social, Machine e: **BIOSOMA**
Biological Society e: **BS**
Biological Society of Washington e: **BSW**
Biological Stain Commission e: **BSC**
Biological Standards Control Laboratory
   e: **BSCL**
Biological Station, Fisheries and Oceans
   Canada e: **NBAB**
Biological Synoptic Ocean Prediction e:
   BIOSYNOP
Biological Technical Assistance Group e:
   BTAG
Biological Therapies in Dentistry e: **BTD**
biological threshold limit value e: **btlv**
Biological Trace Element Research e:
   Biol. Trace Elem. Res.
biological transformations e: **BIOTRANS**
biological urge e: **bu**
biologic[al] value e: **bv**
Biological Warfare e: **BIOWAR**
biological warfare e: **bw**
Biological Warfare/Chemical Warfare e:
   BW/CW
Biological Warfare Defense e: **BWD**
Biological War[fare] Laboratory e: **BWL**
Biological Warfare Rapid Warning System
   e: **BWRS**, e: **BWRWS**
Biological Warfare Research Center e:
   BWRC
Biological Warfare Research Establishment
   e: **BWRE**
Biological Warfare Weapons e: **B.W.W's**

Biological Weapon e: **BW**
Biological Weapons e: **BIOLWPN**
Biological Weapon[s] System e:
   BIOLWPNSYS, e: **BWS**
biologically clean e: **bioclean**
Biologically Important Trace Species e:
   BITS
Biologically Liberated Organo-Beasties e:
   BLOB
Biologicheskie Nauki R: **Biol Nauki**
Biologie d: **BI**, d: **Biol.**
Biologie in unserer Zeit d: **BIO IN UNS
   ZEIT**
Biologie und Technik d: **Bionik**
Biologin d: **Biol.**
biologisch d: **B**, d: **biol.**
Biologisch-Archaeologisch Instituut van de
   Rijksuniversiteit te Groningen n: **BAI**
biologisch falsch positive Reaktion d: **BFP**
biologisch-technische Angestellte d: **BTA**
biologisch-technischer Angestellter e:
   BTA
Biologische Anstalt Helgoland d: **BAH**
Biologische Bundesanstalt für Land- und
   Forstwirtschaft d: **BBA**
Biologische Einheit[en] d: **BE**
Biologische Kampfmittel d: **BiKM**
biologische Kampfmittel d: **BK**
biologische Lösung d: **Bllg.**
Biologische-Mechanische
   Behandlungsanlage d: **BMA**
biologische Prozeßsteuerungsmittel d:
   BPM
Biologische Reichsanstalt d: **Biol.R.-A.**
Biologische Reichsanstalt für Land- und
   Forstwirtschaft d: **BRA**, d: **BRfLF**
Biologische Rundschau d: **Biol. Rundsch.**
Biologische Schutzgemeinschaft Hunte-
   Weser-Ems e.V. d: **BSH**
biologische Trockensubstanz d: **bTS**
biologische Wertigkeit d: **BW**
Biologische Zentralanstalt d: **BZA**
Biologischer Arbeitsplatztoleranzwert d:
   BAT
biologischer Sauerstoffbedarf in n Tagen
   d: **BSBn**
biologischer Wirkungsherd d: **BWH**
biologisches Humusgas d: **BIHU-Gas**
Biologisches Institut d: **Biol**
Biologisches Institut Metelen d: **BIM**
Biologisches Zentralblatt d: **Biol. Zent.bl.**
biologi[sk] a: **biol**
Biologiske Meddelelser Kongelige Danske
   Videnskabernes Selskab a: **KVBMAS**
Biologist d: **BIOL**
Biologiya Morya R: **Biol. Morya**
Biology e: **BIO**, e: **Biol.**
Biology Abstracts and Zoological Records
   e: **BIOSIS**
Biology and Fertility of Soils e: **Biol.
   Fertil. Soils**
Biology Branch Herbarium, Biological &
   Chemical Research Institute e: **DAR**
biology classroom activity checklist e:
   bcac
biology + electronics e: **bionics**
Biology genus e: **gen.**
Biology of Reproduction e: **Biol Reprod**,
   e: **BOR**
Biology of the Cell e: **Biol Cell**
Biology of the Neonate e: **Biol Neonate**
Biološki Institut se: **BI**
biomedical e: **biomed**

Biomedical Analog[ue] Signal Processor
   e: **BASP**
Biomedical and Environmental Assessment
   Group e: **BEAG**
Biomedical and Environmental Sciences e:
   Biomed Environ Sci
Biomedical Application Team[s] e: **BAT**
Biomedical Applications e: **JCBADL**
Biomedical Applications of Computers e:
   BAC
Biomedical Chromatography e: **Biomed
   Chromatogr**, e: **BMC**
Biomedical Communications Inventory e:
   BCI
Biomedical Communications Network e:
   BCN
Biomedical Computer Program[me] e:
   BMD
Biomedical Computing Council of
   California Universities e: **BCCCU**
Biomedical Computing Society e: **BCS**
Biomedical Computing Technology
   Information Center e: **BCTIC**
Biomedical Data e: **BMD**
Biomedical Data Processing e: **BMDP**
Biomedical Display Unit e: **BDU**
Biomedical Engineering e: **Biomed. Eng.**,
   e: **BMT**
Biomedical Engineering and the Research
   to AID Persons with Disabilities e:
   BME/RAPD
Biomedical Engineering Research
   Corporation e: **BERC**
Biomedical Engineering Society e: **BMES**
Biomedical & Environmental Science
   Laboratory e: **BE**
Biomedical Equipment Assessment and
   Management e: **BEAM**
Biomedical Equipment Technician (or
   Technology) e: **BMET**
Biomedical Equipment Technicians e:
   BMETs
Biomedical Experiment Scientific Satellite
   e: **BESS**
Biomedical Experiment Support Satellite
   e: **BESS**
Biomedical Information Processing
   Organization e: **BIO**
Biomedical Information System of the
   Andean Region e: **SIBRA**
Biomedical Instrumentation and
   Technology e: **Biomed Instrum
   Technol**
Biomedical Instrumentation Consultant e:
   BIC
Biomedical Interdisciplinary Curriculum
   Project e: **BICP**
Biomedical Library Acquisitions Bulletin
   e: **BLAB**
Biomedical Measurement and Control Panel
   e: **BMCP**
Biomedical Monitoring System e: **BMS**
Biomedical Office e: **MD**
Biomedical Optics Society e: **BiOS**
Biomedical Recovery Capsule e: **BRC**
Biomedical Research Database e: **BRD**
Biomedical Research Education Trust e:
   BRET
Biomedical Research in Progress e: **BRIP**
Biomedical Science & Technology e: **BST**
Biomedical Sciences Corporation e: **BSC**
Biomedical Science[s] Corps e: **BSC**

Biomedical Sciences Instrumentation *e:*
Biomed Sci Instrum
Biomedical Sciences Instrumentation
Symposium *e:* **BSIS**
Biomedical Science[s] Support Grant *e:*
BSSG
Biomedical Simulations Resource *e:*
BMSR
Biomedical Urine Sampling System *e:*
BUSS
biomedicine *e:* **biomed**
Biomedicine and Pharmacotherapy *e:*
Biomed Pharmacother
Biomedicinska Dokumentationscentralen
r: **BMDC**
biomedizinische Datenbank *d:* **BIOMED**
Biomedizinische Technik *d:* **Biomed
Tech**, *d:* **BMT**
Biometrie und Informatik in der Biologie
und Medizin *d:* **Biom. Inform. Biol.
Med.**
Biomonitoring of Environmental Status and
Trends *e:* **BEST**
bionomics, environment, plasmodium,
treatment, immunity *e:* **beptl**
Bioorganic and Medicinal Chemistry *e:*
Bioorg Med Chem
Biopedagogical Research Organization on
Intensive Learning Environment
Reactions *e:* **BROILER**
Biosafety in Microbiological and
Biomedical Laboratories *e:* **BMBL**
Bioscience[s] Information Service of
Biological Abstracts *e:* **BIOSIS**
Biosphere Aspects of the Hydrological
Cycle [Program] *e:* **BAHC**
Biosphere-Atmosphere Chemistry *e:* **BAC**
Biosphere-Atmosphere-Chemistry *e:*
BACH
Biosphere-Atmosphere Exchange of
Pollutants *e:* **BIATEX**
Biosphere-Atmosphere Exchange of Trace
Gases *e:* **BIATEX**
Biosphere-Atmosphere Interactions in the
Tropics *e:* **BAIT**
Biosphere-Atmosphere Interactions project
e: **BAI**
Biosphere Atmosphere Research and
Training *e:* **BART**
Biosphere-Atmosphere Stable Isotope
Network *e:* **BASIN**
Biosphere-Atmosphere Trace Gas Exchange
in the Tropics *e:* **BATGE**
Biosphere-Atmosphere Transfer Scheme *e:*
BATS
Biosphere-Atmosphere Transfer Scheme
Version 1e *e:* **BATS1E**
Biosphere-Atmosphere Transfers and
Ecological Research in Situ Studies in
Amazonia *e:* **BATERISTA**
Biotechnology and Biological Science[s]
Research Council *e:* **BBSRC**
Biotechnology Orbital Laboratory *e:* **BOL**
bipolar *d:* **bi**
Bipolar *d:* **BIPO**
bipolar *e:* **bp**
Bipolar Active-plastic Cell *e:* **BAC**
Bipolar Affective Disorder *e:* **BPAD**
Bipolar Coagulation Probe *d:* **BICAP**
Bipolar Integrated Technology Inc *e:* **BIT**
Bipolar Line Unit *e:* **BLU**
Bipolar Memory Technology *e:* **BMT**
Bipolar Non-Return-to-Zero *e:* **BPNRZ**

Bipolar Offset Binary Code *e:* **BOB
CODE**
Bipolar Operational Power Supplies *e:*
BOP's
Bipolar Operational Power Supply *e:* **BOP
Supply**
Bipolar Read-Only Memories *e:* **BROMs**
Bipolar Read-Only Memory *e:* **BROM**
Bipolar Return to Zero *e:* **BPRZ**
Bipolar Twos-Complement Code *e:* **BTC
Code**
Bipolar Violation *e:* **BPV**
Birds Protection Act *e:* **BPA**
Birmingham Medical Institute *e:* **BMI**
Birmingham Natural History Society *e:*
BNHS
Birmingham University Railway and Inland
Waterway Society *e:* **BURIWS**
Birmo AG Gewinnung und Vertrieb von
natürlichem Bitterwasser *d:* **Birmo**
Biro za geodetske radove, Zagreb *kr:*
Geobiro
Bistatic Spaceborne Radar *e:* **BSR**
Bit Space *e:* **BS**
Bitter Lake National Wildlife Refuge *e:*
BLNWR
Biulleten Eksperimentalnoi Biologii i
Meditsiny *R:* **Biull Eksp Biol Med**
Black Sea *e:* **Euxine Sea**
Black Sea Berth Contract [Grain] *e:*
Russcon
Black Sea Economic Cooperation Zone *e:*
BSEC
Black Sea Environmental Programme *e:*
BSEP
Black Sea Fisheries Commission *e:* **BSCF**,
e: **BSFC**
Blackbeard Island National Wildlife Refuge
e: **BINWR**
Blackwater National Wildlife Refuge *e:*
BNWL, *e:* **BNWR**
Bladder Observation *e:* **BLOBS**
Blank Space *e:* **BS**
Blast Environment Wave Simulator *e:*
BEWS
Bleid Commissie Remote Sensing *e:*
BCRS
Block-level Intercensal Geographic
Changes and Transactions *e:* **BIGCAT**
Block Protection Unit *e:* **BPU**
Blockorientiertes Automatisierungssystem
d: **BAS**
Blood Wasserman *e:* **BW**
Bloque Nacionalista Popular Galego *s:*
B.N.P.G.
Blount Memorial Hospital, Medical Library,
Maryville *e:* **TMaryB**
Blue Hill Meteorological Observatory *e:*
BHMO
Blue Mountain Seismological Observatory
e: **BMSO**
Blue Sea Line *e:* **BSL**
Blue Shield Medical Care Plans *e:*
BSMCP
Board for Certified Consulting
Meteorologists *e:* **BCCM**
Board of Certification in Emergency
Medicine *e:* **BCEM**
Board of Certified Healthcare Safety
Management *e:* **BCHSM**
Board of Coast and Geodetic Survey *e:*
BCGS
Board of Geographic Names *e:* **BGN**

Board of Health *e:* **B of H**
Board of Medical Examiners *e:* **BOME**
Board of Medical Quality Assurance *e:*
BMQA
Board of Medicine [National Academy of
Sciences] *e:* **BOM**
Board of Podiatric Medicine *e:* **B o PM**
Board of Registration of Medical
Auxiliaries *e:* **B.R.M.A.**
Board of Schools of Medical Technology
e: **BSMT**
Board of Sport Fisheries and Wildlife *e:*
BOSFW
Board on Agriculture and Natural Resources
e: **BA**
Board on Atmospheric Science and Climate,
National Research Council *e:* **BASC**
Board on Geographic[al] Names *e:* **BGN**
Boardman Atmospheric Radiation Flux
Experiment *e:* **BARFEX**
Boden-Wetter-Radaranlage *d:* **BWR**
Bodenbiologische Standort-Klassifikation
d: **BBSK**
Bodenheizung, Bodendämpfung und
Unterflurbewässerung-System *d:*
BEDU-System
Bodenklimazahl *d:* **BKZ**
Bodenkundliche Kartieranleitung, 4. Aufl.
d: **KA 4**
Bodensee-Wasserversorgung *d:* **BWV**
Bodenseewerk British Aerospace GmbH *d:*
BBG
body water *e:* **bw**
Boeing Aerospace Company *e:* **BAC**
Bogen-Wasserzeichen *d:* **Bg-Wz.**
Boiler Feedwater *e:* **BFW**
Boiler, Hot Water *e:* **BHW**
Boiler Space *e:* **BS**
Boiler Water *e:* **BOWR**
Boiler, Water Supply *e:* **BWS**
boiling heavy water *e:* **bhw**
Boiling Heavy Water Reactor *e:* **BHWR**
Boiling Light-Water Tank *e:* **BLWT**
Boiling Water [nuclear] Reactor *e:* **BWR**
Boiling Water Proof *e:* **BWP**
Boiling Water Reactor Experiment *e:*
BORAX
Boiling Water Reactor-Full Lenght
Emergency Cooling Heat Transfer Test
e: **BWR-FLECHT**
Boiling Water Reactor, Type 6 *e:* **BWR/6**
Boiling Water Resistant *e:* **BWR**
Boletim do Instituto de Ciências Naturais.
Univ. do Rio Grande do Sul. Pôrto Alegre
p: **ICN/B.**
Boletim Geográfico. Instituto Brasileiro de
Geografia e Estatística. Conselho
Nacional de Geografia. Rio de Janeiro *p:*
IBGE/B.
Boletin-Asociacion Medica de Puerto Rico
s: **Bol Asoc Med P R**
Boletin de Estudios Medicos y Biologicos
s: **Bol Estud Med Biol**
Boletin. Sociedad Geografica de Lima *s:*
SGL/B
Boletín del Instituto de Estudios Médicos y
Biológicos. Univ. Nacional Autónoma de
México *s:* **IEMB/B.**
Bollettino della Società ticinese di scienze
naturali *i:* **Boll. soc. tic. sci. nat.**
Bollettino-Società Italiana Biologia
Sperimentale *i:* **Boll Soc Ital Biol Sper**
Bomb Orbital Strategic System *e:* **BOSS**

Bomb Orbital Strategic System - Weapon Development Glide Entry e: **BOSS-Wedge**

Bombay Hook National Wildlife Refuge e: **BHNWR**, e: **Bombay Hook**

Bombay Natural History Society e: **B.N.H.S.**

Bond Molecular Orbital[s] e: **BMO**

Bond Order Orbital e: **BOO**

Bond van Adverteerders n: **BVA**

Bond van Ambtenaren bij de Waterschappen in Nederland n: **BAWN**

Bond van Bierhandelaren en Mineraalwaterfabrikanten n: **BBM**

Bond van Verenigingen van Afgestudeerden van Middelbaar-Technische Scholen in Nederland n: **BMT**

Bonding Bond Orbital e: **BBO**

Bonding Molecular Orbital e: **BMO**

Bonheur Children's Medical Center, Health Sciences Library, Memphis e: **TMLBC**

Bookmakers' Protection Association e: **B.P.A.**

Books-Across-the-Sea [project] e: **BAS**

Books-Across-the-Sea-project e: **BAS project**

Boost Protective Cover e: **BPC**

Booster Orbiter e: **B/O**

Boot and Shoe Manufacturers' Association and Leather Trades Protection Society e: **B.A.S.M.A.**

Borated Water Storage Tank e: **BWST**

Bord-zu-Erde d: **BzE**

Border Environment Cooperation Commission e: **BECC**

Bordet-Wassermann Reaktion d: **BW Reaktion**

Boreal Ecosystem[s] Atmosphere Study e: **BOREAS**

Borehole Water e: **BW**

Bosque Apache National Wildlife Refuge e: **BANWR**

Boston College Environmental Affairs Law Review e: **B.C. Envtl. Aff. L. Rev.**

Boston Society of Natural History e: **BSNH**

Boston Society of Natural History, Proceedings e: **Boston Soc of Nat Hist Proc**

Boston University School of Medicine e: **BUSM**

Botanische Jahrbücher für Systematik, Pflanzengeschichte und Pflanzengeographie d: **Bot. Jahrb. Syst. Pflanzengesch. Pflanzengeogr.**

Botswana Protectorate Federal Party e: **BPFP**

Bottom Environmental Sensing System e: **BESS**

Bottom Settlings and Water e: **BS and W**

Bottom Settlings plus Water e: **BS + W**

Boulder Atmospheric Observatory e: **BAO**

Boulder Remote Data Collection and Control System e: **BOULD**

Boulder Upslope Cloud Observation Experiment e: **BUCOE**

Boundary Water Canoe Area e: **BWCA**

Bounded Cellular Space e: **BCS**

Bournemouth Naturalists' and Scientific Society e: **B.N.S.S.**

Bovine Animals [Records, Identification and Movement] Order e: **BARIMO**

Bowater Paper Corp. Ltd. e: **B**

Bowater Tutt Industries Pty Ltd. e: **Tutts**

Bowdoin National Wildlife Refuge e: **BNWL**, e: **BNWR**

Bowman Gray School of Medicine e: **BGSM**

Bowman Gray School of Medicine, Winston-Salem e: **NBG**

BPC Hydrocunsult e: **BPCHYDRO**

Brackish Water Arrival Draft e: **BWAD**

Brackishwater Aquaculture Information System e: **BRAIS**

Brake Specific Hydrocarbon[s] e: **BSHC**

Branch Hydrographic Office e: **BHO**, e: **BRANCHHYDRO**

Branching Process with Markovian Environments e: **BPME**

Branching Process with Random Environments e: **BPRE**

Brandenburger Wasserspar-GmbH d: **Brawas**

Brandenburgisches Wassergesetz d: **BbgWG**

Brassboard Fault Tolerant Spaceborne Computer e: **BFTSC**

Brauchwasserspeicher d: **BWS**

Braunerde d: **B**

Braunton Burrows National Nature Reserve e: **BBNNR**, e: **BRNNR**

Brazilian Commission for/of Space Activities e: **COBAE**

Brazilian environmental agency e: **IBAMA**

Brazilian Institute for Space Research e: **INPE**

Brazilian Institute of Environment and Renewable Natural Resources e: **IBMARNR**

Brazilian Journal of Medical and Biological Research e: **Braz J Med Biol Res**

Brazilian Marine Geology Programme e: **PBGM**

Brazilian Oceanographic Data Centre e: **BNDO**

Brazilian 12-passenger transport honoring frontier pioneers e: **Bandeirante**

Brazilian Remote Sensing Experiment e: **BRESEX**

Brazilian Society for Cartography, Geodesy, Photogrammetry, and Remote Sensing e: **SBC**

Brazilian Space Agency e: **INPE**

Breakwater e: **BKw.**, e: **Bkwr**, e: **brkwtr**

Breakwater Fort e: **BWF**

Breathers for the Reduction of Atmospheric Hazards to the Environment e: **BREATHE**

Brems-Pferdestärke d: **BPS**

Brevet Technique des Métiers f: **BTM**

Bridge Remote Control e: **BRC**

Bridgewater College e: **BC**

Bridgewater College, Bridgewater e: **ViBrC**

Brigada da Estudos Geológicos do Estado da India, Junta de Investigações do Ultramar p: **BEGEI**

Brigada de Estudos Agronómicos para Cabo Verde p: **BEACV**

Brigada de Geologia a S. Tomé, Junta de Investigações do Ultramar p: **BGST**

Brigade Medical Officer e: **BMO**

Brigade Remote Computer Center e: **BRCC**

Brigade Routière f: **B.R.**

Brigade Routiére Motorisée f: **B.R.M.**

Brigantine National Wildlife Refuge e: **BNWL**, e: **BNWR**

Brigham Young University Science Bulletin, Biological Series e: **Brigham Young Univ. Sci. Bull.**

Brighton and Hove Natural History and Philosophical Society e: **BHNHPS**

Brikettierung d: **Brikettier.**

Brillantmont, École intere f: **BM**

Bristol Aerospace Ltd. e: **BAL**

Bristol Ice and Snow Cover Algorithm e: **BRISCA**

Bristol Naturalists' Society e: **BNS**

Britain Nepal Medical Trust e: **BNMT**

British Aearospace's Reinforced and Microwave Plastics e: **RMP**

British Aerospace e: **BAE**

British Aerospace Aircraft Group e: **BAAG**

British Aerospace Commercial Aircraft e: **BACA**

British Aerospace Corporation e: **BAC**

British Aerospace Dynamics Group e: **BADG**

British Aerospace PLC e: **HQ**

British Aerospace Simulation Ltd. e: **BAeSL**

British Aerospace Staff Association e: **BASA**

British Aerospace Systems & Equipment Ltd. e: **BASE**

British Aircraft Corporation Commercial Habitat Under the Sea e: **BACCHUS**

British Animal Medicine Makers' and Allied Traders' Association e: **BAMMATA**

British Antarctic Survey Medical Unit e: **BASMU**

British Approvals Service for Electrical Equipment in Flammable Atmospheres e: **BASEEFA**

British Association for Accident and Emergency Medicine e: **BAEM**

British Association for Biological Anthropology and Osteoarchaeology e: **BABAO**

British Association in Forensic Medicine e: **B.A.F.M.**

British Association in/of Forensic Medicine e: **BAFM**

British Association of Cosmetic Surgeons e: **BACS**

British Association of Homoeopathic Veterinary Surgeons e: **BHAVS**

British Association of Manipulative Medicine e: **BAMM**

British Association of Medical Managers e: **BAMM**

British Association of Oral and Maxillofacial Surgeons e: **BAOMS**

British Association of Oral Surgeons e: **BAOS**

British Association of P[a]ediatric Surgeons e: **BAPS**

British Association of Physical Medicine e: **BA Phys Med**, e: **BAPM**

British Association of Physical Medicine and Rheumatology e: **BAPM&R**

British Association of Plastic[s] Surgeons e: **BAPS**

British Association of Remote Sensing Companies e: **BARSC**

British Association of Sport [and] Medicine
  e: **BASM**
British Association of Urological Surgeons
  e: **BAUS**
British Atmosphere *e:* **Br. atm.**
British Central Africa Protectorate *e:*
  B.C.A.P.
British College of Obstetricians and
  Genaecologists *e:* **B.C.O.G.**
British Columbia Environmental
  Information Network *e:* **BCEIN**
British Columbia Geographic System *e:*
  BCGS
British Columbia Health Association *e:*
  BCHA
British Columbia Hydro and Power
  Authority *e:* **BCHPA**, *e:* **BCHPH**
British Columbia Medical Association *e:*
  BCMA
British Columbia Veterinary Medical
  Association *e:* **BCVMA**
British Columbia Wildlife Federation *e:*
  BCWF
British Committee for ECOR [Engineering
  Committee on Ocean Resources
  UNESCO] *e:* **BC-ECOR**
British Commonwealth Geographical
  Liaison Office *e:* **BCGLO**
British Copyright Protecting (or Protection)
  Association *e:* **BCPA**
British Crop Protection Council *e:* **BCPC**
British defense-notice system for protecting
  state secrets with the cooperation of the
  press *e:* **D-notice system**
British Dental Health Foundation *e:*
  BDHF
British Ecological Society *e:* **BES**
British Empire Naturalists' Association *e:*
  B.E.N.A.
British Entomological and Natural History
  Society *e:* **BENHS**
British Fire Protection Systems Association
  e: **BFPSA**
British Frontier Service *e:* **BFS**
British Geological Survey *e:* **BGS**
British Geomorphological Research Group
  e: **BGRG**
British Geotechnical Society *e:* **BGS**
British Healthcare Internet Association *e:*
  BHIA
British Herbal Medicine Association *e:*
  BHMA
British Holistic Medical Association *e:*
  BHMA
British Hydrological Society *e:* **BHS**
British Hydromechanical (or
  Hydromechanics) Research Association
  e: **BHRA**
British Hydromechanics Research
  Association *e:* **BHMRA**
British Ice Hockey Association *e:* **BIHA**
British Indian Ocean Territories *e:* **BIOT**
British Indian Ocean Territory *e:* **IOT**
British Industrial Biological Research
  Association *e:* **BIBRA**
British Journal of Biomedical Science *e:*
  Br J Biomed Sci
British Journal of Healthcare Computing
  and Information Management *e:*
  BJHC&IM
British Journal of Hospital Medicine *e:* **Br
  J Hosp Med**

British Journal of Industrial Medicine *e:*
  Br. J. Ind. Med.
British Journal of Medical Psychology *e:*
  BJMPs, *e:* **Br J Med Psychol**
British Journal of Obstetrics and
  Gynaecology *e:* **BJOG**, *e:* **Br J Obstet
  Gynaecol**
British Journal of Sports Medicine *e:* **Br J
  Sports Med**
British Junior Naturalists' Association *e:*
  BJNA
British Library of Wildlife Sounds *e:*
  BLOWS
British Medical Acupuncture Society *e:*
  BMAS
British Medical Association *e:* **BMA**
British Medical Association's Deputising
  Service *e:* **BMADS**
British Medical Battalion *e:*
  BRITMEDBATT
British Medical Board *e:* **BMB**
British Medical Bulletin *e:* **BMB**, *e:* **Br.
  Med. Bull.**
British Medical Council *e:* **BMC**
British Medical Informatics Society *e:*
  BMIS
British Medical Journal *e:* **BMJ**, *e:* **Br.
  Med. J.**
British Medical Pilots Association *e:*
  BMPA
British Medical Representatives
  Association *e:* **BMRA**
British Medical Research Council *e:*
  B.M.R.C.
British Medical Society *e:* **BMS**
British Medical Students Association *e:*
  BMSA
British Medical Students Journal *e:* **BMSJ**
British Medical Union *e:* **BMU**
British Meteorological Office *e:* **BMO**
British Museum of Natural History, London
  e: **BMNH**
British National Committee for Geography
  e: **BNCG**
British National Committee for
  Oceanographic Research *e:* **BNCOR**
British National Committee for/of Ocean
  Engineering *e:* **BNCOE**
British National Committee for/on Space
  Research *e:* **BNCSR**
British National Committee on Ocean
  Engineering *e:* **ENCOE**
British National Health Insurance *e:*
  B.N.H.I.
British National Health Service *e:* **BNHS**
British National Institute for Medical
  Research *e:* **BNIMR**
British National Remote Sensing Centre *e:*
  BNRSC
British National Space Centre *e:* **BNSC**
British National Space Council *e:* **BNSC**
British Natural Hygiene Society *e:* **BNHS**
British Naturalists' Association *e:* **BENA**,
  e: **BNA**
British Naturopathic and Osteopathic
  Association *e:* **BNOA**
British Nuclear Medicine Society *e:*
  BNMS
British Oceanographic Data Center *e:*
  BODC
British Oceanographic Data Service[s] *e:*
  BODS
British Photobiology Society *e:* **B.P.S.**

British Polarographic Research Institute *e:*
  BPRI
British Postgraduate Medical Federation *e:*
  BpMF
British Psychological Society, Medical
  Section *e:* **B.P.S.M.S.**
British Radiological Protection Association
  e: **BRPA**
British Small Animal[s] Veterinary
  Association *e:* **BSAVA**
British Social Biology Council *e:* **BSBC**
British Society for Allergy, Environmental
  and Nutritional Medicine *e:* **BSAENM**
British Society for Cell Biology *e:*
  B.S.C.B.
British Society for Disability and oral
  Health *e:* **BSDH**
British Society for International Health
  Education *e:* **BSIHE**
British Society for/of Developmental
  Biology *e:* **BSDB**
British Society of Animal Production *e:*
  BSAP
British Society of Animal Science *e:*
  BSAS
British Society of Medical and Dental
  Hypnosis *e:* **BSMDH**
British Solomon Islands Protectorate *e:*
  BSIP
British Space Development *e:* **BSD**
British Space Development Company, Ltd.
  e: **BSDC**
British Underwater Test and Evaluation
  Centre *e:* **BUTEC**
British Water and Effluent Treatment Plant
  Association *e:* **BWETPA**
British Water Research Association *e:*
  BWRA
British Waterways *e:* **BW**
British Waterways Board *e:* **BWB**
British Waterworks Association *e:* **BWA**,
  e: **B.W.W.A.**
British Young Naturalists Association *e:*
  BYNA
Brittany Oceanological Center *e:* **BOC**
Broad Ocean Area *e:* **BOA**
Broad Ocean Area - Missile Impact
  Locating SYstem *e:* **BOA-MILS**
Broad Ocean Scoring System *e:* **BOSS**
Broadband Observatory for the Localization
  of Transients *e:* **BOLT**
Broadband Remote Line Unit *e:* **BRLU**
Broadband Remote Oculometer *e:* **BRO**
Brock University's Geological (or
  Geoscience) Department *e:* **BGS**
Brody Medical Science Building *e:* **MS**
Broek in Waterland *n:* **B.I.W.**
Broken [sea] *e:* **B**
bromohydrosis *e:* **bromidrosis**
Brooke Army Medical Center *e:* **BAMC**
Brookhaven Medical Research Center *e:*
  BMRC
Brookhaven Medical Research Reactor *e:*
  BMRR
Brookhaven's Medical Reactor *e:* **BMR**
Brown Animal Sanitary Institution *e:*
  B.A.S.I.
Brtish Medical Protection Society *e:*
  BMPS
Brunswick/Glynco Naval Air Station
  [Georgia] *e:* **KNEA**
Brussels Institute for Management of the
  Environment *e:* **BIM**

Brussels Research Unit for Environmental, Geochemical and Life Sciences Studies *e:* **BRUEGEL**

Buffalo Environmental Law Journal *e:* **BELJ**, *e:* **Buff. Envtl. L.J.**

Buffalo Lake National Wildlife Refuge *e:* **BLNWR**

Buffalo Society of Natural History *e:* **BSNH**

Buffalo Society of Natural Sciences *e:* **BSNS**

Buffalo Society of Natural Sciences, Buffalo Museum of Science, Buffalo *e:* **NBuB**

Buffered Distilled Water *e:* **BDW**

Buffered Hydro Fluoric acid *e:* **BHF**

Building Environmental Performance Assessment Criteria *e:* **BEPAC**

Building for Environmental and Economic Sustainability *e:* **BEES**

Building Research Establishment Environmental Assessment Method *e:* **BREEAM**

Building Waterproofers Association *e:* **BWA**

Buildings, Antennas, Spans, Earth formations *e:* **BASE**

Built from the HYPO water boiler nuclear reactor *e:* **SUPO**

Built-in Logic Block Observation *e:* **BILBO**

Bulgarian Geological Society *e:* **BGS**

Bulk Water *e:* **BW**

Bulletin Board, Geographic Information System *e:* **BBGIS**

Bulletin d'alerte climatique *f:* **BAC**

Bulletin de la Société des Sciences Medicales du Grand-Duche de Luxembourg *f:* **Bull Soc Sci Med Grand Duche Luxemb**

Bulletin de la société fribourgeoise des sciences naturelles *f:* **Bull. soc. fribg. sci. nat.**

Bulletin de la Société Géologique de France *f:* **Bull. Soc. Géol. Fr.**

Bulletin de la société neuchâteloise des sciences naturelles *f:* **Bull. soc. neuchâtel. sci. nat.**

Bulletin de la Société royale forestière de Belgique *f:* **Bull. Soc. r. for. Belg.**

Bulletin de la Société Vaudoise des sciences naturelles *f:* **Bull. Soc. Vaud. sci. nat.**

Bulletin des Neuesten und Wissenswürdigsten aus der Naturwissenschaft *d:* **Hermbstädt's Bull.**

Bulletin. Freshwater Fisheries Research Laboratory *e:* **TSKHAY**

Bulletin Geological Society of America *e:* **Bull. Geol. Soc. Am.**

Bulletin Geological Survey of Canada *e:* **Bull. Geol. Surv. Can.**

Bulletin. Kyoto Educational University. Series B. Mathematics and Natural Science *e:* **KBSEA**

Bulletin of Animal Behaviour *e:* **Bull. Anim. Behav.**

Bulletin of Aquatic Biology *e:* **Bull. Aquat. Biol.**

Bulletin of Environmental Education *e:* **BEE**

Bulletin of Experimental Biology and Medicine *e:* **Bull. Exp. Biol. Med**

Bulletin of Freshwater Fisheries Research Laboratory *e:* **Bull. Freshwater Fish. Res. Lab.**

Bulletin of Mathematical Biology *e:* **Bull Math Biol**

Bulletin of the Academy of Sciences of the USSR, Geologic Series *e:* **Bull. Acad. Sci. USSR, Geol. S**

Bulletin of the American Meteorological Society *e:* **BAMS**, *e:* **Bull. Amer. Meteorol. Soc.**

Bulletin of the Biogeographical Society of Japan *e:* **Bull. Biogeogr. Soc. Jpn.**

Bulletin of the British Museum of Natural History, Botany *e:* **Bull. Br. Mus. Nat. Hist., Bot.**

Bulletin of the Geisinger Medical Center *e:* **Bull. Geisinger Med. Cent.**

Bulletin of the Geological Society of Finland *e:* **Bull. Geol. Soc. Finl.**

Bulletin of the Georgia Academy of Science *e:* **Bull. Ga. Acad. Sci.**

Bulletin of the History of Medicine *e:* **Bull Hist Med**

Bulletin of the Institute of Maritime and Tropical Medicine in Gdynia *e:* **Bull Inst Marit Trop Med Gdynia**

Bulletin of the International Association of Scientific Hydrology *e:* **Bull. Int. Assoc. Sci. Hydrol.**

Bulletin of the Islamic Medical Association of South Africa *e:* **BIMA**

Bulletin of the Medical Library Association *e:* **BMLA**, *e:* **Bull. Med. Libr. Ass.**

Bulletin of the New York Academy of Medicine *e:* **Bull. N.Y. Acad. Med.**

Bulletin of the Wildlife Society *e:* **Bull. Wildl. Soc.**

Bulletin of the World Health Organization *e:* **Bull. Wld. Hlth. Org.**, *e:* **Bull World Health Organ**

Bulletin of Tokyo Medical and Dental University *e:* **Bull Tokyo Med Dent Univ**

Bulletin Peabody Museum of Natural History, Yale University *e:* **Bull. Peabody Mus. Nat. Hist., Yale Univ.**

Bulletin Trimestriel. Société de Geographie et d'Archeologie de La Province d'Oran *f:* **Soc Geo A Oran**

Bullpup All-Weather Guidance System *e:* **BAGS**

Bund angestellter Akademiker technisch-naturwissenschaftlicher Berufe *d:* **BaA**

Bund Architektur und Baubiologie e.V. *d:* **BAB**

Bund der Leiter der Gas-, Wasser- und Elektrizitätswerke, Straßen- und Kleinbahnen Deutschlands e.V. *d:* **BLW**

Bund der Technischen Beamten-Gewerkschaft Technik und Naturwissenschaft im öffentlichen Dienst *d:* **BTB**

Bund der Umweltschützer *d:* **BdU**

Bund der Wasser- und Kulturbauingenieure e.V. *d:* **BWK**

Bund für Naturschutz und Umwelt in Deutschland *d:* **BUND**

Bund in Deutschland approbierter Medizinalpersonen *d:* **Bidam**

Bund-Länder-Arbeitsgemeinschaft Umweltchemikalien *d:* **BLAU**

Bund/Länder-Arbeitskreis Umweltinformationssysteme *d:* **BLAK**

Bund-Länder-Arbeitskreis Umweltinformationssysteme *d:* **BLAK-UIS**

Bund Natur- und Umweltschutz *d:* **BNU**

Bund Natur- und Umweltschutz Rheinland Pfalz e.V. *d:* **BNR**

Bund Naturschutz in Bayern *d:* **BN**, *d:* **BNS**

Bund Naturschutz Ostertal e.V. *d:* **BNO**

Bundes-Tierärzteordnung *d:* **BTÄO**

Bundes-Wasser- und Schiffahrtsverwaltung *d:* **BW**

Bundes-Wasserstraßengesetz *d:* **BWaStG**

Bundesamt für gesundheitlichen Verbraucherschutz und Veterinärmedizin *d:* **BgVV**

Bundesamt für Gesundheit[swesen] *d:* **BAG**

Bundesamt für Kartographie und Geodäsie *d:* **BKG**

Bundesamt für Naturschutz *d:* **BfANL**, *d:* **BfN**

Bundesamt für Seeschiffahrt und Hydrographie *d:* **BSH**

Bundesamt für Seeschiffahrt und Hydrologie *d:* **BSH**

Bundesamt für Umwelt, Wald und Landschaft *d:* **BUWAL**

Bundesamt für Umweltschutz *d:* **BUS**

Bundesamt für Wasser und Geologie *d:* **BWG**

Bundesamt für Wasser und Geologie/Landeshydrologie und -geologie *d:* **BWG/LHG**

Bundesanstalt für Arbeitsschutz und Arbeitsmedizin *d:* **BAuA**

Bundesanstalt für Geowissenschaften und Rohstoffe *d:* **BAGR**, *d:* **BAGuR**, *d:* **BfGR**

Bundesanstalt für Geowissenschaft[en] und Rohstoffe *d:* **BGR**

Bundesanstalt für Gewässerkunde *d:* **BAfG**, *d:* **BfG**

Bundesanstalt für Naturschutz und Landschaftspflege *d:* **BANL**

Bundesanstalt für Wasser-, Boden- und Lufthygiene *d:* **Wabolu**

Bundesanstalt für Wasserbau *d:* **BAW**

Bundesanstalt für Wasserschutz *d:* **BAW**

Bundesarbeitsgemeinschaft für Verbraucherfragen im Gesundheitswesen e.V. *d:* **BAVG**

Bundesberufsfortbildungszentrum wassergefährdende Stoffe GmbH *d:* **BwS**

Bundesdeutscher Arbeitskreis für Umweltbewußtes Management *d:* **B.A.U.M.**

Bundesfachverband Medizinprodukteindustrie e.V. *d:* **BVMed**

Bundesfachverband Wasseraufbereitung e.V. *d:* **BFWA**

Bundesflächendatenbank für Naturschutz und Landschaftspflege *d:* **BDNL**

Bundesforschungsanstalt für Kleintierzucht *d:* **BFAK**

Bundesforschungsanstalt für Naturschutz und Landschaftsoekologie *d:* **BFANL**

Bundesforschungsanstalt für Viruskrankheiten der Tiere in Tübingen *e:* **BFAV**

Bundesgesundheitsamt *e:* **BGA**
Bundesgesundheitsblatt *d:* **BuGBl**
Bundesinstitut für Arzneimittel und
Medizinprodukte *d:* **BfArM**
Bundesminister für Gesundheitswesen *d:*
BMGes
Bundesministerium für Arbeit, Gesundheit
und Soziales *d:* **BMAGS**
Bundesminister[ium] für Atomkernenergie
und Wasserwirtschaft *d:* **BMAt**
Bundesministerium für Gesundheit *d:*
BMG
Bundesminister[ium] für Jugend, Familie
und Gesundheit *d:* **BMJFG**
Bundesnaturschutzgesetz *e:* **BNatSchG**
Bundestierärztekammer *d:* **BTK**
Bundesumweltministerium *d:* **BMU**
Bundesverband Biologischer Produkte *d:*
BBP
Bundesverband Bürgerinitiativen
Umweltschutz e.V. *e:* **BBU**
Bundesverband der Deutschen Gas- und
Wasserwirtschaft e.V. *d:* **BGW**
Bundesverband der deutschen Luft- und
Raumfahrt- und Ausrüstungsindustrie
e.V. *d:* **BDLI**
Bundesverband der Naturwerkstein-
Fachbetriebe *d:* **BNF**
Bundesverband der Tierversuchsgegner *d:*
BTVG
Bundesverband der Tierzucht- und
Besamungstechniker e.V. *d:* **BTB**
Bundesverband für fachgerechten Natur-
und Artenschutz *d:* **BNA**
Bundesverband Medizintechnik *d:* **BMT**
Bundesverband praktischer Tierärzte *d:*
BpT
Bundesverband Schwimmbad,- Sauna- und
Wassertechnik *d:* **BSSW**
Bundesverband von Fachgroßhändlern des
Bedarfs für Heizungs-, Lüftungs- und
Klimaanlagen e.V. *d:* **BVH**
Bundesvereinigung der Firmen im Gas- und
Wasserfach e.V. *d:* **FIGAWA**
Bundesvereinigung der Industrieverbände
Heizungs-, Klima- und Sanitärtechnik
e.V. *d:* **BHKS**
Bundeswasser- und Schiffahrtsverwaltung
d: **BWSV**
Bundeswasserstraßengesetz *d:* **WaStrG**
Bundeszentrale für gesundheitliche
Aufklärung *d:* **BZgA**
Buoy Underwater Sound Signal *e:* **BUSS**
bupivacaine hydrochloride *e:* **bupiv**
Buque de Observación Voluntaria *s:* **BOV**
Buque geográfico auxiliar *s:* **AGS**
Buque Meteorológico Oceánico *s:* **OWS**
Bureau Agricole et Forestier Guyanais *f:*
BAFOG
Bureau Artisanal des Matières *f:* **B.A.M.**
Bureau Central Météorologique *f:* **B.C.M.**
Bureau d'Audiences Publiques sur
l'Environnement *f:* **BAPE**
Bureau de Contrôle Médical *f:* **B.C.M.**
Bureau de Liaison des Sanatoriums
Universitaires et de Protection Anti-
Tuberculeuse des Étudiants *f:* **Inter-SU**
Bureau de Liaison d'Information Religieuse
pour l'Océan Indien *f:* **BLIROI**
Bureau de l'industrie et de l'environnement
f: **BIE**
Bureau de Normalisation de l'Aéronautique
et de l'Espace *f:* **BNAE**

Bureau de Normalisation de l'Industrie
Papetiére *f:* **BNIP**
Bureau de Normalisation de Matières
Plastiques *f:* **BNMP**
Bureau de Recherches Geologique et
Minieres *f:* **BRGM**
Bureau de Recherches Géologiques et
Géophsyques *f:* **B.R.G.G.**
Bureau de Recherches Géologiques,
Géophysiques et Minières *f:* **BRGGM**
Bureau des Constations Médicales *f:*
B.C.M.
Bureau d'Information pour l'Environnement
f: **BIE**
Bureau d'information sur les changements
climatiques *f:* **IUCC**
Bureau d'Études de Standardisation et de
Technique en arboriculturefruitière *f:*
BEST
Bureau d'Études et de Recherches
Géotechniques *f:* **BERG**
Bureau d'Études Géologiques et Minières
Coloniales *f:* **B.E.G.M.C.**
Bureau Européen de l'Environnement *f:*
BEE
Bureau Européen d'Information pour le
Développement de la Santé Animale *f:*
DSA
Bureau for/of Oceans [and] International
Environment[al] and Scientific Affairs [of
State Department] *e:* **OES**
Bureau for/of Overseas Medical Service *e:*
BOMS
Bureau Français des Transports Routiers *f:*
BFTR
Bureau Frontière *f:* **B.F.**
Bureau Hydrographique International[e] *f:*
BHI
Bureau International Permanent de Chimie
Analytique pour les matiéres destinées à
l'alimentation de d'home et des animaux
f: **BIPCA**
Bureau International pour la Protection de
la Propriété Industrielle *f:* **B.I.P.P.I.**
Bureau International pour la Protection des
Œuvres Littéraires et Artistiques *f:*
BIPOLA
Bureau Nationale des Données Océaniques
f: **BNDO**
Bureau of Animal Industry *e:* **BAI**, *e:*
B.A.Ind.
Bureau of Aviation Medicine *e:* **BAM**
Bureau of Biological and Physical Sciences
e: **BBPS**
Bureau of Biologics *e:* **BB**, *e:* **BOB**
Bureau of Community Environmental
Management *e:* **BCEM**
Bureau of Community Health Services *e:*
BoCHS
Bureau of Disease Prevention and
Environment[al] Control *e:* **BDPEC**
Bureau of Economic Geology *e:* **BEG**
Bureau of Environmental Statistics *e:* **BES**
Bureau of Health Care Delivery and
Assistance *e:* **BHCDA**
Bureau of Health Insurance *e:* **BHI**
Bureau of Health Insurance, Social Security
Administration *e:* **BHISSA**
Bureau of Health Manpower *e:* **BHM**, *e:*
BoHM
Bureau of Health Manpower Education *e:*
BHME

Bureau of Health Planning and Resource
Development *e:* **BHPRD**
Bureau of Health Planning and Resources
Development *e:* **BoHP&RD**
Bureau of Health Professions *e:* **BHPr**
Bureau of Health Professions Education and
Manpower Training *e:* **BEMT**
Bureau of Health Protection Services. State
of Nevada. *e:* **BHPS**
Bureau of Health Resources Development
e: **BHRD**
Bureau of Health Services *e:* **BHS**
Bureau of Information and Research on
Student Health *e:* **BIRSH**
Bureau of Medical Devices *e:* **BMD**, *e:*
BoMD
Bureau of Medical Devices and Diagnostic
Products *e:* **BMDDP**
Bureau of Medical Services *e:* **BMS**, *e:*
BoMS
Bureau of Medical Statistics *e:* **BMS**
Bureau of Medicine *e:* **BM**
Bureau of Medicine and Surgery *e:* **BMS**,
e: **BUMED**, *e:* **BUM&S**
Bureau of Medicine and Surgery,
Department of the Navy *e:* **MS**
Bureau of Medicine and Surgery Hospital
Corps Publication *e:* **NMSHC**
Bureau of Medicine and Surgery
Publications *e:* **NM & S**
Bureau of Meteorological Research Center
e: **BMRC**
Bureau of Meteorology *e:* **BM**, *e:* **BOM**
Bureau of Meteorology and Oceanographic
Services *e:* **METOC**
Bureau of Meteorology. Bulletin [Australia]
e: **Met Bur Bull**
Bureau of Meteorology. Meteorological
Study [Australia] *e:* **Met Bur Met
Study**, *e:* **Meteorol Stud Meteorol B**
Bureau of Meteorology. Meteorological
Summary [Australia] *e:* **Met Bur Met
Summ**
Bureau of Meteorology. Project Report
[Australia] *e:* **Met Bur Proj Rep**
Bureau of Meteorology Research Center *e:*
BMRC
Bureau of Meteorology Research Centre *e:*
BMRC
Bureau of Meteorology Training Centre *e:*
BMTC
Bureau of Meteorology. Working Paper
[Australia] *e:* **Met Bur Working Paper**
Bureau of Mineral Resources. Geological
Map [Australia] *e:* **Min Res Bur Geol
Map**
Bureau of Mineral Resources, Geology and
Geophysics *e:* **BMR**
Bureau of Mineral Resources. Geophysical
Observatory Report [Australia] *e:* **Min
Res Bur Geophys Obs Rep**
Bureau of Mineral Resources. 1 Mile
Geological Series [Australia] *e:* **Min
Res Bur 1 Mile Geol Ser**
Bureau of Mines and Geosciences *e:* **BMG**
Bureau of Natural Gas *e:* **BNG**
Bureau of Oceans and International
Environmental and Scientific Affairs *e:*
BOIESA
Bureau of Oceans and International
Environmental and Scientific
Affairs/Environmental and Population
Affairs *e:* **OES/ENP**

Bureau of Oceans and International Environmental and Scientific Affairs/Ocean and Fishery Affairs *e:* **OFS/OFA**

Bureau of Oceans and International Environmental and Scientific Affairs/Scientific and Technological Affairs *e:* **OES/SCI**

Bureau of Oceans, Fisheries and Scientific Affairs *e:* **BOFSA**

Bureau of Ordnance and Hydrography *e:* **BOH**

Bureau of Primary Health Care *e:* **BPHC**

Bureau of Radiological Health *e:* **BRH**

Bureau of Radiological Health, Division of Electronics Products *e:* **BRH/DEP**

Bureau of Radiological Health, Division of Environmental Radiation *e:* **BRH/DER**

Bureau of Radiological Health, Division of Medical Radiation Exposure *e:* **BRH/DMRE**

Bureau of Radiological Health, North Eastern Radiological Health Laboratory *e:* **BRH/NERHL**

Bureau of Radiological Health, Office of Regional Operations *e:* **BRH/ORO**

Bureau of Radiological Health, South-Eastern Radiological Health Laboratory *e:* **BRH/SERHL**

Bureau of Radiological Health, South-Western Radiological Health Laboratory *e:* **BRH/SWRHL**

Bureau of Sport Fisheries and Wildlife *e:* **BOSFW,** *e:* **BSFW**

Bureau of Veterinary Medicine *e:* **BVM**

Bureau pour l'Application des Renseignements Météorologiques aux activités économiques et Agricoles, *f:* **BARMA**

Bureaux Internationaux Réunis pour la protection de la Propriéte Intellectuelle *f:* **BIRPI**

Bureaux Internationaux réunis pour la Protection de la Propriété, Littéraire et Artistique *f:* **BIPPILA**

Bürgeraktion Umweltschutz Bonn *d:* **BUB**

Bürgeraktion Umweltschutz Rhein-Neckar e.V. *d:* **BURN**

Bürgeraktion Umweltschutz Zentrales Oberrheingebiet *d:* **BUZO**

Bürgerinitiative Energieplanung Umweltschutz *d:* **BEU**

Bürgerinitiative für Demokratie und Umweltschutz *d:* **BIDU Mölln**

Bürgerinitiative für Gesundheitsschutz am Arbeitsplatz *d:* **BIGA**

Bürgerinitiative Umweltschutz *d:* **BIU**

Bürgerinitiative Umweltschutz Augsburg *d:* **BUA**

Bürgerinitiative Umweltschutz Barnstorf *d:* **BUB**

Bürgerinitiative Umweltschutz Lauenburg *d:* **BUL**

Bürgerinitiative Umweltschutz Rheinfelden *d:* **BUR**

Bürgerinitiative Umweltschutz Unterelbe *d:* **BUU**

Bürgerunion Umweltschutz *d:* **BUU**

burial at sea *e:* **deep 6**

Burma Frontier Force *e:* **B.F.F.**

Burnable Poison Water Reactor *e:* **BPWR**

Büro für Umwelt-Pädagogik, Göttingen *d:* **BUP**

Büro für Umweltschutz *d:* **BU**

Burroughs Remote Job Entry *e:* **BRJE**

Burton-on-Trent Natural History and Archaeological Society *e:* **B.N.H.A.S.**

Businees Environment Risk Information *e:* **Beri**

Business Geographics Conference *e:* **BGC**

Business in the Environment *e:* **BiE**

Business Risk and Value of Operation in Space *e:* **BRAVO**

Butanol-Acetic-acid Water *e:* **BAW**

Buteshire Natural History Society *e:* **B.N.H.S.**

Butterworths Medico-Legal Reports *e:* **B.M.L.R .**

Butylhydroxianisol *d:* **E 320**

Butylhydroxitoluol *d:* **E 321**

Byrd Polar Research Center *e:* **BPRC**

bíogeology *e:* **biogeo**

C

C & GS [Coast and Geodetic Survey] Automated Data System *e:* **COGADS**

CAA [Civil Aeronautics Administration] High-Altitude Remote Monitoring (or Monitor[s]) *e:* **CHARM**

CAB International Insitute of Biological Control *e:* **CIBC**

Cabinet for Health Services *e:* **CHS**

Cable-controlled Underwater Research (or Recovery) Vehicle *e:* **CURV**

Cable Signal Fault Signature *e:* **CSFS**

Cableless Underwater Television *e:* **CUT,** *e:* **CUTV**

Cableless Underwater Television Link *e:* **CUT Link**

CAD Geometry Data Exchange *e:* **CADEX**

Caerlaverock National Nature Reserve *e:* **CNNR**

Cahiers de Sociologie et de Demographie Medicales *f:* **Cah Sociol Demogr Med**

Cairngorm Summit Automatic Weather Station *e:* **CSAWS**

Cairngorms National Nature Reserve *e:* **CNNR**

Cairns and Far North Environment Council *e:* **CFNEC**

Caisse de Retraites des Industries de Matières Colorantes *f:* **C.R.I.M.C.**

Caisse des Écoles *f:* **C.E.**

Caisse Forestière de Crédit Agricole Mutuel et de garantie incendie forestier *f:* **C.F.C.A.M.**

Caisse Interdépartementale des Assurances Sociales *f:* **CIAS**

Caisse Médicale Chirurgicale Mutuelle *f:* **CMCM**

Calcium- and Magnesium-Free Synthetic [Sea] -Water *e:* **CMFSW**

Calciumhydrogensulfit *d:* **E 227**

Calciumhydroxid *d:* **E 526**

Calcul. of Reactor Accident Consequences with effects of Containment, Meteorology, & Evacuation *e:* **CRACOME**

Calcutta School of Tropical Medicine *e:* **CSTM**

California Academy of Sciences Geology Type Collection *e:* **CASGTC**

California Association for Medical Laboratory Technology *e:* **CAMLT**

California Association of Acupuncture and Oriental Medicine *e:* **CAAOM**

California Association of Reclamation Entities of Water *e:* **AQUACARE**

California Biomedical Research Association *e:* **CBRA**

California Board of Medical Quality Assurance *e:* **CBMQA**

California College of Medicine *e:* **CCM**

California Comprehensive Ocean Area Plan *e:* **COAP**

California Cooperative Oceanic Fisheries Investigation[s] *e:* **CALCOFI**

California Cooperative Oceanic Fisheries Investigations *e:* **CCOFI,** *e:* **COFI**

California Cooperative Remote Sensing Project *e:* **CCRSP**

California Council for Geographic Education *e:* **CCGE**

California Department of Water Resources *e:* **CDWR**

California Division of Mines and Geology *e:* **CDMG**

California Ecology Corpsmen *e:* **CECs**

California Environmental Protection Program Fund *e:* **CEPPF**

California Environmental Quality Act *e:* **CEQA**

California Environmental Resource[s] Evaluation System *e:* **CERES**

California Healthcare Association *e:* **CHA**

California Integrated Remote Sensing System *e:* **CIRSS**

California Medical Association *e:* **CMA**

California Medical Facility *e:* **CMF**

California Medicine *e:* **Calif. Med.**

California Mental Health Analysis *e:* **CMHA**

California Natural Gas Association *e:* **CNGA**

California Occupational Safety and Health Administration *e:* **CAL-OSHA**

California Parks and Wildlife Initiative *e:* **CalPAW**

California Porter-Cologne Water Quality Control Act *e:* **CPCWQCA**

California Remote Sensing Council *e:* **CRSC**

California Space Institute *e:* **CalSpace**

California State Water Resources Control Board *e:* **CSWRCB**

California Universities Council on Space Sciences *e:* **CUCOSS**

California Veterinary Medical Association *e:* **CVMA**

California Water Resources Association *e:* **CWRA**

California Water Service *e:* **CWS**

California Wildlife Federation *e:* **CWF**

CAM [Complementary and Alternative Medicine] Citation Index *e:* **CCI**

Camas National Wildlife Refuge *e:* **CNWR**

Cambridge and Isle of Ely Naturalist Trust *e:* **CIENT**

Cambridge Atmospheric Density Numerical Integration Program[me] *e:* **CADNIP**

Cambridge Geological Data System *e:* **CGDS**

Cambridge Healthtech Institute *e:* **CHI**

Cambridge Observation Error Analysis *e:* **COBERA**

Cambridge Observatory *e:* **Camb.Obs.**

Cambridge Quarterly of Healthcare Ethics
 e: **Camb Q Healthc Ethics**, *e:* **CQ**

Cambridge Radio Observatory Committee
 e: **CAMROC**

Campagne Océanographique Française *f:*
 COF

Campaign for Earth Federation *e:* **CEF**

Campaign for Integrated Observations of
 Solar Flares *e:* **CINOF**

Canada Centre for Geomatics *e:* **CCG**

Canada Centre for Inland Waters *e:* **CCIW**

Canada Centre for Inland Waters,
 Burlington, Ontario *e:* **OBUC**

Canada Centre for Remote Sensing, Energy,
 Mines and Resources Canada Ottawa,
 Ontario *e:* **OOCCR**

Canada-France-Hawaii Observatory *e:*
 CFHO

Canada France Ocean Optics Experiment
 e: **CFOX**

Canada (or Canadian) Space Agency *e:*
 CSA

Canada South Pacific Ocean Development
 Project *e:* **CSPODP**

Canadian Advisory Committee on Remote
 Sensing *e:* **CACRS**

Canadian Aeronautics and Space Institute
 e: **CASI**

Canadian Aerospace Institute *e:* **CASI**

Canadian Air-Ground Environment *e:*
 CAGE

Canadian Air-Sea Transportable Brigade
 e: **CAST**

Canadian Alliance of Community Health
 Center Associations *e:* **CACHCA**

Canadian Armament Research and
 Development Establishment, Valcartier
 e: **CARDE**

Canadian Armed Forces Institute of
 Environmental Medicine *e:* **CFIEM**

Canadian Army Medical Corps *e:* **CAMC**

Canadian Association for Clinical
 Microbiology and Infectious Diseases *e:*
 CACMID

Canadian Association for Environmental
 Analytical Laboratories *e:* **CAEAL**

Canadian Association for Health, Physical
 Education and Recreation *e:* **CAHPER**

Canadian Association for Laboratory
 Animal Science *e:* **CALAS**

Canadian Association for Underwater
 Sciences *e:* **CAUS**

Canadian Association of General Surgeons
 e: **CAGS**

Canadian Association of Geographers *e:*
 CAG

Canadian Association of
 Geographers/Association Candienne des
 Géographes *e:* **CAG/ACG**

Canadian Association of Medical
 Microbiologists *e:* **CAMM**

Canadian Association of Medical
 Oncologists *e:* **CAMO**

Canadian Association of Medical Radiation
 Technologists *e:* **CAMRT**

Canadian Association of Medical Radiation
 Technologists, Ottawa, Ontario *e:*
 OOCAM

Canadian Association of Medical Students
 and Interns *e:* **CAMSI**

Canadian Association of Paediatric
 Surgeons *e:* **CAPS**

Canadian Association of Physicians for the
 Environment *e:* **CAPE**

Canadian Center (or Centre) for Remote
 Sensing *e:* **CCRS**

Canadian Centre for Geoscience Data *e:*
 CCGD

Canadian Centre for Inland Waters *e:*
 CCIW

Canadian Centre for Occupational Health
 and Safety *e:* **CCOHS**

Canadian Centre for Occupational Health
 and Safety compact disk *e:* **CCINFO**

Canadian Centre for Occupational Health
 and Safety Hamilton, Ontario *e:*
 OHOHS

Canadian Children's Environmental Health
 Network *e:* **CCEHN**

Canadian Chiropractic Protective
 Association *e:* **CCPA**

Canadian Circumpolar Institute *e:* **CCI**

Canadian Circumpolar Library *e:* **CCL**

Canadian Climate Centre *e:* **CCC**

Canadian Climate Program *e:* **CCP**

Canadian Climate Research Network *e:*
 CCRN

Canadian College of Medical Geneticists
 e: **CCMG**

Canadian College of Microbiologists *e:*
 CCM

Canadian College of Naturopathic Medicine
 e: **CCNM**

Canadian College of Physicists in Medicine
 e: **CCPM**

Canadian Committee on Ecological Land
 Classification *e:* **CCELC**

Canadian Committee on History of
 Geological Sciences *e:* **CANHIGEO**

Canadian Coordinating Office for Health
 Technology Assessment *e:* **CCOHTA**

Canadian Corporation for University Space
 Science *e:* **CCUSS**

Canadian Council for Human Resources in
 the Environment Industry *e:* **CCHREI**

Canadian Council of Resource and
 Environment Ministers *e:* **CCREM**

Canadian Council on Animal Care *e:*
 CCAC

Canadian Council on Geographic Education
 e: **CCGE**

Canadian Council on Geomatics *e:* **CCOG**

Canadian Council on Geomatics
 Interchange Format *e:* **CCOGIF**

Canadian Council on Health Services
 Accreditation *e:* **CCHSA**

Canadian Council on Smoking and Health
 e: **CCSH**

Canadian Deuterium natural Uranium
 heavy-water reactor *e:* **CANDU**

Canadian Earth Observation Network *e:*
 CEONet

Canadian Earth Resources Evaluation
 Satellite *e:* **CERES**

Canadian Environmental Assessment
 Research Council *e:* **CEARC**

Canadian Environmental Certification
 Approvals Board *e:* **CECAB**

Canadian Environmental Law Association
 e: **CELA**

Canadian Environmental Law Research
 Foundation *e:* **CELRF**

Canadian Environmental Network *e:* **CEN**

Canadian Environmental Protection Act *e:*
 CEPA

Canadian Federation of Biological Societies
 e: **CFBS**

Canadian Field-Naturalist *e:* **Can. Field-
Nat.**

Canadian Forces Aerospace and Navigation
 School, Canadian Forces Base Winnipeg,
 Westwin, Manitoba *e:* **MWCF**

Canadian Forces Environmental Medicine
 Establishment *e:* **CFEME**

Canadian Forces Institute of Aviation
 Medicine *e:* **CFIAM**

Canadian Forces Medical Council *e:*
 CFMC

Canadian Forces Medical Service *e:*
 CFMS

Canadian Geographic Board *e:* **CGB**

Canadian Geographic[al] Information
 System *e:* **CGIS**

Canadian Geographical Journal *e:* **Canad
Geog J**

Canadian Geographic[al] Journal *e:* **Can.
Georg. J.**

Canadian Geographical Journal *e:* **CGJ**

Canadian Geographical Names Data Base
 e: **CGNDB**

Canadian Geographical Society *e:* **CGS**

Canadian Geological Foundation *e:* **CGF**

Canadian Geologic[al] Survey *e:* **CGS**

Canadian Geomorphology Research Group
 e: **CGRG**

Canadian Geophysical Union *e:* **CGU**

Canadian Geoscience Council *e:* **CGC**

Canadian Geoscience Information Centre
 e: **CGIC**

Canadian Geospatial Data Infrastructure *e:*
 CGDI

Canadian Geotechnical Journal *e:* **Can.
Geotech. J.**, *e:* **Can. Geotechn. J.**

Canadian Geotechnical Society *e:* **CGS**

Canadian Global Ocean Ecosystems
 Dynamics programme *e:* **GLOBEC**

Canadian Health Economics Research
 Association *e:* **CHERA**

Canadian Health Education Society *e:*
 CHES

Canadian Health Libraries Association *e:*
 CHLA

Canadian Health Network *e:* **CHN**

Canadian Health Services Research
 Foundation *e:* **CHSRF**

Canadian Health[care] Association *e:*
 CHA

Canadian Heart Health Initiative-Ontario
 Project *e:* **CHHIOP**

Canadian Hydrographic Association *e:*
 CHA

Canadian Hydrographic Service *e:* **CHS**

Canadian Institute for Climate Studies *e:*
 CICS

Canadian Institute for Health Information
 e: **CIHI**

Canadian Institute for Research in
 Atmospheric Chemistry *e:* **CIRAC**

Canadian Institute of Child Health *e:*
 CICH

Canadian Institute of Geomatics *e:* **CIG**

Canadian Institute of Public Health
 Inspectors *e:* **CIPHI**

Canadian Institutes of Health Research *e:*
 CIHR

Canadian International Health Education
 Network *e:* **CIHEN**

Canadian Journal of Animal Science *e:* **Can. J. Anim. Sci.**

Canadian Journal of Earth Science *e:* **Can. Journ. Earth Sci.**

Canadian Journal of Earth Sciences *e:* **Can. J. Earth Sci.**, *e:* **CJES**

Canadian Journal of Medical Technology *e:* **Can. J. Med. Technol.**

Canadian Journal of Public Health *e:* **Can J Public Health**

Canadian Journal of Remote Sensing *e:* **Can. J. Remote Sens.**

Canadian Journal of Rural Medicine. *e:* **CJRM**

Canadian Library of Family Medicine *e:* **CLFM**

Canadian Medical Acupuncture Society *e:* **CMAS**

Canadian Medical and Biological Engineering Society *e:* **CMBES**

Canadian Medical Association *e:* **CMA**

Canadian Medical Association Journal *e:* **Can. Med. Assoc. J.**, *e:* **CMAJ**

Canadian Medical Association, Ottawa, Ontario *e:* **OOCMA**

Canadian Medical Protective Association *e:* **CMPA**

Canadian Medical Students Association *e:* **CMSA**

Canadian Mental Health Association *e:* **CMHA**

Canadian Meteorological and Oceanographic Society *e:* **CMOS**

Canadian Meteorological and Oceanographic Study *e:* **CMOS**

Canadian Meteorological Centre *e:* **CMC**

Canadian Meteorological Service *e:* **Can Met Ser**

Canadian Minimum Navigation Performance Specification Airspace *e:* **CMNPS**

Canadian Museum of Health and Medicine *e:* **CMHM**

Canadian Museum of Nature *e:* **CMN**

Canadian National Committee for Earthquake Engineering *e:* **CANCEE**

Canadian Nature Federation *e:* **CNF**

Canadian Naturopathic Association *e:* **CNA**

Canadian Network for Environmental Education and Communication *e:* **EECOM**

Canadian Nurses Protective Society *e:* **CNPS**

Canadian Ocean Escort Vessel *e:* **COEV**

Canadian Oceanographic Data Center *e:* **CODC**

Canadian Oceanographic Data Centre *e:* **CODC**

Canadian Oceanographic Identification Centre *e:* **COIC**

Canadian Organisation (or Organization) for Advancement of Computers in Health *e:* **COACH**

Canadian Organization of Medical Physicists *e:* **COMP**

Canadian Park Service, Environment Canada, Cornwall, Ontario *e:* **OCN**

Canadian Park Service, Environment Canada, Quebec, Quebec *e:* **QQPCQ**

Canadian Permanent Committee on Geographical Names *e:* **CPCGN**

Canadian Petroleum Geology *e:* **CPG**

Canadian Polar Commission *e:* **CPC**

Canadian Polar Information System *e:* **CPIS**

Canadian Prostate Health Council *e:* **CPHC**

Canadian Public Health Association *e:* **CPHA**

Canadian Radiation Protection Association *e:* **CRPA**

Canadian Register of Health Service Providers in Psychology *e:* **CRHSPP**

Canadian Remote Sensing Society *e:* **CRSS**

Canadian Rural Medicine Network *e:* **CaRMeN**

Canadian Society for Cell Biology *e:* **CSBC**, *e:* **CSCB**

Canadian Society for Engineering in Agriculture, Food and Biological Systems *e:* **CSAE**

Canadian Society for International Health *e:* **CSIH**

Canadian Society for Medical Laboratory Science *e:* **CSMLS**

Canadian Society for the Prevention of Cruelty to Animals *e:* **CSPCA**

Canadian Society of Addiction Medicine *e:* **CSAM**

Canadian Society of Animal Production *e:* **CSAP**

Canadian Society of Animal Science *e:* **CSAS**

Canadian Society of Biochemistry and Molecular & Cell Biology *e:* **CSBMCB**

Canadian Society of Diagnostic Medical Sonographers *e:* **CSDMS**

Canadian Society of Exploration Geophysicists *e:* **CSEG**

Canadian Society of Microbiologists *e:* **CSM**

Canadian Society of Petroleum Geologists *e:* **CSPG**

Canadian Society of Telehealth *e:* **CST**

Canadian Society of Wildlife and Fishery Biologists *e:* **CSWFB**

Canadian Space Agency Engineering Support Center *e:* **CESC**

Canadian Space Centre *e:* **CSC**

Canadian Space Geodesy Forum *e:* **CANSPACE**

Canadian Speech Research Environment *e:* **CSRE**

Canadian Task Force on Preventive Health Care *e:* **CTFPHC**

Canadian Veterinary Medical Association *e:* **CVMA**

Canadian Water Resources Association *e:* **CWRA**

Canadian Wildlife Federation *e:* **CWF**

Canadian Wildlife Service *e:* **CWS**

Canadian Wildlife Service, Environment Canada Ottawa, Ontario *e:* **OOECW**

Canadian Wildlife Service, Environment Canada Sackville, New Brunswick *e:* **NBSACW**

Canadian Wildlife Service, Environment Canada Winnipeg, Manitoba *e:* **MWECW**

Canadian Wildlife Service, Environment Canada Yellowknife, Northwest Territories *e:* **NWYECW**

Canadian Women's Health Network *e:* **CWHN**

Canal Zone Biological Area *e:* **CZBA**

Canandaigua Veterans Administration Medical Center Library, Canandaigua *e:* **VQC**

Canberra Deep Space Communications Complex *e:* **CDSCC**

Canberra Sar Sea Imaging Experiment *e:* **CASSIE**

Cancer Chemotherapy and Biological Response Modifiers *e:* **Cancer Chemother Biol Response Modif**

Cantieri Navale Apuania S.A. *i:* **C.N.A.S.A.**

Cantieri Navale dell'Elba *i:* **C.N.E.**

Cantieri Navale Luigi Orlando *i:* **CNLO**

Cantieri Navali del Levante *i:* **C.Na.L.**

Cantieri Navali del Tirreno e Riuniti *i:* **CNTR**

Cantieri Navali e Officine Meccaniche di Venezia *i:* **CNOMV**

Cantieri Navali e Officine Meccaniche di Venezia S.p.a. *i:* **C.N.O.M.V.**

Cantieri Navali Italiani *i:* **CNI**

Cantieri Navali Riuniti *i:* **CNR**

Cantieri Navaltechnica *i:* **CN**

Cantieri Riuniti dell'Adratico, Monfalcone *i:* **C.R.D.A.**

Cantieri Riuniti dell'Adriatico *i:* **Cant**

Capa límite atmosférica *s:* **ABL**

capable of underwater missile launchings *e:* **C-class**

Capacity Bale Space *e:* **T.cc.bl.**

Capacity Increase Lower airspace *e:* **CILO**

Cape Canaveral Reference Atmosphere *e:* **CCRA**

Cape Clear Bird Observatory *e:* **CCBO**

Cape Cod Experiment *e:* **CCE**

Cape Grim Baseline Atmospheric Pollution Station *e:* **CGBAPS**

Cape Kennedy Reference Atmosphere *e:* **CCR**, *e:* **CKRA**

Cape Kennedy Space Network, Incorporated *e:* **CKSNI**

Cape Romain National Wildlife Refuge *e:* **CRNWR**

Cape Verde Computer Communication Project *e:* **CVCCP**

Cape Verde Islands *e:* **CVI**, *e:* **Verds**

Cape York Space Agency *e:* **CYSA**

Cape York Space Base *e:* **CYSB**

Cape York Space Facility *e:* **CYSF**

Cape York Space Port *e:* **CYSP**

Capillary Water Barrier *e:* **CWB**

Capsule Observation Panel *e:* **COP**

Captain Fishery Protection *e:* **CFP**

Captive Animals Protection Society *e:* **CAPS**

Capture Orbit Vehicle Assembly Mode *e:* **COVAM**

CARBA AG [Industrie- und Medizinalgase] *d:* **CARBA**

Carbo medicinalis vegetabilis *l:* **E 153**

Carbon, Hydrogen and Nitrogen *e:* **CHN**

Carbon Hydrogen Nitrogen Analyzer *e:* **CHN Analyzer**

Carbon, Hydrogen, Nitrogen, Oxygen, Phosphorus, and Sulfur *e:* **CHNOPS**

carbon, hydrogen, nitrogen, oxygen, phosphorus, sulfur *e:* **C-H-N**

Carbon Hydrogen Oxidant experiment *e:* **CHOX**

Carboxymethylhydroxyäthyl-Cellulose *d:* **CMHEC**

Card and Printer Remote Interface e: **CAPRI**

Card Information Space e: **CIS**

Cardiff Naturalists' Society e: **CNS**

cardiolipin natural lecithin e: **cnl**

Cardiothoracic and Vascular Surgeons e: **CTVS**

cardiovascular observation unit e: **cvou**

Care How Others Keep the Environment e: **CHOKE**

Care-Oriented Medical Record e: **COMREC**

Career Medical Officers Association e: **CMOA**

Caribbean Community Ocean Sciences Network e: **CCOSNET**

Caribbean Environment Programme e: **CAR**

Caribbean Environment Program[me] e: **CEP**

Caribbean Environmental Health Institute e: **CEHI**

Caribbean Environmental Information Center e: **CEIC**

Caribbean Environmental Network project e: **CEN**

Caribbean Federation for Mental Health e: **CFMH**

Caribbean Institute for Meteorology and Hydrology e: **CIMH**

Caribbean Marine Biological Institute e: **C.M.B.I.**

Caribbean Marine Biological Institute (Netherlands Antilles) e: **CARMABI**

Caribbean Meteorological Institute e: **CMI**

Caribbean Meteorological Organization e: **CMO**

Caribbean Natural Resources Institute e: **CANARI**, e: **CNRI**

Caribbean Operational Hydrology Institute e: **COHI**

Caribbean Plant Protection Commission (or Committee) e: **CPPC**

Caribbean Sea and Adjacent Regions e: **CSAR**

Caribbean Sea Project e: **CSP**

Caring for the Earth e: **CFE**

Carnegie Geophysical Laboratory e: **CGL**

Carnegie Institution of Washington Geophysical Laboratory e: **CIWGL**

Carnegie Museum of Natural History. Special Publication e: **SPCHDX**

Carnegie Observatories e: **TCO**

Carnegie Southern Observatory e: **CARSO**

Carolina Geological Society e: **CGS**

Carolina Sandhills National Wildlife Refuge e: **CSNWR**

Carpathian Balkan Geological Association e: **CBGA**

Carriage of Goods by Sea Act e: **COGSA**

Carribean Sea Frontier e: **CARIBSEAFRON**, e: **CSF**

Carrier All-Weather Flying e: **CAWF**

Carrier Pigeon e. **CP**

CART Data Environment e: **CDE**

Carte Générale Bathymétrique des Océans f: **GEBCO**

Cartesian to Polar e: **C-P**

Cartesian-to-Polar Converter e: **CPC**

Cartier-McNamara-Mannix-Morrison & Knudson e: **CMMMK**

Cartographic and Geodetic Processing Squadron e: **CGPSq**

Cartography and Geographic Information Science e: **CaGIS**

Cartography and Geographic Information Society e: **CAGIS**

Cartography and Geographic Information Systems e: **CaGIS**

Cartography Special Group, Association of American Geographers e: **CSG**

Cartotheque, Departement de Geographie, Universite de Montreal, Quebec f: **QMUGC**

Cartotheque, Departement de Geographie, Universite de Sherbrooke, Quebec f: **QSHERUGC**

Cartotheque, Departement de Geographie, Universite du Quebec, Trois-Rivieres, Quebec f: **QTUGC**

Cartotheque, Institut de Geologie, Universite de Montreal, Quebec f: **QMUGL**

Cascade Natural Gas Corporation e: **CGC**

Case-Wester Reserve School of Medicine e: **CWRSM**

Case Western Reserve University, Cleveland Health Sciences Library, Cleveland e: **OClW-H**

Cases in Chancery Tempore George II e: **Temp Geo II**

Caspian Sea Level e: **CSL**

cassetten-orientiertes modulares Buchungssystem d: **COMB**

Casualty Surgeons Association e: **CSA**

Catalan Agency for Health Technology Assessment e: **CAHTA**

Catalog of Environmental Resource Data e: **CERD**

Catalogue des Actes Médicaux f: **CdAM**

Catalogue et Index des Sites Médicaux Francophones f: **CISMeF**

Catalogue Multilingual Natural Language Access/Linguistic Server e: **CANAL/LS**

Catchment and Land Protection e: **CALP**

Catchment Areas Protection Board e: **CAPB**

cathodic protection e: **capac.**

Cathodic Protection Survey Kit e: **CPSK**

Catholic Health Association of Canada e: **CHAC**

Catholic Health Association of Canada, Ottawa, Ontario e: **OOCHAC**

Catholic Health Association of the United States e: **CHA**

Catholic Health Association of Wisconsin e: **CHA-W**

Catholic Health Australia e: **CHA**

Catholic Knights of Saint George e: **C.K.St.G.**

Catholic Medical Mission Board e: **CMMB**

Catholic Study Circle for Animal Welfare e: **CSCAW**

Cats Protection League e: **CPL**

Caucho Natural s: **NR**

Cayambe-Coca Ecological Reserve [Ecuador] e: **RECAY**

CCD Airborne Experimental Scanner for Applications in Remote Sensing e: **CAESAR**

CDOS Software Support Environment e: **CSSE**

CEGEP de La Pocatiere, Quebec e: **QPCE**

Cell Atmosphere Processing System e: **CAPS**

Cell Biology and Toxicology e: **Cell Biol Toxicol**

Cell Biology International e: **Cell Biol Int**

Cell for Monitoring and Analysis of Sea-level e: **CMAS**

Cell-Medicated Lympholysis e: **CML**

Cell Space Simulation Language e: **CESSL**

Cell Water Removal Mechanism e: **CWRM**

Cellular and Molecular Biology e: **Cell Mol Biol**

Cellular and Molecular Biology Research e: **Cell Mol Biol Res**

Cellular and Molecular Neurobiology e: **Cell Mol Neurobiol**

Cellular Geographic Service(or Serving) Area e: **CGSA**

Cellule Interrégionale de l'Environnement f: **CELINE**

Cement/Water e: **c/w**

Cement/Water Ratio e: **C/W Ratio**

Cenozoic Investigations of the Western Ross Sea e: **CIROS**

Cenozoic Reef Evolution in Space and Time e: **CREST**

CENTAG Medical Working Party e: **CMWP**

Centaur Operations at the Space Station e: **COSS**

Center for Advanced Medical Informatics at Stanford e: **CAMIS**

Center For Advanced Molecular Biology and Immunology e: **CAMBI**

Center for Advanced Training in Cell and Molecular Biology e: **CATCMB**

Center for Advanced Training in Cell and Molecular Biology/Catholic University of America e: **CATCMB/CUA**

Center for Aerospace Doctrine, Research and Education e: **CADRE**

Center for Agricultural, Resource and Environmental Systems e: **CARES**

Center for Alternatives to Animal Testing e: **CAAT**

Center for Analysis of Dynamics of Atmospheric Regions e: **CADRE**

Center for Analysis of Environmental Change e: **CAEC**

Center for Animal Alternatives e: **CAA**

Center for Animal Disease and Information Analysis e: **CADIA**

Center for Animal Health and Productivity e: **CAHP**

Center for Animal Health Monitoring e: **CAHM**

Center for Applications of Remote Sensing e: **CARS**

Center for Applied Development of Environmental Technologies e: **CADET**

Center for Astrophysics and Space Scientists e: **CASS**

Center for Atmospheric and Remote Sounding Studies e: **CARSS**

Center for Biologics Evaluation and Research e: **CBER**

Center for Cell Regulation and Enhancement of Biology/Biomaterial Interfaces e: **CREBBI**

Center for Climate System Research e: **CCSR**

Center for Climatic and Environmental Assessment e: **CCEA**

Center for Clouds, Chemistry and Climate e: **C4**, e: **CCCC**, e: **CH**

Center for Coastal and Marine Environmental Research e: **TERRAMARE**

Center for Cold Ocean Research Engineering e: **C-CORE**

Center for Devices and Radiological Health e: **CDRH**

Center for Earth and Environmental Sciences e: **CEES**

Center for Earth and Planetary Studies e: **CEPS**

Center for Energy and Environmental Assessment e: **CEEA**

Center for Energy and Environmental Information e: **CEEI**

Center for Energy and Environmental Management e: **CEEM**

Center for Energy and Environmental Studies, Princeton University e: **CEES**

Center for Enhancement of the Biology/Biomaterial Interfaces e: **CEBBI**

Center for Environment Commerce and Energy e: **CECE**

Center for Environmental and Regulatory Systems e: **CERIS**

Center for Environmental Conflict Resolution e: **RESOLVE**

Center for Environmental Education e: **CFEE**

Center [for] Environmental Education, Inc. e: **CEE**

Center for Environmental Health & Injury Control e: **CEHIC**

Center for Environmental Information e: **CEI**

Center for Environmental Information and Statistics e: **EPA**

Center for Excellence for Space Data and Information Sciences e: **CESDIS**

Center for Geographic Information e: **CGI**

Center for GIS [Geograph[ical] Information System] e: **CGIS**

Center for Global Environmental Studies e: **CGES**

Center for Health Administration Studies e: **CHAS**

Center for Health and Gender Equity e: **CHANGE**

Center for Health Applications of Aerospace Related Technologies e: **CHAART**

Center for Health Care Strategies e: **CHCS**

Center for Health Management Research e: **CHMR**

Center for Health Resources Planning Information e: **CHRPI**

Center for Health Services e: **CHS**

Center for Healthcare Environmental Management e: **CHEM**

Center for Healthcare Ethics e: **CHCE**

Center for Healthcare Information Management e: **CHIM**

Center for Human Radiobiology e: **CHR**

Center for Indigenous Peoples Nutrition and Environment e: **CINE**

Center for Information Biology e: **CIB**

Center for Integration of Natural Disaster Information e: **CINDI**

Center for International and Environmental Research e: **CICERO**

Center for International Climate and Energy Research e: **CICERO**

Center for International Earth Sciences Information Network e: **CIESIN**

Center for International Environment Information e: **CIEI**

Center for International Environmental Cooperation e: **INENCO**

Center for International Environmental Law e: **CIEL**

Center for International Health Information e: **CIHI**

Center for International Meeting on Biology e: **CIMB**

Center for Legislative Energy & Environmental Research e: **CLEER**

Center for Male Medicine e: **CMM**

Center for Marine and Environmental Studies e: **CMES**

Center for Medical Consumers and Health Care Information e: **CMC**

Center for Mental Health Services e: **CMHS**

Center for Minority Health e: **CMH**

Center for National Space Studies f: **CNES**

Center for Ocean Atmospheric Modeling e: **COAM**

Center for Ocean, Land and Atmospheric Interactions e: **COLAI**

Center for Ocean-Land-Atmosphere Studies e: **COLA**

Center for/of Environmental Research Information e: **CERI**

Center for Optimum Environments e: **COE**

Center for Orbit Determination in Europe e: **CODE**

[Center for] Population, Health and Nutrition e: **PHN**

Center for Preventive Medicine e: **CPM**

Center for Protection Against Corrosion e: **CPAC**

Center for Public Health Practice e: **CPHP**

Center for Radiophysics and Space Research e: **CRSR**

Center for Remote Sensing and Environmental Optics e: **CRSEO**

Center for Research in Ambulatory Health Care Administration e: **CRAHCA**

Center for Research in Water Resources e: **CRWR**

Center for Scientific Review. National Institutes of Health e: **CSR**

Center for Space and Advanced Technology e: **CSAT**

Center for Space Environmental Health e: **CSEH**

Center for Space Research e: **CSR**

Center for Telemedicine Law e: **CTL**

Center for the Advancement of Community Based Public Health e: **CACCBPH**

Center for the Advancement of Electronic Health Records e: **CAEHR**

Center for the Advancement of Health e: **CFAH**

Center for the Assessment & Monitoring of Forest & Environmental Resources e: **CAMFER**

Center for the Health Effects of Environmental Contamination e: **CHEEC**

Center for the Integrative Study of Animal Behavior e: **CISAB**

Center for the Study of Earth from Space e: **CSES**

Center for the Study of Environmental Endocrine Effects e: **CSEEE**

Center for the Study of Non-Medical Drug Use e: **CSNMDU**

Center for the Study of Random Geophysical Phenomena e: **CEPRAG**

Center for Toxicology and Environmental Health e: **CTEH**

Center for Urban Environmental Studies e: **CUES**

Center for Veterinary Biologics e: **CVB**

Center for Veterinary Medicine e: **CVM**

Center for Water Quality e: **CWQ**

Center for Wildlife Ecology e: **CFE**, e: **CWE**

Center of Health Technology e: **CHT**

Center of the earth e: **O**

Center (or Centre) for Earth Observation e: **CEO**

Center (or Centre) for Environmental Studies (or Study) e: **CES**

Center (or Centre) for Geographical Information and Analysis e: **CGIA**

Center (or Centre) for Technical Geoscience e: **CTG**

Center Weather Advisories e: **CWA**

Center Weather Advisory e: **CWA**

Center Weather Service Unit e: **CWSU**

Center[s] for Epidemiology and Animal Health e: **CEAH**

Centers for Medicare and Medicaid Services e: **CMS**

Center[s] for [the] Commercial Development of Space e: **CCDS**

Centra de Sensores Remotes i: **CSR**, s: **CSR**

Centraal Waterschaps-Kantoor voor de Vorstenlanden op Java n: **CWK**

Central Advisory Water Committee e: **CAWC**

Central Aero-Hydrodynamical Institute e: **CAHI**

Central Aero-Hydrodynamics Institute e: **TsAGI**

Central Aerohydrodynamics Institute e: **TAGSI**

Central Aerological Observatory e: **CAO**

Central African Journal of Medicine e: **Cent Afr J Med**

Central Africa[n] Regional Program for the Environment e: **CARPE**

Central Air Medical Board e: **C.A.M.B.**

Central Aircrew Medical Review Board e: **CAMRB**

Central Airspace Reservation Federation e: **CARF**

Central America Health Rights Network e: **CAHRN**

Central American Commission for Environment and Development e: **CCAD**

Central American Federation of Medical Students e: **CAFMS**

Central American Protected Areas System e: **CAPAS**

Central Arctic Geological Expedition Association Sevmorgeologia e: **CAGE**

Central Asian Republics' Network on Health Care Reforms e: **CARNET**

Central Association of Obstetricians and Gynecologists e: **CAOG**

Central Atlantic Regional Ecological Test Site project *e:* **CARETS**

Central Coast Public Health Unit *e:* **CC PHU**

Central Command for Land, Sea and Air Forces *e:* **CCLSAF**

Central Committee for Community Medicine *e:* **CCCM**

Central Committee for Hospital Medical Services *e:* **CCHMS**

Central Council for British Naturism *e:* **C.C.B.N.**

Central Council for Health Education *e:* **C.C.H.E.**

Central Council for Rivers Protection *e:* **C.C.R.P.**

Central Editorial Board for the International Geological/Geophysical Atlases of the Atlantic and Pacific Oceans, short name: GAPA Central Editor *e:* **CEB-GAPA**

Central Electricity and Water Administration *e:* **CEWA**

Central Environmental Committee *e:* **CEC**

Central Environmental Satellite Computer System *e:* **CEMSCS**

Central Environmental Satellite Data System *e:* **CEMSDS**

Central Europe/Inland Waterways Transport *e:* **CE/IWT**

Central European Environmental Data Request Facility *e:* **CEDAR**

Central European Journal of Public Health *e:* **Cent Eur J Public Health**

Central Fire Liaison Panel [British Insurance Association, Chief Fire Officers Association, Confederation of British Industry, Fire Protection Association] *e:* **CFLP**

Central Flow Weather Service Unit *e:* **CFMWP**

Central Geographic Data Base *e:* **CGDB**

Central Geological Survey *e:* **CGS**

Central Groundwater Board *e:* **CGB**

Central Health Monitoring Unit *e:* **CHMU**

Central Health Outcomes Unit *e:* **CHOU**

Central Health Services *e:* **CHS**

Central Ice Data Exploration *e:* **CIDEX**

Central Indian Medicinal Plants Organization *e:* **CIMPO**

Central Information Service on occupational health and safety *e:* **CIS**

Central Institute for Physics of the Earth *e:* **CIPE**

Central Kansas Medical Center Great Bend *e:* **KGbMC**

Central Laboratory for Geodesy *e:* **CLG**

Central Medical Board *e:* **CMB**

Central Medical Emergency Dispatcher *e:* **CMED**

Central Medical Equipment Depot *e:* **CMED**

Central Medical Establishment *e:* **CME**

Central Medical Establishment, Aviation *e:* **CMEA**

Central Medical Library Association *e:* **CMLA**

Central Medical War Committee *e:* **C.M.W.C.**

Central Meteorological Observatory *e:* **CMO**

Central Meteorological Office *e:* **CMO**

Central North American Water Project *e:* **CeNAWP**

Central of Georgia Railroad Co. *e:* **C of GA**

Central of Georgia Railway *e:* **CGARY**

Central of Georgia Railway Co. *e:* **CG**

Central Office for Environmental Protection *e:* **COEP**

Central Ohio Biomedical Engineering Community Council *e:* **COBECC**

Central Public Health Engineering Research Institute *e:* **CPHERI**

Central Public Health Laboratory *e:* **CPHL**

Central Public Health Library *e:* **CPHL**

Central Research Institute for Animal Science *e:* **PUSLITBANGNAK**

Central Region Headquarters, Atmospheric Environment Service, Environment Canada Winnipeg, Manitoba *e:* **MWEAE**

Central Seismological Observatory *e:* **CSO**

Central States Society of Industrial Medicine and Surgery *e:* **CSSIMS**

Central Station Electrical Protection (or Protective) Association *e:* **CSEPA**

Central Tierversicherungs-Gesellschaft AG *d:* **CTVH**

Central Unit on Environmental Pollution *e:* **CUEP**

Central United States Earthquake Consortium *e:* **CUSEC**

Central Water Advisory Committee *e:* **CWAC**

Central Water and Power Commission *e:* **CWPC**

Central Water and Power Department (or Development) *e:* **C.W.P.D.**

Central Water and Power Research Station *e:* **CWPRS**

Central Water Planning Unit *e:* **CWPU**

Central Waterpower, Irrigation and Navigation Research Station *e:* **CWINRS**

Central Waterways, Irrigation and Navigation Commission *e:* **CWINC**

Central Weather Bureau *e:* **CWB**

Central Weather Processor *e:* **CWP**

Central Weather Service Unit *e:* **CWSU**

Central West Public Health Unit *e:* **CWPHU**

Central Western Queensland Division Medical Division *e:* **CWQDGP**

Centrale Bibliotheek van Landsverdediging *n:* **APDB**

Centrale Commissie van Georganiseerd Overleg in Ambtenarenzaken *n:* **C.C.G.O.A.**

Centrale Commission voor Georganiseerd Overleg *n:* **CCGO**

Centrale Coopérative des Productions Animales *f:* **CCPA**

Centrale d'Achats des Miroitiers français *f:* **CAMIR**

Centrale des Auberges de Jeunesse Luxembourgeoises *f:* **CAJL**

Centrale des Auberges Luxembourgeoises de Jeunesse *f:* **A.L.J.**

Centrale Laitière Haute-Normandie *f:* **CLHN**

Centrale Luxembourgeoise du Sport pour Chiens d'Utilité *f:* **C.L.S.C.U.**

Centralised Information Service for Complementary Medicine *e:* **CISCOM**

Centralized Environmental Facility *e:* **CEF**

Centralized Online Processing Environment *e:* **COPE**

Centralized Service Observation *e:* **CSO**

Centralna Medicinska Knjižnica *S:* **CMK**

Centralny Urząd Geodezji i Kartografii *P:* **CUGiK**

Centralny Urząd Geologii *P:* **CUG**

Centre Administratif Technique Interdépartemental *f:* **C.A.T.I.**

Centre African de Documentation et d'Information en matiere de Brevets *f:* **CADIB**

Centre Algérien de Recherches et Expérimentations Forestières *f:* **CAREF**

Centre Belgo-Luxembourgeois d'Information de l'Acier *f:* **CBLIA**

Centre Canadien d'Information sur la Geoscience *f:* **CCIG**

Centre Climatologique Régional *f:* **CCR**

Centre commun d'analyse des données environnementales *f:* **JEDA**

Centre d'Accueil et d'Observation *f:* **CAO**

Centre d'Animation Pedagogique, Conseil des Ecoles Separees Catholiques d'Ottawa, Ontario *f:* **OOCESC**

Centre de Biologie Marine *f:* **MBC**

Centre de Distribution de Médicaments Vétérinaires *f:* **CDMV**

Centre de Documentation, Bureau de la Protection Civile du Quebec, Ste.-Foy, Quebec *f:* **QSFPC**

Centre de Documentation, Charette, Fortier, Hawey, Touche, Ross, Montreal, Quebec *e:* **QMCFH**

Centre de Documentation, Direction de l'Environnement, Hydro-Quebec, Montreal, Quebec *f:* **QMHDE**

Centre de Documentation Géographique *f:* **C.D.G.**

Centre de Documentation, Hydro-Québec International, Montreal, Québec *f:* **QMHI**

Centre de Documentation, INRS-Georessources, Ste.-Foy, Quebec *f:* **QSFIG**

Centre de Documentation, Institut de Technologie Agro-Alimentaire de La Pocatiere, Quebec *f:* **QPES**

Centre de Documentation, Redaction et Terminologie, Hydro-Quebec, Montreal, Quebec *f:* **QMHRT**

Centre de Documentation Tiers-Monde[-Mission] *f:* **CDTM**

Centre de Documentation, Verification Generale, Hydro-Quebec, Montreal, Quebec *f:* **QMHVG**

Centre de Documentation, École Secondaire de Plantagenet, Ontario *f:* **OPES**

Centre de Découverte de la Nature du Parc Naturel Régional de Brotonne *f:* **CEDENA**

Centre de Formation des Conducteurs Routiers *f:* **C.F.C.R.**

Centre de Formation et Documentation sur l'Environnement industriel *f:* **CFDE**

Centre de Liaison pour l'Environnement *f:* **CLE**

Centre de liaison pour l'environnement International *f:* **CLEI**

Centre de Productivité et d'aciton Forestière de l'Aquitaine *f:* **CPFA**

Centre de Protection Infantile *f:* **CPI**

Centre de Protection Maternelle et Infantile *f:* **C.P.M.I.**

Centre de Recherche en Geomatique *f:* **CRG**

Centre de recherche et de développement sur le bovin laitier et le porc *f:* **CRL**

Centre de Recherche International de Nutrition Animale *f:* **CRINA**

Centre de Recherche sur l'Amerique Latine et le Tiers-Monde *f:* **CETRAL**

Centre de Recherches Atmosphériques *f:* **CRA**

Centre de Recherches Biologiques *f:* **C.R.B.**

Centre de Recherches Biologiques Tropicales *f:* **CRBT**

Centre de Recherches en Astronomie Astrophysique et Géophysique *f:* **CRAAG**

Centre de Recherches en Physique de l'Environment terrestre et planetaire *f:* **CRPE**

Centre de Recherches en Physique de l'Environnement terrestre et solaire *f:* **CRPE**

Centre de Recherches et d'Information Tiers-Monde *f:* **CRI T-MONDE**

Centre de Recherches et d'Études Océanographiques *f:* **CREO**

Centre de Recherches Géodynamiques *f:* **CRG**

Centre de Recherches Géophysiques *f:* **CRG**

Centre de Recherches Océanographiques *f:* **CRO**

Centre de Recherches Océanographiques et des Pêches *f:* **CROP**

Centre de Recherches Pétrographiques et Géochimiques *f:* **CRPG**

Centre de Recherches Routières *f:* **CRR**

Centre de Recherches sur les Ressources Biologiques Terrestres *f:* **CRBT**

Centre de Recherches sur les trypanosomiases Animales *f:* **CRIA**

Centre de Ressources, École Secondaire Algonquin, North Bay, Ontario *f:* **ONBA**

Centre de récherche en Géochimie Isotopique et en Géochronologie at UQAM *f:* **GEOTOP**

Centre de Récherches Minérales, Ministère des Richesses Naturelles, Québec *f:* **QU**

Centre d'Ecologie des Ressources Renouvelables *f:* **CERR**

Centre d'Enseignement de la Météorologie Nationale *f:* **CEMN**

Centre des Nations unies pour les ressources naturelles, l'Énergie et les Transports *f:* **CNERT**

Centre d'Essai Biochimique (ou biologique) *f:* **C.E.B.**

Centre d'Etudes et de Rechereches Geodynamiques et Astronomiques *f:* **CERGA**

Centre d'Examen Médical du Personnel Navigant *f:* **C.E.M.P.N.**

Centre d'Expertise Médicale du Personnel Navigant de l'Aéronautique *f:* **C.E.M.P.N.A.**

Centre d'Exploration et de Recherche Médicale par Emission de Positons *f:* **CERMEP**

Centre d'Information des Services Médicaux des Entreprises *f:* **CISME**

Centre d'Information et de Documentation tiers-monde *f:* **CID**

Centre d'Information et d'Orientation Médicale *f:* **CIOM**

Centre d'Information Geographique et Foncière Ministre de l'Energie et des Ressources *f:* **CIGF**

Centre d'Information Médicale et d'Éducation Sanitaire *f:* **CIMES**

Centre d'Information sur l'Energie et l'Environnement *f:* **CIELE**

Centre d'Information sur l'Environnement International *f:* **CIEI**

Centre d'Information Tiers-Monde *f:* **CITM**

Centre d'Instruction du Service Biologique et Vétérinaire des Armées *f:* **CISBVA**

Centre d'Investigations Médico-Pharmaceutiques *f:* **CIMEPHA**

Centre dobservation de El Niño *f:* **ENMOC**

Centre d'Observation Public d'Éducation Surveillée *f:* **COPES**

Centre d'Observation Économique *f:* **COE**

Centre d'orbitographie opérationnel *f:* **COO**

Centre du droit de l'environnement *f:* **CDE**

Centre d'Éducation Médicale pour des Enfants Arrières *f:* **CEMEA**

Centre d'étude de la chimie du climat marin *f:* **COCC**

Centre d'étude du climat *f:* **CAC**

Centre d'Étude et de Développement de l'Informatique Médicale du Hainaut Occidental *e:* **CEDIMHO**

Centre d'Étude et de Recherche sur la Pollution Atmosphérique *f:* **CERPA**

Centre d'Études Biologiques des Animaux Sauvages *f:* **CEBAS**

Centre d'Études d'Applications Médico-Pédagogique *f:* **CEAMP**

Centre d'Études de Biologie Rurale *f:* **CEBER**

Centre d'Études de Droit International Médical *f:* **CEDIM**

Centre d'Études de Geographie Tropical *f:* **CEGET**

Centre d'Études de la Météorologie Spatiale *f:* **CEMS**

Centre d'Études de Recherches et d'Actions Techniques et Économiques des Métiers *f:* **CERATEM**

Centre d'Études de Recherches et d'Applications Biologiques *f:* **CERAB**

Centre d'Études des Matières Plastiques *f:* **CEMP**

Centre d'Études des matières Plastiques *f:* **CEP**

Centre d'Études des Pays de l'Océan Indien *f:* **CEPOI**

Centre d'Études des Phenomenes Aleatoires Geophysiques *f:* **CEPHAG**

Centre d'Études des Supports d'Information Médical *f:* **CESSIM**

Centre d'Études des Techniques Forestières *f:* **CETEF**, *f:* **CETF**

Centre d'Études Economiques et Sociales de l'Environnement *f:* **CEESE**

Centre d'Études et Aménagement des Ressources Naturelles *f:* **CEARN**

Centre d'Études et de Perfectionnement de l'Artisanat des Métiers *f:* **CEPAM**

Centre d'Études et de Realisations Cartographiques Geographiques *f:* **CERCG**

Centre d'Études et de Recherche sur l'Économie et l'Organisation des Productions Animales *f:* **CEREOPA**

Centre d'Études et de Recherches de Biologie Alimentaire *f:* **CERBA**

Centre d'Études et de Recherches de Biologie et d'Océanographie Médicale *f:* **CERBOM**

Centre d'Études et de Recherches de Géographie Active sur le Sous-Développement *f:* **CERGASD**

Centre d'Études et de Recherches de l'Environnement *f:* **CERE**

Centre d'Études et de Recherches de Matériel Médical *f:* **CEREM**

Centre d'Études et de Recherches Eco-Geographiques *f:* **CEREG**

Centre d'Études et de Recherches en Biologie Humaine et Animale *f:* **CERBHA**

Centre d'Études et de Recherches Géologiques et Hydrogéologiques *f:* **CERGH**

Centre d'Études et de Recherches sur les Sociétés de l'Ocean Indien *f:* **CERSOI**

Centre d'Études et Promotion des Métiers Artisanaux de l'Ile-de-France *f:* **CEPMAIF**

Centre d'Études et Recherches de la Géologie et de ses Applications *f:* **CERGA**

Centre [d'Études] Européen pour les Problèmes de l'Environnement Marin *f:* **CEPEM**

Centre d'Études Francophones de l'Ocean Indien *f:* **CERFOI**

Centre d'Études Géologiques et Minières *f:* **CEGM**

Centre d'Études Physiosociologiques et Écologiques *f:* **CEPE**

Centre d'Études Politiques et Juridiques du Tiers-Monde *f:* **C.E.P.J.T.M.**

Centre d'Études pour la Gestion des Ressources Naturelles *f:* **CEGERNA**

Centre d'Études pour le Développement des Recherches Appliquées à la protection du potentiel *f:* **CERDAR**

Centre d'Études Techniques et Économiques des Matières grasses élémentaires *f:* **CETEMA**

Centre d'Études Économiques et Sociales du Tiers Monde *f:* **CEESTM**

Centre Europe Tiers-Monde *e:* **CETIM**

Centre Europe-Tiers Monde *f:* **CETIM**

Centre Européen Associé de Biologie Humaine *f:* **CEABH**

Centre Européen de Culture, de Recherche et d'Éducation Permanente "Wildpeace" *f:* **Wildpeace CECREP**

Centre Européen de Recherches et d'Applications Medicales Bruxelles *f:* **CERAMBRUX**

Centre Européen des constructeurs de matériel de Comptage et de Distribution des hydrocarbures *f:* **CECOD**

Centre Européen des Observations par Sondage *f:* **CEROS**

Centre européen d'information, de coordination pour le respect des personnes handicapees, de la nature et de l'environnement *f:* **HNE**

Centre Européen d'information pour la conservation de la nature *f:* **CEICN**

Centre Européen d'Écologie Humaine *f:* **CEEH**

Centre Européen pour les Prévisions Météorologiques à Moyen Terme *f:* **CEPMMT**

Centre for Addiction and Mental Health. Centre de toxicomanie et de santé mentale *f:* **CAMH**

Centre for Advanced Studies in Environment *e:* **CASE**

Centre for Agrobiological Research *e:* **CABO**

Centre for Applied Geology *e:* **CAG**

Centre for Applied Health Research *e:* **CAHR**

Centre for Applied Microbiology and Research *e:* **CAMR**

Centre for Development and Environment *e:* **CDE**

Centre for Earth Resource Management Applications *e:* **CERMA**

Centre for Economic and Environmental Development *e:* **CEED**

Centre for Economic and Social Studies on the Environment *e:* **CESSE**

Centre for Environment and Development for/in the Arab Region and Europe *e:* **CEDARE**

Centre for Environment, Fisheries and Aquaculture Science *e:* **CEFAS**

Centre for Environmental and Estuarine Studies *e:* **CEES**

Centre for Environmental Health *e:* **CEH**

Centre for Environmental Mechanics *e:* **CEM**

Centre for Evidence-Based Medicine *e:* **CEBM**

Centre for Evidence Based Mental Health *e:* **CEBMH**

Centre for Global Environmental Research *e:* **CGER**

Centre for Health Economics *e:* **CHE**

Centre for Health Economics and Policy Analysis *e:* **CHEPA**

Centre for Health Evidence *e:* **CHE**

Centre for Health Informatics *e:* **CHI**

Centre for Health Informatics in Medical Education *e:* **CHIME**

Centre for Health Informatics & Multiprofessional Education *e:* **CHIME**

Centre for Health Information Management Research *e:* **CHIMR**

Centre for Health Information Quality *e:* **CHIQ**

Centre for Health Policy *e:* **CHP**

Centre for Health Program Evaluation *e:* **CHPE**

Centre for Health Services and Policy Research *e:* **CHSPR**

Centre for Integrated Resource Management and Environmental Science *e:* **CIRMES**

Centre for International Cooperation in Health and Development *e:* **CCISD**

Centre for International Environmental Law *e:* **CIEL**

Centre for Medical *e:* **CMERD**

Centre for Medicines Research International *e:* **CMR**

Centre for Natural Resources, Energy and Transport *e:* **CNRET**

Centre for Ocean Analysis and Prediction *e:* **COAP**

Centre for Ocean Climate Chemistry (Institute of Ocean Sciences, Canada) *e:* **COCC**

Centre for Offshore and Remote Medicine *e:* **MEDICOR**

Centre for Postgraduate and Continuing Medical Education *e:* **CPCME**

Centre for Protection Against Corrosion *e:* **CPAC**

Centre for Rehabilitation of Wildlife *e:* **CROW**

Centre for Research in Experimental Space Science *e:* **CRESS**

Centre for Research in Women's Health *e:* **CRWH**

Centre for Resource and Environmental Studies *e:* **CRES**

Centre for Sanitary Engineering and Environmental Sciences *e:* **CSEES**

Centre for Social and Economic Research on the Global Environment *e:* **CSERGE**

Centre for the Study of Environmental Change *e:* **CSEC**

Centre for Tropical Veterinary Medicine *e:* **CTVM**

Centre Française de Protection de l'Enfance *f:* **CFPE**

Centre Fribourgeois de Documentation Pédagogique *f:* **CFDP**

Centre Inter-Médical *f:* **CIM**

Centre Intercontinental des Études de Techniques Biologiques *f:* **CIETB**

Centre Interdisciplinaire d'étude du Milieu naturel et de l'Aménagement rural *f:* **CIMA**

Centre Interdépartemental de Microscopie Électronique *f:* **CIME**

Centre interdépartemental d'Étude des Terrains Instables *f:* **CETI**

Centre Intergouvernemental de Documentation sur l'Habitat et l'Environnement pour les pays de la Commission Économique pour l'Europe des Nations unies *f:* **CIDHEC**

Centre International d l'Environnement *f:* **CIE**

Centre International de Documentation "Georges Dopagne" *f:* **CIDGD**

Centre international de gestion des ressources aquatiques biologiques *f:* **ICLARM**

Centre International de Liaison des Écoles de Cinéma et de Télévision *f:* **CILECT**

Centre International de l'Industrie et pour l'Environnement *f:* **CIIE**

Centre International de Recherche Biologique *f:* **CIRB**

Centre International de Recherche Médicales de Franceville *f:* **CIRMF**

Centre International de Recherches sur l'Environnement et le Développement *f:* **CIRED**

Centre international d'Information sur le Gaz naturel et tous hydrocarbures gazeux *f:* **CEDIGAZ**

Centre International du Film Médical et Chirurgical *f:* **CIFMC**

Centre International pour la Formation et les Échanges Geologiques *f:* **CIFEG**

Centre International pour la Formation et les Études Geologiques *f:* **CIFEG**

Centre interprofessional Technique d'Études de la Pollution Atmosphérique *f:* **CETEPA**

Centre Interprofessionnel d'Études et d'examens Médicaux *f:* **CIEM**

Centre Interprofessionnel Laitier *f:* **C.I.L.**

Centre Interprofessionnel Laitier de l'Anjou *f:* **CILA**

Centre Interprofessionnel Technique d'Études de la Pollution Atmosphérique *f:* **CITEPA**

Centre Latino-Américain des sciences Biologiques *f:* **CLAB**

Centre Lorrain d'Information pour le Développement collectif tiers-monde de Nancy *f:* **CLID**

Centre Meteorologique de Concentration et de Diffusion, French Air Force *f:* **LFYF**

Centre mondial de climatologie des précipitations *f:* **GPCC**

Centre mondial de surveillance continue de la conservation de la nature *f:* **WCMC**

Centre Médical *f:* **C.M.**

Centre Médical de la Défense Nationale *f:* **CMDN**

Centre Médical Inter-entreprise de la Publicité *f:* **CMIP**

Centre Médico-Chirurgical *f:* **C.M.C.**

Centre Médico-Psycho-Pédagogique *f:* **C.M.P.P.**

Centre Médico-Social *f:* **C.M.S.**

Centre Météorologique de NATO *f:* **CM-NATO**

Centre Météorologique Principal *f:* **CMP**

Centre Météorologique Régional *f:* **CMR**

Centre National d'Astronomie, d'Astrophysique et de Géophysique *f:* **CNAAG**

Centre National de Données Climatiques *f:* **NCDC**

Centre National de Données Océanographiques des Etats-Unis *f:* **USNODC**

Centre National de Données Océanographiques du Viet Nam *f:* **VNODC**

Centre National de l'Information Géographique *f:* **CNIG**

Centre National de Prévention et de Protection *f:* **CNPP**, *f:* **C.N.P.P.**

Centre National de Recherche Atmosphérique *f:* **NCAR**

Centre National de Recherches de l'Espace *f:* **CNRE**

Centre National de Recherches et d'Application des Géosciences *f:* **CRAG**

Centre National de Recherches et Expérimentations Forestiéres *f:* **CNREF**

Centre National de Recherches Forestières *f:* **C.N.R.F.**

Centre National de Recherches Geomorphologiques *f:* **CNRG**

Centre National de Recherche Météorologiques *f:* **CNRM**

Centre National de Ressources sur le Tourisme en Espace Rural *f:* **CNRTER**

Centre National de Tri d'Oceanographie Biologique *f:* **CENTOB**

Centre National des Biologistes *f:* **CNB**

Centre National des Métiers de France *f:* **CNMF**

Centre national des Recherches scientifiques et techniques pour l'Industrie Cimentière *f:* **CRIC**

Centre National d'Information pour la Protection des candidats à la construction familiale *f:* **CNIP**

Centre National d'Information Routière *f:* **CNIR**

Centre National d'Instruction de la Protection Contre l'Incendie *f:* **CNIPCI**

Centre National d'Observation de Fresnes *f:* **C.N.O.F.**

Centre National d'Études Techniques de Géomètres Experts Fonciers *f:* **CNETGEF**

Centre National Interprofessionnel de l'Économie Laitière *f:* **CNIEL**

Centre National pour l'Exploitation des Oceans *f:* **CNEXO**

Centre Naturiste International de la Méditerranée *f:* **C.N.I.M.**

Centre Océanographique du Pacifique *f:* **COP**

Centre Océanographique National *f:* **NOC**

Centre Océanologique de Bretagne *f:* **COB**

Centre Odontologique de Médicométrie et d'Évaluation *f:* **COME**

Centre of Industrial Microbiological Investigationes *e:* **CIMI**

Centre of Information and Documentatioin in Medical Education and Health Care *e:* **CIDEMS**

Centre of Marine Geological Survey Data (Russian Federation) *e:* **CMGD**

Centre on Environment for the Handicapped *e:* **CEH**

Centre Panaméricain de formation à l'Évaluataion des Ressources Naturelles *f:* **CEPERN**

Centre panaméricain de la technique sanitaire et des sciences de l'environnement *f:* **CEPIS**

Centre Permanent de Défense de l'École publique *f:* **C.P.D.E.**

Centre Permanent d'Initiation à l'Environnement *f:* **CPIE**

Centre pour la Protection Sociale de Développement Sociale Asie Pacifique *f:* **CPSDSAP**

Centre pour l'Accroissement de la Productivité des Entreprises Laitières *f:* **CAPEL**

Centre pour l'Environnement et la Développement pour la Région Arabe et l'Europe *f:* **CEDARE**

Centre pour les Ressources Naturelles, l'Énergie et les Transports *f:* **CNRET**

Centre pour les ressources naturelles, l'énergie et les transports *f:* **CRNET**

Centre Principal d'Expertises Médicales du Personnel Navigant *f:* **C.P.E.M.P.N.**

Centre Psycho-Médico-Social *f:* **C.P.M.S.**

Centre Regional de Formation et d'Application en Agrométéorologie et Hydrologie Opérationnelle *f:* **AGRHYMET**

Centre Routier International *f:* **C.R.I.**

Centre Régional de Biologie Marine *f:* **CRBM**

Centre régional de biologie tropicale *f:* **BIOTROP**

Centre régional de biologie tropicale de la SEAMEO *f:* **BIOTROP**

Centre Régional de formation en matière d'Économie alimentaire de Nutrition Appliquée *f:* **CRECENA**

Centre régional de formation et d'application en Agrométéorologie et Hydrology operationnelle *f:* **Centre AGRHYMET**

Centre Régional de Gestion d'études et d'Information de l'Artisanat et des Métiers *f:* **CREGAM**

Centre Régional de la Propriété Forestière *f:* **CRPF**

Centre Régional d'Information et de Coordination Routière *f:* **CRICR**

Centre Régional d'Études pour la Protection et l'Aménagement de la Nature *f:* **CREPAN**

Centre scientifique et Médical de l'Université Libre de Bruxelles en Afrique Centrale *f:* **CEBUMAC**

Centre scientifique et Médical de l'Université libre de Bruxelles en Afrique Centrale *f:* **CEMUBAC**

Centre socialiste de Documentation et d'Études sur les problèmes du Tiers Monde *f:* **CEDETIM**

Centre Suisse de Documentation en matière d'enseignement et d'éducation *f:* **CESDOC**

Centre Technique de l'Industrie du Décolletage *f:* **CTID**

Centre Technique et de Promotion des Laitiers de Haut Fourneau *f:* **C.T.P.L.**

Centre Technique Forestier *f:* **C.T.F.**

Centre Technique Forestier Tropical *f:* **CTFT**

Centre Textile de Conjonctures et d'Observation Économique *f:* **CTCOE**

Centres Administratifs et Techniques Interdépartementaux *f:* **CATI**

Centro Africano de Aplicaciones Meteorológicas para el Desarrollo *s:* **ACMAD**

Centro Alemán de Datos Oceanográficos *s:* **DOD**

Centro Argentino de Datos Oceanográficos *s:* **CEADO**

Centro Australiano de Datos Oceanográficos *s:* **AODC**

Centro Bibliografico Medico *i:* **C.B.M.**

Centro Biológico del Oceano Indico *s:* **CBOI**

Centro Brasileño de Datos Oceanográficos *p:* **BNDO**

Centro Británico de Datos Oceanográficos *s:* **BODC**

Centro Coreano de Datos Oceanográficos *s:* **KODC**

Centro de Asistencia Médica para Enfermos Pobres *s:* **CAMEP**

Centro de Biología Aquática Tropical *p:* **CBAT**

Centro de Biología Marina *s:* **MBC**

Centro de Biología Piscatória *s:* **CBP**

Centro de Control de área Oceánica *s:* **OAC**

Centro de Coordinación de Investigaciónes de Recursos Naturales y su Aplicación *s:* **CECIRNA**

Centro de Datos del Subprograma Oceanográfico [para el GATE] *s:* **OSDC**

Centro de Datos Oceanográficos del Japón *s:* **JODC**

Centro de Datos sobre Estudios de Geología Marina *s:* **CMGD**

Centro de Estudio del Clima *s:* **CAC**

Centro de Estudios Costeira e Oceanica *s:* **CECO**

Centro de Estudos de Cabo Verde *p:* **CECV**

Centro de Geografia do Ultramar *p:* **CGU**

Centro de Geografía Tropical *s:* **CGT**

Centro de Investigaciones de Plantas y Animales Medicinales *s:* **CIPAM**

Centro de Investigaciones Geotecnicas Department *s:* **CIG**

Centro de Investigaciones Oceanológicas *s:* **CRO**

Centro de Investigaciones Pesqueras y Oceanográficas *s:* **CRHO**

Centro de Investigación de Biología Marina *s:* **CIBIMA,** *s:* **CIBM**

Centro de Medicina Andina *s:* **CMA**

Centro de Observación de El Niño *s:* **ENMOC**

Centro de Orbitología Operativa *s:* **COO**

Centro de Preclasificación Oceánica de México *s:* **CPOM**

Centro de Recursos Microbiológicos *s:* **MIRCEN**

Centro de Recursos Naturales *s:* **CENREN**

Centro de Recursos Naturales, Energía y Transportes *s:* **CNRET,** *s:* **CRNET**

Centro de Servicios de Constatación Animal *s:* **CENAPA**

Centro de Servicios de Diagnóstico en Salud Animal *s:* **CENASA**

Centro de Utilización de Datos Meteorológicos *s:* **MDUC**

Centro di Geodesia Spaziale *i:* **CGS**

Centro do Estudos de Antropobiologia *p:* **CEA**

Centro Espacial de Lanzamientos para la Prospección Atmosférica *s:* **CELPA**

Centro Español de Datos Oceanograficos *s:* **CEDO**

Centro Europeo de Previsiones Meteorológicas a Plazo Medio *s:* **ECMWF**

Centro Interamericano de Desarrollo Integras de Aguas y Tierra *s:* **CIDIAT**

Centro Interamericano para el Desarrollo Integral de Aguas y Tierras *s:* **CIDIAT**

Centro Internacional de Documentación Georges Dopagne *s:* **CIDGD**

Centro Internacional de Ecologia Tropical *s:* **CIET**

Centro Internacional para la Ordenación de los Recursos Acuáticos Biológicos *s:* **ICLARM**

Centro Internazionale di Ipnosi Medica e Psicologica *i:* **CIIMP**

Centro Internazionale Radio-Medico *i:* **CIRM**

Centro Italiano per lo Studio e lo Sviluppo dell'Agopuntura Moderna e dell'altra Medicina *i:* **CISSAM**

Centro Latinoamericano de Estudios y Difusión de la Construcción en Tierra *s:* **CLEDTIERRA**

Centro Lationamericano de Ciencias Biológicas *s:* **CLAB**

Centro Meteorologico *i:* **C.M.**

Centro Meteorológico Canadiense *s:* **CMC**

Centro Meteorológico Especializado de la
ASEAN s: **ASMC**

Centro Meteorológico Mundial s: **CMM**

Centro Meteorológico Nacional s: **CMN**

Centro Meteorológico Regional s: **CMR**

Centro Meteorológico Regional
Especializado s: **CMRE**

Centro Multinacional de Documentación
Científica sobre Geología, Geofisica de
Colombia s: **CEMDOC**

Centro Mundial de Climatología de las
Precipitaciones s: **CMCP**

Centro Médico Argentino-Británico s:
CMAB

Centro Nacional de Datos Oceanograficos
s: **CENADA**

Centro Nacional de Datos Oceanográficos
s: **NODC**

Centro Nacional de Datos Oceanográficos
de China s: **CNODC**

Centro Nacional de Datos Oceanográficos
de Colombia s: **CECOLDO**

Centro Nacional de Datos Oceanográficos
de la República Popular Democrática de
Corea s: **KNODC**

Centro Nacional de Documentación e
Información en Medicina y Ciencias de la
Salud s: **CENDIM**

Centro Nacional de Estudios e
Investigaciones Oceanográficas s:
CNERO

Centro Nacional de Informação Cientifica
en Microbiologia p: **CENIM**

Centro Nacional de Informacão Geografica
p: **CNIG**

Centro Nacional de Investigaciones
Atmosféricas s: **NCAR**

Centro Nacional de Investigaciones
Oceanográficas s: **CNRO**

Centro Nacional de Investigaciones
Oceanográficas y Pesqueras s: **CNROP**

Centro Nacional de Patología Animal s:
CNPA

Centro Nacional Helénico de Datos
Oceanográficos s: **HNODC**

Centro Nacional Iraní de Oceanografía s:
INCO

Centro Nazionale di/per la Fisica
dell'Atmosfera e Meteorologia i:
CENFAM

Centro Oceanográfico Nacional s: **NOC**

Centro Panamericano de Entrenamiento
para la Evaluación de los Recursos
Naturales s: **CEPERN**

Centro Panamericano de Estudios e
Investigaciones Geográficas s:
CEPEIGE

Centro Regional de Biología Tropical s:
BIOTROP

Centro Regional de Formación Profesional
Meteorológica s: **CRFPM**

Centro Regional del Clima s: **CRC**

Centro Studi Problemi Medici i: **C.S.P.M.**

Centrul de Documentare Medicala ru:
CDM

Centrum voor Agribiologisch Onderzoek
n: **CABO-DLO**

Centrum voor Onderzoek Waterkeringen
n: **COW**

Ceramic Oceanographic Buoy e: **COB**

Ceramic to Metal Sea e: **CTMS**

Cercle Namurois d'Informatique Médicale
f: **CeNIM**

Cercles des Jeunes Naturalistes f: **CJN**

cerebrospinal fluidWassermann reaction e:
csf Wr

Cerro Tolo Interamerican Observatory e:
CTIO

Certifed Medical Assistant Administrative
and Clinical e: **CMAAC**

Certificate in Health Services Management
e: **Cert HSM**

Certificate in Industrial Health e: **CIH**

Certificate in Public Health e: **CPH**

Certificate of General Aviation Medicine
e: **Cert.Gen.Av.Med**

Certificate of the Royal College of
Surgeons e: **CRCS**

Certificate of Underwater Medicine of the
Royal Navy e: **Cert.Un.Med[RN]**

Certified Clinical Mental Health Counselors
e: **CCMHC**

Certified Correctional Health Professional
e: **CCHP**

Certified Environmental Trainer e: **CET**

Certified Health Education Specialists e:
CHES

Certified Health Physicist e: **CHP**

certified inhalation protection e: **cip**

Certified Medical Assistant e: **CMA**

Certified Medical Manager e: **CMM**

Certified Medical Representatives Institute
e: **CMR**

Certified Medical Transcriptionist e: **CMT**

Certified Professional in Healthcare Quality
e: **CPHQ**

Certified Remote Management Engineer e:
CRME

Ceylon Medical Journal e: **Ceylon Med J**

Chair of Economic Geology e: **CEG**

Chamberlain Armor Protection System e:
CHAPS

Chambre Belge des Pédicures Médicaux f:
CBPM

Chambre de Métiers d'Alsace f: **CMA**

Chambre des Métiers f: **CM**

Chambre des Métiers de France f: **C.M.F.**

Chambre des Métiers de la Seine f: **C.M.S.**

Chambre des Métiers Interdépartementale
de Paris f: **CMIP**

Chambre Interdépartementale des Notaires
de Paris f: **CINP**

Chambre Syndicale Belge des Fabricants et
Distributeurs de Produits Naturels et
Diététiques f: **PRONADI**

Chambre Syndicale de la Phytopharmacie et
de la protection des plantes f: **CSP**

Chambre Syndicale des Courtiers en
Valeurs f: **C.S.C.V.**

Chambre Syndicale des Emballages en
Matières Plastiques f: **CSEMP**

Chambre Syndicale du Commerce en Gros
des Produits Laitiers et Avicoles du
Marché d'Intérêt National de Rungis f:
SYCLOPA

Chambre Syndicale Nationale des Industries
de Protection f: **CSNIP**

Chambre Syndicale pour la Protection des
Inventeurs f: **C.S.P.I.**

Chandra X-Ray Observatory e: **CXO**

Chandraprabha Wildlife Sanctuary e:
CWS

Chang Keng I Hsueh [Chang Gung Medical
Journal] ch: **Chang Keng I Hsueh**

Changements de l'environnement planétaire
f: **GEC**

Changeout e: **C/O**

Changeover Point e: **CHOP**

Changeover Time e: **CT**

Chantier de Construction Navale f:
CHACONA

Chantier Naval f: **C.N.**

Chantiers Aéro-Maritimes de la Seine f:
C.A.M.S.

Chantiers Aéronautique de Normandie f:
CAN

Chantiers de France-Dunkerque f: **CFD**

Chantiers du nord et de la Méditerranée f:
NORMED

Chantiers Navale de La Ciotat f: **CNC**

Chantiers Navals et Industriels de la
Méditerranée f: **CNIM**

Chantiers Navals Franco-Belges f: **CNFB**

Charged Particle Lunar Environment
Experiment e: **CPLEE**

Charles E. Drew Postgraduate Medical
School e: **Drew**

Charles M. Russell National Wildlife Range
e: **CMRNWR**

Charlottenburger Wasser- und
Industriewerke AG d: **CharlWass**, d:
ChWIW

Chartered Institute of Environmental Health
e: **CIEH**

Chartered Society of Massage and Medical
Gymnastics e: **C.S.M.M.G.**

Chassahowitzka National Wildlife Refuge
e: **CNWR**

Chatauqua National Wildlife Refuge e:
CNWR

Chaudiere Branch, Departmental Library,
Environment Canada Ottawa, Ontario e:
OOPAC

Cheap Access To Space e: **CATS**

Check-list of the Freshwater Fishes of
Africa e: **CLOFFA**

Checkout Atmospheric Science Experiment
Set e: **CASES**

Chemical Agent Remote Monitor System
e: **CARMS**

Chemical and Biological e: **C and B**, e:
CB

Chemical and Biological Accident and
Incident Control Plan e: **CBAICP**

Chemical and Biological Arms Control
Institute e: **CBACI**

Chemical and Biological Defence
Establishment e: **CBDE**

Chemical and Biological Defense
Information Analysis Center e: **CBIAC**

Chemical and Biological Information
Handling e: **CBIH**

Chemical and Biological Medical Treatment
Symposia e: **CBMTS**

Chemical [and] Biological Munition[s] e:
CBM

Chemical and Biological Warfare e: **CBW**

Chemical and Biological Weapons e:
CBW, e: **CBWs**

Chemical-Biological Acti vities e: **CBAC**

Chemical-Biological Activities e: **CBA**

Chemical, Biological, and Radiation
Laboratories e: **CBRL**

Chemical, Biological and Radiological e:
CBR

Chemical, Biological and Radiological
Center e: **CBRC**

Chemical, Biological and Radiological
Element e: **CBRE**

Chemical, Biological and Radiological Section e: **CBRS**

Chemical, Biological, and Radiological Warfare e: **CBRW**

Chemical, Biological and Radiological [Warfare] e: **CEBAR**

Chemical-Biological Coordination Center e: **CBCC**

Chemical & Biological Defense Agency e: **CBDA**

Chemical Biological, Radiological Agency e: **CBRA**

Chemical, Biological, Radiological and Nuclear e: **CBRN**

Chemical, Biological, Radiological Control Center e: **CBRCC**

Chemical-Biological-Radiological Engineering Group e: **CBREG**

Chemical, Biological, Radiological Officer e: **CBRO**

Chemical, Biological, Radiological Operations Center e: **CBROC**

chemIcal-biological warfare e: **cbw**

Chemical/Biological [weapons] Defense e: **C/BD**

Chemical Corps Biological Laboratories e: **CMLCBL**

Chemical Geology e: **Chem. Geol.**

Chemical Groundwater e: **CGW**

Chemical Health & Safety e: **CH&S**

Chemical Industry Safety and Health [Council] e: **CISHEC**

Chemical Orbit-to-Orbit Shuttle e: **COOS**

chemical protective clothing e: **cpc**

chemical, radiological, biological e: **crb**

Chemical Release Observation e: **CRO**

Chemical Research and Environmental Needs e: **CREN**

Chemical Surface Water e: **CSW**

Chemical Underwater Explosive e: **CUE**

Chemical Warfare Protective Equipment e: **CWPE**

chemical warfarebiological warfare e: **cw-bw**

Chemical[ly] & Biologically Protective Shelter e: **CBPS**

Chemically Induced Dynamic Nuclear Polarization e: **CIDNP**

Chemically Rigidized Space Structure e: **CRSS**

Chemico-Biological Interactions e: **Chem Biol Interact**

Chemin de Fer Congo-Océan f: **CFCO**

Chemistry and Climate Change Working Group e: **CCCWG**

Chesapeake Bay Center for Environmental Studies e: **CBCES**

Chesapeake Biological Laboratories e: **CBL**

Chester and North Wales Medical Society e: **C.N.W.M.S.**

Chester Society of Natural Sciences, Literature and Art e: **C.S.N.S.L.A.**

Chicago College of Osteopathic Medicine e: **CCOM**

Chicago Hydrometeorological Area Project e: **CHAP**

Chicago Medical School e: **CMS**

Chicago Medical School Quarterly e: **Chicago Med. Sch. Quart.**

Chicago Museum of Natural History e: **ChMNH**

Chicago Natural History Museum e: **CNHM**

Chief Administrative Medical Officer e: **CAMO**

Chief [Hydrologist] e: **CH**

Chief Medical Officer e: **Ch Med O**, e: **CMO**

Chief of the Bureau of Medicine e: **ChBuMed**

Chief of the Bureau of Medicine and Surgery e: **CHBUMED**, e: **ChBuMedSurg**

Chief Polaris Executive [missiles] e: **CPE**

Chief Superintendent Naval Meteorology e: **C.S.N.M.**

Chief Superintendent of Hydrographic Supplies e: **CSHS**

Chief Surgeon e: **Chf Surg**, e: **CS**

Chief Surgeon's Office e: **CSO**

Chief Water Tender e: **CWT**

Child: Care, Health and Development e: **Child Care Health Dev**

Child Family Health International e: **CFHI**

Child Health and Nutrition e: **CH/N**

Child Health Associate Program e: **CHAP**

Child Health Bulletin e: **Child Health Bul**

Child Health Clinic e: **CHC**

Child Health Magazine e: **Child Health M**

Child Health Surveillance e: **CHS**

Child Online Privacy Protection Act e: **COPPA**

Child Protection Case Management Team e: **CPCMT**

Child Protection Register e: **CPR**

Child Protection Services e: **CPS**

Child[ren] Online Protection Act e: **COPA**

Children with Special Health Care Needs e: **CSHCN**

Children's Alliance for Protection of the Environment e: **CAPE**

Children's Environmental Health Network e: **CEHN**

Children's Environments Advisory Service, Canada Mortgage and Housing Corp. Ottawa, Ontario e: **OOCMC**

Children's Health Development Foundation e: **CHDF**

Children's Health Environmental Coalition e: **CHEC**

Children's Health Information Network e: **CHIN**

Children's Health Insurance Program e: **CHIP**

Children's Health Services Division e: **CHSD**

Children's Healthcare Options Improved through Collaborative Efforts and Services e: **CHOICES**

Children's Hospital Medical Center e: **CHMC**

Children's Medical Relief International e: **CMRI**

Childrens Medical Research Foundation e: **CMRF**

Chilean National Union for the Environment e: **PNUMA**

Chilean Space Studies Committee e: **CEE**

Chilled Drinking Water e: **CDW**

chilled drinking water return e: **c dwr**

chilled water e: **chw**

Chilled Water Supply e: **CWS**

Chilled Water System e: **CWS**

Chiller, Water, Fan/coil e: **CWF**

Chiller, Water, Refrigerated e: **CWR**

China Accreditation Committee for Environmental management system certification Bodies e: **CACEB**

China Historical Geographic Information System e: **CHGIS**

China Medical Board e: **CMB**

China Medical Board of New York e: **CMBNY**

China Medical Informatics Association e: **CMIA**

China Meteorological Administration e: **CMA**

China Meteorological Agency e: **CMA**

China National Oceanographic Data Center e: **CNODC**

China Ocean Mineral Resources [Research] and Development Association e: **COMRA**

China Ocean Shipping Company e: **COSCO**

China Ocean Shipping Corporation e: **COSCO**

Chincoteague National Wildlife Refuge e: **CNWR**

Chinese Academy of Geological Sciences e: **CAGS**

Chinese Academy of Medical Sciences e: **CAMS**

Chinese Academy of Meteorological Science e: **CAMS**

Chinese Academy of Space [and] Technology e: **CAST**

Chinese Advisory Committee for Polar Research e: **CACPR**

Chinese American Medical Society e: **CAMS**

Chinese Brazilian Earth Resources Satellite e: **CBERS**

Chinese Ecological Research Network e: **CERN**

Chinese Geodetical Star Catalogue e: **CGSC**

Chinese Geophysical Soicety e: **CGS**

Chinese Medical Association e: **CMA**

Chinese Medical Journal e: **Chin Med J**

Chinese Medical Sciences Journal e: **Chin Med Sci J**

Chinese National Committee on Oceanic Research e: **CNCOR**

Chinese Operational Earth Resources Satellite e: **COFRS**

Chinese Society of Geophysics e: **CGS**

Chinese Society of Oceanology and Limnology e: **CSOL**

Chinese Solar-Geophysical Data e: **CSGD**

Chinese weather satellite e: **Feng Yun I**

Chlorierte Kohlenwasserstoffe d: **CKW**

Chlorinated Hydrocarbon e: **CHC**

chlorinated organics in wastewater e: **cow.**

Chlorkohlenwasserstoff e: **CKW**

Chockpit Geometry Evaluation e: **CGE**

Cholesteryl Ester Hydrolase e: **CEH**

Choline Dehydrogenase e: **CDH**

Christ Hospital Institute of Medical Research, Research Library, Cincinnati e: **OCCIM**

Christelijke Bond van Gepensioneerden n: **C.B.G.**

Christian Frontier Council e: **C.F.C.**

Christian Health Association of Liberia e: **CHAL**

Christian Medical and Dental Society *e:*
CMDS

Christian Medical Commission *e:* **CMC**

Christian Medical Council *e:* **CMC**

Christian Medical &Dental Associations *e:*
CMDA

Christian Medical Fellowship *e:* **CMF**

Christian Medical Society *e:* **CMS**

Christians in Health Care *e:* **CHC**

chromatiert *d:* **c**

Chromosome[s] and Plant Cell Division in
Space [Experiment] *e:* **CHROMEX**

Chronic Biological False-Positive *e:*
CBFP

Chronobiology International *e:*
Chronobiol Int

Chrysler Corporation Space Division *e:*
CCSD

Chukchi Sea Circulation Study *e:* **CSCS**

Chung-Hua Fu Chan Ko Tsa Chih [Chinese
Journal of Obstetrics and Gynecology]
ch: **Chung Hua Fu Chan Ko Tsa Chih**

Chung-Hua I Hsueh Tsa Chih [Chinese
Medical Journal] *ch:* **Chung Hua I
Hsueh Tsa Chih**

Chung-Hua Min Kuo Wei Sheng Wu Chi
Mien I Hsueh Tsa Chih [Chinese Journal
of Microbiology and Immunology] *ch:*
**Chung Hua Min Kuo Wei Sheng Wu
Chi Mien I Hsueh Tsa Chih**

Chung-Hua Nei Ko Tsa Chih [Chinese
Journal of Internal Medicine] *ch:* **Chung
Hua Nei Ko Tsa Chih**

Chung-Hua Yu Fang I Hsueh Tsa Chih
[Chinese Journal of Preventive Medicine]
ch: **Chung Hua Yu Fang I Hsueh Tsa
Chih**

Chung-Kuo Chung Yao Tsa Chih [Chinese
Journal of Chinese Materia Medica] *ch:*
Chung Kuo Chung Yao Tsa Chih

Chung-Kuo I Hsueh Ko Hsueh Yuan Hsueh
Pao [Acta Academiae Medicinae Sinicae]
ch: **Chung Kuo I Hsueh Ko Hsueh Yuan
Hsueh Pao**

Ciencias Oceánicas en relación con los
Recursos no Biológicos *s:* **OSNLR**

CIM Implementation Addressing Levels of
Integration in Various Environments *e:*
CIM-ALIVE

CIME Computing Environment: Integrating
CNMA *e:* **CCE-CNMA**

CINC NORAD Remote Display Information
Terminal *e:* **CREDIT**

Cincinnati Society of Natural History *e:*
CSNH

Cinta Internacional de Meteorología
Marítima *s:* **IMMT**

Circular High Acceptance [magnetic] Orbit
Spectrometer *e:* **CHAOS**

Circular Parking Orbit *e:* **CPO**

Circular Terminal Orbit *e:* **CTO**

Circulating Raw Water *e:* **CRW**

Circulating Raw-Water Pump *e:* **CRWP**

Circulating Water *e:* **CW**

Circulating Water Pump *e:* **CWP**

Circulating Water System *e:* **CWS**

circumpolar *e:* **cp**

Circumpolar Active Layer Monitoring
[Program] *e:* **CALM**

Circumpolar Active Layer Permafrost
System *e:* **CAPS**

Circumpolar Arctic Paleo-Environments *e:*
CAPE

Circumpolar Deep Water *e:* **CDW**

Circumpolar Intermediate Water *e:* **CPIW**

Circumpolar Protected Area Network *e:*
CPAN

Circumpolar Seabird Working Group *e:*
CSWG

Circumpolar Universities Association *e:*
CUA

Cislunar Interorbital Transportation *e:*
CIT

Cislunar Space *e:* **CLS**

Cities-Aerospace Industry Coalition *e:*
CAIC

Citizens and Scientists Concerned About
Dangers to the Environment *e:*
CASCADE

Citizens Armed Forces Geographical Unit
e: **CAFGU**

Citizens Association for the Care of
Animals *e:* **CACA**

Citizens Committee on Natural Resources
e: **CCNR**

Citizens' Environmental Coalition *e:* **CEC**

Citizens for a Better Environment *e:* **CBE**

Citizens Medical Reference Bureau *e:*
CMRB

Citizens Organized to Defend the
Environment *e:* **CODE**

Citizens Protection Society *e:* **CPS**

Citizens to End Animal Suffering and
Exploitation *e:* **CEASE**

City of Hope National Medical Center *e:*
CHNMC

Civic Leaders for Ecological Action and
Responsibility *e:* **CLEAR**

Civil Aeromedical Agricultural Research
Institute *e:* **CARI**

Civil Aeromedical Institute *e:* **CAMI**

Civil Aerospace Medical Association *e:*
C.A.M.A.

Civil Air Surgeon *e:* **CAS**

Civil Aviation Medical Association *e:*
CAMA

Civil Aviation Medicine *e:* **CAM**

Civil Earth Remote Sensing System *e:*
CERSS

Civil Space Technology Initiative *e:* **CSTI**

Civilian Employees Health Service *e:*
CEHS

Civilian Health and Medical Program *e:*
CHAMP

Civilian Health and Medical Program of the
Department of Veterans Affairs *e:*
CHAMPVA

Civilian Health and Medical Program of the
Uniformed Services *e:* **CHAMPUS**, *e:*
CHAMPUS

Civilian Help and Medical Program *e:*
CHAMP

Civilian Medical Personnel *e:* **C.M.P.**

Civilian Medical Practitioner *e:* **CMP**

Civilian National Commission on Space
Activities *e:* **CONAE**

Clarence Environment Centre *e:* **CEC**

Clarence Rhode National Wildlife Range
(or Refuge) *e:* **CRNWR**

Clark County Department of Health *e:*
CCDH

Classe Préparatoire aux Grandes Ecoles *f:*
CPGE

Classified Intelligence Handling
Environment *e:* **CHIVE**

Classified Matter Protection and Control
e: **CMPC**

Classified Scientific and Technical
Aerospace Report[s] *e:* **CSTAR**

Classroom Observation System for
Analyzing Depression *e:* **COSAD**

Clay Pigeon Shooting Association *e:*
CPSA

Clean Air and Environmental Reporting
Division *e:* **CAERD**

Clean Urban River Environment Project *e:*
CURE Project

Clean Urban River Environments *e:*
CURE

Clean Water Act *e:* **CWA**

Clean Water Act[ion] Project *e:* **CWAP**

Clean Water Commission *e:* **CWC**

Clearinghouse for Occupational Safety and
Health Information *e:* **COSHI**

Clearwater Correctional Center, Resident
Library, Forks *e:* **WaForC-R**

Clearwater Correctional Center, Staff
Library, Forks *e:* **WaForC**

Clearwater Forest District *e:* **DCL**

CLEM Grapple Changeout Facility *e:*
CGCF

Clerkship Directors in Internal Medicine
e: **CDIM**

Cleveland Clinic Journal of Medicine *e:*
CCJM

Cleveland Department of Water *e:* **CDW**

Cleveland Health Museum *e:* **CHM**

Cleveland Health Sciences Library *e:*
CHSL

Cleveland Museum of Natural History *e:*
CMNH

Cleveland Museum of Natural History,
Cleveland *e:* **OCIMN**

Client-Server Environment *e:* **CSE**

Clima Commerce International *e:* **CCI**

Clima y Variabilidad del Atlántico Nordeste
s: **CLIVA**

Climat et variabilité de l'Atlantique Nord-
Est *f:* **CLIVA**

Climate *e:* **CLIM**

Climate Action Network *e:* **CAN**

Climate Action Network Europe *e:* **CAN-
Europe**

Climate Air-Sea Interaction Drifter *e:*
CASID

Climate Alert Bulletin *e:* **BAC**

Climate Analysis Center (or Centre) *e:*
CAC

Climate Analysis Section *e:* **CAS**

Climate and Cryosphere *e:* **CLIC**

Climate and Environmental Data Retrieval
and Archive *e:* **CERA**

Climate and Global Change Impacts of the
Maghreb Countries *e:* **CLIMAGH**

Climate and Global Change Program *e:*
C&GC, *e:* **CGCP**

Climate and Global Dynamics Division *e:*
CGD

Climate and Variability of the North-East
Atlantic *e:* **CLIVA**

Climate Applications Project *e:* **CLIMAP**

Climate Applications Referral System *e:*
CARS

Climate Assistance Service *e:* **CLASS**

Climate Change Action Fund *e:* **CCAF**

Climate Change Action Plan *e:* **CCAP**

Climate Change and Assessment Working
Group *e:* **CCAWG**

Climate Change and Carrying Capacity e: **CCCC**, e: **CCCC PICES-GLOBEC**

Climate Change Database e: **CLIM**

Climate Change Detection Project e: **CCDP**

Climate Change Experiment e: **CLIMEX**

Climate Change Information Exchange Programme e: **CC:Info**

Climate Change Prediction Program e: **CCP**, e: **CCPP**

Climate Change [project] e: **CLI**

Climate Change Training Programme e: **CC:Train**

Climate Computing e: **CLICOM**

Climate Computing [Project] e: **CLICOM**

Climate Data Assimilation System e: **CDAS**

Climate Data Center e: **CDC**

Climate Data Service for West Africa e: **WACLIM**

Climate Database for the World Oceans e: **CLIWOC**

Climate Diagnostics Center e: **CDC**

Climate Diagnostics Center Laboratory e: **CDCL**

Climate Dynamics e: **Clim. Dyn.**

Climate Dynamics and Experimental Prediction e: **CDEP**

Climate-Hydrology-Ecosystems Interrelation[s] in Mountainou[s] Region[s] e: **CHESMO**

Climate Impact and Response Strategies Network e: **CIRSNet**

Climate Impact Assessment Division e: **CIAD**

Climate Impacts Assessment and Management Program for Commonwealth Countries e: **COMCIAM**

Climate Impacts Centre e: **CIC**

Climate Impacts Research Centre e: **CIRC**

Climate Information and Prediction Services e: **CLIPS**

Climate Interest Group e: **CIG**

Climate Inventory and Catalog e: **CLIC**

Climate-Leaf Analysis Multivariate Program e: **CLAMP**

Climate: Long-range Investigation, Mapping, [Analysis] and Prediction [project] e: **CLIMAP**

Climate Longrange Investigation, Mapping, and Prediction Study e: **CLIMAPS**

Climate Mapping e: **CLIMAP**

Climate Modeling, Analysis, and Prediction [program] e: **CMAP**

Climate Modeling and Analysis Program e: **CMAP**

Climate Modeling and Diagnostics Laboratory e: **CMDL**

Climate Modeling Experiment e: **CME**

Climate Modeling Section e: **CMS**

Climate Modelling Programme e: **CMP**

Climate Monitoring and Diagnostic[s] Laboratory e: **CMDL**

Climate Monitoring Bulletin e: **CMB**

Climate Network Europe e: **CNE**

Climate Observing System Fund e: **COSF**

Climate of the 17th-18th-19th-20th centuries e: **CSENT**

Climate (or Climatic) Impact Assessment Program e: **CIAP**

Climate Prediction and Agriculture e: **CLIMAG**

Climate Prediction Center e: **CPC**

Climate Research e: **Clim. Res.**

Climate Research Centre e: **CRC**

Climate Research Committee e: **CRC**

Climate Research Data Center e: **CRDC**

Climate Research Data tools e: **CRDtools**

Climate Research Institute e: **CRI**

Climate Research Program e: **CRP**

Climate Sensitivity and CO2 Research Group e: **CSCORG**

Climate Services e: **CS**

Climate Simulation Laboratory e: **CSL**

Climate Simulation Laboratory Allocation Panel e: **CSLAP**

Climate System Laboratory e: **CSL**

Climate System Model e: **CSM**

Climate System Modeling Program e: **CSMP**

Climate System Monitoring [Project] e: **CSM**

Climate Systems Modeling and Information Program e: **CSMIP**

Climate Systems Modeling Initiative e: **CSMI**

Climate Test Chamber e: **CTC**

Climate Variability and Predictability [program] e: **CLIVAR**

Climate Variability Study e: **CLIVAR**

Climate Variability Working Group e: **CVWG**

climate, vegetation, productivity e: **cvp**

Climates and Environments of the Last Interglacial in the Arctic e: **CELIA**

Climates of the Past e: **CLIP**

Climatic e: **CLIM**

Climatic Change e: **Clim. Chang.**

Climatic Data Analysis Program[me] e: **CDAP**

Climatic Data for the World e: **W**

Climatic Extremes of the Past e: **CLIMEX**

Climatic Impact Assessment Program e: **CIAP**

Climatic Laboratory e: **CL**

Climatic Mapping of Australia and New Zealand e: **CLIMANZ**

Climatic Research Unit e: **CRU**

Climatic Variation Analysis e: **CVA**

climatographer e: **cltgr**

climatological e: **climat**

Climatological e: **CLTGL**

Climatological Aerological Reference Data Set e: **CARDS**

Climatological and Historical Analysis of Clouds for Environmental Simulations e: **CHANCES**

Climatological Data e: **CD**

Climatological Data National Summary e: **CDNS**

Climatological Data Set (or Sheet) e: **CDS**

Climatological Dispersion Model e: **CDM**

Climatological Dispersion Model with calibration and source Contribution e: **CDMQC**

climatological prediction by model statistics e: **CPMS**

Climatologie Etendue des Nuages et des Aerosols f: **CENA**

Climatologist e: **CLIMAT**

climatology e: **climat**

Climatology e: **Climatol**

Climatology and Persistence e: **CLIPER**

Climax Materials Interaction Test e: **CMIT**

Climax Mine [Nevada] e: **NYM**

climax stock quartz monsonite e: **csqm**

Clinch Valley College.of the University of Virginia, Wise e: **ViWisC**

Clinical Accountability Service Planning and Evaluation specialist healthcare training group e: **CASPE**

Clinical and Experimental Obstetrics and Gynecology e: **Clin Exp Obstet Gynecol**

Clinical and Investigative Medicine e: **CIM**, e: **Clin Invest Med**

Clinical Classifications for Health Policy Research e: **CCHPR**

Clinical Environmental Laboratory e: **CEL**

Clinical Journal of Sport Medicine e: **Clin J Sport Med**

Clinical Medical Officer e: **CMO**

Clinical Medicine e: **Clin. Med.**

Clinical Microbiology Procedures Handbook e: **CMPH**

Clinical Microbiology Reviews e: **Clin Microbiol Rev**, e: **CMR**

Clinical Nuclear Medicine e: **Clin Nucl Med**

Clinical Obstetrics and Gynecology e: **Clin. Obstet. Gynecol.**

Clinical Practice of Medicine e: **CPM**

Clinical Society of Genito-Urinary Surgeons e: **CSGUS**

Clinics in Chest Medicine e: **Clin Chest Med**

Clinics in Geriatric Medicine e: **Clin Geriatr Med**

Clinics in Laboratory Medicine e: **Clin Lab Med**

Clinics in Podiatric Medicine and Surgery e: **Clin Podiatr Med Surg**

Clinics in Sports Medicine e: **Clin Sports Med**

Clio Medica l: **Clio Med**

Close Observation Platoon e: **COP**

Close Protection e: **CP**

Closed Ecological LifeSupport System e: **CELSS**

Closed-Loop Cooling Water System e: **CLCWS**

Closed-Loop Ecological Cycle e: **CLEC**

Closed-Loop Service Water System e: **CLSWS**

Closed Orbit e: **CO**

Closely Spaced Basing e: **CSB**

Cloud and Aerosol Remote Sensing Radiometer e: **CARSR**

Cloud Climate Interactions Group e: **CCIG**

Cloud Photopolarimeter e: **CPP**

Cloud Physics Observatory e: **CPO**

Cloud Water Content e: **CWC**

Clouds and Climate Program e: **CCPR**

Clouds and [the] Earth's Radiant Energy System e: **CERES**

Clouds in Climate Program e: **CCP**

Club for Young Friends of Animals e: **C.Y.F.A.**

Co-orbital Intercepter Scoring Technique e: **CIST**

Co-orbiting Platform e: **COP**

Co-orbiting Satellite e: **COS**

Co-ordinated Information.System on the State of the Environment and Natural Resources e: **CORINE**

Co-ordinating Committee for Oceanographic Research, Science Cooperating Division *e:* **CCOR**

Co-oriented Information of the European Environment *e:* **CORINE**

Co-Polar Attenuation *e:* **CPA**

Coal Consumers Protective Association *e:* **CCPA**

Coal-Water Fuel *e:* **CWF**

Coalition for Biomedical & Health Research *e:* **CBHR**

Coalition for Earth Science Education *e:* **CESE**

Coalition for Environmentally Responsible Economies *e:* **CERES**

Coalition for Healthier Cities and Communities *e:* **CHCC**

Coalition for National Health Education Organizations *e:* **CNHEO**

Coalition for the Medical Rights of Women *e:* **CDRR**, *e:* **CMRW**

Coalition for the Peaceful Uses of Space *e:* **CPUS**

Coalition of Spanish-Speaking Mental Health Organizations *e:* **COSSMHO**

Coalition pour la Recherche Biomédicale et en Santé *f:* **CRBS**

Coalition to Cease Ocean Dumping *e:* **CCOD**

Coalition to Protect Social Security *e:* **SOS**

Coast and Geodetic Magnetic Observatory *e:* **CGMO**

Coast and Geodetic Survey *e:* **CGS**

Coast and Geodetic Survey [Electro] Magnetic *e:* **CGSM**

Coast and Geodetic Survey Electrostatic *e:* **CGSE**

Coast and Geodetic Survey Electrostatic System *e:* **CGSE System**

Coast and Geodetic Tide Station *e:* **CGTS**

Coast Earth Station *e:* **CES**

Coast Geodetic Survey *e:* **Co Geo Surv**

Coast Guard Oceanographic Unit *e:* **CGOU**

Coast Orbital Insertion *e:* **COI**, *e:* **COL**

Coast Survey Marine Observation System *e:* **COSMOS**

Coastal and Estuarine Oceanography Branch *e:* **CEOB**, *e:* **COEB**

Coastal and Marine Environment Management Information System *e:* **COMEMIS**

Coast[al] and Shelf Ecology of the Antarctic Sea Ice Zone *e:* **CS-EASIZ**

Coastal Ballast Water Guidelines Working Group *e:* **CBWGWG**

Coastal Douglas Fir [Biogeoclimatic] Zone *e:* **CDF**

Coastal Environment Management Plans *e:* **CEMP**

Coastal Environment Research Demonstration Areas *e:* **CERDA**

Coastal Environmental Assessment Studies *e:* **CEAS**

Coastal Frontier *e:* **Cf**, *e:* **COFRON**

Coastal Geology Program *e:* **CGP**

Coastal Health Library Information Consortium *e:* **CHLIC**

Coastal Minesweeper (Underwater Locator) *e:* **AMCU**

Coastal Observation and Simulation with Topography *e:* **COAST**

Coastal Observation Program, Engineering *e:* **COPE**

Coastal Ocean Dynamics Applications Radar *e:* **CODAR**

Coastal Ocean Dynamics Experiment *e:* **CODE**

Coastal Ocean Management, Planning and Assessment System *e:* **COMPAS**

Coastal Ocean Observing System *e:* **COOS**

Coastal Ocean Prediction Systems Program[me] *e:* **COPS**

Coastal Ocean Processes *e:* **CoOP**

Coastal Ocean Program *e:* **COP**

Coastal Ocean Reponse Experiment *e:* **CORE**

Coastal Oceans Monitoring Satellite System *e:* **COMSS**

Coastal Ocean[s] Probing Experiment *e:* **COPE**

Coastal Radio Station *e:* **CRS**

Coastal Watershed Assessment Procedure *e:* **CWAP**

Coburger Lehrmittelanstalt-Medien für die Gesundheitserziehung *d:* **CLA**

Cochise Resource Center for Environmental Education *e:* **CRCEE**

Cochrane Ecological Institute *e:* **CEI**

Cocos Island Animal Quarantine Station *e:* **CIAQS**

Cod and Climate Change *e:* **CCC**

Code and Climate Change Programme *e:* **CCC ICES-GLOBEC**

Code für die weltweite, gleichzeitige Beobachtung der meteorologischen Elemente *e:* **SYNOP**

Coded Label Additional Security and Protection System *e:* **CLASPS**

COGLA [Canada Oil and Gas Lands Administration] Ocean Mining Resource Centre, Ottawa, Ontario *e:* **OOCOG**

Coherent Acceleration and Velocity Observations in Real Time *e:* **CAVORT**

Cold Acclimated *e:* **CA**

Cold and Hot Water *e:* **CHW**

Cold Ocean Warm Land *e:* **COWL**

Cold Region Automatic Weather Stations *e:* **CRAWS**

Cold Sanitary Water *e:* **CSW**

Cold Spring Harbor Symposia on Quantitative Biology *e:* **Cold Spring Harbor Symp. Quant**

Cold Water *e:* **CW**

Cold water component of Watercolors *e:* **ICECOLORS**

Cold Water Resistant *e:* **CWR**

Cold Water Rinse *e:* **CWR**

Cold Water Soluble *e:* **CWS**

Cold Water Supply *e:* **CWS**

Cold Weather Injury *e:* **CWINJ**

Cold-Weather Landing Exercise *e:* **COWLEX**

Cold Weather Materiel Test Unit *e:* **CWMTU**

Cold Weather Operations *e:* **CWOP**

Cold Weather Protection *e:* **CWP**

Cold Weather Training Center *e:* **CWTC**

Coleford Nature Reserve *e:* **CNR**

Collaboration of Australia and Nippon for a Gamma Ray Observatory in the Outback *e:* **CANGAROO**

Collaboration on Advanced Multispectral Earth Observation *e:* **CAMEO**

Collaborative Health Informatics Centre *e:* **CHIC**

Collaborative Model for Multiscale Atmospheric Simulation *e:* **COMMAS**

Collaborative Radiological Health Laboratory *e:* **CRHL**

Collaborative Virtual Prototyping Environment *e:* **CVPE**

Collection of Scientific Works. Faculty of Medicine. Charles University *e:* **SVLKAO**

Collective Protection Equipment *e:* **CPE**

Collège académique international de l'environnement *f:* **ACADEVIR**

Collège Canadien des Microbiologistes *f:* **CCM**

Collège de France Géologie *f:* **C.F.Gé**

College de Ste.-Anne, La Pocatiere, Quebec *f:* **QPC**

Collège des Praticiens Spécialistes en Information et Communication Médicales *e:* **COPSICOM**

Collège Française de Rédaction et de Communication Médicale *f:* **CFRCM**

Collège International du Tiers-Monde *f:* **CITM**

Collège National des Gynécologues et Obstétriciens Français *f:* **CNGOF**

College of African Wildlife Management *e:* **CAWM**

College of Earth and Mineral Sciences *e:* **CEMS**

College of Earth and Minerals *e:* **CEM**

College of Geographic Sciences *e:* **COGS**

College of Health Sciences *e:* **CHS**

College of Healthcare Information Management Executives *e:* **CHIME**

College of Human Ecology *e:* **CHE**

College of Medical Evangelists *e:* **CME**

College of Medicine and Dentistry of New Jersey, Newark *e:* **NJN**

College of Mines and Earth *e:* **CME**

College of Osteopathic Medicine and Surgery *e:* **COMS**

College of Osteopathic Medicine of the Pacific *e:* **COMP**

College of Osteopathic Physicians and Surgeons *e:* **COPS**

College of Physicians and Surgeons-Columbia University *e:* **CPSCU**

College of Physicians and Surgeons of New Brunswick *e:* **CPSNB**

College of Physicians and Surgeons of Nova Scotia *e:* **CPSNS**

College of Physicians and Surgeons of Ontario *e:* **CPSO**

College of Staten Island, St. George Campus Library, Staten Island *e:* **VSI**

College of Surgeons of Australasia *e:* **CSA**

College of the Sea *e:* **C.O.S.**

Collège Rhône-Alpin de l'Information Médicale *f:* **CRAIM**

Collège Régional de l'Information Médicale *f:* **CRIM**

Collège Régional des Départements d'Information Médicale du Nord-Pas de Calais *e:* **COREDIM**

Collegio Professionale Interprovinciale Tecnici Sanitari di Radiologia Medica *i:* **TSRM**

Collegio Universitario Aspiranti Medici Missionari *i:* **CUAMM**

Collegium Medicorum Theatri *l:* **COMET**

Colombia Geográfica. Revista del Instituto Geográfico Agustín Codazzi. Bogotá *s:* **IGAC/CG.**

Colombian Internal Medical Congress *e:* **CIMC**

Colonial Medical Department *e:* **C.M.D.**

Colonial Medical Research Committee *e:* **CMRC**

Colonial Medical Service *e:* **C.M.S.**

Colonial Microbiological Research Institute *e:* **CMRI**

Colonial Office Scrub Typhus Research Unit, Institute for Medical Research *e:* **COSTRU**

Colonial Plant and Animal Products *e:* **Colon. Plant Anim. Prod.**

Colonial Waterbirds *e:* **Colon. Waterbirds**

Coloquio Internacional sobre Oceanografía Operacional para la Pesca *s:* **ISOFO**

Colorado Center for Environmental Management *e:* **CCEM**

Colorado Committee for Environmental Information *e:* **CCEI**

Colorado Department of Health *e:* **CDH**

Colorado Division of Wildlife *e:* **CDOW,** *e:* **TPCWDL**

Colorado Foundation for Medical Care *e:* **CFMC**

Colorado Geological Survey *e:* **CGS**

Colorado Journal of International Environmental Law and Policy *e:* **Colo. J. Int'l Envtl. L.&Pol'y**

Colorado Medical Device Association *e:* **CMDA**

Colorado River Ecology Alliance *e:* **CREA**

Colorado River Municipal Water District *e:* **CRMWD**

Colorado State Medical Society *e:* **CSMS**

Colorado State University Regional Atmospheric Modeling System *e:* **CSU-RAMS**

Colorado University Long Term Ecological Research *e:* **CULTER**

Colorado Veterinary Medical Association *e:* **CVMA**

Colorado Water Data Bank System *e:* **CWDBS**

Columbia Journal of Environmental Law *e:* **Colum. J. Envtl. L.**

Columbia National Wildlife Refuge *e:* **CNWR**

Columbia-Presbyterian Medical Center *e:* **CPMC**

Columbia University, Biological Sciences Library, New York *e:* **NNC-B**

Columbia University, Lamont-Doherty Geological Observatory, Palisades *e:* **NNC-G**

Columbia University School of Medicine *e:* **CUSM**

Columbus Polar Platform *e:* **PPF**

columnar water vapor *e:* **CWV**

Comando der Luchtverdediging *n:* **CLV**

Combat Air Forces Weather Software Package *e:* **CAFWSP**

Combat Electromagnetic Environment Simulator *e:* **CEESIM**

Combat Medical Badge *e:* **CMB**

Combat Net Radio Environment *e:* **CNRE**

Combat Observation Lasing Team *e:* **COLT**

Combat Systems Oceanographic Performance Assessment *e:* **CSOPA**

Combat Underwater Exploitation System *e:* **CUES**

Combat Weather System *e:* **CWS**

Combination of Forward Combustion and Waterflooding *e:* **COFCAW**

Combined Allied Naval Forces Southwest Pacific Ocean Area Operating Plan *e:* **CANFSWPAOPPLAN**

Combined Environment Centrifuge *e:* **CEC**

Combined Environment Groups *e:* **CEG**

Combined Environmental Chamber *e:* **CEC**

Combined Environmental Data Information System *e:* **CEDIS**

Combined Environmental Reliability Test *e:* **CERT**

Combined Environmental Reliability Test[s] *e:* **CERTs**

Combined Environmental Test *e:* **CET**

Combined Environmental, Vibration, Acceleration, Temperature *e:* **CEVAT**

Combined Health Information Database *e:* **CHID**

Combined Homestation Ops in Combat Environment *e:* **CHOICE**

Combined Meteorological Committee *e:* **CMC**

Combined Neutral and Earth *e:* **c.n.e.**

Combined Orbital Maneuvering and Abort System *e:* **COMAS**

combustion space monitor *e:* **csm**

Comisia pentru Ocrotirea Monumentelor Naturii *ru:* **CMN**

Comisión Columbiana de Oceanografia *s:* **CCO**

Comisión de Aplicaciónes Expeciales de la Meteorología y de la climatología *s:* **CAEM**

Comisión de Ciencias Atmosféricas *s:* **CCA**

Comisión de Climatología *s:* **CCl**

Comisión de Cooperación Ecológica Fronteriza *s:* **COCEF**

Comisión de Ecología *s:* **CE**

Comisión de Geología Marina *s:* **CMG**

Comisión de Instrumentos y Métodos de Observación *s:* **CIMO**

Comisión de Meteorología Aeronáutica *s:* **CMAe**

Comisión de Meteorología Agrícola *s:* **CMAg**

Comisión de Meteorología Marina *s:* **CMM**

Comisión de Pesca para el Océano Indico *s:* **CPOI**

Comisión del Mapa Geológico del Mundo *s:* **CGMW**

Comisión Internacional Permanente de Medicina del Trabajo *s:* **CIPMT**

Comisión Nacional de Ecología *s:* **CNE**

Comisión Oceanográfica Intergubernamental *s:* **COI**

Comisión para la Regularización de la Tenencia de la Tierra *s:* **CORETT**

Comisión Protectora de Bibliotecas Populares *s:* **CPBP**

Comissão Nacional Portuguesa para Investigação Oceanográfico *p:* **CNPIO**

Comitato Collaborazione Medica *i:* **CCM**

Comitato dei Geografi Italiani *i:* **COGEI**

Comitato del commercio dei Cereali e degli Alimenti per animali della CEE *i:* **COCERAL**

Comitato per la Difesa Atomica, Biologica e Chimica *i:* **COMABC**

Comite Internationale Catholique des Infirmieres et Assistantes Medico-Sociales *f:* **CICIAMS**

Comité Antarctique Français de l'Année Géophysique *f:* **CAFAG**

Comité Asesor de Investigaciones Meteorólogicas Oceánicas *s:* **CAIMO**

Comité CEE de l'Union Internationale des Agents Commerciaux et des Courtiers *f:* **COMACEE**

Comité Central de la Propriété Forestière de la CEE *f:* **CCPF**

Comité Central des Sociétés Forestières *f:* **CCSF**

Comité central d'Océanographie et d'Étude des Côtes *f:* **COEC**

Comité Científica para las Investigaciones Oceánicas *s:* **SCOR**

Comité Científico de Investigaciones Oceánicas *s:* **CCIO**

Comité COI-OMM-PNUE pour le Système mondial d'observation de l'océan , Comité pour le GOOS *f:* **I-GOOS**

Comité COI-OMM-PNUMA para el Sistema Mundial de Observación de los Océanos , Comité para el GOOS *s:* **I-GOOS**

Comité Consultatif de la Recherche Météorologique Océanique *f:* **CCRMO**

Comité Consultatif d'Hydrologie Opérationnelle *f:* **CCHO**

Comité Consultatif en matière d'Information et de Documentation *f:* **CCID**

Comité Consultatif International de la Recherche dans le Programme des Sciences Exactes et Naturelles *f:* **CCIRPSEN**

Comité consultatif pour les applications et les données climatologiques *f:* **CCADC**

Comité consultatif sur la protection des mers *f:* **ACOPS**

Comité Consultatif[s] de Protection des Personnes se prêtant à des Recherches Biomédicales *f:* **CCPPRB**

Comité d'Action pour la Sauvegarde des Libertés Forestière *f:* **CASLF**

Comité d'Action Technique contre la Pollution Atmosphérique *f:* **CATPA**

Comité d'Action École et Vie Rurale *f:* **CAEVR**

Comité de Ciencia y Tecnología en los Países en Desarrollo/Red Internacional de Ciencias Biológicas *s:* **COSTED/RIB**

Comité de Coordinación para el Programa Mundial sobre el Clima *s:* **CCPMC**

Comité de Coordination de la Politique Internationale de l'Environnement *f:* **CCPIE**

Comité de Coordination de la Production Fruitière *f:* **CCPF**

Comité de coordination de la Production Fruitière française *f:* **C.P.F.**

Comité de coordination de la Recherche Forestière Méditerranéenne *f:* **CRFM**

Comité de Coordination de l'Espace Aérien Européen *f:* **CCEAE**

Comité de coordination pour la protection de la couche d'ozone *f:* **CCOL**

Comité de coordination pour le Programme climatologique mondial *f:* **CCPCM**

Comité de Coordination pour l'Environnement *f:* **CCE**

Comité de coordination sur le conditionnement atmosphérique pour les essais *f:* **ATCO**

Comité de la COI sobre Intercambio Internacional de Datos e Información Oceanográficos, Comité de la COI sobre IODE *s:* **COI-IODE**

Comité de la COI sobre los Procesos Oceánicos y el Clima *s:* **COI-OPC**

Comité de la COI sur les processus océaniques et le climat *f:* **COI-OPC**

Comité de la Protection de l'Enfance *f:* **CPE**

Comité de la Protection du Milieu Marin *f:* **CPMM**

Comité de la Recherche Géologique et Minière *f:* **CRGM**

Comité de la Recherche Océanologique *f:* **CRO**

Comité de lenvironnement *f:* **EC**

Comité de Liaison des Geometres-Experts Européens *f:* **CLGEE**

Comité de Liaison et d'Action des syndicats Médicaux Européens *f:* **CELAME**

Comité de Liaison Intersyndical des transformateurs de matières Plastiques et Similaires *f:* **CLIPS**

Comité de Oceanografía Física *s:* **POC**

Comité de Protection des Obtentions Végétales *f:* **CPOV**

Comité de Rapprochement Belgo-Néerlando-Luxembourgeois *f:* **CRBNL**

Comité de Recursos Naturales *s:* **CRN**

Comité de Recyclage des matières valorisables par l'Innovation *f:* **C.R.I.**

Comité de Santé Environnementale du Québec *f:* **CSE**

Comité de Transports Routiers *f:* **CTR**

Comité d'Entente des Écoles d'Auxiliares de Puériculture *f:* **CEEAP**

Comité d'Entente des Écoles de Puéricultrices *f:* **CEEP**

Comité d'Entente des Écoles d'Infirmières Anesthésistes Diplômés d'État *f:* **CEEIADE**

Comité des Informations Météorologiques *f:* **MIC**

Comité des institutions de développement international pour l'environnement *f:* **CIDIE**

Comité des Jeux Internationaux des Écoliers *f:* **CJIE**

Comité des Ressources Naturelles *f:* **CRN**

Comité des utilisations pacifiques de l'espace extra-atmosphérique *f:* **COPUOS**

Comité d'experts pour la constitution du réseau écologique paneuropéen *f:* **STRA-REP**

Comité d'Exploitation des Océans *f:* **COMEXO**

Comité d'Organisation des Transports Routiers *f:* **C.O.T.R.**

Comité du commerce et de l'environnement *f:* **CTE**

Comité du Conseil constitué à étudier la question de la protection des Minorités *f:* **CCM**

Comité d'Étude de la Corrosion et de la Protection des Canalisations *f:* **CEOCOR**

Comité d'Étude dc la Répartition géographique des Stations radioélectriques *f:* **CORESTA**

Comité d'Études et d'Action pour l'École Unique *f:* **CEAEU**

Comité d'Études pour le Développement de l'Industrie Morutiére *f:* **CEDIM**

Comité Editorial Central de los Atlas Geológicos/Geofísicos Internacionales de los Océanos Atlántico y Pacífico *f:* **CEB-GAPA**

Comité Editorial del Mapa Batimétrico Internacional del Mediterráneo y sus Colecciones Geológicas/Geofísicas, Comité Editorial del IBCM *s:* **EB-IBCM**

Comité Europeo de Ciencias Oceánicas y Polares *s:* **ECOPS**

Comité Européen de Contrôle Laitier *f:* **CECL**

Comité Européen de Contrôle Laitier-Beurrier *f:* **CECLB**

Comité Européen des associations d'entreprises spécialisées dans le Revêtement et le Traitement des matériaux pour le compte de tiers *f:* **CERT**

Comité Européen permanent de recherches pour la protection des populations contre les risques d'Intoxication à long terme *f:* **EUROTOX**

Comité Européen pour la Protection des Animaux à Fourrure *f:* **CEPAF**

Comité Européen pour la Protection des Phoques et autres Animaux à Fourrure *f:* **CEPPAF**

Comité Européen pour la Sauvegarde de la Nature et des Ressources Naturelles *f:* **CDSN**

Comité Fédératif National de Contrôle Laitier *f:* **CFNCL**

Comité Interaméricain de Protection Agricole *f:* **CIPA**

Comité Intergubernamental sobre las Ciencias Oceánicas y los Recursos Biológicos *s:* **OSLR**

Comité interinstitutions du Programme d'action pour le climat *f:* **CIPAC**

Comité Interministériel d'Action pour la Nature et l'Environnement *f:* **CIANE**

Comité Interministériel de la Sécurité Routière *f:* **CISR**

Comité Interministériel de l'Éspace Aérien *f:* **CIEA**

Comité Internacional de Geofísica *s:* **CIG**

Comité Internacional de Medicina y Farmacia Militares *s:* **CIMFM**

Comité International de Géophysique *f:* **CIG**

Comité International de Liaison des Gynécologues et Obstétriciens *f:* **CILOPGO**

Comité International de Photobiologique *f:* **CIP**

Comité International de Standardisation en Biologie *f:* **CISBH**

Comité International d'Historiens et Géographes de Langue Française *f:* **CIHGLF**

Comité International pour le Contrôle de la Productivité Laitière du Bétail *f:* **CICPLB**

Comité Interorganismos sobre la Acción para el Clima *s:* **CIOAC**

Comité Interprofessionnel des Vins Doux Naturels *f:* **CIVDN**

Comité Interprofessionnel du Machinisme Forestier *f:* **CIMAFOR**

Comité Intersecretarial de Programas Científicos relacionados con la Oceanografía *s:* **ICSPRO**

Comité Mixta sobre Programas Científicos Relacionados con la Oceanografía *s:* **CMPCO**

Comité Médical Départemental *f:* **C.M.D.**

Comité Médical Permanent Européen *f:* **CMPE**

Comité Médical pour les Exilés *f:* **COMEDE**

Comité Météorologique *f:* **MET**

Comité Météorologique International *f:* **CMI**

Comité National d'Action pour la Sauvegarde de la Vie et l'Équilibre Biologique *f:* **CNASVEB**

Comité National de Géographie *f:* **CNG**

Comité National de Propagande des Produits Laitiers Français *f:* **CNPPLF**

Comité National de propagande en faveur des Produits Laitier *f:* **CNPL**

Comité National des Exploitants Agricoles Forestiers *f:* **CNEAF**

Comité National Fançais de Recherches dans l'Espace *f:* **CNFRE**

Comité National Français de Géodesie et de Géophysique *f:* **CNFGG**

Comité National Français de Recherche Océanique *f:* **CNFRO**

Comité National Malgache de Recherche Océanique, Centre d'océanographie et des pêches de Nosy Bé *f:* **CNMRO**

Comité National Permanent des Chambres d'Agriculture, des Chambres de Commerce et d'Industrie et Chambres de Métiers *f:* **CNPCACCICM**

Comité National Routier *f:* **C.N.R.**

Comité national sur les dimensions humaines des changements de l'environnement planétaire *f:* **NHDP**

Comité Oceanográfico Nacional *s:* **CONA**, *s:* **NOC**

Comité Océanographique National *f:* **NOC**

Comité para el Almacenamiento, el Tratamiento Automático y la Recuperación de Datos Geológicos *s:* **COGEODATA**

Comité Paritaire National de la Visite Médicale *f:* **CNPVM**

Comité Permanent Canadien des Noms Géographiques *f:* **CPCNG**

Comité Permanent de la Presse Médicale Européenne *f:* **MEDICA EUROPRESS**

Comité Permanent d'organisation des Expositions de l'ouest parisien des industries et métiers *f:* **COPEX**

Comité permanent pour la protection du saumon de la mer Baltique *f:* **BSSSC**

Comité pour les Changements Climatiques et l'Océan *f:* **CCCO**

Comité pour l'Organisation de l'École Paysanne *f:* **C.O.E.P.**

Comité pour l'Utilisation des Résultats de l'Année Géophysique Internationale *f:* **CURAGI**

Comité Régional d'Arboriculture Fruitière du bassin parisien *f:* **CRAF**

Comité Scientifique Chargé des Problèmes de l'Environnement *f:* **SCOPE**

Comité Scientifique de l'Année Géophysique Internationale *f:* **CSAGI**

Comité scientifique pour le Programme international sur la géosphère et la biosphère *f:* **SC-IGBP**

Comité Scientifique pour les Problémes de l'Environnement *f:* **CSPE**

Comité Scientifique pour les Recherces Océaniques *f:* **CSRO**

Comité scientifique pour les recherches océaniques *f:* **SCOR**

Comité sobre Satélites de Observación de la Tierra *s:* **CEOS**

Comité Spécial du Programme Biologique International *f:* **CSPBI**

Comité sur la protection de l'environnement *f:* **CEP**

Comité sur les satellites d'observation de la Terre *f:* **CEOS**

Comité Technique Régional de l'Information Médicale *f:* **COTRIM**

Comité Économique du Médicament *f:* **CEM**

Comitétul National al Geologilor din RSR *ru:* **C.N.G.R.S.R.**

Command and Observation Post *e:* **COP**

Command Flight Medical Officer *e:* **CFMO**

Command Meteorological Centre *e:* **CMC**

Command Post/Observation Post *e:* **CPOP**

Command Surgeon *e:* **SG**

Command Surgeon's Microcomputer Program *e:* **CSMP**

Command Surveillance and Weather *e:* **CSW**

Commandant des troupes du Quartier-Maître *f:* **CQM**

Commandant Supérieur des Forces Françaises du Sud de l'Océan Indien *f:* **C.S.F.F.S.O.I.**

Commandement des Écoles de l'Armee de l'Air *f:* **CEAA**

Commandement Supérieur des Écoles et Centres d'Instruction *f:* **C.S.E.C.I.**

Commander Alaskan Sea Frontier *e:* **COMALSEAFRON**

Commander Black Sea Defence Sector *e:* **COMBLACKBASE**

Commander Caribbean Sea Frontier *e:* **CCSF**, *e:* **COMCARIBSEAFRON**

Commander Central Section/Western Sea Frontier *e:* **COMCENSECT/WESTSEAFRON**

Commander, Eastern Sea Frontier *e:* **CESF**, *e:* **COMEASTFRON**

Commander Eastern Sea Frontier *e:* **COMEASTSEAFRON**

Commander, German Naval Forces North Sea Subarea *e:* **COMGERNORSEA**

Commander, German North Sea *e:* **COMGRNORSEA**

Commander Hawaiian Sea Frontier *e:* **COMHAWSEAFRON**

Commander-in-Chief, Aerospace Defense Command *e:* **CINCAD**

Commander-in-Chief, Channel [and South North Sea] *e:* **CINChan**

Commander-in-Chief North American Aerospace Defense Command *e:* **CINCNORAD**

Commander-in-Chief, Pacific Fleet and Pacific Ocean Areas *e:* **CINCPAC-CINCPOA**

Commander-in-Chief, Pacific Ocean Areas Headquarters, Pearl Harbor *e:* **CINCPOAHEDPEARL**

Commander-in-Chief, Pacific Ocean (or Operation) Area *e:* **CINCPOA**

Commander-in-Chief, Space Command *e:* **CINCSPACE**

Commander International Ice Patrol *e:* **COMINTICEPAT**

Commander Military Sea Transport Service, Far East *e:* **COMSTSFE**

Commander Military Sea Transport Service, Pacific *e:* **COMSTSPAC**

Commander Military Sea Transport[ation] Service *e:* **COMSTS**

Commander Military Sea Transport[ation] Service, Atlantic [Area] *e:* **COMSTSLANT**

Commander, Military Sea Transportation Service, Atlantic Area *e:* **COMSTSLANTAREA**

Commander Military Sea Transportation Service, Eastern Atlantic and Mediterrane Area *e:* **COMSTSELMAREA**

Commander Military Sea Transportation Service Gulf Subarea *e:* **COMSTSGULFSUBAREA**

Commander Military Sea Transportation Service Mid-Pacific Subarea *e:* **COMSTSMIDPACSUBAREA**

Commander Military Sea Transportation Service Northern Pacific Subarea *e:* **COMSTSNORPACSUBAREA**

Commander Military Sea Transportation Service Pacific Area *e:* **COMSTSPACAREA**

Commander Military Sea Transportation Service, Southeast Asia *e:* **COMSTSSEA**

Commander Military Sea Transportation Service West Pacific Area *e:* **COMSTSWESTPACAREA**

Commander, Moroccan Sea Frontier Force *e:* **COMORSEAFRON**

Commander, Naval Division North Sea *e:* **COMNAVDIV NORSEA**

Commander Naval Sea Systems Command *e:* **COMNAVSEASYSCOM**

Commander, Naval Space Command *e:* **COMNAVSPACECOM**

Commander North Sea Subarea [Centre Europe] *e:* **COMNORSEACENT**

Commander Northern Section/Western Sea Frontier *e:* **COMNORSECT/WESTSEAFRON**

Commander, Ocean Atlantic Subarea *e:* **COMOCEANLANT**, *e:* **COMOCEATLANT**

Commander Ocean Subarea Atlantic *e:* **COMOCEANLANT**

Commander Oceanographic Systems, Atlantic *e:* **COMOCEANSYSTLANT**

Commander Oceanographic Systems, Atlantic/Pacific *e:* **COSL/P**

Commander Oceanographic Systems, Pacific *e:* **COMOCEANSYSPAC**

Commander, Oceanographic Systems, Pacific *e:* **COSP**

Commander [of] Central European Sea Forces *e:* **CCESF**

Commander of Northern European Sea Forces *e:* **CNESF**

Commander, Panama Sea Frontier *e:* **COMPASEAFRON**

Commander Panama Section/Caribbean Sea Frontier *e:* **COMPASECTCARIBSEAFRON**

Commander Panama Section/Western Sea Frontier *e:* **COMPASECT/WESTSEAFRON**

Commander Puerto Rico Section/Caribbean Sea Frontier *e:* **COMPUERTORICOSECT/CARIBSEAFRON**

Commander Sea Area South *e:* **COMSARSOUTH**

Commander, Sea Frontier *e:* **COMSEAFRON**

Commander Sea Training *e:* **CST**

Commander Southern European Sea Forces *e:* **CSESF**

Commander Southern Section/Western Sea Frontier *e:* **COMSOSECT/WESTSEAFRON**

Commander Sub-Frontier Defense *e:* **COMSUBFRONDESF**

Commander Sub-Frontier Defense/Delaware Group *e:* **COMSUBFRONDEF/DELGRU**

Commander, Submarine Sea Training *e:* **CSST**

Commander, US Amphibious Force, Northwest African Waters *e:* **COMPHIBNAW**

Commander, US Naval Forces, Northwest African Waters *e:* **COMNAVNAW**

Commander Western Sea Frontier *e:* **COMWESTSEAFRON**, *e:* **CWSF**

Commanding General, Pacific Ocean Areas *e:* **COMGENPOA**

Commanding General United States Army in the Caribbean [Sea Area] *e:* **COMGENUSARCARIB**

Commercial Earth Station *e:* **CES**

Commercial Light-Water (nuclear) Reactor *e:* **CLWR**

Commercial Space Center *e:* **CSC**

Commerciale de produits Métallurgiques et matières premières pour l'industrie *f:* **COMETAL**

Commercially Developed Space Facility *e:* **CDSF**

Commissie Grondwaterwet Waterleidingsbedrijven *n:* **CoGroWa**

Commissie inzake Wateronttrekking aan de Bodem *n:* **CoWaBo**

Commissie Onderzoek Landbouwwaterhuishouding Nederland *n:* **COLN**

Commissie voor Georganiseerd Overleg in Politieamtenarenzaken *n:* **CGOP**

Commission Administrative Mixte Belgo-Luxembourgeoise *f:* **CAMBEL**

Commission Climatologique Internationale *f:* **CCI**

Commission consultative de la Traite des Femmes et de la protection des Enfants *f:* **CTFE**

Commission Consultative Médicale *f:* **CCM**

Commission de Climatologie *f:* **C.C.,** *f:* **CCe**

Commission de climatologie *f:* **Ccl**

Commission de la Carte Géologique du Monde *f:* **CCGM**

Commission de la Météorologie Synoptique *f:* **CMS**

Commission de la Projection des Cartes Météorologiques *f:* **CPMC**

Commission de l'Information et de la Documentation en matière d'Orientation Scolaire et Professionnelle *e:* **CIDOSP**

Commission de météorologie Agricole *f:* **CAg**

Commission de Météorologie Agricole *f:* **CMAg**

Commission de Météorologie Aéronautique *f:* **CMAé**

Commission de Météorologie Hydrologique *f:* **CMH**

Commission de Météorologie Maritime *f:* **CMM**

Commission des Applications Biologiques et Médicales *f:* **CABM**

Commission des Applications Spéciales de la Météorologie et de la Climatologie *f:* **CASMC**

Commission des instruments et des méthodes d'observation *f:* **CIMO**

Commission des Nations Unies pour l'Utilisation Pacifique de l'Espace Extra-Atmosphérique *f:* **CNUUPEE**

Commission des Pêches pour l'Océan Indien *f:* **CPOI**

Commission des Sciences de l'Atmosphère *f:* **CSA**

Commission des stratégies et de la planification de l'environnement *f:* **CSPE**

Commission des Tarifs Médicaux *f:* **CTM**

Commission d'hydrologie *f:* **CHy**

Commission du droit de l'environnement /UICN/ *f:* **CDDE**

Commission d'Études pour Relais à Environnements Sévères *f:* **CERES**

Commission d'Études Pratiques d'Océanographie *f:* **CEPOC**

Commission Européenne des Communes Forestières et communes de montagne *f:* **CECF**

Commission Exécutive Hydroélectrique du Lempa *f:* **C.E.H.L.**

Commission for Aeronautical Meteorology *e:* **CAeM**

Commission for Agricultural Meteorology *e:* **CAgM**

Commission for Biological Education *e:* **CBE**

Commission for Climatology *e:* **CCI,** *e:* **CCl**

Commission for Climatology and Applications of Meteorology *e:* **CCAM**

Commission for Environmental Cooperation *e:* **CEC**

Commission for European Airspace Coordination *e:* **CEAC**

Commission for Geographical Education *e:* **GCE**

Commission for Health Improvement *e:* **CHI,** *e:* **CHIMP**

Commission for Health Improvements *e:* **CHIP**

Commission for Hydrology *e:* **Chy**

Commission for International Coordination of Space Techniques for Geodesy and Geodynamics *e:* **CSTG**

Commission for Marine Geology *e:* **CMG**

Commission for Marine (or Maritime) Meteorology *e:* **CMM**

Commission for/on Atmospheric Science[s] *e:* **CAS**

Commission for/on Instrumentation (or Instruments) and Methods of Observation[s] *e:* **CIMO**

Commission for/on Marine Geology *e:* **CMG**

Commission for Special Applications of Meteorology and Climatology *e:* **COSAMC**

Commission for Synoptic Meteorology *e:* **CMS,** *e:* **CSM**

Commission for Synoptic Weather Information *e:* **CSWI**

Commission for the Geological Map of the World *e:* **CGMW**

Commission Forestière pour l'Amérique du Nord *f:* **CFAN**

Commission Genevoise d'Observation du Français *f:* **COGOF**

Commission Geologique du Canada *f:* **CGC**

Commission hydrographique de la mer Baltique *f:* **CHMB**

Commission hydrographique de la mer du Nord *f:* **CHMN**

Commission hydrographique de la mer Méditerranée et de la mer Noire *f:* **CHMMN**

Commission hydrographique de l'Asie orientale *f:* **CHAO**

Commission Inter-Européene des Communes Forestières et des communes de montagne *f:* **CIECF**

Commission Interdépartementale du Développement Durable *f:* **CIDD**

Commission Interdépartementale Romande de Coordination de l'Enseignement *f:* **CIRCE**

Commission Interfaculté Médicale Suisse *f:* **CIMS**

Commission International pour la Protection des Régions Alpines *f:* **CIPRA**

Commission Internationale de la Météorologie Polaire *f:* **CIMP**

Commission internationale de l'hydrologie du bassin du Rhin *f:* **CHR**

Commission internationale de l'Hydrologie du Rhin *f:* **CHR**

Commission Internationale de Lutte Biologique contre les animaux et les plantes nuisibles *f:* **CILB**

Commission Internationale de Lutte Biologique contre les ennemis des cultures *f:* **CILB**

Commission Internationale de Météorologie Aéronautique *f:* **CIMA,** *f:* **CIMAé**

Commission Internationale de Protection contre les Radiations ionisantes *f:* **CIPR**

Commission Internationale Médico-Physiologique *f:* **CIMP**

Commission Internationale pour la Protection des Alpes *f:* **CIPRA International**

Commission Internationale pour la Protection des Eaux du Leman contre la pollution *f:* **CIPEL**

Commission Mixte Internationale pour les expériences relatives à la protection des lignes de télécommunications et des canalisations sousterraines *f:* **CMI**

Commission mondiale sur l'environnement et le développement, Commission Brundtland *f:* **CMED**

Commission Médicale Chrétienne *f:* **CMC**

Commission Médicale d'Établissement *f:* **CME**

Commission Médico-Pédagogique Départementale *f:* **CMPD**

Commission Médico-Pédagogique et Psycho-Sociale *f:* **MMPS**

Commission Météorologique *f:* **C.M.**

Commission Météorologique Départementale *f:* **CMD**

Commission Météorologique Régionale *f:* **CMR**

Commission Nationale des Tarifs Médicaux en sécurité sociale *f:* **C.N.T.**

Commission Océanographique Intergouvernementale *f:* **COI**

Commission on Accreditation of Allied Health Education Programs *e:* **CAAHEP**

Commission on Accreditation of Medical Transport Systems *e:* **CAMTS**

Commission on African Animal Trypanosomiasis *e:* **COAT**

Commission on Biological Nomenclature *e:* **CBN**

Commission on Chemical and Biological Warfare *e:* **CCBW**

Commission on Ecology *e:* **COE**

Commission on Education in Agricultural and Natural Resources *e:* **CEANAR**

Commission on Environmental, Economic and Social Policy *e:* **CEESP**

Commission on Environmental Economics, Strategy and Policy *e:* **CEESP**

Commission on Environmental Law *e:* **CEL**

Commission on Environmental Planning *e:* **CEP**

Commission on Environment[al] Policy, Law and Administration *e:* **CEPLA**

Commission on Environmental Strategy and Planning *e:* **CESP**

Commission on Geography in Education *e:* **CGE**

Commission on Geological Documentation *e:* **COGEODOC**

Commission on Geological Sciences Environmental Planning *e:* **CGSEP**

Commission on Geology Teaching *e:* **CGT**

Commission on Global Continental Palaeohydrology *e:* **INQUA/GLOCOPH**

Commission on Health Research for Development *e:* **CHRD**

Commission on Human Ecology *e:* **CHE**

Commission on Human Evolution and Palaeoecology *e:* **INQUA,** *e:* **INQUA/HEP**

Commission on Man and Environment *e:* **CME**

Commission on Measurement[s] and Theory Application in Geomorphology *e:* **COMTAG**

Commission on National Parks and Protected Areas e: **CNPPA**

Commission on Palaeoclimate e: **INQUA**, e: **INQUA/PC**, e: **PALCLIM**

Commission on Present Day Geomorphic Process e: **CPDGP**

Commission on Resources and the Environment e: **C.O.R.E.**

Commission on Sea Level Changes and Coastal Evolution e: **INQUA**, e: **INQUA/SLCCE**

Commission on Standardization of Biological Stains e: **CSBS**

Commission on Storage, Automatic Processing and Retrieval of Geological Data e: **COGEODATA**

Commission on Study of the Earth's Deep Interior e: **SEDI**

Commission on the Paleoecology of Early Man e: **INQUA**

Commission on the Paleogeographic Atlas of the Quaternary e: **INQUA**

Commission on Undergraduate Education in [the] Biological Sciences e: **CUEBS**

Commission (or Committee) of/on Atmospheric Chemistry and Global Pollution e: **CACGP**

Commission (or Committee) of/on the Peaceful Uses of Outer Space e: **COPUOS**

Commission pour la Coopération Multilatérale dans l'Observation des Satellites Artificiels de la Terre f: **INTEROPS**

Commission pour la protection du milieu marin de la Baltique, Commission d'Helsinki f: **HELCOM**

Commission pour la Protection Internationale de la Propriété Industrielle f: **C.P.I.P.I.**

Commission Romande d'Observation du Français f: **COROF**

Commission Régionale des Opérations Immobilières de l'Architecture et des Espaces Protégés f: **CROIAEP**

Commission Régionale d'Évaluation Médicale f: **CREM**

Commission Régionale d'Évaluation Médicale des Établissements f: **CREME**

Commission Régulatrice Routière f: **C.R.R.**

Commission sur les systèmes côtiers f: **CCS**

Commission Technique de la prospection et de l'exploitation des hydrocarbures en Mer f: **COTEM**

Commission Technique et de Promotion des Laitiers f: **CTPL**

Commission Technique et de Promotion des Laitiers de Haute Fourneau f: **C.T.P.L.**

Commission Technique Européenne des Transmissions Hydromécaniques f: **CTETH**

Commission Épiscopale pour l'École Catholique f: **CEEC**

Commissione delle Tariffe Mediche i: **CTM**

Commissione Geodetica Italiana i: **CGI**

Commissione Interfacoltaria Medica Svizzera i: **CIMS**

Commissione Italiana del Comitato Internazionale di Geofisica i: **CICIG**

Commissione Medica i: **CM**

Commissione Medica Ospedaliera i: **CMH**

Commissione per l'Aggiornamento medico ad hoc i: **CFC**

Commissione per lo studio dei Problemi Relativi alla Medicina i: **CEPREM**

Commissioners of Medical Services e: **C.M.S.**

Committee for an International Program in the Atmospheric Sciences and Hydrology e: **CIPASH**

Committee for Aquatic Microbiology e: **CAM**

Committee for Automated Weather Information Systems e: **CAWIS**

Committee for Aviation & Space Industry Development e: **CASID**

Committee for Biological Pest Control e: **Comm Bio Pest**

Committee for Environmental Conservation e: **CoEnCo**

Committee for Environmental Information e: **CEI**

Committee for European Air Space Coordination e: **CEASC**

Committee for European Marine Biological Symposia e: **CEMBS**, e: **EMBS**

Committee for Evaluating the Feasibility of Space Rocketry e: **CEFSR**

Committee for Exploitation of the Oceans e: **COMEXCO**

Committee for Freedom of Choice in Medicine e: **CFCM**

Committee for Geographical Names in Australia e: **CGNA**

Committee for Geophysical Data e: **CGD**

Committee for Global Ocean Observing System e: **I-GOOS IOC**

Committee for Health in Southern Africa e: **CHISA**

Committee for Leaving the Environment of America Natural e: **CLEAN**

Committee for Medical Aid to Central America e: **COMACA**

Committee for National Accreditation of Environmental Laboratories e: **CNAEL**

Committee for National Health Insurance e: **CNHI**

Committee for/of European Airspace Coordination e: **CEAC**

Committee for/on Climate (or Climatic) Change[s] and/on the Ocean[s] e: **CCCO**

Committee for/on Environmental Protection e: **CEP**

Committee for/on Solar and Space Physics e: **CSSP**

Committee for Proprietary Medicinal Products e: **CPMP**

Committee for the National Institute for the Environment e: **CNIE**

Committee for the Nation's Health e: **CNH**

Committee for the Reform of Animal Experimentation e: **CRAE**

Committee for Upgrading Environmental Radiation Data e: **CUERD**

Committee for Veterinary Medicinal Products e: **CVMP**

Committee for Wildlife on the Last Frontier e: **WOLF**

Committee of an Advanced Nature e: **CAN**

Committee of Earth Sciences e: **CES**

Committee of Experts for the Pan-European Ecological Network e: **STRA-REP**

Committee of International Development Institutions for/of/on the Environment e: **CIDIE**

Committee of/on Safety of Medicines e: **CSM**

Committee on Aeronautical Meteorological Problems e: **CAMP**

Committee on Agrometeorology e: **NCA**

Committee on Air and Water Conservation e: **CAWC**

Committee on Allied Health Education and Accreditation e: **CAHEA**

Committee on Application of Polarized Headlights e: **CAPH**

Committee on Atmosphere and Oceans e: **CAO**

Committee on Atmospheric Chemistry e: **CAC**

Committee on Atmospheric Problems of Aerospace Vehicles e: **CAPAV**

Committee on Aviation Medicine e: **CAM**

Committee on Biological Sciences Information e: **COBSI**

Committee on Chemical and Biological Warfare e: **C.C.B.W.**

Committee on Earth and Environmental Sciences e: **CEES**, e: **CEES US**

Committee on Earth Observation[s] (or Observing) Satellites e: **CEOS**

Committee on Earth Observing Sensors e: **CEOS**

Committee on Earth Observing Systems e: **CEOS**

Committee on Emergency Medical Identification e: **CEMI**

Committee on Environment[al] and Natural Resources e: **CENR**

Committee on Environmental Quality e: **CEQ**

Committee on Extension of the Standard Atmosphere e: **COESA**

Committee on Geological Sciences e: **CGS**

Committee on Geophysical Environmental Data e: **CGED**

Committee on Geostationary Meteorological Satellite System e: **CGMS**

Committee on Global Ecology Concern e: **CGEC**

Committee on International Environmental Activities e: **CIEA**

Committee on International Ocean Affairs e: **CIEA**

Committee on International Policy in the Marine Environment e: **CIPME**

Committee on International Reference Atmosphere e: **CIRA**

Committee on Man's Underwater Activities e: **CMU/WA**

Committee on Medical Aspects of Food Policy e: **COMA**

Committee on Medical Aspects of Radiation in the Environment e: **COMARE**

Committee on Medical Research e: **CMR**

Committee on Medicine and Computers e: **COMAC**

Committee on Meteorological Analysis, Prediction and Research e: **CMAPR**

Committee on Meteorological Effect of Stratospherical Aircraft e: **COMESA**

Committee on Mineral Resources and the Environment e: **COMRATE**

Committee on Natural Gas Fluids Measurement e: **COGM**

Committee on Natural Resource Information Management e: **CONRIM**

Committee on Natural Resources e: **CNR**

Committee on Nucleation and Atmospheric Aerosols e: **CNAA**

Committee on Ocean Processes and Climate e: **OPC**

Committee on Oceanography and GARP e: **COG**

Committee on Polar Research e: **CPR**

Committee on Radiation Protection and Public Health e: **CRPPH**

Committee on Remote Sensing Programs for Earth Resource Surveys e: **CORSPERS**

Committee on Research in Medical Economics e: **CRME**

Committee on Space Programs for Earth Observations e: **COSPEAR**

Committee on Space Research e: **COSPAR**, e: **COSR**

Committee on the Application of Aerospace Technology to Society e: **AATS**

Committee on the Cost of Medical Care e: **CCMC**

Committee on the Formation of the National Biological Survey e: **CFNBS**

Committee on the Human Environment e: **CHEK**

Committee on the Interplay of Engineering with Biology and Medicine e: **CIEBM**

Committee on the Medical Effects of Air Pollutants e: **COMEAP**

Committee on the Status of Endangered Wildlife in Canada e: **COSEWIC**

Committee on Trade and Environment e: **CTE**

Committee on Veterans Medical Problems e: **CVMP**

Committee on Water e: **COW**

Committee on Water Research e: **COWAR**

Committee on Water Resources e: **COWAR**

Committee on Water Resources Research e: **COWRR**

Committee on[of] Earth Science[s] e: **CES**

Committee to Protect Journalists e: **CPJ**

Committee to Protect Our Children's Teeth e: **CPOCT**

Committee to Remove Unnatural Deposits from the Environment e: **CRUDE**

Commodore, Arabian Sea and Persian Gulf e: **COMAS**

Common Aviation Weather Subsystem e: **CAWS**

Common Desktop Environment e: **CDE**

Common Desktop Operating Environment e: **CDOE**

Common Operating Environment e: **COE**

Common Property and Environment e: **COPE**

Common Property and Environmental Policy in Comparative Perspective e: **COPE**

Common Queue Space e: **CQS**

Common Runtime Environment e: **CORE**

Common Services Agency for the Scottish Health Service e: **CSASHS**

Common Wadden Sea Secretariat e: **CWSS**

Commons, Open Spaces and Footpaths Preservation Society e: **C.O.S.F.P.S.**

Commonwealth Bureau of Animal Breeding and Genetics e: **CBABG**

Commonwealth Bureau of Animal Breeding and Genetics. Technical Communication e: **TCBAAQ**

Commonwealth Bureau of Animal Health e: **CBAH**

Commonwealth Bureau of Animal Nutrition e: **CBAN**

Commonwealth Bureau of Animal Nutrition. Technical Communication e: **TCANAQ**

Commonwealth Caribbean Medical Research Council e: **CCMRC**

Commonwealth Consultative [Group] on Mineral Resources and Geology e: **CCMRG**

Commonwealth Department of Health e: **C.D.H.**

Commonwealth Environment Protection Agency e: **CEPA**

Commonwealth Geographical Bureau e: **CGB**

Commonwealth Geological Liaison Office e: **CGLO**

Commonwealth Human Ecology Council e: **CHEC**

Commonwealth Institute of Biological Control e: **CIBC**

Commonwealth Institute of Health e: **CIH**

Commonwealth Medical Association e: **CMA**

Commonwealth Medical Association Trust e: **ComMAT**

Commonwealth Meteorology Research Centre e: **CMRC**

Commonwealth of Australia Bureau of Meteorology e: **CABM**

Commonwealth Office of Space Science and Applications e: **COSSA**

Commonwealth Regional Health Community Secretariat for East, Central and Southern Africa e: **CRHCS**

Communauté Internationale des Obtenuers de Plantes Ornementales et fruitières de Reproduction Asexuée f: **CIOPORA**

Communication, Electronic and Meteorological Equipment Status e: **CEMES**

Communication in Behavioral Biology e: **CBB**

Communication/ Navigation/Meteorological e: **COM/NAV/MET**

Communications and Computer Applications in Public Health e: **CCAPH**

Communications and Replenishment At Sea e: **RAS**

Communications/Aural Protective System e: **CAPS**

Communications by Meteor Trails e: **COMET**

Communications Electronics- Meteorological e: **CEM**

Communications-Electronic[s]- Meteorological Board e: **CEMB**

Communications Electronics Meteorological Program Implementation Man. System e: **CEMPIMS**

Communications-Electronics-Meteorology Program Aggregate Code e: **CEMPAC**

Communications Spacecraft Operations Center e: **COMSOC**

Communikation in natürlicher Sprache mit dialog-orientiertem Retrievalsystem d: **CONDOR**

Community and Child Health e: **CCH**

Community-Based Environmental Project e: **CBEP**

Community-Based Environmental Protection e: **CBEP**

Community Based Public Health e: **CBPH**

Community Based Public Health Initiative e: **CBPHI**

Community Breast Health Project e: **CBHP**

Community-Campus Partnerships for Health e: **CCPH**

Community Climate Model e: **CCM**

Community Climate Model one e: **CCM1**

Community Climate Model two e: **CCM2**

Community Climate System Model e: **CCSM**

Community Dental Health e: **CDH**

Community Environmental Council e: **CEC**

Community Environmental Health Concerns e: **CENC**

Community Environmental Service Teams e: **CEST**

Community Health Accreditation and Standards Program e: **CHASP**

Community Health Accreditation Program e: **CHAP**

Community Health Action Planning Service e: **CHAPS**

Community Health Air Monitoring Program e: **CHAMP**

Community Health and Environmental Surveillance Studies e: **CHESS**

Community Health and Environmental Surveillance System e: **CHESS**

Community Health Association e: **CHA**

Community Health Center e: **CHC**

Community Health Council e: **CHC**

Community Health Department, Lakeshore General Hospital, Pointe-Claire, Quebec e: **QMLGC**

Community Health Department, Montreal General Hospital, Quebec e: **QMGHC**

Community Health Education Project e: **CHEP**

Community Health Index e: **CHI**

Community Health Information Classification and Coding e: **CHIC**

Community Health Information [Network] e: **CHIN**

Community Health Information Partnerships e: **CHIP**

Community Health Information Technology Alliance e: **CHITA**

Community Health Management Information Systems e: **CHMIS**

Community Health Nurse e: **CHN**

Community Health Promotion Network Atlantic e: **CHPNA**

Community Health Purchasing Alliance e: **CHIPAS**

Community Health Research & Training Unit e: **CHRTU**

Community Health Service e: **CHS**

Community Health Status Indicators e: **CHSI**

Community Health Worker e: **CHW**

Community Mental Health Center e:
CMHC
Community Mental Health Center Program
e: **CMHCP**
Community Mental Health Centers Act e:
CMHCA
Community Mental Health Journal e:
Community Ment Health J
Community Mental Health Program e:
CMHP
Community Mental Health Team e:
CMHT
Community-Oriented Program[me]s
Environment Scale e: **COPES**
Community Outreach Health Information
System e: **COHIS**
Community Watershed Guidelines e:
CWG
Community Wholistic Health Center e:
CWHC
Community-wide Coordination of
Information of the European Environment
e: **CORINE**
COMNAVMAR Environmental Quality
Control e: **CEQC**
Compact Air-Launched Ice Beacon e:
CALIB
Compact Meteorological & Oceanographic
Drifter e: **CMOD**
Compact Orbital Gears, Ltd. e: **COG**
Compacted Earth e: **CE**
Compacted Earth Sodium Treated e:
CEST
compagnia pontieri ausiliari i: **cp.pt.aus.**
Compagnie Africaine Forestière et de
Allumettes f: **CAFAL**
Compagnie Agricole et Forestière f: **CAF**
Compagnie Agricole et Forestière du
Cameroun f: **CAFC**
Compagnie Automobile de Protection Anti-
Aérienne f: **C.A.P.A.A.**
Compagnie d'Assurance Médicale et
Chirurgicale f: **C.A.M.C.**
Compagnie d'Aérostiers de Campagne f:
CAC
Compagnie de Ballons de Protection f:
C.B.P.
Compagnie de Circulation Routière f:
C.C.R.
Compagnie de Défense et de Protection f:
C.D.P.
Compagnie de Gestion Médicale
Hospitalière f: **CGMH**
Compagnie de Mortiers f: **Cie Mor,** f:
C.M.
Compagnie de Mortiers Lourds f: **C.M.L.**
Compagnie de Prospection Géophysique
Française f: **CPGF**
Compagnie de Protection en Algérie f:
CPA
Compagnie de Quartier Général f: **C. de
Q.G.,** f: **Cie Q.G.**
Compagnie de Quartier général f: **C.Q.D.**
Compagnie de Quartier-Maître f: **Cie Q.M.**
Compagnie de Réparation d'Avions légers
d'Observation d'Artillerie f:
C.R.A.L.O.A.
Compagnie de satellites dobservation de la
Terre f: **EOSAT**
Compagnie de transport et de Quartier
Général f: **C.t.Q.G.**
Compagnie de Transports Routiers et de
Messageries f: **CTRM**

Compagnie des Tramways Strasbourgeois
f: **CTS**
Compagnie des Transports Strasbourgeois
f: **CTS**
Compagnie d'Essence Routière f: **C.E.R.**
Compagnie d'Exploitation Forestière de
Divo f: **CEFDI**
Compagnie d'études et d'exploitation des
techniques Océans f: **COCEAN**
Compagnie Forestière de Gabon f: **CFG**
Compagnie Forestière du Congo f: **CFC**
Compagnie forestière du Golfe du Guinée
f: **CFGG**
Compagnie Forestière du Sud-Gabon f:
CFSG
Compagnie Forestière et Industrielle du
Congo f: **COFORIC**
Compagnie Forestière Gabonaise f:
COFORGA
Compagnie Forestière Sangha-Oubangui f:
CFSO
Compagnie Française de Nutrition Animale
f: **C.O.F.N.A.**
Compagnie Française de Protection
Électrique f: **CFPE**
Compagnie Française des Matières
Colorantes f: **CFMC**
Compagnie Fruitière d'Orgeval f:
COFROR
Compagnie Generale de Geophysique f:
CGG
Compagnie Générale de Travaux, de
Recherches et d'Exploitation Océaniques
f: **CGTREO**
Compagnie Générale des Matières
nucléaires f: **COGEMA**
Compagnie Géologique et Minière des
Ingénieurs et Industriels Belges f:
GEOMINES
Compagnie Géologique et Minière du
Ruanda-Urundi f: **GEORUNDA**
Compagnie Industrielle des Matières
Premières f: **CIMAP**
Compagnie Internationale Fruitière f: **CIF**
Compagnie Ivoirienne de Transports
Routiers f: **CITR**
Compagnie Luxembourgeoise de Banque
S.A. f: **CLB**
Compagnie Luxembourgeoise de
Radiodiffusion f: **CLR**
Compagnie Luxembourgeoise de
Télédiffusion f: **CLT**
Compagnie Luxembourgeoise de
Télédiffusion/ Radio-Télé-Luxembourg
f: **CLT/RTL**
Compagnie Malienne de Transports
Routiers f: **CMTR**
Compagnie Marocaine de Transit et
Transport International Routier f:
COMATTIR
Compagnie Minière et Phosphatière f:
COMIPHOS
Compagnie Mixte de Mortiers f: **C.M.M.**
Compagnie Mixte de Mortiers de la Légion
Étrangère f: **C.M.M.L.E.**
Compagnie Médicale f: **C.M.**
Compagnie Médicale de Corps d'Armée f:
C.M.C.A.
Compagnie Nationale des Experts Forestiers
f: **CNEF**
Compagnie Nationale des Transports
Routiers f: **CNTR**

Compagnie Parachutistes de Martiers f:
C.P.M.
Compagnie pour la Protection Intégrale des
Matériaux f: **COPIM**
Compagnie Routière f: **C.R.**
Compagnie Routière Divisionnaire f:
C.R.D.
Compagnie Universelle du Canal
Interocéanique f: **C.U.C.I.**
Compagnie Étrangère Parachutiste de
Mortiers Lourds f: **C.E.P.M.L.**
Compañía de Satélites de Observación de la
Tierra s: **EOSAT**
Comparative Biochemistry and Physiology.
Part B, Biochemistry and Molecular
Biology e: **Comp Biochem Physiol B
Biochem Mol Biol**
Comparative Immunology, Microbiology
and Infectious Diseases e: **Comp
Immunol Microbiol Infect Dis**
Comparative Planetology and the Early
Earth e: **CPEE**
Compatible High Density Bipolar e:
CHDB, e: **CHDE**
Compatible High Density Bipolar Code e:
CHDB Code
Competitive Medical Plan e: **CMP**
Compiler Oriented for Multiprogramming
and Multiprocessing Environments e:
COMMEN
Complementary and Alternative Medicine
e: **CAM**
Complete Active-Space Self-Consistent
Field e: **CASSCF**
Complete (or Complex) Atmospheric
Energetics Experiment e: **CAENEX**
Completely Denatured e: **CD**
Completely Denatured Alcohol e: **CDA**
Completely Self-Protected e: **CSP**
Complex Geometry of Nature e: **CGN**
Complex Orbital Near-Earth Observations
of the Solar Activity e: **CORONAS**
Complex Problem Solving Environment e:
CPSE
Compliance Safety and Health Officer e:
CSHO
Complimentary and Alternate Medicine e:
CAAM
Component Cooling Water e: **CCW**
Component Cooling Water System e:
CCWS
Componente Oceanográfico del PMIC s:
PMIC-O
Composante de FRIENDS concernant
l'hydrologie alpine et méditerranéenne f:
AMHY
Composite Health Care System e: **CHCS**
Composite Launch & Spacecraft
Program[me] e: **CLASP**
Composite Lightweight Affordable
Spacecraft Structure e: **CLASS**
Composite Medical Facility e: **CMF**
Compound Animal Feedingstuffs
Manufacturers National Association e:
CAFMNA
Comprehensive Automation of the
Hydrometeorological Service[s] e:
CAHS
Comprehensive Economic Environmental
Policy Evaluation System e: **CEEPES**
Comprehensive Environmental Assessment
and Response Program e: **CEARP**

Comprehensive Environmental Assessment Response *e:* **CERCLA**

Comprehensive Environmental Evaluation *e:* **CEE**

Comprehensive Environmental Response, Compensation, and Liability Act *e:* **CERCLA**

Comprehensive Environmental Response, Compensation and Liability Information System *e:* **CERCLIS**

Comprehensive Environmental Restoration Program *e:* **CERP**

Comprehensive (groundwater) Monitoring Evaluation *e:* **CME**

Comprehensive [groundwater] Monitoring Evaluation Log *e:* **CMEL**

Comprehensive Health Insurance Plan *e:* **CHIP**

Comprehensive Health Planning *e:* **CHP**

Comprehensive Health Planning Service *e:* **CHPS**

Comprehensive Healthcare Analysis and Management Program *e:* **CHAMP**

Comprehensive Ice Reconnaissance *e:* **CIR**

Comprehensive Ice Reconnaissance System *e:* **CIRES**, *e:* **CIRS**

Comprehensive Integrated Remote Sensing *e:* **CIRS**

Comprehensive Long-Term Environmental Action, Navy *e:* **CLEAN**

Comprehensive Medical Plans *e:* **CMP**

Comprehensive Medical Society *e:* **CMS**

Comprehensive Ocean Area Plan *e:* **COAP**

Comprehensive Ocean-Atmosphere Data Set *e:* **COADS**

Comprehensive State Ground Water Protection Program *e:* **CSGWPP**

Comprehensive Water-quality Management Planning *e:* **COWAMP**

Compressed Natural Gas *e:* **CNG**

Compressor Protect and Control System *e:* **CPCS**

Comptes Rendus des Seances de la Société de Biologie et de Ses Filiales *f:* **C R Seances Soc Biol Fil**

Comptoir de commerce et de Représentation pour l'Océan Indien *f:* **COROI**

Comptoir d'Exportation de Vanille de l'Océan Indien *f:* **CEVOI**

Comptoir Industriel de Décolletage et Outillage *f:* **CIDECOU**

Comptoir Strasbourgeois d'Aciers Spéciaux *f:* **COSAS**

Compton Gamma Ray Observatory *e:* **GRO**

Compton Observatory Science Support Center *e:* **COSSC**

Computation of Miss-Between Orbits *e:* **COMBO**

Computation-Universal Cellular Space *e:* **CUCS**

Computer-Aid of Environmental Legislative Data System *e:* **CELDS**

Computer Aided Community Oral Health Information System *e:* **CACOHIS**

Computer Aided Design Environment *e:* **COMRADE**

Computer-aided Environmental Legislation Data System *e:* **CELDS**

Computer-Aided Geometry Modeling Symposium *e:* **CAGMS**

Computer-Aided Learning in Meteorology *e:* **CALMET**

Computer-Aided Medical Diagnostics System *e:* **CAMDS**

Computer-Aided Remote Maintenance *e:* **CARM**

Computer Architecture for Production Information Systems in a Competitive Environment *e:* **CAPISCE**

Computer-Assisted Artillery Meteorology *e:* **CAAM**

Computer Assisted Software Development Environment *e:* **CASDE**

Computer-Assisted Virtual Environment *e:* **CAVE**

Computer-Assisted Virtual Environment Research Network *e:* **CAVERN**

Computer Automatic Virtual Environment *e:* **CAVE**

Computer-based Patient Record Institute-Healthcare Open Systems and Trials *e:* **CPRI-HOST**

Computer Driven Simulation Environment *e:* **CDSE**

Computer Environment Energy Control System *e:* **CEECS**

Computer for Advanced Space Systems *e:* **COMPASS**

Computer Geoscience Section *e:* **CGS**

Computer-Integrated Polarization Microscopy *e:* **CIP**

Computer Language for Aeronautics and Space Programming *e:* **CLASP**

Computer Methods and Programs in Biomedicine *e:* **Comput Methods Programs Biomed**

Computer Orientated Geological Software *e:* **COGS**

Computer-Oriented Geological Society *e:* **COGS**

Computer-orientierte Methode für Planung und Ablauf-Steuerung in Seehäfen *d:* **COMPASS**

Computer Polarization Holography *e:* **CPH**

Computer Program protection Manager *e:* **CPM**

Computer Science for Environment Protection *e:* **CSEP**

Computer Support for Environmental Impact Assessment [Conference] *e:* **CSEIA**

Computer System for Medical Information Services *e:* **COSMIS**

Computer to External Environments Interface *e:* **CXE**

Computer Umwelt-Projekt *d:* **CUP**

computerassistierte Emissionstomographie *d:* **ECAT**

Computerbearbeitung chemischer und biologischer Forschungsergebnisse *d:* **CCBF**

Computerized Aerospace Ground Equipment *e:* **CAGE**

Computerized Environmental Legislative Data System *e:* **CELDS**

Computerized Environmental Resources Data System *e:* **CERDS**

Computerized Exploration and Technical Underwater Surveyor *e:* **CETUS**

Computerized Geographic Information System *e:* **CGIS**

Computerized Health Education Assessment Program *e:* **CHEAP**

Computerized Image Processing System for Meteorological Applications *e:* **CIPSMAP**

Computerized Information Network for Community Health *e:* **CINCH**

Computerized Medical Imaging and Graphics *e:* **Comput Med Imaging Graph**

Computerized Medical Imaging Society *e:* **CMIS**

Computerized Natural Resources, Inc. *e:* **CNR**

Computerized Occupational Health Program *e:* **COHP**

Computerized Occupational Health Program Coronary Artery Risk Evaluation *e:* **COHP/CARE**

Computerized Problem-Oriented Medical Record *e:* **CPOMR**

Computerorientierte Ausbildung *d:* **EDUTRONICS**

computerorientierte Informationstechnik *d:* **COI**

computerorientiertes Informationssystem *d:* **CIS**

computerorientiertes Management-Informationssystem *d:* **CMIS**

Computers and Biomedical Research *e:* **Comput. Biomed. Res.**

Computers and Medicine *e:* **C & M**

Computers Environment and Urban Systems *e:* **CEUS**

Computers in Aerospace Conference *e:* **CAC**

Computers in Biology and Medicine *e:* **Comput Biol Med**

Computers in Mental Health *e:* **CIMH**

Comtté Panamericano de Ciencias Geoficicas *s:* **CPCG**

Concentrated Animal Feeding Operations *e:* **CAFO**

Concentrated Animal Feedlot *e:* **CAFO**

Concentrated Sea Water *e:* **CSW**

Concentrated Space *e:* **CS**

Concentration of Hydrogen *e:* **CH**

Concentric-Orbit Rendezvous *e:* **COR**

Conceptual Models of the Mission Space *e:* **CMMS**

Concours Spécial technique d'Accès aux Grandes Écoles d'ingénieurs *f:* **COSAGE**

concrete deepwater structure[s] *e:* **condeep(s)**

Condensate Water Servicing Unit *e:* **CWSU**

Condensed Water *e:* **CW**

Condiciones meteorológicas *s:* **WX**

Condiciones Meteorológicas de vuelo por Instrumentos *s:* **IMC**

Condiciones Meteorológicas de vuelo Visual *s:* **VMC**

Conditions of Roads and Weather *e:* **CROW**

Confederación Médica Panamericana *s:* **CMP**

Confederación Sudamericana de Medicina del Deporte *s:* **CONSUMED**

Confederation of African Medical Associations and Societies *e:* **CAMAS**

Confederation of Health Service Employees *e:* **CHSE**, *e:* **C.O.H.S.E.**

Confederation of Medical Associations in/of Asia and Oceania *e:* **CMAAO**

Conference for Health Council Work *e:* **CHCW**

Conference Internationale des Facultes, instituts et École s de Pharmacie d'Expression Française *f:* **CIFPEF**

Conference of Baltic Oceanographers *e:* **CBO**

Conference of Biological Editors *e:* **CBE**

Conference of Biology Editors *e:* **C.B.E.**

Conference of Fire Protection Associations *e:* **CFPA**

Conference of Latin Americanist Geographers *e:* **CLAG**

Conference of Local Environmental Health Administrators *e:* **CLEHA**

[Conference of] Medical Informatics *e:* **MEDINFO**

Conference of Municipal Public Health Engineers *e:* **CMPHE**

Conference of Postgraduate Medical Deans *e:* **COPMED**

Conference of Presidents and Officers of State Medical Associations *e:* **CPOSMA**

Conference of Public Health Laboratorians *e:* **CPHL**

Conference of Public Health Laboratory directors *e:* **CPHL**

Conference of Public Health Veterinarians *e:* **CPHV**

Conference of Research Workers in Animal Disease[s] *e:* **CRWAD**

Conference of State and Provincial Health Authorities of North America *e:* **CSPH**

Conference of State and Provincial Public Health Laboratory Directors *e:* **CSPPHLD**

Conference of State and Territorial Directors of Public Health Education *e:* **CSTDPHE**

Conference of State and Territorial Health Officers with Public Health Service *e:* **CSTHOPHS**

Conference of State Health and Environmental Managers *e:* **CSHEM**

Conference of the Parties to the Convention on Biological Diversity *e:* **COP**

Conference of the Parties to the Framework Convention on Climate Change *e:* **COP/FCCC**

Conference of the Parties (to the United Nations Framework Convention on Climate Change) *e:* **COP**

Conference on Computational Molecular Biology *e:* **RECOMB**

Conference on Global Impacts of Applied Microbiology *e:* **GIAM**

Conference on Optical Metrology Applied to Medicine and Biology *e:* **OPTIMED**

Conference on Protective Equipment *e:* **COPE**

Conference on Remote Sensing Education *e:* **CORSE**

Conference on Scientific Ocean Drilling *e:* **COSOD**

Conference on the Inhabitants of the Ocean *e:* **CIO**

Conferencia Mundial sobre el Clima *s:* **CMC**

Conferenza Mondiale degli Istituti Secolari *i:* **CMIS**

Configurable Environment for Robust Vision in Industrial Processes *e:* **CERVIP-CP94-1263**

Confined Space *e:* **CS**

Confined Space Entry *e:* **CSE**

Confined Space Training *e:* **CST**

Confinement Protection Limit *e:* **CPL**

Conformal Space Projection *e:* **CSP**

Confédération Luxembourgeoise des Syndicats Chrétiens *f:* **CLSC**

Confédération des Associations et Sociétés Medicales d'Afrique *f:* **CASMA**

Confédération des Syndicats Médicaux *f:* **C.S.M.**

Confédération des Syndicats Médicaux [des médecins] Français *f:* **CSMF**

Confédération Générale des Syndicats Médicaux de France *f:* **C.G.S.M.F.**

Confédération Interallié des Officiers-Médicaux de Reserve *f:* **CIOMR**

Confédération Internationale des Associations de Medecines Alternatives Naturelles *f:* **CIAMAN**

Confédération Médicale Panaméricaine *f:* **CMP**

Confédération Nationale de l'Artisanat et des Métiers *f:* **C.N.A.M.**

Confédération Nationale des Chauffeurs Routiers *f:* **CNCR**

Confédération Nationale des Métiers d'Arts et de Décoration *f:* **CNMAD**

Confédération Nationale des Syndicats Médicaux *f:* **CNSM**

Confédération Nationale Laitière *f:* **CNL**

Conférence des Nations Unies sur l'environnement et le développement *f:* **CNUED**

Conférence des Parties (à la Convention-cadre des Nations Unies sur les changements climatiques) *f:* **COP**

Conférence Européenne de Biologie Moléculaire *f:* **CEBM**

Conférence Européenne des Experts Météorologistes de l'Aéronautique *f:* **CEEMA**

Conférence Interministérielle de l'Environnement *f:* **CIE**

Conférence Internationale des Matières premières *f:* **C.I.M.**

Conférence Internationale des Matières Premières *f:* **CIMP**

Conférence internationale sur l'eau et l'environnement: Le développement dans la perspective du XXIe siècle *f:* **ICWE**

Conférence internationale sur l'environnement côtier méditerranéen *f:* **MEDCOAST**

Conférence internationale sur une plate-forme scientifique pour l'environnement et le développement jusqu'au XXIe siècle *f:* **ASCEND-21**

Conférence ministérielle africaine sur l'environnement *f:* **CMAE**

Conférence mondiale sur le climat *f:* **CMC**

Conférence Suisse des Directeurs d'École s professionnelles et de métiers *f:* **CSD**

Conférence traitant les transports Maritimes dans l'Océan indien *f:* **CIMACOREM**

Conférences Régionales de Métiers *f:* **COREM**

Congregation des Pretres des Ecoles de Charite *f:* **Institut Cavanis**

Congrès Géologique International *f:* **CGI**

Congrès International de Géographie *f:* **CIG**

Congreso Geológico Internacional *s:* **CGI**

Congreso International de Medicina Tropical y Paludismo *s:* **CIMTP**

Congreso Panamericano de Ingeniería de Minas y Geología *s:* **CPIM**

Congress of Neurological Surgeons *e:* **CNS**

Congress on Optimum Population and Environment *e:* **COPE**

Congress on Sedimentary Geology *e:* **CSG**

Conical Earth Sensor *e:* **CES**

Conjugated Diene Hydroperoxide *e:* **CDHP**

Connaissance de l'Environnement *f:* **CE**

Connaître et Protéger la Nature *f:* **CPN**

Connected Family Environment *e:* **CFE**

Connecticut Geological and Natural History Survey *e:* **CGNHS**

Connecticut Medicine *e:* **Conn. Med.**

Connecticut Natural Gas [Corporation] *e:* **CNG**

Connecticut River Watershed Council *e:* **CRWC**

Connecticut Society of Emergency Medical Services Instructors *e:* **CSEMSI**

Connecticut State Medical Society *e:* **CSMS**

Connection of Health Data and General Practice *e:* **CHDGP**

Connector Environmental Test Stand *e:* **CETS**

Conseil canadien des ressources humaines de l'industrie de l'environnement *f:* **CCRHIE**

Conseil Canadien des Écoles de Bibliothécaires *f:* **CCEB**

Conseil de la coopération internationale en matière d'étude et d'utilisation de l'espace extra-atmosphérique *f:* **INTERCOSMOS**

Conseil de la Recherche et du Développement Forestiers *f:* **CRDF**

Conseil de Préfecture Interdépartemental *f:* **C.P.I.**

Conseil de Recherches en Sciences Naturelles et en Génie du Canada *f:* **CRSNG**

Conseil de Recherches Médicales du Canada *f:* **CRM**

Conseil des Observations Astronautiques *f:* **COA**

Conseil des Organisations Internationales des Sciences Médicales *f:* **COISM**

Conseil des Productions Animales du Québec *f:* **CPAQ**

Conseil des Écoles Polytechniques Fédérales *f:* **CEPF**

Conseil en Architecture, Urbanisme et Environnement *f:* **CAUE**

Conseil Européen du Droit de l'Environnement *f:* **CEDE**

Conseil inter-Etats d'hydrométéorologie de la Communauté d'Etats indépendants *f:* **CIH CEI**

Conseil International de Coordination des Associations d'Études et d'Action en Matière de Viellissement *f:* **CICAV**

Conseil international de liaison pour une Autorité mondiale de l'environnement *f:* **CILAME**

Conseil International des Organisations des Sciences Médicales *f:* **CIOSM**

Conseil International des Transports Routiers *f:* **C.I.T.R.**

Conseil international pour l'application des moyens Audio-Visuels à l'environnement *f:* **AUDIVIR**

Conseil International pour le Droit de l'Environnement *f:* **CIDE**

Conseil Intersecrétariats des Programmes Scientifiques Relatifs à l'Océanographie *f:* **CIPSRO**

Conseil Médical du Québec *f:* **CMQ**

Conseil National de la Formation Médicale Continue *f:* **CNFMC**

Conseil National de l'Information Géographique *f:* **CNIG**

Conseil National des Grandes Écoles *f:* **CNGE**

Conseil National pour la Gestion de l'Environnement *f:* **CONAGESE**

Conseil pour la Coordination des Congrès Internationaux des Sciences Médicales *f:* **CCCISM**

Conseil pour la Stratégie paneuropéenne de la Diversité biologique et paysagère *f:* **STRA-CO**

Conseil Suisse des Écoles de Service Social *f:* **CSESS**

Conseil Supérieur de la Météorologie *f:* **CSM**

Conseil Supérieur des Professions Para-Médicales *f:* **CSPPM**

Consejo Interestatal de Hidrometeorología de la Comunidad de Estados Independientes *s:* **CIH CEI**

Consejo Latinoamericano de Oceanografía *s:* **CLAO**

Conservation and Natural Resources *e:* **CNR**

Conservation and Wildlife Studies *e:* **CAWS**

Conservation Biology *e:* **Conserv. Biol.**

Conservation Division, Environment Canada Ottawa, Ontario *e:* **OOEOB**

Conservation of Clean Air and Water in Western Europe *e:* **CONCAWE**

Conservatoire National des Arts et Métiers *f:* **CNAM**

Conservatoire nationale des Arts et Métiers *f:* **CAM**

Consistent Office Environment *e:* **COE**

Consolidated Aerospace Equipment List *e:* **CAEL**

Consolidated Aerospace Ground Equipment List *e:* **CAGEL**

Consolidated Aerospace Supplier Evaluation *e:* **CASE**

Consolidated Natural Gas [Company] *e:* **CNG**

Consolidated Space Operations Center *e:* **CSOC**, *e:* **CSOC**

Consolidated Space Test Center *e:* **CSTC**

Consortium for Environmental Education in Medicine *e:* **CEEM**

Consortium for International Crop Protection *e:* **CICP**

Consortium for International Earth Science Information Network[s] *e:* **CIESIN**

Consortium for Oceanographic Research and Education *e:* **CORE**

Consortium of Regional Environmental Education Councils *e:* **CREEC**

Consortium on the Ocean's Role in Climate *e:* **CORC**, *e:* **CORC SIO-LDEO**

Constant Hot Water *e:* **CHW**

Constellation Observing System for Meteorology, Ionosphere, and Climate *e:* **COSMIC**

Constrained and Unconstrained Testing Environment *e:* **CUTE**

Construction Mécanique et Décolletage *f:* **COMED**

Construction Occupational Health-Safety-Environment Forum *e:* **COHSEF**

Constructive Solid Geometry *e:* **CGS**

Constructive Solid Geometry Consulting Services Group *e:* **CSG**

Constructive Solid[s] Geometry *e:* **CSG**

Consultants' Environmental Liability *e:* **CEL**

Consultative Committee for [on] Space Data Systems *e:* **CCSDS**

Consultative Committee on Exotic Animal Diseases *e:* **CCEAD**

Consultative Environmental Review *e:* **CER**

Consultative Group on Biological Diversity *e:* **CGBD**

Consultative Group on Ocean Mapping *e:* **CGOM**

Consultative Group on Potentially Harmful Effects of Space Experiments *e:* **CGOPHEOSE**

Consumer Affairs Medical Quality Assurance Board *e:* **CAMQAB**

Consumer and Environmental Health Services Administration *e:* **CEHSA**

Consumer and Patient Health Information Section. Medical Library Association *e:* **CAPHIS**

Consumer Assessment of Health Plans *e:* **CAHPS**

Consumer Credit Protection Act *e:* **CCPA**

Consumer Health Informatics (or Information) *e:* **CHI**

Consumer Health Information Program and Service[s] *e:* **CHIPS**

Consumer Protection Advisory Committee *e:* **CPAC**

Consumer Protection and Environmental Health Service *e:* **CPEHS**

Consumer Protection Association *e:* **CPA**

Consumers' Health Forum of Australia *e:* **CHF**

Consumer's Health Forum of Australia *e:* **CHFA**

Contact, Help, Advice, Information, Network for Effective Health Care *e:* **C.H.A.I.N**

Contact Signature Generator *e:* **CSG**

Containment Atmosphere Dilution *e:* **CAD**

Containment Atmosphere Recirculation System *e:* **CARS**

Containment Water Storage *e:* **CWS**

Contaminated Water Removal and Storage System *e:* **CWRSS**

Contemporary Topics in Immunobiology *e:* **Contemp Top Immunobiol**

Content Protection for Recordable Media *e:* **CPRM**

Content Standard for Digital Geospatial Metadata *e:* **CSDGM**

Continental Aerospace Defense Command *e:* **CONAD**

Continental Atlantic Tidewater and Cities *e:* **CATC**

Continental Geographic[al] Information System *e:* **CGIS**

Continental Hydrologic Processes *e:* **CHP**

Continental Margin Environment and Mineral Resources Sub-programme *e:* **COMEMIR**

Continental Meteorological Data System *e:* **COMEDS**

Continental Oil, Atlantic Refining, Tidewater Oil, Cities Service *e:* **C.A.T.C.**

Continental Polar *e:* **cP**

Continental Polar Air *e:* **cP Air**

continental polar air mass *e:* **cpam**

continental shelf of a continent extending into the sea before it descends sharp *e:* **cont shelf**

Contingency Orbit Insertion *e:* **COI**

Continuation Operational Sea Training *e:* **COST**

Continuing Medical Education *e:* **CME**

Continuous Automatic Remote Display *e:* **CARD**

Continuous Orbital Guidance Sensor *e:* **COGS**

Continuous Orbital Guidance System *e:* **COGS**

Continuous Wave Separated Orbit Cyclotron *e:* **CWSOC**

Continuous Wave Space Duplexed *e:* **CWSD**

Contract Employment Program for Aboriginal People in Natural and Cultural Resource Management *e:* **CEPANCRM**

Contract [or]-Furnished Aerospace Equipment *e:* **CFAE**

Contract Surgeon *e:* **Cont Surg**, *e:* **CS**, *e:* **CSN**

Contributions. Department of Geology and Mineralogy. Niigata University *e:* **NDRCAJ**

Contributions. Institute of Geology and Paleontology. Tohoku University *e:* **TDRCAH**

Contributions. Laboratory of Vertebrate Biology. University of Michigan *e:* **UNIVBA6**

Contributions to Gynecology and Obstetrics *e:* **Contrib Gynecol Obstet**

Contributions to Microbiology and Immunology *e:* **Contrib Microbiol Immunol**

Control and Protection System *e:* **CPS**

Control de Transito Areo Oceanico *s:* **ZOZ**

Control Execution Environment *e:* **CEE**

Control of Sea Ice Information *e:* **ICECON**

Control of Substances Hazardous to Health *e:* **COSHH**

Controllability\Observability\and Maintenance Engineering Technic *e:* **COMET**

Controlled Air Space *e:* **CAS**

Controlled Airspace *e:* **CTA**

Controlled Atmosphere *e:* **CA**

Controlled-Atmosphere Brazing *e:* **CAB**

Controlled Atmosphere Packaging *e:* **CAP**

Controlled Atmosphere Transfer *e:* **CAT**

Controlled Environment Agriculture *e:* **CEA**

Controlled Environment and Life Support System e: **CELS**

Controlled Environment [and] Life Support System e: **CELSS**

Controlled Environment Enclosure e: **CEE**

Controlled Environment Enclosures e: **CEEs**

Controlled Environment Research Laboratory e: **CERES**

Controlled Environmental System e: **CES**

Controlled Environmental Test[ing] e: **CET**

Control[led] Environment[al] Vault e: **CEV**

Controlled Environments Ltd., Winnipeg, Manitoba e: **MWCE**

Controlled Helium Atmosphere Plant e: **CHAP**

Controlled Library Environment and Resources e: **CLEAR**

Controlled Recirculation Boiling Water Reactor e: **CRBR**

Controlled Space-Charge Limited Resistor e: **CSCLR**

Controls Astrophysics Structures Experiment in Space e: **CASES**

Controls for Environmental Pollution, Inc. e: **CEP**

CONUS Meteorological Environmental Distribution System e: **COMEDS**

Convective Airspace Guidance e: **CAG**

Convective Meteorology Section e: **CMS**

Convective precipitation over water e: **CW**

Convenio sobre la Diversidad Biológica s: **CBD**

Convention concerning the protection of the world cultural and natural heritage e: **World Heritage Convention**

[Convention for] Long-Term Ecological Research e: **LTER**

Convention for/on International Trade in Endangered Species of Wild Fauna and Flora e: **CITES**

Convention Internationale pour la Protection des Végétaux f: **CIPV**

Convention internationale pour la prévention de la pollution des eaux de la mer par les hydrocarbures f: **OILPOL**

Convention internationale sur la préparation, la lutte et la coopération en matière de pollution par les hydrocarbures f: **OPRC**

Convention internationale sur la responsabilité civile pour les dommages dus à la pollution par les hydrocarbures f: **CLC**

Convention on Biological Diversity e: **Biodiversity, e: CBD**

Convention on International Regulation[s] for Preventing Collisions at Sea e: **COLREG[S]**

Convention on the conservation of European wildlife and natural habitats e: **Berne Convention**

Convention on the Conservation of European Wildlife and Natural Habitats e: **CCEWNH**

Convention on the Conservation of Migratory Species of Wild Animals e: **CMS**

Convention on the contract for the international carriage of passengers and luggage by inland waterway e: **CVN**

Convention on the protection of the marine environment of the Baltic Sea area e: **Helsinki Convention**

Convention on Wetlands of International Importance Especially as Waterfowl Habitat e: **Wetlands**

Convention on Wetlands of International Importance Especially as Waterfowl Habitats e: **RAMSAR**

Convention pour la protection des phoques de l'Antarctique f: **CCAS**

Convention sur la diversité biologique f: **CBD**

Convention sur la Diversité Biologique f: **CDB**

Conventional Combustion Environmental Assessment e: **CCEA**

Conventional Geometry Smart Projectile e: **CGSP**

Conventional Launch Sea Wolf e: **CLSW**

Conventions for the protection of the marine environment of the North-East Atlantic e: **OSPENEA**

Conversational Remote Batch e: **CREB**

Conversational Remote Batch Entry e: **CRBE**

Conversational Remote Job Entry e: **CRJE**

Conversation[al] System[s] with Online Remote Terminals e: **CONSORT**

converter remote off e: **ROFF**

converter remote on e: **RON**

Convicts' Association for a Good Environment e: **CAGE**

Cook College Remote Sensing Center e: **CCRSC**

Cookeville General Hospital, Stephen Farr Health Sciences Library, Cookeville e: **TCooH**

Cooled Atmospheric Spectrometer e: **CATMOS**

Cooler, Air, chilled Water e: **CAW**

Cooling Water e: **CW**

Cooling Water Association e: **CWA**

Cooling Water Gamma Monitor e: **CWGM**

Cooling Water Return e: **CWR**

Cooling Water Supply e: **CWS**

Cooling Water System e: **CWS**

Cooperative Atmosphere Surface Exchange Study e: **CASES**

Cooperative Development Environment e: **CDE**

Cooperative Distributed Interactive Atmospheric Catalogue e: **CODIAC**

Cooperative Ecological Research Project e: **CERP**

Cooperative Environmental Management e: **CEM**

Cooperative Florida Meteorological Experiment e: **COFMEX**

Cooperative Geographic Information System e: **CoGIS**

Cooperative Health Statistics System e: **CHSS**

Cooperative Healthcare Networks e: **CHN**

Cooperative Huntsville Meteorological Experiment e: **COHMEX**

Cooperative Inst. for Applied Meteorology e: **CIAM**

Cooperative Institute for Applied Remote Sensing e: **CIARS**

Cooperative Institute for Climate Studies e: **CICS**

Cooperative Institute for Geodata Management and Applications e: **CIGMA**

Cooperative Institute for Geoscience Management and Applications e: **CIGMA**

Cooperative Institute for Marine and Atmospheric Studies e: **CIMAS**

Cooperative Institute for Meteorological Training and Applied Research e: **CIMTAR**

Cooperative Institute for/of Mesocale Meteorological Studies e: **CIMMS**

Cooperative Institute for/of Meteorology Satellite Studies e: **CIMSS**

Cooperative Institute for Research in the Atmosphere e: **CIRA**

Cooperative Institute for Research in [the] Environmental Sciences e: **CIRES**

Cooperative Internationale de Recherche et d'action en matiere de Communication f: **CIRCOM**

Cooperative Investigation of the Northern Central West Indian Ocean e: **CINCWIO**

Cooperative Investigations of a Large Ocean Gyre e: **CILOG**

Cooperative Marine Science Programme for the Black Sea e: **COMSBLACK**

Cooperative Medical Advertising Bureau e: **C.M.A.B.**

Cooperative Meteorological Rocket Network e: **CMRN**

Cooperative Observational and Modeling Project for the Analysis of Severe Storms e: **COMPASS**

Cooperative Observations Program e: **COOP**

Cooperative (or Coordinated) Observations of Polar Electrodynamics e: **COPE**

Cooperative Program for Operational Meteorology, Education and Training e: **COMET**

Cooperative Programme in Europe for Research on Nature and Industry through Coordinated University Studies e: **COPERNICUS**

Cooperative Research Centre for Catchment Hydrology e: **CRCCH**

Cooperative Research Centre for Freshwater Ecology e: **CRCFE**

Cooperative Research Centre for Southern Hemisphere Meteorology e: **CRCSHM**

Cooperative Spacecraft System e: **CSS**

Cooperative Wildlife Research Laboratory e: **CWRL**

Coopers Allied Water Committee e: **CAWF**

Coopération Géophysique Internationale f: **CGI**

Coopérative agricole de production bananière et Fruitière de Côte-d'Ivoire f: **COFRUCI**

Coopérative Bananière et Fruitière f: **COBAFRUIT**

Coopérative des Planteurs de Caféiers de Mbouda f: **CPCAM**

Coopérative Ouvrière de Géomètres pour l'Étude, le Relevé et l'Aménagement du Territoire f: **COGERAT**

Coordinador de una Zona Meteorológica s: **CZM**

Coordinamento di Iniziative Popolari di Solidarieta Internazionale *i:* **CIPSI**

Coordinated Accident Rescue Endeavor-State of Mississippi *e:* **CARE-SOM**

Coordinated Air-Sea Experiment *e:* **CASE**

Coordinated Eiscat and Balloon Observations *e:* **CEBO**

Coordinate[d] Geometry *e:* **COGO**

Coordinate[d] Geometry Language *e:* **COGO Language**

Coordinated Information on the European Environment *e:* **CORINE**

Coordinated Proposal Ice-Sheet Research with ERS-1 *e:* **ISR-ERS-1**

Coordinated Research and Environmental Surveillance Programme *e:* **CRESP**

Coordinated Studies in Polar Stratospheric Clouds *e:* **COSPOC**

Coordinating Committee for Earthquake Prediction *e:* **CCEP**

Coordinating Committee for the World Climate Programme *e:* **CCWCP**

Coordinating Committee of the Societies of Mineral-Deposit Geologists *e:* **CCSMDG**

Coordinating committee on atmospheric conditioning for testing *e:* **ATCO**

Coordinating Committee on Great Lakes Basic Hydraulic and Hydrologic Data *e:* **CCGLBHHD**

Coordinating Committee on Oceanography *e:* **CCO**

Coordinating Council on Medical Education *e:* **CCME**

Coordinating Group for the Tactical Weather Net *e:* **CGTWN**

Coordinating Research Council-Environmental Protection Agency *e:* **CRC-EPA**

Coordination de l'aménagement de l'Ouest lausannois et des Hautes Écoles *f:* **COH**

Coordination et Pilotage des Chantiers de Bâtiment *f:* **COPIBATA**

Coordination Group for Meteorological Studies *e:* **CGMS**

Coordination Group of Non Governmental Organizations in the Field of Man-Made Environment *e:* **COG**

Coordination of Information on the Environment *e:* **CORINE**

Coordination of/on Geostationary Meteorological Satellites *e:* **CGMS**

Coordination of Space Techniques for Geodesy and Geodynamics *e:* **CSTC**

Coordination of Space Techniques for Geodesy and Geophysics *e:* **CSTGAG**

Coordination pour l'Oceanie des Recherches sur les Arts, les Idees et les Litteratures *f:* **CORAIL**

Copyright Protection Technical Working Group *e:* **CPTWG**

Coral Sea Islands *e:* **CSI**

Core Auxiliary Cooling Water System *e:* **CACWS**

Core Dynamics and the Earth's Dynamo *e:* **CDED**

Core Project 1, the Global Description of the world ocean *e:* **CP1**

Core Project 2, the Southern Ocean Experiment *e:* **CP2**

Core Protection Calculator *e:* **CPC**

Core Protection Computer *e:* **CPC**

Core Water-Recycling System *e:* **CWRS**

Cornell Geological Sciences *e:* **CGS**

Cornell Institute for Research in Chemical Ecology *e:* **CIRCE**

Cornell Medical Community Computer Project *e:* **CMCCP**

Cornell Medical Index *e:* **CMI**

Cornell Medical Index Questionnaire *e:* **CMIQ**

Cornell University Department of Geological Sciences *e:* **CUDGS**

Cornell University, Medical College, New York *e:* **VYC**

Cornish Water Wheels Preservation Society *e:* **CWWPS**

Corometrics Medizin Elektronik GmbH Perinatologie und Notfallmedizin *d:* **CME**

Coronal Helium Abundance Spacelab Experiment *e:* **CHASE**

Coronary Care Intensive Medical *e:* **CCIM**

Corps Air Space Management Element *e:* **CAME**

Corps de Protection Civile *f:* **C.P.C.**

Corps Medical Centre *e:* **CMC**

Corps of Engineers, Colorado Citizens Coordinating Committee on Environmental Planning *e:* **CECEP**

Corps of Engineers Waterborne Commerce Statistics Center *e:* **CEWCSC**

Corpus Christi Geological Society *e:* **CCGS**

Corrected Geomagnetic Latitude *e:* **CGL**

Corrected Geomagnetic Time *e:* **CGT**

Correctional Medical Systems *e:* **CMS**

Corrective Optics Space Telescope Axial Replacement *e:* **COSTAR**

Correlation Interferometer for the Measurement of Atmosphere Trace Species *e:* **CIMATS**

Correlation Protected Instrument Landing System *e:* **CPILS**

Correlation Protected Integrated Landing System *e:* **CPILS**

Corridor Aerogeophysics South East Ross Transect Zone *e:* **CASERTZ**

Corriente Circumpolar Antártica *s:* **CCA**

Corrosion and Cathodic Protection *e:* **CACP**

Corrosion and Protection Association *e:* **CAPA**

Corrosion and Protection Centre, Industrial Services Unit *e:* **CAPCIS**

Corvallis Environmental Research Laboratory *e:* **CERL**

COSPAR [Committee on Space Research] International Reference Atmosphere *e:* **CIRA**

Cotacachi-Cayapas Ecological Reserve [Ecuador] *e:* **RECC**

Cotteswold Naturalists' Field Club *e:* **C.N.F.C.**

Couche limite atmosphérique *f:* **ABL**

Council for Biology in Human Affairs *e:* **CBHA**

Council for Environmental Education *e:* **CEE**

Council for Environmental Science and Engineering *e:* **CESE**

Council for Heads of Medical Schools *e:* **CHMS**

Council for Interdisciplinary Communication in Medicine *e:* **CIDCOMED**

Council for International Organizations of Medical Sciences *e:* **COIMS**

Council for Medical Affairs *e:* **CFMA**

Council for Nature *e:* **CfN**

Council for Postgraduate Medical Education *e:* **CPME**

Council for Postgraduate Medical Education in England and Wales *e:* **CPMEEW**

Council for Professions Supplementary to the Medicine Act *e:* **CPSM**

Council for the Co-ordination of International Congresses of Medical Sciences *e:* **CCICMS**

Council for the Education and Training of Health Visitors *e:* **CETHV**

Council for [the] International Organisations (or Organizations) of Medical Sciences *e:* **CIOMS**

Council for the Pan-European Biological and Landscape Diversity Strategy *e:* **STRA-CO**

Council for the Protection of Rural England *e:* **CPRE**

Council for the Protection of Rural Wales *e:* **CPRW**

Council of Arab Ministers Responsible for the Environment *e:* **CAMRE**

Council of Biology Editors *e:* **CBE,** *e:* **Coun Biology Eds**

Council of British Fire Protection Equipment Manufactures *e:* **CBFPEM**

Council of British Geography *e:* **COBRIG**

Council of Community Health Services *e:* **CCHS**

Council of Defense and Space Industry Associations *e:* **CODIA**

Council of Defense Space Industries Association[s] *e:* **CODSIA**

Council of Directors of Tropical Medicine Institutes in Europe *e:* **TROPMEDEUROP**

Council of Emergency Medicine Residency Directors *e:* **CORD**

Council of Health Organizations *e:* **COHO**

Council of Industrial Health *e:* **C.I.H.**

Council of Medical Genetics Organizations *e:* **COMGO**

Council of Medical Specialty Societies *e:* **CMSS**

Council of Nature Conservation Ministers *e:* **CONCOM**

Council of [the] Baltic Sea States *e:* **CBSS**

Council of United States Universities for Soil and Water Development in Arid and Subhumid Areas *e:* **CUSU[S]WASH**

Council on Atmospheric Studies *e:* **CAS**

Council on Biological Information *e:* **COBI**

Council on Biological Sciences Information *e:* **COBSI**

Council on Education for Public Health *e:* **CEPH**

Council on Education in the Geological Sciences *e:* **CEGS**

Council on Environmental Quality *e:* **CDQ,** *e:* **CEQ**

Council on Family Health *e:* **CFH**

Council on Graduate Medical Education *e:* **COGME**

Council on Health Information and Education *e:* **CHIE**

Council on Health Research for Development *e:* **COHRED**

Council on International Cooperation in the Study and Utilization of Outer Space e: **INTERCOSMOS**

Council on Medical Student Education Education in Pediatrics e: **COMSEP**

Council on Medical Television e: **CMT**

Council on Medication and Hospitals e: **CMEH**

Council on Ocean Law e: **COL**

Council on Oceanographic Laboratory Directors e: **COLD**

Council on Podiatric Medical Education e: **CPME**

Council on Pollution and Environment e: **COPE**

Council on Population and Environment e: **COPE**

Council on Resident Education in Obstetrics and Gynecology e: **CREOG**

Counter Low Observables e: **CLO**

Country Towns Water Supply Improvement Program e: **COWSIP**

County Medical Association e: **CMA**

County Medical Services e: **CMS**

County Naturalist Trust e: **CNT**

County Public Health Unit e: **CPHU**

County Water Authority e: **CWA**

Couple to Couple League for natural family planning e: **CCL**

Couple Years Protection e: **CYP**

Coupled atmosphere/ocean GCM e: **A/OGCM**

Coupled Carbon Cycle Climate Model Intercomparison Project e: **C4MIP**

Coupled Climate Systems Program e: **CCSP**

Coupled Energetics and Dynamics of the Atmospheric Regions e: **CEDAR**

Coupled Hydrosphere-Atmosphere Research Model e: **CHARM**

Coupled [Ocean-atmosphere] General Circulation Model e: **CGCM**

Coupled Ocean Atmosphere Mesoscale Prediction System e: **COAMPS**

Coupled Ocean-Atmosphere Regional Experiment e: **COARE**

Coupled Ocean-Atmosphere Response Experiment e: **COARE**

Coupled ocean-land-atmosphere 1-dimensional e: **COLA1D**

Coupled Oceanographic and Atmospheric Model e: **COAMPS**

Coupling, Energetics and Dynamics of Atmospheric Regions e: **CEDAR**

Courrier de l'environnement de l'INRA f: **Courr. environ. INRA**

Coventry Health and Safety Movement e: **CHASM**

Covert Survivable In-Weather Reconnaissance/Strike e: **CSIRS**

Cowater International, Inc., Ottawa, Ontario e: **OOCOW**

Crab Orchard National Wildlife Refuge e: **CONWR**

Craniofacial Biology Group of the International Association for Dental Research e: **CBG**

Crayon, Water Color and Craft Institute e: **CWCCI**

Creeping Environmental Problems e: **CEP**

Crescent Lake National Wildlife Refuge e: **CLNWR**

Crescent Medical Aid e: **CMA**

Crew Habitability and Protection e: **CH & P**

Crew Health Care System e: **CHeCS**

Crew Medical Restraint System e: **CMRS**

Crimean Astrophysical Observatory e: **CAO**

Crisis Action Weather Support System e: **CAWSS**

Crisis Environments Training Initiative e: **CETI**

Critical Appraisal for Medical Students e: **CAMS**

Critical Aquifer Protection Area e: **CAPA**

Critical Care Medicine e: **Crit Care Med**

Critical Infrastructure Protection e: **CIP**

Critical Reviews In Biochemistry and Molecular Biology e: **Crit Rev Biochem Mol Biol**

Critical Reviews in Biomedical Engineering e: **Crit Rev Biomed Eng**

Critical Reviews in Microbiology e: **Crit Rev Microbiol**

Critical Reviews in Neurobiology e: **Crit Rev Neurobiol**

Critical Reviews in Oral Biology and Medicine e: **Crit Rev Oral Biol Med**

Critical Sea Tests e: **CST**

Croisière biologique américaine au large de la Basse-Californie f: **MESCAL**

Crop Environment Resource Synthesis e: **CERES**

Crop Estimation through Resource and Environment Synthesis e: **CERES**

Crop Identification Technology Assessment for Remote Sensing e: **CITARS**

Crop Protection Institute e: **CPI**

Crop Protection Product e: **CPP**

Cross-chain Loran Atmospheric Sounding System e: **CLASS**

Cross Creeks National Wildlife Refuge e: **CCNWR**

Cross Cultural Health Care Program e: **CCHCP**

Cross-Polarization e: **XP**, e: **X-POL**

Cross-Polar[ization] Decoupling e: **XPD**

Cross Polar[ization] Discrimination e: **XPD**

Cross-Polarization Interference e: **XPI**

Cross Polarization Interference Canceller e: **XPIC**

Cross Polarization - Magic Angle Spinning e: **CP/MAS**

cross-polarization/magic angle spinning conditions e: **CPMAS**

Cross-Polarized Light e: **XPL**

Croydon Natural History and Scientific Society e: **C.N.H.S.S.**

Crucero Biológico Norteamericano Frente a las Costas de la Baja California s: **MESCAL**

Cruelty to Animals Inspectorate e: **CAI**

Crusade for a Cleaner Environment e: **CCE**

cryobiological[ly] e: **cryobio**

cryobiologist e: **cryobio**

cryobiology e: **cryobio**

Cryogenic Infrared Spectrometer[s] [and] Telescope[s] for [the] Atmosphere e: **CRISTA**

Cryogenic on Orbit Liquid Depot Storage, Acquisition, Transfer e: **COLD-SAT**

cryosurgeon e: **cryosurg**

Crypto Remote Control Unit e: **CRCU**

CSIRO [Commonwealth Scientific and Industrial Research Organisation]/Division of Atmospheric Research e: **CSIRO/DAR**

CSIRO [Commonwealth Scientific and Industrial Research Organisation] Office of Space Science and Applications e: **CSIRO OSSA**

CSIRO Office of Space Science and Applications e: **COSSA**

CSU Regional Atmospheric Modeling System e: **CSU-RAMS**

Cuatemalan Health Rights Support Project e: **GHRSP**

Cubic Feet Cylinder C /X-Disbursement Account Delivered at Frontier e: **CUFT CyC/XD/ADAF**

Culture and Nature Visitor e: **CNV**

Culture, Medicine and Psychiatry e: **Cult Med Psychiatry**

Cumberland Plateau Seismological Observatory e: **CPSO**

Cumulated Index Medicus e: **CIM**

Cumulative Hydrologic Impact Assessment e: **CHIA**

Cumulative Index to Nursing and Allied Health Literature e: **CINAHL**

Cumulative Techniques and Procedures in Clinical Microbiology e: **CUMITECHS**

Current Aerospace Research Activities e: **CARA**

Current Awareness in Biological Sciences e: **CABS**

Current Bibliographies in Medicine e: **CBM**

Current Biology e: **Curr Biol**

Current Geographical Publications e: **CGP**, e: **CGPs**

Current List of Medical Literature e: **CLML**

Current Medical Diagnosis & Treatment e: **CMDT**

Current Medical Information and Terminology e: **CMIT**

Current Medical Research and Opinion e: **Curr Med Res Opin**

Current Medical Terminology e: **CMT**

Current Ocean Detecting and Ranging e: **CODAR**

Current Opinion in Cell Biology e: **Curr Opin Cell Biol**

Current Opinion in Neurobiology e: **Curr Opin Neurobiol**

Current Opinion in Obstetrics and Gynecology e: **Curr Opin Obstet Gynecol**

Current Opinion in Structural Biology e: **Curr Opin Struct Biol**

Current Topics in Developmental Biology e: **Curr Top Dev Biol**

Current Topics in Medical Mycology e: **Curr Top Med Mycol**

Current Topics in Microbiology and Immunology e: **CTMI**, e: **Curr Top. Microbiol. Immunol.**

Current Workspace Pointer e: **CWP**

Custom Editing and Display of Reduced Information in Cartesian space e: **CEDRIC**

Cutter Protein Hydrolysate, 5% in Water e: **CPH 5**

Cyberspace Description Format e: **CDF**

Cyberspace Research and Education Center
 e: **CYREC**
Cycle Postrgade en Sciences de
 l'Environnement f: **CPSE**
Cycloidal Activities in Two Oceans
 [program] e: **CATO**
Cylindrical Hydrophone Array e: **CHA**
Cyperspace Developer Kit e: **CDK**
Cyprus Geographical Association e: **CGA**
Cyprus Marine Environment Protection
 Association e: **CYMEPA**
cytoecologic[al][ly] e: **cytoeco**
cytoecologist e: **cytoeco**
Czech Environment Management Center e:
 CEMC
Czech Ministry of Environment e: **CME**
Cía Chilena de Navegación Interoceanica
 s: **CCNI**

D

Daily Historical Climate Network e:
 DHCN
Daily Water Flow e: **D.W.F.**
Daimler-Benz-Aerospace d: **DASA**
Dairy and Ice Cream Equipment
 Association e: **DICE**
Dakar Medical e: **Dakar Med**
Dalhousie Earth Sciences e: **DES**
Dalhousie Ocean Studies Program e:
 DOSP
Dalhousie Ocean Studies Programme,
 Dalhousie University, Halifax, Nova
 Scotia e: **NSHDOS**
damage by sea water e: **s.w.d.**
Damage microstructures in fusion [reactor]
 environments e: **DMFE**
Damage Protection Plan e: **DPP**
damage protection plan e: **DPP-charges**
Dangerous Environment Electrical
 Protection system e: **DEEP**
Danger[ous] Space e: **DS**
Danish Association of Medical Imaging e:
 DRO
Danish Centre for Atmospheric Research
 e: **DCAR**
Danish Cooperation for Environment and
 Development e: **DANCED**
Danish Medical Bulletin e: **Dan Med Bull**
Danish Medical Society e: **DMS**
Danish Meteorological Institute Limited
 Area Model e: **DMI-LAM**
Danish National Committee of the
 International Association on Water
 Pollution Research and Control e:
 DNCIAWPRC
Danish Natural Science Research Council
 e: **SNF**
Danish Polar Center e: **DPC**
Danish Radiation Protection Authority e:
 SIS
Danish Society for Medical Informatics e:
 DSMI
Danish Space Research Institute e: **DSRI**
Danish Water Quality Institute e: **VKI**
Danmarks Geologiske Undersøgelse a:
 DGU
Danmarks Meteorologiske Institut a: **DMI**
Danmarks Natur- og Lågevidenskabelige
 Bibliotek a: **DNLB**
Dansk Forening for Medicinsk Fysik a:
 DFMF

Dansk Geofysisk Forening a: **DGF**
Dansk Geoteknisk Forening a: **DGF**
Dansk Medicinsk Selskab a: **DMS**
Dansk Naturist Union a: **DNU**
Dansk Olie & Naturgas A/S a: **D.O.N.G.**
Dansk Olie og Naturgas a: **DONGAS**
Dansk Olje Og Naturgas a: **DONG**
Dansk Selskab for Almen Medicin a:
 DSAM
Dansk Selskab for Intern Medicin a:
 DSIM
Dansk Selskab for Klinisk Fysiologi og
 Nuklear Medicin a: **DSKFNM**
Dansk Selskab for Medicinsk Informatik
 a: **DSMI**
Dansk Selskab for Trafikmedicin og
 Ulykkesforebyggelse a: **DSTM**
Dansk Ski- og Orientieringsforbund a:
 D.S.O.F.
Danske Interne Medicineres Organisation
 a: **DIMO**
Danske Meteorologiske Institut a: **DMI**
Danube Sea Container Service e: **DSCS**
Dardo de Investigación Meteorológica s:
 DIM
Darling National Wildlife Refuge e:
 DNWR
Darnell Army Hospital, Medical Library,
 Fort Hood e: **TxFhH**
DASAG Deutsche Naturasphalt GmbH der
 Limmer und Vorwohler Grubenfelder d:
 DASAG
Data Analysis System e: **DAS**
Data and Remote control Terminal e:
 DART
Data Base Environment e: **DBE**
Data Center for Marine Geology e: **DCMG**
Data Consistency Orbit e: **DACO**
Data Enhancement for Accountability and
 Leadership in Maternal and Child Health
 e: **DEAL-MCH**
Data Exception Error Protection e: **DEEP**
Data Integration and Collection
 Environment e: **DICE**
Data Meteorological Satellite Program[me]
 e: **DMSP**
Data on Environmentally Significant
 Chemicals Network e: **DESCNET**, e:
 DESNET
Data Protection Act e: **DPA**
Data Protection Agency e: **DPA**
Data Protection Authority e: **DPA**
Data Protection Commission e: **DPC**
Data Protection Committee e: **DPC**
Data Quality Objectives/Observational
 Approach e: **DQO/OA**
Data System Environment Simulator e:
 DASYS
Data Terminal Environment e: **DTE**
Data Up-Date Procedure at a Remote
 Terminal e: **DUPART**
Database and monitoring network in
 CADDIA on environmental, agricultural
 and urban development e: **RESEAU**
Database Application Remote Interface e:
 DARI
Database Management Environment e:
 DBME
Database program for carbonate, interstitial
 water, gas chromatography, and Rock-
 Eval analysis results e: **CHEMDB**
Data:.Network on Environmentally
 Significant Chemicals e: **D E S C N E T**

Daten der Fernerkundung der Erde d: **DFE**
Datenbank Dokumentationen im Bereich
 Umweltschutz d: **Endoc**
Datenbank Floristische Kartierung d:
 FLORKAT
Datenbank Forschungsvorhaben
 Umweltschutz d: **ENREP**
Datenbank für wassergefährdende Stoffe
 d: **DABAWAS**
Datenfernverarbeitungsorientierte
 Abwicklung von Industrieanlagen-
 Projekten im Seetransport d: **DAVIS**
Datenfolgeorganisation d: **DSORG**
datieren d: **dat.**
datiert d: **dat.**, d: **dd**
Datos meteorológicos en forma de valores
 reticulares s: **GRID**
dauernde gesundheitliche Bedenken d:
 DGB
David Dunlap Observatory e: **DDO**
David Lloyd George e: **DLG**
Davis Department of Geology e: **DDG**
Day/Night Adverse weather Pilotage
 System e: **D/NAPS**
Day One SMS [Synchronous
 Meteorological Satellite] System e:
 DOSS
Days at Sea e: **DAS**
Dayton Museum of Natural History, Dayton
 e: **ODaMNH**
Dazian Foundation for Medical Research
 e: **DFMR**
de-ice d: **di**
De-ionized water e: **DI-water**
De-Mineralized Water e: **DMW**
De Natura Deorum l: **Nat D**
de Rerum Natura l: **DRN**
De Soto National Wildlife Refuge e:
 DSNWR
Dead [air] Space e: **DS**
Dead Animal Removal e: **DAR**
dead flat in the water e: **dfitw**
Dead in the Water e: **DIW**
Dead Space Free e: **DSF**
Dead space gas e: **D**
dead space volume e: **VD**
Deaerating Cold Weather Oil System e:
 DCWOS
Debt-for-Nature Swap e: **DFNS**
Decadal to Centennial Climate Variability
 e: **DecCen**
Decade of North American Geology project
 e: **DNAG**
Decca-Langstreckenflächenüberdeckung
 d: **DELRAC**
Decenio Internacional para la Reducción de
 los Desastres Naturales s: **DIRDN**
DECHEMA Environmental Technology
 Equipment Data Bank e: **DETEQ**
Decision Support Systems for Health and
 Social Care e: **CARE SUPPORT-CP94-
334**
Decision Tree for Exploration Applications
 of Remote Sensing by Dekker and Dams
 e: **DEAR DAD**
Decisions of the Water Courts [South
 Africa] e: **Krummeck**
Deck Working Space e: **DWS**
Decommissioning and Environmental
 Operations e: **DEO**
Dedicated All-Weather aircraft e: **DAW**
Dee Weather Radar Project e: **DWRP**

Deep Observation and Sampling of the Earth's Continental Crust, Inc. *e:* **DOSECC**

Deep Observation Wells *e:* **DOW**

Deep Ocean Environment *e:* **DOE**

Deep Ocean Floor *e:* **DOF**

Deep Ocean Installation *e:* **DOI**

Deep Ocean Laboratory *e:* **DOL**

Deep Ocean Logging Profiler Hydrographic Instrumentation and Navigation *e:* **DOLPHIN**

Deep Ocean Manned Instrument[ed] Station[s] *e:* **DOMAINS**

Deep Ocean Mining [and] Environmental Study *e:* **DOMES**

Deep Ocean Mining Co.Ltd. *e:* **Domco**

Deep Ocean Mining Company *e:* **DOMCO**

Deep Ocean Mining Experimental Study *e:* **DOMES**

Deep Ocean Object Location and Recovery *e:* **DOOLAR**

Deep Ocean Optical Measurement *e:* **DOOM**

Deep Ocean Ordnance *e:* **DOO**

Deep Ocean Research Vehicle *e:* **DORV**

Deep Ocean Resources Development Co. Ltd. [India] *e:* **DORD**

Deep Ocean Search System *e:* **DOSS**

Deep Ocean Sediment Probe *e:* **DOSP**

Deep Ocean Sediment Probes *e:* **DOSPs**

Deep Ocean Technology *e:* **DOT**

Deep Ocean Test-In-Place and Observation System *e:* **DOTIPOS**

Deep Ocean Test Instrument Placement and Observation System *e:* **DOTIPOS**

Deep Ocean Tracer Experiment *e:* **DOTREX**

Deep Ocean Transponder *e:* **DOT**

Deep Ocean Trough *e:* **DOT**

deep ocean work boat *e:* **dowb**

Deep Oceanic Turbulence *e:* **DOT**

Deep Oceanographic Survey Vehicle *e:* **DOSV**

Deep Sea Diving Project *e:* **DSDP**

Deep Sea Diving School *e:* **DSDS**

Deep Sea Drilling Program[me] *e:* **DSDP**

Deep Sea Drilling Project [France, Germany, Japan, UK, USA, former USSR] *e:* **DSDP**

Deep Sea Exploration Association *e:* **DSEA**

Deep Sea Production System *e:* **DSPS**

Deep-Sea Research *e:* **Deep-Sea Res.**

Deep-Sea Research and Oceanographic Abstracs *e:* **Deep-Sea Res. Oceanogr. Abstr.**

Deep-Sea Research, Part B *e:* **Deep-Sea Res. B**

Deep-Sea Research, PartA *e:* **Deep-Sea Bes. A**

Deep Sea Reversing Thermometer *e:* **DSRT**

Deep-Sea Sediments *e:* **DSS**

Deep Sea Submergence Project *e:* **DSSP**

Deep-Sea System for Evaluating Acoustic Transducers *e:* **DEEPSEAT,** *e:* **DSSEAT**

Deep Sea Vehicle *e:* **DSV**

Deep Sea Winch *e:* **DSW**

Deep Space *e:* **DS**

Deep Space Aerial *e:* **DSA**

Deep Space Antenna *e:* **DSA**

Deep Space Communications Complex *e:* **DSCC**

Deep Space Instrument[ation] Facility *e:* **DSIF**

Deep Space Measurement *e:* **DSM**

Deep Space Net[work] *e:* **DSN**

Deep Space Object *e:* **DSO**

Deep Space Probe *e:* **DSP**

Deep Space Station *e:* **DSS**

Deep Space Station Complex *e:* **DSSC**

Deep Space Surveillance Radar *e:* **DSSR**

Deep Space Surveillance System *e:* **DS3**

Deep Space Tracking System *e:* **DSTS**

Deep Space Warning Radar *e:* **DSWR**

Deep Underwater Measuring Device *e:* **DUMD**

Deep Underwater Missile *e:* **DUM**

Deep Underwater Muon and Neutrino Detection (or Detector) *e:* **DUMAND**

Deep Underwater Nuclear Counter (or Counting) *e:* **DUNC**

Deep Underwater Nuclear Counting Device *e:* **DUNC Device**

Deep Water *e:* **DW**

Deep Water Fording Kit *e:* **DWFK**

Deep Water Isotopic Current Analyzer *e:* **DWICA**

Deep-Water Sediments *e:* **DWS**

Deepwater Escort Hydrofoil *e:* **DEH**

Deepwater Motion Picture System *e:* **DMPS**

deepwater port *e:* **dwp**

Deepwater Ports Act *e:* **DPA**

Deepwater Rice *e:* **DWR**

Deer Environment Ecology and Resources *e:* **DEER**

Deer Flat National Wildlife Refuge *e:* **DFNWR**

Defence & Aerospace Publishing Services SA *e:* **DAPS**

Defence and Civil Institute of Environmental Medicine *e:* **DECIEM**

Defence Chemical, Biological and Radiation Establishment *e:* **DCBRE**

Defence Chemical, Biological, and Radiation Laboratories *e:* **DCBRL**

Defence Imagery & Geospatial Organisation *e:* **DIGO**

Defence Medical and Dental Services Advisory Board *e:* **DMDSAB**

Defence Medical Equipment Depot *e:* **DMED**

Defence Medical Services *e:* **DMS**

Defence Nuclear, Biological and Chemical School *e:* **DNBC**

Defence (or Defense) and Civil Institute of Environmental Medicine *e:* **DCIEM**

Defence (or Defense) Mapping Agency Hydrographic Topographic Center *e:* **DMAHTC**

Defence (or Defense) Meteorological Satellite Program[me] *e:* **DMSP**

Defence Radiological Protection Service *e:* **DRPS**

Defence Research Establishment Valcartier *e:* **DREV**

Defence Research Establishment Valcartier, Canada Department of National Defence Courcelette, Québec *e:* **QQC**

Defence Research Medical Laboratory *e:* **DRML**

Defence & Space Talks *e:* **DST**

Defenders of Animals *e:* **D of A**

Defenders of Wildlife *e:* **DOW,** *e:* **DW**

defensa biológica *s:* **DB**

Defense Aid Vessels and Other Watercraft *e:* **DAV & OW**

Defense and Space *e:* **D&S**

Defense and Space Center *e:* **D & SC**

Defense Environmental Network and Information Exchange *e:* **DENIX**

Defense Environmental Quality Program Policy Memorandum *e:* **DEQPPM**

Defense Environmental Restoration Account *e:* **DERA**

Defense Environmental Restoration and Waste Management fund type code *e:* **TE**

Defense Environmental Restoration Information System *e:* **DERPMIS**

Defense Environmental Restoration (or Restriction) Program *e:* **DERP**

Defense Environmental Status Report *e:* **DESR[EP]**

Defense Fire Protection Association *e:* **DFPA**

Defense Health Agency *e:* **DHA**

Defense Health and Welfare Service *e:* **D.H.W.S.**

Defense Health Program *e:* **DHP**

Defense Hydrographic Initiative Laboratory *e:* **DHI**

Defense Info Infrastructure Common Operating Environment *e:* **DIICOE**

Defense Mapping Agency Aerospace Center *e:* **DMAAC**

Defense Mapping Agency Hydrographic Center *e:* **DMAHC**

Defense Mapping Agency Inter-American Geodetic Survey *e:* **DMAIAGS**

Defense Medical Activity *e:* **DMSA**

Defense Medical Facilities Office *e:* **DMFO**

Defense Medical Materiel Board *e:* **DMMB**

Defense Medical Regulating Information System *e:* **DMRIS**

Defense Medical Supply Center *e:* **DMSC**

Defense Medical System[s] Support Center *e:* **DMSSC**

Defense Personnel Support Center, Directorate of Medical Material Library, Philadelphia, PA *e:* **PPDef-M**

Defense Space Council *e:* **DSC**

Defense Space Operations Committee *e:* **DSOC**

Defense Waste and Environmental Restoration [program] *e:* **DWER**

Definierte geometrische Punkte *d:* **A\ B\ C\ D\ E**

Definitive Atmospheric Buoyant Boundary Layer Experiments *e:* **DABBLE**

definitive observation unit *e:* **dou**

Definitive Orbit Determination System *e:* **DODS**

Defueling Water Cleanup System *e:* **DWCS**

11-dehydrocorticosterone *e:* **compound A**

Dehydroepiandrosteron[e] *d:* **DEA**

Dehydroepiandrosteronsulfat *d:* **DS**

DeIonized [water] *e:* **DI**

deionized water *e:* **DIW**

Deionized Water *e:* **DW**

Deionized water System *e:* **DIS**

Dekrementieren *d:* **DEC**

Delaware, Florida, Georgia, Maryland, North Carolina, South Carolina, Virginia and West Virginia e: **South Atlantic States**

Delaware Geological Survey e: **DGS**

Delaware Health and Social Services e: **DHSS**

Delaware Medical Journal e: **Del Med J**

Delaware Museum of Natural History e: **Del Mus Nat Hist**, e: **DMNH**

Delaware Water Gap between New Jersey and Pennsylvania e: **Water Gap**

Delaware Water Gap National Recreation e: **DEWA**

Delaware Water Gap National Recreation Area e: **DWGNRA**

Delayed Action Space Missile e: **DASM**

Delayed Hydrogen Cracking e: **DHC**

Delayed Impact Space Missile e: **DISM**

Delayed Weather e: **DW**

Delft Atmospheric Research Radar e: **DARR**

Delivering Information in a Cellular Environment e: **DICE**

Deliwa-Verein e.V., Berufsverein für das Energie- und Wasserfach d: **Deliwa**

Delta Environmental Advisory Committee e: **DEAC**

Delta Instituut voor Hydrobialogisch Onderzoelk n: **DIIIO**

Delta National Wildlife Refuge e: **DNWR**

delta-wing orbiter e: **dwo**

Deltaic Watercourse e: **WTCD**

Demineralization Water e: **DEW**

Demineralized Water e: **DW**

Demineralized Water Storage Tank e: **DWST**

Demineralized Water System e: **DWS**

Demineralized Water Tank e: **DWT**

Demographic [and] Health Survey[s] e: **DHS**

demontieren d: **dem.**

Denaturated e: **DNTRD**

Denaturated DNA [Desoxyribonucleic Acid] e: **D-DNA**

denatured e: **denat**

Denatured e: **DNTRD**

Denatured molten salt reactors e: **DMSR**

Denaturierung d: **Denaturier.**

Denkschriften der Schweizerischen naturforschenden Gesellschaft d: **Denkschr. Schweiz. nat.forsch. Ges.**

Denmark Environment Centre e: **DEC**

Density of Water e: **DOW**

Dental Health International e: **DHI**

Dental health Maintenance Organization e: **DMO**

Dental Health Services Research Unit e: **DHSRU**

Dental Surgeon e: **DS**

Dental Surgeon [or Surgery] e: **D Surg**

Dentariae Medicinae Doctor e: **DMD**

Denver Museum of Natural History e: **DMNH**

Deo volente, weather permitting e: **Dvwp**

Deorbit e: **DEORB**

Deorbit, Entry and Landing e: **DEL**

Deorbit/Landing e: **D/L**

Departamento de Inspecao de Produtos de Origem Animal p: **DIPO**

Departamento de Microbiología s: **INTA**

Departamento de Prevenção e Combate as Calamidades Naturais p: **DPCCN**

Departamento Estadual de Geografia e Catografia p: **DEGC**

Departamento Medico Legal p: **DML**

Departamento Nacional de Geología s: **DENAGEO**

Departement de Geographie, Universite de Sherbrooke, Quebec f: **QSHERUG**

Departement de Geographie, Universite du Quebec, Chicoutimi, Quebec f: **QCUG**

Departement de Geologie et de Mineralogie, Universite Laval, Quebec, Quebec f: **QQLAGM**

Departement de Recherches Forestieres f: **DRF**

Department Innere Medizin d: **DIM**

Department of Aerophysics and Aerospace Engineering e: **AASE**

Department of Agriculture and Natural Resources e: **DANR**

Department of Animal Regulation e: **DAR**

Department of Civil and Environmental Engineering e: **DCEE**

Department of Civil and Geological Engineering e: **DCGE**

Department of Community & Health Services, Tasmania e: **DCHS**

Department of Community Services and Health e: **DCSH**

Department of Conservation and Environment e: **DCE**

Department of Conservation and Environment, Victoria e: **VDCE**

Department of Conservation and Natural Resources e: **DCNR**

Department of Consumer Protection e: **DCP**

Department of Defense - Council of Defense and Space Industry Associations e: **DOD-CODSIA**

Department of Defense Environmental Contamination e: **DODEC**

Department of Defense Manned Spaceflight e: **DDMS**

Department of Defense Medical Examination Review Board e: **DODMERB**

Department of Earth and Environmental Sciences e: **DEES**

Department of Earth and Space Sciences e: **DESS**

Department of Earth Atmospheric and Planetary Sciences e: **DEAPS**

Department of Earth Sciences e: **DES**

Department of Ecology e: **DOE**

Department of Ecology/Washington State e: **DOEC**

Department of Energy and Natural Resources e: **DENR**

Department of Energy environmental Checklist e: **DEC**

Department of Energy Headquarters, Environment & Health e: **DOE/HQ-EH**

Department of Energy Office of Environment, Safety and Health e: **DOE/EH**

Department of Energy, Office of Environmental Audit e: **DOE EH-24**

Department of Energy-Remote Console e: **DOE/RECON**

Department of Energys Voluntary Protection Program e: **DOE-VPP**

Department of Environment e: **DOE**

Department of Environment and Land Management e: **DELM**

Department of Environment and Natural Resources e: **DENR**

Department of Environment and Planning e: **DEP**

Department of Environment/ Atmospheric Environment Service e: **DOE/AES**

Department of Environment, Heritage and Aboriginal Affairs e: **DEHAA**

Department of Environment, Housing, and Community Development e: **DEHCD**

Department of Environment, Land and Planning e: **DELP**

Department of Environmental and Geographical Sciences e: **DEGS**

Department of Environmental Conservation e: **DEC**

Department of Environmental Management e: **DEM**

Department of Environmental Protection e: **DEP**

Department of Environmental Quality e: **DEQ**

Department of Environmental Regulation e: **DER**

Department of Environmental Resources e: **DER**

Department of Environmental Resources Management e: **DERM**

Department of Fish & Wildlife e: **DOFW**

Department of Fisheries and Oceans e: **DFO**

Department of Fish[eries] and Wildlife e: **DFW**

Department of Forest Management and Forest Geodesy e: **DFMFG**

Department of Geodesy and Geomatics Engineering e: **DGGE**

Department of Geographic Information e: **DGI**

Department of Geography, Bishop's University, Lennoxville, Quebec e: **QLBG**

Department of Geography, Lakehead University, Thunder Bay, Ontario e: **OPALG**

Department of Geography, Memorial University, St. John's, Newfoundland e: **NFSMG**

Department of Geography, Queen's University, Kingston, Ontario e: **OHQG**

Department of Geography, Sir George Williams Campus, Concordia University, Montreal, Quebec e: **QMGG**

Department of Geography, University of Manitoba, Winnipeg, Manitoba e: **MWUG**

Department of Geography, University of Regina, Saskatchewan e: **SRUG**

Department of Geography, University of Western Ontario, London e: **OLUG**

Department of Geological Scienc[es] e: **DGS**

Department of Geological Sciences e: **DOGS**

Department of Geological Sciences, McGill University, Montreal, Quebec e: **QMMGS**

Department of Geological Sciences Queens University, Kingston, Ontario e: **OKQGS**

Department of Geological Sciences Web
  Server e: **DGSWS**
Department of Geological Survey   e: **DGS**
Department of Geological Survey and
  Exploration e: **DGSE**
Department of Geology e: **DOG**
Department of Geology and Geography e:
  DGG
Department of Geology and Geophysics e:
  DGG, e: **DOGG**
Department of Geology and Petroleum
  Geology e: **DGPG**
Department of Geology and Planetary
  Sciences e: **DGPS**
Department of Geophysics and Astronomy
  e: **DGA**
Department of Geothermal Energy e: **DGE**
Department of Health e: **DH**, e: **DOH**
Department of Health and Community
  Services e: **DHCS**
Department of Health and Environmental
  Control e: **DHEC**
Department of Health and Environmental
  Science e: **DHES**
Department of Health and Family Services
  e: **DH&FS**
Department of Health and Hospitals e:
  DHH
Department of Health and Human Services
  e: **DHHS**, e: **DHHS**
[Department of] Health and Human
  Services e: **HHS**
Department of Health and Human Services.
  National Institute of Mental Health.
  Science Monographs e: **NSMOD2**
Department of Health and Mental Hygiene
  e: **DHMH**
Department of Health and Social Security
  e: **DHSC**, e: **DHSS**
Department of Health and Social Services
  e: **DHSS**
Department of Health, Education and
  Welfare e: **DHEW**
[Department of] Health, Education and
  Welfare e: **HEW**
Department of Health for Scotland e:
  D.H.S.
Department of Health, Housing and
  Community Services e: **DHHCS**
[Department of] Health, Housing, Local
  Government and Community Services e:
  HHLGCS
Department of Health & Human Resources
  e: **DHHR**
[Department of Health & Human Services]
  Office of Inspector General e: **OIG**
Department of Health Regulations e: **DHA**
Department of Health Sciences e: **DHS**
Department of Health Services e: **DHS**
Department of Health Toll Free MCH
  Number e: **TEL-LINK**
Department of Home Affairs and
  Environment e: **DHAE**
Department of Human Services and Health
  e: **DHSH**
Department of International Health-Johns
  Hopkins University e: **DIHJHU**
Department of Justice Land and Natural
  Resources Division e: **DJLNRD**
Department of Land and Natural Resources
  e: **DLNR**
Department of Land and Water
  Conservation e: **DLCW**, e: **DLWC**

Department of Land Surveying and
  Geoinformatics e: **DLSG**
Department of Lands, Forests and Waters
  e: **DLFW**
Department of Lands, Planning and
  Environment e: **DLPE**
Department of Legal Medicine e: **DLM**
Department of Mechanical and Aerospace
  Engineering e: **ME/AEROSPACE**
Department of Medical Assistance e:
  DMA
Department of Medical Education e: **DME**
Department of Medical Radiology e:
  D.M.R.
Department of Medicine and Surgery e:
  DMS
Department of Mental Health e: **DMH**
Department of Microbiology and
  Immunology e: **DMI**
Department of National Health and
  Population Development e: **DNHPD**
Department of National Health and Welfare
  e: **DNHW**
Department of Natural Resources e:
  DONR
Department of Natural Resources and
  Conservation e: **DNRC**
Department of Natural Resources and
  Energy e: **DNRE**
Department of Natural Resources and
  Environment e: **DNRE**
Department of Natural Resources and
  Environmental Control e: **DNREC**
Department of Natural Resources and
  Environmental Protection e: **DNREP**
Department of Natural Resources
  [Queensland] e: **SUNMAP**
Department of Occupational Health, Safety
  and Welfare e: **DOHSWA**
Department of Ocean Engineering e: **DOE**
Department of Oceanography e: **DO**
Department of Public Health e: **DPH**
Department of Public Safety -Emergency
  Medical Service e: **DPS-EMS**
Department of Rangeland Ecology and
  Management e: **DREM**
Department of Social and Health Services
  e: **DSHS**
Department of Space e: **DOS**
Department of the Army Panel on
  Environmental Psychology e: **DAPEP**
Department of the Arts, Heritage &
  Environment e: **DAHE**
Department of the Arts, Sport[s], the
  Environment, Tourism and Territories e:
  DASET[T]
Department of the Environment e: **DE**, e:
  DOE, e: **DoE**, e: **D of E**, e: **DOTE**
Department of [the] Environment and
  Heritage e: **DEH**
Department of the Environment, Sport and
  Territories e: **DEST**
Department of the Environment, Transport
  and the Regions e: **DETR**
Department of the Medical Director-
  General e: **D.M.D.G.**
Department of Theoretical Production
  Ecology e: **TPE**
Department of Urban Geology e: **DOUG**
Department of Water Affairs and Forestry
  e: **DWAF**
Department of Water and Power [of a city]
  e: **DWP**

Department of Water Resources e: **DWR**
Department of Water Supply e: **DWS**
Department of Water Supply, Gas and
  Electricity e: **DWSGAE**
Department of Water Supply, Gas, and
  Electricity e: **DWSG & E**
Department of Waters e: **DW**
Department of Wildlife and Fisheries,
  Louisiana Stream Control Commission,
  Baton Rouge e: **LBrWF-S**
Departmental Library, Environment Canada
  Ottawa, Ontario e: **OOFF**
DePaul Journal of Health Care Law e:
  DePaul J. Health Care L.
Dependent Meteorological Office e: **DMO**
Dependents' Medical Care Act e: **DMCA**
Deployable Advanced Fire Observation
  Simulator e: **DAFOS**
Deployable Medical System[s] e:
  DEPMEDS
Depolarization Aerosol and Backscatter
  Unattended Lidar e: **DABUL**
Depolarization Current e: **DC**
Depolarized Light Mixing e: **DLM**
Deposition of Biogeochemical[ly]
  Important Trace Species e: **DEBITS**
Deproteinated Natural Rubber e: **DP-NR**
Depth to Water, Recharge, Aquifer Media,
  Soil Media, Topography, Impact of the
  Vadose Zone, Conductivity e:
  DRASTIC
Deputy Assistant Chief Hydrologist e:
  DACH
Deputy Assistant Director-General of
  Medical Services e: **D.A.D.G.M.S.**
Deputy Assistant Director of Army Health
  e: **DADAH**
Deputy Assistant Director of Inland Water
  Transport Service e: **D.A.D.I.W.T.**
Deputy Assistant Director of Medical
  Service e: **DADMS**
Deputy Assistant Director of Medical
  Services e: **D.A.D.M.S.**
Deputy Assistant Secretary for Health e:
  DASH
Deputy Commander for Space Operations
  e: **DCSO**
Deputy Commander [of] Aerospace
  System[s] e: **DCAS**
Deputy Commissioner, Medical Services
  e: **DCMS**
Deputy Commissioner of Medical Services
  e: **D.C.M.S.**
Deputy Director General of Medical Service
  e: **DDGMS**
Deputy Director-General of Royal Air Force
  Medical Service e: **D.D.G.M.S.**
Deputy Director of Army Health e: **DDAH**
Deputy Director of Medical Organization
  for War e: **DDMOW**
Deputy Director of Medical Services e:
  DDMS
Deputy Director of Sea Transport e: **DD of
  ST**
Deputy for Space Launch Systems e: **YV**
Deputy Medical Director-General of the
  Navy e: **DMDGN**
Deputy Medical Officer e: **DMO**
Deputy of Space Systems e: **DSS**
Deputy Principal Medical Officer e:
  DPMO
Deputy Regional Medical Officer e:
  DRMO

Deputy Sea Transport Officer *e:* **DSTO**
Deputy Surgeon-General *e:* **DSG**
Derivati Biologici S.p.A. *e:* **DE BI**
Des Lacs National Wildlife Refuge *e:*
 DLNWR
Desarrollo para el Acceso a la Red
 Internacional en Observación *s:* **DARIO**
DesBrisay Museum and National Exhibit
 Centre, Bridgewater, Nova Scotia *e:*
 NSBDM
Descending Node Orbit *e:* **DNO**
Descent Orbit Insertion *e:* **DOI**
Descriptive Geometry Language *e:* **DGL**
Desert National Wildlife Refuge *e:*
 DNWR
Desert Protective Council *e:* **DPC**
Design Base Earthquake[s] *e:* **DBE**
Design Environmental Simulator *e:* **DES**
Design for Environment, Safety and Health
 e: **DfESH**
Design for [the] Environment *e:* **DFE**
Design Knowledge Acquisition and
 Redesign Environment *e:* **DEKLARE**
Design-To-Manufacture Environment *e:*
 DTME
Designated Agency Safety and Health
 Official *e:* **DASHO**
Designated Medical Examiner *e:* **DME**
Designated Official[s] for Environmental
 Matters *e:* **DOEM**
designation for an ice core drilled in 1977 at
 Law Dome, Antarctica *e:* **DE08**
Designation of an ice core drilled in 1977 at
 Law Dome, Antarctica *e:* **BHD**
Designed for Environment *e:* **DfE**
Designed Load Waterline *e:* **D.L.W.L.**
Designed Water Line *e:* **DWL**
Destacamento de enlace y observación *s:*
 DEO
Det Danske Geografiske Selskab *a:* **DGS**
Det Kongelige Danske Geografiske Selskab
 a: **DKDGS**
Det Norske Meteorologiske Institutt *N:*
 DNMI
detailed Atmospheric Radiation model *e:*
 ATRAD
Detection in Cluttered Environments
 programme *e:* **DICE**
Detection Radar Environmental Display *e:*
 DRED
Determination d'Orbite et
 Radiopositionement Intégré (ou Integres)
 par Satellite *f:* **DORIS**
Determination of Biological Characteristics
 e: **BIO-ASSAY**
Determination of the Ecological
 Consequences of Dredged Material
 Emplacement *e:* **DECODE**
Deterministic Bounded Cellular Space *e:*
 DBCS
Deuterated Hydrocyanic Acid *e:* **DCN**
Deuterated Hydrogen Y *e:* **DHY**
Deutscber Bauerndienst
 Tierversicherungsgesellschaft aG *d:*
 DBD
Deutsch-Brasilianische Gesellschaft für
 Medizin e.V. *d:* **DBGM**
Deutsch-österreichische tierärztliche
 Wochenschrift *d:* **DötW**
Deutsche Abwasser-Klärung *d:* **Deak**
Deutsche Aerospace [Administration] *d:*
 DASA

Deutsche Agentur fur
 Raumfahrtangelegenheiten GmbH *d:*
 DARA
Deutsche Akkreditierungs- und
 Zulassungsgesellschaft für
 Umweltgutachter *d:* **DAU**
Deutsche Akkreditierungsstelle Chemie
 GmbH *d:* **DACH**
Deutsche Akkreditierungsstelle für
 Informations- und
 Telekommunikationstechnik *d:*
 DEKITZ
Deutsche Akkreditierungsstelle Mineralöl
 GmbH *d:* **DASMIN**
Deutsche Akkreditierungsstelle Stahlbau
 und Energietechnik *d:* **DASET**
Deutsche Akkreditierungsstelle Technik *d:*
 DATech
Deutsche Arztgemeinschaft für
 Medizinische Zusammenarbeit *d:* **DAZ**
Deutsche Bundesstiftung Umwelt *d:* **DBU**
Deutsche Dokumentations Zentrale Wasser
 e.V. *d:* **DZW**
Deutsche Einheitsverfahren zur Wasser-,
 Abwasser- und Schlammuntersuchung *d:*
 DEV
Deutsche Erde *d:* **DE**
Deutsche Forschungs- und Versuchsanstalt
 für Luft- und Raumfahrt e.V. *d:* **DFVLR**
Deutsche Forschungsanstalt für Luft- und
 Raumfahrt e.V. *d:* **DFLR**, *d:* **DLR**
Deutsche Forschungsanstalt für Luft und
 Raumfahrttechnik *d:* **DFL**
Deutsche Geodätische Kommission *d:*
 DGK
Deutsche Geologische Beratergruppe El
 Salvador *d:* **DGBES**
Deutsche Geologische-Geophysikalische
 Mission [in Brasilien] *d:* **DGGM**
Deutsche Geologische Gesellschaft *d:*
 DGG
Deutsche Geologische Landesanstalt *d:*
 DGL
Deutsche Geologische Mission in
 Afghanistan *d:* **DGMA**
Deutsche Geologische Mission in Jordanien
 d: **DGMJ**
Deutsche Geologische Mission in Tansania
 d: **DGMT**
Deutsche Geophysikalische Gesellschaft
 e.V. *d:* **DGG**
Deutsche Geseilschaft für Anästhesie und
 Intensivmedizin *d:* **DGAI**
Deutsche Gesellschaft für Agrar- und
 Umweltpolitik *d:* **DGAU**
Deutsche Gesellschaft für
 Allgemeinmedizin *d:* **DEGAM**
Deutsche Gesellschaft für Arbeitsmedizin
 d: **DGAM**
Deutsche Gesellschaft für
 Bewässerungswirtschaft e.V. *d:* **DGBW**
Deutsche Gesellschaft für Biomedizinische
 Technik *d:* **DGBMT**
Deutsche Gesellschaft für
 Gesundheitsvorsorge e.V. *d:* **DGGV**
Deutsche Gesellschaft für Hydrokultur *d:*
 DGHK
Deutsche Gesellschaft für Hygiene und
 Mikrobiologie e.V. *d:* **DGHM**
Deutsche Gesellschaft für Innere Medizin
 d: **DGIM**
Deutsche Gesellschaft für
 Laboratoriumsmedizin *d:* **DGLM**

Deutsche Gesellschaft für Luft- und
 Raumfahrt e.V. *d:* **DGLR**
Deutsche Gesellschaft für Luft- und
 Raumfahrtmedizin *d:* **DGLRM**
Deutsche Gesellschaft für Manuelle
 Medizin *d:* **DGMM**
Deutsche Gesellschaft für Medizinische
 Dokumentation, Informatik und Statistik
 d: **DGMDS**
Deutsche Gesellschaft für Medizinische
 Dokumentation, Informatik und Statistik
 e.V. *d:* **GMDS**
Deutsche Gesellschaft für Medizinische
 Dokumentation und Statistik *d:* **DGMD**,
 d: **DMDS**
Deutsche Gesellschaft für Medizinische
 Informatik, Biometrie und Epidemiologie
 d: **GMDS**
Deutsche Gesellschaft für Medizinische
 Physik *d:* **DGMP**
Deutsche Gesellschaft für Medizinische
 Soziologie in der BRD e.V. *d:* **DGMS**
Deutsche Gesellschaft für Medizinische
 Tumortherapie *d:* **DGMR**
Deutsche Gesellschaft für Natur- und
 Völkerkunde Ostasiens *d:* **OAG**
Deutsche Gesellschaft für Nuklearmedizin
 d: **DGN**
Deutsche Gesellschaft für Perinatale
 Medizin *d:* **DGPM**
Deutsche Gesellschaft für Polarforschung
 d: **DeGePo**, *d:* **DGPL**
Deutsche Gesellschaft für
 Psychosomatische Medizin e.V. *d:*
 DGPM
Deutsche Gesellschaft für Raketentechnik
 und Raumfahrt *d:* **DGRR**
Deutsche Gesellschaft für Rechtsmedizin
 d: **DGRM**
Deutsche Gesellschaft für Sozialmedizin
 d: **DGS**
Deutsche Gesellschaft für Sozialmedizin
 und Prävention *d:* **DGSMP**
Deutsche Gesellschaft für Ultraschall in der
 Medizin *d:* **DGUM**
Deutsche Gesellschaft für Ultraschall in der
 Medizin e.V. *d:* **DEGUM**
Deutsche Gesellschaft für Umweltschutz
 e.V. *d:* **DGU**
Deutsche Gesellschaft für Verkehrsmedizin
 d: **DGVM**
[Deutsche Gesellschaft für Wehrmedizin
 und Wehrpharmazie e.V.]-Vereinigung
 ehemaliger Sanitätsoffiziere *d:* **VdSO**
Deutsche Gesellschaft für
 Weltraumforschung *d:* **DGfW**
Deutsche Gesellschaft für
 Wohn[ungs]medizin *d:* **DGW**
Deutsche Gesellschaft zur Förderung der
 Medizinischen Diagnostik *d:* **DGFMD**
Deutsche Gesundheitshilfe *d:* **DGH**
Deutsche Gewässerkundliche Mitteilungen
 d: **Dtsch. Gewässerk. Mitt.**
Deutsche Hydrographische Zeitschrift *d:*
 DHZ, *d:* **Dtsch. Hydrogr. Z.**
Deutsche Immobilien-Investierungs-AG *d:*
 DII
Deutsche interdisziplinäre Vereinigung für
 Intensivmedizin *d:* **DIVI**
Deutsche Kommission für Ozeanographie
 d: **DKfO**
Deutsche Kommission für
 Weltraumforschung *d:* **DKfW**

Deutsche Liga für Luft- und Raumfahrt e.V.
  d: **DLLR**
Deutsche Luft- und Raumfahrt,
  Forschungsbericht d: **DLR-FB**
Deutsche Medizinalzeitung d: **DMZtg**
Deutsche Medizinische
  Arbeitsgemeinschaft für Herd- und
  Regulationsforschung e.V. d: **DAH**
Deutsche Medizinische
  Arbeitsgemeinschaft für Herdforschung
  und Herdbekämpfung d: **D.A.H.**
Deutsche Medizinische Wochenschrift d:
  DMW, d: **Dtsch. Med. Wochenschr.**
Deutsche Medizinische Zeitschrift d:
  DMZ
Deutsche Meteorologische Gesellschaft e.V.
  d: **DMG**
Deutsche Naturfilm-Gesellschaft d:
  Dt.Nat.-F.
Deutsche Naturwissenschaftliche
  Gesellschaft e.V. d: **D.N.G. e.V.**
Deutsche Ozean-Reederei d: **D.O.R.**
Deutsche Pelztierzüchter Vereinigung d:
  DPV
Deutsche Phytomedizinische Gesellschaft
  e.V. d: **DPG**
Deutsche Raumfahrtagentur d: **DRA**
Deutsche Richtervereinigung für
  Pferdeleistungsprüfungen d: **DRV**
Deutsche Röntgengesellschaft -
  Gesellschaft für Medizinische Radiologie,
  Strahlenbiologie und Nuklearmedizin e.V.
  d: **DRG**
Deutsche Rundschau für Geographie d:
  DRG
Deutsche Rundschau für Geographie und
  Statistik d: **DRGS**
Deutsche Tierärzteschaft e.V. d: **DT**
Deutsche tierärztliche Wochenschrift d:
  DtäW
Deutsche Tierärztliche Wochenschrift d:
  Dtsch. Tierärztl. Wochenschr., d: **DTW**
Deutsche Tierschutzjugend e.V. d: **DTJ**
Deutsche Tiersperma Im- und Export-
  GmbH d: **Spermex**
Deutsche Tropenmedizinische Gesellschaft
  e.V. d: **DTG**
Deutsche Umwelt-Aktion d: **DUA**
Deutsche Union der Geologischen
  Wissenschaften d: **DUGW**
Deutsche Union für Geodäsie und
  Geophysik d: **DUGG**, d: **DUGG-West**
Deutsche Verband für Wasserwirtschaft und
  Kulturbau e.V. d: **DVWK**
Deutsche Vereinigung der Erdölgeologen
  and Erdölingenieure d: **DVGI**
Deutsche Versuchanstalt für Luft- und
  Raumfahrt d: **DLR**
Deutsche Versuchsanstalt für Luft- und
  Raumfahrt e.V. d: **DVL**
Deutsche Veterinärmedizinische
  Gesellschaft e: **DVMG**
Deutsche Veterinärmedizinische
  Gesellschaft e.V. d: **DVG**
Deutsche Wasserwirtschaft d: **DWassW**,
  d: **DWW**
Deutsche Zeitschrift für die gesamte
  gerichtliche Medizin e: **DZggM**
Deutsche Zeitschrift für Tiermedizin e:
  DZTM
Deutsche Zentrale für
  Volksgesundheitspflege e.V. d: **DZV**

Deutsche Zentren für Medizinische
  Vorsorge GmbH & Co. d: **DMZ**
Deutsche Zentren für medizinische
  Vorsorge GmbH & Co. KG d: **DZM**
Deutscher Anteil bei Advisory Group for
  Aerospace Research and Development d:
  DtA AGARD
Deutscher Anteil beim Hauptquartier Allied
  Forces Central Europe d: **DtA HQ
  AFCENT**
Deutscher Arbeitskreis Wasser e.V. d:
  DAW
Deutscher Arbeitskreis Wasserforschung
  d: **DZW**
Deutscher Arbeitskreis Wasserforschung
  e.V. d: **DAW**
Deutscher Ausschuss für den
  mathematischen und
  naturwissenschaftlichen Unterricht d:
  Damnu
Deutscher Bund für naturgemäße Lebens-
  und Heilweise [Naturheilbund] e.V. d:
  Naturheilbund
Deutscher Dachverband für Geoinformation
  d: **DDGI**
Deutscher Eisenbahn-Tiertarif d: **DETT**
Deutscher Geodätentag,
  Arbeitsgemeinschaft Deutsches
  Großteleskop d: **DGT**
Deutscher Grosshändlerverband für
  Heizungs-, Lüftungs- und Klimabedarf
  d: **DGH**
Deutscher Großhändlerverband für
  Heizungs-, Lüftungs- und Klimabedarf
  e.V. d: **DGH**
Deutscher Jugendbund für
  Naturbeobachtung d: **DJN**
Deutscher Kälte- und Klimatechnischer
  Verein e.V. d: **DKV**
Deutscher Landesausschuß für das
  Internationale Geophysikalische Jahr d:
  DL.-IGJ
Deutscher Medizinischer
  Informationsdienst e.V. d: **DMI**
Deutscher Medizinischer
  Informationsdienst-Nachrichten d: **DMI-
  Nachrichten**
Deutscher Militärgeographischer Dienst d:
  DMG
Deutscher Naturkundeverein e.V. d: **DNV**
Deutscher Naturschutzring e.V. d: **DNR**
Deutscher Pferdesport-Verband d: **DPV**
Deutscher Tierschutzbund d: **DTSchB**
Deutscher Tierschutzverein d: **DTV**
Deutscher Umwelttag d: **DUT**
Deutscher Unterwasserclub d: **DUC**
Deutscher Verband für Angewandte
  Geographie e.V. d: **DVAG**
Deutscher Verband für Wandern,
  Bergsteigen und Orientierungslauf d:
  DWBO
Deutscher Verband für Wasserwirtschaft
  e.V. d: **DVWW**
Deutscher Verband Medizinischer
  Bibliothekare d: **DVMD**
Deutscher Verband Medizinischer
  Dokumentare e.V. d: **DVMD**
Deutscher Verband neutraler
  Klassifizierungsunternehmen für
  Schlachttierkörper d: **DVK**
Deutscher Verband Technischer Assistenten
  in der Medizin d: **Dvta**

Deutscher Verband unabhängiger
  Überwachungsgesellschaften für
  Umweltschutz e.V. d: **DVÜ**
Deutscher Verein des Gas- und
  Wasserfaches e.V. d: **DVGW**, d: **GW**
Deutscher Verein für Gesundheitspflege d:
  DE VAU GE, d: **DVG**
Deutscher Verein für öffentliche
  Gesundheitspflege d: **DVföG**
Deutscher Verein von Gas- und
  Wasserfachmännern e.V. d: **DVGW**
Deutscher Verein zur Förderung des
  Mathematisch-Naturwissenschaftlichen
  Unterrichts e.V. d: **MNU**
Deutscher Wetterdienst d: **DW**
Deutscher Wetterdienst, Offenbach a.M. e:
  DWD
Deutscher Wetterdienst/Seewetteramt d:
  DWD/SWA
Deutscher Wetterdienst, Seewetteramt d:
  DWS
Deutsches Akkreditierungssystem
  Prüfwesen GmbH d: **DAP**
Deutsches Archiv für innere Medizin d:
  DAiM
Deutsches Archiv für klinische Medizin d:
  DaklM
Deutsches Fernerkundungs-Datenzentrum
  bei der Deutschen Forschungs- und
  Versuchsanstalt für Luft- und Raumfahrt
  d: **DFD/DFVLR**
Deutsches Geodätisches Forschungsinstitut
  d: **DGFI**
Deutsches Gesundheitsmuseum d: **DGM**
Deutsches Hydrographisches Institut d: **HI**
Deutsches Hydrographisches Institut,
  Hamburg d: **DHI**
Deutsches Institut für medizinische
  Dokumentation und Information d:
  DIMDI
Deutsches Institut für medizinische
  Dokumentation und Information Netz d:
  DIMDINET
Deutsches Kaltblutpferde-Leistungsbuch
  d: **DKLB**
Deutsches Klima-Rechenzentrum GmbH
  d: **DKRZ**
Deutsches Kollegium für psychosomatische
  Medizin e.V. d: **DKPM**
Deutsches Medizin Forum d: **DMF**
Deutsches Medizinisches Journal d:
  Dtsch. Med. J.
Deutsches Meteorologisches Jahrbuch d:
  DMJ
Deutsches Meteorologisches Jahrbuch für
  Bayern d: **DMJB**
Deutsches Ozeanographisches
  Datenzentrum, Hamburg e: **DOD**
Deutsches Zentralinstitut für
  Arbeitsmedizin d: **DZA**
Deutsches Zentrum für Klimaüberwachung
  d: **DZK**
Deutsches Zentrum für Luft- und Raumfahrt
  e.V. d: **DLR**
Deutschland, Europa, mobil, offen, kritisch,
  risikoreich, international, talentiert -
  Fördereinrichtung der Alexander-von-
  Humboldt-Stiftung d: **Demokrit**
Development Boiling Water Reactor e:
  DBWR
Development Investigations in Military
  Orbiting Systems e: **DEIMOS**

Development of Implementation Strategies for Approximation in Environment e: **DISAE**

Development of marine environment management technology e: **EUROMAR**

Development of Minicomputers Applications in an Environment of Scientific and Technological Information Centers e: **DOMESTIC**

Development of Polar Industries e: **DIPOL**

Development of Second Generation Expert Systems for Environmental Toxicology e: **EST-CP94-1029**

Development Platform for Unified Access to Enabling Environments e: **ACCESS**

Development Signature Approval e: **DSA**

Development Signature Approval - Fabrication Order e: **DSA/FO**

Developmental Biology e: **Dev Biol**

Developmental Biology Center e: **DBC**

Developmental Fast Hydrofoil e: **DFH**

Developmental Medicine and Child Neurology e: **Dev Med Child Neurol**

Developmental Medicine and Child Neurology. Supplement e: **Dev Med Child Neurol Suppl**

Developmental Orbital Research Laboratory e: **DORL**

Developmental Psychobiology e: **Dev Psychobiol**

Developmental Software Support Environment e: **DSSE**

Developmental Software Support Environment Plan e: **DSSEP**

Developments in Agricultural and Managed-forest Ecology e: **DAME**

Developments in Atmospheric Science e: **DAS**

Developments in Biological Standardization e: **Dev Biol Stand**

Developments in Economic Geology e: **DEG**

Developments in Geomathematics e: **DGM**

Developments in Geotechnical Engineering e: **DGE**

Developments in Geotectonics e: **DG**

Developments in Solar System and Space Science e: **DSSSS**

Developments in Solid Earth Geophysics e: **DSEG**

Developments in Water Science e: **DWS**

Dever Water Cont. e: **DWC**

Device for Automatic Remote Data Collection e: **DARC**, e: **DARDC**

Dextrose and Water e: **D/W**

Dextrose in Distilled Water e: **D/DW**

Dextrose 5% in Water e: **D5W**

Dezernat Militärhydrographie d: **DezMilHydro**

Di-Hydrogen e: **Di-H**

Diabetic Medicine e: **Diabet Med**

Diagnostic Imaging in Clinical Medicine [Germany] e: **Diagn. Imaging Clin. Med.**

Diagnostic Microbiology and Infectious Disease e: **Diagn Microbiol Infect Dis**

Dialogorientierte Daten-Ermittlungs-Methode d: **DIADEM**

Dialogorientierte Datenverarbeitung im Krankenhaus d: **DOUIK**

Dialogorientiertes Energie-Abrechnungs-System d: **DEAS**

Diaminohydroxypirimidin e: **DAHP**

Dianetics the Modern Science of Mental Health e: **DMSMH**

Diatomeenerde d: **DE**

Dickinson Journal of Environmental Law & Policy e: **Dick. J. Envtl. L.&Pol'y**

Dictionary of Abbreviations in Medicine e: **DAM**

Dictionary of Aeronautics and Aerospace Technology Abrreviations e: **DAATA**

Dictionary of Biological Sciences e: **DBS**

Dictionary of Geography e: **DGeogr**

Dictionary of Geological Terms e: **DGT**

Dictionary of Geology e: **DGeol**

Dictionnaire des Médicaments Vétérinaires f: **DMV**

die von Natriumdampf emittierte gelbe Spektrallinie d: **D-Linie**

Die Wasserkraft d: **WassKr**

Die Wasserwirtschaft d: **WassW**

died a natural death e: **dnd**

Dienst Umwelt/Bundesamt für Statistik d: **UW/BFS**

Dienstbeschwerde d: **D.-Beschw.**

Diethylaminopropyl Chloride Hydrochloride e: **DEPC**

Difesa Aerea Costiera i: **DACOS**

difesa costiera i: **D.C.**

Different Orbitals for Different Spin e: **DODS**

differential absorption remote sensing e: **dars**

Differential Geometry e: **DG**

Differential Orbit Correction and Ephemeris Tables e: **DOCET**

Differential Orbit Improvement e: **DOI**

Differential Pressure Sea Water e: **DPSW**

Differential Puls[e] Polarography e: **DPP**

differential space justifier e: **dsj**

Differentially Pumped Environmental Chamber e: **DIFPEC**

differentielle Puls-Polarographie d: **DPP**

Diffusion et Prospection médicale en Afrique f: **DPA**

diffusionsselbstjustiert d: **DSA**

Digests of Environmental Impact Statements e: **EIS**

Digital Alarm, Remote Telemetry System e: **DARTS**

Digital Automatic Weather and NOTAM System e: **DAWNS**

Digital Automatic Weather Network e: **DAWN**

Digital Communication through Orbiting Needles e: **DICON**

Digital Electronic Signature Test e: **DIGEST**

Digital Geobailistic Computer e: **DCBC**

Digital Geoballistic Computer e: **DGBC**, e: **DGC**

Digital Geographic Information Exchange Standard e: **DGIES**

Digital Geographic Information Exchange Standards e: **DIGEST**

Digital Geographic Information Working Group e: **DGIWG**

Digital Geographic Research Corporation e: **DGRC**

Digital-Geometrie-orientiertes System d: **DIGOS**

Digital Geospatial Data Files e: **DGDF**

Digital Geospatial Metadata e: **DGM**

Digital Ice Forecast and Analysis System e: **DIFAS**

Digital Image Processing Of Remotely Sensed Data e: **DIPORS**

digital implementierte Analogverarbeitung e: **DIAP**

Digital Imposition Geometry e: **DIG**

Digital Library for Earth System Education e: **DLESE**

Digital Oceanographic Data Acquisition System e: **DODAS**

Digital Optical Protection System e: **DOPS**

Digital Orbiting Voice Encoder e: **DOVE**

Digital Remote Antenna Driver e: **DRAD**

Digital Remote Measurement Unit e: **DRMU**

Digital Signature Algorithm e: **DAS**

Digital Space Trajectory Measurement [System] e: **DISTRAM**

Digital Space Trajectory Measurement System e: **DISTRAMS**, e: **DISTRAM System**

Digital Transmission Content Protection e: **DTCP**

Digital Voice Protection e: **DVP**

Digital Weather Processing System e: **DWIPS**

Digitale Umweltqualitätskarte Dormund d: **UQUADO**

Digitally Integrated Geographic Information Technologies e: **DIGIT**

dihydro-dimethyl-benzopyran butyric acid e: **dba**

Dihydrodiphosphopyridine Nucleotide, Reduced Form e: **DPNH**

Dihydrofolsäure-Reduktase d: **DR**

Dihydropteridinreduktase d: **DPHA**

Dihydrostreptomycin d: **DSM**, d: **DST**

Dihydrouridine e: **hU**

Dilated Space e: **DS**

DIMDI [Deutsches Institut für medizinische Dokumentation und Information] Datenbank d: **DDBG**

DIMDI [Deutsches Institut für medizinische Dokumentation und Information] Information Research System d: **DIRS**

DIMDI [Deutsches Institut für medizinische Dokumentation und Information] Listen d: **DLPG**

Dinas Hidro Oceanografi in: **DISHIDROS**

Dinámica de los Ecosistemas y los Recursos Biológicos s: **EDLR**

Dinámica de los Océanos y el Clima s: **ODC**

Diotamaceous Earth e: **DE**

Dipioma in Medical Radiology e: **DMR**

Diplom-Biologe d: **Dipl.-Biol.**

Diplom-Geograph d: **Dipl: Geogr.**

Diplom-Geologe d: **Dipl.-Geol.**

Diplom-Geophysiker d: **Dipl: Geophys.**

Diplom-Hydrologe d: **Dipl.-Hydrol.**

Diplom-Meteorologe d: **Dipl: Met.**

Diploma-Health Service Administration e: **DHSA**

Diploma in Aviation Medicine e: **D.Av.Med.**

Diploma in Ayurvedic Medicine e: **DAM**

Diploma in Ayurvedic Medicine and Surgery e: **Dip AMS**

Diploma in Basic Medical Sciences e: **Dip BMS**

Diploma in Child Health *e:* **DCH,** *e:* **DCHID.C.H.**

Diploma in Clinical Medicine of [the] Tropics *e:* **DCMT**

Diploma in Dental Public Health *e:* **DDPH**

Diploma in Dermatological Medicine *e:* **DDM**

Diploma in Forensic Medicine *e:* **DFM**

Diploma in General Medicine *e:* **DGM**

Diploma in Genito-Urinary Medicine *e:* **Dip.G-Um**

Diploma in Geriatric Medicine *e:* **Dip.Ger.Med**

Diploma in Gynaecology and Obstetrics *e:* **DGO,** *e:* **Dip G & O**

Diploma in Health and Social Welfare *e:* **DipHSW**

Diploma in Health Services Management *e:* **DipHSM**

Diploma in History of Medicine and Scientific Arts *e:* **DHMSA**

Diploma in Industrial Health *e:* **DIH**

Diploma in Medical Care in Catastrophes *e:* **DMCC**

Diploma in Medical Jurisprudence *e:* **DMJ**

Diploma in Medical Laboratory Technology *e:* **DMLT**

Diploma in Medical Pathology and Bacteriology *e:* **DMPB**

Diploma in Medical Psychology *e:* **DMP**

Diploma in Medical Radio-Diagnosis *e:* **DMRD**

Diploma in Medical Radio-Therapy *e:* **DMRT**

Diploma in Microbiology *e:* **Dip.Micr.,** *e:* **Dip Micro**

Diploma in Naturopathy *e:* **ND**

Diploma in Obstetrics and Gynaecology *e:* **DipO & G**

Diploma in Obstetrics of the Royal College of Obstetricians and Gynaecologists *e:* **D.Obst.R.C.O.G.**

Diploma in Occupational Health and Safety *e:* **DOHS**

Diploma in/of Industrial Health *e:* **DIH**

Diploma in/of Medical Services Administration *e:* **DMSA**

Diploma in/of Public Health *e:* **DPH**

Diploma in Ophthalmic Medicine and Surgery *e:* **D.O.M.S.**

Diploma in Physical Medicine *e:* **D Phys Med**

Diploma in Psychological Medicine *e:* **DPM,** *e:* **DPM/D.P.M.**

Diploma in Public Health Dentistry *e:* **DPHD**

Diploma in Public Health Nursing *e:* **DPHN**

Diploma in the History of Medicine of the Society of Apothecaries of London *e:* **DHMSA**

Diploma in [the] Medical Radiology and Electology *e:* **D.M.R.E.**

Diploma in the Philosophy of Medicine of the Society of Apothecaries of London *e:* **DPMSA**

Diploma in Tropical Medicine and Hygiene *e:* **DTM&H**

Diploma in Tropical Medicine[s] *e:* **DTM**

Diploma in Tropical Public Health *e:* **DTPH**

Diploma in Tropical Veterinary Medicine *e:* **DTVM**

Diploma in Veterinary Public Health *e:* **DVPH**

Diploma in Veterinary State Medicine *e:* **D.V.S.M.**

Diploma in[of] Dental Health *e:* **DDH**

Diploma of Community Child Health *e:* **DCCH**

Diploma of Meteorology *e:* **DMet**

Diploma of the College of Obstetricians and Gynaecologists *e:* **DCOG**

Diploma of the Royal College of Obstetricians and Gynaecologists *e:* **DRCOG**

Diploma of the Royal College of Obstetrics and Gynaecology *e:* **Dip.Obst.RCOG**

Diploma of Veterinary State Medicine *e:* **DVSM**

Diplomagrarbiologe *d:* **Dipl.Agr.Biol.**

Diplomate of the National Board of Medical Examiners *e:* **DNB**

Diplomate of the Royal College of Obstetricians and Gynaecologists *e:* **D Obst RCOG**

Diplomate of Tropical Medicine and Hygiene *e:* **DTMH**

Diplombiologe *d:* **Dipl.Biol.**

Diplôme de l'École Supérieure Technique *f:* **DEST**

Diplomgeometer *d:* **Dipl.-Geom.**

Diplomgeophysiker *d:* **Dipl.-Geoph.**

Diplommedizin-pädagoge *d:* **Dipl.-Med.-Päd.**

Diplommediziner *d:* **Dipl.-Med.**

Diplomozeanograph *d:* **Dipl.-Ozeanogr.**

Direção Nacional de Geografia e Cadastro *p:* **DINAGECA**

Direccão de Servicos de Geologia e Minas *p:* **DSGM**

Direccão Nacional de Geografia e Cadastro *p:* **Dinageca**

Direccion de Geológia de la Nación [Argentina] *s:* **DGN**

Dirección de Geologia, Minas y Petrolio *s:* **DGMP**

Dirección de Geología de la Nación *s:* **DGN**

Dirección de Recursos Naturales Renovables *s:* **DRNR**

Dirección del Servicio Geografico Militar *s:* **DSGM**

Dirección General de Geografía *s:* **DGG**

Dirección General de Geografía y Meteorología *s:* **DGGM**

Dirección General de Geologia y Minas *s:* **DGGM**

Dirección General de Meteorología del Uruguay *s:* **DGMU**

Dirección General de Minas y Geologia *s:* **DGMG**

Dirección General de Oceanografia *s:* **DGO**

Dirección General de Oceanografia y Senalamiento Maritimo *s:* **DGOSM**

Dirección General de Recursos Naturales [Honduras] *s:* **DGRN**

Dirección General de Recursos Naturales Renovables *s:* **DIRENIARE**

Dirección General del Servicio Nacional Meteorológico *s:* **DGSNM**

Dirección Nacional de Mineria y Geologia *s:* **DMMG**

Dirección Nacional de Recursos Naturales Renovables *s:* **RENARE**

Direct Access Device [for] Space Management *e:* **DADSM**

Direct Access Storage Space Allocation *e:* **DASSA**

Direct Access to Remote Data-bases Overseas *e:* **DARDO**

Direct Current Polarography *e:* **DCP**

Direct Current Reverse Polarity *e:* **DCRP**

Direct Geodetic Constraint *e:* **DGC**

Direct Geodetic Constraint Method *e:* **DGCM**

Direct Machine Environment *e:* **DME**

Direct Read-Out Weather Satellite *e:* **DROWS**

Direct Readout Equatorial Weather Satellite *e:* **DREWS**

Directed Cyclic Biologic *e:* **DCB**

Directed Information Communications Environment *e:* **DICE**

Directia Economiei Forestiere *ru:* **DEF**

Directia Generală a Producției Animale *ru:* **DGPA**

Directia Generala Geo-Topografică si de Organizare a Tertoriului *ru:* **DGGTOT**

Directia Generala Productiei Animale *i:* **DGPA**

Direction de la Geologie et des Mines *f:* **DGM**

Direction de la Geologie [Morroco] *f:* **MDG**

Direction de la Géologie et de la Prospection Minière *f:* **DGPM**

Direction de la Météorologie Nationale *f:* **DMN**

Direction de la protection et de la sécurité de défense *f:* **DPSD**

Direction de la Protection et de la Sécurité de la Défense *f:* **D.P.S.D.**

Direction de la Technologie de l'Environnement Industriel et des Mines *f:* **DITEIM**

Direction de l'Amernagement du Territoire et de la Protection de l'Environnement *f:* **DATPE**

Direction de l'Hygiène du Milieu /Environmental Health Directorate *f:* **DHM/EHD**

Direction des Mines et de la Geologie *f:* **SDMG**

Direction des Mines et de la Géologie *f:* **DMG**

Direction des Recherches Géologiques et Minires *f:* **DRGM**

Direction des Routes et de la Circulation Routière *f:* **DRCR**

Direction des Services Médicaux et Sociaux *f:* **DSMS**

Direction du Service Géologique National *f:* **DSGN**

Direction Départementale de la Protection Civile *f:* **DDPC**

Direction Générale de la Protection de la Santé *f:* **DGP,** *f:* **DGPS**

Direction Générale des Quartiers, Travaux et Fortifications *f:* **D.G.Q.T.F.**

Direction Interdepartementale de l'Industrie *f:* **DII**

Direction Interdépartementale des Anciens Combattants et vicitimes de la guerre *f:* **DIAC**

Direction Régionale de l'Environnement *f:* **DIREN**

Direction Régionale de l'Industrie, de la
Recherche de l'Environnement *f:*
DRIRE

Direction supérieure des quartiers de
travaux *f:* **DSQT**

Direction Technologique de
l'Environnement Industriel et des Mines
f: **DTEIM**

Directional Ocean Wave Spectrum *e:*
DOWS

Director-General, Joint Medical Services
e: **DGJMS**

Director-General, Medical Services [Air]
e: **DGMS[Air]**

Director General of Army Medical Services
e: **DGAMS**

Director-General of Emergency Medical
Service[s] *e:* **D.G.E.M.S.**

Director General of Medical Services *e:*
DGMS

Director General of Weapons [Underwater
Division] *e:* **DGW[U]**

Director-General, [Royal Air Force]
Medical Services *e:* **D.G.M.S.**

Director General Underwater Weapons *e:*
DGUW

Director General, Underwater Weapons *e:*
DGUW[N]

Director of Aviation Medicine *e:* **DAMed**

Director of Base Medical Services *e:*
DBMS

Director of Biological Research *e:* **D.B.R.**

Director of Control Environment Operations
e: **DCEO**

Director of Health and Safety *e:* **HSDir**

Director of Health & Human Services *e:*
DH&HS

Director of Inland Water Transport *e:*
D.I.W.T.

Director of Medical Acitivities *e:* **DMEDA**

Director of Medical and Health Services *e:*
D.M.H.S.

Director of Medical Education *e:* **DME**

Director of Medical Services *e:* **D.M.S.**

Director of Naval Sea Transport *e:* **DNST**

Director of Orbital Verification *e:* **DOV**

Director of Sea Transport[ation] *e:* **DST**

Director of the Office of Oceanography *e:*
DOO

Director of Undersurface [or Underwater]
Warfare *e:* **DUSW**

Director of Underwater Weapon Material
Department *e:* **D.U.W.M.**

Director of Underwater Weapon[s] Material
Department *e:* **DUWM**

Director-Office of Oceanography *e:* **DOO**

Directoraat Generaal Telecommunicatie en
Post van het Ministerie van Verkeer en
Waterstaat *e:* **DGTP**

Directorate General of Geological Surveys
e: **DGGS**

Director[ate]-General of Royal Air Force
Medical Service *e:* **D.G.R.A.F.M.S.**

Directorate General XI [Environment,
Nuclear Safety and Civil Protection] of
the European Commission *e:* **DG XI**

Directorate Meteorological Office *e:* **DMO**

Directorate of Aerospace Combat Systems
e: **DACS**

Directorate of Aerospace Safety *e:* **DAS**

Directorate of Biological Operations *e:*
DBO

Directorate of Conservation and
Environment *e:* **DCE**

Directorate of Environmental Geology *e:*
DEG

Directorate of Geographic Affairs *e:* **DAG**

Directorate of Geophysics Research *e:*
DGR

Directorate of Hydrography and Navigation
e: **DHN**

Director[ate] of Medical and Sanitary
Services *e:* **DMSS**

Directorate of Medical Research *e:* **DMR**

Directorate of Medical Systems *e:* **SG**

Director[ate] of Naval Medical Services *e:*
DNMS

Director[ate] of Naval Weather Service[s]
e: **DNWS**

Directorate of Strategic Military
Geographic Information *e:* **DSMGI**

Director[ate] of Underwater Weapons *e:*
DUW

Directoria da Produção Animal *p:* **DIPAN**

Director's Health & Fitness Award *e:*
DHFA

Directors of Nordic Hydrological Institutes
e: **CHIN**

Directorship of National Parks and Wildlife
e: **DNPW**

Directory of Environmental Resources *e:*
DER

Direktorat for Naturforvaltning *N:* **DN**, *N:*
DNF

Direktorat Geologi *in:* **DGI**

Direktorat Geologie *d:* **DGI**

Diretoria de Hidrografia e Navegaçao *p:*
DHN

Disaster Medical Assistance Team *e:*
DMAT

Discovery of Natural Latent Ability *e:*
DNLA

Discrete and Computational Geometry *e:*
Discrete Comput. Geom.

Discrete Space and Discrete Time *e:*
DSDT

Discrete-Space Discrete-Time *e:* **DSDT**

Discrete Transient Protection *e:* **DTP**

Disease Management & Health Outcomes
e: **DMHO**

disease of medical progress *e:* **DOMP**

Disease Vector Ecology and Control Center
e: **DVECC**

Disk Operated Search System for
Information Executed Remotely *e:*
DOSSIER

Disk Remote Operating System *e:* **DROS**

Disk Space Management *e:* **DSM**

Disk Space Manager *e:* **DSM**

Diskussionsforum Medizinische Ethik *d:*
Diskussionsforum Med Ethik

Dismounted Battlespace Battle Lab *e:*
DBBL

Dismounted Warfighting Battlespace
Laboratory *e:* **DWBL**

Displaced Workers Health Benefits Program
e: **DWHBP**

Displacement Waterline *e:* **D.W.L.**

Disposable Eye Respiratory Protection *e:*
DERP

disposing of anything unwanted in at least
six fathoms of water *e:* **deep 6**

Dispositif de Protection Urbaine *f:* **D.P.U.**

Distant Space Radio Center *e:* **DSRC**

distilled water *e:* **dw**

Distribución de datos meteorológicos *s:*
MDD

Distributed Application Programming
Environment *e:* **DAPE**

Distributed Audio Video Environment *e:*
DAVE

Distributed Computing Environment
Remote Procedure Call *e:* **DCE-RPC**

Distributed coordination Function
Interframe Space *e:* **DIFS**

Distributed Geographical Information
Systems *e:* **DISGIS**

Distributed Integrated Multimedia
Publishing Environment *e:* **DIMPE**

Distributed Interactive Processing
Environment *e:* **DIPE**

Distributed Interactive Virtual Environment
e: **DIVE**

Distributed Management and Coordination
of Scheduling System in a Multisite
Production Environment *e:* **DISCO**

Distributed Management Environment *e:*
DME

Distributed Object Environment *e:* **DOE**

Distributed Object Management
Environment *e:* **DOME**

Distributed Ocean Data System *e:* **DODS**

Distributed Oceanographic Data System *e:*
DODS

Distributed System[s] Environment *e:*
DSE

Distributed Virtual Environment *e:* **DVE**

Distribution of Oceanographic Data on
Isotropic Levels *e:* **DODIS**

Distribution Register of organic Pollutants
in water *e:* **WDROP**

District Health Authority *e:* **DHA**

District Health Committee *e:* **DHC**

District Health Committee News *e:* **DHC
News**

District Health Office[r] *e:* **DHO**

District Medical Committee *e:* **DMC**

District Medical Officer *e:* **DISTMEDO**,
e: **DMO**

District of Columbia Health Science
Information Network *e:* **DOCHSIN**

District of Columbia Health Sciences
Information Network *e:* **DOCHSINE**

District Sea Transport Officer *e:* **DSTO**

Ditch [Intracoastal Waterway] *e:* **Ditch**

Divers' Environmental Survey *e:* **DES**

Dividends from Space *e:* **DFS**

Diving Medical Advisory Committee *e:*
DMAC

Divisao de Defesa Sanitaria Animal *p:*
DDSA

Divisão de Geologia e Mineralogia *p:*
DGM

Divisão de Inspecão de Produtos de Origem
Animal *p:* **DIPOA**

Divisão de Inspeção e Fiscalização de
Produtos de Origem Animal *p:* **DIFPOA**

Divisao de Nutricao Animal e Agrostologia
p: **DINAGRO**

Divisão Nacional de Vigilância Sanitária
Medicamentos [Brazil] *p:* **Dimed**

divisie verdeelplaats *n:* **divvpl**

Division Air Space Management Element
e: **DAME**

Division Airspace Management Element
System *e:* **DAMES**

Division des Gites Mineraux de l'Association Geologique du Canada *f:* **DGM**

Division for Ocean Affairs and the Law of the Sea *e:* **DOALOS**

Division for Physical and Health Disabilities *e:* **DPHD**

Division Medical Operations Center *e:* **DMOC**

Division Medical Supply Officer *e:* **DMSO**

Division of Adolescent and School Health *e:* **DASH**

Division of Allied Health Monpower *e:* **DAHM**

Division of Atmospheric Research *e:* **DAR**

Division of Atmospheric Sciences *e:* **ATM**

Division of Atmospheric Surveillance *e:* **DAS**

Division of Biological Standard[s] *e:* **DBS**

Division of Biologics Standards *e:* **DBS**

Division of Biology and Medicine *e:* **DBM**

Division of Cancer Biology and Diagnosis *e:* **DCBD**

Division of Cancer Biology, Diagnosis and Centers *e:* **DCBDC**

Division of Consumer Protection *e:* **DCP**

Division of Earth Sciences *e:* **DES**

Division of Emergency Health Services *e:* **DEHS**

Division of Energy and Environmental Assessment *e:* **DEEA**

Division of Environment Information and Assessment of UNEP *e:* **DEIA**

Division of Environmental Health Laboratory Sciences *e:* **EHLS**

Division of Environmental Impact Analysis *e:* **DEIA**

Division of Environment[al] Information and Assessment *e:* **DEIA**

Division of Environmental Protection *e:* **DEP**

Division of Environmental Radiation *e:* **DER**

Division of Environmental Sciences *e:* **DES**

Division of General Medical Sciences *e:* **DGMS**

Division of General Practice Central Sydney Area Health Service *e:* **DGPCSAHS**

Division of Geological and Geophysical Surveys *e:* **DGGS**

Division of Geology and Land Survey *e:* **DGLS**

Division of Geothermal Energy *e:* **DGE**

Division of Geothermal Research *e:* **DGR**

Division of Health Assessment and Consultation *e:* **DHAC**

Division of Health Examination Statistics *e:* **DHES**

Division of Health Manpower Educational Services *e:* **DHMES**

Division of Health Studies *e:* **DHS**

Division of Healthcare Quality Promotion *e:* **DHQP**

Division of Indian Health *e:* **DIH**

Division of International Medical Education *e:* **DIME**

Division of Marine Meteorology and Oceanography *e:* **DMMO**

Division of Medical Radiation Exposure *e:* **DMRE**

Division of Medical Standards *e:* **DMS**

Division of Medical Technology *e:* **DMT**

Division of Mental Health & Developmental Disabilities *e:* **DMHDD**

Division of Microbiology and Infectious Diseases *e:* **DMID**

Division of Mines and Geology *e:* **DMG**

Division of Natural Resources *e:* **DNR**

Division of Natural Resource[s] Review and Coordination *e:* **DNRRC**

Division of Occupational Safety & Health *e:* **DOSH**

Division of Oceanic Sciences *e:* **OCE**

Division of Oceanography *e:* **DO**

Division of Polar Programs *e:* **DPP**

Division of Radiological Health *e:* **DRH**

Division of Regional Medical Programs *e:* **DRMP**

Division of Reproductive Health *e:* **DRH**

Division of Sea Fisheries *e:* **DSF**

Division of Space Nuclear Systems *e:* **DSNS**

Division of Technology and Environmental Education *e:* **DTEE**

Division of Veterinary Services and Animal Industry *e:* **DVSAI**

Division of Water Planning *e:* **DWP**

Division of Water Pollution Control *e:* **DWPC**

Division of Water Resources *e:* **DOWR**, *e:* **DWR**, *e:* **DWRM**

Division of Wildlife *e:* **DOW**

Division of Wildlife and Ecology *e:* **DWE**, *e:* **W&E**

Division of Wildlife Resources *e:* **DWR**

Divisional Sea Transport Office[r] *e:* **DSTO**

Divisions-Medizinalpunkt *d:* **DMP**

Divisionsmedizinpunkt *d:* **DVP**

División de Conservación de Recursos Naturales *s:* **DICOREN**

Dixie College, St. George, UT *e:* **UStgD**

DNA and Cell Biology *e:* **DNA Cell Biol**

Doctor medicinae *l:* **Dr med**

doctor medicinae dentariae *l:* **Dr. med. deot**

Doctor medicinae universae *l:* **Dr med univ**

Doctor medicinae veterinariae *l:* **Dr med vet**

Doctor of Biological Chemistry *e:* **D.Bi.Chem.**, *e:* **Dr Bi Ch**, *e:* **Dr Bi Chem**

Doctor of Biological Engineering *e:* **D Bi E**, *e:* **D Bi Eng**

Doctor of Biological Physics *e:* **D Bi Phy**

Doctor of Biological Sciences *e:* **D Bi S**, *e:* **D Bi Sc**

Doctor of Comparative Medicine *e:* **DCM**, *e:* **MCD**

Doctor of Dental Medicine *e:* **DDM**, *e:* **D.M.D.**, *e:* **MDD**

Doctor of Environment *e:* **DEnv**

Doctor of Environmental Design *e:* **DED**, *e:* **DEnvDes**

Doctor of Environmental Studies *e:* **DES**

Doctor of Geography *e:* **Dr Geo**

Doctor of Geological Engineering *e:* **D Ge E**, *e:* **D Ge Eng**

Doctor of Geological Sciences *e:* **DGS**

Doctor of Geology *e:* **Dr Ge**

Doctor of Geopolitics *e:* **Dr GP**

Doctor of Health and Safety *e:* **HSD**

Doctor of Health Science[s] *e:* **D.H.S.**

Doctor of Medical Dentistry *e:* **DMD**

Doctor of Medical Jurisprudence *e:* **DMJ**, *e:* **MJD**

Doctor of Medical Science *e:* **DMedSc**, *e:* **DM Sc**, *e:* **Med Sc D**, *e:* **MSD**

Doctor of Medical Science[s] *e:* **DMS**

Doctor of Medical Sciences *e:* **Sc D Med**

Doctor of Medical Technology *e:* **DMT**

Doctor of Medicine *e:* **D.M.**, *e:* **DMed**, *e:* **Dr Med**, *e:* **M.D.**

Doctor of Meteorology *e:* **D. Meteor.**

Doctor of Microbiology *e:* **D Mic**, *e:* **MIC D**

Doctor of Natural History *e:* **N.H.D.**

Doctor of Natural Philosophy *e:* **Dr N Ph**, *e:* **N.Ph.D.**

Doctor of Natural Science *e:* **Dr Nat.Sci**, *e:* **Nat. Sc.D.**

Doctor of Natural Sciences *e:* **Dr Sci Nat**, *e:* **DScNat**

Doctor of Naturopathy *e:* **D Nat**, *e:* **NMD**

Doctor of Oriental Medicine *e:* **OMD**

Doctor of Osteopathic Medicine *e:* **DO**

Doctor of Pediatric Medicine *e:* **D.P.M.**

Doctor of philosophiae naturalis *l:* **Dr phil nat**

Doctor of Philosophy [Medicine] *e:* **PhD [Med]**

Doctor of Physical Biology *e:* **DPB**

Doctor of Physical Medicine *e:* **DPM**

Doctor of Podiatric Medicine *e:* **DPM**

Doctor of Prevent[at]ive Medicine *e:* **Dr Pr M**

Doctor of Public Health *e:* **D.P.H.**, *e:* **DrPH**, *e:* **PHD**

Doctor of Public Health and Hygiene *e:* **Dr PH Hy**

Doctor of Public Health Education *e:* **DPH Ed**

Doctor of Public Health Engineering *e:* **DPHE**, *e:* **DPH Eng**

Doctor of Public Health Nursing *e:* **DPHN**

Doctor of Science in Geological Engineering *e:* **DS in Ge Engr**

Doctor of Science in Geophysical Engineering *e:* **DS in Gp Engr**

Doctor of Science in Industrial Medicine *e:* **DSIM**

Doctor of Science in Veterinary Medicine *e:* **D Sc in VM**

Doctor of the Natural Sciences *e:* **Dr N Sc**

Doctor of Tropical Medicine *e:* **Dr T Med**, *e:* **DTM**

Doctor of Veterinary Medicine *e:* **DMV**, *e:* **D Vet Med**, *e:* **DVM**, *e:* **M.D.**, *e:* **M.D.V.**, *e:* **MVD**, *e:* **VMD**

Doctor of Veterinary Medicine and Surgery *e:* **DVM and S**, *e:* **DVMS**

doctor philosophiae naturalis *l:* **Dr. phil. nat.**

Doctor rerum naturalium *l:* **Dr rer nat**

doctor rerum naturalium technicarium *l:* **Dr. nat. techn.**

Doctor rerum naturalium technicarum *l:* **Dr nat techn**

Doctor scientiarum naturalium *l:* **Dr sc nat**

Document Application Processing in a Heterogeneous Network Environment *e:* **DAPHNE**

Documentation Centre, George Etienne Canier House, Parks Canada, Montreal, Quebec *e:* **QMPCG**

Documentation Géographique Militaire *f:*
DGM

Documentation Oceanique *f:*
DOCOCEAN

Documentazione Geografica Militare *i:*
DGM

DOD Manager for Space Shuttle Support
e: **DDMS**

Dodge City Weather Forecast Office *e:*
DDC

Dodumentation Medizinische Technik *d:*
MEDITEC

DOE Environmental Checklist *e:* **DEC**

DOE-HQ Environmental *e:* **DHE**

DOE/Office of Environmental Restoration
and Waste Management, Germantown *e:*
DOE/EM

DOE/Westinghouse School for
Environmental Excellence *e:* **DWSEE**

Dogger Bank in the North Sea off England's
east coast *e:* **Dogger**

Doklady Biological Sciences *e:* **Dokl.
Biol. Sci.**

Doktor der Medizin *d:* **Dr Med**

Doktor der medizinischen Wissenschaften
d: **Dr. sc. med.**

Doktor der Naturwissenschaften *d:*
Dr.phil.nat., *d:* **Dr. rer. nat.**, *d:*
Dr.rer.nat.

Doktor der Tierheilkunde *d:* **Dr. med. vet.**,
d: **Dr. vet.**

Doktor für Naturwissenschaften *d:*
Dr.sc.nat.

Dokumentation Wasser *d:* **DW**

Dokumentations- und Informationsstelle für
Umweltfragen der Kinderärzte *d:* **DISU**

Dokumentationsdienst der medizinischen
Forschung *d:* **DOKDI**

Dokumentationsdienst der Schweizerischen
Akademie der Medizinischen
Wissenschaft[en] *d:* **DOKDI**

Dokumentationsstelle für Biologie *d:* **DSB**

Dokumentationszentrale Wasser der
Fraunhofer Gesellschaft *d:* **DZW**

dokumentiert *d:* **dok.**

Domain Oriented Natural Language
Understanding *e:* **DONAU**

Dome-Space Fire *e:* **DSF**

Domestic Animal Diversity *e:* **DAD**

Domestic Animal Diversity Information
System *e:* **DAD-IS**

Domestic Animal Endocrinology *e:*
Domest Anim Endocrinol

Domestic Geographic Name *e:* **DGN**

Domestic Geographic Names Report *e:*
DGNR

Domestic Hot Water *e:* **DHW**

Domestic Water *e:* **DW**

Dominion Astronomical (or Astrophysical)
Observatory *e:* **DAO**

Dominion Observatory *e:* **DO**

Dominion Radio Astrophysical Observatory
e: **DRAO**

Donau-Wasserkraft AG *d:* **DWK**

Door Operator and Remote Controls
Manufacturers Association *e:*
DORCMA

Dopamine Beta-Hydroxylase Inhibitor *e:*
DBHI

Doppelt Notierte Einheitsklassifikation *d:*
DONEK

Doppler Electronic Weather Sensor *e:*
DEWS

[Doppler] Lidar [or Laser] Atmospheric
Wind Sounder *e:* **LAWS**

Doppler Orbit and Radio Positioning
Integration by Satellite *e:* **DORIS**

Doris Orbitography and Geopotential
Evaluation *e:* **DOGE**

Dorland's Illustrated Medical Dictionary *e:*
DIMD

Dorset Natural Historical and
Archaeological Society *e:* **D.N.H.A.S.**

Dorset Natural History and Archaeological
Society. Proceedings *e:* **Proc Dorset Soc**

Dortmunder Energie- und
Wasserversorgung GmbH *d:* **DEW**

Doses via Environmental Transport of
Radionuclides *e:* **DETRA**

DOT Climatic Impact Assessment Program
e: **DOT/CIAP**

Dotierung *d:* **DOT**

Dotierung von Elektrolytkupfer für
Leitzwecke *d:* **DEL**

Double Atmospheric Density *e:* **DAD**

Double Braid[ed] Weather Proof *e:* **DBWP**

Double Precision Orbit Determination
Program *e:* **DPODP**

Double Space *e:* **DS**

Double Zeta Polarization *e:* **DZP**

doublecolumn inch *e:* **dci**

Doubly Labeled Water *e:* **DLW**

Douglas Space Physics Laboratory *e:*
DSPL

Douglas Space Vehicle *e:* **DSV**

Downstate Medical Center *e:* **VVD**

Dr. Otto Schaefer Health Resource Centre,
Yellowknife, Northwest Territories *e:*
NWYOS

Dr. William M. Scholl College of Podiatric
Medicine, Chicago *e:* **JAV**

Draft Environmental Impact Statement *e:*
DEIS

Draft Environmental impact Statement *e:*
DES

Draft Environmental Impact Statement *e:*
DIES

Draft Environmental Report *e:* **DER**

Draft Environmental Statement *e:* **DES**

Draft Generic Environmental Impact
Statement *e:* **DGEIS**

Draft International Convention on Liability
and Compensation for Damage in
Connection with the Carriage of
Hazardous and Noxious Substances by
Sea *e:* **HNS**

Draft programmatic environmental impact
statement *e:* **DPEIS**

Drainage and Water Supply Office[r] *e:*
DWSO

Drift-card Experiment in the Mediterranean
Sea *e:* **DRIFTEX**

Drifting Automatic Radio-Meteorological
Station *e:* **DARMS**

Drilling, Observation and Sampling of the
Earth's Continental Crust *e:* **DOSECC**

dringliche medizinische Hilfe *d:* **DMH**

Drinking Water *e:* **DW**

Drinking Water Criteria Documents *e:*
DWCDs

Drinking Water Equivalent Level *e:*
DWEL

Drinking Water Quality Research Center
e: **DWQRC**

Drinking Water Standard[s] *e:* **DWS**

Drinking Water State Revolving Fund *e:*
DWSRF

drinking water tank *e:* **dw tk**

Driving Instrumentation Vehicle for
Environmental and Acoustic Research *e:*
DIVEAR

Droit Naturel *f:* **DN**

Dropping Last Outwards Sea Pilot *e:*
DLOSP

Dropping Off Last Sea Pilot *e:* **DOLSP**

Druck-Hydrogenium-Kracken *d:* **DHC**

Druck-Hydrogenium-Raffination *d:* **DHR**

Druckwasser *d:* **WaD**

Druckwasserreaktor *d:* **DWR**

Dry Ice *e:* **DI**

Dry Water Content *e:* **DWC**

Dry Weather Flow *e:* **DWF**

DSIF [Deep Space Instrumentation Facility]
Maintenance Facility *e:* **DMF**

DSIF [Deep Space Instrumentation Facility]
Monitor and Control Subsystem *e:*
DMC, *e:* **DMC Subsystem**

DSIF [Deep Space Instrumentation Facility]
Supply Depot *e:* **DSD**

DSIF [Deep Space Instrumentation Facility]
Telemetry and Command Subsystem *e:*
DTC Subsystem

DSN/Multi-leavin Remote Job Entry *e:*
DSN/MRJE

DSS [Deep Space Station] Communications
Equipment Subsystem *e:* **DCES**

DSS [Deep Space Station] Communications
Terminal Subsystem *e:* **DCT**

DTW. Deutsche Tierärztliche
Wochenschrift *d:* **DTW Dtsch Tierärztl
Wochenschr**

dual aerospace servoamplifier *e:* **dasa**

Dual Axis Radiographic Hydrodynamic
Test *e:* **DARHT**, *e:* **DE DARHT**

Dual Driver Protective Service *e:* **DDPS**

Dual Environment Safety Switch *e:* **DESS**

Dual Frequency Dual Polarization SAR *e:*
DFDPSAR

Dual Linear Polarization Radar *e:* **DLPR**

Dual Path Protection Arrangement *e:*
DUPPA

Dublin Naturalists' Film Club *e:* **D.N.F.C.**

Dublin Society for the Prevention of
Cruelty to Animals *e:* **DSPCA**

Duke Environmental Law & Policy Forum
e: **Duke Envtl. L.&Pol'y F.**

Duke University Medical Board *e:*
DUMBO

Duke University Medical Center *e:* **DUMC**

Dungeon Master *e:* **DM**

Dungeon Master's Guide *e:* **DMG**

Dungeon Module *e:* **DM**

Duplex Multi-Environment Real Time *e:*
DMERT

Durable Medical Equipment *e:* **DME**

Durable Medical Equipment Regional
Carriers *e:* **DIWERC**, *e:* **DMERC**

durchkontaktierte Leiterplatte *d:* **DICL**

Durham Geological Sciences *e:* **DGS**

Durham Natural History Society *e:*
D.N.H.S.

Durrell Institute of Conservation and
Ecology *e:* **DICE**

Dust Indicators and Records from
Terrestrial and Marine Paleoenvironments
e: **DIRTMAP**

Dutch Prognostics & Health Management
Consortium *e:* **DPCC**

Dutchess County Mental Health Center, Poughkeepsie e: **NPDCM**

Duty Orbital Analyst e: **DOA**

Duty Space Surveillance Officer e: **DSSO**

Dynamic Environment & Terrain e: **DET**

Dynamic Environmental Conditioning e: **DEC**

Dynamic Environmental Effects Model e: **DEEM**

Dynamic Environmental Laboratory Test e: **DELT**

Dynamic Environment[al] Simulator e: **DES**

Dynamic Global Phytogeography Model e: **DOLY**

Dynamic Integrated Climate Economy e: **DICE**

Dynamic Manned Orbital Weapon System e: **DYNA-MOWS**

Dynamic memory relocation and protection system e: **DRPS**

Dynamic Nuclear Polarization e: **DNP**

Dynamic Object Rendering Environment e: **DORE**

Dynamic Ocean Track System e: **DOTS**

Dynamic Ocean Tracking System e: **DOTS**

Dynamic Response of the Forest-Tundra Ecotone to Environmental Change e: **DART**

Dynamic Special-Use Airspace e: **DSUA**

Dynamic Synthetic Environment e: **DSE**

Dynamic Weather Display e: **DWD**

Dynamics, Acoustics and Thermal Environment e: **DATE**

Dynamics Adapted Network for the Atmosphere e: **DYANA**

Dynamics Environment Measurement System e: **DEMS**

Dynamics of Atmospheres and Oceans n: **Dyn. Atmos. Oceans**

Dynamics of the Solid Earth e: **DOSE**

Dynamique des Espaces Géographiques f: **DEG**

Dynamique des océans et climat f: **ODC**

Dynamique et Chimie Atmosphérique en Forêt Equatoriale f: **DECAFE**

Dystonia Medical Research Foundation e: **DMRF**

Dzerhinskiy All-Union Institute of Health Engineering e: **VTI**

Décennie Hydrologique Internationale f: **DHI**

Décennie internationale de la prévention des catastrophes naturelles f: **DIPCN**

Décret de Naturalisation f: **DN**

Délivrance Naturelle Complète f: **DNC**

Délégation à l'Espace Aérien f: **DEA**

Département de Protection Sanitaire f: **DPS**

Département des Travaux, Recherches et de l'Exploitation Océaniques f: **DTREO**

Département fédéral de l'Environnement, des Transports, de l'Énergie et de la Communication e: **DETEC**

Dépôt de Quartier-Maître f: **Dép.Q.M.**

Dépôts Océan Congo f: **DOC**

Dépérissement des Forets Attribué a la Pollution Atmosphérique f: **DEFORPA**

Détachement Atomique [service médical] f: **Dét At**

Détachement de Circulation Routière f: **D.C.R.**

Détachement de Liaison et d'Observation [d'artillerie] f: **DLO**

Détachement de Régulation Routière f: **D.R.R.**

Détachement d'Observation f: **D.O.**

détachement médical f: **dét.méd.**

Détachement Opérationnel de Protection f: **D.O.P.**

Día Meteorológico Mundial s: **DMM**

Díploma in Pharmaceutical Medicine f: **D.Ph:M.**

E

Eagle Ocean Transport e: **EOT**

Earle's Lactalbumin Hydrolysate e: **ELAH**

Early After Depolarisation e: **EAD**

Early Capability Orbital Manned Station e: **ECOMS**

Early Open Water e: **e.o.w.**

Early Page Space Allocation e: **EPSA**

Earth e: **E**, e: **Ea**

Earth and Atmospheric Sciences e: **EAS**

Earth and Environmental Science Building e: **EESB**

Earth and Environmental Science[s] e: **EES**

Earth and Environmental Sciences Center e: **EESC**

Earth and Life Sciences Editors e: **ELSE**

Earth and Mineral Sciences e: **EMS**

Earth and Ocean Dynamic Applications Program[me] e: **EODAP**

Earth and Ocean Dynamics Program e: **EODP**

Earth and Ocean Physics e: **EOP**

Earth and Ocean Physics Application Program e: **EOPAP**

Earth and Planetary Science Letters e: **Earth Planet Sci Lett**

Earth and Planetary Science Letters [Netherlands] n: **Earth Planet. Sci. Lett.**

Earth and Planetary Sciences e: **EPS**

Earth and Space Data Computing Division e: **ESDCD**

Earth Aspect Sensor e: **EAS**

Earth Awareness Fair e: **EAF**

Earth Awareness Foundation e: **EAF**

Earth-Based Radio Guidance e: **EBRG**

earth-based tug e: **ebt**

Earth Centered Earth Fixed e: **ECEF**

Earth Centered Inertial e: **ECI**

Earth-Centered Inertial System e: **ECIS**

Earth Centered Rotating e: **ECR**

Earth Central Angle e: **ECA**

Earth Central Inertial e: **ECI**

earth closet e: **ec**

Earth Colonization Research Center e: **ECRC**

Earth Comet e: **EC**

Earth Communications Office e: **ECO**

Earth Continuity Conductor e: **ECC**

Earth Council e: **EC**

Earth Coverage antenna e: **EC**

Earth Coverage Antenna e: **ECA**

Earth Coverage Horizon Measurement e: **ECH**, e: **ECHM**

Earth Coverage to Earth Coverage e: **EC-EC**

Earth Coverage to Narrow Coverage/Area Coverage e: **EC-NC/AC**

Earth-Crossing Asteroids e: **ECA**

Earth Crust Formation e: **ECF**

Earth Current e: **EC**

Earth Curvature e: **EC**

Earth Data Analysis Center e: **EDAC**

Earth Data System Reference Application e: **EDSRA**

Earth Data Systems e: **EDS**

Earth-Dawn e: **ED**

Earth Departure Window e: **EDW**

Earth Detector e: **ED**

Earth Ecology Foundation e: **EEF**

Earth Entry Module e: **EEM**

Earth Environment and Resources Conference e: **EERC**

Earth Environment Satellite Initiative e: **EESI**

Earth Environment Space Initiative[s] e: **EESI**

Earth Equatorial Plane e: **EEP**

Earth Exploration Satellite e: **EES**

Earth Exploration Satellite Service e: **EESS**

Earth Far Horizon e: **EFH**

earth fixed coordinate e: **efc**

Earth Fixed Coordinate System e: **EFCS**

Earth Fixed System e: **EFS**

earth geodetic satellite e: **ergs**

Earth Horizon Scanner e: **EHS**

Earth Images Catalog e: **EIC**

Earth Imaging Working Group e: **EIWG**

Earth Inductor e: **EI**

Earth Inductor Compass e: **EIC**

Earth-Ionosphere Cavity e: **EIC**

Earth Island Institute e: **EII**

Earth-Jupiter Orbiter Transfer Flight e: **EJOTF**

Earth Landing Control Area e: **ELCA**

Earth Landing Sequence Controller e: **E LSC**

Earth Landing System e: **EIS**, e: **ELS**

Earth Landmark e: **ELDMK**

Earth Launch Date e: **ELD**

Earth Launch Vehicle e: **ELV**

Earth Launch Window e: **ELW**

Earth Limb Infrared Atmospheric Structure e: **ELIAS**

Earth Limb Measurement Satellite e: **ELMS**

Earth-Limb Radiance Experiment e: **ELRAD**

Earth-Lunar Horizon Sensor e: **ELHS**

Earth-Mars-Earth e: **EME**

Earth Mass e: **EM**

Earth Mean Orbital Speed e: **EMOS**

Earth Monitoring Educational System e: **EMES**

Earth, Moon, and Mars e: **EMM**

Earth, Moon and Planets n: **Earth Moon Planets**

Earth-Moon-Earth (Connection) e: **EME**

Earth-Moon Space Exploration Study e: **ESES**

Earth Near Horizon e: **ENH**

Earth Negotiations Bulletin e: **ENB**

Earth Net Dial e: **END**

Earth Observation e: **EO**

Earth Observation Advisory Committee e: **EOAC**

Earth Observation Aircraft Program e: **EOAP**

Earth Observation Center (or Centre) e: **EOC**

Earth Observation Experiment e: **EOE-1**

Earth Observation Images *e:* **EOI**

Earth Observation Magazine *e:* **EOM**

Earth Observation Mission[s] *e:* **EOM**

Earth Observation (or Observatory, or Observing) Satellite[s] *e:* **EOS**

Earth Observation [or Observing] Data Center [or Centre] *e:* **EODC**

Earth Observation (or Observing) Data Group *e:* **EODGRU**

Earth Observation (or Observing) Data Mobile Unit *e:* **EODMU**

Earth Observation (or Observing) Data Technical Center *e:* **EODTECHCTR**

Earth Observation (or Observing) System *e:* **EOS**

Earth Observation Preparatory Programme *e:* **EOPP**

Earth Observation Program *e:* **EOP**

Earth Observation Research Center *e:* **EORC**

Earth Observation Satellite and Modular Platform *e:* **ERDSAT**

Earth Observation Satellite Co. *e:* **EOSAT**

Earth Observation Satellite System *e:* **EOSS**

Earth Observation Satellites Program *e:* **EOSP**

Earth Observation Scientific and Technical Advisory Group *e:* **EOSTAG**

Earth Observation Working Group *e:* **EOWG**

Earth Observation[s] Commercialization Application[s] Program *e:* **EOCAP**

Earth Observation[s] Data Management Systems *e:* **EODMS**

Earth Observations Division *e:* **EOD**

Earth Observation[s] International Coordination Working Group *e:* **EO-ICWG**

Earth Observation[s] Laboratory *e:* **EOL**

Earth Observations Science Committee *e:* **EOSC**

Earth Observatory Laboratory *e:* **EOL**

Earth Observed Time *e:* **EOT**

Earth Observing Radar *e:* **EOR**

Earth Observing Scanning Polarimeter *e:* **EOSP**

Earth Observing System Afternoon Crossing Mission *e:* **EOS PM**

Earth Observing System-Chemistry *e:* **EOS-CHEM**

Earth Observing System-Color *e:* **EOS-COLOR**

Earth Observing System Satellite Synthetic Aperture Radar *e:* **EOS SAR**

Earth Orbit *e:* **EO**

Earth Orbit Ejection *e:* **EOE**

Earth Orbit Equipment *e:* **EOE**

Earth Orbit Escape Device *e:* **EOED**

Earth Orbit Insertion *e:* **EOI**

Earth Orbit Insertion Monitor *e:* **EOI Monitor**

Earth Orbit Launch *e:* **EOL**

earth orbit plane *e:* **eop**

Earth Orbit Rendezvous *e:* **EOR**

Earth Orbital Flight *e:* **EOF**

Earth Orbital Launch Configuration *e:* **EOLC**

Earth Orbital Military Satellite *e:* **EOMS**

Earth Orbital Mission *e:* **EOM**

earth orbital rendezvous *e:* **eor**

Earth Orbital Space Station *e:* **EOSS**

Earth Orbiting Recoverable Biological Satellite *e:* **EORBS**

Earth Orbiting Satellite *e:* **EOS**

Earth Orbit[ing] Shuttle *e:* **EOS**

Earth-Orbiting Thermal Emission Spectrometer *e:* **E-TES**

Earth Orientation Service *e:* **EOS**

Earth-Oriented Research Working Group *e:* **ERG**

Earth Parking Orbit *e:* **EPO**

Earth Path Indicator *e:* **EPI**

Earth Penetrating *e:* **EP**

Earth Penetrating Manoeuvring Re-entry Vehicle *e:* **EPMaRV**

Earth-Penetrating Warhead *e:* **EPW**

Earth Penetrating Weapon *e:* **EPW**

Earth Penetrator Warhead *e:* **EPW**

Earth Penetrator Weapon *e:* **EPW**

Earth Physics and Physical Oceanography Program *e:* **EPPO**, *e:* **EPPO Program**

Earth Physics Branch *e:* **EPB**

Earth Physics Branch, Energy, Mines and Resources Canada Ottawa, Ontario *e:* **OOO**

Earth Physics Program *e:* **EPP**

Earth-Physics Satellite Observation (or Observing) Campaign *e:* **EPSOC**

Earth Plate *e:* **EP**

Earth-Pointing Instrument Carrier *e:* **EPIC**

Earth Potential Compensation *e:* **EPC**

Earth Potential Difference *e:* **EPD**

Earth Potential for Manned Flight Computation *e:* **EPMFC**

Earth Prelaunch Calibration *e:* **EPC**

Earth-Pressure Balanced Shield *e:* **EPBS**

Earth Probe *e:* **EP**

Earth-Probe-Mars *e:* **EPM**

Earth-Probe-Sun Angle *e:* **EPS Angle**

Earth Protectors *e:* **EP**

Earth Radiation Budget *e:* **ERB**

Earth Radiation Budget [Experiment] *e:* **ERBE**

Earth Radiation Budget Experiment Non-Scanner *e:* **ERBE-NS**

Earth Radiation Budget Experiment Scanner *e:* **ERBE-S**

Earth Radiation Budget Explorer Satellite *e:* **ERBES**

Earth Radiation Budget Instrument *e:* **ERBI**

Earth Radiation Budget Package *e:* **ERB-PACK**

Earth Radiation Budget Satellite *e:* **ERBS**

Earth Radiation Budget Satellite System *e:* **ERBSS**

Earth Radiometer Backscatter Experiment *e:* **ERBE**

Earth Radius *e:* **ER**

Earth Rate Compensation *e:* **ERC**

Earth Rate Directional Reference *e:* **ERDR**

Earth Rate Unit *e:* **ERU**

Earth Recources Survey *e:* **ERS**

Earth Recovery Subsystem *e:* **ERS**

Earth Reentry Module *e:* **ERM**

Earth Reference Point *e:* **ERP**

Earth Reference Pulse *e:* **ERP**, *e:* **ERTP**

Earth Regeneration and Reforestation Association *e:* **TERRA**

Earth Regeneration Society *e:* **ERS**

Earth Remote Sensing *e:* **ERS**

Earth Remote-Sensing Satellite *e:* **ERSS**

Earth Research From Space *e:* **ERS**

Earth Resistivity Meter *e:* **ERM**

Earth Resource Data System *e:* **ERDS**

Earth Resource Mapping *e:* **ERM**

Earth Resource Survey Satellites *e:* **ERSATS**

Earth Resources Aircraft Facility *e:* **ERAF**

Earth Resources Aircraft Program *e:* **ERAP**

Earth Resources Aircraft Project *e:* **ERAP**

Earth Resources Consultants *e:* **ERC**

Earth Resources Corporation *e:* **ERC**

Earth Resources Data *e:* **ERD**

Earth Resources Data Analysis System[s] *e:* **ERDAS**

Earth Resources Data Center *e:* **ERDC**

Earth Resources Digital Analysis system Software *e:* **ERDAS**

Earth Resources Experiment Package (or Packaging) Program *e:* **EREPP**

Earth Resources Experiment[al] Package *e:* **EREP**

Earth Resources Experimental Program *e:* **EREP**

Earth Resources Experiment[s] Package *e:* **EREP**

Earth Resources Flight Data Processor *e:* **ER FDP**

Earth Resources Infomation System *e:* **ERIS**

Earth Resources Information Network *e:* **ERIN**

Earth Resources Information Storage, Transformation, Analysis and Retrieval *e:* **ERISTAR**

Earth Resources Interactive Processing System *e:* **ERIPS**

Earth Resources Inventory System *e:* **ERIS**

Earth Resources Laboratory *e:* **ERL**

Earth Resources Laboratory Application Software *e:* **ERLAS**

Earth Resources Laboratory Applications Software *e:* **ELAS**

Earth Resources Management System *e:* **ERMAN System**

Earth Resources Observation (or Observing) Satellite *e:* **EROS**

Earth Resources Observation Systems Data Center *e:* **EDC**

Earth Resources Observation Systems Program *e:* **EROSP**

Earth Resources Observation[s] (or Observing) System[s] *e:* **EROS**

Earth Resources [or Remote Sensing] Satellite *e:* **ERS**

Earth Resources [or Remote Sensing] Satellite-1 *e:* **ERS-1**

Earth Resources Package *e:* **EREP**

Earth Resources Program *e:* **ERP**

Earth Resources Research *e:* **ERR**

Earth Resources Research Data Facilities *e:* **ERRDF**

Earth Resources-2 (satellite) *e:* **ER2**

Earth Resources Satellite Data Analysis Center *e:* **ERSDAC**

Earth Resources Satellite Data and Information System *e:* **ERSDIS**

Earth Resources Satellite Survey *e:* **ERSS**

Earth Resources Satellite System *e:* **ERSS**

Earth Resources Shuttle Imaging Radar *e:* **ERSIR**

Earth Resources Spaceflight Program *e:* **ERSP**

Earth Resources Spectral Information System *e:* **ERSIS**

Earth Resources Survey *e:* **ERS**

Earth Resources Survey Flights Program *e:* **ERSFP**

Earth Resource[s] Survey Operational Satellite *e:* **ERSOS**

Earth Resources Survey Operation[al] System *e:* **ERSOS**

Earth Resources Survey Program *e:* **ERSP**

Earth Resources Survey Program Review Committee *e:* **ERSPRC**

Earth Resources Survey Satellite[s] *e:* **ERSS**

Earth Resources Survey System *e:* **ERS[S]**

Earth Resources Synthetic Aperture Radar *e:* **ERSAR**

Earth Resources Technology *e:* **ERT**

Earth Resources Technology Satellite *e:* **ERST**

Earth Resource[s] Technology Satellite[s] *e:* **ERTS**

Earth Return *e:* **ER**

Earth Return Module *e:* **ERM**

earth rotation in lunar distances *e:* **erild**

Earth Satellite Corporation *e:* **EARTHSAT**

Earth Satellite Dedicated to Oceanographic Applications *e:* **SEASAT**

Earth Satellite Vehicle *e:* **ESV**

Earth Satellite Weapon System[s] *e:* **ESWS**

Earth Science and Applications Data System *e:* **EASDS**

Earth Science [and] Applications Division *e:* **ESAD**

Earth Science and Related Information Selected Annotated Titles *e:* **ESRISAT**

Earth Science Catalogue Gopher *e:* **ESCG**

Earth Science Curriculum Project Newsletter *e:* **ESCP Newsletter**

Earth-Science Data Acquisition *e:* **ESDA**

Earth-Science Data Acquisition Guidelines *e:* **ESDAG**

Earth Science Data and Information System *e:* **ESDIS**

Earth Science Data Directory *e:* **ESDD**

Earth Science Education Conference *e:* **ESEC**

Earth Science Geostationary Platform *e:* **ESGP**

Earth Science Image Processing Package *e:* **ESIPP**

Earth Science Index *e:* **ESI**

Earth Science Information Manager *e:* **ESIM**

Earth Science Information Network *e:* **ESIN**

Earth Science Information Office *e:* **ESIO**

Earth Science Information System *e:* **ESIS**

Earth Science Journals Online *e:* **ESJO**

Earth Science Links *e:* **ESL**

Earth Science Research *e:* **ESR**

Earth-Science Reviews *n:* **Earth-Sci. Rev.**

Earth-Science Shelf *e:* **ESS**

Earth Science Teacher Preparation Project *e:* **ESTPP**

Earth Science Technical Plan *e:* **ESTP**

Earth Sciences and Map Library *e:* **EART**

Earth Sciences and Research Laboratory *e:* **ESRL**

Earth Sciences and Resources Institute *e:* **ESRI**

Earth Sciences Associates *e:* **ESA**

Earth Science[s] Curriculum Project *e:* **ESCP**

Earth Sciences Data Standards Council *e:* **ESDA**

Earth sciences dimension to TIGER *e:* **TIGGER**

Earth Sciences Division *e:* **ES**, *e:* **ESD**

Earth Sciences Information *e:* **ESI**

Earth Science[s] Information Center (or Centre) *e:* **ESIC**

Earth Science[s] Joint Working Group *e:* **ESJWG**

Earth Sciences Laboratories *e:* **ESL**

Earth Sciences Review Group *e:* **ESRG**

Earth Sciences Technologies Association *e:* **ESTA**

Earth Search Sciences Incorporated *e:* **ESSI**

Earth Sensor Assembly Module *e:* **ESAM**

Earth-Sighting Simulator *e:* **ESS**

Earth Station *e:* **ES**

Earth Station-Arabia *e:* **ESA**

Earth Station-Brazil *e:* **ESB**

Earth Station-Chile *e:* **ESCH**

Earth Station-Columbia *e:* **ESCO**

Earth Station-Congo *e:* **ESC**

Earth Station Database *e:* **ESDB**

Earth Station-Ecuador *e:* **ESEC**

Earth Station - Egypt *e:* **ESEG**

Earth Station-Greece *e:* **ESG**

Earth Station - Hong Kong *e:* **ESHK**

Earth Station-Iran *e:* **ESI**

Earth Station - Israel *e:* **ESIS**

Earth Station-Ivory Coast *e:* **ESIC**

Earth Station-Jordan *e:* **ESJ**

Earth Station-Kenya *e:* **ESK**

Earth Station-Libya *e:* **ESL**

Earth Station-Marocco *e:* **ESMO**

Earth Station-Mexico *e:* **ESM**

Earth Station on Board Vessel *e:* **ESV**

Earth Station Remote *e:* **ESR**

Earth Station-Scandinavia *e:* **ESSC**

Earth Station-Senegal *e:* **ESSE**

Earth Station-South Africa *e:* **ESSA**

Earth Station-Sudan *e:* **ESS**

Earth Station-Syria *e:* **ESSY**

Earth Station-Turkey *e:* **EST**

Earth Station-Venezuela *e:* **ESV**

Earth Station-Yugoslavia *e:* **ESY**

Earth-Surface Potential *e:* **ESP**

Earth Surface Processes and Landforms *e:* **Earth Surf. Process. Landf.**, *e:* **Earth Surf. Process. Landf.**

Earth Surveillance and Reconnaissance Simulator *e:* **ESARS**

Earth Surveillance and Rendezvous Simulator *e:* **ESARS**

Earth Switch *e:* **ES**

Earth System Data and Information Management *e:* **ESDIM**

Earth System History *e:* **ESH**

Earth System Model Information System *e:* **ESMDIS**

Earth System Model of Intermediate Complexity *e:* **EMIC**

Earth System Science Center *e:* **ESSC**

earth system science division *e:* **SG**

Earth System Science Education *e:* **ESSE**

Earth System Science Information System *e:* **ESSIS**

Earth System Science Pathfinders *e:* **ESSP**

Earth System Science[s] *e:* **ESS**

Earth Systems Institute *e:* **ESI**

Earth Systems Model *e:* **ESM**

Earth Systems Program *e:* **ESP**

Earth Systems Science Committee *e:* **ESDD**

Earth System[s] Science[s] Committee *e:* **ESSC**

Earth Terminal *e:* **ET**

Earth Terminal Complex *e:* **ETC**

Earth Terminal Control Station *e:* **ETCS**

Earth Terminal Measurement System *e:* **ETMS**

Earth Terrain Camera *e:* **ETC**

Earth Tide *e:* **ET**

Earth to Orbit *e:* **ETO**

Earth-Venus Transit *e:* **EVT**

Earth Viewing Application[s] Laboratory *e:* **EVAL**

Earth Viewing Module *e:* **EVM**

earth watch *e:* **ew**

Earth Works Group Inc. *e:* **EWG**

Earthcare Network *e:* **EN**

Earthfax Engineering Incorporated *e:* **EFEI**

Earthmovers and Contractors Association *e:* **ECA**

earthmoving equipment *e:* **EM equipment**

Earthmoving machin[e] *e:* **EM machine**

Earthnet ERS-1 Central Facility *e:* **EECF**

Earthnet Info Server *e:* **EIS**

Earthnet Programme Office *e:* **EPO**

Earthquake *e:* **EQ**

earthquake and war damage *e:* **eq & wd**

Earthquake Controller Lateral *e:* **ECL**

Earthquake Controller, Vertical *e:* **ECV**

Earthquake Engineer[ing] *e:* **EE**

Earthquake Engineering and Structural Dynamics *e:* **Earthq. Eng. Struct. Dyn.**

Earthquake Engineering Research Center *e:* **EERC**

Earthquake Engineering Research Institute *e:* **EERI**

Earthquake Engineering Research Laboratory *e:* **EERL**

Earthquake Finger Gateway *e:* **EFG**

Earthquake Hazard Maps *e:* **EHM**

Earthquake Information Center *e:* **EIC**

Earthquake Information Requests *e:* **EIR**

Earthquake Locator *e:* **EQL**

Earthquake Maps and Reports *e:* **EMR**

Earthquake Mechanisms Laboratory *e:* **EML**

Earthquake Monitoring System *e:* **EMS**

Earthquake Phenomena Observation System *e:* **EPOS**

Earthquake Prediction Observation Center *e:* **EPOC**

Earthquake Preparedness Center of Expertise *e:* **EQPCE**

Earthquake Research Institute *e:* **ERG**

Earthquake Risk Analysis *e:* **ERA**

Earthquake Seismology Research *e:* **ESR**

earthquake[s] *e:* **quake[s]**

Earth's self-sustaining Biosphere *e:* **GAIA**

Earthwide Internet Education and Information Organization *e:* **EIEIO**

Earthwork/Center for Rural Studies *e:* **ECRS**

Easily Hydrolyzable *e:* **EH**

East Africa Protectorate *e:* **EAP**

East Africa Regional Remote Sensing Management Committee *e:* **EARCOM**

East African Freshwater Fisheries (or Fishery) Research Organization e: **EAFFRO**

East African Institute for Medical Research e: **EAIMR**

East African Medical Journal [Nairobi] e: **East Afr Med J**

East Africa[n] Medical Research Council e: **EAMRC**

East African Meteorological Department e: **EAMD**

East African National Health Service e: **EANHS**

East African Natural History Society e: **E.A.N.H.S.**

East African Natural Resources Research Council e: **EANRRC**

East African Wildlife Society e: **EAWLS**, e: **EAWS**

East Antarctic Ice Sheet e: **EAIS**

East Asia Hydrographic Commission e: **EAHC**

East Carolina University, Health Sciences Library, Greenville e: **NEH**

East Center e: **EC**

East Coast Conference on Aerospace and Navigational Electronics e: **ECCANE**

East Coast Migrant Health Project e: **ECMHP**

East-Ocean Meeting Point e: **EASTOMP**

East Pakistan Water and Power Development Authority e: **EPWAPDA**

East Tennessee Chapter Health Physics Society e: **ETCHPS**

East Tennessee Geological Society e: **ETGS**

East Tennessee Natural Gas e: **ETNG**

East Tennessee State University, Medical Library, Johnson City e: **TJoS-M**

Eastern Atlantic, Channel and North Sea [Orders for Ships] e: **ECNOS**

Eastern Atlantic Hydrographic Commission e: **EAtHC**

Eastern Caribbean Natural Area Management Program e: **ECNAP**

Eastern Environmental Radiation Facilities (or Facility) Sample Data Base e: **EERF**

Eastern Environmental Radiation Laboratory e: **EERL**

Eastern Goldfields Medical Division of General Practice e: **EGMDGP**

Eastern Kentucky Health Science Information Network e: **EKHSIN**

Eastern Neck National Wildlife Refuge e: **ENNWR**

Eastern Ocean Margin e: **EOM**

Eastern Pacific Ocean e: **EPAC**

Eastern Pacific Ocean Climate Study e: **EPOCS**

Eastern Pacific Ocean[ic] Conference e: **EPOC**

Eastern Pacific Oceanographic Conference e: **EPOC**

Eastern Region[al] Remote Sensing Applications Center e: **ERRSAC**

Eastern Sea Frontier e: **EASTSEAFRON**, e: **ESF**

Eastern Sea Road Service e: **ESS**

Eastern Space and Missile Center e: **ESMC**, e: **ESMCETR**, e: **ESME**

Eastern State Hospital, Medical Lake e: **WaMeH**

Eastern Tropical Pacific Ocean e: **ETPO**

Eastern Virginia Medical Authority, Norfolk e: **VNN**

Eastern Virginia Medical School, Norfolk e: **ViNE**

Eastman Kodak Co., Health and Safety Laboratory, Library, Rochester e: **VQK**

Eccentric Geophysical Observatory e: **EGO**

Eccentric Orbiting Geophysical Observatory e: **EGO**, e: **EOGO**

Echange de polluants entre l'atmosphère et les océans f: **INTERPOLL**

Échelons Régionaux du Service Médical f: **ERSM**

Echo Integration-MidWater Trawl e: **EIMWT**

Echo Protect Time e: **EPT**

Echtzeit-Steuerprogrammsystem, festplattenspeicherorientiert d: **ESFO**

Eclogae Geologicae Helvetiae l: **Eclogae Geol. Helv.**

ECMWF Meteorological Operational System e: **EMOS**

Eco 3. Energies, Environnement, Matieres Premieres f: **NRE**

Eco-sondeo geológico inclinado de largo alcance s: **GLORIA**

ecogeographer e: **ecogeo**

ecogeographic[al][ly] e: **ecogeo**

Ecolabelling Schemes e: **ELS**

École f: **E**, f: **EC**, f: **Eco**, f: **Ele**

École Administrative f: **EA**

École Africaine de la Météorologie et de l'Aviation Civile f: **EAMAC**

École africaine de la Météorologie et de l'Aviation Civile f: **EMAC**

École Africaine et Mauricienne d'Architecture et d'Urbanisme f: **EAMAU**

École Africaine et Mauricienne dArchitecture et dUrbanisme f: **EAMU**

École Catholique d'Arts et Métiers f: **E.C.A.M.**

École Centrale f: **EC**

École Centrale de Pyrotechnique f: **E.C.P.**

École Centrale des Arts de Manufactures de Paris f: **E.C.P.**

École Centrale des Arts et des Métiers f: **E.C.A.M.**

École Centrale des arts et manufactures f: **Centr.**

École Centrale Lyonnaise f: **E.C.L.**, f: **ECLY**

École Coloniale d'Agriculture de Tunis f: **ECAT**

École Coloniale des Parachutistes f: **E.C.P.**

École Commerciale de Jeunes Filles f: **ECJF**

École Communale f: **EC**, f: **E.Com.**

École d' Agriculture Algerienne f: **EAA**

École d'Administration de la Marine f: **E.A.M.**

École d'Administration et de Direction des Entreprises f: **ECADE**

École d'Administration Militaire f: **E.A.M.**

École d'Administration Pénitentiaire f: **EAP**

École d'Agriculture f: **EA**

École d'Agriculture de la Touche f: **EAT**

École d'Agriculture d'Hiver f: **E.A.H.**

École d'Analyse et de Programmation Appliquées f: **ECAPA-ENI**

École d'Application f: **EA**

École Dapplication de l'Administration f: **EAA**

École d'Application de l'Armée Blindée et Cavalerie f: **E.A.A.B.C.**

École d'Application de l'Armée de l'Air f: **E.A.A.A.**

École d'Application de l'Aviation Légère de l'Armée de Terre f: **E.A.A.L.A.T.**

École d'Application de l'Infanterie f: **EAI**

École d'Application des Hauts Polymères f: **EAHP**

École d'Application des Manufactures d'État f: **EAME**

École d'Application des Transmissions f: **E.A.T.**

École d'Application du Génie Maritime f: **E.A.G.M.**

École d'Application du Matériel f: **E.A.M.**

École d'Application du Service de Santé f: **E.A.S.S.**

École d'Application du Service de Santé Militaire f: **EASSM**

École d'Application du Train f: **E.A.T.**

École d'Application Militaire de l'Énergie Atomique f: **E.A.M.E.A.**

École d'Apprentissage f: **EA**

École d'Apprentissage Maritime f: **E.A.M.**

École d'Appui Aérienne f: **E.A.A.**

École darchitecture f: **Ear**

École d'Artillerie f: **E.A.**

École d'Artillerie Autiaérienne f: **E.A.A.**

École d'Arts Appliqués f: **EAA**

École d'Arts et Métiers de Reims f: **AMR**

École d'Aviation Civile f: **EAC**

École de Bibliothéconomie, Universite de Montreal, Quebec f: **QMUEB**

École de Chauffage Industriel f: **E.C.I.**

École de Chauffage Rationnel Industriel f: **E.C.R.I.**

École de Chimie f: **EC**

École de chimie f: **Ech**

École de Chimie, Geneva, Switzerland f: **SzGE**

École de Combat et d'Appui Tactique f: **ECAT**

École de Culture Générale f: **ECG**

École de Degré Diplôme f: **EDD**

École de Droit f: **ED**

École de Formation des Officiers de Réserve f: **E.F.O.R.**

École de Formation des Sous-officiers du Personnel Navigant f: **E.F.S.P.N.**

École de Formation d'Officiers f: **EFO**

École de Formation Initiale des Sous-Officiers f: **EFISO**

École de Formation Initiale du Personnel Navigant f: **E.F.I.P.N.**

École de Formation Technique de l'Aéronautique f: **EFTA**

École de Formation Technique Normale f: **EFTN**

École de Haut Enseignement Commercial pour les Jeunes Filles f: **EHECJF**

École de Haute Montagne f: **E.H.M.**

École de Journalisme f: **E.J.**

École de la Guerre des Mines f: **EGUERMIN**

École de l'Air et École Militaire de l'Air e: **EA-EMA**

École de l'Aviation Civile et de la Météorologie f: **EACM**

École de Législation Professionnelle *f:*
  ELP
École de Maistrance *f:* **E.M.**
École de Management international et de
  Communication *f:* **ESM**
École de Médecine *f:* **E.M.**
École de Notariat de Paris *f:* **ENP**
École de Parents et des Éducateurs *f:*
  E.P.E.
École de Perfectionnement *f:* **EP**
École de Pharmacie *f:* **EP**
École de Physique et Chimie Industrielle de
  Paris *f:* **E.P.C.I.**
École de physique et de chimie industrielle
  f: **EPC**
École de Pilotage Avancée *f:* **EPA**
École de Pilotage du Rhin *f:* **E.P.R.**
École de Pilotage Elémentaire *f:* **EPE**
École de Pilotage Transitaire *f:* **EPT**
École de Plein Air *f:* **EPA**
École de Préparation à la Pratique des
  Affaires *f:* **EPPA**
École de Préparation aux Examens
  Comptables *f:* **EPEC**
École de Préparation des Sous-Lieutenants
  f: **E.P.S.L.**
École de Publicité de Presse et de Relations
  Publiques *f:* **EPPREP**
École de Puériculture *f:* **EP**
École de Puériculture de la Faculté de
  Médecine de Paris *f:* **E.P.F.**
École de Service de Santé *f:* **E.S.S.**
École de Service de Santé de Bordeaux *f:*
  E.S.S.B.
École de Service de Santé de la Marine *f:*
  ESSM
École de Service de Santé de Lyon *f:*
  E.S.S.L.
École de Specialisation *f:* **ES**
École de Specialisation de la Cooperation
  Agricole *f:* **ESCA**
École de Spécialisation de l'Artillerie
  Antiaérienne *f:* **E.S.A.A.**
École de Sécrétariat Moderne *f:* **ESM**
École de Techniques Notariales Apliquées
  f: **ETNA**
École de Technologie Superieure,
  Universite de Quebec, Montreal, Quebec
  f: **QMUQET**
École de Tir *f:* **E.T.**
École de Viticulture et d'Oenologie *f:*
  EVO
École d'Enseignement Général de l'Armée
  de l'Air *f:* **E.E.S.G.A.A.**
École d'Enseignement Technique de
  l'Armée de Terre *f:* **E.E.T.A.T.**
École d'Enseignement Technique Féminin
  f: **ETAF**
École d'Entraînement Physique Militaire *f:*
  E.E.P.M.
École des Affaires de Paris *f:* **EAP**
École des Apprentis de l'Air *f:* **E.A.A.**
École des Apprentis Marins *f:* **E.A.M.**
École des Apprentis Mécaniciens de la
  Flotte *f:* **E.A.M.F.**
École des Apprentis Mécaniciens de
  l'Armée de l'Air *f:* **E.A.M.A.A.**
École des Arts Appliqués à l'Industrie *f:*
  E.A.A.
École des Arts Décoratifs *f:* **E.A.D.**
École des Arts Décoratifs de Strasbourg *f:*
  EADS

École des Arts et Métiers d'Erquelines *f:*
  A.M.E.R.
École des Arts Visuels, Universite Laval,
  Quebec, Quebec *f:* **QQLAAV**
École des Attachés de Direction *f:* **EAD**
École des Beaux-Arts *f:* **E.B.A.**
École des Beaux-Arts, Montreal, Quebec
  e: **QMBA**
École des Bibliothécaires, Archivistes et
  Documentalistes *f:* **EBAD**
École des Cadres de Commerce *f:* **EDC**
École des Elèves Ingénieurs Mécaniciens
  f: **E.E.I.M.**
École des Filles *f:* **F**
École des Forces Armées *f:* **EFA**
École des Hautes Alpes *f:* **EHA**
École des Hautes Etudes Commerciales,
  Montreal, Quebec *f:* **QMHE**
École des Hautes Études Administratives
  f: **HEA,** *f:* **H.E.Ad.**
École des Hautes Études Agraires *f:* **HEA**
École des Hautes Études Commerciales *f:*
  EDHEC, *f:* **E.H.E.C.,** *f:* **H.E.C.**
École des Hautes Études en Sciences
  Sociales *f:* **EHESS**
École des Hautes Études Industrielles *f:*
  E.H.E.I., *f:* **HEI**
École des Hautes Études Internationales *f:*
  EHEI
École des Hautes Études Militaires *f:*
  HEM
École des Hautes Études Navales *f:* **HEN**
École des Hautes Études Sociales *f:*
  E.H.E.S., *f:* **HES**
École des Hélicoptères de l'Armée de Terre
  f: **E.H.A.T.**
École des Industries Agricoles *f:* **E.I.A.**
École des Ingenieurs Agricoles *f:* **EINIA**
École des Langues Orientales Vivantes *f:*
  E.L.O.V.
École des Mines *f:* **EM**
École des Mines d'Ales *f:* **EMA**
École des Mines de Paris *f:* **EMP**
École des Mines de Paris Mineralogy
  Museum *e:* **EMPMM**
École des Mines de Saint-Etienne *f:*
  EMSE
École des Mines et de Géologie *f:* **EMIG**
École des Mousses *f:* **E.M.**
École des Métiers *f:* **EM**
École des métiers *f:* **Emét**
École des Pupilles de la Marine *f:* **E.P.M.**
École des Sciences de l'Information *f:* **ESI**
École des Sciences Politiques *f:* **ESP**
École des Secrétaires de Direction *f:*
  E.S.D.
École des Sous-Officiers *f:* **E.S.O.**
École des Sous-Officiers de Réserve *f:*
  E.S.O.R.
École des Techniciens de l'Équipement *f:*
  TE
École des Techniques Nouvelles *f:* **ETN**
École de[s] Transmissions *f:* **E.Tr.**
École des Troupes Aéroportées, Pau *f:*
  E.T.A.P.
École des Troupes Blindées *f:* **E.T.B.**
École des Élèves-Officiers de Marine *f:*
  E.E.O.M.
École des Élèves-Officiers de Réserve *f:*
  E.E.O.R.
École d'Ingénieurs de l'Etat de Vaud *f:*
  EINEV
École d'Ingénieurs de Marseille *f:* **E.I.M.**

École d'Ingénieurs Hydrauliciens de
  Grenoble *f:* **E.I.H.G.**
École d'Ingénieurs mécaniciens de la
  Marine Militaire *f:* **E.I.M.M.**
École du Commissariat de la Marine *f:*
  E.C.M.
École du Génie Civil *f:* **E.G.C.**
École du Génie Rural *f:* **EGR**
École du Personnel Féminin de l'Armée de
  Mer *f:* **E.P.F.A.M.**
École du Personnel Navigant *f:* **E.P.N.**
École du Personnel Navigant d'Essais et de
  Reception *f:* **EPNER**
École du Personnel Navigant d'Essais et de
  Réception *f:* **E.P.N.E.R.**
École du Service de Santé Militaire *f:*
  E.S.S.M.
École du Service du Matériel *f:* **E.S.M.**
École du service électrique et de la
  signalisation *f:* **ESES**
École du Travail de la Viande *f:* **ETRAVI**
École d'Éducateurs Spécialisés *f:* **EES**
École d'Électricité et de Mécanique
  Industrielle *f:* **E.E.M.I.**
École d'Électricité Industrielle de Marseille
  f: **E.E.I.M.**
École d'Électricité Industrielle de Paris *f:*
  E.E.I.P.
École d'État-Major *f:* **E.E.M.**
École d'État-Major de l'Air *f:* **E.E.M.A.**
École Enfantine *f:* **EE**
École enfantine *f:* **Eenf**
École et Centre de formation
  Professionnelle *f:* **ECEP**
École Française d'Afrique *f:* **EFA**
École Française de Gestion Commerciale
  f: **EFGC**
École Française de Meunerie *f:* **E.F.M.**
École Française de Radio-électricité *f:*
  EFR
École Française de Radio Électricité et
  d'électronique *f:* **EFRE**
École Française de Tannerie *f:* **EFT**
École Française d'Enseignement
  Paramédical *f:* **EFEP**
École Française des Grandes Surfaces de
  Vente *f:* **EFGSV**
École Française d'Extrême-Orient *f:*
  E.F.E.O.
École Française d'Information et de
  Marketing *f:* **EFIM**
École Française d'Orthopédie et Massage
  f: **EFOM**
École Fédérale de Sport de Macolin *f:* **EFS**
École Gratuite *f:* **EG**
École Instrument de la Paix *f:* **EIP**
École Inter-états des Sciences et Médecine
  Vétérinaires *f:* **EISMV**
École inter-états d'Ingénieurs de
  l'Équipement Rural *f:* **EIER**
École Interaméricaine de Bibliothéconomie
  f: **EIAB**
École Interarmée de Perfectionnement
  d'Officiers *f:* **E.I.P.O.**
École Interarmée des Sports *f:* **E.I.S.**
École Interarmées des Personnels Militaire
  Féminins *f:* **E.I.P.M.F.**
École Internationale de Bordeaux *f:* **EIB**
École Internationale d'Enseignement
  Infirmier Supérieur *f:* **EIEIS**
École Libre *f:* **EL**
École libre de Marketing et de Publicité *f:*
  EMP

École Libre des Sciences Politiques *f:* **ELSP**

École Libre Paroissiale *f:* **ELP**

École Maternelle *f:* **EM**

École maternelle *f:* **Emat**

École Militaire *f:* **E.M.**

École Militaire d'Administration de Vincennes *f:* **Vinc.**

École Militaire de Haute Montagne *f:* **E.M.H.M.**

École Militaire de l'Administration *f:* **E.M.A.**

École Militaire de Spécialisation Atomique *f:* **EMSA**

École Militaire de Strasbourg *f:* **E.M.S.**

École Militaire des Armes Spéciales *f:* **E.M.A.S.**

École Militaire du Corps Technique et Administratif *f:* **E.M.C.T.A.**

École Militaire Inter-Armes Camerounaise *f:* **EMIAC**

École Militaire Préparatoire de la Réunion *f:* **EMPR**

École Militaire Royale *f:* **E.M.R.**

École Militaire Spéciale *f:* **EMS**

École Militaire Supérieure Technique des Transmissions *f:* **EMSTT**

École Moyenne *f:* **EM**

École Municipale *f:* **EM**

École Municipale de Physique et Chimie Industrielle de Paris *f:* **E.M.P.C.I.**

École Municipale de Physique et de Chimie *f:* **E.M.P.C.**

École municipale professionnelle *f:* **EMP**

École Ménagère *f:* **EM**

École Ménagère Agricole *f:* **E.M.A.**

École Météorologique *f:* **EM**

École National des Mines *f:* **ENM**

École National Supérieur d'Agronomie *f:* **ENSA**

École Nationale *f:* **EN**

École Nationale Agronomique Féminine *f:* **ENAF**

École Nationale Annexe des Sous-Officiers d'Active *f:* **E.N.A.S.O.A.**

École Nationale d'Administration *f:* **ENA**

École Nationale d'Administration Municipale *f:* **ENAM**

École Nationale d'Administration Publique *f:* **E.N.A.P.**

École Nationale d'Administration Publique, Universite du Québec, Montreal, Québec *f:* **QMUQEN**

École Nationale d'Administration Publique, Universite du Québec, Québec, Québec *f:* **QQUQEN**

École Nationale d'Agriculture *f:* **ENA,** *f:* **ENAre**

École Nationale d'Agriculture d'Alger *f:* **ENAA**

École Nationale d'Alpinisme *f:* **E.N.Alp.**

École Nationale d'art Décoratif de Nice *f:* **ENDN**

École Nationale d'Assurances *f:* **ENA,** *f:* **ENASS**

École Nationale d'Assurances de Paris *f:* **E.N.A.P.**

École Nationale d'Aéronautique Civile *f:* **E.N.A.C.**

École Nationale d'Aéronautique Navale *f:* **ENAN**

École Nationale de Chimie de Paris *f:* **ENC**

École Nationale de Commerce *f:* **ENC**

École Nationale de Commercialisation des Produits de la Mer *f:* **ENCPM**

École Nationale de Conduite Automobile *f:* **E.N.C.A.**

École Nationale de Formation Agronomique *f:* **ENFA**

École Nationale de Formation des Personnels de l'Éducation Surveillée *f:* **ENFPES**

École Nationale de Formation et de Perfectionnement de Patrons de Pêche et de Mécaniciens *f:* **ENFPPM**

École Nationale de la Coopération *f:* **ENC**

École Nationale de la France d'Outre-Mer *f:* **ENFOM**

École Nationale de la Jeunesse et de lEducation Populaire *f:* **ENJEP**

École Nationale de la Magistrature *f:* **ENM**

École Nationale de la Marine Marchande *f:* **ENMM**

École Nationale de la Météorologie *f:* **ENM**

École Nationale de la Protection Civile *f:* **E.N.P.C.**

École Nationale de la Pédagogie Relationnelle du Language *f:* **ENPRL**

École Nationale de la Santé *f:* **ENS,** *f:* **E.N.S.**

École Nationale de la Santé Publique *f:* **ENSP**

École Nationale de la Statistique et de l'Administration Économique *f:* **ENSAE**

École Nationale de la Visite Médicale *f:* **ECNAVM**

École Nationale de l'Aviation Civile *f:* **ENAC**

École Nationale de l'Éducation Physique Militaire *f:* **E.N.E.P.M.**

École Nationale de Musique *f:* **E.N.Mus.**

École Nationale de Navigation Maritime *f:* **E.N.N.M.**

École Nationale de Navigation Sous-Marine *f:* **E.N.S.M.**

École Nationale de Perfectionnement pour l'Enfance Inadaptée *f:* **ENPEI**

École Nationale de Police *f:* **E.N.P.**

École Nationale de Promotion Sociale *f:* **ENPS**

École Nationale de Radiotechnique et d'Électricité Appliquée *f:* **ENREA**

École Nationale de Santé et dActions Sociales *f:* **ENSAS**

École Nationale de Ski et d'Alpinisme *f:* **ENSA**

École Nationale de Trésor *f:* **ENT**

École Nationale de Voile *f:* **E.N.V.**

École Nationale dEconomie Appliquée *f:* **ENEA**

École Nationale d'Enseignement Ménager *f:* **E.N.E.M.**

École Nationale d'Enseignement Ménager et Agricole de Rennes *f:* **ENEMA**

École Nationale d'Enseignement Technique Aéronautique *f:* **ENETA**

École Nationale d'Entraînement Physique Militaire *f:* **ENEPM**

École Nationale des Arts Décoratifs *f:* **ENAD**

École [nationale] des Arts et Métiers *f:* **A.M.**

École Nationale des Beaux-Arts *f:* **ENBA**

École Nationale des Cadres des Entreprises *f:* **ENCA**

École Nationale des Cadres Techniques *f:* **ENCT**

École Nationale des Chartes *f:* **ENC**

École Nationale des Douanes *f:* **END**

École Nationale des Eaux-et-Forêts *f:* **ENEF**

École Nationale des Haras *f:* **ENH**

École Nationale des Impôts *f:* **ENI**

École Nationale des Industries Agricoles *f:* **E.N.I.A.**

École Nationale des Industries Agricoles et Alimentaires *f:* **ENIAA**

École Nationale des Ingénieurs de Construction Aéronautique *f:* **ENICA**

École Nationale des Ingénieurs des Travaux Agricoles *f:* **ENITA**

École Nationale des Jeunes Aveugles *f:* **E.N.J.A.**

École Nationale des Langues Orientales *f:* **E.N.L.O.**

École Nationale des Langues Orientales Vivantes *f:* **E.N.L.O.V.**

École Nationale des Mines *f:* **ENM**

École Nationale des Moteurs *f:* **E.N.M.**

École Nationale des Officiers de Réserve du Service d'État-Major *f:* **ENORSEM**

École Nationale des Ponts-et-Chaussées *f:* **ENPC**

École nationale des ponts et chaussées *f:* **EPC**

École Nationale des Sciences Géographiques *f:* **ENSG**

École Nationale des Services Vétérinaires *f:* **ENSV**

École Nationale des Sourds-Muets *f:* **ENSM**

École Nationale des Sous-Officiers d'Active *f:* **E.N.S.O.A.**

École Nationale des Techniques Industrielles et des Mines *f:* **ENTIM**

École Nationale des Travaux Aéronautiques *f:* **E.N.T.A.**

École Nationale des Travaux de l'Air *f:* **E.N.T.A.**

École Nationale des Travaux Publics *f:* **ENTP**

École Nationale des Travaux Publics de l'Est *f:* **E.N.T.P.E.**

École Nationale des Vétérinaires *f:* **E.N.V.**

École Nationale d'Horlogerie *f:* **ENH**

École Nationale d'Horticulture *f:* **ENH**

École Nationale d'Ingenieurs *f:* **ENI**

École Nationale d'Ingenieurs des Techniques des Industries Agricoles et Alimentaires *f:* **ENITIAA**

École Nationale d'Ingenieurs des Travaux Agricoles Option Horticulture *f:* **ENITAI**

École Nationale d'Ingénieurs Arts et Métiers *f:* **ENIAM**

École Nationale d'Ingénieurs de Strasbourg *f:* **ENIS**

École Nationale d'Ingénieurs de Travaux *f:* **ENIT**

École Nationale d'Ingénieurs de Travaux Agricoles Horticoles *f:* **ENITAH**

École Nationale d'Ingénieurs de Travaux Eaux et Forêts *f:* **ENITEF**

École Nationale d'Ingénieurs de Travaux Ruraux et Techniques Sanitaires *f:* **ENITRTS**

École Nationale d'Ingénieurs des
    Techniques des Industries Agricoles et
    Alimentaires *f:* **ENITAA**
École Nationale d'Ingénieurs des Travaux
    Ruraux et des Techniques Sanitaires *f:*
    E.N.I.T.R.
École Nationale d'Ingénieurs Spécialisés en
    Agriculture *f:* **ENISA**
École Nationale d'Informatique *f:* **ENI**
École Nationale d'Optique Appliquée *f:*
    ENOA
École Nationale d'Organisation Économique
    et Sociale *f:* **E.N.O.E.S.**
École Nationale du Cadastre *f:* **ENC**
École Nationale du Génie Rural, des Eaux
    et Forêts *f:* **ENGREF**
École Nationale d'Électrotechnique
    Hydraulique et Radio *f:* **ENEHR**
École Nationale d'Équitation *f:* **E.N.E.**
École Nationale Forestiere d'Ingenieurs *f:*
    ENFI
École Nationale Féminine d'Agronomie *f:*
    ENFA
École Nationale Laitière *f:* **ENL**
École Nationale Professionnelle *f:* **ENP**
École Nationale Professionnelle de l'Air *f:*
    ENPA
École Nationale Superieure d'Agronomique
    de Montpellier *f:* **ENSAM**
École Nationale Superieure de Saint Etienne
    f: **ENSMSE**
École Nationale Superieure des Industries
    Agro Alimentaires du Cameroun *f:*
    ENSIAAC
École Nationale Superieure d'Horticulture
    f: **ENSI**
École Nationale Supérieur des Officier
    Sapeur-Pompier *f:* **ENSOSP**
École Nationale Supérieure Agronomique
    f: **E.N.S.A.**
École Nationale Supérieure Agronomique
    de Grignon *f:* **E.N.S.A.G.**
École Nationale Supérieure Agronomique
    de Nancy *f:* **ENSAN**
École Nationale Supérieure Agronomique
    de Rennes *f:* **ENSAR**
École Nationale Supérieure Agronomique
    de Toulouse *f:* **ENSAT**
École Nationale Supérieure d'Agronomie et
    des Industries Alimentaires *f:* **ENSAIA**
École Nationale Supérieure d'Agronomie
    pour Jeunes Filles *f:* **ENSAJF**
École Nationale Supérieure d'Architecture
    et des Arts Décoratifs *f:* **ENSAD**
École Nationale Supérieure de
    Bibliothécaires *f:* **ENSB**
École Nationale Supérieure de Biologie
    Appliquée à la Nutrition et à
    l'Alimentation *f:* **ENSBANA**
École Nationale Supérieure de Brasserie *f:*
    E.N.S.B.
École Nationale Supérieure de Chimie de
    Bordeaux *f:* **ENSCB**
École Nationale Supérieure de Chimie de
    Caen *f:* **ENSCC**
École Nationale Supérieure de Chimie de
    Clermond Ferrand *f:* **ENSCCF**
École Nationale Supérieure de Chimie de
    Lille *f:* **ENSCL**
École Nationale Supérieure de Chimie de
    Montpellier *f:* **ENSCM**
École Nationale Supérieure de Chimie de
    Paris *f:* **ENSCP**

École Nationale Supérieure de Chimie de
    Rouen *f:* **ENSCR**
École Nationale Supérieure de Chimie de
    Strasbourg *f:* **ENSCS**
École Nationale Supérieure de Chimie de
    Toulouse *f:* **ENSCT**
École Nationale Supérieure de
    Chronométrie et Micromécanique *f:*
    ENSCM
École Nationale Supérieure de Céramique
    f: **E.N.S.C.**
École Nationale Supérieure de Céramique
    Industrielle *f:* **ENSCI**
École Nationale Supérieure de Fontenay-
    aux-Roses *f:* **ENSF**
École Nationale Supérieure de Géologie *f:*
    ENSG
École Nationale Supérieure de Géologie
    Appliquée et de Prospection Minière *f:*
    ENSGAPM
École Nationale Supérieure de Géologie
    Appliquée et de Prospection Minière de
    Nancy *f:* **E.N.S.G.A.N.**
École Nationale Supérieure de
    l'Aéronautique *f:* **E.N.S.A.**, *f:* **E.N.S.Aé.**
École Nationale Supérieure de
    l'Aéronautique et de l'Espace *f:* **ENSAE**
École Nationale Supérieure de
    l'Électronique et de ses Applications *f:*
    ENSEA
École Nationale Supérieure de Meunerie et
    des Industries Céréalières *f:* **ENSMIC**
École Nationale Supérieure de Mécanique
    f: **ENSM**
École Nationale Supérieure de Mécanique et
    Aéronautique *f:* **ENSMA**
École Nationale Supérieure de Mécanique et
    d'Aérotechnique de Poitiers *f:*
    E.N.S.M.A.P.
École Nationale Supérieure de Métallurgie
    et d'Industrie des Mines *f:* **ENSMIM**
École Nationale Supérieure de Navigation
    f: **ENSN**
École Nationale Supérieure de Physique *f:*
    ENSP
École Nationale Supérieure de Techniques
    Avancées *f:* **ENSTA**
École Nationale Supérieure d'Enseignement
    Technique Agricole Féminine *f:*
    ENSETAF
École Nationale Supérieure des Arts
    Décoratifs *f:* **E.N.S.A.D.**
École Nationale Supérieure des Arts et
    Industries de Strasbourg *f:* **ENSAIS**
École Nationale Supérieure des Arts et
    Industries Textiles *f:* **ENSAIT**
École Nationale Supérieure des Beaux-Arts
    f: **ENSBA**
École Nationale Supérieure des Industries
    Agricoles et Alimentaires *f:* **ENISA**, *f:*
    ENSIAA
École Nationale Supérieure des Industries
    Chimiques de Nancy *f:* **E.N.S.I.C.N.**
École Nationale Supérieure des Mines *f:*
    ENSM
École Nationale Supérieure des Mines de
    Nancy *f:* **E.N.S.M.N.**
École Nationale Supérieure des Mines de
    Paris *f:* **ENSMP**
École nationale supérieure des Mines de
    Saint-Etienne *f:* **EMSE**
École Nationale Supérieure des Mines de
    Saint-Étienne *f:* **ENSME**

École Nationale Supérieure des Officiers de
    Réserve du Service d'État-Major *f:*
    ENSORSEM
École Nationale Supérieure des PTT
    [Postes, Télégraphes, Téléphones] *f:*
    ENSPTT
École Nationale Supérieure des Sciences
    Agronomiques Appliquées *f:* **ENSAA**, *f:*
    ENSSAA
École Nationale Supérieure des Sciences de
    l'Information et des Bibliothèques *f:*
    ENSSIB
École Nationale Supérieure des Travaux
    Publics *f:* **ENSTP**
École Nationale Supérieure des Travaux
    Publics de l'État *f:* **ENTPE**
École Nationale Supérieure des
    Télécommunications *f:* **ENST**
École Nationale Supérieure des
    Télécommunications de Bretagne *f:*
    ENSTBr
École Nationale Supérieure d'Horticulture
    f: **ENSH**
École Nationale Supérieure d'Hydraulique
    f: **ENSH**
École Nationale Supérieure d'Industrie
    Chimique *f:* **ENSIC**
École Nationale Supérieure d'Informatique
    et de Mathématique Appliquée *f:*
    ENSIMA
École Nationale Supérieure d'Ingénieurs *f:*
    ENSI
École Nationale Supérieure d'Ingénieurs des
    Études et Techniques de l'Armement *f:*
    E.N.S.I.E.T.A.
École Nationale Supérieure du Génie
    Maritime *f:* **E.N.S.G.M.**
École Nationale Supérieure du Paysage *f:*
    ENSP
École Nationale Supérieure du Pétrole *f:*
    ENSP
École Nationale Supérieure du Pétrole et
    des Moteurs à Combustion Interne *f:*
    ENSPM
École Nationale Supérieure d'Éducation
    Physique de Jeunes Gens *f:* **ENSEPJG**
École Nationale Supérieure d'Électricité et
    de Mécanique *f:* **ENSEM**
École Nationale Supérieure d'Électricité et
    de Mécanique de Nancy *f:* **E.N.S.E.M.N.**
École Nationale Supérieure d'Électrochimie
    et d'Électrométallurgie de Grenoble *f:*
    ENSEEG, *f:* **ENSEG**
École Nationale Supérieure
    d'Électrométallurgie et d'Électrochimie
    f: **ENSEE**
École Nationale Supérieure d'Électronique
    et de Radio-électricité *f:* **ENSER**
École Nationale Supérieure d'Électronique
    et d'Électricité de Caen *f:* **ENSEEC**
École Nationale Supérieure
    d'Électrotechnique, d'Hydraulique et de
    Radio-Électricité de Grenoble *f:*
    ENSEHR
École Nationale Supérieure
    d'Électrotechnique et de Génie Physique
    f: **ENSEGP**
École nationale supérieure
    délectrotechnique et dhydraulique *f:*
    ENSEH
École Nationale Supérieure
    d'Électrotechnique et d'Hydraulique de
    Grenoble *f:* **E.N.S.E.H.G.**

École Nationale Supérieure
d'Électrotechnique et d'Hydraulique de
Toulouse *f:* **E.N.S.E.H.T.**

École Nationale Supérieure
d'Électrotechnique, Électronique,
Informatique et Hydraulique de Toulouse
f: **ENSEEIHT**

École Nationale Supérieure Féminine
d'Agronomie *f:* **ENSFA**

École Nationale technique des Sous-
officiers d'Active Armées *f:* **E.N.S.O.A.**

École Nationale Technique des Sous-
Officiers d'Active armées *f:*
E.N.T.S.O.A.

École Nationale Veterinaire de Lyon *f:*
ENVL

École Nationale Veterinaire de Nantes *f:*
ENVN

École Nationale Veterinaire de Toulouse *f:*
ENVT

École Nationale Vétérinaire d'Alfort *f:*
E.N.V.A.

École Nationale Ágricole de Arroz et
Formation *f:* **ENA**

École Navale *f:* **E.N.**

École Normale *f:* **EN**

École Normale Catholique *f:* **ENC**

École Normale de Représentation
Technique *f:* **E.N.R.T.**

École Normale d'Enseignement Technique
f: **E.N.E.T.**

École Normale d'Instituteurs *f:* **E.N.I.**

École Normale d'Éducation Physique *f:*
E.N.E.P.

École Normale d'Éducation Physique
Féminine et Catholique *f:* **ENEPFC**

École Normale Jacques Cartier *f:* **ENJC**

École Normale M. L. Duplessis, Trois-
Rivieres, Quebec *e:* **QTE**

École Normale Mixte *f:* **ENM**

École Normale Nationale d'Apprentissage
f: **ENNA**

École Normale Ouvrière *f:* **ENO**

École Normale Primaire *f:* **ENP**

École Normale Primaire d'Instituteurs *f:*
E.N.P.I.

École Normale Préparatoire de
l'Enseignement dans les Collèges *f:*
E.N.P.E.C.

École Normale Secondaire de Jeunes Filles
f: **E.N.S.J.F.**

École Normale Sociale *f:* **ENS**

École Normale Supérieure *f:* **ENS**

École Normale Supérieure de lAfrique
Centrale *f:* **ENSAC**

École Normale Supérieure de
l'Enseignement *f:* **E.N.S.E.**

École Normale Supérieure de
l'Enseignement Primaire *f:* **E.N.S.E.P.**

École Normale Supérieure d'Enseignement
Secondaire *f:* **ENSES**

École Normale Supérieure d'Enseignement
Technique *f:* **ENSET**

École Normale Supérieure des Jeunes Filles
f: **ENSJF**

École Normale Supérieure d'Éducation
Physique *f:* **E.N.S.E.P.**

École Normale Supérieure d'Éducation
Physique et Sportive *f:* **ENSEPS**

École Nouvelle d'Organisation Économique
et Sociale *f:* **ENOES**

École nouvelle d'organisation économique
et sociale *f:* **OES**

École Nouvelle Préparatoire *f:* **ENP**

École Polytechnique *f:* **EP**, *f:* **P.**

École Polytechnique d'Assurances *f:* **EPA**

École Polytechnique de Lausanne *f:* **EPL**

École Polytechnique de l'Université de
Lausanne *f:* **EPUL**

École Polytechnique de Montreal *f:* **EPM**

École Polytechnique de Vente *f:* **E.P.V.**

École Polytechnique de Zürich *f:* **EPZ**

École Polytechnique de Zurich *f:* **PZ**

École Polytechnique Fédérale *f:* **EPF**

École Polytechnique Fédérale de Lausanne
f: **EPFL**

École Polytechnique Fédérale de Zurich *f:*
EPFZ

École Polytechnique Féminine *f:* **E.P.F.**

École Polytechnique, Montreal, Quebec *f:*
QMEP

École Pratique de l'Alliance Française *f:*
EPAF

École Pratique de Représentation *f:* **EPR**

École Pratique de Service Social *f:*
E.P.S.S.

École Pratique de Sous-Marins *f:* **E.P.S.M.**

École Pratique d'Enseignement Programmé
f: **EPEP**

École Pratique des Hautes Études *f:* **EPHE**

École Pratique d'Infirmières *f:* **E.P.I.**

École Primaire *f:* **EP**

École primaire *f:* **Epr**

École Professionnelle *f:* **EP**

École Professionnelle d'Apprentissage
Maritime *f:* **EPAM**

École Professionnelle de Dessin Industriel
f: **EPDI**

École Professionnelle de la Société
Industrielle et Commerciale *f:* **EPSIC**

École professionnelle de soudure *f:* **EPS**

École Professionnelle Supérieure de
l'Informatique *f:* **EPSI**

École Préparatoire *f:* **EP**

École Préparatoire de Gendarmerie *f:*
E.P.G

École Quebecoise du Meuble et du Bois
Ouvre, College de Victoriaville, Quebec
f: **QVCEMBO**

École Romande de Typographie *f:* **ERT**

École Royale Militaire *f:* **ERM**

École Régionale d'Agriculture *f:* **ERA**

École Régionale d'Organisation Scientifique
du Travail *f:* **EROST**

École Régionale postuniversitaire
d'Aménagement et de gestion Intégrée des
Forêts Tropicales *e:* **ERAIFT**

École Secondaire Champlain, Ottawa,
Ontario *f:* **OOESC**

École Secondaire le Caron,
Penetanguishene, Ontario *f:* **OPENE**

École Secondaire Nicolas-Gatineau,
Gatineau, Quebec *f:* **QGNG**

École Secondaire Saint-Stanislas, Montreal,
Quebec *f:* **QMES**

École Secondaire St.-Francois, Sherbrooke,
Quebec *f:* **QSHERSF**

École Secondaire St.-Joseph, Hull, Quebec
f: **QHESJ**

École Spéciale d'Architecture *f:* **ESA**

École Spéciale de Langues Orientales
Vivantes *f:* **E.S.L.O.V.**

École Spéciale de l'Architecture des Jardins
f: **ESAJ**

École Spéciale de Mécanique et
d'Electricité *f:* **E.S.M.E.**

École [spéciale] des Langues Orientales
[vivantes] *f:* **E.L.O.**

École Spéciale des Travaux Aéronautiques
f: **ESTA**

École Spéciale des Travaux Publics *f:* **ETP**

École Spéciale Militaire *f:* **E.S.M.**

École Spéciale Militaire Interarmes *f:*
E.S.M.I.A.

École Spécialisée et Sociale des Retraités
f: **ESSOR**

École Suisse d'Aviation et de Transport *f:*
ESAT

École Suisse de Tourisme *f:* **EST**

École Suisse d'Ingenieurs et Techniciens du
Bois *f:* **ESIB**

École Superieure des Mines *f:* **ESM**

École Supérieure *f:* **EcSup**

École Supérieure Aéronautique *f:* **E.S.A.**

École Supérieure d'Agriculture *f:* **ESA**, *f:*
E.S.A.

École Supérieure d'Agriculture d'Angers *f:*
ESAA

École Supérieure d'Agriculture de Purpan
f: **ESAP**

École Supérieure d'Agriculture de Tunis *f:*
ESAT

École Supérieure d'Agronomie Tropicale *f:*
ESAT

École Supérieure d'Application
d'Agriculture Tropicale *f:* **E.S.A.A.T.**

École Supérieure d'Application du Matériel
f: **ESAM**

École Supérieure d'Approvisionnement *f:*
ESA, *f:* **ESAP**

École Supérieure d'Aéronautique *f:*
Supaéro

École Supérieure de Brasserie et de Malterie
f: **ESBM**

École Supérieure de Cadres pour
l'Économie et l'Administration *f:*
ESCEA

École Supérieure de Chimie *f:* **ESC**

École Supérieure de Chimie Appliquée *f:*
ESCA

École Supérieure de Chimie de Mulhouse
f: **ESCM**

École Supérieure de Chimie Industrielle *f:*
ESCIL

École Supérieure de Chimie Industrielle de
Lyon *f:* **E.S.C.I.L.**

École Supérieure de Chimie Organique et
Minérale *f:* **ESCOM**

École Supérieure de Commerce *f:* **ESC**

École Supérieure de Commerce de Dijon *f:*
ESCD

École Supérieure de Commerce de Lyon *f:*
ESCL

École Supérieure de Commerce de Marseille
f: **ESCM**

École Supérieure de Commerce de Paris *f:*
ESCP

École Supérieure de Commerce de Toulouse
f: **ESCT**

École supérieure de commerce et
d'administration des entreprises *f:*
E.S.C.A.E.

École Supérieure de Commerce et
d'Administration des Entreprises de
Rouen *f:* **ESCAER**

École Supérieure de Comptabilité *f:* **ESC**

École Supérieure de Couture *f:* **ESC**

École Supérieure de Filature de Mulhouse
f: **E.S.F.M.**

École Supérieure de Filature et Textile *f:*
E.S.F.T.

École Supérieure de Filature et Tissage de
l'Est *f:* **ESFTE**

École supérieure de fonderie *f:* **ESF**

École Supérieure de Formation Agricole *f:*
ESFA

École supérieure de Guerre Aérienne *f:*
E.S.G.A.

École Supérieure de Guerre Interarmée *f:*
E.S.G.I.

École Supérieure de Guerre Navale *f:*
ESGN

École Supérieure de la Marine *f:* **E.S.M.**

École Supérieure de l'Intendance Militaire
f: **E.S.I.M.**

École Supérieure de l'Électronique de
l'Armée de Terre *f:* **ESEAT**

École Supérieure de Pharmacie *f:* **E.S.P.**

École Supérieure de Physique et Chimie
Industrielle de Paris *f:* **ESPCI**

École Supérieure de Publicité *f:* **ESP**

École Supérieure de Publicité et de
Marketing *f:* **ESPM**

École Supérieure de Secrétariat *f:* **E.S.S.**

École Supérieure de Soudure Autogène *f:*
E.S.S.A.

École Supérieure de Technologie Électrique
f: **ESTE**

École Supérieure de Travaux Aéronautiques
f: **E.S.T.A.**

École Supérieure de Télévision *f:* **EST**

École Supérieure des Arts Modernes *f:*
ESAM

École Supérieure des Dirigeants
d'Entreprises *f:* **ESDE**

École Supérieure des Géomètres et
Typographes *f:* **ESGT**

École Supérieure des Industries Agricoles et
Alimentaitres *f:* **ESIAA**

École Supérieure des Industries de
Vêtement *f:* **ESIV**

École Supérieure des Industries Laitières *f:*
E.S.I.L.

École Supérieure des Industries Textiles de
Mulhouse *f:* **ESIT**, *f:* **ESITM**

École Supérieure des Mines *f:* **E.M.**

École supérieure des Mines de la Géologie
de la Communauté économique de
l'Afrique de l'Ouest *f:* **EMIG**

École Supérieure des Métiers de la Viande
f: **ESMV**

École Supérieure des Officiers de Réserve
du Service d'Etat-Major *f:* **E.S.O.R.E.M.**

École Supérieure des Postes, Télégraphes et
Téléphones [Télécommunications] *f:*
E.S.P.T.T.

École supérieure des postes-télégraphes-
téléphones *f:* **ESPTT**

École Supérieure des Sciences
Commerciales Appliquées *f:* **ESSCA**

École Supérieure des Sciences
Commerciales d'Augers *f:* **ESSCA**

École supérieure des sciences économiques
et commerciales *f:* **ESSEC**

École Supérieure des Sciences
Économiques et Commerciales *f:*
E.S.S.E.C.

École Supérieure des Techniques de
Biologie Appliquée *f:* **ESTBA**

École Supérieure des Techniques de Brest
f: **ESTB**

École Supérieure de[s] Transmissions *f:*
ES&T

École Supérieure des Transports *f:* **EST**

École Supérieure des Travaux Publics *f:*
E.S.T.P.

École Supérieure des Travaux Publics et
Bâtiments Industriels *f:* **ESTPBI**

École Supérieure d'Information
Documentaire *f:* **ESID**

École Supérieure d'Informatique *f:* **ESI**

École Supérieure d'Informatique,
d'Électrotechnique et d'Automatisme *f:*
ESIEA

École Supérieure d'Informatique
Professionnelle *f:* **E.S.I.P.**

École Supérieure d'Ingénieurs de Marseille
f: **ESIM**

École Supérieure d'Ingénieurs en
Électrotechnique et Électronique *f:*
ESIEE

École Supérieure d'Ingénieurs et
Techniciens pour l'Agriculture *f:*
ESITPA

École Supérieure d'Intendance *f:* **ESI**

École Supérieure d'Interpretation et de
Traduction *f:* **ESIT**

École Supérieure d'Interprètes et
Traducteurs *f:* **ESIT**

École Supérieure du Bois *f:* **ESB**

École Supérieure du Génie Militaire *f:*
ESGM

École Supérieure du Génie Rural *f:*
E.S.G.R.

École Supérieure du Journalisme *f:* **ESJ**

École Supérieure du Laboratoire *f:* **ESL**

École Supérieure du Textile *f:* **ES&T**

École Supérieure d'Éducation Physique [et
sportive] *f:* **E.S.E.P.**

École Supérieure d'Électricité *f:* **E.S.E.**, *f:*
Sup, *f:* **Sup. Elect.**

École Supérieure d'Électronique de l'Ouest
f: **ESEO**

École Supérieure et Technique d'Arceuil *f:*
ESTA

École Supérieure Féminine Agricole *f:*
E.S.F.A.

École Supérieure Interafricaine de
l'Électricité *f:* **ESIE**

École Supérieure Internationale de
Journalisme de Yaoundé *f:* **ESIJY**

École Supérieure Internationale de la
Coopération *f:* **ESIC**

École Supérieure Physique/Chimie *f:*
ESPC

École Supérieure Polytechnique *f:* **ESP**

École Supérieure Technique des
Transmissions *f:* **E.S.T.T.**

École Supérieure Technique du Génie *f:*
E.S.T.G.

École Technique Coopérative *f:* **E.T.C.**

École Technique d'Aéronautique et de
Construction Automobile *f:* **ETACA**

École Technique de formation à l'Efficacité
dans les Relations et les Communications
f: **ETERC**

École Technique de la Conserve *f:* **ETC**

École Technique de l'Aéronautique et
Construction Automobile *f:* **ETECA**

École Technique de Photo et du Cinéma *e:*
E.T.P.C.

École Technique de Publicité *f:* **E.T.P.**

École Technique des Métiers de
l'Alimentation *f:* **ETMA**

École Technique des Surintendantes
d'Usines et de Services Sociaux *f:*
E.T.S.U.S.S.

École Technique du Bois *f:* **ETB**

École Technique et de Normalisation
Bancaire *f:* **ETNB**

École Technique Normale *f:* **E.T.N.**

École Technique Officielle *f:* **ETO**

École Technique Secondaire Superieure
d'Agriculture *f:* **ETSA**

École Technique Supérieure *f:* **ETS**

École Technique Supérieure de Dessin
Appliqué *f:* **ETSDA**

École Technique Supérieure de la Marine
f: **E.T.S.M.**

École Technique Supérieure de l'Armement
f: **E.T.S.A.**

École Technique Supérieure de l'Industrie
Graphique *f:* **ESIG**

École Technique Supérieure des
Constructions et Armes Navales *f:*
ETSCAN

École Technique Supérieure d'Ingénieurs
Industriels *f:* **ETSII**

École Technique Supérieure du Laboratoire
f: **ETSL**

École Universitaire d'Ingénieurs de Lille *f:*
EUDIL

École universitaire par correspondance *f:*
EUC

École Vaudoise en Mutation *f:* **EVM**

École vétérinaire d'Alfort *f:* **EA**

École Vétérinaire d'Alfort *f:* **EVA**

École Élémentaire *f:* **E.El.**

Écoles d'Agriculture *f:* **E.A.**

Écoles d'Application *f:* **E.A.**

Écoles d'Apprentissage *f:* **E.A.**

Écoles d'Assistantes Sociales *f:* **E.A.S.**

Écoles de Métiers *f:* **E.M.**

Écoles de Perfectionnement des Sous-
Officiers de Réserve *f:* **E.P.S.O.R.**

Écoles des Sages-Femmes *f:* **E.S.F.**

Écoles Libres Paroissiales *f:* **E.L.P.**

Écoles Maternelles *f:* **E.M.**

Écoles Municipales *f:* **E.M.**

Écoles Ménagères *f:* **E.M.**

Écoles Nationales d'Agriculture *f:* **E.N.Ag.**

Écoles Nationales d'Arts et Métiers *f:*
E.N.A.M.

Écoles Nationales de Médecine Vétérinaire
f: **E.N.M.V.**

Écoles Nationales d'Industries Laitères *f:*
ENIL

Écoles Nationales Professionnelles *f:*
E.N.P.

Écoles Nationales Supérieures
Agronomiques *f:* **ENSA**

Écoles Normales Primaires *f:* **E.N.P.**

Ecoles Polytechniques Fédérales *f:* **EPF**

Écoles Pratiques de Commerce et
d'Industrie *f:* **E.P.C.I.**

Ecoles Primaires Confessionnelles *f:* **EPC**

Écoles Primaires pour Filles *f:* **E.P.F.**

Écoles Primaires pour Garçons *f:* **E.P.G**

Écoles Primaires Supérieures *f:* **EPS**

Écoles Primaires Élémentaires *f:* **E.P.E.**

Écoles Professionnelles de la Ville de Paris
f: **E.P.V.P.**

Écoles Professionnelles Industrielles et
Artisanales *f:* **EPIA**

Écoles Régimentaires *f:* **E.R.**

Écoles Régionales d'Agriculture *f:* **E.R.A.**

Écoles sans Frontières *f:* **ESF**

Écoles Techniques *f:* **E.T.**
Écoles Vétérinaires *f:* **E.V.**
Écolier *f:* **Ec**
Ecologia Mediterranea *e:* **Ecol. Mediterr.**
Ecological *e:* **ECO,** *e:* **ECOL**
Ecological Agriculture Project *e:* **EAP**
Ecological and Physical Sciences Study
  Center *e:* **EPSSC**
Ecological and Toxicological Association
  of the Dyes and Pigments Manufacturers
  e: **ETAD**
Ecological Applications *e:* **Ecol. Appl.**
Ecological Centre of Study and Protection
  of the East-European [Tundra] *e:* **ECET**
Ecological Classification System *e:* **ECS**
Ecological Coalition on the Law of the Sea
  e: **ECOLOS**
Ecological Consortium *e:* **ECOCO**
ecological criticism *e:* **ecolcrit**
Ecological Entomology *e:* **Ecol. Entomol.**
Ecological Genetics *e:* **EG**
Ecological Information and Analysis Center
  e: **EIAC**
Ecological Integrity *e:* **EI**
Ecological Management of Arid and Semi
  Arid Rangelands in Africa, the Near East
  and Middle East *e:* **EMASAR**
Ecological Modelling *e:* **Ecol. Model.**
Ecological Monitoring and Assessment
  Network *e:* **EMAN**
Ecological Monitoring Coordinating Office
  e: **EMCO**
Ecological Monitoring of the Oceans
  Programme [Russian Federation] *e:*
  ECOMONOC
Ecological Monographs [of Ecological
  Society of America] *e:* **Ecol. Monogr.**
Ecological Optics for Surfaces *e:*
  REALISE-NSF-EC-US056
Ecological (or Ecology) Society of America
  e: **ESA**
Ecological Planning and Assessment *e:*
  EPA
Ecological Planning and Assessment Group
  e: **EPAG**
Ecological Rates of Change *e:* **EROC**
Ecological Research *e:* **Ecol. Res.**
Ecological Research and Investigations *e:*
  ERG
Ecological Research and Investigations
  Group *e:* **ERIG**
Ecological Research Division *e:* **ERD**
Ecological Research Information System
  Kiel *e:* **EcoRISK**
Ecological Research Network *e:* **ERN**
Ecological Research Project *e:* **ERP**
Ecological Response to Change *e:* **EROC**
Ecological Review *e:* **SKENAN**
Ecological Risk Assessment *e:* **ERA**
Ecological Science Centre *e:* **ESC**
Ecological Science Centres *e:* **ESCs**
Ecological Science Co-operative *e:* **ESC**
Ecological Science Co-operatives *e:* **ESCs**
Ecological Sciences Information System *e:*
  ESIC
Ecological Society of America *e:* **Ecol Soc
  Am**
Ecological Society of Australia *e:* **ESA**
Ecological Society of Equatorial South
  America *e:* **ESA**
Ecological Statistics Package *e:* **ESP**
Ecological Studies *e:* **Ecol. Stud.**
Ecological Study Center *e:* **ESC**

ecological system economic system *e:* **eco
  system**
Ecological Vegetation Class *e:* **EVC**
ecologically ideal utopia[n] *e:* **ecotopia[n]**
Ecologically Sustainable Development *e:*
  ESD
Ecologically Sustainable Development
  Intersectoral Issues Report *e:* **ESDIIR**
Ecologically Sustainable Development
  Steering Committee *e:* **ESDSC**
Ecologically Sustainable Forest
  Management *e:* **ESFM**
Ecologically Sustainable Society *e:* **ESS**
Ecologie des côtes et du plateau continental
  de la zone de la glace de mer antarctique
  f: **CS-EASIZ**
ecologist *e:* **eco**
Ecologist *e:* **ECOL**
ecology *e:* **ecol**
Ecology Action *e:* **E/A**
Ecology Action Educational Institute *e:*
  EAEI
Ecology and Analysis of Trace
  Contaminants *e:* **EATC**
Ecology and Environment, Inc., Buffalo *e:*
  NBuEE
Ecology and Epidemiology Laboratory *e:*
  EEL
Ecology and Evolution Home Page *e:*
  EEHP
Ecology Center *e:* **EC**
Ecology Center Communications Council
  e: **ECCC**
Ecology Center Kiel *e:* **ECK**
Ecology Council of America *e:* **ECA**
ecology critic *e:* **ecolcrit**
Ecology Ethology and Evolution *e:* **EEE**
Ecology for Mineral Industries *e:* **EMI**
ecology fuel *e:* **ecofuel**
Ecology International Corporation *e:* **EIC**
Ecology of Knowledge Network *e:* **EKN**
Ecology of the Antarctic Sea Ice Zone *e:*
  EASIZ
Ecology of the Continental Margins *e:*
  ECOMARGE
Ecology on the Internet *e:* **EOTI**
Ecology Party *e:* **Eco Pty,** *e:* **EP**
ecology signal *e:* **eco**
Ecología de la Costa y la Plataforma
  Continental de la Zona de Hielo Marino
  del Antártico *s:* **CS-EASIZ**
EcoNet Environmental Directory *e:* **ENED**
Economic Analysis of Water Supply *e:*
  WATER
Economic and Applied Microbiology *e:*
  EAM
Economic Evaluation of Natural Resources
  e: **EENR**
Economic Geographic Information
  Reference Tape *e:* **EGIRT**
Economic Geographic Reference File *e:*
  EGRF
Economic Geography *e:* **Econ Geog,** *e:*
  EG
Economic Geology and the Bulletin of the
  Society of Economic Geologists *e:* **Econ
  Geol.**
Economic Geology [of Society od
  Economic Geologists] *e:* **Econ. Geol.**
Economic Geology Series *e:* **EGS**
Ecosystem Dynamics and the Atmosphere
  e: **EDA**

Ecosystem Dynamics and the Atmosphere
  Section *e:* **EDAS**
Ecotoxicology and Environmental Safety
  e: **Ecotoxicol. Environ. Saf.,** *e:*
  Ecotoxicol Environ Saf, *e:* **EES**
Edge of Earth *e:* **EOE**
Edinaja Sistema Naucnoj Medicinskoj
  Informacii Socialisticeskih Stran *R:*
  ESNMI
Edinburgh Department of Geology *e:* **EDG**
Edinburgh Geological Society *e:* **EGS**
Edinburgh Geology and Geophysics *e:*
  EGG
Edinburgh Medical Missionary Society *e:*
  EMMS
Edinburgh Remote Terminal Emulator *e:*
  ERTE
Édition des Vedettes Autorité Auteur dans
  le Système Medicis *f:* **EDIVED**
Éditions de l'École du Chant *f:* **EDUC**
Éditions Médicales Et Universitaires *f:*
  EMU
Editorial Board for the International
  Bathymetric Chart of the Caribbean Sea
  and the Gulf of Mexico, short name:
  Editorial Board for IBCCA *e:* **EB-
  IBCCA**
Editorial Board for the International
  Bathymetric Chart of the Mediterranean
  and its Geological/ Geophysical Series
  e: **EB-IBCM**
Editorial Board for the International
  Bathymetric Chart of the Western Indian
  Ocean, short name: Editorial Board for
  the IBCWIO *e:* **EB-IBCWIO**
Edmonton Space Sciences Foundation *e:*
  ESSF
Educacion Medica y Salud *e:* **Educ Med
  Salud**
Education à l'Environnement, bien sûr *f:*
  EE
Education and Communication on
  Environment and Development *e:* **ECO-
  ED**
Education and Neighborhood Action for
  Better Living Environment *e:* **ENABLE**
Education Career Services/Health Career
  Service *e:* **ECS/HCS**
Éducation Médicale Continue *f:* **EMC**
Educational Commission for Foreign
  Medical Graduates *e:* **ECFMG**
Educational Council for Foreign Medical
  Students *e:* **ECFMS**
Educational Council for/of Foreign Medical
  Graduates *e:* **ECFMG**
Educational Excellence for Children with
  Environmental Limitations *e:* **EEXCEL**
Educational Resources Information
  Center/Clearinghouse for Science,
  Mathematics, and Environmental
  Education *e:* **ERIC/SMEAC**
Education's Leadership Georgia *e:* **ELG**
Educazione Continua in Medicina *i:* **ECM**
Edward Henry Kraus Natural Science
  Building *e:* **N S**
Eerste Centrale Organisatie ter Nivellering
  van Angemotiveerde Overwinstmarges
  n: **ECONOOM**
Effective Biological Dose *e:* **EBD**
Effective Medical Practice and Managed
  Care *e:* **EMPMC**
effektive Pferdestärke *d:* **ePS**
Efficacité Biologique Relative *f:* **EBA**

   Abkürzungen und Akronyme in Ökologie, Umwelt, Geowissenschaften

efficacité biologique relative *f:* **EBR**

Efficient Water Management Practice *e:*
EWMP

Effluent and Water Advisory Committee *e:*
EWAC

Effluent and Water Treatment Journal *e:*
Effluent Water Treat. J.

EFMC International Symposium on
Medicinal Chemistry *e:* **EFMC-ISMC,**
e: **ISMC**

Egyptian Journal of Biomedical
Engineering [of National Information and
Dokumentation Center, Egypt] *e:* **Egypt.
J. Biomed. Eng.**

Egyptian Medical Association *e:* **EMA**

Egyptian National Committee of the
International Association on Water
Pollution Research and Control *e:*
ENCIAWPRC

Egyptian Remote Sensing Center *e:* **ERSC**

Egyptian Society of Animal Production *e:*
ESAP

El Paso Natural Gas Co., Technical
Information Center, El Paso *e:* **TxENG**

Eidgenössische Anstalt für
Wasserversorgung, Abwasserreinigung
und Gewässerschutz *d:* **EAWAG**

Eidgenössische Forschungsanstalt für
Agrikulturchemie und Umwelthygiene
d: **FAC**

Eidgenössische Militärpferdeanstalt *d:*
EMPFA

Eidgenössische Natur- und Heimatschutz-
Kommission *d:* **NHK**

Eidgenössische Natur- und
Heimatschutzkommission *d:* **ENHK**

Eidgenössisches Amt für Wasserwirtschaft
d: **A+W**

Eidgenössisches Departement für Umwelt,
Verkehr Energie und Kommunikation *d:*
UVEK

Eigenkontroll-Verordnung (Abwasser) *e:*
EKVO

Eilat Gulf Coral Reef Nature Reserve *e:*
EGCRNR

Ein Gedi Nature Reserve *e:* **EGNR**

Einfache Wetterbedingungen am Tag *d:*
TE

Einflüsse der Küste auf Atmosphäre und
Meer *d:* **EKAM**

Einheitlicher Meteorologischer
Datenspeicher, Potsdam *e:* **EMDS**

Einheitliches astronomisch - geodätisches
Netz *d:* **EAGN**

einheitliches Kontrollsystem
Wasserwirtschaft *d:* **EKS
Wasserwirtschaft**

Einjähriges Wildgras *d:* **EW**

Einstein Medical Center *e:* **EMC**

Einstein Observatory [HEAO-2] Solid State
Spectrometer *e:* **SSS**

Einstein Observatory Monitoring
Proportional Counter *e:* **MPC**

Einwohnerwert *d:* **EW**

Einzeltier *d:* **ET**

Eisenerzreduktion im flüssigwerdendem
Zustand *d:* **FIOR-Verfahren**

El Niño and the Southern Oscillation
[coupled oceanic-atmospheric change] *e:*
ENSO

El Niño et loscillation australe [Une étude
de linteraction océan/atmosphère] *f:*
ENSO

El Paso Geological Sciences *e:* **EPGS**

El Paso Natural Gas *e:* **EPNG**

El Paso Natural Gas Company *e:* **El G**

Elastic Space Vehicle *e:* **ESV**

Elasto-Hydrodynamic Lubrication *e:* **EHL**

Elastohydrodynamic[al] *e:* **EHD**

Electric Consumers Protection Act *e:*
ECPA

Electric Geospace Shuttle *e:* **EGS**

electric hot water service *e:* **ehws**

Electric Polarization Vector *e:* **EPV**

Electric Space Heating and Air
Conditioning [Committee] *e:* **ESHAC**

Electric Water Systems Council *e:* **EWSC**

Electrical Aerospace Ground Equipment *e:*
EAGE

Electrical, Environmental and
Communications *e:* **EECOM**

Electrical, Environmental and Consumables
System Engineer *e:* **EECOMP**

Electrical, Environmental, Consumables
and Mechanical [Systems] *e:* **EECOM**

Electrical, Mechanical, and Environmental
Systems *e:* **EMES**

Electrical Output Spaces *e:* **EOS**

electrical remediation at contaminated
environments *e:* **ERACE**

Electrical Techniques in Medicine and
Biology *e:* **ETMB**

Electro-Hydrodynamic Power Generation
e: **EHG**

Electro-Hydrolic Actuator *e:* **EHA**

Electro-Hydrostatic Actuator *e:* **EHA**

Electro-magnetic Environment Simulator
e: **EES**

Electro-magnetic Test Environment *e:*
EMTE

Electro-Medical Agreement Group *e:*
EMEDCA

Electro Medical Trade Association *e:*
EMTA

Electro-Optic Electromagnetic Environment
Monitoring System *e:* **EO-EMS**

Electro-Optics Meteorology *e:* **EOMET**

Electroacoustic Dewatering *e:* **EAD**

Electrochemical Depolarized (Module) *e:*
EDC(M)

Electrochemical Hydrogen Cracking *e:*
EHC

Electrochemistry in Industrial Processing
and Biology *R:* **Electrochem. Ind.
Process. Bio**

Electrocinetógrafo geomagnético *s:* **GEK**

Electrodynamics of the Middle Atmosphere
e: **EMA**

Electrohydrodimerization *d:* **EHD**

Electrohydrodynamic Atomization *e:*
EHDA

Electrohydrodynamic Heat Pipe *e:*
EHDHP

Electrohydrodynamic[s] *e:* **EHD**

Electrolyzed Water *e:* **EW**

Electromagnetic Energy Environment
Criteria *e:* **EEEC**

Electromagnetic Environment *e:* **EME**

Electromagnetic Environment Analysis *e:*
EEA

Electromagnetic Environment Experiment
e: **EEE**

Electromagnetic Environment Generator *e:*
EMEG

Electromagnetic Environmental Effect *e:*
EEE

Electromagnetic Environmental Effects *e:*
E3

Electromagnetic Environmental Test
Facility *e:* **EETF**

Electromagnetic Environment[al] Test
Facility *e:* **EMETF**

Electromagnetic Modeling and Simulation
Environment for Systems *e:* **EMSES**

Electromagnetic Pulse Protection *e:*
EMPP

Electromagnetic Pulse Radiation
Environznent Simulator for Ships *e:*
EMPRESS

Electromagnetic Signature Identification
and Data Evaluation *e:* **EMSIDE**

Electromechanical and Environmental
Systems Division *e:* **EESD**

Electromedical Equipment *e:* **EME**

Electromedicinsk Apparat Compagni *a:*
EMACO

Electromolecular Instrument Space
Simulator *e:* **EMISS**

Electron Beam Cold-Hearth Refining *e:*
EBCHR

Electron Ionization-Chemical Ionization
Changeover *e:* **EI-CI Changeover**

Electronic and Aerospace Report *e:* **EAR**

Electronic and Aerospace Systems
Conference *e:* **EASCON**

Electronic and Geodetic Ranging Satellite
e: **EGRS**

Electronic British Medical Journal *e:*
eBMJ

Electronic Combat Threat Environment
Description *e:* **ECTED**

Electronic Computing Health-Oriented
Organization *e:* **ECHO**

Electronic Countermeasures Environment
e: **ECMC,** *e:* **ECME**

Electronic Data Interchange Messaging
Environment *e:* **EDIME**

Electronic Data Remote Communications
Complex *e:* **EDRCC**

Electronic Document Gathering
Environment *e:* **EDGE**

Electronic Environment Simulator *e:* **EES**

Electronic Environmental Test Facility *e:*
EEFT, *e:* **EETF**

Electronic Equipment Environment Surey
e: **EEES**

Electronic Frontier Foundation *e:* **EFF**

Electronic Frontier Norway *e:* **EFN**

Electronic Frontier Society *e:* **EFS**

Electronic Frontiers Japan *e:* **EFJ**

Electronic Geographic Coordinate
Navigation *e:* **EGECON**

Electronic Geographic Coordinate
Navigation System *e:* **EGECON System**

Electronic Health Economics Analysis
Letters *e:* **EHEAL**

Electronic Health Economics Letters *e:*
EHEL

electronic Journal of Medical Genetics *e:*
eJMG

Electronic Journal of Surgery and
Specialistic Medicine *e:* **EJS**

Electronic Medical Record *e:* **EMR**

Electronic Medical Record System *e:*
EMRS

Electronic Medical System *e:* **EMS**

electronic Medicines Compendium *e:* **eMC**

Electronic Ocean Reconnaissance Satellite
e: **EORSAT**

Electronic Pack Remote Display Unit e: **EPRDU**

Electronic Public Health Development Project e: **EPHDP**

Electronic Space Products, Incorporated e: **ESPI**

Electronic Spacecraft Simulator e: **ESCS**

Electronic Systems Precision Orbit Determination e: **ESPOD**

Electronic Terms for Space Age Language e: **ETSAL**

Electronic Warfare Ground Environment Threat Simulator e: **EWGETS**

Electronic Warfare Tactical Environment Simulation e: **EWTES**

Electronic Warfare Threat Environment Simulation Facility e: **EWTES**

Electronics and Aerospace Systems Convention and Exposition e: **EASCON**

Electronic[s] Command Meteorological Support Agency e: **ECMSA**

Electronics & Space Corporation of Canada Ltd. e: **ESCAN**

Electrophoresis Operations in Space e: **EOS**

Elektro-Hydro-Thermo d: **EHT**

Elektrohydrodynamik d: **EHD**

Elektrohydrodynamisch d: **EHD**

Elektrohydrothermo-Koagulation d: **EHT-Koagulation**

Elektrohydrothermosonde d: **EHT**

elektromagnetische Orientierung [und Erkennung] d: **EMAGO**

Elektromagnetische Verträglichkeit zur Umwelt d: **EMVU**

Elektromedizin d: **EM**

Elektronisches Wasserstrassen-Informationssystem für die Binnenschifffahrt d: **ELWIS**

Elevated Environmental Risk Summary e: **EERS**

Elevated Water Storage Tank e: **EWST**

Eli Whitney Meteorology Center e: **EWMC**

ELINT Ocean Reconnaissance Satellite e: **EORS**, e: **EORSAT**

Elisabeth Bruyere Health Center Ottawa, Ontario e: **OOEB**

Elk Mountain Observatory e: **EMO**

Elliot Automation Space and Advanced Military System e: **EASAMS**

Elliott-Automation's Space and Advanced Military System e: **ESAMS**

Elliptical Earth Orbit e: **EEO**

Elliptical Orbit e: **EO**

Elliptical Orbiting Geological Observatory e: **EOGO**

Elliptically Polarized Wave[s] e: **EPW**

Elsevier Oceanographic Series e: **EOS**

Elsevier Oceanography Series e: **EOS**

Elsevier Publishing Earth Sciences Department e: **EPESD**

Embarkation Medical Official e: **EMO**

Embedded Advanced Sampling Environment e: **EASE**

Emergency Advisory Committee for Natural Gas e: **EACNG**

Emergency Changeover Acknowledgement Signal e: **ECA Signal**

Emergency Changeover Order Signal e: **ECO Signal**

Emergency Community Water Assistance Grants e: **ECWAG**

Emergency Core Cooling Water e: **ECCW**

Emergency Deorbit System e: **EDS**

Emergency Earth Orbital Escape Device e: **EEOED**

Emergency Exchanger Cooling Water e: **EECW**

Emergency Feed-Water System e: **EFWS**

Emergency Feedwater e: **EFW**

Emergency Food and Medical Program e: **EFMP**

Emergency Health Preparedness Advisory Committee e: **EHPAC**

Emergency Health Service e: **EHS**

Emergency Managers' Weather Information Network e: **EMWIN**

Emergency Medical Advisory Service e: **EMAS**

Emergency Medical Command and Communications System e: **EMCCS**

Emergency Medical Doctor e: **EMD**

Emergency Medical Hologram e: **EMH**

Emergency Medical Kit e: **EMK**

Emergency Medical Response e: **EMR**

Emergency Medical Response Agency e: **EMRA**

Emergency Medical Response Team e: **EMRT**

Emergency Medical Service[s] e: **EMS**

Emergency Medical Services Communications e: **EMSCOM**

Emergency Medical Services Communications System e: **EMSCOM System**

Emergency Medical Services for Children e: **EMSC**

Emergency Medical Services Instructor e: **EMSI**

Emergency Medical Services System[s] e: **EMSS**

Emergency Medical Services Systems Act e: **EMSS Act**

Emergency Medical Tag e: **EMT**

Emergency Medical Team e: **EMT**

Emergency Medical Technican Paramedic e: **EMT-P**

Emergency Medical Technician [Ambulance] e: **EMT**

Emergency Medical Technician-Ambulance e: **EMT-A**

emergency medical technique f: **emt**

Emergency Medical Technologist e: **EMT**

Emergency Medical Transport e: **EMT**

Emergency Medical Treatment e: **EMT**

Emergency Medical Treatment and Active Labor Act e: **EMTALA**

Emergency Medicine Bulletin Board System e: **EMBBS**

Emergency Medicine Clinics of North America e: **Emerg Med Clin North Am**

Emergency Medicine Foundation e: **EMF**

Emergency Medicine Journal e: **EMJ**

Emergency Medicine Residents' Association e: **EMRA**

Emergency Raw Cooling Water e: **ERCW**

Emergency Raw Water e: **ERW**

Emergency Service Water e: **ESW**

Emergency Service Water System e: **ESWS**

Emergency Shutdown Water System e: **ESWS**

Emergency Water Supply e: **EWS**

Emergency Watershed Protection e: **EWP**

Emergency Weather Station e: **EWS**

emeritiert d: **em.**

Emission Line Polarimeter e: **ELP**

Emissions of Volatiles into the Atmosphere e: **EVA**

emittiert d: **em.**

Emory University, A. W. Calhoun Medical Library e: **GEU-M**

Employee Health Assistance Program e: **EHAP**

Employee Health Maintenance Examination e: **EHME**

Employee Safety, Health and Environmental Concerns Response System e: **ESHECRS**

Employment Agencies Protective Association of the United States e: **EAPAUS**

Employment Medical Advisory Service e: **EMAS**

EMT-Wilderness e: **EMT-W**

Encasement Hydrotest Riser e: **EHR**

Enclosed Space Detector System e: **ESDS**

Encounter in Health Education e: **ENHE**

Encyclopedia of Environmental Science e: **EES**

Encyclopédie Medico-Chirurgicale f: **EMC**

End System Operating Environment e: **ESOE**

Endangered Species Protection Act e: **ESP**, e: **ESP Act**

Endangered Species Protection Board e: **ESPD**

Endangered Wildlife Trust e: **EWT**

Endo-Atmospheric Decoy e: **EAD**

Endo-atmospheric Non-nuclear Kill e: **ENK**

Endoatmospheric e: **ENDO**

Endoatmospheric Non-Nuclear Kill e: **ENNK**

Energetically-Active Zones of the Ocean e: **EAZO**

Energetically Active Zones of the Ocean and Climate Variability e: **SECTIONS**

Energie- und Umweltzentrum am Deister e.V. d: **E.u.U.Z.**

Energy Active Zones of the Ocean e: **EAZO**

Energy and Environment Division e: **EED**

Energy and Environment Group e: **EEG**

Energy and Environment Information e: **EEI**

Energy and Environment Research e: **EER**

Energy and Environment Study Conference e: **EESC**

Energy and Environmental Analysis e: **EEA**

Energy and Environmental Applications e: **EEA**

Energy and Environmental Assessment e: **EEA**

Energy and Environmental Engineering Center e: **EEEC**

Energy and Environmental Response Center e: **EERC**

Energy and Environmental Studies e: **EES**

Energy and Environmental Technologies e: **E&ET**

Energy and Natural Resources e: **ENR**

Energy and Water Development Appropriations Act e: **EWDAA**

Energy Data Geographical Explorer e: **EDGE**

Energy difference between the Highest Occupied Molecular Orbital and the Lowest Unoccupied Molecular Orbital *e:* **HOMO/LUMO gap**

Energy Economics and Environment *e:* **EEE**

Energy, Economics and Environment Institute *e:* **EEEI**

Energy Efficient Environments *e:* **EEE**

Energy, Environment and Development *e:* **EED**

Energy, Environment and Economics *e:* **E-Cubed**

Energy & Environmental Systems Co. *e:* **E&ES**

Energy, Matter, Personality, Space, Time *e:* **EMPST**

Energy Supply and Environmental Coordination Act *e:* **ESECA**

Enfant Naturel *f:* **EN**

Enfermedades Infecciosas y Microbiologia Clinica *e:* **Enferm Infecc Microbiol Clin**

Engeharia de Pecursos Naturais *p:* **ERN**

Engin Blinde Mortier Canon *e:* **EMC**, *f:* **EMC**

Engine Environment Protection *e:* **EEP**

Engine Health Monitoring *e:* **EHM**

Engine Health Monitoring System *e:* **EHMS**

Engineering and Scientific Committee on Water *e:* **ESCOW**

Engineering Aspects of Magnetohydrodynamics *e:* **EAMHD**

Engineering Commission on Ocean Resources *e:* **ECOR**

Engineering Committee on Ocean[ic] Resources *e:* **ECOR**

Engineering, Design and Geosciences Group *e:* **EDGe**

Engineering Geologist *e:* **EG**

Engineering Geology *e:* **EG**

Engineering Geology Group *e:* **EGG**

Engineering Hydrology *e:* **EH**

Engineering in Medicine *e:* **Eng. Med.**

Engineering in Medicine and Biology *e:* **EMB**

Engineering in Medicine and Biology Magazine [of Institute of Electrical and Electronics Engineers] *e:* **Eng. Med. Biol. Mag.**

Engineering in Medicine and Biology Society *e:* **EMBS**

Engineering Waterways Experiment Station *e:* **EWES**

English National Board for Nursing, Midwifery and Health Visiting *e:* **ENB**

Enhanced Hearing Protector *e:* **EHP**

Enhanced Interactive Business Integrating Environment Manager *e:* **EIBIEM**

Enhanced Radar Environmental Simulation (or Simulator) System *e:* **ERESS**

Enhanced Stream Water Quality Model *e:* **QUAL2E**

Enhanced Stream Water Quality Model with Uncertainty Analysis *e:* **QUAL2EU**

Enhanced Surface Water Treatment Rule *e:* **ESWTR**

Enhanced Weatherization Program *e:* **WX**

Eniwetok Marine Biological Laboratory *e:* **EMBL**

ENMOD Convention: Convention on the Prohibition of Military or Any Other

Hostile Use of Environmental Modification Techniques *e:* **ENMOD**

Enol-Lactone Hydrolase *e:* **ELH**

Ensearch Environmental Corporation *e:* **EEC**

Ente Nazionale per le Biblioteche Popolari e Scolastiche *i:* **ENBPS**

Ente Nazionale Previdenza ed Assistenza Medici *i:* **ENPAM**

Ente Nazionale Protezione Animali *i:* **ENPA**

Entente des Hôpitaux Luxembourgeois *f:* **EHL**

Entente Européenne pour l'Environnement *f:* **EEE**

Entente Laitiere e Agricole du Centre *f:* **ELAC**

Entente Médicale Méditerranéenne *f:* **EMM**

Entering Water Temperature *e:* **EWT**

Enterprise Nationale de Géophysique *f:* **ENAGEO**

entmineralisiertes Wasser *d:* **E-Wasser**

Entomology Environmental Laboratory *e:* **EEL**

Entraide Médicale Internationale *f:* **EMI**

Entrance Cable Protector Ground Bar *e:* **ECPGB**

Entreprise Agricole et Forestière *f:* **ENAF**

Entreprise Forestière de Bois Africains Centrafrique *f:* **EFBACA**

Entreprise Forestière des Bois Africains *f:* **EFBA**

Entreprise Générale de Travaux Routiers SA *f:* **EGTR**

Entreprise Torestiere des Bois Africains Centralafrique *f:* **ETBACA**

Entscheidungsunterstützendes System Umweltverträglichkeitsprüfung *d:* **EUSUVP**

entwässern *d:* **entw.**

entwässert *d:* **entw.**

Entwässerung *d:* **Entw.**, *d:* **Entwässer.**

Entwässerungskanal *d:* **Entw. Kan.**

Entwicklung dialogorientiertes Anwendersystem *d:* **EDA**

Entwicklungsring für Luft- und Raumfahrt *d:* **ELR**

Entwurfwasserlinie *d:* **EWL**

Environic Foundation International *e:* **EFI**

Environinental Protection Agency *e:* **EPA**

Environment *e:* **ENV**

Environment Actions Plan *e:* **EAP**

Environment and Behavior *e:* **EB**

Environment and Coastal Resource Project *e:* **ENCORE**

Environment and Conservation Organisations *e:* **ECO**

Environment and Development in the Third World *e:* **ENDA TW**

Environment and Development Service for NGOs *e:* **Both ENDS**

Environment and Energy Directory *e:* **EED**

Environment and Heredity *e:* **E & H**

Environment and History *e:* **Environ. Hist.**

Environment [and] Land Management *e:* **ELM**

Environment and Land Management Sector *e:* **ELMS**

Environment and National Development in Africa *e:* **ENDA**

Environment and Natural Resources *e:* **ENR**

Environment and Natural Resources Information Center *e:* **ENRIC**

Environment and Resources Integrated Management System for Cray (Korea Inst. of Science & Technology) *e:* **C-ERIMS**

Environment and Safety Data Exchange *e:* **ESDX**

Environment and School Initiatives [Project] *e:* **ENSI**

Environment Assessment *e:* **EA**

Environment Assessment Technical Report *e:* **EATR**

Environment Assistance Program *e:* **EAP**

Environment Atmospheric Environment Service *e:* **EAES**

Environment Australia *e:* **EA**

Environment Australia Online Service *e:* **EAOS**

Environment Canada *e:* **EC**

Environment Canada Atlantic *e:* **ECA**

Environment Canada Dartmouth, Nova Scotia *e:* **NSDE**

Environment Canada Data Dictionary *e:* **ECDD**

Environment Canada, Environment Update *e:* **Environ. Can. Environ. Update**

Environment Canada, Notice of Publications *e:* **Environ. Can. Notice Publ.**

Environment Centre *e:* **EC**

Environment Centre [Northern Territory] *e:* **EC[NT]**

Environment Centre of the Northern Territory *e:* **ECNT**

Environment Code of Ethics for Rangeland Managers *e:* **ECERM**

Environment Committee *e:* **EC**

Environment Condition *e:* **EC**

Environment Conservation Authority *e:* **ECA**

Environment Control Table *e:* **ECT**

Environment Control Workstation *e:* **ECWS**

Environment Coordination Board *e:* **ECB**

Environment Council of Alberta *e:* **ECA**

Environment Decision[-making] Support System *e:* **EDSS**

Environment Division, Newfoundland Department of Consumer Affairs and Environment, St. John's, Newfoundland *e:* **NFSCAEE**

Environment Effects Statement *e:* **EES**

Environment, Environmental *e:* **ENVIR**

Environment for Sequential-to-Parallelprocessing *e:* **E/SP**

Environment for Verifying and Evaluating Software *e:* **EVES**

Environment Funds *e:* **EF**

Environment Generation & Analysis *e:* **EGA**

Environment Generator *e:* **EG**

Environment Health and Pesticide Services Section *e:* **EHPSS**

Environment, Health, and Safety *e:* **EH&AMPS**

Environment, Health and Safety Division *e:* **EHSD**

Environment Health Safety Program *e:* **EHSP**

Environment, Housing, and Community Development *e:* **EHCD**

Environment in Latin-America Network *e:* **ELAN**

Environment Information Bureau *e:* **EIB**

Environment Information Center *e:* **EIC**

Environment Information Network *e:* **EIN**

Environment Information System *e:* **EIS**

Environment Institute *e:* **EI**

Environment Institute of Australia *e:* **EIA**

Environment International *e:* **Environ. Int.**

Environment Law and Machinery Unit *e:* **ELMU**

Environment Liaison Board *e:* **ELB**

Environment Liaison International *e:* **ELI**

Environment Library Integrated Automated System *e:* **ELIAS**

Environment Management and Review Program *e:* **ERMP**

Environment Management Industries *e:* **EMI**

Environment Management Industry Association of Australia *e:* **EMIAA**

Environment Management Program *e:* **EMP**

Environment-Mapped Bump Mapping *e:* **EMBM**

Environment Mining Model *e:* **EMM**

Environment Modification Convention *e:* **ENMOD**

Environment Near Death *e:* **END,** *e:* **ND**

Environment One Corporation *e:* **EOC**

Environment Planning Authority *e:* **EPA**

Environment Policy and Technology Project *e:* **EPT**

Environment Policy Coordinating Committee *e:* **EPCC**

Environment Priorities and Coordination Group *e:* **EPCG**

Environment Protection Agency *e:* **EPA**

Environment Protection [Alligator Rivers Region] Act *e:* **EP[ARR] Act**

Environment Protection and Biodiversity Conservation Bill *e:* **EP&BC**

Environment Protection Council *e:* **EPC**

Environment Protection Equipment Manufacturers Association *e:* **EPEMA**

Environment Protection [Impact of Proposals] Act *e:* **EP[IP]**

Environment Protection Policy *e:* **EPOC**

Environment quality and natural resources *e:* **DG XI-D**

Environment Remote Sensing Analysis Facility *e:* **ERSAF**

Environment Reporter *e:* **ER**

Environment Research Programme *e:* **CEC-JRC**

Environment Resources Management Association *e:* **ERMA**

Environment Round Table *e:* **ERT**

Environment, Safety and Economics *e:* **ESE**

Environment, Safety, and Health *e:* **ES&AMPH**

Environment, Safety and Health Division *e:* **ESHD**

Environment, Safety and Health Information Portal *e:* **TIS, US-DOE**

Environment, Safety, Health and Quality Assurance *e:* **ESQA**

Environment, Safety, Health and Quality Committee *e:* **ESHQC**

Environment, Science and Technology *e:* **ES&T**

Environment, Science and Technology Resources [statistical package] *e:* **ESTR**

Environment Sensitive Cracking *e:* **ESC**

Environment Specific Inter-ORB Protocol *e:* **ESIOP**

Environment Sport and Territories *e:* **EST**

Environment Strategies Division *e:* **ESD**

Environment Teachers Association *e:* **ETA**

Environment Technical Advisory Committee *e:* **ETAC**

Environment Virtual Library *e:* **EVL**

Environment[al] *e:* **ENVIR**

environment[al] *e:* **environ.**

Environment[al] *e:* **ENVMT,** *e:* **ENVR**

Environmental Acceptance Test *e:* **EAT**

Environmental Action *e:* **EA**

Environmental Action Coalition *e:* **EAC**

Environmental Action Committee *e:* **EAC**

Environmental Action for Survival *e:* **ENACT**

Environmental Action Foundation *e:* **EAF**

Environmental Action Plan *e:* **EAP**

Environmental Action Programme for Central and Eastern Europe *e:* **EAP**

Environmental Activities Reporting System *e:* **EARS**

Environmental Adaptation Research Group *e:* **EARG**

Environmental Advisory Committee *e:* **EAC**

Environmental Affairs Committee *e:* **EAC**

Environmental Affairs Program *e:* **EAP**

Environmental Agency *e:* **EA**

Environmental ALARA Memorandum *e:* **EAM**

Environmental ALARA Review *e:* **EAR**

Environmental ALARA Review Letter *e:* **EARL**

Environmental Alliance for Senior Involvement *e:* **EASI**

Environmental Analog[ue] Recording System *e:* **EARS**

Environmental Analysis *e:* **ENVANAL**

Environmental Analysis and Assessment Section *e:* **EAAS**

Environmental Analysis and Monitoring *e:* **EA&M**

Environmental Analysis and Planning *e:* **EAP**

Environmental Analysis and Remote Sensing *e:* **EARS**

Environmental Analysis Section *e:* **EAS**

Environmental Analytical Laboratory *e:* **EAL**

Environmental and Ecological Reserach Institute *e:* **EERI**

Environmental and Ecological Statistics *e:* **Environ. Ecol. Stat.**

Environment[al] and Energy Study Institute *e:* **EESI**

Environmental and Energy Systems Division *e:* **EESD**

Environmental and Experimental Botany *e:* **Environ. Exp. Bot.**

Environmental and GeoGraphical Science *e:* **EGGS**

Environmental and Geographical Science *e:* **EGS**

Environmental and Health Compliance Division *e:* **E&HCD**

Environmental and Health Protection Division *e:* **E&HPD**

Environmental and Molecular Mutagenesis *e:* **Environ Mol Mutagen**

Environmental [and] Molecular Sciences Laboratory *e:* **EMSL**

Environmental and Monitoring Office *e:* **EMO**

Environment[al] and Natural Resources Information Network[s] (or Networking) *e:* **ENRIN**

Environment[al] and Natural Resource[s] Management *e:* **ENRM**

Environmental and Occupational Risk Management *e:* **EORM**

Environmental and Occupational Safety Division *e:* **E&OSD**

Environmental and Preventive Medicine Unit *e:* **EPMU**

Environmental and Radiological Monitoring *e:* **ERM**

Environmental and Safety Activities *e:* **ESA**

Environmental and Social Systems Analyst *e:* **ESSA**

Environmental and Societal Impacts Group *e:* **ESIG**

Environmental Appeal Board *e:* **EAB**

Environmental Area Characterization Report *e:* **EACR**

Environmental Aspects of Mining *e:* **EAM**

Environmental Aspects Report *e:* **EAR**

Environmental Assesment Center *e:* **EAC**

Environmental Assessment Act *e:* **EAA**

Environmental assessment and Evaluation *e:* **EE**

Environmental Assessment and Review Process *e:* **EARP**

Environmental Assessment and Review Program *e:* **EARP**

Environmental Assessment Council, Inc. *e:* **eac**

Environmental Assessment Data System[s] *e:* **EADS**

Environmental Assessment Determination *e:* **EAD**

Environmental Assessment Office *e:* **EAO**

Environmental Assessment Review Panel *e:* **EARP**

Environmental Assessment team *e:* **EA**

Environmental Assessment Worksheet *e:* **EAW**

Environmental Assessments *e:* **EAs**

Environmental Assessments Group *e:* **EAG**

Environmental Assurance *e:* **EA**

Environmental Audio Extensions *e:* **EAX**

Environmental Audit finding observation *e:* **EAU**

Environmental Audit[ing] *e:* **EA**

Environmental Auditing Roundtable *e:* **EAR**

Environmental Awareness Reading List *e:* **EARL**

Environmental Ballistics Associates *e:* **EBA**

Environmental Baseline Survey *e:* **EBS**

Environmental Bill of Rights *e:* **EBR**

Environmental Biology of Fishes *e:* **Environ. Biol. Fishes**

Environmental Biology Program *e:* **EBP**

environmental buoy *e:* **eb**

Environmental Capacity *e:* **EC**

Environmental Carcinogen Information Center *e:* **ECIC**

Environmental Center of Excellence *e:* **ECE**

Environmental Chamber *e:* **EC**

Environmental Chamber Shroud *e:* **ECS**

Environmental Change in Africa *e:* **ECA**

Environmental Change Network *e:* **ECN**

Environmental Change Unit *e:* **ECU**

Environmental Characterization Projects Office *e:* **ECPO**

Environmental Characterization Report *e:* **ECR**

Environmental Chemical Laboratory *e:* **ECL**

Environment[al] Chemical[s] Data and Information Network *e:* **ECDIN**

Environmental Chemistry *e:* **EC**

Environmental Chemistry and Biology *e:* **ECB**

Environmental Chemistry Division *e:* **ECD**

Environmental Chemistry Laboratory *e:* **ECL**

Environmental Cleanup Responsibility Act *e:* **ECRA**

Environmental Clearinghouse, Incorporated *e:* **ECI**

Environmental Coal Mining *e:* **ECM**

Environment[al] Coalition for North America *e:* **ENCONA**

Environmental Coalition on Nuclear Power *e:* **ECNP**

Environmental Communications Network *e:* **ECN**

Environmental Compatability Assurance Program[me] *e:* **ECAP**

Environmental Compliance *e:* **EC**

Environmental Compliance Assessment and Management Program *e:* **ECAMP**

Environmental Compliance Assurance *e:* **ECA**

Environmental Compliance Group *e:* **ECG**

Environmental Compliance Manual *e:* **ECM**

Environmental Compliance Officer *e:* **ECO**

Environmental Compliance Online System *e:* **ECOS**

Environmental Compliance Order *e:* **ECO**

Environmental Compliance Plan *e:* **ECP**

Environmental Compliance Program *e:* **ECP**

Environmental Compliance Section *e:* **ECS**

Environmental Compliance Support *e:* **ECS**

Environmental Compliance Task Force *e:* **ECTF**

Environmental Compliance Tracking System *e:* **ECTS**

Environmental Compliance Unit *e:* **ECU**

Environmental Compliance Verification *e:* **ECV**

Environmental Compliance Verification Program *e:* **ECVP**

Environmental Concerns and Safety *e:* **EN-CAS**

Environmental Conditioning System *e:* **ECS**

Environmental Conditions Determination *e:* **ECD**

Environmental Conservation *e:* **Environ. Conserv.**

Environmental Conservation Acreage Reserve Program *e:* **ECARP**

Environmental Conservation Board *e:* **ECB**

Environmental Conservation Hotlinks *e:* **ECHO**

Environmental Conservation Library of Minnesota *e:* **ECOL**

Environmental Conservation [Program] *e:* **ENCON**

Environmental Conservation Service *e:* **ECS**

Environmental Consulting Engineering *e:* **ECE**

Environmental Contaminants Authority *e:* **ECA**

Environmental Control *e:* **EC**

Environmental Control Administration *e:* **ECA**

Environmental Control and Life Support *e:* **ECLS**

Environmental Control and Life Support Systems *e:* **ECLSS**

Environmental Control and Processing Module *e:* **ECPM**

Environmental Control Assembly *e:* **ECA**

Environmental Control Council *e:* **ECC**

Environmental Control Equipment *e:* **ECE**

Environmental control limit *e:* **ECL**

Environmental Control/Nuclear, Biological & Chemical *e:* **EC/NBC**

Environmental Control Organization *e:* **ECO**

Environmental Control Shroud *e:* **ECS**

Environment[al] Control System[s] *e:* **ECS**

Environmental Control Technology *e:* **ECT**

Environment[al] Control Unit *e:* **ECU**

Environmental Cooperation with Asia Program *e:* **ECAP**

Environmental Coordinating Group *e:* **ECG**

Environmental Coordinator *e:* **EC**

Environmental Council of Lenawee *e:* **ECOL**

Environmental Council of [the] States *e:* **ECOS**

Environmental Crack Model Development *e:* **EDEAC**

Environmental Crimes Unit *e:* **ECU**

Environmental Crisis Operation *e:* **ECO**

Environmental Criteria and Assessment Office *e:* **ECAO**

Environmental Damage *e:* **ED**

Environmental Damage [and its] Assessment *e:* **EDA**

Environmental Data Acquisition Sub-System *e:* **EDASS**

Environmental Data and Ecological parameters *e:* **EDE**

Environmental Data and Information Management Systems *e:* **EDIMS**

Environmental Data and Information Service *e:* **EDIS**

Environmental Data Base Directory *e:* **EDBD**

Environmental Data Book *e:* **EDB**

Environmental Data Buoy *e:* **EDB**

Environmental Data Center *e:* **EDC**

Environmental Data Collection and Processing Facility *e:* **EDCPF**

Environmental Data Directory *e:* **EDD**

Environmental Data Index *e:* **ENDEX**, *e:* **ENDIX**

Environmental Data Management Center *e:* **EDMC**

Environmental Data Manager *e:* **EDM**

Environmental Data Network *e:* **EDN**

Environmental Data Planning Associates, Inc. *e:* **EDPA**

Environmental Data Remedial Tracking System *e:* **EDRTS**

Environmental Data Research Institute *e:* **EDRI**

Environmental Data Service[s] *e:* **EDS**

Environmental Data Services [Limited] *e:* **ENDS**

Environmental Data Service[s] Technical Memoranda *e:* **EDSTM**

Environmental Database Gateway *e:* **EDG**

Environmental Decision Alignment Process *e:* **EDAP**

Environmental Defense Fund *e:* **ECSSID**

Environmental Defense Fund, Inc. *e:* **EDF**

Environmental Department *e:* **JENV**

Environmental Descriptor Manager *e:* **EDM**

Environmental Design Library *e:* **ENVI**

Environment[al] Design Research Association *e:* **EDRA**

Environmental Designation for Noise Abatement *e:* **EDNA**

Environmental Development Administration *e:* **EDA**

Environmental Development Agency *e:* **EDA**

Environmental Development Plan *e:* **EDP**

Environmental Devices, Inc., Sacramento, California *e:* **E/D**

Environmental Discrimination Circuit *e:* **EDC**

Environmental Dispute Coordination Commission *e:* **EDCC**

Environmental Disruption *e:* **ED**

Environmental division *e:* **ENV**

Environmental Document Managment Center *e:* **EDMC**

Environmental Dose Modeling and Analysis System *e:* **EDMAS**

Environmental Dynamics Incorporated *e:* **EDII**

Environmental Easement Program *e:* **EEP**

Environmental Ecological and Support Laboratory *e:* **EESL**

Environmental-Ecological Education *e:* **EEE**

Environmental Economics *e:* **ENVEC**

environmental education *e:* **ee**

Environmental Education Act *e:* **EEA**

Environmental Education and Information Committee *e:* **EEIC**

Environmental Education Group *e:* **EEG**

Environmental Education Link *e:* **EEL**

Environmental Education Network *e:* **EEN**

Environmental Education Server *e:* **EES**

Environmental Education, Training and Information Network *e:* **EETIN**

Environmental Effects for Distribution Interactive Simulation *e:* **E2DIS**

Environmental Effects Laboratory *e:* **EEL**

Environmental Effects of Nuclear War, Nuclear Winter Ecology Group *e:* **ENUWAR**

Environmental Effects, Transport and Fate Committee *e:* **EETFC**

Environmental Elements Corporation *e:* **EEC**

Environmental Emergencies Technology Division *e:* **EETD**

Environmental Emergency Response Unit *e:* **EERU**

Environmental Engineer *e:* **EnvE**

Environmental Engineer[ing] *e:* **EE**

Environmental Engineering *e:* **Environ. Eng.**

Environmental Engineering and Geotechnology Function *e:* **EE&GF**

Environmental Engineering and Technology *e:* **EE&T**

Environmental Engineering Exhibition *e:* **ENVIREX**

Environmental Engineering Group *e:* **EEG**

Environmental Engineering Intersociety Board *e:* **EEIB**

Environmental Engineering Studies *e:* **EES**

Environmental Engineering Technologist *e:* **EET**

Environmental Engineering Technology *e:* **EET**

Environmental Engineering Test Facility *e:* **EETF**

Environmental Engineering Unit *e:* **EEU**

Environmental Engineers Group *e:* **EEG**

Environmental Enterprises Assistance Fund *e:* **EEAF**

Environmental Entomology *e:* **Environ. Entomol.**

Environmental Equipment Division *e:* **EED**

Environmental Equipment Institute *e:* **EEI**

Environmental Equipments Ltd., Wokingham *e:* **EE**

Environmental Evaluation *e:* **EE**

Environmental Evaluation Group *e:* **EEG**

Environmental Evaluation Unit *e:* **EEU**

Environmental Expenditure on Protection and Abatement *e:* **EEPA**

Environmental Experiments Program *e:* **EEP**

Environmental Facility Compliance *e:* **EFC**

Environmental Fate Data Bases *e:* **EFDB**

Environmental Field Services *e:* **EFS**

Environmental Field Services Group *e:* **EFSG**

Environmental Financial Advisory Board *e:* **EFAB**

Environmental Financing Authority *e:* **EFA**

Environmental Financing Information Network *e:* **EFIN**

Environmental Flow Requirements of Australias Waterways *e:* **EFR**

Environmental Flows Decision Support System *e:* **EFDSS**

environmental force unit *e:* **efu**

Environmental Forecast Center *e:* **EPC**

Environmental Functional Appraisal *e:* **EFA**

Environmental Fund *e:* **TEF**

Environmental Fund for Georgia *e:* **EFG**

Environmental Geochemistry *e:* **EGC**

Environmental Geochemistry and Health *e:* **Environ. Geochem. Health**

Environmental Geology *e:* **Environ. Geol.**

Environmental Geology and Water Sciences *e:* **Environ. Geol. Water Sci.**

Environmental Geology Group *e:* **EGG**

Environmental Geology Notes *e:* **EGN**

Environmental Geology Page *e:* **EGP**

Environmental Governance in Asia *e:* **EGA**

Environmental Graphic Designer *e:* **EGD**

Environmental Graphical Information *e:* **EGI**

Environmental Group, Pacific Command *e:* **EGPACOM**

Environmental Grouping - Australia, Canada, Japan, New Zealand and the USA *e:* **A-CAP**

Environmental Hazard Safety Classification *e:* **EHSC**

Environmental Hazards and Health Effects *e:* **EHHE**

Environmental Hazards Management *e:* **EHM**

Environmental Hazards Management Institutes *e:* **EHMI**

Environmental Health *e:* **EH,** *e:* **Environ. Health**

Environmental Health Agency *e:* **EHA**

Environmental Health and Safety *e:* **EHS**

Environmental Health Center *e:* **EHC**

Environmental Health Committee *e:* **EHC**

Environmental Health Conferences *e:* **EHC**

Environmental Health Criteria *e:* **EHC**

Environmental Health Directorate *e:* **EHD**

Environmental Health Directorate, Health Protection Branch, Department of National Health and Welfare Ottawa, Ontario *e:* **OONHH**

Environmental Health Engineering Services *e:* **EHES**

Environmental Health Forum *e:* **EHF,** *e:* **EHM**

Environmental Health Information Services *e:* **EHIS**

Environment[al] Health Laboratory *e:* **EHL**

Environmental Health Network *e:* **EHN**

Environmental Health Officer[s] *e:* **EHO**

Environmental Health [Officers] Association *e:* **EHA**

Environmental Health Perspective[s] *e:* **EHP**

Environmental Health Perspectives *e:* **Environ Health Perspect**

Environmental Health & Pesticides Services *e:* **EH&PS**

Environmental Health Program *e:* **EHP**

Environmental Health Project *e:* **EHP**

Environmental Health Regional Information Network *e:* **CEHA**

Environmental Health Research Staff *e:* **EHRS**

Environmental Health Review *e:* **EHR**

Environmental Health & Safety Research *e:* **EH&SR**

Environmental Health Sciences *e:* **EHS**

Environmental Health Service[s] *e:* **EHS**

Environmental Health Standard[s] *e:* **EHS**

Environmental Health System *e:* **EHS**

Environmental Health Watch *e:* **EHW**

Environmental Hearing Board *e:* **EHB**

Environmental Hearings Office *e:* **EHO**

Environmental History *e:* **EH**

Environmental History Newsletter *e:* **Environ. Hist. Newsl.**

[Environmental] Hot Cell Expansion *e:* **HCE**

Environmental Hydro Systems *e:* **EHS**

Environmental Hygiene Agency *e:* **EHA**

Environment[al] Illness *e:* **EI**

Environmental Imaging Spectrometer *e:* **EIS**

Environmental Impact *e:* **EI**

Environmental Impact Analysis *e:* **EIA**

Environmental Impact Analysis Process (or Project) *e:* **EIAP**

Environmental Impact Analysis Report *e:* **EIAR**

Environmental Impact Appraisal *e:* **EIA**

Environmental Impact Assessment *e:* **EIP**

Environmental Impact Assessment of Mineral Resource Exploitation and Exploration in Antarctica *e:* **EAMREA**

Environment[al] Impact Assessment[s] *e:* **EIA**

Environmental Impact Computer System *e:* **EICS**

Environmental Impact Planning *e:* **EIP**

Environment[al] Impact Report[s] *e:* **EIR**

Environmental Impact Reports *e:* **EIRs**

Environmental Impact Statement *e:* **EIS,** *e:* **MÁU**

Environmental Impact Statements *e:* **EISs**

Environmental Impact Study *e:* **EIS**

Environmental Impacts and Criteria Development Project *e:* **EICDP**

Environmental Impacts Division *e:* **EID**

Environmental Impacts on Water Resources *e:* **WAT**

Environmental Impairment Liability *e:* **EIL**

Environmental Improvement Board *e:* **EIB**

Environmental Improvement Commission *e:* **E.I.C.**

Environmental Improvement Program *e:* **EIP**

Environmental Industries (or Industry) Council *e:* **EIC**

Environmental Information Abstracts *e:* **EIA**

Environmental Information Analysis Center *e:* **EIAC**

Environmental Information and Documentation Centres On-line Directory *e:* **ENDOC**

Environmental Information and Retrieval System *e:* **ENVIR**

Environmental Information and Support Network *e:* **EISN**

Environment[al] Information Center (or Centre) *e:* **EIC**

Environmental Information Division *e:* **EID**

Environmental Information Index *e:* **EII**

Environmental Information Management *e:* **EIM**

Environmental Information Management Plan *e:* **EIMP**

Environmental Information Management Unit *e:* **EIMU**

Environmental Information Online *e:* **ENVIROLINE**

Environmental Information Science [of Center for Environmental Information Science, Japan] *j:* **Environ. Inf. Sci.**

Environmental Information Service[s] *e:* **EIS**

Environmental Information Society of
Ontario e: **EISO**
Environmental Information System e: **EIS**
Environmental Information System[s]
Office e: **EISO**
Environmental Initiative for the Americas
e: **EIA**
Environmental Innovation Program e: **EIP**
Environmental Institute Task Force e:
EITF
Environmental Instrumentation
Measurement and Monitoring e:
EIMAM, e: **EIM&M**
Environmental Interaction Theory of
Personality e: **EIT**
environmental interaction theory of
personality e: **eitp**
Environmental Interface Processor e: **EIP**
Environment[al] Investigation Agency e:
EIA
Environmental Investigation and
Instructions e: **EI&I**
Environmental Investigations Instruction
e: **EII**
Environmental Labelling Schemes e: **ELS**
Environmental Laboratories Information
Retrieval Technique e: **ELIRT**
Environmental Law Alliance e: **ELA**
Environmental Law and Management e:
E.L.M.
Environmental Law Center e: **ELC**
Environmental Law Information System e:
ELIS
Environmental Law Institute e: **ELI**
Environmental Law Library e: **ELL**
Environmental Law Monthly e: **Env. L.M.**
Environmental Law Reporter e: **ELR**
Environmental Law Reports e: **Env. L.R.**
Environmental Law Service e: **ELS**
Environmental Law Society e: **EIS**, e:
ELS
Environmental Legal Information Base e:
ELIB
Environment[al] Liaison Center e: **ELC**
Environment[al] Liaison Center
International e: **ELCI**
Environmental Librarian's Network e:
ELN
Environmental Libraries Automated System
e: **ELIAS**
Environmental Library of Minnesota e:
ELM
Environmental, Life and Social Sciences e:
ELSS
Environmental Life Support Assembly e:
ELSA
Environmental Life Support System e:
ELSS
Environmental Literacy Council e: **ELC**
Environmental Living Zone e: **ELZ**
Environmental Loan Unit e: **ELU**
Environmental Management Agency e:
EMA
Environmental Management and
Enrichment Facilities e: **EMEF**
Environmental Management and Planning
Information System e: **EMPIS**
Environmental Management Appraisal e:
EMA
Environmental Management Association
e: **EMA**
Environmental Management Association of
Malaysia e: **ENSEARCH**

Environmental Management Audit e:
EMA
Environmental Management Audit Scheme
e: **EMAS**
Environmental Management Bureau e:
EMB
Environmental Management Career
Opportunities for Minorities e:
EMCOM
Environmental Management Center e:
EMCP
Environmental Management Center
Opportunities Resource e: **EMCORE**
Environmental Management Committee e:
EMC
Environmental Management Division e:
EMD
Environmental Management/Environmental
Health e: **EM/EH**
Environmental Management Framework e:
EMF
Environmental Management, Incorporated
e: **EMI**
Environmental Management of Enclosed
Coastal Seas e: **EMECS**
Environmental Management Office e:
EMO
Environmental Management Performance
Report e: **EMPR**
Environmental Management Plan e: **EMP**
Environmental Management Program
Integrating Contractor e: **EPIC**
Environmental Management Programs e:
EMP
Environmental Management Questionnaire
e: **EMQ**
Environmental Management Report e:
EMR
Environmental Management Service e:
EMS
Environmental Management System e:
EMS
Environmental Mapping and Assessment
Program e: **EMAP**
Environmental Measurement Experiment[s]
e: **EME**
Environmental Measurement Payload e:
EMP
Environmental Measurements, Incorporated
e: **EMI**
Environmental Measurements Laboratory
e: **EM**
Environmental Measurement[s] Laboratory
e: **EML**
Environmental Measuring Laboratory e:
EML
Environmental Media Association e: **EMA**
Environmental Media Evaluation Guide e:
EMEG
Environmental Mediation Association e:
EMA
Environment[al] Mediation International
e: **EMI**
Environmental Medicine Officer e: **EMO**
Environmental Meteorological Support Unit
e: **EMSU**
Environmental Methods Testing Site e:
EMTS
Environmental Mine Engineering e: **EME**
Environmental Modeling Center e: **EMC**
Environmental Modifcation e: **Enmod**
Environmental Monitoring e: **EM**

Environmental Monitoring and Analysis
Program e: **EMAP**
Environmental Monitoring and Assessment
e: **EMA**, e: **Environ. Monit. Assess.**
Environmental Monitoring and Assessment
Program e: **EMAP**
Environmental Monitoring and Compliance
e: **EMC**
Environmental Monitoring and Compliance
Department e: **EM&CD**
Environmental Monitoring and Mitigation
Plan e: **EMMP**
Environmental Monitoring and Prediction
e: **EMP**
Environment[al] Monitoring and Research
Programme e: **EMRP**
Environmental Monitoring and Services
Center e: **EMSC**
Environmental Monitoring [and] Support
Laboratory e: **EMSL**
Environmental Monitoring and Surveillance
Laboratory e: **EMSL**
Environmental Monitoring Center e: **EMC**
Environmental Monitoring Management
Information System e: **EMMIS**
Environmental Monitoring Methods Index
e: **EMMI**
Environmental Monitoring Plan e: **EMP**
Environmental monitoring Plan e: **EP**
Environmental Monitoring Satellite e:
EMS
Environmental Monitoring Stations e:
EMS
Environmental Monitoring System e: **EMS**
Environmental Monitoring Systems
Division e: **EMSD**
Environmental Monitoring Systems
Laboratory e: **EMSL**
Environmental Monitoring Systems
Laboratory at Las Vegas e: **EMSL-LV**
Environmental Monitoring Systems
Upgrade e: **EMSU**
Environmental Monitoring Testing Site e:
EMTS
Environmental Monitoring Unit e: **EMU**
Environmental Mutagen Information Center
e: **EMIC**
Environmental Mutagen Society e: **EMS**
Environmental Mutagenesis e: **Environ.
Mutagenesis**
Environmental News Network e: **ENN**
Environment[al] Noise Control Committee
e: **ENCC**
Environment[al] Non-Governmental
Organization[s] e: **ENGO**
Environmental Observation Division e:
EOD
Environmental Officer e: **EO**
Environmental Operations Division e:
EOD
Environmental Operations Specification
Document e: **EOSD**
Environmental Oxygen Interaction with
Materials e: **EOIM**
Environmental Park e: **EP**
Environmental Performance Agreement e:
EnPA
Environmental Performance Evaluation e:
EPE
Environmental Periodicals Bibliography e:
EPB
Environmental Periodicals Bibliography
e: **EPB**

Environmental Pesticide Act *e:* **EPA**

Environmental Photographic Interpretation Center *e:* **EPIC**

Environmental Physics Research Laboratories *e:* **EPRL**

Environmental Physiology *e:* **EP**

Environmental Planning and Management *e:* **EPM**

Environmental Planning and Programming Language *e:* **EPPL**

Environmental Planning Authority *e:* **EPA**

Environmental Planning Data[base] System *e:* **EPDS**

Environmental Policy Act *e:* **EPACT**

Environmental Policy Center *e:* **EPC**

Environmental Policy Database *e:* **EPD**

Environmental Policy Institute *e:* **EPI**

Environmental Policy Research *e:* **EPR**

Environmental Policy Unit *e:* **EPU**

Environmental Pollution *e:* **Environ. Pollut.,** *e:* **EP**

Environmental Pollution Control *e:* **Envir. Poll. Contr.**

Environmental Pollution Control Exhibition *e:* **ENPOCON**

Environmental Pollution Licensing *e:* **EPL**

Environmental Pollution Monitoring and Research Programme *e:* **ENV**

Environmental Pollution Processors Corporation *e:* **EPPCO**

Environmental Processes and Effects Research [program] *e:* **EPER**

Environmental Productivity Index *e:* **EPI**

Environmental Professional [of National Association of Environmental Professionals] *e:* **Environ. Prof.**

Environmental Professional Page *e:* **EPP**

Environmental Professions Intern Center *e:* **EPIC**

Environmental Profile[s] *e:* **EP**

Environmental Program Information System *e:* **EPIS**

Environmental Program Manager *e:* **EPM**

Environmental Program/Projects *e:* **EP/P**

Environmental Programme for Europe *e:* **EPE**

Environmental Programme for the Mediterranean *e:* **EPM**

Environmental Programs Assistance Act[ion] *e:* **EPAA**

Environmental Progress [of American Institute of Chemical Engineers] *e:* **Environ. Prog.**

Environmental Project *e:* **EP**

Environmental Project Manager *e:* **EPM**

Environmental Project on Central America *e:* **EPOCA**

Environmental Projects Working Group *e:* **EPWG**

Environmental Proof Test *e:* **EPT**

Environmental Protection *e:* **EP**

Environmental Protection Act *e:* **EPA**

Environmental Protection Administration *e:* **EPA**

Environmental Protection Agency Acquisition Regulation[s] *e:* **EPAAR**

Environmental Protection Agency/Air and Waste Management Association *e:* **EPA/AWMA**

Environmental Protection Agency Chemical Activities Status Report *e:* **EPACASR**

Environmental Protection Agency Circulation System *e:* **EPACIR**

Environmental Protection Agency-District of Columbia *e:* **EPA-DC**

Environmental Protection Agency Document Control System *e:* **EPADOC**

Environmental Protection Agency Information Retrieval System *e:* **EPAIRS**

Environmental Protection Agency on Global Warming, Washington *e:* **EPA**

Environmental Protection Agency Payroll System *e:* **EPAYS**

Environmental Protection Agency, Region V *e:* **EPA-V**

Environmental Protection Agency Regulations *e:* **EPAR**

Environmental Protection Agency Report System *e:* **EPANTS**

Environmental Protection Agency/Toxic Substance Control Act *e:* **EPA/TSCA**

Environmental Protection Agency Translation System *e:* **EPATR**

Environmental Protection and Education Club *e:* **EPEC**

Environmental Protection Assurance System *e:* **EPAS**

Environment[al] Protection Authority *e:* **EPA**

Environmental Protection Committee *e:* **EPC**

Environmental Protection Control *e:* **EPC**

Environmental Protection Data Base *e:* **EPDA,** *e:* **EPDB**

Environmental Protection Deviation Report *e:* **EPDR**

Environmental Protection Devices *e:* **EPD**

Environmental Protection Division *e:* **ENVPD,** *e:* **EPD**

Environmental Protection Encouragement Agency *e:* **EPEA**

Environmental Protection Engineering *e:* **Enriron. Prot. Eng.**

Environmental Protection Evaluation *e:* **EPE**

Environmental Protection Facility *e:* **EPF**

Environmental Protection Group *e:* **EPG**

Environmental Protection Implementation Plan *e:* **EPIP**

Environmental Protection Information Bulletin *e:* **EPIB**

Environmental Protection Initiative *e:* **EPI**

Environmental Protection Limit *e:* **EPL**

Environmental Protection Manual *e:* **EPM**

Environmental Protection Officer *e:* **EPO**

Environmental Protection Oil Sands System *e:* **EPOSS**

Environmental Protection Program Implementation Plan *e:* **EPPIP**

Environmental Protection Research Institute *e:* **EPRI**

Environmental Protection, Safety and Emergency Planning *e:* **EPSEP**

Environmental Protection Safety and Emergency Preparedness *e:* **EPSED**

Environmental Protection Service *e:* **EPS**

Environmental Protection Service, Environment Canada Montreatl, Quebec *e:* **QMEE**

Environmental Protection Service, Environment Canada Regina, Saskatchewan *e:* **SREEP**

Environmental Protection Service, Environment Canada Winnipeg, Manitoba *e:* **MWEEP**

Environmental Protection Specialist *e:* **EPS**

Environmental Protection System *e:* **EPS**

Environmental Protective Plan *e:* **EP**

Environmental Pulse Radiation Environment Simulator for Ships *e:* **EMPRESS**

Environmental Qualification *e:* **EQ**

Environmental Qualification Test *e:* **EQT**

Environmental Quality *e:* **EQ**

Environmental Quality Abstracts *e:* **EQA**

Environmental Quality Act *e:* **EQA**

Environmental Quality Administration *e:* **EQA**

Environmental Quality Advisory Agency *e:* **EQAA**

Environmental Quality Advisory Board *e:* **EQAB**

Environmental Quality Assurance *e:* **EQA**

Environmental Quality Board *e:* **EQB**

Environmental Quality Control *e:* **EQC**

Environmental Quality Council *e:* **EQC**

Environmental Quality Incentives Program *e:* **EQIP**

Environmental Quality Index *e:* **EQI**

Environmental Quality Information Panel *e:* **EQIP**

Environmental Quality Laboratory *e:* **EQL**

Environmental Quality Magazine *e:* **EQM**

Environmental Quality Modeling *e:* **EQM**

Environment[al] Quality Objective *e:* **EQO**

Environmental [quality] Protection Program *e:* **EPP**

Environmental Quality Standard *e:* **EQS**

Environmental Quality Standard Agency *e:* **EQSA**

Environmental Quality Study Council *e:* **EQSC**

Environmental Quarterly *e:* **Environ. Quart.**

Environmental Radiation Ambient Monitoring System *e:* **ERACF,** *e:* **ERAMS**

Environmental Radiation Exposure Advisory Committee *e:* **EREAC**

Environmental Radiation Protection *e:* **ERP**

Environmental Radiochemistry Analysis *e:* **ERA**

Environmental Radiofrequency Data Base *e:* **ERDB**

Environmental Record Editing and Statistics *e:* **ERES**

Environmental Recording Data Set *e:* **ERDS**

Environmental Recording Editing and Printing *e:* **EREP**

Environmental Records and Information Services *e:* **ERIS**

Environmental Regulation Steering Committee *e:* **ERSC**

Environmental Release Summary *e:* **ERS**

Environmental Release System *e:* **ERS**

Environmental Remedial Action Project *e:* **ERAP**

Environmental Remediation [or Restoration] Disposal Facility *e:* **ERDF**

Environmental Remote Sensing Analysis Laboratory *e:* **ERSAL**

Environmental Remote Sensing Applications Centre *e:* **ERSAC**

Environmental Remote Sensing Applications Consultants Ltd. *e:* **ERSAC**

Environmental Remote Sensing Applications Laboratory *e:* **ERSAL**

Environmental Remote Sensing Center *e:* **ERSC**

Environmental Remote Sensing Unit *e:* **ERSUN**

Environmental Report *e:* **ELR**, *e:* **ER**

Environmental Reports *e:* **EVR**

Environmental Requirement *e:* **ER**

Environmental Requirements Advanced Technology *e:* **ERAT**

Environmental Requirements/Capabilities Management Information System *e:* **ERCMIS**

Environmental Research *e:* **Environ. Res.**

Environmental Research Aircraft [and] Sensor Technology *e:* **ERAST**

Environmental Research and Information Center *e:* **ERIC**

Environmental Research and Technology *e:* **ERT**

Environmental Research Center *e:* **ERC**

Environmental Research Chemistry Laboratory *e:* **ERCL**

Environmental Research Consortium *e:* **ERC**

Environmental Research, Development and Demonstration Authorization Act *e:* **DRD&DAA**, *e:* **ERD&DAA**

Environmental Research Group, Inc. *e:* **ERG**

Environmental Research Institute *e:* **ERG**

Environmental Research Institute of Michigan *e:* **ERIM**

Environmental Research Laboratories (or Laboratory) *e:* **ERL**

Environmental Research Laboratories Technical Memorandum *e:* **ERLTM**

Environmental Research Laboratory Corvallis *e:* **ERL-C**

Environmental Research Laboratory Gulf Breeze *e:* **ERL-GB**

Environmental Research Laboratory Narragansett *e:* **ERLN**

Environmental Research Laboratory, University of Arizona *e:* **ERLUA**

Environmental Research Literature Search and Storage *e:* **ER-LSS**

Environmental Research News *e:* **ERN**

Environmental Research Paper[s] *e:* **ERP**

Environmental Research Parks *e:* **ERP**

Environmental Research Program *e:* **ERP**

Environmental Research Project *e:* **ERP**

Environmental Research Projects in the European Communities *e:* **ENREP**

Environmental Research Satellite *e:* **ERS**

Environmental research ship *e:* **AGER**

Environmental Research Systems Institute *e:* **ERSI**

Environmental Research & Technology Division *e:* **ERTD**

Environmental Resistance *e:* **ER**

Environmental Resistance Inherent in Equipment *e:* **ERIE**

Environmental Resource *e:* **ER**

Environmental Resource Institute *e:* **ERG**

Environmental Resource Research Institute *e:* **ERRI**

Environmental Resource Studies *e:* **ERS**

Environmental Resources Analysis *e:* **ERA**

Environmental Resource[s] Center *e:* **ERC**

Environmental Resource[s] Information Network *e:* **ERIN**

Environmental Resources Information System *e:* **ERIS**

Environmental Resources Library *e:* **ERL**

Environmental Resources Limited *e:* **ERL**

Environmental Resources Mapping System [software] *e:* **ERMS**

Environmental Resource[s] Network *e:* **ERN**

Environmental Resources of Australia *e:* **ERA**

Environmental Resources Services *e:* **ERS**, *e:* **ESR**

Environmental Response and Referral Service *e:* **ERRS**

Environmental Response Branch *e:* **ERB**

Environmental Response Centre *e:* **ERC**

Environmental Response Organization *e:* **ERO**

Environmental Response Team *e:* **ERT**

Environmental Restoration *e:* **ER**

Environmental Restoration and Facilities Update *e:* **ERFU**

Environmental Restoration and Facilities Upgrade [Program] *e:* **ERFU**

Environmental Restoration and Remedial Action Information System *e:* **ERRAIS**

Environmental Restoration and Waste Management *e:* **EM**, *e:* **ER&WM**

Environmental Restoration and Waste Management Programs *e:* **ERWMP**

Environmental Restoration and Waste Management Technology Development *e:* **ERWMTD**

Environmental Restoration Contract[or] *e:* **ERC**

Environmental Restoration D&D *e:* **ERD&D**

Environmental Restoration Division *e:* **ERD**

Environmental Restoration Document Management Center *e:* **ERDMC**

Environmental Restoration Engineering *e:* **ERE**

Environmental Restoration Group *e:* **ERG**

Environmental Restoration Information System *e:* **ERIS**

Environmental Restoration Management Contract[or] *e:* **ERMC**

Environmental Restoration Monitoring and Assessment Program *e:* **ERMA**

Environmental Restoration Operations *e:* **ERO**

Environmental Restoration Organization *e:* **ERO**

Environmental Restoration Program *e:* **ERP**

Environmental Restoration Program Information Center *e:* **EPIC**

Environmental Restoration Program Support *e:* **ERPS**

Environmental Restoration Remedial Action *e:* **ERRA**

Environmental Restoration Storage & Disposal Facility *e:* **ERSDR**

Environmental Retraining and Internship *e:* **EnRI**

Environmental Retrieval Online *e:* **ENVIRON**

Environmental Review *e:* **Environ. Rev.**

Environmental Review and Documentation Program *e:* **ERDP**

Environmental Review and Documentation System *e:* **ERDS**

Environmental Review and Integration *e:* **ER&I**

Environmental Review Board *e:* **ERB**

Environmental Risk *e:* **ER**

Environmental Risk Assessment *e:* **ERA**

Environmental Risk Management Authority *e:* **ERMA**

Environmental Safety *e:* **ES**

Environmental Safety and Economic *e:* **ESECOM**

Environmental Safety and Economic Aspects of Fusion Energy *e:* **ESEAFE**

Environment[al] Safety and Health *e:* **ESH**

Environment[al], Safety and Health Compliance [Directorate] *e:* **ESHC**

Environmental, Safety and Health Concerns Hotline *e:* **ESHCH**

Environmental, Safety and Health Upgrade *e:* **ESHU**

Environmental, Safety, and Security *e:* **ES&S**

Environment[al], Safety, Health, and Quality. *e:* **ESH&Q**

Environmental Safety, Health, and Quality Assurance *e:* **ESH&QA**

Environmental, Safety, & Quality Assurance *e:* **ESQ**

Environmental Safety Quality Data department *e:* **ESQD**

Environmental Sampling Group *e:* **ESG**

Environmental Sampling Procedure *e:* **ESP**

Environment[al] Sanitation Information Center [Centre] *e:* **ENSIC**

Environmental Satellite Data System *e:* **ESDS**

Environmental Satellite Distribution/Interactive Processing Center *e:* **ESD/IPC**

Environmental Scanning Electron Microscop[y|e] *e:* **ESEM**

Environmental Science *e:* **EvS**

Environmental Science and Engineering *e:* **ESE**

Environmental Science [and] Information Center *e:* **ESIC**

Environmental Science and Pollution Research *e:* **Environ. Sci. Pollut. Res.**

Environmental Science and Society *e:* **ESS**

Environmental Science and Technology *e:* **ES&T**

Environmental Science and Technology [of American Chemical Society] *e:* **Environ. Sci. Technol.**

Environmental Science Citation Index *e:* **ESCI**

Environmental Science Data Integration and Management *e:* **ESDIM**

Environmental Science Index *e:* **ESI**

Environmental Science Index On Line *e:* **ENVIROLINE**

Environmental Science Research consortia *e:* **ERC**

Environmental Science Resources *e:* **ESR**

Environmental Science Section *e:* **ESS**

Environmental Science Series *e:* **ESS**

Environmental Science Services *e:* **ESS**

Environmental Science Services Administration *e:* **ESSC**, *e:* **ESSS**

Environmental Science Services Administration Satellites *e:* **ESSA Satellites**

Environmental Science Services Agency *e:* **ESSA**

Environmental Science & Services Corporation *e:* **ESSCO**

Environmental Sciences Catalog *e:* **ESC**

Environmental Sciences Division *e:* **ESD**

Environmental Sciences Division Complex *e:* **ESDC**

Environmental Science[s] Research Center *e:* **ESRC**

Environmental Sciences Research Laboratory *e:* **ESRL**

Environmental Sciences Research Unit *e:* **ESRU**

Environmental Science[s] Service[s] Administration *e:* **ESSA**

Environmental Seience and Technology A *e:* **Environ. Sci. Technol. A**

Environmental Self-Assessment Program *e:* **ESAP**

Environmental Sensing Device *e:* **ESD**

Environmental-Sensitive Fracture Processes *e:* **ESFP**

Environmental Sensor Kit *e:* **ESK**

Environmental Services *e:* **ES**

Environmental Services Agency *e:* **ESA**

Environmental Services Assistance Team *e:* **ESAT**

Environmental Services Association *e:* **ESA**

Environmental Services Branch *e:* **ESB**

Environmental Services Department *e:* **ESD**

Environmental Services Division *e:* **ESD**

Environmental Service[s] Section *e:* **ESS**

Environmental Simulation Equipment *e:* **ESE**

Environmental Simulation Program *e:* **ESP**

Environmental Simulator *e:* **ENSIM**

Environmental Site Assessment *e:* **ESA**

Environmental Site of the Week *e:* **ESW**

Environmental Sketches in Perspective *e:* **ESP**

Environmental Software *e:* **Environ. Softw.**

Environmental Space Sciences *e:* **Environ. Space Sci.**

Environmental Specimen Banking *e:* **ESB**

Environmental Standard Review Plan[s] *e:* **ESRP**

Environmental Stress Crack[ing] *e:* **ESC**

Environmental Stress-Cracking Resistance *e:* **ESCR**

Environmental Stress Screening *e:* **ESS**

Environmental Studies *e:* **ES**

Environmental Studies Association of Canada *e:* **ESAC**

Environmental Studies Board *e:* **ESB**

Environmental Studies Institute *e:* **ESI**

Environmental Studies Program *e:* **ESP**

Environmental Studies Research Fund *e:* **ESRF**

Environmental Studies Resources *e:* **ESR**

Environmental Studies Revolving Fund[s] report *e:* **ESRF**

Environmental Study Center *e:* **PSL**

Environmental Study Conference *e:* **ESC**

Environmental Supercomputer Center *e:* **ESC**

Environmental Support Facility *e:* **ESF**

Environmental Support Group *e:* **ESG**

Environmental Support Solutions *e:* **ESS**

Environmental Support System *e:* **ESS**

Environmental Surveillance Database *e:* **ESD**

Environmental Surveillance & Monitoring *e:* **ES&M**

Environmental Surveillance Procedure *e:* **ESP**

Environmental Surveillance report *e:* **ESI**

Environmental Surveillance Report *e:* **ESR**

Environmental Survey *e:* **ES**

Environmental Survey Manual *e:* **ESM**

Environmental Survey Satellite *e:* **ESS**, *e:* **ESSA**

Environmental System and Effects Division *e:* **ESED**

Environmental System Test *e:* **EST**

Environmental System Test-Phase I *e:* **EST-I**

Environmental System Test-Phase II *e:* **EST-II**

Environmental Systems Applications Center *e:* **ESAC**

Environmental Systems Laboratory *e:* **ESL**

Environmental Systems Monitor *e:* **ESM**

Environmental Systems Research Institute *e:* **ESRI**

Environmental Systems Test Facility *e:* **ESTF**

Environmental Task Force *e:* **ETF**

Environmental Technical Application[s] Center *e:* **ETAC**

Environmental Technical Information Center *e:* **ETIC**

Environmental Technical Information System *e:* **ETIS**

Environmental Technical Specification *e:* **ETS**

Environmental Technics *e:* **Envitec**

Environmental Technologies Group *e:* **ETG**

Environmental Technologist *e:* **ET**

Environmental Technology *e:* **Envitec**, *e:* **ET**

Environmental Technology and Assessment *e:* **ETA**

Environmental Technology Building *e:* **ETB**

Environmental Technology Center *e:* **ETC**

Environmental Technology Information Center *e:* **ETIC**

Environmental Technology Information Services *e:* **ETIS**

Environmental Technology Initiative *e:* **ETI**

Environmental Technology Laboratory *e:* **ETL**

Environmental Technology Letters *e:* **Environ. Technol. Lett.**

Environmental Technology Programs *e:* **ETP**

Environmental Technology Seminar *e:* **ETS**

Environmental Technology Verification Program *e:* **ETV**

Environmental Tectonics Corporation *e:* **ETC**

Environmental Teratology Information Center *e:* **ETIC**

Environmental Test *e:* **ET**

Environmental Test Area *e:* **ENTA**

Environmental Test Article *e:* **ETA**

Environmental Test Chamber *e:* **ETC**

Environmental Test Control Centre *e:* **ETCC**

Environmental Test Facility *e:* **ETF**

Environmental Test Program[me] *e:* **ETP**

Environmental Test Report *e:* **ETR**

Environmental Test Satellite *e:* **ARENTS ARPA**

Environmental Testing Advisory Board *e:* **ETAB**

Environmental Testing Corporation *e:* **ETC**

Environmental Threshold of Measurement Accuracy *e:* **ETOMA**

Environmental Tolerance Indices *e:* **ETIs**

Environmental Toxicology and Chemistry *e:* **Environ. Toxicol. Chem.**

Environmental Tracking System *e:* **ETS**

Environmental Training Program *e:* **ENDA**

Environmental Triage *e:* **ENTR**

Environmental Tritium Model *e:* **ETMOD**

Environmental Unit Leader *e:* **EUL**

Environmental Use Permit *e:* **EUP**

Environmental Vapor Monitor *e:* **EVM**

Environmental Virtual Information Library *e:* **EVIL**

Environmental Voting Records *e:* **EVR**

Environmental Web Resources *e:* **EWR**

Environmental Workforce Coordinating Committee *e:* **EWCC**

Environmental Working Group *e:* **EWG**

Environmental Writing Program *e:* **EWP**

Environmental Youth Congress *e:* **EYC**

environmentalism *e:* **environ.**

environmentalist *e:* **environ.**, *e:* **greeny**

Environmentalist[s] *e:* **Env.**

Environmentalists *e:* **Envs.**

environment[al][ly] *e:* **env**

Environmentally Compatible Energy Strategies [project] *e:* **ECS**

Environmentally Conscious Manufacturing *e:* **ECM**

Environmentally Conscious Manufacturing Integrated Demonstration *e:* **ECMID**

Environmentally Conscious Manufacturing Strategic Initiative Group *e:* **ECM-SIG**

Environmentally-Mediated Intellectual Decline *e:* **Emid**

Environmentally Sensitive Area[s] *e:* **ESA**

Environmentally Sensitive Investment System *e:* **ESIS**

Environmentally Sound and Sustainable Development *e:* **ESSD**

Environmentally Sound Products *e:* **ESP**

Environments and Threats Directorate *e:* **ETD**

Environnement de Controle et de Décision *f:* **ECD**

Environnement et Développement du Tiers Monde *f:* **ENDA**, *f:* **ENDA-TM**

Environnement et Développement en Afrique *f:* **ENDA**

Environnement Intégré de Données Techniques *f:* **EIDT**

Environnement Psychosociologique et Architecture *f:* **EPSA**

E.O. Hulburt Center for Space Research *e:* **HCSR**

EOS Atmospheric Global LIDAR Experiment *e:* **EAGLE**

EOS [Earth Observing System] Aerosol Mission *e:* **EOS-AERO**

EOS [Earth Observing System] Altimetry Mission *e:* **EOS-ALT**

EOS [Earth Observing System] Data Information System on Distributed Data Centers *e:* **EOSDIS**

EOS [Earth Observing System] Handbook *e:* **EOSH**

EOS [Earth Observing System] Morning Crossing Mission *e:* **EOS-AM**

EOS Polar Ground Stations *e:* **EPGS**

EOS Transactions of the American Geophysical Union *e:* **EOS Trans. Am. Geophys. Union**

EPI Quarterly Report [of Environmental Policy Institute] *e:* **EPI Q. Rep.**

Epidemiologie, Mikrobiologie, Imunologie *d:* **Epidemiol Mikrobiol Imunol**

epigeous *e:* **epig**

Epigraphica Anatolica. Zeitschrift für Epigraphik und historische Geographie Anatoliens *d:* **Epig[r]Anat**

Epilepsy on-Line Institutes of Health, National Institute of Neurological and Communicative Disorders and Stroke *e:* **EPILEPSYLINE**

Episcopal Conference of the Indian Ocean *e:* **CEDOI**

Epithelial Cell Biology *e:* **Epithelial Cell Biol**

Epoxidized Natural Rubber *e:* **ENR**

Epoxytetrahydrophthalmic Anhydride *e:* **ETHPA**

Equal Area SSMI Earth *e:* **EASE**

Equal Area SSMI Earth Grid *e:* **EASE-Grid**

Equal Error Protection *e:* **EEP**

Equally Spaced *e:* **EQL SP**

equally spaced *e:* **eq sp**

Equate Operand Spaces *e:* **EOS**

Equator Earth Terminal *e:* **EET**

Equatorial Islands in the central and South Pacifc Ocean, also called the Line Islands *e:* **Equatorials**

Equatorial Middle Atmosphere Dynamics *e:* **EMAD**

Equatorial Pacific Interocean Circulation *e:* **EPIC**

Equatorial Pacific Ocean Climate Studies *e:* **EPOCS**

Equilibrium Orbit *e:* **EO**

Equilibrium Vegetation Ecology *e:* **EVE**

Equipe de Biologia e Pesca de Agua Doce *p:* **EBPAD**

Équipes Médico-Sociales Itinérantes *f:* **EMSI**

Equitorial Mount with Mirrors for Acceleration with Water Spray *e:* **EMMAQUA**

Equivalent Bond Orbital *e:* **EBO**

Erase Protected *e:* **E**

Erase Unprotected to Address *e:* **EUA**

ERDA: Division of Biomedical and Environmental Research *e:* **DBER**

ERDA Remote Console *e:* **ERDA-RECON**

Erde *d:* **E**, *d:* **earth**

Erde International [of Aloe Technology Association] *e:* **Erde Int.**

Erde-Mars-Erde *d:* **EME**

Erde-Mond-Erde *d:* **EME**

Erd[e]funkstelle *d:* **EFuSt**, *d:* **ErdFuSt**

Erdeinschießziel *d:* **Erdei.**

Erderkundungs-Daten & Informations System *d:* **EDIS**

Erderkundungs-Daten-Service *d:* **EDS**

Erderkundungsexperimentepaket *d:* **EREP**

Erderkundungsflugzeug *d:* **EKUF**

Erdészeti Tudományos Intézet *H:* **ERTI**

Ergänzende klimatologische Daten *e:* **EKDA**

Ergebnisse der exakten Naturwissenschaften *d:* **EeN**

Ergebnisse der gesamten Medizin *d:* **EgM**

Ergebnisse der inneren Medizin und Kinderheilkunde *e:* **EiMKh**

Ergebnisse der medizinischen Strahlenforschung *d:* **EmStr**

Erie Area Health Information Library Cooperative *e:* **EAIHILC**

Erie County Medical Center *e:* **ECMC**

Erie National Wildlife Refuge *e:* **ENWR**

Erim Ocean Model *e:* **EOM**

Erlanger Medical Center, I. C., Thompson's Children's Pediatric Library, Chattanooga *e:* **TCEC-P**

Erlanger Medical Center, Medical Library, Chattanooga, *e:* **TCEC**

Erlanger Medical Center, Nursing School, Chattanooga *e:* **TCEC-N**

ERNO Spacelab Product Assurance Department *e:* **SLA**

erprobter fortgeschrittener Druckwasserreaktor *d:* **EFDR**

erstes offenes Wasser *d:* **e.o.W.**

Erwärmung im Wasserbad *d:* **EW**

Es wird ein Skript abgearbeitet, welches beschreibt, wie und mit wem die Verbindung aufgebaut werden soll. *e:* **Dialout-Mode**

ESA Bulletin [of European Space Agency, France] *f:* **ESA Bull.**

ESA [European Space Agency] Remote Sensing Satellite *e:* **ERS**

ESA Features [of European Space Agency, France] *f:* **ESA Feat.**

ESA Journal [of European Space Agency Technical Center] *n:* **ESA J.**

ESA Space Documentation Service *e:* **ESA/SDS**

ESA Space Information Systems *e:* **ESIS**

Escadron de Quartier Général *f:* **E.Q.G.**

ESCAP Division for Shipping, Ports and Inland Waterways *e:* **SPIW**

Escuela Interamericana de Bibliotecologia *s:* **EIAB**

Escuela Interamericana de Bibliotecología *s:* **EIB**

Escuela Interamericana de Bibliotecología Medellin *s:* **EIBM**

Escuela Nacional de Ciencias Biológicas *s:* **ENCB**

Escuela Universitaria de Bibliotecología y Ciencias Afines *s:* **EUBCA**

ESF/European Palaeoclimate and Man Project *e:* **ESF/EPC**

ESF [European Science Foundation] Consortium for Ocean Drilling *e:* **ECOD**

Espace Intercostal *e:* **EIC**

Espace Produit Technologie *f:* **EPT**

Espace Économique Européen *f:* **EEE**

ESRO [European Space Research Organization] Advanced Imaging Detector *e:* **EAID**

ESRO [European Space Research Organization] Technical (or Technology) Center (or Centre) *e:* **ESTEC**

ESRO Geostationary Earth Orbiting Satellite *e:* **ESGEO**

ESRO Space Documentation Service *e:* **ESRO-SDS**

ESSA [Environmental Science Service[s] Administration] Weather Wire Service *e:* **EWWS**

Essays in International Business. Published by the Institute of International Business in cooperation with Georgia State College, School of Business *e:* **IIB/EIB.**

Essential Cooling Water *e:* **ECW**

Essential Cooling Water System *e:* **ECWS**

Essential National Health Research *e:* **ENHR**

Essential Procedures for Clinical Microbiology *e:* **EPCM**

Essential Services Cooling Water System *e:* **ESCWS**

Essential Technical Medical Data *e:* **ETMD**

Essex Naturalists' Trust *e:* **ENT**

Estação Experimentál de Biologia e Piscicultura de Perassununga *p:* **EEBP**

Estacion Biologica de Donana *s:* **EBD**

Estación Biológica de las Bermudas *s:* **BBS**

Estación Climatológica de Referencia *s:* **ECR**

Estación de Biologia Marina *s:* **EBM**

estación meteorológica *s:* **E/Meteo**

Estación Meteorológica Oceánica *s:* **OWS**

Estatuto Jurídico del Personal Médico *s:* **EP Med**

Estimated Environmental Concentrations *e:* **EECs**

Estimating Water Treatment Costs *e:* **CULP**

Estonian Meteorological and Hydrological Institute *e:* **EMHI**

Estrategia Integrada de Observación Mundial *s:* **EIOM**

Estuarine and Brackish-Water Biological Association *e:* **EBBA**

Estuarine and Brackish-Water Sciences Association *e:* **EBSA**

Estuarine Water Quality Model *e:* **ES001**

Estudio de Archivos sobre la Historia del Clima *s:* **ARCHISS**

Estudio de Evaluación de Modelos de Transporte Atmosférico *s:* **ATMES**

Estudio de los Flujos Oceánicos Biogeoquímicos *s:* **BOFS**

Estudio de Mejoras en la Protección frente a descargas Atmosféricas en Estaciones bases *e:* **EMPATE**

Estudio Geoquímico de Secciones Oceánicas *s:* **GEOSECS**

Estudio Japonés del Clima en el Océano Pacífico *s:* **JAPACS**

Estudios de la Interacción Océano-Atmósfera-Clima *s:* **OACIS**

Estudios sobre el Clima del Océano Pacífico Ecuatorial *s:* **EPOCS**

Établissement d'Études et de Recherches Météorologiques *f:* **EERM**

Établissement d'Utilité Agricole à Compétence Interdépartementale *f:* **E.U.A.C.I.**

Établissement National pour l'Exploitation Météorologique et Aéronautique *f:* **ENEMA**

Établissement Principal Service Hydrographique et Océanographique de la Marine *f:* **EPSHOM**

Établissements Médico-Sociaux *f:* **EMS**

Etat côtier *f:* **CS**

Ether Water *e:* **EW**

Ethiopian Institute of Geological Survey *e:* **EIGS**

Ethiopian Mapping and Geography Institute *e:* **EMGI**

Ethiopian Medical Journal *e:* **Ethiop Med J**

Ethiopian Water Resources Authority *e:* **EWRA**

Ethno-, Geo-, Polycentric *e:* **EGP**

Ethnobiological Institute of Australia *e:* **INEA**

Ethyl-acetate Pyridine-Water *e:* **EPW**

ETR Biological Shielding *e:* **EBS**

Étude de Processes dans l'Ocean Pacifique Equatorial *f:* **EPOPE**

Etude des variations climatiques sur une longue période avec établissement de cartes et de prévisions *f:* **CLIMAP**

Etude du système climatique de l'Arctique *f:* **ACSYS**

Etude japonaise sur le climat de l'océan Pacifique *f:* **JAPACS**

Etude sur l'évaluation des modèles de transport atmosphérique *f:* **ATMES**

Études Climatiques dans l'Atlantique Tropical *f:* **ECLAT**

Études et Constructions Electro-mécaniques et Médicales *f:* **ECEM**

Études et Réalisations d'Équipements Médicaux *f:* **EREM**

Études Médicales *f:* **EM**

Etudes sur l'interaction océan-atmosphère-climat *f:* **OACIS**

Étudiants, Manipulateurs, Techniciens en Electro-Radiologie Médicale *f:* **EMTERM**

Eufaula National Wildlife Refuge *e:* **ENWR**

Eugene Water and Electric Board *e:* **EWEB**

Eumetsat Polar System *e:* **EPS**

EUREKA project on an ecological and economic European tanker *e:* **TANKER**

EUREKA project on an economically efficient and environmentally friendly road traffic system *e:* **PROMETHEUS**

Euro-Arab Sea Trailer-Line *e:* **EAST**

Euromarket Federation of Animal Protein Importers *e:* **EFAPI**

Euromarket Federation of Animal Protein Importers and Traders *e:* **EFAPIT**

Europaeum Medicum Collegium *l:* **EMC**

Europäische Akademie für Medizinische Fortbildung *d:* **EAMF**

Europäische Hilfeorganisation für Tiere in Not *d:* **EHOTN**

Europäische Konferenz für Molekularbiologie *f:* **EKMB**

Europäische Konferenz für Molekularbiologie, Heidelberg *d:* **EMBC**

Europäische Naturstein-Union *d:* **ENU**

Europäische Organisation für Molekularbiologie *d:* **EMBO**

Europäische Organisation für Weltraumforschung *d:* **ESR0**

Europäische Tierschutzunion *d:* **EUPA**

Europäische Union gegen den Missbrauch der Tiere *d:* **EUMT**

Europäische Vereinigung der Geophysiker für Bodenuntersuchungen *d:* **EAEG**

Europäische Vereinigung für Tierzucht *d:* **EVT**

Europäische Weltraumforschungs-organisation, Paris *d:* **ESRO**

Europäischer Umweltdienst e.V. *d:* **EUD**

Europäisches Abwasser- und Abfall-Symposium *d:* **EAS**

Europäisches Experiment zum Transport und zur Umwandlung umwelt-relevanter Spurenstoffe in der Troposphäre über Europa *d:* **EUROTRAC**

Europäisches Forschungskomitee für den Schutz der Bevölkerungen vor chronisch-toxischen Umweltschäden *d:* **EUROTOX**

Europäisches Laboratorium für Molekularbiologie *d:* **ELM**

Europäisches Laboratorium für Molekularbiologie, Heidelberg *d:* **EMBL**

Europäisches Meteorologisches Rechen-Zentrum *d:* **EMRZ**

Europäisches Naturschutzjahr 1970 *d:* **ENJ 1970**

Europäisches Umweltschutzbüro *e:* **EEB**

Europäisches Zentrum für mittelfristige Wettervorhersage *d:* **EZMW**

Europäisches Zentrum für mittelfristige Wettervorhersagen *d:* **ECMWF**

European Advisory Committee for Medical Research *e:* **EACMR**

European Advisory Committee on Health Research *e:* **EACHR**

European Aeronautic Defence & Space Company *e:* **EADS**

European Aerospace Industries Association *e:* **EUROSPACE**

European Agency for the Evaluation of Medicinal Products *e:* **EMEA**

European Agreement Concerning the Carriage of Dangerous Goods by Inland Waterways *e:* **AND**

European Airborne Remote Sensing Capabilities *e:* **EARSEC**

European Airborne Remote Sensing Facility *e:* **EARSF**

European American Phytomedicines Coalition *e:* **EAPC**

European [and Mediterranean] Plant Protection Organisation (or Organization) *e:* **EPPO**

European and Mediterranean Plant Protection Organization *e:* **EMPPO**

European Association for Animal Production *e:* **EAAP**

European Association for Earthquake Engineering *e:* **EAEE**

European Association for Earthquake Prediction *e:* **EAEP**

European Association for Free Nature Reserves *e:* **EUREL**

European Association for Health Information and *e:* **EAHIL**

European Association for/of Gynaecologists and Obstetricians *e:* **EAGO**

European Association for Oral Medicine *e:* **EAOM**

European Association for the International Space Year *e:* **EURISY**

European Association of Dental Public Health *e:* **EADPH**

European Association of Earth Science[s] Editors *e:* **EDITERRA**

European Association of Editors of Biological Periodicals *e:* **EAEBP**, *e:* **ELSE**

European Association of Environmental and Resource Economists *e:* **EAERE**

European Association of Exploration Geophysicis *e:* **EACG**

European Association of Exploration Geophysicists *e:* **EAGS**

European Association of Exploration[al] Geophysicists *e:* **EAEG**

European Association of Geoscientists and Engineers *e:* **EAGE**

European Association of Internal Medicine *e:* **AEMIE**

European Association of Nuclear Medicine *e:* **EANM**

European Association of Oral Surgeons *e:* **EAOS**

European Association of Passive Fire Protection *e:* **EAPFP**

European Association of Perinatal Medicine *e:* **EAPM**

European Association of Petroleum Geologists *e:* **EAPG**

European Association of Petroleum Geoscientists *e:* **EAPG**

European Association of Petroleum Geoscientists and Engineers *e:* **EAPGE**

European Association of Programmes in Health Service Studies *e:* **EAPHSS**

European Association of Remote Sensing Companies *e:* **EARSC**

European Association of Remote Sensing Laboratories *e:* **EARSEL**

European Association of Scientists in Environmental Pollution *e:* **EUROSEP**

European Association of Training Programmes in Hospital and Health Services Administration *e:* **EATPHHSA**

European Biological and Landscape Diversity Strategy *e:* **EBLDS**

European Board and College of Gynecology and Obstetrics *e:* **EBCOG**

European Butylated Hydroxytoluene-BHT-Manufacturers Association *e:* **EBMA**

European Cell Biology Organisation (or Organization) *e:* **ECBO**

European Center for Geodynamics and Seismology *e:* **ECGS**

European Center (or Centre) for Medium-Range Weather Forecasting (or Forecasts) *e:* **ECMWF**

European Centre for Environment and Health *e:* **ECEH**

European Centre for Environment[al] Communication *e:* **ECEC**

European Centre for Human Ecology *e:* **ECHE**

European Centre for Medical Demography and Health Economics *e:* **EUCEMEC**

European Centre for Medium Range Weather Forecasting *e:* **EECMWF**

European Centre for Medium-Range Weather Forecasts e: **ECMRWF**

European Centre for Nature Conservation e: **ECNC**

European Centre for Space Law e: **ECSL**

European Chemical Industry Ecology and Toxicology Center e: **ECETOC**

European Climate and Hydrological Project on Interactions between Vegetation, Atmosphere and Land Surface e: **ECHIVAL**

European Climate Support Network e: **ECSN**

European Coastal and Marine Ecological Network e: **ECMEN**

European Committee for Intrusion and Fire Protection e: **ESCIF**

European Committee for the Conservation of Nature and Natural Resources e: **ECCNR**

European Committee for the Protection of the Population against the Hazards of Chronic Toxicity e: **EUROTOX**

European Committee for Water Resources Management e: **ECOWARM**

European Committee of Crop Protection e: **ECP**

European Committee on Ocean[ic] and Polar Science[s] e: **ECOPS**

European Communities (or Community) Biologists Association e: **ECBA**

European Confederation for Plant Protection Research e: **ECP**

European Confederation of Medical Suppliers Association[s] e: **EUCOMED**

European Conference of Meteorological Experts for Aeronautics e: **ECMEA**

European Conference on Molecular Biology e: **ECMB**

European Cooperation Space Environment Committee e: **ECOSEC**

European Coordinating Committee of the Radiological and Electromedical Industries e: **COCIR**

European Corporation for Laboratory Medicine e: **ECLM**

European Council for Animal Welfare e: **ECAW**

European Council for Environmental Law e: **ECEL**

European Council for Laboratory Medicine e: **ECLM**

European Council on Environmental Law e: **CEDE**

European Deep Sea Transect e: **EURODEST**

European Developmental Biology Organization e: **EBDO**

European Directory of Marine Environmental Data[sets] e: **EDMED**

European Directory of Marine Environmental Research Projects e: **EDMERP**

European Dry Ice Association e: **EDIA**

European Earth Observation System e: **EEOS**

European Ecological Centre e: **EEC**

European Ecological Federation e: **EEF**

European Ecological Network e: **EECONET**

European Economic Space e: **EES**

European Environment and Health Committee e: **EEHC**

European Environment Foundation e: **EEF**

European Environment Information and Observation Network e: **EIONET**

European Environment Monitoring Satellite e: **EEMS**

European Environment[al] Agency e: **EEA**

European Environment[al] Bureau e: **EEB**

European Environmental Database e: **EED**

European Environmental Information System e: **EEIS**

European Environmental Law Review e: **E.E.L.R.**

European Environmental Management Association e: **EEMA**

European Environmental Mutagen Society e: **EEMS**

European Environmental Programme e: **EUEP**

European Experiment for/on Transport and Transformation of Environmentally Relevant Trace Constituents in the Troposphere over Europe e: **EUROTRAC**

European Experiment on Transport and Transformation of Environmentally Relevant Trace Constituents in the Troposphere over Europe e: **EUROTRAC T**

European Federation for Medical Informatics e: **EFTMI**

European Federation for/of Medical Chemistry e: **EFMC**

European Federation for/of Medical Information e: **EFMI**

European Federation for the Protection of Waters e: **EFPA**, e: **EFPW**

European Federation for the Study of Ultrasound in Medicine and Biology e: **EFSUMB**

European Federation of Association[s] of Health Product Manufacturers e: **EHPM**

European Federation of Associations of Industrial Safety and Medical Officers e: **FAS**

European Federation of Naturopaths e: **E.F.N.**

European Federation of Organisations for Medical Physics e: **EFOMP**

European Federation of Sea Anglers e: **EFSA**

European Federation of Societies for Ultrasound in Medicine and Biology e: **EFSUMB**

European Forum on Nature Conservation and Pastoralism e: **EFNCP**

European Geo-Traverse e: **EGT**

European Geographic Information Infrastructure e: **EGII**

European Geographical Information Symposia e: **EGIS**

European Geographical Information System[s] e: **EGIS**

European Geophysical Society e: **EGS**

European Geophysical Society Working Group on Tsunami e: **EGSWG**

European Geostationary Navigation Overlay Service (or System) e: **EGNOS**

European Global Ocean Observing System e: **EuroGOOS**

European Group for Ecological Action e: **ECOROPA**

European Group for Ecological Policy e: **Policy**

European Group on Ocean Stations e: **EGOS**

European Health Policy Forum e: **EHPF**

European Health Telematics Observatory e: **EHTO**

European Healthcare Management Association e: **EHMA**

European Ice-Sheet Modelling Initiative e: **EISMINT**

European Information Center for Explosion Protection e: **EUROPEX**

European Information Technology Observatory e: **EITO**

European Initiative in Library and Information in Aerospace e: **EURILIA**

European Institute for Water e: **EIW**

European Institute of Ecology and Cancer e: **INEC**

European Institute of Environmental Cybernetics e: **EIEC**

European Institute of Women's Health e: **EIWH**

European International Project on Climate and Hydrological Interactions between Vegetation, Atmosphere and Landsurfaces e: **EFEDA**

European Journal of Cell Biology e: **EJCB**, e: **Eur J Cell Biol**

European Journal of Cell Biology. Supplement e: **Eur J Cell Biol Suppl**

European Journal of Clinical Microbiology and Infectious Diseases e: **Eur J Clin Microbiol Infect Dis**

European Journal of Gynaecological Oncology e: **Eur J Gynaecol Oncol**

European Journal of Nuclear Medicine e: **Eur J Nucl Med**

European Journal of Obstetrics and Gynecology and Reproductive Biology e: **EJOGR**

European Journal of Obstetrics, Gynecology, and Reproductive Biology e: **Eur J Obstet Gynecol Reprod Biol**

European Land-Ocean Interaction Studies e: **ELOISE**

European large-orbiting instrumentation for solar experimentation e: **Eloise**

European Large Orbiting Instrumentation for Solar Experiments e: **ELOISE**

European Launcher for Geostationary Orbit e: **ELGO**

European Local Environmental Information Clearing House e: **ELEICH**

European Marine and Polar Science Secretariat e: **EMaPS**

European Marine Biological Association e: **EMBA**

European Medical Electronic Data Interchange e: **EMEDI**

European Medical Graduate Exchange e: **EMGE**

European Medical Informatics Society e: **EMIS**

European Medical Laser Association e: **EMLA**

European Medical Research Council e: **EMRC**

European Medical Students Association e: **EMSA**

European Medicine Evaluation Agency e: **EMEA**

European Mediterranean Commission on Water Planning e: **EMCWP**

European Meteorological Data System *e:*
EMDS

European Meteorological Data systems *e:*
EURMEDS

European Meteorological Satellite *e:*
EMOS, *e:* **EUMETSTAT**, *e:*
METEOSTAT

European Meteorological Satellite
[Organisation] (or Organization) *e:*
EUMETSAT

European Meteorological
Telecommunications Network *e:* **EMTN**

European Microwave Signature Laboratory
e: **EMSL**

European Molecular Biology Conference
e: **EMBC**

European Molecular Biology Data Network
e: **EMBnet**

European Molecular Biology Laboratory
e: **EMBL**

European Molecular Biology Organisation
(or Organization) *e:* **EMBO**

European Multimedial Medical Journal *e:*
EMMJ

European Natural Heritage Fund *e:*
EURONATUR

European Natural Hygiene Society *e:*
ENHS

European Natural Sausage Casings
Association *e:* **ENSCA**

European Nature Information System *e:*
EUNIS

European Near-Earth Asteroids Search
Observatories *e:* **EUNEASO**

European Network for Development of
Multiprofessional Education [in Health
Sciences] *e:* **EMPE**

European Network of Ocean Stations *e:*
ENOS

European Neuromuscular Centre for the
Coordination of Medical and Scientific
Affairs *e:* **ENMC**

European Nuclear Medicine Society *e:*
ENIMS, *e:* **ENMS**

European Ocean[ographic] Association *e:*
EUROCEAN

European Office of Aerospace Research *e:*
EOAB

European Office of Aerospace Research and
Development *e:* **EOARD**

European Office of [the Office of]
Aerospace Research *e:* **EOAR**

European Organisation for the Exploitation
of Meteorological Satellites *e:* **EOEMS**,
e: **EUMESAT**

European Organization for Aid to Animals
in Distress *e:* **EOAAD**

European Organization for the Development
and Construction of Space Vehicle
Launchers *e:* **ELDO**

European Palaeoclimate and Man Project
e: **EPC**

European Partners for the Environment *e:*
EPE

European Polar Forum *e:* **EPF**

European Polar Ice Coring in Antarctica *e:*
EPICA

European Polar[-Orbiting] Platform *e:*
EPOP

European Polar Platform *e:* **EPP**

European Polar Segment *e:* **EPS**

European Polar System *e:* **EPS**

European Polarstern Study *e:* **EPOS**

European Processurized Watercooled
Reactor *e:* **EPR**

European Program in Chemistry of the
Atmosphere *e:* **EUROPICA**

European Program[me] on Climate (or
Climatology) and [natural] Hazards *e:*
EPOCH

European Public Health Alliance *e:* **EPHA**

European Remote Sensing Aircraft Facility
e: **ERSAF**

European Remote Sensing Program *e:*
ERSP

European Remote Sensing Satellite *e:*
ERS, *e:* **ERSS**

European Remote Sensing Satellite
Programme *e:* **ERSSP**

European Remote Sensing System *e:* **ERS**

European Retrievable Orbiting System *e:*
EUROS

European River Ocean System *e:* **EROS**

European River-Ocean Systems Programme
e: **EROS-2000**

European Satellite Agency *e:* **ESA**

European Science and Technology
Observatory *e:* **ESTO**

European Society for Animal Blood-Group
Research *e:* **ESABR**

European Society for Biomedical Research
on Alcoholism *e:* **ESBRA**

European Society for Cllinical
Microbiology *e:* **ESCM**

European Society for Comparative Skin
Biology *e:* **ESCSB**

European Society for Infectious Diseases in
Obstetrics and Gynecology *e:* **ESIDOG**

European Society for Magnetic Resonance
in Medicine and Biology *e:* **ESMRMB**

European Society for/of Animal Cell
Technology *e:* **ESACT**

European Society for/of Medical Oncology
e: **ESMO**

European Society for/of Medical Sociology
e: **ESMS**

European Society for Radiation Biology *e:*
ESRB

European Society for Radiation Protection
e: **ESRP**

European Society of Cataract and
Refractive Surgeons *e:* **ESCRS**

European Society of Chronobiology *e:*
ESC

European Society of Foot and Ankle
Surgeons *e:* **ESFAS**

European Society of Gynaecological
Oncology *e:* **ESGO**

European Society of Limnology and
Oceanography *e:* **ESLO**

European Southern Observatory *e:* **ESO**

European Space Agency *e:* **ES**, *e:* **ESA**, *f:*
ASE

European Space Agency Environmental
Satellite *e:* **ENVISA**, *e:* **ENVISAT**

European Space Agency Geosynchronous
Meteorological Satellite *e:* **METEOSAT**

European Space Agency [Information]
Network *e:* **ESANET**

European Space Agency Information
Retrieval Service *e:* **ESA/IRS**

European Space Agency information
retrieval service *e:* **ESA-IRS**

European Space Agency - Information
Retrieval System *e:* **ESA IRS**

European Space Agency Remote Sensing
Satellite *e:* **ERS-1**

European Space Agency Technical Center
e: **ESATC**

European [Space Agency] X-ray
Observation Satellite *e:* **EXOSAT**

European Space Agencys Earth Resources
e: **ESAER**

European Space Agencys X-ray
Observatory *e:* **Exosat**

European Space Association *e:* **ESA**

European Space Conference *e:* **ESC**

European Space Data Analysis Center [or
Centre] *e:* **ESDAC**

European Space Data Center *e:* **ESDAC**

European Space Information System *e:*
ESIS

European Space Launcher Organization *e:*
ESLO

European Space [Launching] Range *e:*
ESRANGE

European Space Operation[s] Center (or
Centre) *e:* **ESOC**

European Space Operations Centre *e:*
ESOP, *e:* **FSOC**

European Space Organization *e:* **ESO**

European Space Power Conference *e:*
ESPC

European Space Research Group *e:*
EUROSPACE

European Space Research Institute *e:*
ESRI, *e:* **ESRIN**

European Space [research] Laboratories (or
Laboratory) *e:* **ESLAB**

European Space [Research] Laboratory *e:*
ESLA

European Space Research Organisation *e:*
ESA

European Space Research Organisation (or
Organization) Satellite *e:* **ESRO**

European Space Research Organization *e:*
ESR0

European Space Research [Range] *e:*
ESRANGE

European Space Satellite Tracking and
Telemetry Network *e:* **ESTRACK**

European Space Study Group *e:*
EUROSPACE

European Space Technology Centre *e:*
ESTC

European Space Technology Institute *e:*
ESTI

European Space Tracking *e:* **ESTRACK**

European Space Tribology Center *e:*
ESTC

European Space Tribology Laboratory *e:*
ESTL

European [Space Vehicle] Launcher
Development Organization *e:* **ELDO**

European Space Vehicle Launcher
Development Organization *e:*
EUR/SV/LDO

European Station for Time-Series in the
Ocean, Canary Islands *e:* **ESTOC**

European Station for Time-Series
Observations in the Ocean *e:* **ESTOC**

European Stress Physiology and Climate
Experiment *e:* **ESPACE**

European Subpolar Ocean Programme *e:*
ESOP

European Symposium on Polar Platform
Opportunities and Instrumentation for
Remote Sensing *e:* **ESPOIR**

European Teaching Group of Orthopaedic Medicine *e:* **Etgom**

European Technical Association for/of Protective Coatings *e:* **ETAPC**

European Technical Office for Medicinal Products *e:* **ETOMEP**

European Telephony Numbering Space *e:* **ETNS**

European Topic Centre on Nature Conservation *e:* **ETC / NC**

European Trade Union Technical Bureau for Health and Safety *e:* **TUTB**

European Umbrella Organisation (or Organization) for Geographic[al] Information *e:* **EUROGI**

European Undersea[s] Bio-medical Society *e:* **EUBS**

European Underwater Federation *e:* **EUF**

European Union for Packaging and the Environment *e:* **EUPE**

European Union for the Prevention of Cruelty to Animals *e:* **UEMTA**

European Union for the Protection of Animals *e:* **EUPA**

European Union of Dental Medicine Practitioners *e:* **EUD**

European Union of Geosciences *e:* **EUG**

European Union of School and University Health and Medicine *e:* **EUSUHM**

European Water Pollution Control Association *e:* **EWPCA**

European Water Sectoral Committee *e:* **EWSC**

European Weather Central *e:* **EWC**

European Weather Graphics System *e:* **EWGS**

European X-ray Observatory *e:* **EXO**

Europese Verdedigingsorganisatie *n:* **EVO**

Œuvre Nationale d'Aide et de Protection *f:* **ONAP**

Evaluating Fallout Protection in Homes *e:* **EFPH**

evaluation basis earthquake *e:* **EBE**

Evaluation by Computer of the Learning Environment *e:* **ECOLE**

Evaluation de limpact sur lenvironnement *f:* **EIE**

Évaluation et Suivi de la Production Agricole en Fonction du Climat et de lEnvironment *f:* **ESPACE**

Evaluation of Strategies to Address Climate Change by Adapting to and Preventing Emissions *e:* **ESCAPE**

Evaluation SAGE [Semi-Automatic Ground Environmernt] Sector *e:* **ES**

Evangelical Environmental Network *e:* **EEN**

evaporative water loss *e:* **ewl**

Everett General Hospital, Medical Library, Everett *e:* **WaEG**

Evidence-Based Health Care *e:* **EBHC**

Evidence Based Medicine *e:* **EBM**

Evidence Based Medicine Reviews *e:* **EBMR**

Evidence for Community Health Organization *e:* **ECHO**

Evolutionary Biology *e:* **EB**, *e:* **Evol. Biol.**

Evolutionary Ecology *e:* **EE**, *e:* **Evol. Ecol.**

Evolving Natural Language Information Model *e:* **ENALIM**

Ex-Containment Chilled Water *e:* **ECCW**

Exabiology and Radiation Assembly *e:* **ERA**

Examen Médical Sérologique *f:* **E.M.S.**

Examining Medical Officer *e:* **EMO**

Excerpta Medica *e:* **Excrpt Med**, *e:* **EXM**

Excerpta Medica Broader Tags *e:* **EMTAGS**

Excerpta Medica Classifcation System *e:* **EMCLASS**

Excerpta Medica Computer System *e:* **EMCS**

Excerpta Medica Data Base *e:* **EMBASE**

Excerpta-Medica-Datenbank *d:* **EM-Datenbank**

Excerpta Medica Foundation *e:* **EMF**

Excerpta Medica On Line *e:* **EMOL**

Excerpta Medica Physicians' Information Retrieval and Education Service *e:* **EMPIRES**

Exchange Core Polarization *e:* **ECP**

Exe Estuary National Wildlife Refuge *e:* **EENWR**

Execution Orbital Analysis Engineer *e:* **XOAE**

Executive Board of the International Association of Microbiological Societies *e:* **EBIAMS**

Executive Committee's Panel on Meteorological Aspects of Ocean Affairs *e:* **ECPMACA**

Exerpta Medica *l:* **ExMed**

Exo-Earth Discoverer *e:* **EED**

Exo-Earth Imager *e:* **EEI**

Exoatmospheric *e:* **EXO**

Exoatmospheric Defense System *e:* **XDS**

Exoatmospheric Discrimination Simulation *e:* **XoDiS**

Exoatmospheric-Endoatmospheric Interceptor *e:* **E2I**

Exoatmospheric Penetration Aid *e:* **EPA**

Exoatmospheric Re-entry Vehicle Interception System *e:* **ERVIS**

Exoatmospheric Reentry Interceptor Subsystem *e:* **ERIS**

Exoatmospheric Reentry Interceptor System *e:* **ERIS**

Exoatmospheric Reentry Vehicle Interceptor Subsyst[em] *e:* **ERIS**

exoatmosphericjettisonable control wafer *e:* **exopac**

exobiologic[al][ly] *e:* **exobio**

exobiologist *e:* **exobio**

exobiology *e:* **exobio**

Exoterrestrial Biology *e:* **EXOBIOLOGY**

Exotic Animal Disease [preparedness] Consultative Council *e:* **EXANDIS**

Exotic-Diseases Sub-Committee of Animal Health Committee *e:* **EDSC**

Expandable Remote-Operated Weather Station *e:* **EROWS**

Expanded Mid-Ocean Dynamics Experiment *e:* **POLY-MODE**

Expanded Program on Immunization. Pan American Health Organization *e:* **EPI**

expected repository environment[s] *e:* **ere**

Expedición Internacional al Océano Indico *s:* **EIOI**

Expedición Oceanográfica Internacional al Mar de Weddell *s:* **IWSOE**

Expedite the Processing of Experiments to Space Station *e:* **EXPRESS**

Expeditions Astrophysiques et Géophysiques Belges *f:* **EAGB**

expendable bathy thermograph (water dropped temperature device) *e:* **XBT**

Experienced Library and Information Personnel in Asia and Oceania *e:* **ELIPA**

Experiment Operator (Spacelab) *e:* **EXO**

Experiment Terminal (Operator Console on Spacelab) *e:* **EXT**

Experimental Aerospace Multiprocessor *e:* **EXAM**

Experimental Biology and Medicine *e:* **EBM**

Experimental Biology Online *e:* **EBO**

Experimental Boiling-water Reactor *e:* **EBWR**

Experimental Cartography Unit [of Natural Environment Research Council] *e:* **ECU**

Experimental Center for Mesoscale Ocean Predictions *e:* **ECMOP**

Experimental Ecological Reserves *e:* **EER**

Experimental Environmental Reporting Buoy *e:* **XERB**

Experimental Farm, Agriculture Canada La Pocatiere, Quebec *e:* **QPAG**

Experimental Geodetic Payload *e:* **EGP**

Experimental Geodetic Satellite *e:* **EGS**

Experimental Geophysical Orbiting *e:* **EGO**

Experimental Health Service[s] Delivery System *e:* **EHSDS**

Experimental Inter-American Meteorological Rocket Network *e:* **EXAMETNET**

Experimental Land Observation System *e:* **ELOS**

Experimental Man[ned] Space Station *e:* **EMSS**

Experimental Medical Care Review Organization *e:* **EMCRO**

Experimental Medicine and Microbiology *e:* **Exp. Med. Microbiol.**

Experimental Medicine and Surgery *e:* **Exp. Med. Surg.**

Experimental Meteorological sounding rocket research Network *e:* **EXMETNET**

Experimental Meteorology Laboratory *e:* **EML**

Experimental Prototype Automatic Meteorological System *e:* **EPAMS**

Experimental Reflector Orbit[al] Shot *e:* **EROS**

Experimental Remote Maneuvering Unit *e:* **ERMU**

Experimental SAGE [Semi-Automatic Ground Environment] Sector *e:* **ES**

Experimental/SAGE [Semi-Automatic Ground Environment] Sector *e:* **ESS**

Experimental Satellite Communication[s] Earth Station *e:* **ESCES**

Experimental Space Communication Earth Station *e:* **ESCES**

Experimental Space Laboratory *e:* **XSL**

Experimental Space Station *e:* **XSS**

Experimental Underwater Pump Jet *e:* **EUPJ**

experimentelle geodätische Nutzlast *d:* **EGP**

experimentieren *d:* **exp.**

Experimento de Simulación del Sistema de Observación *s:* **OSSE**

Experimento del Balance de Radiación de la Tierra *s:* **ERBE**

Experimento del Sistema de Observación s: **OSE**

Experimento Integral sobre la Energía Atmosférica s: **CAENEX**

Experimento Meteorologico del Verano p: **EMVER**

Experimento Meteorológico Francés con Globos de Nivel Constante y Comunicación por Satélite s: **EOLE**

Experimento Meteorológico Mundial s: **GWE**

Experimento Oceanográfico en el Atlántico Noreste s: **POLYGON**

Experimento Oceanográfico y Meteorológico de Barbados s: **BOMEX**

Experimento Piloto Hidrológico y Atmosférico s: **HAPEX**

Experimento Polar Hemisferio Norte s: **POLEX Norte**

Experimento Polar Hemisferio Sur s: **POLEX Sur**

Experimento sobre la Capa Límite Atmosférica s: **ABLE**

Expert Dungeons & Dragons e: **ED&D**

Expert Field Medical Badge e: **EFMB**

Expert Field Medicine Badge e: **EFMB**

Expert System for Accessing Remotely Sensed Data e: **ESARS**

Expert-System for Computer Aided Environmental Planing Tasks e: **EXCEPT**

Expert System for Spacecraft Operation Planning and Execution e: **ESSOPE**

Expertensystem Umweltgefährlichkeit von Altlasten d: **XUMA**

Experts Group for Command Application Environment e: **EG-CAE**

Explanation of Medicare Benefits e: **EOMB**

Exploidation Forestiere du Gabon f: **EXFOGA**

Exploration and Mining Geology e: **EMG**

Exploration Geochemist[ry] e: **EG**

Exploration Geochemistry e: **EGC**

Exploration Geophysicist e: **EG**

Exploration Geophysics e: **EG**, e: **EGP**, e: **Explor. Geophys.**

Exploring Human Nature e: **EHN**

Expédition Internationale de l'Océan Indien f: **EIOI**

Expérience complète sur l'énergétique de l'atmosphère f: **CAENEX**

Expérience concernant les systèmes d'observation f: **OSE**

Expérience de simulation des systèmes d'observation f: **OSSE**

Expérience pilote sur les relations entre les facteurs hydrologiques et atmosphériques f: **HAPEX**

Expérience sur la couche limite atmosphérique f: **ABLE**

Expérience sur la réponse du système couplé océan-atmosphère f: **COARE**

Expérience surface terrestre processus climatiques dans l'hémisphère Nord f: **NOPEX**

Extendable Integration Support Environment e: **EISE**

Extended Air Defence Ground Environment e: **EADGE**

Extended Cold Weather e: **ECW**

Extended Cold Weather Clothing System e: **ECWCS**

Extended Cold Weather Sleep System e: **ECWSS**

Extended Duration Orbiter e: **EDO**

Extended Generalized Programming Environment e: **EGPE**

Extended Hückel Molecular Orbit e: **XHMO**

Extended Hückel Molecular Orbit[al] e: **EHMO**

Extended Hückel Molecular Orbital Method e: **EHMO Method**

Extended Inter Frame Space e: **EIFS**

Extended Lunar Orbital Rendezvous e: **ELOR**

Extended Lunar Orbital Rendezvous Mission e: **ELORM**

Extended Polar Satellite e: **EPS**

Extended Range and Space Communication e: **ERSC**

Extended Remote Copy e: **XRC**

Extended Remote Job Entry e: **ERJE**

Extended Remote Operator Control Panel e: **EROCP**

Extended Twin-Engine Overwater Operations e: **ETOPS**

Extended Virtual Environment e: **EVE**

Extensible Display Geometry Engine e: **EDGE**

External Environment e: **EE**

External Environment Interface e: **EEI**

External Hydrogen/Oxygen Tank e: **EHOT**

External Oxygen and Hydrogen Tanks e: **EOHT**

External Polarization Modulation e: **EPM**

Extra Space Design e: **XSD**

Extracellular Water e: **ECW**

Extraterrestrial Biological Entity e: **EBE**

Extravascular Space e: **EVS**

extravaskuläres Lungenwasser d: **EVLW**

Extravehicular Space Suit e: **EVSS**

Extravehicular Space Unit e: **EVSU**

extreme-high-water-level spring tides e: **ehws**

Extreme Low Water e: **ELW**

Extreme Low Water of Spring e: **ELWS**

Extremely Elliptical Orbit e: **EEO**

Extreme[ly] High Water e: **EHW**

Eye Health Council of Canada e: **EHCC**

F

FAA [Federal Aviation Administration] Lincoln Laboratory Operational Weather Studies e: **FLOWS**

Fabrikantenvereinigung der Medizin-Mechanik d: **FdM**

Fachausstellung der Heizungs-, Isolierungs-Lüftungs/Klima-, Sanitär- und Automatikbranche d: **HILSA**

Fachausstellung Sanitär-, Heizungs-, Klimatechnik d: **SHK**

Fachbereich Biologie d: **FB BI**

Fachbereich Landeskultur und Umweltschutz d: **FB LU**

Fachinformationssystem [für Boden, Geologie, Hydrologie, Geochemie] d: **FIS**

Fachinstitut Gebäude-Klima d: **FGK**

Fachmesse für medizinische Ausrüstung d: **Salmed**

Fachnormenausschuß Materialprüfung/Arbeitsausschuß Klimaprüfung d: **FNM/Klima**

Fachnormenausschuß Medizin d: **FNMed**

Fachnormenausschuß Wasserwesen im Deutschen Normenausschuß d: **FNW**

Fachschaft Geologie/Mineralogie d: **GeoMin**

Fachsektion Hydrogeologie der Deutschen Geologischen Gesellschaft d: **FH-DGG**

Fachverband Elektromedizinische und Strahlentechnische Geräte d: **FESG**

Fachverband Schweizerischer Süssgetränke- und Mineralwasser-Industrien d: **SSM**

Facilities and Environment Measurement Compared Parts List e: **FEMCPL**

Facilities and Environmental Measuring System[s] e: **FEMS**

Facility and Environment e: **F&E**

Facility Effluent Monitoring Plan [and Environmental Restoration] e: **FEMP**

Facility for Atmospheric Remove Sensing e: **FARS**

Facility Remote Control Panel e: **FRCP**

Faculdade de Medicina Veterinaria e Zootecnia p: **FMVZ**

Faculdade de Medicina Veterinária da Universidade de Sao Paulo p: **FMV**

Faculdade de Medicina Veterinária e Agronomia de Jaboticabal p: **FMVAJ**

Facultad de Ciencias Astronomicas y Geofisicas s: **FCAG**

Facultad de Ciencias Astronomicas y Geofisicas de La Plata s: **FCAGLP**

Facultad de Medicinas de la Universidad Francisco Marroquín s: **FMUFM**

Faculte de Foresterie et Geodesie f: **FFG**

Faculty of Accident and Emergency Medicine e: **FAEM**

Faculty of Anaesthetists of the Royal Australian College of Surgeons e: **FARACS**

Faculty of Anaesthetists of the Royal College of Surgeons of England e: **FARCS**

Faculty of Natural Sciences and Mathematics e: **FNSM**

Faculty of Occupational Medicine of Royal College of Physicians e: **FOM**

Faculty of Pharmaceutical Medicine e: **FPharmM**

Faculty of Physicians and Surgeons e: **FPS**

Faculty of Public Health Medicine e: **FPHM**

Faculty of Surgeons of England e: **FSE**

Fagforeningernes Verdensføderation a: **FVF**

Fahlerde d: **F**

Fahrwasser d: **Fahrw.**, d: **Fhrw.**, d: **Fhrwss**, d: **Fw.**

Fair Isle Bird Observatory Trust e: **FIBOT**

Fair Weather Current e: **FWC**

Fairbanks Museum of Natural Science, St. Johnsbury e: **VtStjF**

Fairfield Health Service Division of General Practice e: **FHSDGP**

Fakulta Biologická c: **FB**

Fakulta Geologicko-Geografická c: **FGG**

Fakultät für Naturwissenschaften d: **FNW**

Fallout Protection in Homes [or Houses] e: **FPHS**

Fallout Studies Branch, Division of Biology & Medicine e: **FSB**

falls soweit anders nicht notiert d: **E.A.O.N.**

Family and Health Section *e:* **FHS**
Family [and] Medical Leave Act *e:* **FMLA**
Family Environment Scale *e:* **FES**
Family Health Insurance Plan *e:* **FHIP**
Family Health International *e:* **FHI**
Family Health Plan *e:* **FHP**
Family Health Services *e:* **FHS**
Family Health Services Authority *e:*
FHSA
Family Medical Doctor *e:* **FMD**
Family Medicine *e:* **Fam-Med**
Family Medicine Literature Index *e:*
FAMLI
Family Medicine Program *e:* **FMP**
Family Medicine Research Centre *e:*
FMRC
Family Protection Law *e:* **FPL**
Family Protection League of USA *e:* **FPL**
Fann Water Supply Grant *e:* **FWSG**
Far East Hydrometeorological Institute,
State Committee on Hydrometeorology,
Vladivostok *e:* **DVNIGMI**
Far Eastern Association of Tropical
Medicine *e:* **FEATM**
Far Eastern Regional Hydrometeorological
Research Institute *e:* **FERHI**
Far Infrared Observation *e:* **FIO,** *e:* **FIRO**
Far-Infrared Space Telescope *e:* **FIRST**
Far Ultraviolet Space Telescope *e:* **FAUST**
Faraday Dark Space *e:* **FDS**
Farm Animal Reform Movement *e:* **FARM**
Farm Animal Welfare Council *e:* **FAWC**
Farm Animal[s] Welfare Advisory
Committee *e:* **FAWAC**
Farm Operations, Plant Protection and
[Pest] Surveillance *e:* **FOPPS**
Farm Workers Family Health Center *e:*
FWFHC
Farming and Wildlife Advisory Group[s]
e: **FWAG**
Farmland Protection Policy Act *e:* **FPPA**
FASCODE for the Environment *e:* **FASE**
FASEB Journal [of Federation of American
Societies for Experimental Biology] *e:*
FASEB J.
Fast Atmosphere (or Atmospheric)
Signature Code *e:* **FASCODE**
Fast Atmospheric Pulsation *e:* **FAP**
Fast-millisecond-long Atmospheric-light
Pulsations *e:* **FAPS**
Fast Ocean-Atmosphere Model *e:* **FOAM**
fast on-orbit recording of transient events
e: **FORTE**
Fast Running Interpreter Enabling Natural
Diagnosis *e:* **FRIEND**
Fast Space Charge Wave *e:* **FSCW**
Fate of Atmospheric Pollutants Study *e:*
FAPS
Fault Tolerant Spaceborne Computer *e:*
FTSC
FDF Orbital and Mission Aids
Transformation System *e:* **FORMATS**
Feature Extraction Environment *e:* **FEE**
Feature Space Iterative Clustering *e:* **FSIC**
Federacion de Trabajadores de la Tierra *s:*
FTT
Federación Boliviana de Médicos
Veterinarios *s:* **FBMV**
Federación de Estudiantes de Medicina
Centroamericanos *s:* **FEMCA**
Federación Española de Trabajadores de la
Tierra *s:* **F.E.T.T.**

Federación Internacional de la Industria del
Medicamento *s:* **FIIM**
Federación Internacional de Medicina
Fisica *s:* **FIMF**
Federación latinoamericana de Sociedades
Científicas de Estudiantes de Medicina
s: **FELSOCEM**
Federación Mundial Protectora de Animales
s: **FMPA**
Federación Nacional de Trabajadores
Agropecuarios, Recursos Naturales
Renovables, Jardineros y Similares *s:*
FETRANJAS
Federación Naturista Internacional *s:* **FNI**
Federación Panamericana de Asociaciones
de Facultades y Escuelas de Medicina *s:*
FEPAFEM
Federación para la Naturaleza y los Parques
Nacionales de Europa *s:* **FNNPE**
Federación Sindical de Trabajadores de la
Silvicultura, Madera, Ambiente y
Recursus Naturales de Guatemala *s:*
FESITRASMAR
Federal Advisory Committee on
Occupational Safety and Health *e:*
FACOSH
Federal Advisory Council on Medical
Training Aids *e:* **FACMTA**
Federal Agency for Geodesy and
Cartography *e:* **RosKarto-grafiya**
Federal Agency for Hydrometeorology and
Environmental Monitoring *e:*
RosHydro- Met
Federal Air Surgeon *e:* **FAS**
Federal Air Weather Service *e:* **FAWS**
Federal Aviation Administration Office of
Aviation Medicine *e:* **AAM**
Federal Aviation Administration-Office of
Aviation Medicine *e:* **FAA-AM**
Federal Aviation Administration-Office of
Environment and Energy *e:* **FAA-EE,** *e:*
FAA-OEE
Federal Aviation Administration-Office of
Environmental Quality *e:* **FAA-EQ**
Federal Centre for AIDS [Acquired Immune
Deficiency Syndrome], Health Protection
Branch, Health and Welfare Canada,
Ottawa, Ontario *e:* **OONHAC**
Federal Centre of Geoecological Systems
e: **FCGS**
Federal Committee for Meteorological
Services and Supporting Research *e:*
FCMSSR
Federal Coordinator for Geology *e:* **FCG**
Federal Coordinator for Marine
Environmental Prediction *e:* **FCMAREP**
Federal Coordinator for Meteorological
services and supporting research *e:*
FCM
Federal Coordinator for Meteorological
Services and Supporting Research *e:*
FCMSSR
Federal Coordinator for Ocean Mapping and
Prediction *e:* **FCOMP**
Federal Coordinators Office of Meteorology
e: **FCOM**
Federal Employee Occupational Safety and
Health *e:* **FEOSH**
Federal Employees Health Benefit[s] *e:*
FEHB
Federal Employees Health Benefits Act *e:*
FEHBA

Federal Employees Health Benefits Program
e: **FEHBP**
Federal Environmental Assessment Review
Office *e:* **FEARO**
Federal Environmental Assessment Review
Office, Ottawa, Ontario *e:* **OOFE**
Federal Environmental Assessment Review
Process *e:* **FEARP**
Federal Environmental Executive *e:* **FEE**
Federal Environmental Pesticide[s] Control
Act *e:* **FEPCA**
Federal Environmental Pollution Control
Act *e:* **FEPCA**
Federal Environmental Protection Agency
e: **FEPA**
Federal Facility Environmental
Improvement Initiatives *e:* **FFEII**
Federal Firearms Owners Protection Act *e:*
FFOPA
Federal Geodetic Control Committee *e:*
FGCC
Federal Geodetic Control Subcommittee *e:*
FGCS
Federal Geographic Data Commission (or
Committee) *e:* **FGDC**
Federal Geographic Data Committee *e:*
FDGC
Federal Geographic Data Products *e:*
FGDP
Federal Geographic Exchange Format *e:*
FGEF
Federal Geographic Technology *e:* **FGT**
Federal Geologic Mapping Project *e:*
FEDMAP
Federal Geospatial Data Clearinghouse *e:*
FGDC
Federal Health Programs Service *e:* **FHPS**
Federal Meteorological Handbook *e:* **FMH**
Federal Meteorological Handbook, Volume
1 *e:* **FMH-1**
Federal Mine Safety and Health *e:* **FMSH**
Federal Mine Safety and Health Review
Commission *e:* **FMSHRC**
Federal Oceanographic Fleet Coordination
Council *e:* **FOFCC**
Federal Office of Military Health Service
e: **OFSAN**
Federal Protection Service *e:* **FPS**
Federal Protective Officer *e:* **FPO**
Federal Sea Safety and Surveillance Centre
(Australia) *e:* **COASTWATCH**
Federal Security Agency, Health,
Education, and Welfare *e:* **FSHEW**
Federal Service Campaign for National
Health Agencies *e:* **FSCNHA**
Federal Services Podiatric Medical
Association *e:* **FSPMA**
Federal-State Cooperative Geologic
Mapping *e:* **COGEOMAP**
Federal Water Policy *e:* **FWP**
Federal Water Pollution [and] Control Act
e: **FWPCA**
Federal Water Pollution [and] Control
Administration *e:* **FWPCA**
Federal Water Quality Administration *e:*
FWQA
Federal Water Quality Association *e:*
FWQA
Federal Water Quality Criteria *e:* **FWQC**
Federal Water Resources Assistance
Program *e:* **FWRAP**
Federal Water Resources Council *e:*
FWRC

Federal Wildlife Permit Office *e:* **FWPO**

Federally Qualified Health Center *e:* **FQHC**

Federated Council for Internal Medicine *e:* **FCIM**

Federated Natural Resources Corporation *e:* **FNRC**

Federation for International Cooperation of Health Services and Systems Research Centers *e:* **FICOSSER**

Federation for/of Astronomical and Geophysical Permanent Services *e:* **FAGS**

Federation International Gynecological Obstetrics *e:* **FIGO**

Federation internationale des quartiers anciens *f:* **Civitas Nostra**

Federation of African Medical Students' Associations *e:* **FAMSA**

Federation of American Health Systems *e:* **FAHS**

Federation of American Societies for/of Experimental Biology *e:* **FASEB**

Federation of Animal Science Societies *e:* **FASS**

Federation of Asian and Oceanian Biochemists *e:* **FAOB**

Federation of Asian and Oceanian Biochemists and Molecular Biologists *e:* **FAOBMB**

Federation of Associations of Health Regulatory Boards *e:* **FAHRB**

Federation of Associations of Mental Health Workers *e:* **FAMHW**

Federation of Associations on the Canadian Environment *e:* **FACE**

Federation of Astronomical, Geodetical and Geophysical Services *e:* **FAGGS**

Federation of Australian Underwater Instructors *e:* **FAUI**

Federation of British Columbia Naturalists *e:* **FBCN**

Federation of Computer Users in the Medical Sciences *e:* **FCUMS,** *e:* **FOCUS**

Federation of Environmental Technologists *e:* **FET**

Federation of European Delegation Associations of Scientific Equipment Manufacturers, Importers, and Dealers in the Laboratory, Industrial and Medical Fields *e:* **FEDAS**

Federation of European Laboratory Animal Science Association[s] *e:* **FELASA**

Federation of European Microbiological Societies *e:* **FEMS**

Federation of Feminist Health Centers *e:* **FFHC**

Federation of Immunological Societies of Asia-Oceania *e:* **FIMSA**

Federation of Institutions Concerned with the Study of the Adriatic Sea *e:* **FICSAS**

Federation of Islamic Medical Associations *e:* **FIMA**

Federation of Medical Women of Canada *e:* **FMWC**

Federation of Mental Health Centers *e:* **FMHC**

Federation of Mental Health Workers *e:* **FMHW**

Federation of Nature and National and Natural Parks of Europe *e:* **FNNPE**

Federation of Nurses and Health Professionals *e:* **FNHP**

Federation of Ontario Naturalists *e:* **FON**

Federation of Podiatric Medical Boards *e:* **FPMB**

Federation of Remote Sensing Companies of India *e:* **FORSCI**

Federation of State Medical Boards [of the United States] *e:* **FSMB**

Federation of State Medical Boards of the United States *e:* **FSMBUS**

Federation of World Health Foundations *e:* **FWHF**

Federation Proceedings [Federation of American Societies for Experimental Biology] *e:* **FP**

Federazione dei medici svizzeri *i:* **FMI**

Federazione dei Medici Svizzeri *i:* **FMS**

Federazione Italiana dei Gruppi Professionali e Sindacali Medici Igienisti *i:* **F.I.M.I.**

Federazione Italiana delle Biblioteche Popolari *i:* **FIBP**

Federazione Italiana delle Societa di Protezione Animali *i:* **FISPA**

Federazione Medico-Sportiva Italiana *i:* **FMSI**

Federazione Nazionale degli Ordini dei Medici *i:* **FNOM,** *i:* **FNOOMM**

Federazione Nazionale pro Natura *i:* **FEDERNATURA**

feed and water *e:* **f & w**

Feed Water *e:* **FDW,** *e:* **FW**

Feed Water Heater Manufacturers Association *e:* **FWHMA**

Feedback Analysis for GCM Intercomparison and Observation[s] *e:* **FANGIO**

feeding and watering *e:* **f & w**

Feedwater Pump *e:* **FWP**

Feedwater Regulation Valve *e:* **FRV**

Feet of Fresh Water *e:* **FFW**

Feet of Salt Water *e:* **FSW**

feet of sea water *e:* **fsw**

Feldwetterstation *d:* **FWSt**

Feldwetterwarte *d:* **Fewewa,** *d:* **FWW**

Felicidades Wildlife Foundation *e:* **FWF**

Fellow in Dental Surgery of the Royal College of Physicians and Surgeons of Glasgow *e:* **FDSRCPS Glas,** *e:* **FDSRCPS Glas[g]**

Fellow in Dental Surgery of the Royal College of Surgeons in England *e:* **FDSRCSEng**

Fellow in Dental Surgery of the Royal College of Surgeons of Edinburgh *e:* **FDSRCSEd,** *e:* **FDSRCS Edin**

Fellow in Dental Surgery of the Royal College of Surgeons of England *e:* **FDSRCS**

Fellow of the Academy of Gynaecology and Obstetrics *e:* **F.A.G.O.**

Fellow of the American Academy of Medicine *e:* **FAAOM**

Fellow of the American Academy of Orthopaedic Surgeons *e:* **FAAOS**

Fellow of the American College of Foot Surgeons *e:* **FACFS**

Fellow of the American College of Health Administrators *e:* **FACHA**

Fellow of the American College of Obstetricians and Gynecologists *e:* **FACOG**

Fellow of the American College of Obstetrics and Gynecology *e:* **FACOG**

Fellow of the American College of Preventive Medicine *e:* **FACPM**

Fellow of the American College of Sports Medicine *e:* **FACMS,** *e:* **FACSM**

Fellow of the American College of Surgeons *e:* **FACS**

Fellow of the American Geographical Society *e:* **FAGS**

Fellow of the American Medical Association *e:* **FAMA**

Fellow of the American Occupational Medicine Association *e:* **FAOMA**

Fellow of the American Public Health Association *e:* **FAPHA**

Fellow of the Association of Public Health Inspectors *e:* **FAPHI**

Fellow of the Australian College of Dental Surgeons *e:* **FACDS**

Fellow of the Australian College of Emergency Medicine *e:* **FACEM**

Fellow of the Australian Society of Animal Production *e:* **FASAP**

Fellow of the Australian Society of Microbiologists *e:* **FASM**

Fellow of the Canadian Aeronautics and Space Institute *e:* **FCASI**

Fellow of the Canadian Association of Medical Radiation Technologists *e:* **FCAMRT**

Fellow of the Canadian College of Medical Genetics *e:* **FCCMG**

Fellow of the College of Medicine and Surgery *e:* **FCMS**

Fellow of the College of Obstetricians and Gynaecologists *e:* **FCOG**

Fellow of the College of Obstetrics and Gynaecology *e:* **F.C.O.G.**

Fellow of the College of Physicians and Surgeons *e:* **FCPS**

Fellow of the College of Physicians and Surgeons and Obstetricians of South Africa *e:* **FCPSO[SoAf]**

Fellow of the College of Physicians and Surgeons [of] South Africa *e:* **FCPSA**

Fellow of the College of Surgeons of Hong Kong *e:* **FCSHK**

Fellow of the College of Surgeons of South Africa *e:* **FCS[SoAf]**

Fellow of the Faculty of Anaesthetists of the Royal Australian College of Surgeons *e:* **FFARACS**

Fellow of the Faculty of Anaesthetists of the Royal College of Surgeons *e:* **FFARCS**

Fellow of the Faculty of Anaesthetists of the Royal College of Surgeons in Ireland *e:* **FFARCSI**

Fellow of the Faculty of Anaesthetists of the Royal College of Surgeons of England *e:* **FFARCS Eng**

Fellow of the Faculty of Community Medicine *e:* **FFCM**

Fellow of the Faculty of Dental Surgeons *e:* **FFD**

Fellow of the Faculty of Dental Surgery [of the] Royal College of Surgeons *e:* **FFDRCS**

Fellow of the Faculty of Dentistry of the Royal College of Surgeons in Ireland *e:* **FFDRCSI,** *e:* **FFDRCS Irel**

Fellow of the Geographical Society e:
FGS

Fellow of the Geographical Society of
America e: **FGSA**

Fellow of the Geological Society e: **FGS**

Fellow of the Geological Society of
America e: **FGSA**

Fellow of the Indian Academy of Medical
Sciences e: **F.A.M.S.**, e: **FIAMS**

Fellow of the Industrial Medical
Association e: **FIMA**

Fellow of the Institute of Biology e: **FIB**,
e: **FI Bio**, e: **FIBio[l]**, e: **FInstBiol**, e:
FIBiol

Fellow of the Institute of Health Education
e: **FIHE**

Fellow of the Institute of Health Service
[Administrators] e: **FHA**

Fellow of the Institute of Medical
Laboratory Technology e: **FIMLT**, e:
F.I.M.L.T.

Fellow of the Institute of the Aerospace
Sciences e: **F.I.A.S.**

Fellow of the Institution of Occupational
Safety and Health e: **FIOSH**

Fellow of the Institution of Public Health
Engineers e: **FIPHE**

Fellow of the Institution of Water Engineers
e: **FIWE**

Fellow of the International College of
Surgeons e: **FICS**, e: **FICS**

Fellow of the Medical Council e: **FMC**

Fellow of the Medical Society e: **F.M.S.**

Fellow of the Meteorological Society e:
FMS

Fellow of the National Institute of Medical
Herbalists e: **FNIMH**

Fellow of the Royal Academy of Medicine
e: **FRAM**

Fellow of the Royal Austral[as]ian College
of Surgeons e: **FRACS**

Fellow of the Royal Australian College of
Dental Surgeons e: **FRACDS**

Fellow of the Royal Canadian Geographical
Society e: **FRCGS**

Fellow of the Royal College of Medicine
e: **FRCM**

Fellow of the Royal College of
Obstetricians and Gynaecologists e:
FRCOG

Fellow of the Royal College of Paediatrics
and Child Health e: **FRCPCH**

Fellow of the Royal College of Physicians
and Surgeons of Glasgow e:
FRCPS[Glasg]

Fellow of the Royal College of Surgeons
in[of] Ireland e: **FRCSI**

Fellow of the Royal College of Surgeons of
Canada e: **FRCS Can**

Fellow of the Royal College of Surgeons of
Edinburgh e: **FRCS E[d][in]**

Fellow of [the] Royal College of Surgeons
[of England] e: **FRCS**

Fellow of the Royal College of Surgeons of
England e: **FRCSE**, e: **FRCS Eng**

Fellow of the Royal College of Surgeons of
Glasgow e: **FRCS[Glasg]**

Fellow of the Royal College of Surgeons of
London e: **FRCSL**

Fellow of the Royal College of University
Surgeons e: **FRCUS**

Fellow of the Royal College of Veterinary
Surgeons e: **F.R.C.V.**

Fellow of the Royal College [of] Veterinary
Surgeons e: **FRCVS**

Fellow of the Royal Dublin Society for
Promoting Natural Knowledge e: **FRDS**

Fellow of the [Royal] Faculty of Physicians
and Surgeons e: **FFPS**

Fellow of the Royal Faculty of Physicians
and Surgeons e: **FRFPS**

Fellow of the [Royal] Faculty of Physicians
and Surgeons [Glasgow] e: **FFPSG**

Fellow of the Royal Faculty of Physicians
and Surgeons of Glasgow e: **FRFPSG**

Fellow of the Royal Faculty of Surgeons e:
F.R.F.S.

Fellow of [the] Royal Geographical Society
e: **FRGS**

Fellow of the Royal Geographical Society
of Australia e: **F.R.G.S.A.**

Fellow of the Royal Geographical Society
of Canada e: **FRGSC**

Fellow of the Royal Geographical Society,
Scotland e: **FRGSS**

Fellow of the Royal Imperial Geographical
Society e: **FRIGS**

Fellow of the Royal Institute of Public
Health e: **FRIPH**

Fellow of the Royal Institute of Public
Health and Hygiene e: **FAIPHH**, e:
FRIPHH, e: **FRIPHH**

Fellow of the Royal Medical and
Chirurgical Society, London e:
FRMCSL

Fellow of the Royal Medical Society e:
FRMedSoc

Fellow of the Royal Medico-Chirurgical
Society e: **FRMCS**

Fellow of the Royal Meteorological Society
e: **FRMetS**, e: **FR Met Soc**, e: **FRMS**

Fellow of the Royal Scottish Geographic[al]
Society e: **FRSGS**

Fellow of the Royal Society [for the
Promotion] of Health e: **FRSH**

Fellow of the Royal Society [of London for
Promoting Natural Knowledge] e: **FRS**

Fellow of the Royal Society of London [for
Promoting Natural Knowledge] e: **FRSL**

Fellow of the Royal Society of Medicine e:
FRSM, e: **FRSocMed**

Fellow of the Royal Society of Physicians
and Surgeons e: **FRSPS**

Fellow of the Royal Society of Tropical
Medicine and Hygiene e: **FRSTM**, e:
FRSTM&H

Fellowship for Freedom in Medicine e:
FFM

Fellowship of the American Academy of
Neurological and Orthopaedic Surgeons
e: **FAANaOS**

Feminist Resources on Energy and Ecology
e: **FREE**

Feminist Women's Health Center e:
FWHC

Feminist Women's Health Center/Women's
Choice Clinic e: **FWHC/WCC**

Feministische Frauen-Gesundheitszentrum
e.V. d: **FFGZ**

FEMS Circular [of Federation of the
European Microbiological Societies] e:
FEMS Circ.

FEMS Ecology [of Federation of the
European Microbiological Societies] e:
FEMS Ecol.

FEMS Immunology and Medical
Microbiology e: **FEMS Immunol Med
Microbiol**

FEMS Microbiology Letters [of Federation
of the European Microbiological
Societies] e: **FEMS Microbiol Lett.**

FEMS Microbiology [of Federation of the
European Microbiological Societies] e:
FEMS Microbiol.

FEMS Microbiology Reviews e: **FEMS
Microbiol Rev**

Fenómeno Meteorológico y Oceanográfico
frente a la Costa Occidental de América
del Sur s: **EL NIñO**

Ferme de Recherche sur le Mouton, La
Pocatière f: **FRMLP**

fermentieren d: **ferm**

fermentiert d: **f**, d: **ferm.**

Fermes-Écoles f: **F.E.**

Fernald Environmental Management
Program (or Project) e: **FEMP**

Feuille d'Observation f: **FO**

Fibre Optic[al] Communications for
Aerospace Systems e: **FOCAS**

Fichier de données intégrales sur les
interactions océan-atmosphère f:
COADS

FID Commission for Asia and Oceania e:
FID/CAO

FID Committee on Medical Documentation
e: **FID/MD**

Fiducial Laboratories for an International
Natural Science[s] Network e: **FLINN**

Field Ambulance, Royal Army Medical
Corps e: **FARAMC**

Field Army Airspace Utilization Study e:
FAAUS

Field Artillery Meteorological Acquisition
System e: **FAMAS**

Field Conference Guidebook. New Mexico
Geological Society e: **NMGGA**

Field Forcing Protective e: **FFP**

Field Headspace Analysis e: **FHA**

Field Medical Card e: **FMC**, e: **FM-Card**

Field Medical Unit e: **FMU**

Field Museum of Natural History e:
FMNH

Field Naturalist e: **Field Nat.**

Field Naturalists' Club of Victoria e:
F.N.C.V.

Field Naturalists' Society of South Australia
e: **FNSSA**

Field Service Manual for Army Medical
Services e: **F.S.M.A.M.S.**

Fighter Squadron - All Weather e: **VF AW**

Fiji School of Medicine e: **FSM**

Fiji Waterside Workers and Seamens Union
e: **FWWSU**

Filchner-Ronne Ice Shelf Programme e:
FRISP

File Protect Memory e: **FPM**

File Protect Mode e: **FPM**

Filter Response Analysis for Continuously
Accelerating Spacecraft e: **FRACAS**

Filtered Water e: **FW**

Final Environmental Impact Statement e:
FEIS

Final Environmental Statement e: **FES**

Final Environmental Survey e: **FES**

Final Feedwater Temperature Reduction e:
FFWTR

Final Meteorological Radiation e: **FMR**

Final Meteorological Radiation Tape e: **FMRT**

Final Protective Line e: **FPL**

Final Space Utilization Plan e: **FSUP**

Fine Mesh-cover Protected e: **FMPROT**

Finite Element of Water Flow through Aquifers e: **FEWA**

Finite Element Surface Water Model System e: **FESWMS**

finite-element three-dimensional ground water e: **fe3dgw**

Finite Geometry e: **FG**

Finnish Environment Institute e: **FEI**

Finnish gaussian short-range meteorological dispersion model e: **YDINO**

Finnish Geodetic Institute e: **FGI**

Finnish Geographical Information System e: **FINGIS**

Finnish Laboratory Animal Scientists e: **FinLAS**

Finnish Meteorological Institute e: **FMI**

Finnish Museum of Natural History e: **FMNH**

Finnish National Committee of the International Association on Water Pollution Research and Control e: **FNCIAWPRC**

Finnish Office for Health Care Technology Assessment e: **FinOHTA**

Finnish research programme on atmospheric changes e: **SILMU**

Fire Information Systems Research in the Ecology, Socio-Culture and History of the Mediterranean Environment e: **FIRESCHEME**

Fire Protection Association e: **FPA**

Fire Protection Association of Australia e: **FPAA**

Fire Protection Association of Southern Africa e: **FPASA**

Fire Protection Industry Association of Australia e: **FPIAA**

Fire Protection Officer e: **FPO**

Fire Protection Relay e: **FPR**

Fire Protection Research International e: **FPRI**

Fire Protection Stick Relay e: **FPSR**

Fire Protection Technician e: **FPT**

Fire [protection] Water e: **FW**

Fire Protection Water Tank e: **FPWT**

fire-resistive protected e: **Xp**

fire-resistive, unprotected e: **Xu**

Fire-, Water-, Weather-, Mildew-Resistant e: **FWWMR**

Fire Weather Index e: **FWI**

Fire-Weather Warning Service e: **FWWS**

First Aid and Water Safety [Red Cross] e: **FAWS**

First Aid/Medical Aid Station e: **FA**

First-Aid, Small Craft and Water Safety e: **FASCWS**

First Air-Sea Interaction Experiment e: **FASINEX**

First Airborne Telescopic and Spectrographic Observatory e: **FATSO**

First American Health Concepts, Inc. e: **FAHC**

first American high-energy launch vehicle for space exploration-D-Series Atlas b e: **Atlas-Centaur**

first Chinese space satellite e: **Chicom 1**

First GARP [Global Atmospheric Research Program] Global Experiment[s] e: **FGGE**

First German Spacelab e: **SL-D1**

First Global Weather Experiment e: **FGWE**

First International Biological Experiment e: **FIBEX**

First International Design for Extreme Environments Assembly e: **IDEEA ONE**

First International Saturation Study of Herring and Hydroacoustics e: **FISSHH**

First ISCCP [International Satellite Cloud Climatology Project] Regional Experiment e: **FIRE**, e: **FIREIFO**

First ISCCP [International Satellite Cloud Climatology Project] Regional Experiment [Phase 2] e: **FIRE-2**

First ISCCP [Intitute Satellite Cloud Climatology Project] Regional Experiment e: **FIRE**

First ISLSCP [International Satellite Land Surface Climatology Project] Field Experiment e: **FIFE**

First Lunar Observatory e: **FLO**

First Manned Orbital Flight e: **FMOF**

First Manned Orbital Flight With EVA e: **FMOFEV**

First Manned Orbital Flight With Payload e: **FMOFPL**

First Medical Devices Corporation e: **FMDC**

First meeting of the ad hoc technical expert group on marine and coastal protected areas e: **TEMCPA**

First Nations Environmental Assessment e: **FNEA**

First Open Water e: **FOW**

first open water chartering e: **f.o.w.**

First Orbit Penetration System e: **FOPS**

First Orbital Flight e: **FOF**

First Orbital Vehicle e: **FOV**

First orbiting X-ray satellite. e: **Uhuru**

First-Pass In-Weather Attack e: **FPIWA**

First Polar Platform Mission e: **FPM**

First Regional Observational Study of the Troposphere e: **FROST**

First Sea Level Test e: **FSLT**

First Sea Lord e: **FSL**

first Soviet space shuttle e: **Buran**

First Spacelab Payload e: **FSLO**, e: **FSLP**

First Spacelab[oratory] Payload e: **FSLP**

Fischgesundheitsdienst der DDR d: **FGD**

Fish and Wildlife Advisory Team e: **FWAT**

Fish and Wildlife Coordination Act e: **FWCA**

Fish and wildlife reference service e: **FWRS**

Fish and Wildlife Resources e: **FWR**

Fish and Wildlife Service e: **FWS**

Fish and Wildlife Service/Office of Biological Services e: **FWS/OBS**

Fish Springs National Wildlife Refuge e: **FSNWR**

Fisheries and Oceans e: **F&O**

Fisheries and Oceans Canada Halifax, Nova Scotia e: **NSHF**

Fisheries and Oceans Canada Moncton, New Brunswick e: **NBMOF**

Fisheries and Oceans Canada Ottawa, Ontario e: **OOFI**

Fisheries and Oceans Research and Advisory Council e: **FORAC**

Fisheries-Oceanography Cooperative (or Coordinated) Investigations e: **FOCI**

Fisheries Oceanography Cooperative Users System e: **FOCUS**

Fishery-Oceanography Experiment e: **FOX**

Fishery Protection e: **FP**

Fishery Protection Cruiser e: **FPC**

Fishery Protection Service e: **FPS**

Fishery Protection Squadron e: **FPS**

Fishery Protection Vessel e: **FPV**

Fishing, Hunting, Wildlife and Associated Recreation e: **FHWAR**

Fitzherbert's Natura Brevium e: **Nat Brev**

Fitzsimons Army Medical Center e: **FAMC**

Five Colleges Radio Astronomy Observatory e: **FCRAO**

Five-liter resealable container for ethanol-water solutions e: **jeroboam**

Fixed Link Aerospace to Ground e: **FLAG**

flageolet e: **flag.**

Flames Analysis & Reduction Environment e: **FLARE**

Flanders Environmental Library Network e: **FELNET**

Flank Observation e: **FO**

Flare-Activated Radiobiological Observatory e: **FARO**

Flare Remote Control e: **FRC**

Flat Earth Research Society International e: **FERSI**

Flat Earth Society e: **FES**

Flatland Atmospheric Observatory e: **FAO**

Flatland Meteorological Observatory e: **FMO**

Fleet Air Meteorological Observation Satellite e: **FAMOS**

Fleet All-Weather Training Unit e: **FAWTU**, e: **FltAllWeaTraU**

Fleet All-Weather Training Unit, Atlantic e: **FAWTULANT**, e: **FltAllWeaTraULant**

Fleet All-Weather Training Unit, Pacific e: **FAWTUPAC**, e: **FltAllWeaTraUPac**

Fleet Application[s] of Meteorological Observations for/from Satellites e: **FAMOS**

Fleet Dental Surgeon e: **FDS**

Fleet Environmental Support System e: **FESS**

Fleet Medical Officer e: **FMO**

Fleet Meteorological Officer e: **FMETO**

Fleet Numerical Meteorology and Oceanography Center e: **FNMOC**

Fleet Numerical Oceanographic (or Oceanography) Center e: **FNOC**

Fleet Numerical Weather Center e: **F.N.W.C.**

Fleet Numeric[al] Weather Central e: **FNWC**

Fleet Numerical Weather Facilities e: **FNWF**

Fleet Observation of Oceanographic Data e: **FLOOD**

Fleet Ocean Surveillance Information Center e: **FOSIC**

Fleet Ocean Surveillance Information Facility e: **FOSIF**

Fleet ocean tug e: **ATF**

Fleet Seawater e: **FSW**

Fleet Surgeon *e:* **FltSurg,** *e:* **FS**
Fleet Weather Center *e:* **FLEWEACEN,**
 e: **FLTWEACEN**
Fleet Weather Center (or Central) *e:* **FWC**
Fleet Weather Facility *e:* **FLEWEAFAC,**
 e: **FWF**
Fleet Weather & Oceanographic Centre *e:*
 FWOC
Fleet Weather & Oceanographic Centre
 Computer Equipment Replacement *e:*
 FWOCCER
Fleischbeschau Verordnung Haarwild und
 Kaninchen *d:* **FlVHK**
flektiere *d:* **flekt.**
flektiert *d:* **fl.,** *d:* **flekt.**
Flemish Aerospace Group *e:* **FLAG**
Flexible Interactive Remote Sensing Data
 Information and Management System *e:*
 FIRSDIMS
Flexible Space Garment *e:* **FSG**
Flexible Use of Airspace *e:* **FUA**
fließend kalt[es] und warm[es] Wasser *d:*
 fl.k.u.w.W.
fließend[es] Wasser *d:* **fl. W.**
Flight Advisory Weather Service *e:* **FAWS**
Flight Computer Operating System
 (Orbiter) *e:* **FCOS**
Flight in a Radiation Environment *e:*
 FIRE
Flight Investigation of Apollo Reentry
 Environment *e:* **FIARE**
Flight Investigation Reentry Environment
 e: **FIRE**
Flight Management Geographic Information
 System *e:* **FMGIS**
Flight Medical Officer *e:* **FMO**
Flight Medicine Clinic *e:* **FMC**
Flight Space *e:* **FLSP**
Flight Surgeon *e:* **FLS,** *e:* **FltSurg,** *e:* **FS**
Flight Surgeon Badge *e:* **FltSurgBad**
Flinders Earth Sciences *e:* **FES**
Flinders Institute for/of Atmospheric and
 Marine Sciences *e:* **FIAMS**
Flinders University School of Earth
 Sciences *e:* **FUSES**
Flint Area Health Science Library Network
 e: **FAHSLN**
Flint Area Health Sciences Libraries
 Association *e:* **FAHSLA**
Flint Hills National Wildlife Refuge *e:*
 FHNWR
Floating Ice Detection Experiment *e:*
 FIDEX
Floating Ocean Research and Development
 Station *e:* **FORD,** *e:* **FORDS,** *e:* **FORD**
 Station
Floating Spherical Gaussian Orbitals *e:*
 FSGO
Flood Disaster Protection Act *e:* **FDPA**
Flora and Fauna Protection Board *e:* **FFPB**
Florida Area Cumulus Experiment *e:*
 FACE
Florida Automated Weather Network *e:*
 Fawn
Florida Climate and Control System *e:*
 FLACCS
Florida Department of Environmental
 Regulation *e:* **FDER**
Florida Emergency Medicine Foundation
 e: **FEMF**
Florida Environmental Reader *e:* **FER**
Florida Game & Fresh Water Fish
 Commission *e:* **FG&FWFC**

Florida Geological Survey *e:* **FGS**
Florida Institute of Oceanography *e:* **FIO**
Florida Keys Wildlife Refuge[s] *e:* **FKWR**
Florida Medical Association *e:* **FMA**
Florida Medical Library Association *e:*
 FMLA
Florida Museum of Natural History *e:*
 FMNH
Florida Ocean Sciences Institute *e:* **FOSI**
Florida Public Health Association *e:*
 FPHA
Florida Society of Oral and Maxillofacial
 Surgeons *e:* **FSOMS**
Florida Space Coast Writers Conference *e:*
 FSCWC
Florida State Oriental Medical Association
 e: **FSOMA**
Florida Veterinary Medical Association *e:*
 FVMA
Flota Oceanica Brasileira *p:* **Flota**
Flow of Steam/Flow of Water *e:* **FS/FW**
Flower Gardens Ocean Research Center *e:*
 FGORC
Flugmedizinisches Institut der Luftwaffe
 d: **FlMedInstLw**
Flugwetterberatungsdienst *d:* **FAWS**
Flugwetterdienst *d:* **FWD**
Flugwettervorhersage *d:* **FIFOR**
Flugwetterwarte *d:* **DMO**
Flugzeuglidar für Ozeanographie und
 Hydrologie *d:* **FLOH**
Flugzeugwasserbombe *d:* **FlWB**
Fluid Thermal and Aerospace Sciences *e:*
 FTAS
Fluidic Environmental Sensor *e:* **FES**
Fluor Ocean Services, Engineering Library,
 Houston *e:* **TxHFO**
Fluorchlorkohlenwasserstoffe *d:* **FCKW**
Fluoride Wastewater Treatment *e:* **FWT**
Fluorine One-Stage Orbital Space Truck *e:*
 FLOSOST
Fluorkohlenwasserstoff[e] *d:* **FKW**
flush armor balanced watertight hatch *e:* **fl**
 abwth
Flush Armo[u]r Balanced Watertight Hatch
 e: **FlABWtH**
Flush Quick-Acting Watertight *e:*
 FQAWT
Flush Water-Tight Hatch *e:* **FWTH**
Flush Water-Tight Manhole *e:* **FWTMH**
Flußbiologie *d:* **Flußbiol.**
Flußorientierungs-ESR *d:* **FOESR**
Flux de Matière dans l'Ocean *f:* **FMO**
Fluxes in the Deep Ocean Instrument *e:*
 FIDO
flyable orbital vehicle *e:* **fov**
Flyg- och Navalmedicinska Nämnden *r:*
 FMN
Flygvapnets Medicinska
 Undersökningscentral *r:* **FMU**
Flying Infrared Signatures Technology
 Aircraft *e:* **FISTA**
Flying Medical Samaritans *e:* **FMS**
FM-CW Atmospheric Doppler Radar
 System *e:* **FADRS**
FMIT Water Test Loop *e:* **FWTL**
FMS Patuxent Wildlife Research Center
 Financial Management System *e:*
 PWRC
FNWF Ocean History Information Retrieval
 System *e:* **FOIDRS**
Foam Removal for Environmentally Safe
 Housing *e:* **FRESH**

focal length of image space *e:* **f**
focal length of object space *e:* **f**
Focus on Atmospheric Aerosols *e:* **FAA**
Föderation Europäischer Gewässerschutz
 d: **FEG**
Foederatio Medicorum Helveticorum *l:*
 FMH
Fog over Sea *e:* **F.S.**
Fogarty International Center. John E.
 Fogarty International Center for
 Advanced Study in the Health Sciences.
 National Institutes of Health *e:* **FIC**
Fogg Dam Protected Area *e:* **FDPA**
foilborne waterline *e:* **fwl**
Foire Internationale de l'Artisanat et des
 Métiers *f:* **FIAM**
folded-and-gathered signatures *e:* **f & g's**
Folia Facultatis Scientarum Naturalium
 Universitatis Prkkynianae Brunensis,
 Physica *c:* **Folia Fac. Sci. Nat. Univ.**
 Pur
Folia Geobotanica et Phytotaxonomica *l:*
 Folia Geobot. Phytotaxon.
Folia Histochemica et Cytobiologica *s:*
 Folia Histochem Cytobiol
Folia Medica *l:* **Folia Med**
Folia Medica Cracoviensia *e:* **Folia Med**
 Cracov
Folia Microbiologica *e:* **Folia Microbiol**
 [Praha]
Folklore Americano. Instituto
 Panamericano de Geografía e Historia,
 Comisión de Historia, Comité de
 Folklore. México *s:* **IPGH/FA.**
Follow-on Wild Weasel *e:* **FOWW,** *e:*
 FWW
Fonctionnaire chargé des questions
 denvironnement *f:* **DOEM**
Fond d'Action Médico Sanitaire *f:*
 FONAMES
Fondation européenne Anne Andre pour la
 securite et la protection de l'enfance *f:*
 Fondation Anne Andre, *f:* **Foundation**
 Anne Andre
Fondation Européenne des Metiers de
 l'Image et du Son *f:* **FEMIS**
Fondation Européenne pour l'Education à
 l'Environnement *f:* **FEEE**
Fondation Médicale de l'Université de
 Louvain au Congo *f:* **FOMULAC**
Fondation pour la Protection des
 Consommateurs *f:* **FPC**
Fondation pour la Recherche Médicale *f:*
 FRM
Fondation pour la Recherche Médicale
 Française *f:* **FRMF**
Fondation pour la Sauvegarde de la Nature
 f: **FPSN**
Fondation suisse d'Éducation pour
 l'Environnement *f:* **FEE**
Fondazione di Medicina Sociale e
 Preventiva *i:* **FMSP**
Fondo de Cooperación Oceanográfica
 Internacional *s:* **COI-F**
Fondo Especial en Depósito para
 Actividades sobre el Clima y el Medio
 Ambiente Atmosférico *s:* **CAEA**
Fondo Mundial para la Naturaleza *s:*
 WWF
Fondo Nacional para la Tierra *s:*
 FONATIERRA

Fondo para el Sistema Mundial de Observación del Clima *s:* **COSF**, *s:* **GCOSF**

Fonds commun pour la recherche sur le climat *f:* **FCRC**

Fonds d'Affectation Spéciale des Nations Unies pour la Planification et des Projections en matière de Développement *f:* **FASNUPPD**

Fonds d'affectation spéciale pour les activités consacrées au climat et à l'environnement atmosphérique *f:* **CAEA**

Fonds de Recherches et de Développement Forestier *f:* **FRDF**

Fonds de Recherches Forestieres. Universite Laval. Contribution *f:* **QLFCAE**

Fonds de Recherches Forestieres. Universite Laval. Note Technique *f:* **NTFLDX**

Fonds de Soutien des Hydrocarbures *f:* **FSH**

Fonds des Conseils de Parents d'Élèves des École s publiques *f:* **FCPE**

Fonds des Nations Unies pour les Activités en matière de Population *f:* **FNUAP**

Fonds d'Intervention et d'Action pour la Nature et l'Environnement *f:* **FIANE**

Fonds d'Investissement Routier *f:* **F.I.R.**

Fonds Forestier *f:* **F.F.**

Fonds Forestier National *f:* **F.F.N.**

Fonds Français pour la Nature et l'Environnement *f:* **FFNE**

Fonds international d'indemnisation pour les dommages dus à la pollution par les hydrocarbures *f:* **FIPOL**

Fonds mondial pour la nature *f:* **WWF**

Fonds Médical Tropical *f:* **FOMETRO**

Fonds pour le Système mondial d'observation du climat *f:* **COSF**, *f:* **GCOSF**

Fonds pour l'Environnement Mondial *f:* **FEM**

Fonds Reine Elisabeth pour l'Assistance Médicale aux Indigènes du Congo, Bruxelles *f:* **FOREAMI**

Fonds Routiers *f:* **F.R.**

Fonds Spécial d'Investissement Routier *f:* **FSIR**

Food and Environmental Quality Laboratory *e:* **FEQL**

Food Animal Concerns Trust *e:* **FACT**

Food Animal Integrated Research *e:* **FAIR**

Food Animal Residue Avoidance Databank *e:* **FARAD**

Food Quality Protection Act *e:* **FQPA**

Food Reserve[s] on Space Trip *e:* **FROST**

Food Trades Protection Society *e:* **FTPS**

Food, Water and Waste *e:* **FWW**

Food, Water and Waste Management *e:* **FWWM**

Food, Water and Waste Management System *e:* **FWWMS**

for Environmental Studies (or Study) *e:* **CES**

For NASA [National Aeronautics and Space Administration] Personnel Only *e:* **FNPO**

Forbes Biological Station *e:* **FBS**

Force de protection des Nations Unies *f:* **FORPRONU**

Force Océanique Stratégique *f:* **FOST**

Forced-Oil and Forced-Water *e:* **FOW**

Forces Armées de la Zone Sud de l'Océan Indien *f:* **F.A.Z.S.O.I.**

Forces Françaises du Sud de l'Océan Indien *f:* **F.F.S.O.I.**

Forces Hydroélectriques de l'Andorre *f:* **FHASA**

Ford Aerospace *e:* **FA**

Ford Aerospace and Communications Corporation *e:* **FACC**

Ford Aerospace Corporation Communication satellite *e:* **FORDSAT**

Ford Aerospace Satellite Services *e:* **FASS**

Ford Aerospace Satellite Services Corporation *e:* **FASSC**

Förderrichtlinien der Wasserwirtschaftsverwaltung *d:* **FöRiWWV**

Forecast of Conflict Environment *e:* **FORCE**

Forecasting Ocean-Atmosphere Model *e:* **FOAM**

Foreign Aerospace Science and Technology [Directorate] Center *e:* **FASTC**

Foreign Bondholders Protective Council *e:* **FBPC**

Foreign Medical Graduate *e:* **FMG**

Foreign Medical Graduates *e:* **FMG's**

Foreign Medical Graduates Examination in the Medical Sciences *e:* **FMGEMS**

Foreign Medical Graduation *e:* **FMG**

Foreign National Weather Agency *e:* **FNWA**

Foreign Sea Duty *e:* **FSD**

Foreign Service and Sea Duty Allowance *e:* **FS&SD**

Foreningen af Danske Medicinfabrikker *a:* **MEFA**

forensic medicine *e:* **foren**, *e:* **for med**

Forensic Medicine Consultant-Advisor *e:* **FMCA**

forensisch *d:* **forens**

Forest and Bird Protection Society *e:* **FBPS**

Forest and Bird Protection Society [of New Zealand] *e:* **FBPS**

Forest and Wildlands Conservation Information System *e:* **FOWCIS**

Forest Assessment and Monitoring Environment *e:* **FAME**

Forest Biology *e:* **FB**

Forest Ecology and Management *e:* **For. Ecol. Manage.**

Forest Ecology Management *e:* **Forest Ecol. Manage.**

Forest Environment and Resource Information Analysis System *e:* **FERIAS**

Forest Environment and Resources Information System *e:* **FERIS**

Forest Health Committee *e:* **FHC**

Forest Hydrology Laboratory *e:* **FHL**

Forest, Range and Watershed Laboratory *e:* **FRWL**

Forest Range Environmental Production Analytical System *e:* **FREPAS**

Forest Range Environmental Study *e:* **FRES**

Forest Resource Geographic Information system *e:* **FORGIS**

Forest Resources and Environment Collective *e:* **FREColl**

Forestry Branch, Saskatchewan Department of Natural Resources, Prince Albert, Saskatchewan *e:* **SPAF**

Forestry Canada Remote Sensing Working Group *e:* **FCRSWG**

Forestry Committee on Remote Sensing *e:* **FORCORS**

Forestry Remote Sensing Laboratory *e:* **FRSL**

Forestry, Wildlife and Wildland Working Group *e:* **FWW**

Forges et Chantiers de la Méditerranée *f:* **F.C.M.**

Forma Binaria Universal de Representación de Datos Meteorológicos *s:* **BUFR**

Formal Environmental Assessment *e:* **FEA**

Format for the Archival of Sea-Ice Data in Digital Form *e:* **SIGRID**

Format Space Planning Language *e:* **FOSPLAN**

Format zum Austausch geometrischer Informationen *d:* **VDAFS**

Formation Médicale Continue *f:* **FMC**

Formato de Intercambio de Datos Geofísicos Marinos *s:* **MGD77**

Formular-Orientiertes Interaktives Datenbanksystem *d:* **FIDAS**

Formularorientiertes Interaktives Ablaufvariantes Titelaufnahmesystem *d:* **FLIRT**

formularorientiertes interaktives Datenbanksystem *d:* **FIDA System**

Forschungen zur Deutschen Geodäsie *d:* **FDG**

Forschungs- und Berater Informationssystem. Forschungsergebnisse in Umweltbereichd *e:* **INFOR**

Forschungsamt für Schiffahrt, Gewässerund Bodenkunde, Bielefeld *d:* **FA-Schiff**

Forschungsanstalt der Bundeswehr für Wasserschall und Geophysik *d:* **FWG**

Forschungsanstalt für Schiffahrt, Wasserund Grundbau *d:* **FAS**

Forschungsgesellschaft für angewandte Naturwissenschaften *d:* **FGAN**

Forschungsgruppe Satellitengeodäsie *d:* **FGS**

Forschungsinstitut für Anwendungsorientierte Wissensverarbeitung *d:* **FAW**

Forschungsinstitut für biologischen Landbau *d:* **FIBL**

Forschungsinstitut für die Biologie landwirtschaftlicher Nutztiere *d:* **FBN**

Forschungsinstitut für Medizinische Diagnostik *d:* **FMD**

Forschungsinstitut und Naturmuseum Senckenberg, Frankfurt am Main *d:* **FIS**

Forschungsleitplan des Forschungsvorhabens "Klimaänderung und Küste" *d:* **FLP**

Forschungsprojekt "Schadstoffe in der Luft und ihr Einfluss auf Wasser- und Boden-Ökosysteme" *d:* **WaBoLu**

Forschungszentrum Borstel, Zentrum für Medizin und Biowissenschaften, Borstel *d:* **FZB**

Forschungszentrum für Management im Gesundheitswesen *d:* **FMIG**

Forschungszentrum für Marine Geowissenschaften *d:* **GEOMAR**

Forschungszentrum für Umwelt und Gesundheit GmbH *d:* **GSF**

Forschungszentrum Karlsruhe GmbH Technik und Umwelt *d:* **FZK**

Forschungzentrum für Medizintechnik und Biotechnologie e. V. *d:* **FZMB**

Försökscentralens Flygmedicinska Laboratorium i Malmslätt r: **FC/FM**

Forstlich- naturwissenschaftliche Zeitschrift d: **Forstl.-nat.wiss. Z.**

Försvarsmedicinska Forskningsdelegationen r: **FMFO**

Fort Frederica National Monument on Saint Simon's Island off Brunswick, Georgia e: **Fort Frederica**

Fort Niobrara National Wildlife Refuge e: **FNNWR**

Fort Sanders Regional Medical Center Knoxville e: **TKFSM**

Fort Worth Geological Society e: **FWGS**

Fortbildungszentrum für Technik und Umwelt d: **FTU**

fortgeschrittener Druckwasserreaktor d: **FDR**

Forth Individuals' Recursive Environment e: **FIRE**

Fortschritte auf dem Gebiet der Röntgenstrahlen und der Nuklearmedizin, Diagnostik d: **Fortschr. Geb. Röntgenstr. Nuk**

Fortschritte der Chemie Organischer Naturstoffe d: **Fortschr Chem Org Naturst**

Fortschritte der Geologie und Paläontologie d: **FGP**

Fortschritte der Medizin d: **FMed**, d: **Fortschr Med**, d: **Fortschr. Med.**

Fortschritte der Medizin. Monographie d: **Fortschr Med Monogr**

Fortschritte der Medizin. Supplement d: **Fortschr Med Suppl**

Fortschritte der naturwissenschaftlichen Forschung d: **FnatF**

Forum Européen des Courtiers en Assurances f: **FECA**

Forum for Acoustic Ecology e: **FACE**

Forum for Climate and Global Change e: **ProClim**

Forum for Medical Affairs e: **FMA**

Forum für Klima und globale Umweltveränderung d: **ProClim**

Forum International de l'Instrumentation et de l'Information Géographiques f: **FI3G**

Forum of Environmental Journalists of Bangladesh e: **FEJB**

Forum on Allied Health Data e: **FAHD**

Forward Area Water Point Supply System e: **FAWPSS**

Forward Environmental Protection Device e: **FEPD**

Forward Flying Observation System e: **FFOS**

Forward [Looking Infrared and] Lidar Atmospheric Propagation in the Infrared e: **FLAPIR**

Forward Medical Equipment Depot e: **FMED**

Forward Medical Officer e: **FMO**

Forward Observation e: **FO**

Forward Observation Battery e: **FO Bty**

Forward Observation & Reconnaissance Thermal Imaging System e: **FORTIS**

Forward Observation Unit, Royal Artillery e: **F.O.U.R.A.**

Forward Observer Remote Target Acquisition System e: **FORTAS**

Forward Space Block e: **FSB**

Foster Medical Corp. e: **FMED**

Foundation for Biomedical Research e: **FBR**

Foundation for Environmental Conservation e: **FEC**

Foundation for Environmental Development and Education in Nigeria e: **FEDEN**

Foundation for Environmental Education e: **FEE**

Foundation for Environmental Education in Europe e: **FEEE**

Foundation for Genetic Medicine e: **FGM**

Foundation for Health e: **FFH**, e: **FH**

Foundation for Health Care Evaluation e: **FHCE**

Foundation for Health Care Quality e: **FHCQ**

Foundation for Health Services Research e: **FHSR**

Foundation for Innovation in Medicine e: **FIM**

Foundation for International Environmental Law and Development e: **FIELD**

Foundation for Medical Care e: **FMC**

Foundation for Medical Technology e: **FMT**

Foundation for Microbiology e: **FFM**, e: **FMB**

Foundation for North American Wild Sheep e: **FNAWS**

Foundation for Ocean Research e: **FOR**

Foundation for Oceanographic Research and Education e: **FORE**

Foundation for Research on Economics and the Environment e: **FREE**

Foundation for Research on the Nature of Man e: **FRNM**

Foundation for Social and Preventive Medicine e: **FMSP**, e: **FSPM**

Foundation for Sports Medicine Education and Research e: **FSMER**

Foundation for the Advancement of Innovative Medicine e: **FAIM**

Foundation for the Advancement of Innovative Medicine Education Fund e: **FAIM-ED**

Foundation for the Preservation and Protection of the Przewalski Horse e: **FPPPH**

Foundation for the Support of International Medical Training e: **FSIMT**

Foundation for Traditional Chinese Medicine e: **FTCM**

Foundation for Women's Health Research and Development e: **FORWARD**

Foundation Health Federal Services e: **FHFS**

Foundation of the American Association of Gynecologic Laparoscopists e: **FAAGL**

Fourier Transform-Chemically Induced Dynamic Electron Polarization e: **FT-CIDEC**

Fra Fysikkens Verden N: **Fra Fys. Verden**

Fractal Geometry and Spatial Phenomena e: **FGSP**

Fraction of Waste Water Treated Anaerobically e: **FWWTA**

fragmentierte Chromosomenbruchstücke d: **F-Chromosomen**

Frame-Space-Bandwidth product e: **FSBW**

Frame Space Bandwidth Product e: **FSBW Product**

Framed Access Command Environment e: **FACE**

Framework Convention on Climate Change[s] e: **FCCC**

Framework for Development of Environmental Statistics e: **FDES**

Français Océan Climat en Atlantique Équatorial f: **FOCAL**

France Nature Environnement f: **FNE**

France Routiers e: **FR**

France's Institute for Protection and Nuclear Safety e: **IPSN**

Frankfurt Army Regional Medical Center e: **FARMC**

Frankfurter Geographische Gesellschaft e.V. d: **FGG**

Fraternitas Medicorum l: **FM**

Fraternite tiers monde, Centre d'Études et de Recherches Apliquées pour la Cooperation au Développement Integral f: **CERACODI**

Fraunhofer-Arbeitsgruppe für Toxikologie und Umweltmedizin d: **ATU**

Fraunhofer-Institut für Atmosphärische Umweltforschung d: **IFU**

Fraunhofer-Institut für Biomedizinische Technik d: **IBMT**

Fraunhofer-Institut für Hydroakustik d: **IHAK**

Fraunhofer-Institut für Naturwissenschaftlich-Technische Trendanalysen d: **INT**

Fraunhofer-Institut für Umweltchemie und Ökotoxikologie d: **IUCT**

Fraunhofer line characteristic of hydrogen e: **C**

Fred Lawrence Whipple Observatory e: **FLWO**

Free China Fund for Medical and Refugee Aid e: **FCF**

Free Flight Air Space e: **FFAS**

Free Oceanographic Instrument Float e: **FOIF**

Free Polar Corticosteroid[s] e: **FPCS**

Free Radical Biology and Medicine e: **Free Radic Biol Med**

Free Route Airspace e: **FRA**

Free Space e: **FRSPC**

Free Space Loss e: **FSL**

Free Space Management e: **FSM**

Free Space Microwave Interferometer e: **FSMWI**

Free Space Reactor e: **FSR**

Free Surface Water Tunnel e: **FSWT**

Free Water Damage e: **FWD**

Free Water Surface e: **FWS**

Freiburger Geographische Hefte d: **Freibg. Geogr. Hefte**

Freight Equipment Environmental Sampling Test Program e: **FEEST**

French-American Mid-Ocean Undersea Study e: **FAMOUS**

French group for Analysis, Validation, and Investigation of Satellite Oceanography e: **AVISCO**

French Group for Analysis, Validation and Investigation of Satellite Oceanography e: **AVISO**

French Group for Processing ERS-1 low-bit-rate data from ocean areas e: **CERSAT**

French Group for Processing ERS-1 low-bit-rate oceanic data e: **C**

French Guiana Space Centre e: **CSG**

French Guyana Space Center e: **GUY**

French-Language Society of Medical Psychology e: **FLSMP**

French Meteorological Experiment with Constant Level Balloons and Satellite Communication e: **EOLE**

French Meteorological Society e: **FMS**

French Ocean-Climat Atlantique Equatorial e: **FOCAL**

French Water Study Association e: **FWA**

Frequency Reference Protection e: **FRP**

Frequency Space Characteristic Impedance e: **FSCI**

Frequent Traveller Medical Card e: **FREMEC**

Fresh water e: **Fr. wa.**

Fresh Water e: **FW**

Fresh Water Arrival Draft e: **FWAD**

Fresh Water Damage e: **FWD**

Fresh Water Departure Draft e: **FWDD**

Fresh Water Drain Collecting Tank e: **FWDCT**

Fresh Water Fish Wholesalers Association e: **FWFWA**

Fresh Water Flux e: **FWF**

Fresh Water Generator e: **FWG**

Fresh Water Institute e: **FWI**

Fresh Water Pump e: **FWP**

Fresh Water Tank e: **FWT**

freshwater e: **f**

Freshwater and Aquaculture Contents Tables e: **FACT**

freshwater ballast e: **fw ball.**

Freshwater Biological Association e: **FBA**

Freshwater Biological Association. Occasional Publication e: **OPFAEI**

Freshwater Biological Association of the British Empire e: **FBABE**

Freshwater Biological Investigation Unit e: **FBIU**

Freshwater Biological Society e: **F.B.S.**

Freshwater Biology e: **Freshwater Biol.**

Freshwater Draught e: **F.W.D.**

Freshwater Ecosystems e: **FWE**

Freshwater Fish Marketing Corporation e: **FFMC**

Freshwater Fish of Illinois e: **FFI**

Freshwater Fisheries Advisory Council e: **FFAC**

Freshwater Fisheries Management Plans e: **FFMOP**

Freshwater Institue, Fisheries and Oceans Canada Winnipeg, Manitoba e: **MWFW**

Freshwater Institute Numeric Database e: **FIND**

Friendly Societies Health Services e: **FSHS**

Friendly Societies Medical Association e: **FSMA**

Friends' Health Connection e: **FHC**

Friends of Aerospace Supporting Science and Technology e: **FASST**

Friends of Animals e: **FOA**

Friends of Ecological Reserves e: **FER**

Friends of George Sand e: **FGS**

Friends of Nature e: **FN**

Friends of the Earth e: **FE**, e: **FOE**, e: **F of E**

Friends of the Earth Foundation e: **FEF**

Friends of the Earth-France e: **FOEF**

Friends of the Earth-Hong Kong e: **FOEHK**

Friends of the Earth International e: **FOEI**

Friends of the Earth-Portugal e: **FOEP**

Friends of the National Library of Medicine e: **FNLM**

Friends of the Sea Lion e: **FSL**

Friends of the Sea Lion Marine Mammal Center e: **FSLMMC**

Friends of the Sea Otter e: **FSO**

Friends of the Wilderness e: **FOW**

Frinton-on-Sea e: **F-o-S**

Frischwasser d: **FrW**, d: **FW**

Frischwasserfreibord d: **F**

Frischwassergebiet d: **F**, d: **Fwgb.**

Frischwassertank d: **Fr.W.T.**, d: **FWT**

Frisian islanders or the Frisian Islands in the North Sea e: **Frisians**

from the Caspian Sea and the Caucasus Mountains to the Ural Mountains e: **Eurasia**

Front Uni Libérateur de la Guinée Portuguesa et des Isles du Cap Verde f: **FUL**

Frontage Protection Zone e: **FPZ**

Frontal Air-Sea Interaction Experiment e: **FASINEX**

Frontier e: **Front.**

Frontier Airline[s] e: **FAL**

Frontier Airlines e: **FL**

Frontier Armed and Mounted Police e: **FAMP**

Frontier Force[s] e: **FF**

Frontier Inspections Service e: **FIS**

Frontier Mounted Police e: **FMP**

Frontier Nursing Service e: **FNS**

Frontier School Division, Winnipeg, Manitoba e: **MWFSD**

frontier set of e: **Fr**

Frontiera Orientale i: **FO**

Frontiers in Neuroendocrinology e: **Front Neuroendocrinol**

Frontiers International e: **FI**

Frontiers of Biology e: **FOB**

Frontiers of Medical and Biological Engineering e: **Front Med Biol Eng**

Frontiers of Radiation Therapy and Oncology e: **Front Radiat Ther Oncol**

Frontwetterwarte d: **Fr.W.W.**

FSL X-window AWIPS-Like Prototype for Hydrometeorological Applications e: **FX-ALPHA**

Fuchs Gas- und Wassertechnik d: **F.G.W.**

Fuel Geoscience Unit e: **FGU**

Fuel handling and remote maintenance e: **FH&RM**

Fuel Oil and Water Heater Manufacturers Association e: **FOWHM**

Fuel Preburner (Space Shuttle Main Engine) e: **FPB**

Fuel/Water Storage & Pump Modules e: **SIXCONS**

Fueling-at-Sea e: **FAS**

Fuerza Aeromóvil del Ejército de Tierra s: **FAMET**

Fukuoka Igaku Zasshi. Fukuoka Acta Medica j: **Fukuoka Igaku Zasshi**

Fukushima Journal of Medical Science e: **Fukushima J Med Sci**

Full Space Output e: **FSO**

Fully Remote Data Acquisition e: **FREDA**

Fully Remote Data Acquisition System e: **FREDA System**

Functional Ecology e: **Funct. Ecol.**

Functionally Related Observable Differences e: **FROD**

Fund for Animals e: **FfA**

Fund for Integrative Biomedical Research e: **FIBER**

Fund for International Oceanographic Cooperation e: **IOC-F**

Fund for Renewable Energy and the Environment e: **FREE**

Fund for the Replacement of Animals in Medical Experiments e: **FRAME**

Fundação Brasileira para e Conservação da Natureza p: **FBCN**

Fundação Instituto de Estatistica e Geografia p: **FIGBE**

Fundación de Informática Médica s: **FIM**

Fundación Defensores de la Naturaleza s: **FDN**

Fundación La Salle de Ciencias Naturales s: **FLS**

Fundación Oceanográfica Internacional s: **IOF**

Fundación para Defensa de la Naturaleza s: **FUDENA**

Fundamental Astronomy by Space Techniques Consortium e: **FAST**

Fungal Genetics and Biology e: **FG&B**

Funkfeuer mit rotierendem Strahl d: **FFm.r.S.**

Funkwetter-Beobachtungsstelle d: **Fub**

Furnish Fuel and Water e: **FF & W**

futterbedarfsorientierte Grossvieheinheit d: **fGV**

Future Control Zone [Hanford Site Defense Waste Environmental Impact Statement Terminology] e: **FCZ**

Future European Space Transportation Investigation Programm d: **FESTIP**

Future of Ocean Research e: **FORE**

Fuze/Munitions Environment Characterization Symposium e: **FES**

Fuzzy Interface Development Environment e: **FIDE**

Fuzzy System Standard Environment e: **FSSE**

Fédération Bananière et Fruitière de la Côte d'Ivoire, Abidjan f: **FEDERBAN**

Fédération Belge de la Carrosserie et des métiers connexes f: **FEBELCAR**

Fédération belge des exploitants forestiers et Marchands de bois de mine et papeterie f: **FEDEMAR**

Fédération Belge des Exploitants Forestiers et Marchands de Bois de Mine et Papeterie f: **FEDEMtAR**

Fédération belgo-luxembourgeoise des industries de tabac f: **FEDETAB**

Fédération Compagnonnique Régionale des Métiers du Bâtiment f: **FCRMB**

Fédération de la Vulgarisation Forestière de l'Est f: **FVFE**

Fédération de l'Industrie Cimentière f: **FIC**

Fédération de l'Industrie Granitière Européenne f: **FIGE**

Fédération des anciens élèves de l'École Nationale d'Administration f: **FDENA**

Fédération des Associations Canadiennes sur l'Environnement f: **FACE**

Fédération des Associations de Communes Forestières Françaises f: **FACFF**

Fédération des Associations d'Ingenieurs et Anciens Eleves des Ecoles Superieures d'Agriculture Privees f: **FAP**

Fédération des Associations Fribourgeoises d'Enseignants f: **FAFE**

Fédération des Experts Forestiers f: **FEF**

Fédération des Grossistes en Produits Laitiers *f:* **FGPL**

Fédération des Gynécologues et Obstétriciens de Langue Française *f:* **FGOLF**

Fédération des Industriels Luxembourgeois *f:* **FIL**

Fédération des Industries de Matieres Premieres et des Ameliorants pour la Boulangerie et la Patisserie dans la CEE *f:* **FEDIMA**

Fédération des Industries de Matieres premieres et des ameliorants pour la boulangerie et la patisserie dans la CEE *f:* **FIDIMA**

Fédération des Industries Luxembourgeois *f:* **FEDIL**

Fédération des Jeunes Chambres Economiques d'Afrique et de l'Océan Indien *f:* **FJCEAOI**

Fédération des Maisons Médicales et Collectifs de Santé Francophones *e:* **FMMCSF**

Fédération des Parcs Naturels de France *f:* **FPNF**

Fédération des Parcs Naturels et Nationaux d'Europe *f:* **FNNPE**

Fédération des Parcs Naturels Régionaux de France *f:* **FPNRF**

Fédération des Services Astronomiques et Géophysiques *f:* **FSAG**

Fédération des services d'Analyse de données astronomiques et Géophysiques *f:* **FAGS**

Fédération des Sociétés des Anciens Élèves des Écoles Techniques de la Suisse Occidentale *f:* **FAETSO**

Fédération des Syndicats Libres des Travailleurs Luxembourgeois *f:* **FSL**

Fédération des Syndicats Médicaux *f:* **FSM**

Fédération des Transports Routiers *f:* **FTR**

Fédération des Écoles Normales *f:* **FEN**

Fédération des Écoles Techniques *f:* **FET**

Fédération des Étudiants en Grandes Écoles Privées *f:* **FEGEP**

Fédération d'Écoles Supérieures d'Ingénieurs et Cadres *f:* **FESIC**

Fédération Européene d'Informatique Médicale *f:* **FEIM**

Fédération Européenne d'Associations Medicales (ou de Medecins) Catholiques *f:* **FEAMC**

Fédération Européenne de la Santé Animale *e:* **FEDESA**

Fédération Européenne de la Tannerie et des métiers connexes *f:* **FEDETAN**

Fédération Européenne des Fabricants d'Adjuvants pur la Nutrition Animale *f:* **FEFANA**

Fédération Européenne des Professionnels de l'Environnement *f:* **FEPE**

Fédération Européenne des Syndicats d'Agrobiologistes *f:* **FESA**

Fédération Européenne des Écoles *f:* **FEDE**

Fédération Européenne pour la Protection des Eaux *f:* **FEPE**

Fédération Francaise de la Cooperation Fruitiere, Legumiere et Horticole *f:* **FELCOOP**

Fédération Française de la Coopération Fruitière, Légumière et Horticole *f:* **FFCFLH**

Fédération Française de Naturisme *f:* **F.F.N.**

Fédération Française de Syndicats de Courtiers marchandises et grains *f:* **FFSC**

Fédération Française des Papetiers Spécialistes *f:* **FFPS**

Fédération Française des Sociétés de Protection de la Nature *f:* **FFSPN**

Fédération Française du Yoga sous contrôle médical *f:* **FFY**

Fédération Horticole Professionnelle Luxembourgeoise *f:* **FHPL**

Fédération Intercommunale pour la Sauvegarde de l'Environnement de la Région Grenobloise *f:* **FISERG**

Fédération Interdépartementale des Chasseurs de l'Essonne et Val de l'Oise Yvelines *f:* **FICEVY**

Fédération Internationale de Gynecologie Infantile et Juvenile *f:* **FIGIJ**

Fédération Internationale de Gynécologie et d'Obstétrique *f:* **FIGO**

Fédération Internationale de Gynécologie Infantile et Juvénile *f:* **FIGI**

Fédération Internationale de la Documentation Commission for Asia and Oceania *f:* **FID/CAO**

Fédération Internationale de l'Industrie du Médicament *f:* **FIIM**

Fédération Internationale de l'Électronique Médicale *f:* **FIEM**

Fédération Internationale de Médicine Manuelle *f:* **FIMM**

Fédération Internationale de Psychothérapie Médicale *f:* **FIPM**

Fédération internationale des associations pour la sauve-garde du patrimoine culturel et naturel de l'Europe *f:* **Europa Nostra**

Fédération Internationale des Géomètres *f:* **FIG**

Fédération Internationale des Mouvements d'École Moderne *f:* **FIMEM**

Fédération Internationale des Organismes de Psychologie Médicale *f:* **FIOPM**

Fédération Internationale des Écoles de Parents et Éducateurs *f:* **FIEP**

Fédération Internationale du Sport Médical pour l'Aide à la Recherche Cancerologique *f:* **FISMARC**

Fédération Internationale du Thermalisme et du Climatisme *f:* **FITC,** *f:* **FITEC**

Fédération Internationale pour la Protection des Populations *f:* **FIPP**

Fédération Internationale Routière *f:* **FIR**

Fédération Latière Neuchâteloise *f:* **FLN**

Fédération Luxembourgeoise de Football *f:* **FLF**

Fédération Mondiale pour l'Enseignement Médical *f:* **FMEM**

Fédération Mutualiste interdépartementale de Paris *f:* **FMP**

Fédération Médicale Belge *f:* **FEMEB,** *f:* **FMB**

Fédération Nationale Agro-Alimentaire et Forestiere *f:* **FNAF**

Fédération Nationale Artisanale des Métiers d'Art et de Création du Bijou et de l'Horlogerie *f:* **FNAMAC**

Fédération Nationale Belge des Transporteurs Routiers *f:* **FNBTR**

Fédération Nationale Conseils de Parents d'Élèves des Écoles Publiques *f:* **FNCPEEP**

Fédération Nationale d'Agriculture Biologique *f:* **FNAB**

Fédération Nationale de Cheminots, Travailleurs du Transport, Fonctionnaires et Employés Luxembourgeois *f:* **FNCTTFEL**

Fédération Nationale de Défense de l'Agriculture Biologique *f:* **FNDAB**

Fédération Nationale de l'Industrie Laitière *f:* **FNIL**

Fédération Nationale des Anciens de Grandes Écoles *f:* **FNAGE**

Fédération Nationale des Associations des Grandes Écoles *f:* **FNAG**

Fédération Nationale des Associations d'Élèves des Grandes Écoles *f:* **F.N.A.G.E.**

Fédération Nationale des Associations d'Élèves des Lycées et Grandes Écoles *f:* **FNALGE**

Fédération nationale des Auto-Écoles professionnelles de Belgique *f:* **FAB**

Fédération Nationale des Cafetiers Limonadiers *f:* **FNCL**

Fédération Nationale des Chorales Universitaires des Grandes Écoles *f:* **FNCUGE**

Fédération Nationale des Coopératives Laitières *f:* **F.N.C.L.**

Fédération Nationale des Détaillants de Produits Laitiers *f:* **FNDPL**

Fédération Nationale des Groupements de Protection des Cultures *f:* **FNGPC**

Fédération Nationale des Hôteliers, Restaurateurs et Cafetiers du Grand Duché de Luxembourg *f:* **HORESCA**

Fédération Nationale des Maîtres Artisans et Petites Enterprises des Métiers Graphiques *f:* **FNMAPEMG**

Fédération Nationale des Métiers Giraphiques *f:* **FNMG**

Fédération Nationale des Observatoires Régionaux de la Santé *f:* **FNORS**

Fédération Nationale des Organismes de Controle Laitier *f:* **FNOCL**

Fédération Nationale des Petits Rentiers de la Caisse de Retraite *f:* **F.N.P.R.C.R.**

Fédération Nationale des Praticiens de Thérapeutiques Naturelles *f:* **FNPTN**

Fédération Nationale des Propriétaires Forestiers Sylviculteurs *f:* **FNPFS**

Fédération Nationale des Recoltants Familiaux de Fruits et Producteurs d'Eau-de-Vie Naturelle *f:* **FNRFF**

Fédération Nationale des Sociétés de Sciences Naturelles *f:* **FNSSN**

Fédération Nationale des Syndicats de Détaillants en Produits Laitiers *f:* **FNSDPL**

Fédération Nationale des Syndicats de Proprietaires Forestiers Sylviculteurs *f:* **FHSPFS**

Fédération Nationale des Syndicats de Propriétaires Forestiers Sylviculteurs *f:* **FNSPFS**

Fédération Nationale des Syndicats des industries de l'Alimentation Animale *f:* **FENSYAA**

Fédération Nationale des Syndicats des Industries de l'Alimentation Animale *f:* **FNSIAA**

Fédération nationale des syndicats des patrons confiseurs et chocolatiers de Belgique *f:* **FENACO**

Fédération Nationale des Syndicats d'Exploitants Forestiers, Scieurs et Industriels du Bois *f:* **FNSEF**

Fédération Nationale des Syndicats d'Industriels Laitiers *f:* **FNSIL**

Fédération Nationale des Transporteurs Routiers *f:* **FNTR**

Fédération Nationale des Étudiants Luxembourgeois *f:* **FNEL**

Fédération Nationale du Commerce des Produits Laitiers et Avicoles *f:* **FNCPLA**

Fédération Nationale pour la Protection et Réadaptation Sociale des Handicapés Mentaux et Physiques *f:* **FNPR**

Fédération Nationale pour l'Utilisation Naturelle des Fruits *f:* **FNUNF**

Fédération Naturiste Internationale *f:* **FNI**

Fédération Rhône-Alpes de Protection de la Nature *f:* **FRAPNA**

Fédération Romande des Maîtres Menuisiers Ebénistes, Fabricants de Meubles, Charpentiers de Parqueteurs *f:* **FRM**

Fédération Romande des Écoles de Conduite *f:* **FRE**, *f:* **FREC**

Fédération Routière Belge *f:* **FRB**

Fédération Routière Internationale *f:* **FRI**

Fédération Routière Suisse *f:* **FRS**

Fédération royale des Géomètres Experts Indépendants *f:* **FGEI**

Fédération Régionale des Organisations Syndicales de l'Artisanat et des Métiers de Basse Normandie *f:* **FROSAM**

Fédération Suisse des Cafetiers, Restaurateurs et Hôteliers *f:* **FSCRH**

Fédération suisse des École s privées *e:* **FSEP**

Fédération suisse des Écoles de Parents *f:* **FEP**

Fédération Thermale et Climatique *f:* **F.T.C.**

Fédération Thermale et Climatique de Bretagne *f:* **FTCB**

Fédération Thermale et Climatique Française *f:* **FTCF**

Féedération Mondiale pour la Protection des Animaux *f:* **FMPA**

G

G7 Environment and Natural Resources Management Project *e:* **G7 ENRM project**

G7 Global Environmental Information Locator Service *e:* **GELOS**, *e:* **G7 GELOS**

G Report.Saskatchewan Research Council. Geology Division *e:* **G Rep Sask Res Counc Geol Div**

Gaceta Ecológica *s:* **GE**

Gaceta Medica de Mexico *e:* **GMMEA**, *s:* **Gac Med Mex**

Gale Environmental Sourcebook *e:* **GES**

GALE Oceanographic Temperature Studies *e:* **GOTS**

Gallium Neutrino Observatory *e:* **GNO**

Gamma-Ray Astronomy Observatory *e:* **GRAO**

Gamma Ray Environmental Mapping Spectrometer *e:* **GEMS**

Gamma Ray Large Area Space Telescope *e:* **GLAST**

Gamma Ray [orbiting] Observatory *e:* **GRO**

Garantie Incendie Forestière *f:* **GIF**

garantiert rein *d:* **GR**

Gareth Mills' Geoscience Related Links *e:* **GMGRL**

Garnet-rutile-ilmenite-plagioclase-silica [geobarometer] *e:* **GRIPS**

GARP [Global Atmospheric Research Program] Atlantic Tropical Experiment *e:* **GATE**

GARP [Global Atmospheric Research Program] International Sea Trial *e:* **GIST**

Gas Chromatography in Biology and Medicine *e:* **GCBM**

Gas Companies' Protection Association *e:* **G.C.P.A.**

Gas-Cooled Heavy Water Moderated Reactor *e:* **GCHWR**

Gas, Electricity, Water *e:* **GEW**

Gas, Elektrizität, Wasser *d:* **GEW**

Gas-, Elektrizitäts- und Wasserwerke *d:* **GEW**, *d:* **GEW-Werke**

Gas-, Elektrizitäts- und Wasserwerke AG *d:* **GEWAG**

Gas-Filled Hydrophobic Region *e:* **GFHR**

Gas Gathering Pipelines [North Sea] Ltd. *e:* **GGP**

Gas Hot Water Service *e:* **GHWS**

Gas Hour Space Velocity *e:* **GHSV**

Gas Industry. Natural Gas Edition *e:* **GINGA**

Gas Natural *s:* **GN**

Gas Natural Licuado *s:* **GNL**

Gas Naturale Liquido *i:* **GNL**

Gas Recycle Hydrogenation *e:* **GRH**

Gas und Wasser *d:* **GW**

Gas- und Wasserfach *d:* **GuWf**, *d:* **gwf**

Gas, Wasser, Abwaser *d:* **GWASA**

Gas, Wasser, Abwasser. Schweizerische Monatszeitschrift für Gasförderung und Siedlungswasserwirtschaft *d:* **GHA**

Gas, Wasser, Elektrizität *d:* **GWE**

Gas-, Wasser- und Elektrizitätswerke *d:* **GWE-Werke**

Gas-, Wasser- und Fernwärmeversorgung der Stadt Bern *d:* **GWB**

gas-water contact *e:* **gwc**

Gas-Water Module Storage *e:* **GWMS**

Gaseous Hydrogen *e:* **GH**

Gastroenterologie Clinique et Biologique *f:* **Gastroenterol Clin Biol**

Gateway Medical Systems, Incorporated *e:* **GMSI**

Gauceng Oral Health Services *e:* **GOHS**

Gauss Hypergeometric Equation *e:* **GHE**

Gaussian Orbitals *e:* **GO**

Gay Men's Health Crisis *e:* **GMHC**

Gay Public Health Workers Caucus *e:* **GPHW**

Gaz Naturel Liquéfié *f:* **GNL**

Gazette Médicale de France *f:* **GMF**

GCOS/GTOS Terrestrial Observation Panel *e:* **TOP**

Geautomatiseerde Administratie *n:* **G.A.**

Gebieds Gebonden Onderdelen *n:* **GGO**

Gedeputeerde Staten *n:* **G.S.**

Geesthacht Simulation Model of the Atmosphere *e:* **GESIMA**

Geesthachter Simulationsmodell der Atmosphäre *d:* **GESIMA**

Gefahrgutverordnung Binnenschiffahrt [Verordnung über die Beförderung gefährlicher Güter auf Binnengewässern] *d:* **GGVBinSch**

gefärbt konvertierbar *d:* **fbk**

gegen Warmwetterfronten empfindlicher Konstitutionstyp *d:* **W-Typ**

Geisinger Medical Center, Medical Library, Danville *e:* **GEI**

Gekombineerde Zwemvereniging Winschoten *n:* **GZVW**

Gelsenberg-Mannesmann-Umweltschutz GmbH *d:* **GMU**

Gemeente-Waterleiding *n:* **GW**

Gemeinsames Bund/Länder-Meßprogramm für die Küstengewässer der Nordsee *e:* **BLMP**

Gemeinschaft zur Förderung der Luftfahrt in Bayern *d:* **GFL**

Gemini Earth Station *e:* **GES**

Gemini Environmental Control System *e:* **GECS**

Gemini Spacecraft Project Office *e:* **GSPO**

Gene Geography *e:* **Gene Geogr**

General Architecture for Medical Expert Systems *e:* **GAMES**

General Association of Municipal Health and Technical Experts *e:* **GAMHTE**

General Aviation Forecast (Weather) *e:* **GAFOR**

General Bathymetric Chart of the Ocean[s] *e:* **GEBCO**

General Circulation Model [National Center for Atmospheric Research] *e:* **GCM**

General Council of Medical Education and Registration *e:* **G.C.M.E.R.**

General Dynamics/ Convair Aerospace Division, Fort Worth *e:* **TxFG**

General Dynamics Space Systems *e:* **GDSS**

General Election Coordinating Committee for Animal Protection *e:* **GECCAP**

General Electric BWR [Boiling Water Reactor] Thermal Analysis Branch *e:* **GETAB**

General Electric Co., Missile and Space Vehicle Department, Aerosciences Laboratory, Philadelphia, PA *e:* **PPGE-M**

General Electric Medical Systems *e:* **GEMS**

General Electric Miniature Aerospace Navigator *e:* **GEMAN**

General Electric Missile and Space Vehicle Department *e:* **GE-MSD**

General Electric Missile Space Vehicle Department *e:* **GEMSVD**

General Electric Satellite Orbit Control *e:* **GESOC**

General Environmental Data Base System *e:* **GEDS**

General Environmental Impact Statement on the Use of Mixed Oil Fuel *e:* **GESMO**

General Environmental Statement for Missed Oxide Fuel *e:* **GFSMO**

General Environment[al] Statement for/on Mixed Oxide Fuel *e:* **GESMO**

General Environmental Verification
Specification e: **GEVS**

General Establishment of Geology and
Mineral Resources e: **GEGMR**

General Format No 3 [A General
Oceanographic Data Exchange Format]
e: **GF3**

General Health e: **GH**

General Health Queslionnaire e: **GHQ**

General Health Questionnaire e: **GHO**

General Hydrocarbons of Minnesota e:
GHYD

General Hydrological Model e: **GHM**

General Indexing in Reciprocal Lattice
Space d: **GIRLS**

General Information Environment e:
GENIE

General Medical e: **GM**

General Medical Council e: **GMC**

General Medical Intelligence e: **GMI**

General [Medical] Laboratory e: **GL**

General Medical Officer e: **GMO**

General Medical Practice e: **GMP**

General Medical Practitioner e: **GMP**

General Medical Problem e: **GMP**

General Medical Sciences and Atomic
Energy Commission e: **GeMSAEC**

General Medical Services e: **GMS**

General Medical Services Committee (or
Council) e: **GMSC**

General Medicine e: **GM**

General Medicine and Surgery e: **GM+S**

General Meteorological (or Meteorology)
Package e: **GEMPAK**

General NORAD [North American Air
Defense] Environment Simulation and
Subsystem e: **GENESIS**

General NORAD [North American Air
Defense] Environment Simulation
Subsystem Executive Program e:
GENEX

General Ocean Research e: **GOR**

General Optronics Line of Sight
Atmospheric Lightwave Communication
System e: **GOALS**

General Organisation[al] [and] (or
Organization[al]) Environment e:
GEORGE

General Organization of Remote Sensing
e: **GORS**

General Overhauser Orbitals e: **GOO**

General Preventive Medicine e: **GPM**

General Protection e: **GP**

General Protection Fault (or Failure) e:
GPF

general-purpose aerospace equipment e:
gpae

General Purpose Remote Machining Center
e: **GPRMC**

General Purpose Remote Sensor System e:
G P R S S

General Purpose Scientic Ducoment Water
e: **GPSDW**

General-Purpose Simulation Environment
e: **GPSE**

General Remote Network Processor e:
GRNP

General Research in the Environment for
Eastern European Nations e: **GREEN**

General Sea Harvest e: **GSP**

General Short Arc Geodetic Reduction e:
GSAGR

General Space Planner e: **GSP**

General Staff Geographical Section maps
covering Africa, Asia, the East Indies and
Europe e: **GSGS maps**

General Water-Quality Engineering e:
GWQE

Generalised [Generalized] Architecture for
Languages, Encyclopaedias and
Nomenclatures in Medicine e: **GALEN**

Generalized Aerospace Program e: **GASP**

Generalized Diatomic Orbital e: **GDO**

General[ized] Euclidean Geometry e:
GEG

Generalized Geometric Optics
Approximation e: **GGOA**

Generalized Geometry Hold-up e: **GGH**

Generalized Hartree-Fock/Natural
Orbital/Configuration Interactions e:
GHF-NO-CI

Generalized Hybrid Orbital e: **GHO**

Generalized Projective Geometries e:
GPG

Generalized Remote Access Data base
System e: **GRADS**

General[ized] Remote Access Database e:
GRADB

Generalized Remote Acquisition and Sensor
Processing e: **GRASP**

Generalsekretariat des Eidgenössischen
Departements für Umwelt, Verkehr,
Energie und Kommunikation d:
GS/UVEK

Generating Station Protection System e:
GSPS

Generation Animalium [of Aristotle] e:
Gen An

Generation II Model For Environmental
Dose Calculations e: **GENII**

Generator Earth Orbital Scene e: **GEOS**

Generator Environmental Tester e: **GET**

Generic Application Environment e: **GAE**

Generic Environmental Evaluation e: **GEE**

Generic Environmental Impact Assessment
e: **GEIA**

Generic Environmental Impact Statement
[or Study] e: **GEIS**

Generic Environmental Statement e: **GES**

Generic VHSIC Spaceborne Computer e:
GVSC

Genesee Hospital, Stabins Health Science
Library, Rochester e: **VQO**

Genesis Health Ventures e: **GHVI**

Genesis of Atmosphere Lows Experiment
e: **GALE**

Genetic Data Environment e: **GDE**

Genetic Psychology Monographs, Child
Behavior, Animal Behavior, and
Comparative d: **Genet.Psychol.Monogr.**

Genetics and Biology of Drosophila e:
Genet Biol Drosophila

Geneva Convention for the Amelioration of
the Condition of the Wounded, Sick and
Shipwrecked Members of the Armed
Forces at Sea e: **GWS Sea**

Geneva Convention Relative to Protection
of Civilian Persons in Time of War e:
GC

Genie Biologique et Medical f: **Geaie Biol
Med**

Génie Climatique International f: **GCI**

Génie Hydrotechnique f: **G.H.**

Genito-Urinary Medicine e: **GUM**

Genitourinary Medicine e: **GEMEE2**, e:
Genitourin Med

Genotype x Environment interaction e:
GxE

GenRad's Environment for Strategy-
Independent Software e: **GENESIS**

Geo Abstracts and Indexes e: **Geo
Abs&Indexes**

Geo Abstracts. B. Climatology and
Hydrology e: **Geo Abstr B Climatol
Hydrol**

Geo Abstracts. C. Economic Geography e:
Geo Abstr C Econ Geog

Geo Abstracts. D. Social and Historical
Geography e: **Geo Abstr D Soc Hist
Geog**

Geo Abstracts. E. Sedimentology e: **Geo
Abstr E Sedimentology**

Geo Abstracts. F. Regional and Community
Planning e: **Geo Abstr F Reg Com Plan**

Geo Abstracts. G. Remote Sensing,
Photogrammetry and Cartography e:
**Geo Abstr G Remote Sensing Pho
Cartogr**

Geo-Archeologia Periodico
dell'Associazione Geo-Archeologica
Italiana i: **Geo-Archeologia**

Geo-Based Information System e: **GBIS**

Geo-Centers Incorporated e: **GEOCI**

Geo-Common Subsystem e: **GCS**

Geo-Data International e: **GED**

Geo-Data System e: **GDS**

Geo facilities Data Base Support e: **GDBS**

Geo-Heat Center. Quarterly Bulletin e:
GCQBD, e: **Geo Heat Cent Q Bull**

Geo-Heat Utilization Center. e: **Geo-Heat
Util Center Q Bull**

Geo Journal e: **Geo J**

Geo-Located Multisource Exploitation
system e: **GLMX**

Geo-Marine Letters e: **Geo-Mar Let**

Geo Marine Technology e: **GMT**

Geo-Processing e: **Geo-Process**

Geo Requirements Working Group e:
GRWG

Geo-Stationary Satellite e: **GSS**

Geo-synchronous Earth Orbit e: **GEO**

GEO Transfer Orbit e: **GTO**

Geo- und Kosmoswissenschaften d: **GK**

Geo-Urban-Eco-System-Simulation e:
GUESS

GeoAgenda e: **GeoAgenda**

Geoanomaly Interactive Data Analysis
System e: **GIDAS**

Geoaphic Systems Laboratory e: **GSL**

Geoastrophysics e: **Geoastrophys.**

Geoballistic Input Unit e: **GIU**

Geobios [Lyon] e: **GEBSAJ**

Geobotanica selecta e: **Geobot. sel.**

Geobotany e: **GEOBD2**

GeoBusiness Association e: **GBA**

Geocarto International [Hong Kong] e:
Geocarto Int.

Geocartographics Subdivison e: **GCG**

Geocbemical Journal e: **GEJOBE**

geocentric e: **geo**

Geocentric Coordinated Time e: **TCG**

Geocentric Datum of Australia e: **GDA**, e:
GGDA

Geocentric Dust Cloud e: **GDC**

Geocentric Dust Converter e: **GDC**

Geocentric Pendulum Control e: **GPC**

Geocentric Reference System e: **GRS**

Geocentric Solar Ecliptic [System] e: **GSE**

Geocentric Solar Ecliptic System e: **GSES**

Geocentric Solar Magnetospheric e: **GSM**

Geocentric Solar Magnetospheric System
  e: **GSMS**

Geocentric Vertical Reference e: **GVR**

Geochemical e: **GEOCHEM**

Geochemical Interactive Systems Analysis
  e: **GISA**

Geochemical Journal e: **Geochem J**

Geochemical Journal [Geochemical Society
  of Japan] e: **Geochem J [Geochem Soc
  Jap]**

Geochemical Journal [Nagoya] e:
  Geochem J [Nagoya]

Geochemical Journal [Tokyo] e: **Geochem
  J [Tokyo]**, e: **Geohem J [Tokyo]**

Geochemical Logging Tool e: **GLT**

Geochemical, Microbiological and
  Hydrological Experiment e: **GEM-HEX**

Geochemical Model e: **MINTEQ**

Geochemical News e: **Geochem News**

Geochemical News [Geochemical Society]
  e: **Geochem News**

Geochemical Ocean Section Study e:
  GOESECS

Geochemical Ocean Studies e: **GOS**

Geochemical Ocean[s] Section Study e:
  GEOSECS

Geochemical Society e: **GS**

Geochemical Society of India e: **Geohem
  Soc India Bull**

Geochemical Society of India. Bulletin e:
  Geochem Soc India Bull

Geochemie d: **Geochem.**

Geochemie. Geocbemical Methods and Data
  e: **Geochem Geochem Metbods Data**

Geochemist e: **GEOCHEM**

Geochemist[ry] e: **Gc**

Geochemistry e: **GECHB**

geochemistry e: **geo**

Geochemistry e: **GEOCHEM**

Geochemistry International e: **Geochem
  Int**

Geochimica e: **GEOCD**

Geochimica et Cosmochimica Acta l:
  GCA

Geochimica et Cosmochimica Acta
  [Geochemical Society] l: **Geochim.
  Cosmochim. Acta**

Geochron Laboratories Inc. e: **GX**

Geochronique e: **GECHD**

Geochronology e: **Gc**

Geocodage Multivarie f: **GEOMULTI**

Geocode Service Center e: **GSC**

Geocoded Emissions Modeling and
  Projections e: **GEMAP**

Geocoded Image Correction System e:
  GICS

Geocoding and Compositing [System] e:
  GEOCOMP

Geocryologie d: **Geocrypol.**

Geodaetisk Danmark a: **GID**

Geodaetisk Institut a: **GI**, a: **GID**

Geodäsie d: **geo**, d: **Geod.**

Geodät d: **Geod.**

GeoData Products Index e: **GDPI**

Geodätische Forschung d: **GF**

Geodätische und Geophysikalische
  Veröffentlichungen. Reihe III d: **Geodät
  Geophys Veröffentlicbungen Reihe III**

Geodätisches Forschungszentrum d: **GFZ**

Geodätisches Institut d: **Geod**

Geodätisches Kolloquium d: **GK**

geodætisk a: **geod.**

Geode Speciality Growers Association e:
  GSGA

Geoderma e: **GEDMAB**

Geodesic e: **geod**

Geodesic Isotensoid e: **GI**

Geodesic Line e: **GL**

Geodesist e: **GEOD**

geodesy e: **geo**

Geodesy e: **GEOD**

Geodesy and Aerophotography [USSR] e:
  Geod Aerophotogr [USSR]

Geodesy and Geodynamics Laboratory e:
  GGL

Geodesy and Geographic Information e:
  GGI

Geodesy Intelligence and Mapping
  Research and Development Agency e:
  GIMA, e: **GIMBADA**

Geodesy, Intelligence and Mapping
  Research and Development Agency e:
  GIMRA[N]DA

Geodesy, Mapping and Photogrammetry e:
  Geodes Mapp Photogramm, e: **Geod
  Mapp Pbotogram**

Geodesy, Mapping and Photogrammetry.
  English Translation e: **Geod Mapp
  Photogramm Engl Transl**

Geodesy Program[me] System e: **GEOPS**

Geodesy Research Group e: **GRT**

Geodesy Satellite e: **GEOSAT**, e: **Geosat**

geodetic e: **geo**

Geodetic e: **GEOD**

Geodetic Communications and Electronia
  Squadron e: **GCES**

Geodetic Communications and Electronics
  Squadron e: **GCESq**

Geodetic Coordinate Conversion e: **GCC**

Geodetic Data Center e: **GDC**

Geodetic Data Reduction e: **GDR**

Geodetic Data Site e: **GDS**

Geodetic Datum Point e: **Geo Dat Pt**

Geodetic Distance Measurement e: **GDM**

Geodetic [Earth-]Orbiting Satellite e:
  GEOS

Geodetic Earth-Orbiting Satellite e: **GESO**

Geodetic Engineer e: **Geod E**

Geodetic Estimate[s] from Orbital
  Perturbations of Satellites e: **GEOPS**

Geodetic & Geophysical e: **G&G**

Geodetic/Geophysical Satellite e:
  GEOSAT

Geodetic Inertial Survey and Horizontal
  Alignment e: **GEISHA**

Geodetic Infrastructure for Antarctica e:
  GIANT

Geodetic Institute e: **GI**

Geodetic LASER Survey System e:
  GLASS

Geodetic Observation Satellite e: **GEOS**

Geodetic Operations Control Center e:
  GOCC

Geodetic Optical System e: **GOS**

Geodetic Receiver e: **GEOCEIVER**

Geodetic Reference System e: **GRS**

Geodetic Reference System of 1980 e:
  GRS 80

Geodetic Research and Development
  Laboratory e: **GRDL**

Geodetic Satellite e: **GEOS**

Geodetic Satellite in Polar Geosynchronous
  Orbit e: **GENOPAUSE**, e: **GEOPAUSE**

Geodetic Satellite Mission e: **Geos-3**

Geodetic Satellite Policy Board e: **GSPB**

Geodetic Satellite Program e: **GSP**

Geodetic Satellites Data Center e: **GSDC**

Geodetic Satellites Data service e: **GSDS**

Geodetic Service General Survey e: **GSGS**

Geodetic Society of Japan. Journal e:
  Geod Soc Jap J

Geodetic Space Craft e: **GSC**

Geodetic Stationary Satellite e: **GSS**

Geodetic Survey Division e: **GSD**

Geodetic Survey Institute e: **GSI**

Geodetic Survey Marks Register e:
  GESMAR

Geodetic Survey of Canada e: **GSC**

Geodetic [Survey] Satellite e: **GS**

Geodetic Survey Squadron e: **GSS**, e:
  GSSq

Geodeticky a Kartograficky Obzor c:
  Geod Kartogr Obzor

Geodeticky a Kartograficky Podnik v Praze
  c: **GKP**

Geodetska Glavna Uprava se: **GGU**

Geodetska Srednja Tehnička Škola se:
  GSTŠ

Geodetska Uprava se: **GU**

Geodetska Uprava Narodne Republika
  Bosne i Hercegovine se: **GU NR BiH**

Geodetska Zveza S: **GZ**

Geodezia es Kartografa H: **Geod Kartogr**

Geodezia es Kartografia [Budapest] H:
  Geod Kartogr [Budap]

Geodezia, Kartografia, i Aerofotos'emka
  [Ukrainian SSR] U: **Geod Kartogr
  Aerofotos**

Geodeziia, Kartografia i Aerofotos'emka
  R: **GKAEA**

Geodezija i Kartografja R: **GK**

Geodezijos Darbai [Lithuanian SSR] li:
  Geod Darb

Geodic Isotensoid e: **GI**

Geodome Resources Ltd. e: **GOE**, e:
  GOED

GEODSS Test Site e: **GTS**

Geodynamic Experimental Ocean Satellite
  e: **GEOSAT**

Geodynamic Meter e: **gdm**

geodynamics e: **geo**

Geodynamic[s] e: **GEOD**

Geodynamics Corp. e: **GDYN**

Geodynamic[s] Experimental Ocean
  Satellite e: **GEOS**

Geodynamics [or Geoscience] Laser
  Ranging System e: **GLRS**

Geodynamics Series [American
  Geophysical Union] e: **Geodyn. Ser.**

geodynamischer Meter d: **gdm**

Geodyne Resources, Inc. e: **GDR**, e:
  GEODRS

Geodéziai és Kartográfiai Egyesület H:
  GKE

Geodéziai és Kartográfiai Intézet H: **GKI**

Geoelectric e: **geoelectr.**

Geoelectric Effect e: **GEE**

Geoelectricity e: **Geoelectr.**

Geoelectrokinetograph e: **GEK**

geoelektrischer Effekt d: **GEE**

Geoexploration e: **Geoexplor**

Geoexploration Monographs e: **Geoexplor
  Monogr**

Geoffrion, Leclerc, Inc. e: **GFL**

Geofisica e Meteorologia i: **Geofis
  Met[eorol]**, s: **Geofis Met**

Geofisica International *e:* **Geofis Int**

Geofisica Pura e Applicata *e:* **Geofis Pur Appl**, *i:* **Geofis Pur[a] Appl**

Geofisica Pura e Applicata [Italy] *i:* **Geofis Pura Appl**

Geofizicheskaya Apparatura *R:* **Geofiz App[ar]**

Geofizicheskaya Razvedka *R:* **Geofiz Razved**

Geofizicheskie Issledovaniya pri Reshenii Geologicheskikh Zadach v Vostochnoi Sibiri *R:* **Geofiz Issled Reshenii Geol Zadach Vost Sib**

Geofizicheskie Metody Razvedki v Arktike *R:* **Geofiz Metody Razved Arkt**

Geofizicheskii Sbornik [Kiev] *R:* **Geofiz Sb [Kiev]**

Geofizicheskii Sbornik [Sverdlovsk] *P:* **Geofíz Sb [Sverdlovsk]**

Geofizicheskii Zhurnal *R:* **Geofiz Zh**

Geofizicheskoe Priborostroenie *R:* **Geofiz Pribomstr**

Geofizikai Koezlemenyek *H:* **Geofiz Kozl[emenyek]**, *H:* **Geof Koezl**, *P:* **Geofíz Kozl**

Geofizyka i Geologia Naftowa *P:* **Geofiz Geol Naft**

Geoforschungszentrum *d:* **GFZ**

Geoforschungszentrum Potsdam *d:* **GFZP**

Geoforum *d:* **GEOF**, *e:* **GEFO**

Geofysikalni Sbornik *P:* **Geofys Sb**

Geofysiske Publikasjoner *r:* **Geof[ys] Publ**

Geofyzikální Ústav při ČSAV *c:* **GFÚ-ČSAV**

Geofzicheskie Issledovaniya *P:* **Geofiz Issled**

Geofzicheskii Zhurnal *R:* **GEZHD**

Geogafisk Tidsskrift *P:* **Geog Tidsstr**

Geogical Investigation Series. Geological Survey of Pakistan. Interim Geological Report *e:* **Geol Invest Ser Geol Surv Pak Interim Geol Rep**

geognosy *e:* **geo**

Geognosy *e:* **GEOGNOS**

geograf *N:* **geogr**

Geografcheskii Sbornik Penzenskogo Otdeleniya Geografcheskogo Obshchestva SSSR *R:* **Geogr Sb Penz Otd Geogr O-va SSSR**

Geografia *P:* **GEO**, *a:* **GEOG**

Geograficheskii Sbornik Penzenskogo Otdeleniya Geograficheskogo Obshchestva SSSR *R:* **GSPGAF**

Geografie *d:* **GEO**, *d:* **Geogr.**

geografisch *d:* **geo**

Geografisch Tijdschrift *N:* **Geogr Tjds**

Geografisch Tijdschrift. Nieuwe Reeks *N:* **GET**

Geografische Basiseenheid *n:* **GBE**

geografische Breite *d:* **geogr.Br.**

geografische Datenbanksoftware *d:* **GDBS**

Geografische Mijl *n:* **G.M.**

geografischer Punkt *d:* **G.P.**

Geografisches Netzinformationssystem *d:* **GEONIS**

geografi[sk] *a:* **geogr.**

Geografisk Orientering *a:* **GO**

Geografisk Tidsskrift *N:* **GGTI-A**, *a:* **GT**

Geografisk Tidsskrift. Det Kongelige Danske Geografiske Selskab. Copenhagen *a:* **KDG/GT.**

Geografisk Tídsskrift *N:* **GETD**

Geografiska Annaler *a:* **Geog Annaler**, *e:* **Geogr A**, *e:* **Geogr Ann**, *e:* **Geogr Annlr**

Geografiska Annaler. Series A *r:* **GGFA**

Geografiska Annaler. Series B. *e:* **Geogr Ann Ser B Hum Geogr**

Geografiska Annaler. Series B. Human Geography *a:* **Geogr Ann [Ser] B [Hum Geogr]**, *e:* **Geogr Ann B**

Geografiska Förbundet *r:* **GF**

Geografiske Casopis *c:* **Geogr Cas**

geografiskt referenssystem *r:* **Georef**

Geografiya Ezhegodnogo Geograficheskogo Obshchestva Litovskoi SSR *P:* **Geogr Ezheg Geogr Ova Lit SSR**

Geografiya Raka v Turkmenii *P:* **Geogr Raka Turkm**

Geografiya v Shkole *R:* **Geogr Shk**

Geografnis Metrastis *P:* **Geogr Metrastis**

geograf[sk] *a:* **geogr**

Geografski Glasnik *P:* **Geogr Glas**, *c:* **Geogr Glas[n]**, *se:* **GGI**

Geografski Institut Jugoslovenske Narodne Armije *se:* **GIJNA**

Geografski Institut Srpske Akademije Nauka *se:* **GISAN**

Geografski Pregled *P:* **Geogr Pregl**

Geografski Vestnik *S:* **GV**, *c:* **Geogr Vestn**

Geografsko Društvo *se:* **GD**

Geografíceskij Sbornik *P:* **Geogr Sb**

Geograpaphische Zeitschrift *d:* **Geogr Z**

Geographe Canadien *f:* **Geogr Can**

Geographenkalender *d:* **GK**

geographer *e:* **geo**, *e:* **geog**

Geographer *e:* **GEOGR**

Geographia *e:* **Geogr**, *l:* **GEOG**

Geographia Medica *e:* **GMDCB4**, *l:* **Geogr Med**

Geographia [of Ptolemy] *e:* **Geog**

Geographia Polonica *l:* **Geogr Pol**

Geographic *e:* **GEO**

Geographic Access *e:* **GA**

Geographic Air Surveys Ltd. *e:* **GSL**

Geographic Analysis *e:* **GA**

Geographic Analysis and Display System *e:* **GADS**

Geographic and Cartographic Research and Applications Section *e:* **GCRA**

Geographic and Land Information Society *e:* **GLIS**

Geographic Application Program *e:* **GAP**, *e:* **GA-PROGRAM**

Geographic Areas Reference Manual *e:* **GARM**

Geographic Base File[s] *e:* **GBF**

Geographic Base File[s]/Dual Independent Map Encoding *e:* **GBF/DIME**

Geographic Base Information System *e:* **GBIS**

Geographic-based Information Management System *e:* **GIMS**

Geographic-Catalog of Political and Statistical Areas *e:* **GEO-CAT**

Geographic Coordinate Transformation Package *e:* **GCTP**

Geographic Coordinate[s] Data Base *e:* **GCDB**

Geographic Correlator Exploration Machine *e:* **GCEM**

Geographic Correspondence Engine *e:* **Geocorr**

Geographic Cross-Reference Data *e:* **GEOBASE**

Geographic Data Analysis System *e:* **GDA**

Geographic Data Committee *e:* **GDC**

Geographic Data Council *e:* **GDC**

Geographic Data File[s] *e:* **GDF**

Geographic Data Format *e:* **GDF**

Geographic Data Management and Image Processing System *e:* **GEOMIPS**

Geographic Data Management System *e:* **GDMS**

Geographic Data, Overlay and Manipulation System *e:* **GEODOM**

Geographic Data Products *e:* **GDP**

Geographic Data Service *e:* **GDS**

Geographic Data Service Center *e:* **GDSC**

Geographic Data Technology, Incorporated *e:* **GDT**

Geographic Design and Implementation System *e:* **GEODIS**

Geographic Digest *e:* **GD**

Geographic Distribution *e:* **GD**

Geographic Distribution of Federal Funds Information System *e:* **GDFF**

Geographic Districting Information System for Maryland *e:* **GeoDIS**

Geographic Division *e:* **GEO**

Geographic Education National Implementation Project *e:* **GENIP**

Geographic Enforcement Initiative *e:* **GEI**

Geographic Entry System *e:* **GES**

Geographic Equivalent *e:* **GE**

Geographic File *e:* **GEOFILE**

Geographic Identification Code Scheme *e:* **GICS**

Geographic Incremental Plotting System *e:* **GIPSY**

Geographic Information *e:* **GI**

Geographic Information and Analysis Laboratory *e:* **GIAL**

Geographic Information and Modeling System *e:* **GIMS**

Geographic Information and Resource Technology Conference *e:* **GIRTC**

Geographic Information and Spatial Data Exposition and Conference *e:* **GISDEX**

Geographic Information Board *e:* **GIB**

Geographic Information Coordinating Committee *e:* **GICC**

Geographic Information Database *e:* **GIDB**

Geographic Information For Multiple Application *e:* **GEOMAP**

Geographic Information Index *e:* **GII**

Geographic Information Management Systems Committee *e:* **GIMS**

Geographic Information Management Technology *e:* **GIMT**

Geographic Information Mapping and Management System *e:* **GIMMS**

Geographic Information Officer *e:* **GIO**

Geographic Information Retrieval and Analysis *e:* **GIRA**

Geographic Information Retrieval and Analysis System *e:* **GIRAS**

Geographic Information Starter System *e:* **GISTARS**

Geographic Information System *e:* **GEOIS**

Geographic Information System Client Support Team *e:* **GISCST**, *e:* **GISSC**

Geographic Information System for Transportation *e:* **GIST**

Geographic Information System Laboratory *e:* **GISL**

Geographic Information System Steering Committee *e:* **GISWG**

Geographic Information System Toolkit *e:* **GIST**

Geographic Information System Tutorial *e:* **GIST**

Geographic Information Systems Bulletin Board *e:* **GISNET**

Geographic Information Systems Division *e:* **GISD**

Geographic Information Systems Interest Group *e:* **CISIG**

Geographic [information systems] Jobs Clearinghouse *e:* **GJC**

Geographic Information Visualisation (or Visualization) *e:* **GIV**

Geographic Intelligence and Topographic System *e:* **GIANT**

Geographic Investigations Office *e:* **GIO**

Geographic Location *e:* **GL**

Geographic Location Code *e:* **GEOLOC**

Geographic Location Profile *e:* **GLP**

Geographic Locations Code File System *e:* **GEOFILE**

Geographic Locator *e:* **GELO**

Geographic Macro Language *e:* **GML**

Geographic Map Attribute Enhancement *e:* **GEOMATE**

Geographic Measurement Systems *e:* **GMS**

Geographic Monitoring System *e:* **GEMS**

Geographic Names Information Service *e:* **GNIS**

Geographic Names Information System *e:* **GNIS**

Geographic Navigation *e:* **GEONAV**

Geographic OPAREA [Operating Area] Coordinates *e:* **GOAC**

Geographic or true *e:* **GEO**

Geographic Pactice Cost Index *e:* **GPCI**

Geographic Point *e:* **GP**

geographic position *e:* **gp**

Geographic Position Locator *e:* **G P L**

Geographic Processor System *e:* **GPS**

Geographic Query Language *e:* **GQL**

Geographic Reference *e:* **GECREF**

Geographic Reference File *e:* **GRF**

Geographic Reference File-Names *e:* **GRF-N**

Geographic Reference Identification Number *e:* **GRIN**

Geographic Reference Manual *e:* **GRM**

Geographic Reference System *e:* **GEOREF System**

Geographic Research Division *e:* **GRD**

Geographic Resources Center *e:* **GRC**

Geographic Scanning *e:* **GEOSCAN**

Geographic Sciences Laboratory *e:* **G S L**

Geographic Security *e:* **GEOSEC**

Geographic Snow Information System *e:* **GSIS**

Geographic Society of Chicago. Bulletin *e:* **Geog Soc Chicago B**

Geographic Support System *e:* **GSS**

Geographic survey data *e:* **GSD**

Geographic Survey Institute *e:* **GSI**

Geographic Systems Analysis *e:* **GSA**

Geographic Systems Corporation *e:* **GSC**

Geographic Systems, Incorporated *e:* **GSI**

Geographic Tabulation Unit Base *e:* **GTUB**

Geographic Town Management System *e:* **GeoTMS**

Geographic Township *e:* **GEOTp**

Geographic Underwriting System *e:* **GUS**

Geographic Update System *e:* **GUS**

Geographic Visualization *e:* **GVIS**

Geographic Web Resource Locator *e:* **GWRL**

Geographica *e:* **Geogr**

Geographica Bernensia *l:* **Geogr. Bern.**

Geographica Helvetica *e:* **GGHVA4,** *l:* **Geogr Helv**

Geographica [Lisbon] *p:* **GeoL**

geographic[al] *e:* **geog**

Geographic[al] *e:* **GEOGR**

geographical *e:* **geograph**

Geographical Abstracts *e:* **GeoAb,** *e:* **Geo Abstr,** *e:* **Geogr Abstr,** *e:* **Geogrl Abstr**

Geographical Analysis *e:* **Geogr Anal,** *e:* **Geogr Anal[r]**

Geographical and Topoaphical Texts of the Old Testament *e:* **GTT**

Geographical Association *e:* **GA**

Geographical Band Segmentation *e:* **GBS**

Geographical Bulletin *e:* **Geog Bul,** *e:* **Geogr B**

Geographical Computer Aided Design System *e:* **GCAD**

geographical coordinates *e:* **gc**

Geographical Data Description Directory *e:* **GDDD**

Geographical Data of Sweden *e:* **GSD**

Geographical Education *e:* **Geogr Ed,** *e:* **Geogr Ed[uc]**

Geographical Enforcement System *e:* **GES**

Geographical Engineering Field Division *e:* **GEFD**

Geographical Field Group *e:* **GFG**

Geographical Fluid Dynamics *e:* **GFD**

Geographical Full-Time *e:* **GFT**

Geographic[al] Information [and] Analysis *e:* **GIA**

Geographical Information Display System *e:* **GEOGRID**

Geographical Information Group *e:* **GIG**

Geographical Information Processing System *e:* **GIPS**

Geographic[al] Information System[s] *e:* **GIS**

Geographic[al] Information Systems International Group *e:* **GISIC**

Geographical Inter-University Resource Management Seminar *e:* **GIRMS**

Geographical Journal *e:* **GEJO,** *e:* **Geog J,** *e:* **Geogr J,** *e:* **Geogrl J,** *e:* **GGJOA,** *e:* **GJ,** *e:* **GJG,** *e:* **GJL**

Geographical Journal [London] *e:* **Geogr J [Lond]**

Geographical Knowledge [Peking] *e:* **Geogr Knowl [Peking]**

Geographical Location *e:* **GEOLOC,** *e:* **G. Loc.**

Geographical Magazine *e:* **GeM,** *e:* **GEMA,** *e:* **Geog M,** *e:* **GGMA-A,** *e:* **GM**

Geographical Magazine [London] *e:* **Geogr Mag [Lond]**

Geographical Names Register *e:* **GNR**

Geographical Observatories Programme *e:* **GOP**

Geographic[al] Operating Environment *e:* **GOE**

Geographical (or Geological) Long-Range Inclined ASDIC [Antisubmarine Detection Investigation Committee] *e:* **GLORIA**

Geographical Paper. Canada Department of Environment *e:* **GEPACDE**

Geographical Pole *e:* **GP**

Geographic[al] Position *e:* **GP**

Geographical Positioning System *e:* **GPS**

Geographical Problem Type Reports *e:* **GPTR**

Geographic[al] Reference System *e:* **GEOREF**

Geographical Referenced Data Storage and Retrieval *e:* **GRDSR**

Geographical Resource Analysis Software Package *e:* **GRASP**

Geographic[al] Resource[s] Analysis Support[ing] System *e:* **GRASS**

Geographical Review *e:* **Geog R,** *e:* **Geog Rev,** *e:* **Geogrl Rev,** *e:* **Geogr R,** *e:* **Geogr R[ev],** *e:* **Geo R,** *e:* **GEORAD,** *e:* **GR**

Geographical Review. American Geographical Society *e:* **AGS/GR**

Geographical Review [New York] *e:* **Geogr Rev [New York]**

Geographical Review of *e:* **GRIN-A**

Geographical Review of India *e:* **Geog R Ind,** *e:* **Geogr RI**

Geographical Review of Japan *e:* **Geogr Rev Jap**

Geographical Review of India *e:* **GRI**

Geographical Rotation *e:* **GEOROT**

Geographical Section [of the] General Staff *e:* **GSGS**

Geographical Situation *e:* **GEO/SIT**

Geographical Situation Display *e:* **GSD**

Geographical Society *e:* **GS**

Geographical Society of America *e:* **GSA**

Geographical Society of Chicago *e:* **GSC**

Geographical Society of Ireland *e:* **G.S.I.**

Geographical Society of Philadelphia *e:* **Geog Soc Phila,** *e:* **GSP**

Geographical Society of Philadelphia. Bulletin *e:* **Geog Soc Phila B**

Geographical Society of Philadelphia, Philadelphia, PA *e:* **PPGeo**

Geographical Specialist Team *e:* **GST**

Geographical statistics program *e:* **GSP**

Geographical Studies *e:* **Geogr Stud**

Geographical Survey *e:* **GS**

Geographical Survey Department *e:* **G.S.D.**

Geographical Survey Institute *e:* **GSI**

Geographical Teacher *e:* **GEOG T**

Geographically detailed Model *e:* **GEOM**

Geographically Disadvantaged States *e:* **GDS**

Geographically Impossible *e:* **GI**

Geographically Referenced Data Storage and Retrieval *e:* **G R D S R**

Geographically Referenced Data Storage and Retrieval System *e:* **GRDRS,** *e:* **GRDSR**

Geographically Separated Unit[s] *e:* **GSU**

Geographici Graeci Minores *e:* **GGM**

Geographic[s] Resources Information and Data System *e:* **GRIDS**

Geographie *d:* **geo,** *d:* **GEOG,** *d:* **Geogr.,** *d:* **GG,** *e:* **GG**

Geographie et Recherche *f:* **Georgr et Rech**

Geographie Physique et Quaternaire *f:* **Geog Phys et Quat**

geographisch *d:* **geogr.**

Geographisch-Ethnographische Gesellschaft Zürich d: **GEGZ**

Geographisch-Ethnologische Gesellschaft Basel d: **GEG**

geographische Breite d: **ge. B.**, d: **ge. Br.**, d: **geogr. Br.**

Geographische Gesellschaft d: **GG**

Geographische Gesellschaft in München. Jahresbericht d: **Geog Ges München Jber**

Geographische Gesellschaft Wien d: **GGW**

Geographische Gesellschaft zu Hannover d: **GGH**

Geographische Informationen d: **Geogr Inf**

geographische Lage d: **ge.L.**

Geographische Rundschau d: **Geog Rdsch**, d: **Geogr Rdsch**, d: **Geogr R[un]d[sch]**, d: **Geog Rund**

Geographische Zeitschrift d: **Geog Z**, d: **GgrZ**, d: **GZ**

Geographischer Jahresbericht aus Österreich d: **Geogr Jber Österr**

geographischer Katalog d: **GEOK**

geographischer Nord d: **ge. N.**

Geographisches Informationssystem d: **GIS**

Geographisches Jahrbuch d: **GJ**, d: **GJb**

Geographisches Jahrbuch aus Österreich d: **GJbÖ**

Geographisches Landinformationssystem d: **GEOLIS**

Geographisches Referenzsystem d: **GEOREF**

Geographisches Taschenbuch d: **Geogr TB**

Geographski Institut se: **GI**

geography e: **geo**

Geography e: **GEOG**, e: **Geogr**, e: **GGHY-A**, e: **GGHYAD**

Geography and Map [Division] e: **GM**

Geography and Map Division Bulletin e: **Geog Map Div Bull**

Geography Association of Thailand e: **GAT**

Geography Database for the United States e: **GeoB**

Geography Department, Carleton University, Ottawa, Ontario e: **OOCCG**

Geography Division e: **GEO**

Geography Markup Language e: **GML**

Geography Program e: **GP**

Geography Remote Sensing Unit e: **GRSU**

Geography Teacber e: **Geogr Teach**

Geography Teachers Association e: **GTA**

Geograpic Base System e: **GBS**

geográfico s: **Geo**

Geográfico o verdadero s: **GEO**

Geohydrodynamics and Environment Research e: **GHER**

Geohydrologic Information System e: **GIS**

Geohydrologic Map Editor e: **GME**

geohygiene e: **geohy**

GeoInfo Network e: **GIN**

GeoInfo Systems Magazine e: **GISM**

Geojournal e: **GEOJDQ**, e: **Geojournal**

Geokhimicheskie Issledovaniya P: **Geokhim Issled**

Geokhimicheskie Metody Poiskov. Nefti i Gaza R: **Geokhim Metody Poiskov Nefti Gaza**

Geokhimicheskie Metody pri Poiskakh i Razvedke Rudnykh Mestorozhdenii R: **Geokhim Metody Poiskakh Razred Rudn Mestorozhd**

Geokhimicheskii Sbornik P: **Geokhim Sb**, R: **GKSBA**

Geokhimiya P: **Geokhim**

Geokhimiya i Rudoobrazovanie P: **Geokhim Rudoobraz**

Geokhimiya, Mineralogiya i Petrologiya R: **Geokhim Mineral Petrol**

Geokinetic Data Acquisition System e: **GDAS**

Geokinetics e: **GEOK**

Geolagical Society of London. Transactions. Proceedings. Quarterly Journal e: **G Soc London Tr Pr Q J**

Geologe d: **Geol.**

geologi a: **geol**

Geologi [Helsinki] F: **GEOHAH**

Geologia Applicata e Idrogeologia e: **Geol Appl Idrogeol**

Geologia Colombiana e: **Geol Colomb**

Geologia e Metalurgia [Sao Paulo] p: **Geol Metal [Sao Paulo]**

Geologia Sudetica e: **GLSDA6**, l: **Geol Sudetica**

Geologia Sudetica [Warsaw] P: **Geol Sudetica [Warsaw]**

Geologia Tecnica i: **Geol Tec**

Geologia y Metalurgia [Bolivia] s: **Geol Metal**

Geologia y Metalurgia [San Luis Potosi] s: **Geol Metal [San Luis Potosi]**

Geologial, Mining and Metallurgical Society of India. Quarterly Journal e: **Geol Min Metall Soc India Q J**

Geologial Repons. Shimane Univetsity e: **Geol Rep Shimane Unir**

Geologial Society of Malaysia. Bulletin e: **Geol Soc Malays Bull**

Geologian Tutkimuskeskus F: **GT**

geologic e: **geol**

Geologic Aspects of Rivers e: **GAR**

Geologic Atlas of Pennsylvania e: **Geol Atlas PA**

Geologic Division e: **GD**

Geologic Inquiries Group e: **GIG**

Geologic Map e: **GM**

Geologic Map and Mineral Resources. Summary [State of Tennessee] e: **Geol Map Miner Resour Summ [State Tennessee]**

Geologic Map. Deputy Ministry for Mineral Resources [Kingdom of Saudi Arabia] e: **Geol Map Deputy Minist Miner Resour [Saudi Arabia]**, e: **Geol Map Deputy Minist Miner Resour [Saudi Arabia]**

Geologic Map Index e: **GMI**

Geologic Map. Montana Bureau of Mines and Geology e: **Geol Map Montana Bur Mina Geol**, e: **Geol Map Montana Bur Mines Geol**

Geologic Map Standards Committee e: **GMSC**

Geologic Mapping and Framework Studies e: **GMFS**

Geologic Mapping and Framework Studies Group e: **GMFSG**

Geologic Names Committee e: **GNC**

Geologic Names of the United States e: **GEONAMES**

Geologic Names Unit e: **GNU**

Geologic Names Unit Lexicon e: **GNULEX**

Geologic Quadrangle e: **GQ**

Geologic Quadrangle Maps e: **GQM**

Geologic Record of Global Change e: **GRGC**

Geologic Records and Samples Library e: **GRSL**

Geologic Remote Sensing Field Experiment e: **GRSFE**

Geologic Report. State of Alaska Department of Natural Resources e: **Geol Rep State Alaska Dep Nat Resour**

Geologic repository operations area e: **GROA**

Geologic Review Group e: **GRG**

Geologic Satellite [program] e: **Geosat**

Geologic Section Program e: **GSP**

Geologic Spatial Analysis e: **GSA**

Geologic Surface Model e: **GSM**

Geologic Synthetic Aperture Radar e: **GEOSAR**

Geologica Balcania e: **GE8AD2**

Geologica Balcanica e: **Geol Balc**

Geologica Bavarica e: **GEBAAX**, e: **Geol Bav**, l: **Geol Bav[arica]**

Geologica et Palaeontologica e: **Geol Palaeontol**

Geologica Hungarica e: **Geol Hung**

Geologica Hungarica. Series Palaeontologica e: **GHPADP**, l: **Geol Hung Ser Palaeontol**

Geologica Romana e: **Geol Rom**, e: **Geol Roman**, l: **Geol Rom[an]**, l: **GROMAL**

Geologica Ultriectina i: **Geol Ultriectina**

Geologic[al] e: **GEOL**

Geological Abstracts e: **Geol Abstr**

Geological Analysis Aid Package e: **GAAP**

Geological and Geophysical Sciences e: **GAGS**

Geological and Mining Society e: **G M Soc Am Univ Y Bk**

Geological and Planetary Sciences e: **GPS**

Geological and Scientific Bulletin e: **G Sc B**

Geologic[al] Applications of Remote Sensing e: **GARS**

Geological Assistance for Siting Solid Waste Facilities e: **GASSWF**

Geological Association e: **G.A.**

Geological Association of Canada e: **GAC**, e: **Geol Assoc Can**, e: **Geol Assoc Can**

Geological Association of Canada. Cordilleran Section. Programme and Abstracts e: **Geol Assoc Can Cordilleraa Sect Programme Abstr**

Geological Association of Canada. Proceedings e: **Geol Assoc Canada Proc**

Geological Association of Canada. Special Papers e: **Geol Assoc Can Spec Pap**

Geological Bulletin. e: **Geol Bull Natl Geol Surv China**

Geological Bulletin. National Geological Survey of China [China] e: **Geol Bull Nat Geol Surv China**

Geological Bulletin. Punjab University e: **Geol Bull Punjab Univ**

Geological Bulletin. University of Peshawar e: **Geol Bull Univ Peshawar**

Geological Center. Research Series *e:*
Geol Center Research Ser, *e:* **Geol
Center Res Ser**

Geological Characterization Report *e:*
GCR

Geological Correlation *e:* **Geol Correl**

Geological Curators Group *e:* **GCG**

Geological Data Center *e:* **GDC**

Geologic[al] Depository *e:* **GD**

Geologic[al] Disposal Technology Program
e: **GDTP**

Geological Echo Profiler *e:* **GEP**

Geological Editor of Field Notes *e:* **GEOF**

Geological Engineer *e:* **Ge Eng,** *e:* **Ge
Engr,** *e:* **Geol E**

Geological Engineer[ing] *e:* **GE**

Geological Engineering Technologist *e:*
GET

Geological Engineering Technology *e:*
GET

Geological Enginneering Geology and
Geophysics *e:* **GEGG**

Geological, Exploration and Development
Information System *e:* **GEDIS**

Geological Exploration and Mapping
System *e:* **GEMS**

Geologic[al] Exploration Department *e:*
GED

Geological Image Analysis Program
Package *e:* **GIAPP**

Geological Information and Name
Tabulating System *e:* **GIANT,** *e:*
GIANT System

Geological Information Group *e:* **GIG**

Geological Information System[s] *e:* **GIS**

Geological Institute *e:* **GI**

Geological Journal *e:* **Geol J,** *e:* **Geol. J.**

Geological Journal [Liverpool] *e:* **Geol J
[Liverpool]**

Geological Journal. Liverpool Geological
Society and the Manchester Geological
Association. Liverpool *e:* **LGS/GJ.**

Geological Journal of Queen Mary College
e: **Geol J Queen Mary Coll**

Geological Laboratory, Saskatchewan
Depanment of Energy and Mines, Regina,
Saskatchewan *e:* **SRSEMG**

Geological Magazine *e:* **GEMGA4,** *e:*
Geol M, *e:* **Geol M[ag],** *e:* **Geol.Mag.,** *e:*
GM, *e:* **G Mag**

Geological Map of Japan *e:* **GMJ**

Geological Memoirs. Geological Survey of
China. Series A *e:* **Geol Mem Geol Surv
China Ser A**

Geological Memoirs. Geological Survey of
China.Series B *e:* **Geol Mem Geol Surv
China Ser B**

Geological, Mining and Metallurgical
Society of India *e:* **GMMSI**

Geological, Mining and Metallurgical
Society of Liberia. Bulletin *e:* **Geol Min
Met[all] Soc Liberia Bull**

Geological Museum of Great Britain *e:*
GM

Geological Notes and Local Details for
1:10\000 Sheets. Institute of Geological
Sciences *e:* **Geol Notes Local De
1:10000 Sheets Inst Geol Sci**

Geological Paper. Carleton *e:* **Geol Pap
Carleton**

Geological Paper. Carleton University.
Department of Geology *e:* **Geol Pap
Carleton Univ Dep Geol**

Geological Paper. Mineral Resources
Division [Manitoba] *e:* **Geol Pap Miner
Resour Dir [Manitoba]**

Geological Papers. Geological Survey of
Malaysia *e:* **Geol Pap Geol Surv
Malaysia**

Geological Prospecting *e:* **GP**

Geological Publishing House *e:* **GPH**

Geological Records Unit *e:* **GRU**

Geological Reference File [Database] *e:*
GEOREF

Geological Reference [System] *e:*
GEOREF

Geological Report. Hiroshima University
e: **Geol Rep Hiroshima Univ**

Geological Report. Mineral Resources
Division [Manitoba] *e:* **Geol Rep Miner
Resour Dir [Manitoba],** *e:* **Geol Rep
Miner Resour Div [Manitoba]**

Geological Reports *e:* **Geo Rep**

Geological Reports. Department of Natural
Resources [Quebec] *e:* **Geol Rep Dep
Nat Resour [Queb]**

Geological Reports. Shimane University *e:*
Geol Rep Shimane Univ

Geological Resource Study *e:* **GEROS**

Geological Review [Beijing] *e:* **Geol Rev
[Beijing]**

Geological Sciences Gopher Server *e:* **GSGS**

Geological Section. Bulletin. Libya
Ministry of Industry *e:* **Geol Sect Bull
Libya Minist Ind**

Geological Service *e:* **GS**

Geological Socety of America. Bulletin *e:*
Geol Soc Bull

Geological Society Newsletter *e:* **GSN**

Geological Society. Newsletter [London]
e: **Geol Soc [Lond] Newsl**

Geological Society of Africa *e:* **GSA**

Geological Society [of America] *e:* **GS**

Geological Society of America *e:* **GSA**

Geological Society of America. Abstracts
Programms *e:* **Geol Soc Am Abstr
Programs**

Geological Society of America. Abstracts
with Programs *e:* **Geol Soc Am Abst
Programs,** *e:* **Geol Soc America Abs
with Prog**

Geological Society of America. Annual
Meeting. Field Trip Guidebook *e:* **Geol
Soc Am Annu Meet Field Trip Guideb**

Geological Society of America. Bulletin *e:*
Geol S Am B, *e:* **Geol Soc Am Bull,** *e:*
Geol Soc Am[er] Bull, *e:* **G Soc Am B**

Geological Society of America. Cordilleran
Section. Annual Meeting Guidebook *e:*
**Geol Soc Am Cordilleran Sect Annu
Meet Guideb**

Geological Society of America. Engineering
Geology Case Histories *e:* **Geol Soc
Amer Eng Geol Case Hist**

Geological Society of America Inc. *e:*
GSAI

Geological Society of America. Map and
Chart Series *e:* **Geol Soc Am Map
Chart Ser**

Geological Society of America. Memoir *e:*
Geol Soc Am[er] Mem, *e:* **GSAMAQ**

Geological Society of America. Memoir[s]
e: **Geol Soc Am Mem**

Geological Society of America. Microform
Publicalion *e:* **Geol Soc Am Microform
Publ**

Geological Society of America. Proceedings
e: **Geol Soc Am Proc,** *e:* **Geol Soc Proc**

Geological Society of America.
Sootheastern Section Guidebook *e:* **Geol
Soc Am Southeast Sect Guideb**

Geological Society of America. Special
Paper *e:* **Geol Soc America Spec Paper,**
e: **Geol Soc Am[er] Spec Pap**

Geological Society of America. Special
Paper [Regional Studies] *e:* **Geol Soc
Am Spec Pap [Reg Stud],** *e:* **GSAPAZ**

Geological Society of Australia *e:* **GSA**

Geological Society of Australia Journal *e:*
Geol Soc Australia J

Geological Society of Chicago *e:* **GSC**

Geological Society of China *e:* **G.S.C.**

Geological Society of China. Proceedings
e: **Geol Soc China Proc**

Geological Society of Dublin. Journal *e:* **G
Soc Dublin J**

Geological Society of Edinburgh *e:* **GSE**

Geological Society of Egypt. Annual
Meeting. Abstracts *e:* **Geol Soc Egypt
Annu Meet Abstr**

Geological Society of Finland. Bulletin *e:*
Geol Soc Finl Bull

Geologica[l] Society of Flemish Americans
e: **GSFA**

Geological Society of Glasgow *e:* **GSG**

Geological Society of Glasgow.
Transactions *e:* **G Soc Glas Tr**

Geological Society of Great Britain *e:*
GSGB

Geological Society of Greece. Bulletin *e:*
Geol Soc Greece Bull

Geological Society of India. Bulletin *e:*
Geol Soc India Bull

Geological Society of India Journal *e:*
Geol Soc India Jour

Geological Society of India. Memoir *e:*
Geol Soc India Mem

Geological Society of India.Bulletin *e:*
GSIBAX

Geological Society of Iraq. Journal *e:* **Geol
Soc Iraq J**

Geological Society of Jamaica Journal *e:*
Geol Soc Jam J

Geological Society of Japan. Journal *e:*
Geol Soc Jap J

Geological Society of Korea. Journal *e:*
Geol Soc Korea J

Geological Society of London *e:* **G.L.S.**

Geological Society of London. Journal *e:*
Geol Soc Lond J

Geological Society of London. Memoirs *e:*
Geol Soc London Mem

Geological Society of London.
Miscellaneous Paper *e:* **Geol Soc Lond
Misc Pap**

Geological Society of London. Quarterly
Journal *e:* **Geol Soc Lond Q J**

Geological Society of London. Special
Report *e:* **Geol Soc Lond Spec Rep**

Geological Society of Malaysia. *e:* **Geol
Soc Malays**

Geological Society of Malaysia *e:* **GSM**

Geological Society of Malaysia Bulletin *e:*
Geol 5oc Malays Bull

Geological Society of Malaysia. Bulletin
e: **GSMBBK**

Geological Society of Malaysia. Newsletter
e: **Geol Soc Malays Newsl**

Geological Society of Malaysia Newsletter
e: **GSMNBM**

Geological Society of New Jersey. Report
e: **Geol Soc NJ Rept**

Geological Society of New Zealand. *e:*
Geol Soc NZ

Geological Society of New Zealand *e:*
GSNZ

Geological Society of New Zealand.
Newsletter *e:* **Geol Soc NZ Newsl**

Geological Society of Norfolk. Bulletin *e:*
Geol Soc Norfolk Bull

Geological Society of Pennsylvania.
Transactions *e:* **G Soc PA Tr**

Geological Society [of] South Africa *e:*
GSSA

Geological Society of South Africa.
Congress Abstracts *e:* **Geol Soc S Afr
Congr Abstr**

Geological Society of South Africa.
Quarterly News Bulletin *e:* **Geol Soc S
Afr Q News Bull,** *e:* **GSQNA**

Geological Society of South Africa. Special
Publication *e:* **Geol Soc S Afr Spec
Publ**

Geological Society of South Africa.
Transactions *e:* **Geol Soc S Afr Trans**

Geological Society of South Africa.
Transactions and Proceedings *e:* **Geol
Soc So Africa Trans**

Geological Society of. Special Publication
e: **Geol Soc Zimbabwe Spec Publ**

Geological Society of the Oregon Country.
Newsletter *e:* **Geol Soc Oregon
Country Newsl**

Geological Society of the Philippines.
Journal *e:* **Geol Soc Philipp J**

Geological Society of Tokyo. Journal *e:* **G
Soc Tokyo J**

Geological Society of Zimbabwe *e:* **GSZ**

Geological Survey *e:* **Geol Surv,** *e:* **GS**

Geological Survey Analytical Data Sorage
and Retrieval System *e:* **GEODAT**

Geological Survey and Mines Department
e: **GSMD**

Geological Survey and Mining Authority
e: **EGSMA**

Geological Survey and Museum of Practical
Geology of Great Britain and Northern
Ireland *e:* **GSGB**

Geological Survey Bulletin *e:* **Geol. Surv.
Bull.**

Geological Survey Circular *e:* **Geol Surv
Circ**

Geological Survey Department *e:* **GSD**

Geological Survey Department [Jamaica,
West Indies]. Occasional Paper *e:* **Geol
Surv Dep [Jam West Indies] Occas Pap**

Geological Survey Department [Jamaica,
West Indies]. Bulletin *e:* **Geol Surv Dep
[Jam] Bull**

Geological Survey [Department of the
Interior] *e:* **G.S.**

Geological Survey Division *e:* **GSD**

Geological Survey Institute *e:* **GSI**

Geological [survey] Local Area Network
e: **GEOLAN**

Geological Survey. Mineral Industry of
New South Wales [A publication] *e:*
Geol Surv NSW Miner Ind NSW

Geological Survey of Alabama *e:* **GS,** *e:*
GSA

Geological Survey of British Guiana. *e:*
Geol Surv Br Guiana Bull

Geological Survey of Canada *e:*
GEOSCAN, e: GSC

Geological Survey of Canada. Bulletin *e:*
Geol Surv Can Bull

Geological Survey of Canada. Economic
Geology Report *e:* **Geol Surv Can Econ
Geol Rep**

Geological Survey of Canada. Memoir *e:*
Geol Surv Can Mem, *e:* **GSCM**

Geological Survey of Canada Ottawa,
Ontario *e:* **OOG**

Geological Survey of Canada. Paper *e:*
Geol Surv Can Pap, *e:* **GSCP**

Geological Survey of Canada.Bulletin *e:*
GSCB[ul]

Geological Survey of Ceylon. Memoir *e:*
Geol Surv Ceylon Mem

Geological Survey of Denmark. II Series
e: **Geol Surv Den II Ser**

Geological Survey of Denmark. III Series
e: **Geol Surv Den III Ser**

Geological Survey of Denmark. Report *e:*
Geol Surv Den Rep

Geological Survey of Denmark. Serie A *e:*
Geol Surv Den Ser A

Geological Survey of Denmark. Serie B *e:*
Geol Surv Den Ser B

Geological Survey of Denmark. Yearbook
e: **Geol Surv Den Yearb**

Geological Survey of Estonia *e:* **GSE**

Geological Survey of Finland *e:* **GSF,** *e:*
GTK

Geological Survey of Finland. Bulletin *e:*
Geol Surv Finl Bull, *e:* **GSFNAK**

Geological Survey of Georgia Bulletin *e:*
Geol Surv GA Bull

Geological Survey of Great Britain *e:*
GSGB

Geological Survey of Great Britain and
Museum of Practical Geology *e:* **GSM**

Geological Survey of Great Britain.
Memoirs of the Geological Survey
[Scotland] *e:* **Geol Surv GB Mem Geol
Surv [Scotl]**

Geological Survey of Greenland *e:* **GGU**

Geological Survey of Greenland. Report *e:*
Geol Surv Greenland Rep

Geological Survey of Guyana. Bulletin *e:*
Geol Surv Guyana Bull

Geological Survey of India. *e:* **Geol Surv
India**

Geological Survey of India *e:* **GSI**

Geological Survey of India. Miscellaneous
Publication *e:* **Geol Surv India Misc
Publ**

Geological Survey of India News *e:* **Geol
Surv India News**

Geological Survey of Inland. Bulletin *e:*
GSFB

Geological Survey of Iran *e:* **GSI**

Geological Survey of Iran. Report *e:* **Geol
Surv Iran Rep,** *e:* **Geol Surv Iran Rep**

Geological Survey of Ireland *e:* **GSI**

Geological Survey of Ireland. Bulletin *e:*
Geol Surr Irel Bull, *e:* **Geol Surv Irel
Bull**

Geological Survey of Israel *e:* **GSI,** *e:* **IGS**

Geological Survey of Israel. Bulletin *e:*
Geol Surv Isr Bull

Geological Survey of Japan. *e:* **Geol Surv
Jap**

Geological Survey of Japan *e:* **GSJ**

Geological Survey of Japan.
Hydrogeological Maps of Japan *e:* **Geol
Surv Jap Hydrogeol Maps Jap**

Geological Survey of Japan. Report *e:*
Geol Surv Jap Rep, *e:* **Geol Surv Jpn
Rep**

Geological Survey of Kenya *e:* **GSK**

Geological Survey of Kenya. Bulletin *e:*
Geol Surv Kenya Bull

Geological Survey of Kenya. Report *e:*
Geol Surv Kenya Rep

Geological Survey of Korea. Technical
Paper *e:* **Geol Surv Korea Tech Pap**

Geological Survey of Malaysia. Annual
Report *e:* **Geol Surv Malays Annu Rep**

Geological Survey of Malaysia. District
Memoir *e:* **Geol Surv Malays Dist Mem**

Geological Survey of Malaysia. Geological
Papers *e:* **Geol Surv Malays Geol Pap**

Geological Survey of Malaysia.District
Memoir *e:* **GSMMBJ**

Geological Survey of Malaysia.Geological
Papers *e:* **GSMPAR**

Geological Survey of Namibia *e:* **GSN**

Geological Survey of New South Wales.
Bulletin *e:* **Geol Surv NSW Bull**

Geological Survey of New South Wales.
Department of Mines. The Mineral
Industry of New South Wales *e:* **Geol
Surv of NSW Miner Ind NSW**

Geological Survey of New South Wales.
Geological Survey Report *e:* **Geol Surv
NSW Geol Surv Rep,** *e:* **Geol Surv NSW
Rep**

Geological Survey of Nigeria. Bulletin *e:*
Geol Surv Nigeria Bull

Geological Survey of Northern Ireland *e:*
GSNI

Geological Survey of Pakistan *e:* **GSP**

Geological Survey of Queensland *e:* **GSQ**

Geological Survey of Queensland.
Publication *e:* **Geol Surv Queensl Pub,**
e: **Geol Surv Queensl Publ**

Geological Survey of Queensland. Report
e: **Geol Surv Queensl Rep**

Geological Survey of Sierra Leone. Bulletin
e: **Geol Surv Sierra Leone Bull**

Geological Survey of Sweden *e:* **SGU**

Geological Survey of Tanzania. Builetin *e:*
Geol Surr Tanzania Bull

Geological Survey of Tanzania. Bulletin *e:*
Geol Surv Tanzania Bull

Geological Survey of Tasmania. Bulletin
e: **Geol Surv Bull Tasmania**

Geological Survey of Uganda. Memoir *e:*
Geol Surv Uganda Mem

Geological Survey of Uganda. Report *e:*
Geol Surv Uganda Rep

Geological Survey of Victoria *e:* **GSV**

Geological Survey of Victoria. Bulletin *e:*
Geol Surv Victoria Bull

Geological Survey of Victoria. Memoir *e:*
Geol Surv Victoria Mem

Geological Survey of West Malaysia.
District Memoir *e:* **Geol Surv West
Malaysia Dist Mem**

Geological Survey of Western Australia *e:*
GSWA

Geological Survey of Western Australia.
Bulletin *e:* **Geol Surv W Aust Bull,** *e:*
Geol Surv West Aust Bull

Geological Survey of Wyoming *e:* **GSW**

Geological Survey of Wyoming. Bulletin
  e: **Geol Surv Wyo Bull**

Geological Survey of Wyoming County
  Resource Series *e:* **Geol Surv Wyo C
  Resour Ser**

Geological Survey of Wyoming. Memoir
  e: **Geol Surv Wyo Mem**

Geological Survey of Wyoming.
  Preliminary Report *e:* **Geol Surv Wyo
  Prelim Rep**

Geological Survey of Wyoming. Report of
  Investigations *e:* **Geol Surv Wyo Rep
  Invest**

Geological Survey of Zambia *e:* **GSZ**

Geological Survey Open-File Report *e:*
  GSORD

Geological Survey Paper. Department of
  Mines. Tasmania *e:* **Geol Surv Pap Tas
  Dep Mines**

Geological Survey Papua New Guinea *e:*
  GSPNG

Geological Survey Report. Department of
  Mines [New South Wales] *e:* **Geol Surv
  Rep Dep Mines [NSW]**

Geological Survey Research Committee *e:*
  GSRC

Geological Survey, Reston *e:* **GSR**

Geological Survey Triga Reactor *e:* **GSTR**

Geological Survey-Water Resources
  Division *e:* **GS-WRD**

Geological Survey, Water Resources
  Division, Helena *e:* **GIH**

Geological Testing Consultant *e:* **GTC**

Geological Time Scale *e:* **GTS**

Geologically-Related Web Resources *e:*
  GRWR

Geologicargia Speakers Association *e:*
  GSA

Geologicheskaya Izuchennost SSR *R:*
  Geol Izuch SSR

Geologicheskaya Literatura SSSR
  Bibliografioheskiy Yezhegodnik *R:*
  Geol Lit SSSR Bibliogr Yezhegodnik

Geologicheskii Sbornik *R:* **Geol Sbornik**

Geologicheskii Sbornik [Lvov] *R:* **Geol Sb
  [Lvov]**

Geologicheskii Sbornik [Tiflis] *R:* **Geol
  Sb [Tiflis]**

Geologicheskii Zhurnal [Kiev] *R:* **Geol Zh**

Geologicheskii Zhurnal [Russian Edition]
  R: **Geol Zb [Russ Ed]**

Geologicheskii Zhurnal [Russian Editíon]
  R: **Geol Zh [Russ Ed]**

Geologicheskoe Stroenie i Poleznye
  Iskopaemye Kalmytskoi ASSR *R:* **Geol
  Str Poleznye Iskop Kalmytskoi ASSR**

Geologichnii Zhurnal [Ukrainian Edition]
  U: **Geol Zh [Ukr Ed]**

Geologicke Prace *c:* **Geol Pr**

Geologicke Prace [Bratislava] *P:*
  GE0PA7, *c:* **Geol Pr [Bratisl],** *c:*
  GEOPA[B]

Geologicke Prace. Zpravy *c:* **Geol Prace Zpr**

Geologicky Pruzkum *P:* **Geol Pruzkum,**
  P: **GEYPA**

Geologicky Zbornik *c:* **Geol Zb,** *c:*
  GESBA, *c:* **GESBAJ**

Geologicky Zbornik-Geologica Carpathica
  c: **Geol Zb Geol Carpathica**

Geologicky Zbornik-Geologica Carpathica.
  Slovenska Akademia Vied *c:* **Geol Zb
  Slov Akad Vied**

Geologicky Ústav Dionyz Stur *c:* **GUDS**

Geologie *d:* **Geol**

Geologie Alpine *d:* **Geol Alp**

Geologie Appliquee et Prospection Miniere
  f: **Geol Appl Prospect Miniere**

Geologie. Beihefte *d:* **Geol Beih**

Geologie. Bulletin de la Société Belge de
  Geologie *f:* **Geol Bull Soc Belge Geol**

Geologie de la France *f:* **Geol Fr**

Geologie en Mijnbouw *n:* **GEMIA[A],** *n:*
  Geologie Mijnb

Geologie en Mijnbouw. Koninklijk
  Nederlands Geologisch Minjnbouwkundig
  Genootschap. The Hague *n:*
  KMGMG/GM.

Geologie en Mijnbouw [Netherlands] *n:*
  Geol. Mijnb.

Geologie Mediterraneenne *f:* **Geol
  Mediter**

Geologie und Bauwesen *d:* **Geol Bauwes**

Geologiese Vereniging van Suid-Afrika.
  Kwartaallikse Nuusbulletin *A:* **Geol Ver
  S-Afr Kwart Nuusbull**

Geologija *R:* **Geol**

Geologija. Razprave in Porocila *P:* **Geol
  Razpr Porocila**

Geologikai Anagnoriseis Ekthesis *H:* **Geol
  Anagoriseis Ekthesis**

Geologikai kai Geofizikai Meletai *H:* **Geol
  Geohz Meletai**

Geologikai kaí Geofizikai Meletai *P:* **Geol
  Geofiz Meletai**

geologisch *d:* **geol.,** *d:* **geolog.**

Geologisch Mijnbouwkundige Dienst van
  Suriname *n:* **GMD**

Geologische Blaetter für Nordost-Bayern
  und *d:* **Geol BI**

Geologische Blätter für Nordost-Bayern und
  Angrenzende Gebiete *d:* **Geol Bl
  [Nordost-Bayern Angrenzende Geb]**

Geologische Bundesanstalt *d:* **GB,** *d:*
  GBA, *d:* **Geol.B.A.**

Geologische Expedition in die Shackleton
  Range *d:* **GEISHA**

Geologische Forschung und Erkundung *d:*
  GFE

Geologische Landesanstalt *d:* **Geol. L.A.,**
  d: **GLA**

Geologische Reichs-Museum in Leiden.
  Sammlungen *n:* **G Reichs-Mus Leiden
  Samm**

Geologische Rundschau *d:* **GeolR,** *d:* **Geol
  Rundsch,** *d:* **GERUA,** *d:* **GRundschau**

Geologische Staatsanstalt *d:* **Geol. St.A.**

Geologische Substratherkunft *d:* **GEH**

Geologische Übersichtskarte *d:* **GÜK**

Geologische und paläontologische
  Abhandlungen *d:* **GPAbh**

Geologische Vereinigung *d:* **Geol.V.**

Geologisches Archiv *d:* **GeolA**

Geologisches Landesamt Baden-
  Württemberg *d:* **GLAB-W**

Geologisches Landesamt Bayern *d:* **GLAB**

Geologisches Landesamt des Saarlandes *d:*
  GLAS

Geologisches Landesamt Nordrhein-
  Westfalen *e:* **GLAN-W**

Geologisches Landesamt NRW *e:* **GLA**

Geologisches Landesamt Rheinland-Pfalz
  d: **GLR-P**

Geologisches Landesamt Schleswig-
  Holstein *d:* **GLAS-H**

geologisk *a:* **geol**

Geologiska Foereningens i Stockbolm.
  Foerhandlingar *r:* **Geol Foer[en]
  St[ockh] Foerh**

Geologiska Foereningens i Stockholm.
  Foerhandlingar *r:* **GFF**

Geologiska Foereningens i Stockholm.
  [Foerhandlingar] *r:* **G Foeren
  Stockholm Foerh**

Geologiska Foereningens i Stockholm.
  Foerhandlingar *r:* **GFSFA**

Geologiska Forskningsanstalten *r:* **GF**

Geologist *e:* **GEO**

geologist *e:* **geol**

Geologist *e:* **GLGST**

Geologist [New York] *e:* **GLGSA**

Geologist Registration Act *e:* **GRA**

Geologists and Geophysicists Board of
  Registration *e:* **G&GBR**

Geologists' Association *e:* **GA**

Geologists' Association [London].
  Proceedings *e:* **Geol Assoc [Lond] Proc**

Geologists' Association London.
  Proceedings *e:* **Geologists' Assoc
  [London] Pro**

Geologiya i Geofizika *P:* **Geol i Geofíz,** *R:*
  Geol. Geofiz., *R:* **GGASA**

Geologiya i Geokhimiya *P:* **Geol
  Geokhim**

Geologiya i Geokhimiya Goryuchikh
  Iskopaemykh *R:* **Geol Geokhim
  Goryuch Iskop**

Geologiya i Geokhimiya Mestorozbdenii
  Tverdykh Goryuchikh Iskopaemykh *R:*
  **Geol Geokhim Mestorozhd Tverd
  Goryucb Iskop**

Geologiya i Geokhimiya Neftyanskh i
  Gazovykh Mestorozhdenii *R:* **Geol
  Geolthlm Neft Gazor Mestorozhd**

Geologiya i Mineralogiya *R:* **Geol
  Mineral**

Geologiya i Neftegazonosnost
  Turkmenistana *R:* **GNTUD**

Geologiya i Polezne Iskopaemye Urala *R:*
  Geol Polezn Iskop Urala

Geologiya i Polezne Iskopaemye
  Zapadnogo Kazakhstana *R:* **Geol Polezn
  Iskop Zapadn Kaz**

Geologiya i Razvedka Gazovykh i
  Gazokondensatnykh Mestornzhdenii *R:*
  **Geol Razred Gazov Gazokondens
  Mestorozhd**

Geologiya i Rudonosnost Yuga Ukrainy *R:*
  Geol Rudonosn Yuga Ukr, *R:* **Geol
  Rudonosn Yuga Ukr**

Geologiya Mestorozhdenii Redkikh
  Elementov *R:* **Geol Mestorozhd Redk
  Elem**

Geologiya. Metodika i Tekhnika Razvedki.
  Laboratorye Raboty *R:* **Geol Metod
  Tekh Razved Lab Rab**

Geologiya Morya *R:* **Geol Morya**

Geologiya Nefti *R:* **Geol Nefti**

Geologiya Nefti i Gaza *P:* **Geol Nefti
  Gaza,** *R:* **GENGA,** *R:* **Geol Nefti [i]
  Gaza**

Geologiya Nefti i Gaza Severo-Vostoka
  Evropeiskoi Chasti SSSR *R:* **Geol Nefti
  Gaza Ser Vostoka Evr Chasti SSSR**

Geologiya Poberezh'ya i Dna Chernogo i
  Azovskogo Morei v Predelakh Ukrainskoi
  SSR *R:* **Geol Poberezh'ya Dna Chern
  Azovskogo Morei Predela**

Geologiya, Poiski i Razvedka Nerudnykh Poleznykh Iskopaemykh *R:* **Geol Poiski Rasved Nerudn Polezn Iskop**, *R:* **GPRID**

Geologiya Rudnykh Mestorozhdenii *R:* **Geol Rud[n] Mestorozbd**, *R:* **Geol Rud Mestorozhd**, *R:* **GRMAA**

Geologiya SSSR *R:* **Geol SSSR**

Geologiya Zakaspiya *P:* **Geol Zakaspiya**

Geologlya i Geofizika *e:* **Geol Geofiz**

Geologues *f:* **GEOLB**

geology *e:* **geo**

Geology *e:* **GEOL**

Geology and Geophysic. Academy of Sciences *e:* **GGR**

Geology and Geophysics *e:* **Geol. Geophys.**

Geology and Geophysics Index *e:* **GGI**

Geology and Geophysics Number Crunchers Forum *e:* **GGNCF**

Geology and Palaeontology of Southeast Asia *e:* **Geol Palaeontol Southeast Asia**

Geology Archive [Database] *e:* **GEOARCHIVE**

Geology at Radford University *e:* **GRU**

Geology [Boulder] *e:* **GLGYBA**

Geology Club of Puerto Rico. *e:* **Geology Club Puerto Rico**

Geology Club of Puerto Rico. Bulletin *e:* **Geology Club Puerto Rico Bull**

Geology Digital Inventory *e:* **GEOLIN**

Geology. Exploration and Mining in British Columbia *e:* **Geol Explor Min BC**

Geology Facts on File *e:* **GFF**

Geology Gems from Winona *e:* **GGW**

Geology Gems from Winona State University *e:* **GGWSU**

Geology Map and Mineral Resources Summary. North Carolina Geological Survey *e:* **Geol Map Miner Resour Summ North Carolina Geol Sur**

Geology of Pennsylvania *e:* **G PA**

Geology Oriented Database System *e:* **GEODAS**

Geologíja *P:* **Geol**

Geolokhi Glasnik *se:* **Geol G1as**

Geoloski Glasnik. Posebna Izdanja *se:* **Geol G1as Posebna Izd**

Geoloski Glasnik [Titograd] *se:* **Geol Glas [Titograd Yugosl]**

Geološki Institut Jugoslavije *se:* **G.I.J.**

Geoloski Vjesnik *se:* **GEVJA**, *se:* **GEVJAO**

Geoloski Vjesnik [Zagreb] *P:* **Geol Vjesn [Zagreb]**

Geološki Zavod *kr:* **GZ**

Geološki Zavod Slovenije *S:* **GZS**

Geolshki Anali Balkanskoga Poluostrva *P:* **Geol An Balk Poluostrva**

Geomagnetic *e:* **GM**

Geomagnetic Bulletin. Institute of Geological Sciences *e:* **Geomagn Bull Inst Geol Sci**

Geomagnetic Daily Variations *e:* **GDV**

Geomagnetic Data Center *e:* **GDC**

geomagnetic electrokinetograph *e:* **geek**

Geomagnetic Electrokinetograph *e:* **GEK**

Geomagnetic Indices Bulletin *e:* **GIB**

Geomagnetic Information Node[s] *e:* **GIN**

Geomagnetic Observing System *e:* **GOS**

geomagnetic planetary index *e:* **kp**

Geomagnetic Polarity Timescale *e:* **GPTS**

geomagnetic pulsation *e:* **psc**

geomagnetic pulsations *e:* **pc**

Geomagnetic Reversal Time Scale *e:* **GRTS**

Geomagnetic Series. Earth Physics Branch *e:* **Geomagn Ser Earth Pbys Branch**

Geomagnetic Series, Earth Physics Branch [Energy, Mines and Resources, Canada] *e:* **Geomagn. Ser. Earth Phys. Branch.**

Geomagnetic Tail Laboratory *e:* **GTL**

Geomagnetically Induced Current *e:* **GIC**

Geomagnetism *e:* **GEOMAG**, *e:* **Geomagn.**

Geomagnetism and Aernnomy *e:* **GMARA**

Geomagnetism and Aeronomy *e:* **Geomagn. Aeron.**, *e:* **Geomagn and Aeron**

Geomagnetism and Aeronomy [USSR] *R:* **Geomagn and Aeron [USSR]**, *e:* **Geom Aeron.**

Geomagnetism and Paleomagnetism Home Page *e:* **GPHP**

Geomagnetism Group Home Page *e:* **GGHP**

Geomagnetismus *d:* **Geomagn.**

Geomagnetizim i Aeronomiya [USSR] *R:* **Geom Aeron.**

Geomagnetizm and Aeronomy [USSR] *R:* **Geomagn Aeron [USSR]**

Geomagnetizm i Aeronomiya *R:* **GEAEA**, *R:* **Geomagg Aer**, *R:* **Geomagn Aeron**, *R:* **Geomagn and Aeron**

Geomaque Explorations Ltd. *e:* **GMVIO**, *f:* **GMQ**

Geomatics Association of Nova Scotia *e:* **GANS**

Geomatics Industry Association of Canada *e:* **GIAC**

Geomatics Industry Association of New Brunswick *e:* **GIANB**

Geomechania Computing Programme *e:* **Geomech Comput**

Geomechanica Computing Programme *e:* **Geomech Comput Progm**

Geomechanics Abstracts [Royal School of Mines] *e:* **GMA**

Geometer *d:* **Geom.**

Geometriae Dedicata *e:* **Geom Dedicata**

geometric *e:* **geom**

Geometric and Positional Tolerance *e:* **GPT**

Geometric and Technical Draughting *e:* **GTD**

Geometric Arithmetic Parallel Processor *e:* **GAPP**

Geometric Correction Data *e:* **GCD**

Geometric Data Base *e:* **GBD**

Geometric Database *e:* **GDB**

Geometric Degradation of Position *e:* **GDOP**

Geometric Dilution of Precision *e:* **GDOP**

Geometric Dimensioning and Tolerancing *e:* **GD&T**

Geometric Editor *e:* **G E O M E D**

Geometric External Amplification Ratio *e:* **GEAR**

Geometric Information for Targets *e:* **GIFT**

Geometric Interpolation Grid *e:* **GIG**

Geometric Invariance in Computer Vision *e:* **VIVA-NSF-EC-US021**

Geometric Manipulation Package *e:* **GEOMPAK**

Geometric Math Model *e:* **GMM**

Geometric Mean *e:* **GM**, *e:* **GMT**

Geometric Mean Diameter *e:* **GMD**

Geometric Mean Distance *e:* **GMD**

Geometric Mean Error *e:* **GME**

Geometric Mean Radius *e:* **GMR**

Geometric Mean Relative Absolute Error *e:* **GMRAE**

Geometric Mean Time to Repair *e:* **GMMTTR**

Geometric Mean Titre *e:* **G M T**

Geometric Modeling Application Program *e:* **GMAP**

Geometric Modeling Application[s] Project *e:* **GMAP**

Geometric Modeling System *e:* **GMS**

Geometric Modeller *e:* **GEOMOD**

Geometric Modelling Project *e:* **GMP**

Geometric Modulation Transfer Function *e:* **GMTF**

Geometric On-Line Definition *e:* **G O L D**

Geometric Operations *e:* **GO**

Geometric Optics *e:* **GO**

Geometric Optimization *e:* **GO**

Geometric Position Error *e:* **GPE**

Geometric Progression *e:* **GP**

Geometric Rectification Expert System *e:* **GERES**

Geometric scan *e:* **GM**

Geometric Spot Analysis System *e:* **GSPOT**

Geometric Standard Deviation *e:* **GSD**

Geometric Standard Error *e:* **GSE**

Geometric[al] *e:* **GEOM**

Geometric[al] [and] Technological Language *e:* **GTL**

Geometrical and True Positioning *e:* **GTPT**

Geometrical and True Positioning Tolerance *e:* **GTPT**

Geometric[al] Data Processing *e:* **GDP**

Geometrical Mean Free Path *e:* **GMFP**

Geometrical Optical Analysis of Lens Systems *e:* **G O A L S**

geometrical progression *e:* **g.p.**

Geometric[al] Stochastic Automaton *e:* **GSA**

Geometrical Technological *e:* **GTL**

Geometrical Technological Language *e:* **GTL**

Geometric[al] Theory of Diffraction *e:* **GTD**

Geometrically Close-Packed *e:* **GCP**

Geometrician *e:* **GEOM**

Geometrics, Derivatives, Moments and Noise *e:* **GEDEMON**

Geometrics Industry Association of America *e:* **GIAA**

Geometrie *d:* **Geom.**

geometrisch *d:* **geom.**

geometrische Datenverarbeitung *d:* **GDV**

geometrisk *a:* **geom.**

Geometrodynamics *e:* **GMD**

Geometry *e:* **G**

geometry *e:* **geo**

Geometry *e:* **GEOM**

Geometry Adjustment *e:* **GEOM.ADJ.**

Geometry and Topology *e:* **GT**

Geometry Definition System *e:* **GDS**

Geometry-Driven Diffusion in Vision *e:* **DIFFUSION-EC-US022**

Geometry of Fractal Sets *e:* **GFS**

Geometry of the Wake Experiment *e:* **GOWEX**

Geometry-Optimized e: **GO**
Geometry Technology Module e: **GTM**
Geometry Theorem Prover e: **GTP**
Geometry Transfer Engine e: **GTE**
Geomicrobiology Journal e: **GEJODG**, e: **Geomicrobiology J**
Geomimet e: **GEOMD**
Geomorphic Response Unit[s] e: **GRU**
geomorphologic[al] e: **geomorph**
Geomorphological Abstracts e: **Geomorph Abstr**
Geomorphologie d: **Geomorph.**
geomorphologist e: **geomorph**
geomorphology e: **geomorph**
Geomorphology e: **GM**
Geon [exoecaria agallocha] Timber e: **GEO Timber**
Geon Process Butadiene e: **GPB**
Geonet Names Server e: **GNS**
Geonex Corp. e: **GEOX**
Geonuclear Nobel Paso e: **GNP**
Geophex Airborne Unmanned Survey System e: **GAUSS**
Geophysial Monograph. American Geophysical Union e: **Geophys Monogr Am Geophys Union**
Geophysica Norvegica e: **GPNOA**
Geophysica Norvegica [Norway] N: **Geophys. Nor.**
geophysical e: **geophy**
Geophysical e: **GEOPHYS**
Geophysical Abstracts e: **GEAB**, e: **Geophys Abstr**
Geophysical and Astrophysical Fluid e: **Geol Astrophys Fluid Dyn**
Geophysical and Astrophysical Fluid Dynamics e: **Geophys [and] Astrophys Fluid Dyn**
Geophysical and Environmental Research Corporation e: **GERC**
Geophysical and Environmental Research Imaging Spectrometer e: **GERIS**
Geophysical and Polar Research Center e: **GPRC**
Geophysical Associates International e: **GAI**
Geophysical Case Histories e: **Geophys Case Histories**
Geophysical Company of Norway e: **GECO**
Geophysical Consulting Services e: **GCS**
Geophysical Data Center e: **GDC**
Geophysical Data Management System e: **GDMS**
Geophysical Data Record e: **GDR**
Geophysical Data System e: **GEODAS**
Geophysical Engineer e: **Gp E**, e: **Gp En**, e: **Gp Eng[r]**
Geophysical Environmental Research Inc. Spectroradiometer e: **GERS**
Geophysical Exploration Manned Mobile Submersible e: **GEMMS**
Geophysical Exploration [Society of Exploration Geophysicists of Japan] j: **Geophys. Explor.**
Geophysical Exploration Technology e: **GET**
Geophysical Fleet Mission Program Library e: **GFMPL**
Geophysical Fluid Dynamics e: **Geophys Fluid Dyn**
Geophysical Fluid Dynamics Institute e: **GFDI**

Geophysical Fluid Dynamic[s] Laboratory e: **GFDL**
Geophysical Fluid Dynamics Program e: **GFDP**
Geophysical Fluid Flow Cell Experiment e: **GFFC**
Geophysical Focus Area e: **GFA**
Geophysical Incentive System e: **GIS**
Geophysical Institute e: **GI**
Geophysical Institute. Faculty of Science. Tokyo University. Geophysical Notes. Supplement [Japan] e: **Geophys Inst Fac Sci Tokyo Univ Geophys Notes Supp**
Geophysical Institute, University of Alaska e: **GIA**
Geophysical Institute. University of Alaska. UAG Report Series e: **GIUAG R**
Geophysical Institute. University of Alaska.Contribution Series e: **GIUAC**
Geophysical Investigations Maps e: **GIM**
Geophysical Journal e: **Geophys J**, e: **Geophys J[our]**, e: **GJOUD**
Geophysical Journal International e: **Geophys. J. Int.**
Geophysical Journal of the Royal Astronomical Society e: **Geophys.J.Roy.Astron.Soc.**
Geophysical Journal. Royal Aslronomical Society e: **GEOJA**
Geophysical Journal. Royal Astronomical e: **Geophys J R Astr Soc**
Geophysical Journal. Royal Astronomical Society e: **Geopbys J R**, e: **Geophys J R [Astronom Soc]**
Geophysical Magazine e: **Geophys Mag**
Geophysical Magazine [Japan Meteorological Agency] j: **Geophys. Mag.**
Geophysical Memoirs [London] e: **Geophys Mem [Lond]**
Geophysical Models for Data Interpretation e: **GMDI**
Geophysical Monitoring for Climate (or Climatic) Change[s] e: **GMCC**
Geophysical Monitoring Satellite e: **GMS**
Geophysical Monograph e: **Geophys Monogr**, e: **GPMGAD**
Geophysical Monograph Series [American Geophysical Union] e: **Geophys. Monogr. Ser.**
Geophysical Note [Tokyo] e: **Geophys Note [Tokyo]**
Geophysical Observatories and Mapping Program e: **GOMP**
Geophysical Processor System e: **GPS**
Geophysical Products System e: **GPS**
geophysical properties tool e: **GEOPROPS**
Geophysical Prospecting e: **GPP**, e: **GPPRA**
Geophysical Prospecting [European Association of Exploration Geophysicists, Netherlands] n: **Geophys. Prosp.**
Geophysical Prospecting [The Hague] n: **Geophys Prospect [The Hague]**
Geophysical Report e: **GEO**
Geophysical Research Board e: **GRB**
Geophysical Research Bulletin e: **Geophys R B**, e: **GRBUD**
Geophysical Research Directorate e: **GRD**
Geophysical Research Letters e: **GRL**

Geophysical Research Letters [American Geophysical Union] e: **Geophys. Res. Lett.**
Geophysical Research Mission e: **GRM**
Geophysical Research Papers e: **Geophys Res Pap**
Geophysical Research program e: **GRP**
Geophysical Satellite e: **GEOS**
Geophysical Sciences Laboratory e: **GSL**
Geophysical Service[s], Incorporated e: **GSI**
Geophysical Service[s] International e: **GSI**
Geophysical Signal e: **GS**
Geophysical Signal Analysis e: **GSA**
Geophysical Society of Tulsa Proceedings e: **Geophys Soc Tulsa Proc**
Geophysical Statistics Project e: **GSP**
Geophysical Survey Data Processing System e: **GSDP**
Geophysical Survey System e: **GEOSS**
Geophysical Surveys e: **Geophys Surv**, e: **GPSVA**
Geophysical Transactions [Hungary] H: **Geophys. Trans.**
Geophysical Turbulence Program e: **GTP**
Geophysical Well Log e: **WL**
Geophysicist e: **GEOPHYS**
geophysics e: **geo**, e: **geoph**, e: **geophy**
Geophysics e: **GEOPHYS**, e: **GP**, e: **GPH**, e: **GPYSA**
Geophysics and Astronomy e: **G&A**
Geophysics and Astrophysics Monographs e: **Geophys Astrophys Monogr**
Geophysics and Space Data Bulletin e: **Geophys Space Data Bull**, e: **GSDB**
Geophysics and Tectonia Abstracts e: **Geophys Tecton Abstr**
Geophysics Collection, Geological Survey of Canada, Ottawa, Ontario e: **OOO**
Geophysics Corporation of America e: **GCA**
Geophysics Fluid Dynamics Laboratory e: **GFDL**
Geophysics Laboratory e: **GL**
Geophysics Magnetometer e: **GMAG**
Geophysics Research Board e: **GRB**
Geophysics Research Directorate e: **GRD**
Geophysics Technology Transfer Initiative e: **GTTI**
Geophysik d: **Geophs.**, d: **Geophys.**
Geophysik und Geologie d: **Geophys Geol**
geophysikalisch d: **geophys.**
Geophysikalische Beratergruppe d: **GeophysBGrp**
Geophysikalische Beratungsstelle d: **GeophysBSt**
Geophysikalischer Beratungsdienst der Bundeswehr d: **GeophysBDBw**
Geophysiker d: **Geophys.**
Geophysícal Fluid Dynamics e: **Geophys Fluid Dyn**
Geophysícal Magazine [Tokyo] e: **GEOMA**
Geophysícal Research Letters e: **Geophys R L**
Geophysícs e: **Geophys**
Geophythology e: **GPHTAR**
geopolitical e: **geopol**
Geopolitical Code e: **GC**
geopolitics e: **geo**, e: **geopol**
Geopolities e: **Geopol**
Geopotential Decameter e: **GPDM**

Geopotential Meter e: **GPM**

Geopotential [or Geoid] Satellite e: **GEOSAT**

Geopotential Research Explorer Mission e: **GREM**

Geopotential Research Mission e: **GRM**

Geopotential Unit e: **GPU**

geopotentielles Meter d: **gpm**

Geopower Technologies Incorporated e: **GTI**

Geopposserde [Defendant] [Netherlands] [Legal term] n: **Geopp**

Geoprocessing Map Call e: **GP.MC**

Geoprocessing Map Call Deamon program e: **GP.MCD**

Geoquímica del Océano Indico s: **INDIGO**

Georesources, Incorporated e: **GEOI**

Georg-Agricola-Gesellschaft zur Förderung der Geschichte der Naturwissenschaften und der Technik d: **GAG**

Georg Thieme, Verlag für Medizin und Naturwissenschaften d: **GTL**

Georg-von-Neumayer-Station, Antarktis e: **GvN**

Georganiseerd Overleg n: **GO**

Georganiseerde Werkloozenzorg n: **GW**

George Air Force Base e: **GAFB**

George Bernard Shaw e: **P-Shaw**, e: **Shaw**

George Brown College e: **GB COLL**

George C. Marshall Research Foundation e: **GCMRF**

George C. Marshall Space Flight Center e: **MSFC**

George C. Marshall Spaceflight Center e: **GCMSC**

George Eastman House, Rochester e: **NRGE**

George Emerson's Old Grandmother Rode a Pig Home e: **GEOGRAPHY**

George Institute of Technology e: **GIT**

George Marshall Spaceflight Center e: **GMSFC**

George Mason University, Fairfax e: **VGM**

George Orwell Society e: **GOS**

George Remote Terminal Interrogative Environment e: **GERTIE**

George Rogers Clark National Historical Park e: **GERO**

George Santayana, Jorge Augustín Nicolás Ruiz de Santayana [1863-1952] Santiago s: **Santayana**

George Washinglon Journal of lnternational Law and Economics e: **JIL**

George Washington Journal of International Law and Economic e: **George Washington J Internat Law and Econ**

George Washington Journal of International Law and Economics e: **Geo Wash J Ind L[and Econ]**

George Washington University, Medical Library e: **GWM**

George Wasington's Birthday e: **Washington's**

George's Mississippi Digest e: **Geo Dig**

Georgetown e: **SYGC**, e: **SYGT**

Georgetown Clinical Research Institute e: **GCRI**

Georgetown College Observatory e: **GCO**

Georgetown Dental Journal e: **Georgetown Dent J**

Georgetown International Environmental Law Review e: **Geo. Int'l Envtl. L. Rev.**

Georgetown Journal of Legal Ethics e: **Geo. J. Legal Ethics**

Georgetown Journal on Fighting Poverty e: **Geo. J. Fighting Poverty**

Georgetown Law Journal e: **Georgetown IJ**, e: **Georgetown Law J**

Georgetown Medical Bulletin e: **Georgetowm Med Bull**, e: **Georgetown Med Bull**, e: **GTMBAQ**

Georgetown/Timehri Internacional e: **SYTM**

Georgetown Univelsity, Medical Center Library e: **GTU**

Georgetown University. Monograph Series on Languages e: **GMSLL**

Georgetown University. School of Dentistry. Mirror e: **Georgetown Univ Sch Dent Mirror**

Georgia Academy for the Blind e: **GAB**

Georgia Academy of Science e: **GAS**

Georgia Accrediting Commission e: **GAC**

Georgia Advisory Council on Education e: **GACE**

Georgia Advisory Council on Libraries e: **GACL**

Georgia Aeronautics and Space Administration e: **GASA**

Georgia Agricultural Research e: **GEARA**

Georgia Architectural and Engineering Society e: **G.A.&E.S.**

Georgia Art Education Association e: **GAEA**

Georgia Association for Community Education e: **GACE**

Georgia Association for Supervision and Curriculum Development e: **GASCD**

Georgia Association of Alternative Educators e: **GAAE**

Georgia Association of American Industrial Arts Student Association e: **GAAIASA**

Georgia Association of Colleges e: **GAC**

Georgia Association of Curriculum and Instructional Supervisors e: **GACIS**

Georgia Association of Educational Leaders e: **GAEL**

Georgia Association of Educators e: **GAE**

Georgia Association of Elementary School Principals e: **GAESP**

Georgia Association of Independent Schools e: **GAIS**

Georgia Association of Junior Colleges e: **GAJC**

Georgia Association of Middle School Principals e: **GAMSP**

Georgia Association of School Business Officials e: **GASBO**

Georgia Association of School Psychologists e: **GASP**

Georgia Association of Secondary School Principals e: **GASSP**

Georgia Association of the Technology Student Association e: **GATSA**

Georgia Association of Young Children e: **GAYC**

Georgia Baptist Hospital e: **GABH**

Georgia Basic Skills Test e: **GBST**

Georgia Bight Experiment e: **GABEX**

Georgia Board of Education e: **GBOE**

Georgia Bureau of Investigation e: **GBI**

Georgia Center for Advanced Telecommunications Technology e: **GCATT**

Georgia College Educators' Network e: **GC EduNET**

Georgia Commercial Flower Growers Association Inc. e: **GCFGA**

Georgia Compensatory Education Leaders e: **GCEL**

Georgia Council of Administrators of Special Education e: **G-CASE**

Georgia Decisions e: **Geo Dec**

Georgia Dental Hygienists' Association e: **GDHA**

Georgia Department of Education e: **GDE**

Georgia Department of Education, Atlanta e: **GSL**

Georgia Department of Public Safety e: **GDPS**, e: **GDSP**

Georgia Division, Lockheed Aircraft Corporation e: **GEIAC**, e: **GELAC**

Georgia Division of Public Health e: **GDPH**

Georgia Education Leadership Academy e: **GELA**

Georgia Educational Network Exchanging School Information State-Wide e: **GENESIS**

Georgia Educational Research Association e: **GERA**

Georgia Emergency Medical Services e: **GAEMS**

Georgia-Florida Coastal Plain e: **GAFL**

Georgia. Forest Research Council. Report e: **GFRRA**

Georgia Forestry Association e: **GFA**

Georgia Geologic Survey e: **GGS**

Georgia Green Industry Association e: **GGIA**

Georgia Gulf Corp. e: **GGLF**

Georgia Gulf Corporation e: **GGC**

Georgia Health Sciences Library Association e: **GHSLA**

Georgia Information Dissemination Center e: **GIDC**, e: **GIDS**

Georgia Institute of Technology e: **GAT**, e: **GTEC**, e: **GTI**

Georgia Institute of Technology Integrated Civil Engineering System e: **GTICES**

Georgia Institute of Technology Research Reactor e: **GTRR**

Georgia Institute of Technology School of Information Science e: **GITSIS**

Georgia Institute of Technology School of Information Sciences e: **GITIS**

Georgia Institute of Technology Technical Information Service e: **GATTIS**

Georgia Journal of International and Comparative Law e: **Ga. J. Int'l&Comp. L.**, e: **Georgia J Int Comp L**

Georgia Journal of Science e: **GJSCD**

Georgia Law Review e: **GLR**

Georgia Library Information Network e: **GLIN**

Georgia Media Specialist Evaluation Program e: **GMSEP**

Georgia Mental Health Institute e: **GMH**

Georgia Mining and Mineral Research Institute e: **GMMRI**

Georgia Nuclear Aircraft Laboratory e: **GNAL**

Georgia Nuclear Laboratories e: **GNL**

Georgia Online Database e: **GOLD**

Georgia-Pacific Corp. e: **GP**

Georgia-Pacific Plywood Co. *e:* **G-P**, *e:* **GXP**

Georgia Project for Assistive Technology *e:* **GPAT**

Georgia Psychoeducational Network *e:* **GPN**

Georgia Public Health Association *e:* **GPHA**

Georgia Satellite Academic and Medical System *e:* **GSAMS**

Georgia School Counselors Association *e:* **GSCA**

Georgia School Food Service Association *e:* **GSFSA**

Georgia School of Technology *e:* **GST**

Georgia School Psychologist Evaluation Program *e:* **GSPEP**

Georgia School Public Relations Association *e:* **GSPRA**

Georgia School Social Worker Evaluation Program *e:* **GSSWEP**

Georgia State Florists Association *e:* **GSFA**

Georgia Superintendent Evaluation Instrument *e:* **GSEI**

Georgia Tech Research Institute *e:* **GTI**

Georgia Technical Research Institute *e:* **GTRI**

Georgia Telecommunications Network *e:* **TELNET**

Georgia-Tennessee Regional Health Commission, Chattanooga *e:* **TCGT**

Georgia Textile Manufacturers Association *e:* **GTMA**

Georgia University *e:* **Ga Univ**

Georgia Warm Springs Foundation *e:* **GWSF**

Georgia World Congress Center *e:* **GWCC**

Georgia Youth Science and Technology Centers *e:* **GYSTC**

Georgian Bay Township Public Library, Mactier, Ontario *e:* **OMGB**

Georgian College of Applied Arts and Technology, Barrie, Ontario *e:* **OBAGC**

Georgian College Resource Centre, Owen Sound, Ontario *e:* **OOWGC**

Georgian Red Cross Society *e:* **GRC**

Georgian Soviet Socialist Republic *e:* **GSSR**

Georgia's Effective Teaching Strategies *e:* **GETS**

Geos. Canada Department of Energy, Mines and Resources *e:* **GEOQ**

Geos Corp. *e:* **GEOS**

GEOS [Geodetic Earth-Orbiting Satellite] Data Adjustment Program[me] *e:* **GDAP**

Geosat Exact Repeat Mission *e:* **GEOSAT-ERM**

Geosat Follow-on *e:* **GFO**

Geosat Oceans Applications Program *e:* **GOAP**

Geoscan Image Processing System *e:* **GIPSY**

Geoscience *e:* **Geosc.**

Geoscience Abstracts *e:* **Geosci Abstr**, *e:* **Geoscience Abs**

Geoscience Airborne Laser Altimeter *e:* **GALA**

Geoscience and Man *e:* **Geosci Man**

Geoscience and Remote Sensing Society *e:* **GRSS**

Geoscience Canada *e:* **Geosci Can**, *e:* **GOCA**

Geoscience Centre *e:* **GSC**

Geoscience Conference Calendar *e:* **GCC**

Geoscience Data Evaluation System *e:* **GEODES**

Geoscience Data Index for Alberta *e:* **GEODIAL**

Geoscience Data Referral System *e:* **GDRS**

Geoscience Documentation *e:* **GSDCB**

Geoscience Electronics *e:* **GE**, *e:* **GEO**

Geoscience Expedition to Dronning Maud Land *e:* **GEOMAUD**

Geoscience Information Society *e:* **GIS**

Geoscience Information Society. Proceedings *e:* **Geoscience Ini Soc Proc**, *e:* **GISPA**

Geoscience Laser Altimeter System *e:* **GLAS**

Geoscience Laser Altimetry/Ranging System *e:* **GLARS**

Geoscience Laser Ranging System-Altimeter *e:* **GLRS-A**

Geoscience Laser Ranging System-Ranger *e:* **GLRS-R**

Geoscience Research Corporation *e:* **GRC**

Geoscience Research Drilling Office *e:* **GRDO**

Geoscience Research Graphics Environment-3 Dimensional *e:* **GEORGE-3D**

Geoscience Research Institute *e:* **GRI**

Geoscience Studies [Japan] *e:* **Geosci Stud**

Geosciences Computing Laboratory *e:* **GCL**

Geosciences data analysis toolkit *e:* **GEODAT**

Geosciences Data Center *e:* **GDC**

Geosciences Directorate *e:* **GEO**

Geosciences group *e:* **GEOS**

Geosciences Information Center *e:* **GEOFIZ**

Geoscience[s] Information Group *e:* **GIG**

Geoscientific Resource Data Base *e:* **GRDB**

Geoscope *e:* **GEOS**

GEOSECS Operations Group *e:* **GOG**

GeoSim Information Server *e:* **GSIS**

Geospace Environment Modeling [Program] *e:* **GEM**

Geospace Interorbital Transportation *e:* **GIT**

Geospace Swing Station *e:* **GSS**

Geospatial Analysis. *e:* **GSA**

Geospatial Analysis of Glaciated Environments *e:* **GAGE**, *e:* **GAGE**

Geospatial Data *e:* **GD**

Geospatial Data and Exploration System *e:* **GEODESY**

Geospatial Data Clearinghouse *e:* **GDC**

Geospatial Data Management *e:* **GDM**

Geospatial Information & Technology Association *e:* **GITA**

Geospatial Metadata Application Profile *e:* **GEO**

Geospatial Prototype Facility *e:* **GPF**

Geospatial Standards Management Committee *e:* **GSMC**

Geosphere-Biosphere Model[s] *e:* **GBM**

Geosphere-Biosphere Observatories *e:* **GBO**

Geosrience Documentation *e:* **Geosci Doc**

Geostandards Newsletter *e:* **Geostand Newsl**

Geostar Mining Corporation *e:* **GMC**

Geostarionary Earth Orbit *e:* **GEO**

GeoStat Groundwater Modelling *e:* **GSGM**

geostatic *e:* **geo**

Geostational Day *e:* **GD**

Geostationaly Technology Satellite *e:* **GTS**

geostationärer Satellit *d:* **GEOS**

Geostationary Airglow Monitor *e:* **GAM**

Geostationary Archival and Retrieval System *e:* **GARS**

Geostationary Atmospheric Profiler *e:* **GAP**

Geostationary Backscatter Ultraviolet *e:* **GBUV**

Geostationary Communications Satellite *e:* **GCS**

Geostationary Data Collection Platform *e:* **GDCP**

Geostationary Earth Climate Sensor *e:* **GECS**

Geostationary Earth Observation *e:* **GEO**

Geostationary Earth Observation Satellite *e:* **GEOS**

Geostationary Earth Observatories *e:* **GEO**

Geostationary Earth Orbit (Satellite) *e:* **GEO**

Geostationary Earth Orbiter *e:* **GEO**

Geostationary Earth Orbiting Nadir Etalon Sounding Spectrometer *e:* **GEONESS**

Geostationary Earth-Orbiting Satellite *e:* **GEOS**

Geostationary Earth Processes Spectrometer *e:* **GEPS**

Geostationary Earth Radiation Budget *e:* **GERB**

Geostationary Environmental Operational Satellite *d:* **GEOS**, *e:* **GEOSAT**

Geostationary Environmental Satellite System *e:* **GESS**

Geostationary European Meteorological Satellite *e:* **GEMS**

Geostationary Experimental Temperature and Moisture Sounder *e:* **GETMS**

Geostationary Launch Vehicle *e:* **GSLV**

Geostationary Meteorological Satellite System *e:* **GMSS**

Geostationary Meteorological Satellite[s] *e:* **GMS**

Geostationary Microwave Precipitation Radiometer *e:* **GMPR**

Geostationary Mobile Radio *e:* **GMR**

Geostationary Multispectral Electroscanning Radiometer *e:* **GEOMER**

Geostationary Operational Environmental Satellite *e:* **GEOS**

Geostationary Operational Environment[al] Satellite *e:* **GOES**

Geostationary Operational Environmental Satellite *e:* **GOFS/DCP**

Geostationary Operational Environmental Satellite-A *e:* **GOES-A**

Geostationary Operational Environmental Satellite Data Collection Platform *e:* **GOES/DCP**

Geostationary Operational Environmental Satellites *e:* **GOESs**

Geostationary Operational Imager *e:* **GOI**

Geostationary Operational Meteorological Satellite[s] *e:* **GOMS**

Geostationary Operational Sounder e:
GOS
Geostationary Orbit e: **GEO**, e: **GSO**
Geostationary Orbit-Infrared Sensor e:
GEO-IRS
Geostationary Orbital Earth Satellite e:
GOES, e: **GOFS**
Geostationary Orbiting Environmental
Satellite[s] e: **GOES**
Geostationary Orbiting Meteorological
Satellite e: **GOMS**
Geostationary Satellite e: **GEOSAT**, e:
GSS
Geostationary Satellite Orbit e: **GSO**
Geostationary Satellite Precipitation Data
Centre e: **GSPDC**
Geostationary Search and Rescue e:
GEOSAR
Geostationary Test Satellite e: **GTS**
Geostationary Transfer Orbit e: **GTO**
Geostationary Very High Resolution
Radiometer e: **GVHRR**
Geostatistical Environmental Exposure
Assessment Software e: **GEEAS**
Geostatistical Evaluation of Mines e:
GEM
GeoStatistical Library e: **GSL**
Geostatistical Orebody Modelling e: **GOM**
Geosynchmnous Solar Electric Propulsion
Stage e: **GEOSEPS**
Geosynchrnnous Synthetic Aperture Radar
e: **GEOSAR**
Geosynchronons earth Orbit e: **GSO**
Geosynchronous Communication Satellites
e: **GCS**
Geosynchronous Earth Observation System
e: **GEOS**
Geosynchronous Earth Orbit e: **GEO**
Geosynchronous Earth Orbit Satellites e:
GEOS
Geosynchronous Earth Orbit Synthetic
Aperture Radar e: **GEOSAR**
Geosynchronous Gas Filter Radiometer e:
GGFR
Geosynchronous Launch Vehicle e: **GSLV**
Geosynchronous Operational
Environmental Satellite[s] e: **GOES**
Geosynchronous Orbit High Resolution
Earth Monitoring Satellite e: **GOHREM**
Geosynchronous Orbital Environmental
Satellite e: **GOES**
Geosynchronous Orbiting Earth Satellite
e: **GOES**
Geosynchronous Orbit[s] e: **GSO**
Geosynchronous Oribtal Earth Satellite e:
GOES
Geosynchronous Satellite Launch Vehicle
e: **GSLV**
Geosynchronous Transfer Orbit e: **GTO**
Geosynchronous Very High Resolution
Radiometer e: **GVHRR**
Geosynthesis e: **GS**
Geosynthetic Clay Liner e: **GCL**
Geosynthetics e: **GS**
Geotbermal Resources Council.
Transactions [China] e: **Geotherm Res
Counc Trans**
Geotech Capital e: **GEO**
Geotechnical Abstracts e: **Geotech Abstr**
Geotechnical Aquifer Test e: **GAQ**
Geotechnical Consultant e: **GTC**
Geotechnical Engineering e: **Geotech Eng**
Geotechnical Engineer[ing] e: **GTE**

GeoTechnical Engineering Group e:
GTEG
Geotechnical Engineering Groups e: **GEG**
Geotechnical Engineering Laboratory e:
GEL
Geotechnical Fabrics Report e: **GFR**
Geotechnical Field Drilling e: **GFD**
Geotechnical Groundwater Stabilized e:
GGS
Geotechnical Logging Society e: **GLS**
Geotechnical-Map e: **GMA**
Geotechnical Mapping Unit e: **GMU**
Geotechnical Micromorphology and
Microanalysis Centre e: **GMMC**
Geotechnical News [Canadian Geotechnical
Society] e: **Geotech. News**
Geotechnical-Physical Analysis e: **GPA**
Geotechnical Project e: **GTP**
Geotechnical Project Design e: **GTPD**
Geotechnical Research Center (or Centre)
e: **GRC**
Geotechnical Science Laboratories e:
GSL, e: **GTSL**
Geotechnical Services e: **GS**
GeoTechnical Services e: **GTS**
Geotechnical Testing Journal [American
Society for Nondestructive Testing] e:
Geotech. Test. J.
Geotechnical-Well Construction e: **GWC**
Geotechnik d: **Geotech.**
Geotechnique f: **GEOTECHNIQ**
Geotechnique [Engtand] e: **GTNQA**
Geotechnisches Institut, Wien d: **GI**
Geotectonics e: **Geotecton**, e: **GT**
Geotek Industries, Inc. e: **GOTK**
Geoteknillisia Julkaisuja F: **Geotek Julk**
Geotektonika R: **Geotekton**, s: **GTKTA**
Geotektonika Tektonofizika i Geodinamika
R: **Geotektonika Tektonofiz
Geodinamika**
Geotektonische Forschungen d:
Geotekton Forsch, d: **Geotektonische
Forsch**
Geotel, Inc. e: **GETE**
geothermal e: **geo**
Geothermal Energy e: **Geotherm Energy**,
e: **GTE**
Geothermal Energy Magazine e:
Geotherm Energy Mag
Geothermal Energy New Zealand Limited
e: **GENZL**
Geothermal Energy Update e: **Geotherm
Energy Update**, e: **GEU**
Geothermal Engineer[ing] e: **GE**
Geothermal Heat Pump Consortium e:
GHPC
Geothermal Hot Line e: **Geotherm Hot
Line**, e: **GHI.lD**, e: **GHLID**
Geothermal Loop Experimental Facility e:
GLEF
Geothermal Metallogenesis East Pacific e:
Geometep
Geothermal Report e: **Geotherm Rep**, e:
GERED
Geothermal Report. Mineral Resourcess
Department [Fiji] e: **Geotherm Rep
Miner Resour Dep [Fiji]**
Geothermal Resource Interactive Temporal
Simulation e: **GRITS**
Geothermal Resource[s] Council e: **GRC**
Geothermal Resources Council. Special
Report e: **Geotberm Res Counc Spec
Rep**

Geothermal Resources International e:
GRI
Geothermal Resources International, Inc.
e: **GEO**, e: **GEOW**
Geothermal Technology e: **Geotherm
Technol**
Geothermal Test Facility e: **GTF**
Geothermal World Information Center e:
GWIC
GeothermalReport e: **Gertherm Rep**
Geothermia l: **Geotherm**
Geothermics e: **Geotherm**
Geothermics . e: **GTMCA**
Geotimes e: **GEOTA**
Geotronics Service Center e: **GSC**
GeoVision Systems Limited e: **GVSL**
GeoVision Vision e: **GVV**
GeoWaste, Inc. e: **GEOW**
Geowissenschaften in Unserer Zeit d: **Geo
Unserer Zeit**, d: **Geo Uns Zeit**
Geowissenschaftliche
Gemeinschaftsaufgaben d: **GGA**
Geowissenschaftliche Literaturinformation
d: **GWL**
Geoworks Ensemble Operating System e:
GEOS
GeoWorks Snail Mail Network e:
GWSMN
geozentrisch d: **geoz.**
geozyklisch d: **geoz.**
Gerakan Indonesi Merdek in: **GIM**
Gerätewagen-Umweltschutz d: **GW-U**
Gerätewagen-Wasserrettung d: **GW-W**
Gerätschaften und Mittel zur Abwehr von
Gewässergefährdungen d: **GMAG**
Gereformeerd Geologisch Tijdschrift n:
GerefTTS
Gereformeerde Politieke Jeugdstudieclubs
n: **GPJC**
Gerequireerde n: **Gereq**
Geriatric & Medical Centers, Inc. e:
GEMC
gerichtliche Medizin d: **ger.Med.**
Gerichtsmedizin[er] d: **Ger.-Med.**
Gerlands Beiträge zur Geophysik
[Germany] d: **Gerlands Beitr. Geophys.**
German Air Defence (or Defense) Ground
Environment e: **GEADGE**
German Air Defense Ground Environment
System e: **GADGES**
German Airborne Environment e:
GEAEGIS
German Application Environment e: **GAE**
German Association for Infant Mental
Health e: **GAIMH**
German D-1 Spacelab Payload e: **BMFT**
German Environmental Information
Network e: **GEIN**
German Geological Mission in Jordan e:
G.G.M.J.
German Hydrographic Institute e: **GHI**
German Medical Monthly e: **German Med
Monthly**, e: **Ger Med Mon**, e: **GRMMA**
German Medicament e: **Germed**
German Medicine e: **Ger Med**
German Military Geographical Office e:
GMGO
German Military Geophysical Office e:
GMGO
German National Center for the
Documentation and Evaluation of
Alternatives to Animal Experiments e:
ZEBET

German North Sea *e:* **GNS**
German North Sea Port *e:* **GNSP**
German North Sea Sub-Area *e:* **GNSSA**
German Oceanic Lidar System *e:* **GOLS**
German Oceanographic Data Centre *e:* **DOD**
German Pharma Health Fund e.V. *e:* **GPHF**
German Pressurized Water Reactor *e:* **GPWR**
German Society for Rocket Technology and Space Travel *e:* **GSRTST**
German Space Operation Center (or Centre) *e:* **GSOC**
German Spacelab *e:* **SL-D**
German Spacelab Contractor *e:* **ERNO**
German Spacelab Mission *e:* **SPACELAB-D**
German Water Engineering GmbH *e:* **GWE**
German Zonal Meteorological Organization *e:* **GZMO**
Germany. Bundesanstalt für Bodenforschnng und Geologische Landesämter. Geologisches Jahrbuch. Beiheft *d:* **Ger Bundesanst Bodenforscb Geol Jahrb Beih**
Gerrnan Medicine *e:* **GRMDA**
Gesellschafr für Naturkunde in Württemberg. Jahreshefte *d:* **Ges Naturkd Württemb Jahresh**
Gesellschaft der Tierärzte in Wien *d:* **GTW**
Gesellschaft Deutscher Naturforscher und Ärzte *d:* **GND,**
Gesellschaft Deutscher Naturforscher und Ärzte e. V. *d:* **GDNÄ**
Gesellschaft Deutscher Naturforscher und Ärzte. Wissenschaftliche Konferenz *d:* **Ges Dtsch Naturforsch Ärzte Wiss Konf**
Gesellschaft Deutscher Tierfotografen *d:* **GDT**
Gesellschaft für Akkreditierung und Zertifizierung von chemischen Laboratorien GmbH *d:* **GAZ**
Gesellschaft für Angewandte Datenverarbeitung und Automation in der Medizin *d:* **GADAM**
Gesellschaft für Bergbau, Metallurgie, Rohstoff- und Umwelttechnik *d:* **GDMB**
Gesellschaft für Biologische Anthropologie, Eugenik und Verhaltensforschung *d:* **GBAEV**
Gesellschaft für biologische Anthropologie, Eugenik und Verhaltensforschung e.V. *d:* **GfbAEV**
Gesellschaft für Biologische Chemie e.V. *d:* **GBCh**
Gesellschaft für Biologische Sicherheit *d:* **G.b.S.**
Gesellschaft für Ernährungsphysiologie der Haustiere *d:* **GfEaH**
Gesellschaft für Geologische Wissenschaften *d:* **GGW**
Gesellschaft für geophysikalische Vermessungen mbH *d:* **GGV**
Gesellschaft für Hydrid- und Wasserstofftechnik mbH *d:* **HWT**
Gesellschaft für Innere Medizin *d:* **G.I.M.**
Gesellschaft für Kältetechnik-Klimatechnik mbH & Co. *d:* **GfKK**
Gesellschaft für Katastrophen- und Unfallhilfe, Katastrophenmedizin und Umweltschutz *d:* **GfKU**

Gesellschaft für Kläranlagen und Wasserversorgung mbH, Mannheim *d:* **GKW**
Gesellschaft für Klima- und lufttechnische Anlagen mbH *d:* **GKL**
Gesellschaft für Klimatechnik bmH & Co. KG *d:* **gkk**
Gesellschaft für Lüftungstechnik, Klimatechnik und Luftreinigung mbH *d:* **GLK**
Gesellschaft für Medizin und Forschung in Afrika *d:* **AMREF-D**
Gesellschaft für medizinische Ausbildung *d:* **GMA**
Gesellschaft für medizinische Datenerfassung und Auswertung mbH *d:* **GEMEDA**
Gesellschaft für medizinische Dokumentation und Statistik *d:* **GMD**
Gesellschaft für medizinische Information *d:* **GMI**
Gesellschaft für Medizinische Radiologie *d:* **GMR**
Gesellschaft für Medizintechnik mbH *d:* **GMT**
Gesellschaft für Molekularbiologische Forschung *d:* **GMB,** *d:* **GMBF**
Gesellschaft für Natur- und Umweltschutz Cuxhaven e.V. *d:* **G.N.U.**
Gesellschaft für Qualitätsmanagement in der Gesundheitsversorgung *d:* **GQMG**
Gesellschaft für Strahlen und Umweltforschung mbH *d:* **GSF**
Gesellschaft für Synthese der Medizin *d:* **G.S.M.**
Gesellschaft für Technologie und Umwelt mbH *d:* **GTU**
Gesellschaft für Technologie- und Umweltschutzberatung *d:* **GTU**
Gesellschaft für Umwelt-Mutationsforschung e.V. *d:* **GUM**
Gesellschaft für Umweltmessungen und Umwelterhebungen mbH in Karlsruhe *d:* **UMEG**
Gesellschaft für Umweltschutz mbH *d:* **REIKA**
Gesellschaft für Versuchstierkunde *d:* **GV**
Gesellschaft für Versuchstierkunde-Society of Laboratory Animal Science *d:* **GV-SOLAS**
Gesellschaft für Weltraumforschung mbH *d:* **GfW**
Gesellschaft für Weltraumforschung und Raumfahrt *d:* **GWR**
Gesellschaft für Weltraumforschung und Raumfahrt der Deutschen Demokratischen Republik *d:* **GWR/DDR**
Gesellschaft Naturforschender Freunde zu Berlin. Sitzungsberichte *d:* **Ges Naturf Freund Berlin Szb**
Gesellschaft Schweizerischer Tierärzte *d:* **GST**
Gesellschaft Umweltmanagement e.V. *d:* **GUM**
Gesellschaft: Zahngesundheit der Jugend *d:* **G:ZJ**
Gesellschaft zur Aufklärung von Umweltgefahren e.V. *d:* **GAU**
Gesellschaft zur Beförderung der Gesammten Naturwissenschaften zu Marburg. Schriften *d:* **Ges Naturw Marburg Schrift**

Gesellschaft zur Erhaltung alter und gefährdeter Haustierrassen *d:* **GEH**
Gesellschaft zur Förderung der Abwassertechnik e.V. *d:* **GFA**
Gesellschaft zur Förderung der kernphysikalischen Forschung e.V. *d:* **GFKF**
Gesellschaft zur Herstellung umweltfreundlicher Abfallbeseitigungsanlagen mbH *d:* **GUA**
Gesetz über den deutschen Wetterdienst *d:* **DWD-Gesetz**
Gesetz über die Erhebung einer Abgabe für Grundwasserentnahmen *d:* **HGruWAG HE**
Gesetz über die Erhebung einer Abgabe für Grundwasserentnahmen (Hessen) *e:* **GruWAG HE**
Gesetz über die Erhebung einer Gebühr für Grundwasserentnahmen *d:* **GruwaG HA**
Gesetz über die Erhebung einer Grundwasserentnahmegebühr *d:* **BremGruWEGG BR**
Gesetz über die Erhebung einer Grundwasserentnahmegebühr (Bremen) *e:* **GruWEGG BR**
Gesetz über die innerdeutsche Rechts- und Amtshilfe in Strafsachen *d:* **RHilfeG**
Gesetz über die soziale Wohnraumförderung *d:* **WoFG**
Gesetz über die Umweltverträglichkeitsprüfung *d:* **UVPG**
Gesetz über die Vereinheitlichung des Gesundheitswesen *d:* **GVG**
Gesetz über die vermögensrechtlichen Verhältnisse der Bundeswasserstraßen *d:* **WaStrVermG**
Gesetz über Umweltstatistiken *d:* **UstatG**
Gesetz überden unmittelbaren Zwang bei Ausübung öffentlicher Gewalt durch Vollzugsbeamte *e:* **UZwG**
Gesetz zur Änderung des Medizinproduktegesetzes *d:* **MPG-ÄndG**
Gesetz zur Durchführung der Rechtsakte der Europäischen Gemeinschaft über die besondere Etikettierung von Rindfleisch und Rindfleischerzeugnissen [Rindfleischetikettierungsgesetz] *d:* **RiFlEtikettG**
Gesetz zur Übertragung von Verwaltungsaufgaben auf dem Gebiet der Raumfahrt [Raumfahrtaufgabenübertragungsgesetz] *d:* **RAÜG**
Gestion Environnement Agronomie *e:* **GENAGRO,** *f:* **GENAGRO**
Gestion et d'Etude des Information Spectroscopiques Atmospheriques *e:* **GEISA**
Gestion et Etude des Informations Spectroscopiques Atmospheriques *f:* **GEIBA**
Gestion et Étude des Informations Spectroscopiques Atmosphériques *f:* **GEISA**
Gesunde Pflanzen *e:* **Gesunde Pfl[anz]**
Gesundheit *d:* **Ges.,** *d:* **Gesund.,** *d:* **Gesundh.**
Gesundheit-Presse-Dienst *d:* **GPD**
Gesundheit und Wohlfahrt *e:* **Gesundh Wohlf[ahrt]**

Gesundheits-, Arbeits- und Brandschutz *d:*
  GAB, *d:* **GABS**
Gesundheits-Ingenieur *d:* **GEINA**, *d:* **Ges-Ing**, *d:* **Gesundh.-Ing.**, *d:* **Gesund-Ing**,
  e: **Gesundh[eits]-Ing**
Gesundheits-Ingenieur. Haustechnik-Bauphysik-Umwelttechnik *e:* **Gesund-Ing Haustech-Bauphys-Umwelttech**
Gesundheits-Überwachungs-Vorsorge *d:*
  GÜV
Gesundheits- und Arbeitsschutz *d:* **GAS**,
  d: **GuA**
Gesundheits Verträglichkeitsprüfung *d:*
  GVP
Gesundheitsamt *d:* **GesA**
Gesundheitsberatung *d:* **GHB**
Gesundheitsdienst *d:* **GD**, *e:* **Gesundhd**
Gesundheitsdienstgesetz *d:* **GDG**
Gesundheitsdirektion des Kantons Zürich
  d: **GD-ZH**
Gesundheitserziehung *d:* **GE**
Gesundheitsführung *d:* **Gesundheitsführ.**
Gesundheitsführung des Deutschen Volkes
  d: **Gesundheitsführ Dtsch Volkes**
Gesundheitsfürsorge *e:* **Gesundh Fürs**
Gesundheitskarte *d:* **G-Karte**
Gesundheitskarteikarte *d:* **GKK**
Gesundheitsminister-Konferenz *d:* **GMK**
Gesundheitspolitischer Kongreß *d:* **GPK**
Gesundheitsreformgesetz *d:* **GRG**
Gesundheitsschutz in den Betrieben *d:*
  GSB
Gesundheitsstrukturgesetz *d:* **GSG**
Gesundheitstechnische Gesellschaft *d:*
  GTG
Gesundheitswesen *d:* **Gesundheitswes.**
Gesundheitswesen und Desinfektion *d:*
  GEDEAL, *e:* **Gesundheitw und Desinfekt**
Gesundheitszeugnis *d:* **GZ**
Gesundheitszeugnisverordnung *d:* **GZV**,
  d: **GZVO**
Gewässer *d:* **Gew**
Gewässergüteüberwachungssystem *d:*
  GÜS
Gewässerinformationssystem *d:* **GEWIS**
Gewässerschutzamt Basel Stadt *d:* **GSA**
Gewässerüberwachungssystem
  Niedersachsen *d:* **GÜN**
Gewässerunterhaltungs- und
  Meliorationsverband *d:* **GUM**
GEWEX [Global energy and Water Cycle
  Experiment] Cloud System Study *e:*
  GCSS
GEWEX Hydrometeorological Panel *e:*
  GHP
GEWEX Water Vapour Project *e:* **GVaP**
GFF [Geologiska Foreningen i Stockholm
  Forhandlingar] *r:* **GFF [Geol Foren Stockholm Forhandl]**
Ghana. Animal Research Institute. Annual
  Report *e:* **Ghana Anim Res Inst Annu Rep**
Ghana Geographical Association *e:*
  G.G.A.
Ghana Geographical Association. Bulletin
  e: **GGAB**
Ghana Medical Journal *e:* **Ghana Med J**,
  e: **GHMJA**, *e:* **GHMJA[Y]**
Ghana Water and Sewage Corporation *e:*
  GWSC
Giant Earth Mover *e:* **GEM**

Gidrobiologicheskii Zhurnal *R:* **Gidrobiol Zh**
Gidrobiologicheskii Zhurnal/
  Hydrobiological Journal *R:* **Gidrobiol Zh Hydrogiol J**
Gidrogeologicheskii Sbornik *R:* **Gidrogeol Sb**
Gidrogeologiya i Gidrogeokhimiya *R:*
  Gidrogeol Cidrogeokhim
Gidrogeologiya i Karstoverdenie *R:*
  Gidrogeol Karstoved
Gidrogeoloya i Gidrogeokhimiya *R:*
  Gidrogeol Gidrogeokhim
Gidrometeorologiya Azerbaidzhana i
  Kaspiiskogo.Morya *R:* **Gidromet Azerb Kasp Mory**
Giessener Geographische Schriften *d:*
  Giess. Geogr. Schr.
Gießener Geologische Schriften *d:*
  Gießener Geol Schr
Giessener Geologische Schriften *d:* **Giess. Geol Schr**
Gießener Schriftenreihe Tierzucht und
  Haustiergenetik *d:* **Gießener Schriftenr Tierz Haustiergenet**, *d:* **GSTHA4**
Giornale Italiano di Medicina del Lavoro
  i: **G Ital Med Lav**
Gippsland Regional Environmental Study
  e: **GRES**
Gippsland Waters Coalition *e:* **GWC**
Gir Wildlife Sanctuary *e:* **GWS**
GIS Newsletter [Geoscience Information
  Society] *e:* **GIS Newsl.**
Gish Biomedical, Inc. *e:* **GISH**
Give Our Animals Time *e:* **GOAT**
Gl. Haustechnik, Bauphysik,
  Umwelttechnik *d:* **GHBUD**
Glacial Geomorphology *e:* **GGM**
Glacier Natural History Association.Special
  Bulletin *e:* **Glacier Nat History Assoc Special Bull**
Glacier-Ocean-Atmosphere *e:* **GOA**
Glaciers, Ice Sheets and Sea Level *e:*
  GISSL
Glas. Srpska Akademija Nauka i Umetnosti
  Odeljenje Medicinskih Nauka *S:*
  SUGMAW
Glas. Srpska Akademija Nauka I Umetnosti,
  Odeljenje Medicinskih Nauka *se:* **Glas Srp Akad Nauka [Med]**
Glasgow Medical Journal *e:* **Glasg Med J**,
  e: **Glasgow Med J**
Glasgow Naturalist *e:* **GGNTAS**, *e:* **Glasg Nat**, *e:* **Glasg[ow] Nat**
Glasgow Obstetrical and Gynaecological
  Society *e:* **G.O.G.S.**
Glasnik. Bioloske Sekcije. *P:* **Glasn Biol Sekc Hrv Prir Dr**
Glass Oceanographic Buoy *e:* **GOAT**, *e:*
  GOB
Glasson Moss National Nature Reserve *e:*
  GMNNR
Glavna Uprava Medicinske Proizvodnje
  se: **GUMP**
Glavnaya Astronomicheskaya
  Observatoriya *R:* **GAO**
Glavnaya Geofizicheskaya Observatoriya
  R: **GGO**
Glavnaya Geofzicheskaya Observatory *R:*
  GGO
Glavnoe Upravlenie Geodezii i Kartografii
  R: **GUGK**

Glavnoe Upravlenie po Geodezia i
  Kartografia i Kadaster *R:* **GUGKK**
Glavnoje Upravlenije Geodesii i Kartografii
  R: **G G U G K**
Glavnoje Upravlenije
  Gidrometeorologicheskoi Sluzhby *R:* **G U G M S**
Glazed Earthenware *e:* **GEW**
Glazialgeologie *d:* **Glazialgeol.**
gleichwertiger Wasserstand *d:* **GLW**
Gleitkomma-Interpretiersystem *d:* **GIPS**
Glen Canyon Environmental Studies *e:*
  GCES
Glen on the Public Health Laws *e:* **Glen Pub H**
Global Air-ocean in-situ System *e:*
  GAINS
Global Air [or Atmospheric] Sampling
  Program *e:* **GASP**
Global Alliance for Women's Health *e:*
  GAWH
Global and Remote Observations Section
  e: **GRO**
Global Atmosphere (or Atmospheric) Gases
  Experiment *e:* **GAGE**
Global Atmosphere (or Atmospheric)
  Research Program[me] *e:* **GARP**
Global Atmosphere (or Atmospheric) Watch
  e: **GAW**
Global Atmospheric Aerosol Radiation
  Experiment *e:* **GAAREX**
Global Atmospheric and Aerosol Radiation
  Study *e:* **GAARS**
Global Atmospheric Chemical (or
  Chemistry) Survey *e:* **GLOCHEM**
Global Atmospheric Chemistry *e:* **GAC**
Global Atmospheric Measurements
  Experiment[s] of/on Tropospheric
  Aerosols and Gases *e:* **GAMETAG**
Global Atmospheric Measurements Program
  e: **GAMP**
Global Atmospheric Prediction Model *e:*
  GAPM
Global Atmospheric Radionuclide
  Detection System *e:* **GARDS**
Global Atmospheric Research Programme.
  Publications Series *e:* **Global Atmos Res Programme Publ Ser**
Global Atmospheric Sampling Laboratory
  e: **GASLAB**
Global Biogeochemical Cycles *e:* **Glob. Biogeochem. Cycles**
Global biome model-biogeochemical cycle
  e: **BIOME-BGC**
Global Change and Ecological Complexity
  e: **GCEC**
Global Change Climate and History *e:*
  GCH
Global Change Observation (or Observing)
  System *e:* **GCOS**
Global Climate Change Digest *e:* **GCCD**
Global Climate Change [Program] *e:* **GCC**
Global Climate Change Program *e:* **GCCP**
Global Climate Coalition *e:* **GCC**
Global Climate Convention *e:* **GCC**
Global Climate Model *e:* **GCM**
Global Climate Modeling Group *e:*
  GCMC, *e:* **GCMG**
Global Climate Observing System *e:*
  GCOS
Global Climate Observing System Fund *e:*
  GCOSF

Global Climate Perspectives System e:
GCPS

Global Community Health e: **GCH**

Global Computer Network for Environment,
Peace and Human Rights e: **GreenNet**

Global Continental Palaeohydrology Project
e: **GLOCOPH**

Global Crop Protection Federation e:
GCPF

Global Digital Sea-Ice Data Bank e:
GDSIDB

Global Ecology and Biogeography Letters
e: **Glob. Ecol. Biogeogr. Lett.**

Global Ecology and Water Cycle
Experiment e: **GWEX**

Global Ecology Honors Program e: **GEHP**

Global Electro-Optical Systems
Environment Matrix e: **GEOSEM**

Global Emergency Medicine Archives e:
GEMA

Global Emergency Observation and
Warning System e: **GEOWARN**

Global Energy and Water [Cycle]
Experiment e: **GEWEX**

Global Environment and Trade Study e:
GETS

Global Environment Facility/UNDP as the
Implementing Agencie[y] e:
GEF/UNDP

Global Environment Information Centre e:
GEIC

Global Environment Monitoring System e:
GEMB

Global Environment Outlook e: **GEO**

Global Environment Outlook-2 Process e:
GEO-2

Global Environment Research Group e:
GERG

Global Environment Research Office e:
GER

Global Environmental and Ecological
Simulation of Interactive Systems e:
GENESIS

Global Environment[al] Change e: **GEC**

Global Environmental Change and Human
Security [project] e: **GECHS**

Global Environmental Change Programme
e: **GECP**

Global Environment[al] Change Report e:
GECR

Global Environmental Corp. e: **GLEN**

Global Environmental Data Directory e:
GEDD

Global Environmental Epidemiology
Network e: **GEENET**

Global Environment[al] Facility e: **GEF**

Global Environment[al] Fund e: **GEF**

Global Environmental Information Locator
Service e: **GELOS**

Global Environmental Management
Initiative e: **GEMI**

Global Environmental Monitoring Service
e: **GEMS**

Global Environmental Monitoring
Service/Programme Activity Centre e:
GEMS/PAC

Global Environment[al] Monitoring
System[s] e: **GEMS**

Global Environmental Network e: **GNN**

Global Environmental Network for
Information Exchange e: **GENIE**

Global Environmental Network[s] e: **GEN**

Global Environment[al] Outlook
[Programme] e: **GEO**

Global Environmental Research e: **GER**

Global Environmental Research
Organization e: **GERO**

Global Environmental Trust Fund e:
GETF

Global Epidemiological Surveillance and
Health Situation Assessement e: **GES**

Global Geocryological Database e: **GGD**

Global Geodynamics Project e: **GGP**

Global Geoscience Transects e: **GGT**

Global Geospace Science Polar Spacecraft
e: **Polar**

Global Geospace Science Program e: **GGS**

Global Geospace Science satellite Wind e:
GGS-Wind

Global Geospace Study e: **GGS**

Global Geosynchronous Science e: **GGS**

Global Geosynchronous Science Thermal
Ions Dynamics Experiment e:
GGSTIDE

Global Health and Environment Library
Network e: **GELNET**

Global Health Council e: **GHC**

Global Health Data Viewer e: **GHDV**

Global Health Disaster Network e:
GHDNet

Global Health Equity Initiative e: **GHEI**

Global Health Foundation e: **GHF**

Global Health Network e: **GHNet**

Global Health Sciences Fund e: **GHS**

Global Historical Climate (or Climatology)
Network e: **GHCN**

Global Impacts (or Implications) of Applied
Microbiology e: **GIAM**

Global Information Environment e: **GIE**

Global Inland Waters Assessment
programme e **GIWA**

Global Interdependence Center e: **GIC**, e:
IGIC

Global Investigation of/on Pollution in the
Marine Environment e: **GIPME**

Global Investigation of Pollution in the
Marine Environment e: **GIMPE**

Global Land-Ocean River Inputs database
e: **GLORI**

Global Learning and/by Observation[s] to
Benefit the Environment e: **GLOBE**

Global Legislators' Organisation (or
Organization) for a Balanced
Environment e: **GLOBE**

Global Legislators Organization for a
Balanced Environment e: **GLOBE
Europe**

Global Low Orbit Message Relay [Satellite]
e: **GLOMR**

Global Mean Water Line e: **GMWL**

Global [Meteorological Ground]
Telecommunications System e: **GTS**

Global Meteorological Satellite System
Program e: **GMSS**

Global Modelling of Atmospheric
Chemistry e: **GLOMAC**

Global Natural Resources, Inc. e: **GNR**

Global Natural Resources Properties Ltd.
e: **GNRP**

Global Network for Environmental
Monitoring e: **GNEM**

Global Network of Environment and
Technology e: **GNET**

Global Observation Information Network
e: **GOIN**

Global Observation Research Initiative in
Alpine Environments e: **GLORIA**

Global Observation Station e: **G.O.S.**

Global Observation Surveillance System e:
GLOSS

Global Observation System e: **GOS**

Global Observations and Modeling Project
e: **GOM**

Global Observations, Modeling and Optical
Techniques Section e: **GOMOT**

Global Observations of Forest Cover e:
GOFC

Global Observing Systems Space Panel e:
GOSSP

Global Ocean-Atmosphere-Land-Surface
Interactions e: **GOALS**

Global Ocean Atmosphere Land System e:
CLIVAR GOALS

Global Ocean Camers Ltd e: **GIBLOCN**

Global Ocean Carbon Research Program e:
GORC

Global Ocean Carriers Ltd. e: **GLBIN**, e:
GLO

Global Ocean Color e: **GOC**

Global Ocean Data Assimilation
Experiment e: **GODAE**

Global Ocean Database 1996 e: **GODB96**

Global Ocean-Ecosystem Coupling e:
GLOBEC

Global Ocean Euphotic Zone Study e:
GOEZS

Global Ocean-Floor Analysis and Research
e: **GOFAR**

Global Ocean Flux e: **GOF**

Global Ocean Flux Study e: **GOFS**

Global Ocean Monitoring e: **GOM**

Global Ocean Monitoring Payload Studies
e: **GOMPS**

Global Ocean Monitoring Satellite e:
GOMS

Global Ocean Observing System e: **GOOS**

Global Ocean Sea Surface Temperature e:
GOSST

Global Ocean Sea Surface Temperature
Computation e: **GOSSTCOMP**

Global Ocean Surface Temperature Atlas
e: **GOSTA**

Global Ocean Surveillance System Glossary
e: **GLOSS**

Global Ocean Velocity Pilot Project e:
GOVPP

Global [Oceanographic and] Meteorological
Experiment e: **GLOMEX**

Global Oceanographic Data Archaeology
and Rescue Project e: **GODAR**

Global Oceans Ecosystems Dynamics e:
GOED, e: **GOES**

Global Omnibus Environmental Survey e:
GOES

Global [Orbiting and] Navigation Satellite
System e: **GLONASS**

Global Orbiting Defence System e: **GODS**

Global Paleoclimate Observing System e:
GPOS

Global Positioning System-Integrated
Precipitable Water e: **GPS-IPW**

Global Precipitation Climatology Center (or
Centre) e: **GPCC**

Global Precipitation Climatology Program
(or Project) e: **GPCP**

Global Precipitation Climatology Project-
Algorithm Intercomparison Project e:
GPCP-AIP

Abkürzungen und Akronyme in Ökologie, Umwelt, Geowissenschaften

Global Programme of Action for the Protection of the Marine Environment from Land-based Activities e: **GPA**, e: **GPA-LBA**

Global Protectinn Against Accidental Launch System e: **GPAALS**

Global Protection against Accidental Launch System e: **GPALS**

Global Protection against Limited Strike e: **GPAIS**

Global Protection System e: **GPS**

Global RADAR for Ocean Waves e: **GLOW**

Global Redevelopment with Energy Environment Sustainability e: **GREENS**

Global Sea Ice and Sea Surface Temperature e: **GISST**

Global Sea Level Monitoring Programme e: **GSLMP**

Global Sea-Level Observing System e: **GLOSS**

Global Security Environment e: **GSE**

Global Sedimentary Geology Program e: **GSG**, e: **GSGP**

Global Services Space Systems e: **GSSS**

Global Space Transport e: **GST**

Global Spectral Ocean Wave Model e: **GSOWM**

Global Telecommunications System [of the World Weather] e: **G.T.S.**

Global Telecommunication[s] System [of the World Weather Watch] e: **GTS**

Global Theater Weather Analysis and Prediction System e: **GTWAPS**

Global Tropospheric Experiment/Transport and Atmospheric Chemistry near the Equator e: **GTE/TRACE**

Global User Environment e: **GLUE**

Global Water e: **GW**

Global Water Partnership e: **GWP**

Global Water Quality Monitoring Programme e: **GEMS/ WATER**

Global Weather Center e: **GWC**

Global Weather Central e: **GWC**

Global Weather Dynamics Inc. e: **GWDI**

Global Weather Experiment e: **GWE**

Global Weather Facsimile Network e: **GWFN**

Global Weather Intercept Position e: **GWIP**

Global [weather] Observing Systems e: **GOS**

Globale Atmosphärenüberwachung d: **GAW**

Globales Energie- und Wasserkreislauf Experiment d: **GEWEX**

Globalisation, Ecology and Economy e: **GEE**

GLOBEC Southern Ocean Programme e: **SO-GLOBEC**

Glycobiology (Oxford) e: **Glycobiology**

Glynn on Water Powers e: **Glynn Wat Pow**

GMI Short Paper. Oregon Department of Geology and Mineral Industries e: **GMI Short Pap Oreg Dep Geol Miner Ind**

GMIL Spaceffight Tracking and Data Network e: **GMIL Sp**

GMT of Orbital Midnight e: **TOM**

GN Geodesics and Mask e: **GSMASK**

GNSS [combined GPS and GLONASS positioning systems] Receiver for Atmospheric Sounding e: **GRAS**

GO. Revista de Atualizacao em Ginecologia e Obstetricia i: **GORABE**

GO. Revista de Atualizacaoem Ginecologiaa e Obstetricia e: **GO Rev Atualizacao Ginecol Obs**

GOAL Ground Operations Aerospace Language e: **GOAL Gr**

GOAL [Ground Operations Aerospace Language] Language Processor e: **GLP**

GOAL [Ground Operations Aerospace Language] Processing Language e: **GPL**

GOAL [Ground Operations Aerospace Language] Program Control Block e: **GPCB**

GOAL [Ground Operations Aerospace Language] Test Procedurc Update Request e: **GPUR**

Goddard Earth Model e: **GEM**

Goddard Earth Observing System e: **GEOS**

Goddard Geophysical and Astronomical Observatory e: **GGAO**

Goddard Inst. for Space Studies-Indiana State University Remote Sensing Laboratory e: **GISS-ISURSL**

Goddard Institute for/of Space Studies e: **GISS**

Goddard Institute for Space Sciences e: **GISS**

Goddard Institute for Space Studies e: **GI for SS**

Goddard Laboratory for/of Atmospheric Science[s] e: **GLAS**

Goddard Laboratory for [of the] Atmospheres e: **GLA**

Goddard Manned Space Flight e: **GMSF**

Goddard Space Flight Center (or Centre) e: **GSFC**

Godden Memorial Medical Centre e: **GMMC**

Godisnjak Bioloskog Instituta Universiteta u Sarajevu se: **God Biol Inst Univ Sarajevu**

Godisnjak Vojnomedicinske Akademije se: **God Vojnomed Akad**

GOES Geostationary Operational Environment Satellite e: **GOES Ge**

GOES-Meteosat Relay e: **GMR**

Gold Bondholders Protective Council e: **GBPC**

Gold Coast Environment Centre e: **GCEC**

Gold Coast Geological Survey.Bulletin e: **Gold Coast Geol Surv Bull**

Gold PlacerDeposits at the Food of the Eastern Cordillera of Bolivia e: **Gold Placer Deposits Foot East**

Goldstone Deep Space Communications Complex e: **GDSCC**

Goldstone-SFOF [Space Flight Operations Facility] Microwave Assembly e: **GSMA**

Goodland Weather Forecast Office e: **GLD**

Goodyear Aerospace Corporation e: **GAC**

Gordon Environmental Studies Laboratory e: **GEVST**

Gorgas Memorial Institute of Tropical and Preventive Medicine e: **GMITPM**

Gosudarstvennaja Central'naja Naučnaja Medicinskaja Biblioteka R: **GCNMB**

Goteborg Universitet. Naturgeografiska Institutionen.Rapport r: **Goteborg Univ Naturgeogr Inst Rapp**

Göteborgs Medicinska Högskola r: **Gbg Med HS**

Goteborgs Naturhistoriska Museum Arstryck r: **Goteb Naturhist Mus Arstryck**

Goteborgs Universitet Naturgeografiska Institutionen r: **GUNI**

Göttingen Geochemical Institute e: **GGI**

Göttinger Arbeiten zur Geologie d: **Goett Arb Geol Palaeontol**

Göttinger Arbeiten zur Geologie und Paläontologie d: **Gött Arb Geol Paläontol**

Göttingisches Journal der Naturwissenschaften d: **Goething J Naturw**, d: **Götting J Naturw**

Gould in Waters e: **Gould Wat**

Gould, Inc., Ocean Systems Information Center, Cleveland e: **OGO**

Gould Medical Dictionary e: **GMD**

Governing Council for Environmental Programmes e: **G C E P**

Governing Council for Environmental Programs e: **GCEP**

Government Employees Health Fund e: **GEHF**

Government-Furnished Aernspace Equipment e: **GFAE**

Government-Furnished Aerospace Ground Equipment e: **GFAGE**

Government Geologists Database Policy Advisory Committee e: **GGDPAC**

Government Medical Office[r] e: **GMO**

Government of Canada, Environment Canada e: **GC ENV**

Government Relations Office, Spar Aerospace Ltd., Ottawa, Ontario e: **OOSAR**

Governor Bacon Health Center e: **GBHC**

GPS Geoscience Instrument e: **GGI**

GPS/Meteorological Satellite e: **GPS/MET**

Grade Crossing Protection Device e: **GCPD**

Graduate Aerospace Mechanical Engineering e: **GAM Engineering**

Graduate Diploma for Science Teachers [Geology] e: **GradDipGeol**

Graduate Diploma in Environmental and Municipal Engineering e: **GradDipEnv&MunEng**

Graduate Diploma in Health Information Management e: **GradDipHIM**

Graduate Diploma in Health Services Management e: **GradDipHealthServMgmt**

Graduate Diploma in Metal Finishing and Surface Protection e: **GradDipSurFin**

Graduate Diploma in Occupational Health and Safety e: **GradDipOH&S**

Graduate in Homoeopathic Medicine and Surgery e: **GHMS**

Graduate Medical Education e: **GME**

Graduate Medical Education National Advisory Committee e: **GMENAC**

Graduate of the London School of Tropical Medicine e: **G.L.S.T.M.**

Graduate Program in Ecology e: **GPE**

Graduate School of Biomedical Sciences e: **GSBS**

Graduate School of Integrative Medicine e: **GSIM**

Graduate School of Oceanography e: **GSO**

Graduates of Italian Medical Schools *e:* **GIMS**

Graecolatina et Orientalia *l:* **GeO**

Graham and Waterman on New Trials *e:* **Grah&W New Trials**

Graham-Field Health Products, Inc. *e:* **GRHMFL**

Gram[s] of Water in Air *e:* **GWA**

Grand Canyon Natural History Association.Bulletin *e:* **Grand Canyon Nat History Assoc Bull**

Grand Challenge Computational Environment *e:* **GRACCE**

Grand Island Biological Company *e:* **GIBCO**

Grand prix international de l'environnement marin *f:* **GPIEM**

Grand Quartier Général *f:* **GQG**

Grand Quartier-Général des Armées *f:* **G.Q.G.A.**

Grandeur Nature *f:* **GN**

Grant Tensor Geophysical *e:* **GRNT**

Graphic Environment Operating System *e:* **GEOS**

Graphic Remote Interface Display *e:* **GRLD**

Graphic Weather Display System *e:* **GWDS**

Graphical Airspace Design Environment *e:* **GRADE**

Graphical Natural Interference System *e:* **GRANIS**

Graphic[al] (or Graphics) Environment Manager *e:* **GEM**

Graphics Environment Manager *e:* **GEM**

Graphite Moderated Water Cooled *e:* **GMWC**

graphitiert *d:* **graph.**

Graphitierung *d:* **Graphitier.**

Grasslands Ecology Program *e:* **GEP**

Graver Water Conditioning Company. Technical Reprint *e:* **Graver Water Cond Co Tech Repr**

Graves Medical Audiovisual Library *e:* **GMAL**

Gravina's De Jure Naturale Gentium, Etc. *l:* **Grav De Jur Nat Gent**

Gravitational Redshift Space Probe *e:* **GP**, *e:* **GRAVR**

Gravity Field and Steady-State Ocean Circulation Explorer *e:* **GOCE**

Gravity Recovery and Climate Experiment *e:* **GRACE**

Grays Harbor College Aberdeen *e:* **WaAG**

Great Basin Naturalist *e:* **Great Basin Nat**, *e:* **Gt. Basin Nat.**

Great Basin Naturalist. Memoirs *e:* **Great Basin Nat Mem**

Great Hungarian Plain *e:* **GHP**

Great Lakes and Marine Waters Center *e:* **GLMWC**

Great Lakes Environmental [Data and] Information Center *e:* **GLEDIC**

Great Lakes Environmental Information Sharing *e:* **GLEIS**

Great Lakes Environmental Research Laboratory *e:* **GLERL**

Great Lakes Environmental Wire *e:* **GLEW**

Great Lakes Protection Fund *e:* **GLPF**

Great Lakes Water *e:* **GLW**

Great Lakes Water Quality Agreement[s] *e:* **GLWQA**

Great Lakes Water Quality Board *e:* **GLWQB**

Great Lakes Waterways Development Association *e:* **GLWDA**

Great Space Handshake *e:* **GSH**

Great Swamp National Wildlife Refuge *e:* **GSNWR**

Great Water Holt *e:* **GWH**

Great White Heron National Wildlife Refuge *e:* **GWHNWR**

Greater Baltimore Medical Center *e:* **GBMC**

Greater North Central Natural Resources Journal *e:* **Greater N. Cent. Nat. Resources J.**

Greater Underwater Propulsion Power *e:* **GUPPY**

Greater Winnipeg Water District *e:* **GWWD**

Greek Army Geographic Service *e:* **GAGS**

Green Bank Observatory *e:* **GBO**

Green Disk Environmental Journal *e:* **GDEJ**

Green Institute of Geophysics and Planetary Physics *e:* **GIGPP**

Greenhouse Climate Response Index *e:* **GCRI**

Greenland Environment Research Institute *e:* **GM**

Greenland Environmental Research Institute *e:* **GERI**

Greenland Geologiske Undersoegelse.Bulletin *a:* **Greenland Geol Unders Bull**

Greenland Geoscience *e:* **Greenl Geosci**

Greenland Geoscience.Meddelelser om Gronland *a:* **GRGSC**

Greenland Ice Cap Aeromagnetic Survey *e:* **GICAS**

Greenland Ice-core Program *e:* **GRIP**

Greenland Ice[-core] Project *e:* **GRIP**

Greenland Ice Sheet *e:* **GIC**

Greenland Ice Sheet Program *e:* **GISP**

Greenland Ice Sheet Project *e:* **GISP**

Greenland Sea Project *e:* **GSP**

Greenland.Geologiske Undersoegelse.Rapport *a:* **Greenland Geol Unders Rapp**

Greenwich Royal Observatory *e:* **GRO**

GREMP [Geothermal Reservoir Engineering Management Program] News *e:* **NGRPD**

Grenoble. Faculte des Sciences. Laboratoire de Geologie.Memoires *f:* **Grenoble Fac Sci Lab Geol Mem**

Grenzgebiete der Medizin *d:* **Grenzgeb Med**

Gridded Meteorological Data Extraction System *e:* **GMDES**

Griffith Observatory *e:* **GOC**

Griffith Observatory and Planetarium *e:* **GO&P**

Groenlands Geologiske Undelsoegelse. Rapport *a:* **GGUR**

Groenlands Geologiske Undersoegelse. Bulletin *a:* **GGUB**, *a:* **Groenlnds Geol Unders Bull**

Groenlands Geologiske Undersoegelse. Miscellaneous Papers *a:* **GGUMP**

Groenlands Geologiske Undersoegelse.Miscellaneous Papers *a:* **Groenlands Geol Unders Misc Pap**

Groenlands Geologiske Undersoegelse.Rapport *a:* **Groenl Geol Unders Rap**

Grondboor en Hamer [Nederlandse Geologische Verening Tijdschrift] *n:* **Grondboor Hamer**

Grønlands Geologiske Undersøgelser *a:* **GGU**

Großversuchseinrichtung zur Grundwasser- und Altlastensanierung *d:* **VEGAS**

Großwetterlage *d:* **GWL**

Ground and Environment[al] *e:* **G&E**

Ground-based Atmospheric Profiling Experiment *e:* **GAPEX**

Ground-based Earth Observing Network *e:* **GEONET**

Ground-based Electro-Optical Deep Space Surveillance System *e:* **GEODESS System**

Ground-Based Electro-Optical Deep-Space Surveillance [System] *e:* **GEODSS**

Ground-based Electro-Optical Deep Space Surveillance System *e:* **GEODSSS**

Ground-Based Electro-Optical Deep Space Surveillance System *e:* **GEODSS System**

Ground-Control[led] Space System[s] *e:* **GCSS**

Ground Detection Radarmeteorology *e:* **GDR**

Ground Earth Station *e:* **GES**

Ground Environment Complex *e:* **GEC**

Ground Environment Equipment *e:* **GEE**

Ground Environment Installation *e:* **GES**

Ground Environment Program *e:* **GEP**

Ground Environment Technical Information System *e:* **GETIS**

Ground Environment Technical Installation System *e:* **GETIS**

Ground Environmental Control System *e:* **GECS**

Ground Environmental Development *e:* **GED**

Ground Environment[al] Team of the International Staff *e:* **GETIS**

Ground Identification of Missions in Space *e:* **GIMS**

Ground Launched Optical Observation Platform *e:* **GLOOP**

Ground Meteorological Detector *e:* **GMD**

Ground Meteorological Device *e:* **GMD**

Ground Meteorological Site *e:* **GMD**

Ground Observation Post *e:* **GOP**

Ground Observation Reporting System *e:* **GORS**

Ground Operational Equipment for the Orbiting Astronomical Observatory *e:* **GOE for OAO**

Ground Operations Aerospace Language *e:* **GOAL**

Ground Protection *e:* **GP**

Ground Protection Against Limited Strike[s] *e:* **GPALS**

Ground Protective *e:* **GP**

Ground-Protective Relay *e:* **GP Relay**

Ground Radar Environment *e:* **GRE**

Ground, Remotely-Sensed and Documentary Data Bank *e:* **GRSDDB**

Ground Spaceflight Tracking and Data Network *e:* **GSTDN**

Ground System Development Environment *e:* **GSDE**

Ground Test Accelerator/Neutral Particle Beam Space Experiment *e:* **GTA/NPBSE**

Ground Up-to-Space *e:* **GUTS**

Ground Water *e:* **GW**

Ground Water Age *e:* **Groond Wat**

Ground Water Assessment *e:* **GWA**

Ground Water Council *e:* **GCS,** *e:* **GWC**

Ground Water Development Bureau *e:* **GWDB**

Ground Water Disinfedtion Rule *e:* **GWDR**

Ground Water Heat Pump Journal *e:* **Gmand Water Heat Pump J,** *e:* **GWHJD**

Ground-Water Information *e:* **GWI**

Ground Water Institute *e:* **GWI**

Ground Water Level *e:* **GWL**

Ground Water Management District *e:* **GWMD**

Ground Water Monitor[ing] *e:* **GWM**

Ground Water Monitoring Plan *e:* **GMP**

Ground Water Monitoring Review *e:* **Gronnd Water Monit Rer**

Ground Water Protection Act *e:* **GWPA**

Ground Water Protection Management Program Plan *e:* **GWPMPP**

Ground Water Protetion Council *e:* **GWPC**

Ground Water Research Institute *e:* **GWRI**

Ground Water Resources Institute *e:* **GWRI**

Ground Water Table *e:* **GWT**

Ground Water Technology Division *e:* **GWTD**

Ground Water Travel Time *e:* **GWTT**

Ground Water Treatment Rule *e:* **GWTR**

Ground Water Under the Influence *e:* **GWUI**

Groundwater Activated Carbon *e:* **GAC**

Groundwater and Environmental Geology *e:* **GEG**

Groundwater and Soil Cleanup *e:* **GW/S**

Groundwater Characterization Project *e:* **GCP**

Groundwater Contamination Indicators *e:* **GWCI**

Groundwater Data Analysis System *e:* **GDAS**

Groundwater Flow *e:* **GWF**

Groundwater Flow and Transport Modelling Page *e:* **GFTMP**

Groundwater Management Caucus *e:* **GMC**

Groundwater Management Districts Association *e:* **GMDA**

Groundwater Modelling Department *e:* **GMD**

Groundwater Modelling Software Internet Resources *e:* **GWSIR**

Groundwater Monitoring Review *e:* **GWMR**

Groundwater Monitoring System *e:* **GWMS**

Groundwater Monitoring Wells *e:* **GMW**

Groundwater Policy and Management Staff *e:* **GWPMS**

Groundwater Protection Management Plan *e:* **GPMP**

Groundwater Protection Management Program *e:* **GPMP**

Groundwater Protection Management Program Plan *e:* **GPMPP**

Groundwater Protection Standard[s] *e:* **GWPS**

Groundwater Protection Strategy *e:* **GPS,** *e:* **GWPS**

Groundwater Pumping Incentives Scheme *e:* **GPIS**

Groundwater Remedial Guidance Level *e:* **GRGL**

Groundwater Remediation Field Laboratory *e:* **GRFL**

Groundwater Residue Guidance Level *e:* **GRGL**

Groundwater Resource Protection Regulatory Compliance *e:* **GRPRC**

Groundwater Resources and Protection *e:* **GRP**

Groundwater Site Inventory *e:* **GWSI**

Groundwater Surveillance *e:* **GWS**

Groundwater Task Force *e:* **GWTF**

Groundwater Technology, Incorporated *e:* **GWTI**

Groundwater Well Services *e:* **GWS**

Groundwater Working Group *e:* **GWG**

Group Climate Questionnaire *e:* **GCQ**

Group Environment Scale *e:* **GES**

Group for Environmental Education *e:* **GEE**

Group Health Association of America *e:* **GHAA**

Group Health Cooperative *e:* **GHC**

Group Health Insurance *e:* **GHI**

Group Health Journal *e:* **Group Health J**

Group Health Program *e:* **GHP**

Group 77 [meaning a group of 77 underdeveloped countries] *e:* **G77**

Group Medical Report *e:* **GMR**

Group Medicare Cooperative Society *e:* **GMCS**

Group Meteorological Officer *e:* **GMetO**

Group of Experts Monitoring of Radioactive Substances in the Baltic Sea *e:* **MORS**

Group of Experts on Environmental Pollutants *e:* **GEEP**

Group of Experts on Ocean Processes and Climate *e:* **GE-OPC**

Group of Experts on Pollution of the Ocean Originating on Land *e:* **POOL**

Group of Experts on Responsible National Oceanographic Data Centres [RNODCs] and Climate Data Services *e:* **GE-RCDS**

Group of Experts on Responsible National Oceanographic Data Centres [RNODCs] and Global Programmes *e:* **GERGP**

Group of Experts on [the] Global Sea-level Observing System *e:* **GE-GLOSS**

Group of Experts on the Scientific Aspects of Marine Environmental Protection *e:* **GESAMP**

Group of Specialists on Cenozoic Paleoenvironments of the Southern High Latitudes *e:* **GOSC**

Group of Specialists on Environmental Affairs and Conservation *e:* **GOSEAC**

Group of Specialists on Southern Ocean Ecology *e:* **GOS-SOE**

Group on Geoscience Electronics *e:* **G-GE**

Group spécialisé des ingénieurs du génie Rural et Géomètres *f:* **GRG**

Groupe Aérien d'Observation *f:* **GAO**

Groupe Aérien d'Observation d'Artillerie *f:* **GAOA**

Groupe chargé de la mise en place du Système d'observation de l'océan *f:* **OOSDP**

Groupe consultatif de la COI sur la cartographie des océans *f:* **CGOM**

Groupe Consultatif de la Recherche et de l'Enseignement Forestier pour l'Amérique Latine *f:* **GACIFAL**

Groupe d'Aide Médico-Sociale aux Vieillards *f:* **GAMSAV**

Groupe de Coordination des Satellites Météorologiques *f:* **CGMS**

Groupe de coordination du Système d'observation composite de l'Atlantique Nord *f:* **CGC**

Groupe de Protection et de Sécurité du Président de la République *f:* **GPSP**

Groupe de Protection Urbaine *f:* **GPU**

Groupe de Rapporteurs en Matière de Freinage *f:* **GR**

Groupe de Rapporteurs sur les Casques Protectives *f:* **GRP**

Groupe de Recherche Appliquée en Macroécologie *f:* **GRAME**

Groupe de Recherche de Géodésie Spatiale *f:* **GRGS**

Groupe de Recherche en Biologie de la Reproduction *f:* **GRBR**

Groupe de Recherche en Biologie Spatiale *f:* **GRBS**

Groupe de Recherche en Environnement Agricole *f:* **GREA**

Groupe de Recherche en Recyclage Biologique et Aquiculture *f:* **GREREBA**

Groupe de recherche et de Réalisations pour le Développement Rural dans le tiers monde *f:* **GRDR**

Groupe de Recherche sur les Aspects Sociaux de la Santé et de la Prévention. Health and Prevention Social Research Group *e:* **GRASP**

Groupe de Recherches de Géodésie Speciale *f:* **GRGS**

Groupe de Recherches et d'Études en Océanographie Spatiale *f:* **GREOS**

Groupe de Recherches pour l'Informatique Médicale *f:* **GRIM**

Groupe de Travail de la Détection des Changements Climatiques *f:* **GTDCC**

Groupe de travail Romand et tessinois de l'Audiovisuel à l'École *f:* **GRAVE**

Groupe de travail sur les tsunamis de la Société Européenne de Géophysique *f:* **EGSWG**

Groupe des organismes de parrainage des systèmes mondiaux d'observation *f:* **G3OS**

Groupe des Systèmes mondiaux d'Observation chargé des questions Spatiales *f:* **GOSSP**

Groupe des Écoles d'Armes *f:* **GEDAR**

Groupe des Écoles de Mécaniciens *f:* **G.E.M.**

Groupe des Écoles des Missiliers Artillerie *f:* **G.E.M.A.**

Groupe d'Experts de la COI sur le Système mondial d'observation du niveau de la mer *f:* **GE-GLOSS**

Groupe d'experts de la COI sur le Système mondial d'observation du niveau de la mer, Groupe d'experts sur le GLOSS *f:* **GE-GLOSS**

Groupe d'experts de la gestion de l'environnement pour la lutte antivectorielle *f:* **PEEM**

Groupe d'experts Intergouvernemental sur l'Évolution du Climat *f:* **GIEC**

Groupe d'experts sur les aspects météorologiques de l'océan *f:* **MAOA**

Groupe d'Experts sur les Centres Nationaux de Données Océanographiques Responsables [CNDOR] et les Programmes Mondiaux *f:* **GERGP**

Groupe d'Experts sur les Centres Nationaux de Données Océanographiques Responsables [CNDOR] et les Services de Données Climatologiques *f:* **GE-RCDS**

Groupe d'Experts sur les Processus Océaniques et le Climat *f:* **GE-OPC**

Groupe d'Information Madagascar Océan Indien *f:* **GIMOI**

Groupe directeur d'Experts sur le Programme sur l'Océanologie et les Ressources non vivantes *f:* **GGE-OSNLR**

Groupe d'Observation Dispersée *f:* **GOD**

Groupe d'Observation du Français *f:* **GOF**

Groupe du Conseil exécutif pour l'étude des Aspects Météorologiques des Questions Océaniques *f:* **AMQO**

Groupe d'Étude et Recherches, sur Test Matérieux dans l'Espace *f:* **GERME**

Groupe d'Études de Recherches Critiques d'Espace *f:* **ERCE**

Groupe d'Études en Réanimation Médicale de l'Enfant *f:* **GERME**

Groupe d'Études et de Recherches en Espace de la Créolophonie *f:* **GEREC**

Groupe d'Études pour la Protection de la Nature *f:* **GEPN**

Groupe européen de l'industrie papetiere pour les affaires sociales *f:* **PEGS**

Groupe Européen sur les Stations Océaniques *f:* **EGOS**

Groupe GSC pour l'élaboration du module concernant la santé de l'océan *f:* **HOOP**

Groupe Géographique *f:* **G.G.**

Groupe Hygiène Naturelle *f:* **GHN**

Groupe international de coordination sur la couleur de l'océan *f:* **IOCCG**

Groupe international des Importateurs de Gaz Naturel Liquéfié *f:* **GIGNL**

Groupe International des Importateurs de Gaz Naturel Liquéfié *f:* **GIIGNL**

Groupe interorganisations de la biométéorologie agricole *f:* **IGAB**

Groupe Interuniversitaire des Recherches Océanographiques du Québec *f:* **GIROQ**

Groupe mixte d'Experts chargé d'étudier les Aspects Scientifiques de la Protection de l'environnement Marin *f:* **GESAMP**

Groupe mixte sur les tables et les normes océanographiques *f:* **JPOTS**

Groupe Météorologique du Comité Militaire *f:* **MCMG**

Groupe Parisien des Anciens Élèves de l'École Polytechnique *f:* **GPX**

Groupe Permanent d'Étude des Marchés de Chauffage et de Climatisation *f:* **GPEMCC**

Groupe Romand de l'École Moderne *f:* **GREM**

Groupe Spécialisé des ingénieurs Forestiers *f:* **GSF**

Groupe sur la santé des océans *f:* **HOTO**

Groupe sur les Observations Océaniques pour l'étude du Climat *f:* **OOPC**

Grouped Communication-Electronics and Meteorological Reporting System *e:* **ESR**

Groupement cantonal genevois des Associations de Parents d'élèves des École s Primaires et enfantines *f:* **GAPP**

Groupement d'Ateliers Modernes de Métiers d'Art *f:* **GAMMA**

Groupement d'Aviation Légère de l'École de l'Air *f:* **GALEA**

Groupement de l'Information Médicale des Établissements Privés *f:* **Gimep**

Groupement de Quartier Général et de Transit *f:* **G.Q.G.T.**

Groupement de Recherches Coordonnées sur l'interaction laser-matières *f:* **GRECO**

Groupement des Associations de Défense des Sites de l'Environnement de la Côte d'Azur *f:* **GADSECA**

Groupement des Fabricants et Représentants des Adjuvants en Nutrition Animale *f:* **FRANA**

Groupement des Industries Sidérurgiques Luxembourgeoises *f:* **GISL**

Groupement des Laboratoires internationaux de recherche et d'Industrie du Medicament *f:* **LIM**

Groupement des Organisations de Formation et d'Information Médicales Continues *f:* **GOFIMEC**

Groupement des Transporteurs professionnel routiers de Voyageurs de la Loire *f:* **GTVL**

Groupement des Écoles Préparatoires *f:* **GEP**

Groupement d'Exportation des Constructeurs Français de Matériels Météorologiques *f:* **GEXMET**

Groupement d'Interet Économique pour la Gestion des Navires Océanologiques *f:* **GENAVIR**

Groupement d'intérêt scientifique, Économie Mondiale, tiers monde, Développement *f:* **GEMDEV**

Groupement Départemental des Transports Routiers *f:* **GDTR**

Groupement d'Éspace Fonctionnel *f:* **GEF**

Groupement Européen d'Action Écologique *f:* **ECOROPA**

Groupement Européen des Sources d'Eaux Minérales Naturelles *f:* **GESEM**

Groupement Interdépartemental de l'Apprentissage *f:* **GIDA**

Groupement Interdépartemental des Distillateurs Artisanaux *f:* **GIRAC**

Groupement Interdépartemental des Distillateurs Artisanaux de Calvados *f:* **GIDAC**

Groupement International d'Editeurs Scientifiques, Techniques, et Medicaux *f:* **STM**

Groupement Interprofessionnel d'Action en Faveur du Centre d'Étude des Matières Plastiques *f:* **GIACE**

Groupement Intersyndical pour l'Équipement des Industries du Pétrole, du Gaz Naturel et de la Pétrochimie *f:* **GEP**

Groupement National des Associations Professionnelles Régionales des

Commissionaires Affrêteurs-Routiers *f:* **GNAPRCAR**

Groupement National des Industries de l'Alimentation Animale *f:* **GNIAA**

Groupement National des Papetiers Répartiteurs Spécialisés *f:* **PRS**

Groupement National des Transporteurs Routiers de Denrées et Produits Périssables *f:* **GRDP**

Groupement pour l'Encouragement à la Recherche en Nutrition Animale *f:* **GERNA**

Groupement Professionnel Routier *f:* **G.P.R.**

Groupement Régional d'Animation et d'Initiation à la Nature et à l'Environnement *f:* **GRAINE**

Groupement Tactique Régimentaire Luxembourgeois *f:* **G.T.R.L.**

Groupement Unité Sécurité Protection *f:* **G.U.S.P.**

Groupement École *f:* **GE**

Groupes Géographiques de l'Armée Française *f:* **GGF**

Groupes Régionaux d'Observation de la Grippe *e:* **GROG**

Groupment Observation Post *e:* **Gpmt OP**

Growth of Strategic Materials in Space *e:* **GSMS**

Growth Space Station *e:* **GSS**

Grumman Aerospace Corporation *e:* **GAC**

Grundlagenmedizin *d:* **Grumed**

Grundwasser *d:* **Grdw,** *d:* **Grundw.,** *d:* **Gr.-W.,** *d:* **GW**

Grundwasserabgabengesetz (Schleswig-Holstein) *d:* **GruWAG SH**

Grundwasserflurabstand *d:* **GWF**

Grundwasserneubildung *d:* **GWN**

Grundwasseroberfläche *d:* **GWO**

Grundwasserspiegel *d:* **Grdw.-Sp.,** *d:* **Grundw. Sp.,** *d:* **G.-Sp.,** *d:* **Gwsp.,** *d:* **GW-Spiegel**

Grüne Liste Umweltschutz *d:* **GLU**

Grüne Liste Umweltschutz und Demokratie *d:* **GLD**

Grüne Liste-Wählerinitiative für Umweltschutz und Demokratie *d:* **GLW**

Grüne Listen Umwelt *d:* **GLU**

Grüne Reihe des Bundesministeriums für Gesundheit und Umweltschutz *d:* **Grüne Reihe Bundesminist Gesund Umweltschutz**

Grüne Stadt. Naturschutz in der Großstadt *d:* **Grüne Stadt Natur Großstadt**

Grupo de Coordinación para el Sistema Mixto de Observación para el Atlántico Norte *s:* **CGC**

Grupo de Coordinación sobre Satélites Meteorológicos *s:* **CGMS**

Grupo de Expertos de la COI sobre el Sistema Mundial de Observación del Nivel del Mar, Grupo de Expertos sobre el GLOSS *s:* **GE-GLOSS**

Grupo de Expertos sobre Centros Nacionales Responsables de Datos Oceanográficos [RNODC] y Programas Mundiales *s:* **GERGP**

Grupo de Expertos sobre Centros Nacionales Responsables de Datos Oceanográficos [RNODC] y Servicios de Datos relativos al Clima *s:* **GE-RCDS**

Grupo de Expertos sobre los Procesos Oceánicos y el Clima *s:* **GE-OPC**

Grupo de Orientación de Expertos COI-Naciones Unidas/DOALOS sobre el Programa de Ciencias Oceánicas en relación con los Recursos no Biológicos *s:* **GGE-OSNLR**

Grupo de Patrocinadores para los Sistemas Mundiales de Observación *s:* **G3OS**

Grupo de Trabajo sobre Comercialización de los Servicios Meteorológicos e Hidrológicos [Consejo Executivo de la OMM] *s:* **GTCOM**

Grupo de Trabajo sobre Meteorología del Antártico *s:* **GTMA**

Grupo de Trabajo sobre Tsunamis de la Sociedad Europea de Geofísica *s:* **EGSWG**

Grupo des Comité Ejecutivo Encargado de los Aspectos Meteorológicas de las Asuntos Océanicos *s:* **AMAO**

Grupo Ecológico de Organización y Solidaridad *s:* **GEOS**

Grupo Executivo do Atlas Geoeconomico *s:* **GEAGE**

Grupo Interinstitucional sobre Biometeorología Agrícola *s:* **IGAB**

GSA Bulletin [Geological Society of America] *e:* **GSA Bull.**

GSA [Geolial Society of America] Special Paper [Regional Studies] *e:* **GSA Spec Pap [Reg Stud]**

GSF-Forschungszentrum für Umwelt und Gesundheit GmbH *d:* **GSF**

GSFC Spaceflight Tracking and Data Network Station (KSC) Merritt Island *e:* **MIL**

Guam Remote Ground Terminal *e:* **GRGT**

Guanidine Hydrochloride *e:* **GHCI**

Guardia Medica *i:* **G.M.**

Guardians of Hydrocephalus Research Foundation *e:* **GHRF**

Guggenheim Center for Aviation Health and Safety *e:* **GCAHS**

Guiana Space Center *e:* **GSC**

Guidance and Orbit Determination *e:* **GOD**

Guidance and Orbit Determination for Solar Electric Propulsion *e:* **G O D**, *e:* **GODSEP**

Guidance Attitude Space Position Indicator *e:* **GASPI**

Guidance-Pilotage Orbital *e:* **GPO**

Guide Star Production Operations Environment *e:* **GSOPS**

Guide to Environmental Resources *e:* **GER**

Guidebook Series. Geological Institute [Bucharest] *e:* **Guideb Ser Geol Inst [Bucharest]**

Guidebook to the Geology of Utah *e:* **Guideb Geol Utah**

Guidebook.Annual Field Conference. Montana Geological Society *e:* **Guideb Anna Field Conf Mont Geol Soc**

Guided Missile and Aerospace Intelligence Committee *e:* **GMAIC**

Guided Space Vehicle *e:* **GSV**

Guidelines in Medicine *e:* **Guidel Med**

Guiding Group of Experts on the Programme of Ocean Science in Relation to Non-Living Resources *e:* **GGE-OSNLR**

Guild of Natural Science Illustrators *e:* **GNSI**

Guild of Public Health Inspectors *e:* **GPHI**

Guinea Pig Anti-Bovine Protection *e:* **GPABP**

Gulf Breeze Environmental Research Laboratory *e:* **GBERL**

Gulf Centre for Remote Sensing *e:* **GCRS**

Gulf Coast Association of Geological Societies *e:* **GCAGS**

Gulf Coast Association of Geological Societies. Field Trip Guidebook *e:* **GCGGA**

Gulf Coast Association of Geological Societies. Transactions *e:* **Gulf Coast Assoc Geol Socs Trans**

Gulf Coast Hydroscience Center *e:* **GCHC**

Gulf Coast Low Water Datum *e:* **GCLWD**

Gulf Energy and Environmental Systems *e:* **GEES**

Gulf Environmental Measurements Program *e:* **GEP**

Gulf Environmental Systems Inc. *e:* **GES**

Gulf Geographic Information System *e:* **G-GIS**

Gulf Intracoastal Waterway *e:* **GIW**, *e:* **GIWW**

Gulf Offshore Weather Observing Network *e:* **GOWON**

Gulf Sea Frontier *e:* **GSF**, *e:* **GULFSEAFRON**

Gulf-Stream Atmospheric Gradient Exchange *e:* **GAGE**

Gulf UnderwaterFlare Experiment *e:* **GUFEX**

Gundle Environmental Systems, Inc. *e:* **GUN**, *e:* **GUNDLE**

Gunma Journal of Medical Sciences *e:* **Gunma J Med Sci**

Gunma Journal of Medical Sciences. Supplementum *e:* **Gunma J Med Sci Suppl**

Gunma Reports of Medical Sciences *e:* **Gnma Rep Med Sci**

Gunners Quoin and Quoin Channel north of Mauritius in the Indian Ocean *e:* **Quoins**

Guyana Geology and Mines Commission *e:* **GGMC**

Guyana.Geological Survey Department. Report *e:* **Guyana Geol Surv Dep Rep**

Guyana.Ministry of Agriculture and Natural Resources. Agriculture and Land Development Departments. Annual Report *e:* **Guyana Minist Agric Nat Resour Agric Land Dev Ann Rep**

Guyana.Ministry of Agriculture and Natural Resources. Geological Survey Department.Report *e:* **Guyana Minist Agric Nat Resour Geol Surv Dep Rep**

Guy's Forensic Medicine *e:* **Guy For Med**

Guy's Medical Jurisprudence *e:* **Guy Med Jur**

GWA: Gewässerschutz, Wasser und Abwasser [Germany] *d:* **GWA Gewässerrschutz Wasser Abwasser**

GWE [Global Weather Experiment] Operational Year *e:* **GOY**

Gwent Trust for Nature Conservation *e:* **OWL**

Gwent Wildlife Trust *e:* **OWL**

GWF [Gas- und Wasserfach] Wasser-Abwasser *d:* **GWF Wasser-Abwasser**

GWF. Gas- und Wasserfach: Wasser/Abwasser *d:* **GWWAA**

Gynecologic and Obstetric Investigation *e:* **Gynecol Obstet Invest**

Gynecologic Cancer Foundation *e:* **GCF**

Gynecologic Investigation *e:* **Gynecol Inv[est]**

Gynecologic Oncologists of Canada *e:* **GOC**

Gynecologic Oncology *e:* **Gynecol Oncol**, *e:* **GYNOA**

Gynecologic Oncology Group *e:* **GOG**

Gynecological Endocrinology *e:* **Gynecol Endocrinol**

Gynecologie et Obstetrique *f:* **Gynecol Obstet**

Gynecologie et Obstetrique de Langue Française *f:* **GYOBA**

Gynecologie Pratique *f:* **Gynecol Prat**

Gynecology *e:* **Gyn, GYN**

Gynecology, Obstetrics, & Reproductive Medicine *e:* **GORM**

Gyrocompassing Geosynchron Geosynchronous Operational Environmental Satellite *e:* **GYROCOMP**

Gyromagnetic Polarizing Interferometer *e:* **GYMPI**

GZA Geo-Environmental Technologies, Inc. *e:* **GZEA**

H

H-2 Orbiting Space Plane *e:* **HOPE**

H & Q Healthcare Investors *e:* **HQH**

H20. Tijdschrift voor Watervoorsiening en Afvalwaterbehandeling *n:* **HTW**

habilitierter Doktor *d:* **Dr. habil.**

habilitierter Doktor-Ingenieur *d:* **Dr. Ing. habil.**

Habitat International Journal [World Environment and Resources Council, Belgium] *e:* **Habitat Int J**

Hackensack Water Co. *e:* **HWA**

Hadassah-Hebrew University Medical Center *e:* **HHUMC**

Hadassah Medical Relief Association *e:* **HMRA**

Hadley Centre for climate prediction and research *e:* **HC**

Haemohydrometry *e:* **HHM**

Hagerman National Wildlife Refuge *e:* **HNWR**

Hahnemann Medical College and Hospital *e:* **HMC&H**

Hahnemann Medical College and Hospital, Philadelphia, PA *e:* **PPHa**

Haitian Medical Association Abroad *e:* **HMAA**

Halden Boiling [heavy] Water Reactor *e:* **HBWR**

Hale Observatories *e:* **HO**

Half Demurrage Weather Time Saved *e:* **HDWTS**

half-plane half-satellite space shuttle *e:* **Orbiter**

Halieutic Radar Experiment Mediterranean Sea *e:* **HAREM**

Halifax Ocean Meeting Point *e:* **HOMP**

Hall Geological Society *e:* **HGS**

Halliburton Geophysical Services *e:* **HGS**

Halo Orbit Space Station *e:* **HOSS**

Halogenated Cyclic Hydrocarbons *e:* **HCH**

Halogenated hydrocarbons *e:* **HH**

Halogenkohlenwasserstoffe *d:* **HKW**

Hamburg-Mannheimer Stiftung für Informationsmedizin *d:* **HMSI**

Hamburg Model of the Ocean Carbon Cycle *e:* **HAMOCC**

Hamburger Notierungen *d:* **HN**

Hamburger Umweltinformationssystem *d:* **HUIS**

Hamburger Wasserwerke *d:* **HWW**

Hamilton Aerospace *e:* **HA**

Hand Emplaced Remote Monitoring Electronic Surveillance System *e:* **HERMES**

Handbok för medicinalpersonal inom krigsmakten *r:* **H med K**

Handbook of Consumer Protection Program *e:* **HCPP**

Handbook of Instructions for Aerospace Personnel Subsystem Designers *e:* **HIAPSD**

Handbook of Instructions for Aerospace Systems Design[ers] *e:* **HIASD**

Handbook of Instructions for Aerospace Vehicle Equipment Design *e:* **HIAVED**

Handford Meteorologie Surveys *e:* **HMS**

Hands Off Wildlife *e:* **HOWL**

Handshake Transceiver Unit-Remote Terminal End *e:* **HTU-R**

Handy Dandy Orbital Computer *e:* **HDOC**

Hanford [basalt] ground water *e:* **Hgw**

Hanford Defense Waste Environmental Impact Statement *e:* **HDW-EIS**

Hanford Environmental Action League *e:* **HEAL**

Hanford Environmental Baseline *e:* **HEB**

Hanford Environmental Compliance-Environmental Assessment *e:* **HEC-EA**

Hanford Environmental Compliance Line Item *e:* **HECLI**

Hanford Environmental Compliance Plan *e:* **HECP**

Hanford Environmental Compliance Report *e:* **HECR**

Hanford Environmental Data System *e:* **HEDS**

Hanford Environmental Dose Overview Panel *e:* **HEDOP**

Hanford Environmental Dose Reconstruction [project] *e:* **HEDR**

Hanford Environmental Health Development Laboratory *e:* **HEDL**

Hanford Environmental Health Foundation *e:* **HE**, *e:* **HEHF**

Hanford Environmental Information System *e:* **HEIS**

Hanford Environmental Management Plan (or Program) *e:* **HEMP**

Hanford Environmental Manager Program Plan *e:* **HEMPP**

Hanford Environmental Manager Program-Program Manager *e:* **HEMP-PM**

Hanford Environmental Oversight *e:* **HEO**

Hanford Environmental Oversight Program *e:* **HEOP**

Hanford Environmental Science and Engineering consortium *e:* **HESEC**

Hanford Geographic Information System *e:* **HGIS**

Hanford Geotechnical Sample Library *e:* **HGSL**

Hanford Health Information Network *e:* **HHIN**

Hanford Health Services *e:* **HHS**

Hanford Medical Scheduling *e:* **HMS**

Hanford Meteorological System *e:* **HMS**

Hanford Meteorology Survey *e:* **HMS**

Hanford Occupational Medical system *e:* **HOM**

Hanford Protective Clothing and Equipment Committee *e:* **HPCEC**

Hanford Remedial Action Environmental Impact Statement and Comprehensive Land Use Plan *e:* **HRA-EIS**

Hanford [Site] Environmental Compliance [project] *e:* **HEC**

Hanford [Site] environmental program implementation plan *e:* **HIP**

Hanford [Site] Groundwater Database *e:* **HGWDB**

Hanford [Site] Meteorological Station *e:* **HMS**

Hanford [Site] Meteorology Surveys *e:* **HMS**

Hanford [Site] Regional Historic[al] Earthquake *e:* **HRHE**

Hank's Lactalbuminhydrolysate *e:* **HLAH**

Hannover Environmental Information System *e:* **HEINS**

Hanseatische Präzisions- und Orbittechnik GmbH *d:* **HPO**

Harbor Branch Oceanographic Institution, Fort Pierce, Florida *e:* **HBOI**

Harbor View Medical Center *e:* **HVMC**

Hard Water *e:* **HW**

hardwater *e:* **hard**

Hardwood Weather Board *e:* **HWWB**

Harlem Hospital Center, Health Sciences Library, New York *e:* **VXA**

Harmful Environment *e:* **HE**

Harmonization Ecological Monitoring in Biosphere *e:* **HEMiBioR**

Harmonization of Environmental Measurements Information System *e:* **HEMIS**

Harmonization[s] of Environmental Measurement [program] *e:* **HEM**

HARRIS Ada Programming Support Environment *e:* **HAPSE**

Harsh Environment[al] Recorder *e:* **HER**

Hartbeestehoek Radio Space Research Station *e:* **HRSRS**

Hartree-Fock Orbital *e:* **HFO**

Harvard College Observatory *e:* **HCO**

Harvard Community Health Plan *e:* **HCHP**

Harvard Department of Earth and Planetary Science *e:* **HDEPS**

Harvard Environmental Law Review *e:* **Harv. Envtl. L. Rev.**

Harvard Medical School *e:* **HMS**

Harvard Radio Meteor Project *e:* **HRMP**

Harvard School of Dental Medicine *e:* **HSDM**

Harvard School of Public Health *e:* **HSPH**

Harvard-Smithsonian Reference Atmosphere *e:* **HSRA**

Harvard Underwater Sound Laboratory *e:* **HUSL**

Hastings Environment Council *e:* **HEC**

Hastings West-Northwest Journal of Environmental Law & Policy *e:* **West-Northwest**

Haulage Emergency Link Protection *e:* **HELP**

Hauptabteilung Sicherheit - Abteilung Umweltschutz *e:* **HS-US**

Hauptkwartier *n:* **H.K.**

Hauptverband für Zucht und Prüfung deutscher Pferde *d:* **HDP**

Hauptverwaltung des Hydrometeorologischen Dienstes, Moskau *d:* **GUGMS**

Hauptwetterwarte *d:* **Hauwewa**

Haustier[e] *d:* **HsT**

Haute École Populaire Internationale *f:* **HEPI**

Haute École Spécialisée *f:* **HES**

Hauterythemdosis *d:* **HED**

Hauts fonctionnaires responsables de l'environnement des pays de l'ANASE *f:* **ASOEM**

Havard Public Health Alumni Bulletin *e:* **HPHBA**

Havasu Lake National Wildlife Refuge *e:* **HLNWR**

Hawaii Deep Water Cable *e:* **HDWC**

Hawaii Environmental Area Rapid Transport [system] *e:* **HEART**

Hawaii Environmental Area Rapid Transport System *e:* **HEART System**

Hawaii Institute of Marine Biology *e:* **HIMB**

Hawaii Medical Journal *e:* **Hawaii Med J**, *e:* **HWMJA**

Hawaii Medical Library, Inc. *e:* **HML**

Hawaii Medical Service Association *e:* **HMSA**

Hawaii Natural Energy Institute *e:* **HNEI**

Hawaii Ocean Science and Technology Park *e:* **HOST**

Hawaii Ocean Time-Series *e:* **HOTS**

Hawaii Public Health Internet Virtual Emporium *e:* **HiPHIVE**

Hawaii Territorial Medical Association *e:* **HTMA**

Hawaii Underwater Research Laboratory *e:* **HURL**

Hawaii Volcano Observatory [of Geological Survey] *e:* **HVO**

Hawaiian Environmental Analysis and Prediction System *e:* **HEAPS**

Hawaii[an] Institute of Geophysics *e:* **HIG**

Hawaiian Islands National Wildlife Refuge *e:* **HBNWR**, *e:* **HINWR**

Hawaiian Ocean Time [series] *e:* **HOT**

Hawaiian Sea Frontier *e:* **HAWSEAFRON**, *e:* **HSF**

Hazardous Air Pollutant Health Effects Fact Sheets *e:* **HAPFACT**

Hazardous Atmospheric Release Model *e:* **HARM**

Hazardous Constituents, Hydrocarbon *e:* **HC**

Hazardous Environment Machine *e:* **HEM**

Hazardous hydrocarbons *e:* **HH**

Hazardous Inflight Weather Advisory Service *e:* **HIWAS**

Hazardous Substance Release/Health Effects Database *e:* **HazDat**

Hazardous Waste Groundwater Task Force *e:* **HWGTF**, *e:* **HWGWTF**

Hazardous Waste Groundwater Test Facility *e:* **HWGTF**, *e:* **HWGWTF**

HCO [Harvard College Observatory] Announcement Cards *e:* **HAC**

Head, Heart, Hands and Health *e:* **HHHH**

Heads of European Veterinary Regulatory Authorities for medicinal products *e:* **HEVRA**

Headspace *e:* **HS**

Headspace Analysis e: **HSA**
Headspace Sampling-Gas Chromatography
  e: **HS-GC**
Headwater Basin e: **BSNH**
Health e: **HLT**
Health Access Project e: **HAP**
Health Accreditation Programme for New
  Zealand e: **HAPNZ**
Health Action Information Network e:
  HAIN
Health Action International e: **HAI**
Health Action Network Society e: **HANS**
Health Action Overseas e: **HAO**
Health Action Zone e: **HAZ**
Health Activities Recommendation Panel
  e: **HARP**
Health Administration Center e: **HAC**
Health Administration Responsibility
  Project e: **HARP**
Health Advisories e: **HA**
Health Advisory Service e: **HAS**
Health Advocacy Services e: **HAS**
Health Advocates for Older People e:
  HAFOP
Health Affairs e: **Health Aff**, e: **Health
  Aff [Millwood]**
Health Affairs Library e: **HAL**
Health Alliances e: **HA**
Health and Accidence Insurance e: **H&A
  Ins**
Health and Accident e: **H&A**
Health [and accident] Insurance Logistics
  Automated e: **HILA**
Health and Air Research Program e:
  HARP
Health and Beauty Aids e: **HABA**
Health [and] Behavior Information Transfer
  e: **HABIT**
Health and Canadian Society e: **HCS**
Health and Education [department or
  ministry] e: **HEED**
Health and Energy Institute e: **HEI**
health and environment e: **hev**
Health and Environment Library Modules
  e: **HELM**
Health and Environmental Effects Data
  Analysis e: **HEEDA**
Health and Environmental Effects
  Document e: **HEED**
Health and Environmental Effects
  Documents e: **HEEDs**
Health and Environmental Effects Profile
  e: **HEEP**
Health and Environmental Effects Profiles
  e: **HEEPs**
Health and Environmental Research
  Advisory Committee e: **HERAC**
Health and Environmental Review Division
  e: **HERD**
Health and Environmental Study Audit
  Program e: **HESAP**
Health and Fault Management e: **HFM**
Health and Healing Ministries e: **HHM**
Health and Human Resource Center e:
  HHRC
Health and Human Resources e: **HHR**
Health and Human Services e: **HHS**
Health and Hurnan Services e: **HHS**
Health and Medical Informatics Digest e:
  HMID
Health and Nutrition Examination Survey
  e: **HANES**

Health and Population Perspectives and
  Issues e: **HPPIDE**
Health and Psychosocial Instruments e:
  HaPI
Health and Rehabilitation Services e: **HRS**
Health and Rehabilitative Library Services
  Division e: **HRLSD**
Health and Research Employees'
  Association e: **HREA**
Health and Safety e: **HS**, e: **Safety**
Health and Safety Assurance e: **HSA**
Health and Safety at Work e: **Health
  Safety Work**
Health and Safety at Work Act e:
  HASAWA, e: **HSWA**
Health and Safety Authority e: **HSA**
Health and Safety Code e: **HSC**
Health and Safety Commission e: **HSC**
Health and Safety Department e: **HSD**, e:
  JSFT
Health and Safety Directive e: **HSD**
Health and Safety Division e: **HS**
Health and Safety, Environmental
  Protection and Safeguards e: **HSEPS**
Health and Safety Execurive e: **HSE**
Health and Safety Executive e: **H and SE**
Health and Safety Executive Mining
  Approvals e: **HSE[M]**
Health and Safety Executive Online e:
  HSELINE
Health and Safety Hazard Program e:
  HSHAP
Health and Safety in Industry and
  Commerce e: **Health Saf Ind Commer**
Health and Safety Inspection Report System
  e: **HSIRS**
Health and Safety Laboratories e: **HASL**,
  e: **HSL**
Health and Safety Manual e: **HSM**
Health and Safety Officer e: **HSO**
Health and Safety Plan e: **HASP**, e: **HSP**
Health and Safety Program e: **HASP**
Health and Safety Program Plan e:
  H&SPP
Health and Safety Project Leader e:
  H&SPL
Health and Safety Research and Test Center
  e: **HSRTC**
Health and Safety Science Abstracts e:
  HSSA
Health and Safety Technician e: **HST**
Health and Safety Training e: **HST**
Health and Service Command e: **HSC**
Health and Social Services e: **HSS**
Health and Social Services Journal e:
  HSSJB
Health and Social Work e: **Health Soc
  Work**
Health and Society e: **HSY**
Health and Usage Monitoring e: **HUM**
Health and Usage Monitoring System e:
  HUMS
Health and Welfare Canada e: **HWC**
Health Aspects of Pesticides e: **HAPS**
Health Aspects of Pesticides Abstract
  Bulletin e: **HAPAB**
Health Assessment e: **HA**
Health Assessment Document e: **HAD**
Health Assessment Documents e: **HADs**
Health Associated Representatives e:
  HEAR
Health Authority e: **HA**
Health Based Level e: **HBL**

Health Behaviour in School-Aged Children
  e: **HBSC**
Health Belief Model e: **HBM**
Health Benefit Advisor e: **HBA**
Health Benefit Groups e: **HBG**
Health Benefit Organizations e: **HBOs**
Health Benefits e: **HB**
Health Benefits Counselor e: **HBC**
Health Benefits Program e: **HBP**
Health Benefits Program Information
  Officer e: **HBPIO**
Health Board e: **HB**
Health Bulletin e: **Health Bull [Edinb]**
Health Canada e: **HC**
Health Canada Health Protection Branch e:
  HPB
Health Canada. Population and Public
  Health Branch e: **PPHB**
Health Canada/Santé Canada e: **HC/SC**
Health Care Administration e: **HCA**
Health Care Administrators e: **HCAD**
Health Care Advanced Networked System
  Architectures: Three Demonstrators for
  Eastern Europe e: **HANSA-3DEMO-
  CP96-96**
Health Care Advisors Association e:
  HCAA
Health Care Advisory Board e: **HCAB**
Health Care Analysis e: **HCA**
Health Care Compare Corp. e: **HCCC**
Health Care Consumers Association e:
  HCCA
Health-care Convention and Exhibitors
  Association e: **HCEA**
Health Care Corporation e: **HCC**
Health Care Delivery Simulator for Urban
  Population[s] e: **HEADS-UP**
Health Care Delivery System e: **HCDS**
Health Care Demand Plan e: **HCDP**
Health Care Finance Administration e:
  HCFA
Health Care Financial Management
  Association e: **HFMA**
Health Care Financing e: **HCF**
Health Care Financing Study Group e:
  HCFSG
Health Care for the Homeless e: **HCH**
Health Care Industry Group e: **HCIG**
Health Care Information System. British
  Library. e: **HCIS**
Health Care Liability Alliance e: **HCLA**
Health Care Literature Information Network
  e: **HECLINET**
Health Care Management e: **HCM**
Health Care Management Review e:
  Health Care Manage Rev
Health Care Occupational Health and Safety
  Association e: **HCOHSA**
Health Care of Australia e: **HCoA**
Health Care on the Internet e: **HCI**
Health Care Plan Medical Center, West
  Seneca e: **NWsHeaC**
Health Care Practitioner e: **HCP**
Health Care Prepayment Plan e: **HCPP**
Health Care Professionals Discussion Group
  e: **HCPDG**
Health Care Provider Records e: **HCPR**
Health Care Quality Improvement Program
  e: **HCQIP**
Health Care Research and Educational
  Foundation e: **HCREF**
Health Care Research Division e: **HCRD**

Health Care Resource Management Society
e: **HCRMS**

Health Care Studies Division e: **HCSD**

Health Care Support e: **HCS**

Health Care System e: **HCS**

Health Care Technology e: **HCT**

Health Care Technology Study Section e:
HCTSS

Health Care Telecommunications
Corporation e: **HTC**

Health Care Without Harm e: **HCWH**

Health Category e: **HC**

Health Certificate e: **HC**

Health Check e: **HC**

Health-Chem Corp. e: **HCH**

Health Communication[s] Network e:
HCN

Health Computer Information Bureau e:
HCIB

Health Concepts IV, Inc. e: **HCFI**

Health Conference for Business and
Industry e: **HCBI**

Health Coordinating Council e: **HCC**

Health Correspondence Schools
International e: **HCSI**

Health Cost Index Database e: **HCID**

Health Cost Index Report e: **HCIR**

Health Council e: **HC**

Health Crisis 2000 [United States] e:
Health [US]

Health Data Recorder e: **HDR**

Health Development Agency e: **HDA**

Health Development Services, Incorporated
e: **HSI**

Health Disk Operating System e: **HDOS**

Health Division e: **H**

Health Economic Service e: **HES**

Health Economics e: **HE**, e: **Health Econ**

Health Economics Analysis Letters e:
HEAL

Health Economics Research Center e:
HERC

Health Education e: **HE**

Health Education and Adult Literacy e:
HEAL

Health Education and Promotion
Information System e: **HEAPS**

Health, Education and Welfare Procurement
Regulations e: **HEWPR**

Health Education Assets Library e: **HEAL**

Health Education Assistance Loans e:
HEAL

Health Education Authority e: **HEA**

Health Education Board for/of Scotland e:
HEBS

Health Education Council e: **HEC**

Health Education Division, Newfoundland
Department of Health, St. John's,
Newfoundland e: **NFSHE**

Health Education Foundation e: **HEF**

Health Education Information Retrieval
System e: **HEIRS**

Health Education Library for People e:
HELP

Health Education Materials Information
Service e: **HEMIS**

Health Education Media Association e:
HEMA

Health Education Network e: **HEN**

Health Education Officer e: **HEO**

Health Education Professional Resources
e: **HEPR**

Health Education Quarterly e: **Health
Educ Q**, e: **HEQ**

Health Education Quarterly. Supplement
e: **Health Educ Q Suppl**

Health Education Research Service e:
HERS

Health Education Resource Organization
e: **HERO**

Health Education Technologies e: **HET**

Health-Education Telecommunications e:
HET

Health Educational Robot e: **HERO**

Health Educator Council e: **HEC**

Health Edutech, Inc. e: **HEDT**

Health Effects and Life Science Research
Division e: **HELSRD**

Health Effects Assessment e: **HEA**, e:
HEAS

Health Effects Assessment Summary Tables
e: **HEAST**

Health Effects Institute e: **HEI**

Health Effect[s] of Environment[al]
Pollutants e: **HEEP**

Health Effects of Environmental Pollution
e: **HEEP**

Health Effects Research Division e:
HERD

Health Effects Research Laboratory e:
HERL

Health Effects Research Laboratory
Management Information System e:
HERL/MIS

Health Electronic Data Interchange
Corporation e: **HEDIC**

Health Emergency and Dispensary, Inc. e:
HEAD

Health Enhancement Research Organization
e: **HERO**

Health, Environment, Safety, and Security
e: **HESS**

Health, Environment & Work e: **HE&W**

Health Evaluation and Referral Service e:
HERS

Health Evaluation and Risk Tabulation e:
HEART

Health Evaluation through Logical
Processing e: **HELP**

Health Evidence Application and Linkage
Network e: **HEALNet**

Health Examination Survey e: **HES**

Health Facilities Management e: **HFM**

Health Facilities Planning and Construction
Service e: **HFPCS**

Health Food Manufacturers Association e:
HFMA

Health Hazard Assessment e: **HHA**

Health Hazard Evaluation [program] e:
HHE

Health Hazards Assessment Report e:
HHAR

Health Improvement Programme e: **HImP**,
e: **HIP**

Health Inca Tea e: **HIT**

Health Indication Test e: **HIT**

Health Industries Association e: **HIA**

Health Industries Institute e: **HII**

Health Industry Advisory Committee e:
HIAC

Health Industry Bar Code Council e:
HIBCC

Health Industry Business Communications
Council e: **HIBCC**

Health Industry Distributors Association
e: **HIDA**

Health Industry Manufacturers Association
e: **HIMA**

Health Industry Number e: **HIN**

Health Industry Representatives
Association e: **HIRA**

Health Industry Wage and Salary
Committee e: **HIWSC**

Health Informatics Australia e: **HIA**

Health Informatics Australia-NSW e:
HIANSW

Health Informatics Europe e: **HIE**

Health Informatics Society Australia e:
HISA

Health Informatics System Planning Panel
e: **HISPP**

Health Information and Decision Support
Workbench e: **HEALTHBENCH**

Health Information and Surveillance
Systems Board e: **HISSB**

Health Information Base System e: **HIBS**

Health Information Center e: **HIC**

Health Information Foundation e: **HIF**

Health Information Infrastructure e: **HII**

Health Information Libraries of Westchester
e: **HILOW**

Health Information Library Network of
Northeastern Pennsylvania e: **HILNNEP**

Health Information Library Program[me]
e: **HILP**

Health Information Management e: **HIM**

Health Information Management
Association of Australia e: **HIMAA**

Health Information Network e: **HIN**

Health Information Network of the Pacific
e: **HINOP**

Health Information Network Services e:
HINS

Health Information Research Unit e:
HIRU

Health Information Resource Center e:
HIRC

Health Information Resources [and]
Service[s] e: **HIRS**

Health Information Series e: **HIS**

Health Information Services e: **HIS**

Health Information Sharing Project e:
HISP

Health Information System e: **HIS**

Health Information Systems Incorporated
e: **HISI**

Health Information Technologies and
Education Center e: **HITEC**

Health Inspector e: **HI**

Health Instrument Division e: **H.I.**

Health Insurance e: **HI**

Health Insurance Advocacy Program e:
HIAP

Health Insurance Associate e: **HIA**

Health Insurance Association of America
e: **HIAA**

Health Insurance Association of Australia
e: **HIAA**

Health Insurance Benefit e: **H.I.B.**

Health Insurance Benefits Advisory Council
e: **HIBAC**

Health Insurance Commission e: **HIC**

Health Insurance Council e: **HIC**

Health Insurance Counseling and Advocacy
Program e: **HICAP**

Health Insurance Enrollment e: **HIE**

Health Insurance Institute e: **HII**

Health Insurance Manual *e:* **HIM**

Health Insurance Master Record *e:* **HIMR**

Health Insurance Network Hinck Hinckley *e:* **HIN**

Health Insurance of Vermont, Inc. *e:* **HIVT**

Health Insurance Plan *e:* **HIP**

Health Insurance Portability and Accountability Act *e:* **HIPAA**

Health Insurance Purchasing Cooperative *e:* **HIPC**

Health Insurance Registration Board *e:* **HIRB**

Health Insurance Restricted Membership Association of Australia *e:* **HIRMAA**

Health Interview Survey [National Institute of Health] *e:* **HIS**

Health Laboratory Science *e:* **Health Lab.Sci.**

Health Labour Relations Association *e:* **HLRA**

Health Level Seven *e:* **HL7**

Health Level Seven Enterprise Communications Framework *e:* **HL7ECF**

Health Libraries Association of British Columbia *e:* **HLABC**

Health, Literature, Library and Information Service *e:* **HELLIS**

health locus of control *e:* **hlc**

Health Maintenance Facility *e:* **HMF**

Health Maintenance Organisation (or Organization) *e:* **HMO**

Health Maintenance Organization Act *e:* **HMOA**

Health Maintenance Organization Service *e:* **HMOS**

Health Maintenance Organizations *e:* **HMOs**

Health Management Associates *e:* **HMA**

Health Management Board *e:* **HMB**

Health Management Information Service *e:* **HELMIS**

Health Management Information System *e:* **HMIS**

Health Management Plan *e:* **HMP**

Health Management Quarterly *e:* **Health Manage Q**, *e:* **HMQ**

Health Management Teams *e:* **HMT**

Health Manpower Advisory Council *e:* **HMAC**

Health Manpower Shortage Area Placement Opportunity List *e:* **HPOL**

Health Matrix: Journal of Law-Medicine *e:* **Health Matrix: J.L.-Med.**

Health Media Education *e:* **HME**

Health Ministers Council *e:* **HMC**

Health Mobilization Series *e:* **HMS**

Health Monitor Computer *e:* **HMC**

Health Monitoring *e:* **HM**

Health Monitoring Unit *e:* **HMU**

Health-Mor, Incorporated *e:* **HMI**

Health News Institute *e:* **HNI**

Health Occupations *e:* **HO**

Health Occupations Students of America *e:* **HOSA**

Health of Munition Workers Committee *e:* **HMWC**

Health of Ocean Module *e:* **HOOP**

Health of the Oceans *e:* **HOTO**

Health Office[r] *e:* **HO**

Health Omnibus Programs Extension Legislation *e:* **HOPE**

Health on the Net Foundation *e:* **HON**

Health Online Service *e:* **HOS**

Health Opinion Survey *e:* **HOS**

Health Opportunities for People Everywhere *e:* **HOPE**

Health Organization of the League of Nations *e:* **H.O.L.N.**

Health Organization to Preserve the Environment *e:* **HOPE**

Health-Oriented Physician Education *e:* **HOPE**

health, physical education and recreation *e:* **hper**

Health Physicist *e:* **HP**

Health Physics *e:* **HP**

Health Physics Analysis Laboratory *e:* **HPAL**

Health Physics and Medical Division *e:* **HPM**

Health Physics Center *e:* **HPC**

Health Physics Field Change Request *e:* **HPFCR**

Health Physics Great Ideas Database *e:* **HPGIDB**

Health Physics Information Center *e:* **HPIC**

Health Physics Network *e:* **HPN**

Health Physics Program *e:* **HPP**

Health Physics Quality Safety Tracking Database *e:* **HPQSTDB**

Health Physics Radiation Work Permit Database *e:* **HPRWP**

Health physics records storage *e:* **HPRS**

Health Physics Research Abstracts *e:* **HPRA**

Health Physics Research Reactor *e:* **HPRB**, *e:* **HPRR**

Health Physics Society *e:* **HPS**

Health Physics Society Standards Committee *e:* **HPSSC**

Health Physics Station *e:* **HPS**

Health Physics Surveillance *e:* **HPS**

Health Physics Technician *e:* **HPT**

Health Plan Purchasing Cooperatives *e:* **HPPC**

Health Policy Advisory Center *e:* **HAC**, *e:* **HPAC**

Health Policy and Economic Research Unit *e:* **HPERU**

Health Policy Council *e:* **HPC**

Health Policy Quarterly *e:* **HPOQ**

Health Policy Support Program *e:* **HPSP**

Health Policy Tracking Service *e:* **HPTS**

Health Post and Drug Retailers *e:* **HEPODRUG**

Health Professional Incorporated *e:* **HPI**

Health Professionals New Zealand *e:* **HPNZ**

health professions *e:* **hlth prof**

Health Professions Council of South Africa *e:* **HPCSA**

Health Professions Regulatory Advisory Council *e:* **HPRAC**

Health Professions Scholarship Program *e:* **HPSP**

Health Professions Stress Inventory *e:* **HPSI**

Health Professions Student Loans *e:* **HPSL**

Health Programs Management Information System *e:* **HPMIS**

Health Programs Systems Center *e:* **HPSC**

Health Promotion and Disease Prevention Initiative *e:* **HPDPI**

Health Promotion Council of Southeastern Pennsylvania *e:* **HPC**

Health Promotion England *e:* **HPE**

Health Promotion Foundation *e:* **FFS**

Health Promotion Monographs *e:* **HPRM**

Health Promotion Online *e:* **HPO**

Health Promotion Practice *e:* **HPP**

Health Promotion Research Internet Network *e:* **HPRIN**

Health Protection Branch, Canada Department of National Health and Welfare Montreal, Quebec *e:* **QMNHH**

Health Protection Computer System *e:* **HPCS**

Health Protection Technician *e:* **HPT**

Health Psychology *e:* **Health Psychol**, *e:* **HPSY**

Health Query Language *e:* **HQL**

health record *e:* **hel rec**

Health Record *e:* **HREC**

Health Record[s] *e:* **HELREC**

Health & Rehabilitation Properties Trust *e:* **HRP**

health-related facilities *e:* **hrf's**

Health Reports *e:* **Health Rep**

Health Research Council of New Zealand *e:* **HRC**

Health Research Group *e:* **HRG**

Health Research Groups *e:* **HRGs**

Health Research, Incorporated *e:* **HRI**

Health Research Laboratory *e:* **HRL**, *e:* **TA-43**

Health Resources Administration *e:* **HRA**

Health Resources and Services Administration *e:* **HRSA**

Health Resources Statistics *e:* **HRS**

Health Risk Appraisal *e:* **HRA**

Health Risk Assessment *e:* **HRA**

Health Safety and Analysis Center *e:* **HSAC**

Health, Safety, and Environment Advisory Committee *e:* **HSEAC**

Health, Safety, and Environment [Division] *e:* **HSE**

Health, Safety, and Environment Remark *e:* **HSER**

Health Safety and Environmental *e:* **HSE**

Health, Safety and Fire *e:* **HSF**

Health & Safety in Employment *e:* **HSE**

Health Schools Australia *e:* **HSA**

Health Science Cluster Program *e:* **HSCP**

Health Science Libraries Information Cooperative *e:* **HSLIC**

Health Science Libraries of Central Georgia *e:* **HSLCG**

Health Sciences Advancement Award *e:* **HSAA**

Health Sciences Center *e:* **HSC**

Health Sciences Communication Association *e:* **HSCA**

Health Science[s] Communication[s] Association *e:* **HESCA**

Health Sciences Computing Facility *e:* **HSCF**

Health Sciences Consortium *e:* **HSC**

Health Sciences Education and Training Command *e:* **HSETC**

Health Sciences Information Centre, Jewish Rehabilitation Hospital Chomedey, Quebec *e:* **QCHJC**

Health Sciences Information Network *e:* **HSIN**

Health Sciences Information Service *e:* **HSIS**

Health Science[s] Librarians of Illinois *e:* **HSLI**

Health Sciences Libraries Consortium *e:* **HSLC**

Health Sciences Libraries of Minnesota *e:* **HSLM**

Health Sciences Library *e:* **HSL**

Health Sciences Library, Centracare Saint John, Inc., New Brunswick *e:* **NBSC**

Health Sciences Library, General & Marine Hospital, Owen Sound, Ontario *e:* **OOWGM**

Health Sciences Library Management Internal Program *e:* **HSLMIP**

Health Sciences Library, McMaster University, Hamilton, Ontario *e:* **OHMB**

Health Sciences Library, Memorial University, St. Johns, Newfoundland *e:* **NFSMM**

Health Sciences Library, Miramichi Hospital, Newcastle, New Brunswick *e:* **NBNM**

Health Sciences Library, Mississauga Hospital, Ontario *e:* **OMH**

Health Sciences Library, Plains Health Centre, Regina, Saskatchewan *e:* **SRHS**

Health Sciences Library, University of Ottawa Ontario *e:* **OOUH**

Health Sciences Library, Victoria General Hospital, Halifax, NovaScotia *e:* **NSHVGH**

Health Science[s] Resource Centre *e:* **HSRC**

Health Sciences Training and Education Command *e:* **HSTEC**

Health Security Action Council *e:* **HSAC**

Health Service Action *e:* **HSA**

Health Service Advisory Committee *e:* **HSAC**

Health Service Agreement *e:* **HSA**

Health Service Area[s] *e:* **HSA**

Health Service Command *e:* **HSC**

Health Service Commissioner *e:* **HSC**

Health Service Guidance *e:* **HSG**

Health Service Indicators *e:* **HSI**

Health Service Journal *e:* **HSJ**

Health Service Laboratory *e:* **HS Lab**

Health Service Logistics Support System *e:* **HSLSS**

Health Service Plan *e:* **HSP**

Health Service Region *e:* **HSR**

Health Service Support *e:* **HSS**

Health Service Support Air Land Battle *e:* **HSSALB**

Health Service System *e:* **HSS**

Health Services *e:* **HSI**

Health Services Administration *e:* **HSA**

Health Services Administration. Publications *e:* **HSA**

Health Services and Mental Health Administration *e:* **HSM,** *e:* **HSMHA**

Health Services and Mental Health Admlnistration. Publications *e:* **HSM**

Health Services and Mental Health Association *e:* **HSMHA**

Health Services and Promotion Branch, Department of National Health and Welfare Ottawa, Ontario *e:* **OONHHS**

Health Services Centre *e:* **HSC**

Health Services Command *e:* **HSC**

Health Services Department *e:* **HSD**

Health Services Incorporated *e:* **HSI**

Health Services International *e:* **HSI**

Health Service[s] Laboratory *e:* **HSL**

Health Services Library, Halifax Infirmary, Nova Scotia *e:* **NSHHI**

Health Services Management Centre *e:* **HSMC**

Health Services Management Inspectors *e:* **HSMI**

Health Services Officer *e:* **HSO**

Health Services Report *e:* **HSRPA**

Health Services Research *e:* **Health Serv Res,** *e:* **HSR**

Health Services Research and Development *e:* **HSRD**

Health Services Research and Development Service *e:* **HSR&D**

Health Services Research and Training Program *e:* **HSRTP**

Health Services Research Center *e:* **HSRC**

Health Services Research Projects in Progress *e:* **HSRPROJ**

Health Services Research Unit *e:* **HSRU**

Health Services Support Officer *e:* **HSSO**

Health Services, Technology, Administration and Research *e:* **HealthSTAR**

Health Services/Technology Assessment Research *e:* **HSTAR**

Health Services/Technology Assessment Texts *e:* **HSTAT**

Health Services Utilization and Research Commission *e:* **HSURC**

Health Stabilization Program *e:* **HSP**

Health Standard[s] and Quality Bureau *e:* **HSQB**

Health Status Questionnaire *e:* **HSQ**

Health Study *e:* **HS**

Health Surveillance System *e:* **HSS**

Health Surveillance System for Communicable Diseases *e:* **HSSCD**

Health Systems Agency *e:* **HSA**

Health Systems Development Unit *e:* **HSDU**

Health Systems Plan *e:* **HSP**

Health Systems Research Institute *e:* **HSRI**

Health Systems Trust *e:* **HAST,** *e:* **HST**

Health Systems Vendors Association *e:* **HSVA**

Health Technology Assessment *e:* **Health Technol Assess,** *e:* **HTA**

Health Technology Board for Scotland *e:* **HTBS**

Health Underserved Rural Areas *e:* **HURA**

Health Understanding and Education *e:* **HUE**

Health Unit Co-ordinator *e:* **HUC**

Health Unlimited *e:* **HU**

Health & Usage Monitoring Computer *e:* **HUMC**

Health Values.Achieving High Level Wellness *e:* **HVHW**

Health Vest SBI *e:* **HVT**

Health Visitor *e:* **HV**

Health Visitor Teacher *e:* **HVT**

Health Visitors' Association *e:* **HVA**

Health Visitor's Certificate *e:* **HVC,** *e:* **HVCBrt**

Health Volunteers Overseas *e:* **HVO**

Health Ways Systems, Incorporated *e:* **HWSI**

Health & Welfare *e:* **H&W**

Healthcare Association of New York State *e:* **HANYS**

Healthcare Computing and Communications *e:* **Healthc Comput Commun**

Healthcare Cost and Utilization Project *e:* **HCUP**

Healthcare Electronic Data Interchange Trading Partner *e:* **HEDITP**

Healthcare Evaluation Unit *e:* **HCEU**

Healthcare Financing Study Group *e:* **HFSG**

Healthcare Informatics Society of Ireland *e:* **HISI**

Healthcare Information and Management Systems Society *e:* **HIMSS**

Healthcare Information Management & Communication Canada *e:* **HIM&CC**

Healthcare Information Network *e:* **HCIN**

Healthcare Information Systems Sharing Group *e:* **HISSG**

Healthcare Integrity and Protection Data Bank *e:* **HIPDB**

Healthcare International, Incorporated *e:* **HII**

Healthcare Marketing Report *e:* **Healthcare**

Healthcare Open Systems and Trials *e:* **HOST**

Healthcare Product *e:* **HP**

Healthcare Professional Shortage Area *e:* **HPSA**

Healthcare Quality Certification Board *e:* **HQCB**

Healthcare Quality Head Quarters *e:* **HQHQ**

Healthcare Resource Groups *e:* **HRG**

Healthcare Services Group, Inc. *e:* **HCSG**

Healthcare Services of America, Incorporated *e:* **HSAI**

Healthplan Employer Data and Information Set *e:* **HEDIS**

Healthplex, Inc. *e:* **HPLX**

Healthsouth Rehabilitation Corporation *e:* **HRC**

Healthtrust-Hospital Co. *e:* **HTI**

Healthworld Online *e:* **HWOL**

Healthy America *e:* **HA**

Healthy Mothers, Healthy Babies Coalition *e:* **HMHB**

Hearing Health Care Research Unit *e:* **HHCRU**

Hearing Protective Device *e:* **HPD**

Hearth Electric Furnace *e:* **HEF**

Hearth Furniture Interim Industrial Council *e:* **H.F.I.I.C.**

Heat Exchanger, Water *e:* **HXW**

Heat Protection System *e:* **HPS**

Heated Biological Input *e:* **HBI**

Heater Unit, Water *e:* **HUW**

Heater, Water, Electric *e:* **HWE**

Heater, Water, Gas *e:* **HWG**

Heater, Water, Steam *e:* **HWS**

Heath, Environment, Safety & Quality Assurance *e:* **HESQA**

Heating Water System *e:* **HWS**

heavenly body's polar distance *e:* **PX**

Heavy Earth-Moving Machinery *e:* **HEMM**

Heavy Environment *e:* **HI**

Heavy Hydrogen *e:* **HH**

Heavy Observation Aircraft e: **HOA**

Heavy Seal [Sea-Air-Land] Support Craft
e: **HSSC**

Heavy Water e: **HW**

Heavy Water Components Test Reactor e:
HWTCR

Heavy Water Component[s] Test Reactor
[Savannah River Plant] e: **HWCTR**

Heavy Water Deuterium Oxide e: **HEATH**

Heavy Water Gas-Cooled Reactor e:
HWGCR

Heavy-Water-moderated e: **HWGCH**

Heavy-Water moderated, Boiling Light-
Water cooled Reactor e: **HWBLW[R]**

Heavy-Water-Moderated Gas-Cooled
Reactor e: **HWGCB**

Heavy Water Moderated Light-Water
Cooled Reactor e: **HWLWB**, e:
HWLWR

Heavy Water[-moderated] Organic-Cooled
Reactor e: **HWOCR**

Heavy Water[-moderated] Organic-cooled
Reactor e: **HWOR**

Heavy-Water Moderated Organic-Cooled
Reactor e: **HWROCR**

Heavy Water-moderated Reactor e: **HWR**

Heavy Water Plant [Savannah River] e:
HWP

Heavy Water Processing Facility e:
HWPF

Heavy Water Project e: **HWP**

Heavy Water Reactor Facility e: **HWRF**

Heavy Weather Patrol Boats e: **HWPB**

Heereswetterzentrale d: **HWZ**

Height above Spherical Earth e: **HS**

Heimat-Pferdelazarett d: **H.Pf.Laz.**

Heineman Medical Research Center e:
HMRC

Heißwassererzeuger d: **HWE**

Heißwasserfraktion der Stärke d: **HWS**

heißwasserlösliche Kohlenstofffraktion d:
Chwl

Heißwasserrakete d: **HWR**

Heißwasserspeicher d: **HS**

Heizung, Lüftung, Klima, Kälte d: **HLKK**

Heizung, Lüftung, Klima, Kälte,
Energiesummen d: **HLKKES**

Heizung, Lüftung, Klima, Kälte, Grafik d:
HLKKGR

Heizung, Lüftung, Klima, Kälte, Lasten und
Leistung d: **HLKKL**

Heizung, Lüftung, Klimatechnik d: **HLK**

Heizung-Lüftung-Klimatechnik-
Haustechnik [Verein Deutscher
Ingenieure, Germany] d: **HLH**

Helicopter Adverse Weather Fire
Control/Acquisition Radar e:
HAWFCAR

Helicopter Adverse Weather Target
Acquisition and Destruction System e:
HAWTADS

Helicopter Ambulance Medical Detachment
e: **HAMD**

Helicopter Assault Survivability in a Threat
Environment e: **HASTE**

Helicopter Emergency Medical Services e:
HEMS

Helicopter Operations in a Selected Radar
Environment e: **HELORADE**

Helicopter Personnel Escape Protection and
Survival e: **HEPS**

Helicopter Protected Zone e: **HPZ**

Helicopter Remote Classification and
Localization System e: **HERCULES**

Helicopter Remote Wind Sensor e: **HRWS**

Helicopter Sea Control Wing e: **HSCW**

Helicopter Targets in Bad Weather e:
HTBW

Helicopter Targets in Clear Weather e:
HTCW

Helicopter Underwater Escape Trainer e:
HUET

Helicoptere d'Observation Radar et
d'Investigation sur Zone f: **HORIZON**

Heliocentric Orbit Rendezvous Horizon e:
HOB

Heliocentric Orbit Rendezvous [Horizontal]
e: **HOR**

HELIOS Observation System e: **HOS**

Helium Underwater Speech Translating
Equipment e: **HUSTLE**

Hellenic Aerospace Industry Ltd. e: **HAI**

Hellenic Hydrobiological Institute e: **HHI**

Hellenic Marine Environment[al] Protection
Association e: **HELMEPA**

Hellenic Military Geographical Service e:
HMGS

Hellenic National Oceanographic Data
Centre e: **HNODC**

Helsinki Commission for the Protection of
the Baltic Marine Environment e:
HELCOM

Helsinki Commission/Monitoring of
Radioactive Substances in the Baltic Sea
e: **HELCOM/MORS**

Henry George Foundation of Great Britain
e: **H.G.F.G.B.**

Henry George School of Social Science e:
HGSSS

H(erbert) G(eorge) Wells -English author
e: **Wells**

Herbs, Spices and Medicinal Plants e:
HSMPE8

Hercules on Water e: **HOW**

Hercules-Over-Water e: **HOW**

Herd Health Declaration Scheme e: **HHDS**

Herdeinfalldosis d: **HED**

Herder Buchgemeinde für Jugend und Haus
d: **HBG**

Herder-Institut e.V. d: **HI**

Heredity and Environment e: **H&E**

Heritage Climate Data Collection e:
HCDC

Herma Ness National Nature Reserve e:
HNNNR

Hervormd Gereformeerde Partij n: **HGP**

Hervormd Gereformeerde Staatspartij n:
HGS

Hessische Arbeitsgemeinschaft für
Gesundheitserziehung d: **HAGE**

Hessische Gesellschaft für Ornithologie und
Naturschutz d: **HGON**

Hessische Landesanstalt für Umwelt,
Wiesbaden d: **HLfU**

Hessische Zucht- und Absatzgenossenschaft
für Zuchttiere GmbH d: **HZA**

Hessisches Ministerium für
Landesentwicklung, Wohnen,
Landwirtschaft, Forsten und Naturschutz
d: **HMFAS**

Hessisches Ministerium für Umwelt,
Landwirtschaft und Forsten d: **HMULF**

Hessisches Wassergesetz d: **HWG**

Heterogeneous Environment for Remote
Execution e: **THERE**

Heterogeneous Network Computing
Environment e: **HENCE**

Heteropowered Earth Launched Interorbital
Spacecraft e: **HELIOS**

Hexahydrophthalic Anhydride e: **HHPA**

Hexahydroxybenzene e: **HHB**

hexane and higher hydrocarbons e: **C6+**

Hic Locus Sepulturae Hererdem Non
Sequetur l: **H.L.S.H.N.S**

Hickling Broad National Nature Reserve e:
HBlYNR, e: **HBNNR**

Hidrometeorološki Observatorij se: **HMO**

Hidrometeorološki Zavov se: **HZ**

Hierarchical Environmental Retrieval for
Management Access and Networking e:
HERMAN

High Accuracy Spacecraft Separation
System e: **HASSS**

High-Altitude Airborne Observation e:
HAAO

High-Altitude Integrated Airborne Platform
for Environmental Research e: **HIAPER**

High-Altitude Learjet Observatory e:
HALO

High Altitude Low Observable e: **HALO**

High Altitude Observatory e: **HAO**

High Altitude Orbital Space Station e:
HAOSS

High-Altitude Platform e: **HAP**

High Altitude Radiation Environment Study
e: **HARES**

High Altitude Space Platform e: **HASP**

High-Altitude Space Probe e: **HASP**

High-Altitude Space Velocity Radar e:
HASVR

High Altitude Weather Aircraft Data
System e: **HAWADS**

High Cross Range Orbiter e: **HCRO**

High Density Air Space Control Zone e:
HIDACZ

High Density Bipolar Code e: **HDBC**, e:
HDB Code

High-Density Hydrocarbon[s] e: **HDHC**

High Earth Orbit [Satellite] e: **HEO**

High-Elliptic-inclined Orbit Satellite e:
HEOS

High Elliptical Orbiting Scientific e:
HEDS

High Elliptical Orbiting Scientific Program
e: **HEDS Program**

High Endoatmospheric Defence
Intercept[or] e: **HEDI**

High Endoatmospheric Defense System e:
HEDS

High-Energy Astronomical (or Astronomy)
Observatory e: **HEAO**

High Energy Astronomy Observatory 1 e:
HEAO 1

High Energy Astrophysical Observatory e:
HEAO

High-Energy Orbit e: **HEO**

High Environment[al] Test System e:
HETS

High Fidelity Interactive Visual
Environment e: **HIFIVE**

High Frontier e: **HF**

High Geographic Aerospace Search Radar
e: **HIGH GASSER**

High Ignition Temperature Propellants-Self
Extinguishing at Atmospheric Pressure
e: **HITP-SEAP**

High Institute of Public Health e: **HIPH**

High Integrity Protective System[s] *e:* **HIPS**

High Interference Signalling Environment *e:* **HISE**

High-level [Flight weather] Forecast *e:* **HIFOR**

High Level Radioactive Waste Risk Model Environmental Pathways *e:* **WESPDOSE2**

High Orbital Bombardment System *e:* **HOBS**

High Order Assembly Language for Shuttle [flight] (or Spacelab usage) *e:* **HAL/S**

High Performance Army Observation Aircraft *e:* **HPAOA**

High Performance Computing in Geosciences, Safety of Constructions with Respect to Rock Deformations and Movements *e:* **HIPERGEOS-CP94-820**

High Performance Signal Processing for Laboratory Environments *e:* **HPSPLE**

High Performance Space Feed *e:* **HIPSF**

High Plains Regional Climate Center *e:* **HPRCC**

High Polar Latitude *e:* **HPL**

High Power Water Boiler *e:* **HYPO Water Boiler**

High-Power Water-Boiler Reactor *e:* **HYPO**

High-Precision Geodetic Network *e:* **HPGN**

High-pressure Demineralized Water *e:* **HDW**

High-pressure Filtered Water *e:* **HPFW**

High-Pressure Fire Protection *e:* **HPFP**

High Pressure Hot Water *e:* **HPHW**

High Pressure Oceanographic Equipment *e:* **HIPOE**

High-pressure Raw Water *e:* **HPRW**

High Pressure Service Water *e:* **HPSW**

High-Pressure Service Water System *e:* **HPSWS**

High-Purity Water *e:* **HPW**

High Quality Environment *e:* **HQE**

High Rate Geographical Areas *e:* **HRGA**

High [Resolution] Earth Processes Imager *e:* **HEPI**

High-Resolution Evaluation of Radiances from Meteorological Satellites *e:* **HERMES**

High-Resolution Remote Tracking Sonar *e:* **HRBTS**, *e:* **HRRTS**

High Resolution Solar Observatory *e:* **HRSO**

High School for Health Professions *e:* **HSHP**

High School Geography Project *e:* **HSGP**

High Sea Fleet *e:* **HSF**

High Sea State Container Transfer System *e:* **HISEACOTS**

High Speed Bipolar Technologie *e:* **HSBT**

High-speed Integrated Space Transportation Evaluation Program[me] *e:* **HI-STEP**

High-Speed Remote Influence Sweep *e:* **HSRIS**

High Speed Remote Job Entry *e:* **HSRJE**

High-Speed Surface Craft, Incorporating Hovering Craft and Hydrofoil *e:* **HSSC**

High Technology Medicine *e:* **HTM**

High-Temperature-Superconductivity Space Experiment *e:* **HTSSE**

High Temperature Water *e:* **HTW**

High Test Hydrogen-Peroxide *e:* **HTHP**

High-Test Hydrogen-Peroxide *e:* **HTP**

High Vacuum Environment *e:* **HVE**

High Vacuum Orbital Simulation (or Simulator) *e:* **HIVOS**

High Velocity Ballistic Protection *e:* **HVBP**

high water *e:* **hi wat**

High Water *e:* **HW**

High-Water-Based Fluid *e:* **HWBF**

High-Water-Content Fluid *e:* **HWCF**

High Water Full and Change *e:* **HWF&C**

High Water Inequality *e:* **HWIQ**

High Water Interval *e:* **HWI**

High Water Level *e:* **HWL**, *e:* **HW Level**

High Water Line *e:* **HWL**

High Water Line Mark *e:* **HWLM**

High Water London Bridge *e:* **HWLB**

High-Water Lunitidal Interval *e:* **HWLI**

High Water Mark *e:* **HWM**

high-water mark neap tide *e:* **hwmnt**

high-water mark ordinary neap tide *e:* **hwmont**

high-water mark ordinary spring tide *e:* **hwmost**

high-water mark spring tide *e:* **hwmst**

high-water neap tide *e:* **hwnt**

High-Water Neaps *e:* **HWN**

High Water of Ordinary Neap Tides *e:* **HWONT**

High Water [of] Ordinary Spring Tides *e:* **HWOST**

High Water of Spring Tide *e:* **HWS**

high-water ordinary springs *e:* **hwos**

High Water Quadrature *e:* **HWQ**

High Water Speed Technology Demonstrator *e:* **HWSTD**

High Water, Spring Tide *e:* **HWST**

Higher High Water *e:* **HHW**

Higher High Water Interval *e:* **HHWI**

higher low water *e:* **hlw**

Higher Low Water Interval *e:* **HLWI**

Higher Medical Training *e:* **HMT**

Highest Filled Molecular Orbital *e:* **HFMO**

highest low-water neap tides *e:* **hlwn**

Highest Low Water of Neap [tides] *e:* **HLWN**

Highest Occupied Molecular Orbital[s] *e:* **HOMO**

Highest Occupied Molecular Orbitals *e:* **HOMOs**

Highland Hospital, Williams Health Science Library, Rochester, *e:* **VQP**

Highly Distributed Environment *e:* **HDE**

Highly Eccentric Orbit Satellite *e:* **HEOS-A2**

Highly Electric Orbit *e:* **HEO**

Highly Elliptical Orbit Satellite *e:* **HEOS**

High[ly] Excentric[ity] Orbit[ing] Satellite *e:* **HEOS**

High[ly-inclined] Elliptic[al] [satellite] Orbit *e:* **HEO**

Highly Instrumented Orbiting Primate Experiment *e:* **HOPE**

Highly Maneuverable Experimental Spacecraft *e:* **HIMES**

Highly Optimized Microscope Environment *e:* **HOME**

Highly Protected Risk *e:* **HPR**

Highly Unusual Geophysical Operation[s] *e:* **HUGO**

Highly Usable Geophysical Observation *e:* **HUGO**

Highway Controller/Health Monitor *e:* **HCHM**

HilisdaleCollege *e:* **MiHilC**

Himal Hydropower & Construction Pr. Lmt. Com. *e:* **HHPCL**

Himalayan Climate Centre *e:* **HCC**

Himalayan Interdisciplinary Paleoclimate Project *e:* **HIPP**

Himmel und Erde *d:* **HuE**

Hiroshima Journal of Medical Sciences *e:* **Hiroshima J Med Sci**

Hispanic Health and Nutrition Examination Survey *e:* **HHANES**

Histochemistry and Cell Biology *e:* **Histochem Cell Biol**

Historic Environment Information Resources *e:* **HEIRs**

Historical Canadian Climate Database *e:* **HCCD**

Historical Climatology Network *e:* **HCN**

Historical Climatology Network-Daily *e:* **HCND**

Historical Sea Surface Temperature Data Project *e:* **HSSTD**

Historie, Geografi, Naturfagene *a:* **HGN-fagene**

Historisches Institut, Abteilung Geschichte der Naturwissenschaften und Technik *d:* **HistNT**

History of Earth Sciences Society *e:* **HESS**

History of Medicine *e:* **H.M.**

History of Medicine Division. National Library of Medicine *e:* **HMD**

History of medicine Online *e:* **HISTLINE**

History of Science, Technology and Medicine *e:* **HSTM**

Hitchhiker [Goddard Space Flight Center] *e:* **HH-G**

Hitchhiker, MSFC [Marshall Spaceflight Center] *e:* **HH-M**

HITRAN Atmospheric Workstation *e:* **HAWKS**

HJW GeoSpatial, Inc. *e:* **HJW**

Hlavní Správa Geologického Průzkumu *c:* **HSGP**

HO [Harvard Observatory] Annals *e:* **HA**

Hoch-Elliptischer Orbit-Satellit *d:* **HEOS**

Hochschul-Sammlung Naturwissenschaft Informatik *d:* **HochschulSammlung Naturwiss Informat**

Hochschul Umwelt Informationen *d:* **HUI**

Hochschuldidaktik der Naturwissenschaften *d:* **Hochschuldidaktik Naturwiss**

Höchster Schiffahrtswasserstand *d:* **HSW**

Höchster schiffbarer Wasserstand *d:* **HschWst**

Höchster Wasserstand *d:* **HWS**

Hochwasser *d:* **Hochw**, *d:* **HW**

Hochwasserbett *d:* **HW-Bett**

Hochwasserhöhe *d:* **HWH**

Hochwasserintervall *d:* **HWI**

Hochwassermenge *d:* **HW Menge**

Hochwasserquantität *d:* **HQ**

Hochwasserschutz *d:* **HWS**

Hochwasserstand *d:* **Hochw-St**

Hochwasserzeit *d:* **HWZ**

HOH Water Technology Corp. *e:* **HOHI**

Höheres Niedrigwasser *d:* **HNW**

Hokkaido Igaku Zasshi. Hokkaido Journal of Medical Science *j:* **Hokkaido Igaku Zasshi**

Holarctic Ecology *e:* **Holarct. Ecol.**

Hole Full of Water *e:* **HFW**

Holistic Health Havens *e:* **HHH**

Holistic Health Organizing Committee *e:* **HHOC**

Holla Bend National Wildlife Refuge *e:* **HBNWR**

Holland-on-Sea *e:* **H-o-S**

Holmes Junge Protected Area *e:* **HJPA**

Holographic Ice Surveying System *e:* **HISS**

Holographic Labelling Techniques for Automatic Identification in CIM Environments *e:* **HIDCIM**

Holston Valley Community Hospital, Health Science Library, Kingsport *e:* **TKiH**

Holy Sea *e:* **HS**

Holz-Frischwasser-Tropenfreibord *d:* **HFT**

Home Environment Aid for Living *e:* **HEAL**

Home Environment and Living Program *e:* **HELP**

Home Fallout Protection Survey *e:* **HFPS**

Home Geographic Monthly *e:* **Home Geog.Mo.**

Home Health Agency *e:* **HHA**

Home Health Care Classification *e:* **HHCC**

Home Health Care of America *e:* **HHCA**

Home Health Care Services Quarterly *e:* **Home Health Care Serr Q**

Home Health Journal *e:* **Home Health J**

Home Health Nurse *e:* **Home Health Nurse**

Home Health Review *e:* **Home Health Rev**

Home Health Services and Staffing Association *e:* **HHSSA**

Home Health Services Association *e:* **HHSA**

Home Healthcare Nurses Association *e:* **HHNA**

Home Observation for Measurement of the Environment *e:* **HOME**

Home Oncology Medical Extension *e:* **HOME**

Home Sea Service *e:* **HSS**

Home Surgeon *e:* **HS**

Homeopathic Academy of Naturopathic Physicians *e:* **HANP**

Homeopathic Doctor of Medicine *e:* **H.M.D.**

Homeopathic Medical Doctor *e:* **MD[H]**

Homoeopathiae Medicinae Doctor *l:* **H.M.D.**

Homogeneous Multipolar Equivalent Generator *e:* **HMEG**

Homophile Effort for Legal Protection *e:* **HELP**

Homopolar Disk Dynamo *e:* **HDD**

Homopolar Generator *e:* **HG**

Homopolar Linear Synchronous Motor *e:* **HLSM**

Homopolar Pulse Welding *e:* **HPW**

Hong Kong Association of Sports Medicine & Sports Science *e:* **HKASMSS**

Hong Kong Geographical Association *e:* **HKGA**

Hong Kong Medical Association *e:* **HKMA**

Honolulu Magnetic and Seismological Observatory *e:* **HMSO**

Honolulu Magnetic Observatory *e:* **HMO**

Honoraires Médicaux *f:* **H.M.**

Honorary Associate of the Royal College of Veterinary Surgeons *e:* **HARCVS**

Honorary Fellow of the Royal College of Physicians and Surgeons *e:* **FRCPS[Hon]**

Honorary Surgeon Lieutenant-Colonel *e:* **HON SURG LIEUT COL**

Honorary Surgeon of the King *e:* **HSK**

Honorary Surgeon to the Queen *e:* **HSQ**

Honorary Surgeon to the Viceroy of India *e:* **VHS**

Hoofd Geuniformeerde Dienst *n:* **HGD**

Hoofddirectie Telecommunicatie en Post [van het Ministerie van Verkeer en Waterstaat] *n:* **HDTP**

Hoofdkwartier *n:* **HK**

Hook, Oil and Fresh Water Damage *e:* **HO&FWD**

Hôpital Sans Frontière *f:* **HSF**

Horicon National Wildlife Refuge *e:* **HNWR**

Horizon Health Corporation *e:* **HORC**

Horizontal and Vertical Adjustment of Geodetic Observations *e:* **HAVAGO**

Horizontal component of the earth's magnetism [symbol] *e:* **H**

Horizontal Earth Rate *e:* **HER**

Horizontal Polarization *e:* **HORIZ**

Horizontal Transmit-Horizontal Receive Polarization *e:* **HH**

Horizontal Transmit - Vertical Receive Polarization *e:* **HV**

Horizontal Weather Depiction *e:* **HWD**

Horizontally Polarized Shear Wave *e:* **HPSW**

Horn Point Environmental Laboratories *e:* **HPL**

Horn Point Environmental Laboratory *e:* **HPEL**

Horsemen's Benevolent and Protective Association *e:* **HBPA**

Horses and Ponies Protection Association *e:* **HPPA**

Horton Hydrocarbons, Incorporated *e:* **HHI**

Hospital and Community Health Services *e:* **HCSC**

Hospital and Health Care *e:* **Hosp Hlt Care**

Hospital and Health Management *e:* **Hosp Hlt Man**

Hospital and Health Services *e:* **HHS**

Hospital and Health Services Administration *e:* **Hosp and Health**, *e:* **Hosp Health Serv Adm[in]**

Hospital and Health Services Review *e:* **Hosp Health Serv Rev**

Hospital and Medical Care Association *e:* **HMCA**

Hospital dos Servidores do Estado. Revista Medica *s:* **Hosp Servidores Estado Rev Med**

Hospital Employee Health *e:* **Hosp Employ Health**

Hospital Health Care Newsletter *e:* **Hosp Health Care Newsl**

Hospital Medical Office[r] *e:* **HMO**

Hospital Medical Record *e:* **HMR**

Hospital Medical Records Institute *e:* **HMRI**

Hospital Medical Staff *e:* **Hosp Med Statf**

Hospital Medical Staff Advocate *e:* **Hosp Med Staff Advocate**

Hospital Medicine *e:* **Hosp Med**

Hospital-Oriented Programmed Environment *e:* **HOPE**

Hospital Surgeon *e:* **HS**

Hospital-Surgical-Medical *e:* **HSM**

Hospitals and Health Networks *e:* **Hosp Health Netw**

Hospitals for a Healthy Environment *e:* **H2E**

Hospitals & Health Networks *e:* **H&HN**

Host Remote Node Entry System *e:* **HRNES**

Hostile Environment Machine *e:* **HEM**

Hostile Observation Post *e:* **HOP**

Hot and Cold Running Water *e:* **HCRW**

Hot and Cold [Water] *e:* **H&C**

Hot and Cold Water *e:* **H&C Water**

Hot Climate Physiological Research Unit *e:* **HCPRU**, *e:* **HOCPRU**

Hot Creek Radio Astronomy Observatory *e:* **HCRAO**

Hot Hydrogen Nozzle *e:* **HHN**

Hot Ultrapure Water *e:* **HUPW**

Hot Water *e:* **HW**

Hot Water Circulating *e:* **HWC**

Hot-Water-cure Motar *e:* **HWM**

Hot Water Heater *e:* **HWH**

Hot Water Line *e:* **HWL**

Hot Water-Insoluble Nitrogen *e:* **HWIN**

Hot Water Oxidizer *e:* **HWO**

Hot Water Quenching *e:* **HOWAQ**

Hot Water Return *e:* **HWR**

Hot Water Service System *e:* **HWSS**

Hot Water Soluble *e:* **HWS**

Hot Water Supply *e:* **HWS**

hot water tank *e:* **hwt.**

Hot Water Temperature *e:* **HWT**

Hot Water Treatment *e:* **HWT**

Hot Weather Battle Dress Uniform *e:* **HWBDU**

Hot Weather Battle Fluid *e:* **HWBDU**

Hotel-Dieu Medical-Nursing Educational Media Center, E Paso *e:* **TxEHD**

Houches. École d'Ete de Physique Theoretique *f:* **Houches Ec Ete Phys Theor**

House Committee on Science, Space, and Technology *e:* **HCSS&T**

House [of Representatives] Committee on Space and Astronautics *e:* **HCSA**

House of Representatives Standing Committee on Environment and Conservation *e:* **HORSEC**

House of Representatives Standing Committee on the Environment, Recreation and the Arts *e:* **HORSCERA**

House Space Committee *e:* **HSC**

House Spacecraft *e:* **HS/C**

House Surgeon *e:* **HS**

Houston Academy of Medicine for Texas Medical Center, Houston *e:* **TMC**, *e:* **TxHAM**

Houston Academy of Medicine, Houston *e:* **TxHMC**

Houston Academy of Medicine-Texas Medical Center Library *e:* **HAM-TMC**

Houston Aerospace Language *e:* **HAL**

Houston Automatic Spooling Priority with Remote Job Entry *e:* **HASP/RJE**

Houston Biomedical, Inc. *e:* **HBII**

Houston Environmental Foresight *e:* **HEF**

Houston Geographic [information system] Society *e:* **HOGS**

Houston Geological Society. Bulletin e: **Houston Geol Soc Bull**

Houston Medical Center Building e: **HMC**

Houston Natural Gas Corporation e: **HNG**

Hovering Craft and Hydrofoil e: **Hov Craft Hydrof**

Hovering Craft & Hydrofoil e: **HC&H**

Hovik Medical e: **HVK**

How to Evaluate Health Programs e: **How Eval Health Programs**

Howard Hughes Medical Institute e: **HHMI**

HRLSD [Health and Rehabilitative Library Services Division] Journal e: **HRLSDJ**

Hrvatska Meteorološka Služba kr: **HMS**

Hrvatski Geografski Glasnik kr: **H.G.G.**

HSL [Health and Safety Executive Library] Abstract e: **HSLA**

HSMHA [Health Services and Mental Health Administration] Health Report e: **HSHRA**

HSMHA [Health Services and Mental Health Administration] Health Reports e: **HSMHA Health Rep.**

Hua-hsi I Ko Ta Hsueh Hsueh Pao [Journal of West China University of Medical Sciences] ch: **Hua Hsi I Ko Ta Hsueh Hsueh Pao**

Hubble Space Telescope e: **HAST**, e: **HST**, e: **Hubble**

Hudson River Sloop Clearwater e: **HRSC**

Huftier[e] d: **Hft**

Hughes Earth Station e: **HES**

Hughes Medical Institute e: **HMI**

Hughes NADGE [NATO Air Defense Ground Environment] Consortium e: **HUCO**

Hughes Satellite Earth Station e: **HSES**, e: **HSFS**

Hughes Spin Stabilized Spacecraft e: **SYNCOM**

Huile Animale f: **HA**

Huleh Swamp Nature Reserve e: **HSNR**

Hull University. Occasional Papers in Geography e: **Hull Univ Occas Pap Geogr**

Human Activity and Global Environment e: **HAGE**

Human Biology e: **HUBIA**, e: **Human Biol**, e: **Hum Biol**

Human Biology Council e: **HBC**

Human Biology in Oceania e: **Hum Biol Oceania**

Human Counter 1 [permits accurate determination of the body burden of fission products and naturally ocurring radioisotopes] e: **HUMCO 1**

Human Dimension of Global Environmental Change[s] e: **HDGEC**

Human Dimension[s] for/of Global Environmental Change Program[me] e: **HDP**

Human Dimensions of Global Environmental Change Program[me] e: **HDGECP**

Human Dimensions of Global Environmental Change Programme Data and Information System e: **HDP-DIS**

Human Ecology e: **Human Ecol**, e: **Hum Ecol**

Human Ecology Action League e: **HEAL**

Human Ecology Forum e: **Hum Ecol Forum**

Human Ecology Fund e: **HEF**

Human Ecology Research Service e: **HERS**

Human Environment in Sweden e: **Hum Environ Swed**

Human Environment Scientists Committee e: **HESC**

Human Environmental Services e: **HES**

Human Exploration and Development of Space e: **HEDS**

Human Frontier Science Program e: **HFSPO**

Human Frontier Science Program[me] e: **HFSP**

Human Health and [the] Environment e: **HHE**

Human Health Assessment Group e: **HHAG**

Human Health Costs e: **HHC's**

Human Life and Natural Family Planning Foundation e: **HLNFPF**

Human Nature Cooperative e: **HNC**

Human Nature Council e: **HNC**

Human Neurnbiology e: **HUNEDR**

Human Neurobiology e: **Hum Neurob**, e: **Hum Neurob[iol]**

Human Noise and Wildlife e: **HNW**

human observation[al] blunder e: **hob**

Human Reproductive Medicine e: **HRM**, e: **Human Reprod Med**

Human Rights Protection Party e: **HRPP**

Human Space Flight e: **HSF**

Humanmedizin d: **HM**

Humidifier, Air, Water-spray e: **HAW**

Humidity Exchange Over the Sea e: **HEXOS**

Hungarian Association for the Protection of Industrial Property e: **MIE**

Hungarian Medical Archives e: **Hung Med Arch**

Hungarian Medical Bibliograaphy e: **Hung Med Biblio**

Hungarian Medical Journal e: **Hung Med J**

Hungarian Meteorological Service e: **HMS**

Hungarian National Committee of the International Association on Water Pollution Research and Control e: **HNCIAWPRC**

Hungarica Acta Biologica l: **HABiol.**

Hunter Environmental Services, Incorporated e: **HESI**

Hunter Natural History e: **Hunter Nat Ht**

Hunter Post Graduate Medical Institute e: **HPGMI**

Hunter Public health Unit e: **HUN PHU**

Huntington Medical Research Institutes e: **HMRI**

Husband's Forensic Medicine e: **Husb For Med**

Hutton Lake National Wildlife Refuge e: **HLNWR**

Hybrid Analog-Switcbing Attitude Control System for Space Vehicles e: **HYACS**

Hybrid Collective Protection Equipment e: **HCPE**

Hybrid Earth Station e: **HES**

Hybrid Orbital e: **HO**

Hybrid Orbital Rehybridization Method e: **HORM**

Hybridization Protection Assay e: **HPA**

Hycor Biomedical, Inc. e: **HYBD**

hydraulic/pneumatic hydr hydrographer e: **hyd/pnu**

Hydraulique Villageoise et Pastorale f: **HVP**

Hydrazine and Water Treatment. Proceedings of the International Conference e: **Hydrazine Water Treat Proc Int Conf**

Hydro-acoustic Impact Timing System e: **HITS**

Hydro-Chemical Form Die e: **HCFD**

Hydro-Dynamic[s] Welding e: **HDW**

Hydro-Electric Commission of Ontario e: **HECO**

Hydro-Electric Physics Laboratory e: **HEPC**

Hydro-Electric Power Commission e: **HEPC**

Hydro-Electric Power Commission Approved e: **HEPC App**

Hydro-Electric Power Commission of Ontario e: **HEPCO**, e: **HEPO**, e: **HEP X**

Hydro Electric Power [Japan] e: **Hydro Electr Power**

Hydro-Electric Securities Corporation e: **HES Corporation**

Hydro-Electric Unit[s] e: **HEU**

Hydro Electric[ity] Commission e: **HEC**

Hydro-Electricity Commission of Tasmania e: **HECT**

Hydro-Electro-Presses SA f: **HEPSA**

Hydro Flame Corp. e: **HFLM**

Hydro Home Appliances Ltd. e: **HHA**

Hydro-Lab Journal e: **Hydro Lab J**

Hydro Mechanical Power Train e: **HMPT**

Hydro-Mechanical Power Transmission e: **HMPT**

Hydro-Mechanical Unit e: **HMU**

Hydro- og Aerodynamik Laboratorium a: **HyA**

Hydro Optics, Inc. e: **HOPC**

1-Hydro-Penta-Fluoropropylene e: **HFPE**

Hydro-Press Accessory e: **HPAC**

Hydro-Press Form e: **HPFM**

Hydro-Quebec, Bibliotheque e: **HQM**

Hydro-Quebec Institute of Research e: **HQIR**

Hydro-Quebec International e: **HQI**

Hydro-Quebec, Montreal, Quebec e: **QMH**

Hydro-Québec f: **HQ**

Hydro Reconnaissance Experimental e: **HRE**

Hydro Research System e: **HRS**

Hydro-Shift Gun e: **HSG**

Hydro-Shock Munition e: **HSM**

Hydro-Space Technology, Inc. e: **HSt**

Hydroacoustic Data Acquisition System e: **HYDAS**

Hydroacustic Information System e: **HAIS**

Hydroaphic e: **HYD**

Hydrobiological Bulletin e: **Hydrobiol Bull**

Hydrobiological Journal e: **Hydrobiol.J.**

Hydrobiological Journal [English Translation of Gidrobiologicheskii Zhurnal] e: **Hydrobiol J [Engl Transl Gidrobiol Zh]**

Hydrobiological Studies e: **Hydrobiol Stud**

Hydrobiologie d: **Hydrobiol**

Hydrobiology e: **Hydrobiol**

Hydrocarbon e: **HCB**

Hydrocarbon and Rosin Resins Producers Association e: **HARRPA**

Hydrocarbon Oxidation Studies e: **HOS**

Hydrocarbon Processing e: **Hydrocarbon Process, e: Hydroc Proc**

Hydrocarbon Processing and Petroleum Refiner e: **HPPRA, e: Hydrocarbon Process Pet Refiner**

Hydrocarbon Processing Industry e: **HPI**

Hydrocarbon Research Group e: **HRG**

Hydrocarbon Reservoir Management e: **HRM**

Hydrocarbon Subcommittee e: **HSC**

Hydrocarbon[s] e: **HC**

Hydrocarbons e: **HCs**

Hydrocarbure e: **HYDCA**

Hydrocarbures Aromatiques Polycycliques f: **HAP**

Hydrocephalus News & Notes e: **HNN**

Hydrochemical Institute e: **GKhI**

Hydrochemie d: **Hydrochem**

Hydrochloric Acid e: **HCA**

Hydrochloric Peroxide Mix e: **HPM**

Hydrochlorothiazid[e] e: **HCT**, e: **HCTZ**, e: **HCZ**

Hydroclimate Data Network e: **HCDN**

Hydrocollator Pack e: **HY**

Hydrocolloid Impression e: **HcImp**

Hydrocortison d: **HCS**

Hydrocortisonacetat d: **HCA**

Hydrocortisone e: **HC**

Hydrocyanic-acid, Normal e: **HCN**

Hydrocyclones. Papers Presented at the International Conference e: **Hydrocyclones Pap Int Conf**

Hydrocylic Pressure Testing e: **HPT**

Hydrodealkylation d: **HDA**

Hydrodemetalation e: **HDM**

Hydrodenitrogenation e: **HDHNH**, e: **HDN**

Hydrodensimeter d: **HDM**

Hydrodesulphurization Process e: **HDS Process**

Hydrodynamic Analysis Tool e: **HYDAT**

Hydrodynamic Chromatography e: **HDC**

Hydrodynamic Core Disruptive Accident e: **HCDA**

hydrodynamic group of hydrodynamics e: **hydro**

hydrodynamic head e: **h**

Hydrodynamic Journal Bearing e: **HJB**

Hydrodynamic Machining e: **HDM**

Hydrodynamic Model e: **DYNHYD4**

Hydrodynamic Modulation e: **HDIV1**

Hydrodynamic Modulation Transfer Function e: **HMTF**

Hydrodynamic Technology e: **HDT**

Hydrodynamic Test System e: **HTS**

Hydrodynamic Test Unit e: **HTU**

Hydrodynamic Yield e: **HYM**

Hydrodynamic[al] e: **HYDRODYN**

Hydrodynamics e: **H**, e: **HD**

Hydrodynamic[s] e: **HYDRO**

Hydrodynamics e: **HYDRODYN**

Hydrodynamics Laboratory e: **HL**

Hydrodynamik d: **Hydrodyn**

Hydroelectric e: **HYDRELC**

hydroelectric e: **hydro**

Hydroelectric e: **hydro elec**

Hydroelectric Department e: **HE Dept**

Hydroelectric Engineer e: **Hydroelec Engr**

Hydroelectric Plant e: **HEP**

Hydroelectric Power e: **HEP**, e: **HYD**

Hydroelectric Power Plant e: **HEPP**

Hydroelectric Power Station e: **HEPS**

Hydroelectric Research and Technical Services e: **HRTS**

Hydroelectric Research and Technical Services Group e: **HRTSG**

hydroelectric[al] e: **hydel**

hydroelectrical e: **hydro**

Hydroelectric[ity] e: **HE**

Hydrofluic Stability Augmentation System e: **Hy S A S**

Hydrofluidic Stability Augmentation System e: **HYSAS**

Hydrofluomcarbon e: **HFC**

Hydrofluoric acid e: **HF**

Hydrofluoric Acid e: **HF Acid**

Hydrofluoric Acid Reprocessor Return System e: **HFRR**

Hydrofluosilicic Acid e: **HFSA**

Hydrofoil e: **HYF**

Hydrofoil Advanced Research Study Program e: **HARPY**

Hydrofoil Amphibious Tracked Vehicle e: **HATV**

Hydrofoil Analysis and Design e: **HANDE**

Hydrofoil Collision Avoidance and Tracking System e: **HYCATS**

hydrofoil motor torpedo boat e: **PTH**

Hydrofoil Ocean Combatant e: **HOC**

Hydrofoil-Operated Rocket Submarine e: **HORSE**

Hydrofoil Patrol Craft, Medium e: **PHM**

Hydrofoil research ship e: **AGEH**

Hydrofoil Ship e: **HS**

Hydrofoil Small Waterplane Area Ship e: **HYSWAS**

Hydrofoil Special Trials Unit e: **HYSTO**, e: **HYSTU**

Hydrofoil Stabilization Device e: **HYSTAD**

hydrofoil stabilizing device e: **hystad**

Hydrofoil Supported Catamaran e: **HYSUCAT**

Hydrofoil Tactical Data System e: **HTDS**

Hydrofoil Test Craft e: **HTC**

hydrofon r: **Hf**, r: **Hfn**

hydrofonbojgrupp r: **Hfnbojgrp**

hydrofonmatroser r: **Hfm**

hydrofonskola r: **Hf [school]**

hydrofonstation r: **Hfstn**

hydrofontjänst r: **Hfntj**

Hydroformylated Linseed Oil e: **HYFLO**

Hydrogaphic e: **HYDROG**

Hydrogasification e: **HYAS**

Hydrogen e: **H**, e: **H2**

Hydrogen Absorption Reaction e: **HAR**

Hydrogen-Active Species e: **HAS**

Hydrogen Actuation System e: **HAS**

Hydrogen Assisted Cracking e: **HAC**

Hydrogen-Assisted Stress-Corrosion Cracking e: **HASCC**

Hydrogen-Assisted Stress Corrosion Cracking e: **HSCC**

Hydrogen Bomb e: **HB**, e: **H-Bomb**

Hydrogen Check Valve e: **HCV**

Hydrogen Chemisorption e: **HC**

Hydrogen Chloride e: **HCl**

Hydrogen Control e: **HC**

Hydrogen Convection Zone e: **HCZ**

Hydrogen Cyanide e: **AC**, e: **HCN**

Hydrogen Defect Shallow Donors e: **HDSD**

Hydrogen Detection System d: **HDS**

Hydrogen/Deuterium/Tritium e: **HJD/T**

Hydrogen/Deuterium/Tritium [Ratio] e: **H/D/T**

Hydrogen Drain e: **HD**

Hydrogen Economy Miami Energy e: **THEME**

Hydrogen Electrode e: **HE**

Hydrogen Embrittlement e: **HE**, e: **HEM**

Hydrogen Embrittlement Cracking e: **HEC**

Hydrogen Embrittlement Proof e: **HEP**

Hydrogen Energy Progress [International Association for Hydrogen Energy] e: **Hydrogen Energy Prog**

Hydrogen Engineering Applications Ltd. e: **HEA**

Hydrogen Environment[al] Embrittlement e: **HEE**

Hydrogen Event-Containment Transient Response e: **HECTR**

Hydrogen Evolution e: **HE**

Hydrogen Evolution Reaction e: **HEB**, e: **HER**

Hydrogen Extraction Column e: **HXC**

Hydrogen Fill e: **HF**

Hydrogen Flame Ionisation [Ionization] Detection (or Detector) e: **HFID**

Hydrogen Flame Ionization e: **HFI**

Hydrogen Flouride e: **HF**

Hydrogen Fluid Distribution System e: **HFDS**

Hydrogen Fluoride Laser e: **HFL**

Hydrogen Forward-scattering Spectrometry e: **HFS**

Hydrogen Gas d: **HG**, e: **HG**

Hydrogen Gas Embrittlement e: **HGE**

Hydrogen Gas Saver e: **HGS**

Hydrogen Gas Valve e: **HGV**

Hydrogen Gasification e: **HYGAS**

Hydrogen Generator e: **HG**

Hydrogen in Metals e: **Hydrogen Met**

Hydrogen-Induced Blister Cracking e: **HIBC**

Hydrogen-Induced Cracking e: **HIC**

Hydrogen-Induced Deformation Experiment e: **HIDE**

Hydrogen-Induced Delayed Cracking e: **HIDC**

Hydrogen-Induced Stress-Corrosion Cracking e: **HISCC**

Hydrogen Injection e: **HI**

Hydrogen Iodide e: **HI**

Hydrogen Ion e: **H Ion**

hydrogen-ion concentration e: **pH**

Hydrogen Leak Detection System e: **HLDS**

Hydrogen Line e: **HL**

Hydrogen Line Emission e: **HLE**

Hydrogen Manual Valve e: **HMV**

Hydrogen Maser e: **HM**

Hydrogen Maser for Navigation Satellite e: **HYMNS**

Hydrogen Mitigation Controlled Exhaust System e: **HMCES**

Hydrogen-mitigation design-basis accident e: **HMBDA**

Hydrogen Mitigation System e: **HMS**

Hydrogen mitigation system source term e: **HMSST**

Hydrogen Mixing Studies e: **HMS**

Hydrogen Mixing Study/Transient Reactor Analysis Code e: **HMS/TRAC**

Hydrogen Organization for Progress, Education and Cooperation e: **HOPEC**

Hydrogen Overpotential e: **HOP**

Hydrogen-Oxygen e: **HO**, e: **HYDROX**

Hydrogen-Oxygen Fuel System e: **HOFS**

Hydrogen-Oxygen Primary Extraterrestrial e: **HOPE**

Hydrogen-Oxygen Primary Extraterrestrial Fuel Cell e: **HOPE Fuel Cell**

Hydrogen-Oxygen Primary Extraterrestrial Fuel Cell Program e: **HOPE Fuel Cell Program**

Hydrogen-Oxygen Recombination Device e: **HORD**

Hydrogen/Oxygen Second Stage e: **HOSS**

Hydrogen-Oxygen Turbine Super-High Operating Temperatures e: **HOT-SHOT**

Hydrogen Peroxide e: **H2O2**, e: **HTP**

Hydrogen Pressure Regulator e: **HPR**

Hydrogen Pressure Relief Valve e: **HPRV**

Hydrogen Progress [United States] e: **Hydrogen Prog**

Hydrogen Purifier e: **HP**

Hydrogen Recombination and Purge System e: **HRPS**

Hydrogen Recombiner e: **HR**

Hydrogen Relief e: **HR**, e: **Hydrogen Re**

Hydrogen Saturated Vacancy e: **HSV**

Hydrogen Seal Oil e: **HSO**

Hydrogen Storage e: **HYSTOR**

Hydrogen Stress Cracking e: **HSC**

Hydrogen Sulfide e: **H2S**

Hydrogen Swelling e: **HS**

Hydrogen Technology Evaluation Center e: **HTEC**

Hydrogen Thermal Electrochemical Converter e: **HYTEC**, e: **HYTREC**

Hydrogen Uranyl Phosphate e: **HUP**

Hydrogen Vent e: **HV**

Hydrogen Vent Header e: **HVH**

Hydrogen Ventilated Enclosure e: **HYVE**

Hydrogenated Amorphous Carbon e: **HAC**

Hydrogenated Anthracene Oil e: **HAO**

hydrogenated coconut oil e: **hco**

Hydrogenated Fatty Acid e: **HYFAC**

Hydrogenated Fish Oil e: **HFO**

Hydrogenated Nitrile Butadiene Rubber e: **H-NBR**

Hydrogenated Styrene Butadiene Block Copolymer e: **H-SB-BL**

Hydrogenation e: **HYD**

Hydrogenation of Pyrolysis Naphtha e: **HPN**

Hydrogendeuterium e: **HD**

Hydrogenic Atoms in Molecules e: **HAM**

Hydrogenic Effective Mass e: **HEM**

Hydrogenium d: **H**

Hydrogenium-Bombe d: **H-Bomb**, d: **H-Bombe**

Hydrogenous Exponential Liquid Experiment e: **HELEX**

Hydrogenous Gas Delivery System e: **HGS**

Hydrogeological Information Systems with Spatial Reference e: **HISSR**

Hydrogeologicke Informace [Csechoslovakia. Ustav Geologickeho Inzenyrstvi] c: **Hydrogeol Inf [Czech]**

Hydrogeologie d: **Hydrogeol**

Hydrogeology e: **HG**

Hydrogeology Research Laboratory e: **HRL**

Hydrograph d: **Hydrogr**

Hydrograph[er] e: **HYD**

Hydrographer e: **Hydr**

Hydrograph[er] e: **HYDRO**

Hydrographer e: **HYDROG**

Hydrographer of the Navy e: **H of N**, e: **Hydrog**

Hydrographer to the navy e: **H**

hydrographic e: **hydro**, e: **hyd[rog]**

Hydrographic Airborne Laser Sounder e: **HALS**

Hydrographic Automated Data Acquisitioning and Processing System e: **HADARS**

Hydrographic Automated (or Automatic) Data Logging and Processing System e: **HADLAPS**

Hydrographic Automated System e: **HAS**

Hydrographic Bulletin e: **Hydrog Bull**

Hydrographic Center e: **HC**

Hydrographic Chart Raster Format e: **HCRF**

Hydrographic Data Acquisition System e: **HYDAS**

Hydrographic Data Aquisition Systems e: **HDAS**

Hydrographic Data Logging and Plotting System e: **HYDLAPS**

Hydrographic Data Logging and Processing Systems e: **HYDLAPS**

Hydrographic Department e: **HD**

Hydrographic Department, Admiralty e: **HDA**

Hydrographic Department of Japan e: **HDJ**

Hydrographic Digital Positioning and Depth Recording [System] e: **HYDRA**

Hydrographic Digital Positioning and Depth Recording System e: **HYDRAS**

Hydrographic Image Exploitation System e: **HIES**

Hydrographic Information Committee e: **HIC**

Hydrographic Information for the Atlantic e: **HYDROLANT**

Hydrographic Information for the Pacific e: **HYDROPAC**

Hydrographic Journal [Hydrographic Society] e: **Hydrogr J**

Hydrographic Oceanographic Data Sheets e: **HODS**

Hydrographic Office e: **HO**, e: **HYDRO**

Hydrographic Office. Publication e: **HO Publ**

Hydrographic Office Publication[s] e: **HOP**

Hydrographic Office Scale e: **HOS**

Hydrographic Office-Washington e: **HO-W**

Hydrographic Personnel e: **HYPER**

Hydrographic Precision Scanning Echo Sounder e: **HYPSES**

Hydrographic Review e: **Hydrog Rev**

Hydrographic Society e: **HS**, e: **THS**

Hydrographic Society of South Africa e: **HSSA**

Hydrographic Survey Assistance Program e: **HYSAP**

Hydrographic Survey Platform System e: **HSPS**

Hydrographic Survey[ing] and Charting [System] e: **HYSURCH**

Hydrographic Survey[ing] and Charting System e: **HYSURCH System**

Hydrographic Topographic Center e: **HTC**

Hydrographic Warning-Atlantic Ocean e: **HYDROLANT**

Hydrographic Warning-Pacific Ocean e: **HYDROPAC**

Hydrographic[al] e: **HYD**

Hydrographical Department e: **HYDRO**

Hydrographie d: **Hydrogr**

hydrographisch d: **hydrogr**

Hydrography e: **HY**

hydrography e: **hyd**

Hydrography e: **Hydr**, e: **HYDRO**

Hydrograph[y] e: **Hydrog**

Hydrography of the Atlantic Ocean e: **HYDROLANT**

Hydrography of the Indian Ocean e: **HYDROIND**

Hydrography of the Pacific Ocean e: **HYDROPAC**

Hydrolic Institute e: **HI**

Hydrolisierzahl d: **HZ**

Hydrolize[d] e: **HYD**

Hydrologe d: **Hydr**, d: **Hydrol**

Hydrologic e: **HYDROL**

Hydrologic Analysis e: **HYDRA**

Hydrologic Assessment Report e: **HAR**

Hydrologic Atlas e: **HA**

Hydrologic-Atmospheric Pilot Experiment-Modelisation du Bilan Hydrique e: **HAPEX-MOBILHY**

Hydrologic Bench Mark e: **HBM**

Hydrologic Bench Mark Network e: **HBMN**

Hydrologic Data Laboratory e: **HDL**

Hydrologic Engineering Center e: **HEC**

Hydrologic Evaluation of Landfill Performance Model e: **HELP MOD**

Hydrologic field assistant e: **HF**

Hydrologic Information System e: **HIS**

Hydrologic Information Unit e: **HIU**

Hydrologic Instrumentation Facility e: **HIF**

Hydrologic Investigations Atlas e: **HIA**

Hydrologic Rainfall Analysis Project e: **HRAP**

Hydrologic Reports. State Bureau of Mines and Mineral Resources [New Mexico] e: **Hydrol Rep St Bur Mines Miner Resour [New Mexico]**

Hydrologic Resonance Management Program e: **HRMP**

Hydrologic Study Area e: **HSA**

Hydrologic Transport Model e: **HTM**

Hydrologic Unit Area e: **HUA**

Hydrologic Unit Code e: **HUC**

Hydrologic Unit Map e: **HUM**

Hydrological and Atmospheric Pilot Experiment in the Sahel e: **HAPEX**

Hydrological Atmospheric Pilot Experiment e: **HAPEX-Sahel**, e: **MOBILHY**

Hydrological Communications Satellite e: **HCS**

Hydrological Cycle Observing System e: **HYCOS**

Hydrological Data Bank e: **HYDABA**

Hydrological Emscher Radar Project e: **HERP**

Hydrologic[al] Growing Season e: **HGS**

Hydrological Information Referral Service e: **INFOHYDRO**

Hydrologic[al] Information Storage and Retrieval System e: **HISARS**

Hydrological Institute and Belgrade University e: **HIBU**

Hydrological Journal e: **Hydrol J**

Hydrological Operational Multipurpose
Subprogramme e: **HOMS**

Hydrological Operational Multipurpose
System e: **HOMS**

Hydrological Processes e: **Hydrol Process**

Hydrological Processes and Climate e:
HPC

Hydrological Rearch Laboratory e: **HRL**

Hydrologic[al] Research Unit e: **HRU**

Hydrological Sciences and Technology
[American Institute of Technology] e:
Hydrol Sci Technol

Hydrological Sciences Bulletin e: **Hydrol.
Sci. Bull.**

Hydrological Sciences. Bulletin des
Sciences Hydrologiques f: **Hydrol Sci
Bull Sci Hydrol**

Hydrological Sciences Bulletin.
International Association of Hydrological
Sciences e: **Hydrol Sci Bull Int Assoc
Hydrol Sci**

Hydrological Sciences Journal e: **Hydrol.
Sci. J.**, e: **Hydro Sci J**

Hydrological Sciences Journal
[International Association of
Hydrological Sciences, Netherlands] e:
Hydrol Sci J

Hydrologic[al] Sensing Satellite e: **HSS**

Hydrological Series. Australian Water
Resources Council e: **Hydrol Ser Aust
Wat[er] Resour Counc**

Hydrological Simulation Program e:
HSPF

Hydrologie d: **Hydr**, d: **Hydrol**

hydrologisch d: **hydr**, d: **hydrol**

Hydrologische Bibliographie d: **Hydrol
Bibl**

Hydrologische Datenbank d: **HYDABA**

Hydrologische Staatanstalt d: **HydrStA**

Hydrologische Staatsanstalt d: **Hydr.St.A.**

Hydrologischer Dienst d: **HD**

Hydrologiska Byrån r: **HB**

hydrologist in charge e: **hic**

Hydrology e: **HYD**

hydrology e: **hydro**, e: **Hydrol**

Hydrology and Water Resources in Arizona
and the Southwest e: **Hydrol Water
Resor Ariz Southwest**

Hydrology and Water Resources
Programme e: **HWR**

Hydrology and Water Resources
Program[me] e: **HWRP**

Hydrology Laboratory e: **HL**

Hydrology Overview Committee e: **HOC**

Hydrology Symposium e: **Hydrol Symp**

Hydrology Symposium. Proceedings
[Ottawa] e: **Hydrol Symp Proc
[Ottawa]**

Hydrolyse d: **Hydr**, d: **Hydrol**

Hydrolysed Vegetable Protein e: **HYP**

Hydrolysis e: **H**

hydrolytisch d: **hydrolyt**

Hydrolyzable Tannin Level e: **HT**

Hydrolyzed Plant Protein e: **HPP**

Hydrolyzed Polar Lipid Fraction e: **HPLF**

Hydrolyzed Vegetable Protein e: **HVP**

Hydromagnetic e: **HM**

Hydromagnetic Emission[s] e: **HE**

hydromagnetic[s] e: **hydromag**

Hydromechanical e: **HM**

Hydromechanical Control System e: **HCS**

Hydromechanical Fuel Control Unit e:
HFCU

Hydromechanical Test Facility e: **HTF**

hydromechanics e: **hydrom**

Hydromechanics and Hydraulic Engineering
Abstracts e: **Hydromech&Hydraul
Engng Abstr**

hydromechanisch d: **hydromech**

Hydromer, Incorporated e: **HYDI**

Hydrometallurgist e: **HM**

Hydrometallurgy e: **HM**

Hydrometals, Ind. e: **HYD**

Hydrometeor Erosion & Recessing Test e:
HEART

Hydrometeor Free Atmosphere e: **HYFA**

Hydrometeorological Applications CSCI
e: **HM**

Hydrometeorological Automated Data
System e: **HADS**

Hydrometeorological Automatic Recording
and Telemetering System e: **HARTS**

Hydrometeorological Prediction Center e:
HPC

Hydrometeorological Processes Division
e: **HPD**

Hydrometeorology Research Division e:
HRD

Hydrometer d: **HYDM**

Hydrometer Videosonde e: **HYVIS**

hydrometrisch d: **hydrom**

Hydromorphieflächentyp d: **HFT**

Hydronautics Ship Model Basin e: **HSMB**

Hydronic Radiant Heating Association e:
HRHA

Hydronics Institute e: **HI**

Hydropak-Belebtschlamm-Biologie d:
HBB

Hydropathic e: **HYDRO**

hydrophile/lipophile number e: **h/l
number**

Hydrophilic Group e: **HG**

Hydrophilic Lipophilic Balance e: **HLB**

Hydrophobe organische
Kohlenstoffverbindungen d: **HOC**

Hydrophobic Organic Compound[s] e:
HOC

Hydrophobic Tail e: **HT**

Hydrophone e: **HYPH**

Hydrophone Effect e: **HE**

Hydropneumatic e: **H Pn**, e:
HYDROPNEU

Hydropneumatic Suspension Device e:
HSD

Hydropneumatic Suspension System[s] e:
HSS

Hydropneumatic Trailer e: **HPT**

Hydropneumatic Vehicle Suspension e:
HPVS

Hydroponic Society of America e: **HSA**

Hydroquench Thrust Termination System
e: **HTTS**

Hydroquinone Monomethyl Ether e:
HMME, e: **HQMME**

Hydroscience Associates, Incorporated e:
HAI

hydroskimmer e: **skmr**

Hydrospace e: **Hydrosp**

Hydrospace Target Recognition, Evaluation
and Control e: **HYTREC**

Hydrosphere Resource Consultants e:
HRC

Hydrostatic e: **HYDRO**, e: **HYDRST**

Hydrostatic Balanced Loading e: **HBL**

Hydrostatic Deformation Potential e: **HDP**

Hydrostatic Equilibrium e: **HSE**

Hydrostatic Equilibrium System e: **HSFS**

Hydrostatic Extrusion e: **HSE**

hydrostatic gage e: **hg**

Hydrostatic-Gauging Technology e: **HGT**

Hydrostatic Head Monitoring Station e:
HHMS

Hydrostatic Impact Rocket e: **HIR**

Hydrostatic Indifference Point e: **HIP**

Hydrostatic Interface Unit e: **HIU**

Hydrostatic Pressure e: **HP**, e: **HSP**

Hydrostatic Pressure Test Certification e:
HPTC

Hydrostatic Research System e: **HRS**

Hydrostatic Tank Gauging e: **HTG**

Hydrostatic Transmission e: **HST**

hydrostatic[al] e: **hyd**

Hydrostatic[s] e: **HS**, e: **HYD**, e: **HYDR**,
e: **HYDRO**

hydrostatics e: **hydros**

Hydrotechnical Construction e:
Hydrotech Constr

Hydrotechnik d: **Hydrotech**

Hydrotechnique Association e: **HA**

Hydrotherapy e: **HT**, e: **HYDRO**

hydrotherapy e: **hydrot**

Hydrothermal Coal Process e: **HCP**

Hydrothermal Cyclis Shear Test e: **HCST**

Hydrothermal Power Company e: **HPC**

Hydrothermal Processing e: **HTP**

Hydrothermal Processing Unit e: **HPU**

Hydrothermal Reaction e: **HTR**

Hydrothermal Vent e: **HTV**

Hydrothermally Treated e: **HT**

Hydrous e: **HYD**

hydrous aluminum fluorosilicate e: **topaz**

hydrous copper silicate e: **chrysocolla**

hydrous magnesium silicate e: **talc**

Hydroviscous Drive e: **HVD**, e: **HYD**

Hydroxide d: **HYDX**

hydroxide[s] e: **hydx**

Hydroxprolin e: **HYP**

Hydroxy Methyl Cystosine e: **HMC**

2-Hydroxy-5-Nitrobenzyl Bromide e:
HNBB

Hydroxy Polycyclic Aromatic Hydrocarbon
e: **HPAH**

Hydroxy Polycyclic Aromatic Nitrogen
Heterocycle e: **HPANH**

Hydroxy Polycyclic Aromatic Sulfur
Heterocycle e: **HPASH**

Hydroxy Terminated Polyisobutylene e:
HTPIB

Hydroxyaminoguanidine e: **HAG**

Hydroxyapatite Crystal e: **HAC**

Hydroxybenzene e: **HB**

Hydroxybenzeneazo Benzoic Acid e:
HBABA

Hydroxybenzoic Acid e: **HBA**

Hydroxybenzylpindolol e: **HYP**

Hydroxycitronellal Diethyl Acetal e: **HDA**

Hydroxydaunomycin, Oncovin, Prednisone
e: **HOP**

Hydroxyheptadecatrienoic Acid e: **HHT**

Hydroxyindol[e]-O-Methyltransferase e:
HIOMT

Hydroxyindole O-Methyltransferase e:
HOMT

Hydroxyiodoquinolinesulfonic Acid e:
HIQSA

Hydroxyisophthalyl Dihydroxarnic Acid e:
HIPDA

Hydroxyl Terminated Liquid e: **HTL**

Hydroxyl Terminated Polybutyiene e: **HTR**

Hydroxyl Value e: **HV**

Hydroxylamine Acid Sulfate e: **HARTRAN**, e: **HAS**

Hydroxylamine Sulfate e: **HS**

Hydroxylaminsulfat d: **HS**

Hydroxylapatite-Polylactic Acid e: **HA-PLA**

Hydroxylcarbonate Apatite e: **HCA**

Hydroxyline e: **hydrox**

Hydroxylysin d: **HYL**

Hydroxylysine d: **Hyl**, e: **Hylys**

Hydroxylzahl d: **HOZ**

Hydroxymercurbenzoate e: **HMBA**

Hydroxymethyl Cellulose e: **HEC**

Hydroxymethyl Diacetone Acrylamide e: **HMDAA**

Hydroxymethyl Uracil e: **HMU**

Hydroxymethylfuraldehyde e: **HMF**

Hydroxymethylglutaryl d: **HMG**

Hydroxynaphthoic Acid e: **HNA**

Hydroxyndole Acetic Acid e: **HIA**

Hydroxyoxo-lnorvaline e: **HON**

Hydroxyphenyl Ethyl Aminoethyl Tetralone e: **HEAT**

Hydroxyphenyl Pyruvate e: **HPP**

Hydroxypmline-Rich Glycoprotein e: **HRGP**

Hydroxyprolin d: **Hypro**

Hydroxyproline e: **HP**

Hydroxyprolin[e] e: **HYP**

hydroxyproline e: **hypro**

Hydroxypropylcellulose d: **E 463**, e: **HPC**

Hydroxypropylmethylcellulose d: **E 464**

Hydroxypyrenetrisulfonate e: **HPT**

Hydroxypyrenetrisulfonic Acid e: **HPTS**

Hydroxyquinoline Oxide e: **HQO**

Hydroxyquinolinesulfonic Acid e: **HQSA**

Hydroxysteroid Dehydrogenase e: **HSD**

Hydroxytryptophan d: **HTP**

Hydroxytyptophane e: **HTP**

Hydroxyurea e: **HU**, e: **HYD**, e: **HYDREA**

Hygiene und Medizin d: **Hyg Med**

Hygienisch-medizinische Untersuchungsstelle d: **HygUSt**

Hygienisch-medizinische Untersuchungsstelle im Wehrbereich d: **HygUStWB**

Hygienisch-medizinisches Institut des Wehrmedizinalamtes d: **Hyg.Inst.**

Hyogo University of Teacher Education. Journal.Series 3.Natural Sciences, Practical Life Studies e: **Hyogo Univ Tech Educ J Ser 3**

Hyper-Environmental Radar e: **HER**

Hyper-Environmental Test Station e: **HETS**

Hyper-Environment[al] Test System e: **HETS**

Hyperbaric Environmental Control Assembly e: **HECA**

Hyperfiltration Wash Water Recovery System e: **HWWS**

Hypergeometric Group Testing e: **HGT**

Hypermedia Geographical Information Systems e: **HGIS**

Hypermedia Presentations of Integrated Medical Data e: **HYPERMEDATA-CP94-943**

Hyperpolarization e: **HP**

Hypersonic Aerospace Sizing Analysis e: **HASA**

Hypersonic Flight Environmental Simulator e: **HYFES**, e: **HYPES**

Hypersonic Integral Boundary Layer Analysis of Reentry Geometries e: **HI-BLARG**

Hypersonic Lifting Entry Aerospace Program e: **Hy Leap**

Hypersonic Orbital Research and Utilization System e: **HORUS**

Hypersonic Orbital Upper Stage e: **HORUS**

Hypodermic e: **H**

Hélicoptères d'Appui Protection f: **HAP**

Héritiers Indivis f: **H.I.**

I

I Receiving Water Model e: **RECEIV-I**

IAEA Marine Environment Laboratory e: **IMEL**

IAEA Marine Environment[al] Laboratory e: **IAEA-MEL**

IAHS [International Associa- tion of Hydrological Sciences] International Commission on Continental Erosion e: **IAHS-ICCE**

IAHS [International Associa- tion of Hydrological Sciences] International Commission on Groundwater e: **IAHS-ICGW**

IAHS [International Associa- tion of Hydrological Sciences] International Commission on Water Quality e: **IAHS-ICWQ**

IAHS [International Association of Hydrological Sciences] Publication e: **IAHS Publ.**

IAMAP Commission on Dynamic Meteorology e: **ICDM**

IAMAP-International Association of Hydrological Science[s] e: **IAMAP-IAHS**

IAMG Newsletter [International Association for Mathematical Geology] e: **IAMG Newsl**

Ibero-American Society for Cell Biology e: **IASCB**

ICAO Standard Atmosphere e: **ISA**

Ice and Climate Experiment e: **ICEX**

Ice Center Environment Canada e: **ICEC**

Ice core Circum-Arctic Paleoclimate Programme e: **ICAPP**

Ice Sheet Mass Balance and Sea-level Contributions e: **ISMASS**

Ice Shelf Water e: **ISW**

Ice Water Content e: **IWC**

ice water path e: **IWP**

Iceland Ocean Meeting Point e: **ICOMP**

Iceland-Scotland Overflow Water e: **ISOW**

Icelandic Medical Association e: **L.I.**

Icelandic Meteorological Office e: **IMO**

Icelandic Radiation Protection Institute e: **IRPI**

ICSU Inter-Union Commission for Geodynamics e: **IICG**

Idaho Bureau of Mines and Geology e: **IBMG**

Idaho Department of Health and Welfare e: **IDHW**

Idaho Department of Water Resources e: **IDWR**

Idaho Geological Survey e: **IGS**

Idaho Museum of Natural History e: **IMNH**

Idaho National Engineering and Environmental Laboratory e: **INEEL**

Idaho Water and Energy Resources Research Institute e: **IWERRI**

Idlewild, New York [Kennedy International Airport] e: **IDL**

IEEE Aerospace and Electronic Systems Magazine [IEEE Aerospace and Electronics Systems Society] e: **IEEE Aerosp Electron Syst Mag**

IEEE Engineering in Medicine and Biology Magazine [Institute of Electrical and Electronics Engineers] e: **IEEE Eng Med Biol Mag**

IEEE [Institute of Electrical and Electronic Engineers] Aerospace and Electronic Systems e: **IAES**

IEEE [Institute of Electrical and Electronics Engineers] Biomedical Engineering e: **IEBM**

IEEE [Institute of Electrical and Electronics Engineers] Geoscience Electronics e: **IEGE**

IEEE [Institute of Electrical and Electronics Engineers] Group Aerospace and Electronics Society e: **IEEE G-AES**

IEEE [Institute of Electrical and Electronics Engineers] Transactions on Geoscience Electronics e: **IEEE Trans Geosci Electron**

IEEE Journal of Oceanic Engineering [IEEE Oceanic Engineering Society] e: **IEEE J Ocean Eng**

IEEE Proceedings of Conference on Engineering in Medicine and Biology e: **IEEE Proc Conf Eng Med Biol**

IEEE Transactions on Aerospace and Electronic Systems e: **IEEE AER EL**

IEEE Transactions on Aerospace and Electronic Systems [Institute of Electrical and Electronics Engineers] e: **IEEE Trans Aerosp Electron Syst**

IEEE Transactions on Bio Medical Engineering e: **IEEE BIOMED**

IEEE Transactions on Biomedical Engineering [Institute of Electrical and Electronics Engineers] e: **IEEE Trans Biomed Eng**

IEEE Transactions on Geoscience and Remote Sensing [IEEE Geoscience and Remote Sensing Society] e: **IEEE Trans Geosci Remote Sens**

IEEE Transactions on Geoscience Electronics e: **IEEE GEOSCI**

IEEETransactions on Medical Imaging [Institute of Electrical and Electronic Engineers] e: **IEEE Trans Med Imaging**

IES Monograph Series [Institution of Environmental Engineers] e: **IES Monogr Ser**

IES Proceedings [Institution of Environmental Engineers] e: **IES Proc**

Igaku Kenkyu. ACTA Medica [Fukuoka] e: **Igaku Kenkyu**

Igloo Environment Control Subsystem e: **IECS**

Igneous and Geothermal Processes e: **IGP**

IGOSS [Integrated Global Ocean Station System] Data Processing Services System *e:* **IDPSS**

IGOSS Pilot Project on Altimetric Sea-surface Topography Data *e:* **IPAST**

IGOSS Sea-Level Pilot Project in the North and Tropical Atlantic *e:* **ISLPP-NTA**

IGOSS Sea-Level Pilot Project in the Pacific Ocean *e:* **ISLPP**

IGOSS Sea-Level Programme *e:* **ISLP**

IGOSS Sea-Level Programme in the Pacific *e:* **ISLP-PAC**

IGOSS Sea Level Project *e:* **ISLP**

IGOSS Sea Level Project in the Pacific *e:* **ISLP-Pac**

Ikatan Ahli Geologi Indonesia *in:* **IAGI**

Ikatan Pendukung Kemerdekaan Indonesia *in:* **IPKI**

Illawarra Public Health Unit *e:* **ILL PHU**

Illegal Frontier Crosser *e:* **IFC**

Illinois Association for Infant Mental Health *e:* **ILAIMH**

Illinois College of Podiatric Medicine *e:* **ICPM**

Illinois Department of Mental Health and Developmental Disabilities, Library Services Network *e:* **DMHDD/LISN**

Illinois Department of Natural Resources *e:* **IDNR**

Illinois Department of Public Health *e:* **IDPH**

Illinois Geographic Information System *e:* **IGIS**

Illinois Geologic Mapping Advisory Committee *e:* **IGMAC**

Illinois Geologic Quadrangle *e:* **IGQ**

Illinois Geological Mapping Advisory Committee *e:* **IGMAP**

Illinois Geological Survey *e:* **IGS**

Illinois Groundwater Consortium *e:* **IGC**

Illinois Groundwater Protection Act *e:* **IGPA**

Illinois-Indiana Sea Grant Program *e:* **IISGP**

Illinois Institute for Environmental Quality *e:* **IIBQ,** *e:* **IIEQ**

Illinois Journal of Health, Physical Education and Recreation *e:* **ILHP**

Illinois Medical Journal *e:* **Ill Med J**

Illinois Natural History Survey *e:* **INHS**

Illinois Nature Conservancy *e:* **INC**

Illinois State Geological Survey *e:* **ISGS**

Illinois State Geological Survey, Urbana *e:* **IUrG**

Illinois State Medical Society *e:* **ISMS**

Illinois State Veterinary Medical Association *e:* **ISVMA**

Illinois State Water Survey *e:* **ISWS,** *e:* **M-ISWS**

Illinois State Water Survey, Urbana *e:* **IUrW**

Illinois Water Reserves Center *e:* **IWRC**

Illness-Correctional Environments *e:* **ICE**

[Illustrierte] Rundschau der medizinisch-chirurgischen Technik *d:* **Rdsch.d.m.chir.Techn.**

IMA Journal of Mathematics Applied in Medicine and Biology *e:* **IMA J Math Appl Med Biol**

Image Analysis and Graphic Facility for Ecological Studies *e:* **IMAGES**

Image-Based Analysis of Geographic Data *e:* **IMAGED**

Image-Based Geographic Information System *e:* **IBGIS**

Image Dynamics in Science and Medicine *e:* **Image Dyn Sci Med**

Images from the History of Medicine. National Library of Medicine *e:* **IHM**

Imaging Middle-Atmosphere Geophysical Radar *e:* **IMAGER**

Imaging Photo-Polarimeters *e:* **IPPs**

Imaging Spectoscopic Observatory *e:* **ISO**

Imaging Spectrometer Observatory *e:* **ISO**

Imaging Spectrometric Observatory *e:* **ISO**

imitieren *d:* **imit**

imitiert *d:* **im,** *d:* **imit**

Immediate Danger to Life and Health *e:* **IDLH**

Immediately Dangerous to Life and/or Health *e:* **IDLH**

Immigratie- en Naturalisatiedienst *n:* **IND**

Immigration and Naturalization Reporter *e:* **I&N Reporter**

Immigration and Naturalization [Service] *e:* **I&N**

Immigration and Naturalization Service *e:* **I&NS**

Immunobiologie *d:* **Immunobiol**

Immunobiology Research Institute *e:* **IRI**

Immunology and Cell Biology [Adelaide] *e:* **Immunol Cell Biol**

Impact des activités humaines sur les éco-systèmes côtiers et estuariens *f:* **MICE**

Impact Signature Training Practice Warhead *e:* **ISTPW**

Imperial College of Science, Technology and Medicine *e:* **ICSTM**

Imperial Ethiopian Mapping and Geographical Institute *e:* **MGI**

Imperial Ethiopian Mapping and Geography Institute *e:* **IEMGI**

Imperial National Wildlife Refuge *e:* **INWR**

Implementation Air Space Task Force Group A *e:* **IAS-TFA**

Implementation Air Space Task Force Group B *e:* **IAS-TFB**

Implementation and Effectiveness of International Environmental Commitments *e:* **IEC**

Implementation and Effectiveness of International Environmental Committee *e:* **IEC**

Implementing Secure Health Telematics Applications in Europe *e:* **ISHTAR**

importieren *d:* **imp**

importiert *d:* **imp**

Improved Atmospheric Sounding Interferometer *e:* **IASI**

Improved Benevolent [and] Protective Order of Elks of the World *e:* **IBPOEW**

Improved Cycle Boiling Water Reactor *e:* **ICBWR,** *e:* **ICBWVR**

Improved [or Infrared] Limb Atmospheric Spectrometer *e:* **ILAS**

Improved Performance Space Motor *e:* **IPSM**

Improved Remote Area Anti-Armor Mine *e:* **IRAAM**

Improved Replenishment-at-Sea Program *e:* **IRP**

Improved SAGE [Semi-Automatic Ground Environment] Manned Intercept System *e:* **ISMIS**

Improved Space Manned Interceptor *e:* **ISMI**

Improved Television and Infrared Observation Satellite *e:* **ITOS**

Improved TIBOS [Television [and] Infrared Observation Satellite] Operational Satellite (or System) *e:* **ITOS**

Improved UK Air Defence Ground Environment Command and Control System *e:* **ICCS**

Improved United Kingdom Air Defence Ground Environment *e:* **IUKADGE**

Improved Virtual Orbitals *e:* **IVO**

Improved Water Analysis Kit *e:* **IWAK**

Improved Weather Reconnaissance *e:* **IWR**

Improved Weather Reconnaissance System *e:* **IWRS**

Improved Weather Reconnaissance System Program Council *e:* **IWRPC**

Improvend Biological Detection System *e:* **IBDS**

Improving Our Health Odds *e:* **IOHO**

Improving the multidisciplinary co-operation on globalisation, economy and ecology *e:* **ERPNET**

Impulse Transfer Orbit *e:* **ITO**

In-Containment Chilled Water *e:* **ICCW**

In Defense of Animals *e:* **IDA**

in der Medizin meist für Therapie *d:* **Th**

In-Flight Aeromedical Evacuation Team *e:* **IAET**

In-Flight Operational Evaluation of [a] space [System] *e:* **INFOES**

In-Flight Operational Evaluation of a Space System *e:* **INFOES System**

In-Flight Operational Evaluation of Space Systems *e:* **INFOESS**

In Ocean By Mistake *e:* **IOBM**

In-Orbit Checkout and Calibration *e:* **IOC**

In-Orbit Plane *e:* **IOP**

In-Orbit Test Antenna *e:* **IOT**

In-Orbit Test[ing] *e:* **IOT**

In-Place Inactivation and Natural Restoration Technologies *e:* **IINERT**

In Rotating Water Spinning Process *e:* **INBOWASP,** *e:* **INROWASP**

In-Space Ground Support Equipment *e:* **IGSE**

In Space Maintenance *e:* **ISM**

In Vitro Cellular and Developmental Biology *e:* **In Vitro Cell Dev Biol**

In Vitro Cellular and Developmental Biology. Animal *e:* **In Vitro Cell Dev Biol Anim**

Inactive Aerospace Vehicle *e:* **IA**

Inactive Aerospace Vehicle [or Aircraft] Authorization *e:* **IAA**

Inactive Aerospace Vehicle [orAircraft] Inventory *e:* **IAI**

Incendiary Torch Remote Opening Device *e:* **ITROD**

inch of water *e:* **in. H2O**

Inch[es] of Water *e:* **in w**

Inch[es] of Water Gauge *e:* **IN WG**

Incident at Sea *e:* **INCSEA**

Incineration at Sea Site Monitoring and Permits File *e:* **IAS**

Inclination of a Plane to the Plane of the Earth's Equator *e:* **IPEE**

Incoming Trunk Service Observation *e:* **ITSO**

Incorporated Liverpool School of Tropical Medicine e: **ILSTM**

Incorporated Society of Registered Naturopaths e: **ISRN**

Incredible Natural Abundance Double Quantum Transfer Experiment e: **INADEQUATE**

Independent Data Unit Protection Generic Security Service Application Programming Interface e: **IDUP-GSS-API**

Independent Duty Medical Technician e: **IDT**

Independent Group for Health in Africa e: **IGHA**

Independent Health Food e: **IHF**

Independent Health Insurance Institute e: **IHII**

Independent Investor Protective League e: **IIPL**

Independent Medical Distributors Association e: **IMDA**

Independent Medical Evaluation e: **IME**

Independent Medical Examiner e: **IME**

Independent Natural Gas Association of America e: **INGAA**

Independent Order of Foresters International Oceanographic Foundation e: **IOF**

Independent Pet and Animal Transportation Association e: **IPATA**

Independent Protectionist e: **IndProt**

Independent Scientific Committee on Smoking and Health e: **ISCSH**

Independent Snowmobile Medical Research [association] e: **ISMR**

Independent Space Experiment Systems e: **ISES**

Independent Space Research Group e: **ISRG**

Independent Union of Plant Protection Employees e: **IUPPE**

Independent Union of Plant Protection Employees in the Electrical and Machine Industry e: **PPE**

Independent World Commission on the Oceans e: **IWCO**

Indescor Hydrodynamics, Inc. e: **IHS**

Index Medicus e: **IM**, e: **Ind Med**

Index Medicus Africain f: **IMA**

Index Medicus for Eastern Mediterranean Region e: **IMEMR**

Index Medicus for South-East Asia Region e: **IMSEAR**

index of environmental quality e: **ieq**

Index of Medieval Medical Images in North America e: **IMMI**

Index of Watershed Indicators e: **IWI**

Index of Wilderness Quality e: **IWQ**

Index to Geologic Maps e: **IGM**

Index to Health Information e: **IHI**

Indexed References to Biomedical Engineering Literature e: **IRBEL**

India Board of Alternative Medicine e: **IBAM**

India Meteorological Department e: **IMD**

Indian Academy of Sciences. Proceedings. Section A. Earth and Planetary Sciences e: **Proc Indian Acad Sci Sect A Earth Planetary Sci**

Indian Agricultural Research International, Water Technology Center e: **IARI-WTC**

Indian Air Defence Ground Environment System e: **IADGES**

Indian Army Medical Corps e: **IAMC**

Indian Association for Radiation Protection e: **IARP**

Indian Association on Water Pollution Research and Control e: **IAWPRC**

Indian-built Remote Sensing satellite e: **IRS-IA**

Indian cean GEOSECS Program e: **INDOCHEM**

Indian Condition Evaluation e: **ICEV**

Indian Council of Medical Research e: **ICMR**

Indian Deep Water e: **IDW**

Indian earth Research Satellite e: **IRS**

Indian earth resources satellite e: **BHASKARA**

Indian Forest Records. Wild Life and Recreation e: **IWLRAA**

Indian Geographical Society e: **I.G.S.**

Indian Geostationary Meteorological Satellite e: **INSAT**

Indian Geotechnical Journal e: **Indian Geotech J**

Indian Health Service[s] e: **IHS**

Indian Institute of Biochemistry and Experimental Medicine e: **IIBEM**

Indian Institute of Experimental Medicine e: **IIEM**

Indian Institute of/for Tropical Meteorology e: **IITM**

Indian Institute of Geomagnetism e: **IIG**

Indian Institute of Remote Sensing e: **IIRS**

Indian Journal of Chemistry. Section B. Organic Chemistry, Including Medicinal e: **Indian J Chem B**

Indian Journal of Experimental Biology e: **Indian J Exp Biol**

Indian Journal of Medical Research e: **Indian J Med Res**

Indian Journal of Medical Sciences e: **Indian J Med Sci**

Indian Journal of Meteorology and Geophysics e: **Indian J Meteorol Geophys**

Indian Journal of Pathology and Microbiology e: **Indian J Pathol Microbiol**

Indian Journal of Public Health e: **Indian J Public Health**

Indian Journal of Radio and Space Physics e: **Indian J Radio Space Phys**

Indian Landsat Earth Station e: **ILES**

Indian Medical Academy e: **I.M.A.**

Indian Medical Association e: **IMA**

Indian Medical Department e: **I.M.D.**

Indian Medical Gazette e: **Ind Med Gaz**

Indian Medical Record e: **Ind Med Rec**

Indian Medical Service e: **I.M.S.**

Indian Meteorological Department e: **I.M.D.**

Indian Meteorology Department e: **IMD**

Indian Middle Atmosphere Programme e: **IMAP**

Indian National Committee for Space Research e: **INCOSPAR**

Indian National Committee of the International Association on Water Pollution and Control e: **INCIAWPBC**

Indian National Committee on Oceanic Research e: **INCOR**

Indian National Oceanographic Data Centre e: **INODC**

Indian Ocean e: **Ind**, e: **Ind O**, e: **IO**

Indian Ocean and Southern Hemisphere Anaylsis Centre [or Center] e: **INOSHAC**

Indian Ocean Biological Centre [or Center] e: **IOBC**

Indian-Ocean Cable Management Committee e: **ICMC**

Indian Ocean Commission e: **InOC**, e: **IOC**

Indian Ocean Conventional Target List e: **IOCTL**

Indian Ocean Expedition e: **IOE**

Indian Ocean Experiment e: **INDEX**, e: **INDOEX**, e: **INOEX**

Indian Ocean Fisheries Commission e: **IOFC**

Indian Ocean Geochemistry e: **INDIGO**

Indian Ocean Marine Affairs Cooperation e: **IOMAC**

Indian Ocean Panel e: **IOP**

Indian Ocean Planning Group e: **IOPG**

Indian Ocean Rank e: **IOR**

Indian Ocean Region e: **INO**, e: **IOR**

Indian Ocean Ship e: **IOS**

Indian Ocean Site e: **IOS**

Indian Ocean Standard Net e: **IOSN**

Indian Ocean Station Support e: **IOSS**

Indian Ocean Territories e: **IOTs**

Indian Ocean Territory e: **IOT**

Indian Ocean Tuna Commission e: **IOTC**

Indian Ocean Zone of Peace e: **IOPZ**

Indian Rare Earths Limited e: **IRE**

Indian Remote-sensing Satellite e: **IRS**

Indian Remote Sensing Satellite e: **IRSS**

Indian School of Mines and Applied Geology e: **ISMAG**

Indian Society for Medical Statistics e: **ISMS**

Indian Society for Nuclear Techniques in Agricullure and Biology. Newsletter e: **ISNTANV**

Indian Society of Naturalists e: **INSONA**

Indian Space Commission e: **ISC**

Indian Space Research Organisation (or Organization) e: **ISRO**

Indian Space Research Organization and Massachusetts Institute of Technology Studies on the Indian National Satellite project e: **ISRO-MIT[INSAT]**

Indian Space Tracking Network e: **ISTRACK**

Indian Spring Low Water e: **ISLW**

Indian Spring Low Water Time e: **ISLW Time**

Indian Subordinate Medical Department e: **ISMD**

Indiana Geological Survey e: **IGS**

Indiana-Kentucky Geological Society e: **IKGS**

Indiana Medicine [Indianapolis] e: **Indiana Med**

Indiana State Department of Health e: **ISDH**

Indiana State Medical Association e: **ISMA**

Indiana State University Remote Sensing Laboratory e: **ISURL**, e: **ISURSL**

Indiana University Medical Center e: **IUMC**

© K · G · Saur, München

Abkürzungen und Akronyme in Ökologie, Umwelt, Geowissenschaften

Indiana University, School of Medicine *e:*
IUM

Indiana Veterinary Medical Association *e:*
IVMA

Indianapolis Water *e:* **IWTR**

Indians into Medicine *e:* **INMED**

Indigenous Council for the Environment *e:*
ICE

Indirectly-Bonded Carbon-Hydrogen *e:*
INCH

Individual Medical Account *e:* **IMA**

Individual Medical Record *e:* **IMR**

Individual Medical Report *e:* **IMR**

Individual Protection Laboratory *e:* **IPL**

Individual Protective Equipment *e:* **IPE**

Individual Resource Protection System *e:*
IRPS

Indo-Pacific Sea Level Network *e:* **IPSLN**

Indonesia Space Experiment *e:* **INSPEX**

Indonesian Marine Environment Remote
Sensing Experiments *e:* **IMERSE**

Indonesian Wildlife Forum *e:* **WAHLI**

Indoor Environmental Quality *e:* **IEQ**

Induced Environment Contamination
Monitor *e:* **I ECM**

Induced Polarization Method *e:* **IP**
Method

Indus Water Treaty *e:* **IWT**

Industrial Applications Centers [of National
Aeronautics and Space Administration]
e: **IAC**

Industrial Central Atmosphere Monitoring
System *e:* **ICAMS**

Industrial City Water *e:* **ICW**

Industrial Energy and Environmental
Analysis *e:* **IEEA**

Industrial Environmental Association *e:*
IEA

Industrial Environmental Research
Laboratory *e:* **IERL**

Industrial Facilities Protection Program *e:*
IFPP

Industrial Fire Protection Association of
Great Britain *e:* **IFPA**

Industrial Health *e:* **Ind Health**

Industrial Health Advisory Council *e:*
IHAC

Industrial Health and Safety Branch *e:*
IHSB

Industrial Health and Safety [Committee]
e: **IHS**

Industrial Health Engineering Association
e: **IHEA**

Industrial Health Foundation *e:* **IHF**

Industrial Health Research Board *e:*
I.H.R.B.

Industrial Launch Vehicle [Space] *e:* **ILV**

Industrial Medical Administrators'
Association *e:* **IMAA**

Industrial Medical Association *e:* **IMA**

Industrial Medical Officer *e:* **I.M.O.**

Industrial Medical Service *e:* **I.M.S.**

Industrial Medicine *e:* **I.M.**

Industrial Medicine and Surgery *e:* **IMS,**
e: **Ind Med Surg**

Industrial Organisation and Health *e:* **Ind**
Org Hlth

Industrial Research Geological Survey *e:*
I.R.G.S.

Industrial Safety and Fire Protection *e:*
IS&FP

Industrial safety and health *e:* **IS&H**

Industrial Safety & Health Program
Services *e:* **ISH**

Industrial Scientific and Medical Apparatus
e: **ISM Apparatus**

Industrial, Scientific and Medical
[Applications] *e:* **ISM**

Industrial, Scientific and Medical
frequencies *e:* **ISM frequencies**

Industrial, Scientific and Medical Purposes
e: **ISM Purposes**

Industrial, Scientific and Medical
Wavelengths *e:* **ISM Wavelengths**

industrial, scientific, medical wave length
e: **ism**

Industrial Space Facility *e:* **ISF**

Industrial Transformation and Global
Environmental Change *e:* **IT**

Industrial Water Conditioning Institute *e:*
IWCI

Industrial Water Engineering *e:*
IWEGA[A]

Industrial Water Supply *e:* **IWS**

Industrial Water System *e:* **IWS**

Industrials Scientific-Medical *e:* **ISM**

Industrias Biologicas Mexicana *s:* **IBM**

Industrie Laitière *f:* **I.L.**

Industriegewerkschaft Bau, Steine, Erden
d: **BSE**

Industriegewerkschaft Bauen-Agrar-
Umwelt *d:* **BAU**

Industrieprojektierung *d:* **IPRO**

Industrieverband Heimtierbedarf e.V. *d:*
IVH

Industry and environment *e:* **DG XI-E**

Industry and Environment Office *e:* **IE,** *e:*
IEO, *e:* **IEP**

Industry and Environment Program Activity
Centre *e:* **IE/PAC**

Industry and Environment [United Nations
Environment Programme] *e:* **Ind**
Environ

Industry Committee for Packaging and the
Environment *e:* **INCPEN**

Industry Cooperative for Ozone Layer
Protection *e:* **ICOLP**

Industry, Human Settlements and
Environment Division *e:* **IHE**

Industry Missile and Space Conference *e:*
IMSC

Industry Resource Protection *e:* **IRP**

Inert Nitrogen Protection *e:* **INP**

Inertial Range Atmospheric Turbulence
Entrainment *e:* **IRATE**

Inferior Joint Space *e:* **IJS**

Inflatable Microsmeteoroid Paraglid[er] *e:*
IMP

Inflight Medical Support System *e:* **IMSS**

Informaciones Geograficas. Universidad de
Chile *s:* **UC/IG**

Informaciones Geográficas. Univ. de Chile,
Depto. de Geografía. Santiago *s:* **Inf**
Geogr/Santiago.

Información Meteorológica para aeronaves
en vuelo *s:* **VOLMET**

Información Meteorológica relativa a las
Operaciones *s:* **OPMET**

Información Sistema Médico *s:* **ISM**

Informal Natural Language Access to Navy
Data *e:* **INLAND**

Information action tiers-monde Aquitaine
f: **IATMA**

Information Center for the Environment *e:*
ICE

Information Centre of Tropical Plant
Protection *e:* **INTROP**

Information Circular. Bureau of Mines and
Geo-Sciences [Philippines] *e:* **Inf Circ**
Bur Mines Geosci [Philipp]

Information Content Natural Unit *e:* **NAT**

Information et Diffusion en éducation à
l'environnement *f:* **IDée**

Information Exchange System on Country
Activities on Climate Change *e:*
CLIMEX

Information exchange system on industrial
health and safety *e:* **JANUS**

Information for the Management of
Healthcare *e:* **IFM**

Information Management and Decision
Support in High Dependency
Environments *e:* **INFORM**

Information Market Observatory *e:* **IMO**

Information Necessary for Optimum
Resource Management and Protection *e:*
INFORMAP

Information Network for Public Health
Officials *e:* **INPHO**

Information on Mining, Metallurgy and
Geological Exploration *e:* **IMMAGE**

Information Protection Task Force *e:*
IPTF

Information Resource for the Release of
Organisms into the Environment *e:*
IRRO

Information Resources Center, Manitoba
Health, Winnipeg, Manitoba *e:* **MWHP**

Information Santé Multimédia *s:* **ISM**

Information Service on Toxicity and
Biodegradability [Water Pollution
Research Laboratory] *e:* **INSTAB**

Information System [and] Software Update
Environment *e:* **ISSUE**

Information System for Hazardous Organics
in Water [Database] *e:* **ISHOW**

Information System for Improved Plant
Protection *e:* **ISIPP**

Information System Medical *e:* **ISM**

Information system within CADDIA for
veterinary services on animal health
inspection at EC external border posts *e:*
SHIFT

Information Technology in Community
Health *e:* **ITCH**

Information Unit on Climate Change *e:*
IUCC

Informationen zur Umweltpolitik *d:* **IzU**

Informations- und Kommunikationssystem
gefährliche und umweltrelevante Stoffe
d: **IGS**

Informations-vermittlungsstelle Medizin
d: **IVS-Medizin**

Informationsberichte des Bayerischen
Landesamtes für Wasserwirtschaft *d:*
Inf.ber. Bayer. Landesamtes
Wasserwirtsch.

Informationsdienst Naturschutz
Niedersachsen *d:* **Inf.dienst Nat.schutz**
Niedersachs.

Informationsdienstkartei-selektiert *d:*
IDK-S

Informationssystem der Gesundheitsbericht-
erstattung des Bundesinstitut für
Medizinische Statistik, Dokumentation
und Datenverarbeitung *d:* **IMSDD**

Informationssystem für die Medizin *d:*
ISM

Informationssystem für
Umweltchemikalien, Chemieanlagen und
Störfälle des Umweltbundesamtes d:
INFUCHS

Informationssystem zur Klimaforschung d:
INFOKLIF

Informationszentrum Gas/Wasser d:
IGAWA

Informatique Geologique. Sciences de la
Terre f: **Inf Geol Sci Terre**

Informe de observación batitermográfico
s: **BATHY**

Informe de Observación proveniente de una
Boya a la Deriva s: **DRIFTER**

Informe meteorológico aeronáutico especial
seleccionado s: **SPECI**

Informe Meteorológico Aeronáutico
ordinario s: **METAR**

Informe meteorológico de aeronave s:
AIREP

Informe meteorológico especial s:
SPECIAL

Informer, Aider, Developper le Tiers Monde
f: **IAD**, f: **IAD Tiers Monde**

Infra-Red Signature Suppression e: **IRSS**

Infra-Red Space Interferometry Mission e:
IRSI

Infra-Red Telescope on Spacelab e: **IRTS**

Infrared Atmospheric and Signature
Prediction Model e: **IASPM**

Infrared Atmospheric Band Airglow
Radiometer e: **IRA**

Infrared Atmospheric Sounding Instrument
e: **IASI**

Infrared Atmospheric Sounding
Interferometer e: **IASI**

Infrared Background Signature
Study/Chemical Release Observation e:
IBSS/CRO

Infrared Background Space Surveillance
Experiment e: **IBSS**

Infrared Laser Atmospheric Monitoring
System e: **ILAMS**

Infrared Signatures e: **IRSIGS**

Infrared Small Astronomical Spacecraft e:
ISAS

Infrared Space Observatory e: **ISO**

Infrared Telescope in Space e: **IRTS**

Infrastructure Ground Environment Sub-
Committee e: **IGESUCO**

Infusionstherapie und Transfusionsmedizin
d: **Infusionsther Transfusionsmed**

Ingenieurbiologie Mitteilungsblatt d:
Ing.biol. Mitt.bl.

Ingenieurbüro für Gesundheitstechnik d:
IGT

Ingenieurgeologe d: **Ingenieurgeol**

Ingenieurplanung Technischer
Gebäudeausrüstung Heizung, Lüftung,
Klima, Sanitär, Elektro d: **ingplan**

Ingenieurs et Technologues Sans Frontieres
f: **ITSF**

Ingenieurverband der Wasser- und
Schiffahrtsverwaltung e.V. d: **IWSV**

Ingenieurvereinigung Wasser-Abwasser-
Abfall e.V. d: **IWAA**

Ingénierie et Management de
l'Environnement f: **IME**

Ingénieur Breveté de l'École Navale f:
IBEN

Ingénieur des Travaux Géographiques de
l'État f: **ITGE**

Ingénieur Forestier f: **IF**

Ingénieur Hydrographe f: **IgH**, f:
Ing.Hydr.

Ingénieur[s] Hydrographe[s] f: **IH**

Inidian Territorial Force Medical Corps e:
ITFMC

Initial Environment Evaluation e: **IEE**

Initial Environmental Assessment e: **IEA**

Initial Mass in Earth Orbit e: **IMEO**

initial mass in earth orbit e: **imieo**

Initial Memory Protection e: **IMP**

Initial Observation Period e: **IOP**

Initial Orbit Time e: **IOT**

Initial Orbitial Configuration e: **IOC**

Initial Orbiting Capability e: **IOC**

Initial Sea Training e: **IST**

Initial Space Station e: **ISS**

Initiative on the development of anetwork
of consultative medical centres e:
MACNET

Initiative to aid internal and external border
regions overcome problems of
development caused by their comparative
remoteness e: **INTERREG**

Initiativgruppe Umweltschutz d: **IGU**

Initiativgruppe Umweltschutz Hanau, d:
IUH

Iniut Circumpolar Conference e: **ICC**

injectio hyperdermica l: **inj hyp**

Injury Control & Emergency Health
Services Section, American Public Health
Association e: **ICEHS**

Inland Fisheries, Forestry and Wildlife
Sectors of [the] SADC e: **IFFWS**

Inland Water Petroleum Carriers
Association e: **IWPCA**

Inland Water Transport e: **IWT**

Inland Water Transport Authority e:
I.W.T.A.

Inland Water Transport Corporation e:
IWTC

Inland Water Transport Department e:
IWTD

Inland Water Transport Department Section
e: **IWTDS**

Inland Waters, Coastal and Ocean
Information Network e: **ICOIN**

Inland Waters Directorate, Environment
Canada Regina, Saskatchewan e:
SREIW

Inland Waterway Operation e: **IWO**

Inland Waterway Service e: **IWS**

Inland Waterway[s] e: **IW**, e: **IWW**

Inland Waterways Amenity Advisory
Council e: **IWAAC**

Inland Waterways Association e: **IWA**

Inland Waterways Common Carriers
Association e: **IWCCA**

Inland Waterways Corporation e: **IWC**

Inland Waterways Directorate e: **IWD**

Inland Waterways Reconnaissance Device
e: **IWWRD**

Inland Waterway[s] Transport e: **IWT**

Inland Waterways Working Group e:
IWT-WG

Inner German Frontier e: **IGF**

Inner Mongolia Grasland-Atmosphere
Surface Study e: **IMGRASS**

Innovationsförderungs- und
Technologietransfer Zentrum d: **ITZ**

Innovative Nuclear Space Power Institute
e: **INSPI**

Inosine Monophosphate Dehydrogenase e:
IMPDH

Input-Output Remote Terminal e: **IORT**

Inquiry into Pollution and Environmental
Conservation e: **INSPECT**

Insect Biochemistry and Molecular Biology
e: **Insect Biochem Mol Biol**

Insect Molecular Biology e: **Insect Mol
Biol**

Insects Affecting Man and Animals
Laboratory e: **IAMAL**

Insensible Water Loss e: **IWL**

Insensitive Nuclear enhanced by
Polarization Transfer e: **INEPT**

Insensitive Nuclear Enhanced by
Polarization under Composite Refocusing
e: **INEPT CR**

Inshore Underwater Warfare e: **IUW**

Insitut für Hydrologie e: **IfH**

Inspection des Denrées Animales et
d'Origine Animale f: **IDAOA**

Inspection Générale de l'Environnement f:
IGE

Inspection Médicale du Travail f: **IM&T**

Inspection Médicale Scolaire f: **I.M.S.**

Inspection Technique du Service
Biologique et Vétérinaire de l'Armée f:
ITSBVA

Inspector-General of Waterguard e:
I.G.W.

Inspector General, Pacific Fleet and Pacific
Ocean Areas e: **INSGENPAC**

Inspector, Naval Medical Activity e:
InspNavMedActy

Inspector of Medical Services e: **IMS**

Inspector under Cruelty to Animals Act e:
I.C.A.A.

Inspectorate of the Ministry of Health e:
I.M.H.

Inspekteur des Sanitäts- und
Gesundheitswesens d: **InspSan**

Inspektion des Sanitäts- und
Gesundheitswesens d: **InSan**

Inspéction Médicale f: **I.M.**

Installations, Logistics & Environment e:
ILE

Instandsetzungswerkstatt für medizinische
Geräte d: **IWMed**

Instant Ocean Culture System e: **IOCS**

Instantaneous Geographic Fov e: **IGFOV**

Instantaneous Geometric Field of View e:
IGFOV

Instantaneous Geometric Fov e: **IGFOV**

Instantaneous Unit Hydrograph e: **IHU**, e:
IUH

Institut Archéologique Liégeois f: **IAL**

Institut Belgo-Luxembourgeois du Change
f: **I.B.L.C.**

Institut Biologique Physico-Chimique f:
IBPC

Institut Bruxellois pour la Gestion de
l'Environnement f: **IBGE**

Institut Canadien d' Information sur la
Santé/Canadian Institute for Health
Information e: **ICIS/CIHI**

Institut Canadien de la Santé
Infantile/Canadian Institute of Child
Health e: **ICSI/CICH**

Institut Catholique d'Arts et Métiers f:
ICAM

Institut Coopératif de l'École Moderne f:
ICEM

Institut de Biologie f: **IB**

Institut de Biologie Appliquée à la Nutrition
et l'Alimentation f: **IBANA**

Institut de biologie des mers du sud *f:* **IBSS**

Institut de Biologie et d'Expérimentation *f:* **IBEX**

Institut de Biologie Expérimentale Lyonnais *f:* **IBEL**

Institut de biologie marine des Caraïbes *f:* **CARMABI**

Institut de Calcul des Effets de la Croissance industrielle sur l'environnement socio-économique *f:* **ICEC**

Institut de Formation et de Recherche en Education à l'Environnement *f:* **IFREE**

Institut de Geographie, Universite Laval, Quebec, Quebec *f:* **QQLAG**

Institut de Génie de l'Environnement *f:* **IGE**

Institut de Génétique et de Biologie Moléculaire et Cellulaire *f:* **IGBMC**

Institut de Géographie *f:* **I.G.**

Institut de Géographie Alpine *f:* **IGA**

Institut de Géomatique *f:* **IGEO**

Institut de la Médicine du Travail et de l'Environnement *f:* **IMTE**

Institut de l'Energie et de l'Environnement de la Francophonie *f:* **IEPF**

Institut de l'Environnement *f:* **IE**

Institut de Météorologie et de Physique du Globe d'Algérie *f:* **IMPGA**

Institut de Physique Météorologique *f:* **IPM**

Institut de Protection et de Sûreté Nucléaire *f:* **IPSN**

Institut de Préparation aux Grandes Écoles *f:* **IPGE**

Institut de Recherche d'Hydro-Quebec, Varennes, Quebec *f:* **QVAH**

Institut de Recherche en Biologie Appliquée de Guinée *f:* **IRBAG**

Institut de Recherche sur l'Environnement Construit *f:* **IREC**

Institut de Recherches Agronomiques et Forestieres *f:* **IRAF**

Institut de Veille Sanitaire. National Institute for Public Health Surveillance *e:* **InVS**

Institut des Frères des Écoles Chrétiennes *f:* **IFEC**

Institut des Parcs Nationaux et des Réserves Naturelles du Katanga *f:* **IPNRK**

Institut des ressources naturelles des Caraïbes *f:* **CANARI**

Institut des Sciences et des Techniques de l'Equipement et de l'environnement pour le Développement *f:* **ISTED**

Institut d'Hydrologie et de Climatologie *f:* **I.H.C.**

Institut d'Observation Économique *f:* **I.O.E.**

Institut d'études biologiques appliquées à la médecine des collectivités *f:* **IBMC**

Institut d'Études Internationales de la Communication sur l'Environnement *f:* **COMUVIR**

Institut d'Études Supérieures Industrielles et d'Économie Laitière *f:* **IESEL**

Institut Européen des Recherches et Applications Médicales *f:* **IERAM**

Institut Européen d'Écologie et de Cancérologie *f:* **INEC**

Institut Fiziki Atmosfery *R:* **IFA**

Institut for Advanced Research in Asian Science and Medicine *e:* **IARASM**

Institut for Geography and Geoecology *e:* **IGG**

Institut Français de l'Environnement *f:* **IFEN**

Institut Français de Recherches Fruitières d'Outre- Mer *f:* **IFRFOM**

Institut Français des Visiteurs Médicaux *f:* **IFVM**

Institut Français d'Océanie *f:* **I.F.O.**

Institut Franco-Allemande de Recherche sur l'Environnement *f:* **IFARE**

Institut für Aerobiologie *d:* **IAe**

Institut für angewandte Geodäsie *d:* **IAG**

Institut für Angewandte Geodasie *d:* **IIAG**

Institut fur Angewandte Geodasie *e:* **IfAG**

Institut für Angewandte Geodäsie, Frankfurt *d:* **IFAG**

Institut für angewandte Isotopen-, Gas- und Umweltuntersuchungen *d:* **IGU**

Institut für Anwendungen der Geodäsie im Bauwesen *e:* **GeodB**

Institut für Arbeitsmedizin *e:* **IfAM**

Institut für Atmosphärenphysik an der Universität Rostock, Kühlungsborn *e:* **IAP**

Institut für Atmosphärische Radioaktivität *d:* **IAR**

Institut für Atmosphärische Umweltforschung *d:* **IAU**

Institut für Bioklimatologie, Universität Göttingen *d:* **IBK**

Institut für Biologie landwirtschaftlicher Nutztiere *d:* **IBN**

Institut für biologische Forschung GmbH *d:* **INBIFO**

Institut für Biomedizinische Technik *e:* **BiomedT**

Institut für Bodensanierung, Wasser- und Luftanalytik GmbH *d:* **IBWL**

Institut für Chemie und Biologie des Meeres *d:* **ICBM**

Institut für das Gesundheitswesen *d:* **IfG**

Institut für die Pädagogik der Naturwissenschaften *d:* **IPM**

Institut für die Pädagogik der Naturwissenschaften an der Universität Kiel, Kiel *e:* **IPN**

Institut für Dokumentation und Information über Sozialmedizin und öffentliches Gesundheitswesen *d:* **IDIS**

Institut für Energie- und Umweltforschung Heidelberg e.V. *d:* **IFEU**

Institut für Europäische Umweltpolitik *d:* **IEUP**

Institut für Geodäsie & Photogrammetrie *d:* **IGP**

Institut für Geographie *e:* **Geogr**

Institut für Geographie und Geoökologie *d:* **IGG**

Institut für Geologie und Paläontologie *d:* **Geol**

Institut für Geometrie und Praktische Mathematik *d:* **IGPM**

Institut für Geophysik *d:* **IfG**, *e:* **Geophys**

Institut für Geotechnik *e:* **GrundB**

Institut für Geschichte der Medizin *d:* **IGM**

Institut für Geschichte der Naturwissenschaften der Universität Hamburg *d:* **IGN**

Institut für Geschichte der Naturwissenschaften der Universität München *d:* **IGN**

Institut für Gesundheits-System-Forschung *d:* **IGSF**

Institut für Gesundheits- und Sozialforschung *d:* **IGES**

Institut für Gesundheitswissenschaften *e:* **IfG**

Institut für Gewässerökologie und Binnenfischerei, Berlin *d:* **IGB**

Institut für Gewässerschutz und Wassertechnologie *d:* **IGW**

Institut für gewerbliche Wasserwirtschaft und Luftreinhaltung, Köln *d:* **IWL**

Institut für industrielle und biologische Forschung GmbH *d:* **Inbifo**

Institut für Informationsverarbeitung in Technik und Biologie *d:* **IITB**

Institut für Kernenergetik und EnergiesystemeAbteilung Heizung, Lüftung, Klimatechnik *d:* **HeizLüft**

Institut für Landesplanung und Raumforschung [der Universität Hannover] *d:* **ILR**

Institut für Landschaftsforschung und Naturschutz *d:* **ILN**

Institut für Medizinische Biochemie *d:* **IBIO**

Institut für Medizinische Datenverarbeitung *d:* **IMD**

Institut für Medizinische Informatik und Biometrie *e:* **IMIB**

Institut für Medizinische Mikrobiologie *e:* **IMIKRO**

Institut für Medizinische Psychologie *d:* **IMP**

Institut für Medizinische Statistik *d:* **IMS**

Institut für Medizinische Statistik und Dokumentation *d:* **IMSD**

Institut für medizinische und pharmazeutische Prüfungsfragen *d:* **IMPP**

Institut für Meteorologie und Klimaforschung *e:* **IMK**

Institut für Mikrobiologie *e:* **Mikrobiol**

Institut für Naturheilkunde AG *d:* **IFN**

Institut für naturwissenschaftlich-technische Dienste GmbH *d:* **Natec**

Institut für Neurobiologie *d:* **IFN**, *d:* **INB**

Institut für niederdeutsche Sprache *d:* **INS**

Institut für physikalische Medizin und Rehabilitation *d:* **IPMR**

Institut für Polarökologie *e:* **IPÖ**

Institut für praxisorientierte Sozialforschung *d:* **IPOS**

Institut für Radiometeorologie und maritime Meteorologie an der Univerität Hamburg *d:* **IRM**

Institut für Raumfahrtsysteme *e:* **RaumfAntr**

Institut für Raumfahrttechnik *d:* **IR**

Institut für Rechtsmedizin *e:* **IfRM**

Institut für Siedlungswasserbau, Wassergüte- und Abfallwirtschaft *e:* **SiedlWB**

Institut für Sozialmedizin und Epidemiologie *d:* **SOZEP**

Institut für Statik und Dynamik der Luft- und Raumfahrtkonstruktionen *d:* **StaDynL**

Institut für Statik und Dynamik der Luft- und Raumfahrtkonstruktionen, Universität Stuttgart *d:* **ISD**

Institut für Thermodynamik der Luft- und Raumfahrt *e:* **ThermL**

Institut für Tierzuchtforschung *d:* **IfT**

Institut für Umweltforschung und Entwicklungsplanung *d:* **SYSTEMPLAN**

Institut für Umweltschutz und Umweltgüteplanung, Dortmund *d:* **INFU**

Institut für Umwelttechnik *d:* **IfU**

Institut für Umweltverfahrenstechnik *d:* **IUV**

Institut für Veterinärmedizin-Robert-von-Ostertag-Institut *d:* **VETMED**

Institut für Wasser-, Boden- und Lufthygiene des Umweltbundesamtes in Berlin *d:* **WaBoLu**

Institut für Wasserforschung GmbH *d:* **IfW**

Institut für wassergefährdende Stoffe *d:* **IWS**

Institut für Wasserwirtschaft *d:* **IfW**

Institut für Wehrmedizin und Hygiene *d:* **WehrMedInst**

Institut für Wehrmedizinalstatistik und Berichtswesen *d:* **WehrMedStatInst**

Institut für Wissenschaftsinformation in der Medizin *d:* **IWIM**

Institut für Zoo- und Wildtierforschung, Berlin *e:* **IZW**

Institut Fédéral de Recherches en Matière de Réacteurs *f:* **IFR**

Institut Geographique de Burkina Faso *f:* **IGBF**

Institut Geographique de Burundi *f:* **IGEBU**

Institut Geographique de la Cote d'Ivoire *f:* **IGCI**

Institut Geographique du Zaire *f:* **IGZa**

Institut Geographique National *f:* **IGNB**

Institut Geographique National Belgique *f:* **IGNB**

Institut Geographique National Burundi *f:* **IGNB**

Institut Geographique National Congolaise *f:* **IGNC**

Institut Geographique National Guineen *f:* **INCG**

Institut Geographique Nationale *f:* **IGN**

Institut Géographique de France *f:* **I.G.F.**

Institut Géographique du Congo Belge *f:* **IGCB**

Institut Géographique Militaire *f:* **IGM**

Institut Géographique Militaire, Belgique *f:* **IGMB**

Institut Géographique National *f:* **I.G.N.**

Institut Géographique National de France *f:* **IGNF**

Institut Géographique National de France-Cadastre du Luxembourg *f:* **IGNF.CL**

Institut hydrographique des Forces armées chiliennes *f:* **IHA**

Institut Interdépartementale des Barrages Réservoirs du bassin de la Seine *f:* **IIBR**

Institut International de Gestion et de Genie de l'Environnement *f:* **IIGGE**

Institut international de génie biomédical *f:* **IIGBM**

Institut International de l'Environnement *f:* **IIE**

Institut international de recherche sur la prévision du climat *f:* **IRICP**

Institut International d'étude et de documentation en matière de Concurrence Commerciale *f:* **IICC**

Institut international pour l'environnement et le développement *f:* **IIED**

Institut international pour les sciences et les technologies de la terre, de la mer et de l'environnement *f:* **IIEM**

Institut Mondial de l'Environnement *f:* **IME**

Institut Mondial d'Écologie et de Cancérologie *f:* **IMEC**

Institut Mondial pour la Protection de la Haute Qualité Alimentaire *f:* **I.M.P.H.Q.A.**

Institut Montaire Lunxembourgeois *f:* **IML**

Institut Municipal d'Investigación Médica *s:* **IMIM**

Institut Médico-Légal *f:* **I.M.L.**

Institut Médico-Pédagogique *f:* **I.M.P.**

Institut National d'Astronomie et de Géophysique *f:* **INAG**

Institut National de la Sante et de la Recherche Medicale *f:* **INSEBM**

Institut National de la Santé et de la Recherche Médicale. French Institute of Health and Medical Research *f:* **INSERM**

Institut National de l'Environnement Industriel et des Risques *e:* **INERIS**, *f:* **INERIS**

Institut National de Recherches en Hydrologie *f:* **INRH**

Institut National de Recherches Forestières *f:* **INRF**

Institut National d'Océanographie *f:* **NIO**

Institut National d'Océanographie et de pêche *f:* **NIOF**

Institut national pour le développement de la pêche [Cape Verde] *f:* **INDP**

Institut National Scientifique et Technique d'Oceanographie et de Peche *f:* **INSTOP**

Institut Océanographique [de Paris] *f:* **IO**

Institut pour la Protection de la Nature au Congo Belge *f:* **I.P.N.C.B.**

Institut pour la Repression des Ravageurs Forestiers *f:* **IRRF**

Institut pour le Développement Forestier *f:* **IDF**

Institut Professionnel de Contrôle et de Recherche en Alimentation Animale *f:* **IPCAA**

Institut Professionnel de Contrôle et de Recherches Scientifiques des Industries de l'Alimentation Animale *f:* **IPCIAA**, *f:* **IPCRSIAA**

Institut Royal des Sciences Naturelles de Belgique *f:* **IRScNB**, *f:* **IRSNB**, *f:* **ISNB**

Institut Royal Meteorologique de Belgique Bulletin Trimestriel Observations d'Ozone [Belgium] *f:* **Inst R Meteorol Belg Bull Trimest Obs Ozone**

Institut Royal Météorologique à Uccle *f:* **IRMU**

Institut Royal Météorologique de Belgique *f:* **I.R.M.**

Institut Royal pour la Gestion durable des ressources naturelles et la promotion des Technologies propres *f:* **IRGT**

Institut Superieur de Gestion Tiers Monde *f:* **ISG TIERS MONDE**

Institut voor Marien en Atmosferisch Onderzoek Utrecht *n:* **IMAU**

Institut za Biološka Istraživanja *se:* **IBI**

Institut za Geodeziju i Fotogrametriju *se:* **IGF**

Institut za Geološka istraživanja *se:* **IG**

Institut Zairois pour la Conservation de la Nature *f:* **INZN**

Institut Équatorial de Recherches et d'Études Géologiques et Minières *f:* **IEREGEM**

Institut Équatorial de Recherches Géologiques et Minières *f:* **IERGM**

Institute for Aerospace Studies *e:* **IAS**

Institute for Airspace Science *e:* **IAS**

Institute for Animal Disease Research *e:* **IADR**

Institute for Animal Health *e:* **IAH**

Institute for Atmospheric Optics and Remote Sensing *e:* **IFAORS**

Institute for Atmospheric Radioactivity *e:* **IAR**

Institute for Atmospheric Sciences *e:* **IAS**

Institute for Biomedical Communication *e:* **IBC**

Institute for Biomedical Engineering Research *e:* **IBER**

Institute for Burn Medicine *e:* **IBM**

Institute for Chemistry and Biology of the Marine environment *e:* **ICBM**

Institute for Child Health Policy *e:* **ICHP**

Institute for Comparative and Environmental Toxicology *e:* **ICET**

Institute for Complementary Medicine *e:* **ICM**

Institute for Earth Education *e:* **IEE**

Institute for Earth Sciences *e:* **IES**

Institute for Ecological Economics *e:* **IEE**

Institute for Ecological Policies *e:* **IEP**

Institute for Ecological Problems of the North, Russia *e:* **IEPS**

Institute for Engineering Research in the Oceans *e:* **IERO**

Institute for Environment and Health *e:* **IEH**

Institute for Environmental Awareness *e:* **IEA**

Institute for Environmental Research *e:* **IER**

Institute for Environmental Research Technical Memorandum *e:* **IERTM**

Institute for Environmental Science and Management *e:* **ESAM**

Institute for Environmental Toxicology *e:* **IET**

Institute for Forensic Medicine *e:* **IFM**

Institute for Geography `Augustin Codazzi' [Colombia] *e:* **IGAC**

Institute for Grassland and Animal Production *e:* **IGAP**

Institute for Groundwater Research *e:* **IGR**, *e:* **IGWR**

Institute for Health and Productivity Management *e:* **IHPM**

Institute for Health Care Studies *e:* **IHCS**

Institute for Health Services Research *e:* **IHSR**

Institute for Healthcare Improvement *e:* **IHI**

Institute for Human-Animal Relationships *e:* **IHAR**

Institute for Hydrogen Studies *e:* **IHS**

Institute for Hydrogen Systems *e:* **IHS**

Institute for Hydrogen Systems, Mississauga, Ontario *e:* **OMIHS**

Institute for International Cooperation in Animal Biologics *e:* **IICAB**

Institute for International Studies of Communication in Environmental Matters *e:* **COMUVIR**

Institute for Labor and Mental Health *e:* **ILMH**

Institute for Laboratory Animal Research *e:* **ILAR**

Institute for Marine and Atmospheric Resesarch *e:* **IMAU**

Institute for Marine Environmental Research *e:* **IMER**, *e:* **IMMER**

Institute for Medical Literature *e:* **IML**

Institute for Medical Record Economics *e:* **IMRE**

Institute for Medical Research *e:* **IMR**

Institute for Medical Research and Medicinal Plants Studies *e:* **IMRMPS**

Institute for Mental Health Initiatives *e:* **IMHI**

Institute for Natural Products Research *e:* **INPR**

Institute for Natural Resources in Africa *e:* **INRA**

Institute for Naval Oceanography *e:* **INO**

Institute for Oceanography *e:* **IO**

Institute for/of Antarctic and Southern Ocean Studies *e:* **IASOS**

Institute for/of Environmental Sciences *e:* **IES**

Institute for/of Remote Sensing Application[s] *e:* **IRSA**

Institute for/of Space Studies *e:* **ISS**

Institute for Petroleum Resources and Geophysics *e:* **IPRG**

Institute for Plant Protection, Moscow *e:* **VIZR**

Institute for Polar Research and Technology *e:* **IFRTP**

Institute for Reparative Medicine and Vascular Surgery *e:* **IRMVS**

Institute for Reproductive Health *e:* **IRH**

Institute for Research in Animal Behavior *e:* **IRAB**

Institute for Research on Animal Diseases *e:* **IRAD**

Institute for Resource and Environmental Studies *e:* **IRES**

Institute for Rural Environmental Health [Colorado State University] *e:* **IREH**

Institute for Safe Medication Practices *e:* **ISMP**

Institute for Scientific Information, Biomedical Online *e:* **ISI/BIOMED**

Institute for Security and Cooperation in Outer Space *e:* **ISCOS**

Institute for Social Studies and Medical Care *e:* **ISSMC**

Institute for Space and Security Studies *e:* **ISSS**

Institute for Space and Terrestrial Science *e:* **ISTS**

Institute for Space Research, Moscow *e:* **ISR**

Institute for the Advancement of Health *e:* **IAH**

Institute for [the] Advancement of Medical Communication *e:* **IAMC**

Institute for the Human Environment *e:* **IHE**

Institute for the Management of Renewable Natural Resources *e:* **INRENARE**

Institute for the Study of Animal Behavior *e:* **ISAB**

Institute for the Study of Animal Problems *e:* **ISAP**

Institute for the Study of Earth and Man *e:* **ISEM**

Institute for the Study of Earth Oceans and Space *e:* **EOS**

Institute for Traditional Medicine *e:* **ITM**

Institute for Unmanned Space Experiments Force Flyer *e:* **USEF**

Institute for Water Resources *e:* **IWR**

Institute for Water Resources. University of Alaska. Report *e:* **IWRUAR**

Institute for Wetland and Waterfowl Research *e:* **IWWR**

Institute for Wildlife Research *e:* **IWR**

Institute for Work & Health. Institut de Recherche sur le Travail et la Santé *e:* **IWH**

Institute of Action Research for Community Health *e:* **IARCH**

Institute of Aeronautics and Space *e:* **LAPAN**

Institute of Aerospace *e:* **IAS**

Institute of Aerospace Safety and Management *e:* **IASM**

Institute of Aerospace Sciences *e:* **IAeS**

Institute of Agricultural Remote Sensing Laboratory *e:* **IARSL**

Institute of Agriculture & Natural Resources *e:* **IANR**

Institute of Animal Behavior *e:* **IAB**

Institute of Animal Genetics *e:* **IAG**

Institute of Animal Physiology *e:* **IAP**, *e:* **IAPhys**

Institute of Animal Physiology and Genetics Research *e:* **IAPGR**

Institute of Animal Resource Ecology *e:* **IARE**

Institute of Animal Sciences *e:* **IAS**

Institute of Animal Technicians *e:* **IAT**

Institute of Animal Technology *e:* **IAT**

Institute of Applied Biology Research of Guinea *e:* **IABRG**

Institute of Applied Geology *e:* **IAG**

Institute of Applied Natural Science *e:* **IANS**

Institute of Applied Physiology and Medicine *e:* **IAPM**

Institute of Applied Tropical Medicine *e:* **IATM**

Institute of Arctic and Alpine Geochronological Research *e:* **IAAGB**

Institute of Arctic Biology *e:* **IAB**

Institute of Atmospheric Physics *e:* **IAP**

Institute of Atmospheric Physics, Academy of Sciences, Moscow *e:* **IFA**

Institute of Australian Geographers *e:* **IAG**

Institute of Aviation Medicine *e:* **IAM**

Institute of Biological Engineering *e:* **IBE**

Institute of Biology *e:* **IB**, *e:* **IBiol**, *e:* **IOB**, *e:* **I of B**

Institute of Biology of the Southern Seas *e:* **IBSS**

Institute of Biomedical Engineering *e:* **IBME**

Institute of Biomedical Science *e:* **IBMS**

Institute of British Geographers *e:* **IBG**

Institute of British Geographers (Liverpool). Transactions and Papers *e:* **Trans Papers (L) Brit G**

Institute of Certified Healthcare Business Consultants *e:* **ICHBC**

Institute of Child Health *e:* **ICH**

Institute of Coastal Oceanography and Tides *e:* **ICOT**

Institute of Comparative Biology *e:* **ICB**

Institute of Contemporary Russian Studies Medical Reports *e:* **ICRS Medical Reports**

Institute of Continuing Legal Education in Georgia *e:* **GICLE**

Institute of Critical Care Medicine *e:* **ICCM**

Institute of Earth and Planetary Physics *e:* **IEPP**

Institute of Earth Physics *e:* **IEP**

Institute of Ecology *e:* **IOE**

Institute of Environment and Offshore Medicine *e:* **IEOM**

Institute of Environmental Action *e:* **IEA**

Institute of Environmental Engineers *e:* **IEE**

Institute of Environmental Managers *e:* **IEM**

Institute of Environmental Medicine and Physiology *e:* **IEMP**

Institute of Environmental Science and Management *e:* **IESAM**

Institute of Environmental Sciences *e:* **I Env S**

Institute of Environmental Sciences. Technical Meeting. Proceedings *e:* **Inst Environ Sci Tech Meet Proc**

Institute of Epidemiology and Behavioral Medicine *e:* **IEBM**

Institute of Experimental Medicine and Surgery *e:* **IEMS**

Institute of Experimental Meteorology *e:* **IEM**

Institute of/for Environmental Education *e:* **IEE**

Institute of/for Environmental Studies *e:* **IES**

Institute of/for European Environment[al] Policy *e:* **IEEP**

Institute of/for Laboratory Animal Resources *e:* **ILAR**

Institute of/for Physics of the Atmosphere *e:* **IPA**

Institute of/for Rural Water *e:* **IRW**

Institute of/for Terrestrial Ecology [Natural Environment Research Council] *e:* **ITE**

Institute of Geography *e:* **IG**

Institute of Geological Science Report *e:* **Inst Geol Sci Rep**

Institute of Geological Sciences *e:* **IGS**

Institute of Geological Studies *e:* **IGS**

Institute of Geology [and] Mineral Exploration *e:* **IGME**

Institute of Geology and Palaeontology *e:* **IGP**

Institute of Geomantic Research *e:* **IGR**

Institute of Geophysics *e:* **IG**

Institute of Geophysics and Interplanetary Physics *e:* **IGIP**

Institute of Geophysics and Planetary Physics *e:* **IGPP**

Institute of Geophysics and Planetary Physics at Scripps *e:* **IGPPS**

Institute of Global Climate and Ecology *e:* **IGCE**

Institute of Global Environment and Society *e:* **IGES**

Institute of Health and Care Development
e: **IHCD**

Institute of Health Economics and
Technology Assessment *e:* **IHETA**

Institute of Health Education *e:* **IHDP,** *e:*
IHE

Institute of Health Promotion Research *e:*
IHPR

Institute of Health Record Information and
Management *e:* **IHRIM**

Institute of Health Sciences *e:* **IHS**

Institute of Health Service Administrators
e: **IHSA**

Institute of Health Service Managers (or
Management) *e:* **IHSM**

Institute of Hydrology *e:* **IH,** *e:* **I of H**

Institute of International Health *e:* **IIH**

Institute of International Medical Education
e: **IIME**

Institute of Man and the Amazon
Environment *e:* **IMAZON**

Institute of Marine Biology *e:* **I.M.B.**

Institute of Marine Biology of Crete *e:*
IMBC

Institute of Marine Biomedical Research *e:*
IMBR

Institute of Marine Geology and Geophysics
[Russian Federation] *e:* **IMGG**

Institute of Medical and Biological
Illustration *e:* **IMBI**

Institute of Medical and Veterinary Science
e: **IMVS**

Institute of Medical Illustrators in Scotland
e: **IMIS**

Institute of Medical Laboratory Sciences
e: **IMLS**

Institute of Medical Laboratory Technology
e: **IMLT**

Institute of Medical Psychology *e:* **I.M.P.**

Institute of Medical Research *e:* **I.M.R.**

Institute of Medicine *e:* **IM,** *e:* **I of M,** *e:*
IOM

Institute of Medicine. National Academy of
Sciences *e:* **IOM**

Institute of Medicine of Chicago *e:* **IMC**

Institute of Meteorology *e:* **IM**

Institute of Microbiology *e:* **I.M.B.,** *e:*
INMI

Institute of Microbiology, Rutgers
University *e:* **IMRU**

Institute of Molecular Biology *e:* **IMB**

Institute of Molecular Medicine for the
Prevention of Human Diseases *e:* **IMM**

Institute of Museum Services-Health,
Education and Welfare *e:* **IMS/HEW**

Institute of National Parks of the Ministry
of Environment and Renewable Natural
Resources of the Republic of Venezuela
e: **INPARQUES**

Institute of Natural Resources *e:* **INR**

Institute of Natural Resources and
Environment *e:* **INRE**

Institute of Natural Resources, Division of
Environmental Management, Chicago *e:*
ISNR-E

Institute of Natural Resources, Energy
Information Library, Springfield *e:*
ISNR

Institute of Nature Conservation *e:* **IN,** *e:*
INC

Institute of Nature Conservation and
Resources *e:* **INCR**

Institute of Naval Medicine *e:* **INM,** *e:*
MSch[N]

Institute of Neurobiology *e:* **IN**

Institute of North Industrial Ecology
Problems *e:* **INEP**

Institute of Nuclear Medicine and Allied
Sciences *e:* **INMAS**

Institute of Occupational and
Environmental Health *e:* **IOEH**

Institute of Occupational Medicine *e:* **IOM**

Institute of Ocean *e:* **IOS**

Institute of Oceanographic Science *e:* **IOS**

Institute of Oceanographic Sciences. Data
Report *e:* **IOS Data Report**

Institute of Oceanographic Sciences,
Deacon Laboratory *e:* **IOSDL**

Institute of Oceanographic Services *e:* **IOS**

Institute of Oceanography, Nova Scotia
[Canada] *e:* **IONS**

Institute of Oceanography, University of
British Columbia *e:* **IOIUBC**

Institute of Oceanography-University of
British Columbia *e:* **IOUBC**

Institute of Pathology and Tropical
Medicine *e:* **IPTM**

Institute of Physical Medicine and
Rehabilitation *e:* **IPMR**

Institute of Physical Sciences in Medicine
e: **IPSM**

Institute of Physics of the Earth *e:* **IPE**

Institute of Physics of the Earth (Moscow)
e: **VNIIG**

Institute of Planetary and Space Science *e:*
IPSS

Institute of Polar Studies *e:* **IPS**

Institute of Polar Studies [Ohio]. Reports
ISPOUSC *e:* **ISPOR**

Institute of Post-Graduate Medical
Education and Research *e:* **IPMER**

Institute of Problems of Evolutionary
Ecology *e:* **IPEE**

Institute of Rehabilitation Medicine [New
York University] *e:* **IRM [NYU]**

Institute of Religion, Texas Medical Center,
Houston *e:* **TxHIR**

Institute of Sedimentary and Petroleum
Geology *e:* **ISPG**

Institute of Space and Astronautical Science
of Japan *e:* **ISAS**

Institute of Space and Atmospheric Science
e: **ISAS**

Institute of Space and Atmospheric Studies
e: **ISAS**

Institute of Space Engineering *e:* **ISE**

Institute of Space Engineers *e:* **I.S.E.**

Institute of Space Sciences *e:* **I.S.S.**

Institute of [the] Aerospace Science[s] *e:*
IAS

Institute of Tropical Medicine *e:* **ITM**

Institute of Tropical Meteorology *e:* **ITM**

Institute of Urban and Environmental
Studies *e:* **UEST**

Institute of Water Engineers *e:* **IWE**

Institute of Water Pollution Control *e:*
InstWPC, *e:* **IWPC**

Institute of Water Research *e:* **IWR**

Institute of Water Study *e:* **IWS**

Institute (or Institution) of Occupational
Safety and Health *e:* **IOSH**

Institute (or Institution) of Public Health
Engineers *e:* **IPHE**

Institute (or Institution) of Water Engineers
e: **Inst WE**

Institute Royal Météorologique de Belgique
f: **IRMB**

Institutes for Oceanography *e:* **IOC**

Institute[s] of Environmental Research *e:*
IER

Institutes of Religion and Health *e:* **IRH**

Institution of Environmental Engineers *e:*
I.E.E.

Institution of Environmental Health
Offlcers *e:* **IEHO**

Institution of Geologists *e:* **IG**

Institution of Mining and Metallurgy,
Transactions, Section B, Applied Earth
Sci *e:* **Inst Min Metall, Trans, Se**

Institution of Physics and Engineering in
Medicine and Biology *e:* **IPEMB**

Institution of Water and Environmental
Management *e:* **IWEM**

Institution of Water Engineers *e:* **I.W.,** *e:*
I.W.E.

Institution of Water Engineers and
Scientists *e:* **IWEM**

Institutional Animal Care and Use
Committee *e:* **IACUC**

Institutional Dimensions of Global
[environmental] Change *e:* **IDGC**

Institutional Dimensions of Global
Environmental Change *e:* **IDGEC**

institutional, environmental and safety *e:*
ie&s

Institutional Space Inventory Technique
System *e:* **INSITE,** *e:* **INSITE System**

Instituto Alfred Wegener de Investigaciones
Polares y Marinas *s:* **AWI**

Instituto Argentino de Oceanografía *s:*
IADO

Instituto Brasileiro de Geografia e
Estadistica *p:* **IBGE**

Instituto Cubano de Geodesia y Cartografia
s: **ICGC**

Instituto de Astronomia e Geofisica da
Universidade de São Paulo *p:* **IAGUSP**

Instituto de Biologia *p:* **EGB**

Instituto de Biologia e Pesquisas
Tecnológicas *p:* **IBPT**

Instituto de Biología de los Mares Australes
s: **IBSS**

Instituto de Biología Marina del Caribe *s:*
CARMABI

Instituto de Biología Marina, San Antonio
e: **IBM**

Instituto de Biológia y Medicína
Experimental *s:* **IBME**

Instituto de Biológia, Universidad de
México *s:* **IBM**

Instituto de Ciencia Animal *s:* **ICA**

Instituto de Ciencias Naturales *s:* **ICN-
MHN**

Instituto de Ciencias Oceanográficas *s:*
IOS

Instituto de Ciencias Oceanográficas,
Canadá *s:* **IONS**

Instituto de Estudios de la Contaminación
Atmosférica *s:* **I.C.A.**

Instituto de Fisiografia y Geológica *s:* **IFG**

Instituto de Geociencias e Astronomia *p:*
IGA

Instituto de Geofísica de Hawai *s:* **HIG**

Instituto [de] Geografía `Agustin Codazzi'
s: **IGAC**

Instituto de Geología Marina *s:* **MGI**

Instituto de Geología y Geofísica Marinas
s: **IMGG**

Instituto de Higiene y Fomento de la
Producción Animal s: **IHFPA**
Instituto de Informacion y Documentacion
en Biomedicina s: **IBIM**
Instituto de Investigação Médica de Angola
p: **IIMA**
Instituto de Investigação Médica de
Moçambique p: **IIMM**
Instituto de Investigaciones en Biomedicina
y Ciencias Aplicadas s: **IIBCA**
Instituto de Investigaciones Geologico
Mineras s: **INGEOMINAS**
Instituto de Investigaciones Químicas y
Biológicas s: **IIQB**
Instituto de Investigación de Recursos
Naturales s: **IREN**
Instituto de Investigaciónes Geologicas
Edafologicas y Agrobiologicas de Galicia
s: **IIGEAG**
Instituto de Investigaciónes Geológicas s:
IIG
Instituto de Investigaciónes Médicas de la
Universidad de Los Andes s: **IIMUA**
Instituto de Medicina Tropical p: **IMT**
Instituto de Médicos Especialistas p: **IME**
Instituto de Produção Animal p: **IPA**
Instituto de Recursos Naturales del Caribe
s: **CANARI**
Instituto del Minifundio y de las Tierras
Indivisas s: **IMTI**
Instituto Ecuatoriano de Antropología y
Geográfica s: **IEAG**
Instituto Ecuatoriano de Ciencias Naturales
s: **IECN**
Instituto Español de Oceanográfia s: **IEO**
Instituto Geofísico del Perú s: **IGP**
Instituto Geografico e Cadastral s: **IGCP**
Instituto Geografico e Cadastral Portugal
p: **IGCP**
Instituto Geografico e Geologico de São
Paulo p: **IGGSP**
Instituto Geografico Militar e: **ICM**
Instituto Geografico Nacional Tommy
Guardia s: **IGNTG**
Instituto Geografico Universitario s: **IGU**
Instituto Geográfico de Costa Rica s:
IGCR
Instituto Geográfico e Geológico p: **IGG**
Instituto Geográfico e Histórico da Bahia
p: **I.G.H.B.**
Instituto Geográfico Militar s: **IGM**
Instituto Geográfico Nacional s: **IGN**
Instituto Geologico Minero y Metalurgico
s: **INGEMMET**
Instituto Geologico y Minero de España s:
IGME
Instituto Geológico Nacional s: **IGN**
Instituto Geominero Argentino s:
INGEMAR
Instituto Historico e Geografico p: **IHG**
Instituto Histórico e Geográfico Brasileiro
p: **IHGB**
Instituto Histórico e Geográfico de Santa
Catarina s: **IHGSC**
Instituto Histórico e Geográfico do Rio
Grande do Norte s: **I.H.G./R.N.**
Instituto Interamericano de Geografía e
Historio s: **IIGH**
Instituto Internacional de Investigación
sobre la Predicción del Clima s: **IRICP**
Instituto Internacional para las Ciencias y
Tecnologías de la Tierra, el Medio
Ambiente y el Mar s: **IIEM**

Instituto Meteorológico del Caribe s: **CMI**
Instituto Meteorológico Internacional s:
IMI
Instituto Mexicano de Recursos Naturales
Renovables s: **IMRNR**
Instituto Nacional de Biología Animal s:
INBA
Instituto Nacional de Ecología s: **INE**
Instituto Nacional de Estadisticas,
Geografia e Informática p: **INEGI**
Instituto Nacional de Geografía p: **ING**
Instituto Nacional de Geologia p:
INAGEO, s: INGM
Instituto Nacional de Investigaciones
Geologico-Mineras s: **INGEO-MINAS**
Instituto Nacional de Investigaciones
Geológico-Mineras s: **INGENOMINAS**
Instituto Nacional de Investigaciónes
Biológico-Pesqueras s: **INIBP**
Instituto Nacional de Medicina Veterinaria
s: **INMV**
Instituto Nacional de Meteorologia s: **INM**
Instituto Nacional de Meteorologia e
Geofisica p: **INMG**
Instituto Nacional de Meteorologia y
Hidrologia s: **INMH**
Instituto Nacional de Meteorología e
Hidrología s: **INAMHI**
Instituto Nacional de Meteorología y
Geofísica s: **INMG**
Instituto Nacional de Oceanografía s: **NIO**
Instituto Nacional de Oceanográphia y
Pesca s: **NIOF**
Instituto Nacional de Sismología,
Vulcanología, Meteorología e Hidrología
s: **INSIVUMEH**
Instituto Nacional para la Conservación de
la Naturaleza s: **ICONA**
Instituto Nigeriano de Oceanografía e
Investigación Marina s: **NIOMR**
Instituto Oceanográfico da Úniversidade de
São Paulo p: **IOUSP**
Instituto Oceanográfico de Bedford s: **IOB**
Instituto Oceanográfico de Florida s: **FIO**
Instituto Oceanográfico de Valparaíso s:
IOV
Instituto Panamericano de Geografía e
Historia s: **IPGH, s: IPOH**
Instituto panamericano de geografía e
historia. México s: **Inst panamer geog
hist.**
Instituto panamericano de geografía e
historia, México s: **Inst pan geog e hist.**
Instituto Panamericano de Ingeniería de
Minas y Geología s: **IPIMIGEO**
Instituto Regional de Ecologia Andina s:
IRINEA
Instituts-Informationssystem (Sanitäts- und
Gesundheitswesen) d: **IIS**
Institutt for Fiskeribiologi N: **IFB**
Institutt for Marin Biologi N: **IMBO**
Institutul de Cercetäri Forestiere ru: **I.C.F.**
Institutul de Cercetari Forestiere ru:
INCEF
Institutul de Geodezie, Fotogrammetrie,
Cartografie si Organizarea Teritoriului
ru: **IGFCOT**
Institutul de Geologie si Geofizica ru:
IGG
Institutul de Patalogie şi Igienă Animala
ru: **I.P.I.A.**
Institutul Medico-Farmaceutic ru: **I.M.F.**

Institutul pentru Perfectionarea şi
Specializarea Medicilor şi Farmaciştilor
ru: **IPSMF**
Instituut voor Biologisch en Scheikundig
Onderzoek van Landbouwgewassen n:
IBS
Instituut voor Cultuurtechniek en
Waterhuishouding n: **ICW**
Instituut voor Toegepast Biologisch
Onderzoek in de Natuur n: **ITBON**
Instituut voor Toegepast Biologisch
Onderzoek in de Natuur. Mededeling e:
MIBNAU
Instituto de Quimico Biológico p: **IQB**
instruction-curriculum environment e: **ice**
Instructions for Superintending Sea
Transport Officers e: **I.S.S.T.O.**
Instrument [Flight] Meteorological
Condition[s] e: **IMC**
Instrument Flight Rules Weather e: **IFR
Weather**
Instrument Landing System Radio
Environmental Monitor e: **ILSREM**
Instrument Meteorological Conditions-
Instrument Flight Rules e: **IMC-IFR**
Instrument Meteorological Control e: **IMC**
Instrumentation and Protective Service e:
I&PS
Instrumentation for Aerospace Simulation
Facilities Committee e: **IASFC**
Instrumentation for/in Aerospace
Simulation Facilities e: **IASF**
Instrumentation Graphics Environment e:
IGE
instrumentieren d: **instr**
instrumentiert d: **instr**
Instrumentierung d: **Instr, d: Instrum**
Instrumento de observación del color de los
mares s: **OCM**
Instrumentos de control y medición s:
ICM
Instruments and Methods of Observation
Programme e: **IMOP**
Instument Airport Weather e: **IAW**
Instytut Biologii Doswiadczalnej P: **IBD**
Instytut Geograficzny Uniwersytetu
Łódzkiego P: **IGU**
Instytut Geografii P: **IG**
Instytut Geografii i Przestrzennego
Zagospodarowania P: **IGiPZ**
Instytut Geografii Polskiej Akademii Nauk
P: **IG PAN**
Instytut Geografii Uniwersytetu
Warszawskiego P: **IGUW**
Instytut Geologiczny P: **IG**
Instytut Hodowli i Aklimatyzacji Roslin P:
IHAR
Instytut Meteorologii i Gospodarki Wodnej
P: **IMGW**
Insuatrial Safety [Protective Equipment]
Manufactures Association Spectroscopy
e: **IS[PE]MA**
Intake Cooling Water e: **ICW**
INTECOL Bulletin [International
Association for Ecology] e: **INTECOL
Bull**
INTECOL Newsletter [International
Association for Ecology] e: **INTECOL
Newsl**
Integral and Ditierential Monitoring e:
IDM
Integral Protective Entrances e: **IPE**

Integrated Atmospheric Deposition Network
  e: **IADN**

Integrated Climate Change Analysis Model
  e: **ICCAM**

Integrated Closed Loop Environmental
  Control System e: **ICECS**

Integrated Computer-Enhanced Remote
  Viewing System e: **ICERVS**

Integrated Design and Analysis
  Environment for Advanced Magnetic
  Devices e: **IDAM**

Integrated Development and Debugging
  Environment e: **IODE**

Integrated Development & Debugging
  Environment e: **IDDE**

Integrated Development Environment
  configuration e: **IDE**

Integrated Environmental Control e: **IEC**

Integrated Environmental Design e: **IED**

Integrated Environmental Management
  Division e: **IEMD**

Integrated Environmental Management
  Project e: **IEMP**

Integrated Environmental, Safety and
  Health Management System e: **ISMS**

Integrated Flood Observation and Warning
  System e: **IFLOWS**

Integrated Forest Study on the Effects of
  Atmospheric Deposition e: **IFS**

Integrated Geographic[al] Information
  System e: **IGIS**

Integrated Geophysical System e: **IDS**, e:
  IGS

Integrated Geophysics Corporation e: **IGC**

Integrated Global Observating Strategy e:
  IGOS

Integrated Global Ocean Monitoring e:
  IGOM

Integrated Global Ocean Services (or
  Serving) System e: **IGOSS**

Integrated Global Ocean Station System e:
  IGLOSS, e: **IGOSS**

Integrated Health Delivery System e:
  IHDS

Integrated Health & Usage Monitoring
  System e: **IHUMS**

Integrated Healthcare Advisory Group e:
  IHAG

Integrated Healthcare Association e: **IHA**

Integrated Hydrographic Survey System e:
  IHSS

Integrated Instrumentation Environment e:
  IIE

Integrated Lake-Watershed Acidification
  Study e: **ILWAS**

Integrated Land and Water Information
  System e: **ILWIS**

Integrated Land and Watershed
  [Management] Information System e:
  ILWIS

Integrated Language Environment e: **ILE**

integrated liquid water e: **ILW**

Integrated Mapping and Geographic
  Encoding System e: **IMAGE**

Integrated Medical and Behavioral
  Laboratory Management e: **IMBLM**

Integrated Medical and Behavioral
  Laboratory Measurement System e:
  IMPLMS

Integrated Medical [and] Behavio[u]ral
  Laboratory Measurement System e:
  IMBLMS

Integrated Medical Curriculum e: **IMC**

Integrated Medical Services e: **IMS**

Integrated Meteo-Database in Cala e: **IMC**

Integrated Meteorological System e:
  IMETS, e: **IMS**

Integrated Model of Plumes and
  Atmosphere in Complex Terrain e:
  IMPACT

Integrated Modelling Environment e: **IME**

Integrated Modelling of Renewable Natural
  Resources e: **IRENE**

Integrated Observation Device e: **IOD**

Integrated Observation System e: **IOS**

Integrated Ocean Surveillance System e:
  IOSS

Integrated Operational Hydrological System
  e: **IOHS**

Integrated Orbital Operations Simulation
  Facility e: **IOOSF**

Integrated Orbital Service System e: **IOSS**

Integrated Personal Protection System e:
  IPPS

Integrated Power and Environment[al]
  Control System e: **IPECS**

integrated pressurized water reactor e:
  IPWR

Integrated Program[me] for Aerospace-
  vehicle Design e: **IPAD**

Integrated Programmes for Aerospace-
  vehicle Desgin e: **IPAD**

Integrated Programming Environment e:
  IPE

Integrated Programming Support
  Environment e: **IPSE**

Integrated Regional Environmental
  Management [Project] e: **IREM**

Integrated Remote Interface Control
  Element e: **IRICE**

Integrated Sensor Underwater System e:
  ISUS

Integrated Services System for Low Bitrate
  Environments e: **ISSLOW**

Integrated Space Experiment e: **ISE**

Integrated Space Technology
  Demonstration e: **ISTD**

Integrated Space Technology Flights e:
  ISTF

Integrated Spacecraft Avionics System e:
  ISAS

Integrated Spacecraft Operations Plan e:
  ISOP

Integrated Submarine Cornmunications
  System Polaris/Poseidon e: **ISCSP2**

Integrated System for Automated
  Hydrography e: **ISAH**

Integrated [system] of Environmental and
  Economic Accounting e: **IEEA**

Integratcd Tactical Environment Modeling
  System e: **ITEMS**

Integrated Target Weather System e:
  ITWS

Integrated Terminal Weather Information
  System e: **ITWIS**

Integrated Terminal Weather System e:
  ITWS

Integrated Thermal Micrometeorid Garment
  e: **ITMG**

Integrated Underwater Surveillance System
  e: **IUSS**

Integrated Waste Water Treatment e: **IWT**

Integrated Water Treatment System e:
  IWTS

Integrated Water Vapor e: **IWV**

Integrated Watershed Management Plan e:
  IWMP

Integrated Wildlife-Intensive Forestry
  Research e: **IWIFR**

Integration and Verification Test
  Environment e: **IVTE**

Integrierte Vermeidung und Verminderung
  von Umweltschäden d: **IVU**

Integrierter Druckwasserreaktor d: **IDWR**

integriertes dialogorientiertes Testsystem
  d: **IDT**

Integriertes Meß- und Informationssystem
  [zur Überwachung] der
  Umweltradioaktivität d: **IMIS**

Integriertes System für die Projektierung
  optimaler Schiffe d: **ISPOS**

integrity basis earthquake e: **ibe**

Intelligence Center, Pacific Ocean Areas
  e: **ICPOA**, e: **INTELCENPAC**

Intelligence Data Analysis System for
  Spacecraft e: **IDASS**

intelligence preparation of the battlespace
  e: **IPB**

[Intelligent] Cartography in Mountain
  Environment e: **CIME**

Intelligent Geographic[al] Information
  System e: **IGIS**

Intelligent Remote Batch Terminal e:
  IRBT

Intelligent Remote Station Support e:
  IRSS

Intelligent Robot Operating Environment
  e: **IROE**

Intelligent System Operating Environment
  e: **ISOE**

Intelligent Systems for Molecular Biology
  e: **ISMB**

Intelligent Training Systems in Industrial
  Environment e: **ITSIE**

International Journal of Nautical
  Archaeology and Underwater Exploration
  e: **J Naut Arch**

Intensely Supportive Learning Environment
  e: **ISLE**

Intensity, Hue and Saturation Colour Space
  e: **IHS**

Intensive Care Medicine [New York] e:
  Intensive Care Med

intensive care unit [medical] e: **icu**

Intensive Field Observation[s] e: **IFO**

Intensive Observation (or Observing)
  Period e: **IOP**

Intensive therapy observation unit e: **IOU**

Intensivmedizin d: **ITMZBJ**

Inter-African Advisory Committee for
  Animal Health and Production e:
  IACAHP

Inter-African Bureau for Animal Health e:
  IBAH

Inter-African Bureau for Animal Health and
  and Protection e: **IBAHP**

Inter-African Bureau for/of Animal
  Resources e: **IBAR**

Inter-African Committee on Traditional
  Practices affecting the Health of Women
  and Children e: **IAC**

Inter-Agency Climate Change Committee
  e: **IACCC**

Inter-Agency Committee on Geomatics e:
  IACG

Inter-Agency Committee on Global
  Environmental Change e: **IACGEC**

Inter-Agency Committee on Oceanography *e:* **IAO,** *e:* **ICO**

Inter-Agency Committee on Remote Sensing *e:* **IACRS**

Inter-agency Committee on the Climate Agenda *e:* **IACCA**

Inter-Agency Committee on Water Resources *e:* **ICEWATER**

Inter-Agency Consultative Group [for Space Science] *e:* **IACG**

Inter-Agency Space Debris Coordination Committee *e:* **IADC**

Inter-American Association of Sanitary and Environmental Engineering *e:* **IAASEE**

Inter-American Association of Sanitary Engineering and Environmental Sciences *e:* **IAASEES**

Inter-American Centre for the Integral Development of Water and Land Resources *e:* **CIDIAT**

Inter-American Commit. on Space Research *e:* **IACOSPAR**

Inter-American Committee for Space Research *e:* **ICSR**

Inter-American Geodetic Survey [Defense Mapping Agency] *e:* **IAGS**

Inter-American Institute of Ecology *e:* **IAIE,** *e:* **IIE**

Inter-American Underwater Festival *e:* **IAUF**

Inter-Armes, École Spéciale Militaire *f:* **I.A.**

Inter-Association Committee on Health *e:* **IACH**

Inter-comparison of Land-Surface Codes in Climate Models *e:* **ICLCCM**

Inter Frame Space *e:* **IFS**

Inter-Governmental Committee on the Convention on Biological Diversity *e:* **IGCCBD**

Inter-Islamic Network in/on Space Science[s] and Technology *e:* **ISNET**

Inter-Islamic Network on Oceanography *e:* **INOC**

Inter-Ministerial Committee for Environment *e:* **IMCE**

Inter-NASA [National Aeronautics and Space Administration] Data Exchange *e:* **INDEX**

Inter-ocean[ic] Canal Study Commission *e:* **ICSC**

Inter-Orbit Link *e:* **IOL**

Inter Orbit Transfer and Logistics Vehicle *e:* **IOTLV**

Inter-Parliamentary Commission for Environment and Development *e:* **CICAD**

Inter-Professional Ad Hoc Group for Environmental Information Sharing *e:* **IPAHGEIS**

Inter-Range Instrumentation Group-Meteorological Working Group *e:* **IRIG-MWG**

Inter-Secretariat Committee for Scientific Programs (or Problems) Relating to Oceanography *e:* **ICSPRO**

Inter-secretariat Group on Water Resources *e:* **ISGWR**

Inter-State Ecological Council *e:* **IEC**

Inter-Sun-Earth Explorer *e:* **ISSE**

Inter-Union Commission of/on Frequency Allocations for Radio Astronomy and Space Science *e:* **IUCAF**

Inter-Union Commission on Frequency Allocations [for Radio Astronomy and Space Science] *e:* **IUCFA**

Inter-Union Commission on Geodynamics *e:* **ICG,** *e:* **IUCOG**

Inter-Union Commission on Radio Meteorology *e:* **IUCRM**

Inter-Union Geodynamics Commission *e:* **IGC**

Inter-University Biology Teaching Project *e:* **IUBTP**

Interacción Tierra-Océano en las Zonas Costeras *s:* **LOICZ**

Interactive Design and Evaluation of Advanced Spacecraft *e:* **IDEAS**

Interactive Development Environments, inc *e:* **IDE**

Interactive Geo-facilities Graphic Support *e:* **IGGS**

Interactive Geographical Index *e:* **IGI**

Interactive Geological Interpretation System *e:* **IGIS**

Interactive Health Care Eligibility Benefits Inquiry *e:* **IHCEBI**

Interactive Health Care Eligibility Benefits Response *e:* **IHCEBR**

Interactive Health Care System *e:* **IHCS**

Interactive Health Communication *e:* **IHC**

Interactive Health Ecology Access Links *e:* **IHEAL**

Interactive Healthcare Information System *e:* **IHIS**

Interactive Hydrographic Map *e:* **IHM**

Interactive Medical Communications *e:* **IMC**

Interactive Menu-Assisted Graphics Environment *e:* **IMAGE**

Interactive Meteorological Information Access in a Graphic Environment *e:* **IMAGE**

Interactive Multi-Activity Graphics Environment Software *e:* **IMAGE Software**

Interactive Remote Job Entry *e:* **IRJE**

Interactive Remote Sensing Software Package *e:* **IRSSP**

Interactive System for Investigation by Graphics of Hydrological Trends *e:* **INSIGHT**

Interactive Tactical Environment Management System *e:* **ITEMS**

Interagency Advisory Committee on Water Data *e:* **IACWD**

Interagency Climate-Aerosol Radiative Uncertainties and Sensitivities [Program] *e:* **ICARUS**

Interagency Collaborative Group on Environmental Carcinogenesis *e:* **ICGEC**

Interagency Commission on Ocean Resources *e:* **ICOR**

Interagency Committee for Applied Meteorological Research *e:* **ICAMR**

Interagency Committee for International Meteorological Programs *e:* **ICIMP**

Interagency Committee for/on Meteorological Services and Supporting Research *e:* **ICMSSR**

Interagency Committee for [the] World Weather Program[s] *e:* **ICWWP**

Interagency Committee on Climate Services and Research *e:* **ICCSR**

Interagency Committee on Environment and Development *e:* **IACED**

Interagency Committee on Global Environmental Change *e:* **IAGEC**

Interagency Committee on Marine Environmental Prediction *e:* **ICMAREP**

Interagency Committee on Ocean Exploration and Environmental Services *e:* **OEES,** *e:* **OEFS**

Interagency Committee on Radiological Protection *e:* **ICRA**

Interagency Committee on Water Resources *e:* **ICWR**

Interagency Coordinating Committee for Earth Resource[s] Survey Program *e:* **ICCERSP**

Interagency Geographic Data Committee *e:* **IGDC**

Interagency Geothermal Coordinating Council *e:* **IGCC**

Interagency Group on Agricultural Biometeorology *e:* **IGAB**

Interagency Group on International Programs in Atmospheric Science *e:* **IGIPAS**

Interagency Life Sciences supporting space research and technology Exchange *e:* **ILSE**

Interagency Monitoring of Protected Visual Environment[s] *e:* **IMPROVE**

Interagency Office of Environmental Technology *e:* **IETO**

Interaktive geometrisch/ graphische Software *d:* **IGGS**

Interaktives Graphisches System [für Wettervorhersage] *d:* **IGS**

Interamerican College of Physicians and Surgeons *e:* **ICPS**

Interational Institute for Research and Development on Natural and Holistic Therapies *e:* **IRENATH**

Interavia Aerospace Review *e:* **Interavia Aerosp Rev**

Interavia Space Markets *e:* **ISM**

Intercambio Internacional de Datos e Información Oceanográficos *s:* **IODE**

Intercept during Exo-atmospheric Fall *e:* **IDEF**

Intercept System Environment *e:* **ISE**

Interchange of Pollutants between the Atmosphere and the Oceans *e:* **INTERPOLL**

Interchurch Medical Assistance *e:* **IMA**

Intercollegiate Ice Hockey Association *e:* **IIHA**

Intercom (Orbiter to Ground via Hardline) *e:* **IC**

Intercomparison of Operational Hydrological Network Design Techniques *e:* **HYNET**

Intercomparison of Radiation Codes for/in Climate Models *e:* **ICRCCM**

Intercontinental Aerospacecraft Range Unlimited System *e:* **ICARUS**

Intercontinental Medical Book Corp. *e:* **IMB**

Intercontinental Medical Statistics Ltd. *e:* **IMS**

interdecadal climate variability *e:* **ICV**

Interdendritic *e:* **ID**

Interdenominational Advisory Committee on Army Chaplaincy Services *e:* **I.A.C.A.C.S.**

Interdenominational African Ministers Federation e: **I.D.A.M.F.**

Interdenominational Church Ushers Association e: **ICUA**

Interdenominational Foreign Mission Association of North America e: **IFMA**

Interdepartementale Arbeitsgruppe Aktenführung in der Administration d: **AIDA**

Interdepartementale Commissie Duurzame Ontwikkeling n: **ICDO**

Interdepartementale Zwemgroep n: **IDZ**

Interdepartment Committee on Search and Rescue e: **ICSAR**

Interdepartmental e: **ID**, e: **INTERDEPT**

Interdepartmental Advisory and Development Committee e: **IADC**

Interdepartmental Advisory Committee e: **IAC**

Interdepartmental Air Traffic Control Board e: **IATCB**

Interdepartmental Billing e: **IDB**

Interdepartmental Billing Form e: **IBF**

Interdepartmental Commission on Interplanetary Communications e: **ICIC**

Interdepartmental Commission on Military-Technical Co-operation e: **ICMTC**

Interdepartmental Committee e: **IDC**, e: **INDEC**

Interdepartmental Committee for Atmospheric Sciences [of Federal Council for Science and Technology] e: **ICAS**

Interdepartmental Committee for Computer Processing in Departmental Libraries e: **INTERLIB**

Interdepartmental Committee for Meteorological Services e: **ICMS**

Interdepartmental Committee for/on Applied Meteorological Research e: **ICAMR**

Interdepartmental Committee of Futures Research e: **ICFR**

Interdepartmental Committee of/on External Relations e: **ICER**

Interdepartmental Committee on Aerial Surveys e: **ICAS**

Interdepartmental Committee on Air Pollution Research e: **ICAPR**

Interdepartmental Committee on Commercial Policy e: **ICCP**

Interdepartmental Committee on Energy Development and Research e: **ENCORD**

Interdepartmental Committee on Internal Security e: **ICIS**

Interdepartmental Committee on Labour Requirements e: **ICLR**

Interdepartmental Committee on Land e: **ICL**

Interdepartmental Committee on Manpower Requirements e: **MRC**

Interdepartmental Committee on Nutrition for National Defense e: **ICNND**

Interdepartmental Committee on Scientific and Cultural Cooperation e: **S.C.C.**

Interdepartmental Committee on Scientific Research and Development e: **ICSRD**

Interdepartmental Committee on Space e: **ICS**

Interdepartmental Committee on the Redevelopment of Contaminated Land e: **ICRCL**

Interdepartmental Committee on the Status of Women e: **ICSW**

Interdepartmental Committee on Toxic Chemicals e: **ICTC**

Interdepartmental Committee on Weather Modification e: **ICWM**

Interdepartmental Communication e: **IDC**

Interdepartmental Communication for Atmospheric Science e: **ICAS**

Interdepartmental Coordinating Committee for/on Scientific and Technical Informatio e: **ICCSTI**

interdepartmental cypher e: **idc**

Interdepartmental Electronic Mail e: **IDEM**

Interdepartmental Group e: **ID**, e: **IG**

Interdepartmental Hurricane Conference e: **IHC**

Interdepartmental Intelligence Conference e: **ICC**

Interdepartmental Intelligence Unit e: **IDIU**

Interdepartmental Liaison Forum e: **ILF**

Interdepartmental Meeting e: **IDM**

Interdepartmental Meteorological Data Exchange System e: **IMDES**

Interdepartmental Packaging Co-ordinating Committee e: **IPCC**

Interdepartmental Planning Committee on Germany e: **IPCOG**

Interdepartmental Procurement Request e: **IPR**

Interdepartment[al] Radio Advisory Committee e: **IRAC**

Interdepartmental Regional Group e: **IRG**

Interdepartmental Savings Bond Committee e: **ISBC**

Interdepartmental Screw Thread Committee e: **ISTC**

Interdepartmental Sub-committee for Component Co-ordination e: **ISCC**

Interdepartmental Work Release Order e: **IWRO**

Interdepartmental Workers' Compensation Task Force e: **IWCTF**

Interdepartmental Working Group e: **IDWG**

Interdepartmental Working Group on the Greenhouse Effect e: **IWGGE**

Interdisciplinary Climate Systems e: **ICS**

Interdisciplinary Committee for Environmental Research e: **ICER**

Interdisciplinary Health Research Group e: **IHRG**

Interdisciplinary Natural Resources Development and Management Program e: **INRDM**

Interdisciplinary Panel on Climate Change e: **IRAP**

Interdisciplinary Sciences-Land Surface Climatology e: **IDS-LSC**

Interessengemeinschaft Biologischer Umweltschutz d: **IBU**

Interessengemeinschaft für Weltraumforschung d: **IGW**

Interessengemeinschaft Luft- und Raumfahrt d: **IGLR**

Interféromètre Michelson pour sondage passif de l'atmosphère f: **MIPAS**

Intergovernment Committee on Ecologically Sustainable Development e: **ICESD**

Intergovernmental Agreement on the Environment e: **IAG**, e: **IGAE**

Intergovernmental Committee [Commission] on Oceanography e: **ICO**

Intergovernmental Committee for Ocean Science and Living Resources e: **OSLR**

Intergovernmental Committee for/on the Convention on Biological Diversity e: **ICCBD**

Intergovernmental Committee on the Convention of Biological Diversity e: **ICCBC**

Intergovernmental Conference on Oceanic Research e: **ICOR**

Intergovernmental Conference on Oceanographic [Research] e: **INCOR**

Intergovernmental Council for/of the International Hydrological Programme e: **IHP**

Intergovernmental Documentation Center on Housing and Environment e: **IDCHE**

Intergovernmental Documentation Centre on Housing and Environment of the Countries of the United Nations Economic Commission for Europe e: **IDCHEC**

Intergovernmental Forum on Forests under the United Nations Commission on the Protection of Forests in Europe e: **UNCSD/IFF**

Intergovernmental Health Policy Project e: **IHPP**

Intergovernmental Meeting of Scientific Experts on Biological Diversity e: **ISE**

Intergovernmental Meeting on the World Climate Programme e: **IGM-WCP**

Intergovernmental Negotiating Committee for a Framework Convention on Climate Change e: **INC-FCCC**

Intergovernmental Negotiating Committee for Framework Convention on Climate Change e: **IGM/WCP**

Intergovernmental Negotiating Committee [for the Framework Convention on Climate Change] e: **INC**

Intergovernmental Oceanographic Commission-Bureau and Consultative Council e: **IOC/B&CC**

Intergovernmental Oceanographic Commission Committee for Training, Education, and Mutual Assistance in the Marine Sciences e: **IOC-TEMA**

Intergovernmental Oceanographic Commission/Executive Council e: **IOC/EC**

Intergovernmental Oceanographic Commission Regional Committee for the Central Eastern Atlantic e: **IOCEA**

Intergovernmental Oceanographic Commission Regional Committee for the Central Indian Ocean e: **IOCINDIO**

Intergovernmental Oceanographic Commission Sub-commission for the Caribbean and Adjacent Regions e: **IOCARIBE**

Intergovernmental Oceanographic Commission. Technical Series e: **IOCTAH**

Intergovernmental Oceanographic Commission/Voluntary Assistance Program e: **IOV/VAP**

Intergovernmental Oceanographic Commission Voluntary Cooperation Program e: **IOC-VCP**

Intergovernmental Oceanographic Council [or Commission] *e:* **IOC**

Intergovernmental Panel of Experts on Radioactive Waste Disposal at Sea/LC/ *e:* **IGPRAD**

Intergovernmental Panel on Climate Change/Subgroup *e:* **IPCC Sg**

Intergovernmental Panel on Climate Change/Working Group *e:* **IPCC WG**

Intergovernmental Panel on Climate (or Climatic) Change *e:* **IPCC**

Intergovernmental Technical Working Group on Animal Genetic Resources for Food and Agriculture *e:* **ITWG-AnGR**

Interim Biogeographical Regionalisation for Australia *e:* **IBRA**

Interim Committee on Medical and Biological Abstracting *e:* **SAMB**

Interim Earth Penetrator Weapon *e:* **IEPW**

Interim Meteorological Satellite *e:* **IMS**

Interim National Space Surveillance Control Center *e:* **INSSCC**

Interim Operation Meteorological System *e:* **IOMS**

Interim Pacific Oceanographic Support System *e:* **IPOSS**

Interim Sea Control Ship *e:* **ISCS**

Interim Standard Atmosphere *e:* **ISA**

Interim Terminal Test Environment *e:* **ITTE**

Interim Wilderness Committee *e:* **IWC**

Interior Fish, Forestry, Wildlife Guidelines *e:* **IFFWG**

Interior Geographic Data Committee *e:* **IGDC**

Interior Space International *e:* **ISI**

Interlake Schcol, Staff Library, Medical Lake *e:* **WaMel**

Intermediate Circular [Earth] Orbit *e:* **ICO**

Intermediate Main Meteorological Office *e:* **IMMO**

Intermediate Water Depth *e:* **IWD**

Intermediate Water Depth Mine *e:* **IWDM**

intermedica e.V.-medikamentenhilfe für entwicklungsländer *d:* **intermedica**

Intermedics, Inc. *e:* **ITM**

Interministerial Commission for the Resources of the Sea *e:* **CIRM**

Interministerieller Ausschuß für Umweltschutz *d:* **IMAU**

intermittieren[d] *d:* **interm**

intermittierendes Luftstrahltriebwerk *d:* **IL**

Intermittierendes Luftstrahltriebwerk *d:* **IL-Triebwerk**

Intermountain Regional Medical Program *e:* **IRMIP**

Intermountain Regional Medical Program[me] *e:* **IRMP**

Intermountain Veterinary Medical Association *e:* **IVMA**, *e:* **WVC**

Internacia Geografa Asocio *eo:* **IGA**

Internacia Naturista Organizo Esperantista *eo:* **INOE**

Internaitonal Centre for/of Insect Physiology [and] Ecology *e:* **ICIPE**

Internal Environment *e:* **IE**

Internal Environment[al] Simulator *e:* **IES**

Internal Hydrogen Embrittlement *e:* **IHE**

Internal Medicine *e:* **IM**, *e:* **Intern Med**

internal medicine *e:* **int med**

Internal Medicine Group Practice *e:* **IMGP**

Internal Thermal Environment Management *e:* **ITEM**

Internally Generated Electronic Environment *e:* **INGEE**

Internatioinal Organization for Marine Geology *e:* **Intermorgeo**

Internationaal Biologisch Contact- en Informatiebureau voor Nederland *n:* **IBCIN**

Internationaal Biologisch Programma *n:* **I.B.P.**

Internationaal Geofysisch Jaar *n:* **IGEJA**

Internationaal Geophysisch Jaar *n:* **IGJ**

International Abstracts of Biological Sciences *e:* **IABS**

International Academic College of the Environment *e:* **ACADEVIR**

International Academy for/of Environmental Safety *e:* **IAES**

International Academy of Aviation and Space Medicine *e:* **IAASM**

International Academy of Biological Medicine *e:* **IABM**

International Academy of Chest Physicians and Surgeons *e:* **IACPS**

International Academy of Gynecological Cytology *e:* **IAGC**

International Academy of Health Care Professionals *e:* **IAHCP**

International Academy of Law and Mental Health *e:* **IALMH**

International Academy of Legal Medicine *e:* **IALM**

International Academy of Medicine *e:* **IAM**

International Academy of Medicine and Psychology *e:* **IAMP**

International Academy of Osteopathic Medicine *e:* **IAOM**

International Academy of Preventive Medicine *e:* **IAPM**

International Academy of Reproductive Medicine *e:* **IARM**

International Academy of the History of Medicine *e:* **IAHM**

International Action Programme on Water and Sustainable Agricultural Development *e:* **IAP-WASAD**

International Advisory Committee for Biological Standardization *e:* **IABS**

International Advisory Committee for/on Biological Control *e:* **IACBC**

International Advisory Committee [on Research in the Natural Sciences] *e:* **IAC**

International Aerosol Climatology Project *e:* **IACP**

International Aerospace Abstracts *e:* **IAA**

International Aerospace Business Advisors *e:* **IABA**

International Aerospace Hall of Fame *e:* **IAHF**

International Aerospace Technologies [Processing System] *e:* **IAT**

International Agency for Earth Resources Experiments *e:* **IAFEREX**

International Agency for Research on Cancer of the World Health Organization *e:* **IARC**

International Agreement Regarding the Maintenance of Certain Lights in the Red Sea *e:* **IARMCLRS**

International Alliance of Healthcare Educators *e:* **IAHE**

International Animal Exchange *e:* **IAE**

International Animal Husbandry Association *e:* **IAHA**

International Animal Rights Alliance *e:* **IARA**

International Antarctic Meteorological Research Centre *e:* **IAMRC**

International Archives of Occupational and Environmental Health [Berlin] *e:* **Int Arch Occup Environ Health**

International Arctic Environment[al] Data Directory *e:* **ADD**

International Arctic Ocean Expedition *e:* **IAOE**

International Argyrothecologists' Club *e:* **IAC**

International Arts Medicine Association *e:* **IAMA**

International Assembly of Non-Governmental Organizations concerned with the Environment *e:* **INASEN**

International Associanon of Microbiologists *e:* **IAM**

International Associatinn for/of Medicine and Biology of [the] Environment *e:* **IAMBE**

International Association Ayurveda and Naturopathy *e:* **IAAN**

International Association for a Natural Economic Order *e:* **INWO**

International Association for Accident and Traffic Medicine *e:* **IAATM**

International Association for Adolescent Health *e:* **IAAH**

International Association for Aerobiology *e:* **IAA**

International Association for Colon Hydrotherapy *e:* **I-ACT**

International Association for Disability and Oral Health *e:* **IADH**

International Association for Ecology *e:* **IAE**

International Association for Environmental Hydrology *e:* **IAEH**

International Association for Food Protection *e:* **IAFP**

International Association for Hydrogen Energy *e:* **IAHE**

International Association for Maternal and Neonatal Health *e:* **IAMANEH**

International Association for Mathematical Geology *e:* **IAMG**

International Association for Medical Assistance to Travelers *e:* **IAMAT**

International Association for Medical Research and Cultural Exchange *e:* **IAMR**

International Association for/of Aquatic Animal Medicine *e:* **IAAAM**

International Association for/of Biological Oceanography *e:* **IABO**

International Association for/of Biological Standardization *e:* **IABS**

International Association for/of Earthquake Engineering *e:* **IAEE**

International Association for/of Ecology *e:* **INTECOL**

International Association for/of Engineering Geologists (or Geology) *e:* **IAEG**

International Association for/of Geochemistry and Cosmochemistry *e:* **IAGC**

International Association for/of Hydrological Scienc[es] *e:* **IAHS**

International Association for/of Hydrology
  e: **IAH**
International Association for/of Landscape
  Ecology *e:* **IALE**
International Association for/of
  Meteorology and Atmospheric Physics
  e: **IAMAP**
International Association for/of Physical
  Oceanogaphy *e:* **IAPO**
International Association for/of [the]
  Physical Sciences of the Ocean[s] *e:*
  IAPSO
International Association for/of Water Law
  e: **IAWL**
International Association for/on Water
  Pollution Research and Control *e:*
  IAWPRC
International Association for Quality
  Assurance in Health Care *e:* **ISQA**
International Association for Sea Survival
  Training *e:* **IASST**
International Association for the
  Advancement of Earth and Environmental
  Sciences *e:* **IAAEES**
International Association for the Promotion
  and Protection of Private Foreign
  Investments *e:* **APPI**
International Association for the Protection
  of Industrial Property *e:* **IAPIP**, *e:*
  IVfgR
International Association for the Study of
  Traditional Environments *e:* **IASTE**
International Association of Accident and
  Health Underwriters *e:* **IAAHU**
International Association of Aeronomy and
  Geomagnetism *e:* **IAAG**, *e:* **IAEA**
International Association of Agricultural
  Medicine and Rural Health *e:* **IAAMRH**
International Association of Coroners and
  Medical Examiners *e:* **IACME**
International Association of Earthquake
  Engineers *e:* **IAEE**
International Association of Endocrine
  Surgeons *e:* **IAES**
International Association of Engineering
  Geology. Bulletin *e:* **Int Assoc Engng
  Geol Bull**
International Association of Environmental
  Analytical Chemistry *e:* **IAEAC**
International Association of Environmental
  [Coordinators] *e:* **IAEC**
International Association of Environmental
  Mutagen Societies *e:* **IAEMS**
International Association of Environmental
  Testing Laboratories (or Laboratory) *e:*
  IAETL
International Association of Fish and
  Wildlife Agencies *e:* **IAFWA**
International Association of Geodesy *e:*
  IAG
International Association of Geologists *e:*
  IAG
International Association of Geology *e:*
  IAG
International Association of Geomagnetism
  and Aeronomy *e:* **IAGA**
International Association of Geomagnetism
  and Agronomy *e:* **IAGA**
International Association of Geomagnetism
  and Cosmochemistry *e:* **IAGC**
International Association of
  Geomorphologists *e:* **IAG**

International Association of Geophysical
  Contractors *e:* **IAG**, *e:* **IAGC**
International Association of Gerontology
  [European Biological Section] *e:*
  IAGEBS
International Association of Health Policy
  e: **IAHP**
International Association of Health
  Underwriters *e:* **IAHU**
International Association of Holistic Health
  Practitioners *e:* **IAHHP**
International Association of Human
  Biologists *e:* **IAHB**
International Association of
  Hydrogeologists *e:* **IAH**
International Association of Hydrologists
  e: **IAH**
International Association of Ice Cream
  Manufacturers *e:* **IAICM**
International Association of Machinists
  [and Aernspace Workers] *e:* **IAM**
International Association of Machinists and
  Aerospace Workers *e:* **IAMA**, *e:*
  IAMAW
International Association of
  Macrobiologists *e:* **IAMB**
International Association of Manufacturers
  of Aerospace Equipment *e:* **IAAM**
International Association of Medical
  Esperantists *e:* **IAME**
International Association of Medical
  Laboratory Technologists *e:* **AMLT**, *e:*
  IAMLT
International Association of Medical
  Museums *e:* **IAMM**
International Association of Medical
  Prosthesis Manufacturers *e:* **IAPM**
International Association of Meteorological
  and Atmospheric Physics *e:* **IAMAP**
International Association of Meteorology
  [and Atmospheric Physics] *e:* **IAM**
International Association of Meteorology
  and Atmospheric Science[s] *e:* **IAMAS**
International Association of
  Microbiological Societies *e:* **IAMS**
International Association of
  Microbiological Studies *e:* **IAMS**
International Association of
  Microbiologists *e:* **IAMB**
International Association of Milk, Food and
  Environmental Sanitarians *e:* **IAMFES**
International Association of Natural
  Resource Pilots *e:* **IANRP**
International Association of Olympic
  Medical Officers *e:* **IAOMO**
International Association of/on Water
  Pollution Research [and Control] *e:*
  IAWPR
International Association of/on Water
  Quality *e:* **IAWQ**
International Association of Oral and
  Maxillofacial Surgeons *e:* **IAOMS**
International Association of Oral Surgeons
  e: **IAOS**
International Association of Physical
  Geography *e:* **IAPG**
International Association of Plant Breeders
  for the Protection of Plant Varieties *e:*
  IAPBPPV
International Association of Professional
  Natural Hygienists *e:* **IAPNH**
International Association of Scientific
  Hydrology *e:* **IASH**

International Association of Seismology
  and Physics of the Earth's Interior *e:*
  IAS, *e:* **IASPE**, *e:* **IAS-PEI**
International Association of Space
  Philatelists *e:* **IASP**
International Association of Teachers of
  Veterinary Preventive Medicine *e:*
  IATVPM
International Association of Testing and
  Environmental Laboratories *e:* **IATEL**
International Association of Underwater
  Games *e:* **IAOUG**
International Association of Volcanology
  (or Vulcanology) and Chemistry of the
  Earth's Interior *e:* **IAVCEI**
International Association of Water Polo
  Referees *e:* **AIWP**
International Association of Waterworks in
  the Rhine Basin Area *e:* **IAWRBA**
International Association `Rurality-
  Environment-Development' *e:* **RED**
International Association[s] Against Painful
  Experiments on Animals *e:* **IAAPEA**
International Asssociation of Hydrological
  Sciences *e:* **AHS**
International Asthmological Medical
  Association *e:* **INTERASMA**
International Atmospheric Research
  Program *e:* **IARP**
International Atmospheric Surveillance
  Program *e:* **IASP**
International Baltic Sea Fishery
  Commission *e:* **IBSF**, *e:* **IBSFC**
International Bathymetric Chart of the
  Caribbean Sea and the Gulf of Mexico *e:*
  IBCCA
International Bathymetric Chart of the
  Mediterranean and its
  Geological/Geophysical Series *e:* **IBCM**
International Bathymetric Chart of the Red
  Sea and Gulf of Aden *e:* **IBCRSGA**
International Bathymetric Chart of the
  Western Indian Ocean *e:* **IBCWIO**
International Bio-Environmental
  Foundation *e:* **IBEF**
International Biodiversity Observation Year
  2001-2002 *e:* **IBOY**
International Biological
  Program/Productivity-Marine Section *e:*
  IBP/PM
International Biological Program[me] *e:*
  IBP
International Biological Programme
  Conservation of Terrestrial Biological
  Communities *e:* **IBP/CT**
International Biological Program[me]--
  Human Adaptability *e:* **IBP-HA**
International Biological Program[me]--
  Productivity in Freshwater *e:* **IBP-PF**
International Biological Year *e:* **IBY**
International Biomedical Expedition to the
  Antarctic *e:* **IBEA**
International Biosphere-Geosphere
  Programme *e:* **IBGP**
International Board of Medicine and
  Psychology *e:* **IBMP**
International Border Environmental Plan
  e: **IBEP**
International Bottled Water Association *e:*
  IBWA
International Boundary and Water
  Commission *e:* **IBC**

International Boundary [and] Water Commission e: **IBWC**

International Boundary and Water Commission e: **IBWG**

International Boundary and Water Commission-Planning and Reports Branch e: **IBWC-PRB**

International Boundary and Water Commission, United States and Mexico e: **IBWCUSMEX**

International Buoy Programme for the Indian Ocean e: **IBPIO**

International Bureau for Protection and Investigation e: **IBPI**

International Bureau of Atmospheric Ozone e: **OZONE**

International Business Earth Stations e: **IBES**

International Cable Protection Committee e: **ICPE**

International Cell Biology [International Federation of Cell Biology, Canada] e: **Int Cell Biol**

International Center for Aerospace Science and Technology e: **ICAST**

International Center for Biological Control e: **ICBC**

International Center for Environmental Research e: **Intl Ctr Envir**

International Center for Family Medicine e: **ICFM**

International Center for Interdisciplinary Studies of Immunology at Georgetown e: **ICISI**

International Center for Medical Environmental Sciences and Future Research e: **MEDICEF**

International Center for Medical Research e: **ICMR**

International Center for Medical Research and Training e: **ICMRT**

International Center for Medical Specialties e: **ICMS**

International Center for Medicine and Law e: **ICML**

International Center for the Environment e: **ICE**

International Center for [the] Industry and the Environment e: **ICIE**

International Center for the Protection of European Culture in Africa e: **ICPECA**

International Center for the Solution of Environmental Problems e: **ICSEP**

International Center (or Centre) of Medical and Psychological Hypnosis e: **ICMPH**

International Center (or Centre) of Studies for the Protection of Human Rights e: **ICSPHR**

International Centre for Alpine Environments e: **ICALPE**

International Centre for Coastal and Ocean Policy Studies e: **ICCOPS**

International Centre for Earth Tides e: **ICET**

International Centre for Equatorial Atmospheric Research, Indonesia e: **ICEAR**

International Centre for Eye Health e: **ICEH**

International Centre for Insect Pest Ecology e: **ICIPE**

International Centre for Ocean Development e: **ICOD**

International Centre for Ocean Development, Halifax, Nova Scotia e: **NSHIC**

International Centre for Training and Exchanges in Geosciences e: **CIFEG**

International Centre of Landscape Ecology within Geography e: **ICOLE**

International Centre of Research Youth, Violence, Environment e: **ICRYVE**

International Centre on Protected Landscapes e: **ICPL**

International Child Health Nursing Alliance e: **ICHNA**

International Christian Medical and Dental Association e: **ICMDA**

International Circumpolar Arctic Ice Drilling Project e: **ICAP**

International Classification of Diseases and Related Health Problems e: **ICD**

International Classification of Functioning, Disability and Health e: **ICF**

International Classification of Procedures in Medicine e: **ICPM**

International Clearinghouse for Ground Water Models e: **ICGWM**

International Clearinghouse of Health System Reform Initiatives e: **ICHSRI**

International Climate Change Partnership e: **ICCP**

International Climate Zone e: **ICZ**

International Climatic Research Program e: **ICRP**

International Climatological Commission e: **ICC**

International Co-ordination Group for the Global Investigation of Pollution in the Marine Environment e: **ICG-GIPME**

International College of Advanced Longevity Medicine e: **ICALM**

International College of Psychosomatic Medicine e: **ICPM**

International College of Surgeons e: **ICS**

International Commission [Committee] on Radiation Protection e: **ICRP**

International Commission for Medical Equipment e: **ICME**

International Commission for/of Health Professionals for Health and Human Rights e: **ICHP**

International Commission for/on Environmental Assessment e: **ICEA**

International Commission for/on Protection against Environmental Mutagens and Carcinogens e: **ICPEMC**

International Commission for Scientific Exploration of the Mediterranean Sea e: **CIESM**

International Commission for the Hydrology of the Rhine Basin e: **CHR**

International Commission for the Hydrology of the River Rhine Basin e: **DHR**

International Commission for the Protection of Lake Constance e: **ICPLC**

International Commission for the Protection of the Alps e: **CIPRA**

International Commission for the Protection of the Moselle against Pollution e: **ICPMP**

International Commission for the Protection of the Rhine against Pollution e: **ICPBAP**

International Commission for the Protection of the Rhine Against Pollution e: **ICPRAP**

International Commission for the Protection of the Rhine against Pollution e: **ICPRP**

International Commission for the Scientific Exploration of the Mediterranean Sea e: **ICSEMS**

International Commission Internationale pour la Protection des Alpes f: **CIPRA**

International Commission of Health Professionals for Health and Human Rights/Commission Internationales des Professionals de la Santé e: **ICHP/CINPROS**

International Commission of/on Snow and Ice e: **ICSI**

International Commission on Atmospheric Chemistry and Global Pollution e: **ICACGP**

International Commission on Atmospheric Electricity e: **IACE**, e: **ICAE**

International Commission on Climate e: **ICCL**

International Commission on Dynamic Meteorology e: **ICDM**

International Commission on Groundwater e: **ICGW**

International Commission on Laboratory Animals e: **ICLA**

International Commission on Microbiological Specifications for Food e: **ICMSF**

International Commission on Microbiological Specifications for Food[s] e: **ICMSF**

International Commission on National Parks and Protected Areas e: **ICNPPA**

International Commission on Non-Ionizing Radiation Protection e: **ICNIRP**

International Commission on Oceanography e: **ICO**

International Commission on Planetary Atmospheres and their Evolution e: **ICPAE**

International Commission on Polar Meteorology e: **ICPM**

International Commission on Radiological Protection e: **CRP**, e: **ICRC**, e: **ICRP**, e: **IRCP**

International Commission on Remote Sensing and Data Transmission [for Hydrology] e: **ICRSDT**

International Commission on Surface Water e: **ICSW**

International Commission on the Biological Effects of Noise e: **ICBEN**, e: **ICBN**

International Commission on the History of the Geological Science[s] e: **INHIGEO**

International Commission on [the] Meteorology of the Upper Atmosphere e: **ICMUA**

International Commission on Water Quality e: **ICWQ**

International Commission on Water Resources Systems e: **ICWRS**

International Commission (or Committee) on Atmosphere-Soil-Vegetation Relations e: **ICASVR**

International Commission (or Congress) of/on Occupational Health e: **ICOH**

International Committee [Commission] on Microbial Ecology e: **ICOME**

International Committee for Biological Control e: **ICBC**

International Committee for Bird Protection e: **ICBP**

International Committee for Earth Sciences e: **ICES**

International Committee for Life Assurance Medicine e: **ICLAM**

International Committee for Microbiological and Immunological Documentation e: **ICMID**

International Committee for Natural Therapeutics e: **ICNT**

International Committee for Recording the Productivity of Milk Animals e: **ICRPMA**

International Committee for Research and Study of/on Environmental Factors e: **ICEF**

International Committee for Standardization in Human Biology e: **ICSHB**

International Committee of Aerospace Activities e: **ICA**

International Committee of French-Speaking Historians and Geographers e: **ICFSHG**

International Committee of Geophysics e: **ICG**

International Committee of Medical Journal Editors e: **ICMJE**

International Committee of Military Medicine and Pharmacy e: **CMMP**

International Committee of/on Aerospace Activities e: **ICAA**

International Committee of/on Military Medicine and Pharmacy e: **ICMMP**

International Committee on Economic and Applied Microbiology e: **ICEAM**

International Committee on Food Microbiology and Hygiene e: **ICFMH**

International Committee on/for Outer Space Onomastics e: **ICOSO**

International Committee on Laboratory Animals e: **ICLA**

International Committee on Laboratory Animals Bulletin e: **ICLA Bulletin**

International Committee on Laser Atmospheric Studies e: **ICLAS**

International Committee on Medical Chemistry e: **ICMC**

International Committee on Microbial Ecology e: **ICME**

International Committee on Occupational Mental Health e: **ICOMH**

International Committee on Ocean Exploration and Environmental Services e: **ICOEES**

International Committee on Polar Viruses e: **ICPV**

International Committee on Radionuclide Meteorology e: **ICRM**

International Committee on the Organization of Traffic at Sea e: **ICOTAS**

International Conference on an Agenda of Science for Environment and Development into the 21st Century e: **ASCEND-21**

International Conference on Emergency Medicine e: **ICEM**

International Conference on Environmental Sensing and Assessment e: **ICESA**

International Conference on Geochronology e: **ICOG**

International Conference on Geoscience Information e: **ICGI**

International Conference on Heavy Metals in the Aquatic Environment e: **ICHMAE**

International Conference on Indoor Air Quality and Climate e: **ICIAQC**

International Conference on Mechanics in Medicine and Biology e: **ICMMB**

International Conference on Medical and Biological Engineering e: **ICMBE**

International Conference on Medical Computer Science e: **MEDCOMP**

International Conference on Medical Electronics e: **ICME**

International Conference on Medical Physics e: **ICMP**, e: **IDMP**

International Conference on Numerical Methods in Geomechanics e: **ICONMIG**

International Conference on Paleoceanography e: **ICP**

International Conference on Polymers in Medicine e: **ICPM**

International Conference on Port and Ocean Engineering under Arctic Conditions e: **POAC**

International Conference on the Analysis of Geological Materials e: **INTERAN**

International Conference on the Biology of Lipids e: **ICBL**

International Conference on the Combined Effects of Environmental Factors e: **ICCEF**

International Conference on the Internal and External Protection of Pipes e: **ICPP**

International Conference on the Mediterranean Coastal Environment e: **MEDCOAST**

International Conference on Water and the: Development Issues for the 21st Century e: **ICWE**

International Conference (or Congress) on Instrumentation in Aerospace Simulation Facilities e: **ICIASF**

International Conference[s] on Environmental Future e: **ICEF**

International Congress for Microbiology. Symposia e: **SICMAU**

International Congress for/on Tropical Medicine and Malaria e: **ICTMM**

International Congress of Animal Health Information Specialists e: **ICAHIS**

International Congress of Aviation and Space Medicine e: **ICASM**

International Congress of Carboniferous Stratigraphy and Geology s: **ICC**

International Congress of Ecology e: **ICE**

International Congress of Industrial Waste Water and Wastes e: **ICIWWW**

International Congress of Medical Laboratory Technologists e: **ICMLT**

International Congress of/on Systematic and Evolutionary Biology e: **ICSEB**

International Congress of Physical Medicine e: **ICPM**

International Congress of Scientists on the Human Environment e: **HESC**

International Congress on Computing in Medicine e: **MEDCOMP**

International Congress on Medical Librarianship e: **ICML**

International Congress on Rapid Methods and Automation in Microbiology and Immunology e: **RAMI**

International Consortium for Medical Imaging Technology e: **ICMIT**

International Convention for Saving[Safety] of Life at Sea e: **ICSLS**

International Convention for the Prevention of Pollution of the Sea by Oil e: **OILPOL**

International Coordinating Council of Aerospace Industries Assiciations e: **ICCATA**

International Coordinating Council of Aerospace Industries (or Industry) Association[s] e: **ICCAIA**

International Coordination of Oceanographic Research within the Antarctic Zone e: **AnZone**

International Coordination Working Group for Earth Observation e: **ICWG-EO**

International Correspondence Society of Obstetricians and Gynecologists e: **ICSOG**

International Council for Health, Physical Education, and Recreation e: **ICHPR**

International Council for Laboratory Animal Science e: **ICLAS**

International Council for Local Environmental Initiatives e: **ICLEI**

International Council for/of Environmental Law e: **ICEL**

International Council for/on Health, Physical Education and Recreation e: **ICHPER**

International Council for Radiation Protection e: **ICRP**

International Council for the Exgloration of the Sea e: **ICES**

International Council for the Exploration of the Sea. Cooperative Research Report. Series A e: **IXSAAZ**

International Council for the Exploration of the Sea. Cooperative Research Report. Series B e: **IXSBBS**

International Council of Aerospace Sciences e: **ICAS**

International Council of Medical Acupuncture and Related Technique[s] e: **ICMART**

International Council of Prison Medical Services e: **ICPMS**

International Council of Scientific Unions Advisory Committee on the Environment e: **ICSU-ACE**

International Council of Space Union e: **ICSU**

International Council on Environmental Design e: **ICED**

International Council on Metals and the Environment e: **ICME**

International Decade for Natural Disaster Reduction e: **IDNDR**

International Decade of Natural Hazard Reduction e: **IDNHR**

International Decade of Ocean Exploration e: **IDOE**

International Deepwater Rice Yield Nursery e: **IDRYN**

International Defence Equipment & Aerospace Exhibition e: **IDEA**

International Defenders of Animals e: **IDA**

Abkürzungen und Akronyme in Ökologie, Umwelt, Geowissenschaften

International Dental Health Foundation e:
IDHF
International Desalination and
Environmental Association e: **IDEA**
International Design for Extreme
Environments Association e: **IDEEA**
International Development Cooperation
Program of the Swedish Radiation
Protection Institute e: **SIUS**
International DN Ice Yacht Racing
Association e: **IDNIYRA**
International Donkey Protection Trust e:
IDPT
International Drinking Water Supply and
Sanitation Decade e: **IDWSSD**
International Earth Observation (or
Observing) System e: **IEOS**
International Earth Observation Satellite
Committee e: **IEOSC**
International Earth Observation Satellite
Missions e: **IEOSM**
International Earth Reference System e:
IERS
International Earth Rotation Service e:
IERS
International Ecological Engineering
Society e: **IEES**
International Ecology Society e: **IES**
International Electronic & Aerospace
Report e: **I/EAR**
International Electronic and Aerospace
Report e: **IEAR**
International Electronics Energy and
Aerospace Exhibition e: **RIENA**
International Environment and
Development Service e: **IEDS**
International Environment Assistance e:
IEA
International Environment Bureau e: **IEB**
International Environment Forum e: **IEF**
International Environment Technology
Transfer Advisory Board e: **IETTAB**
International Environmental and Natural
Resource Assessment Information Service
e: **INTERAISE**
International Environmental Bureau [of the
Non-Ferrous Metals Industry] e: **IEB**
International Environmental Education
Program[me] e: **IEEP**
International Environment[al] Facility e:
IEF
International Environmental Information
System e: **IEIS**
International Environmental Information
System Global Environmental Information
Exchange Network e: **INFOTERRA**
International Environmental Institute e:
IEI
International Environmental Protection
Union e: **IU**
International Environmental Technology
Centre e: **IETC**
International Equation of State of Seawater,
1980 e: **EOS-80**
International Esperantist Organization of
Naturists e: **IEON**
International Federation for Family Health
e: **IFFH**
International Federation for Hydrocephalus
and Spina Bifida e: **if**, e: **IFHSB**
International Federation for Hygiene,
Preventive and Social Medicine e:
FHPSM, e: **IFHPSM**

International Federation for Medical and
Biological Engineering e: **IFMBE**
International Federation for/of Medical
Electronics e: **IFME**
International Federation for/of Medical
Psychotherapy e: **IFMP**
International Federation of Aerospace
Technology and Engineering e: **IFATE**
International Federation of American
Homing Pigeon Fanciers e: **IF**, e:
IFAHPF
International Federation of Associations for
the Protection of Europe's Cultural and
Natural Heritage e: **Europa Nostra**
International Federation of Cell Biology e:
IFCB
International Federation of Clinical
Chemistry and Laboratory Medicine e:
IFCC
International Federation of Environmental
Health e: **IFEH**
International Federation of Gynaecology
and Obstetrics e: **IFGO**
International Federation of Gynecologic
Endoscopists e: **IFGE**
International Federation of Gynecology and
Obstetrics e: **FIGO**
International Federation of Health Funds
e: **FHF**
International Federation of Health Plans e:
iFHP
International Federation of Health
Professionals e: **IFHP**
International Federation of Health Records
Organizations e: **FHRO**, e: **IFHRO**, e:
IFRHO
International Federation of Hydrotherapy
and Climatotherapy e: **IFHAC**
International Federation of Infantile and
Juvenile Gynecology e: **IFIJG**, e: **IFJG**
International Federation of Manual
Medicine e: **IFMM**
International Federation of Medical
Students' Associations e: **IFMSA**
International Federation of Oral Medicine
e: **IFOM**
International Federation of Physical
Medicine e: **IFPM**
International Federation of Physical
Medicine and Rehabilitation e: **IFPMR**
International Federation of Practitioners of
Natural Therapeutics e: **IFPNT**
International Federation of Societies of
Economic Geologists e: **IFSEG**
International Federation of [the]
Psychological-Medical Organizations e:
IFPMO
International Federation of Thermalism and
Climatism e: **IFTC**
International Federation of Voluntary
Health Service Funds e: **IFVHSF**
International Federation of École Moderne'
Movements e: **Pedagogy Freinet**
International Ferderation of Computer
Sciences e: **IFCS**
International Flat Earth Research Society
e: **IFERS**
International Floating Rice Observational
Nursery e: **IFRON**
International Forum on/for Earth
Observations Using Space Station
Elements e: **IFEOS**

International Foundation for Earth
Construction e: **IFEC**
International Friends of Nature e: **IFN**
International Fund for Animal Welfare e:
IFAW
International Fund for the Aral Sea e:
IFAS
International Geochemical Congress e:
IGC, e: **IGES**
International Geochemical Exploration
Symposium e: **IGES**
International Geodynamics Project e: **IGP**
International Geographic Information
Foundation e: **IGIF**
International Geographic Information
System e: **IGIS**
International Geographic Institute e: **IGN**
International Geographical Association e:
IGA
International Geographical Union e: **IGU**
International Geographical Union
Newsletter e: **IGU Newsletter**
International Geographics e: **IGE**
International Geologic[al] Congress e:
IGC
International Geological Congress Report
e: **IGC**
International Geological Correlation
Program[me] e: **IGCP**
International Geological Correlation
Programme Age and Isotopes of South
American Ores [1992-1996] e: **IGCP
Project 342**
International Geological Correlation
Programme Alkaline and Carbonatitic
Magmatism e: **IGCP Project 314**
International Geological Correlation Pro-
gramme Andean Lithospheric Evolution
[1993-1997] e: **IGCP Project 345**
International Geological Correlation
Programme Anthropogenic Impact on
Weathering Processes [1996-2000] e:
IGCP Project 405
International Geological Correlation
Programme Biosedimentology of
Microbial Buildups [1995-1999] e:
IGCP Project 380
International Geological Correlation
Programme Biotic Recoveries from Mass
Extinctions [1993-1997] e: **IGCP
Project 335**
International Geological Correlation
Programme Caledonide Orogen e: **IGCP
Project 27**
International Geological Correlation
Programme Caribbean Volcanic Arcs and
Ophiolites [1994-1998] e: **IGCP Project
364**
International Geological Correlation
Programme Carpatho-Balkan Plate
Tectonics and Metallogeny [1993-1997]
e: **IGCP Project 356**
International Geological Correlation
Programme Circum-Arctic Palaeozoic
Vertebrates [1996-2000] e: **IGCP
Project 406**
International Geological Correlation
Programme Circum-Pacific Jurassic e:
IGCP Project 171
International Geological Correlation
Programme Circumalpine Quaternary
Correlations [1994-1997] e: **IGCP
Project 378**

International Geological Correlation Programme Coastal Evolution in the Quaternary [1988-1993] *e:* **IGCP Project 274**

International Geological Correlation Programme Continental Shelves in the Quaternary [1996-2000] *e:* **IGCP Project 396**

International Geological Correlation Programme Correlation of Caledonian Stratabound Sulphides *e:* **IGCP Project 60**

International Geological Correlation Programme Correlation of Ganges-Brahmaputra Sediments [1995-1999] *e:* **IGCP Project 347**

International Geological Correlation Programme Correlation of Tethyan, Circum-Pacific and Marginal Gondwanan Permo-Triassic [1993-1997] *e:* **IGCP Project 359**

International Geological Correlation Programme Cretaceous Environmental Change in East and Southeast Asia [1993-1997] *e:* **IGCP Project 350**

International Geological Correlation Programme Cretaceous of Latin America *e:* **IGCP Project 242**

International Geological Correlation Programme Early Paleozoic Evolution in NW Gondwana [1993-1997] *e:* **IGCP Project 351**

International Geological Correlation Programme Earth's Glacial Record *e:* **IGCP Project 260**

International Geological Correlation Programme East Asia Activated Zones [1993-1997] *e:* **IGCP Project 361**

International Geological Correlation Programme Ecological Aspects of the Cambrian Radiation [1994-1997] *e:* **IGCP Project 366**

International Geological Correlation Programme Economic Superaccumulations of Metals in Lithosphere [1995-1999] *e:* **IGCP Project 354**

International Geological Correlation Programme Events of the Mid-Cretaceous [1974-1985] *e:* **IGCP Project 58**

International Geological Correlation Programme Fluvial Environments *e:* **IGCP Project 158A**

International Geological Correlation Programme Genesis and Correlation of Marine Polymetallic Oxides *e:* **IGCP Project 318**

International Geological Correlation Programme Geochemical Event Markers in the Phanerozoic *e:* **IGCP Project 293**

International Geological Correlation Programme Geodynamics of Continental Rifting [1996-2000] *e:* **IGCP Project 400**

International Geological Correlation Programme Geoenvironmental Evaluation of Coastal Belts in Arab Countries [1995-1999] *e:* **IGCP Project 389**

International Geological Correlation Programme Geological Events at the Eocene-Oligocene Boundary *e:* **IGCP Projcet 174**

International Geological Correlation Programme Geology, Climate, Hydrology and Karst Formation [1990-1994] *e:* **IGCP Project 299**

International Geological Correlation Programme Geotectonic Evolution and Metallogeny in the Eastern Mediterranean and Western Asia *e:* **IGCP Project 169**

International Geological Correlation Programme Global Biological Events in Earth History *e:* **IGCP Project 216**

International Geological Correlation Programme Global Geochemical Baselines [1993-1997] *e:* **IGCP Project 360**

International Geological Correlation Programme Global Limnology *e:* **IGCP Project 324**

International Geological Correlation Programme Global Paleogeography of the Late Precambrian and Early Paleozoic [1992-1996] *e:* **IGCP Project 319**

International Geological Correlation Programme Gondwana Dispersion and Asian Accretion [1991-1995, 1996] *e:* **IGCP Project 321**

International Geological Correlation Programme Gondwanaland Sutures and Fold Belts [1990-1995, 1996] *e:* **IGCP Project 288**

International Geological Correlation Programme Impact and Extraterrestrial Spherules [1996-2000] *e:* **IGCP Project 384**

International Geological Correlation Programme International Geochemical Mapping *e:* **IGCP Project 259**

International Geological Correlation Programme Intraplate Magmatism and Metallogeny [1992-1996] *e:* **IGCP Project 336**

International Geological Correlation Programme Jurassic Events in South America [1992-1996] *e:* **IGCP Project 322**

International Geological Correlation Programme Karst Processes and the Carbon Cycle [1995-1999] *e:* **IGCP Project 379**

International Geological Correlation Programme Late Quaternary Coastal Records of Rapid Change: Application to Present and Future Conditions [1994-1999] *e:* **IGCP Project 367**

International Geological Correlation Programme Late Quaternary Sea-Level Changes: Measurements, Correlations and Future Applications *e:* **IGCP Project 200**

International Geological Correlation Programme Laurentian-Gondwanan Connections [1994-1998] *e:* **IGCP Project 376**

International Geological Correlation Programme Lower Crustal Processes *e:* **IGCP Project 304**

International Geological Correlation Programme Lower Proterozoic of the Sub-Equatorial Africa [1994-1998] *e:* **IGCP Project 363**

International Geological Correlation Programme Metamorphism and Geodynamics *e:* **IGCP Project 235**

International Geological Correlation Programme Mire Environments, established in 1976 *e:* **IGCP Project 158B**

International Geological Correlation Programme Neogene of the Paratethys [1992-1996] *e:* **IGCP Project 329**

International Geological Correlation Programme Neogeodynamica Baltica [1994-1997] *e:* **IGCP Project 346**

International Geological Correlation Programme Neoproterozoic Events and Resources [1991-1996] *e:* **IGCP Project 320**

International Geological Correlation Programme Neritic Middle-Upper Eocene [1996-2000] *e:* **IGCP Project 393**

International Geological Correlation Programme North Atlantic Precambrian [1994-1998] *e:* **IGCP Project 371**

International Geological Correlation Programme Oligocene-Miocene Transition in the Northern Hemisphere [1992-1996] *e:* **IGCP Project 326**

International Geological Correlation Programme Organics and Mineral Deposits [1993-1997] *e:* **IGCP Project 357**

International Geological Correlation Programme Origin and Evolution of the Archaean Continental Crust *e:* **IGCP Project 92**

International Geological Correlation Programme Origin of Anorthosite and Related Rocks *e:* **IGCP Project 290**

International Geological Correlation Programme Pacific Neogene *e:* **IGCP Project 114**

International Geological Correlation Programme Palaeogene of South America [1991-1995, 1996] *e:* **IGCP Project 301**

International Geological Correlation Programme Palaeohydrology of the Temperate Zone During the Last 15,000 Years *e:* **IGCP Project 158**

International Geological Correlation Programme Palaeostress, Neotectonics, Geodynamics and Natural Hazards in West Pacific/Asia [1996-2000] *e:* **IGCP Project 383**

International Geological Correlation Programme Palaeoweathering Records and Paleosurfaces [1991-1995, 1996] *e:* **IGCP Project 317**

International Geological Correlation Programme Paleoclimatology and Palaeoceanography from Laminated Sediments [1994-1998] *e:* **IGCP Project 374**

International Geological Correlation Programme Paleozoic Microvertebrates [1991-1995, 1996] *e:* **IGCP Project 328**

International Geological Correlation Programme Past and Future Evolution of Deserts *e:* **IGCP Project 252**

International Geological Correlation Programme Perithethyan Rift Basins [1994-1998] *e:* **IGCP Project 369**

International Geological Correlation Programme Proterozoic Events in East Gondwana Deposits [1995-1999] *e:* **IGCP Project 368**

International Geological Correlation
Programme Quaternary Deserts and
Climatic Change/Desert Margins and
Paleomonsoons in the Old World/Desert
Margins e: **IGCP Project 349**

International Geological Correlation
Programme Quaternary Glaciations in the
Northern Hemisphere e: **IGCP Project
24**

International Geological Correlation
Programme Quaternary Stratigraphy of
Asia and the Pacific e: **IGCP Project
296**

International Geological Correlation
Programme Rapakivi Granites and
Related Rocks [1991-1995, 1996] e:
IGCP Project 315

International Geological Correlation
Programme Response of the
Ocean/Atmosphere System to Past Global
Changes [1996-2000] e: **IGCP Project
386**

International Geological Correlation
Programme Sand Accumulations and
Groundwater in the Sahara [1995-1999]
e: **IGCP Project 391**

International Geological Correlation
Programme Sea-levels of the Last 15,000
years e: **IGCP Project 61**

International Geological Correlation
Programme Seismotectonics and Seismic
Hazard Assessment of the Mediterranean
Basin [1996-2000] e: **IGCP Project 382**

International Geological Correlation
Programme South Atlantic Mesozoic
Correlations [1995-1999] e: **IGCP
Project 381**

International Geological Correlation
Programme Southern Hemisphere Paleo-
and Neoclimates [1993-1997] e: **IGCP
Project 341**

International Geological Correlation
Programme Stratigraphic Analysis of
Perithethyan Basins [1992-1996] e: **IGCP
Project 343**

International Geological Correlation
Programme Stratigraphic Correlation in
South-East Asia [1992-1995, 1996] e:
IGCP Project 306

International Geological Correlation
Programme Termination of the
Pleistocene [1989, 1990-1994] e: **IGCP
Project 253**

International Geological Correlation
Programme Terrestrial Carbon in the Past
125 ka [1996-1999] e: **IGCP Project
404**

International Geological Correlation
Programme Tethyan and Boreal
Cretaceous [1993-1997] e: **IGCP
Project 362**

International Geological Correlation
Programme The Mozambique and Related
Belts [1993-1997] e: **IGCP Project 348**

International Geological Correlation
Programme The Structure and
Metallogenesis of Central African Late
Proterozoic Belts e: **IGCP Project 302**

International Geological/Geophysical
Atlases of the Atlantic and Pacific Oceans
e: **GAPA**

International Geological-Geophysical
Cruise Inventory e: **IG-GCI**

International Geology Review e: **Int Geol
Rev**

International Geomagnetic Reference Field
e: **IGRF**

International Geophysical Bulletin e: **IGB**

International Geophysical Committee e:
IGC

International Geophysical Cooperation e:
IGC

International Geophysical Extension e:
IGE

International Geophysical Month e: **IGM**

International Geophysical Union e: **IGU**

International Geophysical Year e: **IGY**

International Geophysical Year-World Data
Centre (or Center) e: **IGY-WDC**

International Geophysics Bulletin e:
I.G.B.

International Geophysics Committee e:
CIG

International Geoscience and Remote
Sensing Society e: **IGARSS**, e: **IGRSS**

International Geoscience and Remote
Sensing Symposium e: **IGARSS**

International Geosphere-Biosphere (or
Global Change) Program e: **IGBP**

International Geosphere-Biosphere (or
Global Change) Programme-Data and
Information System e: **IGBP-DIS**

International Geosphere- Biosphere (or
Global Change) Programme Scientific
Advisory Committee e: **IGBP-SAC**

International Geosphere-Biosphere
Programme e: **IGAC**

International Geosphere-Biosphere
Programme/Global Change System for
Analysis, Research and Training e:
IGBP/ START

International Geosphere-Biosphere
Programme System for Analysis,
Research and Training e: **IGBP-START**

International Geosphere Biosphere Project
e: **IGBP**

International Geotechnical Classification
e: **IGC**

International Geotextile Society e: **IGS**

International Geothermal Association e:
IGA

International Global Atmosphere
Programme e: **IGAP**

International Global Atmospheric
Chemistry Program e: **IGACP**

International Global Atmospheric
Chemistry Program[me] e: **IGAC**

International Global Atmospheric
Chemistry Project e: **IGAC**

International Global Ocean Ecosystem
Dynamics Programme e: **GLOBEC-INT**

International Global Ocean Services System
e: **IGOSS**

International Global Ocean Station System
e: **IGOSS**

International Global Positioning System
Geodynamic Service e: **IGS**

International GPS Service [for
Geodynamics] e: **IGS**

International Greenland Sea Project e:
IGSP

International Ground Environment
Interrupted Continuous Wave e:
IGESUCO

International Ground Environment
[Subcommittee] e: **IGESUCO**

International Ground Water Modelling
Centre/Center e: **IGWMC**

International Group of Protection and
Indemnity Associations e: **P and I**

International Group of Scientific, Technical
and Medical Publishers e: **STM**

International Health and Temperance
Association e: **IHTA**

International Health Board e: **IHB**

International Health Centre of Socio-
Economics Researches and Studies e:
IHCSERS

International Health Conference e: **IHC**

International Health Council e: **IHC**

International Health Division e: **IHD**

International Health Economics and
Management Institute e: **IHEMI**

International Health Economics Association
e: **IHEA**

International Health Evaluation Association
e: **IHEA**

International Health Exchange e: **IHDP**

International Health Foundation e: **IHF**

International Health Geographics
Conference e: **IHGC**

International Health Human Resources
Registry e: **IHHRR**

International Health Human Resources
Registry/Registre des Ressources
Humaines en Santé Internationale e:
IHHRR/RRHSI

International Health Industries Association
e: **IHIA**

International Health Organization e: **IHO**

International Health Policy and
Management Institute e: **IHPMI**

International Health Policy Program e:
IHPP

International Health Program Office e:
IHPO

International Health Research Network e:
IHRN

International Health Society e: **IHS**

International Healthcare Opportunities
Clearinghouse e: **IHOC**

International Healthcare Safety Professional
Certification Board e: **IHSPCB**

International Healthy Cities Foundation e:
IHCF

International Historical Association of the
Indian Ocean e: **IHAIO**

International Human Dimensions of Global
Environmental Change Programme e:
IHDP

International Hydro-Elec. System e: **IH Pr**

International Hydrocarbon Intercomparison
Committee e: **IHIC**

International Hydrofoil Society e: **IHS**

International Hydrographic Bulletin
[Bureau Hydrographique International,
Monaco] e: **Int Hydrogr Bull**

International Hydrographic Bureau e: **IHB**

International Hydrographic Organisation (or
Organization) e: **IHO**

International Hydrographic Program[me]
e: **IHP**

International Hydrographic Review [Bureau
Hydrographique International, Monaco]
e: **Int Hydrogr Rev**

International Hydrologic Decade e: **IHD**

International Hydrological Program/
Operation Hydrological Program e:
IHP/OHP

International Hydrological Program[me] e:
IHP

International Hydron Corp. e: **HYD**

International Ice Cream Association e:
IICA

International Ice Hockey Federation e:
IIHF

International Ice Patrol e: **IIC**, e: **IIP**, e:
IP

International Indian Ocean Expedition e:
IIOE

International Indian Ocean Survey e: **IIOS**

International Institute for Aerial
[Aerospace] Survey and Earth Sciences
e: **IIASES**

International Institute for Aerial (or
Aerospace) Survey and Earth Science[s]
e: **ITC**

International Institute for Biological and
Botanical Research e: **IIBBR**

International Institute for Earth,
Environmental and Marine Sciences and
Technologies e: **IIEM**

International Institute for Environmental
Affairs e: **IIEA**

International Institute for Environment[al]
and Development e: **IIED**

International Institute for Environmental
Studies e: **IIES**

International Institute for Hydraulic and
Environmental Engineering e: **HE**, e:
IHE

International Institute for Hydrologic and
Environmental Engineering e: **IHE**

International Institute for Infrastructure,
Hydraulic and Environmental Engineering
e: **IHE**

International Institute for Medical
Electronics and Biological Engineering
e: **IIMEBE**

International Institute for the Urban
Environment e: **IIUE**

International Institute of Biological Control
e: **IIBC**

International Institute of Biological
Husbandry e: **IIBH**

International Institute of Children's Nature
and Their Rights e: **IICNTR**

International Institute of Geophysics e:
I.I.G.

International Institute of Health Care,
Ethics and Human Values e: **IIHCEHV**

International Institute of Islamic Medicine
e: **IIIM**

International Institute of Physical
Oceanography e: **IIPO**

International Institute of Practical
Geomancy e: **IIPG**

International Institute of Seismology and
Earthquake e: **IIS**

International Institute of Seismology and
Earthquake Engineering e: **IIS&EE**

International Institute of Space Law e:
IISL

International Interdependent Research and
Development e: **IIRD**

[International] Interplanetary Space Travel
Research Association e: **ISTRA**

International Irrigated Rice Observational
Nursery e: **IIRON**

International Joint Commission on
Boundary Waters e: **IHC**

International Journal for Disability and Oral
Health e: **IJDH**

International Journal for Numerical and
Analytical Methods in Geomechanics e:
Int J Numer Anal Methods Geomech

International Journal for Quality in Health
Care e: **Int J Qual Health Care**

International Journal of Bio-Medical
Computing [Limerick] e: **Int J Biomed
Comput**

International Journal of Bio-Medical
Computing [Netherlands] n: **Int J Bio-
Med Comput**

International Journal of Biochemistry and
Cell Biology e: **Int J Biochem Cell Biol**

International Journal of Biological
Macromolecules e: **Int J Biol
Macromol**

International Journal of Biological
Macromolecules [Guildford] e: **Int J
Biiol Macromol**

International Journal of Biological Markers
[Milano] e: **Int J Biol Markers**

International Journal of Biometeorologie
[R] e: **Int. J. Biometeorol.**

International Journal of Biometeorology
[Amsterdam] e: **Int J Biometeorol**

International Journal of Biometeorology
[International Society of Biometeorology,
Switzerland] e: **Int J Biomet**

International Journal of Climatology e: **Int
J Climatol**

International Journal of Developmental
Biology e: **Int J Dev Biol**

International Journal of Earthquake and
Structural Dynamics [Japan] j: **Int J
Earthquake Eng Struct Dyn**

International Journal of Environmental
Analytical Chemistry [International
Association of Environmental Analytical
Chemistry, Switzerland] e: **Int J
Environ Anal Chem**

International Journal of Environmental
Health Research e: **IJEHR**

International Journal of Environmental
Studies e: **Int J Environ Stud**

International Journal of Food Microbiology
[International Union of Microbiological
Societies] e: **Int J Food Microbiol**

International Journal of Geographical
Information Systems e: **IJGIS**, e: **Int J
Geogr Int Syst**

International Journal of Gynaecology and
Obstetrics [Limerick] e: **Int J Gynaecol
Obstet**

International Journal of Gynecological
Cancer e: **Int J Gynecol Cancer**

International Journal of Gynecological
Pathology e: **Int J Gynecol Pathol**

International Journal of Health Services e:
HS, e: **Int J Health Serv**

International Journal of Hydrogen Energy
e: **Int J Hydrog Energy**

International Journal of Legal Medicine
[Heidelberg] e: **Int J Legal Med**

International Journal of Medical
Microbiology e: **Int J Med Microbiol**

International Journal of Medical
Microbiology, Virology, Parasitology and
Infectious Diseases e: **Int J Med
Microbiol Virol Parasitol Infect Dis**

International Journal of Mental Health e:
Internat J Mental Health

International Journal of Mine Water
[International Mine Water Association,
Spain] s: **Int J Mine Water**

International Journal of Nautical
Archaeology and Underwater Exploration
e: **IJNA**

International Journal of Nuclear Medicine
and Biology [Elmsford] e: **Int J Nucl
Med Biol**

International Journal of Occupational
Medicine and Environmental Health e:
Int J Occup Med Environ Health

International Journal of Psychiatry in
Medicine e: **IJPM**, e: **Int J Psychiatry
Med**

International Journal of Quantum
Chemistry, Quantum Biology Symposium
e: **Int J Quantum Chem\ Quantum Biol
Symp**

International Journal of Radiation
Applications and Instrumentation. Part B,
Nuclear Medicine and Biology [Oxford]
e: **Int J Rad Appl Instrum [B]**

International Journal of Radiation Biology
and Related Studies in Physics e: **Int J
Radiat Biol**

International Journal of Radiation
Oncology, Biology, Physics e: **IJROBP**,
e: **Int J Radiat Oncol Biol Phys**

International Journal of Remote Sensing e:
Int J Remote Sens

International Journal of Rock Mechanics
and Mining Sciences and Geomechanics
Abstracts e: **Int J Rock Mech Min Sci
Geomech Abstr**

International Journal of Sports Medicine
[Stuttgart] e: **Int J Sports Med**

International Journal of Systematic
Bacteriology [International Union of
Microbiological Societies] e: **Int J Syst
Bacteriol**

International Journal of Technology
Assessment in Health Care e: **Int J
Technol Assess Health Care**

International Juridical Institute for Animal
Protection e: **IJIAP**

International Juridical Organization for
Environment and Development e: **IJO**

International Laboratory for Research
into/on/of Animal Disease[s] e: **ILRAD**

International Lake Environmental
Preservation Committee e: **ILEC**

International Land Surface Climatology
Project e: **ISLSCP**

International Latitude Observatory e: **ILO**

International League for Animal Rights e:
ILAR

International League for the Protection of
Cetaceans e: **ILPC**

International League for the Protection of
Horses e: **ILPH**, e: **ILPIH**

International League for the Protection of
Native Races e: **ILPNR**

International Liaison Committee on Medical
Physics e: **ILCMP**

International Liaison Council for a World
Environment Authority e: **CILAME**

International Lifesaving Museum and Water
Safety Center e: **ILMWSC**

International Loan Fund /for Health and
Family Projects e: **ILF**

International Long-Term Ecological
Research [Network] e: **ILTER**

International Lookout for Infectious Animal Disease e: **ILIAD**

International Low Water e: **ILW**

International Marine Animal Trainers Association e: **IMATA**

International Marine Environment Award e: **GPIEM**

International Marine Meteorological Punch Card e: **IMMPC**

International Maritime Meteorological Tape e: **IMMT**

International Medical and Research Foundation e: **IMRF**

International Medical Assistance Society e: **IMA**

International Medical Association for Radio and Television e: **IMART**

International Medical Corps e: **IMC**

International Medical Engineering and Automation Exhibition e: **MEDEA**

International Medical Exchange e: **IME**

International Medical Graduates e: **IMG**

International Medical Implant e: **IMI**

International Medical Informatics Association e: **IMI**, e: **IMIA**

International Medical Information Center (or Centre) e: **IMIC**

International Medical Journal e: **IMJ**

International Medical Libraries Ring e: **IML**

International Medical Parliamentarians Organization e: **IMPO**

International Medical Regulatory and Shipping Association e: **IMRSA**

International Medical Rehabilitation Association e: **IMRA**

International Medical Research e: **I.M.R.**

International Medical Sciences Academy e: **IMSA**

International Medical Society for Motor Disturbances e: **ISMD**

International Medical Society of Paraplegia e: **IMSOP**, e: **IMSP**

International Medical Volunteers Association e: **IMVA**

International Medico-Athletic and Scientific Association e: **I.M.A.S.A.**

International Meeting of Animal Nutrition Experts e: **RITENA**

International Meeting of Medical Advisers in the Pharmaceutical Industry e: **IMMAPI**

International Meteor Organization e: **IMO**

International Meteorological Center (or Centre) e: **IMC**

International Meteorological Committee e: **IMC**

International Meteorological Consultant[s] Service e: **IMCOS**

International Meteorological Educational Program e: **IMEP**

International Meteorological Institute e: **IMI**

International Meteorological Organisation (or Organization) e: **IMO**

International Meteorological Service Program e: **IMSP**

International Meteorological Teleprinter Network [in] Europe e: **IMTNE**

International Meteorological Vocabulary e: **IMV**

International Microbiological Education Committee e: **MEC**

International Mine Water Association e: **IMWA**

International Natural Rubber Agreement e: **INRA**

International Natural Rubber Organization e: **INRO**

International Natural Sausage Casing Association e: **INSCA**

International Nature Friends e: **INF**

International Naturist Federation e: **INF**

International Naturopathic Association e: **INA**

International Network for Environmental Management e: **INEM**

International Network for Religion and Animals e: **INRA**

International Network for the History of Public Health e: **INHPH**

International Network of Agencies for Health Technology Assessment e: **INAHTA**

International Normal Atmosphere e: **INA**

International Northern Sea Route Programme e: **INSROP**

International Observations e: **INTEROBS**

International Ocean Color Coordination Group e: **IOCCG**

International Ocean Data Exchange e: **IODE**

International Ocean Disposal Symposium e: **IODS**

International Ocean Institute e: **IOI**

International Ocean Racing e: **IOR**

International Ocean Rule e: **IOR**

International Ocean Towage Agreement (Daily Hire) e: **TOWHIRE**

International Ocean Towage Agreement (Lumpsum) e: **TOWCON**

International Oceanographic Committee [or Commission] e: **IOC**

International Oceanographic Data and Information Exchange e: **IODE**

International Oceanographic Data Exchange Working Group e: **IODE**

International Oceanographic Foundation e: **IOF**

International Office for the Protection of Nature e: **IOPN**

International Office for Water e: **IOW**

International Office for Water Education e: **IOWE**

International Office of Documentation on Military Medicine e: **IODMM**

International Office of Military Medicine Documentation e: **IOMMD**

International Office of Public Health e: **IOPH**

International Offshore and Polar Engineering Conference e: **ISOPE**

International Organisation for/of Medical Physics e: **IOMP**

International Organization for Biological Control of Noxious Animals and Plants e: **IOBC**

International Organization for Cooperation in Health Care e: **IOCHC**

International Organization for Human Ecology e: **IOHE**

International Organization for Marine Geology e: **INTERMARGEO**

International Organization for Marine Geology [Council for Mutual Economic Assistance] e: **IHTERMORGEO**

International Organization for Medical Cooperation e: **IOMC**

International Organization for Standardization Development Environment e: **ISODE**

International Organization for Technical Cooperation in Geology e: **Intergeotechnika**, e: **IOTCG**

International Organization of Space Communication[s] e: **Intersputnik**

International Oxidative Medicine Association e: **IOMA**

International Paleoclimate Database e: **PKDB**

International Paleoclimatic Data Network e: **IPDN**

International Peace, Economy and Ecology e: **IPEE**

International Petroleum Industry Environmental Conservation Association e: **IPIECA**

International Phase of Ocean Drilling e: **IPOD**

International Physicians Commission for the Protection of Prisoners e: **IPCPP**

International Physicians for Equitable Healthcare e: **IPEH**

International Pigeon Board e: **I.P.B.**

International Pigeon Federation e: **IPF**

International Plant Protection Center (or Centre) e: **IPPC**

International Plant Protection Convention e: **IPPC**

International Polar Commission e: **I.P.C.**

International Polar Institute e: **IPI**

International Polar Motion Service e: **IPMS**

International Polar-Orbiting Meteorological Satellite Group e: **IPOMS**

International Polar Orbiting Platform e: **POP**

International Polar Transportation Conference e: **IPTC**

International Polar Year e: **IPY**

International Polaris Energy Corp. e: **IPS**

International Post conference Symposium on Low Cost and Energy Saving Wastewater Treatment Technologies e: **ISLEWTT**

International Post-Partum Mental Health Network e: **IPPMHN**

International Primate Protection League e: **IPPL**

International Professional Association for Environmental Affairs e: **IPREA**

International Professional Association for/of Environmental Affairs e: **IPRE**

International Program[me] of Ocean Drilling e: **IPOD**

International Project in Dendroclimatology e: **IPID**

International Public Health Office e: **IPHO**

International Radiation Commission [of the International Association of Meteorology and Atmospheric Physics] e: **IRC**

International Radiation Protection Association e: **IRPA**

International Rainfed Lowland Rice Observational Nursery e: **IDRON**, e: **IRLON**

International Rainfed Rice Shallow Water Observational Nursery e: **IRRSWON**

International Rainfed Rice Shallow Water Observational Nursery-Early e: **IRRSWON-E**

International Rainfed Rice Shallow Water Observational Nursery-Medium e: **IRRSWON-M**

International Rainfed Rice Shallow Water Yield Nursery-Early e: **IRRSWYN-E**

International Rainfed Rice Shallow Water Yield Nursery-Medium e: **IRRSWYN-M**

International Reference Center [or Centre] [for Community Water Supply and Sanitation] e: **IRC**

International Reference Centre [or Center] for Water Disposal e: **IRCWD**

International Reference Organization in Forensic Medicine [and Sciences] e: **INFORM**

International Reference Preparation [WHO Expert Committee on Biological Standardization] e: **IRP**

International Register for Sources of Environmental Information e: **INFOTERRA**

International Rehabilitation Medicine Association e: **IRMA**

International Remote Sensing Institute e: **IRSI**

International Research and Information Network on Children's Health Environment and Safety e: **INCHES**

International Research Career Development Program [Public Health Service] e: **IRCDP**

International Research Institute for Climate Prediction e: **IRI**, e: **IRICP**

International REST [Restricted Environmental Stimulation Techniques] Investigators Society e: **IRIS**

International Review of Neurobiology e: **Int Rev Neurobiol**

International Rice Acid Lowland Soils Observational Nursery e: **IRALON**

International Rice Boro Observational Nursery e: **IRBON**

International Rice Deep Water Observational Nursery e: **IRDWON**

International Rice Deep Water Yield Nursery e: **IRDWYN**

International Rice Finegrain Aromatic Observational Nursery e: **IRFAON**

International Rice Hybrid Observational Nursery e: **IRHON**

International Rice Observational Nursery e: **IRON**

International Rice Observational Nursery-Early e: **IRON-E**

International Rice Observational Nursery-Medium e: **IRON-M**

International Rice Observational Nursery-Very Early e: **IRON-VE**

International Rice Salinity and Alkalinity Tolerance Observational Nursery e: **IRSATON**

International Rice Salinity Tolerance Observational Nursery e: **IRSTON**

International Rice Slender Grain Observational Nursery e: **IRSGON**

International Rice Temperate Observational Nursery e: **IRTON**

International Safety and Health Exhibition e: **ISHE**

International Satellite Cloud Climate [or Climatology] Project [or Program] e: **ISCCP**

International Satellite Geodesy Experiment[s] e: **ISAGEX**

International Satellite Land Surface Climatology Program e: **ISLSCP**

International Satellite Land Surface Climatology Project e: **ISLSCP**

International Scientific, Educational, Medical & Industrial Laboratory Equipment Exhibition e: **SEMLAB**

International Sea-Bed Area e: **ISBA**

International Sea-Bed Authority e: **ISBA**

International Sea Mapping e: **ISM**

International Secretariat for Water e: **SIE**

International Service Association for Health e: **INSA**

International Service of/for Geomagnetic Indices e: **ISGI**

International Shipbrokers & Agents Protect & Indemnity Club Ltd. e: **ISBACLUB**

International Society Biomedical Research and/on Alcoholism e: **ISBRA**

International Society for a Complete Earth e: **ISCE**

International Society for Aerosols in Medicine e: **ISAeM**, e: **ISAM**

International Society for Animal and Human Mycology e: **ISAHM**

International Society for Animal Blood Group Research e: **ISABGR**, e: **ISABR**

International Society for Animal Genetics e: **ISAG**

International Society for Animal Rights e: **ISAR**

International Society for Chronobiology e: **ISC**

International Society for Development of Psychobiology e: **ISDP**

International Society for Ecological Economics e: **ISEE**

International Society for Ecological Modelling e: **ISEM**

International Society for Ecosystem Health e: **ISEH**

International Society for Environmental Education e: **ISEE**

International Society for Environmental Epidemiology e: **ISEE**

International Society for Environmental Toxicology and Cancer e: **ISETC**

International Society for Geometry and Graphics e: **ISGG**

International Society for Geothermal Engineering e: **ISGE**

International Society for Magnetic Resonance in Medicine e: **ISMRM**

International Society for Medical and Psychological Hypnosis e: **ISMPH**

International Society for Mountain Medicine e: **ISMM**

International Society for/of Bioclimatology and Biometeorology e: **ISBB**

International Society for/of Cell Biology e: **ISCB**

International Society for/of Disaster Medicine e: **ISDM**

International Society for/of Human and Animal Mycology e: **ISHAM**

International Society for/of Internal Medicine e: **ISIM**

International Society for/of Oncodevelopmental Biology and Medicine e: **ISOBM**

International Society for/of Photogrammetry [and] Remote Sensing e: **ISPRS**

International Society for/of Plant Molecular Biology e: **ISPMB**

International Society for/of Respiratory Protection e: **ISRP**

International Society for/of Technology Assessment in Health Care e: **ISTAHC**

International Society for Orbital Disorders e: **ISOD**

International Society for Orthomolecular Medicine e: **ISOM**

International Society for Quality in Health Care e: **ISQua**

International Society for Telemedicine e: **IsfT**

International Society for the Advancement of Humanistic Studies in Gynecology e: **ISFAHSIG**

International Society for the History of Islamic Medicine e: **ISHIM**

International Society for the History of Medicine e: **ISHM**

International Society for the Prevention and Mitigation of Natural Hazards e: **NHS**

International Society for the Prevention of Water Pollution e: **ISPWP**

International Society for the Protection of Animals e: **ISPA**

International Society for the Protection of Horses e: **ISPH**

International Society for the Protection of Mustangs and Burros e: **ISPMB**

International Society for the Study of Subtle Energies and Energy Medicine e: **ISSSEEM**

International Society for the Study of the Human-Companion Animal Bond e: **ISSHCAB**

International Society for Tropical Ecology e: **ISTE**

International Society of Animal License Collectors e: **ISALC**

International Society of Arthroscopy, Knee Surgery, and Orthopaedic Sports Medicine e: **ISAKOS**

International Society of Behavioural Medicine e: **ISBM**

International Society of Biometeorology e: **ISB**

International Society of Biophysical Medicine e: **ISBM**

International Society of Cardiovascular Surgeons e: **ISCVS**

International Society of Chemical Ecology e: **ISCE**

International Society of Complex Environmental Studies e: **ISCES**

International Society of Computers in Obstetrics, Neonatology, Gynecology e: **ISCONG**

International Society of Cranio-Facial Biology e: **ISCFB**

International Society of Cybemetic Medicine e: **ISCM**

International Society of Dermatology: Tropical, Geographic and Ecologic e: **ISD**

International Society of Development[al]
Biologists e: **ISDB**

International Society of Doctors for the
Environment e: **ISDE**

International Society of Ecotoxicology and
Environmental Safety e: **SECOTOX**

International Society of Emergency Medical
Services e: **ISEMS**

International Society of Environmental
Micropaleontolgy, Microbiology, and
Meiobenthology e: **ISEMMM**

International Society of Ethnobiology e:
ISE

International Society of Free Space
Colonizers e: **I5FSC**, e: **ISFSC**

International Society of Geographic
Ophthalmology e: **ISGO**

International Society of Geographical
Pathology e: **ISGP**

International Society of Healthcare
Executives e: **ISHE**

International Society of Indoor Air Quality
and Climate e: **ISIAQ**

International Society of Mathematical
Biology e: **ISMB**

International Society of Medical Hydrology
[and Climatology] e: **ISMH**

International Society of Medical Hydrology
and Climatology e: **ISMHC**

International Society of Mediterranean
Ecology e: **ISOMED**

International Society of Naturalists e:
INSONA

International Society of Naturopathic
Physicians e: **ISNP**

International Society of Oncodevelopmental
Biology and Medicine e: **ISOMB**

International Society of Plastic Surgeons
e: **ISPS**

International Society of Police Surgeons e:
ISPS

International Society of Prenatal and
Perinatal Psychology and Medicine e:
ISPP

International Society of Psychiatric-Mental
Health Nursing e: **ISPN**

International Society of Psychosomatic
Obstetrics and Gynaecology e: **ISPOG**

International Society of Radiobiology e:
ISR

International Society of Reproductive
Medicine e: **ISRM**

International Society of Travel Medicine
e: **ISTM**

International Socio-Ecological Union e:
ISEU

International Solar Polar [Mission] e: **ISP**

International Solar Polar Mission e: **ISPM**

International Southern Ocean Studies (or
Study) e: **ISOS**

International Space Congress e: **ISC**

International Space Corporation e: **ISC**

International Space Explorer e: **ISE**

International Space Observatory e: **ISO**

International Space Research Group e:
ISRG

International Space Station e: **ISS**

International Space Station Alpha e: **ISSA**

International Space Technology Assessment
Program e: **ISTAP**

International Space University e: **ISU**

International Space Year e: **ISY**

International Standard Atmosphere e: **ISA**

International Standard Statistical
Classification of Aquatic Animals and
Plants e: **ISSCAAP**

International Standards Organization
standards on environmental management
systems e: **ISO 14000**

International Standing Committee for the
Study of Corrosion and Protection of
Underground Pipelines e: **ICC**

International Standing Committee on Water
Quality and Treatment e: **ISCWQT**

International Statistical Ecology
Program[me] e: **ISEP**

International Study Group for Waterworks
in the Rhine Catchment Area e:
ISGWRCA

International Sun-Earth Explorer e: **ISEE**

International Sun Earth Explorer e: **ISSE**

International Sun Earth Explorer Satellite
e: **ISEE Satellite**

International Sun-Earth Physics Program
e: **ISEPP**

International Sun-Earth Physics Satellite
e: **ISEPS**

International Sun Earth Physics Satellites
Program e: **ISEPS Program**

International Sun Earth Physics Satellites
Program[me] e: **ISEPS Program[me]**

International Symposium on Aerospace
Nuclear Propulsion e: **ISASNP**

International Symposium on Ecological
Aspects of Tree-Ring Analysis e:
ISEATRA

International Symposium on Environmental
Biogeochemistry e: **ISEB**

International Symposium on Environmental
Pollution e: **ISEP**

International Symposium on Identification
and Measurement of Environmental
Pollutants e: **ISIMEP**

International Symposium on Medical
Imaging and Image Interpretation e:
ISMIII

International Symposium on Operational
Fisheries Oceanography e: **ISOFO**

International Symposium on Rocket and
Satellite Meteorology e: **ISRSM**

International Symposium on Space
Electronics e: **ISSET**

International Symposium on Space
Technology and Science e: **ISTS**

International Symposium on the Transport
of Dangerous Goods by Sea and Inland
Waterways e: **ISTDG**

International Technical Conference on [the]
Protection of Nature e: **ITCPN**

International Technieal Conference on the
Protection of Nature e: **ICCPN**

International Technogeographical Society
e: **ITS**

International Technology Environmental
[data base] Management [system] e:
ITEM

International Tidal Wetland Rice
Observational Nursery e: **ITRON**

International Tide-Prone Rice
Observational Nursery e: **ITPRON**

International TOGA [Tropical Ocean Global
Atmosphere] Project Office e: **ITPO**

International Tourist Health Association e:
ITHA

International Traffic Medicine Association
e: **ITMA**

International Training Center (or Centre)
for Water Resources Management e:
ITCWRM

International Training Centre for Water
Resources Management e: **CEFIGRE**

International Training in Health [Program]
e: **INTRAH**

International Training Network for Low-
Cost [Water] Supply and Sanitation e:
ITN

International Travelers Health Institute e:
ITHI

International Tribunal for the Law of the
Sea e: **ITLOS**

International Ultraviolet Explorer [space
vehicle] e: **IUE**

International Underwater Contractors, Inc.
e: **IUC**

International Underwater Research
Corporation e: **IURC**

International Underwater Spearfishing
Association e: **IUSA**

International Union for Circumpolar Health
e: **IUCH**

International Union for Conservation [of
Nature and Natural Resources] e: **IUC**

International Union for Conservation of
Nature and Natural Resources. Technical
Meeting e: **IUCN**

International Union for Health Education
e: **IUHE**

International Union for Health Promotion
and Education e: **IUHPE**

International Union for Nature and Natural
Resources-Primate Specialists Group e:
IUCNPSG

International Union for/of Biochemistry and
Molecular Biology e: **IUBMB**

International Union for/of Geodesy and
Geophysics e: **IUGG**

International Union for/of Pure and Applied
Biology e: **IUPAB**

International Union for Physical and
Engineering Sciences in Medicine e:
IUPESM

International Union for Protecting Public
Morality e: **IUPM**, e: **I.U.P.P.M.**

International Union for [the] Conservation
of Nature and Natural Resources e:
IUCNNR

International Union for the Conservation of
Nature/Environmental Law Centre e:
IUCN/ELC

International Union for the Conservation of
Nature/European Regional Office e:
IUCN/ERO

International Union for the Conservation of
Nature General Assembly e: **IUCNGA**

International Union for the Conservation of
Nature/Office for Central Europe e:
IUCN/CERO

International Union for the Conservation of
Nature/Office for the Commonwealth of
Independent States e: **IUCN/CIS**

International Union for the Protection of
Industrial Property e: **IIPIP**, e: **IUPIP**

International Union for the Protection of
Literary and Artistic Works e: **IUPLAW**

International Union for the Protection of
Nature e: **IUPN**

International Union for Thermal Medicine
and Climatothalassotherapy e: **IUTCT**,
e: **IUTMCT**

International Union of Biological Sciences
e: **IIUBS**, *e:* **IUBS**, *e:* **UBS**, *e:* **UIBS**

International Union of Game Biologists *e:*
IUGB

International Union of Geodesy and
Geophysics. Newsletter *e:* **IUGG Newsl**

International Union of Geological Sciences
Commission for Marine Geology *e:*
IUGS/CGM

International Union of Geological Sciences
Commission on Geological
Documentation *e:* **IUGS/COGEODOC**

International Union of Geological Sciences
Commission on Storage, Automatic
Processing and Retrieval of Geological
Data *e:* **IUGS/COGEODATA**

International Union of Geological Sciences
Commission on Tectonics *e:*
IUGS/COMTEC

International Union of Geological Services
[or Sciences] *e:* **IUGS**

International Union of Geophysical
Sciences *e:* **IUGS**

International Union of Medical Automobile
Clubs *e:* **IUMAC**

International Union of Microbiological
Societies-Bacteriological (or
Bacteriology) Division *e:* **IUMSBD**

International Union of Microbiological
Societies [or Sciences] *e:* **IUMS**

International Union of Radioecologists *e:*
IUR

International Union of Railway Medical
Services *e:* **IURMS**, *e:* **UIMC**

International Union of School and
University Health and Medicine *e:*
IUSUHM

International Union of Societies for the Aid
of Mental Health *e:* **IUSAMH**

International Union of the Medical Press
e: **IUMP**

International Union of United Automobile,
Aerospace and Agricultural Implement
Workers of America *e:* **IUUAAAIWA**

[International Union of] United
Automobile, Aerospace and Agricultural
[Implement] Workers of America *e:*
UAW

International Union, United Automobile,
Aerospace, and Agricultural Implement
Workers of America *e:* **United Auto
Workers**

International Union[s] for [the]
Conservation of Nature and Natural
Resources *e:* **IUCN**

International University of New Medicine
e: **IUNM**

International Upland Rice Observational
Nursery *e:* **IURON**

International Upland Rice Observational
Nursery-Early *e:* **IURON-E**

International Upland Rice Observational
Nursery-Medium *e:* **IURON-M**

International Veterinary Academy on
Disaster Medicine *e:* **IVADM**

International Veterinary Association for
Animal Production *e:* **IVAAP**

International Water Association *e:* **IWA**

International Water Information System *e:*
IWIS

International Water Management Institute
e: **IWMI**

International Water Power and Dam
Construction *e:* **Int Water Power Dam
Constr**, *e:* **IWPCD**

International Water Resources Association
e: **IWRA**

International Water Supply Association *e:*
IWSA

International Water Supply Association of
South-Central and West Asian Countries
e: **ASCEW**

International Water Treatment and Shipping
Consulting Engineers GmbH *e:* **IWTS**

International Water Tribunal *e:* **IWT**

International Water Works Association *e:*
IWWA

International Waterfowl [and Wetlands]
Research Bureau *e:* **IWRB**

International Waterfowl and Wetlands
Research Bureau *e:* **IWWRB**

International Waterfowl Research Institute
e: **IWRI**

International Waterpolo Board *e:* **IWP**

International Waterproofing Association *e:*
IWA

International Waterways and Docks *e:*
IWD

International Weddell Sea Oceanographic
Expedition *e:* **IWSOE**

International Wild Life Protection *e:*
IWLP

International Wild Rice Association *e:*
IWRA

International Wild Waterfowl Association
e: **IWWA**

International Wildcat Resources *e:* **IWC**

International Wilderness Leadership
Foundation *e:* **IWLF**

International Wildfowl Research Bureau *e:*
IWRB

International Wildfowl Research Institute
e: **IWRI**

International Wildlife *e:* **Int Wildlife**

International Wildlife Coalition *e:* **IWC**

International Wildlife Rehabilitation
Council *e:* **IWRC**

International Wildrose Resources, Inc. *e:*
IWS

International Women's Health Coalition *e:*
IWHC

International Year of the Oceans *e:* **IYO**

International Young Nature Friends *e:*
IYNF

International Youth Federation [for
Environmental Studies and Conservation]
e: **IYF**

Internationale Arbeitsgemeinschaft der
Wasserwerke im Rheineinzugsgebiet *d:*
IAWR

Internationale Assoziation für
Geomagnetismus und Aeronomie *d:*
IAGA

Internationale Ausstellung für Heiz-, Kühl-
und Klimatechnik *d:* **INTERKLIMA**

Internationale Ausstellung für
Krankenhausausstattung und
Medizinische Instrumente *d:* **MEDIC-
ASIA**

Internationale Chrétienne Professionnelle
pour les Industries Graphiques et
Papetières *f:* **ICPIGP**

Internationale des Amis de la Nature *f:*
IAN

Internationale des Jeunes Amis de la Nature
f: **IJAN**

Internationale Fachausstellung Kälte- und
Klimatechnik *d:* **IKK**

Internationale Fachmesse für Abwasser-
und Abfalltechnik *d:* **IFAT**

Internationale Fachmesse für Arbeitsschutz,
Feuerverhütung, Bewachung und
Umweltschutz *d:* **SCHUTZ**

Internationale Fachmesse für Heizung,
Klima, Kälte *d:* **INTERCLIMA**

Internationale Fachmesse für
Umweltgestaltung *d:* **public design**

Internationale Fachmesse Sanitär, Heizung,
Klima *d:* **ISH**

Internationale Fachmesse
Wasserversorgung *d:* **IFW**

Internationale Geographische Union *d:*
IGU

Internationale Gesellschaft für Aerosole in
der Medizin *d:* **IGAeM**

Internationale Gesellschaft für
Allgemeinmedizin *d:* **IGAM**

Internationale Gesellschaft für Prospektive
Medizin *d:* **IGPM**

Internationale Gesellschaft für
Radiobiologie *d:* **I.G.R.**

Internationale Gesundheitsvorschriften *d:*
IGV

Internationale Gewässerschutzkommission
für den Bodensee *d:* **IGKB**

Internationale Hydrographische
Organisation *d:* **IHO**

Internationale Hydrologische Dekade *d:*
IHD

Internationale Indische-Ozean-Expedition
d: **IIOE**

Internationale Klassifikation der Prozeduren
der Medizin, German Extension *d:*
ICPM-GE

Internationale Kommission für die
Hydrologie des Rheingebietes *d:* **KHR**

Internationale Liga Ärzte für die
Abschaffung der Tierversuche" *d:*
ILÄAT

Internationale Luft- und
Raumfahrtausstellung *d:* **ILA**

Internationale Medizinische Publikationen
d: **I.M.P.**

Internationale Messe und Kongreß für
Medizin *d:* **MEDICIN**

Internationale Meteorologische
Organisation *d:* **IMO**

Internationale Naturistenföderation *d:* **INF**

Internationale Normalatmosphäre *d:* **INA**

Internationale Orientierungslauf-Föderation
d: **IOF**

Internationale Orientierungslauf-
Föderation, Wissenschaftliche
Arbeitsgruppe *d:* **IOFWA**

Internationale Pflanzengeographische
Exkursion *d:* **I.P.E.**

Internationale Revue der gesamten
Hydrobiologie und Hydrographie *d:*
IRgHydr.

internationale Standardatmosphäre *d:* **ISA**

Internationale Technogeographische
Gesellschaft e.V. *d:* **ITG**

Internationale Tierärztliche Vereinigung für
Tierproduktion *d:* **ITVTP**

Internationale Tierärztliche Vereinigung für
Zootechnik *d:* **ITVZ**

Internationale Umweltschutzunion *d:* **IU**

Internationale Union für die Erhaltung der Natur und der natürlichen Hilfsquellen *d:* **IUCN**

Internationale Union für Geodäsie und Geophysik *d:* **IUGG**

Internationale Vereinigung für Natürliche Wirtschaftsordnung *d:* **INWO**

Internationale Wassersportausstellung *d:* **INTERBOOT**

Internationale Wassertransport-Gesellschaft *d:* **IWTG**

Internationaler Austausch ozeanographischer Daten und Informationen *d:* **IODE**

Internationaler Ferderation of Information Processing *e:* **IFIP**

Internationaler Förderkreis für Raumfahrt Hermann Oberth-Werner von Braun *d:* **IFR**

Internationaler Kurdienst, Gesellschaft für medizinischen Tourismus *d:* **IKD**

Internationaler Praktikantenaustausch für Studierende der naturwissenschaftlich-technischen Studiengänge *d:* **IAESTE**

Internationaler Tierärztlicher Kongreß *d:* **I.T.K.**, *d:* **ITK**

Internationaler Verband für wasserbauliches Versuchswesen *d:* **IVWV**

Internationales Archiv für Arbeitsmedizin *d:* **Int Arch Arbeitsmed**

Internationales Biologisches Programm *d:* **IBP**

Internationales Centrum für Anlagenbau, Verkehr, Bau- und Umwelttechnik *d:* **ICA**

Internationales Dokumentationssystem [für Informationsquellen über die Umwelt] *d:* **INFOTERRA**

Internationales geologisches Programm der UNESCO *d:* **IGCP**

Internationales Geophysikalisches Jahr *d:* **IGJ**

Internationales Geosphären-Biosphären Programm *d:* **IGBP**

Internationales Geosphären-Biosphärenprogramm/ Internationales Änderungssystem zur Analyse, Forschung und Fortbildung *d:* **IGBP/START**

Internationales Hydrographisches Büro *d:* **IHB**

Internationales Hydrologisches Programm der UNESCO *d:* **IHP**

Internationales Institut für Baubiologie *d:* **IBR**

Internationales Institut für Umwelt und Gesellschaft *d:* **IIUG**

Internationales Quelenorientiertes Informationssystem *d:* **IQIS**

Internationales Tierseuchenamt *d:* **ITA**

Internationales Transferzentrum für Umwelttechnologie *d:* **ITUT**

Internet Display and Remote Access Project *e:* **INDRA Project**

Internet Health Resources *e:* **IHR**

Internet Health Watch *e:* **IHW**

Internet Healthcare Coalition *e:* **IHC**

Internet Journal of Health Promotion *e:* **IJHP**

Internet Journal of Public Health Education *e:* **I-JPHE**

Internet Medicine *e:* **IM**

Internet Operating Environment *e:* **IOE**

Internet remote job entry *e:* **IRJE**

Internet Weather Report *e:* **IWR**

Interocean Line *e:* **IL**

Interoceanic Regional Authority [Panama] *e:* **ARI**

Interorbital Space Vehicle *e:* **IOSV**, *e:* **ISV**

Interorbital Vehicle Assembly Mode *e:* **IVAM**

Interplanetary Meteoroid Experiment *e:* **IME**

Interplay of Engineering with Biology and Medicine *e:* **IEBM**

Interpretation Division, Environment Canada-Parks, Ottawa, Ontario *e:* **OOEIB**

interpretieren *d:* **interpr**

interpretiert *d:* **interpr**

Interprocess Communication Environment *e:* **IPCE**

Interprofessional Commission on Environmental Design *e:* **ICED**

Interprofessional Council of Environmental Design[ers] *e:* **ICED**

Interregional Cell for the Environment *e:* **IRCEL**

Intersessional Working Group on IOC's Possible Role in Relation to the United Nations Convention on the Law of the Sea *e:* **IOC-LOS**

Intersociety Council on Continuing Medical Education *e:* **ICCME**

Intersociety Council on Laboratory Medicine of Canada *e:* **ICLMC**

Intersociety Safety and Health Committee *e:* **ISHC**

Interspace *e:* **IS**

Interstate Clearing House on Mental Health *e:* **ICHMH**

Interstate Conference on Water Policy *e:* **ICWP**

Interstate Conference on Water Problems *e:* **ICWP**

Interstate Council on Hydrometeorology of the Countries of the Commonwealth of Independent States *e:* **ICH CIS**

Interstate Council on the Problems of the Aral Sea *e:* **ICAS**

Interstate Natural Gas Association *e:* **INGA**

Interstate Natural Gas Association of America *e:* **INGAA**

Interstate Postgraduate Medical Association of North America *e:* **IPMANA**

Interstitial Water *e:* **ISE**, *e:* **ISW**, *e:* **IW**

Intervirology [International Union of Microbiological Societies] *e:* **Intervirol**

Interwest Medical Corporation *e:* **IMCO**

Intracellular Water *e:* **ICW**

Intracoastal Waterway *e:* **IWW**

Intracostal Space *e:* **ICS**

Intraseasonal Atmospheric Oscillation *e:* **ISO**

Intreprindere de Lucrari Forestiere *ru:* **ILF**

Introduction to Biomedical Research Program *e:* **IBRP**

Inuit Circumpolar Conference *e:* **ICC**

Inventario Internacional de Cruceros Geológicos y Geofísicos *s:* **IG-GCI**

Inventory of the EDI Information Systems in the Baltic Sea Countries *e:* **EDI-Baltic-S-82326**

invertieren *d:* **inv**

invertiert *d:* **inv**

investieren *d:* **inv**

investiert *d:* **inv**

Investigaciones Biológicas sobre las Poblaciones y los Sistemas Marinos del Antártico *s:* **- f**

Investigation of the Geothermal Potential of the UK. British Geological Survey *e:* **Inrest Geotherm Potential UK Br Geol Surv**

Investigational New Animal Drug Application *e:* **INADA**

Involuntary Second SEA [Southeast Asia] Tour *e:* **ISST**

IOC Black Sea Regional Committee *e:* **IOC-BSRC**

IOC Committee for Global Ocean Observing System *e:* **I-GOOS**

IOC Committee on International Oceanographic Data and Information Exchange *e:* **IOC-IODE**

IOC Committee on Ocean Processes and Climate *e:* **IOC-OPC**

IOC International Oceanographic Data and Information Exchange *e:* **IODE**

IOC Regional Committee for the Cooperative Investigation in the North and Central Western Indian Ocean *e:* **IOCINCWIO**

IOC Regional Committee for the Southern Ocean *e:* **IOCSOC**

IOC [UNESCO] Working Committee on International Oceanographic Data Exchange *e:* **IODE**

Iowa Department of Public Health *e:* **IDPH**

Iowa Foundation for Medical Care *e:* **IFMC**

Iowa Geological Survey *e:* **IGS**

Iowa Geological Survey Bureau *e:* **IGSB**

Iowa Geological Survey Web Server *e:* **IGSWS**

Iowa Medicine *e:* **Iowa Med**

Iowa Natural Areas nventory *e:* **INAI**

Iowa State Medical Society *e:* **ISMS**

Iowa State Water Resources Research Institute *e:* **ISRRI**, *e:* **ISWRRI**

Iowa Veterinary Medical Association *e:* **IVMA**

Iowa Water Resources Data System *e:* **IWARDS**

Iranian National Centre for Oceanography *e:* **INCO**

Iraq Natural History Museum. Report *e:* **IRNRAJ**

IRCS [International Research Communications System] Medical Science. Library Compendium *e:* **IRLCAW**, *e:* **IRLCD**

IRE [Institute of Radio Engineers] Transactions on Telemetry and Remote Control *e:* **IRE Trans Telem Remote Control**

IRE Transactions on Bio-Medical Electromics *e:* **IRE Trans Bio Med Electron**

Irish Fisheries Investigations. Series A. Freshwater *e:* **Ir Fish Invest Ser A Freshwater**

Irish Free State Medical Union *e:* **IFSMU**

Irish Geographical Bulletin *e:* **Ir Geogr B**

Irish Georgian Society *e:* **IGS**

Irish Georgian Society. Bulletin *e:* **Irish Georgisn Soc Bull**

Irish Georgian Society. Quarterly Bulletin
e: **Irish Georgian Soc Qly Bull**

Irish Journal of Medical Science e: **Irish J Med**

Irish Journal of Medical Science [Dublin]
e: **Ir J Med Sci**

Irish Journal of Psychological Medicine e:
Ir J Psychol Med

Irish Journal of Psychotherapy and
Psychosomatic Medicine e: **Ir J Psychother Psychosom Med**

Irish Medical Association e: **I.M.A.**

Irish Medical Journal e: **Irish Med J**

Irish Medical Journal [Dublin] e: **Ir Med J**

Irish Medical Times e: **Irish Med Times**

Irish Medicines Board e: **IMB**

Irish Naturalists' Journal e: **Ir Nat J**

Irish Naturist Association, Dublin e: **INA**

Irish Society of Travel Medicine e: **ISTM**

Irish Underwater Council e: **IUC**

Irish Water Spaniel Club of America e:
IWSCA

Irish Wildfowl Committee. Publication e:
Irish Wildfowl Comm Publ

Iroquois National Wildlife Refuge e:
INWR

IRPA Bulletin [International Radiation
Protection Association, France] f: **IRPA Bull**

Irrespirable Atmosphere e: **IA**

Irrigation and Water Supply Commission
e: **IWSC**

Irvine Ranch Water District e: **IRWD**

ISA [Instrument Society of America
Proceedings. National Aerospace
Instrumentation Symposium e: **ISA Proc Natl Aerosp Instrum Symp**

Isarco Hydro-Electric Company e: **IHY MAT**

ISCE Newsletter [International Society of
Chemical Ecology] e: **ISCE Newsl**

ISDN Remote Power Control[ler] e: **IRPC**

ISGE [International Society for Geothermal
Engineering] Transactions and
Geothermal World Journal e: **ISGE Trans Geotherm World J**

ISGE [International Society or Geothermal
Engineering] Transactions and the
Geothermal Journal e: **ISGE Trans Geotherm J**

ISIS Gesellschaft für biologische Aquarien-
und Terrarienkunde zu München e.V. d:
ISIS

Islamic Medical Association of North
America e: **IMANA**

Islamic Medical Association [of South
Africa] e: **IMA**

Islamic Network of Water Resources
Development and Mangement e:
INWARDAM

Islamic Organization for Medical Sciences
e: **IOMS**

Islamic Republic of Iran Meteorological
Organization e: **IRIMO**

Island-Pferde-Züchter- und Besitzer-
Vereinigung d: **IPZV**

islands of South Pacific from Madagascar in
Indian Ocean to Hawaiian Islands in e:
Austronesia

Isles of the Sea e: **IoS**

ISO-Imaging Photopolarimeter e:
ISOPHOT

Isoplanar Integrated Injection Logic II 3-
Micron (Second Generation) High
Performance Bipolar Technology e: **I³L-II**

Isotope and Radiation Research on Animal
Diseases and Their Vectors. Proceedings
e: **Isot Radiat Res Anim Dis Vec**

Isotope Geology e: **IG**

Isotope Geoscience e: **Isot Geosci**

Isotopes in the Hydrological Cycle e:
ISOHYC

Isozymes. Current Topics in Biological and
Medical Research e: **Isozymes Curr Top Biol Med Res**

ISPRS Journal of Photogrammetry and
Remote Sensing [International Society of
Photogrammetry and Remote Sensing,
Netherlands] n: **ISPRS J Photogramm Remote Sens**

Israel Aerospace Medicine Institute e:
IAMI

Israel Association of Environmental
Engineers e: **IAEE**

Israel Centre for Waterworks Appliances
e: **ICWA**

Israel Geographical Society e: **IGS**

Israel Geological Society. Annual Meeting
e: **Isr Geol Soc Annu Meet**

Israel. Geological Survey. Bulletin e:
ISGBBC, e: **Isr Geol Surv Bull**

Israel. Geological Survey. Geological Data
Processing Unit. Report e: **Isr Geol Surv Geol Data Process Unit Rep**

Israel. Geological Survey. Report e: **Isr Geol Surv Rep**

Israel. Hydrological Service. Report e: **Isr Hydrol Serv Rep**

Israel Institute for Biological Research e:
IIBR

Israel. Institute of Animal Science.
Scientific Activities e: **Isr Inst Anim Sci Sci Act**, e: **SAISDP**

Israel. Institute of Plant Protection.
Scientific Activities e: **Isr Inst Plant Prot Sci Act**

Israel. Institute of Soils and Water.
Scientific Activities e: **Isr Inst Soils Water Sci Act**

Israel Journal of Dental Medicine e: **Isr J Dent Med**

Israel Journal of Earth-Sciences e: **Isreal J Earth Sci**, e: **Isr J Earth-Sci**

Israel Journal [of] Experimental Medicine
e: **Isr J Exp Med**

Israel Journal of Medical Sciences e:
IJMS, e: **Israel J Med Sc**, e: **Isr J Med S[ci]**

Israel Journal of Medical Sciences [Tel
Aviv] e: **Isr J Med Sci**

Israel Journal of Veterinary Medicine e:
Isr J Vet Med

Israel Medical Association e: **I.M.A.**

Israel Medical Journal e: **ISMJAV**, e: **Isr Med J**

Israel. Ministry of Agriculture. Water
Commission. Hydrological Service.
Hydrological Paper e: **Isr Min Agr Water Comm Hydrol Serv Hydrol Paper**

Israel National Committee for
Oceanographic Research e: **INCOR**

Israel National Committee on the Biosphere
and Environment e: **INCBE**

Israel Oceanographic and Limnological
Research. Annual Report e: **Isr Oceanogr Limnol Res Annu Rep**

Israel Space Agency e: **ISA**

Israel Space Agency Investigation About
Hornets e: **ISAIAH**

Issledovaniya po Geomagnetizmii,
Aeronomii i Fizike Solntsa R: **Issled Geomagn Aeron Fiz Solntsa**

Issledovaniya po Mikrobiologii R: **Issled Mikrobiol**

Issue Based Indian Ocean Network e:
IBION

Issues in Health Care of Women e: **Issues Health Care Women**

Issues in Law and Medicine [Terre Haute]
e: **Issues Law Med**

Issues in Mental Health Nursing e: **Issues Ment Health Nurs**

Istanbul Medical Faculty Medical Bulletin.
Istanbul University e: **Istanbul Med Fac Med Bull Istanbul Univ**

Istanbul Universitesi Fen Fakultesi
Hidrobiologi Arastirma Enstitusu
Yayinlari z: **Istanbul Univ Fen Fak Hidrobiol Arastirma Enst Yayin**

Istanbul Universitesi Observatuari Yazilari
z: **Istanbul Univ Obs Yazilari**

Istanbul Universitesi Veteriner Fakultesi
Dergisi/Journal of the Faculty of
Veterinary Medicine. University of
Istanbul z: **Istanbul Univ Vet Fak Derg J Fac Vet Med Univ Istanbul**

Istanbul University. Medical Bulletin e:
Istanbul Univ Med Bull

Istanbul University. Medical Faculty.
Medical Bulletin e: **Istanbul Univ Med Fac Med Bull**

Istanbul University. Review of the
Geographical Institute. International
Edition e: **Istanbul Univ Rev Geog Inst Internat Ed**

Istituto di Fisica dell'Atmosfera i: **IFA**

Istituto di Medicina Aeronautica i: **I.M.A.**

Istituto di Medicine Sociale i: **IMS**

Istituto di Microbiologia Agraria e Tecnica
i: **IMAT**

Istituto Geografico Agustin Codazzi i: **IGAC**

Istituto Geografico de Agostini i: **IGA**, s: **IGA**

Istituto Geografico Militare i: **IGM**

Istituto Geografico Militare Italiano i:
IGMI

Istituto Nazionale Geodetico i: **ING**

ISWS Bulletin. Illinois Water Survey e:
ISWS Bull III Water Surv

It aims to achieve, through closer cooperation among enterprises and research
institutes, progress on projects which
mainly concern environment e:
EUREKA

Italia Medica i: **Ital Med**

Italian Association for Medical Oncology
e: **AIOM**

Italian Journal of Medicine e: **Ital J Med**

Italian National Agency for New
technology, Energy and the Environment
e: **ENEA**

Italian Space Agency e: **ISA**

Italian Space Commission e: **ISC**

Italy. Ministero dell'Agricoltura e delle
Foreste Collana Verde i: **Italy Minist Agric For Collana Verde**

ITC Journal [International Institute for Aerial Survey and Earth Sciences, Netherlands] *n:* **ITC J**

Iterative Orbit Calculator *e:* **IOC**

Itogi Nauki Biologicheskie Ul'trastruktury *R:* **Itogi Nauki Biol Ultrastrukt**

ITT [International Telephone and Telegraph] Space Communications, Incorporated *e:* **ITTSPC**

IUCN [International Union for Conservation of Nature and Natural Resources] Bulletin *e:* **IUCN Bull**

IUCN [International Union for Conservation of Nature and Natural Resources] Publications. New Series *e:* **IUCN Publ New Ser**

IUCN [International Union for Conservation of Nature and Natural Resources] Yearbook *e:* **IUCN Yearb**

IUGG [International Union of Geodesy and Geophysics] Chronicle *e:* **IUGG Chron**

IUGG [International Union of Geodesy and Geophysics] Committee on Atmospheric Sciences *e:* **IUGG/CAS**

IUGG [International Union of Geodesy and Geophysics] Tsunami Commission *e:* **IUGG-TC**

IUGS Commission for Marine Geology *e:* **GMG**

Ivy Medical, Incorporated *e:* **IVMI**

Iz Istorii Biologii *R:* **Iz Istor Biol**

Izvestiia Akademii Nauk SSSR. Geograficheskaia. Moscow *R:* **Izv Ak Nauk SSSR.**

Izvestiia Akademii Nauk SSSR. Seriia Biologicheskaia [Moskva] *R:* **Izv Akad Nauk SSSR [Biol]**

Izvestija Akademii Nauk SSSR Serija Fizika Atmosfery i Okeana *R:* **Izv Akad Nauk SSSR Ser Fiz Atmosfer i Okeana**

Izvestiya Academy of Sciences USSR, Atmospheric and Oceanic Physics *R:* **Izv Acad Sci USSR, Atmos Ocean Phys**

Izvestiya Academy of Sciences USSR, Physics of the Solid Earth *R:* **Izv Acad Sci USSR, Phys Solid Earth**

Izvestiya Akademii Nauk Estonskoi SSR. Biologiia *R:* **Izv Akad Nauk Est SSR Biol**

Izvestiya Akademii Nauk SSSR, Fizika Atmosfery i Okeana [USSR] *R:* **Izv Akad Nauk SSSR, Fiz Atmos Okeana**

Izvestiya Akademii Nauk Turkmenskoi SSR, Fiziko-Tekhnicheskikh Khimicheskikh i Geologicheskikh Nauk *R:* **Izv Akad Nauk Turkm SSR, Fiz-Tekh Khim Geol**

Izvestiya Glavnoi Astronomicheskoi Observatorii v Pulkove *R:* **Izv Gl Astron Obs Pulkove**

Izvestiya Krymskoi Astroficheskoi Observatorii *R:* **Izv Krym Astrofiz Obs**

J

J. N. [Ding] Darling National Wildlife Refuge *e:* **JNDNWR**

JAAMI Journal. Association for the Advancement of Medical Instrumentation *e:* **JAAMI J Assoc Adv Med Instrum**

Jaarboek. Instituut voor Biologisch en Scheikundig Ondenoek van Landbouwgewassen *e:* **Jaarb Inst Biol Scheih Onden Landb Gewss**

Jacket [of] Water *e:* **JW**

jacket water after cooled *e:* **jwac**

Jackson Country Medical Society *e:* **JCMS**

Jackson County Medical Society, Kansas City *e:* **MoKJ**

Jackson's Index to the Georgia Reports *e:* **Jack Geo Ind**

Jacobsen's Law of the Sea *e:* **Jac Sea laws**

Jagd und Natur *d:* **Jagd Nat.**

Jahrbuch der St. Gallischen Naturwissenschaftlichen Gesellschaft *d:* **Jahrb. St. Gallische Nat.wiss. Ges.**

Jahrbuch der Geologischen Bundesanstalt *d:* **JGBA**

Jahrbuch der geologischen Reichsanstalt Wien *d:* **JGRAW**

Jahrbuch der Naturwissenschaftlichen Gesellschaft, St. Gallen *d:* **JNGSG**

Jahrbuch der Preussischen Geologischen Landesanstalt *d:* **JPGLA**

Jahrbuch der Preußischen Geologischen Landesanstalt *d:* **JPrGLA**

Jahrbuch der Schweizerischen naturforschenden Gesellschaft *d:* **Jahrb. Schweiz. nat.forsch. Ges.**

Jahrbuch der St. Gallischen Naturwissenschaftlichen Gesellschaft *d:* **Jahrb. St. Gallische Nat.wiss. Ges.**

Jahrbuch der wissenschaftlichen und praktischen Tierzucht *d:* **JwpTZ**

Jahrbuch des Schweizerischen Wasserwirtschaftsverbandes *d:* **Jahrb. Schweiz. Wasserwirtschafts-verb.**

Jahrbuch des Umwelt- und Technikrechts *d:* **JbUTR,** *d:* **UTR**

Jahrbuch des Vereins für Niederdeutsche Sprachforschung *d:* **JVndSp,** *d:* **JVNS**

Jahrbuch des Vereins zum Schutze der Alpenpflanzen und -Tiere *d:* **Jahrb. Ver. Schutz Alp.pflanzen -Tiere**

Jahrbuch für Mineralogie und Geologie *d:* **JfMuG**

Jahrbuch Schweizerische Akademie der Naturwissenschaften *d:* **Jahrb. Schweiz. Akad. Nat.wiss.**

Jahrbücher der Literatur. Verhandlungen des naturhistorisch-medicinischen Vereins zu Heidelberg *d:* **Heidelberg, Jahrb.Lit.**

Jahrbücher. Nassauischer Verein für Naturkunde *d:* **Jahrb Nassau Ver Naturkd**

Jahresbericht der Geographisch-Ethnographischen Gesellschaft, Zürich *d:* **JbGEGZ**

Jahresbericht der Naturforschenden Gesellschaft Graubünden *d:* **Jahresber. Nat.forsch. Ges. Graubünden**

Jahresbericht der Naturforschenden Gesellschaft, Hannover *d:* **JNGH**

Jahresbericht des Oberrheinischen Geologischen Vereins *d:* **JORhGV**

Jahresbericht. Naturwissenschaftlicher Verein zu Wuppertal *d:* **Jber Narw Ver Wuppertal**

Jahresbericht/Schweizerische Akademie der Medizinischen Wissenschaften *d:* **Jahresber Schweiz Akad Med Wiss**

Jahresbericht über die Leistungen auf dem Gebiete der Veterinär-Medizin *d:* **Jahresb Leistung Vet-Med**

Jahresbericht Veterinär-Medizin *d:* **Jahresb Vet Med**

Jahresberichte der Wetterauischen Gesellschaft für die Gesamte Naturkunde zu Hanau *d:* **Jahresber Wetterauischen Ges Gesamte Naturkd Hanau**

Jahresheft. Geologisches Landesamt in Baden Württemberg *d:* **Jahresh Geol Landesamtes Baden Württemb**

Jahresheft. Verein für Vaterländische Naturkunde in Württemberg *d:* **J Ver Vaterl Naturk Württ**

Jahreshefte des Vereins für vaterländische Naturkunde in Württemberg *D:* **Jahresh. Ver. vaterl. Nat.kd. Württ.**

Jahreshefte. Gesellschaft für Naturkunde in Württemberg *d:* **Jahresh Ges Naturkd Württemb**

Jakarta Mandate on Marine and Coastal Biodiversity (or Biological Diversity) *e:* **JM**

Jamaica Geological Information System *e:* **JAMGIS**

Jamaica. Geological Survey Departmenl. Publication *e:* **Jamcaia Geol Survey Pub**

Jamaica. Geological Survey Department. Annual Report *e:* **Jamaica Geol Survey Dept Ann Rept**

Jamaica. Geological Survey Department. Bulletin *e:* **Jamaica Geol Survey Dept Bull**

Jamaica. Geological Survey Department. Economic Geology Report *e:* **Jam Geol Surv Dep Econ Geol Rep**

Jamaica. Geological Survey Department. Occasional Paper *e:* **Jamaica Geol Survey Dept Occ Pap**

Jamaica. Geological Survey Department. Short Paper *e:* **Jamaica Geol Survey Dept Short Pap**

Jamaica Medical Review *e:* **Jam Med Rev**

Jamaica. Mines and Geology Division. Special Publication *e:* **Jam Mines Geol Div Spec Publ**

Jamaica Water Properties *e:* **JWAT**

Janus Earth Observation Satellite *e:* **JEOS**

Japan Animal Wellfare Society *e:* **JAWS**

Japan Area Defence Environment *e:* **JADE**

Japan-Asia Sea Cable *e:* **JASC**

Japan Association for Medical Informatics *e:* **JAMI**

Japan Chemical Industry Ecology-Toxicology & Information Center *e:* **JETOC**

Japan Council for Quality Health Care *e:* **JCQHC**

Japan Earth Remote Sensing Satellite *e:* **JERS**

Japan Earth Resources Satellite *e:* **JERS-1**

Japan/East Sea *e:* **JES**

Japan Environment Agency *e:* **JEE**

Japan Environmental Agency *e:* **JEA**

Japan Environmental Systems *e:* **JES**

Japan ERS [Earth Resources Satellite] *e:* **JERS**

Japan Geological Survey. Bulletin *e:* **Jap Geol Surv Bull**

Japan Geological Survey. Report *e:* **Jap Geol Surv Rep**

Japan Geothermal Energy Association. Journal *e:* **Jap Geotherm Energy Ass J**

Japan-Germany Medical Reports *e:* **Jpn-Ger Med Rep**

Japan Hydrographic Office *e:* **JHO**

Japan Industrial Safety and Health Association *e:* **JISHA**

Japan International Biological Program *e:* **JIBC**

Japan International Biological Programme *e:* **JIBP**

Japan Journal of Water Research [Japan] *e:* **Jpn. J. Water Res.**

Japan Manned Space Systems Corporation *e:* **JAMSS**

Japan Medical Association *e:* **JMA**

Japan Medical Congress *e:* **JMC**

Japan Medical Depot *e:* **JMD**

Japan Medical Gazette *e:* **Japan Med Gaz**

Japan Medical Programming System *e:* **JAMPS**

Japan Medical Research Foundation. Publication *e:* **JMRPDC**, *e:* **Jpn Med Res Found Publ**

Japan Medical Society *e:* **JMS**

Japan Medical World *e:* **Japan Med World**

Japan Meteorological Agency *e:* **JMA**

Japan Meteorological Agency. Volcanological Bulletin *e:* **Jap Meteorol Agency Volcanol Bull**

Japan Meteorological Association *e:* **JMA**

Japan. National Institute of PolarResearch. Memoirs. Special Issue *e:* **JNIPRMSI**

Japan Overseas Christian Medical Cooperative Service *e:* **JOCS**

Japan Research Committee of Environmental Remote Sensing *e:* **JACERS**

Japan Science Review. Medical Sciences *e:* **Jpn Sci Rer Med Sci**

Japan Sea *e:* **JAP S**

Japan Sea Cable *e:* **JASC**

Japan Sea-Farming Association *e:* **JASFA**

Japan Society for Aeronautical and Space Sciences *e:* **JSASS**

Japan Society for Aeronautical and Space Sciences. Transactions *e:* **Jpn S Aeronaut Space Sci Trans**

Japan Society of Medical Electronics and Biological Engineering *e:* **JSMEBE**

Japan Society of Photogrammetry and Remote Sensing *e:* **JSPRS**

Japan Society of Snow and Ice *e:* **JSSI**

Japan Society of Ultrasonics in Medicine *e:* **JSUM**

Japan Society on Water Pollution Research *e:* **JSWPR**

Japan-U.S. Tropical Ocean Study *e:* **JUSTOS**

Japanese Air Defence Environment *e:* **JADE**

Japanese Archives of Internal Medicine *e:* **Jpn Arch Intern Med**

Japanese Archives of Intemal Medicine *e:* **Jap Arch Int Med**

Japanese Association for Acute Medicine *e:* **JAAM**

Japanese Association for Laboratory Animal Medicine *e:* **JALAM**

Japanese Association for Microbiology *e:* **JAM**

Japanese Association of Mineralogists Petrologists, and Economic Geologists. Journal *e:* **Jap Assoc Mineral Petrol Econ Geol J**

Japanese Asuka spacecraft *e:* **ASCA**

Japanese B Encephalitis [Medicine] *e:* **JBE**

Japanese Cloud and Climate Study *e:* **JACCS**

Japanese Earth Observation System *e:* **JEOS**

Japanese Earth Observing Satellite *e:* **JEOS**

Japanese Earth Remote-sensing Satellite-1 *e:* **JERS-1**

Japanese Earth Resource Remote-Sensing Satellite *e:* **JERS**

Japanese Earth Resources Satellite *e:* **JERS**

Japanese Earth Resources Satellite-OPS Sensor *e:* **JERS-OPS**

Japanese Earth Resources Sensing Satellite 1 *e:* **JERS-1**

Japanese Earthquake Prediction Plan *e:* **JEPP**

Japanese Expedition[s] of the Deep Sea *e:* **JEDS**

Japanese Geomorphological Union *e:* **JGU**

Japanese Hydrographic Office *e:* **J.H.O.**

Japanese Joumal of Aerospace Medicine and Psychology *e:* **KUISA**

Japanese Journal of Aerospace Medicine and Psychology *e:* **Jgn J Aerosp Med Psychol**

Japanese Journal of Animal Reproduction *e:* **Jpn J Anim Reprod**

Japanese Journal of Astronomy and Geophysics *e:* **Jap J Astr Geophys**, *e:* **Jpn J Astron Geohys**

Japanese Journal of Clinical and Experimental Medicine *e:* **Jpn J Clin Exp Med**

Japanese Journal of Clinical Medicine *e:* **Jap J Clin Med**, *e:* **Jpn J Clin Med**

Japanese Journal of Constitutional Medicine *e:* **Jpn J Const Med**

Japanese Journal of Ecology *e:* **Jap J Ecol**, *e:* **Jpn J Ecol**

Japanese Journal of Experimental Medicine *e:* **Jap J Exp M[ed]**

Japanese Journal of Experimental Medicine [Tokyo] *e:* **Jpn J Exp Med**

Japanese Journal of Geology and Geoaphy *e:* **Jpn J Geol Geogr**

Japanese Journal of Geology and Geography *e:* **Japanese Jour Geology and Geography**, *e:* **Jap J Geol Geogr**

Japanese Journal of Geophysics *e:* **Jap J Geophys**

Japanese Journal of Industrial Health *e:* **Jpn J Ind Health**

Japanese Journal of Medical Electronics and Biological Engineering *e:* **Jap J Med Electron & Biol Eng**, *e:* **Jpn J Med Electron Biol Eng**

Japanese Journal of Medical Electronics and Biological Engineering [Japan Society of Medical Electronics and Biological Engineering] *e:* **Jpn. J. Med. Electron. Biol. Eng.**

Japanese Journal of Medical Science and Biology *e:* **Jap J Med S[ci Biol]**

Japanese Journal of Medical Science and Biology [Tokyo] *e:* **Jpn J Med Sci Biol**

Japanese Journal of Medical Sciences. Part 1 *e:* **Jpn J Med Sci 1**

Japanese Journal of Medical Sciences. Part 6. Bacteriology and Parasitology *e:* **Jpn J Med Sci 6**

Japanese Journal of Medical Sciences. Part 2. Biochemistry *e:* **Jpn J Med Sci 2**

Japanese Journal of Medical Sciences. Part 3. Biophysics *e:* **Jpn J Med Sci 3**

Japanese Journal of Medical Sciences. Part 13. Dermatology and Urology *e:* **Jpn J Med Sci 13**

Japanese Journal of Medical Sciences. Part 10. Ophthalmology *e:* **Jpn J Med Sci 10**

Japanese Journal of Medical Sciences. Part 12. Oto-Rhino-Laryngology *e:* **Jpn J Med Sci 12**

Japanese Journal of Medical Sciences. Part 4. Pharmacology *e:* **Japan J Med Sc Pt 4 Pharmacol**

Japanese Journal of Medical Sciences. Part 9. Surgery, Onhopedy and Odontology *e:* **Jpn J Med Sci 9**

Japanese Journal of Medicine *e:* **Jap J Med**

Japanese Journal of Medicine [Tokyo] *e:* **Jpn J Med**

Japanese Journal of Michurin Biology *e:* **Jpn J Michurin Biol**

Japanese Journal of Microbiology *e:* **Jap J Micro[b]**, *e:* **Jpn J Microbiol**

Japanese Journal of Nuclear Medicine *e:* **Jpn J Nucl Med**

Japanese Journal of Obstetrics and Gynecology *e:* **Jpn J Obstet Gynecol**

Japanese Journal of Oral Biology *e:* **Jpn J Oral Biol**

Japanese Journal of Pedatric Surgery and Medicine *e:* **Jpn J Pediat Surg Med**

Japanese Journal of Physical Fitness and Sports Medicine *e:* **Jpn J Phys Fitess Sports Med**, *e:* **TAKAAN**

Japanese Journal of Psychosomatic Medicine *e:* **Jpn J Psychosom Med**, *e:* **SHIGD4**

Japanese Journal of Public Health *e:* **NKEZA4**

Japanese Journal of Tropical Medicine and Hygiene *e:* **Jpn J Trop Med Hyg**

Japanese Journal of Water Pollution Research [Japan] *e:* **Jpn. J. Water Pollut. Res.**

Japanese Journal ofGeology and Geography *e:* **Japan J Geol & Geog**

Japanese Language Environment *e:* **JLE**

Japanese Medical Abstract Scanning System *e:* **JAMASS**

Japanese Medical Abstracts Scanning System *e:* **JAMAS**

Japanese Medical Journal *e:* **Jpn Med J**

Japanese Meteorological Agency *e:* **J.M.A.**

Japanese National Oceanographic Data Centre [or Center] *e:* **JNODC**

Japanese Nuclear Medicine *e:* **JANMA**, *e:* **Jpn Nucl Med**

Japan[ese] Ocean[ographic] Data Center (or Centre) *e:* **JODC**

Japanese Pacific Climate Studies [or Study] *e:* **JAPACS**

Japanese Polar[-Orbiting] Platform *e:* **JPOP**

Japanese Progress on Climatology *e:* **Jap Prog Climatol**

Japanese Remote Sensing [satellite] *e:* **JRS**

Japan[ese] Resources Observation System Organization *e:* **JAROS**

Japanese Society for Laboratory Animal and Environment *e:* **JSLAE**

Japanese Society of Medical Imaging Technology *e:* **JAMIT**

Japanese Society of Medical Research on Alcoholism *e:* **JSMRA**

Japanese Space Shuttle Utilization Program *e:* **JSSUP**

Japanese Spacelab Mission *e:* **SPACELAB-J**

Japnese Journal of Medical Sciences. Part 8. Internal Medicine, Pediatry and Psychiatry *e:* **Jpn J Med Sci 8**

Japnese Journal of Medical Sciences. Part 5. Pathology *e:* **Jpn J Med Sci 5**

Japnese Journal of Medical Sciences. Part 7. Social Medicine and Hygiene *e:* **Jpn J Med Sci 7**

JAR on Medical *e:* **JAR-MED**

JARE [Japanese Antarctic Research Expedition] Scientific Reports. Series E. Biology *e:* **JARE Sci Rep Ser E Biol**

Jasmine Application Development Environment *e:* **JADE**

Java Api for XML-based Remote Procedure Call *e:* **JAX-RPC**

Java Card Workstation Development Environment *e:* **JCWDE**

Java Development Environment *e:* **JDE**

Java Interface for Geospatial Information *e:* **JIGI**

Java Remote Method Protocol *e:* **JRMP**

Javelin Experimental and Theoretical Physics Protection Oil Sands System *e:* **JEPOSS**

Jawaharlal Institute of Postgraduate Medical Education and Research *e:* **JIPMER**

JCI Health, Safety & Environmental Department *e:* **JHSE**

Jefferson Community College, Library, Water-town *e:* **VND**

Jefferson Medical College *e:* **JMC**

Jefferson Medical College of Philadelphia *e:* **JMCP**

Jeju University Journal. Natural Sciences *e:* **J Nat Sci**

Jenaische Zeilschrift für Medizin und Natuissenschaft *d:* **Jen Z Med Naturws**

Jenaische Zeitschrift für Medizin und Naturwissenschaft *d:* **Jenaische Z[ei]tschr[ift] [Med u Naturw]**

Jenaische Zeitschrift für Naturwissenschaft *d:* **Jenaische Ztschr Naturw**, *d:* **Jena Z Naturw[iss]**, *d:* **JZNw**

Jersey Wildlife Preservation Trust *e:* **JWM**, *e:* **JWPT**

Jet Propulsion Laboratory/Pilot Ocean Data System *e:* **JPL/PODS**

Jet Propulsion Laboratory. Space Programs Summary *e:* **JPL Space Programs Summ**

Jeunes Pour la Nature *f:* **JPN**

Jewish Association for the Protection of Girls, Women and Children *e:* **J.A.P.G.W.C.**

Jewish Health Organization of Great Britain *e:* **J.H.O.G.B.**

Jews for Animal Rights *e:* **JAR**

Jiangsu Medical Journal *e:* **Jiangsu Med J**

Jikeikai Medical Journal *e:* **Jikeitai Med J**

Jikken Dobustu. Experimental Animals [Tokyo] *j:* **Jikken Dobutsu**

Jindalee Ocean Surveillance Expert [System] *e:* **JOSE**

Jinsen Medical Journal *e:* **Jinsen Med J**

Job Safety and Health *e:* **Job Safe & H**, *e:* **JOSH**

Job Safety & Health Quarterly *e:* **JSHQ**

Jodrell Bank Observatory *e:* **JBO**

JOGN [Journal of Obstetric, Gynecologic and Neonatal Nursing] Nursing *e:* **JOGNB**

JOGN [Journal of Obstetric Gynecologic and Neonatal Nursing] Nursing *e:* **JOGN Nurs**

John C. Stennis Space Center *e:* **SSC**

John Curtin School of Medical Research *e:* **JCSMR**

John F. Kennedy Space Center Florida, Inc. *e:* **KSC**

John F. Kennedy Spaceflight Center *e:* **JFKSC**

John H. Burrows & Sons Ltd., Southend-On-Sea, United Kingdom *e:* **UkSsB**

John H. Nelson Environmental Study Area *e:* **NESA**

John Lawrence Interdisciplinary Symposium on the Physical and Biomedical Sciences *e:* **John Lawrence Interdiscip Symp Phys Biomed Sci**

John Muir Institute [for Environnental Studies] *e:* **JMI**

Johns Hopkins Medical Institutions *e:* **JHMI**

Johns Hopkins Medical Journal *e:* **Johns H Med**, *e:* **Johns Hopkins Med J**

Johns Hopkins Medical Journal. Supplement *e:* **Johns Hopkins Med J Suppl**

Johns Hopkins Oceanographic Studies *e:* **JHOS**, *e:* **Johns Hopkins Oceanogr Stud**

Johns Hopkins University, George Peabody Library, Baltimore *e:* **MdBJ-P**

Johns Hopkins University School of Hygiene and Public Health *e:* **JHUSHPH**

Johns Hopkins University, School of Hygiene and Public Health, Maternal and Child Health-Population Dynamics Library, Baltimore *e:* **MdBJ-H**

Johns Hopkins University School of Medicine *e:* **JHUSM**

Johns Hopkins University. Studies in Geology *e:* **Johns Hopkins Univ Studies in Geology**

Johns Hopkins University, Welch Medical Library *e:* **JHW**

Johns Hopkins University, William H. Welch Medical Library, Baltimore *e:* **MdBJ-W**

Johnson City Medical Center Hospital, Learning Resources Center, Johnson City *e:* **TJoMC**

Johnson County Mental Health Center, Mission *e:* **KMiJ**

Johnson-Sea-Link I *e:* **JSLI**

Johnson Space Center *e:* **JBC**

Johnson Space Center Payload Operations Center *e:* **JPOC**

Joint Agriculture-Weather Facility *e:* **JAWF**

Joint Air-Force NASA [National Aeronautics and Space Administration] *e:* **JAFNA**

Joint Air-Sea Interaction Program *e:* **JASIN**

Joint Air-Sea Interaction Program[me] *e:* **JASIN Program[me]**

Joint Air-Sea Interaction Project *e:* **JASIN**

Joint Airport Weather Studies (or Study) [project] *e:* **JAWS**

Joint Airworthiness Requirement on All Weather Operations *e:* **JAR-AWO**

Joint All-Weather Seeker *e:* **JAWS**

Joint Animal Welfare Council *e:* **JAWC**

Joint Approach Central Meteorological Advisory Service *e:* **JACMAS**

Joint Archive for Sea Level *e:* **JASL**

Joint Arctic Weather Stations *e:* **JAWS**

Joint Army-Navy-Air Force Sea Transport[ation] [Message] *e:* **JANAST**

Joint Army-Navy-Air-Force Sea Transportation Message *e:* **JANAST Message**

Joint Army-Navy Ocean Terminal *e:* **JANOT**

Joint Automated Weather Observing (or Observation) Program *e:* **JAWOP**

Joint Battlespace Infosphere *e:* **JBI**

Joint Board of Remote Sensing Activities *e:* **JOBRESA**

Joint Center for Research in the Management of Ocean Data *e:* **JCRMOD**

Joint Centre for Earth System Science *e:* **JCESS**

Joint Climate Program/Projects Office *e:* **JCP/PO**

Joint Climate Research Fund *e:* **JCRF**

Joint Commission for Black Sea Fisheries *e:* **JCBSF**

Joint Commission for Ocean and Marine Measurements *e:* **JCOMM**

Joint Commission [on] Accreditation of Healthcare Organizations *e:* **JCAHO**

Joint Commission on Allied Health in Ophthalmology *e:* **JCAHPO**

Joint Commission on Allied Health Personnel in Ophthalmology *e:* **JCAHPO**

Joint Commission on Competitive Safeguards and the Medical Aspects of Sports *e:* **JCCSMAS**

Joint Commission on Cooperation in the Field of Environmental Protection *e:* **JCCFEP**

Joint Commission on Healthcare Organizations *e:* **JCHO**

Joint Commission on Mental Health of Children *e:* **JCMHC**

Joint Commission on Mental Illness and Health *e:* **JCMIH**

Joint Commission on Sports Medicine and Science *e:* **JCSMS**

Joint Committee for Higher Medical Training *e:* **JCHMT**

Joint Committee of the Nordic Natural Science Research Council[s] *e:* **JCNNSRC**

Joint Committee on Cooperation in Studies of the World Ocean *e:* **JCCSWO**

Joint Committee on Health Policy [of the United Nations Children's Fund] *e:* **JCHP**

Joint Committee on Higher Professional Medical Education *e:* **JCHPME**

Joint Committee on Higher Training in Accident & Emergency Medicine *e:* **JCHT**

Joint Committee on Medicine and Biology *e:* **JCMB**

Joint Conference on Medical Conventions *e:* **JCMC**

Joint Continental Aerospace Defense Integration Staff *e:* **JCADIS**

Joint Coordinating Committee for Environmental Restoration and Waste Management *e:* **JCCEM**

Joint Council to Improve Health Care of the Aged *e:* **JCIHCA**

Joint Defense Space Communications Station *e:* **JDSCS**

Joint Documentation Service of European Space Research Organisation, Èuropean Industrial Space Group and the European Organizations *e:* **EURODOC**

Joint Environmental Data Analysis Center *e:* **JEDA**

Joint Environmental Department *e:* **JENV**

Joint Environmental Effects Program *e:* **JEEP**

Joint Environmental Monitoring *e:* **JEM**

Joint Environmental Research Unit *e:* **JERU**

Joint Environmental Service *e:* **JES**

Joint Environment[al] Simulator *e:* **JES**

Joint European Development of Tunable Diode Laser Absoprtion Spectometry for the Measurement of Atmospheric Gases *e:* **JETDLAG**

Joint European Medical Research Board *e:* **JEMRB**

Joint Executive Committee on Medicine and Biology *e:* **JECMB**

Joint Exercise Observation File *e:* **JEOF**

Joint Expeditions in the Indian Ocean Sector of the Southern Ocean *e:* **JEISSO**

Joint Experimental Committee on Medicine and Biology *e:* **JECMB**

Joint force Meteorological and oceanographic Forecast Unit *e:* **JMFU**

Joint force Meteorological and Oceanographic officer *e:* **JMO**

Joint Global Ocean Flux Study Global Synthesis *e:* **JGOFS GS**

Joint Global Ocean Flux Study Photosynthetic Measurements [task team] *e:* **JGOFS PM**

Joint Global Ocean Flux Study [Program] *e:* **JGOFS**

Joint Global Ocean Flux Study Scientific and Technical Committee *e:* **J-GOOS**

Joint Global Ocean Flux Study Scientific Steering Committee *e:* **JGOFS-SSC**

Joint Ice Center *e:* **IC**

Joint Ice Center/US Navy-NOAA/ *e:* **JIC**

Joint ICSU-UATI Coordinating Committee on Water Research *e:* **COWAR**

Joint Institute for Marine and Atmospheric Research [University of Hawaii] *e:* **JIMAR**

Joint Institute for [the] Study of the Atmosphere and Ocean *e:* **JISAO**

Joint Intelligence Center, Pacific Ocean Areas *e:* **JICPOA**

Joint International Climate Projects/Planning Office *e:* **JICP/PO**

Joint IOC-UNEP Intergovernmental Panel for the Global Investigation of Pollution in the Marine Environment, short name: Joint IOC-UNEP Intergovernment *e:* **IGP-GIPME**

Joint Kinematics and Geometry *e:* **JOKING**

Joint Medical Mobilization Office *e:* **JMMO**

Joint Medical Regulating Office *e:* **JMRO**

Joint Meteorological Board *e:* **JMB**

Joint Meteorological Committee *e:* **JMC**

Joint Meteorological Group *e:* **JMG**

Joint Meteorological Observing Facility *e:* **JMOF**

Joint Meteorological Radio Propagation Committee *e:* **JMRP**, *e:* **JMRP Committee**

Joint Meteorological Radio Propagation Subcommittee *e:* **JMRPS**

Joint Meteorological Rocket Network Steering Committee *e:* **JMRNSC**

Joint Meteorological Satellite Advisory Committee *e:* **JMSAC**

Joint Meteorological Satellite Communication *e:* **JMSC**

Joint Meteorological Satellite Program Office *e:* **JMSPO**

Joint Military Medical Command *e:* **JMMC**

Joint Mission Processing Environment *e:* **JMPE**

Joint North Sea Information System[s] [Group] *e:* **JONSIS**

Joint North Sea Wave [Analysis] Project *e:* **JONSWAP**

Joint North Sea Wave Atmosphere Program *e:* **JONSWAP**

Joint Numerical Weather Prediction Unit *e:* **JNWPU**

Joint Observation for Cometary Research *e:* **JOCR**

Joint Ocean Shipping Procedure[s] *e:* **JOSPRO**

Joint Ocean Surface Study *e:* **JOSS**

Joint Ocean Surveillance Information Centre *e:* **JOSIC**

Joint Ocean Wave Investigation Project *e:* **JOWIP**

Joint Oceanographic Assembly *e:* **JOA**

Joint Oceanographic Institutes (or Institution) for Deep Earth Sampling[s] *e:* **JOIDES**

Joint Oceanographic Institutions Deep Earth Sampling Program *e:* **JOIDESP**

Joint Oceanographic Institutions for Deep Earth Sampling Journal *e:* **JOIDES J[ournal]**

Joint Oceanographic North Sea Data Acquisition Program (or Project) *e:* **JONSDAP**

Joint Oceanographic Research Group *e:* **JORG**

Joint Oceanographic[s] Institutions, Inc. *e:* **JOI**

Joint Operational Climatological Support *e:* **JOCS**

Joint Operations Radar Airspace Control *e:* **JORAC**

Joint Organization for Solar Observations *e:* **JOSO**

Joint Organizing Committee [Global Atmospheric Research Program] *e:* **JOC**

Joint Panel on Oceanographic Tables and Standards *e:* **JPOTS**

Joint Regional Medical Planning Office *e:* **JRMPO**

Joint Review Committee for Ophthalmic Medical Personnel *e:* **JRCOMP**

Joint Review Committee for the Ophthalmic Medical Assistant[s] *e:* **JRCOMA**

Joint Review Committee on Education in Diagnostic Medical Sonography *e:* **JRCDMS**

Joint Review Committee on Educational Programs for the EMT [Emergency Medical Technician]-Paramedic *e:* **JRCEMT-P**

Joint Review Committee on Educational Programs in Nuclear Medicine Technology *e:* **JRCNMT**

Joint Scientific Committee for the WCRP [World Climate Reseach Programme] *e:* **JSC**, *e:* **JSC-WCRP**

Joint Sea-Air Interaction Experiment *e:* **JASIN**

Joint Service Medical Rehabilitation Unit *e:* **JSMRU**

Joint Service Software Engineering Environment *e:* **JSSEE**

Joint Space Command Intelligence Center *e:* **JSIC**

Joint Space Narrowing *e:* **JSN**

Joint Spacelab Working Group *e:* **JSLWG**

Joint Steering Committee of the World Climate Research Programme *e:* **JSC/WCRP**

Joint Unit for Research on the Urban Environment *e:* **JURUE**

Joint University Libraries, George Peabody College for Teachers, Nashville *e:* **TNJ-P**

Joint University Libraries, Vanderbilt Medical Center, Nashville *e:* **TNJ-M**

Joint Working Group ATMOS *e:* **JWGA**

JOM. Journal of Occupational Medicine [United States] *e:* **JOM J Occup Med**

Jones Medical Industries, Inc. *e:* **JMED**

Jones Spacelink Ltd. *e:* **SPLK**

Jonrnal. Medical Association of Formosa *e:* **J Med Ass Form**

Jordan Medical Journal *e:* **Jordan Med J**

Jordan National Geographic Centre *e:* **JNGC**

Jornal Brasileiro de Ginecologia *p:* **J Bras Ginecol**

Jornal Brasileiro de Medicina *p:* **J Bras Med**, *p:* **JBRMA**

Jornal de Medicina de Pernambuco *p:* **J Med Pernambuco**

Jornal do Medico *s:* **J Med**

Jornal do Medico [Porto] *p:* **J Med [Porto]**

Jornal. Sociedade das Ciencias Medicas de Lisboa *p:* **J Soc Cienc Med Lisb**

Joul of Experimental Psychology Animal Behavior *e:* **J Exp Psy A**

Joullial. College of Surgeons of Australasia *e:* **J Coll Surgeons Australasia**

Joulnal of Medical Entomology. Supplement *e:* **J Med Entomol Suppl**

Jounal. Society of Occupational Medicine *e:* **J Soc Occup Med**

Journal. Academy of Natural Sciences of Philadelhia *e:* **J Acad Nat Sci Phila**

Journal. Aero Medical Society of India *e:*
AMSJAX, *e:* **J Aero Med Soc India**

Journal. Aerospace Transpon Division.
American Society of Civil Engineering
e: **J Aerosp Trans Div Am Soc Civ Eng**

Journal. Aichi Medical University
Association *e:* **J Aichi Med Univ Assoc**

Journal. Alaska Geological Society *e:*
JAG

Journal. Alberla Society of Petroleum
Geologists *e:* **J Alberta Soc Pet Geol**

Journal. Albert Einstein Medical Center *e:*
JAEMA

Journal. Albert Einstein Medical Center
[Philadelphia] *e:* **JAEMAL**

Journal. All India Institute of Medical
Sciences *e:* **JAISDS,** *e:* **J All India Inst
Med Sci**

Journal. All India Institute of. Mental
Health *e:* **J All India Inst Ment Health**

Journal. Alumni Associatioon College of
Physicians and Surgeons [Baltimore] *e:*
**J Alumni Ass Coll Phys and Surg
[Baltimore]**

Journal. American Animal Hospital
Association *e:* **JAAHBL,** *e:* **J Am Anim
Hosp Assoc**

Journal. American Association of Medical
Record Librarians *e:* **J Am Ass Med Rec
Libr**

Journal. American College Health
Association *e:* **JAHAA,** *e:* **JAHAAY,** *e:*
J Am Coll H, *e:* **J Am Coll Health. Ass**

Journal. American College of Emergency
Physicians and the University Association
for Emergency Medical Services *e:*
JACEP

Journal. American Health Care Association
e: **J Am Health Care As**

Journal. American Medical Association *e:*
J Am Med A[ssoc]

Journal. American Medical Record
Association *e:* **J Am Med Rec Assoc**

Journal. American Medical Technologists
e: **JAMDAY,** *e:* **J Am Med Technol**

Journal. American Medical Women's
Association *e:* **J Am Med Wom[en's]
Ass[oc],** *e:* **JAMWA[N]**

Journal. American Podiatric Medical
Association *e:* **JAPAEA**

Journal. American Society of
Psychosomatic Dentistry and Medicine
e: **J Am Soc Psychosom Dent [Med]**

Journal. American Veterinary Medical
Association *e:* **J Amer Vet Med Ass,** *e:*
J Am Vet Me[d Ass], *e:* **JAVMA[4]**

Journal. American Water Works
Association *e:* **J Am Water [Works
Ass],** *e:* **JAWWA**

Journal. Animal Technicians Association
e: **J Anim Tech Ass[oc],** *e:* **JATAAQ**

Journal. Arab Vetennary Medical
Association *e:* **J Arb Vet Med As**

Journal. Arkansas Medical Society *e:*
JAMSA, *e:* **J Arkan Med Soc**

Journal. Association for Hospital Medical
Education *e:* **J Assa Hosp Med Educ**

Journal. Association for the Advancement
of Medical Instrumentation *e:* **J Ass
Advan Med Instrum,** *e:* **J Assoc Adv
Med Instrum**

Journal. Association for the Care of
Children's Health *e:* **J Assoc Care Child
Health**

Journal. Association Medicale Canadienne
f: **J Assoc Med Can**

Journal. Association of American Medicai
Colleges *e:* **J Assoc Am Med Coll**

Journal. Association of Medical Illustrators
e: **J Assoc Med Illus**

Journal. Bethune Umversity of Medical
Sciences *e:* **J Bethune Univ Med Sci**

Journal. Biolglical Board of Canada *e:* **J
Biol Board Cn**

Journal. Biological Photographic
Association *e:* **J Biol Phorogr Ass[oc],**
e: **J Biol Phot,** *e:* **J Biol Phot Assn,** *e:*
JBPAA

Journal. Bombay Natural History Society
e: **J Bombay Nat Hist Soc**

Journal. Bowman Gray School of Medicine.
Wake Forest College *e:* **J BowmBn
Grsy Scb Med Wake For Coll**

Journal. British Waterworks Association *e:*
J Br Waterworks As

Journal. Busan Medical College *e:* **J
Busan Med Coll**

Journal Canadien de la Recherche
Forestiere *f:* **J Can Rech For**

Journal Canadien de Microbiologie *f:* **J
Can Microbiol**

Journal Capital Institute of Medicine *e:* **J
Cap Inst Med**

Journal. Catholic Medical College *e:* **J
Cathol Med Coll**

Journal. Central Bureau for Animal
Husbandry and Dairying in India *e:* **J
Cent Bur Anim Husb Dairy India**

Journal. Ceylon Branch. British Medical
Association *e:* **J Ceylon Br Brit Med
Ass**

Journal. Ceylon Obstetric and
Gynaecological Association *e:* **Journ
Ceyl Obstet Gyn Ass**

Journal. Changchun College of Geology *e:*
J Changcbun Col! Geol

Journal. Changchun Geological Institute *e:*
J Cbangcbun GI Inst, *e:* **J Changchun
Geol Inst**

Journal. Changchun University of Earth
Science *e:* **J Cbangchun Univ Earth
Sci**

Journal. Chiba Medical Society *e:* **J Chiba
Med S**

Journal. Chinese Rare Earth Society *e:* **J
Chin Rare Earth Soc**

Journal. Chosen Medical Association *e:* **J
Chosen Med Assoc**

Journal. Christian Medical Association of
India *e:* **J Christ Med Assoc India**

Journal College of Arts and Sciences. Chiba
University. Natural Science [Japan] *e:* **J
Coll Arts Sci Chiba Univ Nat Sci**

Journal. College of Dairying. Natural
Science [Ebetsu] *e:* **J Coll Dairy Nat
Sci [Ebetsu]**

Journal. Connecticut State Medical Society
e: **J Conn State Med Soc**

Journal de Biologie Buccale *f:* **J Biol Bua**

Journal de Biologie Buccale [Paris] *f:* **J
Biol Buccale**

Journal de Biologie et de Medecine
Nucleaires *f:* **JBMNA**

Journal de Chimie Medicale, de Pharmacie
et de Toxicologie *f:* **J Chim Med Pha
Toxil**

Journal de Chimie Physique et de Physico-
Chimie Biologique *e:* **Journ Chim Phys
Chim**

Journal de Chimie Physique et de Physico-
Chimie Biologique [Société de Chimie
Physique, France] *f:* **J. Chim. Phys.
Phys.-Chim. Biol.**

Journal de Chimie Physique et de Physique
Chimie Biologique *f:* **J Chim Phys [Phy
Chim Biol]**

Journal de Gynecologie, Obstetrique et
Biologie de la Reproduction *f:* **J
Gynecol Obstet Biol Reprod [Paris]**

Journal de Gynologie, Obstetrique et
Biologie de la Reprodudion *f:* **JGOBA**

Journal de l'Association Médicale
Canadienne *f:* **JAMC**

Journal de Mecanique et Physique de
l'Atmosphere *f:* **J Mecan Phys Atm,** *f:* **J
Mec Phys Atmos**

Journal de Medecine de Poitiers *f:* **J Med
Poitiers**

Journal de Microscopie et de Biologie
Cellulaire *f:* **JMBCD,** *f:* **J Microsc B[iol
Cell]**

Journal de Physique, de Chimie, d'Histoire
Naturelle et des Arts *f:* **J Phy**

Journal de Recherche Oceanographique *f:*
J Rech Oceanogr

Journal de Recherches Atmospheriques
[France] *f:* **J. Rech. Atmos.**

Journal. Department of Geography.
National University of Malaysia *e:* **J
Dep Geogr Natl Univ Malaysia**

Journal des Connaissances Medico-
Chirurgicales *f:* **J Conn Med Chir**

Journal des Sciences Medicales de Lille *f:*
J Scl Med Lille

Journal. Devon Trust for Nature
Conservation *e:* **J Devon Trust Nat
Conserv**

Journal d'Urologie Medicale et Chirurgicale
f: **J Urol Med Chir**

Journal. East Africa Natural History Society
e: **J Ea Afr Nat Hist S**

Journal. East Africa Natural History Society
and National Museum *e:* **J East Afr Nat
Hist Soc Natl Mus**

Journal. Egyptan Public Health Association
e: **JEGPA**

Journal. Egyptian Medical Association *e:*
J Egypt M[ed] A[ssoc], *e:* **JEMAA**

Journal Egyptian Medical Society *e:* **J
Egypt Med Soc**

Journal. Egyptian Public Health Association
e: **J Egypt Public Health Assoc**

Journal. Egyptian Veterinary Medical
Association *e:* **J Egypt Vet Med Ass**

Journal. Environmental Engineering
Division. American Society of Civil
Engineers *e:* **J Envir Eng,** *e:* **J Environ
Eng Dir A[m] S[oc] C[iv] E[ng]**

Journal. Environmental Engineering
Division. Proceedings of the American
Society of Civil Engineering *e:* **J
Environ Engng Dir Proc ASCE**

Journal. Environmental Engineering
Division. Proceedings of the American
Society of Civil Engineers *e:* **JEED**

Journal. Environmental Protection Society [Republic of China] *e:* **J Environ Prot S [Repub China]**

Journal Europeen de Pathologe Forestiere *f:* **J Eur Pathol For**

Journal Europeen de Radiotherapie, Oncologie, Radiophysique Radiobiólogie *f:* **J Eur Radiother**

Journal. Faculty of Applied Biological Science. Hiroshima University *e:* **J Fac Appl Biol Sci Hirosbima Univ**

Journal. Faculty of Education. Natural Sciences. Tottori University *e:* **J Fac Educ Nat Sci Tottori Univ**

Journal. Faculty of Fisheries and Animal Husbandry. Hiroshima University. *e:* **J Fac Fish Anim Husb Hiroshima Univ**

Journal. Faculty of Liberal Arts. Shinshu University. Part II Natural Sciences *e:* **J Fac Lib Arts Shinshu Univ Part II Nat Sci**

Journal. Faculty of Medicine [Baghdad] *e:* **J Fac Med [Baghdad]**

Journal. Faculty of Medicine. Chulalongkorn University [Bangkok] *e:* **J Fac Med Chulalongkorn Univ [Bangkok]**

Journal. Faculty of Medicine. Shinshu University *e:* **J Fac Med Shin Univ**

Journal. Faculty of Medicine. University of Ankara *e:* **J Fac Med Univ Ankara**

Journal. Faculty of Medicine. University of Ankara. Supplement *e:* **J Fac Med Univ Ankara Suppl**

Journal. Faculty of Oceanography. Tokai University *e:* **J Fac Oceanogr Tokai Univ**

Journal. Faculty of Science. Hokkaido Imperial University. Series 4. Geology and Mineralogy *e:* **J Fac Sci Hokkaido Imp Univ Ser 4**

Journal. Faculty of Science. Hokkaido University. Series IV. Geology and Mineralogy *e:* **J Fac Sci Hokkaido Univ Ser IV**

Journal. Faculty of Science. Hokkaido University. Series VII Geophysics *e:* **J Fac Sci Hokkaido Univ Ser VII**

Journal. Faculty of Science. Imperial University ofTokyo. Section II Geology, Mineralogy, Geography, Seismology *e:* **J Fac Sci Imp Univ Tokyo Sect II**

Journal. Faculty of Science. University of Tokyo. Section II Geology, Mineralogy, Geography, Geophysics *e:* **J Fac Sci Univ Tokyo Sect II General Mineral Geogr Geophys**

Journal. Faculty of Textile Science and Technology. Shinshu University. Series A. Biology *e:* **J Fac Text Sci Technol Shinshu Univ Ser A**

Journal. Faculty of Veterinary Medicine. University of Anka *e:* **J Fac Vet Med Univ Tokyo**

Journal. Florida Medical Association *e:* **J Fla Med Ass**, *e:* **J Florida MA**, *e:* **JFMA**

Journal for Water and Wastewater Research *e:* **JWABAQ**, *e:* **J Water Wastewater Res**

Journal Forestier Suisse *f:* **J For Suisse**

Journal. Formosan Medical Association *e:* **J Formosan Med Ass**

Journal. Fudan University. Natural Science *e:* **J Fudan Univ Nat Sci**

Journal. Fujian Teachers University. Natural Science Edition *e:* **J Fujinn TeBcb Univ Nat Sci Ed**

Journal für Medizinische Kosmetik *d:* **J Med Kosmet**

Journal. Gakugei Tokushima University. Natural Science *e:* **J Gakugei Tokushima Univ Nat Sci**

Journal. Geochemical Society of India *e:* **J Geochem Soc India**

Journal Geographica *i:* **J Geog**

Journal. Geological Society of Australia *e:* **J Geol Soc Aust[ralia]**

Journal. Geological Society of India *e:* **J Geol Soc In**

Journal. Geological Society of Iraq *e:* **J Geol Soc Iraq**

Journal. Geological Society of Japan *e:* **J Geol Soc Jpn**

Journal. Geological Society of London *e:* **J Geol Soc london**, *e:* **JGSLA**

Journal. Geological Society of Thailand *e:* **J Geol Soc Thailand**

Journal. Geological Society of the Philippines *e:* **J Geol Soc Philipp**

Journal. Geological Society of Tokyo *e:* **J Geol Soc Tokyo**

Journal. Geological Society [Seoul] *e:* **J Geol Soc [Seoul]**

Journal. Georgia Dental Association *e:* **GDAJA**

Journal. Georgia Dental Assonation *e:* **J GA Dent Assoc**

Journal. Georgia Entomological Society *e:* **GENSA**, *e:* **J GA Ent[omol] Soc**

Journal. Geotechnicai Engineering Division. Proceedings of the American Society of Civil Engineers *e:* **J Ceotech Engng Dir Proc ASCE**

Journal Geotechnical Engineering Division. American Society of Civil Engineers *e:* **J Geotech Engng Div ASCE**

Journal. Geotechnical Engineering Division. Proceedings of the American Society of Civil Engineers *e:* **J Geotech Eng Dir Amer Soc Civil Eng Proc**

Journal. Geothermal Energy Research and Development Company, Limited *e:* **J Geotherm Energy Res Dev Co Ltd**

Journal. Gyeongsang National University. Natural Sciences *e:* **J Gyeongsang Ntl Univ Nat Sci**, *e:* **NKTAD**

Journal. Hanyang Medical College [South Korea] *e:* **J Hanyang Med Coll**

Journal. Hebei University. Natural Science Edition *e:* **J Hebei Univ Nat Sci Ed**

Journal. Hiroshima Medical Association [Japan] *e:* **J Hiroshim Med Asc**

Journal. Hokkaido Gynecology and Obstetrical Society *e:* **J Hokkaido Gynecol Obstet Soc**

Journal. Hongkóng University. Geographical, Geological and Archaeologcal Society *e:* **JGGAS**

Journal. Hopeh University. Natural Science *e:* **J Hopeh Univ Nat Sci**

Journal. Hungrian Veterinary Surgeons *e:* **J Hung Vet Surg**

Journal. Hyderabad Geological Survey *e:* **J Hyderabad Geol Surv**

Journal. Hyogo College of Medicine *e:* **J Hyogo Coll Med**

Journal. Indian Academy of Geoscience *e:* **J Indian Acad Geosci**

Journal. Indian Geophysical Union *e:* **J Indian Geophys Union**

Journal. Indian Geoscience Association *e:* **J Indian Gesci Assoc**

Journal. Indian Institute of Science. Section C. Biological Sciences *e:* **J Indian Inst Sci Sect C Biol Sci**

Journal. Indian Medical Association *e:* **J Indian M[ed] A[ssoc]**

Journal. Indiana State Medical Association *e:* **JIDXA**, *e:* **J Indiana MA**, *e:* **J Indian State Med Assoc**

Journal. Institute of Animal Technicians *e:* **J Inst Anim Tech**

Journal. Institute of Geology. Vikram University *e:* **J Inst Geol Vikram Univ**

Journal. Institute of Polytechnics. Osaka City University. Series D. Biology *e:* **J Inst Polytech Osaka City Univ Ser D**

Journal. Institute of Polytechnics. Osaka City University. Series G. Geoscience *e:* **J Inst Polytech Osaka City Univ Ser G**

Journal. Institution of Engineers [India]. Environmental Engineering Division *e:* **J Inst Eng [India] Environ Eng Div**

Journal. Institution of Engineers [India]. Public Health Engineering Division *e:* **J Inst Eng [India] Pub[lic] Health Eng Div**

Journal. Institution of Public Health Engineers *e:* **J Inst Public Health Eng**

Journal. Institution of Water Engineers *e:* **J Instn Wat Engrs**, *e:* **J Inst Water Eng**

Journal. Institution of Water Engineers and Scientists *e:* **J Instn Water Engnrs Sci**, *e:* **J Instn Wat[er] Engrs Sci[entists]**, *e:* **J Inst Water Eng[rs &] Sci**

Journal. International Academy of Preventive Medicine *e:* **J Int Ad Pre Med**

Journal International Associalion for Mathematical Geology *e:* **J Int Ass Math Geol**

Journal. International Association for Mathematical Geology *e:* **J Int Ass Mat**, *e:* **J Internat Assoc Math[ematical] Geol**

Journal. International College of Surgeons *e:* **J Internat Coll Surgeons**

Journal. International College of Surgeons [United States] *e:* **J Int Coll Surg**

Journal. International Federation of Gynaecology and Obstetrics *e:* **J Int Fed Gynael Obstet**

Journal. International Institute for Aerial Survey and Earth Sciences *e:* **J Int Inst Aerial Surv Earth Sci**

Journal. Iowa Medical Society *e:* **J Iowa Med S**

Journal. Iowa State Medical Society *e:* **J Iowa State Med Soc**

Journal. Irish Colleges of Physicians and Surgeons *e:* **J Ir Coll Physicians Surg**, *e:* **J Irish CP**

Journal. Irish Medical Association *e:* **JIMSA**, *e:* **J Irish MA**, *e:* **J Ir Med Assoc**

Journal. Islamic Medical Association of the United States and Canada *e:* **J IMA**

Journal. Israel Medical Association *e:* **J Isr Med Assoc**

Journal. Iwate Medical Association *e:* **J Iwate Med Assoc**

Journal. Japan Health Physics Society *e:* **J Jpn Health Phys Soc**

Journal. Japan Veterinary Medical Association *e:* **J Jpn Vet Med Asc**

Journal. Japan Water Works Association *e:* **JWWJA**

Journal. Japanese Association of Physical Medicine, Balneology and Climatology *e:* **J Jpn Assoc Phys Med Bineol ClimBtol**

Journal. Japanese Obstelrics and Gynecology *e:* **J Jpn Obstet Gynecol**

Journal. Kanazawa Medical University *e:* **J Kanazawa Med Univ**

Journal. Kansai Medical School [Japan] *e:* **J Kansai Med Sch**

Journal. Kansai Medical University *e:* **J Kansai Med Univ**

Journal. Kansas Geological Survey *e:* **J Kansas Geol Surv**

Journal. Kansas Medical Society *e:* **J Kan Med Soc,** *e:* **J Kansas Med Soc,** *e:* **J Kans Med Soc,** *e:* **JKMSA**

Journal. Keio Medical Society [Japan] *e:* **J Keio Med Soc**

Journal. Kentucky State Medical Association *e:* **J Ky State Med Assoc**

Journal. Kerala Academy of Biology *e:* **J Kerala Ad Biol**

Journal. Kirin University. Natural Science *e:* **J Kirin Univ Nt i**

Journal. Korea Merchant Marine College. Natural Sciences Series *e:* **J Korea Merch Mar Coll Nat Sci Ser,** *e:* **JMMSD**

Journal. Korean Association for Radiation Protection *e:* **J Korean Ass Radit Prot**

Journal. Korean Institute of Mining Geology *e:* **J Korean Inst Min Geol**

Journal. Korean Medical Association *e:* **J Korean Med Assoc**

Journal. Korean Meteorological Society *e:* **J Korean Meteorol Soc**

Journal. Korean Oriental Medical Society *e:* **J Korean Orient Med Soc**

Journal. Korean Society for Microbiology *e:* **J Korean Soc Microbiol**

Journal. Kumamoto Medical Society *e:* **J Kumamoto Med Soc**

Journal. Kurume Medical Association *e:* **J Kurume Med Assoc**

Journal. Kuwait Medical Association *e:* **J Kuwait Med Ass**

Journal. Kyorin Medical Society *e:* **J Kyorin Med Soc**

Journal. Kyoto Medical Assocation *e:* **J Kyoto Med Assoc**

Journal. Kyoto Prefectural Medical University *e:* **J Kyoto Prefect Med Univ**

Journal. Kyoto Prefectural University of Medicine *e:* **J Kyoto Prefect Univ Med**

Journal. Lanchow University. Natural Sciences *e:* **J Lanchow Univ Nat Sci**

Journal . London School of Tropical Medicine *e:* **J London School Trop Med**

Journal. Louisiana State Medical Society *e:* **J LA Med S,** *e:* **J LA State Med Soc,** *e:* **J Louis St Med Soc,** *e:* **JLSMA**

Journal. Madras University. Section B. Contributions in Mathematics, Physical and Biological Science *e:* **J Madras Univ B**

Journal. Maine Medical Association *e:* **J Maine Med Assoc,** *e:* **JMMAA**

Journal. Malayan Branch. British Medical Association *e:* **J Mal Br Brit Med Ass,** *e:* **J Malgya Branch Br Med Assoc**

Journal. Malayan Veterinary Medical Association *e:* **J Ml Vet Med Ass**

Journal. Manchester Geographical Society *e:* **J Manch Geogr Soc**

Journal. Manchester Geological Association *e:* **J Manch Geol Ass**

Journal. Marine Biological Association [India] *e:* **J Mar Biol Assoc [India]**

Journal. Marine Biological Association [United Kingdom] *e:* **J Mar[ine] Biol Ass[oc] [UK]**

Journal. Mechanical Engineers Association of Witwatersrand *e:* **J Mech Eng Assoc Witwatersrand**

Journal. Medical and Dental Association of Botswana *e:* **J Med Dent Assoc Botswana**

Journal. Medical and Pharmaceutical Society for Wakan-Yaku *e:* **J Med Pharm Soc Wkan Yaku**

Journal. Medical Assiation of Israel *e:* **J Med Assoc Isr**

Journal Medical Association of Eire *e:* **J Med Ass[oc] Eire**

Journal. Medical Association of Georgia *e:* **J Med Ass[oc] GA**

Journal. Medical Association of Iwate Prefectural Hospital [Japan] *e:* **J Med Assoc Iwate Prefect Hosp**

Journal. Medical Association of Okayama *e:* **J Med Ass Ok**

Journal. Medical Association of South Africa *e:* **J Med Assoc S Afr,** *e:* **J Med Ass S[outh] Afr[ica]**

Journal. Medical Association of Thailand *e:* **J Med Ass[oc]Thai[land]**

Journal. Medical Association of the State of Alabama *e:* **J Med Ass[oc State] Ala[bama]**

Journal. Medical Assoriation of Jamaica *e:* **J Med Assoc JBm**

Journal. Medical College in Keijo *e:* **J Med Coll Keijo**

Journal Medical de Bruxelles *f:* **J Med Brux**

Journal Medical Francais *f:* **J Med Franc**

Journal Medical Haitien *e:* **J Med Hait**

Journal Medical Libanais. Lebanese Medical Journal *e:* **J Med Liban**

Journal. Medical Professions Association *e:* **J Med Prof Ass**

Journal. Medical Society of New Jersey *e:* **J Med Soc N[ew] J[ersey],** *e:* **JMSNA**

Journal. Medical Society of Toho University *e:* **J Med Soc Toho Univ**

Journal. Medical Women's Federation *e:* **J Med Wom Fed**

Journal Medico-Chirurgical *e:* **J Med Chir**

Journal. Mental Health Administlation *e:* **J Ment Health Adm**

Journal. Meteorological Society of Japan *e:* **J Meteorol Soc Jpn,** *e:* **J Met Soc Jap**

Journal. Michigan State Medical Society *e:* **J Mich [State] Med Soc**

Journal. Mie Medical College *e:* **J Mie Med Coll**

Journal. Mining College. Akita University. Series A. Mining Geology *e:* **J Min Coll Akita Unir Ser A**

Journal. Ministry of Health *e:* **J Minist Health**

Journal. Mississippi State Medical Association *e:* **J Miss[issippi] Med Ass**

Journal. Missouri Water and Sewerage Conference *e:* **J Mo Water Sewerage Conf**

Journal. Mysore Medical Association *e:* **J Mysore Med Assoc**

Journal. Nagasaki Earth Science Association *e:* **J Nagasaki Earth Sci Ass**

Journal. Nagasaki Public Health Society *e:* **J Nagasaki Public Health Soc**

Journal. Nagoya City University Medical Association [Japan] *e:* **J Nagoy City Univ Med Ass**

Journal. Nagoya Medical Association *e:* **J Nagoya Med Assoc**

Journal. Nanjing University. Natural Science Edition *e:* **J Nanjing Univ Nat Sci Ed**

Journal. Nara Gakugei University. Natural Science *e:* **J Nara Gakugei Univ Nat Sci**

Journal. Nara Medical Association *e:* **J Nara Med Ass[oc]**

Journal. National Academy of Sciences [Republic ofKorea]. Natural Sciences Series *e:* **J Natl Acad Sci [Repub Korea] Nat Sci Ser**

Journal. National Defense Medical College *e:* **J Natl Def Med Coll**

Journal. Natural Science Research Institute. Yonsei University *e:* **J Nat Sci Res Inst Yonsei Unir**

Journal. Natural Science Research Institute. Yonsei University [Republic of Korea] *e:* **J Nat Sci Res Inst**

Journal. Natural Scientific Society. Ichimura Gakuen Junior College *e:* **J Nat Sci Soc Ichimura Gakuen J Coll**

Journal. New England Water Pollution Control Association *e:* **J N Engl Water Pollut Control Assoc**

Journal. New England Water Works Association *e:* **J N Engl Water Works Assoc,** *e:* **J New Engl Water Works Ass**

Journal. New York Medical College. Flower and Fifth Avenue Hospitals *e:* **J NY Med Coll Flower [and] Fifth Ave Hosp**

Journal. New Zealand Institute of Medical Laboratory Technology *e:* **JNZ Inst Med Lab Technol**

Journal. Newark Beth Israel Medical Center *e:* **J Newark Beth Isr Med Cent**

Journal. Nihon University Medical Association *e:* **J Nihon Univ Med Ass,** *e:* **NICHAS**

Journal. North Carolina Section of the American Water Works Association and North Carolina Water Pollution Control Association *e:* **J NC Sect Am Water Works Assoe NC Water PollutConhol Assoc**

Journal. Northamptonshire Natural History Society and Field Club *e:* **J Northamptonshire Natur Hist Soc Field Club**

Journal. Northwest University. Natural Science Edition e: **J Northwest Univ Nt Sci Ed**

Journal. Norwegian Medical Association e: **J Norw Med Ass**

Journal. Oceanographical Society of Japan e: **J Oceanogr Soc Jpn**

Journal. Oceanological Society of Korea e: **J Oceanol Soc Kor**

Journal of Accident and Emergency Medicine e: **J Accid Emerg Med**

Journal of Accidental Medicine e: **J Accidental Med**

Journal of Adolescent Health e: **J Adolesc Health**

Journal of Adolescent Health Care e: **JAHCD9**

Journal of Adolesnt Health Care e: **J Adolesc Health Care**

Journal of Aerosol Medicine [International Society for Aerosols in Medicine] e: **J. Aerosol Med.**

Journal of Aerospace Science e: **JAS**

Journal of African Earth Sciences e: **JAES**, e: **J Afr Earth Sci**

Journal of African Earth Sciences and the Middle East e: **J Afr Earth Sci Middle East**

Journal of Agricultural Meteorology e: **J Agric Meteorol**, e: **NOKIAB**

Journal of Agricultural Meteorology [Japan] e: **J Agr Meteorol [Japan]**

Journal of Agricultural Meteorology [Tokyo] e: **J Agric Met [Tokyo]**

Journal of Agriculture and Water Resources Research e: **J Agric Water Resour Res**, e: **JAWRFS**

Journal of Allied Health e: **JAHEDF**

Journal of Allied Health [Thorofare] e: **J Allied Health**

Journal of Alternative and Complementary Medicine e: **JACM**

Journal of American College Health e: **JACH**, e: **JACHEY**

Journal of Animal Breeding and Genetics e: **JABREG**, e: **J Anim Breed Genet**

Journal of Animal Ecology e: **JAECAP**, e: **J Animal Ecol[ogy]**, e: **J. Anim. Ecol.**

Journal of Animal Morphoiogy and Physiology e: **J Anim Morph[ol] Physiol**

Journal of Animal Morphology and Physiology e: **JAMPA2**

Journal of Animal Physiology and Animal Nutrition e: **J Anim Physiol Anim Nutr**, e: **JAPNEF**

Journal of Animal Production of the United Arab Republic e: **J Anim Prod U[n] A[rab] R[epub]**

Journal of Animal Production Research e: **J Anim Prod Res**, e: **JAPRDQ**

Journal of Animal Science e: **J Animal Sci**, e: **J. Anim. Sc.**, e: **J Anim Sci**, e: **JANSA[G]**

Journal of Applied Biology e: **J Appl Biol**

Journal of Applied Ecology e: **JAPEAI**, e: **J Ap Ecol**, e: **J App Ecol**, e: **J Appl Ecol**, e: **J Applied Ecology**

Journal of Applied Medicine e: **J Appl Med**

Journal of Applied Meteorology e: **J Ap Meterol**, e: **J Appl Met**, e: **J Appl Meteorol**, e: **J App Meteor**

Journal of Applied Meteorology [American Metereological Society] e: **J. Appl. Meteorol.**

Journal of Applied Microbiology and Biotechnology [Sweden] e: **J Appl. Microbiol. Biotech.**

Journal of Applied Physiology Respiratory, Environmental and Exercise Physiology e: **J Appl Physiol Respir Environ Exerc[ise] Physiol**

Journal of Aquatic Animal Health e: **J. Aquat. Anim. Health.**

Journal of Arid Environments e: **J Arid Environ**

Journal of Association of Exploration Geophysicists [Center of Exploration Geophysics, India] e: **J. Assoc. Explor. Geophys.**

Journal of Atmospheric and Terrestrial Physics e: **J Atm[os] [and] Terr P[hys]**, e: **J. Atmos. Terrest. Phys.**, e: **J Atmos Terr Phys**, e: **Journ Atm Terr Phys**

Journal of Atmospheric Chemistry e: **J Atmos Chem**

Journal of Audiological Medicine e: **JAM**

Journal of Audiovisual Media in Medicine e: **J Audiov Media Med**

Journal of Avian Biology e: **J. Avian Biol.**

Journal of Aviation Medicine e: **J Aviation Med**

Journal of Bacteriology [American Society for Microbiology] e: **J. Bacteriol.**

Journal of Basic Microbiology e: **J Basic Microbiol**

Journal of Behavioral Health Services & Research e: **JBHS&R**

Journal of Behavioral Medicine e: **JOBM**

Journal of Behavioral Medicine [New York] e: **J Behav Med**

Journal of Biochemical and Microbiological Technology and Engineering e: **Journ Biochem MicrTech Eng**

Journal of Biochemical and Microbiological Technology and Enginring e: **J Biochem Microbiol Tech Eng**

Journal of Biochemistry, Molecular Biology and Biophysics e: **JBMBB**

Journal of Biogeography [Including Global Ecology & Biogeography Letters and Biodiversity Letters] e: **J Biogeography**

Journal of Biogeography. Oxford e: **J Biogeogr.**

Journal of Biological Chemistry e: **JBC**, e: **J Bioi Chem**, e: **Journ Biol Chem**

Journal of Biological Chemistry [American Society for Biochemistry and Molecular Biology] e: **J. Biol. Chem.**

Journal of Biological Education e: **J Biologicl Ed**

Journal of Biological Photography [Durham] e: **J Biol Photogr**

Journal of Biological Physics e: **J Biol Phys**, e: **JBPI**

Journal of Biological Psychology e: **J Biol Psychol**

Journal of Biological Regulators and Homeostatic Agents [Milano] e: **J Biol Regul Homeost Agents**

Journal of Biological Response Modifers e: **JBRM**

Journal of Biological Response Modifiers e: **J Biol Response Mod[if]**

Journal of Biological Rhythms e: **J Biol Rhythms**

Journal of Biological Rhythms [New York] e: **J Biol Rhythms**, e: **JBR**

Journal of Biological Sciences e: **J Biol Sci**

Journal of Biological Sciences [Baghdad] e: **J Biol Sci [Baghdad]**

Journal of Biological Sciences [Bombay] e: **J Biol Sci [Bombay]**

Journal of Biological Sciences Research e: **J Biol Sci Res**, e: **JBSRES**

Journal of Biological Sciences Research Publication e: **J Biol Sci Res Publ**

Journal of Biological Standardization e: **J Biol Stan[d]**, e: **JBSTD**

Journal of Biological Standardization [International Union of Microbiolgical Societies] e: **J. Biol. Stand.**

Journal of Biology [Bronx] e: **J Biol [Bronx NY]**

Journal of Biology. Osaka City University e: **J Biol Osaka City Univ**

Journal of Bioluminescence and Chemiluminescence e: **J Biolumin Chemilumin**

Journal of Biomedical Engineering [Guildford] e: **J Biomed Eng**

Journal of Biomedical Materials Research e: **J Biomed M[at] R[es]**

Journal of Biomedical Materials Research. Biomedical Materials Symposium e: **J Biomed Mater Res Biomed Mater Symp**

Journal of Biomedical Materials Research [New York] e: **J Biomed Mater Res**

Journal of Biomedical Materials Research [Society for Biomaterials] e: **J. Biomed. Mater. Res.**

Journal of Biomedical Systems e: **J Biomed Syst**

Journal of Cardiovascular Medicine e: **JCMEDK**

Journal of Cardovascular Medicine e: **J Cardiovasc Med**

Journal of Cell Biology e: **JCB**

Journal of Cell Biology [American Society of Cell Biology] e: **J. Cell Biol.**

Journal of Central China Normal University [Natural Sciences] e: **J. Cent. China Norm. Univ. [Nat. Sci.]**

Journal of Chemical Ecology [International Society of Chemical Ecology] e: **J. Chem. Ecol.**

Journal of Child and Adolescent Psychiatric and Mental Health Nursing e: **JCPN**

Journal of Chinese Medicine e: **JCM**

Journal of Chromatography. B, Biomedical Applications e: **J Chromatogr B Biomed Appl**

Journal of Climate [American Meteorological Society] e: **J. Clim.**

Journal of Climate and Applied Meteorology e: **J Clim and Appl Meteorol**, e: **J. Clim. Appl. Meteorol.**

Journal of Climatology e: **J. Climatol.**, e: **J Climtol**

Journal of Clinical and Experimental Medicine [Tokyo] e: **J Clin Exp Med [Tokyo]**

Journal of Clinical Laser Medicine and Surgery e: **JCLMS**

Journal of Clinical Medicine e: **J Clin Med**

Journal of Clinical Microbiology *e:* **J Clin Micr**, *e:* **JCM**, *e:* **JCMID**

Journal of Clinical Microbiology [American Society for Microbiology] *e:* **J. Clin. Microbiol.**

Journal of Clinical Microbiology [Washington, DC] *e:* **J Clin Microbiol**

Journal of Community Health *e:* **J Commun Health**, *e:* **JOCH**

Journal of Community Health [New York] *e:* **J Community Health**

Journal of Community Health Nursing *e:* **J Community Health Nurs**

Journal of Comparative Medicine and Veterinary Archives *e:* **J Comp Med and Vet Arcb**

Journal of Comparative Physiology. B, Biochemical, Systemic and Environmental Physiology [Berlin] *e:* **J Comp Physiol [B]**

Journal of Compliance in Health Care *e:* **JCHC**, *e:* **J Compliance Health Care**

Journal of Computational Biology *e:* **J Comput Biol**

Journal of Contaminant Hydrology *e:* **J. Contam. Hydrol.**

Journal of Contemporary Health Law and Policy *e:* **J Contemp Health Law Policy**

Journal of Contemporary Health Law & Policy *e:* **J. Contemp. Health L.&Pol'y**

Journal of Continuing Education in Obstetrics and Gynecology *e:* **J Contin Educ Obstet Gynecol**

Journal of Continuing Education in the Health Professions *e:* **JCEHP**

Journal of Correctional Health Care *e:* **JCHC**

Journal of Craniofacial Genetics and Developmental Biology [Copenhagen] *e:* **J Craniofac Genet Dev Biol**

Journal of Craniofacial Genetics and Developmental Biology. Supplement [New York] *e:* **J Craniofac Genet Dev Biol Suppl**

Journal of Crustacean Biology *e:* **J Crustacean Biol**, *e:* **Jnl Crustscean Biol**

Journal of Cultural Geography. Popular Culture Assn., American Culture Assn., Bowling Green State Univ., Bowling Green *e:* **J Cult Geogr.**

Journal of Dental Health [Tokyo] *e:* **J Dent Health [Tokyo]**

Journal of Dental Medicine *e:* **J Dent Med**

Journal of Diagnostic Medical Sonography *e:* **JDMS**

Journal of Differential Geometry *e:* **J Differential Geom[etry]**

Journal of Earth Sciences *e:* **J Earth Sci**

Journal of Earth Sciences. Nagoya University *e:* **J Earth Sci Nagoya Unir**

Journal of Earth Sciences. Royal Dublin Society *e:* **J Earth Sci R Dublin S**, *e:* **Jnl Eartb Sci R Dublin Soc**

Journal of Ecology *e:* **J Ecol**

Journal of ecology, British Ecological Society *e:* **Jour of ecology.**

Journal of Ecology. British Ecological Society. London *e:* **Jour ecol.**

Journal of Economic Biology *e:* **J Econ Biol**

Journal of Emergency Medical Services *e:* **J Emerg Med Serv**, *e:* **JEMS**

Journal of Emergency Medicine *e:* **J Emerg Med**

Journal of Energy Law, Natural Resources & Environmental Law *e:* **J. Energy Nat. Res.&Envtl. L.**

Journal of Environmenlal Biology *e:* **J Environ Biol**

Journal of Environmental Economics and Management *e:* **JEE**, *e:* **JEEMD**, *e:* **JEM**, *e:* **J Enriron Econ Manage**

Journal of Environmental Economics and Management [Association of Environmental and Resource Economists] *e:* **J. Environ. Econ. Manage.**

Journal of Environmental Education *e:* **J Env Educ**, *e:* **J Environ Educ**, *e:* **JEVED**

Journal of Environmental Engineering [American Society of Civil Engineers] *e:* **J. Environ. Eng.**

Journal of Environmental Health *e:* **J Environ Health**

Journal of Environmental Law *e:* **J.Env.L.**

Journal of Environmental Law and Litigation *e:* **J. Envtl. L.&Litig.**

Journal of Environmental Management *e:* **J Envir Mgm**, *e:* **J. Environ. Manage.**

Journal of Environmental Pathology and Toxicology *e:* **J Environ Pathol Toxicol**

Journal of Environmental Pathology, Toxicology and Oncology *e:* **J Environ Pathol Toxicol Oncol**

Journal of Environmental Pathology, Toxicology and Oncology [Cambridge] *e:* **JEPTO**

Journal of Environmental Planning and Pollution Control *e:* **J Environ Plan Pollut Control**

Journal of Environmental Pollution Control [Tokyo] *e:* **J Environ Pollut Control [Tokyo]**

Journal of Environmental Polymer Degradation *e:* **J. Environ. Polym. Degrad.**

Journal of Environmental Psychology *e:* **Jnl of Environmental Psychology**

Journal of Environmental Quality *e:* **J Envir Q[uality]**, *e:* **JEVQA**

Journal of Environmental Quality [Soil Science Society of America] *e:* **J. Environ. Qual.**

Journal of Environmental Radioactivity *e:* **J. Environ. Radioact.**

Journal of Environmental Science and Health *e:* **J Envir Sci Hlth**

Journal of Environmental Science and Health. Part A. Environmental Science and Engineering *e:* **J Environ Sci Health Part A [Environ Sci Eng]**

Journal of Environmental Science and Health. Part B. Pesticides, Food Contaminants and Agricultural Wastes *e:* **J Enrimn Sci Health Part B [Pestic Food Contam Agric Wastes]**

Journal of Environmental Science and Health. Part B: Pesticides, Food Contaminants and Agricultural Wastes *e:* **J Environ Sci Health B**

Journal of Environmental Science and Health. Part C. Environmental Health Sciences *e:* **J Environ Sci Health [C]**

Journal of Environmental Sciences *e:* **J Envir Sci**

Journal of Environmental Sciences [Beijing, China] *e:* **J Environ Sci [Beijing]**

Journal of Environmental Sciences [Institute of Environmental Sciences] *e:* **J. Environ. Sci.**

Journal of Environmental Systems *e:* **J Environ Syst[ems]**, *e:* **JET**, *e:* **JEVSB**

Journal of Epidemiology and Community Health *e:* **JECH**, *e:* **J Epidemiol Community Health**

Journal of Equine Medicine and Surgery *e:* **J Equine Med Surg**

Journal of Ethnobiology. Center for Western Studies. Flagstaff, *e:* **J Ethnobiol.**

Journal of Ethnobiology [Society of Ethnobiology] *e:* **J. Ethnobiol.**

Journal of Eukaryotic Microbiology *e:* **J Eukaryot Microbiol**

Journal of Experimental Animal Science [Jena] *e:* **J Exp Anim Sci**

Journal of Experimental Biology *e:* **JEB**, *e:* **J Exper Biol**

Journal of Experimental Biology and Medicine *e:* **J Exp Biol Med**

Journal of Experimental Biology [London] *e:* **J Exp Biol**

Journal of Experimental Biology [R] *e:* **J. Exp. Biol.**

Journal of Experimental Botany [Society for Experimental Biology, GB] *e:* **J. Exp. Bot.**

Journal of Experimental Marine Biology *e:* **J Exp Marine Biol**

Journal of Experimental Marine Biology and Ecology *e:* **J. Exp. Mar. Biol. Ecol.**, *e:* **J Exp Mr B[iol Ecol]**

Journal of Experimental Medical Sciences *e:* **J Exp Med Sci**

Journal of Experimental Medicine *e:* **JEM**, *e:* **J Exper Med**

Journal of Experimental Psychology Animal Behavior Processes *e:* **JEPABP**

Journal of Experimental Psychology. Animal Behavior Processes *e:* **J Exp Psychol Anim Beb**

Journal of Experimental Psychology: Animal Behavior Processes *e:* **J Exp Psychol Anim Behav Process**

Journal of Experimental Psychology: Animal Behavior Processes [Washington] *e:* **J Exp Psychol [Anim Behav]**

Journal of Experimetnal Medicine [New York] *e:* **J Exp Med**

Journal of Exposure Analysis and Environmental Epidemiology *e:* **J Expo Anal Environ Epidemiol**

Journal of Fish Biology *e:* **J Fish Biol**

Journal of Foetal Medicine *e:* **J Foetal Med**

Journal of Food Protection *e:* **J Food Prot[ect]**, *e:* **JFPRD**

Journal of Forensic Medicine *e:* **J Forensic Med**, *e:* **J For M**

Journal of Forensic Medicine [Istanbul] *e:* **J Forensic Med [Istanbul]**

Journal of Free Radicals in Biology and Medicine *e:* **J Free Radic[als] Biol [&] Med**

Journal of Freshwater *e:* **J Fresbwater**

Journal of Freshwater Ecology *e:* **J Freshw[ater] Ec[ol]**

Journal of Gas Lighting, Water Supply and Sanitary Improvement *e:* **J Gas Light Water Supply Sanit Improv**

Journal of General and Applied Microbiology *e:* **J Gen A[ppl] Mic[robiol]**

Journal of General Internal Medicine *e:* **JGIM**

Journal of General Internal Medicine [Philadelphia, PA] *e:* **J Gen Intern Med**

Journal of General Microbiology *e:* **J Gen Micro[biol]**, *e:* **JGM**

Journal of General Microbiology [London] *e:* **J Gen Microbiol**

Journal of Genetic Psychology, Child Behavior, Animal Behavior and Problems of A *e:* **J. Genet. Psychol.**

Journal of Geobotany *e:* **J Geobot**

Journal of Geochemical Exploration *e:* **JGCEA**, *e:* **J Geochem E[xplor]**

Journal of Geodynamics *e:* **J. Geodyn.**

Journal of Geoelectricity *e:* **J. Geolectr.**

Journal of Geography *e:* **JG**, *e:* **J Geog**, *e:* **JOGG A**

Journal of Geography in Higher Education *e:* **J Geo Higher Educ**

Journal of Geography. National Council of Geographic Education *e:* **NCGE/J**

Journal of Geography. National Council of Geographic Education. Menasha *e:* **J Geog[r].**

Journal of Geography [Tokyo] *e:* **J Geogr [Tokyo]**

Journal of Geological Education *e:* **J Geol Educ**, *e:* **Jour Geol Eductihon**

Journal of Geological Sciences. Applied Geophysics *e:* **J Geol Sci Appl Geophys**

Journal of Geological Sciences. Palaeontology *e:* **J Geol Sci Palaeontol**

Journal of Geological Sciences. Technology, Geochemistry [Prague] *e:* **J Geol Sci Technol Geochem [Prague]**

Journal of Geological Society *e:* **J. Geol. Soc.**

Journal of Geology *e:* **JG**, *e:* **J Geo**, *e:* **J Geol**

Journal of Geology. Chicago *e:* **JG.**

Journal of geology. Chicago *e:* **Jour geol.**

Journal of Geology. Ukrainian Academy of Sciences. Institute of Geology *e:* **J Geol Ukr Aad Sci Inst Geol**

Journal of Geology. United Arab Republic *e:* **J Geol UAR**

Journal of Geomagnetism and Geoelectricity *e:* **J Geomagn [&] G[eoelec]**

Journal of Geomagnetism and Geoelectricity [Japan] *e:* **J. Geomagn. Geoelectr.**

Journal of Geometry *e:* **J Geom**, *e:* **J Geometry**

Journal of Geometry and Physics [Italy] *e:* **J. Geom. Piys.**

Journal of geomorphology. New York City *e:* **Journal geomorph.**

Journal of Geophysical Prospecting *e:* **J Geophys Prospect**

Journal of Geophysical Research *e:* **J Geoph Res**, *e:* **J. Geophy. Res.**, *e:* **J Geophys Res**, *e:* **J. Geophys. Res.**, *e:* **JGR**

Journal of Geophysical Research A [American Geophysical Union] *e:* **J. Geophys. Res. A**

Journal of Geophysical Research [American Geophysical Union] *e:* **J. Geophys. Res.**

Journal of Geophysical Research. Atmospheres *e:* **J Geophys Res**

Journal of Geophysical Research B [American Geophysical Union] *e:* **J. Geophys. Res. B**

Journal of Geophysical Research C [American Geophysical Union] *e:* **J. Geophys. Res. C**

Journal of Geophysical Research. Series B *e:* **J Geophys Res B**

Journal of Geophysical Research. Series C. Oceans *e:* **J Geophys Res C Oceans**, *e:* **J Geophys Res Oceans**

Journal of Geophysical Research. Series C. Oceans and Atmospheres *e:* **J Geo R-OA**, *e:* **JGR C**

Journal of Geophysical Research. Series C. Oceans Atmospheres *e:* **J Geophys Res C Oceans Atmos**

Journal of Geophysical Research. Series D. Atmospheres *e:* **J Geophys Res D Atm**

Journal of Geophysical Research. Space Physics *e:* **J Geo R-SP**

Journal of Geophysics *e:* **JGEOD**, *e:* **J Geophys**

Journal of Geosciences. Osaka City University *e:* **J Geosci Osska City Univ**

Journal of Geotechnical Engineering *e:* **GT**, *e:* **J. Geotech. Eng.**

Journal of Gynaecolagical Endacrinology *e:* **Gyneacol Endocr**

Journal of Gynaecological Endocrinology *e:* **Gynaecol Endocr**, *e:* **J Gynecol Endocr**

Journal of Gynecological Practice [Japan] *e:* **J Gynecol Pract**

Journal of Health Administration Education *e:* **J Health Adm Educ**

Journal of Health and Hospital Law *e:* **J. Health&Hosp. L.**

Journal of Health and Human Behavior. Texas Christian Univ., Fort Worth *e:* **J Health Hum Behav.**

Journal of Health and Human Resources Administration *e:* **J Health Hum Resour[ce] Adm[in]**, *e:* **JHH**

Journal of Health and Social Behavior *e:* **J Health [&] Soc[ial] [Behav]**

Journal of Health and Social Behavior [Washington, DC] *e:* **J Health Soc Behav**

Journal of Health Care Finance *e:* **J Health Care Finance**

Journal of Health Care for the Poor and Underserved [Nashville] *e:* **J Health Care Poor Underserved**

Journal of Health Care Marketing *e:* **JHCM**, *e:* **J Health Care Mark[et]**

Journal of Health Care Technology *e:* **J Health Care Technol**

Journal of Health Economics *e:* **JOHE**

Journal of Health, Physical Education, Recreation *e:* **J Helth Phys Ed Rec**, *e:* **JOHPER**

Journal of Health Physics and Radiation Protection *e:* **J Health Phys Radiat Prot**

Journal of Health Politics, Policy and Law *e:* **J Health Pol[it Policy Lw]**, *e:* **JHPL**

Journal of Health Politics, Policy, and Law *e:* **JHPPL**

Journal of Health Politics, Policy and Law [Durham] *e:* **J Health Polit Policy Law**

Journal of Health, Population and Nutrition *e:* **JHPN**

Journal of Health Toxicology *e:* **J Health Toxicol**, *e:* **J Toxicol**

Journal of Healthcare Education and Training *e:* **J Healthc[are] Educ Train**

Journal of Healthcare Material Management *e:* **J Healthc Mater Manage**

Journal of Healthcare Protection Management *e:* **J Healthc Prot Manage**

Journal of Historical Geography *e:* **J Hist G[eogr]**

Journal of Historical Geography. London, New York *e:* **J Hist Geogr.**

Journal of Holistic Health *e:* **JOHH**

Journal of Holistic Medicine *e:* **JHMEDL**, *e:* **J Holistic Med**

Journal of Hydrogeology *e:* **J Hydrogeol**

Journal of Hydrological Sciences.[Poland] *e:* **J Hydrol Sci**

Journal of Hydrology *e:* **J. Hydrol.**

Journal of Hydrology [Amsterdam] *e:* **JHYDA7**

Journal of Hydrology. Amsterdam *e:* **J Hydrol.**

Journal of Hydrology [Amsterdam] *e:* **J Hydrol [Amst]**

Journal of Hydrology [Dunedin] *e:* **J Hydrol [Dunedin]**, *e:* **JLHYAD**

Journal of Hydrology [Netherlands] *e:* **J Hydrol [Neth]**

Journal of Hydronautics *e:* **J Hydronaut**

Journal of Hydroscience and Hydraulic Engineering *e:* **J. Hydrosci. Hydraul. Eng.**

Journal of Hygiene, Epidemiology, Microbiology and Immunology [Praha] *e:* **J Hyg Epidemiol Microbiol Immunol**

Journal of Indiana State Medical Association *e:* **J. Indiana State Med. Assoc.**

Journal of Industrial Microbiology *e:* **JIM**, *e:* **J Indust Microbiol**

Journal of Industrial Microbiology [Society for Industrial Microbiology] *e:* **J. Ind. Microbiol.**

Journal of Intensive Care Medicine *e:* **J Intensiv Care Med**

Journal of Internal Medicine [Oxford] *e:* **J Intern Med**

Journal of Internal Medicine. Supplement [Oxford] *e:* **J Intern Med Suppl**

Journal of International Biomedical Information and Data *e:* **J Int Biomed Inf Data**

Journal of International Law and Economics. George Washington Univ., The National Law Center. Washington *e:* **J Int Law Econ.**

Journal of International Medical Research *e:* **JIMR**

Journal of International Medical Research [Northampton, Eng] *e:* **J Int Med Res**

Journal of Investigative Medicine *e:* **JIM**, *e:* **J Investig Med**

Journal of Jinsen Medical Sciences *e:* **J Jinsen Med Sci**

Journal of Korean Medical Science [Seoul] *e:* **J Korean Med Sci**

Journal of Laboratory and Clinical Medicine *e:* **J Lab Clin Med**, *e:* **J La Cl Med**, *e:* **JLCM**

Journal of Land Use and Environmental Law *e:* **J. Land Use&Envtl. L.**

Journal of Law and Medicine *e:* **JLM**

Journal of Law, Medicine & Ethics *e:* **JLME**

Journal of Legal Medicine *e:* **J Leg Med**, *e:* **J L Med**

Journal of Leukocyte Biology *e:* **J Leukocyte Biol**

Journal of Leukocyte Biology [New York] *e:* **J Leukoc Biol**

Journal of Leukocyte Biology. Supplement *e:* **J Leukoc Biol Suppl**

Journal of Liberal Arts and Natural Sciences. Sapporo Medical College *e:* **J Lib Arts Nat Sci Sapporo Med Coll**

Journal of Liberal Arts and Sciences. Sapporo Medical College *e:* **J Lib Arts Sci Sapporo Med Coll**

Journal of Light and Visual Environment [Illuminating Engineering Institute of Japan] *e:* **J. Light Vis. Environ.**

Journal of Inferential and Deductive Biology *e:* **J Inferential Deductive Biol**

Journal of International Medical Research *e:* **J Int Med R**

Journal of Managed Care Medicine *e:* **JMCM**

Journal of Mathematical Biology [Berlin] *e:* **J Math Biol**

Journal of Mayan Linguistics. Dept. of Geography and Anthropology, Louisana State Univ., Baton Rouge *e:* **J Mayan Linguist.**

Journal of Medical and Veterinary Mycology [Abingdon] *e:* **J Med Vet Mycol**

Journal of Medical Education *e:* **JMEDA**, *e:* **J Med Ed[uc]**, *e:* **J M Educ**

Journal of Medical Eleclronics *e:* **J Med El[ectron]**

Journal of Medical Engineering and Technology *e:* **J Med Eng [and] Technol**, *e:* **J Med Eng Technol**, *e:* **J. Med. Eng. Technol.**

Journal of Medical Engineering and Technology [London] *e:* **J Med Eng Technol**

Journal of Medical Entomology [Lawrence, KS] *e:* **J Med Entomol**

Journal of Medical Enzymology *e:* **J Med Enzymol**

Journal of Medical Ethics *e:* **JME**

Journal of Medical Ethics [London] *e:* **J Med Ethics**

Journal of Medical Genetics *e:* **JM Cenet**, *e:* **J. Med. Genet.**, *e:* **JMG**

Journal of Medical Genetics [London] *e:* **J Med Genet**

Journal of Medical Humanities and Bioethics *e:* **J Med Humanit Bioeth[ics]**

Journal of Medical Imaging *e:* **JMI**

Journal of Medical Internet Research *e:* **JMIR**

Journal of Medical Laboratory Technology *e:* **J Med Lab Technol**

Journal of Medical Microbiology *e:* **J Med Micro[biol]**

Journal of Medical Microbiology [Edinburgh] *e:* **J Med Microbiol**

Journal of Medical Primatology *e:* **J Med Prim[atol]**, *e:* **JMPMA**

Journal of Medical Primatology [Copenhagen] *e:* **J Med Primatol**

Journal of Medical Sciences *e:* **J Med Sci**

Journal of Medical Sciences. Banaras Hindu University *e:* **J Med Sci Banaras Hindu Univ**

Journal of Medical Screening *e:* **J Med Screen**

Journal of Medical Systems *e:* **J Med Syst**

Journal of Medical Technology *e:* **J M Technol**

Journal of Medical Technology [Tokyo] *e:* **J Med Technol [Tokyo]**

Journal of Medical Virology *e:* **J Med Virol**, *e:* **J M Virol**

Journal of Medicinal and Pharmaceutical Chemistry *e:* **J Med Pharm Chem**

Journal of Medicinal Chemistry *e:* **JMC**

Journal of Medicinal Chemistry [American Chemical Society] *e:* **J. Med. Chem.**

Journal of Medicinal Plant Research. Planta Medica *e:* **J M Plant Res**

Journal of Medicine *e:* **J Med**

Journal of Medicine and Philosophy *e:* **J Med Phil[os]**

Journal of Medicine and Philosophy [Dordrecht] *e:* **J Med Philos**

Journal of Medicine [Cincinnati] *e:* **J Med [Cincinnati]**

Journal of Medicine. Experimental and Clinical *e:* **J Med Exp Clin**

Journal of Medicine. Experimental and Clinical [Basel] *e:* **J Med [Basel]**

Journal of Medicine. Mie Prefectural University *e:* **J Med Mie Prefect Univ**

Journal of Medicine [Westbury, New York] *e:* **J Med [Westbury NY]**

Journal of Membrane Biology *e:* **J Membr[ane] Biol**

Journal of Mental Health *e:* **J Ment Health**

Journal of Metamorphic Geology *e:* **J Metamorph Geol**, *e:* **JMG**

Journal of Meteorological Research [Japan] *e:* **J Meteorol Res**

Journal of Meteorology *e:* **J Met**, *e:* **J. Met.**, *e:* **J. Meteorol.**

Journal of Meteorology. American Meteorological Society. Lancaster *e:* **Jour meteorology.**

Journal of Meteorology [UnitedStates] *e:* **J Meteorol**

Journal of Microbiological Methods *e:* **J Microbiol Meth**, *e:* **JMM**

Journal of Microbiological Methods [Netherlands] *e:* **J. Microbiol. Methods**

Journal of Microbiology [Chaoyang, People's Republic of China] *e:* **J Microbiol [Chaoyang Peoples Repub China]**

Journal of Microbiology, Epidemiology and Immunobiology *e:* **J Microbiol Epidem Immunobiol**

Journal of Microbiology, Epidemiology and Immunobiology. English Translation *e:* **J Microbiol Epidemiol Immunobiol Engl Transl**

Journal of Microbiology, Epidemiology and Immunobiology [USSR] *e:* **J Microbiol Epidemiol Immunobiol [USSR]**

Journal of Microbiology of the United Arab Republic *e:* **J Microbiol UAR**

Journal of Microscopy and Natural Science *e:* **J Micr and Nat Sc**

Journal of Mineralogy, Petrology and Economic Geology *e:* **J Mineral Petrol Econ Geol**

Journal of Mining and Geology [Nigeria] *e:* **J Min Geol**

Journal of Molecular Biology *e:* **JMB**, *e:* **J. Mol. Biol.**

Journal of Molecular Medicine *e:* **J Mol Med**

Journal of Natural History *e:* **J Nat Hist**, *e:* **J Natl Hist**

Journal of Natural Products *e:* **JNPRD**

Journal of Natural Products [Columbus, OH] *e:* **J Nat Prod**

Journal of Natural Products [Lloydia] *e:* **J Nat Prod [Lloydia]**

Journal of Natural Resources & Environmental Law *e:* **J. Nat. Resources&Envtl. L.**

Journal of Natural Resources Management and Interdisciplinary Studies *e:* **JNRM**

Journal of Natural Rubber Research *e:* **JNRREQ**

Journal of Natural Rubber Research [Rubber Research Institute of Malay:sia] *e:* **J. Nat. Rubber Res.**

Journal of Natural Science. Chonnam Natianal University *e:* **JNCUD**

Journal of Natural Sciences and Mathematics *e:* **J Nat Sci Math**, *e:* **J Natur Sci [and] Math**

Journal of Natural Sciences and Mathematics [Lahore] *e:* **J Nat Sci Math [Lahore]**

Journal of Natural Sciences. College of General Studies. Seoul National University *e:* **J NBt Sci Coll Gen Stud Seoul Nstl Uoiv**

Journal of Natural Sciences. Yeungnam University *e:* **J Nat Sci Yeungnam Univ**

Journal of Neurobiology [New York] *e:* **J Neurobiol**

Journal of Nuclear Agriculture and Biology *e:* **JNABD**, *e:* **J Nucl Agric Biol**

Journal of Nuclear Biology and Medicine [Torino] *e:* **J Nucl Biol Med**

Journal of Nuclear Medicine *e:* **J Nuclear Med**

Journal of Nuclear Medicine and Allied Sciences *e:* **JNMSD**, *e:* **J Nucl Med Allied Sci**

Journal of Nuclear Medicine [New York] *e:* **JNM**

Journal of Nuclear Medicine. Pamphlet *e:* **J Nucl Med Pam**

Journal of Nuclear Medicine [Society of Nuclear Medicine] *e:* **J. Nucl. Med.**

Journal of Nuclear Medicine. Supplement *e:* **J Nucl Med Suppl**

Journal of Nuclear Medicine Technology *e:* **JNMT**

Journal of Nuclear Medicine Technology [Society of Nuclear Medicine] *e:* **J. Nucl. Med. Technol.**

Journal of Nutritional and Environmental Medicine *e:* **JNEM**

Journal of Obstetric, Gynecologic and Neonatal Nursing [Philadelphia] *e:* **JOGNN**

Journal of Obstetric, Gynecologic, and Neonatal Nursing [Philadelphia, PA] *e:* **J Obstet Gynecol Neonatal Nurs**

Journal of Obstetrics and Gynaecology *e:* **J Obstet Gynaecol**

Journal of Obstetrics and Gynaecology of India *e:* **J Obstet Gyneecol India**

Journal of Obstetrics and Gynaecology of the British Commonwealth *e:* **J Obstet Gynaec Br[it] Commonw,** *e:* **J. Obstet. Gynaecol. Br. Commonw.**

Journal of Obstetrics and Gynaecology of the British Empire *e:* **J Obstet Gynaecol Br Emp**

Journal of Occupational and Environmental Medicine *e:* **J Occup Environ Med,** *e:* **JOEM**

Journal of Occupational Health and Safety-Australia and New Zealand *e:* **J Occup Health Safety**

Journal of Occupational Health and Safety in Australia *e:* **J Occ Health Safety Aust**

Journal of Occupational Medicine *e:* **J Occ[upa] Med,** *e:* **J Occup Med,** *e:* **JOCMA,** *e:* **JOM,** *e:* **JOOM**

Journal of Ocean Technology *e:* **J Ocean Technol**

Journal of Oncology. Tianjin Medical Journal. Supplement *e:* **J Onenl Tianjin Med J Suppl**

Journal of Oral Medicine *e:* **J Oral Med**

Journal of Oral Pathology and Medicine [Copenhagen] *e:* **J Oral Pathol Med**

Journal of Orthomolecular Medicine *e:* **JOM**

Journal of Paediatrics and Child Health [Melbourne] *e:* **J Paediatr Child Health**

Journal of Perinatal Medicine [Berlin] *e:* **J Perinat Med**

Journal of Petroleum Geology [England] *e:* **J Pet[rol] Geol**

Journal of Petrology and Geology *e:* **J. Petrol. Geol.**

Journal of Pharmaceutical and Biomedical Analysis *e:* **J Pharm B,** *e:* **J Pharm Biomed Anal**

Journal of Pharmaceutical Medicine *e:* **J Pharm Med**

Journal of Photochemistry and Photobiology. B, Biology [Lausanne] *e:* **J Photochem Photobiol B**

Journal of Physical Oceanography [American Meteorological Society] *e:* **J. Phys. Oceanogr.**

Journal of Physics of the Earth *e:* **J Phys Earth**

Journal of Physics of the Earth [Japan] *e:* **J. Phys. Earth**

Journal of Planning and Environment Law *e:* **JPEL,** *e:* **J.P.E.L.,** *e:* **J Plan[ing] [and] Environ[ment] Law,** *e:* **J Pln Envir[on] [&] L[aw]**

Journal of Plant Diseases and Protection *e:* **J Plant Dis Prot**

Journal of Plant Protection *e:* **J Plant Prot**

Journal of Podiatric Medical Education *e:* **J Poditr Med Educ**

Journal of Population. Behavioral, Social, and Environmental Issues *e:* **J Popul Behar Soc Environ Issues**

Journal of Postgraduate Medicine [Bombay] *e:* **J Postgrad Med,** *e:* **J Postgrad Med [Bombay]**

Journal of Prison Health *e:* **JPRH**

Journal of Protective Coatings and Linings *e:* **J. Prot. Coatings Linings**

Journal of Psychiatric & Mental Health Nursing *e:* **J Psychiatr Mental Health Nurs**

Journal of Psychiatric Nursing and Mental Health Services *e:* **JPNNB,** *e:* **J Psychiatr Nurs**

Journal of Psychological Medicine and Medical Jurisprudence *e:* **Jour Ps Med,** *e:* **J Psychologic Medicine**

Journal of Psychosocial Nursing and Mental Health Services *e:* **J Psychos Nurs Ment Health Serv,** *e:* **J Psychosoc[ial] Nurs**

Journal of Psychosocial Nursing and Mental Health Services [Thorofare] *e:* **J Psychosoc Nurs Ment Health Serv**

Journal of Psychosomatic Obstetrics and Gynaecology *e:* **JPOGDP,** *e:* **J Psychosom Obstet Gynaecol**

Journal of Psychosomatic Obstetrics and Gynecology *e:* **JPOG**

Journal of Public Health *e:* **J Public Health**

Journal of Public Health and Medical Technology. Korea University *e:* **J Public Health Med Technol Korea Univ**

Journal of Public Health Dentistry *e:* **JPHD**

Journal of Public Health Dentistry [Raleigh] *e:* **J Public Health Dent**

Journal of Public Health Medicine [Oxford] *e:* **J Public Health Med**

Journal of Public Health Policy *e:* **JPHP**

Journal of Public Health Policy [Burlington] *e:* **J Public Health Policy**

Journal of Public Health Practice [Japan] *e:* **J Public Health Pract**

Journal of Radiological Protection *e:* **J. Radiol. Prot.**

Journal of Religion and Health *e:* **J Regional Health,** *e:* **J Rel Hth,** *e:* **J Relig H[ealth]**

Journal of Remote Sensing *e:* **J Remote Smsing**

Journal of Reproductive Biology and Comparative Endocrinology *e:* **JRBEDZ,** *e:* **J Reprod Biol Comp Endocrinol**

Journal of Reproductive Medicine *e:* **JRM**

Journal of Reproductive Medicine [Chicago] *e:* **J Reprod Med**

Journal of Research in Indian Medicine *e:* **J Res Indian Med**

Journal of Research in Indian Medicine, Yoga and Homoeopathy *e:* **J Res Indian Med Yog Homoeopthy,** *e:* **JRI,** *e:* **JRIM**

Journal of Research. United States Geological Survey *e:* **J Res US Geol Surv,** *e:* **J Res US Geo Surv,** *e:* **J Res US GS**

Journal of Rural Health *e:* **JRH**

Journal of School Health *e:* **JOSH,** *e:* **JSHEA**

Journal of School Health [Kent] *e:* **J Sch Health**

Journal of Science and Health Policy *e:* **Scipolicy**

Journal of Science. Hiroshima University. Series C. Geology and Mineralogy *e:* **J Sci Hiroshima Univ Ser C [Geol Mineral]**

Journal of Science Technology [Aberdeen, Scotland] *e:* **J Sci Technol [Aberdeen Scotl]**

Journal of Scientific Research in Plants and Medicines *e:* **J Sci Res Plants & Med**

Journal of Small Animal Practice *e:* **J Small Anim Pract,** *e:* **J Sm Anim P,** *e:* **J Smll Anim Prct**

Journal of Soil and Water Conservation *e:* **J Soil & Water Conser,** *e:* **J Soil [&] Wat[er Conserv],** *e:* **JSWC**

Journal of Soil and Water Conservation in India *e:* **J Soil Water Conserv India**

Journal of Soil Biology and Ecology *e:* **J Soil Biol & Etnl**

Journal of South American Earth Sciences. Earth Sciences and Resources Institute, Univ. of South Carolina. New York *e:* **J South Am Earth Sci.**

Journal of Space and Astronomy Research [Iraq] *e:* **J. Space Astron. Res.**

Journal of Space Law *e:* **J. Space L.,** *e:* **J Space L[aw]**

Journal of Spacecraft and Rockets *e:* **J. Spacecraft Rockets,** *e:* **J Spacecr [and] Rockets,** *e:* **J Spac Rock,** *e:* **JSR**

Journal of Spacecraft and Rockets [American Institute of Aeronautics and Astronautics] *e:* **J. Spacecr. Rockets**

Journal of Spinal Cord Medicine *e:* **J Spinal Cord Med**

Journal of Sports Medicine *e:* **J Sports Med**

Journal of Sports Medicine and Physical Fitness *e:* **J Sport Med,** *e:* **J Sports Med [and] P[hys] Fit[ness]**

Journal of State Medicine *e:* **J St Med**

Journal of Steroid Biochemistry and Molecular Biology [Oxford] *e:* **J Steroid Biochem Mol Biol**

Journal of Structural Biology *e:* **J Struct Biol**

Journal of Structural Geology *e:* **J. Struct. Geol.**

Journal of Technical Methods and Bulletin. International Association of Medical Museums *e:* **J Techn Meth**

Journal of the Aero/Space Sciences *e:* **J Aero/Space Sci**

Journal [of the] Albert Einstein Medical Center *e:* **J.Albert Einstein Med.Cent.**

Journal of the Alliance of Medical Internet Professionals *e:* **JAMIP**

Journal of the American Academy of Orthopaedic Surgeons *e:* **JAAOS**

Journal of the American Animal Hospital Association *e:* **JAAHA**

Journal of the American Association of Gynecologic Laparoscopists *e:* **JAAGL**

Journal of [the] American College of Health *e:* **J Am Coll Health**

Journal of the American College of Surgeons *e:* **J Am Coll Surg**

Journal [of the] American Medical Association *e:* **JAMA**

Journal of the American Medical Association *e:* **J. Amer. Med. Assoc.**

Journal of the American Medical College
e: **J.A.M.Coll.**

Journal of the American Medical Directors
Association e: **JAMDA**

Journal of the American Medical
Informatics Association e: **JAMIA**, e: **J
Am Med Inform Assoc**

Journal of the American Medical Womens
Association e: **J Am Med Wom Assoc**,
e: **JAMWA**

Journal [of the] American Podiatric Medical
Association e: **J Am Podiatr Med
Assoc**

Journal of the American Veterinary Medical
Association e: **J. Amer. Vet. Med.
Assoc.**, e: **J Am Vet Med Assoc**, e:
JAVMA

Journal [of the] American Water Works
Association e: **J.Amer.Water Works
Assoc.**

Journal of the American Water Works
Association e: **J. Am. Water Works
Assoc.**

Journal [of the] Arkansas Medical Society
e: **J Ark[ansas] Med Soc**

Journal of [the] Atmospheric Science[s] e:
JAS

Journal of the Atmospheric Sciences e: **J
Atmos[pheric] Sci**

Journal of [the] Atmospheric Sciences
[American Meteorological Society] e: **J.
Atmos. Sci.**

Journal of the Biological Inorganic
Chemistry Society [] e: **J Biol Inorg
Chem Soc**

Journal of the Biological Photographic
Association e: **J. Biol. Photogr. Assoc.**

Journal of the Earth and Space Physics
[Tehran] e: **J Earth SPace Phys
[Tehran]**

Journal of the Environmental Satellite
Amateur Users' Group e: **JESAUG**

Journal of the Florida Medical Association
e: **J Fla Med Assoc**, e: **JFMA**

Journal of the Formosan Medical
Association e: **J Formos Med Assoc**

Journal of the Geological Society of
Australia e: **J. Geol. Soc. Aust.**

Journal of the Geological Society of India
e: **J. Geol. Soc. India**

Journal [of the] Geological Society of
Jamaica e: **J. Geol. Soc. Jam.**

Journal of the History of Biology e: **J Hist
Biol**

Journal of the History of Medicine e:
JHM, e: **Jour Hist Med**

Journal of the History of Medicine and
Allied Sciences e: **J Hist Med [Allied
Sci]**

Journal of the History of Medicine and
Allied Sciences, Department of the
History of Medicine. Yale University.
New Haven e: **J Hist Med Allied Sci.**

Journal of the Indian Medical Association
[Calcutta] e: **J Indian Med Assoc**

Journal of the Indian Medical Associations
[Calcutta] e: **JIMA**

Journal of the Indian Medical Profession
e: **J Indian Med Prof**

Journal of the Indian Waterworks
Association e: **J. Indian Waterworks
Assoc.**

Journal of the Institution of Engineers
[India], Public Health Engineering
Division e: **J. Inst. Eng. [India], Publ.
Health Eng. Div.**

Journal of the Institution of Water
Engineers and Environmental
Management e: **J. Inst. Water Eng.
Environ. Manage.**

Journal of the Iraqi Medical Professions e:
J Iraqi Med Prof

Journal of the Islamic Medical Association
of South Africa e: **JIMASA**

Journal of the Israel Medical Association
e: **JIMA**

Journal of the Japan Society for
Aeronautical and Space Sciences e: **J.
Jpn. Soc. Aeronaut. Space Sci.**

Journal of the Japan Water Works
Association e: **J. Jpn. Water Works
Asc.**

Journal of the Kansas Medical Society e:
J. Kans. Med. Soc.

Journal of the Kentucky Medical
Association e: **J Ky Med Assoc**

Journal of the Louisiana State Medical
Society e: **J La State Med Soc**

Journal of the Manchester Geographical
Society e: **J MAN GS**

Journal of the Marine Biological
Association e: **J.M.B.A.**

Journal of the Medical Association of
Georgia e: **J Med Assoc Ga**

Journal of the Medical Association of
Thailand e: **J Med Assoc Thai**

Journal of the Medical Library Association
e: **JMLA**

Journal of the Medical Society of New
Jersey e: **J. Med. Soc. N.J.**

Journal of the Mississippi State Medical
Association e: **J Miss State Med Assoc**

Journal of the National Medical Association
e: **J Natl Med Assoc**, e: **JNMA**

Journal of the Nepal Medical Association
e: **JNMA**

Journal of the Oklahoma State Medical
Association e: **J. Okla. State Med.
Assoc.**

Journal of the Royal Army Medical Corps
[London] e: **J R Army Med Corps**

Journal of the Royal College of Surgeons of
Edinburgh e: **J R Coll Surg Edinb**

Journal of the Royal Geographical Society
e: **JRGS**

Journal of the Royal Naval Medical Service
[Alverstoke] e: **J R Nav Med Serv**

Journal [of the] Royal Society of Health
[London] e: **J R Soc Health**

Journal of the Royal Society of Medicine
e: **JRSM**

Journal [of the] Royal Society of Medicine
[London] e: **J R Soc Med**

Journal of the Society for Health Systems
[Norcross, GA] e: **J Soc Health Syst**

Journal of the Society of Environmental
Engineers e: **J. Soc. Environ. Eng.**

Journal of the South Carolina Medical
Association e: **J. S. C. Med. Assoc.**

Journal of the Walter Roth Museum of
Archaeology and Anthropology. Ministry
of Education, Social Development and
Culture. Georgetown e: **J Walter Roth
Mus.**

Journal of the Water Pollution Control
Federation e: **J. Water Pollut. Contr.
Fed.**, e: **J. Water Pollut. Control Fed.**,
e: **JWPCF**

Journal of the Waterways and Harbors
Division, Proceedings of the American
Socie e: **J. Waterways Harbors Div.,
Ame**

Journal of Theoretical Biology e: **JTB**, e:
J Theor[et] Bio[l]

Journal of Theoretical Biology [London]
e: **J Theor Biol**

Journal of Theoretical Neurobiology e: **J
Theor N**

Journal of Thermal Biology e: **J Therm
Bio[l]**

Journal of Tongji Medical University
[Wuhan] e: **J Tongji Med Univ**

Journal of Toxicological and Environmental
Chemistry [Switzerland] e: **J. Toxicol.
Environ. Chem.**

Journal of Toxicology and Environmental
Health e: **J Tox Env H**, e: **J Toxicol
Environ Health**

Journal of Trace Elements in Experimental
Medicine e: **J Trace Elem Exp Med**

Journal of Traditional Chinese Medicine e:
JTCMEC

Journal of Traditional Chinese Medicine
[Beijing] e: **J Tradit Chin Med**

Journal of Transportation Medicine [Japan]
e: **J Transp Med**

Journal of Tropical Geography e: **JTG**, e:
JTGG-A, e: **JTGGAA**, e: **J Trop[ical]
Geog[raphy]**

Journal of Tropical Geography. Depts. of
Geography, Univ. of Singapore and
University of Malaya e: **J Trop Geogr.**

Journal of Tropical Medicine and Hygiene
e: **JTM&H**

Journal of Tropical Medicine and Hygiene
[London] e: **J Trop Med and Hyg
[London]**

Journal of Tropical Medicine and Hygiene
[Oxford] e: **J Trop Med Hyg**

Journal of Tropical Medicine [London] e:
J Trop Med [London]

Journal of Tropical Pediatrics and African
Child Health e: **J Trop Pediatr Afr
Child Health**

Journal of Tropical Pediatrics and
Environmental Child Health e: **J Trop
Pediatr Environ Child Health**

Journal of Tropical Pediatrics and
Environmental Child Health. Monograph
e: **J Trop Pediatr Environ Child Health
Monogr**

Journal of Ultrasound in Medicine
[Rockville] e: **J Ultrasound Med**

Journal of UOEH [University of
Occupational and Environmental Health]
[Japan] e: **J UOEH**

Journal of Veterinary and Animal
Husbandry Research [India] e: **J Vet
Anim Husb Res [India]**

Journal of Veterinary Internal Medicine
[Philadelphia] e: **J Vet Intern Med**

Journal of Veterinary Medical Education
e: **J Vet Med Educ**, e: **JVME**

Journal of Veterinary Medical Science
[Tokyo] e: **J Vet Med Sci**

Journal of Veterinary Medicine A e: **J Vet
Med A**

Journal of Veterinary Medicine B e: **J Vet Med B**

Journal of Veterinary Medicine. Series A e: **J Vet Med Ser A**, e: **JVMAE6**

Journal of Veterinary Medicine. Series B e: **J Vet Med Ser B**, e: **JVMBE9**

Journal of Virology [American Society for Microbiology] e: **J. Virol.**

Journal of Volcanology and Geothermal Research e: **J Volanol Geotherm Res**

Journal of Water and Waste e: **J. Water Waste**

Journal of Water and Waste [Japan] e: **J Water Waste**

Journal of Water Resources e: **J Water Resour**, e: **JWREEG**

Journal of Weather Modification [Weather Modification Association] e: **J. Weather Modif.**

Journal of Wildlife Diseases e: **JWIDA**

Journal of Wildlife Diseases [Ames] e: **J Wildl Dis**

Journal of Wildlife Managemenl e: **J Wildl Man[age]**

Journal of Wildlife Management e: **J. Wildlife Manage.**, e: **J Wildlife Mgt**, e: **J. Wildl. Manage.**, e: **JWIM**

Journal of Wildlife Management [Washington] e: **J Wildl Manage**

Journal of Xiamen University [Natural Science] [China] e: **J. Xianten Univ. [Nat. Sci.]**

Journal of Zoo Animal Medicine e: **J Zoo Anim Med**

Journal ofHealth and Social Behavior e: **JHSB**

Journal ofMedicine and Interriational Medical Abstracts and Reviews e: **J Med Int Med Absb Rev**

Journal. Okayama Medical Society e: **J Okayama Med Soc**

Journal. Okayama Medical Society. Supplement e: **J OkayamB Med Soc Suppl**

Journal-Oklahoma State Medical Association e: **J Okla State Med Assoc**

Journal. Osaka City Medical Center e: **J Osaka City Med Cent**

Journal. Osaka Industrial University. Natural Sciences e: **J Osaka Ind Univ Nat Sci**

Journal. Osaka Medical College [Japan] e: **J Osak Med Coll**

Journal. Pakistan Medical Association e: **J Pak Med Ass[oc]**

Journal. Palestinca Arab Medical Association e: **J Palest Arab Med Ass**

Journal. Pangasinan Medical Society e: **J Pang Med S**, e: **J Pang Med Soc**

Journal. Pennsylvania Water Works Operators' Assiation e: **J PA Water Works Oper Assoc**

Journal. Philippine Federation of Private Medical Practitioners e: **J Philipp Fed Priv Med Pract**

Journal. Philippine Islands Medical Association e: **J Philipp Isl Med Assoc**

Journal. Philippine Medical Association e: **J Philippine MA**, e: **J Philipp Med Assoc**, e: **JPMEA**

Journal. Philippine Veterinary Medical Association e: **J Philipp Vet Med Assoc**

Journal. Polarographic Society e: **JPLSA**

Journal Polarographic Society [England] e: **J Polar Soc**

Journal pour l'Avancement des Soins Medicaux d'Urgence f: **JASMU**

Journal. Pusan Medical College e: **J Pusan Med Coll**

Journal. Rakuno Gakuen University. Natural Science e: **J Rakuno Gakuen Univ Nt Sci**

Journal. Research Institute of Medical Science of Korea e: **JRes Inst Med Sci Kor**

Journal. Royal Army Medical Corps e: **JRAMA**, e: **J R Army Med Corps**

Journal. Royal College of Surgeons in Ireland e: **J R Coll Surg Irel**

Journal. Royal College of Surgeons of Edinburgh e: **J R Coll Surg Edinb[urg]**, e: **JRCSA**

Journal. Royal Institute of Public Health and Hygiene e: **J R Inst Public Health Hyg**

Journal. Royal Institute of Public Health [England] e: **J R Inst Public Health**

Journal. Royal Meteorological Society e: **JRMS**

Journal. Royal Naval Medical Service e: **JRNMA**

Journal. Royal Society of Health e: **JRSH**

Journal. Sailama University. Faculty of Education. Mathematics and Natural Science e: **J Sailama Univ Fac Ed Math Natur Sci**

Journal. Sailama University. Natural Science [Japan] e: **J Sailama Univ Nt Sci**

Journal. Saint Barnabas Medical Center e: **J St Barnnbas Med Cent**

Journal Scientifque de la Meteorologie f: **J Sci Meteorol**

Journal. Scottish Association of Geography Teachers e: **J Scott As Geogr Teach**

Journal. Severance Union Medical College e: **J Severance Union Med Coll**

Journal. Shanghai Science Institute. Section 4. Experimental Biology and Medicine e: **J Shanghai Sci Inst Sect 4**

Journal. Shanghai Science Institute. Section 2. Geology Palaeontology, Mineralogy and Petrology e: **J Shanghai Sci Inst Sect 2**

Journal. Shanghai Science Institute. Section 1. Mathematics, Astronomy, Physics, Geophysics, Chemistry and Allied Sciences e: **J Shanghai Sci Inst Sect 1**

Journal. Shanghai Science Institute. Section 3. Systematic and Morphological Biology e: **J Shanghai Sci Inst Sect 3**

Journal. Shanxi University. Natural Science Edition e: **J Shanxi Univ Nat Sci Ed**

Journal. Shimane Medical Association [Japan] e: **J Shimane Med Assoc**

Journal. Showa Medical Association [Japan] e: **J Showa Med Assoc**

Journal. Society for Radiological Protection e: **J Soc Radiol Prot**

Journal. Society for the Bibliography of Natural History e: **J Soc Bibliogr Nat Hist**

Journal. Society for Undetwater Technology e: **J Soc Underwater Technol**

Journal. Society of Environmental Engineers e: **J Soc Enriron Eng**, e: **J Soc Env Engrs**, e: **J Soc Environ Engrs**

Journal. Société des Oceanistes f: **JSO**, f: **JSOc**, f: **J Soc Ocean[istes]**

Journal. South African Biological Society e: **J S Afr Biol S**

Journal. South African Veterinary Medical Association e: **J S Afr Vet Med Assoc**, e: **J South Afr Vet Med Ass**, e: **J Sth Afr Vet Med Ass**

Journal. South Carolina Medical Association e: **JSCMA**, e: **J SC Med Assoc**

Journal. Southeastern Section. American Water Works Association e: **J Southeast Sect Am Water Works Ass**

Journal. Southern African Wildlife Management Association e: **J South Afr Wildl Manage Ass**

Journal. Student American Medical Association e: **J Stud Amer Med Ass**

Journal Sul-Americano de Medicina s: **J Sul-Am Med**

Journal. Tennesse Medical Assiation e: **JTMMA**

Journal. Tennessee Medical Association e: **J Tenn Med Ass[oc]**

Journal. Tokyo Medical Association e: **J Tokyo Med Assoc**

Journal. Tokyo Medical College e: **J Tokyo Med Coll**

Journal. Tokyo Women s Medical College e: **J Tokyo Women's Med Coll**

Journal. Travis County Medical Society e: **J Travis County Med Soc**

Journal. University Geological Society [Nagpur] e: **J Unir Geol Soc [Nagpur]**

Journal. University of Sheffield. Geological Society e: **J Univ Sheffield Geol Soc**

Journal. University of Sydney. Medical Society e: **J Univ S Med S**

Journal. Urban Living and Health Association [Japan] e: **J Urban Living Health Assoc**

Journal Wakayama Medical Society e: **J Wakyama Med Soc**

Journal Watch: Women's Health e: **JMWH**

Journal. Water Pollution Control Federation e: **J Water PC**, e: **J Water Pollut Contr[ol] Fed**, e: **JWP[FA]**

Journal. Water Resources Planning and Management Division. Proceedings of the American Society of Civil Engineers e: **J Water Resour Planning & Manage Div Proc ASCE**, e: **J Water Resour Plann Manage Div Am Soc Civ Eng**

Journal. Water ResourcesPlanning and Management Division. Proceedings of the American Society of Civil Engineers e: **J Water Resour Plann Manage Div ASCE**

Journal. Water Works Association [Japan] e: **J Water Works Assoc**

Journal. Waterways and Harbors Division. American Society of Civil Engineers e: **J Waterw Harbors Div Am Soc Civ Eng**

Journal. Waterways, Harbors and Coastal Engineering Division. American Society of Civil Engineers e: **J Waterway**

Journal. Waterways, Ports, Coastal and Ocean Division. American Society of Civil Engineers e: **J Waterw Port Coastal Ocean Div ASCE**

Journal. Waterways, Ports, Coastal and Ocean Division. American Society of

Civil Engineers. Proceedings e: **J Waterway Port Coastal Ocean Div Amer S Civil Eng Proc**, e: **J Waterway Port Coastal & Ocean Div Proc ASCE**

Journal. Won Kwang Public Health Junior College e: **J Won Kwang Public Health JrColl**

Journal. Yonago Medical Association e: **J Yonago Med Assoc**

Journal. Zhejiang Medical University e: **J Zhejiang Med Univ**, e: **ZYDXDM**

Journal École Polytechnique f: **J Ec Polytech**

Journalism and Geological Information System Interest Group e: **JAGIS**

Journal of Biological Education e: **J Biol Educ**

Journals of Gerontology. Series A, Biological Sciences and Medical Sciences e: **J Gerontol A Biol Sci Med Sci**

Journees Medicales de France et de l'Union Francaise f: **Journ Med Fr**

JPMA. Journal of the Pakistan Medical Association [Karachi] e: **JPMA J Pak Med Assoc**

JSC [Johnson Space Center] Manual e: **JSCM**

JSC [Johnson Space Center] Payload Operations Center e: **J**

Judge Advocate Civil Law, Environmental e: **JACE**

Jugend Aktion Natur und Umweltschutz Niedersachsen d: **JANUN**

Jugendaktionskongress Umwelt und Natur in Nordrhein-Westfalen d: **JAU**

Jugendumweltbüro d: **JUB**

Jugendumweltjahrmarkt d: **JUMJA**

Jugendumweltkongress d: **JUKSS**

Jugendumweltwerkstatt d: **JUW**

Juneau Ice Field Research Project e: **JIRP**

Jungle Environmental Survival Training [School] e: **JEST**

Jungle Environmental Survival Training School e: **JEST School**

Junior Hospital Medical Officer e: **JHMO**

Junior Observers of Meteorology e: **JOOM**, e: **JOOMS**

Junior Ocean Group e: **JOG**

Junior Resident Medical Officer e: **JRMO**

Junta das Missões Geográficas e de Investigações do Ultramar p: **JMGIU**

Jupiter Atmospheric Probe e: **JAP**

Jupiter Orbiter e: **JO**

Jupiter Orbiter Probe e: **JOp**

Jupiter Orbiter Probe-Galileo e: **JOP**

Jupiter Orbiter Satellite Lander e: **JO/SL**

Jupiter Orbiting Vehicle for Exploration e: **JOVE**

Justice's Sea Law e: **Just SL**

Jute-Protected Cable e: **JP Cable**

Jutendo Medicine [Japan] e: **Jutendo Med**

Juvenile Water e: **JW**

Juventude Ecológica Angolana p: **JEA**

K

Kabinet pro Geomorfologii c: **KG**

Kabinet pro Historickou Geografii c: **KHG**

Kagoshima Space Center e: **KSC**

Kagoshima Space Center [Japan] e: **KAG**

Kaiser Foundation Medical Bulletin e: **Kaiser Fdn Med Bull**, e: **Kaiser Found Med Bull**

Kaiser Foundation Medical Bulletin. Abstract Issue e: **Kaiser Found Med Bll Abstr Issue**

Kaiserlicbe Akademie der Wissenschaften. Mathematische-Naturwissenschaftliche Klasse. Sitzungsberichte d: **K Ak Wiss Mat-Nt CI Szb**

Kaiserlich-Königliche Naturhistorische Hofmuseum Annalen e: **K-K Naturh Hofmus An**

Kaiserlich Leopoldinische Deutsche Akademie der Naturforscher d: **K.L.D.A.N.**

Kaku Igaku = Japanese Journal of Nuclear Medicine [Tokyo] j: **Kaku Igaku**

Kalamazoo Medicine e: **Kalamazoo Med**

Kalamazoo Nature Center e: **KNC**

Kaliningradskgo Gosudarstvennogo Universitet Diffierencial'naja Geometrija Mogoobrazii Figur R: **Klainingrad Gos Univ Differencial'naja Geom Mnogoobraz Figur**

Kaliumhydrogensulfit d: **E 228**

Kaliumhydroxid d: **E 525**

Kaliumsulfat, Kaliumhydrogensulfat d: **E 515**

Kälte-Klima-Praktiker d: **Kälte-Klima-Prakt**

Kälte und Klimatechnik d: **Kälte Klimatech**

Kälte-Wärme-Klima d: **KWK**

Kälte-Wärme-Klimatechnik GmbH d: **KWK**

kaltes Wasser d: **k.W.**

Kältetechnik-Klimatisierung d: **Kältetech-Klim**

Kaltwasser d: **KW**

Kaltwasserfraktion der Stärke d: **KWS**

Kaltwassersatz d: **KS**

Kamera für Erderkundung d: **ETC**

Kananaskis Centre for Environmental Research e: **KCER**

Kangaroo Protection Committee e: **KPC**

Kangaroo Protection Foundation e: **KPF**

Kano, Nigeria (Remote Site) e: **KNO**

Kansas Association for Infant Mental Health e: **KAIMH**

Kansas City College of Osteopathic Medicine, Kansas City e: **MoKCO**

Kansas City Medical Journal e: **Kansas Ci Med J**

Kansas City Weather Forecast Office e: **EAX**

Kansas Cosmosphere and Space Center e: **KCSC**

Kansas Department of Health and Environment e: **KDHE**

Kansas Environmental Health Services Bulletin e: **Kans Environ Health Serv Bull**

Kansas Geological Society e: **KGS**

Kansas Geological Survey e: **KGS**

Kansas Geological Survey. Bulletin e: **Kans Geol Surv Bull**

Kansas Geological Survey Map e: **Kansas Geol Survey Map**

Kansas Geological Survey. Series on Spatial Analysis e: **Kans Geol Surv Ser Spat Anal**

Kansas Ground Water. Basic-Data Release e: **Kans Ground Water Basic-Data Release**

Kansas Medical Society e: **KMS**

Kansas Medicine e: **Kans Med**

Kansas-Nebraska Natural Gas Company, Inc. e: **KNB**

Kansas Public Health Association e: **KPHA**

Kansas School Naturalist e: **Kans Sch Nat**

Kansas State Geological Survey. Bulletin e: **Kans State Geol Suvr Bull**

Kansas State Geological Survey. Computer Contribution e: **Kans State Geol Surv Comput[er] Contrib**

Kansas State Geological Survey. Special Distribution Publication e: **Kans State Geol Surv Spec Distrib[ution] Publ[ication]**

Kansas State University, Veterinary Medicine Library, Manhattan e: **KMK-V**

Kansas State Water Resources Board. Bulletin e: **Kansas Water Resources Bull**

Kansas Universily. Museum of Natural History. Miscellaneous Publication e: **Kansas Univ Mus Nat History Misc Pub**

Kansas University. Museum of Natural History. Publications. Paleontological Contributions. Science Bulletin e: **Kans Univ Mus Nat History Pub Paleont Contr Sci Bull**

Kansas Veterinary Medical Association e: **KVMA**

Kansas Water Resources Board. Bulletin e: **Kans Water Res Board Bull**

Kansas Water Resources Research Institute e: **KWRRI**

Kao-Hsiung I Hsueh Ko Hsueh Tsa Chih [KaoHsiung Journal of Medical Sciences] [Kaohsiung] ch: **Kao Hsiung I Hsueh Ko Hsueh Tsa Chih**

Karger Biobehavioral Medicine Series e: **Karger Biobehav Med Ser**, e: **KBMEDO**

Karlsruhe Atmospheric Mesoscale Model e: **KAMM**

Karlsruher Geographische Hefte d: **Karlsruber Geogr Hefte**

Karnataka Medical Journal e: **Karnataka Med J**

Katalog Umweltrelevanter Daten d: **KURD**

Katastrofmedicinska Organisationskommitté[n] r: **KAMEDO**

katastrophale Hochwasserquantität d: **KHQ**

katastrophischer Hochwasserstand d: **KHW**

Katedra Matematiky a Deskriptivní Geometrie c: **KMDG**

Katholische Arbeitsgemeinschaft für Volksgesundung d: **KAVG**

Katholische deutsche Schwestern-Vereinigung für Gesundheitsund Wohlfahrtsdienste e.V. d: **K.D.S.V.**

Kawaki Medical Journal e: **KAMJD**

Kawasaki Medical Journal e: **Kwasaki Med J**

Kaziranga Wildlife Sanctuary e: **KWS**

Keeping Abreast of Medical Transcription e: **KAMT**

Keilschrifttexte Medizinischen lnhalts d: **KMI**

Keio Journal of Medicine j: **Keio J Med**

Kellogg Biological Station e: **KBS**

Kenkyu Hokoku. Journal. Faculty of Education. Tottori University. Natural Science e: **Kenkyu Hokoku J Tottori Univ Nat Sci**

Kennedy Space Center e: **KDC**

Kennedy Space Center Area Permit e: **KSCAP**

Kennedy Space Center Atmospheric Boundary Layer Experiment e: **KABLE**

Kennedy Space Center Avionics Test Set e: **KATS**

Kennedy Space Center Data Management System e: **KDMS**

Kennedy Space Center DOD Payloads Plan/Requirement e: **K-DPM**

Kennedy Space Center IUS Plan/Requirement e: **K-IUSM**

Kennedy Space Center Landing Site, Florida e: **TAC**

Kennedy Space Center Notice e: **KNO**

Kennedy Space Center Spacelab Plan (or Requirement) e: **K-SLM**

Kennedy Space Center Station Set Specification e: **KSSS**

Kennedy Space Center/Unmanned Launch Operations e: **KSC/ULO**

Kennedy Space Center-Western Test Range Operations Division e: **KSC-WTROD**

Kennedy Space[flight] Center e: **KSC**

Kenting Earth Sciences e: **KENTING**

Kenton Natural Resources Corp. e: **KNN**

Kentucky Academy of Sciences and Kentucky State Nature Preserves Commission e: **KAS-KSNPC**

Kentucky Children's Health Insurance Program e: **KCHIP**

Kentucky Department for Environmental Protection e: **KDEP**

Kentucky. Department of Fish and Wildlife Resources. Fisheries Bulletin e: **KY Dep Fish Wildl Resour Fish Bull**

Kentucky. Department of Mines and Minerals. Geological Division. Series 8. Bulletin e: **KY Dep Mines Miner Geol Div Ser 8 Bull**

Kentucky Environmental Education Program e: **KEEP**

Kentucky. Geoiogical Sutvey. Series 10. Report of Investigation e: **KY Geol Surv Ser 10 Rep Invest**

Kentucky Geological Survey e: **KGS**

Kentucky. Geological Survey. Bulletin e: **Kentucky Geol Surv[ey] Bull**

Kentucky. Geological Survey. Bulletin. Information Circular. Report of Investigations. Special Publications e: **KY Geol Survey Bull Inf Circ Rept Inv Special Pub**

Kentucky. Geological Survey. County Report e: **Kentucky Geol Survey County Rept**

Kentucky. Geological Survey. Information Circular e: **Kentucky Geol Survey Inf Circ**

Kentucky. Geological Survey. Report of Investigations e: **Kentucky Geol Survey Rept Inv**, e: **KY Geol Surv Rep Invest**

Kentucky. Geological Survey. Report of Progress. Bulletin e: **KY GS Rg Prog B**

Kentucky. Geological Survey. Series 9. Bulletin e: **KY Geol Surv Ser 9 Bull**

Kentucky. Geological Survey. Series 10. County Report e: **KY Geol Surv Ser 10 Cty Rep**

Kentucky. Geological Survey. Series 9. Report of Investigation e: **KY Geol Surv Ser 9 Rep Invest**

Kentucky. Geological Survey. Series 9. Special Publication e: **KY Geol Surv Ser 9 Spec Publ**

Kentucky. Geological Survey. Special Publication e: **Kentucky Geol Surrey Sec Pub**, e: **Ky Geol Surv Spec Publ**

Kentucky. Geological Survey. Thesis Series e: **KY Geol Surv Thesis Ser**

Kentucky Medical Insurance Co. e: **KYMD**

Kentucky Medical Journal e: **Kentucky Med J**

Kentucky Natural Resources Information System e: **KNRIS**

Kentucky. Nature Preserves Commission. Technical Report e: **KY Nat Preserv Comm Tech Rep**

Kentucky-Ohio-Michigan Regional Medical Library e: **KOMRML**

Kentucky State Medical Association e: **KSMA**

Kentucky State Nature Preserves Commission e: **KSNPC**

Kentucky Veterinary Medical Association e: **KVMA**

Kentucky Water Resources Research Institute e: **KWRRI**

Kenya and East African Medical Journal e: **Kenya and East African Med J**

Kenya. Colony and Protectorate. Geological Survey. Memoir e: **Kenya Colony Prot Geol Surv Mem**

Kenya Department of Resources Surveys and Remote Sensing e: **KREMU**

Kenya Energy and Environment Organisations e: **KENGO**

Kenya Journal of Science and Technology. Series B. Biological Sciences e: **KSTSDG**

Kenya Medical Journal e: **Kenya Med J**

Kenya Rangeland Ecological Monitoring Unit e: **KREMU**

Kenya Wildlife Service e: **KWS**

Kenyan Medical Research Institute e: **KEMRI**

Keoladeo Ghana Wildlife Sanctuary e: **KGWS**

Kern-, bakteriologische [ober biologische] und chemische Waffen d: **KBC-Waffen**

Kern County Water Agency e: **KCWA**

Kern-Pixley National Wildlife Refuge e: **KPNWR**

Kernstrahlungs-, chemische und biologische Aufklärung d: **KCB-Aufklärung**

Kernstrahlungs-, chemische und biologische Beobachtung d: **KCB-Beobachtung**

Kerr's Water and Mineral Cases e: **Kerr W&M Cas**

Kesselspeisewasser d: **KSW**

Keuringsinstituut voor Waterleidingsartikelen n: **KIWA**

Key Asset Protection Program e: **KAPP**

Key Geographic Location e: **KGL**

Key to Oceanographic Records Documentation e: **Key Oceanogr Rec Doe**, e: **KORADQ**

Key West National Wildlife Refuge e: **KWNWR**

Key Word Index of Wildlife Research e: **Key Word Index Wildl Res**

Keystone Medical Corporation e: **KMEC**

Keyword Index for the Medical Literature e: **Keyword Index Med Lit**

Keyword Index in Internal Medicine e: **Keyword Index Intern Med**

Khidrologiya i Meteorologiya R: **KHMEA**

Khidrologiya i Meteoroloya R: **Khidrol Met[eorol]**

Khigiena. Epidemiologiya i Mikrobiologiya R: **Khig Epidemiol Mikrobiol**

Kiev Universitet Visnik Serya Geografi R: **Kiev Univ Visn Ser Geogr**

KIGAM [Korea Research Institute of Geoscience and Mineral Resources] Bulletin e: **KIGAM Bull**

Kill All Animals e: **KAA**

Kilogramm pro Pferdestärke-Stunde d: **kg/PSh**

Kilometer-Wave Orbiting Telescope e: **KWOT**

Kimmins Environmental Service Corp. e: **KEVN**

Kimmins Environmental Services e: **KVN**

Kinder-Aktion-Umweltschutz d: **KAKTUS**

Kindness in Nature's Defense e: **KIND**

Kinematic Simulation, Monitoring and Off-Line Programming Environment for Telerobotics e: **KISMET**

Kinetic Experiment[s] on Water Boiler Reactor e: **KEWB Reactor**

Kinetic Experiment[s] on Water Boiler[s] e: **KEWB**

King Abdulaziz Medical Journal e: **King Abdulaziz Med J**

King Faisal Specialist Hospital. Medical Journal e: **King Faisl Spec Hosp Med J**

King Mahendra Trust for Nature Conservation e: **KMTNC**

Kingston Geology Review e: **Kingston Geol Rev**

Kintyre Antiquarian and Natural History Society. Magazine e: **Kintyre Antiqu Nat Hist Soc Mag**

Kirin University Journal. Natural Sciences e: **Kirin Univ J Nat Sci**

Kirkenes Verdensråd N: **KV**

Kirschner Medical Corporation e: **KMDC**

Kiruna Geophysical Observatory e: **KGO**

Kirwin National Wildlife Refuge e: **KNWR**

Kitakanto Medical Journal e: **Kitakanto Med J**

Kitano Hospital Journal of Medicine e: **Kitano Hosp J Med**

Kitasato Archives of Experimental Medicine [Tokyo] j: **Kitasato Arch Exp Med**

Kitasato Medicine e: **Kitasato Med**

Kitt Peak National Observatory Arizona e: **KPNO**

Kitt Peak National Observatory Library, Tucson e: **KPNO**

Kitt Peak National Observatory [Tucson] e: **KPNO[B]**

Kitt Peak National Observatory, Tucson e: **KPO**

Klamath Basin National Wildlife Refuges e: **KBNWR**

Kleine Naturwissenschaftliche Bibliothek
  d: **Kleine Naturwiss Bibliothek**
Kleintier-Praxis *d:* **KLEPA**
Kleintierkunde *d:* **Kleintierkd.**
Kleinwasserzuschlag *d:* **KWZ**
Klima in historischen Zeiten [Projekt] *d:*
  KIHZ
Klima , Kälte , Heizung *d:* **Klima Kälte**
  Heiz
Klima -Kälte -Technik *d:* **Klima -Kälte-**
  Tech
Klima-Schnellmeldedienst *d:* **Klima Schn**
  D
Klima-Technik *d:* **Klima-Tech.**, *d:* **Klima-**
  Techn.
Klima und Kälte Ingenieur *d:* **Klim Kälte**
  Ing
Klima und Kälteingenieur *d:* **Klima**
  Kälteing
Klimaänderung und Bodden *d:* **KLIBO**
Klimaanlage *d:* **Klima**
Klimabündnis niedersächsischer Schulen
  e.V. *d:* **KlinSch**
Klimadatenbank *d:* **KLIBADA**, *d:*
  KLIDABA, *e:* **KLIDABA**
Klimaheilkunde *d:* **Klimaheilkd.**
Klimainformationssystem *d:* **KLIS**
Klimakunde *d:* **Klimakde.**
Klimameßzahl *d:* **KMZ**
Klimarechenzentrum, Hamburg *d:* **KRZ**
Klimatechnische Gesellschaft *d:* **KTG**
Klimathermokammer *d:* **KTK**
Klimatisacija Grejanje Hladenje *c:* **Klim**
  Grej Hlad
Klimatische Wasserbilanz *d:* **KWB**
Klimatologie *d:* **Klimatol.**
Klinik und Poliklinik für Innere Medizin
  e: **KIM**
Klinik und Poliklinik für Nuklearmedizin
  e: **KNuk**
Klinik und Poliklinik für Psychosomatik
  und Psychotherapeutische Medizin *d:*
  KPM
Klinische Medizin *d:* **Klin. Med.**
Klinische Medizin [Vienna] *d:* **Klin Med**
  [Vienna]
Kliniska un Eksperimentala Medicina *a:*
  Klin Eksp Med
Knight Commander of the Order of St
  Michael and St George *e:* **KCMG**
Knight of Saint Michael and Saint George
  e: **KSM&SG**
Knihovna Státního Ústavu Geologického
  Československé Republiky *c:*
  KSÚGČSR
Knihovna Ustredniho Ustavu Geologickeho
  c: **Knih Ushed Ust[avu] Geol**, *c:* **Knih**
  Ustred Ust Geol
Know Problems of Hydrocephalus *e:* **KPH**
Knowledge Based Geographical
  Information System *e:* **KBGIS**
Knowledge-Based Planning and Control in
  Manufacturing Environments *e:*
  FLEXPLAN
Knowledge Engineering Environment *e:*
  KEE
Knowledge Enneering Environment *e:*
  KEE
Knowledgeable Observation Analysis
  Advisory System *e:* **KOALAS**
Known Geological Structure *e:* **KGS**
Known Geothermal Resource[s] Area[s] *e:*
  KGRA

Knoxville Academy of Medicine, Knoxville
  e: **TKAM**
Knoxville Area Health Science Consortium
  e: **KAHSLC**
Knuckeys Lagoon Protected Area *e:*
  KLPA
Kobe Journal of Medical Sciences *e:*
  KJMDA, *e:* **Kobe J Med Sci**
Kobe Journal of Medical Sciences (Kobe)
  e: **Kobe J Med Sci**
Kobe Marine Observatory *e:* **KMO**
Kobe University Medical Mission to
  Indonesia *e:* **KUMMI**
Kodaikanal Observatory Bulletin. Series A
  [India] *e:* **Kodaikanal Obs Bull [Ser] A**
Kodaikanal Observatory Bulletin. Series B
  [India] *e:* **Kodaikanal Obs Bull B**
Koeltechniek/Klimaatregeling *r:* **NVK**
Kohlenwasserstoff *d:* **KW-Stoff**
Kohlenwasserstoffe *d:* **HC**
Kohlenwasserstoff[e] *d:* **KW**
Kohlenwasserstoffe mit Methan *e:* **CHCH**
Kohlenwasserstoffe (ohne Methan) *d:* **CH**
Kohlenwasserstoffgase *d:* **KWG**
Kokoxili Suture *e:* **KS**
Kolff Medical, Inc. *e:* **KOLF**
Kollektiv sozialistische Medizin *d:*
  Kosomed
Kölner Geographische Arbeiten *d:* **Kö**
  Geogr Arb
Kölner Geologische Hefte *d:* **Köln Geol H**
Kölner Observatorium für Submillimeter
  Astronomie *d:* **KOSMA**
Kometen, Planetoiden, Meteore *d:* **KPM**
Komitet Geograficzny Polskiej Akademii
  Nauk *P:* **KGPAN**
kommentiert *d:* **komm.**
Kommission des Abgeordnetenhauses *d:*
  K.D.A.
Kommission für Bildungsfragen im
  Gesundheitswesen *e:* **KBG**
Kommission für die Bewertung
  wassergefährdender Stoffe *d:* **KBwS**
Kommission für elektronische Bauelemente
  für Raumfluggeräte *d:* **KEBR**
Kommission für Raumfahrttechnik *d:* **KfR**
Kommission für Umwelt, Raumplanung und
  Energie *d:* **UREK**
Kommunale Energie- und
  Wasserversorgungs-AG *d:* **KEW**
Kommunikationsorientiertes
  Echtzeitbetriebssystem *d:* **TRAX**
Kommutierungskondensator *d:* **KK**
Komplementäre Medizin: Homöopathie *d:*
  HOM
Kompostierung *d:* **Komp.**
Konferenz der Internationalen Gesellschaft
  für Biologische Rhythmusforschung *d:*
  Konf Int Ges Biol Rhythm Forsch
konfrontieren *d:* **konfr.**
konfrontiert *d:* **konfr.**
Kongelige Danske Videnskabemes Selskab.
  Biologiske Skrifter *a:* **K Dan Vidensk**
  Selsk Biol Skr
Kongelige Danske Videnskabernes Selskab.
  Skrifter. Naturvidenskabelig ug Mathe-
  matisk Afdeling *a:* **K Dan Vidensk**
  Selsk Skr Naturvidensk Mat Afd
Kongres Buruh Islamic Merdeka *ma:*
  KBIM
Kongreßzentralblatt für die Gesamte Innere
  Medizin und ihre Grenzgebiete *d:*
  Kong[r] Z[entral]bl Ges Inn[ere] Med

Königlich Belgisches Institut für
  Naturwissenschaften *d:* **KBIN**
Königlich-Böhmische Gesellschaft der
  Wissenschaften in Prag. Mathematisch-
  Naturwissenschaftliche Klasse.
  Sitzungsberichte *e:* **K-Böhm Ges Wiss**
  Mat-Nat CI Szb
Koninklijk Magnetisch en Meteorologisch
  Observatorium *n:* **K.M.M.O.**
Koninklijk Meteorologisch Instituut van
  België *n:* **KMI**
Koninklijk Museum voor Midden-Afrika
  [Tervuren, Belgie]. Annalen. Reeks in
  Octavo. Geologische Wetenschappen *n:*
  K Mus Midden-Afr [Tervuren Belg]
  Ann Reeks OctBvo Geol Wet
Koninklijk Museum voor Midden-Afrika
  [Tervuren, Belgie]. Rapport Annuel.
  Departement de Geologie et de
  Mineralogie *n:* **K Mus Midden-Afr**
  [Tervuren Belg] Rapp Annu Dep Geol
  Mineral
Koninklijk Nederlands Geologisch
  Mijnbouwkundig Genootschap *n:*
  KNGMG
Koninklijk Nederlands Meteorologisch
  Instituut *n:* **KNMI**
Koninklijk Nederlandsch Geologisch-
  Mijnbouwkundig Genootschap
  Verhandelingen. Geologische Serie *n:* **K**
  Nederlandsch Geol-Mijn Genootschap
  Verh Geol Ser
Koninklijk Verbond van de Industrie van
  Waters en Frisdranken *n:* **VIWF**
Koninklijke Nederlande Espace Sociétéit
  n: **KNES**
Koninklijke Nederlandse Akademie van
  Wetenschappen. Proceedings Series B.
  Palaeontology, Geology, Physics, and
  Chemistry *n:* **K Ned Akad Wet Proc**
  Ser B Palaeontol Geol Phys Chem
Koninklijke Nederlandse Akademie van
  Wetenschappen. Proceedings. Series C.
  Biolocal and Medical Sciences *n:* **K Ned**
  Akad Wet Proc Ser C
Koninklijke Nederlandse Akademie voor
  Naturwetenschappen *n:* **KNAN**
Koninklijk[e] Nederlandse
  Natuurhistorische Vereeniging
  [Vereeniging voor Veldbiologie] *n:*
  KNNV
Konstante Pixelanzahl der und derer
  zugeordneten Flächen im Raster der
  CCD-Matrix *e:* **Const pix**
konstatieren *d:* **konst.**
Konstitutionelle Medizin *d:* **KM**, *d:*
  Konstit Med
Konstitutionelle Medizin und
  Neuraltherapie *d:* **Konstit Med Neur**
  Ther
Konstruktionswasserlinie *d:* **D.W.L.**, *d:*
  KWL
kontinentale Polarluft *d:* **cP**, *d:* **KPL**
kontingentieren *d:* **kont.**
kontingentiert *d:* **kont.**
Kontingent[ierung] *d:* **Kont[g]**
Kontinuierlicher Abfluß und Stofftransport
  Integrierte Modellierung unter Nutzung
  von Geoinformationssystemen *d:* **ASGi**
kontrastieren *d:* **kontr.**
kontrastiert *d:* **kontr.**
Kontrolliert biologischer Anbau *d:* **KbA**
konvertierbar *d:* **konv.**, *d:* **konvert.**

Konvertierbarkeit *d:* **Konv.**

Konvertierung *d:* **Konv.**

Konvertierungs-, Moratoriums- und Transfer-Risiko *d:* **KMT-Risiko**

Konvertierungs- und Transferrisiko *d:* **KT-Risiko**

Konza Prairie Research Natural Area *e:* **KPRNA**

konzertierte Aktion im Gesundheitswesen *d:* **KAiG**

Kooperative Abteilung Tierproduktion *d:* **KAT**

kooptieren *d:* **koop.**

Koordinationszentrum für geologische Ausrüstungen und Erkundungsmethoden *d:* **Intergeotechnika**

Koordinierungskomitee für die atmosphärischen Bedingungen beim Prüfen *d:* **ATCO**

Korea Aerospace Research Institute *e:* **KARI**

Korea Association for Radiation Protection *e:* **KARP**

Korea. Geological and Mineral Institute. Report of Geological and Mineral *e:* **Korea Geol and Miner Inst Rep of Geol Miner Explor**

Korea Institute for Population and Health *e:* **KIPH**

Korea Medical Journal *e:* **Korea Med J**

Korea Ocean Research and Development Institute *e:* **KORDI**

Korea Oceanographic Data Centre [or Center] *e:* **KODC**

Korea Research Institute of Geoscience and Mineral Resources. KIGAM Bulletin *e:* **Korea Res Inst Geosci Miner Resour KIGAM Bull**

Korea University. Medical Journal *e:* **Korea Univ Med J**

Korea Water Resources Development Corporation *e:* **KOWACO**

Korean Central Journal of Medicine *e:* **Korean Cent J Med**

Korean Geological Survey *e:* **KGS**

Korean Institute of Geology, Mining and Minerals *e:* **KIGAM**

Korean Journal of Animal Sciences *e:* **Korean J Anim Sci**

Korean Journal of Applied Microbiology and Bioengineering *e:* **Korean J Appl Microbiol Bioeog**

Korean Journal of Environmental Health Society *e:* **Korean J Environ Health Soc**

Korean Journal of Internal Medicine (Seoul) *e:* **Korean J Intern Med**

Korean Journal of Microbiology *e:* **Korean J Microbiol**

Korean Journal of Nuclear Medicine *e:* **Korean J Nucl Med**

Korean Journal of Obstetrics and Gynecology *e:* **Korean J Obstet Gyneenl**

Korean Journal of Plant Protection *e:* **Korean J Plant Prot**

Korean Journal of Public Health *e:* **Korean J Public Health**

Korean Medical Abstracts *e:* **KOMAB**

Korean Medical Association of America *e:* **KMAS**

Korean Medicine *e:* **Kor Med**

Korean Ministry of Environment *e:* **KMOE**

Korean National Committee of the International Association on Water Pollution Research and Control *e:* **KNCIAWPRC**

Korean National Oceanographic Data Centre *e:* **KNODC**

Korean (or Korea's) Meteorological Administration *e:* **KMA**

Korean Society of Animal Nutrition and Feedstuffs *e:* **Korean S Anim Nutr & Feedstuffs**

Korean Society of Water Pollution Research and Control *e:* **KSWPRC**

Korpspferdepark *d:* **K.Pf.P.**

Korrespondenz Abwasser *d:* **Korresp Abwasser**

Korrespondenzblatt des Vereins für Niederdeutsche Sprachforschung *d:* **Niederdt Kbl**

Korrespondenzblatt. Verein für Niederdeutsche Sprachforschung *d:* **Kbl**

Korrespondenzblätter des Naturforscher-Vereins Riga *d:* **KoBlNFVR**

Kosmicheskaya Biologiya i Aviakosmicheskaya Meditsina *R:* **KBAMA,** *R:* **Kosm B[iol] Av[ikosm] M[ed]**

Kosmicheskaya Biologiya i Meditsina *R:* **KBMEA,** *R:* **Kosm Biol Med**

Kosmobiologische Akademie Aalen *d:* **KAA**

Kosmos. Die Zeitschrift für alle Freunde der Natur. Stuttgart *d:* **KOSMOS.**

Kosmos. Seria A. Biologia [Warsaw] *P:* **KOSBA,** *P:* **Kosmos Ser A [Biol] [Warsaw]**

Kostenverordnung zum Bundesnaturschutzgesetz *d:* **BNatSchGKostV**

Kotierung *d:* **Kot.**

Kredietbank Luxembourgeoise *f:* **KBL**

Kreisinspektion Gesundheitsschutz *d:* **KIG**

Kreisnaturschutzbeauftragte[r] *d:* **KNB**

Kreisnaturschutzring Harburg-Land e.V. *d:* **KNR**

Kreisnaturschutzverwaltung *d:* **KNV**

Kresge Medical Research Institute *e:* **K M R I**

KSC [Kennedy Space Center] Automated Payloads Project *e:* **K-APPS**

KSC [Kennedy Space Center] Handbook *e:* **KHB**

KSC [Kennedy Space Center] Management Instruction *e:* **KMI**

KSC [Kennedy Space Center] MMSE [Multiuse Mission Support Equipment] Notice *e:* **K-MMSEN**

KSC [Kennedy Space Center] MMSE [Multiuse Mission Support Equipment] Project Specifcation *e:* **K-MMSEPS**

KSC [Kennedy Space Center] Notice *e:* **KN**

KSC [Kennedy Space Center] Operation Instruction *e:* **KOI**

KSC [Kennedy Space Center] Organizational Manual *e:* **KOM**

KSC [Kennedy Space Center] Shuttle Management *e:* **KM**

KSC [Kennedy Space Center] Shuttle Project Notice *e:* **K-SPN**

KSC [Kennedy Space Center] Shuttle Project Specifcation *e:* **K-SPS**

KSC [Kennedy Space Center] Shuttle Project Station Set Specification *e:* **K-SSS**

KSC [Kennedy Space Center] Shuttle Test Station Notice *e:* **K-STSN**

KSC [Kennedy Space Center] Shuttle Test Station Project Specification *e:* **K-STSPS**

KSC [Kennedy Space Center] Space Transportation System Management *e:* **K-STSM**

KSC [Kennedy Space Center] Spacelab Notice *e:* **K-SLN**

KSC [Kennedy SpaceCenter] Spacelab Project Specifcation *e:* **K-SLPS**

KSC [KennedySpace Center] Automated Payloads Notice *e:* **K-APN**

Ku-Ring-Cai Bushland and Environmental Society [Australia] *e:* **KUBES**

Kühlwasser *d:* **Kühlw.,** *d:* **KW**

Kühlwasseroptimierung *d:* **KWOP**

Kuiper Airborne Observatory *e:* **KAO**

Kulturgeografi, Tidsskrift for Befolkningsgeografi. Bebyggelsesgeografi Erhvervsgeographi. Politish Geografi. København *a:* **Kulturgeografi.**

Kumamoto Joumal of Science. Biology *e:* **Kumamoto J Sci Biol**

Kumamoto Journal of Science. Geology *e:* **Kumamoto J Sci Geol**

Kumamoto Journal of Science. Senes B. Section 2. Biology *e:* **KJSBA**

Kumamoto Journal of Science. Series B. Section 2. Biology *e:* **Kumamoto J Sci Ser B Sect 2 Biol**

Kumamoto Journal of Science. Series B. Section 1. Geology *e:* **Kumamoto J Sci Ser B Sect 1**

Kumamoto Medical Joumal *e:* **Kumamoto Med J**

Kumamoto Medical Journal *e:* **KUMJA**

Kumamoto University. Faculty of Education. Memoirs. Natural Science *e:* **Mem Fac Ed Kumamoto Univ Natur Sci**

Kungliga Svenska Vetenskapsakademiens. Avhandlingar i Naturskyddsarenden *r:* **K Sven Vetenskapsakad Avh Naturskyddsarenden**

Kungliga Svenska Vetenskapsakademiens. Skrifter i Naturskyddsarenden *r:* **K Sven Vetenskapsakad Skr Naturskyddsarenden**

Kuratorium für Wasser- und Kulturbauwesen e.V. *d:* **KWK**

Kuratorium für Wasserwirtschaft *d:* **KfW**

Kurme Medical Journal *e:* **KRMJA,** *e:* **Kurme Med J**

Kurume Medical Journal *e:* **Kurume Med J**

Kuwait Medical Student International Committee *e:* **KuMSIC**

Kuwait Oil-Fire Smoke Atmospheric Measurements Program *e:* **KOSAMP**

Kvinnenes Verdensråd *N:* **KV**

Kvinnens Demokratiske Verdensforbund *N:* **KDV**

Kwajalein Standard Atmosphere *e:* **KSA**

Kwaliteitseisen voor Hout voor Bouwkundige en Waterbouwkundige Doeleinden *n:* **KVH**

Kwartalnik Geologiczny *P:* **Kwart[alnik] Geol**, *P:* **KWGEA**

Kwartalnik Geologiczny [Poland. Instytut Geologiczny] *P:* **Kwart Geol [Pol Inst Geol]**

KwaZulu Department of Nature Conservation *e:* **KDNC**

KwaZulu Self-Protection Forces *e:* **KZSPF**

Kyorin Journal of Medicine and Medical Technology *e:* **Kyorin J Med Med Technol**

Kyoto Protocol to the United Nations Framework Convention on Climate Change *e:* **Climate Change-Kyoto Protocol**

Kyoto University. Faculty of Science. Memoirs. Series of Geology and Mineralogy *e:* **Kyoto Univ Fac Sci Mem Ser Geol Mineral**

Kyoto University. Geophysical Research Station. Reports *e:* **Kyoto Univ Geophys Res Stn Rep**

Kytingpook University. Medical Journal *e:* **KUMJB**

Kyung Hee Nepal Friendship Medical Center *e:* **KYUNGHEE**

Kyung Hee University. Oriental Medical Journal *e:* **Kyung Hee Univ Orient Med J**

Kyungpook University. Medical Journal *e:* **Kyungpooh Univ Med J**

Kyushu Journal of Medical Science *e:* **Kyush J Med Sci**

Kyushu University. College of General Education. Reports on Earth Science *e:* **Kyushu Univ Coll Gen Educ Rep Earth Sci**

Kyushu University. Department of Geology. Science Reports *e:* **Kyushu Univ Dep Geol Sci Rep**

Kyushu University. Faculty of Science. Memoirs. Series D. Geology *e:* **Kyushu Univ Fac Sci Mem Ser D**

L

L-Cystein, L-Cysteinhydrochlorid *d:* **E 920**

La-Crosse Boiling Water Reactor *e:* **LABWR**

La Crosse Boiling Water Reactor *e:* **LCBWR**

La Geographie *f:* **La Geog**

La Palma Observatory *e:* **LPO**

Lab Animal Allergy *e:* **LAA**

Labor Medizin *d:* **Labor Med**

Labor Occupational Health Program *e:* **LOHP**

Labor Occupational Safety & Health program *e:* **LOSH**

Labor-Praxis in der Medizin *d:* **Labor Praxis Med**

Labor Service Medical Depot Company *e:* **LSMDC**

Laboratoire Associe de Meteorologie Physique *f:* **LAMP**

Laboratoire de Biologie Animale *f:* **L.B.A.**

Laboratoire de Biologie Végétale *f:* **LBV**

Laboratoire de Biotechnologie Environnementale *f:* **LBE**

Laboratoire de Génie Chimique et Biologique *f:* **LGCB**

Laboratoire de Génie Médical *f:* **LGM**

Laboratoire de Géologie *f:* **GEOLEP**

Laboratoire de l'environnement marin de l'AIEA, Laboratoire de Monaco *f:* **LEM**

Laboratoire de Meteorologie *f:* **LMA**

Laboratoire de Météorologie Dynamique *f:* **LMD**

Laboratoire de Météorologie Dynamique, version iv-Laboratoire de Modelisation du Climat et de l'Environnement *f:* **LMDiv-LMCE**

Laboratoire de Physique de l'Atmosphère *f:* **LPA**

Laboratoire de Pollution Atmosphérique et Sol *f:* **LPAS**

Laboratoire de Sondages Électromagnetiques de l'Environnement Terrestre *f:* **LSEET**

Laboratoire des Produits Forestiers de l'Est [Canada]. Rapport *f:* **Lab Prod For Est [Can] Rapp**

Laboratoire d'Essai des Matériaux de l'École Polytechnique de l'Université de Lausanne *f:* **LEMEPUL**

Laboratoire d'Hydrologie et Aménagements *f:* **HYDRAM**

Laboratoire d'Océanographie Dynamique et de Climatologie *f:* **LODYC**

Laboratoire d'Optique Atmospherique *f:* **LOA**

Laboratoire National de Contrôle des Médicaments *f:* **L.N.C.M.**

Laboratoire pour le Contrôle des Médicaments *f:* **L.C.M.**

Laboratoř Agrometeorologická *c:* **LAM**

Laboratoř Mikrobiologická *c:* **LM**

Laboratoř pro Biologii Rozmnožování Hospodářskýck Zvířat *c:* **LBZ**

Laboratoř pro Elektronovů Mikroskopii v Biologii *c:* **LEMB**

Laboratories for Astrophysics and Space Research *e:* **LASR**

Laboratorio de Dinámica de Fluidos Geofísicos *s:* **GFDL**

Laboratorio Deacon del Instituto de Ciencias Oceanográficas *s:* **IOSDL**

Laboratorio Goddard de Ciencias Atmosféricas *s:* **GLAS**

Laboratorio Oceanográfico y Meteorológico del Atlántico *s:* **AOML**

Laboratoriums Medizin *d:* **Lab Medizin**

Laboratoriumsblätter für die Medizinische Diagnostik E. V. Behring *d:* **Laboratoriumsbl Med Diagb E Behring**

Laboratory and Research Methods in Biology and Medicine [New York] *e:* **Lab Res Methods Biol Med**

Laboratory Animal Breeders' Association *e:* **LABA**

Laboratory Animal Care *e:* **Lab Anim Care**

Laboratory Animal Data Bank *e:* **LADB**

Laboratory Animal Handbooks *e:* **Lab Anim Handb**

Laboratory Animal Management and Business Systems *e:* **LAMBS**

Laboratory Animal Management Association *e:* **LAMA**

Laboratory Animal Science *e:* **LBASA**

Laboratory Animal Science [Joliet] *e:* **Lab Anim Sci**

Laboratory Animal Symposia *e:* **Lab Anim Symp**

Laboratory Animal Veterinary Association *e:* **LAVA**

Laboratory Animals *e:* **Lab Anim**, *e:* **LBANA**

Laboratory Animals Bureau *e:* **LAB**

Laboratory Animals Centre *e:* **LAC**

Laboratory Animal[s] Science Association *e:* **LASA**

Laboratory Centre for Disease Control, Health Protection Branch, Department of National Health and Welfare Ottawa, Ontario *e:* **OONHL**

Laboratory de Géologie-Géomorphologie Structurale et Télédétection *f:* **LGGST**

Laboratory Environment Model *e:* **LEM**, *e:* **LFM**

Laboratory Environmental Review Committee *e:* **LERC**

Laboratory Experience in Atmospheric Research *e:* **Project LEARN**

Laboratory Experience in Atmospheric Research at NCAR *e:* **LEARN**

Laboratory for Agricultural Remote Sensing *e:* **LARS**

Laboratory for Applications of Remote Sensing Forest Resource Information System *e:* **LARSFRIS**

Laboratory for Application[s] of Remote Sensing System [for Aircraft Analysis] *e:* **LARSSYAA**

Laboratory for Applications of Remote Sensing System for Aircraft Analysis *e:* **LARSYSAA**

Laboratory for Atmosphere (or Atmospheric) and Space Physics *e:* **LASP**

Laboratory for Energy-Related Health Research *e:* **LEHR**

Laboratory for Environmental Data Research *e:* **LEDR**

Laboratory for Environmental Studies *e:* **LES**

Laboratory for Experimental Medicine and Surgery in Primates *e:* **LEMSIP**

Laboratory for Geology/ Geomorphology and Remote Sensing *e:* **LGGST**

Laboratory for Meteorology and Earth Sciences *e:* **LLMES**

Laboratory for Research on Animal Diseases *e:* **LRAD**

Laboratory for Resource and Environmental Information Systems *e:* **LREIS**

Laboratory for Space Research *e:* **LSR**

Laboratory Medicine *e:* **Lab Med**

Laboratory of Atmospheric Physics *e:* **LAP**

Laboratory of Atmospheric Science[s] *e:* **LAS**

Laboratory of Biomedical and Environmental Sciences *e:* **LBES**

Laboratory of Ice Core and Cold Regions Environment *e:* **LICCRE**

Laboratory of Meteorological Dynamics *e:* **LMD**

Laboratory of Meteorology and Earth Sciences *e:* **LMES**

Laboratory of Nuclear Medicine and Radiation Biology *e:* **LNMRB**

Laboratory of Radiation Biology *e:* **LRB**

Laboratory of Radiobiology and Environmental Health *e:* **LREH**

Laboratory of Regional Geodynamics *e:* **LARGE**

Laboratory of Research in Human and Social Ecology e: **LAREHS**

Laboratory of the Department of Earth Sciences, University of Wales, Cardiff e: **ABER**

Laboratory Studies of the Chemistry of Atmospheric Ozone e: **LACTOZ**

Laboratory Techniques in Biochemistry and Molecular Biology e: **Lab Tech Biochem Mol Biol**

Labormodul Columbus Orbital Facility e: **COF**

Labortechnik für Mikrobiologie und Biotechnologie, Fernwald d: **Tecnomara**

Labrador Ice Dynamics Experiment e: **LIDEX**

Labrador Ice Margin Experiment e: **LIMEX**

Labrador Sea Water e: **LSW**

Lacassine National Wildlife Refuge e: **LNWR**

Lacreek National Wildlife Refuge e: **LNWR**

LaCrosse Boiling Water Reactor e: **LACBWR**

Lade-Wasserlinie d: **LWL**

Lady Davis Institute for Medical Research, Jewish General Hospital, Montreal, Quebec e: **QMJGL**

Lagrange Point 4 240,000 mile Earth orbit e: **L4**

Laguna Atascosa National Wildlife Refuge e: **LANWR**

Lake Andes National Wildlife Refuge e: **LANWR**

Lake County Medical Society e: **LCMS**

Lake Erie Environmental Studies e: **LEES**, e: **LEFS**

Lake George [Uganda] e: **HULA**

Lake Ilo National Wildlife Refuge e: **LINWR**

Lake Tahoe Environmental Education Consortium e: **LTEEC**

Lake Woodruff National Wildlife Refuge e: **LWNWR**

Lakeland Village School, Medical Lake e: **WaMeL**

Lakeshore Mental Health Institute, Staff Library, Knoxville e: **TKLMl**

Lakey Clinic Medical Center e: **LC**

Lamont-Doherty Earth Observatory of Columbia University e: **LDEO**

Lamont Doherty Geological Observatory e: **Lamont**

Lamont-Doherty Geological [or Geology] Observatory [Columbia University] e: **LDGO**

Lamont Geological Observatory e: **LGO**

Lamont Geological Observatory, Columbia University e: **L**

Lanchow University Journal. Natural Sciences [People's Republic of China] e: **Lanchow Univ J Nat Sci**

Land and Approach System for Space Vehicles e: **LASSV**

Land and Environment Notes e: **LEN**

Land and Natural Resources Division e: **LNRD**

Land and Sea Interaction Laboratory e: **LASIL**

Land and Water Conservation Fund e: **LCWS**, e: **LWCF**

Land and Water Law Review e: **Land&Water L. Rev.**

Land and Water Management Plan e: **LWMP**

Land and Water Resources and Economic Models System e: **LAWREMS**

Land and Water Resources Research and Development Corporation e: **LWRRDC**

Land-Atmosphere-Ice-Interactions e: **LAII**

Land-Atmosphere Interactions Dynamics e: **LAID**

Land Disposal Restrictions [Envimnmental Protection Agency] e: **LDR**

Land [earth resources] Remote Sensing Satellite[s] e: **LANDSAT**

Land Earth Station e: **LES**

Land Ecosystem Atmosphere Feedback e: **LEAF**

Land Observation Satellite e: **LOS**

Land-Ocean-Climate Satellite e: **LOCS**

Land Ocean Climate Satellite System e: **LOCSS**

Land-Ocean Interactions in the Coastal Zone e: **LOTREX**

Land-Ocean-Interactions in the Coastal Zone [Project] e: **LOICZ**

Land-Ocean Interactions in the Russian Arctic e: **LOIRA**

Land-Ocean Interaction[s] Study e: **LOIS**

Land Protection Incentives Scheme e: **LPIS**

Land Remote Sensing Assembly e: **LRSA**

Land Remote Sensing Satellite[s] e: **Landsat**

Land-Sea-Air Interaction Laboratory e: **LASAIL**

Land Sea Rescue e: **LSR**

Land-surface Transfer scheme, a component of climate models e: **LSX**

Land Use and Climate Change e: **LUCC**

Land Use and Climate Impacts on Fluvial Systems during the Period of Agriculture e: **LUCIFS**

Land Use and Environment Law Review e: **Land Use and Env L Rev**

Land Use and Environmental Management Authority e: **LUEMA**

Land Use and Environmental Regulation e: **LUER**

Land Use and Natural Resource Information System e: **LUNR**

Landcare and Environment Action Plan (or Program) e: **LEAP**

Landelijke Organisatie van Vermeerderaars n: **LOV**

Länder-Arbeitsgemeinschaften Wasser und Abfallbeseitigung d: **LAWA**

Länderarbeitsgemeinschaft Naturschutz, Landschaftspflege und Erholung d: **LANA**

Länderarbeitsgemeinschaft Wasser [und Abwasser] d: **LAWA**

Landes-Umweltinformationssystem [in Brandenburg] d: **LUIS**

Landesamt für Naturschutz und Landespflege d: **LN**

Landesamt für Umwelt und Natur d: **LAUN**

Landesamt für Umwelt[schutz] d: **LAU**

Landesamt für Umweltschutz (Baden-Württemberg) d: **LfU**

Landesamt für Umweltschutz und Gewerbeaufsicht Rheinland-Pfalz, Oppenheim d: **LfUG**

Landesamt für Wasser und Abfall d: **LWA**

Landesamt für Wasserhaushalt und Küsten d: **LWK**

Landesamt für Wasserwirtschaft Rheinland-Pfalz, Mainz d: **LfW**

Landesanstalt für Umwelt d: **LfU**

Landesanstalt für Umweltschutz Baden-Württemberg, Karlsruhe d: **LfU**

Landesanstalt für Umweltschutz, Informationstechnisches Zentrum d: **ITZ**

Landesgemeinschaft Naturschutz und Umwelt [Nordrhein-Westfalen] d: **LNU**

Landesgesundheitsamt d: **LGA**

Landesgrundwasserdienst d: **LGD**

Landeshydrologie und -geologie, Mitteilung d: **Landeshydrol. -geol., Mitt.**

Landesinformationssystem Umwelt, Agrar und Forst d: **LISUAF**

Landesmedizinalrat d: **LMedR**, d: **LMR**

Landesnaturschutzverband d: **LNV**

Landesumweltamt d: **LUA**

Landesumweltamt Brandenburg d: **LUA**

Landesumweltamt Nordrhein-Westfalen, Essen d: **LUA**

Landesverband Bürgerinitiativen Umweltschutz d: **LBU**

Landesverband Bürgerinitiativen Umweltschutz, Berlin d: **LBU Berlin**

Landeswassergesetz d: **LWassG**, d: **LWG**

Landing Barge Water e: **LBW**

Landing Craft and Bases, Northwest African Waters e: **LANCRABNAW**, e: **LANDCRABNAW**

Landing Craft, Hydrofoil, Experimental e: **LVHX**

Landing Vehicle, Hydrofoil e: **LVH**

Landlocked and Geographically Disadvantaged States e: **LLGDS**

Landowners for Responsible Natural Resource Management e: **LRNRM**

Landsat On-Line Earthnet Data Availability Database e: **LEDA**

Landsat Signature Development Program e: **LSDP**

Landscape Ecology e: **Landsc. Ecol.**

Landschaftsentwicklung und Umweltforschung d: **Landsch.entwickl. Umweltforsch.**

Landschaftsinformationssystem [der Bundesforschungsanstalt für Naturschutz und Landschaftsökologie] d: **LANIS**

Landschaftsökologie und Umweltforschung e: **Landsch.ökol. Umweltforsch.**

Landsurface-Atmosphere (or Atmospheric)-Vegetation Interaction Programme e: **LAVIP**

Länge in der Wasserlinie d: **LWL**

Langkawi International Maritime & Aerospace Exhibition e: **LIMA**

Langley Space Flight Center e: **LSFC**

Language Definition Environment e: **LADE**

L'Annee Biologique f: **L'Annee Biologique**

Lanterne Medicale l: **Lanterne Med**

Lanzhou Institute of Glaciology and Geocryology e: **LIGG**

LARC Medical e: **LARC Med**

Large Amplitude Multi-mode Aerospace Research Simulator e: **LAMARS**

Large Amplitude SLOSH [Sea, Lake, Overland Surge from Hurricanes] e: **LAMPS**

Large Amplitude Space Simulator *e:* **LASS**

Large Animal *e:* **LA**

Large-Animal Anesthesia Machine *e:* **LA of Alta Bul**

Large Animal Exposure Facility *e:* **EPRI 1 & 2**

Large Astronomical Observatory Satellite *e:* **LAOS**

Large Atmospheric Multipurpose Lidar *e:* **LAMP**

Large Climate-Moderating Envelope *e:* **LCME**

Large Earth-based Solar Telescope *e:* **LEST**

Large Earth Terminals *e:* **LETs**

Large Group Health Plan *e:* **LGHP**

Large Inventory Top-Tier Site *e:* **LITTS**

Large Optical Tracker-Aerospace *e:* **LOTAS**

Large Orbital (or Orbiting) Research Laboratory *e:* **LORL**

Large Orbital Telescope *e:* **LOT**

Large Orbital X-ray Telescope *e:* **LOXT**

Large Orbiting Earth Resources Observatory *e:* **LOERO**

Large Orbiting Telescope *e:* **LOT**

Large-Probe Atmospheric Structure *e:* **LAS**

Large Radio Observatory *e:* **LRO**

Large-scale Atmospheric Moisture Balance of Amazonia using Data Assimilation *e:* **LAMBADA**

Large Scale Biological-Atmosphere Experiment Amazonia *e:* **LBA**

Large Scale Disturbance and Recolonization Experiment *e:* **DISCOL**

large-scale ecological destruction *e:* **ecodoom**

Large-scale Geostrophic *e:* **LSG**

Large Solar Observatory *e:* **LSO**

Large Space Photography *e:* **LSP**

Large Space Structures *e:* **LSS**

Large Space System Technology Program *e:* **LSST**

Large Space Telescope *e:* **LST**

Large Space Telescope Project *e:* **LST Project**

Large Volume water samples *e:* **LV**

Las Vegas Valley Water District *e:* **LVVWD**

Laser-Activated Geodetic Satellite *e:* **LAGS**

Laser-Activated Reflecting Geodetic[al] Optical Satellite *e:* **LARGOS**

Laser Aerospace Communications Experiment *e:* **LACE**

Laser Applications in Medicine and Biology *e:* **Laser Appl Med Biol**

Laser Atmospheric Sounder and Altimeter *e:* **LASA**

Laser Atmospheric Transmission Test *e:* **LATT**

Laser Atmospheric Visibility and Contamination System *e:* **LAVAC System**

Laser Atmospheric Wind Sounder *e:* **LAWS**

Laser Environmental Active Fluorosensor *e:* **LEAF**

Laser Geodetic [Earth Orbiting] Satellite *e:* **LAGEOS**

Laser Geodynamic Earth Orbiting Satellite *e:* **LAGEOS**

Laser Geodynamic Satellite *e:* **LAGEO**

Laser-Induced Fluorescence and Environmental Sensing *e:* **LIFES**

Laser Induced Fluorescence of the Environment *e:* **LIFE**

Laser Integrated Space Experiment *e:* **LISE**

Laser Interferometer Gravitational-Wave Observatory *e:* **LIGO**

Laser Interferometric Gravity Wave Observatory *e:* **LIGO**

Laser Interferometry Gravitational Wave Observatory *e:* **LIGO**

Laser (or Lidar) Atmospheric Sensing Experiment *e:* **LASE**

Laser (or Lidar) Atmospheric Sounder Experiment *e:* **LASE**

Laser [or Lidar] In Space Technology Experiment *e:* **LITE**

Laser Synchronization [of Clocks] from Stationary Orbit Experiment *e:* **LASSO**

Laser Weather Identifier *e:* **LWI**

Lasers for Medicine, Incorporated *e:* **LFMI**

Lasers in Medical Science *e:* **Lasers Med Sci,** *e:* **LMSCEZ**

Lasers in Surgery and Medicine [New York] *e:* **Lasers Surg Med**

Lasers in Surgery and Medicine. Supplement [New York] *e:* **Lasers Surg Med Suppl**

Last Open Water *e:* **LOW**

Last Pre-Midcourse Orbit *e:* **LAPM Orbit**

Late Quaternary Ocean Palaeocirculation and Climate Change *e:* **LOPACC**

Lateral Observation *e:* **L Obsn**

Laterally Archiving Containment, Health, Environment & Safety System *e:* **LACHESIS**

Latin America and Caribbean Hydrological Cycle and Water Resources Activities Observation and Information System *e:* **LACHYCOS**

Latin American and Caribbean Health Sciences Information Center *e:* **BIREME**

Latin American Association of Environmental Mutagens, Carcinogens and Teratogens *e:* **ALAMCTA**

Latin American Association of Environmental Mutagens, Carcinogens and Teratogens Societies *e:* **LAAEMCTS**

Latin American Biological Network *e:* **RELAB**

Latin-American Federation of Societies for Ultrasound in Medicine and Biology *e:* **FLAUS**

Latin American Federation of Surgeons *e:* **FELAC**

Latin American Federation of Thermalism and Climatism *e:* **LAFTC**

Latin American Office of Aerospace Research *e:* **LAOAR**

Latin American Research Network in Animal Production Systems *e:* **RISPAL**

Latin Ameriran Association of Medical Schools and Faculties *e:* **LAAMSF**

Latin and Mediterranean Group for Sport Medicine *e:* **LMGSM**

Latin Mediterranean Medical Union *e:* **LMMU**

Launceston Environment Centre *e:* **LEC**

Launch Environment, Mission, Type, Design Number and Series [Missiles] *e:* **LTDNS**

Launch Environmental Simulator *e:* **LES**

Laundau Orbital *e:* **LOFER**

Laura Ingalls Wilder Memorial Society *e:* **LIWMS**

Laurence-Moon-Biedl [Medicine] *e:* **LMB**

Laurentide ice sheet *e:* **LIS**

Laval Medical *e:* **LAMEA,** *f:* **Laval Med**

Laval University Medical Center *e:* **LUMC**

Lavalin Environment, Inc., Montreal, Quebec *e:* **QMLAVE**

Lavalin Environnement, Montreal, Quebec *e:* **QMAMA**

Law Enforcement Aerial Observation *e:* **LEAO**

Law for Federal Marine Protection *e:* **FPMA**

Law, Medicine and Health Care *e:* **Law Med [&] Health Care,** *e:* **L Med and Health**

Law of the Sea *e:* **LOS**

Law of the Sea Conference *e:* **LOSC,** *e:* **LSC**

Law of the Sea Information System *e:* **LOSIS**

Law of the Sea Institute *e:* **LSI**

Law of the Sea Treaty *e:* **LOST**

Law on Protection of Personal Data *e:* **LORTAD**

Lawyers Committee for the Enforcement of Animal Protection Law *e:* **LCEAPL**

Lawyer's Medical Journal *e:* **Law Med J**

Lawyers Protecting People from Malicious and Unjustified Lawsuits *e:* **LPPMUL**

Layer-cake Geology *e:* **LCG**

Lead Hydrogen Purge System *e:* **LHPS**

Leading Medical Assistant *e:* **LMA**

Leaf Water Content Index *e:* **LWCI**

Leaf Water Potential *e:* **LWD,** *e:* **LWP**

League for Ecological Democracy *e:* **LED**

League of Nations. Bulletin of the Health Organization *e:* **League Nations Bull Health Org**

Learning in a Free Environment *e:* **LIFE**

Learning Resource Center, Taubman Medical Library *e:* **LRC**

Learning Resources Centre, Georgian College of Applied Arts and Technology, Orillia, Ontario *e:* **OORIGC**

Learning to Manage Health information *e:* **LTM**

Least Restrictive Environment *e:* **LRE**

Leaving Water Temperature *e:* **LWT**

Lebanese Medical Journal *e:* **Leban Med J**

Leben und Umwelt [Wiesbaden] *d:* **Leben Umwelt [Wiesb]**

Lebendige Erde *d:* **Leben Erde**

Lecture Notes in Earth Sciences *e:* **Lect. Notes Earth Sci.**

Lectures. Colloquium on Environmental Protection in Mechanial Engineering *e:* **Lect Colloq Environ Prot Mech Eng**

Lectures Notes in Medical Informatics *e:* **Lectures Notes in Med Inform**

Lectures on the Scientific Basis of Medicine *e:* **Lect Sci Basis Med**

Leeds Medico-Chirurgical Society e: **L.M.C.S.**

Left Intercostal Space e: **LIS**

Left Observation Post e: **LOP**

Lega Italiana Naturisti i: **LIN**

Legal Environment of Business e: **LEB**

Legal Maxims with observations by George Frederick Wharton e: **Whart.**

Legal Medicine e: **Leg Med**, e: **LM**

Legal Questions Relating to Scientific Investigations in the Ocean e: **LEG**

Legal Services, Environment Canada Ottawa, Ontario e: **OOELS**

Legal sub-division, a geographic referencing system used in Canada and USA e: **LSD**

Legion of Frontiersmen e: **L.F.**

Legislative Action on Smoking and Health e: **LASH**

Legislative Environmental Impact Statement e: **LEIS**

Leguas: Revista Argentina de Geografía. Univ. Nacional de Cuyo, Facultad de Filosofía y Letras. Mendoza s: **Leguas/Mendoza.**

leichtflüchtige, aromatische Kohlenwasserstoffe e: **BTX**

Leichtflüchtige Chlorkohlenwasserstoffe d: **LCKW**

Leichtflüchtige Halogenkohlenwasserstoffe d: **LHKW**

Leichtwasser-Brutreaktor d: **LWBR**

Leichtwasser graphitmoderierter Reaktor d: **LWGR**

Leichtwasserreaktor-Kernkraftwerk d: **LWR-KKW**

Leichtwasserreaktor[en] d: **LWR**

Leichtwasserreaktoren d: **LWRn**

Leipzig Institute of Meteorology e: **LIM**

Leitender Heeresmeteorologe d: **LHM**

Leitender Regierungsmedizinaldirektor d: **LRMed Dir**

Leitungswasser d: **Lw**

Lembaga Geografi Nasional in: **LGN**

Length at/on Waterline e: **LWL**

Length Waterline e: **Length WL**

Leningrad Association of Soviet Polar Explorers e: **LASPOL**

Leningrad Hydrometeorological Institute e: **LGMI**

Leningrader Medizinisches Institut d: **LMI**

Leninsk-Baikonur Space Centre e: **LBSC**

L'Entreprise Forestiere Camerounaise f: **EEC**, f: **EFC**

L'Equilibre Biologique f: **OHB**

Lesbian and Gay Medical Association e: **LGMA**

Lesbian & Gay Veterinary Medical Association e: **LGVMA**

Lesotho Department of Mines and Geology e: **LDMG**

Lethal Concentration in environment resulting in 50% mortality e: **LC50**

Lethal Dose where 50 Percent of Animals Die e: **LD50**

Letterman Army Medical Center e: **LAMC**

Letters in Applied Microbiology e: **LAMIE7**, e: **Lett Appl Microbiol**

Lettres de Naturalisation f: **LN**

Levantine Intermediate Water e: **LIW**

Levtech Medical Technologies Ltd. e: **LMT**

Lewis Space Flight Center e: **LSPC**

Ley General de Equilibrio Ecológico (o Ecología) y la Protección al Ambiente s: **LGEEPA**

Ley para Racionalización de la estructura y de la Acción protectora de la Seguridad Social s: **LRSS**

Liaison Committee on Graduate Medical Education e: **LCGME**

Liaison Committee on Medical Education e: **LCME**

Liaison Report. Commonwealth Geological Liaison Office e: **Liaison Rep Commonw Geol Liaison Off**

Liberal Geological Society. Cross Sections. Type Log e: **Liberl Geol Soc Cross Sec Type Log**

Liberian Frontier Force e: **LFF**

Liberian Geological Survey e: **LGS**

Liberian Water and Sewer Corporation e: **LWSC**

Liberty [geographical division] e: **LIB**

Liberté sans Frontières [fondation] f: **LSF**

Libraries: Electronic Remote Access to Information over Networks e: **LIBERATION**

Library Extends Catalog Access and New Delivery System [Georgia Institute of Technology] e: **LENDS**

Library of Congress Geography and Map Division e: **LCGMD**

Library Services Division, Health Protection Branch, Health and Welfare Canada Ottawa, Ontario e: **OONHHP**

Library Services, Health Sciences Centre, Winnipeg, Manitoba e: **MWHS**

Library Services, Policy, Communications and Information Branch, Health and Welfare Canada Ottawa, Ontario e: **OONHPP**

Library, United States Weather Bureau e: **DWB**

Libya. Ministry of Industry. Geological Section. Bulletin e: **Libya Minist Ind Geol Sec[t] Bull**

Libyan American Joint Service for Agriculture and Natural Resources e: **LAJS**

Libyan Journal of Earth Science e: **Libyan J Earth Sci**

Licensed Animal Slaughter and Salvage Association e: **LASSA**

Licentiate All-India Monthly Journal of Medicine and Surgery e: **Licentiate All-India Mon J Med Surg**

Licentiate and Licentiate in Midwifery of the Royal College of Surgeons e: **LLMRCS**

Licentiate in Dental Surgery in the Royal College of Surgeons e: **LDSRCS**

Licentiate in Dental Surgery of the Royal College of Physicians and Surgeons e: **LDSRCPS**

Licentiate in Dental Surgery of the Royal College of Physicians and Surgeons of Glasgow e: **LDSRCPS Gls**

Licentiate in Dental Surgery of the Royal College of Surgeons in Ireland e: **LDSRCS Irel**

Licentiate in Dental Surgery of the Royal College of Surgeons of Edinburgh e: **LDSRCS Edin**

Licentiate in Dental Surgery of the Royal College of Surgeons of England e: **LDSRCS Eng**

Licentiate in Dental Surgery, Royal Faculty of Physicians and Surgeons [Glasgow] e: **L.D.S.R.F.P.S.[G.]**

Licentiate in Health, Dublin e: **LHD**

Licentiate in Medicine e: **Lic Med**, e: **L.M.**, e: **L Med**, e: **ML**

Licentiate in Medicine and Surgery of the Society of Apothecaries e: **LMSSA**

Licentiate in/of Medicine and Surgery e: **LMS**

Licentiate in/of Tropical Medicine e: **L.T.M.**

Licentiate Member of the Royal Society for the Promotion of Health e: **LMRSH**

Licentiate of the Australian College of Health Service Administrators e: **LACHSA**

Licentiate of the College of Physicians and Surgeons of America e: **LCP&SA**

Licentiate of the College of Physicians and Surgeons of Ontario e: **L.C.P.&S.O.**

Licentiate of the Faculty of Physicians and Surgeons e: **LFPS**

Licentiate of the Faculty of Physicians and Surgeons, Glasgow e: **LFPG**, e: **L.F.P.S.G.**

Licentiate of the Institute of Health Service Administrators e: **LHA**

Licentiate of [the] Medical Council of Canada e: **LMCC**

Licentiate of the Medical Council of the United Kingdom e: **LMC**

Licentiate of the Royal College of Physicians [and the College of] Surgeons [of Edinburgh and of the Faculty of Physicians and Surgeons of Glasgow] e: **LRCP&S**

Licentiate of the Royal College of Surgeons e: **LRCS**

Licentiate of the Royal College of Surgeons, Edinburgh e: **LRCSE**

Licentiate of the Royal College of Surgeons, Glasgow e: **L.R.C.S.G.**

Licentiate of the Royal College of Surgeons, Ireland e: **LRCSI**

Licentiate of the Royal College of Veterinary Surgeons e: **LRCVS**

Licentiate of the Royal Faculty of Physicians and Surgeons e: **LRFPS**

Licentiate of the Royal Faculty of Physicians and Surgeons of Glasgow e: **LRFPSG**

Licht-, Kraft- und Wasserwerke Kitzingen GmbH d: **LKW**

Lick Observatory e: **LO**

Lidar Atmospheric Wind Sounder e: **LAWS**

LIDAR [Light of Detection and Ranging] Atmospheric Sounder and Altimeter e: **LASA**

Lidar Multispectral Earth Observation System e: **LIMES**

Liechtensteinische Gesellschaft für Umweltschutz d: **LGU**

Life and Earth Environment e: **LEE**

Life and Environment [Japan] e: **Life Environ**

Life and Environmental Sciences Committee e: **LESC**

Life and Medical Sciences Online e: **LAMSO**

Life Core Biomedical, Inc. e: **LCBM**

Life-Cycle Software Support Environment *e:* **LCSSE**

Life Environmental Testing *e:* **LET**

Life [Health and Accident] Cases [Commerce Clearing House] *e:* **Life C[as]**

Life, Health and Accident Insurance Cases. Second. Commerce Clearing House *e:* **Life Health&Accid Ins Cas 2d CCH**

Life Insurance Medical Research Fund *e:* **LIMRF**

Life Sciences and Biomedical Engineering Branch [Aerospace Medical Association] *e:* **LSEB**

Life Sciences and Space Research *e:* **LSSR**

Life Sciences and Space Research [Netherlands] *e:* **Life Sci Space Res**

Life Sciences. Part II. Biochemistry. General and Molecular Biology *e:* **Life Sci Part II**, *e:* **Life Sci Part II Biochem Gen Mol Biol**

Life Sciences Space Laboratory *e:* **LSS L**

Life Space *e:* **Lsp**

Life Support and Environmental Control System *e:* **LSECS**

Lifeline Healthcare Group, Ltd. *e:* **LLMD**

Lifetime Health Advisory *e:* **LHA**

Lifetime Medical Television *e:* **LMT**

Liga Medicorum Homoeopathica Internationalis *l:* **LMHI**

Light All-Weather Missile *e:* **LWM**

Light and Lighting and Environmental Design *e:* **Light [and] Light [an] Environ [Des]**

Light boiling water cooled graphite moderated pressure tube reactor *e:* **RBMK**

Light Hydrocarbon *e:* **LHC**

Light Low Water Line *e:* **LLWL**

Light Observation Aircraft *e:* **LOA**

Light Observation Helicopter Target Acquisition Designation System *e:* **LOHTADS**

Light Observation Helicopters *e:* **LOHs**

Light Observation Utility Helicopter *e:* **LOUH**

Light Rare-earth Element[s] *e:* **LREE**

Light SEAL [Sea, Air and Land] Support Craft *e:* **LSSC**

Light-Water Breeder Reactor *e:* **LWBR**

Light Water-cooled [and moderated] Reactor *e:* **LWR**

Light-Water-Cooled, Graphite-Moderated Reactor *e:* **LGR**

Light-Water-Cooled Graphite-Moderated Reactor *e:* **LWGR**

Light Water Gas Cooled Reactor *e:* **LWGCR**

Light Water-moderated Organic-cooled Reactor *e:* **LWOR**

Light Water Reactors *e:* **LWRs**

Lightning Cloud-to-Water *e:* **LTGCW**

Lightning Location and Protection *e:* **LLP**

Lightning Protection Institute *e:* **LPI**

Lightweight Artillery Meteorological System *e:* **LAMS**

Lightweight Remote Procedure Call[s] *e:* **LRPC**

Lightweight Universal Night Observation System *e:* **LUNOS**

Lightweight Weather Radar Set *e:* **LWRS**

Ligue Française pour la Protection des Oiseaux *f:* **LFPO**

Ligue française pour la Protection des Oiseaux *f:* **L.P.O.**

Ligue Intentationale des Droits de l'Animal *f:* **LIDA**

Ligue Internationale pour l'Ordre Economique Naturel *f:* **INWO**

Ligue Luxembourgeoise Contre le Cancer *f:* **LLCC**

Ligue Luxembourgeoise pour la Protection de la Nature et des Oiseaux *f:* **LLPNO**

Ligue pour la Protection des Mères Abandonnées *f:* **LPMA**

Ligue Protectrice des Animaux *f:* **L.P.A.**

Ligue suisse pour la protection de la nature *f:* **LSPN**

Lille Medical *e:* **Lille Med**

Lille Medical Actualites *e:* **Lille Med Act**

Limb-Atmospheric Infrared Spectrometer *e:* **LAS**

Limited Airport Weather Reporting System *e:* **LAWRS**

Limited Area Remote Collector *e:* **LARC**

Limited Aviation Weather Reporting Station *e:* **LAWRS**

Limited Egress/Confined Space *e:* **LE/CS**

Limited Environmental Test *e:* **LET**

Limited Space Charge Accumulation *e:* **LSCA**

Limited Underwater Breathing Apparatus *e:* **LUBA**

Limited Weather Observation *e:* **LWO**

limitieren *d:* **lim**

limitiert *d:* **lim**

Limnology and Oceanography *e:* **Limn Ocean**, *e:* **Limnol. Oceanogr.**, *e:* **LO**

Limnology and Oceanography. Supplement *e:* **Limnol Oceanogr Suppl**

Lincoln Health Sciences Library Group *e:* **LHSLG**

Lincoln Near Earth Asteroid Research *e:* **LINEAR**

Lindenberg Inhomogeneous Terrain, Fluxes between Atmosphere and Surface *e:* **LITFASS**

Lindisfarne National Nature Reserve *e:* **LNNR**

Linea Ecologica *p:* **Linea Ecologica**

Linear Combination of Gaussian Orbitals *e:* **LCGO**

Linear Natural Density Filter *e:* **LNDF**

Linksniederrheinische Entwässerungsgenossenschaft *d:* **LINEG**

Linnean Society. Biological Journal *e:* **Linnean Soc Biol J**

Linnean Society of London. Biological Journal *e:* **Linn Soc Lond Biol J**

L'Instrument Financier pour l'Environnement *f:* **LIFE**

Linus Pauling Institute of Science and Medicine *e:* **LPI**

Liofilizzazione Criobiologia Applicazioni Criogeniche *i:* **Liofilizzazione Criobiol Appl Criog**

Lipid Hydrocarbon *e:* **LH**

Lippincott's Medical Science *e:* **Lippincott's Med Sci**

Liquefied Natural Gas Tanker *e:* **LNGT**, *e:* **LNG Tanker**

Liquefied Natural Petroleum *e:* **LNP**

Liquefield Natural Gas *e:* **LNG**

Liquefield Natural Gas Ship *e:* **LNG Ship**

Liquid Conditioned Microclimate System *e:* **LCMCS**

Liquid Hourly Space Velocity *e:* **LHSV**

Liquid Hydrogen *e:* **LH**, *e:* **LHY**

Liquid Hydrogen Container *e:* **LHC**

Liquid Hydrogen fuel *e:* **LH2**

Liquid Hydrogen System Complex *e:* **LHSC**

Liquid Hydrogen Vessel *e:* **LHV**

Liquid Metal Magnethohydrodynamic *e:* **LMMHD**

Liquid Natural Gas Carrier *e:* **LNGC**

Liquid Natural Rubber *e:* **LNR**

Liquid Observation Well *e:* **LOW**

Liquid Oxygen and Liquid Hydrogen *e:* **LOX/LH**

liquid oxygen/liquid hydrogen *e:* **lox**

Liquid Water in Grams *e:* **LWG**

Liquified Natural Gas *e:* **LGN**

Liquified Natural Gases *e:* **LNG**

List of Journals Indexed in Index Medicus *e:* **LJI**

List of Molecular Biology databases *e:* **LIMB**

Liste de Noms Geographiques *f:* **LNG**

Lister Hill National Center for Biomedical Communication *e:* **ELIHILL**

Lister Hill National Center for Biomedical Communications *e:* **LHNCBC**

Lister Institute of Preventive Medicine *e:* **L.I.P.M.**

Lisuride Hydrogen Maleate *e:* **LHM**

Liter-Atmosphere *e:* **lat**, *e:* **latm**

Literatmosphäre *d:* **latm**

Literatmosphäre, technische *d:* **lat**

Literature and Medicine *e:* **L and M**, *e:* **L&M**

Literature and Medicine [Baltimore] *e:* **Lit Med**

Literature Service in Medicine and Environment [Austrian National Institute for Public Health] *e:* **LID**

Lithospheric Investigation in the Ross Sea Area *e:* **LIRA**

Litologiya, Geokhimiya i Paleogeografiya Neftegazonosn Osadochnyhh Formatsii Uzbekistana *R:* **Litol Geokhim Paleogeogr Neftegazonosn Osad Form Uzb**

Little Ice Age *e:* **LIA**

Littoral Environment Observation [Program] *e:* **LEO**

Live Animals Board *e:* **LAB**

Live Environment Testing with SAGE *e:* **LETS**

Livermore Water Boiler *e:* **LIWB**

Livermore Water Boiler Reactor *e:* **LIWB Reactor**

Livermore Water Reclamation Plant *e:* **LWRP**

Liverpool and Manchester Geological Joumal *e:* **Liverp Manch Geol J**

Liverpool and Manchester Geological Journal *e:* **Liverpool and Manchester Geol Jour**, *e:* **LMGJ**

Liverpool Geographical Society. Transactions and Annual Report of the Council *e:* **Liverpool Geog Soc Tr An Rp**

Liverpool Geological Association. Transactions. Journal *e:* **Lirerpool G As Tr J**

Liverpool Geological Society. Proceedings *e:* **Liverpool G Soc Pr**

Liverpool Marine Biology Committee *e:* **LMBC**

Liverpool Medical Institution. Transactions and Reports *e:* **Liverpool Med Inst Trans Rep**

Liverpool Medico-Chirurgical Journal *e:* **Liv Med Chir J**

Liverpool School of Tropical Medicine *e:* **L.S.T.M.**

Liverpool School of Tropical Medicine. Memoirs *e:* **Lirerpool School Trop Med Mem**

Living Conditions and Health *e:* **Liv Condit Health**

Llacta. Instituto Ecuatoriano de Antropología y Geografía. Quito *s:* **IEAG/L.**

Lloydia. A Quarterly Journal of Biological Science. Cincinnati *e:* **Lloydia, a quart journ of biological science.**

Lloydia. Journal of Natural Products *e:* **Lloydia J Nat Prod**

Lloyds [Register of Shipping] Ocean Engineering Platform System *e:* **LOPS**

Lloyd's Reports: Medical *e:* **Lloyd's Rep.Med.**

Load Water Line *e:* **LWL**

Load Water Plane *e:* **LWP**

Loads/Environmental Spectra Survey *e:* **L/ESS**

Lobo Wildlife Lodge [Tansania] *e:* **HTLO**

L'Observatoire du Sahara et du Sahel *f:* **OSS**

Local Address Space *e:* **LAS**

Local Area Underwater Navigation System *e:* **LAUNS**

Local Authority Ecologists *e:* **LAEs**

Local Authority Health Services *e:* **LAHS**

Local Board of Health *e:* **L.B.H.**

Local Climatological Data *e:* **LCD**

Local Earth Observation *e:* **LEO**

Local Environment Plan *e:* **LEP**

Local Environmental Health Action Plan *e:* **LEHAP**

Local Environmental Protection and Water Management Funds *e:* **LEPWMF**

Local Geomagnetic Time *e:* **LGT**

Local Government Environmental Information Exchange Scheme *e:* **LGEIES**

Local Health Authority *e:* **LHA**

Local Health Department *e:* **LHD**

Local Health Office[r] *e:* **LHO**

Local Health Unit *e:* **LHU**

Local Medical Committee *e:* **LMC**

Local Medical Doctor *e:* **LMD**

Local Medical Officer *e:* **LMO**

Local Medical Officers Advisory Committee *e:* **LMOAC**

Local Medical Workforce Advisory Groups *e:* **LMWAGS**

Local Ocean Area *e:* **LOA**

Local Space Rectangular *e:* **LSR**

Local System Environment *e:* **LSE**

Local Vertical and Orbit Plane *e:* **LVOP**

Local Weather Dissemination Systems *e:* **LWDS**

Location Geological Characterization Report *e:* **LGCR**

Loch Leven National Natural Reserve *e:* **LLNNR**

Lockheed-Georgia Co., Scientific and Technical Information Department *e:* **GMarLG**

Lockheed Martin Advanced Environmental Systems *e:* **LMAES**

Lockheed Missiles and Space Company *e:* **LMSC**

Lockheed Space Operations Company *e:* **LSOC**

Lockheed Space Systems *e:* **LSS**

Lockheed Symposia on Magnetohydrodynamics *e:* **Lockheed Symp Magnetohydrodyn**

Lockheed Underwater Missile Facilities *e:* **LUMF**

Logarithm Natural *e:* **LN**

Logarithmus Naturalis *d:* **ln**

Logistics Chain Multidimensional Design Toolbox with Environmental Assessment *e:* **LOCOMOTIVE**

Logistics Research Project, George Washington University *e:* **LRP/GWU**

Logistics-Transport by Sea *e:* **LOGSEA**

Loi Canadienne sur la Protection de l'Environnement *f:* **LCPE**

Loi fédérale sur les Hautes Écoles Spécialisées *f:* **LHES**

Lommen Health Science Library, University of South Dakota, Vermillion *e:* **USF**

London and Counties Medical Protection Society *e:* **L.&C.M.P.S.**

London Association for the Protection of Trade *e:* **LAPT**

London Clinic Medical Journal *e:* **Lond Clin Med J**

London Environmental Economics Centre *e:* **LEEC**

London Health News *e:* **London Hlth News**

London Hospital Medical College *e:* **LHMC**

London Medical Gazette *e:* **Lond Med Gaz**

London Medical Group *e:* **LMG**

London Medical Research Council *e:* **LMRC**

London Medical Schools *e:* **LMS**

London Medical Society *e:* **L.M.S.**

London Medical Studies *e:* **Lond.Med.St.**

London Meteorological Office *e:* **LMO**

London Natural History Society *e:* **LNHS**

London School of Hygiene and Tropical Medicine *e:* **LSHTM**

London School of Medicine for Women *e:* **LSMW**

London School of Tropical Medicine *e:* **L.S.T.M.**

London School of Tropical Medicine. Research Memoir Series *e:* **Lond School Trop Med Research Mem Ser**

London Waterguard *e:* **L.W.**

London Weather Centre *e:* **LWC**

Long Acting Thyroid Stimulator-Protector *e:* **LATS-P**

Long Duration Orbital Simulator *e:* **LDOS**

Long Hydrographic Sections Program[me] *e:* **LONGLINES**

Long Island Biological Association *e:* **LIBA**

Long Lake National Wildlife Refuge *e:* **LLNWR**

Long Life Space System *e:* **LLSS**

Long-Life Space System *e:* **L²S²**

Long Point Bird Observatory. Annual Report *e:* **Long Point Bird Obs Annu Rep**

Long-Range Aerospace Observation Platform *e:* **LRAOP**

Long-Range Earth Current [Communications] *e:* **LOREC**

Long-Range Earth Current Communications System *e:* **LOREC Communications System**

Long-Range Earth Sensor *e:* **LRES**

Long-Range Environmental Studies *e:* **LORES**

Long-range Open Ocean Patrol *e:* **LOOP**

Long-Range Overwater Diffusion *e:* **LROD**

Long-Range Reconnaissance & Observation System *e:* **LORROS**

Long-Range Transport of Atmospheric Pollution *e:* **LRTAP**

Long Rate Night Observation Device *e:* **LRNOD**

Long, Rolling Sea *e:* **L**

Long-Term and Expanded Program of Oceanic Research and Exploration *e:* **LEPORE**

Long-term and Expanded Program[me] of Oceanic Exploration and Research [Intergovernmental Oceanographic Commission] *e:* **LEPOR**

Long-term Carbon and Water Flux Network *e:* **FLUXNET**

Long-term Ecological Modelling Activity *e:* **LEMA**

Long-Term Ecological Research program [National Science Foundation] *e:* **LTER**

Long-Term Ecological Research Project *e:* **LTER**

Long-term Funding for the Environment Through Technology *e:* **LIFETECH**

Long-term Ocean Bottom Settlement Test for Engineering Research *e:* **LOBSTER**

Long-Term Research in Environmental Biology *e:* **LTREB**

Long Term Space Plan *e:* **LTSP**

Long-Term Upper Ocean Study, Woods Hole, 1983 *e:* **LOTUS**

Lookout Mountain Observatory *e:* **LMO**, *e:* **LMS**

Los Alamos Area Office/Environment, Safety & Health Branch *e:* **LAAO-ES&H**

Los Alamos Health Care Plan *e:* **LAHCP**

Los Alamos Medical Center *e:* **LAMC**

Los Alamos Space and Science Committee *e:* **LASSC**

Los Alamos Water Boiler *e:* **LAWB**

Los Amigos de la Tierra Internacional *s:* **FoEI**

Los Angeles County Medical Association *e:* **LACMA**, *e:* **LACMedA**

Los Angeles County Museum of Natural History. Quarterly *e:* **Los Angeles County Mus Nat History Quart**

Los Angeles Department of Water and Power *e:* **LADWP**

Los Angeles Geographic Society *e:* **LAGS**

Los Angeles Medical Journal *e:* **L Ang**

Los Angeles Society of Internal Medicine *e:* **LASIM**

Löschwasser-Rückhalte-Richtlinie *e:* **LöRüRL**

Loss of Coolant Protection *e:* **LOCP**

Loss of Feedwater *e:* **LOF**, *e:* **LOFW**
Loss of River Water *e:* **LORW**, *e:* **LRW**
Loss-on-ignition, often used in palynology and palaeoecology as a means of measuring organic matter content of samples *e:* **LOI**
Lost in Space Fannish Alliance *e:* **LISFA**
Lostwood National Wildlife Refuge *e:* **LNWR**
Loteni Nature Reserve *e:* **LNR**
Louisiana. Bureau of Scientific Research and Statistics. Geological Bulletin *e:* **La Bur Sci Res Stat Geol Bull**
Louisiana Depaltment of Health and Human Resources, Policy Planning and Evaluation Office, Baton Rouge *e:* **LBrHR**
Louisiana Department of Conservation. Bureau of Scientific Research. Minerals Division. Geological Bulletin *e:* **La Dep Conserv Bur Sci Res Miner Div Geol Bull**
Louisiana Department of Conservation. Geological Survey and Department of Public Works. Water Resources Pamphlet *e:* **La Dep Conserv Gel Surv Dep Public Works Water Resour Pam**
Louisiana. Department of Conservation. Geological Survey. Mineral Resources Bulletin *e:* **LA Dep Conserv Geol Surv Miner Bull**
Louisiana Department of Environmental Quality *e:* **LDEQ**
Louisiana Department of Health and Human Resources, Office of Youth Services, Baton Rouge *e:* **LBrHR-Y**
Louisiana. Department of Public Works. Water Resources Pamphlet *e:* **LA Dept Public Works Water Res Pampb**
Louisiana Geographic Information Center *e:* **LAGIC**
Louisiana Geographic Information Systems Council *e:* **LGISC**
Louisiana Geological Survey *e:* **LGS**
Louisiana. Geological Survey and Department of Public Works. Water Resources Bulletin *e:* **LA Geol Surv Water Resour Bull**
Louisiana. Geological Survey and Department of Public Works. Water Resours Pamphlet *e:* **LA Geol Surv Water Resour Pam**
Louisiana. Geological Survey. Bulletin *e:* **Louisiana Geol Surv Bull**
Louisiana Geological Survey. Clay Resoues Bulletin *e:* **LA Geol Surv Clay Ressour Bull**
Louisiana. Geological Survey. Geological Bulletin *e:* **LA Geol Surv Geol Bull**
Louisiana. Geological Survey. Mineral Resources Bulletin *e:* **LA Geol Surv Miner Ressour Bull**
Louisiana State Department of Conservation. Geological Bulletin *e:* **LA State Dep Conserv Geol Bull**
Louisiana State Experiment Stations. Geology and Agriculture of Louisiana *e:* **LA St Exp St G Agr LA**
Louisiana State Medical Society *e:* **LSMS**
Louisiana State Medical Society. Journal *e:* **LA State Med Soc J**
Louisiana State University Institute of Environmental Studies *e:* **LSU-IES**

Louisiana State University. Studies. Biological Science Series *e:* **LA State Univ Stud Biol Sci Ser**
Louisiana Veterinary Medical Association *e:* **LVMA**
Louisiana Water Resources Research Institute. Bulletin *e:* **LA Water Resour Res Inst Bull**, *e:* **Louisiana Water Resources Research Inst Bull**
Louisville Medical Library *e:* **KyloM**
Louisville Medical News *e:* **Louisville Med News**
Louisville Medicine *e:* **Louisville Med**
Louvain Medical *e:* **Louv Med**
Lovelace Foundation for Medical Education and Research *e:* **LF**, *e:* **LFMER**
Lovelace [Foundation for Medical Education and Research] Aerosol Particle Separator *e:* **LAPS**
Loveland Geographic Information/Cartographic System *e:* **LOGIC**
Low-Altitude Observation *e:* **LA**, *e:* **LALO**
Low-Altitude Space Platform *e:* **LASP**
Low Atmospheric (or Atmosphere) Composition and Temperature Experiment *e:* **LACATE**
Low-Cost Modular Spacecraft *e:* **LCMS**
Low Cross-Range Orbiter *e:* **LCRO**
Low Earth Orbit Satellite[s] *e:* **LEOS**
Low Earth Orbit Search and Rescue *e:* **LEOSAR**
Low Earth Orbit Synthetic Aperture Radar *e:* **LEOSAR**
Low Earth Orbiting Nadir Etalon Sounding Spectrometer *e:* **LEONESS**
Low Earth Orbiting Satellite *e:* **LEO Satellite**
Low Earth Orbit[ing] [satellites] *e:* **LEO**
Low Endoatmospheric Defence *e:* **LED**
Low Endoatmospheric Defence Interceptor *e:* **LEDI**
Low Enrichment Ordinary Water Reactor *e:* **LEO Water Reactor**
Low-Frequency Accelerometer POGO [Polar Orbiting Geophysical Observatory] *e:* **LFAP**
Low Gravity Orbit *e:* **LGO**
Low-Income Weatherization Assistance Program *e:* **LIWAP**
Low-Income Weatherization Program *e:* **WX**
Low-Level Earthquake *e:* **LLE**
Low-Level Tritiated Water Processing Subsystem *e:* **LLTWP**
Low Lunar Orbit *e:* **LLO**
Low Mars Orbit *e:* **LMO**
Low-Molecular-Weight Hydrocarbon *e:* **LMWHC**
Low-Observability Reentry Vehicle *e:* **LORV**
Low-Observable Weapon Airframe Technology *e:* **LOWAT**
Low Observation Visibility *e:* **LOV**
Low Orbital Reentry Vehicle *e:* **LORV**
Low-power Atmospheric Compensation Experiment satellite *e:* **LACE**
Low-Pressure Filtered Water *e:* **LPFW**
Low-Pressure Raw Water *e:* **LPRW**
Low Pressure Service Water *e:* **LPSW**
Low-Temperature Heavy-Water Reactor *e:* **LTHWR**

Low Temperature Science. Series B. Biological Sciences *e:* **Low Temp Sci Ser B Biol Sci**
low water *e:* **lowat**
Low Water *e:* **LW**
Low Water Date *e:* **LWD**
Low Water Datum *e:* **LWD**
Low Water Equinoctal Spring Tide *e:* **LWEST**
Low Water Full and Change *e:* **LWF&C**
Low Water Interval *e:* **LWI**
Low Water Level *e:* **LWL**, *e:* **LW Level**
Low Water Line *e:* **LWL**
Low-Water Mark *e:* **L.W.M.**
Low Water of Ordinary Spring *e:* **LWOS**
Low Water [of] Ordinary Spring Tides *e:* **LWOST**
Low Water Ordinary Neap Tide *e:* **LWONT**
Low Water Plane *e:* **LWP**
Low Water Quadrature *e:* **LWQ**
Low Water Sensitivity *e:* **LWS**
Low Water Spring Tide[s] *e:* **LWST**
Lowell Observatory *e:* **LO**
Lowell Observatory Near-Earth Object Search *e:* **LONEOS**
Lower Airspace *e:* **LAS**
Lower Atmosphere Research Satellite *e:* **LARS**
Lower Atmosphere Wind Profiler *e:* **LAWP**
Lower High Water *e:* **LHW**
Lower High-Water Interval *e:* **LHWI**
Lower Low Water *e:* **LLW**
Lower Low-Water Interval *e:* **LLWI**
Lower Mississippi River Environmental Program *e:* **LMREP**
Lowest Observable Effect Level *e:* **LOEC**
Lowest Observable Frequency *e:* **LOF**
Loxahatchee National Wildlife Refuge *e:* **LNWR**
Lubricant, Arctic Weather *e:* **LAW**
Lucas Aerospace Power Transmission Corp. *e:* **LAPTC**
Luchtmacht Meteorologische Groep *n:* **LMG**
Luft-, Klima- und Kältetechnik GmbH *d:* **LKK**
Luft- und Klimatechnische Montage-Gesellschaft *d:* **LKM**
Luft- und Raumfahrtindustrie *d:* **LRI**
Luft, Wasser, Sand GmbH & Co. KG *d:* **LUWASA**
Luftfahrttechnik-Raumfahrttechnik *d:* **LRT**
Lukuru Wildlife Research Project *e:* **LWRP**
Lunar and Planetary Institute [University Space Research Association] *e:* **LPI**
Lunar Applications of a Spent Stage in Orbit *e:* **LASSO**
Lunar Atmosphere Detector *e:* **LAD**
Lunar Atmosphere (or Atmospheric) Composition Experiment *e:* **LACE**
Lunar Dust and Earth Return *e:* **LUSTER**
Lunar Ejecta and Meteorites *e:* **LEAM**
Lunar Ejecta and Micrometeorites *e:* **LEAM**
Lunar Environment Construction and Operations Simulator *e:* **LECOS**
Lunar-Environment Sample Container *e:* **LESC**
Lunar Geological Camera *e:* **LGC**

Lunar Geological Equipment e: **LGE**
Lunar Geological Exploration Camera e: **LGEC**
Lunar Geology Experiment e: **LGE**
Lunar Geology Investigation e: **LGI**
Lunar Geophysical Surface e: **LGS**
Lunar Geoscience Observer e: **LGO**
Lunar Meteoroid Analyzer e: **LMA**
Lunar Meteoroid Detector e: **LMD**
Lunar Meteoroid Detector-Analyzer e: **LMDA**
Lunar Orbit and Landing Approach Simulator e: **LOLA Simulator**
Lunar Orbit Injection e: **LOI**
Lunar Orbit Insertion Burn e: **LOIB**
Lunar Orbit Plane e: **LOP**
Lunar Orbit Plane Change e: **LOPC**
Lunar Orbit Space Station e: **LOSS**
Lunar Orbit Staging Facility e: **LOSF**
Lunar Orbital Map e: **LOM**
Lunar Orbital Mission e: **LOM**
Lunar Orbital Missions e: **LOMs**
Lunar Orbital Photo Craft e: **LOPC**
Lunar Orbital Photographic Project e: **LOPP**
Lunar Orbital Photographic System e: **LOPS**
Lunar Orbit[al] Rendezvous e: **LOR**
Lunar Orbital Survey System e: **LOSS**
Lunar Orbiter e: **LO**
Lunar Orbiter Data Conversion System e: **LODCS**
Lunar Orbiter Photographic System e: **LOPS**
Lunar Orbiter Spacecraft e: **LOS**
Lunar Orbiting Photograph e: **LOP**
Lunar Orbiting Photographic System e: **LOPS**
Lunar Orbiting Photographic Vehicle e: **LOP Vehicle**
Lunar Orbiting Reconnaissance System e: **LORS**
Lunar Orbiting Satellite e: **LOS**
Lunar Orbiting Spacecraft e: **LOS**
Lunar Orbiting Vehicle for Emergency Rescue e: **LOVER**
Lunar Parking Orbit e: **LPO**
Lunar Science Natural Language Information System e: **LSNLIS**
Lunar Ultraviolet Observatory e: **LUVO**
Lund University Library Building 2. Lund Institute of Technology, Mathematics and Natural Sciences and Faculty of Medicine e: **UB2**
L'Universo. Institúto Geografico Militare. Florence i: **Universo/Florence.**
L'Universo. Rivista bimestrale dell'Istituto Geografico Militare. Firenze i: **IGM/U.**
Luther Medical Products, Inc. e: **LUTH**
Lutheran Institute of Human Ecology e: **LIHE**
Lutheran Medical Center e: **LMC**
Lutheran Medical Mission Association e: **LMMA**
Lutherske Verdensforbund N: **LVF**
Lutte Biologique contre les Locustes et les Sauterelles f: **LUBILOSA**
Luxemburger Natur- und Vogelschutzliga d: **LNVL**
Lyndon B. Johnson Space Center e: **JSC**, e: **LBJSC**
Lyndon B. Johnson Tropical Medical Center e: **LBJTMC**

Lynx Geosystems Incorporated e: **LGI**
L'École de Criminologie, Universite de Montreal, Quebec f: **QMUEC**

M

Maastricht Upper Airspace Center e: **MAS UAC**
MAC Aeromedical Evacuation System e: **J-54**
MacDonnell Douglas Aerospace Corporation e: **MDAC**
Machine Area Cooling Water System e: **MACWS**
Madigan Army Medical Center e: **MAMC**
Madras Geographical Association e: **M.G.A.**
Madrid Deep Space Communications Complex e: **MDSCC**
Magnesiumhydroxid d: **E 528**
Magnetic Environment Measuring Equipment e: **MEME**
Magnetic Resonance in Medicine e: **Magn Reson Med**
Magnetic Signature Measurement System e: **MSMS**
Magneto-, Hydro-, Radiative Dynamics Research e: **MHRDR**
Magnetohydrodynamic e: **Magnetohydrodyn.**
Magnetohydrodynamic code e: **SNUBS**
magnetohydrodynamics e: **hydromagnetics**
Magnetohydrodynamics code e: **FLX**
Magnetohydrodynamik d: **Magnetohydrodyn.**
Magnetospheric, Ionospheric and Solar-Terrestrial Environment e: **MIST Environment**
Magyar Biológiai Társaság H: **MBT**
Magyar Geofizikusok Egyesülete H: **M.G.E.**
Magyar Mikrobiológiai Társaság H: **MMT**
Maharashi University of Natural Law e: **MUNL**
Maharish Heaven on Earth Development Corporation e: **Mahedco**
Main Administration of Geodesy and Cartography [Russian Federation] e: **GUGK**
Main Feedwater and Condensate System e: **MFWCS**
Main Geophysical Obervatory e: **GGO**
Main Geophysical Observatory e: **MGO**
Main Meteorological Office e: **MMO**
Main Sea Level e: **MSL**
Maine Criminal Justice Academy, Waterville e: **MEJ**
Maine Department of Environmental Protection e: **MDEP**
Maine Department of Inland Fisheries and Wildlife, Fishery Research Management Division e: **MDIF&W**
Maine Geological Survey e: **MGS**
Maine Medical Association e: **MMA**
Maine Meteorological Office e: **MMO**
Maine Veterinary Medical Association e: **MEVMA**, e: **MVMA**
Mainly about Nature e: **M.A.N.**
Maintenance and Logistics Space e: **MALOS**
Maintenance and Logistics Space System e: **MALOS System**

Maintenance Environmental and Engineering Services e: **ME&ES**
MAJCOM On-Line Aerospace Vehicle Training Report System e: **MOATRS**
Major Environmental Category e: **MEC**
Makapuu Oceanic Center e: **MOC**
Make-Up Water Treatment e: **MWT**
Makeup Water e: **MW**
Malayan Journal of Topical Geography e: **Malayan J. Trop. Geogr.**
Malayan Nature Journal e: **Malayan Nat. J.**
Malayan Nature Society e: **MNS**
Malaysian Air Defence Ground Environment e: **MADGE**
Malaysian Centre for Remote Sensing e: **MACRES**, e: **MCRS**
Malaysian Medical Association e: **MMA**
Malaysian [natural] Rubber Producers' Research Association e: **MRPRA**
Malcolm Bliss Mental Health Center e: **MBMHC**
Maleatdehydrogenase d: **MDH**
males of various animals e: **toms**
Malheur National Wildlife Refuge e: **MNWR**
Man in Space e: **MIS**
Man-in-Space Program e: **MISP**
Man in Space Simulator e: **MISS**
Man-in-Space-Soonest e: **MISS**
Man in Space Sophisticated e: **MISSOPH**
Man-in-the-Sea Program e: **MITS**, e: **MITS Program**
Man-out-of-Space Easiest e: **MOOSE**
Man-Year-Space e: **MYD**, e: **MYS**
Managed Behavioral Healthcare Organization e: **MBHO**
Managed Health Care e: **MHC**
Management Analysis Reporting Information on the Naval Environment e: **MARINE**
Management Analysis Reporting Information on the Naval Environment System e: **MARINE System**
Management and Study of Atmospheric Spectroscopic Information e: **GEISA**
Management Applications in a Computer Environment e: **MACE**
Management, Medical & Security e: **MM&S**
Management Observation Assessment Program e: **MOAP**
Management of Atmospheric Data for Evaluation and Research e: **MADER**
Management of Information through Natural Discourse e: **MIND**
Management Sciences for Health Inc. e: **MSH**
Management Unit of the Mathematical Model of the North Sea and Scheldt Estuary e: **MUMM**
Managing Engineering Safety Health e: **MESH**
Manas Wildlife Sanctuary e: **MWS**
Manchester Geographical Society e: **M.G.S.**
Manchester Geological and Mining Society e: **MGMS**
Manchester Medical Society e: **M.M.S.**
Maneuverable and Recoverable Space Vehicle e: **MRSV**
Maneuvering & Sea Keeping Basin e: **MASK**

Manitoba Centre for Health Policy & Evaluation e: **MCHPE**

Manitoba Department of Environment, Workplace Safety and Health, Winnipeg, Manitoba e: **MWEWSH**

Manitoba Environmental Management Division, Winnipeg, Manitoba e: **MWEM**

Manitoba Health Organizations, Winnipeg, Manitoba e: **MWHO**

Manitoba Health Services Commission, Winnipeg, Manitoba e: **MWHSC**

Manitoba Hydro, Winnipeg, Manitoba e: **MWH**

Manitoba Medical Association e: **M.M.A.**

Manitoba Museum of Man & Nature, Winnipeg, Manitoba e: **MWMM**

Manitoba Naturalists Society e: **MNS**

Manitoba Workplace Safety and Health Division, Winnipeg, Manitoba e: **MWWSH**

Manned Aerodynamic Reusable Spaceship e: **MARS**

Manned Astronomical Space Telescope e: **MAST**

Manned Deep Space Vehicle e: **MDSV**

Manned Earth Observatory e: **MEO**

Manned Earth Orbit e: **MEO**

Manned Earth Orbit Mission e: **MEOM**

Manned Earth-Orbiting Laboratory e: **MEOL**

Manned Earth Reconnaissance [Naval Air Electronic Systems Command project] e: **MER**

Manned Environmental Systems Assessment e: **MESA**

Manned Interceptor SAGE [Semi-Automatic Ground Environment] Evaluation Routine e: **MISER**

Manned Lunar Orbiter e: **MLO**

Manned Maneuverable Space System e: **MMSS**

Manned Open Sea Experiment[ation] Station e: **MOSES**

Manned Orbital Development e: **MOD**

Manned Orbital Development Station e: **MOD Station**

Manned Orbital Facility e: **MOF**

Manned Orbital Flight e: **MOF**

Manned Orbital Laboratory e: **MMOL**, e: **MOL**

Manned Orbital Maneuvering Vehicle e: **MOMV**

Manned Orbital Oceanographic Survey System Experiment e: **MOOSSE**

Manned Orbital Operations Safety Equipment e: **MOOSE**

Manned Orbital [or Orbiting] Development Station (or System) e: **MODS**

Manned Orbital (or Orbiting) Station e: **MOS**

Manned Orbital Platform e: **MOP**

Manned Orbital Research and Development System e: **MORDS**

Manned Orbital Research Laboratory e: **MORL**

Manned Orbital Solar Telescope e: **MOST**

Manned Orbital Space Laboratory e: **MOSL**

Manned Orbital Space Station e: **MOSS**

Manned Orbital Space System e: **MOSS**

Manned Orbital Telescope e: **MOT**

Manned Orbital Transfer Vehicle e: **MOTV**

Manned Orbital Weapon[s] Station (or System) e: **MOWS**

Manned Orbiter e: **MO**

Manned Orbiting Mission e: **MOM**

Manned Orbiting Module e: **MOM**

Manned Orbiting Vehicle e: **MOV**

Manned Reusable Spacecraft e: **MRS**

Manned Scientific Orbital Laboratory e: **MSOL**

Manned Space Flight e: **MSF**

Manned Space Flight Data Processing System e: **MSFDPS**

Manned Space Flight Experiments Board e: **MSFEB**

Manned Space Flight Headquarters e: **MSFH**

Manned Space Flight Laboratory e: **MSFL**

Manned Space Flight Network Operations Center e: **MSFNOC**

Manned Space Flight Network[s] e: **MSFN**

Manned Space Flight Operations e: **MSFO**

Manned Space Flight Program e: **MSFP**

Manned Space Flight Subcommittee e: **MSFS**

Manned Space Flight Support Group e: **MSFSG**

Manned Space Flight Support Requirements Documentation e: **MSFSRD**

Manned Space Flight System e: **MSFS**

Manned Space Laboratory e: **MSL**

Manned Space Network e: **MSN**

Manned Space Station e: **MSS**

Manned Space Station Communications System e: **MSSCS**

Manned Space System e: **MSS**

Manned Space Vehicle e: **MSV**

Manned Space Vehicles e: **MSVs**

Manned Spacecraft [Center] e: **MSC**

Manned Spacecraft Operations e: **MSCO**, e: **MSO**

Manned Spacecraft Operations Building e: **MSOB**

Manned Spacecraft Test Center e: **MSTC**

Manned Spaceflight Control Center e: **MSCC**

Manned Spaceflight Control Squadron e: **MSCS**

Manned Spaceflight Support Project Office e: **MASSPO**

Manned Static Space Simulator e: **MSSS**

Manned Test Space Station e: **MTSS**

Manned Underwater Station e: **MUS**, e: **MUWS**

Mannesmann-Veba-Umwelttechnik d: **MVU**

Manpower for a Clean Environment [Water Pollution Control Federation] e: **MANFORCE**

Man's Environments-Display Implication and Applications e: **MEDIA**

Manual, Alternative and Natural Therapy Index System e: **MANTIS**

Manual-Changeover-Acknowledgement Signal e: **MCA Signal**

Manual Intervention and Observation Simulator e: **MINOS**

Manual Mode Space Simulator e: **MMSS**

Manual of Clinical Microbiology, 6th Edition e: **MCM6**

Manual of Federal Geographic Data Products e: **MFGDP**

Manual of Medical Aspects of Chemical Warfare e: **M.M.A.C.W.**

Manual of the Medical Department e: **MANMED**, e: **MANMEDDEPT**, e: **MMD**

Manual Remote Rebroadcast Box e: **MRRB**

Manufacturing Automation Protocol/Technical Office Protection e: **MAPTOP**

Manufacturing Technology for Complex Geometries based on Rational Splines e: **MATRAS**

Maori policy section of the Ministry of the Environment e: **Maruwhenua**

Map and Geography Round Table e: **MAGERT**

Map Publishing Environment e: **MPE**

Mapa Batimétrico Internacional del Mediterráneo y sus Colecciones Geológicas/Geofísicas s: **IBCM**

mapped atmosphere-plant-soil system e: **MAPSS**

Mapping and Geodesy e: **M and G**, e: **M & G**

Mapping and Geographic Information Centre e: **MAGIC**

Mapping and Geography Institute e: **MGI**

Mapping Cartography, Geodesy & Imagery e: **MCG&I**

Mapping, Charting and Geodesy e: **MC and G**, e: **MC&G**

Mapping, Charting, Geodetic Data and Imagery e: **MCG&I**

Mapping Experiment From Space e: **MAPEX**

Mapping, Geodesy and Military Geographic Intelligence e: **MG/MGI**

Mar Egeo s: **Egeo**

Maracay/Centro Nacional de Comunicaciones/Meteorologicos, Aragua s: **SVMR**

Marconi Mobile Satellite Earth Terminal e: **MARMOSET**

Marconi Space [and] Defence (or Defense) Systems e: **MSDS**

Marconi Space and Defence Systems e: **MSDA**

Marconi Underwater Systems Ltd. e: **MUSL**

Marginal Ice Zone e: **MIZ**

Marginal Ice Zone Experiment e: **MIZEK**, e: **MIZEX**

Marginal Sea Flux Experiment [in the West Pacific] e: **MASFLEX**

Marin County Medical Society e: **MCMS**

Marine Advisory Service [National Oceanic and Atmospheric Administration] e: **MAS**

Marine & Aerospace Engineering Pty Ltd. e: **MAE**

Marine All Weather Fighter Attack Squadron e: **VMFA [AW]**

Marine All-Weather Fighter Squadron e: **VMF[AW]**

Marine and Atmospheric Sciences Directorate e: **MASD**

Marine and Estuarine Protected Area e: **MEPA**

Marine and Inland Waters Advisory Committee e: **MIWAC**

Marine Arctic Geological Expedition, Murmansk Association Sevmorgeologia e: **MAGE**

Marine Atmospheric Boundary Layer e: **MABL**

Marine Attack Squadron [All-Weather] e: **VMA[AW]**

Marine Automatic Meteorological Observing Station e: **MAMOS**

Marine Automatic Telephone Weather Answering Service e: **MATWAS**

Marine Biological Association e: **MBA**

Marine Biological Association [of the United Kingdom] e: **M.B.A.**

Marine Biological Association of the United Kingdom e: **MBAUK**

Marine Biological Centre e: **MBC**

Marine Biological Laboratory e: **MBL**

Marine Biological Laboratory, Woods Hole e: **MWhB**

Marine Biology e: **Mar. Biol.**

Marine Biology Letters e: **Mar. Biol. Lett.**

Marine Biology (New York)/(Berlin) e: **Mar. Biol. (NY)/(Berl.)**

Marine Biomedical Institute e: **MBI**

Marine Climatological and related Ocean Data Base e: **MCODB**

Marine Climatological Summaries Scheme e: **MCSS**

Marine Corps Environmentally Controlled Medical System e: **MCEMS**

Marine Corps Logistics Base Albany, Georgia e: **MCLBA**

Marine Corps Meteorological Mobile Facility e: **METMF**

Marine Ecological Database System e: **MEDS**

Marine Ecological Institute e: **MEI**

Marine Ecology Progress Series e: **Mar. Ecol. Prog. Ser.**

Marine Environment Protection Committee e: **MEPC**

Marine Environment Protection Committee Baltic Maritime Coordinating Meeting e: **MEPC BMCM**

Marine Environment Remote-Controlled Measuring and Integrated Detection e: **MERMAID**

Marine Environment Studies Laboratory e: **MESL**

Marine Environmental Data Information Referral System. IOC Secretariat e: **MEDI**

Marine Environmental Data Service (Canada) e: **MEDS**

Marine Environmental Management Office e: **MEMO**

Marine Environmental Prediction Task Group e: **MAREP**

Marine Environmental Quality e: **MEQ**

Marine Environmental Quality Committee e: **MEQC**

Marine Environmental Response e: **MER**

Marine Environmental Services e: **MES**

Marine Environmental Survey Capability e: **MESC**

Marine Environmental Testing and Electro-Optical Radiation e: **METEOR**

Marine Fighter Squadron [All-Weather] e: **VMF[AW]**

Marine Firemen, Oilers, Watertenders and Wipers e: **MFOWW**

Marine Gas Emissions, Atmospheric Chemistry, and Climate e: **MAGE**

Marine Geological Institute [Indonesia] e: **MGI**

Marine Geology and Geophysics [Report] e: **MGG**

Marine Geophysical Data Exchange Format e: **MGD77**

Marine Geophysical Survey e: **MGS**

Marine-Hauptquartier-Informationssystem d: **MHQI**

Marine Hydrophysical Institute e: **MHI**

Marine Hydrophysical Institute, Ukraine Academy of Sciences Sevastopol e: **MGI**

Marine Mammal[s] Protection Act e: **MMPA**

Marine Meteorological Services e: **MAMS**, e: **MARMETS**, e: **MMS**

Marine Meteorological Services System e: **MMSS**

Marine Meteorology Programme e: **MMP**

Marine National Nature Reserve e: **MNNR**

Marine Observation Squadron e: **VMO**

Marine Observation Squadron [Artillery Spotting] e: **VMO[AS]**

Marine Observation[al] (or Observations) Satellite e: **MOS**

Marine Pollution Monitoring Center [including LIPI's Network of the Center for Research and Development in Oceanography] e: **LIPI**

Marine Protected Area e: **MPA**

Marine Protection, Research, and Sanctuaries Act e: **MPRSA**

Marine Radioecology Working Group e: **MARECO**

Marine Remote Area Approach [and] Landing System e: **MRAALS**

Marine Remote Sensing Experiment e: **MARSEN**

Marine Remote Sensing Information System [for Regional European Seas] e: **MARSIS**

Marine Resources and Environment Management Programme e: **MAREMP**

Marine-Unterwasserregelanlagen-Planungsgesellschaft d: **MUG**

Marine Weather Service e: **MWS**

Marinehauptquartier d: **MHQ**

Mariner V Spacecraft e: **MV Spacecraft**

Maritime Aircraft Weather Code e: **MAWEC**

Maritime Orbital Test Satellite e: **Marots**

Maritime Orbital Test Satellite[s] e: **MAROTS**

Maritime Orbiter Technology Satellite e: **MAROTS**

Maritime Polar e: **mP**

Maritime Polar Air e: **mP Air**

maritime Polarluft d: **mP**, d: **MPL**

Maritime Safety and Environmental Strategy e: **MS&ES**

Maritimes Forest Research Centre, Environment Canada Fredericton, New Brunswick e: **NBFE**

Mark Twain National Wildlife Refuge e: **MTNWR**

Marmonization of Environmental Measurement e: **HEM**

Maroc Informations Médicales f: **MIM**

Mars Atmosphere Density Sensor e: **MADS**

Mars Atmosphere Probe e: **MAP**

Mars Atmospheric Water Detection e: **MAWD**

Mars Climate Orbiter e: **MCO**

Mars Orbit Ejection e: **MOE**

Mars Orbit Inertion e: **MOI**

Mars Orbital Rendezvous e: **MOR**

Mars spacecraft e: **MARS**

Marshall Space Flight Center Information Retrieval and Display System e: **MIRADS**

Marshall Space Flight Center System for Aerospace Systems Simulation e: **MARSYAS**

Marshall Space Flight System e: **MSFS**

Marshfield Medical Research Foundation e: **MMRF**

Martens Polarization Photometer e: **MPP**

Martin Marietta Aerospace e: **MMA**

Martin Marietta Manned Space System e: **MMMS**

Martin Marietta Orlando Aerospace e: **MMOA**

Maryland Automated Geographic Information System e: **MAGI**

Maryland Department of the Environment e: **MDE**

Maryland Environmental Service e: **MES**

Maryland Geological Survey e: **MGS**

Maryland Institute Emergency Medical Services e: **MIEMSS**

Maryland Medical Journal e: **Md Med J**

Maryland Veterinary Medical Association e: **MDVMA**, e: **MVMA**

Masonic Medical Research Laboratory, Utica e: **NUtMM**

Mass Balance of Arctic Glaciers and Ice Sheets in relation to Climate and Sea Level Changes e: **MAGICS**

Mass in Earth Orbit e: **MEO**

Mass Observation e: **MO**

mass of biological material e: **biomass**

Massachusettensis Medicinae Societatis Socius l: **MMSS**

Massachusetts Basic Data Report. Ground Water Series e: **Mass Basic Data Rep Ground Water Ser**

Massachusetts Department of Environmental Quality e: **MDEQ**

Massachusetts Department of Natural Resources. Division of Marine Fisheries. Monographs Series e: **Mass Dep Nat Resour Div Mar Fish Monogr Ser**

Massachusetts Department of Public Health e: **MDPH**

Massachusetts Environmental Protection Act e: **MEPA**

Massachusetts Health Journal e: **Mass Health J**

Massachusetts Institute of Technology and Woods Hole Oceanographic Institution. Papers e: **Mass Inst Technology and Woods Hole Oceanog Inst Paper**

Massachusetts Institute of Technology. School of Engineering. Department of Civil Engineering Hydrodynamics Laboratory. Report e: **Mass Inst Tech Dep Civ Eng Hydrodyn Lab Rep**

Massachusetts Institute of Technology. School of Engineering. Department of Civil Engineering Research in Earth Physics. Research Report e: **Mass Inst Tech Dep Civ Eng Res Earth Phys Res Rep**

Massachusetts Institute of Technology. School of Engineering. Ralph M. Parsons Laboratory for Water Resources and

Hydrodynamics. Report e: **MIT Ralph M Parsons Lab Water Resour Hydrodyn Rep**

Massachusetts Institute of Technology Sea Grant Program e: **MITSG**

Massachusetts Medical Journal e: **Mass Med J**

Massachusetts Medical Society e: **MMS**

Massachusetts Society for Medical Research e: **MSMR**

Massachusetts University. College of Food and Natural Resources. Agricultural Experiment Station. Research Bulletin e: **Mass Univ Coll Food Nat Resour Agric Exp Stn Res Bull**

Massachusetts University. Department of Geology and Mineralogy. Special Department Publication e: **Mass Univ Dept Geology and Mineralogy Special Dept Pub**

Massachusetts University. Department of Geology. Contribution e: **Mass Univ Dep Geol Contrib**

Massachusetts Veterinary Medical Association e: **MAVMA**, e: **MVMA**

Massstaborientierte Einheitliche Raumbezugsbasis für Kommunale Informations-Systeme d: **MERKIS**

Master Geographical Reference Area e: **MGRA**

Master in Professional Geophysics e: **M Pr Gph**

Master Index Remote Access Capability e: **MIRAC**

Master List of Medical Indexing Terms e: **MALIMET**, e: **MALIMIT**

Master [Mistress] of Veterinary Medicine e: **M.Vet.Med.**

Master of Biological Chemistry e: **M Bi Ch**, e: **M Bi Chem**

Master of Biological Engineering e: **M Bi E**, e: **M Bi Eng**

Master of Biological Physics e: **M Bi Phy**

Master of Biological Sciences e: **M Bi S**

Master of Biomedical Engineering e: **MBiomedE**

Master of Community Health e: **M Comm H**

Master of Emergency Medical Services e: **MEMS**

Master of Engineering [Public Health] e: **M.E.[P.H.]**, e: **ME [Pub. Health]**

Master of Environmental Science e: **MEnvSc**

Master of Environmental Studies e: **MEnvS[t][ud]**, e: **MSES**

Master of Geological Engineering e: **M.G.E.**, e: **M Ge E**, e: **M Ge E[ng]**, e: **M Geol E**, e: **M Geol E[ng]**

Master of Gynaecology and Obstetrics e: **M.G.O.**, e: **M.Gyn. and Obs.**

Master of Health Administration e: **MHA**

Master of Health Personnel Education e: **MHPEd**

Master of Health, Physical Education and Recreation e: **MH PE & R**

Master of Health Planning e: **MHP**

Master of Health Sciences e: **MHS**

Master of Industrial Health e: **M.I.H.**

Master of Internal Medicine e: **M Int Med**

Master of Laboratory Animal Sciences e: **MLAS**

Master of Medical Science e: **M Med Sc[i]**, e: **M.M.S.**, e: **MM Sc**, e: **MSM**, e: **MS Med**

Master of Medical Technology e: **MMT**

Master of Medicine e: **M Med**

Master of Medicine [Paediatrics] e: **MMedPaed**

Master of Microbiology e: **M Mic**

Master of Natural Resources e: **MNatRes**

Master of Obstetrics and Gynaecology e: **MO and G**, e: **MO & G**

Master of Occupational Health e: **MOH**

Master of Physical Biology e: **MPB**

Master of Physical Education and Health e: **MPH**

Master of Physical Health and Tropical Medicine e: **MPHTM**

Master of Preventive Medicine e: **M Pr M**

Master of Professional Studies-Hospital and Health Services Administration e: **MPS-HHSA**

Master of Psychological Medicine e: **MPM**, e: **M Psy Med**

Master of Public Health Education e: **MPH Ed**

Master of Public Health Engineering e: **MPHE**, e: **MPH Eng**

Master of Public Health Nursing e: **MPHN**

Master of Science in Agriculture and Animal Husbandry e: **M Sc Agr & AH**

Master of Science in Animal Husbandry e: **M Sc AH**

Master of Science in Biological Sciences e: **MS in Bl Sc**

Master of Science in Geological Engineering e: **M.S.G.E.**

Master of Science in Geology e: **SM Geol**

Master of Science in Geophysical Engineering e: **MS in Gp Engr**

Master of Science in Health and Physical Education e: **MSH & Ph Ed**

Master of Science in Health Physics e: **MSHP**

Master of Science in Medical Science e: **M Sc Med Sc**

Master of Science in Medicine e: **M Sc Med**, e: **MS in Med**

Master of Science in Public Health e: **MS in PH**, e: **MSPH**

Master of Science in Public Health Education e: **MSPH Ed**

Master of Science in Public Health Engineering e: **MSPHE**

Master of Science [Medical] e: **MSc[Med]**

Master of the Science of Medicine e: **M Sc M**

Master of Veterinary Medicine e: **MDV**, e: **MVM**

Master Surgeon Dentist e: **MSD**

Master Water Data Index e: **MWDI**

Master[s] in Public Health e: **MPH**

Materia Medica Polona e: **Mater Med Pol**

Material Exposure in Low Earth Orbit e: **MELEO**

Materialauswahl Umweltschutz d: **MAUS**

Materialien der Komission für Mineralogie und Geochemie. Karpato-Balkanische Geologische Assoziation d: **Mater Kom Mineral Geochem Karpato Balk Geol Assoz**

Materially and Geometrically Non-Linear Analysis e: **MAGNA**

Materials Processing in Space e: **MPS**

Materials Protection e: **Mater Prot**

Materials Protection and Performance e: **Mater. Protect. Performance**, e: **Mater Prot Perform[ance]**

Material[s] Science and Manufacturing in Space e: **MS/MS**

Materiaux pour la Geologie de la Suisse. Geophysique f: **Mater Geol Suisse Geophys**

Materiaux pour le Leve Geobotanique de la Suisse f: **Mater Leve Geobot Suisse**

Maternal and Child Health Bureau e: **MCHB**

Maternal and Child Health Funds through Social Security Act e: **TITLE V**

Maternal and Child Health Journal e: **MCHJ**

Maternal and Child Health Program e: **MCHP**

Maternal and Child Health [Service] e: **MCH**

Maternal and Child Health Service e: **MCHS**

Maternal and Neonatal Health e: **MNH**

Maternal, Child and Women's Health e: **MCWH**

Maternal & Child Health Policy Research Center e: **MCHPRC**

Mathematical Geologists of the United States e: **MGUS**

Mathematik für Ingenieure, Naturwissenschaftler, Ökonomen und Landwirte d: **Math Ingen Naturwiss Ökonom Landwirte**

Mathematik für Ingenieure, Naturwissenschaftler, Ökonomen und Sonstige Anwendungsorientierte Berufe d: **Math Ingen Naturwiss Ökonom Sonstige Anwendungsorient Berufe**

Mathematik für Naturwissenschaft und Technik d: **Math Naturwiss Tech**

Mathematik und Naturwissenschaften d: **NAT**

Mathematisch-Naturwissenschaftliche Bibliothek d: **Math-Naturwiss Bibliothek**

Mathematisch-naturwissenschaftliche Blätter d: **MNBl**

Mathematisch-Naturwissenschaftliche Fakultät e: **MNF**

Mathematisch-naturwissenschaftliche Mitteilungen d: **MnM**

Mathematisch-Naturwissenschaftliche Taschenbücher d: **Math-Naturwiss Taschenb**

Mathematischer und Naturwissenschaftlicher Unterricht d: **Math Naturw[iss] Unterr**

Matiere Azotee Totale f: **MAT**

Matrix Biology e: **Matrix Biol**

Matrix of/for Environmental Residuals for Energy Systems e: **MERES**

Mattamuskeet National Wildlife Refuge e: **MNWR**

Matter, Energy, Space and Time e: **MEST**

Matériaux pour la Carte Géologique de la Suisse f: **Matér. Carte Géol. Suisse**

Matériaux pour le levé géobotanique de la Suisse f: **Matér. levé géobot. Suisse**

Matériel pour l'Etude des Phénomènes Interéssant la Solidification sur Terre et en Orbite f: **MEPHISTO**

Mauna Kea Observatory e: **MKO**

Mauna Loa Observatory *e:* **MLO**

Mauna Loa Observatory Photochemical Experiment *e:* **MLOPEX**

Mauna Loa Solar Observatory *e:* **MLSO**

Maurice Lamontagne Institute, Fisheries and Oceans Canada, Mont-Joli, Quebec *e:* **QQPSM**

Maury Center for Ocean Science *e:* **MC**

Max-Delbrück-Centrum für Molekulare Medizin, Berlin *d:* **MDC**

Max-Planck-Institut für Medizinische Forschung, Heidelberg *d:* **GyHeM**

Max-Planck-Institut für Meteorologie *d:* **MPIM**

Max Planck Institut für Meteorologie, Hamburg *d:* **MPI**

Max-Planck-Institut für Meteorologie, Hamburg *e:* **MPI-HH**

Max-Planck Institute for Meteorology *e:* **MPI**

Maxey Flats Radioactive Protective Association *e:* **MFRPA**

Maximale Immissionskonzentration [für Schadstoffe in bodennahen Schichten der Atmosphäre] *d:* **MIK**

Maximum Access to Diagnosis and Therapy: The Electronic Library of Medicine *e:* **MAXX**

Maximum Contaminant Level Goal [Environmental Protection Agency] *e:* **MCLG**

Maximum Envelope of Water *e:* **MEOW**

Maximum Health *e:* **MXH**

Maximum Space-Charge-Limited Emission *e:* **MSCLE**

Maximum Water Level *e:* **MWL**, *e:* **MW Level**

May Institute of Medical Research *e:* **MIMR**

Mayor Atmospheric Gamma-ray Imaging Cherenkov Telescope *e:* **MAGIC Telescope**

McDonald Observatory *e:* **McDO**, *e:* **McD Obs**

McDonald Observatory Library *e:* **McD**

McDonnell Douglas Aerospace Information Services *e:* **MDAIS**

McDonnell Douglas Space Systems Company *e:* **MDSSC**

McGill University, Medical Library *e:* **GLM**

McGill Weather Observatory *e:* **MWO**

MCM Tactical Environmental Data System *e:* **MTEDS**

McMaster University Medical Center *e:* **McMUMC**, *e:* **MUMC**

Meadowview Wild Life Preserve *e:* **MWLP**

Mean diurnal high water inequality *e:* **DHQ**

mean diurnal low-water inequality *e:* **dlp**

Mean diurnal low water inequality *e:* **DLQ**

Mean Effective Depth of the Atmosphere Duct *e:* **MEDAD**

Mean High Water *e:* **MHW**

Mean High Water Level *e:* **MHWL**

Mean High Water Line *e:* **MHWL**

Mean High Water Lunitidal Interval *e:* **MHWLI**

Mean High Water, Neap Tide *e:* **MHWNT**

Mean High Water, Neaps *e:* **MHWN**

Mean High Water, Spring Tide *e:* **MHWST**

Mean High Water, Springs *e:* **MHWS**

Mean Higher High Water *e:* **MHHW**

Mean Higher High Water Line *e:* **MHHWL**

Mean Higher Low Water *e:* **MHLW**

Mean Low Water *e:* **MLW**

Mean Low Water Level *e:* **MLWL**

Mean Low Water Lunitidal Interval *e:* **MLWLI**

Mean Low Water, Neap Tide *e:* **MLWNT**

Mean Low Water, Neaps *e:* **MLWN**

Mean Low Water, Spring Tide *e:* **MLWST**

Mean Low Water, Springs *e:* **MLWS**

Mean Lower High Water *e:* **MLHW**

Mean Lower Low Water *e:* **MLLW**

Mean range [between mean high and mean low water] *e:* **Mn**

Mean Sea Level *e:* **MSL**

Mean Sea Level Pressure *e:* **MSLP**

Mean Temperature Water *e:* **MTW**

Mean Water Level *e:* **MWL**, *e:* **MW Level**

mean water neap tide *e:* **mwnt**

Mean Water Pressure *e:* **MWP**

Mean Water Temperature *e:* **MWT**

Measurement of Air Pollution from Space *e:* **MAPS**

Measurement of Atmospheric Pollution from Satellites *e:* **MAPS**

Measurements of Earth Data for Environmental Analysis *e:* **MEDEA**

Measuring Air Pollution from Space *e:* **MAPS**

Meat Animal Research Center *e:* **MARC**

Mechanical Aerospace Ground Equipment *e:* **MAGE**

Mechanical and Aerospace Engineer[ing] *e:* **MAE**

Mechanical Endurance Load on Environment Test Apparatus *e:* **MELETA**

Mechanical Impact System Design for Advanced Spacecraft *e:* **MISDAS**

Mechanical Transport Water Tank Company *e:* **M.T.W.T.Co.**

Mechanisch-biologische Restmüllbehandlung *d:* **MBR**

Mechanized Infantry in a Smoke Environment *e:* **MISE**

Meddelanden fra Dansk Geologiske Forendlingen *a:* **Medd Dansk Geol Forend**

Meddelelser fra Dansk Geologisk Forening *a:* **Medd Dan Geol Foren**

Meddelelser om Groenland. Geoscience *a:* **Medd Groenl Geosci**

Medecine et Biologie *f:* **Med Bipl**

Medic-Alert Foundation International *e:* **MAFI**

Medica-Legal Papers *e:* **Med Leg Pap**

Medicaid Managed Care Program *e:* **MMCP**

Medicaid Management Information System *e:* **MMIS**

Medical *e:* **M**, *e:* **MED**

medical *e:* **med**

Medical *e:* **MEDL**

Medical Abstainers' Association *e:* **M.A.A.**

Medical Abstract Service *e:* **Med Abstr**

Medical Academic Staff Committee *e:* **MASC**

Medical Access and Retrieval System *e:* **MEDARS**

Medical Accessories Kit *e:* **MAK**

Medical Accounting *e:* **MEDAC**

Medical Acupuncture Research Foundation *e:* **MARF**

Medical Administration Management System *e:* **MAMS**

Medical Administrative Control System *e:* **MEDACS**

Medical Administrative Corps *e:* **M.A.C.**, *e:* **Med Adm C**

Medical Administrative Management System-Revision *e:* **MAMS-R**

Medical Advanced Technology Management Office *e:* **MATMO**

Medical Advisers Support Centre *e:* **MASC**

Medical Advisory Board *e:* **M.A.B.**

Medical Advisory Committee *e:* **MAC**

Medical Advisory Service [Civil Service Department] *e:* **MAS**

Medical Advisory Services for Travellers Abroad *e:* **MASTA**

Medical Advisory System *e:* **MAS**

Medical Afairs *e:* **Med Aff**

Medical Aid [federal program] *e:* **MEDICAID**

Medical Aid for Indochina *e:* **MAI**

Medical Aid for Palestinians *e:* **MAP**

Medical Aid of California *e:* **MEDI-CAL**

Medical Aid Post *e:* **MAP**

Medical Air *e:* **MA**

Medical Air Evacuation *e:* **MAE**

Medical Analysis of Days of Care *e:* **MADOC**

Medical and Actuarial Research Foundation *e:* **MARF**

Medical and Biological Electronics *e:* **MBE**

Medical and Biological Engineering *e:* **Med [and] Biol Eng**, *e:* **Med Bio Eng**, *e:* **Med. Biol. Eng.**, *e:* **Med Biol Engng**

Medical and Biological Engineering and Computing *e:* **Med [and] Biol Eng [and] Comput**, *e:* **Med Biol Eng Comput**

Medical and Biological Illustration *e:* **Med Bio Ill**, *e:* **Med Biol Illus[tr]**

Medical and Blood Products Management *e:* **MEDBLD**

Medical and Chirurgical Faculty of the State of Maryland. Baltimore *e:* **MdBM**

Medical and Dental Defence Union of Scotland *e:* **MDDUS**

Medical and Dental Education Levy *e:* **MADEL**

Medical and Dental Education Network *e:* **MADEN**

Medical and Dental Supply Office *e:* **MDSO**

Medical and Endoscopical Television Appliances *e:* **METVA**

Medical and Health Department *e:* **MHD**

Medical and Health Related Sciences Thesaurus *e:* **MHRST**

Medical and Health Research Association of New York City *e:* **MHRA**

Medical and Hospital Department *e:* **M&HDA**

Medical and Nursing [Red Cross Disaster Services] *e:* **M&N**

Medical and Occupational Radiation Program *e:* **MORP**

Medical and Other Applications Proceedings. International Congress on

Isozymes e: **Med Other Appl Proc Int Congr Isozymes**

Medical and Pediatric Oncology e: **Med Pediatr Oncol**, e: **MPO**

Medical and Pediatric Oncology. Supplement e: **Med Pediatr Oncol Suppl**

Medical and Personnel Planning Factors Report e: **MEDPERFAC**

Medical and Philosophical Commentaries e: **Med and Phil Comment**

Medical and Physial Journal e: **Med Phys J**

Medical and Professional Woman's Journal e: **Med Prof Womans J**

Medical and Psychological Previews e: **PREV**

Medical and Surgical e: **M&S**

Medical and Technical Assistant e: **MTA**

Medical and Veterinary Entomology e: **Med Vet Entomol**

Medical Annals of the District of Columbia e: **Med Ann DC**, e: **Med Ann Distr Columbia**

Medical Annual [England] e: **Med Annu**

Medical Anthropology e: **Med Anthro[pol]**

Medical Anthropology Newsletter e: **Med Anthropol Newsletter**

Medical Anthropology Quarterly e: **Med Anthropol Q**

Medical Application Service Provider e: **MASP**

Medical Application Software Quality Enhancement by Standards e: **MASQUES**

Medical Art e: **Med Art**

Medical Artists Association [of Great Britain] e: **MAA**

Medical Artists Association of Great Britain e: **MAAGB**

Medical Arts and Sciences e: **Med Ar Sci**

Medical Aspects of Human Sexuality e: **Med Aspec Hum Sex**

Medical Assistance Administration e: **MAA**

Medical Assistance Advisory Council e: **MAAC**

Medical Assistance for the Aged e: **MAA**

Medical Assistance Program[me], International e: **MAP**

Medical Assistant e: **MA**

Medical Assisted Facility e: **MAF**

Medical Association for [the] Prevention of War. e: **MAPW**

Medical Association of Eire e: **M.A.E.**

Medical Association of Georgia e: **MAG**

Medical Association of Jamaica e: **MAJ**

Medical Association of Malta e: **MAM**

Medical Association of New Zealand e: **MANZ**

Medical Association of South Africa e: **M.A.S.A.**

Medical Association of South East Asian Nations e: **MASEAN**

Medical Association of the State of Alabama e: **MASA**

Medical Association of the State of Alabama. Journal e: **Med Assoc State Ala J**

Medical Audit Advisory Group e: **MAAG**

Medical Audit Statistics e: **MAS**

Medical Augmentation e: **MEDAUG**

Medical Authorization e: **MA**

Medical Automation Intelligence [System] e: **MAIN**

Medical Automation Intelligence System e: **MAIN System**

Medical Badge e: **MBAD**, e: **MEDBAD**

Medical Badge Pay e: **MedBP**

Medical Battalion e: **MB**, e: **MEDBN**

Medical Benefits Fund e: **MBF**

Medical Bioengineering Research and Development Laboratory e: **MBRDL**

Medical Biology e: **Med Biol**

Medical Biology [Helsinki] e: **Med Biol [Helsinki]**

Medical Blood e: **MEDBLOOD**

Medical Board e: **M.B.**, e: **MEB**

Medical Books for China International e: **M.B.C.I.**

Medical Branch e: **M.B.**, e: **MEDBR**

Medical Bulletin e: **MB**

Medical Bulletin. Exxon Corporation and Affliated Companies e: **Med Bull Exxon Corp Affil Co**

Medical Bulletin. Fukuoka University e: **Med Bull Fukuoka Univ**

Medical Bulletin. Istanbul Faculty of Medicine. Istanbul University e: **Med Bull Istanbul Fac Med Istanbul Univ**

Medical Bulletin. Istanbul Medical Faculty e: **Med Bull Istanbul Med Fac**

Medical Bulletin. Istanbul Medical Faculty. Istanbul University e: **Med Bull Istanbul Med Fac Istanbul Univ**

Medical Bulletin. Istanbul University e: **Med Bull Istanbul Univ**

Medical Bulletin. National Medical Center [Seoul] e: **Med Bull Natl Med Cent [Seoul]**

Medical Bulletin of Northern Virginia e: **Med Bull No Virginia**

Medical Bulletin. Providence Hospital [Soulhfield, Michigan] e: **Med Bull Providence Hosp [Southfield Mich]**

Medical Bulletin. Standard Oil Company [New Jersey] and Affliated Companies e: **Med Bull Stand Oil Co [NJ] Affil Co**

Medical Bulletin [United States Army] e: **Med Bull [US Army]**

Medical Bulletin. University of Cincinnati e: **Med Bull Univ Cincinnati**

Medical Bulletin. US Army [Europe] e: **Med Bull US Army [Eur]**

Medical Bulletin. Veterans Administration e: **Med Bull Vet Adm**

Medical Cabinet e: **MC**

Medical Campaign Against Nuclear Weapons e: **MCANW**

Medical Care e: **Med Care**, e: **MEDICARE**

Medical Care International, Inc. e: **MEDC**

Medical Care Research and Review e: **MCRR**

Medical Care Review e: **Med Care Rev**

Medical Care Support Equipment e: **MEDCASE**

Medical Career Research Group e: **MCRG**

Medical Center e: **MC**, e: **Med. Cen.**, e: **Med. Ctr.**

Medical Center for Family Planning [Ecuador] e: **CEMOPLAF**

Medical Center for Federal Prisoners e: **MCFP**

Medical Center Journal. University of Michigan e: **Med Cent J Univ Mich**

Medical Certificate e: **MC**

Medical Civic Action Teams e: **MEDCAT**

Medical Civil Action Program e: **Med CAP**

Medical Clinics of North America e: **Med.Clin.N.Amer.**

Medical Coding System e: **MCS**

Medical College e: **MC**

Medical College Admission Test e: **MCAT**

Medical College of Georgia e: **MCG**

Medical College of Georgia, Augusta e: **GXM**

Medical College of Pennsylvania e: **MCP**

Medical College of Pennsylvania, Philadelphia, PA e: **PPWM**

Medical College of South Carolina e: **MCSC**

Medical College of Virginia e: **MCV**

Medical College of Virginia. Quarterly e: **Med C Virg**

Medical College of Wisconsin e: **MCOW**

Medical Command e: **MEDCOM**

Medical Commanding Officer e: **MC Off.**

Medical Commission of the International Olympic Committee e: **IOC**

Medical Commission on Accident Prevention e: **MCAP**

Medical Committee against the Abuse of Prisoners by Drugging e: **MCAPD**

Medical Committee for Civil Rights e: **MCCR**

Medical Committee for Human Rights e: **MCHR**

Medical Communications e: **Med Commun**

Medical Communications System e: **MEDICOM System**

Medical Company e: **Med Co**

Medical Computer Journal e: **Med Comp J**

Medical Computer Services e: **MCS**

Medical Computer Services Administration e: **MCSA**

Medical Construction Liaison Office[r] e: **MCLO**

Medical Consultant Staff [Social Security Administration] e: **MCS**

Medical Consultation and New Remedies e: **Med Consult New Remedies**

Medical Consultative Board e: **M.C.B.**

Medical Consumers Association of Australia e: **MCAA**

Medical Contact Lens and Ocular Surface Association e: **MCLOSA**

Medical Contact Lens Association e: **MCLA**

Medical Contingency Report e: **MEDCON**, e: **MEDCON Report**

Medical Continuity of Operations Plan e: **MEDCOOP**, e: **MEOOP**

Medical Control Agency e: **MCA**

Medical Corporation e: **M.C.**

Medical Corps e: **MC**, e: **Md C**, e: **Med C**, e: **MEDCORPS**

Medical Corps, Merchant Marine, General Service e: **MCMR**

Medical Corps, Merchant Marine, Special Service e: **MCMS**

Medical Corps, Special Service e: **MCS**

Medical Corps, Women's Reserve e: **MCW**

Medical Corpsman e: **MEDIC**

Medical Correctional Association e: **MCA**

Medical Council and Registration Office e: **M.C.R.O.**

Medical Council of Australia e: **MCA**

Medical Council of Canada e: **M.C.C.**

Medical Council of New Zealand e: **MCNZ**

Medical Council on Alcoholism e: **MCA**

Medical Counterpoint e: **Med Counterpoint**

Medical Crew Director e: **MCD**

Medical Crisis Center e: **MCC**

Medical Data Acquisition System e: **MDAS**

Medical Data Limited e: **MDL**

Medical Data Specialist e: **MEDDS**

Medical Data System e: **MDS**

Medical Data System for Analysis of Clinical Information e: **MEDAAC**

Medical Data System/Joint Camera Computer e: **MDS/JCC**

Medical Decision Making e: **MDM**, e: **Med Decision Making**, e: **Med Decis Making**

Medical Defence e: **MD**

Medical Defence Association of Victoria e: **MDAV**

Medical Defence (or Defense) Union e: **MDU**

Medical Defence Union e: **M.D.U.**

Medical-Dental e: **MED-DENT**

Medical, Dental and Hospital Consultants e: **MDHC**

Medical-Dental Committee on Evaluation of Fluoridation e: **MDCEF**

Medical Dental Division e: **MED-DENT**

Medical-Dental-Hospital Bureaus of America e: **MDHBA**, e: **MHBA**

Medical/Dental Journal e: **Med Dent J**

Medical Dental Service e: **MDS**

Medical Department e: **MD**, e: **MED**

Medical Department Activity e: **MEDDAC**

Medical Department Personnel Support Agency e: **MEDDPERSA**

Medical Department Representative e: **MDR**

Medical Depot e: **Med. Dep.**

Medical Depot Company e: **Med Dep Co**

Medical Device and Diagnostic Industry e: **Med Device & Dign Ind**

Medical Device Directive e: **MDD**

Medical Device Directorate e: **MDD**

Medical Devices Agency e: **MDA**

Medical Devices Reports [Commerce Clearing House] e: **Med Devices Rep [CCH]**

Medical Diagnostics Imagery System e: **MDIS**

Medical Dietary Information System e: **MEDIS**

Medical Dimensions e: **Med Dimensions**

Medical Director-General e: **M.D.G.**

Medical Director General of the Royal Canadian Navy e: **MDG RCN**

Medical Directors' Association e: **MDA**

Medical Directory of Australia e: **MDA**

Medical Discharge e: **MD**, e: **Med. Dis.**

Medical Display Analysis and Recording System e: **MEDDARS**

Medical Distributing Station e: **MDS**

Medical Doctor e: **M.D.**

Medical Documentation Service e: **MDS**

Medical Documentation Systems e: **MEDDOC**

Medical Documents [Eccles Health Sciences Library University of Utah] e: **MEDOC**

Medical Dosimetrists Certification Board e: **MDCB**

Medical Dosimetry e: **Med Dosim**

Medical Early Direct Commissioning Program e: **MEDCOMP**

Medical Economics for Surgeons e: **Med Econ Surgeons**

Medical Education e: **Med Educ**

Medical Education Cooperation with Cuba e: **MEDICC**

Medical Education for National Defense e: **MEND**

Medical Education Online e: **MEO**

Medical Education Preparatory Program [of Southern Illinois University] e: **MEDPREP**

Medical Education Program e: **MEP**

Medical Electronic Data Aquisition and Control e: **MEDAC**

Medical Electronic Data Interpretation and Correlation e: **MEDIC**

Medical Electronics and Data Society e: **MEDS**

Medical Electronics Society e: **MES**

Medical Emergency Decisions Assistance System e: **MEDAS**

Medical Emergency Development International Committee e: **MEDIC**

Medical Emergency Radiological Response Team e: **MERRT**

Medical Emergency Relief Care for Youth e: **MERCY**

Medical Emergency Relief International e: **MERLIN**

Medical Emergency Report e: **MEDMER**

Medical Emergency Service Associates e: **MESA**

Medical Engineering and Physics e: **Med Eng Phys**

Medical Entomology Research and Training Unit, University de Valle e: **MERTU**

Medical Environmental Development with Air Assistance e: **MEDAIR**

Medical Equipment Display and Conference e: **MEDAC**

Medical Equipment Management Office e: **MEMO**

Medical Equipment Management Office/Maintenance e: **MEMO/MAINT**

Medical Equipment Repair Center e: **MERC**

Medical Equipment Research and Development Laboratory e: **MERDL**

Medical Equipment Test and Evaluation Division e: **MET&E**

Medical Ethics Resource Network of Michigan e: **MERN**

Medical Evacuation e: **MEDEVAC**

Medical Evacuation Vehicle e: **MEV**

Medical Evaluation e: **MEDEVAL**

Medical Evaluation Data System e: **MEDS**

Medical Evidence Disaggregated Direct Input of Costs Database e: **MEDDIC**

Medical Evidence [Medical Record] e: **ME [MR]**

Medical Examination Centre e: **MEC**

Medical Examiner e: **ME**

Medical Examiners and Coroners Alert Project e: **MECAP**

Medical Examining Board e: **M.E.B.**, e: **MEBD**

Medical Exhibitors Association e: **MEA**

Medical Expedition to Easter[n] Island e: **METEI**

Medical Expense and Performance Report e: **MEPR**

Medical Expense and Performance Reporting System e: **MEPRS**

Medical Expert e: **MEDEX**

Medical Eye History e: **MEH**

Medical Field Activity e: **Med. Fld. Actv.**

Medical Field Assistance Branch e: **MEDFAD**

Medical Field Book e: **MFB**

Medical Field Manual e: **MFM**

Medical Field Service School e: **MFSS**

Medical Field Service School, Fort Sam Houston e: **TxFshM**

Medical Field Service Technician e: **MFT**

Medical First Aid Guide for use in Accidents Involving Dangerous Goods e: **MFAG**

Medical follow up e: **MFU**

Medical Force 2000 e: **MF2K**

Medical Forward Treatment Unit e: **MFTU**

Medical Function Control System e: **MFCS**

Medical Functional Requirements Group e: **MFRG**

Medical Geniculate Nucleus e: **MGN**

Medical Group Management Association e: **MGMA**

Medical Group Management Journal e: **MGM**

Medical Group Practice Council e: **M.G.P.C.**

Medical Gymnast e: **MG**

Medical History e: **Med Hist**, e: **M/H**

Medical History Sheet e: **MHS**

Medical History. Supplement e: **Med Hist Suppl**

Medical Hospitals Association e: **M.H.A.**

Medical Hypotheses e: **Med Hypotheses**

Medical Illustration Service for Museum Design e: **MISMD**

Medical Illustrator e: **MI**

Medical Imaging and Radiation Oncology Data Alliance e: **MIRODA**

Medical Impairment Bureau e: **MIB**

Medical Incident Report e: **MIR**

Medical Informatics e: **Med Inf [Lond]**, e: **MINFDZ**

Medical Informatics Cultural Literacy Project e: **MICLP**

Medical Information e: **MEDINFO**

Medical Information [and] Communications System e: **MEDICS**

Medical Information and Intelligence Agency e: **MIIA**

Medical Information Bureau e: **MIB**

Medical Information Center e: **MIC**

Medical Information Group e: **MIG**

Medical Information Management System e: **MIMS**

Medical Information Network e: **MINET**

Medical Information Science Section e: **MISS**

Medical Information Service via Telephone *e:* **MIST**

Medical Information Storage and Retrieval System *e:* **MEDISTARS**

Medical Information System *e:* **MEDIS**

Medical Information System[s] *e:* **MIS**

Medical Information System[s] Program[me] *e:* **MISP**

Medical Inspection *e:* **MI**

Medical Inspection Room *e:* **MIR**

Medical Inspector of Seamen *e:* **MIS**

Medical Institutions' Financial Accounting System *e:* **MIFACS**

Medical Instrument Society of Japan *e:* **MISJ**

Medical Instrument[s] Calibration System *e:* **MICS**

Medical Intelligence *e:* **MEDINT**

Medical Intelligence Office *e:* **MIO**

Medical Intensive Care Unit *e:* **MICU**

Medical Interfraternity Conference *e:* **MIC**

Medical Internal Radiation Dose [Committee] [Society of Nuclear Medicine] *e:* **MIRD**

Medical International Cooperation [Organization] *e:* **MEDICO**

Medical Journal. Armed Forces [India] *e:* **Med J Armed For [India]**

Medical Journal. Cairo University *e:* **Med J Cairo Univ**

Medical Journal. Chulalongkorn Hospital Medical School [Bangkok] *e:* **Med J Chulalongkorn Hosp Med Sch [Bangkok]**

Medical Journal [English Translation of Lijecnicki Vjesnik] *e:* **Med J [Engl Transl Lijec Vjesn]**

Medical Journal Finder *e:* **MJF**

Medical Journal for Communication *e:* **Med J Commun**

Medical Journal for the Netherlands Indies *e:* **Med J Neth Indies**

Medical Journal. Fraternity Memorial Hospital *e:* **Med J Fraternity Mem Hosp**

Medical Journal. Han-Il Hospital *e:* **Med J Han-Il Hosp**

Medical Journal. Hiroshima University [Japan] *e:* **Med J Hiroshima Univ**

Medical Journal. Kagoshima University *e:* **Med J Kagoshima Univ**

Medical Journal. Kinki University *e:* **Med J Kinki Univ**

Medical Journal. Kobe University *e:* **Med J Kobe Univ**

Medical Journal. Minami Osaka Hospital [Japan] *e:* **Med J Minami Osaka Hosp**

Medical Journal. Mutual Aid Association [Japan] *e:* **Med J Mutual Aid Assoc**

Medical Journal National Hospitals and Sanatoriums of Japan *e:* **Med J Natl Hosp Sanat Jpn**

Medical Journal of Australia *e:* **Med J Aust**, *e:* **MJA**

Medical Journal of Australia. Supplement *e:* **Med J Aust Supp**

Medical Journal of Malaysia *e:* **Med J Malays[ia]**

Medical Journal of Osaka University *e:* **Med J Osaka Univ**

Medical Journal of Zambia *e:* **Med J Zamb**

Medical Journal. Osaka University *e:* **Med J Osaka Univ**

Medical Journal. Osaka University [English Edition] *e:* **Med J Osaka Univ [Engl Ed]**

Medical Journal .Osaka University [Japanese Edition] *e:* **Med J Osaka Univ [Jpn Ed]**

Medical Journal. Shinsu University *e:* **Med J Shinsbu Univ**

Medical Journal. Siamese Red Cross *e:* **Med J Siamese Red Cr**

Medical Journal. South West *e:* **Med J South West**

Medical Journal [Ukraine] *e:* **Med J [Ukr]**

Medical Jurisprudence *e:* **MED JUR**

Medical Knowledge Self-Assessment Program *e:* **MKSAP**

Medical Laboratory *e:* **MED LAB**, *e:* **ML**

Medical Laboratory Advisory Service *e:* **Med Laboratory Advisory**

Medical Laboratory Contract Reports *e:* **MLCR**

Medical Laboratory Observer *e:* **Med Lab Observer**, *e:* **MLO**

Medical Laboratory Sciences *e:* **Med Lab Sci**

Medical Laboratory Scientific Officer *e:* **MLSO**

Medical Laboratory Technology *e:* **Med Lab Tec**, *e:* **Med Lab Technol**

Medical Laboratory World *e:* **Med Lab World**

Medical Law International *e:* **Med.L.I.**

Medical Law Reports *e:* **Med.L.R.**

Medical Law Review *e:* **Med.L.Rev.**

Medical Leave of Absence *e:* **MLOA**

Medical Letter *e:* **ML**

Medical Letter on Drugs andTherapeutics *e:* **Med Lett DrugsTher**

Medical Liability Advisory Service *e:* **Med Liability Advisory**

Medical Liability Commission *e:* **MLC**

Medical Liberation Front *e:* **MLF**

Medical Libraries *e:* **Med Libr**

Medical Library Assistance Act *e:* **MLAA**

Medical Library Association *e:* **MLA**

Medical Library Association. Bulletin *e:* **Med Lib Assn Bul[l]**

Medical Library Association, Section on Mental Health Libraries *e:* **MLA-SMHL**

Medical Library, Bristol-Myers Pharmaceutical Group, Ottawa, Ontario *e:* **OOBMM**

Medical Library Center *e:* **MLC**

Medical Library Center of New York *e:* **MLCNY**

Medical Library Center of New York, New York *e:* **NNMLC**, *e:* **VVZ**

Medical Library Group of Southern California and Arizona *e:* **MLGSCA**

Medical Library, Hoechst Canada, Inc., Montreal, Quebec *e:* **QMHC**

Medical Library McGill University, Montreal, Quebec *e:* **QMMM**

Medical Library, Pfizer Canada, Inc., Kirkland, Quebec *e:* **QKPC**

Medical Library, Ross Memorial Hospital Lindsay, Ontario *e:* **OLRM**

Medical Library, South Street Campus, Victoria Hospital Corp., London, Ontario *e:* **OLVH**

Medical Library, Syntex, Inc., Mississauga, Ontario *e:* **OMSM**

Medical Library, Tom Baker Cancer Center, Calgary, Alberta *e:* **ACRBC**

Medical Library, University of Manitoba, Winnipeg, Manitoba *e:* **MWM**

Medical Library, University of Saskatchewan, Saskatoon, Saskatchewan *e:* **SSUM**

Medical Library, Yarmouth Regional Hospital, Nova Scotia *e:* **NSYR**

Medical Literature Analysis and Retreival System *e:* **MEDLARS**

Medical Lobby for Appropriate Marketing *e:* **MaLAM**

Medical Logistics *e:* **MEDLOG**, *e:* **ML**

Medical Logistics and Contingency Planning system *e:* **LOGCON**

Medical Maintenance Unit *e:* **MMU**

Medical Malpractice Cost Containment Journal *e:* **Med Malpract Cost Containment J**

Medical Malpractice Insurance Association *e:* **MMIA**

Medical Malpractice Lawsuit Filings *e:* **MEDMAL**

Medical Management Information System *e:* **MEDMIS**

Medical Manpower Standing Advisory Committee *e:* **MMSAC**

Medical Marketing and Media *e:* **Med Market Media**

Medical Marketing and Media *e:* **Med Mark Media**, *e:* **Med Mkt**

Medical Material Mission Reserve *e:* **MMMR**

Medical Materiel Accounting System *e:* **MMAS**

Medical Materiel Advice Code *e:* **MMAC**

Medical Materiel Management Center *e:* **MMMC**

Medical Materiel Management System *e:* **MEDMATS**, *e:* **MMMS**

Medical Materiel Management System On-Line *e:* **MMMS-OL**

Medical Materiel Program for Defense against Biological and Chemical Agents *e:* **MMPDABC**

Medical Materiel Program for Nuclear Casualties *e:* **MMPNC**

Medical Meetings *e:* **Med Meetings**

Medical Member *e:* **Med. Mbr.**

Medical Mentor *e:* **Med Mentor**

Medical Microbiology *e:* **Med Microbiol**

Medical Microbiology and Immunology *e:* **Med Microbi**, *e:* **Med Microbiol Immunol**, *e:* **Med Microbiol Immunol [Berl]**

Medical Microbiology Interdisciplinary Committee *e:* **MEMIC**

Medical Milk Commission *e:* **M.M.C.**

Medical Mission Planner *e:* **MMP**

Medical Missionaries of Mary *e:* **MMM**

Medical Mobilization for Soviet Jewry *e:* **MMSJ**

Medical Monitor *e:* **MDM**

Medical Mycological Society of the Americas *e:* **MMSA**

Medical Necessity Program *e:* **MNP**

Medical Neuropsychiatric Research Unit *e:* **MNRU**

Medical Neurosecretory brain Cell *e:* **MNC**

Medical News e: **Med News**
Medical Nutrition Laboratory e: **MNL**
Medical Officer e: **M.O.**
Medical Officer [England] e: **Med Officer**
Medical Officer in Charge e: **MOIC**
Medical Officer-in-Command e: **MEDOFCOM**
Medical Officer in Command e: **MOIC**
Medical Officer of Health e: **M.O.H.**
Medical Officer of Schools e: **SMO**
Medical Officer of the Day e: **MOD**
Medical Officer Report e: **MOR**
Medical Officers' Health Service e: **M.O.H.S.**
Medical Officers' Information Service e: **M.O.I.S.**
Medical Officers of Health e: **M.Os.H.**
Medical Officers of Schools Association e: **M.O.S.A.**
Medical Officers' Reserve Corps e: **Med.O.R.C.**, e: **M.O.R.C.**
Medical Oncology e: **Med Oncol**
Medical Oncology and Tumor Pharmacotherapy e: **Med Oncol Tumor Pharmacother**
Medical Operations Requirements Document e: **MORD**
Medical Opinion and Review e: **Med Opin Rev**
Medical Opportunities in Michigan e: **MOM**
Medical Outcomes Study e: **MOS**
Medical Passport Foundation e: **MPF**
Medical Patient Accounting and Reporting e: **MEDPAR**
Medical Personnel Priority Committee e: **MPPC**
Medical Physics e: **Med Phys**
Medical Physics Handbooks e: **Med Phys Handb**
Medical Planning & Execution System e: **MEPES**, e: **MPES**
Medical Planning Module e: **MPM**
Medical Planning Program e: **MPP**
Medical Post [Canada] e: **Med Post**
Medical Practice Informant e: **MPI**
Medical Practices Committee e: **MPC**
Medical Practitioners' Union e: **MPU**
Medical Preoptic Area e: **MPOA**
Medical Prescibing Adviser e: **MPA**
Medical Press e: **Med Press**
Medical Press and Circular e: **Med Press and Circ**
Medical Press of Egypt e: **Med Press Egypt**
Medical Problems of Performing Artists e: **Med Probl Performing Artists**
Medical Proceedings e: **Med Proc**
Medical Procurement Agency e: **MPA**
Medical Products Sales e: **Med Prod Sales**, e: **MPS**
Medical Products Salesman e: **Med Prod Salesman**
Medical Proficiency Training e: **MPT**
Medical Program Review Committee e: **MPRC**
Medical Progress [New York] e: **Med Prog [NY]**
Medical Progress through Technology e: **Med Prog Technol**, e: **Med Pr Tech**
Medical Properties, Inc. e: **MEDPRP**
Medical Protection Society e: **M.P.S.**
Medical Provisioning Point e: **MPP**

Medical Quality Assurance Board e: **MQAB**
Medical Quarterly e: **L Med Q**
Medical Quarterly. Indiana University. School of Medicine e: **Med Q Indiana Univ Sch Med**
Medical Questionnaire e: **MQ**
Medical Radiation Technologists Board e: **MRTB**
Medical Radiography and Photography e: **Med Radiogr Photogr**
Medical Radioisotope Program e: **MRP**
Medical Radioisotopes Research Program e: **MRRP**
Medical Radiology [USSR] e: **Med Radiol [USSR]**
Medical Readiness Assemblage Medical System e: **MEDRAMS**
Medical Readiness Division, Office of the Joint Chiefs of Staff e: **J-4/JCS**
Medical Readiness Exercise e: **MEDREX**
Medical Readiness Report e: **MEDRED Report**
Medical Readiness Report Capability e: **MEDRED**
Medical Readiness System e: **MRS**
Medical Readiness Training Exercises e: **MEDRETES**
Medical Receiving Station e: **MRS**
Medical Reception Station e: **MRS**
Medical Record e: **Med Rec**, e: **MR**
Medical Record and Annals e: **Med Rec Ann**
Medical Record and Health Care Inforrnation Journal e: **Med Rec Health Care Inf J**
Medical Record Information Service e: **MRIS**
Medical Record [New York] e: **Med Rec [NY]**
Medical Record News e: **Med Rec News**
Medical Record of Mississippi e: **Med Rec Mississippi**
Medical Records Department e: **MRD**
Medical Records Institute e: **MRI**
Medical Records Librarian e: **MRL**
Medical Records Library e: **MRL**
Medical Records Officer e: **MRO**
Medical Red Flag e: **MRF**
Medical Reference Department e: **MRD**
Medical Reference Services Quarterly e: **Med Ref Serv Q**, e: **MRSQ**
Medical Registration Council of Ireland e: **MRCI**
Medical Regulating Office e: **MRO**
Medical Regulating Officer e: **MRO**
Medical Regulating (or Regulation) e: **MEDREG**
Medical Rehabilitation Unit e: **MRU**
Medical Relief International e: **MERIT**
Medical Replacement Training Center e: **MRTC**
Medical Reports. Charles University Medical Faculty at Hradec Kralove e: **Med Rep Charles Univ Med Fac Hradec Kralove**
Medical Repository e: **Med Reposit**
Medical Requirements Model e: **MEDREQ**, e: **MEDRTS**
Medical Research and Development Command e: **MR and DC**, e: **MRDC**
Medical Research and Nutrition Laboratory e: **MRNL**

Medical Research Centre [Nairobi]. Annual Report e: **Med Res Cent [Nairobi] Annu Rep**
Medical Research Council [Great Britain]. Special Report Series e: **Med Res Counc [GB] Spec Rep Ser**
Medical Research Council e: **MEDRESCO**, e: **MRC**
Medical Research Council [Great Brilain]. Laboratory Animals Centre. Symposia e: **Med Res Counc [GB] Lab Anim Cent Symp**
Medical Research Council [Great Britain]. Annual Report e: **Med Res Counc [GB] Annu Rep**
Medical Research Council [Great Britain]. Industrial Health Research Board Report e: **Med Res Counc [GB] Ind Health Res Board Rep**
Medical Research Council [Great Britain]. Laboratory Animals Centre. Manual Series e: **Med Res Counc [GB] Lab Anim Cent Man Ser**
Medical Research Council [Great Britain]. Memorandum e: **Med Res Counc [GB] Memo**
Medical Research Council [Great Britain] Monitoring Report e: **Med Res Counc [GB] Monit Rep**
Medical Research Council Laboratories e: **MRCL**, e: **MRC LABS**
Medical Research Council of Canada e: **MRCC**
Medical Research Council of Canada/Conseil de Recherches Médicales du Canada e: **MRC/CRM**
Medical Research Council of Ireland e: **M.R.C.I.**
Medical Research Council of New Zealand e: **MRCNZ**
Medical Research Council of Zimbabwe e: **MRCZ**
Medical Research Council [or Committee] [or Center] e: **M.R.C.**
Medical Research Engineering e: **Med.Res.Eng.**
Medical Research Information System e: **MRIS**
Medical Research Institute e: **MERI**, e: **MRI**
Medical Research Institute of Chemical Defense e: **MRICD**
Medical Research Institute of Worcester e: **MRIW**
Medical Research Institute. Tokyo Medical and Dental University. Annual Report e: **Med Res Inst Tokyo Med Dent Univ Annu Rep**
Medical Research Laboratory e: **MRL**
Medical Research Library of Brooklyn, Brooklyn e: **NBM**
Medical Research Modernization Committee e: **MRMC**
Medical Research Organization e: **MRO**
Medical Research Projects e: **Med Res Proj**
Medical Research Reactor e: **MRR**
Medical Research Society e: **M.R.S.**
Medical Researches for Photosensitizing Dyes e: **Med Res Phorosensit Dyes**
Medical Reserve Corps e: **MEDRC**, e: **Med Res C**, e: **M.R.C.**

Medical Resources Consortium of Central New Jersey e: **MEDCORE**

Medical Responsibility Center Manager Cost Center Report e: **MRCMCCR**

Medical Resupply Requirements Module e: **MRRM**

Medical Resupply Set Model e: **MRS**

Medical Review Officer e: **MRO**

Medical Review Officer Certification Council e: **MROCC**

Medical Room Assistant e: **MRA**

Medical School e: **Med Sch**, e: **MS**

Medical School Building e: **MSB**

Medical School Rounds e: **Med SchI**

Medical Schools of [the] University of London e: **M.S.U.L.**

Medical Schools of the University of London e: **MSU Lond**

Medical Science e: **Med Sci**, e: **MSC**

Medical Science Doctor e: **MSD**

Medical Science Research e: **Med Sri Res**

Medical Sciences Bulletin e: **MSB**

Medical Self-Help e: **MSH**

Medical Seminars International e: **MSI**

Medical Service e: **M.**, e: **Med Serv**

Medical Service Activity e: **MEDSAC**

Medical Service Commission e: **MSC**

Medical Service Corps e: **MEDSERVC**, e: **MSC**

Medical Service Corps, Office of the Surgeon General e: **MSCOTSG**

Medical Service Research and Development Plan e: **MSRDP**

Medical Service School e: **MSS**

Medical Service Warrant e: **MEDSERWRNT**

Medical Services e: **MS**

Medical Services Account e: **MSA**

Medical Services Accountable Officer e: **MSAO**

Medical Services Administration e: **MSA**

Medical Services Journal [Canada] e: **Med Serv[ices] J [Canada]**

(medical) signs and symptoms e: **Sx**

Medical Social Services e: **MSS**

Medical Social Worker e: **MSW**

Medical Society Executives Association e: **MSEA**

Medical Society for the Study of Radiesthesia e: **MSSR**

Medical Society for the Study of Venereal Diseases e: **MSSVD**

Medical Society of London e: **M.S.L.**

Medical Society of New Jersey e: **MSNJ**

Medical Society of the County of New York e: **MSCNY**

Medical Society of the State of New York e: **MSSNY**

Medical Society of the State of Pennsylvania e: **MSSP**

Medical Society of the State of Pennsylvania. Transactions e: **Med Soc PA Tr**

Medical Society of the United States and Mexico e: **MSUSM**

Medical Society of Victoria e: **MSV**

Medical Society of Virginia e: **MSV**

Medical Socioeconomic Research Sources. American Medical Association e: **MedS**, e: **MEDSOC**

Medical Software Reviews [newsletter] e: **MSR**

Medical Sourcing Model e: **MSM**

Medical Specialist Corps e: **MEDSPECC**, e: **MSC**, e: **MSPC**

Medical Specialist Preference Blank e: **MSPB**

Medical Staff e: **MS**, e: **MS[or m.s.]**

Medical Staff Corps e: **MSC**

Medical Staff Hospital Joint venture e: **MSHJ**

Medical Statistical System e: **MEDSTAT**

Medical Statistics Agency e: **MSA**

Medical Stenographer e: **STT**

Medical Sterile Products Association e: **MEDISPA**

Medical Stock Control System e: **MEDSTOCK**

Medical Student JAMA e: **MSJAMA**

Medical Students For Choice e: **MSFC**

Medical Students' Representative Council e: **M.S.R.C.**

Medical Subject Heading[s] (Thesaurus) e: **MESH**

Medical Superintendent e: **Med Supt**

Medical Superintendents Society e: **MSS**

Medical Supply e: **MS**

Medical Supply Depot e: **MEDSUPDEP**, e: **MSD**

Medical Supply, Optical and Maintenance Unit e: **MEDSOM**

Medical Supply Section e: **MSS**

Medical Support Equipment e: **MSE**

Medical Support Services e: **MSS**

Medical Support Unit e: **MSU**

Medical-Surgical Manufacturers Association e: **MSMA**

Medical Survey e: **MS**

Medical System Hanover e: **MSH**

Medical Systems Network e: **MEDNET**

Medical Technician e: **Med Tech**

Medical Technologist e: **Med Tech**, e: **MT**

Medical Technologist of the American Society of Clinical Pathologists e: **MTASCP**

Medical Technology e: **Med. Tech.**, e: **Med. Techn.**

Medical Technology and Practice Patterns Institute e: **MTPPI**

Medical Test Cabinet e: **MTC**

Medical Testing System e: **MTS**

Medical Training Center e: **MTC**

Medical Training Establishment e: **MTE**

Medical Training Establishment Journal e: **MTE Journal**

Medical Transcription e: **MT**

Medical Transport[ation] Officer e: **MTO**

Medical Treatment Facility e: **MTF**

Medical Treatment Facility System e: **MTFS**

Medical Unit e: **Med.U.**

Medical Unit, Self-contained, Transportable e: **MUST**

Medical University College of Medicine e: **MUCM**

Medical University of South Carolina e: **MUSC**

Medical University of South Carolina, Charleston e: **ScCM**

Medical University of South Carolina, Charleston, SC e: **ScCM**

Medical University of South Carolina Library, Charleston e: **SMC**

Medical University of Southern Africa e: **MEDUNSA**, e: **MUSA**

Medical Vacuum e: **MVAC**

Medical War Reserve Automated Process e: **MED-WRAP**

Medical War Reserve Materiel Quality Assurance Subsystem e: **MWRMQAS**

Medical Waste Incinerator e: **MWI**

Medical Waste Leachate e: **MWL**

Medical Waste Tracking Act e: **MWTA**

Medical Women's Federation e: **M.W.F.**

Medical Women's International Association e: **MWIA**

Medical Workforce Standing Advisory Committee e: **MWSAC**

Medical Workforce Standing Advisory Group e: **MWSAG**

Medical Workstations for Intelligent Interactive Acquisition and Analysis of Digital Medical Images e: **MIMI**

Medical World News e: **Med. World News**, e: **Med.World News**, e: **MWN**

Medically Orientat[ed] Data System e: **MODS**

Medically Oriented Language e: **MEDOL**

Medicamentos de Actualidad s: **Med Actual**

Medicare Continuous History Sample File e: **MCHSF**

Medicare Managed Care Contract e: **MMCC**

Medicare Payment Advisory Commission e: **MedPAC**

Medicare Physician Identification and Eligibility System e: **MPIES**

Medicare Provider Analysis and Review e: **MEDPAR**

Medicare Provider Identifier e: **MPI**

Medicare Supplement Insurance e: **Medigap**, e: **Medsupp**

Medicare Transaction System e: **MTS**

Medicare Volume Performance Standard e: **MVPS**

Medicat Liability Reporter e: **Med Liab R**

Medications e: **MEDS**

medications, medicines e: **meds, MEDS**

Medicina [Bogota] s: **Med [B]**

Medicina, Cirugia, Farmacia s: **Med Cir Farm**

Medicina Clinica e: **Med Clin [Barc]**, s: **Med Clin**

Medicina Clinica e Sperimentale s: **Med Clin Sper**

Medicina Colonial [Madrid] s: **Med Colon [Madr]**

Medicina Contemporanea p: **Med Cont[emp]**

Medicina Contemporanea [Lisbon] p: **Med Contemp [Lisbon]**

Medicina Cutanea s: **Med Cut[anea]**

Medicina Cutanea Ibero-Latino-Americana s: **Med Cutan Iber Lat Am**

Medicina de los Paises Calidos s: **Med Pises Calidos**

Medicina del Lavorno i: **Med Lav**

Medicina del Lavoro s: **MELAA**

Medicina e Cultura s: **Med Cult**

Medicina e Morale i: **Med Morale**

Medicina Espanola s: **Medna Esp**

Medicina et Phannacologia Experimentalis. International Journal of Experimental Medicine e: **Med Pharmacol Exp Int J Exp Med**

Medicina et Pharmacologia Experimentalis l: **Med Pharmacol Exp**

Medicina Interna *e:* **Med Interna**

Medicina Legale e delle Assicurazioni *i:* **Med Leg Assicur**

Medicina [Lisbon] *p:* **Med [L]**

Medicina Moderna *i:* **Med Mod**

Medicina Nucleare. Radiobiologica Latina *l:* **Med Nucl Radiobtol Lat**

Medicina Nucleare. Radiobiologica Latina. Supplement [Italy] *l:* **Med Nucl Radiobiol Lat Suppl**

Medicina [Parma] *i:* **Med [P]**

Medicina Pratica [Napoli] *i:* **Med Prat [Napoli]**

Medicina Psicosomatica *i:* **Med Psicosom**

Medicina Revisla Mexicana *s:* **Med Rev Mex**

Medicina Sociale [Turin] *i:* **Med Soc [Turin]**

Medicina y Cirugia *s:* **Med Cir**

Medicina y Cirugia de Guerra *s:* **Med Cir Gu**

Medicina y Seguridad del Trabajo [Madrid] *s:* **Med Segur Trab [Madr]**

Medicinae Baccalaureus *l:* **M.B.**

Medicinae Doctor *l:* **M.D.**

Medicinae Doctor Chirurgia Magister *l:* **MDCM**

Medicinae Doctor Et Professor Publicus *l:* **MED D.ET.P.P**

Medicinae Licentiatus *l:* **MED.LIC**, *l:* **M.L.**

Medicinal and Aromatic Plants Research Station *e:* **SCPMA**

Medicinal Chemistry A Series of Monographs *e:* **Med Chem Ser Monogr**

Medicinal Chemistry A Series of Reviews *e:* **Med Chem Ser Rev**

Medicinal Research *e:* **Med Res**

Medicinal Research A Series of Monographs *e:* **Med Res Ser Monogr**

Medicinal Research Reviews *e:* **Med Res Rev**

Medicinalkårexpedition *r:* **ME**

medicinalstyrelsen *r:* **MedStyr**

Medicinalstyrelsen *r:* **M. S.**

Medicine *e:* **M**, *e:* **MED**, *e:* **MEDS**

Medicine and Biology [Tokyo] *e:* **Med Biol [Tokyo]**

Medicine and Computer *e:* **Med and Comp**

Medicine and Duty *e:* **M and D**

Medicine and Law *e:* **Med & Law**, *e:* **MELA**

Medicine and Science in Sports *e:* **Med Sci Spt**

Medicine and Science in Sports and Exercise *e:* **Med [and] Sci Sport[s] Exerc**, *e:* **Med Sci Sports Exerc**

Medicine and Surgery *e:* **M and S**, *e:* **M&S**

Medicine and Surgery Bureau *e:* **MSB**

Medicine and War *e:* **Med War**

Medicine Australia-The Online Journal of Medicine *e:* **MedAu**

Medicine, Bachelor of *e:* **MB**

Medicine Cabinet Manufacturers Council *e:* **MCMC**

Medicine Lake National Wildlife Refuge *e:* **MLNWR**

Medicine, Law and Public Policy *e:* **Med L & Pub Pol**

Medicine on the Midway *e:* **Med Midway**

Medicine-Pediatrics Program Directors Association *e:* **MPPDA**

Medicine Radiation *e:* **MR**

Medicine, Science and the Law *e:* **Med Sci [&] L[aw]**

Medicines *e:* **Meds**

Medicines Act Veterinary Information Service *e:* **MAVIS**

Medicines Commission *e:* **MC**, *f:* **MC**

Medicine[s] Control Agency *e:* **MCA**

Medicines Control Council *e:* **MCC**

Medicinical *e:* **Med**

Medicinimportørernes Forening *a:* **MEDIF**

medicin[sk] *r:* **Med**

Medicinsk Arbog *a:* **Med Arb**

Medicinska Föreningen *r:* **MF**

Medicinska Föreningen i Göteborg *r:* **MFG**

Medicinska Föreningen i Stockholm *r:* **MFS**

Medicinska Högskolornas Organisationskommitté *r:* **MHO**

Medicinska Istraživanja *R:* **Med Istraz**

Medicinska Istraživanja. Supplementum *R:* **Med Istraz Suppl**

Medicinska Undersökningscentral *r:* **Muc**

Medicinski Arhiv *R:* **Med Arh**

Medicinski Podmladak *c:* **Med Podmladak**

Medicinski Pregled *se:* **Med Pregl**

Medico *e:* **Med**

Medico-Chirurgical *e:* **M-C**

Medico-Chirurgical Society *e:* **M.C.S.**

Medico-Legal and Criminological Review *e:* **Med-Leg [&] Crim[inol] Rev**

Medico-Legal Bulletin *e:* **Med Leg Bull**

Medico-Legal Journal *e:* **Med-Legal J**, *e:* **Med Leg J**

Medico-Legal Journal [London] *e:* **Med-Leg J [London]**

Medico-Legal Journal [New York] *e:* **Med-Leg J [NY]**

Medico-Legal News *e:* **Med Leg N**, *e:* **Med LN**

Medico-Legal Papers *e:* **Med LP**

Medico-Legal Society *e:* **M.L.S.**

Medico-Legal Society of Victoria. Proceedings *e:* **Med Leg Vic Proc**, *e:* **Proc Med-Leg Soc Vic**

Medico-Legal Society. Transactions *e:* **Med-Legal Soc'y Trans**

Medicos del Mundo *s:* **MDM**

Medicus *l:* **MED**

Medicus Ludi Matutini *l:* **MED.LVD.MAT**

Medicus Mundi Internationalis *l:* **MMI**

Medicus Mundi Schweiz *d:* **MMS**

Medicus Mundi Suisse *f:* **MMS**

Medicus Mundi Switzerland *e:* **MMS**

Medicus Ordinarius *l:* **MED.ORD**

Medicus Tuticus *l:* **MED.TUC**

Medicus Veterinarius *l:* **M.V.**

Medicus Veterinarius Doctor *l:* **MVDr**

Mediko-Biologichni Problemi *R:* **Med Biol Probl**

Mediterranean and Black Seas Hydrographic Commission *e:* **MBSHC**

Mediterranean Association for Marine Biology and Oceanology *e:* **MAMBO**

Mediterranean Association of Marine Biological Oceanography *e:* **MAMBO**

Mediterranean Development and Environment Observatory *e:* **MEDO**

Mediterranean Environment Technical Assistance Programme *e:* **METAP**

Mediterranean Global Sea-Level Observing System *e:* **MEDGLOSS**

Mediterranean Hydrological Cycle Observing System *e:* **MED-HYCOS**

Mediterranean Military Sea Transportation Service Space Assignment Committee *e:* **MSTSPACOM**

Mediterranean Oceanic Data Base *e:* **MOBD**

Mediterranean Oceanographic Project *e:* **MEDOC**

Mediterranean Scientific Association for Environmental Protection *e:* **MSAEP**

Mediterranean Scientific Association of Environmental Protection *e:* **MESAEP**

Mediterranean Sea *e:* **Med**, *e:* **Med. S.**

Mediterranee Medicale *l:* **Mediterr Med**

Medium Altitude Critical Atmospheric Turbulence *e:* **MEDCAT**

Medium-altitude Earth Orbit *e:* **MEO**

Medium Earth Orbit *e:* **MEO**

Medium Earth Orbit Satellites *e:* **MEOS**

Medium-energy Light-Water-Moderated industrial nuclear reactor *e:* **MLWM**

Medium Energy Research Light-water-moderated Industrial Nuclear Reactor *e:* **MERLIN Reactor**

Medium Energy Research Light-water-moderated Industrial Nuclear Source *e:* **MARLIN Source**, *e:* **MERLIN Source**

Medium Observation Aircraft *e:* **MOA**

Medium Orbiting Earth Resources Observatory *e:* **MOERO**

Medium Range Remotely Piloted Vehicle *e:* **MRRPV**

Medium SEAL [Sea, Air and Land] Support Craft *e:* **MSSC**

Medizin Aktuell *d:* **Med Aktuell**

Medizin-, Labor- und Wägetechnik *d:* **MLW**

Medizin Mensch Gesellschaft *d:* **MMG**

Medizin-Technische Gesellschaft mbH *d:* **METEC**

Medizin und Chemie [Leverkusen, Germany] *d:* **Med Chem [Leverkusen Ger]**

Medizin und Sport *d:* **MuS**

Medizin- und Sportsoziologie *d:* **MSS**

Medizin und Veterinärmedizin *d:* **MED**

Medizinal-Abteilung *d:* **MA**

Medizinalassistent[in] *d:* **MA**

Medizinaldezernent *d:* **Med.-Dez.**

Medizinaldirektor *d:* **Med.-Dir.**

Medizinalpraktikant *d:* **MP**

Medizinalrat *d:* **Med.-R.**, *d:* **MR**

Medizin[er] *d:* **Med.**

Medizinhistorisches Journal *d:* **Medzinhist J**

medizinisch *d:* **med**, *d:* **mediz.**

Medizinisch-Naturwissenschaftliche Gesellschaft *d:* **MNG**

Medizinisch-naturwissenschaftliches Archiv *d:* **MNA**

Medizinisch-Psychologische Untersuchungsstelle[n] *d:* **MPU**

Medizinisch-Psychologisches Institut *d:* **MPI**

Medizinisch-statistischer Jahresbericht über die Stadt Stuttgart *d:* **M.Stat.Jber.Stuttg.**

medizinisch-statistisches Büro d: **MSB**

Medizinisch-technisch d: **MT**

Medizinisch-Technische Verlags- und
Handelsgesellschaft mbH d: **CEDIP**

medizinisch-technische[r] Assistent[in] d:
MTA

Medizinisch-Technisches Zentrum d: **MTZ**

Medizinische Akademie d: **MA**

Medizinische Akademie Dresden d: **MAD**

Medizinische Akademie Erfurt d: **MAE**

Medizinische Blätter d: **Med Bl**

Medizinische Fakultät d: **FME**, d: **MEF**

Medizinische Fakultät Stuttgart d: **MFS**

Medizinische Fakultät Stuttgart Aussagen
d: **MFSA**

Medizinische Fakultät Stuttgart Statistik d:
MFSS

Medizinische Fakultät Stuttgart Text d:
MFST

Medizinische Forschungsanstalt d: **MFA**

Medizinische Geräte-Fabrik d: **MGF**

Medizinische Geräteverordnung d:
MedGV

Medizinische Hilfsberufe d: **MHB**

Medizinische Hochschule d: **MedH**, d:
MeH, d: **MH**

Medizinische Hochschule Hannover d:
MHH

Medizinische Hochschule, Hannover-
Krefeld d: **GyHanM**

Medizinische Informatik d: **MI**

Medizinische Klinik d: **MEKLA**, d: **MK**,
d: **MKl**

Medizinische Klinik [Berlin] d: **Med Klin
[Berlin]**

Medizinische Klinik [München] d: **Med
Klin [Müncben]**, d: **Medsche Klin
[München]**

Medizinische Monatsschrift d: **Med
Monatsschr**, d: **MEMOA**

Medizinische Monatsschrift für
Pharmazeuten d: **Med Monatsschr
Pharm**

Medizinische Monatsschrift [Stuttgart] d:
Med Mschr [Stuttg]

Medizinische Prisma d: **Med Prisma**

Medizinische Statistik der SUVA d:
SUMEST

Medizinische Statistik der VESKA d:
MSV

Medizinische und Pädagogische
Jugendkunde d: **Med Pädgog Jugendkd**

Medizinische Universität d: **MU**

Medizinische Welt d: **Med. Welt**

Medizinische Welt [Stuttgart] d: **Medsch
Welt [Stuttg]**

Medizinische Woche d: **MedW**

Medizinischer Assistent d: **MA**

Medizinischer Dienst d: **MD**

Medizinischer Dienst der
Krankenversicherung d: **MDK**

Medizinischer Dienst des Verkehrswesens
d: **MDV**

Medizinischer Fakultätentag der
Bundesrepublik Deutschland d: **MFT**

Medizinischer Literaturdienst d: **MLD**

Medizinischer Monatsspiegel d: **Med
Monatssp**

Medizinisches Conversationsblatt d: **Med
Convers Bl**

Medizinisches Correspondenz-Blatt
Bayerischer Ärzte d: **Med Cor-Bl Bayer
Ärzte**

Medizinisches Correspondenz-Blatt
Rheinischer und Westfälischer Ärzte d:
Med Cor-Bl Rhein u Westfäl Änte

Medizinisches Correspondenz-Blatt.
Württembergischer Ärztlicher
Landesverein d: **Med Cor-Bl Württemb
Ärztl Landesver**

Medizinisches Correspondenz-Blatt.
Württembergischer Ärztlicher Verein d:
Med Cor-Bl Württemb Ärztl Ver

medizinisches Informationssystem
Danderyd-Spital d: **MIDAS**

Medizinisches Institut d: **MedInst**

Medizinisches Institut für Umwelthygiene
an der Heinrich-Heine-Universität
Düsseldorf d: **MIU**

Medizinisches Laboratorium d: **Med Lab**

Medizinisches Laboratorium [Stuttgart] d:
Med Lab [Stuttg]

medizinisches Schutzpäckchen d: **MSP**

Medizinprodukte- Betreiberverordnung d:
MPBetreibV

Medizinprodukte-Gesetz d: **MPG**

Medizinrecht d: **MedR**

Medizinsoziologie d: **MS**

Medizinstudent d: **Med.-St.**

Medizinstudium d: **Med.-St.**

Medizintechnik Leipzig d: **MEDI**

Medizintechnisches Servicezentrum d:
MSZ

MEDLARS [Medical Literature Analysis
and Retrieval System] On-Line e:
MEDLINE

Medycyna Doswiadczalna i Mikrobiologia
[Translation] P: **Med Dosw Mikrobiol
[Transl]**

Meeresbiologie d: **Meeresbiol.**

Meeresumweltdatenbank d: **MUDAB**

Mees Solar Observatory e: **MSO**

Meeting of European Geological Societies
e: **MEGS**

Meeting of experts on marine and coastal
biological diversity e: **JMEM**

Meeting of the CBD-UNESCO consultative
working group of experts on biological
diversity education and public awareness
e: **GEEPA**

Meeting on the Interconnection of
Molecular Biological (or Biology)
Databases e: **MIMBD**

Megacity Impact on Regional and Global
Environments e: **MIRAGE**

Mehany Medical College, Nashville e:
TNM

Meharry Medical College e: **MMC**

Meharry Medical College, Nashville e:
TMD

Melanges d'Archeologie et d'Histoire. École
Francaise du Rome f: **Melanges d'Arch**

Member of the Academy of Natural
Sciences e: **MANS**

Member of the Association of Public Health
Inspectors e: **MAPHI**

Member of the British College of
Obstetricians and Gynaecologists e:
M.C.O.G.

Member of the British Naturopathic and
Osteopathic Association e: **MBNOA**

Member of the College of Physicians and
Surgeons e: **MCPS**

Member of the Faculty of Anaesthetists of
the Royal College of Surgeons e:
M.F.A.R.C.S.

Member of the Faculty of Community
Medicine e: **M.F.C.M.**

Member of the Faculty of Occupational
Medicine e: **MFOccM**

Member of the Faculty of Pharmaceutical
Medicine e: **MFPharmM**

Member of the Faculty of Physicians and
Surgeons e: **MFPS**

Member of the Faculty of Public Health
Medicine e: **MFPHM**

Member of the Institute of Biology e:
M.I.Biol.

Member of the Institute of Health Education
e: **MIHE**

Member of the Institute of Psionic Medicine
e: **MIPsiMed**

Member of the Institute of Water Engineers
e: **MInstWE**

Member of the Institute of Water Pollution
Control e: **MIWPC**

Member of the Institution of Occupational
Safety and Health e: **MIOSH**

Member of the Institution of Public Health
Engineers e: **M.I.P.H.E.**

Member of the Institution of Water
Engineers e: **MIWE**

Member of the Medical Faculty e: **MMF**

Member of the Mining, Geological and
Metallurgical Institute of India e:
MMGI

Member of the National Institute of Medical
Herbalists e: **MNIMH**

Member of the Punjab Irregular Frontier
Force e: **Piffer**

Member of the Royal College of
Obstetricians and Gynaecologists e:
MRCOG

Member of the Royal College of Paediatrics
and Child Health e: **MRCPCH**

Member of the Royal College of Physicians
and Surgeons of Glasgow e: **MRCPGlas**

Member of the Royal College of Surgeons
e: **M.R.C.S.**

Member of the Royal College of Surgeons,
Edinburgh e: **MRCSE**

Member of the Royal College of Surgeons
of Ireland e: **MRCSI**

Member of the Royal College of Veterinary
Surgeons e: **MRCVS**

Member of the Royal Geographical Society
e: **MRGS**

Member of the Royal Institute of Painters in
Water Colours e: **MRIPWC**

Member of the Royal Institute of Public
Health and Hygiene e: **MRIPHH**

Member of the Royal Society for the
Promotion of Health e: **MRSPH**

Member of the Royal Society of Health e:
MRSH

Member of the Royal Society of Medicine
e: **MRSM**

Member of the Royal Society of Painters in
Water-Colours e: **MRSPWC**

Memoils. Geological Survey of Great
Britain. England and Wales Explanation
Sheet e: **Mem Geol Surr GB Engl
Wales Explan Sheet**

Memoir. American Association of
Petroleum Geologists e: **Mem Am Assoc
Pet Geol**

Memoir. Canadian Society of Petroleum
Geologists e: **Mem Can Soc Pet Geol**

Memoir. Department of Geological Sciences. Virginia Polytechnic Institute and State University e: **Mem Dep Geol Sci Va Polytech Inst State Univ**

Memoir. Geological Society of America e: **Mem Geol Soc Am**

Memoir. Geological Society of China e: **Mem Geol Soc Chin**

Memoir. Geological Survey of Northern Ireland e: **Mem Geol Surv North Irel**

Memoir. Geological Survey of South West Africa e: **Mem Geol Surv South West Afr**

Memoir. Geological Survey of Wyoming e: **Mem Geol Surv Wyo**

Memoir. Montana Bureau of Mines and Geology e: **Mem Mont Bur Mines Geol**

Memoir. South Africa Geological Survey e: **Mem S Afr Geol Surv**

Memoires. Bureau de Recherches Geologiques et Minieres [France] f: **Mem BRGM**, f: **Mem Bur Rech Geol Minieres**

Memoires. Museum National d'Histoire Naturelle f: **Mem Mus Natl Hist Nat**

Memoires. Museum National d'Histoire Naturelle [Paris]. Serie C. Sciences de la Terre f: **Mem Mus Inst Nat [Paris] Ser C**

Memoires. Museum National d'Histoire Naturelle. Serie A. Zoologie f: **Mem Mus Natl Hist Nat Ser A Zool**

Memoires. Museum National d'Histoire Naturelle. Serie A. Zoologie [Paris] f: **Mem Mus Natl Hist Nat Ser A [Paris]**

Memoires. Museum National d'Histoire Naturelle. Serie B. Botanique f: **Mem Mus Natl Hist Nat Ser B Bot**

Memoires. Museum National d'Histoire Naturelle. Serie C. Geologie f: **Mem Mus Natl Hist Nat Ser C Geol**

Memoires. Museum National d'Histoire Naturelle. Serie C. Sciences de la Terre [Paris] f: **Mem Mus Natl Hist Nat Ser C [Paris]**

Memoires. Museum National d'Histoire Naturelle. Serie D. Sciences Physico-Chimiques [Paris] f: **Mem Mus Natl Hist Nat Ser D [Paris]**

Memoires pour Servira l'Explication des Cartes Geologiques et Minieres de la Belgique f: **Mem Explic Cartes Geol Min Belg**

Memoires. Société des Sciences Naturelles et Archeologiques de la Creuse f: **Mem Creuse**

Memoirs. Boston Society of Natural History e: **Mem Boston Soc Nat Hist**

Memoirs. College of Agriculture. Kyoto University. Animal Sciences Series e: **Mem Coll Agric Kyoto Univ Anim Sci Ser**

Memoirs. College of Medicine. National Taiwan University e: **Mem Coll Med Natl Taiwan Univ**

Memoirs. College of Science. Univetsity of Kyoto. Series B. Geology and Biology e: **Mem Coll Sci Univ Kyoto Ser B Geol Biol**

Memoirs. Commonwealth Solar Observatory. Australia e: **Mem Comm Solar Observ Aust**

Memoirs. Ecological Society of Australia e: **Mem Ecol Soc Aust**

Memoirs. Ehime University. Natural Science. Series A e: **Mem Ehime Univ Natur Sci Ser A**

Memoirs. Ehime University. Natural Science. Series B [Biology] e: **Mem Ehime Univ Nat Sci Ser B [Biol]**

Memoirs. Ehime University. Natural Science. Series C e: **Mem Ehime Univ Nat Sci Ser C**

Memoirs. Ehime University. Section 2. Natural Science. Series C. Chemistry e: **Mem Ehime Univ Sect 2 Ser C**

Memoirs. Faculty of Education. Akita University. Natural Science e: **Mem Fac Educ Akita Univ Nat Sci**

Memoirs. Faculty of Education. Kumamolo University. Natural Science e: **Mem Fac Educ Kumamoto Univ Nat Sci**

Memoirs. Faculty of Education. Kumamoto University. Section 1 [Natural Science] e: **Mem Fac Educ Kumamoto Univ Sect 1 [Nat Sci]**

Memoirs. Faculty of Education. Kumamoto Univetsity. Section 1 [Natural Science] e: **Mem Fac Ed Kumamoto Univ Sect 1**

Memoirs. Faculty of Education. Shiga University. Natural Science e: **Mem Fac Educ Shiga Univ Nat Sci**

Memoirs. Faculty of Education. Shiga University. Natural Science and Pedagogic Science e: **Mem Fac Educ Shiga Univ Nat Sci Pedagog Sci**

Memoirs. Faculty of Liberal Arts and Education. Akita University. Natural Science e: **Mem Fac Lib Arts Educ Aki Univ Nat Sci**

Memoirs. Faculty of Liberal Arts and Education. Pait 2. Mathematics and Natural Sciences. Yamanashi University e: **Mem Fac Lib Arts Educ Part 2 Yamanashi Univ**

Memoirs. Faculty of Literature and Science. Shimane University. Natural Sciences [Matsue] e: **Mem Fac Lit Sci Shimane Univ Natur Sci**

Memoirs. Faculty of Science. Kochi University. Series D. Biology e: **Mem Fac Sci Kochi Univ Ser D Biol**

Memoirs. Faculty of Science. Kyoto University. Series of Biology e: **Mem Fac Sci Kyoto Univ Ser Biol**

Memoirs. Faculty of Science. Kyoto University. Series of Geology and Mineralogy e: **Mem Fac Sci Kyoto Univ Ser Geol Mineral**

Memoirs. Faculty of Science. Kyoto University. Series of Physics, Astrophysics, Geophysics and Chemistry e: **Mem Fac Sci Kyoto Univ Ser Phys Astrophys Geophys Chem**

Memoirs. Faculty of Science. Kyushu University. Series D Geology e: **Mem Fac i Kyshu Univ Ser D Geol**

Memoirs. Faculty of Science. Kyushu University. Series D. Geology e: **Mem Fac Sci Kyushu Univ Ser D**

Memoirs. Faculty of Science. Kyushu University. Series E. Biology e: **MEKEA**, e: **Mem Fac Sci Kyshu Univ Ser E**

Memoirs. Geological Survey Department [Sudan] e: **Mem Geol Surv Dep [Sudan]**

Memoirs. Geological Survey of Canada e: **Mem Geol Surv Can**

Memoirs. Geological Survey of China. Series A e: **Mem Geol Surv China Ser A**

Memoirs. Geological Survey of Great Britain e: **Mem Geol Surv Gt Br**

Memoirs. Geological Survey of Great Britain [Scotland] e: **Mem Geol Surv GB [Scotl]**

Memoirs. Geological Survey of Great Britain. Special Reports on the Mineral Resources of Great Britain e: **Mem Geol Surv GB Spec Rep Miner Resour GB**

Memoirs. Geological Survey of India e: **Mem Geol Surv India**

Memoirs. Geological Survey of New South Wales e: **Mem Geol Surv NSW**

Memoirs. Geological Survey of New South Wales. Department of Mines. Geology e: **Mem Geol Surv of NSW Geol**

Memoirs. Geological Survey of New South Wales. Palaeontology e: **Mem Geol Surv NSW Palaeontol**

Memoirs. Geological Survey of Papua New Guinea e: **Mem Geol Surv Papua New Guinea**

Memoirs. Geological Survey of South Africa e: **Mem Geol Surv S Afr**

Memoirs. Geological Survey of Victoria e: **Mem Geol Surv Vic[t]**

Memoirs. Geological Survey of Victoria [Australia] e: **Mem Geol Survey Vic**

Memoirs. Geological Survey of Western Australia e: **Mem Geol Surv West Aust**

Memoirs. International Association of Hydrogeologists e: **Mem Int Assoc Hydrogeol**

Memoirs. Kakioka Magnetic Observatory [Japan] e: **Mem Kakioka Magn Obs**

Memoirs. Kobe Marine Observatory [Kobe, Japan] e: **Mem Kobe Mar Obs [Kobe Jpn]**

Memoirs. Kumamoto University. Faculty of General Education. Natural Sciences e: **Mem Fac Gen Ed Kumamoto Univ Natur Sci**

Memoirs. National Institute of Polar Research. Series E. Biology and Medical Science e: **Mem Natl Inst Polar Res Ser E Biol Med Sci**

Memoirs. Niihama Technical College. Natural Sciences e: **Mem Niihama Tech Coll Nat Sci**

Memoirs of Mineral Resources Geological Survey of Szechuan e: **Mem Miner Resour Geol Surv Szechuan**

Memoirs of Natural and Cultural Researches of theSan-ln Region e: **Mem Nat Cult Res San-ln Reg**

Memoirs of the Geological Society e: **MGS**

Memoirs of the Geological Society of America e: **MGSA**

Memoirs of the Geological Society of London e: **MGSL**

Memoirs of the Geological Survey e: **MGS**

Memoirs of the Geological Survey of India e: **MGSI**

Memoirs of the India Meteorological Department e: **Mem.I.M.D.**

Memoirs. Osaka Kyoiku University. III. Natural Science and Applied Science e: **Mem Osaka Kyoiku Univ III Nat[ur] Sci Appl Sci**

Memoirs. Osaka University of Liberal Arts and Education. B. Natural Science e: **Mem OsakB Umr Lib Arts Educ B Natur Sci**

Memoirs. Palaeontology Series. Geological Survey [New South Wales] e: **Mem Palaeontol Ser Geol Surv [NSW]**

Memorandum. Medical Research Council [London] e: **Memo Med Res Counc**

Memorandum. University College of Wales. Department of Geography e: **Memo Univ Coll Wales Dept Geogr**

Memoria. Asociacion Latinoamericana de Produccion Animal s: **Mem Assoc Latinoam Prod Anim**

Memoria. Congreso Medico Latino-Americano [Buenos Aires] s: **Mem Cong Med Latino-Am [Buenos Aires]**

Memorial de la Meteorologie Nationale f: **Meml Meteorol Natl**

Memorial University of Newfoundland. Occaional Papers in Biology e: **Memorial Univ Newfoundland Occas Pap Biol**

Memory Expansion [and Protection] Unit e: **MEU**

Memory Management and Protection Unit e: **MMPU**

Memory Protect Override e: **MPO**

Memory Protect[ion] Key e: **MPK**

Memphis and Mid-South Medical Journal e: **Memphis Mid-South Med J**

Memphis and Shelby County Health Department, Memphis e: **TMSCH**

Memphis Journal of the Medical Sciences e: **Memphis J Med Sci**

Memphis Light, Gas, and Water Division Library, Memphis e: **TMLG**

Memphis Medical Monthly e: **Memphis Med Month**

Mennonite Health Assembly e: **MHA**

Mennonite Hospital Health Sciences Library, Bloomington e: **JAT**

Menorah Medical Center, Kansas City e: **MoKMM**

Mensch-Technik-Umwelt d: **MTU**

Mensch-Technik-Umwelt-Systeme d: **MTU-Systeme**

Mental Health e: **MH**

Mental Health Act Commission e: **MHAC**

Mental Health Administration e: **MHA**

Mental Health and Institutional Workers' Journal e: **MHIW Journal**

Mental Health Association e: **MHA**

Mental Health Association of Oregon e: **MHAO**

Mental Health Authority e: **MHA**

Mental Health Branch e: **MHB**

Mental Health Centre, Penetanguishene, Ontario e: **OPENM**

Mental Health/Chemical Dependency e: **MH/CD**

Mental Health Commission e: **MHC**

Mental Health Digest e: **MHD**

Mental Health Enquiry e: **MHE**

Mental Health Film Board e: **MHFB**

Mental Health Foundation e: **MHF**

Mental Health Foundation of New Zealand e: **MHFNZ**

Mental Health Institute e: **MHI**

Mental Health Materials Center e: **MHMC**

Mental Health Net e: **MHN**

Mental Health Project e: **MHP**

Mental Health Research Fund e: **MHRF**

Mental Health Research Institute e: **M H R I**

Mental Health Research Institute of Victoria e: **MHRI**

Mental Health Special Interest Section [American Occupational Therapy Association] e: **MHSS**

Mental Health Statistical Note e: **Ment Health Stat Note**

Mental Health/Substance Abuse e: **MH/SA**

Mental Health Worker e: **MHW**

Mental Observation e: **MO**

Menthal Health Professional e: **MHP**

Menthal Health Psychologist e: **MHP**

Merced National Wildlife Refuge e: **MNWR**

Mercer County Health Center e: **MCHC**

Mercury-Atlas Spacecraft e: **MA Spacecraft**

Mercury Scout Spacecraft e: **MS Spacecraft**

Mercury Surface, Space Environment, Geochemistry and Ranging Mission e: **MESSENGER**

Mercury, Venus, Earth, Mars, Saturn, Jupiter e: **MEVEMSJ**

Mercy Hospital and Medical Center e: **MHMC**

Mercy Hospital, Library, Watertown e: **VNA**

Meridian Ocean Systems e: **MOS**

Merkblatt für Umweltverträglichkeitsprüfungen im Strassenbau d: **MUVS**

Merritt Island National Wildlife Refuge e: **MINWR**

Mesa Verde National Park e: **MEVE**, e: **MVNP**

Mesoscale Air-Sea Exchange [Experiment] e: **MASEX**

Mesoscale and Microscale Meteorology division e: **M3**, e: **MMM**

Mesoscale Atmospheric Processes Research Program e: **MAPRP**

Mesoscale Atmospheric Simulation Sensor e: **MASS**

Mesoscale Atmospheric Transport Studies e: **MATS**

Mesoscale Climate Model Garmisch-Partenkirchen e: **McGAP**

Mesoscale Convective System e: **MCS**

Mesoscale Meteorological Model-Version 4 [Pennsylvania State University] e: **MM4**

Mesoscale Meteorological Preprocessor Program e: **MESOPAC**

Message d'observation bathythermique f: **BATHY**

Message dobservation provenant dune bouée dérivante f: **DRIFTER**

Meßtechnik für Umweltschutz GmbH [München] d: **MFU**

Metal and nonmetal mine health and safety e: **MNMHS**

Metal Ions in Biological Systems e: **Met Ions Biol Syst**

Metal Speciation for Equilibrium for Surface and Ground Water e: **MINTEQA2**

Metallogenicheskie i Geologicheskie Issledovaniya R: **Metallog Geol Issled**

Meteor d: **Met.**

Meteor Burst Communication System e: **MBCS**

Meteor Burst Communications e: **MBC**

Meteor Communications Corporation e: **MCC**

Meteor Echo Detection and Collection System e: **MEDAC**

Meteor Echoes-No Transmitter-Only Receivers e: **MENTOR**

Meteor Forschungsergebnisse. Reihe A. Allgemeines, Physik und Chemie des Meeres d: **Meteor Forschungsergeb Reihe A**

Meteor Forschungsergebnisse. Reihe B. Meteorologie und Aeronomie d: **Meteor Forschungsergeb Reihe B**

Meteor Forschungsergebnisse. Reihe C. Geologie und Geophysik d: **Meteor Forschungsergeb Reihe C**

Meteor Forschungsergebnisse. Reihe D. Biologie d: **Meteor Forschungsergeb Reihe D Biol**

Meteor Ionizing Efficiency e: **MIE**

Meteor Scatter Applications e: **MSA**

Meteor Simulation Vehicle e: **MSV**

Meteor Trail Communications System e: **MTCS**

Meteoric Water Line e: **MWL**

Meteorid d: **Met.**

Meteorid Penetration Probe e: **MPP**

Meteorid Protection e: **MP**

Meteorite Observation and Recovery Project e: **MORP**

Meteoritic Impact Origin e: **MIO**

Meteoritical e: **METEORIT**

Meteoritical Society e: **MS**

Meteoritical Society. Contributions e: **Meteorit Soc Contr**

Meteoroid Detection Satellite e: **MDS**

Meteoroid Exposure Module e: **MEM**

Meteoroid Technology [Satellite] e: **METEC**

Meteoroid Technology Satellite e: **MTS**

Meteorologe d: **Met.**

Meteorologica [Classical studies] l: **Mete**

Meteorologic[al] e: **M**

Meteo[rological] e: **MET**

meteorologic[al] e: **meteo.**

Meteorological e: **Meteorol**, e: **Metgl.**, e: **METRL**, e: **METRO**, e: **MT**

Meteorological Abstracts e: **MA**

Meteorological Abstracts and Bibliography e: **Meteorol Abst and Biblio**

Meteorological Acquisition and Display System e: **METADS**

Meteorological Actual Report e: **METAR**

Meteorological & Aeronautical Presentation System e: **MAPS**

Meteorological Aid Service e: **MetA**

Meteorological Aids Service e: **MAS**

Meteorological Aids Station e: **SM**

Meteorological Airborne Data System e: **MADS**

Meteorological Airborne Radar Data System e: **MARS**

Meteorological Analysis Software Package e: **METPAK**

Meteorological and Climate Services Project e: **MSCP**

Meteorological and Environmental Data Services e: **MEDS**

Meteorological and Geoastrophysical Abstracts e: **Meteor & Geoastrophys**

Abstr, *e:* **Meteorol Geoastrophys Abstr,** *e:* **Met & Geo Ab,** *e:* **MGA**

Meteorological and Geoastrophysical Titles *e:* **MGT**

Meteorological and Geophysics Agency *e:* **BMG**

Meteorological and Oceanographic *e:* **METOC**

Meteorological and Oceanographic Equipment Program *e:* **MOEP**

Meteorological and oceanographic Forecast Center *e:* **MFC**

Meteorological and Oceanographic Phenomenon off the West Coast of South America *e:* **EL NIñO**

Meteorological and Oceanographic Sensing System *e:* **M/O**

Meteorological and Omega Data Digitizer *e:* **MODD**

Meteorological Applications *e:* **MA**

Meteorological Applications Branch *e:* **MAB**

Meteorological Atmospheric Turbulence *e:* **MAT**

Meteorological Automatic Reporting Station *e:* **MARS**

Meteorological Automatic Reporting System *e:* **MARS**

Meteorological Auxiliary Sea Current Observation Transmitter *e:* **MASCOT**

Meteorological Aviation Report[s] *e:* **METAR**

Meteorological Balloon Tracking System *e:* **MBTS**

Meteorological Broadcast[s] *e:* **MET Broadcast[s]**

Meteorological Codes *e:* **MC**

Meteorological Communications Centre [or Center] *e:* **MCC**

Meteorological Communications Package *e:* **MCP**

Meteorological Company *e:* **Met Co**

Meteorological Conditions *e:* **Met. Condns.**

Meteorological Conversion Process *e:* **PAME**

Meteorological Coordinating Committee *e:* **METCO**

Meteorological Coordination Office[r] *e:* **METCO**

Meteorological Data Acquisition System *e:* **MDAS,** *e:* **MEDAS**

Meteorological Data Analysis System *e:* **METDAS**

Meteorological Data Collection *e:* **MDC**

Meteorological Data Collection and Reporting System *e:* **MDCRS**

Meteorological Data Collection and Transmission System *e:* **MDCTS**

Meteorological Data Dissemination *e:* **MDD**

Meteorological Data Distribution *e:* **MDD**

Meteorological Data Handling System *e:* **MDHS**

Meteorological Data Sounding System *e:* **MDSS**

Meteorological Data System *e:* **MDS**

Meteorological Data Systems *e:* **MEDS**

Meteorological Data Utilization Centre [or Center] *e:* **MDUC**

Meteorological Data Utilization Station *e:* **MDUS**

Meteorological Datum Plane *e:* **MDP**

Meteorological Department *e:* **MD**

Meteorological Distribution System *e:* **MDS**

Meteorological Equipment Improvement Program *e:* **METIMP**

Meteorological Equipment Terminal and Representative Observation *e:* **METRO**

Meteorological Event Oriented Reporting System *e:* **METEOR**

Meteorological Group *e:* **MG**

Meteorological Hydrogen Generator *e:* **MHG**

Meteorological Impact Statement *e:* **MIS**

Meteorological Information *e:* **Met. Inf.,** *e:* **MIF**

Meteorological Information [and] Data Acquisition System *e:* **MIDAS**

Meteorological Information and Dose Acquisition System *e:* **MIDAS**

Meteorological Information Committee *e:* **MIC**

Meteorological Information Extraction Center (or Centre) *e:* **MIEC**

Meteorological Information for Aircraft in Flight *e:* **VOLMET**

Meteorological Information System *e:* **METIS**

Meteorological Institute of the University of Uppsala *e:* **MIUU**

Meteorological Institute Stockholm University *e:* **MISU**

Meteorological Interactive Data Display System *e:* **MIDDS**

Meteorological Interactive Display Data System/Man Computer Interactive Data Access System *e:* **MIDDS/MEIDAS**

Meteorological Interactive Software System for Image Data Analysis *e:* **MISS-IDA**

Meteorological long-range trajectory and dispersion model *e:* **TRADOS**

Meteorological Magazine *e:* **Meteor Mag,** *e:* **Meteorol Mag**

Meteorological Measuring System *e:* **MMS**

Meteorological Model to Calculate Concentrations on Elevated Terrain *e:* **VALLEY**

Meteorological Monitoring Plan *e:* **MMP**

Meteorological Monographs *e:* **Meteorol Monogr**

Meteorological Observation and Data Assimilation Center *e:* **MODAC**

Meteorological Observer *e:* **MO**

Meteorological Observing Station, Extremely Simple *e:* **MOSES**

Meteorological Office *e:* **Met O,** *e:* **M.O.**

Meteorological Office Data-Logging Equipment *e:* **MODLE**

Meteorological Office. Joint Meteorological Radio Propagation Sub-Committee *e:* **MOJMRP**

Meteorological Office [or Committee] *e:* **MET**

Meteorological Office Weather Observing System *e:* **MOWOS**

Meteorological Officer *e:* **METO**

Meteorological Operational Programme *e:* **MOP**

Meteorological Operational Telecommunications Network *e:* **MOTN**

Meteorological Operational Telecommunication[s] Network of Europe *e:* **MOTNE**

Meteorological Operational [Weather] Satellite *e:* **METOP**

Meteorological Orbiting Platform *e:* **METOP**

Meteorological Penetration Detection Development *e:* **MPDD**

Meteorological Prediction Center *e:* **MPC**

Meteorological Profiler System *e:* **MPS**

meteorological radar station *e:* **WXD**

Meteorological Report *e:* **Met. Rep.**

Meteorological Research Committee *e:* **M.R.C.**

Meteorological Research Flight *e:* **MRF,** *e:* **MR Flight**

Meteorological Research, Incorporated *e:* **MRI**

Meteorological Research Institute *e:* **MRI**

Meteorological Research Laboratory *e:* **MRL**

Meteorological Rocket *e:* **METROC**

Meteorological Rocket Facility *e:* **MRF**

Meteorological Rocket Network *e:* **MRN**

Meteorological Rocket Network Committee *e:* **MRNC**

Meteorological Satellite *e:* **MET,** *e:* **METEOR,** *e:* **METSAAT,** *e:* **METSAT**

Meteorological Satellite Activities *e:* **MSA**

Meteorological Satellite Center *e:* **MSC**

Meteorological Satellite Information System *e:* **METSIS**

Meteorological Satellite Laboratory *e:* **MSL**

Meteorological Satellite Program Review Board *e:* **MSPRB**

Meteorological Satellite Section *e:* **MSS**

Meteorological-Satellite Service *e:* **MetS**

Meteorological Satellites *e:* **METSATs**

Meteorological Service *e:* **LLBD,** *e:* **Met Serv**

Meteorological Service of Canada *e:* **MSC**

Meteorological Services Department *e:* **MSD**

Meteorological Services to Marine Activities *e:* **MSMA**

Meteorological Society *e:* **MS**

Meteorological Society of Japan *e:* **MSJ**

Meteorological Sounding Rocket *e:* **MSR**

Meteorological Squadron *e:* **VJ**

Meteorological Study *e:* **Meteorol Stud**

Meteorological symbol *e:* **Cb**

Meteorological Synthesising Centre *e:* **MSC**

Meteorological Systems Management Section *e:* **MSMS**

Meteorological Terminal Aviation Routine Weather Report *e:* **METAR**

Meteorological Terminal Aviation Weather Forecast *e:* **METAF**

Meteorological Training Center *e:* **MTC**

Meteorological Transmission Satellite Service *e:* **METRASAT**

Meteorological Watch *e:* **MET Watch**

Meteorological Watch Advisory *e:* **MWA**

Meteorological Watch Office *e:* **MWO**

Meteorological Working Group *e:* **MWG**

Meteorologicke Zpravy *c:* **Meteorol Zpr**

Meteorologie *d:* **M,** *d:* **Met.**

Meteorolog[i]e *d:* **Meteo**

Meteorologie *d:* **Meteorol.**

Meteorologie Consult GmbH *d:* **METEO**

Meteorologija, Klimatologija i Gidrologija *R:* **Meteor Klimat Gidrol**

Meteorologin *d:* **Met.**

meteorologisch d: **met.**, d: **meteo.**, d: **meteor.**

Meteorologische Abhandlungen. Institut für Meteorologie und Geophysik d: **Meteorol. Abh. Inst. Meteorol**

Meteorologische Rundschau d: **Meteorol Rundsch**, d: **Meteor Rund**

Meteorologische Weltorganisation d: **MWO**

Meteorologische Zeitschrift d: **Meteorol. Z.**, d: **MetZ**

Meteorologische Zentralanstalt d: **MZA**

Meteorologischer Dienst d: **MD**

Meteorologischer Dienst der Deutschen Demokratischen Republik Veröffentlichungen d: **Meteorol Dienst DDR Veröff**

Meteorologischer und Hydrologischer Dienst d: **MHD**

Meteorologisches Amt d: **MetA**

Meteorologisches Amt für Nordwestdeutschland d: **MANWD**

Meteorologisches Informationssystem d: **MIS**, d: **MISAWI**

Meteorologisches Informationssystem [Rheinland-Pfalz] d: **METIS**

Meteorologisches Institut der Universität Hamburg d: **MI**

Meteorologisches Institut der Universität München d: **MIM**

Meteorologisches Observatorium Hamburg d: **MOH**

Meteorologisches Observatorium Hohenpeißenberg d: **MOHp**

Meteorologisches Observatorium Lindenberg d: **MOL**

Meteorologisches Observatorium Potsdam d: **MOP**

Meteorolog[i][sk] N: **Met**

Meteorologiska Byrån r: **MB**

Meteorologiske Annaler a: **Met A**, a: **Met Ann**, a: **Meteorol Ann**

Meteorologist e: **M**, e: **MET**

meteorologist e: **meteo.**

Meteorologist e: **Metgst.**

Meteorologist-in-charge e: **MIC**

Meteorologist Technician e: **METEC**, e: **Met Tec**

Meteorologist Tracking Computer e: **METRACOM**

Meteorologist Weather Processor e: **MWP**

Meteorologiya i Gidrologiya R: **Meteorol Gidrol[og]**, R: **Meteorol i Gidrol**

Meteorology e: **M**, e: **MET**, e: **METEOR**, e: **METEOROL**, e: **Meteorolo.**, e: **METR**, e: **metrl**, e: **METRO**

Meteorology and Atmospheric Physics e: **Meteorol. Atmos. Phys.**

Meteorology and Earth Observation Satellite e: **MERSAT**

Meteorology and Geophysics Agency e: **BMG**

Meteorology and Hydrology [UnitedStates] e: **Meteorol Hydrol**

Meteorology Engineering Center e: **MEC**

Meteorology Laboratory e: **ML**

Meteorology on Stamps Study Unit e: **MSSU**, e: **MSU**

Meteorology (or Meterological) and Environmental Protection Administration e: **MEPA**

Meteorology Panel e: **MP**

Meteorology Research, Incorporated e: **MRI**

Meteorology Station e: **METEOS**

Meteorología s: **MET**, s: **Meteo[r]**, s: **Mgía**

Meteorológico s: **MET**

Meteorólogo s: **Met**

Meteosat Argos Extended Dissemination Service e: **MAEDS**

Meteosat Exploitation Project e: **MEP**

Meteosat Infrared & Microwave Sounder e: **MIMS**

Meteosat [Meteorological Satellite] Ground Computer (or Computing) Station (or System) e: **MGCS**

Meteosat Operational Programme e: **MOP**

Meteosat Second Generation e: **MSG**

Meteosat Visible and InfraRed Instrument e: **MVIRI**

Meter-Wassersäule d: **MWS**

Metering Water Dispenser e: **MWD**

Meteroid Protective Garment e: **MPG**

Meters below sea level e: **Mbsl**

Meters of Water Equivalent e: **MWE**

Meters Water Depth e: **MWD**

Methane emitted from animal manure e: **MMCH4**

Methanol Dehydrogenase e: **MDF**

Methanol/Water e: **M/W**

Method of Measuring Chlorine Residual in Water e: **DPD**

Methodist Hospital, Stratton Medical Library, Memphis e: **TMMH**

Methodologies to Estimate Social, Environmental, and Economic Consequences e: **MESEEC**

Methods in Cell Biology e: **Methods Cell Biol**

Methods in Geochemistry and Geophysics e: **MGG**

Methods in Geomathematics e: **MG**

Methods in Membrane Biology e: **MEMBBM**

Methods in Molecular Biology e: **Methods Mol Biol**

Methods of Information in Medicine e: **Meth.Inf.Med.**, e: **Methods Inf Med**

Methods of Investigation of the Dead Sea Scrolls and the Khirbet Qumran Site e: **MIDSS**

Methoxy-Hydroxy-Mandelic Acid e: **MHMA**

Methylene Diphosphonate e: **MDP**

Metre [or Meter] Water Head e: **MWH**

Metres above sea level e: **M.a.s.l.**

Metres of Fresh Water e: **MFW**

Metres of Salt Water e: **MSW**

Metres of Sea Water e: **MSW**

Metropolitan Association of Urban Designers and Environmental Planners e: **MAUDEP**

Metropolitan College Mental Health Association e: **MCMHA**

Metropolitan Detroit Medical Library Group e: **MDMLG**

Metropolitan Meteorological Experiment e: **METROMEX**

Metropolitan Police Surgeons' Association e: **M.P.S.A.**

Metropolitan Water Board e: **M.W.B.**

Metropolitan Water District e: **MWD**

Metropolitan Water Works Authority e: **MWWA**

Metropolitan Waterworks and Sewerage System e: **MWSS**

Metropolitan Waterworks Authority of Thailand e: **MWA**

Metropolitian Medical Strike Team e: **MMST**

Mexican environmental agency e: **SEDESOL**

Mexican Foundation for Environmental Education e: **FUNDEA**

Mexican Oceanic Sorting Centre e: **CPOM**

Mexican Water Plan e: **MWP**

Miami Nature Biotechnology Winter Symposium e: **MNBWS**

Michael Reese Hospital and Medical Center e: **MRHMC**

Michaelson Interferometer for Coordinated Auroral Doppler Observations e: **MICADO**

Michelson Interferometer [for] Passive Atmospheric Sounding [Sounder] e: **MIPAS**

Michigan Association for Infant Mental Health e: **MAIMH**

Michigan Community Health Electronic Library e: **MCHEL**

Michigan Department of Community Health e: **MDCH**

Michigan Department of Conservation. Geological Survey Division. Publication e: **Mich Dep Conserv Geol Surv Div Publ**

Michigan Department of Conservation. Geological Survey Division. Water Investigation e: **Mich Dep Conserv Geol Surr Div Water Invest**

Michigan. Geological Survey Annual Statistical Summary e: **Michigan Geol Survey Ann Statistical Summ**

Michigan. Geological Survey. Bulletin e: **Mich Geol Surv Bull**

Michigan Geological Survey Division e: **MGSD**

Michigan. Geological Survey Division. Bulletin e: **Mich Geol Surv Div Bull**

Michigan. Geological Survey Division. Miscellany e: **Mich Geol Surv Div Misc**

Michigan. Geological Survey Division. Publication e: **Mich Geol Surv Div Publ**

Michigan. Geological Survey Division Water Investigation e: **Mich Geol Surv Div Water Invest**

Michigan. Geological Survey. Michigan State Board of Geological Survey. Report e: **Mich G S Rp**

Michigan. Geological Survey. Report of Investigation e: **Mich Geol Surv Rep Invest**, e: **Michigan Geol Survey Rept Inv**

Michigan. Geologieal Survey. Water Investigation e: **Michigan Geol Survey Water Inv**

Michigan Health & Hospital Association e: **MHA**

Michigan Health Sciences Libraries Association e: **MHSLA**

Michigan Medicine e: **Michigan Med**, e: **Mich Med**

Michigan Natural Features Inventory e: **MNFI**

Michigan Natural Resources Magazine e: **Mich Nat Resour Mag**

Michigan Occupational Safety and Health Act e: **MIOSHA**

Michigan Public Health Association e: **MPHA**

Michigan Public Health Institute e: **MPHI**

Michigan Pure Water Council e: **MPWC**

Michigan Society for Medical Research e: **MISMR**

Michigan State Medical Society e: **MSMS**

Michigan State University Pre-Veterinary Medical Association e: **MSU-PVMA**

Michigan Water Resources Commission. Report e: **Mic Water Res Comm Rept**

Michigan Women for Medical Control of Abortion e: **MWMCA**

Michin. Geological Survey Division. Progress Report e: **Mich Geol Surv Div Prog Rep**

Micmform Publication. Geological Society of America e: **Microform Publ Geol Soc Am**

Micro-Climate Cooling Unit e: **MCCU**

Micro-Computer Based Advanced System for Environmental Analysis With Remote Sensing Data e: **MICRO-ASEAN**

Micro Earth Station e: **MES**

Micro Geographic Information System e: **MGIS**

Micro-Meteoric Erosion e: **MME**

Micro-Station Foundation and Modular GIS Environment e: **MGE**

Microbial Ecological Monitoring System e: **MEMS**

Microbial Ecology e: **Microb Ecol**

Microbial Ecology Evaluation Device e: **MEED**

Microbial Ecology of the Phylloplane. Papers Read at the International Symposium on the Microbiology of Leaf Surfaces e: **Microb Ecol Phylloplane Pap Int Symp Microbiol Leaf Surf**

Microbial Environment Exposure Device e: **MEED**

Microbial Geochemistry e: **Microb Geochem**

Microbiologia Espanola s: **Microbiol Esp**

Microbiological e: **MICROBIOL**

Microbiological Abstracts e: **Microbiol Abstr**

Microbiological Food Surveillance Group e: **MFSG**

Microbiological Research e: **Microbiol Res**

Microbiological Research Department e: **MRD**

Microbiological Research Establishment e: **MRE**

Microbiological Resources Center (or Centre) e: **MIRCEN**

Microbiological Reviews e: **Microbiol Rev**

Microbiological Sciences e: **Microbiol Sci**

Microbiologically Induced Corrosion e: **MIC**

microbiologie d: **Microb**

Microbiologie, Aliments, Nutrition e: **Microbiol Aliments Nutr**

Microbiology e: **MIC**, e: **MICR**, e: **MICROBIOL**, e: **Microbiolog**

Microbiology and Immunology [Japan] e: **Microbiol Immunol**

Microbiology and Infectious Diseases Research Committee e: **MIDRC**

Microbiology and Molecular Biology Reviews e: **Microbiol Mol Biol Rev**, e: **MMBR**

Microbiology [English Translation of Mikrobiologiya] e: **Microbiology [Engl Transl Mikrobiologiya]**

Microbiology of Fish and Meat Curing Brines. Proedings. International Symposium on Food Microbiology e: **Microbiol Fish Met Curing Brines Proc Int Symp**

Microecology and Therapy e: **Microecol Ther**

Microlensing Observations in Astrophysics e: **MOA**

Micrometeoride Exposure Module e: **MEM**

Micrometeoroid Explorer e: **ME**

Micrometeoroid Explorer Satellite e: **ME Satellite**

Microscale Meteorology Section e: **MMS**

Microscopia Electronica y Biologia Celular s: **Microsc Electron Biol Cel**

Microwave Aerospace Navigation e: **MAN**

Microwave Ice Accretion Measurement Instrument e: **MIAMI**

Microwave Interference Protection e: **MIP**

Microwave & Millimeter Wave Advanced Computer Environment e: **MMACE**

Microwave Remote Sensing Experiment e: **MRSE**

Microwave Remote Sensing Laboratory e: **MIRSL**

Microwave Remote Sensor for the Ocean Surface e: **MIROS**

Microwave Space Relay e: **MISRE**

Microwave Space Research Facility e: **MSRF**

Microwave Water Substance Radiometer e: **MWSR**

Mid-America Remote Sensing Center e: **MARC**

Mid-Atlantic Council of Watershed Associations e: **MACWA**

Mid-Continent Association for Agriculture, Biomedical Research and Education e: **MAABRE**

Mid-Continent Wildcatters Association e: **MCWA**

Mid-Course Space Experiment e: **MSX**

Mid-Eastern Regional Medical Library Service e: **MERMLS**

Mid-Latitude Ecosystems as Sources and Sinks for Atmospheric Oxidants e: **MILOX**

Mid-latitude Standard Atmosphere e: **MLSA**

Mid-Ocean Dynamic Experiment e: **MODA**

Mid-Ocean Meeting Place e: **MOMP**

Mid-Ocean Ridge e: **MOR**

Mid-ocean-ridge Basalt e: **MORB**

Mid-Ocean Target Array e: **MOTA**

Mid-Ocean[ic] Dynamic[s] Experiment [National Science Foundation] e: **MODE**

Midcontinent Ecological Science Center e: **MESC**

Midcontinental Chapter of the Medical Library Association e: **MCMLA**

Midcontinental Regional Medical Library e: **MCRML**

Midcourse Space Experiment e: **MSX**

Middle Air Space e: **MAS**

Middle and High Latitude[s] Oceanic Variability Study e: **MAHLOVS**

Middle Atlantic Underwater Council e: **MAUC**

Middle-Atmosphere Chemistry, Radiation and Transport program e: **MACRAT**

Middle Atmosphere Community Climate Model, Version 2 e: **MACCM2**

Middle Atmosphere Cooperation e: **MAC**

Middle Atmosphere Cooperation/Summer in Northern Europe e: **MAC/SINE**

Middle Atmosphere in the Climate System e: **MACS**

Middle Atmosphere Program/Winter in Northern Europe [Project] e: **MAP/WINE**

Middle Atmosphere Program[me] e: **MAP**

Middle Atmosphere Research Initiative e: **MARI**

Middle Atmosphere Responses to Change[s] e: **MARC**

Middle Atmosphere Science Initiative e: **MASI**

Middle Atmospheric Sounder e: **MAS**

Middle-Earth Role Playing e: **MERP**

Middle East Environmental Research and Education Committee e: **MEEREC**

Middle East Medical Advisory Committee e: **MEMAC**

Middle Georgia College e: **MGC**

Middlesex Hospital Medical School e: **M.H.M.S.**

Midget Ocean Racing Class e: **MORC**

midpoint of denaturization e: **Tm**

Midwest Climate Center e: **MCC**

Midwest College of Medical Assistants, Kansas City e: **MoKMC**

Midwest Integrated Systems Laboratories, Inc. [Watertown] e: **MIS LABS**

Midwest Migrant Health Information Office e: **MMHIO**

Midwestern Climate Information System e: **MICIS**

Midwestern State University, George Moffett Library, Wichita Falls e: **TMI**

Międzynarodowa Unia Geograficzna P: **MUG**

Międzynarodowa Współpraca Geofizyczna P: **MWG**

Migrant & Seasonal Worker Protection Act e: **MSPA**

Migration of Radioisotopes in the Geosphere e: **MIRAGE**

Migratory Animal Pathological Survey e: **MAPS**

Mikrobiologicheskaya Promyshlennost Referativnyi Sbornik R: **Mikrobiol Prom Ref Sb**

Mikrobiologicheskie Protsessy v Pochvakh Moldavii R: **Mikrobiol Protsessy Pochrakh Mold**

Mikrobiologicheskii Sintez Sbornik Informatsii Malerialov R: **Mikrobiol Sint Sb Inf Mater**

Mikrobiologichnyi Zhurnal R: **Mikrobiol Zh**

Mikrobiologická Společnost Československá c: **MSČ**

Mikrobiologie d: **Mikrobiol.**

Mikrobiologiya R: **Mikrobiol**

Mikrobiolohichnyi Zhurnal R: **Mikrobiol Z**

Mikroorganizmy i Rasteniya Trudy Instituta Mikrobiologii Akademii Nauk Latviiskoi SSR *R:* **Mikroorg Rast Trudy Inst Mikrobiol Akad Nauk Latvii SSR**

Milchsäuredehydrogenase (LDH) *d:* **MDH**

Militair Geografisch Instituut *n:* **M.G.I.**

Militärgeographische Dienststelle *d:* **MilGeoDSt**

Militärgeographische Dokumentation *d:* **MGD**

Militärgeographisches Amt *d:* **MilGeoA**

Militärhydrographische Dienststelle *d:* **MilHydroDSt**

militärische Benutzung der Wasserstraßen *d:* **MBdW**

Militarized Multimission Modular Spacecraft *e:* **MMMS**

Militærkontoret ved Norges Geografiske Oppmåling *N:* **MK/NGO**

Militärmedicinsk Undersökningscentral *r:* **MMUC**

Militärmedizin *d:* **Militärmed.**

Militärmedizinische Sektion *d:* **MMS**

Military Aircraft Voice Weather Code *e:* **MAVWC**

Military and Aerospace Connector Manufacturers Association *e:* **MACMA**

Military Assistance Advisory Group, Army Branch, Logistics-Medical *e:* **MAGARLM**

Military Committee Meteorological Group *e:* **MCMG**

Military Community Oral Health Managers *e:* **MCOHM**

Military Computer Basic Environment for Test Handling *e:* **MCBETH**

Military Effectiveness in a Toxin Environment *e:* **METOXI**

Military Evaluation of Geographic Areas *e:* **MEGA**

Military Experience Directed into Health Careers [project] *e:* **MEDIHC**

Military Geographic Documentation *e:* **MGD**

Military Geographic Information *e:* **MGI**

Military Geographic Information and Documentation *e:* **MGID**

Military Geographic Information System *e:* **MGIS**

Military Geographic Intelligence *e:* **MGI**

Military Geography *e:* **Mil. Geo.**

Military Geography Specialist Team *e:* **MGST**

Military Health Service[s] System *e:* **MHSS**

Military Health System *e:* **MHS**

Military Indoctrination for Medical Service Officers *e:* **MIMSO**

Military Information Environment *e:* **MIE**

Military Interdepartmental Purchase (or Procurement) Request *e:* **MIPR**

Military Interdepartmental Purchase Request *e:* **MIRP**

Military Medical Benefits Property *e:* **MMBP**

Military Medical Manual *e:* **MMM**

Military Medical Mobilization *e:* **MMM**

Military Medical Research and Services Program *e:* **MMR&S**

Military Medical Supply Agency *e:* **MMSA**

Military Medicine *e:* **Mil. Med.**, *e:* **MM**

Military Meteorological System *e:* **MILIMETS**

Military Ocean Terminal *e:* **MOT**

Military Ocean Terminal Bay Area *e:* **MOTBA**

Military Ocean Terminal, Bayonne *e:* **MOTBY**

Military Ocean Terminal, King's Bay *e:* **MOTKI**

Military Ocean Terminal, Sunny Point *e:* **MOTSU**

Military Oceanographic Information Center *e:* **MOIC**

Military Oceanography *e:* **MILOC**

Military Oceanography Subcommittee *e:* **MOS**

Military Orbital Development Station *e:* **MODS**

Military Orbital Development System *e:* **MODS**

Military Provincial Health Assistance Program *e:* **MILPHAP**

Military Public Health *e:* **MPH**

Military Sea Transport Service, Far East *e:* **MSTSFE**

Military Sea Transport Union *e:* **MSTU**

Military Sea Transportation Service, Eastern Atlantic and Mediterranean *e:* **MSTSELM**

Military Sea Transportation Service Office Vietnam *e:* **MSTSOV**

Military Sealift Command Auxiliary General Ocean Surveillance *e:* **T-AGOS**

Military Sealift Command Oceanographic Research Ship *e:* **TAGOR**, *e:* **Tagos**

Military Space Surveillance Control Center *e:* **MSSCC**

Military Space Systems Technology Model *e:* **MSSTM**

Military Test Space Station *e:* **MTSS**

Military Weather Warning Center *e:* **MWWC**

Milk Ingredient Water *e:* **MIW**

Milli-Earth Rate Unit *e:* **MERU**

Millimeter Wassersäule *d:* **mmWS**

Millimeter-Wave Atmospheric Sounder-Space Shuttle *e:* **MAS-SS**

Millimeter Wave Observatory *e:* **MWO**

Millimetric Ice Mapping Instrument *e:* **MIMI**

Millstone Hill Observatory *e:* **MHO**

Milton Helpern Institute of Forensic Medicine *e:* **MHIFM**

Mimeoaph Series. Georgia Agricultural Experiment Station *e:* **Mimeogr Ser GA Agr[ic] Exp Stn**

Minature Flow Cytometer *e:* **MiniFCM**

MIND [Management of Information through Natural Discourse] Grammar Rule Language *e:* **MGRL**

Mine Clearance & Armour Protection *e:* **MCAP**

Mine Environment Neutralization Draining *e:* **MEND**

Mine & Ice Detection/Avoidance System *e:* **MIDAS**

Mine Medical Officers' Association of South Africa *e:* **MMOA**

Mine Safety and Health Administration, Denver, Denver *e:* **ULM**

Mine Safety and Health Administration (or Agency) *e:* **MSHA**

Mine warfare Environmental Decision Air Library *e:* **MEDAL**

Mined Geologic Disposal System Requirements *e:* **MGDSR**

Mineral Assessment Report. Institute of Geological Sciences *e:* **Miner Assess Rep Inst Geol Sci**

Mineral Brief British Geological Survey *e:* **Miner Brief Br Geol Surv**

Mineral Deposits Circular. Ontario Geological Survey *e:* **Miner Deposits Circ Ontrio Geol Surv**

Mineral Deposits Division, Geological Association of Canada *e:* **MDD**

Mineral Economics Series [Indiana Geological Survey] *e:* **Miner Econ Ser [Indiana Geol Surv]**

Mineral Industry Surveys. Natural Graphite *e:* **MIS Graph**

Mineral Reconnaissance Programme Report. British Geological Survey *e:* **Miner Reconnaissance Programme Rep Br Geol Surv**

Mineral Reconnaissance Programme Report. Institute o Geological Sciences *e:* **Miner Reconnaissance Programme Rep Inst Geol Sci**

Mineral Resource Circular [University of Texas at Austin. Bureau of Economic Geology] *e:* **Miner Resour Circ [Univ Tex Austin Bur Econ Geol]**

Mineral Resource Report. Pennsylvania Topographic and Geologic Survey *e:* **Miner Resour Rep PA Topogr Geol Surv**

Mineral Resources Bulletin [Geological Survey of Western Australia] *e:* **Miner Resour Bull [Geol Surv West Aust]**

Mineral Resources Bulletin. Louisiana Geological Survey *e:* **Miner Resour Bull LA Geol Surv**, *e:* **Miner Resour Bull Louisiana Geol Surv**

Mineral Resources Pamphlet. Geological Survey of Guyana *e:* **Miner Resour Pam Geol Surv Guynna**

Mineral Resources Report. Botswana Geological Survey Department *e:* **Miner Resour Rep Botswna Geol Surv Dep**

Mineral Resources Report. Bureau of Mineral Resources. Geology and Geophysics *e:* **Miner Resour Rep**

Mineral Resources Report. Commonwealth Geological Liaison Office *e:* **Miner Resour Rep Commonw Geol Liaison Off**

Mineral Resources Report. Geological Survey Department [Botswana] *e:* **Miner Resour Rep Geol Surv Dep [Botswna]**

Mineral Resources Series. Division of Geology [South Carolina] *e:* **Miner Resour Ser Div Geol [SC]**

Mineral Resources Series. Rhodesia Geological Survey *e:* **Miner Resour Ser Rhod Geol Surv**

Mineral Resources Series. West Virginia Geological and Economic Survey *e:* **Miner Resour Ser WV Geol Econ Surv**

Mineral Water Company of Canada *e:* **MWCC**

Mineralogiyai Geokhimiya [USSR] *R:* **Mineral Geokhim**

Mineralöl-Kohlenwasserstoffe *d:* **MKW**

Minerals and the Environment *e:* **Miner Environ**

Minerva Biologica *e:* **Minerr Biol**

Minerva Ginecologica *s:* **Minerva Ginecol**

Minerva Medica *s:* **Minerva Med**

Mines Geologic Disposal System *e:* **MGDS**

Minesweeper, Ocean *e:* **MSO**

Mingo National Wildlife Refuge *e:* **MNWR**

Miniature Eyesafe Laser Infrared Observation Set *e:* **MELIOS**

Miniature Interferometer Terminals for Earth Survey *e:* **MITES**

miniaturized version of the ground-based atmospheric emitted radiance interferometer *e:* **UAV-AERI**

Minidoka National Wildlife Refuge *e:* **MNWR**

Minimal Orbit Unmanned Satellite Experiment *e:* **MOUSE**

Minimalwasserspiegel *d:* **Min.Wsp.**

Minimization of Earthworks Vertical Alignment *e:* **MINERVA**

Minimum Biological Acceptable Levels *e:* **MBALs**

Minimum Floor Space *e:* **MFS**

Minimum Navigation Performance Specifications Airspace *e:* **MNPSA**

Minimum number of Animal Units *e:* **MAU**

Minimum Variance Orbit Determination *e:* **MINIVAR**

Mining and Geological Institute *e:* **MGI**

Mining and Geological Institute of India *e:* **M.G.I.**

Mining and Geological Journal *e:* **Min Geol J**, *e:* **Min & Geol J**

Mining and Water Cases, Annotated *e:* **M & W Cas**

Mining, Geological and Metallurgical Institute [of India] *e:* **MGMI**

Mining Geology [Japan] *e:* **Min Geol**

Mining Geology [Society of Mining Geologists of Japan] Journal *e:* **Min Geol [Soc Min Geol Jap]**

Mining Geology [Society of Mining Geologists of Japan] Special Issue [Tokyo] *e:* **Min Geol Spec Issue [Tokyo]**

Minister für Natur, Umwelt und Landesentwicklung *d:* **MNUL**

Minister für Natur, Umwelt und Landesentwicklung, Schleswig-Holstein *d:* **MinNUL S-H**

Minister für Umwelt, Raumordnung und Bauwesen *d:* **MURB**

Minister für Umwelt, Raumplanung und Landwirtschaft *d:* **MURL**

Minister of State for Population and Research Environment, Indonesia *e:* **KLH**

Minister of State for Population and Research Environment [Indonesia] *e:* **LIPI**

Ministere de l'Environnement, Ste-Foy, Quebec *f:* **QQEN**

Ministère de la Protection de la Nature et de l'Environment *f:* **MDPNE**

Ministère de l'Environnement *f:* **ME**

Ministère de l'Environnement et de la Faune *f:* **MEF**

Ministere de l'Environnement, Montreal, Quebec *f:* **QMEN**

Ministerial Conference of Western and Central African States on Sea Transport *e:* **MCWCS**

Ministerial Conference on the Protection of Forests in Europe *e:* **MCPFE**

Ministerie van Landsverdediging *n:* **MLV**

Ministerie van Verkeer en Waterstaat *n:* **MVenW**

Ministerie van Waterstaat *n:* **MINVW**

Ministerio del Ambiente y los Recursos Naturales Renovables *s:* **MARNR**

Ministerium für Außen- und Innerdeutschen Handel *d:* **MfAuI**

Ministerium für Gesundheitswesen *d:* **MfG**, *d:* **MfGe[s.]**

Ministerium für Innerdeutschen Handel, Außenhandel und Materialversorgung *d:* **MIAM**

Ministerium für Landwirtschaft, Umweltschutz und Raumordnung des Landes Brandenburg *d:* **MLUR**

Ministerium für Umwelt, Energie und Verkehr *d:* **MUEV**

Ministerium für Umwelt, Naturschutz und Raumordnung [des Landes Brandenburg] *d:* **MUNR**

Ministerium für Umwelt und Gesundheit *d:* **MUG**

Ministerium für Umweltschutz und Wasserwirtschaft *d:* **MUW**

Ministero della Cultura Popolare, Roma *i:* **MINCULPOP**

Ministerstvo Geologii SSSR *R:* **MGSSSR**

Ministry for Civil Defence, Emergencies and Elimination of Consequences of Natural Disasters [Russian Federation] *e:* **TsENTROSPAS**

Ministry for the Environment *e:* **MFE**

Ministry of Agriculture and Natural Resources. Central Agricultural Station. Research Report [Guyana] *e:* **Minist Agric Nat Resour Cent Agric Stn Res Rep [Guyana]**

Ministry of Agriculture and Water *e:* **MAW**

Ministry of Agriculture/Department of Livestock Development & Animal Health *e:* **MOA/DLDAH**

Ministry of Agriculture, Nature Conservation and Fisheries *e:* **LNV**

Ministry of Energy and Natural Resources *e:* **MENR**

Ministry of Environment *e:* **ENVICAN**

Ministry of Environment and Energy *e:* **MOEE**

Ministry of Environment and Science *e:* **MST**

Ministry of Environment, Lands and Parks *e:* **MELP**, *e:* **MOELP**

Ministry of Environmental Protection and Regional Development *e:* **MEPRD**

Ministry of Forests and Environment *e:* **MOFE**

Ministry of Forests and Environment/ Department of Forests *e:* **MOFE/DOF**

Ministry of Forests and Environment/ Department of Medicinal Plants *e:* **MOFE/DOMP**

Ministry of Forests and Environment/ Department of National Parks & Wildlife Conservation *e:* **MOFE/DNPWC**

Ministry of Forests and Environment/ Department of Soil Conservation *e:* **MOFE/DOSC**

Ministry of Forests and Environment/Forest Products Development Board *e:* **MOFE/FPDB**

Ministry of Forests and Environment/ Timber Corporation of Nepal *e:* **MOFE/TCN**

Ministry of Health *e:* **M.H.**, *e:* **MINSA**, *e:* **MOHE**

Ministry of Health/Amp Pipal Hospital *e:* **MOHE/APH**

Ministry of Health and Social Services [Northern Ireland] *e:* **MHSS[NI]**

Ministry of Health and Welfare *e:* **MHW**

Ministry of Health/Central Health Laboratory *e:* **MOHE/CHL**

Ministry of Health/Department of Ayurveda *e:* **MOHE/DAU**

Ministry of Health/Department of Water Supply and Sanitation *e:* **MOHE/DWSS**

Ministry of Health Inspectorate *e:* **M.H.I.**

Ministry of Health, Legal Branch *e:* **M.H.L.B.**

Ministry of Health, Medical Branch *e:* **M.H.M.B.**

Ministry of Health/National Centre For Aid & Standard Control *e:* **MOHE/NCAID**

Ministry of Health/National [Health] Education, Information and Communication *e:* **MOHE/HICC**

Ministry of Health. New Zealand *e:* **MOH**

Ministry of Health/Nutritious Food Programme Management Committee *e:* **MOHE/NFPMC**

Ministry of Health/Okhaldhunga Hospital *e:* **MOHE/OH**

Ministry of Health/Patan Hospital *e:* **MOHE/PA**

Ministry of Health/Public Health Division *e:* **MOHE/PHD**

Ministry of Health/public Health Division *e:* **MOH/PHD**

Ministry of Health/Royal Drugs Research Laboratory *e:* **MOHE/RDRL**

Ministry of Health/Tansen Hospital *e:* **MOHE/TS**

Ministry of Health/Western Regional Hospital *e:* **MOHE/WRH**

Ministry of Housing and Physical Planning/Department of Hydrology and Meteorology *e:* **MOHPP/DHM**

Ministry of Housing and Physical Planning/Department of Water Supply and Sewerage *e:* **MOHPP/DWSS**

Ministry of Housing and Physical Planning/Nepal Water Supply Corporation *e:* **MOHPP/NWSC**

Ministry of Industry/ Department of Mines and Geology *e:* **MOI/DMG**

Ministry of Information and Communication/Department of Mines and Geology *e:* **MOI/DMG**

Ministry of Land and Natural Resources *e:* **MLNR**

Ministry of Lands, Survey and Natural Resources *e:* **TMLS**

Ministry of Local Development/Remote Area Development Committee *e:* **MOLD/RADC**

Ministry of Natural Resources [Canada] *e:* **MNR**

Ministry of Planning and Environment *e:*
MPE

Ministry of Population and Environment *e:*
MOPE

Ministry of Protection of the Environment
and Natural Resources of the Russian
Federation *e:* **MINPRIRODI**

Ministry of Public Health *e:* **MOPH**

Ministry of Public Health and Medical
Industry *e:* **MinZdravMedProm**

Ministry of Science, Technology and
Environment *e:* **MOSTE**

Ministry of [the] Environment *e:* **MOE**

Ministry of the Environment and Natural
Resources *e:* **MARNR**

Ministry of the Protection of Nature and the
Environment *e:* **MDPNE**

Ministry of Water and Irrigation *e:* **MWI**

Ministry of Water Resources *e:* **MOWR**

Ministry of Water Resources/Department of
Irrigation *e:* **MOWR/DOI**

Ministry of Water Resources/Department of
Meteorology and Hydrology *e:*
MOWR/DOMH

Ministry of Water Resources/Ground Water
Resources Development Board *e:*
MOWR/GWRDB

Ministry of Water Resources/Marsyangdi
Hydroelectric Development Board *e:*
MOWR/MHDB

Ministry of Water Resources/Nepal
Electricity Authority *e:* **MOWR/NEA**

Ministry of Water Resources/Small Hydro
Power Department *e:* **MOWR/SHDP**

Ministry of Water Resources/Water
Resources Development Board *e:*
MOWR/GROUND

Minneapolis Center for Microbiological
Investigations *e:* **MCMI**

Minnesota Academy of Natural Sciences.
Bulletin *e:* **Minn Ae N Sc B**

Minnesota Atmospheric Boundary Layer
Experiments *e:* **MABLE**

Minnesota. Department of Conservation.
Division of Waters. Bulletin. Technical
Paper *e:* **Minn Dept Conn Div Waters
Bull Tech Paper**

Minnesota Department of Health *e:* **MDH**

Minnesota. Department of Natural
Resources. Division of Fish and Wildlife.
Section of Wildlife. Wildlife Research
Quarterly *e:* **Minn Dep Nat Resour Div
Fish Wildl Sect Wildl Wildl Res Q**

Minnesota. Department of Natural
Resources. Division of Game and Fish.
Section of Technical Services.
Investigational Report *e:* **Minn Dep Nat
Resour Div Game Fish Sect Tech Serv
Invest Rep**

Minnesota. Department of Natural
Resources. Game Research Project.
Quarterly Progress Report *e:* **Minn Dep
Nat Resour Game Res Proj Q Prog Rep**

Minnesota Department of Natural
Resources. Section of Fisheries.
Investigational Report *e:* **Minn Dep Nat
Resour Sect Fish Invt Rep**

Minnesota. Division of Waters. Bulletin *e:*
Minn Div Waters Bull

Minnesota Environmental Control Citizens
Association *e:* **MECCA**

Minnesota. Geological and Natural History
Survey *e:* **Minn G S**

Minnesota Geological Survey *e:* **MGS**, *e:*
Minn Geol Surv

Minnesota. Geological Survey. Bulletin *e:*
Minn Geol Surv Bull

Minnesota. Geological Survey.
Miscellaneous Map *e:* **Minnesota Geoll
Survey Misc Map**

Minnesota. Geological Survey. Report of
Investigations *e:* **Minnesota Geol
Survey Rept Inv**, *e:* **Minn Geol Surv
Rep Invest**

Minnesota. Geological Survey. Special
Publication Series *e:* **Minnesota Geol
Survey Spec Pub Ser**, *e:* **Minn Geol
Surv Spec Publ Ser**

Minnesota Medicine *e:* **Minnesota Med**,
e: **Minn Med**

Minnesota Public Health Association *e:*
MPHA

Minnesota State Medical Association *e:*
MSMA

Minnesota. University. Water Resources
Research Center Bulletin *e:* **Minn Univ
Water Resour Res Cent Bull**

Minnesota Veterinary Medical Association
e: **MVMA**

Minority Association for Animal Protection
e: **MAAP**

Minority Biomedical Research Support
Program *e:* **MBRS**

Minority Health Initiative *e:* **MHI**

MIRACL/Sea Lite Beam Director *e:*
MIRACL/SLBD

Miramichi Natural History Society,
Chatham, New Brunswick *e:* **NBCM**

Miscellaneous Information Listing
Program[me] Apollo Spacecraft *e:*
MILPAS

Miscellaneous Paper. Ontario Geological
Survev *e:* **Misc Pap Ont Geol Surv**

Miscellaneous Paper. Oregon Department of
Geology and Mineral Industries *e:* **Misc
Pap Oreg Dep Geol Miner Ind**

Miscellaneous Paper. United States Army
Engineers. Waterways Experiment Station
e: **Misc Pap US Army Eng Waterw Exp
Stn**

Miscellaneous Papers. Gronlands
Geologiske Undersogelse *a:* **Misc Pap
Gronl Geol Unders**

Miscellaneous Publications. Geological
Survey of India *e:* **Misc Publ Geol Surv
India**

Miscellaneous Report. Ohio Division of
Geological Survey *e:* **Misc Rep Ohio
Div Geol Surv**

Miscellaneous Reports. Research Institute
for Natural Resources [Tokyo] *e:* **Misc
Rep Res Inst Nat Resourc [Tokyo]**

Miscellaneous Series. North Dakota
Geological Survey *e:* **NDGXA**

Miseellaneous Series. North Dakota
Geological Survey *e:* **Misc Ser ND Geol
Surv**

Misericordia Hospital, Medical Library,
Bronx *e:* **VMH**

Misión de Investigaciones Geofísicas *s:*
GRM

Missão de Biologia Marítima, Junta de
Investigações do Ultramar *p:* **MBM**

Missão de Estudos Broceanólogicas e de
Pesca de Angola *p:* **MEBPA**

Missão de Geografia Física e Humana do
Ultramar *p:* **MGFHU**

Missão Geo-Hidrográfica da Guiné *p:*
MGHG

Missão Geográfica de Angola *p:* **MAG**

Missão Geográfica de Angola, Junta de
Investigações do Ultramar *p:* **MGA**

Missão Geográfica de Moçambique, Junta
de Investigações do Ultramar *p:* **MGM**

Missão Geográfica de Timor, Junta de
Investigações do Ultramar *p:* **MGT**

Missão Hidrográfica do Arquipélago de
Cabo Verde *p:* **MHCV**

Missile and Space Council *e:* **MSC**

Missile and Space Intelligence Center *e:*
MSIC

Missile and Space-Vehicle Department *e:*
MSVD

Missile and Space Vehicle Office *e:* **MSVO**

Missile Environment[al] Testing Study *e:*
METS

Missile Sea Level *e:* **MSL**

Missile, Space and Range Pioneers *e:*
MSRP

Missile & Space System Division *e:*
M&SSD

Missile Warning and Space Operations
Center *e:* **MWSOC**

Mission Analysis Branch [Manned
Spacecraft Center] *e:* **MAB**

Mission Control Center-National
Aeronautics and Space Administration *e:*
MCC-NASA

Mission de Documentation de Géographie
Militaire *f:* **M.D.G.M.**

Mission de l'Environnement Rural et Urbain
f: **MERU**

Mission Display Board Assembly [Space
Flight Operations Facility] *e:* **MDB**

Mission Environment Tape *e:* **MET**

Mission From Planet Earth *e:* **MFPE**

Mission Hydrographique l'Atlantique *f:*
MHA

Mission Jupiter Orbit *e:* **MJO**

Mission Modes and Space Analysis *e:*
MIMOSA

Mission Modular Spacecraft *e:* **MMS**

Mission Oceanographique de la
Mediterranée *f:* **MOM**

Mission to Deep Sea Fishermen *e:* **MDSF**

Mission to Planet Earth *e:* **MPE**

Mission to Planet Earth [program] *e:*
MTPE

Mississippi-Alabama Sea Grant Consortium
e: **MASGC**

Mississippi. Board of Water
Commissioners. Bulletin *e:* **Miss Board
Water Comm Bull**

Mississippi Bureau of Geology *e:* **MGB**

Mississippi. Geological, Economic and
Topographical Survey. Bulletin *e:* **Miss
Geol Surv Bull**, *e:* **Mississippi Geol
Econ and Topog Survey Bull**

Mississippi. Geological, Economic and
Topographical Survey. Information Series
MGS *e:* **Miss Geol Ecn Topogr Surv
Inf Ser MGS**

Mississippi Geological Society *e:* **M.G.S.**

Mississippi. Geological Survey. Bulletin
e: **Miss G S B**

Mississippi Geology *e:* **Miss Geol**

Mississippi Medical Record *e:* **Mississippi
Med Rec**

Mississippi National Wildlife Refuge *e:* **MNWR**

Mississippi State Department of Health *e:* **MSDH**

Mississippi State Geological Survey. Bulletin *e:* **Miss State Geol Surv Bull**

Mississippi State Geological Survey. Bulletin. Circular *e:* **Miss State Geol Survey Bull Circ**

Mississippi State Medical Association *e:* **MSMA**

Mississippi Valley Medical Journal *e:* **Miss V Med J**

Mississippi Valley Medical Society *e:* **MVMS**

Missouri Department of Natural Resources *e:* **MDNR**

Missouri Division of Geology and Land Survey *e:* **MDGLS**

Missouri Environmental Law and Policy Review *e:* **Mo. Envtl. L.&Pol'y Rev.**

Missouri. Geological Survey and Water Resources. Educational Series *e:* **Missouri Geol Survey and Water Resources Educ Ser**

Missouri. Geological Survey and Water Resources. Information Circular *e:* **Missouri Geol Survey and Water Resources Inf Circ**

Missouri. Geological Survey and Water Resources. Report *e:* **Missouri Geol Survey and Water Resources Report**

Missouri. Geological Survey and Water Resources. Report of Investigations *e:* **Missouri Geol Survey and NVater Resources Rept Inv**

Missouri. Geological Survey and Water Resources. Special Publication *e:* **Missouri Geol Survey and Water Resources Spec Pub**

Missouri Medicine *e:* **Miss Med**, *e:* **Missouri Med.**, *e:* **Mo Med**

Missouri Natural Heritage Inventory *e:* **MoNHI**

Missouri State Medical Association *e:* **MSMA**

Missouri Veterinary Medical Association *e:* **MVMA**

MIT Interdepartmental Laboratory *e:* **MAC**

MIT [Massachusetts Institute of Technology] Hydrodynamics Laboratory. Technical Report *e:* **MIT Hydrodyn Lab Tech Rep**

Mitchell's Modern Geography *e:* **Mitch Mod Geog**

Mitteilung Steiermärkisches Landesmuseum [Graz]. Museum für Bergbau, Geologie und Technik *d:* **Mitt Steiermärkisches Landesmus [Graz] Mus Bergbau Geol Tec**

Mitteilungen aus den Grenzgebieten der Medizin und Chirurgie *d:* **MGgMCh**, *d:* **MGrenzg.**

Mitteilungen aus der Biologischen Bundesanstalt für Land- und Forstwirtschaft *d:* **Mitt. Biol Bundesanst. Land- Forstwirtsch.**

Mitteilungen aus der Biologischen Bundesanstalt für Land- und Forstwirtschaft, Berlin-Dahlem *d:* **Mitt. Biol Bundesanst. Land- Forstwirtsch., Berl.-Dahl.**

Mitteilungen der Aargauischen naturforschenden Gesellschaft *d:* **Mitt. Aargau. nat.forsch. Ges.**

Mitteilungen der Arbeitsgemeinschaft Geobotanik in Schleswig-Holstein und Hamburg *d:* **Mitt. Arb.gem. Geobot. Schlesw.-Holst. Hambg.**

Mitteilungen der Biologischen Reichsanstalt *d:* **MBRA**

Mitteilungen der Deutschen Gesellschaft für Natur- und Völkerkunde Ostasiens *d:* **MDGNVO**

Mitteilungen der Deutschen Gesellschaft für Natur- und Volkskunde Ostasiens *d:* **MGNVO**

Mitteilungen der Geographisch-Ethnographischen Gesellschaft, Basel *d:* **MGEGB**

Mitteilungen der Geographisch-Ethnographischen Gesellschaft, Zürich *d:* **MGEGZ**

Mitteilungen der Geographisch-Ethnographischen Gesellschaft Zürich *d:* **Mitt. Geogr.-Ethnogr. Ges. Zür.**

Mitteilungen der Geographischen Gesellschaft, Hamburg *d:* **MGGH**

Mitteilungen der Geographischen Gesellschaft in München *d:* **MGGM**

Mitteilungen der Geographischen Gesellschaft und des naturhistorischen Museums, Lübeck *d:* **MGGL**

Mitteilungen der Geographischen Gesellschaft, Wien *d:* **MGGW**

Mitteilungen der geologischen Gesellschaft, Berlin *d:* **MgeolGB**

Mitteilungen der geologischen Gesellschaft, Wien *d:* **MgeolGW**

Mitteilungen der Gesellschaft für Tierpsychologie *d:* **MGTPs**

Mitteilungen der kaiserlich und königlichen Geographischen Gesellschaft in Wien *d:* **MGG**

Mitteilungen der Landesanstalt für Wasserhygiene *d:* **MLAWHy**

Mitteilungen der Naturforschenden Gesellschaft des Kantons Glarus *d:* **Mitt. Nat.forsch. Ges. Kanton Glarus**

Mitteilungen der Naturforschenden Gesellschaft des Kantons Solothurn *d:* **Mitt. Nat.forsch. Ges. Kanton Solothurn**

Mitteilungen der Naturforschenden Gesellschaft in Bern *d:* **Mitt. Nat.forsch. Ges. Bern**

Mitteilungen der Naturforschenden Gesellschaft Luzern *d:* **Mitt. Nat.forsch. Ges. Luzern**

Mitteilungen der Naturforschenden Gesellschaft Schaffhausen *d:* **Mitt. Nat.forsch. Ges. Schaffhausen**

Mitteilungen der Naturwissenschaftlichen Gesellschaft Thun *d:* **Mitt. Nat.wiss. Ges. Thun**

Mitteilungen der Naturwissenschaftlichen Gesellschaft Winterthur *d:* **Mitt. Nat.wiss. Ges. Winterthur**

Mitteilungen der Thurgauischen Naturforschenden Gesellschaft *d:* **Mitt. Thurgau. Nat.forsch. Ges.**

Mitteilungen der Versuchsanstalt für Wasserbau, Hydrologie und Glaziologie an der Eidg. Technischen Hochschule Zürich *d:* **Mitt. Vers.anst. Wasserbau Hydrol. Glaziol. Eidgenöss. Tech. Hochsch. Zür.**

Mitteilungen des Arbeitskreises Wald und Wasser *d:* **Mitt. Arb.kr. Wald Wasser**

Mitteilungen des Badischen Landesvereins für Naturkunde und Naturschutz *d:* **Mitt. Bad. Landesver. Nat.kd. Nat.schutz**

Mitteilungen des Deutschen Wasserwirtschaftsverbandes *d:* **MDWWV**, *d:* **MDWwV**

Mitteilungen des Instituts für allgemeine Biologie, Hamburg *d:* **MIaBH**

Mitteilungen des naturwissenschaftlichen Vereins an der Universität Wien *d:* **MnatVW**

Mitteilungen des Vereins der Geographen an der Universität Leipzig *d:* **MVGUL**

Mitteilungen des Vereins zur Verbreiterung naturwissenschaftlicher Kenntnis nördlich der Elbe *d:* **M.d.V.z.V.n.K.**

Mitteilungen zur Geschichte der Medizin *d:* **MGM**

Mitteilungen zur Geschichte der Medizin und Naturwissenschaften *d:* **MGMNw**

Mittelhochwasser *d:* **MHW**

Mittelkleinwasser *d:* **M.Kl.W.**

Mittelmaßstäbige landwirtschaftliche Standortkartierung *d:* **MMK**

Mitteltidehochwasser *d:* **MTHW**

Mitteltideniedrigwasser *d:* **MTNW**

Mittelwasser *d:* **M.W.**

Mittelwasserbett *e:* **MW Bett**

Mittelwasserquantität *d:* **MQ**

Mittelwasser[stand] *d:* **MW**

mittlerer Pulmonalarteriendruck *d:* **PpA**

mittlere Hochwasserhöhe *d:* **MHWH**

mittlere Hochwasserquantität *d:* **MHQ**

mittlere medizinische Kraft *d:* **Mmk**

mittlere Niedrigwasserhöhe *d:* **M.N.W.H.**

mittlere Niedrigwasserquantität *d:* **MNQ**

mittlere tägliche Hochwasserungleichheit *d:* **DHQ**

mittlere tägliche Niedrigwasserungleichheit *d:* **DLQ**

mittlerer Hochwasserstand *d:* **MHWSt**

mittlerer medizinischer Beruf *d:* **MmB**

mittlerer Niedrigwasserstand *d:* **MNW**

mittleres Kleinwasser *d:* **M. kl. W.**

mittleres Niedrigwasser *d:* **M.N.W.**

mittleres Tidehochwasser *d:* **MThw**

mittleres Tideniedrigwasser *d:* **MTnw**

Mixed Commission for Black Sea Fisheries *e:* **MCBSF**

Mixed Medical Commission *e:* **M.M.C.**

Mixed Type of Ice Formation *e:* **MX**

Mobile Aeromedical Staging Facilities (or Facility) *e:* **MASF**

Mobile Aeromedical Staging Flights *e:* **MASF**

Mobile/Aerospace [Alabama] *e:* **KBFM**

Mobile Air & Space Defense *e:* **MASD**

Mobile Air Traffic Control and All-Weather Landing System *e:* **MATCALS**

Mobile Autonomous Robot in an Industrial Environment *e:* **MARIE**

Mobile Earth Station *e:* **MES**

Mobile Earth Station Facility *e:* **MESF**

Mobile Electrical Network Testing, Observation and Recording *e:* **MENTOR**

Mobile Electronic Robot Manipulator and Underwater Television *e:* **MERMUT**

Mobile Environmental Team[s] *e:* **MET**

Mobile Ionospheric Observatory [Boston University] *e:* **MIO**

Mobile Meteorological Equipment *e:* **MME**

Mobile Micrometeorological Observation System *e:* **MMMOS,** *e:* **MMOS**

Mobile Ocean Basing System *e:* **MOBS**

Mobile Oceanography Support System *e:* **MOSS**

Mobile Protected Gun *e:* **MPG**

Mobile Protected Gun System *e:* **MPGS**

Mobile [Remote-Controlled] Robot *e:* **MOBOT**

Mobile Satellite Photometric Observatory *e:* **MOSPO**

Mobile Sea Range *e:* **MSR**

Mobile Station for Environmental Services *e:* **MOSES**

Mobile Underwater Surveillance Teams *e:* **MUST**

Mobile Underwater Test vehicle *e:* **MUST**

Mobile Underwater Vehicle *e:* **MUV**

Mobile Water Mine *e:* **MOWAM**

Mobiles Umweltschutzkommando *d:* **MUK**

Mobility Environmental Research Study *e:* **MERS**

Moccasin Bend Mental Health Institute, Chattancoga *e:* **TCMI**

MODEC [Mitsui Ocean Development and Engineering Company] Anchor Piling System *e:* **MAPS**

Model Evaluation Consortium for Climate Assessment [project] *e:* **MECCA**

Model for Atmospheric Chemistry and Transport *e:* **MATCH**

Model for Evaluating Missile Observation *e:* **MEMO**

Model for Intertheater Deployment by Air & Sea *e:* **MODAS**

Model of Acidification of Groundwater in Catchment *e:* **MAGIC**

Model of the Global Universal Tracer Transport in the Atmosphere *e:* **MOGUNTIA**

Modèle Agrométéorologique d'Évaporation et de Temperature *f:* **MAGRET**

Modèle de circulation atmosphérique générale *f:* **AGCM**

modelling framework of the health impact assessment of man-induced atmospheric changes *e:* **MIASMA**

Modelling Global Biogeochemical Cycles *e:* **MGBC**

Modelling Natural Images for Synthesis and Animation *e:* **MONALISA**

Modelo de Circulación Atmosférica General *s:* **AGCM**

Moderate-Resolution Atmospheric Radiance and Transmittance Model *e:* **MODTRAN**

Moderator Circulating Water System *e:* **MCWS**

Moderne Medizin. Zeitschrift für Wissenschaft und Soziologie *d:* **Mod.M.**

Modified Advanced Research Environmental Test Satellite *e:* **MARENTS**

modifiziertes Naturprodukt *d:* **MN**

Modoc National Wildlife Refuge *e:* **MNWR**

Modular Automated Weather System *e:* **MAWS**

Modular Electronic Solid-State Aerospace Ground Equipment *e:* **MESSAGE**

Modular Environment for Data Systems *e:* **MEDS**

Modular Hydrologic Modeling System *e:* **MHMS**

Modular Multi-Mission Remotely Piloted Vehicle *e:* **MMMRPV**

Modular Ocean Model *e:* **MOM**

Modular Space Station *e:* **MSS**

Modular Toxic Environment Protective Suit *e:* **MODTEPS**

Modular Underwater Measurement System *e:* **MUMS**

Modules and Apparatus (Spacelab D-1 Experiment) *e:* **MEDEA**

MOL [Manned Orbiting Laboratory] Environmental Shelter *e:* **MES**

Molecular and Cell Biology of Human Diseases Series *e:* **Mol Cell Biol Hum Dis Ser**

Molecular and Cellular Biology *e:* **MCB,** *e:* **Mol Cell Biol**

Molecular Aspects of Medicine *e:* **Mol Aspects Med**

Molecular Biology *e:* **MOL,** *e:* **Mol Biol,** *e:* **Molec Biol**

Molecular Biology an International Series of Monographs and Textbooks *e:* **Mol Biol Int Ser Monogr Textb**

Molecular Biology [and] Evolution *e:* **Mol Biol Evol**

Molecular Biology and Medicine *e:* **Mol Biol & Med**

Molecular Biology, Biochemistry and Biophysics *e:* **Mol Biol Biochem Biophys**

Molecular Biology. English Translation of Molekulyarnaya Biologiya [Moscow] *e:* **Mol Biol Engl Transl Mol Biol [Mosc]**

Molecular Biology of the Cell *e:* **Mol Biol Cell**

Molecular Biology of the Mammalian Genetic Apparatus *e:* **Mol Biol Mamm Gene Appar**

Molecular Biology. Proceedings. International Conference *e:* **Mol Biol Proc Int Conf**

Molecular Biology Reports *e:* **Mol Biol R[e]p**

Molecular Cell Biology Research Communications *e:* **MCBRC**

Molecular Ecology *e:* **MOLE,** *e:* **Mol Ecol**

Molecular Ecology [R] *e:* **Mol. Ecol.**

Molecular Environmental Science *e:* **MES**

molecular environmental science synchrotron radiation *e:* **MES-SR**

Molecular Marine Biology and Biotechnology *e:* **Mol Mar Biol Biotechnol**

Molecular Medicine *e:* **Mol Med**

Molecular Membrane Biology *e:* **Mol Membr Biol**

Molecular Microbiology *e:* **Mol Microbiol**

Molecular Neurobiology *e:* **Mol Neurobiol**

Molecular Spin Orbital *e:* **MSO**

Molekularbiologie *d:* **Mol.-Biol.,** *d:* **Molekularbiol.**

Molekuliarnaia Biologiia *R:* **Mol Biol [Mosk]**

Molekuliarnaia Genetika, Mikrobiologia, i Virusologa *e:* **Mol Gen Mikrobiol Virusol**

Molekülorbital-Theorie *d:* **MO-Theorie**

Molekulyarnaya Biologiya *R:* **Mol Biol**

Molekulyarnaya Biologiya [Kiev] *R:* **Mol Biol [Kiev]**

Molekulyarnaya Biologiya [Moscow] *e:* **Mol Biol [Mosc]**

Molekulyarnaya Genetika, Mikrobiologia i Virusologiya *R:* **Mol Genet Mikrobiol Virusol**

Molonglo Observatory Synthesis Telescope *e:* **MOST**

Monaco Oceanographic Institute *e:* **MOI**

Monatsberichte der Deutschen Geologischen Gesellschaft *d:* **MbDGG**

Monatshefte für den Naturwissenschaftlichen Unterricht Aller Schulgattungen und Natur und Schule *d:* **Monatsh Naturwiss Unterr Aller Schulgattungen Natur Sch**

Monatshefte für praktische Tierheilkunde *d:* **MhpTh**

Monatshefte für Praktische Tierheilkunde *f:* **Monatsh Prakt Tierh**

Monatshefte für Tierheilkunde *d:* **Monatsh Tierheilkd**

Monatshefte für Veterinärmedizin *d:* **Monatsh Vet[erinärmed]**

Monatsschrift für naturwissenschaftlichen Unterricht *d:* **MnU**

Monatsschrift für praktische Tierheilkunde *d:* **MprTh**

Monatsschrift für Unfallheilkunde und Versicherungsmedizin *d:* **MUV**

Monatsschrift für Unfallheilkunde. Versicherungs-, Versorgungs- und Verkehrsmedizin *d:* **Monatsschr Unfallheilkd Versicher-Versorg Verkehrsmed**

Monde Medical [Paris] *f:* **Monde Med [Paris]**

Monegasque Association for the Protection of Nature *e:* **AMPN**

Monitor and Control System [Deep Space Instrumentation Facility] *e:* **MCS**

Monitore Ostetrico-Ginecologico *i:* **Monit Ostet-Ginecol**

Monitore Ostetrico-Ginecologico di Endocrinologia e del Metabolismo *i:* **Monit Ostet-Ginecol Endocrinol Metab**

Monitoring Agriculture by/with Remote Sensing *e:* **MARS**

Monitoring Agro-Ecological Resources with Remote Sensing and Simulation *e:* **MARS**

Monitoring Earth's Rotation and Intercomparison of Techniques *e:* **MERIT**

Monitoring Environmental Progress *e:* **MEP**

Monitoring in Complex Environments *e:* **MICE**

Monitoring [of] the Sun-Earth Environment [International Council of Scientific Unions] *e:* **MONSEE**

Monitoring River Health *e:* **MRH**

Monitoring River Health Initiative *e:* **MRHI**

Monitoring Transport of Ocean Currents *e:* **MTOC**

Monmouth County Medical Society. Newsletter *e:* **Monmnuth County Med S Newsletter**

Monograph. British Crop Protection Council e: **MonogrBr Crop Prot Counc**

Monograph. Geological Survey of Alabama e: **Monogr Geol Surv Alabama**

Monographiae Biologicae l: **Monographiae Biol**, l: **Monogr Biol**

Monographie Annuelle. Société Francaise de Biologie Clinique f: **Monogr Annu Soc Fr Biol Clin**

Monographies Medicales et Scientifiques f: **Monogr Med Sci**

Monographs. Academy of Natural Sciences of Philadelphia e: **Monogr Acad Nat Sci Phila**

Monographs and Surveys in Water Resource Engineering e: **Monographs Surveys Water Res Engrg**

Monographs in Developmental Biology e: **Monogr Dev Biol**

Monographs in Population Biology e: **Monographs Population Biol**, e: **Monogr Popul Biol**

Monographs on Nuclear Medicine and Biology e: **Monogr Nucl Med Biol**

Monographs on Nuclear Medicine and Biology Series e: **Monogr Nucl Med Biol Ser**

Monographs on Oceanographic Methodology e: **Monogr Oceanogr Methodol**

Monopoles, Astrophysics, and Cosmic Ray Observatory e: **MACRO**

Monroe Community Hospital, Medical-Nursing Library, Rochester e: **VQU**

Monroe County Department of Health, Library, Rochester e: **VQV**

Monroe County Pure Water Agency e: **MCPWA**

Monsoon Climatological Index e: **MCI**

Montana Bureau of Mines and Geology e: **MBMG**

Montana Energy and Magneto-Hydro-dynamics Research Institute e: **MERDI**

Montana Veterinary Medical Association e: **MVMA**

Montana Water Resources Research Center e: **MWRRC**

Montane Spruce [Biogeoclimatic] Zone e: **MS**

Montangeologie d: **Montangeol.**

Monte Vista National Wildlife Refuge e: **MVNP**, e: **MVNWR**

Montefiore Hospital and Medical Center e: **MHMC**

Montezuma National Wildlife Refuge e: **MNWR**

Monthly Bulletin. Emergency Pubtic Health Laboratory Service [Great Britain] e: **Mon Bull Emerg Public Health Lab Serv**

Monthly Bulletin. Ministry of Health and the Public Health Laboratory e: **Mon Bull Minist Health Public Health Lab**

Monthly Bulletin. Ministry of Health and the Public Health Laboratory Service [England] e: **Mon Bull Minist Health Public Health Lab Serv**

Monthly Bulletin. Ministry of Mines and Hydrocarbons [Caracas] e: **Mon Bull Minst Mines Hydrocarbons [Caracas]**

Monthly Bulletin of thc Ministry of Health and the Public Health Laboratory Service e: **MBMH**

Monthly Climate Data for the World e: **MCDW**

Monthly Depot Space and Operating Report e: **MDSOR**

Monthly Health Bulletin e: **Mon Health Bull**

Monthly Index of Medical Specialities e: **MIMS**

Monthly Vital Statistics Report. Health Interview Survey e: **Vital S HI**

Monthly Vital Statistics Report. Health Statistics e: **Vital S HS**

Monthly Weather Review e: **Mon. Weather Rev.**, e: **M WeatherR**, e: **M Weath Rer**

montieren d: **mont.**

montiert d: **mont.**

Montierung d: **Mont.**

Montserrat Volcano Observatory e: **MVO**

Moon-Earth-Plane e: **MEP**

Moon Landing Site e: **MLS**

Moon Orbiting Observatory e: **MORO**

Moore School Air Space Simulation Effort e: **MASE**

Moosehorn National Wildlife Refuge e: **MNWR**

MORS [Monitoring of Radioactive Substances in the Baltic Sea] Project e: **MORS-PRO**

Mort Naturelle f: **MN**

Mortier a Injection Regeneratrice d'Ergol Liquide f: **MIREL**

Morton Wildlife Refuge e: **MWR**

Most Intense Earthquake e: **MIE**

Most Probable Earthquake e: **MPE**

Mother and Child Health Centre[s] e: **M.C.H.**

Motion Picture & Medical Television Department e: **MP&MTD**

Motor Water Lighter e: **MWL**

Motorpferdestärke d: **Mot. PS**, d: **MPS**

Motorpferdestärke/Stunde d: **MPS/h**

Mount Palomar Observatory e: **Mt P O**

Mount Sinai Journal of Medicine e: **Mt Sinai J Med**

Mount Sinai School of Medicine of the City University of New York, New York e: **VVL**

Mount Washington Observatory e: **MWO**

Mount Wilson Observatory e: **MtWO**, e: **MtW Obs.**, e: **MWO**

Mountain Climate Model e: **MT-CLIM**

Mountain Environment and Natural Resources Information System e: **MENRIS**

Mountain Sinai Medical Center e: **MSMC**

Mounted Battlespace Battle Lab e: **MBBL**

Mouvement d'Autodéfense des Usagers Routiers f: **MADUR**

Mouvement d'Écologie Politique f: **MEP**

Mouvement Guyanais de Décolonisation f: **Moguyde**

Mouvement Italien pour la Protection de la Nature f: **MIPN**

Movimento Italiano per la Protezione della Natura i: **MIPN**

Movimento Popolare Monarchico i: **MPM**

Movimiento Pro-Tierra s: **MPT**

Mt Hopkins Observatory e: **Hopkins**

Mt. Palomar Mountain Observatory near San Diego California e: **Palomar**

Mudamalai Wildlife Sanctuary e: **MWS**

Mullard Radio Astronomy Observatory e: **MRAO**

Mullard Space Science Laboratory e: **MSSL**

Multi-center Airborne Coherent Atmospheric Wind Sensor e: **MACAWS**

Multi-Channel Sea Surface Temperature e: **MCSST**

Multi-Cultural Environmental Science Education Centers e: **MESEC**

Multi-Dimensional Random Sea Facility e: **MDRSF**

Multi-Dimensional Reconstruction and Imaging in Medicine e: **MURIM**

Multi-disciplinary Interest in Rural and General Health Education e: **MIRAGE**

Multi-Effect Distillation plant for sea-water desalination e: **MED**

Multi Language Environment e: **MLE**, e: **MLEM**

Multi-Leaving Remote Terminal Processor e: **MLRTP**

Multi-Module Space Station e: **MMSS**

Multi Observation Satellite Image Correction System e: **MOSAICS**

Multi-purpose Electromagnetic Environment Simulator e: **MEES**

Multi-Unit Space Transport and Recovery Device e: **MUSTARD**

Multi-user Object-Oriented environment e: **MOO**

Multichannel Ocean Colour Sensor e: **MOCS**

Multicultural Association of Medical Interpreters of Central New York e: **MAMI**

Multicultural Health Communication Service e: **MHCS**

Multidisciplinary Earth Observation Satellite System e: **MEOS**

Multidisciplinary Integrated Research Activities in Complex Laboratory Environments e: **MIRACLE**

Multienvironmental Electron Microscope e: **MEM**

Multilateral Environmental Agreement[s] e: **MEA**

Multilateral Environmental Agreements e: **MEAs**

Multimedia Environment for Mobiles e: **MEMO**

Multimedia Environmental Pollutant (or Pollution) Assessment System e: **MEPAS**

Multimedia Remote Interactive Electronic Documents e: **MURIEL**

Multimedial Medical Diagnostic Assistant e: **MEDICA**

Multimission Modular Spacecraft e: **MMS**

Multiphase Analysis of Groundwater, Nonaqueous Phase Liquid, Chemical and Soluble Components in Three Dimensions e: **MAGNAS3**

Multiphase Atmospheric Chemistry e: **MAC**

Multiphasic Health Testing Centre e: **MHTC**

Multiple Access Space Test Inertia Facility e: **MASTIF**

Multiple Earthed Neutral e: **M.E.N.**

Multiple Environment Overstress Tests e: **MEOST**

Multiple Environment Real Time *e:*
MERT

Multiple Experiment Transporter into Earth
Orbit and Return *e:* **METEOR**

Multiple Input Signature Register *e:* **MISR**

Multiple Mirror Telescope Observatory *e:*
MMTO

Multiple Opening Closing Net [and]
Environmental Sampling System *e:*
MOCNESS

Multiple Orbit/Multiple Satellite *e:*
MOMS

Multiple Orbit[al] Bombardment System
e: **MOBS**

Multiple Protective Earthing *e:* **m.p.e.**

Multiple Remote Terminal Unit *e:* **MRTU**

Multipulse Observation Sizing Technique
[Southwest Research Institute] *e:* **MOST**

Multipurpose In-Space Throttleable Engine
e: **MIST**

Multisensor module of the space station
MIR *e:* **PRIRODA**

Multiservice Health Facility Association *e:*
MSHFA

Multispectral Airborne System for
Environmental Research *e:* **MASER**

Multispectral Data Analysis System for
Earth Resources *e:* **MDASER**

Multistack Meteorological Model in EPA
UNAMAP Series *e:* **PTMTP**

Multistage Atmospheric Power Production
Pollution Study *e:* **MAP3S**

Multistate Atmospheric Power Production
Pollution Study/Precipitation Chemistry
Network *e:* **MAP3S/PCN**

Multitype Branching Process in a Random
Environment *e:* **MBPRE**

Münchener Medizin Mechanik *d:* **MMM**

Münchener Medizinische Wochenschrift
d: **MMW**, *d:* **Mü.M.W.**, *d:* **München.
Med. Wochenschr.**

Münchener Tierärztliche Gesellschaft *d:*
MTG

Münchner Notierungen *d:* **MN**

Municipal Environmental Research
Laboratory *e:* **MERL**

Municipal Waste Water *e:* **MWW**

Murmansk Association Sevmorgeologia *e:*
MAGE

Murmansk Marine Biological Institute,
Kola Scientific Centre, Russian Academy
of Sciences *e:* **MMBI KNC RAN**

Murmansk Regional Environmental Affairs
Committee *e:* **MREAC**

Murray-Darling Freshwater Research
Centre *e:* **MDFRC**

Murray Geological Basin Native Vegetation
Clearance Policy *e:* **MGBNVCP**

Museo de Biologia de la Universidad
Central de Venezuela *s:* **MBUCV**

Museo del Instituto Oceanografico de la
Universidad de Oriente *s:* **MIOUDO**

Museo Nacional de Historia Natural *s:*
MNHN

Museo Nacional de Historia Natural in
México *s:* **MNHNM**

Museum Association of the American
Frontier *e:* **MAAF**

Museum National d'Histoire Naturelle.
Notulae Systematicae *f:* **NOSYAV**

Museum of Man and Nature *e:* **MMN**

Museum of Natural History *e:* **MNH,** *e:*
Mus.Nat.Hist.

Museum of Practical Geology *e:* **M.P.G.**

Museum of Southwestern Biology *e:* **MSB**

Museum of the International College of
Surgeons *e:* **MICS**

Musée Océanographique Monaco *f:* **MOM**

Muséum National d'Histoire Naturelle *f:*
M.N.H.N.

mutieren *d:* **mut.**

Mutual Climatic Range *e:* **MCR**

Mykrobiolchichniyi Zhurnal *R:*
Mykrobiol Zh

Myonj-Ji University. Journal of Natural
Science *e:* **Myonj-Ji Univ J Nat Sci**

Mysore. Department of Mines and Geology.
Geol Studies *e:* **Mysore Dep Mines
Geol Geol Stud**

Médecin de quartier *f:* **MQ**

Médecins Sans Frontières *f:* **M.S.F.**

Médecins Sans Frontières Belgium *f:*
MSF-B

Médecins Sans Frontières France *f:* **MSF-
F**

Médecins Sans Frontières Netherlands *f:*
MSF-H

Médecins Sans Frontières Spain *f:* **MSF-S**

Médicos Sin Fronteras *s:* **MSF**

Mélanges d'archéologie et d'histoire de
l'École Française de Rome *f:* **Mél.**

Mémoires de la Société vaudoise des
Sciences Naturelles *f:* **Mém. Soc. vaud.
Sci. Nat.,** *f:* **Mém. Soc. vaud. Sci. Nat.**

Métier *f:* **Met**

Métier Manuel *f:* **MM**

Météorologie Nationale *f:* **M.N.**

N

N-Hydroxysuccinimidyl Palmitate *e:*
NHSP

N-Methylhydroxylamine *e:* **NMH**

NAACOG: the Organization for Obstetric,
Gynecologic and Neonatal Nurses *e:*
NAACOG

Nachrichten der Arbeitsgemeinschaft für
das Gesundheitswesen *d:* **Nachr Arb
Gem Ges Wes**

Nachrichten der Deutschen Gesellschaft für
Natur- und Völkerkunde Ostasiens *d:*
NOAG

Nachrichten der Gesellschaft für Natur und
Völkerkunde Ostasiens *d:* **Nachr Ges N
Vk Ostas**

Nachrichten der Gesellschaft für Natur- und
Völkerkunde Ostasiens *d:* **NGNVO**

Nachrichten der Tropischen Medizin
[Tiflis] *d:* **Nachr Trop Med [Tiflis]**

Nachrichten. Gesellschaft der
Wissenschaften zu Göttingen.
Mathematisch-Physikalische Klasse.
Fachgruppe 6. Biologie *d:* **Nachr Ges
Wiss Göttingen Math Phys Kl
Fachgruppe 6**

Nachrichten. Gesellschaft der
Wissenschaften zu Göttingen.
Mathematisch-Physikalische Klasse.
Fachgruppe 4. Geologie *d:* **Nachr Ges
Wiss Göttingen Math Phys Kl
Fachgruppe 4**

Nachrichten. Gesellschaft der
Wissenschaften zu Göttingen.
Mathematisch-Physikalische Klasse.
Fachgruppe 2. Physik, Astronomie,
Geophysik, Technik *d:* **NWGPA**

Nachrichten. Naturwissenschaftliches
Museum der Stadt [Aschaffenburg] *d:*
**Nachr Naturwiss Mus Stadt
[Aschaffenburg],** *d:* **Nachr Naturw Mus
[Aschaffenb]**

NADGE [NATO Air Defense Ground
Environment] Policy Board *e:* **NPB**

Nadir Climate Interferometer Spectrometer
e: **NCIS**

Nagasaki Medical Journal *e:* **Nagasaki
Med J**

Nagoya Journal of Medical Science *e:* **Nag
J Med Sci,** *e:* **Nagoya J Med Sci**

Nagoya Medical Journal *e:* **Nagoya Med J**

Nagoya University. Department of Earth
Sciences. Collected Papers on Earth
Sciences *e:* **Nagoya Univ Dep Earth Sci
Collect Pap Earth Sci**

Nagoya University. Journal of Earth
Sciences *e:* **Nagoya Univ Jour Earth
Sci**

Nährung. Chemie, Biochemie,
Mikrobiologie, Technologie *d:* **Nähr**

Nairobi Journal of Medicine *e:* **Nairobi J
Med**

Namulonge Agrometeorology Station
[Uganda] *e:* **HUNA**

Nansen Environmental and Remote Sensing
Center *e:* **NERSC**

Nansen Remote Sensing Centre *e:* **NRSC**

Nanyang University. Journal. Part III.
Natural Sciences *e:* **Nanyang Univ J
Part III**

Narrative, Immersive, Collaborative
Environment *e:* **NICE**

Narrow Coverage/Area Coverage to Earth
Coverage *e:* **NC/AC-EC**

NAS [National Academy of Sciences]
Committee for International
Environmental Programs *e:* **IEPC**

NAS [National Academy of Sciences]
Committee on Atmospheric Science *e:*
NASCAS

NAS [National Academy of Sciences]
Committee on Oceanography *e:* **NASCO**

NAS [National Academy of
Sciences]/Committee on Water *e:*
NAS/COW

NASA Climate Data System *e:* **NCDS**

NASA Earth Resources Data Annotation
System *e:* **NERDAS**

NASA [National Aeronautics and Space *e:*
NMI

NASA [National Aeronautics and Space
Administration] Aerospace Safety
Information Systems *e:* **NASIS**

NASA [National Aeronautics and Space
Administration] Communications
Network *e:* **NASCOM Network**

NASA [National Aeronautics and Space
Administration] Conference Publication
e: **NASA Conf Publ**

NASA [National Aeronautics and Space
Administration] Contractor Report *e:*
NASA Contract Rep, *e:* **NSCRA**

NASA [National Aeronautics and Space
Administration] Document *e:* **ND**

NASA [National Aeronautics and Space
Administration] Dryden Flight Research
Center *e:* **NASA DFRC**

NASA [National Aeronautics and Space
Administration] Energy-Cost Analysis
Program *e:* **NECAP**

NASA [National Aeronautics and Space Administration]/ Environmental Data Centre e: **NASA/EDC**

NASA [National Aeronautics and Space Administration]/ Goddard Space Flight Center e: **NASA/GSFC**

NASA [National Aeronautics and Space Administration]-Kennedy Space Center e: **NASA-KSC**

NASA [National Aeronautics and Space Administration] Large Space Telescope e: **NASA LST**

NASA [National Aeronautics and Space Administration]-Manned Spacecraft Center e: **NASA-MSC**

NASA [National Aeronautics and Space Administration] Marshall Space Flight Center e: **NASA-MSFC**

NASA [National Aeronautics and Space Administration] Memorandum e: **NASA Memo**

NASA [National Aeronautics and Space Administration] Planning Studies e: **NPS**

NASA [National Aeronautics and Space Administration] Policy Directive e: **NPD**

NASA [National Aeronautics and Space Administration] Procurement Circular e: **NPC**

NASA [National Aeronautics and Space Administration] Publication Control e: **NPC**

NASA [National Aeronautics and Space Administration] Quality Control e: **NQC**

NASA [National Aeronautics and Space Administration] Reference Publication e: **NASA Ref Publ**

NASA [National Aeronautics and Space Administration] Scientific and Technical Aerospace Reports e: **NASA STAR**

NASA [National Aeronautics and Space Administration]/ Scientific and Technical Information Facility e: **NASA/STIF**

NASA [National Aeronautics and Space Administration] Space Network e: **NSN**

NASA [National Aeronautics and Space Administration] Special Publications e: **NASA Spec Publ**, e: **NSSPA**

NASA [National Aeronautics and Space Administration] Test Support e: **NTS**

NASA [National Aeronautics and Space Administration] Unmanned Launch Operation[s] e: **NULO**

NASA [National Aeronautics and Space Administration]/ VAFB [Vandenberg Air Force Base] Payload Operations Working Group e: **NVPOWG**

NASA National Space Science Data Center e: **NNSDC**

NASA Ocean Data Service e: **NODS**

NASA Ocean Data System e: **NODS**

NASA Orbital Debris Observatory e: **NODO**

NASA Orbital Support Plan e: **NOSP**

NASA Polar [Orbiting] Platform e: **NPOP**

NASA Resource Protection e: **NRP**

NASA Space and Earth Sciences Computing Center e: **NSESCC**

Nassau County Medical Center, Plainview Division, Plainview e: **NPIMC**

Nassauischer Verein für Naturkunde. Jahrbücher d: **Nassauischer Ver Naturk Jb**

NASTRAN [National Aeronautics and Space Administration Structural Analysis] Systems Management Office e: **NSMO**

Natal/KwaZulu Association for Geographical Information Systems e: **NAGIS**

Natal Medical Corps e: **NMC**

Nation River Observatory e: **NRO**

Nationaal Verbond der Geteisterden van België n: **N.V.G.B.**

Nationaal Werk van de Oudstrijders [Verzetsstrijders, Politieke Gevangenen, Weggevoerden en Werkweigeraars] n: **N.W.O.S.**

National Aboriginal Health Organisation e: **NAHO**

National Academy of Clinicians and Holistic Health e: **NACH**

National Academy of Engineering Aeronautics and Space Engineering Board e: **NAE-ASEB**

National Academy of Engineering Committee on Ocean Engineering e: **NAECOE**

National Academy of Engineering Navy Environmental Protection Program Study Group e: **NAE-NEPP**

National Academy of Geosciences e: **NAG**

National Academy of Medical Sciences [India]. Annals e: **Natl Acad Med Sci [India] Ann**

National Academy of Sciences. Committee on Polar Research. Report of United States Antarctic Research Activities. Report e: **Natl Acad Sci Comm Polar Res Rep US Antarc Res Act**

National Academy of Sciences/Environmental Studies Board e: **NAS/ESB**

National Academy of Sciences/Geophysical Research Board e: **NAS/GRB**

National Academy of Sciences Institute of Medicine e: **IOM**

National Academy of Sciences/Ocean Affairs Board e: **NAS/OAB**

National Academy of Sciences/Ocean Sciences Board e: **NAS/OSB**

National Accreditation Commission for Schools and Colleges of Acupuncture and Oriental Medicine e: **NACSCAOM**

National Accreditation Council for Environmental Health Curricula e: **NACEHC**

National Acupuncture and Oriental Medicine Alliance e: **NAOMA**

National Adolescent Reproductive Health Partnership e: **NARHP**

National Advisory Committee for/on Environmental Policy and Technology e: **NACEPT**

National Advisory Committee on Health Manpower e: **NACHM**

National Advisory Committee on Microbiological Criteria for Foods e: **NACMCF**

National Advisory Committee on Occupational Safety and Health e: **NACOSH**

National Advisory Committee on Oceanography e: **NACO**

National Advisory Committee on Oceans and Atmosphere e: **NACOA**

National Advisory Committee on Research in the Geological Sciences e: **Natl Advisory Comm Research Geol Sci**

National Advisory Committee on Water Resources Research e: **NACWRR**

National Advisory Council on Occupational and Environmental Health e: **NACOEH**

National Advisory Health Council e: **NAHC**

National Aerometic Data Bank [Evironmental Protection Agency] e: **NADB**

National Aerometric Data Information System [Environmental Protection Agency] e: **NADIS**

National Aeronautical and Space Administration, Institute for Space Studies, New York e: **NNNASA**

National Aeronautics and Space Administration e: **NAA**

National Aeronautics and Space Administration Act e: **NASAA**

National Aeronautics and Space Administration, Johnson Space Center, Houston e: **NAJ**

National Aeronautics and Space Administration, Langley Research Center, Hampton e: **ViHaNASA**

National Aeronautics and Space Administration, Lewis Research Center, Cleveland e: **OCINASA**

National Aeronautics and Space Administration, Manned Spacecraft Center, Technical Library, Houston e: **TxHNASA**

National Aeronautics and Space Council e: **NASC**

National Aerospace and Defense Contractors Accreditation Procedures e: **NADCAP**

National Aerospace Development Agency of Japan e: **NASDA**

National Aerospace Education Council e: **NAEC**

National Aerospace Electronics Conference. Proceedings e: **Natl Aerosp Electron Conf Proc**

National Aerospace Laboratory e: **NAL**, e: **NLR**

National Aerospace Research Laboratory e: **NARL**

National Aerospace Standards Committee e: **NASC**

National AHEC [Area Health Education Centers] Organization e: **NAO**

National Air [and] Radiation Environmental Laboratory e: **NAREL**

National Air and Space Museum Library e: **NASML**

National Air Data Branch [Environmental Protection Agency] e: **NADB**

National Air Raid Precautions Animals Committee e: **NARPAC**

National Airspace Analysis e: **NAA**

National Airspace Communications System e: **NASCOM**

National Airspace Data Interchange Network e: **NADIN**

National Airspace Performance Reporting System e: **NAPRS**

National Airspace System Performance Analysis Capability e: **NASPAC**

National Airspace System Program Office
  e: **NASPO**
National Alliance for Animal Legislation
  e: **NAAL**
National Alliance for Hydroelectric Energy
  e: **NAHE**
National Ambient Water Quality Criteria
  e: **NAWQC**
National Ambulatory Medical Care Survey
  e: **NAMCS**
National Analytical Facility [National
  Oceanic and Atmospheric Administration]
  e: **NAF**
National and Aviation Meteorological
  Faxmile Network *e:* **NAMFAX**
National Animal Control Association *e:*
  NACA
National Animal Damage Control
  Association *e:* **NADCA**
National Animal Disease Center (or Centre)
  e: **NADC**
National Animal Disease Laboratory *e:*
  NADL
National Animal Genome Research Program
  e: **NAGRP**
National Animal Health Information System
  e: **NAHIS**
National Animal Health Monitoring
  System[s] *e:* **NAHMS**
National Animal Husbandry Research
  Institute *e:* **NAHRI**
National Animal Poison Control Center *e:*
  NAPCC
National Animal Serum Bank *e:* **NASB**
National Annual Medic Improvement
  Program *e:* **NAMIP**
National Archive for Computerized Data on
  Aging [Department of Health and Human
  Services] *e:* **NACDA**
National Asian Womens Health
  Organization *e:* **NAWHO**
National Assembly of Chief Livestock
  Health Officials *e:* **NACLHO**
National Assembly of National Voluntary
  Health and Social Welfare Organizations
  e: **NANVH & SWO**
National Assembly on School-Based Health
  Care *e:* **NASBHC**
National Association for BioMedical
  Research *e:* **NABR**
National Association for Biomedical
  Research *e:* **NARB**
National Association for Environmental
  Education *e:* **NAEE**
National Association for Healthcare Quality
  e: **NAHQ**
National Association for Humane and
  Environmental Education *e:* **NAHEE**
National Association for Medical
  Equipment Services *e:* **NAMES**
National Association for Mental Health *e:*
  NAMH
National Association for/of Black
  Geologists and Geophysicists *e:*
  NABGG
National Association for/of Healthcare
  Recruitment *e:* **NAHCR**
National Association for/on a Standard
  Medical Vocabulary *e:* **NASMV**
National Association for Public Health
  Statistics and Information Systems *e:*
  NAPHSIS

National Association for Rural Mental
  Health *e:* **NARMH**
National Association for Safety and Health
  in the Arts and Crafts *e:* **NASHAC**
National Association for Statewide Health
  and Welfare *e:* **NASHAW**
National Association for the Rescue of
  Animals *e:* **NARA**
National Association Medical Staff Services
  e: **NAMSS**
National Association of Advisers (or
  Advisors) for the Health Professions *e:*
  NAAHP
National Association of Advisors for the
  Health Professions *e:* **NAAPH**
National Association of Air National Guard
  Health Technicians *e:* **NAANGHT**
National Association of Animal Breeders
  e: **NAAB**
National Association of Biological
  Engineering *e:* **NABE**
National Association of Biology Teachers
  e: **NABT**
National Association of Community Health
  Centers *e:* **NACHC**
National Association of Continuing Medical
  Education Meetings and Seminars *e:*
  NACMEMS
National Association of County and City
  Health Officials *e:* **NACCHO**
National Association of County Health
  Facility Administrators *e:* **NACHFA**
National Association of County Health
  Officials *e:* **NACHO**
National Association of Emergency Medical
  Technicians *e:* **NAEMT**
National Association of Employers on
  Health Care Action *e:* **NAEHCA**
National Association of Employers on
  Health Care Alternatives *e:* **NAEHCA**
National Association of EMS [Emergency
  Medical Service] Educators *e:*
  NAEMSE
National Association of EMS [Emergency
  Medical Service] Physicians *e:*
  NAEMSP
National Association of Environmental
  Professionals *e:* **NAEP**
National Association of Flood and Storm
  Water Management Agencies *e:*
  NAFS[W|MA
National Association of Foreign Medical
  Graduates *e:* **NAFMG**
National Association of Geology Teachers
  e: **NAGT**
National Association of Geoscience
  Teachers *e:* **NAGT**
National Association of Health and Welfare
  Ministries of the United Methodist
  Church *e:* **NAHWMUMC**
National Association of Health Authorities
  e: **NAHA**
National Association of Health Authorities
  & Trusts *e:* **NAHAT**
National Association of Health Career
  Schools *e:* **NAHCS**
National Association of Health Data
  Organizations *e:* **NAHDO**
National Association of Health Services
  Executives *e:* **NAHSE**
National Association of Health
  Underwriters *e:* **NAHU**

National Association of Health Unit Clerks-
  Coordinators *e:* **NAHUC**
National Association of Healthcare
  Recruiters *e:* **NAHCR**
National Association of Home Health
  Agencies *e:* **NAHHA**
National Association of Inland Waterway
  Carriers *e:* **NAIWC**
National Association of Jewish Family,
  Children's and Health Professionals *e:*
  NAJFCHP
National Association of Jewish Family,
  Children's, and Health Services *e:*
  NACHES
National Association of Local Boards of
  Health *e:* **NALBOH**
National Association of Medical-Dental
  Bureaus *e:* **NAMDB**
National Association of Medical Examiners
  e: **NAME**
National Association of Medical Legal
  Nurse Consultants *e:* **NAMLNC**
National Association of Naturopathic
  Physicians *e:* **NANP**
National Association of Neighborhood
  Health Centers *e:* **NANHC**
National Association of Nurse Practitioners
  in Reproductive Health *e:* **NANPRH**
National Association of Nurse Practitioners
  in Women's Health *e:* **NPWH**
National Association of Occupational
  Health Nurses *e:* **NAOHN**
National Association of Physicians for the
  Environment *e:* **NAPE**
National Association of Postgraduate
  Medical Education Centre Administration
  e: **NAPMECA**
National Association of Precollege
  Directors *e:* **NAPD**
National Association of Professional
  Environmental Communicators *e:*
  NAPEC
National Association of Public Hospitals
  [and Health Systems] *e:* **NAPH**
National Association of Soft Water Service
  Operators *e:* **NASWSO**
National Association of Soil and Water
  Conservation Districts *e:* **NACD**
National Association of Specialist
  Obstetricians & Gynaecologists *e:*
  NASOG
National Association of State [and
  Territorial] Public Health Veterinarians
  e: **NASPHV**
National Association of State and
  Territorial Public Health Veterinarians
  e: **NASTPHV**
National Association of State Boards of
  Geology *e:* **NASBOG**
National Association of State
  Environmental Programs Agencies *e:*
  NASEPA
National Association of State Mental Health
  Program Directors *e:* **NASMHPD**
National Association of Water Companies
  e: **NAWC**
National Association of Water Institute
  Directors *e:* **NAWID**
National Association of Women's Health
  Professionals *e:* **NAWHP**
National Astronomical Observatory *e:*
  NAO

National Astronomical Observatory of Japan *e:* **NAOJ**

National Astronomical Space Observatory *e:* **NASO**

National Atmospheric Background Network *e:* **NABN**

National Atmospheric Data Bank *e:* **NADB**

National Atmospheric Deposition Program *e:* **NADP**

National Atmospheric Deposition Program/National Trends Network *e:* **NADP/NTN**

National Atmospheric Radiation Centre *e:* **NARC**

National Atmospheric Research Institute *e:* **NARI**

National Atmospheric Sciences Program *e:* **NASP**

National Atmospherie Chemistry Database *e:* **NATCHEM**

National Atomic Research Spaceship Testing and Information Bureau *e:* **NARSTI**

National Aviation Weather Advisory Committee *e:* **NAWAC**

National Aviation Weather Advisory Unit *e:* **NAWAU**

National Aviation Weather Processing Facility *e:* **NAWPF**

National Aviation Weather Products Generator *e:* **NAWPG**

National Aviation Weather Program Council *e:* **NAWPC**

National Aviation Weather Program Plan *e:* **NAWPP**

National Aviation Weather System *e:* **NAWS**

National Aviation Weather System Study *e:* **NAVWESS**

National Benchmark Network for Agrometeorology *e:* **NBNA**

National Biological Information Infrastructure *e:* **NBII**

National Biological Service *e:* **NBS**

National Biological Standards Laboratory *e:* **NBSL**

National Biological Survey *e:* **NABIS**

National Biological Survey, [National Bureau of Standards] *e:* **NBS**

National Biomedical Research Foundation *e:* **NBRF**

National Biomedical Sciences Instrumentation Symposium. Proceedings *e:* **Natl Biomed Sci Instrum Symp Proc**

National Biomedical Tracer Facility *e:* **NBTF**

National Black Health Planners Association *e:* **NBHPA**

National Black Women's Health Project *e:* **NBWHP**

National Board Examination Committee for Veterinary Medicine *e:* **NBEC**

National Board for Nursing, Midwifery and Health Visiting for Scotland *e:* **NBS**

National Board of Examiners for Osteopathic Physicians and Surgeons *e:* **NBEOPS**

National Board of Medical Examiners *e:* **NBME**

National Board of Osteopathic Medical Examiners *e:* **NBOME**

National Board of Podiatric Medical Examiners *e:* **NBPME**

National Board of Roads and Water *e:* **NBR**

National Bone Health Campaign *e:* **NBHC**

National Cartographic and Geographic Information Center *e:* **NCGIC**

National Cartographic Information Center [United States Geological Survey] *e:* **NCIC**

National Cat Protection Society *e:* **NCPS**

National Catholic Society for Animal Welfare *e:* **NCSAW**

National Center for a Barrier Free Environment *e:* **NCBFE**

National Center for Atmospheric Research *e:* **NCAR**

National Center for Atmospheric Research. Quarterly *e:* **NCAR Q**

National Center for Atmospheric Research Quarterly *e:* **NCAR Quarterly**

National Center for Atmospheric Research/University Corporation for Atmospheric Research *e:* **NCAR/UCAR**

National Center for Biomedical Communications *e:* **NCBC**

National Center for Chronic Disease Prevention and Health Promotion *e:* **NCCDPHP**

National Center for Complementary and Alternative Medicine *e:* **NCCAM**

National Center for Devices and Radiological Health *e:* **NCDRH**

National Center for Drugs and Biologics *e:* **NCDB**

National Center for Earthquake Engineering Research *e:* **NCEE**, *e:* **NCEER**

National Center for Earthquake Research *e:* **NCER**

National Center for Ecological Analysis and Synthesis *e:* **NCEAS**

National Center for Education in Maternal and Child Health *e:* **NCEMCH**

National Center for Emergency Medicine Informatics *e:* **NCEMI**

National Center for Environmental Assessment *e:* **NCEA**

National Center for Environmental Health *e:* **NCEH**

National Center for Environmental Health and Injury Control *e:* **NCEHIC**

National Center for Environmental Health Strategies *e:* **NCEHS**

National Center for Environmental Publications and Information *e:* **NCEPI**

National Center for Exploitation of the Oceans *e:* **NCEO**

National Center for Ground Water Research *e:* **NCGWR**

National Center for Health Care Technology *e:* **NCHCT**

National Center for Health Education *e:* **NCHE**

National Center for Health Promotion and Aging *e:* **NCHPA**

National Center for Health Services Research and Development *e:* **HSRD**, *e:* **NCHSR & D**

National Center for Health Services Research and Health Care Technology Assessment *e:* **NCHSR**

National Center for Health Statistics *e:* **NCHS**

National Center for Laboratory Animal Sciences *e:* **NCLAB**

National Center for Radiological Health *e:* **NCRH**

National Center for Synthesis in Experimental Biology *e:* **NCSEB**

National Center for the Advancement of Blacks in the Health Professions *e:* **NCABHP**

National Center for Urban and Industrial Health *e:* **NCUI[H]**

National Center for Urban Environmental Studies *e:* **NCUES**

National Center of Preventive and Stress Medicine *e:* **NCPSM**

National Center on Minority Health and Health Disparities *e:* **NCMHD**

National Center (or Centre) for Geographic Information and Analysis *e:* **NCGIA**

National Centers Advanced Weather Interactive Processing System *e:* **N-AWIPS**

National Centers for Health and Medical Information, Inc. *e:* **NCHMI**

National Center[s] (or Centre) for/of Environmental Prediction *e:* **NCEP**

National Central American Health Rights Network *e:* **NCAHRN**

National Centre for Classification in Health *e:* **NCCH**

National Centre for Epidemiology and Population Health *e:* **NCEPH**

National Centre for Fishery and Oceanographic Research (Mauritania) *e:* **CNROP**

National Centre for Human Settlements and Environment *e:* **NCHSE**

National Centre for Medium Range Weather Forecasting *e:* **NCMRWF**

National Centre for Oceanographic Study and Research (Morocco) *e:* **CNERO**

National Certification Agency for Medical Laboratory Personnel *e:* **NCA**

National Certification Commission for Acupuncture and Oriental Medicine *e:* **NCCAOM**

National Charting & Geodetic Survey *e:* **NC&GS**

National Chicano Health Organization *e:* **NCHO**

National Child Health and Education Study *e:* **NCHES**

National Children's Dental Health Month *e:* **NCDHM**

National Citizens Committee for the World Health Organization *e:* **NCCWHO**

National Clearinghouse for Mental Health Education *e:* **NCMHE**

National Clearinghouse for Mental Health Information *e:* **NCMHI**

National Clearinghouse on Family Violence, Health and Welfare Canada, Ottawa, Ontario *e:* **OONHFV**

National Clearinghouse on Tobacco and Health *e:* **NCTH**

National Climate and Global Change Program *e:* **NCGCP**

National Climate Archive *e:* **NCA**

National Climate Center (or Centre) *e:* **NCC**

National Climate Climotological Center *e:* **NCCC**

National Climate (or Climatic) Data Center (or Centre) *e:* **NCDC**

National Climate Program Coordinating Office *e:* **NCPCO**

National Climate Program Office *e:* **NCPO**

National Climate Program[me] *e:* **NCP**

National Climate Project Office *e:* **NCPO**

National Climate Research Committee *e:* **NCRC**

National Climatic Center, Ashville *e:* **OAQ**

National Climatic Research Program *e:* **NCRP**

National Climatological Center *e:* **NCA**

National Clinical Mental Health Counseling Examination *e:* **NCMHCE**

National Coalition for Disease Prevention and Environmental Health *e:* **NCDPEH**

National Coalition for Health Professional Education in Genetics *e:* **NCHPEG**

National Coalition of Hispanic Health and Human Services Organizations *e:* **NCHHSO**

National Coalition of Hispanic Mental Health and Human Services Organizations *e:* **NCHMHHSO**

National Coalition on Health Care *e:* **NCHC**

National Coalition to Stop Food and Water Irradiation *e:* **NCSFWI**

National College of Foot Surgeons *e:* **NCFS**

National Collegiate Emergency Medical Services Foundation *e:* **NCEMSF**

National Commission for Health Certifying Agencies *e:* **NCHCA**

National Commission for Health Education Credentialing *e:* **NCHEC**

National Commission for Wildlife Conservation and Development *e:* **NCWCD**

National Commission on Allied Health Education *e:* **NCAHE**

National Commission on Community Public Health Services *e:* **NCCHS**

National Commission on Confidentiality of Health Records *e:* **NCCHR**

National Commission on Correctional Health Care *e:* **NCCHC**

National Commission on Radiological Protection *e:* **NCRP**

National Commission on Space Research *e:* **CNIE**

National Commission on Water Quality *e:* **NCWQ**

National Commission to Preserve Social Security and Medicare *e:* **NCPSSM**

National Committee for Careers in Medical Technology *e:* **NCCMT**

National Committee for Careers in the Medical Laboratory *e:* **NCCML**

National Committee for Climate Change and Atmospheric Sciences *e:* **NCCAS**

National Committee for Oceanic Sciences *e:* **NCOS**

National Committee for/on Oceanographic Research *e:* **NCOR**

National Committee for/on Space Research *e:* **NCSR**

National Committee for/on Vital and Health Statistics *e:* **NCVHS**

National Committee for Quality Health Care *e:* **NCQHC**

National Committee for the Environment *e:* **NCE**

National Committee on Agrometeorology *e:* **NCA**

National Committee on Geographic Names *e:* **KPMA**

National Committee on Human Dimensions of Global Environmental Change *e:* **NHDP**

National Committee on Maternal Health *e:* **NCMH**

National Committee (or Council) for Geodesy and Geophysics *e:* **NCGG**

National Committee (or Council) on Radiation Protection and Measurement[s] *e:* **NCRPM**

National Compendium of Freshwater Fish & Water Temperature Data *e:* **FISHTEM**

National Conference for Cooperation in Health Education *e:* **NCCHE**

National Conference for Individual Onsite Wastewater Systems. Proceedings *e:* **Natl Conf Individ Onsite Wastewater Syst Proc**

National Conference of Health, Welfare and Pension Plans, Trustees and Administrators *e:* **NCHWPPTA**

National Conference of Local Environmental Health Administrators *e:* **NCLEHA**

National Conference on Earth Science. Papers [Alberta University] *e:* **Natl Conf Earth Sci Pap [Alberta Univ]**

National Conference on Mental Health Statistics *e:* **NCMHS**

National Conference on Standards for Environmental Improvement *e:* **NCSEI**

National Conference on the Challenge of Health and Safety *e:* **NCCHS**

National Congress of Animal Trainers and Breeders *e:* **NCATB**

National Consortium for Child Mental Health Services *e:* **NCCMHS**

National Consortium of/on Health Science and Technology Education *e:* **NCHSTE**

National Consultative Committee on Animal Welfare *e:* **NCCAW**

National Coordinating Centre for Health Technology Assessment *e:* **NCCHTA**

National Coordinating Committee for/on Aviation Meteorology [Federal Coordinating Group] *e:* **NACCAM**

National Coordinating Committee on Human Environment *e:* **NCCHE**

National Council Against Health Fraud *e:* **NCAHF**

National Council for Animal Welfare *e:* **NCAW**

National Council for Community Behavioral Healthcare *e:* **NCCBH**

National Council for Environmental Balance *e:* **NCEB**

National Council for Geocosmic Research *e:* **NCGR**

National Council for Geographic Education *e:* **NCGA**

National Council for Geographie Education *e:* **NCGE**

National Council for/of Health Care Services *e:* **NCHCS**

National Council for/on International Health *e:* **NCIH**

National Council for Reliable Health Information *e:* **NCRHI**

National Council of Community Mental Health Centers *e:* **NCCMHC**

National Council of Geography Teachers *e:* **NCGT**

National Council of Health Centers *e:* **NCHC**

National Council of Homemakers and Home Health Aids *e:* **NCHHA**

National Council of/on Radiation Protection [and Measurement[s]] *e:* **NCRP**

National Council of State Emergency Medical Services Training Coordinators *e:* **NCSEMSTC**

National Council of the Paper Industry for Air and Stream Improvement. Atmospheric Pollution Technical Bulletin *e:* **NCASI Atm Poll Tech Bull**

National Council of the Paper Industry for Air and Stream Improvement. Technical Bulletin. Atmospheric Quality Improveme *e:* **NCASI Tech Bull Atmos Qual Improv Tech Bull**

National Council on Alternative Health Care Policy *e:* **NCAHCP**

National Council on Graduate Medical Education *e:* **NCGME**

National Council on Health Laboratory Services *e:* **NCHLS**

National Council on Health Planning and Development *e:* **NCHPD**

National Council on Medical Technology Education *e:* **NCMTE**

National Council on Naturalization and Citizenship *e:* **NCONAC**

National Council on Radiation Protection and Measurements *e:* **CRP**

National Council on Radiation Protection and Measurements. Annual Meeting *e:* **Natl Counc Radiat Prot Meas Annu Meet**

National Council on Wholistic Therapeutics and Medicine *e:* **NCWTM**

National Crop Protection Center *e:* **NCPC**

National Defence Medical Centre, Department of National Defence Ottawa, Ontario *e:* **OONDM**

National Defence (or Defense) Medical Center (or Centre) *e:* **NDMC**

National Defense Medical Journal [Tokyo] *e:* **Natl Def Med J [Tokyo]**

National Demonstration Water Project *e:* **NDWP,** *e:* **NWP**

National Dental Health Conference *e:* **Natl Dent Health Conf**

National Diploma in Health *e:* **NDH**

National Disaster Medical Operations Center *e:* **NDMOC**

National Disaster Medical System *e:* **NDMS**

National Disaster Medical System Operations Support Center *e:* **NDMSOSC**

National d'Observation des Polluants Atmosphériques *f:* **NABEL**

National Drinking Water Advisory Council *e:* **NDWAC**

National Earth Observation[s] Center *e:* **NEOC**

National Earth Satellite Data and Information System *e:* **NESDIS**

National Earth Satellite Service *e:* **NESS**

National Earth Science Teachers
   Association e: **NESTA**

National Earth Shelter Builders Association
   e: **NESBA**

National Earthquake Early Reporting
   System e: **NEERS**

National Earthquake Hazard[s] Reduction
   Program e: **NEHRP**

National Earthquake Information Center e:
   NEIC

National Earthquake Information Service
   e: **NEIS**

National Earthquake loss reduction Program
   e: **NEP**

National Earthquake Prediction Evaluation
   Council e: **NEPEC**

National Earthquake Strategy Working
   Group e: **NESW**

National Eclectic Medical Quarterly e:
   Natl Eclectic Med Q

National Ecological Research Laboratory
   e: **NERL**

National Ecology Center e: **NEC**

National Ecology Research Center e:
   NERC

National Education Center for
   Paraprofessionals in Mental Health e:
   NEC

National Education, Health and Allied
   Workers' Union e: **NEHAWU**

National Electronic Library for Health e:
   NeLH

National Emergency Medical Service e:
   N.E.M.S.

National Emergency Medical Services
   Information Network e: **NEMSINET**

National Emergency Medicine Political
   Action Committee e: **NEMPAC**

National EMS [Emergency Medical
   Service] Pilots Association e:
   NAEMSPA, e: **NEMSPA**

National Energy Protection Board e:
   NEPB

National Enginemen and Firemen's
   Protection Society e: **NEFPS**

National Environment and Renewable
   Natural Resources Institute e: **IBAMA**

National Environment Awareness Trust e:
   NEAT

National Environment Fund [Bolivia] e:
   FONAMA

National Environment Management Plans
   e: **NEMPs**

National Environment Management
   Strategies (or Strategy) program e:
   NEMS

National Environment Policy Plan e:
   NEPP

National Environment Protection Authority
   e: **NEPA**

National Environment Protection Council
   e: **NEPC**

National Environment Protection Measure
   e: **NEPM**

National Environment Protection Measures
   e: **NEPMs**

National Environment Protection Plan e:
   NEPP

National Environment Resource Council e:
   NERC

National Environment, Satellite, Data [and]
   Information Service e: **NESDIS**

National Environment Secretariat e: **NES**

National Environment[al] Action Plan e:
   NEAP

National Environmental Action Plans e:
   NEAPs

National Environmental Balancing Bureau
   e: **NEBB**

National Environmental Board e: **NEB**

National Environmental Controls, Inc. e:
   NECT

National Environmental Council e:
   CONAM, e: **CONEN**

National Environmental Council [Peru] e:
   CONAM

National Environmental Data and
   Information Service e: **NEDIS**

National Environmental Data Referential
   Service e: **NEDRES**

National Environmental Data Referral
   Service e: **NESDRES**

National Environmental Development
   Association e: **NEDA**

National Environmental Development
   Association/Ground Water Project e:
   NEDA/GRND

National Environmental Development
   Association Groundwater Project e:
   NEDA/Ground

National Environmental Education
   Development [Program of National Park
   Service] e: **NEED**

National Environmental Education
   Landmarks [Department of the Interior]
   e: **NEEL**

National Environmental Enforcement
   Council e: **NEEC**

National Environmental Enforcement
   Journal e: **NEEJ**

National Environmental Engineering
   Research Institute e: **NEERI**

National Environmental Group e: **NEG**

National Environmental Group, Inc. e:
   NATENV

National Environmental Health Action Plan
   e: **NEHAP**

National Environmental Health Association
   e: **NEHA**

National Environmental Indicators
   Programme e: **NEIP**

National Environmental Information
   Symposium e: **NEIS**

National Environmental Laboratories e:
   NELS

National Environmental Monitoring and
   Prediction System e: **NEMPS**

National Environmental Performance
   Partnership System e: **NEPPS**

National Environmental Policy e: **NEP**

National Environmental Policy Act e:
   NEPA, e: **NEPAN**

National Environmental Policy
   Act/categorical exclusion e: **NEPA-CX**

National Environmental Policy
   Administration e: **NEPA**

National Environmental Policy Institute e:
   NEPI

National Environmental Protection Act e:
   NEPA, e: **NEPAN**

National Environmental Protection Agency
   e: **NEPA**

National Environment[al] Research Center
   (or Centre) e: **NERC**

National Environmental Research Institute
   e: **NERI**

National Environmental Research Park e:
   NEPP, e: **NEPR**, e: **NERP**

National Environmental Research Park
   System e: **ParkNet**

National Environmental Satellite Center e:
   NESC

National Environmental Satellite Center
   Technical Memoranda e: **NESCTM**

National environmental Satellite data and
   Information service e: **NSI**

National Environmental Satellite Data
   Information System e: **NESDIS**

National Environment[al] Satellite Service
   e: **NESS**

National Environmental Services
   Administration Committee e: **NFSAC**

National Environmental Specialist
   Association e: **NESA**

National Environmental Specimen Bank e:
   NESB

National Environment[al] Studies Project
   e: **NESP**

National Environmental Study Area[s] e:
   NESA

National Environmental Supercomputing
   Center e: **NESC**

National Environmental Systems
   Contractors Association e: **NESCA**

National Environmental Technology
   Applications Corporation e: **NETAC**

National Environmental Training
   Association e: **NETA**

National Environmental Trust Fund e:
   NETF

National Examining Board in Occupational
   Safety and Health e: **NEBOSH**

National Extreme Weather Systems e:
   NEWS

National Eye and Health Foundation e:
   NEHF

National Eye Health Education Program e:
   NEHEP

National Family Planning and Reproductive
   Health Association e: **NFPRHA**

National Federation of Cold Storage and Ice
   Trades e: **NFCSIT**

National Fertilizer and Environmental
   Research Center e: **NFERC**

National Fish and Wildlife Foundation e:
   NFWF, e: **NMFWF**

National Fish and Wildlife Service e:
   NFWS

National Fish Health Research Laboratory
   e: **NFHRL**

National Flotation Health Care Foundation
   e: **NFHCF**

National Foot Health Council e: **NFHC**

National Forum on Hospital and Health
   Affairs e: **Natl Forum Hosp Health Aff**

National Foundation for Conservation and
   Environmental Officers e: **NFCEO**

National Foundation for Environmental
   Control e: **NFEC**

National Foundation for Health, Physical
   Education and Recreation e: **NFHPER**

National Foundation for Long Term Health
   Care e: **NFLTHC**

National Foundation for Research in
   Medicine e: **NFRM**

National Foundation for Rural Medical Care
   e: **NFRMC**

National Fund for Environmental Protection
   and Water Management e: **NFEPWM**

National Fund for Medical Education e:
NFME
National Geo Data Information e: **NGDI**
National Geochemical Data Bank e:
NGDB
National Geodetic and Cartographic Service
  e: **NGCS**
National Geodetic Data Base e: **NGDB**
National Geodetic Information Branch e:
NGIB
National Geodetic Information Center e:
NGIC
National Geodetic Reference System e:
NGRS
National Geodetic Satellite Program e:
NGSP
National Geodetic Survey e: **NGS**
National Geodetic Survey Information
  Center e: **NGSIC**
National Geodetic Survey Operations
  Center e: **NGSCO**
National Geodetic Vertical Datum e:
NGVD
National Geographic Atlas of the World e:
NGAW
National Geographic Data Center e:
NGDC
National Geographic Magazine e: **Nat
Geog**, e: **Nat.Geog.M.**, e: **Nat Geog
Mag**, e: **Nat Geog[r] M[ag]**, e: **Natl
Geogr[aphic] Mag**, e: **Natl Geogr Mag**,
e: **Natn Geogr Mag**, e: **N.Geo.M.**, e:
NGM
National Geographic Magazine. National
  Geographic Society e: **NGS/NGM**
National Geographic Names Data Base e:
NGN
National Geographic Research e: **NAGR**,
e: **Nat Geog R**, e: **NatGeogRes**, e: **Natl
Geogr Res**, e: **NGREEG**
National Geographic Society Education
  Foundation e: **NGSEF**
National Geographic Society Library e:
NGSL
National Geographic Society. National
  Geographic Monographs e: **Nat Geog
Soc Nat Geog Mon**
National Geographic Society [or Service]
  e: **NGS**
National Geographic Society. Research
  Reports e: **Natl Geogr Soc Res Rep**
National Geographic World e: **Nat Geog
World**
National Geographical Association e:
NGA
National Geographical Journal of India
  [Varanasi] e: **Nat Geog J Ind**
National Geographical Society of India e:
NGSI
National Geography Institute e: **NGI**
National Geologic Map Database e:
NGMBD
National Geological Survey of China.
  Special Report e: **Natl Geol Surv China
Spec Rep**
National Geomagnetic Information Center
  e: **NGIC**
National Geophysical and Solar-Terrestrial
  Data Center e: **NGSDC**, e: **NGSTDC**
National Geophysical Data Center e:
NGDC
National Geophysical [Research] Institute
  e: **NGRI**

National Geophysical Research Institute
  [Hyderabad, India]. Bulletin e: **Natl
Geophys Res Inst [Hyderabad India]
Bull**
National Geoscience Mapping Agency e:
NGMA
National Geospatial Data Clearinghouse e:
NGDC
National Geospatial Data Files e: **NGDF**
National Ground Water Information Center
  e: **NGWIC**
National Ground Water Quality
  Symposium. Proceedings e: **Natl
Ground Water Qual Symp Proc**
National Health Accounts e: **NHA**
National Health Advisory Committees e:
NHAC
National Health Agencies e: **NHA**
National Health Agencies for the Combined
  Federal Campaign e: **NHACFC**
National Health and Environmental Effects
  Research Laboratory e: **NHEERL**
National Health and Medical Research
  Council e: **NHMR**, e: **NH&MRC**
National Health and Medical Research
  Council [Canberra]. Medical Research e:
**Natl Health Med Res Counc [Canberra]
Med Res**, e: **NHMDAP**
National Health and Medical Research
  Council [Canberra]. Medical Research
  Projects e: **Natl Health Med Res Counc
[Canberra] Med Res Proj**
National Health and Medical Research
  Council [Canberra]. Report e: **Natl
Health Med Res Counc [Canberra] Rep**
National Health and Medical Research
  Council of Australia e: **NHMRCA**
National Health and Nutrition Examination
  Study e: **NHANES**
National Health and Safety Awareness
  Center e: **NHSAC**
National Health and Welfare e: **NHW**
National Health and Welfare Retirement
  Association e: **NHWRA**
National Health Assembly e: **N.H.A.**
National Health Association e: **NHA**
National Health Awareness Center e:
NHAC
National Health Bill e: **N.H.B.**
National Health Board e: **NHB**
National Health Care Anti-Fraud
  Association e: **NHCAA**
National Health Care Campaign e: **NHCC**
National Health Care Corporation e:
NHCC
National Health Care Expenditures Study
  e: **NHCFS**
National Health Care for the Homeless
  Council e: **HCH**, e: **NHCHC**
National Health Care Foundation for the
  Deaf e: **NHCFD**
National Health Care Skill Standards
  Project e: **NHCSSP**
National Health Care Survey e: **NHCS**
National Health Care Systems, Inc. e:
NHCS
National Health Corporation e: **NHCC**
National Health Council e: **NHC**
National Health Data Advisory Council e:
NHDAC
National Health Education Foundation e:
NHEF

National Health Enhancement Systems, Inc.
  e: **NHES**
National Health Examination Survey e:
NHES
National Health Federation e: **NHF**
National Health Federation Bulletin e:
NHF Bull
National Health Foundation e: **NHF**
National Health Information Center e:
NHIC
National Health Information Clearinghouse
  e: **NHIC**
National Health Information
  Knowledgebase e: **NHIK**
National Health Information Resource
  Center e: **NHIRC**
National Health Information System of
  South Africa e: **NHIS/SA**
National Health Institute e: **NHI**
National Health Institute [Dominican
  Republic] e: **INSALUD**
National Health Insurance e: **NHI**
National Health Insurance Joint Committee.
  Medical Research Committee [Great
  Britain]. Special Report Series e: **Natl
Health Insur Jt Comm Med Res Comm
[GB] Spec Rep Ser**
National Health Insurance Reports e: **Natl
Health Insur Rep**
National Health Investors e: **NHI**
National Health Laboratories, Inc. e: **NH**
National Health Law Program e: **NHeLP**
National Health Lawyers Association e:
NHLA
National Health & Medical Research
  Council e: **NHMRC**
National Health Planning and Resource
  Development Act e: **NHRD**
National Health Planning Information
  Center e: **NHPIC**
National Health Policy Forum e: **NHPF**
National Health Professions Placement
  Network e: **NHPP**
National Health Provider Inventory e:
NHPI
National Health Research and Development
  Program e: **NHRDP**
National Health Resources Advisory
  Committee e: **NHRAC**
National Health Screening Council for
  Volunteer Organizations e: **NHSCVO**
National Health Service Act e: **NHSA**
National Health Service Administrative
  Register e: **NHSAR**
National Health Service Audit Staff e:
NHSAS
National Health Service Central Register
  e: **NHSCR**
National Health Service Corps e: **NHSC**
National Health Service Economic
  Evaluation Database e: **NHSEED**
National Health Service Ethical Health Unit
  e: **NHSEHU**
National Health Service Executive e:
NHSE
National Health Service for Coding and
  Classification e: **NHSCCC**
National Health Service in Scotland e:
NHS[S]
National Health Service Information
  Authority e: **NHSIA**
National Health Service Information Centre
  e: **NHSIMC**

National Health Service Litigation
  Authority e: **NHSLA**
National Health Service Management
  Executive e: **NHSME**
National Health Service Supplies e: **NHSS**
National Health Service Training
  Directorate e: **NHSTD**
National Health Service Training Unit e:
  NHSTU
National Health Service Trust e: **NHST**
National Health Service Trust Federation
  e: **NHSTF**
National Health Service-Wide Clearing
  Service e: **NWCS**
National Health Service[s] e: **NHS**
National Health Services Information
  Bulletin e: **Nat Health Serv Inf Bul**
National Health Society e: **N.H.S.**
National Health Statistics Center e: **NHSC**
National Health Survey Division e: **NHSD**
National Healthcare Antifraud Association
  e: **NHAS**
National Healthcare, Incorporated e:
  NHCI
National Healthcare Staffing Association
  e: **NHSA**
National Healthcorp Ltd. e: **NHC**
National Hellenic Oceanographic Society
  e: **NHOS**
National Hispanic Medical Association e:
  NHMA
National Home Health Care e: **NHHC**
National Hospital Health Care e: **Natl
  Hosp Health Care**
National Hurricane [and] Experimental
  Meteorology Laboratory e: **NHEML**
National Hydrography Dataset e: **NHD**
National Hydrology Research Center (or
  Centre) e: **NHRC**
National Hydrology Research Institute e:
  NHRI
National Hydrology Research Institute.
  Paper e: **NHRI Paper**
National Hydrology Rsearch Centre,
  Environment Canada Saskatoon,
  Saskatchewan e: **SSEH**
National Hydrometeorological
  Development System e: **NHDA**, e:
  NHDR, e: **NHDW**
National Hydropower Association e: **NHA**
National Ice Association e: **NIA**
National Ice Center (or Centre) e: **NIC**
National Ice Centre e: **NIC US**
National Ice Core Curatorial Facility e:
  NICCF
National Ice Core Laboratory e: **NICL**
National Ice Cream and Yogurt Retailers
  Association e: **NICYRA**
National Ice Cream Mix Association e:
  NICMA
National Ice Cream Retailers Association
  e: **NICRA**
National Indian Health Board e: **NIHB**
National Indoor Environmental Institute e:
  NIEI
National Industrial Space Committee e:
  NISC
National Information Center on Health
  Services Research and Health Care
  Technology e: **NICHSR**
National Information Service for
  Earthquake Engineering e: **NISEE**

National Institute for Aerospace
  Technology e: **INTA**
National Institute for Biological Standards
  and Control e: **NIBSC**
National Institute for Burn Medicine e:
  NIBM
National Institute for Environmental
  Studies e: **NIES**
National Institute for Geology and Mining
  Research e: **NIGMR**
National Institute for Global Environmental
  Change e: **NIGEC**
National Institute for Medical Research e:
  N.I.M.R.
National Institute for Medical Research On-
  line Data-base e: **NIMROD**
National Institute for Occupational Safety
  and Health, Cincinnati e: **OCNIOS**
National Institute for/of Environmental
  Health Science[s] e: **NIEHS**
National Institute for/of Occupational
  Safety and Health e: **NIOSH**
National Institute for/of Polar Research e:
  NIPR
National Institute for Radiation Protection
  e: **NIRP**
National Institute for Space Research e:
  INPE
National Institute for Space Research-
  Instituto de Pesquisas Espacias, Brazil e:
  NISR-INPE
National Institute for the Conservation of
  Nature e: **ICONA**
National Institute for the defense of
  Competition and the Protection of
  Intellectual Property e: **INDECOPI**
National Institute for the Environment e:
  NIE
National Institute for Urban Wildlife e:
  NIUW
National Institute for Water Research e:
  NIWR
National Institute for Water Supply
  [Netherlands]. Quarterly Report e: **Natl
  Inst Water Supply [Neth] Q Rep**
National Institute of Agro-Environmental
  Studies e: **NIAES**
National Institute of Agrobiological
  Resources e: **NIAR**
National Institute of Animaal Health.
  Quarterly e: **NIAHAI**
National Institute of Animal Agriculture e:
  NIAA
National Institute of Animal Health e:
  NIAH
National Institute of Animal Health.
  Quarterly e: **Nat I Anim**, e: **Natl Inst
  Anim Health Q**
National Institute of Animal Health.
  Quarterly [Yatabe] e: **Natl Inst Anim
  Health Q [Yatabe]**
National Institute of Animal Industry e:
  NIAI
National Institute of Atmospheric Research
  e: **NIAR**
National Institute of Biology e: **NIB**
National Institute of Biomedical Imaging
  and Bioengineering e: **NIBIB**
National Institute of Biotechnology and
  Applied Microbiology e: **BIOTECH**
National Institute of Child Health and
  Human Development e: **NICHD**, e:
  NICHHD

National Institute of Dental Health e:
  NIDH
National Institute of Environmental Science
  e: **NIES**
National Institute of General Medical
  Sciences e: **NIGMS**
National Institute of Health Administration
  and Education e: **NIHAE**
National Institute of Health and Human
  Development e: **NIHHD**
National Institute of Health and Science
  Research e: **INSERM**
National Institute of Health. Bulletin.
  United States Public Health Service e:
  **National Inst Health Bull US Pub
  Health Serr**
National Institute of Health Class Library
  e: **NIHCL**
National Institute of Health, Division of
  Research Grants e: **NRSA-NIOD DRG**
National Institute of Health Record e: **NIH
  Record**
National Institute of Health Sciences, Japan.
  e: **NIHS**
National Institute of Marine Medicine and
  Pharmacology e: **NIMMP**
National Institute of Medical Health e:
  NIMH
National Institute of Medical Herbalists e:
  NIMH
National Institute of Mental Health and
  Neuro Sciences e: **NIMHANS**
National Institute of Mental Health, Clinical
  Research Center Medical Library, Fort
  Worth e: **TxFNIMH**
National Institute of Oceanography e: **NIO**
National Institute of Oceanography and
  Fisheries e: **NIOF**
National Institute of Oceanology e: **N.I.O.**
National Institute of Polar Research.
  Memoirs. Series A. Aeronomy e:
  NIPRMAA
National Institute of Polar Research.
  Memoirs. Series B. Meteorology e:
  NIPRMBMT
National Institute of Polar Research.
  Memoirs. Series C. Earth Sciences e:
  **Natl Inst Polar Res Mem Ser C Earth
  Sci**, e: **NIPRMCFS**
National Institute of Polar Research.
  Memoirs. Series E. Biology and Medical
  Science e: **NIPRMEB**
National Institute of Polar Research.
  Memoirs. Series F. Logistics e:
  NIPRMFL
National Institute of Polar Research.
  Memoirs. Special Issue e: **Natl Inst
  Polar Res Mem Spec Issue**, e: **NIPRM**,
  e: **NIPRMS**
National Institute of Polar Research.
  Special Map Series e: **NIPRSMS**
National Institute of Polar Research
  [Tokyo]. Antarctic Geological Map Series
  e: **Natl Inst Polar Res [Tokyo] Antarct
  Geol Map Ser**
National Institute of Polarology e: **NIP**
National Institute of Public Health e:
  NIPH
National Institute of Water and Atmosphere
  (or Atmospheric) Research Ltd. e:
  NIWAR
National Institute[s] of/for Mental Health
  e: **NIMH**

National Institutes of Health *e:* **HEW-nih**

National Institutes of Health. Consensus Development Conference. Summaries *e:* **Natl Inst Health Consensus Dev Conf Summ**

National Institute[s] of Health, Japan *e:* **NIHJ**

National Institutes of Health. Publications *e:* **NIH**

National Interagency Council on Smoking and Health [Inactive] *e:* **NICSH**

National Interdepartmental Seminar *e:* **NIS**

National Interim Primary Drinking Water Regulations *e:* **NIPDWR**

National Interim Primary Drinking Water Standards *e:* **NIPDWS**

National Jewish Center for Immunology and Respiratory Medicine *e:* **NJCIRM**

National Land and Water Resources Audit *e:* **NLWRA**

National Land and Water Resources Audit Advisory Committee *e:* **NLWRAAC**

National Legal Center for the Medically Dependent and Disabled *e:* **NLCMDD**

National Legal Resource Center for Child Advocacy and Protection *e:* **NLRCAP**, *e:* **NLR[C]CAP**

National Library for the Environment *e:* **NLE**

National Library of Medicine *e:* **HEW-na**, *e:* **NLM**

National Library of Medicine-Biomedical Communications Network *e:* **NLM-BCN**

National Library of Medicine. Current Catalog *e:* **NLMC**

National Library of Medicine. News *e:* **NLM News**

National Library of Medicine Specialized Information Services *e:* **NLM SIS**, *e:* **SIS**

National Library of Medicine. Technical Bulletin *e:* **NLM Tech Bull**

National Library of Medicine's Full-Text Retrieval System *e:* **FTRS**

National Local Government Environmental Resource Network *e:* **NLGERN**

National Managed Health Care Congress *e:* **NMHCC**

National Manufacturers of Soda Water Flavors *e:* **NMSWF**

National Marine Environmental Forecasting Center (or Centre) *e:* **NMEFC**

National Marine Water Quality Laboratory *e:* **NMWQL**

National Maternal and Child Health Clearinghouse *e:* **NMCHC**

National Maternal and Child Oral Health Resource Center *e:* **NMCOHRC**

National Maternal and Infant Health Survey *e:* **NMIHS**

National Medic-Card [Society] *e:* **NMCS**

National Medical Advisory Committee *e:* **NMAC**

National Medical and Dental Association *e:* **NAMDA**, *e:* **NMDA**

National Medical Association Foundation *e:* **NMAF**

National Medical Association[s] *e:* **NMA**

National Medical Audiovisual Center [of the National Library of Medicine] *e:* **NMAC**

National Medical Care *e:* **NMC**

National Medical Care Expenditures Survey *e:* **NMCES**

National Medical Care, Inc. *e:* **NMD**

National Medical Care Utilization and Expenditure Survey *e:* **Natl Med Care Utilization and Expenditure Survey**, *e:* **NMCUES**

National Medical Center *e:* **NMC**

National Medical Device Coalition *e:* **NMDC**

National Medical Enterprises *e:* **NME**

National Medical Expenditure Survey *e:* **NMES**

National Medical Fellowship[s] *e:* **NMF**

National Medical Foundation for Eye Care *e:* **NMFEC**

National Medical Journal *e:* **Nat. M. J.**

National Medical Journal of China [Peking] *e:* **Natl Med J China [Peking]**

National Medical Journal of India *e:* **Natl Med J India**

National Medical Library and Center for [Medical] Documentation *e:* **NMLCD**

National Medical Review *e:* **Nat. M. Rev.**

National Medical Service *e:* **N.M.S.**

National Medical Utilization Committee *e:* **NMUC**

National Medicare Education Program *e:* **NMEP**

National Medicine Society *e:* **NMS**

National Medico-Dental Conference for the Evaluation of Fluoridation *e:* **NMDCEF**

National Mental Health Association *e:* **N.M.H.A.**

National Mental Health Consumer Self Help Clearinghouse *e:* **NMHCSHC**

National Mental Health Consumers' Association *e:* **NMHCA**

National Mental Health Foundation *e:* **NMHF**

National Mental Health Institute on Deafness *e:* **NMHID**

National Mental Health Services Knowledge Exchange Network *e:* **KEN**

National Mental Health Strategy *e:* **NMHS**

National Meteorological Center[s] (or Centre) *e:* **NMC**

National Meteorological Institute of Athens *e:* **NMIA**

National Meteorological Operations Centre *e:* **NMOC**

National Meteorological Rocket Network *e:* **NMRN**

National Meteorological Satellite System *e:* **NMSS**

National Meteorological Service *e:* **NMS**

National Meteorologicial and Hydrological Service *e:* **NMHS**

National Military Fish and Wildlife Association *e:* **NMFWA**

National Mine Health and Safety Academy *e:* **NMHSA**

National Mine Health and Safety Academy, Beckley *e:* **UDM**

National Minority Health Association *e:* **NMHA**

National Minority Medical Suppliers Association *e:* **NMMSA**

National Multi-purpose Space Station *e:* **NMSS**

National Museum of Canada. Natural History Papers *e:* **Natl Mus Can Nat Hist Pap**

National Museum of Natural History *e:* **NMNH**

National Museum of Natural Sciences *e:* **NMNS**

National Museum of Natural Sciences, Ottawa, Ontario *e:* **OONMNS**

National Museum of Natural Sciences [Ottawa]. Publications in Biological Oceanography *e:* **Natl Mus Nat Sci [Ottawa] Publ Biol Oceanogr**

National Museum of Natural Sciences [Ottawa]. Publications in Botany *e:* **Natl Mus Nat Sci [Ottawa] Publ Bot**

National Museum of Natural Sciences [Ottawa]. Publications in Natural Sciences *e:* **Natl Mus Nat Sci [Ottawa] Publ Nat Sci**

National Museum of Natural Sciences [Ottawa]. Publications in Palaeontology *e:* **Natl Mus Nat Sci [Ottawa] Publ Palaeontol**

National Museum of Natural Sciences [Ottawa]. Publications in Zoology *e:* **Natl Mus Nat Sci [Ottawa] Publ Zool**

National Museums of Canada. Publications in Biological Oceanography *e:* **NMCPBO**

National Museums of Canada. Publications in Natural Sciences *e:* **NMCPNS**

National Natural Landmarks Program *e:* **NNLP**

National Natural Resource Management System *e:* **NNRMS**

National Natural Resources Information System *e:* **NNRIS**

National Natural Science Foundation *e:* **NNSF**

National Nature Reserve[s] *e:* **NNP**, *e:* **NNR**

National Nature Reserves *e:* **NNRs**

National Naval Medical Center *e:* **Natl Nav Med Cen**, *e:* **NATNAVMEDCEN**, *e:* **NNMC**

National Network for Environmental Management Studies *e:* **NNEMS**

National Network of Libraries of Medicine *e:* **NN/LM**

National New Professional Health Workers *e:* **NNPHW**

National Occupant Protection Use Survey *e:* **NOPUS**

National Occupational Health and Safety Commission (or Committee) *e:* **NOHSC**

National Occupational Health Survey of Mining *e:* **NOHSM**

National Ocean Access Project *e:* **NOAP**

National Ocean Agency Headquarters *e:* **NOAH**

National Ocean Communications Network *e:* **NOCN**

National Ocean Data System *e:* **NODS**

National Ocean Industries Association *e:* **NOIA**

National Ocean Policy Study *e:* **NOPS**

National Ocean Pollution Planning Act *e:* **NOPPA**

National Ocean Pollution Protection Act *e:* **NOPPA**

National Ocean Satellite System *e:* **NOSS**

National Ocean Science and Technology Agency *e:* **NOSTA**

National Ocean Sciences AMS Facility *e:* **NOSAMS**

National Ocean Sediment Coring Program
 e: **NOSCP**
National Ocean Service *e:* **NOS**
National Ocean Survey *e:* **NOS**
National Ocean Survey Analytical Plotter
 e: **NOSAP**
National Ocean Survey Lake Survey Center
 e: **NOS-LSCR**
National Ocean Survey System *e:* **NOSS**
National Ocean Survey Tide Station *e:*
 NOSTS
National Oceanic and Atmosphere (or
 Atmospheric) Administration *e:* **NOAA**
National Oceanic and Atmospheric
 Administration *e:* **MAP**, *e:* **NAOO**, *e:*
 NMRNOAA, *e:* **NPAA**
National Oceanic and Atmospheric
 Administration Data Network *e:*
 NOADN
National Oceanic and Atmospheric
 Administration Earth System Data
 Directory *e:* **NOAADIR**
National Oceanic and Atmospheric
 Administration Environmental Services
 Data Directory *e:* **NOAADIR**
National Oceanic and Atmospheric
 Administration Joint Tsunami Research
 Effort *e:* **NOAA-JTRE**
National Oceanic and Atmospheric
 Administration, Miami *e:* **OAO**
National Oceanic and Atmospheric
 Administration, Miami Branch, Miami *e:*
 OAL
National Oceanic and Atmospheric
 Administration network *e:* **NOAAnet**
National Oceanic and Atmospheric
 Administration Pacific Marine
 Environmental Laboratory *e:* **NOAA-
 PMEL**
National Oceanic and Atmospheric
 Administration, Rockville *e:* **OLA**
National Oceanic and Atmospheric
 Administration Technical Report *e:*
 NOAA Tech. Rep.
National Oceanic and Atmospheric
 Administration [United States]. Circular
 e: **Natl Oceanic Atmos Adm [US] Circ**
National Oceanic and Atmospheric
 Administration [United States]. Fishery
 Bulletin *e:* **Natl Oceanic Atmos Adm
 [US] Fish Bull**
National Oceanic and Atmospheric
 Administration [United States]. Special
 Scientific Report. Fisheries *e:* **Natl
 Oceanic Atmos Adm [US] Spec Sci Rep
 Fish**
National Oceanic Satellite System *e:*
 NOSS
National Oceanic Survey Satellite *e:*
 NOSS
National Oceanographic Center (or Centre)
 e: **NOC**
National Oceanographic Committee *e:*
 NOC
National Oceanographic Council *e:* **NOC**
National Oceanographic Data Center
 Advisory Board *e:* **NODCAB**
National Oceanographic Data Center (or
 Centre) *e:* **NODC**
National Oceanographic Facility *e:* **NOF**
National Oceanographic Foundation *e:*
 NOF

National Oceanographic Hazard Survey *e:*
 NOHS
National Oceanographic Instrumentation
 Center *e:* **NOIC**
National Oceanographic Laboratory System
 e: **NOLS**
National Oceanographic Office *e:* **NOO**
National Oceanographic (or Oceanography)
 and Maritime Institute *e:* **NOAMI**
National Oceanographic (or Oceanography)
 Association *e:* **NOA**
National Oceanographic Program[me] *e:*
 NOP
National Oceanographic Records Center *e:*
 NORC
National Oceanographic Research Centre
 (Madagascar) *e:* **CNRO**
National Oceanographic Satellite System
 e: **NOSS**
National Oceanographiic Reference Station
 Network *e:* **NORSNET**
National Oceans Systems Center *e:* **NOSC**
National Office of Animal Health *e:*
 NOAH
National Open Hearth [Steel] Committee
 e: **NOHC**
National Operational Environmental
 Satellite Service *e:* **NOES**
National Operational Environmental
 Satellite System *e:* **NOESS**
National Operational Meteorological
 Satellite System *e:* **NOMSS**
National Operational Weather radar *e:*
 NOWrad
National Optical Astronomical (or
 Astronomy) Observatories *e:* **NOAO**
National Optical Astronomy Observatones
 e: **NOAOs**
National Oral Health Information
 Clearinghouse *e:* **NOHIC**
National Oral Health Surveillance System
 e: **NOHSS**
National Orbiting Space Station *e:* **NOSS**
National Organization for Public Health
 Nursing *e:* **NOPHN**
National Parent Consortium on Maternal
 and Child Health *e:* **NPCMCH**
National Park Service. Natural Resources
 Report *e:* **NRUSDD**
National Parks and Wildlife [Act] *e:* **NPW**
National Parks and Wildlife Conservation
 Act *e:* **NPWC**, *e:* **NPWC Act**
National Parks and Wildlife Service *e:*
 NPWS
National Photographic Index of Australian
 Wildlife *e:* **NPIAW**
National Pigeon Association [and
 Marketing Conference, Ltd.] *e:* **NPA**
National Plan to Combat Pollution of the
 Sea by Oil *e:* **NATPLAN**
National Plant Protection Association *e:*
 PPA
National Podiatric Medical Association *e:*
 NPMA
National Polar Orbiter Environmental
 Satellite System *e:* **NPOESS**
National Presbyterian Health and Welfare
 Association *e:* **NPHWA**
National Primary Drinking Water
 Regulation[s] *e:* **NPDWR**
National Program for Responding to
 Greenhouse Climate Change *e:*
 NPRGCC

National Programme for Remote Sensing
 e: **NPRS**
National Progressive Primary Health Care
 Network *e:* **NPPHCN**
National Public Health Partnership *e:*
 NPHP
National Public Health Program Reporting
 System *e:* **NPHPRS**
National Public Relations Council of Health
 and Welfare Services *e:* **NPRC**
National Publicity Council for Health and
 Welfare Services *e:* **NPC**, *e:* **NPCHWS**
National Pure Water Association *e:*
 NPWA
National Radiation Protection Board *e:*
 NRPB
National Radio Astronomical Observatory
 e: **NRAO**
National Radio Astronomy Observatory *e:*
 NRAS
National Radio Astronomy Observatory,
 Charlottesville *e:* **ViCRA**
National Radio Astronomy
 Observatory,Charlottesville *e:* **RAO**
National Radiological Protection Board *e:*
 NRPB
National Registry of Domestic Animal
 Pathology *e:* **NRDAP**
National Registry of Emergency Medical
 Technicians *e:* **NREMT**
National Registry of Environmental
 Professionals *e:* **NREP**
National Registry of Medical Secretaries
 e: **NRMS**
National Registry of Radiation Protection
 Technologists *e:* **NRRPT**
National Remote Sensing Agency *e:*
 NRSA
National Remote Sensing Centre *e:* **NRSC**
National Remote Sensing Program[me] *e:*
 NRSP
National Research and Development Centre
 for Welfare and Health *e:* **STAKES**
National Research Council Division of
 Earth Sciences *e:* **NRCDES**
National Research Council of Canada.
 Associate Committee on Ecological
 Reserves. Newsletter *e:* **NRCE**
National Research Council of Canada.
 Associate Committee on Geodesy and
 Geophysics. Proceedings of Hydrology
 Symposium *e:* **Nat Res Counc Can Ass
 Comm Geod Geophys Proc Hydrol
 Symp**
National Research Council of Canada.
 Associate Committee on Geotechnical
 Research Technical Memorandum *e:* **Nat
 Res Counc Can Ass Comm Geotech Res
 Tech Memo**
National Research Council of Canada.
 Associate Committee on Geotechnical
 Research. Technical Memorandum *e:*
 NRCAGTM
National Research Council of Canada.
 Associate Committee on Scientific
 Criteria for Environmental Quality.
 Publication *e:* **Natl Res Counc Can
 Assoc Comm Sci Criter Environ Qual
 Publ**, *e:* **NRCEBF**
National Research Council of Canada.
 Environmental Secretariat. Publication
 e: **Natl Res Counc Can Environ Secr
 Publ**

National Research Institute for Earth
Science and Disaster Prevention *e:*
NIED
National Research Institute for
Occupational Diseases. South African
Medical Research Council. Annual Report
e: **Natl Res Inst Occup Dis S Afr Med
Res Counc Annu Rep**
National Research Institute for Oceanology
e: **NRIO**
National Research Laboratory of
Meteorology *e:* **NRLM**
National Resource Ecology Laboratory *e:*
NREL
National River Health Program *e:* **NRHP**
National Round Table on the Environment
and the Economy *e:* **NRTEE**
National Rural and Environmental Studies
Association *e:* **NRESA**
National Rural Health Alliance *e:* **NRHA**
National Rural Health Association *e:*
NRHA
National Rural Health Care Association *e:*
NRHCA
National Rural Health Network *e:* **NRHN**
National Rural Water Association *e:*
NRWA
National Safety Congress. Occupational
Health Nursing Section. Transactions *e:*
Natl Saf Congr Trans
National Satellite Land Remote Sensing
Data Archives *e:* **NSLRSDA**
National Science Council. Proceedings. Part
2. Biological, Medical and Agricultural
Sciences [Taiwan] *e:* **Natl Sci Counc
Proc Part 2 [Taiwan]**
National Science Council [Taipei].
Proceedings Part 1. Natural and
Mathematical Sciences *e:* **Natl Sci
Counc [Taipei] Proc Part 1 Nat Math
Sci**
National Science Foundation Office for the
International Decade of Ocean
Exploration *e:* **NSF/IDOE**
National Science Museum. Bulletin. Series
C. Geology [Tokyo] *e:* **Natl Sci Mus
Bull Ser C [Tokyo]**
National Science Museum [Tokyo].
Bulletin. Series C. Geology and
Paleontology *e:* **Natl Sci Mus [Tokyo]
Bull Ser C Geol Paleontol**
National Scientific Committee on
Oceanography *e:* **NSCO**
National Sea Grant Program *e:* **NSGP**
National Sea Rescue Institute *e:* **NSRI**
National Sea Training School[s] *e:* **NSTS**
National Sea Training Trusts *e:* **NSTT**
National Secondary Drinking Water
[Regulations] *e:* **NSDWR**
National Security Council
Interdepartmental Group *e:* **NSCIG**
National Snow and Ice Data Center (or
Centre) *e:* **NSIDC**
National Society for Animal Protection *e:*
NSAP
National Society for Medical Research *e:*
NSMR
National Society for Medical Research.
Bulletin *e:* **Nat Soc Med Res Bull**
National Society for Protection of
Environment & Children *e:* **NSPEC**
National Society for the Prevention of
Cruelty to Animals *e:* **NSPCA**

National Society of Biomedical Equipment
Technicians *e:* **NSBET**
National Society of Medical Technologists
e: **NSMT**
National Solar Observatory *e:* **NSO**
National Solar Space Observatory *e:*
NSSO
National Space Activities Council *e:*
NSAC
National Space Agency of Ukraine *e:*
NSAU
National Space and Aeronautics Agency *e:*
NSAA
National Space [and] Technology
Laboratories (or Laboratory) *e:* **NSTL**
National Space Biomedical Research
Institute *e:* **NSBRI**
National Space Club *e:* **NSC**
National Space Council *e:* **NSC**, *e:* **NSpC**
National Space Development Agency *e:*
NSDA
National Space Development Center (or
Centre) *e:* **NSDC**
National Space Institute *e:* **NSI**
National Space Policy Directive *e:* **NSPD**
National Space Program *e:* **NSP**
National Space Science Data Center *e:*
NSSDC
National Space Society *e:* **NSS**
National Space Station *e:* **NSS**
National Space Station Planning Sub-Panel
e: **NSSPSP**
National Space Surveillance Center *e:*
NSSC
National Space Surveillance Control Center
e: **NSSCC**
National Space Surveillance System *e:*
NSSS
National Space Technology Program[me]
e: **NSTP**
National Space Transportation System *e:*
NSTS
National Space Transportation System
Program Office *e:* **NSTSPO**
National Space Weather Program *e:*
NSWP
National Sports Medicine Institute [of the
United Kingdom] *e:* **NSMI**
National States Geographic Information
Council *e:* **NSGIC**
National Strategy for/and Ecologically
Sustainable Development *e:* **NSESD**
National Stream Water Quality Accounting
Network *e:* **NASQUAN**
National Student Health Association *e:*
NSHA
National Study of Graduate Education in
Internal Medicine *e:* **NaSGIM**
National Surface Water Survey *e:* **NSWS**
National Surfave Water Survey *e:* **NSWS**
National Survey of Oral Health in School
Children *e:* **NSOHSC**
National Survey of Personal Health
Practices and Consequences *e:* **NSPHPC**
National Symposium on Hydrology *e:*
Natn Symp Hydrol
National Symposium on Space Electronics
and Telemetry *e:* **NSSET**
National Task Force on Healthcare Reform
e: **NTFHR**
National Transit Geographic Information
System *e:* **NTGIS**

National Tribal Environmental Council *e:*
NTEC
National Trust for Places of Historic
Interest or Natural Beauty *e:* **NT**
National Undergraduate Research
Observatory *e:* **NURO**
National Underwater Accident Data Center
e: **NUADC**
National Underwater and Marine Agency
e: **NUMA**
National Underwater Laboratory System *e:*
NULS
National Underwriter [Life and Health
Insurance Edition] *e:* **Natl Underwrit
[Life Health], *e:* Natl Underwrit [Life
Health Insur Ed], *e:* Nat Underw [Life],
e: Nat Underw [Life Ed], *e:* NULH**
National Union of Mineral Water
Manufacturers Associations *e:*
N.U.M.W.M.A.
National Union of Petroleum and Natural
Gas Workers *e:* **NUPENG**
National Union of Water Works Employees
e: **NUWWE**
National Union of Waterworks Employees
e: **N.U.W.E.**
National Veterinary Medical Association
e: **NVMA**
National Veterinary Medical Association of
Great Britain and Ireland Publication *e:*
NVMA Publications
National Veterinary Medicine Association
e: **N.V.M.A.**
National voluntary body monitoring
heritage and environment *e:* **An Taisce**
National Voluntary Health Agencies *e:*
NVHA
National Water Alliance *e:* **NWA**
National Water and Soil Conservation
Authority *e:* **NWSCA**
National Water and Soil Conservation
Organisation (or Organization) *e:*
WASCO
National Water and Soil Conservation
Organization *e:* **NWASCO**, *e:* **NWSCO**
National Water Authority *e:* **NWA**
National Water Carriers Association *e:*
NWCA
National Water Center *e:* **NWC**
National Water Commission *e:* **NWC**
National Water Companies (or Company)
Conference *e:* **NWCC**
National Water Conditions *e:* **Natl. Water
Cond.**
National Water Conservation Order *e:*
NWCO
National Water Council *e:* **NWC**
National Water Data Exchange *e:*
NAWDEX
National Water Data System *e:* **NWDS**
National Water Information Clearinghouse
e: **NWIC**
National Water Information System *e:*
NWIS
National Water-Level Observation Network
e: **NWLON**
National Water Lift Co. *e:* **NWL**
National Water Project *e:* **NWP**
National Water Purification Foundation *e:*
NWPF
National Water Quality *e:* **NWQ**
National Water Quality Assessment *e:*
NAWQUA

National Water Quality Data Bank [Environment Canada] *e:* **NAQUADAT**

National Water Quality Inventory *e:* **NWQI**

National Water Quality Laboratory *e:* **NWQL**

National Water Quality Management Strategy *e:* **NWQMS**

National Water Quality Surveillance System *e:* **NWQSS**

National Water Research Institute *e:* **NWRI**

National Water Resources Association *e:* **NWRA**

National Water Resources Committee *e:* **NWRC**

National Water Resources Council [Philippines] *e:* **NWRC**

National Water Slide Association *e:* **NWSA**

National Water Supply Improvement Association *e:* **NWSIA**

National Water Well[s] Association *e:* **NWWA**

National Waterbed Retailers Association *e:* **NWRA**

National Waterfowl Council *e:* **NWC**

National Watermen and Lightermen's Federation *e:* **NWLF**

National Watershed Congress *e:* **NWC**

National Waterways Conference *e:* **NWC**

National Waterways Study *e:* **NWS**

National Waterways Transport Association [British] *e:* **NWTA**

National Weather Analysis Center *e:* **NAWAC**, *e:* **NWAC**

National Weather Association *e:* **NWA**

National Weather Digest *e:* **Natl. Weather Dig.**

National Weather Facsimile Network *e:* **NATFAX**

National Weather Institute *e:* **NWI**

National Weather Records Center *e:* **NWRC**

National Weather Satellite Center *e:* **NWSC**

National Weather Satellite System *e:* **NWSS**

National Weather Service Center *e:* **NWSC**

National Weather Service Employees Organization *e:* **NWSEO**

National Weather Service Forecast Office *e:* **NWSFO**

National Weather Service Headquarters *e:* **NWSH**

National Weather Service Modernization, Test and Integration System River Forecast Office *e:* **NMTR**

National Weather Service Modernization, Test and Integration System Weather Forecast Office *e:* **NMTW**

National Weather Service River Forecast System *e:* **NWSRFS**

National Weather Service Technical Training Center *e:* **NWSTTC**

National Weather Service Telecommunications [Gateway] *e:* **NWSTG**

National Weather Service Training Center System 1, River Forecast Center *e:* **NTCA**

National Weather System [or Services] [or Service] *e:* **NWS**

National Wild and Scenic River Act *e:* **NWSRA**

National Wild and Scenic Rivers System *e:* **NWSRS**

National Wild Turkey Federation *e:* **NWTF**

National Wilderness Inventory *e:* **NWI**

National Wilderness Preservation System *e:* **NWPS**

National Wildflower Research Center *e:* **NWRC**

National Wildhorse Research Center *e:* **NWRC**

National Wildlife *e:* **Natl Wildl**, *e:* **Nat Wildlife**

National Wildlife Centre *e:* **NWC**

National Wildlife Defence Council *e:* **NWDC**

National Wildlife Federation *e:* **NWF**

National Wildlife Federation Corporate Conservation Council *e:* **NWFCCC**

National Wildlife Health Center *e:* **NWHC**

National Wildlife Health Foundation *e:* **NWHF**

National Wildlife Health Laboratory *e:* **NWHL**

National Wildlife Protection Act *e:* **NWPA**

National Wildlife Protection Unit *e:* **NWPU**

National Wildlife Refuge Association *e:* **NWRA**

National Wildlife Refuge [System] *e:* **NWR**

National Wildlife Refuge System *e:* **NWRS**

National Wildlife Rehabilitators Association *e:* **NWRA**

National Wildlife Rescue Team *e:* **NWRT**

National Wildlife Research Center *e:* **NWRC**

National Wildlife Research Centre, Canadian Wildlife Service, Environment *e:* **OOECWN**

National Wildlife Reserve *e:* **NWR**

National Womens Health Information Center *e:* **NWHIC**

National Women's Health Network *e:* **NWHN**

National Women's Health Resource Center *e:* **NWHRC**

Nationale Arbeitsgemeinschaft für Qualitätsförderung im Gesundheitswesen *d:* **NAQ**

Nationale Arbeitsgruppe Marine Umweltqualitätsziele *d:* **AG MQZ**

Nationale Belgische Federatie der Baanvervoerders *n:* **NBFBV**

Nationale Confederatie der Groeperingen der Geteisterden van België *n:* **NACOGGEB**

Nationale Klimadatenbank *d:* **NKDB**

Nationale Vereniging der Waterleidingsbedrijven *n:* **NAVEWA**

Nationales Komitee für Geodäsie und Geophysik *d:* **NKGG**

Native American Graves Protection and Repatriation Act *e:* **NAGPRA**

Native Americans for a Clean Environment *e:* **NACE**

NATO Acoustic and Remote Sensing Shallow Water Experiment *e:* **NARSHA**

NATO [North Atlantic Treaty Organization] ASI [Advanced Science Institutes] Series. Series G. Ecological Sciences *e:* **NASGEJ**, *e:* **NATO ASI [Adv Sci Inst] Ser Ser G Ecol Sci**

NATO Sea Sparrow Project Office *e:* **NSPO**

NATO Sea Sparrow Project Steering Committee *e:* **NSPSC**

Natriumhydrogensulfit *d:* **E 222**

Natriumhydroxid *d:* **E 524**

Natriumsulfat, Natriumhydrogensulfat *d:* **E 514**

Natur *d:* **Nat.**

Natur Jutlandica *l:* **Nat Jutlandica**

Natur och Kultur, bokförlag *r:* **NoK**

Natur og Museum [Arhus] *a:* **Natur Mus [Arhus]**

Natur und Heimat *d:* **Nat Heimat**

Natur und Land *d:* **Nat Land**

Natur und Landschaft *d:* **Nat. Landsch.**, *d:* **Nat Landschaft**, *d:* **Natur Landsch**, *d:* **NL**

Natur- und Landschaftsschutzgebiete Baden-Württembergs *d:* **Nat.-Landsch.schutzgeb. Baden-Württ.**

Natur und Mensch *d:* **Nat. Mensch**

Natur und Museum *d:* **Nat Mus**, *d:* **Natur u Mus**

Natur und Museum [Frankfurt] *d:* **Natur Mus [Frankf]**

Natur und Museum. Senckenbergische Naturforschende Gesellschaft *d:* **Nat Mus Senckenb Naturforsch Ges**

Natur und Naturschutz in Mecklenburg *d:* **Nat. Nat.schutz Mecklenbg.**

Natur und Recht *d:* **NuR**

Natur und Technik *d:* **Nat Tech**

Natur- und Umwelt-Führungsinformationssystem *d:* **NUFIS**

Natur- und Umweltinformationssystem Schleswig Holstein *d:* **NUIS-SH**

Natur und Volk *d:* **Natur u Volk**

Natur und Volk [Frankfurt] *d:* **Nat Volk [Frankf]**

Natura Energy Corp. *e:* **NATU**

Natura Jutlandica *l:* **Nat Jutl**

Natura Mosana *f:* **Nat Mosana**

Natura Mosana. Supplement B. Botanique *f:* **Nat Mosana Suppl B Bot**

Natura Mosana. Supplement CD. Zoologie *f:* **Nat Mosana Suppl CD Zool**

Natura. Serie Biologie *d:* **Nat Biol**

Natural *e:* **NAT**

Natural Alternatives, Inc. *e:* **NATA**

Natural and Accelerated Biomediation Research *e:* **NABIR**

Natural and Applied Science Bulletin *e:* **Nat Appl Sci Bull**

Natural and Synthetic *e:* **NATSYN**

Natural Area Council *e:* **NAC**

Natural Areas Association *e:* **NAA**

Natural Areas Journal *e:* **Nat Areas J**

Natural Areas of Canadian Significance *e:* **NACS**

Natural Asphalt Mine-Owners' and Manufacturers' Council *e:* **NAMMC**

Natural Assessments Group *e:* **NAG**

Natural Axis *e:* **N**

Natural Background Clutter *e:* **NBC**

Natural Binary *e:* **NB**

Natural Binary-Coded Decimal *e:* **NBCD**

Natural Biological Information System *e:*
BIOS

Natural Birth Control *e:* **NBC**

Natural Bridges National Monument *e:*
NABR

Natural Bridges National Monument in
Southeastern Utah *e:* **Natural Bridges**

Natural Casing Institute *e:* **NCI**

Natural Circulation Reactor *e:* **NCR**

Natural Circulation Verification Program
e: **NCVP**

natural contour theory *e:* **nct**

Natural Convection *e:* **NC**

Natural Convection Boiling Loops *e:*
NCBL

Natural Convection in the Stationary
Condition *e:* **NAKOSTA**

Natural Convection in the Stationary
Condition Program *e:* **NAKOSTA
Program**

natural convector *e:* **nc**

Natural Daylight *e:* **NDL**

Natural Death *e:* **ND**

Natural Disaster and Drought Relief
Policies *e:* **NDDRP**

Natural Disaster Hospital *e:* **NDH**

Natural Disaster Relief Arrangements *e:*
NDRA

Natural Disaster Warning *e:* **NADWARN**

Natural Disaster Warning Survey *e:*
NADWAS

Natural Disaster Warning System *e:*
NADWARN System

Natural Disasters Organization *e:* **NDO**

Natural Disturbance Type *e:* **NDT**

Natural Division *e:* **N**

Natural Draft Cooling Tower *e:* **NDCT**

Natural Draft Heat *e:* **NDH**

Natural Draught *e:* **ND**

Natural Energy Association *e:* **NEA**

natural energy electric vehicle *e:* **neev**

Natural Environment Research Council.
Institute of Terrestrial Ecology. Annual
Report *e:* **Nat Environ Res Counc Inst
Terr Ecol Annu Rep**

Natural Environment Research Council.
News Journal *e:* **Nat Environ Res
Counc News J**

Natural Environment Support Room *e:*
NESR

Natural Environment[al] Research Council
e: **NERC**

Natural Family Planning *e:* **NFP**

Natural Food *e:* **NF**

Natural Food and Farming *e:* **Natural
Food Fmg, e: NF & F**

Natural Food Associates *e:* **NFA**

Natural Food Colors Association *e:*
NATCOL

Natural Food Institute *e:* **NFI**

Natural forest biomass burned onsite *e:* **Bs**

Natural forest biomass used for energy *e:*
En

natural frequency *e:* **f**

Natural Frequency *e:* **nat. freq., e: NF**

Natural Gamma Ray *e:* **NGR**

Natural gamma-ray logging tool *e:* **GR**

natural gamma ray units *e:* **API units**

Natural-gamma Spectrometry Tool *e:*
NGT

Natural Gardening *e:* **Natural Gard**

Natural Gas *e:* **Nat Gas, e: NG**

Natural Gas and Gas Liquids Tax *e:*
NGGLT

Natural Gas and Gasoline Journal *e:* **Nat
Gas Gasoline J**

Natural Gas Annual *e:* **Nat Gas A**

Natural Gas Association of America *e:*
NGAA

Natural Gas Association of America.
Proceedings *e:* **Nat Gas As Am Pr**

Natural Gas for Industry *e:* **Natural Gas
Ind**

Natural Gas/Fuel Forecast. Series A.
Geographic *e:* **Nat Gas/Fuel Forecast
Ser A**

Natural Gas/Fuel Forecast. Series B.
Industrial *e:* **Nat Gas/Fuel Forecast Ser
B**

Natural Gas Industrial Technology *e:* **Nat.
Gas Ind. Technol.**

Natural Gas Industry *e:* **Nat Gas Ind**

Natural Gas Liquid[s] *e:* **NGL**

Natural Gas Magazine *e:* **Nat Gas Mag**

Natural Gas Pipeline Safety Act *e:*
NGPSA

Natural Gas Plant Liquids *e:* **NGPL**

Natural Gas Policy Act *e:* **NGPA**

Natural Gas Supply Association *e:* **NGSA**

Natural Gas Supply Committee *e:* **NGSC**

Natural Gas Vehicle Technology
Partnership *e:* **NGVTP**

Natural Gasoline Supply Men's Association
e: **NGSMA**

Natural Ground Level *e:* **NGL**

Natural Ground Surface *e:* **NGS**

Natural Hazards *e:* **Nat. Hazards**

Natural Hazards [R] *e:* **Nat. Hazards**

Natural Hazards Research and Applications
Information Center *e:* **NHRAIC**

Natural Heritage and Endangered Species
Program *e:* **NHESP**

Natural Heritage Trust *e:* **NHT**

Natural Heritage Trust Advisory Committee
e: **NHTAC**

Natural History *e:* **Nat Hist, e: Natural
Hi, e: Natur Hist, e: NH**

Natural History Bulletin. Siam Society *e:*
Nat Hist Bull Siam Soc

Natural History Information Retrieval
System *e:* **NHIR, e: NHIR System**

Natural History Magazine *e:* **Nat Hist
Mag**

Natural History Magazine [Chicago] *e:*
Nat Hist Misc [Chic]

Natural History Museum *e:* **NHM**

Natural History Museum, London *e:* **BM**

Natural History Museum of Los Angeles
County. Contributions in Science *e:* **Nat
Hist Mus Los Ang Cty Contrib Sci**

Natural History Museum of Los Angeles
County. Science Bulletin *e:* **Nat Hist
Mus Los Ang Cty Sci Bull**

Natural History Museum of Los Angeles
County. Science Series *e:* **Nat Hist Mus
Los Ang Cty Sci Ser**

Natural History [New York] *e:* **Nat Hist
[NY]**

Natural History of Rennell Island, British
Solomon Islands *e:* **Nat Hist Rennell Isl
Br Solomon Isl**

Natural History of the National Parks of
Hungary *e:* **Nat Hist Natl Parks Hung**

Natural History Park *e:* **NHP**

Natural History Press *e:* **NHP**

Natural History Review *e:* **NH Rv**

Natural History Society *e:* **N.H.S.**

Natural History Society of New Brunswick.
Bulletin *e:* **NH Soc NB B**

Natural Hydrocarbon *e:* **NHC**

Natural Immunity *e:* **Nat Immun**

Natural Immunity and Cell Growth
Regulation *e:* **Nat Imman Cell Growth
Regul**

Natural Intelligence *e:* **NI**

Natural Interference to Transmission or
Reception *e:* **QRS**

Natural Iteration Method *e:* **NIM**

Natural Killer Cells *e:* **CD56**

Natural Land and Water Reserves System
e: **NLWRS**

Natural Law Forum *e:* **Nat LF, e: Natural
L F**

Natural Law Society *e:* **NLS**

Natural Learning Acquisition *e:* **NAT-
LAB**

Natural Liquid Fuel *e:* **NLF**

Natural Logarithm *e:* **ln**

natural logarithm *e:* **loge**

Natural Logarithm *e:* **NALOG**

natural logarithm *e:* **nat log**

Natural Magnetic Orbital *e:* **NMO**

Natural Magnetic Remanence *e:* **NMR**

Natural Metal Finish *e:* **NMF**

Natural Moisturizing Factor *e:* **NMF**

Natural Natural Resource[s] Information
System *e:* **NRIS**

Natural Orbital *e:* **NO**

Natural Order *e:* **Nat Ord, e: NO**

Natural Organic Farmers Association *e:*
NOFA

Natural Organics Corp. *e:* **NAOR**

Natural Parity Exchange *e:* **NPE**

Natural Particulate Matter *e:* **NPM**

Natural Period in Heave *e:* **NPH**

Natural Phenomena *e:* **NP**

Natural Phenomena Hazard *e:* **NPH**

Natural Philosopher *e:* **Nat Philos**

natural philosophy *e:* **nat phil**

Natural Process Limits *e:* **NPL**

Natural Product Broker Association *e:*
NPBA

Natural Product Data Base *e:*
NAPRALERT

Natural Product Reports *e:* **NPRRDF**

Natural Products *e:* **NPs**

Natural Products Alert [University of
Illinois at Chicago] [Information service
or system] *e:* **NAPRALERT**

Natural Product[s] Reports *e:* **Nat. Prod.
Rep.**

Natural Radioactive Nuclides *e:* **NRN**

Natural Rale Hypothesis *e:* **NRH**

Natural Remanent Magnetism [or
Magnetization] *e:* **NRM**

Natural Resources Department, Office of
Forestry, Baton Rouge *e:* **LBrNR-F**

Natural Research Institute *e:* **NRI**

Natural Resource Authority of Jordan *e:*
NRAJ

Natural Resource-based Products *e:* **NRBP**

Natural Resource Conservation Service *e:*
NRCS

Natural Resource Damage *e:* **NRD**

Natural-Resource Damage Assessment *e:*
NRDA

Natural Resource Ecology Laboratory *e:*
NREL

Natural Resource Management *e:* **NRM**

Natural Resource Management Unit *e:* **NRMU**

Natural Resource Unit *e:* **NRU**

Natural Resource Usage Normal *e:* **NRUN**

Natural Resource Valuation *e:* **NRV**

Natural Resources *e:* **NATR**, *e:* **NR**

Natural Resources and Earth Sciences. Abstract Newsletter *e:* **Nat Resour Earth Sci**

Natural Resources and Energy Agency *e:* **NREA**

Natural Resources and Environmental Education Center *e:* **NREEC**

Natural Resources Audit Council *e:* **NRAC**

Natural Resources Board *e:* **NRB**

Natural Resources Canada *e:* **NRC**, *e:* **NRCan**

Natural Resources Center *e:* **NRC**

Natural Resources Conservation Authority *e:* **NRCA**

Natural Resources Conservation League *e:* **N.R.C.L.**

Natural Resources Conservation League of Victoria *e:* **NRCLV**

Natural Resource[s] Conservation Service *e:* **NRCS**

Natural Resources Conservation Service *e:* **NRCSM**

Natural Resources Conservatiopn League *e:* **NRCL**

Natural Resources Council of America *e:* **NRC**, *e:* **NRCA**

Natural Resources Data Directory *e:* **NRDD**

Natural Resource[s] Defense Council *e:* **NRDC**

Natural Resources Department, Research and Development Library, Baton Rouge *e:* **LBrNR**

Natural Resources District *e:* **NRD**

Natural Resources Districts *e:* **NRD's**

Natural Resources Division *e:* **NRD**

Natural Resources, Energy and Environment *e:* **NRES**

Natural Resources Forum *e:* **Nat Resour Forum**, *e:* **Natur Resources Forum**, *e:* **NRFOD**

Natural Resources Forum Library *e:* **Nat Resour Forum Libr**

Natural Resources Inventory *e:* **NRI**

Natural Resources Journal *e:* **Nat Res J**, *e:* **Nat Resources J**, *e:* **Nat Resources Jour**, *e:* **Natural Resources J**, *e:* **Natural Resources Jnl**, *e:* **Natur Res J**, *e:* **Natur Resources J**, *e:* **NRJ**

Natural Resources Law *e:* **Nat Res Law**

Natural Resources Law Newsletter *e:* **Nat Resources L Newsl**

Natural Resources Lawyer *e:* **Nat Res Lawyer**, *e:* **Nat Resources Law**, *e:* **Nat Resour Lawyer**, *e:* **Natural Resources Law**, *e:* **Natur Res L**, *e:* **Natur Resou**

Natural Resource[s] Management [and] Development Project *e:* **NRMDP**

Natural Resource[s] Management Strategy [or System] *e:* **NRMS**

Natural Resources Research Division *e:* **NRRD**

Natural Resources Research Institute *e:* **NRRI**

Natural Resources Research [Paris] *e:* **Nat Resour Res [Paris]**

Natural Rights Center *e:* **NRC**

Natural Rubber Development *e:* **Nat. Rubber Dev.**

Natural Rubber News *e:* **Nat Rubber**, *e:* **Nat. Rubber News**, *e:* **Nat Rubb News**

Natural Rubber Procedures Research Association Strain Tester *e:* **NRPRA Strain Tester**

Natural Rubber Producers' Research Association *e:* **NRPRA**

Natural Rubber Shippers Association *e:* **NRSA**

Natural Rubber Technology *e:* **N R Technol**

Natural Sausage Casings Manufacturers' Association *e:* **NSCMA**

Natural Science *e:* **Nat. Sc.**

Natural Science Association of Staten Island. Proceedings *e:* **Nat Sc As Staten Island Pr**

Natural Science Bulletin. University of Amoy *e:* **Nat Sci Bull Univ Amoy**

Natural Science Doctor *e:* **Nat. Sc. D.**

Natural Science for Youth Foundation *e:* **NSYF**

Natural Science Foundation of China *e:* **NSFC**

Natural Science Report. Ochanomizu University *e:* **Nat Sci Rep Ochanomizu Univ**, *e:* **Natur Sci Rep Ochanomizu Univ**

Natural Science Research Council *e:* **NSRC**

Natural Science Research. Natural Science Institute. Chosun University *e:* **Nat Sci Res Nat Sci Inst Chosun Univ**

Natural Science Tripos *e:* **NS Tripos**

Natural Science[s] *e:* **Nat Sci**, *e:* **NSC**

Natural Sciences [and] Engineering *e:* **NSE**

Natural Science[s] and [Engineering] Research Council [of Canada] *e:* **NSERC**

Natural Sciences and Engineering Research Council of Canada *e:* **NSERCC**

Natural Sciences and Engineering Research Council of Canada, Ottawa, Ontario *e:* **OONSE**

Natural Sciences [Department of UNESCO] *e:* **NS**

Natural Stupidness *e:* **NS**

Natural Systems Group *e:* **NSG**

Natural Toxins *e:* **Nat Toxins**

Natural Toxins Research Center *e:* **NTRC**

Natural Transition Orbitals *e:* **NTO**

Natural Uranium Fuel *e:* **NUF**

Natural Valence-Band Offset *e:* **NVBO**

Natural Variability, Resilience and Buffer Capacity of the Bodden Ecosystem *e:* **NAVAREP**

Natural Vegetable Powder *e:* **NVP**

natural wavelength *e:* **nwl**

Naturalia Hispanica *s:* **Nat Hisp**

Naturalia Monspeliensia *l:* **Nat Monspel**

Naturalia Monspeliensia. Serie Botanique *l:* **Nat Monspeliensia Ser Bot**, *l:* **Nat Monspel Ser Bot**, *l:* **Naturalia Monspel Ser Bot**

Naturalia Monspeliensia. Série Botanique *f:* **NMBQAA**

naturalisieren *d:* **natur.**

naturalisiert *d:* **natur.**

naturalist *d:* **natur**, *e:* **nat**

Naturalista Siciliano *i:* **Nat Sicil**, *i:* **NTSIAI**

Naturaliste Canadien *e:* **Nat. Can.**, *f:* **Nat. Can.**, *f:* **Naturaliste Can**

Naturaliste Canadien (Québec) *f:* **Nat. Can. (Qué.)**

Naturaliste Malgache *f:* **Nat Malgache**

Naturalistes Belges, *e:* **Nat. Belg.**

Naturalist's Library *e:* **NL**

NATURALISÉ FRANÇAIS *f:* **NF**

Naturalization *e:* **Nat**

Naturalization Test *e:* **NT**

Naturalized *e:* **Nat**

naturalized citizens *e:* **Nats**

naturally *e:* **natch**, *e:* **naty**

Naturally Aspirated *e:* **N**

Naturally Flat *e:* **NF**

Naturally Occurring Mutants *e:* **NM**

Naturally Occurring Top Component *e:* **NTC**

Naturally Radioactive *e:* **NR**

Naturally Radioactive Product *e:* **NRAP**

Naturalwirtschaft *d:* **Nat.-Wirtsch.**

Naturdenkmal *d:* **ND**

nature *e:* **nat**

Nature *e:* **NATRA**

Nature and Earth United with Science *e:* **NEXUS**

Nature and Landscape Conservation *e:* **NLC**

Nature and Life in Southeast Asia *e:* **Nat Life Southeast Asia**, *e:* **Nature and Life SE Asia**

Nature and Resources *e:* **NAREB**, *e:* **Nat Resour**, *e:* **Nat. Resources**

Nature and Science Education Review *e:* **Nature and Sci Ed R**

Nature and System *e:* **Nature Syst**

Nature Canada *e:* **Nat Can**, *e:* **Nat Canada**, *e:* **NTCNB**

Nature Canada [Ottawa] *e:* **Nat Can [Ottawa]**

Nature Conservancy *e:* **Nat Con**, *e:* **NC**, *e:* **TNC**

Nature Conservancy Council. Research Reports Digest *e:* **NCC Res Rep Dig**

Nature Conservancy News *e:* **Nat Conserv News**

Nature Conservation Branch. Transvaal Bulletin *e:* **Nat Conserv Branch Transtvaal Bull**

Nature Conservation Council *e:* **NCC**

Nature Conservation Council of New South Wales *e:* **NCCNSW**

Nature Conservation Review *e:* **NCR**

Nature Conservation Society of South Australia *e:* **NCSSA**

Nature et Progrès *f:* **Nat. Prog.**

Nature Farming International Research Foundation *e:* **NFIRF**

Nature Friends of America *e:* **NFA**

Nature Friends of Israel *e:* **NFI**

Nature Genetics *e:* **Nat Genet**

Nature in Cambridgeshire *e:* **Nat Cambs**

Nature in Wales *e:* **Nat W**

Nature Information *e:* **Nat. Inf.**

Nature/Land Cover information package *e:* **NATLAN**

Nature [London] *e:* **Na**

Nature [London]. New Biology *e:* **Nature [London] New Biol**

Nature [London]. Physical Science *e:*
Nature [London] Phys Sci

Nature Lovers League *e:* **NLL**

Nature Magazine *e:* **Nature M.**, *e:* **Nature Mag**

Nature Malaysiana *e:* **Nat Malays**

Nature Medicine *e:* **Nat Med**

Nature: New Biology *e:* **Nat New Biol**, *e:* **Nature New Biol**

Nature New Biology *e:* **NNB**

Nature: New Biology *e:* **NNBYA**

Nature of Action *e:* **NOA**

Nature [or Naturalist] *e:* **Nat**

Nature, Paris [R] *e:* **Nature (Paris)**

Nature: Physial Science *e:* **NPS**

Nature: Physical Science *e:* **Nature: Phys Sci**

Nature Reserve *e:* **NR**

Nature. Science Progress *e:* **Nat Sci Prog**

Nature Structural Biology *e:* **Nat Struct Biol**

Nature Study *e:* **Nat Study**

Nature Study Society *e:* **N.S.S.**

Nature Vivante *f:* **Nat Vivante**

Naturegraph Ocean Guide Books *e:* **Naturegp Ocean Guide Books**, *e:* **Naturegr Ocean Guide Books**

Naturel *f:* **Nat**

Naturens Verden *a:* **Naturens Verd**, *a:* **Nat Verden**

Nature's Sunshine Products, Inc. *e:* **NATR**

naturfarben *d:* **natfarb.**, *d:* **nf**

Naturfaser *d:* **Na**

Naturforschende Gesellschaft des Kantons Glarus *d:* **NGG**

Naturforschende Gesellschaft in Basel. Verhandlungen *d:* **Naturf Gesell Basel Verh**, *d:* **Naturforsch Ges Basel Verh**

Naturforschende Gesellschaft in Bern *d:* **NGB**

Naturforschende Gesellschaft in Zürich *d:* **NGZ**

Naturforschende Gesellschaft in Zürich. Vierteljahresschrift *d:* **Naturf Gesell Zürich Vierteljahrsschr**

Naturforschende Gesellschaft in Zürich. Vierteljahrsschrift *d:* **Naturforsch Ges Zürich Vierteljahrsschr**

Naturforschende Gesellschaft Luzern *d:* **NGL**

Naturforscher *d:* **Nat.-Forsch.**, *d:* **Ntf.**

Naturforschung *d:* **Nat.-Forsch.**, *d:* **Ntfg.**

Naturforschung und Medizin in Deutschland *d:* **NF Med Dt**

Naturfreunde-Internationale *d:* **NFI**

Naturfreundejugend *d:* **Intercultur**, *d:* **NFJ**

Naturfreundejugend Deutschlands *d:* **NFJD**

Naturgeschichte *d:* **Naturgesch.**

naturhistorisch *d:* **naturhist.**

Naturhistorisch-Medizinischer Verein zu Heidelberg. Verhandlungen *d:* **Naturh-Med Ver Heidelberg Verh**

Naturhistorische Gesellschaft e.V. *d:* **NHG**

Naturhistorischer Verein der Preussischen Rheinlande und Westphalens. Verhandlungen *d:* **Naturh Ver Preus Rheinl Verb**

Naturhistorischer Verein der Preussischen Rheinlande. Verhandlungen [Niederrheinische Gesellschaft für Natur und Heilkunde] *d:* **Naturh Ver Preus Rheinl Verh [Niederrhein Ges Bonn] Szb**

Naturhistorisches Museum in Wien. Annalen *d:* **Naturhist Mus Wien Ann**

Naturhistorisk-Antropologisk-Etnografiska Sällskapet i Moskva *r:* **N.A.E.S.**

Naturhistoriska Riksmuseet Stockholm *r:* **NRS**

Naturistenbund Köln e.V. *d:* **N.B.K.**

Naturkautschuk *d:* **Naturkautsch.**

Naturkunde *d:* **Nat**, *d:* **Naturkd.**

naturkundliches Bildungszentrum *d:* **NBZ**

Naturlehre *d:* **Naturl.**

natürliche Größe *d:* **Nat.Gr.**

natürliche Standorteinheit *d:* **NSTE**

natürliche[r] Größe *d:* **n. Gr.**

Natürliches Kohlenstoffisotopenverhältnis *d:* **nat. CIR**

Naturopa *e:* **Naturopa**

Naturopathic Doctor *e:* **N.D.**

Naturpark Pfälzerwald *d:* **NPW**

Naturprodukt *d:* **N**

Naturschutz *d:* **Nat.-Sch.**

Naturschutz heute *e:* **Nat.schutz heute**

Naturschutz und Landschaftspflege in Hamburg *d:* **Nat.schutz Landsch.pfl. Hambg.**

Naturschutz und Landschaftspflege in Niedersachsen *d:* **Nat.schutz Landsch.pfl. Niedersachs.**

Naturschutz und Landschaftsplanung *d:* **Nat.schutz Landsch.plan.**

Naturschutz- und Naturparks *d:* **Natursch Naturp**

Naturschutzbund Deutschland *d:* **Nabu**

Naturschutzgebiet *d:* **NSG**

Naturschutzgesetz *d:* **NatSchG**

Naturschutzjugend *d:* **NAJU**

Naturschutzverband Niedersachsen *d:* **NVV**

Naturschutzzentrum *d:* **NZ**

Naturschutzzentrum Hessen *d:* **NSH**, *d:* **NZH**

Naturumlauf *d:* **NU**

Naturvännernas Internationella Turistförening *r:* **NIT**

naturvidenskabelig *a:* **nat.**

Naturvidenskabeligt Forskningsråd *a:* **NFV**

Naturwissenschaft und Medizin *d:* **Naturwissenschaft Med**, *d:* **Naturwiss Med**, *d:* **NM**

Naturwissenschaft[en] *d:* **Naturwiss.**

Naturwissenschaften *d:* **Naturwissen**

Naturwissenschaften im Unterricht. Physik/Chemie/Biologie *d:* **Naturwiss Unterr Phys Chem Biol**

Naturwissenschaften im Unterricht [Teil] Physik/Chemie *d:* **Naturwiss Unterr Phys/Chem**

Naturwissenschaft[ler] *d:* **Naturw.**, *d:* **Naturwiss.**, *d:* **Nat.-Wiss.**, *d:* **Ntw.**

naturwissenschaftlich *d:* **naturw.**, *d:* **naturwiss.**, *d:* **natw.**, *d:* **natwiss.**

Naturwissenschaftlich-technische Fachsprache *d:* **NTF**

Naturwissenschaftliche Fakultät Münchner Universität. Inaugural-Dissertation *d:* **Naturwiss Fak Münich Univ Inaug-Diss**

Naturwissenschaftliche Monatshefte *d:* **NwMh**

Naturwissenschaftliche Monatshefte für den Biologischen, Chemischen, Geographischen, und Geologischen Unterricht *d:* **Naturwiss Monatsh Biol Chem Geogr Geol Unterr**

Naturwissenschaftliche Rundschau *d:* **Naturwiss Bundsch**, *d:* **Naturwiss. Rundsch.**, *d:* **Naturwiss. Rundschau**, *d:* **Naturw Rdsch**, *d:* **Nat.wiss. Rundsch.**, *d:* **NR**, *d:* **NwR**

Naturwissenschaftliche Rundschau [Stuttgart] *d:* **Naturw Rdsch [Stuttg]**

Naturwissenschaftliche Umschau der Chemiker Zeitung *d:* **Naturwiss Umsch Chem Ztg**

Naturwissenschaftliche Wochenschrift *d:* **Naturw Wchnschr**, *d:* **Naturw. Wo.**, *d:* **Naturw Wochensch**, *d:* **NwW**

Naturwissenschaftliche Zeitschrift für Forst- und Landwirtschaft *d:* **Naturwiss Z Forst Landwirtsch**, *d:* **Naturw Z Forst u Landw**, *d:* **NZFL**

Naturwissenschaftliche Zeitschrift für Land- und Forstwirtschaft *d:* **Naturw Z Land-u Forstw**, *d:* **NatZLF**

Naturwissenschaftlicher Lesesaal *d:* **NLS**

Naturwissenschaftlicher Verein *d:* **NWV**

Naturwissenschaftlicher Verein, Elberfeld *d:* **NVE**

Naturwissenschaftlicher Verein für Neuvorpommern und Rügen in Greifswald. Mitteilungen *d:* **Naturw Ver Neuvorpommern und Rügen in Greifswald Mitt**

Naturwissenschaftlicher Verein für Schleswig-Holstein. Schriften *d:* **Naturwiss Ver Schleswig-Holstein Schr**

Naturwissenschaftlicher Verein [Halle]. Jahresberichte *d:* **Naturw Ver [Halle] Jber**

Naturwissenschaftliches Forschungszentrum der N.V. Philips Gloeilampen-Fabrieken, Eindhoven *d:* **NATLAB**

Nauchnaya Konferentsiya po Yadernoi Meteorologii [Obninsk] *R:* **Nauch Konf Yadern Meteor [Obninsk]**

Nauchnyi Ezhegodnik Odesskii Gosudarstvennyi Universitet Biologicheskii Fakul'tet *R:* **Nauchn Ezheg Odess Gos Univ Biol Fak**

Naučno-Issledovatel'skii Institut Geologii Artiki *R:* **NIIGA**

Naučnyj Eżegodnik Odesskii Gosudarstvennyi Universitet Biologicheskii Fakul'tet *R:* **Naučn Eżeg Odess Gos Univ Biol Fak**

Nautilus Environmedic *e:* **NENV**

Naval Aeronautical Medical Center *e:* **NAVAEROMEDCEN**

Naval Aerospace and Regional Medical Center *e:* **NARMC**

Naval Aerospace Medical Center *e:* **NAMC**

Naval Aerospace Medical Institute *e:* **NAMI**, *e:* **NAVAEROSPMEDINST**, *e:* **NAVMED**

Naval Aerospace Medical Research Institute *e:* **NAVAEROSPMEDRSCHINST**

Naval Aerospace [Medical] Research Laboratory *e:* **NAMRL**

Naval Aerospace Research Facility *e:* **NARF**

Naval Air All Weather Flight Squadron e: **NAAWFS**

Naval Air Development Center-Aerospace Crew Equipment Department e: **NADC-AC**

Naval Air Development Center-Aerospace Medical Research Department e: **NADC-MR**

Naval Air Development Center-Aviation Medical Acceleration Laboratory e: **NADC-Ma**, e: **NADC-ML**

Naval All-Weather Testing Program e: **NAWTP**

Naval All Weather Testing Program Detachment e: **NAWTPD**

Naval Atlantic Meteorology and Oceanography Center e: **NLMOC**

Naval Automated Medical Logistics System e: **NAMLS**

Naval Aviation Medical Center e: **NAVAVNMEDCEN**

Naval Aviation School of Medicine e: **NASM**

Naval Aviator/Flight Surgeon e: **NA/FS**

Naval Biological Laboratory e: **NAVBIOLAB**, e: **NBL**

Naval Biomedical Research Laboratory e: **NBRL**

Naval Branch Oceanographic Offices e: **NBOO**

Naval Command, Control and Ocean Surveillance Center Research, Development, Test and Evaluation (RDT&E) Division e: **NRaD** **(NCCOSC)**

Naval Command, Control & Ocean Surveillance Center e: **NCCOSC**

Naval Command, Control & Ocean Systems Center e: **NCCOSC**

Naval Control and Protection of Shipping e: **NCAPS**

Naval Electronic[s] Environment[al] Training System e: **NEETS**

Naval Energy and Environmental Support Activity e: **NEESA**

Naval Environmental Bulletin Board System e: **NEBBS**

Naval Environmental Command Tactical Aid e: **NECTA**

Naval Environmental Compliance Information System e: **NECIS**

Naval Environmental Data System e: **NEDS**

Naval Environmental Display Station e: **NEDS**

Naval Environmental Display System e: **NEDS**

Naval Environmental Prediction Research Facility e: **NAVENVPREDRSCHFAC**, e: **NEPRF**

Naval Environmental Protection Act National Estuarine Research Reserve System e: **NELC**

Naval Environmental Protection Support Service e: **NEPSS**

Naval Environmental Support Office e: **NESCO**

Naval European Meteorology and Oceanography Center e: **NEMOC**

Naval Experimental Manned Observatory e: **NEMO**

Naval Health Research Center e: **NAVHLTHRSCHC**, e: **NHRC**

Naval Ice Center e: **NAVICECEN**

Naval Institute of Oceanology e: **NIO**

Naval Medical Center e: **NMC**

Naval Medical Command e: **NAVMEDCOM**, e: **NMC**

Naval Medical Data Service Center e: **NAVMEDATASERVCEN**, e: **NMDSC**

Naval Medical Depot e: **NMD**

Naval Medical Field Research Laboratory e: **NMFRL**

Naval Medical Information Management Center e: **NMIMC**

Naval Medical Information System e: **NAVMEDIS**

Naval Medical Materiel Support Command e: **NAVMEDMATSUPPCOM**

Naval Medical Neuropsychiatric Research Unit e: **NMNRU**

Naval Medical Program for Nuclear Casualties e: **NMPNC**

Naval Medical Publication e: **NMP**

Naval Medical Research and Development Command e: **NMRDC**

Naval Medical Research Institute e: **NMR**, e: **NMRI**

Naval Medical Research Institute Detachment e: **NAMRID**

Naval Medical Research Laboratory e: **NMRL**

Naval Medical Research Unit e: **NAVMEDRSCHU**, e: **NMRU**, e: **NRMI**

Naval Medical School e: **NAVMEDSCOL**, e: **NMS**

Naval Medical Supply Depot e: **NMSD**

Naval Medical Unit e: **NavMedU**

Naval Medicine e: **NAVMED**

Naval Meteorological Branch e: **N.M.B.**

Naval Meteorological Service e: **NMS**

Naval Meteorology and Oceanography Command e: **NMOC**

Naval Mobile Environmental Team e: **NMET**

Naval Observatory e: **NAVOBS**, e: **NO**, e: **NOBS**, e: **NOBSY**

Naval Observatory Flagstaff [Arizona] Station e: **NAVOBSYFLAGSTAFFSTA**

Naval Ocean Intelligence Center e: **NOIC**

Naval Ocean Research and Development Activity e: **NORDA**

Naval Ocean Research and Development Agency e: **NORDA**

Naval Ocean Surveillance Information Center e: **NOSIC**

Naval Ocean System[s] Center e: **NOSC**

Naval Oceanic Vertical Aerosol Model e: **NOVAM**

Naval Oceanographic and Atmospheric Research Laboratory e: **NOARL**

Naval Oceanographic and Meteorological Support System e: **NOMSS**

Naval Oceanographic Command e: **NOC**

Naval Oceanographic Data Center e: **NODC**

Naval Oceanographic Data Distribution and Expansion System e: **NODDES**

Naval Oceanographic Data Distribution System e: **NODDS**

Naval Oceanographic Distribution Center e: **NODC**

Naval Oceanographic District Office e: **NAVOCEANDISTO**

Naval Oceanographic Office e: **NAVO**, e: **NAVOCEANO[FC]**, e: **NAVOCEAO**, e: **NOC**

Naval Oceanographic Office Instruction e: **OCEANAVINST**

Naval Oceanographic Office Special Publication e: **NOO-SP**

Naval Oceanographic Processing Center e: **NOPF**

Naval Oceanographic Program e: **NOP**

Naval Oceanographic Publication e: **NOP**

Naval Oceanographic Research and Development Administration e: **NORDA**

Naval Oceanography Command Center/Joint Typhoon Warning Center e: **NOCC/JTWC**

Naval Oceanography Command Detachment e: **NAVOCEANCOMDET**

Naval Oceanography Command Support System e: **NAVOCEANCOM**

Naval (or Navy) Medical Research Unit e: **NAMRU**

Naval [or Navy] Underwater Sound Laboratory e: **NUSL**

Naval [or Navy] Underwater Sound Reference Laboratory e: **NUSRL**

Naval [or Navy] Weather Service e: **NWS**

Naval Pacific Meteorology and Oceanography Center e: **NPMOC**

Naval Polar Oceanographic (or Oceanography) Center e: **NPOC**

Naval Preventive Medical Unit e: **NavPreventMedU**, e: **NAVPVNTMEDU**

Naval Radio Research Observatory e: **NRRO**

Naval Regional Medical Center e: **NAVREGMEDCEN**, e: **NRMC**

Naval Remote Ocean Sensing System e: **N-ROSS**

Naval Research Oceanographic Satellite System e: **N-ROSS**

Naval School of Aviation Medicine e: **NSAM**

Naval School of Health Sciences e: **NSHS**

Naval Sea Data Support Activity e: **NSDSA**

Naval Sea Logistics Center, Detachment e: **NSLCD**

Naval Sea Systems Command identifier e: **SEA**

Naval Sea Systems Command Technical Representative e: **NSTR**

Naval Space Projects Office e: **NSPO**

Naval Space Surveillance System e: **NSSS**

Naval Submarine Medical Center e: **NAVSUBMEDCEN**, e: **NSMC**

Naval Submarine Medical Research Laboratory e: **NAVSUBMEDRSCHLAB**, e: **NSMRL**

Naval Underwater Ordnance Laboratory e: **NUOL**

Naval Underwater Ordnance Station e: **NavUnderwaterOrdnSta**, e: **NUOS**

Naval Underwater Sound Laboratory e: **NAVUWSOUNDLAB**

Naval Underwater Systems Center e: **NUSC**

Naval Underwater Systems Center Aluminum e: **NUSCAL**

Naval Underwater Systems Center, New London e: **NUSC/NL**

Naval Underwater Systems Center, Newport e: **NUSC/NPT**

Naval Underwater System[s] Engineering
Center e: **NUSEC**
Naval Underwater Warfare Center e:
NUWC
Naval Underwater Weapons Evaluation
Station e: **NUWES**, e: **NUWFS**
Naval Underwater Weapons Research and
Engineering Station e: **NUWRES**
Naval Underwater Weapons [Research and
Engineering] Station e: **NUWS**
Naval Underwater Weapons Systems
Engineering Center e: **NUWSEC**
Naval Weather Research Facility e:
NWRF
Naval Weather Service Association e:
NWSA
Naval Weather Service [Command] e:
NAVWEASERV
Naval Weather Service Command e:
NWSC
Naval Weather Service Command
Representative e:
NAVWEASERVCOMREP
Naval Weather Service Command
Representative, Atlantic e:
NAVWEASERVCOMREPLANT
Naval Weather Service Command
Representative, Europe and
Mediterranean e:
NAVWEASERVCOMREPEUR/MED
Naval Weather Service Command
Representative, Pacific e:
NAVWEASERVCOMREPPAC
Naval Weather Service Detachment [or
Division] e: **NWSD**
Naval Weather Service Environmental
Detachment e: **NWSED**
Naval Weather Service Office e: **NWSO**
Naval [Worldwide] Environmental Data
Network e: **NEDN**
Navigable General-Purpose Unterwater
Surveyor e: **ANGUS A**
Navigation and Ocean Development e:
NOD
Navigation in Australian waters e:
NavAus
Navigation in the Indian Ocean e: **NavInd**
Navigational and Meteorological Warning
Broadcast Service e: **NAVTEX**
Navy Branch Oceanographic Office e:
NAVBROCEANOS
Navy Deep Sea Oceanographic System e:
NDSOS
Navy Environmental and Preventive
Medicine Unit e: **NEPMU**
Navy Environmental Operational
Nowcasting System e: **NEONS**
Navy Environmental Protection Data Base
e: **NEPDB**
Navy Environmental Remote Sensing
Program e: **NERSP**
Navy Environmental Support Office e:
NESO
Navy Hydrographic Office e: **NHO**
Navy Integrated Space Program e: **NISP**
Navy Medical Administrative Unit e:
NAVMEDADMINU
Navy Medical Center e: **NAVMEDCEN**
Navy Medical Field Research Laboratory
e: **NAVMEDFLDRSCHLAB**
Navy Medical Neuropsychiatric Research
Unit e: **NAVMEDNPRSCHU**

Navy Medical Research Institute e:
NAVMEDRSCHINST
Navy Medical Research Laboratory e:
NAVMEDRSCHLAB
Navy Medical Support Unit e:
NAVMEDSUPPU
Navy Numerical Weather Problems [Group]
e: **NANWEP**
Navy Occupational Health Information
Management System e: **NOHIMS**
Navy Occupational Safety and Health e:
NAVOSH
Navy Ocean Experimental Acoustic Data
Bank e: **NAVDAB**
Navy Ocean Modeling and Prediction
Program e: **NOMP**
Navy Ocean Surveillance Information
Center e: **NOSIC**
Navy Ocean Surveillance Satellite e:
NOSS
Navy Oceanographic [and[Meteorological
[Automatic] Device e: **NOMAD**
Navy Oceanographic Observations from
Space e: **NOOS**
Navy Oceanographic Office e: **NOO**
Navy Oceanographic Vertical Aerosol
Model e: **NOVAM**
Navy Operational Global Atmospheric
Prediction System e: **NOGAPS**
Navy Operational Regional Atmospheric
Prediction System e: **NORAPS**
Navy Regional Medical Center e: **NRMC**
Navy Remote [Ocean] Sensing Satellite [or
System] e: **N-ROSS**
Navy Space Project e: **NSP**
Navy Space Systems Activity e: **NSSA**
Navy Underwater Sound Laboratory e:
NASL, e: **NASU**
Navy Underwater Sound Reference
Laboratory e:
NAVUWTRSOUNDREFLAB
Navy Weather & Oceanographic Center e:
NWOC
Navy Weather Research Facility e:
NAVWEARSCHFA
Navy Weather Service Command e:
NAVWEASERVCOM
NCAR [National Center for Atmospheric
Research] GARP [Global Atmospheric
Research Program] Task Group e:
NGTG
NCAR [National Center for Atmospheric
Research] Quarterly e: **NCAR Quart.**,
e: **NCAR Q[uart][erly]**
NCHS [National Center for Health
Statistics] Advance Data e: **NCHS [Natl
Cent Health Stat] Adv Data**
Near-Coast Matter- and Energy Fluxes: The
Transition between Land/Sea in the
South-eastern North Sea e: **KUSTOS**
Near Coastal Waters Program e: **NCWP**
Near-Earth Asteroid e: **NEA**
Near Earth Asteroid Prospector e: **NEAP**
Near Earth Asteroid Rendezvous e: **NEAR**
Near Earth Asteroid Tracking e: **NEAT**
Near-Earth Instrumentation Facility e:
NEIF
near-earth magnetospheric satellite e:
nems
Near-Earth Object e: **NEO**
Near-Earth Orbit e: **NEO**
Near-Earth Phase e: **NEP**

Near-Earth Tracking and Data System e:
NETDS
Near East Animal Health Institute e:
NEAHI
Near Space e: **NS**
Near Space Instrumentation Facility e:
NSIF
Near-Surface Geological Disposal e:
NSGD
Near Term Active Protection System e:
NTAPS
Nebraska Behavioral Biology Group e:
NBBG
Nebraska Geological Survey. Bulletin e:
Nebr Geol Surv Bull
Nebraska Geological Survey. Paper e:
Nebraska Geol Survey Paper
Nebraska Medical Journal e: **Nebr Med J**
Nebraska Natural Resources Information
System e: **NNRIS**
Nebraska State Medical Association e:
NSMA
Nebraska State Medical Journal e: **Nebr
State Med J**, e: **Nebr St Med J**
Nebraska Veterinary Medical Association
e: **NVMA**
Nebraska Water Resource[s] Center e:
NWRC
Nebraska Water Survey Paper e: **Nebr
Waber Surv Pap**
Necedah National Wildlife Refuge e:
NNWR
Nechako Environmental Coalition e: **NEC**
Nederlands Geologisch Mijnbouwkundig
Genootschap [Koninklijk].
Verhandelingen n: **Ned Geol
Mijnbouwkd Genoot Verh**
Nederlands Instituut voor Technisch-
Biologisch Onderzoek in de Natuur n:
NITBON
Nederlands Onderwater Bond e: **NOB**, n:
NOB
Nederlands Verkoopkantoor voor
Wasserijproducten n: **NVW**
Nederlands-vlaamse Vereniging voor
ecologie n: **NecoV**
Nederlandsch Tijdschrift voor Hygien,
Microbiologie, en Serologie n: **Ned
Tijdschr Hyg Microbiol Serol**
Nederlandsch Tijdschrift voor Hygiene,
Microbiologie, en Serologie n: **NETHA**
Nederlandsch Tijdschrift voor Verloskunde
en Gynaecologie n: **Ned Tijdschr
Verloskd Gynaecol**, n: **Ned Ts Verlosk**,
n: **NTVGA**
Nederlandse Ecologen Vereniging n: **NEV**
Nederlandse Federatie van
Naturistenverenigingen n: **NFN**
Nederlandse Vereniging tegen Water-,
Bodem- en Luchtverontreiniging n:
WBL
Nederlandse Vereniging van Producenten
en Importeurs van Wegen- en
Waterbouwmaterialen n: **VPI**
Nederlandse Vereniging voor
Afvalwaterzuivering n: **NVA**
Nederlandse Vereniging voor Geodesie n:
NVG
Nederlandse Vereniging voor Microbiologie
n: **NVvM**
Nederlandse Vereniging voor de Handel in
Pluimvee en Wild n: **VHP**

Nederlandse Verniging voor de Handel en Verwerking van Pluimvee, Wild en Tamme Konijnen *n:* **VHVP**

Neftegazovaya Geologiya i Geofizika *R:* **Neftegazov Geol Geofiz**

negativ dotiertes Silizium *d:* **NDS**

Negative Logarithm of Hydrogen-Ion Activity *e:* **pH**

Negative Polarity Operation *e:* **NPO**

Negative Pressure Chilled Circulating Water *e:* **NPCCW**

Negative Pressure Chilled Water *e:* **NPCW**

Neighborhood Environmental Evaluation and Decision System [Health Services and Mental Health Administration] *e:* **NEEDS**

Neighborhood environmental watch network *e:* **NEWNET**

Neighborhood Environmental Workshops *e:* **NEWS**

Neighborhood Environmental Workshops Program *e:* **NEWS Program**

Neighborhood Health Center *e:* **NHC**

Neighborhood Health Program *e:* **NHP**

Neighborhood Voluntary Associations and Consumer Protection *e:* **NVACP**

Nennleistung in Pferdestärken *d:* **NgPS**

Nennleistung, mittlere in Pferdestärke[n] *d:* **Nm/PS**

Neonatal-Perinatal Medicine *e:* **NPM**

Neoterik Health Technologies, Inc. *e:* **NTRK**

Nepal Forum of Environmental Journalists *e:* **NFEJ**

Nepal Water Supply and Sewerage Corporation *e:* **NWSSC**

NERC Isotope Geosciences Laboratory *e:* **NIGL**

NESDIS [National Environmental Satellite Data and Information Service] Environmental Inventory *e:* **NESDIS [Natl Environ Satell Data Inf Serv] Environ Inventory**

NESP [National Environmental Studies Project] Report *e:* **NESP Rep**

Net Environmental Benefits *e:* **NEB**

Net Present Value for Space Shuttle *e:* **NPVSH**

Netherlands Agency for Aerospace Programmes *e:* **NIVR**

Netherlands Association on Wastewater Treatment and Water Pollution Control *e:* **NAWTWPC**

Netherlands Development Corporation for Energy and the Environment *e:* **NOVEM**

Netherlands' Ecological Society *e:* **NES**

Netherlands. Geologische Dienst. Toelichting bij de Geologische Kaart van Nederland 1:50\000 *n:* **Neth Geol Dienst Toelichting Geol Kaart Ned 1:50\000**

Netherlands. Institute for Sea Research. Publication Series *e:* **Neth Inst Sea Res Publ Ser**

Netherlands Institute for Sea Research. Publication Series *e:* **NSRPDU**

Netherlands Institute of Ecology *e:* **NIE**

Netherlands Institute of Ocean Sciences *e:* **NIOZ**

Netherlands Interdepartmental Working Community for the Application of Remote Sensing Techniques *e:* **NIWARS**

Netherlands Journal of Medicine *e:* **Neth J Med,** *e:* **NLJMA**

Netherlands Journal of Sea Research *e:* **Neth J Sea,** *e:* **Neth J Sea Res,** *e:* **NJSRB**

Netherlands National Committee of the International Association on Water Pollution Research and Control *e:* **NNCIAWPRC**

Netherlands National Institute of Public Health and Environmental Protection *e:* **RIVM**

Netherlands Observatory of Science and Technology *e:* **NOWT**

Netherlands. Rijks Geologische Dienst. Jaarverslag *n:* **Neth Rijks Geol Dienst Jaarversl**

Network for Continuing Medical Education *e:* **NCME**

Network for Environment and Sustainable Development for Africa *e:* **NESDA**

Network [for] Environmental Technology Transfer [association] *e:* **NETT**

Network for Industrial Environmental Management *e:* **NIEM**

Network Medical Information Services *e:* **NMIS**

Network of Animal Health *e:* **NOAH**

Network of Community-Oriented Educational Institutions for Health Sciences *e:* **NCOEIHS**

Network Operating System/Batch Environment *e:* **NOS/BE**

Network Protective Devices *e:* **NPDs**

Network Remote Procedure Call *e:* **NetRPC**

Neue Denkschriften der Schweizerischen Naturforschenden Gesellschaft *d:* **NDSchNG**

Neues Jahrbuch für Geologie und Palaeontologie, Abhandlungen *d:* **Neues Jahrb. Geol. Palaeontol.**

Neues Jahrbuch für Geologie und Palaeontologie, Monatshefte *d:* **Neues Jahrb. Geol. Palaeontol.**

Neujahrsblatt der Naturforschenden Gesellschaft in Zürich *d:* **Neujahrsbl. Nat.forsch. Ges. Zür.**

Neujahrsblatt der Naturforschenden Gesellschaft Schaffhausen *d:* **Neujahrsbl. Nat.forsch. Ges. Schaffhausen**

Neujahrsblatt Herausgegeben von der Naturforschenden Gesellschaft in Zürich *d:* **Neujahrsbl Naturforsch Ges Zürich**

Neujahrsblatt. Naturforschende Gesellschaft in Zürich *d:* **NNGZB**

Neujahrsblatt. Naturforschenden Gesellschaft in Zürich *d:* **Neujahrsbl Naturforsch Ges Zür**

Neurnlogy and Neurobiology *e:* **NEUND**

neurobiological *e:* **neurobio**

Neurobiologie *d:* **Neurobiol.**

neurobiologist *e:* **neurobio**

Neurobiology *e:* **NBBMAN**

neurobiology *e:* **neurobio**

Neurobiology, Biochemistry and Morphology *e:* **Neurobiol Biochem Morphol**

Neurobiology of Aging *e:* **Neurobiol Aging**

Neurobiology of Learning and Memory *e:* **Neurobiol Learn Mem**

Neurologia Medico-Chirurgica *e:* **Neurol Med Chir [Tokyo]**

Neurology and Neurobiology [New York] *e:* **Neurol Neurobiol [NY]**

Neuromedical Technologies, Inc. *e:* **NMTI**

Neuropathology and Applied Neurobiology *e:* **NANED,** *e:* **Neurop Ap N,** *e:* **Neuropathol Appi Neurobiol,** *e:* **Neuropathol Appl Neurobiol**

Neurosurgeon *e:* **NS,** *e:* **NSURG**

Neutral-Atmosphären-Temperatur-Experiment *d:* **NATE,** *d:* **NAT Experiment**

Neutral Atmosphere Temperature Experiment *e:* **NATE**

Neutral Particle Beam Space Experiment *e:* **NPBSE**

Neutral Particle Beam Space Vehicle *e:* **NPBSV**

Neutralatmosphärentemperatur *d:* **NATE**

neutronendotiertes Silizium *d:* **NDS**

Nevada Academy of Natural Sciences *e:* **NANS**

Nevada Applied Ecology Group *e:* **NAEG**

Nevada Applied Ecology Information Center [Department of Energy] *e:* **NAEIC**

Nevada Bureau of Mines and Geology *e:* **NBMG**

Nevada. Bureau of Mines and Geology. Bulletin *e:* **Nev Bur Mines Geol Bull**

Nevada. Bureau of Mines and Geology. Report *e:* **Nev Bur Mines Geol Rep**

Nevada. Department Conservation and Natural Resources. Water Resources Information Series *e:* **Nev Dep Conserv Nat Resour Water Resour Inf Ser**

Nevada Department of Conservation and Natural Resources *e:* **NDCNR**

Nevada. Department of Conservation and Natural Resources. Water Resources Bulletin *e:* **Nev Dep Conserv Nat Resour Water Resour Bull**

Nevada. Department of Conservation and Natural Resources. Water Resources Reconnaissance Series *e:* **Nev Dep Conserv Nat Resour Water Resour Recoanaissance Ser**

Nevada Department of Health *e:* **NDH**

Nevada Department of Natural Resources and Conservation *e:* **NDNRC**

Nevada Department of Wildlife *e:* **NDW**

Nevada Department (or Division) of Environmental Protection *e:* **NDEP**

Nevada Division of Occupational Safety and Health *e:* **NDOSH**

Nevada Division of Radiological Health *e:* **NDRH**

Nevada Division of Water Planning *e:* **NDWP**

Nevada Division of Water Resources *e:* **NDWR**

Nevada. Division of Water Resources. Water Resources Bulletin *e:* **Nev Div Water Resour Water Resour Bull**

Nevada. Division of Water Resources. Water Resources Reconnaissance Series *e:* **Nev Div Water Resour Water Resour Reconnaissance Ser**

Nevada Division of Wildlife *e:* **NDOW**

Nevada Environmental Advisory Group *e:* **NEAG**

Nevada. Office of the State Engineer. Water Resources Bulletin *e:* **Nev Off State Eng Water Resour Bull**

Nevada. State Engineer. Water Resources Bulletin *e:* **Nev State Eng Water Resour Bull**

Nevada. State Engineers Office. Water Resources Bulletin *e:* **Nev State Engineer's Office Water Res Bull**

Nevada State Health & Coordinating Council *e:* **NSHCC**

Nevada University. Department of Geology and Mining Bulletin *e:* **Nev Univ Dp G M B**

Nevada University. Desert Research Institute. Center for Water Resources Research. Project Report *e:* **Nevada Univ Center Water Resources Research Proj Rept**

Nevada Wildlife *e:* **Nev Wildl**

New Animal Drug Application [Food and Drug Administration] *e:* **NADA**

New Biological Nomenclature *e:* **NBN**

New Biologist *e:* **New Biol.**

New Biology *e:* **NB,** *e:* **New Biol**

New Brunswick Department of Natural Resources and Energy Fredericton, New Brunswick *e:* **NBFNR**

New Brunswick. Department of Natural Resources. Mineral Resources Branch. Report of Investigation *e:* **NB Dep Nat Resour Miner Resour Branch Rep Invest**

New Brunswick. Department of Natural Resources. Mineral Resources Branch. Topical Report *e:* **NB Dep Nat Resour Miner Resour Branch Top Rep**

New Brunswick Department of Natural Resources. Reprint *e:* **NB Dep Nat Resour Repr**

New Caledonia. Bulletin Geologique *e:* **Nea Caledonia Bull Geol**

New Dimensions in Medicine *e:* **NDM**

New Directions for Mental Health Services *e:* **New Dir Ment Health Serv**

New Ecological Paradigm *e:* **NEP**

New Ecologist *e:* **NECG,** *e:* **New Ecol**

New England Interstate Environmental Training Center *e:* **NEIETC**

New England Interstate Water Pollution Control Commission *e:* **NEIWPCC**

New England Journal of Medicine *e:* **Ne Engl J Med,** *e:* **NEIMAG,** *e:* **NEJM,** *e:* **NEJMA,** *e:* **NEngJ Med,** *e:* **N England J Med,** *e:* **N Engl J Med,** *e:* **New Engl J Med**

New England Journal of Medicine. Medical Progress Series *e:* **N Engl J Med Med Prog Ser**

New England Medical Center *e:* **NEMC**

New England Medical Center Hospitals *e:* **NEMCH**

New England Medical Gazette *e:* **N. Eng. M. Gaz.**

New England Offshore Mining Environmental Study *e:* **NOMES**

New England Plant, Soil and Water Laboratory *e:* **NEPSWL**

New England Regional Medical Library Service *e:* **NERMLS,** *e:* **NRMLS**

New England Water Works Association *e:* **NEWWA**

New England Water Works Association. Journal *e:* **NEWAJ,** *e:* **New England Water Works Assoc Jour**

New England Waterworks Association *e:* **NEWA**

New England Wild Flower Preservation Society *e:* **NEWFPS**

New England Wild Flower Society *e:* **NEWFS,** *e:* **NEWS**

New Geographical Dictionary *e:* **NGD**

New Hampshire Medical Association *e:* **NHMA**

New Hampshire Medical Society *e:* **NHMS**

New Hebrides. Geological Survey. Annual Report *e:* **New Hebrides Geol Surv Annu Rep**

New Hebrides. Geological Survey. Report *e:* **New Hebrides Geol Surv Rep**

New Jersey Association of Healthcare Recruiters *e:* **NJAHR**

New Jersey. Bureau of Geology and Topography. Bulletin *e:* **NJ Bur Geol Topogr Bull,** *e:* **NJ Geol Topogr Bull**

New Jersey. Department of Conservation and Economic Development. Geologic Report Series *e:* **NJ Dep Conserv Econ Develop Geol Rep Ser**

New Jersey Department of Environmental Protection *e:* **NJDEP**

New Jersey Department of Environmental Protection and Energy *e:* **NJDEPE**

New Jersey. Department of Environmental Protection. Division of Natural Resources. Bureau of Geology and Topography. Bul *e:* **NJ Dep Environ Prot Div Nat Resour Bur Geol Topogr Bull**

New Jersey. Division of Water Policy and Supply. Special Report *e:* **NJ Div Water Policy Supply Spec Rep**

New Jersey. Division of Water Policy and Supply. Water Resources Circular *e:* **NJ Div Water Policy Supply Water Resour Cir**

New Jersey. Division of Water Resources. Special Report *e:* **NJ Div Water Resour Spec Rep,** *e:* **NJ Water Resour Spec Rep**

New Jersey. Geological Survey *e:* **NJ G S**

New Jersey Health and Sanitary Association *e:* **NJHSA**

New Jersey Medical School *e:* **NJMS**

New Jersey Medicine *e:* **N J Med**

New Jersey Veterinary Medical Association *e:* **NJVMA**

New Medical Journal *e:* **New Med J**

New Mexico. Bureau of Mines and Mineral Resources. Geologic Map. New Mexico Institute of Mining and Technology *e:* **New Mexico Bur Mines and Mineral Resources Geol Map**

New Mexico. Bureau of Mines and Mineral Resources. Ground Water Report *e:* **NM Bur Mines Miner Resour Ground Water Rep**

New Mexico. Bureau of Mines and Mineral Resources Hydrologic Report *e:* **NM Bur Mines Miner Resour Hydrol Rep**

New Mexico Department of Health *e:* **NMDOH**

New Mexico Environment Department *e:* **NMED**

New Mexico Environment Division *e:* **NMED**

New Mexico Environmental Improvement Board *e:* **NMEIB**

New Mexico Environmental Improvement Division *e:* **NMEID**

New Mexico Geological Society. Annual Field Conference Guidebook *e:* **NM Geol Soc Annu Field Conf Guideb**

New Mexico Geological Society. Field Conference Guidebook *e:* **NM Geol Soc Field Conf Guideb**

New Mexico Geological Society. Guidebook of Annual Field Conference *e:* **NM Geol Soc Guideb Annu Field Conf**

New Mexico Geological Society. Special Publication *e:* **New Mexico Geol Soc Spec Pub,** *e:* **NM Geol Soc Spec Publ**

New Mexico Geology *e:* **New Mex Geol,** *e:* **N Mex Geol,** *e:* **NM Geol**

New Mexico Regulations Governing Water Supplies *e:* **NMRGWS**

New Mexico State Bureau of Mines and Mineral Resources. Geologic Map *e:* **NM State Bur Mines Miner Resour Geol Map**

New Mexico University. Bulletin. Geological Series *e:* **N Mex Univ B G S**

New Mexico University. Publications in Geology. Publications in Meteoritics *e:* **N Mex Univ Pubs Geology Pubs Meteoritics**

New Mexico University. Publications in Meteoritics *e:* **New Mexico Univ Pubs Meteoritics**

New Mexico Water Quality Control Commission Regulations *e:* **NMWQCCR**

New Mexico Water Quality Regulations *e:* **NMWQR**

New Mexico Wildlife *e:* **NM Wildl**

New Microbiologica *e:* **New Microbiol**

New Millennium Observatory *e:* **NEMO**

New Natura Brevium *e:* **New Nat Brev,** *e:* **New NB,** *e:* **NNB**

New Opportunities for Animal Health scientists *e:* **NOAH**

New Orleans Geographical Society. Log *e:* **NOGS Log**

New Orleans Medical and Surgical Journal *e:* **New Orleans Med Surg J,** *e:* **N Orl Med and S J,** *e:* **N.Orl.M.&S.J.,** *e:* **N. Orl. N. & S. J.**

New Production Heavy-Water Reactor *e:* **NP-HWR**

New Production Light-Water Reactor *e:* **NP-LWR**

New Professionals Section of the American Public Health Association *e:* **NPSAPHA**

New Source and Environmental Questionnaire *e:* **NS/EQ**

New South Waks Association for Mental Health *e:* **NSWAMH**

New South Wales. Department of Agriculture. Biological and Chemical Research Institute. Annual Plant Disease Survey *e:* **NSW Dep Agric Biol Chem Res Inst Annu Plant Dis Surv**

New South Wales Department of Land and Water Conservation *e:* **NSW LWC**

New South Wales. Department of Mines. Geological Survey. Bulletin *e:* **NSW Dep Mines Geol Surv Bull**

New South Wales. Department of Mines. Geological Survey. Mineral Industry of New South Wales e: **NSW Dep Mines Geol Surv Miner Ind NSW**

New South Wales. Department of Mines. Geological Survey. Report e: **NSW Dep Mines Geol Surv Rep**

New South Wales. Department of Mines. Memoirs of the Geological Survey of New South Wales. Geology e: **NSW Dep Mines Mem Geol Surv NSW Geol**

New South Wales. Department of Mines. Memoirs of the Geological Survey of New South Wales. Palaeontology e: **NSW Dep Mines Mem Geol Surv NSW Palaeontol**

New South Wales Environment Protection Authority e: **NSWEPA**

New South Wales. Geological Survey. Bulletin e: **NSW Geol Surv Bull**

New South Wales. Geological Survey. 1 :250\000 Geological Series e: **NSW Geol Surv 1:250000 Geol Ser**

New South Wales. Geological Survey. Memoirs. Geology e: **Mem Geol Surv NSW Geol**, e: **NSW Geol Surv Mem Geol**

New South Wales. Geological Survey. Memoirs. Palaeontology e: **NSW Geol Surv Mem Palaeontol**

New South Wales. Geological Survey. 4-Mile Geological Series e: **NSW Geol Surv 4-Mile Geol Ser**

New South Wales. Geological Survey. Mineral Industry of New South Wales e: **NSW Geol Surv Mineral Industry of NSW**

New South Wales. Geological Survey. Mineral Resources e: **Miner Resour Geol Surv NSW**, e: **NSW Geol Survey Mineral Resour**, e: **NSW Geol Surv Miner Resour**, e: **NSW Geol Surv Min Res**

New South Wales. Geological Survey. Quarterly Notes e: **NSW Geol Surv Q Notes**

New South Wales. Geological Survey. Records e: **NSW Geol Surv Rec**

New South Wales. Geological Survey. Report e: **NSW Geol Surv Rep**

New South Wales Health Commission e: **NSWHC**

New South Wales National Parks and Wildlife Service e: **NSWNPWS**

New South Wales. Water Conservation and Irrigation Commission. Survey of Thirty New South Wales River Valleys. Report e: **NSW Watt Conserv Irrig Comm Surv Thirty NSW River Valleys Re**

New South Wales Waterways e: **NSWW**

New South Wales Weather Report e: **NSW Weath Rep**

New Techniques in Biophysics and Cell Biology e: **New Tech Biophys Cell Biol**

New Version Ocean Container Control e: **NVOCC**

New Water-Tube Boiler e: **NWTB**

New Water-Tube Donkey Boiler[s] e: **NWTDB**

New Wilderness Foundation e: **NWF**

New York Academy of Medicine e: **NYAM**

New York Academy of Medicine, New York e: **NNNAM**, e: **VVK**

New York City Health and Hospitals Corporation e: **HOSCORP**

New York City Medical Examiners Office e: **NYCMEO**

New York College of Osteopathic Medicine, Old Westbury e: **NOwNC**

New York Conservation Department. Water Resources Commission. Bulletin e: **New York Water Resources Comm Bull**

New York Conservation Department. Water Resources Commission. Report of Investigation e: **New York Water Resources Comm Rept Inv**

New York Consumer Protection Board e: **NYCPB**

New York Cooperative Wildlife Research Unit e: **NYCWRU**

New York County Medical Society Library e: **NYCMSL**

New York Downstate Medical Center e: **NYDMC**

New York Geological State Geological Survey e: **NYSGS**

New York Geological Survey e: **NY G S**

New York Health and Safety Laboratory e: **NYHSL**

New York Hospital-Cornell Medical Center e: **NYH-CMC**

New York Institute of the Aerospace Sciences e: **NYIAS**

New York Journal of Medicine e: **NYork J Med**

New York Medical and Physical Journal e: **NY Med Phys J**

New York Medical and Surgical Brief e: **N.Y.M. & S. Brief**

New York Medical Association e: **NYMA**

New York Medical College e: **NYMC**

New York Medical College, Flower and Fifth Avenue Hospitals, New York e: **NNNM**

New York Medical College, New York e: **VVF**

New York Medical College, Westchester Medical Center, Valhalla e: **VVO**

New York Medical Journal e: **NY Med J**, e: **N York Med J**

New York Medical Society e: **N.Y.M.S.**

New York Medicine e: **NY Med**

New York Ocean Science Laboratory, Montauk e: **NMoN**

New York Ocean[s] Science Laboratory e: **NYOSL**

New York Online Access to Health e: **NOAH**

New York Sea Grant Institute e: **NYSGI**

New York Sea Grant Law and Policy Journal e: **NY Sea Grant L and Pol'y J**

New York State Atomic and Space Development Authority e: **NYSASDA**

New York State Cabinet of Natural History. Annual Report. Regents University e: **NY St Cab An Rp**

New York State Department of Environmental Conservation. Bulletin e: **NY State Dep Environ Conserv Bull**

New York State Department of Environmental Consevation e: **NYSDEC**

New York State Department of Health e: **NYSDH**

New York State Department of Health, Albany e: **VXN**

New York State Department of Health, Division of Laboratories and Research, Albany e: **NAlDH**

New York State Department of Health. Division of Laboratories and Research. Annual Report e: **NY State Dep Health Div Lab Res Annu Rep**

New York State Department of Health. Division of Laboratories and Research. Operations Data e: **NY State Dep Health Lab Res Oper Data**

New York State Geologist. Annual Report e: **NY St G An Rp**

New York State Journal of Medicine e: **NY J Med**

New York State Journal of Medicine e: **New York J Med**, e: **N.Y. State J. Med.**, e: **NY St J Med**

New York State Museum of Natural History. Annual Report e: **NY St Mus An Rp**

New York State Psychiatric Institute, Medical Library Center of NewYork, NewYork e: **ZPI**

New York State Society of Industrial Medicine e: **NYSSIM**

New York State Society of Orthopaedic Surgeons e: **NYSSOS**

New York State Water Power and Control Commission. Bulletin e: **NY Water Power Control Comm Bull**

New York State Water Resources Commission. Basin Planning Report e: **NY State Water Resour Comm Basin Plann Rep**

New York State Water Resources Commission. Bulletin e: **NY Water Resour Comm Bull**

New York Tuberculosis and Health Association e: **NYTHA**

New York University Environmental Law Journal e: **N.Y.U. Envtl. L.J.**

New York University, Institute of Environmental Medicine, Tuxedo Park e: **NNU-IEM**

New York University Medical Center e: **NYUMC**, e: **VVU**

New York University Medical Center, New York e: **NNU-M**

New York University School of Medicine e: **NYUSM**

New York Upstate Medical Center e: **NYUMC**

New York Water Power and Control Commission. Bulletin e: **NY Water Power and Control Comm Bull**

New ZAMCA Army Medical Corps e: **NZAMC**

New Zealand Association of Health, Physical Education and Recreation e: **NZAHPER**

New Zealand Committee for Water Pollution Research and Control e: **NZCWPRC**

New Zealand. Department of Health. Special Report Series e: **NZ Dep Health Spec Rep Ser**

New Zealand. Department of Internal Affairs. Wildlife Publication e: **NZ Dep Intern Aff Wildl Publ**

New Zealand. Department of Scientific and Industrial Research. Geological Survey. Paleontological Bulletin *e:* **NZ Dep Sci Ind Res Geol Surv Paleontol Bull**

New Zealand. Department of Scientific and Industrial Research. Geophysics Division. Report *e:* **NZ Dep Sci Ind Res Geophys Div Rep**

New Zealand. Department of Scientific and Industrial Research. Geophysics Division. Technical Note *e:* **NZ Dep Sci Ind Res Geophys Div Tech Note**

New Zealand Ecological Society *e:* **NZES**

New Zealand Ecological Society. Proceedings *e:* **NZ Ecol Soc Proc**

New Zealand Environment *e:* **NZ Environ**

New Zealand Federation of Freshwater Anglers *e:* **NZFFA**

New Zealand Geochemical Group. Newsletter *e:* **NZ Geochem Group Newsl**

New Zealand Geographer *e:* **NZ Geogr**, *e:* **NZGGA**

New Zealand Geographical Society *e:* **N.Z.G.S.**

New Zealand Geological Society *e:* **NZGS**

New Zealand Geological Survey *e:* **NZGS**

New Zealand Geological Survey Antarctic Expedition *e:* **NZGSAE**

New Zealand. Geological Survey. Bulletin *e:* **New Zeal Geol Surv Bull**, *e:* **NZ Geol Surv Bull**

New Zealand. Geological Survey. Industrial Minerals and Rocks *e:* **NZ Geol Surv Ind Miner Rocks**

New Zealand. Geological Survey. Miscellaneous Series. Map *e:* **NZ Geol Surv Misc Ser Map**

New Zealand. Geological Survey. Report *e:* **NZ Geol Surv Rep**

New Zealand Geophysics Division *e:* **NZGD**

New Zealand Health Information Service *e:* **NZHIS**

New Zealand Health Technology Assessment *e:* **NZHTA**

New Zealand Hydrological Society *e:* **NZHS**

New Zealand Institute of Medical Photography *e:* **NZIMP**

New Zealand Journal of Ecology *e:* **NZ J Ecol**

New Zealand Journal of Geography *e:* **NZ J Geogr**

New Zealand Journal of Geology and Geophysics *e:* **New Zealand Jour Geology and Geophysics**, *e:* **New Zeal J Geol Geophys**, *e:* **NZ J Geol**, *e:* **NZ J Geol Geophys**

New Zealand Journal of Health, Physical Education and Recreation *e:* **NZJHPER**, *e:* **NZ J Phys Educ**

New Zealand Journal of Marine and Freshwater Research *e:* **NZ J Mar Freshwater Res**, *e:* **NZ J Mar Freshw Res**, *e:* **NZ J Mar Res**

New Zealand Journal of Medical Laboratory Technology *e:* **NZ J Med Lab Technol**

New Zealand Journal of Sports Medicine *e:* **NZ J Sports Med**

New Zealand Medical Association *e:* **NZMA**

New Zealand Medical Corps *e:* **N.Z.M.C.**

New Zealand Medical Journal *e:* **New Zealand MJ**, *e:* **New Zeal Med J**, *e:* **NZ Med J**, *e:* **NZMJ**, *e:* **NZMJA**

New Zealand Medical Journal. Supplement *e:* **NZ Med J Suppl**

New Zealand Medical Research Council *e:* **NZMRC**

New Zealand Meteorologieal Service *e:* **NZMS**

New Zealand National Committee of the International Association on Water Pollution Research and Control *e:* **NZNCIAWPRC**

New Zealand National Committee on Oceanic Research *e:* **NZNCOR**

New Zealand National Health Committee *e:* **NHC**

New Zealand National Institue for Water and Atmospheric Research *e:* **NIWA**

New Zealand. National Radiation Laboratory. Environmental Radioactivity. Annual Report *e:* **NZ Natl Radiat Lab Environ Radioact Annu Rep**

New Zealand Natural Sciences *e:* **NZ Nat Sci**

New Zealand Nature Conservation Council *e:* **NZNCC**

New Zealand Oceanographic Institute *e:* **NZOI**

New Zealand Oceanographic Institute. Collected Reprints *e:* **NZ Oceanogr Inst Collect Repr**

New Zealand Oceanographic Institute. Memoir *e:* **NZ Oceanogr Inst Mem**

New Zealand Oceanographic Institute. Oceanographic Field Report *e:* **NZOI Oceanographic Field Report**

New Zealand Post Graduate Medical Federation *e:* **NZPGMF**

New Zealand Sea Frontier *e:* **NZ Sea Fron**

New Zealand Society of Animal Production *e:* **NZSAP**

New Zealand Underwater Association *e:* **NZUA**

New Zealand Water Safety Council *e:* **NZWSC**

New Zealand Water Ski Association *e:* **NZWSA**

New Zealand Waterside Workers Federation *e:* **NZWWF**

New Zealand Wildlife Service *e:* **NZWS**

Newfoundland Forest Research Centre, Environment Canada St. John's, Newfoundland *e:* **NFSEC**

Newfoundland Geological Survey. Information Circular. [Report] *e:* **Newfoundland Geol Survey Inf Circ Rept**

Newfoundland. Geological Survey. Report *e:* **Newfoundland Geol Surv Rep**

Newfoundland Industrial Health and Safety Association *e:* **NIHSA**

Newfoundland Institute for Cold Ocean Science *e:* **NICOS**

Newfoundland Journal of Geological Education *e:* **Newfoundland J Geol Educ**

Newfoundland Ocean Industries Association *e:* **NOIA**

Newfoundland Ocean[s] Research and Development Corporation *e:* **NORDCO**

Newport Natural History Society. Proceedings *e:* **Newport N H Soc Pr**

News of Geothermal Energy Conversion Technology *e:* **News Geotherm Energy Convers Technol**

Newsletter. American Academy of Health Administration *e:* **Newsl Am Acad Health Adm**

Newsletter. Australian and New Zealand Society of Nuclear Medicine *e:* **Newsl Aust NZ Soc Nucl Med**

Newsletter. Commonwealth Geological Liaison Office *e:* **Newsl Commw Geol Liaison Off**

Newsletter. Commonwealth Science Council. Earth Sciences Programme *e:* **Newsl Commonw Sci Counc Earth Sci Programme**

Newsletter. Environmental Mutagen Society *e:* **NEMSB**, *e:* **Newsl Environ Mutagen Soc**

Newsletter for Research in Mental Health and Behavioral Sciences *e:* **Nl Res Men Health & Behav Sc**

Newsletter. Geological Society [London] *e:* **Newsl Geol Soc [London]**

Newsletter. Geological Society of New Zealand *e:* **Newsl Geol Soc NZ**

Newsletter. Geological Society of Zambia *e:* **Newsl Geol Soc Zambia**

Newsletter. Geoscience Information Society *e:* **Newsl Geosci Inf Soc**

Newsletter. International Geological Correlation Programme. Project 167 *e:* **Newsl-IGCP Proj 167**

Newsletter. International Geological Correlation Programme. Project 156. Phosphorites *e:* **Newsl Int Geol Correl Programme Proj I56 Phosphorites**

Newsletter. International Union of Biological Sciences *e:* **Newsl Int Union Biol Sci**

Newsletter of Biomedical Safety and Standards *e:* **Newsl Biomed Saf Stand**

Newsletter of the Army Medical Department *e:* **NAMD**

Newsletter of the Environmental Mutagen Society *e:* **Newslett. Environ. Mutagen Soc**

Newsletter on the Application of Nuclear Methods in Biology and Agriculture *e:* **Newsl Appl Nucl Methods Biol Agric**

Newsletter. Wildlife Disease Association *e:* **Newsl Wildl Dis Assoc**

NEXRAD Weather Service Forecast Office *e:* **NWSFO**

Next Generation Space Telescope *e:* **NGST**

Next Generation Water Level Measurement system *e:* **NGWLM**

Next Generation Water Level Measurement System *e:* **NGWLMS**

NFSDIS [National Environmental Satellite Data and Information Service] Environmental Inventory *e:* **NEINEI**

NHANES [National Health and Nutritional Examination Survey] Epidemiologic Followup Study *e:* **NHEFS**

Nicaragua Medica *e:* **Nicar Med**

Nicaragua Medical Aid *e:* **NMA**

Nice Medical *e:* **Nice Med**

Nicholls State University. Professional Papers Series. Biology *e:* **Nicholls State Univ Prof Pap Ser Biol**

Nichtzucker zu Wasser-Verhältnis *d:* **N/W-Verhältnis**

Niederdeutsche Zeitschrift für Volkskunde *d:* **Niederdt.Zs.,** *d:* **NZV**

Niederrheinische Gas- und Wasserwerke [GmbH] *d:* **NGW**

Niederrheinische Gesellschaft für Natur und Heilkunde zu Bonn. Sitzungsberichte *d:* **Niederrhein Ges Bonn Szb**

Niedersächsisches Landesamt für Wasser und Abfall *d:* **NLWA**

Niedersächsisches Umwelt-Landesamt *d:* **NULA**

Niedersächsisches Umweltinformationssystem *d:* **NUMIS**

Niedersächsisches Wassergesetz *d:* **NWG**

Niederwasserbett *d:* **NW-Bett**

Niederwassermenge *d:* **NW Menge**

Niederwasserspiegel *d:* **NW-Sp**

Niederwasserstand *d:* **NW-Stand**

Niederwasserzeit *d:* **NWZ**

niedrigste Niederwasserquantität *d:* **NNQ**

niedrigster Niedrigwasserstand *d:* **N.N.W.**

niedrigstes Hochwasser *d:* **NHW**

niedrigstes Niedrigwasser *d:* **NNW**

niedrigstes Tideniedrigwasser *d:* **NNTnw**

Niedrigstwasserstand *d:* **NW**

Niedrigwasser *d:* **Nd-Was,** *d:* **Nd-Wss,** *d:* **N.W.**

Nigeria. Annual Report. Geological Survey Department *e:* **Niger Annu Rep Geol Surv Dep**

Nigeria Federation. Annual Report. Geological Survey *e:* **Niger Fed Annu Rep Geol Surv**

Nigeria Geological Survey Division. Annual Report *e:* **Niger Geol Surv Div Annu Rep**

Nigerian Geographical Journal *e:* **NGJ,** *e:* **Nigeria Geogr J**

Nigerian Institute for Oceanography and Marine Research *e:* **NIOMR**

Nigerian Medical Association *e:* **NMA**

Nigerian Medical Journal *e:* **Nigerian Med J,** *e:* **Niger Med J**

Nigerian Society for Photogrammetry and Remote Sensing *e:* **NSPRS**

Nigerian Society of Remote Sensing *e:* **NISORS**

Night Observation [Surveillance] sight *e:* **NOS**

Night Observation System *e:* **NOS**

Night Observation Television in a Pod *e:* **NOTIP**

NIH [National Institutes of Health] Consensus Development. Conference Summary *e:* **NIH Consensus Dev Conf Summ**

NIH [National Institutes of Health] Consensus Statement *e:* **NIH Consens Statement**

NIHAE [National Institute of Health Administration and Education] Bulletin *e:* **NIHAE Bull**

Nihon Juishikai Zasshi/Journal. Japan Veterinary Medical Association *j:* **Nihon Juishikai Zasshi J Jap Vet Med Assoc**

Nihon University. Journal of Medicine *e:* **Nihon Univ J Med,** *e:* **NUMDA**

Nihon University. Journal of Radiation Medicine and Biology *e:* **Nihon Univ J Radiat Med Biol**

Nihon University. Mishima College of Humanities and Sciences. Annual Report of the Researches. Natural Sciences *e:* **Nihon Univ Mishima Coll Humanit Sci Annu Rep Res Nat Sci**

Niigata Medical Journal *e:* **Niigata Med J**

Niigata University. Science Reports. Series E [Geology and Mineralogy] *e:* **Niigata Univ Sci Rep Ser E**

Nimbus Arctic Ice Reconnaissance *e:* **NAIREC**

Nimbus [Cloud] *e:* **NB**

Nimbus Meteorological Radiation Tape *e:* **NMRT**

Nimbus Observations Processing System *e:* **NOPS**

Nimbus Weather Satellite *e:* **NWS**

Ninepipe and Pablo National Wildlife Refuge *e:* **N & PNWR**

NIOSH [National Institute for Occupational Safety and Health] Pocket Guide to Chemical Hazards *e:* **NPG**

NIPH [National Institute of Public Health] Annals *e:* **NIPH Ann**

NIPH [National Institute of Public Health] Annals [Oslo] *e:* **NIPH [Natl Inst Public Health] Ann [Oslo]**

Nippon Hoigaku Zasshi. Japanese Journal of Legal Medicine *j:* **Nippon Hoigaku Zasshi**

Nippon Institute for Biological Science *e:* **NIBS**

Nippon Institute for Biological Science Bulletin *e:* **NIBS Bulletin**

Nippon Koshu Eisei Zasshi [Japanese Journal of Public Health] *j:* **Nippon Koshu Eisei Zasshi**

Nippon Naika Gakkai Zasshi. Journal of Japanese Society of Internal Medicine *j:* **Nippon Naika Gakkai Zasshi**

Nippon Rinsho. Japanese Journal of Clinical Medicine *j:* **Nippon Rinsho**

Nippon Sanka Fujinka Gakkai Zasshi. Acta Obstetrica et Gynaecologica Japonica *j:* **Nippon Sanka Fujinka Gakkai Zasshi**

NMCS [National Military Command System] Environmental Support System *e:* **NESS**

NMR in Biomedicine *e:* **NMR Biomed**

No Change in Weather *e:* **NCW,** *e:* **NCWX**

No More to Be Done [Medicine] *e:* **NMTBD**

No Observable Adverse Effect Level *e:* **NOAEL**

No Observable (or Observed) Effect[s] Level *e:* **NOEL**

No Risk Till Water Borne *e:* **NRTWB**

no signature *e:* **no sig**

NOAA Earth Watch Service *e:* **NEWS**

NOAA N-ROSS/ERS-1 Environmental Data Development *e:* **NNEEDD**

NOAA [National Oceanic and Atmospheric Administration] Accounting Manual *e:* **NAM**

NOAA [National Oceanic and Atmospheric Administration] Administrative Order *e:* **NAO**

NOAA [National Oceanic and Atmospheric Administration] Corps [Operations] *e:* **NC**

NOAA [National Oceanic and Atmospheric Administration] Earth Science Data Directory *e:* **NESDD**

NOAA [National Oceanic and Atmospheric Administration] Environmental Watch *e:* **NEW**

NOAA [National Oceanic and Atmospheric Administration] Geophysical Fluid Dynamics Laboratory, Princeton *e:* **OAY**

NOAA [National Oceanic and Atmospheric Administration] Interoceanic Canal Project *e:* **NICP**

NOAA [National Oceanic and Atmospheric Administration] Library and Information Network *e:* **NLIN**

NOAA [National Oceanic and Atmospheric Administration]-LISD Seattle Center, Seattle *e:* **OAE**

NOAA [National Oceanic and Atmospheric Administration] Ocean Wave [Model] *e:* **NOW**

NOAA [National Oceanic and Atmospheric Administration] Oceanographic Data Distribution System *e:* **NODDS**

NOAA [National Oceanic and Atmospheric Administration] Operational Telecommunications Coordinator *e:* **NOTC**

NOAA [National Oceanic and Atmospheric Administration] Operational Telecommunications System *e:* **NOTS**

NOAA [National Oceanic and Atmospheric Administration] Operational VAS Assessment Program *e:* **NOVA**

NOAA [National Oceanic and Atmospheric Administration] Technical Report. NMFS [National Marine Fisheries Service] Circular *e:* **NOAA Tech Rep NMFS Circ**

NOAA [National Oceanic and Atmospheric Administration] Undersea Research Program *e:* **NURP**

NOAA [National Oceanic and Atmospheric Administration] Virtual Data System *e:* **NVDS**

NOAA [National Oceanic and Atmospheric Administration] Water Vapor Project *e:* **NVAP**

NOAA [National Oceanic and Atmospheric Administration] Weather Radio *e:* **NWR**

NOAA [National Oceanic and Atmospheric Administration] Weather Wire Service *e:* **NWWS**

Nobel Medical Institute *e:* **N.M.I.**

Nobeyama Radio Observatory *e:* **NRO**

NODC [National Oceanographic Data Center] Index for Instrument Measured Subsurface Current Observation *e:* **NIMSCO**

NODC [National Oceanographic Data Center] Ocean Science Information Exchange *e:* **NOSIE**

Noise Protection Transformer *e:* **NPT**

Nomenclature des Actes de Biologie Médicale *f:* **NABM**

Nomenklatur für Medizinprodukte *d:* **UMDNS**

Nomina Geographica Flandrica *l:* **NGF**

Nomina Geographica Neerlandica *l:* **NGN**

Nominal Protection Rate *e:* **NPR**

Non-All Weather *e:* **NAW**

Non-Community Water System *e:* **NCWS**

Non-Essential Service Water *e:* **NESW**

Non-Geostationary Satellite Orbit *e:* **NGSO**

Non-medical Education and Training *e:* **NMET**

Non-Methane Hydrocarbon Intercomparison Experiment *e:* **NOMHICE**

Non-Rejected Earth Radiance *e:* **NRER**

Non-sea-salt *e:* **Nss**

non-selfpropelled water barge *e:* **YWN**

Non-transient Non-community Water System *e:* **NTNC**

Non-Transient Non-Community Water System *e:* **NTNCWS**

Non-Virtual Ocean *e:* **NVO**

Non-Voice/Non-Geostationary *e:* **NV/NG**

Non-Volatile Ocean Container Control *e:* **NVOCC**

Non-Weathering *e:* **NW**

Noncontact Cooling Water *e:* **NCCW**

Nonessential Services Chiled Water System *e:* **NESCWS**

Nonhydroxylated Fatty Acid *e:* **NFA**

Nonlinear Sea Surface Temperature *e:* **NLSST**

Nonmethane Total Hydrocarbons *e:* **NMTHC**

Nonpaired Spatial Orbitals *e:* **NPSO**

Nonpenetrating Orbit *e:* **NPO**

Nonpolarized Return-to-Zero *e:* **RTZ[NP]**, *e:* **RZ[NP]**

Nonreal-Time Conversion Subsystem [Space Flight Operations Facility] *e:* **NRTC**

Nonrotating Earth *e:* **NRE**

nonwatertight *e:* **nwt**

Nonwatertight Door *e:* **NWTD**

Nordic Association for Hydrology *e:* **NAH**

Nordic Association of Applied Geophysics *e:* **NAAG**

Nordic Cooperation in Polar Research *e:* **NOCOPOR**

Nordic Coordinating Committee of Hydrology *e:* **KOHYNO**

Nordic Council for Animal Protection *e:* **NCAP**

Nordic Council for Arctic Medical Research *e:* **NCAMR**

Nordic Council for Marine Biology *e:* **NCMB**

Nordic Council for Physical Oceanography *e:* **NCPO**

Nordic Council for Wildlife Research *e:* **NCWB**, *e:* **NCWR**

Nordic Council on Medicine[s] *e:* **NCM**

Nordic Environment Finance Corporation *e:* **NEFCO**

Nordic Federation for Medical Education *e:* **NFME**

Nordic Geodetic Commission *e:* **NGC**

Nordic Hydrological Association *e:* **NHF**

Nordic Hydrological Programme *e:* **NHP**

Nordic Hydrology *e:* **NOHY**, *e:* **Nord Hydrol**, *e:* **Nordic Hydrol**

Nordic Integrated Hydrographic System *e:* **NORDIHS**

Nord[ic] Medico-Statistical Committee *e:* **NOMESCO**

Nordic Polar Research Committee *e:* **NPRC**

Nordic Radiation Protection Society *e:* **NRPS**

Nordic Society Against Painful Experiments on Animals *e:* **NSAPEA**

Nordic Society for Cell Biology *e:* **NSCB**

Nordic Society for Radiation Protection *e:* **NSRP**

Nordic Society for Space Research *e:* **NSSR**

Nordic Subarctic-Subalpine Ecology *e:* **NSSE**

Nordic Union for Health and Work *e:* **NUHW**

Nordic Universities Group on Physical Oceanography *e:* **NUGPO**

Nordisk Förening för Medicinsk Radiologi *N:* **NFfMR**

Nordisk Förening för Tillämpad Geofysik *r:* **NOFTIG**

Nordisk Hydrologisk Forening *r:* **NHF**

Nordisk Kollegium for Fysisk Oceanografi *r:* **NKFO**

Nordisk Kollegium for Marinbiologi *N:* **NKMB**

Nordisk Medicin *a:* **NM**, *r:* **Nord Med**

Nordisk Medicinhistorisk Aarsbok *a:* **Nord Medicinhist Arsb**

Nordisk Medicinsk Tidskrift *r:* **Nord Med Tidskr**

Nordisk Samkatalog foer Seriella Medicinska Publikationer *r:* **Nordser**

Nordisk Tidskrift foer Medicoteknik *r:* **Nord Tidskr Medicotek**

Nordisk Veterinaermedicin *r:* **Nord Veterinaermed**, *r:* **Nord Vetmed**

Nordisk Veterinaermedicin. Supplementum *r:* **Nord Veterinaermed Suppl**

Nordiska Kommissionen for Geodesi *N:* **NKG**

Nordiska Medicinska Statistiska *a:* **NOMESKO**

Nordiska Publiceringsnamnden for Naturvetenskap *r:* **NOP-N**

Nordiska Samarbetsorganisationen för Teknisk-Naturventenskaplig Forening *N:* **NORDSFORSK**

Nordiska Samarbetsorganisationen för Teknisk-Naturvetenskaplig Forskning *r:* **NORDFORSK**

Nordiskt Medicinskt Arkiv *r:* **N.M.A.**, *r:* **Nord Med Ark**

Nordiskt Medicinskt Arkiv Afdeling 2. Inre Medicine Arkiv foer Inre Medicin *r:* **Nord Med Ark Afd 2 Med**

Nordostatlantisches Monitoring Programm *d:* **NOAMP**

Nordpolarsequenz *d:* **NPS**

Norfolk and Norwich Institute for Medical Education *e:* **NANIME**

Norfolk County Medical Society, Inc., Norfolk *e:* **ViNM**

Norges Geografiske Oppmåling *N:* **NGO**

Norges Geologiske Undersoekelse *N:* **Nor Geol Unders**

Norges Geologiske Undersoekelse. Bulletin *N:* **Nor Geol Unders Bull**

Norges Geologiske Undersoekelse [Publikasjoner] *N:* **Norg Geol Unders [Publ]**

Norges Geologiske Undersoekelse. Skrifter *N:* **Nor Geol Unders Skr**

Norges Geologiske Undersøkelser *N:* **NGU**

Norges Geologjske Undersoekelse *N:* **NOGU**

Norges Geotekniske Institutt *N:* **NGI**

Norges Hydrodynamiske Laboratorier *N:* **NHL**

Norges Teknisk-Naturvitenskapelige Forskningsråd *N:* **NTNF**

Norges Teknisk Naturvitenskapelige Forskningsrad. Metallurgisk Komite. Meddelelse *N:* **Nor Tek Naturvitensk Forskningsrad Metall Kom Medd**

Norges Teknisk-Naturvitenskapelige Universitet *N:* **NTNU**

Normal Environmental Control System *e:* **NECS**

Normal Environmental Temperature *e:* **NET**

normal gravity acceleration at sea-level *e:* **g0**

Normal Hourly Space Velocity *e:* **NHSV**

Normal Water Level *e:* **NWL**

normal water surface *e:* **nws**

normale Atmosphäre *d:* **An**

Normalisatieraad *N:* **NR**

Norme d'Echange de Données en Environnement RTC *f:* **NEDER**

Normenausschuss Grundlagen des Umweltschutzes *d:* **NAGUS**

Normenausschuß Medizin im DIN [Deutsches Institut für Normung] e.V. *d:* **NAMed**

Normenausschuß Wasserwesen im DIN [Deutsches Institut für Normung] e.V. *d:* **NAW**

Norsk Forening for Medicinisk Radiologi *N:* **NFMR**

Norsk Geodetisk Forening *N:* **NGF**

Norsk Geofysisk Forening *N:* **NGF**

Norsk Geologisk Forening *N:* **NGF**

Norsk Geologisk Tidsskrift *a:* **Nor. Geol. Tidsskr.**

Norsk Geoteknisk Forening *N:* **NGF**

Norsk Hydro AS *N:* **NHY**

Norsk Meteorologforening *N:* **NMF**

Norsk Polarinstitutt *N:* **Nor Pol**, *N:* **NP**

Norsk Polarinstitutt Skrifter *N:* **Nor. Polarinst. Skr.**

Norsk Polarinstitutt Temakart *N:* **Nor. Polarinst. Temakart**

Norsk Polarnavigasjon A/S *N:* **NPN**

Norsk Samfunnsgeografisk Forening *N:* **NSGF**

Norske Meteorologiske Institutt *N:* **NMI**

Norske Meteorologiske Institutt. Meteorologiske Annaler *N:* **NMIA**, *N:* **NMIMA**

Norske Naturhistoriske Museers Landsforbund *N:* **NNML**

Norske Videnskaps-Akademi i Oslo. Matematisk-Naturvidenskapelig Klasse. Skrifter *N:* **Norske Vid-Akad Oslo Mat-Natur Kl Skr**

Norske Videnskaps-Akademi i Oslo. Matematisk-Naturvidenskapelig Klasse. Skrifter. Ny Serie *N:* **Nor Vidensk-Akad Oslo Mat Natur Kl N Ser**

Norte Geográfico *s:* **NG**

North African Medical Section *e:* **NAMED**

North African Waters *e:* **NAW**

North Alabama Biomedical Information Network *e:* **NABIN**

North American Academy of Manipulative Medicine *e:* **NAAMM**

North American Academy of Musculoskeletal Medicine *e:* **NAAMM**

North American Agreement for/on Environmental Cooperation *e:* **NAAEC**

North American Association for/of
Environmental Education *e:* **NAEE**

North American Association for the
Protection of Predatory Animals *e:*
NAAPPA

North American Atmospheric Observing
System *e:* **NAOS**

North American Aviation Space and
Information Division *e:* **NAA S & ID**

North American Aviation Space Division
e: **NAASD**

North American Biologicals, Inc. *e:* **NAB**,
e: **NBIO**

North American Biologicals, Incorporated
e: **NBI**

North American Commission for
Environmental Cooperation *e:* **NACEC**

North American Commission on the
Environment *e:* **NACE**

North American Environmental Fund *e:*
NAEF

North American Environmental, Inc. *e:*
NAE

North American Forest Biology Workshop
e: **North Am For Biol Workshop**

North American Fund for Environmental
Cooperation *e:* **NAFEC**

North American Land Mammal Age *e:*
NALMA

North American Nutrition and Preventive
Medicine Association *e:* **NANPMA**

North American Plant Protection
Organization *e:* **NAPPO**

North American Slope Water *e:* **NASW**

North American Society for Oceanic
History *e:* **NASOH**

North American Water and Power Alliance
e: **NAWAPA**, *e:* **NAWPA**, *e:* **NOWAPA**

North American Weather Consultants *e:*
NAWC

North American Wilderness Survival
School *e:* **NAWSS**

North American Wildlife Foundation *e:*
NAWF

North American Wildlife Park Foundation
e: **NAWPF**

North Atlantic Deep Water *e:* **NADW**

North Atlantic Deepwater Oil Terminal *e:*
NADOT

North Atlantic Health Sciences Libraries
e: **NAHSL**

North Atlantic Mid-Ocean-Ridge Basalt *e:*
NAMORB

North Atlantic Naval Coastal Frontier *e:*
NANCF

North Atlantic Ocean *e:* **Ln-**, *e:* **NAO**

North Atlantic Ocean Prediction Systems
e: **NAOPS**

North Atlantic Ocean Region *e:* **N.A.O.R.**

North Atlantic Ocean Regional Planning
Board *e:* **NAORPB**

North Atlantic Ocean Regional Planning
Group *e:* **NAORPG**

North Atlantic Ocean Station *e:* **NAOS**

North Atlantic Ocean Station[s] Program
e: **NAOSP**

North Atlantic Polar Front *e:* **NAPF**

North Atlantic Regional Medical Center *e:*
NARMC

North Atlantic Treaty Organization-Military
Oceanography Group *e:*
NATOMILOCGRP

North Atlantic Treaty Planning Board on
Ocean Shipping *e:* **NAPBOS**

North Carolina. Department of
Conservation and Development. Division
of Mineral Resources. Geologic Map
Series *e:* **North Carolina Div Mineral
Resources Geol Map Ser**

North Carolina. Department of Natural and
Economic Resources. Groundwater
Section. Report of Investigation *e:* **NC
Dep Nat Econ Resour Groundwater
Sect Rep Invest**

North Carolina. Department of Natural and
Economic Resources. Regional Geology
Series *e:* **NC Dep Nat Econ Resour Reg
Geol Ser**

North Carolina. Department of Water and
Air Resources. Division of Ground Water.
Ground Water Bulletin *e:* **North
Carolina Div Ground Water Ground
Water Bull**

North Carolina. Department of Water
Resources. Division of Stream Sanitation
and Hydrology. Bulletin *e:* **NC Div
Water Resour Div Stream Sanit Hydrol
Bull**

North Carolina. Division of Ground Water.
Ground Water Bulletin *e:* **NC Div
Ground Water Ground Water Bull**

North Carolina. Division of Ground Water.
Ground Water Circular *e:* **NC Dir
Ground Water Ground Water Circ**

North Carolina. Division of Resource
Planning and Evaluation. Mineral
Resources Section. Regional Geology
Series *e:* **NC Div Resour Plann Eval
Miner Resour Sect Reg Geol Ser**

North Carolina. Division of Resource
Planning and Evaluation. Regional
Geology Series *e:* **NC Div Resour
Plann Eval Reg Geol Ser**

North Carolina Geological Survey *e:*
NCGS

North Carolina Geological Survey. Bulletin
e: **NCGS B**

North Carolina Healthcare Information and
Communications Alliance *e:* **NCHICA**

North Carolina Medical Journal *e:* **N C
Med J**, *e:* **North Car Med J**

North Carolina Medical Society *e:* **NCMS**

North Carolina. Mineral Resources Section.
Regional Geology Series *e:* **NC Miner
Resour Sect Reg Geol Ser**

North Carolina Natural Gas Corp. *e:*
NCNG

North Carolina State University, School of
Veterinary Medicine, Raleigh *e:* **NRV**

North Carolina Veterinary Medical
Association *e:* **NCVMA**

North Central Watershed Research Unit
[Department of Agriculture] *e:* **NCWRU**

North Coast Environment Centre *e:* **NCEC**

North Coast Public Health Unit *e:* **NCPHU**

North Dakota Atmospheric Resources
Board *e:* **NDARB**

North Dakota Geological Society *e:* **NDGS**

North Dakota Geological Survey *e:* **NDGS**

North Dakota. Geological Survey. Biennial
Report *e:* **N Dak G S Bien Rp**

North Dakota. Geological Survey. Bulletin
e: **N Dak Geol Surv Bull**, *e:* **ND Geol
Surv Bull**, *e:* **North Dakota Geol Survey
Bull**

North Dakota. Geological Survey. Circular
e: **N Dak Geol Surv Circ**, *e:* **ND Geol
Surv Circ**

North Dakota. Geological Survey.
Educational Series *e:* **ND Geol Surv
Educ Ser**

North Dakota. Geological Survey.
Miscellaneous Map *e:* **ND Geol Surv
Misc Map**, *e:* **North Dakota Geol
Survey Misc Map**

North Dakota. Geological Survey.
Miscellaneous Series *e:* **N Dak Geol
Surv Misc Ser**, *e:* **ND Geol Surv Misc
Ser**, *e:* **North Dakota Geol Survey Misc
Ser**

North Dakota. Geological Survey. Report of
Investigations *e:* **N Dak Geol Surv Rep
Invest**, *e:* **North Dakota Geol Survey
Rept Inv**

North Dakota Natural Heritage Inventory
e: **NDNHI**

North Dakota State Health Department,
Bismarck *e:* **NdBHD**

North Dakota State Medical Association *e:*
NDSMA

North Dakota Water Resources Research
Institute *e:* **NDWRRI**

North Devon Water Board *e:* **NDWB**

North East Atlantic Palaeooceanography
and Climate Change *e:* **NEAPACC**

North East Frontier Agency *e:* **NEFA**

North East Frontier Tract *e:* **NEFT**

North-East Radio Observatory Corporation
e: **NEROC**

North Indian Intermediate Water *e:* **NIIW**

North Liberty Radio Observatory *e:*
NLRO

North Medicine *e:* **North Med**

North of 60. Environmental Studies *e:*
NES

North of Scotland Hydro-Electric Board *e:*
NSHB, *e:* **NSHEB**

North of Scotland Hydroelectric Board *e:*
NOSHEB

North Okanagan Health Region *e:* **NOHR**

North Pacific Central Mode Water *e:*
NPCMW

North Pacific Deep Water *e:* **NPDW**

North Pacific Intermediate Water *e:* **NPIW**

North Pacific Ocean Monitoring for Climate
Research *e:* **TRANSPAC**

North Polar Distance *e:* **NPD**

North Polar Region *e:* **NPR**

North Polar Sequence *e:* **NPS**

North Queensland Naturalist *e:* **North
Queensl Nat**, *e:* **N QD Nat**, *e:* **N Qld
Nat**, *e:* **N Queensl Nat**

North Queensland Naturalists Club *e:*
NQNC

North Sea *e:* **NS**

North Sea ACMI Range *e:* **NSAR**

North Sea Assets *e:* **NSA**

North Sea Coastal Engineering Group *e:*
NSCEG

North Sea Conference *e:* **NSC**

North Sea Environmental Study Group *e:*
NSESG

North Sea Ferries *e:* **NSFe**

North Sea Hydrographic Commission *e:*
NSHC

North Sea Hyperbaric Centre *e:* **NSHC**

North Sea International Chart Commission
e: **NSICC**

North Sea Island Group *e:* **NSIG**

North Sea Mine Force Association *e:*
NSMFA

North Sea-Nonrigid Airship *e:* **NS**

North Sea Observer *e:* **NSR**

North Sea Oceanographic[al] Study Group
e: **NSOSG**

North Sea Oil Information Sheet *e:* **North
Sea Oil Inf Sheet**

North Sea Special Programme of Action *e:*
NORSPA

North Sea Spectrum *e:* **NORSPEC**

North Sea Subarea *e:* **NORSEACENT**

North Sea Task Force *e:* **NSTF**

North Slope of Alaska and Adjacent Arctic
Ocean *e:* **NSA/AAO**

North Wales Naturalists' Trust *e:* **NWNT**

North Water *e:* **NOW**

North-West Atlantic Fisheries Centre,
Fisheries and Oceans Canada St. John's,
Newfoundland *e:* **NFSF**

North West European Microbiological
Group *e:* **NWEMG**

North West Frontier Fellowship *e:* **NWFF**

North West Frontier, Pakistan *e:* **NWF
Pak**

North-West Frontier Province *e:* **NWFP**

North-West Underwater Research Group
e: **NWURG**

North-West Water Authority *e:* **NWWA**

North Western Atlantic Environmental
Study *e:* **NORWESTLANT**

North Western Naturalists' Union *e:*
NWNU

North Westland Wildlife Corridor *e:*
NWWC

Northamptonshire Natural History Society
and Field Club *e:* **N.N.H.S.**

Northeast Area Remote Sensing System
Association *e:* **NEARSS**

Northeast Atlantic Deep Water *e:*
NEADW

Northeast Microbial Physiologists,
Ecologists and Taxonomists *e:*
NEMPET

Northeast Water *e:* **NEW**

Northeast Water Polynya Project, land
based *e:* **NEWLAND**

Northeast Water Resources Information
Terminal *e:* **NEWRIT**

Northeast Watershed Research Center *e:*
NWRC

Northeastern Consortium for Health
Information *e:* **NECHI**

Northeastern Environmental Science *e:*
Northeast Environ Sci

Northeastern Geology *e:* **Northeast Geol**

Northeastern Ohio Regional Medical
Program *e:* **NEORMP**

Northeastern Ohio University, College of
Medicine, Rootstown *e:* **ONE**

Northeastern Radiological Health
Laboratory *e:* **NERHL**

Northern Biosphere Observation and
Modelling Experiment *e:* **NBIOME**

Northern California and Nevada Medical
Group *e:* **NCNMLG**

Northern California Occupational Health
Center *e:* **NCOHC**

Northern Districts Public Health Unit *e:*
NDPHU

Northern Environmental Council *e:*
NOREC

Northern Environmental Studies Revolving
Fund *e:* **NESRF**

Northern Hemisphere Climate Process
Land-Surface Experiment *e:* **NOPEX**

Northern Hemisphere Observatory *e:* **NHO**

Northern Hydrographic Group *e:* **NHG**

Northern Illinois Library for Mental Health,
Rockford *e:* **IRoN**

Northern Illinois Meteorological Research
on Downbursts University of Chicago *e:*
NIMROD

Northern Institute for Environmental and
Minority Law *e:* **NIEM**

Northern Ireland Centre for Health Care Cooperation and Development *e:* **NICARE**

Northern Ireland. Government. Ministry of
Commerce. Memoirs. Geological Survey
e: **North Irel Gov Minist Commer Mem
Geol Surv**

Northern Ireland. Memoirs. Geological
Survey *e:* **North Irel Mem Geol Surv**

Northern Natural Gas [Company] *e:* **NNG**

Northern New Mexico Environmental
Information Exchange *e:* **NENIX**

Northern Prairie Wildlife Research Center
e: **NPWRC**

Northern Prairie Wildlife Research Center,
Jamestown *e:* **UDJ**

Northern Projects Journal. British Columbia
Hydro *e:* **NPJO**

Northern Remote Sensing Laboratory *e:*
NRSL

Northern Rhodesia. Department of
Geological Survey. Bulletin *e:* **North
Rhod Dep Geol Surv Bull**

Northern Rhodesia. Geological Survey.
Bulletin *e:* **North Rhod Geol Surv Bull**

Northern Rhodesia. Geological Survey.
Report *e:* **North Rhod Geol Surv Rep**

Northern Sea Route *e:* **NSR**

Northern Seas Environmental Control
Agency *e:* **NORSECA**

Northern State College Library, Aberdeen
e: **NOS**

Northern Sydney Public Health Unit *e:* **NS
PHU**

Northern Territory Aerial Medical Service
e: **NTAMS**

Northern Territory Medical Service *e:*
NTMS

Northern Tier Integration Project *e:*
NOTIP

Northern Wisconsin Area Health Education
Center *e:* **NAHEC**

Northern Wisconsin Health Science Library
Cooperative *e:* **NWHSLC**

Northrop Space Laboratories (or
Laboratory) *e:* **NSL**

Northrop University. Law Journal of
Aerospace, Energy and the Environment
e: **Northrop ULJ**, *e:* **Northrop ULT
Aero Energy and Envt**

Northumbrian Water Authority *e:* **NWA**

Northwater. Institute of Water Resources.
University of Alaska *e:* **NOWR**

Northwest African Waters *e:* **NAW**

Northwest AHEC [Area Health Education
Center]-Bowman Gray School of
Medicine, Taylorsville *e:* **NBF**

Northwest Atlantic Mid-Ocean Canyon *e:*
NAMOC

Northwest Environmental Journal *e:*
Northwest Environ J

Northwest Geology *e:* **Northwest Geol**

Northwest Medical Service *e:* **NWMS**

Northwest Medical Teams International *e:*
NWMT

Northwest Medicine *e:* **Northwest Med**, *e:*
Northw Med

Northwest Pacific Oceanographers *e:*
NWPO

Northwest Sea Frontier *e:* **NWSF**

Northwestern Sea Frontier *e:*
NORWESSEAFRON

Northwestern Sector, Western Sea Frontier
e: **NORWESSEC**

Northwestern University. Department of
Geography. Studies in Geography *e:*
**Northwestern Univ Dept Geography
Studies Geography**

Norton-Children's Hospital Medical
Library, Louisville *e:* **KLN**

Norway. Geologiske Undersoekelse.
Bulletin *N:* **Norway Geol
Undersoekelse Bull**

Norwegian Geotechnical Institute.
Publication *e:* **Norw Geotech Inst Publ**

Norwegian Institute for Nature Research *e:*
NINA

Norwegian Institute for Water Research *e:*
NIVA

Norwegian Maritime Remote Sensing
Programme *e:* **NORMARSEN**

Norwegian National Committee of the
International Association on Water
Pollution Research and Control *e:*
NNCIAWPRC

Norwegian Natural Science Research
Council *e:* **NAVF**

Norwegian Polar Institute *e:* **NP**

Norwegian Polar Research Institute *e:*
NPRI

Norwegian Radiation Protection Authority
e: **NRPA**

Norwegian Remote Sensing Experiment
Programme *e:* **NORSEX**

Norwegian Remote Sensing Spectroscopy
for Mapping and Monitoring of Algal
Blooms and Pollution *e:* **NORSMAP**

Norwegian Sea Overflow Water *e:* **NSOW**

Norwegian Space Center (or Centre) *e:*
NSC

Norwegian Underwater Institute *e:* **NUI**

Norwegian Underwater Technology Center
e: **NUTEC**

Norwegian Water Association *e:* **NWA**

Nos Oiseaux. Bulletin de la Société
Romande pour l'Etude et la Protection des
Oiseaux *f:* **Nos Oiseaux Bull Romande
Etude Prot Oiseaux**

Noss National Nature Reserve *e:* **NNNR**

Notas Biologicas. Facultad de Ciencias
Exactas, Fisicas, y Naturales. Universidad
National del Nordeste. Corrientes Zool
s: **NBNZAK**

Notas de Geometria y Topologia *s:* **Notas
Geom Topol**

Notas Preliminares e Estudos. Servico
Geologico e Mineralogico do Brazil *s:*
**Notas Prelim Estud Serv Geol Mineral
Braz**

Notationes Biologicae *l:* **Not Biol**

Note. Laboratorio di Biologia Marina e
Pesca-Fano *i:* **Note Lab Biol Mar
Pesca-Fano**

Note Technique. Centre Technique Forestier Tropical [Nogent-Sur-Marne, France] *f:* **Note Tech Cent Tech For Trop [Nogent Sur Marne Fr]**

Note technique Groupement technique forestier *f:* **Note tech. Group. tech. for.**

Notes and Memoirs. United Arab Republic. Hydrobiological Department *e:* **Notes Mem UAR Hydrobiol Dep**

Notes du Service Geologique du Maroc *f:* **Notes Serv Geol Maroc**

Notes et Memoires du Service Geologique [Rabat] *f:* **Notes Mem Serv Geol [Rabat]**

Notes et Memoires. Service Geologique du Maroc *f:* **Notes Mem Serv Geol Maroc**

Notes on Water Pollution [Stevenage] *e:* **Notes Water Pollut [Stevenage]**

Notes on Water Research *e:* **Notes Water Res**

Notes Techniques en Hydrologie *f:* **Notes Tech Hydrol**

Notgemeinschaft Abwassergeschädigter [Bergische Bäche und der unteren Wupper] e.V. *d:* **NAG**

Notice of Exception Oceanographic Foundation *e:* **NOE**

Noticia Geomorfologica *i:* **Notic Geomorfol**

Noticiario Mensual. Museo National de Historia Natural *s:* **Not Mens Mus Nac Hist Nat**

notieren *d:* **not.**

Notulae Naturae. Academy of Natural Sciences of Philadelphia *e:* **Not Nat Acad Nat Sci Philadelphia**

Notulae Naturae [Philadelphia] *l:* **Not Nat [Phila]**

Nouveautes Medicales *f:* **Nouv Med**

Nouvel Observateur *f:* **N O**

Nouvelle Compagnie Forestière et Industrielle du Bois *f:* **COFIBOIS**

Nouvelle Presse Medicale *f:* **Nouv Presse**, *f:* **Nouv Presse Med**

Nouvelle Société Forestière du Gabon *f:* **NSFG**

Nouvelles der Landeshydrologie und -geologie *d:* **Nouv. Landeshydrol. -geol.**

Nova Acta Regiae Societatis Scientiarum Upsaliensis. Seria C. Botany, General Geology, Physical Geography, Paleontology, *l:* **Nova Acta Regiae Soc Sci Ups Ser C**

Nova Guinea. Geology *e:* **Nova Guinea Geol**

Nova Natural Resources Corp. *e:* **NOVA**

Nova Scotia Department of Natural Resources *e:* **NSDNR**

Nova Scotia Department of the Environment, Halifax, Nova Scotia *e:* **NSHDE**

Nova Scotia Institute of Natural Science. Proceedings and Transactions *e:* **NS Inst N Sc Pr Tr**

Nova Scotia Medical Bulletin *e:* **Nova Scotia Med Bull**, *e:* **NS Med Bull**

Novametrix Medical Systems, Inc. *e:* **NMTX**

Novdades Cientificas. Contribuciones Ocasionales del Museo de Historia Natural La Salle [Caracas]. Serie Botanica *s:* **NCMBBJ**

Novenyvedelem Idoszeru Kerdesei *H:* **Novenyved Idoszeru Kerdesei**

Novoe v Zhizni, Nauke, Tekhnike. Seriya Biologiia *R:* **Nov Zhizni Nauke Tekh Ser Biol**

Novosti Neftyanoi i Gazovni Tekhniki. Geologiya *R:* **Nov Neft Gazov Tekh Geol**

Novosti Neftyanoi Tekhniki. Geologiya *R:* **Nov Neft Tekh Geol**

Novye Dannye po Geologii i Poleznym Iskopaemym Zapadnoi Sibiri *R:* **Nov Dannye Geol Polezn Iskop Zapadn Sib**

Növényvédelem Időszaki Kérdései *H:* **NIK**

Noxubee National Wildlife Refuge *e:* **NNWR**

NPDES Water Compliance System *e:* **WACO**

NR [Natural Rubber] Technical Bulletin *e:* **NR Tech Bull**

NRAO [National Radio Astronomy Observatory] Pulsar *e:* **NP**

NRI [Nomura Research Institute] Symposia on Modern Biology *e:* **NRI Symp Mod Biol**

NTIS Environmental Pollution Control [of National Technical Information Service] *e:* **NTIS Environ. Pollut. Control**

NTM. Schriftenreihe für Geschichte der Naturwissenschaften, Technik, und Medizin *d:* **NTM**, *d:* **NTMSB**, *d:* **NTM Schr Geschichte Natur Tech Medizin**

Nuc Compact. Compact News in Nuclear Medicine *e:* **Nuc Compact Compact News Nucl Med**

Nucleaire, Biologische en Chemische School *n:* **NBCS**

Nuclear Aerospace Research Facility *e:* **NARF**

Nuclear Aerospace Research Institute *e:* **NARI**

Nuclear and Environmental Safety Council *e:* **NESC**

Nuclear-Armed Sea-Launched Cruise Missile *e:* **TLAM/N**

Nuclear, Biological [and] Chemical *e:* **NBC**

Nuclear, Biological, and Chemical Contamination *e:* **NBCC**

Nuclear, Biological and Chemical Defense Control Element *e:* **NBCDCE**

Nuclear, Biological and Chemical Defense Exercise *e:* **NBCDX**

Nuclear, Biological and Chemical Element *e:* **NBCE**

Nuclear, Biological and Chemical Warfare *e:* **NBC Warfare**

Nuclear, Biological and Chemical [Warfare] Defense *e:* **NBCD**

Nuclear, Biological and Chemical Warfare Operations *e:* **NUBICWOPS**

Nuclear, Biological, Ballistic Missile & Chemical *e:* **NB[2]C**

Nuclear, Biological, Chemical and Damage *e:* **NBCD**

Nuclear, Biological, Chemical & Fire *e:* **NBCF**

Nuclear, Biological & Chemical Protective Cover *e:* **NBCPC**

Nuclear-Biological-Chemical Reconnaissance System *e:* **NBCRS**

Nuclear, Biological & Chemical Shelter System *e:* **NBCSS**

Nuclear, Biological, Chemical Warfare *e:* **NBCW**

Nuclear, Biological, Chemical Warfare Reporting System *e:* **NBCWRS**

Nuclear, Biológico y Químico *s:* **NBQ**

Nuclear Component Cooling Water System *e:* **NCCWS**

Nuclear Effects from Analysis of Residual Signatures *e:* **NEFARS**

Nuclear-Electric Unmanned Spacecraft *e:* **NEUS**

Nuclear, Electronic, Biological *e:* **NEB**

Nuclear Energy Propulsion Space Test Program *e:* **NEPSTP**

Nuclear Energy Waste Space Transportation and Removal *e:* **NEWSAR**

Nuclear Environment Protection *e:* **NEP**

Nuclear Exoatmospheric Burst *e:* **NEB**

Nuclear Institute for Agriculture and Biology *e:* **NIAB**

Nuclear Island Closed Cooling Water *e:* **NICCW**

Nuclear Island Closed Cooling Water System *e:* **NICCWS**

Nuclear Medical Research Detachment Europe *e:* **NMRDE**

Nuclear Medical Science *e:* **NMS**

Nuclear Medicine *e:* **NM**

nuclear medicine *e:* **N-medicine**

Nuclear Medicine *e:* **NMIMAX**, *e:* **Nucl Med**

Nuclear Medicine and Biology *e:* **Nucl Med Biol**

Nuclear Medicine Annual *e:* **NMANDX**, *e:* **Nucl Med Annu**

Nuclear Medicine Communications *e:* **NMC**, *e:* **Nucl Med C**, *e:* **Nucl Med Commun**

Nuclear Medicine Department *e:* **NMD**

nuclear-medicine technician *e:* **N-med tech**

Nuclear Medicine Technology *e:* **NMT**

Nuclear Medicine Technology Certification Board *e:* **NMTCB**

Nuclear Medizin. Supplementum *d:* **Nucl Med Suppl**

Nuclear Optical & Radar Signature Estimation *e:* **NORSE**

Nuclear Orbit-to-Orbit Shuttle *e:* **NOOS**

Nuclear Orbit Transfer Stage *e:* **NOTS**

Nuclear Polarization *e:* **NP**

Nuclear-Powered Ocean Engineering Vehicle *e:* **NPOEV**

Nuclear River Service Water *e:* **NRSW**

Nuclear safety and civil protection *e:* **DG XI-C**

Nuclear Safety Protection System *e:* **NSPS**

Nuclear Science and Applications. Series A. Biological Science *e:* **NSAAB**

Nuclear Science & Engineering & Health Physics *e:* **NSEHP**

Nuclear Service Raw Water *e:* **NSRW**

Nuclear Service Water System *e:* **NSWS**

Nuclear Services Cooling Water System *e:* **NSCWS**

Nuclear Underwater Sound Source *e:* **NUSOS**

Nuclear Waste Geotechnical Projects *e:* **NWGP**

Nuestra Tierra. Paz y Progreso *s:* **Nuestra Tierra**

Nuffield Institute for Health *e:* **NIH**

Nuffield Institute of Comparative Medicine *e:* **NICM**

Nuffield Observatory, Jodrell Bank *e:*
N.O.

Nuffield Unit of Tropical Animal Ecology
e: **NUTAE**

Nuisances et Environnement *f:* **Nuisances
Environ**

Nuklearmedizin *d:* **Nuklearmed.**

Null-Reflecting Water *e:* **NRW**

Numerical Master Geometry [System] *e:*
NMG

Numerical Master Geometry System *e:*
NMG System

Numerical Oceanographic Prediction *e:*
NOP

Numerical Weather and Oceanographic
Forecasting Center *e:* **NWOFC**

Numerical Weather Facility *e:* **NWF**

Numerical Weather Prediction *e:* **NWP**

Numerical Weather Prediction Model *e:*
NWPM

Numerical Weather Prediction Operational
Grid *e:* **NWPOG**

Nurse Practitioners in Reproductive Health
e: **NPRH**

Nurses and Army Medical Specialists *e:*
NAMS

Nurses Association of the American College
of Obstetricians and Gynecologists (or
Gynecology) *e:* **NAACOG**

Nurses Observation Scale for Inpatient
Evaluation *e:* **NOSIE**

Nursing and Health Care *e:* **Nurs Hlth
Care**

Nutrient Enhanced Coastal Ocean
Productivity [Program] *e:* **NECOP**

Nutrient Requirements of Domestic
Animals *e:* **Nutr Requir Domest Anim**

Nutrition and Dental Health *e:* **Nutr Dent
Health**

Nutrition and Health *e:* **Nutr Health**

Nutrition and Health.A Journal of
Preventive Medicine *e:* **NUAH**

Nutrition for Optimal Health Association
e: **NOHA**

Nutrition in Health and Disease *e:* **Nutr
Health Dis**

NVG Operations Weather Software *e:*
NOWS

NWSIA [National Water Supply
Improvement Association] Journal *e:*
NWSIA J

NWT [Northwest Territories, Canada]
Wildlife Notes *e:* **NWTWN**

NWT [Northwest Territories, Canada]
Wildlife Service. Completion Reports *e:*
NWTWSCR

NWT [Northwest Territories, Canada]
Wildlife Service. Contact Reports *e:*
NWTWSCT

NWT [Northwest Territories, Canada]
Wildlife Service. File Reports *e:*
NWTWSFR

NWT [Northwest Territories, Canada]
Wildlife Service. Progress Reports *e:*
NWTWSPR

Nyasaland Protectorate. Geological Survey
Department. Memoir *e:* **Nyasal Geol
Surv Dep Mem**

Nyasaland Protectorate Law Reports *e:*
NPLR

Nystagmus [Medicine] *e:* **NYST**

Nytest Environmental, Inc. *e:* **NYTS**

Nytt Magasin foer Naturvidenskapene *N:*
Nytt Mag Naturvid, *N:* **Nytt Mag
Naturvidensk**

NZOI [New Zealand Oceanographic
Institute] Records *e:* **NZOI Rec**

Núcleo de Estudos de Farmacologia das
Plantas Medicinais do Ultramar, Junta de
Investigações do Ultramar, Lisboa *p:*
NEFPMU

O

Oak Ridge National Laboratory/Distributed
Active Archive Center for
Biogeochemical Dynamics *e:*
ORNL/DAAC

Oberdeutsche Zeitschrift für Volkskunde
d: **O.Zs.f.V.**

Oberflächenwasser *d:* **OW**

Obermedizinalrat *d:* **Ob.-Med.-R.,** *d:*
OMedR, *d:* **OMR**

Oberregierungsgeologe *d:* **ORGeol**

Oberregierungsmedizinalrat *d:* **Ob.-Reg.-
Med.-R.,** *d:* **ORegMedR,** *d:* **ORegMR,** *d:*
ORMedR, *d:* **ORMR**

Oberste Behörde für die Prüfungen von
Warm- und Kaltblutpferden *d:* **OBWK**

Oberwasser *d:* **OW**

Oberwasserlinie *d:* **OWL**

Oberwasserspiegel *d:* **O.W.Sp.,** *e:* **OW**

Oberwasserstand *d:* **OW**

Obesity and Bariatric Medicine *e:* **Obesity
& Bariatric Med**

Object-Oriented Distributed Computing
Environment *e:* **OODCE**

Object Remote Procedure Call *e:* **ORPC**

Object Space *e:* **OS**

Objektorientierte Implementierung *d:* **OOI**

Objektorientierte Programmierung *d:* **OOP**

O'Brien Environmental Energy *e:*
OBRIEN, *e:* **OBS**

observación *s:* **Obs**

Observación *s:* **Obsn,** *s:* **RMK**

observador *s:* **Obs**

Observador *s:* **Obsdr**

observasjon *N:* **Obs**

observasjonsbatteri *N:* **obs. btt.**

observasjonsplass *N:* **obs. pl.**

Observasjonsplass *N:* **Opl**

observasjonspost *N:* **obs. p.**

Observasjonspost *N:* **OP**

Observatie Team *n:* **OT**

Observation *e:* **OB,** *e:* **OBS,** *e:* **OBSERV,**
e: **OBSN,** *e:* **OBSR**

observation *e:* **obsv**

Observation [Aircraft] *e:* **O**

Observation and Assessment *e:* **O& A**

Observation and Fields of Fire, Cover and
Concealment, Obstacles, Key Terrain,
Avenues of Approach *e:* **OCOKA**

Observation and Listening *e:* **O and L**

Observation Balloon *e:* **OB,** *e:* **OBBO**

Observation Balloon System *e:* **OBS**

Observation Car *e:* **OC**

Observation, Conclusion, Temporary Data
e: **OCTD**

Observation Control Optimization *e:*
OBCOOP

Observation Deck *d:* **OB DK**

Observation Fighter Squadron *e:* **VOF**

Observation Group *e:* **OG**

Observation Helicopter *e:* **HO**

Observation Landplane *e:* **OLP**

Observation Line *e:* **OBSN L**

Observation Markup Format *e:* **OMF**

Observation (or Observing) Simulation
System Experiment[s] *e:* **OSSE**

Observation-Orientation-Decision-Action
e: **OODA**

Observation Patrol *e:* **OBS PAT,** *e:* **OP**

Observation Plane *e:* **OBS PL,** *e:* **OP,** *e:*
VO

Observation Plane Squadron *e:* **VOG**

Observation Point [or Post] *e:* **OP**

Observation Post *e:* **O.P.**

Observation Post Vehicle *e:* **OPV**

Observation Preparation Branch *e:* **OPB**

Observation Report Conversion [program]
e: **ORCON**

Observation Requirement Data Sheet *e:*
ORDS

Observation Residue[s] *e:* **ORES**

Observation Schedule and Records *e:*
OSCAR

Observation Scout Plane *e:* **VOS**

Observation Set *e:* **OBSET**

Observation Squadron *e:* **OBSRON,** *e:*
OS, *e:* **VO**

Observation Station *e:* **OBS Station,** *e:*
OBS Stn, *e:* **OS,** *e:* **O. Stn.**

Observation System Simulation *e:* **OSS**

Observation Ward *e:* **OW**

Observational Approach *e:* **OA**

Observational Nursery *e:* **ON**

Observational (or Observing) Facilities
Advisory Panel *e:* **OFAP**

Observational Test and Development Center
e: **OTDC**

Observational Yield Test *e:* **OYT**

Observational Yield Trial *e:* **OYT**

observations- *r:* **o-**

observation[s] *r:* **obs**

Observations Astronomiques *f:* **O.A.**

Observations Météorologiques *f:* **O.M.**

Observations sur la Physique, sur l'Histoire
Naturelle, et sur les Arts *f:* **Obs sur
Phys**

observationslinje *r:* **olinje**

Observationsplats *r:* **Oplats**

Observationsplatsvärn *r:* **Ovärn**

Observationspost *r:* **Op**

observationspost *r:* **opost**

Observatoire *f:* **Obs.**

Observatoire de Haute Provence *f:* **OHP**

Observatoire de la Chirurgie Française *f:*
OCF

Observatoire de la Faune, de la Flore et des
Habitats *f:* **OFFH**

Observatoire de la géosphère et de la
biosphère *f:* **GBO**

Observatoire de Meudon *f:* **O.M.**

Observatoire des Technologies pour
l'éducation en Europe *f:* **OTE**

Observatoire du Parc de Montsouris *f:*
O.P.M.

Observatoire du Sahara et du Sahel *f:* **OSS**

Observatoire Européen des Drogues et des
Toxicomanies *f:* **OEDT**

Observatoire français des conjonctures
économiques *f:* **OFCE**

Observatoire Français des Drogues et des
Toxicomanies *f:* **OFDT**

Observatoire Français des Techniques
Avancées *f:* **OFTA**

Observatoire méditerranéen de l'environnement et du développement *f:* **OMED**

Observatoire Régional de la Santé *f:* **ORS**

Observatoire Régional de la Santé d'Ile-de-France *f:* **ORSIF**

Observatoire Régional Emploi Formation *f:* **OREF**

Observatoire Social Européen *f:* **OSE**

Observatoires Régionaux de la Santé *f:* **ORS**

Observatør *a:* **O**

Observator *d:* **OBS**, *d:* **Observ.**

observatorio *s:* **Obs**

Observatorio *s:* **Obsio**, *s:* **Obst**, *s:* **Obto**

Observatorio Astronomico de la Universidad Nacional de La Plata. Serie Astronomica *s:* **Obs Astronom Univ Nac La Plata Ser Astronom**

Observatorio Astronomico de Quito *s:* **OAQ**

Observatorio Avanzado *s:* **Obs Avdo**

Observatorio de la Geosfera y la Biosfera *s:* **OGB**

Observatorio del Desarrollo y el Medio Ambiente del Mediterráneo *s:* **MEDO**

Observatorio Lateral *s:* **OBSLAT**

Observatorium *d:* **Obs.**

Observatory *e:* **O**, *e:* **OBS**

observatory *e:* **observ**, *e:* **obsv**

Observatory *e:* **OBSY**

Observatory of Fauna, Flora and Habitats *e:* **OFFH**

Observatory of the Sahara and the Sahel *e:* **OSS**

Observe (u Observado, u Observación) *s:* **OBS**

Observing and Modelling of Eddy Scale Geostrophic and Ageostrophic Circulation *e:* **OMEGA**

Obshchaya Ekologiya, Biotsenologiya, Gidrobiologiya *R:* **Obshch Ekol Biotsenol Gidrobiol**

Obstetria and Gynecology *e:* **Obst Gynec**

Obstetric, Gynecologic and Neonatal *e:* **OGN**

Obstetrica si Ginecologia *l:* **Obstet Ginecol**

Obstetrica si Ginecologia [Bucharest] *l:* **Obstet Ginecol [Buchar]**

Obstetrical and Gynecological Survey *e:* **Obstet Gynecol Surv**, *e:* **Obstet Gynec Surv**, *e:* **Obst Gynec Surv**

Obstetrical and Gynecological Therapy [Japan] *e:* **Obstet Gynecol Ther**

Obstetrical-Gynecological *e:* **OB-GYN**

Obstetricia y Ginecologia Latino-Americanas *s:* **Obstet Ginecol Lat-Am**

Obstetrician-Gynaecologist *e:* **Ob-G**

Obstetrician-Gyn[a]ecologist *e:* **OB-GYN**

Obstetrics and Gynecology *e:* **OBGNA**, *e:* **Obstet Gyn[ec]**

Obstetrics and Gynecology. Annual *e:* **Obstet Gynecol Annu**

Obstetrics and Gynecology Clinics of North America *e:* **Obstet Gynecol Clin North Am**

Obstetrics and Gynecology [Tokyo] *e:* **Obstet Gynecol [Tokyo]**

Obstetrics-Gyn[a]ecology *e:* **OB-GYN**

Obstetrics-Gynecology *e:* **OBG**, *e:* **OG**

Obstáculo Natural *s:* **Obst Nat**

Occasional Papers. Bell Museum of Natural History. University of Minnesota *e:* **Occas Pap Bell Mus Nat Hist Univ Minn**

Occasional Papers. Buffalo Society of Natural Sciences *e:* **Occas Pap Buffalo Soc Nat Sci**, *e:* **OPBSDH**

Occasional Papers. C. C. Adams Center for Ecological Studies. Western Michigan University *e:* **Occas Pap C C Adams Cent Ecol Stud West Mich Univ**

Occasional Papers. Department of Biology. University of Guyana *e:* **Occ Pap Dep Biol Univ Guyana**

Occasional Papers. Department of Biology. University of Puget Sound *e:* **Occas Pap Dep Biol Univ Puget Sound**

Occasional Papers. Geological Survey of Nigeria *e:* **Occ Pap Geol Surv Nig**

Occasional Papers. Geological Survey of Uganda *e:* **Occ Pap Geol Surv Ug**

Occasional Papers in Geography *e:* **Oc P Geog**

Occasional Papers. Minnesota Museum of Natural History *e:* **Occas Pap Minn Mus Nat Hist**

Occasional Papers. Museum of Natural History. University of Kansas *e:* **Occas Pap Mus Nat Hist Univ Kans**

Occasional Papers. Museum of Natural History. University of Puget Sound *e:* **Occas Pap Mus Nat Hist Univ Puget Sound**

Occasional Papers. National Museums and Monuments of Rhodesia. Series B. Natural Sciences *e:* **Occas Pap Natl Mus Monum Rhod Ser B Nat Sci**

Occasional Papers. San Diego Society of Natural Hislory *e:* **Occas Pap San Diego Soc Nat Hist**

Occasional Publications. Institute of Health Administration. Georgia State University *e:* **Occas Publ Inst Health Adm GA State Univ**

Occupational and Environmental Health Laboratory *e:* **OEHL**

Occupational and Environmental Health Unit, University of Toronto *e:* **KOC**

Occupational and Environmental Medicine *e:* **Occup Environ Med**

Occupational and Environmental Protection *e:* **O&EP**

Occupational & Environmental Health Library *e:* **OEH**

Occupational Health *e:* **Occup. Health**, *e:* **Occup Hlth**

Occupational Health Administration *e:* **OHA**

Occupational Health and Hygiene *e:* **OHH**

Occupational Health and Safety *e:* **Occ Health & Sfty**, *e:* **Occup Health and Saf**, *e:* **Occup Health Saf**, *e:* **OH&S**, *e:* **OHSAD**

Occupational Health and Safety Act *e:* **OHSA**

Occupational Health and Safety Branch *e:* **OHSB**

Occupational Health and Safety Commission (or Committee) *e:* **OHSC**

Occupational Health and Safety Division *e:* **OHSD**

Occupation[al] Health and Safety Staff *e:* **OHSS**

Occupational Health Australia and New Zealand *e:* **Occ Heal ANZ**

Occupational Health Bulletin [Ottawa] *e:* **Occup Health Bull [Ottawa]**

Occupational Health Center *e:* **OHC**

Occupational Health Facility *e:* **OHF**

Occupational Health Institute *e:* **OHI**

Occupational Health Labels *e:* **OC-HLTHLB**

Occupational Health Laboratory *e:* **OHL**

Occupational Health [London] *e:* **Occup Health [Lond]**

Occupational Health Management Information System *e:* **OHMIS**

Occupational Health Monitoring and Evaluation System *e:* **OHMES**

Occupational Health Nurse *e:* **OHN**

Occupational Health Nursing *e:* **Occ Health Nurs**, *e:* **Occup Health Nurs**, *e:* **Occup Hlth Nurs**

Occupational Health Nursing Certificate *e:* **OHNC**

Occupational Health Nursing [New York] *e:* **Occup Health Nurs [NY]**

Occupational Health Nursing Officer *e:* **OHNO**

Occupational Health Nursing Sister *e:* **OHNS**

Occupational Health Physician *e:* **OHP**

Occupational Health Review *e:* **Occup Health Rev**, *e:* **Occup Hlth Rev**

Occupational Health/Safety Programs Accreditation Commission *e:* **OHSPAC**

Occupational Health & Safety Technician *e:* **OHST**

Occupational Health Service *e:* **OHS**

Occupational Health Services Material Safety Data Sheets *e:* **OHS MSDS**

Occupational Health Site *e:* **TA-59**

Occupational Medical Administrators' Association *e:* **OMAA**

Occupational Medical Association of Canada *e:* **OMAC**

Occupational Medical Association of Connecticut *e:* **OMAC**

Occupational Medical Corporation of America, Inc. *e:* **OMCA**

Occupational Medicine *e:* **OCC MED**, *e:* **Occup Med**, *e:* **Occup Med [Oxf]**, *e:* **OCMEA**, *e:* **OM**

Occupational Medicine and Hygiene *e:* **O.M.H.**

Occupational Medicine and Hygiene Laboratory *e:* **OMHL**

Occupational Medicine/ Environmental Health Evaluation Center *e:* **OM/EH**

Occupational Medicine Office *e:* **OMO**

Occupational Medicine Self-Assessment Program *e:* **OMSAP**

Occupational Safety and Health *e:* **Occup Saf Health**, *e:* **Occup Saf Hlth**

Occupational Safety and Health Act *e:* **OSHA**

Occupational Safety and Health Act[ivity] *e:* **OSHA**

Occupational Safety and Health Administration *e:* **OSHA**

Occupational Safety and Health Administration Subscription Service *e:* **Occup. Sat Health Admin. Sub Serv.**

Occupational Safety and Health Administration. Subscription Service. Volumes 1 and 4 *e:* **Occup Saf Hlth Admin Sub Service Vols 1 & 4**

Occupational Safety and Health Administration, Technical Data Center, Washington *e:* **ULO**

Occupational Safety and Health Agency *e:*
OSHA

Occupational Safety and Health Branch,
Labour Canada Ottawa, Ontario *e:*
OOLAP

Occupational Safety and Health
[Conference] *e:* **OSH**

Occupational Safety and Health Control
Report *e:* **OCR**

Occupational, Safety and Health Institute
e: **OSHI**

Occupational Safety and Health Review
Commission *e:* **OSAHRC**

Occupational Safety and Health Review
Commission (or Committee) *e:* **OSHRC**

Occupational Safety and Health Scheme *e:*
OSHS

Occupational Safety and Health Series.
International Labour Office *e:* **Occup
Saf Health Ser Int Labour Off**

Occupational Safety and Health Standards
Act *e:* **OSHSA**

Occupational Safety & Health Worker
Protection Pilots *e:* **OSHWPP**

Occupational Therapy in Health Care *e:*
Occup Ther Health Care

Occupational Therapy in Mental Health *e:*
Occup Ther Ment Health

Ocean *e:* **O**, *e:* **OC**, *e:* **OCE**

Ocean Acoustic Tomography *e:* **OAT**

Ocean Acre *e:* **OA**

Ocean Acre Project *e:* **OCAC**

Ocean Affairs Advisory Committee *e:*
OAAC

Ocean Affairs Board *e:* **OAB**

Ocean Aids to Navigation *e:* **OAN**

Ocean Airways, Inc. *e:* **OCN**

Ocean All-Source Information System *e:*
OASIS

Ocean and Lake Surveys *e:* **O and LS**, *e:*
O & LS

Ocean and Rail *e:* **O and R**, *e:* **O & R**

Ocean and Shoreline Management *e:*
Ocean & Shoreline Manage

Ocean Area Reconnaissance Satellite *e:*
OARS

Ocean-Atmosphere Carbon Exchange Study
e: **OACES**

Ocean Atmosphere Climate Interaction
Studies *e:* **OACIS**

Ocean Atmosphere Exchange of Trace
Compounds *e:* **OAXTC**

Ocean-Atmosphere Exchange Processes *e:*
OAMEX

Ocean-Atmosphere-Ice Interactions *e:*
OAII

Ocean, Atmosphere, Research and
Investigation with Acoustic Techniques
e: **OCARINA**

Ocean Atmosphere Response Studies *e:*
OARS

Ocean Atmospheric Surveillance and
Information System *e:* **OASIS**

Ocean Beach *e:* **OB**, *e:* **Ocn Bch**

Ocean Bill of Lading *e:* **OB/L**, *e:* **OC B/L**

Ocean Bio-Chem, Incorporated *e:* **OBCI**

Ocean Boarding Vessel *e:* **OBV**

Ocean Bottom *e:* **OB**

Ocean Bottom Communications System *e:*
OBCS

Ocean Bottom Scanning Sonar *e:* **OBSS**

Ocean Bottom Seismograph *e:* **OBS**

Ocean Bottom Seismographic Station *e:*
OBS Station

Ocean Bottom Seismometer *e:* **OBS**

Ocean Bottom Station *e:* **OBS**

Ocean Bottom Suspension *e:* **OBS**

Ocean Carbon Cycle Model *e:* **OCCM**

Ocean Carbon-Cycle Model
Intercomparison Project *e:* **OCMIP**

Ocean Cargo Line *e:* **OCL**

Ocean Catalog Group *e:* **OCG**

Ocean Chemistry Division *e:* **OCD**

Ocean Circulation [and] Climate Advanced
Modelling [programme] *e:* **OCCAM**

Ocean Circulation and Climate Advanced
Modelling Project *e:* **OCCAM**

Ocean Circulation Model *e:* **OCM**

Ocean Climate Data Workshop *e:* **OCDW**

Ocean Climate Observing System *e:*
OCOS

Ocean Climate Research Committee *e:*
OCRC

Ocean Climate Research Division *e:*
OCRD

Ocean Color and Temperature Sounder *e:*
OCTS

Ocean Color Environment Archive Network
e: **OCEAN**

Ocean Color Working Group *e:* **OCWG**

Ocean Colour and Temperature Sensor *e:*
OCTS

Ocean Colo[u]r [and] Thermal Scanner *e:*
OCTS

Ocean Colour European Archive Network
e: **OCEAN**

Ocean Colo[u]r Experiment *e:* **OCE**

Ocean Colour Imager *e:* **OCI**

Ocean Colour Monitor *e:* **OCM**

Ocean Colour Radiometer *e:* **OCR**

Ocean Colour Scanner *e:* **OCS**

Ocean Colour Techniques for Observation,
Processing and Utilization Systems *e:*
OCTOPUS

Ocean Container Zebrugge *e:* **OCZ**

Ocean Control Authority *e:* **OCA**

Ocean Coordinating Committee *e:* **OCC**

Ocean Covered Earth *e:* **OCE**

Ocean Crust Boundary *e:* **OCB**

Ocean Culture Product *e:* **OCP**

Ocean Culture System *e:* **OCS**

Ocean Data Acquisition System[s] *e:*
ODAS

Ocean Data and Information Network *e:*
ODIN

Ocean Data and Information Network for
Eastern Africa *e:* **ODINEA**

Ocean Data Buoy *d:* **ODB**

Ocean Data Environmental Science[s]
Service[s] Acquisition *e:* **ODESSA**

Ocean Data Equipment Corporation *e:*
ODEC

Ocean Data Station *e:* **ODS**

Ocean Data Station Buoy *e:* **ODSB**

Ocean Data Systems, Incorporated *e:*
ODSI

Ocean Data Transmitter *e:* **ODT**

Ocean Design Engineering Corporation *e:*
ODEC

Ocean Development and International Law
e: **Oc Dev and Int L**, *e:* **Ocean
Dev[el]&Int L**, *e:* **Ocean Develop Int
Law**, *e:* **Ocean Development and
Internat Law**, *e:* **Ocean Dev I**, *e:* **Ocean
Dev & Int L**

Ocean Development and International Law
Journal *e:* **Ocean Dev and Intl LJ**

Ocean Development & International Law
e: **Ocean Dev.&Int'l L.**

Ocean Drilling and Exploration Company,
New Orleans, La. *e:* **ODECO**

Ocean Drilling & Exploration Co. *e:* **ODR**

Ocean Drilling Program[me] *e:* **ODP**

Ocean Dumping Ban Act *e:* **ODBA**

Ocean Dumping Control Act *e:* **ODCA**

Ocean Dumping Permits *e:* **ODUMP**

Ocean Dumping Surveillance System *e:*
ODSS

Ocean Dynamic Satellite *e:* **SEASAT**

Ocean Dynamics Advisory Subcommittee
e: **ODAS**

Ocean Dynamics and Climate *e:* **ODC**

Ocean Dynamics Information System *e:*
ODIS

Ocean Economics and Technology Branch
e: **OETB**

Ocean Economics and Technology Office
e: **OETO**

Ocean Education Project *e:* **OEP**

Ocean Engineer *e:* **OceanE**

ocean engineer[ing] *e:* **oceaneer[ing]**

Ocean Engineering *e:* **Ocean Eng**, *e:*
Ocean Engng

Ocean Engineering Centre *e:* **OEC**

Ocean Engineering Centre, Memorial
University, St. John's, Newfoundland *e:*
NFSMO

Ocean Engineering Division *e:* **OED**

Ocean Engineering Information Centre *e:*
OEIC

Ocean Engineering. Information Series *e:*
Ocean Eng Inf Ser

Ocean Engineering System Development
e: **OESD**

Ocean Environment Research Division *e:*
OERD

Ocean Floor Analysis Division *e:* **OFAD**

Ocean Floor Drilling *e:* **OFD**

Ocean Freight Reimbursement *e:* **OFR**

Ocean General Circulation Model *e:*
OGCM, *e:* **OPYC**

Ocean Going *e:* **OG**

Ocean Heat Transport Experiment *e:*
OHTEX

Ocean Highway Association *e:* **OHA**

Ocean History Panel *e:* **OHP**

Ocean Industries Association *e:* **OIA**

Ocean Industries Capital Assistance
Program *e:* **OICAP**

Ocean Industries Development Office *e:*
OIDO

Ocean Industry *e:* **Ocean Ind**

Ocean Industry. Engineering, Construction
and Operations *e:* **OCI**

Ocean Information Center *e:* **OCEANIC**

Ocean Information System Baseline
Upgrade *e:* **OBU**

Ocean Instrumentation Engineering Office
e: **OIEO**

Ocean-island Basalt *e:* **OIB**

Ocean Living Institute *e:* **OLI**

Ocean Management *e:* **Ocean Manage**, *e:*
Ocean Mgt, *e:* **OCM**

Ocean Management [Apublication] *e:*
Ocean Man

Ocean Management Incorporated *e:* **OMI**

Ocean Map *e:* **OCNMAP**

Ocean Mapping *e:* **OM**

Ocean Mapping Group e: **OMG**
Ocean Margin Drilling e: **OMD**
Ocean Margin Drilling Project [or Program] e: **OMDP**
Ocean Margin Exchange[s] Experiment (or Study) e: **OMEX**
Ocean Margins Exchange e: **OMEX**
Ocean Margins Program e: **OMP**
Ocean Marine Technology e: **OMT**
Ocean Materials Criteria Branch e: **OMCB**
Ocean Measurement and Array Technology e: **OMAT**
Ocean Minerals Company e: **OMCO**
Ocean Minesweeper e: **OMS**
Ocean Mining Administration e: **OMA**
Ocean Mining Associates e: **OMA**
Ocean Mixed Layer e: **OML**
Ocean Mixed Layer Depth e: **MLD**
Ocean Mixed Layer Experiment e: **OMLET**
Ocean Model Intercomparison Project e: **OMIP**
Ocean Movement Designator e: **OMD**
Ocean Observing System e: **OOS**
Ocean Observing System[s] Development Panel e: **OOSDP**
Ocean Outlook e: **OO**
Ocean Patrol Ship e: **OPS**
Ocean Pearl Button Manufacturers Association e: **OPBMA**
Ocean Personal Computer Project e: **OCEAN-PC**
Ocean Platform Station e: **OPS**
Ocean Policy Committee e: **OPC**
Ocean Pollution Data and Information Network e: **OPDIN**
Ocean Prediction through Observation, Modeling and Analysis e: **OPTOMA**
Ocean Pressure Laboratory e: **OPL**
Ocean [Pressure] Simulation Facility e: **OSF**
Ocean Process Analysis Laboratory e: **OPAL**
Ocean Production Enhancement Network e: **OPEN**
Ocean Products Center e: **OPC**
Ocean Radar-Station Ship e: **YAGR**
Ocean Range Vessel e: **ORV**
Ocean Range Vessels e: **ORVs**
Ocean Reef Airways Club e: **ORA**
Ocean [region] e: **OCE**
Ocean Rescue 2000 e: **OR2000**
Ocean Research Buoy e: **ORB**
Ocean Research Equipment, Inc. e: **ORE**
Ocean Research Institute e: **ORI**
Ocean Research [Seoul] e: **Ocean Res [Seoul]**
Ocean Resource Coordination and Assessment e: **ORCA**
Ocean Resources Conservation Association e: **O.R.C.A.**
Ocean Resources Engineering e: **ORE**
Ocean Resources Institute e: **ORI**
Ocean Ridge Crest Processes e: **ORCP**
Ocean Sampling and Environmental Analysis System e: **OSEAS**
Ocean Science and Engineering e: **Ocean Sci Eng**, e: **OSE**
Ocean Science and Surveys e: **OSS**
Ocean Science and Technology Advisory Committee e: **OSTAC**
Ocean Science and Technology Group e: **OSTG**

Ocean Science Committee e: **OSC**
Ocean Science Division-Naval Research Laboratory e: **OSDNRL**
Ocean Science in Relation to Living Resources e: **OSLR**
Ocean Science Laboratory e: **OSCILAB**
Ocean Science News e: **OSN**
Ocean Science [or Service] in Relation to Non-Living Resources e: **OSNLR**
Ocean Sciences Board e: **OSB**
Ocean Sciences Center e: **OSC**
Ocean Sediment Coring Program e: **OSCP**
Ocean Seismic Network e: **OSN**
Ocean Shipping Act e: **OSA**
Ocean Shipping and Enterprises e: **OSE**
Ocean Shipping Procedures e: **OSPRO**
Ocean State Business e: **Ocean St B**
Ocean Station e: **OS**
Ocean Station Vessel e: **OSV**
Ocean Studies Board e: **OSB**
Ocean Studies Satellite e: **OCEANSAT**
Ocean Subarea [Atlantic] e: **OCEANLANT**
Ocean Surface Current Radar e: **OSCR**
Ocean Surface Roughness Measurement System e: **OSRMS**
Ocean Surface Temperature e: **OST**
Ocean Surveillance e: **OSUS**
Ocean Surveillance Air Patrol e: **OSAP**
Ocean Surveillance Data Base e: **OSDB**
Ocean Surveillance Information System e: **OSIS**
Ocean Surveillance Product e: **OCP**, e: **OSP**
Ocean Surveillance Product Dissemination Service e: **OSPDS**
Ocean Surveillance Satellite e: **OSS**
Ocean Surveillance Ship e: **AGOS**, e: **TAGOS**
Ocean Survey Advisory Panel e: **OSAP**
Ocean Survey Program e: **OSP**
Ocean Survey Vessel e: **OSV**
Ocean Systems, Atlantic e: **OCEANSYSLANT**
Ocean Systems Engineering Corporation e: **OSEC**
Ocean Systems Operations e: **OSO**
Ocean Systems [or Search], Incorporated e: **OSI**
Ocean Systems, Pacific e: **OCEANSYSPAC**
Ocean Technology Division e: **OTD**
Ocean Temperature Large Antenna Microwave Radiometer e: **OTLAMR**
Ocean Test Fixture e: **OTF**
Ocean Test Ranges and Instrumentation [Conference] e: **OTRAN**
Ocean Thermal Energy Conservation e: **OTEC**
Ocean Thermal Energy Conversion e: **OTEC**
Ocean Thermal Energy Conversion Research and Development e: **OTEC R&D**
Ocean Thermal Energy Conversion System e: **OTECS**
Ocean Thermal Gradient System e: **OTGS**
Ocean Transport and Trading e: **OTT**
Ocean Transport and Trading Limited e: **Ocean**
Ocean Transportation e: **OT**
ocean transshipment cargo e: **otc**
Ocean Travel Development e: **OTD**

Ocean Science Committee e: **OSC**
Ocean University of Qingdao e: **OUQ**
ocean view e: **oc vu**
ocean wave profile recorder e: **owpr**
Ocean Weather Service e: **OSW**, e: **O.W.S.**
Ocean Weather Ship e: **OSW**, e: **OWS**
Ocean Weather Ship Meteorological Summary e: **OWS Meteorological Summary**
Ocean Weather Ship Service e: **OWSS**
Ocean Weather Station e: **OSW**, e: **OWS**
Ocean Yearbook e: **Ocean Yearb**
Oceaneering International, Inc. e: **OLL**
Oceaneering Technology [Integration] e: **OTECH**
Oceania e: **Oc**, e: **OCE**, e: **OCN**
Oceania National Olympic Committees e: **ONOC**
oceanic e: **o**
Oceanic Abstracts e: **OA**, e: **OceanAb**
Oceanic Affairs Committee e: **OAC**
Oceanic Air Roule Tracking System e: **OARTS**
Oceanic Air Traffic Center e: **OATC**
Oceanic Air Traffic Control e: **O.A.T.C.**
Oceanic Air-traffic Control e: **OCAC**
Oceanic and Atmospheric Research e: **OAR**
Oceanic and Atmospheric Satellite Imaging System e: **OASIS**
Oceanic and Atmospheric Scientific Information System e: **OASIS**
Oceanic Area e: **OCA**
Oceanic Area Control e: **OAC**
Oceanic Area Control Centre [or Center] e: **OACC**
Oceanic Area System Improvement Study e: **OASIS**
Oceanic Control Area e: **OCA**, e: **OCTA**
Oceanic Control Center e: **OCC**
Oceanic Data Assimilation System e: **ODAS**
Oceanic Data Link e: **ODL**
Oceanic Display and Planning System e: **ODAPS**
Oceanic Educational Foundation e: **OEF**
Oceanic Engineering e: **OE**
Oceanic Engineering Society e: **OES**
Oceanic Flight Information Region e: **OFIR**
Ocean[ic] Industries Association e: **OIA**
Oceanic Institute of Hawaii e: **OIH**
Oceanic Linguistics e: **Ocean Ling**, e: **OcL**
Oceanic Monitoring, Assessment and Prediction e: **OMAP**
Oceanic Navigational Error Report e: **ONER**
Oceanic Operators e: **OO**
Oceanic Remote Sensing Assembly e: **ORSA**
Oceanic Research Foundation e: **ORF**
Oceanic Ridge Basalts e: **ORB**
Oceanic Scanning Spectrophotometer e: **OSS**
Oceanic Society e: **OS**
Oceanic Society Expeditions e: **OSE**
Oceanic Space Subcommittee e: **OSS**
Oceanic Steamship Company e: **O**
Oceanic System Development and Support e: **OSDA**
Oceanic Trade Alliance Council International e: **OTAC**

© K · G · Saur, München

Oceanic Traffic Planning System *e:* **OTPS**

Oceanic Transition Route *e:* **OTR**

Oceanografiska Institute *r:* **Ocean Inst**

Oceanografía Física del Mediterráneo
  Oriental *s:* **POEM**

Oceanographer *e:* **OCEANOGR**

Oceanographer of the U.S. Navy *e:*
  OCEANAV

Oceanographic *e:* **OCEANOGR**

Oceanographic Advisory Committee *e:*
  OAC

Oceanographic Air Survey Unit *e:* **OASU**

Oceanographic and Atmospheric Master
  Library *e:* **OAML**

Oceanographic and Atmospheric Support
  and Information System *e:* **OASIS**

Oceanographic and Environmental Service
  Laboratory *e:* **OESL**, *e:* **OFSL**

Oceanographic and Meteorological *e:* **OM**

Oceanographic, Boarding and Diving
  Officer *e:* **OBDO**

Oceanographic Commission of Washington
  e: **OCW**

Oceanographic Committee *e:* **OCC**

Oceanographic Community Modeling Effort
  e: **OCME**

Oceanographic, Coordination, Evaluation,
  and Analysis Network *e:* **OCEAN**

1983 Oceanographic cruise along 0°
  Meridian into Weddell Sea *e:* **AJAX**

Oceanographic cruise in the South Pacific,
  1968 *e:* **SCORPIO**

oceanographic cutter *e:* **WAGO**

Oceanographic Data *e:* **OD**

Oceanographic Data and Information Centre
  e: **ODIC**

Oceanographic Data Center *e:* **ODC**

Oceanographic Data Facility *e:* **ODF**

Oceanographic Data for the Environmental
  Science Services Administration *e:*
  ODESSA

Oceanographic Data in Subtrial Areas *e:*
  ODISTA

Oceanographic Data Information System
  e: **ODIS**

Oceanographic Data Processing and Control
  System[s] *e:* **ODPCS**

Oceanographic Data Station *e:* **ODS**, *e:*
  OD Station

Oceanographic data system, formerly
  Equatorial Pacific Information Collection
  e: **EPIC**

Oceanographic Database and Environmental
  Satellite System Application *e:*
  ODESSA

Oceanographic Datastation *e:* **OD**

Oceanographic development squadron *e:*
  VXN

Oceanographic Devices *e:* **OC**

Oceanographic Digital Data System *e:*
  ODDS

Oceanographic Equipment Evaluation
  Range *e:* **OEER**

Oceanographic Experiment in the North-
  East Atlantic *e:* **POLYGON**

Oceanographic Facility *e:* **OF**

Oceanographic Institute of Hawaii *e:* **OIH**

Oceanographic Institute of Washington *e:*
  OIW

Oceanographic Institute of Wellington *e:*
  OIW

Oceanographic Instrumentation Center *e:*
  OIC

Oceanographic Lidar System *e:* **OLS**

Oceanographic Observations of the Pacific
  e: **OOP**

Oceanographic Office *e:* **OO**

Oceanographic Program of the USSR *e:*
  SECTIONS

Oceanographic Research Buoy *e:* **ORB**

Oceanographic Research Equipment *e:*
  ORE

Oceanographic Research for Defense
  Application *e:* **ORDA**

Oceanographic Research Institute *e:* **ORI**

Oceanographic Research Institute [Durban].
  Investigational Report *e:* **Oceanogr Res
  Inst [Durban] Invest Rep**

Oceanographic Research Ship *e:* **ORS**

Oceanographic Services, Incorporated *e:*
  OSI

Oceanographic Sub-programme [for GATE]
  Data Centre *e:* **OSDC**

Oceanographic Survey Recorder *e:* **OSR**

Oceanographic Technical Data Handling
  Committee *e:* **OTDHC**

Oceanographical Cruise Report. Division of
  Fisheries and Oceanography.
  Commonwealth Scientific and Industrial
  Research Organisation *e:* **Oceanogrl
  Cruise Rep Div Fish Oceanogr CSIRO**

Oceanographical Cruise Report. Institute of
  Marine Research [Djakarta] *e:*
  **Oceanogr Cruise Rep Inst Mar Res
  [Djakarta]**

Oceanographical Magazine *e:* **OCMAA**

Oceanographical Magazine [Tokyo] *e:*
  Oceanogr Mag [Tokyo]

Oceanographical Society of Japan. Journal
  e: **Oceanogr Soc Jap J**

Oceanographical Station List. Division of
  Fisheries and Oceanography.
  Commonwealth Scientific and Industrial
  Research Organisation *e:* **Oceanogrl Stn
  List Div Fish Oceanogr CSIRO**

oceanography *e:* **oceanog**

Oceanography *e:* **OCEANOGR**

Oceanography and Fisheries Committee *e:*
  OFC

Oceanography and Marine Assessment *e:*
  OMA

Oceanography and Marine Biology *e:*
  Oceanogr Mar Biol

Oceanography and Marine Biology: An
  Annual Review *e:* **Oceanogr Mar Biol
  Annu Rev**

Oceanography and Marine Technology *e:*
  OMT

Oceanography and Meteorology *e:* **OM**

Oceanography & Hydrographic Ship *e:*
  OHS

Oceanography Section *e:* **OS**

Oceanorraphy and Marine Biology Annual
  Review *e:* **Oceanogr. Mar. Biol. Annu.
  Rev.**

Oceanologia Acta *f:* **Oceanol. Acta**

Oceanologia et Limnologia Sinica *f:*
  Oceanol. Limnol. Sin., *l:* **Oceanol Limn
  Sin**

Oceanologica et Limnologia Sinica *l:*
  Oceanol Limnol Sin

Oceanological Research Centre (Abidjan,
  Côte d'Ivoire) *e:* **CRO**

oceanologic[al][ly] *e:* **oceano**

Oceanologist *e:* **OCEANO**

oceanology *e:* **oceano**

Oceanology *e:* **Oceanol**

Oceanology International *e:* **Oceanol Int**,
  e: **OI**

Oceanroutes, Inc., Palo Alto *e:* **OCU**

Oceans and Coastal Areas Programme *e:*
  OCAP

Oceans and Coastal Areas Programme
  Activity Centre *e:* **OCA/PAC**

Ocean[s]-based Measurements Working
  Group *e:* **OMWOG**

Oceans Magazine *e:* **Oceans Mag**

Ocean[s] Observation Panel for Climate *e:*
  OOPC

Oceans of Canada *e:* **OCOC**

Ochanomizu Medical Journal [Japan] *j:*
  Ochanomizu Med J

Ocherki po Geologii Sovetskikh Karpat *R:*
  Ocherki Geol Sov Karpat

Ocotillo Water League *e:* **OWL**

Ocrotirea Naturii *l:* **Ocrotirea Nat**

Ocrotirea Naturii si a Mediului Inconjurator
  l: **Ocrotirea Nat Med Inconjurator**

Octanol/Wasser-Verteilungskoeffizient *d:*
  KOW

Octanol-water partition coefficient *e:* **Kow**

Océan Glacial Nord *f:* **OGN**

Océan Glacial Sud *f:* **OGS**

odd hydrogen *e:* **HOx**

O'Dea's Medical Experts *e:* **O'Dea Med
  Exp**

Odessa Ocean Line *e:* **OOL**

ODP Nankai Downhole Observatory *e:*
  ONDO

ODPHP Health Information Center *e:*
  OHIC

ODPHP [Office of Disease Prevention and
  Health Promotion] National Health
  Information Center *e:* **ONHIC**

OECD [Organization for Economic
  Cooperation and
  Development]/Environment Committee
  e: **OECD/EN[C]**

Oecologia Plantarum *l:* **Oecol Plant**

Oekologia Plantarum *l:* **Oekol. Plant.**

Öffentliche Gesundheitsdienst *d:* **Oeff GD**

Öffentliche Gesundheitswesen *d:* **Oeff
  Gesundheitswes**, *d:* **OEGWA**, *d:* **Off
  Gesundheitswes**

Office Canadien de Coordination de
  l'Évaluation des Technologies de la
  Santé/Canadian Coordinating Office for
  Health Technology Assessment *e:*
  OCCETS/CCOHTA

Office Cantonal de l'Industrie, des Arts et
  Métiers et du Travail *f:* **OCIAMT**

Office Central de Coopération à l'Ecole *f:*
  OCCE

Office, Chief Surgeon *e:* **OCSurg**

Office de Biologie, Ministere du Loisir, de
  la Chasse et de la Peche, Montreal,
  Quebec *e:* **QMOB**

Office de la Circulation Routière *f:* **O.C.R.**

Office de la Protection du Consommateur,
  Quebec, Quebec *e:* **QQOPC**

Office de Protection contre les Radiations
  Ionisantes *f:* **OPRI**

Office de Protection de la Maternité et de
  l'Enfance *f:* **O.P.M.E.**

Office des Transports Routiers *f:* **O.T.R.**

Office Environment *e:* **Off. Environ.**

Office for Dependents' Medical Care *e:*
  ODMC

Office for Ocean Affairs and the Law of the Sea e: **OALOS**

[Office for] Oceanographic Facilities and Support e: **OFS**

Office for/of Human Research Protections e: **OHRP**

Office for/of Interdisciplinary Earth Studies e: **OIES**

Office for/of Protection from Research Risks e: **OPRR**

Office for/of Remote Sensing of/for Earth Resources e: **ORSER**

Office for the Advancement of Telehealth e: **OAT**

Office Français d'Aide Médicale aux Campeurs f: **OFAMAC**

Office Français de Protection des Refugies et Apatrides f: **OFPRA**

Office Fédéral de l'Environnement, des Forêts et du Paysage f: **OFEFP**

Office Fédérale de l'Industrie des Arts et Métiers et du Travail f: **OFIAMT**

Office Intercantonal de Contrôle des Médicaments f: **OICM**

Office International pour la Protection de la Nature f: **OIPN**

Office Mondial d'Information sur les Problèmes d'Environment f: **OMIPE**

Office Médico-Légal f: **O.M.L.**

Office Météorologiques f: **O.M.**

Office national de Développement et d'Exploitation des ressources Forestières f: **ODEF**

Office National de la Coopération à l'École f: **O.N.C.E.**

Office National des Travaux Forestiers f: **ONTF**

Office National des Universités et Écoles Françaises f: **ONUEF**

Office National des Élèves des Écoles Supérieures de Commerce et d'Administration des Entreprises f: **O.N.E.E.S.-C.A.E.**

Office National d'Hydrocarbures f: **ONAH**

Office National Interprofessionnel des Plantes à Parfum, Aromatiques et Médicinales f: **ONIPPAM**

Office National Météorologique f: **O.N.M.**

Office Nationale de la Geologie f: **ONIG**

Office of Acid Deposition, Environmental Monitoring and Quality Assurance e: **OADEMQA**

Office of Aeronautical and Space Research e: **OASR**

Office of Aeronautical and Space Technology (or Aeronautics) [and] Space Technology e: **OAST**

Office of Aerospace Medicine e: **OAM**, e: **OASM**

Office of Aerospace (or Air) Research Automatic Computer e: **OARAC**

Office of Aerospace Research e: **OER**

Office of Air and Water Measurement e: **OAWM**

Office of Air and Water Programs e: **OAWP**

Office of Alternative Medicine e: **OAM**

Office of Animal Care and Use e: **OACU**

Office of Applied Studies. Substance Abuse and Mental Health Statistics e: **OAS**

[Office of] Assistant Manager Environmental Management e: **AME**

Office of Assistant Secretary of Health e: **OASH**

Office of Atmospheric Water Resources e: **OAWR**

Office of Aviation Medicine e: **OAM**

Office of Basic Energy Science/Geosciences e: **OBESG**

Office of Biological and Environmental Research e: **OBER**

Office of Biological Education e: **OBE**

Office of Biological Service[s] e: **OBS**

Office of Charting and Geodetic Services e: **C&GS**

Office of Chemical and Biological Controls & Treaty Compliance e: **CBCTC**

Office of Chemical, Biological and Missile Proliferation, Nonproliferation Bureau, Department of State e: **CBM**

Office of Coastal Environment e: **OCE**

Office of Commercial Space Transportation e: **OCST**

Office of Cooperative Environmental Management e: **OCEM**

Office of Defense and Health Welfare Service[s] e: **ODHWS**

Office of Disease Prevention and Health Promotion e: **ODPHP**

Office of Drinking Water EPA e: **ODW**

Office of Earth Science[s] Applications e: **OESA**

Office of Earthquake Studies e: **OES**

Office of Earthquakes, Volcanoes and Engineering e: **OEVE**

Office of Environment, Safety and Health e: **EH**

Office of Environmental Affairs e: **OEA**

Office of Environmental Analysis e: **OEA**

Office of Environmental and Health Affairs e: **OEHA**

Office of Environmental and Health Protection e: **EHP**

Office of Environmental Assurance, Permits and Policy e: **EAP**

Office of Environmental Compliance e: **OEC**

Office of Environmental Engineering and Technology e: **OEET**

Office of Environmental Engineering and Technology Demonstration e: **OEETD**

Office of Environmental Guidance e: **OEG**

Office of Environmental Health Hazard Assessment e: **OEHHA**

Office of Environmental Health & Safety e: **OEHS**

Office of Environmental Management e: **EM**

Office of Environmental Mediation e: **OEM**

Office of Environmental Policy e: **OEP**

Office of Environmental Policy and Planning e: **OEPP**

Office of Environmental Process[es] and Effects Research e: **OEPER**

Office of Environmental Project Review e: **OEPR**

Office of Environmental Quality Control e: **OEQC**

Office of Environmental Regulatory Research e: **OERR**

Office of Environmental Restoration e: **EM-40**, e: **ER**, e: **OER**

Office of Environmental Restoration and Waste Management e: **EM**

Office of Environmental Technology e: **OET**

Office of/for/of the Civilian Health and Medical Program of the Uniformed Services e: **OCHAMPUS**

Office of/for Space Science[s] and Application[s] e: **OSSA**

Office of Geographic Data Coordination e: **OGDC**

Office of Geography e: **OG**

Office of Geologic Repositories e: **OGR**

Office of Ground Water e: **OGW**

Office of Ground Water and Drinking Water e: **OGWDW**

Office of Ground Water Protection e: **OGWP**

Office of Hanford Environment e: **OHE**

Office of Hazardous Wastes Hydrology e: **OHW**

Office of Health Affairs e: **OHA**

Office of Health [and] Environmental Assessments e: **OHEA**

Office of Health and Environmental Research e: **OHER**

Office of Health and Environmental Science e: **OHES**

Office of Health and Human Services e: **HHS**

Office of Health and Safety Information System e: **OHASIS**

Office of Health Economics e: **OHE**

Office of Health Maintenance Organization e: **OHMO**

Office of Health Research e: **OHR**

Office of Health Technology Assessment e: **OHTA**

Office of Hydrology e: **OH**

Office of Indian Water Rights e: **OIWR**

Office of Integrated Environmental Analysis e: **OIEA**

Office of Interim Space Station Program e: **OISSP**

Office of International Geology e: **OIG**

Office of International Health Relations e: **OIHR**

Office of International Hydrology e: **OIH**

Office of International Public Health e: **OIPH**

Office of Interoceanic Canal Studies e: **OICS**

Office of Laboratory Animal Welfare e: **OLAW**

Office of Land Use and Water Planning e: **OLUWP**

Office of International Health e: **OIH**

Office of Manned Space Flight e: **OMSF**

Office of Marine and Estuarine Protection e: **OMEP**

Office of Marine Geolog e: **OMG**

Office of Marine Geology e: **OMG**

Office of Medical Applications of Research e: **OMAR**

Office of Medical Education Research and Development e: **OMERAD**

Office of Medical Services e: **MED**

Office of Mental Health e: **OMH**

Office of Meteorological Observations e: **OMO**

Office of Meteorology e: **OM**

Office of Minority Health e: **OMH**

Office of Minority Health Resource Center e: **OMH-RC**

Office of National Environmental Board e:
ONEB

Office of National Geodetic Survey e:
ONGS

Office of Naval Weather Service e:
OFFNAVWEASERV, e: ONWS

Office of Ocean Affairs e: **OOA**

Office of Ocean Engineering e: **OOE**

Office of Ocean Management e: **OOM**

Office of [Oceanic and] Atmospheric
Research e: **OAR**

Office of Oceanic and Atmospheric
Services e: **OAS**

Office of Oceanography e: **O.O.**

Office of Oceanography and Limnology
[Smithsonian Institution] e: **OOL**

Office of/on Women's Health e: **OWH**

Office of Planning and Environment e:
OPE

Office of Polar Programs e: **OPP**

Office of Prepaid Health Care e: **OPHC**

Office of Professional Medical Conduct e:
OPMC

Office of Protective Intelligence e: **OPI**

Office of Public Health and Science e:
OPHS

Office of Rare Diseases, National Institutes
of Health e: **ORD**

Office of Research and
Development/Hazardous Waste
Environmental Research Laboratory e:
ORD/HWERL

Office of Research on Minority and
Women's Health e: **ORMWH**

Office of Research on Minority Health e:
ORMH

Office of Research on Women's Health
computers e: **ORWH**

Office of River Protection e: **ORP**

Office of Rural Health Policy e: **ORHP**

Office [of] Saline Water e: **OSW**

Office of Sea Grant e: **OSG**

Office of Sea Grant Development e:
OSGD

Office of Sea Grant Programs e: **OSGP**

Office of Space and Terrestrial
Application[s] e: **OSTA**

Office of Space Biology and Medicine e:
OSBM

Office of Space Communications e: **OSC**

Office of Space Data Processing and
Distribution e: **OSDPD**

Office of Space Flight e: **OSF**

Office of Space Flight Development e:
OSFD

Office of Space Operations e: **OSO**

Office of Space Science[s] e: **OSS**

Office of Space Systems e: **OSS**

Office of Space Systems Development e:
OSSD

Office of Space Tracking and Data Systems
e: **OSTDS**

Office of Space Transportation Operations
e: **OSTO**

Office of Space Transportation Systems e:
OSTS

Office of Space Vehicles e: **OSV**

Office of Spacecraft and Flight Missions
e: **OSFM**

Office of Spaceflight Programs e: **OSFP**

Office of Special Health Issues e: **OSHI**

Office of Statewide Health Planning and
Development e: **OSHPD**

Office of Substance Abuse Prevention in the
Alcohol, Drug Abuse and Mental Health
Administration e: **OSAP**

Office of Surface Water e: **OSW**

Office of Surgeon General e: **OSG**

Office of the Assistant Chief Hydrologist
e: **OACH**

Office of the Chief Hydrologist e: **OCH**

Office [of the] Chief Surgeon e: **OCS**

Office of the Federal Coordinator for
Meteorological Services and Research e:
OFCM

Office of the Federal Inspector for the
Alaska Natural Gas Transportation
System e: **FA**

Office of the Inspector-General of
Waterguard e: **O.I.G.W.**

Office of the Intergovernmental
Oceanographic Commission and Marine
Science Related Issues e: **IOC-MRI**

Office of the Oceanographer of the Navy
e: **OCNAV**

Office of the Regional Hydrologist e:
ORH

Office of the Regional Research
Hydrologist e: **ORRH**

Office of [the] Space Station e: **OSS**

Office of the Surgeon General e: **OTSG**

Office of the Theater Chief Surgeon e:
OTCS

Office of Tropical Medicine and
International Research e: **OTMIR**

Office of Vocational Rehabilitation, Health,
Education, and Welfare Department e:
OVR

Office of Water e: **OW**

Office of Water and Hazardous Materials
e: **OWHM**

Office of Water Data Coordination e:
OWDC

Office of Water Enforcement and Permits
e: **OWEP**

Office of Water Policy [or Programs] e:
OWP

Office of Water Program Operations e:
OWPO

Office of Water Regulations and Standards
e: **OWRS**

Office of Water Research and Technology
e: **OWRT**

Office of Water Resources and Research e:
OWRR

Office of Water Resources Technology e:
OWRT

Office of Water Services e: **OFWAT**

Office of Weather Research and
Modification e: **OWRM**

Office of Wetlands, Oceans and Watersheds
e: **OWOW**

Office of Wetlands Protection e: **OWP**

Office of World Weather Systems e:
OWWS

Office Privé de Préparation aux Professions
de la Propagande Médico-pharmaceutique
f: **O.P.P.M.**

Office Professionnel des Transports
Routiers f: **O.P.T.R.**

Office Space Allocation Plan e: **OSAP**

Official Journal. Research Institute of
Medical Science of Korea e: **Off J Res
Inst Med Sci Korea**

Official Records. World Health
Organization e: **Off Rec WHO**

Offshore Biological Programme e: **OBP**

Offshore Ecology Investigation e: **OEI**

Offshore Labrador Biological Studies e:
OLABS

Offshore North Sea Technology Conference
e: **ONS**

Offshore. The Journal of Ocean Business
e: **OFS**

Oficial de enlace con el ejército de tierra s:
OET

Oficina Australiana de Meteorología s:
ABOM

Oficina de la Comisión Oceanográfica
Intergubernamental y Cuestiones
relacionadas con las Ciencias del Mar s:
IOC-MRI

Oficina de Vigilancia Meteorológica s: **MWO**

Oficina Internacional de Información y
Observación del Español s: **OFINES**

Oficina Internacional Permanente de
Quimica Analitica para los Alimentos
Humanos y Animales s: **OIPQA**

Oficina meteorológica auxiliar s:
OF/MET/AUX

Oficina meteorológica principal s:
OF/MET/P

Oficina Nacional de Datos Oceanográficos
s: **BNDO**

Oficina Nacional de Evaluación de
Recursos Naturales s: **ONERN**

Ogston's Medical Jurisprudence e: **Ogs
Med Jur**

Ohio Aerospace Institute Neural Networks
e: **OAINN**

Ohio Biological Survey. Biological Notes
e: **Ohio Biol Surv Biol Notes**

Ohio Biological Survey. Bulletin e: **Ohio
Biol Surv Bull**

Ohio Biological Survey. Informative
Circular e: **Ohio Biol Surv Inf Circ**

Ohio Conference on Water Purification.
Annual Report e: **Ohio Conf Water
Purif Annu Rep**

Ohio Department of Health e: **ODH**

Ohio Department of Natural Resources e:
ODNR

Ohio. Department of Natural Resources.
Division of Geological Survey.
Miscellaneous Report e: **Ohio Dep Nat
Resour Div Geol Surv Misc Rep**

Ohio Division of Geological Survey e:
ODGS

Ohio. Division of Geological Survey.
Bulletin e: **Ohio Div Geol Surv Bull**

Ohio. Division of Geological Survey.
Information Circular e: **Ohio Div Geol
Surv Inform Circ**

Ohio. Division of Geological Survey.
Miscellaneous Report e: **Ohio Div Geol
Surv Misc Rep**

Ohio. Division of Geological Survey.
Report of Investigations e: **Ohio Div
Geol Surv Rep Invest**

Ohio. Division of Water. Bulletin e: **Ohio
Div Water Bull**

Ohio. Division of Water. Information
Circular [Apublication] e: **Ohio Div
Water Inform Circ**

Ohio. Division of Water. Ohio Water Plan
Inventory. Report e: **Ohio Div Water
Ohio Water Plan Inrent Rep, e: Ohio
Div Water Ohio Water Plan Inventory
Reg**

Ohio. Division of Water. Report on Ohio Water Table Survey e: **Ohio Div Water Rep Ohio Water Table Surv**

Ohio. Division of Water. Technical Report e: **Ohio Div WaterTech Rep**

Ohio Enviromental Protection Agency e: **OEPA**

Ohio Environmental Agency e: **OEA**

Ohio Environmental Protection Agency Library, Columbus e: **OEN**

Ohio Fish and Wildlife Report e: **Ohio Fish Wildl Rep**

Ohio Geographically Referenced Information Program e: **OGRIP**

Ohio. Geological Survey. Bulletin e: **Ohio G S B**

Ohio Health Information Management Association e: **OHIMA**

Ohio Medical Education Network e: **OMEN**

Ohio Naturalist. Ohio State University e: **Ohio Nat**

Ohio River Valley Water Sanitation Commission e: **ORSANCO**

Ohio State Medical Journal e: **Ohio State Med J**

Ohio State University. Institute of Polar Studies. Report e: **Ohio State Univ Inst Polar Stud[ies] Rep[t]**

Ohio State University Radio Observatory e: **OSURO**

Ohio Valley Regional Medical Program e: **OVRMP**

Ohio Veterinary Medical Association e: **OVMA**

Ohio Water Pollution Control Board e: **OWPCB**

Ohio Watershed Network e: **OWN**

Ohio Watersheds Online e: **OWO**

Oil and Gas Geology e: **Oil Gas Geol**

Oil and Hazardous Materials Simulated Environmental Test Tank e: **OHMSETT**

Oil and Natural Gas Commission e: **ONGC**

Oil Companies International Study Group for Conservation of Clean Air and Water e: **OCISGCCAW**

Oil Companies International Study Group for Conservation of Clean Air and Water in Europe e: **CONCAWE**

Oil Geophysical Prospecting e: **Oil Geophys Prospect**

Oil-Immersed, Water-Cooled e: **OIWC**

Oil-in-Water e: **O-W**

Oil-Insulated, Water-Cooled e: **OIWC**

Oil Remaining after Waterflooding e: **ORAW**

Oil Sands Environmental Research Program e: **OSERP**

Oil Sands Environmental Study Group e: **OSESG**

Oil Shale Environmental Advisory Panel e: **OSEAP**

Oil-Water Contract e: **OWC**

Oil/Water Emulsion e: **O/W Emulsion**

Oil, Water, Gas e: **OWG**

oil/water ratio e: **o/w**

Oil Water Separator e: **OWS**

Oil/Water Type e: **O/W Type**

Okefinokee National Wildlife Refuge e: **ONWR**

Okefinokee National Wildlife Refuge and the Okefinokee Swamp e: **Okefinokee**

Oklahoma Alliance for Geographic Education e: **OKAGE**

Oklahoma Climatological Society e: **OCS**

Oklahoma Climatological Survey e: **OKCS**

Oklahoma Department of Environmental Quality e: **ODEQ**

Oklahoma. Department of Geology and Natural History. Biennial Report e: **Okla Dp G N H Bien Rp**

Oklahoma. Division of Water Resources. Bulletin e: **Okla Div Water Resour Bull**

Oklahoma Environmental Information and Media Center e: **OEIMC**

Oklahoma Geographic Information Retrieval System e: **OGIRS**

Oklahoma Geological Survey e: **OGS**

Oklahoma. Geological Survey e: **Okla G S**

Oklahoma. Geological Survey. Bulletin e: **Okla Geol Surv Bull**

Oklahoma. Geological Survey. Circular e: **Okla Geol Surv Circ**

Oklahoma. Geological Survey. Guidebook e: **Oklahoma Geol Survey Guidebook**

Oklahoma. Geological Survey. Map e: **Okla Geol Surv Map**, e: **Oklahoma Geol Survey Map**

Oklahoma. Geological Survey. Mineral Report e: **Okla Geol Surv Miner Rep**

Oklahoma Geology Notes e: **Okla Geol Notes**

Oklahoma Geology Notes Oklahoma Geological Survey e: **Oklahoma Geology Notes**

Oklahoma Health Planning Commission e: **OHPC**

Oklahoma Medical News Journal e: **Okla Med Ne J**

Oklahoma Medical Research Foundation e: **OMRF**

Oklahoma Medical Research Institute e: **OMRI**

Oklahoma Natural Gas Company e: **ONG**

Oklahoma State Department of Health e: **OSDH**

Oklahoma State Medical Association e: **OSMA**

Oklahoma Veterinary Medical Association e: **OVMA**

Oklahoma Water Resources Board e: **OWRB**

Oklahoma. Water Resources Board. Bulletin e: **Okla Water Res Board Bull**

Oklahoma Water Resources Research Institute e: **OWRRI**

Ökosystem Boddengewässer-Organismen und Stoffhaushalt d: **ÖKOBOD**

Öl-in-Wasser-Emulsion d: **O/W-Emulsion**

Old Dominion Journal of Medicine and Surgery e: **Old Dominion J Med and S**

Old Natura Brevium e: **Old Nat Brev**, e: **ONB**, e: **Vet Na B**, e: **Vet N Br**

Old Watercolour Society e: **O.W.S.**

Omaha System for Community Health Nursing e: **Omaha System**

Omega Environmental e: **OMEG**

Omega Hydrocarbons Ltd. e: **OMH**

Omega Upper Atmospheric Sounding Systems e: **OUASS**

Omnia Medica l: **Omnia Med**

Omnia Medica et Therapeutica l: **Omnia Med Ther**

Omnia Medica. Supplemento l: **Omnia Med Suppl**

Omniforce Spatial Environment e: **OSE**

Omond's Law of the Sea e: **Om Sea**

On-Board Energy and Environmental Systems e: **BEES**

On-Camera Meteorologist e: **OCM**

On-line Medical Dictionary e: **OMD**

On-Line Remote Compile System e: **ORCS**

On-Line Remote Job Entry Terminal System e: **ORJETS**

On Orbit e: **O/O**

On-Orbit Flight Technique Meeting e: **OFTM**

On-orbit Segment e: **US**

On-Orbit Station e: **OOS**, e: **OS**

On-Orbit Station Distribution Panel e: **OOSDP**

On-Orbit Support e: **OOS**

on-Sea e: **o-S**

Onboard Electronics Operating Basis Earthquake e: **OBE**

Onboard Health Monitoring System e: **OHMS**

Oncodevelopmental Biology and Medicine e: **OBIMD**, e: **Oncodev Biol Med**

Onderdeels Coördinatie Centrum n: **OCC**

Onderstepoort Journal of Veterinary Science and Animal Industry e: **Onderstepoort J Vet Sci**, e: **Onderstepoort J Vet Sci Anim Ind**

One-Way Polar e: **OWP**

Online Images from the History of Medicine Division e: **OLI/HMD**

Online Medical Employment Center e: **OMEC**

Online Mendelian Inheritance in Animals e: **OMIA**

Onsala Atmospheric Measurements e: **ONSAM**

Ontario Association for Remote Sensing e: **OARS**

Ontario Association of Medical Laboratories e: **OAML**

Ontario Association of Medical Radiation Technologists e: **OAMRT**

Ontario Biological Aeration Tillage Association e: **OBATA**

Ontario Centre [or Center] for Remote Sensing e: **OCRS**

Ontario Department of Health e: **ODH**

Ontario. Department of Mines and Northern Affairs. Geological Report e: **Ont Dep Mines North Aff Geol Rep**

Ontario. Department of Mines. Geological Circular e: **Ont Dep Mines Geol Circ**

Ontario. Department of Mines. Geological Report e: **Ontario Dept Mines Geol Rept**, e: **Ont Dep Mines Geol Rep**

Ontario. Department of Mines. Preliminary Geochemical Map e: **Ontario Dept Mines Prelim Geochem Map**

Ontario. Department of Mines. Preliminary Geological Map e: **Ontario Dept Mines Prelim Geol Map**

Ontario. Division of Mines. Geological Report e: **Ont Div Mines Geol Rep**

Ontario. Division of Mines. Geoscience Report e: **Ont Div Mines Geosci Rep**

Ontario. Division of Mines. Preliminary Map. Geological Series e: **Ont Div Mines Prelim Map Geol Ser**

Ontario. Division of Mines. Preliminary Map. Geophysical Series *e:* **Ont Div Mines Prelim Map Geophys Ser**

Ontario Field Biologist *e:* **Ont Field Biol,** *e:* **Ont Fld Biol**

Ontario Fish and Wildlife Review *e:* **Ont Fish Wildl Rev**

Ontario Food Protection Association *e:* **OFPA**

Ontario Geography *e:* **Ont Geography**

Ontario Geological Society *e:* **OGS**

Ontario Geological Survey *e:* **OGS**

Ontario. Geological Survey. Miscellaneous Paper *e:* **Ont Geol Surv Misc Pap**

Ontario Health Care Evaluation Network *e:* **OHCEN**

Ontario Health Resources Development Program *e:* **OHRDP**

Ontario Health Services Insurance Plan *e:* **OHSIP**

Ontario Hydro *e:* **OH**

Ontario Hydro Design and Development Division *e:* **OHDDD**

Ontario Hydro/Design and Development Division-Generation *e:* **OH/D&D-G**

Ontario Hydro Library *e:* **OHL**

Ontario Hydro/Nuclear Materials Management Department *e:* **OH/NMMD**

Ontario Hydro-Research *e:* **OHR**

Ontario Hydro Research Division *e:* **OHRD**

Ontario Hydro Research Division/Tritium Systems Test Assembly *e:* **OHRD/TSTA**

Ontario Hydro-Research News *e:* **OHRNA,** *e:* **Ont Hydro-Res News**

Ontario Hydro-Research News. Review *e:* **Ont Hydro Res Rev**

Ontario Hydro-Research Quarterly *e:* **Ont Hydro-Res Q**

Ontario Medical Association *e:* **OMA**

Ontario Medical Review *e:* **Ontario Med Rev,** *e:* **Ont Med Rev**

Ontario Medical Secretaries Association *e:* **OMSA**

Ontario Medical Surgical Insurance Plan *e:* **OMSIP**

Ontario Ministry of Health *e:* **OMH**

Ontario Ministry of Natural Resources *e:* **OMNR**

Ontario Ministry of Natural Resources, Maple, Ontario *e:* **OMAPFW**

Ontario Ministry of the Environment *e:* **OME**

Ontario Municipal Health and Safety Association *e:* **OMHSA**

Ontario Naturalist *e:* **ONNA**

Ontario Paramedic Association *e:* **OPA**

Ontario Public Health Association *e:* **OPHA**

Ontario Veterinary Medical Association *e:* **OVMA**

Ontario Water Resources Commission *e:* **OWRC**

Open-File Report. Geological Survey of Northern Ireland *e:* **Open File Rep Geol Surv North Irel**

Open-File Report. United States Geological Survey *e:* **Open-File Rep US Geol Surv**

Open Geodata Interoperability Specification *e:* **OGIS**

Open Geospatial Datastore Interface *e:* **OGDI**

Open Hearth and Basic Oxygen Steel Conference. Proceedings *e:* **Open Hearth Basic Oxygen Steel Conf Proc**

Open Hearth Furnace *e:* **OH Furnace**

Open Hearth Proceedings. Metallurgical Society of AIME [American Institute of Mining, Metallurgical and Petroleum Engineers]. Iron and Steel *e:* **Open Hearth Proc AIME**

Open Marsh Water Managed *e:* **OMWM**

Open Ocean Mining *e:* **OOM**

Open Ocean Monitoring [Payload] Studies *e:* **OOM[P]S**

Open Ocean Release *e:* **OOR**

Open Partial Agreement on the Prevention of, Protection Against and Organization of Relief, in Major Natural and Technological Disasters *e:* **PP-ORMNT**

Open Software Foundation Distributed Computing Environment *e:* **OSF/DCE**

Open Space Action Committee *e:* **OSAC**

Open Space Institute *e:* **OSI**

Open-Space Program *e:* **OSP**

Open System Environment profile for Imminent Acquisitions *e:* **OSEIA**

Open Systems Environment *e:* **OSA,** *e:* **OSE**

Open Systems Environment Implementors Workshop *e:* **OIW**

Open Systems [Interconnection] Environment *e:* **OSIE**

Opera Collecta. Centrum voor Bosbiologisch Onderzoek. Bokrijk-Genk *n:* **Opera Collecta Cent Bosbiol Onderz Bokrijk-Genk**

Operating-Basis Earthquake *e:* **OBE**

Operating Space/Allowance Equipage List *e:* **OS/AEL**

Operating Space Item *e:* **OSI**

Operating System/Environment *e:* **OS/E**

Operation System Function/Distributed Management Environment *e:* **OSF/DME**

Operational Applications of Satellite Snowcover Observations *e:* **OASSO**

Operational Biomedical Harness *e:* **OBH**

Operational Biomedical Sensors *e:* **OBS**

Operational Biomedical System[s] *e:* **OBS**

Operational Climate Prediction and Services *e:* **OCLIPS**

Operational Climatic Testing *e:* **OCT**

Operational Earth Resources System *e:* **OERS**

Operational Experiment on Mesoscale Meteorology *e:* **OEMM**

Operational Geographer [of Canadian Association of Geographers] *e:* **Oper. Geogr.**

Operational Groundwater Monitoring Network *e:* **OGWMN**

Operational Health Physics *e:* **OHP**

Operational Health Physics Site Surveillance *e:* **OHPSS**

Operational Hydrological Programme *e:* **OHP**

Operational Hydrology Program[me] *e:* **OHP**

Operational Hydromet Data Management System *e:* **OHDMS**

Operational Land Observation System *e:* **OLOS**

Operational Maneuver from the Sea *e:* **OMFTS**

Operational Meteorological Information *e:* **OPMET**

Operational Meteorological Satellite *e:* **OMS**

Operational [meteorological] Satellite Improvement Program *e:* **OSIP**

Operational Meteorological Satellite System for Specific European Requirements *e:* **OMSS**

Operational Mission Environment *e:* **OME**

Operational Oceanography Center *e:* **OOC**

Operational Orbit Determination Centre *e:* **COO**

Operational Sea Training *e:* **OST**

Operational Synchronous Earth Observatory Satellite *e:* **OSEOS**

Operational TIROS [Television Infrared Observation Satellite] *e:* **OT**

Operational Weather Satellite *e:* **METEOR**

Operational Weather Support *e:* **OSW**

Operational World Weather Watch Systems Evaluation *e:* **OWSE**

Operational World Weather Watch Systems Evaluation for Africa *e:* **OWSE-AF**

Operational World Weather Watch Systems Evaluation-North America *e:* **OWSE-NA**

Operations [or Operational] Weather Support *e:* **OWS**

Operations Research in Agriculture and Water Resources *e:* **ORAGWA**

Operative Machine Needle Makers' Protection Society *e:* **OMNMPS**

Ophthalmology Medical Group *e:* **OMG**

Opinions of the Attorney General of Georgia *e:* **Op GA Att'y Gen**

Opthalmic Medical Practitioner *e:* **OMP**

Optical Atmospheric Quality in Europe *e:* **OPAQUE**

Optical Fibers in Medicine *e:* **Opt Fibers Med**

Optical Nuclear Polarization *e:* **ONP**

Optical Processing of Airborne Remote Sensing *e:* **OPTIPARES**

Optical Remote Sensing of the Land *e:* **ORLA**

Optical Space-Division Multiplexing *e:* **OSDM**

Optical Space Surveillance System [or Subsystem] *e:* **OSSS**

Optical Tracking Aid [Deep Space Instrumentation Facility] *e:* **OTA**

Optically Pumped Polarized Ion Source *e:* **OPPIS**

Optimale Datenmodelle und Algorithmen für Ingenieur- und Naturwissenschaften *d:* **ODIN**

Optimization Program for Economical Remote Trunk Arrangement and TSPS [Traffic Service Positions System] Operator Arrangements *e:* **OPERATORS**

Optimized Magnetohydrodynamic Conversion *e:* **OMACON**

Optimum Orbital Attitude *e:* **OOA**

Options for Animals Foundation *e:* **OAF**

Opuscula Medica *l:* **Opusc Med**

Opuscula Medica. Supplementum *l:* **Opusc Med Suppl**

Oral Health Education Foundation *e:* **OHEF**

Oral Health Maintenance Program *e:* **OHMP**

Oral Health Research Institute *e:* **OHRI**

Oral Health Status Index *e:* **OHSI**

Oral Nitroglycerine [Medicine] *e:* **ONTG**

Oral Surgeon *e:* **ORS**

Oral Surgery. Oral Medicine. Oral Pathology *e:* **Oral Surg. Oral Med. Oral Pa**

Oral Surgery, Oral Medicine, Oral Pathology, Oral Radiology and Endodontics *e:* **Oral Surg Oral Med Oral Pathol Oral Radiol Endod**

Orbit Analyse *e:* **OA**

Orbit and Altitude *e:* **O and A**

Orbit Attitude and Maneuvering System *e:* **OAMS**

Orbit, Ballistic Impact and Trajectory *e:* **ORBIT**

Orbit Data Editor Assembly *e:* **ODE Assembly**

Orbit Determination *e:* **OD**

Orbit Determination Group *e:* **ORDET**

Orbit Frequency Utilization Simulation *e:* **OFUS**

Orbit Frequency Utilization Simulation-Mobile *e:* **OFUS-M**

Orbit Insertion Maneuver *e:* **OIM**

Orbit International Corp. *e:* **ORBT**

Orbit Maneuvering Propulsion System *e:* **OMPS**

Orbit Modification *e:* **OM**

Orbit Navigation Analysis Program *e:* **ONAP**

Orbit-on-Demand Vehicle *e:* **OODV**

Orbit [or Orbital] Insertion *e:* **OI**

Orbit Rate Display-Earth and Lunar *e:* **ORDEAL**

Orbit Readiness Test *e:* **ORT**

Orbit Replaceable Unit *e:* **ORU**

Orbit Stay Time *e:* **OST**

Orbit-to-Air Intercept *e:* **ORTAI**

Orbit-to-Orbit Shuttle *e:* **OOS**

Orbit-to-Orbit Stage *e:* **OOS,** *e:* **OTOS**

Orbit-to-Orbit Vehicle *e:* **OOV**

Orbital *e:* **ORB**

Orbital Acceleration Research Experiment *e:* **OARE**

Orbital Analysis *e:* **ORAN**

Orbital Analysis Engineer *e:* **OAE**

Orbital Angular Momentum *e:* **L**

Orbital Assembly *e:* **OA**

Orbital Assembly Support Vehicle *e:* **OASV**

Orbital Astronomy Support Facility *e:* **OASF**

Orbital Check *e:* **OC**

Orbital Circularization Technique *e:* **OCT**

Orbital Correction Program *e:* **OCP**

Orbital Data Systems special upper-air observing site *e:* **ORB**

Orbital Emergency Arresting System *e:* **OEAS**

Orbital-Escape System *e:* **OES**

Orbital Facilities *e:* **O.F.**

Orbital Flight *e:* **O/F**

Orbital Flight Instrumentation *e:* **OFI**

Orbital Flight Test *e:* **OFT**

Orbital Flight Test Data System *e:* **OFTDS**

Orbital Flight Test Requirement *e:* **OFTR**

orbital frequency *e:* **Fo**

Orbital Horizontal Ground Vibration Test *e:* **OHGVT**

Orbital Imaging Corporation *e:* **ORBIMAGE**

Orbital Improvement Program *e:* **OIP**

Orbital Launch Operations *e:* **OLOs**

Orbital Launch Vehicle *e:* **OLV**

Orbital Maneuvering Engine *e:* **OM,** *e:* **OME**

Orbital Maneuvering System [or Subsystem] *e:* **OMS**

Orbital Maneuvering Unit *e:* **OMU**

Orbital Maneuvering Vehicle *e:* **OMV**

Orbital Mapping System *e:* **OMS**

Orbital Mode/Data *e:* **OM/D**

Orbital Multifunction Satellite *e:* **OMS**

Orbital [or Orbiter] Flight System *e:* **OFS**

Orbital [or Orbiter] Main Engine *e:* **OME**

Orbit[al] [or Orbiter] Transfer Vehicle *e:* **OTV**

Orbital [or Orbiting] International Laboratory *e:* **OIL**

Orbital [or Orbiting] Space Station *e:* **OSS**

Orbital Period *e:* **OP**

Orbital-Plane Experiment[al] Package *e:* **OPEP**

Orbital Polarized Hartree-Fock *e:* **OPHF**

Orbital Position Indicator *e:* **OPI**

Orbital Probe *e:* **OP**

Orbital Propellant Storage Facility *e:* **OPSF**

Orbital Propellant Storage Subsystem *e:* **OPSS**

Orbital Reentry Vehicle *e:* **ORV**

Orbital Refueling System *e:* **ORS**

Orbital Remote Maneuvering Unit *e:* **ORMU**

Orbital Rendezvous Base System *e:* **ORBS**

Orbital Rendezvous Positioning, Indexing and Coupling System *e:* **ORPICS**

Orbital Rendezvous Procedure *e:* **ORP**

Orbital Rendezvous Radar *e:* **ORR**

Orbital Rendezvous Technique *e:* **ORT**

Orbital Repair and Maintenance *e:* **ORAM**

Orbital Replacement Unit *e:* **ORU**

Orbital Replacement Unit[s] [Carrier] *e:* **ORUC**

Orbital Requirements Document *e:* **ORD**

Orbital Rescue Vehicle *e:* **ORV**

Orbital Research Centrifuge *e:* **ORC**

Orbital Return Vehicle *e:* **ORV**

Orbital Sciences Corporation *e:* **OSC**

Orbital Sequence of Events *e:* **OSE**

Orbital Service Module *e:* **OSM**

Orbital Servicing *e:* **OS**

Orbital Servicing Vehicle *e:* **OSV**

Orbital Solar Observation *e:* **OSB,** *e:* **OSO**

Orbital Solar Observatory *e:* **OSO**

Orbital Space Station Study [or Studies] *e:* **OSSS**

Orbital Space Station System *e:* **OSSS**

Orbital Space Surveillance Subsystem *e:* **OSSS**

Orbital Spacecraft Consumables Resupply System *e:* **OSCRS**

Orbital Support Plan *e:* **OSP**

Orbital Support Vehicle *e:* **OSV**

Orbital System *e:* **MIR**

orbital technical satellite *e:* **ots**

Orbital Technology Satellite *e:* **OTS**

Orbit[al] Test Direction *e:* **OTD**

Orbit[al] Test Directive *e:* **OTD**

Orbital Test Flight *e:* **OTF**

Orbital Test Satellite *e:* **OTS**

Orbital Test Satellite/ European Communications Satellite *e:* **OTS/ECS**

Orbital Transport and Rocket AG *e:* **OTRAG**

Orbital Transport System[s] *e:* **OTS**

Orbital Transport- und Raketen-Aktiengesellschaft *d:* **OTRAG**

Orbital Utility Light *e:* **OUL**

Orbital Valence Force Field *e:* **OVFF**

Orbital Vehicle *e:* **OV**

Orbital Vehicle Assembly Mode *e:* **OVAM**

Orbital Vehicle Reentry Simulator *e:* **OVERS**

Orbital Vety Long Baseline Interferometer *e:* **OVLBI**

Orbital Weapon System *e:* **OSW**

Orbital Weightless Flight *e:* **OWF**

Orbital Workshop *e:* **OSW,** *e:* **OWS**

Orbiter *e:* **ORB**

Orbiter Access Arm *e:* **OA**

Orbiter Aeroflight Simulator *e:* **OAS**

Orbiter Aft Flight Deck *e:* **OAFD**

Orbiter Air Flight Deck *e:* **OAFD**

Orbiter Alternate Airfield *e:* **OAA**

Orbiter Ancillary *e:* **OANC**

Orbiter Atmospheric Drag *e:* **OAD**

Orbiter Atmospheric Flight Test Office *e:* **OAFTO**

Orbiter Atmospheric Simulator *e:* **OAS**

Orbiter Automatic Landing System *e:* **OALS**

Orbiter Avionics Software Control Board *e:* **OASCB**

Orbiter Avionics System *e:* **OAS**

Orbiter Camera Payload System *e:* **OCPS**

Orbiter CEI Specification *e:* **OS**

Orbiter Cloud Photopolarimeter *e:* **OCPP**

Orbiter Critical Design Review *e:* **OCDR**

Orbiter Electron Temperature Probe *e:* **OETP**

Orbiter Experiments *e:* **OEX**

Orbiter/External Tank *e:* **O/ET**

Orbiter Flight Program *e:* **OFP**

Orbiter Flight Test *e:* **OFT**

Orbiter Greenwich Mean Time *e:* **OGMT**

Orbiter Infrared Radiometer *e:* **OIR**

Orbiter Insertion Stage *e:* **OIS**

Orbiter Instrumentation *e:* **OI**

Orbiter Instrumentation Systems *e:* **OIS**

Orbiter Integrated Test *e:* **OIT**

Orbiter Interface Adaptor [or Adapter] *e:* **OIA**

Orbiter Interface Box *e:* **OIB**

Orbiter Interface Verification Set *e:* **OIVS**

Orbiter Ion Mass Spectrometer *e:* **OIMS**

Orbiter Lift-Off Weight *e:* **OLOW**

Orbiter Magnetometer *e:* **OMAG**

Orbiter Main Engine *e:* **OM**

Orbiter Maintenance and Checkout *e:* **OMC**

Orbiter Maintenance and Checkout Facility *e:* **OMCF**

Orbiter Maintenance and Refurbishment Facility *e:* **OMRF**

Orbiter Maintenance Down Period *e:* **OMDP**

Orbiter Maintenance Engineering Working Group *e:* **OMEWG**

Orbiter Maintenance Man-Hours *e:* **OMMH**

Orbiter Management Review *e:* **OMR**

Orbiter Mating Device *e:* **OMD**

Orbiter Midbody Umbilical Unit   e: **OMBUU**

Orbiter Mission Elapsed Time   e: **OMET**

Orbiter Modification and Refurbishment Facility   e: **OMRF**

Orbiter Mold Line   e: **OML**

Orbiter Neutral Buoyancy Trainer   e: **ONBT**

Orbiter Neutral Mass Spectrometer   e: **ONMS**

Orbiter On-Dock   e: **OOD**

Orbiter [or Orbital] Landing Facility   e: **OLF**

Orbiter Payload Interrogator   e: **OPI**

Orbiter Payload Work Station   e: **OPWS**

Orbiter Plasma Analyzer   e: **OPA**

Orbiter Preflight Checklist   e: **OPFC**

Orbiter Prime Item Specification   e: **OPIS**

Orbiter Processing and Landing Facility   e: **OPLF**

Orbiter Processing Facility   e: **OPF**

Orbiter Processing Support Building   e: **OPSB**

Orbiter Project Parts List   e: **OPPL**

Orbiter Project Schedules   e: **OPS**

Orbiter Project[s] Office   e: **OPO**

Orbiter Project[s] Parts Authorization Request   e: **OPPAR**

Orbiter Radar   e: **ORAD**

Orbiter Reduction Data Center   e: **ORDC**

Orbiter Relay Simulator   e: **ORS**

Orbiter Structural Body Reference, X-Axis   e: **XO**

Orbiter Subsystem[s] Requirements Handbook   e: **OSSRH**

Orbiter Support Equipment   e: **OSE**

Orbiter Support Trolley   e: **OST**

Orbiter System Definition Handbook   e: **OSDH**

Orbiter Systems Operating Procedures   e: **OSOP**

Orbiter Test Conductor   e: **OTC**, e: **OTS**

Orbiter Test Director   e: **OTD**

Orbiter Thermal Control Model   e: **OTCM**

Orbiter Thermal Effects Simulator   e: **OTES**

Orbiter Timeline Constraints   e: **OTLC**

Orbiter Utilities Tray   e: **OUT**

Orbiter Vehicle   e: **OV**

Orbiting and Launch Approach Flight Simulator   e: **OLAFS**

Orbiting [and] Retrievable Far and Extreme Ultraviolet Spectrometer   e: **ORFEUS**

Orbiting Astronomical Explorer   e: **OAE**

Orbiting Astronomical Observatory   e: **OAO**, e: **OOAO**

Orbiting Astronomical Support Facility   e: **OASF**

Orbiting Deep Space Relay Station   e: **ODSRS**

Orbiting Geophysical Observatory   e: **OGO**

Orbiting Geosurvey Observatories   e: **OGO**

Orbiting Large Engineering Observatory   e: **Oleo**

Orbiting Lunar Station   e: **OLS**

Orbiting Manoeuvring System   e: **OMS**

Orbiting Meteorological Observatory   e: **OMO**

Orbiting Military Laboratory   e: **OML**

Orbiting Observatory   e: **OO**

Orbiting [or Orbital] Research Laboratory   e: **ORL**

Orbiting [or Orbital] Space Laboratory   e: **OSL**

Orbiting Planetary Observatory   e: **OPO**

Orbiting Primate Experiment   e: **OPE**

Orbiting Primate Spacecraft   e: **OPS**

Orbiting Radio Beacon Ionospheric Satellite   e: **ORBIS**

Orbiting Radio Beacon Ionospheric Satellite for Calibration   e: **ORBISCAL**

Orbiting Radio Emission Observatory   e: **OREO**

Orbiting Reentry Experiment   e: **OREX**

Orbiting Rendezvous Base System   e: **ORBS**

orbiting research satellite   e: **ors**

Orbiting Satellite Observer   e: **OSO**

Orbiting Satellite[s] Carrying Amateur Radio   e: **OSCAR**

Orbiting Scientific Observatory   e: **OSO**

Orbiting Servicing Vehicle   e: **OSV**

Orbiting Solar Laboratory   e: **OSL**

Orbiting Space Laboratory   e: **OSL**

Orbiting System Test Plan   e: **OSTP**

Orbiting Tanker Base   e: **OTB**

Orbiting Vehicle   e: **OV**

Orbiting Vehicle Assembly Building   e: **OVAB**

Orbiting Vehicle Checkout Procedure   e: **OVCP**

Orbiting Vehicle Integrating Contractor   e: **OVIC**

Orbiting Vehicle Limited Maintenance Area   e: **OVLMA**

Orbiting Vehicle Requirements   e: **OVR**

Orbiting Vehicle Support Building   e: **OVSB**

Orbiting Vehicle System   e: **OVS**

Orbiting Velocity Meter   e: **OVM**

Orbiting Wide-Angle Light Collectors   e: **OWL**

Orbiting X-ray Observatory   e: **OXO**

Orbiting Zoological Observatory [to Track Animals]   e: **OZO**

Orbits per Minute   e: **OPM**

Ordinance Environmental Support Office   e: **OESO**

Ordinary High Water Mark   e: **OHWM**

Ordinary Hydrodynamic   e: **OHD**

Ordinary Low Water Mark   e: **OLWM**

Ordine Cantonale dei Medici   i: **OCM**

Ordine dei Medici del Canton Ticino   i: **OMCT**

Ordnance Medical Department   e: **OMD**

Ordnance Systems Command Hydroballistics Advisory Committee   e: **ORDHAC**

Oregon Biomedical Research Association   e: **OBRA**

Oregon Department of Fish and Wildlife [Research and Development Section]   e: **ODFW**

Oregon Health Division   e: **OHD**

Oregon Health Sciences University   e: **OHSU**

Oregon State University, Institute of Marine Biology, Coos Bay   e: **OrCS-MB**

Oregon Water Resources Department   e: **OWRD**

Organic and Atmospheric Mass Spectrometer   e: **OAMS**

Organic Geochemistry   e: **OG**

Organic Geochemistry Group   e: **OGG**

Organic Material Hydrocarbon Equivalent   e: **OMHCE**

Organic Weather Team   e: **OWT**

Organisasi Papua Merdeka   in: **OPM**

(Organisatie voor) Toegepast-NaturwetenschappelijkOnderzoek   n: **TNO**

Organisation de Defense de l'Environnement et de la Faune Africaine   f: **ODEFA**

Organisation de Distribution Agricole et Laitière   f: **ODAL**

Organisation europeenne de la protection du credit textile   f: **TEXTIL CREDIT**

Organisation Européenne de Biologie Moléculaire   f: **OEBM**

Organisation Européenne de/pour la Biologie Cellulaire   f: **OEBC**

Organisation européenne des compagnies pétrolières pour la protection de l'environnement et de la santé   f: **CONCAWE**

Organisation Européenne et Méditerranéenne pour la Protection des Plantes   f: **EPPO**

Organisation Européenne et méditerranéenne pour la Protection des Plantes   f: **OEPP**

Organisation Européenne et Méditerranéenne pour la Protection des Plants   f: **OEPP**

Organisation Hydrographique Internationale   f: **OHI**

Organisation Internationale de Lutte Biologique [contre les Animaux et les Plantes Nuisibles]   f: **OILB**

Organisation Internationale de Protection Civile   f: **OIPC**

Organisation Internationale Météorologique   f: **OIM**

Organisation Internationale pour la Coopération Médicale   f: **OICM**

Organisation Internationale pour la Protection des œuvres d'Art   f: **OIPA**

Organisation mondiale des parlementaires pour la protection de l'environnement   f: **GLOBE**

Organisation Mondiale pour la Protection des Aveugles   f: **OMPA**

Organisation Mondiale pour la Protection Sociale des Aveugles   f: **OMPSA**

Organisation Météorologique Internationale   f: **OMI**

Organisation Météorologique Mondiale   f: **OMM**

Organisation Nationale de/pour la Sécurité Routière   f: **ONSER**

Organisation Naturiste Suisse   f: **ONS**

Organisation of European Laboratories testing Medical Devices   e: **EUROMEDTEST**

Organising Medical Networked Information   e: **OMNI**

Organisme de Protection d'Établissement   f: **OPE**

Organismo de Meteorología y Protección del Medio Ambiente   s: **MEPA**

Organismo Meteorológico del Japón   s: **JMA**

Organização das Mulheres de Cabo Verde   p: **OMCV**

Organizacion de los Estados Americanos. Programa Regional de Desarrollo

Cientifico y Tecnologico. Serie de
Biologia. Monografia *s:* **OEBMAL**

Organización Europea para la Explotación
de Satélites Meteorológicos *s:*
EUMETSAT

Organización Internacional de Lucha
Biológica *s:* **OILB**

Organización Meteorológica de la
República Islámica del Irán *s:* **IRIMO**

Organización Meteorológica del Caribe *s:*
CMO

Organización Meteorológica Mundial *s:*
OMM

Organization for Indian Ocean Marine
Affairs Cooperation *e:* **IOMAC**

Organization for the Protection and
Advancement of Small Telephone
Companies *e:* **OPASTCO**

Organization Health Survey *e:* **OHS**

Organization of Biological Field Stations
e: **OBFS**

Organization [or Organisation] Health
Program Officer *e:* **OHPO**

Organization Pro-Démocratique pour la
Défense de la Nature *f:* **OPDN**

Organizzazione Meteorologica Mondiale *i:*
OMM

Oribi Gorge Nature Reserve *e:* **OGNR**

Oriel College\Oxford *e:* **ORIEL**

Oriented Space Vehicle *e:* **OSV**

orientieren *d:* **or**, *d:* **orient.**

orientiert *d:* **orient.**

Orientierung *d:* **Or**, *d:* **Orient.**, *d:*
Orientier.

Orientierungspunkt *d:* **OP**, *d:* **O-Punkt**

Orientierungspunktskizze *d:* **OP-Skizze**

Original Water Depth Mine *e:* **OWDM**

Origins of Plasma in [the] Earth's
Neighborhood *e:* **OPEN**

Orlando Aerospace *e:* **OA**

Orleans Parish Medical Society , New
Orleans *e:* **LNOP**

Országos Erdészeti Egyesület *H:* **OEE**

Országos Erdészeti Főigazgatóság *H:* **OEF**

Országos Geodéziai Adattár *H:* **OGA**

Orthopaedic Surgeon *e:* **OS**

Orthopedic Foundation for Animals *e:*
OFA

Orthopedic Surgeon *e:* **ORS**

Ortszeit auf der geografischen Länge vnn
Greenwich, nach dem NATO-Alphabeth
sogenannte "Zulu-Zeit" *d:* **Z-Zeit**

Osaka City Medical Journal *e:* **Osaka City
Med J**

OSIS [Ocean Surveillance Information
System] Baseline System *e:* **OBS**

Osler Medical Journal *e:* **OMJ**

Oslo [1972] and Paris [1974] Conventions
for Protection of the Marine Environment
of the North-East Atlantic *e:* **OSPAR**

Oslo Geofysikers Forening *N:* **OGF**

Oslo Underwater Club *e:* **OUC**

OSMH Health Sciences Library, Orillia
Soldiers' Memorial Hospital, Ontario *e:*
OORISMH

Osservatorio Geofisico Sperimentale *i:*
OGS

Ostdeutscher Naturwart *d:* **OdNtw**

Osteopathic Medicine and Surgery *e:* **OM
& S**

Österreichische Gesellschaft für
Raumforschung und Raumplanung *d:*
OeGRR

Österreichische Gesellschaft für
Weltraumforschung und
Flugkörpertechnik *d:* **OeGWFT**

Österreichische Wasser- und
Abfallwirtschaft *d:* **Österr. Wasser-
Abfallwirtsch.**

Österreichisches Bundesinstitut für
Gesundheitswesen *d:* **OBIG**

Osteuropa Naturwissenschaft *d:* **Osteur.
Naturwiss.**

Ostschweizerische Gesellschaft für
Allgemeinmedizin *d:* **OSGAM**

OSW Sludge Program-Health Impacts *e:*
SPHI

Ottawa National Wildlife Refuge *e:*
ONWR

Ouray National Wildlife Refuge *e:* **ONWR**

Outdoor Biology Instructional Strategies
e: **OBIS**

Outer Atmospheric Temperature *e:* **OAT**

Outer Continental Shelf Environmental
Assessment *e:* **OCSEA**

Outer Continental Shelf Environment[al]
Assessment Program *e:* **OCSEAP**

Outer Continental Shelf Environmental
Assessment Program. Arctic Project
Bulletin *e:* **OCSAPB**

Outer Continental Shelf Environmental
Assessment Program. Arctic Project
Special Bulletin *e:* **OCSAPSB**

Outer Continental Shelf Environmental
Assessment Program. Bering Sea-Gulf of
Alaska Newsletter *e:* **OCSB**

Outer Continental Shelf Environmental
Studies Advisory Commission *e:*
OCSEAC

Outer Space *e:* **OS**

Outer Space Affairs Division *e:* **OSAD**

Outer Space Committee *e:* **OSC**

Outer Space Treaty *e:* **OST**

Outstanding National Resource Waters *e:*
OMRB

Over-Ocean Communications *e:* **OOC**

Over Pressurization Protection Switch *e:*
OPPS

Over-Pressurization Protection System *e:*
OPPS

Over-Voltage Load Protection *e:* **OVLP**

Over-Voltage Protection *e:* **OVP**

over water *e:* **ow**

Over-Water Jet Transport *e:* **OJT**

Over Water Line *e:* **OWL**

Overlake Hospital, Medical Library,
Bellevue *e:* **WaBOH**

Overpressure [or Overpressurization]
Protection System *e:* **OPS**

Overseas Development Natural Resources
Institute Newsletter *e:* **Overseas Devt.
Nat. Resourc. Inst. Newsl.**

Overseas Development [of] Natural
Resources Institute *e:* **ODNRI**

Overseas Geological Survey *e:* **OGS**

Overtemperature Protection *e:* **OTP**

Overvoltage Protection Unit *e:* **OVPU**

Owens Valley Radio Observatory *e:*
OVRO

Owens Valley Radio Observatory
Millimeter Array *e:* **OVRO Millimeter
Array**

Oxford Medical Manuals *e:* **OMM**

Oxford Medical Oxford University Press
e: **Ox M OUP**

Oxford Medical Publications *e:* **OMP**

Oxidizing Capacity of the Troposphere
Atmosphere *e:* **OCTA**

Oxygen-Activated Sludge Environmental
System *e:* **OASES**

Oxygen and Hydrogen *e:* **O&H**

Oxygen at Atmospheric Pressure *e:* **OAP**

Oxygen Enriched Atmosphere *e:* **OEA**

Ozean *d:* **O**, *d:* **OZ**

Ozean-Eis-Atmosphäre *d:* **OEA**

Ozean + Technik *d:* **O + t**

Ozeanboden-Seismometer *d:* **OBS**

Ozeanographische Forschungsanstalt der
Bundeswehr *d:* **OFBw**

Ozeanographische Forschungsstelle der
Bundeswehr *d:* **OzFStBw**

Ozone ARCAS [All-purpose Rocket for
Collecting Atmospheric Soundings] *e:*
OZARC

ozone-atmosphere rocket *e:* **ozarc**

P

p-Hydroxibenzoesäure-methylester *d:* **E
218**

p-Hydroxibenzoesäure-methylester,
Natriumverbindung *d:* **E 219**

p-Hydroxibenzoesäure-n-propylester *d:* **E
216**

p-Hydroxibenzoesäure-n-propylester,
Natriumverbindung *d:* **E 217**

p-Hydroxibenzoesäureethylester *d:* **E 214**

p-Hydroxibenzoesäureethylester,
Natriumverbindung *d:* **E 215**

p-Hydroxymercuribenzoate *e:* **PMB**

P-Methane Hydroperoxide *e:* **PMHP**

PA A Low-Level Radioactive Waste
Environmental Transport and Risk *e:*
PRESTO-E

Pace Environmental Law Review *e:* **Pace
Envtl. L. Rev.**

Pacific Aerospace Corporation Ltd. *e:*
PAC

Pacific Aerospace Index *e:* **PAI**

Pacific Aerospace Library *e:* **PAL**

Pacific Animal Therapy Society *e:* **PATS**

Pacific Area Ground Environment
Electronic Installation Agency *e:*
PACGEEIA

Pacific Basin Extended Climate Study *e:*
PBECS

Pacific Biological Station *e:* **P.B.S.**

Pacific Care Health Systems, Inc. *e:* **PHSY**

Pacific Coast Marine Firemen, Oilers,
Watertenders and Wipers Association *e:*
MFOW

Pacific Environmental Group *e:* **PEG**

Pacific Equatorial Ocean Dynamics
[Program] *e:* **PEQUOD**

Pacific Geoscience Center *e:* **PGC**

Pacific Health Information Network *e:*
PHI

Pacific Institute of Geography *e:* **PIG**

Pacific Island Climate Change Assistance
Programme *e:* **PICCAP**

Pacific Marine Environmental Laboratories
e: **PMEL**

Pacific Marine Environmental Laboratory
e: **PMEL**

Pacific Medical Center *e:* **PMC**

Pacific Meteorological Distribution
Systems *e:* **PACMEDS**

Pacific Meteorological Network *e:*
PACMETNET

Pacific Northern Naval Coastal Frontier *e:* **PNNCF**

Pacific Northwest Chapter of the Medical Library Association *e:* **PNC MLA**

Pacific Northwest Environmental Research Laboratory *e:* **PNERL**

Pacific Northwest Regional Visibility Experiment using Natural Tracers *e:* **PREVENT**

Pacific Northwest Waterways Association *e:* **PNWA**

Pacific Ocean *e:* **Pacific,** *e:* **Pac. O.,** *e:* **Pac. Oc.,** *e:* **PO**

Pacific Ocean Area *e:* **POA**

Pacific Ocean Areas Headquarters Pearl Harbor *e:* **POAHEDPEARL**

Pacific Ocean Division Engineers *e:* **PODE**

Pacific Ocean Fisheries Investigations *e:* **P.O.F.I.**

Pacific Ocean Region *e:* **POR**

Pacific Ocean Remote Sensing Conference *e:* **PORSEC**

Pacific Ocean Ship *e:* **POS**

Pacific Ocean Territories *e:* **Pac Ocean Terr**

Pacific Oceanographic Group *e:* **POG**

Pacific Oceanographic Research Laboratories *e:* **PORL**

Pacific Oceanography Laboratories *e:* **PAL,** *e:* **POL**

Pacific Oceanological Institute *e:* **POI**

Pacific Oceanological Institute, Far East Department of the USSR Academy of Sciences (Vladivostok) *e:* **TOI**

Pacific Range Electromagnetic Signature Studies [or System] *e:* **PRESS**

Pacific Range Electromagnetic Signature System *e:* **PRESS**

Pacific Scientific Research Institute of Fisheries and Oceanography *e:* **TINRO**

Pacific Sea Council *e:* **PSC**

Pacific Sea Grant Advisory Program *e:* **PASGAP**

Pacific Southwest Regional Medical Library *e:* **PSRMLS**

Pacific Tsunami Observation Program *e:* **PacTOP**

Pacific Weather Centre *e:* **PWC**

Pacific Weather Graphics System *e:* **PWGS**

Package for Analysis and Visualization of Environmental Data *e:* **PAVE**

Packaged Ice Association *e:* **PIA**

packaged reefer space unit *e:* **PRS**

Packaging and Remote Technology Development *e:* **PRTD**

PACOM [Pacific Area Command] Air Defense Ground Environment Requirements Committee *e:* **PADGERC**

Page Free Space *e:* **PFS**

Paging Area Memory Space *e:* **PAMS**

paiement en nature *f:* **PN**

Pair Natural Orbital *e:* **PNO**

Pair Natural Orbital Configuration Interaction *e:* **PNO-CI**

Pakistan Animal Husbandry Research Institute *e:* **PAHRI**

Pakistan Army Medical Corps *e:* **PAMC**

Pakistan Medical Association *e:* **PMA**

Pakistan Medical Research Council *e:* **PMRC**

Palaeoclimate Commission *e:* **INQUA**

Palaeoclimate[s] from/of Arctic Lakes and Estuaries *e:* **PALE**

Palaeoclimates of the Northern and Southern Hemispheres *e:* **PANASH**

Palaeoclimates of the Southern Hemisphere *e:* **PASH**

Palaeoecological Analysis of Circumpolar Treeline [project] *e:* **PACT**

Palaeoenvironmental Multiproxy Analysis and Mapping Project *e:* **PMAP**

Palaeoenvironments from Ice Cores *e:* **PICE**

Palaeogeography Palaeoclimatology Palaeoecology *e:* **Palaeogeogr. Palaeoclimatol. Palaeoecol.**

Palaeogeography, Palaeoclimatology, Palaeoecology *e:* **Palaeo III**

Paleo Environment and Climate History of the Russian Arctic *e:* **PECHORA**

Paleo-Network for Geological and Environmental Data *e:* **PANGAEA**

Paleoclimate (or Paleoclimatological, or Paleoclimatic) Model[ling] Intercomparison Project *e:* **PMIP**

Paleoclimate Reconstructions of Climate Modeling [Observatory] *e:* **PRCM**

Paleoclimate Reconstructions of Climate Modeling Observatory *e:* **PRCMO**

Paleoclimate Research *e:* **Paleoclim. Res.**

Paleoecological Reconstruction of Recent Lake Acidification *e:* **PIRLA**

Paleoecology *e:* **PE**

Paleoenvironmental Database of China *e:* **PDC**

Paleogeomorphology *e:* **PGM**

Paleolimnological Investigations of Salinity, Climatic and Environmental Shifts *e:* **PISCES**

Palliative Medicine *e:* **Palliat Med**

Palmer Hydrological Drought Index *e:* **PHDI**

Palo Alto Medical Research Foundation *e:* **PAMRF**

Palo Verde Junior College *e:* **PVJC**

Palomar Mountain Observatory *e:* **PMO**

Palomar Observatory *e:* **Pal Obs**

Palomar Observatory Sky Survey *e:* **POSS**

PAM, Atlas-Centaur Class Spacecraft *e:* **PAM-A**

PAM, Delta Class Spacecraft *e:* **PAM-D**

Pan-African Network for a Geological Information System *e:* **PANGIS**

PAN AM Environmental *e:* **PENV**

Pan-American Center for Geographical Studies and Research *e:* **PACGSR**

Pan American Center for Human Ecology and Health *e:* **ECO/PAHO/WHO,** *e:* **ECO/PAHWHO**

Pan American Centre for Human Ecology and Health (Mexico) *e:* **WHIO-PAHO-ECO**

Pan American Centre for Sanitary Engineering and Environmental Sciences *e:* **CEPIS**

Pan-American Climate Studies *e:* **PACS**

Pan-American Federation of Associations of Medical Schools *e:* **PAFAMS**

Pan-American Health and Education Foundation *e:* **PAHEF**

Pan-American Health [Care] Organization *e:* **PAHO**

Pan-American Health Organization Center for Development Studies *e:* **PAHOCENDES**

Pan-American Homeopathic Medical Congress *e:* **PAHMC**

Pan-American Institute of Geography and History *e:* **PAIGH,** *e:* **PIGH**

Pan American Institute of Mining Engineering and Geology *e:* **IPIMIGEO**

Pan-American Institute of Mining, Engineering, and Geology *e:* **PAIMEG**

Pan-American Medical Association *e:* **PAMA**

Pan-American Medical Women's Alliance *e:* **PAMWA**

Pan-American Meteorological Station *e:* **Pan Met**

Pan-European Biological and Landscape Diversity Strategy *e:* **PEBLDS**

Pan-European Ecological Network *e:* **PEEN**

Pan-Indian Ocean Science Association *e:* **PIOSA**

Panama Canal Watershed *e:* **PCW**

Panama Sea Frontier *e:* **Pan Sea Fron,** *e:* **PSF**

Panel de Observación del Océano en relación con el Clima *s:* **OOPC**

Panel Espacial de los Sistemas Mundiales de Observación *s:* **GOSSP**

Panel for International Programs and International Cooperation in Ocean Affairs *e:* **PIPICO**

Panel Mixto sobre Tablas y Normas Oceanográficas *s:* **JPOTS**

Panel of Experts on Climatic Change *e:* **PECC**

Panel of Experts on Environmental Management for Vector Control *e:* **PEEM**

Panel of Experts on Environmental Pollution *e:* **PEEP**

Panel on Air Space Management & Control System *e:* **PAMCS**

Panel on Geological Site Criteria *e:* **PGSC**

Panel on Meteorological Aspects of Ocean Affairs *e:* **MAOA**

Panel on Oceanography *e:* **POO**

Panel on Operational Meteorological *e:* **POMS**

Panel on Operational Meteorological Satellites *e:* **POMS**

Panel on the Environment [President's Science Advisory Committee] *e:* **POE**

Panel para el Desarrollo del Sistema de Observación de los Océanos *s:* **OOSDP**

Panellinios Syndesmos Exagogeon *e:* **PSE**

Panellinios Synomospondia Enoseon Georgikon Synetairismon *g:* **PASEGES**

Panhellenic Medical Association *e:* **PMA**

pankreatische Xanthindehydrogenase *d:* **PXDH**

Panminerva Medica *e:* **Panminerva Med**

Pantone Open Color Environment *e:* **POCE**

Papua New Guinea Medical Journal *e:* **P N G Med J**

Para-Methane Hydroperoxide *e:* **PMHP**

Paracel Islands in the South China Sea east of Vietnam *e:* **Paracels**

Parachute Medical Rescue Service *e:* **PMRS**

Parahydrogen *e:* **PH**

Parallel Climate Model e: **PCM**

Parallel Computing Applied to Geographic Information Systems e: **GIS-PAC-ITDC-135**

parallel ocean-climate model e: **POCM**

Parallel Ocean Program e: **POP**

Paramedic e: **PARA**

Parameter Signature Identification e: **PSI**

Parametric Evaluation Geometric System e: **PEGS**

Paraplegics on Independent Nature Trails e: **POINT**

Paraplegics on Independent Nature Trails, Dallas e: **POINT**

Parents' Alliance to Protect Our Children e: **PAPOC**

Parents League of American Students of Medicine Abroad e: **PLASMA**

Paris Commission for the Environmental Protection of the North East Atlantic e: **PARCOM**

Paris International Aviation and Space Salon e: **PIASS**

Paritätische Umweltkommission d: **PUKO**

Park Management Library, Manitoba Department of Natural Resources, Winnipeg, Manitoba e: **MWPNR**

Park Ridge Hospital, Medical Library, Rochester e: **NRPH**, e: **VQX**

Parkbahn um die Erde d: **EPO**

Parker River National Wildlife Refuge e: **PRNWR**

Parkers Marsh Natural Area e: **PMNA**

Parking Orbit e: **P/O**

Parking Orbit Injection e: **POI**

Parks and Wildlife Service e: **PWS**

Parks Service Environment Canada, Quebec e: **QQCPQ**

Parliamentary Commissioner for the Environment e: **PCE**

Parque Nacional Henri Pittier s: **PNHP**

Partei für Frieden und Umweltschutz d: **PFU**

Parti des Ecologistes f: **ECOLO**, f: **PECO**

Parti des Ecologistes Guinéens f: **PEG**

Parti pour la Protection de l'Environnement f: **PPE**

Partially Hydrolyzed Polyacrylamide e: **PHPA**

Particle Environment Monitor e: **PEM**

Particularly Sensitive Sea Area e: **PSA**

Particularly Sensitive Sea Areas e: **PSSAs**

Partido Nacional Ecologista de Angola p: **PNEA**

Partido Verde Ecologista Mexicano s: **PVEM**

partielle mechanische Innenkontaktierung d: **PMI**

Partitioned Emulation Programming-Local/Remote e: **PEP-LR**

Partito Monarchico Popolare i: **P.M.P.**

Partito Operaio Unificato Popolare i: **POUP**

Partito Popolare Italiano i: **P.P.I.**

Partnership for Environmental Technology Education e: **PETE**

Partnership for Health Reform e: **PHR**

Partnership for Safe Water e: **PSW**

Partnerships for Environmental Education and Research e: **PEER**

Party for the Protection of the Environment e: **PPE**

Party of Ecologists e: **ECOLO**

Pasadena Foundation for Medical Research e: **PFMR**

passenger space ratio e: **psr**

Passive and Remote Crosswind Sensor e: **PRCS**

Passive Anti-Submarine Warfare Environmental Protection System e: **PASWEPS**

Passive Geodetic [Earth-Orbiting] Satellite e: **Pageos**

Passive Geodetic Satellite e: **PGS**

Passive Infrared Remote Observation System e: **PIROS**

Passive Ocean Colour Subsystem e: **POCS**

Passive Underwater Fire-control Feasibility Study e: **PUFFS**

Password Protection e: **PP**

Past Global Environmental Changes e: **PAGES**

Past Medical History e: **PMH**

Past Medical Illness e: **PMI**

Pastoral and Agricultural Geographic Information System e: **PAGIS**

Pasture Systems and Watershed Management Research Laboratory e: **PSWMRL**

Pasture Systems and Watershed Management Research Unit e: **PSWMRU**

patent medicine e: **pat. med**

patentieren d: **pat.**

patentiert d: **pat.**

Pathfinder and Helicopter Operation in a Toxic Environment e: **PHOTOXE**

Pathfinder Instruments for Cloud and Aerosol Spaceborne Observations e: **PICASSO**

Pathologie Biologie f: **Pathol Biol**

Patient Computer Medical Record e: **PCMR**

Patient Protective Wrap e: **PPW**

Patienten-Administration und medizinisches Informationsregister d: **PAMIR**

Patients Protection Law Commission e: **PPLC**

Patrol Craft, Hydrofoil e: **PCH**

Patrol Gunboat, Hydrofoil e: **PGH**

Patrol Hydrofoil Missile Ship e: **PHM Ship**

Patrol Hydrofoil Missile Ship[s] e: **PHMS**

Patrol Missile Hydrofoil e: **PMH**

Patuxent Wildlife Research Center e: **PWRC**

Pay Record[s] and Health Record[s] e: **PAHEL**

Payload Changeout Room e: **PRC**

Payload Environmental Transportation System e: **PETS**

Państwowy Instytut Biologii Doświadczalnej P: **PIBD**

Państwowy Instytut Geologiczny P: **PIG**

Państwowy Instytut Hydrologiczno-Meteorologiczny P: **PIHM**

Państwowy Instytut Meteorologiczny P: **PIM**

Peabody Museum of Natural History e: **PMNH**

Peace Officers Association of Georgia e: **POAG**

Peace on Earth e: **POE**

Peace on Earth Research Center e: **PERC**

Peak Health Care, Incorporated e: **PHCI**

Pediatria Medica e Chirurgica e: **Pediatr Med Chir**

Pediatric Critical Care Medicine e: **PCCM**, e: **PedsCCM**

Pediatric Pathology and Laboratory Medicine e: **Pediatr Pathol Lab Med**

Peer-to-Peer Remote Copy e: **PPRC**

Peking University Remote Sensing Information System e: **PURSIS**

Pele Medical Corporation e: **PEMC**

Pen and Pocket Blade Forgers' and Smithers' Protective Society e: **PPBFSPS**

Peninsula Environmental Network e: **PEN**

Penmarch Radar Oceanographic Microwave Experiment on Signature Studies e: **PROMESS**

Pennsylvania Analysis of Decompression for Undersea and Aerospace e: **PADUA**

Pennsylvania Animal Network e: **PAN**

Pennsylvania Department of Environmental Projection e: **PDEP**

Pennsylvania Department of Environmental Resources e: **PADER**

Pennsylvania Medicine e: **Pa Med**

Pennsylvania Society for Biomedical Research e: **PSBR**

Pennsylvania State University Radio Astronomy Observatory e: **PSURAO**

Pennsylvania Substance Abuse and Health Information e: **PennSAHIC**

Pennsylvania Veterinary Medical Association e: **PAVMA**

Pension Protection Act e: **PPA**

Pentanol Acedic-acid Water e: **PAW**

People, Access, Coastal Environment e: **PACE**

People Against Cruel Animal Transport e: **PACAT**

People and Physical Environmental Research e: **PAPER**

People-Animals-Love e: **PAL**

People for Environmentally Sustainable Transport e: **PEST**

People for Open Space e: **POS**

People for the Ethical Treatment of Animals e: **PETA**

People of the Earth e: **POE**

People & Resources Identified for Distributed Environments e: **PRIDE**

People's Dispensary for Sick Animals e: **P.D.S.A.**

People's Dispensary for Sick Animals Associate e: **PDSA Associate**

People's Dispensary for Sick Animals of the Poor e: **P.D.S.A.P.**

People's League of Health e: **P.L.H.**

People's Medical Society e: **PMS**

Peptone Water e: **PW**

per vias naturales l: **p.v.n.**

(per) weather permitiing day e: **w.p.d.**

per weather working day e: **p.w.w.d.**

(per) weather working day e: **W.W.D.**

per weather working hour e: **p.w.w.h.**

per workable hatch and weather working day e: **wh**, e: **whww day**, e: **wwd**

per workable hatch and working day, weather permining e: **wh wd wp**

per workable hatch per weather working day e: **p.w.h.w.w.d., pwhwwd**

0.7 percent of natural uranium e: **U235**

perdendosi i: **perden.**

perdenosi i: **perd**

Perdeuterated e: **DAST d-26**
Performance Assessment of Geologically
   Isolated Systems e: **PAGIS**
Performance Assessment of the Geological
   Disposal Medium-level and Alpha Waste
   in a Clay Formation in Belgium e:
   PACOMA
Performance Evaluation of Amplifiers from
   a Remote Location e: **PEARL**
Performing and Captive Animals Defence
   League e: **PADL**
Performing Animal Television Star of the
   Year e: **PATSY**
Performing Arts Center for Health e:
   PACH
Periodic Environmental Test e: **PET**
Periodic Orbital Theory e: **POT**
Periodical Holdings in the Library of the
   School of Medicine e: **PHILSOM**
Periodical Holdings in the Library of the
   School of Medicine Network e:
   PHILSOM Network
Periyar Wildlife Sanctuary e: **PWS**
Permafrost and Climate in Europe e:
   PACE
Permanent Automatic Ground Environment
   e: **PAGE**
Permanent Commission and International
   Association on Occupational Health e:
   PCIAOH
Permanent Committee on Biological
   Standards e: **PCBS**
Permanent Committee on Geographical
   Names e: **PCGN**
Permanent Committee on Tides and Mean
   Sea-Level e: **PCTMSL**
Permanent GPS Geodetic Array e: **PGGA**
Permanent International Bureau of
   Analytical Chemistry of Human and
   Animal Food e: **PIBAC**
Permanent International Commission on
   Industrial Medicine e: **PICIM**
Permanent Large Array of Terrestrial
   Observatories e: **PLATO**
Permanent Manned Orbital Station e:
   PMOS
Permanent Medical Member e: **Perm Med
   Mbr**
Permanent Orbital Station e: **POS**
Permanent reorganisiertes
   Informationssystem merkmalorientierter
   Anwendearten d: **PRISMA**
Permanent Section of Microbiological
   Standardization e: **PSMS**
Permanent Service for Geomagnetic Indices
   e: **PSGI**
permanent service on earth tides e: **pset**
Permanent Service on Geomagnetic Indices
   e: **PSGI**
Permanent Space-Based Logistics System
   e: **PSBLS**
Permanently Open Ocean Zone e: **POOZ**
Pernament Service for Mean Sea Level e:
   PSMSL
Perpendicular Ocean Platform e: **P.O.P.**
Perpendicular-to-Orbit Plane e: **POP**
Persistent Internal Polarization e: **PIP**
persistierende generalisierte
   Lymphadenopathie d: **PGL**
persistierende Proteinurie d: **PPU**
Personal Computer University College
   Dublin Geographic Information System
   e: **PCUCDGIS**

Personal Earth Station e: **PES**
personal effects protection e: **pep.**
Personal Environment Modules e: **PEM**
Personal Health Summary e: **PHS**
Personal Health Summary System e: **PHSS**
personal injury protection e: **pip**
Personal Medical Services e: **PMS**
personal ozone protection e: **pop.**
Personal Protection (or Protective)
   Equipment e: **PPE**
Personal Protection Order e: **PPO**
Personal Protection Squad e: **PPS**
Personal Protection Weapon e: **PPW**
Personal Protective Armor Association e:
   PPAA
Personal Protective Equipment Unit e:
   PPEU
Personal Security Environment e: **PSE**
Personal Terminal Environment e: **PTE**
Personal Water Purifier e: **PWP**
Personal Watercraft e: **PWC**
Personality, Matter, Energy, Space, Time
   e: **PMEST**
personne naturalisée f: **PN**
Personnel Féminin Médical de l'Armée de
   l'Air f: **PFMAA**
Personnel Hazards Associated with Space
   Radiation e: **PHASR**
Personnel Orbit Transfer Vehicle e: **POTV**
Personnel Protection e: **PP**
Personnel Protection and Communication
   Services e: **PPCS**
Perspectives in Biology and Medicine e:
   Perspect.Biol.Med.
Perspectives on Developmental
   Neurobiology e: **Perspect Dev
   Neurobiol**
Perthshire Society of Natural Science e:
   PSNS
Perturbation by East Asia Continental Air
   Mass to Pacific Oceanic Troposphere e:
   PEACAMPOT
Perturbative Configuration Interaction
   using Localized Orbitals e: **PCILO**
Perturbative Configuration Interaction
   Using Localized Orbitals for Crystal
   Calculation e: **PCILOCC**
Período de Observación Intensiva s: **IOP**
Pesticides Abstracts [of Environmental
   Protection Agency] e: **PESTAB**
Pesticides in Groundwater Strategy e:
   PIGS
Pesticides in Groundwater Systems e:
   PIGS
Pet Health Council e: **PHC**
Pet Owners' Protective Association e:
   POPA
Petawawa National Forestry Institute,
   Canadian Forestry Service, Environment
   Canada Chalk River, Ontario e: **OCKE**
Pete Waterman Limited e: **PWL**
Petermanns Geographische Mitteilungen
   d: **PGM**
Petroleum and Geosystems Engineering e:
   PGE
Petroleum Association for Conservation of
   the Canadian Environment e: **PACE**
Petroleum Association for the Conservation
   of the Environment e: **PACE**
Petroleum Environmental Research Forum
   e: **PERF**
Petroleum Geology e: **Pet.Geol.**
Petroleum Hydrocarbon e: **PHC**

Petroleum Industry Environmental
   Conservation Executive e: **PIECE**
Petroleum Training Association-North Sea
   e: **PETANS**
Pets and Wildlife e: **PAW**
Peugeot Owners' Club e: **POC**
Pfälzischer Verein für Naturkunde und
   Naturschutz d: **Pollichia**
Pferdearzt d: **Pfaz**
Pferdedepot d: **Pf.D.**
Pferdekraft d: **PK**
Pferdelazarett d: **Pf.-Laz.**
Pferde[leistungs]stunde[n] d: **Ph**
Pferdestärke d: **PS**, d: **Pst.**
Pferdestärke, abgebremste d: **PSab**
Pferdestärke, effektiv d: **PSef**
Pferdestärke effektive d: **PSe**
Pferdestärke, indizierte d: **PSi**
Pferdestärkenstunde d: **PS/h**
Pferdestärkenstunden d: **PShn**
Pferdestärkesekunde d: **PSs**, d: **PS/sec**
Pferdestärkestunde d: **PSst**
Pferdetage d: **PT**
Pferdezuchtverband d: **Pfzvb.**
Pferdezuchtverband Rheinland-Pfalz-Saar
   d: **PRPS**
Phantom Group Orbital e: **PGO**
Pharmaceutical and Healthcare Industries
   News Database e: **PHIND**
Pharmaceutical and Healthcare Industry
   News e: **PHIN**
Pharmaceutical Industry Medical Advisers
   Group e: **PIMAG**
Pharmaciens Sans Frontières f: **PSF**
Pharmaco-Medical Documentation, Inc. e:
   PMD
Pharos of Alpha Omega Alpha Honor
   Medical Society e: **Pharos**
phenol-hydroquinone e: **p-q**
Phenylephrine Hydrochloride e:
   PHENYLEPH
Phenylmercuric Hydroxide e: **PMH**
Phenylpropanolamin-hydrochlorid d: **PPA**
Phenylpropanolamine[hydrochloride] e:
   PPA, e: **PPH**, e: **PPM**
Philadelphia Academy of Natural Sciences
   e: **PANS**
Philadelphia College of Osteopathic
   Medicine, Philadelphia, PA e: **PPCO**
Philadelphia County Medical Society,
   Philadelphia, PA e: **PPCM**
Philadelphia Tuberculosis and Health
   Association, Philadelphia, PA e:
   PPPHC
Philadelphia Water Department e: **PWD**
Philippine Atmospheric, Geophysical and
   Astronomical Services Administration e:
   PAGASA
Philippine Council for Agriculture,
   Forestry, and Natural Resources Research
   and Development e: **PCARRD**
Philippine Earth Terminal e: **PET**
Philippine Geothermal, Incorporated e:
   PGI
Philippine Medical Association e: **P.M.A.**
Philippine National Committee of the
   International Association on Water
   Pollution Research and Control e:
   PNCIAWPRC
Philippine Sea Frontier e:
   PHILSEAFRON, e: **PSF**
Philippine Sea Frontier Headquarters e:
   PSFHQ

Philippine Veterinary Medical Association
  e: **PVMA**
Philips Environmental Protection *e:* **PEP**
Philips Environmental Protection
  Programme *e:* **PEP Programme**
Phillips Laboratory, Geophysics Directorate
  e: **PL/GP**
Philosophical Transactions of the Royal
  Society of London. Series B: Biological
  Sciences *e:* **Philos Trans R Soc Lond B
  Biol Sci**
Phoenix Real-time Instrumentation for
  Surface Meteorological Studies network
  e: **PRISMS**
Phosphate Dehydrogenase *d:* **PDH**
Photo Hydrography System *e:* **PHS**
Photochemical and Photobiological
  Reviews *e:* **PPHRD**
Photodermatology, Photoimmunology and
  Photomedicine *e:* **Photodermatol
  Photoimmunol Photomed**
photogeography *e:* **photogeog**
Photogrammetric Engineering and Remote
  Sensing [of American Society of
  Photogrammetry] *e:* **Photogramm. Eng.
  Remote Sens.**
Photogrammetric Engineering & Remote
  Sensing *e:* **PE&RS**
Photogrammetric Ocean Survey Equipment
  e: **POSE**
Photographic Applications in Science.
  Technology and Medicine *e:* **Photogr.
  Appl. Sci. Technol.**
Photographic Geology *e:* **PHOTOGEOL**
Photographic Protection Plan Position
  Indicator *e:* **PPPPI**
Photometric Eclipse Polar Plume Imager *e:*
  PEPPI
Photopolarimeter-Radiometer *e:* **PPA**
photopolarimeter radiometer *e:* **PPR**
Photopolarimeter Spectrometer *e:* **PPS**
Phototype Environment Buoy *e:* **PEB**
phototype environmental buoy *e:* **peb**
Photovoltaic Array Space Power Plus
  Diagnostics *e:* **PASP Plus**
Phuket Marine Biological Center *e:*
  PMBC
Physical Control Space *e:* **PCS**
Physical Geography *e:* **PG**
Physical & Health Education *e:* **PHED**
Physical Hydrogen Cracking *e:* **PHC**
Physical Hydrology Division *e:* **PHD**
physical medicine *e:* **phys med**
Physical Medicine *e:* **P/M**
Physical Medicine and Rehabilitation *e:*
  PMR
Physical Medicine and Rehabilitation
  Service *e:* **PMRS**
Physical Medicine Centre *e:* **PMC**
Physical Movement of Spacecraft *e:*
  PMOS
Physical Oceanographic Real-Time System
  e: **PORTS**
Physical Oceanography *e:* **PHYSOCEAN,**
  e: **PO**
Physical Oceanography Committee *e:*
  POC
Physical Oceanography of the Eastern
  Mediterranean *e:* **POEM**
Physical[ly-protected] Control Zone *e:*
  PCZ
Physician Reservists in Medical
  Universities and Schools *e:* **PRIMUS**

Physicians and Surgeons *e:* **Phys.&Surg.,**
  e: **P&S**
Physicians and Surgeons Hospital *e:*
  PHYSH
Physicians' Association for
  Anthroposophical Medicine *e:* **PAAM**
Physicians Committee for Responsible
  Medicine *e:* **PCRM**
Physician's Evaluation and Educational
  Review in Emergency Medicine *e:*
  PEER
Physicians for a National Health Program
  e: **PNHP**
Physicians' Health Association *e:* **P.H.A.**
Physicochemical Hydrodynamics *e:*
  Physicochem. Hydrodyn.
Physics and Chemistry of Earth Materials
  e: **PACEM**
Physics and Chemistry of the Atmosphere
  e: **PACA**
Physics in Medicine and Biology [Institute
  of Physics] *e:* **Phys. Med. Biol.**
Physics of Colloids in Space *e:* **PCS**
Physics of the Earth and Planetary Interiors
  e: **Phys. Earth Planet. Inter.**
Physics of the Solid Earth *e:* **Phys. Solid
  Earth**
Physikalisch-Bioklimatische
  Forschungsstelle *d:* **PBF**
Physikalisch-Meteorologisches
  Observatorium Davos *d:* **PMOD**
Physikalisch Technische Prüfanstalt für
  Radiologie und Elektromedizin *d:* **PTP**
Physiological Chemistry and Physics and
  Medical NMR *e:* **Physiol Chem Phys
  Med NMR**
Physiology and Ecology Japan *e:* **Physiol.
  Ecol. Jpn.**
Physiology of Chimpanzees in Orbit *e:*
  POCO
Physische Geographie *d:* **Phys. Geogr.**
Phytogeography *e:* **Phytogeog.**
Piedmont National Wildlife Refuge *e:*
  PNWR
Piedmont Natural Gas Company, Inc. *e:*
  PNY
Pig Health Control Association *e:*
  P.H.C.A.
Pig Health Monitoring Scheme *e:* **PHMS,**
  e: **PIGMON**
Pig Herd Health Management Scheme *e:*
  PHHMS
Pigeon *e:* **PGN**
Pilot Airborne Recovery Device [Goodyear
  Aerospace Corporation] *e:* **PARD**
Pilot Climate Data System *e:* **PCDS**
Pilot Ocean Data System *e:* **PODS**
Pilot Ocean Monitoring Study *e:* **POMS**
Pilot Project on Baseline Studies and
  Monitoring of Oil and Petroleum
  Hydrocarbons in Marine Waters *e:* **MED
  POL-I**
Pilot Radiation Observation Experiment *e:*
  PROBE
Pilot Radiation Observations Experiment
  e: **PROBE**
Pilot Weather Briefing *e:* **PWB**
Pilot [weather] Report *e:* **PIREP**
Pilots Automatic Telephone Weather
  Answering Service *e:* **PATWAS**
Pine Lodge Correctional Center, Resident
  Library, Medical Lake *e:* **WaMeP-R**

Pine Lodge Correctional Center, Staff
  Library, Medical Lake *e:* **WaMeP**
Pines to Palms Wildlife Committee *e:*
  PPWC
Pion Generator for Medical Irradiation *e:*
  PIGMI
Pioneer Jupiter Orbit *e:* **PJO**
Pioneer Natural Gas Co. *e:* **PNA**
Pioneer Venus Orbiter *e:* **PVO**
Pipe Break Automatic Protective System
  e: **PBAPS**
Pipe Line Under the Ocean *e:* **PLUTO**
pipecolylxylidine *e:* **PPX**
Pipeline Under Mother Earth *e:* **PLUME**
Pit Ponies' Protection Society *e:* **P.P.P.S.**
Pitch Pine Naturalist *e:* **PPNADY**
Pittsburgh Academy of Medicine,
  Pittsburgh, PA *e:* **PPiAM**
Pittsburgh, Chartiers & Youghiogheny
  Railway Co. *e:* **PCY**
Pittsburgh Health Research Institute *e:*
  PHRI
Plakat[ierungs]steuer *d:* **Pl.-St.**
plan providing medical care for the elderly
  e: **Eldercare**
Planar Halogenated Hydrocarbon *e:* **PHH**
Plane Polarized *e:* **pp**
Plane-Polarized Wave *e:* **PPW**
Plane Wave Orbital *e:* **PWO**
Planen-Prüfen-Investieren *d:* **PPI**
Planen-Prüfen-Investieren [Technischer
  Verlag Resch KG] *d:* **PPI**
Planetary and Space Science *e:* **Planet
  Space Sci**
Planetary Atmosphere *e:* **P/A**
Planetary Atmosphere Experimental Test
  e: **PAET**
Planetary Atmosphere Experiments Test
  Vehicle *e:* **PAET Vehicle**
Planetary Atmosphere Experiments Tests
  e: **PAETs**
Planetary Landing Observation Package *e:*
  PLOP
Planetary Manned Space Flight Network *e:*
  PMSFN
Planetary Microbiological Assay *e:* **PMA**
Planetary Observation Geometry and
  Science Instrument Sequence Program *e:*
  POGASIS
Planetary Orbit *e:* **PO**
Planetary Orbit Determination *e:* **PLOD**
Planetary Orbit Determination Program[me]
  e: **PLOD Program[me]**
Planetary Rocket Ocean Platform *e:* **PROP**
Planetary Space Vehicle *e:* **PSV**
Plankton Rate Processes in Oligotrophic
  Oceans *e:* **PRPOOS**
Plankton Reactivity in the Marine
  Environment *e:* **PRIME**
Planned Environment and Education
  Research Institute *e:* **PEER**
Planned Interdependency Incentive Method
  e: **PIIM**
Planned Ocean Logistic System *e:* **POLS**
Planners Remote Offline Form Image Tape
  e: **PROFIT**
Planning and Coordinating Committee for
  Environmental Studies *e:* **PCCES**
Planning and Environmental Review Board
  e: **PERB**
Planning and Geographic Information
  Systems *e:* **PAGIS**

Planning Board for Ocean Shipping *e:*
PBOS

Planning for the Employment of the Army
in a Conflict-free Environment *e:*
PEACE

Plant and Animal Products Department *e:*
PAOD, *e:* **P.A.P.D.**

Plant Biological Institute *e:* **PBI**

Plant, Cell and Environment *e:* **Plant Cell
Environ.**

Plant Control and Protection System *e:*
PCAPS

Plant Ecology *e:* **Plant Ecol.**

Plant Health and Seeds Inspectorate *e:*
PHSI

Plant Health Committee *e:* **PHC**

Plant Molecular Biology *e:* **PMB**

Plant Molecular Biology Association *e:*
PMBA

Plant Molecular Biology [of International
Society for Plant Molecular Biology] *e:*
Plant Mol. Biol.

Plant Molecular Biology Reporter [of
International Society for Plant Molecular
Biology] *e:* **Plant Mol. Biol. Rep.**

Plant Nuclear Protection System *e:* **PNPS**

Plant Population Biology Section *e:* **PPBS**

Plant Protection *e:* **PP**

Plant Protection and Quarantine *e:* **PP/Q**

Plant Protection and Quarantine Program
e: **PP/Q Program**

Plant Protection Committee for the South
East Asia and Pacific Region *e:*
PPCSEAPR

Plant Protection Quarterly *e:* **PPQUE8**

Plant Protection Research Institute *e:*
PPRI

Plant Protection System *e:* **PPS**

Plant Variety Protection *e:* **PVP**

Plant Variety Protection Office *e:* **PVPO**

Planta Medica *e:* **Planta Med**

Planung Umwelt Statistik *d:* **PLUS**

Planungs-Programmierungs-Budgetierungs-
System *d:* **PPB**

Planungs-, Programmierungs- und
Budgetierungs-System *d:* **PPBS**

Plasma Physics and Environmental
Perturbation *e:* **PPEP**

plastic surgeon *e:* **p surg**

Plastics Environment Council *e:* **PEC**

Plastohydrodynamic[s] *e:* **PHD**

Plateau State Water Board *e:* **PSWB**

Platform Environment Profile *e:* **PEP**

Platform for Atmospheric Data in Real-
Time *e:* **PADIRT**

Platform Observables *f:* **PLATO**

Platform Observables Subassembly *e:*
PLATO

Plattieraluminium *d:* **PlAl**

plattiert *d:* **pl**

plattiertes Duralumin *d:* **Duralplat**

Plug-in Development Environment *e:* **PDE**

Plum Island Animal Disease Center *e:*
PIADC

Plum Island Animal Disease Laboratory *e:*
PIADL

Plutonium Finishing Plant Environmental
Impact Statement *e:* **PFP-EIS**

Plutonium Protection System *e:* **PPS**

Pneumatic Energy Detector with Remote
Optics *e:* **PEDRO**

Pod Integrated Localisation, Observation,
Transmission *e:* **PILOT**

Point Coordination Inter Frame Space *e:*
PIFS

Point InterFrame Space *e:* **PIFS**

Polar *e:* **P**, *e:* **POL**

Polar Acquisition and Control Subsystem
e: **PACS**

Polar Air and Snow Chemistry Programme
e: **PASC**

Polar Air-Show Experiment *e:* **PASE**

Polar Amateur Radio Club of Alaska
Certificate *e:* **PARCAC**

Polar Anglo-American Conjugate
Experiment [Permafrost and Climate in
Europe] *e:* **PACE**

Polar Area Index *e:* **PAI**

Polar Atlantic *e:* **PA**, *e:* **POLAT**

Polar Atmosphere Snow Experiment *e:*
PASEX

Polar Atmospheric and Snow Chemistry *e:*
PASC

Polar Atmospheric Chemistry *e:* **PAC**

Polar Automatic Weather Station *e:*
PAWS

Polar Beacon Experiments and Auroral
Research [satellite] *e:* **Polar BEAR**

Polar Bear Association *e:* **PBA**

Polar Bear Club-USA *e:* **PBC-USA**

Polar Biomedical Research *e:* **PBR**

Polar Branch, Research Environmental
Science Division *e:* **PBRESD**

Polar Cap Absorption *e:* **PCA**

Polar Cap Observatory *e:* **PCO**

Polar Cap Radar *e:* **PCR**

Polar-Cartesian *e:* **P-C**

Polar Circling Balloon Observatory *e:*
POCIBO

Polar Climate Working Group *e:* **PCWG**

Polar Continental *e:* **PC**, *e:* **POLCO**

polar continental air *e:* **cP**

polar continental air warmer than
underlying surface *e:* **cPw**

Polar Continental Shelf Project *e:* **PCSP**

Polar Coordinates Navigation System *e:*
PCNS

Polar Crane *e:* **PC**

Polar DAAC Advisory Group *e:* **PoDAG**

Polar Density Function *e:* **PDF**

Polar Distance *e:* **PD**, *e:* **P. Dist.**

Polar Environmental Officers Network *e:*
PEON

Polar Equatorial Index *e:* **PEI**

Polar Equatorial Near-Vertical-Incidence
Experiment *e:* **PENEX**

Polar Exchange at the Sea Surface *e:*
POLES

Polar Experiment *e:* **POLEX**

Polar Experiment, atmospheric *e:* **POLEX**

Polar Experiment in the Northern
Hemisphere *e:* **POLEX-NORTH**

Polar Experiment in the Southern
Hemisphere *e:* **POLEX-SOUTH**

Polar Experiment Network for Geophysical
Upper-atmosphere Investigations *e:*
PENGUIN

Polar Front *e:* **PF**

Polar Front Zone *e:* **PFZ**

Polar Ice Core Drilling Office *e:* **PICO**

Polar Ice Coring Office *e:* **PICO**

Polar Ice Extent *e:* **PIE**

Polar Ice Mapping Radiometer *e:* **PIMR**

Polar Ice Prediction System *e:* **PIPS**

Polar Ice Sheet Program *e:* **PISP**

Polar Icebreaker Canadian Design Group
e: **PICDG**

Polar Inductor *e:* **PI**

Polar Information Program *e:* **PIP**

Polar Institute of Marine Fishery and
Oceanography *e:* **PINRO**

Polar Ionosphere Beacon Satellite *e:* **PIBS**

Polar Ionosphere [or Ionospheric] Beacon
e: **PIB**

Polar Ionospheric Trough *e:* **PIT**

Polar Libraries Colloquy *e:* **PLC**

Polar Marine Geosurvey Expedition *e:*
PMGE

Polar Mesopause Summer Echo *e:* **PMSE**

Polar Mesosphere Summer Echo *e:* **PMSE**

Polar Mesospheric Cloud *e:* **PMC**

Polar North Atlantic Margins [Programme]
e: **PONAM**

Polar Oceans and the Law of the Sea Project
e: **POLOS**

Polar Operational Meteorological Satellite
e: **POMS**

Polar-Optical *e:* **PO**

Polar Orbiter Effective Rainfall Monitoring
Integrative Technique *e:* **PERMIT**

Polar Orbiter Remapping and
Transformation Application Library *e:*
PORTAL

Polar Orbiting Earth Monitoring *e:* **POEM**

Polar-Orbiting Earth[-observation] Mission
e: **POEM**

Polar Orbiting Geomagnetic Satellite *e:*
POGS

Polar Orbiting Geophysical Observatories
(or Observatory) *e:* **POGO**

Polar Orbiting Meteorological Satellite *e:*
POMS

Polar-Orbiting [Operational] Environmental
Satellite[s] *e:* **POES**

Polar [Orbiting] Platform *e:* **POP**

Polar Orbiting Platform Element *e:* **POPE**

Polar Orbiting Satellite *e:* **POS**

Polar Orbiting Satellite System *e:* **POSS**

Polar Orbiting Satellite System-University
of Michigan *e:* **POSSUM**

Polar Ozone Aerosol Monitor *e:* **POAM**

Polar Ozone and Aerosol Measurement *e:*
POAM

Polar Ozone Lidar Experiment *e:* **POLE**

Polar Pacific *e:* **POLPA**, *e:* **PP**

Polar Patrol Balloons *e:* **PPB**

Polar Plasma Laboratory *e:* **POLAR**

Polar Platform *e:* **PPF**

Polar Platform Utilisation Study *e:* **P-
PLUS**

Polar Public Access Catalog *e:* **PolarPAC**

Polar-Reflection Faraday Effect *e:* **PRFE**

Polar Regions Award *e:* **PRA**

Polar Regions Award [amateur radio] *e:*
PRA

Polar Research *e:* **Polar Res.**

Polar Research and Development Center *e:*
PR&DC

Polar Research Board *e:* **PRB**

Polar Research Cell *e:* **PRC**

Polar Research Committee-Chinese
Academy of Sciences *e:* **PRC-CAS**

Polar Research Institute of China *e:* **PRIC**

Polar Research Laboratory *e:* **PRL**

Polar Satellite Data Processing Centre *e:*
PSDPC

Polar Satellite Launch Vehicle *e:* **PSLV**

Polar Satellite Precipitation Data Centre *e:* **PSPDC**

Polar Science Center *e:* **PSC**

Polar Stereographic *e:* **PS**

Polar Stratospheric Clouds *e:* **PSC**

Polar Sunrise Experiment *e:* **PSE**

Polar-to-Cartesian *e:* **PC**

Polar-To-Rectangular *e:* **PTR**

polare deutsche Bodenstation *d:* **P-DBS**

Polarimetric Active Radar Calibrator *e:* **PARC**

Polarimetric Diversity [Doppler] Radar *e:* **POLDIRAD**

Polarimetric Instrument for Solar Eclipse-98 *e:* **POISE-98**

Polarimetric Radar Control and Data Aquisition *e:* **PRACDA**

Polarimetric Scatterometer *e:* **POLARSCAT**

Polaris Accelerated Change Operation *e:* **PACO**

polaris accelerated flight *e:* **paf**

Polaris Acceleration Test *e:* **PAT**

Polaris Control and Information Center *e:* **PC&IC**

Polaris correction *e:* **Q**

Polaris Engineering Technical Service *e:* **PETS**

Polaris Executive Plan *e:* **PEPLAN**

Polaris Fleet Ballistic Missile Force *e:* **PFBMF**

Polaris Improvement Program *e:* **PIP**

Polaris Integrated Test Team *e:* **PITT**

Polaris Material Office *e:* **PMO**

Polaris Material Office, Atlantic Fleet *e:* **PMOLANT**

POLARIS Missile Assembly Facility *e:* **PMAF**

Polaris Missile Facility *e:* **PMF**, *e:* **POMF**

Polaris Missile Facility, Atlantic Fleet *e:* **POMFLANT**

Polaris Missile Facility, Pacific *e:* **PMF-PAC**, *e:* **POMPAC**

Polaris Missile Facility, Pacific Fleet *e:* **POMFPAC**

Polaris Missile System *e:* **PMS**

Polaris Operational Performance Surveillance Engineering Report *e:* **POPSER**

Polaris Operational Readiness Instrumentation *e:* **PORI**

Polaris Operations Support Task Group *e:* **POST**

Polaris-Poseidon Intelligence Digest *e:* **PPID**

Polaris/Poseidon Material Management System *e:* **PPMMS**

Polaris Resources, Inc. *e:* **POLA**

Polaris Star Tracker *e:* **PST**

Polaris Tactical Missile *e:* **PTM**

Polaris Target Card Computing System *e:* **PTCCS**

Polaris Task Group *e:* **PTG**

POLARIS Technical Information Bulletin *e:* **POTIB**

Polaris Tender Management Computer *e:* **PTMC**

Polarisation *d:* **P**, *d:* **Pol.**

Polarisationspunkt *d:* **Pol.-P.**, *d:* **Pol.-Pkt.**

Polarisationsstrom *d:* **Pol.-Str.**

Polarisationsweiche *d:* **PolWe**, *d:* **PW**

polarisieren *d:* **pol.**

polarisierend *d:* **pol.**

polarisiert *d:* **pol.**

Polarisierung *d:* **Pol.**

Polarität *d:* **Pol.**

Polaritätswechsel *d:* **PW**

Polarity *e:* **P**, *e:* **Plrt**, *e:* **PLRTY**, *e:* **PO**, *e:* **POL**

polarity *e:* **polar**

Polarity Coefficient *e:* **PC**

Polarity Coincidence Correlation receiver *e:* **PCC**

Polarity Correlation Function *e:* **PKF**

Polarity Health Institute *e:* **PHI**

Polarity Reversal Unit *e:* **PRU**

Polarity Selector *e:* **PS**

Polarizability *e:* **P**

Polarization *e:* **P**, *e:* **POL**, *e:* **POLAR**

Polarization-Agile Instrumentation Radar *e:* **PAIR**

Polarization and Directionality of the Earth's Reflectance[s] *e:* **POLDER**

polarization angle *e:* **polang**

Polarization Differential Reflectance *e:* **PDR**

Polarization Diversity Array *e:* **PDA**

Polarization Image Detector *e:* **PID**

Polarization Independent Narrow Channel *e:* **PINC**

Polarization-Maintaining *e:* **PM**

Polarization Microscope *e:* **PM**

Polarization Mode Dispersion *e:* **PMD**

Polarization Modulation *e:* **PM**

Polarization Modulation Fourier Transform Infrared *e:* **PM-FTIR**

Polarization Optical Time-Domain Reflectometry *e:* **POTDR**

Polarization-Preserving *e:* **PP**

Polarization-Preserving Fiber *e:* **PPF**

Polarization Radar Illinois Rainfall Experiments *e:* **PRAIRE**

Polarization Ratio *e:* **PR**

Polarize *e:* **POLAR**

Polarized *e:* **POL**

Polarize[d] *e:* **POLAR**

Polarized Airborne Laser Imaging Sensor *e:* **PALIS**

Polarized Angle-Resolved Infrared Spectroscopy *e:* **PARIS**

Polarized[-field] Frequency Relay *e:* **PFR**

Polarized Light *e:* **PL**

Polarized Light Microscopy *e:* **PLM**

Polarized Orbital Approximation *e:* **POA**

Polarized Platen Viewer *e:* **PPV**

Polarized Relay *e:* **PR**

Polarized Return-to-Zero *e:* **RTZ[P]**, *e:* **RZ[P]**

Polarized X-Ray *e:* **PXR**

Polarizer *e:* **P**

Polarizer Compensator Analyzer *e:* **PCA**

Polarizer-Compensator Sample Analyzer *e:* **PCSA**

Polarizer/Diplexer *e:* **P/D**

Polarizer-retarder-sample-analyzer *e:* **PRSA**

Polarizing Beamsplitter *e:* **PBS**

Polarkoordinaten *d:* **PK**

Polarografický Ústav při ČSAV *c:* **PÚ-ČSAV**

polarographische Serumfiltrat-Reaktion *d:* **PSF-Reaktion**

Polaroid Colo[u]r Pack Camera *e:* **PCP Camera**

Polaroid Corp. *e:* **PRD**

Polaroid Stereoscopic Chroncyclegraph *e:* **PSC**

Police de l'Air et des Frontières *f:* **P.A.F.**

Police Protective League *e:* **PPL**

Police Routière *f:* **P.R.**

Policy Coordinating Committee for Oceans and International Environmental and Scientific Affairs *e:* **PCC/OES**

Policyholders Protective Association of America *e:* **PPA**

Polish Institute of Hydrology and Meteorology *e:* **PIHM**

Polish National Committee of the International Association on Water Pollution Research and Control *e:* **PLNCIAWPRC**

Polish Ocean Lines *e:* **POL**

Polish Review of Radiology and Nuclear Medicine *e:* **Pol. Rev. Radiol. Nucl. Med.**

Polish Sea League of America *e:* **PSLA**

Polish Society of Social Medicine *e:* **PSSM**

Political-Military Interdepartmental Group *e:* **PMIG**

Politie te Water *n:* **RPTW**

Pollutant Response in Marine Animals *e:* **PRIMA**

pollution abatement and environmental control technology *e:* **paect**

Pollution and Natural Resources Program *e:* **PNRP**

Pollution Atmospherique *e:* **Pollut. Atmos.**

Pollution Control and Ecology Commission *e:* **PCEC**

Pollution Control Ecology *e:* **PCE**

Pollution of Oceans Originating on Land *e:* **POOL**

Polskie Linie Oceaniczne *P:* **PLO**

Polskie Towarzystwo Balneologii, Bioklimatologii i Medycyny Fizykalnej *P:* **PTBBiMF**

Polskie Towarzystwo Geofizyczne *P:* **PTGeof**

Polskie Towarzystwo Geologiczne *P:* **PTG**

Polskie Towarzystwo Hydrobiologiczne *P:* **PTH**

Polskie Towarzystwo Mikrobiologiczne *P:* **PTM**

Polyclitic Aromatic Hydrocarbons *e:* **PHAs**

Polycyclic Organic Hydrocarbons *e:* **POHC**

Polygon Midocean Dynamic Experiment *e:* **POLYMODE**

Polymerized Trimethyl Dihydro Quinoline *e:* **PTDQ**

Polymerized Water *e:* **Polywater**

Polymethylhydrosiloxane *e:* **PMHS**

polynuclear aromatic hydrocarbon *e:* **PNA**

Polynuclear Aromatic Hydrocarbons *e:* **PAHs**, *e:* **PNA**, *e:* **PNAH**

Ponderosa Pine [Biogeoclimatic] Zone *e:* **PP**

Ponding Water Depth *e:* **PWD**

pondus Hydrogenii *l:* **pH**

Pondus Hydrogenii Value *e:* **pH Value**

Pool Water Treatment Advisory Group *e:* **PWTAG**

Population and International Health *e:* **PIH**

Population, Health and Nutrition *e:* **PHN**

Population Health Research Unit *e:* **PHRU**

Population Health Summary System *e:* **PHSS**

Population Protection and Resources Management *e:* **PPRM**

Population Reports. Series L, Issues in World Health *e:* **Popul Rep L**

Population, Resources and Environment Program *e:* **PREP**

pore-water sampler *e:* **PWS**

Port and Ocean Engineering Under Arctic Conditions *e:* **POAC**

Port Health Authority *e:* **PHA**

Port Health Officer *e:* **PHO**

Port Medical Officer *e:* **PMO**

Port Meteorological Officer *e:* **PMO**

Portable Apparatus for Rapid Acquisition of Bidirectional Observations of Land and Atmosphere *e:* **PARABOLA**

Portable Atmospheric Noise Data Acquisition *e:* **PANDA**

Portable Automated Remote Inspection System *e:* **PARIS**

Portable Automatic Weather Observing Station *e:* **PAWOS**

Portable Collective Protection System *e:* **PCPS**

Portable Common Tool Environment *e:* **PCTC,** *e:* **PIMB**

Portable Common Tools Environment *e:* **PCTE**

Portable Earth Resources Ground Station *e:* **PERGS**

Portable Environment for Real-time Control *e:* **PERC**

Portable Environmental Assessment and Research Laboratory *e:* **PEARL**

Portable Environmental Control System *e:* **PECS**

Portable Environmental Measuring System *e:* **PEMS**

Portable Operating System Environment *e:* **POSE**

Portable Operating Systems for Computer Environments *e:* **POSIX**

Portable Oprating System Environment Standard *e:* **POSIX**

Portable Remote Observations of the Environment *e:* **PROBE**

Portable Remote Terminal *e:* **PRT**

Portable Water Intake *e:* **PWI**

Portable Water System *e:* **PWS**

Porte Mortier *f:* **PM**

Portfolio of Environment Sport and Territories *e:* **EST**

Portier *d:* **Port.**

Ports and Beaches and Inland Waterways Transports *e:* **PB/IWT**

Ports and Waterways Safety Act *e:* **PWSA**

Portuguese Association on Water, Wastewater and Solid Wastes Research *e:* **PAWWSWR**

Portuguese National Committee of the International Association on Water Pollution Research and Control *e:* **PNCIAWPRC**

Portuguese national meteorological institute *e:* **IM-PT**

Portuguese Water Dog Club of America *e:* **PWDCA**

Position of Earth Satellites in Digital-display *e:* **POESID**

Position Operational, Meteorological Aircraft Report *e:* **POMAR**

Positioning Ocean Sea Earth and Ice Dynamics and Orbiting Navigator *e:* **POSEIDON**

Positive Control[led] Airspace *e:* **PCA**

Positive Pressure Chilled Circulating Water *e:* **PPCCW**

Post-Graduate Institute of Health Training *e:* **PGIHT**

Post Loss-of-Coolant Accident Protection *e:* **PLOCAP**

Post Orbit *e:* **PO**

Posterior Odds Processing [weather forecasting] *e:* **POP**

Postgraduate and Continuing Medical Education *e:* **PGCME**

Postgraduate Center for Mental Health *e:* **PCMH**

Postgraduate Medical and Dental Education *e:* **PGMDE**

Postgraduate Medical Institute *e:* **Postgrad Med Inst**

Postgraduate Medical Journal *e:* **PMJ,** *e:* **Postgrad. Med. J.**

Postgraduate Medicine *e:* **Postgrad. Med.**

Postinsertion Deorbit Preparation *e:* **PDP**

Potable water *e:* **POT [able]**

Potable Water *e:* **POT W,** *e:* **PW**

potassa [potassium hydroxide] *e:* **pot.**

Potassium Dihydrogen Arsenate *e:* **KDA**

Potassium Dihydrogen Arsenates *e:* **KDAs**

Potassium Dihydrogen Phosphates *e:* **KDPs**

Potassium Hydrogen Phthalate *e:* **KHP**

Potassium Hydroxide *e:* **KOH**

Potassium [K], Rare Earth Elements and Phosphorus *e:* **KREEP**

potential of Hydrogen *e:* **pH**

Potsdam-Institut für Klimafolgenforschung e.V. *d:* **PIK**

Potsdam Land-Atmosphere Interaction Model *e:* **PLAI**

Power and Water Authority *e:* **PAWA**

Power for Underwater Logistics and Living *e:* **PULL**

Power On/Off Protection *e:* **POP**

Power Open Environment *e:* **POE**

Power Remote Control Panel *e:* **PRCP**

Powered Underwater Research Vehicles *e:* **PURVs**

P.P. Shirshov Institute of Oceanology, Academy of Sciences, Moscow *e:* **IOAN**

Prace Geologiczno-Mineralogiczne. Acta Universitatis Wratislaviensis *c:* **Pr Geol-Mineral Acta Univ Wratislav**

Prace Instytutu Geologii *P:* **PRIGA**

Prace Instytutu Jedwabiu Naturalnego *P:* **Pr Inst Jedwabiu Nat**

Prace Instytutu Meteorologii i Gospodarki Wodnej *P:* **Pr Inst Meteorol Gospod Wodnej**

Prace Morskiego Instytutu Rybackiego. Seria A. Oceanografia i Biologia Rybacka *P:* **Pr Morsk Inst Rybackiego Ser A**

Prace Naukowe Instytutu Geotechniki Politechniki Wroclawskiej *P:* **Pr Nauk Inst Geotech Politech Wroclaw**

Prace Statneho Geologickeho Ustavu [Bratislava] *c:* **Pr Statneho Geol Ustavu [Bratisl],** *c:* **Pr Statneho Geol Ustavu [Bratislava]**

Prace Ustavu Geologickeho Inzenyrstvu *c:* **Pr Ustavu Geol Inz**

Practice of Medicine [Philadelphia] *e:* **Pract Med [Phila]**

Prager medizinische Wochenschrift *d:* **PmW**

Prager Medizinische Wochenschrift *d:* **Prager Med Wochenschr**

Prairie Institute of Environmental Health. Report PIEH *e:* **Prairie Inst Environ Health PIEH**

Prairie Migratory Bird Research Centre, Ganadian Wildlife Service, Environment Canada Saskatoon, Saskatchewan *e:* **SSECW**

Prairie Naturalist *e:* **Prairie Nat**

Prairie Provinces Water Board *e:* **PPWB**

Prairie University Biological Seminars *e:* **PUBS**

Praktika. Hellenic Hydrobiological Institute *e:* **Prakt Hell Hydrobiol Inst**

Praktische Tierarzt *d:* **Prakt Tier,** *d:* **Prakt Tierarzt**

Präsentierung *d:* **Präs.**

Pratica del Medico *i:* **Pratica Med**

Pratsi i Materiali Pershogo Kharkivs'kogo Derzhavnogo Medichnogo Institutu *R:* **Pr Mater Pershogo Khark Derzh Med Inst**

Pratsi Institut Geologii Korisnikh Kopalin Akademiya Nauk Ukrains'koi RSR *R:* **Pr Inst Geol Korisnikh Kopalin Akad Nauk Ukr**

Pratsi Institutu Gidrobiologii Akademiya Nauk Ukrains'koi RSR *R:* **Pr Inst Gidrobiol Akad Nauk Ukr RSR**

Pratsi Odeskogo Deržavnogo Universitetu Seriya Biologičnich Nauk *U:* **Pratsi Odes Derž Univ Ser Biol Nauk**

Pratsi Odes'kogo Gidrometeorologichnogo Institutu *R:* **Pr Odes Gidrometeorol Inst**

Pratsi Vinnits'kogo Derzhavnogo Medichnogo Institutu *R:* **Pr Vinnits'k Derzh Med Inst**

Pratt on Sea Lights *e:* **Pratt SL**

Praxis Biologics, Inc. *e:* **PRXS**

Praxis der Naturwissenschaften *d:* **Prax Naturw**

Praxis der Naturwissenschaften. Physik *d:* **Prax Naturwiss Phy**

Praxis der Naturwissenschaften. Physik im Unterricht der Schulen *d:* **Prax Naturwiss Phys Unterr Sch**

Praxis der Naturwissenschaften. Teil 3. Chemie *d:* **Prax Naturwiss Teil 3,** *d:* **Pr Naturwiss Teil 3**

Pre-Storm Oklahoma-Kansas Preliminary Regional Experiment-Stormscale Operational Research and Meteorology *e:* **O-K**

Pre-university Orbital Information Tracker Equipment and Recorder *e:* **POINTER**

Preboot Execution Environment *e:* **PXE**

Precambrian Paleobiology Research Group *e:* **PPRG**

precipitable water *e:* **PW**

precipitable water vapor *e:* **PWV**

precipitation-environment *e:* **p-e**

Precipitation Water Content *e:* **PWC**

Precise Orbit Determination *e:* **POD**

Precise Orbit Determination System *e:* **PODS**

Precise Orbit Positioning Satellite *e:* **POPSAT**

Precise Position System- Precise Orbit Determination System *e:* **PPS-PODS**

Precision Earth Pointing System *e:* **PEPSY**

Precision Integrator for Meteorological Echoes *e:* **PRIME**

Precision Optical Interferometer in Space *e:* **POINTS**

Precision Orbit Determination Experiment *e:* **POD**

Precision Remote Bathythermograph *e:* **PRBT**

Precision Underwater Navigation *e:* **PUN**

Predel no Dopustimye Kontsentratsii Atmosfernykh Zagryaznenii *R:* **Predel no Dopustimye Konts Atmos Zagryaz**

Predicasts. Water Treatment Chemicals Industry Study 165 *e:* **Predi 165**

Predicción Meteorológica Numérica *s:* **PMN**

Predicted Environmental Concentration *e:* **PEC**

Predicted Orbit *e:* **PROR**

predictor[s] of large-scale ecological destruction *e:* **ecodoomster[s]**

Preduzeće za geološke istražne radove *se:* **Geoistrage**

prefix for specimens from American Museum of Natural History *e:* **AMNH**

Preflight Acceptance Checkout Equipment for Spacecraft *e:* **PACE-S/C**

Prehistoire Ariegeoise *f:* **Prehist Arieg**

Prehospital and Disaster Medicine *e:* **PDM**

Preisnotierung *d:* **Pr.-Not.**

Preliminary Automated Ground Environment *e:* **PAGE**

Preliminary Draft Environmental Impact Statement *e:* **PDEIS**

Preliminary Draft Environmental Statement *e:* **PDES**

Preliminary Environmental Impact Statement *e:* **PEIS**

Preliminary Mid-Ocean Dynamics Experiment *e:* **PREMODE**

Preliminary Natural Resources Survey *e:* **PNRS**

Preliminary Orbit Determination Method *e:* **PODM**

Preliminary Orbit Determination Method Computer *e:* **PODM Computer**

Preliminary Protective Concentration Limits *e:* **PPCL**

Preliminary Reference Earth Model *e:* **PREM**

Preliminary Research Experiment-Stormscale Operational and Research Meteorology *e:* **PRE-STORM**

Preliminary Space Utilization Plan *e:* **PSUP**

premedical *e:* **pre-med**

Premier Acte Médical *f:* **P.A.M.**

Premier Quartier *e:* **PQ**

Premodulation Processor-Deep Space-Voice *e:* **PDV**

Premote Hemodynamics and Metabolism in an Orbiting Satellite *e:* **PHAMOS**

Prensa Medica Argentina *s:* **Prensa Med Argent**

Prensa Medica Mexicana *s:* **Prensa Med Mex**

Preparatory Commission for the International Seabed Authority and for the International Tribunal for the Law of the Sea *e:* **PREPCOM**

Prepositioned War Reserve Requirements for Medical Facilities *e:* **PWRR-MF**

Prepositioned War Reserve Stocks for Medical Facilities *e:* **PWRS-MF**

Preprints. Annual Scientific Meeting. Aerospace Medical Association *e:* **Prepr Annu Sci Meet Aerosp Med Assoc**

Preprints of Papers Presented at National Meeting. Division of Environmental Chemistry. American Chemical Society *e:* **Prepr Pap Natl Meet Div Environ Chem Am Chem Soc**

Preprints of Papers Presented at National Meeting. Division of Water, Air and Waste Chemistry. American Chemical Society *e:* **Prepr Pap Natl Meet Dir Water Air Waste Chem Am Chem Soc**

Preprints. Scientific Program. Aerospace Medical Association *e:* **Prepr Sci Program Aerosp Med Assoc**

Preprocessing of Airborne Remote Sensing Data *e:* **PARES**

Presbytarian Health, Education and Welfare Association *e:* **PHEWA**

Presbyterian-St. Luke's Hospital. Medical Bulletin *e:* **Presbyt-St. Luke's Hosp Med Bull**

Prescription-Only Medicines *e:* **POM**

Present Atmospheric Level *e:* **PAL**

Present Weather Sensor *e:* **PWS**

Presentation Environment for Multi-Media Objects *e:* **PREMO**

Presentation Space Application Programming Interface *e:* **PSAPI**

Presentation Space Identifier *e:* **PSID**

President of the Geographical Society *e:* **PGS**

President of the Geological Society *e:* **PGS**

President of the Meteorological Society *e:* **PMS**

President of the Royal College of Obstetricians and Gynaecologists *e:* **P.R.C.O.G.**

President of the Royal College of Surgeons *e:* **P.R.C.S.**

President of the Royal Geographical Society *e:* **PRGS**

President of the Royal Institute of Painters in Water Colours *e:* **PRI**

President of the Royal Scottish Water Colour Society *e:* **PRSW**

President of the Royal Society for the Promotion of Health *e:* **PRSH**

President of the Royal Society of Painters in Water Colours *e:* **PRWS**

Presidential Protective Division *e:* **PPD**

President's Advisory Commission on Recreation and Natural Beauty *e:* **PACRNB**

President's Advisory Panel on Timber and the Environment *e:* **PAPTE**

President's Council on Environmental Quality *e:* **PCEQ**

President's Environmental Quality Council *e:* **PEQC**

President's Scientific Advisory Committee Panel on Oceanography *e:* **PSACPOO**

Presión atmosférica a la elevación del aeródromo *s:* **QFE**

Presquile National Wildlife Refuge *e:* **PNWR**

Presse Medicale *f:* **Presse Med**, *s:* **PRMEA**, *s:* **Pr Med**

Presse Medicale Belge *f:* **Presce Med Belge**

Presse Thermale et Climatique *f:* **Presse Therm Clim**

Pressure Environment Equipment *e:* **PEE**

Pressure in Atmosphere *e:* **BARA**

Pressure Protection Valve *e:* **PPV**

Pressurised-Water Reactor *e:* **PWR**

Pressurized Heavy and Light Water Reactor *e:* **PHLWR**

Pressurized Heavy Water *e:* **PHW**

Pressurized Heavy-Water Reactor *e:* **PHWR**

Pressurized Heavy Water Reactor-Homogenized [Type] *e:* **PHWRH**

Pressurized Light Water Reactor *e:* **PLWR**

Pressurized Water Reactor-Flexible Assembly *e:* **PWR-FA**

Pressurized Water Reactor-Full Length Emergency Cooling Heat Transfer *e:* **PWR-FLECHT**

Prestige Saltwater Fly Anglers *e:* **PSWFA**

Pretoria, Witwatersrand, Vereeniging Industrial Area *e:* **PWV**

Pretty Good Protection *e:* **PGP**

Preußisches Wassergesetz *d:* **Pr. WG**

Prevention Routiere Internationale *e:* **PRI**

Preventive Intervention Research Center for Child Health *e:* **PIRC**

Preventive Medicine *e:* **PM**, *e:* **Prev Med**, *e:* **PVNTMED**

Preventive Medicine, Preventive Maintenance *e:* **PM**

Preventive Medicine Unit *e:* **PMU**, *e:* **PREMEDU**, *e:* **PREVMEDU**

Preventive Veterinary Medicine *e:* **Prev Vet M**, *e:* **Prev Vet Med**

Previous Medical Illness *e:* **PMI**

Pribilov Islands in the Bering Sea off Alaska *e:* **Pribilovs**

Price Waterhouse *e:* **PW**

Price Waterhouse Review *e:* **Price Waterhouse R**, *e:* **Price Waterhouse Rev**

PricewaterhouseCoopers *e:* **PWC**

Pricing Review to Intensify Competitive Environment *e:* **PRICE**

Pride Institute. Journal of Long Term Home Health Care *e:* **Pride Inst J Long Term Home Health Care**

Prikladnaja Geometrija i Inzenernaja Grafika *R:* **Prikl Geom i Inzener Grafika**

Prikladnaya Biokhimiya i Mikrobiologiya *R:* **Prikl Biokhim Mikrobiol**

Prikladnaya Geofizika *R:* **Prikladnaya Geofiz**, *R:* **Prikl Geofiz**

Primary Cooling Water *e:* **PCW**

Primary Cooling Water Reactor *e:* **PCW Reactor**

Primary Drinking Water Standards *e:* **PDWS**

primary [earthquake] waves *e:* **p waves**

Primary Environment Care *e:* **PEC**

Primary Health Care *e:* **PHC**

Primary Health Care Operations Research *e:* **PRICOR**

Primary Health Care Specialist Group *e:* **PHCSG**

Primary Health Care Team *e:* **PHCT**

Primary Health Care Technology Project *e:* **PRITECH**

Primary Integrated Platform Environment *e:* **PIPE**

Primary Medical care for the Uniformed Services *e:* **PRIMUS**

Primary Medical Group *e:* **PMG**

Primary Mental Health Project *e:* **PMHP**

Primary Oceanographic Prediction System *e:* **POPS**

Primary Providers' Training and Education in Reproductive Health *e:* **PRIME**

Primates in Medicine *e:* **Primates Med**

Prime Medical Aid *e:* **PMA**

Prime Medical Services *e:* **PMSI**

Primenenie Matematicheskikh Metodov v Biologii *R:* **Primen Mat Metodov Biol**

Prince George Forest District *e:* **DPG**

Prince George Forest Region *e:* **RPG**

Prince George Free-Net Association *e:* **PGFNA**

Princeton Ocean Model *e:* **POM**

Princeton University Observatory *e:* **PUO**

Principal Clinical Medical Officer *e:* **PCMO**

Principal Colonial Medical Officer *e:* **PCMO**

Principal Conical Polar Curve *e:* **PCPC**

Principal Deputy Assistant Secretary for Health *e:* **PDASH**

Principal Medical Officer *e:* **P.M.O.**

Principal Regional Medical Officer *e:* **P.R.M.O.**

Principal Sea Transport Officer *e:* **P.S.T.O.**

Principal Vertical Polar Curve *e:* **PVPC**

Principal Veterinary Surgeon *e:* **PVS**

Printers' Medical Aid and Friendship Society *e:* **P.M.A.**

Printers' Medical Aid and Sanatorial Association *e:* **PMASA**

Printing Economy Remote Terminal *e:* **PERT**

Printing Industry Association of Georgia *e:* **PIAG**

Priorities and Protection Team *e:* **PPT**

Priority Delayed Weather *e:* **PDW**

Priority Health Training Programs *e:* **PHTP**

Prison Medical Reform Council *e:* **P.M.R.C.**

Prisoner[s] of Watergate *e:* **P o W**

Pritikin Health Association of Australia *e:* **PHAA**

Privacy Protection Act *e:* **PPA**

Privacy Protection Study Commission *e:* **PPSC**

Private Anation Weather Station *e:* **PAWS**

Private Aviation Weather Research Station *e:* **PAWRS**

Private Medical Communication *e:* **PMC**

Private Medical Doctor *e:* **PMD**

Private Medical Insurance *e:* **PMI**

Privately-Owned Stored Water *e:* **POSW**

Privy Council for Medical Research *e:* **P.C.M.R.**

Pro Medico *e:* **Pro Med**

Pro Natura *e:* **Pro Nat**

Probable Hydrologic Consequences *e:* **PHC**

Problem-Oriented Medical Information System *e:* **PROMIS**

Problem-Oriented Medical Record *e:* **POMR**

Problem-Oriented Medical Records *e:* **POMR**

Problem-oriented veterinary medical record *e:* **POVMR**

Problem-Solving Environment *e:* **PSE**

Problem-Solving In Medical Physiology, Logically Explained *e:* **PSIMPLE**

Problemorientierte Informationsausgabe *d:* **POI**

problemorientierte Programmiersprache *d:* **PPS**, *d:* **PPSpr**

problemorientierte Programmiersprache für mittlere Datentechnik *d:* **PROMIDA**

problemorientierte Programmiersprachen *d:* **PPSprn**

problemorientierte Prozedur *d:* **PO-Prozedur**

problemorientierte Prozedur[en] *d:* **POP**

problemorientierte Prozeduren-Bibliothek *d:* **POP-Bibliothek**

problemorientierte Routine *d:* **POR**

problemorientierte Systemunterlagen *d:* **POS**

problemorientierter Baustein *d:* **POB**

problemorientiertes medizinisches Informationssystem *d:* **PROMIS**

Problems in Biology *e:* **Probl Biol**

Problems in Geometry in the Key Word Index [Moscow] *e:* **Problems in Geometry**

Problems of Biocybernetics and Biomedical Engineering *e:* **Probl Biocybern Biomed Eng**

Problems of Ecology and Biocenology *e:* **Probl Ecol Biocenol**

Problems of Radiobiology *e:* **Probl. Radiobiol.**

Problems Related to Ionospheric Modeling and Observations Project *e:* **PRIMO**

Problemy Biologie Krajiny *R:* **Probl Biol Krajiny**

Problemy Fiziki Atmosfery *R:* **Probl Fiz Atmos**

Problemy Geokhimii *R:* **Probl Geokhim**

Problemy Geologii Nefti [USSR] *R:* **Probl Geol Nefti**

Problemy Inzhenernoi Geologii Severnogo Kavkaza *R:* **Probl Inzh Geol Sev Kavk**

Problemy Kontrolya i Zashchita Atmosfery ot Zagryazneniya *R:* **Probl Kontrolya Zashch Atmos Zagryaz**

Problemy Kosmicheskoi Biologii *R:* **Probl Kosm Biol**

Problemy Kosmicheskoi Biologii Akademiya Nauk SSSR *R:* **Problemy Kosmich Biol Akad Nauk SSSR**

Problemy Obshchei i Molekulyarnoi Biologii *R:* **Probl Obshch Mol Biol**

Problemy Osadochnoy Geologii Dokembriya *R:* **Probl Osad Geol Dokembr**

Problemy Sovetskoi Geologii [USSR] *R:* **Probl Sov Geol**

Procaine hydrochloride *e:* **PROC**

Procedures for Air Navigation Service[s]/Meteorology *e:* **PANS/MET**

Proceedings. Academy of Natural Sciences of Philadelphia *e:* **Proc Acad Nat Sci Phila**

Proceedings. Academy of Sciences. Georgian SSR. Biological Series *e:* **Proc Acad Sci Georgian SSR Biol Ser**

Proceedings. Academy of Sciences of the USSR. Geochemistry Section *e:* **Proc Acad Sci USSR Geochem Sect**

Proceedings. American Society of Animal Production. Western Section *e:* **Proc Amer Soc Anim Pro W Sect**

Proceedings. American Society of Animal Science. Western Section *e:* **Proc Amer Soc Anim Sci W Sect**

Proceedings. American Veterinary Medical Association *e:* **Proc Am Vet Med Ass**, *e:* **Proc Am Vet Med Assoc**

Proceedings. American Water Works Association *e:* **Proc Am Water Works Assoc**

Proceedings and Abstracts. Society of Biological Chemists *e:* **Proc Abstr Soc Biol Chem**

Proceedings and Abstracts. Society of Biological Chemists [Bangalore] *e:* **Proc Abstr Soc Biol Chem [Bangalore]**

Proceedings and Papers. International Union for the Conservation of Nature and Natural Resources *e:* **Proc Pap Int Union Conserv Nature Nat Resour**

Proceedings and Reports. Belfast Natural History and Philosophical Society *e:* **Proc Rep Belfast Nat Hist Philos Soc**

Proceedings and Transactions. British Entomological and Natural History Society *e:* **Proc Trans Br Entomol Nat Hist Soc**

Proceedings and Transactions. Croydon Natural History and Scientific Society *e:* **Proc Trans Croydon Natur Hist Sci Soc**

Proceedings and Transactions. Liverpool Biological Society *e:* **Proc [and] Tr[ans] Liverp[ool] Biol Soc**, *e:* **Proc and Tr Liverpool Biol Soc**, *e:* **Proc Trans Liverp Biol Soc**

Proceedings. Animal Care Panel *e:* **Proc Anim Care Panel**

Proceedings. Annual AlChE [American Institute of Chemical Engineers] Southwestern Ohio Conference on Energy and the Environment *e:* **Proc Annu AlChE Southwest Ohio Conf Energy Environ**

Proceedings. Annual Arkansas Water Works and Pollution Control Conference and Short School *e:* **Proc Annu Arkansas Water Works Pollut Control Conf Short Sch**

Proceedings. Annual Biology Colloquium *e:* **Proc A Biol Colloq**

Proceedings. Annual Biology Colloquium [Oregon State University] *e:* **Proc Annu Biol Colloq [Oreg State Univ]**

Proceedings. Annual Biomedical Sciences Instrumentation Symposium *e:* **Proc Annu Biomed Sci Instrum Symp**

Proceedings. Annual Conference. Maryland-Delaware Water and Sewage Association *e:* **Proc Annu Conf MD Del Water Sewage Assoc**

Proceedings. Annual Conference on Biological Sonar and Diving Mammals *e:* **Proc Annu Conf Biol Sonar Diving Mamm**, *e:* **Proc Annu Conf Biol Sonar Diving Mammals**

Proceedings. Annual Conference on Environmental Chemicals. Human and Animal Health e: **Proc Annu Conf Environ Chem Hum Anim Health**

Proceedings. Annual Conference on Research in Medical Education e: **Proc Annu Conf Res Med Educ**

Proceedings. Annual Conference. Southeastern Association of Fish and Wildlife Agencies e: **Proc Annu Conf Southeast Assoc Fish Wildl Agencies**

Proceedings. Annual Convention. Natural Gas Processors Association. Technical Papers e: **Proc Annu Conv Natur Gas Process Ass Tech Pap**

Proceedings. Annual Convention. Natural Gasoline Association of America. Technical Papers e: **Proc Annu Conv Nat Gasoline Assoc Am Tech Pap**

Proceedings. Annual Convention. Western Canada Water and Sewage Conference [1960-1975] e: **Proc Annu Conv West Can Water Sewage Conf**

Proceedings. Annual Engineering Geology and Soils Engineering Symposium e: **Proc Annu Eng Geol Soils Eng Symp**

Proceedings. Annual Engineering Geology Symposium e: **Proc Annu Eng Geol Symp**

Proceedings. Annual Environmental and Water Resources Engineering Conference e: **Proc Annu Environ Water Resour Eng Conf**

Proceedings. Annual Fall Meeting California Natural Gasoline Association e: **Proc Annu Fall Meet Calif Nat Gasoline Assoc**

Proceedings. Annual Forestry Symposium. Louisiana State University. School of Forestry and Wildlife Management e: **Proc For Symp LA Sch For**

Proceedings. Annual Meeting. American Society of Animal Science. Western Section e: **Proc Annu Meet Am Soc Anim Sci West Sect**

Proceedings. Annual Meeting Medical Section. American Council of Life Insurance e: **Proc Annu Meet Med Sect Am Counc Life Insur**

Proceedings. Annual Meeting. Medical Section. American Life Convention e: **Proc Annu Meet Med Sect Am Life Conv**

Proceedings. Annual Meeting. Medical Section. American Life Insurance Association e: **Proc Annu Meet Med Sect Am Life Insur Assoc**

Proceedings. Annual Meeting. National Council on Radiation Protection and Measurements e: **Proc Annu Meet Natl Counc Radiat Prot Meas**

Proceedings. Annual Meeting of the Medical Section of the American Council of Life Insurance e: **Proc Annu Meet Med Sect Am Counc Life Insur**

Proceedings. Annual Meeting. United States Animal Health Association e: **Proc Annu Meet US Anim Health Assoc**

Proceedings. Annual Symposium on Engineering Geology and Soils Engineering e: **Proc Annu Symp Eng Geol Soils Eng**

Proceedings. Annual Tall Timbers Fire Ecology Conference e: **Proc Annu Tall Timbers Fire Ecol Conf**

Proceedings. Annual Technical Meeting. Institute of Environmental Sciences e: **Proc Annu Tech Meet Inst Environ Sci**

Proceedings. Annual WWEMA [Water and Wastewater Equipment Manufacturers Association] Industrial Pollution Conference e: **Proc Annu WWEMA Ind Pollut Conf**

Proceedings. Association for Plant Protection of Kyushu e: **Proc Assoc Plant Prot Kyushu**, e: **Proc Ass Plant Prot Kyushu**

Proceedings. Association of Economic Biologists e: **Proc Ass Econ Biol**

Proceedings. Association of Plant Protection of Hokuriku e: **Proc Ass Plant Prot Hokuriku**

Proceedings. Australian Society for Medical Research e: **Proc Aust Soc Med Res**

Proceedings. Australian Society of Animal Production e: **Proc Aust Soc Anim Prod**

Proceedings. Biological Society of Washington e: **Proc Biol Soc Wash**

Proceedings. Bristol Naturalists Society e: **Proc Bristol Nat Soc**

Proceedings. 1980 British Crop Protection Conference. Weeds e: **Proc Br Crop Prot Conf**

Proceedings. British Society of Animal Production e: **Proc Br Soc Anim Prod**

Proceedings. Canadian Federation of Biological Societies e: **Proc Can Fed Biol Soc**

Proceedings. Cardiff Medical Society e: **Proc Cardiff Med Soc**

Proceedings. College of Medicine. University of the Philippines e: **Proc Coll Med Univ Philipp**

Proceedings. College of Natural Sciences. Section 4. Biological Sciences. Seoul National University e: **Proc Coll Nat Sci Sect 4 Biol Sci Seoul Natl Univ**

Proceedings. College of Natural Sciences. Section 3. Chemistry. Seoul National University e: **Proc Coll Nat Sci Sect 3 Seoul Nat Univ**

Proceedings. College of Natural Sciences. Section 5. Geology Meteorology and Oceanography. Seoul National University e: **Proc Coll Nat Sci Sect 5 Seoul Nat Univ**

Proceedings. College of Natural Sciences. Section 4. Life Sciences. Seoul National University e: **Proc Coll Nat Sci Sect 4 Seoul Nat Univ**

Proceedings. College of Natural Sciences. Section 2. Physics, Astronomy. Seoul National University e: **Proc Coll Nat Sci Sect 2 Seoul Nat Univ**

Proceedings. College of Natural Sciences [Seoul] e: **Proc Coll Nat Sci [Seoul]**

Proceedings. College of Natural Sciences. Seoul National University e: **Proc Coll Nat Sci Seoul Natl Univ**

Proceedings. Conference of Engineering in Medicine and Biology e: **Proc Conf Eng Med Biol**

Proceedings. Conference on Remote Systems Technology e: **Proc Conf Remote Syst Technol**

Proceedings. Congres Annuel. Corporation des Ingenieurs Forestiers [Quebec] e: **Proc Congr Ann Corp Ingen For [Quebec]**

Proceedings. Congress of the Hungarian Association of Microbiologists e: **Proc Congr Hung Assoc Microbiol**

Proceedings. Convention. International Association of Fish and Wildlife Agencies e: **Proc Conv Int Assoc Fish Wildl Agencies**

Proceedings. Cotteswold Naturalists' Field Club e: **Proc Cotteswold Natur Fld Club**

Proceedings. Coventry District Natural History and Scientifc Society e: **Proc Coventry Dist Natur Hist Sci Soc**

Proceedings. Croydon Natural History Science Society e: **Proc Croydon Nat Hist Sci Soc**

Proceedings. Cumberland Geological Society e: **Proc Cumberland Geol Soc**

Proceedings. Department of Horticulture and Plant Health. Massey University e: **Proc Dep Hortic Plant Health Massey Univ**

Proceedings. Dorset Natural History and Archaeological Society e: **Proc Dorset Natur Hist Arch[aeol] Soc**

Proceedings. Ecological Society of Australia e: **Proc Ecol Soc Aust**

Proceedings. Environmental Engineering and Science Conference e: **Proc Environ Eng Sci Conf**

Proceedings. First Livestock by Ocean Conference e: **Proc First Livest Ocean Conf**

Proceedings. Forest Microclimate Symposium. Canada Department of Fisheries and Forestry e: **Proc For Microclim Symp Can Dep Fish For**

Proceedings. Forum on Fundamental Surgical Problems. Clinical Congress of the American College of Surgeons e: **Proc Forum Fundam Surg Probl Clin Congr Am Coll Surg**

Proceedings. [Fourth] New Zealand Geographical Conference e: **Proc [Fourth] NZ Geogr Conf**

Proceedings. Frontiers in Education Conference e: **Proc Front Educ Conf**

Proceedings. General Meeting of the Society for Industrial Microbiology e: **Proc Gen Meet Soc Ind Microbiol**

Proceedings. Geoinstitut e: **Proc Geoinst**

Proceedings. Geological Association e: **Proc Geol Ass**

Proceedings. Geological Association of Canada e: **Proc Geol Ass Can**

Proceedings. Geological Society of China e: **Proc Geol Soc China**

Proceedings. Geological Society of London e: **Proc Geol Soc Lond**

Proceedings. Geological Society of South Africa e: **Proc Geol Soc S Afr**

Proceedings. Geologists' Association e: **Proc Geol Assoc**

Proceedings. Geologists' Association of London e: **Proc Geol Assoc London**

Proceedings. Geophysical Society of Tulsa e: **Proc Geophys Soc Tulsa**

Proceedings. Geoscience Information Society e: **Proc Geosci Inf Soc**

Proceedings. Health Policy Forum *e:* **Proc Health Policy Forum**

Proceedings. Hydrology Symposium *e:* **Proc Hydrol Symp**

Proceedings. ICMR [International Center for Medical Research, Kobe University] Seminar *e:* **Proc ICMR Semin**

Proceedings. Indian Academy of Sciences. Animal Sciences *e:* **Proc Indian Aad Sci Anim Sci**

Proceedings. Indian Academy of Sciences. Earth and Planetary Sciences *e:* **Proc Indian Acad Sci Earth and Planet Sci**, *e:* **Proc Indian Acad Sci Earth Planetary Sci**, *e:* **Proc Indian Acad Sci Earth Planet Sci**

Proceedings. Indian National Science Academy. Part B. Biological Sciences *e:* **Proc Indian Natl Sci Acad Part B Biol Sci**

Proceedings Indian National Science Academy. Part B. Biological Sciences *e:* **Proc Indian Natl Sci Acad Part B**

Proceedings. Institute of Environmental Sciences *e:* **Proc Inst Environ Sci**

Proceedings. Institute of Medicine of Chicago *e:* **Proc Institute Med Chicago**, *e:* **Proc Inst Med Chic**, *e:* **Proc Inst Med Chicago**

Proceedings. Institute of Natural Sciences. Nihon University *e:* **Proc Inst Nat Sci Nihon Univ**

Proceedings. Institute of Oceanography and Fisheries. Bulgarian Academy of Sciences *e:* **Proc Inst Oceanogr Fish Bulg Acad Sci**

Proceedings. International ISA [Instrument Society of America] Biomedical Sciences Instrumentation Symposium *e:* **Proc Int ISA Biomed Sci Instrum Symp**

Proceedings. International Meeting of Biological Standardization *e:* **Proc Int Meet Biol Stand**

Proceedings. International Symposium of the Institute for Biomedical Research. American Medical Association Education and Research Foundation *e:* **Proc Int Symp Inst Biomed Res Am Med Assoc Educ Res Found**

Proceedings. International Symposium on Fresh Water from the Sea *e:* **Proc Int Symp Fresh Water Sea**

Proceedings. International Symposium on Medical Mycology *e:* **Proc Int Symp Med Mycol**

Proceedings. International Symposium on Remote Sensing of Environment *e:* **Proc Int Symp Remote Sens[ing] Environ**

Proceedings. International Union of Biological Sciences *e:* **Proc Int Union Biol Sci**

Proceedings. International Union of Biological Sciences. Series B *e:* **Proc Int Union Biol Sci Ser B**

Proceedings. Koninklijke Nederlandse Akademie van Wetenschappen. Series C. Biological and Medical Sciences *e:* **Proc K Ned Akad Wet Ser C**, *e:* **Proc K Ned Akad Wet Ser C Biol Med Sci**

Proceedings. Liverpool Geological Society *e:* **Proc Liverpool Geol Soc**

Proceedings. Maryland-Delaware Water and Pollution Control Association *e:* **Proc MD Del Water Pollut Control Assoc**

Proceedings. Medico-Legal Society of Victoria *e:* **Proc Medico-Legal Soc Vict**

Proceedings. Meeting of the Animal Husbandry Wing. Board of Agriculture and Animal Husbandry in India *e:* **Proc Meet Anim Husb Wing Board Agric Anim Husb India**

Proceedings. Meeting of the Japanese Society for Medical Mass Spectrometry *e:* **Proc Meet Jpn Soc Med Mass Spectrom**

Proceedings. Microbiological Research Group. Hungarian Academy of Science *e:* **Proc Microbiol Res Group Hung Acad Sci**

Proceedings. Mine Medical Officers Association *e:* **Proc Mine Med Off Assoc**

Proceedings. Mine Medical Officers Association of South Africa *e:* **Proc Mine Med Off Assoc SA**

Proceedings. National Academy of Sciences [India]. Section B. Biological Sciences *e:* **Proc Nat Acad Sci [India] Sect B**, *e:* **Proc Natl Acad Sci [India] Sect B**, *e:* **Proc Natl Acad Sci [India] Sect B Biol Sci**

Proceedings. National Academy of Sciences [United States of America]. Biological Sciences *e:* **Proc Nat Acad Sci [USA] Biol Sci**

Proceedings. National Biomedical Sciences Instrumentation Symposium *e:* **Proc Natl Biomed Sci Instrum Symp**

Proceedings. National Conference for Individual Onsite Wastewater Systems *e:* **Proc Natl Conf Individ Onsite Wastewater Syst**

Proceedings. National Council on Radiation Protection and Measurements *e:* **Proc Natl Counc Radiat Prot Meas**

Proceedings. National Institute of Sciences [India]. Part B Biological Sciences *e:* **Proc Natl Inst Sci [India] Part B**

Proceedings. National Institute of Sciences [India]. Part B. Biological Sciences *e:* **Proc Natl Inst Sci [India] Part B Biol Sci**

Proceedings. National Meeting on Biophysics and Medical Engineering in Finland *e:* **Proc Natl Meet Biophys Med Eng Finl**

Proceedings. National Open Hearth and Basic Oxygen Steel Conference *e:* **Proc Natl Open Hearth Basic Oxygen Steel Conf**

Proceedings. National Symposium on Radioecology *e:* **Proc Natl Symp Radioecol**

Proceedings. Natural Gas Processors Association *e:* **Proc Natur Gas Processors Ass**

Proceedings. Natural Gas Processors Association. Annual Convention *e:* **Proc Nat Gas Processors Assoc Annu Conv**

Proceedings. Natural Gas Processors Association. Technical Papers *e:* **Proc Nat Gas Process Assoc Tech Pap**

Proceedings. New Zealand Ecological Society *e:* **Proc NZ Ecol Soc**

Proceedings. New Zealand Society of Animal Production *e:* **Proc NZ Soc Anim Proc**

Proceedings of the Annual Symposium on Computer Applications in Medical Care *e:* **Proc Annu Symp Comput Appl Med Care**

Proceedings of the Australian Society for Medical Research *e:* **Proc. Aust. Soc. Med. Res.**

Proceedings of the Australian Society of Animal Production *e:* **Proc. Aust. Soc. Anim. Prod.**

Proceedings of the Bristol Naturalists Society *e:* **PBNS**

Proceedings of the Geological Society *e:* **PGS**

Proceedings of the Indian National Science Academy, Part B, Biological Sciences *e:* **Proc. Indian Natl. Sci. Acad.,**

Proceedings of the Institute of Medicine of Chicago *e:* **Proc. Inst. Med. Chicago**

Proceedings of the Institution of Mechanical Engineers. Part H, Journal of Engineering in Medicine *e:* **Proc Inst Mech Eng [H]**

Proceedings of the International Congress of Ecology *e:* **Proc. Int. Congr. Ecol.**

Proceedings of the Liverpool Geological Society *e:* **PLGS**

Proceedings of the Royal Geographical Society *e:* **PRGS**, *e:* **PRGS**

Proceedings of the Royal Society of London Series B: Biological Sciences *e:* **Proc. R. Soc. Lond. Ser. B Biol. Sci.**

Proceedings of the Royal Society of Medicine *e:* **Proc. Roy. Soc. Med.**

Proceedings of the Society for Experimental Biology and Medicine *e:* **Proc. Soc. Exp. Biol. Med.**, *e:* **Proc Soc Exp Biol Med**, *e:* **PSEBM**

Proceedings of the Society for Water Treatment and Examinations *e:* **PSWTE**

Proceedings of the Yorkshire Geological Society *e:* **PYGS**

Proceedings. Osaka Prefecture Institute of Public Health. Edition of Food Sanitation *e:* **Proc Osaka Prefect Inst Public Health Ed Food Sanit**

Proceedings. Osaka Prefecture Institute of Public Health. Edition of Industrial Health *e:* **Proc Osaka Prefect Inst Public Health Ed Ind Health**

Proceedings. Osaka Prefecture Institute of Public Health. Edition of Mental Health *e:* **OKHED4**, *e:* **Proc Osaka Prefect Inst Public Health Ed Ment Health**

Proceedings. Osaka Prefecture Institute of Public Health. Edition of Pharmaceutical Affairs *e:* **OFKYDA**, *e:* **Proc Osaka Prefect Inst Public Health Ed Pharm Aff**

Proceedings. Osaka Prefecture Institute of Public Health. Edition of Public Health *e:* **OKEHDW**, *e:* **Proc Osaka Prefect Inst Public Health Ed Public Health**

Proceedings. Osaka Public Health Institute *e:* **Proc Osaka Public Health Inst**

Proceedings. Public Health Engineering Conference *e:* **Proc Public Health Eng Conf**

Proceedings. Remote Systems Technology Division of the American Nuclear Society *e:* **Proc Remote Syst Technol Div ANS**

Proceedings. Research Institute for Nuclear Medicine and Biology *e:* **PRNBA**, *e:* **Proc Res Inst Nucl Med Biol**

Proceedings. Research Institute for Nuclear Medicine and Biology. Hiroshima University e: **Proc Res Inst Nucl Med Biol Hiroshima Univ**

Proceedings. Research Institute of Atmospherics. Nagoya University e: **Proc Res Inst Atmos Nagoya Univ**

Proceedings. Research Institute of Oceanography and Fisheries [Varna] e: **Proc Res Inst Oceanogr Fish [Varna]**

Proceedings. Royal Geographical Society of Australasia. South Australian Branch e: **Proc R Geogr Soc Australas S Aust Br**, e: **Proc R Geogr Soc Aust[ralas] S[outh] Aust Br[anch]**

Proceedings Royal Geographical Society of Australia. South Australian Branch e: **Proc Roy Geog Soc Austral**

Proceedings. Royal Irish Academy. Section B. Biological, Geological and Chemical Science e: **PRIBA**

Proceedings. Royal Irish Academy. Section B Biological, Geological and Chemical Science e: **PRIBAN**

Proceedings. Royal Irish Academy. Section B. Biological, Geological and Chemical Science e: **P R Ir Ac B**, e: **Proc R Ir Acad Sect B**, e: **Proc R Ir Acad Sect B Biol Geol Chem Sci**, e: **Proc R Irish Acad Sect B**

Proceedings. Royal Society of Edinburgh. Section B. Biological Sciences e: **PREBA3**, e: **Proc Roy Soc Edinb B**, e: **Proc R Soc Edinburgh B**, e: **Proc R Soc Edinburgh Biol Sci**

Proceedings. Royal Society of Edinburgh. Section B. Biology e: **Proc R Soc Edinb Biol**, e: **Proc R Soc Edinb Sect B Biol**

Proceedings. Royal Society of Edinburgh. Section B. Natural Environment e: **Proc R Soc Edinb Nat Environ**, e: **Proc R Soc Edinb Sect B Nat Environ**, e: **P RS Edin B**

Proceedings. Royal Society of London. Series B. Biological Science e: **Proc R Soc Lond Biol**

Proceedings. Royal Society of London. Series B. Biological Sciences e: **Proc Roy Soc B**, e: **Proc Roy Soc London S B**, e: **Proc R Soc B**, e: **Proc R Soc Lond**, e: **Proc R Soc Lond B Biol Sci**, e: **P Roy Soc B**

Proceedings. Royal Society of Medicine e: **Proc Roy Soc Med**, e: **Pr[oc] R[oy] S[oc] Med**, e: **Proc R Soc Med**, e: **Proc Soc Med**, e: **P Roy S Med**, e: **Pr RS Med**, e: **PRSM**

Proceedings. Royal Society of Medicine. Supplement e: **Proc R Soc Med Suppl**

Proceedings. Royal Soeiety of Edinburgh. Section B. Biological Science e: **Proc R Soc Edinb Sect B**

Proceedings. Rudolf Virchow Medical Society in the City of New York e: **Proc Rudolf Virchow Med Soc[iety] NY**

Proceedings. San Diego Biomedical Symposium e: **Proc San Diego Biomed Symp**

Proceedings. Sea Grant Conference e: **Proc Sea Grant Conf**

Proceedings Series. American Water Resources Association e: **Proc Ser Am Water Resour Assoc**

Proceedings. Society for Experimental Biology and Medicine e: **Proc Soc Exp Biol Med**, e: **Proc Soc Exper Biol Med**, e: **Proc Soc Exp[er] Biol Med**, e: **Pr Soc Exp Biol Med**

Proceedings. Society for Experimental Biology and Medicine [New York] e: **Proc Soc Exp Biol [NY]**

Proceedings. Society for Industrial Microbiology e: **Proc Soc Ind Microbiol**

Proceedings. Society for the Study of Industrial Medicine e: **Proc Soc Study Ind Med**

Proceedings. Society for Water Treatment and Examination e: **Proc Soc Water Treat Exam**, e: **Pro Soc Water Treat Exam**

Proceedings. Society of Biological Chemists e: **Proc Soc Biol Chem**

Proceedings. Society of Biological Chemists of India e: **Proc Soc Biol Chem India**

Proceedings. Somerset Archaeology and Natural History Society e: **Proc Somerset Arch Natur Hist Soc**

Proceedings. South African Society of Animal Production e: **Proc S Afr Soc Anim Proc**

Proceedings. South London Entomological and Natural History Society e: **Proc South Lond Entom and Nat Hist Soc**

Proceedings. Southeast Asian Regional Seminar on Tropical Medicine and Public Health e: **Proc Southeast Asian Reg Semin Trop Med Public Health**

Proceedings. Southern Water Resources and Pollution Control Conference e: **Proc South Water Resour Pollut Control Conf**

Proceedings. Symposium on the Biology of Skin e: **Proc Symp Biol Skin**

Proceedings. Tall Timbers Conference on Ecological Animal Control by Habitat Management e: **Proc Tall Timbers Conf Ecol Anim Control Habitat Manage**

Proceedings. Tall Timbers Fire Ecology Conference e: **Proc Tall Timbers Fire Ecol Conf**

Proceedings. Technical Meeting. International Union for Conservation of Nature and Natural Resources e: **Proc Tech Mtg Int Union Conserv Nature**

Proceedings. Texas Water and Sewage Works Short School e: **Proc Tex Water Sewage Works Short Sch**

Proceedings. Texas Water Utilities Short School e: **Proc Tex Water Util Short Sch**

Proceedings. University of Missouri. Annual Conference on Trace Substances in Environmental Health e: **Proc Univ MO Annu Conf Trace Subst Environ Health**

Proceedings. University of Otago Medical School e: **Proc Univ Otago Med Sch**

Proceedings. Virchow-Pirquet Medical Society e: **Proc Virchow-Pirquet Med Soc**

Proceedings. Washington Animal Nutrition Conference e: **Proc Wash Anim Nutr Conf**

Proceedings. Western Poultry Disease Conference and Poultry Health Symposia e: **Proc West Poult Dis Conf Poult Health Symp**

Proceedings. Yorkshire Geological Society e: **Proc Yorks[hire] Geol Soc**

Proces-Verbaux des Seances. Société des Sciences Physiques et Naturelles de Bordeaux e: **Proces-Verb Seances Soc Sci Phys Nat Bordeaux**

Procesos de Hielo Marino, Ecosistemas y Clima del Antártico s: **ASPECT**

Process and Assembly Computerized Environment e: **PACE**

Process Cooling Water e: **PCW**

Process Cooling Water Returns e: **PCWR**

Process Oriented Observation Program e: **POOP**

Process Water e: **PW**

Process Water Diesel Generator e: **PWDG**

Process Water Gamma Monitor e: **PWGM**

Process Water Purification System e: **PWPS**

Process Water System e: **PWS**

Processed and Geocoded SAR data e: **L1B**

Processes and Resources of the Bering Sea Shelf e: **PROBES**

Processing and Manufacturing in Space [European Space Agency] e: **PAMIS**

Processing Graph Support Environment e: **PGSE**

Processor Interface Butier e: **PIB**

Processus de la glace de mer, écosystèmes et climat de l'Antarctique f: **ASPECT**

Produccion Animal s: **Produccion Anim**

Production Assurance/ Environment, Safety, and Health e: **PA/ES&H**

Production Environmental Test[s] [or Testing] e: **PET**

Production Laitiere Moderne f: **Prod Lait Mod**

Production Possibility Frontier e: **PPF**

produits naturels f: **PN**

Produktionsgenossenschaft werktätiger Pelztierzüchter d: **PwP**

Produktionswasser d: **PW**

Produzione Animale i: **Prod Anim**

Proeedings. Arkansas Water Works and Pollution Control Conference and Short School e: **Proc Arkansas Water Works Pollut Control Conf Short Sch**

Proeeedings. Brown University Symposium on the Biology of Skin e: **Proc Brown Univ Symp Biol Skin**

Profession Allied to Medicine e: **PAM**

Profession Medicale i: **Profession Med**

Professional Aeromedical Transport Association e: **PATA**

Professional Association of Georgia Educators e: **PAGE**

Professional Drivers Council for Safety and Health e: **PROD**

Professional Ecologist e: **PE**

Professional Geographer e: **Prof Geog**, e: **Prof Geogr**

Professional Geologist e: **PG**, e: **PGeol**, e: **Prof Geologist**

Professional Geophysicist e: **PG**

Professional Group on Medical Electronics e: **PGME**

Professional Group on Radio Telemetry and Remote Control e: **PGRTRC**

Professional Group on Space Electronics and Telemetry *e:* **PGSET**

Professional Group on Telemetry and Remote Control *e:* **PGTRC**

Professional Health Care of America, Inc. *e:* **PRCR**

Professional Medical Assistant *e:* **Prof Med Assist**

Professional Medical Film *e:* **PMF**

Professional Papers Series. Florida Department of Natural Resources. Marine Research Laboratory *e:* **Prof Pap Ser Fla Dep Nat Resour Mar Res Lab**

Professional Papers. United States Geological Survey *e:* **Prof Pap Geol Surv**, *e:* **Prof Pap US Geol Surv**

Professional Protector and Legal Defense Fund *e:* **PPLDF**

Professional Register of Traditional Chinese Medicine *e:* **PRTCM**

Professional Technical Group on Aerospace *e:* **PTGAS**

Professional Technical Group on Aerospace and Navigational Electronics *e:* **PTGANE**

Professions Supplementary to Medicine *e:* **PSM**

Professor of Aerospace Studies *e:* **PAS**

Profile of Medical Practice *e:* **Profile Med Pract**

Profile Telemetry of Upper Ocean Currents *e:* **PROTEUS**

profitieren *d:* **prof.**

profitiert *d:* **prof.**

PROFS Operational Weather Education and Research *e:* **POWER**

Prog Neuropsychopharmacol Biol Psychiatry *e:* **Progress in Neurobiology**

Progess in Neurobiology *e:* **Prog Neurobiol**

Program and Environmental Management *e:* **PEM**

Program Director for Weather and Flight Service Stations *e:* **ANW**

Program Environment[al] Checkout System *e:* **PECOS**

Program for Astronomical Research and Scientific Experiments Concerning Space *e:* **PARSECS**

Program for Climate Model Diagnosis and Intercomparison *e:* **PCMDI**

Program for Ecological Research *e:* **PER**

Program for Evaluation of Ground Environment *e:* **PEGE**

Program for Health Policy in Economies under Stress *e:* **PHPES**

Program for In-Orbital Rendezvous *e:* **PRIOR**

Program for Orbit Development *e:* **PROD**

Program for Rapid Earth-to-Space Trajectory Optimization *e:* **PRESTO**

Program for the Advancement of Geoscience Education *e:* **PAGE**

Program for the Refinement of Orbital Parameters *e:* **PROP**

Program Logical Address Space *e:* **PLAS**

Program Notes. Association of University Programs in Health Administration *e:* **Program Notes Assoc Univ Programs Health Adm**

Program Office Safety and Environmental Cost System *e:* **POSECS**

Program on water tables and irrigation *e:* **WHATIF**

Program Protect Flag *e:* **PPF**

Programa Biológico de Alta Mar *s:* **OBP**

Programa Biológico Internacional *s:* **PBI**

Programa de Acción Mundial para la Protección del Medio Marino Frente a las Actividades Realizadas en Tierra *s:* **GPA-LBA**

Programa de Aplicaciones de la Dinámica de la Tierra y el Océano *s:* **EODAP**

Programa de Aplicaciones de la Meteorología *s:* **PAM**

Programa de Cooperación para la Vigilancia y la Evaluación del Transporte de los Contaminantes Atmosféricos a Larga Distancia en Europa *s:* **EMEP**

Programa de Ecología, Pesquerías y Oceanografía del Golfo de México *s:* **EPOMEX**

Programa de Estudio y Observaciones Mundiales en Beneficio del Medio Ambiente *s:* **GLOBE**

Programa de Geología Marina del Brasil *s:* **PBGM**

Programa de Instrumentos y Métodos de Observación *s:* **PIMO**

Programa de Investigación sobre Meteorología Tropical *s:* **PIMT**

Programa de Investigación sobre Predicción Meteorológica a Corto y Medio Plazo *s:* **PPCP**

Programa de Investigación sobre Predicción Meteorológica a Largo Plazo *s:* **PPLP**

Programa de Meteorología Aeronáutica *s:* **PMAe**

Programa de Meteorología Agrícola *s:* **PMAg**

Programa de Meteorología Marina *s:* **PMM**

Programa de Reordenación Urbana y Protección Ecológica *s:* **PRUPE**

Programa de Resúmenes de Climatología Marina *s:* **MCSS**

Programa de Satélites Meteorológicos de Defensa *s:* **DMSP**

Programa de Servicios Meteorológicos al Público *s:* **PSMP**

Programa de Vigilancia Ecológica de los Océanos *s:* **ECOMONOC**

Programa Europeo de Climatología y Riesgos Naturales *s:* **EPOCH**

Programa Internacional de Correlación Geológica *s:* **PICG**

Programa Internacional sobre Cosechas de Tierras Aridas *s:* **IPALAC**

Programa Internacional sobre la Geosfera y la Biosfera Estudio de los Cambios a Escala Mundial *s:* **IGBP**

Programa Mundial de Estudios del Impacto del Clima *s:* **PMEC**

Programa Mundial de Evaluación de Impacto y Estrategias de Respuesta sobre el Clima *s:* **PMEIERC**

Programa Mundial sobre el Clima *s:* **PMC**

Programa Nacional sobre el Clima *s:* **PNC**

Programa Oceanográfico Nacional *s:* **NOP**

Programa Regional Meteorológico Marítimo *s:* **PRMM**

Programa sobre Oceanografía Física y Clima *s:* **POCCAR**

Programm des regionalen Anwendungs-zentrums für Agrometeorologie und operative Hydrologie und deren Anwendungsgebiete *d:* **AGRHYMET**

Programmable Etalon Spectrometer for Twilight Observations *e:* **PRESTO**

Programmable Remote Operation *e:* **PRO**

Programmatic Environmental Impact Statement *e:* **PEIS**

Programme biologique au large *f:* **OBP**

Programme Biologique International[e] *f:* **PBI**

Programme Climatologique Mondial *f:* **PCM**

Programme climatologique national *f:* **PCN**

Programme concerté de surveillance continue et dévaluation du transport à longue distance des polluants atmosphériques en Europe *f:* **EMEP**

Programme consacré à la recherche atmosphérique et à l'environnement *f:* **PRAE**

Programme Coordination Unit of the Black Sea Environmental Programme *e:* **PCU**

Programme d'action communautaire en matière de mobilité des étudiants *f:* **ERASMUS**

Programme d'action mondial pour la protection du milieu marin contre la pollution due aux activités terrestres *f:* **GPA-LBA**

Programme d'aménagement côtier *f:* **PAC**

Programme d'Analyse des Troupeaux Laitiers du Québec *f:* **PATLQ**

Programme d'assistance technique pour l'environnement méditerranéen *f:* **METAP**

Programme de formation concernant les changements climatiques *f:* **CC:Train**

Programme de Médicalisation des Systèmes d'Information Hospitaliers *f:* **PMSI**

Programme de recherche et de surveillance concernant la pollution de l'environnement *f:* **ENV**

Programme de recherches sur l'atmosphère globale *f:* **GARP**

Programme de résumés de climatologie maritime *f:* **MCSS**

Programme des instruments et des méthodes d'observation *f:* **PIMO**

Programme des Nations Unies pour l'environnement *f:* **PNUE**

Programme d'hydrologie et de mise en valeur des ressources en eau *f:* **PHRE**

Programme d'hydrologie opérationnelle *f:* **PHO**

Programme d'échange d'informations sur les changements climatiques *f:* **InfoCC**

Program[me] Environment[al] Control *e:* **PEC**

Programme européen en matière de climatologie et de risques naturels *f:* **EPOCH**

Program[me] for Algebraic Sequences Specifically of/on Input-Output Nature *e:* **PASSION**

Programme for an Operational Meteorological Information System *e:* **PROMIS**

[Programme for] Environmentally Sound Management of Inland Water[s] *e:* **EMINWA**

Program[me] for Geographiccal Display *e:* **PGD**

Program[me] for Investigation of Global Atmospheric Processes *e:* **PIGAP**

Program[me] for Linguistic Analysis of Natural Plants *e:* **PLANIT**

Program[me] for/of International Polar Oceans Research *e:* **PIPOR**

Program[me] for Rapid Earth-to-Space Trajectory Optimization *e:* **PRESTO**

Programme for the Promotion of Environmental Health *e:* **PEH**

Programme Hydrologique International *f:* **PHI**

Programme international concernant la chimie de l'atmosphère à l'échelle du globe *f:* **IGAC**

Programme International de Correlation Geologique *e:* **PICG**

Programme International de Corrélation Géologique *f:* **PICG**

Programme International d'Éducation relative à l'Environnement *f:* **PIEE**

Programme International sur la Géosphère et la Biosphère *f:* **PIGB**

Programme international sur les dimensions humaines des changements de l'environnement planétaire *f:* **IHDP**

Program[me] Logical Address Space *e:* **PLAS**

Programme mondial concernant l'étude des incidences du climat *f:* **PMIC**

Programme Mondial de Recherche sur le Climat *f:* **PMRC**

Programme mondial de surveillance du système climatique *f:* **PMSSC**

Programme mondial des applications et des services climatologiques *f:* **PMASC**

Programme mondial des données climatologiques et de surveillance du climat *f:* **PMDSC**

Programme mondial d'éducation et d'observation pour la défense de l'environnement *f:* **GLOBE**

Programme mondial d'évaluation des incidences du climat et de formulation de stratégies de parade *f:* **PMICSP**

Programme National de Recherche et de Développement en matière de Santé *f:* **PNRDS**

Programme National d'Études de la Dynamique du Climat *f:* **PNEDC**

Programme Océanographique National *f:* **PON**

Programme of Ecology, Fisheries and Oceanography of the Gulf of Mexico *e:* **EPOMEX**

Programme of International Nature management *e:* **PIN**

Programme of the Regional Training Centre for Agrometeorology and Operational Hydrology and their Applications *e:* **AGRHYMET**

Programme Officiel. Journce Interregionale de Recolte Mechanique du Mais-Grain *f:* **Progr Offic Journee Interreg Recolte Mec Mais-Grain**

Programme on Biological Diversity *e:* **DIVERSITAS**

Programme on Coastal Ocean Advanced Science and Technology Study *e:* **COASTS**

Programme on Coastal Ocean Circulation Dynamics and Fluxes *e:* **COCDYF**

Programme on Marine Arctic Ecology *e:* **PROMARE**

Programme on Physical Oceanography and Climate *e:* **POCCAR**

Programme on Short and Medium-Range Weather Prediction Research *e:* **PSMP**

Program[me] Operation and Environment Transfer *e:* **POET**

Programme pour l'environnement dans la Méditerranée *f:* **PEM**

Programme pour l'environnement de la mer Rouge et du golfe d'Aden *f:* **PERSGA**

Programme pour l'environnement des Caraïbes *f:* **CEP**

Programme régional océanien de l'environnement *f:* **PROE**

Programme sur l'environnement de la mer Noire *f:* **BSEP**

Programme sur les changements climatiques de l'Atlantique *f:* **ACCP**

Programme sur les dimensions sociales des changements de l'environnement planétaire *f:* **HDGECP**

Programme sur l'océanographie physique et le climat *f:* **POCCAR**

Programme that allows one to use a remote computer *e:* **telnet**

Programme zur Kontrolle des Medizinischen Sachbedarfs im Krankenhaus *d:* **PROMESA**

Programme Élargi et à Long terme d'exploration et de Recherches Océaniques *f:* **PELRO**

Programmed International Computer Environment *e:* **PRINCE**

Program[me][s] for Appropriate Technologies (or Technology) in Health *e:* **PATH**

Programming Environment *e:* **PE**

Programming Support Environment *e:* **PSE**

Progres en Obstetrique et Gynecologie *f:* **Prog Obstet Gynecol**

Progres en Virologie Medicale *f:* **Prog Virol Med**

Progres Medical *e:* **Prog Med**

Progres Medical [Paris] *f:* **Progres Med [Paris]**, *f:* **Progr Med [Paris]**

Progreso Medico [Habana] *s:* **Progreso Med [Habana]**

Progress in Aerospace Sciences *e:* **Prog Aerosp Sci**

Progress in Animal Biometeorology *e:* **Prog Anim Biometeorol**

Progress in Atomic Medicine *e:* **Prog At Med**

Progress in Biometeorology *e:* **Prog Biometeorol**

Progress in Biometeorology. Division A. Progress in Human Biometeorology *e:* **Prog Biometeorol Div A**

Progress in Biometeorology. Division B. Progress in Animal Biometeorology *e:* **Prog Biometeorol Div B**

Progress in Biophysics and Molecular Biology *e.* **Prog Biophys and Mol Biol**, *e:* **Prog Biophys Mol Biol**

Progress in Clinical and Biological Research *e:* **Prog Clin Biol Res**

Progress in Clinical Biochemistry and Medicine *e:* **Prog Clin Biochem Med**

Progress in Critical Care Medicine *e:* **Prog Crit Care Med**

Progress in Geography *e:* **Prog Geogr**

Progress in Gynecology *e:* **Prog Gynecol**

Progress in Human Biometeorology *e:* **Prog Hum Biometeorol**

Progress in Human Geography. International Review of Current Research *e:* **Progr Hum Geogr**

Progress in Immunobiological Standardization *e:* **Prog Immunobiol Stand**

Progress in Industrial Microbiology *e:* **Prog Ind Microbiol**, *e:* **Progr Indust Microbiol**

Progress in Leukocyte Biology *e:* **Prog Leukocyte Biol**

Progress in Medical Genetics *e:* **Prog Med Ge**, *e:* **Prog Med Genet**, *e:* **Progr. Med. Genet.**

Progress in Medical Parasitology in Japan *e:* **Prog Med Parasitol Jpn**

Progress In Medical Virology *e:* **Prog Med Vi**

Progress in Medical Virology *e:* **Prog Med Virol**, *e:* **Progr Med Virol**

Progress in Medicinal Chemistry *e:* **Prog Med Chem**

Progress in Medicine [Tokyo] *e:* **Prog Med [Tokyo]**

Progress in Molecular and Subcellular Biology *e:* **Prog Mol Subcell Biol**

Progress in Neuro-Psychopharmacology and Biological Psychiatry *e:* **Prog Neuro-Psychopharmacol&Biol Psychiatry**

Progress in Neurobiology [New York] *e:* **Prog Neurobiol [NY]**

Progress in Neurobiology [Oxford] *e:* **Prog Neurobiol [Oxf]**

Progress in Nuclear Energy. Series 6. Biological Sciences *e:* **Progr Nucl Energy Ser 6**

Progress in Nuclear Energy. Series 12. Health Physics *e:* **Prog Nucl Energy Ser 12**

Progress in Nuclear Energy. Series 7. Medical Sciences *e:* **Prog Nucl Energy Ser 7 Med Sci**

Progress in Nuclear Medicine *e:* **Prog Nucl Med**

Progress in Nucleic Acid Research and Molecular Biology *e:* **Prog Nucleic Acid Res Mol Biol**, *e:* **Progr. Nucl. Acid Res. Mol. Bi**

Progress in Oceanography *e:* **Prog Oceanogr**

Progress in Physical Geography *e:* **Prog Phys Geogr**

Progress in Psychobiology and Physiological Psychology *e:* **Prog Psychobiol Physiol Psychol**

Progress in Reproductive Biology *e:* **Prog Reprod Biol**

Progress in Reproductive Biology and Medicine *e:* **Prog Reprod Biol Med**

Progress in the Biological Sciences in Relation to Dermatology *e:* **Prog Biol Sci Relat Dermatol**

Progress in the Science and Technology of the Rare Earths *e:* **Progr. Sci. Technol. Rare Eart**, *e:* **Prog Sci Technol Rare Earths**

Progress in Theoretical Biology *e:* **Prog Theor Biol**

Progress in Underwater Science *e:* **Prog Underwater Sci**

Progress in Veterinary Microbiology and Immunology *e:* **Prog Vet Microbiol Immunol**

Progress in Water Technology *e:* **Prog Water Technol**

Progress Notes. Walter Reed Army Medical Center *e:* **Prog Notes Walter Reed Army Med Cent**

Progress Observation and Corrective Action *e:* **POCA**

Progressive Animal Welfare Society *e:* **PAWS**

progressive Pflegeordnung *d:* **PPO**

Progressive Space Forum *e:* **PSF**

Progresso Medico [Rome] *i:* **Prog Med [Rome]**

Progressus Medicinae [Istanbul] *l:* **Prog Med [Istanbul]**

Project Aerospace Plane *e:* **PAP**

Project for Estimation of Long-Term Variability in Ice Concentration *e:* **PELICON**

Project for Health Information Dissemination *e:* **PHID**

Project for Public Spaces *e:* **PPS**

Project. International Union for Conservation of Nature. World Wildlife Fund. Joint Project Operations *e:* **Project IUCN/Wld Wildl Fund**

Project: Long-term Dioxide and Water Vapour Fluxes of European Forests and Interactions with the Climate System *e:* **EUROFLUX EC**

Project Manager, Remotely Piloted Vehicle *e:* **PM-RPV**

Project on cross-national collaboration between adjacent border regions on the environment, tourism and transport *e:* **PAMINA**

Project on the development of renewable natural resources *e:* **RES**

Project Safety & Health Review *e:* **PSHR**

Project supported by the European Commission to evaluate the radiological impact of natural and anthropogenic radioactivity in the sea and to provide an overall view of the radiological exposure of the populations to sources of radioactivity in the sea *e:* **Marina**

Projected Intensity Triplet Space *e:* **PITS**

Projects in Controlled Environments *e:* **PRINCE**

Projekt Optische Geräte in der Medizin *d:* **OGM**

Projektgruppe Bayern zur Erforschung der Wirkung von Umweltschadstoffen *e:* **PBWU**

Projektierung *d:* **Proj.**

Projektierungs-, Konstruktions- und Montagebüro *d:* **PKM**

Projektierungs-, Konstruktions- und Montagebüro für Kohleverarbeitung *d:* **PKM-Kohleverarbeitung**

Projektierungs- und Konstruktionsbüro *d:* **PKB**

Projektierungs- und Konstruktionsbüro Kohle *d:* **PKB Kohle**

Projektierungsprozeß *d:* **PP**

projektierungsprozeßbezogener Datenspeicher *d:* **PDSP**

Projektierungsstufe *d:* **PS**

Projektierungssystematik *d:* **PS**

Projektierungsvorschrift *d:* **PV**

Projet de détection des changements climatiques *f:* **CCDP**

Projet de Gestion des Ressources Naturelles *f:* **PGRN**

Projet de Recherche pour l'Observation et la Gestion des Ressources Terrestres *f:* **PROGERT**

Projet d'Observation, de Surveillance et d'Études Intégrées de la Dynamique des Océans *f:* **POSEIDON**

Projet international d'établissement d'une climatologie des nuages à l'aide de données satellitaires *f:* **ISCCP**

Projet international d'établissement d'une climatologie des terres émergées au moyen de satellites *f:* **ISLSCP**

Projet majeur interrégional de l'UNESCO sur la recherche et la formation en vue de l'aménagement intégré des systèmes côtiers *f:* **COMAR**

Projet mondial de climatologie des précipitations *f:* **GPCP**

Projet pilote de surveillance continue de la pollution des mers [hydrocarbures] *f:* **MAPMOPP**

Projet pilote sur les études de base et la surveillance continue du pétrole et des hydrocarbures pétroliers dans les eaux marines *f:* **MED POL-I**

Projet pour une Agriculture Écologique *f:* **PAE**

Projet régional de recherche et de formation sur les systèmes côtiers de l'Amérique latine et des Caraïbes et leurs relations avec le plateau continen *f:* **COSALC**

Projet régional de recherche et de formation sur les systèmes côtiers marins en Afrique *f:* **COMARAF**

Projet `Services d'information sur le climat et prévision climatologique' *f:* **CLIPS**

Projeto RADAMBRASIL [Radar da Amazonia, Brasil]. Levantamento de Recursos Naturais *p:* **Proj RADAMBRAS Levantamento Recursos Nat**

Promet-Meteorologische Fortbildung *d:* **Promet-Meteorol Fortbild**

Promethazine Hydrochloride *e:* **PROMETH**

Promoting Ecological and Integral Development *e:* **PROECODI**

Promoting Health *e:* **PROH**, *e:* **Promot Health**

Promotion of Environmental Health *e:* **PEH**

Promotion of the Role of Women in Water and Environmental Sanitation Services *e:* **PROWESS**

Proof Test Orbiter *e:* **PTO**

Proof Test Spacecraft *e:* **PT-S/C**

Propagating Space Charge *e:* **PSC**

Propagation en Air Clair et Meteorologie *f:* **PACEM**

Propane-Vacuum-Hydrogen *e:* **PVH**

Propellant Engine Research Environmental Facility *e:* **PEREF**

propelling [water] screw *e:* **PROP, prop., prop**

Property Owners' Protection Association *e:* **P.O.P.A.**

Property Protected Area *e:* **PPA**

Property Protection Insurance *e:* **PPI**

Proposed Final Environmental Statement *e:* **PFES**

Propulsion Environmental Chamber *e:* **PEC**

Propulsion Research and Openwater Testing of Experimental Underwater System *e:* **PROTEUS**

Propulsion Research Environmental Chamber *e:* **PREC**

Propulsion Research Environmental Facility *e:* **PREF**

Prospect Hill Millimeter Wave Observatory *e:* **PHMWO**

Prospects for Extra-Mural and Clinical Information Systems Environment *e:* **PRECISE**

Prostaglandins and Medicine *e:* **Prostaglandins Med**

Prostaglandins, Leukotrienes and Medicine *e:* **Prostaglandins Leukotrienes Med**

Protección del Medio Ambiente para lograr una Tierra más Limpia *s:* **PEACE**

Protect *e:* **PR**, *e:* **PROT**, *e:* **PTCT**

Protect America's Children *e:* **PAC**

Protect Appalachian Wilderness *e:* **PAW**

Protect as Restricted Data *e:* **PARD**

Protect Each Other *e:* **PEO**

Protect Error *e:* **PTE**

Protect Life in All Nations *e:* **PLAN**

Protect Our Mountain Environment *e:* **POME**

Protect Our Nation's Youth *e:* **PONY**

Protect Our Pelican Society *e:* **POPS**

Protect Status *e:* **PS**

Protect the Innocent *e:* **PTI**

Protect the Queen *e:* **PTQ**

Protect Your Environment [groups] *e:* **PYE**

Protectable Mobilization Reserve Material Requirements *e:* **PMRMR**

Protectable Mobilization Reserve Materiel Objective *e:* **PMRMO**

Protecte Payments System *e:* **PPS**

protect[ed] *e:* **p**

Protect[ed] *e:* **prot**

Protected Area Information *e:* **PAI**

Protected Area Management Board *e:* **PAMB**

Protected Area Resource Centres *e:* **PARC**

Protected Area[s] *e:* **PA**

Protected Areas and Landscapes Programme *e:* **PALP**

Protected Areas Boundary Advisory Team *e:* **PABAT**

Protected Areas Co-ordinating Team *e:* **PACT**

Protected Areas Data Unit *e:* **PADU**

Protected Areas Programme *e:* **PROP**

Protected Areas Strategy *e:* **PAS**

Protected Areas Virtual Library *e:* **PAVL**

Protected Cable System *e:* **PCS**

Protected Code *e:* **P-Code**

Protected Difference Fat *e:* **PDF**

Protected Difference Milk *e:* **PDM**

Protected Distribution System *e:* **PDS**

Protected Extra Low Voltage *e:* **PELV**

Protected Home Circle Life Insurance Society *e:* **PHCLIS**

Protected Infantry Combat Vehicle *e:* **PICV**

Protected Natural Area Programme *e:* **PNAP**

Protected Natural Area programme e: **PNA programme**

Protected Outlet Box e: **POB**

Protected Partition Area e: **PPA**

Protected Personnel Carrier e: **PPC**

Protected Private Land e: **PPL**

Protected Process Cooling Water e: **PPCW**

Protected Process Water e: **PPW**

Protected Queue Area e: **PQA**

Protected Service Routine e: **PSR**

Protected Ship e: **PS**

Protected Storage e: **PS**

Protected Storage Address e: **PSA**

Protected Store e: **PS**

protected terminal block e: **PTB**

Protected Voice Portable Communications System e: **PVPCS**

Protected Wire[line] Distribution System e: **PWDS**

Protected Zone Joint Authority e: **PZJA**

Protecteur du Citoyen du Quebec, Ste.-Foy e: **QSTFP**

Protecting Steel with Zinc Dust Paints. Papers. Seminar e: **Prot Steel Zinc Dust Paints Pap Semin**

Protectio Vitae i: **Prot Vitae**

Protection e: **P**, e: **PRO**, e: **PROT**, e: **PROTEC**, e: **PRTCT**

Protection Actual e: **PROTA**

Protection & Advocacy e: **P&A**

Protection Aerienne f: **Prot Aer**

Protection Against Aircraft e: **PAC**

Protection, Amélioration, Conservation, Transformation de l'habitat [organisation] f: **PACT**

Protection and Defence Systems e: **PDS**

Protection and Indemnity e: **P and I**

protection and indemnity e: **p & i**

Protection and Indemnity Associations e: **P&I Clubs**

Protection and Indemnity Clause e: **P and I Clause**, e: **P & I Clause**

Protection and Indemnity club e: **P and I club**

Protection and Indemnity Club[s] e: **P&I Club[s]**

Protection and Indemnity of Oil Pollution Indemnity Clause e: **PIOPIC**

Protection and Preservation of the Marine Environment e: **PPME**

Protection Ballistic Limit e: **PBL**

Protection by Reflection Optics of Xerographic Images e: **PROXI**

Protection Civile f: **P.C.**

Protection Civile et Securite Industrielle f: **Prot Civ Secur Ind**

Protection Civile et Sécurité Industrielle f: **PCSI**

Protection Civile Française f: **PCF**

Protection de la Jeune Fille [Œuvre] f: **P.J.F.**

Protection de la nature f: **Prot. nat.**

Protection de l'enfance f: **PE**

Protection de l'environnement pour une Terre plus saine f: **PEACE**

Protection des Plantes et Environnement f: **PPE**

Protection des Végétaux f: **PV**

Protection Development International Corporation e: **PDIC**

Protection d'Établissement f: **PE**

Protection Earth e: **PE**

Protection Earth Neutral e: **PEN**

Protection Ecology e: **Prot Ecol**

Protection Engineers Group e: **PEG**

Protection et Defense de la Nature f: **PRODFINA**

Protection Factor e: **PF**

Protection Identification Key e: **PIT**

Protection & Indemnity e: **P&I**

Protection Index 3 e: **PI3**

Protection Interval e: **PI**

Protection Key e: **PK**

protection maternelle et infantile f: **PMI**

Protection Maternelle et Infantile [assistantes] f: **PMI**

Protection Mode Indicator e: **PMI**

Protection of Environment for Assuring Cleaner Earth e: **PEACE**

Protection of Metals e: **Prot Met**, e: **Prot Metals**

Protection of Metals [Union of Soviet Socialist Republics] e: **Prot Met [USSR]**

Protection of Persons Undergoing Medical Examination e: **POPUMET**

Protection of Reefs and Islands from Degradation and Exploitation e: **PRIDE**

Protection of the Arctic Marine Environment e: **PAME**

Protection of the Sea Levy e: **PSL**

Protection Survey Kit e: **PSK**

Protection System e: **POP**

Protection Technology Hanford e: **PTH**

Protection Technology Idaho e: **PTI**

Protection Technology Los Alamos e: **PTLA**

Protection Technology of Los Alamos e: **PT**

Protection Training Unit e: **PTU**

Protection Unearthed e: **PU**

Protection Water Quality Management e: **PWQM**

Protective e: **P**, e: **PROT**, e: **PROTCT**

Protective Action Zone e: **PAZ**

Protective Agent e: **PA**

protective antireflection [coating] e: **PVAR**

Protective Barrier Development Program e: **PBDP**

Protective Barrier Test Facility e: **PBTF**

Protective Clothing Arrangement e: **PCA**

Protective Coatings on Metals e: **PRCMC**, e: **Prot Coat Met**

Protective Connecting Arrangement e: **PCA**

Protective Cover e: **PRCR**

Protective Custody Unit e: **PCU**

Protective Device e: **PROT DEV**

Protective Dose e: **PD**

Protective Earth e: **PE**

Protective Equipment Decontamination e: **PED**

Protective Equipment Decontamination Facility e: **PEDF**

Protective Equipment Decontamination Section e: **PEDS**

Protective Force e: **PF**

Protective Force Services Subcontractor e: **PFSS**

Protective Ground e: **PG**

Protective Guideline e: **PG**

Protective Integrated Hood Mask e: **PIHM**

Protective Life Corp. e: **PROT**

Protective Maintenance e: **PM**

Protective Maintenance Procedure e: **PMP**

Protective Maintenance System e: **PMS**

Protective Mobilization Plan e: **PMP**

Protective Multiple Earthing e: **PME**

Protective Packaging Inc e: **PPI**

Protective Packaging Incorporated e: **PPI**

protective partial reflector e: **PPR**

Protective Reaction e: **PR**

Protective Research Section e: **PRS**

Protective Reservation Equipment e: **PRE**

protective response inducing substance e: **PRIS**

Protective Response Recommendation e: **PRR**

Protective Security e: **PS**

Protective Serum Dilution e: **PSD**

Protective Service Operations e: **PSO**

Protective Shielding Program e: **PSP**

protective silver e: **PS**

Protective Structures Development Center e: **PSDC**

Protective Structures Division e: **PSD**

Protective Work for Combat Areas e: **PROCOM**

Protector l: **PRO**, l: **PROT**, l: **PRT**

Protector Domesticus l: **PRO.DOM**

Protectorate e: **PROT**, e: **Protec**

Protectorate Regiment e: **PR**

Protectors of Our Rights e: **POOR**

Protestant Health and Welfare Assembly e: **PHWA**

Protides of the Biological Fluids. Proceedings of the Colloquium e: **Protides Biol Fluids Proc Colloq**

Protides of the Biological Fluids. Proceedings of the Colloquium [Bruges] e: **Protides Biol Fluids Proc Colloq [Bruges]**

Proto-Environmental Model e: **PEM**

Protocol Data Unit Programming Environment e: **PDUPE**

Protocol on Environment Protection of the Antarctic Treaty e: **PEPAT**

Protocol on Environmental Protection e: **PEP**

Protocol on Environmental Protection to the Antarctic Treaty e: **Antarctic-Environmental Protocol**

Protocol on Space requirements for Special Trade Passenger Ships e: **SPACE STP**

Proton Event Start Forecast [solar weather information] e: **PESTF**

Proton Polar Zone e: **PPZ**

Prototype Hydrofoil Gunboat e: **PHG**

Prototype Lunar Geologist Tool e: **PLGT**

Prototype Ocean Surveillance Terminal e: **POST**

Prototype Radiation Observation Experiment e: **PROBE**

Prototype Regional Observation and Forecasting Service e: **PROFS**

Proudman Oceanographic Laboratory e: **POL**

Provence Universite. Annales. Geologie Mediterraneenne f: **Provence Univ Ann Geol Mediterr**

Providence Hospital of Detroit. Medical Bulletin e: **Providence Hosp Detroit Med Bull**

Providence Hospital [Southfield, Michigan]. Medical Bulletin e: **Providence Hosp [Southfield Mich] Med Bull**

Providence-Saint Margaret Health Center, Kansas City e: **KKcP**

Provincial Association of Geography Teachers e: **PAGT**

Provincial Health Assistance Program e: **PHAP**

Provincial Public Health Nursing Services, Winnipeg, Manitoba e: **MWPPH**

Provincial Water Conservancy Bureau e: **PWCB**

Provinciale Intercommunale Drinkwatermaatschappij van de Provincie Antwerpen n: **PIDPA**

Provinciale Waterstaat n: **PW**

Provisional National Council for Mental Health e: **P.N.C.M.H.**

Proyecto de Cooperación en materia de Investigaciones Ecológicas s: **CERP**

Proyecto de Servicios de Información y Predicción del Clima s: **SIPC**

Proyecto Internacional de Arqueología y Recuperación de Datos Oceanográficos s: **GODAR**

Proyecto Internacional para Elaborar una Climatología de la Superficie Terrestre mediante Datos Satelitales s: **ISLSCP**

Proyecto Internacional para Elaborar una Climatología de las Nubes mediante Datos Satelitales s: **ISCCP**

Proyecto Mundial de Climatología de las Precipitaciones s: **GPCP**

proyector para observación en el mar s: **Proy O**

Prozesse im Schadstoffkreislauf Meer-Atmosphäre d: **PRISMA**

Prüflingsadaptierung d: **PLA**

Przedsiębiorstwo Geofizyki Przemysłu Naftowego P: **PGPN**

Przedsiębiorstwo Geologiczne P: **PG**

Przeglad Geofizyczny P: **PRGEA**, P: **Przegl Geofiz**

Przeglad Geograficzny P: **Przeglad Geog**, P: **Przegl Geogr**

Przeglad Geograficzny/Polish Geographical Review P: **Przegl Geogr Pol Geogr Rev**

Przeglad Geologiczny P: **Przegl Geol**, P: **PRZGA**

Przeglad Meteorologiczny i Hydrologiczny P: **Przegl Met Hydrol**

Prévention Routière Internationale f: **PRI**

Prévision Ameliorée et Techniques d'affinement de la Climatologie f: **PATAC**

Pseudoephedrine Hydrochloride e: **PSEUDOEPH**

Psychiatrie, Neurologie und medizinische Psychologie d: **Psychiat. Neurol. med. Psychol**

Psychiatrische Observationsklinik d: **POK**

psychobiological e: **psychobio**

psychobiologist e: **psychobio**

psychobiology e: **psychobio**

psychogeographer e: **psychogeog**

Psychogeographic e: **PSYCHOGEOG**

psychogeographlc[al] e: **psychogeog**

psychogeography e: **psychogeog**

Psychological, Atmospheric and Weather Sciences e: **PAWS**

Psychological Medicine e: **Psychol Med**

Psychological Medicine. Monograph Supplement e: **Psychol Med Monogr Suppl**

Psychological & Medico-Legal Journal e: **Psych.&M.L.J.**

Psychologisch-Medizinische Untersuchungsstelle d: **PMU**

Psychosomatic Medicine e: **Psychosom Med**

Psychosomatische Medizin d: **PYM**, e: **PSM**

Psychosoziale Medizin e: **PSZ**

Psychosurgeon e: **PSYCHOSURG**

Psychotherapeutische Medizin e: **PTH**

Psychotherapie, Psychosomatik, Medizinische Psychologie d: **Psychother Psychosom Med Psychol**

PTS-WAF-Symposium für Wasser- und Umwelttechnik d: **PTS-WAF**

Public Broadcasting Environment Center e: **PBEC**

Public Citizen Health Research Group e: **PCHRG**

Public Environment Report e: **PER**

Public Health e: **PH**

Public Health Act e: **P.H.A.**

Public Health Alliance e: **PHA**

Public Health and Tropical Medicine e: **PHTM**

Public Health Association e: **PHA**

Public Health Association of Australia e: **PHA**

Public Health Bibliography e: **PHB**

Public Health Cancer Association of America e: **PHCAA**

Public Health Committee e: **PHC**

Public Health Common Data Set e: **PHCDS**

Public Health Department e: **PHD**

Public Health Doctor e: **P.H.D.**

Public Health Education e: **PHE**

Public Health Education and Research Program e: **PHERP**

Public Health Engineer e: **P.H.E.**, e: **PH Eng**

Public Health Engineering Abstracts e: **PHEA**

Public Health Evaluation e: **PHE**

Public Health Evaluation Manual e: **PHEM**

Public Health Foundation e: **PHF**

Public Health Image Library e: **PHIL**

Public Health Inspector e: **PHI**

Public Health Institute e: **P.H.I.**

Public Health Institute-London Action Group e: **PHILAG**

Public Health Laboratory e: **PHL**

Public Health Laboratory Information System e: **PHLIS**

Public Health Laboratory Service e: **PHLS**

Public Health Laboratory Service Board e: **PHLSB**

Public Health Law e: **PHL**

Public Health Leadership Institutes e: **PHLI**

Public Health Library e: **PUBL**

Public Health Network e: **PHN**

Public Health Nurse e: **PHN**

Public Health Nursing e: **PHN**, e: **Public Health Nurs**

Public Health Plan e: **PHP**

Public Health Policy Unit e: **PHPU**

Public Health Practice Program Office e: **PHPPO**

Public Health Prevention Service e: **PHPS**

Public Health Reports e: **PHR**, e: **Public Health Rep**

Public Health Research Institute e: **PHRI**

Public Health Resource Unit e: **PHRU**

Public Health Review Evaluation Database e: **PHRED**

Public Health Reviews e: **Public Health Rev**

Public Health Risk e: **PHR**

Public Health Risk Evaluation Data Base e: **PHRED**

Public Health Service e: **PHS**, e: **USPHS**

Public Health Service Act e: **PHSA**

Public Health Service, Court Decisions e: **Pub. Health U.S.**

Public Health Service Publications e: **PHSP**

Public Health Standards e: **PHS**

Public Health Statement e: **PHS**

Public Health Training Network e: **PHTN**

Public Health Unit e: **PHU**

Public Protection and Disaster Relief e: **PDDR**, e: **PPDR**

Public Remote-Access Computer Standards Association e: **PRACSA**

Public Responsibility in Medicine and Research e: **PRIM&R**

Public Safety and Resource Protection Program e: **PSRPP**

Public Voice for Food and Health Policy e: **PVFHP**

Public Water Supply e: **PWS**

Public Water Supply System e: **PWSS**

Public Water System e: **PWS**

Public Water System Supervision Program e: **PWSSP**

Public Weather Services Programme e: **PWSP**

Publication. Utah Geological Association e: **UGAPB**

Publications de l'École Moderne Française f: **PEMF**

Publications. Dominion Observatory e: **ODOPA**

Publications in Climatology e: **PC**

Publicity-Owned [wastewater] Treatment Works e: **POTW**

Publizistische Arbeitsgemeinschaft für Medizin d: **PAM**

Puerto Rican (or Rico) Water Resources Authority e: **PRWRA**

Puerto Rico Commonwealth. Water Resources Bulletin e: **PR Commonw Water Resour Bull**

Puerto Rico Health Bulletin e: **PR Health Bull**

Puerto Rico Health Sciences Journal e: **PR Health Sci J**

Puerto Rico Information and Decision Environment e: **PRIDE**

Puerto Rico. Water Resources Bulletin e: **PR Water Resour Bull**

Puesto de mando y observación s: **PMO**

Puesto de observación s: **PO**, s: **POBS**

Puesto de observación antiaéreo s: **POAA**

Puesto de observación aérea s: **PO AER**

Puesto de observación costero s: **POC**

Puesto de observación de la red de observadores terrestres s: **POOT**

Puesto de observación de minas s: **PO Min**

Puesto de observación ingeniero s: **POI**

Puesto de observación móvil s: **PO Mov**

Puesto de observación técnica s: **POT**

Puesto de recolección de la técnica s: **PRTA**

Puesto secreto [de observación] s: **P Sec**

Puffendorf's Law of Nature e: **Puffendorf.**

Puffendorf's Law of Nature and Nations e: **Puf.**, e: **Puffendorf.**

Pulaski Area Geographic Information System e: **PAGIS**

Pulletop Nature Reserve e: **PNR**

Pulsated Overheated [Hot] Water Rocket e: **POHWARO**

pulse-code modulated/polarized light e: **pcm/pl**

Pulse-Polarized Binary Modulation e: **PPBM**

Pulse Polarography e: **PP**

Pulse Power MagnetoHydrodynamic e: **PPMMHD**

Pulse RADAR Intelligent Diagnostic Environment e: **PRIDE**

Pulse Signature Classification System e: **PSCS**

Pulsed Plasma Magnetohydrodynamic e: **PPMHD**

Pump, Chilled Water e: **PCW**

Pump, Coolant Water e: **PCW**

Pump, Deionized Water e: **PDW**

Pump, Domestic Hot water e: **PDH**

Pump, Hot Water e: **PHW**

Pump, Sealant Water e: **PSW**

Pungo National Wildlife Refuge e: **PINWR**, e: **PNWR**

Pupil Observation Survey e: **POS**, e: **POSR**

Purchase Request/Military Interdepartmental Purchase Request e: **PR/MIPR**

Purdue Remote On-line Console System e: **PROCSY**

Purdue University's Weather Processor software for analyzing and displaying meteorological data e: **WXP**

Pure and Applied Geophysics. Basel e: **PAGEOPH**

Pure Water Preservation Society e: **PWPS**

Purge Water Activity Database e: **PWADB**

Purge Water Treatment and Storage Facility e: **PWTSF**

Purley Natural History and Scientific Society e: **P.N.H.S.S.**

Puromycin Dihydrochloride e: **PDH**

Puromycindihydrochlorid d: **PDH**

Purple Mountain Observatory, Academia Sinica, Nanjing e: **PMO**

Pusat Penelitian dan Pengembangan Biologi in: **PPPB**

Pusat Penelitian dan Pengembangan Geologi in: **PPPG**, ma: **PPPG**

Pushbroom Airborne Infrared Remote Sensor e: **PAIRS**

Put Under Observation e: **PUO**

Putnam Memorial Hospital, Medical Library, Bennington e: **VtBennP**

Pyrrolidone Hydrotribromide e: **PHT**

Pyruvate Dehydrogenase e: **PDH**

Pyruvate Kinase/Lactic Dehydrogenase d: **PK/LDH**

Période d'observation intensive f: **IOP**

Période d'observation spéciale f: **POS**

Q

Qatar Sea Arm e: **QSA**

QJM [Quarterly Journal of Medicine]: Monthly Journal of the Association of Physicians e: **QJM**

Quaderni de Clinica Ostetrica e Ginecologica i: **Quad Clin Ostet Ginecol**

Quaderni di Clinica Ostetrica e Ginecologica i: **Quad Clin Ostet**

Quaderni di Geofisica Applicata i: **Quad Geofis Appl**

Quaderni di Storia della Scienza e della Medicina. Universita degli Studi di Ferrara i: **Quad Storia Sci Med Univ Studi Ferrara**

Quaderni. Sezione Perugina. Societa Italiana di Biologia Sperimentale i: **Quad Sez Perugina Soc Ital Biol Sper**

Quadrangle Series 1:50.000. Geological Survey of Japan e: **Quadrangle Ser 1:50000 Geol Surv Jap**

Quadripartite Chemical, Biological, Radiological Standardization Committee e: **QCSC**

Quadripartite Working Group on Surveillance and Target Acquisition/Night Observation e: **QWG/STANO**

Quaestiones Geobiologicae l: **Quaest Geobiol**

Quaestiones Naturales e: **QNat**

Qualified Medicare Beneficiary e: **QMB**

Qualified Mental Health Professional e: **QMHP**

Quality and Safety in Health Care e: **QSHC**

Quality Assurance and Environmental Monitoring Laboratory e: **QAEML**

Quality Assurance Environment[al] Test[ing] e: **QAET**

Quality Assurance of Medical Standards e: **QAMS**

Quality Assurance Spacecraft Acceptance Center e: **QASAC**

Quality Control of Medicines. Proceedings. International Congress of Pharmaceutical Sciences e: **Qual Control Med Proc Int Congr Pharm Sci**

Quality Criteria for Water e: **QCW**

Quality, Environment, Safety & Health Assurance Division e: **QESHA**

Quality, Environmental, and Safety Tracking system e: **QUEST**

Quality Health New Zealand e: **QHNZ**

Quality in Health Care e: **QHC**

Quality of Groundwater. Proceedings. International Symposium e: **Qual Groundwater Proc Int Symp**

Quality of water e: **QW**

Quality, safety and health programs division e: **QSH**

Quality Use of Medicine e: **QUM**

Quantitative Environmental Science and Technology e: **QUEST**

Quantitative Oceanographic Data e: **QOD**

Quantity of biomass cleared annually from natural forests e: **Fr**

quantity of water discharged e: **Q**

Quantum Health Resources e: **QHRI**

Quantum HydroDynamic e: **QHD**

Quantum Statistical Mechanics in the Natural Sciences e: **Quantum Stat Mech Nat Sci**

Quarantine and Animal Health Committee e: **QAHC**

Quarries and Mines Other than Coal. Health and Safety e: **Quarries Mines Coal Health Saf**

quarter ocean net e: **qon**

Quarter-orbit Magnetic Altitude Control e: **QMAC**

Quarter Orbit Magnetic Attitude Control e: **QOMAC**

Quarterdeck d: **Q**, d: **QD**

Quarterdeck Office Systems e: **QDEK**

Quarterdeck Qemm e: **.QDK**

Quarterdeck's Antivirus Research Center e: **QUARC**

Quarterdeck[s] Expanded (or Extended) Memory Manager e: **QEMM**

Quarterly Bulletin. Geo-Heat Utilization Center e: **Q Bull Geo-Heat Util Cent**

Quarterly Bulletin. Health Organisation. League of Nations e: **Q Bull Health Organ League Nations**

Quarterly Bulletin. Indiana University. Medical Center e: **Q Bull Indiana Univ Med Cent**

Quarterly Bulletin. Northwestern University. Medical School e: **Q Bull Northwest Univ Med Sch**, e: **Q Bull NWest Univ Med Sch**, e: **Q[uart] Bull Northwest[ern] Univ M[ed] Sch[ool]**

Quarterly Bulletin. Sea View Hospital e: **Q Bull Sea View Hosp**

Quarterly Cumulative Index Medicus e: **QCIM**, e: **Q.C.Ind.Med.**, e: **Q Cum Index Med**

Quarterly Journal. Geological, Mining and Metallurgical Society [India] e: **Q J Geol Min Metall Soc [India]**

Quarterly Journal. Geological Society of London e: **Q J Geol Soc Lond[on]**

Quarterly Journal of Engineering Geology e: **QJ Eng Geol**

Quarterly Journal of Experimental Physiology and Cognate Medical Sciences e: **Q J Exp Physiol**, e: **Q J Exp Physiol Cogn Med Sci**

Quarterly Journal of Medicine e: **Q J Med**, e: **Quaart J Med**

Quarterly Journal of medicine e: **Quart.Journ.of med.**

Quarterly Journal of Nuclear Medicine e: **Q J Nucl Med**

Quarterly Journal of the Royal Meteorological Society e: **QJRMS**

Quarterly Journal of Veterinary Science in India and Army Animal Management e: **Quart J Vet Sc India**

Quarterly Journal. Royal Meteorological Society e: **Q Jl R Met Soc**, e: **QJRMA**, e: **Q J R Meteo[rol Soc]**, e: **Quart J Roy Meteorol Soc**

Quarterly. Los Angeles County Museum of Natural History. Los Angeles e: **LACMNH/Q.**

Quarterly Medical Review e: **Q Med Rev**

Quarterly. National Fire Protection Association e: **Q Natl Fire Prot Assoc**

Quarterly News Bulletin. Geological Society of South Africa e: **Q News Bull Geol Soc S Afr**

Quarterly Newsletter. Special Committee on Environmental Law e: **Q Newl-Spec Comm Env L**

Quarterly Review of Biology e: **QRB**, e: **QRBIA**, e: **Q R Biol**, e: **Quar R Biol**, e: **Quart Rev Biol**

Quarterly Review of Medicine e: **Q Rev Med**

Quarterly Review of Obstetrics and Gynecology e: **Q Rev Obstet Gynecol**

Quarterly Review of Surgery. Obstetrics and Gynecology e: **Q Rev Surg Obstet Gynecol**

Quarterly Review on Environment e: **Q Rev Environ**

Quartermaster Water-Repellent Clothing e: **QUARPEL**

quartermaster waterrepellent e: **quarpel**

Quartier d: **Q**, d: **Qu.**, d: **Quart.**

quartier f: **Q-r**

Quartier de Securité Renforcée f: **QSR**

Quartier General e: **QG**

Quartier Generale i: **QG**

Quartier Général f: **QG**

Quartier Général d'Armée f: **Q.G.A.**

Quartier général de guerre f: **QGG**

Quartier Général de la Défense Nationale f: **QGDN**

Quartier Général de la Région du Nord f: **QGRENOR**

Quartier Général des Forces Atlantiques f: **Q.G.F.A.**

Quartier Latin f: **QL**

Quartiermeister d: **Q**, d: **QM**, d: **Q.-Mstr.**, d: **Qu.**

Quartiermeister-Material d: **Qm.-Material**

Quartiermeistertruppenschule d: **QMTrS**

quartiers excentriques f: **QE**

Quartierzentrum Kanzlei d: **QZK**

Quasi-Geostrophic Analysis e: **QG**

Quasi-Nonhydrostatic model e: **QNH**

Quaternary Environment[s] of the Eurasian North e: **QUEEN**

Quaternary Geological Atlas e: **QGA**

Quebec. Conseil de la Recherche et du Développement Forestiers. Rapport f: **Que Cons Rech Dev For Rapp**

Quebec. Conseil de la Recherche et du Développement Forestiers. Rapport Annuel f: **Que Cons Rech Dev For Rapp Annu**

Quebec. Department of Natural Resources. Geological Report e: **Que Dep Natur Resour Geol Rep**

Quebec. Department of Natural Resources. Preliminary Report e: **Quebec Dept Nat Resources Prelim Rept**, e: **Que Dep Natur Resour Prelim Rep**

Quebec. Department of Trade and Commerce. Geographical Service. Publication e: **Quebec Dept Trade and Commerce Geog Service Pub**

Quebec. Direction de la Geologie. Travaux sur le Terrain f: **Que Dir Geol Trav Terrain**

Quebec Hydro-Electric Commission e: **Q**

Quebec Laitier e: **Qu Lait**

Quebec. Ministere de l'Energie et des Ressources. Service de la Recherche Forestiere. Memoire f: **Que Minist Energ Ressour Serv Rech For Mem**

Quebec. Ministere de l'Industrie et du Commerce. Service de Biologie. Rapport Annuel f: **Que Minist Ind Commer Serv Biol Rapp Annu**

Quebec. Ministere des Richesses Naturelles. Etude Speciale f: **Que Minist Richesses Nat Etude Spec**

Quebec [Province]. Department of Natural Resources. Special Paper e: **Qu [Prov] Dep Nat Resour Spec Pap**

Quebec [Province]. Ministere des Richesses Naturelles. Rapport Preliminaire e: **Que [Prov] Minist Richesses Nat Rapp Prelim**

Quebec Society for the Protection of Plants e: **QSPP**

Quebec Society for the Protection of Plants. Report e: **Que Soc Prot Plants Rep**, e: **Que Soc Prot Plants Rep**

Quebec Sturgeon River Mines Ltd. e: **QSR**, e: **QSRT**

Queen's Honorary Dental Surgeon e: **QHDS**

Queen's Honorary Surgeon e: **Q.H.S.**

Queen's Polar Medal e: **QPM**

Queen's University, Medical Library e: **QUM**

Queensland Association for Mental Health e: **QAMH**

Queensland Conservation Council and Environment Centre e: **QCCEC**

Queensland Department of Environment and Heritage e: **QDEH**

Queensland. Department of Mines. Geological Survey of Queensland. Publication e: **Queensl Dep Mines Geol Surv Queensl Publ**

Queensland. Department of Mines. Geological Survey of Queensland. Report e: **Queensl Dep Mines Geol Surv Queensl Rep**

Queensland. Department of Primary Industries. Division of Animal Industry. Bulletin e: **Queensl Dep Primary Ind Div Anim Ind Bull**

Queensland Environmental Program e: **QEP**

Queensland Geographical Journal e: **Qd Geogr J**, e: **Q Geog J**, e: **Qld Geogr J**, e: **Queensl Geogr J**

Queensland. Geological Survey 1:250 000 Geological Series e: **Qd Geol Surv 1:250 000 Geol Ser**

Queensland. Geological Survey. 1:250.000 Geological Series e: **Queensl Geol Surv 1:250000 Geol Ser**

Queensland. Geological Survey. Publication e: **Queensl Geol Surv Publ**

Queensland. Geological Survey. Report e: **Qd Geol Surv Rep**, e: **Queensl Geol Surv Rep**

Queensland Geology e: **Queensl Geol**

Queensland Institute of Medical Research e: **QIMR**

Queensland Journal of Agricultural and Animal Sciences e: **Qd J Agric Anim Sci**, e: **QJAAS**, e: **Queensland J Agr Anim Sci**, e: **Queensl J Agric Anim Sci**

Queensland National Parks and Wildlife Authority e: **QNPWA**

Queensland National Parks and Wildlife Service e: **QNPWS**

Queensland Naturalist e: **Qd Nat**, e: **Qld Nat**, e: **Queensl Nat**

Queensland Naturalists' Club e: **Q.N.C.**

Queensland Remote Sensing Information Note e: **QRSIN**

Queensland Space Frontier Society e: **QSFS**

Queensland University. Department of Geology. Papers e: **Queensl Univ Dep Geol Pap**

Queensland Women's Health Network e: **QWHN**

Queensland's Health e: **Q Health**, e: **Qld Health**

Quellenorientiertes Informationssystern d: **QIS**

quellenorientiertes Informationszentrum d: **QIZ**

Query Optimization in a Protective Environment e: **QOPE**

Quest Medical, Inc. e: **QMED**

Quetico-Superior Wilderness Research Center. Annual Report e: **Quetico-Super Wilderness Res Cent Annu Rep**

Quetico-Superior Wilderness Research Center. Technical Note e: **Quetico-Super Wilderness Res Cent Tech Note**

Quick Medical Reference e: **QMR**

Quick-Reaction Space Laboratory e: **QRSL**

quiet observation aircraft e: **Q-star**

Quinnipiac Health Law Journal e: **Quinnipiac Health L.J.**

Quinte Health Care e: **QHC**

quittieren d: **quitt.**

Quittieren Hörmelder d: **QH**

Quittieren Sichtmelder d: **QS**

quittiert d: **qu.**, d: **quitt.**

quittierter Erstwert d: **QEW**

quittierter Neuwert d: **QN**

Quittierung d: **Q**

Quivira National Wildlife Refuge e: **QNWR**

R

Raboty i Issledovaniya. Institut Meteorologii i Gidrologii. Chast 2. Gidrologiya R: **Rab Issled Inst Meteorol Gidrol Chast 2**

Raboty Tyan-Shan'skoi Fiziko-Geograficheskoi Stantsii. Akademiya Nauk Kirgizskai SSR R: **Rab Tyan-Shan Fiz-Geogr Sta**

Raboty Tyan-Shan'skoi Fiziko-Geograficheskoi Stantsii. Akademiya Nauk Kirgizskoi SSR R: **Rab Tyan Shan'skoi Fiz Geogr Stn Akad Nauk Kirg SSR**

Raccoglitore Medico Fano Forli i: **Raccoglitore Med Forli**

rack for space stage group for digital exchange 5 e: **R:SSG:DE5**

Rada Ochrony Powietrza Atmosferycznego P: **ROPA**

RADAR Automatic Weather System e: **RAWS**

Radar d'Observation et de Designation d'Objectifs f: **RODEO**

Radar Environment Simulation e: **RES**

Radar Environment Simulator e: **RES**

Radar Environment Simulator System e: **RESS**

Radar-equipped Ocean Reconnaissance Satellites e: **RORSATS**

Radar Observation of Bird Intensivity and Notification e: **ROBIN**

Radar Ocean Reconnaissance Satellite e: **RORS**, e: **RORSAT**

Radar Ocean Surveillance Satellite e: **RORSAT**

Radar Protection System e: **RAPS**

Radar Remote Weather Display System e:
RRWDS
Radar Sea Clutter e: **RSC**
Radar Sea State Analyser [or Analyzer] e:
RASSAN
Radar-Signatur-Mess- und Analyseanlage
d: **RaSigma**
Radar Signature Analysis e: **RSA**
Radar Target Signature Analysis e: **RTSA**
Radar weather Report e: **RAREP**
RADARSAT International Remote Sensing
Institute e: **RSI**
Radiation and Environmental Biophysics
e: **Radiat and Environ Biophys**, e:
Radiat Env, e: **Radiat Environ Biophys**
Radiation and Meteoroid Satellite e: **RMS**
Radiation Biological Effectiveness e: **RBE**
Radiation Biological Equivalent e: **RBE**
Radiation Biology e: **Radiat Biol**
Radiation Biology Institutes e: **RBI**
Radiation Biology Laboratory e: **RBL**
Radiation Control for Health and Safety Act
e: **RCHSA**
Radiation Health Information Project e:
RHIP
Radiation Hydrodynamics e: **RH**
Radiation-Induced Thermally Activated
Depolarization e: **RITAD**
Radiation Medicine e: **Radiat Med**
Radiation Medicine Centre e: **RMC**
Radiation Meteorid Satellite e: **RM**
Satellite
Radiation/Meteoroid e: **R/M**
Radiation Office [Environmental Protection
Agency] e: **RO**
Radiation Polarization Measurement e:
RPM
Radiation protection e: **DG XI-C1**, e: **DG**
XII-F6
Radiation Protection e: **Radiat Prot**, e:
RP
Radiation Protection Act e: **RPA**
Radiation Protection Advisor e: **RPA**
Radiation Protection Bureau e: **RPB**
Radiation Protection Dosimetry e: **Radiat**
Prot Dosim
Radiation Protection Guide e: **RPG**
Radiation Protection. ICRP e: **Radiat Prot**
ICRP Publ
Radiation Protection in Australia e:
Radiat Prot Aust
Radiation Protection Officer e: **RPO**
Radiation Protection Program e: **RPP**
Radiation Protection [Seoul] e: **Radiat**
Prot [Seoul]
Radiation Protection Standard e: **RPS**
Radiation Protection Supervisor e: **RPS**
Radiation Protection [Taiyuan,People's
Republic of China] e: **Radiat Prot**
[Taiyuan People's Repub China]
Radiation Protection Technician (or
Technologist) e: **RPT**
Radiation Safety Section, Dept. of Health &
Community Services e: **RSS**
Radiation Signature Measurement e: **RSM**
Radiative-Convective-Atmospheric e:
RCA
Radiative Input from the Sun to the Earth
Program e: **SunRISE**
Radiative Inputs from Sun to Earth e:
RISE
Radiatsionnaia Biologiia, Radioecologiia
R: **Radiats Biol Radioecol**

Radical Community Medicine e: **Radiral**
Commun Med
Radio and Space Research e: **R and SRE**,
e: **R&SRE**
Radio and Space Research Station e:
RSRS
Radio Astronomical Observatory e: **RAO**
Radio Astronomical Space System of
Aperture Synthesis e: **RASSAS**
Radio Atmospheric Study Centre e: **RASC**
Radio-Frequency Protection Guide e:
RFPG
Radio Ice Cerenkov Experiment e: **RICE**
Radio North-Sea International e: **RNI**
Radio Optical Observatory e: **ROO**
Radio Remote Control e: **RRC**
Radio remote PickUp system e: **RPU**
Radio-Sonde Observation e: **RSO**
radio subscriber number protection e:
RASNP
radio telemetry and remote control e: **rtrc**
Radio Telescope in Orbit e: **RATIO**
Radio Weather Intercept Element e:
RAWIE
Radioactive Health Data e: **RHD**
Radioactive Waste Disposal. Research
Series. Institute of Geological Sciences
e: **Radioact Waste Disposal Res Ser Inst**
Geol Sci
Radioactivity in the Sea e: **Radioact Sea**
Radioactivity (or Radioactive)
Environmental Monitoring e: **REM**
Radioatmospherics e: **RA**
Radiobiologia-Radioterapia p:
Radiobiol-Radiother, p: **Radiobiol-**
Radiother [Berlin]
Radiobiologia si Biologia Moleculara e:
RABMA
Radiobiologia,Radioterapia e Fisica Medica
p: **Radiobiol Radioter Fis Med**
Radiobiologica Latina l: **Radiobiol Lat**
Radiobiological Research Unit e: **RRU**
Radiobiologiya Informatsionnyi Byulleten'
R: **Radiobiol Inf Byull**
Radiobiology e: **RADBIOL**, e: **RB**
Radiobiology/Environmental Health
Laboratory e: **RE**
Radiobiológiya R: **Radiobiol**
Radioecology Programme e: **RAD**
Radioecology research program e: **RAD**
Radioekologiya Vodnykh Organizmov R:
Radioekol Vodn Org
radiofrequencypolarography e: **RFP**
Radioisotope Medicine e: **RIM**
Radiologia Clinica et Biologica p:
RCBOA
Radiologia Medica e: **RAMEA**, i: **Radiol**
Med
Radiological Advisory Medical Team e:
RAMT
Radiological and Environmental Sciences
Laboratory e: **RESL**
Radiological-Chemical-Biological Warfare
e: **RCBW**
Radiological Emergency Medical Teams e:
REMT
Radiological Environmental Monitoring
Laboratory e: **REML**
Radiological Ground Water e: **RGW**
Radiological Health e: **RH**
Radiological Health Data and Reports e:
Radiol. Health Data Rep., e: **RHD and**
R, e: **RHD&R**

Radiological Health Laboratory e: **RHL**
Radiological North Sea Project e:
RANOSP
Radiological Protection e: **RP**
Radiological Protection Mexican
Association e: **SMSR**
Radiological Protection Service e: **RPS**
Radiology Assembly of Medical Group
Management Association e: **RA**
Radiometeorograph Observation e:
RAOBS
Radioprotection e: **RAPRB**
Radiosonde Observation e: **RAOB**, e:
RASONDE
Radiosonde-observation Data e: **RADAT**
Radiosonde Observation Icing at ... e:
RAICG
Rahmenübereinkommen der Vereinten
Nationen über Klimaänderungen d:
UNFCCC
Raid Air Protection e: **RAP**
Rail and Ocean e: **R and O**
rail and ocean e: **r&o**
Rail and Water e: **R and W**
rail and water e: **r&w**
Rail International Design [and]
Environment e: **RIDE**
Rail-Water e: **RAWA**, e: **R-W**
Rail-Water-Rail e: **RAWARA**
rail-water-rail e: **r-w-r**
Rain Water Pipe e: **RWP**
Rainforest Health Project e: **RHP**
rainwater conductor e: **rwc**
raised quarterdeck[ing] e: **r qd**
raised watertight hatch e: **R.W.T.H.**
Rajasthan Medical Journal e: **Rajasthan**
Med J
Rajput Frontier Force Rifles e: **R.F.F.**
Rifles
Raketentechnik und Raumfahrtforschung
d: **Raketentech Raumfahrtforsch**
Raketenwasserbombe d: **RWB**
Raketenwasserbomben-Abschußgerät d:
RWBAg
Raman Water Vapor Lidar e: **RWVL**
RAMCON, Inc., Environmental
Engineering Library, Memphis e: **TMRI**
RAMM Branch Advanced Meteorological
Satellite Demonstration and Interpretation
System e: **RAMDIS**
Rammed Earth Institute International e:
REEI
Rancho California Water District e:
RCWD
Rand Water Board e: **RWB**
Random Signal Vibration Protector e:
RSVP
Rand's Omnibus Calculator of the Kinetics
[or Kinematics] of Earth Trajectories e:
ROCKET
Range Commanders Council Meteorological
Group e: **RCC/MG**
Ranger Rick's Nature Club e: **RRNC**
Ranger Uranium Environmental Inquiry e:
RUEI
Ranges and Space Ground Support e:
RSGS
Rapid Aerospace Vehicle Evaluation
System e: **RAVES**
Rapid Changing Environment e: **RCE**
Rapid Environmental Surveying Using
Mobile Equipment e: **RESUME**

Rapid Information Display and
Dissemination in Library Environments
e: **RIDDLE**
Rapid Optical Ocean Surveillance Testbed
e: **ROOST**
Rapid Protective Works *e:* **RPW**
Rapidly Installed Breakwater *e:* **RIB**
Rapport. Activite du Bureau Voltaique de le
Geologie et des Mines *f:* **Rapp Act Bur
Voltaique Geol Mines**
Rapport Annuel. Service Geologique
[Malagasy] *f:* **Rapp Annu Serv Geol
[Malagasy]**
Rapport. Bureau de la Nutrition Animale et
de l'Elevage *f:* **Rap Bur Nutr Anim
Elev**
Rapport d'Activite. Service Geologique
[Madagascar] *f:* **Rapp Act Serv Geol
[Madagascar]**
Rapport d'Activite. Service Geologique
[Malagasy] *f:* **Rapp Act Serv Geol
[Malagasy]**
Rapport. Geologique. Ministere de l'Energie
et des Ressources [Quebec] *f:* **Rapp
Geol Minist Energie Ressour [Quebec]**
Rapport. Laboratoire des Produits Forestiers
de l'Est [Canada]] *f:* **Rapp Lab Prod
For Est [Can]**
Rapport Preliminaire. Ministere des
Richesses Naturelles [Quebec] *f:* **Rapp
Prelim Minist Richesses Nat [Que]**
Rapport Statistique Canadien sur
l'Hydrographie et les Sciences
Oceaniques *f:* **Rapp Stat Can Hydrogr
Sci Oceaniques**
Rapports Scientifques et Techniques.
CNEXO [Centre National pour
l'Exploitation des Oceans] *f:* **Rapp Sci
Tech CNEXO**
Rare Animal Relief Effort *e:* **RARE**
Rare Earth *e:* **R**, *e:* **RE**
Rare-Earth Alloy *e:* **REA**
Rare Earth Boride *e:* **REB**
Rare-Earth Cobalt *e:* **RAECO**, *e:* **REC**
Rare Earth Device *e:* **RED**
Rare Earth Elements *e:* **REE**
Rare-Earth Elements *e:* **REEs**
Rare-Earth Exchanged *e:* **REX**
Rare-Earth Garnet *e:* **REG**
Rare-Earth Information Center *e:* **REIC**
Rare-earth Information Center *e:* **RIC**
Rare-Earth Iron Garnets *e:* **REIG**
Rare Earth Laser *e:* **REL**
Rare Earth Laser Device *e:* **RELD**
Rare-Earth Metal *e:* **REM**
Rare Earth-Muffin-Tin Sphere *e:* **RE-MTS**
Rare-Earth Oxide *e:* **REO**
Rare-Earth Oxides *e:* **REOS**
Rare-Earth Oxysulfide *e:* **REOS**
Rare Earth Research Conference *e:* **RERC**
Rare-earth scandium garnet *e:* **RESG**
Rare Earth/Transition Metal *e:* **RE/TM**
Rare-Earth Transition-Metal *e:* **R-T**
Rare Earth Transition Metal Alloy *e:* **RETMA**
RARE [Rare Animal Relief Effort] Center
Tropical Bird Conservation *e:* **RCTBC**
Rassega di Medicina Industriale *i:* **Rass
Med Ind**
Rassegna di Medicina Applicata al Lavoro
Industriale *i:* **Rass Med Appl Lav Ind**
Rassegna di Medicina Industriale e di
Igiene del Lavoro *i:* **Rass Med Ind Ig
Lav**

Rassegna di Medicina Sperimentale *i:*
Rass Med Sper
Rassegna Giuliana di Medicina *i:* **Rass
Giuliana Med**
Rassegna Italiana di Chirurgia e Medicina
i: **Rass Ital Chir Med**
Rassegna Medica *i:* **Rass Med**
Rassegna Medica-Convivium Sanitatis *i:*
Rass Med Convivium Sanit
Rassegna Medica e Culturale *i:* **Rass Med
Cult**
Rassegna Medica Sarda *i:* **Rass Med
Sarda**
Rassegna Medica Sarda. Supplemento *i:*
Rass Med Sarda Suppl
Rastitelna Zashtita/Plant Protection *R:*
Rastit Zasht Plant Prot
Rate Gyro Assembly-Orbiter *e:* **RGAO**
Ration, Cold Weather *e:* **RCW**
rationiert-repartiert *d:* **r.**
RATS Open Systems Environment *e:*
ROSE
Raumfahrtelektronik *d:* **rfe**
Raumfahrtforschung *d:* **RFF**
Raumflug-Planetarium *d:* **RFP**
Raumflug-Planetarium mit direkter
Programmierung *d:* **RFP-DP**
Raumflugkörper *d:* **RFK**
Raumforderung *d:* **RF**
Raumforschung und Raumordnung *d:*
Raumforsch und Raumordnung, *e:*
Raumforsch u-Ordnung
Ravalli National Wildlife Refuge *e:*
RNWR
Raw Water *e:* **RW**
Raw Water Intake Structure *e:* **RWIS**
Raw Water System *e:* **RWS**
Rawinsonde Observation *e:* **RAOB**
Rayonnements Ionisants. Techniques de
Mesures et de Protection *e:* **Rayonnem
Ionis Tech Mes Prot**
Ray's Medical Jurisprudence of Insanity *e:*
Ray Ins, *e:* **Ray Ins. [or Med. Jur.]**, *e:*
Ray Med Jur
Razvedochnaya Geofizika *R:* **RAGEA**, *R:*
Razved Geofiz
Razvedochnaya i Promyslovaya Geofizika
R: **Razved Promysl Geofis**
RBM. Revue Europeenne de Biotechnologie
Medicale *f:* **RBM Rev Eur Biotechnol
Med**
Reaction Control/Orbital Insertion *e:*
RC/OI
Réaction de Wassermann *f:* **RW**
Reactive Atmosphere Process *e:* **RAP**
Reactive Hydrocarbon Analyzer *e:* **RHA**
Reactive Hydrocarbon[s] *e:* **RHC**
Reactor Building Closed Coolant Water *e:*
RBCCW
Reactor Building Closed Cooling Water *e:*
RBCCW
Reactor Building Closed Cooling Water
System *e:* **RBCCW System**
Reactor Building Closed Loop Cooling
Water *e:* **RBCLCW**
Reactor Building Cooling Water System *e:*
RBCWS
Reactor Building Hydrogen Purge Fan *e:*
RBHPF
Reactor Building Protection *e:* **RBP**
Reactor Development and Technology
Remote Data Transmitter *e:* **RDT**
Reactor Low Water Level *e:* **RLWL**

Reactor Make-Up Water System *e:*
RMWS
Reactor Plant River Water Pump *e:*
RPRWP
Reactor Protection Control Rod System *e:*
RPCRS
Reactor Protection Logic System *e:* **RPLS**
Reactor Protection System *e:* **RPS**
Reactor Protective System Motor Generator
e: **RPSMG**
Reactor safety, waste management and
radiation protection research program *e:*
SOS
Reactor Vessel Water Level Indication
System *e:* **RVLIS**
Reactor Water Clean-up System *e:* **RWCU
System**
Reactor Water Cleanup System *e:* **RWCS**
Reactor Water Cleanup Unit *e:* **RWCU**
Reactor Water Level *e:* **RWL**
Read-Access Key Remote Access Key *e:*
RAK
Read Natural Childbirth Foundation *e:*
RNCF
Ready for Sea *e:* **RFS**
reaktives Ionenplattieren *d:* **RIP**
Real Academia de Ciencias
Medicas,Fisicas,y Naturales de la Habana.
Anales *s:* **R Ac Cienc Habana An**
Real Estate and Space Management
Information System *e:* **RSMIS**
Real Sociedad de Historia Natural *s:*
R.S.H.N.
Real Time DSN [Deep Space Network]
Monitor Software Assembly *e:*
RTDMSA
Real-Time Environmental Arctic
Monitoring *e:* **R-TEAM**
Real-Time Environmental Measures *e:*
RTEM
Real Time Geometry *e:* **RTG**
Real-Time Hydrological Forecasting *e:*
RTHF
Reale Comitato Geologico d'Italia.
Bolletino *i:* **R Comitato G Italia B**
Realläroverkets Naturvetenskapliga
Förening *r:* **R.N.F.**
Rear Area Protection *e:* **RAP**
Rear Area Protection Operations Extended
e: **RAP-EX**
Reason-Oriented Modeling Environment
e: **ROME**
Rebated Weather Boards *e:* **RWB**
Receive-Only Earth Station *e:* **RES**
Receive-Only Ship-Earth Station *e:*
ROSES
Receiver Site [Nevada] [US Geologial
Survey] *e:* **NYR**
Receiving Array Hydrophone *e:* **RAH**
Recent Advances in Animal Nutrition *e:*
RAANES
Recent Advances in Community Medicine
e: **RCOMD6**
Recenti Progressi in Medicina *i:* **Recenti
Prog Med**
Recherche et formation sur les systèmes
côtiers dans le Sud-Est asiatique et dans
le Pacifique *f:* **COMARASP**
Recherche et Informations pour le Tiers-
monde en Matiere d'Environnement et de
Sante *f:* **RITMES**
Recherches Géologiques *f:* **R.G.**

rechnerunterstützter Arbeitsplatz für
  Projektierung d: **RAP**
Rechtsbeschwerde d: **RB**, d: **R.-Beschw.**
Rechtsgeleerde Adviezen n: **RA**
Rechtsrheinische Gas- und
  Wasserversorgung AG d: **RGW**
Recirculated Cooling Water e: **RCW**
Recommended Area and Protection e:
  RAP
Recommended Area and Protection under
  the protected natural areas programme e:
  RAP
Recommended Areas for Protection e:
  RAPs
Reconnaissance by Orbiting Ship-
  Identification Equipment e: **ROSIE**
Recoverable Booster Space System e:
  RBSS
Recoverable Interplanetary Space Probe e:
  RISP
Recoverable Orbital Launch System e:
  ROLS
rectangular midwater trawl e: **RMT**
Rectilinear Polarization e: **R**
Recueil de données climatologiques
  anciennes f: **HCDC**
Recuperation Assistee des Hydrocarbures
  f: **RAH**
Recycle Water e: **REW**
Recycled Water Coordination Committee
  e: **RWCC**
red brown earth e: **RBE**
Red Básica de Observación en Altitud s:
  BUAN
Red de Ciencias Oceánicas de la
  Comunidad del Caribe s: **CCOSNET**
Red de Datos e Información Oceanográficos
  s: **ODIN**
Red de Datos e Información Oceanográficos
  para Africa Oriental s: **ODINEA**
Red de telecomunicaciones meteorológicas
  para las operaciones en Europa s:
  MOTNE
Red del Impacto del Clima y Estrategias de
  Respuesta s: **RICEP**
Red Europea de Apoyo al Clima s: **ECSN**
Red Internacional de Ciencias Biológicas
  s: **RIB**
Red Legged Earth Mite e: **RLEM**
Red Oceanográfica Interislámica s: **INOC**
Red Rock Lakes National Wildlife Refuge
  e: **RRLNWR**
Red Sea and Gulf of Aden Environment
  Programme e: **PERSGA**
Red Sea Container Line e: **RECON**, e:
  RECONLINE
Red Sea Development Corporation e:
  RODOPA
Red Sea Express e: **R.S.E.**
Red Sea Mission Team e: **RSMT**
Rediative Transfer [RT] model for
  Television Infrared Orbiting Satellite
  [TIROS] Operational Vertical Sounder
  [TOVS] e: **RTTOV**
Reduced Exoatmospheric Cross-Section e:
  REX
Reduced Gravity Environment e: **RGE**
Reducing Kernel Hilbert Space e: **RKHS**
Reentry Environment and Systems
  Technology e: **REST**
Reentry Environmental Systems Division
  e: **RESD**

Reentry System Environmental Protection
  e: **RESEP**
Reentry System Evaluation Radar
  [aerospace] e: **RESER**
Reentry Vehicle Test and Observables e:
  RVTO
Reference Climate Station e: **RCS**
Reference Geological Regime e: **RGR**
Reference Hydrologic Basin Network e:
  RHBN
Références Médicales Opposables f: **RMO**
reflector in space e: **RIS**
Reflector Orbital Equipment e: **ROE**
reflektieren d: **refl.**
reflektierend d: **refl.**
reflektiert d: **refl.**
Reflexionsfaktor des ersten Vollfilters seits
  des Lichteinfalles, zugeordnet zur k-ten
  Partialfläche einer Partialfilterung d:
  R\k
Refractory Technology Aerospace
  Components e: **RTAC**
Refrigerated Sea Water e: **RSW**
Refueling At Sea e: **RAS**
Refuelling Water Storage Tank e: **RWST**
Refugee Medical Assistance e: **RMA**
Refuse[s] Medical Assistance e: **RMA**
Regar Memorial Museum of Natural History
  e: **RMMNH**
Regensburger Energie- und
  Wasserversorgung AG d: **REWAG**
Régie de l'Assurance Médicale du Québec
  f: **RAMQ**
Regierungsbiologierat d: **RBiolR**
Regierungsgeologe d: **R.-Geol.**
Regierungsmedizinaldirektor d: **RMD**, d:
  RMedDir
Regierungsmedizinalrat d: **RMedR**, d:
  RMP
Regierungsobermedizinalrat d: **ROMedR**
Régime forestier f: **RF**
Regimental Medical Offcer e: **RMO**
Regimental Medical Officer e: **Regtl MO**
Regimental Medical Post e: **R.M.P.**
Regiments-Medizinpunkt d: **RMP**
Regio-Klima-Programm d: **REKLIP**
Region 2 Environmental Map Catalog
  System e: **MAPS**
Region 7 NPDES Water Compliance
  System e: **WACO**
Region 2 Water Quality Models e: **HAR03**
Regional Airspace Control Plan e: **RACP**
Regional and Mesoscale Meteorology e:
  RAMM
Regional Animal Health Advisory
  Committee e: **RAHAC**
Regional Associations' Working Groups on
  Hydrology e: **RAWG/Hydrology**
Regional Atmospheric Measurement and
  Analysis Network e: **RAMAN**
Regional Atmospheric Modeling System e:
  RAMS
Regional Atmospheric (or Atmosphere)
  Modeling System e: **RAMS**
Regional Atmospheric Pollution Study e:
  RAPS
Regional Atmospheric Transport Code for
  Hanford Emission Tracking e:
  RATCHET
Regional Aviation Weather Products
  Generator e: **RAWPG**
Regional Center for Tropical Meteorology
  e: **RCTM**

Regional Centre for Science in Surveying,
  Mapping and Remote Sensing e:
  RCSSMRS
Regional Centre for Training in Aerospace
  Surveys e: **RECTAS**
Regional Climate Center (or Centre) e:
  RCC
Regional Climate Model e: **RCM**, e:
  RegCM
Regional Climate Model, Version Two e:
  RegCM2
Regional Climate Modelling and Integrated
  Global Change Impact Studies in the
  European Arctic e: **CLIMPACT**
Regional Climate Project e: **REKLIP**
Regional Commission on Land and Water
  Use in the Near East e: **LWU**, e:
  RCLWUNE
Regional Control Officer, North-East
  Weather Region e: **RCO NE Wea Reg**
Regional Cooperation in Scientific
  Information Exchange in the Western
  Indian Ocean e: **RECOSCIX-WIO**
Regional Cooperative Network for
  Education in Agriculture and Renewable
  Natural Resources e: **REDCA**
Regional Coordination of Biomedical
  Information Resources Program[me] e:
  RECBIR Program[me]
Regional Environment Centre e: **REC**
Regional Environment Employment
  Program e: **REEP**
Regional Environmental Applications
  Program e: **REAP**
Regional Environmental Center for Central
  and Eastern Europe e: **REC**
Regional Environmental Information
  System e: **REIS**
Regional Environmental Management
  Allocation Process e: **REMAP**
Regional Environmental Mapping and
  Assessment Program e: **R-MAP**
Regional Environmental Technical
  Assistance e: **RETA**
Regional Environmental Training and
  Research Organization e: **RETRO**
Regional Federation of Health Informatics
  Societies in Latin America and the
  Caribbean e: **IMIA-LAC**
regional geographic information system e:
  RGIS
Regional Geographical Information System
  e: **REGIS**
Regional Geological Project Manager e:
  RGPM
Regional Health Administrator e: **RHA**
Regional Health Authority e: **RHA**
Regional Health Authority [Teaching] e:
  RHA[T]
Regional Health Director e: **RHD**
Regional Health Information Network e:
  RHIN
Regional Health Organisation of Southern
  Africa e: **RHOSA**
Regional Home Health Intermediary e:
  RHHI
Regional Hydro-Ecological Simulation
  System e: **RHESSys**, e: **RHIESSys**
Regional Hydrologist e: **RH**
Regional Integrated Lake-Watershed
  Acidification Study e: **RILWAS**
Regional Integrated Protected Areas System
  e: **RIPAS**

Regional Interactions of Climate and Ecosystems *e:* **RICE**

Regional International Organisation (or Organization) for Plant Protection and Animal Health *e:* **RIOPPAH**

Regio[nal]-Klima-Projekt *d:* **REKLIP**

Regional Library of Medicine *e:* **RLM**

Regional Marine Biological Centre *e:* **RMBC**

Regional Medical Library *e:* **RML**

Regional Medical Library Network *e:* **RMLN**

Regional Medical Library Program *e:* **RMLP**

Regional Medical Officer *e:* **R.M.O.**

Regional Medical Program *e:* **RMP**

Regional Medical Programs Service *e:* **RMPS**

Regional Medical Training Centers *e:* **RMTCs**

Regional Mental Health Center of Oak Ridge, Oak Ridge *e:* **TOMH**

Regional Meteorological Center (or Centre) *e:* **RMC**

Regional Meteorological Training Centre *e:* **RMTC**

Regional Observation Monitoring Program *e:* **ROMP**

Regional Observational Cooperative *e:* **ROC**

Regional Oceanographic Data Center *e:* **RODC**

Regional Oil Combating Centre for the Mediterranean Sea *e:* **ROCC**

Regional OPMET [Operational Meteorological Information] Bulletin Exchange Scheme *e:* **ROBEX**

Regional Organization for the Protection of the Marine Environment *e:* **ROPME**

Regional Political Ecology *e:* **RPE**

Regional Protected Area Team *e:* **RPAT**

Regional Research Hydrologist *e:* **RRH**

Regional Research Networks Oceania *e:* **RRN OCE**

Regional Space Support Center *e:* **RSSC**

Regional/Specialized Meteorological Centers (or Centre) *e:* **RSMC**

Regional Urban Environment *e:* **RUE**

Regional Water Authorit *e:* **RWA**

Regional Water Authorities *e:* **RWAs**

Regional Water Authority *e:* **RWA**

Regional Water Quality Control Board *e:* **RWQCB**

Regional Weather Service *e:* **RWS**

Regionsjukhuset, Medicinska Biblioteket *r:* **SwOrM**

Register for the Ascertainment and Prevention of Inherited Diseases [of the Medical Research Council] *e:* **RAPID**

Registered Animal Nursing Auxiliary *e:* **RANA**

Registered Diagnostic Medical Sonologist *e:* **RDMS**

Registered Environmental Manager *e:* **REM**

Registered Health Underwriter *e:* **RHU**

Registered Medical Assistants *e:* **RMA**

Registered Medical Officer *e:* **R.M.O.**

Registered Medical Practitioner *e:* **RMP**

Registered Protective Circuitry *e:* **RPC**

Registered Technician-Nuclear Medicine *e:* **R.T.N.**

Registry of Medical Technologists *e:* **RMT**

Reglaje de la subescala del altímetro para obtener elevación estando en tierra *s:* **QNH**

Reglement General du Protection du Travail *f:* **RGPT**

Règlement International concernant le transport des marchandises (ou matières) Dangereuses par chemin[s] de fer *f:* **RID**

Reglementierung *d:* **Regl.**

Règlements routiers *f:* **RR**

Regular Geophysical Day *e:* **RGD**

Regulated Medical Wastes *e:* **RMW**

Regulations for Her Majesty's Sea Transport Service *e:* **RHMSTS**

Regulations for Medical Services of the Army *e:* **Rgs M.S.A.**

Regulations of the Medical Services of the Army *e:* **RMSA**

Regulations to Prevent and Control the Contamination of the Sea from the Disposal of Rubbish and Other Materials *e:* **RPCCMBDM**

Regulations under the Natural Gas Act *e:* **RNG**

Regulator Pressure, Water *e:* **RPW**

Rehabilitation Medicine Service *e:* **RMS**

Rehabilitierungsgesetz *d:* **RehaG**

Reichsgesundheitsamt *d:* **RGA**, *d:* **RGesA**, *d:* **RGsuA**, *d:* **RGusA**

Reichsgesundheitsblatt *d:* **RGusBl**

Reichsgesundheitsrat *d:* **RGesR**

Reichskommissar für Pferdesport und Pferdezucht *d:* **RKPf**

Reichsnaturschutzgesetz *d:* **RNatSchG**, *d:* **RNG**

Reichsstelle für Wetterdienst *d:* **RfW**

Reichstierärzteordnung *d:* **RTÄO**, *d:* **RTO**

Reichsverband des Deutschen Gas- und Wasserfachs *d:* **RVGW**

Reichsverband für Prüfung des Warmblutpferdes *d:* **R.V.**

Reichswasserschutz *d:* **RWS**, *d:* **RWSch**

Reichswasserstraßenverwaltung *d:* **RWV**

Reichswetterdienst *d:* **RWD**

Reindeer Herders Association *e:* **RHA**

Reindeer Upper-atmosphere Device for Open-air Linear Flight *e:* **RUDOLF**

Reisegepäck- und Expreßgutsortierung *d:* **RESI**

Reklame-, Plakatierungs- und Ankündigungs-Unternehmen rGmbH *d:* **Rapag**

Relational Advanced Visual Environment *e:* **RAVE**

Relative Biological Effect *e:* **RBE**

Relative Biological Effectiveness *e:* **RBE**

Relative Biological Effectiveness Linear Energy Transfer *e:* **RBELET**

Relative Biological Effects *e:* **RBE**

Relative Biological Efficiency *e:* **RBE**

Relative Biological Value *e:* **RBV**

relative biologische Dosis *d:* **RBD**

relative biologische Effektivität *d:* **RBE**

relative biologische Wirksamkeit *d:* **EBR**, *d:* **RBW**

Relative Jostle Biological Effectiveness *e:* **RJBE**

Relative Mean Sea Level *e:* **RMSL**

Relative Sea Level *e:* **RSL**

Relative Sensitivity Factor Remote Support Facility *e:* **RSF**

Relative Water Level *e:* **RWL**

Relative Water-Level Recorder *e:* **RWLR**

Relativistic and Spin-Orbit *e:* **RSO**

Relay Reliability Panel of Electronic Parts [Committee of Aerospace Industries Association of America] *e:* **RRP**

Release Remote File *e:* **RRF**

Reliable Earth Terminal *e:* **RET**

Remnant Vegetation Protection Scheme *e:* **RVPS**

Remote *e:* **R**, *e:* **REM**, *e:* **RM**, *e:* **RMTE**

remote *e:* **RMT**

Remote Abstract Windows Toolkit *e:* **RAWT**

Remote Access *e:* **RA**, *e:* **RAC**

remote access *e:* **R.A.X.**

Remote Access and Control *e:* **RAAC**, *e:* **RAC**

Remote Access and Test Equipment *e:* **RATES**

Remote access Application Programming Interface *e:* **RAPI**

Remote access audio *e:* **RAA**

Remote Access Audio Device *e:* **RAA Device**

Remote Access Calibration System *e:* **RACS**

remote access computer *e:* **RAC**

Remote Access Computer System *e:* **RACS**

Remote Access Computer Technique *e:* **RACT**

Remote Access Computing System *e:* **RACS**, *e:* **RAC System**, *e:* **RAX**

Remote Access Concentrator *e:* **RAC**

Remote Access Dial-In User Server *e:* **RADIUS**

Remote Access Editing System *e:* **RAES**, *e:* **RAE System**

Remote-access Editing System *e:* **RES**

Remote Access Execution *e:* **RAX**

Remote Access Gateway *e:* **RAG**

Remote Access-Immediate Response *e:* **RA-IR**

Remote Access Information *e:* **REACTION**

Remote Access Information System *e:* **REACTION System**

Remote Access Interactive Debugger *e:* **RAID**, *e:* **RAID**

Remote Access Key *e:* **RAK**

Remote Access Key Station *e:* **RAK Station**

Remote Access Maintenance Protocol *e:* **RAMP**

Remote Access Modem *e:* **RAM**

Remote Access Monitor *e:* **RAM**

Remote Access Multi-User System *e:* **RAMUS**

Remote Access Multiplexer *e:* **RAM**

Remote Access Outsourcing *e:* **RAO**

Remote Access Planning for Institutional Development *e:* **RAPID**

Remote Access Point *e:* **RAP**

Remote Access Power Support [system] *e:* **RAPS**

Remote Access Procedure for Interactive Design *e:* **RAPID**

Remote Access Server *e:* **RAS**, *e:* **RAS/Exchange**

Remote Access Service *e:* **RAS**

Remote Access Service Application Programming Interface *e:* **RASAPI**

Remote Access Software *e:* **RAS**
Remote Access Switching and Patching *e:* **RASP**
Remote-Access System *e:* **RAS**
Remote Access Terminal *e:* **RAX**
remote access unit *e:* **RAU**
remote access unit version A nn [nn = 12 or 04] *e:* **RAUAnn**
Remote Access Verification Environment *e:* **RAVE**
Remote Acoustic Doppler System *e:* **RADS**
Remote Acquisition *e:* **REMAC**
Remote Acquisition and Checkout Unit *e:* **RACU**
Remote Acquisition and Command Unit *e:* **RACU**
Remote Acquisition Station *e:* **RAS**
Remote Acquisition Unit *e:* **RAU**
Remote Acquisition Unit Interconnecting Station *e:* **RAUIS**
Remote Activated Stores System *e:* **RASS**
Remote Active Spectrometer *e:* **RAS**
Remote Aerosol-Mapping System *e:* **RAMS**
Remote Afloat Terminal System *e:* **RATS**
Remote Air Battle Station *e:* **RABS**
Remote Air-Ground Facility *e:* **RAGF**
Remote AirborneTelevision Display of Ground RADAR Coverage via TACAN *e:* **RATAC**
Remote Alarm Indication *e:* **RAI**
Remote alarm setpoint panel *e:* **RASP**
Remote Alarm Signal *e:* **RAI**
Remote Alarm Transmission System *e:* **RATS**
Remote Amplifier [acquisition] and Advisory box *e:* **RAAB**
Remote Analog Submultiplexer *e:* **RASM**
Remote Analysis Computer *e:* **RAAC**
Remote Analysis System *e:* **RAS**
Remote Antenna Driver *e:* **RAD**
Remote Antenna Driver/Remote Antenna Signal Processor *e:* **RAD/RASP**
Remote Antenna Signal Processor *e:* **RASP**
Remote Antenna Units *e:* **RAU**
Remote Anti-Armore Mine Systems *e:* **RAAMS**
Remote Antiarmor Assault System *e:* **RAAA**
Remote Antiarmor Mine *e:* **RAAM**
Remote Approach Control *e:* **RAPCON**
Remote Arctic Measuring System *e:* **RAMS**
Remote Arctic Measuring System Buoy *e:* **RAMS Buoy**
Remote Area Conflict Information Center *e:* **RACIC**
Remote Area Instrument Landing Sensor *e:* **RAILS,** *e:* **RAILS**
Remote Area Instrument Landing System *e:* **RAILS,** *e:* **RAILS**
Remote Area Landing *e:* **RAL**
Remote Area Mobility Study *e:* **RAMS**
Remote area monitor *e:* **RYD**
Remote Area Monitoring *e:* **RAM**
Remote Area Monitoring System *e:* **RAMS**
Remote Area Navigation *e:* **RNAV**
Remote Area Nurse *e:* **RAN**
Remote Area Power Supply Investigation Branch *e:* **RAPSI**

Remote Area Support *e:* **RAS**
Remote Area Tactical System *e:* **RATS**
Remote Area Television Service *e:* **RATS,** *e:* **RATV**
Remote Area Terminal *e:* **RAT**
Remote Area Terminal System *e:* **RATS**
Remote Area Weather Station *e:* **RAWS,** *e:* **RWAS**
Remote ARIA [Apollo Range Instrumentation Aircraft] Control Center *e:* **RACC**
Remote Arm Reset *e:* **RAR**
Remote Arming Common Element System *e:* **RACES**
Remote Army Set *e:* **RAS**
Remote Assistance *e:* **RA**
Remote Associates Test *e:* **RAT**
Remote Associations Test *e:* **RAT**
Remote Atmosphere & Ionospheric Detection System *e:* **RAIDS**
Remote Atmospheric Measurements Program *e:* **RAMP**
Remote Atmospheric Measurements Systems *e:* **RAMS**
Remote Atmospheric Monitoring Project *e:* **RAMP**
Remote Attitude Measurement Sensor *e:* **RAMS**
Remote Augmented Lift System *e:* **RAIS,** *e:* **RALS**
Remote Authentication Dial-In User Service *e:* **RADIUS**
Remote Automated Color Video Observing System *e:* **ROVOS-C**
Remote Automatic Calibration *e:* **RAAC**
Remote Automatic Calibration System *e:* **RACS**
Remote Automatic Computing Equipment *e:* **RACE**
Remote Automatic Control System *e:* **RACS**
Remote Automatic Detection of Contingencies *e:* **RADOC**
Remote Automatic Meteorological Observing Station *e:* **RAMOS**
Remote Automatic Multipurpose Station *e:* **RAMS**
Remote Automatic Parts Input for Dealers *e:* **RAPID**
Remote Automatic Telemetry Equipment *e:* **RATE**
Remote Automatic Weather Station *e:* **RAWS**
Remote Automation Connection Manager *e:* **RACMan**
Remote Automation Objects *e:* **RAO**
Remote Autoranging Picoammeter *e:* **RAP**
remote axis admittance *e:* **RAA**
Remote Balance Control *e:* **RBC**
Remote Bar Code System *e:* **RBCS**
Remote Batch *e:* **RB**
Remote Batch Access Method *e:* **RBAM**
Remote Batch Address method *e:* **RBA**
Remote Batch Address Method *e:* **RBAM**
Remote Batch Business Package *e:* **RBBP**
Remote Batch Entry *e.* **RBE**
Remote Batch Facility *e:* **RBF**
Remote Batch Module *e:* **RBM**
Remote Batch Processing *e:* **RBP**
Remote Batch Processor *e:* **RBP**
Remote-batch Station Program *e:* **RESP**
Remote-batch Station Program[me] *e:* **RESP**

Remote Batch System *e:* **RBS**
Remote Batch Terminal *e:* **RBT**
Remote Batch Terminal Emulator *e:* **RBTE**
Remote Batch Terminal Module *e:* **RBTM**
Remote Battle System *e:* **RBS**
Remote Bridge Hub *e:* **RBH**
Remote Bridge Management Software *e:* **RBMS**
Remote Buffer Unit *e:* **RBU**
Remote Bulletin Board System *e:* **RBBS**
Remote Call Forwarding *e:* **RCF**
Remote Carrier-Controlled Modem *e:* **RCCM**
Remote Carrier Module *e:* **RCM**
Remote Cell Unit *e:* **RCU**
Remote Center Air/Ground *e:* **RCAG**
Remote Center Air-Ground Facility *e:* **RCAG Facility**
Remote Center Compliance *e:* **RCC**
Remote channel *e:* **RC**
Remote Checkout Umbilical Array *e:* **RCUA**
Remote Client Application *e:* **RCA**
Remote Clinical Communication System *e:* **RCCS**
remote cloud sensing *e:* **RCS**
Remote Cluster Controller *e:* **RCC**
Remote Cluster Executive *e:* **RCX**
Remote Cluster Facility *e:* **RCF**
Remote Commercial Radio Services *e:* **RCRS**
remote commercial television services *e:* **RCTS**
Remote Common Gateway Interface *e:* **RCGI**
Remote Communication Air-to-Ground System *e:* **RCAG System**
Remote Communication Facility *e:* **RCF**
Remote Communications Air-to-Ground *e:* **RCAG**
Remote Communications Center *e:* **RCC**
Remote Communications Central *e:* **RCC**
Remote Communications Complex *e:* **RCC**
Remote Communications Concentrator *e:* **RCC**
Remote Communications Console *e:* **RCC**
Remote Communication[s] Message *e:* **RCOM**
Remote Communications Monitoring Unit *e:* **RCMU**
Remote Communications Outlet *e:* **RCO**
Remote Communications Processor *e:* **RCP**
Remote Community Demonstration Program *e:* **RCDP**
Remote Compensation Unit *e:* **RCU**
Remote Computer *e:* **R/C**
Remote Computer-Access Communications [Service] *e:* **RCAC**
Remote Computer Access Communications Service *e:* **RCAC Service**
Remote Computer Center *e:* **RCC**
Remote computer communication access method *e:* **RCAM**
Remote Computer Communication Access Method *e:* **RCCAM**
Remote Computer-controlled Hardware Monitor *e:* **RCHM**
Remote Computer Interface Subsystem *e:* **RCIS**
Remote Computer Interface Unit *e:* **RCIU**

Remote Computer Output Room *e:* **RCOR**
Remote Computing *e:* **RC**
Remote Computing Capability *e:* **RCC**
Remote Computing Program[me] *e:* **RC Program[me]**
Remote Computing Service *e:* **RCS**
Remote Computing System *e:* **RCS**
Remote Concentration Unit. *e:* **RCU**
Remote Concentrator *e:* **r.c.**
remote concentrator unit *e:* **RU**
Remote Connection Service *e:* **RCS**
Remote Console *e:* **RECON**
Remote Contact Sensor *e:* **RCS**
Remote Control *e:* **R/C,** *e:* **R/CONT,** *e:* **RECON,** *e:* **RMC**
remote control *e:* **RMCTR**
Remote Control Adapter *e:* **RCA**
Remote Control/All-Terrain Vehicle *e:* **RC/ATV**
Remote Control Amplifier *e:* **RCA**
Remote Control and Monitoring System *e:* **RCMS**
Remote control center *e:* **RCC**
Remote Control Complex *e:* **RCC**
Remote control console *e:* **RCC**
Remote Control Equipment *e:* **RCE**
Remote Control Indicator *e:* **RCI**
Remote Control Interface *e:* **RCI**
Remote Control Interface Adapter *e:* **RCIA**
Remote Control Location *e:* **RCL**
Remote Control Mine Disposal System *e:* **RCMDS**
Remote control module *e:* **RCM**
Remote Control & Monitoring Unit *e:* **RCMU**
remote control observation *e:* **RCO**
Remote Control of Mines *e:* **RECO**
Remote Control Office *e:* **RCO**
Remote Control Office[r] *e:* **RCO**
Remote Control On-Line Information Service *e:* **RECON**
remote-control oscillator *e:* **rco**
Remote Control Panel *e:* **RCP**
Remote Control Pool *e:* **RCP**
Remote control rack *e:* **RCR**
Remote Control Radio Service *e:* **RCRS**
Remote Control Recovery System *e:* **RCRS**
Remote Control-Rod Cluster Assembly *e:* **RCC**
Remote-Control Secure Voice System *e:* **REMSEVS**
Remote Control Set *e:* **RCS**
Remote Control Station *e:* **RCS**
Remote control switch *e:* **RCS**
Remote Control [System] *e:* **RC[S]**
Remote Control Terminal *e:* **RCT**
Remote[-control] Underwater Manipulator *e:* **RUM**
Remote Control Unit *e:* **RCU**
Remote Control Units *e:* **RCUs**
Remote Control User Part *e:* **RCUP**
Remote Control Video Switch *e:* **RCVS**
Remote Control Water Sampler *e:* **RCWS**
Remote-Controlled Aerial Target *e:* **RCAT**
Remote Controlled Aiming Package *e:* **RECAP**
Remote Controlled Air-Ground Communication *e:* **RCAGC**
Remote Controlled Air-Ground Facility *e:* **RCAG Facility**

Remote-Control[led] Air-to-Ground *e:* **RCAG**
Remote-Controlled Anti-Armor system *e:* **RCAAS**
Remote Controlled Anti-Armor System *e:* **RECAAS**
Remote Controlled Defence Unit *e:* **RCDU,** *e:* **RCOU**
Remote-Controlled Equipment *e:* **RCE**
Remote Controlled Identification Vehicle *e:* **RCIV**
Remote Controlled Inking *e:* **RCI**
Remote-controlled transport vehicle *e:* **RCTV**
Remote Controller *e:* **REMCON**
Remote Copy *e:* **RCP**
Remote Copy Program *e:* **RCP**
Remote Core Sampler *e:* **RCS**
Remote Data Access Object *e:* **RDAO**
Remote Data Access Unit *e:* **RDAU**
Remote [data] Acquisition and Checkout Unit[s] *e:* **RACU**
Remote Data Acquisition Chart *e:* **RDAC**
Remote Data Acquisition Subsystem *e:* **REMAC Subsystem**
Remote Data Acquisition Unit *e:* **RDAU**
Remote Data, Analysis, and Archive Center *e:* **RDAAC**
Remote Data Base Access *e:* **RDBA**
Remote Data Collection *e:* **RDC**
remote data concentration *e:* **RDC**
Remote Data Concentrator *e:* **RDC**
Remote Data Connector *e:* **RDC**
Remote Data Control *e:* **RDC**
Remote data entry *e:* **RDE**
Remote Data Entry System *e:* **RDES**
Remote Data Input *e:* **RDI**
Remote Data Module *e:* **RDM**
Remote Data Object[s] *e:* **RDO**
Remote Data Processing *e:* **RDP**
Remote Data Processor *e:* **RDP**
Remote Data Processors *e:* **RDPs**
Remote Data Recovery *e:* **RDR**
Remote Data Service *e:* **RDS**
Remote Data Services *e:* **RDS**
Remote Data Station *e:* **RDS**
Remote Data Terminal *e:* **RDT**
Remote Data Transmission *e:* **RDT**
Remote Data Transmission Subsystem *e:* **RDTS**
Remote Data Transmitter *e:* **RDT**
Remote Data[base] Access *e:* **RDA**
Remote Database Management System *e:* **RDBMS**
Remote Decoder Unit *e:* **RDU**
Remote Defect Identification *e:* **RDI**
Remote Defect Incicator-Path Level *e:* **RDI-P**
Remote Defect Indication (or Indicator) *e:* **RDI**
Remote Degassing Station *e:* **RDS**
Remote Demolition Mine *e:* **RDM**
Remote Desktop *e:* **RD**
Remote Desktop Protocol *e:* **RDP**
Remote Detection and Controls *e:* **REDAC**
Remote Detonation Capability *e:* **RDC**
Remote Device Control *e:* **RDC**
Remote Device Handler *e:* **RDH**
Remote Device Interface Unit *e:* **RDIU**
Remote Diagnosis *e:* **RD**
Remote Diagnostic Center *e:* **RDC**
Remote Diagnostic Manager *e:* **RDM**
Remote Digital Loopback *e:* **RDL**

Remote Digital Multiplexer *e:* **RDM**
Remote Digital Readout *e:* **RDR,** *e:* **RDRD**
Remote Digital Terminal *e:* **RDT**
remote digital trunk *e:* **RDT**
Remote Disassembly Machine *e:* **RDM**
Remote disconnect *e:* **RD**
Remote Disk Operating System *e:* **REMDOS**
Remote Disk Station *e:* **RDS**
Remote Display/Alarm *e:* **RDA**
Remote Display Interface *e:* **RDI**
Remote Display Link *e:* **RDL**
Remote Display Protocol *e:* **RDP**
Remote Display Unit *e:* **RDU**
Remote Distributed Terminal Controller *e:* **RDTC**
Remote Docking Procedure Simulator *e:* **RDPS**
Remote Dual Copy *e:* **RDC**
Remote Electric Drive-Turret *e:* **RED-T**
Remote Electric Drive Turret System *e:* **REOT**
Remote Electrical Alphanumeric Display *e:* **READ**
Remote Electrical Block Energization Clock Control Arrangement *e:* **REBECCA**
Remote Electrical Manipulator System *e:* **REMS**
Remote Electronic Alphanumeric Display *e:* **READ**
Remote Electronic Control of Ordnance *e:* **RECO**
Remote Electronic Desktop Integration *e:* **REDI**
Remote Electronic Microfilm in Storage Transmission and Retrieval *e:* **REMSTAR**
Remote Emergency Monitoring and Control System *e:* **REMACS**
Remote Emergency Power *e:* **REP**
Remote Emergency Power Off *e:* **REPO**
Remote Emergency Salvage and Clean-Up Equipment *e:* **RESCUE**
Remote Emergency Satellite Rescue Unit *e:* **RESCU**
Remote Emitter System *e:* **RES**
Remote Emitter Unit *e:* **REU**
Remote Enable *e:* **REN**
Remote Energy Monitor/Alarm System *e:* **REMAS**
Remote Engagement Target System *e:* **RETS**
Remote Engineering *e:* **REENG**
Remote Entry Acquisition Package *e:* **REAP**
Remote Entry Flexible Security *e:* **REFS**
Remote Entry Services *e:* **RES**
Remote Entry Subsystem *e:* **RES**
Remote Entry System *e:* **RES**
Remote Entry Unit *e:* **REU**
Remote Environmental Automatic Data Acquisition Concept *e:* **READAC**
Remote Equipment Decontamination Cell *e:* **REDC**
Remote Equipment Kit *e:* **REK**
Remote Equipment Module *e:* **REM**
Remote Ethernet Bridge *e:* **REB**
Remote Excavation System *e:* **RES**
Remote Exchange *e:* **RX**
Remote Executable *e:* **REXEC**
Remote Execution *e:* **REXEC**
Remote Execution Server *e:* **RES**

Remote Execution Service e: **RES**
Remote Exhaust [concept] e: **REX**
Remote Experiment Station e: **RES**
Remote Explosive Disposal Falkland
  Islands,Royal Engineers e: **REDFIRE**
Remote Facility Inquiry e: **RFI**
Remote Feature Control e: **RFC**
Remote Feeding Telecommunication e:
  RFT
Remote-Fiber Fluorometry e: **RFF**
Remote-Field Eddy Current e: **RFEC**
Remote File e: **RF**
Remote File Access e: **RFA**
Remote File Access Monitor e: **RFAM**
Remote File Inquiry e: **RFI**
Remote File Management System e:
  RFMS
Remote File Server e: **RFS**
Remote File Service e: **RFS**
Remote File Sharing e: **RFS**
Remote File System e: **RFS**
Remote File Transfer System e: **RFTS**
Remote Fire Unit e: **RFU**
Remote Fluvial Experimental Series e:
  REFLEX
Remote Foreign Office e: **RFO**
Remote Frame Buffer e: **RFB**
Remote Frame Handler e: **RFH**
Remote Frequency Channel Indicator e:
  RFCI
Remote Front Panel e: **RFP**
Remote Fuel Pin Identification System e:
  RFPIS
Remote Fuels Refabrication Laboratory e:
  RFRL
Remote Function Call e: **RFC**
Remote Gain Amplifier e: **RGA**
Remote Gas Filter Correlation e: **RGFC**
Remote Generalized Application Language
  e: **REGAL**
Remote Geophysical Monitor e: **RGM**
Remote Global Computer Access Service
  e: **RGCAS**
Remote Graphic Instruction Set e: **REGIS**
Remote Graphics Processor e: **RGP**
Remote Ground Switching e: **RGS**
Remote Ground Terminal e: **RGT**
Remote Guidance and Control e: **RGC**
Remote Guidance System e: **RGS**
Remote Gun Flash Detection e: **RGFD**
Remote Gyro Sight e: **RGS**
Remote-Handled Transuranic[s] e: **RH-
TRU**
Remote-Handled [waste] e: **RH**
Remote Handling e: **RH**
Remote Handling Facility e: **RHF**
Remote Handset e: **RHS**
Remote Hardware Monitoring e: **RHM**
Remote Hellfire Electronics e: **RHE**
Remote Highway Coupler e: **RHC**
Remote Host Option e: **RHO**
Remote Identifier e: **RID**
Remote Image (or Imaging) Processing e:
  RIP
Remote Image (or Imaging) Protocol e:
  RIP
Remote Image Transceiver system e: **RIT**
Remote Imagery Transceiver e: **RIT**
Remote Independently Operable
  Transceiver e: **RIOT**
Remote Information Center e: **RIC**
Remote Information Exchange e: **RIX**

Remote Information Management System
  e: **RIMS**
Remote information management system.
  e: **RINIS**
Remote Information Processing Center e:
  RIPC
Remote Information Processing System e:
  RIPS
Remote Information Query System e:
  RiQS
Remote Information Retrieval and
  Management System e: **RIRMS**
Remote Information System e: **RIS**
Remote Information Systems Center e:
  RISC
Remote Infrared Surveillance System e:
  RISS
Remote Initial Program Loading e: **RIPL**
Remote Input Message Processor e:
  RIMP, e: **RIMP**
Remote input/output e: **RIO**
Remote Input/Output Control[ler] e:
  RIOC
Remote Input/Output System e: **RIOS**
Remote Input/Output Terminal e: **RIOT**
Remote Input/Output Unit e: **RIO Unit**
Remote Input Terminal System e: **RITS**
Remote Inquiry Unit e: **RIU**
Remote Installation and Maintenance e:
  RIM
Remote Installation Service e: **RIS**
Remote Instrument Package e: **RIP**
Remote Integrated Services Line Unit e:
  RISLU
Remote Integrity Monitoring Station e:
  RIMS
Remote Intelligence Acquisition e: **RIA**
Remote Intelligent Network e: **RIN**
Remote Interactive Communication e:
  RIC
Remote Interactive Terminal e: **RIT**
Remote Intercomputer Communications
  Interface e: **RICC**
Remote Interface Unit e: **RIU**
Remote Interrogation Information Exchange
  Subsystem e: **RIIXS**
Remote Job Entry e: **REJEN**, e: **RJE**
Remote Job Entry Executive e: **RJEX**
Remote Job Entry Facility e: **RJEF**
Remote Job Entry Function e: **RJEF**
Remote job entry system e: **RES**
Remote Job Entry System e: **RJES**
Remote Job Entry Terminal e: **RJET**
Remote Job Initiation e: **RJI**
Remote Job Output e: **RJO**
Remote Job Processing e: **RJP**
Remote Job Processor e: **RJP**
remote junction alarm e: **RJA**
Remote Keying Variable e: **RKV**
Remote-Konzentrator d: **RK**
Remote LAN Node e: **RLN**
Remote Landing Site Tower e: **RLST**
Remote Language Teaching e: **ReLaTe**
Remote Laser Controlled Exploder System
  e: **RELACES**
Remote Latch Unit e: **RLU**
Remote Learning System e: **RLS**, e: **RSL**
Remote Lift Fan e: **RLF**
Remote Line Adapter e: **RLA**
remote line circurt e: **RLC**
Remote Line Concentrator e: **RLC**
Remote Line Module e: **RLM**
remote line signalling e: **RLSIG**

Remote Line Switch e: **RLS**
Remote Line Test e: **RLT**
Remote Line Unit e: **RLU**
Remote Load Controller e: **RLC**
Remote/Local e: **R/L**
Remote Location e: **RL**
Remote Login e: **RLOGIN**
Remote Loop e: **RL**
Remote Loop Adapter e: **RLA**
Remote Loop Group Multiplexer e:
  RLGM
Remote Loopback e: **RL**
Remote Magnetic Anomaly Detection e:
  REMAD
Remote Magnetic Heading System e:
  RMHS
Remote Magnetic Indicator e: **RMI**
Remote Maintenance Administration and
  Traffic System e: **RMATS**, e: **RMATS**
Remote Maintenance Analysis e: **RMA**
Remote Maintenance and Testing System
  e: **RMATS**
Remote Maintenance Control System e:
  RMCS
Remote Maintenance Demonstration Test
  e: **RMDT**
Remote Maintenance Equipment e: **RME**
Remote Maintenance Evaluation Facility
  e: **RMEF**
Remote Maintenance Line e: **RML**
Remote Maintenance Monitor e: **RMM**
Remote Maintenance Monitoring e: **RMM**
Remote Maintenance Monitoring System
  e: **RMMS**
Remote Maintenance Processor e: **RMP**
Remote Maintenance Protocol e: **RMP**
Remote Maintenance Service e: **RMS**
Remote Maintenance System e: **RMS**
Remote Maintenance Vehicle e: **RMV**
Remote Management Agent e: **RMA**
Remote Management Facility e: **RMF**
Remote Maneuvering System e: **RMS**
Remote Maneuvering Unit e: **RMU**
Remote Manipulating System e: **RMS**
Remote Manipulation System e: **RMS**
Remote Manipulation System[s] e:
  ROMANS
Remote Manipulator e: **RM**
Remote Manipulator Arm e: **RMA**
Remote Manipulator [Sub]system e: **RMS**
Remote Manipulator Subsystem
  Verification Plan e: **RMSVP**
Remote-Manual e: **REM**
Remote Manual e: **RM**
Remote Manual Control e: **RMC**
Remote Manual Switch e: **RMS**
Remote Map Generator e: **ROMAG**
Remote Map Reader e: **RMR**
Remote Marshalling Base e: **REMAB**
Remote Measurement of Vehicle Emission
  e: **REMOVE**
Remote Measurements Laboratory e: **RML**
Remote Measuring Unit e: **RMU**
Remote Mechanical e: **RM**
Remote Mechanical A e: **RMA**
Remote Mechanical B e: **RMB**
Remote Mechanical C e: **RMC**
Remote Mechanical Investigator e: **RMI**
Remote Memory Administration System e:
  RMAS
Remote Memory Port Interface e: **RMPI**
Remote Message Concentrator e: **RMC**
Remote Message Register e: **RMR**

Remote Messaging Interface *e:* **RMI**
Remote Meter Reading *e:* **RMP**, *e:* **RMR**
Remote Method Invocation *e:* **RMI**
Remote Micro Facility *e:* **RMF**
Remote Microphone Network *e:* **RMN**
Remote Minehunting System *e:* **RMS**
Remote Mobile *e:* **RM**
Remote Monitoring Ballistic Area
    Surveillance System *e:* **REMBASS**
Remote Monitoring [Sub]system *e:* **RMS**
Remote Multiplexer *e:* **RM**, *e:* **RMX**
Remote Multiplexer Combiner *e:* **RMC**
Remote Multiplexer System *e:* **RMS**
Remote Multiplexing Unit *e:* **RMU**
Remote Network *e:* **RNET**
Remote Network Access *e:* **RNA**
Remote Network Access Controller *e:*
    RNAC
Remote (Network) Monitoring *e:* **RMON**
Remote Network Monitoring Management
    Information Base *e:* **RMONMIB**
Remote Network Processor *e:* **RNP**
Remote Network User Identification *e:*
    RNUI
Remote Node Service for ISDN *e:* **RNSI**
Remote Object Communications *e:* **ROC**
Remote Object Data Base *e:* **RODB**
Remote Object Proxy Engine *e:* **ROPE**
Remote Observation *e:* **REMOB**
Remote Observations of Sea Surface and
    Atmosphere *e:* **ROSSA**
Remote Obstacle Breaching Assault Tank
    e: **ROBAT**
Remote Ocean Sensing Satellite *e:* **ROMS**,
    e: **ROSS**
Remote Ocean Surface Measuring Sensors
    e: **ROMS**
Remote Office Branch Office *e:* **ROBO**
Remote Office Test Line *e:* **ROTL**
Remote On-Line Business Information
    Network *e:* **ROBIN**
Remote On-line Print Executive System *e:*
    ROPES
Remote On-Line Subsystem *e:* **ROLS**
Remote On-Line System *e:* **ROLS**
Remote On-Line Testing System *e:*
    ROLTS
Remote On-Line Transaction Processing *e:*
    ROLTP
Remote Online Communication System *e:*
    ROCS
Remote OPCM *e:* **ROPCOM**
Remote Operated Door[s] *e:* **ROD**
Remote-Operated Hoisted Platform *e:*
    ROHP
Remote Operated Radiographic Inspection
    System *e:* **RORIS**
Remote Operating Facility, Airborne *e:*
    ROFA
Remote Operating System *e:* **ROS**
Remote Operating System Conversational
    Online Environment *e:* **ROSCOE**
Remote Operating System Conversational
    Operating Environment *e:* **ROSCOE**
Remote Operation *e:* **ROP**
Remote Operation Control Center *e:*
    ROCC
Remote Operation Facility *e:* **ROF**
Remote Operation System *e:* **ROS**
Remote Operational Control Unit *e:*
    ROCU
Remote Operations *e:* **RO**
Remote Operations Error *e:* **ROER**

Remote Operations Invoke *e:* **ROIV**
Remote Operations Microprocessor *e:*
    ROMP
Remote Operations Protocol Machine *e:*
    ROPM
Remote Operations Reject *e:* **RORJ**
Remote Operations Response *e:* **RORS**
Remote Operations Return Error *e:* **RORE**
Remote Operations Service *e:* **ROP**, *e:*
    ROPS
Remote Operations Service Element *e:*
    ROSE
Remote Operation[s] Service Element
    [protocol] *e:* **ROSE**
Remote Operations Service Entity *e:*
    ROSE
Remote Operator Console Facility *e:*
    ROCF
Remote Operator Control Facility *e:*
    ROCF
Remote Operator Control Panel *e:* **ROCP**
Remote Operator Facility *e:* **ROF**
Remote Operator Task Station *e:* **ROTS**
Remote Operator's Console *e:* **ROC**
Remote Optical Character Recognition *e:*
    ROCR
Remote Optical System *e:* **ROS**
Remote Optical Viewing *e:* **ROV**
Remote Optical Viewing System *e:* **ROVS**
Remote Optronics Director *e:* **ROD**
Remote Order Buffer *e:* **ROB**
Remote Ordnance Neutralization Device *e:*
    ROND
Remote Parameter Control *e:* **RPC**
Remote Passphrase Authentication *e:* **RPA**
Remote Password Generator *e:* **RPG**
Remote Payload Operations Center *e:*
    RPOC
remote P[E]CVD *e:* **RPECVD**
Remote Performance Monitor *e:* **RPM**
Remote Performance Monitoring *e:* **RPM**
Remote Performance Monitoring and
    Control *e:* **RPMC**
Remote Peripheral Access *e:* **RPA**
Remote Peripheral Equipment *e:* **RPE**
Remote Phrase Authentication *e:* **RPA**
Remote Pick-up *e:* **RP**
Remote Pickup Unit *e:* **RPU**
Remote-Piloted Vehicle Experiment *e:*
    RPVX
Remote Plan Position Indicator *e:* **RPPI**
Remote Plasma Assisted Oxidation *e:*
    RPAO
Remote Plasma-Enhanced Chemical Vapor
    Deposition *e:* **RPCVD**
Remote Plasma Nitridation *e:* **RPN**
Remote Pointing Protocol *e:* **RPP**
Remote Port Module *e:* **RPM**
Remote Position Control *e:* **RPC**
Remote Positioning Unit *e:* **RPU**
Remote Positioning Valve *e:* **RPV**
Remote Power Control *e:* **RPC**
Remote Power Controller *e:* **RPC**
Remote Power Controllers *e:* **RPCs**
Remote Power Feeding *e:* **RPF**
remote power supply for local modem for
    asynchron peripheral *e:* **RPSRMAP**
Remote Power Unit *e:* **RPU**
Remote Printer *e:* **RPRINTER**
Remote Printer Management *e:* **RPM**
Remote Printing System *e:* **RPS**
Remote Private Branch Exchange *e:* **RPB**
Remote Procedure Call *e:* **RPC**

Remote Procedure Call Language *e:*
    RPCL
Remote Procedure Error *e:* **RPE**
Remote Procedure Load *e:* **RPL**
Remote Procedure Services *e:* **RPS**
Remote Process Management *e:* **RPM**
Remote Processing Service *e:* **RPS**
Remote Processing System *e:* **RPS**
Remote Processor *e:* **RP**
Remote processor controller *e:* **RPC**
Remote Product Generator *e:* **RPG**
Remote Program Link *e:* **RPL**
Remote Program Loader *e:* **RPL**
Remote Programming Box *e:* **RPB**
Remote Radar Head *e:* **RRH**
Remote Radar Integrating Station *e:* **RRIS**
Remote Radar Integration Station *e:* **RRIS**
Remote Radar Operator *e:* **REMO**, *e:*
    REMRO
Remote Radar Tracking Station *e:* **RRTS**
Remote Radar Tracking System *e:* **RRTS**
Remote Radio Controlled Vehicle *e:*
    RRCV
Remote Radioactive Cleaning Facility
    MASF *e:* **DECON-I**
Remote Readable Counter *e:* **RRC**
Remote Reading High-Intensity Constant
    Monitoring Device *e:* **RRHICMD**
Remote Readout Experiment *e:* **REREX**
Remote Readout Unit *e:* **RROU**, *e:* **RRU**
Remote Rebroadcast Box *e:* **RRB**
Remote Reconnaissance Vehicle *e:* **RRV**
Remote Record Access *e:* **RRA**
Remote Record Address *e:* **RRA**
Remote Recovery Data Facility *e:* **RRDF**
Remote Refueling Systems *e:* **RRS**
Remote Relay Station *e:* **RRS**
remote request handler *e:* **RRH**
Remote-Request Interface *e:* **RRI**
Remote Request Number *e:* **RRN**
remote safing switch *e:* **rss**
Remote Sampling System. *e:* **RSS**
Remote Scanner and Encoder Unit *e:*
    RSEU
Remote scannIng online retrieval system.
    e: **RESORS**
Remote Scientific Computing *e:* **RSC**
Remote Scripting *e:* **RS**
Remote Security Station *e:* **RSS**
Remote Sensing *e:* **R/S**
Remote Sensing and Image Processing *e:*
    RSIP
Remote Sensing and Meteorological
    Applications Division *e:* **RSMAD**, *e:*
    RSMD
Remote Sensing and Photogrammetry
    Association of Australia *e:* **RSPAA**
Remote Sensing and Photogrammetry
    Association of Australia Ltd. *e:*
    RS&PAA
Remote Sensing Applications Center *e:*
    RSAC
Remote Sensing Applications Laboratory
    e: **RSAL**
Remote-Sensing Association of Australia
    e: **RSAA**
Remote Sensing Center *e:* **CLIRSEN**, *e:*
    RSC
Remote Sensing Center/Texas A&M
    University *e:* **RSC/TAMU**
Remote Sensing Chemical Agent Alarm *e:*
    RSCAAL
Remote Sensing Data Base *e:* **RSDB**

Remote Sensing Facility *e:* **RSF**
Remote Sensing Imagery *e:* **RSI**
Remote Sensing Institute *e:* **RSI**
Remote Sensing Laboratory *e:* **RSL**
Remote Sensing Oceanography *e:* **RSOC**
Remote Sensing of Earth Resources *e:*
  RSER
Remote Sensing of Environment *e:*
  Remote Sens. Environ.
Remote Sensing of Mediterranean
  Desertification and Environment Stability
  e: **RESMEDES**
Remote Sensing On-Line Retrieval System
  e: **RESORS**, *e:* **RSORS**
Remote Sensing project of agriculture and
  forestry in Europe *e:* **AGRESTE**
remote sensing public access center *e:*
  RSPAC
Remote Sensing Research Center *e:* **RSRC**
Remote Sensing Science Council *e:* **RSSC**
Remote Sensing Series *e:* **Remote Sens.**
  Ser.
Remote Sensing Society *e:* **RSS**
Remote Sensing System *e:* **RSS**
Remote Sensing Task Force *e:* **RSTF**
Remote Sensing Technology Center *e:*
  RESTEC
Remote Sensing Technology Center of
  Japan *e:* **RESTEC**
Remote Sensing Units *e:* **RSU**
Remote Sensor *e:* **REMS**
Remote Sensor Communication and
  Navigation *e:* **REMSCAN**
Remote Sensor Platforms *e:* **RSP**
Remote Sequenced Packet Exchange *e:*
  RSPX
Remote Service Access Point *e:* **RSAP**
Remote Service Call *e:* **RSC**
Remote Service Facility *e:* **RSF**
Remote Service Unit *e:* **RSU**
Remote Services Center *e:* **RSC**
Remote Session Access *e:* **RSA**
Remote Session Manager *e:* **RSM**
Remote Shell *e:* **REMSH**, *e:* **RSH**
Remote Shutdown Panel *e:* **RSDP**
Remote Shutdown System *e:* **RSS**
Remote Side *e:* **R/S**
remote signalling alarm *e:* **RSA**
Remote Single-layer *e:* **RS**
Remote Single-layer Embedded *e:* **RSE**
Remote Site *e:* **RS**
Remote Site Data-Processing *e:* **RSD**
Remote Site Data Processing *e:* **RSDP**
Remote-Site Data Processor *e:* **RSDP**
Remote Site Network Connectivity *e:*
  RSNC
Remote-Site Simulation Unit *e:* **RSSU**
Remote-Site Simulator Console *e:* **RSSC**
Remote Site Subsystem *e:* **RSS**
Remote Size Reduction *e:* **RSR**
Remote Slave Set *e:* **RSS**
Remote Smearing and Analysis System *e:*
  RSAS
Remote Software Update *e:* **RSU**
Remote Source Control System *e:* **RSCS**
Remote Source Route Bridging *e:* **RSRB**
Remote Speaker Control *e:* **RMT SPKR**
  CNT
Remote Spooling and Communications
  Subsystem *e:* **RSCS**
Remote Spooling and Control Subsystem
  e: **RSCS**

Remote Spooling Communications System
  e: **RSCS**
remote spooling control system *e:* **RSCS**
Remote Spooling Vector Processor *e:*
  RSVP
Remote Spoolout Processor *e:* **RSP**
Remote Sprint Launching *e:* **RSL**
Remote Start Relay *e:* **RSR**
Remote Station *e:* **RS**, *e:* **RST**
Remote Station Alarm *e:* **RSA**
Remote Station Communication[s] Interface
  Equipment *e:* **RSCIE**
Remote Station Data Terminal *e:* **RSDT**
Remote Storage Activities *e:* **RSA**
Remote Storage Controller *e:* **RSC**
Remote Storage Management *e:* **RSM**
Remote Store Controller *e:* **RSC**
Remote Subscriber Line Module *e:* **RSLM**
remote subscriber unit control and analog
  lines version A *e:* **RCAL1A**
remote subscriber unit control part 1A [full
  equipped] *e:* **RCPT1A**
remote subscriber unit control part 2A
  [under equipped] *e:* **RCPT2A**
remote subscriber unit control part version
  A *e:* **RCPA16**
remote subscriber unit interface module *e:*
  RIM
remote subscriber unit module *e:* **RSUM**
Remote Subscriber Units *e:* **RSU**
Remote Supervisory Station *e:* **RSS**
Remote Support Facility *e:* **RSF**
Remote Support Function *e:* **RSF**
Remote Surveillance System *e:* **RSS**
Remote Switch Subsystem *e:* **RSS**
Remote Switching Module *e:* **RSM**
Remote Switching System *e:* **RSS**
Remote Switching Unit *e:* **RSU**
Remote Symbiont Interface *e:* **RSI**
Remote Synchronous Terminal Control
  Program[me] *e:* **RSTCP**
Remote System Base *e:* **RSB**
Remote System Data Terminal *e:* **RSDT**
Remote System Manager *e:* **RSM**
Remote System Services Control Point *e:*
  RSSCP
Remote System Verification Program[me]
  e: **RSVP**
Remote Systems Applications *e:* **RSA**
Remote Systems, Incorporated *e:* **RSI**
Remote Systems Scanner *e:* **RSS**
Remote Tactical Airborne SIGINT System
  e: **RTASS**
Remote Tactical Airborne Signals System
  e: **RTASS**
Remote Takeover System *e:* **RTS**
Remote Tank Inspection *e:* **RTI**
Remote Tape Control System *e:* **RTCS**
Remote Target System *e:* **RETS**
Remote Targeting System *e:* **RTS**
Remote Task Force *e:* **RTF**
Remote technical assistance *e:* **RTA**
Remote Technical Assistance and
  Information Network *e:* **RETAIN**
Remote Telecommunication Access Method
  e: **RTAM**
Remote Telemetry Module *e:* **RTM**
Remote Teleprocessing Access Method *e:*
  RTAM
Remote Telerobotic Vehicle for Intelligent
  Remediation *e:* **RETRVIR**
Remote-Teleserviceadapter *d:* **RTSA**
Remote Television *e:* **RTV**

Remote Temperature Detector *e:* **RTD**
Remote Terminal *e:* **RMT**, *e:* **RT**
Remote Terminal Access *e:* **RTA**
Remote Terminal Access Method *e:*
  RTAM
Remote Terminal Controller *e:* **RTC**
Remote Terminal Emulation *e:* **RTE**
Remote Terminal Emulator *e:* **RTE**
Remote Terminal Identification *e:* **RTI**
Remote Terminal Input/Output *e:* **RTIO**
Remote Terminal Interface *e:* **RTI**
Remote Terminal Interface Package *e:*
  RTIP
Remote Terminal Network *e:* **RTN**
Remote Terminal Processor *e:* **RTP**
Remote Terminal Routine Package *e:*
  RTRP
Remote Terminal Scanning *e:* **RTS**
Remote Terminal Scanning System *e:* **RTS**
  System
Remote Terminal Site *e:* **RTS**
Remote Terminal Supervisor *e:* **RTS**
Remote Terminal System *e:* **RTS**
remote terminal unit *e:* **rtu**
Remote Terminal[s] *e:* **RT**
Remote Test Access *e:* **RTA**
Remote Test and Analysis. *e:* **RTA**
remote test control *e:* **REMOCONT**
Remote Test Facility *e:* **RTF**
remote test for maintenance *e:*
  REMOMAINT
Remote Test Module *e:* **RTM**
Remote Test Processor *e:* **RTP**
Remote Test System *e:* **RTS**
Remote Test Unit *e:* **RTU**
Remote Timing and Data Distribution *e:*
  RTDD
Remote Tracking Network *e:* **RTN**
Remote Tracking Site *e:* **RTS**
Remote Tracking Station *e:* **RTS**
Remote Transaction Input/Output *e:* **RTIO**
Remote Transaction Program Name *e:*
  RTPN
Remote Transfer Point *e:* **RTP**
Remote Transfer Service Element *e:*
  RTSE
Remote Transmit Select System *e:* **RTSS**
Remote Transmitter/Receiver *e:* **RTR**
Remote Transparent Monitor *e:* **RTM**
Remote Triaxial Sensors *e:* **RTS**
Remote Trigger *e:* **RT**
Remote Trigger Activator Device *e:*
  RTAD
Remote Trunk Arrangement *e:* **RTA**
Remote Tuning Technique *e:* **RTT**
Remote-Überwachungseinheit *d:* **RUE**
Remote Ultralow Light Level Imaging *e:*
  RULLI
Remote Ultrasonic Stream Gage *e:* **RUSG**
Remote Underwater Fisheries Assessment
  System *e:* **RUFAS**
Remote Underwater Manipulator *e:* **RUM**
Remote Underwater Manipulator System
  e: **RUMS**
Remote Underwater Mine Countermeasures
  e: **RUMIC**
Remote Underwater System *e:* **RUWS**
Remote Underwater Work System *e:*
  RUWS
Remote Unit *e:* **RU**
Remote Unit Monitor *e:* **RUM**
Remote Unit of Work *e:* **RUOW**, *e:* **RUW**
Remote Unit Power Assembly *e:* **RUPA**

Remote Unit Processor *e:* **RUP**
Remote Unmanned Work Subsystem *e:*
  RUWS
Remote Unmanned Work System *e:*
  RUWS
Remote User Access Centers *e:* **RUAC**
Remote User Agent *e:* **RUA**
Remote User Information Program *e:*
  RUIP
Remote User Module *e:* **RUM**
Remote Use[r] of Shared Hardware *e:*
  RUSH
Remote Use[r] of Standard Hardware *e:*
  RUSH
Remote Utilization Monitor *e:* **RUM**
Remote Variant Selection Algorithm *e:*
  RVSA
Remote Vehicle *e:* **RV**
Remote Vehicle Checkout Facility *e:*
  RVCF
Remote Vehicle Survey Tool *e:* **RVST**
Remote Video Terminal *e:* **RVT**
Remote Viewing System *e:* **RVS**
Remote Virtual Disk *e:* **RVD**
Remote Visual Inspection *e:* **RVI**
Remote Voltage Adjustment *e:* **RVA**
Remote Volume Control *e:* **REVOCON,**
  e: **RVC**
Remote Wake Up *e:* **RWU**
Remote Weight Indicator *e:* **RWI**
Remote Winsock *e:* **RWS**
Remote Work Package *e:* **RWP**
Remote Work Vehicle *e:* **RWV**
Remote workstation *e:* **RWS.**
Remote Write Protocol *e:* **RWP**
Remotely Activated Command and Control
  e: **RACC**
Remotely Augmented Vehicle *e:* **RAV**
Remotely Controlled Agile Target *e:*
  RECAT
Remotely-Controlled Explosive Cutter *e:*
  RCEC
Remote[ly-]Controlled Intelligence System
  e: **RCIS**
Remotely-Controlled Mine Disposal
  Vehicle *e:* **RCMDV**
Remotely Controlled Reconnaissance
  Monitor *e:* **RECORM**
Remote[ly] Controlled Vehicle *e:* **RCV**
Remotely Delivered Mine *e:* **RDM**
Remotely Deployable Mission Support
  System *e:* **RDMSS**
Remotely Independently Operable
  Transceiver *e:* **RIOT**
Remotely Initiated Illuminating Perimeter
  Rocket *e:* **RIPER**
Remotely Manned Vehicle *e:* **RMV**
Remotely Measured Target *e:* **RMT**
Remotely Monitored Battlefield Area
  Sensor System *e:* **REMBASS**
Remotely Monitored Battlefield Sensor
  System *e:* **REBASS**
Remotely observed signatures in the
  thermosphere of explosive releases *e:*
  ROSTER
Remotely Operated Control Vehicle
  Weapon Recovery *e:* **ROVWR**
Remotely Operated Geophysical Explorer
  e: **ROGER**
Remotely Operated Longwall Face *e:*
  ROLF
Remotely Operated Manipulator *e:*
  ROMAN

remotely operated mobile manipulator *e:*
  roman
Remotely Operated Platform for Ocean
  Science *e:* **ROPOS**
Remotely-Operated Special Equipment *e:*
  ROSE
Remotely operated Standoff Lightweight
  Antiarmor Munition *e:* **RSLAM**
Remotely Operated Vehicle[s] *e:* **ROV**
remotely-operated vehicles *e:* **rov's**
Remotely-Operated Volume Damper *e:*
  ROVD
Remotely-Piloted Aerial Observation
  Designation System *e:* **RPAODS**
Remotely Piloted Aircraft *e:* **RPA**
Remotely-Piloted Helicopter *e:* **RPH**
Remotely Piloted Mini-Blimp *e:* **RPMB**
Remotely Piloted Mini-Blimps *e:* **RPMBs**
Remotely Piloted Miniature Blimp *e:*
  RPMB
Remotely Piloted Munition *e:* **RPM**
Remotely Piloted Observation Aircraft
  Designator System *e:* **RPOADS**
Remotely Piloted Observer/Designator
  System *e:* **RPODS**
Remotely Piloted Research Aircraft *e:*
  RPRA
Remotely-Piloted Research Vehicle *e:*
  RPRV
Remotely-Piloted Vehicle *e:* **RPV**
Remotely Programmable Conference
  Arranger *e:* **RPCA**
Remotely Receiving Station *e:* **RRS**
Remotely Sensed Imagery *e:* **RSI**
Remotely Submitted Transaction *e:* **RST**
Remoteness Seeker *e:* **RS**
Rendezvous Compatible Orbit *e:* **RCO**
Rene Dubos Center for Human
  Environments *e:* **RDCHE**
Renewable Energy and Environmental
  Conservation Association in Developing
  Countries *e:* **REECA**
Renewable Natural Resources Center *e:*
  RNRC
Renewable Natural Resources Foundation
  e: **RNRF**
Renseignement-Action-Protection
  [Deuxième Bureau] *f:* **R.A.P.**
repartiert *d:* **r,** *d:* **rep.**
Repatriation Department. Medical Research
  Bulletin [Australia] *e:* **Med Res Bull**
  Rept Dept
Répertoire Opérationnel des Métiers et
  Emplois *f:* **ROME**
repetieren *d:* **rep.**
repetiert *d:* **rep.**
repetitive ventricular premature
  depolarization *e:* **RVPD**
Replenishment at Sea *e:* **RAS**
Replenishment at Sea Corrective Action
  Program *e:* **RASCAP**
Replenishment at Sea Working Party *e:*
  RASWP
Report of a Drifting-Buoy Observation *e:*
  DRIFTER
Report of Investigations. University
  ofTexas at Austin. Bureau of Economic
  Geology *e:* **TUGRA**
Report on Observations/Samples Collected
  by Oceanographic Programs *e:*
  ROSCOP
Report. Sado Marine Biological Station.
  Niigata University *e:* **NRFHE8**

Report. Texas Water Development Board
  e: **TWDRA**
Reported Significant Observation *e:* **RSO**
reporting on the state of the environment
  e: **ROSE**
Reports of the Witwatersrand High Court
  [Transvaal, South Africa] *e:* **TL**
Reports on Health and Social Subjects *e:*
  Rep Health Soc Subj
Representative Association of Medical
  Schemes *e:* **RAMS**
Representative in Medical Council *e:*
  RMC
Representative Observation Site *e:* **ROS**
Representative Shuttle Environmental
  Control System *e:* **RECS,** *e:* **RSECS**
Reproducing Kernel Hilbert Space *e:*
  RKHS
Reproductive and Primary Health Care *e:*
  RH/PHC
Reproductive Biological Research
  Foundation *e:* **RBRF**
Reproductive Health *e:* **RH**
Reproductive Health Care Center *e:*
  RHCC
Reproductive Health Care Center/Planned
  Parenthood *e:* **RHCC/PP**
Reproductive Health Hazards Program *e:*
  RHHP
Reproductive Health Online *e:* **ReproLine**
Republic Health Corp. *e:* **REPH**
Republic Observatory, Johannesburg *e:*
  ROJ
República de Cabo Verde *p:* **Rep Cabo**
  Verde
Required Space *e:* **RSP**
Required Space character *e:* **RSP**
Requirements Engineering Environment *e:*
  REE
Rerum Naturalium Doctor *l:* **RNDr.**
Rescue and Weather Reconnaissance Wing
  e: **RWRW**
Rescue Convention of Sea *e:* **RCS**
Research Aircraft for Visual Environment
  e: **RAVE**
Research and training programme on remote
  handling in hazardous nuclear
  environments *e:* **TELEMAN**
Research Animal Alliance *e:* **RAA**
Research Animal Diagnostic and
  Investigative Laboratory *e:* **RADIL**
Research Animal Holding Facility *e:*
  RAHF
Research Applications Program
  Thunderstorm Weather *e:* **RAPTSTM**
  WX
Research Association of Applied Geometry
  e: **RAAG**
Research Aviation Facility [National Center
  for Atmospheric Research] *e:* **RAF**
Research Aviation Medicine *e:* **RAM**
Research Center for Marine Geoscience *e:*
  GEOMAR
Research Center for Urban and
  Environmental Planning *e:* **RCUEP**
Research Center of Isotropic Geochemistry
  and Geochronology *e:* **RCIGG**
Research Centre for Fisheries and
  Oceanography (Cameroon) *e:* **CRHO**
Research, Conservation and Monitoring
  Project of Migratory Arctic Birds on the
  Baltic Sea and the White Sea *e:*
  RECMAB

Research Council for Complementary
    Medicine e: **RCCM**
Research Earth Borer e: **REB**
Research Hospital and Medical Center,
    Kansas City e: **MoKRes**
Research in Experimental Medicine e: **Res
    Exp Med**
Research in Laboratory Animal Medicine
    and Care e: **RILAMAC**
Research in Microbiology e: **Res
    Microbiol**
Research in Nursing and Health e: **Res
    Nurs Health**
Research in Supersonic Environment e:
    RISE
Research Institute for Agrobiology and Soil
    Fertility e: **AB-DLO**
Research Institute for Animal Production
    e: **RIAP**
Research Institute for Environmental
    Medicine e: **RIEM**
Research Institute for Mediciane and
    Chemistry e: **RIMAC**
Research Institute for Nature Conservation
    of Arctic and the North e: **RINCAN**
Research Institute for the Natural Sciences
    e: **RINS**
Research Institute for Water Resource
    Information Systems e: **VodNIIInform-
    Project**
Research Institute of Agricultural
    Microbiology, Moscow Department e:
    VNIISHMM
Research Institute of Agricultural
    Microbiology, St.-Petersburg e:
    VNIISHM
Research Institute of Animal Science e:
    RIAS
Research Institute of Atmospherics e: **RIA**
Research Institute of Environmental
    Conservation e: **VNIIPriroda**
Research Institute of Hydrogeology and
    Engineering Geology e: **VSEGINGEO**
Research Natural Area e: **RNA**
Research Notes and Memoranda of Applied
    Geometry for Prevenient Natural
    Philosophy e: **RAAG Res Notes**
Research on Orbital Plasma
    Electrodynamics e: **ROPE**
Research Programme on Landsurface
    Processes and Climate e: **PLSPC**
Research Report/Health Effects Institute e:
    Res Rep Health Eff Inst
Research Review [Office of Aerospace
    Research] e: **Res. Rev. [Office Aerosp.
    Res.]**
Research Satellite for Geophysics e: **RSG**
Research Scanning Polarimeter e: **RSP**
Research School of Biological Sciences e:
    RSBS
Research Society for Natural Therapeutics
    e: **RSNT**
Research Space Surveillance Network e:
    RSSN
Research Unit for Hospital Administration
    and Medical Care Organization e:
    RUHAMCO
Researth-Cottrell, Inc. e: **RC**
Réseau de Liaison et d'échange de
    l'Information Environnementale
    Francophone f: **RELIEF**
Réseau de stations de surveillance de la
    pollution atmosphérique f: **BAPMoN**

Réseau de surveillance de la pollution de
    fond de l'air f: **BAPMoN**
Réseau d'Echanges Multidisciplinaire pour
    l'Environnement et le Développement f:
    REMED
Réseau d'Education à l'Environnement
    Breton f: **REEB**
Réseau d'Information en Sciences
    Biologiques pour l'Amérique Latine et les
    Caraïbes f: **RIBLAC**
Réseau d'information specialise dans
    l'introduction des nouvell technologies de
    l'information dans les Écoles f:
    EURYCLEE
Réseau d'Information Tiers-Monde f:
    RITIMO
Réseau d'Information Tiers-Monde des
    centres de documentation pour le
    développement f: **RITIMO**
Réseau d'Observatoires de Surveillance
    Ecologique Long Terme f: **ROSELT**
Réseau d'ONG africaines sur
    l'environnement f: **ANEN**
Réseau d'éducation à l'environnement
    urbain f: **Citéphile**
Réseau européen dappui climatologique f:
    ECSN
Réseau Européen des Télécommunications
    Opérationnelles Météorologiques f:
    RETOM
Réseau européen dobservation et
    d'information sur lenvironnement f:
    EIONET
Réseau International d'Education à
    l'Environnement f: **RIEE**
Réseau National de Ressources en Sciences
    Médico-Sociales f: **RNRSMS**
Réseau National de Surveillance
    Aérobiologique f: **RNSA**
Réseau pour l' Environnement et le
    Développement durable en Afrique f:
    REDDA
Réseau pour l'évaluation des incidences du
    climat et la formulation de stratégies de
    parade f: **CIRSNet**
reserve feed water e: **R.F.W.**
Reserve of Medical Officers e: **R.M.O.**
Reserve Officers' Training Course Medical
    Units e: **ROTCMU**
Réserves Naturelles de France f: **RNF**
Residency Review Committee for
    Emergency Medicine e: **RRCEM**
Resident Aerospace Medicine e: **RAM**
Resident Apollo Spacecraft Program Office
    e: **RASPO**
Resident Apollo Spacecraft Project Office
    e: **RASPO**
Resident Medical Officer e: **R.M.O.**
Resident Space Shuttle Project Office[r] e:
    RSSPO
Residential Space Planners International e:
    RSPI
Residents Organized for Better and
    Beautiful Environmental Development
    e: **ROBBED**
Residual Analysis Program [Space Flight
    Operations Facility] e: **RAP**
Residual Heat Removal Service Water e:
    RHRSW
Residual Polarization Error e: **RPE**
Residuals-Environmental Quality
    Management e: **REQM**

Resource Appraisal Group Library, United
    States Geological Survey e: **GIR**
Resource Centre, Ecology Action Centre,
    Dalhousie University, Halifax, Nova
    Scotia e: **NSHDEA**
Resource Ecology and Fisheries
    Management e: **REFM**
Resource Protection well e: **RP**
Resource-sharing in a Distributed
    Environment Network e: **RIDE
    Network**
Resource System Time
    Sharing/Environment e: **RSTS/E**
Resources for Cross Cultural Health Care
    e: **RCCH**
Resources Protection Board e: **RPB**
respektieren d: **resp.**
respektiert d: **resp.**
Respiratory Health Network of Centres of
    Excellence. Réseau des Centres
    d'Excellence en Santé Respiratoire e:
    INSPIRAPLEX
Respiratory Medicine e: **Respir Med**
Respiratory Protective Device e: **RPD**
Respiratory Protective Equipment e: **RPE**
Responsible Medical Officer e: **RMO**
Responsible National Oceanographic Data
    Center (or Centre[s]) e: **RNODC**
Responsible National Oceanographic Data
    Centre for the Indian Ocean e: **RNODC-
    INDO**
Responsive Environment Programmed
    Laboratory e: **REPLAB**
Ressources naturelles f: **RN**
Restructuring the Undergraduate Learning
    Environment e: **RULE**
Resultierende d: **R**
Results on Marine Biological Investigations
    e: **ROMBI**
Retired Serviceman's Family Protection
    Plan e: **RSFPP**
Retiro Interdenominacional de Pastores
    Evangélicos de Nicaragua s: **RIPEN**
retrocardial space e: **RCS**
Retroreflector in Space e: **RIS**
Return to Earth e: **RTE**
Return-to-Earth Digital e: **RTED**
Return-to-Zero-Nonpolarized e: **RZ-NP**
Return-to-Zero-Polarized e: **RZ-P**
Returnd Account Weather e: **RAWX**
returned account of weather e: **rawx**
Reunión Intergubernamental sobre el
    Programa Mundial sobre el Clima s:
    RIG-PMC
Réunion intergouvernementale sur le
    Programme climatologique mondial f:
    IGM-WCP
Reunión Internacional de Técnicos de la
    Nutrición Animal f: **RITENA**
Reusable Aerodynamic Space Vehicle e:
    RASV
Reusable Aerospace Passenger Transport
    e: **RAPT**
Reusable Aerospace Vehicle e: **RASV**
Reusable Multi-purpose Spacecraft e:
    RMS
Reusable Multilingual Lexica for Natural
    Language Processing e: **AQUILEX-EC-
    US004**
Reusable One-stage Orbital Space Truck e:
    ROOST
Reusable Orbital Carrier e: **ROC**
Reusable Orbital Carriers e: **ROCs**

Reusable Orbital Module Booster and Utility Shuttle e: **ROMBUS**

Reusable Orbital Transport e: **ROT**

Reusable Orbital Transport System e: **ROTS**

Reusable Orbital Transport Vehicle e: **ROTV**

Reusable Orbital Transporter e: **ROT**

Reusable Space Shuttle System e: **RSSS**

Reusable Space Transportation Cargo Vehicle e: **RSTCV**

Reuters Health Information Services e: **RHIS**

Revenue Enforcement and Protection Program e: **REAP**

Reverse-Osmosis Water e: **ROW**

Reverse Osmosis Water Purification e: **ROWPU**

Reverse Osmosis Water Purification Unit e: **ROWPU**

Reverse Polarization Transfer e: **RPT**

Reverse Video Space e: **RVS**

Reversible Hydrogen Electrode e: **RHE**

Review of Allied Health Education e: **RAHE**

Review of Environmental Effects of Pollutants e: **REEP**

Review of European Community and International Environmental Law e: **R .E.C.I.E.L.**

Review of Geophysics and Space Physics e: **RGSP**

Reviews of Environmental Contamination and Toxicology e: **Rev Environ Contam Toxicol**

Reviews of Geophysics and Space Physics e: **Rev. Geophys. Space Phys.**

Reviews on Environmental Health e: **Rev Environ Health**

Revision Advisor-An Integrated Quality Support Environment e: **RA-IQSE**

Revision Control Unifying Related Environments e: **RECOURSE**

Revista. Academia de Ciencias Exactas,Fisico-Quimicas,y Naturales de Zaragoza s: **RACZA**

Revista Argentina de Microbiologia s: **Rev Argent Microbiol**

Revista Brasileira de Biologia p: **Rev Bras Biol**

Revista Brasileira de Estatística. Ministério do Planejamento e Coordenação Geral, Instituto Brasileiro de Geografia e Estatística. Rio de Janeiro p: **IBGE/RBE.**

Revista Brasileira de Geociencas p: **RBGCA**

Revista Brasileira de Geografia p: **R Brasil Geogr**

Revista Brasileira de Geografia. Conselho Nacional de Geografia, Instituto Brasileiro de Geografia e Estadística. Rio de Janeiro p: **IBGE/R.**

Revista Chilena de Histona y Geografa s: **RChil Hist Geogr**

Revista Chilena de Historia y Geografa s: **RCHG**

Revista Chilena de Obstetricia y Ginecologia s: **RCOBA**, s: **Rev Chil Obstet Ginecol**

Revista Costanicense de Ciencias Medicas s: **RCCMEF**

Revista Cubana de Medicina Tropical s: **Rev Cubana Med Trop**

Revista Cubana de Obstetricia y Ginecologia s: **RCOGB**

Revista Cubana de Reproduccion Animal s: **RCRADJ**

Revista da Associacao Medica Brasileira p: **Rev Assoc Med Bras**

Revista da Sociedade Brasileira de Medicina Tropical p: **Rev Soc Bras Med Trop**

Revista de Biologia Tropical s: **Rev Biol Trop**

Revista de Ciencias Biologicas s: **RCIBDB**

Revista de Historia de las Ideas. Instituto Panamericano de Geografía e Historia. Editorial Casa de la Cultura Ecuatoriana. Quito s: **IPGH/RHI.**

Revista de la Facultad de Ciencias Medicas/Universidad Nacional de Cordoba s: **Rev Fac Cien Med Univ Nac Cordoba**

Revista de Medicina de la Universidad de Navarra s: **Rev Med Univ Navarra**

Revista de Medicina Veterinaria s: **RMV**

Revista del Instituto Histórico y Geográfico del Uruguay. Montevideo s: **IHGU/R.**

Revista do Hospital das Clinicas, Faculdade de Medicina da Universidade de Sao Paulo p: **Rev Hosp Clin Fac Med Sao Paulo**

Revista do Instituto de Medicina Tropical de Sao Paulo p: **Rev Inst Med Trop Sao Paulo**

Revista do Instituto Geográfico e Geológico. São Paulo p: **IGG/R.**

Revista do Instituto Geográfico e Geológico. Secretaria da Agricultura, Indústria e Comércio. São Paulo p: **I G G. O I.G.G.**

Revista do Instituto Geográfico e Histórico da Bahia. Salvador [Bahia] p: **IGHB/R.**

Revista do Instituto Histórico e Geográfico Brasileiro. [Departamento de Imprensa Nacional]. Rio de Janeiro p: **IHGB/R.**

Revista do Instituto Histórico e Geográfico de Alagoas. Maceió p: **IHGA/R.**

Revista do Instituto Histórico e Geográfico de Minas Gerais. Belo Hostizonte p: **IHGMG/R.**

Revista do Instituto Histórico e Geográfico de Sergipe. Aracajú p: **IGHS/R.**

Revista do Instituto Histórico e Geográfico de Sergipe. Aracajú [Sergipe] p: **IHGS/R.**

Revista do Instituto Histórico e Geográfico Guarujá-Bertioga. São Paulo p: **IHGGB/R.**

Revista do Instituto Histórico e Geográfico. Instituto Histórico e Geográfico, Guarujá-Bertioga. São Paulo p: **IHGSP/R.**

Revista do Instituto Histórico, Geográfico e Etnográfico Paranaense. Curitiba p: **IHGEP/R.**

Revista. Facultad de Ciencias Medicas. Universidad Nacional del Litoral Rosario s: **RCMLAO**

Revista Geográfica. Instituto Geográfico Militar del Ecuador, Departamento Geográfico. Quito s: **IGME/RG.**

Revista Latinoamericana de Microbiologia s: **Rev Latinoam Microbiol**

Revista Medica de Chile s: **Rev Med Chil**

Revista Medica de Panama s: **Rev Med Panama**

Revista Medico-Chirurgicala a Societatii de Medici si Naturalisti din Iasi ru: **Rev Med Chir Soc Med Nat Iasi**

Revista. Museo Argentino de Ciencias Naturales Bernardino Rivadavia e Instituto Nacional de Investigacion de las Ciencia s: **RABBAR**

Revista. Museo de la Plata. Universidad Nacional de La Plata. Facultad de Ciencias Naturales y Museo s: **UNLPM/R**

Revista Paulista de Medicina p: **Rev Paul Med**

Revista. Real Academia de Ciencias Exactas, Fisicas, y Naturales de Madrid s: **RCFNA**

Revolutions per Orbit e: **RPO**

Revolving Fund for Natural Resources Exploration e: **RFNRE**

Revue Canadienne de Biologie f: **RCanad Biol**, f: **RCBIA**

Revue Canadienne de Geographie f: **R Canad Geogr**

Revue de Cytologie et de Biologie Vegetales-La Botaniste f: **RCBBDA**

Revue de médicine f: **Rev. de méd.**

Revue Française de Gynecologie et d'Obstetrique f: **Rev Fr Gynecol Obstet**

Revue Medicale de Bruxelles f: **Rev Med Brux**

Revue Medicale de la Suisse Romande f: **Rev Med Suisse Romande**

Revue Medicale de Liege f: **Rev Med Liege**

Revue Naturiste Internationale f: **R.N.I.**

Revue suisse d'Hydrologie f: **Rev. suisse Hydrol.**

Revue Tiers-Monde f: **TMC**

Revues de Formation Médicale Continue f: **RFMC**

Reynolds Hydrodynamic Theory e: **RHT**

Rheinisch-Bergischer Naturschutzverein d: **RBN**

Rheinwasserschutz d: **RWS**

Rhine Medical Depot e: **RMD**

Rhodamine Experiment in the North Sea e: **RHENO**

Rhode Island Medical Journal e: **R.I. Med. J.**

Rhode Island Medical Society e: **RIMS**

Rhode Island Medicine e: **R I Med**

Rhode Island Veterinary Medical Association e: **RIVMA**

Ribitdehydrogenase d: **RDH**

Ribitol-dehydrogenase e: **RDH**

Rice Lake National Wildlife Refuge e: **RLNWR**

Richard Abr. Herder GmbH, Solingen d: **RAHSOL**

Richmond Academy of Medicine, Richmond e: **ViRA**

Richmond-Cape Henry Environmental Laboratory e: **RICHEL**

Richtlinie der Zentralstelle für Unfaliverhütung und Arbeitsmedizin d: **Z-Richtlinie**

Richtlinie für das Errichten von wasser- und abwassertechnischen Einrichtungen bei der Deutschen Bundespost d: **Richtl Wasser**

Rickenbach & Co. AG, Luft- und Klimatechnik *d:* **rico**
Rideout Pyrohydrolysis *e:* **RPH**
Riedel Environmental Technologies, Incorporated *e:* **RETI**
Rieselwasser *d:* **RiWa**
Rigas Medicinas Instituuts *le:* **RMI**
Right Circular Polarization (or Polarizer) *e:* **RCP**
Right Circularly Polarized Light *e:* **RCPL**
Right Hand Circular Polarization (or Polarized) *e:* **RHCP**
Right Hand Elliptically Polarized *e:* **RHEP**
Right-Hand polarized Mode *e:* **RHM**
Right[-handed] Circular Polarization *e:* **RCP**
Right Medical Rectus *e:* **RMR**
right medical rectus muscle *e:* **RMR**
Right Observation Post *e:* **ROP**
Rigid Space Structure *e:* **RSS**
Rijks Geologische Dienst *n:* **RGD**
Rijks Zuivel-Agrarische Afvalwaterdienst *n:* **RAAD**
Rijksinstituut voor Veldbiologisch Onderzoek in Nederland *n:* **RIVON**
Rijksinstituut voor Veldbiologisch Onderzoek ten behoeve van het Natuurbehoud *n:* **RIVON**
Rijksinstituut voor Zuivering van Afvalwater *n:* **RIZA**
Rijksinstituut voor Zuivering van Afvalwater en Verontreiniging van Openbare Wateren *n:* **RIZA**
Rijkswaterstaat *n:* **RWS**
Rijncommissie Waterleidingbedrijven *n:* **RIWA**
Rindfleischetikettierungsgesetz *d:* **RiFlEtikettG**
Rio Branco/Presidente Medici [Brazil] *p:* **SBRB**
Rise-of-Water *e:* **ROW**
Rising Observational Sounding Equipment *e:* **ROSE**
Risk-Aversion Linear Program Model for Deriving an E V efficiency frontier *e:* **MOTAD**
Risk: Issues in Health & Safety *e:* **Risk Issues Health&Safety**
Riso Integrated Environmental Project *e:* **RIMI**
River Dee valley around Aberdeen *e:* **Deeside**
River Ice Breaker *e:* **RIB**
River Input to Ocean Systems *e:* **RIOS**
River Protection Project *e:* **RPP**
River Road Environmental Technology Centre, Environment Canada Ottawa, Ontario *e:* **OOEAPT**
River Water *e:* **RW**
River Water Supply System *e:* **RWSS**
River Water System *e:* **RWS**
Rivista Critica di Clinica Medica *i:* **RCCMA**
Rivista di Biologia *i:* **RBILA**, *i:* **Riv Biol**
Rivista di Idrobiologia *i:* **Riv. Idrobiol.**
Rivista Europea per le Scienze Mediche e Farmacologiche *i:* **Riv Eur Sci Med Farmacol**
Rivista Geografica Italiana. Societa di Studi Geografici e Coloniali *i:* **SSG/RGÌ**
RL Environmental surveillance Inspection *e:* **REI**

RMA [Rückgewinnung von Metallen aus Abwasser]-System Firma Dornier GmbH *d:* **RMA**
Road Space *e:* **RS**
Roaded Natural *e:* **RN**
Rob and Bessie Welder Wildlife Foundation, Sinton *e:* **TxSiW**
Robert S. Kerr Environmental Research Laboratory *e:* **RSKERL**
Robot Independent Programming Environment *e:* **RIPE**
Robust Biological Equations *e:* **RBE**
Roche Institute of Molecular Biology *e:* **RIMB**
Rock in Water *e:* **RKW**
Rockefeller Institute for Medical Research *e:* **RIMR**
Rockefeller University, Population Council, Bio-Medical Library, New York *e:* **NNRU-P**
Rocket Orbital Bomber *e:* **ROBO**
Rocket Orbital Bomber Project *e:* **ROBO Project**
Rockets launched up to the upper atmosphere for soundings of the earth *e:* **SOUNDING ROCKETS**
Rocks in Water *e:* **RKSW**
Rocky Flats Environmental Monitoring Council *e:* **RFEMC**
Rocky Flats Environmental Technology Site, Golden, Colorado *e:* **RFETS**
Rocky Mountain Association of Geologists *e:* **RMAG**
Rocky Mountain Center for Occupational and Environmental Health *e:* **RMCOEH**
Rocky Mountain Center on [the] Environment *e:* **ROMCOE**
Rocky Mountain Medical Corp. *e:* **RMED**
Rocky Mountain Medical Journal *e:* **Rocky Mt. Med. J.**
Rocky Mountain Natural Gas Co. *e:* **RGAS**
Rocky Mountains Association of Petroleum Geologists *e:* **R.A.P.G.**
Roentgen Equivalent Biological *e:* **REB**
Role of Clouds, Energy, and Water In global change program *e:* **ROCEW**
Roll Over Protection Standards *e:* **ROPS**
Roll-over Protection System *e:* **ROPS**
Roll-Over-Protective and Falling-Object-Protective Structure *e:* **ROPS-FOPS**
Roll-Over-Protective Structure *e:* **ROPS**
Rollin' Rock Club of Texas and Any Other State or Country of the World and Outer Space *e:* **RRCOTAAOSOCOTWAOS**
Romanian Journal of Internal Medicine *e:* **Rom J Intern Med**
[Romberg] Tiburon Center for Environmental Studies *e:* **TCES**
Röntgen- und elektromedizinische Apparate *d:* **RÖMED**
Roosevelt Hospital, Medical Library, New York *e:* **VVQ**
Roots Effects on the Atmosphere, Carbon and Hydrology *e:* **REACH**
Rosensteil School of Marine and Atmospheric Sciences, Miami *e:* **RSMAS**
Ross Ice Shelf Ecosystem *e:* **RISE**
Ross Ice Shelf Program *e:* **RISP**
Ross Sea Ice Shelf Project *e:* **RISP**
Ross Sea Marginal Ice Zone Ecology *e:* **ROSSMIZE**

Rotary Hearth Furnace *e:* **RHF**
Rotating Biological Contractor *e:* **RBC**
Rotating Biological Contractors *e:* **RBC**
Rotating Linear Polarization *e:* **RLP**
Rotating Observation Platform *e:* **ROP**
Rotating Water Atomization Process *e:* **ROWAP**
rotation, geographical *e:* **rot., geogr.**
Rotational Air Weather Squadron *e:* **ROT AWS**
Rote Zelle Medizin *d:* **Rotzmed**
rotierend *d:* **rot.**
rotierendes Abreißen *d:* **rA**
Rotor-Burst Protection Program *e:* **RBPP**
Rough Sea *e:* **R**
Roumanian Archives of Microbiology and Immunology *e:* **Roum Arch Microbiol Immunol**
Route Forestière *f:* **R.F.**
Routine Environmental High-Volume Air Samples *e:* **REHVAS**
Routine for Executing Biological Unit Simulations *e:* **REBUS**
Routine Seed Health Test *e:* **RSHT**
Routing and Remote Access Service *e:* **RRAS**
Routing Remote Access Service *e:* **RRAS**
Royal Academy of Medicine, Dublin *e:* **R.A.M.D.**
Royal Accounting System [United States Geological Survey] *e:* **RAS**
Royal Aerospace Establishment *e:* **RAE**
Royal Air Force Institute of Aviation Medicine *e:* **R.A.F.I.A.M.**
Royal Air Force Institute of Community Medicine *e:* **RAF ICM**
Royal Air Force Institute of Dental Health & Training *e:* **RAF IDHT**
Royal Air Force Medical Services *e:* **R.A.F.M.S.**
Royal and Ancient Society of Polar Bears *e:* **RASPB**
Royal Army Medical College *e:* **RAMC**
Royal Army Medical Corps *e:* **R.A.M.C.**
Royal Army Medical Corps Depot *e:* **RAMCD**
Royal Army Medical Corps Magazine *e:* **RAMC Magazine**
Royal Army Medical Corps,Territorials *e:* **RAMCT**
Royal Army Medical Service *e:* **R.A.M.S.**
Royal Australasian College of Dental Surgeons *e:* **RACDS**
Royal Australasian College of Medical Administrators *e:* **RACMA**
Royal Australasian College of Surgeons *e:* **R.A.C.S.**
Royal Australian Air Force Medical Officer *e:* **R.A.A.F.M.O.**
Royal Australian Air Force Medical Service *e:* **R.A.A.F.M.S.**
Royal Australian and New Zealand College of Obstetricians and Gynaecologist *e:* **RANZCOG**
Royal Australian Army Medical Corps *e:* **R.A.A.M.C.**
Royal Australian College of Obstetricians and Gynaecologists *e:* **RACOG**
Royal Belgian Institute of Natural Sciences *e:* **RBINS**
Royal Canadian Air Force Medical Bulletin *e:* **RCAF Medical Bulletin**

Royal Canadian Army Medical Corps *e:* **RCAMC**

Royal Canadian Army Medical Personnel *e:* **RCAMP**

Royal Canadian Geographical Society *e:* **RCGS**

Royal Canadian Geological Society *e:* **RCGS**

Royal Canadian Sea Cadets *e:* **R.C.S.C.**

Royal Canadian Sea Cadets Corps *e:* **RCSCC**

Royal Canadian Veterinary Surgeon *e:* **RCVS**

Royal College of Dental Surgeons *e:* **RCDS**

Royal College of Obstetricians and Gynaecologists *e:* **R.C.O.G.**

Royal College of Paediatrics and Child Health *e:* **RCPCH**

Royal College of Physicians and Surgeons *e:* **RCPS**

Royal College of Physicians and Surgeons of Canada *e:* **RCP[C],** *e:* **RCPSC**

Royal College of Physicians and Surgeons of Glasgow *e:* **RCPGlas,** *e:* **RCPGlass,** *e:* **RCPS Glas,** *e:* **R.C.P.S.Glasg.,** *e:* **RSPS[Glasg]**

Royal College of Surgeons *e:* **R.C.of S.,** *e:* **R.C.S.**

Royal College of Surgeons, Edinburgh, United Kingdom *e:* **UkERCS**

Royal College of Surgeons of Canada *e:* **RCSC,** *e:* **RCS Can**

Royal College of Surgeons of Edinburgh *e:* **RCSE,** *e:* **R.C.S.E[din].**

Royal College of Surgeons of England *e:* **R.C.S.[Eng.]**

Royal College of Surgeons of England, London, United Kingdom *e:* **UkLRCS**

Royal College of Surgeons of Ireland *e:* **RCSI**

Royal College of Veterinary Surgeons *e:* **R.C.V.S.**

Royal Commission on Environmental Pollution *e:* **RCEP**

Royal Environmental Health Institute of Scotland *e:* **R.E.H.I.S.**

Royal Faculty of Physicians and Surgeons *e:* **RFPS**

Royal Faculty of Physicians and Surgeons of Glasgow *e:* **RFPS [G[las]]**

Royal Forest and Bird Protection Society Inc. *e:* **F&B**

Royal Geographical Society, England *e:* **RGS**

Royal Geographical Society, London *e:* **RGSoc**

Royal Geographical Society of Australasia *e:* **R.G.S.A.**

Royal Geographical Society of Australasia. South Australian Branch. Proceedings *e:* **Proc S Aust Brch R Geogr Soc Australas**

Royal Geographical Society of Australia *e:* **RGSA**

Royal Geographical Society. Proceedings *e:* **GSP**

Royal Geographical Society Research Series *e:* **RGS Research Series**

Royal Greenwich Observatory *e:* **RGO,** *e:* **RGrOb**

Royal Institute for the sustainable management of Natural resources and the promotion of clean Technology *e:* **RINT**

Royal Institute of Painters in Water Colours *e:* **R.I.**

Royal Institute of Public Health and Hygiene *e:* **RIPH,** *e:* **R.I.P.H.H.**

Royal Institute of Public Health and Hygiene. Journal. London *e:* **PH and H journal**

Royal Interocean Lines *e:* **R.I.L.**

Royal Interocean Lines, Amsterdam *e:* **RIL**

Royal Medical and Chirurgical Society *e:* **RMCS**

Royal Medical Benevolent Fund *e:* **R.M.B.F.**

Royal Medical Officer *e:* **R.M.O.**

Royal Medical Society *e:* **R.M.S.**

Royal Medicine Society *e:* **RMedSoc**

Royal Medico-Psychological Association *e:* **R.M.P.A.**

Royal Meteorological Society *e:* **R Met S,** *e:* **RMetS[oc],** *e:* **R.M.S.**

Royal National Mission to Deep-Sea Fishermen *e:* **R.N.M.D.S.F.**

Royal Naval Hydrographic Department *e:* **R.N.H.D.**

Royal Naval Medical Corps *e:* **RNMC**

Royal Naval Medical School *e:* **R.N.M.S.**

Royal Naval Medical Service *e:* **RNMS**

Royal Naval Volunteer Reserve Pigeon Service *e:* **R.N.V.R.P.S.**

Royal Navy Medical Corps *e:* **R.N.M.C.**

Royal Navy Polaris School *e:* **RNPS**

Royal Netherlands Meteorological Institute *e:* **RNMI**

Royal New Zealand Army Medical Corps *e:* **R.N.Z.A.M.C.**

Royal New Zealand Society for the Health of Women and Children *e:* **RNZSHWC**

Royal Observatory *e:* **R.O.**

Royal Observatory, Edinburgh *e:* **ROE**

Royal Observatory, Greenwich *e:* **R.O.G.**

Royal Observatory Technical Memoirs *e:* **RO Technical Memoirs**

Royal Ocean Racing Club *e:* **R.O.R.C.**

Royal Pigeon Racing Association *e:* **RPRA**

Royal Postgraduate Medical School *e:* **RPMS**

Royal Protection Branch *e:* **RPB**

Royal Provident Fund for Sea Fishermen *e:* **R.P.F.S.F.**

Royal School of Medicine *e:* **RSM**

Royal School Society for the Prevention of Cruelty to Animals *e:* **R.S.S.P.C.A.**

Royal Scottish Geographical Society *e:* **R.S.G.S.**

Royal Scottish Water-Colour Society *e:* **R.S.W.S.**

Royal Society for Nature Conservation *e:* **RSNC**

Royal Society for Protection of Birds *e:* **RSPB**

Royal Society for the Health of Women and Children *e:* **RSHWC**

Royal Society for the Prevention of Cruelty to Animals *e:* **R.S.P.C.A.**

Royal Society for the Promotion of Health *e:* **R.S.H.,** *e:* **RSPH**

Royal Society for the Protection and Care of Animals *e:* **RSPCA**

Royal Society for the Protection of Rats *e:* **RSPR**

Royal Society of Health *e:* **R.S.H.**

Royal Society of London for Improving Natural Knowledge *e:* **Royal Society**

Royal Society of Medicine *e:* **R.S.M.,** *e:* **RSMA**

Royal Society of Medicine, London, United Kingdom *e:* **UkLRSM**

Royal Society of Painters in Water Colours *e:* **R.S.P.W.[C.]**

Royal Society of Tropical Medicine and Hygiene *e:* **RSTM&H**

Royal Water Colour Society *e:* **RWCS**

Royal West African Frontier Force *e:* **R.W.A.F.F.**

RPV [Remotely Piloted Vehicle] Simulation Evaluation Program[me] *e:* **RSEP**

RRN Oceania *e:* **RRN OCE**

Rubber-Covered and Weather-Proof *e:* **RCWP**

Rubber Covered, Braided and Weather-Proof *e:* **RCBWP**

Rubber-Covered Weather-Proof Wire *e:* **RCWP Wire**

Rubber Glove/Remote Button *e:* **RG/RB**

Rubber Hydrocarbon *e:* **RHC**

Rubber Hydrocarbon Content *e:* **RHC Content**

Ruby Lake National Wildlife Refuge *e:* **RLNWR**

Rufus River Groundwater Interception Scheme *e:* **RRGIS**

Rugged Glen Nature Reserve *e:* **RGNR**

Ruhrtal-Elektrizitätsgesellschaft *d:* **REG**

Run Time Environment *e:* **RTE**

Runway Protection Zone *e:* **RPZ**

Rural Clean Water Program *e:* **RCWP**

Rural Environmental Assistance Program *e:* **REAP**

Rural Environmental Conservation Program *e:* **RECP**

Rural Health Care Corporation *e:* **RHCC**

Rural Health Office[r] *e:* **RHO**

Rural Health Program *e:* **RHP**

Rural Information Center Health Services *e:* **RICHS**

Rural Nature Conservation Program *e:* **RNCP**

Rural Oxidants in the Southern Environment *e:* **ROSE**

Rural Ozone in a Southern Environment *e:* **ROSE**

Rural Ozone in Southern Environment-Aircraft *e:* **ROSE-AIR**

Rural Water Commission *e:* **RWC**

Rural Water Pricing Policy *e:* **RWPP**

Rural Water Supply & Sanitation Development Fund Board *e:* **RWSSDFB**

Rurality-Environment-Development *e:* **RED**

Russian Academy of Space Sciences *e:* **IKI**

Russian Environmental Federation Information Agency *e:* **REFIA**

Russian Hydrometeorological Institute *e:* **RSHMI**

Russian manned space station *e:* **MIR**

Russian Ministry for Civil Defense, Emergencies and the Elimination of Consequences of Natural Disasters *e:* **EMERCOM**

Russian Navy, Department of Navigation and Oceanography *e:* **GUNIO**

Russian pressurized light-water reactor *e:* **VVER**

Russian programme studying the influences of pollution on the Arctic environment *e:* **ICGP**

Russian Research and Production Centre of Geoinformation *e:* **RosGeoInform**

Russian Space Agency *e:* **RSA**

Russian Space Research Institute *e:* **IKI**

Russian space research reactor *e:* **TOPAZ**

Russian Space Science Internet *e:* **RSSI**

Russian Space Station *e:* **MIR**

Russian State Committee for Geology and Mineral Resources *e:* **RosComNedra**

Russian State Committee for Hydrometeorology *e:* **RosComhydromet**

Russian State Committee for Water Resources *e:* **Ros ComVod**

Russian State Committee on Geology and the Use of Underground Resources *e:* **ROSKOMNEDRH**

Russian State Hydrometeorological Institute *e:* **RGGI**, *e:* **RSHI**

Russia's Ministry of Environment *e:* **RMENR**

Rüstwagen-Umweltschutz *d:* **RW-U**

Rüstwagen-Wasserrettung *d:* **RW-W**

Rutherford's Institutes of Natural Law *e:* **Ruth. Inst.**

Ryan's Medical Jurisprudence *e:* **Ry. Ed. Jur.**, *e:* **Ry. Med. Jur.**

S

S-band Polar Ultra *e:* **SPU**

S-Band Polarization Diversity *e:* **SPD**

S. L. Ross Environmental Research, Ottawa, Ontario *e:* **OOSLR**

Saarberg-Hölter Umwelttechnik GmbH *d:* **SHU**

Saarländische Naturschutzgesetz *d:* **SaNatSchG**

Saarländisches Wassergesetz *e:* **SWG**

Sabine National Wildlife Refuge *e:* **SNWR**

Sachgebietsorientierte Programmsprache *d:* **SOPS**

sachgebietsorientiertes Programmiersystem *d:* **SOPS**

sachgebietsorientiertes Programmiersystem betriebliche Materialwirtschaft *d:* **SOPS MAWI**

sachgebietsorientiertes Programmpaket *d:* **SOPP**

Sachs-Georgi Reaktion *d:* **SGR**

Sachs-Georgi Test *d:* **S-GT**, *e:* **S-G Test**

Sächsisches Wassergesetz *d:* **SächsWG**, *e:* **SächsWG**

Sachverständigenorganisation zum Umgang mit wassergefährdenden Stoffen *d:* **SwS**

Sachverständigenrat für Umweltfragen *d:* **SRU**

Sacramento Medical Society *e:* **SMS**

Sacramento National Wildlife Refuge *e:* **SNWR**

Sacramento Peak Observatory *e:* **SPO**

Sado Marine Biological Station. Niigata University. Special Publication *e:* **NDRHFA**, *e:* **Sado Mar Biol Stn Niigato Univ Spec Publ**, *e:* **Sado Mar Biol Stn Niigato Univ Spec Publ**

Safe Drinking Water Act *e:* **SDWA**

Safe Drinking Water Information System *e:* **SDWIS**

Safe Medical Device Act *e:* **SMDA**

Safe Medical Devices Act *e:* **SMDA**

Safe, R and QA, and Protective Services *e:* **SF**

Safe Shutdown Earthquake *e:* **SSE**

Safe Water Coalition *e:* **SWC**

Safe Water Enforcement Tracking *e:* **SWETS**

Safeguards and accountability remote terminal *e:* **SART**

Safety and Environment *e:* **S&E**

Safety and Environmental Advisory Council *e:* **SEAC**

Safety and Environmental Division *e:* **SED**

Safety and Environmental Division/Environmental Oversight Branch *e:* **SED/EOB**

Safety and Environmental Division/Nuclear Facility Safety Branch *e:* **SED/NFS**

Safety and Environmental Division/Occupational Safety & Emergency Preparedness Branch *e:* **SED/OSE**

Safety and environmental engineering *e:* **S&EE**

Safety and Environmental Protection Division *e:* **SAF**

safety and health *e:* **S&H**

Safety and Health Administration *e:* **SHA**

Safety and Health Bulletin *e:* **Saf Hlth Bull**

Safety and Health Data Sheet *e:* **SHDS**

Safety and Health Five-Year Plan *e:* **S&H FYP**

Safety and Health Hall of Fame International *e:* **SHHOFI**

Safety and Health Management Division *e:* **SHMD**

Safety and Health Regulations for Construction *e:* **SHRC**

Safety and Health Standards Management Board *e:* **SHSMB**

Safety and occupational health *e:* **S&OH**

Safety appraisal/audit finding/observation *e:* **SAF**

safety at sea *e:* **SAS**

Safety At Sea International, Maritime Electronics Exhibition *e:* **SASMEX**

Safety At Sea & Marine Electronics Exhibition and Conference *e:* **SASMEX `88**

Safety Control Water System *e:* **SCWS**

Safety Environmental and Emergency Actions *e:* **SE&EA**

Safety Fire Protection Survey *e:* **SFP**

Safety Function Earthquake *e:* **SFE**

Safety, Health and Environment Intra Industry Benchmarking Association *e:* **SHEiiBA**

Safety, health and the environment *e:* **SHE**

Safety, Health and Welfare *e:* **Saf Health Welfare**

safety, health and welfare *e:* **shw**

Safety Injection and Refueling Water *e:* **SIRW**

Safety Injection and Refueling Water Tank *e:* **SIRWT**

Safety Injection Reserve Water Tank *e:* **SIRWT**

Safety Observation Station *e:* **SOS**

Safety Observation Station Display Console *e:* **SOSC**

Safety of Life at Sea [conference (or convention)] *e:* **SOLAS**

Safety on Sea *e:* **SOS**

Safety Shutdown Earthquake *e:* **SSE**

Safety Training and Observation Program *e:* **STOP**

Safety Weather Probability Study *e:* **SWEPS**

Safugetierkundliche Mitteilungen *d:* **Safugetierkd Mitt**

SAGE [Semi-Automatic Ground Environment] Air Traffic Integration *e:* **SATIN**

SAGE [Semi-Automatic Ground Environment] Analytics International, Incorporated *e:* **SAII**

SAGE [Semi-Automatic Ground Environment] Back-up *e:* **SABU**

SAGE [Semi-Automatic Ground Environment] Battery Routing Equipment *e:* **SABRE**

SAGE [Semi-Automatic Ground Environment] Computer Program[me] (or Project) *e:* **SCP**

SAGE [Semi-Automatic Ground Environment] Computer Programming Training *e:* **SCPT**

SAGE [Semi-Automatic Ground Environment] Control Center *e:* **SCC**

SAGE [Semi-Automatic Ground Environment] Data Generator *e:* **SADGE**

SAGE [Semi-Automatic Ground Environment] Division Commander *e:* **SDC**

SAGE [Semi-Automatic Ground Environment] Evaluation Exercise *e:* **SEE**

SAGE [Semi-Automatic Ground Environment] Evaluation Library Tape *e:* **SELT**

SAGE [Semi-Automatic Ground Environment] Experimental Display Generator *e:* **SEDGE**

SAGE (Semi-Automatic Ground Environment) Improvement Program *e:* **SIP**

SAGE (Semi-Automatic Ground Environment) Intercept Target Simulation *e:* **SITS**

SAGE (Semi-Automatic Ground Environment) Interceptor Simulator *e:* **SIS**

SAGE (Semi-Automatic Ground Environment) Interceptor System *e:* **SIS**

SAGE (Semi-Automatic Ground Environment) Main Distributing Frame *e:* **SMDF**

SAGE (Semi-Automatic Ground Environment) Maintenance Control *e:* **SMC**

SAGE (Semi-Automatic Ground Environment) Operation Analysis Project *e:* **SOAP**

SAGE [Semi-Automatic Ground Environment] Strobe Training Operator *e:* **SASTRO**

SAGE (Semi-Automatic Ground Environment) System Status Report *e:* **SSSR**

SAGE (Semi-Automatic Ground Environment) System Training Unit *e:* **SSTU**

SAGE [Semi-Automatic Ground Environmental] Direction Center *e:* **SDC**

SAGE [Semiautomatic Ground Environment] Tracking and Guidance Evaluation System e: **STRANGE**

Saginaw Health Sciences Library e: **MiSHS**

Saguenay Medical e: **Sague Med**

Sahara and Sahel Observatory e: **OSS**, e: **SSO**

Said Medical Journal e: **Said Med J**

Saint Elirabeth Medical Center Covington e: **KyCovStE**

Saint Elisabeth Hospital Health Science Library, Beaumont e: **TxBeaSE**

Saint Francis Hospital, Medical Library, Memphis e: **TMStF**

Saint-Georges-De-L'Oyapock f: **SOOG**

Saint Joseph Hospital , Medical and Nursing Library, Fort Worth e: **TxFSJ**

Saint Joseph's Hospital, School of Nursing and Medical Library, Syracuse e: **NSySJ**

Saint Lawrence University. Geological Information and Referral Service. Bulletin e: **Saint Lawrence Univ Geol Inf and Referral Serrice Bull**, e: **Saint Lawrence Univ Geol Inf and Referral Service Bull**

Saint Marks National Wildlife Refuge e: **SMNWR**

Saint Mary's Hospital, Henegen Medical Library, Streator e: **IstrSMH**

Saint Mary's Medical Center, Medical Library, Knoxville e: **TKSMC**

Saint Mary's Medical Center, Nursing School Library, Knoxville e: **TKSMC-N**

Saint Simons Island off the coast of Brunswick, Georgia e: **S'n Simons**

Saint Thomas Hospital, Health Sciences Library, Nashville e: **TNStT**

Saint Vincents Medical Center of Richmond, Staten Island e: **NSiSV**

Saito Ho-On Kai Museum of Natural History. Research Bulletin e: **Saito Ho-On Kai Mus Nat Hist Res Bull**, e: **SHKBDX**

Sal Oceanic Area Control Center e: **GVSC**

Sales Environment Learning Laboratory e: **SELL**

Sales Order and Ledger Accounting (using) Computerline Environment e: **SOLACE**

Salick Health Care, Incorporated e: **SHCI**

Salicylhydroxamic Acid e: **SHAM**

Salicylideniminobenzohydroxamic Acid e: **SIBH**

Saline Water Conversion e: **SWC**

Saline Water Conversion Corporation e: **SWCC**

Saline Water Conversion Program [Department of the Interior] e: **SWCP**

Salisbury Medical Bulletin e: **Salisbury Rev**

Salk Institute for Biological Sciences e: **SIBS**

Salk Institute for Biological Studies e: **SIBS**

Sallskapet for Agronomisk Hydroteknik a: **SAHT**

Sällskapet for Agronomisk Hydroteknik r: **SAHT**

Salmon Protection Association of Western Newfoundland e: **SPAWN**

Salomon Islands in the Chagos Archipelago in the Indian Ocean e: **Salomons**

Salon International de l'Exploitation des Océans f: **OCEANEXPO**

Salon International de l'Équipement Laitier f: **SIEL**

Salon International de Techniques du Chauffage, du Froid et de la Climatisation f: **INTERCLIMA**

Salon international des Techniques Papetières et Graphiques f: **TPG**

Salt Lake City Weather Forecast Office e: **SLC**

Salt Plains National Wildlife Refuge e: **SPNWR**

salt water e: **sw**

salt water average draft e: **s.w.a.d.**

Salt Water Average Draft (or Draught) e: **SWAD**

Salt-Water Circulating Pump e: **SWCP**

Salt-Water Cooling System e: **SWCS**

Salt Water Departure Draft e: **SWDD**

Salt Water Draft (or Draugth) e: **SWD**

salt water gauge e: **S.W.G.**

Salt Water Igniter e: **SWI**

Salt Water Leak Check e: **SWLC**

Salt-Water Pump e: **SWP**

Salt Water System e: **SWS**

Saltee Islands in St George's Channel off Wexford, Ireland e: **Saltees**

Salute Italia Medica i: **Salute Italia Med**

Salvadoran Development and Natural Resources Research Program e: **PRISMA**

Salvadoran Medical Relief Fund e: **SMRF**

Salvation Army Medical Fellowship e: **SAMF**

Samarbetsnamnden for de Nordiska Naturvetenskapliga Forskningraden r: **NOS-N**

Same Sea and Country e: **SS & C**

same sea and country or coast e: **S.S.a.C.**

Same Sea and Country (or Coast) e: **SS and C**

Samenwerking documentatie op het gebied van verontreiniging van Bodem, Water en Lucht n: **BOWAL**

Sami Medica. Journal. Sami Medical Association e: **SAMJ**

Sammlung Geologischer Führer d: **Samml Geol Führer**

Samoa Observatory e: **SMO**

Sample Polarity Coincidence Correlator e: **SPCC**

Sampling Aernspace Nuclear Debris e: **SAND**

Sampling Aerospace Nuclear Debris e: **SAND**

Sampling & Identification of Biological & Chemical Agents e: **SIBCA**

San Andreas Fault Observatory at Depth e: **SAFOD**

San Andreas Geological Observatory e: **SAO**

San Antonio Joint Military Medical Command e: **SAJMMC**

San Bernardino County Medical Society. Bulletin e: **San Bernardino County Med Soc Bull**, e: **San Bernardino County Med Soc Bull**

San Clemente Ocean Probing Experiment e: **SCOPE**

San Diego Aerospace Museum e: **SDAM**

San Diego Biomedical Research Institute e: **SDBRI**

San Diego Biomedical Symposium. Proceedings e: **San Diego Biomed Symp Proc**

San Diego County Medical Society e: **SDCMS**

San Diego County Water Authority e: **SDCWA**

San Diego Ecology Center e: **SDEC**

San Diego Foundation for Medical Care e: **SDFMC**

San Diego Institute for Burn Medicine e: **SDIBM**

San Diego Museum of Natural History e: **SDMNH**

San Diego Natural History Museum e: **SDNHM**

San Diego Oceanic Coordinating Committee e: **SANDOCC**

San Diego Society of Natural History e: **SDSNH**

San Diego Society of Natural History. Memoirs e: **San Diego Soc Nat Hist Mem**, e: **San Diego Soc Nat Hist Mem**

San Diego Society of Natural History. Occasional Papers. Transactions e: **San Diego Soc Nat History Occasional Paper Trans**

San Diego Society of Natural History. Transactions e: **San Diego Soc Nat History Trans**, e: **San Diego Soc N H Tr**

San Diego Symposium for Biomedical Engineering e: **SDSBE**

San Diego Wild Animal Park e: **SDWAP**

San Francisco Institute of Automotive Ecology e: **SFIAE**

San Francisco Medical Center e: **SFMC**

San Francisco Medical Society e: **SEMS**

San Francisco Medicine e: **San Francisco Med**

San Juan County Water Conservation District e: **SJC-WCD**

San Luis National Wildlife Refuge e: **SLNWR**

San Miguel Sea Lion Virus e: **SMSV**

Sand-Braunerde d: **sB**

Sand Lake National Wildlife Refuge e: **SLNWR**

Sand-Rosterde d: **sR**

Sandia Controllability Observability Analysis Program[me] e: **SCOAP**

Sanierung der Atmosphäre d: **SANA**, e: **SANA**

Sanierung der Atmosphäre über den Neuen Bundesländern d: **SANA**, e: **SANA**

Sanitary Engineering and Environmental Health Research Laboratory e: **SEEHRL**

Sanitary Wastewater Consolidation System e: **SWCS**

Sanitary wastewater systems consolidation e: **SWSC**

Sanitary Water e: **SW**

Sanitation Handbook of Consumer Protection Programs e: **SHCPP**

Santa Ana National Wildlife Refuge e: **SANWR**

Santa Barbara Citizens for Environment Defense e: **SBCED**

Santa Barbara Museum of Natural History e: **SBMNH**

Santa Barbara Museum of Natural History Contributions in Science e: **St Barbara Mus Nat Hist Contrib Sci**

Santa Barbara Museum of Natural History. Department of Geology. Bulletin *e:* **Santa Barbara Mus Nat History Dept Geology Bull**

Santa Barbara Society of Natural History. Bulletin *e:* **Santa Barbara Soc N H B**, *e:* **Santa Barbara Soc N H B**

Santee National Wildlife Refuge *e:* **SNWR**

Santo Tomas Journal of Medicine *e:* **Santo Tomas J Med**, *e:* **St Tomas J Med**

Sao Nicolau, Sao Nicolau Island [Kap Verden] *e:* **GVSN**

Sao Paulo. Instituto Geografico e Geologico. Boletim *p:* **Sao Paulo Inst Geogr Geol Bol**

Sao Paulo. Instituto Geografico e Geologico. Relatorio *p:* **Sao Paulo Inst Geogr Geol Relat**

Sao Paulo. Universidade. Instituto de Geociencias. Boletim *p:* **Sao Pulo Univ Inst Geocienc Bol**, *p:* **Sao Pulo Univ Inst Geocienc Bol**

Sao Paulo. Universidade. Instituto de Geografa. Geografia e Planejamento *p:* **Sao Paulo Univ Inst Geogr Geogr Planejamento**, *p:* **Sao Paulo Univ Inst Geogr Geogr Planejamento**

Sao Paulo. Universidade. Instituto de Geografa. Serie Teses e Monografias *p:* **Sao Paulo Univ Inst Geogr Ser Teses Monogr**, *p:* **Sao Paulo Univ Inst Geogr Ser Teses Monogr**

Sao Paulo. Universidade. Instituto de Geografia. Geomorfologia *p:* **Sao Paulo Univ Inst Geogr Geomorfol**, *p:* **Sao Paulo Univ Inst Geogr Geomorfol**

Sao Vicente, Sao Vicente Island [Kap Verden] *e:* **GVSV**

SAR and QSAR in Environmental Research *e:* **SAR QSAR Environ Res**

SAR AND QSAR IN ENVIRONMENTAL RESEARCH (READING) *e:* **SAR QSAR Environ Res**

Sariska Wildlife Sanctuary *e:* **SWS**

Saskatchewan Department of Health, Regina, Saskatchewan *e:* **SRPH**

Saskatchewan Department of the Environment, Regina\Saskatchewan *e:* **SRE**

Saskatchewan Geological Society *e:* **SGS**

Saskatchewan Meteorological Inspection Office *e:* **SMIO**

Saskatchewan Museum of Natural History *e:* **SMNH**

Saskatchewan Outdoor and Environmental Education Association *e:* **SOEEA**

Saskatchewan Water Resources Commission, Regina, Saskatchewan *e:* **SRWR**

Satellit *d:* **Sat**

Satellite *d:* **SAT**, *e:* **S**, *e:* **SAT**

satellite *e:* **sate**

Satellite *e:* **Satel**, *e:* **SATL**, *e:* **STL**, *e:* **STLT**

Satellite Access Network *e:* **SAN**

Satellite accumulation area *e:* **SAA**

Satellite Action Plan *e:* **SAP**

Satellite Action Plan Regulatory Group *e:* **SAP-REG**

Satellite Active Archive *e:* **SAA**

Satellite Active Nullifier *e:* **SATAN**

Satellite Aeromedical Research Vehicle *e:* **SARV**

Satellite-Aided Search and Rescue Project *e:* **SARSAT**

Satellite-Aided Search and Rescue System *e:* **SASRS**

Satellite-Aided Search & Rescue System *e:* **SASRS**

Satellite Airlift Control Center *e:* **SALCC**

Satellite Alert Force Employment *e:* **SAFE**

Satellite Analog Tie Trunk *e:* **S/ATT**

Satellite and Computer Communications *e:* **SCC**

Satellite and Mesometeorology Research Project University of Chicago *e:* **SMRP**

Satellite and Missile Observation Station *e:* **SAMOS**

satellite and missile observation system *e:* **SAMOS**

Satellite and Physicians Office Testing *e:* **SPOT**

Satellite and Production Services *e:* **SPS**

Satellite Angular Radiometer *e:* **SARA**

Satellite Antenna Test System *e:* **SATS**

Satellite Application Centre *e:* **SAC**

Satellite Application Facility *e:* **SAF**

Satellite Applications Centre *e:* **SAC**

Satellite Array for International and National Telecommunications *e:* **SAINT**

Satellite Assembly Building *e:* **SAB**

Satellite [ATM] *e:* **SAT**

Satellite Attack Sensor *e:* **SAS**

Satellite Attack Warning and Assessment Flight Experiment *e:* **SAWAFE**

Satellite Attack Warning and Verification *e:* **SAWV**

Satellite Attack Warning System *e:* **SAWS**

Satellite Attitude Acquisition *e:* **SAA**

Satellite Attitude Acquisition Technique *e:* **SAAT**

Satellite Attitude-Conlrol Simulator *e:* **SACS**

Satellite Attitude-Control Simulator *e:* **SACS**

Satellite Auction Network, Inc. *e:* **SATL**

Satellite Auto-Monitor System *e:* **SAMS**

Satellite Automatic Monitoring System *e:* **SAMS**

Satellite Automatic Terminal Rendezvous and Coupling *e:* **SATRAC**

Satellite AutomatIc Tracking Antenna *e:* **SATA**

Satellite Automatic Tracking Antenna *e:* **SATAN**

Satellite Automation System *e:* **SAMS**

Satellite-Based Advanced Air Traffic Management System *e:* **SAATMS**

Satellite-Based Advanced Air Traffic Management System [Department of Transporta *e:* **SAATMS**

Satellite-Based Advanced Air Traffic Management System [Department of Transportation] *e:* **SAATMS**

Satellite Based Atomic Energy Detection System *e:* **SBAEDS**

Satellite Based Augmentation System *e:* **SBAS**

Satellite Based Interceptor System *e:* **SBIS**

satellite-based interceptor systems *e:* **sbis**

Satellite-Based Maritime Search and Bescue System *e:* **SAMSARS**

Satellite-based Maritime Search and Rescue System *e:* **SAMSARS**

Satellite based text only communication system *e:* **INMARSAT C**

Satellite-Borne Instrumentation *e:* **SBI**

Satellite Broadcast Network *e:* **SBN**

Satellite Broadcast System *e:* **SBN**

Satellite Broadcasters Association *e:* **SBA**

Satellite Broadcasting and Communications Association *e:* **SBCA**

Satellite Broadcasting Interface *e:* **SBI**

Satellite Business System *e:* **SBS**

Satellite Business Systems *e:* **SBS**

Satellite Cable Audio Networks *e:* **SCAN**

Satellite Capture and Retrieval *e:* **SCAR**

Satellite Carriers *e:* **SC**

Satellite Charging at High Altitude *e:* **SCATHA**

Satellite Chromosome *e:* **SAT Chromosome**

Satellite Cloud Photograph *e:* **SCP**

Satellite Collection Buoy Observations *e:* **SCOBO**

Satellite Collection of Meteorological Observations *e:* **SCOMO**

Satellite Command *e:* **SATCOM**

Satellite Committee Agency *e:* **SCA**

Satellite Communication *e:* **SAT-COM**

Satellite Communication Agency *e:* **SATCOM**

satellite communication centre *e:* **satcom**

Satellite Communication Concentrator *e:* **SCC**

Satellite Communication Control Facility *e:* **SCCF**

Satellite Communication System *e:* **SATCOM**, *e:* **SCS**

Satellite Communication Terminals *e:* **SCOTs**

Satellite Communications *e:* **SATCOM**, *e:* **Satell Commun**, *e:* **Satellite**, *e:* **SC**

Satellite Communications Agency *e:* **SATCOM**, *e:* **SATCOMA**, *e:* **SATCOM AGEN**, *e:* **SCA**

Satellite Communications and Data Handling *e:* **C&DH**

Satellite Communications Contingency Planning Group *e:* **SCCPG**

Satellite Communications Control *e:* **SCC**

Satellite Communications Control Centre *e:* **SCCC**

Satellite Communications Control Facility *e:* **SCCF**

Satellite Communications Control Office *e:* **SCC**

Satellite Communications Control Processor *e:* **SCCP**

Satellite Communications Control SyStem *e:* **SCCS**

Satellite Communications Controller *e:* **SCC**

Satellite Communications for Learning. *e:* **SCOLAR**

Satellite-Communications On-board Terminal *e:* **SCOT**

Satellite Communications. Satellite Industry Directory *e:* **Satel Dir**

Satellite Communications Sub-Group *e:* **SCSG**

Satellite Communications System *e:* **SATCOM**, *e:* **SATCOM System**

Satellite Communications System Control *e:* **SCSC**

Satellite Communication[s] Terminal *e:* **SCOT**

Satellite Communications Test Operations Center *e:* **SCTOC**

Satellite Communications Users Conference e: **SCUC**

Satellite Communications Working Group e: **SCWG**

Satellite Computer e: **SC**

Satellite Computer-Operated Readiness Equipment e: **SCORE**

Satellite Condition e: **SATCON**

Satellite Conference Network e: **SCN**

Satellite Configuration Control Element e: **SCCE**

Satellite Control and Test Station e: **SCTS**

Satellite Control Center e: **SCC**

Satellite Control Centre e: **SCC**

Satellite Control Department e: **SCD**

Satellite Control Engineering Office e: **SCEO**

Satellite Control Facility e: **SCF**

Satellite Control Network e: **SCN**

Satellite Control Officer e: **SATLCONO**

Satellite Control Satellite e: **SCS**

Satellite Control Site e: **SCS**

Satellite Control Squadron e: **SACS**

satellite control system e: **scs**

Satellite Control Terminal e: **SCT**

Satellite d'application technologique f: **ATS**

Satellite Data e: **SATDAT**

Satellite Data Access and Management format e: **SDAM**

Satellite Data Analysis Center e: **SDAC**

Satellite Data Area e: **SDA**

Satellite Data Broadcast Networks, Inc. e: **SATNET**

Satellite Data Exchange e: **SDX**

Satellite Data for Fallout e: **SATFAL**

Satellite Data Handling System e: **SDHS**

Satellite Data Link Standard e: **SDLS**

Satellite Data Reduction e: **SADAR**, e: **SDR**

Satellite Data Services Branch e: **SDSB**

Satellite Data Services Division e: **SDSD**

Satellite Data System e: **SDS**

Satellite Data System Spacecraft e: **SDSS**

satellite data to be decoded in the satellite data recorder e: **SIN**

Satellite Data Transmission System e: **SDTS**

Satellite Data Unit e: **SDU**

Satellite Databank e: **SATELDATA**

Satellite de géodésie f: **GEOSAT**

Satellite de mesure du bilan radiatif de la Terre f: **ERBS**

Satellite de pointe d'observation de la planète f: **ADEOS**

Satellite de Recherches et d'Environment Technique f: **SRET**

Satellite Delay Compensation Unit e: **SDCU**

satellite des recherches et etudes technologiques f: **SRET**

Satellite Development Trust. e: **SDT**

Satellite d'exploitation géostationnaire pour l'étude de l'environnement f: **GOES**

Satellite dexploration des ressources terrestres f: **ERS**

Satellite Digital and Analog Display System e: **SDADS**

Satellite Digital and Anlog[ue] Display e: **SDAD**

Satellite Digital and Display System e: **SDADS**, e: **SDAS**

Satellite Digital Audio Broadcasting e: **S-DAB**

Satellite Digital Audio Radio e: **SDAR**

Satellite Digital Tie Trunk e: **S/DTT**

Satellite Distribution Frame e: **SDF**

Satellite d'observation de la Terre f: **EOS**

Satellite d'observation marine f: **MOS-1**

Satellite d'étude des interactions climatiques terre-océan f: **LOCS**

Satellite détude du milieu f: **ESSA**

Satellite Early Warning e: **SEW**

Satellite Early Warning System e: **SEWS**

Satellite Earth Station e: **SES**

Satellite Earth Stations and Systems e: **SES**

Satellite Educational and Informational Television e: **SEIT**

Satellite Educational Resources Consortium e: **SERC**

Satellite Electrostatic Triaxial Accelerometer e: **SETA**

Satellite Emission Range Inferred Earth Surveying e: **SERIES**

Satellite Engineering Cabin e: **SEC**

Satellite Equipment Room e: **SER**

Satellite Experiment Plot Package e: **SEPP**

Satellite Experiments Simultaneous with Antarctic Measurements programme e: **SESAME**

Satellite expérimental de géodynamique des océans f: **GEOS-3**

Satellite Field Distribution Facility e: **SFDF**

Satellite Field Office e: **SFO**

Satellite Field Services Stations e: **SFSS**

satellite fix e: **sat. fix.**

Satellite for Aerospace Research e: **SATAR**

Satellite for Earth Observations e: **SEO**

Satellite for Electric Rocket Test e: **SERT**

Satellite for Measurement of Background Anisotropies e: **SAMBA**

Satellite for Orientation, Navigation and Geodesy e: **SONG**

Satellite for Research in Environmental Technology e: **SRET**

Satellite Grand Link System e: **SGLS**

satellite graphic job processor e: **SGJP**

Satellite Gravity Gradiometry e: **SGG**

Satellite Ground Controlled Interception e: **SAT GCI**

Satellite Ground Controlled Intereeption e: **SATGCI**

Satellite Ground Terminal e: **SGT**

Satellite Ground Terminal System e: **SGTS**

Satellite géostationnaire indien f: **INSAT**

Satellite Housing Integrated Programmed Support e: **SHIPS**

Satellite Imagery Dissemination System e: **SIDS**

Satellite Imagery Processing System e: **SIPS**

Satellite Imaging Experiment e: **SIE**

Satellite Imaging Spectrometer Experiment e: **SISEX**

Satellite in Orbit e: **SIO**

Satellite Inertial Navigation Determination e: **SIND**

Satellite Information Center e: **SIC**

Satellite Information Message Protocol e: **SIMP**

Satellite Information Processor e: **SIP**

Satellite Information Processor Operational Program e: **SIPOP**

Satellite Information Processor Operational Program[me] Office e: **SIPOPO**

Satellite Information Service e: **SIS**

Satellite Information System Company e: **SISCOM**

Satellite Information Systems Co. e: **SATI**

Satellite Infra-Red Experiment e: **SIRE**

Satellite Infra-red Radiation Spectrometer e: **SIRS**

Satellite Infrared Spectrometer e: **SIS**

Satellite Infrared Spectrometry e: **SIRS**

Satellite Input to Numerical Analysis and Prediction e: **SINAP**

Satellite Input to Numerical Analysis and Procedure e: **SINAP**

Satellite Inspection e: **SATIN**

Satellite Inspection Program e: **SIP**

Satellite Inspection Technique e: **SAINT**, e: **SATIN Technique**

Satellite Inspector and Satellite Interceptor e: **SAINT**

Satellite Inspector/Interceptor & Negation e: **SAINT**

Satellite Inspector Program e: **SIP**

Satellite Inspector System e: **SATIN**, e: **SATIN System**

Satellite Inspector Target e: **SIT**

Satellite Instructional Television Experiment e: **SITE**

satellite instructional television experirnent e: **STTE**

Satellite Instrumentation Processor System e: **SIPS**

Satellite Integrated Buoy e: **SIB**

Satellite Intensity Analysis e: **SIA**

Satellite Interactive Terminal e: **SIT**

Satellite Interceptor e: **SAINT**

Satellite Interceptor Navigation System e: **SINS**

Satellite Interceptor Program e: **SIP**

Satellite Intercept[or] System e: **SIS**

Satellite Interface Message Processor e: **SIMP**

Satellite International Television Center e: **SITC**

Satellite-Interrogated Automatic Weather Station e: **SIAWS**

Satellite Interrogated Environmental Buoy e: **SIEB**

satellite ionospheric beacon(s) e: **sib**

Satellite Ionospherie Beacon e: **SIB**

Satellite Italiano Ricera Industriale Orienta i: **SIRIO**

Satellite japonais d'exploration des ressources terrestres f: **JERS-1**

Satellite Kill e: **SKILL**

Satellite Laboratory e: **SATELLAB**

Satellite Landing Ground e: **SLG**

Satellite Landing System e: **SLS**

Satellite LASER Communication e: **SLC**

Satellite LASER Ranging e: **SLR**

Satellite LASER Ranging System e: **SLRS**

Satellite Launch and Repair e: **SLR**

Satellite Launch Dispenser Communications e: **SLEDCOM**

Satellite [launched from a] Balloon e: **SALON**

Satellite Launch[ing] Vehicle e: **SLV**

Satellite Library Information Network e: **SALINET**

Satellite Like e: **SL**

Satellite-Like Virus *e:* **SL**
Satellite Like Virus *e:* **SL Virus**
Satellite Line Link *e:* **SLL**
Satellite Link Adapter *e:* **SLA**
Satellite Low Orbit Bombardment *e:* **SLOB**
Satellite Lucerne Transient Streak Virus *e:* **sLTSV**
Satellite Maintenance and Repair Technique[s] *e:* **SMART**
Satellite Master Aerial Television *e:* **SMATV**
Satellite Master Antenna Television *e:* **SMATV**
Satellite Materials Hardening *e:* **SMATH**
Satellite Mediated Controlled Experiment for Continuing Education and Monitoring Doctors *e:* **SATDOC**
Satellite Militaire de la Reconniassance Orbitale *f:* **SAMRO**
Satellite-Missile Observation Satellite *e:* **SAMOS**
Satellite Monitoring System *e:* **SAMOS**
Satellite Monsoon Index *e:* **SMI**
Satellite Motion Simulator *e:* **SMS**
Satellite Multi Services *e:* **SMS**
Satellite Multiservice Systems *d:* **SMS**
Satellite Multiservice Transponder *e:* **SMT**
Satellite Music Network, Incorporated *e:* **SMNI**
Satellite Mutual Visibility *e:* **SMV**
Satellite météorologique des Etats-Unis *f:* **NIMBUS**
Satellite météorologique d'exploitation géostationnaire *f:* **GOMS**
Satellite météorologique géostationnaire *f:* **GMS**
Satellite météorologique géostationnaire de l'ASE *f:* **METEOSAT**
Satellite Navigation *e:* **SATNAV**
Satellite Navigation Alert Plotter *e:* **SNAP**
Satellite Navigation Map *e:* **SNM**
Satellite Navigation [position location] System *e:* **TRANSIT**
satellite navigation system *e:* **Satnav**
Satellite Navigation System *e:* **SNS**
satellite navigator *e:* **satnav**
Satellite Network *e:* **SATNET**
Satellite Network Control Station *e:* **SNCS**
Satellite Network of Columbia *e:* **SATCOL**
Satellite Networking Associates, Inc. *e:* **SNA**
Satellite News *e:* **Satel News**
Satellite News Channel *e:* **SNC**
satellite news gathering *e:* **SNG**
Satellite News Vehicle *e:* **SNV**
Satellite Nuclear Auxiliary Power *e:* **SNAP**
Satellite Nuclear Power Station *e:* **SNPS**
Satellite Object Number *e:* **SONO**
Satellite Observation System *e:* **SOS**
Satellite Observations *e:* **SATOBS**
Satellite Ocean Analysis for Recruitment *e:* **SOAR**
Satellite Ocean Data Systems Scientific Working Group *e:* **SODSSWG**
Satellite Ocean Research Program *e:* **SOREP**
Satellite Ocean Surveillance Evaluation Center *e:* **SOSEC**
Satellite Ocean Surveillance System *e:* **SOSS**

Satellite Oceanic Control Center *e:* **SOCC**
Satellite of Love *e:* **SOL**
Satellite On-board Attack Warning System *e:* **SORAS**
Satellite Onboard Attack Report[ing] System *e:* **SOARS**
Satellite Online Searching Training Interactive Conferencing Experiment *e:* **SOLSTICE**
Satellite Operation Command and Control *e:* **SOCC**
Satellite Operation Planning and Data Analysis System *e:* **SODAS**
Satellite Operations Center *e:* **SO, SOC**
Satellite Operations Control Center *e:* **SOCC**
Satellite Operations Graup *e:* **SAOG**
Satellite Operations Group *e:* **SOG**
Satellite Operators and Users Technical Committee *e:* **SOUTC**
Satellite Optical Surveillance Station *e:* **SOSS**
Satellite opérationnel TIROS perfectionné *f:* **ITOS**
Satellite Orbit Control *e:* **SOC**
Satellite Orbit Control Program *e:* **SOCP**
Satellite Orbital Debris Characterization Impact Test *e:* **SOCIT**
Satellite Orbital Track and Intercept *e:* **SORTI**
Satellite Paper Tape Transfer *e:* **SATPATT**
Satellite Parametric Reduction *e:* **SPR**
Satellite Personal Communication Services *e:* **S-PCS**
Satellite Personal Communications Network *e:* **S-PCN**
Satellite Personnel Activity *e:* **SPA**
Satellite Photo-Electric (or Electronic) Analog Rectification System *e:* **SPEARS**
Satellite Picture *e:* **SATPIC**
Satellite Position Adjusting Rocket *e:* **SPAR**
Satellite Position and Display System *e:* **SPADS**
Satellite-position Prediction and Display *e:* **SPAD**
Satellite Positioning and Tracking *e:* **SPOT**
Satellite Positive-Ion-Beam System *e:* **SPIBS**
Satellite pour Astronomie Radio Amateur *e:* **SARA,** *f:* **SARA**
Satellite pour l'Observation de la Terre *f:* **SPOT**
Satellite Power System *e:* **SPS**
Satellite Precipitation and Cloud Experiment *e:* **SPACE**
Satellite Probatoire d'Observation de la Terre *f:* **SPOT**
Satellite Processing Center *e:* **SPC**
satellite processor *e:* **SP**
satellite processor access method *e:* **SPAM**
Satellite Program Services *e:* **SPS**
Satellite Program[ming] Network *e:* **SPN**
Satellite Protection for Area Defense *e:* **SPAD**
Satellite Protection for Area (or Air) Defense *e:* **SPAD**
Satellite Purchasing Program[me]s Administrator *e:* **SPPA**
Satellite Racing Development *e:* **SRD**

Satellite Radar Station *e:* **SRS**
Satellite Radiation Budget Climatology Project *e:* **SRBCP**
Satellite Readout Equipment *e:* **SROE**
Satellite Readout Station *e:* **SRS**
satellite receiving antenna *e:* **Sat An**
Satellite Receiving Station *e:* **SRS**
Satellite Reconnaissance Advance Notice *e:* **SATRAN**
Satellite Reconnaissance Radio *e:* **SRR**
Satellite Reentry Vehicle *e:* **SRV**
Satellite Regional Warning Center *e:* **SRWC**
Satellite remote -sensing for Lake Monitoring *e:* **SALMON**
Satellite Search & Rescue System *e:* **SARSAT**
Satellite Service Centre *e:* **SSC**
Satellite Services, Incorporated *e:* **SSI**
Satellite Servicing Vehicle *e:* **SSV**
Satellite Serving System *e:* **SSS**
Satellite Simulation *e:* **SATSIM**
Satellite Situation Display Room *e:* **SSDR**
Satellite Situation Report *e:* **SSR**
Satellite Solar Power Station *e:* **SSPS**
Satellite Solar Power System *e:* **SSPS**
Satellite Stratospheric Monitor *e:* **SSM**
Satellite Subscription Television *e:* **SSTV**
Satellite Supply Operations Officer *e:* **SSOO**
Satellite Surveillance Program *e:* **SURSAT**
Satellite Surveillance System *e:* **SSS**
Satellite Surveillance Technology *e:* **SST**
Satellite-Switched *e:* **S-S**
Satellite switched *e:* **SSW**
Satellite Switched-FDMA *e:* **SS-FDMA**
Satellite Switched TDMA (Time Division Multiple Access) *e:* **SS-TDMA**
Satellite-Switched Time-Diwsion Multiple Access *e:* **SSTDMA**
Satellite Switching *e:* **SS**
Satellite Switching Center *e:* **SSC**
Satellite Switching Office *e:* **SSO**
Satellite switchstream. *e:* **SATSTREAM**
Satellite Switchstream Service *e:* **SATSTREAM**
Satellite Syndicated Systems *e:* **SSSN**
Satellite Syndicated Systems Inc. *e:* **SSS**
Satellite System *e:* **SS**
Satellite System Development *e:* **SSD**
Satellite System for Precise Navigation *e:* **SSPN**
Satellite System Monitor *e:* **SSM**
Satellite System Monitoring Equipment *e:* **SSME**
Satellite System Operational Center *e:* **SSOC**
Satellite System Operational Guide *e:* **SSOG**
Satellite System Receiver *e:* **SSR**
Satellite system useful for surface characterization *e:* **LANDSAT**
Satellite Systems Corporation *e:* **SSC**
Satellite Systems Division *e:* **SSD**
Satellite Systems Engineering, Inc. *e:* **SSE**
Satellite Systems Monitoring Group *e:* **SSMG**
Satellite Systems Operations Evaluation Group *e:* **SSOEG**
Satellite Systems Operations Guide *e:* **SSOG**
Satellite Systems Operations Plan *e:* **SSOP**

Satellite Technical and Operational
Committee *e:* **STOC**

Satellite technologique canadien *f:* **CTS**

Satellite Technologique d'Applications et de
Relais *f:* **STAR**

Satellite technologique de télédétection des
ressources terrestres *f:* **ERTS**

Satellite Technology Management, Inc. *e:*
STM

Satellite Telecommunications Analysis and
Modeling Program *e:* **STAMP**

Satellite Telecommunications Center *e:*
STC

Satellite Telecommunications Company *e:*
SATELCO

Satellite Telecommunications Experimental
Project *e:* **STEP**

Satellite Telecommunications Subdivision
e: **SATELCOMM**

Satellite Telecommunications with
Automatic Routing *e:* **STAR**

Satellite Telemetry and Computer System
e: **STACS**

Satellite Telemetry Automatic Reduction
System *e:* **STARS**

Satellite Telemetry Interagency Working
Group *e:* **STIWG**

Satellite Telemtry Interagency Working
Group *e:* **STIWG**

Satellite Television Antenna Systems Ltd.
e: **SATVRN**

Satellite Television Asia Region *e:* **STAR**

Satellite Television Corporation *e:* **STC**

Satellite Television Network *e:* **STN**

Satellite Terminal Guidance *e:* **STG**

Satellite Test Annex *e:* **STA**

Satellite Test Center *e:* **STC**

Satellite test of Remote Ultralow Light
Level Imaging *e:* **RULLI/SAT**

Satellite Test of the Equivalence Principle
e: **STEP**

Satellite Test Vehicle *e:* **STV**

Satellite Theater Network *e:* **STN**

Satellite Ticket Printer *e:* **STP**

Satellite-to-Earth Missile *e:* **SEM**

Satellite To Host *e:* **STH**

Satellite-to-Satellite *e:* **STS**

Satellite to Satellite communication
frequency *e:* **KuBand**

Satellite-to-Satellite Tracking *e:* **SST**

Satellite-to-Space Vehicle *e:* **STSV**

Satellite Tobacco Necrosis Virus *e:* **STNV**

Satellite Tobacco Ringspot Virus *e:*
STobRV

Satellite Tool Kit *e:* **STK**

Satellite-Tracked Submarine-Launched
Antimissile *e:* **SATSLAM**

Satellite Tracking *e:* **SATRACK**

Satellite Tracking and Data Acquisition
Department *e:* **STADAD**

Satellite Tracking and Data Acquisition
Network *e:* **STADAN**

Satellite Tracking Center *e:* **STC**

Satellite Tracking Committee *e:* **STC**

Satellite Tracking Facility *e:* **STF**

Satellite Tracking Network *e:* **STN**

Satellite Tracking of Balloons and
Emergencies *e:* **STROBE**

Satellite Tracking Orbit Determination
Program *e:* **SATODP**

Satellite Tracking Program [of the
Smithsonian Institution's Astrophysical
Laboratory] *e:* **STP**

Satellite Tracking & Ranging Station *e:*
STARS

Satellite Tracking Section *e:* **STS**

Satellite Tracking Set *e:* **STS**

Satellite Tracking Station *e:* **STS**

Satellite Transfer Vehicle *e:* **STV**

Satellite Transit System *e:* **STS**

Satellite Transmission and Reception
Specialist *e:* **STARS**

Satellite Transmission Effects Simulations
e: **STRESS**

Satellite Transmission Experiment Linking
Laboratories *e:* **STELLA**

Satellite Transmission Systems Inc. *e:*
STS

Satellite Transponder Addressable Receiver
e: **STAR**

Satellite Transponder Leasing Corporation
e: **STLC**

Satellite under Test *e:* **SUT**

Satellite Undetected Duds *e:* **SUDS**

Satellite Unfurlable Antenna *e:* **SUA**

Satellite used to telemeter data to shore
stations *e:* **ARGOS**

Satellite User Mapping Register *e:* **SUMR**

satellite vehicle *e:* **SV**

Satellite Video Exchange Society *e:* **SVES**

Satellite Virus *e:* **SV**

Satellite Weather Information System *e:*
SWIS

Satellite Wide Area Network *e:* **SWAN**

Satellite Wildlife Research Project *e:*
SWRP

Satellite X-ray *e:* **SAX**

Satellite X-ray Test Facility *e:* **SXTF**

Satelliten- *d:* **SAT-**

Satelliten Füllfaktor Klausel *d:* **SFK**

Satelliten für Telekommunikation,
Anwendung und Raumforschung *d:*
STAR

SATelliten-KOMmunikation *d:* **SatKom**

Satelliten-Kommunikations-Anlage *d:*
SKA

Satelliten-Kommunikations-
Empfangseinrichtung *d:* **SKE**

Satelliten-Mehrdienstsystem *d:* **SMS**

Satelliten-Zwischenfrequenz *d:* **Sat-ZF**

Satellitendatenverarbeitung *d:* **SDVA**

Satellitendirektfernsehen *d:* **SDF**

Satellitenprogramm *d:* **SAP**

Satellitenrechner *d:* **SR**

Satellitensystem *d:* **SS**

Satellitenvermittler *d:* **SAV**

Satellitenvirus *d:* **SV**

Satellites, Balloons and Rockets *e:*
SABAR

Satellites de Télécommunications,
d'Application et de Recherches *f:* **STAR**

Satellites for Health and Rural Education
e: **SHARE**

Satellites for Telecommunication[s]
Application[s] and Research *e:* **STAR**

Saturated Hydroxy-Terminated
Polybutadiene *e:* **SHTPB**

Saturn-Launched Meteoroid Satellite *e:*
SLMS

Saturn Orbiter *e:* **SO**

Saturn orbiter and Titan probe *e:*
CASSINI

Saturn Orbiter Probe *e:* **SOP**

Saturn Orbiter Satellite Lander *e:* **SO/SL**

Saturn Orbiter/Titan Probe *e:* **SOTP**

Satélite de observación de la Tierra *s:*
EOS

Satélite de Observación Marina *s:* **MOS-1**

Satélite del Balance de Radiación de la
Tierra *s:* **ERBS**

Satélite del Clima del Océano y el Suelo *s:*
LOCS

Satélite Geodésico *s:* **GEOSAT**

Satélite Geoestacionario Indio *s:* **INSAT**

Satélite Geoestacionario Operacional de
Estudio del Medio Ambiente *s:* **GOES**

Satélite Meteorológico de los Estados
Unidos *s:* **NIMBUS**

Satélite Meteorológico Geoestacionario *s:*
GMS

Satélite Meteorológico Geoestacionario del
ESA *s:* **METEOSAT**

Satélite Meteorológico Operativo
Geoestacionario *s:* **GOMS**

Satélite Oceánico Experimental de
Geodinámica *s:* **GEOS-3**

Satélite Perfeccionado para la Observación
de la Tierra *s:* **ADEOS**

Saudi Arabia. Directorate General of
Mineral Resources. Geologic Map *e:*
**Saudi Arabia Dir Gen Miner Resour
Geol Map**

Saudi Arabia. Directorate General of
Mineral Resources. Geologic Map GM
e: **Saudi Arabia Dir Gen Miner Resour
Geol Map GM**

Saudi-Sudanese Red Sea Joint Commission
e: **SSRSJC**

Sauerstoff- und Wasser-Werke AG, Luzern
d: **SWWL**

Sauerstoffbedarf für biologisch abbaubare
Substanzen *d:* **BSB**

Sauerstoffbedarf für biologisch abbaubare
Substanzen nach 5 Tagen *d:* **BSB5**

sauerstoffhaltige Kohlenwasserstoffe *e:*
CHO

Säugetier *d:* **Sgt**

Saugetierkundliche Mitteilungen *d:*
Saugertierkd Mitt

Säugetierkundliche Mitteilungen *d:*
Säugetierkd Mitt

Saugetierkundliche Mitteilungen *d:*
Saugetierkundliche Mitt

Säugetierkundliche Mitteilungen *d:*
STKMBC

Savannah, Georgia *e:* **SAV**

Savannah [Georgia] Area Law Enforcement
System *e:* **SALES**

Savannah National Wildlife Refuge *e:*
SNWR

Savannah River Ecology Laboratory *e:*
SREL

Savannah River Region Health Information
System *e:* **SRRHIS**

Savannah State College [Georgia] *e:* **SSC**

Save All Valley Environment *e:* **SAVE**

Save Animals from Extinction *e:* **SAFE**

Save Animals from Extinction
[organization] *e:* **SAFE**

Save, Help Animals Man Exploits *e:*
SHAME

Save Life on Earth *e:* **SLOE**

Save Maine's Only Official State Animal
e: **SMOOSA**

Save Our Cities from Environmental Mess
e: **SOCEM**

Save Pound Animals from Research
Experiments *e:* **SPARE**

Save the Environment from Atomic
Pollution e: **SEAP**

Save the Hawkesbury's Unique River
Environment e: **SHURE**

Save Us from Formaldehyde Environmental
Repercussions e: **SUFFER**

Save Your Afterdeck e: **SYA**

Savez Geografskih Drustava Hrvatske S:
SGDH

Savezna Geodetska Uprava se: **SGU**

Savezna Uprava Hidrometeorološke Službe
se: **SUHS**

Savezna Uprava za Geološka Istraživanja
se: **SUGI**

Savezni Hidrometeorološki Zavod se:
SHMZ, se: **SHZ**

Saville Advanced Remote Keying e: **SARK**

Saving and Preserving Arts and Cultural
Environment e: **SPACES**

Savings in Space Operations e: **SSO**

Saw Grinders' Trade Protective Society e:
SGTPS

SBl [Space Based Interceptor]-system
Concept and Integrated Technology e:
SCIT

Sbomik Geologickych Ved. Paleontologie
c: **Sb Geol Ved Paleontol**

Sbornik Aspirantskikh Rabot Kazanskii
Gosudarstvennyi Universitet
Estestvennye Nauki Biologiya R: **Sb
Aspir Rab Kazan Gos Univ Estest
Nauki Bio**

Sbornik Ceskoslovenske Akademie
Zemedelskych Ved. Veterinarni Medicina
c: **Sb Cesk Akad Zemed Ved Vet Med**

Sbornik Geologickych Ved. Geologie S:
SGVGA, c: **Sb Geol Ved Geol**

Sbornik Geologickych Ved. Hydrogeologie,
Inzenyrska, Geologie c: **Sb Geol Ved
Hydrogeol Inz Geol**

Sbornik Geologickych Ved. Loziskova
Geologie S: **SGVLA**, c: **Sb Geol Ved
Loriskova Geol**

Sbornik Geologickych Ved. Loziskova
Geologie. Mineralogie c: **Sb Geol Ved
Lozishova Geol Mineral**

Sbornik Geologickych Ved. Rada
Loziskova Geologie c: **Sb Geol Ved
Rada Loziskova Geol**

Sbornik Geologickych Ved. Rada P:
Paleontologie c: **Sb Geol Ved Rada P
Paleontol**

Sbornik Geologickych Ved. Rada Uzita
Geofyzika c: **Sb Geol Ved Rada Uzita
Geofyz**

Sbornik Geologickych Ved. Technologie,
Geochemie c: **Sb Geol Ved Technol
Geochem**

Sbornik Geologickych Ved. Uzita
Geofyzika S: **SGVUA**, c: **Sb Geol Ved
Uzita Geofyz**

Sbornik Nauchno-Issledovatel'skii Institut
Gidrometeorologicheskogo
Priborostroeniya R: **Sb Nauchno Issled
Inst Gidrometeorol Priborostr**

Sbornik Nauchnogo Studencheskogo
Obshchestva Geologicheskii Fakul'tet
Moskovskii Gosudarstvennyi Universitet
R: **Sb Nauchn Stud Ova Geol Fak Mosk
Gos Uni**, R: **SSGMB**

Sbornik Nauchnykh Rabot Moldavskogo Ot.
Vses. Nauchn. Obsh. Mikrobiologov,
Epidemiologov, i Infekt. R: **SOMIA8**

Sbornik Nauchnykh rudov Institut Biologii
Akademiya Nauk Belorusskoi SSR R: **Sb
Nauchn Tr Inst Biol Akad Nauk BSSR**

Sbornik Nauchnykh Soobshchenii Kafedry
Zoologii Biologii Khimii Dagestanskogo
Universiteta R: **Sb Nauchn Soobshch
Kafedry Zool Biol Khim Dagest Univ**

Sbornik Nauchnykh Trudov Glavgeologii
Uzbekskoi SSR i Tashkentskogo
Politekhnicheskogo Instituta R: **Sb
Nauchn Tr Glavgeologii Uzb SSR
Tashk Politekh Inst**

Sbornik Nauchnykh Trudov Instituta
Geologii i Geofiziki Akadeii Nauk
Uzbekskoi SSR R: **Sb Nauchn Tr Inst
Geol Geofiz Akad Nauk Uzb SSR**

Sbornik Nauchnykh Trudov Vsesoyuznyi
Nauchno-Issledovatel'skii Institut
Gidrogeologii i Inzhenernoi Geologii R:
**Sb Nauchn Tr Vses Nauchno Issled Inst
Gidrogeol Inzh Geo**

Sbornik Rabot Ashkhabadskoi
Gidrometeomlogicheskoi Observatorii
R: **Sb Rab Ashkhab Gidrometeorol Obs**

Sbornik Rabot Basseinovoi Gidrometeoro-
logicheskoi Chernogo i Azovskogo Morei
R: **Sb Rab Basseinovoi Gidrometeorol
Obs Chern Azorskogo Morei**

Sbornik Rabot Gor'kovskoi Volzhskoi i
Rybinskoi Gidrometeomlogicheskikh
Observatorii R: **Sb Rab Gor'k Volzh
Rybinsk Gidrometeorol Obs**

Sbornik Rabot Kurskoi
Gidrometeorologicheskoi Observatorii
R: **Sb Rab Kursk Gidrometeorol Obs**

Sbornik Rabot po Biologii. Tekhnike
Rybolovstva i Tekhnologii R: **Sb Rab
Biol Tekh Rybolov Tekhnol**

Sbornik Rabot po Ikhtiologii i Gidrobiologii
R: **Sb Rab Ikhtiol Gidrobiol**

Sbornik Statei po Geologii i Gidrogeologii
R: **Sb Statei Geol Gidrogeol**

Sbornik Statei po Gidrogeologii i Geotermii
R: **Sb Statei Gidrogeol Geoterm**

Sbornik Statniho Geologickeho Ustavu
Ceskoslovenski Republiky c: **Sb
Statniho Geol Ustavu Cesk Repub**

Sbornik Trudov Kafedry Mikrobiologii
Orenburgskogo Meditsinskogo Instituta
R: **Sb Tr Kafedry Mikrobiol Orenb
Med Ins**

Sbornik Trudov Khar'kovskii
Gidrometeorologicheskii Institut R: **Sb
Tr Khar'k Gidrometeorol Inst**

Sbornik Trudov Kirgizskii Nauchno-
Issledovatel'skii Institut Epidemiologii,
Mikrobiologii, i Gigieny R: **Sb Tr Kirg
Nauchno-Issled Inst Epidemiol
Mikrobiol Gig**

Sbornik Trudov Sektor Radiobiologii
Akademiya Nauk Armyanskoi SSR R:
**Sb Tr Sekt Radiobiol Akad Nauk Arm
SSR**

Sbornik Trudov Vladivostokskogo
Nauchno-Issledovatel'skogo Instituta
Epidemiologii, Mikrobiologii, i Gigieny
R: **Sb Tr Vladivost Nauchno Issled Inst
Epidemiol Mikrobiol Gig**

Sbornik Ustredniho Ustavu Geologickeho
c: **Sb Ustred Ustavu Geol**, c: **SUUG**

Sbornik Ustredniho Ustavu Geologickeho.
Oddil Geologicky c: **Sb Ustred Ustavu
Geol Oddil Geol**

Sbornik Vedeckych Praci Vysoke Skoly
Banske v Ostrave. Rada Hornicko-
Geologicka c: **Sb Ved Pr Vys Sk
Banske Ostrave Rada Horn-Geo**

Sbornik Vysoka Skola Zemedelska v Praze
Provozne Ekonomicke Fakulty v Ceskych
Budejovicich Biologicka Rada c:
SVRBAR

SBZ Sanitär-, Heizungs- und Klimatechnik
d: **SBZ Sanit Heiz Klimatech**

Scalable Object Processing Environment
e: **SCOPE**

Scales of Creativity and Learning
Environment e: **SCALE**

Scandinavian Association of Obstetricians
and Gynaecologists e: **SSOG**

Scandinavian Association of Paediatric
Surgeons e: **ScAPS**

Scandinavian Federation for Laboratory
Animal Science e: **SCANDLAS**

Scandinavian Journal of Medicine and
Science in Sports e: **Scand J Med Sci
Sports**

Scandinavian Journal of Primary Health
Care e: **Scand J Prim Health Care**

Scandinavian Journal of Primary Health
Care. Supplement e: **Scand J Prim
Health Care Suppl**

Scandinavian Journal of Rehabilitation
Medicine e: **Scand J Rehabil Med**, e:
Scand J Rehabil Med, e: **Scand J Rehab
Med**

Scandinavian Journal of Rehabilitation
Medicine. Supplement e: **Scand J
Rehabil Med Suppl**

Scandinavian Journal of Social Medicine
e: **Scand J Soc Med**

Scandinavian Journal of Social MedicIne.
Supplement e: **Scand J Soc Med Suppl**

Scandinavian Journal of Work,
Environment and Health e: **Scand J
Work Environ Health**

Scandinavian Journal of Work Environment
and Health e: **SWEHO**

Scandinavian Red Sea Service e: **Scanred**

Scandinavian Society of Forensic Medicine
e: **SSFM**

Scandinavian Underwater Technology e:
SUTEC

Scanner for Earth Radiation Budget e:
ScaRaB

Scanning Electron Microscopy for
Polarization Analysis e: **SEMPA**

Scanning Hydrographic Operational
Airborne Lidar Survey e: **SHOALS**

Scanning Hydrographic Operational
Airborne Lidar System e: **SHOALS**

Scanning Imaging Absorption Spectrometer
for Atmospheric Cartography e:
SCIAMACHY

Scanning Imaging Absorption Spectrometer
for Atmospheric Chemistry e:
SCIAMACHY

Scanning Infrared Remote Alarm e: **SIRA**

Scanning Ocean Bottom SONAR e: **SOBS**

scanning spectral polarimeter e: **SSP**

SCAR Group of Specialists on Southern
Ocean Ecology e: **GOSSOE**

Scenario Analysis for VTOL Vehicles using
an Interactive Environment e: **SAVVIE**

Scenario Toolkit & Generation
Environment e: **STAGE**

Schalenwildeinheit d: **SWE**

schattiert *d:* **schatt.**

Schaum-Wasserwerfer auf Anhänger *d:* **SWW**

Schaum-Wasserwerferanhänger *d:* **SWA**

Scheduled Weather Broadcast *e:* **SWB**

Schiffahrtmedizinisches Institut der Marine *d:* **SchiffMed-InstM**

Schiffsinspektion und Wasserschutz *d:* **SuW**

schlagwettergeschützt *d:* **fp**

Schlagwetterschutz *d:* **Sch**

schlagwettersicher *d:* **s,** *d:* **sch.**

Schlechtwettergeld *d:* **SWG**

Schlesische Jahrbücher für Geistes- und Naturwissenschaft *d:* **SJGN**

schmutziges Wasser *d:* **schm. W**

Schneepflug Bauart Klima *d:* **SPK**

schnelle medizinische Hilfe *d:* **SMH**

School for Resource and Environmental Studies/CDN *e:* **SRES**

School Health Additional Referral Program [Public Health Service] *e:* **SHARP**

School Health Education Study *e:* **SHES**

School Health Resource Services *e:* **SHRS**

School/Home Observational Referral System *e:* **SHORS**

School Natural Science Society *e:* **SNSS**

School Nature Study Union *e:* **S.N.S.U.**

School of Aerospace Medicine *e:* **SAM,** *e:* **SCHAVMED,** *e:* **SCOLAVNMED**

School of Aerospace Medicine, Brooks AFB *e:* **TBM**

School of Aerospace Medicine Color Threshold Test *e:* **SAMCTT**

School of Allied Health Sciences *e:* **SAHS**

School of Applied Aerospace Sciences *e:* **SAAS**

School of Applied Health *e:* **SAH**

School of Aviation Medicine *e:* **SAM,** *e:* **SCHAVMED,** *e:* **SCOLAVNMED**

School of Aviation Medicine-Brooks *e:* **SAM-B**

School of Aviation Medicine-Brooks AFB *e:* **SAMB**

School of Aviation Medicine-Brooks AFB [Air Force Base] *e:* **SAMB**

School of Aviation Medicine Brooks Air Force Base *e:* **SAMB**

School of Community and Allied Health Resources *e:* **SCAHR**

School of Environment, Resources and Development *e:* **SERD**

School of Health and Related Research *e:* **ScHARR**

School of Health Care Sciences *e:* **SHCS**

School of Health Care Sciences, United States Air Force *e:* **SHCS USAF**

School of Natural Sciences *e:* **SNS**

School of Public Health *e:* **SPH**

School of Resource and Environmental Management *e:* **SREM**

School of Resources and Environmental Studies, Dalhousie University, Halifax, Nova Scotia *e:* **NSHDIR**

School of Underwater Medicine *e:* **SUM**

Schools of the Pacific Rainfall Climate Experiment *e:* **SPaRCE**

Schriftenreihe Bayerisches Landesamt für Umweltschutz *d:* **Schr.reihe Bayer. Landesamt Umweltschutz**

Schriftenreihe der Landesstelle für Naturschutz und Landschaftspflege in Nordrhein-Westfalen *d:* **Schr.reihe**

Landesstelle Nat.schutz Landsch.pfl. Nordrh.-Westfal.

Schriftenreihe des Vereins für Wasser-, Boden-, und Lufthygiene *d:* **Schriftenr Ver Wasser Boden Lufthyg**

Schriftenreihe für Landschaftspflege und Naturschutz *d:* **Schr.reihe Landsch.pfl. Nat.schutz**

Schriftenreihe Umwelt *d:* **Schr.reihe Umw.**

Schubpferdestärke *d:* **SPS**

Schule für Wehrgeophysik *d:* **Swgeophys**

SchülerInnen Aktion Umweltschutz *d:* **SAU**

Schulzahnärztlicher Gesundheitsdienst *d:* **SZGD**

Schutzgemeinschaft Deutsches Wild *d:* **SDWild**

Schutzgemeinschaft Gesunde Umwelt *d:* **SGU**

Schwefelwasserstoff *d:* H_2S, *d:* **Schwfwst**

Schweize rische Rundschau für Medizin Praxis *d:* **Schweiz Rundsch Med Prax**

Schweizer Archiv für Tierheilkunde *d:* **SATHA,** *d:* **SchAT,** *d:* **Schweiz Arch Tierheilkd**

Schweizer Medizinische Wochenschrift *d:* **SchMW**

Schweizer Monatsschrift für Zahnmedizin *d:* **Schweiz Monatsschr Zahnmed**

Schweizer Naturisten-Föderation *d:* **SNF**

Schweizer Naturschutz *d:* **Schweiz. Nat.schutz**

Schweizer Unterwassersportverband *d:* **SUV**

Schweizerische Akademie der medizinischen Wissenschaften *d:* **SAMW**

Schweizerische Akademie der Medizinischen Wissenschaften *e:* **SAMW**

Schweizerische Akademie der Naturwissenschaften *d:* **SANW,** *d:* **SNG**

Schweizerische Arbeitsgemeinschaft für Raumfahrt *d:* **SAFR**

Schweizerische Arbeitsgemeinschaft für Umweltforschung *d:* **SAGUF**

Schweizerische Ärztegesellschaft für Manuelle Medizin *d:* **SAMM**

Schweizerische Geodätische Kommission *d:* **SGK**

Schweizerische Geographische Gesellschaft *d:* **SGgG**

Schweizerische Geologische Gesellschaft *d:* **SGG**

Schweizerische Geologische Kommission *d:* **SGK**

Schweizerische Geophysikalische Kommission *d:* **SGpK**

Schweizerische Geotechnische Kommission *d:* **SGtK**

Schweizerische Gesellschaft für Allgemeinmedizin *d:* **SGAM**

Schweizerische Gesellschaft für Angewandte Geographie *d:* **SCAP,** *d:* **SGAG**

Schweizerische Gesellschaft für Balneologie und Bioklimatologie *d:* **SGBB**

Schweizerische Gesellschaft für biologischen Landbau *d:* **SGBL**

Schweizerische Gesellschaft für Biomedizinische Technik *d:* **SGBT**

Schweizerische Gesellschaft für die zahnmedizinische Betreuung Behinderter und Betagter *e:* **SGZBB**

Schweizerische Gesellschaft für ein Soziales Gesundheitswesen *d:* **SGSG**

Schweizerische Gesellschaft für ein volkswirtschaftlich orientiertes Gesundheitswesen *e:* **SGVOG**

Schweizerische Gesellschaft für Geschichte der Medizin und der Naturwissenschaften *d:* **SGGMN**

Schweizerische Gesellschaft für Gesundheitspolitik *d:* **SGGP**

Schweizerische Gesellschaft für Innere Medizin *d:* **SGIM**

Schweizerische Gesellschaft für Intensivmedizin *d:* **SGI**

Schweizerische Gesellschaft für Medizinische Genetik *d:* **SGMG**

Schweizerische Gesellschaft für Medizinische Informatik *d:* **SGMI**

Schweizerische Gesellschaft für Physikalische Medizin und Rheumatologie *d:* **SGPMR,** *d:* **SHPMR**

Schweizerische Gesellschaft für Phytomedizin, Info *d:* **Schweiz. Ges. Phytomed., Info**

Schweizerische Gesellschaft für Radiologie und Nuklearmedizin *d:* **SGRNM**

Schweizerische Gesellschaft für Sozial- und Präventivmedizin *d:* **SGSPM**

Schweizerische Gesellschaft für Sportmedizin *d:* **SGSM**

Schweizerische Gesellschaft für Tropenmedizin und Parasitologie *d:* **SGTP**

Schweizerische Gesellschaft für Ultraschall in der Medizin und Biologie *d:* **SGUMB**

Schweizerische Gesellschaft für Umweltschutz *d:* **SGU**

Schweizerische Gesellschaft für Unfallmedizin und Berufskrankheiten *d:* **SGUB**

Schweizerische Gesellschaft für Unterwasser- und Hyperbarmedizin *d:* **SGUHM**

Schweizerische Gesundheitsligen Konferenz *d:* **GELIKO**

Schweizerische Kommission für biologische Sicherheit in Forschung und Technik *d:* **SKBS**

Schweizerische Kommission für die Erhaltung der Wildflora *d:* **SKEW**

Schweizerische Kommission für Gesundheitsstatistik *d:* **KOGES**

Schweizerische Medizinische Interfakultätskommission *d:* **SMIFK**

Schweizerische Medizinische Wochenschrift *d:* **Schweiz Med Wochenschr,** *d:* **SMWOA**

Schweizerische Meteorologische Anstalt des EDI (Schweiz) in Zürich *d:* **SMA**

Schweizerische Naturforschende Gesellschaft *d:* **SNG**

Schweizerische Rundschau für Medizin *d:* **SchRM**

Schweizerische Stiftung für Gesundheitsförderung *d:* **SSGF**

Schweizerische Union für Laboratoriums Medizin *d:* **SULM**

Schweizerische Vereinigung der Gemeindekranken- und Gesundheitspflege *d:* **SVGO**

Schweizerische Vereinigung der
Hauspflegeorganisationen *d:* **SVHO**
Schweizerische Vereinigung für
Arbeitsmedizin, Arbeitshygiene und
Arbeitssicherheit *d:* **SVAAAA**
Schweizerische Vereinigung für
Gesundheitsrecht *d:* **SVGR**
Schweizerische Vereinigung für
Gesundheitstechnik *d:* **SVG**
Schweizerische Vereinigung für
Gewässerschutz *d:* **SVGS**
Schweizerische Vereinigung für
Kleintiermedizin *d:* **SVK**
Schweizerische Vereinigung für
Medizinische Ausbildung *d:* **SVMA**
Schweizerische Vereinigung für Qualität im
Gesundheitswesen *d:* **VQG**
Schweizerische Vereinigung für Tierzucht
d: **SVT**
Schweizerische Vereinigung Medizinisch
Technischer Radiologieassistenten *d:*
SVMTRA
Schweizerische Zeitschrift für Hydrologie
d: **Schweiz. Z. Hydrol.**, *d:* **SZHYA**
Schweizerischer Bund für Naturschutz *d:*
SBN, *d:* **SNB**
Schweizerischer Fachverband der
Diplomierten Medizinischen
Laborantinnen und Laboranten *d:*
SFDMLL
Schweizerischer Gesellschaft für
Psychosomatische Medizin *d:* **SGPSM**
Schweizerischer Patentjäger- und
Wildschutzverband *d:* **SPW**
Schweizerischer Pferdezuchtverband *d:*
SPV
Schweizer[ischer] Tierschutz *d:* **STS**
Schweizerischer Tierschutzverband *d:*
STV
Schweizerischer Verband der
Berufsorganisationen im
Gesundheitswesen *d:* **SVBG**
Schweizerischer Verband der Leiter
medizinisch analytischer Laboratorien *d:*
FAMH
Schweizerischer Verband des Mineral- und
Tafelwasserhandels *d:* **MITA**
Schweizerischer Verband für Pferdesport
d: **SVP**
Schweizerischer Verein von Gas- und
Wasserfachmännern *d:* **SVGW**
Schweizerischer Verein von Wärme- und
Klimaingenieuren *d:* **SWKI**
Schweizerischer Wasserwirtschaftsverband
d: **SWV**
Schweizerischer Zentralverband für
Pferdesport *d:* **SZP**
Schweizerisches Institut für Alternativen zu
Tierversuchen *d:* **SIAT**
Schweizerisches Zentrum für
Umwelterziehung *d:* **SZU**
schwere Kohlenwasserstoffe *d:* **SKW**
Schwerflüchtige
Halogenkohlenwasserstoffe *d:* **SHKW**
Schwerkraft-Warmwasserheizung *d:*
SWWH
Schwerwasser-Druckwasserreaktor *d:*
SDWR
Schwerwasser-Materialprüfreaktor *d:*
DEMETER
Schwierige Wetterbedingungen *d:* **SWB**
Schwierige Wetterbedingungen am Tag *d:*
TS

SCICON's Patrolling Underwater Robot *e:*
SPUR
Science Advisory Committee on Terrestrial
Environmental Monitoring and
Assessment *e:* **SACTEMA**
Science and Application Manned Space
Platform *e:* **SAMSP**
Science and Application Space Platform *e:*
SASP
Science and Applications Space Platform
e: **SASP**
Science and Geography Education *e:*
SAGE
Science and technology aerospace reports
e: **STAR**
Science and Technology for Environmental
Protection *e:* **STEP**
Science and Technology for the Protection
of the Environment. *e:* **STEP**
Science, Engineering, Medicine and
Technology *e:* **SEMT**
Science Frontiers *e:* **SF**
Science in China. Series B, Chemistry, Life
Sciences and Earth Sciences *e:* **Sci
China B**
Science, Mathematics and Environmental
Education Information Analysis Center
e: **SMEAC**
Science of Anticipation Recognition
Evaluation Control of Health Risks *e:*
SAREC
Science of the Total Environment *e:* **Sci
Total Environ**
Science Panel on Interactive
Communication and Health *e:* **SciPICH**
Science Planning Intelligent Knowledge-
Based Environment *e:* **SPIKE**
Science Reports. Niigata University. Series
E. Geology and Mineralogy *e:* **NSEGB4**
Science Reports. Tohoku University.
Seventh Series. Geography *e:* **SRTG-A**
Science Reports Yokohama National
University. Section II. Biology and
Geology *e:* **SYUBAT**
Sciences Library, Natural Sciences Centre,
University of Western Ontario, London
e: **OLUM**
Sciences Naturelles *f:* **S.N.**
Sciences Physiques, Chimiques, Naturelles
f: **S.P.C.N.**
Scientia Sinica. Series B. Chemical,
Biological, Agricultural, Medical\and
Earth Sciences *e:* **SSBSEF**
Scientifc and Technical Aerospace Reports
Abstract *e:* **STA Rept Abstr**
Scientific Advisory Committee on
Biological Diversity *e:* **SACBD**
Scientific American Medicine *e:* **SAM**
Scientific and Technical Aerospace Reports
e: **Sci. Tech. Aerosp. Rep.**, *e:* **STAR**
Scientific and Technical Assessment of
Environmental Pollutants *e:* **STAEP**
Scientific and Technological Aspects of
Materials Processing in Space *e:*
STAMPS
Scientific Aspects of International Ocean
Research Working Party *e:* **SAIOR**
Scientific Authority for Animals *e:* **SAA**
Scientific Committee for Animal Health and
Welfare *e:* **SCAHAW**
Scientific Committee for International
Geosphere-Biosphere Programme *e:* **SC
IGBP**

Scientific Committee for/on Ocean[ic]
Research [of International Council of
Scientific Unions] *e:* **SCOR**
Scientific Committee for/on Problems of the
Environment *e:* **SCOPE**
Scientific Committee for Veterinary
Measures relating to Public Health *e:*
SCVMPH
Scientific Committee on Problems of the
Environment *e:* **SCOPL**
Scientific Committee on Science and
Technology for Environmental Protection
e: **SCOSTEP**
Scientific Committee on Water Research
e: **SCOWAR**, *e:* **SCWR**
Scientific Current Aerospace Notices *e:*
SCAN
Scientific Ecology Group, Inc., Oak Ridge,
Tennessee *e:* **SEG**
Scientific Event Alert Network [in the
National Museum of Natural History,
Smithsonian Institution] *e:* **SEAN**
Scientific Group for Space Research *e:*
SGSR
Scientific, Industrial and Medical
Photographic Laboratories *e:* **SIMPL**
[Scientific] Institute of Public Health *e:*
IPH
Scientific Instrument Protective Enclosure
e: **SIPE**
Scientific & Medical Instruments *e:* **SMI**
Scientific & Medical Publications of
France, Inc. *e:* **SMPF**
Scientific Organization of Laboratory
Animal Societies *e:* **SOLAS**
Scientific Parameters for Health and the
Environment, Retrieval and Estimation
e: **SPHERE**
Scientific Personal Interactive Computing
Environment *e:* **SPICE**
Scientific Pollution and Environmental
Control Society *e:* **SPEC**
Scientific Report. Laboratory for
Amphibian Biology. Hiroshima
University *e:* **SRLUDT**
Scientific Steering Committee for Ocean-
Atmosphere-Ice Interactions *e:*
SSCOAII
scientific technical and medical *e:* **STM**
Scientific, Technical and Medical
Publishers *e:* **STMP**
Scientific-Technical-Medical Book News
e: **S.T.M. Book News**
Scientific Wild Aim Guess *e:* **SWAG**
Scientific Wild-Aim Guess System *e:*
SWAGS
Scientific Wild Assessed Guess *e:* **SWAG**
Scientific Works. Research Institute of
Animal Production at Nitra *e:* **VPVZB9**
Scientists' Center for Animal Welfare *e:*
SCAW, *e:* **SCAW**
Scientists for Health and Research for
Development *e:* **SHARED**
Scientists' Group for Reform of Animal
Experimentation *e:* **SGRAE**
Scientists in the Sea Program *e:* **SITS**
Scion's Patrollin Underwater Robot *e:*
SPUR
scopolamine hydrochloride *e:* **SCOP**
Scott on Naturalization of Aliens *e:* **Sco.
Nat.**
Scott Polar Research Institute, Cambridge
e: **SPRI**

Scottish Advisory Committee on Computers in the Health Service e: **SACCHS**

Scottish Advisory Committee on the Computers in the Health Service e: **SACCHS**

Scottish Amateur Ice Speed Skating Association e: **SAISSA**

Scottish Association fo Mental Health e: **SAMH**

Scottish Association for Mental Health e: **SAM**, e: **SAMH**

Scottish Association for/of Mental Health e: **SAMH**

Scottish Association of Cold Storage and Ice Trades e: **SACSIT**

Scottish Association of Geography Teachers e: **SAGT**

Scottish Association of Health Councils e: **SAHC**

Scottish Board of Health e: **S.B.H.**

Scottish Clay Pigeon Association e: **SCPA**

Scottish Committee Action on Smoking and Health e: **SCASH**

Scottish Council for Postgraduate Medical and Dental Education e: **SCPMDE**

Scottish Department of Health e: **S.D.H.**, e: **SODoH**

Scottish Environmental Protection Agency e: **SEPA**

Scottish Federation of Sea Anglers e: **SFSA**

Scottish Geographical Magazine e: **Scot Geog M**, e: **Scot Geog Mag**, e: **SGM**

Scottish Health Advisory Service e: **SHAS**

Scottish Health Authorities Revenue Equalisation e: **SHARE**

Scottish Health Education Coordinating Committee e: **SHECC**

Scottish Health Education Group e: **SHEG**

Scottish Health on the Web e: **SHOW**

Scottish Health Purchasing Information Centre e: **SHPIC**

Scottish Health Service Planning Council e: **SHSPC**

Scottish Health Services Centre e: **SHSC**

Scottish Health Visitors Association e: **SHVA**

Scottish Home and Health Department e: **S.H.H.D.**

Scottish Home Office and Health Department e: **SOHHD**

Scottish Inland Waterways Association e: **SIWA**

Scottish Marine Biological Association e: **S.M.B.A.**

Scottish Medical Aid for Nicaragua e: **SMAN**

Scottish Medical Journal e: **Scott Med J**

Scottish Meteorological Society e: **S.M.S.**

Scottish Royal Geographical Society e: **S.R.G.S.**

Scottish Sea Fishers' Union e: **S.S.F.U.**

Scottish Society for the History of Medicine e: **SSHM**

Scottish Society for the Prevention of Cruelty to Animals e: **SSPCA**

Scottish Society for the Protection of Wild Birds e: **S.S.P.W.B.**

Scottish Water Ski Association e: **SWSA**

Scottish Wild Land Group e: **SWLG**

Scottish Wildlife Trust e: **SWT**

Scout Observation Service Unit e: **SOSU**

Scouting-Observation e: **SO**

Scouting, Observation and Sniping e: **SO & S**

Scouting-Observation Plane e: **SO**

Scripps Cooperative Oceanic Productivity Expedition e: **SCOPE**

Scripps Institute (or Institution) of Oceanography University of California at San Diego e: **SIO**

Scripps Institution of Oceanography e: **SCRIPPS**

Scripps Institution of Oceanography, La Jolla, California e: **SIO**

Scripps Institution of Oceanography University of California e: **Scripps**

Scripps Oceanographic Institution e: **SOI**

Scripps Orbit and Permanent Array Center e: **SOPAC**

Scripps Tuna Oceanographic Research e: **S.T.O.R.**

Scripta Geobotanica p: **Scr. Geobot.**

Scrolls from the Wilderness of the Dead Sea. Smithsonian Institution Exhibit Catalogue e: **SWDS**

Sculpture in the Environment e: **SITE**

Scuola Internazionale di Oncologia e Medicina Sperimentale i: **SIOMS**

Scuola Superiore di Oncologia e Scienze Biomediche (Genua) i: **SSOSB**

sea-air-landand- underwater targets e: **salut**

Sea Environment Acquisition System e: **SEAS**

Sea Environmental Monitoring System e: **SEAMOS**

Sea Frontier e: **SEAFRON**

Sea Ice Ecology and Flux Study e: **SIEFS**

Sea Ice Extent e: **SIE**

Sea Ice Mechanics Initiative e: **SIMI**

Sea Ice Microbial Colony e: **SIMCO**

sea-ice model developed at Los Alamos National Laboratory e: **CICE**

Sea Ice Monitoring Site e: **SIMS**

Sea Ice Numerical Experimentation Group e: **SINEG**

Sea Ice Ocean Modelling e: **SIOM**

Sea Ice Penetrometer e: **SIP**

Sea Level Atmosphere Pressure e: **QNF**

Sea Level Instrumentation and Observation Network e: **SEALION**

Sea Level Pilot Project-Southern Ocean e: **SLPP-SO**

Sea level Response to Ice Sheet Evolution e: **SeaRISE**

sea observation e: **sea-obs**

sea water e: **SW**, e: **s/w**

Sea-Water Acetic Acid Test e: **SWAAT**

Sea Water Activated Release System e: **SEWAWRS**

Sea-Water Conversion Laboratory e: **SWCL**

Sea Water Feed e: **SWF**

Seabrook Sea Island Cotton e: **SBSI**

Seafarers' International Union of North America [AFL-CIO]-Atlantic, Gulf, Lakes, and Inland Waters District e: **SIU-AGLI[W]**

Seafarers' International Union of North America [AFL-CIO], Atlantic, Gulf, Lakes and Inland Waters District e: **SIU-AGLIW**

Seafarers' International Union of North America [AFL-CIO]-Pacific Coast Marine Firemen, Oilers, Watertenders, and Wipers e: **SIU-MFOW**

Seafloor Geosciences Division e: **SGD**

Seal Beach Wildlife Refuge e: **SBWR**

SEAL [Subsea Equipment Associates Limited] Atmospheric System e: **SAS**

Sealant and Waterproofers Institute e: **SWI**

Sealant Waterproofing and Restoration Institute e: **SWRI**

Sealing Water e: **SW**

Seamen's Protection Society e: **SPS**

Seamen's United Protection Society e: **SUPS**

SEAMEO [South East Asian Ministers of Education Organization] Regional Center (or Centre) for Tropical Biology e: **BIOTROP**

Search Natural Resources, Inc. e: **SRCH**

Searth and Release e: **SAR**

SEASAT [Sea Satellite]-A Scatterometer System e: **SASS**

Seashore Environmental Alliance e: **SEA**

Seasonal Climate Outlook e: **SCO**

Seasonal High Water Level e: **SHWL**

Seasonal Ice Zone e: **SIZ**

Seasonal Ice-Zone Experiment e: **SIZEX**

Seasonal-to-interannual Climate Prediction Program e: **SCPP**

Seaspeed Sea Services Unit e: **SSSU**

Seattle Environmental Arts Museum e: **SEAM**

Seattle Ocean Services Unit e: **SOSU**

Seawater Microbial Community Model e: **SWAMCO**

seawater treatment plant e: **stp**

Secolul XX e: **SXX**

Second German Spacelab e: **SL-D2**

Second Greenland Ice Sheet Program (or Project) II e: **GISP II**

Second International Biological Experiment e: **SIBEX**

Second Large ESRO (European Space Research Organization) Project e: **SLEP**

Second Life Insurance of Georgia e: **SLIC**

Second Sea Lord e: **SSL**

Second Sea Lord's Office for Appointments e: **S.S.L.O.A.**

Second-Tier Securities Market e: **SSM**

Second World Climate Conference e: **SWCC**

secondary (earthquake) waves e: **s waves**

Secours en Nature f: **S.N.**

Secours Routier Français f: **S.R.F.**

Secretaria de Recursos Naturales s: **SRN**

Secretariat for Dental Health in Africa e: **SEDHA**

Secretariat for European Medicine e: **SEM**

Secretariat for the Convention on International Trade in Endangered Species of Wild Fauna and Flora e: **CITES Secretariat**

Secretariat for the Environment of the Presidency of the Federative Republic of Brazil e: **SEMAM**

Secretariat of Agriculture and Water Resources of the United Mexican States e: **SARH**

Secretariat of the Convention on the Conservation of Migratory Species of Wild Animals e: **CMS, UNEP/CMS**

Secretariat of the Interministerial Commission for the Resources of the Sea e: **SECIRM**

Secretary of Air Force Space Liaison *e:* **SAFSL**

Secretary of Health and Human Services *e:* **SecHHS**

Secretary of the Air Force, Director of Space & SDI Programs *e:* **SAF/AQS**

Secretary of the Air Force Space Liaison *e:* **SAFSL**

Secretary's Advisory Committee on Genetic Testing. National Institutes of Health *e:* **SACGT**

Secretaría de Desarrollo Urbano y Ecología *s:* **SEDUE**

Secretaría del Medio Ambiente, Recursos Naturales y Pesca *s:* **SEMARNAP**

Secteur Côtier des Recherches Agronomiques *f:* **SCRA**

Section de Protection Aérienne *f:* **S.P.A.**

Section de Recherches Forestières du Cameroun *f:* **SRFCAM**

Section de Recherches Forestières du Gabon *f:* **SRFG**

Section des Transports Routiers *f:* **S.T.R.**

Section d'Oceanographie d'Universite de Quebec a Rimouski *f:* **SOUQAR**

Section for Magnetic Resonance Technologists of the International Society for Magnetic Resonance in Medicine *e:* **SMRT**

Section Géographique de l'Armée Française *f:* **S.G.A.F.**

Section of Medical Information Science *e:* **SMIS**

Section on Experimental Psychology and Animal Behaviour *e:* **SEPAB**

secundum naturam *l:* **sec. nat.**, *l:* **s.n.**

Securable Remote Control Unit *e:* **SRCU**

Secure Automated Facility Environment *e:* **SAFE**

Secure Co-operative Processing Environment *e:* **SCOPE**

Secure Communications Processing Environment *e:* **SCPE**

Secure Communications Processor Environment *e:* **SCPE**

Secure Operating Environment *e:* **SOE**

Secure Remote Control Unit *e:* **SRCU**

Secure Remote Password authentication *e:* **SRP**

Securities Investor Protection Act *e:* **SIPA**

Securities Investor Protection Corp. *e:* **SIP**

Securities Investor Protection Corporation *e:* **SIPC**

Security/data protection *e:* **SEC**

Security Military Space Program *e:* **SMSP**

Sedgwick County Geological Information System *e:* **SCGIS**

Seedskadee National Wildlife Refuge *e:* **SNWR**

Seehydrographischer Dienst *d:* **SHD**

Seewasser *d:* **Seew.**, *d:* **Sw**

Seewasserkühlung *d:* **SK**

Seewasserstraßenordnung *d:* **SWO**

Segmentiersystem *d:* **SEGSYS**

Seismic Research Observatory *e:* **SRO**

Seismic Sea Wave Warning System *e:* **SSWS**

Seismic Sea-Wave Warning System *e:* **SSWWS**

Seismic Underwater Explorer *e:* **SUE**

Sektion Gesundheit *d:* **GES/BFS**

Sektion Überwachung der Radioaktivität des Bundesamtes für Gesundheitswesen *d:* **SUeR**

selbständige medizinische Abteilung *d:* **smA**

Selbstinterpretierende Programme *d:* **SIP**

Selbstinterpretierender Programmgenerator *d:* **SIP**

Select Committee on Ocean Policy *e:* **SOPS**

Selected Current Aerospace Notices *e:* **SCAN**

Selected Legally Protected Animals *e:* **SLPA**

Selected Natural Diamond *e:* **SND**

Selected Natural Diamond-Metal Bond *e:* **SND-MB**

Selected References on Environmental Quality as it Relates to Health *e:* **SROEQ**

Selected Water Resources Abstracts *e:* **SWRA**

Self Consistent Field Molecular Orbital *e:* **SCFMO**

Self Contained Adverse-Weather Night Attack *e:* **SCANA**

Self-Contained Adverse-Weather Night Attack *e:* **SCAWNA**

Self-Contained All-Weather Landing and Taxiing *e:* **SALT**

Self-Contained Ancillary Modular Platform [Woods Hole Oceanographic Institution] *e:* **SCAMP**

Self-Contained Atmosphere Protective (or Atmospheric Protection) Ensemble (or Ensembly) *e:* **SCAPE**

Self-Contained Atmospheric Personnel Ensemble *e:* **SCAPE**

Self-Contained Atmospheric Protective Ensemble *e:* **SCAPE**

Self Contained Atmospheric Protective Ensemble Suit *e:* **SCAPE**

Self-Contained Underwater Breathing Apparatus *e:* **SCUBA**

Self-Deploying Space Station *e:* **SDSS**

Self-Earth Ethic *e:* **SEE**

Self-Erecting Space Laboratory *e:* **SESL**

Self-Ferrying Trans-Ocean Rotary-Wing Crane *e:* **STORC**

Self Gated In-water Photography *e:* **SEGAIP**

Self Observation and Report Technique *e:* **SORT**

Self-Propelled Underwater *e:* **SPU**

Self-Propelled Underwater Missile *e:* **SPU Missile**

Self-Propelled Underwater Research Vehicle *e:* **SPURV**

Self Protection Aid Device *e:* **SPAD**

Self Protection Aid Devices *e:* **SPADs**

Self-Protection/Air Defense Suppression *e:* **SP/ADS**

Self-Protection EW Suite *e:* **SPEWS**

Self-Protection Subsystem *e:* **SPS**

Self Protection System *e:* **SPS**

Self Protection Weapon *e:* **SPW**

Self-Protective Anti-Tank *e:* **SPAT**

Self-Protective Anti-Tank Weapon *e:* **SPAT Weapon**

Self-Sealing Aerospace Vehicle *e:* **SSAV**

selfpropelled water barge *e:* **YW**

Selpropelled Remotely Operated Acoustic Magnetic Minesweep *r:* **SAM**

Sel'skokhozyaistvennaya Biologiya *R:* **S-Kh Biol**, *R:* **SSBLA**

Seltene Erden *d:* **SE**

SEM with polarization analysis *e:* **SEMPA**

SEMATECH Cell Application Learning Environment *e:* **SCALE**

Semi-airspace. *e:* **SAS**

Semi automated indexing of natural language *e:* **SAINT**

Semi-Automatic Business Environment Research *e:* **SABER**

Semi-Automatic Business-Related Environment *e:* **SABRE**

Semi-Automatic Business Research Environment *e:* **SABRE**

Semi-Automatic Decentralized Intercept Environment *e:* **SADIE**

Semi-Automatic Ground Environment *e:* **SAGE**

Semi-Automatic Ground Environment and Back-up Interceptor Control *e:* **SAGE-BUIC**

Semi-Automatic Ground Environment and Back-Up Interceptor Control *e:* **SAGE/BUIC**

Semi-Automatic Ground Environment Computer *e:* **SAGE Computer**

Semi-Automatic Indexing of Natural Language *e:* **SAINT**

Semi-Autonomous Underwater Vehicle *e:* **SAUV**

Semi-Submarine Ice-breaking Tanker *e:* **SSIT**

Semiautomated Business Research Environment *e:* **SABRE**

Semiautomatic BOMARC Local Environment *e:* **SABLE**

Semiautomatic Defense Intercept Environment *e:* **SADIE**

Semiautomatic Tactical Control and Airspace Management System *e:* **SATCAMS**

Semiconductor Bipolar Processor *e:* **SBP**

Semiempirical Natural Orbital *e:* **SNO**

Semigeostrophic *e:* **SG**

Semihydroascorbat *d:* **SDA**

Seminars in Cancer Biology *e:* **Semin Cancer Biol**

Seminars in Cell Biology *e:* **Semin Cell Biol**

Seminars in Nuclear Medicine *e:* **Semin. Nucl. Med.**

Seminars in Veterinary Medicine and Surgery [Small Animal] *e:* **Semin Vet Med Surg [Small Anim]**

Semioccupied Molecular Orbital *e:* **SOMO**

Semipolar *e:* **SP**

SEMMS [Solar Electric Multiple-Mission Spacecraft] Coordinating Group *e:* **SCG**

Senate Aeronautical and Space Sciences Committee *e:* **SASSC**

Senate Committee on Environment, Recreation and the Arts *e:* **SCERA**

Senate Environment and Public Works Committee *e:* **SEPWC**

Senator für Stadtentwicklung und Umweltschutz *d:* **SfSU**

Senatsausschuß für Umweltforschung *d:* **SAUF**, *d:* **SAUF**, *e:* **SAUF**

Senatsausschuß für Umweltfragen *d:* **SAUF**, *e:* **SAUF**

Senckenbergische Naturforschende Gesellschaft *d:* **SNG**

Seneca Underwater Test and Evaluation Center *e:* **SUTEC**

Seney National Wildlife Refuge *e:* **SNWR**

Senior Action in a Gay Environment e: **SAGE**

Senior Advisors [to ECE-Governments] on Environmental Problems e: **SAEP**

Senior Citizen's Medical Clinic e: **SCMC**

Senior Clinical Medical Officer e: **SCMO**

Senior Environmental Employee e: **SEE**

Senior Environmental Employment e: **SEE**

Senior Flight Surgeon e: **SFS**

Senior Flight Surgeon Badge e: **SRFLSBAD**, e: **SrFltSurgBad**

Senior Health Officer e: **SHO**

Senior Health Physics Technician e: **SHPT**

Senior Hospital Medical Officer e: **SHMO**

Senior Interdepartmental Group e: **SIG**

Senior Level Weapons Protection Group e: **SLWPG**

Senior Management Observation Program e: **SMOP**

Senior Medical Consultant e: **SMC**

Senior Medical Investigator e: **SMI**

Senior Medical Officer e: **SMO**, e: **SMO (mil)**

Senior Medical Officer of Health e: **SMOH**

Senior Medical Technician e: **SMT**

Senior Meteorological and Oceanographic Officer e: **SMO**

Senior Meteorological Officer e: **S Met O**

Senior Principal Medical Officer e: **SPMO**

Senior Resident Medical Doctor e: **SRMD**

Sense Amplitier-Blocking Oscillator e: **SA-BO**

Sensitive Wildlife Information System e: **SWIS**

Sensitivity of Water Resources e: **SOWR**

Sensor, Signatures, Signal & Information Processing e: **S3I**

Separated Orbit Cyclotron e: **SO**

separated orbit cyclotron e: **SOC**

Separated-Orbit Cyclotron Experiment e: **SOCE**

Separated Orbits e: **SO**

Sequence Number Protection e: **SNP**

Sequential Environmental Stress e: **SES**

Serbian American Medical and Dental Society e: **SAMDS**

Serendipity Association for Research and Implementation of Holistic Health and World Peace e: **SARIHHWP**

Series of American manned spacecraft e: **APOLLO**

Serum Hydroxybutyrate Dehydrogenase e: **SHBD**

Serum Lactate (or Lactic) Dehydrogenase e: **SLD**, e: **SLDH**

Serum Malic Dehydrogenase e: **SMD**

Serum-Milchsäure-Dehydrogenase d: **SMDH**

Serum Wassermann Reaction e: **SWR**

Serum-Wassermann-Reaktion d: **SWR**

serum X-hydroxy-butyrate dehydrogenase e: **shbd**

Serumlaktatdehydrogenase d: **SLD**, d: **SLDH**

Server-Natural Format e: **SNF**

Servic Médical d'Urgence de réanimation f: **SMUR**

Service and Health Records e: **SERVHEL Records**

Service Central de Protection contre les Radiations Ionisantes f: **SCPRI**

Service Central de Protection contre les Rayonnements Ionisants f: **SCPRI**

Service Central Hydrographique f: **S.C.H.**

Service Central Hydrographique de la Marine f: **S.C.H.M.**

Service Central Hydrologique f: **SCH**

Service Central Météorologique f: **S.C.M.**

Service Clarified Water e: **SCW**

Service Creation Environment e: **SCE**

Service Creation Environment Function e: **SCEF**

Service Creation Environment Point e: **SCEP**

Service d'Aide Médicale Urgente f: **SAMU**

Service de la Carte Géologique de France f: **SCGF**

Service de la Météorologie Nationale f: **S.M.N.**

Service de l'environnement atmosphérique f: **SEA**

Service de l'Inspection de l'Organisation et des Écoles f: **SIOE**

Service de l'Inventaire Forestier National f: **IFN**

Service de Protection de la Jeunesse f: **SPJ**

Service de Santé et de Secours Médical f: **SSSM**

Service des Renseignements de l'Observation du Terrain f: **SROT**

Service des Études et Recherches de la Circulation routière f: **S.E.R.C.**

Service d'Information Géologique f: **SIG**

Service d'information international sur les évaluations de l'environnement et des ressources naturelles f: **INTERAISE**

Service d'information sur les données hydrologiques f: **INFOHYDRO**

Service d'Orientation Médicale f: **SOM**

Service d'Utilité Agricole à Compétence Interdépartementale f: **SUACI**

Service d'Échange et de Diffusion d'Images Médicales Européen f: **SEDIME**

Service Départemental de la Protection Civile f: **S.D.P.C.**

Service Environment Power e: **SEPS**

Service Geographique National f: **SGN**, f: **SSGN**

Service Geologique Belgique f: **SGB**

Service Geologique de l'Armee f: **SGA**

Service Geologique de Luxembourg f: **SGL**

Service Geologique du Gabon f: **SGG**

Service Geologique National f: **SGN**

Service Géographique f: **S.G.**

Service Géographique de l'Armée f: **G.A.**, f: **S.G.A.**

Service Géographique, Forces Françaises en Allemagne f: **SGFFA**

Service Géographique Militaire f: **S.G.M.**

Service Géologique f: **S.G.**

Service Géologique de Madagascar f: **SGM**

Service Hydrographique de la Marine f: **S.H.M.**, f: **SKM**

Service hydrographique du Canada f: **SHC**

Service Hydrographique d'Études et de Documentation f: **S.H.E.D.**

Service Hydrographique et Océanographique de la Marine f: **SHOM**

Service Interministeriel des Affaires Civiles et Economiques de Défense et de Protection Civile f: **SIACEDPC**

Service Interministeriel Régional des Affaires Civiles et Economiques de Défense et de Protection Civile f: **SIRACEPDC**

Service Interminsteriel de Défense et de Protecton Civile f: **SIDPC**

Service International du Système GPS pour la Géodynamique f: **SIG**

Service Juridique de Protection de l'Enfance f: **S.P.E.**

Service Logic Execution Environment e: **SLEE**

Service Medico-Social f: **S.M.S.**

Service Médical f: **S.M.**

Service Médical de la Seine f: **S.M.S.**

Service Médical Interentreprise f: **S.M.I.**

Service Médical Provincial du Ruanda-Urundi f: **SM du RU**

Service Météorologique f: **S.M.**

Service Météorologique National des Etats-Unis f: **NWS**

Service National de la Protection Civile f: **S.N.P.C.**

Service national de satellites, de données et d'information en matière d'environnement f: **NESDIS**

Service national des satellites pour l'étude de l'environnement f: **NESS**

Service National d'Information et de Protection f: **SNIP**

Service Observance Bureau e: **SOB**

Service Observation Board e: **SOBD**

Service, Pay and Health Records e: **SERVPAHEL Records**

service protection network e: **SPN**

Service Water e: **SW**

Service Water Booster Pump e: **SWBP**

Service Water Pressurization Pump e: **SWPP**

Service Water Pump e: **SWP**

Service Water Reservoir e: **SWR**

Service Water Storage Tank e: **SWST**

Service Water System e: **SWS**

Service Women in Non-Traditional Environmental Roles e: **SWINTER**

Services Consultance en Observation de la Terre f: **SCOT**

Services Hydrographiques f: **S.H.**, f: **S.Hydr.**

Services Médicaux du Travail f: **S.M.T.**

Servicio de Pesca y Animales Salvajes de los Estados Unidos s: **USFWS**

Servicio del Medio Ambiente Atmosférico s: **AES**

Servicio Geodésico Interamericano s: **SGI**

Servicio Geografico del Ejercito s: **SGE**

Servicio Geografico Militar s: **SGM**

Servicio Geologico de Bolivia s: **GEOBAL**, s: **SGB**

Servicio Geológica Nacional s: **SGN**

Servicio Geológico de Bolivia s: **GEOBOL**

Servicio Internacional de Estudio de Rotación de la Tierra s: **IERS**

Servicio Internacional de Información Ambiental y de Evaluación de Recursos Naturales s: **INTERAISE**

Servicio Medico para Empleados Departamentales s: **SEMEDE**

Serviço Meteorológico de Moçcambique p: **S.M.M.**

Servicio Meteorológico Militar s: **SMM**, s: **SMN**

Servicio Meteorológico Nacional s: **S.M.N.**

Servicio Meteorológico Nacional de los EE.UU. s: **NWS**

Servicio Médico Forense s: **SEMEFO**

Servicio Nacional de Geología y Minería s: **SERNAGEOMIN**, s: **SNGM**

Servicio Nacional de Instrumentación Oceanográfica (Mexico) s: **SNIO**

Servicio Nacional de Meteorología e Hidrología s: **SNMH**

Servicio Oceanografico y de Pesca s: **SOYP**

Serviços Geológicos de Portugal p: **SGP**

Servicios Nacionales de Meteorología y Aerofotografía s: **SNMA**

Servico de Estudos e Planejamentos Agronómicos e Biológicos s: **SEPAB**

Servico de Inspeção de Produtos de Origem Animal p: **SIPOA**

Serviço de Pesquisas de Patologia Animal p: **SPPA**

Serviço Meteorologica de Angola p: **SEMA**

Serviço Meteorologica de Mozambique p: **SEMMO**

Serviço Meteorológico de Angola p: **S.M.A.**

Serviço Meteorológico de Moçambique p: **SMM**

Serviço Meteorológico Nacional p: **S.M.N.**

Servizio Geologico d'Italia i: **SGI**

Servizio Tecnico Geografico i: **STEGEO**

Servizio Telecommunicazione e Meteorologico dell'Aeronautica i: **ITAVI**

Session Management Protect e: **SMP**

Sever Environment Workstation e: **SEWS**

Severe Acoustic Noise Environment e: **SANE**

Severe Environment and Tempest e: **SET**

Severe Environment Controller System e: **SECS**

Severe Environment Memory Series e: **SEMS**

Severe Environment Memory System e: **SEMS**

Severe Environment Nosetip Test e: **SENT**

Severe Environment Power System e: **SEPS**

Severe Environment Systems Company e: **SESCO**

Severe Environmental Air Launch Study e: **SEALS**

Severe Environmental Storms and Mesoscale Experiment [National Science Foundation and National Oceanic and Atmospheric Administration] e: **SESAME**

severe noise environment e: **snc**

Severe Noise Environment e: **SNE**

Severe Weather Avoidance Plan e: **SWAP**

Severe Weather Avoidance Procedures (or Program) e: **SWAP**

Severe weather forecast alert e: **AWW**

Severe Weather Threat e: **SWEAT**

Severe Weather Warning e: **SWW**

Severe Weather Warning Center e: **SWWC**

Severe Weather Watch bulletin e: **WW**

Severe WeatherAvoidance Nationwide e: **SWAN**

Sexual Medicine Today e: **SMT**

SF-36 Health Survey e: **SF-36**

SFOF [Space Flight Operations Facility] Communications Terminal Subsystem e: **SCTS**

Shallow Resources, Inc. [Environmental Protection Agency] e: **SWO**

Shallow Underwater Missile e: **SUM**

Shallow Underwater Missile System e: **SUMS**

Shallow Underwater Mobile e: **SUM**

Shallow Water e: **SW**

Shallow Water Acoustic Tracking System e: **SWATS**

Shallow Water Acoustics e: **SWA**

Shallow Water Active Classification e: **SWAC**

Shallow Water Anti-Submarine Warfare e: **SWASW**

Shallow Water Anti-Traffic Mine e: **SWATM**

Shallow-water Assault Breaching e: **SABRE**

Shallow-Water Assault Breaching System e: **SABRE**

Shallow Water Attack Craft e: **SW**

Shallow Water Attack Craft, Light e: **SWAC**, e: **SWAL**

Shallow Water Attack Craft, Medium e: **SWAM**

Shallow Water Diver e: **SW**

Shallow-Water Environmental Cell Experiment e: **SWELLEX**

shallow-water equations e: **SWE**

Shallow-Water Evaluation Cell e: **SWELL**

Shallow Water MCM e: **SWMCM**

Shallow Water Mine Countermeasures e: **SWMCM**

Shallow-Water Oceanographic Research Data System e: **SWORDS**

Shallow Water Oceanographic Research Data System e: **SWORD System**

Shallow Water Oceanographic Research Data [System] [Naval Ordnance Laboratory and Naval Oceanographic Office] e: **SWORD**

Shallow Water SONAR e: **SWS**

Shanghai Environmental Sciences e: **Shanghai Environ Sci**

Shanghai Ocean Shipping Company e: **SOSC**

Shantung Medical Journal e: **Shantung Med J**

Shanxi Medical and Pharmaceutical Journal e: **Shanxi Med Pharm J**

Shanxi University. Journal. Natural Science Edition e: **Shanxi Univ J Nat Sci Ed**

Shared Graphics Work Space e: **SGWS**

Shared Medical Systems Corp. e: **SMED**

Shared Remote Control Unit e: **SRCU**

Shawnee Medical Center Medical Library, e: **KSM**

Shawnee. Mission Medical Center, Merriam e: **KMrS**

SHDSL Transceiver Unit-Remote Terminal End e: **STU-R**

Sheer Idiots Monopurpose Programming Language Environment e: **SIMPLE**

Sheet Metal Occupational Health Institute e: **SMOHI**

Sheffield Sawmakers' Protection Society e: **SSPS**

Sheffield University. Geological Society. Journal e: **Sheffield Univ Geol Soc J**

Shell public health and agricultural news, London e: **Span**

Shenandoah Natural History Association e: **SNHA**

Shepard Commemorative Volume. Papers on Marine Geology e: **Shepard Commem Vol Pap Mar Geol**

Sherburne National Wildlife Refuge e: **SNWR**

Shetland Health Board e: **SHB**

Shiawasse National Wildlife Refuge e: **SNWR**

Shielded Diatomic Orbitals e: **SDO**

Shielded Environmental Radiometallurgy Facility e: **SERF**

Shielded Environmental Radiometric Facility Cask e: **SERFC**

Shielded Environmental Research Facility e: **SERF**

Shielded Hydrothermal Testing Facility e: **SHTF**

Shiga University. Faculty of Education Memoirs. Natural Science e: **Mem Fac Ed Shiga Univ Natur Sci**

Shih Yen Sheng Wu Hsueh Pao [Acta Biologiae Experimentalis Sinica] ch: **Shih Yen Sheng Wu Hsueh Pao**

Shikimate Dehydrogenase e: **SKD**, e: **SKDH**

Shikoku Acta Medica l: **Shikoku Acta Med**

Shikoku Medical Journal e: **Shikoku Med J**

Shimane Journal of Medical Science e: **Shimane J Med Sci**, e: **SJSCDM**

Shimane University. Faculty of Education. Memoirs. Natural Science e: **Mem Fac Ed Shimane Univ Natur Sci**

Shinshu Medical Journal e: **Shinsbu Med J**

Ship Environmental Support Office[r] e: **SESO**

Ship Launched Underwater Transponder Target e: **SLUTT**

Ship Signals Exploitation Space e: **SSES**

Ship Technical Operation Protective e: **STOP**

ship-to-earth stations e: **SESe**

Shipboard Environmental [data] Acquisition System e: **SEAS**

Shipboard Equipment Environmental Design Study e: **SEEDS**

Shipboard Ice Navigation Support System e: **SINSS**

Shipboard Integrated Membrane Wastewater Treatment System e: **SHIMWTS**

Shipboard Meteorological and Oceanographic Observing Sensor e: **SMOOS**

Shipboard Meteorological Satellile Readout Station e: **SMSRS**

Shipboard Occanographic Survey System e: **SOSS**

Shipboard Tactical Airborne Remote Piloted Vehicle e: **STAR**

Shipboard Toxicological Operational Protective System e: **STOPS**

Shipborne Ice Alert and Monitoring e: **SIAM**

Shippers for Competitive Ocean Transportation e: **SCOT**

Shipping, Ports and Inland Waterways e: **SPIW**

Ship's Earth Station *e:* **SES**

Ships Tactical Environmental Control Receiver *e:* **STECR**

Ship's Toxicological Protective System *e:* **STOP**

Shirshov Institute of Oceanology *e:* **SIO**

Shizenshi-Kenkyu Occasional Papers. Osaka Museum of Natural History *e:* **Shizenshi-Kenkyu Occas Pap Osaka Mus Nat Hist**

Shock Hydrodynamic Elastic Plastic *e:* **SHEP**

Shock Protection System *e:* **SPS**

Shokubutsu Boeki/Plant Protection *e:* **Shokubutsu Boeki Plant Prot**

Short and Medium-Term Priority Environmental Action Programme *e:* **SMAP**

Short-Arc Geodetic Adjustment *e:* **SAGA**

short form for the Farasan Islands of the Red Sea off Saudi Arabia *e:* **Farasans**

Short Inter Frame Space *e:* **SIFS**

Short-Range All-Weather Air-Defense System *e:* **SHORADS**

Short-range Combined Observation, Uncooled Thermal *e:* **SCOUT**

Short Report. Rhodesia Geological Survey *e:* **Short Rep Rhod Geol Surv**

Shorthand Programming Language in COBOL Environment *e:* **SPCICE**

Shorthand programming language in Cobol environment *e:* **SPLICE**

Shuttle Atmospheric Science Experiment *e:* **SASE**

Shuttle Compatible Orbital Transfer Subsystem *e:* **SCOTS**

Shuttle Environment Monitoring System *e:* **SEMS**

Shuttle Induced Atmosphere *e:* **SIA**

Shuttle Orbit-Injection Propulsion System Analysis *e:* **SOPSA**

Shuttle Orbital Application *e:* **SOA**

Shuttle Orbiter Medical System *e:* **SOMS**

Shuttle Upper Atmosphere Mass Spectrometer *e:* **SUMS**

Shuttte Orbital Applications and Requirements *e:* **SOAR**

SIA/Groupe Specialise des Ingenieurs Forestiers *f:* **SIA/GSF**

Sibirskii Geograficheskii Sbornik *R:* **Sib Geogr Sb**

Sicherheit in Chemie und Umwelt *d:* **Sicherheit Chem Umwelt**

Sicherheitserde *d:* **SE**

Sicula Oceanic S.A. *e:* **SIOSA**

Side Impact Protection *e:* **SIP**

Side Water Depth *e:* **SWD**

Sidereal Polar Axis Celestial Equipment *e:* **SPACE**

Siding Spring Observatory, Australia *e:* **Siding Spring**

Sieboldia Acta Biologica *l:* **SIEBA**

Siedewasser-Versuchsreaktor *d:* **EBWR**

Siedewasserreaktor *d:* **SWR**

Siedewasserreaktoren *d:* **SWRn**

Siena Health Services, Inc. *e:* **SIE**

Sierra Health Services, Inc. *e:* **SIERHS**

Sierra Leone Agricultural Division. Ministry of Agriculture and Natural Resources. Report *e:* **Sierra Leone Agric Div Minist Agric Nat Resour Rep**

Sierra Leone. Report on the Geological Survey Division *e:* **Sierra Leone Rep Geol Surv Div**

Siglo Medico *l:* **Siglo Med**

Sign Signature *e:* **S/S**

SIGNAAL Command Oriented Programming Environment *e:* **SCOPE**

Signal Communications by Orbiting Relay Equipment *e:* **SCORE**

Signal Regenerator Unit-Remote *e:* **SRU-R**

Signal Underwater Exploding *e:* **SUE**

Signal Underwater Sound *e:* **SUS**

Signalisation Routière Internationale *f:* **S.R.I.**

Signals Communications by Orbital Relay Experiment *e:* **SCORE**

Signatur *d:* **SIG**, *d:* **Sign.**

Signature *e:* **S**, *e:* **SG**, *e:* **SGNR**, *e:* **.sig**, *e:* **Sign**

signature *e:* **sign(e)**

Signature *e:* **SIGNRE**

Signature Analysis *e:* **SA**, *e:* **SigAn**

Signature Analysis Methods for Mission Identifcation *e:* **SAMMI**

Signature Analysis Methods for Mission Identification *e:* **SAMMI**

Signature and Propagation Laboratory *e:* **SPL**

Signature Authority Hazmat Driver-Highway *e:* **SAHDH**

Signature Authority Manager *e:* **SAMGR**

Signature Authority System *e:* **SAS**

Signature Authorization Card *e:* **SAC**

Signature Authorization Chart *e:* **SAC**

Signature Book *e:* **SB**

Signature Library Intelligence Catalogue *e:* **SLIC**

Signature Managed Air Traffic Control Approach & Landing System *e:* **SMATCALS**

Signature Missing *e:* **Sig Mis**

Signature of Fragmented Tanks *e:* **SOFT**

Signature Overlap Range Prediction *e:* **SORAP**

Signature Overlay Range Prediction *e:* **SORP**

Signature Security Service *e:* **SSS**

Signature Unknown *e:* **Sig Unk**

Signature Verification *e:* **SV**

signatures *e:* **SGNTS**

Signaturfile *d:* **.ctx**

Signaturgesetz *d:* **SiG**, *d:* **SIGG**

Signaturverordnung *d:* **SIGV**

Signed Out Against Medical Advice *e:* **SOMA**

signes biologiques *f:* **S.B.**

Significant Hydrologic Resources *e:* **SHR**

Significant Meteorological Advisory *e:* **SIGMET**

Significant Meteorological Information *e:* **SIGMET Information**

Significant Meteorological Messages *e:* **SIGMET**

Significant Natural Area *e:* **SNA**

Significant Opportunities in Atmospheric and Research Sciences *e:* **SOARS**

Significant Weather *e:* **SIGWX**

significant weather chart *e:* **SWC**

Silent Solid-state Environmental Control System *e:* **SSEC**

Silhouetting Underwater Detecting System *e:* **SUDS**

Silicon Blpolar-MOS. *e:* **SBI MOS**

Silicon Capacitive Sensors for Biomedical Applications *e:* **CASE-CP96-136**

Silicon Cate Bipolar *e:* **SIGBIP**

Silicones Health Council *e:* **SHC**

Simple Communications Programming Environment *e:* **SCOPE**

Simple Environment Factor *e:* **SEF**

Simple Virtual Environment *e:* **SVE**

Simplex[ed] Remote Communications Central (or Centre) *e:* **SRCC**

Simplified Boiling Water Reactor *e:* **SBWR**

Simplified Pressurized Water Reactor *e:* **SPWR**

Simply Extended and Modified Batch Environmental Graphical System *e:* **SEMBEGS**

Simulated Ab-initio Molecular Orbital *e:* **SAMO**

Simulated Ab Initio Molecular Orbitals *e:* **SAMO**

Simulated Ab Inito Molecular Orbitals *e:* **SAMO**

Simulated Area Weapons Effects-Nuclear, Biological & Chemical *e:* **SAWE-NBC**

Simulated EMP (Electromagnetic Pulse) Ground Environment *e:* **SIEGE**

Simulated Natural Gas *e:* **SNG**

Simulated Remote Sites *e:* **SRS**

Simulated Remote Sites Subsystem *e:* **SRSS**

Simulated Remote Station *e:* **SRS**

Simulated Remote Station Control Center *e:* **SRSCC**

Simulated Remote Station Control Console *e:* **SRSCC**

Simulated Spacecraft *e:* **SSC**

Simulated Waste Access to Ground Water *e:* **SWAG**

Simulated Water Entry Test *e:* **SWET**

Simulating Accelerator Radiation Environment *e:* **SARE**

Simulating Medical Reasoning *e:* **SMR**

Simulation Algorithm for Water flow in Aqueous in Habitats *e:* **SAWAH**

Simulation Data Conversion Center [Space Flight Operations Facility] *e:* **SDCC**

Simulation of Closure and Rendezvous Approach Techniques for Early Spacecraft *e:* **SOCRATES**

Simulation Support Environment *e:* **SSE**

Simulation von Tier- und Organversuchen in der Lehre *d:* **STOL**

Simulations of Spacelab Missions *e:* **SIMS**

simulator atmospheric boundary layer environment *e:* **SABLE**

Simulator fiür elektromagnetische Umweltparameter *d:* **EES**

Simulator for Water Resources in Rural Basins *e:* **SWRRB**

Simulator Ueberwasserwaffen Schiessverfahren *d:* **SUES**

Simultaneous Adjustment of Photogrammetric and Geodetic Observations *e:* **SAPGO**

Simultaneous Auroral Multi-Balloons Observations *e:* **SAMBO**

Simultaneous Observations *e:* **SIMOBS**

Sindacato Nazionale Autonomo Medici Italiani *i:* **SNAMI**

Sindacato Nazionale Medici *i:* **SNM**

Singapore Aerospace *e:* **SAe**

Singapore Aerospace Maintenance Company *e:* **SAMCO**

Singapore Aerospace Warehousing and
   Supplies Pte *e:* **SAWS**
Singapore Journal of Tropical Geography
   e: **Singapore J Trop Geogr**, *e:* **SJTGD5**
Singapore Medical Association *e:* **SMA**
Singapore Medical Journal *e:* **SIMJA**, *e:*
   Singapore Med J, *e:* **Singapore MJ**
Singapore National Committee of the
   International Association on Water
   Pollution Research and Control *e:*
   SNCIAWPRC
Singapore Public Health Bulletin *e:* **Sing
   Pub Health B**
Single-Carrier Space-Charge-Limited
   Current *e:* **SCSCLC**
single-column version of the Community
   Climate Model *e:* **SCCM3**
Single Crystal Meteorite *e:* **SCM**
Single Integrated Medical Logistics
   Manager *e:* **SIMLM**
Single Layer Environment *e:* **SLE**
Single Linear Polarization *e:* **SLP**
Single Orbit Computation *e:* **SO**, *e:* **SOC**
Single-Point Orbit Calculator *e:* **SPOC**
Single Precision Orbit Determination
   Program[me] *e:* **SPODP**
Single Space *e:* **SS**
Single Stack Meteorological Model in EPA
   UNAMAP Series *e:* **PTDIS**
Single Stack Meteorological Model in EPA
   UNAMAP series *e:* **PTMAX**
Single-stage Earth-orbital Reusable Vehicle
   e: **SERV**
Single-Stage Hydrocracker *e:* **SSHC**
Single-Stage to Orbit *e:* **SSTO**
Single Underwater Sound *e:* **SUS**
Single Wire Earth Return *e:* **SWER**
Sino-American Medical Rehabilitation
   Association *e:* **SAMBA**
Sintered Hydroxyapatite *e:* **SHAP**
Sinusoidal Hydrodynamic Modulation *e:*
   SHM
Siouxland Health Sciences Consortium *e:*
   SHSLC
Sir George Williams Campus, Concordia
   University, Montreal, Quebec *e:* **QMG**
Sir George Williams College *e:* **S.G.Wms.**
Sistema de Administración de Datos
   Geofísicos *s:* **GEODAS**
Sistema de Análisis y Modificación de la
   Utilización de la Tierra *s:* **LUCAS**
Sistema de aproximación dirigida desde
   tierra *s:* **GCA**
Sistema de Datos Geofísicos *s:* **GEODAS**
Sistema de Datos Oceanográficos
   Descentralizados *s:* **DODS**
Sistema de Información Geográfica *s:*
   GIS, *s:* **SIG**
Sistema de Medición del Nivel del Mar de
   Nueva Generación *s:* **NGWLM**
Sistema de Observación de los Océanos *s:*
   OOS
Sistema de Observación del Ciclo
   Hidrológico *s:* **HYCOS**
Sistema de Observación del Ciclo
   Hidrológico en el Mediterráneo *s:* **MED-
   HYCOS**
Sistema de Observación del IGOSS *s:* **IOS**
Sistema de Observación e Información
   sobre el Ciclo Hidrológico y las
   Actividades sobre Recursos Hídricos en
   América Latina y el Caribe *s:*
   LACHYCOS

Sistema de Orbitografía de Precisión y
   Localización Exacta de Balizas Instalado
   a bordo de Satélite *s:* **DORIS**
Sistema de Procesamiento de Información
   Oceanográfica y Atmosférica *s:* **AOIPS**
Sistema de Transmisión Automático de
   Observaciones de Aeronaves *s:* **AARS**
Sistema Global Integrado de Estaciónes
   Océanicas *s:* **SGIEO**
Sistema Mixto de Observación para el
   Atlántico Nortes *s:* **COSNA**
Sistema Mundial de Observación *s:* **SMO**
Sistema Mundial de Observación de la
   Tierra *s:* **GTOS**
Sistema Mundial de Observación de los
   Océanos *s:* **GOOS**
Sistema Mundial de Observación del Clima
   s: **SMOC**
Sistema Mundial de Observación del Nivel
   del Mar *s:* **GLOSS**
Sistema Mundial de Observación del Nivel
   del Mar Mediterráneo *s:* **MEDGLOSS**
Sistema Mundial de Observación del Ozono
   s: **GOOS**
Sistema Nacional de Informacão Geografica
   p: **SNIG**
Sistema Nacional de Información
   Ambiental y Recursos Naturales *s:*
   SNIARN
Sistema Polar Europeo *s:* **EPS**
Sistemas de Acquisición de Datos
   Oceánicos *s:* **SADO**
Sistemas de Informacion Geografica S.A.
   s: **SIGSA**
Site health and Safety Coordinator *e:*
   SHSC
Site Index Biogeoclimatic Ecosystem
   Classification *e:* **SIBEC**
Site of Special Biological Interest *e:* **SSBI**
Site of Special Wildlife Interest *e:* **SSWI**
Site Personnel Protection *e:* **SPP**
Site Safety and Health Officer *e:* **SSHO**
Site Safety and Health Plan *e:* **SSHP**
Site Space Surveillance Monitor *e:* **SSSM**
Site Specific Health and Safety Plan *e:*
   SSHSP
Site-Specific Natural Isotope Fractionation
   e: **SNIF**
Site-Specific Water Quality Criteria *e:*
   SSWQC
Site-Wide Environmental Impact Statement
   e: **SWEIS**
SITS (SAGE (Semi-Automatic Ground
   Environment) Intercept Target
   Simulation) Prob *e:* **SPODAC**
Situation/Ready for Sea, Identification *e:*
   SIT/RFS IDEN
Sitzungsberichte. Akademie der
   Wissenschaften der DDR. Mathematik-
   Naturwiss.-Technik. *d:* **Sitzungsber
   Akad Wiss DDR Math-Naturwiss Tech**
Sitzungsberichte. Bayerische Akademie der
   Wissenschaften. Mathematisch-
   Naturwissenschaftliche Klasse *d:*
   **Sitzungsber Bayer Akad Wiss Math-
   Naturwiss Kl**
Sitzungsberichte. Gesellschaft
   Naturforschender Freunde zu Berlin *d:*
   Sber Ges Naturf Freunde Berl, *d:*
   **Sitzungsber Ges Naturforsch Freunde
   Berlin**
Sitzungsberichte. Gesellschaft zur
   Beförderung der Gesamten

Naturwissenschaften zu Marburg *d:*
   **Sitzungsber Ges Befoerd Ges Naturwiss
   Marburg**
Sitzungsberichte. Gesellschaft zur
   Beförderung der Gesamten
   Naturwissenschaften zu Marburg *d:*
   SBGMA
Sitzungsberichte. Heidelberg Akademie der
   Wissenschaften. Mathematisch-
   Naturwissenschaftliche Klasse *d:*
   **Sitzungsber Heidelb Akad Wiss Math-
   Natur KI**, *d:* **Sitzungsber Heidelb Akad
   Wiss Math-Naturwiss KI**
Sitzungsberichte. Oesterr. Akad. der Wiss.
   Math.-Naturwiss. Klasse. Abt. II.
   Meteorologie, und Technik *d:*
   **Sitzungsber Oesterr Akad Wiss Math-
   Naturwiss KI Abt II**
Sitzungsberichte. Saechsische Akademie
   der Wissenschaften (Leipzig).
   Mathematisch-Naturwiss. Klasse *d:*
   **Sitzungber Saechs Akad Wiss (Leipzig)
   Math-Natur Kl**
Sizing Aerospace Vehicle Structures *e:*
   SAVES
Sizing of Aerospace Vehicle Structures *e:*
   SAVES
Skånes Natur Stockholm, tidskrift *r:* **Sk.N.**
Skid Jacket Water Cooling Pump *e:*
   SJWCP
Skidaway Institute of Oceanography *e:*
   SIO
Skin Protection Factor *e:* **SPF**
Skrifter fran Mineralogisk och
   Paleontologisk-Geologiska
   Institutionerna *N:* **Skr Mineral
   Paleontol Geol Inst**
Skrifter. Norske Videnskaps-Akademi i
   Oslo. I. Matematisk-Naturvidenskapelig
   Klasse *N:* **Skr Nor Vidensk-Akad Oslo
   I Mat-Naturvidensk Kl**
Skrifter Utgitt. Norske Videnskaps-
   Akademi i Oslo. I. Matematisk-
   Naturvidenskapelig Klasse *N:* **Skr
   Norske Vid-Akad Oslo I**, *N:* **Skr Nor
   Vidensk-Akad Oslo I**
Skylab Medical Experiments Altitude Test
   e: **SMEAT**
Skylab Operational Environment *e:* **SOE**
Skylab Orbit-Deorbit System *e:* **SODS**
Skylab Orbital Workshop *e:* **SOW**
Skywave Observation Timer *e:* **SOT**
Slade National Wildlife Refuge *e:* **SNWR**
Slant Water Vapor *e:* **SWP**
slant water vapor *e:* **SWV**
Slater Orbital Exponents *e:* **SOE**
Slater-Type Orbital *e:* **STO**
Sliding Watertight Door *e:* **SWD**
Slocan Valley Watershed Alliance *e:*
   SVWA
Slosson Post-Observational Testing Screen
   e: **SPOTS**
Slosson Pre-Observational Record Screen
   e: **SPORS**
slot space *e:* **slot sp**
Slovak Medical Society *e:* **SLS**
Slovak Office of Geodesy and Cartography
   e: **SUGK**
Slow Space Charge Wave *e:* **SSCW**
Slowly varying absorption, Polar cap
   absorption, Auroral substorm,
   Zusatzraketen *e:* **SPAZ**
Sludge Program-Health Impacts *e:* **SPHI**

Sluzby Kwatermistrzewske *P:* **SK**

Small Aerial Vehicle for Observation, Intelligence & Reconnaissance *e:* **SAVOIR**

Small animal *e:* **SA**

Small Animal *e:* **Sm. An.**

Small-Animal Anesthesia Machine *e:* **SAAM**

Small Animal Care Hospital *e:* **SACH**

Small Arms Remote Target System *e:* **SARTS**

Small Arms Remote Targets *e:* **SARTS**

Small Hydro Costing Program *e:* **SHYDRO**

Small Hydro Society *e:* **SHS**

Small-Inventory Top-Tier Site *e:* **SITTS**

Small, Light [water-cooled], Graphite-moderated Reactor *e:* **SLGR**

Small Magnetospheric Observatory *e:* **SMO**

Small (or stationary) Pressurized-Water Reactor *e:* **SPWR**

Small Orbital Laboratory *e:* **SOL**

Small Orbiting Earth Resources Observatory *e:* **SOERO**

Small Payload Ejection and Recovery for the Space Shuttle *e:* **SPEAR**

Small Pelagic Fishes and Climate Change *e:* **SPACC**

Small-Probe Atmospheric Structure *e:* **SAS**

Small-Size Pressurized Water Reactor *e:* **SSPWR**

Small Spacecraft Technology Initiative Program *e:* **SSTI**

Small Unit Rehearsal Environment *e:* **SURE**

Small Volume water samples *e:* **SV**

Small Waterplane Area Air Cushion Ships *e:* **SWAACS**

Small Waterplane Area Ship *e:* **SWAS**

Small-Waterplane-Area Twin-Hull Ship *e:* **SWATH**

Small Weather Terminal *e:* **SWT**

Smaller Manufacturers Medical Device Association *e:* **SMMDA**

Smallest Space Analysis *e:* **SSA**

Smatt-Scale Hydroelectric Project *e:* **SSH**

Smelter Environmental Improvement Project *e:* **SEIP**

Smith on Forensic Medicine *e:* **Sm For Med**

Smith's Inquiry into the Nature and Causes of the Wealth of Nations *e:* **Smith Wealth Nat**

Smithsonian Air and Space Museum *e:* **SASM**

Smithsonian Air and Space Museum *e:* **SASM**

Smithsonian Astrophysical Observatory *e:* **SAO**

Smithsonian Contributions to Paleobiology *e:* **Smithson Contrib Paleobiol**

Smithsonian Contributions to the Earth Sciences *e:* **Smithson Contrib Earth Sci**, *e:* **Smithson Contrib Earth Sciences**

Smithsonian earth physics satellite *e:* **SEPS**

Smithsonian Environmental Research Center *e:* **SERC**

Smithsonian Institute/Astrophysical Observatory *e:* **SI/AO**

Smithsonian Institution. Astrophysical Observatory *e:* **SAO**

Smithsonian Institution-Peace Corps Environmental Program *e:* **SI-PCEP**

Smithsonian Oceanographic Sorting Center *e:* **SOSC**

smoke + ice *e:* **smice**

Smoking and Health Bulletin *e:* **S and H Bull**

Smoking and Health Reporter *e:* **SMHR**

Smooth Sea *e:* **S**

Smoothed-Particle Hydrodynamics *e:* **SPH**

SNA Remote Job Entry *e:* **SRJE**

Snap Lock Environmental *e:* **SLE**

Sniping, Observation and Scouting *e:* **SOS**

Snow and Ice Distributed Active Archive Center *e:* **SIDAAC**

Snow and Ice on Runways *e:* **SIR**

Snow, Ice and Permafrost Research Establishment *e:* **SIPRE**

snow survey and remote telemetry *e:* **SNOTEL**

Snow-Water Equivalent *e:* **SWE**

Snowwater Resources Ltd. *e:* **SNW**

Snowy Mountains Hydro-Electric Authority *e:* **SMHEA**

Soap and Water *e:* **S & W**

Sociai Biology Films *e:* **SB**

Social Biology *e:* **SOBIA**, *e:* **Soc. Biol.**, *e:* **Social Biol**

Social Biology and Human Affairs *e:* **SBHAD7**, *e:* **Soc Biol Hum Aff**

Social Health Authority *e:* **SHA**

social health insurance *e:* **SHI**

Social Health Maintenance Organization *e:* **SHMO**

Social, Natural, and Agricultural Resources Information Laboratory *e:* **SNARIL**

Social Science and Medicine *e:* **Social Sc M**, *e:* **Soc Sci and Med**, *e:* **Soc Sci Med**, *e:* **Soc Sci Medic**

Social Science and Medicine Africa Network *e:* **SOMA-Net**

Social Science and Medicine (Medical Anthropology) *e:* **Soc Sci Med (Med Anthropol)**

Social Science and Medicine (Medical Geography) *e:* **Soc Sci Med (Med Geogr)**

Social Science and Medicine (Medical Psychology Medical Sociology) *e:* **Soc Sci Med (Med Psychol Med Sociol)**

Social Science and Medicine. Part A. Medical Psychology and Medical Sociology *e:* **Soc Sci & Med Part A Med Psychol & Med Sociol**, *e:* **SSMSDZ**

Social Science and Medicine. Part A. Medical Sociology *e:* **Soc Sci Med A**

Social Science and Medicine. Part B. Medical Anthropology *e:* **Soc Sci Med B**, *e:* **Soc Sci & Med Part B Med Anthropol**

Social Science and Medicine. Part C. Medical Economics *e:* **Soc Sci Med C**, *e:* **Soc Sci Med Med Econ**, *e:* **Soc Sci & Med Part C Med Econ**

Social Science and Medicine. Part D. Medical Geography *e:* **Soc Sci Med D**, *e:* **Soc Sci & Med Part D Med Geogr**

Social Science and Medicine. Part E. Medical Psychology *e:* **Soc Sci & Med Part E Med Psychol**

Social Science and Medicine. Part F. Medical and Social Ethics *e:* **Soc Sci & Med Part F Med & Soc Ethics**

Social security and medicare *e:* **Soc. Sec.**

Social Security Benefit Protection Service *e:* **SSBPS**

Social Services National Coordination Council/Health Coordination Committee *e:* **SSNCC/HCC**

Social Work in Health Care *e:* **Soc Work Health Care**, *e:* **SWHC**

Social Workers' Association of Georgia *e:* **SWAG**

Socialist Environment and Resources Association *e:* **SERA**

Socialist Health Association *e:* **SHA**

Socialist Medical Association *e:* **S.M.A.**

Socially and Ecologically Responsible Geographers *e:* **SERGE**

Socialmedicinsk Tidskrift *r:* **SMT**

Sociedad Andaluza de Medicina Intensiva y Unidades Coronarias *e:* **SAMIUC**, *s:* **SAMIUC**

Sociedad Argentina de Biología *s:* **SAB**

Sociedad Argentina de Medicina Nuclear *s:* **SADMN**

Sociedad Argentina de Minería y Geología *s:* **SAMG**

Sociedad Chilena de Historia Natural *s:* **S.Ch.H.N.**

Sociedad Chilena de Historia y Geografía *s:* **SCHHG**

Sociedad Chilena de Producción Animal *s:* **SCHPA**

Sociedad Colombiana de Obstetricia y Ginecologia *s:* **SCOG**

Sociedad Colombiana de Recursos Naturales *s:* **SCRN**

Sociedad Columbia de Recursos Naturales *s:* **SCRN**

Sociedad Cubana de Historia Natural. Memorias *s:* **Soc Cubana Historia Nat Mem**

Sociedad de Ciencias Naturales la Salke *s:* **SVCS**

Sociedad de Ciencias Naturales La Salle *s:* **SCNS**

Sociedad de Estudiantes de Medicina *s:* **S.E.M.**

Sociedad de Geografia y Estadistica de La Republica Mexicana. Boletin *s:* **Soc Geog Mex B**

Sociedad Espanola de Historia Natural. Anales *s:* **Soc Espanola H N An**

Sociedad Espanola de Historia Natural. Boletin. Seccion Geologica *s:* **Soc Espan Hist Nat Bol Secc Geol**

Sociedad Española de Informática Médica *s:* **SEIM**

Sociedad Española de Microbiología *s:* **SEM**

Sociedad Española de Radiología y Electrología Médicas y de Medicina Nuclear *s:* **S.E.R.M.**

Sociedad Española de Radiología y Electrología Médicas y Medicina Nuclear *s:* **SEREM**

Sociedad Europea de Geofísica *s:* **EGS**

Sociedad Geografica. Boletin (Madrid) *s:* **Soc Geogr Bol (Madrid)**

Sociedad Geografica de Lima. Boletin *s:* **Soc Geog Lima Bol**

Sociedad Geográfica de Colombia *s:* **SGC**

Sociedad Geologica del Peru. Boletin s:
Soc Geol Peru Bol

Sociedad Geologica Mexicana. Boletin s:
Soc Geol Mex Bol, s: **Soc Geol Mexicana Bol**, s: **Soc G Mex B**

Sociedad Geológica Boliviana s: **SGB**

Sociedad Geológica de Chile s: **SGCH**

Sociedad Geológica del Perú s: **SGP**

Sociedad Iberoamericana de Biología Celular s: **SIABC**

Sociedad Ibérica de Nutrición Animal s: **SINA**

Sociedad Internacional de Biología Clínica s: **SIBC**

Sociedad Internacional de Evaluación de Tecnologías de la Salud s: **ISTAHC**

Sociedad Internacional de Micología Humana y Animal s: **SIMHA**

Sociedad Internacional de Patología Geográfica s: **SIPG**

Sociedad Medica Orizabeña s: **SMO**

Sociedad Meteorológica de Bolivia s: **SMB**

Sociedad Mexicana de Geografa y Estadistica. Boletin s: **Soc Mex Geog Estadistica B**, s: **Soc Mexicana Geografa y Estadistica Bol**

Sociedad Mexicana de Geografía y Estadística s: **SMGE**

Sociedad Mexicana de Historia Natural s: **SMHN**

Sociedad Mexicana de Historia Natural. Revista s: **Soc Mexicana Historia Nat Rev**

Sociedad Mexicana de Medicina y Cirugía Zootécnicas s: **SMMCZ**

Sociedad Médico-Quirúrgica de Zulia s: **SMQZ**

Sociedad Venezolana de Ciencias Naturales s: **SVCN**

Sociedad Venezolana de Ciencias Naturales. Boletin s: **Soc Venez Cienc Nat Bol**, s: **Soc Venezolana Ciencias Natar Bol**

Sociedad Venezolana de Geólogos s: **SVG**

Sociedade Brasileira de Geologia p: **SBG**

Sociedade Brasileira de Medicina Veterinaria p: **SBMV**

Sociedade de Geografia de Lisboa p: **SGL**

Sociedade de Protecao de Recursos Naturais p: **SOPREN**

Sociedade Geográfica Brasileira p: **SGB**

Sociedade Geologica de Portugal. Boletim p: **Soc Geol Port Bol**

Sociedade Portuguesa de Estomatologia e Medicina Dentaria p: **SPEMD**

Sociedade Portuguesa de Geotecnia p: **SPG**

Sociedade Portuguesa de Medicina Fisica e Reabilitação p: **S.P.M.F.R.**

Sociedade Portuguesa de Medicina Laboratorial p: **SPML**

Sociedád Argentina de Biologia s: **SAB**

Sociedád Argentina de Mineria y Geologia s: **SAMG**

Società Culturale Italiana Veterinari per Animali da Compagnia i: **SCIVAC**

Società di Studi Geografici i: **S.S.G.**

Società Ecologica Friulana i: **S.E.F.**

Società Elvetica di Scienze Naturali i: **SESN**

Società Esercizio Cantieri SpA i: **SEC**

Società Geografica Italiana i: **S.G.I.**

Società Geologica Italiana i: **SGI**, i: **S.G.I.**

Società Geologica Italiana. Bollettino i: **Soc G Italiana B**

Società Geologica Italiana. Memorie i: **Soc Geol Ital Mem**

Società Internazionale di Radiobiologia i: **S.I.R.**, i: **SIRB**

Società Italiana di Biogeografia i: **S.I.B.**

Società Italiana di Biologia e Medicina Nucleare i: **SIBMN**

Società Italiana di Biologia Marina i: **S.I.B.M.**

Società Italiana di Biologia Sperimentale i: **S.I.B.S.**, i: **S.I.B.Sp.**

Società Italiana di Ecologia i: **SItE**

Società Italiana di Ecologia, Atti i: **Soc. Ital. Ecol., Atti**

Società Italiana di Ginnastica Medica\Medicina Fisica e Riabilitazione i: **SIGM**

Società Italiana di Medicina i: **SIM**, i: **SIM**

Società Italiana di Medicina del Lavoro i: **SIML**

Società Italiana di Medicina del Traffico i: **SIMT**

Società Italiana di Medicina Fisica e Riabilitazione i: **S.I.M.F.E.R.**

Società Italiana di Medicina Interna i: **SIMI**

Società Italiana di Medicina Legale e delle Assicurazioni i: **SIMLA**

Società Italiana di Medicina Preventiva e Sociale i: **SIMPS**

Società Italiana di Medicina Psicosomatica i: **SIMP**

Società Italiana di Medicina Sociale i: **SIMS**

Società Italiana di Medicina Subacquea ed Iperbarica i: **SIMSI**

Società Italiana di Meteorologia Applicata i: **SIMA**

Società Italiana di Microbiologia i: **SIM**, i: **SIM**

Società Italiana di Ostetria e Ginecologia i: **Soc.It.Ost. e Gin.**

Società Italiana di Ostetricia e Ginecologia i: **SIOG**

Società Italiana di Patologia e Medicina Orale i: **SIPMO**

Società Italiana di Radiologia e Medicina Nucleare i: **SIRMN**

Società Italiana di Radiologia Medica i: **SIRM**

Società Italiana di Radiologia Medica e Medicina Nucleare i: **SIRMN**

Società Italiana di Scienze Naturali i: **SISN**

Società Italiana di Scienze Naturali e Museo Civico di Storia Naturale di Milano. Atti i: **Soc Ital Sci Nat Mus Civ Stor Nat Milano Atti**

Società Italiana di Scienze Naturali in Milano. Atti i: **Soc Italiana Sc Nat Milano Atti**

Società Italiana di Statistica Medico-Sanitaria i: **SISMES**, i: **SISMES**

Società Italiana di Storia della Medicina i: **S.I.S.MED.**

Società Italiana Medica del Training Autogeno i: **S.I.M.T.A.**

Società Italiana Medici e Operatori Geriatrici i: **SIMOG**

Società Italiana per le Scienze Ambientali: Biometeorologia, Bioclimatologia ed Ecologia i: **S.I.S.A.**

Società Laziale-Abruzzese Marchigiana Molisana di Ostetricia e Ginecologia i: **L.A.M.**

Societa Ligustica di Scienze Naturali e Geografiche. Atti i: **Soc Ligustica Sc Nat Geog Atti**

Società Ostetrica e Ginecologia i: **SOG**

Società Protettrice degli Animali i: **S.P.A.**

Società Ricerche Esperienze Meteorologiche i: **SO.R.E.M.**

Società Svizzera degli Ingegneri Termici e Climatici i: **SITC**

Società Toscana di Scienze Naturali i: **STSN**

Società Toscana di Scienze Naturali. Atti. Memorie. Serie A i: **Soc Toscana Sci Nat Atti Mem Ser A**

Societa Veneziana de Scienze Naturali Lavori i: **Soc Ven Sci Nat Lav**

Società Veneziana de Scienze Naturali Lavori i: **Soc Ven Sci Nat Lav**

Societas Geographica Fenniae. Acta Geographica l: **Soc Geog Fenniae Acta Geog**

Societas Internationalis Historiæ Medicinæ l: **SIHM**

Societas Internationalis Medicinae Generalis l: **SIMG**

Societas Medicinae Sinensis f: **SMS**

Societatis Medicae Londoniensis Socius l: **S.M.Lond.Soc.**

Society American Gastrointestinal Endoscopic Surgeons e: **SAGFS**

Society and Natural Resources e: **Soc Nat Resour**

Society, Environment and Energy Development Studies e: **SEEDS**

Society for Academic Emergency Medicine e: **SAEM**

Society for Adolescent Medicine e: **SAM**

Society for Advanced Medical Systems e: **SAMS**

Society for Animal Protective Legislation e: **SAPL**

Society for Animal Rights e: **SAR**

Society for Animal Welfare in Israel e: **SAWI**

Society for Biological Rhythm e: **SBR**

Society for Cell Biology e: **SCB**

Society for CIyobiology e: **SC**

Society for Clean Environment, Bombay e: **SOCLEEN**

Society for Clinical Ecology e: **SCE**

Society for Companion Animal Studies e: **SCAS**

Society for Computer Science in Biology and Medicine e: **SCSBM**

Society for Computing in Critical Care, Pulmonary Medicine and Anesthesia e: **SCCCPMA**

Society for Conservation Biology e: **SCB**

Society for Cryobiology e: **SC**

Society for Developmental Biology e: **SDB**

Society for Earthquake and Civil Engineering Dynamics e: **SECED**

Society for Ecological Restoration e: **SER**

Society for Education and Research in Psychiatric-Mental Health Nursing e: **SERPN**

Society for Environmental Education e:
  SEE
Society for Environmental Improvement e:
  SEI
Society for Environmental Stabilization e:
  SES
Society for Environmental Stress Analysis
  e: **SESA**
Society for Environmental Therapy e: **SET**
Society for Experimental Biology e: **SEB**,
  e: **Soc Exp Biol**
Society for Experimental Biology Seminar
  Series e: **Soc. Exp. Biol. Semin. Ser.**
Society for Gynecologic Investigation e:
  SGI
Society for Health and Human Values e:
  SHHV
Society for Health Education e: **SHE**
Society for Health Services Research in
  Radiology e: **SHSRR**
Society for Healthcare Consumer Advocacy
  e: **SHCA**
Society for Healthcare Epidemiology of
  America e: **SHEA**
Society for in Vitro Biology e: **SIVB**
Society for Indecency to Naked Animals e:
  SINA
Society for Industrial Biology e: **SIB**
Society for Industrial Microbiology e:
  SIM
Society for Integrative and Comparative
  Biology e: **SICB**
Society for Laboratory Animal Science e:
  SOLAS
Society for Low Temperature Biology e:
  SLTB
Society for Medical Anthropology e: **SMA**
Society for Medical Decision Making e:
  SMDM
Society for Natural Philosophy e: **SNP**
Society for Nature Conservation in the
  Netherlands e: **VBNN**
Society for Northwestern Vertebrate
  Biology e: **SNVB**
Society for Occupational and
  Environmental Health e: **SOEH**
Society for/of Biological Rhythm e: **SBR**
Society for/of Environmental Toxicology
  and Chemistry e: **SETAC**
Society for/of Experimental Biology and
  Medicine e: **SEBM**
Society for/of Geology Applied to Mineral
  Deposits e: **SGA**
Society for/of Nuclear Medicine-Europe e:
  SNME
Society for/of Teachers of Emergency
  Medicine e: **STEM**
Society for/of Underwater Technology e:
  SUT
Society for Private and Commercial Earth
  Stations e: **SPACE**
Society for Radiological Protection e: **Soc
  Radiol Prot**, e: **SRP**
Society for Radiological Protection. Journal
  e: **Soc Radiol Prot J**
Society for Reproductive Surgeons e: **SRE**
Society for Research into Hydrocephalus
  and Spina Bifida e: **SRHB**, e: **SRHSB**
Society for Research on Biological
  Rhythms e: **SRBR**
Society for Respiratory Protection e: **SRP**
Society for Sedimentary Geology e:
  SEPM

Society for Social Work Administrators in
  Health Care e: **SSWAHC**
Society for the Advancement of Breeding
  Research in Asia and Oceania e:
  SABRAO
Society for the Advancement of Breeding
  Researches in Asia and Oceania e:
  SABRAO
Society for the Advancement of Breeding
  Researct in Asia and Oceania e:
  SABRAO
Society for the Advancement of Space
  Travel e: **SAST**
Society for the Area of Biological and
  Chemical Overlap d: **SABCO**
Society for the Conservation of Biology e:
  SCB
Society for the Exploration and
  Development of Space e: **SEDS**
Society for the Internet in Medicine e:
  SIM
Society for the Perpetration of Outrageous
  Farces e: **SPOOF**
Society for the Preservation of Natural
  History Collections e: **SPNHC**
Society for the Preservation of the
  Rainforest Environment e: **SPORE**
Society for the Prevention of Cruelty to
  Animals e: **S.P.C.A.**
Society for the Promotion of Nature
  Conservation e: **SPNC**
Society for the Promotion of Nature
  Preserves e: **S.P.N.P.**
Society for the Promotion of Nature
  Reserves e: **SPNR**
Society for the Protection of Ancient
  Buildings e: **S.P.A.B**
Society for the Protection of Animals e:
  S.P.A.
Society for the Protection of Animals
  Abroad e: **SPANA**
Society for the Protection of Animals in
  North Africa e: **SPANA**
Society for the Protection of Beer from the
  Wood e: **SPBW**
Society for the Protection of Children in
  India e: **SPCI**
Society for the Protection of Children in
  India Quarterly e: **SPCI Quarterly**
Society for the Protection of Fast Asians'
  Human Rights e: **SPEAHR**
Society for the Protection of Life from Fire
  e: **S.P.L.F.**
Society for the Protection of Nature in
  Israel e: **SPNI**
Society for the Protection of New
  Hampshire Forests e: **SPNHF**
Society for the Protection of Old Fishes e:
  SPOOF
Society for the Protection of Science and
  Learning e: **SPSL**
Society for the Protection of the Unborn
  Child[ren] e: **SPUC**
Society for the Protection of the Unborn
  through Nutrition e: **SPUN**
Society for the Protection of Whitey e:
  SPW
Society for the Protection, Preservation and
  Propagation of the Queensland Cane Toad
  e: **SPPPQCT**
Society for the Relief of Medical Men e:
  S.R.M.M.

Society for the Scientific Study of the Sea
  e: **SSSS**
Society for the Social History Medicine e:
  Soc Soc Hist Med
Society for the Social History of Medicine
  e: **SSHM**
Society for the Social History of Medicine.
  Bulletin e: **Soc Soc Hist Med Bull**
Society for the Study and Conservation of
  Nature e: **SSCN**
Society for the Study of Human Biology e:
  SSHB
Society for the Study of Medical Ethics e:
  SSME
Society for the Study of Social Biology e:
  SSSB
Society for Tropical Veterinary Medicine
  e: **STVM**
Society for Underwater Historical Research
  e: **SUHR**
Society for Vector Ecology e: **SVE**
Society for Veterinary Epidemiology and
  Preventive Medicine e: **SVEPM**
Society for Veterinary Medical Ethics e:
  SVME
Society of Aerospace Material and Process
  Engineers e: **SAMPE**
Society of Afghan Doctors & Health
  Personnel Outside Afghanistan e: **SAD**
Society of Air Line Meteorologists e:
  SALM
Society of American Gastrointestinal
  Endoscopic Surgeons e: **SAGES**
Society of Animal Artists e: **SAA**
Society of Applied Biology e: **S.A.B.**
Society of Australasian Specialists/Oceania
  e: **SASO**
Society of Behavioral Medicine e: **SBM**
Society of Biological Psychiatry e: **SBP**,
  e: **SOBP**
Society of Biological Rhythm e: **SBR**
Society of Biomedical Equipment
  Technicians e: **SBET**
Society of British Aerospace Companies e:
  SBAC, e: **SMAC**
Society of British Aerospace Companies
  Ltd. e: **SBAC**
Society of British Neurological Surgeons
  e: **SBNS**
Society of Catholic Medical Missionaries,
  Inc. e: **SCMM**
Society of Community Medicine e: **SCM**
Society of Critical Care Medicine e:
  SCCM
Society of Critical Medicine e: **SCCM**
Society of Diagnostic[s] Medical
  Sonographers e: **SDMS**
Society of Economic Geologists e: **SEG**
Society of Economic Geology e: **SEG**
Society of Emergency Medicine Physician
  Assistants e: **SEMPA**
Society of Environmental Engineering e:
  SEE
Society of Environmental Engineers e:
  SEE
Society of Environmental Graphic
  Designers e: **SEGD**
Society of Environmental Journalists e:
  SEJ
Society of Ethnobiology e: **SE**
Society of Exploration Geologists e: **SEG**
Society of Exploration Geophysicists e:
  SEG, e: **Soc Explor Geophys**

Society of Exploration Geophysicists. Annual International Meeting. Abstracts *e:* **Soc Explor Geophys Annu Int Meet Abstr**

Society of Exploration Geophysicists of Japan *e:* **SEGJ**

Society of Exploration Geophysics *e:* **SEG**

Society of Eye Surgeons *e:* **SES**

Society of Fire Protection Engineers *e:* **SFPE**

Society of Fire Protection Specialists *e:* **SFPS**

Society of Fire Protection Technicians *e:* **SFPT**

Society of General Internal Medicine *e:* **SGIM**

Society of General Microbiology *e:* **SGM**

Society of General Surgeons *e:* **SGS**

Society of Gynecologic Nurse Oncologists *e:* **SGNO**

Society of Gynecologic Oncologists *e:* **SGO**

Society of Gynecological Oncology *e:* **SGO**

Society of Head and Neck Surgeons *e:* **SHNS**

Society of Health and Beauty Therapists *e:* **SHBTh**

Society of Independent Professional Earth Scientists *e:* **SIPES**, *e:* **Soc Indep Prof Earth Sci**

Society of Independent Professional Earth Scientists. Bulletin *e:* **Soc Indep Prof Earth Sci Bull**

Society of Indian Aerospace Technologies & Industries *e:* **SIATI**

Society of Industrial Microbiology *e:* **SIM**

Society of Japanese Aerospace Companies Inc. *e:* **SJAC**

Society of Laparoendoscopic Surgeons *e:* **SLS**

Society of Latin American Remote Sensing Specialists *e:* **SELPER**

Society of Medical Administrators *e:* **SMA**

Society of Medical Authors *e:* **SOMA**

Society of Medical Consultants to the Armed Force[s] *e:* **SMCAF**

Society of Medical-Dental Management Consultants *e:* **SMD**, *e:* **SMDMC**

Society of Medical Jurisprudence *e:* **SMJ**

Society of Medical Officers of Health *e:* **S.M.O.H.**

Society of Military Orthopaedic Surgeons *e:* **SMOS**, *e:* **SOMOS**

Society of Military Otolaryngologists-Head and Neck Surgeons *e:* **SMOHNS**

Society of Neurological Surgeons *e:* **SNS**

Society of Nuclear Medicine *e:* **SNM**, *e:* **Soc Nucl Med**

Society of Nuclear Medicine (or Medical) Technologists *e:* **SNMT**

Society of Nuclear Medicine. Southeastern Chapter. Continuing Education Lectures *e:* **Soc Nucl Med Southeast Chapter Contin Educ Lect**

Society of Nuclear Medicine-Technologist Section *e:* **SNMTS**

Society of Obstetricians and Gynaecologists of Canada *e:* **SOGC**

Society of Occupational Medicine *e:* **Soc Occup Medicine**, *e:* **S.O.M.**

Society of Occupational Medicine. Journal *e:* **Soc Occup Medicine J**

Society of Pelvic Surgeons *e:* **SPS**

Society of Philippine Surgeons in/of America *e:* **SPSA**

Society of Plant Protection of North Japan. Special Report *e:* **Soc Plant Prot North Jpn Spec Rep**

Society of Plastic Surgeons *e:* **SPS**

Society of Pollution and Environmental Control *e:* **SPEC**

Society of Power Industry Biologists *e:* **SPIB**

Society of Practising Veterinary Surgeons *e:* **SPVS**

Society of Prospective Medicine *e:* **SPM**

Society of Public Health *e:* **SPH**

Society of Public Health Education (or Educators) *e:* **SOPHE**

Society of Senior Aerospace Executives *e:* **SSAE**

Society of State Directors of Health, Physical Education and Recreation *e:* **SSDHPER**

Society of Teachers of Family Medicine *e:* **STFM**

Society of Thoracic and Cardiovascular Surgeons of Great Britain and Ireland *e:* **STCVS**

Society of Thoracic Surgeons *e:* **STS**

Society of United States Air Force Flight Surgeons *e:* **SUSAFFS**, *e:* **USAF/EDA**, *e:* **USAFSAM/ED**, *e:* **USAFSAM/VN**

Society of University Otolaryngologists-Head and Neck Surgeons *e:* **SUO-HNS**

Society of University Surgeons *e:* **SUS**

Society of Vascular Medicine and Biology *e:* **SVMB**

Society of Vector Ecologists *e:* **SVE**

Society of Wildlife Artists *e:* **SWLA**

Society of Wildlife Artists of Australasia *e:* **SWAA**

Society of Woman (or Women) Geographers *e:* **SWG**

Society to Rescue Animals you've Surrendered *e:* **STRAYS**

Societá Italiana Coloranti Naturali Affini *i:* **SCNA**

Socio-Economic-Environmental Information System *e:* **SEEIS**

Socio-Economic Model of the Planet Earth *e:* **SEMPE**

Socio-Economic Research Division, Parks Canada Program, Environment Canada Ottawa, Ontario *e:* **OOEPSE**

sociobiologic(al)(ly) *e:* **sociobio**

sociobiologist *e:* **sociobio**

sociobiology *e:* **sociobio**

socioecologic(al)(ly) *e:* **socioecol**

socioecologist *e:* **socioecol**

socioecology *e:* **socioecol**

Socioeconomic Issues of Health *e:* **Socioecon Issues Health**

Socioeconomic Report. California Medical Association *e:* **Socioecon Rep**

Sociol Social Science and Medicine. Part A. Medical Sociology *e:* **Soc Sci & Med Part A Med**

Sociology of Health and Illness *e:* **Sociol Health Illn**, *e:* **Sociol Health Illness**

Société Africaine de Produits Laitiers *f:* **SAPRO-LAIT**

Société africaine de transformation de matières plastiques *f:* **PLASTAFRIC**

Société Africaine de Transports Routiers *d:* **SAT**, *f:* **SAT**

Société Africaine des Produits Laitiers *f:* **SAPRO-LAIT**

Société Africaine Forestière *f:* **SAF**

Société Africaine Forestière et Agricole *f:* **SAFA**

Société Africaine pour le Droit de l'Environnement *f:* **SADE**

Société Agricole Forestière Industrielle pour l'Afrique *f:* **SAFIA**

Société Agro Animale Benino-Lybienne *f:* **SABLI**, *s:* **SABLl**

Société Algérienne de Géophysique *f:* **ALGEO**

Société Allemande de Radiobiologie et de Médicine Nucléaire *f:* **SARMN**, *f:* **SARMN**

Société Amicale des Géologues Amateurs *f:* **SAGA**

Société Anonyme Forestière et Agricole *f:* **SAFA**

Société Anonyme Luxembourgeoise de Gestion et d'Administration, Luxembourg *f:* **Salgad**

Société Anonyme Luxembourgeoise d'Exploitations Minières *f:* **SALEM**

Société Belge d'Astronomie, de Meteorologie et de Physique du Globe SBASI *f:* **SBAMPG**

Société Belge d'Astronomie, de Météorologie et de Physique du Globe *f:* **SBA**, *f:* **SBAMPG**

Société Belge de Biologie *f:* **SBB**, *f:* **SBB**

Société Belge de Biologie Clinique *f:* **SBBC**, *f:* **SBBC**

Société Belge de Géologie *f:* **SBG**

Société Belge de Géologie. Bulletin *f:* **Soc Belge G[eol] B[ull]**

Société Belge d'Informatique Medicale *f:* **M.I.M.**

Société Belge du Congrès Européen de Médicine Périnatale *f:* **EUROPERI-NATALE**

Société Belge d'Études Geographiques. Bulletin *f:* **Soc Belge d'Études Geog Bull**

Société Bernoise des Maîtres des Écoles Moyennes *f:* **SBMEM**

Société Camerounaise d'Exploitation Forestiére *f:* **SCEF**

Société Camerounaise Forestière et Industrielle *f:* **SOCAFI**

Société Canadienne de Biochimie et de Biologie Moléculaire et Cellulaire *e:* **SCBBMC**, *e:* **SCBBMC**, *f:* **SCBBMC**

Société Canadienne de Météorologie et d'Océanographie *f:* **SCMO**

Société Canadienne de Geologique Petroliers *f:* **SCGP**

Société Canadienne d'Histoire Naturelle *f:* **SCHN**

Société Centr[al]africaine d'Exploitation Forestières et Industrielle *f:* **SOCEFI**

Société Commerciale Transocéanique des Conteneurs *f:* **SCTC**

Société Commission Produits Laitiers *f:* **SCPL**

Société Cooperative Agricole du Mantois et Environs *f:* **SCAME**

Société Cooperative Agricole et Fruitière de Loire Atlantique *f:* **SCAFLA**

Société Coopérative Forestière
d'administration et de gestion *f:*
C.O.O.P.E.F.O.R.

Société Cotonnière Transocéanique *f:* **SCT**

Société d'Alimentation et de Recherch
Biologiques *f:* **SARB**

Société d'Alimentation et de Recherches
Biologiques *f:* **SARB,** *f:* **S.A.R.B.**

Société d'Application Hydro-Mécanique
Moderne *f:* **S.A.H.M.M.,** *f:* **S.A.H.M.M.**

Société d'Application Pharmaceutique et
Biologique *f:* **SAPB,** *f:* **SAPB**

Société d'Applications Techniques
Agricoles et Caoutchoutières *f:* **SATAC**

Société d'Assistance Technique pour
l'Exploitation Forestière *f:* **SATEF**

Société de Biologie de Montréal *f:* **SBM,** *f:*
SBM

Société de Biologie Experimentale *f:* **SBE**

Société de Chimie Biologique *f:* **S.C.B.**

Société de Courtage et de Representation
pour Industrie Laitière *f:* **SCERMA**

Société de Discipline Médicale *f:* **SDM**

Société de Développement des Ressources
Animales *f:* **SODERA**

Société de Développement et d'Exploitation
des Productions Animales *f:* **SODEPA**

Société de Garantie des Entreprises
Laitieres Agricoles et Alimentaires *f:*
SOGAL

Société de Geographie. Bulletin *f:* **Soc
Geog B**

Société de Geographie de Quebec. Bulletin
f: **Soc Geog Que B**

Société de Geographie (Paris). Bulletin *f:*
Soc Geog (Paris) B

Société de Gestion des Informations
Agrobiologiques *f:* **SGIA**

Société de Gestion Forestiere et Fonciere
f: **SGFF**

Société de Gestion Luxembourgeoise *f:*
SOGELUX

Société de Géographie *f:* **SG**

Société de Géologie Appliquée aux Gites
Minéraux *f:* **SGA**

Société de la Psychologie Medicale de
Langue Française *f:* **SPMLF**

Société de Physique et d'Histoire Naturelle
de Geneve. Compte Rendu des Seances
f: **Soc Physique et Histoire Nat Geneve
Compte Rendu**

Société de Production Animales *f:*
SOCAPRA

Société de Produits Laitiers et Alimentaires
f: **SAPLA**

Société de Quebec pour La Protection des
Plantes. Rapport *f:* **Soc Que Prot Plant
Rapp**

Société de Récupération et d'Exploitation
Forestière du Québec *f:* **REXFOR**

Société des Chantiers et Ateliers du Rhin
f: **SCAR**

Société des Cliniques Médicales *f:*
CLINIMED

Société des Grands Travaux Routiers *f:*
GTR

Société des Naturalistes Luxembourgeois
f: **SNL**

Société des Naturalistes Luxembourgeois.
Bulletin *f:* **Soc Nat Luxemb Bull**

Société des Obstétriciens et Gynécologues
du Canada *f:* **SOGC**

Société des Oceanistes. Journal *e:* **Soc
Ocean J**

Société des Produits Laitiers du Togo *f:*
SOR

Société des Recherches Médicales *f:*
FRAM

Société des Sciences Naturelles de L'Quest
de La France. Bulletin *f:* **Soc Sci Nat
Ouest Fr Bull**

Société des Sciences Naturelles de
Neuchatel. Bulletin *f:* **Soc Sc Nat
Neuchatel B**

Société des Sciences Naturelles et
Physiques du Maroc. Comptes Rendus des
Seances Mensuelles *f:* **Soc Sci Nat Phys
Maroc C R Seances Mens**

Société des Transports Automobiles de la
Région Belfort et Environs *f:* **S.T.A.B.E.**

Société des Transports Routiers du Bénin
f: **TRANS- BENIN**

Société des Écoles Polytechniques *f:* **SEP**

Société des Écrivains luxembourgeois de
Langue Française *f:* **SELF**

Société des Études Océaniennes *f:* **S.E.O.**

Société d'Etudes de Protection des
Installations Atomiques *f:* **SEPIA**

Société d'Expansion des Matières Plastiques
f: **SEP**

Société d'Exploitation des Hydrocarbures
d'Hassi R'Mel *f:* **SEHR**

Société d'Exploitation des Plantes
Médicinales et Tropicales *f:* **SEPLA**

Société d'Exploitation des Ressources
Animales du Sénégal *f:* **SERAS**

Société d'Exploitation Forestière du
Cameroun *f:* **SOFECAM**

Société d'Exploitation Forestière du Noum
f: **SEFN**

Société d'Exploitation Forestière[s] et
Industrielle[s] du Cameroun *f:* **SEFIC**

Société d'Exploitation Forestiére et
Agricole du Cameroun *f:* **SEFAC**

Société d'Exploitations Forestieres
Africaines *f:* **SEFA**

Société d'Exploitations Forestières et
Agricoles de la Côte-d'Ivoire *f:* **EFACI**

Société d'Exploitations Forestières et
Industrielles *f:* **SEFI**

Société d'Histoire Naturelle de Toulouse.
Bulletin *f:* **Soc Hist Nat Toulouse Bull**

Société Diamantière de la Côte d'Ivoire *f:*
SODIAMCI

Société d'Importation et d'Exportation de
l'Ocean Indien *f:* **SOCIMEX,** *f:*
SOCIMEX

Société d'Investissement Forestier *f:* **SIF**

Société d'Investissement Laitiers d'Outre-
Mer *f:* **SILOM**

Société d'Obstétrique et du Gynécologie de
Toulouse *f:* **SOGT**

Société d'Éditions Médico-Pharmaceutiques
f: **SEMP**

Société d'Études de Protection des
Installations Atomiques *f:* **SEPIA,** *f:*
SEPIA

Société d'Études et de Participations
Phosphatières *f:* **SEPHOS**

Société d'Études et de Recherches
Biologiques *f:* **S.E.R.B.**

Société d'Études Géographiques,
Économiques et Sociologiques
Appliquées *f:* **SEGESA**

Société d'Études pour la Mise en Valeur du
Gaz Naturel Camerounaise *f:*
SEGAZCAM

Société Européenne de Géophysique *f:*
EGS

Société Européenne de Production de
l'Avion d'École de Combat et d'Appui
Tactique *f:* **SEPECAT**

Société Européenne de Radiobiologie *f:*
SERB

Société financière et industrielle des ateliers
et chantiers de Bretagne *f:* **ACB**

Société Forestière *f:* **SOFOR**

Société Forestière Agricole des Ruraux
Africains *f:* **SOFARA**

Société Forestière Agricole, Industrielle et
Commerciale en Afrique Équatoriale *f:*
FORALAC

Société Forestière de Dolisie *f:* **SFD**

Société Forestière de la Côte-d'Ivoire *f:*
SOFOCI

Société Forestière de la Téné *f:* **SOFOTE**

Société Forestière de l'Ouest Cameroun *f:*
SFOC

Société Forestière du Cameroun *f:*
SOFOCAM

Société Forestière du Dja et Lobo *f:* **SFDL**

Société Forestière du Maine Sénégal *f:*
SFMS

Société Forestière et Industrielle de Belabo
f: **SOFIBEL**

Société Forestière et Industrielle de la
Doumé *f:* **SFID**

Société Forestière et Industrielle de la
Lokoundje *f:* **SFIL**

Société Forestière et Industrielle de la
Sangha *f:* **SFIS**

Société Forestière et Industrielle de l'Azobé
f: **SFIA**

Société Forestière et Industrielle des Bois
Ivoiriens *f:* **SOFIBOI**

Société Forestière Industrielle et
Commerciale *f:* **SOFICA**

Société Forestière Marcel Régnier *f:*
SFMR

Société Forestière Tropicale *f:* **SFT**

Société Française de Biologie Clinique *f:*
SFBC

Société Française de Biologie et de
Dietetique *f:* **SFBD**

Société Française de Gynécologie *f:* **SFG**

Société Française de Gynécologie. Comptes
Rendus *f:* **Soc Fr Gynecol C R**

Société Française de Radioprotection *f:*
SFRP

Société Française de Stockage Géologique
f: **Geostock**

Société Française des Lasers Médicaux *e:*
SFLM

Société Française d'Experimentation
Animale *f:* **SFEA**

Société Française d'Oncologie
Gynécologique *e:* **SFOG**

Société Française d'Électrologie Médicale
f: **SFE**

Société Française d'Électroradiologie
Médicale et Filiales *f:* **SFEMF**

Société Française d'Étude du Comportement
Animal *f:* **SFECA**

Société Française pour l'Application des
Ultrasons à la Médecine et à la Biologie
f: **SFAUMB**

Société Française pour l'Étude et la Protection des Mammifères *f:* **SFEPM**

Société Fribourgeoise des Sciences Naturelles. Bulletin. Memoires *f:* **Soc Fribourgeoise Sc Nat B Mem**

Société Geographique de Liege. Bulletin *f:* **SGLI,** *f:* **Soc Geog Liege Bul**

Société Geologique de Belgique. Annales *f:* **Soc G Belgique An,** *f:* **Soc Geol Belg An,** *f:* **Soc Geol Belgique Annales**

Société Geologique de France. Bulletin *f:* **Soc Geol Fr[ance] Bull**

Société Geologique de France. Bulletin. Memoires *f:* **Soc G France B Mem**

Société Geologique de France. Memoire Hors Serie *f:* **Soc Geol Fr Mem Hors Ser**

Société Geologique de Normandie. Bulletin *f:* **Soc G[eol] Normandie B[ull],** *f:* **Soc G Normandie B**

Société Geologique du Nord. Annales *f:* **Soc Geol Nord Ann**

Société Geologique du Nord. Annales. Memoires *f:* **Soc G Nord An Mem**

Société Geologique et Mineralogique de Bretagne. Bulletin *f:* **Soc Geol et Mineralog Bretagne Bull,** *f:* **Soc Geol Mineral Bretagne Bull**

Société Geoscientifique de l'Atlantique *f:* **SGA,** *f:* **SGA**

Société Génerale des Techniques Hydro-Agricoles *f:* **SOGETHA**

Société Générale de Forgeage Décolletage *f:* **GFD**

Société Générale des Forces Hydroélectriques du Katanga *f:* **SOGEFOR**

Société Géologique de Belgique *f:* **S.G.B.**

Société Géologique de France *f:* **S.G.F.**

Société Géologique de France. Memoires *f:* **Soc Geol Fr Mem**

Société Géologique et Minéralogique de Bretagne *f:* **SGMB**

Société Géologique Suisse *f:* **SGS**

Société Haitienne d'Histoire de Geographie et de Geologie. Revue *f:* **Soc Haitienne Histoire Geographie Geologie Revue**

Société Havraise de Protection des Animaux *f:* **SHPA**

Société Hellénique pour la Protection de la Nature *f:* **SHPN**

Société Helvétique des Sciences Naturelles *f:* **SHSN**

Société Hongroise de Geographie. Abrege du Bulletin *f:* **Soc Hongroise Geog Abrege B**

Société Hydrotechnique de France *f:* **SHF**

Société Imperiale des Naturalistes de Moscou. Bulletin *f:* **Soc Imp Nat Moscou B**

Société Industrielle de Produits Laitiers *f:* **SIPL**

Société Industrielle des Nouvelles Applications des Matières Plastiques *f:* **SNAP**

Société Industrielle et Forestière de Côte d'Ivoire *f:* **SIFCI**

Société Industrielle et Forestiere de Cote d'Ivoire *f:* **SITCI**

Société Industrielle et Forestiere des Allumettes *f:* **SIFA**

Société Industrielle Forestière en Afrique Centrale *f:* **SIFAC**

Société Industrielle Forestière et Commerciale Camerounaise *f:* **SIFCCA**

Société Internationale de Biologie Clinique *f:* **SIBC,** *f:* **SIBIOC**

Société Internationale de Biologie Mathématique *f:* **SIBM**

Société Internationale de Biometeorologie *f:* **SIB**

Société Internationale de Mycologie Humaine et Animale *f:* **SIMHA**

Société Internationale de Médecine Hydrologique *f:* **SIMH**

Société Internationale de Pathologie Géographique *f:* **SIPG**

Société Internationale de Radiobiologie *f:* **S.I.R.B.**

Société Internationale de Technique Hydrothermale *f:* **SITH**

Société Internationale d'Ophtalmologie Geographique *f:* **SIOG**

Société Internationale d'Écologie Tropicale *f:* **SIET**

Société Internationale d'Énergie Hydroélectrique *f:* **SIDRO**

Société Internationale d'Évaluation des Technologies de la Santé *f:* **ISTAHC**

Société Internationale Forestiere et Miniere du Congo *f:* **FORMINIERE**

Société internationale pour la prévention et l'atténuation des risques naturels *f:* **NHS**

Société Internationale pour la Recherche sur les Maladies de Civilisation et l'Environnement *f:* **SIRMCE**

Société Interprofessionnelle Maritime et Fruitiére *f:* **SIMA-FRUIT**

Société Ivoirienne de Climatisation *f:* **SIVOCLIM**

Société Ivoirienne de Construction Médicale *f:* **SICOMED**

Société Ivoirienne de Gestion et d'Exploitation Forestière *f:* **SIGEFOR**

Société Ivoirienne de Matieres Plastiques pour l'Agriculture *f:* **SIMPAGRI**

Société Ivoirienne de Productions Animales *f:* **SIPRA**

Société Ivoirienne de Tâcheronnage et d'Exploitation Forestière *f:* **SITEF**

Société Laitière Industrielle du Gabon *f:* **SLIGA**

Société Languedocienne de Geographie *f:* **Soc Languedoc Geogr**

Société Languedocienne de Geographie. Bulletin *f:* **Soc Languedocienne Geogr Bull**

Société Latière du Niger *f:* **SOLANI**

Société Luxembourgeoise de Biologie Clinique *f:* **SLBC**

Société Luxembourgeoise de Centrales Nucléaires S.A. *f:* **SCN**

Société Luxembourgeoise de Navigation Aérienne *f:* **S.L.N.A.**

Société Luxembourgeoise d'Entreprise et de Constructions S.A. *f:* **Soludec**

Société Luxembourgeoise des Auteurs *f:* **SOLUXA**

Société Luxembourgeoise d'Énergie Nucléaire *f:* **SENU**

Société Malienne d'Exploitation de Matières Plastiques *f:* **PLASMALI**

Société Maritime de Transports Océano-Méditerranéens *f:* **SOMATROM**

Société Marocaine de Navigation Fruitière *f:* **SOFRUMA**

Société Medicale Suisse d'Homéopathie *f:* **SMSH**

Société Medico-Chirurgicale des Hopitaux et Formations Sanitaires des Armees *f:* **Soc Med-Chir Hop Form Sanit Armees**

Société Médical des Hôpitaux de Paris *e:* **SMHP**

Société Médicale Canadienne sur l'Addiction *e:* **SMCA**

Société Médicale de Biothérapie *f:* **SMB**

Société Médicale de la Suisse Romande *f:* **SMSR**

Société Médicale Internationale de Endoscopie et Radiocinématographie *f:* **SMIER**

Société Médicale Internationale de Photocinématographie et Télévision Endoscopique et Radiocinématographique *f:* **SMIPCTER**

Société Médicale Internationale d'Endoscopie et de Radio-cinématographie *f:* **SMER**

Société Médicale Internationale d'Endoscopie et de Radiologie *f:* **SMIER**

Société Médicale Suisse de Psychothérapie *f:* **SMSP**

Société Météorologique de France *f:* **SMF**

Société National de Protection de la Nature et d'Acclimatation de France *f:* **SNPN**

Société Nationale d' Irrigation et de Amenagement Hydro-Agricole *f:* **SONIAH**

Société Nationale d'Acclimatation *f:* **SNA**

Société Nationale d'Acclimatation de France *f:* **S.N.A.F.**

Société Nationale de Développement de la Culture Fruitière *f:* **TOGO-FRUIT**

Société Nationale de la Production Animale *f:* **SONAPA**

Société nationale des Chemins de Fer Luxembourgeois *f:* **CFL**

Société Nationale des Chemins de Fer Luxembourgeois *f:* **SNCL**

Société Nationale des Hydrocarbures *f:* **SNH**

Société Nationale des Transports Maritimes des Hydrocarbures et des Produits Chimiques *f:* **SNTM-HYPROC**

Société Nationale des Transports Routiers *f:* **SNTR**

Société Nationale d'Irrigation et d'Aménagement Hydro-Agricole *f:* **SONIAH**

Société Nationale Française de Medicine Interne *f:* **S.N.F.M.I.**

Société Nationale pour la Recherche, la Production, le Transport, la Transformation et la Commercialisation des Hydrocarbures *f:* **SONA-TRACH**

Société Nationale pour la Renovation et le Développement de la Cacaoyère et de Cafetière Togolaise *f:* **SRCC**

Société Nationale pour le Développement Forestièr *f:* **SNAFOR**

Société Neuchateloise de Geographie. Bulletin *f:* **Soc Neuchatel Geogr Bull**

Société Nigérienne d'Exploitation des Ressources Animales *f:* **SONERAN**

Société Nouvelle de Transports et d'Exploitation Forestière *f:* **SONOTREF**

Société Nouvelle des Ateliers et Chantiera du Havre *f:* **SNACH**

Société pour Exploitation des Procédés S.E.A. *f:* **SEPSEA**

Société pour la Protection de la Nature en Israel *f:* **SPNI**

Société pour la Protection de l'Agriculture *f:* **SOPRA**

Société pour la Protection des Paysages et de l'Esthétique de la France *f:* **SPPEF**

Société pour l'Aménagement Touristique Argentière-Lognan *f:* **S.A.T.A.L.**

Société pour le Développement des Plantations Forestières *f:* **SODEFOR**

Société pour le Développement des Productions Animales *f:* **SODEPRA**

Société pour le Forestière du Heil *f:* **SOFOHI**

Société pour l'environnement du golfe de Finlande *f:* **SULA**

Société Protectrice des Animaux *f:* **SPA**

Société Protectrice des Animaux en Afrique du Nord *f:* **SPAAN**

Société Protectrice Humains *f:* **SPH**

Société Provisoire de l'Économique Laitière *f:* **SPEL**

Société Pédagogique Fribourgeoise Francophone *f:* **SPFF**

Société Romande pour l'étude et protection des Oiseaux *f:* **SRO**

Société Routièr de Côte-d'Ivoire *f:* **SOROCI**

Société Routière Colas de la Côte-d'Ivoire *f:* **SRCI**

Société Routière Colas de l'Ouest Africain *f:* **SRCOA**

Société Routière du Togo *f:* **SRT**

Société Royale Belge de Geographie. Bulletin *f:* **Soc Roy Belge de Geog B**

Société Royale Belge de Géographique *f:* **SRBG**

Société Royale de Géographie d'Égypte *f:* **S.R.G.E.**

Société Royale Forestière de Belgique *f:* **SRFB**

Société Serbe de Geographie. Memoires *f:* **Soc Serbe Geographie Mem**

Société Suisse de Gynécologie *f:* **SSG**

Société Suisse de Géographie Appliquée *f:* **SSGA**

Société Suisse de Médecine Thermale et Climatique *f:* **SSMTC**

Société Suisse des Ingénieurs en Chauffage et Climatisation *f:* **SICC**

Société Suisse des Maîtres Charpentiers *f:* **SSMC**

Société Suisse des Maîtres des Écoles Professionnelles Commerciales *f:* **SMEPC**

Société Suisse d'Histoire de la Médecine et des Sciences Naturelles *f:* **SSHMSN**

Société Suisse d'Industrie Laitière *f:* **SSIL**

Société Suisse pour la Protection de l'Environnement *f:* **SPE**

Société Suisse pour la Protection des Biens Culturels *f:* **SSPBC**

Société suisse pour la Recherche appliquée en matière de Formation Professionnelle *f:* **SRFP**

Société Sénégalaise pour l'Expansion de la Pêche Côtiére, Surgélation et Conditionnement des Aliments *f:* **SENE-PESCA**

Société Tchadienne d'Exploitation des Ressources Animales *f:* **SOTERA**

Société Tchadienne Industrielle et Commerciale de Produits Animales *f:* **STICPA**

Société Technique pour l'Océanologie *f:* **TECHNO-OCEAN**

Société Togolaise des Hydrocarbures *f:* **STH**

Société Tropicale d'Exploitation Forestière *f:* **SOTREF**

Société Tunisienne des Industries Laitières *f:* **Stil**

Société Vaudoise des Sciences Naturelles *f:* **SVSN**

Société Vaudoise des Sciences Naturelles. Bulletin *f:* **Soc Vaudoise Sci Nat Bull**

Société Voltaïque des Transports Routiers *f:* **SVTR**

Société Équipement Laitier et Industriel *f:* **SELI**

Sodium Dihydrogen Phosphate *e:* **SDP**

Sodium Glycodihydrofusidate *e:* **SGDHF**

sodium hydroxide *e:* **SOD HYDROX**

Sodium Hydroxide Addition *e:* **SHA**

Sodium Hydroxide Purge System *e:* **SHPS**

Sodium Hydroxybutyrate *e:* **SHB**

Sodium Taurodihydrofusidate *e:* **STDF**

Sodium-Water Reaction *e:* **SWR**

Sodium-Water Reaction Pressure Relief Subsystem *e:* **SWRPRS**

Sodium Water Reactor *e:* **SWR**

Soeiety of Airline Meteorologists *e:* **SALM**

Soeiété Cimentiere du Congo *f:* **SOCICO**

Software Aided Group Environment *e:* **SAGE**

Software Design Package for Land Mobile Communication Systems in Urban Environments *e:* **TEAMS-CP94-1067**

Software Development and Maintenance Environment *e:* **SDME**

Software Development Environment *e:* **SDE**

Software Development Realized On Natural Language *e:* **SDRONL**

Software Engineering Environment *e:* **SE2**, *e:* **SEE**

Software Environment for the Design of Open Distributed Systems *e:* **SEDOS**

Software in Healthcare *e:* **Softw Healthc**

Software Protection *e:* **SPROE**

Software Support Environment *e:* **SSE**

Software Test Environment *e:* **STE**

Soicété d'Études et de Recherches Biologiques *f:* **SERB**

Soil Airfield Fighter Environment *e:* **SAFE**

Soil and Crop Environment Research Programme *e:* **SCEP**

Soil and Health Foundation *e:* **SHF**

Soil and Health Society *e:* **SHS**

Soil and Water Assessment Tool *e:* **SWAT**

Soil and Water Conservation Act *e:* **SWCA**

Soil and Water Conservation Association of Australia *e:* **SAWCAA**, *e:* **SWCAA**

Soil and Water Conservation District *e:* **SWDC**

Soil and Water Conservation Districts *e:* **Soil & Water Conserv. Dist.**

Soil and Water Conservation Districts Foundation, Davis Conservation Library, League City *e:* **TxLcD**

Soil and Water Conservation Journal *e:* **Soil and Water Conserv Jour**

Soil and Water Conservation News *e:* **Soil and Water Conser News**

Soil and Water Conservation Research Division *e:* **SWCRD**

Soil and Water Conservation Research Division [of Department of Agriculture] *e:* **SWC**

Soil and Water Conservation Society *e:* **SWCS**

Soil and Water Conservation Society of America *e:* **SCSA**

Soil and Water Environmental Enhancement Program *e:* **SWEEP**

Soil and Water Management Association *e:* **SAWA**, *e:* **SAWMA**

Soil and Water Resources Conservation Act *e:* **RCA**

Soil and Water Sciences *e:* **SWS**

Soil Biology and Biochemistry *e:* **Soil Biol and Biochem**, *e:* **Soil Biol B**, *e:* **Soil Biol. Biochem.**

Soil Biology and Microbiology *e:* **Soil Biol Microbiol**

Soil, Environmental, and Agricultural Management System *e:* **SEAMS**

Soil [Microbiology, Soil Science[s]], and Water and Sciences Division *e:* **SWS**

Soil or Soil and Water Conservation District *e:* **SCD/SWDC**

Soil-Plant Atmosphere Computer *e:* **SPAM Computer**

Soil-Plant-Atmosphere Model *e:* **SPAM**

Soil-Plant-Atmosphere Research *e:* **SPAR**

Soil Science, Agrochemistry and Plant Protection *e:* **Soil Sci Agrochem Plant Prot**

Soil Survey Geographical *e:* **SSURGO**

Soil-test Water Probe *e:* **SWP**

Soil-Vegetation-Atmosphere Transfer Model *e:* **SVAT**

Soil-Vegetation Atmosphere Transfer System *e:* **SVATS**

Soil Water and Temperature System *e:* **SWATS**

Soil Water Deficit *e:* **SWD**

Soil, Water, Estuarine Monitoring *e:* **SWEMS**

Soil, Water, Waste *e:* **SWW**

Soins. Gynecologie, Obstetrique, Puericulture *f:* **Soins Gynecol Obst Pueric**

Solar and Atmospheric Structure Satellite *e:* **SRATS**

Solar [and] Heliosphysic[al] Observatory [satellite] *e:* **SOHO**

solar and infrared radiation observation stations *e:* **SIROS**

Solar Array Performance in Piasma Environments *e:* **SAPPE**

Solar Atmospher[ic] Explorer *e:* **SAE**

Solar Atmospheric Gas Experiment *e:* **SAGE**

Solar Atmospheric Tide *e:* **SAT**

Solar Eclipse Atmospheric and Ionospheric Measurements Project *e:* **SEAIMP**

Solar Electric Multi-Mission Spacecraft *e:* **SEMMS**

Solar Electric-Propelled Spacecraft *e:* **SEPS**

Solar Environment Monitor Subsystem *e:* **SEMS**

Solar Environment Simulator *e:* **SES**
Solar Flare X-Ray Polarimeter *e:* **SFEX**
Solar-Geophysical Data *e:* **SGD**
Solar Hydrogen Rocket Engine *e:* **SOHR,**
  e: **SOHR Engine**
Solar Observatory *e:* **SO**
Solar Optical Universal Photopolarimeter
  e: **SOUP**
Solar Optical Universal Polarimeter *e:*
  SOUP
Solar Orbital Communications *e:* **SOCOM**
Solar Perturbation and Atmospheric Density
  Experiments Satellite *e:* **SPADES**
Solar Polar Mission *e:* **SPM**
Solar Polar Monitor *e:* **SPM**
Solar Probe Spacecraft *e:* **SPS**
Solar Proton Alert Network [of Space
  Disturbances Laboratory, National
  Oceanic and Atmospheric Administration]
  e: **SPAN**
Solar Radio Observatory *e:* **SRO**
Solar Sea Power Plant *e:* **SSPP**
Solar Spectrum at earth's surface for
  average weather conditions *e:* **AM2**
Solar Spectrum at earth's surface for
  optimum conditions at sea level, sun at
  zenith *e:* **AM1**
Solar Spectrum Outer Space *e:* **AMO**
Solar-Terrestrial Environment Model *e:*
  STEM
Solar Terrestrial Environmental Research in
  Japan *e:* **Sol Terr Environ Res Jpn**
Solar Terrestrial Observatory *e:* **STO**
Solar-Terrestrial Physics-Meteorology *e:*
  STP-M
Solar Tower Atmospheric Cherenkov Effect
  Experiment *e:* **STACEE**
Solar Water Heating *e:* **SWH**
Solar Weather Seminar *e:* **SWS**
Soldier-Integrated Protective Ensemble *e:*
  SIPE
Solid Amine Water Absorption *e:* **SAWD**
Solid Amine Water Desorbed *e:* **SAWD**
Solid Earth Geophysics *e:* **SEG**
Solid Earth Science and Applications
  Mission Experiment *e:* **SESAME**
Solid-State Logic Protection System *e:*
  SSLPS
Solid State Primary Protectors *e:* **SSOVP**
Solid State Protection System, *e:* **SSPS**
Solid Waste Information Retrieval System
  [Environmental Protection Agency] *e:*
  SWIRS
Solomon Islands Geological Survey *e:*
  SIGS
Soluble Malate Dehydrogenase *e:* **s-MDH**
Soluble, Repository, Dihydrostreptomycin
  e: **SRD**
Solution to Environmental and Economic
  Problems *e:* **STEEP**
Somerset Archaeological and Natural
  History Society *e:* **S.A.N.H.S.**
Somerset Archaeology and Natural History
  e: **SANH,** *e:* **Som A Natur Hist,** *e:*
  Somerset Archaeol Natur Hist, *e:*
  Somerset Arch Nat Hist
Somerset County Library, Bridgewater *e:*
  SOM
Somerset County Vocational and Technical
  School, Bridgewater *e:* **SOV**
Somersetshire Archaeological and Natural
  History Society. Proceedings *e:* **So AS**
Sommermittelwasser *d:* **SMW**

Sonar Environmental & Acoustic Tactical
  Decision Aid *e:* **SEATDA**
Sonar Environmental Prediction and
  Display System *e:* **SEPADS**
Sonderbände des Naturwissenschaftlichen
  Vereins in Hamburg *d:* **Sonderb
  Naturwiss Ver Hamb**
Sonderforschungsbereich "Biologische
  Nachrichtenaufnahme und Verarbeitung"
  d: **SFB 114 "Bionach"**
Songklanagarind Medical Journal [Prince of
  Songkla University, Thailand] *e:* **SMJ**
Sonic Observation of the Trajectory and
  Impact of Missiles *e:* **SOTIM**
Sonic Underwater Navigation System *e:*
  SUNS
Sons of Sherman's March to the Sea *e:*
  SSMS
Soobshcheniya Byurakanskoi Observatorii
  Akademiya Nauk Armyanskoi SSR *R:*
  SBOAA
Soobshcheniya Shemakhinskoi
  Astrofizicheskoi Observatorii Akademiya
  Nauk Azerbaidzhanskoi SSR *R:* **SSAOA**
Soon Chun Hyang Journal of Medicine *e:*
  SHJMD, *e:* **Soon Chun Hyang J Med**
Sorbit *d:* **E 420**
Sorbital Dehydrogenase *e:* **SD**
Sorbitdehydrogenase *d:* **SD,** *d:* **SDH,** *d:*
  SODH, *e:* **SorbD**
Sorbitol Dehydrogenase *e:* **SDH,** *e:* **Sorb D**
Sortier-Misch-Generator *d:* **SMG**
Sortier- und Auswahlprogramm mit
  Mehrfachausgabe zur Organisation von
  Abläufen *d:* **SAMOA**
Sortierautomatik *d:* **SA**
Sortierbegriff *d:* **SB**
Sortiereinheit *d:* **SE**
Sortieren *d:* **SO**
Sortieren und Trennen *d:* **STT**
Sortierer *d:* **So**
Sortierfolge *d:* **SortF**
Sortierkriterium *d:* **SK**
Sortiermaschine *d:* **SM**
Sortierplatz *d:* **SPL**
Sortierprogramm *d:* **SOP,** *d:* **SP**
Sortierschlüssel *d:* **SortSchl**
sortiert *d:* **sort.**
Sortierung *d:* **S**
Sound Ocean Fixing and Ranging *e:* **SOFAR**
Sound Surveillance Underwater System *e:*
  SOSUS
Sound System for Underwater Surveillance
  e: **SOSUS**
Sound Under Water Signals *e:* **SUS**
Sound Underwater Signal Source *e:* **SUSS**
Sound Underwater Source *e:* **SUS**
Source Oriented Medical Information
  System *e:* **SOMIS**
Source Region EMP protection *e:* **SREMP**
Source Water Assessment Program *e:*
  SWAP
Source Water Protection Area *e:* **SWPA**
Source Water Quality Protection
  Partnership Petitions *e:* **SWQPPP**
Sources d'archives pour les recherches sur
  l'histoire du climat *f:* **ARCHISS**
Sources of Ambient MicroSeismic Oceanic
  Noise Experiment *e:* **SAMSON**
Sources of Radioactivity in the Marine
  Environment and their Relative
  Contributors to Overall Dose Assessment
  from Marine Radioactivity *e:* **MARDOS**

Sournal. Medical Association of Croatia *e:*
  J Med Ass Croat
Sous-Commission de Coordination des
  Questions Forestières Méditerranéennes
  f: **SCM**
Sous-groupe des satellites d'observation de
  l'océan et de la télédétection *f:* **OSRS**
Sous-programme sur l'environnement et les
  ressources minérales des marges
  continentales *f:* **COMEMIR**
South Africa [Cape Of Good Hope]
  Degartment of Nature. Conservation
  Report *e:* **S Afr [Cape Good Hope] Dep
  Nat Conserv Rep**
South Africa. Depanment of Mines.
  Geological Survey. Bulletin *e:* **S Afr
  Geol Surv Bull**
South Africa. Department of Agriculture
  and Water Supply. Entomology Memoir
  e: **S Afr Dep Agric Water Supply
  Entomol Mem**
South Africa. Department of Agriculture
  and Water Supply. Technical
  Communication *e:* **S Afr Dep Agric
  Water Supply Tech Commun**
South Africa. Department of Mines.
  Geological Survey. Annals of the
  Geological Survey *e:* **S Afr Dep Mines
  Geol Surv Ann Geol Suv**
South Africa. Department of Mines.
  Geological Survey. Memoir *e:* **S Afr
  Geol Surv Mem**
South Africa. Division of Sea Fisheries.
  Annual Report *e:* **S Afr Div Sea Fish
  Annu Rep**
South Africa. Division of Sea Fisheries.
  Fisheries Bulletin *e:* **S Afr Div Sea Fish
  Fish Bull**
South Africa. Division of Sea Fisheries.
  Investigational Report *e:* **S Afr Div Sea
  Fish Invest Rep**
South Africa. Geological Survey.
  Bibliography and Subject Index of South
  African Geology *e:* **S Afr Geol Surv
  Bibliogr Subj Index S Afr Geol**
South Africa. Geological Survey. Handbook
  e: **S Afr Geol Surv Handb**
South Africa. Geological Survey.
  Seismologic Series *e:* **S Afr Geol Surv
  Seismol Ser**
South Africa. Geological Survey. South-
  West Africa Series *e:* **S Afr Geol Surv
  South-West Afr Ser**
South Africa Lombard Nature Reserve *e:*
  SALNR
South Africa. Report of the Secretary for
  Water Affairs *e:* **S Afr Rep Secr Water
  Affairs**
South Africa. Sea Fisheries Branch.
  Investigational Report *e:* **S Afr Sea Fish
  Branch Invest Rep**
South Africa. Sea Fisheries Institute.
  Investigational Report *e:* **S Afr Sea Fish
  Inst Invest Rep**
South Africa. Sea Fisheries Research
  Institute. Investigational Report *e:* **S Afr
  Sea Fish Res Inst Invest Rep**
South African Association for Marine
  Biological Research *e:* **SAAMBR**
South African Association for Marine
  Biological Rescarch. Bulletin *e:* **S Afr
  Assoc Mar Biol Res Bull**

South African Association of Physicists in Medicine and Biology e: **SAAPMB**

South African Astronomical Observatory e: **SAAO**

South African Climate Change, Analysis, Interpretation and Modelling e: **SACCAIM**

South-African ContainerDepots e: **SACD**

South African Country Study on Climate Change e: **SACSCC**

South African demographic and health survey e: **SADHS**

South African Fire-Atmosphere Research Initiative e: **SAFARI-92**

South African Geographer e: **S Afr Geogr**

South African Geographical Journal e: **S Afr Geogr J**, e: **SAGJ**, e: **South Afr Geogr J**

South African Geographical Society e: **S.A.G.S.**

South African Health and Social Services Organisation e: **SAHSSO**

South African Institute for Medical Research e: **SAIMR**

South African Institute for Medical Research. Annual Report e: **S Afr Inst Med Res Annu Rep**

South African Institute of Environmental Health e: **SAIEH**

South African Institute of Medical Research e: **SAIMR**

South African Journal of Animal Science e: **S Afr J Anim Sci**, e: **SAJAC**

South African Journal of Continuing Medical Eduation e: **S Afr J Contin Med Educ**

South African Journal of Continuing Medical Education e: **SACED**

South African Journal of Geology e: **S Afr J Geol**

South African Journal of Hospital Medicine e: **S Alr J Hosp Med**, e: **SJMED**

South African Journal of Laboratory and Clinical Medicine e: **S Afr J Lab Clin Med**

South African Journal of Medical Laboratory Technology e: **S Afr J Med Lab Technol**, e: **SAJTA**

South African Journal of Medical Sciences e: **S Afr J Med Sci**, e: **SAJMA**

South African Journal of Photogrammetry. Remote Sensing and Cartography e: **S Afr J Photogramm Remote Sensing Cartogr**

South African Journal of WIldlife Research e: **S Afr J Wildl Re**

South African Journal of Wildlife Research e: **S. Afr. J. Wildl. Res.**, e: **S Afr J Wild Res**

South African Law Reports, Witwatersrand High Court e: **W.H.C.**

South African Law Reports, Witwatersrand Local Division e: **W.L.D.**

South African Medical and Dental Council e: **SAMDC**

South African Medical Association e: **SAMA**

South African Medical Corps e: **S.A.M.C.**

South African Medical Equipment News e: **S Afr Med Equip News**

South African Medical Journal e: **S Afr Med J**, e: **S Afr Med J**, e: **SAMJ**, e: **SAMJA**, e: **South African Med J**, e: **South African MJ**

South African Medical Literature e: **SAMED**

South African Medical Record e: **South African Med Rec**

South African Medical Service e: **SAMS**

South African Medical Times e: **S Afr Med Tim**

South African National Committee for Geomagnetism, Aeronomy and Space Sciences e: **SANCGASS**

South African National Committee for Oceanographic Research e: **SANCOR**

South African National Committee of the International Association on Water Pollution Research and Control e: **SANCIAWPRC**

South African Natural Areas Information System e: **SANAIS**

South African Scientific Committee for the International Union of Geological Sciences e: **SACUGS**

South African Society for Photogrammetry, Remote Sensing and Cartography e: **SASPRSC**

South African Society of Animal Production e: **SASAP**

South African Society of Animal Science e: **SASAS**

South African Society of Microbiology e: **SASM**

South African Society of Occupational Health Nursing Practitioners e: **SASOHN**

South African Society of Occupational Medicine e: **SASOM**

South African Underwater Union e: **SAUU**

South African Water Information Center e: **SAWIC**

South African Water Information Centre e: **SAWIC**

South American Journal of Medicine e: **South Am J Med**

South and Central Asian Medicinal and Aromatic Plants Network e: **SCAMAP**

South and Southeast Asia Network for Environmental Education e: **SASANEE**

South Arican Journal of Obstetrics and Gynaecology e: **S Afr J Obstet Gynaecol**

South Asia Cooperative Environment Program e: **SACEP**

South Asia Cooperative Environment Programme e: **SACEP**

South Asia Hydrological Cycle e: **SAHC**

South Australia. Director of Mines and Government Geologist. Annual Report e: **S Aust Dir Mines Gov Geol Annu Rep**

South Australia. Geological Survey. Atlas Series e: **S Aust Geol Atlas Ser**

South Australia. Geological Survey. Bulletin e: **SA Geol Surv Bull**, e: **South Aust Geol Surv Bull**

South Australia. Geological Survey. Geological. Atlas. I MileSeries e: **SA Geol Surv Geol Atlas 1 Mile Ser**

South Australia. Geological Survey. 1:250,000 Geological Series e: **SAust Geol Surv 1:250000 Geol Ser**

South Australia. Geological Survey. 1:250\000 Geological Series e: **South Aust Geol Surv 1:250000 Geol Ser**

South Australia. Geological Survey. Quarterly Geological Notes e: **Q Geol Notes Geol Surv South Aust**, e: **S Aust Geol Surv Q Geol Notes**, e: **South Aust Geol Surv Q Geol Notes**

South Australia. Geological Survey. Report of Investigations e: **SA Geol Surv Rep Invest**, e: **S Aust Geol Surv Rep Invest**, e: **South Aust Geol Surv Rep Invest**

South Australia. Geological Survey. Report of Investigations e: **S Aastralia Geol Surv Rep Invest**

South Australia. Geologiøl Survey. Bulletin e: **S Aust Geol Surv Bull**

South Australian Cell Biology Society e: **SACBS**

South Australian Centre for Remote Sensing e: **SACRS**

South Australian Department of Environment and Land Management e: **SADELM**

South Australian Department of Environment and Planning e: **SADEP**

South Australian Naturalist e: **SA Nat**, e: **SA Naturalist**, e: **S Aust Nat**, e: **South Aust Nat**

South Bay Wildlife Refuge e: **SBWR**

South Carolina Department of Health and Environmental Control e: **SCDHEC**

South Carolina. Division of Geology. Geologic Notes e: **SC Div Geol Geol Notes**, e: **South Carolina Div Geology Geol Notes**

South Carolina. Division of Geology. Mineral Industries Laboratory. Monthly Bulletin e: **SC Div Geology Mineral Industries Lab Monthly Bull**

South Carolina. Division of Geology. Mineral Resources Series e: **SC Div Geol Miner Resour Ser**

South Carolina. Division of Geology. Miscellaneous Report e: **SC Div Geol Misc Rep**, e: **South Carolina Div Geology Mise Rept**

South Carolina Environmental Law Journal e: **S.C. Envtl. L.J.**

South Carolina Geological Survey e: **SCGS**

South Carolina Water Resources Commission e: **SCWRC**

South Central Australia Institute of Medical and Veterinary Science e: **SCAIMVS**

South Central Chapter of the Medical Library Association e: **SCC/MLA**

South Central Regional Medical Library Program e: **TALON**

South China Sea Fisheries Development and Coordinating Program e: **SCSP**

South China Sea Monsoon Experiment e: **SCSMEX**

South Dakota Geological Survey e: **SDGS**

South Dakota Geological Survey and South Dakota Water Resources Commission. Water Resources Report e: **South Dakota Geol Survey Water Resources Rept**

South Dakota. Geological Survey. Guidebook e: **South Dakota Geol Survey Guidebook**

South Dakota. Geological Survey. Report of Investigations e: **South Dakota Geol Survey Rept Inv**

South Dakota. Geological Survey. Special Report *e:* **South Dakota Geol Survey Spec Rept**

South Dakota Journal of Medicine *e:* **S D J Med**

South Dakota Public Health Association *e:* **SDPHA**

South Dakota State Medical Association *e:* **SDSMA**

South-East Asia and Pacific Plant Protection Organization *e:* **SEAPPO**

South-East Asia Association on Seismology and Earthquake Engineering *e:* **SEASEE**

South-East Asia[n] Geotechnical Society *e:* **SEAGS**

South-East Asian Medical Information Centre *e:* **SEAMIC**

South East London Traffic and Environmental Problems *e:* **SELTEP**

South East Public Health Observatory *e:* **SEPHO**

South-East Water Laboratory *e:* **SEWL**

South-Eastern Geological Society *e:* **SEGS**

South-Eastern Mediterranean sea Project *e:* **SEMEP**

South-Eastern Pacific Biological Oceanographic Program *e:* **SEPBOP**

South-Eastern Plant Environment Laboratories *e:* **SEPEL**

South Eastern Public Health Unit *e:* **SEPHU**

South-Eastern Radiological Health Laboratory *e:* **SERHL**

South Eastern Sydney Public health Unit *e:* **SES PHU**

South Georgia *e:* **S Ge**, *e:* **SGG**

South Georgia and the South Sandwich Islands *e:* **S. Georg. & S. Sandwich Is.**

South Georgia Associated Libraries *e:* **SGAL**

South Georgia College *e:* **SGC**

South Georgia Tech *e:* **SGT**

South London Medical Staff Corps *e:* **SLMSC**

South Pacific Action Committee for [the] Human Ecology and the Environment *e:* **SPACHEE**

South Pacific [Applied Geoscience Commission] *e:* **SOPAC**

South Pacific Cosmedical Centre *e:* **SPCC**

South Pacific Deep Water *e:* **SPDW**

South Pacific Environment Protection Convention *e:* **SPREP**

South Pacific Journal of Natural Science *e:* **South Pac J Nar Sci**, *e:* **SPJSEY**

South Pacific Marine Geological Notes *e:* **South Pac Mar Geol Notes**

South Pacific Regional Environmental [Protection] Program[me] *e:* **SPREP**

South Pacific Underwater Medical Society *e:* **SPUMS**

South Polar Cap *e:* **SPC**

south polar distance *e:* **S.P.D.**

South Polar Region *e:* **SPR**

South Pole Observatory *e:* **SPO**

South Rhodesia Geological Survey *e:* **SRGS**

South Sea Evangelical Mission *e:* **S.S.E.M.**

South Texas Geological Society *e:* **STGS**

South Texas Geological Society. Bulletin *e:* **South Texas Geol Soc Bull**

South Vietnam Ocean Shipping Agency *e:* **SVOSA**

South-West Water Authority *e:* **SWWA**

South-Western Idaho Water Conservation Project *e:* **SWIWCP**

South Western Sydney Public Health Unit *e:* **SWS PHU**

South Westland Environmental and Community Advisory Committee *e:* **SWECAG**

Southampton Oceanographic Centre *e:* **SOC**

Southeast Asian Health Project *e:* **SEAHP**

Southeast Asian Journal of Tropical Medicine and Public Health *e:* **Southeast Asian J Trop Med Public Health**

Southeast Asian Regional Centre for Tropical Biology *e:* **SEAMEO-BIOTROP**

Southeast Bering Sea Carrying Capacity *e:* **SEBSCC**

Southeast Michigan Health Association *e:* **SEMHA**

Southeastern Association of Fish and Wildlife Agencies *e:* **SAFWA**

Southeastern Geographer *e:* **Southeast Geogr**

Southeastern Geological Society. Field Conference Guidebook *e:* **Southeast Geol Soc Field Conf Guideb**

Southeastern Geology *e:* **SOGEA**, *e:* **Southeast. Geol.**

Southeastern Geology. Special Publication *e:* **Southeastern Geology Spec Pub**, *e:* **Southeast Geol Spec Publ**

Southeastern Ontario Academic Medical Organization *e:* **SEAMO**

Southeastern Regional Medical Library Program[me] *e:* **SERMLP**

Southeastern Water Use Group *e:* **SEWUG**

Southend-on-Sea *e:* **S-o-S**

Southern African Atmosphere Research Initiative *e:* **SA'ARI**

Southern African Fire Atmosphere (or Atmospheric) Research Initiative *e:* **SAFARI**

Southern African Fire Atmosphere Research Initiative *e:* **SAFARI**

Southern African Fire-Atmospheric Research Initiative *e:* **SAFARI**

Southern African Radiation Protection Association *e:* **SARPA**

Southern African Wildlife Management Association *e:* **SAWMA**

[Southern African] Wildlife Management Association *e:* **WMA**

Southern Arizona Water Resources Associatit *e:* **SAWARA**

Southern Association for the History of Medicine and Science *e:* **SAHMS**

Southern California Coastal Water Research Project *e:* **SCCWRP**

Southern California Coastal Water Research Project. Annual Report *e:* **South Calif Coastal Water Res Proj Annu Rep**

Southern California Coastal Water Research Project. Biennial Report *e:* **South Calif Coastal Water Res Proj Bienn Rep**

Southern California Coastal Water Research Project TR *e:* **SCCWRP TR**

Southern California Earthquake Center *e:* **SCEC**

South[ern] California Earthquake Preparedness Project *e:* **SCEPP**

Southern California Sector, Western Sea Frontier *e:* **SOCAISEC**

Southern California Water Co. *e:* **SWTR**

Southern Chapter of the Medical Library Association *e:* **SC/MLA**

Southern Environmental Law Center *e:* **SELC**

Southern Europe-Inland Water Transport *e:* **SE/IWT**

Southern General Practitionner of Medicine and Surgery *e:* **South Gen Pract Med Surg**

Southern Journal of the Medical and Physical Sciences *e:* **Southern J Med Phys Sc**

Southern Medical Association *e:* **SMA**

Southern Medical Bulletin *e:* **SOMBA**, *e:* **South. Med. Bull.**

Southern Medical Journal *e:* **SMJ**, *e:* **SMJOA**, *e:* **South. Med. J.**, *e:* **South MJ**

Southern Medicine *e:* **South Med**

Southern Medicine and Surgery *e:* **South Med Surg**

Southern Methodist University. Institute for the Study of Earth and Man. Reports of Investigations *e:* **South Methodist Univ Inst Stud Earth Man Rep**

Southern Natural Gas Co. *e:* **SGA**

Southern Natural Resources, Inc. *e:* **NRG**

Southern Nevada Water Authority *e:* **SNWA**

Southern Nevada Water System *e:* **SNWS**

Southern Ocean Cloud Experiment *e:* **SOCEX**

Southern Ocean Float Experiment *e:* **SOFEX**

Southern Ocean-Global Ocean Ecosystems Dynamics Research *e:* **SO-GLOBEC**

Southern Ocean-Joint Global Ocean Flux Study *e:* **SO-JGOFS**

Southern Ocean Racing Conference *e:* **SORC**

Southern Ocean Waves Experiment *e:* **SOWEX**

Southern Oceans Survey *e:* **SOC**

Southern Ontario Health Libraries Information Network *e:* **SOHLIN**

Southern Regional Environmental Education Council *e:* **SREEC**

Southern Regional Medical Consortium *e:* **SRMC**

Southern Rhodesia Geological Society *e:* **S.R.G.S.**

Southern Rhodesia. Geological Survey. Bulletin *e:* **South Rhod Geol Surv Ball**, *e:* **S Rhodesia Geol Surv Bull**

Southern Rhodesia. Geological Survey. Short Report *e:* **South Rhod Geol Surv Short Rep**

Southern Rhodesia Medical Corps *e:* **S.R.M.C.**

Southern Surgeon *e:* **South Surg**

Southern Tier Library System *e:* **STLS**

Southern Water Authority *e:* **SWA**

Southern Water Authority SWA Southern Woodwork Association *e:* **SWA**

Southern Water Resources Scientific Information Center *e:* **SWRSIC**

Southwest Biomedical Research Institute *e:* **SBRI**

Southwest Center for Environmental
Research and Policy e: **SCERP**
Southwest Foundation for Biomedical
Research e: **SFBR**
Southwest New Jersey Consortium for
Health Information Services e: **SWNJ**
Southwest Sea Frontier e:
SOWESSEAFRON
Southwest Water Company e: **SWWC**
Southwest Water Works Journal e:
Southwest Water Works J
Southwestern Association of Clinical
Microbiology e: **SWACM**
Southwestern Association of Petroleum
Geologists. Bulletin e: **Southwestern As
Petroleum G B**
Southwestern Medicine e: **SOMDA**, e:
Southwest Med
Southwestern Naturalist e: **Southwest Nat**,
e: **SWest Nat**
Southwestern Naturalist [United States] e:
SWNAA
Southwestern Radiological Health
Laboratory e: **SRHL**, e: **SWRHL**
Southwestern University, Georgetown e:
TxGeoS, e: **TXX**
Sovetskaya Geologiya R: **Sovet
Geol[ogiya]**, R: **Sov Geol**, R: **SVGLA**
Soviet all-weather jet fighter aircraft called
Fishpot by NATO e: **SU-9**
Soviet-American Committee on Health
Cooperation e: **SACHC**
Soviet-American Symposium on the
Comprehensive Analysis of the
Environment e: **Sov Am Symp Compr
Anal Environ**
Soviet Black Sea Ore Charter e: **Sovietore**
Soviet Geography. Review and Translations
e: **SGRT**, e: **Sov Geogr**, e: **Sov Geogr R**
Soviet Geology and Geophysics e: **Sov
Geol and Geophys**, e: **Sov Geol Geophys**
Soviet Health Protection in Turkomen e:
Sov Health Prot Turkomen
Soviet Hydrology. Selected Papers e:
SHSPB, e: **Sov Hydrol**, e: **Sov Hydrol
Sel Pap**
Soviet Hydrometeorological Service e:
SHS
Soviet Indian Ocean Squadron e:
SOVINDRON
Soviet Journal of Developmental Biology
e: **SJDBA**, e: **Sov J Dev Biol**
Soviet Journal of Ecology e: **SJECA**, e:
Soviet J Ecol, e: **Sov J Ecol**
Soviet Journal of Marine Biology e: **Sov.
J. Mar. Biol.**
Soviet Journal of Marine Biology (English
Translation of Biologiya Morya) e: **Sov.
J. Mar. Biol. (Engl. Transl. Biol.
Morya)**
Soviet Meteorology and Hydrology e: **Sov
Meteorol and Hydrol**, e: **Sov Meteorol
Hydrol**
Soviet Ocean Surveillance System e:
SOSS, e: **SSOS**
Soviet Oceanographic Surveillance e: **SOS**
Soviet Oceanography e: **Sov Oceanogr**
Soviet Public Health e: **Sov Public Health**
Soviet Roundwood Charter Party. For
Pulpwood Pitwood Roundwood and Logs
from Baltic and White Sea Ports ofthe
U.S.S.R. e: **Sovconround**

Soviet Scientific Reviews. Section D.
Biology Reviews e: **Sov Sci Rev Sect D
Biol Rev**, e: **SRSRDL**
Soviet Scientific Reviews. Section E.
Astrophysics and Space Physics Reviews
e: **Sov Sci Rev Sect E**
Soviet Space Event Support Ships e:
SSFSS
Sovmestnaya Sovetsko-Mongol'skaya
Nauchno-Issledovatel'skaya
Geologicheskaya Ekspeditsiya Trudy R:
**Sovmestnaya Sov-Mong Nauchno-Issled
Geol Eksped Tr**
Sovremennye Problemy Radiobiologii R:
Sovrem Probl Radiobiol
Sowerby Centre for Health Informatics at
Newcastle e: **SCHIN**
Soy Protein Hydrolyzate e: **SPH**
Sozial- und Praeventivmedizin d: **SZPMA**
Sozial- und Präventivmedizin d: **Soz
Präventivmed**
Sozialistisches Arbeitskollektiv Biologie
d: **Sabi**
Sozialmedizinische und Paedagogische
Jugendkunde d: **Sozialmed Paedagog
Jugendkd**
Sozialwissenschaftliches Institut für
Katastrophen- und Umweltforschung d:
SIFKU
Space e: **S**
space e: **SP**
Space e: **SPA**
Space Acceleration Measurement System
e: **SAMS**
Space Acceleration Measurement System
for Free Flyers e: **SAMS-FF**
Space Acceleration Measurement System
for International Space Station e:
SAMS-II
Space Acquisition Defense Equipment e:
SPADE
Space Acquisitions Defence Experiment e:
SPADE
Space Active Vibration Isolation e: **SAVI**
Space Activities Commission e: **SAC**
Space Activities Promotion Council e:
SAPC
Space Activity Suit e: **SAS**
Space Adaptation Syndrome e: **SAS**
Space Adaptation Syndrome Experiment e:
SASE
Space Adaptation Tests and Observation e:
SATO
Space Aeronautics e: **SA**, e: **SA**
Space/Aeronautics e: **Space/Aeronaut**, e:
SPAEA
Space After e: **SPACEA**
Space Age Microcircuits e: **SAM**
Space Age News e: **SAN**
Space Age Review e: **SAR**
Space Aged Access Count e: **SAAC**
Space Agency Forum for/on the
International Space Year e: **SAFISY**
Space Agency Forum for the International
Space Year e: **SAFISY**
Space Agency Forum on International
Space Year e: **SAFISY**
Space Agency Forum on the International
Space Year e: **SAFISY**
Space Air Force STS Liaison Office e: **SP-
AF**
Space Air Force Support Office e: **SP-AF**

Space Air Relay Communications e:
SPARC
Space-Air Vehicle e: **SAV**
Space-Alternating Generalized EM e:
SAGE
Space Amateur Radio Experiment e:
SAREX
Space Analyst Intervention Display System
e: **SAIDS**
Space and Aeronautics Orientation Class
e: **SAOC**
Space and Astronautics Orientation Course
e: **SAOC**
Space and Component Log e: **SACL**
Space and Defense Power Systems Program
e: **SP-100**
Space and Earth Sciences Advisory
Committee e: **SESAC**
Space and Electronic Warfare e: **SEW**
Space and Electronic Warfare Commander
e: **SEWC**
Space and Flight Equipment d: **SAFE**
Space and Flight Equipment Association
e: **SAFE**, e: **SAFEA**, e: **SFEA**
Space and Information System e: **SIS**
Space and Information System(s) e: **S & IS**
Space and Information Systems Division
e: **SAID**, e: **SID**, e: **SISD**
Space and Missile System Organization e:
SAMSO
Space and Missile Systems e: **SAMS**
Space and Missile Systems Center e: **SMC**
Space and Missile Systems Office e:
SAMSO
Space and Missile Systems Organisation e:
SAMSO
Space and Missile Systems Organisation (or
Organization) e: **SAMSO**
Space and Missile Systems Organization e:
SAMSO
Space and Missile Systems Organization
Regulation e: **SAMSOR**
Space and Missile Systems Organization
(USAF) e: **SAMSO**
Space and Missile Test Center e:
SAMTEC
Space and Missile Test Center Detachment
1 e: **SAMTEC/DET**
Space and Missile Test Center Manual e:
SAMTEC
Space and Missile Test Center (VAFB, CA)
e: **SAMTEC**
Space and Missile Test Organisation e:
SAMTO
Space and Missile Test Organization e:
SAMTO
Space and Missile Test Organization
(VAFB) e: **SAMTO**
Space and Missiles Systems Organization
e: **SAMSO**
Space and MissileTest Center Manual e:
SAMTECM
Space and Naval Warfare System Command
e: **SNWSC**
Space and Naval Warfare systems command
e: **SPAWAR**
Space and Naval Warfare Systems
Command e: **SPAWARCOM**, e:
SPAWARS
Space and Naval Warfare Systems
Command-Naval Warfare Systems
Architecture & Engineering e:
SPAWAR/30

Space and Power e: **SP**

Space and Reentry Systems e: **SRS**

Space and Siting Committee e: **SSC**

Space and Strategic Defense Command e: **SSDC**

Space and Tactical System Corporation e: **SPACETAC**

Space and Technology Agency e: **STA**

Space and Terrestrial Applications Advisory Committee e: **STAAC**

Space and Unexplained Celestial Events Research Society e: **SAUCERS**

Space and Upper Atmosphere Research Commission e: **SUPARCO**

Space and Upper Atmospheric Research Committee e: **SUPARCO**

Space and Warfare Command e: **SPAWAR**

Space and Warfare Systems Command e: **S & W S C**

Space Antenna Diversity e: **SAD**

Space Antennae Diversity e: **SAD**

Space Applications Advisory Committee e: **SAAC**

Space Applications Board e: **SAB**

Space Applications Center e: **SAC**

Space Applications & Research Centre e: **SPARC**

Space Assembly and Maintenance Study e: **SAMS**

Space Assembly Maintenance and Servicing Study e: **SAMSS**

Space Assets Supply System e: **SASS**

Space Assignment Committee e: **SPASCOMT**

Space Assignments & Capital Improvements Committee e: **SACI**

Space Astronomy Laboratory e: **SAL**

Space astrophysics laboratory e: **ASTRO**

space at will e: **saw.**

Space Available e: **S/A**

Space-Available Mail e: **SAM**

Space Available Travel e: **SAT**

Space-Bandwidth product e: **SBW**

Space Base e: **SB**

Space-Base Wide Area Surveillance e: **SBWAS**

Space-Based Antimissile e: **SBAM**

Space Based Augmentation System e: **SBAS**

Space-Based Chemical Laser e: **SBCL**

Space-Based Experimental System e: **SBES**

Space-Based Experimental Version e: **SBEV**

Space-Based Free-Electron Laser e: **SBFEL**

Space-based Global Change Observation System e: **S-GCOS**

Space-based Global Change Observing System e: **S/COS**

Space-Based Hypervelocity Experiment e: **SBHe**

Space-Based Hypervelocity Rail Gun e: **SBHRG**

Space Based Infrared System e: **SBIRS**

Space-Based Interceptor e: **SBI**

Space Based KiII Vehicle e: **SBKV**

Space-Based Kinetic Energy Weapon e: **SBKEW**

Space-Based Kinetic Energy Weapon System e: **SBKEWS**

Space Based Kinetic KiII Vehicie e: **SBKKV**

Space-Based Kinetic Kill Vehicle e: **SBKKV**

Space-Based Laser e: **SBL**

Space-Based Laser/Ballistic Missile Defense e: **SBL/BMD**

Space-Based LASER Weapon e: **SLW**

Space-Based Neutral Particle Beam e: **SBNPB**

Space-based Observation Panel e: **SOP**

Space-Based Particle Beam e: **SBPB**

Space-Based Radar e: **SBR**

Space-Based Radar/Infra-Red e: **SBR/IR**

Space-based short Wavelength Chemical Laser e: **SWCL**

Space-Based Surveillance e: **SBS**

Space-Based Surveillance System e: **SBSS**

Space-Based Tug e: **SBT**

Space-Based Visible e: **SBV**

Space-Based Wide Area Surveillance e: **SBWAS**

Space Before e: **SPACEB**

space between the walls of concentric cylinders, in drilling, the space between the hole wall or casing and the drill string. e: **annulus**

Space Biology and Medicine e: **SBMEA**

Space Biology and Medicine [English Translation] e: **Space Biol Med [Engl Transl]**

Space Biomedical Research Institute e: **SBRI**

Space Bioreactor e: **BI0**

Space Biospheres Venture e: **SBV**

Space Biospheres Ventures e: **SBV**

Space Block Map e: **SBM**

Space Booster e: **SB**

Space Borne Computer e: **SBC**

Space-borne Data Conditioning System e: **SDCS**

Space Borne Programmer e: **SBP**

space brothers e: **sb's**

Space Business Daily e: **SBD**

Space Business Development Operation e: **SBDO**

Space Cabin Simulator e: **SCS**

Space Capsule e: **S/C**

Space Capsule Regulator and Monitor e: **SCRAM**

Space Cargo Handler and Manipulator for Orbital Operations e: **SCHMOO**

Space Chamber Analyzer-Thermal Environment e: **SCATE**

Space Chamber Complex e: **SCC**

space character e: **sp**

space charge e: **esc**

Space Charge e: **SC**

Space Charge Atomizing Precipitater e: **SCAP**

Space Charge Grid e: **SCG**

Space Charge Layer e: **SCL**

Space Charge Limited e: **SCL**

Space-Charge Recombination e: **SCR**

Space-Charge Wave e: **SCW**

Space Checkout and Launch Equipment e: **SCALE**

Space City News e: **Space Cit**

Space Combat Weapon System e: **SCWS**

Space Command e: **SPACECOM**

Space Command and Control System e: **SPACCS**

Space Command Center e: **SPACC**

space command station e: **scs**

Space Commerce Bulletin e: **Space Comm**

Space Communication and Tracking e: **SCAT**

Space Communications e: **SC**

Space Communication[s] e: **SPACECOM**

Space Commuicatons and Tracking e: **SCAT**

Space Communications Company e: **SPACECOM**

Space Communications Corporation e: **SCC**

Space Communications Division e: **SPCD**

Space Communications Network e: **SPAN**

Space Communications Station Operation e: **SCSO**

Space Communications System e: **SCS**

Space Components f: **SPACECOMPS**

Space Components Coordination Committee e: **SCCC**

Space Congress e: **Space Congr**

Space Congress. Proceedings e: **Space Congr Proc**, e: **SPCPB**

Space Construction Automated Fabrication Experiment Definition Study e: **SCAFEDS**

Space Construction Base e: **SCB**

Space Consultative Committee e: **SCC**

Space Control e: **SPACON**

Space Control Center e: **SPACC**

Space Control Document e: **SCD**

Space-Controlled Army Measurements Probe e: **SCAMP**

Space Council e: **SC**

Space-Craft Operational Performance Evaluation e: **SCOPE**

Space Daily e: **SD**

Space Data Analysis Center e: **SDAC**

Space Data Corporation e: **SDC**

Space Data Network e: **SDN**

Space Defence Operational Center e: **SPADOC**

Space & defense e: **S&D**

Space Defense Center e: **SDC**

Space Defense Command e: **SDC**

Space Defense Command and Control System e: **SPADCCS**

Space Defense Corporation e: **SDC**

Space Defense Initiative e: **SDI**

Space Defense Operations Center e: **SDOC**, e: **SPADOC**

Space Defense Operations Center, block 4 e: **SPADOC 4**

Space Defense Project Office e: **SDPO**, e: **SPDO**

Space Defense System e: **SDS**

Space Defense System Program e: **SDSP**

Space Delimited File e: **.sdf**

Space Delimited Format e: **SDF**

Space Detection and Tracking e: **SDT**

Space Detection and Tracking Center e: **SPADAT**

Space Detection and Tracking System e: **SPADATS**, e: **SPADETS**

Space Detection and Tracking System Center e: **SPADATSC**

Space Detection and Tracking System Improved e: **SPADATSIMP**

Space Detection and Tracking System Sensor e: **SPADATSS**

Space Detection Network e: **SPADETS**

Space Detection System e: **SPADETS**

Space Development Conference e: **SPC**

Space Development Corporation *e:* **SDC**
Space Development Office *e.* **SDO**
Space Digest *e:* **SD**
Space Digital Computer *e:* **SDC**
Space Disturbance Center *e:* **SDC**
Space Disturbance Forecast Center *e:* **SDFC**
Space Disturbance Monitoring Facility [Environmental Science Services Administration] *e:* **SDMF**
Space Disturbances Laboratory *e:* **SDL**
Space Division Evaluator *e:* **SDE**
Space Division Multiple Access *e:* **SDMA**
Space-Division Multiplexing *e:* **SDM**
Space Division Regulation *e:* **SDR**
Space Division Shuttle Simulator *e:* **SDSS**
Space Documentation Service/ESRO *e:* **SDS/ESRO**
Space Documentation Service [of the European Space Agency] *e:* **SDS**
Space Dynamics Laboratory *e:* **SDL**
Space Early Warning *e:* **SEW**
Space Education and Foundation *e:* **SEF**
Space Education Foundation *e:* **SEF**
Space Electric [or Electronic] Rocket Test *e:* **SERT**
Space Electric Power Office *e:* **SEPO**
Space Electric Ramjet *e:* **SERJ**
Space Electrochemical Research and Technology *e:* **SERT**
Space Electronic Rocket Test *e:* **SERT**
space electronic roeket test *e:* **sert**
Space & Electronic Warfare *e:* **SEW**
Space & Electronic Warfare/Intelligence *e:* **SEW/I**
Space & Electronic Warfare Simulation *e:* **SEWSIM**
Space Electronics and Telemetry *e:* **SET**
Space Electronics Corporation *e:* **SEC**
Space Electronics Detection System *e:* **SEDS**
Space Electronic[s] Package *e:* **SEP**
Space Emergency Reentry Vehicle *e:* **SERV**
Space Engineering Document *e:* **SED**
Space Entry Recovery Vehicle in Commercial Environments *e:* **SERVICE**
Space Environment information service *e:* **ENVIROnet**
Space Environment Laboratory *e:* **SEL**
Space Environment Monitoring *e:* **SEM**
Space Environment Monitoring System *e:* **SPEMS**
Space Environment Monitors *e:* **SEMs**
Space Environment Services Center *e:* **SESC**
Space Environment Simulator *e:* **SES**
Space Environmental Center *e:* **SEC**
Space Environmental Chamber *e:* **SEC**
Space Environmental Control System *e:* **SECS**
Space Environmental Facility *e:* **SEF**
Space Environmental Laboratory Data Acquisition and Display System *e:* **SELDADS**
Space Environmental Monitor *e:* **SEM**
Space Environmental Research Facility *e:* **SERF**
Space Environment[al] Simulation Laboratory *e:* **SESL**
Space Environmental Support Project Office[r] *e:* **SESPO**

Space Environmental Support System *e:* **SESS**
Space Environmental Technology Transition *e:* **SETT**
Space Equivalent *e:* **SE**
Space Erectable Structure *e:* **SES**
Space Event Conference *e:* **SEC**
Space Event Support Ship *e:* **SESS**
Space Experiment and Flight Support Program *e:* **SEFSP**
Space Experiment Facility *e:* **SEF**
Space Experiment on Relativistic Theories of Gravitation *e:* **SERTOG**
Space Experiment Support Program *e:* **SESP**
Space Experiments Division *e:* **SED**
Space Experiments Laboratory *e:* **SEL**
Space Experiments with Particle Accelerators *e:* **SEPAC**
Space Exploration *e:* **SE**
Space Exploration Initiative [Program] *e:* **SEI**
Space Exploration Initiative Program *e:* **SEIP**
Space Exploration Program Council *e:* **SEPC**
Space-Exposed Experiment Developed for Students *e:* **SEEDS**
Space Flight *e:* **SF**
Space Flight Acceleration Profile Simulator *e:* **SFAPS**
Space Flight and Ground Systems Office *e:* **SP-FGS**
Space Flight Awareness *e:* **SFA**
Space Flight Center *e:* **SFC**
Space Flight Ground Environment Panel *e:* **SFGEP**
Space Flight Instrumentation *e:* **SFI**
Space Flight Operations *e:* **SFO**
Space Flight Operation[s] Center *e:* **SFOC**
Space Flight Operations Complex *e:* **SFOC**
Space Flight Operations Director *e:* **SFOC**
Space Flight Operations Facility *e:* **SFOF**
Space Flight Operations Memorandum *e:* **SFOM**
Space Flight Operations Plan *e:* **SFOP**
Space Flight Project *e:* **SFP**
Space Flight Systems *e:* **SFS**
Space Forecast Center *e:* **SFC**
Space Frame and Unit Integrating System *e:* **SF/UIS**
Space Frame RADOME [Radar Dome] *e:* **SFR**
Space-General *e:* **S-G**
Space-General Corporation *e:* **S-G C**
Space Geodesy Altimetry Study *e:* **SGAS**
Space-Ground Link *e:* **SGL**
Space-Ground Link Station *e:* **SGLS**
Space Ground Link System *e:* **SGLSY**
Space Ground Support Operations *e:* **SGSO**
Space Group *e:* **SG**, *e:* **SPG**
Space Guidance Computer *e:* **SGC**
Space Habitat Modules *e:* **SPACEHAB**
Space Hammer *e:* **SPAMMER**
Space Hand Tool *e:* **SHT**
Space Heater *e:* **SPH**
Space Heaters *e:* **SPHs**
Space Identification Device System *e:* **SIDS**
Space Image Rectification Centre, Toulouse (France) *e:* **CRIS-T**

Space Imbalanced Military Occupational Specialty *e:* **SIMOS**
Space Impact Hand Tool *e:* **SIHT**
Space Impact Tool *e:* **SIT**
space in a containership occupied by one container *e:* **slot**
Space Industrialization *e:* **SI**, *e:* **Space Ind**
Space Industries, Incorporated *e:* **SII**
Space Inertial Reference Equipment *e:* **SPIRE**
Space Influences on the Terrestrial Environment *e:* **SITE**
Space Informatics Network Experiment *e:* **SPINE**
Space Information-2 Meter Data *e:* **SPIN-2**
Space Information Systems Division *e:* **SPISD**
Space Infra-Red Telescope Facility *e:* **SIRTF**
Space Infrared Telescope Facility *e:* **SIRTF**
Space Inspection *e:* **SPIN**
Space Institute *e:* **SI**
Space Integrated Control Experiment *e:* **SPICE**
Space Integrated Logistics Support Office *e:* **SP-ILS**
Space Intelligence *e:* **SI**
Space Intercept *e:* **SPIN**
Space Interceptor Missile *e:* **SIM**
Space Interface Unit *e:* **SCIU**
Space Interferometer Mission *e:* **SIM**
Space Intruder Detector *e:* **SID**
Space-Invariant Point-Spread Function *e:* **SIPSF**
Space Inventory and Utilization System *e:* **SILUS**, *e:* **SIUS**
Space Inventory System *e:* **SIS**
Space Investigations Documentation System *e:* **SIDS**
Space Isotope Program *e:* **SIP**
Space Isotope Project *e:* **SIP**
Space Key Code *e:* **SKC**
Space Laboratory *e:* **S/L**, *e:* **Spacelab**
Space Laboratory Module *e:* **SLM**
Space Laboratory Simulator *e:* **SLS**
Space Laser Energy Detector *e:* **SLED**
Space Lattice *e:* **SL**
Space Launch Complex *e:* **SLC**
Space Launch System *e:* **SLS**
Space-Launched Air Missile *e:* **SLAM**
Space-Launched Ballistic Missile *e:* **SLBM**
Space Launcher *e:* **SL**
Space Launch[er] Vehicle *e:* **SLV**
Space Law *e:* **Space L.**
Space Life Sciences *e:* **SLS**, *e:* **Space Life Sci**, *e:* **SPLSA**
space light modulator. *e:* **SLM**
Space-Like Vector *e:* **SLV**
space link access protocol *e:* **SLAP**
Space Logistics Maintenance and Repair (or Rescue) *e:* **SLOMAR**
Space Logistics Maintenance and Repair (or Rescue) Vehicle *e:* **SLOMAR Vehicle**
Space Logistics Maintenance and Rescue *e:* **SOLMAR**
Space Logistics Management Office *e:* **SP-LMO**
Space Maintenance Analysis Center *e:* **SMAC**
Space Maintenance and Repair Technique[s] *e:* **SMART**

Space Management and Retail Tracking System *e:* **SMART**

Space Management Information System *e:* **SMIS**

Space Management Page *e:* **SMP**

Space Manufacturing Facility *e:* **SMF**

Space Markets *e:* **Space Marke**

Space Medicine *e:* **SM**

Space Medicine Advisory Group *e:* **SPAMAG**

Space Meteorology Branch *e:* **SMB**

Space Microwave Laboratories, Incorporated *e:* **SMLI**

Space Migration, Intelligence and Life Extension *e:* **SMILE**

Space & Missile Systems Organization *e:* **SAMSO**

Space & Missile Test Organisation *e:* **SMTO**

Space Missiles Aircraft Computer *e:* **SMAC**

Space & Missiles Test Center *e:* **SMTC**

Space Mission Simulator *e:* **SMS**

Space Mission Survivability Implementation Plan *e:* **SMSIP**

Space Missions Group *e:* **SMG**

Space-Monitoring System *e:* **SMS**

Space-Monitoring System/Continuous Air Monitor *e:* **SMS/CAM**

Space Motion Sickness *e:* **SMS**

Space & naval Warfare Systems Command *e:* **SPAWARSYSCOM**

Space Navigation *e:* **SPAN**

Space Navigation Network *e:* **SPAN NET**

Space Navigation System *e:* **SNS**

Space Network *e:* **SN**

Space Network Anomaly Report *e:* **SNAR**

Space Network Loading *e:* **SNL**

Space Nuclear Applications Program *e:* **SNAP**

Space Nuclear Auxiliary Power *e:* **SNAP**

Space Nuclear Electric Propulsion Test *e:* **SNEPT**

Space Nuclear Propulsion *e:* **SNP**

Space Nuclear Propulsion Office *e:* **SNPO**

Space Nuclear Propulsion Office, Albuquerque *e:* **SNPOA**

Space Nuclear Propulsion Office, Cleveland *e:* **SNPOC**

Space Nuclear Propulsion Office, Nevada *e:* **SNPON**

Space Nuclear System *e:* **SNS**

Space Nuclear Systems Office *e:* **SNSO**

Space Nuclear Thermal Propulsion *e:* **SNTP**

space object identification *e:* **soi**

Space Object Identification Central Analysis System *e:* **SOICAS**

Space Object Identification Summary *e:* **SOISCUM**

Space Object Identification System *e:* **SOIS**

Space Oblique Mercator *e:* **SOM**

Space-Occupying Lesion *e:* **SOL**

Space Off-Site Offices *e:* **SP-OSO**

Space Operation Center *e:* **SPOC**

Space Operation Command System *e:* **SOCS**

Space Operation service *e:* **SO**

Space Operation Service *e:* **SOS**

Space Operational Intelligence Center *e:* **SOIC**

Space Operations and Flight Techniques *e:* **SOFT**

Space Operations and Scientific Investigations *e:* **SOSI**

Space Operations Center *e:* **SO**

Space Operations Center(or Centre) *e:* **SOC**

Space Operations Controller *e:* **SOC**

Space Operations Intelligence Center *e:* **SOIC**

Space Operations Management Office *e:* **SOMO**

Space Operations Management System *e:* **SOMS**

Space Operations Planning and Integration Office *e:* **SP-OPI**

Space Operations Support *e:* **SPAOPSUP**

Space Operations Support Center *e:* **SOSC**

Space Orbital Bomber *e:* **SOB**

Space Ordnance Systems, Inc. *e:* **SOS**

Space Organization Method *e:* **SOM**

Space Pallet Satellite *e:* **SPAS**

Space Parts Control Center *e:* **SPCC**

Space Parts Working Group *e:* **SPWG**

Space Patrol *e:* **SP**

Space Patrol Active Defense *e:* **SPAD**

Space Patrol Air Defense *e:* **SPAD**

Space Patrol Antimissile Defense *e:* **SPAD**

Space Patrol for Air Defense *e:* **SPAD**

Space Performance Management Systems Office *e:* **SP-PMS**

Space Performance Test Battery *e:* **SPTB**

Space Philatelists International Society *e:* **SPIS**

Space Physics and Analysis Network *e:* **SPAN**

Space Physics Laboratory *e:* **SPL**

Space Physics Research Laboratory *e:* **SPRL**

Space Physiology Experiment *e:* **SPE**

Space Planning Bureau *e:* **SPB**

Space Planning Council *e:* **SPC**

Space Planning System *e:* **SPS**

Space Plasma Analysis Network *e:* **SPAN**

Space Plasma High-Voltage Interaction Experiment *e:* **SPHINX**

Space Plasma Laboratory-1 *e:* **SPL-1**

Space [Platform] *e:* **SP**

Space platform (SPAS) and earth observation payload (ARGUS) *e:* **ARGUS-SPAS**

Space Plume Experiment *e:* **SPX**

Space Pointing, Acquisition and Tracking Experiment *e:* **SPARTE**, *e:* **SPATE**

Space Polar Power Station *e:* **SPPS**

Space Power Advanced Reactor *e:* **SPAR**

Space Power and Electric Propulsion Division *e:* **SPEPD**

Space Power Experiments Aboard Rocket *e:* **SPEAR**

Space Power Facility *e:* **SPF**

Space Power Internal Combustion Engine *e:* **SPICE**

Space Power Program *e:* **SPP**

Space Power System *e:* **SPS**

Space-Power System Architecture Studies *e:* **SPAS**

Space Power Systems Conference *e:* **SPSC**

Space Power Systems Division *e:* **SPSD**

Space Power Systems Project *e:* **SPSP**

Space Power Tool *e:* **SPT**

Space Power Unit Reactor *e:* **SPUR**

Space Precision Altitude Reference System *e:* **SPAR**

Space Precision Attitude Reference System *e:* **SPARS**

Space Prediction Attitude Reference System *e:* **SPARS**

Space Principles, Applications and Doctrine *e:* **SPAD**

Space Probe *e:* **SP**

Space Probe Optical Recording Telescope *e:* **SPORT**

Space Probe Radar Altimeter *e:* **SPRA**

Space Probe Radar Torch *e:* **SPRA**

Space Processing Applications Rocket *e:* **SPAR**

Space Processing Applictions *e:* **SPA**

Space Processing Equipment *e:* **SPE**

Space Program *e:* **SP**

Space Program Advisory Council *e:* **SPAC**

Space Program American Citizens' Effort *e:* **SPACE**

Space Program Analysis and Review Council *e:* **SPARC**

Space Program[me] (or Programming) Language Implementation Tool *e:* **SPLIT**

Space Programming Language *e:* **SPL**

Space Programming Language Machine *e:* **SPLM**

Space Programming Language Machine Language *e:* **SPLML**

Space Programs Laboratory *e:* **SPL**

Space Project Applications Rocket *e:* **SPAR**

Space Project Assessment and Integration Staff *e:* **SP-PAI**

Space Project Control Office *e:* **SP-PCO**

Space Projects Center *e:* **SPC**

Space Propellant *e:* **SP**

Space Propulsion *e:* **SP**

Space Propulsion and Power Division *e:* **SPPD**

Space Propulsion Automated Synthesis Modeling *e:* **SPASM**

Space Propulsion Automated Synthesis Modeling Program *e:* **SPAST Program**

Space Propulsion Research Facility *e:* **SPRF**

Space Propulsion Synergy Group *e:* **SPSG**

Space Qualified Booster *e:* **SQB**

Space Qualified Booster Charger *e:* **SQBC**

Space Qualified LASER *e:* **SQL**

Space Radar Laboratory *e:* **SRL**

Space Radiation Analysis Group *e:* **SPAG**, *e:* **SRAG**

Space Radiation Assembly Demonstration *e:* **SRAD**

Space Radiation Effects Laboratory *e:* **SREL**

Space Radiation Evaluation System *e:* **SPARES**

Space Range Radar *e:* **SPANDAR**

Space Reactor Power Supply *e:* **SRPS**

Space reactor Prototype *e:* **SP-100**

Space Recovery System *e:* **SRS**

Space Recovery Vehicle *e:* **SRV**

Space Reference Unit *e:* **SRU**

Space Remote Sensing Center *e:* **SRSC**

Space Replaceable Unit *e:* **SRU**

Space Request Routine *e:* **SRR**

Space Requirement Forms *e:* **SRF**

Space Requirement Program *e:* **SRP**

Space Rescue Vehicle *e:* **SRV**

Space Research e: **Space Res**, e: **SR**
Space Research [Advisory Group] e: **SR**
Space Research and Remote Sensing
  Organisation e: **SPARRSO**
Space Research and Technology e:
  SPART
Space Research Capsule e: **SPARC**
Space Research Conic e: **SPARC**
Space Research Coordination Center e:
  SRCC
Space Research Corp., Mansonville, Quebec
  e: **QMASRC**
Space Research Corporation e: **SRC**
Space Research Corporation of Quebec e:
  SRC-Q
Space Research Council e: **SRC**
Space Research Facilities Branch [National
  Research Council of Canada] e: **SRFB**
Space Research in Bulgaria e: **Space Res
  Bulg**, e: **SRBUD**
Space Research Institute e: **SRI**
Space Research Management Unit e:
  S.R.M.U., e: **SRNIU**
Space Research Organization of the
  Netherlands e: **SRON**
Space Research Service e: **SRS**
Space Resolving Framing Spectrograph e:
  SPREFS
Space Satellite Power Station e: **SSPS**
Space Saver Spare Tyre e: **SSS Tyre**
Space Science Analysis and Command
  [team] e: **SSAC**
Space Science Analysis Area e: **SSAA**
Space Science and Engineering Center e:
  SSEC
Space Science and Engineering Laboratory
  e: **SSEL**
Space Science and Technology Center e:
  SSTC
Space Science and Technology Division e:
  SST
Space Science Board e: **SPB**, e: **SSB**
Space Science Committee e: **SSC**
Space Science Data Center e: **SSDC**
Space Science Department e: **SSD**
Space Science Development Facility e:
  SSDF
Space Science Development Facility-North
  American Aviation e: **SSDF-NAA**
Space Science Fiction Magazine e: **SSM**
Space Science Instrumentation e: **Space
  Sci Instrum**
Space Science Radioastronomy Program e:
  SSRP
Space Science Reviews e: **Space Sci R[ev]**
Space Science Steering Committee e:
  SSSC
Space Science[s] e: **SS**
Space Sciences Division e: **SSD**
Space Sciences Laboratory e: **SSL**
Space Sciences Office e: **SSO**
Space Section Control Center e: **SSCC**
Space Selector Terminal e: **SST**
Space Services Incorporated e: **SSI**
Space Services Incorporation of America
  e: **SSI**
Space Settlement Studies Program e: **SSSP**
Space Settlers' Society e: **SSS**
Space Sextant e: **SXT**
Space Shift Elimination e: **Sp S Elim**, e:
  SSE
Space Ship Experimental e: **SSX**
Space Shuttle e: **S/S**

Space Shuttle Access Tower e: **SSAT**
Space Shuttle Atlantis e: **STS**
Space Shuttle Cargo Handling System e:
  SSCHS
Space Shuttle Crew Safety Panel e:
  SSCSP
Space Shuttle Display e: **SSD**
Space Shuttle Display and Simulation e:
  SSDS
Space Shuttle Engine e: **SSE**
Space Shuttle Engineering and Operations
  Support e: **SSEOS**
Space Shuttle Flight and Ground System
  Specification e: **SSFGSS**
Space Shuttle Functional Simulator e:
  SSFS
Space Shuttle Main Engine e: **SSME**
Space Shuttle Main Engine Controller e:
  SSM EC
Space Shuttle Main Engine Controller
  Assembly e: **SSMECA**
Space Shuttle Maintenance Baseline e:
  SSM B
Space Shuttle Mission e: **SSM**
Space Shuttle Observation Project e:
  SSEOP
Space Shuttle Operator's Manual e: **SSOM**
Space Shuttle Orbiter e: **SSO**
Space Shuttle Payload Data Activity e:
  SSPDA
Space Shuttle Payload Data Study e:
  SSPDS
Space Shuttle Payload Planning Steering
  Group e: **SSPPSG**
Space Shuttle Program e: **SSP**
Space Shuttle Program Ground Support
  Equipment e: **SSPGSE**
Space Shuttle Program Manager e: **SSPM**
Space Shuttle Program Office e: **SSPO**
Space Shuttle Program Resident Office e:
  SSPRO
Space Shuttle Program Schedule e: **SSPS**
Space Shuttle Simulation e: **SSS**
Space Shuttle Simulation Display e: **SSSD**
Space Shuttle Synthesis Program e: **SSSP**
Space Shuttle System e: **SSS**
Space Shuttle System Segment e: **SSSS**
Space Shuttle System Specification e:
  SSSS
Space Shuttle Task Force e: **SSTF**
Space Shuttle Task Group e: **SSTG**
Space Shuttle Test Conductor e: **SSTC**
Space Shuttle Vehicle e: **SSV**
Space Shuttle Vehicle/Guidance, Control
  and Navigation e: **SSV/GC & N**
Space Shuttle Vehicles e: **SSVs**
Space Simulation Facility e: **SSF**
Space Simulation Laboratory e: **SSL**
Space Simulation. Proceedings of a
  Symposium e: **Space Simal Proc Symp**
Space Simulation Test Facility e: **SSTF**
Space Simulator e: **SS**
Space Site Management Office e: **SP-
  SMO**
Space snd Missile Test and Evaluation
  Center e: **SAMTEC**
Space Solar Power Review e: **Space Sol
  Power Rer**
Space, Stack Pointer, System Program e:
  SP
Space Station e: **SS**
Space Station Airlock Trainer e: **SSAT**
Space Station Control Board e: **SSCB**

Space Station Control Center e: **SSCC**
Space Station Data Management System e:
  SSDMS
Space Station Data System e: **SSDS**
Space Station Environmental Control
  System e: **SSECS**
Space Station Fred e: **SSF**
Space Station Freedom e: **FRED**, e: **SSF**,
  e: **S.S. Freedom**
Space Station Freedom Integrated Logistics
  Support System e: **SSFILSS**
Space Station Freedom Manned Base e:
  SSFMB
Space Station Freedom Program e: **SSFP**
Space Station Furnace Facility e: **SSFA**, e:
  SSFF
Space Station Hazardous Processing
  Facility e: **SSHPF**
Space Station Heat Pipe Advanced
  Radiation e: **SHARE**
Space Station Heat Pipe Advanced Radiator
  Element e: **SHARE**
Space Station Information System e: **SSIS**
Space Station Mathematical Model e:
  SSMM
Space Station Module e: **SSM**
Space Station Operations Task Force e:
  SSOTF
Space Station Planning Group, EN e:
  SPGEN
Space Station Polar Platform e: **SSPP**
Space Station Processing Facility e: **SSPF**
Space Station Program e: **SSP**
Space Station Program Element e: **SSPE**
Space Station Program Office e: **SSPO**
Space Station Remote Manipulating System
  e: **SSRMS**
Space Station Science and Applications
  Advisory Subcommittee e: **SSSAAS**
Space Station Simulator e: **SSS**
Space Station Support Center e: **SSSC**
Space Station Systems Division e: **SSSD**
Space Station Systems Trainer e: **SSST**
Space Station Task Force e: **SSTF**
Space Station Training Facility e: **SSTF**
Space Station Utilization Office e: **SSU**
Space Station Work Package e: **SSWP**
Space Stations Present and Future.
  Proceedings. International Astronautical
  Congress e: **Space Stn Present Future
  Proc Int Astronaut Congr**
Space Stories e: **SPS**
Space & Strategic Defense Command e:
  SSDC
Space Studies Board e: **SSB**
Space Studies Institute e: **SSI**
Space Subsystem Control Facility e: **SSCF**
Space Suit Assembly e: **SSA**
Space Suit Communications System e:
  SSCS
Space Suit Communicator e: **SSC**
Space Summary Program[me] e: **SSP**
Space Support Wing e: **SSW**
Space Surveillance e: **SPASUR**
Space Surveillance and Tracking System
  e: **SSTS**
Space Surveillance Center e: **SSC**
Space Surveillance Control Center e:
  SSCC
Space Surveillance Facility, Naval Weapons
  Laboratory, Dahlgren e: **SPASUR**
Space Surveillance Network e: **SPA SUR**,
  e: **SSN**

Space Surveillance Operations Center *e:* **SSOC,** *e:* **SSOC**

Space Surveillance System *e:* **SPASUR,** *e:* **SPASUR System,** *e:* **SSS**

Space Surveillance Technology *e:* **SST**

Space Surveillance Working Group *e:* **SVWG**

Space Switch *e:* **SS,** *e:* **SSW**

Space Switching Memory, Even *e:* **SSME**

Space Switching Memory, Odd *e:* **SSMO**

Space Synchro *e:* **SPASYN**

Space-Syncromesh *e:* **SPASYN**

Space System *e:* **SS**

Space System Development Agreement *e:* **SSDA**

Space System Effectiveness Model *e:* **SSEM**

Space System for Search of Distress Vessels *e:* **COSPAS**

Space Systems and Applications *e:* **SS & A**

Space Systems Center *e:* **SSC,** *e:* **SST**

Space Systems Cost Analysis Group *e:* **SSCAG**

Space Systems Division *e:* **SSD**

Space Systems Operating Procedure *e:* **SSOP**

Space Systems Operational Design Criteria Manual *e:* **SSODCM**

Space Systems Support Squadron *e:* **SSSS**

Space Systems Test and Evaluation Facility *e:* **SSTEF**

Space Systems Test Capability *e:* **SSTC**

Space Taking Entities *e:* **STEs**

Space Taking Entity *e:* **STE**

Space Target Measurement Program *e:* **STMP**

Space Task Group *e:* **STG**

Space Technical Information Control *e:* **STIC**

Space Technology *e:* **ST**

Space Technology Analysis and Mission Planning *e:* **STAMP**

Space Technology and Advanced Reentry Test Program *e:* **START**

Space Technology and Advanced Research *e:* **STAR**

Space Technology and Reentry Test(s) *e:* **START**

Space Technology and Research Center *e:* **STAR**

Space Technology Applications *e:* **STA**

Space Technology Applications and Research Laboratoty *e:* **STARLAB**

Space Technology Applied to Rural Papago Advanced Health Care *e:* **STARPAHC**

Space Technology Center *e:* **STC**

Space Technology Experiments Platform *e:* **STEP**

Space Technology, Incorporated *e:* **STI**

Space Technology Initiative *e:* **STI**

Space Technology Institute *e:* **STI**

Space Technology Interdependence Group *e:* **STIG**

Space Technology Laboratory, Inc. *e:* **STL**

Space Technology Operations and Research Laboratory *e:* **STORLAB**

Space Technology Payload *e:* **STP**

Space Technology Program *e:* **STP**

Space Technology Requirements Engineering Test of Component *e:* **STRETCO**

Space Technology Requirements Engineering Test of Component Hardware *e:* **STRETCH**

Space Technology Research Vehicle *e:* **STRV**

Space Technology Satellite *e:* **STS**

Space Telescope *e:* **ST**

Space Telescope data base *e:* **STDB**

Space Telescope Data Capture Facility *e:* **STDCF**

Space Telescope Decision Support System *e:* **STDSS**

Space Telescope European Coordinating Facility *e:* **ST-ECF**

Space Telescope for Analysis of Resources *e:* **STAR**

Space Telescope Guidance *e:* **STG**

Space Telescope Imaging Spectrograph *e:* **STIS**

Space Telescope Imaging Spectrometer *e:* **STIS**

Space Telescope Infrared Spectrograph *e:* **STIS**

Space Telescope Operations Control Center *e:* **STOCC**

Space Telescope Science Data Analysis System *e:* **STSDAS**

Space Telescope Science Institute *e:* **ST SCI,** *e:* **STSI**

Space Telescope Task Team *e:* **STTT**

Space Terminal Auxiliary Reactor *e:* **STAR**

Space Terminal Evaluation Program *e:* **STEP**

Space Test and Evaluation Facility *e:* **STEF**

Space Test and Reentry Technology *e:* **START**

Space Test Center *e:* **STC**

Space Test Experiments Platform *e:* **STEP**

Space Test Group *e:* **STESTG**

Space Test Operations Section *e:* **STOS**

Space Test Payload *e:* **STP**

Space Test Program *e:* **STP**

Space Test Vehicle *e:* **STV**

Space Thermal Vacuum Chamber *e:* **STVC**

Space Thermionic Auxiliary Reactor *e:* **STAR**

Space Thermo-Electric Power *e:* **STEP**

Space Threat Conference *e:* **STC**

Space Three-Axis Accelerometer for Research *e:* **STAR**

Space Thrust Evaluation and Disposal Investigation *e:* **STEDI**

Space Time *e:* **ST**

Space, Time and Beyond *e:* **STAB**

Space-Time Autoregressive *e:* **STAR**

Space-Time Autoregressive Integrated Moving Average *e:* **STARIMAR**

Space-Time Continuum *e:* **STC**

Space Time Division Multiple Access *e:* **STDMA**

Space-Time Moving Average *e:* **STMA**

Space-Time-Space *e:* **S-T-S**

Space Time Space Network *e:* **STSN**

Space-Time-Space switch *e:* **STS**

Space-Time Structure *e:* **STS**

Space-Time Unit *e:* **STU**

Space Time Yield *e:* **STY**

Space-to-Ground Link Subsystem *e:* **SGLS**

Space-to-Ground Link System *e:* **SGLS**

Space to Ground Link Terminal *e:* **SGLT**

Space to Letters *e:* **S Lt,** *e:* **Sp-Ltrs**

Space-to-Letters *e:* **STL**

Space Tool for Extravehicular Emergencies *e:* **STEVE**

Space Topics Study Group *e:* **STSG**

Space Toy Information Center *e:* **STIC**

Space Track Facility *e:* **STF**

Space Track Interim Fire Control *e:* **STIFC**

Space Tracking *e:* **SPACETRACK**

Space Tracking and Acquisition Network *e:* **STADN**

Space Tracking and Data Acquisition Network *e:* **STADAN**

Space Tracking Center *e:* **STC**

Space Tracking Pty Ltd *e:* **STPL**

Space Trajectory Error Analysis Program[me] *e:* **STEAP**

Space Trajectory Radiation Exposure Procedure *e:* **STREP**

Space Transfer Vehicle *e:* **STV**

Space Transport and Reentry Test(s) *e:* **START**

Space Transportation Air-Breathing Technology Evaluation *e:* **STATE**

Space Transportation Architecture *e:* **STA**

Space Transportation Architecture Study *e:* **STAS**

Space Transportation Booster Engine *e:* **STBE**

Space Transportation Company *e:* **STC**

Space Transportation Main Engine *e:* **STME**

Space Transportation System *e:* **SFCA,** *e:* **STS**

Space Transportation System Cost Model *e:* **STSCM**

Space Transportation Systems Division *e:* **STSD**

Space Ultra-reliable Modular Computer *e:* **SUM-C**

Space Ultravacuum Research Facility *e:* **SURF**

Space Ultraviolet Radiation Environment *e:* **SURE**

Space Unit *e:* **SU**

Space Utilization Research Center *e:* **SURV**

Space-Variant Point-Spread Function *e:* **SVPSF**

Space Vehicle *e:* **S/V**

Space Vehicle Booster *e:* **SVB**

Space Vehicle Booster Test *e:* **SVBT**

Space Vehicle Code *e:* **SVC**

Space Vehicle Data Systems Synthesizer *e:* **SVDSS**

Space Vehicle Dynamic Simulator *e:* **SVDS**

Space Vehicle Electronics *e:* **SVE**

Space Vehicle Mission Analysis *e:* **SVMA**

Space Vehicle Motor *e:* **SVM**

Space Vehicle Operations *e:* **SVO,** *e:* **VO**

Space Vehicle Sectoring Code *e:* **SVSC**

Space Vehicle Simulator *e:* **SVS**

Space Vehicle System *e:* **SVS**

Space Vehicle Test *e:* **SVT**

Space Vehicle Test (Supervisor) *e:* **SVT(S)**

Space Vehicle-to-Space Vehicle *e:* **SVTSV**

Space Vehicles Division *e:* **SVD**

Space Velocity *e:* **SV**

Space Vision System *e:* **SVS**

Space Visualization *e:* **SV**

Space Visualization Contralateral Use *e:* **SVCU**

Space Visualization Test *e:* **SVT**

Space VLBI *e:* **SVLBI**

Space VLBI Assistance Software *e:* **SPAS**

Space VLBI Principal Investigator Software *e:* **SVPIS**

Space Warfare Center *e:* **SWC**

Space Warning and Control System *e:* **SWACS**, *e:* **SWCS**

Space Wave *e:* **SW**

Space Weapon *e:* **SW**

Space Weapon System[s] *e:* **SWS**

Space, Weight and Power *e:* **SWP**

Space Wing *e:* **SPW**, *e:* **SWG**

Spaceborne *e:* **SBN**

Spaceborne Advanced Warning System *e:* **SAWS**

Spaceborne Aerosols and Cloud Lidar Earthprobe *e:* **SPARCLE**

Spaceborne Computer Engineering Conference *e:* **SCEC**

Spaceborne Earth Applications Ranging System *e:* **SPEAR**, *e:* **SPEARS**

Space[borne] Imaging Radar *e:* **SIR**

Spaceborne Infrared Tracker *e:* **SIT**

Spaceborne Intensified Radiometer for Imaging Vetroviolet Spectroscopy *e:* **SIRIVS**

Spaceborne LASER Ranging *e:* **SBLS**

Spaceborne Programming Language *e:* **SPL**

Spaceborne Rawinsonde *e:* **SPAR**

Spaceborne Reconnaissance System *e:* **SRS**

Spaceborne Symbolic Processor *e:* **SSP**

Spacecraft *e:* **S/C**

Spacecraft Adapter *e:* **S/A**, *e:* **S/CA**

Spacecraft Adapter Simulator *e:* **SCAS**

Spacecraft Analysis *e:* **SPAN**

Spacecraft Antenna System *e:* **SAS**

Spacecraft Array for Michelson Spectral Inferometry *e:* **SAMSI**

Spacecraft Assembly and Ecapsulation Building *e:* **SAEB**

Spacecraft Assembly and Encapsulation Building *e:* **SAEB**

Spacecraft Assembly and Encapsulation Facility *e:* **SAEF**

Spacecraft Assembly Building *e:* **SAB**

Spacecraft Assembly Facility *e:* **SAF**

Spacecraft Assessment Report *e:* **SCAR**

Spacecraft Attitude Display *e:* **SAD**

Spacecraft Attitude Display Systems Allocation Document *e:* **SACS**

Spacecraft Attitude Precision Pointing and Slewing Adaptive Control *e:* **SAPPSAC**

Spacecraft/Capsule *e:* **S/C**

Spacecraft Charging at High Altitude *e:* **SCATHA**

Spacecraft Charging at High Altitudes *e:* **SCATHA**

Spacecraft-Charging-At-High Altitudes-Sateilite *e:* **SCATHA**

spacecraft charging at high[er] altitude[s] *e:* **scatha**

Spacecraft Checkout Facility *e:* **SCF**

Spacecraft Command Control Unit *e:* **SCCU**

Spacecraft Communicator *e:* **SC**

Spacecraft Control Center *e:* **SCC**

Spacecraft Control Facility *e:* **SCF**

Spacecraft Control System *e:* **SCS**

Spacecraft Data Analysis Team *e:* **SDAT**

Spacecraft Data Handling Equipment *e:* **SDHE**

Spacecraft Database *e:* **SCDB**

Spacecraft Design Book *e:* **SDB**

Spacecraft Design Specification *e:* **SDS**

Spacecraft Equipment Module *e:* **SEM**

Spacecraft flying *e:* **SeaStar**

Spacecraft Glow Experiment *e:* **SGX**

Spacecraft GOSS [Ground Operational Support System] Interface Test System *e:* **SGITS**

Spacecraft Ground Controlled Approach *e:* **SGCA**

Spacecraft Ground Elapsed Time *e:* **SGET**

Spacecraft Handling Equipment *e:* **SHE**

spacecraft identification code *e:* **SIC**

Spacecraft Incorporated *e:* **SCI**

Spacecraft Information Viewing Device *e:* **SIVD**

Spacecraft Instrumentation Test Equipment *e:* **SITE**

Spacecraft Integration Project Office *e:* **SIPO**

Spacecraft Interface Unit *e:* **SciU**

Spacecraft Landing Strut *e:* **SLS**

Spacecraft LM (Lunar Module) Adapter *e:* **SLA**

Spacecraft Location/Attitude Tape *e:* **SLAT**

Spacecraft Magnetic Test Facility [Goddard Space Flight Center] *e:* **SMTF**

Spacecraft Maneuver Engine Transients *e:* **SMET**

Spacecraft Meteorology Group *e:* **SMG**

Spacecraft Observer *e:* **S/CO**

Spacecraft Oceanography *e:* **SPOC**

Spacecraft Oceanography Project *e:* **SPOC**, *e:* **SPOC Project**

Spacecraft Operational Data Book *e:* **SODB**

Spacecraft Operations *e:* **SCO**

Spacecraft Operations and Checkout Facility *e:* **SOCF**

Spacecraft Operations Control Center *e:* **SOCC**

Spacecraft Operations Manual *e:* **SOM**

Spacecraft Operations Planning Section *e:* **SOPS**

Space[craft (or -flight)] Tracking and Data Network *e:* **STDN**

Spacecraft Orientation Control *e:* **SOC**

Spacecraft Orientation Control System *e:* **SOCS**

Spacecraft Oscillograph Recording System *e:* **SORS**

Spacecraft Performance Analysis and Command *e:* **SPAC**

Spacecraft Performance Analysis Area *e:* **SPAA**

Spacecraft Performance and Flight Path Analysis Directorate *e:* **SPFPAD**

Spacecraft, Planet, Instruments, C Matrix, Events *e:* **SPICE**

Spacecraft, Planetary & Probe Ephemeris, Instrument, C-Matrix, Event File *e:* **SPICE**

Spacecraft Platform *e:* **SCP**

Spacecraft Prelaunch Automatic Checkout Equipment *e:* **SPACE**

Spacecraft Propulsion System *e:* **SPC**, *e:* **SPS**

Spacecraft Protective Landing Area for the Advancement of Science and Humanities *e:* **SPLAASH**

Spacecraft Research Foundation *e:* **SRF**

Spacecraft Sextant *e:* **SXT**

Spacecraft Simulation Equipment *e:* **SSE**

Spacecraft Software Division *e:* **SSD**

Spacecraft Support Planning Section *e:* **SSPS**

Spacecraft Support Unit *e:* **SSU**

Spacecraft Switched Time Division Multiple Access *e:* **SSTDMA**

Spacecraft System *e:* **SCS**

Spacecraft System Console *e:* **SSC**

Spacecraft System Integration *e:* **SSI**

Spacecraft System Integration Support *e:* **SSIS**

Spacecraft System Integration Support Service *e:* **SSISS**

Spacecraft System Support *e:* **SSS**

Spacecraft System Test Console *e:* **SSTC**

Spacecraft Systems Controller Unit *e:* **SSCU**

Spacecraft Systems Monitor *e:* **SCSM**, *e:* **SSM**

Spacecraft Systems Officer *e:* **SSO**

Spacecraft Systems Test *e:* **SST**

Spacecraft Technical Control Center *e:* **STCC**

Spacecraft Technology and Advance Reentry Test *e:* **START**

Spacecraft Technology and Advanced Reentry Test[s] *e:* **START**

Spacecraft Technology Division *e:* **STD**

Spacecraft Telecommunications System *e:* **STS**

Spacecraft Telemetry Command Data Handling System *e:* **STCDHS**

Spacecraft Telemetry Regenerator *e:* **STR**

Spacecraft Television-Ground Data Handling System *e:* **SCTV-GDHS**

Spacecraft Television Video Data *e:* **STVD**

Spacecraft Terminal Thrust *e:* **STT**

Spacecraft Test Conductor *e:* **SCTC**, *e:* **STC**

Spacecraft Test Engineering *e:* **STE**

Spacecraft Test Equipment *e:* **STE**

Spacecraft Test Facility *e:* **STF**

Spacecraft Test Operations Language *e:* **PSTOL**

Spacecraft Tracking Station *e:* **STS**

Spacecraft Vicinity Equipment *e:* **SCVE**

spaced antenna *e:* **SA**

spaced antenna imaging Doppler interferometer *e:* **SAIDI**

Spaced Armour *e:* **SA**

Spaced Array *e:* **SA**

Spaced Doubled *e:* **SD**

Spaced Doublet *e:* **SD**

Spaceflight Meteorology Group *e:* **SMG**

Spaceflight Tracking and Data Network Station *e:* **MIL GSFC**

Spaceflight Tracking and Data Network (STDN) Station (KSC) *e:* **GMIL**

Spacelab *e:* **S/L**

Spacelab Ancillary Data Tape *e:* **SANC**

Spacelab Configuration Management *e:* **SLCC**

Spacelab Contract Administration *e:* **SLCA**

Spacelab Data Processing Facility *e:* **SLDPF**

Spacelab Disposition Record e: **SDR**

Spacelab Engineering e: **SLE**

Spacelab Engineering Model Unit e: **SLEMU**

Spacelab Experiment Channel Tape e: **SECT**

Spacelab Experiment Data Tape e: **SEDT**

Spacelab Experiment Interface Device e: **SEID**

Spacelab I/O Data Tape e: **SIDT**

Spacelab Infrared Telescope Facility e: **SIRTF**

Spacelab Input Processing System e: **SIPS**

Spacelab Integration e: **SLI**

Spacelab Integration and Test e: **SLI**, e: **SLI ERNO**

Spacelab Japan e: **SL-J**

Spacelab Late Access Kit e: **SLAK**

Spacelab Life Sciences e: **SLS**

Spacelab Middeck Experiments e: **SMIDEX**

Spacelab Mission Development e: **SMD**

Spacelab Operations e: **SLO**, e: **SLO ERNO**

Spacelab Operations Directorate e: **CS**

Spacelab Opportunity Payload e: **SOP**

Spacelab Orbiter Common Hardware e: **SOCH**

Spacelab/Orbiter Interface Simulator e: **SOIS**

Spacelab/Orbiter Interface Simulator Station e: **Sols**

Spacelab Output Processing System e: **SOPS**

Spacelab Pallet System e: **SPS**

Spacelab Payload e: **SLN**, e: **SLN ERNO**

Spacelab Payload Accommodations Handbook e: **SPAH**

Spacelab Payload Integration and Coordination e: **SPIC**

Spacelab Payload Integration and Coordination in Europe e: **SPICE**

Spacelab Payload Project Office e: **SPPO**

Spacelab Payload Standard Modular Electronics e: **SPSME**

Spacelab Payloads Processing Project e: **SPPP**

Spacelab Planning and Ground Rule e: **PGR**

Spacelab Processing Facility e: **SPF**

Spacelab Product Assurance Department e: **SLA**, e: **SLA ERNO**

Spacelab Program Board e: **SLPB**

Spacelab Program office e: **SLP**

Spacelab Program Office e: **SLP ERNO**, e: **SPO**

Spacelab Project Control e: **SLC**

Spacelab Projects Office e: **CP-SPO**

Spacelab Simulator e: **SLS**

Spacelab Stored Program Command e: **SSPC**

Spacelab Subsystems e: **SL-SS**

Spacelab Subsystem[s] Segment e: **SL-SSS**

Spacelab Support Module Simulator e: **SLSMS**

Spacelab Systems e: **SL-SS**

Spacelab Technology e: **SLT**, e: **SLT ERNO**, e: **ST**

Spacelab Transfer Tunnel e: **STT**

Spacelab Ultraviolet Telescope e: **SUOT**

Spacelab Utility Kit e: **SLUK**

Spacelab Window Adapter Assembly e: **SWAA**

Spacer e: **S**, e: **SPC**, e: **SPCR**, e: **SPR**

Spacers e: **Sp**

Spacesaver Material Accounting Resource Terminal e: **SMART**

Spain. Estacion Centro de Ecologia. Boletin p: **Spin Estac Cent Ecol Bol**

Spain. Instituto Geologico y Minero. Boletin Geologsco y Minero s: **Spain Inst Geol Min Bol Geol Min**

Spain. Instituto Geologico y Minero. Memorias s: **Spain Inst Geol Min Mem**

Span-America Medical Systems, Inc. e: **SPAN**

SpAN. Shell Public Health and Agricultural News e: **SPAN**

SPAN [Space Physics Analysis Network] Ocean Network Information Center e: **SONIC**

Spanish-America Medical Systems, Inc. e: **SPAN**

Spanish Association for Purification ofWater and Wastewater e: **SAPWW**

Spanish national meteorological institute e: **INM-ES**

Spanish Speaking Mental Health Research Center e: **SSMHRC**

Spar Aerospace Ltd. e: **SPZ**

Spare Medical Gas e: **SMG**

SPASUR [Space Surveillance] Command and Control Center e: **SCCC**

Spatial Signature Analysis e: **SSA**

SPB GSSS Operations Environment e: **SPBOPS**

Special Access Space e: **SAS**

Special Air Launch Environment e: **SALE**

Special Airborne Medical Care Unit e: **SAMCU**

Special Airspace Management System/Military Airspace Management System e: **SAMS/MAMS**

Special Areas and Particularly Sensitive Sea Areas e: **PSSAs**

Special Assistant for Environmental Services e: **SAES**

Special Astrophysics Observatory e: **SAO**

Special Commission for the Amazonian Environment e: **CEMAA**

Special Commission on Weather Modification e: **SCWC**, e: **SCWM**

Special Committee for/on the International Biological Program[me] e: **SCIBP**

Special Committee for the Geosphere-Biosphere e: **SCGB**

Special Committee for the International Biological Programme [of International Council of Scientific Unions] e: **SCIBP**

Special Committee for the International Decade for Natural Disaster Reduction e: **SC-IDNDR**

Special Committee for the International Geosphere-Biosphere Programme e: **IGBP**

Special Committee for the International Geosphere-Biosphere Programme: A Study of Global Change e: **IGPB**

Special Committee on Ocean[ograph][ic] Research e: **SCOR**

Special Committee on Problems of the Environment [of International Council of Scientific Unions] e: **SCOPE**

Special Committee on Space Research e: **SCOSPAR**

Special Committee on Space Technology e: **SCOST**

Special Committee on Water Research e: **SCOWR**

Special Contributions. Geophysical Institute. Kyoto University e: **Spec Contrib Geophys Inst Kyoto Univ**

Special Contributions. Institute of Geophysics. National Central University [Miaoli, Taiwan] e: **Spec Contrib Inst Geophys Natl Cent Univ [Miaoli Taiwan]**

Special Economic Series. Maine Geological Survey e: **Spec Econ Ser Maine Geol Surv**

Special Environmental Radiometallurgy Facility e: **SERF**

Special Environmental Report e: **Spec Environ Rep**

Special Environmental Report. World Meteorological Organization e: **Spec Environ Rep WMO**

Special Environmental Sample Container e: **SESC**

Special Health Authority e: **SHA**

Special Interdepartmental Committee on Protection Against Violence e: **SIDC-PAV**

Special Interest Group/Biological and Chemical Information Systems e: **SIG/BC**

Special Interest Group on Biomedical Computing e: **SIGBIO**

Special Interest Group on Biomedical Computing [of the Association for Computing Machinery] e: **SIGBIO**

Special Interest Group on Biomedical Information Processing e: **SIG/BIOM**, e: **SIG/BIOM**

Special Interest Group on Medical Records e: **SIGMR**

Special Interest Groups of the American Society for Information Science-BC: Biological and Chemical e: **SIGs-ASIS**

Special Interest Groups of the American Society for Information Science-MR: Medical Records e: **SIGs-ASIS**

Special Liasson Report. Commonwealth Geological Liaison Office [London] e: **Spec Liaison Rep Commonw Geol Liaison Off**

Special Libraries Association. Biological Sciences Division. Reminder e: **SLA Biol Sci Div Reminder**

Special Libraries Association. Geography and Map Division. Bulletin e: **SLA Geog & Map Div Bul**

Special Libraries Association Geography & Map Division e: **SLAGMD**

Special Libraries Association. Georgia Chapter. Bulletin e: **SLA GA Chap Bul**

Special Libraries Committee on Environmental Information e: **SCEI**

Special Moment-Resisting Space Frame e: **SMRSF**

Special Ocean Wave Model e: **SOWM**

Special Operations Naval Mobile Environment Team e: **SONMET**

Special Operations Waterproof Bag e: **SOWB**

Special Operations Weather Team *e:* **SOWT**

Special Operations Weather Team/Tactical Element *e:* **SOWT/TE**

Special Paper. Geological Association of Canada *e:* **Spec Pap Geol Ass Can**, *e:* **Spec Pap Geol Assoc Can**

Special Paper. State of Oregon Department of Geology and Mineral Industries *e:* **Spec Pap State Ore Dep Geol Min Ind**

Special Papers. Department of Natural Resources *e:* **Spec Pap Dep Nat Resour [Qd]**

Special Protected Areas Regional Activity Centre *e:* **SPA / RAC**

Special Protection Area under the EC Birds Directive *e:* **SPA**

Special Protection Zone *e:* **SPZ**

Special Protection Zones *e:* **SPZs**

Special Protective Coating *e:* **SPC**

Special Publication. Academy of Natural Sciences. Philadelphia *e:* **Spec Publ Acad Nat Sci Phila**

Special Publication. Association of Exploration Geochemists *e:* **Spec Publ Assoc Explor Geochem**

Special Publication. British Ecological Society *e:* **Spec Publ Br Ecol Soc**

Special Publication. Bureau of Mines and Geology [Montana] *e:* **Spec Publ Bur Mines Geol**

Special Publication. College of Earth and Mineral Sciences. Pennsylvania State University *e:* **Spec Publ Coll Earth Miner Sci Pa State Univ**

Special Publication. Colorado Geological Survey *e:* **Spec Publ Colo Geol Surv**

Special Publication. Colorado Geologieal Survey *e:* **Spec Publ Colorado Geol Surv**

Special Publication, Geological Society of Australia *e:* **Spec. Publ.\ Geol. Soc. Aust.**

Special Publications Series. British Ecological Society *e:* **SPBSES**

Special Publications. Seto Marine Biological Laboratory. Series IV *e:* **SPSBDR**

Special Purpose Integrated Remote Intelligence Terminal *e:* **SPIRIT**

Special Purpose Test Vehicle for Atmospheric Research *e:* **SPTVAR**

Special Report Series. Medical Research Committee [London] *e:* **Special Rep Ser Med Research Com [London]**

Special Report. University of Illinoisat Urbana-Champaign. Water Resources Center *e:* **Spec Rep Univ Ill Urbana Champaign Water Resour Cent**

Special Rules Airspace *e:* **SRA**

Special Scientific Report. Florida Department of Natural Resources. Marine Research Laboratory *e:* **Spec Sci Rep FL Dep Nat Resour Mar Res Lab**

Special Scientific Report. Wildlife. United States Fish and Wildlife Service *e:* **Spec Sci Rep Wildlife US Fish Wildlife Serv**

Special Sensor Microwave Imager Scanning Spectral Polarimeter *e:* **SSM/I SSP**

special sensor microwave water vapor sounder *e:* **SSM/T2**

Special Series. Internalional Association of Volcanology and Chemistry of the Earth's

Interior *e:* **Spec Sel Int Assoc Volcanol Chem Earths Inter**

Special Services Protection *e:* **SSP**

Special Signal Exploitation Spaces *e:* **SSES**

Special Staff United States for Atlas-Centaur Class Spacecraft *e:* **SSUS-A**

Special Staff United States for Delta Class Spacecraft *e:* **SSUS-D**

Special Studies. Utah Geological and Mineral Survey *e:* **Spec Stud Utah Geol Miner Sarv**

Special Symposium on Natural Radiation Environment *e:* **Spec Symp Nat Radiat Environ**

Special Trust Fund for Climate and Atmospheric Environment Activities *e:* **CAEA**

Special-Use Airspace *e:* **SUA**

Special Water Dispenser *e:* **SWD**

Special Water Reactor *e:* **SWR**

Special Weather Intelligence *e:* **SWI**

Special World Geophysical Centre *e:* **SWGC**

Specialised (or Specialized) Oceanographic Center (or Centre) *e:* **SOC**

Specialist in Community Medicine *e:* **SCM**

Specialist in Microbiology *d:* **SpM**

Specialist Periodical Reports. Aliphatic and Related Natural Product Chemistry *e:* **Spec Period Rep Aliphatic Relat Nat Prod Chem**

Specialist Periodical Reports. Environmental Chemistry *e:* **Spec Period Rep Environ Chem**

Specialist, Pigeon Trainer *e:* **SPXPI**

specially denatured *e:* **S.D.**

Specially Denatured Alcohol *e:* **SDA**

Specially Protected Areas and Wildlife *e:* **SPAW**

Specialty Conference on Atmospheric Deposition. Proceedings *e:* **Spec Conf Atmos Deposition Proc**

Specialty Conference on Toxic Substances in the Air Environment. Proceedings *e:* **Spec Conf Toxic Subst Air Environ Proc**

Specialty Law Digest. Health Care Monthly *e:* **Spec Law Dig Health Care Mon**

Specific Living Space *e:* **SLS**

specific polarization index *e:* **spi**

specific water content *e:* **swc**

Specification Environment for Communications Software *e:* **SPECS**

Spectral Mapping (of climate parameters) *e:* **SPECMAP**

spectrally scanning polarimeter *e:* **SSP**

Spectro-Radiometer for Ocean Monitoring *e:* **SROM**

Spectroscopy of the Atmosphere using Far-Infrared Emission *e:* **SAFIRE**

Spectrum Signature *e:* **S/S**

Speed Made Good Through the Water *e:* **STW**

Speicherröhre/Intermittierende Filmschaltung-Verfahren *d:* **SI-Verfahren**

Speisewasser *d:* **Sp**, *d:* **SpW**

Speisewasserbehälter *d:* **SpWB**

Speisewasserpumpe *d:* **SpP**

Speleothem-PEP project, a component of PEP, derives palaeoclimatic information from speleothems *e:* **SPEP**

Spent Fuel Test-Climax *e:* **SFT-C**

Sperimentale. Archivio di Biologia Normale e Patologica *i:* **Sper Arch Biol Norm Patol**

spezielles geodätisches Netz *d:* **SGN**

spezifisch-pathogenfreie Tiere *d:* **SPF-Tiere**

Spherical Polar *e:* **SP**

Sphinkterdehnung *d:* **SD**

Spin-Orbit Coupling *e:* **SOC**

Spin Orbital *e:* **SO**

Spin-Orbital Coupling *e:* **SO**

Spin Polarised Electron Energy Loss Spectroscopy *e:* **SPEELS**

Spin Polarised Inverse Photoemission Spectroscopy *e:* **SPIPES**

Spin Polarised Low Energy Electron Diffraction *e:* **SPLEED**

Spin Polarised Ultraviolet Photoelectron Spectroscopy *e:* **SPUPS**

Spin Polarised X-ray Photoelectron Spectroscopy *e:* **SPXPS**

Spin Polarized *e:* **SP**

Spin Polarized Hartree-Fock *e:* **SPHF**

Spin-Polarized Invene Photoemission *e:* **SPIPE**

Spin-Polarized Low Energy Electron Diffraction *e:* **SLEED**

Spin-Polarized Low-Energy Electron Microscopy *e:* **SPLEEM**

Spin-Polarized Photoelectron Diffraction *e:* **SPPD**

Spin Stabilized Spacecraft *e:* **SSS**

Spinning Space Station *e:* **SSS**

Spiral Point Drill Geometry *e:* **SPDG**

Spiritual Frontiers Fellowship *e:* **SFF**

Spithead Channel joining The Solent and Southampton Water between the Isle of Wight and Portsmouth *e:* **Spit**

Splitierrakete *d:* **SplRak**

Splitierwirkung *d:* **SW**

Spontaneous Polarization *e:* **SP**

Sporadic radiant emission from the upper atmosphere over middle and high latitudes *e:* **AURORA**

Sport Medicine Council of Canada *e:* **SMCC**

Sport- und Gesundheitszentrum *d:* **SGZ**

Sport- und Naturfreunde e.V. *d:* **SUN**

Sports Science and Medical Council *e:* **SSMC**

Sports Science and Medical Council Executive Committee *e:* **SSMCEC**

Spouse Observation Checklist *e:* **SOC**

Spreading Ocean Floor *e:* **SOF**

Springer Series on Health Care and Society *e:* **SHCS**

Springer Series on Health Gare and Soiety *e:* **Springer Ser Health Care Soc**

Springer Tracts in Natural Philosophy *e:* **Springer Tracts Nat Philos**

Springhochwasser *d:* **Sp.H.W.**

Springniedrigwasser *d:* **Sp.N.W.**

Springtidehochwasser *d:* **SpThw**

Springtidenhochwasser *d:* **SprThw**

Spruehprüfung mit Salzwasser *d:* **SW**

Squadron Medical Element *e:* **SME**

Squadron Medical Officer *e:* **SMO**

Square Wave Polarograph *e:* **SWP**

Squaw Creek National Wildlife Refuge *e:* **SCNWR**

Sreden Medicinski Rabotnik *R:* **Sred Med Rab**

Sri Lanka Environmental Journalists Forum
  e: **SLEJF**
Sri Lanka Geological Survey Department
  e: **SLGSD**
Sri Lanka. Geological Survey Department.
  Economic Bulletin *e:* **Sri Lanka Geol
  Surv Dep Econ Bull**
Sri Lankan Environmental Journalists
  Forum *e:* **SEJF**
Srpsko Biološko Društvo *se:* **SBD**
Srpsko Geografsko Društvo *se:* **SGD**
Srpsko Geološko Društvo *se:* **SGD**
St. Andrew's Waterside Church Mission for
  Sailors *e:* **S.A.W.C.M.S.**
St. Barnabas Medical Staff Library,
  Livingston *e:* **VYB**
St. George Division of General Practice *e:*
  SGDGP
St. George Minerals *e:* **SGG**
St. George's Society of New York *e:*
  SGSNY
St. Jude Medical, Inc. *e:* **STJM**
St. Jude medical prosthesis *e:* **SJMP**
St Lawrence and Great Lakes Waterway *e:*
  SLGLW
St. Louis Medical Society *e:* **SLMS**
St. Louis Metropolitan Medicine *e:* **St
  Louis Metropol Med**
St. Luke's Hospital, Bolling Medical
  Library, New York *e:* **VVY**
St. Marianna Medical Journal [Japan] *e:* **St
  Marianna Med J**
51st Medical Battalion Association *e:*
  FMBA
St. Paul Medical Journal *e:* **St Paul Med J**
St. Petersburger Medizinische
  Wochenschrift *d:* **St Petersb Med
  Wchnschr**
Staatkundig Gereformeerde Partij *n:* **SGP**
Staatliches Amt für Technische
  Akkreditierung *d:* **SWEDAC**
Staatliches Amt für Umwelt und Natur *d:*
  STAUN
Staatliches Amt für Wasser[-] und
  Abfall[wirtschaft] *d:* **StAWA**
Staatliches Tierärztliches
  Untersuchungsamt Aulendorf *d:* **STUA**
Staatliches Umweltamt *d:* **StUA**
Staatliches Veterinärmedizinisches
  Prüfungsinstitut *d:* **SVP**
Staatlisches Institut für Gesundheit und
  Umwelt *e:* **SIGU**
Staatsamt für Volksgesundheit *d:* **VGesA**
Stabilised Long-range Observation System
  e: **SLOS**
Stable Ocean Platform *e:* **STOP**
Stable-Orbit Rendezvous *e:* **SOR**
Stabsquartier *d:* **St.-Q.**, *d:* **St.-Qu.**
Staff Meteorological Officer *e:* **S.MET.O.**
Staff Surgeon *e:* **SS**
Staff Weather Advisor *e:* **SWA**
Staff Weather Officer *e:* **SWO**, *e:* **SWXO**
Staged in Orbit *e:* **SIO**
STAL. Sciences et Techniques de l'Animal
  de Laboratoire *f:* **STAL Sci Tech Anim
  Lab**
Stall Protection & Incidence-Limiting
  System *e:* **SPILS**
Standard Abwasser
  Meßwertverarbeitungssystem *d:*
  SAMSY
Standard Apple Numeric Environment *e:*
  SANE

Standard Apple Numerics Environment *e:*
  SANE
standard atmosphere *e:* **std atm**
Standard Authoring Facility Environment
  e: **SAFE**
Standard Automated Remote-to-AUTODIN
  Host *e:* **SARAH**
Standard Communication Environment *e:*
  SCE
Standard Earth Observation Satellite *e:*
  S/EOS
Standard Geographic Base *e:* **SGB**
Standard Geographical Classification *e:*
  SGC
Standard Georgia Practice *e:* **Stand GA
  Prac**
Standard Hydrogen Electrode *e:* **SHE**
Standard Hydrogen Monitoring System *e:*
  SHMS
Standard Hydrometeorological Exchange
  Format *e:* **SHEF**
Standard Manned Space Flight Initiator *e:*
  SMSI
standard mean ocean water *e:* **smor**
Standard Mean Ocean Water *e:* **SNOW**
Standard Mean Oeean Water *e:* **SMOW**
Standard Medical Examination *e:* **SME**
Standard Normal Ocean Water *e:* **SNOW**
Standard Operating Environment *e:* **SOE**
Standard Operating Procedure-
  Meteorological Plan *e:* **SOPMET**
Standard Orbital Parameter Message *e:*
  SOPM
Standard Protective Item *e:* **SPI**
Standard RADAR Environment *e:* **SRE**
Standard Reference Water Sample *e:*
  SRWS
Standard Remote Terminal *e:* **SHT**, *e:*
  SRT
Standard Seawater Service *e:* **SSS**
Standard Support and Environmental
  Impact Statement *e:* **SSEIS**
Standard-Umweltbedingung *d:* **STU**
Standard Underwater Research Vehicle *e:*
  SURV
Standard Underwater Research Vessel *e:*
  SURV
Standard Water Column Model *e:*
  SWACOM
Standard Water-Crossing Equipment *e:*
  S.W.C.E.
Standard Weather Messages Command and
  Control System *e:* **SWMCCS**
Standardization in Europe on Semantical
  Aspects in Medicine *e:* **SESAME**
Standardized Red Green Blue [colorspace]
  e: **SRGB**
Standard[ized] Space Guidance System *e:*
  SSGS
Standard[ized] Space Launch System *e:*
  SSLS
Standard[ized] Space Launch Vehicle *e:*
  SSLV
Standard[ized] Space Launch Vehicles *e:*
  SSLVs
Standby Auxiary Feedwater Pump *e:*
  SBAFWP
Standby Auxiliary Feed Water Pump *e:*
  SBAFWP
Standby Service Water *e:* **SSW**, *e:* **SW**
Standby Service Water System *e:* **SSWS**
Ständige Impfkommission des
  Bundesgesundheitsamtes *d:* **STIKO**

Ständige Konferenz Chemie und Umwelt
  [der Gesellschaft Deutscher Chemiker]
  d: **SKCU**
Ständige Konferenz der Hochschullehrer für
  Psychosomatik, Psychotherapie,
  Medizinische Psychologie und
  Medizinische Soziologie *d:* **HPPS**
Ständiger Ausschuss für Geographische
  Namen *d:* **StAGN**
Standing Committee for International
  Congresses of Military Medicine and
  Pharmacy *e:* **ICMMP**
Standing Committee of Analysts to review
  methods for Quality Control of the Water
  Cycle *e:* **SCA**
Standing Committee of Ocean Data Stations
  e: **SCODS**
Standing Committee of Presidents of
  International NGOs Concerned with
  Mental Health Issues *e:* **PCMH**
Standing Committee on Environment
  Protection *e:* **SCEP**
Standing Committee on International
  Geoscientific Relations *e:* **SCIGR**
Standing Committee on Ocean Data
  Stations *e:* **SCODS**
Standing Committee on Pollution Clearance
  at Sea *e:* **SCOPCAS**
Standing Committee on Postgraduate
  Medical Education *e:* **SCOPME**, *e:*
  SCPME
Standing Group Meteorological Committee
  e: **SGMC**
Standing Group on Health Technology *e:*
  SGHT
Standing Group on Undergraduate Medical
  and Dental Education and Research *e:*
  SGUMDER
Standing Interdepartmental Committee on
  Censorship *e:* **SCC**
Standing Medical Advisory Committee *e:*
  S.M.A.C.
Standing Operating Procedure-
  Meteorological Plan *e:* **SOPMET**
Standing State Advisory Committee [of
  Water Resources Council] *e:* **SSAC**
Standing Technical Advisory Committee on
  Water Quality *e:* **STACWV**
Stanford Environmental Annual *e:* **Stan.
  Env't. Ann.**
Stanford Environmental Law Annual *e:*
  Stan. Envt'l L. Ann.
Stanford Environmental Law Journal *e:*
  Stan. Envt'l L. J.
Stanford Geological Survey *e:* **SGS**
Stanford Medical Bulletin *e:* **Stanford M
  Bull**, *e:* **Stanford Med Bull**
Stanford Medical Student Survival Guide
  e: **MSSG**
Stanford Natural History Museum *e:*
  SNHM
Stanford Studies in Medical Sciences *e:*
  Stanford Stud Med Sci
Stanford University Medical College *e:*
  SUMC
Stanford University Medical Experiment
  e: **SUMEX**
Stanford University Medical Experiment-
  Applications of Artificial Intelligence to
  Medical Research *e:* **SUMEXAIM**
Stanford University Medical Experimental
  Computer *e:* **SUMEX Computer**

Stanford University Network for Space Telescience Applications Research *e:* **SUNSTAR**

Stanford University. Publications in the Geological Sciences *e:* **Stanford Univ Publ Geol**, *e:* **Stanford Univ Publ Geol Sci**

Stanford University. Publications. University Series. Biological Sciences *e:* **Stanford Univ Publ Univ Ser Biol Sci**

Stanford University. Publications. University Series. Medical Sciences *e:* **Stanford Univ Publ Univ Ser Med Sci**

Stanford Worldwide Acquisition of Meteorological Information *e:* **SWAMI**

Stang Hydronics *e:* **STGH**

star + earthquake *e:* **starquake**

Star Frontiers *e:* **SF**

Star Trek, fifth movie/'The Final Frontier' *e:* **STV / ST-TFF**

stark tocopherolhaltige Extrakte natürlichen Ursprungs *d:* **E 306**

State Agency Remote Sensing Data Management *e:* **SARSDM**

State Board of Health *e:* **SBH**

State Board of Medicai Examiners *e:* **SBME**

State Board of Medical Examiners *e:* **SBME**

State Children's Health Insurance Program *e:* **SCHIP**

State Committee for Hydrometeorology *e:* **SCHM**

State Department of Natural Resources *e:* **SDNR**

State Earthquake Administration *e:* **SEA**

State Environmental Education Coordinators Association *e:* **SEECA**

State Environmental Goals and Improvement Project *e:* **SEGIP**

State Environmental Impact Statement *e:* **SEIS**

State Environmental Policy Act *e:* **SEPA**

State Environmental Protection Act *e:* **SEPA**

State Environmental Protection Agency *e:* **SEPA**

State Environmental Quality Act *e:* **SEQA**

State Exotic Animal Disease Emergency Management Plan *e:* **SEADAMP**

State Geodesy and Cartography Board *e:* **SGCB**

State Geographic Database *e:* **STATSGO**

State Geologic Agencies *e:* **SGA**

State Geologists Journal *e:* **State Geologists Jour**

State Health Care Authority *e:* **HCA**

State Health Office *e:* **SHO**

State Health Office Emergency Support Operations Center *e:* **SHOESOC**

State Health Plan *e:* **SHP**

State Health Planning and Development Agency *e:* **SHPDA**

State Hydroelectric Department *e:* **SHD**

State Hydrological Institute *e:* **SHI**

State Inspectorate for Environmental Protection *e:* **PIOS**

State Institute of Applied Ecology *e:* **GIPE**

State Local Education and Medical *e:* **SLEM**

State Medicaid Agencies *e:* **SMA**

State Medicaid Directors Association *e:* **SMDA**

State Medical Association of Texas *e:* **SMAT**

State Medical Facilities Plan *e:* **SMFP**

State Medical Journal Advertising Bureau *e:* **SMJAB**

State Medical Service *e:* **S.M.S.**

State Medical Society *e:* **SMC**

State Medical Society of Wisconsin *e:* **SMSW**

State Meteorology Administration *e:* **SMA**

State Mining and Geology Board *e:* **SMGB**

State Oceanic Administration *e:* **SOA**

State Oceanographic Institute, State Committee on Hydrometeorology, Moscow *e:* **GOIN**

State of Health *e:* **SOH**

State of Illinois. Division of the State Geological Survey. Bulletin *e:* **State Ill Div State Geol Surv Bull**

State of New Jersey. Department of Conservation and Economic Development. Division of Water Policy and Supply. Special Report *e:* **New Jersey Div Water Policy and Supply Spec Rept**

State of New Jersey. Department of Conservation and Economic Development. Division of Water Policy and Supply. Water Resources Circular *e:* **New Jersey Div Water Policy and Supply Water Resources Circ**

State of Oregon Water Resources Department *e:* **SOWRD**

State of Polarisation (or Polarization) *e:* **SOP**

State of the Arctic Environment Report *e:* **SOAER**

State of the Art Reviews. Occupational Medicine *e:* **State of the Art Rev Occup Med**

State-of-the-Atmosphere Variable *e:* **SAV**

state-of-the-atmosphere variables *e:* **SAV**

State of the Environment *e:* **SOE**

State of the Environment Education Kit *e:* **SEEK**

State of the Environment Report *e:* **SER**, *e:* **SOER**

State of the Environment Reporting Information System *e:* **SERIS**

State of the Marine Environment Reporting *e:* **SOMER**

State of Washington Department of Ecology *e:* **ECOLOGY**

State Offices of Rural Health *e:* **SORH**

State Planning and Environment Commission. Technical Bulletin *e:* **State Plann and Environ Comm Tech Bull**

State Research and Innovation Centre of Geoinformation Systems and Technologies *e:* **GosGISCentre**

State Rural Health Associations *e:* **SRHA**

State Science, Environment and Technology Department *e:* **SSET**

State Soil Geographic *e:* **STATSGO**

State Space *e:* **SS**

State Space Analysis *e:* **SSA**

State Space Method *e:* **SSM**

State Space Model *e:* **SSM**

State University of New York at Stony Brook, Health Sciences Library, Stony Brook *e:* **VZB**

State University of New York Biomedical Communication Network *e:* **SUNY BCN**

State University of New York, College of Environmental Science and Forestry, Syracuse *e:* **VXF**

State University of New York, College of Environmental Sciences and Forestry at Syracuse University, Syracuse *e:* **NSySU-F**

State University of New York, Health Sciences Library, Buffalo *e:* **SBH**

State University of New York, Health Sciences Library, Buffalo,NY *e:* **SBH**

State University of New York, Upstate Medical Center, Syracuse *e:* **NSySU-M**

State University System of Florida Institute of Oceanography *e:* **SUSIO**

State Water Control Board *e:* **SWCB**

State Water Plan *e:* **SWP**

State Water Pollution Control Board *e:* **SWPCB**

State Water Project *e:* **SWP**

State Water Resources Control Board *e:* **SWRCB**

State Wildlife Advisory News Service *e:* **SWANS**

State Wildlife Reserve *e:* **SWR**

Statens Meteorologisk-Hydrografiska Anstalt *r:* **SMHA**

Statens Meteorologisk-Hydrografiska Institut *r:* **SMHI**

Statens Naturvärdsverk *r:* **SNV**

Statens Naturvetenskapliga Forskningsgråd *r:* **NFR**

Statens Naturvetenskapliga Forskningsrad Ekologikommitter Bulletin *r:* **Statens Naturvetensk Forskningsrad Ekologikomm Bull**

Statens Naturvidenskabelige Forskninsgrad *r:* **SNF**

Statens Veterinärmedicinska Anstalt, Stockholm *r:* **SVA**

Statewide Health Coordinating Council *e:* **SHCC**

Static Feed Water Electrolysis (Module) *e:* **SFWE(M)**

Static Groundwater Level *e:* **SGL**

Static Pressure Water Gage *e:* **SPWG**

Static Water Level *e:* **SWL**

Static Water Supply *e:* **SWS**

Station biologique des Bermudes *f:* **BBS**

Station de Biologie Marine. Grande Riviere, Quebec. Rapport Annuel *f:* **Stn Biol Mar Grande Riviere Que Rapp Annu**

Station de Recherches Forestieres *f:* **SRF**

Station de Renseignements et d'Observations *f:* **SRO**

Station de Renseignements et d'Observations Météorologiques *f:* **S.R.O.M.**

Station d'Ecoute de Sateilite Meteorologique *f:* **SESAME**

Station d'Hydrobiologie Continentale *f:* **SHC**

Station Earth Ground Point *e:* **SEGP**

Station Identification Symbol, Orbiter X-Axis *e:* **ZO**

Station Internationale de Géobotanique Méditerranéenne et Alpine *f:* **SIGMA**

Station Medical Group *e:* **Sta Med Gp**

Station Note. Forest, Wildlife and Range Experiment Station (Moscow , Idaho) *e:* **Sta Note For Exp Sta (Idaho)**

Station Paper. Forest, Wildlife and Range
Experiment Station (Moscow, Idaho) e:
Sta Pap For Exp Sta (Idaho)

Station Service Water Pump e: **SSWP**

Station Weather Officer e: **Sta Wea Off**

Stationary Earth Orbit Satellite e: **SEOS**

Stationary Meteorological Satellite e:
SMS

Stationary Orbit e: **SO**

Stationary Remotely Piloted Vehicle e:
SRPV

Statistical Ecology Series e: **Statist
Ecology Ser**

Statistical Methods in Medical Research e:
Stat Methods Med Res

Statistical Notes for Health Planners e:
Stat Notes Health Plann

Statistics in Medicine e: **STAM**, e: **Stat
Med**

Statistics in the Computer Environment e:
STATICE

Statiuhea de Cercetari pentru Plante
Medicinale si Aromatice in: **SCPMA**

Staying Healthy after Fifty e: **SHAF**

Steady-State Natural Circulation e: **SSNC**

Steam and Feedwater Rupture Control
System e: **SFRCS**

Steam and water utility operations e:
S&WUO

steam-cooled light water marine reactor e:
SCLMR

Steam-Generating, Heavy-Water e:
SGHW

Steam-Generating Heavy-Water-Moderated
Reactor e: **SGHWR**

Steam Generator Water Level Control e:
SGWLC

Steam/Water e: **S/W**

Stean-Cooled Heavy Water Reactor e:
SCHWR

Steel Non-Watertight e: **SNWT**

Steel Watertight e: **SWT**

Steerable Hydrophone Army, Nonlinear
Element e: **SHANE**

Steering and Hydroplane e: **S & H**

Steierische Wasserkraft- und Elektrizitäts-
AG d: **STEWEAG**

Steirische Beitraege zur Hydrogeologie d:
Steirische Beitr Hydrogeol

Stellar X-ray polarimeter e: **SXRP**

Stenographer, Medical e: **STT**

Stereo Wave Observation Project e:
SWOP

Sterile Environmental Control Technology
Applications to Medicine e: **SECTAM**

Sterile Nitrogen Atmosphere Processing e:
SNAP

Sterile Water e: **SW**

sterile water for injection e: **SWFI**

Sterling Medical Systems, Inc. e: **SSYS**

Steuerpferdestärke d: **StPS**

Steuerprogrammsystem für ökonomische
Aufgaben, kernspeicherorientiert d:
SOEK

Steuerprogrammsystem für ökonomische
Aufgaben, trommelorientiert d: **SOET**

Steve's Homemade Ice Cream, Inc. e:
STVE

Steward Observatory e: **SO**

Stichting Katholieke
Gerepatriërdenzorganisatie n:
S.K.G.Z.

Stichting Medeleven met Gedupeerden van
Misdrijven n: **MGM**

Stichting tot Bevordering van de
Vakopleiding voor de Handel in
Pluimvee, Wild en Tamme Konijnen n:
VOP

Stichting tot Exploitatie van Mechanische
Reproductierechten der Auteurs n:
STEMRA

Stiftung Europäisches Naturerbe d: **SEN**

Stiftung Gesunde Schweiz jetzt d: **GSJ**

Stiftung Schweizerische Ausbildungsstätte
für Natur und Umweltschutz d: **SANU**

Still Water Bending Moments e: **SWBM**

Still Water Level e: **SWL**

Still Water Surface e: **SWS**

Still Waters Foundation e: **SWF**

Stillwater e: **SWO**

Stillwater National Wildlife Management
Area e: **SNWMA**

Stillwater Public Library, Stillwater, OK
e: **STW**

Stimulated Learning by Automated
Typewriter Environment e: **SLATE**

Stink on Ice e: **SOI**

Stirred Tank Biological Reactor e: **STBS**

Stock Aitken Waterman e: **SAW**

Stock Point Logistics Integrated
Communications Environment Project e:
SPLICE

Stockholm Contributions in Geology e:
Stockh Contrib Geol, e: **Stockholm
Contrib Geol**

Stockholm Environment Institute e: **SEI**

Stockholms Universitet Naturgeografiska
Institutionen r: **SUNI**

Stone Canyon Observatory e: **STC**

Stop-Everything Environmentalists e: **SEE**

Stop Hospital and Medical Errors e:
SHAME

Stop the Ocean Pollution e: **STOP**

Stop This Outrageous Purge e: **STOP**

Storage and Retrieval of Water-Related
Data e: **STORET**

Storage (or Store) Protection Key e: **SPK**

Storage Protect Local Store e: **SPLS**

Storage Protect Memory e: **SPM**

Storage Protect[ion] e: **SP**

Storage Protection e: **STOP**

storage protection register e: **SPR**

Storage Protector e: **STOP**

Stores Management Sea e: **SMS**

storm-relative environmental helicity e:
SREH

storm water e: **st w**

Storm Water Management Model e:
SWMM

Storm Water Monitoring Program e:
SWMP

Storm Water Pollution Prevention Plan e:
SWPPP

Storm Water Retention Basin e: **SWRB**

Stormscale Observations Regional
Measurement Program Data Assimilation
Working Group e: **STORM DAWG**

Stormscale Observations Regional
Measurement Program-Fronts Experiment
Systems Test e: **STORM-FEST**

Stormscale Operational and Research
Meteorology Program e: **STORM**

Stormwater Drain e: **SWD**

Stowarzyszenie Geodetów Polskich P:
SGP

Stowarzyszenie Naukowo-Techniczne
Geodetów Polskich P: **SNTGP**

Strafrechtliches Rehabilitierungsgesetz d:
StRehaG

Strasbourg Medical f: **Strasb Med**

Strategic Advisory Group on the
Environment e: **SAGE**

Strategic Aerospace Division e: **STRAD**,
e: **STRATAD**

Strategic Aerospace Squadron e: **SASq**

Strategic Aerospace Wing e: **SAWg**

Strategic Air Force, Pacific Ocean Area e:
STRAFPOA

Strategic Earth Orbit System e: **SEOS**

Strategic Environmental Assessment
System e: **SEAS**

Strategic Environmental Research and
Development Program e: **SERDP**

Strategic Environmental Research Program
e: **SERP**

Strategic Environmental Restoration
Program e: **SERP**

Strategic Low-Orbit Bomber e: **SLOB**

strategic network environment. e: **SNE**

Strategic Orbit Point e: **SOP**, e: **STOP**

Strategic Orbital System e: **SOS**

Strategic Orbital System Study e: **SOSS**

Strategic Protection Force e: **SPF**

Strategic & Space Systems e: **S&SS**

Strategic Technology Protection Program
e: **STPP**

Strategien zur Regeneration von
stickstoffbelasteten Agrarökosystemen im
mitteldeutschen Schwarzerdegebiet d:
STRAS

Strategy Environmental Research and
Development Plan e: **SERDP**

Stratospheric Observatory for Infrared
Astronomy e: **SOFIA**

Stratospheric Processes and their Role in
Climate e: **SPARC**

Stratospheric Sounding Unit-United
Kingdom Meteorological Office e: **SSU-
UKMO**

Stratospheric Tracers of Atmospheric
Transport e: **STAT**

Stratégie d'observation mondiale intégrée
f: **SOMI**

Stratégie mondiale pour la diversité
biologique f: **SMDB**

Stratégie Nationale de Gestion de
l'Environnement f: **SNGE**

Stream Environment Transport Protocol e:
SETP

Streamline: Australian Water Research e:
WATR

Streamlined approach for environmental
restoration e: **SAFER**

Strength and Health e: **Streng and H**

strengthened for navigation in ice e: **Str.
nav. ice**

Stress-Oriented Hydrogen-Induced
Cracking e: **SOHIC**

Strictly Localized Orbital e: **SLO**

Structural Fire Protection Association e:
SFPA

Structural Geology e: **SG**

Structural Thermal and Meteorite Protection
System e: **STAMPS**

Structure/Airframe for Rotorcraft in
Battlefield Environment e: **STARBET**

Structure of the Earth's Deep Interior e:
SEDI

Structured and Open Environment *e:*
STONE

Structured Learning and Teaching
Environment *e:* **SLATE**

Structures for Orbiting Radio Telescope *e:*
SORT

Student Action Corps for Animals *e:*
SACA

Student Action Voters for Ecology *e:*
SAVE

Student Action Voters for Ecology
[organization] *e:* **SAVE**

Student American Medical Association *e:*
SAMA

Student American Veterinary Medical
Association *e:* **SAVMA**

Student and Employee Health Services *e:*
SEHS

Student Council on Pollution and
Environment *e:* **SCOPE**

Student Health Center *e:* **SHC**

Student Health Organization *e:* **S.H.O.**

Student Medicine *e:* **Stud Med**

Student National Medical Association *e:*
SNMA

Student National Podiatric Medical
Association *e:* **SNPMA**

Student Naval Flight Surgeon *e:* **SNFS**

Student Osteopathic Medical Association
e: **SOMA**

Studenten-Comitee für Umwelt-Ökonomie
d: **SCO**

Studenten-Comitee für Umweltschutz-
Ökonomie, Hochschule St. Gallen *d:*
SCÖ

Studentische Arbeitsgruppe gegen
"Tierverbrauch" im Studium *d:* **SATiS**

Studentische Initiative Geographie *d:*
STING

Students and Practitioners Interested in
Rural Practice, Health, Education,
etcetera *e:* **SPINRPHEX**

Students Aware of the Natural Environment
e: **SANE**

Students Concerned About a Ravaged
Environment [organization] *e:* **SCARE**

Students Concerned With Public Health *e:*
SCWPH

Students for Ecological Action *e:* **SEA**

Students for the Exploration and
Development of Space *e:* **SEDS**

Students' Health and Welfare Centers
Organization *e:* **SHAWCO**

Students Naturally Opposed to Outrageous
Prying *e:* **SNOOP**

Students toward Environmental
Participation *e:* **STEP**

Students Watching Over Our Planet Earth
e: **SWOOPE**

Students Wildly Indignant (about) Nearly
Everything *e:* **SWINE**

Studi di Medicina e Chirurgia dello Sport
i: **Stud Med Chir Sport**

Studi e Ricerche. Divisione Geomineraria.
Comitato Nazionale per le Ricerche
Nucleari *i:* **Stud Ric Div Geomineraria
Com Naz Ric Nucl**

Studi Micenei ed Egeo-Anatolici *i:* **SMEA**

Studi Sassaresi. Sezione 2. Archivio
Bimestrale di Scienze Mediche e Naturali
i: **SSSEAK**, *i:* **Studi Sassar Sez 2**

Studi Trentini di Scienze Naturali *i:* **Studi
Trentini Sci Nat**

Studi Trentini di Scienze Naturali. Acta
Biologica *i:* **STSBDL**

Studi Trentini di Scienze Naturali. Acta
Geologica *i:* **STSGD2**, *i:* **Studi Trentini
Sci Nat Acta Geol**

Studi Trentini di Scienze Naturali. Sezione
B. Biologica *i:* **Studi Trentini Sci Nat
Sez B Biol**

Studia Biologica. Academiae Scientiarum
Hungaricae *l:* **Stud Biol Acad Sci Hung**

Studia Biologica Hungarica *l:* **Stud Biol Hung**

Studia Geographica. Ceskoslovenska
Akademie Ved. Geograficky Ustav (Brno)
c: **Stud Geogr Cesk Akad Ved Geogr
Ustav (Brno)**

Studia Geologica Polonica *l:* **Stud Geol
Pol**

Studia Geologica. Universidad de
Salamanca *s:* **Stud Geol Salamanca**, *s:*
Stud Geol Univ Salamanca

Studia Geomorphologica Carpatho-
Balcanica *l:* **Stud Geomorphol
Carpatho-Balcanica**

Studia Geophysica et Geodaetica *i:*
SGEGA, *l:* **Stud Geoph**, *l:* **Stud
Geophys Geod**

Studia Geophysica et Geodaetica
(Ceskosloven-Akademie Ved) *l:* **Stud
Geophys Geod (Cesk Akad Ved)**

Studia Geotechnica et Mechanica *l:* **Stud
Geotech Mech**, *l:* **Studia Geotech Mech**

Studia Geotechnica. Politechnika
Wroclawaka *P:* **Stud Geotech**

Studia Medica Szegedinensia *l:* **Stud Med
Szeged**, *l:* **Stud Med Szegedinensia**

Studia Microbiologica *l:* **Stud Microbiol**

Studia Societatis Scientiarum Torunensis.
Sectio C (Geographia et Geologia) *l:*
Stud Soc Sci Torun Sect C (Geogr Geol)

Studia Universitatis Babes-Bolyai. Series
Biologia *l:* **Stud Univ Babes-Bolyai
Biol**, *l:* **Stud Univ Babes-Bolyai Ser
Biol**, *l:* **SUBBA**

Studia Universitatis Babes-Bolyai. Series
Geologia-Geographia *e:* **SBBGA**, *l:*
Stud Univ Babes-Bolyai Geol-Geogr

Studia Universitatis Babes-Bolyai. Series
Geologia-Minerologia *l:* **Stud Univ
Babes-Bolyai Ser Geol Minerol**

Studien-Material zur Weiterbildung
Medizinisch-Technischer
Laborassistenten *d:* **Stud Mater
Weiterbild Med Tech Laborassistenten**

Studien zur Umwelt des Neuen Testament
d: **StUmwNT**, *d:* **St UNT**

Studien zur Umwelt des Neuen Testament
[Goettingen] *d:* **SUNT**

Studienblätter für Technik und
Naturwissenschaft *d:* **STN**

Studienbücher Naturwissenschaft und
Technik *d:* **Studienb Naturwiss Tech**

Studiengesellschaft für Alpenwasserkräfte
in Österreich *d:* **INTERALPEN**

Studies and Observations Group *e:* **SOG**

Studies and Reports in Hydrology.
International Association of Hydrological
Sciences-United Nations Educational,
Scientific and Cultural Organization *e:*
Stud Rep Hydrol IAHS-UNESCO

Studies and Research Institute of
Meteorology and Hydrology. Part 2.
Hydrology *e:* **Stud Res Inst Meteorol
Hydrol Part 2**

Studies Chemotherapeutic Institute for
Medical Research [Japan] *e:* **Stud
Chemother Inst Med Res**

Studies from the Geological and
Mineralogical Institute. Tokyo University
of Education *e:* **Stud Geol Mineral Inst
Tokyo Univ Educ**

Studies in Biology *e:* **Stud Biol**

Studies in Comparative International
Development.Georgia Institute of
Technology *e:* **GIT/SCID**

Studies in Ecology *e:* **Stud Ecol**

Studies in Geology (Tulsa, Oklahoma) *e:*
Stud Geol (Tulsa Okla)

Studies in History of Biology *e:* **Stud Hist
Biol**

Studies in History of Medicine *e:* **Stud
Hist Med**

Studies in Human Ecology *e:* **Stud Hum
Ecol**

Studies in Medical Geography *e:* **Stud
Med Geogr**

Studies in Microbiology *e:* **Stud
Microbiol**

Studies in Natural Sciences (Portales, New
Mexico) *e:* **Stud Nat Sci (Portales NM)**

Studies in Philosophy of Medicine *e:* **Stud
Philos Med**

Studies in Plant Ecology *e:* **SPLEE2**, *e:*
Stud Plant Ecol

Studies in the Natural Sciences *e:* **Stud
Nat Sci**

Studies in Tropical Oceanography. Institute
of Marine Science. University of Miami
e: **Stud Trop Oceanogr Inst Mar Sci
Univ Miami**

Studies in Tropical Oceanography (Miami)
e: **Stud Trop Oceanogr (Miami)**

Studies in Vermont Geology *e:* **Stud VT
Geol**

Studies Institute for Medical Research
(Malaya) *e:* **Stud Inst Med Res
(Malaya)**

Studies of Ocean Upper Layers *e:* **SOUL**

Studies of the Earth's Deep Interior *e:*
SEDI

Studies of the Hydrology, Influence and
Variability of the Asian summer monsoon
e: **SHIVA**

Studies on the Neotropical Fauna and
Environment *e:* **Stud Neotrop Fauna
Environ**

Studii de Geotekhnica. Fundatii si
Constructii Hidrotehnice *c:* **Stud Geoteh
Fund Constr Hidroteh**

Studland Heath National Nature Reserve *e:*
SHNNR

Study Group on Environmental Monitoring
e: **SGEM**

Study Group on Topoclimatological
Investigation and Mapping *e:* **SGTIM**

Study of Accreditation of Selected Health
Educational Programs *e:* **SASHEP**

Study of Critical Environmental Problems
[Massachussettes Institute of Technology]
e: **SCEP**

Study of Environmental Quality
Information Programs *e:* **SEQUIP**

Study of Lunar Orbiter Photographic
Evaluation *e:* **SLOPE**

Study of Man's Impact on the Climate *e:*
SMIC

Study of/on Surgical Services for/in the United States [of the American College of Surgeons] e: **SOSSUS**

Study of One-Atmosphere Manned Underwater Structures e: **SOAMUS**

Study of Protection e: **STOP**

Study of the Last Interglacial Climate and Environment e: **SLICE**

Study of the Transfer of Particulate and Dissolved Phases from Southern South America to the Southwest Atlantic Ocean e: **PARAT**

Study of Tropical Oceans in Climate Models e: **STOIC**

Study on Sea-Air Exchanges e: **SEAREX**

Study on the Indirect and DIrect Climate influences of Anthropogenic Trace gas Emissions e: **SINDICATE**

Study Towards Autonomous Manned Space flight e: **STEAMS**

Sturgeon. Bankrupt Acts e: **Sturg BL**

Stuttgarter Beitraege zur Naturkunde d: **Stutt Beitr Naturk**

Stuttgarter Beiträge zur Naturkunde d: **Stuttg. Beitr. Nat.kd.**, d: **Stuttg Beitr Naturkd**

Stuttgarter Beiträge zur Naturkunde. Serie A (Biologie) d: **Stuttg Beitr Naturkd Ser A (Biol)**

Stuttgarter Beiträge zur Naturkunde. Serie B (Geologie und Palaeontologie) d: **Stuttg Beitr Naturkd Ser B (Geol Palaeontol)**

Stuttgarter Beiträge zur Naturkunde. Serie C Allgemeinverständliche Aufsätze d: **Stuttg Beitr Naturk Ser C Allg Aufsaetze**

Stuttgarter Geographische Studien d: **Stuttg Geogr Stud**

Style Manual for Biological Journals e: **SMBJ**

Státní Hydrologický a Meteorologický Ústav c: **SHMÚ**

Státní Hydrometeorologický Ústav c: **SHÚ**

Státní Meteorologický Ústav c: **SMÚ**

Státní Výzkumný Ústav Rybářský a Hydrobiologický c: **SVÚRH**

Státní Výzkumný Ústav Rybářský a Hydrologický c: **RÚH**

Státní Ústav Hydrologický T.G. Masaryka c: **SÚH**

Státní Ústav Meteorologický c: **SÚM**

Sub-Antarctic Surface Water e: **SAASW**

Sub-committee on Animal Health Laboratory Standards e: **SCAHLS**

Sub-Committee on Animal Welfare e: **SCAW**

Sub-Committee on Veterinary Public Health e: **SCVPH**

Sub-Dirección de Rehabilitación de Tierras s: **SUDRET**

Sub- group of Experts on IGOSS Basic Observations Network Design e: **IBOND**

sub-nanosecond bipolar isolation lateral quaoxide e: **SUBILO**

Sub-Orbital Mission e: **SOM**

Sub-Tropical Mode Water e: **STMW**

subantarctic mode water e: **SAMW**

Subcommission for Tectonic Maps of the Commission for the Geological Map of the World e: **STMCGMW**

Subcommittee on Animal Welfare e: **SCAW**

Subcommittee on Atmospheric Research e: **SAR**

Subcommittee on Geographical Names and Nomenclature of Ocean Bottom Features e: **SCGN**

Subcommittee on Natural Resources e: **SNRIM**

Subcontractor Safety and Environmental Evaluation e: **SSEE**

Subgroup on Ocean Satellites and Remote Sensing e: **OSRS**

Submarine Chaser [Hydrofoil] e: **PCSH**

Submarine Cold-weather and Arctic Material Program e: **SCAMP**

Submarine Medical Center e: **SMC**, e: **SUBMEDCEN**

Submarine Medical Research Laboratory e: **SMRL**

Submarine Mounted Underwater Tracking System e: **SMUTS**

Submarine Ocean Systems Underwater Surveillance e: **SOSUS**

Submarine Oceanographic Observation Program e: **SOOP**

Submarine Water Reactor e: **SWR**

Submedicus l: **S.M**

Submerged Caracterized Sea Floor Mapping Project e: **SCAMP**

Submersible Electric Prototype Ocean Dredge e: **SEPOD**

Submersible Oriented Platform for Deep Ocean Sediment Studies e: **SOPDOSS**

Submersible Underwater Pipeline Repair Apparatus e: **SUPRA**

Submersible Wastewater Pump Association e: **SWPA**

Submersible Water Pump e: **SWP**

Submersible [Water] Quality Monitor e: **sq m**

Suborbital Sequence e: **SOS**

Suborbital Tank Separation e: **SOTS**

Subpolar Intermediate Water e: **SIW**

subpolar mode water e: **SPMW**

Subroutines for Natural Actuarial Processing e: **SNAP**

Subsidia Medica l: **Subsidia Med**

Subsidiary Agreement on Water e: **SAW**

Subsonic Hovering Armament Direction & Observation Window e: **SHADOW**

Subsonic Sea Skimmer e: **SSS**

Substance Abuse and Mental Health Data Archive e: **SAMHDA**

Substance Abuse and Mental Health Services Administration e: **SAMHSA**

Substitute [for] Natural Gas e: **SNG**

Subsurface Geological Laboratory, Regina, Saskatchewan e: **SRSG**

Subsurface Geology e: **SG**

Subsurface Ocean Area e: **SSOA**

Subsystem Operation (in Spacelab) e: **SSO**

Subsystem Storage Protection e: **SSSP**

Subsystem Terminal on Spacelab e: **SST**

Subtransfer Earth Orbit e: **SEO**

Subtropical Atlantic Climate Studies (or Study) e: **STACS**

Subtropical Indian Mode Water e: **SIMW**

subtropical underwater e: **STUW**

Subtropical Water e: **STW**

Succinic Dehydrogenase e: **SDH**, e: **SDHase**

succinic dehydrogenase activity e: **sda**

Succinic Semialdehyde Dehydrogenase e: **SSADH**

Succinodehydrogenase e: **SUDH**

Sud Medical et Chirurgical e: **Sud Med Chir**

Sudan Geological Survey Department. Bulletin e: **Sudan Geol Surv Dep Bull**

Sudan Journal of Veterinary Science and Animal Husbandry e: **Sudan J Vet Sci Anim Husb**

Sudan Medical Corps e: **SMC**

Sudan Medical Journal e: **Sud Med J**

Sudan Medical Research Laboratories e: **SMRL**

Sudbury Neutrino Observatory e: **SNO**

Sudden Changes in the Integrated Intensity of Atmospherics e: **SCIIA**

sudden enhancement of atmospherics e: **SEA**

Sudder Dewanny Adawlut cases, North West Frontier e: **S.A.D.N.W.F.**

SUDENE Boletim do Recursos Naturais p: **SUDENE Bol Recur Nat**

Sudhoffs Archiv für Geschichte der Medizin und der Naturwissenschaften e: **SAGMN**

Suidwest-Afrika Water en Elektrisiteitskorporasie A: **SWAWEK**

Sukzinatdehydrogenase d: **SDH**, d: **SUDH**

Sukzinatdehydrogenaseaktivität d: **SDA**

sulfated hydrogenated castor oil e: **SHCO**

sulfatierte Mukopolysaccharide d: **SMPS**

sulfonated hydrogenated castor oil e: **shco**

Sulfuric acid/hydrogen Peroxide Mixture e: **SPM**

Sullom Voe Environmental Advisory Group e: **SVEAG**

Sulzer Literaturverteilung und Sortierung d: **SULIS**

Sumerian Animal Proverbs e: **SAP**

Sumitomo Bulletin of Industrial Health e: **Sumitomo Bull Ind Health**

Summa Medical Corp. e: **SUMMA**

Summa Medical Corp l: **SUMA**

Summary of Progress Geological Survey Division (Nigeria) e: **Summ Prog Geol Surv Div (Nigeria)**

Summary of Synoptic Meteorological Observations e: **SSMO**

Summer fresh water load line [timber] e: **LF**

Summit Health Ltd. e: **SUMH**

Sun-Earth Observatory and Climatology Satellite e: **SEOCS**

Sun Ice Ltd. e: **SIH**

Sun-Orbiting Relativity Experiment Satellite e: **SOREL**

Sun Photometer Earth Atmosphere Measurements-2 e: **SPEAM-2**

Sun-Planet-Earth e: **SPE**

Sun-Protection Factor e: **SPF**

Sun Protection Required e: **SPR**

Sun Vehicle Earth e: **SVE**

Sundri (heritiera) Timber e: **SUN Timber**

Sunflower Space Power System e: **SSPS**

Sunnybrook Medical Centre, Toronto e: **SMC**

Sunphotometer Earth Atmospheric Measurements e: **SPEAM**

Sunrise Medical, Inc. e: **SNMD**

Sun's Visual Integrated Environment for Workstations e: **SUNVIEW**

Sunshine Coast Environment Council e: **SCEC**

Suomen Geoteknillinen Yhdistys *F:* **SGY**

Super Natural Atiitude Kinctic Enhancement *e:* **SNAKE**

Super Ocean Carrier Conference *e:* **SOCC**

Super Orbit Entry *e:* **SOE**

Super-Orbital Reentry Test Integrated Environment *e:* **SORTIE**

Super Power Water Boiler *e:* **SUPO**

Super VGA Protected Mode Interface *e:* **SVPMI**

Supercircular Orbital Reentry Test Integrated Environment *e:* **SORTIE**

supercooled liquid water *e:* **SLW**

Supercritical Hydrogen *e:* **SCHO**, *e:* **SH2**

Supercritical Water Oxidation *e:* **SCW**, *e:* **SCWO**, *e:* **SWO**

supercritical water reactor *e:* **SCWR**

superdelicious *e:* **supdel**

Superfluid Helium On-Orbit Transfer *e:* **SHOOT**

Superfund Public Health Evaluation Manual *e:* **SPHEM**

Superheat Boiling Water Reactor *e:* **SBWR**

Superintendência de Servicos Medicos *p:* **SUSEME**

Superintendencia de Servicos Medicos *s:* **SUSEME**

Superintendent, Naval Observatory *e:* **SUPTNAVOBSY**

Superintending Sea Transport Officer *e:* **SSTO**

Superior Geocentric Conjunction *e:* **SGC**

Superior Orbital Fissure *e:* **SOF**

Superior Processing Natural Rubber *e:* **SP-NR**

Supernatural Kinetic Enhancement *e:* **SNAKE**

Supersonic Sea Skimmer *e:* **SSS**

Supersonic Sea-Skimming Target *e:* **SSST**

Supersynchronous Transfer Orbit *e:* **STO**

Supervisao de Producao Animal *p:* **SPA**

Supervisao de Recursos Naturais Renovais *p:* **SRNR**

Supervisory and Informations System for local and remote Areas *e:* **SISA**

Supervisory Immigration Patrol Inspector [Immigration and Naturalization Service] *e:* **SIPI**

Supervisory Monitor and Remote Telemetry *e:* **SMART**

Supplement Geophysics *e:* **Suppl Geophys**

Supplement to Collcction of Scientific Works. Charles University Faculty of Medicine. Hradec Kralove *e:* **Suppl Collect Sci Works Charles Univ Fac Med Hradec Kralove**

Supplemental Environmental Impact Statement *e:* **SEIS**

Supplemental Environmental Project *e:* **SEP**

Supplemental Health Manpower Shortage Area Placement Opportunity List *e:* **SHPOL**

Supplemental Medical Report *e:* **SMR**

Supplemental Natural Gas *e:* **SNG**

Supplemental Weather Service Location *e:* **SWSL**

Supplementary Airway Weather Reports *e:* **SAWRS**

Supplementary Aviation Weather Observatories *e:* **SAWRS**

Supplementary Aviation Weather Reporting Station *e:* **SAWRS**, *e:* **SWARS**

Supplementary Aviation Weather Reporting System *e:* **SAWRS**

Supplementary Medical Insurance Program *e:* **SMI**

Supplementary Meteorological Office *e:* **SMO**

Supplementary Protection System *e:* **SPS**

Supplemento alle Ricerche di Biologia della Selvaggina *i:* **Suppl Ric Biol Selvaggina**

Supplementum Acta Universitatis Carolinae Biologica *l:* **Suppl Acta Univ Carol Biol**

Support Air Observation *e:* **SAO**

Support for the Analysts' File Environment *e:* **SAFE**

Support Kit Overhead Protection *e:* **SKOP**

Support of Environmental Requirements Cloud Analysis and Archive *e:* **SERCAA**

Support Package for Aerospace Computer Emulation *e:* **SPACE**

Support Program for Remote Entry of Alphanumeric Displays *e:* **SPREAD**

Supporting Environment for ODP *e:* **SE-ODP**

Suppressor Environment Characterizer *e:* **SEC**

Suppressor Grid Orbitron Gauge *e:* **SGOG**

Supraorbital *e:* **SO**, *e:* **SO**

Suprathermal Plasma Investigation of Cometary Environments *e:* **SPICE**

Supreme Allied Commander Atlantic Ocean *e:* **SACAO**

Sureface-to-Underwater-Naval *e:* **SUW-N**

Surf Observation Report *e:* **SUROB**

Surface Aerospace Technology *e:* **SAT**

Surface Airways Observation *e:* **SAO**

Surface and Atmospheric Radiation Budget *e:* **SARB**

surface and underwater ship-intercept equipment *e:* **susie**

Surface and Underwater Target *e:* **SUT**

Surface-Atmosphere Processes in Hilly Terrain *e:* **SAPHIR**

Surface Automated Meteorological System *e:* **SAMS**

Surface Automated Meteorological Systems *e:* **SAMS**

Surface Aviation Observation *e:* **SAO**

Surface Aviation weather report *e:* **SA**

Surface Effect Fast Sea Lift Ship *e:* **SFS**

Surface Effects Ship of Ocean Commerce *e:* **SESOC**

Surface Environment and Mining Program *e:* **SEALS**

Surface Environment and Mining [Program] *e:* **SEAM**

Surface Environmental Sample Container *e:* **SESC**

Surface Heat Budget of the Arctic Ocean *e:* **SHEBA**

Surface-launched Underwater Guided Weapon *e:* **SUGW**

Surface Launched Underwater Transponder Target *e:* **SLUTT**

Surface Layer Atmospheric Chemistry Experiment *e:* **SLACE**

Surface Meteorological Observation System *e:* **SMOS**

Surface Meteorological Observing Station *e:* **SMOS**

Surface Meteorology *e:* **SMET**

Surface Ocean-Lower Atmosphere Study *e:* **SOLAS**

Surface-to-Underwater *e:* **S/U**

Surface-to-Underwater Missile *e:* **SUM**

Surface to Underwater Missile Launcher *e:* **SUWN-1**

Surface-Underwater Ship Intercept Equipment *e:* **SUSIE**

Surface Vegetation-Atmosphere Transfer model *e:* **SVAT**

Surface Vegetation Atmosphere Transfer Scheme *e:* **SVATS**

Surface Water *e:* **SW**

Surface Water Assessment Model for Back Calculating Reductions in Abiotic Hazardous Waste *e:* **SARAH**

Surface Water Automatic Computer *e:* **SURWAC**

Surface Water Drain *e:* **SWD**

Surface Water Improvement and Management *e:* **SWIM**

Surface Water Quality Bureau *e:* **SWQB**

Surface Water Retention Index *e:* **SWRI**

Surface Water Supply Index *e:* **SWSI**

Surface Water Treatment Rule *e:* **SWTR**

Surge Protective Device[s] *e:* **SPD**

Surge Protector *e:* **SP**

surge voltage protection *e:* **SVP**

surge voltage protector *e:* **SVP**

Surgeon *e:* **S**, *e:* **Sg**, *e:* **SGN**, *e:* **Surg[.]**, *e:* **SURGN**

Surgeon-Captain *e:* **SC**

Surgeon Captain *e:* **Sg C**

Surgeon-Commander *e:* **SC**, *e:* **Sg Cr**

Surgeon-Commander *e:* **Sur Cdr**

Surgeon-Commander *e:* **Surg Cdr**

Surgeon Commander *e:* **Surg Comdr**

Surgeon General *e:* **SG**, *e:* **SG/S.G.**, *e:* **SURGEN**, *e:* **Surg Gen**

Surgeon General Bureau *e:* **SGB**

Surgeon General of the Navy *e:* **SGN**

Surgeon General Requirements *e:* **SG REQ**

Surgeon-General's Office *e:* **S.G.O.**

Surgeon-in-Chief *e:* **S-in-C**

Surgeon Lieutenant *e:* **Surg Lt**

Surgeon Lieutenant-Commander *e:* **Sg L Cr**, *e:* **SLC**, *e:* **Surg Lt Cdr**

Surgeon Lieutenant Commander *e:* **Surg Lt Comdr**

Surgeon Major *e:* **SM**, *e:* **Surg Maj**, *e:* **SURGMAS**

Surgeon of the Air Force *e:* **SAF**

Surgeon [or Surgery or Surgical] *e:* **SURG**

Surgeon Rear-Admiral *e:* **Sg RA**, *e:* **SRA**

Surgeon Vice Admiral *e:* **Sg VA**

Surgeon's Assistant *e:* **SA**

Surgeon's Certificate of Disability *e:* **SCD**

surgery, gynecology and obstetrics *e:* **sgo**

Surgery, Gynecology and Obstetrics *e:* **SGOBA**, *e:* **Surg Gynec and Obst**, *e:* **Surg Gynecol Obstet**, *e:* **Surg Gyn Ob**

Surgery, Gynecology and Obstetrics with International Abstracts of Surgery *e:* **Surg. Gynecol. Obstet.**

Surveillance Alarm & Protection Intelligence EW Naval System *e:* **SAPIENS**

Surveillance Alarm & Protection, Intelligence EW Naval Systems *e:* **SAPIENS**

Surveillance and Missile Observation
Satellite *e:* **SAMOS**

Surveillance and Missile Observation
System *e:* **SAMOS**

Surveillance du système climatique *f:* **SSC**

Surveillance, Target Acquisition, and Night
Observation Master Plan *e:* **STANMAP**

Surveillance, Target Acquisition, and Night
Observation Systems Manager
[Department of the Army] *e:* **STANSM**

Surveillance, Target Acquisition and Night
Observation[s] *e:* **STANO**

Surveillance, Target Acquisition, Night
Observation and Counter-Surveillance *e:*
STANOC

Survey Notes Utah Geological and Mineral
Survey *e:* **Surv Notes Utah Geol Miner
Surv**

Survey of Biological Progress *e:* **Surv Biol
Prog**

Survey Paper. Horace Lamb Centre for
Oceanographical Research. Flinders
University of South Australia *e:* **Surv
Pap Horace Lamb Centre Oceanogr
Res**

Surveying and Mapping Society of Georgia
e: **SAMSOG**

Surveys, Mapping and Remote Sensing
Sector *e:* **SMRS**

Survivable Collective Protection Shelter *e:*
SCPS

Survivable Collective Protection System *e:*
SCPS

Survivable Collective Protection System-
Medical *e:* **SCPS-M**

Susitna Hydro Studies *e:* **SUHS**

Sustainable Environment and Natural
Resources Management activity *e:*
SENREM

Sustainable Environment Fund *e:* **SEF**

Sustainable Land and Water Resources
Management Committee *e:* **SLWRMC**

Sustained Medication *e:* **SM**

Sustained Naval Aviation Operations in
Chemical, Biological and Radiological
Warfare Conditions *e:* **SNAO/CWC**

Svanhovd Environmental Centre *e:* **SEC**

Svensk Geografisk Årsbok *r:* **S.G.Å.**

Svensk Geografisk Arsbok *r:* **Svensk
Geog Arsbok**

Svensk Naturvetenskap *r:* **Sven
Naturvetensk**, *r:* **SVNAB**

Svenska Föreningen för Medicinsk Fysik
och Teknik *r:* **MFT**

Svenska Geofysiska Föreningen *r:* **SGF**

Svenska Geologiska Undersökning *r:* **SGU**

Svenska Geotekniska Föreningen *r:* **SGF**

Svenska Hotell-Portier-Föreningen *r:*
SHPF

Svenska Hydrografisk-Biologiska
Kommissionens Skrifter. Ny Serie.
Biologi *r:* **Sven Hydrogr Biol Komm
Skr Ny Ser Biol**

Svenska Laser-Medicinska Sällskapet *r:*
SLMS

Svenska Naturskyddsföreningen *r:* **SNF**

Svenska Sällskapet för Antropologi och
Geografi *r:* **SSAG**

Sverdrup Measure of water transport *e:* **Sv**

Sveriges Fältbiologiska Ungdomsförening
r: **SFU**

Sveriges Geologiska Undersoekning *r:*
SVGU

Sveriges Geologiska Undersoekning.
Arsbok *r:* **Sver Geol Unders Arsb**

Sveriges Geologiska Undersoekning.
Arsbok. Serie C. Avhandlingar och
Uppsatser *r:* **Sver Geol Unders Arsb
Ser C Avb Uppsatser**, *r:* **Sveriges Geol
Unders Ser C**

Sveriges Geologiska Undersökning *r:*
SGU

Sveriges Lantbruksuniversitet Institutionen
foer Mikrobiologi. Rapport *r:* **Sver
Lantbruksuniv Inst Mikrobiol Rapp**

Sveriges Meteorologiska och Hydrologiska
Institut *r:* **SMHI**

Sveriges Natur *r:* **Sver Nat**

Sveriges Natur Arsbok *r:* **Sver Nat Arsb**

Sveriges Naturist Förbund *r:* **SNF**

Sveriges Naturvetareförbund *r:* **SN**

Sveriges Yngre Medicinska Teoretiker *r:*
S.Y.M.T.

Sveriges Yngre Naturvetares Förening *r:*
SYNF

Svetska Meteorološka Organizacija *se:*
SMO

SWAGMAN program on water tables and
their management *e:* **OPTIONS**

Swan Lake National Wildlife Refuge *e:*
SLNWR

Swaziland. Annual Report. Geological
Survey and Mines Department *e:*
**Swaziland Annu Rep Geol Surv Mines
Dep**

Swaziland. Geological Survey and Mines
Department. Annual Report *e:*
**Swaziland Geol Surr Mines Dep Annu
Rep**

Sweden. Geologiska Undersoekning. Serie
Ae. Geologiska Kartblad i Skala 1:50\000
r: **Swed Geol Unders Ser Ae Geol
Kartbl 1:50000**

Sweden Geologiska Undersoekning. Serie C
r: **Swed Geol Unders Ser C**

Sweden. Geologiska Undersoekning. Serie
Ca. Avhandlingar och Uppsatser *r:* **Swed
Geol Unders Ser Ca Avh Uppsatser**

Swedish Aerospace Industries Association
e: **SAI**

Swedish Board for Space Activities *e:*
SBSA

Swedish Council of Environmental
Information *e:* **SCEI**

Swedish Council on Technology
Assessment in Health Care *e:* **SBU**

Swedish Deep Sea Expedition Reports *e:*
Swedish Deep-Sea Expedition Repts

Swedish Environment Engineering Society
e: **SEES**

Swedish Environmental Research Index *e:*
SERIX

Swedish Environmental Research Institute
e: **IVL**

Swedish Geotechnical Institute *e:* **SGI**

Swedish Geotechnical Institute.
Proceedings *e:* **Swed Geotech Inst Proc**

Swedish Geotechnical Institute Report *e:*
Swed Geotech Inst Rep

Swedish Institute for Geographic
Information Technology *e:* **SIGIT**

Swedish Lloyd North Sea *e:* **SLNS**

Swedish Medical Literature *e:* **SWEMED**

Swedish National Board of Health and
Welfare *e:* **SNBHW**

Swedish National Committee of the
International Association on Water
Pollution Research and Control *e:*
SNCIAWPRC

Swedish National Space Board *e:* **SNSB**

Swedish Natural Science Research Council
e: **SNSRC**

Swedish Polar Research *e:* **SWPR**

Swedish Polar Research Secretariat *e:*
SPRS

Swedish Radiation Protection Institute *e:*
SSI

Swedish Society Against Painful
Experiments on Animals *e:* **SSAPEA**

Swedish Space Corporation *e:* **SSC**

Swedish Space Research Committee *e:*
SSRC

Swedish University of Agricultural
Sciences. Department of Microbiology.
Report *e:* **Swed Univ Agric Sci Dep
Microbiol Rep**

Swedish University of Agricultural
Sciences. Reports in Forest Ecology and
Soils *e:* **Swed Univ Agric Sci Rep For
Ecol For Soils**

Swedish Wildlife Research (Viltrevy) *e:*
Swed Wildl Res (Viltrevy)

Swedish Wildlife Research Viltrevy *e:*
SWRVDT

Sweetwater City-County Library,
Sweetwater *e:* **TxSw**

Sweetwater Mountains of California and
Nevada *e:* **Sweetwaters**

Swiatowa Organizacja Meteorologiczna *P:*
SOM

Swim the Ontario Waterways *e:* **STOW**

Swing Rate Discriminatur *e:* **SRD**

Swiss Academy of Medical Sciences *e:*
SAMS

Swiss Association for Space Technology
e: **SAST**

Swiss Journal of Hydrology *e:* **Swiss J
Hydrol**

Swiss Meteorological Institute *e:* **SMI**

Swiss National Committee of the
International Association on Water
Pollution Research and Control *e:*
SNCIAWPRC

Swiss Society of Tropical Medicine and
Parasitology *e:* **SSTMP**

Swiss Wildlife Information Service *e:*
SWIS

Switched-Access Remote Test System *e:*
SARTS

Sydenham Society, Lexicon of Medicine &
Allied Sciences *e:* **Syd. Soc. Lex.**

Sydney Ocean Meeting Point *e:* **SOMP**

Sydney University Medical Journal *e:*
Syd[ney] Univ Med J

Sydney University. Medical Journal *e:* **Syd
Univ Med J**

Sydney Water Board. Journal *e:* **Sydney
Water Bd J**, *e:* **Syd Wat Bd J**

Sydsvenska Medicinhistoriska Saellskapets
Arsskrift *r:* **Sydsven Medicinhist**

Symbol for magnetic polar *e:* **J**

Symbolic Application Debugging
Environment *e:* **SADE**

Symbolic Programming Environment *e:*
SPE

Symbolic Utilities Revenue Environment
e: **SURE**

Symmetrix Remote Data Facility *e:* **SRDF**

Symmetry, Orbitals and Spectra *e:* **SOS**

Symposia Biologica Hungarica *e:* **Symp Biol Hung**

Symposia for Cell Biology [Japan] *e:* **Symp Cell Biol**

Symposia Genetica et Biologica Italica *i:* **SGBIA**, *l:* **Symp Genet Biol Ital**

Symposia International Society for Cell Biology *e:* **Symp Int Soc Cell Biol**

Symposia Medica Hoechst *e:* **Symp Med Hoechst**

Symposia Series in Immunobiological Standardization *e:* **Symp Ser Immunobiol Stand**

Symposia. Society for Developmental Biology *e:* **Symp Soc Dev Biol**

Symposia Society for Experimental Biology *e:* **Symp Soc Exp Biol**

Symposia. Society for the Study of Human Biology *e:* **Symp Soc Study Hum Biol**

Symposium. British Society for Developmental Biology *e:* **SBSBDV**, *e:* **Symp Br Soc Dev Biol**

Symposium International Union of Biological Sciences Proceedings *e:* **Symp Int Union Biol Sci Proc**

Symposium of the Engineering Aspects of Magnetohydrodynamics *e:* **SEAM**

Symposium on Computer Application in Medical Care *e:* **SCAMC**

Symposium on Computer Applications in Medical Care *e:* **SCAMC**

Symposium on Ecological Research in Humid Tropics Vegetation *e:* **Symp Ecol Res Humid Trop Vegtn**

Symposium on Engineering Geology and Soils Engineering. Proceedings *e:* **Symp Eng Geol Soils Eng Proc**

Symposium on the Application of Geophysics to Engineering and Environmental Problems *e:* **SAGEEP**

Symposium on the Chemistry of Natural Products. Symposium Papers *e:* **Symp Chem Nat Prod Symp Pap**

Symposium on the Engineering Aspects of Magnetohydrodynamics *e:* **SEALS**

Symposium Papers. Symposium on the Chemistry of Natural Products *e:* **Symp Pap Symp Chem Nat Prod**

Symposium. Society for General Microbiology *e:* **Symp Soc Gen Microbiol**

Symptom Medication Diary *e:* **SMD**

Symptom Pattern Observation Technique *e:* **SPOT**

Symptoms, Observations, Assessment, Plan *e:* **SOAP**

Synchrnnous Remote Control *e:* **SRC**

Synchronous-altitude Meteorological Satellite *e:* **SMS**

Synchronous Continuous Orbital Three-dimensional Tracking *e:* **SCOTT**

Synchronous Earth Observation Satellite *e:* **SEOS**

Synchronous Earth Observatory Satellite *e:* **SEOS**

Synchronous Earth Orbiting Shuttle *e:* **SEOS**

Synchronous Equatorial Orbit *e:* **SEO**

Synchronous Equatorial Orbit[er] *e:* **SEO**

Synchronous Meteorological Satellite/Geostationary Operational Environmental Satellite *e:* **SMS/GOES**

Synchronous Meteorological Test Satellite *e:* **SMTS**

Synchronous, Operational Meteorological Satellite *e:* **SOMS**

Synchronous Orbit Communication Relay *e:* **SOCR**

Synchronous Orbit Data Relay Satellite *e:* **SODRS**

Synchronous-Orbit Particle Analyzer *e:* **SOPA**

Synchronous Orbit Satellite *e:* **SOS**

Synchronous Orbital Resonance *e:* **SOR**

Synchronous [orbiting] Communication Satellite *e:* **SYNCOM Satellite**

Synchronous-Orbiting Communications Satellite *e:* **SYNCOM**

Synchronous Orbiting Solar Observatory *e:* **SOSO**

Synchronous Orbiting Tracking Stations *e:* **SOTS**

Synchrotron Orbital Radiation *e:* **SOR**

Synchrotron Orbital Radiation Technology *e:* **SORTEC**

Syndicat de l'Industrie Laitière de l'Est *f:* **SIL**

Syndicat des Constructeurs Français de Matériel pour la Transformation des Matières Plastiques et du Caoutchouc *f:* **MATFORM**

Syndicat des Constructeurs Français de Matériel pour le Caoutchouc et les Matières Plastiques *f:* **SYMACAP**, *f:* **SYMCAP**

Syndicat des Detaillants en Produits Laitiers *f:* **SDP**

Syndicat des Fabricants d'Aliments Composés pour l'alimenation animale *f:* **SYFAC**

Syndicat des Fabricants d'Aliments Composés pour l'Alimentation Animale *f:* **SYFAC**

Syndicat des Fabricants de Produits Laitiers Frais *f:* **SFPLT**

Syndicat des Fabricants d'Émulsions Routières de Bitume *f:* **SFERB**

Syndicat des Importateurs-Exportateurs de Matières Premières Aromatiques *f:* **SIEMPA**

Syndicat des Industries de l'Éctronique[s] Médicale et de la Radiologie *f:* **SEMRAD**

Syndicat des Mines et de la Géologie du Togo *f:* **SYMIGETO**

Syndicat des Postiers du Canada *f:* **SPC**

Syndicat des Professeurs d'Écoles Normales *f:* **SPEN**

Syndicat des Propriétaires Forestiers de France *f:* **SPFF**

Syndicat des Récoltants et Commerçants des Graines de Semences d'Essences Forestières *f:* **SSF**

Syndicat du Commerce d'Exportation de Produits Laitiers et Avicoles *f:* **SYLAITEX**

Syndicat Départemental des Transports Routiers *f:* **S.D.T.R.**

Syndicat Général des Constructeurs d'Équipements pour la Chimie, les Matières Plastiques et le Caoutchouc, l'Alimentation et pour Industries Diverses *f:* **SYGECAM**

Syndicat Médical *f:* **SM**

Syndicat Médical Français *f:* **S.M.F.**

Syndicat National de Décolletage *f:* **SND**

Syndicat National de l'Exploitation d'équipments Thermiques et de la Génie Climatique *f:* **SNEC**

Syndicat National de l'Industrie et des Technologies Médicales *f:* **SNITEM**

Syndicat National des Adjuvants pour Bétons et Mortiers *f:* **SNABM**

Syndicat National des Armateurs de Chalutiers de Grande Pêche *f:* **SNACGP**

Syndicat National des Constructeurs Francais de Materiel d'Equipement Laitier Industriel/F *f:* **SYCOMEL**

Syndicat National des Constructeurs Français de Matériel et Équipement Laitier Industriel *f:* **SYCOMEL**

Syndicat National des Courtiers d'Assurance et de Réassurances *f:* **SNCAR**

Syndicat National des Dénaturateurs d'Alcol *f:* **SNDA**

Syndicat National des Experts Forestiers Patentes *f:* **SNEFP**

Syndicat National des Fabricants de Produits Laitiers Frais *f:* **SYNDIFRAIS**

Syndicat National des Gynécologues Obstétriciens de France *f:* **SYNGOF**

Syndicat national des Importateurs d'Équipements pour les Industries Papetiéres et Graphiques *f:* **SIPAG**

Syndicat National des Industrielle de la Nutrition Animale *f:* **SNIA**

Syndicat National des Industriels de l'Alimentation Animale *f:* **SNIA**

Syndicat National des Industriels Exportateurs Importateurs de Produits Laitiers *f:* **EXI**

Syndicat National des Industries de Récupérations Animales *f:* **SNIRA**

Syndicat National des Industries Transformateurs de Vanille et des Éléments Aromatiques Naturels au Chimiques *f:* **SITVAR**

Syndicat National des Manufacturers d'Articles de Protection *f:* **SYNAMAP**

Syndicat National des Producteurs de Mortiers Industriels *f:* **SNPMI**

Syndicat National des Producteurs, Ramasseurs et Collecteurs de Plantes Médicinales Aromatiques et Industrielles *f:* **SNPRC[P]M**

Syndicat National des Professeurs des Écoles Normales [d'instituteurs] *f:* **SNPEN**

Syndicat National des Régérateurs de Matières Plastiques *f:* **SNRMP**

Syndicat National des Travailleurs des Mines, des Hydrocarbures et de la Géologie *f:* **SYNTRAMHYG**

Syndicat National des Écoles Privées d'Informatique et d'Automatique *f:* **SNEPIA**

Syndicat Nationale des Courtiers Maritimes de France *f:* **SNCMF**

Syndicat Professionel des Amateurs de Navigation Côtière *f:* **SPANCI**

Syndicat Professionnel des Producteurs Auxiliaires de l'Industrie Laitiere *f:* **SPPAIL**

Syndicat Togolais du Personnel de la Météorologie *f:* **STPM**

Syndicats Médicaux *f:* **S.M.**

Syndikaat voor de Verdediging van de Landbouwbelangen *n:* **S.V.L.B.**

Synoptic and Climatological Automatic Weather Stations *e:* **SCAWS**

Synoptic Atmospheric Imager *e:* **SAI**

Synoptic Meteorological Sounding *e:* **SMS**

Synoptic Ocean Prediction Study *e:* **SYNOPS**

Synoptic Oceanographic Data Acquisition System *e:* **SODAS**

Synoptic Oceanographic Data Assimilation System *e:* **SODAS**

Synoptic Weather Network *e:* **SWN**

Synthesized Hydrocarbon Fluid *e:* **SHF**

Synthetic Aperture Radar for Sea Studies *e:* **SEASAR**

Synthetic Environment Data Representation and Interface Specification *e:* **SEDRIS**

Synthetic Environment Rqmts Concept Evaluation & Synthesis *e:* **SERCES**

Synthetic Environments *e:* **SE**

Synthetic Exercise Environment *e:* **SEE**

Synthetic Natural Gas *e:* **SNG**

Synthetic-Natural Hybrid Coding *e:* **SNHC**

Synthetic Ocean Water *e:* **SOW**

Synthetic Operating Environment *e:* **SOE**

Synthetisches Naturgas *d:* **SNG**

System Analysis of Manned Space Operations *e:* **SAMSON**

System Coordination for SAGE [Semi-Automatic Ground Environment] Computer Program *e:* **SCSCP**

System der automatisierten Projektierung *d:* **SAPr**

System der Implementiersprachen *d:* **SIL**

System des Geophysikalischen Beratungsdienstes der Bundeswehr *d:* **SysGeophys-BDBw**

System Development and Maintenance Environment Software *e:* **SDME**

System Development Environment *e:* **SDE**

System, Environment and Threat Simulation *e:* **SETS**

System Environment Recording *e:* **SER**

System Environment Recording and Editing Program *e:* **SEREP**

System Environmental Qualifcation Test *e:* **SEQT**

System Environmental Recording Editing and Printing *e:* **SEREP**

System File Protection *e:* **SFP**

System for Acquisition, Photo-Interpretation & Remote sensing *e:* **SAPHIR**

System for Locating Eruptive Underwater Turbidity and Hydrography *e:* **SLEUTH**

System for Medical and Biological Sciences Information Searching *e:* **SYMBIOSIS**

System for Natural Programming *e:* **SNAP**

System for Nuclear Observation of Possible Explosives *e:* **SNOOPE**

System for Observation & artillery Data Acquisition *e:* **SODA**

System for the Acquisition, Transmission and Processing of Hydrological Data *e:* **SAPHYDATA**

System for the Acquisition Transmission and Processing of Hydrological Data *e:* **SATPHYDATA,** *e:* **SYTPHYDATA**

System for Upper Atmospheric Sounding *e:* **SUA,** *e:* **SUAS,** *e:* **SUUAS**

System Integrated Pressurised Water Reactor *e:* **SIPWR**

System Managed Access Path Protection *e:* **SMAPP**

System network architecture remote job prccessing *e:* **SNARJP**

System of Long-term Monitoring of Coastal and Near-shore Phenomena related to Climate Change *e:* **GCNSMS**

System Queue Space *e:* **SQS**

System Test Environment Input[s] *e:* **STEIN**

System Thermal Air Platform Reconnaissance Signature *e:* **STARS**

System Usage and Performance Environment Report *e:* **SUPER**

System zum Abspeichern und Wiederauffinden [formatierter Datenbestände] *d:* **SAWI**

Systematic and Applied Microbiology *e:* **SAMIDF,** *e:* **Syst Appl Microbiol**

Systematic Process Observation Technique *e:* **SPOT**

Systematics and Biogeography *e:* **SB**

Systematisch-Geobotanisches Institut, Universität Göttingen *d:* **SGI**

Systematized Nomenclature of Human and Veterinary Medicine *e:* **SNOMED**

Systematized Nomenclature of Medicine *e:* **SNOMED**

Système côtier tempéré de l'Amérique du Sud *f:* **COSALC-VII**

Système d'Analyse par Observation Zenithale *e:* **SAOZ**

Système d'Analyse par Observations Zénithales *f:* **SAOZ**

Système d'Analyse par Observation[s] Zénithale[s] *f:* **SAOZ**

Système d'Aquisition de Données Océaniques *f:* **SADO**

Système de localisation des données sur lenvironnement *f:* **ENDEX**

Systeme de Protection d'Information Numerique *f:* **SPIN**

Système de référence pour les applications climatologiques *f:* **CARS**

Système de surveillance à long terme des phénomènes côtiers ou voisins du rivage en rapport avec les changements climatiques *f:* **GCNSMS**

Système de traitement des données atmosphériques et océanographiques *f:* **AOIPS**

Système de transmission automatique des observations d'aéronefs *f:* **AARS**

SystEme de Transport AErobie REcupErable a decollage arterrissage Horizontoux *f:* **STAR**

Système dinformation du droit de lenvironnement *f:* **ELIS**

Système d'information en matière de Placement et de Statistique du marché du travail *f:* **PLASTA**

Système d'Information Geographique *f:* **SIG**

Système d'Information Médicale et de Bureautique Appliqué au Dossier Médical *f:* **SIMBAD**

Système d'Information sur les Matières Dangereuses Utilisées au Travail *f:* **SIMDUT**

Système d'observation composite de l'Atlantique Nord *f:* **COSNA**

Système d'observation des océans *f:* **OOS**

Système d'observation du cycle hydrologique *f:* **HYCOS**

Système d'observation du cycle hydrologique méditerranéen *f:* **MED-HYCOS**

Système d'observation du SMISO *f:* **SOS**

Système d'observation et d'information relatif aux activités se rapportant au cycle hydrologique et aux ressources en eau de l'Amérique latine et des *f:* **LACHYCOS**

Système d'échange d'informations et d'expériences sur l'environnement et le développement *f:* **INTERFACE**

Système hydrologique opérationnel à fins multiples *f:* **SHOFM**

Système international d'information sur l'environnement *f:* **INFOTERRA**

Système mondial de surveillance continue de l'environnement *f:* **GEMS**

Système mondial d'observation *f:* **SMO**

Système mondial d'observation de l'environnement terrestre *f:* **GTOS**

Système mondial d'observation de l'océan *f:* **GOOS**

Système mondial d'observation de l'ozone *f:* **SMOO**

Système mondial d'observation du climat *f:* **SMOC**

Système mondial d'observation du niveau de la mer *f:* **GLOSS**

Système mondial d'observation du niveau de la mer Méditerranée *f:* **MEDGLOSS**

Système Mondial Intégré de Stations Océaniques *f:* **SMISO**

Système national de satellites océaniques *f:* **NOSS**

Systeme pour la Protection Electronique Contre Tous les Rayonnements Adverse *f:* **SPECTRA**

Système pour l'Observation de la Terre *f:* **SPOT**

Système Probatoire d'Observation de la Terre *f:* **SPOT**

Systemes de Traitement et de Transmissions d'Application Generales pour l'Exploitation Militaire en Environment Severe *f:* **STRATEMES**

Systems Analysis of Manned Space Operations *e:* **SAMSO,** *e:* **SAMSON**

Systems Engineering Environments *e:* **SEE**

Systems Environment Team *e:* **SET**

Systems Evaluation code Under Radiation Environment *e:* **SEURE**

Systems Evaluation Code Under Radiation Environrnent *e:* **SECURE**

Systems for Acquisition, Transmission and Processing of Hydrological Data *e:* **SAPHY-DATA**

Systems Integration Environment *e:* **SIE**

Systems/Software Engineering Environment *e:* **S/SEE**

Systéme d'Analyse par Observations Zénithales *e:* **SAOZ**

Systéme pour l'Observation de la Terre *e:* **SPOT**

Szeged Biological Research Centre *e:* **SZBK**

T

T2 Medical, Inc. *e:* **TSQ**

Table Mountain Observatory *e:* **TMO**

Table Mountain Radio Astronomy Observatory *e:* **TMRAO**

Table Ronde Nationale sur l'Environnement et l'Économie *f:* **TRNEE**

table space *e:* **TS**

Tabulae Biologicae *e:* **Tabulae Biol**, *e:* **Tabul Biol**

TACFIRE Remote Terminal *e:* **TRT**

Tactical Advanced Combat Direction and Electronie Warfare Environmental Generation Control System *e:* **TACDEW/EGCS**

Tactical Aeromedical Evacuation System *e:* **TAES**

Tactical Air Base Weather *e:* **TABWX**

Tactical Air Base Weather Dissemination System *e:* **TABWDS**

Tactical Air Base Weather Element *e:* **TABWE**

Tactical Air Base Weather System *e:* **TABWS**

Tactical Air Force Weather Service *e:* **TAWDS**

Tactical Air Observation *e:* **TAO**

Tactical Air Threat Environment Description *e:* **TACAIR TED**

Tactical Airborne Signal Exploitation Space *e:* **TASES**

Tactical Airborne Weather Stations *e:* **TABWS**

Tactical Airspace Integration System *e:* **TAIS**

Tactical All Weather Attack Requirements *e:* **TAWAR**

Tactical and Environmental Support System *e:* **TESS**

Tactical Area Weather Sensor *e:* **TAWS**

Tactical Automated Weather Distribution System *e:* **TAWDS**

Tactical Automatic Weather Station *e:* **TAWS**

Tactical Decision Aid. Ocean environment *e:* **TDA**

Tactical Earth Penetrator *e:* **TEP**

Tactical Electronic Warfare Environment Simulator *e:* **TEWES**

Tactical Environment Satellite Readout *e:* **TESR**

Tactical Environmental Data Support System *e:* **TEDSS**

Tactical Environmental Dissemination and Display System *e:* **TEDDS**

Tactical Exploitation of National Space Capabilities *e:* **TENCAP**

Tactical Infantry Load Carrier Amphibious Remote *e:* **TILCAR**

Tactical Information Processing and Interpretation Total Environment Facility *e:* **TIPITEF**

Tactical Integrated Ocean Surveillance *e:* **TIOT**

Tactical Medical Center *e:* **TMC**

Tactical Observing Weather-Element *e:* **TOBWE**

Tactical Ocean Surveillance Coordinator *e:* **TOSC**

Tactical Oceanographic Warfare Support programme *e:* **TOWS**

Tactical Operations Control Center Weather Element *e:* **TOCCWE**

Tactical Reconnaissance All Weather aircraft *e:* **TRX**

Tactical Remote Receiving System *e:* **TAC-RRS**

Tactical Remote Sensor System *e:* **TRSS**

Tactical Warning and Space Defense *e:* **TW/SD**

Tactical Water Distribution System *e:* **TWDS**

Tactical Weather *e:* **TACWE**

Tactical weather *e:* **TACWX**

Tactical Weather Analysis Center *e:* **TWAC**

Tactical Weather Central *e:* **TACWEACEN**

Tactical Weather Forecast Station *e:* **TWFS**

Tactical Weather Intelligence *e:* **TWI**

Tactical Weather RADAR *e:* **TWR**

Tactical Weather Station *e:* **TWS**

Tactical Weather System *e:* **TACWE**, *e:* **TACWE System**, *e:* **TAWE System**, *e:* **TWS**

Tactically Expendable Remote Navigator *e:* **TERN**

Taeduk Radio Astronomy Observatory *e:* **TRAO**

tägliche Wasserführung *d:* **D.W.F.**

Tagungsbericht. Gesellschaft für Innere Medizin der DDR *d:* **Tagungsber Ges Inn Med DDR**

Tailored Owner Protection System *e:* **TOPS**

Tailwater *e:* **TW**

Taipei Aerospace Technology Exhibition *e:* **TATE**

Taiwan Aerospace Company *e:* **TAC**

Taiwan Air Defence Ground Environment *e:* **TADGE**

Taiwan Environmental Protection Agency *e:* **TEPA**

Taiwan Environmental Sanitation *e:* **Taiwan Environ Sanit**

Taiwan. Fisheries Research Institute. Laboratory of Biology. Report *e:* **Taiwan Fish Res Inst Lab Biol Rep**

Taiwan. Fisheries Research Institute. Laboratory of Fishery Biology. Report *e:* **Taiwan Fish Res Inst Lab Fish Biol Rep**

Taiwan Journal of Veterinary Medicine and Animal Husbandry *e:* **Taiwan J Vet Med Anim Husb**

Takeoff and Landing Critical Atmosphere Turbulence *e:* **TOLCAT**

Takeoff Space Available *e:* **TOSA**

Taking Care. Newsletter of the Center for Consumer Health Education *e:* **TAKC**

taktieren *d:* **takt.**

Taktil-Akustische Seitenorientierung *d:* **TASO**

Taligent Application Environment *e:* **TalAE**

Taligent Development Environment *e:* **TALDE**

Talk Echo Protection *e:* **TEP**

Tamarac National Wildlife Refuge (Minnesota) *e:* **TNWR**

Tamil Nadu Agricultural University, Water Technology Center *e:* **TNAU-WTC**

Tampa Bay Medical Library Network *e:* **TABAMLN**

Tampa/St Petersburg/Clearwater *e:* **TPA**

Tamper-Protected Recording *e:* **TPR**

Tan pronto como sea posible *s:* **SAP**

Tangent Latitude Computer Amplitier *e:* **TLCA**

Tank and Orbiter Weight *e:* **TOW**

Tank, Condensate Water *e:* **TCW**

Tank Observing Post *e:* **TkOP**

Tank Waste Remediation System-Environmental Impact Statement *e:* **TWRS-EIS**

Tank, Water, Chilled *e:* **TWC**

Tank, Water, City *e:* **TWC**

Tank, Water, Cool *e:* **TWC**

Tank, Water, Hot *e:* **TWH**

Tanknology Environmental *e:* **TANK**

Tantawangalo Catchment Protection Association *e:* **TCPA**

Tanzania. Ministry of Industries. Mineral Resources and Power. Annual Report of the Geological Survey Division *e:* **Tanzania Miner Resour Power Annu Rep Geol Surv Div**

Tanzania. Records of the Geological Survey of Tanganyika *e:* **Tanzania Rec Geol Surv Tanganyika**

Tanzania Wildlife Safaris Limited *e:* **TWLS**

Tanzania Wildlife Safaris Ltd., Arusha *e:* **T.W.L.S.**

Tap Water *e:* **TW**

Tap Water Agar *e:* **TWA**

tap-water enema *e:* **twe**

Tape and Butier Index *e:* **TBI**

TAPPI Environmental Conference. Proceedings *e:* **TAPPI Environ Conf Proc**, *e:* **TECPD**

TAPPI Forest Biology-Wood Chemistry Conference. Conference Papers *e:* **TAPPI For Biol Wood Chem Conf Conf Pap**

Tarapur Boiling Water Reactor *e:* **TBWR**

Tarassevich State Research Institute for Standardization and Control of Medical Biological Preparations *e:* **TI**

Target Acquisition Batiery *e:* **TAB**

Target Area Meteorological Sensor System *e:* **TAMSS**

Target Echo Signature Generator *e:* **TESG**

Target Health Hazard Program *e:* **THHP**

Target Insertion Orbit *e:* **TIO**

Target Observation Battery *e:* **TOB**

Target-Rich Environment *e:* **TRE**

Target Signature Analysis *e:* **TSA**

Target Signature Analysis Center *e:* **TSAC**

Target Signature Investigation *e:* **TSI**

Target Weather Information *e:* **TARWI**

Targets and Backgrounds Signature Analysis Center *e:* **TABSAC**

Tarjeta Perforada Internacional de Meteorología Marítima *s:* **IMMPC**

Tarptautinis Geologu Kongresas *li:* **TGK**

Task Force on Observations and Data Management *e:* **TFODM**

Task Force on Scientific Uses of the Space Station *e:* **TFSUS**, *e:* **TFSUSS**

Task Force on the Environment *e:* **TFOE**

Tasmania. Department of Mines. Geological Atlas. 1:250000 Series SK *e:* **Tasmania Dep Mines Geol Atlas 1:250000 Ser SK**

Tasmania. Department of Mines. Geological Survey. Bulletin *e:* **Tasmania Dep Mines Geol Surv Bull**

Tasmania. Department of Mines. Geological Survey. Record *e:* **Tasmania Dep Mines Geol Surv Rec**

Tasmania. Department of Mines. Geological Survey. Report *e:* **Tasmania Dep Mines Geol Surv Rep**

Tasmania. Department of Mines.
Underground Water Supply Paper *e:*
**Tasmania Dep Mines Underground
Water Sapply Pap**

Tasmania. Geological Survey. Bulletin *e:*
**Tasmania Geol Surv Bull, *e:* Tasm Geol
Surv Bull**

Tasmania. Geological Survey. Explanatory
Report *e:* **Tasmania Geol Surv
Explanatory Rep**

Tasmania. Geological Survey. Explanatory
Report. Geological Atlas. Mile Series *e:*
**Tasmania Geol Surv Explan Rep Geol
Atlas 1 Mile Ser**

Tasmania. Geological Survey. Geological
Atlas. 1 Mile Series *e:* **Tasm Geol Surv
Geol Atlas 1 Mile Ser**

Tasmania. Geological Survey. Record *e:*
Tasmania Geol Surr Rec

Tasmania. Geological Survey. Report *e:*
Tasmania Geol Surv Rep

Tasmania. Geological Survey. Underground
Water Supply Paper *e:* **Tasmania Geol
Surv Underground Water Supply Pap,
e: Tasm Geol Surv Undergr Wat
Supply Pap**

Tasmania National Parks and Wildlife
Service *e:* **TNPWS**

Tasmanian Department of Sea Fisheries *e:*
TDSF

Tasmanian Earth Resources Satellite Station
e: **TERSS**

Tasmanian Environment Centre *e:* **TEC**

Tasmanian Geological Survey. Geological
Atlas. 1 Mile Series *e:* **Tas Geol Surv
Geol Atlas 1 Mile Ser**

Tasmanian Journal of Natural Science *e:*
Tasmanian J

Tasmanian Naturalist *e:* **Tas[m] Nat**

Tasmanian Parks and Wildlife Service *e:*
TASPAWS

Tasmanian Wilderness Society *e:* **TWS**

Tätigkeitsbericht. Bundesanstalt für
Geowissenschaften und Rohstoffe *d:*
**Tatigkeitsber Bundesanst Geowiss
Rohst**

Tätigkeitsbericht der Naturforschenden
Gesellschaft Baselland *d:* **Tätigk.ber.
Nat.forsch. Ges. Baselland**

Tätigkeitsbericht. Geologisches Landesamt
Nordrhein-Westfalen *d:* **Tatigkeitsber
Geol Landsamt Nordrhein-Westfal**

Tavistock Institute of Medical Psychology
e: **TIMP**

Taylor's Medical Jurisprudence *e:* **Tayl
Med Jur**

TDRS H,I,J Spacecraft Simulator *e:* **TSE**

Teacher in Space Project *e:* **TISP**

Teacher of Hydrotherapy *e:* **TH, *e:* THT**

Teacher of Massage and Medical
Gymnastics *e:* **TMMG**

Teacher of Medical Electricity *e:* **TME**

Teacher Practices Observation Record *e:*
TPOR

Teachers Exploring Environmental
Management *e:* **TEEM**

Teaching Individual Protective Strategies
and Teaching Individual Positive
Solutions *e:* **TIPS**

Team Oriented Medical Simulation *e:*
TOMS

Teaming With Wildlife *e:* **TWW**

Teatro Popolare Italiano *i:* **TPI**

Tebiwa Journal. Idaho Museum of Natural
History *e:* **Tebiwa J Idaho Mus Nat
Hist**

Tebiwa Miscellaneous Papers. Idaho State
University. Museum of Natural History
e: **Tebiwa Misc Pap Idaho State Univ
Mus Nat Hist**

Technical Advisor Marine Environment
Pollution *e:* **TAMEP**

Technical Advisory Group on
Oceanographic Data Management *e:*
TAGODM

Technical and Economical Studies. Institute
of Geology and Geophysics. Series I.
Mineralogy Petrology *e:* **Tech Econ
Stud Inst Geol Geophys Ser I**

Technical and Managerial Support
Environment *e:* **TEMSE**

Technical and Operational Control Centre
in the Indian Ocean Region *e:* **IOR-
TOCC**

Technical Associate of the Geological
Society *e:* **TechGeol**

Technical Bulletin. Animal Industry and
Agricultural Branch. Department of the
Northern Territory *e:* **Tech Bull Anim
Ind Agric Branch NT**

Technical Bulletin. Animal Industry and
Agriculture Branch. Northern Territory
e: **Tech Bull Anim Ind Agric Br NT**

Technical Bulletin. Canada Inland Waters
Directorate *e:* **Tech Bull Can Inland
Waters Dir**

Technical Bulletin. Commonwealth
Institute of Biological Control *e:* **Tech
Bull Commonw[ealth] Inst Biol
Contr[ol]**

Technical Bulletin. Georgia Agricultural
Experiment Stations. University of
Georgia. College of Agriculture *e:* **Tech
Bull GA Agr Exp Sta**

Technical Bulletin. Institute for Land and
Water Management Research *e:* **Tech
Bull Inst Ld Wat Mgmt Res**

Technical Bulletin Medical *e:* **TB MED**

Technical Bulletin. Registry of Medical
Technologists *e:* **Tech Bull Regist Med
Technol**

Technical Center for Expertise for
Protective Design *e:* **TCX/PD**

Technical Classified Natural Rubber *e:*
TC-NR

Technical Committee on Ocean Processes
and Climate *e:* **TC/OPC**

Technical Communication. Woodland
Ecology Unit. Commonwealth Sientific
and Industrial Research Organisation *e:*
**Tech Commun Woodld Ecol Unit
CSIRO**

Technical Conference on Automated
Meteorological Systems *e:* **TECAMS**

Technical Conference on the Observation
and Measurement of Atmospheric
Pollution *e:* **TECOMAP**

Technical Document. Food and Agriculture
Organization of the United Nations. Plant
Protection Committee for the South Fa
e: **Tech Doc FAO Plant Prot Comm
Southeast Asia Pac Reg**

Technical Integration and Environmental
Education Development *e:* **TIEED**

Technical, Medical and Science Group *e:*
TMSG

Technical Memoranda. Plant Protection
Limited *e:* **Tech Memor Plant
Protechon Ltd**

Technical Memorandum. Division of
Applied Geomechanics. Commonwealth
Scientific and Industrial Research
Organisation *e:* **Tech Memo Div Appl
Geomech CSIRO**

Technical Memorandum. Division of
Wildlife Research. Commonwealth
Scientific and Industrial Research
Organisation *e:* **Tech Memo Div Wildl
Res CSIRO**

Technical Note. Forestry Department
(British Solomon Islands Protectorate] *e:*
**Tech Note For Dep (Brit Solomon
Islands Protect)**

Technical Note. Quetico Superior
Wilderness Research Center *e:* **Tech
Note Quetico-Sup Wild Res Cent**

Technical Observation Point *e:* **TOP**

Technical Observation Points *e:* **TOPs**

Technical Observation Post *e:* **TOP**

Technical Panel on the Earth Satellite
Program *e:* **TPESP**

Technical Paper. Animal Research
Laboratories. Commonwealth Scientific
and Industrial Research Organisation *e:*
Tech Pap Anim Res Lab[s] CSIRO

Technical Paper. [Australia]
Commonwealth Scientific and Industrial
Research Organization Division of
Applied Geomechanics *e:* **Tech Pap
[Aust] CSIRO Div Appl Geomech**

Technical Paper. Australian Water
Resources Council *e:* **Tech Pap Aust
Water Resour Coun, *e:* Tech Pap Aust
Wat Resour Coun**

Technical Paper. Division of Applied
Geomechanics. Commonwealth Scientific
and Industrial Research Organisation *e:*
Tech Pap Div Appl Geomech CSIRO

Technical Paper. Division of Atmospheric
Physics. Commonwealth Scientific and
Industrial Research Organisation *e:*
Tech Pap Div Atmosph Phys CSIRO

Technical Paper. Division of
Meteorological Physics. Commonwealth
Scientific and Industrial Research
Organisation. *e:* **Tech Pap Div
Met[eorol] Phys CSIRO**

Technical Paper. Division of Wildlife
Research. Commonwealth Scientific and
Industrial Research Organisation *e:*
Tech Pap Div Wildl Res CSIRO

Technical Paper. New York State
Department of Environmental
Conservation *e:* **Tech Pap NY State
Dep Environ Conserv**

Technical Papers in Hydrology *e:* **Tech
Pap Hydrol**

Technical Publications. State Biological
Survey of Kansas *e:* **Tech Publ State
Biol Surv Kans**

Technical Report. Bureau of Meteorology
e: **Tech Rep Bur Met[eorol]**

Technical Report. Center for Research in
Water Resources. University of Texas at
Austin *e:* **Tech Rep Cent Res Water
Resour Univ Tex Austin**

Technical Report. Division of Applied
Geomechanics. Commonwealth Scientific

and Industrial Research Organisation *e:*
Tech Rep Div Appl Geomech CSIRO

Technical Report. Hawaii University. Water
Resource Research Center *e:* **Tech Rep
Water Resour Res Cent Hawaii Univ**

Technical Report. Nanyang University.
College of Graduate Studies. Institute of
Natural Sciences *e:* **Tech Rep Nanyang
Univ Coll Grad Stud Inst Nat Sci**

Technical Report. National Space
Development Agency of Japan *e:* **Tech
Rep Natl Space Dev Agency Jpn**

Technical Report on Environmental Aspects
 e: **TREA**

Technical Report Series. World Health
Organisation *e:* **Techn Rep Ser Wld
Hlth Org**

Technical Report. United States Army
Engineers. Waterways Experiment Station
 e: **Tech Rep US Army Eng Waterw Exp
Stn**

Technical Report. University of Texas at
Austin. Center for Research in Water
Resources *e:* **Tech Rep Univ Tex
Austin Cent Res Water Resour**

Technical Reports in Hydrology and Water
Resources *e:* **Tech. Rep. Hydrol. Water
Resour.**

Technical Reprint. Graver Water
Conditioning Company *e:* **Tech Repr
Graver Water Cond Co**

Technical Series. Florida Department of
Natural Resources. Marine Research
Laboratory *e:* **Tech Ser Fla Dep Nat
Resour Mar Res Lab**

Technical Services Division [National
Library of Medicine] *e:* **TSD**

Technical System Engineering Environment
 e: **TSEE**

Technically Enhanced Naturally
Radioactive *e:* **TENR**

Technically Enhanced Naturally
Radioactive Product *e:* **TENRAP**

Technically Specified Natural Rubber *e:*
TSR

Technician Member of the Institute of
Water Pollution Control *e:*
TechMIWPC

Technicien[ne] de l'Information Médicale
 f: **TIM**

Technik und Umweltschutz *d:* **Tech
Umweltschutz**

Technika Poszukiwan Geologianych *S:*
TGEOD

Technika Poszukiwan Geologicznych *P:*
Tech Poszuhiwan Geol, *P:* **Tech
Poszukiwan Geol Geosynoptyka
Geoterm**

Technikon Witwatersrand *e:* **TWR**

Technikum Geodezyjne *P:* **TG**

Technikum Geologiczne *P:* **TG**

Technique Routiere *f:* **Tech Routiere**

Techniques Development Laboratory [of the
Weather Bureau] *e:* **TDL**

Techniques Hospitalieres, MedicoSociales,
et Sanitaires *f:* **Techn Hosp**

Techniques of Measurement in Medicine
 e: **Tech Meas Med**

Techniques Sans Frontieres *f:* **TSF**

Technisch-ökonomische Zielsetzung
[Aufgabenstellung der
Projektierungsmethodik] *d:* **TÖZ**

Technische Advies Commissie voor de
Waterkeringen *n:* **TACW**

technische Atmosphäre *d:* **at**

Technische Federn Sigmund Scherdel
GmbH *d:* **S**

Technische Informationsbibliothek für
Technik und Naturwissenschaften an der
Universität Hannover *d:* **TIB QUICK
2000**

Technische Regel wassergefährdende Stoffe
 d: **TRwS**

Technische Regeln für Biologische
Arbeitsstoffe *d:* **TRBA**

technische und biomedizinische Kybernetik
 d: **TBK**

Technische Universität Berlin Institut für
Raumfahrttechnik *d:* **TUB-IR**

Techno-Economic-Environmental Model
 e: **TEEM**

Technologically-Enhanced Naturally
Occurring Radioactive Material *e:*
TENORM

Technologically Enhanced Naturally
Radioactive *e:* **TENR**

Technologieentwicklung zur Unterstützung
der Umweltverträglichkeitsprüfungen für
die EXPO 2000 *d:* **TTEK**

Technologieorientierte
Unternehmungsgründung *d:* **TOU**

Technologiespezifische und
branchenorientierte Transferzentren *d:*
TTZ

Technologiezentrum Wasser *d:* **TZW**

Technologisch-orientierte
Programmforschung des Eidgenössischen
Technischen Hochschul-Rates *d:* **TOP**

technologische Betriebsprojektierung *d:*
TBP

technologische Planungs- und
Projektierungsaufgabe *d:* **T/P**

Technologist Section of the Society of
Nuclear Medicine *e:* **TSSNM**

Technology and Environment *e:* **Tech
Environ**

Technology and Health Care *e:* **Technol
Health Care**

Technology and Health Services Division
 e: **THSD**

Technology Development Missions Polar
 e: **TDMP**

Technology Development Report EPS
(Canada Environmental Protection
Service) *e:* **Technol Dev Rep EPS (Can
Environ Prot Serv)**

Technology Feasibility Spacecraft *e:* **TFS**

Technology for Aerospace Computers *e:*
TASC

Technology for Environmental Protection-
International Trade Fair and Congress *e:*
ENVITEC

Technology Institute for Medical Devices
Canada *e:* **TIMEC**

Technology, People, Environment *e:* **TPE**

Technology Protection System *e:* **TPS**

Technology, Work and Environment *e:*
TWE

Tecnol Medical Products *e:* **TCNL**

Teenage Health Education Teaching
Assistants *e:* **THETA**

Tehnika Rudarstvo Geologiya i Metalurgija
 P: **Teh Rud Geol Metal**

Tele-Education and Medicine *e:* **TEAM**

Tele Medicine Framework *e:* **TMF**

Telecom Canada Remote Interface
Monitoring and Management System *e:*
TRIMMS

Telecommunication Earth *e:* **TE**

Telecommunications and Electrical
Machinery Protected From Emanations
Security *e:* **TEMPEST**

Telecommunications and Enterprise
Multimedia Platform Environment *e:*
TEMPE

Telecommunications Standards Committee
Interfaces, Network Power & Protection
 e: **T1E1**

Teledyne Airborne Geophysical Services
 e: **TAGS**

Teledyne Geotech Alexandria Laboratories
 e: **TGAL**

Telemedicine and Advanced Technology
Research Center *e:* **TATRC**

Telemedicine and Education Support Team
 e: **TEST**

Telemedicine for Ontario *e:* **TFO**

Telemedicine Information Exchange *e:*
TIE

Telemedicine Technology Area Directorate
 e: **TTAD**

Telemetering Ocean Bottom Seismometer
 e: **TOBS**

Telemetry and Remote Control *e:* **TRC**

Telephone Consumer[s] Protection Act *e:*
TCPA

Telephone-Medical *e:* **Tel-Med**

Telephone Service Observation *e:* **TSO**

Teleprocessing Environmental Simulator
Testing *e:* **TEST**

Telescript Development Environment *e:*
TDE

Televised Images of Gaseous Region in
Interplanetary Space *e:* **TIGRIS**

Television and Infrared Observation
Satellite *e:* **TIROS**

Television and Infrared Observation
Satellite Sounder *e:* **TIROS**

Television Infrared Observation[al] (or
Observing) Satellite *e:* **TIROS**

Television Infrared Orbital Satellite *e:*
TITOS

Television Interface General-purpose
Economy Remote Terminal *e:* **TIGER
Terminal**

Television Receive Only Earth Station *e:*
TVRO

Television Remote Pickup *e:* **TRP**

Television Space Observatory *e:* **TVSO**

Tellus. Series A. Dynamic Meteorology and
Oceanography *e:* **Tellus Ser A Dyn
Meteorol Oceanogr**

Tellus. Series B. Chemical and Physical
Meteorology *e:* **Tellus Ser B Chem
Phys Meteorol**, *e:* **TSBMD**

Tematicheskii Sbornik Vsesoyuznogo
Nauchno-Issledovatel'skogo Inst.
Gidrogeologii Inzhenerskoi Geologii *R:*
**Temat Sb Vses Nauchno Issled Inst
Gidrogeol Inzh Geol**

Temco Home Health Care Products *e:*
TEMC

Temperatur Technik. Zeitschrift für das
Gesamte Temperaturgebiet Kältetechnik,
Klimatechnik und Heizungstechnik *d:*
KUK

Temperature Acceleration Vibration
Environmental Tester *e:* **TAVET**

Temperature-Controlled Animal *e:* **TCA**
Tempered Water *e:* **TW**
Temple Environmental Law & Technology Journal *e:* **Temp. Envtl. L. & Tech. J.**
Temple University, Medical School, Philadelphia, PA *e:* **PPT-M**
Temporal Stability and Activity of Landslide in Europe with respect to Climatic change *e:* **TESLEC**
Temporary Geographic Grid *e:* **TGG**
Temporary Protected Status *e:* **TPS**
Temporary Remote Operating Facility, Airborne *e:* **TROFA**
temporary reserved airs spaces *e:* **TRAS**
Temporary Reserved Airspace *e:* **TRA**
Temporary Restricted Airspace *e:* **TRA**
Ten-Year Oceanographic Program *e:* **TENOC, *e:* TENOC Program**
Ten-Year Plan for Ocean Exploration *e:* **TYPOE**
Tender Loving Care Health Care, Incorporated *e:* **TLCI**
Tennesee-Tombigway Waterway *e:* **TTW**
Tennessee. Department of Conservation. Division of Geology. Bulletin *e:* **Tenn Dep Conserv Div Geol Bull**
Tennessee. Department of Conservation. Division of Geology. Information Circular *e:* **Tenn Dep Conserv Dir Geol Inf Circ**
Tennessee Department of Health *e:* **TDH**
Tennessee Department of Health and Environment *e:* **TDHE**
Tennessee Department of Public Health, Nashville *e:* **TNPH**
Tennessee Department of the Environment and Conservation *e:* **TDEC**
Tennessee. Division of Geology. Bulletin *e:* **Tenn Div Geol Bull**
Tennessee. Division of Geology. Environmental Geology Series *e:* **Tenn Div Geol Environ Geol Ser**
Tennessee. Division of Geology. Geologic Map *e:* **Tennessee Div Geology Geol Map**
Tennessee. Division of Geology. Information Circular *e:* **Tenn Div Geol Inf[orm] Circ**
Tennessee. Division of Geology. Report of Investigations *e:* **Tenn Div Geol Rep Inrest, *e:* Tenn[essee] Div Geology Rept Inv[est]**
Tennessee. Division of Water Resources. Water Resources Series *e:* **Tenn Div Water Resour Water Resour Ser**
Tennessee Health Science Library Association *e:* **THESLA**
Tennessee Health Studies Agreement *e:* **THSA**
Tennessee Natural Resources *e:* **TENN**
Tennessee Occupational Safety and Health Administration *e:* **TOSHA**
Tennessee State Board of Health. Bulletin. Report *e:* **Tenn St Bd Health B Rp**
Tennessee State Geological Survey. Resources of Tennessee. Bulletin *e:* **Tenn G S Res Teno B**
Tennessee State Medical Association *e:* **TSMA**
Tennessee-Tombigbee Waterway *e:* **TENN-TOM**
Tennessee University. Water Resources Research Center. Research Report *e:*

Tenn Univ Water Resour Res Cent Res Rep
Tennessee Water Resources Research Center *e:* **TNWRRI**
Tennessee Wildlife *e:* **Tenn Wildl**
Tennessee Wildlife Resources Agency *e:* **TWRA**
Tension Space *e:* **TS**
Tenth International Symposium on Environmental Biogeochemistry *e:* **ISEB 10**
Teoreticheskie i Prakticheskie Voprosy Mikrobiologii Epidemiologii *R:* **Teor Prakt Vopr Mikrobiol Epidemiol**
Teoreticheskie i Prakticheskie Voprosy Mikrobiologii i Epidemiologii Resp. Mezhvedomstvennyi Sbornik *R:* **Teor Prakt Vopr Mikrobiol Epidemiol Resp Mezhved Sb**
Terapeutica. Revista de Medicina *s:* **Ter Rev Med**
Terec Remote Terminal *e:* **TRT**
Terminal Airspace Visualization Tool *e:* **TAVT**
Terminal Control Address Space *e:* **TCAS**
Terminal Controlled Airspace *e:* **TCA**
Terminal Doppler Weather Radar *e:* **TDWR**
Terminal emulation protocol, a TCP/IP application protocol for remote connection service *e:* **Telnet**
Terminal Environment Module *e:* **TEMOD**
Terminal Environment Network Information System *e:* **TENIS**
Terminal Guidance Environmental Effects Program *e:* **TGEEP**
Terminal Protection Device *e:* **TPD**
Terminal Protective Device *e:* **TPD**
Terminal Weather Doppler Radar *e:* **TWDR**
Terminating Unit Remote *e:* **TUR**
Terra Livre. Associação dos Geógrafos Brasileiros, São Paulo *p:* **Terra Livre.**
Terrain Integrated Rough Earth Model *e:* **TIREM**
Terre de Protection *f:* **TP**
Terre et la Vie. Revue d'Ecologie Appliquee *f:* **Terre Vie Rev Ecol Appl**
Terre Ocean Atmosphere *f:* **TOA**
Terrell's Laboratories Medical Library, Fort Worth *e:* **TxFTM**
Terrestrial and Freshwater Sciences *e:* **TFS**
Terrestrial Biogeochemical Model *e:* **TBM**
Terrestrial Ecological Research Initiative *e:* **TECO**
Terrestrial Ecological Research Programme on Svalbard *e:* **TERRÖK**
Terrestrial Ecosystem Hydrology Model *e:* **TEHM**
Terrestrial Environment Satellites *e:* **CLUSTER**
Terrestrial Environment System *e:* **TES**
Terrestrial Environmental Services *e:* **TERENVSVC, *e:* TERNVSVC**
Terrestrial Initiative in Global Environmental Research [funded by United Kingdom Natural Environmental Research Council] *e:* **TIGER**
Terrestrial Magnetism and Atmospheric Electricity *e:* **Terr Magn, *e:* Terr Magn Atmos Electr**

Terrestrial Observation (or Observing) Panel for Climate *e:* **TOPC**
Terrestrial Observation Panel *e:* **TOP**
Territorial Sea Journal *e:* **Terr. Sea J., *e:* Terr. Sea Journal**
Territorialgewässer *d:* **TG**
Territory Health Services *e:* **THS**
Tert-Butyl Hydroperoxide *e:* **TBHP**
Tertiary-Butyl Hydroperoxide *e:* **TBHP**
Tertiary Butylhydroquinone *e:* **TBHQ**
Tessaral Harmonic Resonance of Orbital Elements *e:* **THROE**
Test Article Protector *e:* **TAP**
Test cell environment and cooling *e:* **TCEC**
Test de Bon Fonctionnement (Spacelab) *e:* **TBF**
Test Environment Support System Enhancement *e:* **TESSE**
Test Environmental Assessment *e:* **TEA**
Test für medizinische Studiengänge *d:* **TMS**
Test in Other Environment *e:* **TIOE**
Test Observation and Training Room *e:* **TOTR**
Testfluginstrumentierung *d:* **DFI**
testieren *d:* **test.**
Testierung *d:* **Test.**
Testing Earth System Models with Palaeoenvironmental Observations *e:* **TEMPO**
Tests of Reasonable Quantitative Understanding of the Environment *e:* **TORQUE**
Tether Applications in Space *e:* **TAS**
Tether Initiated Space Recovery System *e:* **TISRS**
Tethered Orbiting Satellite Simulator *e:* **TOSS**
Tethered Remote Automatic Pipeline Repairer *e:* **TRAPR**
Tethered Remote Camera *e:* **TREC**
Tethered Remotely Operated Vehicle *e:* **TROV**
Tethered Remotely Operational Vehicle *e:* **TROV**
Tetrabutyl-ammoniumhydroxid *d:* **TBAH**
Tetrabutylammonium Hydrogen Sulfate *d:* **TBAHS**
Tetrabutylammonium Hydroxide *d:* **TBAH, *e:* TBAH, *e:* TBA-OH**
tetracaine hydrochloride *e:* **TETRA**
Tetrachlorohydroquinone *e:* **TCHQ, *l:* TCH**
Tetraethylammonium Hydroxide *e:* **TEAOH**
Tetrahydro-isochinolin *e:* **TIQ**
Tetrahydroaminacrine *e:* **TMA**
Tetrahydroimidazobenzodiazepin *e:* **TIBO**
Tetrahydroisochinoline *e:* **TIQ**
Tetrahydroisoquinoline *e:* **TIQ**
Tetrahydroisoquinoline Sulfonamide *e:* **TIS**
Tetrahydroisoquinone *e:* **TIQ**
Tetrahydronaphthylamin *d:* **TNA**
Tetrahydrosisoquinoline *e:* **TIQ**
(Tetrahydrotetramethylnaphlhyl) Naphthoic Acid *e:* **TTNN**
Tetramethylammonium Hydroxide *e:* **TMAH**
Tetramethylammoniumhydroxid *e:* **TMAH**
Tetrapropylammonium Hydroxide *l:* **TPAOH**

Tewaukon National Wildlife Refuge e: **TNWR**

Texas A & M University Medical Sciences Library, College Station e: **TMV**

Texas A & M University, Medical Sciences Library, College Station e: **TxCM-M**

Texas A & M University. Oceanographic Studies e: **Tex A M Univ Oceanogr Stud**

Texas A & M University. Sea Grant College. TAMU-SG e: **TAUTDV**

Texas A & M University Sea Grant College. TAMU-SG e: **Tex A & M Univ Sea Grant Coll TAMU-SG**

Texas Animal Health Commission e: **TAHC**

Texas. Board of Water Engineers. Bulletin e: **Tex[as] Board [of] Water Eng[ineers] Bull**, e: **Tex Board Water Eng Bull**

Texas. Board of Water Engineers. Chemical Composition of Texas Surface Waters e: **Tex Board Water Eng Chem Compos Tex Surf Waters**

Texas Bureau of Economic Geology e: **TBEG**

Texas Climatological Model e: **TCM**

Texas College of Osteopathic Medicine e: **TCOM**

Texas College of Osteopathic Medicine, Fort Worth e: **TOM**, e: **TxFCO**

Texas Committee for Wildlife Protection e: **TCWP**

Texas Cooperative Wildlife Collections e: **TCWC**

Texas Courier Record of Medicine e: **Texas Cour Rec Med**

Texas Department of Health e: **TDH**

Texas Department of Mental Health and Mental Retardation e: **TDMHMR**

Texas Department of Mental Health and Mental Retardation Austin e: **TxAuMH**

Texas Department of Parks and Wildlife, Austin e: **TxAuPW**

Texas Energy and Natural Resources Advisory Council e: **TENRAC**

Texas Geographic Magazine e: **Tex Geogr Mag**

Texas Geographic Society e: **TGS**

Texas. Geological Survey. Report of Progress e: **Tex G S Rp Prog**

Texas Health Letter e: **TXHL**

Texas Intersection Air Quality Model [Environmental Prolection Agency] e: **TEXIN**

Texas Medical Association e: **TMA**

Texas Medical Association, Austin e: **TxAuM**

Texas Medical Center e: **TMC**

Texas Medical Journal e: **Texas MJ**

Texas Medicine e: **Tex[as] Med**, e: **Tex Med**, e: **TXMD**

Texas-Mexico Border Health Coordinating Office e: **TMBHCO**

Texas Natural Heritage Program e: **TNHP**

Texas Natural Resources Information System e: **TNRIS**

Texas Parks Wildlife e: **Tex Parks Wildl**

Texas Public Health Association e: **TPHA**

Texas Reports on Biology and Medicine e: **Texas Rep Biol Med**, e: **Tex Rep Bio**, e: **Tex Rep Biol Med**, e: **TRBM**, e: **TRBMA**

Texas State Journal of Medicine e: **Tex State J Med**

Texas State Medical Library, Austin e: **Tx-M**

Texas System of Natural Laboratories. Index Series e: **TSNL Index Series**

Texas Tech University, School of Medicine at Lubbock, Library of the Health Science, Lubbock e: **TML**

Texas Tech University, School of Medicine at Lubbock, Lubbock e: **TxLTM**

Texas University at Austin. Bureau of Economic Geology. Geological Circular e: **Texas Univ Austin Bur Econ Geology Geol Circ**

Texas University at Austin. Bureau of Economic Geology. Guidebook e: **Texas Univ Austin Bur Econ Geology Guidebook**

Texas University. Bureau of Economic Geology. Geological Circular e: **Tex Univ Bur Econ Geol Geol Circ**

Texas University. Bureau of Economic Geology. Mineral Resource Circular e: **Tex Univ Bur Econ Geol Miner Resour Circ**

Texas University. Bureau of Economic Geology. Publication e: **Tex Univ Bur Econ Geol Publ**

Texas University. Bureau of Economic Geology. Report of Investigations e: **Tex Univ Bur Econ Geol Rep Invest**

Texas University. Bureau of Economic Geology. Research Note e: **Tex Univ Bur Econ Geol Res Note**

Texas University. Center for Research in Water Resources. Technical Report e: **Tex Univ Cent Res Water Resour Tech Rep**

Texas University. Publication. Bureau of Economic Geology. Mineral Resource Circular. Report of Investigation e: **Texas Univ Pub Bur Econ Geology Mineral Res Circ Rept Inv**

Texas Veterinary Medical Association e: **TVMA**

Texas Water Commission e: **TWC**

Texas Water Commission. Bulletin e: **Tex Water Comm Ball**

Texas Water Commission. Circular e: **Tex Water Comm Circ**

Texas Water Commission. Memorandum Report e: **Tex Water Comm Mem Rep**

Texas Water Development Board, Austin e: **TxAuW**

Texas. Water Development Board. Report e: **Texas Water Devel Board Rept**, e: **Tex Water Der Board Rep**

Texas Water Resources Institute e: **TWRI**

26th space-shuttle mission e: **STS-26**

Thai Environmental and Community Development Association e: **TECDA**

Thai Environmental Engineers' Association e: **TEEA**

Thai Medical Informatics Society e: **TMI**

Thai National Committee of the International Association on Water Pollution Research and Control e: **TNCIAWPRC**

Thai Veterinary Medical Association e: **TVMA**

Thailand. Department of Mineral Resources. Ground Water Bulletin e:

Thailand Dep Miner Resour Ground Water Bull

Thailand Meteorological Department e: **TMD**

Thailand National Remote Sensing Programme e: **TNRSP**

Thailand Plant Protection Service. Technical Bulletin e: **Thail Plant Prot Serv Tech Bull**

Thailand Remote Sensing Center (or Centre) e: **TRSC**

Thames Water Authority e: **TWA**

The Air Surgeon e: **TAS**

The American Academy of Neurological and Orthop[a]edic Surgeons e: **TAANOS**

the Arts, Sport, the Environment and Territories e: **ASETT**

The Atlantic Ocean and the Caribbean e: **USACOM**

The Consequence of a Major Nuclear Accident on the Surrounding Environment: Soil and Surface Rehabilitation e: **RESSAC**

The Earth Regeneration and Reforestation Association e: **TERRA**

The Ecological Society of America e: **ESA**

The Environmental Business Association e: **TEBA**

the four liberal arts-arithmetic, astronomy, geography and music e: **quadrivium**

The funniest-named law in meteorology e: **Buys Ballot's Law**

The Human Role in Space e: **THURSIS**

The Hydrographic Society e: **THS**

The Hydrographic Society of America e: **THSOA**

The Image Processing Software/Signature Verification e: **TIPS/SV**

The Institute of Ecology e: **TIE**

The Interactive Graphics Environment for Real-time Systems e: **TIGERS**

The International Hydrographic Review. International Hydrographic Bureau. Monte Carlo e: **Intl Hydro R.**

The Journal of Geography. A Magazine for Schools. The National Council of Geography Teachers. Chicago e: **Jour geog.**

The Madrid Qumran Congress: Proceedings of the International Congress on the Dead Sea Scrolls, Madrid 18-21 March, 1991, Julio Trebolle Barrera and Lu e: **STJD 11 or MQC**

The Magazine of Oceanography, Marine Sciences, and Underwater Defense e: **UST**

The Medical Reporter e: **TMR**

The Natural History Review e: **Nat. Hist. Rev.**, e: **Nat.Hist.Rev.**

The Natural Step e: **TNS**

The Nature Conservancy e: **TNC**

[The] Naturist Society e: **NS**

The New York Medical Journal e: **New York Med. Journ.**, e: **N. York M.J.**

The Ocean [Antarctic, Arctic, Atlantic, Indian, Pacific] e: **Ocean**

The Oceans: A Heritage for the Future [Lisbon International Exposition] [Lisbon, Portugal, 1998] e: **EXPO 98**

The Old Natura Brevium e: **Vet. N. Br.**

The principal deflection in the electrocardiogram, representing ventricular depolarization e: **QRS complex**

The Remote Informer e: **TRI**

The Russian Black Sea and Azoff Charter Party e: **Zernocon**

The space between the Earth and the Moon e: **Cislunar**

The Space Channel e: **TSC**

The Surgeon General e: **TSG**

The Tavistock Institute of Medical Psychology e: **T.I.M.P.**

[The] Tierco Group Inc. e: **TIER**

The Washington Quarterly. Georgetown University, The Center for Strategic and International Studies. Washington e: **Wash. Q.**

[The] Weather Channel e: **TWC**

[The] Wilderness Society e: **TWS**

The Wildlife Society e: **TWS**

The Zia Manual [Zia Co. Health & Safety Manual] e: **TZM**

Theater Army Medical Management Information System e: **TAMMIS**

Theater Army Medical Management Information System-Division e: **TAMMIS-D**

Theater Medical Information System e: **TMIS**

Theater Medical Materiel Management Center e: **TMMMC**

Theater of Operations Medical Support System e: **TOMSS**

Theater Weather Central e: **TWC**

Theoretical and Applied Climatology e: **Theor. Appl. Climatol.**

Theoretical and Experimental Biology e: **Theor Exp Biol**

Theoretical Biology e: **TB**

Theoretical Chemistry. Periodicities in Chemistry and Biology e: **Theor Chem Period Chem Biol**

Theoretical Earth Utilization System e: **THEUS**

Theoretical Medicine e: **Theor Med**

Theoretical Ocean Depth e: **TOD**

Theoretical Population Biology e: **Theoret Population Biol**, e: **Theor Pop B**, e: **Theor Popul Biol**

Theoretical Production Ecology-Wageningen Agricultural University e: **TPE-WAU**

Theoretieal Climatology e: **TC**

Theoretische und Klinische Medizin in Einzeldarstellungen d: **Theor Klin Med Einzeldarst**, d: **Theor Klin Med Einzeldarstell**, d: **TKMEB**

Theory and Experiment in Exobiology e: **Theory Exp Exobiol**

Therapeutische Monatshefte für Veterinaermedizin d: **Therap Monatsh Vet-Med**

Therapeutische Umschau und Medizinische Bibliographie d: **Therap Umsschau**

Thermal and Hydrodynamic Experiment Research Module in Orbit e: **THERMO**

Thermal Array for the Ocean e: **TAO**

Thermal Depolarization Analysis e: **TDA**

Thermal Hydrodealkylation e: **THDA**

Thermal Infrared Observational Satellite e: **TIROS**

Thermal Meteoroid Garment e: **TMG**

Thermal Micrometeorite (or Micrometeoroid) Garment e: **TMG**

Thermal Micrometeoroid Cover e: **TMC**

Thermal Observation and Gunnery Sight e: **TOGS**

Thermal Observation Device e: **TOD**

Thermal Observation & Gunnery System e: **TOGS**

Thermal Protection and Control e: **TP & C**

Thermal Protection Device e: **TPD**

Thermal Protection Investigation e: **TPI**

Thermal Protection Panel e: **TPP**

Thermal Protection [Sub]system e: **TPS**

Thermal Protection Subsystem Experiments e: **TPSE**

Thermal Protection System Selection e: **TPSS**

Thermal Protection System[s] e: **TPS**

Thermal Unit with Rangefinder for Battlefieid Observation e: **TURBO**

Thermal Vacuum Environment e: **TVE**

Thermally Protected Composite e: **TPC**

Thermally Protected Plastic e: **TPP**

Thermally-Stimulated Depolarization e: **TSD**

Thermally Stimulated Depolarization Current e: **TSDC**

Thermally Stimulated Polarization Current e: **TSPC**

Thermally-Stimulated Polarization (Current)/ Depolarization Current e: **TSPC/DC**

Thermedics e: **THERMD**

Thermedics, Inc. e: **TMD**

Thermionic Reactor for Installed Oceanic Service e: **TRIOS**

thermische Wasseraufbereitung d: **TWA**

Thermo Environmental e: **TEV**

Thermochemical Environmental Energy System e: **TEES**

Thermoclima AG, St. Gallen d: **TCA**

Thermodynamic Ocean Prediction System e: **TOPS**

Thermoelectric Environmental Control Unit e: **TECU**

Thermoelectric Outer Plant Spacecraft e: **TOPS**

Thermoplastic Elastomer Based on Natural Rubber e: **TPE-NR**

Thesaurus der Medizin d: **TdM**

Thesaurus des Activités Médicales f: **THESAM**

Thesaurus Naturwissenschaft und Technik d: **TNT**

Thesaurus of Medical Descriptors e: **TMD**

Theses. Catholic Medical College e: **Theses Cathol Med Coll**

Theses. Catholic Medical College (Seoul) e: **Theses Cathol Med Coll (Seoul)**

Theses Collection. Yeungnam University. Natural Sciences e: **Theses Collect Yeungnam Univ Nat Sci**

Theses de Docteur-Ingenieur. Universite de Dakar. Serie Sciences Naturelles f: **Theses Doct Ing Univ Dakar Ser Sci Nat**

Thiamine Tetrahydrofurfuryl Disulfide e: **TTFD**

Thiamintetrahydrofurfuryldisulfid d: **TTFD**

Thick Weather Watch (Coast Guard) e: **T WW**

Thiermedicinische Rundschau d: **Thiermed Rundschau**

Thin-Film Polarizer e: **TFP**

Third Sea Lord and Controller e: **TSLC**

This Mode of Transportation has been Determined to be More Advantageous to the Government e: **TMDAG**

Thompson Medical Co., Inc. e: **TM**

Thoracic and Cardiovascular Surgeon e: **Thorac Cardiovasc Surg**

Thorne Ecological Foundation e: **TEF**

Thorne Ecological Institute e: **TEI**

Thoroughbred Racing Protective Bureau e: **TRPB**

Thread Environment Block e: **TEB**

Threat Environment Description e: **TED**

Threatened Species and Ecological Communities e: **TSEC**

Three-Astronaut Space System Experimental Laboratory e: **TASSEL**

Three Mile Island Environmental Radiation e: **TMI RAD**

three-polar e: **t.p.**

Thrombolysis in Myocardial Infarction (Study) [Medicine] e: **TIMI**

Through Ice Bathymetry System e: **TIBS**, e: **TlBS**

Through-Water Communications System e: **TWCS**

Thrust Assessment Support Environment e: **TASE**

Thrust-Assisted Orbiter Shuttle e: **TAOS**

Thrust-to-Earth Weight Ratio e: **TEWR**

Thumb-Signature Endorsement System e: **TSES**

Thunderstorm Research Project [Environmental Science Services Administration] e: **TRP**

Thüringisches Wassergesetz d: **ThürWG**

Thymidylate Synthetase Dihydrofolate Reductase e: **TS-DHFR**

Tianjin Medical Journal e: **Tianjin Med J**, e: **TIYADG**

Tibetan Plateau Meteorological Experiment e: **TIPMEX**

Tidal Water e: **TW**

Tidbinbilla Deep Space Communications Complex e: **TDSCC**

Tidbinbilla Deep Space Tracking Station e: **TDSTS**

Tide Gauges for Long Term Sea Level Trends e: **GLOSS-LTT**

Tide Gauges for Ocean Circulation Monitoring e: **GLOSS-OC**

Tidehochwasser[stand] d: **Thw**

Tidemittelwasser d: **Tmw**

Tidewater Bermuda Experiment e: **TIBEX**

Tidewater Consortium, Librarians' Networking Committee e: **VTCCHE**

Tidewater, Inc. e: **TDW**

Tidewater Marine Service, Inc. e: **TMS**

Tidewater Nicaragua Project Foundation e: **TNPF**

Tidewater Oil e: **TV**

Tidewater Oil Company e: **TV**

Tidewater Virginia Development Council e: **TVDC**

Tidewater Virginian e: **Tidewtr VA**

Tiefladelinie für Fahrt in Frischwasser d: **F**

Tiefladelinie für Fahrt in Seewasser während des Winters d: **W**

tiefster Wasserspiegel d: **TWSp**

Tiefwasserhäfen-Kommission d: **THK**

Tier d: **T**

Tier-Mensch-Übergangsfeld d: **TMÜ**

Tier und Naturschutz e.V. d: **TUN**

Tieraerztliche Praxis *d:* **Tieraerztl Prax**
Tieraerztliche Rundschau *d:* **Tieraerztl
Rd**, *d:* **Tieraerztl Rundsch**, *d:* **Tieraerztl
Rundschau**
Tieraerztliche Umschau *d:* **Tieraerztl
Umsch**
Tieraerztliche Zeitschrift *d:* **Tieraerztl Z**
Tierarzt *d:* **TA**
Tierärztekammer *d:* **TÄK**
Tierärztliche Hochschule *d:* **TAeH**, *d:*
TÄH, *d:* **T H**, *d:* **TiH**
Tierärztliche Hochschule [Hannover] *d:*
TiHo
Tierärztliche Praxis *d:* **Tierärztl Prax**
Tierärztliche Rundschau *d:* **TierR**
Tierärztliche Vereinigung für Tierschutz
d: **TVT**
Tierärztlicher Hygienedienst *d:* **THD**
Tierärztliches Centralblatt *d:* **TäC**
Tierbergungswagen *d:* **TBW**
Tierbeschaffungsausschuß *d:* **T.-A.**
Tierce *e:* **Tc**
tierce(s) *e:* **tc**
tierces *e:* **tcs**
Tiered Homing Overlay *e:* **THOR**
Tierernaehrung und Fuetterung *d:*
Tierernaehr Fuetter
Tiergarten *d:* **Tgt.**, *d:* **Tierg**
Tiergarten-Gesellschaft Zürich *d:* **TGZ**
Tiergesundheitsamt *d:* **TGA**
Tiergesundheitsdienst *d:* **TGD**
Tierhygienisches Institut *d:* **THI**
tierisch *d:* **tier.**
tierische Rohstoffe *d:* **tR**
Tierisches Archiv *d:* **TA**
tierisches Eiweiß *d:* **TE**
Tierklinik *e:* **TKL**
Tierkörperbeseitigungsanstalt *d:* **TBA**, *d:*
TKBA
Tierkörperbeseitigungsgesetz *d:*
TierBesG, *d:* **TierkBesG**, *d:* **TierKBG**,
d: **TKBG**
Tierkörperverwertungsanstalt *d:* **TKV**, *d:*
TVA
Tiermedizinische Hochschule *d:* **TMH**
Tierpathologisches Institut der
tierärztlichen Fakultät der Universität
München *d:* **Tierp.Inst.**
Tierphysiologie, Tierernaehrung, und
Futtermittelkunde *d:* **Tierphysiol
Tierernaehr Futtermittelk**
Tierra a Aire *s:* **G/A**
Tierra a aire y aire a tierra *s:* **G/A/G**
Tierra adentro *s:* **LAN**
Tierra Amiga. Red de Ecología Social,
Amigos de la Tierra. Montevideo. *s:*
Tierra Amiga.
Tierra del Fuego *s:* **T del F**
Tierra y Sociedad *s:* **Tierra y Soc**
Tiers Monde Sante Solidarité *f:* **TMSS**
Tiers Monde. Universite de Paris. Institut
d'Etude du Développement Economique
et Social (Paris) *f:* **UP/TM**
Tiers Ordre Carmelitaine *f:* **TOC**
Tierschutzgesetz *d:* **TG**, *d:* **TierSchG**, *d:*
TSchG, *d:* **TSG**
Tierschutzverein *d:* **TschV**
Tierseuchenentschädigung *d:* **TSE**
Tierseuchenklasse *d:* **TSK**
Tierversuch *d:* **Tiervers.**, *d:* **TV**
Tierzucht *d:* **TZ**
Tierzucht-Hauptinspektion *d:* **THI**
Tierzuchtgesetz *d:* **TierZG**, *d:* **TZG**

Tierzuchtinspektion *d:* **TI**
Tierzuchtleiter *d:* **TZL**
TIGER Geographic Reference File Names,
1990 *e:* **PUBGRF90**
TIGER [Topologically Integrated
Geographic Resource] Mapping Service
e: **TMS**
Tihanyi Biologiai Kutatointezetenek
Evkoenyve *H:* **Tihanyi Biol
Kutatointezetenek Evkoen**
Tijdschrift voor Economische en Sociale
Geografie *n:* **TEG**, *n:* **TESG**, *n:*
TESGA, *n:* **Tijd Ec Soc**, *n:* **Tijd Ec Soc
Geogr**, *n:* **Tijdschr Econ Soc Geogr**, *n:*
Tijdschrift voor Econ en Soc Geog
Timber Leaflet. Forestry Department
(British Solomon Islands Protectorate) *e:*
**Timb Leafl For Dep (Brit Solomon
Islands Protect)**
Timber, Recreation, Environment,
Aesthetics for a Sustained, Usable,
Resource *e:* **TREASURE**
Time- Alternating Space- Uncentered *e:*
TASU
Time and Effort Measurement through
Periodic Observation *e:* **TEMPO**
Time and Relative Dimensions in Space *e:*
TARDIS
Time and Space Positioning Information *e:*
TSPI
Time and Space Processing *e:* **TSP**
Time of landing first waterborne assault
wave *e:* **H-HOUR**
Time Polarity Control *e:* **TPC**
Time-Space-Position-Information Data
Processor *e:* **TDP**
Time-Space-Time switch *e:* **TST**
Time to Circularize Orbit *e:* **TTC**
Time to Protection *e:* **TTP**
Timed Environment Multipartioned
Operating System *e:* **TEMPOS**
Times Health Supplement *e:* **THS**
Tinley Park Mental Health Center *e:* **ITpM**
TIPHON Remote InterOp *e:* **TRIO**
Tiroler Wasserkraftwerke AG, Innsbruck
d: **TIWAG**
TIROS [Television and Infrared
Observation Satellite] Operational
Vertical Sounder *e:* **TOVS**
TIROS (Television Infrared Observation
Satellite) Ice Reconnaissance *e:* **TIREC**
TIROS (Television Infrared Observation
Satellite) Operational Satellite *e:* **TOS**
TIROS (Television Infrared Observation
Satellite) Operational Satellite System *e:*
TOSS
TIROS (Televison Infrared Observation
Satellite) Operational System *e:* **TOS**
Tishomingo National Wildlife Refuge *e:*
TNWR
Titan Biologic Explorer *e:* **TBE**
Tivoli Management Environment *e:* **TME**
Tobacco and Health Information Services
e: **THIS**
Tobacco and Health Research Institute *e:*
TAHRI
Toccoa Falls College [Georgia] *e:* **TFC**
TOGA Automated Observations *e:* **TAO**
TOGA Sea Level Center *e:* **TSLC**
Tohoku Geophysical Journal. Science
Reports of the Tohoku University. Fifth
Series *e:* **Tohoku Geophys J Sci Rep
Tohoku Univ Fifth Ser**

Tohoku Journal of Experimental Medicine
e: **TJEMA**, *e:* **Toh J Ex Me**, *e:* **Tohoku J
Exp Med**, *e:* **Toh[oku] J Ex[p] Med**
Tohoku Medical Journal *e:* **Tohoku Med J**
Tohoku University. Science Reports.
Geology *e:* **Tohoku Univ Sci Repts
Geology**
Tohoku University. Science Reports. Series
2. Geology *e:* **Tohoku Univ Sci Rep Ser
2**
Tohoku University. Science Reports. Series
3. Mineralogy, Petrology, and Economic
Geology *e:* **Tohoku Univ Sci Rep Ser 3**
Tokai Journal of Experimental and Clinical
Medicine *e:* **TJEMD**, *e:* **Tokai J Exp
Clin Med**
Toko-Ginecologia Practica *e:* **Tokoginecol
Prac**
Tokushima Journal of Experimental
Medicine *e:* **Tokushima J Exp Med**
Tokyo Astronomical Observatory *e:* **TAO**
Tokyo Astronomical Observatory. Kiso
Information Bulletin *e:* **Tokyo Astron
Obs Kiso Inf Bull**
Tokyo Astronomical Observatory. Report
e: **Tokyo Astron Obs Rep**
Tokyo Astronomical Observatory. Time and
Latitude Bulletins *e:* **Tokyo Astron Obs
Time and Latitude Bull**
Tokyo Jikeika Medical Journal *e:* **Tokyo
Jikeika Med J**
Tokyo Journal of Medical Sciences *e:*
Tokyo J Med Sci
Tokyo Kyoiku Daigaku. Science Reports.
Section C. Geology, Mineralogy, and
Geography *e:* **Tokyo Kyoiku Daigaku
Sci Rep Sec C**
Tokyo Medical and Dental University *e:*
TMDU
Tokyo Metropolitan Research Institute for
Environmental Protection. Annual Report.
English Translation *e:* **Tokyo Metrop
Res Inst Environ Prot Annu Rep Engl
Transl**
Tokyo Metropolitan University.
Geographical Reports *e:* **Tokyo Metrop
Univ Geogr Rep**
Tokyo University. Earthquake Research
Institute. Bulletin *e:* **Tokyo Univ
Earthquake Research Inst Bull**
Tololo Astronomical Observatory *e:* **TLL**
Tonerdegel *d:* **TEG**
Tonerdeleichtstein (Baustoff) *d:* **TL**
Tonerdemodul *d:* **TM**
Tonerdeschaumleichtstein *d:* **TSL**
Tonerdeschmelzzement *d:* **TSZ**
Tonerdezement *d:* **TZ**
Tongue of the Ocean *e:* **TOTO**
Tonindustrie-Zeitung und Keramische
Rundschau. Zentralblatt für das
Gesamtgebiet der Steine und Erden *d:*
TIZ
Tons of Cubic Capacity Bale Space *e:*
TCCBL
Tonto Forest Observatory *e:* **TFO**
Tonto Forest Seismological Observatory *e:*
TFSO
Tonto Hills Observatory *e:* **THO**
Too Badly Decomposed/Technician
Destroyed Animal *e:* **TBD/TDA**
Tool to assess regional and global
environmental and health targets for
sustainability *e:* **TARGETS**

Top End and Torres Straight Islander Primary Health Care Network *e:* **TEATSIPHCN**

Top of the Atmosphere *e:* **TOA**, *e:* **TOP**

Top Water Level *e:* **TWL**

Topeka Weather Forecast Office *e:* **TOP**

Topics in Astrophysics and Space Physics *e:* **Top Astrophys Space Phys**

Topics in Emergency Medicine *e:* **Top Emerg Med**

Topics in Environmental Health *e:* **TEH**, *e:* **Top Environ Health**

Topics in Health Care Financing *e:* **THC**, *e:* **THCF**, *e:* **Top Health Care Financ**

Topics in Health Care Materials Management *e:* **THM**

Topics in Health Record Management *e:* **Top Health Rec Manage**, *e:* **TRM**

Topics in Medicinal Chemistry *e:* **Top Med Chem**

Topics in Molecular and Structural Biology *e:* **Top Mol Struct Biol**

Topics in Perinatal Medicine *e:* **Top Perinat Med**, *e:* **TPEMDZ**

Topographisch-geodätische Einheit *d:* **TGE**

Topography [Ocean] Experiment *e:* **TOPEX**

Topological Effect on Molecular Orbitals *e:* **TEMO**

Topologically Integrated Geographic Encoding and Reference/Geographic Identification Code Scheme [United States Census Bureau] *e:* **TIGER/GICS**

Topologically Integrated Geographic Encoding and Reference/Geographic Reference File-Names *e:* **TIGER/GRF-N**

Topological[ly] Integrated Geographic Encoding and Reference (or Referencing) *e:* **TIGER**

Topologically Integrated Geographic Encoding and Referencing/Census Tract Street Index *e:* **TIGER-CTSI**

Topologically Integrated Geographic Encoding and Referencing System, Census *e:* **TIGER**

Topologically Integrated Geographic Resource and Information System *e:* **TIGRIS**

Topologically Integrated Geographic Resource/Line Record Identification Number *e:* **TLID**

Torah Atmosphere *e:* **TA**

Torino Universita Istituto Geologico Pubblicazioni *i:* **Torino Univ Ist Geol Pub**

Tornado Self Protection Jammer *e:* **TSPJ**

tornado vortex signature *e:* **TVS**

Toroidal Space Station *e:* **TSS**

Toronto Classroom Observation Schedule *e:* **TCOS**

Toronto University Institute for Aerospace Studies UTIAS Report *e:* **Toronto Univ Inst Aerosp Stud UTIAS Rep**

Toronto University. Institute for Aerospace Studies. UTIAS Review *e:* **TIRVB**

Toronto University Institute for Aerospace Studies UTIAS Review *e:* **Toronto Univ Inst Aerosp Stud UTIAS Rev**

Toronto University Institute for Aerospace Studies UTIAS Technical Note *e:* **Toronto Univ Inst Aerosp Stud UTIAS Tech Note**

Toronto University Studies Geological Series *e:* **Toronto Univ Studies G S**

Torpedo Boat [Hydrofoil] *e:* **PTH**

torpedo water *e:* **tw**

Torpedo Water Tube *e:* **TWT**

Torres Strait Protected Zone *e:* **TSPZ**

Torres Strait Protected Zone Authority *e:* **TSPZA**

Torry Research Station (Aberdeen, Scotland) Annual Report *e:* **Torry Res Stn (Aberdeen Scotl) Annu Rep**

Torso Back Protective Armo[u]r *e:* **TBPA**

Torso Front Protective Armo[u]r *e:* **TFPA**

Torun Radio Astronomy Observatory *e:* **TRAO**

Torus Water Storage Tank *e:* **TWST**

Totable Tornado Observatory *e:* **TOTO**

Total Aerospace Vehicle [or Aircraft] Authorization *e:* **TAA**

Total Assets Protection, Inc. *e:* **TAPP**

total atmospheric carbon *e:* **TAC**

Total Body Water *e:* **TBW**

total body water *e:* **TW**

Total Earth Resources System for the Shuttle Era *e:* **TERSSE**

Total Electronic and Mechanical Protection against Emission of Spurious Transmission *e:* **TEMPEST**

Total Emergency Medical Services System *e:* **TEMSS**

Total Energy and Environmental Conditioning *e:* **TEEC**

Total Environment Analysis and management *e:* **TEAM**

Total Environment Centre *e:* **TEC**

Total Environment Surveillance Sensors *e:* **TESS**

Total Environmental Action Foundation *e:* **TEAF**

total environmental control *e:* **tec**

Total Environmental Control System *e:* **TECS**

Total Environmental Facility *e:* **TEF**

Total Environmental Protection *e:* **TENPRO**

Total Feedwater Flow *e:* **TFF**

Total Health Information System *e:* **THIS**

Total Health Systems, Inc. *e:* **TLHT**

Total Hospital [Operating] and Medical Information System *e:* **THOMIS**

Total Hydrocarbon *e:* **THC**

Total Hydrocarbon Reforming *e:* **THR**

Total Hydroxyproline *e:* **THYP**

Total Identifiable Chlorinated Hydrocarbons *e:* **TICH**

Total Inactive Aerospace Vehicle Inventory *e:* **TII**

Total Learning Environment *e:* **TLE**

Total Ocean Profiling System *e:* **TOPS**

Total Online Medical Material Integration *e:* **TOMMI**

Total Overall Aerospace Vehicle [or Aircraft] Authorization *e:* **TOAA**

Total Overall Aerospace Vehicle [or Aircraft] Inventory *e:* **TOAI**

Total Ozone Mapping Spectrometer - Earth Probe *e:* **TOMS-EP**

Total Parameter Space *e:* **TPS**

Total Petroleum Hydrocarbon *e:* **TPH**

Total Polar Material *e:* **TPM**

total publishing environment *e:* **TPE**

Total Radiance Spectral Polarization *e:* **TRSP**

Total Rare Earths *e:* **TRE**

Total Recoverable Petroleum Hydrocarbon *e:* **TRPH**

Total Remote Access Center *e:* **TRACE**

Total Remote Assistance Center *e:* **TRACE**

Total Water Burden *e:* **TWB**

Total Water Management *e:* **TWM**

Totally encapsulated chemical protective *e:* **TECP**

Totally Enclosed Air-Water-Cooled *e:* **TEAWC**

Totally Enclosed Air-Water-Cooled Motor *e:* **TEAWC Motor**

Totally Enclosed All-Water-Cooled *e:* **TEWAC**

Totally Enclosed Water-Cooled *e:* **TEWC**

Totally Enclosed Water-Cooled Motor *e:* **TEWC Motor**

Totally Integrated Environment *e:* **TIE**

Totem Ocean Trailer Express (to Alaska) *e:* **TOTE**

Totwassergehalt *d:* **TW**

Touch for Health Foundation *e:* **TFH**, *e:* **TFHF**, *e:* **THF**

Touchdown Protection *e:* **TDP**

Touche Remnant Natural Resources *e:* **TRNR**

Toulouse Medical *e:* **Toulouse Med**

Toulouse Space Center *e:* **CST**

Tour Outer Planet Spacecraft *e:* **TOPS**

Tourelleau d'Observation et d'Intervention *f:* **TOI**

Tourisme en Espace Rural *f:* **TER**

Tourist Observation and Underwater Research Submarine *e:* **TOURS**

Touristenverein "Die Naturfreunde" *d:* **TVDN**, *d:* **TVN**

TOW [Tube-launched Optically Tracked, Wire-Guided] Cover Artillery Protection *e:* **TOW CAP**

TOW [Tube-launched Optically Tracked Wire-Guided] Protective Shelters *e:* **TOWPROS**

Toward a Concurrent Engineering Environment in the Building and Engineering Structures Industry *e:* **ToCEE**

Toward an Electronic Health Record Europe *e:* **TEHRE**

Towards Rural and Outback Health Professionals in Queensland *e:* **TROHPIQ**

Towarzystwo Geofizykow *P:* **TG**

Towarzystwo Geograficzne *P:* **TG**

Towed Acoustic Tactical Underwater Warning System *e:* **TUWS**

Towed Ocean Bottom Instrument *e:* **TOBI**

Towed Oceanographic Data Acquisition System *e:* **TODAS**

Tower Aviation Weather Reporting Station *e:* **TAWRS**

Townsville Naturalist *e:* **Townsville Nat**

Toxicological Agents Protective *e:* **TAP**

Toxicological and Environmental Chemistry *e:* **Toxicol Environ Chem**

Toxicological and Environmental Chemistry Reviews *e:* **Toxicol Environ Chem Rev**, *e:* **TXECB**

Toxicology and Environmental Health Information Program *e:* **TEHIP**

Toxicology and Industrial Health *e:* **Toxicol Ind Health**

Toxicology and Microbiology Division e: **TMD**

Toxicology Information Program [National Library of Medicine] e: **TIP**

Toxicology Information Query Response Center [National Library of Medicine] e: **TIQRC**

Toxline Chemical Dictionary [National Library of Medicine] e: **TCD**

Trabajos Compostelanos de Biologia s: **Trab Compostelanos Biol**

Trabajos de Geologia s: **Trab Geol**

Trabajos de Geologia Oviedo Universidad Facultad de Ciencias s: **Trab Geol Oviedo Univ Fac Cienc**

Trabajos Instituto Cajal de Investigaciones Biologicas s: **Trab Inst Cajal Invest Biol**

Trabajos Instituto de Fisiologia Faculdade de Medicina Universidade do Lisboa p: **Trab Inst Fisiol Fac Med Univ Lisboa**

Trabajos Instituto Espanol de Oceanografia s: **Trab Inst Esp Oceanogr**

Trabajos Instituto Nacional de Ciencias Medicas s: **Trab Inst Nac Cienc Med**

Trabajos Instituto Nacional de Ciencias Medicas (Madrid) s: **Trab Inst Nac Cienc Med (Madrid)**

Trabajos Presentados al Quinto Congreso Medico Latin-Americano s: **Trab 5 Cong Med Latino-Am**

Trabalhos. Instituto Oceanografico Universidade do Recife p: **Trab Inst Oceanogr Univ Recife**

Trabalhos Oceanograficos. Universidade Federal de Pernambuco s: **Trab Oceanogr Univ Fed Pernambuco**

Trace and Atmospheric Chemistry near the Equator-Atlantic e: **TRACE-A**

Trace Atmospheric Gas Analyser e: **TAGA**

trace component of natural uranium e: **U234**

Trace Elements in Man and Animals e: **TEMA**

Trace Elements in Medicine e: **Tr Elem Med**

Trace Elements Investigations [United States Geological Survey] e: **TEI**

Trace Gas Biogeochemistry section e: **TGB**

Trace Gas Exchange between Midlatitude Terrestrial Ecosystems and Atmosphere e: **TRAGEX**

Trace Metabolism in Man and Animals e: **TEM**

Trace Metals, Radiobiology and Cancer Information Retrieval System e: **TRACIRS**

Trace Remote Atmospheric Chemical Evaluation e: **TRACE**

Trace Substances in Environmental Health e: **Trace Subst Environ Health**

Trace Substances in Environmental Health Proceedings University of Missouri Annual Conference e: **Trace Subst Environ Health Proc Univ Mo Annu Conf**

Track Geometry e: **TG**

Tracking Air with Circularly Polarized Radar e: **TRACIR**

Tracking Error Propagation and Orbit Prediction Program e: **TEPOP Program**

Tracking in an Active and Passive Radar Environment e: **TAPRE**

Tracking Overpower Protection System e: **TOPPS**

Tractor Protection Valve e: **TPV**

Tracts in Mathematics and Natural Science e: **Tracts Math Nat Sci**

Trade and Environment Database e: **TED**

Trade-offs among Competing Social, Environmental, and Economic Goals e: **TOCSEEG**

Trade Protection Service e: **TP**

trade-wind-zone oceanography e: **twzo**

Trademark of Earth Computer Technologies e: **Earth Station**

Trader's Environment Demonstration Project for Banks and Investment Companies in Eastern Europe and NIS Countries e: **TREND-CP96-248**

Traditional Chinese Medicine e: **TCM**

Traditional Ecological Knowledge e: **TEK**

Traditional Environmental Knowledge e: **TEK**

Traditional Medical Practice e: **TMP**

Traditional Medicines Evaluation Committee e: **TMEC**

Traditional Medicines Programme e: **TRAMED**

Traditional Medicines Programme [University of Cape Town] e: **TRAMED**

TRADOC [Training and Doctrine Command] Program Integration Office for the Synthetic Training Environment e: **TPIO-STE**

TRADOC [Training and Doctrine Command] Project Office for Constructive Synthetic Training Environment e: **TPO CONSTRUCTIVE**

TRADOC [Training and Doctrine Command] Project Office for Live Training Environment e: **TPO LIVE**

TRADOC [Training and Doctrine Command] Project Office for Virtual Synthetic Training Environment e: **TPO VIRTUAL**

TrägerGemeinschaft Akkreditierung d: **TGA**

Trägergemeinschaft für Akkreditierung GmbH d: **TGA**

Tragkraftspritzenfahrzeug mit Löschwasserbehälter d: **TSF-W**

Trail Riders of the Wilderness e: **TRW**

Trailerable Intracoastal Waterway Aids to Navigation e: **TICWAN**

Trailerless Collective Protective Shelter e: **TRACOPS**

Traill on Medical Jurisprudence e: **Traill Med. Jur.**

Training ICON Environment e: **TIE**

Training Medical Center e: **TMC**

Training Observation e: **TO**

Training Officer, Medical e: **TOM**

Training, Research, Environment and Education e: **TREE**

Training Set, Fire Observation e: **TSFO**

Trajectory and Signature Data e: **TASD**

Trans-Atlantic Geotraverse e: **TAG**

Trans-Caspian Railroad linking the Caspian Sea region with the southern Urals of the USSR e: **Trans-Caspian**

Trans European Natural Gas Pipeline, Finance Company, Ltd. e: **TENP FINCO**

Trans-Frontier Pollution e: **TFP**

Trans-Jordan Frontier Force e: **T.J.F.F.**

Trans-Ocean Containers Ltd. e: **TOC**

Trans-Ocean Leasing Corp. [of California] e: **TOL**

Trans-Ocean News Service e: **TONS**

Trans-Ocean Terminals e: **TOT**

Trans Oceanic Airways Ltd. e: **TOA**, e: **TQ**

Trans-Oceanic Geophysical Investigations e: **TOGI**

Trans Unaturated Fatty Acids e: **TUFA**

Transaction Control System MIDAS (Medizinisches Informationssystem Danderyd-Spit) e: **TCSM**

Transaction Machine Environment e: **TME**

Transactional Analysis of Personality and Environment e: **TAPE**

Transactional Remote Procedure Call e: **TRPC**

Transactions. All-India Institute of Mental Health e: **Trans All-India Inst Ment Health**

Transactions. American Association of Genito-Urinary Surgeons e: **TAAGA**, e: **Tr Am Ass Genito-Urin Surg**, e: **Tr[ans] Am Ass[oc] Genit[o]-Urin Surg**

Transactions. American Association of Obstetricians and Gynecologists e: **Trans Am Assoc Obstet Gynecol**

Transactions. American Association of Obstetricians, Gynecologists, and Abdominal Surgeons e: **Trans Am Assoc Obstet Gynecol Abdom Surg**

Transactions. American Clinical and Climatological Association e: **Trans Aro Clin Climatol Assoc**

Transactions. American Geophysical Union e: **TAGUA**, e: **TAGUA**, e: **T Am Geophy**, e: **Trans Am[er] Geophys Union**, e: **Trans Am Geophys Union**

Transactions. American Gynecological Society e: **Trans Am Gynecol Soc**

Transactions. American Society of Tropical Medicine e: **Tr Am Soc Trop Med**

Transactions and Papers. Institute of British Geographers. London e: **IBG/TP.**

Transactions and Proceedings. Geological Society of South Africa e: **Trans Proc Geol Soc S Afr**

Transactions and Proceedings. Perthshire Society of Natural Science e: **Trans Proc Perthshire Soc Natur Sci**

Transactions and Proceedings. Torquay Natural History Society e: **Trans Proc Torquay Natur Hist Soc**

Transactions. Association of Industrial Medical Officers e: **Trans Assoc Ind Med Off**

Transactions. Association of Life Insurance Medical Directors of America e: **TALIA**, e: **Trans Assoc Life Ins Med Dir Am**

Transactions. Australian Medical Congress e: **Trans Aust Med Congress**

Transactions. Cardiff Naturalists Society e: **Trans Cardiff Nat[ur] Soc**

Transactions. Caribbean Geological Conference e: **TCGCB**

Transactions. College of Medicine of South Africa e: **Trans Coll Med S Afr**

Transactions. Conference on Polysaccharides in Biology *e:* **Trans Conf Polysaccharides Biol**

Transactions. Dumfriesshire and Galloway Natural History and Antiquarian Society *e:* **Transact Dumfries**, *e:* **Trans Dumfries Galloway Nat Hist Andq Soc**, *e:* **Trans Dumfriesshire Galloway Natur Hist Antiq Soc**

Transactions. East Lothian Antiquarian and Field Naturalists' Society *e:* **Trans East Lothian Antiq Field Nat Soc**, *e:* **Trans E Lothian Antiq Fld Natur Soc**

Transactions. Edinburgh Geological Society *e:* **Trans Edinb Geol Soc**, *e:* **Trans Edinburgh Geol Soc**

Transactions. Federal-Provincial Wildlife Conference *e:* **Trans Fed-Prov Wildl Conf**

Transactions. Geological Society of Glasgow *e:* **Trans Geol Soc Glasg**

Transactions. Geological Society of South Africa *e:* **TGSSA**, *e:* **Trans Geol Soc S Afr**

Transactions. Geothermal Resources Council *e:* **Trans Geotherm Resour Counc**

Transactions. Gulf Coast Association of Geological Societies *e:* **TGCGA**, *e:* **Trans Gulf Coast Ass Geol Soc**, *e:* **Trans Gulf Coast Assoc Geol Soc**

Transactions. Gulf Coast Molecular Biology Conference *e:* **Trans Gulf Coast Mol Biol Conf**

Transactions. Hertfordshire Natural History Society and Field Club *e:* **Trans Hertfordshire Nat Hist Field Club**, *e:* **Trans Hertfordshire Nat Hist Soc Field Club**

Transactions. Indiana State Medical Society *e:* **Tr Indiana Med Soc**

Transactions. Institute of British Geographers *e:* **T I Br Geog**, *e:* **Trans Inst Brit Geogr**

Transactions. Institute of British Geographers. London *e:* **IBG/T.**

Transactions. Institute of British Geographers. New Series *e:* **Trans Inst Br Geogr New Ser**

Transactions. Institute of British Geographers. Oxford, England *e:* **Transactions/Oxford.**

Transactions. Institute of Mining and Metallurgy. Mining and Geological Series *e:* **Trans Inst Min Metall Min Geol Ser**

Transactions. Institute of Mining and Metallurgy (Ostrava). Mining and Geological Series *e:* **Trans Inst Min Metall (Ostrava) Min Geol Ser**

Transactions. Institution of Mining and Metallurgy Section B. Applied Earth Science *e:* **Trans Inst Min Metall Sect B Appl Earth Sci**

Transactions. Institution of Water Engineers *e:* **Trans Inst Water Eng**

Transactions. International Society for Geothermal Engineering *e:* **Trans Int Soc Geotherm Eng**

Transactions. Japan Society for Aeronautical and Space Sciences *e:* **TJASA**, *e:* **Trans Jap Soc Aeronaut Space Sci**, *e:* **Trans Jpn Soc Aeronaut and Space Sci**, *e:* **Trans Jpn Soc Aeronaut Space Sci**

Transactions. Leeds Geological Association *e:* **Trans Leeds Geol Assoc**

Transactions. Medical and Physical Society of Bombay *e:* **Tr Med and Phys Soc Bombay**

Transactions. Medical Society of London *e:* **Trans Med Soc Lond**

Transactions. Medico-Legal Society *e:* **Med Leg Soc Trans**

Transactions. Mining, Geological, and Metallurgical Institute of India *e:* **Trans Min Geol Metall Inst India**, *e:* **Trans Mining Geol Met Inst India**

Transactions. Natural History Society of Formosa *e:* **Trans Nat Hist Soc Formosa**

Transactions. Natural History Society of Northumberland, Durham, and Newcastle-Upon-Tyne *e:* **Trans Nat Hist Northumberl Durham Newcastle Upon Tyne**, *e:* **Trans Nat Hist Soc Northumberl Durham Newcastle-Upon-Tyne**

Transactions. Natural History Society of Northumbria *e:* **Trans Nat Hist Soc Northumbria**

Transactions. New England Obstetrical and Gynecological Society *e:* **Trans New Engl Obstet Gynecol Soc**

Transactions. New Jersey Obstetrical and Gynecological Society *e:* **Trans NJ Obstet Gynecol Soc**

Transactions. North American Wildlife and Natural Resources Conference *e:* **Trans N Am Wildl Nat Resour Conf**, *e:* **Trans North Am Wildl Nat Res Conf**, *e:* **Trans North Am Wildl Nat Resour Conf**

Transactions. North American Wildlife Conference *e:* **Trans North Am Wildl Conf**

Transactions of the American Clinical and Climatological Association *e:* **Trans Am Clin Climatol Assoc**

Transactions of the Cardiff Naturalists' Society *e:* **TCNS**

Transactions of the Edinburgh Geological Society *e:* **TEGS**

Transactions of the Geological Society of Glasgow *e:* **TGSG**

Transactions of the Northeast Section. Wildlife Society *e:* **Trans Northeast Sect Wildl Soc**

Transactions on Aerospace and Electronic Systems *e:* **T-AES**, *e:* **Trans. AES**

Transactions on Bio-Medical Engineering *e:* **T-BME**

Transactions on Geoscience Electronics *e:* **T-Ge**, *e:* **Trans. GE**, *e:* **Trans Geosci Electron**

Transactions on Space Electronics and Telemetry *e:* **Trans SET**

Transactions on Telemetry and Remote Control *e:* **Trans TRC**

Transactions. Pacific Coast Obstetrical and Gynecological Society *e:* **Trans Pac Coast Obstet Gynecol Soc**

Transactions. Royal Geological Society *e:* **Trans R Geol Soc**

Transactions. Royal Geological Society (Cornwall) *e:* **Trans R Geol Soc (Corn)**

Transactions. Royal Society of Edinburgh Earth Sciences *e:* **Trans R Soc Edinb Earth Sci**, *e:* **Trans R Soc. Edinburgh Earth Sci**

Transactions. Royal Society of New Zealand Biological Science *e:* **Trans R Soc NZ Biol Sci**

Transactions. Royal Society of New Zealand. Earth Science *e:* **Trans R Soc NZ Earth Sci**

Transactions. Royal Society of New Zealand Geology *e:* **Trans R Soc NZ Geol**

Transactions. Royal Society of Tropical Medicine and Hygiene *R:* **T Rs Trop M**, *e:* **TRSTA**

Transactions. Royal Society of Tropical Medicine and Hyiene *e:* **Tr Roy Soc Trop Med Hyg**

Transactions. Royal Society ofTropical Medicine and Hygiene *e:* **Trans R Soc Trop Med Hyg**

Transactions. San Diego Society of Natural History *e:* **Trans San Diego Soc Nat Hist**

Transactions. Society of Occupational Medizine *e:* **Trans Soc Occup Med**

Transactions. Society of Tropical Medicine and Hygiene *e:* **Tr Soc Trop Med and Hyg**

Transactions. Society ofTropical Medicine and Hygiene (London) *e:* **Tr Soc Trop Med and Hyg (London)**

Transactions. Southwestern Federation of Geological Societies *e:* **Trans Southwest Fed Geol Soc**

Transactions. Suffolk Naturalists' Society *e:* **Trans Suffolk Natur Soc**

Transactions. Woolhope Naturalists' Field Club *e:* **Trans Woolhope Naturalists**, *e:* **Trans Woolhope Natur Fld Club**

transaktionsorientierte Programmierung *d:* **TOP**

Transaktionsorientiertes Anwendungssystem *d:* **TAS**

Transaktionsorientiertes Maschinenüberwachungs-, Datenerfassungs- und Communications-System *d:* **TMIDCS**

transatmospheric vehicle *e:* **TAV**

Transcontinental Geophysical Survey *e:* **TGS**

Transcribed Weather Broadcast *e:* **TWEB**

Transcribed Weather Broadcast Program *e:* **TWBP**

Transdihydrolisuride *l:* **TDHL**

Transearth Coast *e:* **TEC**

Transearth Injection *e:* **TEI**

Transearth Injection Geometry *e:* **TIG**

Transepidermal Water Loss *e:* **TEWL**

Transeuropa-Naturgas-Pipeline GmbH *d:* **TENP**

Transfer of Undertakings, Protection of Employees *e:* **TUPE**

Transfer Orbit Infrared Earth Sensor *e:* **TOIRS**

Transfer Orbit Stage *e:* **TOS**

Transfer Orbit Stage - Shortened Version *e:* **TOS-S**

Transfer Orbit Sun Sensor Assembly *e:* **TOSSA**

Transfer Orbital Insertion *e:* **TOI**

Transferable Water Entitlements *e:* **TWE**

Transformer Environment Overcurrent Monitor *e:* **TEOM**

Transfusion Clinique et Biologique *f:* **Transfus Clin Biol**

Transfusion Medicine e: **Transfus Med**

Transfusion Medicine Reviews e:
Transfus Med Rev

transfusionsmedizinisches
Dispositionssystem d: **TRAMIDIS**

Transient Non-Community Water System
e: **TNCWS**

Transient Protection Limit e: **TPL**

Transient Protective Device e: **TPD**

Transient Synovilis [Medicine] e: **TS**

Transient Tracers in the Ocean/North
Atlantic Study e: **TTO/NAS**

Transient Tracers in the Oceans e: **TTO**

Transient Water System e: **TWS**

Transit Injector Polaris Derived e:
TRIPOD, e: TRIPOLD

Transit Tracers in the Ocean e: **TTO**

Transition. Institute of Development
Studies, University of Guyana, Georgetown, Guyana e: **Transition/Guyana.**

Transition Plan for Implementation of
Airspace Strategy e: **TPIA**

Transitional Environmental Working Group
e: **TEWG**

Transitional Medical Assistance e: **TM**

Transitional Polar e: **TSLPOL**

Transitional Polar Atlantic e: **TSLPOLAT**

Transitional Polar Continental e:
TSLPOLCO

Transitional Polar Pacific e: **TSLPOLPA**

Translational Electromagnetic Environment
Chamber e: **TEMEC**

translitieren d: **transl.**

Transmission Line Environmental Digital
Studies e: **TRENDS**

Transmitier e: **TX**

Transmitier Control Unit e: **TCU**

Transmitier/Receiver e: **TX/RX**

Transmitier/Receiver e: **TR**

Transmitier Waveguide Pressurization
System e: **TWPS**

Transmitting Elementary Dipole with
Optional Polarization e: **XELEDOP**

Transocean Air Lines e: **TAL**

Transocean Airlines e: **TALOA**

Transocean-Europapress
[Nachrichtenagentur] d: **TOEP**

Transocean Gulf Oil Company, Pittsburgh
e: **TOC**

Transocean Leasing (container) Unit e:
TOLU

Transocean Marine Paint Association e:
TMPA

Transoceanic e: **T/O, e: transocean**

Transoceanic Abort Landing e: **TAL**

Transoceanic Airborne Environment e:
TAE

Transoceanic Development Corporation e:
TDC

Transparent Interleaved Bipolar e: **TIB**

transplantieren d: **transpl.**

transplantiert d: **transpl.**

Transport and Atmospheric Chemistry near
the Equator e: **TRACE**

Transport and Atmospheric Chemistry near
the Equator-Atlantic e: **TRACE-A**

Transport and Environment Select
Committee e: **TESC**

Transport Animal e: **TA**

Transport Environment Circulation e:
TEC

Transport Environment Monitoring System
e: **TEMS**

Transport, Environnement, Aménagement
f: **TEA**

Transport Independent Remote Procedure
Call e: **TIRPC**

Transport International Routier f: **TIR**

Transport of Chemistry near the Ocean e:
TRACE

Transport of Equatorial Waters e: **TEW**

Transport - Planning Board Ocean Shipping
e: **T(PBOS)**

Transport Processes in the Atmosphere and
the Oceans e: **TAO**

Transport, Transfer und Transformation von
Biomasse-Elementen in Wattgewässern
d: **TRANSWATT**

Transportable Applications Environment
e: **TAE**

Transportable Automated Control
Environment e: **TRACE**

Transportable Automated Weather
Distribution System e: **TAWDS**

Transportable Collective Protection System
e: **TCPS**

Transportable Earth Station e: **TES**

Transportable Orbital Tracking Station e:
TOTS

Transportable Reflective-Environment
Communications System, Version I e:
TRECS-I

Transportable Remote Analyzer for
Characterization and Environmental
Remediation e: **TRACER**

Transportable Satellite Earth Station e:
TSES

Transportable Standard Remote Terminal
e: **TSRT**

Transportation Environmental Measurement
and Recording System e: **TEMARS**

Transportation Environmental Operations
Group e: **TREOG**

Transportation International Routier e:
TIR

Transportation Protective Service e: **TPS**

Transportes Aereos de Cabo Verde s: **VR**

Transportes Aéreos de Cabo Verde f:
TACV

transportieren d: **tr**

Transportieren d: **Trsp**

Transthoracic Impedance [Medicine] e:
TTI

Transvaal and Witswatersrand Reports e:
Trans & Wit.

Transvaal Nature Conservation Division.
Annual Report e: **Transvaal Nat
Conserv Div Annu Rep**

Transversally Excited Atmospheric[-
pressure] Laser e: **TEA Laser**

transverse relaxation time: mean relaxation
time based on theinteraction of hydrogen
nuclei within a given tissue. e: **T2**

Transversely Excited Atmosphere e: **TEA**

Transverse[ly] Excited Atmospheric
[pressure] e: **TEA**

Transversely Excited Atmospheric Pressure
e: **TEAP**

Transversely-Excited Atmospheric-Pressure
Carbon Dioxide e: **TEA CO2**

Transversely Excited Atmospheric[-
pressure] Laser e: **TEAL**

Transversely Excited Atmospheric[-
pressure] Lasers e: **TEALS**

Transylvania Journal of Medicine e:
Transylvania J Med

Trap-Free Space-Charge-Limited Current
e: **TFSCLC**

Trapped Ions in Space e: **TRIS**

Trauma Registry of the American College
of Surgeons e: **TRACS**

Travaux. Centre de Recherches et d'Études
Oceanographiques f: **Trav Cent Rech
Études Oceanogr**

Travaux. Comité International pour l'Étude
des Bauxites, des Oxydes et des
Hydroxydes d'Aluminium f: **Trav Com
Int Étude Bauxites Oxydes Hydroxydes
Alum**

Travaux d'Oceanographie Spatiale Capteurs
Actifs dans l'Atlantique Nord-Est f:
TOSCANE

Travaux du Bureau Geologique f: **Trav
Bur Geol**

Travaux et Documents de Geographie
Tropicale f: **Trav Doc Geogr Trop**

Travaux Geographique de Liege f: **TGGL-
B**

Travaux Geophysiques f: **Trav Geophys**

Travaux Geophysiques (Prague) f: **Trav
Geophys (Prague)**

Travaux. Institut de Geologie et
d'Anthropologie Prehistorique. Faculte
des Sciences de Poitiers f: **Trav Inst
Geol Anthropol Prehist Fac Sci Poitiers**

Travaux. Institut Scientifique Cherifien.
Serie Botanique et Biologique Vegetale
f: **Trav Inst Sci Cherifien Ser Bot Biol
Veg**

Travaux. Institut Scientifique Cherifien.
Serie Geologie et Geographie Physique
f: **Trav Inst Sci Cherifien Ser Geol
Geogr Phys**

Travaux. Laboratoire de Geologie. Faculte
des Sciences de Grenoble f: **Trav Lab
Geol Fac Sci Grenoble**

Travaux. Laboratoire de Geologie Faculte
des Sciences de Grenoble. Memoires f:
Trav Lab Geol Fac Sci Grenoble Mem

Travaux. Laboratoire de Geologie. Faculte
des Sciences de Lyon f: **Trav Lab Geol
Fac Sci Lyon**

Travaux. Laboratoire de Geologie. Faculte
des Sciences. Universite de Bordeaux f:
Trav Lab Geol Fac Sci Univ Bordeaux

Travaux. Laboratoire de Geologie
Historique et de Paleontologie. Centre
Saint Charles. Université de Provence f:
**Trav Lab Geol Hist Paleontol Cent St
Charles Univ Provence**

Travaux. Laboratoire de Geologie. École
Normale Superieure (Paris) f: **Trav Lab
Geol Ec Norm Super (Paris)**

Travaux. Laboratoire de Microbiologie.
Faculté de Pharmacie de Nancy f: **Trav
Lab Microbiol Fac Pharm Nancy**

Travaux. Laboratoire d'Hydrobiologie et de
Pisciculture. Université de Grenoble f:
Trav Lab Hydrobiol Pscic Univ Grenoble

Travaux. Laboratoire d'Hydrogeologie
Geochimie. Faculte des Sciences
Université de Bordeaux f: **Trav Lab
Hydrogeol Geochim Fac Sci Univ
Bordeaux**

Travaux. Laboratoire Forestier de Toulouse
f: **Trav Lab For Toulouse**

Travaux. Laboratoire Forestier de Toulouse.
Tome I. Articles Divers f: **Trav Lab For
Toulouse Tome I Artic Divers**

Travaux. Laboratoire Forestier de Toulouse. Tome II. Etudes Dendrologiques *f:* **Trar Lab For Toulouse Tome II Etud Dendrol**

Travaux. Laboratoire Forestier de Toulouse. Tome V. Geographie Forestier du Monde *f:* **Trav Lab For Toulouse Tome V Geogr For Monde**

Travaux. Laboratoire Forestier. Université de Toulouse *f:* **Trav Lab For Univ Toolouse**

Travaux. Laboratoires de Matiere Medicale et de Pharmacie Galenique. Faculte de Pharmacie (Paris) *f:* **Trav Lab Matiere Med Pharm Galenique Fac Pharm (Paris)**

Travaux. Museum d'Histoire Naturelle "Grigore Antipa" *f:* **Trav Mus Hist Nat "Gr Antipa"**, *f:* **Trav Mus Hist Nat "Grigore Antipa"**

Travel by Military Aircraft, Military and/or Naval Water Carrier, Commercial Rail and/or Bus Is Authorized *e:* **TBAWRBA**

Travel Industry for the Environment *e:* **TIE**

Travel More Advantageous to the Government *e:* **TMAG**

Traveler Health & Immunization Services *e:* **TH & IS**

Travelers Health Institute *e:* **THI**

Travelers' Protective Association *e:* **TPA**

Travelers' Protective Association of America *e:* **T.P.A.**

Travelers Protective Association of America *e:* **TPAA**

Travellers Medical and Vaccination Centre *e:* **TMVC**

Travelling Medical Board *e:* **TMB**

Travelling Wave Amplitier *e:* **TWA**

Treatises of the Section of Medical Sciences. Polish Academy of Sciences *e:* **Treatises Sect Med Sci Pol Acad Sci**

Treaty Banning Nuclear Weapons Tests in the Atmosphere, in outer Space, and under Water *e:* **NTB**

Trees and Natural Resources *e:* **Trees Nat Resour**

Trends in Atmospheric Constituents Study *e:* **TRACS**

Trends in Ecology and Evolution *e:* **Trend Ecol. Evol.**, *e:* **Trends Ecol. & Evol.**

Trends in Microbiology *e:* **Trends Microbiol**

Treshold Analysis and Remote Access *e:* **TARA**

Tri Coast Environmental Corp. *e:* **TOXY**

Tri-service Medical Information System[s] *e:* **TRIMIS**

Tri-State Medical Journal *e:* **Tri State Med J**, *e:* **Tri State Med J (Greensburo NC)**, *e:* **Tri Stite Med J (Shreveport LA)**

Triacetylhexahydrotriazine *e:* **TRAT**

Triana Medical Claims Information System *e:* **TRIANA**

Triangle Trans-Ocean Buoy Network *e:* **TRITON**

Triaxial Earth Ellipsoid *e:* **TEE**

Tribhuvan University/Institute of Agriculture and Animal Science *e:* **TU/IAAS**

Tribhuvan University/Institute of Medicine *e:* **TU/IOM**

Tribhuwan University/Institute of Medicine *e:* **TC/IM**

Tribromo(hydroxy)benzoic Acid *e:* **TBHBA**

Trichlorohydroxybiphenyls *e:* **TCHB**

Tridont Health Care, Inc. *e:* **THC**

Triglyceride Hydroperoxides *e:* **TGHPO**

Trihydroxybulyrophenone *d:* **TBHP**

trillion cubic feet (natural gas) *e:* **tcf**

Trimethylammonium Hydroxide *e:* **TMAH**

Trimethylanilinium Hydroxide *e:* **TMAH**

Trimethyldihydronapthalene *l:* **TDN**

Trimethyldihydroquinoline Polymer *e:* **TDQP**

Trinational Animal Health Research Project *e:* **TAHRP**

Trinidad-and-Tobago Medical Association *e:* **TTMA**

Trinity High-Water Mark *e:* **THWM**

Trinity House High Water Mark *e:* **T.H.H.M.**

Trinity House High-water Mark *e:* **THWM**

Trinity House highwater mark *e:* **THhwm**

Trinity House low-water mark *e:* **THlwm**

Trinity-House Low Water Mark *e:* **TLWM**

Trinity House water mark *e:* **THwm**

Trinity Low-Water Mark *e:* **TLWM**

Trinkwasser *d:* **TW**, *d:* **Twas**

Trinkwasser-Aufbereitungsverordnung *d:* **TAVO**

Trinkwasser-Verordnung *d:* **Trinkwasser-Verord**, *d:* **TWVO**

Trinkwasserfluoridierungsanlage *d:* **TWF**

Trinkwasserfluorierung *d:* **TWF**

Trinkwasserverordnung *d:* **TrinkwV**, *d:* **TVO**

Triosephosphat-dehydrogenase *e:* **TPDH**

Tripartite Forum on Health and Safety in the Pharmaceutical Industry *e:* **TFPI**

Triphenyltin Hydroxide *e:* **TPTH**

Triphenyltinhydroxide *e:* **TPTH**

triphibious (land, sea, air) *e:* **triphib**

Triple-Braid Weather-Proof *e:* **TBWP**

Triple-Braid Weather-Proof Conductor *e:* **TBWP Conductor**

Triple Molecolar Collision *e:* **TMC**

Triple Space *e:* **TS**

Tripler Army Medical Center *e:* **TAMC**

Tris(fluoromethylhydroxymethylene)camphorato *e:* **TFMC**

Tris(hydroxymelhyl)methylglycine *e:* **TRICINE**

Tritiated Hydrogen *e:* **HT**

Tritiated water *e:* **THO**

Tritium Remote Control and Monitoring System *e:* **TRECAMS**

Trodove na Morskata Biologichna Stantsiya v Stalin *P:* **Tr Morsk Biol Stn Stalin**

Tromura. Tromsoe Museum Rapportserie. Naturvilenskap *n:* **TMRNV**

Tropenmedizin *d:* **TM**

Tropenmedizin und Parasitologie *R:* **Tropenmed P**, *d:* **Tropenmed Parasitol**

Tropenmedizinische Untersuchungsstelle *d:* **TMU**

tropfwassergeschützt *d:* **Dp**, *d:* **drip P**

tropic high-water inequality *e:* **hwq**

Tropic Higher High Water *e:* **TCHHW**

Tropic Higher High Water Interval *e:* **TcHHWI**

tropic higher low water *e:* **TcHLW**

Tropic Lower Low Water *e:* **TCLLW**

Tropic Lower Low Water Interval *e:* **TCLLWI**

tropica waters *e:* **T**

Tropical Aerosol Radiative Forcing Observational Experiment *e:* **TARFOX**

Tropical and Geographical Medicine *e:* **TGMEA**, *e:* **Trop Geogr Med**, *e:* **Trop Geo Me**

Tropical Animal Health and Production *e:* **Trop Anim Health Prod**

Tropical Animal Production *e:* **Trop Anim Prod**

Tropical Application of Meteorology Using Satellite *e:* **TAMSAT**

Tropical Atlantic Biological Laboratory *e:* **TABL**

Tropical Atmosphere-Ocean (array) *e:* **TAO**

Tropical Atmosphere Ocean Implementation Panel *e:* **TIP**

Tropical Climate Monitoring and Research Station Australia *e:* **TCMRS**

Tropical Earth Resources Satellite *e:* **TERS**

Tropical Ecology *e:* **Trop Ecol**

Tropical Ecosystem Environmental Observations by Satellite *e:* **TREES**

Tropical Environmental Data *e:* **TREND**

Tropical Experiment Board [of World Meteorological Organization and International Council on Scientific Unions] *e:* **TEB**

Tropical Experiment Council [of World Meteorological Organization and International Council on Scientific Unions] *e:* **TEC**

Tropical Fresh Water *e:* **TF**, *e:* **TFW**

tropical fresh water load-line *e:* **T.F.**

Tropical Medicine *e:* **TM**, *e:* **Trop Med**

Tropical Medicine and Hygiene News *e:* **Trop Med Hyg News**

Tropical Medicine and International Health *e:* **Trop Med Int Health**

Tropical Medicine and Parasitology *e:* **Trop Med Parasitol**

Tropical Medicine and Public Health Project, Bangkok *e:* **TROPMED**

Tropical Medicine Research Board *e:* **TMRB**

Tropical Medicine Research Cooperation *e:* **TMRC**

Tropical Medicine Research Studies Series *e:* **TMRSDT**, *e:* **Trop Med Res Stud Ser**

Tropical Meteorology Research Programme *e:* **TMRP**

Tropical Ocean and Global Atmosphere Programme Automated Observations *e:* **TAO**

tropical ocean-atmosphere *e:* **TOA**

Tropical Ocean-Atmosphere Newsletter *e:* **TOAN**

Tropical Ocean Climate Study *e:* **TOCS**

Tropical Ocean Global Atmosphere Program *e:* **TOGA**

Tropical Ocean Global Atmosphere Program Coupled Ocean-Atmosphere Response Experiment *e:* **TOGA[-]COARE**

Tropical Ocean Global Atmosphere Program Numerical Experiment Group *e:* **TOGA NEG**

Tropical Oceanographic and Meteorological Experiment *e:* **TROMEX**

Tropical Oceans and Global Atmosphere Programme *e:* **TOGA**

Tropical Oceans and Global Atmosphere Project *e:* **TOGA**

Tropical Oceans Global Atmosphere *e:* **TOGA**

Tropical Pacific Upper Ocean Heat and Mass Budgets *e:* **TROPIC HEAT**

Tropical Rainforest Ecology Experiment *e:* **TREE**

Tropical Research Medical Laboratory *e:* **TRMG**

Tropical Soil Biology and Fertility Programme *e:* **TSBF**

Tropical Urban Climate Experiment *e:* **TRUCE**

Tropical Western Pacific Ocean *e:* **TWPO**

Tropospheric Aerosol Radiative Forcing Observation[al] Experiment *e:* **TARFOX**

Tropospheric Forward-Scatier-Zug *e:* **TropoFwdScZg**

Tropospheric Radiometer for Atmospheric Chemistry and Environmental Research *e:* **TRACER**

Truck, Rail, and Water *e:* **TR and W**, *e:* **TR & W**

Trudy Akademii Nauk Latviiskoi SSR Institut Mikrobiologii *R:* **Tr Akad Nauk Latv SSR Inst Mikrobiol**

Trudy Akademii Nauk Litovskoi SSR Institut Biologii *R:* **Tr Akad Nauk Litov SSR Inst Biol**

Trudy Akademii Nauk Litovskoi SSR. Seriya V. Biologicheskie Nauki *R:* **Tr Akad Nauk Lit SSR Ser V Biol Nauki**

Trudy Akademiia Nauk Kazakhskoi SSR Institut Mikrobiologii i Virusologii *R:* **Tr Akad Nauk Kaz SSR Inst Mikrobiol Virusol**

Trudy Akademiia Nauk SSSR Sibirskoe Otdelenie. Biologicheskii Institut *R:* **Tr Akad Nauk SSSR Sibirsk Otd Biol Inst**

Trudy Akademíia Nauk SSSR Institut Biologii Vnutrennikh Vod *R:* **Tr Akad Nauk SSSR Inst Biol Vnutr Vod**

Trudy Armyanskogo Geologicheskogo Upravleniya *R:* **Tr Arm Geol Upr**

Trudy Belomorskoi Biologicheskoi Stantsii Moskovskogo Gosudarstvennogo Universiteta *R:* **Tr Belomorsk Biol Stn Mosk Gos Univ**

Trudy Biogeokhimicheskoi Laboratorii Akademiya Nauk SSSR *R:* **Tr Biogeokhim Lab Akad Nauk SSSR**

Trudy Biolog-Pochvennogo Instituta Dal'nevostochnyi Nauchnyi Tsentr Akademiya Nauk SSSR *R:* **Tr Biol Pochv Lost Dalnevost Nauchn Tsentr Akad Nauk SSSR**

Trudy Biologicheskogo Instituta Akademiya Nauk SSSR Sibirskoe Otdelenie *R:* **Tr Biol Lost Akad Nauk SSSR Sib Otd**

Trudy Biologicheskogo Instituta Sibirskoe Otdelenie Akademiya Nauk SSSR *R:* **Trudy Biol Inst Sib Otd Akad Nauk SSSR**

Trudy Biologicheskogo Instituta Zapadno-Sibirskogo Filiala Akademii Nauk SSSR *R:* **Tr Biol Inst Zapadno-Sib Fil Akad Nauk SSSR**

Trudy Biologicheskogo Nauchno-Issledovatel'skogo Instituta i Biologicheskoi Stantsii pri Permskom Gosudarstvennom Universit *R:* **Tr Biol Nauchno Issled Inst Biol Stn Permsk Gos Univ**

Trudy Biologicheskogo Nauchno-Issledovatel'skogo Instituta pri Molotovskom Gosudarstvennom Universitete *R:* **Tr Biol Nauchno Issled Inst Molotov Gos Univ**

Trudy Biologicheskoi Stantsii "Borok" Akademiya Nauk SSSR *R:* **Tr Biol Stn Borok Akad Nauk SSSR**

Trudy Dagestanskogo Gosudarstvennogo Pedagogicheskogo Instituta Estestvenno-Geograficheskii Fakul'tet *R:* **Tr Dagest Gos Pedagog Inst Estestv-Geogr Fak**

Trudy Dal'nevostochnogo Filiala Akademii Nauk SSSR. Seriya Geologicheskaya *R:* **Tr Dalnevost Fil Akad Nauk SSSR Ser Geol**

Trudy Dal'nevostochnogo Geologo-Razvedochnogo Tresta *R:* **Tr Dalnevost Geol Razved Tresta**

Trudy Dal'nevostochnogo Gosudarstven-nogo Universiteta. Seriya 8. Biologiya *R:* **Tr Dalnevost Gos Univ Ser 8**

Trudy Dal'nevostochnogo Gosudarstven-nogo Universiteta. Seriya 11. Geologiya *R:* **Tr Dalnevost Gos Univ Ser 11**

Trudy Dal'nevostochnogo Nauchno-Issledovatel'skogo Gidrometeorologicheskogo Instituta R *R:* **Tr Dalnevost Nauchno Issled Gidrometeorol Inst**

Trudy Geofzicheskogo Instituta Akademiya Nauk SSSR *R:* **Tr Geofíz Inst Akad Nauk SSSR**

Trudy Geograficheskogo Fakul'teta Kirgizskogo Universiteta *R:* **Trudy Geogr Fak Kirgiz Univ**

Trudy Geologicheskogo Instituta Akademiya Nauk Gruzinskoi SSR *R:* **Tr Geol Inst Akad Nauk Gruz SSR**

Trudy Geologicheskogo Instituta Akademiya Nauk Gruzinskoi SSR. Geologicheskaya Seriya *R:* **Tr Geoi Inst Akad Nauk Gruz SSR Geol Ser**

Trudy Geologicheskogo Instituta Akademiya Nauk SSSR *R:* **Tr Geol Inst Akad Nauk SSSR**

Trudy Geologicheskogo Instituta (Kazan) *R:* **Tr Geol Inst (Kazan)**

Trudy Geologicheskogo Instituta Akademiya Nauk Gruzinskoi SSR. Mineralogo-Petrograficheskaya Seriya *R:* **Tr Geol Inst Akad Nauk Gruz SSR Mineral Petrogr Ser**

Trudy Geometricheskogo Seminara *R:* **Tr Geom Semin**

Trudy Glavgeologii (Glavnoe Upravlenie Geologii i Okhrany Nedr) Uzbekskoi SSR *R:* **Tr Glavgeologii (Gl Upr Geol Okhr Nedr) Uzb SSR**

Trudy Glavnoi Geofizicheskoi Observatorii Imeni A. I. Voeikova *R:* **Trudy Glav Geofiz Obs**

Trudy Glavnoi Geofzicheskoi Observatorii *R:* **Tr Gl Geo Obs**

Trudy Glavnoi Geofzicheskoi Observatorii [USSR] *R:* **Tr Gl Geofiz Obs**

Trudy Gorno Geologicheskogo Instituta Akademiya Nauk SSSR Ural'skii Filial *R:* **Tr Gorno Geol Inst Akad Nauk SSSR Ural Fil**

Trudy Gorno- Geologicheskogo Instituta Akademiya Nauk SSSR Zapadno-Sibirskii Filial *R:* **Tr Gorno Geol Inst Akad Nauk SSSR Zapadno Sib Fil**

Trudy Inslituta Geologii Akademiya Nauk Tadzhikskoi SSR *R:* **Tr Inst Geol Akad Nauk Tadzh SSR**

Trudy Institut Biologii Akademiya Nauk Latviiskoi SSR *R:* **Tr Inst Biol Akad Nauk Latv SSR**

Trudy Institut Geologii Kori Korisnikh Koplain Akademiya Nauk Ukrains'koi RSR *R:* **Tr Inst Geol Korisnikh Koplain Akad Nauk Ukr RSR**

Trudy Instituta Biologii Akademiya Nauk SSSR Ural'skii Filial *R:* **Tr Inst Biol Akad Nauk SSSR Ural Fil**

Trudy Instituta Biologii Bashkirskogo Universiteta *R:* **Tr Inst Biol Bashk Univ**

Trudy Instituta Biologii Ural'skii Filial Akademiya Nauk SSSR *R:* **Trudy Inst Biol Ural Fil**

Trudy Instituta Biologii Ural'skogo Filiala Akademiya Nauk SSSR *R:* **Tr Inst Biol Ural Fil Akad Nauk SSSR**

Trudy Instituta Biologii Vnutrennikh Vod Akademiya Nauk SSSR *R:* **Tr Inst Biol Vnutr Vod Akad Nauk SSSR**

Trudy Instituta Biologii Yakutskii Filial Sibirskogo Otdeleniya Akademiya Nauk SSSR *R:* **Tr Inst Biol Yakutsk Fil Sib Otd Akad Nauk SSSR**

Trudy Instituta Eksperimental'noi Biologii Akademiya Nauk Estonskoi SSR *R:* **Tr Inst Eksper Biol Akad Nauk Eston SSR**

Trudy Instituta Eksperimental'noi Biologii Akademiya Nauk Kazakhskoi SSR *R:* **Tr Inst Eksp Biol Akad Nauk Kaz SSR**

Trudy Instituta Epidemiologii i Mikrobiologii (Frunze) *R:* **Tr Inst Epidemiol Mikrobiol (Frunze)**

Trudy Instituta Geofiziki Akademiya Nauk Gruzinskoi SSR *R:* **Tr Inst Geofiz Akad Nauk Gruz SSR**

Trudy Instituta Geografi Akademii Nauk SSSR *R:* **Tr Inst Geogr Akad Nauk SSSR**

Trudy Instituta Geologicheskikh Nauk Akademiya Nauk *R:* **TGKZA**

Trudy Instituta Geologicheskikh Nauk Akademiya Nauk Kazakhskoi SSR *R:* **Tr Inst Geol Nauk Akad Nauk Knz SSR**

Trudy Instituta Geologii Akademiya Nauk Estonskoi SSR *R:* **Tr Inst Geol Akad Nauk Est SSR**

Trudy Instituta Geologii i Geofziki Akademiya Nauk SSSR Sibirskoe Otdelenie *R:* **Tr Inst Geol Geofiz Akad Nauk SSSR Sib Otd**

Trudy Instituta Mikrobiologii Akademii Nauk Latviiskoi SSR *R:* **Tr Inst Mikrobiol Akad Nauk Latv SSR**

Trudy Instituta Mikrobiologii Akademii Nauk SSSR *R:* **Tr Inst Mikrobiol Akad Nauk SSSR**

Trudy Instituta Mikrobiologii i Vinrusologii Akademii Nauk Kazakhskoi SSR *R:* **Tr Inst Mikrobiol Virusol Akad Nauk Kaz SSR**

Trudy Instituta Prikladnoi Geofiziki *R:* **TIPCA, *R:* Tr Inst Prikl Geofiz**

Trudy Instituta Teoreticheskoi Geofiziki Akademiya Nauk SSSR *R:* **Tr Inst Teor Geofiz Akad Nauk SSSR**

Trudy Irkutsk Nauchno-Issledovatel'skogo Instituta Epidemiologii i Mikrobiologii *R:* **Tr Irkutsk Nauchno Issled Inst Epidemiol Mikrobiol**

Trudy Kafedry Pochvovedeniya Biologo-Pochvennogo Fakul'teta Khzakhskii Gosudarstvennyi Universitet *R:* **Tr Kafedry Pochvoved Biol Poch Fak Kaz Gos Univ**

Trudy Kazakhskogo Nauchno-Issledovatel'skogo Gidrometeorologicheskogo Instituta *R:* **Tr Kaz Nauchno-Issled Gidrometeorol Inst**

Trudy Kazanskogo Filiala Akademii Nauk SSSR. Seriya Geologicheskikh Nauk *R:* **Tr Kazan Fil Akad Nauk SSSR Ser Geol Nauk**

Trudy Kazanskoi Gorodskoi Astronomiceskoi Observatorii *R:* **Trudy Kazan Gorod Astronom Observator**

Trudy Kazanskoi Gorodskoi Astronomicheskoi Observatorii *R:* **Tr Kazan Gor Astron Obs**

Trudy Kirgizskogo Gosudarstvennogo Universiteta. Seriya Biologicheskikh Nauk Zoologiya-Fiziologiya *R:* **Trudy Kirgiz Gos Univ Ser Biol Nauk**

Trudy Kirgizskogo Instituta Epidemiologii, Mikrobiologii, i Gigieny *R:* **Tr Kirg Inst Epidemiol Mikrobiol Gig**

Trudy Kirgizskogo Universiteta Seriya Biologicheckikh Nauk *R:* **Tr Kirg Univ Ser Biol Nauk**

Trudy Kompleksnoi Yuzhnoi Geologicheskoi Ekspeditsii. Akademiya Nauk SSSR *R:* **Tr Komplekso Yuzhn Geol Eksped Akad Nauk SSSR**

Trudy Laboratorii Biokhimii i Fiziologii Zhivotnykh Instituta Biologii Akademiya Nauk Latviiskoi SSR *R:* **Tr Lab Biokhim Fiziol Zhivotn Inst Biol Akad Nauk Latv SSR**

Trudy Laboratorii Eksperimental'noi Biologii Moskovskogo Zooparka *R:* **Tr Lab Eksp Biol Mosk Zooparka**

Trudy Laboratorii Fiziologii Zhivotnykh Instituta Biologii Akademii Nauk Litovskoi SSR *R:* **Tr Lab Fiziol Zhivotn Inst Biol Akad Nauk Lit SSR**

Trudy Laboratorii Geologii Dokembriya Akademiya Nauk SSSR *R:* **Tr Lab Geol Dokembr Akad Nauk SSSR**

Trudy Laboratorii Geologii Uglya Akademiya Nauk SSSR *R:* **Tr Lab Geol Uglya Akad Nauk SSSR**

Trudy Laboratorii Gidrogeologicheskikh Problem Akademiya Nauk SSSR *R:* **Tr Lab Gidrogeol Probl Akad Nauk SSSR**

Trudy Leningradskii Gidrometeorologicheskii Inslitut *R:* **Tr Leningr Gidrometeorol Inst**

Trudy Leningradskogo Geologicheskogo Upravleniya *R:* **Tr Leningr Geol Upr**

Trudy Leningradskogo Gidrometeorologicheskogo Instituta *R:* **Trudy Leningr Gidromet Inst**

Trudy Leningradskogo Instituta Epidemiologii i Mikrobiologii *R:* **Tr Leningr Inst Epidemiol Mikrobiol**

Trudy Litovskogo Nauchno-Issledovatel'skogo Geologorazvedochnogo Instituta *R:* **Tr Litov Nauchno Issled Geologorasves Inst**

Trudy Moldavskii Nauchno-Issledovatel'skii Inslitut Epidemiologii, Mikrobiologii, i Gigieny *R:* **Tr Mold Nauchno Issled Inst Epidemiol Mikrobiol Gig**

Trudy Moskovskii Institut Epidemiologii, Mikrobiologii, i Gigieny *R:* **Tr Mosk Inst Epidemiol Mikrobiol Gig**

Trudy Moskovskii Nauchno-Issledovatel's-kii Institut Epidemiologii, Mikrobiologii, i Gigieny *R:* **Tr Mosk Nauchno Issled Inst Epidemiol Mikrobiol Gig**

Trudy Moskovskoe Obshchestvo Ispytatelei Prirody Otedel Biologicheskii *R:* **Tr Mosk Obshch Ispyt Prir Otedel Biol**

Trudy Moskovskogo Geologicheskogo Upravlenie *R:* **Tr Mosk Geol Upr**

Trudy Moskovskogo Geologo-Razvedochnogo Instituta *R:* **Tr Mosk Geol Razved Inst**

Trudy Moskovskogo Nauchno-Issledovatel'skogo Instituta Epidemiologii i Mikrobiologii *R:* **Tr Mosk Nauchno-Issled Inst Epidemiol Mikrobiol**

Trudy Moskovskogo Obshchestva Ispytatelei Prirody Otdel Biologicheskii *R:* **Tr Mosk O-Va Ispyt Prir Otd Biol**

Trudy Murmanskogo Morskogo Biologicheskogo Instituta *R:* **Tr Murm Morsk Biol Inst**

Trudy Murmanskoi Biologicheskoi Stantsii *R:* **Tr Murm Biol Stn**

Trudy Nauchno-Issledovatel'skii Institut Gidrometeorologicheskogo Priborostroeniya *R:* **Tr Nauchno Issled Inst Gidrometeorol Priborostr**

Trudy Nauchno-Issledovatel'skogo Gidrometeorologicheskogo Instituta (Alma-Ata) *R:* **Tr Nauchno-Issled Gidrometerol Inst (Alma-Ata)**

Trudy Nauchno-Issledovatel'skogo Instituta Biologii Char'kovskogo Gosudarstvennogo Universiteta *R:* **Tr Nauchno-Issled Inst Biol Khar'k Gos Univ**

Trudy Nauchno-Issledovatel'skogo Instituta Biologii i Biofziki pri Tomskom Gosudarstvennom Universitete *R:* **Tr Nauchno Issled Inst Biol Biofu Tomsk Gos Univ**

Trudy Nauchno-Issledovatel'skogo Instituta Epidemiologii i Mikrobiologii *R:* **Tr Nauchno-Issled Inst Epidemiol Mikrobiol**

Trudy Nauchno-Issledovatel'skogo Instituta Virusologii Mikrobiologii Gigieny *R:* **Tr Nauchno Issled Inst Virusol Mikrobiol Gig**

Trudy Nauchno-Issledovatel'skogo Instituta Geologii Arktiki *R:* **Tr Nauchno-Issled Inst Geol Arktiki**

Trudy Nauchno-Issledovatel'skogo Instituta Geologii i Mineralogii *R:* **Tr Nauchno Issled Inst Geol Mineral**

Trudy Nizhnevolzhskogo Nauchno-Issledovatel'skogo Instituta Geologii i Geofziki *R:* **Tr Nizhnevolzh Nauchno Issled Inst Geol Geofiz**

Trudy Odesskogo Gidrometeorologicheskogo Instituta *R:* **Tr Odess Gidrometeorol Inst**

Trudy Odesskogo Nauchno-Issledovatel'skogo Instituta Epidemiologii i Mikrobiologii *R:* **Tr Odess Nauchno-Issled Inst Epidemiol Mikrobiol**

Trudy Omskogo Gosudarstvennogo Nauchno-Issledovatel'skogo Instituta Epidemiologii Mikrobiologii i Gigieny *R:* **Tr Omsk Gos Nauchno-Issled Inst Epidemiol Mikrobiol Gig**

Trudy Otdela Geologii Buryatskii Filial Sibirskoe Otdelenie Akademiya Nauk SSSR *R:* **Tr Otd Geol Buryat Fil Sib Otd Akad Nauk SSSR**

Trudy Permskogo Biologicheskogo Nauchno-Issledovatel'skogo Instituta *R:* **Tr Permsk Biol Nauchno Issled Inst**

Trudy Petergofskogo Biologicheskogo Instituta. Leningradskii Gosudarstvennyi Universitet *R:* **Tr Petergof Biol Inst Leningr Gos Univ**

Trudy po Prikladnoi Botanike. Genetike i Selektsii. Seriya 1. Sistematika, Geografia, i Ekologia Rastenii *R:* **Tr Prikl Bot Genet Sel Ser I**

Trudy Seminara "Bionika i Matematiches-koe Modelirovanie v Biologii" *R:* **Tr Semin "Bionika Mat Model Biol"**

Trudy Seminara po Vektornomu i Tenzornomu Analizu s ih Prilozenijami k Geometrii. Mehanike i Fizike *R:* **Trudy Sem Vektor Tenzor Anal**

Trudy Sibirskogo Nauchno-Issledovatel'skogo Instituta Geologii, Geofziki, i Mineral'nogo Syr'ya *R:* **Tr Sib Nauchno-Issled Inst Geol Geofiz Miner Syr'ya, *R:* TSIGA**

Trudy Sovmestnaya Sovetsko-Mongol's-kaya Nauchno-Issledovatel'skaya Geologicheskaya Ekspeditsiya *R:* **Tr Sovmestnaya Sov Mong NauChno Issled Geol Eksped**

Trudy Soyuznaya Geologopoiskovaya Kontora *R:* **Tr Soyuzn Geologopoisk Kontora**

Trudy Sredneaziat Nauchno-Issledovatel'skii Gidrometeorologicheskii Institut *R:* **Tr Sredneaziat Nauchno Issled Gidrometeorol Institut**

Trudy Sredneaziatskii Nauchno-Issledovatel'skii Institut Geologii i Mineral'nogo Syr'ya *R:* **Tr Sredneaziat Nauchno Issled Inst Geol Miner Syrya**

Trudy. Sredneaziatskii Nauchno-Issledovatel'skii Institut Geologii i Mineral'nogo Syrya *R:* **TSNGA**

Trudy Sredneaziatskogo Gosudarstvennogo Universiteta. Seriya 7a. Geologiya *R:* **Tr Sredneaziat Gos Univ Ser 7a**

Trudy Stalinabadskoi Astronomicheskoi Observatorii *R:* **Tr Stalinab Astron Obs**

Trudy Tadzhikskoi Astronomicheskoi Observatorii *R:* **Tr Tadzh Astron Obs**

Trudy Tbilisskogo Nauchno-Issledovatel'skogo Gidrometeorologicheskogo Instituta *R:* **Tr Tbilis Nauchno-Issled Gidrometeorol Inst**

Trudy Tsentral'no-Kazakhstanskogo Geologicheskogo Upravleniya *R:* **Tr Tsentr Kaz Geol Upr**

Trudy Tsentral'noi Aerologicheskoi Observatorii *R:* **Tr Tsent Aerol Obs, *R:* Tr Tsentr Aerol Obs**

Trudy Turkmenskogo Nauchno-Issledovatel'skogo Instituta Klimatologii Kurortologii i Fizicheskikh Metodov Lecheniya *R:* **TTKLAJ**

Trudy Ukrainskii Nauchno-Issledovatel'skii Geologo-Razvedochnyi Institut *R:* **Tr Ukr Nauchno Issled Geol Razved Inst**

Trudy Ukrainskii Nauchno-Issledovatel'skii Geologo-Razvedoehnyi Institut *R:* **TRUGA**

Trudy Ukrainskogo Gidrometeorologicheskogo Instituta *R:* **Trudy Ukr Gidromet Inst**

Trudy Ukrainskogo Nauchno-Issledovatel'skogo Gidrometeorologicheskogo Instituta *R:* **Tr Ukr Nauch-Issled Gidrometeorol Inst**

Trudy Upravleniya Geologii i Okhrany Nedr pri Sovete Ministrov Kirgizskoi SSR *R:* **Tr Upr Geol Okhr Nedr Sov Minist Kirg SSR**

Trudy Uzbekskogo Geologicheskogo Upravlenie *R:* **Tr Uzb Geol Upr**

Trudy Vladivostokskogo Nauchno-Issledovatel'skogo Instituta Epidemiologii, Mikrobiologii, i Gigieny *R:* **Tr Vladivost Nauchno Issled Inst Epidemiol Mikrobiol Gig**

Trudy Vostochno-Sibirskogo Geologicheskogo Instituta Akademiya Nauk SSSR Sibirskoe Otdelenie *R:* **Tr Vost Sib Geol Inst Akad Nauk SSSR Sib Otd**

Trudy Vostochno-Sibirskogo Geologicheskogo Upravleniya *R:* **Tr Vost Sib Geol Upr**

Trudy Vsesoyuznogo Aerogeologicheskogo Tresta *R:* **Trudy Vses Aerogeol Tresta**, *R:* **Tr Vses Aerogeol Tresta**

Trudy Vsesoyuznogo Geologo-Razvedochnogo Ob'edineniya *R:* **Tr Vses Geol Razved Obedin**

Trudy Vsesoyuznogo Gidrobiologicheskogo Obshchestva *R:* **Tr Vses Gidrobiol O-Va**

Trudy Vsesoyuznogo Nauchno- Issledovatel'skogo Geologicheskogo Instituta *R:* **Trudy Vses Nauchno-Issled Geol Inst**

Trudy Vsesoyuznogo Nauchno-Issledovatel'skogo Geologicheskogo Instituta *R:* **Tr Vses Nauchno-Issled Geol Inst**

Trudy Vsesoyuznogo Nauchno-Issledovatel'skogo Geologorazvedochnogo Instituta *R:* **Tr Vses Nauchno Issled Geologorazved Inst**

Trudy Vsesoyuznogo Nauchno-Issledovatel'skogo Instituta Sinteticheskikh i Natural'nykh Dushistykh Veshchestv *R:* **Tr Vses Nauchno-Issled Inst Sint Nat Dushistykh Veshchestv**

Trudy Vsesoyuznogo Neftyanogo Nauchno-Issledovatel'skogo Geologorazvedochnogo lnstituta *R:* **Tr Vses Neft Nauchno-Issled Geologorazved Inst**

Trudy Vsesoyuznyi Nauchno-Issledovatel'skii Geologorazvedochnyi Neftyanoi Instituta *R:* **Tr Vses Nauchno-Issled Geologorazved Neft Inst**

Trudy Vsesoyuznyi Nauchno-Issledovatel'skii Institut Geofizicheskikh Metodov Razvedki *R:* **Tr Vses Nauchno Issled Inst Geofiz Metodov Razved**

Trudy Vsesoyuznyi Nauchno-lsstedovatel'skii Institut Yadernoi Geofiziki i Geokhimii *R:* **Tr Vses Nauchno-Issled Inst Yad Geofiz Geokhim**

Trudy Vysokogornyj Geofzicheskij Institut *R:* **Tr Vysokogorn Gefiz Inst**

Trudy Yakutskogo Filiala Akademii Nauk SSSR Seriya Geologicheskaya *R:* **Tr Yakutsk Fil Akad Naok SSSR Ser Geol**

Trudy Yaltinskogo Nauchno-Issledotel'nogo Instituta Fizicheskikh Metodov Lecheniya i Meditsinskoi Klimatologii *R:* **Tr Yalt Nauchno-Issled Inst Fiz Metodov Lech Med Klimatol**

Trudy Zakavkazskogo Nauchno-Issledovatel'skogo Gidrometeorologicheskogo Instituta *R:* **Tr Zakavk Nauchno-Issled Gidrometeorol Inst**

True Polar Wandering *e:* **TPW**

Trunk Automatic Observation *e:* **TAO**

Trusted Information Exchange for Restricted Environment *e:* **TSIX**

Trusted Interoperation of Healthcare Information *e:* **TIHI**

Trusted Network Interpretation Environmental Guideline *e:* **TNIEG**

TRW Environmental Safety Systems, Inc. *e:* **TESS**

TRW Incorporated-Space and Technology Group *e:* **TRW-STG**

TRW Space Log *e:* **TRSLA**, *e:* **TRW SL**

5-Tryptophanhydroxylase *e:* **5-TPH**

TSCA Environmental Release Application *e:* **TERA**

Tsentral'naja Aerologičeskaja Observatorija *R:* **TsO**

Tsentral'nyi Referativnyi Meditsinskii Zhurnal. Seriya A. Biologiya, Teoreticheskie Problemy Meditsiny *R:* **Tsenti Ref Med Zh Ser A**

Tsentral'nyi Referativnyi Meditsinskii Zhurnal. Seriya G. Mikrobiologiya, Gigiena, i Sanitariya *R:* **Tsentr Ref Med Zb Ser G**

Tsentral'nyj Aerologičeskaja Observatorija *R:* **TSAO**

Tsirkulyar Shemakhinskoi Astrofzicheskoi Observatorii *R:* **Tsirk Shemakh Astrofiz Obs**

TSR [Fortune 500 Company that manufactures Dungeons & Dragons] *e:* **TSR**

Tsukuba Atmospheric Boundary Layer Experiment *e:* **TABLE**

Tsukuba Space Center *e:* **TKSC**

Tsukuba University. Institute of Geoscience Annual Report *e:* **Tsukuba Univ Inst Geosci Annu Rep**

Tsukumo Earth Science *e:* **Tsukumo Farth Sci**

Tsunami Warning System [National Oceanic and Atmospheric Administration] *e:* **TWS**

Tube/Sea Differential Pressure Subsystem *e:* **T/SDPS**

Tübinger Geographische Studien. Universität Tübingen *d:* **Tüb. Geogr. Stud.**

Tubman National Institute of Medical Arts *e:* **TNIMA**

Tubular Water Bath *e:* **TWB**

Tucki Nature Reserve (New South Wales) *e:* **TNR**

Tucson Observatory *e:* **TUO**

Tufs Folia Medica *e:* **Tufs Folida Med**

Tufts Health Science Review *e:* **THSRB**, *e:* **Tufts Health Sci Rev**

Tufts University School of Medicine *e:* **TUSM**

Tulane Environmental Law Journal *e:* **Tul. Envtl. L.J.**

Tulane Studies in Geology *e:* **Tulane Stud Geol**

Tulane Studies in Geology and Paleontology *e:* **Tulane Stud Geol Paleontol**

Tulane University, Medical Library, New Orleans *e:* **LNT-M**

Tulsa Geological Society *e:* **TGS**

Tulsa Geological Society. Digest *e:* **TGSDA**, *e:* **Tulsa Geol Soc Dig[est]**

Tulsa Medicine *e:* **Tulsa Med**

Tulsa Weather Forecast Office *e:* **TUL**

Tumor-BearingAnimal *e:* **TBA**

tumor necrosis factor (natural substance killing cancer cells) *e:* **tnf**

Tumour Biology *e:* **Tumour Biol**

Tumwater *e:* **TUM**

Tunable Etalon Remote Sounder *e:* **TERSE**

Tunable Etalon Remote Sounder of Earth *e:* **TERSE**

Tundra Response to Climate Change *e:* **TRECC**

Tungsten Circulating Water System *e:* **TCWS**

Tungsten Water-Moderated Reactor *e:* **TWMR**

Tunisie Medicale *e:* **TUMEA**, *f:* **Tunis Med**

Turbine Building Closed Cooling Water *e:* **TBCCW**

Turbine Building Closed Cooling Water System *e:* **TBCCW System**

Turbine Building Secondary Closed Cooling Water *e:* **TBSCCW**

Turbine-Building Service Water *e:* **TSW**

Turbine-Driven Auxiliary Feedwater Pump *e:* **TDAFWP**

Turbine Driven Auxiliaty Feedwater Pump *e:* **TDAF**

Turbine Driven Emergency Feedwater Pump *e:* **TDEFWP**

Turbulent Air Pilot Environment Research *e:* **TAPER**

Türk Biologi Dergiği *z:* **Türk Biol Derg**

Turk Biologi Dergisi *z:* **Turk Biol Derg**

Türk Hifzissihhave Tecrubi Biologi Mecmuasi *z:* **Türk Hifzissihha Tecr Biol Mecm**

Türkische Zeitschrift für Hygiene und Experimentelle Biologie *d:* **Türk Z Hyg Exp Biol**

Turkish Bulletin of Hygiene and Experimen-tal Biology *e:* **Turk Bull Hyg Exp Biol**

Turkish Electronic Journal of Medicine *e:* **TEJM**

Turkish Journal of Biology *e:* **Turk J Biol**

Turkish National Committee of the International Association on Water Pollution Research and Control *e:* **TNCIAWPRC**

Turkish National Remote Sensing Working Group *e:* **TNRSWG**

Turtle Islands in the Sulu Sea south of the Philippines *e:* **Turtles**

TUSAS Aerospace Industries Inc. *e:* **TAI**

Twin Cities Biomedical Consortium *e:* **TCBC**

twinengine jetliner designed for medical evacuation *e:* **C-9**

Twisted Tape Boiling Water Reactor *e:* **TTBWR**

Two-Carrier Space-Charge-Limited Current *e:* **TCSCLC**

Two-Dimensional Plumes in Uniform Ground Water Flow *e:* **PLUME2D**

Two Main Orbiting Spacecraft *e:* **TMOS**

Two-man spacecraft *e:* **Gemini**

Two-Stage Hydrocracker *e:* **TSHC**

Two Stage to Orbit *e:* **TSTO**

Two-terminal geometry for measuring magnetoresistivity *e:* **Corbino Geometry**

Typenprojektierung *d:* **Typro**

Typical Ocean Model *e:* **TOM**

Tyrosine Hydroxylase *e:* **TOH**

Tyrosinhydroxylase *e:* **TRH**, *e:* **TYR-OH**

Tyrrhenian Sea *e:* **Tyrr. S.**

U

U-Boot-Abwehr-Unterwasserkampfschiff *d:* **UAW-U-Schiff**

U das Technische Umweltmagazin *d:* **U Tech Umweltmag**

überbetrieblicher arbeitsmedizinischer Dienst *d:* **ÜAMD**

Übergeordnete Funkstelle *d:* **ÜfuSt**

Überwasserfahrzeug *d:* **ÜwFzg**

Überwasserwaffen *d:* **ÜwWa**

Überwasserwaffenelektronik *d:* **ÜwWaElo**

Ubihydrochinon *e:* **U**

UCAR [University Corporation for Atmospheric Research] Office of Programs *e:* **UOP**

UCCIS [United States Army in Europe Command and Control Information System] Medical Management Information Subsystem *e:* **UMMIS**

UCD Health *e:* **DHEA**

Ucenye Zapiski. Stavropol'skij Medicinskij Institut *R:* **Uc Zap Stavr Med Inst**

Uchenye Zapiski Leningradskogo Ordena Lenina Gosudarstvennogo Universiteta Imeni A. A. Zhdanova. Seriya Biologicheskikh Nauk *R:* **ULCBAJ**

UCI Medical Affiliates, Inc. *e:* **UCIM**

UCLA Forum in Medical Sciences *e:* **UCLA Forum Med Sci**

UCL.A Forum in Medical Sciences *e:* **UCMSA**

UCLA Journal of Environmental Law and Policy *e:* **UCLA (Univ Cal Los Angeles) J Environmental Law and Policy**

UCLA Symposia on Molecular and Cellular Biology *e:* **UCLA Symp Mol Cell Biol**

UCLA Symposia on Molecular and Cellular Biology. New Series *e:* **UCLA (Univ Calif Los Ang) Symp Mol Cell Biol New Ser**

Ueberwasserstreitkräfte *d:* **UEWK**

Ufficio Centrale di Meteorologia e di Ecologia Agraria *i:* **UCMEA**

Ufficio Federale dell'Industria, delle Arti e Mestieri e del Lavoro *i:* **UFIAML**

Ufficio Intercantonale per il Controllo dei Medicinali *i:* **UICM**

Ufficio Internazionale di Documentazione di Medicina Militare *i:* **UIDMM**

Uganda Community-Based Health Care Association *e:* **UCBHCA**

Uganda Geological Survey and Mines Department *e:* **UGSMD**

Uganda Medical Workers Union *e:* **UMWU**

Uganda Protectorate Law Reports (1904-51) *e:* **Uganda L.R.**

Uganda Protectorate Law Reports *e:* **Ug Pr LR**

Uganda Protectorate Law Reports [1904-51] *e:* **ULR**

Uganda Protectorate Law Reports (1904-51) *e:* **U.P.L.R.**

ugly, threatening weather *e:* **u**

Uinta Basin Observatory *e:* **UBO**

Uinta Basin Seismological Observatory *e:* **UBSO**

Ukrainian Academy of Medical Sciences *e:* **UAMS**

Ukrainian Medical Association of North America *e:* **UMANA**

Ukrainskii Geometriceskii Sbornik *R:* **Ukrain Geometr Sb**, *R:* **Ukrain Geom Sb**

Ukrains'kij Geometričeskij Sbornik *R:* **Ukr[ain] Geom[etr] Sb**

Ukrainskij Geometricheskij Sbornik *R:* **Ukr Geom Sb**

Ulster Medical Journal *e:* **Ulster Med J**, *e:* **UMJOA**

Ulster Sea Fishermen's Association *e:* **USFA**

Ulster Society for the Prevention of Cruelty to Animals *e:* **USPCA**

Ulster Society for the Protection of Birds *e:* **U.S.P.B.**

Ultimate Plant Protection System *e:* **UPPS**

Ultimatist Religious Bodies on Earth *e:* **URBOE**

Ultradeep Water *e:* **UDW**

Ultrapure Water *e:* **UPW**

Ultraschall in der Medizin *d:* **Ultraschall Med**

Ultrasonic Space Grating *e:* **USG**

Ultrasonically Nebulized Distilled Water Challenge *e:* **UNDWC**

Ultrasound in Medicine and Biology *e:* **Ultrasound Med Biol**, *e:* **UMB**

Ultrasound in Obstetrics and Gynecology *e:* **Ultrasound Obstet Gynecol**

ultraviolet-biological *e:* **UV-B**

Ultraviolet Photometric and Polarimetric Explorer *e:* **UPPE**

Ultraviolet Spectrometer and Polarimeter *e:* **UVSP**

Ultraviolett, biologisch wirksame Strahlung *d:* **UV-B**

Umluft-Wasserkühlung *d:* **ULW**

Umwelt *d:* **UMW**

Umwelt-Datenkatalog *d:* **UDK**

Umwelt. Forschung, Gestaltung, Schutz *d:* **UNL**

Umwelt-Forschungs-Datenbank *d:* **UFOR**

Umwelt. Informationen des Bundesministers des Innern zur Umweltplanung und zum Umweltschutz *d:* **Umwelt Inf Bundesminist Innern**

Umwelt-Literatur Datenbank beim Umweltbundesamt *d:* **ULIDAT**

Umwelt-Planungs-Informationssystem [Umweltbundesamt] *d:* **UMPLIS**

Umwelt & Projektwerkstatt *d:* **UmProWe**

Umwelt-Report *d:* **Umwelt-Rep**

Umwelt- und Diagnoselabor Fulda, Fulda *d:* **ULF**

Umwelt- und Planungsrecht *d:* **Umw Planungsrecht**, *d:* **UPR**

Umwelt- und Prognose-Institut *d:* **UPI**

Umwelt- und Prozeßkontroll-GmbH *d:* **UPK**

Umwelt Zeitschrift der Biologischen Station Wilhelminenberg *d:* **Umwelt Z Biol Stn Wilhelminenberg**, *d:* **UMWLA**

Umweltaudit-Gesetz-Beleihungsverordnung *d:* **UAGBV**

Umweltaudit-Gesetz-Gebührenverordnung *d:* **UAGGebV**

Umweltaudit-Gesetz-Zulassungsverordnung *d:* **UAGZV**

Umweltauditgesetz *d:* **UAG**

Umweltbeauftragter *d:* **UB**

Umweltbeobachtungssatellit *d:* **ESSA**

Umweltbundesamt, Berlin *d:* **UBA**

Umweltbundesamt Meßnetz *d:* **UBAMeN**

Umweltdatenkatalog *d:* **UDK**

Umweltforschungs-Datenbank *d:* **UFOR-Datenbank**

Umweltforschungs-Datenbank beim Umweltbundesamt *d:* **UFORDAT**

Umweltforschungs-Informationssystem *e:* **UFIS**

Umweltforschungskatalog *d:* **UFOKAT**

Umweltforschungsplan des Bundesministeriums für Umwelt *d:* **UFOPLAN**

Umweltforschungssatellit *d:* **ERS**

Umweltforschungszentrum *d:* **UFZ**

Umweltforschungszentrum Leipzig-Halle GmbH, Leipzig *d:* **UFZ**

Umweltführungsinformationssystem *d:* **UFIS**

Umweltgutachter- und Standortregistrierungsgesetz *d:* **USG**

Umweltgutachter-Zulassungs- und Standortregistrierungsgesetz *d:* **UZSG**

Umweltgutachterausschuss *d:* **UGA**

Umwelthaftungsgesetz *d:* **UHG**, *d:* **UmweltHG**

Umwelthandlungsziel *d:* **UHZ**

Umweltinformationsgebührenverordnung *d:* **UIGGebV**

Umweltinformationsgesetz *d:* **UIG**

Umweltinformationssystem *d:* **UIS**, *d:* **UMSYS**, *d:* **UMWIS[S]**, *d:* **UWIS**

Umweltinformationssystem Dortmund *d:* **UDO**

Umweltinformationssystem in Bayern *d:* **KUNIS**

Umweltkonfliktsimulationsspiel *d:* **UKOSIM**

Umweltkontroll- und Lebenserhaltungssystem *d:* **ECLSS**

Umweltkontrolleinheit *d:* **ECU**

Umweltkontrollsystem *d:* **ECS**

Umweltlage- und Informationszentrum *d:* **ULIZ**

Umweltliteratur-Datenbank *d:* **ULIT**, *d:* **ULIT-Datenbank**

Umweltmagazin. Fachzeitschrift für Umwelttechnik in Industrie und Kommune *d:* **TUF**

Umweltmanagementsystem *d:* **UMS**

Umweltministerium *d:* **UM**

Umweltministerkonferenz *d:* **UMK**

Umweltplanung Transfer Consulting *d:*
UTC
Umweltpolitik und Umweltplanung *d:*
Umweltpolit Umweltplanung
Umweltqualität *d:* **UWQ**
Umweltqualitäts-Simulationsmodell *d:*
UQUASIM
Umweltqualitätsziel *d:* **UQZ**
Umweltrahmengesetz *d:* **URG**
Umweltrecht in der Praxis *d:* **Umweltrecht
Prax.**
Umweltrelevante Daten *d:* **HYDABA II**
Umweltschutz *d:* **USch**, *d:* **UWS**
Umweltschutz-Dienst *d:* **UWD**
Umweltschutz. Gesundheitstechnik *d:*
Umweltschutz Gesundheitstech
Umweltschutz Hamburg-Unterelbe *d:* **Uhu**
Umweltschutz in der Schweiz *d:*
Umweltschutz Schweiz
Umweltschutz-Informations- und
steuerungssystem *d:* **USCHI**
Umweltschutz - Staedtereinigung *d:*
Umweltschutz-Staedtereinig
Umweltschutz Südpfalz-Regionalverband,
Aktionsgemeinschaft, Germersheim *d:*
UWS
Umweltschutzarzt *e:* **UMS**
Umweltschutzdienst. Informationsdienst für
Umweltfragen *d:* **UNE**
Umweltschutzgesetz *d:* **USG**
Umweltschutzpapier *d:* **UWS-Papier**
Umweltschutztechnik *d:* **UST**
Umwelttoxikologisches
Informationssystemn *d:* **UTOXIS**
Umweltverschmutzung *d:* **UVERS**
Umweltverträglichkeitsprüfung *d:* **UVP**
Umweltverträglichkeitsstudien *d:* **UVS**
Umweltverträglichkeitsuntersuchungen *d:*
UVU
Umweltwissenschaftliches Institut *d:* **UWI**
Unattended Earth Terminal *e:* **UET**
Unattended Machinery Spaces *e:* **UMS**
Unburned Hydrocarbon *e:* **UBHC**
Unburned Hydrocarbons *e:* **UHC**
Undelvoltage Protection *e:* **UVP**
Undelwater Manifold Center *e:* **UMC**
Undenatured Bacterial Antigen *e:* **UBA**
Under Frequency Protector *e:* **UFP**
Under Water Information Bulletin *e:*
Underwater Inf Bull
Under Water Weapons Training *e:* **UWWT**
underdeck shipment *e:* **U/D**
Underdeck Tonnage *e:* **UDT**
underdeduction *e:* **unded**
Underdeveloped Countries *e:* **UDCs**
Underdeveloped Country *e:* **UDC**
Undergraduate Space Training *e:* **UST**
Underground Facilities Protective
Organization *e:* **UFPO**
Underground Hydroelectric Pumped
Storage *e:* **UHPS**
Underground Pumped Hydro *e:* **UPH**
Underground Pumped Hydro Storage *e:*
UPHS
Underground Sources of Drinking Water
e: **USDW**
Underground Space *e:* **UNSPD**
Underground Water Conference of
Australia. Newsletter *e:* **Underground
Water Conf Aust Newsl**
Underground Water Supply Papers
(Tasmania) *e:* **Undergr Wat Supply
Pap (Tasm)**

Undersea and Hyperbaric Medical Society
e: **UHMS**
Undersea and Hyperbaric Medicine *e:*
Undersea Hyperb Med
Undersea Biomedical Research *e:*
Undersea Biomed Res
Undersea Biomedical Society *e:* **UBMS**
Undersea Medical Society, Inc. *e:* **UMS**
Undersea (or Underwater) Long-range
Missile System *e:* **ULMS**
Undersea (or Underwater) Research Vehicle
e: **URV**
Underwater *d:* **UWTR**, *e:* **U**, *e:* **UNDW**
underwater *e:* **U.W.**
Underwater *e:* **W**
Underwater Acoustic Decoupler *e:* **UAD**
Underwater Acoustic Group *e:* **UAG**
Underwater Acoustic Interference
Coordinating Committee *e:* **UAICC**
Underwater Acoustic Propagation *e:*
UWAP
Underwater Acoustic Propagation Channel
e: **UWAP Channel**
Underwater Acoustic Receiving System *e:*
UARS
Underwater Acoustic Resistance *e:* **UAR**
Underwater Acoustic Sound Source System
e: **UASSS**
Underwater Activities *e:* **UWA**
Underwater Actuator *e:* **UA**
Underwater Angle Receptacle *e:* **UAR**
Underwater Antivehicle Mine *e:* **UWAVM**
Underwater Association *e:* **UA**
Underwater Association for Scientific
Research *e:* **UA**, *e:* **UASR**
Underwater Astronaut Trainer *e:* **UAT**
Underwater Battery *e:* **UB**
Underwater Battery Director Indicator *e:*
UBDI
Underwater Battery Fire Control *e:* **UBFC**
Underwater Battery Fire Control System *e:*
UBFCS
Underwater Battery Plot *e:* **UBP**
Underwater Battery Plotting Room *e:*
UBPLOT
Underwater Breathing Apparatus *e:* **UBA**
Underwater Cable System *e:* **UCS**
Underwater Coded Command Release
System *e:* **UCCRS**
Underwater Combat System *e:* **UCS**
Underwater Communications *e:* **UC**, *e:*
UWC
Underwater Communications System *e:*
UCS
Underwater Conservation Society *e:* **UCS**
Underwater Construction Team *e:* **UCT**
Underwater Control Rating 2nd Class *e:*
UC2
Underwater Control Rating 1st Class *e:*
UC1
Underwater Countermeasures and Weapons
Establishment *e:* **UCWE**
Underwater Countermeasures and Weapons
Research Establishment *e:* **UCWRE**
Underwater Crash Locator System *e:*
UCLS
Underwater Damage Assessment Television
System *e:* **UDATS**
Underwater Data Link *e:* **UDL**
Underwater Decompression Computer *e:*
UDC
Underwater Demolition *e:* **UD**
Underwater Demolition School *e:* **UDS**

Underwater Demolition Team *e:* **UDT**
Underwater Demolition Team Detachment
e: **UDTDET**
Underwater Demolition Team/ Explosive
Ordnance Proposal *e:* **UDT/EOD**
Underwater Demolition Teams, Amphibious
Forces, Pacific Fleet *e:* **UDTPHIBSPAC**
Underwater Demolition Unit *e:* **UDU**
Underwater Destruction Team *e:* **UDT**
Underwater Detection and Classification
System *e:* **UDACS**
Underwater Detection Establishment *e:*
UDE
Underwater Development Establishment *e:*
U.D.E.
Underwater Doppler Navigation *e:* **UDN**
underwater dry transfer chamber *e:* **udtc**
Underwater Electrical Potential *e:* **UEP**
Underwater Engineering Group *e:* **UEG**
Underwater Environmental Laboratory *e:*
UEL
Underwater Equipment *e:* **UWE**
Underwater Explorers Society *e:*
UNEXSO
Underwater Explosion Research and
Development Center *e:* **UERDC**
Underwater Explosion test *e:* **UNDEX**
Underwater Explosions Research Division
e: **UERD**
Underwater Explosive Forming *e:* **UEF**
Underwater Explosives Research
Laboratory *e:* **UERL**
Underwater Fire Control *e:* **UWFC**
Underwater Fire Control Computer *e:*
UFCC
Underwater Fire Control Group *e:* **UFCG**
Underwater Fire-Control System *e:* **UFCS**
Underwater Fire Control System *e:*
UWFCS
Underwater Guided Missile *e:* **UGM**
Underwater Habitat *e:* **UWH**
Underwater Institute *e:* **UI**
Underwater Integration Communication *e:*
UNICOM
Underwater Journal *e:* **UnderwaterJ**
Underwater Journal and Information
Bulletin *e:* **Underwater J Inf Bull**, *e:*
Underw J Inf Bull
Underwater LASER Surveying System *e:*
ULSS
Underwater Launch *e:* **UWL**
Underwater Launch Control Energy
Requirements *e:* **ULCER**
Underwater Launch Current and Energy
Recorder *e:* **ULCER**
Underwater Launch Missile *e:* **ULM**
Underwater Letter *e:* **Under Lttr**
Underwater Locator Beacon *e:* **ULB**
Underwater Long-Range Missile *e:* **ULM**
Underwater Long-Range Missile System *e:*
UCMS
Underwater Maintenance Company *e:*
UMC
Underwater Manifold Centre *e:* **UMC**
Underwater Mechanic *e:* **UM**
Underwater Mine *e:* **UMN**
Underwater Mining Institute *e:* **UMI**
Underwater Monitoring System *e:* **UMS**
Underwater Naturalist *e:* **Underwater Nat**
Underwater New Submarine System *e:*
UNS
Underwater Object Location and Search
Operation *e:* **UOLS Operation**

Underwater Object Location and Search Operations e: **UOIS**

underwater object locator e: **uol**

Underwater Ordnance Development Group e: **UODG**

Underwater Ordnance Station e: **UOS**

Underwater Photographers (or Photographic, or Photography) Society e: **UPS**

Underwater Photography e: **UWP**

Underwater Photography Instruction Association e: **UPIA**

Underwater Physiology Subcommittee [Royal Naval Personnel Research Committee] e: **UPS**

Underwater Pipe Cutter e: **UPC**

Underwater Production System[s] e: **UPS**

Underwater Propulsion Device e: **UPD**

Underwater Pump Jet e: **UPJ**

Underwater Range e: **UWR**

Underwater recovery Transponder/Release unit e: **UTR**

Underwater Replenishment Group e: **URGP**

Underwater Rescue Vehicle e: **URV**

Underwater Research Group e: **U.R.G.**

Underwater Science and Technology Journal e: **Underwater Sci Technol J**

underwater search and recovery e: **usr**

Underwater Search, Detection, Classification e: **USDC**

Underwater Security Advance Warnings e: **USAW**

Underwater Skindivers and Fishermen's Association of Australia e: **U.S.F.A.**

Underwater Society of America e: **USA**, e: **USOA**

Underwater Sound Advisory Group e: **USAG**

Underwater Sound Explosive Devices Branch e: **USED**

Underwater Sound Laboratory e: **USL**

Underwater Sound Projection e: **USP**

Underwater Sound Reference Detachment e: **USRD**

Underwater Sound Reference Division e: **USRD**

Underwater Sound Reference Division, Naval Research Laboratory e: **USRD/NRL**

Underwater Sound Source e: **USS**

underwater submarine warfare e: **usw**

Underwater Systems Center e: **USC**

Underwater Systems Group e: **USG**

Underwater Tactical Range, Pacific e: **UTRP**

Underwater Tank Facility e: **UTF**

Underwater Targets & Ranges Group e: **UWTR**

Underwater Team e: **UWTM**

Underwater Technology School e: **UTS**

Underwater Telephone e: **UWT**

Underwater Telephone System e: **UTS**

Underwater Telephony e: **UT**

Underwater Television e: **UTV**, e: **UWTV**

Underwater Television and Inspection System e: **UNIS**

underwater television system e: **Colmek TV**

Underwater Temperature Recorder e: **UTR**

Underwater Terrain Navigation and Reconnaissance Simulator e: **UTNRS**

Underwater Test Facility e: **UTF**

Underwater-to-Air Missile e: **UAM**

Underwater-to-Air-to-Underwater e: **UATU**, e: **UAU**

Underwater-to-Air-to-Underwater Missile e: **UATUM**, e: **UAUM**

Underwater-to-Surface e: **US**

Underwater-to-Surface Guided Weapon e: **USGW**

Underwater-to-Surface-Missile e: **USM**

Underwater-to-Underwater Guided Weapon e: **UUGW**

Underwater-to-Underwater Missile e: **UUM**

Underwater Tracking Equipment e: **UTE**

Underwater Tracking Range e: **UTR**

Underwater Training Centre e: **UTC**

Underwater Training Unit e: **UTU**, e: **UWTU**

Underwater Transponder Releaser e: **UTR**

underwater underway e: **u/w**

Underwater Vehicle e: **UV**

Underwater Warfare Development Division e: **UWDD**

Underwater Weapons e: **UW**, e: **UWW**

Underwater Weapons and Countermeasures Establishment e: **UWCE**

Underwater Weapons Control System e: **UWCS**

Underwater Weapons Department e: **UWD**

Underwater Weapons System Design Disclosure Management System e: **UWSDDMS**

Underwater Weapons Systems Reliability Data e: **UWSRD**

Underwater Welding Habitat e: **UWH**

Underwater Wide Angle Lens e: **UWAL**

Underwatermarked e: **UNWMK**

UnderwaterTarget-Activated Sensor e: **UTAS**

UnderwaterTelephone e: **UQC**

Undetwater Sound Reference Laboratory e: **USRL**

Undulating Oceanogaphic Recorder e: **UOR**

Unearth e: **UNEA**

UNEP Oceans [and] Coastal Area[s] Programme Activity Centre e: **OCA/PAC-UNEP**

UNEP [United Nations Environmental Programme] Regional Office for Latin America e: **UROLA**

Unequal Error Protection e: **UEP**

UNESCO Division of Earth Sciences e: **SC/GEO**

UNESCO Division of Ecological Sciences e: **SC/ECO**

UNESCO Division of Human Settlements and Socio-Cultural Environment e: **SS/ENV**

UNESCO Division of Water Sciences e: **SC/HYD**

UNESCO Regional Office for Science and Technology for Latin America and the Caribbean Sea e: **ROSTLAC**

UNESCO [United Nations Education, Scientific, and Cultural Organization] Division of Earth Sciences e: **UNESCO-SC/GEO**

UNESCO [United Nations Education, Scientific, and Cultural Organization] Division of Ecological Sciences e: **UNESCO-SC/ECO**

UNESCO [United Nations Education, Scientific, and Cultural Organization] Division of Human Settlements and Socio-Cultural Environment e: **UNESCO-SS/ENV**

UNESCO [United Nations Education, Scientific, and Cultural Organization] Division of Water Science[s] e: **UNESCO-SC/HYD**

UNESCO [United Nations Education, Scientific, and Cultural Organization] Natural Resources Research e: **UNESCO Nat Resour Res**

UNESCO [United Nations Education, Scientific, and Cultural Organization] Regional Office for Education in Asia and Oceania e: **UNESCO-ROEAO**

UNESCO [United Nations Education, Scientific, and Cultural Organization] Regional Office for Science and Technology for Latin America and the Caribbean Sea e: **UNESCO-ROSTLAC**

UNESCO [United Nations Educational, Scientific, and Cultural Organization] Regional Office for Education in Asia and Oceania e: **UROEA**

Uneven Level Protection e: **ULP**

Unexpected Wildlife Refuge e: **UWR**

Unexplained Atmospheric Phenomenon e: **UAP**

unflektiert d: **unfl.**

ungesund d: **unges.**

Unhardened Collective Protection System e: **UCPS**

Unhardened Collective Protection System (for Desert Use) e: **UCPS(DU)**

União das Populaçoes de Guinea e Cabo Verde p: **UPGCV**

União Democratica de Cabo Verde p: **UDCV**

União Democrático Caboverdeano p: **UDC**

União dos Naturais da Guiné Portuguesa p: **UNGP**

União dos Povos das Ilhas do Cabo Verde p: **UPICV**

União Geográfico Internacional p: **UGI**

União Nacional dos Trabalhadores de Cabo Verde-Central Sindical p: **UNTC-CS**

Unidad de Valoración Médica de Incapacidades s: **UVMI**

Unidentified Atmospheric Phenomena e: **UAP**

UNIDO Environment Programme e: **UNIDO**

Unified Flexible Spacecraft Simulation e: **UFSS**

Unified Medical Group Association e: **UMGA**

Unified Medical Language System e: **UMLS**

Unified Nimbus Observatory e: **UNO**

Unified Space Applications Mission e: **USAM**

Uniform Ambulatory Medical Case Minimum Data Set e: **UAMCMDS**

Uniform building code-earthquake e: **UBCE**

Uniform Color Space e: **UCS**

Uniform Geometrical .Theory of Diffraction e: **UGTD**

Uniform Medical Expense e: **UMERS**

Uniform Services University of the Health Sciences, Bethesda e: **MdBeU**

Uniform System of Accounts Prescribed for Natural Gas Companies *e:* **USPG**

Uniformed Services Health Benefits *e:* **USHB**

Uniformed Services Health Benefits Program *e:* **USHBP**

Uniformed Services Medical Facilities *e:* **USMF**

Uniformed Services University of the Health Sciences *e:* **USUHS**

Uniformed Services University [of the Health Sciences Library, Bethesda] *e:* **USU**

Uniformed Services University of the Health Services *e:* **USUHS**

Union Allumettière Équatoriale *f:* **UNALOR**

Union Belge des Géomètres-Experts Immobiliers *f:* **UBG**

Union Belge et Luxembourgeoise de Droit Penal *f:* **UBLDP**

Union Bretonne des Industriels Laitiers *f:* **UBIL**

Union Carbide Nuclear Co., Oak Ridge National Laboratories, Biology Library *e:* **TONL-B**

Union Catalog of Medical Monographs and Multimedia *e:* **UCOM**

Union Catalog of Medical Periodicals *e:* **UCMP**

Union catalog of medical periodicals. Database, Medical Library Center of New York . *e:* **UCMP**

Union Coopérative Agricole Laitiére de la Manche *f:* **UCALMA**

Union d'Assistance Technique pour l'Automobile et la Circulation Routière *f:* **UNATAC**

Union de Géodésie et Géophysique Géodési[qu]e et Géophysique Internationale *f:* **UGGI**

Union de la Région Centre des Associations de Formation Médicale Continue *f:* **UCAFORMEC**

Union de l'Industrie Laitière Belge *f:* **UIL**, *f:* **UILB**

Union der Schweizerischen Gesellschaften für Experimentelle Biologie *d:* **USGEB**

Union des cafetiers-limonadiers de la Communauté économique Européenne *f:* **COM-EURO-CAFE**

Union des Chambers Syndicales des Chocolatiers Confiseurs Fabricants Détaillants *f:* **UNICHOCO**

Union des Constructeurs et Importateurs d'Appareils Scientifiques, Médicaux et de Contrôle *f:* **UDIAS**

Union des Coopérateurs Luxembourgeois *f:* **U.C.L.**

Union des Coopératives Agricoles Laitières de l'Yonne et de la Nièvre *f:* **U.C.A.L.Y.N.**

Union des Employeurs Agricoles et Forèstiers *f:* **UNEMAF**

Union des Fabricants pour la Protection Internationale de la Propriété Industrielle et Artistique *f:* **UFPIPIA**

Union des Femmes Luxembourgeoises *f:* **UFL**

Union des Grandes Écoles *f:* **U.G.E.**

Union des Groupements Villageois de l'Oudalan *f:* **UGVO**

Union des Industires de Matériaux Naturels *f:* **UNINA**

Union des Industriels Laitiers de Basse-Normandie *f:* **UBNIL**

Union des Industriels Laitiers des Pays de Loire *f:* **UNILOIRE**

Union des Industriels Laitiers du Sud-Est *f:* **UNILSE**, *f:* **UNlLSE**

Union des Industries de la Protection des Plantes *f:* **UIPP**

Union des Industries de Matériaux Naturels *f:* **UNINAT**

Union des Ingénieurs Diplômés des Ecoles Nationales Supérieures Agronomiques *f:* **UNIA**

Union des Ingénieurs Diplômés des Écoles Nationales Supérieurs Agronomiques *f:* **UNIENSA**

Union des Jeunesses Naturistes *f:* **U.J.N.**

Union des Oceanographes de France *f:* **Union Oceanogr Fr**

Union des Pharmaciens d'Industrie Luxembourgeoise *f:* **UPIL**

Union des Producteurs de Caoutchouc Natural *f:* **UPC**

Union des Producteurs en Produits Laitiers et Avicoles *f:* **UPPLA**

Union des Professeurs de Langues dans les Grandes Écoles *e:* **UPLEGESS**

Union des Remorquers de l'Océan *f:* **URO**

Union des Remorqueurs de l'Océan Gabon *f:* **UROGABON**

Union des Services Routiers des Chemins de Fer Européens *f:* **URF**

Union des Sociétés Francaises d'Histoire Naturelle. Bulletin Trimestriel *f:* **Union Soc Fr Hist Nat Bull Trimest**

Union des Sociétés laitières Coopératives Agricoles du District parisien *f:* **USCAD**

Union des Sociétés pour la Protection de l'Enfance et la Santé des Juifs *f:* **USPESJ**

Union des Sociétés Suisses de Biologie Expérimentale *f:* **USSBE**

Union des Sous-Officiers de Réserve Luxembourgeois *f:* **USORL**

Union des Syndicats de la Transformation des Matières Plastiques *f:* **USTMP**

Union des Syndicats de l'Industrie Routière Française *f:* **USIRF**

Union des transports Ferroviaires et Routiers *f:* **UFR**

Union Européenne de la Conservation Côtière *f:* **EUCC**

Union Européenne des Miroitiers Vitriers *f:* **UEMV**

Union Européenne des Portiers des Grandes Hôtels *f:* **UEPGH**

Union Européenne des Sources d'Eaux Minérales Naturelles du Marché Commun *f:* **UESEM**, *f:* **UNESEM**

Union Européenne du Commerce des Produits Laitiers et Derives *f:* **EUCOLAIT**, *f:* **EUROLAIT**

Union Européenne du Commerce Laitier *f:* **UNECOLAIT**

Union Famille-École *f:* **UFE**

Union financière Luxembourgeoise *f:* **Ufina**

Union for the Protection of new Varieties of plants *e:* **UPOV**

Union for the Protection of the Human Person by International, Social, and Economic Cooperation *e:* **UPHPISEC**

Union Forestière Camerounaise *f:* **UFOCA**

Union Forestière de l'Ogooué *f:* **UFO**

Union Française des Biologistes *f:* **UFB**

Union Française des Géologues *f:* **UFG**

Union Frontier Police *e:* **UFP**

Union Féminine Suisse des Arts et Métiers *f:* **UFSAM**

Union Géographique de la Faculté des Lettres *f:* **U.G.F.L.**

Union Géographique Internationale *f:* **UGI**

Union Hydroelectrique Africaine *f:* **UHEA**

Union Interfédérale des Producteurs, des Coopératives et des Industriels Laitiers *f:* **UPCIL**

Union Internacional de Protection a la Infancia *f:* **UIPI**

Union International des Sociétés d'Ingénieurs Forestiers *f:* **UISIF**

Union Internationale de la Presse Médicale *f:* **UIPM**

Union Internationale de Médecine Thermale et de Climatothalassothérapie *f:* **UIMTCT**

Union Internationale de Protection de l'Enfance *f:* **UIPE**

Union Internationale de Sciences Biologique[s] *f:* **UISB**

Union Internationale de Service Médical de Chemin de Fer *f:* **UIMC**

Union Internationale des Associations de Prevention de la Pollution Atmospherique *f:* **UIAPPA**

Union Internationale des Automobile-Clubs Médicaux *f:* **UIACM**

Union Internationale des Chauffeurs Routieres *f:* **UICR**

Union Internationale des Fédérations de Détaillants en Produits Laitiers *f:* **UIFL**

Union Internationale des Instituts de Recherches Forestières *f:* **UIIRF**

Union Internationale des Organisations de Recherches Forestières *f:* **UIORF**

Union Internationale des Portiers des Grands Hôtels *f:* **UIPGH**

Union Internationale des Radioécologistes *f:* **UIR**

Union Internationale des Sciences Biologiques *f:* **UIBS**

Union Internationale des Sciences Biologiques. Serie A. Générale *f:* **Union Int Sci Biol Ser A Gen**

Union Internationale des Sciences Biologiques. Serie B. Colloques *f:* **Union Int Sci Biol Ser B Colloq**

Union Internationale des Sciences Géologiques *f:* **UISG**

Union Internationale des Sociétés de Microbiologie *f:* **UISM**

Union Internationale des Syndicats des Travailleurs Agricoles et Forestiers et des Organisations des Paysans Travailleurs *f:* **UISTAF**

Union Internationale des Transports Routiers *f:* **UITR**

Union Internationale d'Hygiène et de Médecine Scolaires et Universitaires *f:* **UIHMSU**

Union internationale d'organisations nationales d'hôteliers, restaurateurs et cafetiers *f:* **HORECA**

Union Internationale d'Écoles par Correspondance *f:* **UNIECO**

Union Internationale pour la Conservation de la Nature et de ses Ressources *f:* **IUCN**

Union Internationale pour la Conservation de la Nature [et des Resources] *f:* **UICN**

Union Internationale pour la Protection de la Moralité Publique *f:* **UIMP**

Union Internationale pour la Protection de la Nature *f:* **UIPN,** *f:* **UIPRON**

Union Internationale pour la Protection de la Propriété Industrielle *f:* **UIPPI**

Union Internationale pour la Protection des Obtentions Végétales *f:* **UPOV**

Union Internationales des Sciences Biologiques, Series B, [Colloques] *f:* **UIS**

Union Intersyndicale Autonome de Protection Mutuelle des VRP [Voyageurs Représentants Placiers] *f:* **UNIAPM**

Union Konkreter Umweltschutz *d:* **UNU**

Union Laitière de Bamako *f:* **ULB**

Union Laitière Normande *f:* **ULN**

Union Luxembourgeoise des Consommateurs *f:* **ULC**

Union Medicale du Canada *f:* **Union Med Can,** *f:* **Un Med Can**

Union Medicale (Paris) *f:* **Union Med (Paris)**

Union Memorial Hospital, Finney Medical Library, Baltimore *e:* **MdBUM**

Union mondiale pour la nature *f:* **UICN**

Union Médicale *f:* **Union Med**

Union Médicale Arabe *f:* **UMA**

Union Médicale Arménienne de France *f:* **UMAF**

Union Médicale Balkanique *f:* **UMB**

Union Médicale de la Méditerranée Latine *f:* **UMML**

Union Médicale du Canada *f:* **UMCAA**

Union Médicale Franco-Ibero Americaine *f:* **UMFIA**

Union Nationale de Protection Civile *f:* **U.N.P.C.**

Union Nationale des Analystes Médicales *f:* **UNAM**

Union Nationale des Associations de Formation Médicale Continue *f:* **UNAFORMEC**

Union Nationale des Cafetiers-Limonadiers *f:* **UNCL**

Union Nationale des Centres Permanents d'Initiation à l'Environnement *f:* **UNCPIE**

Union Nationale des Chambres Syndicales d'Entreprises en Génie Climatique *f:* **UNCSEGC**

Union Nationale des Chambres Syndicates d'Enterprises en Génie Climatique *f:* **UCH**

Union Nationale des Coopératives Laitières *f:* **UNCL,** *f:* **UNILAIT**

Union Nationale des Distillateurs Agricoles Luxembourgeois *f:* **UNDAL**

Union Nationale des Entrepreneurs-Menuisiers et Charpentiers *f:* **UNIEM**

Union Nationale des Organisations Syndicales de Transporteurs Routiers Automobiles *f:* **UNOSTRA**

Union Nationale des Pharmaciens Luxembourgeois *f:* **UNAPHAL**

Union Nationale des Syndicats Agricoles Forèstiers, des Bois, de l'Élevage et de la Pêche du Cameroun *f:* **UNASABEC**

Union Nationale des Techniciens Biologistes *f:* **UNATEB**

Union Nationale des Écoles de Chauffe *f:* **UNEC**

Union Nationale Interprofessionnelle de Propagande pour le Lait et les Produits Laitiers *f:* **UNIPLPL**

Union Nationale Interprofessionnelle des Produits Laitiers *f:* **UNIPRO-LAIT**

Union Nationale pour la Protection et Défense des Droits des Auteurs et Compositeurs *f:* **UNPDAC**

Union Naturiste Internationale *f:* **UNI**

Union Normande Laitière *f:* **UNL**

Union Observatory *e:* **UO**

Union of African Water Suppliers *e:* **UAWS**

Union of American Biological Societies *e:* **UABS**

Union of South Africa Water Courts Decisions *e:* **W.S.S.A.**

Union Postale de l'Asie et de l'Océanie *f:* **UPAO**

Union Professionnelle Belge des Transporteurs Routiers Internationaux *f:* **UPTRI**

Union Professionnelle de Commerce de Gros des Produits Laitiers Laitiers Indigènes et d'Importation autre que Beurre et *f:* **UPDAL**

Union Professionnelle des Transports Publics Routiers *f:* **UPR**

Union Professionnelle Internationale des Gynécologistes (ou Gynécologues) et Obstétriciens *f:* **UPIGO**

Union Professionnelle Nationale des Importateurs Négociants, Commissionaires, Courtiers et Agents en Tabac en Feuilles en Belgique *f:* **UPROTAB**

Union Québécoise pour la Conservation de la Nature *f:* **UQCN**

Union Romande des Gérants et Courtiers en Immeubles *f:* **URGCI**

Union Routière *f:* **U.R.**

Union Routière de France *f:* **U.R.F.**

Union Régionale des Centres Permanents d'Initiation à l'Environnement *f:* **URCPIE**

Union Régionale Laitière Agricole Coopératives *f:* **U.R.L.A.C.**

Union Régionale pour la mise en Valeur de la Nature [Côte d'Azur] *f:* **URVN**

Union Suisse des Arts et Métiers *f:* **USAM**

Union Suisse des Métiers de la Décóration d'Intérieur et de la Sellerie *f:* **USDIS**

Union Suisse des Papetiers *f:* **USP**

Union Syndicale des Courtiers en Assurances *f:* **USCA**

Union Syndicale des Fabricants de Matières Colorantes et d'Hydrosulfites *f:* **USFMC**

Union Tank Car Company. Graver Water Conditioning Division. Technical Report *e:* **Union Tank Car Co Graver Water Cond Dir Tech Repr**

Union Économique Belgo-Luxembourgeoise *f:* **UEBL**

Union Évangélique Médicale et Paramédicale *f:* **UEMP**

Unione Bolognese Naturalisti *i:* **U.B.N.**

Unione Europea dei Medici Dentisti *i:* **UEMD**

Unione Europea di Medicina Sociale *i:* **UEMS**

Unione Geografica Internazionale *i:* **UGI**

Unione Medica Mediterranea *i:* **UMM**

Unione Medicale Mediterranea Latina *i:* **UMML**

Unione Naturista Italiana *i:* **UNI**

Unione Nazionale Cantieri e Industrie Nautiche ed Affini *i:* **UCINA**

Unione Popolare Italiana *i:* **UPI**

Unione Svizzera degli Studenti di Medicina *i:* **USEM**

Unipolar *e:* **UNIP**

Unipolar-Bipolar *e:* **UNIBI**

Unipolar Magnetic Regions *e:* **UMR**

Unipolar Straight Binary *e:* **USB**

Unipolar Straight Binary Code *e:* **USB Code**

Unit Commander Observation System *e:* **UCOS**

Unit Environmental Coordinator *e:* **UEC**

Unit for Laboratory Animal Medicine *e:* **ULAM**

Unit of Comparative Plant Ecology *e:* **UCPE**

Unit of Marine Invertebrate Biology *e:* **UMIB**

Unit of Medical Time *e:* **UMT**

United Action for Animals *e:* **UAA**

United Activists for Animal Rights *e:* **UAAR**

United Aerospace Workers *e:* **UAW**

United Against Cruelty to Animals *e:* **UACTA**

United American Healthcare *e:* **UAHC**

United Animal[s] Nations *e:* **UAN**

United Arab Republic. Geological Survey and Mineral Research Department. Papers *e:* **UAR Geol Surv Miner Res Dep Pap**

United Arab Republic. Institute of Oceanography and Fisheries. Bulletin *e:* **UAR Inst Oceanogr Fish Bull**

United Arab Republic. Journal of Animal Production *e:* **UARJ Anim Prod**

United Arab Republic. Journal of Geology *e:* **UARJ Geol**

United Arab Republic. Journal of Microbiology *e:* **UAR J Microbiol**

United Arab Republic (Southern Region). Ministry of Agriculture. Hydrobiological Department. Notes and Memoirs *e:* **UAR (South Reg) Minist Agric Hydrobiol Dep Notes Mem**

United Association for the Protection of Trade *e:* **UAPT**

United Association Protection Traders Information Online Link Credit Database *e:* **UAPT INFOLINK**

United Bargemen and Watermen's Protective Society *e:* **UBWPS**

United Behavioral Health *e:* **UBH**

United Cerebral Palsy of Prince George's and Montgomery Counties *e:* **UCP/PGMC**

United Citizens Coastal Protection League *e:* **UCCPL**

United Coppersmiths Trade Protection Association *e:* **UCTPA**

United Council of the Protected Areas of the Petén *e:* **UNEPET**

United Earth Sciences Exploration Group *e:* **UESEG**

United Food Animal Association *e:* **UFAA**

United Health Foundation *e:* **UHF**

United Healthcare Corp. *e:* **UNH**

United Healthcare Corporation *e:* **UHC**

United International Bureau for the Protection of Intellectual Property *e:* **UIBPIP**

United Kingdom Air Defense Ground Environment *e:* **UKADGE**

United Kingdom. Atomic Energy Authority. Authority Health and Safety Branch. Memorandum *e:* **UK At Energy Auth Auth Health Saf Branch Mem**

United Kingdom. Atomic Energy Authority. Authority Health and Safety Branch. Report *e:* **UK At Energy Auth Auth Health Saf Branch Rep**

United Kingdom. Atomic Energy Authority. Health and Safety Code. Authority Code *e:* **UK At Energy Auth Health Saf Code Auth Code**

United Kingdom. Atomic Energy Research Establishment. Health Physics and Medical Division. Research Progress Report *e:* **UK At Energy Res Establ Health Phys Med Dir Res Prog Rep**

United Kingdom Central Council for Nursing, Midwifery and Health Visiting *e:* **UKCC**

United Kingdom Colonies and Protectorates *e:* **VP**, *e:* **VQ**, *e:* **VR**

United Kingdom Department of the Environment *e:* **UK DoE**

United Kingdom Environmental Law Association *e:* **UKELA**

United Kingdom Environmental Mutagen Society *e:* **UKEMS**

United Kingdom Industrial Space Committee *e:* **UKISC**, *e:* **UKlSC**

United Kingdom Lean Aerospace Initiative *e:* **UKLAI**

United Kingdom Liaison Committee for Sciences Allied to Medicine and Biology *e:* **SAMB**

United Kingdom Mechanical Health Monitoring Group *e:* **UKMHMG**

United Kingdom Medical Research Council *e:* **UKMRC**

United Kingdom Medicines Information *e:* **UKMI**

United Kingdom Meteorological Office *e:* **UKMO**

United Kingdom National Committee of the International Association on Water Pollution Research and Control *e:* **UKNCIAWPRC**

United Kingdom Sea Mist Test[ing] *e:* **UKSMT**

United Kingdom Spacetrack Processor *e:* **UKSP**

United Kingdom Water Industry Research Ltd. *e:* **UKWIR**

United Lightning Protection Association *e:* **ULPA**

United Medical Corp. *e:* **UM**, *e:* **UTMED**

United Medical & Dental Schools *e:* **UMDS**

United Methodist Association of Health and Welfare Ministries *e:* **UMA**

United Nations Angola Observation Mission *e:* **MONUA**

United Nations Centre for Natural Resources, Energy and Transport *e:* **CNERT**

United Nations Centre for Urgent Environmental Assistance *e:* **UNCUEA**

United Nations Committee on Outer Space *e:* **UNCOS**

United Nations Committee on Peaceful Use[s] of Outer Space *e:* **UNCOPUOS**

United Nations Committee on the Peaceful Uses of Outer Space *e:* **UNCPUOS**

United Nations Conference on [the] Environment[al] (or Environments) and Development *e:* **UNCED**

United Nations Conference on the Exploration and Peaceful Uses of Outer Space *e:* **UNISPACE**

United Nations Conference on [the] Human Environment [at Stockholm Conference] *e:* **UNCHE**

United Nations Conference on the Law of the Sea *e:* **UNCLOS**, *e:* **UNCLS**

United Nations Convention on the Law of the Sea *e:* **Law of the Sea**, *e:* **UNCLOS**

United Nations Disengagement Observation (or Observer) Force *e:* **UNDOF**

United Nations Economic Commission for Asia and the Far East. Water Resources Series *e:* **UN Econ Comm Asia Far East Water Resour Ser**

United Nations Environment Fund *e:* **UNEF**

United Nations Environment Programme *e:* **UNDP**

United Nations Environment Program[me] Coordinating Unit for the Mediterranean Action Plan *e:* **UNEP/MEDU**

United Nations Environment Programme-Global Resources Information Database *e:* **UNEP-GRID**

United Nations Environment Programme-Harmonization of Environmental Measurement *e:* **UNEP-HEM**

United Nations Environment Program[me]/Information Unit for Conventions *e:* **UNEP/IUC**

United Nations Environment Programme/International Referral System *e:* **UNEP/IRS**

United Nations Environment Programme/International Referral System *e:* **UNEP/IRS**

United Nations Environment Program[me] Network for Latin America and the Carribean *e:* **UNEPNET-LAC**

United Nations Environment Program[me] of Technical Assistance *e:* **UNEPTA**

United Nations Environment Programme Participation Act *e:* **UNEPPA**

United Nations Environment Program[me]/Regional Office for Europe *e:* **UNEP/ROE**

United Nations Environmental Programme *e:* **UNEP**

United Nations Framework Convention and/on Climate Change *e:* **UNFCCC**

United Nations Framework Convention on Climate Change *e:* **Climate Change**

United Nations Group of Experts on Geographical Names *e:* **UNGEGN**

United Nations India and Pakistan Observation (or Observer) Mission *e:* **UNIPOM**

United Nations Iraq-Kuwait Observation (or Observer) Mission *e:* **UNIKOM**

United Nations Law of the Sea Conference *e:* **UNLOSC**

United Nations Observation (or Observer) Group in Lebanon *e:* **UNOGIL**

United Nations Observer Mission in Georgia *e:* **UNOMIG**

United Nations Ocean Economics and Technology Office *e:* **UNOETO**

United Nations Oceanographic Organization *e:* **UNOO**

United Nations Office of Legal Affairs/Division for Ocean Affairs and the Law of the Sea *e:* **UN/DAOLOS**

United Nations Outer Space Affairs Division *e:* **UNOASD**

United Nations Peace Observation Commission *e:* **UNPOC**

United Nations Preparatory Commission on the International Sea-Bed Authority and for the international Tribunal for the Law of the Sea *e:* **LOS PrepCom**

United Nations Protected Area *e:* **UNPA**

United Nations Protection Force *e:* **UNPROFOR**

United Nations Public Health and Welfare Detachment *e:* **UNPHWD**

United Nations Revolving Fund for Natural Resources Exploloration *e:* **UNRFNRE**

United Nations Scientific Conference on the Conservation and Utilisation (or Utilization) of [Natural] Resources *e:* **UNSCCUR**

United Nations Space Registry *e:* **UNSR**

United Nations Subcommission on the Prevention of Discrimination and the Protection of Minorities *e:* **UNSPDPM**

United Nations Symposium on the Development and Use of Geothermal Resources. Abstracts *e:* **UN Symp Dev Use Geotherm Resour Abstr**

United Nations Symposium on the Development and Use of Geothermal Resources. Proceedings *e:* **UN Symp Dev Use Geotherm Resour Proc**

United Nations Yemen Observation Mission *e:* **UNYOM**

United Ocean Transport *e:* **UOT**

United Operative Bricklayers' Trade Protection Society *e:* **UOBI**

United Presbyterian Health, Education, and Welfare Association *e:* **UPHEWA**

United Scientists for Environmental Responsibility and Protection *e:* **USERP**

United Seniors Health Cooperative *e:* **USHC**

United Ship Scrapers' Protection League *e:* **USSPL**

United Slate Tile and Composition Roofers, Damp, and Waterproof Workers Association *e:* **RDWW**

United Slate, Tile, and Composition Roofers, Damp, and Waterproof Workers Association *e:* **USTCRDWWA**

United Space Alliance *e:* **USA**

United Space Association *e:* **USA**

United Space Booster, Inc. *e:* **USBI**

United States Aerospace Industry Profile *e:* **US Aeros P**

United States. Aerospace Medical Research Laboratory. Technical Report *e:* **US Aerosp Med Res Lab Tech Rep**

United States. Aerospace Medical Research Laboratory. Technical Report. AMRL-TR *e:* **US Aerosp Med Res Lab Tech Rep AMRL-TR**

United States. Aerospace Research Laboratories. Reports *e:* **US Aerosp Res Lab Rep**

United States Air Force Aerospace Medical School *e:* **USAFAMEDS**

United States Air Force Environmental Health Laboratory *e:* **USAFEHL**

United States Air Force Environmental Technical Application[s] Center *e:* **USAFETAC**

United States Air Force Environmental Technical Applications Center *e:* **USAFETAL, *e:* USAFETC**

United States Air Force, Environmental Technical Applications Center, Air Weather Service Technical Library, Scott Air Force Base *e:* **IScAF-E**

United States Air Force Geophysical Laboratory *e:* **USAFGL**

United States Air Force Medical Service *e:* **USAFMS**

United States Air Force, National Aerospace Education Library, Ellington AFB, Houston *e:* **TxHE-NA**

United States Air Force Occupational and Environmental Health Laboratory *e:* **USAFOEHL**

United States Air Force Radiological Health Laboratory *e:* **USAFRHL**

United States Air Force, Regional Hospital, Medical Library, Sheppard AFB *e:* **TxShpM**

United States Air Force, Sacramento Peak Observatory, Sunspot *e:* **NmSuAF**

United States Air Force School of Aerospace Medicine *e:* **USAFSAM**

United States Air Force, School of Aerospace Medicine, Brooks Air Force Base, San Antonio *e:* **TxSaBAM**

United States. Air Force. School of Aerospace Medicine. Technical Report *e:* **UAERA**

United States Air Force School of Applied Aerospace Sciences *e:* **USAFSAAS**

United States Air Force School of Health Care Science *e:* **USAFSCHCS, *e:* USAFSHCS**

United States Air Force Space Biological Laboratory *e:* **USAFSBL**

United States Air Force-Space Division *e:* **USAF-SP**

United States Air Force Surgeon General *e:* **USAFSG**

United States Air Force Water Port Liaison Officer *e:* **USAFWPO**

United States Air Force Water Port Logistics Office *e:* **USAFWPLO**

United States Air Force, Wilford Hall Medicall Center, Lackland AFB *e:* **TxLaM**

United States Airspace System *e:* **USAS**

United States Animal Bank *e:* **USAB**

United States Animal Health Association *e:* **USAHA**

United States. Argonne National Laboratory. Biological and Medical Research Division. Semiannual Report *e:* **US Argonne Nat Lab Biol Med Res Div Semiannu Rep**

United States Armed Forces. Medical Journal *e:* **US Armed Forc[es] Med J**

United States Army Aberdeen Research and Development Center *e:* **USAARDC**

United States Army Aeromedical Center *e:* **USAAMC**

United States Army Aeromedical Research Laboratory *e:* **USAARL, *e:* USARL**

United States Army Aeromedical Research Unit *e:* **USAARU**

United States Army Air Force-Geophysics Laboratory *e:* **USAAF-GL**

United States Army Atmospheric Sciences Laboratory *e:* **USAASL**

United States Army Biological Laboratories *e:* **USABIOLABS**

United States Army Biological Research and Development Laboratory *e:* **USABRDL**

United States Army Biomedical Research and Development Laboratory *e:* **USABRDL**

United States Army Center for Health Promotion and Preventitive Medicine *e:* **USACHPPM**

United States Army Chemical, Biological, and Radiological Weapons Orientation Course Academic Advisory Board *e:* **USACBRWOCAAB**

United States Army Chemical, Biological, and Radiological Weapons Orientation Course (or Court) *e:* **USACBRWOC**

United States Army Chemical, Biological, and Radiological Weapons Orientation Court Academic Advisory Board *e:* **USACBRWOCAAB**

United States Army, Chemical Systems Laboratory, Aberdeen Proving Ground, Aberdeen *e:* **MdApgC**

United States Army Cold Weather and Mountain School *e:* **USACWMS**

United States Army Combat Developments Command Chemical-Biological-Radiological Agency *e:* **USACDCCBRA, *e:* USACDCCRA**

United States Army Combat Developments Command Medical Service Agency *e:* **USACDCMSA**

United States Army Communications Command Communications Agency-Health Services Command *e:* **USACC COMMAGCY-HSC**

United States Army Communications Command-Health Services Command *e:* **USACC-HSC**

United States. Army Corps of Engineers. Waterways Experiment Station. Miscellaneous Paper *e:* **US Army Corps Engineers Waterways Expt Sta Misc Paper**

United States. Army Corps of Engineers. Waterways Experiment Station. Technical Report *e:* **US Army Corps Engineers Waterways Expt Sta Tech Rept**

United States Army Drinking Water Surveillance Program *e:* **USADWSP**

United States Army Engineer Division, Pacific Ocean *e:* **USAEDPO, *e:* USDELPO**

United States Army Engineer, Geodesy, Intelligence, and Mapping Research and Development Agency *e:* **USAEGIMRADA**

United States Army Engineer Waterways Experiment Station *e:* **USAEWES**

United States Army Engineers. Waterways Experiment Station. Technical Report *e:* **US Army Eng Waterw Exp Stn Tech Rep**

United States Army Environmental Center *e:* **USAEC**

United States Army Environmental Health Laboratory *e:* **USAEHL**

United States Army Environmental Hygiene Agency *e:* **USAEHA**

United States Army Force[s] in Pacific Ocean Area[s] *e:* **USAFPOA**

United States Army Geodesy Intelligence and Mapping Research and Development Agency *e:* **USAGIMRADA**

United States Army Health Clinic *e:* **USAHC**

United States Army Health Services Command *e:* **USAHSC**

United States Army Health Services Data Systems Agency *e:* **USAHSDSA**

United States Army Information Systems Command-Health Services Command *e:* **USAISC-HSC**

United States Army Medical Biochemical Research Laboratory *e:* **USAMBRL**

United States Army Medical Bioengineering Research and Development Laboratory *e:* **USAMBRDL**

United States Army Medical Center *e:* **MEDCEN**

United States Army Medical Center, Fort Gordon *e:* **USAMCFG**

United States Army Medical Command *e:* **USAMEDCOM**

United States Army Medical Command, Europe *e:* **USAMEDCOMEUR**

United States Army Medical Corps *e:* **USAMC**

United States Army Medical Department Board *e:* **USAMEDDBD**

United States Army Medical Depot Activity, Ryukyu Island *e:* **USAMDAR**

United States Army Medical Depot Activity, Ryukyu Islands *e:* **USMDAR**

United States Army Medical Environmental Engineering Research Unit *e:* **USAMEERU**

United States Army Medical Equipment and Optical School *e:* **USAMEOS**

United States Army Medical Equipment Research and Development Laboratory *e:* **USAMERDL**

United States Army Medical Field Service School *e:* **USAMFSS**

United States Army Medical Intelligence and Information Agency *e:* **USAMIIA**

United States Army Medical Laboratory *e:* **USAMEDLAB, *e:* USAML**

United States Army, Medical Library, Fort Gordon *e:* **GFML**

United States Army Medical Material (or Materiel) Agency *e:* **USAMMA**

United States Army Medical Materiel Agency, Pacific *e:* **USAMMAPAC**

United States Army Medical Materiel Center *e:* **USAMMC**

United States Army Medical Materiel Command Europe *e:* **USAMMCE**

United States Army Medical Materiel Development Activity *e:* **USA-MMDA**

United States Army Medical Optical and Maintenance Activity e: **USAMOAMA**

United States Army Medical Optical and Maintenance Agency e: **USAMOMA**

United States Army Medical Research Acquisition Agency e: **USAMRAA**

United States Army Medical Research and Development Command e: **USAMRDC**

United States Army Medical Research and Materiel Command e: **USAMRMC**

United States Army Medical Research and Nutrition e: **USAMRN**

United States Army Medical Research and Nutrition Laboratory e: **USAMRNL**

United States Army Medical Research, Development, Acquisition, and Logistics e: **USAMRDAL**

United States Army Medical Research Institute for Chemical Defense e: **USAMRICD**

United States Army Medical Research Institute of Infection (or Infectious) Diseases e: **USAMRIID**

United States Army Medical Research Laboratory e: **USAMRL**

United States. Army. Medical Research Laboratory. Report e: **US Army Med Res Lab Rep**

United States Army Medical Research Unit e: **USAMRU**

United States Army Medical Research Unit - Europe e: **USAMRU-E**

United States Army Medical Service e: **USAMEDS**

United States Army Medical Service Meat and Diary Hygiene School e: **USAMSMADHS**

United States Army Medical Service School e: **USAMSS**

United States Army Medical Service Veterinary School e: **USAMEDSVS**

United States Army Medical Training Center e: **USAMEDTC**

United States Army Medical Unit e: **USAMU**

United States Army Medical Unit, Fort Detrick, Maryland e: **USAMUFD**

United States Army Meteorology and Calibration Center e: **USAMCC**

United States Army Polar Research and Development Center e: **USAPRDC**

United States Army Research Institute of Environmental Medicine e: **USARIEM**

United States Army School of Aviation Medicine e: **USASAM**

United States Army Signal Training Center, Fort Gordon, Georgia e: **USASTC**

United States Army Space and Strategic Defense Command e: **USASSDC**

United States Army Space Command e: **USARSPACE**

United States Army Space Program Office e: **USASPO**

United States Army Space & Strategic Command e: **USASSC**

United States Army TRADOC [Training and Doctrine Command], Ordnance and Chemical School Library Aberdeen Proving Ground e: **TRX**

United States Army Training Medical Center e: **USATMC**

United States Army Transportation Environmental Operations Group e: **USATREOG**

United States Army Troop Medical Clinic e: **USATMC**

United States Army Tropical Research Medical Laboratory e: **USATRML**

United States Army Waterways Experiment Station e: **USAWES**

United States Army, William Beaumont General Hospital, Medical and Technical Library, El Paso e: **TxEWB**

United States-Asia Environmental Partnership e: **US-AEP**

United States-Asia Environmental Partnership Initiative e: **USAEP**

United States Biological Cruise off Baja California e: **MESCAL**

United States Biological Survey e: **UBS**

United States Board on Geographical Names e: **USBGN**

United States Bureau of Biological Survey e: **USBBS**

United States Bureau of Mines and Geology e: **USBMG**

United States Bureau of Sport Fisheries and Wildlife e: **US Bureau Sport Fish Wildl**

United States Bureau of Sport Fisheries and Wildlife. Investigations in Fish Control e: **US Bureau Sport Fish Wildl Invest Fish Control**

United States. Bureau of Sport Fisheries and Wildlife. Investigations in Fish Control e: **US Bur Sport Fish Wildl Invest Fish Control**

United States Bureau of Sport Fisheries and Wildlife. Research Report e: **US Bur Sport Fish Wildl Res Rep**

United States. Bureau of Sport Fisheries and Wildlife. Resource Publication e: **US Bur Sport Fish Wildl Resour Publ**

United States Bureau of Sport Fisheries and Wildlife. Technical Papers e: **US Bur Sport Fish Wildl Tech Pap**

United States Bureau on Geographical Names e: **USBGN**

United States Coast and Geodetic Survey e: **USCANDGS**, e: **USC & G**, e: **USCGC**, e: **USC & GS**

United States Coast and Geodetic Survey, Department of Commerce e: **USC&GS**

United States Coast and Geodetic Survey. Publication e: **US Coast and Geod Survey Pub**

United States Coast and Geodetic Survey Ship e: **USC&GSS**

United States Commander-in-Chief, Space Command e: **USCINCSPACE**

United States Committee for the Global Atmospheric Research Program e: **USC-GARP**

United States Committee for the Oceans e: **USCO**

United States Committee for the World Health Organization e: **USC-WHO**

United States component of WOCE [World Ocean Circulation Experiment] e: **USWOCE**

United States Conference of City Health Officers e: **USCCHO**

United States Conference of Local Health Officers e: **USCLHO**

United States Decade for Natural Disaster Reduction e: **USDNDR**

United States Depart of Health, Education Welfare e: **USDHEW**

United States Department of Agriculture-Animal and Plant Health Inspection Service e: **USDA/APHIS**

United States Department of Agriculture-Bureau of Biological Survey e: **USDA Bur Biol Surv**

United States Department of Agriculture. Bureau of Biological Survey. Bulletin e: **USDA Bur Biol Surv Bull**

United States. Department of Agriculture. Index-Catalogue of Medical and Veterinary Zoology. Special Publication e: **US Dep Agric Index-Cat Med Vet Zool Spec Publ**

United States. Department of Agriculture. Index-Catalogue of Medical and Veterinary Zoology. Supplement e: **US Dep Agric Index-Cat Med Vet Zool Suppl**

United States Department of Agriculture, Plum Island Animal Disease Laboratory Library, Greenport e: **NGrpAg**

United States Department of Commerce. Coast and Geodetic Survey. Magnetograms and Hourly Values e: **US Coast Geod Surv Magnetograms Hourly Values**

United States Department of Defense Manned Spaceflight e: **USDDMS**

United States Department of Energy. Environmental Measurements Laboratory. Environmental Report e: **US Dep Energy Environ Meas Lab Environ Rep**

United States Department of Health and Human Services e: **US Dept HHS**, e: **USDHHS**

United States Department of Health and Human Services, Health Care Financing Administration, Office of Research Demonstrations and Statistics e: **MdBDH**

United States Department of Health and Human Services. National Institute of Mental Health. Science Monographs e: **US Dep Health Hum Serv Natl Inst Ment Health Sci Monogr**

United States Department of Health and Human Services. Publications e: **US Dept HHS Publ**

United States Department of Health, Education, and Welfare e: **US Dept HEW**, e: **USDHE & W**

United States Department of Health, Education and Welfare Annual Report e: **US Dep Health Educ Welfare Annu Rep**

United States. Department of Health, Education and Welfare. DHEW Publication e: **US Dep Health Educ Welfare DHEW Publ**

United States. Department of Health, Education and Welfare. Health Services Administration. Publication e: **US Dep Health Educ Welfare Health Serv Adm Publ**

United States Department of Health, Education and Welfare. National Institute of Mental Health. Science Monographs e: **US Dep Health Educ Welfare Natl Inst Ment Health Sci Monogr**

United States Department of Health,
Education and Welfare Publications *e:*
US Dept HEW Publ

United States. Department of the Interior.
Fish and Wildlife Service. Research Report *e:*
US Dep Inter Fish Wildl Res Rep

United States. Department of the Interior.
Geological Survey. Mineral
Investigations Field Studies Map *e:* **US
Geol Surv Miner Invest Field Stud Map**

United States Department of the Interior,
Natural Resources Library, Washington
e: **UDI**

United States Department of the Interior,
United States Geological Survey, Reston
e: **GIS**

United States District Court for the
Northern District of Georgia *e:* **USDC
ND GA**

United States Earth Satellite *e:* **USES**

United States Element, North American
Aerospace Defense Command *e:*
USELEMNORAD

United States Environment and Resources
Council *e:* **USERC,** *e:* **USREC**

United States Environmental Protection
Agency *e:* **OCEPA,** *e:* **USEPA**

United States Environmental Protection
Agency, Cincinnati *e:* **OEP**

United States Environmental Protection
Agency, Corvallis Environmental
Research Laboratory *e:* **OrCEPA**

United States Environmental Protection
Agency. Ecological Research *e:* **US EPA
Ecol Res**

United States Environmental Protection
Agency. Environmental Health Effects
Research *e:* **US EPA Envir Health Res**

United States. Environmental Protection
Agency. Environmental Monitoring *e:*
US EPA Envir Monit

United States Environmental Protection
Agency. Environmental Protection
Technology *e:* **US EPA Envir Prot
Technol**

United States Environmental Protection
Agency, Kansas City *e:* **MoKEP**

United States. Environmental Protection
Agency. Municipal Construction
Division. Report *e:* **US Environ Prot
Agency Munic Constr Div Rep**

United States Environmental Protection
Agency. National Environmental
Research Center. Ecological Research
Series *e:* **US Environ Prot Agency Natl
Environ Res Cent Ecol Res Ser**

United States Environmental Protection
Agency, Office of Administration,
Library Services Branch, Park, Durham
e: **NcDurEP**

United States Environmental Protection
Agency. Office of Air and Waste
Management *e:* **US Environ Prot
Agency Off Air Waste Manage**

United States Environmental Protection
Agency Office of Air Quality Planning
and Standards. Technical Report *e:* **US
Environ Prot Agency Off Air Qual
Plann Stand Tech Rep**

United States. Environmental Protection
Agency. Office of Pesticide Programs.
Report *e:* **US Environ Prot Agency Off
Pestic Programs Rep**

United States Environmental Protection
Agency. Office of Radiation Programs *e:*
**US Environ Prot Agency Off Radiat
Programs**

United States. Environmental Protection
Agency. Office of Radiation Programs.
Technical Report *e:* **US Environ Prot
Agency Off Radiat Programs Tech Rep**

United States. Environmental Protection
Agency. Office of Research and
Development. Report EPA *e:* **US
Environ Prot Agency Off Res Dev Rep
EPA**

United States Environmental Protection
Agency. Office of Research and
Development. Research Reports.
Ecological Research Series *e:* **US
Environ Prot Agency Off Res Dev Res
Rep Ecol Res Ser**

United States Environmental Protection
Agency. Publication *e:* **US Environ
Prot Agency Publ**

United States. Environmental Protection
Agency. Socioeconomic Environmental
Studies *e:* **US EPA Socioecon Studies**

United States Environmental Science
Services Administration *e:* **USESSA**

United States Environmental Training
Institute *e:* **USETI**

United States Fish and Wildlife Service *e:*
USF & WS

United States Fish and Wildlife Service,
Alaska Area Office, Anchorage *e:* **UDK**

United States Fish and Wildlife Service,
Billings *e:* **UDO**

United States Fish and Wildlife Service.
Biological Report *e:* **US Fish Wildl
Serv Biol Rep**

United States Fish and Wildlife Service.
Biological Services Program *e:* **US Fish
Wildl Serv Biol Serv Program**

United States Fish and Wildlife Service.
Bureau of Commercial Fisheries. Fishery
Leaflet *e:* **US Fish Wildl Serv Bur
Commer Fish Fish Leafl**

United States Fish and Wildlife Service.
Bureau of Commercial Fisheries.
Statistical Digest *e:* **US Fish Wildl Serv
Bur Commer Fish Stat Dig**

United States Fish and Wildlife Service.
Bureau of Sport Fisheries and Wildlife
e: **US Fish Wildl Serv Bur Sport Fish
Wildl**

United States Fish and Wildlife Service.
Circular *e:* **US Fish Wildl Serv Circ**

United States Fish and Wildlife Service,
Department of the Interior *e:* **USFWS**

United States Fish and Wildlife Service.
Fish and Wildlife Leaflet *e:* **US Fish
Wildl Serv Fish Wildl Leafl**

United States Fish and Wildlife Service.
Fish Distribution Report *e:* **US Fish
Wildl Serv Fish Distrib Rep**

United States Fish and Wildlife Service.
Fishery Bulletin *e:* **US Fish and
Wildlife Service Fishery Bull,** *e:* **US
Fish Wildl Serv Fish Bull**

United States Fish and Wildlife Service.
Investigations in Fish Control *e:* **US
Fish Widl Serv Invest Fish Control**

United States Fish and Wildlife Service.
North American Fauna *e:* **US Fish Wildl
Serv N Am Fauna**

United States Fish and Wildlife Service,
Region 2, Albuquerque *e:* **UDE**

United States Fish and Wildlife Service.
Research Report *e:* **US Fish Wildl Serv
Res Rep**

United States Fish and Wildlife Service.
Resource Publication *e:* **US Fish Wildl
Serv Resour Publ**

United States Fish and Wildlife Service,
Science Reference Library, Twin Cities
e: **UDT**

United States Fish and Wildlife Service
Special Scientific Report *e:* **U.S. Fish
Wildl. Serv. Spec. Sci. Rep.**

United States Fish and Wildlife Service.
Special Scientific Report. Fisheries *e:*
US Fish Wildl Serv Spec Sci Rep Fish

United States Fish and Wildlife Service.
Special Scientific Report. Wildlife *e:* **US
Fish Wildl Serv Spec Sci Rep Wildl**

United States Fish and Wildlife Service.
Technical Papers *e:* **US Fish Wildl Serv
Tech Pap**

United States Fish and Wildlife Service.
Wildlife Leaflet *e:* **US Fish Wildl Serv
Wildl Leafl**

United States Fish and Wildlife Service.
Wildlife Research Report *e:* **US Fish
Wildl Serv Wildl Res Rep**

United States. Fish and Wildlife Service.
Wildlife Research Report *e:*
USFWSWRR

United States Foreign Medical Graduate[s]
e: **USFMG**

United States Forest Service. Northern
Region. Forest Environmental Protection
e: **US For Serv North Reg For Environ
Prot**

United States/French Ocean Topography
Satellite Altimeter Experiment *e:*
TOPEX/POSEIDON

United States Geodetic Survey *e:* **USGS**

United States Geodynamics Committee *e:*
USGC

United States Geographic Board *e:* **USGB**

United States Geographical and Geological
Survey of the Rocky Mountain Region *e:*
US Geog G S Rocky Mtn Reg

United States Geographical and Geological
Survey of the Rocky Mountain Region
(Powell) *e:* **US Geog G S Rocky Mtn
Reg (Powell)**

United States Geological and Geographies
Survey of the Territories *e:* **US G Geog
S Terr**

United States Geological and Geographies
Survey of the Territories (Hayden) *e:* **US
G Geog S Terr (Hayden)**

United States Geological Service *e:* **USGS**

United States Geological Survey and
Minerals Management Service *e:*
USGSMMS

United States. Geological Survey. Annual
Report *e:* **US Geol Surv Annu Rep**

United States. Geological Survey. Annual
Report. Professional Paper. Bulletin.
Water-Supply Paper Monograph. Mineral
Resources Geology Atlas *e:* **USGS An
Rp PPB W-S P Mon Min Res G Atlas
Top Atlas**

United States. Geological Survey. Bulletin
e: **US Geol S Bul,** *e:* **US Geol Surv Bull,**
e: **US Geol S[urv][ey] Bul[l],** *e:* **USGSB**

United States. Geological Survey. Circular *e:* **US Geol Surv Circ**

United States Geological Survey. Circular *e:* **US Geol Survey Circ**

United States. Geological Survey. Circular *e:* **USGSC**

United States Geological Survey. Coal Investigations Map *e:* **US Geol Surv Coal Invest Map**

United States. Geological Survey. Geological Quadrangle Map *e:* **US Geol Survey Geol Quad Map**

United States. Geological Survey. Geophysical Investigations Map *e:* **US Geol Survey Geophys Inv Map**

United States. Geological Survey. Geophysical Investigations Map *e:* **US Geol Surv Geophys Invest Map**

United States Geological Survey. Hydrologic Investigations Atlas *e:* **US Geol Survey Hydrol Inv Atlas**

United States Geological Survey. Index to Geologic Mapping in the United States *e:* **US Geol Survey Index Geol Mapping US**

United States Geological Survey, Menlo Park *e:* **USGS-MP**

United States Geological Survey, Metairie *e:* **GIL**

United States Geological Survey. Mineral Investigations Field Studies Map *e:* **US Geol Survey Mineral Inv Field Studies Map**

United States Geological Survey. Mineral Investigations Resource Map *e:* **US Geol Survey Mineral Inv Res Map**

United States Geological Survey. Miscellaneous Field Studies Map *e:* **US Geol Surv Misc Field Stud Map**

United States. Geological Survey. Miscellaneous Geologic Investigations Map *e:* **US Geol Surv[ey] Misc Geol Inv[est] Map,** *e:* **US Geol Surv Misc Geol Invest Map**

United States Geological Survey of the Territories *e:* **USGS Terr**

United States Geological Survey. Oil and Gas Investigations Chart *e:* **US Geol Survey Oil and Gas Inv Chart**

United States Geological Survey. Oil and Gas Investigations Map *e:* **US Geol Surv Oil Gas Invest Map**

United States Geological Survey. Open-File Report *e:* **US Geol Surv Open-File Rep**

United States. Geological Survey. Professional Paper *e:* **US Geol S Professional Pa**

United States Geological Survey. Professional Paper *e:* **US Geol Survey Prof Paper**

United States. Geological Survey. Professional Paper *e:* **US Geol S[urv] Prof[essional] Pa[p]**

United States Geological Survey Professional Paper *e:* **U.S. Geol. Surv. Prof. Pap.**

United States. Geological Survey. Professional Paper *e:* **USGSPP**

United States Geological Survey, Reston, Virginia *e:* **W**

United States. Geological Survey. Trace Elements Memorandum Report *e:* **US Geol Surv Trace Elem Memo Rep,** *e:* **US Geol Surv Trace Elem Memo Rep**

United States Geological Survey, Water Resources Division, Syosset *e:* **NSyoG**

United States Geological Survey. Water-Resources Investigations *e:* **US Geol Surv Water-Resour Invest**

United States Geological Survey, Water Resources Services, New York District, Albany *e:* **NAIGS**

United States. Geological Survey. Water-Supply Paper *e:* **US Geol Survey Water-Supply Paper**

United States Geological Survey. Water-Supply Paper *e:* **US Geol Surv Water-Supply Pap**

United States Geological Society *e:* **USGS**

United States Geosphere/Biosphere Program *e:* **US-IGBP**

United States Health, Incorporated *e:* **USHI**

United States Health Manpower Advisory Council *e:* **USHMAC**

United States Healthcare, Inc. *e:* **USHC**

United States Historical Climatology Network *e:* **USHCN**

United States Hydrograph Laboratory *e:* **USHL**

United States Hydrographic Office *e:* **USHO,** *e:* **US Hydrog Office**

United States Hydrographic Office. Publication *e:* **US Hydrog Office Pub**

United States Imagery and Geospatial Information System *e:* **USIGS**

United States Immigration and Naturalization Officers' Association *e:* **USINOA**

United States Immigration and Naturalization Service *e:* **USI & NS**

United States Indian Health Service *e:* **USIH**

United States Institute for Environmental Conflict Resolution *e:* **USIECR**

United States Institute of Space Studies *e:* **USISS**

United States Inter-Oceanic Sea-Level Canal Commission *e:* **USIOSLCC**

United States Interdepartmental Committee for Atmospheric Sciences. Report *e:* **US Interdep Comm Atmos Sci Rep**

United States International Space Year Association *e:* **US-ISY,** *e:* **US-ISY**

United States-Japan Cooperative Medical Science Program *e:* **USJCMSP**

United States-Japan Cooperative Program in/on Natural Resources *e:* **UJNR**

United States/Japan Natural Resources Panel *e:* **USJNRP**

United States Joint Global Ocean Flux Studies (or Study) *e:* **USJGOFS**

United States Medical Department *e:* **USMD**

United States Medical Doctor *e:* **USMD**

United States Medical Enterprises, Inc. *e:* **USMD**

United States Medical Graduate *e:* **USMG**

United States Medical Intelligence and Information Agency, Frederick *e:* **UAM**

United States Medical Licensing Examination *e:* **USMLE**

United States Medical Nutrition Laboratory *e:* **USMNL**

United States Medicine *e:* **US Med**

United States Merit Systems Protection Board *e:* **USMSPB**

United States Meteorological Satellite *e:* **NIMBUS**

United States-Mexico Border Health Association *e:* **USMBHA**

United States Mexico Border Public Health Association *e:* **USMBPHA**

United States Military Academy Department of Earth, Space, and Graphic Sciences *e:* **USMA/ESGS**

United States National Aeronautics and Space Administration *e:* **USNASA,** *e:* **US Natl Aeronaut Space Admin**

United States. National Aeronautics and Space Administration. Conference Publication *e:* **USNASA Conf Publ**

United States National Aeronautics and Space Administration. Special Publication *e:* **US Natl Aeronaut Space Admin Spec Publ**

United States National Aeronautics and Space Administration, Technical Library, Wallops Island *e:* **ViWiN**

United States National Biological Survey *e:* **USNBS**

United States National Center for Health Statistics *e:* **USNCHS**

United States National Committee for International Hydrological Program *e:* **USNC/IHP**

United States National Committee for/on the History of Geology *e:* **USHIGEO**

United States National Committee for the International Biological Program *e:* **USNC/IBP,** *e:* **USNC/IBP**

United States National Committee for the International Geophysical Year *e:* **USNC-IGY,** *e:* **USNC-IGY**

United States National Committee for the Scientific Committee on Oceanic Research *e:* **USNC/SCOR**

United States National Committee on Scientific Hydrology *e:* **USNCHC,** *e:* **USNC/SH**

United States National Earthquake Center, Golden, Colorado *e:* **USNEC**

United States National Earthquake Predictions Evaluation Council *e:* **USNEPEC**

United States National Environmental Health Sciences Center, Durham *e:* **NcDurHS**

United States National Institutes of Health *e:* **US Natl Inst Health**

United States National Institutes of Health. National Toxicology Program Technical Report Series *e:* **US Natl Inst Health Natl Toxicol Program Tech Rep Ser**

United States National Institutes of Health. Publication *e:* **US Natl Inst Health Publ**

United States National Library of Medicine *e:* **USNLM**

United States National Marine Fisheries Service, Biological Laboratory, Galveston *e:* **TxGUSFW**

United States National Ocean Service *e:* **USNOS**

United States National Ocean Survey *e:* **USNOS**

United States National Ocean-Wide Survey Program *e:* **USNOWSP**

United States. National Oceanic and Atmospheric Administration. Environmental Data Service. Technical

Memorandum e: **US Natl Oceanic Atmos Adm Environ Data Serv Tech Memo**

United States National Oceanic and Atmospheric Administration. Key to Oceanographic Records Documentation e: **US Natl Oceanic Atmos Adm Key Oceanogr Rec Doc**

United States National Oceanic and Atmospheric Administration. Northeast Fisheries Center Sandy Hook Laboratory. Technical Series Report e: **TSNSDH**

United States National Oceanographic Data Center e: **US Natl Oceanog Data Center**

United States National Oceanographic Data Center (or Centre) e: **USNODC**

United States National Oceanographic Data Center. Publication e: **US Natl Oceanog Data Center Pub**

United States National Park Service. Ecological Services Bulletin e: **US Natl Park Serv Ecol Serv Bull**

United States National Park Service. Natural History Handbook Series e: **US Natl Park Service Nat History Handb Ser**

United States National Park Service. Natural Resources Report e: **US Natl Park Serv Nat Resour Rep**

United States Naval Academy Energy-Environment Study Group and Development Team e: **USNA-EPRD**

United States Naval Aerospace Medical Institute e: **US Nav Aerosp Med Inst**, e: **US Naval Aerospace Med Inst**

United States Naval Aerospace Medical Institute. Monograph e: **US Nav Aerosp Med Inst Monogr**

United States Naval Aerospace Medical Research Laboratory e: **US Nav Aerosp Med Res Lab**

United States Naval Aerospace Medical Research Laboratory. Special Report e: **US Nav Aerosp Med Res Lab Spec Rep**

United States Naval Medical Bulletin e: **US Nav[al] Med Bull**, e: **US Nav Med Bull**

United States Naval Medical Research Laboratory e: **US Nav Med Res Lab**

United States Naval Medical Research Laboratory. Report e: **US Nav Med Res Lab Rep**

United States Naval Observatory Automated Data Service e: **USNOADS**

United States Naval Observatory [Library] e: **USNO**

United States Naval Observatory Time Service Division e: **USNO-TS**

United States Naval Ocean Research and Development Activity e: **USNORDA**

United States Naval Oceanographic Office e: **USNOO**

United States Naval Oceanographic Office. Special Publication e: **US Nav Oceanogr Off Spec Publ**

United States Naval School of Aviation Medicine e: **US Nav Sch Aviat Med**

United States Naval School of Aviation Medicine. Monograph e: **US Nav Sch Aviat Med Monogr**

United States Naval School of Aviation Medicine. Research Report e: **US Nav Sch Aviat Med Res Rep**

United States Naval Space Command e: **USNSC**

United States Naval Submarine Medical Center e: **US Naval Submar Med Cent**, e: **US Nav Submar Med Cent**, e: **USNSMC**

United States Naval Submarine Medical Center. Memorandum Report e: **US Nav Submar Med Cent Memo Rep**

United States Naval Submarine Medical Center. Report e: **US Naval Submar Med Cent Rep**

United States. Naval Submarine Medical Center. Report e: **US Nav Submar Med Cent Rep**

United States. Naval Submarine Medical Research Laboratory. Memorandum Report e: **US Nav Submar Med Res Lab Memo Rep**

United States Naval Submarine Medical Research Laboratory. Report e: **US Nav Submar Med Res Lab Rep**

United States Naval Weather Service e: **USNAVWEASERV**

United States Navy Hydrographic Office e: **USNHO**

United States Navy Medical Service Corps e: **USNMSC**

United States Navy Medicine e: **US Navy Med**

United States Navy, Naval Regional Medical Center, Bremerton e: **WaBrNR**

United States Navy Underwater Laboratory e: **USNUWL**

United States Navy Underwater Sound Laboratory e: **USNUSL**

United States Occupational Health Standards e: **USOS**

United States Ocean Survey Plan e: **USOSP**

United States Oceanic and Atmospheric Administration e: **US Natl Oceanic Atmos Adm**

United States Oceanographic Office e: **USOO**

United States of America Aerospace Industries Representatives in Europe e: **USAIRE**

United States. Office of Saline Water Research and Development. Progress Report e: **US Off[ice] Saline Water Res[earch and] Dev[el] Prog[ress] Rep[t]**

United States On-orbit Segment e: **USOS**

United States Pigeon Shooting Federation e: **USPSF**

United States Public Health Report e: **US Publ H Rep**

United States Public Health Service e: **USPHS**, e: **UTSPHS**

United States Public Health Service Clinic e: **USPHSC**

United States Public Health Service Hospital e: **USPHSH**

United States Public Health Service Hospital, Baltimore e: **MdBPH**

United States. Public Health Service. Public Health Monograph e: **US Public Health Serv Public Health Monogr**

United States Public Health Service. Radiological Health Data and Reports e: **US Public Health Serv Radiol Health Data Rep**

United States Public Health Service Reserve e: **USPHSR**

United States Racing Pigeon Association e: **USRPA**

United States Space Administration e: **USSA**

United States Space Command e: **USSPACECOM**

United States Space Command, Paterson Air Force Base, Colorado Springs, Colorado e: **USSC**

United States Space Education Association e: **USSEA**

United States Space Foundation e: **USSF**

United States Space Part Steering Committees e: **USSPC**

United States Standard Atmosphere e: **USSA**

United States Veterans Administration Center, Medical Library, Hampton e: **ViHaV**

United States Veterans Administration. Department of Medicine and Surgery. Bulletin of Prosthetics Research e: **US Veterans Adm Dep Med Surg Bull Prosthet Res**

United States. Veterans Administration (Washington, DC). Department of Medicine and Surgery. Bulletin of Prosthetics Research e: **US Veterans Adm (W) Dep Med Surg Bull Prosthet Res**

United States. Veterans Bureau. Medical Bulletin e: **US Veterans Bureau Med Bull**

United States Water Polo e: **USWP**

United States Waterways Experiment Station e: **US Waterw Exp Stn**

United States. Waterways Experiment Station. Contract Report e: **US Waterw Exp Stn Contract Rep**

United States. Waterways Experiment Station. Miscellaneous Paper e: **US Waterw Exp Stn Misc Pap**

United States. Waterways Experiment Station. Research Report e: **US Waterw Exp Stn Res Rep**

United States. Waterways Experiment Station. Technical Report e: **US Waterw Exp Stn Tech Rep**

United States. Waterways Experiment Station (Vicksburg, Mississippi). Miscellaneous Paper e: **US Waterw Exp Stn (Vicksburg Miss) Misc Pap**

United States. Waterways Experiment Station (Vicksburg, Mississippi). Research Report e: **US Waterw Exp Stn (Vicksburg Miss) Res Rep**

United States Weather-Bureau e: **USWB**

United States Weather Research Program e: **USWRP**

United States Wildlife Service e: **USWLS**

United Underwater Contractors Association e: **UUCA**

United Union of Roofers, Waterproofers and Allied Workers e: **UURWAW**

United Water Resources, Inc. e: **UWR**

Unity Healthcare Holding Co., Inc. e: **UNTY**

Unité Coopérative d'Enseignement [École d'Onex-Bosson] f: **UCE**

Unité de Biostatistique et d'Informatique Médicale f: **UBIM**

Unité de coordination du Programme de l'environnement de la mer Noire *f:* **PCU**

Uniunea Societàtilor de Stiinte Medicale *ru:* **USSM**

Universal Environmental Shelter *e:* **UES**

Universal Geographic Identity *e:* **UGID**

Universal Health Care Ltd. *e:* **UHC**

Universal Health Realty *e:* **UHT**

Universal Health Services, Incorporated *e:* **UHSI**

Universal Medical Assistance International Centre *e:* **UMA**

Universal Medical Buildings, Inc. *e:* **UMB**

Universal Medical Record (London) *e:* **Univ Med Rec (London)**

Universal Polar Stereographic *e:* **UPS**

Universal Polar Stereographic Grid *e:* **UPS**

universal polar stereographic grid *e:* **UPSG**

Universal Processing System for Treasuring Up and Analyzing Images in Remote Sensing *e:* **UPSTAIRS**

Universal Remote Terminal *e:* **URT**

Universal Space Rectangular *e:* **USR**

Universal Synchronous Receiver Transmitier *e:* **USRT**

Universal Underwater Mobile *e:* **UNUMO**

Universal Water Charts *e:* **UWC**

Universal Weather Landing Code *e:* **UCO**

Universala Medicina Esperanto-Asocio *eo:* **U.M.E.A.**

Universe Natural History Series *e:* **Universe Nat Hist Ser**

Universidad Autónoma Potosina. Instituto de Geologia y Metalurgia. Folleto Tecnico *s:* **Univ Auton Potosina Inst Geol Metal Foll Tec**

Universidad de Chile. Facultad de Ciencias Fisicas y Matematicas. Instituto de Geologia. Publicación *s:* **Univ Chile Fac Cienc Fis Mat Inst Geol Publ**

Universidad de Oriente. Instituto Oceanografico. Boletin *s:* **Univ Oriente Inst Oceanogr Bol**

Universidad de Oriente. Instituto Oceanografico. Boletin Bibliografico *s:* **Univ Oriente Inst Oceanogr Bol Bibliogr**

Universidad de Sevilla. Publicaciones. Serie Medicina *s:* **Univ Sevilla Publ Ser Med**

Universidad Hispalense. Anales. Serie Medicína *s:* **Univ Hisp An Ser Med**

Universidad Industrial de Santander. Boletin de Geología *s:* **Univ Ind Santander Bol Geol**

Universidad Nacional Autónoma de México. Instituto de Geologia. Revista *s:* **Univ Nac Auton Mex Inst Geol Rev**

Universidad Nacional Autónoma de México. Instituto de Geología. Anales *s:* **Univ Nac Auton Mex Inst Geol An**

Universidad Nacional Autónoma de México. Instituto de Geología. Boletin *s:* **Univ Nac Auton Mex Inst Geol Bol**

Universidad Nacional de Córdoba. Facultad de Ciencias Medicas. Revista *s:* **Univ Nac Cordoba Fac Cienc Med Rev**

Universidad Nacional de La Plata. Facultad de Ciencias Naturales y Museo. Serie Técnica y Didactica *s:* **Univ Nac La Plata Fac Cienc Nat Mus Ser Tec Didact**

Universidad Nacional de la Plata. Notas del Museo. Geología *s:* **Univ Nac La Plata Notas Mus Geol**

Universidad Nacional de Tucuman. Instituto de Geología y Minería. Revista *s:* **Univ Nac Tucuman Inst Geol Min Rev**

Universidad National Autonoma de Mexico. Instituto de Geologia. Paleontologica Mexicana *s:* **Univ Nac Auton Mex Inst Geol Paleontol Mex**

Universidad Oceánica de Qindgao *s:* **OUQ**

Universidade de Bahia. Escola de Geologia. Publicacao Avulsa *p:* **Univ Bahia Esc Geol Publ Avulsa**

Universidade de São Paulo. Escola Politecnica, Geologia, e Metalurgia. Boletim *p:* **Univ Sao Paulo Esc Politec Geol Metal Bol**

Universidade de São Paulo. Faculdade de Filosofa, Ciencias, e Letras. Boletim. Geologia *p:* **Univ Sao Paulo Fac Filos Cienc Let Bol Geol**

Universidade de São Paulo. Instituto de Geociencias. Boletim IG [Instituto de Geocientias] *p:* **Univ Sao Paulo Inst Geocienc Bol IG**

Universidade de São Paulo. Instituto de Geociencias e Astronomia. Boletim *p:* **Univ Sao Paulo Inst Geocienc Astron Bol**

Universidade do Rio Grande Do Sul. Escola de Geologia. Avulso *p:* **Univ Rio Grande Do Sul Esc Geol Avulso**

Universidade do Rio Grande Do Sul. Escola de Geologia. Boletim *p:* **Univ Rio Grande Do Sul Esc Geol Bol**

Universidade do Rio Grande do Sul. Escola de Geologia. Notas e Estudos *p:* **Univ Rio Grande do Sul Esc Geol Notas Estud**

Universidade Federal de Rio De Janeiro. Instituto de Geociencias. Geologia. Boletim *p:* **Univ Fed Rio De Janeiro Inst Geocienc Geol Bol**

Universidade Federal do Rio De Janeiro. Instituto de Geociencias. Boletim Geologia *p:* **Univ Fed Rio De J Inst Geocienc Bol Geol**

Universidade Federal do Rio De Janeiro. Instituto de Geociencias. Departamento de Geologia. Contribuicao Didatica *p:* **Univ Fed Rio De J Inst Geocienc Dep Geol Contrib Dida**

Universily of Louisville, Health Sciences Library *e:* **KyLoU-HS**

Università degli Studi di Trieste. Facoltà di Scienze. Istituto di Geologia. Pubblicazioni *i:* **Univ Studi Trieste Fac Sci Ist Geol Pubbl**, *i:* **Univ Studi Triest Fac di Sci Ist Geol Pubbl**

Università di Ferrara. Annali. Sezione 6. Fisiologia e Chimica Biologica *i:* **Univ Ferrara Ann Sez 6**

Università di Ferrara. Memorie Geopaleontologiche *i:* **Univ Ferrara Mem Geopaleontol**

Universitaires pour le Tiers Monde *s:* **MONDE-3**

Universität des Saarlandes-Campus-überdeckendes Netz *d:* **UDS-CANTUS**

Universite d'Ankara. Faculte des Sciences. Communications. Serie C. Sciences Naturelles *f:* **Univ Ankara Fac Sci Commun Ser C**

Universite de Yaounde. Faculte des Sciences. Annales. Serie 3. Biologie-Biochimie *P:* **Univ Yaounde Fac Sci Ann Ser 3**

Universite Forestiere et du Bois (Sopron). Publications Scientifiques *f:* **Univ For Bois (Sopron) Publ Sci**

Universiteit van die Witwatersrand *n:* **UW**

Universitet u Geogradu Radovi. Zavoda za Fiziku *se:* **Univ Geograd Radovi Zavoda za Fiz**

Universitetet i Bergen Arbok. Naturvitenskapelig Rekke *N:* **Univ Bergen Arb[ok] Naturv[itensk] R[ekke]**

Universitetet i Oslo, Matematisk-Naturvitenskapelige Fakultet, Oslo, Norway *N:* **NoOU-M**

Universities Council of/on Water Resources Research *e:* **UCOWR**

Universities Council on Water Resources *e:* **UCWR**

Universities Federation for Animal Welfare *e:* **UFAW**

Universities Federation of Animal Welfare Courier *e:* **UFAW Courier**

Universities Global Atmospheric Modelling Programme *e:* **UGAMP**

Universities Global Atmospheric Modelling Project *e:* **UGAMP**

Universities (or University) Space Research Association *e:* **USRA**

Universities Space Automation/Robotics Consortium *e:* **USA/RC**

University Association for Emergency Medical Services *e:* **UAEMS**

University Association for Emergency Medicine *e:* **UA/EM**

University Center for Atmospheric Research *e:* **UCAR**

University Center for Environmental Studies *e:* **UCES**

University College of Physicians and Surgeons *e:* **U.C.P.S.**

University Consortium for Atmospheric Research *e:* **UCAR**

University Consortium for Geographical Information Systems *e:* **UCGIS**

University Cooperation for Atmospheric Research network *e:* **UCARnet**

University Corporation for Atmospheric Research *e:* **UCAR**

University Corporation for Atmospheric Research Foundation *e:* **UCARF**

University Corporation for Atmospheric Research Intellectual Property *e:* **UCARIP**, *e:* **UIP**

University Corporation for Atmospheric Research Intellectual Property Officer *e:* **UCARIPO**

University Corporation for Atmospheric Research Projects Office *e:* **UPO**

University Corporation for Atmospheric Research Scientist's Technical Areas of Research *e:* **USTAR**

University Corporation for Atmospheric Research Software *e:* **UCARSOFT**

University Corporation for Atmospheric Research Trade Secrets *e:* **UCARTS**

University Health Service[s] *e:* **UHS**

University Health Services Support Organizations *e:* **UHSSO**

University Journal. Natural Sciences Series. Busan National University e: **Univ J Nat Sci Ser**

University Map Collection, Department of Geography, Sir George Williams Campus, Concordia University, Montreal, Quebec e: **QMGGM**

University Marine Biological Station, Millport e: **UMBSM**

University Medical Center e: **UMC**

University Medical School Librarians Group e: **UMSLG**

University-National Oceanographic Laboratory System e: **UNOLS**

University National Oceanographic (or Oceanography) Laboratory System e: **UNOLS**

University of Aberdeen e: **U of A**

University of Aberdeen Library e: **UAI**, e: **UAL**

University of Alaska Geophysical Institute e: **UAGI**

University of Alaska. IWR [Institute of Water Resources] Series e: **Univ Alaska IWR [Inst Water Resour] Ser**

University of Allahabad. Studies. Biology Section e: **Univ Allahabad Stud Biol Sect**

University of Arizona College of Medicine [Tucson] e: **UARZ/COM**

University of Arkansas School of Medicine e: **UASM**

University of Baghdad. Natural History Research Center. Annual Report e: **Univ Baghdad Nat Hist Res Cent Annu Rep**

University of Baghdad. Natural History Research Center. Publication e: **Univ Baghdad Nat Hist Res Cent Publ**

University of Baltimore Journal of Environmental Law e: **U. Balt. J. Envtl. L.**

University of Basutoland, Bechuana[land Protectorate], and Swaziland e: **UBBS**

University of British Columbia Institute of Oceanography e: **UBCIO**

University of British Columbia. Programme in Natural Resource Economics. Resources Paper e: **UBCNREP**

University of California at Los Angeles Journal of Environmental Law and Policy e: **UCLA J. Envtl. L. & Pol'y**, e: **UCLA J. Envtl. L.&Pol'y**

University of California (Berkeley). Publications in Public Health e: **Univ Calif (Berkeley) Publ Health**

University of California Center for Animal Alternatives e: **UCCAA**

University of California (Los Angeles). Symposia on Molecular and Cellular Biology e: **Univ Calif (Los Angeles) Symp Mol Cell Biol**

University of California Medical Center e: **UCMC**

University of California Medical School e: **UCSF**

University of California. Publications in Geological Sciences e: **Univ Calif Publ Geol Sci**

University of California. Publications in Public Health e: **Univ Calif Publ Health**

University of California. Sea Water Conversion Laboratory. Report e: **Univ Calif Sea Water Convers Lab Rep**

University of California Space Sciences Laboratoly e: **UCSSL**

University of California. University at Los Angeles. Publications in Biological Sciences e: **Univ Calif Univ Los Angeles Publ Biol Sci**

University of California. Water Resources Center. Contribution e: **Univ Calif Water Resour Cent Contrib**

University of Cambridge. Department of Applied Biology. Memoirs. Review Series e: **Univ Camb Dep Appl Biol Mem Rev Ser**

University of Cambridge. Institute of Animal Pathology. Report of the Director e: **Univ Cambridge Inst Anim Pathol Rep Dir**

University of Chicago/Illinois State Water Survey Radar e: **CHILL**

University of Cincinnati, Biology Library, Cincinnati e: **OCU-B**

University of Cincinnati, Geology-Geography Library, Cincinnati e: **OCU-Geo**

University of Cincinnati, Medical Center, Cincinnati e: **MXC**

University of Cincinnati, School of Medicine, Cincinnati e: **OCU-M**

University of Colorado Health Science Center e: **UCHSC**

University of Colorado Medical Center e: **UCMC**

University of Colorado. Studies. Series D. Physical and Biological Sciences e: **Univ Colo Stud Ser D**

University of Colorado. Studies. Series in Biology e: **Univ Colo Stud Ser Biol**

University of Colorado. Studies. Series in Earth Sciences e: **Univ Colo Stud Ser Earth Sci**

University of Connecticut Health Center e: **UCHC**

University of Connecticut, Health Center Library, Processing Center, Farmington e: **UCP**

University of Connecticut. Occasional Papers. Biological Science Series e: **Univ Conn Occas Pap Biol Sci Ser**

University of Connecticut, Waterbury Branch, Waterbury e: **UBW**

University of Denver Water Law Review e: **U. Denv. Water L. Rev.**

University of Edinburgh. Pfizer Medical Monographs e: **Univ Edinb Pfizer Med Monogr**

University of Florida. Coastal and Oceanographic Engineering Laboratory. Report e: **Univ Fla Coastal Oceanogr Eng Lab Rep**

University of Florida. Publications. Biological Science Series e: **Univ Fla Publ Biol Sci Ser**

University of Florida Water Resources Research Center e: **FWRRC**

University of Florida. Water Resources Research Center. Publication e: **Univ Fla Water Resour Res Cent Publ**

University of Georgia e: **UG**, e: **U of G**

University of Georgia, Athens e: **UGA**

University of Georgia, Experiment Station, Griffin e: **GGriEx**

University of Georgia Libraries e: **U of G Lib**

University of Georgia. Marine Science Center. Technical Report Series e: **Univ GA Mar Sci Cent Tech Rep Ser**

University of Georgia. Monographs e: **UGM**

University of Georgia Press e: **U of G Pr**

University of Georgia, School of Pharmacy e: **GU-P**

University of Hawaii. Hawaii Institute of Geophysics. Biennial Report e: **Univ Hawaii Hawaii Inst Geophys Bienn Rep**

University of Hawaii. Hawaii Institute of Geophysics. Report HIG e: **Univ Hawaii Hawaii Inst Geophys Rep HIG**

University of Hawaii, Leahi Hospital, Hastings H.Walker Medical Library e: **HU-M**

University of Health Sciences-Chicago Medical School e: **UHS-CMS**

University of Illinois at the Medical Center e: **IU-M**

University of Illinois at Urbana-Champaign. Water Resources Center. Research Report e: **Univ III Urbana-Champaign Water Resour Cent Res Rep**

University of Illinois at Urbana-Champaign. Water Resources Center. Special Report e: **Univ Ill Urbana-Champaign Water Resour Cent Spec Rep**

University of Illinois at Urbana/Water Resources Center e: **UILU/WRC**

University of Illinois, Biology Library e: **IU-B**

University of Illinois College of Medicine e: **UICM**

University of Illinois, Illinois Natural History Survey e: **IU-NH**

University of Illinois, Illinois State Geological Survey, Urbana e: **IU-GS**

University of Illinois, Illinois State Water Survey e: **IU-WS**

University of Illinois, Museum of Natural History e: **UIMNH**

University of Illinois, School of Basic Medical Sciences, Library of Public Health Sciences e: **IU-H**

University of Illinois, Urbana/Water Resources Center e: **UILA/WRC**

University of Illinois, Veterinary Medicine Library e: **IU-V**

University of Jyvaskyla. Studies in Sport, Physical Education, and Health e: **Univ Jyvaskyla Stud Sport Phys Educ Health**

University of Kansas Medical Center e: **UKMC**

University of Kansas Medical Library e: **Kkp**

University of Kansas. Museum of Natural History. Missellaneous Publication e: **Univ Kans Mus Nat Hist Misc Publ**

University of Kansas. Museum of Natural History. Monograph e: **Univ Kans Mus Nat Hist Monogr**

University of Kansas. Publications. Museum of Natural History e: **Univ Kans Publ Mus Nat Hist**

University of Kansas School of Medicine e: **UKSM**

University of Kansas, School of Medicine, Kansas City e: **KU-M**

University of Kentucky Medical Center e: **UKMC**

University of Kentucky, Medical Center, Lexington e: **KUM**, e: **KyU-M**

University of Leeds. Medical Journal e: **Univ Leeds Med J**

University of London Animal Welfare Society e: **ULAWS**

University of Iowa. Monographs. Studies in Medicine e: **Univ Iowa Monogr Studies in Med**

University of Iowa. Studies in Natural History e: **Univ Iowa Stud Nat Hist**

University of Maine Medical School e: **UMMS**

University of Manchester Medical School e: **UMMS**

University of Manitoba. Medical Journal e: **UMMJ**

University of Manitoba Medical Library e: **UMM**

University of Manitoba Medical School e: **UMMS**

University of Maryland Center for Environmental and Estuarine Studies e: **UMCEES**

University of Maryland Medical School e: **UMMS**

University of Maryland. Natural Resources Institute. Contribution e: **Univ MD Nat Resour Inst Contrib**

University of Maryland. Sea Grant Program. Technical Report e: **TRMPDU**, e: **Univ MD Sea Grant Program Tech Rep**

University of Maryland. Water Resources Research Center. Technical Report e: **Univ MD Water Resour Res Cent Tech Rep**

University of Maryland. Water Resources Research Center. WRRC Special Report e: **Univ MD Water Resour Res Cent WRRC Spec Rep**

University of Massachusetts at Lowell [Center for Atmospheric Research] e: **UML**

University of Massachusetts. Department of Geology. Contribution e: **Univ Mass Dep Geol Contrib**

University of Massachusetts, Medical Center, Worcester e: **MWMU**

University of Massachusetts Medical School e: **UMMS**

University of Medicine and Dentistry of New Jersey e: **UMD**

University of Medicine and Dentristry of New Jersey e: **UMDNJ**

University of Miami. Rosenstiel School of Marine and Atmospheric Science. Annual Report e: **Univ Miami Rosenstiel Sch Mar Atmos Sci Annu Rep**

University of Miami. Rosenstiel School of Marine and Atmospheric Science. Research Review e: **Univ Miami Rosenstiel Sch Mar Atmos Sci Res Rev**

University of Miami. Sea Grant Program. Sea Grant Field Guide Series e: **Univ Miami Sea Grant Program Sea Grant Field Guide Ser**

University of Miami. Sea Grant Program. Sea Grant Technical Bulletin e: **Univ Miami Sea Grant Program Sea Grant Tech Bull**

University of Michigan Biological Station e: **UMBS**

University of Michigan Health Services e: **UMHS**

University of Michigan Instructional Environment e: **UMIE**

University of Michigan. Medical Bulletin e: **Univ Mich Med Bull**

University of Michigan, Medical Center, Ann Arbor e: **MiU-M**

University of Michigan. Medical Center. Journal e: **UMCJA**, e: **Univ Mich Med Cent J**

University of Michigan Medical School e: **UMMS**

University of Michigan Medical School, Ann Arbor e: **UMMS**

University of Michigan-School of Public Health e: **UMSPH**

University of Minnesota. Continuing Medical Education e: **Univ Minn Contin Med Educ**

University of Minnesota. Graduate School. Water Resources Research Center. Bulletin e: **Minnesota Univ Water Resources Research Center Bull**

University of Minnesota. Medical Bulletin e: **Univ Minn Med Bull**

University of Minnesota Medical School e: **UMMS**

University of Mississippi Medical School e: **UMMS**

University of Missouri at Kansas City, Medical Library, Kansas City e: **MoKU-M**

University of Missouri Medical School e: **UMMS**

University of Montana Medical School e: **UMMS**

University of Nebraska Medical Center e: **UNMC**

University of Nebraska, Medical Center, Omaha e: **UNM**

University of Nevada. Mackay School of Mines. Geological and Mining Series. Bulletin e: **Univ Nev Mackay Sch Mines Geol Min Ser Bull**

University of New Mexico. Bulletin. Biological Series e: **Univ NM Bull Biol Ser**

University of New Mexico. Bulletin. Geological Series e: **Univ NM Bull Geol Ser**

University of New Mexico. Institute of Meteoritics. Special Publication e: **Univ NM Inst Meteorit Spec Publ**

University of New Mexico, Library of the Medical Sciences, School of Medicine and Bernalillo County Medical Society, Albuquerque e: **NmU-M**

University of New Mexico. Publications in Biology e: **Univ NM Publ Biol**

University of New Mexico. Publications in Geology e: **Univ NM Publ Geol**

University of New Mexico. Publications in Meteoritics e: **Univ NM Publ Meteorit**

University of New South Wales. Water Research Laboratory. Report e: **NSW Univ Wat Res Lab Rep**

University of Newcastle Upon Tyne.Medical Gazette e: **Univ Newcastle Tyne Med Gaz**

University of North Dakota, Medical Library, Grand Forks e: **UNF**

University of North Dakota School of Medicine e: **UNDSM**

University of Oklahoma, Health Science Center Library, Oklahoma City e: **OKH**

University of Oklahoma Medical Center e: **UOMC**

University of Oregon, Health Scienes Library, Portland e: **OHS**

University of Pennsylvania. Medical Bulletin e: **Univ PA Med Bull**

University of Pennsylvania School of Medicine e: **UPSM**

University of Pittsburgh, Graduate School of Public Health, Pittsburgh, PA e: **PPiU-PH**

University of Pittsburgh, Maurice and Laura Falk Library of the Health Professions, Pittsburgh, PA e: **PPiU-H**

University of Pittsburgh, Natural Sciences Library, Pittsburgh, PA e: **PPiU-NS**

University of Pretoria. Publications. Series 2. Natural Sciences e: **Univ Pretoria Publ Ser 2**

University of Puerto Rico, Natural Science Library, Rio Piedras, PR e: **PrU-NS**

University of Puerto Rico, School of Medicine, San Juan, PR e: **PrU-M**

University of Queensland, Department of Microbiology, St. Lucia e: **UQM**

University of Queensland. Geology Department. Papers e: **Qd Univ Geol Dep Pap**

University of Queensland. Papers. Department of Geology e: **Univ Queensl Pap Dep Geol**

University of Rhode Island-Graduate School of Oceanography e: **URI-GSO**

University of Rhodesia. Faculty of Medicine Research Lecture Series e: **Univ Rhod Fac Med Res Lect Ser**

University of Rochester Medical Center e: **URMC**

University of Rochester, School of Medicine and Dentistry, Rochester e: **NRU-M**

University of South Carolina, School of Medicine, Columbia e: **SUM**

University of Southern California, Department of Aerospace Engineering e: **USCAE**

University of Southern California Institute for Marine and Coastal Studies. Sea Grant Technical Report Series e: **SGTADY**

University of Sydney. Medical Journal e: **Univ Sydney Med J**

University of Sydney. Postgraduate Committee in Medicine. Annual Postgraduate Oration e: **Syd Univ Post Grad Comm Med Oration**

University of Sydney. Postgraduate Committee in Medicine. Bulletin e: **Syd Univ Post Grad Comm Med Bul**

University of Sydney. Postgraduate Committee in Medicine Bulletin e: **Univ Syd Post Grad Ctee Med Bull**

University of Sydney Students' Geological Society e: **SUGS**, e: **SUSGA**

University of Tasmania. Environmental Studies. Occasional Paper e: **Univ Tasmania Environ Stud Occas Pap**

University of Tasmania. Environmental Studies Occasional Paper e: **UTEPDF**

University of Tasmania. Environmental Studies Working Paper e: **UESPDE**, e: **Univ Tasmania Environ Stud Work Pap**

University of Tennessee Center for the Health Science Library, Stollerman Library, Memphis e: **TU-MS**

University of Tennessee Center for the Health Sciences/Knoxville, Preston Medical Library, Knoxville e: **TU-H**

University of Tennessee, Center for the Health Sciences, Memphis e: **TUM**

University of Tennessee, Center for the Health Sciences/Memphis Department of Family Medicine, Memphis e: **TU-FM**

University of Tennessee Medical Center/Knoxville e: **UTMC/K**

University of Tennessee, Medical Unit e: **UTMU**

University of Tennessee Medical Units, Memphis e: **TU-M**

University of Tennessee Oak Ridge Graduate School of Biomedical Sciences e: **UT-ORGSBMS**

University of Tennessee Space Institute e: **UTSI**

University of Tennessee, Space Institute Library, Tullahoma e: **TU-SI**

University of Texas at Austin. Bureau of Economic Geology. Geologic Quadrangle Map e: **Texas Univ Austin Bur Econ Geology Geol Quad Map**

University of Texas at Austin. Bureau of Economic Geology. Mineral Resource Circular e: **Univ Tex Austin Bur Econ Geol Miner Resour Circ**, e: **Univ Tex Austin Bur Econ Geol Miner Resour Circ**

University of Texas at Austin. Bureau of Economic Geology. Report of Investigations e: **Texas Univ Austin Bur Econ Geology Rept Inv**

University of Texas at Austin. Bureau of Economic Geology. Research Note e: **Univ Tex Austin Bur Econ Geol Res Note**

University of Texas at Austin. Bureau of Esonomic Geology. Handbook e: **Univ Tex Austin Bur Econ Geol Handb**

University of Texas at Austin. Center for Research in Water Resources. Technical Report e: **Univ Tex Austin Cent Res Water Resour Tech Rep**

University of Texas at Austin Institute for Geophysics e: **UT-IG**

University of Texas. Bureau of Economic Geology. Publication e: **Univ Tex Bur Econ Geol Publ**

University of Texas. Bureau of Economlc Geology. Report of lnvestigations e: **Univ Tex Bur Econ Geol Rep Invest**

University of Texas-Graduate School of Biomedical Sciences e: **UT-GSBS**

University of Texas, Health Science Center at Dallas, Dallas e: **TxDaS**

University of Texas Health Science Center at San Antonio e: **UTHSCSA**

University of Texas, Health Science Center at San Antonio, San Antonio e: **TSA**

University of Texas-Houston Health Science Center e: **UT-H**

University of Texas-Houston Health Services e: **UTHS**

University of Texas Institute for Geophysics e: **UTIG**

University of Texas Medical Branch [at Galveston] e: **UTMB**

University of Texas, Medical Branch Library, Galveston e: **TMB**

University of Texas Medical School at San Antonio, San Antonio e: **TxU-STM**

University of Texas, Medical School, Galveston e: **TxU-M**

University of Texas Radio Astronomy Observatory e: **UTRAO**

University of Texas School of Public Health e: **UTSPH**

University of Texas, School of Public Health, Houston e: **TxU-PH**

University of Texas Southwestern Medical School e: **UTSMS**

University of Texas-Southwestern School of Medicine e: **UTSSM**

University of the Philippines-Natural Sciences Research Institute Culture Collection e: **UPCC**

University of the Philippines Training Center for Applied Geodesy and Photogrammetry e: **UPTCAGP**

University of the Witwatersrand. Department of Geography and Environmental Studies. Occasional Paper e: **Univ Witwatersrand Dep Geogr Environ Stud Occas Pap**

University of the Witwatersrand [Johannesburg] e: **UW**

University of Tokyo, Institute of Medical Science e: **UTIMS**

University of Toronto. Biological Series e: **Univ Toronto Biol Ser**

University of Toronto, Institute for Aerospace Studies e: **UtlAS**

University of Toronto. Institute for Environmental Studies. Publication e: **Univ Toronto Inst Environ Stud Publ**

University of Toronto, Institute for/of Aerospace Studies e: **UTIAS**

University of Toronto. Institute of Environmental Sciences and Engineering. Publication e: **Univ Toronto Inst Environ Sci Eng Publ**

University of Toronto. Medical Journal e: **Univ Toronto Med J**

University of Toronto. Studies. Biological Series e: **Univ Toronto Stud Biol Ser**

University of Toronto. Studies. Geological Series e: **Univ Toronto Stud Geol Ser**

University of Utah. Biological Series e: **Univ Utah Biol Ser**

University of Utah College of Medicine e: **UUCM**

University of Utah, Eccles Health Science Library, Salt Lake City e: **UUE**

University of Utah, Library of Medical Sciences, Salt Lake City e: **UU-M**

University of Vermont College of Medicine e: **UVCM**

University of Vermont, College of Medicine, Burlington e: **VtU-Med**

University of Virginia, C. Moore Health Sciences Library, Charlottesville e: **VAM**

University of Virginia Medical Center, Health Sciences Library, Charlottesville e: **ViU-H**

University of Virginia School of Medicine e: **UVSM**

University of Washington. Publications in Biology e: **Univ Wash Publ Biol**

University of Washington. Publications in Geology e: **Univ Wash Publ Geol**

University of Washington. Publications in Oceanography e: **Univ Wash Publ Oceanogr**

University of Washington School of Medicine e: **UWSM**

University of Waterloo e: **U of W**, e: **UOW**, e: **UW**

University of Waterloo. Biology Series e: **Univ Waterloo Biol Ser**

University of Waterloo Cobol e: **WATBOL**

University of Waterloo. Faculty of Environmental Studies. Occasional Paper e: **Univ Waterloo Fac Environ Stud Occas Pap**

University of Waterloo Flood Forecasting System e: **WATFLOOD**

University of Waterloo FORTRAN [Formula Translation] Compiler e: **WATFOR Compiler**

University of Waterloo FORTRAN [Formula Translation] IV e: **WATFIV**

University of Waterloo Interactive Direct Job Enry Terminal System e: **WIDJET System**

University of Waterloo Press e: **UWP**

University of Waterloo, Waterloo, Ontario e: **WAT**

University of Western Ontario. Medical Journal e: **Univ West Ont Med J**, e: **UWOMA6**, e: **UWO Medical Journal**

University of Western Ontario Medical Journal e: **UWO Med J**

University of Wisconsin-Madison, Health Sciences e: **GZH**

University of Wisconsin Medical Centre, Madison e: **UWMC**

University of Wisconsin. Sea Grant College. Technical Report e: **Univ Wis Sea Grant Coll Tech Rep**

University of Wisconsin. Sea Grant Program. Technical Report e: **Univ Wis Sea Grant Program Tech Rep**

University of Wisconsin. Water Resources Center. Eutrophication Information Program. Literature Review e: **Univ Wis Water Resour Cent Eutrophication Inf Prog Lit Rev**

University of Witwatersrand e: **U of W**

University of Witwatersrand Library e: **UWL**

University ofTexas, Health Science Center at Houston, School Public Health, Houston e: **TPH**

University Residence Environment Scale e: **URES**

University Space Experiments e: **USE**

Université d'Abidjan. Departement de Geologie. Serie Documentation f: **Univ Abidjan Dep Geol Ser Doc**

Université Océanique de Qingdao f: **OUQ**

Uniwersytet Imienia Adama Mickiewicza w Poznaniu. Seria Biologia P: **Uniw Adama Mickiewicza Poznaniu Ser Biol**

Uniwersytet imienia Adama Mickiewicza w Poznaniu. Wydzial Biologii i Nauk o Ziemi. Prace. Seria Geologia P: **UPWBA**

Unión Geográfica Internacional s: **UGI**, s: **UGI**

Unión Internacional de Ciencias Biológicas s: **UICB**

Unión Internacional de Ciencias Geológicas s: **UICG**

Unión Internacional de Geodesia y Geofísica s: **UIGG**

Unión Internacional de Geodesia y Geofísica s: **IUGG**

Unión Internacional de la Prensa Médica s: **UIPM**

Unión Internacional de las Sociedades de Microbiología s: **IUMS**

Unión Medica de Mexico s: **Unico Med Mexico**

Unión Mundial para la Naturaleza s: **UICN**

Unión Médica Leonesa s: **UML**

Unknown-Input Observability Subspace e: **UIOS**

Unknown or Variable Composition, Complex Reaction Products, and Biological Materials e: **UVCB**

unlimitiert d: **unl.**

Unmanaged Air Space e: **UMAS**

Unmanned Aerospace Surveillance e: **UAS**

unmanned aerospace vehicle e: **UAV**

Unmanned Geophysical Observatory e: **UGO**

Unmanned Launch Space Vehicle e: **UISV**

Unmanned Launch Space Vehicles e: **ULSV**

Unmanned Lunar Orbiter e: **ULO**

Unmanned Machinery Space e: **UMS**

Unmanned Machinery Space Operation e: **UMS Operation**

Unmanned Orbital e: **UMO**

Unmanned Orbital Laboratory e: **UMOL**

Unmanned Orbital Multifunction Satellite e: **UOMS**

Unmanned Orbital Satellite e: **UOS**

Unmanned Seismic Observatory e: **USO**

Unmanned Seismological Observatory e: **USO**

Unmanned Teleoperator Spacecraft e: **UTS**

Unmanned Underwater Vehicle e: **UUV**

Unmanned Weather Station e: **UWS**

Unnatural Parity Exchange e: **UPE**

Unprotect e: **UNPROT**

Unprotected e: **U.**

Unreasonable Risk to Health e: **URTH**

Unsaturated Hydroxyl-Terminated Polybutadiene e: **UHTPB**

unsortiert d: **unsort.**

unten zitiert d: **u.z.**

unter Naturschutz d: **u. N.**

Unterdecktonne[n] d: **UDT**

untere Wasserstraße d: **UW**

Unternehmensbereich Orbitalsysteme d: **UO**

Unterplattierungsriß d: **UPR**

Unterrichtsblätter für Mathematik und Naturwissenschaften d: **UBlMN**

unterster Wasserstand d: **UW**

Unterwasser- d: **U**

Unterwasser d: **UW**

Unterwasser/Boden d: **U/B**

Unterwasser/Boden-Flugkörper d: **U/B-FK**

Unterwasser-Kamera-Anlage d: **UKA**

Unterwasser/Luft d: **U/L**

Unterwasser/Luft-Flugkörper d: **U/L-FK**

Unterwasser-Motorpumpe d: **UWM-Pumpe**

Unterwasser-Nahkampfmittelabwehr d: **UNA**

Unterwasser/Unterwasser d: **U/U**

Unterwasser/Unterwasser-Flugkörper d: **U/U-F**

Unterwasserabwehr-Schiff d: **UAW-Schiff**

Unterwasseraustiegstrainer d: **UWaT**

Unterwasserduckstrahlmassage d: **UWM**

Unterwasserfahrtausrüstung d: **UF**

Unterwasserfahrzeug d: **UWF**

Unterwasserfernsehen d: **UFS**

Unterwasserhaftladung d: **UWHL**

Unterwasserjagd d: **UJagd**

Unterwasserkräfte d: **UWK**

Unterwasserlaboratorium Helgoland d: **UWLH**

Unterwasserlaboratoriurn d: **UWL**

Unterwassermassage d: **UWM**, d: **UW Massage**

Unterwassermine d: **UWMi**

Unterwassermotorpumpe d: **U-Pumpe**, d: **UWM**

Unterwasserortungsbombe d: **UWOrtBo**

Unterwasserspiegel d: **UW**, d: **UWSp**

Unterwasserstand d: **UW**, d: **UWSt**

Unterwasserstreitkraefte d: **UW**

Unterwassertelefonie d: **UT**

Unterwassertelegrafie d: **UT**

Unterwassertelegrafie-Signal d: **UT-Signal**

Unterwasserwaffe d: **UWa**

Unterwasserwaffenelektronik d: **UWaRlo**

Unterwasserzielbombe d: **UWZBo**

Unterwasserzielrakete d: **UWZRAK**

Untied States Geological Survey e: **USGS**

Unwatermarked e: **UnwmK**, e: **UNWMKD**

Upconing of a Salt-Water/Fresh-Water Interface Below a Pumping Well e: **UPCONE**

Update Protect Checking e: **UPC**

Upper Air Observation e: **UAOB**

Upper Airspace e: **UAS**

Upper Airspace Center e: **UAC**

Upper Airspace Control e: **UAC**

Upper Airspace Control Centre e: **UCC**

Upper Atmosphere e: **UA**

Upper Atmosphere and Space Research Laboratory-University Tohoku e: **UASRL-UT**

Upper Atmosphere Composition e: **UAC**

Upper Atmosphere Geophysics e: **UAG**

Upper Atmosphere Mass Spectrometer e: **UAMS**

upper atmosphere observatory e: **UAO**

Upper Atmosphere Phenomena e: **UAP**

upper atmosphere research e: **uar**

Upper Atmosphere Research Corporation e: **UARC**

Upper Atmosphere Research Program e: **UARP**

Upper Atmosphere Research Satellite e: **UARS**, e: **UNARS**

upper atmosphere vehicle e: **UAV**

Upper Atmosphere Winds e: **UAW**

Upper Atmospheric Facilities Program e: **UAF**

Upper Atmospheric Sounder e: **UAS**

Upper Control Center e: **UCC**

Upper Mississippi River Environmental Management Program e: **UMREMP**

Upper Mississippi River Wildlife and Fish Refuge e: **UMRWFR**

Upper Ocean Panel e: **UOP**

Upper Ocean Thermal e: **UOT**

Upper Souris National Wildlife Refuge e: **USNWR**

Upper Tier Tactical Missile Defense System e: **UTTMDS**

Uppsala University. Geological Institution. Bulletin e: **Upps[ala] Univ G[eol] Inst B[ull]**

Upsala Journal of Medical Sciences e: **Upsala J Med Sci**, e: **Ups J Med Sci**

Upsala Journal of Medical Sciences. Supplement e: **Upsala J Med Sci Suppl**, e: **Ups J Med Sci Suppl**

Upstate Medical Center e: **UMC**

Upstate Medical Center, Syracuse e: **VYQ**

Upstate New York and Ontario Chapter of the Medical Library Association e: **UNYOC**

Upstroke Space e: **Up Sp**, e: **U Sp**

uranium-cased atomic or hydrogen bomb e: **U-bomb**

Urban and Environment Credit Program e: **UE**

Urban and Industrial Health e: **UIH**

Urban Comprehensive Health Care Information System e: **UCHCIS**

Urban Ecology e: **Urban Ecol**, e: **URECD**

Urban Ecology [Netherlands] e: **URBE**

Urban Environment Conference e: **UEC**

Urban Geography e: **UG**

Urban Health e: **URBH**

Urban Hydrology Monitoring System e: **UHMS**

Urban Planning and Environmental Monitoring via GIS in Eastern Europe e: **URBAN-CP96-252**

Urban Waste Water Treatment Directive e: **UWWTD**

Urban Wastewater Toxics Flow Model e: **TOXFLO**

Urban Water Research Association e: **UWRA**

Urban Water Research Association of Australia e: **UWRAA**

Urban Wildlife Research Center e: **UWRC**

Urban Wildlife Society e: **UWS**

Urinal Water Closet e: **URWC**

Urinary Lactic-acid Dehydrogenase e: **ULDH**

Urogynaecologia International Journal e: **UIJ**

Uruguayan National Committee of the International Association on Water Pollution Research and Control e: **UNCIAWPRC**, e: **UNCIAWPRC**

US Army. Natick Laboratories. Technical Report. Microbiology Series e: **US Army Natick Lab Tech Rep Microbiol Ser**

US/Canada Hydrographic Commission e: **US/CHC**

US Department of Health, Education, and Welfare Publications e: **US Dept HEW Publ**

US Environmental Protection Agency. Office of Air and Waste Management. EPA-450 e: **UEPEDY**

US Environmental Protection Agency. Office of Radiation Programs. EPA e: **US Environ Prot Agency Off Radiat Programs EPA**

US Environmental Protection Agency. Office of Radiation Programs. EPA-ORP *e:* **US Environ Prot Agency Off Radiat Programs EPA-ORP**

US Environmental Protection Agency. Publication. AP Series *e:* **US Environ Prot Agency Publ AP Ser**

U.S. Navy's regional weather model *e:* **COAMPS**

usable supply of drinking water *e:* **USDW**

USAF [United States Air Force] Space Tracking System *e:* **SPACETRACK**

User Environment Component *e:* **UEC**

User Interface Design Environment *e:* **UIDE**

User Level Remote Procedure Call *e:* **URPC**

user support environment *e:* **UPS**

User Terminal and Display Subsystem [Space Flight Operations Facility] *e:* **UTD**

USGS Water Resources Division, New York DIstrict, Albany *e:* **UDY**

USMC [United States Marine Corps] All-weather attack squadron *e:* **VMA-[AW]**

USMC [United States Marine Corps] Observation squadron *e:* **VMO**

Uspechi Biologiceskoj Chimii *R:* **Usp Biol Chim**

Uspechi Sovremennoj Biologii *R:* **USB**

Uspekhi Biologicheskoi Khimii *R:* **UBKHA**

Uspekhi Biologicheskoi Khimii [USSR] *R:* **Usp Biol Khim**

Uspekhi Mikrobiologii *R:* **Usp Mikrobiol**

Uspekhi Mikrobioloii *R:* **USMKA**

Uspekhi na Molekulyarnata Biologiya *R:* **Usp Mol Biol**

Uspekhi Sovremennoi Biologii *R:* **USBIA,** *R:* **Usp Sovrem Biol**

USSR. Academy of Science. Proceedings. Geographical Series *e:* **UAG**

USSR Report. Earth Sciences [Arlington] *e:* **USSR Rep Earth Sci**

USSR Research Center for Earth Resources Exploration *e:* **URCERE**

Ústav Fyziologie a Biologie Rostlin *c:* **ÚFBR**

Ústav Stavební Geologie *c:* **ÚSG**

Ústřední Biologický Ústav *c:* **ÚBÚ**

Ústřední SprÁva Geodezie a Kartografie *c:* **ÚSGaK**

Ústřední Ústav Geologický *c:* **ÚÚG**

Ústřední Ústav Polarografický *c:* **ÚÚP**

Usual Health-Care *e:* **UC**

Utah Department of Health *e:* **UDH,** *e:* **UDOH**

Utah Department of Natural Resources *e:* **UDNR,** *e:* **Utah Dep Nat Resour**

Utah. Department of Natural Resources. Division of Water Rights. Technical Publication *e:* **Utah Dept Nat Resources Tech Pub**

Utah. Department of Natural Resources. Technical Publication *e:* **Utah Dep Nat Resour Tech Publ**

Utah. Department of Natural Resources. Water Circular *e:* **Utah Dep Nat Resour Water Cir**

Utah Division of Water Resources *e:* **UDWR**

Utah. Division of Water Resources. Cooperative Investigations Report *e:* **Utah Div Water Resources Coop Inv Rept**

Utah Geological and Mineral Survey *e:* **UGMS**

Utah. Geological and Mineralogical Survey. Bulletin *e:* **Utah Geol and Mineralog Survey Bull,** *e:* **Utah Geol Mineral Surv Bull**

Utah. Geological and Mineralogical Survey. Circular *e:* **Utah Geol and Mineralog Survey Circ,** *e:* **Utah Geol Mineral Surv Circ,** *e:* **Utah Geol Miner Surv Circ**

Utah. Geological and Mineralogical Survey. Quarterly Review *e:* **Utah Geol and Mineralog Survey Quart Rev,** *e:* **Utah Geol Miner Surv Q Rev**

Utah. Geological and Mineralogical Survey. Special Studies *e:* **Utah Geol and Mineralog Survey Spec Studies,** *e:* **Utah Geol Mineral Surv Spec Stud**

Utah. Geological and Mineralogical Survey. Survey Notes *e:* **Utah Geol Miner Surv Surv Notes**

Utah. Geological and Mineralogical Survey. Water Resources Bulletin *e:* **Utah Geol and Mineralog Survey Water Resources Bull,** *e:* **Utah Geol Mineral Surv Water Resour Bull**

Utah Geological Association *e:* **Utah Geol Assoc**

Utah Geological Association. Publication *e:* **Utah Geol Assoc Publ**

Utah Geological Society *e:* **Utah Geol Soc**

Utah Geological Society. Guidebook to the Geology of Utah *e:* **Utah Geol Soc Guidebook to Geology of Utah**

Utah Geology *e:* **Utah Geol**

Utah Medical Bulletin *e:* **Utah Med Bull**

Utah Medical Products, Inc. *e:* **UTMD**

Utah Public Health Association *e:* **UPHA**

Utah State Medical Association *e:* **USMA**

Utah State Medical Journal *e:* **Utah State Med J**

Utah Water Research Laboratory *e:* **UWRL**

Utilitiers Conservation Action Now [Federal Energy Administration] *e:* **UCAN**

Utilitiesman, Water and Sanitation *e:* **UTW**

Utility Library [National Center for Atmospheric Research] *e:* **ULIB**

Utility Water *e:* **UW**

Utilization and Medical Care Assessment Program *e:* **U & MCAP**

Utstredni Sprava Geodezie a Kartografie *c:* **USGK**

Uttar Pradesh. Directorate of Geology and Mining. Monograph *e:* **Uttar Pradesh Dir Geol Min Monogr**

UWD Informationsdienst für Umweltfragen *d:* **UWD**

UWO [University of Western Ontario] Medical Journal *e:* **UWO [Unir West Ont] Med J**

Uzbekskii Biologicheskii Zhurnal *R:* **Uzb Biol Zh,** *R:* **UZBZA**

Uzbekskii Geologicheskii Zhurnal *R:* **Uzbek Geol Zh,** *R:* **UZGZA**

V

Vaccinia Virus: Wild Type *e:* **VV:WT**

Vacuum Hydrogen Furnace *e:* **VHF**

Vacuum Operation of Spacecraft Equipment *e:* **VOSE**

Vakblad voor Biologen *n:* **Vakbl Biol**

Valdosta State College [Georgia] *e:* **VSC**

Valence Atomic Orbital *e:* **VAO**

Valence Orbital Ionization Potential *e:* **VOIP**

Valentine National Wildlife Refuge *e:* **VNWR**

Valero Natural Gas Partners LP *e:* **VLP**

Validating OSA in Industrial CIM Environments *e:* **VOICE**

Validating OSA in Industrial CIM Environments by Integration and Implementation *e:* **VOICE II**

Vallecitos Boiling Water Reactor *e:* **VBWR**

Valley Forge Space Technology Center *e:* **VFSTC**

Valley Health Services Association, Kentville, Nova Scotia *e:* **NSKVH**

valuable-record protector *e:* **vrp**

Value Health Incorporated *e:* **VHI**

Valve Control Amplitier *e:* **VCA**

Valverde *s:* **VDE**

Vancouver Oral Health Index *e:* **VOHI**

Vandenberg Field Office of Aerospace Research *e:* **VFOAR**

Vanderbilt Medical Center, Nashville *e:* **TJM**

Vanderbilt University School of Medicine *e:* **VUSM**

Vanier Reading Room, Place Vanier, Health Protection Branch, Health and Welfare Canada, Ottawa, Ontario *e:* **OONHP**

Vapo[u]r Space Inhibiting *e:* **VSI**

Variabilidad Interdecenal del Clima *s:* **ICV**

Variabilidad y Predictibilidad del Clima *s:* **CLIVAR**

Variability of Coastal Atmospheric Refractivity *e:* **VOCAR**

Variabilité et prévisions climatiques *f:* **CLIVAR**

Variabilité interdécennale du climat *f:* **ICV**

Variable Acuity Remote Viewing System *e:* **VARVS**

Variable Angle Monochromatic Fringe Observation *e:* **VAMFO**

Variable Geometry *e:* **VG**

Variable Geometry Inlet *e:* **VGI**

Variable Geometry Nozzle *e:* **VGN**

Variable Geometry Rotor *e:* **VGR**

Variable Geometry Simulator *e:* **VAGES**

Variable Geometry Structure *e:* **VGS**

Variable geometry supersonic fighter-bomber *e:* **TFX**

Variable Geometry Truss *e:* **VGT**

Variable Geometry Turbocharger *e:* **VGT**

Variable Geometry Wing *e:* **VGW**

Variable Geometry Wing Aircraft *e:* **VGWA**

Variable Hydrologic Source Areas *e:* **VHSA**

Variable Individual Protection *e:* **VIP**

Variable Polarity Plasma Arc *e:* **VPPA**

Vario-Polarization Beacon Aerial *e:* **VPBA**

Vario-Polarization Beacon Antenna *e:* **VPBA**

Vast Integrated Communications Environment *e:* **VICE**

VAX Environment Software Translator *e:* **VEST**

VDSL Transceiver Unit-Remote Terminal *e:* **VTU-R**

VEB Projektierung Wasserwirtschaft *d:* **VEB Prowa**

VEB Wasserversorgung und Abwasserbehandlung *d:* **VEB WAB**

Vector and Image Integration for Remote Sensing and Geographical Information Systems *e:* **VIRGOS-CP94-944**

Vector Biology and Control Office *e:* **VBCO**

Vector Biology Laboratory *e:* **VBL**

Vector Data Butier *e:* **VDB**

Vector Geometry *e:* **VG**

Vegetation Protection Ordinance *e:* **VPO**

Vehicle Ecological System *e:* **VES**

Vehicle for Interplanetary Space Transport Applications *e:* **VISTA**

Vehicle Health Management *e:* **VHM**

Vehicle Ice-Breaking -- Air Cushion *e:* **VIBAC**

Vehicle Magnetic Signature Duplicator *e:* **VEMASD**

Vehicle Parking Protection Services *e:* **VPPS**

Vehicle Protection Factor *e:* **VPF**

Vehicle Radio Remote Control *e:* **VRRC**

Vehicle Space Ground Link Subsystem *e:* **VSGLS**

Vehicle Space Transfer and Recovery *e:* **VSTAR**

Vehicles in Confined Space[s] *e:* **VICS**

Vehicles with Protection Kits *e:* **VPK**

Vehicule d'Observation d'Artillerie *f:* **VOA**

Vehicule Porte Mortier *f:* **VPM**

Vehicule Tracteur de Mortier *f:* **VTM**

Veille de l'atmosphère globale *f:* **VAG**

Veille Météorologique Mondiale *f:* **VMM**

Venecuela. Ministerio de Minas e Hidrocarburos. Direccion de Geologia. Boletin de Geologia *s:* **Venez Min Minas Hidrocarburos Dir Geol Bol Geol**

Venezuela. Direccion de Geologia. Boletin de Geologia *s:* **Venez Dir Geol Bol Geol**

Venezuela. Direccion de Geologia. Boletin de Geologia. Publicacion Especial *s:* **Venez Dir Geol Bol Geol Publ Esp**

Venezuela International Meteorological and Hydrological Experiment[s] [Colorado State University project] *e:* **VIMHEX**

Venezuela. Universidad Central. Escuela de Geología y Minas. Laboratorio de Petrografía y Geoquimica. Informe *s:* **Venez Univ Cent Esc Geol Minas Lab Petrogr Geoquimica Inf**

Venezuelan National Committee of the International Association on Water Pollution Research and Control *e:* **VNCIAWPRC**

Ventech Healthcare Corp., Inc. *e:* **VHC**

Ventricolar Ectopic Depolarization *e:* **VED**

ventricular excitation repolarization phase *e:* **VERP**

Ventricular Premature Depolarization *e:* **VPD**

Venus-Earth-Earth Gravity Assist *e:* **VEEGA**

Venus International Reference Atmosphere *e:* **VIRA**

Venus Orbit Ejection *e:* **VOE**

Venus Orbiter Radiometric Temperature Experiment *e:* **VORTEX**

Venus Orbiting Imaging Radar *e:* **VOIR**

Verband arbeitsmedizinisches Fachpersonal e.V. *d:* **VAF**

Verband Bernischer Schulen im Gesundheitswesen *d:* **VBSG**

Verband der Betriebsbeauftragten für Umweltschutz e.V. *d:* **VBU**

Verband der Deutschen Gas- und Wasserwerke *d:* **VDG**

Verband der Deutschen Gas- und Wasserwerke e.V. *d:* **VGW**

Verband der Deutschen Gemeindetierärzte *d:* **VGT**

Verband der Deutschen Wasserzählerindustrie *d:* **VDDW**

Verband der Diplomingenieure und Naturwissenschaftler in Deutschland *d:* **VDND**

Verband der Hersteller von Großwasserkesseln und anderen Kesselschmiedearbeiten *d:* **GWK**

Verband der Kleingärtner, Siedler und Kleintierzüchter *d:* **VdKSK**, *d:* **VKSK**

Verband der Pelztierzüchter e.V. *d:* **VDP**

Verband der Schweizer Medizinstudenten *d:* **VSM**

Verband Deutscher Biologen *d:* **VDB**

Verband Deutscher Gewässerschutz e.V., Arbeitsgebiet Wasserreinhaltung *d:* **VDG**

Verband Deutscher Kälte-Klima-Fachleute e.V. *d:* **VDKF**

Verband Deutscher Licht- und Wasserfach-Beamten und Angestellten, Dresden *d:* **VDLW**

Verband deutscher Medizinstudenten *d:* **VdM**

Verband Deutscher Meteorologen *d:* **VDM**

Verband Deutscher Meteorologischer Gesellschaften *d:* **VDMG**

Verband Deutscher Naturwein-Versteigerer [der Rheinpfalz] e.V. *d:* **VDNV**

Verband deutscher Schaufensterdekorateure e.V., Stuttgart *d:* **VdS**

Verband Deutscher Tierantfrauen und Tierärztinnen e.V *d:* **VD.l.l.**

Verband Deutscher Tierärztinnen und Tierarztfrauen e.V. *d:* **VDTT**

Verband Deutscher Wasserturbinen-fabriken, Berlin *d:* **VDWT**

Verband für Geoökologie in Deutschland *d:* **VGöD**

Verband für Medizinischer Strahlenschutz in Österreich *d:* **VMSÖ**

Verband für Unabhängige Gesundheitsberatung Deutschland *d:* **UGB**

Verband Landeswasserversorgung *d:* **LWV**

Verband Schweizer Tierarzneimittel-grossisten *d:* **VTG**

Verband Schweizerischer Abwasserfachleute *d:* **VSA**

Verband Schweizerischer Geflügel- und Wild-Importeure *d:* **VSGI**

Verband Schweizerischer Pferdemetzgerein *d:* **VSP**

Verband Schweizerischer Schaufensterdekorateure *d:* **VSD**

Verband Unabhängiger Gesundheitsberater Deutschland e.V., Gießen *d:* **UGB**

Verband zum Schutze der Gewässer in der Nordwestschweiz *d:* **VSGN**

verdecken *d:* **verd.**

verdeckt *d:* **verd.**

verdeckte Gewinnausschüttung *d:* **vGA**

Verdener Maschinen- und Apparatebau GmbH, Verden *d:* **VEMAG**

Verdens Gang *N:* **VG**

Verdens Villmarksfond *N:* **VVF**

verdensrekord *a:* **VR**

Verderben *d:* **Verd.**

Verdet constant *e:* **V**

Verdrag inzake Biologische Diversiteit *n:* **VBD**, *n:* **VDB**

Verdrängungswasserlinie *d:* **D.W.L.**

Vereeniging Leuvense Afgestudeerden in de Psychologie en Paedagogiek *n:* **LAPP**

Verein der Freunde der Naturgeschichte in Mecklenberg Archiv *d:* **Ver Freunde Naturg Mecklenberg Arch**

Verein der Geographen *d:* **VDG**

Verein der Naturfreunde *d:* **V.d.N.-F.**

Verein für Binnenschiffahrt und Wasserstraßen *d:* **VBW**

Verein für Landwirtschaft und Umweltschutz in der Dritten Welt *d:* **VLFU**

Verein für leistungsorientierte Verbraucheraufklärung e.V., Düsseldorf *d:* **VIV**

Verein für Naturforschung und Landespflege e.V. *d:* **Pollichia**

Verein für Umwelt und Arbeitsschutz e.V. *d:* **VUA**

Verein für Vaterländische Naturkunde in Württemberg. Jahreshefte *d:* **Ver Vaterl Naturk Württemberg Jahresh**

Verein Naturschutzpark *d:* **VNP**

Verein Schweizerischer Geographielehrer *d:* **VSGg**

Verein Schweizerischer Geographiestudenten *d:* **VSG**

Verein zur Förderung der Wasser- und Lufthygiene *d:* **VFWL**

Verein zur Verbreitung Naturwissenschaftlicher Kenntnisse in Wien. Schriften *d:* **Ver Verbr Naturwiss Kenntnisse Wien Schr**

Vereinigung der Allergiker und Umweltgeschädigten *d:* **VAU**

Vereinigung der europäischen Hersteller von gasbeheizten Speicherwasserheizern *d:* **ACCUGAZ**

Vereinigung der Fabrikanten im Gas- und Wasserfach *d:* **FAGAWA**

Vereinigung der Freunde der Mineralogie, Paläeontologie und Geologie e.V. *d:* **VFMG**

Vereinigung der Freunde der Mineralogie und Geologie *d:* **VFMG**

Vereinigung der Wasserversorgungsverbände und Gemeinden mit Wasserwerken e.V. *d:* **VEDEWA**

Vereinigung Deutscher Gewässerschutz *d:* **VDG**

Vereinigung Deutscher Gewässerschutz[bund] e.V. *d:* **VDG**

Vereinigung exportierender Elektrizitätsunternehmen *d:* **VEE**

Vereinigung für Allgemeine und Angewandte Mikrobiologie *d:* **VAAM**

Vereinigung für Gewässerschutz und Lufthygiene *d:* **VGL**

Vereinigung für Kristallographie in der Gesellschaft für Geologische Wissenschaften *d:* **VfK**

Vereinigung für Kristallographie in der Gesellschaft für Geologische Wissenschaften der Deutschen Demokratischen Republik d: **VFK/DDR**

Vereinigung medizinischer und betriebswirtschaftlicher Tarifexperten d: **TARMAG**

Vereinigung Österreichischer Kleintiermediziner d: **VÖK**

Vereinigung Schweizerischer Fabriken der Medizinischen Technik d: **FAMED**

Vereinigung schweizerischer Lieferanten von Medical Produkten e: **Asmed**

Vereinigung Schweizerischer Medizinalingenieure d: **VSM**

Vereinigung Schweizerischer Naturwissenschaftslehrer d: **VSN**

Vereinigung Schweizer[ischer] Petroleum-Geologen und -Ingenieure d: **VSP**

Vereinigung Schweizerischer Petroleum-Geologen und Ingenieure. Bulletin d: **Vereinigug Schweizer Petrolium-Gelogen u Ingenieure Bull**, d: **Ver Schweizer Petroleum-Geologen u Ingenieure Bull**, d: **Ver Schweiz Pet-Geol Ing Bull**

Vereinigung Umwelt und Bevölkerung d: **ECOPOP**

Vereinigung Volkseigener Betriebe Elektroprojektierung und Anlagenbau d: **VVB EPA**

Vereinigung Volkseigener Betriebe Geologische Forschung und Erkundung d: **VVB GFE**

Vereinigung Volkseigener Betriebe Tierzucht d: **VVB Tier**

Vereinigung Volkseigener Betriebe Wasserversorgung und Abwasserbehandlung d: **VVB WAB**

Vereinigung Volkseigener Betriebe Zuschlagstoffe und Natursteine d: **VVB ZN**

Vereinigung von Fachhändlern des sanitären Installations-, Gas- und Wasserleitungsbedarfs d: **FSI**

Vereinigung zur Foerderung des Deutschen Brandschutzes. Zeitschrift d: **VFDB Z**

Vereniging Aanemers Grond-Water-en Wegenbouw n: **VAGWW**

Vereniging der grote Verdelingsondernemingen n: **V.G.V.O.**

Vereniging der Publiciteitschefs der Adverteerders van België n: **VPCA**

Vereniging tot Exploitatie eener Proefzuivelboerderij te Hoorn. Verslag n: **Ver Exploit Proefzuivelboerderij Hoorn Versl**

Vereniging van de Europese Fabrikanten van Gasgestookte Warmwatervooradstoestellen n: **ACCUGAZ**

Vereniging van Exploitanten van Waterleidingsbedrijven in Nederland n: **VEWIN**

Vereniging van Gespecialiseerde Schoolleveranciers n: **VGS**

Vereniging van Gespecialiseerde Vloerenbedrijven n: **VGV**

Vereniging van Handel en Industrie op het gbied van Scheepbouw en Watersport n: **HISWA**

Vereniging van Leraren in de Biologie n: **VELEBI**

Vereniging van Officieel gediplomeerde Gidsen n: **VOGEG**

Vereniging van Vis Invoerders n: **VERINVI**

Vereniging van Waterleidingsbelangen in Nederland n: **VWN**

Vereniging van Werkgevers in de Chemische Wasserijen [en Ververijen] n: **VCW**

Vereniging voor Integrale Biologische Architectuur n: **VIBA**

Vereniging voor Medische en Biologische Informatieverwerking n: **VMBI**

vererdet d: **ver.**

verfahrensorientierte Programm[ier]pakete/verfahrensorientierte Programm[ier]s d: **VOPP/VOPS**

verfahrensorientierte Programmiersysteme d: **VOPSe**, d: **VPOSe**

Verfahrensorientierte Programmsprache d: **VOPS**

Verfahrensorientiertes Programmierpaket d: **VOPP**

verfahrensorientiertes Programmiersystem d: **VOPS**

Verfassungsbeschwerde d: **VB**

verfügbare Wasserkapazität d: **VWK**

Verfügungen und Mitteilungen des Ministeriums für Gesundheit d: **VUM**

Verhandelingen. Koninklijke Nederlands Geologisch Mijnbouwkundig Genootschap. Geologische Serie n: **VNGGA**

Verhandelingen. Koninklijke Nederlandse Geologisch Mijnbouwkundig Genootschap n: **Verh K Ned Geol Mijnbouwkd Genoot**

Verhandelingen. Koninklijke Nederlandse Geologisch Mijnbouwkundig Genootschap. Geologische Serie n: **Verh K Ned Geol Mijnbouwkd Genoot Geol Ser**

Verhandelingen. Koninklijke Nederlandse Geologisch Mijnbouwkundig Genootschap. Mijnbouwkundige Serie n: **Verh K Ned Geol Mijnbouwkd Genoot Mijnbouwkd Ser**

Verhandlungen der Geologischen Bundesanstalt in Wien d: **VGBAW**

Verhandlungen der Geologischen Reichsanstalt Wien d: **VGRAW**

Verhandlungen der Gesellschaft Deutscher Naturforscher und Ärzte d: **VDNÄ**

Verhandlungen der Naturforschenden Gesellschaft in Basel d: **Verh. Nat.forsch. Ges. Basel**, d: **VNGB**

Verhandlungen der Schweizerischen naturforschenden Gesellschaft d: **Verh. Schweiz. nat.forsch. Ges.**

Verhandlungen des Internationalen Geographen-Kongresses d: **VIGK**

Verhandlungen des Naturwissenschaftlichen Vereins in Hamburg d: **Verh Naturwiss Ver Hamb**

Verhandlungen. Deutsche Gesellschaft für Experimentelle Medizin d: **Verh Dtsch Ges Exp Med**

Verhandlungen. Deutsche Gesellschaft für Innere Medizin d: **VDGIA**, d: **Verh Dtsch Ges Inn Med**

Verhandlungen. Geologische Bundesanstalt d: **Verhandl Geol Bundesanstalt**, d: **Verh Geol Bundesanst**, d: **VGEBA**

Verhandlungen. Geologische Bundesanstalt Bundesländerserie d: **Verh Geol Bundesanst Bundesländerser**

Verhandlungen. Gesellschaft Deutscher Naturforscher und Ärzte d: **Verhandl Gesellsch Deutsch Naturf u Ärzte**, d: **Verh Ges Dsch Naturfrsch Ärzte**

Verhandlungen. Naturforschender Verein in Brünn d: **Verh Naturforsch Ver Brünn**

Verhandlungen. Naturhistorisch-Medizinischer Verein zu Heidelberg d: **Verh Natur-Med Ver Heidelb**

Verhandlungen. Naturwissenschaftlicher Verein in Hamburg d: **Verhandl Naturw Ver Hamburg**

Verhandlungen. Naturwissenschaftlicher Verein in Karlsruhe d: **Verhandl Naturw Ver Karlsruhe**

Verhandlungen. Physikalisch-Medizinische Gesellschaft in Würzburg d: **Verh Phys-Med Ges Würzburg**

Verhandlungen. Schweizerische Naturforschende Gesellschaft d: **Verhandl Schweiz Naturf Gesellsch**, d: **Verh Schweiz Naturf[orsch] Ges**

Verhandlungen. Schweizerische Naturforschende Gesellschaft. Wissenschaftlicher Teil d: **Verh Schweiz Naturforsch Ges Wiss Teil**

Verificación en tierra s: **GNDCK**

Verification Polarization e: **VP**

Verification Support Environment e: **VSE**

Verkaufsraumfläche d: **VRFL**

Verkehrsmedizin und Ihre Grenzgebiete d: **Verkehrsmed Grenzgeb**, d: **Verkehrsmed Ihre Grenzgeb**

Verkehrsmedizinischer Dienst d: **VMD**

Verkehrsmedizinisches Untersuchungs-, Begutachtungs- und Informationszentrum d: **VMZ**

Verkehrswasserbaubibliothek d: **VtB**

Verkehrswasserwirtschaftliche Daten d: **HYDABA I**

Verlag Georg Westermann, Braunschweig d: **VGW**

Verlag Volk und Gesundheit d: **VuG**

Vermont Center for Geographic Information e: **VCGI**

Vermont Department of Health e: **VDH**

Vermont Geological Survey e: **VGS**

Vermont. Geological Survey. Bulletin e: **V[ermon]t Geol Survey Bull**, e: **VT Geol Surv Bull**

Vermont. Geological Survey. Economic Geology e: **VT Geol Sur Econ Geol**

Vermont. Geological Survey. Water Resources Department. Environmental Geology e: **VT Geol Surv Water Resour Dep Environ Geol**

Vermont Institute of Natural Science e: **VINS**

Vermont Natural Heritage Program e: **VNHP**

Vermont State Geologist. Report e: **VT St G Rp**

Vermont State Medical Society e: **VSMS**

Veröffentlichungen aus den Jahres-Veterinär-Berichten. Beamtete Tierärzte Preußen d: **Veröffentl J-Vet-Ber Beamt Tierärzte Preuß**, d: **Veröffentl J-Vet-Ber Beamt Tierärzte Preuß**

Veröffentlichungen der Landesstelle für Naturschutz und Landschaftspflege in

Baden-Württemberg *d:* **Veröff. Landesstelle Nat.schutz Landsch.pfl. Baden-Württ.**

Veröffentlichungen des Geobotanischen Institutes der Eidg. Technischen Hochschule, Stiftung Rübel in Zürich *d:* **Veröff. Geobot. Inst. Eidgenöss. Tech. Hochsch., Stift. Rübel Zür.**

Veröffentlichungen. Deutsche Geodätische Kommission. Bayerische Akademie der Wissenschaften *d:* **Veröff Dtsch Geod Komm**

Veröffentlichungen. Deutsche Geodätische Kommission. Bayerische Akademie der Wissenschaften. Reihe A *d:* **Veröff Dtsch Geod Komm Reihe A**

Veröffentlichungen für Naturschutz und Landschaftspflege in Baden-Würtemberg *d:* **Veröff Naturschutz Landschaftspflege Baden Württemb**

Veröffentlichungen für Naturschutz und Landschaftspflege in Baden-Württemberg. Beihefte *d:* **Veröff Naturschutz Landschaftspflege Baden-Württemb Beih**

Veröffentlichungen. Geobotanisches Institut. Eidgenössische Technische Hochschule *d:* **Veröff Geobot Inst Eidg Tech Hochsch**

Veröffentlichungen. Geobotanisches Institut. Eidgenössische Technische Hochschule Stiftung Rübel in Zürich *d:* **Veröff Geobot Inst Eidg Tech Hochsch Stift Rübel Zür**

Veröffentlichungen. Geobotanisches Institut Rübel *d:* **Veröff Geobot Inst Rübel**

Veröffentlichungen. Institut für Agrarmeteorologie und des Agrarmeteorologischen Observatoriums.Karl Marx-Universität *d:* **Veröff Inst Agrarmet Univ [Leipzig]**

Veröffentlichungen. Meteorologischer Dienst. Deutsche Demokratische Republik *d:* **Veröff Meteorol Dienstes DDR**

Veröffentlichungen. Meteorologischer und Hydrologischer Dienst. Deutsche Demokratische Republik *d:* **Veröff Meterol Hydrol Dienstes DDR**

Veröffentlichungen Natur-Museum Luzern *e:* **Veröff. Nat.-Mus. Luzern**

Veröffentlichungen. Naturhistorischer Museum [Basel] *d:* **Veröff Naturhist Mus [Basel]**

Veröffentlichungen: Naturhistorischer Museum [Wien] *d:* **Veröff Naturh Mus [Wien]**

Veröffentlichungen. Naturhistorisches Museum *d:* **Veröff Naturh[ist] Mus**

Veröffentlichungen. Reichsgesundheitsamt *d:* **Veröff Reichsgesundheitsamts**

Veröffentlichungen. Schweizerische Gesellschaft für Geschichte der Medizin und der Naturwissenschaft *d:* **Veröffentlich Schweizer Gesellsch Medizin Naturwissensch**

Veröffentlichungen. Zentralinstitut Physik der Erde *d:* **Veröff Zentralinst Phys Erde**

Verordnung über Anforderungen an das Einleiten von Abwasser in Gewässer [Abwasserverordnung] *d:* **AbwV**

Verordnung über Anlagen zum Lagern, Abfüllen und Umschlagen wassergefährdender Stoffe *e:* **VAwS**

Verordnung über das Lagern wassergefährdender Flüssigkeiten *d:* **VLwF**

Verordnung über die freiwillige Beteiligung gewerblicher Unternehmen an einem Gemeinschaftssystem für das Umweltmanagement und die Umweltbetriebsprüfung *d:* **UAVO**

Verordnung über die Genehmigungspflicht für das Einleiten von Abwasser mit gefährlichen Stoffen in öffentliche Abwasseranlagen *d:* **VGS**

Verordnung über energiesparende Anforderungen an den Betrieb von heizungstechnischen Anlagen und Brauchwasseranlagen [Heizungsbetriebs-Verordnung] *d:* **HeizBetrV**

Verordnung über energiesparende Anforderungen an heizungstechnische Anlagen und Brauchwasseranlagen [Heizungsanlagen-Verordnung] *d:* **HeizAnlV**

Verordnung zur Ausführung der Bundestierärzteordnung *d:* **AVBTÄO**

Verordnung zur digitalen Signatur *d:* **SigV**

Versatile Remote Copier *e:* **VRC**

Versuchsanstalt für Wasser- und Erdbau, Eidgenössische Technische Hochschule Zürich *d:* **VAWE**

Versuchsanstalt für Wasserbau, Hydrologie und Glaziologie *d:* **Vers.anst. Wasserbau Hydrol. Glaziol.**

Versuchsanstalt für Wasserbau, Hydrologie und Glaziologie, Eidgenössische Technische Hochschule *d:* **VAW/ETH Zürich**

Versuchsanstalt für Wasserbau, Hydrologie und Glaziologie, Eidgenössische Technische Hochschule Zürich *d:* **VAW/ETHZ, *d:* VAW/ETH [Z][ürich]**

Versuchsanstalt für Wasserbau, Hydrologie und Glaziologie (ETH Zürich) *d:* **VAW**

Versuchsanstalt für Wasserbau und Schiffsbau *d:* **VWS**

Versuchstier *d:* **VT**

Vertical Array Hydrophone *e:* **VAH**

Vertical Axis Hydropower Turbine *e:* **VAHT**

Vertical Earth Rate *e:* **VER**

Vertical Earth Scanning Test *e:* **VEST**

Vertical Launch SEA SPARROW *e:* **VLSS**

Vertical Launch Sea Wolf *e:* **VLSW**

Vertical Observations Involving Convective Exchange Experiment *e:* **VOICE**

Vertical Polarization *e:* **VERT**, *e:* **VP**

Vertical Polarization Mode *e:* **VPM**

Vertical Receiving Array Hydrophone *e:* **VRAH**

Vertical Receiving Hydrophone *e:* **VRH**

Vertical Transmit-Vertical Receive Polarization *e:* **VV**

Vertical Transport and Exchange of material in the upper ocean performed in the California Current *e:* **VERTEX**

vertically polarized *e:* **vp**

Vertically Polarized Dipole *e:* **VPD**

Vertically Polarized Wave *e:* **VPW**

Verwaltungsrat für das UNO - Umweltprogramm *d:* **UNEP**

Verwaltungsrechtliches Rehabilitierungsgesetz *d:* **VwRehaG**

Verwaltungsvorschrift wassergefährdender Stoffe *d:* **VwVwS**

verwildert *d:* **verw.**

Very Deep Water *e:* **VDW**

Very Good Health *e:* **VGH**

Very High Polarization *e:* **VHP**

Very Large Water Carrier *e:* **VLWC**

Very Low Observable *e:* **VLO**

Very Shallow Water *e:* **VSW**

Very Shallow Water Exercise *e:* **VSWEX**

Vessels Lost Due to Weather, Perils of the Sea or Similar Reasons *e:* **LOST/P**

Vest Individual Protective Reflective Adjustable *e:* **VIPRA**

Vestibular Sled (Spacelab D-1 Exp.) *e:* **VS**

Vestnik Belorusskogo Gosudarstvennogo Universiteta. Seriya 2. Biologiya, Khimiya, Geologiya, Geografiya *R:* **Vestn Beloruss Gos Univ Ser 2 Biol Khim Geol Geogr**

Vestnik Khar'kovskogo Universiteta. Geologiya i Geografiya *R:* **Vestn Khar'k Univ Geol Geogr**

Vestnik Khar'kovskogo Universiteta. Seriya Biologicheskaya *R:* **Vestn Khar'k Univ Ser Biol**

Vestnik Khar'kovskogo Universiteta. Seriya Geologicheskaya *R:* **Vestn Khar'k Univ Ser Geol**

Vestnik Leningradskogo Gosudarstvennogo Universiteta. Seriya Biologii *R:* **Vest Leningr Gos Univ Ser Biol**

Vestnik Leningradskogo Universiteta. Biologiya *R:* **Vestn Leningr Univ Biol**

Vestnik Leningradskogo Universiteta. Seriya Biologii *R:* **Vestn Leningrad Univ Ser Biol**

Vestnik Leningradskogo Universiteta. Seriya Biologii, Geografii, i Geologii *R:* **Vestn Lening Univ Ser Biol Geogr Geol**

Vestnik Leningradskogo Universiteta. Seriya Geologii i Geografii *R:* **Vestn Leningr Univ Ser Geol Geogr**

Vestnik Leningrradskogo Universiteta. Geologiya, Geografiya *R:* **Vestn Leningr Univ Geol Geogr**

Vestnik Mikrobiologii, Epidemiologii, i Parazitologii *R:* **Vest Mikrobiol Epidemiol Parazitol, *R:* Vestnik Mikrobiol Epidemiol i Parazitol**

Vestnik Mikrobiologii i Epidemiologii *R:* **Vestnik Mikrobiol i Epidemiol**

Vestnik Moskovskogo Instituta Geografii *R:* **Vest Mosk Inst Geogr**

Vestnik Moskovskogo Instituta. Serija Biologiya, Počvovedenie *R:* **Vest Mosk Inst Biol Počv**

Vestnik Moskovskogo Universiteta. Biologiya, Pochvovedenie *R:* **Vestn Mosk Univ Biol Pochvoved**

Vestnik Moskovskogo Universiteta. Geografiya *R:* **Vestn Mosk Univ Geogr**

Vestnik Moskovskogo Universiteta. Geologiya *R:* **Vestn Mosk Univ Geol**

Vestnik Moskovskogo Universiteta. Serija Geografija *R:* **Vestn Moskov Univ Ser Geogr**

Vestnik Moskovskogo Universiteta. Seriya Biologii, Pochvovedeniya, Geologii, Geografii *R:* **Vest Mosk Univ Ser Biol Pochv Geol Geogr, *R:* Vestn Mosk Univ Ser Biol Pochvoved Geol Geogr**

Vestnik Moskovskogo Universiteta. Seriya 16. Biologiya *R:* **Vestn Mosk Univ Ser 16 Biol**

Vestnik Moskovskogo Universiteta. Seriya 6. Biologiya Pochvovedenie *R:* **Vestn Mosk Univ Ser 6 Biol Pochvoved**

Vestnik Moskovskogo Universiteta. Seriya 6. Biologiya\Pochvovedenie *R:* **VMUBA**

Vestnik Moskovskogo Universiteta. Seriya 5. Geografiya *R:* **Vestn Mosk Univ Ser 5 Geogr,** *R:* **VMOGA**

Vestnik Moskovskogo Universiteta. Seriya 4. Geologiya *R:* **Vestn Mosk Univ Ser 4 Geol,** *R:* **VMUGA**

Vestnik Moskovskogo Universiteta. Seriya 16. Seriya Biologiia *R:* **Vestn Mosk Univ Ser 16 Ser Biol**

Vestnik Nauchno Issledovatel'skogo Instituta Gidrobiologii [Dnepropetrovski] *R:* **Vestn Nauchno-Issled Inst Gidrobiol [Dnepropetr]**

Vestnik Naučno Issledovatel'skogo Instituta Gidrobiologii *R:* **Vestn Naučno-Issled Inst Gidrobiol**

Vestnik Naučnoj Informacii Zabaikal'skogo Filiala Geografičeskogo Obščestva SSSR *R:* **Vestn Naučn Inf Zabaik Fil Geogr Ova SSSR**

Vestnik of the USSR Academy of Medical Sciences *e:* **Vestn. USSR Acad. Med. Sci.**

Vestnik Rossiiskoi Akademii Medicinskich Nauk *R:* **Vestn Ross Akad Med Nauk**

Vestnik Statniho Geologickeho Ústavu Československe Republiky *c:* **Vestn Statniho Geol Ústavu Česk Repub**

Vestnik. USSR Academy of Medical Science *R:* **Vestn USSR Acad Med Sci**

Vestnik Ustredniho Ustavu Geologickeho *c:* **Vestnik Ustredniho Ustavu Geol**

Vestnik Ustredniho Ústavu Geologickeho *c:* **Vestn Ustred Ústavu Geol**

Vestnik Zapadno-Sibirskogo Geologicheskogo Upravleniya *R:* **Vestn Zapadno Sib Geol Upr**

Vestnik Zapadno-Sibirskogo i Novosibirskogo Geologičeskich Upravlenii *R:* **Vestn Zapadno Sib i Norosib Geol Upr**

Veteran Affairs Healthcare *e:* **VAH**

Veterans Administration Medical Center *e:* **VAMC**

Veterans Administration-National Institute of Mental Health *e:* **VA-NIMH**

Veterans Affairs Medical and Regional Office Center *e:* **VAMROC**

Veterans Health Administration *e:* **VHA**

Veteran's Health Care Act *e:* **VHCA**

Veterans Health Services and Research Administration *e:* **VHS & RA**

Veterans Health System Journal *e:* **VHSJ**

Veterans Memorial Medical Center *e:* **VMMC**

Veterans Omnibus Health Care Act *e:* **VOHCA**

Veterinariae Medicinae Doctor *l:* **V.M.D.**

Veterinærmedicinsk Forening *a:* **VMF**

Veterinärmedicinska Föreningen *r:* **VMF**

Veterinärmedizin *d:* **Vet.-Med.**

veterinärmedizinisch-technische(r) Angestellte(r) *d:* **VTA**

veterinärmedizinisch-technische[r] Assistent[in] *d:* **VTA**

Veterinarni Medicina *c:* **Vet Med**

Veterinarni Medicina [Prague] *c:* **Vet Med [Prague]**

Veterinarni Medicina [Praha] *c:* **Vet Med [Praha]**

Veterinäruntersuchungs- und Tiergesundheitsamt *d:* **VU-TGA**

Veterinary and Animal Husbandry Department *e:* **VAHD**

Veterinary Assistant Surgeon *e:* **VAS**

Veterinary Biologics Division *e:* **VBD**

Veterinary Botanical Medicine Association *e:* **VBMA**

Veterinary Clinics of North America. Food Animal Practice *e:* **Vet Clin North Am Food Anim Pract**

Veterinary Clinics of North America [Large Animal Practice] *e:* **Vet Clin North Am [Large Anim Pract]**

Veterinary Clinics of North America [Small Animal Practice] *e:* **Vet Clin North Am [Small Anim Pract]**

Veterinary Medical Assistance Team *e:* **VMAT**

Veterinary Medical Association *e:* **VMA**

Veterinary Medical Association of Ireland *e:* **VMAI**

Veterinary Medical Association of New York City, Inc. *e:* **VMANYC**

Veterinary Medical College Application Service *e:* **VMCAS**

Veterinary Medical Data Program *e:* **VMDP**

Veterinary medical doctor *e:* **VMD**

Veterinary Medical Libraries Section *e:* **VMLS**

Veterinary Medical Libraries Section/Medical Library Association *e:* **VMLS/MLA**

Veterinary Medical (or Medicine) Association of Ireland *e:* **VMAI**

Veterinary Medical Research Council [University of Missouri] *e:* **VMRC**

Veterinary Medical Research Institute *e:* **VMRI**

Veterinary Medical Review *e:* **Vet Med Rev**

Veterinary Medical School Admission Requirements in the United States and Canada *e:* **VMSAR**

Veterinary Medical Science *e:* **Vet Med Sci**

Veterinary Medical Society *e:* **VMS**

Veterinary Medicinal Product *e:* **VMP**

Veterinary Medicine *e:* **Vet,** *e:* **Vet Med**

Veterinary Medicine and Small Animal Clinician *e:* **Vet Med,** *e:* **Vet Med/SAC,** *e:* **Vet Med Small Anim Clin**

Veterinary Medicine Association of Ireland *e:* **VMAI**

Veterinary Medicine, 0ptometry, Podiatry and Pharmacy *e:* **VOPP**

Veterinary Medicines Directorate *e:* **VMD**

Veterinary Microbiology *e:* **Vet Microbiol**

Veterinary Molecular Biology Laboratory *e:* **VMBL**

Veterinary Pharmaceuticals and Biologicals *e:* **VP & B**

Veterinary Public Health Association *e:* **VPHA**

Veterinary Surgeon *e:* **Vet Surg,** *e:* **V.S.**

Veterinary Surgeons Board *e:* **VSB**

Veterinary Surgeons' Health Support Programme *e:* **VSHSP**

Vetus Natura Brevium *l:* **Vet N B,** *l:* **V N B**

VFDB [Vereinigung zur Foerderung des Deutschen Brandschutzes eV] Zeitschrift *d:* **VFDBA,** *d:* **VFDB [Ver Foerd Dtch Brandschutzes] Z**

VHSIC Integrated Environment Workstation *e:* **VIEW**

Vibrating Space Modulator *e:* **VSM**

Vice-President of the Geological Society *e:* **VPGS**

Vice-President of the Royal Geographical Society *e:* **VPRGS**

Vice Presidential Protective Division *e:* **VPPD**

Victor Electrowriter Remote Blackboard *e:* **VERB**

Victor Electrowriter Remote Blackboard System *e:* **VERB System**

Victoria Council on Fitness and General Health *e:* **VICFIT**

Victoria Cross and George Cross Association *e:* **VC&GCA**

Victoria Deep Sea Water Terminal *e:* **VDWT**

Victoria. Fisheries and Wildlife Department. Fisheries Contribution *e:* **Victoria Fish Wildl Dep Fish Contrib**

Victoria. Fisheries and Wildlife Department. Wildlife Contribution *e:* **Victoria Fish Wildl Dep Wildl Contrib**

Victoria. Geological Survey. Bulletin *e:* **Vict Geol Surv Bull,** *e:* **Victoria Geol Bull**

Victoria. Geological Survey. Memoirs *e:* **Vict Geol Surv Mem,** *e:* **Victoria Geol Surv Mem**

Victoria. Mines Department. Groundwater Investigation Program. Report *e:* **Victoria Mines Dep Groundwater Invest Program Rep**

Victoria. Ministry for Conservation. Environmental Studies Program. Project Report *e:* **Proj Rep Victoria Minist Conserv Environ Stud Program,** *e:* **Victoria Minist Conserv Environ Stud Program Proj Rep**

Victoria/New South Wales and Environments, General Practitioners *e:* **VICNSWBEGP**

Victoria. State Rivers and Water Supply Commission. Annual Report *e:* **Victoria State Rivers Water Supply Comm Annu Rep**

Victoria. State Rivers and Water Supply Commission. Technical Bulletin *e:* **St Riv Wat Supply Comm Tech Bull**

Victorian Aboriginal Health Service *e:* **VAHS**

Victorian Environmental Education Council *e:* **VEEC**

Victorian Geographic Data Committee *e:* **VGDC**

Victorian Geographical Journal *e:* **Vic Geogr J,** *e:* **Vict Geogr J**

Victorian Health Promotion Foundation *e:* **VHPF**

Victorian Institute of Animal Science *e:* **VIAS**

Victorian Naturalist *e:* **VicN,** *e:* **Vic Nat,** *e:* **Vic Naturalist,** *e:* **Vict Nat,** *e:* **Vict Naturalist,** *e:* **Victorian Nat**

Victorian Naturalists' Club e: **VNC**

Victorian Water Quality Monitoring Network e: **VWQMN**

Victorian Water Study Group e: **VWSG**

Vida Medica e: **Vida Med**

Vida Sobrenatural e: **VS**

Videnskabelige Meddelelser fra Dansk Naturhistorisk Forening a: **Vidensk Medd Dan Naturhist Foren**

Videnskabelige Meddelelser fra Dansk Naturhistorisk Forening i Khobonhavn a: **Vidensk Medd Dan Naturhist Foren Khobenhavn**

Video Copyright Protection Society e: **VCPS**

Video-Enhanced Contrast Polarization Microscopy e: **VCPM**

Video Ice Particle Sampler e: **VIPS**

Vie et Milieu. Serie A. Biologie Marine f: **Vie Milie A**, f: **Vie Milieu Ser A**, f: **Vie Milieu Ser A Biol Mar**

Vie et Milieu. Serie AB. Biologie Marine et Oceanographie f: **VMSODA**

Vie et Milieu. Serie B. Oceanographie f: **Vie Milie B**, f: **Vie Milieu Ser B Oceanogr**

Vie et Milieu. Serie C. Biologie Terrestre f: **Vie Milie C**, f: **Vie Milieu Ser C Biol Terr**

Vie Medicale f: **Vie Med**

Vie Medicale au Canada Francais f: **Vie Med Can Fr**

Viehbestand und Tierische Erzeugung Land und Forstwirtschaft Fischerei d: **Tier Erzeu**

Vienna, isotopic Standard for Measuring Oxygen and hydrogen isotopes e: **V-SMOW**

Vierteljahreshefte für geographischen Unterricht d: **VjhGU**

Vierteljahresschrift der Naturforschenden Gesellschaft [Zürich] d: **Vj Nat Ges [Zür]**

Vierteljahresschrift der Naturforschenden Gesellschaft Zürich d: **VjNGZ**

Vierteljahresschrift für Gerichtliche Medizin d: **VJGerM**

Vierteljahresschrift für öffentliche Gesundheitspflege d: **Vj öff Gpfl**

Vierteljahrschrift der Naturforschenden Gesellschaft in Zürich d: **Viert Naturf Ges Zürich**

Vierteljahrschrift für Gerichtliche Medizin und Öffentliches Sanitätswesen d: **Vierteljahreschr Gerichtl Med Öff Sanitätswes**

Vierteljahrsschrift. Naturforschende Gesellschaft [Zürich] d: **Vierteljahrsschr Naturforsch Ges [Zürich]**, d: **Vjschr Naturf Ges [Zürich]**

Vietnam Economic Science, Technology, and Environment Network e: **VesteNet**

Vietnam Ocean Shipping Company e: **VOSCO**

Vietnamese National Oceanographic Data Center (or Centre) e: **VNODC**

Viewpoints in Biology e: **Viewpoints Biol**

Vigilancia Meteorológica Mundial s: **VMM**

Vigilantes against Increasing Loss of Environment e: **VILE**

Viking Lander Biological Instrument e: **VLBI**

Viking Orbiter e: **VO**

Viking Orbiter Design Change e: **VODC**

Viking Orbiter System e: **VOS**

Viking Spacecraft e: **V-S/C**

Vikram Sarabhai Space Center (or Centre) e: **VSSC**

Vilas-Oneida Wilderness Society e: **VOWS**

village health worker e: **VHW**

Villanova Environmental Law Journal e: **Vill. Envtl. L.J.**

Vin Doux Naturel f: **VDN**

Vir Devotissimus Protector Lateris Dominici l: **V.D.PT.L.D**

Virchow-Pirquet Medical Society e: **VPMS**

Virchows Archiv für pathologische Anatomie und Physiologie und für klinische Medizin d: **VirchA**

Virchows Archiv für Pathologische Anatomie und Physiologie und für Klinische Medizin d: **Virchows Arch Pathol Anat Physiol Klin Med**

Virgin Islands Ecological Research Station e: **VIERS**

Virgin Islands Medical Institute e: **VIMI**

Virginia Beach Oceana Naval Air Station [Virginia] e: **KNTU**

Virginia Commonwealth University Health Sciences Division, Richmond e: **ViRCU-H**

Virginia Department of Health e: **VDH**

Virginia. Department of Highways. Division of Tests. Geological Yearbook e: **VA Dept Highways Div Tests Geol Yearbook**

Virginia. Division of Geology. Bulletin e: **VA Div Geol Bull**

Virginia. Division of Geology. Bulletin. Reprint Series e: **VA Div Geology Bull Reprint Ser**

Virginia Environmental Law Journal e: **Va. Envtl. L.J.**

Virginia. Geological Survey. Bulletin e: **VA Geol Survey Bull**, e: **VA GSB**

Virginia. Geological Survey. Circular e: **VA Geol Surv Circ**

Virginia. Geological Survey. Reprint Series e: **VA Geol Surv Repr Ser**

Virginia Journal of Natural Resources Law e: **VA J Nat Resourc[es] L[aw]**, e: **VJNRL**

Virginia, Maryland, North Carolina\South Carolina, Georgia e: **Southern Colonies**

Virginia Medical e: **VA Med**

Virginia Medical College e: **VMC**

Virginia Medical Group Management Association e: **VMGMA**

Virginia Medical Information System e: **VAMIS**

Virginia Medical Monthly e: **VA Med Mon**, e: **Virginia M[ed] Month**, e: **VMMOA**

Virginia Medical Quarterly e: **Va Med Q**

Virginia Natural Heritage Program e: **VANHP**

Virginia Polytechnic Institute and State University. School of Forestry and Wildlife Resources. Publication e: **VA Polytechn Inst State Univ Sch For Wildl Resour Publ**

Virginia Polytechnic Institute and State University. Virginia Water Resources

Research Center. Bulletin e: **VA Polytech Inst State Univ VA Water Resour Res Cent Bull**

Virginia Polytechnic Institute and State University. Water Resources Research Center. Bulletin e: **VA Polytech Inst State Univ Water Resour Res Cent Bull**

Virginia Polytechnic Institute-Water Resources Center e: **VPI-WRC**

Virginia Public Health Association e: **VPHA**

Virginia Remote Sensing Study e: **VRSS**

Virginia Rural Health Association e: **VRHA**

Virginia Union List of Biomedical Serials e: **VULBS**

Virginia Veterinary Medical Association e: **VVMA**

Virginia Water Resources Research Center e: **VWRRC**

Virginia Water Resources Research Center Bulletin e: **VA Water Resour Res Cent Bull**

Virginia Wildlife e: **VA Wildl**

Virtual Domain Environment e: **VDE**

Virtual Environment e: **VE**

Virtual Environment Configurable Training Aid e: **VECTA**

Virtual Environments Research Institute e: **VERI**

Virtual Geomagnetic Pole e: **VGP**

Virtual Geomagnetic Pole[s] e: **VGP**

Virtual Health Strore e: **VHS**

Virtual Home Environment e: **VHE**

Virtual Information Environment e: **VIE**

Virtual Interactive Environment Workstation e: **VIEWS**

Virtual Interface Environment Workstation e: **VIEW**

Virtual Learning Environment e: **VLE**

Virtual Machine Environment e: **VME**

Virtual Memory Environment e: **VME**

Virtual Molecular Orbital e: **VMO**

Virtual Protected Mode Interface e: **VPMI**

Virtual Reality in Medicine e: **VIRIM**

Virtual Strike Warfare Environment e: **VSWE**

Virtual System Environment e: **VSE**

Virtual Terminal Environment e: **VTE**

Virtual Visual Environment Display e: **VIVED**

Viša Geodetska Škola se: **VGŠ**

viscous semi-geostrophic e: **VSG**

Visibilidad, nubes y condiciones meteorológicas Ok s: **CAVOK**

Visibility Impairment from Sulfur Transformation and Transport in the Atmosphere e: **VISTTA**

Visible Airglow Experiment-Atmospheric Explorer-C e: **VAE**

Visible and Near Infrared Polarimeter e: **VNIRP**

Visible Atmospheric Sounder e: **VAS**

Visible Emission Observation e: **VEC**

Visible Infrared Spin Scan Radiometer Atmospheric Sounder e: **VAS**

Visible Radiation Polarization Monitor e: **VRPM**

Visiting Medical Officer e: **VMO**

Visiting Medical Practitioner e: **VMP**

Višja Šola za Medicinske Sestre S: **VŠMS**

Visnik Kiivs'kogo Universitetu. Seriya Biologii R: **Visn Kiiv Univ Ser Biol**

Visnik Kiivs'kogo Universitetu. Seriya Geologii ta Geografii R: **Visn Kiiv Univ Ser Geol Geogr**

Visnik L'vivs'kogo Derzhavnogo Universitetu. Seriya Biologichna R: **Visn L'viv Derzh Univ Ser Biol**

Visnik L'vivs'kogo Derzhavnogo Universitetu. Seriya Geologichna R: **Visn L'viv Derzh Univ Ser Geol**

Visnyk Kyyivs'koho Universytetu. Seriya Biolohiyi R: **Visn Kyyiv Univ Ser Biol**

Visnyk L'vivs'koho Universytetu. Seriya Biolohiyi, Heohrafiyi, ta Heolohiyi R: **Visn L'viv Univ Ser Biol Heohr**

Visnyk L'vivs'koho Universytetu. Seriya Biolohiyi Heohrafiyi ta Heolohiyi R: **Visn L'viv Univ Ser Biol Heohr Heol**

Visual Audio Kinetic Unit-Multiples and Environments e: **VAKUME**

Visual BASIC Integrated Development Environment e: **VBIDE**

Visual Development Environment e: **VDE**

Visual Electronic Remote Blackboard e: **VERB**

Visual Emission Observation e: **VEO**

Visual Engineering Environment. e: **VEE**

Visual Environment Simulation System e: **VESS**

visual inspection protection e: **vip**

Visual Interdevice e: **VID**

Visual Medicine e: **Visual Med**

Visual Meteorological Conditions e: **VMC**

visual observation airplane e: **VOS**

Visual Observation Instrumentation Subsystem e: **VOIS**

Visual Observation Instrumentation System e: **VOIS**

Visual Observation Integration Subsystem e: **VOIS**

Visual Programming Environment e: **VPE**

Visual Sonic Medicine e: **Visual Sonic Med**

Visual User Environment e: **VUE**

Visualization and Simulation of Marine environmental Processes e: **VISIMAR**

Vital and Health Statistics. Series 11 e: **VHSKA**

Vital and Health Statistics. Series 3: Analytical and Epidemiological Studies e: **Vital Health Stat 3**

Vital and Health Statistics. Series 3. Analytical Studies e: **Vital Health Stat 3**

Vital and Health Statistics. Series 5: Comparative International Vital and Health Statistics Reports e: **Vital Health Stat 5**

Vital and Health Statistics. Series 2. Data Evaluation and Methods Research e: **Vital Health Stat 2**, e: **Vital Health Statist Ser 2 Data Evaluation Methods Res**

Vital and Health Statistics. Series 10. Data from the National Health Survey e: **Vital Health Stat 10**

Vital and Health Statistics. Series 23. Data from the National Survey of Family Growth e: **Vital Health Stat 23**

Vital and Health Statistics. Series 20. Data from the National Vital Statistics System e: **Vital Health Stat 20**

Vital and Health Statistics. Series 21: Data on Natality, Marriage and di vorce e: **Vital Health Stat 21**

Vital and Health Statistics. Series 14. Data on National Health Resources e: **Vital Health Stat 14**

Vital and Health Statistics. Series 4. Documents and Committee Reports e: **Vital Health Stat 4**

Vital and Health Statistics. Series 1. Programs and Collection Procedures e: **Vital Health Stat 1**

Viticultural and Oecological Research Institute e: **VORI**

Vlaams Ecologisch Netwerk n: **VEN**

Vlaams Waternetwerk n: **VWN**

Vlaamse Geautomatiseerde Centrale Catalogus n: **VLACC**

Vlaamse Vereniging voor Watertoerisme n: **VVW**

VLBI [very long baseline interference] Space Observatory Program. e: **VSOP**

Vocabulario Meteorológico Internacional s: **VMI**

Vocational Consultant/Medical Advisor Services Staff e: **VEMASS**

Voice Data Protection e: **VDP**

Voice Operated Transmitier e: **VOX**

Voivodship environmental funds e: **VEPWMF**

Vojno-Geografski Institut se: **VGI**

Vojno-Medicinska Akademija se: **VMA**

Volatile Halogenated Hydrocarbons e: **VHH**

Volatile Liquid Hydrocarbon e: **VLH**

Volatile Organic Hydrocarbons e: **VOH**

Volcanological Meteorological Bulletin. Japan Meteorological Agency e: **Volcanol Bull Jpn Meterol Agency**

Völkischer Schwimm- und Wassersport-Verband Niederrhein d: **VSWS**

Volksflugzeug Wilden 10 d: **VoWi 10**

Volksgesundheit Schweiz d: **VGS**

Volkstümlicher Wassersport Mannheim [Verein] d: **VWM**

VOLMET-Ausstrahlung [meteorologischer Informationen für Luftfahrzeuge] d: **VOLMET**

voltage impulse protection e: **ViP**

Voltage Protection Relay e: **VPR**

Volumen, Wasser d: **VW**

Voluntary Association for Mental Health e: **VAMH**

Voluntary Effort to Contain Health Care Costs e: **VECHCC**

voluntary environmental organisation e: **VEO**

Voluntary Health Insurance board e: **VHI**

Voluntary Medical Services e: **VMS**

Voluntary Protection Program e: **VPP**

voluntary protection program e: **VVP**

Volunteer Durham Medical Staff Corps e: **VDMSC**

Volunteer Services to Animals e: **VSA**

Volunteering Hydrographic Office e: **VHO**

Volunteers for Medical Engineering, Inc. e: **VME**

Voprosy Biologii R: **Vopr Biol**

Voprosy Biologii i Kraevoi Meditsiny R: **Vopr Biol Kraev Med**

Voprosy Biologii Semennogo Reszmnozheniya R: **Vopr Biol Semennogo Rezmnozheniya**

Voprosy Chetvertechnoi Geologii R: **Vopr Chetvertechn Geol**

Voprosy Fiziologii Rastenii i Mikrobiologii R: **Vopr Fiziol Rast Mikrobiol**

Voprosy Geografii R: **Vopr Geogr**

Voprosy Geografii Dal'nego Vostoka R: **Vopr Geogr Dal'nego Vostoka**

Voprosy Geografii Kazakhstana R: **Vopr Geogr Kaz**

Voprosy Geografii Mordovskoi ASSR R: **Vop Geogr Mordovsk ASSR**, R: **Vopr Geogr Mordov ASSR**

Voprosy Geokhimii i Tipomorfizm Mineralov R: **Vopr Geokhim Tipomorfizm Miner**

Voprosy Geologii i Bureniya Neftyanykh i Gazovykh Skvazhin R: **Vopr Geol Buren Neft Gazov Skvazhin**

Voprosy Geologii i Metallogenii Kol'skogo Poluostrova R: **Vopr Geol Metallog Kol'sk Poluoshova**

Voprosy Geologii i Metodiki Razvedki Zolota R: **Vopr Geol Metod Razved Zolota**

Voprosy Geologii i Mineralogii Kol'skogo Poluostrova R: **Vopr Geol Mineral Kolsk Poluostrova**

Voprosy Geologii i Mineralogii Rudnykh Mestorozhdenii Ukrainy R: **Vopr Geol Mineral Rudn Mestorozhd Ukr**

Voprosy Geologii i Neftegazonosnosti Uzbekistana R: **Vopr Geol Neftegazonsn Uzb**

Voprosy Geologii i Neftenosnosti Srednego Povolzh'ya R: **Vopr GeoI Neftenosn Sredn Povolzh'ya**

Voprosy Geologii Tadzhikistana R: **Vopr Geol Tadzh**

Voprosy Geologii Uzbekistana R: **Vopr Geol Uzb**

Voprosy Geologii Vostochnoi Okrainy Russkoi Platformy i Yuzhnogo Urala R: **Vopr GeoI Vost Okrainy Russ Platformy Yuzhn Urala**

Voprosy Geologii Yuzhnogo Urala i Povolzh'ya R: **Vopr Geol Yuzhn Urala Povolzh'ya**

Voprosy Geomorfologii i Geologii Bashkirii R: **Vopr Geomorfol Geol Bashk**

Voprosy Gidrogeologii i Inzhenernoi Geologii Ukrainy R: **Vopr Gidrogeol Inzh Geol Ukr**

Voprosy Inzhenernoi Geologii i Gruntovedeniya R: **Vopr Inzh Geol Gruntoved**

Voprosy Mikrobiologii R: **Vopr Mikrobiol**

Voprosy Mikrobiologii Akademiya Nauk Armyanskoi SSR R: **Vop Mikrobiol Akad Nauk Armyan SSR**

Voprosy Organicheskoi Geokhimii i Gidrogeologii Neftegazonosnykh Basseinov Uzbekistana R: **Vopr Org Geokhim Gidrogeol Neftegazonosn Basseinov Uzb**

Voprosy Prikladnoi Geokhimii R: **Vopr Prikl Geokhim**

Voprosy Prikladnoi Radiogeologii R: **Vopr Prikl Radiogeol**

Voprosy Radiobiologii R: **Vopr Radiobiol**

Voprosy Radiobiologii. Akademiya Nauk Armyanskoi SSR R: **Vopr Radiobiol Akad Nauk Arm SSR**

Voprosy Radiobiologii i Biologicheskogo
Deistviya Tsitostaticheskikh Prcparatov
R: **Vopr Radiobiol Biol Deistviya
Tsitostatich Prep**

Voprosy Radiobiologii i Biologicheskogo
Dejstviya Tsitostaticheskikh Preparatov
R: **Vopr Radiobiol Biol Dejstv
Tsitostatich Prep**

Voprosy Radiobiologii i Klinicheskoi
Radiologii *R:* **Vopr Radiobiol Klin
Radiol**

Voprosy Radiobiologii. Sbornik Trudov *R:*
Vopr Radiobiol Sb Tr, *R:* **VRARA**

Voprosy Radiobiologii [Yerevan] *R:* **Vopr
Radiobiol [Yerevan]**

Voprosy Razvedochnoi Geofiziki *R:* **Vopr
Razved Geofiz**

Voprosy Regional'noi Geologii i
Metallogenii Zabaikal'ya *R:* **Vopr Reg
Geol Metallog Zabaikal'ya**

Voprosy Rudnoi Geofiziki *R:* **Vopr Rud
Geofiz**, *R:* **Vopr Rudn Geofiz**

Voprosy Rudnoi Geofiziki. Ministerstvo
Geologii i Okhrany Nedr SSSR *R:* **Vopr
Rud Geofiz Minist Geol Okhr Nedr
SSSR**

vor der Höhe, bei geograph. Angaben *d:*
v.d.H.

vororientiert *e:* **vo**

Voters Organized to Think Environment *e:*
VOTE

Voyager Biological Laboratory *e:* **VBL**

Voyager Spacecraft Subsystem *e:* **VSS**

Vrouwenbond voor Informatie en
Verdediging van de Consument *n:*
VIVEC

Vsesojuznnyj Naučno-Issledovatel'skij
Geologičeskij Institut *R:* **VSEGEI**

Vsesojuznoe Geografičeskoe Obščestvo.
Izvestiya *R:* **Vses Geogr O-Vo Izv**

Vsesojuznyj Naučno-Issledovatel'skij
Chimiko-Farmazevtičeskii Institut.
Chimija i Medicina *R:* **Vses Naučno-
Issled Chim Farm Inst Chim Med**

Vsesojuznyj Naučno-Issledovatel'skij
Geologičeskij Institut. Informacionnyj
Sbornik *R:* **Vses Naučno Issled Geol
Inst Inf Sb**

Vsesojuznyj Naučno-Issledovatel'skij
Geologičeskij Institut. Trudy *R:* **Vses
Naučno-Issled Geol Inst Tr**

Vsesojuznyj Naučno-Issledovatel'skij
Geologorazvedočnyj Neftjanoj Institut.
Trudy *R:* **Vses Naučno-Issled
Geologorazved Neft Inst Tr**

Vsesojuznyj Naučno-Issledovatel'skij
Institut Geofizičeskich Metodov
Razvedki. Trudy *R:* **Vses Naučno Issled
Inst Geofiz Metodov Razved Tr**

Vsesojuznyj Naučno-Issledovatel'skij
Institut Gidrogeologii i Inženernoj
Geologii. Trudy *R:* **Vses Naučno Issled
Inst Gidrogeol Inž Geol Tr**

Vsesojuznyj Naučno-Issledovatel'skij
Institut Medicinskoj i mediko-
techničeskoj Informacii *R:* **VNIIMI**

Vsesoyuznoye Geograficheskoye
Obshchestvo. Izvestiya *R:* **Vses Geogr
O-Vo Izv**

Vsesoyuznyi Nauchno-Issledovatel'skii
Institut Geofizicheskikh Metodov
Razvedki. Trudy *R:* **Vses Nauchno
Issled Inst Geofiz Metodov Razved Tr**

Vsesoyuznyi Nauchno-Issledovatel'skii
Geologicheskii Institut. Informatsionnyi
Sbornik *R:* **Vses Nauchno Issled Geol
Inst Inf Sb**

Vsesoyuznyi Nauchno-Issledovatel'skii
Institut Gidrogeologii i Inzhenernoi
Geologii. Trudy *R:* **Vses Nauchno
Issled Inst Gidrogeol Inzh Geol Tr**

Vsesoyuznyy Nauchno-Issledovatel'skiy
Geologorazvedochnyi Neftyanoy
Institut.Trudy *R:* **Vses Nauchno-Issled
Geologorazved Neft Inst Tr**

Vsesoyuznyy Nauchno-Issledovatel'skiy
Geologicheskiy Institut. Trudy *R:* **Vses
Nauchno-Issled Geol Inst Tr**

Vyriausioji Hidrometeorologines Tarnybos
Valdyba *li:* **VHMTV**

Vyriausioji medicinos istaigu aprupinimo
valdyba *li:* **Vyrmedtie kimas**

Vétérinaires Sans Frontières *f:* **VSF**

Vétérinaires sans Frontières *f:* **CSF**

Výzkumný Ústav Geodetický, Topografický
a Kartografický *c:* **VÚGTK**

Výzkumný Ústav Rybářský a
Hydrobilogický při ČSAZV *c:* **VÚR
ČSAZV**

W

W. K. Kellogg Health Sciences Library,
Dalhousie University, Halifax, Nova
Scotia *e:* **NSHDM**

Waclia Institute of Himalayan Geology *e:*
WIHG

Waddell Sea Project *e:* **WASP**

Wadden Sea Project *e:* **DemoWad**

Wadi Amud Nature Reserve *e:* **WANR**

Wadi Bezet Nature Reserve *e:* **WBNR**

Wadi Dishon Nature Reserve *e:* **WDNR**

Wadi Kziv Nature Reserve *e:* **WKNR**

Wadi Tabor Nature Reserve *e:* **WTNR**

Wadkin Automatic Remote Processor
Accessed via Terminal *e:* **WARPAT**

Wadley Medical Bulletin *e:* **Wadley Med
Bull**

wafer environment control *e:* **WEC**

Wagner Earth Bridge *e:* **WEB**

Wahlco Environment Systems *e:* **WAL**

Waiting on Weather *e:* **WOW**

Wakayama Medical Reports *e:*
Wakayama Med Rep

Wake Forest University. Developing
Nations Monograph Series. Series II.
Medical Behavioral Science *e:* **Wake
For Univ Dev Nations Monogr Ser Ser
II Med Behav Sci**

Waksman Institute of Microbiology *e:* **WIM**

Waksman Institute of Microbiology.
Rutgers University. Annual Report *e:*
**Waksman Inst Microbiol Rutgers Univ
Annu Rep**

Waldemar Medical Research Foundation,
Woodbury *e:* **NWbW**

Walker Branch Watershed *e:* **WBW**

Wall-ln-Space *e:* **WIS**

Wallops Island Orbital Tracking Station *e:*
WOTS

Wallops Space Flight Center *e:* **WSFC**

Walter Reed Army Medical Center *e:*
WRAMC

Walter Reed Army Mcdical Center.
Progress Notes *e:* **Walter Reed Army
Med Cent Prog Notes**

Walter Reed General Hospital. Department
of Medicine. Progress Notes *e:* **Walter
Reed Gen Hosp Dep Med Prog Notes**

Wapanocca National Wildlife Refuge
(Arkansas) *e:* **WNWR**

War Agencies Employees Protective
Association *e:* **WAEPA**

War-at-Sea *e:* **WAS**

War Medical Society of India *e:* **W.M.S.I.**

WARC [World Administrative Radio
Conference] for/on Space
Telecommunication[s] *e:* **WARC-ST**

WARC [World Administrative Radio
Conference] for Usage for/of the
Geostationary Satellite Orbit *e:* **WARC-
ORB**

WARC [World Administrative Radio
Conference]-Space Techniques *e:*
WARC-ST

Wardenburg Health Center *e:* **WHC**

Wardenburg Student Health Center *e:*
WSHC

Warm Deep Water *e:* **WDW**

Warm Water Reactor *e:* **WWR**

Warm Water Resistant *e:* **WWR**

Warm Water Rinse *e:* **WWR**

warmes Wasser *d:* **w.W.**

Wärmestrahlung der Atmosphäre *d:* **A**

Wärmestrahlung reflektierendes Glas *d:*
WSR-Glas

Warmwasser *d:* **WW**

Warmwasser-Heizung *d:* **WW-Hzg**

Warmwasser-(Kühlwasser) und
Abgaszusatzheizung in
Verbrennungstriebwagen *d:* **Whzv**

Warmwasserbereiter *d:* **WWB**

Warmwasserboiler *d:* **WWB**

Warmwasserheizung *d:* **Whz**, *d:* **WWH**

Warmwasserheizung mit Kohle- oder
Dampfheizung *d:* **Whzkd**

Warmwasserheizung mit ÖI-, Dampf oder
elektrischer Heizung *d:* **Whzöde**

Warmwasserheizung mit Öl- oder
Dampfheizung mit Frostschutzmittel *d:*
Whzöd-f

Warmwasserheizung mit Ölfeuerung *d:*
Whzö

Warmwasserleitung *d:* **WW**

Warmwasserspeicher *d:* **WS**

Warmwasserverbraucher *d:* **WV**

Warmwasserversorgung *d:* **Wwv**, *d:* **Ww.
Vers.**

Warner & Swasey Observatory *e:* **WSO**

Warning Coordination Meteorologist *e:*
WCM

Warszawskie Przedsiębiorstwo Geodezyjne
P: **WPG**

Wartime Availability of Medical Personnel
upon Mobilization *e:* **WAMPUM**

Wash-Water Recovery System *e:* **WWRS**

Washburn Observatory Library, University
of Wisconsin *e:* **UWis**

Washington Department of Ecology *e:*
WDOE

Washington Department of Health *e:* **WDOH**

Washington Department of Natural
Resources *e:* **DNR**, *e:* **WDNR**

Washington Division of Geology and Earth
Resources *e:* **WDGER**

Washington Environmental Industries
Association *e:* **WEIA**

Washington Forest Protection Association
e: **WFPA**

Washington Health Care Authority *e:* **HCA**

Washington Medical Librarians Association *e:* **WMLA**

Washington Mental Health Counseling Association *e:* **WMHC**

Washington Quarterly. Georgetown University Center for Strategic and International Studies *e:* **GU/WQ**

Washington Sea Grant College Program *e:* **WSGCP**

Washington State Board of Health *e:* **SBOH**

Washington State Department of Ecology *e:* **Ecology**, *e:* **WSDE**

Washington State Department of Health *e:* **WSDOH**

Washington State Department of Natural Resources, Division of Geology and Earth Resources, Olympia *e:* **WaONR**

Washington [State] Industrial Safety and Health Act *e:* **WISHA**

Washington [State] Industrial Safety and Health Administration *e:* **WISHA**

Washington State Library, Ecology Department, Olympia *e:* **Wa-Ec**

Washington State Medical Association *e:* **WSMA**

Washington State Public Health Association *e:* **WSPHA**

Washington State Veterinary Medical Association *e:* **WSVMA**

Washington University School of Medicine *e:* **WUSM**

Washington University School of Medicine Library [St. Louis] *e:* **Wash U Med Lib**

Washington Water Power company *e:* **WWP**

Washington Water Power Company *e:* **WWP Company**

Washita National Wildlife Refuge (Oklahoma) *e:* **WNWR**

Washoe County Water Conservation District *e:* **WCWCD**

Wasser *d:* **H2O**, *d:* **W**, *d:* **Wa.**

Wasser-Bindemittel-Wert *e:* **W/B**

Wasser-Bindemittelwert *d:* **W/B**

Wasser-Boden-Luft *d:* **WaBoLu**

Wasser-Elektrolyt-Haushalt *d:* **WEH**

wasser, energie, luft *d:* **Wasser energ. Luft**

Wasser in Öl *d:* **W/O**

Wasser-in-Öl[-Emulsion] *d:* **W/O**

Wasser-in-Rohöl Emulsion *d:* **W/O Emulsion**

Wasser/Öl Verhältnis *d:* **WÖV**

Wasser- und Abfallwirtschaftliches Informationssystem *d:* **WAWIS**

Wasser- und Abwasserforschungsstelle, München *d:* **WAF**

wasser- und aschefrei *d:* **waf**

Wasser und Boden *d:* **Wasser Boden**

Wasser- und Energieversorgungsgesellschaft *d:* **WEVG**

Wasser- und Energiewirtschaft *d:* **Wasser-Energ.wirtsch.**

Wasser- und Energiewirtschaft, Zürich *d:* **WEW**

Wasser und Gas *d:* **WuG**

wasser- und mineralstofffrei *d:* **wmf**

Wasser- und Schiffahrtsamt *d:* **WSA**

Wasser- und Schiffahrtsdirektion *d:* **WSD**

Wasser- und Schiffahrtsdirektion, Abteilung Binnenschiffahrt *d:* **WSD-B**

Wasser- und Schiffahrtsdirektion Nord *d:* **WSDN**

Wasser- und Schiffahrtsverwaltung *d:* **WSV**

Wasser- und Wegebau-Zeitschrift *d:* **WWZ**

Wasser-Wasser-Wärmepumpe *d:* **WWWP**

Wasser-Wasserenergiereaktor *d:* **WWER**

Wasser-Zement Verhältnis *d:* **W/Z Verhältnis**

Wasser/ Zement-Wert *d:* **W/Z-Faktor**

Wasser/Zement Wert *d:* **W/Z Wert**

Wasserabscheider *d:* **WA**

Wasserabscheider- Zwischenüberhitzer *d:* **WAZÜ**

Wasserabscheidevermögen *d:* **WAV**

Wasserabsorption *d:* **Wa**

Wasseradsorptionskapazität *d:* **WAK**

Wasseralarm *d:* **WA**, *e:* **WA**

Wasseralarmfahrzeug *d:* **WAF**

Wasseralarmzentrale *d:* **WAZ**

Wasseraufbereitung *d:* **Wa**

Wasseraufbereitungsanlage *d:* **WAA**

Wasseraufbereitungsanlage Karlsruhe *d:* **WAK**

Wasseraufnahme *d:* **WA**

Wasseraufnahmefähigkeit *d:* **WAF**

Wasseraufnahmevermögen *d:* **WA**

Wasserbad *d:* **Wssb**

Wasserballast *d:* **WB**

Wasserballasttank *d:* **W.B.T.k.**

Wasserbau *d:* **Wassb**

Wasserbauamt *d:* **W.B.A.**

Wasserbaudirektion *d:* **WBDir**

Wasserbeckenfolie *d:* **WBF**

Wasserbehälter *d:* **Wbh**

Wasserbeständigkeitsklasse *d:* **WBK**

Wasserbezugsort *d:* **Wasbez**

Wasserbindevermögen *d:* **WBV**

Wasserblau [Anilinblau], Eosin, Phloxin [Färbemethode] *d:* **WEP**

Wasserblau-Eosin-Phloxin-Färbung *d:* **WEP-Färbung**

Wasserbombe *d:* **Wabo**, *d:* **WB**

Wasserdamm *d:* **Wd**

Wasserdampf-Kreisprozeß *d:* **WDKP**

Wasserdampfdurchgan *d:* **WDD**

Wasserdampfdurchlässigkeit *d:* **WDD**, *d:* **Wddu**

Wasserdeionisierung *d:* **WD**

wasserdicht *d:* **wd**

wasserdichte Isolierstoff-Kabelarmaturen *d:* **WISKA**

Wasserdruckprüfung *d:* **WDP**

Wassereintrittspunkt *d:* **WEP**

Wassereinzugsgebiet *d:* **WEG**

Wassererwärmer *d:* **WE**

Wasserfahrer *d:* **Wfhr**

Wasserfahrverein *d:* **WFV**

Wasserfall *d:* **Wf.**

Wasserfallen-Transport AG *d:* **Watrag**

Wasserfilterstation *d:* **WFS**

Wasserflugzeug *d:* **W**

wasserfrei *d:* **wf**, *d:* **wfr**

Wassergefährdungsklasse *d:* **WGK**

Wassergehalt *d:* **WG**

Wassergehalt-Saugspannungs-Kurve *d:* **pF-Kurve**

wassergehärtet *d:* **Wgeh**

wassergeschützt *d:* **wg**

Wassergesetz *d:* **WassG**, *d:* **WG**

Wassergesetz für das Land Sachsen-Anhalt *d:* **WGLSA**

Wassergesetz [Mecklenburg-Vorpommern] *d:* **LWaG MV**

Wassergütestelle *d:* **WGSt**

Wasserhaltekapazität *d:* **WHK**

Wasserhaltung *d:* **W**

Wasserhaltungsvermögen *d:* **WH**

Wasserhaushaltsgesetz *d:* **WasHG**, *d:* **WassHG**, *d:* **WHG**

Wasserhaushaltsmodell *d:* **SWATRE**

Wasserheizung *d:* **WH**

Wasserkapazität *d:* **WK**

Wasserkraft *d:* **WK**, *d:* **Wkr.**

Wasserkraftanlage *d:* **WA**, *d:* **WKA**

Wasserkraftwagen *d:* **Wasserkw**

Wasserkraftwerk *d:* **WKW**

Wasserkraftwerke AG, Wien *d:* **WAG**

Wasserkühler *d:* **WK**

Wasserleitfähigkeit *d:* **WL**

Wasserleitfähigkeitskoeffizient in der Darcy-Gleichung *d:* **Kf**

Wasserleitung *d:* **Wltg**

Wasserleitung für Brauchwasser *d:* **WB**

Wasserleitung für Trinkwasser *d:* **WT**

Wasserlinie *d:* **WL**

wasserlöslich *d:* **wasserl.**, *d:* **wasserlösl**, *d:* **wl**, *d:* **wlösl.**

Wassermann *d:* **Wass.**

Wassermann Reaction *e:* **WR**

Wassermann-Reaktion *d:* **WaR**, *d:* **WaR/WAR**, *d:* **WR**

Wassermann-Test *d:* **Wass-Test**

Wassermannsche Reaktion *d:* **WaR**, *d:* **Wa.-Rk.**

Wasserqualitäts-Meßstation *d:* **WQM**

Wasserrahmenrichtlinie *d:* **WRRL**

Wasserreinigungsbau-GmbH *d:* **WABAG**

Wasserreinigungskohle *d:* **WR-Kohle**

Wasserrettungsdienst *d:* **WRD**

Wasserrettungszug *d:* **WRZ**

Wasserrohrkessel *d:* **WK**

Wasserrohrkessel-Verband, Düsseldorf *d:* **WKV**

Wasserrückhaltevermögen *d:* **WRV**

Wassersäule *d:* **WS**

Wasserschall-Nebelsender *d:* **WNS**

Wasserschutzgebiet *d:* **WSG**

Wasserschutzpolizei *d:* **Wapo.**, *d:* **WS**, *d:* **WSchP[ol.]**, *d:* **WSP**, *d:* **W.S.Pol.**

Wasserschutzpolizei-Revier *d:* **WSR**

Wasserschutzpolizei-Revier Schwanenwerder *d:* **WSR Sch**

Wasserschutzpolizei-Revier Spandau *d:* **WSR Sp**

Wasserschutzpolizei-Revier Westhafen/Mitte *d:* **WSR Wh**

Wassersicherstellungsgesetz *d:* **WaSG**, *d:* **WasSG**

Wasserspiegel *d:* **WSp**

Wasserspülung *d:* **W**

Wasserstand *d:* **W**

Wasserstoffperoxid *d:* **WPO**

Wasserstoffperoxyd *d:* **H2O2**

Wasserstraße *d:* **W.Str.**

Wasserstraßen-Jahrbuch *d:* **WassJ**

Wasserstraßen-Reinhaltungsgesetz *d:* **WStrRG**

Wasserstraßenamt *d:* **Wastra**, *d:* **WSA**

Wasserstraßenbevollmächtigter *d:* **WBV**

Wasserstraßendirektion *d:* **WSD**

Wasserstraßenkreuzungsvorschriften *d:* **WKV**

Wasserstraßenselbstanchluß[anlage] *d:*
 Wasa
Wasserstraßenselbstwählanschluß *d:*
 WASA
Wassertank *d:* **WT**
Wasserthermometer *d:* **WT**
Wassertiefe *d:* **WT**
Wassertransport *d:* **WTr**
Wassertransportfahrzeug *d:* **WTF**
Wassertransportkompanie *d:* **WTrspKp**
Wassertrupp *d:* **WT**
Wassertrupp-Führer *d:* **WTF**
Wassertrupp-Mann *d:* **WTM**
Wasserturm *d:* **WT**
Wasserumlauf-Wasserkühlung *d:* **WUW**
wasserunlöslich *d:* **wasserunl.**
Wasserverbandgesetz *d:* **WassVerbG**, *d:*
 WasVbG, *d:* **WasVerbG**
Wasserverbandordnung *d:* **WasVerbO**
Wasserverbandsgesetz *d:* **WVG**
Wasserverbandverordnung *d:* **WasVbV**, *d:*
 WaVbVO, *d:* **WVVO**
Wasserverbund Region Bern *d:* **WVRB**
Wasserversorgung *d:* **Was Vsg**, *d:* **WV**
Wasserversorgung und
 Abwasserbehandlung *d:* **WAB**
Wasserversorgungsbedingungen *d:* **WVB**
Wasserversorgungsunternehmen *d:* **WV**,
 d: **WVU**
Wasservorbereitungsanlage *d:* **Wavo**
Wasserwerfer *d:* **WW**
Wasserwerk *d:* **WW**
Wasserwerk-Beteiligungs GmbH *d:* **WWB**
Wasserwirtschaft-Wassertechnik *d:* **WWT**
wasserwirtschaftliche Nutzfläche *d:* **WN**
Wasserwirtschafts-Gebührenordnung *d:*
 WaGebO
Wasserwirtschaftsamt *d:* **WWA**
Wasserwirtschaftsdirektion *d:* **WWD**
Wasserwirtschaftskommission *d:* **WAKO**
Wasserwirtschaftsprojektierung *d:* **Wapro**
Wasserzahl *d:* **WZ**
Wasserzementfaktor *d:* **WZF**
Wassmann Biological Society *e:* **WBS**
Waste, Analytical and Environmental
 Services *e:* **WAE**
Waste and Wastewater Equipment
 Manufacturers' Association *e:* **WWEMA**
Waste management and environmental
 compliance *e:* **WM&EC**
Waste Remediation and Environmental
 Engineering Section *e:* **WREE**
Waste Water Cluster *e:* **WWC**
Waste Water Outflow *e:* **WWO**
Waste Water Purification Unit *e:* **WWPU**
Waste Water Treating Process *e:* **WWTP**
Waste Water Treatment Plant *e:* **WWTP**
Waste Water Treatment System *e:* **WWTS**
Wastewater and Tank Systems *e:* **WTS**
Wastewater Operations & Maintenance *e:*
 WWTR OPS
Wastewater Planning Users Group *e:*
 WaPUG
Wastewater Plant *e:* **WWT PLT**
Wastewater Research Center *e:* **WRC**
Wastewater Sewage Treatment Plant *e:*
 WS
Wastewater sewage treatment plant *e:*
 WSTP
Wastewater Technology Center *e:* **WTC**
Wastewater Treatment *e:* **WT**, *e:* **WWT**
Wastewater Treatment and Information
 Exchange *e:* **WTIE**

Wastewater Treatment and Information
 Exchange Electronic Bulletin Board
 System *e:* **WTIE/BBS**
Wastewater Treatment System *e:* **WTS**
Wastewater Treatment Test Facility *e:*
 WTTF
Wastewater Treatment Unit *e:* **WTU**, *e:*
 WWTU
Watchdogs on Environment *e:* **WOE**
Water *e:* **H2**, *e:* **H2O**, *e:* **W**, *e:* **WA**, *e:*
 Wtr
Water Absorption Index *e:* **WAI**
water-activated battery *e:* **wab**
Water Agar *e:* **WA**
Water/Air *e:* **W/A**
Water, Air, and Soil Pollution *e:* **WAPLA**
Water-Alcohol Injection *e:* **WAI**
Water Alliances for Environmental
 Efficiency *e:* **WAVE**
Water Alliances for Voluntary Efficiency
 e: **WAVE**
Water Allocation Council *e:* **WAC**
Water-Alternating Gas *e:* **WAG**
Water Analysis Simulation Program *e:*
 WASP4
Water Analyzer Kit *e:* **WAK**
Water and Energy: Atmospheric,
 Vegetative, and Earth Interactions *e:*
 WEAVE
Water and Energy Commission Secretariat
 e: **WECS**
Water and Energy Research Institute of the
 Western Pacific *e:* **WERI**
Water and Environmental Health at London
 and Loughborough *e:* **WELL**
Water and Environmental Sanitation Team
 e: **WET**
Water and Feed *e:* **W and F**, *e:* **W & F**
Water and Hazardous Waste *e:* **WHW**
Water and hazardous waste team *e:*
 WHWT
Water and Land Division *e:* **WLD**
Water and Land Resources Use Simulation
 e: **WALRUS**
Water and Power Development Authority
 e: **WAPDA**
Water and Power Development Consultancy
 Services *e:* **WAPCOS**
Water and Rail *e:* **W and R**
water and rail *e:* **w & r**
Water [and] Resources Advisory Committee
 e: **WRAC**
Water and Sanitation *e:* **WatSan**
Water and Sanitation for Health Project *e:*
 WASH
Water and Sewage Works *e:* **WSW**
Water and Sewage Works Manufacturers
 Association *e:* **WSWMA**
Water and Sewer Distributors of America
 e: **WSDA**
Water and Soil Conservation Organization
 e: **WASCO**
Water and Soil Investigation Department
 e: **WASID**
Water and Steam Program *e:* **WASP**
Water and Toxic Substances Health
 Research Division *e:* **WTSHRD**
Water and Waste Management Monitoring
 Research Division *e:* **WWMMRD**
Water and Waste Management Staff *e:*
 WWMS
Water and Wastes Engineering *e:* **Water
 Wastes Eng.**, *e:* **W&WE**

Water Appeals Commission *e:* **WAC**
Water Audit Working Group *e:* **WAWG**
Water-Augmented Air Jet *e:* **WAAJ**
Water-Augmented Airjet *e:* **WAA**
water-augmented jet *e:* **waj**
Water-Augmented Vehicle *e:* **WAVE**
Water Authorities Association *e:* **WAA**
Water Authority *e:* **WA**
Water Authority of Western Australia *e:*
 WAWA
Water Availability and Vulnerability of
 Ecosystems and Social Structures *e:*
 WAVES
Water Ballast *e:* **WB**
water ballast(ing) *e:* **wb**
Water Bank Program *e:* **WBP**
water barge *e:* **YW**
Water Barge *e:* **YWM**
Water basin concept *e:* **WBC**
Water Basin Storage Facility *e:* **WBSF**
Water Bloom *e:* **WB**
Water Board *e:* **WB**
Water Boat *e:* **WB**
Water-Boiler Neutron Source *e:* **WBNS**
Water Boiler Neutron Source Reactor *e:*
 WBNS Reactor
Water Boiler Reactor *e:* **WBR**
water bottle *e:* **WB**
Water Bound Macadam *e:* **WBM**
Water Box *e:* **WB**
Water Canyon Site *e:* **TA-68**
Water Carriage Pack *e:* **WCP**
Water Carrier *e:* **WC**
Water/Cement *e:* **W/C**
Water/Cement Ratio *e:* **W/C Ratio**
Water Centre for the Humid Tropics of
 Latin America and the Caribbean *e:*
 CATHALAC
water check valve *e:* **wcv**
Water Clearance Authority *e:* **WCA**
Water Closet *e:* **W.C.**
Water Colour Society of Ireland *e:* **WCSI**
Water Colo[u]r Spectrometer *e:* **WCS**
Water column *e:* **WC**
Water Companies' Association *e:* **W.C.A.**
Water Compliance System *e:* **WACO**
Water Conditioning Association
 International *e:* **WCAI**
Water Conditioning Foundation *e:* **WCF**
Water Conditioning Research Council *e:*
 WCRC
Water Conservation Order *e:* **WCO**
Water Content *e:* **WC**
Water Control Board *e:* **WCB**
Water Control Module *e:* **WCM**
Water Coolant Line *e:* **WCL**
Water Coolant Loop *e:* **WCL**
Water Coolant Loop System *e:* **WCLS**
Water Cooled *e:* **WC**
Water-Cooled *e:* **WCLD**
Water cooled and moderated energy reactor
 e: **WWER**
water-cooled copper *e:* **wcc**
Water-Cooled Garment *e:* **WCG**
water-cooled reactor *e:* **wcr**
water-cooled rod *e:* **wcr**
water-cooled tube *e:* **WCT**
water cooler *e:* **wcr**
Water Cooler and Drinking Fountain
 Manufacturers Association *e:*
 WCDFMA
Water Cooler Unit *e:* **WCU**
Water Cooling *e:* **W/C**

Water Cooling Unit *e:* **WCU**
water damage *e:* **wd**
water-damage reduction *e:* **wedar**
Water Data Sources Directory *e:* **WDSD**
Water Data Storage and Retrieval System *e:* **WATSTOR**
Water Department *e:* **WD**
water depth *e:* **WD**
Water Detection Response Team *e:* **WDRT**
Water Development Department, Dar es Salaam *e:* **WDD**
Water Dilution Volume *e:* **WDV**
Water Dispenser/Fire Extinguisher *e:* **WD/FE**
Water Disposal System *e:* **WDS**
water district *e:* **wdi**
Water Division *e:* **WD**
Water Education for Teachers *e:* **WET**
Water Electrolysis Rocket *e:* **WER**
Water Electrolysis System *e:* **WES**
Water Energik voor Lario *n:* **WEL**
Water, Energy, and Biogeochemical Budget *e:* **WEBB**
Water Energy-Vegetation *e:* **WEV**
Water Enforcement Division *e:* **WED**
Water Enforcement National Database *e:* **WENDB**
Water Engineer *e:* **WE**
Water Engineering *e:* **WE**
Water Engineering and Development Centre *e:* **WEDC**
Water Engineering Research Laboratory *e:* **WERL**
Water Engineering Trading *e:* **WET**
Water Environment Federation *e:* **WEF**
Water Environment Research Foundation *e:* **WERF**
Water Equipment Wholesalers and Suppliers *e:* **WEWAS**
Water Equipment Wholesalers and Suppliers Association *e:* **WEWSA**
Water Equivalent *e:* **WE**
Water Erosion Prediction Project *e:* **WEPP**
Water Expansion Pumping System *e:* **WEPS**
Water Expansion System *e:* **WES**
Water Expulsion Vesicle *e:* **WEV**
Water-Extended Polyester *e:* **WEP**
Water-extended polymer *e:* **WEP**
Water Extraction Condenser *e:* **WEC**
Water Facts Consortium *e:* **WFC**
Water Filter *e:* **WF**
Water Finish *e:* **WF**
Water-Finished Paper *e:* **WF Paper**
Water Flow Meter *e:* **WFM**
Water for Peace Office *e:* **WPO**
water gauge *e:* **WG**
Water-Glycol *e:* **W-G**
Water Glycol Service Unit *e:* **WGS**
Water Graphite Reactor Experiment *e:* **WGRE**
Water Hammer *e:* **WH**
water hammer eliminator *e:* **whe**
water heater *e:* **wh**
water horsepower *e:* **whp**
Water Immersion Facility *e:* **WIF**
Water in Hole *e:* **WIH**
water-in-oil *e:* **W/O**
water-in-oil (emulsion) *e:* **wo**
Water-Induced Shift *e:* **WIS**
Water-Industry Specifications. *e:* **WIS**

Water Infiltration in Layered Subfreezing Snow *e:* **WILASS**
Water Information Center [of National Water Council] *e:* **WIC**
Water Information System for Enforcement *e:* **WISE**
Water Injection *e:* **WI**
Water Injection Unit *e:* **WIU**
Water-Insoluble Nitrogen *e:* **WIN**
water installed *e:* **wai**
Water Intrusion *e:* **WI**
Water Jacket *e:* **Wat. Jack.**
Water-Jet Cutting *e:* **WJC**
Water Jet Pump *e:* **WJP**
Water Jet Technology Association *e:* **WJTA**
Water Large Scale Integration *e:* **WLSI**
Water Laser Heat Exchange *e:* **WLHE**
water level *e:* **wl**
Water Level Recorder *e:* **WLR**
Water Line Coefficient *e:* **WL Coeff.**
Water Literature *e:* **WATERLIT**
Water Load *e:* **WL**
Water Management Coordinating Committee *e:* **WMCC**
Water Management District *e:* **WMD**
Water Management Division *e:* **WMD**
Water Management Information System *e:* **WAMIS**
Water Management Research Group *e:* **WMRG**
Water Management Research Laboratory *e:* **WMRL**
Water Management Section *e:* **WMS**
Water Management System *e:* **WMS**
Water Market Reform Working Group *e:* **WMRWG**
Water Meter *e:* **WM**
Water Mill *e:* **WM**
Water Moderated Reactor *e:* **WMR**
Water-Moderated Water-Cooled Reactor *e:* **WWER**
Water Network Distribution Analyzer *e:* **WANDA**
Water, Oil and Gas *e:* **WOG**
Water/Oil Contact *e:* **WOC**
Water-Oil Ratio *e:* **WOR**
Water Operations & Maintenance *e:* **WTR OPS**
water or gas *e:* **wog**
Water Packed *e:* **WP**
Water Phase Salt *e:* **WPS**
Water Pillow Cooling *e:* **WPC**
Water Pipe Ground *e:* **WPG**
water planned *e:* **wap**
Water Planning Division *e:* **WPD**
Water Plant *e:* **WTR PLT**
Water plant communications *e:* **WPC**
Water Point *e:* **W**, *e:* **WP**
Water Policy Committee *e:* **WPC**
Water Policy Office *e:* **WPO**
Water Pollution Committee *e:* **W.P.**
Water Pollution Control *e:* **WPC**
Water Pollution Control Act *e:* **WPCA**
Water Pollution Control Administration *e:* **WPCA**
Water Pollution Control Board *e:* **WPCB**
Water Pollution Control Council *e:* **WPCC**
Water Pollution Control Federation *e:* **WPCF**
Water Pollution Control Federation, Denver *e:* **WPCF**

Water Pollution Control Federation. Journal *e:* **J Water Pollut Control Fed**
Water Pollution Control Research *e:* **WPCR**
Water Pollution Council *e:* **WPC**
Water Pollution Laboratory Performance Evaluation Studies *e:* **WP**
Water Pollution Research *e:* **W.P.R.**
Water Pollution Research Laboratory *e:* **WPR**, *e:* **WPRL**
Water Port Liaison Officer *e:* **WPLO**
Water Port Logistics Office[r] *e:* **WPLO**
Water Port of Debarkation *e:* **WPOD**
Water Port of Discharge *e:* **WPOD**
Water Port of Embarkation *e:* **WPOE**
Water Power *e:* **WAPOA**
Water Pressure Switch *e:* **WPS**
Water Produced *e:* **WPRD**
Water Production Rate *e:* **WPR**
Water Products Promotion Council *e:* **WPPC**
Water Programs Office *e:* **WPO**
Water Propeller *e:* **WP**
Water Publications Digest *e:* **WPD**
Water Pump *e:* **WP**
Water Pump Assembly *e:* **WPA**
Water Pump Package *e:* **WPP**
Water Purification *e:* **WP**
Water-Purification Process *e:* **WPP**
Water Purification System *e:* **WPS**
Water Quality Act *e:* **WQA**
Water Quality Analysis Graphics System *e:* **WATQ**
Water Quality Analysis Simulation Program *e:* **WASP**
Water Quality Analysis Simulation Program, Version 3.1 *e:* **WASP**
Water Quality Analysis System *e:* **WQAS**
Water Quality Analysis Unit-Purification *e:* **WQAU-P**
Water Quality and Aquatic Science Division *e:* **WQASD**
Water Quality and Testing *e:* **WQ&T**
Water Quality and Waste Management. *e:* **WQWM**
Water Quality Association *e:* **WQA**
Water Quality Branch *e:* **WQB**
Water Quality Certification *e:* **WQC**
Water Quality Commission *e:* **WQC**
Water Quality Control Board *e:* **WQCB**
Water Quality Control Commission *e:* **WQCC**
Water quality criteria *e:* **WQC**
Water Quality Criteria Documents *e:* **WQCDs**
Water Quality Database *e:* **WQD**
Water Quality Engineering Division *e:* **WQED**
Water Quality Improvement Act *e:* **W.Q.I.A.**
Water Quality Index *e:* **WQI**
Water Quality Instrument *e:* **WQI**
Water Quality Insurance Syndicate *e:* **WQIS**
Water quality laboratory *e:* **WQL**
Water Quality Management *e:* **WQM**
Water Quality Management Plan *e:* **WQMP**
Water Quality Management Project *e:* **WQMP**
Water Quality Measuring System *e:* **WQMS**
Water Quality Modeling *e:* **WQM4**

Water Quality Modeling Region 4 *e:* **WQM4**

Water Quality Modeling System for the Great Lakes *e:* **WQMSGL**

Water quality modification *e:* **WQM**

Water Quality Monitor[ing] *e:* **WQM**

Water Quality Monitoring Network *e:* **WQMN**

Water Quality Office [of Environmental Protection Agency] *e:* **WQO**

Water Quality Parameter[s] *e:* **WQP**

Water Quality Project *e:* **WQP**

Water Quality Research Council *e:* **WQRC**

Water Quality Standard *e:* **WQS**

Water Quantity Measuring Device *e:* **WQMD**

Water Quench *e:* **WQ**

Water Quench Test *e:* **WQT**

water-quenched *e:* **W.Q.**

Water Quenching *e:* **WQ**

Water-Rail *e:* **WR**

Water Reactor Safety *e:* **WRS**

Water Reactor Safety Information Meeting *e:* **WRSM**

Water reactor safety research *e:* **WRSR**

Water reactors division *e:* **WRD**

Water Recirculation System *e:* **WRS**

Water Recovery and Management *e:* **WRM**

Water Reducing Admixture *e:* **WRA**

Water Relief Valve *e:* **WRV**

Water removal and storage system *e:* **WRSS**

Water Removal Mechanism *e:* **WRM**

water repellency *e:* **wp**

Water Repellency *e:* **WR**

water repellent *e:* **wp**

Water Repellent *e:* **WR**

Water Research *e:* **WR**

Water Research Association *e:* **WRA**

Water Research Association Distribution Analog[ue] Center (or Centre) *e:* **WRADAC**

Water Research Center *e:* **WRC**

Water Research Centre. Notes on Water Research *e:* **NWREDP**

Water Research Centre Report *e:* **WRC Report**

Water Research Commission *e:* **WRC**

Water Research Council *e:* **WRC**

Water Reserve *e:* **WR**

water resistant *e:* **water res**, *e:* **w/r**

Water Resource Division *e:* **WRD**

Water Resource Operations *e:* **WRO**

Water Resource Planning *e:* **WPR**

Water Resources *e:* **WR**, *e:* **WRS**

Water Resources Abstracts *e:* **WRA**

Water Resources and Environmental Monitoring Consortium *e:* **WREMC**

Water Resources Assessment Program *e:* **WRAP**

Water Resources Board *e:* **WRB**

Water resources bulletin *e:* **Water resour. bull.**

Water Resources Center *e:* **WRC**

Water Resources Center Archive *e:* **WRCA**

Water Resources Commission *e:* **WRC**

Water Resources Congress *e:* **WRC**

Water Resources Control Board *e:* **WRCB**

Water Resources Council *e:* **WRC**

Water Resources Department *e:* **WRD**

Water Resources Development Act *e:* **WRDA**

Water Resources Development Department *e:* **WRDD**

Water Resources Division *e:* **WRD**

Water Resources Division, Manitoba Department of Natural Resources, Winnipeg, Manitoba *e:* **MWWR**

Water Resources Document Reference Centre *e:* **WATDOC**

Water Resources Document Reference System *e:* **WATDOC**

Water Resources Forecasting System *e:* **WARFS**

Water Resources Information *e:* **WRI**

Water Resources Information System *e:* **WARIS**

Water Resources Investigation *e:* **WRI**

Water Resources Investigation Report *e:* **WRIR**

Water Resources Management Action Group *e:* **WRMAG**

Water Resources Management Committee *e:* **WRMC**

Water Resources Planning *e:* **WRO**, *e:* **WRP**

Water Resources Planning Act *e:* **WRPA**

Water Resources Planning Commission *e:* **WRPC**

[Water Resources] Planning Committee *e:* **PC**

Water Resources Publication *e:* **WRP**

Water Resources Publications *e:* **WRO**

Water Resources Research *e:* **Water Resour. Res.**

Water Resources Research Act *e:* **WRRA**

Water Resources Research Center *e:* **WRRC**

Water Resources Research Institute *e:* **WRRI**

Water Resources Research Unit *e:* **WRRU**

Water Resources Scientific Information Center *e:* **WARSIC**, *e:* **WRSIC**

water-retention coefficient *e:* **wrc**

Water Rights Office [Bureau of Indian Affairs] *e:* **WRO**

Water Safety *e:* **WS**

Water Safety Instructor *e:* **WSI**

Water Safety Instructor Trainer *e:* **WSIT**

Water Saline Extract *e:* **WSE**

Water Saturation Deficit *e:* **WSD**

Water Science and Technology Board *e:* **WSTB**

Water Separation Index, Modified *e:* **WSIM**

Water Separometer Index *e:* **WSI**

Water Separometer Index, Modified *e:* **WSIM**

Water Servicer *e:* **WS**

Water Servicer Operator *e:* **WSO**

Water Services *e:* **Water Serv.**

Water Servicing Unit *e:* **WSU**

water-side *e:* **ws**

Water Softener and Filter Institute *e:* **WSFI**, *e:* **WSFl**

Water Solenoid Valve *e:* **WSV**

Water Solid *e:* **WS**

Water Solidity Index *e:* **WS**

water soluble *e:* **WS**

water soluble adjuvant *e:* **WSA**

water-soluble base *e:* **wsb**

Water-Soluble Chelating Polymer/ultrafiltration *e:* **WSCP**

Water-Soluble Fraction *e:* **WSF**

Water-Soluble Fractions *e:* **WSFs**

Water Soluble Gum Association *e:* **WSGA**

Water-Soluble Lubricant *e:* **WSL**

Water Space Amenity Commission *e:* **WSAC**

Water Space Amenity Committee *e:* **WSAC**

Water Spectrum *e:* **WASP**

Water Spray Boiler *e:* **WSB**

Water Sterilization Powder *e:* **WSP**

Water Supply *e:* **WS**, *e:* **WSP**, *e:* **WSup**

Water Supply and Sanitation Collaborative Council *e:* **WSSCC**

Water Supply and Sewage Authority, Chittagong *e:* **WASACH**

Water Supply Detachment *e:* **W Sup Det**

Water Supply Evaluation Studies Laboratory Performance *e:* **WS**

Water Supply Improvement Association *e:* **WSIA**

Water-Supply Paper *e:* **WSP**

water supply point *e:* **wsp**

Water Supply Research Laboratory *e:* **WSRL**

Water Supply Simulation Model *e:* **WSSM**

Water Supply Tank *e:* **WST**

Water Supply Violation assessment graphics System *e:* **WSVS**

water-suppression technique *e:* **WST**

Water Surface *e:* **WS**

Water Surface Craft *e:* **S**

Water Surface Profile *e:* **WSPRO**

Water Survey Canada Division *e:* **WSCD**

Water Survey of Canada *e:* **WSC**

Water System *e:* **WTR SYS**

Water Systems Council *e:* **WSC**

Water Table *e:* **WT**

Water Table Depth *e:* **WTD**

Water Tank *e:* **W.T.**, *e:* **WTK**

Water Tank Vessel *e:* **WTV**

water technologist *e:* **watertec**

Water Technologist *e:* **WT**

water technology *e:* **watertec**

Water Technology *e:* **WT**

Water Technology Committee *e:* **WTC**

Water Tender *e:* **WT**

Water Tender Construction Battalion *e:* **WTCB**

Water Terminal Clearance Authority *e:* **WTCA**

Water Terminal Logistic Office *e:* **WTLO**

Water Thermometer *e:* **WT**

Water Tight *e:* **WT**

Water to Energy *e:* **WTE**

Water Tower *e:* **WT**

Water, Toxics, and Pesticides Staff *e:* **WTPS**

Water, Toxics & Pesticides Staff *e:* **WTPF**

Water Traffic Officer *e:* **WTO**

Water Transmission and Communications *e:* **WTC**

Water Transport Association *e:* **WTA**

Water Transport Committee *e:* **WTC**

Water Transportation *e:* **WT**

Water Transportation and Dock, Wharf, Harbour Service *e:* **W.T.D.W.H.S.**

Water treatment *e:* **WT**

Water Treatment Facility *e:* **WTF**

Water Treatment Research Division *e:* **WTRD**

Water Tube *e:* **WT**

Water Tube and Boilermakers Association
  e: **WTBA**
Water-Tube Auxiliary Boiler[s] e:
  WTAauxB
Water Tube Boiler[s] e: **WTB**
water-tube domestic boiler[s] e: **wtdb**
Water TunneI e: **WT**
Water Turbine, Closed-Coupled e: **WTCC**
Water Turbine, Direct e: **WTD**
Water Use Efficiency e: **WUE**
Water use information system e: **WUIS**
Water Users Association e: **WUA**
Water Users Group e: **WUG**
Water Utility Department e: **WUD**
Water Vapor e: **WV**
Water Vapor Content e: **W**
water-vapor electrolysis module e: **wvem**
water vapor flux e: **WVF**
Water Vapor Intensive Observing Period
  e: **WVIOP**
Water vapor nitrogen e: **WVN**
water vapor pressure e: **e**
water vapor profiling e: **WVP**
Water Vapor radiometers e: **WVR**
water vapor regained e: **WVR**
water vapor transfer e: **wvt**
Water Vapour Electrolysis e: **WVE**
Water Vapour Permeability e: **WVP**
Water Vapour Radiometer e: **WVR**
Water Vapo[u]r Sensor e: **WVP**
Water Vapour Sensor e: **WVS**
Water Vapo[u]r Transfer e: **WVT**
Water Vapour Transmission e: **WVT**
Water Vapour Transmission Rate e:
  WVTR
water wall peripheral e: **wwp**
water wall side skegs e: **Wwss**
Water Waste e: **WW**
Water/Waste Management System e:
  W[/]WMS
Water Waste Preventer e: **WWP**
Water Water Reactor e: **WWR**
Water Wave e: **WW**
Water-White e: **WW**
Waterbed Manufacturers (or
  Manufacturing) Association e: **WMA**
Waterbody System e: **WBS**
Waterboiler e: **WB**
Waterborne e: **WB**
Waterborne Commerce of the United States
  e: **WCUS**
Waterborne Intrusion Detection System e:
  WIDS
waterborne logistical craft e: **wablics**
waterborne logistics craft e: **wblc**
Waterborne Special Communications e:
  WSC
Waterbury State Technical Institute e:
  WSTI
watercooler e: **wcl**
Watered Ground e: **WG**
Waterfall e: **FLL**
waterfall[s] e: **fall[s]**
Waterford and Tranmore Railway e: **WTR**
Waterford Education Association e: **WEA**
Waterford Institute of Technology e: **WIT**
Waterford & Tramore e: **W.&T.**
waterfront e: **vvft**, e: **wfnt**, e: **wtf**
Waterfront Commission of New York
  Harbor e: **WCNYH**
waterfront dock facilities e: **wfd**
Waterfront Dock Facility e: **WDF**
Waterfront Guard Association e: **WGA**

Watergate Special Prosecution Force e:
  WSPF
Waterheaters Manufacturers Association
  e: **WMA**
waterholding capacity e: **WHC**
Waterhouse-Friderichsen-Syndrom d:
  WFS
Waterkampioen r: **WAE**
Waterless Electric Biological Toilet. e:
  WEB toilet
Waterless Electrical Data Generating
  Effortless e: **WEDGE**
Waterless Printing Association e: **WPA**
waterline e: **wl**
waterline coefficient e: **wl coef**
Waterline-to-Hatchcoaming e: **WLTOHC**
Waterliterature. Database, South African
  Water Information Centre. e:
  WATERLIT
waterload test e: **WL test**
Waterloo e: **W**
Waterloo Analysis N Design e: **WATAND**
Waterloo and City Railway e: **WCR**
Waterloo Concordance e: **WATCON**
Waterloo FORTRAN (Formula Translation)
  e: **WATFOR**
Waterloo Interactive Direct Job Entry
  Terminal e: **WIDJET**
Waterloo Public Library, Quebec e: **QW**
Waterloo Railroad Company e: **WLO**
Waterloo Research Institute e: **WRI**
Waterloo Resources, Inc. e: **WAL**
Waterloo Systems Language. e: **WSL**
Waterman Marine e: **WACO**
Waterman on Set-Off e: **Wat. Set-Off**
Waterman on the Law of Trespass e: **Wat.
  Tres.**
Waterman Steamship Line e: **W**
Waterman's Justices Manual e: **Wat. Just.**
Waterman's United States Court of Claims
  e: **U.S. Crim. Dig.**
Watermark e: **WM**, e: **Wmk**
Watermark Association of Artisans e:
  WAA
Watermayer's Reports, Supreme Court e:
  W.
Watermelon Growers and Distributors
  Association e: **WGDA**
Watermen and Lightermen's Protective
  Society e: **WLPS**
Watermen's Protective Society e: **WPS**
Watermen's Trade Society e: **WTS**
Watermeyer's Cape of Good Hope Reports
  [S. Africa] e: **Wat. C.G.H.**
Watermeyer's Cape of Good Hope Reports
  (S. Africa) e: **Watermeyer.**
Watermeyer's Cape Of Good Hope Supreme
  Court Reports e: **W**
waterplane coefficient e: **wl**
waterproof e: **W.P.**
Waterproof e: **WTPRF**, e: **WTRPF**, e:
  WTRPR, e: **WTRPRF**
Waterproof Fan-Cooled e: **WPFC**
Waterproof Garment Workers' Trade Union
  e: **W.G.W.T.U.**
waterproof packing e: **w.p.p.**
Waterproof Paper Manufacturers'
  Association e: **WPMA**
waterproof paper packing e: **wpp**
Waterproof Shroud e: **WPS**
Waterproofed e: **wp**
waterproof(ed) e: **wt**
Waterproofing e: **wp**, e: **wpfg**

waterproofing e: **wpg**, e: **wt**
Waters and Rogers e: **Van**
Waters Computing Center e: **WCC**
Watershed e: **WS**
Watershed Assessment Procedure e: **WAP**
Watershed Committee of the Ozarks e:
  WCO
Watershed Data Management System e:
  WDMS
Watershed Foundation e: **WF**
Watershed Information System e: **WIS**
Watershed Integrated Research Program e:
  WIRP
watershed management e: **WS M**
Watershed Management Council e: **WMC**
Watershed Management Program e: **WMD**
Watershed Model e: **WSM**
Watershed Oriented Digital Terrain Model
  e: **WODITEM**
Watershed Protection Approach e: **WPA**
Watershed Protection Initiative e: **WPI**
Watershed Research Unit e: **WRU**
Watershed Restoration Plan e: **WRP**
Waterside Mall e: **WSM**
Waterside Security System e: **WSS**
Waterside Workers' Federation of Australia
  e: **WWF**, e: **WWFA**
waterspout e: **wtspt**
watertight e: **WT**
Watertight e: **WTRTT**
Watertight Bulkhead e: **WTB**
watertight bulkhead e: **WTBhd**
watertight door e: **wtd**
watertight floor e: **WTFI**
Watertight Hatch e: **WTH**
Watertight Manhole e: **WTMH**
watertight quick-acting door e: **wtqad**
Watertight Quick Action e: **WTQA**
Watertight Quick Action Door e: **WTQAD**
watertight tank e: **WTk**
watertime e: **W.T.**
Waterton-Glacier International Peace Park
  e: **WGIPP**
Waterton-Glacier International Peace Park
  on the Alberta-Montana border or
  Waterton Lakes National Park in the same
  area e: **Waterton**
Watertown Arsenal e: **WA**
Watertown Arsenal Laboratory e: **WAL**
Watertown Arsenal Medical Laboratory e:
  WAML
Watertown Operations Office e: **WTO**
Watertransportmaatschappij Rijn-
  Kennemerland n: **WRK**
Watervliet Arsenal e: **WVA**, e: **WVT**
Waterways Bulk Transportation Council e:
  WBTC
Waterways Development, Transport Canada
  Montreal, Quebec e: **QMTR**
Waterways Experiment Station Terrain-
  Analyzer Radar e: **WESTAR**
Waterways Experimental Station e: **WES**
Waterways Freight Bureau e: **WFB**, e:
  WWB
Waterwheel e: **WWHL**
waterworks e: **ww**
Waterworks and water companies e: **Wat.
  wks.**
Waterworks Department e: **WD**
Watson's Medical Jurisprudence e: **Wats.
  Med. Clur.**
Waves in Space Plasma e: **WISP**

Waves in Space Plasma-High Frequency *e:* **WISP-HF**

Waves in Space Plasma-Orbital Maneuvering Vehcle *e:* **WISP-OMV**

Wayne George Encoder Test Set *e:* **WGETS**

Wayne State University Medical Library *e:* **WSUML**

Wayne State University School of Medicine *e:* **WSUSM**

Wayne [University] Remote Access Processor *e:* **WRAP**

Weapons Aerospace Ground Equipment *e:* **WAGE**

Weapons Effect Signature Simulator *e:* **WESS**

Weapons Effectiveness and System Test Environment *e:* **WESTE**

Weather *e:* **W**, *e:* **Wea**, *e:* **Wthr**, *e:* **W/W**

Weather[1] *e:* **WX**

Weather Aircraft Equipped with Meteorological Gear *e:* **W**

Weather Almanac *e:* **WA**, *e:* **WAL**

Weather Amateur Radio Network *e:* **WARN**

Weather Analysis Computer System *e:* **WACS**

Weather and Boil-Proof *e:* **WBP**

Weather and Fixed Map Unit *e:* **WFMU**

Weather and Radar Processor *e:* **WARP**

Weather and Radar Processor systems *e:* **WARP**

Weather Atlas of the United States *e:* **WA**

Weather-Auto Relay Network *e:* **WARN**

Weather Band *e:* **WB**

Weather Base *e:* **WB**

Weather Bomber *e:* **WB**

Weather, Briefing, Advisory, and Warning System *e:* **WBAWS**

weather briefing television *e:* **wbtv**

weather buoy rocket *e:* **webrock**

Weather Bureau *e:* **WB**

Weather Bureau, Air Force and Navy *e:* **WBAN**

Weather Bureau Airport Station *e:* **WBAS**

Weather Bureau Area Forecast Center *e:* **WBAFC**

Weather Bureau Central Office *e:* **WBC**

Weather Bureau Communications Center *e:* **WBC Center**

Weather Bureau Hurricane Forecast Office *e:* **WBHO**

Weather Bureau Meteorological Observation Station *e:* **WBMO**

Weather Bureau/National Weather Records Center *e:* **WB/NWRC**

Weather Bureau Radar Remote System *e:* **WBRR**, *e:* **WBRR System**

Weather Bureau radio thoedolite *e:* **WBRT**

Weather Bureau, Regional Headquarters *e:* **WBRH**

Weather Bureau Regional Office *e:* **WBRO**

Weather Bureau Signal Station *e:* **WB Sig Sta**

Weather Bureau Synoptic and Aviation Reporting Station *e:* **WBSA**

Weather Bureau Technical Memoranda *e:* **WBTM**

Weather Card Data *e:* **WCD**

Weather Center *e:* **WECEN**

Weather Center (or Centre) *e:* **WC**

Weather Communications Processor *e:* **WCP**

Weather Condition *e:* **WC**

Weather Control Research Association *e:* **WCRA**

Weather Current Operations *e:* **WECO**

weather-damage reduction *e:* **wedar**

Weather Decision Aid *e:* **WDA**

Weather Deck *e:* **WDk**

Weather Detector *e:* **WX Detc.**

Weather Division *e:* **WD**

Weather Editing Section *e:* **WES**

Weather Education and Awareness Project *e:* **WEAP**

Weather Facsimile Experiment [Environmental Science Services Administration] *e:* **WEFAX**

Weather Flight *e:* **WF**

Weather Forecast *e:* **WF**, *e:* **WXFCST**

Weather Forecast Office *e:* **WFO**

Weather Forecasting Office Advanced *e:* **FOA**

Weather Graphics System *e:* **WGS**

Weather Group *e:* **WGp**

Weather Half-Working Day *e:* **WHWD**

Weather Image Processing System *e:* **WIPS**

Weather Impact Division Aids *e:* **WIDA**

weather-impacted airspace *e:* **WIA**

Weather Information Branch *e:* **WIB**

weather information display *e:* **WIND**

Weather Information Management System *e:* **WIMS**

Weather Information Network and Display *e:* **WIND**

Weather Information Network and Display System *e:* **WINDS**

Weather Information Network Display System *e:* **WINDS**

Weather Information Network Service *e:* **WINS**

Weather Information Service *e:* **WIS**

Weather Information System *e:* **WIS**

Weather Information Technologies, Inc. *e:* **WITI**

Weather Information Telemetering System *e:* **WITS**

Weather Information Telemetry System *e:* **WITS**

Weather Intelligence Unit *e:* **WIU**

Weather Intercept Control Unit *e:* **WICU**

Weather Information Reporting and Display System *e:* **WIRDS**

Weather Map *e:* **WM**

Weather Mapping System *e:* **WMS**

Weather Message *e:* **WX**

Weather Message Switching Center *e:* **WMSC**

Weather Message Switching Center Replacement *e:* **WMSCR**

Weather Message Switching System *e:* **WMSS**

Weather Mode *e:* **W**

Weather Modification Advisory Board *e:* **WMAB**

Weather Modification Program *e:* **WMP**

Weather Modification Program Office *e:* **WMPO**

Weather-Modification Statistical Research Group *e:* **WMSRG**

Weather Modificiation Association *e:* **WMA**

Weather Network Duty Officer *e:* **WNDO**

Weather Network Management Center *e:* **WNMC**

Weather Non-Working Day[s] *e:* **WNWD**

Weather Observation and Forecasting Control System *e:* **WEARCONS**

Weather Observation Master Plan *e:* **WMOP**

Weather Observation Report *e:* **WXOBS**

Weather Observation Site Building *e:* **WOSB**

Weather Observations Through Ambient Noise *e:* **WOTAN**

Weather Observing Systems Committee *e:* **WOS**

Weather Office in Space Evaluation *e:* **WOSE**

weather outline contour generator *e:* **wocg**

Weather over Target *e:* **WOT**

Weather Permitting *e:* **W.P.**

Weather Permitting Clause *e:* **W.P.Cl.**

Weather Permitting Day *e:* **w.p.d.**

Weather-Proof Company *e:* **WEPCO**

Weather Radar *e:* **WR**

weather radar *e:* **WXR**

Weather Radar Identification of Severe Thunderstorms *e:* **WRIST**

Weather Radar Set *e:* **WRS**

Weather Radar System *e:* **WRS**

Weather radar that is never written out *e:* **GMD-1**

Weather Radio Specific Area Message Encoder *e:* **WRSAME**

weather reconnaissance *e:* **W**

Weather Reconnaissance *e:* **WR**

Weather Reconnaissance Group *e:* **WRG**

Weather Reconnaissance Squadron *e:* **WRS**, *e:* **WRSq**

Weather Reconnaissance Wing *e:* **WRW**, *e:* **WRWg**

Weather Record Processing Center[s] *e:* **WRPC**

Weather Records Processing Center(s) *e:* **WRPC**

Weather Relay Broadcast Center *e:* **WRBC**

Weather Relay Broadcast System *e:* **WRBC**

Weather Relay Center *e:* **WRC**, *e:* **WRC**

Weather Report *e:* **WR**

weather report *e:* **wx**

Weather Research and Forecast *e:* **WRF**

Weather Research Facility *e:* **WEARESFAC**

Weather Research Program *e:* **WRP**

Weather Resistant *e:* **WR**

Weather Review *e:* **W**

Weather Satellite Tracking Parameter Generator *e:* **WEATHER**

weather scenario test tape *e:* **WSTT**

Weather Seal *e:* **WS**, *e:* **WSL**

Weather Search Radar *e:* **WSR**

Weather Service *e:* **WS**

Weather Service Airport Station *e:* **WSAS**

Weather Service Command *e:* **WEASERVCOMM**

Weather Service Communications Center *e:* **WSCC**

Weather Service Cooperating Agencies *e:* **WSCA**

Weather Service Evaluation Officer *e:* **WSEO**

Weather Service Forecast *e:* **WSFO**

Weather Service Forecast Office *e:* **WSFO**

Weather Service Headquarters *e:* **WSH**
Weather Service Meteorological
  Observations *e:* **WSMO**
Weather Service Meteorological
  Observatory *e:* **WSMO**
Weather Service Meteorological Office *e:*
  WSMO
Weather Service Office *e:* **WSO**
Weather Service Office for Agriculture *e:*
  WSO[AG]
Weather Service Office for Aviation *e:*
  WSO[AV]
Weather Service Office for Fire-Weather
  e: **WSO[FW]**
Weather Service Radar *e:* **WSR**
Weather Service Regional Headquarters *e:*
  WSRH
Weather Service Specialist *e:* **WSS**
Weather Service Support Facility *e:* **WSSF**
Weather Services International Corp. *e:*
  WSI
Weather Ship *e:* **WS**
Weather Situation Report *e:* **WXSITREP**
Weather Squadron *e:* **WS,** *e:* **WSq**
Weather Station *e:* **WS,** *e:* **WtStn,** *e:*
  WXStn
Weather Stripping *e:* **WS**
Weather Support Branch *e:* **WSB**
Weather Support for AFHWC *e:*
  WSAFHWC
Weather Support Force *e:* **WSF**
Weather Support Unit *e:* **WSU**
Weather Surveillance Radar *e:* **WSR**
Weather Surveillance Radar-88 Dopplers
  e: **WSR-88D**
Weather Sytems Interface *e:* **WX**
Weather Task Force *e:* **WETAF**
Weather Team *e:* **WETM**
Weather Team/Tactical Air Control Center
  e: **WETEM/TACC**
Weather Time Restraint *e:* **WTR**
Weather Underground Organization *e:*
  WU, *e:* **WUO**
Weather Wing *e:* **WW,** *e:* **WWg**
Weather Wing Pamphlet *e:* **WWP**
Weather Working Day *e:* **WWD**
weather working day(s) *e:* **W.W.**
Weather Working Day[s] *e:* **WW Day[s]**
weather working day(s) *e:* **W.W.D.S.**
Weather Working Days, Sunday and
  Holidays Excepted *e:* **WWDs S & HEx**
weather working days Sundays and holidays
  excluded *e:* **wwdShex**
weather working days, Sundays and
  Holidays included *e:* **W.W.D.S.H.INC.**
weather working days, Sundays & Holidays
  excepted *e:* **W.W.D.S.H.EX.**
Weather Working Days Sundays &
  Holidays Excluded *e:* **W.W.D.S.H.E.X.**
Weatherby Magnum *e:* **WM**
Weatherford College *e:* **WC**
Weatherford College, Weatherford *e:*
  TxWeaC
Weatherford International, Incorporated *e:*
  WII
Weatherford, Mineral Wells and
  Northwestern Railway Company *e:*
  WMWN
Weatherford, Mineral Wells &
  Northwestern *e:* **W M W & NW**
Weatherhead Company *e:* **WHD**
Weatherization *e:* **WX**
weatherization assistance program *e:* **WAP**

Weatherproof *e:* **wp,** *e:* **WTHPRF**
Weatherstrip Research Institute *e:* **WRI**
weathertight *e:* **weat**
Web-Integrated Software metrics
  Environment *e:* **WISE**
Webster's Geographical Dictionary *e:*
  WGD
Weddell Ice Dynamics Experiment *e:*
  WIDE
Weddell Sea Bottom Water *e:* **WSBW**
Weddell Sea Deep Water *e:* **WSDW**
Weddell Sea Project *e:* **WWSP**
Wedge Absorption Remote Sensor *e:*
  WARS
Weekly publication of American
  Geophysical Union *e:* **Eos**
Weekly Web Review in Emergency
  Medicine *e:* **WWREM**
Weeky Weather and Crop Bulletin *e:*
  WWCB
Wegeordnung *d:* **WO**
Wehrbeschwerdeordnung *d:* **WBG**
Wehrmedizinalamt *d:* **WMA**
Wehrmedizinisches Informationssystem *d:*
  WMedInfoSys
Wei Sheng Wu Hsueh Pao [Acta
  Microbiologica Sinica] *ch:* **Wei Sheng
  Wu Hsueh Pao**
Weight before Departure from Mars Orbit
  e: **WDMO**
Weight Hourly Space Velocity *e:* **WHSV**
Weightless Environment Training System
  e: **WETS**
Weightman's Medico-Legal Gazette *e:*
  Weight. Med. Leg. Gaz.
Weiter- und Fortbildungszentrum für
  medizinisches Personal *e:* **WFZ**
Weiterbildungszentrum für
  Gesundheitsberufe *d:* **WE'G**
Welder Wildlife Foundation *e:* **WWF**
Welfare and Health Council *e:* **W&HC**
Welfare for Animals in the Forces Society
  e: **WAIFS**
Well-Spaced Stems per Hectare *e:* **WSSPA**
Wellcome Historical Medical Library *e:*
  WHML
Wellcome Historical Medical Library,
  London, United Kingdom *e:* **UkLW**
Wellcome Institute of the History of
  Medicine *e:* **WIHM**
Wellenpferdestärke *d:* **WPS**
Wellenpferdestärken *d:* **dhp**
Wellhead Protection Area *e:* **WHPA**
Wellhead Protection [Program] *e:* **WHP**
Wellhead Protection Program *e:* **WHPP**
Wellwood's Abridgment of Sea Laws *e:*
  Wellw. Abr.
Welsh Association of Health Authorities
  and Trusts *e:* **WAHAT**
Welsh Board of Health *e:* **W.B.H.**
Welsh Health Common Services Agency
  e: **WHCSA**
Welsh Health Common Services Authority
  e: **WHCSA**
Welsh Health Technical Services
  Organization *e:* **WHTSO**
Welsh Homing Pigeon Union *e:* **WHPU**
Welsh Hospital and Health Services
  Association *e:* **WH&HSA**
Welsh National Board for nursing,
  midwifery and health visiting *e:* **WNB**
Welsh National Water Development
  Authority *e:* **WNWDA**

Welsh Water Authority *e:* **WWA**
Welt-Tier-Organisation *d:* **WTO**
Welt-Tierärztegesellschaft *d:* **WTG**
Welt-Wetter-Organisation *d:* **WWO**
Weltgesellschaft für Geschichte der
  Veterinärmedizin *d:* **WGGVM**
Weltgesundheitsorganisation *d:* **WGO**
Weltnaturfonds *d:* **WWF**
Weltorganisation für Meteorologie *d:*
  WMO, *d:* **WOM**
Weltraumfahrt und Raketentechnik *d:* **WR**
Welttierschutzbund *d:* **WTB**
Weltvereinigung für Tierproduktion *d:*
  WVT
Weltweite Klimabulletins *d:* **CLIMAT**
Weltwetterwacht *d:* **WWW**
Weltzentrum für Niederschlagsklimatologie
  d: **GPCC,** *d:* **WZN**
Wereld-Meteorologische Organisatie *n:*
  WMO
Werkgemeenschap van Gereformeerde
  Jongeren *n:* **WGJ**
Werkstattorientierte Programmierung *d:*
  WOP
Werkstofflabor (Spacelab D-1 Exp.) *d:*
  WL
Wesley Medical Center, Wichita *e:*
  KViWM
Wessex Regional Library and Information
  Service. Medical library *e:* **WRLIS**
West Africa Regional Remote Sensing
  Management Committee *e:*
  WARMCOM
West African College of Surgeons *e:*
  WACS
West African Council for Medical Research
  e: **WACMR**
West African Frontier Force *e:* **W.A.F.F.**
West African Health Community *e:*
  WAHC
West African Health Organization *e:*
  WAHO
West African Health Secretariat *e:* **WAHS**
West African Journal of Medicine *e:* **West
  Afr J Med**
West African Postgraduate Medical College
  e: **WAPMC**
200 West Area Engineering and
  Environmental Distributive Processing
  System *e:* **TWEED**
West Arm Watershed Alliance *e:* **WAWA**
West Georgia College *e:* **WGC**
West Georgia College, Carrollton *e:*
  GCarrWG
West Indian Medical Journal *e:* **West
  Indian Med J**
West Indian Medical Journal. University of
  the West Indies, Mona, Jamaica *e:* **West
  Indian Med. J.**
West Indies Sea Island Cotton Association
  e: **WISICA**
West Siberia Research Geological Oil
  Institute *e:* **WSRGOI**
West Texas Geological Society *e:* **WTGS**
West Virginia Department of Health &
  Human Resources *e:* **WVDHHR**
West Virginia Geological and Economic
  Survey *e:* **WVGES**
West Virginia Medical Journal *e:* **W V
  Med J**
West Virginia Society of Osteopathic
  Medicine *e:* **WVSOM**

West Virginia State Medical Association e: **WVSMA**

West Virginia Veterinary Medical Association e: **WVVMA**

West Virginia Water Resources Division e: **WVAWRD**

West Wales Naturalists Trust e: **WWNT**

West Wales Trust for Nature Conservation e: **WWTNC**

Westchester Academy of Medicine, Purchase e: **NPurW**

Westchester Medical Center, Valhalla e: **NValhM**

Westdeutsche Gesellschaft für Raketentechnik und Raumfahrt e.V. d: **WGRR**

Westdeutscher Medizinischer Fakultätentag e: **WMFT**

Westermann Monatshefte. Georg Westermann Verlag. Braunschweig d: **Westermann Mon.heft.**

West[ern] Antarctic Ice Sheet [project] e: **WAIS**

Western Association of Fish and Wildlife Agencies e: **WAFWA**

Western Association of the Fish and Wildlife Association e: **WAFWA**

Western Atlantic Ocean Experiment e: **WATOX**

Western Atmospheric Deposition Task Force e: **WADTF**

Western Australia Wildlife Research Centre e: **West Aust Wildl Res Cent**

Western Australian Centre for Remote and Rural Medicine e: **WACRRM**

Western Australian Department of Fisheries and Wildlife e: **West Aust Dep Fish Wildl**

Western Australian Environment Protection Authority e: **WAEPA**

Western Australian Natural Gas Proprietary Ltd. e: **WANG**

Western Australian Naturalist e: **WA Nat**, e: **WA Nat[uralist]**

Western Australian Naturalists' Club e: **WANC**

Western Australian Remote Sensing Industry Development and Education Centre e: **WARSIDEC**

Western Australian Water Resources Council e: **WAWRC**

Western Beaufort Sea Ecological Cruise e: **WEBSEC**

Western Biological Laboratories e: **WBL**

Western Canada Wilderness Committee e: **WCWC**

Western Canadian Universities Marine Biological Society e: **WCUMBS**

Western College of Veterinary Medicine e: **WCVM**

Western Division of the Canadian Association of Geographers e: **WDCAG**

Western Earth Sciences Technologies e: **WEST**

Western Equatorial Pacific Ocean Circulation Study e: **WEPOCS**

Western Equatorial Pacific Ocean Climate Studies e: **WEPOCS**

Western European Geological Surveys e: **WEGS**

Western Frontier Force e: **WFF**

Western Geophysical Co., Houston e: **TxHWG**

Western Health Plans, Inc. e: **WHP**

Western Indian Ocean Directory of Marine Science Institutions and Scientists e: **WIODIR**

Western Indian Ocean Marine Applications Project e: **WIOMAP**

Western Indian Ocean Marine Science Association e: **WIOMSA**

Western Indian Ocean Waters e: **WINDOW**

Western Industrial Health Conference e: **WIHC**

Western Industrial Medical Association e: **WIMA**

Western Institute for Health Studies e: **WIHS**

Western Journal of Medicine e: **West J Med**, e: **WJM**

Western Journal of Medicine (electronic) e: **eWJM**

Western Mediterranean Deep Water e: **WMDW**

Western Mental Health Institute, Boliver e: **TBolMH**

Western Missouri Mental Health Center, Kansas City e: **MoKW**

Western Natural Gas Company e: **WNGC**

Western North Pacific Central Water e: **WNPCW**

Western NSW Public Health Unit e: **WN PHU**

Western Ocean Meeting Point e: **WESTOMP**

Western Pacific Air-Sea Interaction Study e: **WPASI**

Western Pacific (ocean or railroad) e: **West Pac**

Western Regional Environmental Education Council e: **WREEC**

Western Sea Frontier e: **WESSEAFRON**, e: **WESTSEAFRON**, e: **WSF**

Western Sector Public Health Unit e: **WS PHU**

Western Society of Naturalists e: **WSN**

Western Society of Oral and Maxillofacial Surgeons e: **WSOMS**

Western South Pacific Central Water e: **WSPCW**

Western Space and Missile Center e: **WSMC**

Western Tasmanian Wilderness National Parks World Heritage Area e: **TWHA**

Western Tropical Pacific Ocean e: **WTPO**

Western Union Space Communications, Incorporated e: **WUSCI**

Western Water and Power Symposium e: **WWPS**

Western·Natural Gas Co., Houston e: **TxHWN**

Westinghouse Aerospace Electrical Division e: **WAED**

Westinghouse Defense and Space Center, Baltimore e: **MdBWe**

Westinghouse Environmental Management Company of Ohio e: **WEMCO**

Westinghouse Pittsburgh Environmental e: **WPE**

Westwater Research Center e: **WRC**

Westworld Community Healthcare, Incorporated e: **WCHI**

Wet Environment Trainer e: **WET**

Wet op de Inkwartieringen n: **Winkw**

Wet Verontreiniging Oppervlaktewater n: **WVO**

Wetterberatungseinheit d: **WeBe**

Wetter d: **W**, d: **Wet**, d: **Wett.**

Wetter und Leben d: **Wetter Leben**

Wetteramt d: **WA**

Wetterauer Jugendclub d: **WJC**

Wetterbeobachtungssatellit d: **WBS**

Wetterbeobachtungsschiff d: **WBS**

Wetterberatung der Bundeswehr d: **WeBBw**

Wetterberatungskanal d: **WeBEK**

Wetterbild-Empfangsstation d: **WES**

Wetterdaten- und Informations-Anzeige-System d: **WIAS**

Wetterdienst d: **WD**, d: **WeDst**, d: **Wett.-D.**

Wetterdienstgesetz d: **WDG**

Wetterdienstreferendar d: **WeDRefd**

Wetterfaksimilesystem d: **WEFAX**

Wetterführungskanal d: **WeFük**

Wetterkarte d: **WK**

Wetterkühler d: **WK**

Wetterlagenklasse Nr. 09 nach der Objektiven Wetterlagenklassifikation des DWD d: **SWAAF**

Wettermessung d: **Wett.-M.**

Wettermodell d: **WM**

Wetterquerschlag d: **WtQu.**

Wetterschacht d: **WS**

Wetterstation d: **Wst**

Wetterstrecke d: **W**

Wettertemperaturbereich d: **WTB**

Wettertrupp (Schallmeß) d: **WeTrp(Schallm)**

Wetterunabhängige Treibladung d: **WUTL**

Wetterwarte d: **Wewa**, d: **WW**

Wexford Slobs Wildfowl Sanctuary e: **WSWS**

WFO Hydrometeorological Forecasting System e: **WHFS**

Whale Protection Act e: **WPA**

Wharton & Stille's Medical Jurisprudence e: **Whar. & St. Med. Jur.**, e: **Whart. & S. Med. Jur.**

Wheel Slide Protection e: **WSP**

Wheeler National Wildlife Refuge (Alabama) e: **WNWR**

Wheeling Medical Park e: **WMP**

Whipple Gamma Ray Observatory e: **WGRO**

White Oak Creek Headwaters e: **WOCH**

White Patriot Witness Protection Program e: **WPP**

White River National Wildtife Refuge e: **WRNWR**

White Sands Air Weather Detachment e: **WSAWD**

White Sands Space Harbor, New Mexico e: **WSSH**

White Sea Biological Station e: **WSBS**

White Sea Canal e: **W.S.C.**

White Sea Wood Charter. White Sea to Great Britain, Ireland and Continent e: **Russwood**

Whitewater Education Association e: **WEA**

Whitewater Resource Toolkit e: **WRT**

Whittaker Health Services e: **WHS**

Whittier College e: **W.C.**

Whittier Law Review e: **Whittier L. Rev.**

WHO International Reference Center for Community Water Supply e: **WIRCCWS**

WHO International Reference Centre for Community Water Supply and Sanitation *e:* **WHO/IRC**

WHO Oral Health Country/Area Profile Programme *e:* **CAPP**

WHO South-East Asia Region Health Literature, Library and Information Services Network *e:* **WHO/SEAR-HELLIS**

WHO Western Pacific Regional Centre for the Promotion of Environmental Planning and Applied Studies *e:* **PEPAS**

Whole Animal Cell Sorting *e:* **WACS**

whole body water *e:* **WBW**

Whole Earth Catalog *e:* **WEC**

Whole Earth Decision Support System *e:* **WEDSS**

Whole Earth Telescope *e:* **WET**

Whole Earth `Lectronic Net *e:* **WELL**

Whole Health Institute International *e:* **WHI**

Wichita Mountains Seismological Observatory *e:* **WMSO**

Wichita Mountains Wildlife Refuge *e:* **WMWR**

Wichita Weather Forecast Office *e:* **ICT**

Wide Area Information Service Ice Core Project *e:* **WAISCORES**

Wide Area Remote Sensors *e:* **WARS**

Wide-Band Remote Switch *e:* **WBRS**

Wide-Range Meteor Burst Gamma Monitoring System *e:* **WRMB-1**

Wideband Electromagnetic Pulse Environment *e:* **WEMPE**

Widely Integrated Distributed Environment *e:* **WIDE**

Widely Interconnected Distributed Environment *e:* **WIDE**

Widow/Orphan [Protection] *e:* **W/O**

Wiener Allgemeines Medizinisches Inforrnationssystem *d:* **WAMIS**

Wiener Archiv für Innere Medizin *d:* **WAIM**

Wiener Archiv für klinische Medizin *d:* **WAklM**

Wiener medizinische Blätter *d:* **WmBl**

Wiener medizinische Presse *d:* **WmPr**

Wiener Medizinische Wochenschrift *d:* **Wien Med Wochenschr**, *d:* **WMW**

Wiener Medizinische Wochenschrift. Supplement *d:* **Wien Med Wochenschr Suppl**

Wiener Plakatierungs- und Anzeigen-GmbH, Wien *d:* **Wipag**

Wiener Tierärztliche Monatsschrift *d:* **WTM**

Wijsbegeerde en Maatschappijwetenschappen *n:* **WM**

Wilbur Hot Springs Health Sanctuary *e:* **WHSHS**

Wild Abortive *e:* **WA**

Wild and Scenic Rivers Act *e:* **WSRA**

Wild Animal Control Act *e:* **WAC**

Wild animal management *e:* **WAM**

Wild Animal Propagation Trust *e:* **WAPT**

Wild animal recovery *e:* **WAR**

Wild Bird Feeding Institute *e:* **WBFI**

Wild Blueberry Association of North America *e:* **WBANA**

Wild Canid Survival and Research Center *e:* **WCSRC**

Wild Cats and Tigers United *e:* **WCTU**

Wild Chimpanzee Foundation *e:* **WCF**

Wild Flowers Preservation Society *e:* **WFPS**

Wild Goose Association *e:* **WGA**

Wild Horse Organized Assistance *e:* **WHOA**

Wild Life Preservation Society of Australia *e:* **W.L.P.S. of A.**

Wild Life Protection Society *e:* **WLPS**

Wild Life Research Institute *e:* **W.L.R.I.**

Wild Life Sanctuary *e:* **WLS**

Wild Life Society of Rhodesia *e:* **WLSR**

wild-type *e:* **wt**

Wild und Hund *d:* **WuH**

Wild Weasel *e:* **WW**

Wild Weasel Augmentation *e:* **WWA**

Wild Weasel Augmentee *e:* **WW**, *e:* **WWA**

Wild Weasel Squadron *e:* **WWS**

Wild West *e:* **West**

Wild, Wonderful West Virginia *e:* **WWWVA**

Wildbiologische Gesellschaft München [Oberammergau] *d:* **WGM**

Wildcat Service Corporation *e:* **WSC**

Wilde-Intelligenztest *d:* **WIT**

wildebeest *A:* **wilde**

Wilder Memorial Library, Weston *e:* **VtWeo**

Wilderness *e:* **W**

Wilderness Act *e:* **WA**

Wilderness Education Association *e:* **WEA**

Wilderness Emergency Medical Services Institute *e:* **WEMSI**

Wilderness Medical Society *e:* **WMS**

Wilderness Society *e:* **WS**

Wilderness Study Area *e:* **WSA**

Wilderness Watch *e:* **WW**

Wilde's Supplement to Barton's Conveyancing *e:* **Wilde Sup. (or Conv.)**

Wildfire *e:* **Wildfire**

Wildfire Coordinating Committee *e:* **WCC**

Wildfire Experiment *e:* **WiFE**

Wildfowl and Wetlands Trust *e:* **WWT**

Wildfowl Foundation *e:* **WF**

Wildfowlers' Association of Great Britain *e:* **WAGB**

Wildfowlers' Association of Great Britain and Ireland *e:* **WAGBI**

Wildfowling Association of Great Britain and Northern Ireland *e:* **WA**

Wildland Resources Center *e:* **WRC**

Wildland Resources Information Display System *e:* **WRIDS**

Wildland Resources Information System *e:* **WRIS**

wildlife and fisheries science *e:* **WFSC**

Wildlife and Inland Waters Library, Environment Canada Ste-Foy, Quebec *e:* **QQE**

Wildlife Clubs of Kenya *e:* **WCK**

Wildlife Conservation Fund of America *e:* **WCFA**

Wildlife Conservation International *e:* **WCI**

Wildlife Conservation Society *e:* **WCS**

Wildlife Conservation Society of Zambia *e:* **WCSZ**

Wildlife Disease Association *e:* **WDA**

Wildlife Division, Nova Scotia Department of Lands and Forests, Kentville, Nova Scotia *e:* **NSKL**

Wildlife Habitat Area *e:* **WHA**

Wildlife Habitat Enhancement Council *e:* **WHEC**

Wildlife Habitat Incentives *e:* **WHI**

Wildlife Information Center *e:* **WIC**

Wildlife Information Network *e:* **WIN**

Wildlife Legislative Fund of America *e:* **WLFA**

Wildlife Management Area *e:* **WMA**

Wildlife Management Institute *e:* **WLMI**, *e:* **WMI**

Wildlife Monographs *e:* **Wildl. Monogr.**

Wildlife Preservation (or Preserve) Society *e:* **WPS**

Wildlife Preservation Society of Australia *e:* **WLPSA**, *e:* **WPSA**

Wildlife Preservation Society of Queensland *e:* **W.P.S.Q.**

Wildlife Preservation Trust International *e:* **WPTl**

Wildlife Protection [Regulations and Exports and Imports] *e:* **WP[REI]**

Wildlife Protection (Regulations and Exports and Imports) Act *e:* **WP(REI)**

Wildlife Rehabilitation Council *e:* **WRC**

Wildlife Rescue Veterinarian Association of Japan *e:* **WRVJ**

Wildlife Research Coordinating Committee *e:* **WRCC**

Wildlife Research Project *e:* **WRO**, *e:* **WRP**

Wildlife Reserve *e:* **WR**

Wildlife Restauration [association] *e:* **WR**

Wildlife Society *e:* **WLS**, *e:* **WS**

Wildlife Sound Recording Society *e:* **WSRS**

Wildlife Trade Monitoring Unit *e:* **WTMU**

Wildlife Tree Committee *e:* **WTC**

Wildlife Tree Patches *e:* **WTP**

Wildlife Trees *e:* **WT**

Wildlife Working Group *e:* **WWG**

Wildlife Youth Service *e:* **WYS**

Wildschadenausgleichskasse *d:* **WAK**

Wilford Hall Medical Center *e:* **WHMC**

Willapa National Wildlife Refuge (Washington) *e:* **WNWR**

William and Mary Environmental Law and Policy Review *e:* **Wm. & Mary Envtl. L. & Pol'y Rev.**

William and Mary Journal of Environmental Law *e:* **Wm. & Mary J. Envtl. L.**

William Beaumont Army Medical Center *e:* **WBAMC**

William Beaumont Medical Center *e:* **WBMC**

William L. Finley National Wildlife Refuge *e:* **WLFNWR**

William Mitchell Environmental Law Journal *e:* **Wm. Mitchell Envtl. L.J.**

Williams Natural Gas Co. *e:* **WNG**

Wilmington Area Biomedical Libraries *e:* **WABLC**

Wiltshire Archaeological and Natural History Society *e:* **W.A.N.H.S.**

Wind and Watermill Section *e:* **WWS**

Wind and Weather *e:* **W and W**, *e:* **W & W**

Wind Imaging Interferometer Remote Analysis Computer *e:* **WINDI RAC**

Wind Observations Through Ambient Noise *e:* **WOTAN**

Wind or current driven opening in winter sea-ice *e:* **Polynya**

Window Atmosphere Sounding Projectile
e: **WASP**

Window Circulating Water System e:
WCWS

Windows File Protection e: **WFP**

Windows, Icons, Mouse and Pull-down
environment e: **WIMP**

Windows Network Environment e: **WNE**

Wing Weather Officer e: **WWO**

Winnebago County Medical Society,
Rockford e: **IRoWM**

Winnebago Mental Health Institute e:
WMHI

Winograde Fourier Transform Algeorithm
e: **WFTA**

Winter Conference on Aerospace and
Electronic Systems e: **WINCON**

Winter Convention [on Aerospace
Electronic Systems] e: **WINCON**

Winter Ice Experiment Beaufort Sea e:
WIEBS

Winter Intermediate Water e: **WIW**

Winter Water e: **WW**

Winter Weddell Sea Project e: **WWSP**

Winterhochwasser d: **WHW**

Wintermittelwasser d: **WMW**

Winterthurer Institut für
Gesundheitsökonomie d: **WIG**

Wire Grid Polarizer e: **WGP**

Wire Strike Protection System e: **WSPS**

Wireless Application Environment e:
WAE

Wirkungsorientiertes Organiations- und
Softwaresystem d: **WIRKOSS**

Wirtschaftsgenossenschaft Deutscher
Pelztierzüchter d: **WDP**

Wirtschaftsgenossenschaft deutscher
Tierärzte d: **W.d.T.**

Wirtschaftsgruppe Gas- und
Wasserversorgung d: **WGUW**

Wirtschaftsverband für Geodäsie und
Kartographie d: **GEO-KART**

Wirtschaftsverwaltungs- und Umweltrecht
d: **WuR**

Wisconsin Department of Health & Family
Services e: **DHFS**

Wisconsin Department of Natural
Resources e: **WDNR**, e: **Wis Dep Nat
Resour**

Wisconsin Environmental Law Journal e:
Wis. Envtl. L.J.

Wisconsin Geological and Natural History
Survey e: **WGNHS**

Wisconsin Health Insurance Risk Sharing
Plan e: **HIRSP**

Wisconsin Health Science Libraries
Association e: **WHSLA**

Wisconsin Medical Journal e: **Wis Med J**

Wisconsin Natural History Society e: **Wis
N H Soc**

Wisconsin Ultraviolet Photopolarimetry
Experiment e: **WUPPE**

Wisconsin Ultraviolet Photopolarimter
Experiment e: **WUPPE**

Wisconsin Veterinary Medical Association
e: **WVMA**

Wissenschaftlich-Technische Gesellschaft
für Geodäsie, Photogrammetrie und
Kartographie d: **WTG GPK**

Wissenschaftliche Arbeitsgemeinschaft für
Raketentechnik und Raumfahrt d:
WARR

Wissenschaftliche Behörde für
Umweltprobleme d: **ESSA**

Wissenschaftliche Gesellschaft für Luft-
und Raumfahrt e.V. d: **WGLR**

Wissenschaftliche Gesellschaft für
Umweltschutz e.V. d: **WGU**

Wissenschaftliche Gesellschaft für
Veterinärmedizin d: **WGV**

Wissenschaftliche Zeitschrift der
Humboldt-Universität zu Berlin,
Mathematisch-Naturwissenschaftliche
Reihe, Berlin d: **Wiss. Z. Humboldt-
Univ. Berlin**

Wissenschaftliche Zeitschrift der
Universität Rostock, Mathematisch-
Naturwissenschaftliche Reihe d: **Wiss.
Z. Univ. Rostock, Math.-**

Wissenschaftlicher Beirat Globale
Umweltveränderungen d: **WBGU**

Wissenschaftliches Komitee für Ozeanische
Forschung d: **SCOR**

Wissenschaftliches Komitee für
Umweltprobleme d: **SCOPE**

Wistar Institute of Anatomy and Biology
e: **WIAB**

Wistar Institute ofAnatomy and Biology,
Philadelphia, PA e: **PPWI**

within vessel's natural segregation e: **wvns**

Witthaus and Becker's Medical
Jurisprudence e: **Witthaus & Becker's
Med. Jur.**

Witwatersrand A: **WWR**, n: **Rand**

Witwatersrand Agricultural Society e:
WAS

Witwatersrand, Johannesburg e: **Witw.**

Witwatersrand Landbougenootskap A:
WLG

Witwatersrand Local Division Reports e: **W**

Witwatersrand Native Labour Association
e: **WENELA**

Witwatersrand Native Labour Association
South Africa e: **WNLA**

Witwatersrand University e: **Wits U**

WOCE Fast Delivery Sea-Level Data
Assembly Centre e: **WSLC**

WOCE Sea Level Center e: **WSLC**

WOCE [World Ocean Circulation
Experiment] Data Management Working
Group e: **WDMWG**

WOCE [World Ocean Circulation
Experiment] Float Program Planning
Committee e: **WFPPC**

WOCE [World Ocean Circulation
Experiment] Hydrographic Program
Implementation Panel e: **WHPIP**

WOCE [World Ocean Circulation
Experiment] Hydrographic Program
Office e: **WHP**, e: **WHPO**

WOCE [World Ocean Circulation
Experiment] Hydrographic Program[me]
e: **WHP**

WOCE [World Ocean Circulation
Experiment] Hydrographic Program[me]
Planning Committee e: **WHPPC**

WOCE [World Ocean Circulation
Experiment] Hydrographic Survey e:
WHP

WOCE [World Ocean Circulation
Experiment] Implementation Plan e:
WIP

WOCE [World Ocean Circulation
Experiment] Scientific Steering Group
e: **WSSG**

Wojewódzkie Biuro Zakwaterowan P:
WBZ

Wojskowy Instytut Geograficzny P: **WIG**

Wolffius, Institutiones Juris Naturae et
Gentium l: **Wolff. Inst.**, l: **Wolff Inst.
Nat.**, l: **Wolffius**, l: **Wolffius\ Inst.**

Womac Army Medical Center e: **WAMC**

Womack Army Hospital Medical Library,
Fort Bragg e: **WAH**

Woman Health International e: **WHI**

Woman in Space Earliest e: **WISE**

Woman's Auxiliary to the American
Medical Association e: **WAAMA**

Women and Children Protection Society e:
W.C.P.S.

Women and Health e: **Women Health**

Women and Health Round Table e: **WHR**

Women, Environment and Development
Network e: **WEDNET**

Women for Healthcare Education, Reform
& Equity e: **WHERE**

Women in Aerospace e: **WIA**

Women in Cell Biology e: **WICB**

Women in Medical Service e: **WMS**

Women in Natural Resources Management
Program e: **WNRM**

Women Investigating Sciences and
Environment e: **WISE**

Women Public Health Officers' Association
e: **W.P.H.O.A.**

Women Sanitary Inspectors' and Health
Visitors' Association e: **W.S.I.H.V.A.**

Women's Addiction Service [National
Institute of Mental Health] e: **WAS**

Women's Auxiliary to the Student American
Medical Association e: **WASAMA**

Women's Council on Energy and the
Environment e: **WCEE**

Women's Environment and Development
Organisation (or Organization) e:
WEDO

Women's Health Action & Mobilization e:
WHAM

Women's Health and Abortion Project e:
WHAP

Women's Health and Action Research
Centre e: **WHARC**

Women's Health and Aging Study e:
WHAS

Women's Health Care House e: **WHCH**

Women's Health Care Nurse Practioner e:
WNP

Womens Health Care Nurse Practitioner e:
WHCNP

Women's Health Care Nurse Practitioner e:
WHNP

Womens Health Data Book e: **Womens
Health Data Book**

Women's Health Information Centre e:
WHIC

Women's Health Information Service e:
WHIN

Women's Health Initiative e: **WHI**

Womens Health Issues e: **Womens Health
Issues**

Women's Health Queensland Wide e:
WHQW

Women's Interagency Health Study e:
WIHS

Women's International Public Health
Network e: **WIPHN**

Women's League of Health and Beauty e:
WLHB

© K · G · Saur, Munich

Women's Medical College *e:* **WMC**

Women's Medical College of Pennsylvania *e:* **WMCP**

Women's Medical Service of India *e:* **W.M.S.I.**

Women's Medical Specialist *e:* **WMS**

Women's Medical Specialists Corps *e:* **WMSC**

Women's Occupational Health Resource Center *e:* **WOHRC**

Women's Reserve, Medical Corps Duties *e:* **W-VS MC**

Women's Veterinary Medical Association *e:* **WVMA**

Wongan Hills Animal Quarantine Station *e:* **WHAQS**

Wood River Township Hospital, Medical Library *e:* **IworH**

Woodman & Tidy on Forensic Medicine *e:* **Woodm. & T. For. Merl.**

Woods Hole Oceanographic Institute (or Institution) *e:* **WHOI**

Woolrych's Law of Waters *e:* **Woolr. Waters**

Worcester Foundation for Experimental Biology *e:* **WFEB**

Word Meteorological Organization *e:* **WMO**

WordPerfect Information System Environment *e:* **WISE**

Work Information Management System-Environmental Subsystem *e:* **WIMS-ES**

Work Programme on the Conservation and Enhancement of Biological and Landscape Diversity in Forest *e:* **WP-CEBLDF**

Work space management report *e:* **WSM**

Worked Three Oceans *e:* **W 3 O**, *e:* **WTO**

Worker Safety and health *e:* **WS**

Workers Health and Safety Centre *e:* **WHSC**

Workers Health and Safety Centre, Don Mills, Ontario *e:* **ODW**

Working Committee on Training, Education, and Mutual Assistance [Intergovernmental Oceanographic Commission] *e:* **TEMA**

Working for Animals used in Research, Drugs, and Surgery *e:* **WARDS**

Working Group for Meteorological Data Management *e:* **WG/ MDM**

Working Group for Next- Generation Weather Radar *e:* **WG/ NGWR**

Working Group for Space Physics Research *e:* **WGSPR**

Working Group for Weather Communications *e:* **WGWC**

Working Group for Weather Plans *e:* **WGWP**

Working Group of Oceanography *e:* **WGO**

Working Group on Air/Sea Fluxes *e:* **WGASF**

Working Group on Antarctic Meteorology *e:* **WGAM**

Working Group on Ballast Water *e:* **WGBW**

Working Group on Biological Effects of Contaminants *e:* **WGBEC**

Working Group on Climate Change Detection *e:* **WGCCD**

Working Group on Geodesy and Geographic Information *e:* **WG-GGI**

Working Group on Inland Water Transport, Military Sub-Group *e:* **IWT/MIL**

Working Group on Sea Ice *e:* **WGSI**

Working Group on Sea-ice Research and Climate *e:* **WGSIC**

Working Group on Shelf Seas Oceanography *e:* **WGSSO**

Working Group on Specialist Medical Training *e:* **WGSMT**

Working Group on the Commercialization of Meteorological and Hydrological Services *e:* **WGCOM**

Working Group on the Paleogeographic Atlases of the Quaternary *e:* **INQUA**, *e:* **INQUA/PAQWG**

Working Panel of Local Authority Ecologists *e:* **WPLAE**

working space. *e:* **WS**

Working Water Pressure *e:* **WWP**

Workplace Environmental Exposure *e:* **WEE**

Workplace Health and Safety Association *e:* **WHSA**

Workshop on biological diversity and Tourism *e:* **WSTOUR**

Workshop on Financing for Biological Diversity *e:* **WSFIN**

Workshop on Forest and Biological Diversity *e:* **WSFBD**

Workshop on Liability and Redress in the context of the Convention on Biological Diversity *e:* **WSLR**

Workshop on Sustainable Use of Biological Diversity *e:* **WSSUSE**

Workshop on the Strategy Plan of the Convention on Biological Diversity *e:* **WSSP**

Workshop on Traditional Knowledge and Biological Diversity *e:* **TKBD**

Workspace *e:* **WS**

Workspace Intrusion Inspection Device *e:* **WIID**

Workspace On-Demand *e:* **WSOD**

Workspace Pointer *e:* **WP**

Workspace-Register Pointer *e:* **WP**

Workstation Support Environment *e:* **WSE**

World Aerospace Education Organisation *e:* **WAEO**

World Animal Organization *e:* **WAO**

World Association for Disaster and Emergency Medicine *e:* **WADEM**

World Association for Emergency and Disaster Medicine *e:* **WAEDM**

World Association for/of Animal Production *e:* **WAAP**

World Association for/of Infant Mental Health *e:* **WAIMH**

World Association for/of Medical Informatics *e:* **WAMI**

World Association for the History of Veterinary Medicine *e:* **WAHVM**

World Association for Transport Animal Welfare and Studies *e:* **TAWS**

World Association of Health, Environment and Culture *e:* **WAHEC**

World Association of Military Surgeons *e:* **WAMS**

World Association of Soil and Water Conservation *e:* **WASWC**

World Association of Veterinary Microbiologists, Immunologists and Specialists in Infectious Diseases *e:* **WAVMI**

World Association of Wildlife Veterinarians *e:* **WAWV**

World Atmosphere Gravity Wave study *e:* **WAGS**

World Bank Environment Department *e:* **WB/ED**

World Bank Monitoring Environmental Progress Database *e:* **WBMEPD**

World Climate Applications and Services Program *e:* **WCASP**

World Climate Applications Program *e:* **WCAP**

World Climate Conference *e:* **WCC**

World Climate Data and Monitoring Program *e:* **WCDMP**

World Climate Data Information and Referral System (or Service) *e:* **INFOCLIMA**

World Climate Data Program *e:* **WCDP**

World Climate Impact Program *e:* **WCIP**

World Climate Impact Studies Program *e:* **WCIP**

World Climate Impacts and Response [Strategies (or Strategy)] Program[me] *e:* **WCIRP**

World Climate Program *e:* **WCP**

World Climate Programme-Water *e:* **WCP-WATER**

World Climate Research Progam[me]-Joint Scientific Committee *e:* **WCRP-JSC**

World Climate Research Progam[me]-Oceanographic component *e:* **WCRP-O**

World Climate Research Program *e:* **WCRP**

World Climate System Monitoring Program *e:* **WCSMP**

World Commission of/on Environment and Development *e:* **WCED**

World Commission on Protected Areas *e:* **WCPA**

World Conference on Earthquake Engineering *e:* **WCEE**

World Conference on Natural Disaster Reduction *e:* **WCNDR**

World Congress of Small Animal Veterinary Associations *e:* **WSAVA**

World Congress of Sports Medicine *e:* **WCSM**

World Council for the Biosphere-International Society for Environmental Education *e:* **WCB-ISEE**

World Data Center-A [Atmospheric trace gases] *e:* **WDC-A**

World Data Center for Marine Geology & Geophysics, Boulder *e:* **WDC for MGG, Boulder**

World Data Centre-A for Marine Geology and Geophysics *e:* **WDC-A**

World Data Centre-A for Oceanography *e:* **WDC-A**

World Data Centre-A for Paleoclimatology *e:* **WDC-A**

World Data Centre A, Marine Geology and Geophysics *e:* **WDC-A-MGG**

World Data Centre A, Meteorology *e:* **WDC-A**

World Data Centre A, Oceanography *e:* **WDC-A**

World Data Centre B, Meteorology *e:* **WDC-B**

World Data Centre B, Oceanography *e:* **WDC-B**

World Digital Data[base] for [the] Environmental Sciences *e:* **WDDES**
World Environment Action Plan *e:* **WEAP**
World Environment and Resources Council *e:* **WERC**
World Environment Center (or Centre) *e:* **WEC**
World Environment Day *e:* **WED**
World Environment Disaster Observation System *e:* **WEDOS**
World Environment[al] Institute *e:* **WEI**
World Federation for Medical Education *e:* **WFME**
World Federation for/of Mental Health *e:* **WFMH**
World Federation for/of Ultrasound in Medicine and Biology *e:* **WFUMB**
World Federation for the Protection of Animals *e:* **WFPA**
World Federation of Associations of Pediatric Surgeons *e:* **WFAPS**
World Federation of Health Agencies for the Advancement of Voluntary Surgical Contraception *e:* **WFHA-AVSC**
World Federation of Nuclear Medicine and Biology *e:* **WFNMB**
World Federation of Proprietary Medicine Manufacturers *e:* **WFPMA**
World Federation of Public Health Associations *e:* **WFPHA**
World Federation of Societies of Biological Psychiatry *e:* **WFSBP**
World Federation of Societies of Intensive and Critical Care Medicine *e:* **WFSICCM**
World Federation of Ultrasonics in Medicine and Biology *e:* **WFUMB**
World Foundation for Environment and Development *e:* **WFED**
World Foundation for Medical Studies in Female Health *e:* **WFFH**
World Geodetic Spheroid *e:* **WGS84**
World Geodetic Survey. *e:* **WGS**
World Geodetic System *e:* **WGS**
World Geophysical Interval *e:* **WGI**
World Health Assembly *e:* **WHA**
World Health Associates *e:* **WHA**
World Health Forum *e:* **World Health Forum**
World Health Foundation *e:* **WHF**
World Health Foundation of the United States of America *e:* **WHF-USA**
World Health Medical Group *e:* **WHMG**
World Health Organisation (or Organization) [of the United Nations] *e:* **WHO**
World Health Organisation Regional Publications. European Series *e:* **WHO Reg Publ Eur Ser**
World Health Organization *e:* **WTO**
World Health Organization Activity Management System *e:* **WHO AMS**
World Health Organization Adverse Reactions Terminology *e:* **WHO-ART**
World Health Organization Bulletin *e:* **WHO Bulletin**
World Health Organization Charter *e:* **W.H.O.Ch.**
World Health Organization European Centre for Environment and Health *e:* **WHO/ECEH**
World Health Organization European Region *e:* **WHO/EURO**

World Health Organization Information Systems Management *e:* **WHO ISM**
World Health Organization Interim Commission *e:* **WHOIC**
World Health Organization International Air Data Base *e:* **WHO-WMO**
World Health Organization International Reference Preparation *e:* **WHOIRP**
World Health Organization-Latin America Cancer Research Information Project *e:* **WHO-PAHO/LACRIP, LACRIP**
World Health Organization Library *e:* **WHO Libr.**
World Health Organization Library Information System *e:* **WHOLIS**
World Health Organization Management Information System *e:* **WHO MIS**
World Health Organization Pesticide Evaluation Scheme *e:* **WHOPES**
World Health Organization/Programme on Substance Abuse *e:* **WHO/PSA**
World Health Organization Regional Office for Europe *e:* **WHO/EURO**
World Health Organization-South-East Asia Region Health Literature, Library and Information Services Network *e:* **WHO/SEAR-HELLIS, SEAR-HELLIS**
World Health Organization Statistical Information System *e:* **WHOSIS**
World Health Organization Summary Information on Global Health Trends *e:* **WHO SIGHT**
World Health Organization Technical Report Series *e:* **World Health Organ Tech Rep Ser**
World Health Organization-Western Pacific Regional Centre for Promotion of Enviroment Planning and Applied Studies *e:* **WHO-PEPAS**
World Health Report *e:* **WHR**
World Health Research Center *e:* **WHRC**
World Health Statistics Quarterly *e:* **World Health Stat Q**
World Hydrological Cycle Observing System *e:* **WHYCOS**
World Ice Sport Organization *e:* **WISO**
World Index of Space Imagery *e:* **WISI**
World Industry Conference on Environmental Management *e:* **WICEM**
World Industry Council for the Environment *e:* **WICE**
World Institute of Ecology and Cancer *e:* **WIEC**
World Institute of Safety Security Health Environment Specialists *e:* **WISSHES**
World International Medical Association *e:* **WIMA**
World Islamic Association for Mental Health *e:* **WIAMH**
World Journal of Microbiology and Biotechnology *e:* **WMB**
World Medical Assembly *e:* **WMA**
World Medical Association *e:* **WMA, *e:* WOMA**
World Medical Association Bulletin *e:* **WMA Bulletin**
World Medical Association for Perfect Health *e:* **WMAFPH**
World Medical Electronics *e:* **WME**
World Medical Mission *e:* **WMM**
World Medical Organization *e:* **WMO**
World Medical Periodicals *e:* **WMP**
World Medical Relief *e:* **WMR**

World Medical Tennis Society *e:* **WMTS**
World Mental Health Year *e:* **WMHY**
World Meteorological Center[s] (or Centre) *e:* **WMC**
World Meteorological Day *e:* **WMD**
World Meteorological Intervals *e:* **WMI**
World Meteorological Office *e:* **WMO**
World Meteorological Organisation *e:* **WMO**
World Meteorological Organization *e:* **WOMO**
World Meteorological Organization Backgrond Air Pollution Monitoring Network *e:* **WMO-BAPMoN BAPMoN**
World Meteorological Organization Bulletin *e:* **WMO Bulletin**
World Meteorological Organization/Global Telecommunication System *e:* **WMO/GTS**
World Meteorological Organization/ Intergovernmental Oceanographic Commission *e:* **WMO/IOC**
World Nature Association *e:* **WNA**
World Ocean and Cruise Liner Society *e:* **WOCLS**
World Ocean Atlas *e:* **WOA**
World Ocean Circulation Experiment *e:* **WOCF**
World Ocean Circulation Experiment/Hydrographic Program *e:* **WOCE/HP**
World Ocean Circulation Experiment/ International Project Office *e:* **WOCE-IPO**
World Ocean Circulation Experiment-Numerical Experimentation Group *e:* **WOCE-NEG**
World Ocean Circulation Experiment program *e:* **WOCE**
World Ocean Circulation Experiment-Scientific Steering Group *e:* **WOCE-SSG**
World Ocean Climate Experiment *e:* **WOCE**
World Ocean Data Centre *e:* **WODC**
World Ocean Watch *e:* **WOW**
World Oceanographic Center (or Centre) *e:* **WOC**
World Oceanographic Data Display *e:* **WODD**
World Oceanographic Data Processing and Services Centre *e:* **WOPC**
World Oceanographic Organization *e:* **WOO**
World Office of Information on Environmental Problems *e:* **WOIEP**
World Organization of Volcano Observatories *e:* **WOVO**
World Radio for Environment and Natural Resources *e:* **WREN**
World Self-Medication Industry *e:* **WSMI**
World Small AnimalVeterinary Association *e:* **WSAVA**
World Society for Protection of Animals *e:* **WSPA**
World Society for the Protection of Animals *e:* **WSPA**
World Space Congress *e:* **WSC**
World Space Directory *e:* **WSD**
World Space Foundation *e:* **WSF**
World Space Organization *e:* **WSO**
World Survey of Climatology *e:* **WSC**

World Underwater Federation *e:* **CMAS,**
  e: **W.U.F.**
World Water Alliance *e:* **WWA**
World Water Conference *e:* **WWC**
World Waterpark Association *e:* **WWA**
World Weather Center *e:* **WWC**
World Weather Organization *e:* **WWO**
World Weather Program *e:* **WWP**
World Weather Research Programme *e:*
  WWRP
World Weather System *e:* **WWS**
World Weather Watch *e:* **WWV,** *e:* **WWW**
World Wide Fund for Nature *e:* **WWF**
World-Wide Fund for Nature *e:* **WWFN**
World Wide Fund for Nature [Australia] *e:*
  WWFA
World Wide Organization for Child Care,
  Health and Hygiene Among Jews *e:*
  World OSE Union
World Wild Web *e:* **WWW**
World Wildlife Federation *e:* **WFF**
World Wildlife Fund-European Policy
  Office *e:* **WWF-EPO**
World Wildlife Fund for Nature *e:* **WWF**
World Wildlife Fund International *e:*
  WWFI
World Wildlife Fund-United States *e:*
  WWF-US
World Wildlife Guide *e:* **WWG**
World Women in the Environment *e:*
  WorldWIDE
World's Greatest Environment Statement
  e: **WGES**
Worlds of Nature *e:* **WN**
Worldwide Atmospheric Gravity Wave
  Study *e:* **WAGS**
Worldwide Dental Health Service *e:*
  WDHS
Worldwide Fund for Nature *e:* **WWF**
Worldwide Organization[al] Structure for
  Army Medical Support *e:* **WORSAMS**
Worldwide What & Where-geographic
  glossary and traveller's guide *e:*
  WWWW
Wreck and Bone Islands Natural Area *e:*
  WBINA
Wright Area Medical Laboratory *e:*
  WAML
Wrightsville Marine Biomedical Laboratory
  e: **WMBL**
write protect. *e:* **WP**
Write Protect *e:* **WPRT**
WRITE PROTECTED *e:* **W**
Write Protected *e:* **WP**
Write Protection *e:* **WP**
Wrong Signature Zero *e:* **WSZ**
Würzburger Abhandlungen [aus dem
  Gesamtgebiet der Medizin] *d:* **WüAbh**
WVF International Socio-Medical
  Information Centre *e:* **WISMIC**
WWB-Wasserwerks-Beteiligungs GmbH
  d: **WWB**
WWMCCS [Worldwide Military Command
  and Control System] Environmental
  Support System *e:* **WESS**
Wydawnictwa Geologiczne *P:* **WG**
Wyoming Geological Association *e:* **WGA**
Wyoming Historical and Geological Society
  e: **WHGS**
Wyoming Infrared Observatory *e:* **WIO,** *e:*
  WIRO
Wyoming State Medical Association *e:*
  WSMA

Wyoming State Medical Society *e:* **WSMS**
Wyoming Water Research Center *e:*
  WWRC
Wyrtki Center for Climate Research and
  Prediction *e:* **WCCRP**
Wytwórnia Sprzętu Geodezyjnego,
  Warszawa *P:* **WSG**
Wytwórnia Urządzeń Klimatyzacyjnych *P:*
  WUK
Wyższa Szkoła Oficerska Sluzb
  Kwatermistrzowskich *P:* **WSOSK**

X

X-Axis of Spacelab *e:* **X**
X/Open Common Application Environment
  e: **X/OCAE**
X window system based Visual/Integrated
  Environment for Workstations *e:*
  XVIEW
Xai-Xai (Mozambique sea-port) *e:* **X-X**
Xanthin-dehydrogenase *e:* **XD**
Xanthine Dehydrogenase *e:* **XDH,** *e:*
  XDHase
xenobiologist *e:* **xenobio**
xenobiology *e:* **xenobio**
Xinjiang Institute of Biology, Pedology and
  Desert Research *e:* **XIBPDR**
XML Namespace Related-resource
  Language *e:* **XNRL**

Y

Y-Axis of Orbiter *e:* **Y**
Y-Axis of Spacelab *e:* **Y**
Yale Journal of Biology and Medicine *e:*
  Yale J Biol Med
Yale on Legal Titles to Mining Claims and
  Water Rights *e:* **Yale Mines**
Yale University Observatory *e:* **YUO**
Yale University School of Medicine, New
  Haven, Connecticut *e:* **YUSM**
Yazoo National Wildlife Refuge *e:* **YNWR**
Year of the Ocean *e:* **YOTO**
Year of the Ocean Foundation *e:* **YOF**
Yearbook. Conference of Latin Americanist
  Geographers, Ball State University,
  Muncie *e:* **Yearbook/CLAG.**
Yearbook of Air and Space Law *e:* **Y.B.**
  Air & Space L., *e:* **Y.B.A.S.L.**
Yearbook of the Association of Pacific
  Coast Geographers. Oregon State
  University Press. Corvallis, Oregon *e:*
  Yearb. Assoc. Pac. Coast Geogr.
Yearbook of the Estonian Naturalist Society
  e: **Yearb. Eston. Nat. Soc.**
yeast alcohol dehydrogenase *e:* **yadh**
Yeast Alcohol Dehydrogenase *e:*
  YADHase
Yerkes Observatory *e:* **Yerk,** *e:* **YO**
Yonsei Medical Journal *e:* **Yonsei Med J**
Yorkshire Geological Society *e:* **Y.G.S.**
Yosemite Natural History Association *e:*
  YNHA
Yosemite Natural History Association *e:*
  YA, *e:* **YNHA**
Yost Ice Arena *e:* **Y I A**
Young Adult Reproductive Health *e:*
  YARH
Young European Environmental Research
  e: **YEER**
Young Europeans and Spacelab *e:* **YES**

Young Naturalists Association *e:* **YNA**
Young Ornithologists' Club-Royal Society
  for the Protection of Birds *e:* **YOC-**
  RSPB
Your Heritage Protection Association *e:*
  YHPA
Youth and Environment Europe *e:* **YEE**
Youth Environmental Programme for West
  Africa *e:* **YEPWA**
Youth for Environment and Service *e:*
  YES
Youth Unit of the Council for
  Environmental Education *e:* **YUCEE**
Yugoslav Association of Small Animal
  Practitioners *e:* **YASAP**
Yugoslav Society for Medical and
  Biological Engineering *e:* **YSMBE**
Yugoslavian National Committee of the
  International Association on Water
  Pollution Research and Control *e:*
  YNCIAWPRC
Yukon Bibliography. Geographical
  database, University of Alberta *e:* **YKB**
Yunnan Observatory, P. R. China *e:* **YnO**

Z

Z-Axis of Orbiter *e:* **Z,** *e:* **ZO**
Z-Axis of Spacelab *e:* **Z,** *e:* **ZL**
Z Local Vertical (Payload Bay Toward
  Earth) *e:* **ZLV**
Z Object Publishing Environment *e:* **ZOPE**
Zackenberg Ecological Research Operations
  e: **ZERO**
Zahnmedizin *d:* **ZM**
Zahnmedizinische Fachhelferin *d:* **ZMF**
zahntechnisch-medizinische Fachkraft *d:*
  ZMF
Zakłady Urządzeń Okrętowych "Hydroster",
  Gdańsk *P:* **ZUO**
Zambia. Department of Wildlife, Fisheries
  and National Parks. Annual Report *e:*
  Zambia Dep Wildl Fish Natl Parks
  Annu Rep
Zambia Geographical Association *e:* **ZGA**
Zambia Geographical Association.
  Magazine *e:* **Zambia Geogr Assoc Mag**
Zambia Geological Survey *e:* **ZGS**
Zambia. Geological Survey. Annual Report
  e: **Zambia Geol Surv Annu Rep**
Zambia. Geological Survey. Department
  Annual Report *e:* **Zambia Geol Surv**
  Dep Annu Rep
Zambia. Geological Survey. Economic
  Report *e:* **Zambia Geol Surv Econ Rep**
Zambia. Geological Survey. Records *e:*
  Zambia Geol Surv Rec
Zambia. Geological Survey. Technical
  Report *e:* **Zambia Geol Surv Tech Rep**
Zambia. Ministry of Lands and Mines.
  Geological Survey Department. Economic
  Report *e:* **Zambia Geol Surv Dep Econ**
  Rep
Zambia. Ministry of Lands and Mines.
  Report of theGeological Survey *e:*
  Zambia Rep Geol Surv
Zambia. Ministry of Lands and Natural
  Resources. Forest Research Bulletin *e:*
  Zambia Minist Lands Nat Resour For
  Res Bull
Zanzibar Protectorate. Annual Report on the
  Medical Department *e:* **Zanzibar**
  Protect Ann Rep Med Dept

Zanzibar Protectorate Law Reports *e:*
Zanzib Prot LR, *e:* **Z.L.R.**
Zapadne Karpaty. Seria Geologia *c:*
Zapadne Karpaty Ser Geol
Zapiski Geograficeskogo Obščestva *se:*
Zap GO
Zapiski Geograficeskogo Obscestva *se:*
Zap GO
Zapiski Kavkazskogo Otdela Russkogo
Geografičeskogo Obščestva *R:* **Zap
KORGO**
Zapiski Zabaikal'skogo Filiala
Geografičeskogo Obščestva SSSR *R:*
Zap Zabaik Fil Geogr Ova SSSR
Zapiski Zabaikal'skogo Otdela
Vsesojuznogo Geografičeskogo
Obščestva *R:* **Zap Zabaik Otd Vses
Geogr O-Va**
Zapisnici Srpskog Geoloskog Drustva *se:*
Zapisnici Srp Geol Drus
Zavod za Geoloska i Geofizicksa
Istrazivanja *se:* **GEOZAVOD**
Zbirnyk Naukovych Prats L'viv'kji
Medichini Institut *U:* **Zb Nauk Pr L'viv
Med Inst**
Zbirnyk Naukovych Robit Charkivs'kogo
Deržavnogo Medičnogo Institutu *U:* **Zb
Nauk Rob Chark Derž Med Inst**
Zbornik Geologicych Vied Zapadne
Karpaty *c:* **Zb Geol Vied Zapadne
Karpaty**
Zbornik Meteoroloskih i Hidroloskih
Radova *c:* **Zb Meteorol Hidrol Rad**
Zbornik Radova. Biološki Institut *se:* **Zb
Rad Biol Inst [Beograd]**
Zbornik Radova. Biološki Institut NR Srbye
Beograd *se:* **Zb Rad Biol Inst NR Srbye
Beogr**
Zbornik Radova. Rudarsko-Geološkog
Fakulteta *se:* **Zb Rad Rud Geol Fak**
Zbornik Radova. Srpska Akademija Nauka
Geološki Institut *se:* **Zb Rad Srp Akad
Nauka Geol Inst**
Zbornik Vojnomedicinske Akademije *se:*
Zb Vojnomed Akad
Zeichenorientierte Fenster-Funktionen *d:*
ZOFF
Zeitner Geological Museum *e:* **ZGM**
Zeitschrifi für die Gesamte Experimentelle
Medizin *d:* **Z Gesamte Exp Med**
Zeitschrift der Deutschen Geologischen
Gesellschaft *d:* **ZDGG,** *d:* **Z. Dtsch.
Geol. Ges.**
Zeitschrift des Deutschen Vereins für
öffentliche Gesundheitspflege *d:*
ZDVöffG
Zeitschrift des Deutschen
Wasserwirtschafts- und
Wasserkraftwerkverbandes *d:* **ZDWWV**
Zeitschrift. Deutsche Geologische
Gesellschaft *d:* **Z Deut Geol Ges,** *d:* **Z
Dt Geol Ges,** *d:* **Z Dtsch Geol Ges**
Zeitschrift fiir Naturforschung *d:* **Z
Naturforsch**
Zeitschrift für Allgemeine Mikrobiologie
e: **Z Allg Mikr**
Zeitschrift für Allgemeine Mikrobiologie.
Morphologie, Physiologie, Genetik, und
Ökologie der Mikrorganismen *e:* **Z Allg
Mikrobiol**
Zeitschrift für Allgemeine Mikrobiologie,
Morphologie, Physiologie und Ökologie
d: **Z. Allg. Mikrobiol.**

Zeitschrift für Allgemeinmedizin *d:* **Z.
Allgemeinmed.,** *d:* **ZFA,** *d:* **Z f Allg Med**
Zeitschrift für Allgemeinmedizin der
Landärzte *e:* **Z Allg Med**
Zeitschrift für Allgemeinmedizin [Stuttgart]
d: **ZFA [Stuttgart]**
Zeitschrift für Angewandte Bäder und
Klimaheilkunde *e:* **Z Angew Bäder
Klimaheilkd**
Zeitschrift für Angewandte Geologie *d:* **Z.
Angew. Geol.,** *d:* **Zeitschr Angew
Geologie,** *e:* **Z Ang Geol**
Zeitschrift für angewandte Geophysik *d:*
ZaGph
Zeitschrift für Angewandte Meteorologie
e: **Z Angew Met**
Zeitschrift für angewandte
Umweltforschung *d:* **ZAU**
Zeitschrift für Bewasserungswirtschaft *d:*
Z Bewasserungswirtsch
Zeitschrift für Biologie *d:* **Z Biol,** *d:*
ZEBLA
Zeitschrift für Biologische Technik und
Methodik *d:* **Z Biol Tech Method**
Zeitschrift für Desinfektion und
Gesundheitswesen *d:* **ZDGW**
Zeitschrift für Desinfektions- und
Gesundheitswesen *d:* **Z Desinfekt
Gesundheitswes**
Zeitschrift für die gesamte experimentelle
Medizin *d:* **ZgeM**
Zeitschrift für die Gesamte Experimentelle
Medizin *d:* **Z Ges Exp Med,** *e:* **ZGEMA**
Zeitschrift für die Gesamte Experimentelle
Medizin einschließlich Experimentelle
d: **Z. Gesam. Exp. Med. einschl. E**
Zeitschrift für die Gesamte Experimentelle
Medizin. Einschliesslich Experimenteller
Chirurgie *d:* **Z Gesamte Exp Med
Einschl Exp Chir**
Zeitschrift für die gesamte gerichtliche und
soziale Medizin *d:* **ZgGSM**
Zeitschrift für die Gesamte Innere Medizin
und Ihre Grenzgebiete *d:* **Z Gesamte
Inn Med,** *d:* **Z Gesamte Inn Med
Grenzgeb,** *d:* **Z Gesamte Inn Med Ihre
Grenzgeb,** *d:* **Z Ges Inn Med**
Zeitschrift für die Gesamte Innere Medizin
und Ihre Grenzgebiete. Klinik,
Pathologie, Experiment *d:* **Z Gesamte
Inn Med Grenzgeb Klin Pathol Exp**
Zeitschrift für die Gesamte Innere Medizin
und Ihre Grenzgebiete. Supplementum
d: **Z Gesamte Inn Med Ihre Grenzgeb
Suppl**
Zeitschrift für die Gesamte Naturwissen-
schaft *d:* **Z Gesamte Naturwiss**
Zeitschrift für die gesamte Wasserwirtschaft
d: **ZGWW**
Zeitschrift für die Gesamten
Naturwissenschaften *d:* **Zs Ges Naturw**
Zeitschrift für Flugwissenschaften und
Weltraumforschung *d:* **Z Flugwiss und
Weltraumforsch,** *d:* **Z Flugwiss
Weltraumforsch,** *d:* **ZFW**
Zeitschrift für Genossenschaftliche
Tierversicherung *d:* **Ztschr
Genossensch Tierversich**
Zeitschrift für Geologische Wissenschaften
e: **Z Geol Wiss**
Zeitschrift für Geomorphologie *d:*
Zeitschr Geomorphologie, *d:* **Z
Geomorph,** *d:* **ZGMPA**

Zeitschrift für Geomorphologie. Gebrüder
Bornträger *d:* **ZG**
Zeitschrift für Geomorphologie. Neue Folge
d: **Zeitschr Geomorphologie Neue
Folge**
Zeitschrift für Geomorphologie
Supplementband. Gebrüder Borntraeger,
Berlin *d:* **Z. Geomorphol. Suppl.bd.**
Zeitschrift für Geophysik *d:* **Zeitschr
Geophysik,** *d:* **ZfGph,** *d:* **Z. Geophys.,** *d:*
ZGPh
Zeitschrift für Geopolitik *d:* **ZGeoP**
Zeitschrift für Gesundheitstechnik und
Städtehygiene *d:* **Z Gesundheitstech
Städtehyg**
Zeitschrift für Gewässerkunde *d:* **ZGK,** *d:*
ZGW
Zeitschrift für Gletscherkunde und
Glazialgeologie *d:* **Zeitschr
Gletscherkunde u Glazialgeologie,** *d:* **Z
Gletscherk Glazialgeol,** *d:* **Z.
Gletsch.kd. Glazialgeol.**
Zeitschrift für Immunitäisforschung.
Immunobiology *d:* **Z Immunitätsforsch
Immunobiol**
Zeitschrift für Immunitäisforschung.
Immunobiology. Supplemente *d:* **Z
Immunitätsforsch Immunobiol Suppl**
Zeitschrift für Infektionskrankheiten,
Parasitäre Krankheiten, und Hygiene der
Haustiere *d:* **Ztschr Infektionskr
Haustiere**
Zeitschrift für Klinische Medizin *d:* **Z
Klin Med**
Zeitschrift für klinische Medizin *d:* **ZKlM**
Zeitschrift für Klinische Medizin [Berlin]
d: **Ztschr Klin Med [Berlin]**
Zeitschrift für Kristallographie,
Kristallgeometrie, Kristallphysik,
Kristallchemie *d:* **Z Kr,** *d:* **Z Krist,** *d:* **Z
Kristall,** *d:* **Z Kristallog Kristallgeom
Krystallphys Kristallchemie,** *d:* **Z.
Kristallogr.,** *d:* **Z Kristallogr
Kristallgeom Kristallphys Kristallchem**
Zeitschrift für Mathematischen und Natur-
wissenschaftlichen Unterricht *d:* **ZMNU**
Zeitschrift für Medizinalbeamte *d:*
Z.f.Med.B., *d:* **ZMB,** *d:*
Zschr.f.M.Beamte
Zeitschrift für Medizinische Chemie *d:* **Z
Med Chem**
Zeitschrift für Medizinische Isotopen-
forschung und deren Grenzgebiete *d:* **Z
Med Isotopenforsch Deren Grenzgeb**
Zeitschrift für Medizinische Laboratoriums-
diagnostik *d:* **Z Med Lab Diagn**
Zeitschrift für Medizinische
Laboratoriumsdiagnostik *d:* **Z Med
Laboratoriumsdiagn**
Zeitschrift für Medizinische Labortechnik
d: **Z. Med. Labortech.,** *d:* **Z. Med.
Labortech.**
Zeitschrift für Medizinische Mikrobiologie
und Immunologie *d:* **Z Med Mikrobiol
Immunol**
Zeitschrift für Medizinische Mikroskopie
d: **Z Med Mikrosk**
Zeitschrift für medizinische Psychologie
und Psycho-Therapie *d:* **ZmPsPth**
Zeitschrift für Medizinstudenten und
Assistenten *d:* **Med Ass**
Zeitschrift für Meteorologie *d:* **Z.
Meteorol.**

Zeitschrift für Militärmedizin *d:* **Z Militärmed**

Zeitschrift für Morphologie der Tiere *d:* **Z Morphol Tiere,** *d:* **Z Morph Tie**

Zeitschrift für Morphologie und Oekologie *d:* **ZMOe**

Zeitschrift für Morphologie und Oekologie der Tiere *d:* **Z. Morphol. Oekol. Tiere**

Zeitschrift für Morphologie und Ökologie der Tiere *d:* **Z Morph Okol Tiere,** *d:* **ZMOTA,** *d:* **Ztschr Morphol u Ökol Tiere**

Zeitschrift für Naturforschung *d:* **Z Nat F,** *d:* **Z. Nat.forsch.,** *d:* **Z Naturforsch,** *d:* **ZNTFA**

Zeitschrift für Naturforschung. A *d:* **Z Naturfo A**

Zeitschrift für Naturforschung. B *d:* **Z Naturfo B**

Zeitschrift für Naturforschung. C *d:* **Z Naturfo C**

Zeitschrift für Naturforschung. Section B. Inorganic Chemistry, Organic Chemistry *d:* **Z Naturforsch Sect B**

Zeitschrift für Naturforschung. Section C. *d:* **Z Naturforsch [C]**

Zeitschrift für Naturforschung. Section C. Biosciences *d:* **Z Naturforsch Sect C Biosci**

Zeitschrift für Naturforschung. Teil A *d:* **Z Naturforsch Teil A**

Zeitschrift für Naturforschung. Teil A. Astrophysik, Physik, und Physikalische Chemie *e:* **Z Naturforsch A**

Zeitschrift für Naturforschung. Teil B *d:* **Z Naturf B**

Zeitschrift für Naturforschung. Teil B. Anorganische Chemie, Organische Chemie *d:* **Z Naturforsch B Anorg Chem Org Chem**

Zeitschrift für Naturforschung. Teil B. Anorganische Chemie, Organische Chemie, Biochemie, Biophysik, Biologie *d:* **Z Naturforsch B Anorg Chem Org Chem Biochem Biophys Biol**

Zeitschrift für Naturforschung. Teil C. Biochemie, Biophysik, Biologie, Virologie *d:* **Z Naturf C,** *d:* **Z Naturforsch C Biochem Biophys Biol Virol,** *d:* **Z Naturforsch Teil C Biochem Biophys Biol Virol**

Zeitschrift für Naturforschung. Teil C. Biosciences *d:* **Z Naturforsch C Biosci,** *d:* **Z Naturforsch Teil C**

Zeitschrift für Naturheilkunde *d:* **Z Naturheilk**

Zeitschrift für Naturwissenschaft *d:* **ZfNw**

Zeitschrift für Naturwissenschaftlich-Medizinische Grundlagenforschung *d:* **Z Naturwiss-Med Grundlagenforsch**

Zeitschrift für Ökologie und Naturschutz *d:* **Z. Ökol. Nat.schutz**

Zeitschrift für Praktische Geologie *d:* **Z Prakt Geol**

Zeitschrift für praktische Geologie *d:* **ZprG**

Zeitschrift für Praktische Geologie *d:* **Zs Prak G**

Zeitschrift für Präventivmedizin *d:* **Z Präventivmed**

Zeitschrift für Psychosomatische Medizin *d:* **ZPSMA,** *d:* **Z Psychosom Med**

Zeitschrift für Psychosomatische Medizin und Psychoanalyse *d:* **Z Psychos M,** *d:* **Z Psychosom Med Psychoanal**

Zeitschrift für Psychotherapie und Medizinische Psychologie *d:* **ZPMPA,** *d:* **Z Psychother Med Psychol,** *d:* **Z Psychot M**

Zeitschrift für Rechtsmedizin *d:* **Z Rechtsmed**

Zeitschrift für Säugetierkunde *d:* **Z Säugetierkd**

Zeitschrift für Schulgesundheitspflege und soziale Hygiene *d:* **ZfSusH**

Zeitschrift für Schulgesundheitspflege [und Soziale Hygiene] *d:* **ZSchGpfl**

Zeitschrift für soziale Medizin *d:* **ZsozM**

Zeitschrift für Technische Biologie *d:* **Z Tech Biol**

Zeitschrift für Tierernährung und Futtermittelkunde *d:* **Z Tierernähr Futtermittelkd**

Zeitschrift für Tiermedizin *d:* **ZTM**

Zeitschrift für Tierphysiologie, Tierernährung, und Futtermittelkunde *d:* **Z Tierphysiol**

Zeitschrift für Tierphysiologie, Tierernährung, und Futtermittelkunde *d:* **Z Tierphysiol Tierernähr Futtermittelk,** *d:* **Z Tierphysiol Tiernaehr Futtermittelkd**

Zeitschrift für Tierpsychologie *d:* **ZT,** *d:* **Z Tierpsychol**

Zeitschrift für Tierpsychologie. Beiheft *e:* **Z Tierpsychol Beih**

Zeitschrift für Tierzüchtung und Züchtungsbiologie *d:* **ZTZü,** *e:* **Z Tierz Züchtungsbiol**

Zeitschrift für Tropenmedizin und Parasitologie *d:* **Z Tropenmed Parasitol,** *d:* **Z Trop Med**

Zeitschrift für Umweltpolitik *d:* **ZEUMD,** *d:* **Z Umweltpolit**

Zeitschrift für Umweltpolitik und Umweltrecht *d:* **ZfU**

Zeitschrift für Umweltrecht *d:* **ZUR**

Zeitschrift für Unfallmedizin und Berufskrankheiten *d:* **Z Unfallmed Berufskr**

Zeitschrift für Versuchstierkunde *d:* **Z Vers Kund,** *d:* **Z Versuchstierkd**

Zeitschrift für Wasser- und Abwasserforschung *d:* **Z Wasser Abwasser Forsch,** *d:* **Z Wasser u Abwasserforsch**

Zeitschrift für Wasser-Versorgung und Abwasserkunde *d:* **Z Wasser Versorg Abwasserkunde**

Zeitschrift für Wasserrecht *d:* **ZfW,** *d:* **Z Wasserrecht**

Zeitschrift für Wirtschaftsgeographie *d:* **Z Wirtschaftsgeog,** *d:* **Z Wirtschaftsgeographie**

Zeitschrift für wissenschaftliche Biologie *d:* **ZwBiol**

Zeitschrift für Wissenschaftliche Biologie. Abteilung A *d:* **ZWBAA,** *d:* **Z Wiss Biol Abt A**

Zeitschrift für wissenschaftliche Geographie *d:* **ZwG**

Zeitschrift für wissenschaftliche Insektenbiologie *d:* **ZwIB**

Zeitschrift für Wissenschaftliche Insektenbiologie *d:* **ZWIBA,** *d:* **Z Wiss InsektBiol,** *d:* **Z Wiss Insektenbiol**

Zeitschrift. Österreichischer Verein von Gas- und Wasserfachmännern *d:* **Z Österr Ver Gas Wasserfachmännern,** *d:* **Z Österr Ver Gas Wasserfachmännern**

Zeitschrift. Tokio Medizinischen Gesellschaft *d:* **Ztschr Tokio Med Gesellsch**

Zeitung für Gesunde *d:* **Ztg Gesunde**

Zement-Wasser Faktor *d:* **ZWF**

zementiert *d:* **zem.**

Zementierung *d:* **Zem.**

Zemleusiroistvo. Planirovka Sel'skikh Naselennykh Punklov i Geodeziya *e:* **Zemleustroistvo Plan Sel'sk Naselennykh Punktov Geod**

Zenana Bible and Medical Mission *e:* **Z.B.M.M.**

Zentimeter Wassersäule *d:* **cmWS**

Zentralamt des Deutschen Wetterdienstes *d:* **ZDW**

Zentralarchiv für Wehrmedizin *d:* **ZAW**

Zentralbibliothek der Medizin *d:* **ZBM**

Zentralbibliothek für Bakteriologie, Parasitenkunde, Infektionskrankheiten, und Hygiene. Erste Abteilung. Originale Reihe A. Medizinische Mikrobiologie und Parasitologie *d:* **ZMMPAO**

Zentralbibliothek für Medizin *d:* **ZBMed**

Zentralblatt der Experimentellen Medizin *d:* **Zentralbl Exp Med**

Zentralblatt für Arbeitsmedizin, Arbeitsschutz, Prophylaxe, und Ergonemie *d:* **Zentralbl Arbeitsmed Arbeitsschutz Prophyl Ergon**

Zentralblatt für Arbeitsmedizin, Arbeitsschutz, Prophylaxe und Ergonomie *d:* **Zentralbl Arbeitsmed Arbeitsschutz Prophyl Ergon**

Zentralblatt für Arbeitsmedizin, Arbeitsschutz, und Prophylaxe *d:* **Zentralbl Arbeitsmed Arbeitsschutz Prophylaxe**

Zentralblatt für Arbeitsmedizin und Arbeitsschutz *d:* **Zbl A Med,** *d:* **Zentralbl Arbeitsmed,** *d:* **Zentralbl. Arbeitsmed. Arbeits,** *d:* **Zentralbl Arbeitsmed Arbeitsschutz**

Zentralblatt für Arbeitsrmedizin, Arbeitsschutz, und Prophylaxe *d:* **Zentralbl Arbeitsmed Arbeitsschutz Prophyl**

Zentralblatt für Bakteriologie, Mikrobiologie, und Hygiene. Abteilung 1. Originale A. Medizinische Mikrobiologie, Infektionskrankheiten, und Parasitol *d:* **Zentralbl Bakteriol Mikrobiol Hyg Abt 1 Orig A**

Zentralblatt für Bakteriologie, Mikrobiologie, und Hygiene. 1 Abteilung. Originale C *d:* **Zentralbl Bakteriol Mikrobiol Hyg 1 Abt Orig C**

Zentralblatt für Bakteriologie, Mikrobiologie, und Hygiene. Serie B. Umwelthygiene, Krankenhaushygiene, Arbeitshygiene, Präventive Medizin *d:* **Zentralbl Bakteriol Mikrobiol Hyg Ser B**

Zentralblatt für Bakteriologie, Mikrobiologie, und Hygiene. Series A. Medical Microbiology, Infectious Diseases, Virology, Parasitology *d:* **Zentralbl Bakteriol Mikrobiol Hyg Ser A**

Zentralblatt für Bakteriologie, Parasitenkunde, Infektionskrankheiten, und

Hygiene. Abteilung 1. Medizinisch-Hygienische Bakteriologie, Virusforschung d: **ZBPHA**

Zentralblatt für Bakteriologie, Parasitenkunde, Infektionskrankheiten, und Hygiene. Abteilung 1. Medizinisch-Hygienische Rakteriologie, Virusforschung d: **Zentralbl Bakteriol Parasitenkd Infektionskr Hyg Abt 1 Ref**

Zentralblatt für Bakteriologie, Parasitenkunde, Infektionskrankheiten, und Hygiene. Erste Abteilung. Originale Reihe A. Medizinische Mikrobiologie und d: **Zentralbl Bakteriol Orig A**

Zentralblatt für Bakteriologie, Parasitenkunde, Infektionskrankheiten, und Hygiene. Naturwissenschaftliche Abteilung d: **Zentralbl Bakteriol Parasitenkd Infektionskrankheiten Hyg II**

Zentralblatt für Bakteriologie, Parasitenkunde, Infektionskrankheiten, und Hygiene. Zweite Naturwissenschaftliche Abteilung. Mikrobiologie der Landwir d: **Zentralbl Bakteriol Naturwiss**

Zentralblatt für Bakteriologie, Parasitenkunde, und Infektionskrankheiten. Abteilung 1. Medizinische-Hygienische Bakteriologie Virusforschung und Tier d: **Zentralbl Bakteriol Parasitenkd Infektionskr Abt 1**

Zentralblatt für Biologische Aerosol-Forschung d: **Zentralbl Biol Aerosol-Forsch**

Zentralblatt für die Gesamte Rechtsmedizin und ihre Grenzgebiete d: **Zentralbl Gesamte Rechtsmed**

Zentralblatt für die medizinischen Wissenschaften d: **Zbl.f.m.Wiss.**

Zentralblatt für Geologie und Paläontologie d: **Zentralbl Geol Paläontol**

Zentralblatt für Geologie und Paläontologie. E. Schweizerbart'sche Verlagsbuchhandlung [Nägele u. Obermiller]. Stuttgart d: **Zent.bl. Geol. Paläontologie.**

Zentralblatt für Geologie und Paläontologie. Teil 1. Allgemeine, Angewandte, Regionale, und Historische Geologie d: **Zentralbl Geol Paläontol Teil 1**

Zentralblatt für Geologie und Paläontologie. Teil 2. Paläontologie d: **Zentralbl Geol Paläontol Teil 2**

Zentralblatt für Hygiene und Umweltmedizin d: **Zentralbl Hyg Umweltmed**

Zentralblatt für Innere Medizin d: **Zentralbl Inn Med**

Zentralblatt für Mikrobiologie d: **ZEMIDI**

Zentralblatt für Mineralogie, Geologie und Paläontologie d: **Zentralbl Mineral Geol Paläontol**

Zentralblatt für Mineralogie, Geologie, und Paläontologie. Teil 2. Gesteinskunde, Lagerstättenkunde, Allgemeine, und Angewandte Geologie d: **Zentralbl Mineral Geol Paläontol Teil 2**

Zentralblatt für Mineralogie, Geologie, und Paläontologie. Teil 3. Historische und Regionale Geologie, Paläontologie d: **Zentralbl Mineral Geol Paläontol Teil 3**

Zentralblatt für Mineralogie, Geologie, und Paläontologie. Teil 1. Kristallographie und Mineralogie d: **Zentralbl Mineral Geol Paläontol Teil 1**

Zentralblatt für Mineralogie. Teil 2. Petrographie, Technische Mineralogie, Geochemie, und Lagerstättenkunde d: **Zentralbl Mineral Teil 2**

Zentralblatt für Verkehrs-Medizin, Verkehrs-Psychologie Luft- und Raumfahrt-Medizin d: **Zentralbl Verkehrs-Med Verkehrs-Psychol Luft-Raumfahrt-Med**

Zentralblatt für Veterinärmedizin d: **Zentralbl Veterinärmed**

Zentralblatt für Veterinärmedizin. Beiheft d: **Zentralbl Veterinärmed Beih**

Zentralblatt für Veterinärmedizin. Reihe A d: **Zbl Vet A**, d: **Zentralbl Veterinärmed [A]**, d: **Zentralbl Veterinärmed Reihe A**

Zentralblatt für Veterinärmedizin. Reihe B d: **Zbl Vet B**, d: **Zentbl Vel Med B**, d: **Zentralbl Veterinärmed [B]**

Zentralblatt für Veterinärmedizin, Reihe B d: **Zentralbl. Veterinärmed., Reih**

Zentralblatt für Veterinärmedizin. Reihe B d: **Zentralbl Veterinärmed Reihe B**

Zentralblatt für Veterinärmedizin. Reihe C d: **Zentralbl Veterinärmed Reihe C**

Zentrale Dokumentation für Geographie d: **ZDG**

Zentrale Dokumentationsstelle für Geographie beim Institut für Landeskunde in der Bundesanstalt für Landeskunde und Raumforschung, Bonn d: **ZDG**

Zentrale Erfassungs- und Bewertungsstelle [für/von Umweltchemikalien im Bundesgesundheitsamt] d: **ZEBS**

Zentrale für Gas- und Wasserverwendung d: **ZfGW**

Zentrale Kommission für Biologische Sicherheit (in der Gentechnologie) d: **ZKBS**

Zentrale Leitstelle für Medizinische Information und Dokumentation d: **ZLMID**

Zentrale Medizin-Meteorologische Forschungsstelle, Freiburg d: **ZMMF**

zentrale Naturschutzverwaltung d: **ZNV**

Zentrale Tierlaboratorien [Freie Universität] d: **ZTL**

Zentrale Umweltschutzgruppe d: **ZUG**

Zentrale Versuchstieranlage [des Bundesgesundheitsamtes] d: **ZVA**

zentrale Wasserversorgungsanlage d: **ZWA**, d: **ZWVA**

Zentrale Wetterdienstgruppe d: **ZWD**

zentraler medizinischer Schreibdienst d: **ZMS**

Zentrales Geologisches Institut d: **ZGI**

Zentrales Hauptquartier d: **ZHQ**

Zentrales Projektierungsbüro der Textilindustrie d: **ZPT**

Zentrales Reserve-Hauptquartier d: **ZRHQ**

Zentrales Umwelt-Kompetenz-System d: **ZEUS**

Zentrales Umwelt- und Klimadaten-Metainformationssystem d: **ZUDIS**

Zentralinstitut für Arbeitsmedizin d: **ZAM**

Zentralinstitut für Mikrobiologie und experimentelle Therapie d: **ZIMET**

Zentralinstitut für Molekularbiologie d: **ZIM**

Zentralinstitut für Seelische Gesundheit d: **ZSG**

Zentralinstitut für Seelische Gesundheit, Mannheim d: **ZI**

Zentralinstitut für Versuchstierzucht. Annual Report d: **Zentralinst Versuchstierzucht Annu Rep**

Zentralinstitut Physik der Erde d: **ZIPE**

Zentralkongreß für Medizinische Assistenzberufe d: **ZMA**

Zentralstelle der Länder für Gesundheitsschutz bei Medizinprodukten d: **ZLG**

Zentralstelle für Luft- und Raumfahrtdokumentation und-information d: **ZLDI**

Zentralstelle für Medizinaltarife d: **ZMT**

Zentralstelle für Naturschutz d: **ZfN**

Zentralstelle für Schiffs- und Maschinentechnik [der Wasser- und Schiffahrtsverwaltung des Bundes] d: **ZSM**

Zentralstelle für Sicherheit von Medizingeräten d: **ZfS**

Zentralstelle für Sicherheitvon Medizingeräten d: **ZfS**

Zentralstelle für Umwelterziehung, Essen d: **ZUE**

Zentralstelle für Unfaliverhütung und Arbeitsmedizin d: **ZeFU**

Zentralstelle zur Erfassung und Bewertung von Ersatz und Ergänzungsmethoden zu Terversuchen des Bundesgesundheitsamtes d: **ZEBET-BGA**

Zentralstelle zur Erfassung und Bewertung von Ersatz- und Ergänzungsmethoden zum Tierversuch d: **ZEBET**

Zentralverband der Ärzte für Naturheilverfahren d: **ZAEN**, d: **ZÄN**

Zentralverband der Medizinischen Fusspfleger Deutschlands d: **ZFD**

Zentralverband Deutscher Pelztierzüchter eV d: **ZDP**

Zentralverband Sanitär-, Heizungs- und Klimatechnik d: **ZVSHK**

Zentralverein für Handelsgeographie zur Förderung deutscher Auslandsinteressen, Berlin d: **Z.f.H.**

Zentralvereinigung Medizintechnik d: **ZMT**

Zentralverwaltung für das Gesundheitswesen d: **ZVG**

Zentrum Biochemie Medizinische Hochschule d: **ZBH**

Zentrum für Angewandte Raumfahrttechnologie und Mikrogravitation d: **ZARM**

Zentrum für Astronomie, Raumfahrt und Meteorologie d: **ZARM**

Zentrum für Flachmeer- Küsten- und Meeresumweltforschung e.V. d: **TERRAMARE**

Zentrum für Innere Medizin d: **ZIM**

Zentrum für Innere Medizin im Klinikum d: **ZIMK**

Zentrum für Luft- und Raumfahrttechnik d: **ZLR**

Zentrum für Medizinische Ethik d: **ZME**

Zentrum für Molekularbiologie und Humangenetik [Heidelberg] d: **ZMBH**

Zentrum für Molekulare Biologie, Heidelberg d: **ZMBH**

Zentrum für Öffentlichkeitsarbeit der Wissenschaftlichen Medizinischen Fachgesellschaften d: **ZÖWMF**

Zentrum für Umweltforschung und Umwelttechnologie *d:* **UFT**

Zentrum zur Dokumentation für Naturheilverfahren *d:* **ZDN**

Zephyr Weather Information Service, Inc. *e:* **Zephyr**

Zero Environment Impact *e:* **ZEI**

zero-gravity environment *e:* **zge**

Zero headspace extractor *e:* **ZHE**

Zero to Space *e:* **Z to Sp**

Zero-To-Space *e:* **ZTS**

Zero-Zero Weather *e:* **ZZW**

Zeszyly Naukowe Akademii Gorniczo-Hutniczej Imienia Stanislawa Staszica. Geologia *P:* **Zesz Nauk Akad Gorn-Hutn Stanislawa Staszica Geot**

Zeszyty Naukowe Akademii Gomiczo-Hutniczej [Krakow]. Geologia *P:* **ZNGGA**

Zeszyty Naukowe Akademii Gorniczo-Hutniczej [Cracow]. Geologia *P:* **Zesz Nauk Akad Gorn Hutn [Cracow] Geol**

Zeszyty Naukowe Akademii Gorniczo-Hutniczej Imienia Stanislawa Staszica. Geologia *P:* **Zesz Nauk Akad Gorn-Hutn Im Stanislawa Staszica Geol**, *P:* **Zesz Nauk Akad Gorn-Hutn Stanisl Staszica Geol**, *P:* **ZNAGD**

Zeszyty Naukowe Akademii Gorniczo-Hutniczej [Krakow]. Geologia *P:* **Zesz Nauk Akad Gorn-Hutn [Krakow] Geol**

Zeszyty Naukowe Uniwersytetu Jagiellońskiego. Prace Biologii Molekularnej *P:* **Zesz Nauk Uniw Jagielloń Pr Biol Mol**, *P:* **ZNUMD**

Zeszyty Naukowe Uniwersytetu Mikolaja Kopernika w Toruniu. Nauki Matematyczno-Przyrodniczne Biologia *P:* **ZMKBA6**

ZFA [Zeitschrift für Allgemeinmedizin] *e:* **ZAMNA**

Zhurnal Eksperimental'noi Biologii i Meditsiny *R:* **Zh Eksp Biol Med**

Zhurnal Geofiziki *R:* **Zh Geofiz**

Zhurnal Gigieny, Epidemiologii, Mikrobiologii, i Immunologii *R:* **ZGEIA**, *R:* **Zh Gig Epidemiol Mikrobiol Immunol**

Zhurnal Mikrobiologii *R:* **Zhurnal Mikrobiol**

Zhurnal Mikrobiologii, Epidemiologii, i Immunobiologii *R:* **Zh Mikrob E**, *R:* **Zh**

Mikrobiol Epidemiol Immunobiol, *R:* **ZMEIA**

Zhurnal Mikrobiologii i Immunobiologii *R:* **Zh Mikrobiol Immunobiol**

Zhurnal Obshchei Biologii *R:* **Zh Obs Biol**, *R:* **Zh Obshch Biol**

Zielfunktionswert bei Start der Sekantenorientierten Stochastik *d:* **ZF0**

Zielorientierte Projektplanung *d:* **ZOPP**

Zimbabwe Environment and Design *e:* **ZED**

Zimbabwe Medical Aid *e:* **ZIMA**

Zinc Atmospheric Tracer *e:* **ZAT**

zinc-sulfide atmospheric tracer *e:* **zsat**

Zirconium-Water Oxidation Kinetics *e:* **ZWOK**

Zisenoxide und -hydroxide *d:* **E 172**

zitieren *d:* **zit.**

zitiert *d:* **zit.**

zitiert nach *d:* **zit.n.**

Ziva. Casopis pro Biologickou Praci *c:* **Ziva**

Zona Agroecológica *s:* **ZAE**

Zona del Frente Polar *s:* **PFZ**

zone de protection *f:* **ZP**

zone de protection du patrimonie urbain architectural et paysager *f:* **ZPPAUP**

Zone de Protection Sapciale *f:* **ZPS**

Zone Naturelle d'Intérêt Ecologique, Faunistique ou Floristique *f:* **ZNIEFF**, *f:* **ZNIEFF**

Zone of Polarising Activity *e:* **ZPA**

zone of polarizing activity *e:* **zpa**

Zone of Protection *e:* **ZP**

Zones expérimentales de recherche sur l'environnement côtier *f:* **CERDA**

Zoo Biology *e:* **ZOBIDX**, *e:* **Zoo Biol**

Zoogeographic[al] *e:* **zoogeog.**

zoogeography *e:* **zoogeog**

Zooiatria Revista de Medicina Veterinaria y Produccion Pecuaria *s:* **Zooiatr Rev Med Vet Prod Pecu**

Zoologia e Biologia Marinha *p:* **Zoo] Biel Mar**

Zoologia e Biologia Marinha [Sao Paulo] [Nova Serie] *p:* **Zool Biol Mar [Sao Paulo] [Nova Ser]**

Zoologische Jahrbücher-Abteilung Allgemeine Zoologie und Physiologie der Tiere *d:* **Zool Jahrb**

Zoologische Jahrbücher. Abteilung für Allgemeine Zoologie und Physiologie der

Tiere *d:* **Zool Jahrb Abt Allg Zool Physiol Tiere**, *d:* **Zool Jb Abt Allg Zool Physiol Tiere**, *d:* **Zool Jhrb Abt Allg Zool Physiol Tiere**

Zoologische Jahrbücher. Abteilung für Anatomie und Ontogenie der Tiere *d:* **Zool Jahrb Abt Anat Ontog Tiere**

Zoologische Jahrbücher. Abteilung für Systematik Ökologie und Geographie der Tiere *d:* **Zool Jahrb Abt Syst Ökol Geogr Tiere**, *d:* **Zool Jb Abt Syst Okol Geog Tiere**

Zoologische Jahrbücher. Abteilung für Systematik Ökologie und Geographie der Tiere [Jena] *d:* **Zool Jahrb Abt Syst [Jena]**

Zoophysiology and Ecology *e:* **Zoophysiol Ecol**

Zootecnica e Nutrizione Animale *i:* **ZNAND**, *i:* **Zootec Nutr Anim**

Zrzeszenie Polskich Nauczycieli Geografii *P:* **ZPNG**

zu ebener Erde *d:* **z.ebn.E.**

zu Pferde *d:* **z.Pf.**

zu viel Wasser *d:* **Wa +**

zu wenig Wasser *d:* **Wa -**

Zucker/Wasser Verhältnis *d:* **Z/W Verhältnis**

Zugeordnete Pixelfläche im Matrixraster *d:* **Azpix**

Zug[haken]-Pferdestärke *d:* **ZPS**

zur Wiederherstellung der Gesundheit *d:* **z.W.d.G.**

Zürcher Geographische Schriften *d:* **Zür. Geogr. Schr.**

Zürich Universität. Biologisches Institut-Eidgenössische Technische Hochschule. Geologisches Institut. Mitteilungen *d:* **Zür Univ Geol Inst-Eidgenöss Tech Hochsch Geol Inst Mitt**

Züricher Bund für Naturschutz *d:* **ZBN**

Zurn Environmental Engineers *e:* **ZEE**

Zurnal Eksperimental'noj i Kliniceskoj Mediciny *R:* **Z Eks Klin Med**

Zurnal Obscej Biologii *R:* **Z Obsc Biol**

Zusatzwasser *d:* **ZW**

Zveva Geografskih Drustev Slovenije *S:* **ZGDS**

Zweigorientiertes Informationszentrum *d:* **ZIZ**

Zwischenraum *d:* **ZWR**

   Abkürzungen und Akronyme in Ökologie, Umwelt, Geowissenschaften

DATE DUE

	PRINTED IN U.S.A.

INFINITE
ICON

A universally understood pictorial language that tells a story
succinctly and with style.

GINGKO PRESS

INFINITE ICON

ISBN 978-1-58423-607-8

First Published in the United States of America by
Gingko Press by arrangement with
Sandu Publishing Co., Ltd.

Gingko Press, Inc.
1321 Fifth Street
Berkeley, CA 94710 USA
Tel: (510) 898 1195
Fax: (510) 898 1196
Email: books@gingkopress.com
www.gingkopress.com

Sponsored by Design 360°
– Concept and Design Magazine

Edited and produced by
Sandu Publishing Co., Ltd.

Book design, concepts & art direction by
Sandu Publishing Co., Ltd.
Chief Editor: Wang Shaoqiang
Design Director: Niu Huizhen

info@sandupublishing.com
www.sandupublishing.com

Printed and bound in China

PREFACE

By_ Joel Lozano
Graphic Designer
Forma & Co

As a graphic design and communication studio, we have been immersed in the market trend that has brought us to the wonderful world of icons in recent years. We believe in synthesis, the essence of things, the concepts, in pure and basic, in simplicity and functionality, in order, in the economy of resources, in austerity and clear and direct messages.

What is an icon? An icon is a graphical schematic representation of a synthetic symbol, real object, or idea. For it to work as such, it must be instantly understandable for as many people as possible. An icon must fulfill its primary function of visually translating, clearly and directly, a concept, but it must also work as part of a family of icons as well as having its own personality.

There are many similarities when compared with the world of typography; icons are also intended to be "read", sometimes are very small, sometimes printed as headings, or on displays; they have different weights, and high or lower contrast with their surroundings affects them. There are many icons on the market, just as there are many typefaces. We find it interesting to create specific families of icons for different needs and create personalities for them that differentiate them from the rest.

An icon by itself is nothing; what is interesting is not the icon itself, but the family. The full set of icons and how they relate to each other is what's truly interesting, and it's important for clients to understand this. The graphic and conceptual coherence of these is very important as they themselves are a visual system, a symphony that should work perfectly. In the same way as a font, each character has the role of representing a letter and as a whole must be seen as part of the same family.

How do we deal with a commission?

The first thing we must know is what the icons' role will be, how and where they will be applied, which are the most important conditions, who will the consumer be, the approximate number of icons in the family, if any hierarchies will be needed, whether they will need to be animated, if they need to be responsive, what will the minimum display size be, the level of abstraction, etc. There are many factors to consider when designing a family of icons. Once these are analyzed, we search for the differentiating traits of the brand or the commission to create a series of essential features that can then be displayed on a grid designed to meet the specific needs of each project.

Why are there so many icons?

In recent years, there has been a growing demand for icons. There has always been a need for icons illustrating signage or instructions, but now the need for user interfaces has increased with the design of new websites, apps, and new devices. It has also changed the kind and speed of information consumption and communication between users, and don't forget the power and universality of an emoticon. This has meant that brands need to have their own icons as an element of their communication. Sometimes iconography must even replace written messages or photographs. An icon will not be worth a thousand words, or have as much detail as a photograph, but will usually enable faster and stronger comprehension.

What makes icon design passionate?

Differentiation. It is very difficult to re-imagine a visualization of a cloud or a sun. We have designed lots of icons, and very often we have to represent the same idea or the same object. The main challenge is to create an icon unique to a brand, with its own DNA, an icon that is theirs and no one else's. If the system is well designed, the sun we draw for them may resemble others but will only fit in the family for which it was designed.

How do we know in the studio if we are on the right path when we are in the process of designing a family of icons?

It's easy, if we feel the need to print a poster with one of the icons we are designing, that means we are going in the right direction.

PREFACE

By_ Maciej Świerczek
Graphic Designer
Jazzy Innovations

Icons are undoubtedly among the most interesting forms of communication. I wholeheartedly agree with the statement that a picture is worth a thousand words. Marketing often places a special emphasis on the brand image, which is communicated, among other ways, through a logo (using a simple, illustrative form as a sigil – also a form of an icon). We encounter icons while traveling or shopping, looking for the bathroom or the way to the airport; in a text message or e mail we use icons (emoticons) as a faster way to express our emotions. In the modern world we are surrounded by visual communication.

Aside from a strictly communicative function, icons can also be decorative, making them attractive for the viewer and creator alike, including me. That may also be the reason why the direction of my designing began to shape itself in this particular sphere. How to create a picture through the design process that is simple, meaningful and eye-catching at the same time? These kinds of questions are why I never find my work boring or mundane. A well-designed icon can convey the essence of a particular issue as well as its character without the need for a comment or translation into another language. It is the universalism of some symbols that makes their beauty so unique. Therefore combining them into new ones is what makes my work most pleasant. That way I can give them a new, wider meaning or stylization – a new character.

My adventure with designing began quite early, although I started working as a professional designer only 10 years ago. At first I studied classical painting and drawing, then I went on to study antiques restoration, only to end my last two years of education at a different college, majoring in graphic design. I had the opportunity to gain knowledge about many patterns and inspirations for designing an image, which highly and positively influenced the way I view my work – how to create, what to avoid. The diversity of styles I was able to familiarize myself and experiment with enhanced my creativity.

I work mostly as a vector graphics designer, in such fields as desktop publishing (DTP), mobile applications or Internet websites. Current trends, as well as the need to finish the project in short amount of time, are among the reasons why the main focus of my work are simple, one-dimensional flat design or linear images. Icons constitute the majority of them. Why is that? It results from the needs of my customers, as well as the development of new technologies, which must be able to communicate with the recipient in a quick and transparent manner. I assume that therein lies the essence of the popularity of icons. Their advantage over traditional, descriptive ways of sending a message, often a complex one, is mostly the clarity of signals – the clarity that is simpler than text or an elaborate outline. With proper experience, the process of creating icons itself is faster (although not in every case, obviously).

Even with the simplest illustrations, being successful requires a lot of time and devotion. Sometimes it manifests in the form of arduous education, sometimes as hard and obstinate work on the commission itself. One needs a lot of patience, particularly in the situations when the whole set of pictographs is needed. The process is similar to typography, which icons have a lot in common with. Typography is another area of my expertise. It is this exact field that taught me how important patience and perseverance are in designing a good set of both letters and pictographs. Sometimes a certain tenet of the concept, which works perfectly well for the first few pictographs, suddenly stops working for the next ones. In such cases, one needs to be creative – or start over from the beginning.

If I were to describe my own style of designing icons, I would say it is more linear and a little more typographic at present. If I am able to, I try to base the shapes on a geometric grid and give meaning to the weight of the stroke I draw my lines with. It is a bit conservative, but is an effective approach. I feel that some aesthetic standards are timeless and they should constitute a foundation for all additional experiments. Without this foundation, the final result will be just an artistic expression of the creator, with a lot of aesthetic shortcomings. These are conclusions I draw from looking at my very first works. The key to good results is a solid knowledge of your craft and the substantial amount of work put into designing. Experience is the only thing we are able to gain and enrich all our life, whilst the need for an artistic expression is more natural and primal. Therefore with every finished project I find myself more experienced and satisfied than the last.

CONTENTS

A STORY SUCCINCTLY AND WITH STYLE.

ICON SETS

CINEMA & KIDS
Design: Irina Kguglova

ORGANIC FOOD
Design: Wojciech Zasina

LEARN VISUAL LEARNING SYSTEM

Design: Klaudia Gal

The way information is presented plays a crucial role in the procedure of processing it. It affects people's memory, logic, and overall attitude toward a certain subject. The Learn Visual project tries to reveal the inherent opportunities for consistent, logical visual design in books, and apply them to school textbooks to create a new, faster, more convenient, and simpler studying experience. The designer presented this system using a history schoolbook which contains all the visual aids, including hundreds of individually designed icons.

The High Mic

oly Roman Emperor) and elected him king. In spring
attacked Hungary but due to Matthias' diplomacy the
defeated and in 1463 a peace treaty was signed. For
ne Holy Crown was returned and in 1464 Matthias was
Holy Crown had been stolen by Ladislas V's mother in
less, a dynastic treaty was also the price for giving back
. They agreed that Frederick or his successors would
ne if Matthias died without an heir.

reforms

lished a strong centralized monarchy following the
so-called 'new monarchs', Charles VII and Louis IX of
ry VII Tudor, based on professional officials, a profes-
i a broad taxing power.

administration

Royal Council as an advisory body. The Chancellery
in institution of administration but Matthias mostly

his attempt he was awarded the dynastic Matthias
ere quite frequent with a greater role for the nobles,
k was basically to vote taxation.
ofessional officials from among even lesser nobility
(e.g. Thomas Bakócz, a prelate of common origins).

finance

the crown were hardly enough for the defence of the
hias started a financial reform: the main income was
osidy (rendkívüli hadiadó), a special war tax (1 florin).
om ordinary revenues were abolished, noblemen
ates had to pay taxes. Revenues were administered
chant, János Ernuszt, who converted to Christianity.
of serfs was introduced: they paid taxes not by estates
nouseholds, the so-called 'füstpénz'. In return Matthias
ght of free movement and forbade unjust taxation.

ns

shed a powerful, reliable and disciplined standing
aries – the Black Army, which came to be called so
of the soldiers' armour. Thus the king was no longer
ne banderia of barons.

King Matthias I an

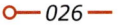

Visual System Elements
colours

The colours play a main role in the system, subconsciously stored in the memory help recalling and differentiating.

patterns

The patterns play a similar role as the colours on a different structural level

icons
/examples

The icons are simple images, leading the readers attention throughout the text, pointing out significant events and data.
These elements together create a visual aid which helps the reader in processing and recollecting information.

Winter   Summer

Autumn   Spring

LOST IN SEASONS

Design: Dylan McDonough

Custom symbol design for Summer, Autumn, Winter, and Spring to represent an "all seasons" retail fashion concept store in South Melbourne.

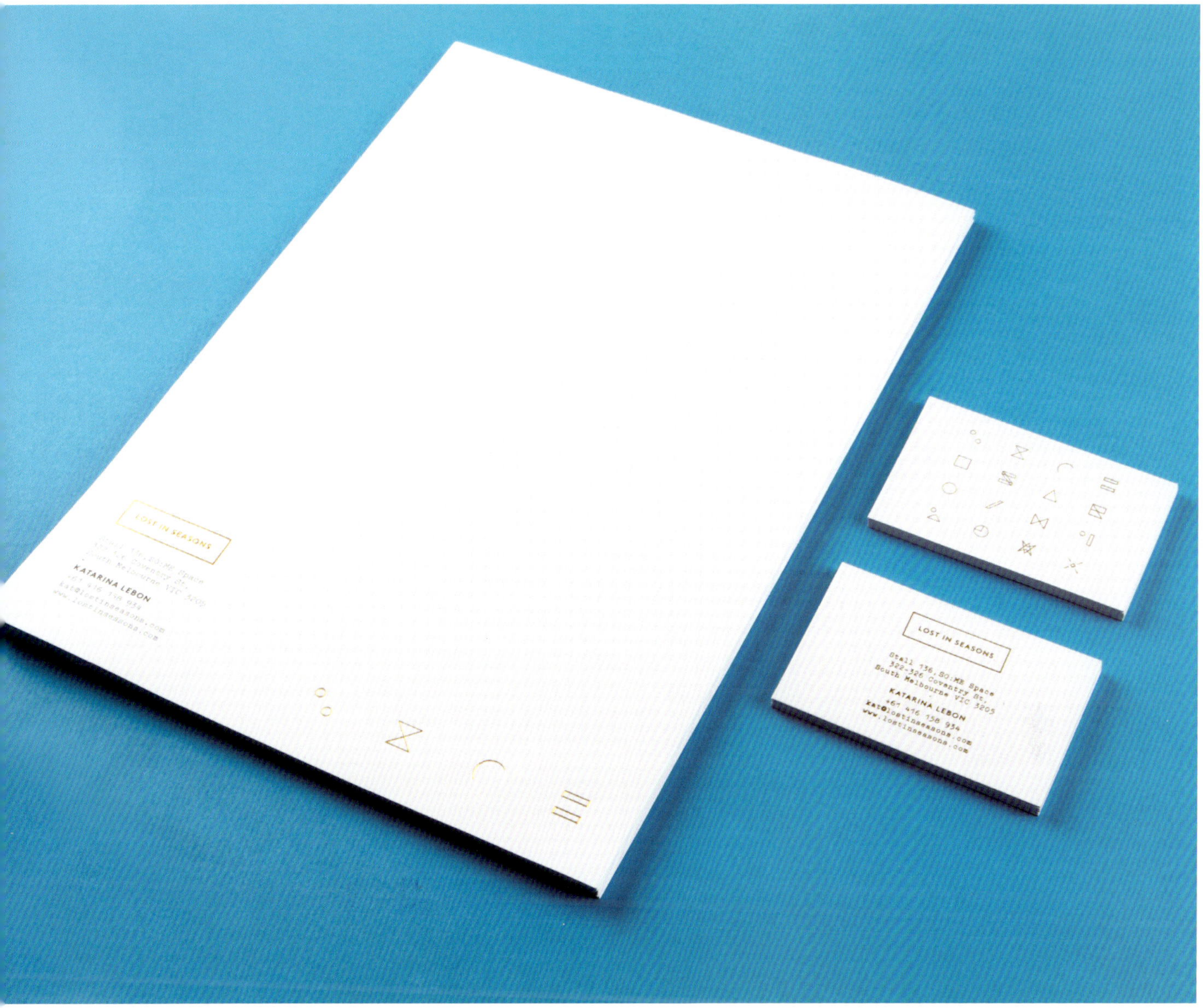
LOST IN SEASONS
KATARINA LEBON
LOST IN SEASONS
KATARINA LEBON

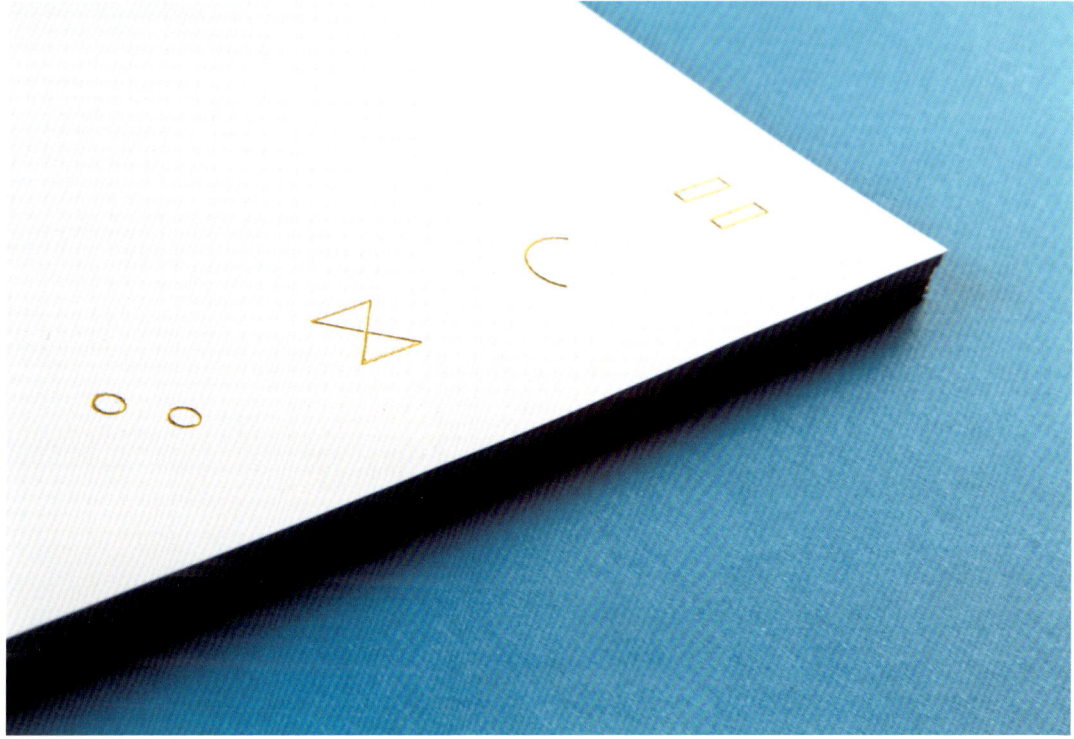

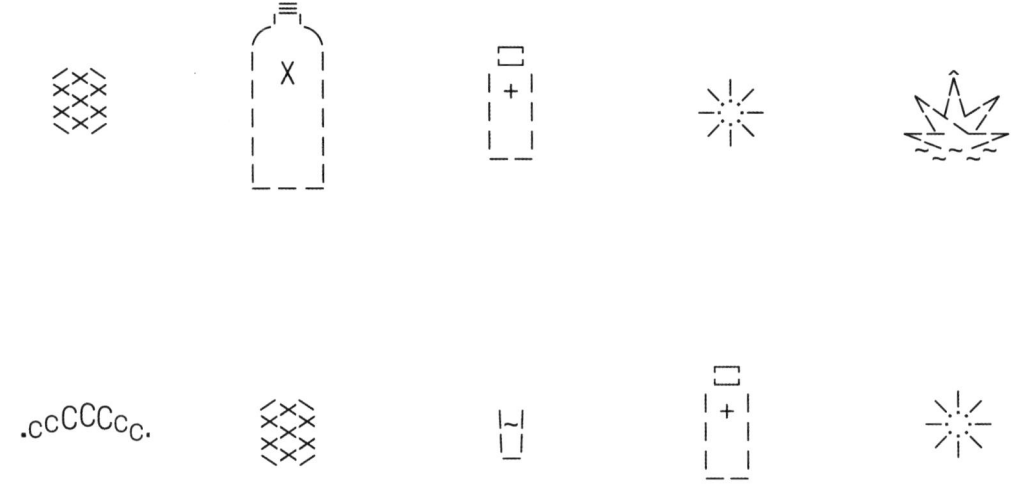

MEZCAL DE BATEO

Design: Futura

"Mezcal de Bateo" is the beverage for those who already know how to drink mezcal, and for those who enjoy it the way it should be. This is the mezcal that people in Mexico have at home and drink daily without affectations or exaggerated rituals. The name makes reference to this "everydayness," and the branding solution is focused on being 100% functional, homogeneous, and informative. A transparent product in every sense. So let's forget about the worm, the salt or the chili-spiced orange slice... a glass of water is the ideal accompaniment for a shot of "Mezcal de Bateo," and that's it.

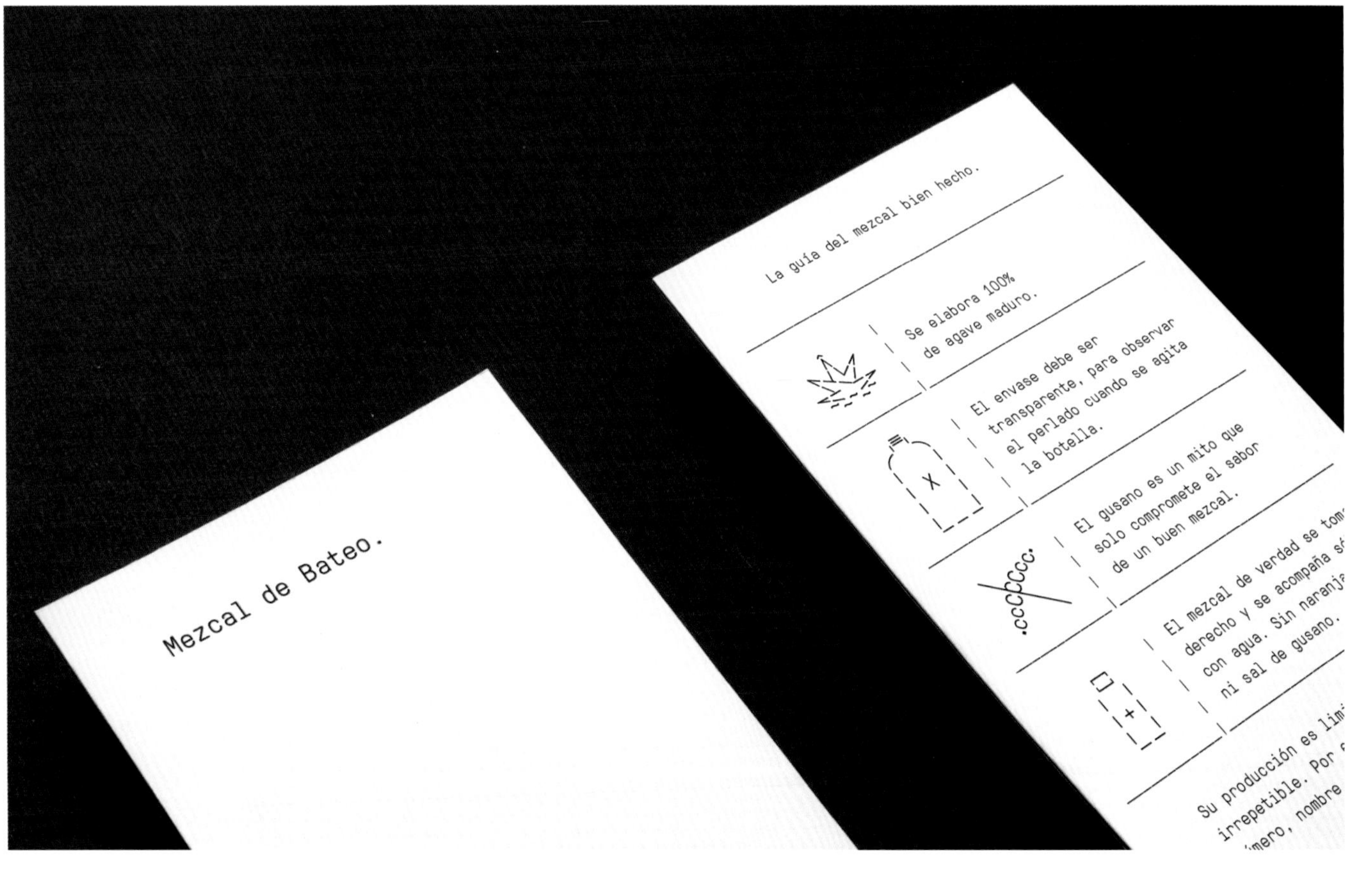

X

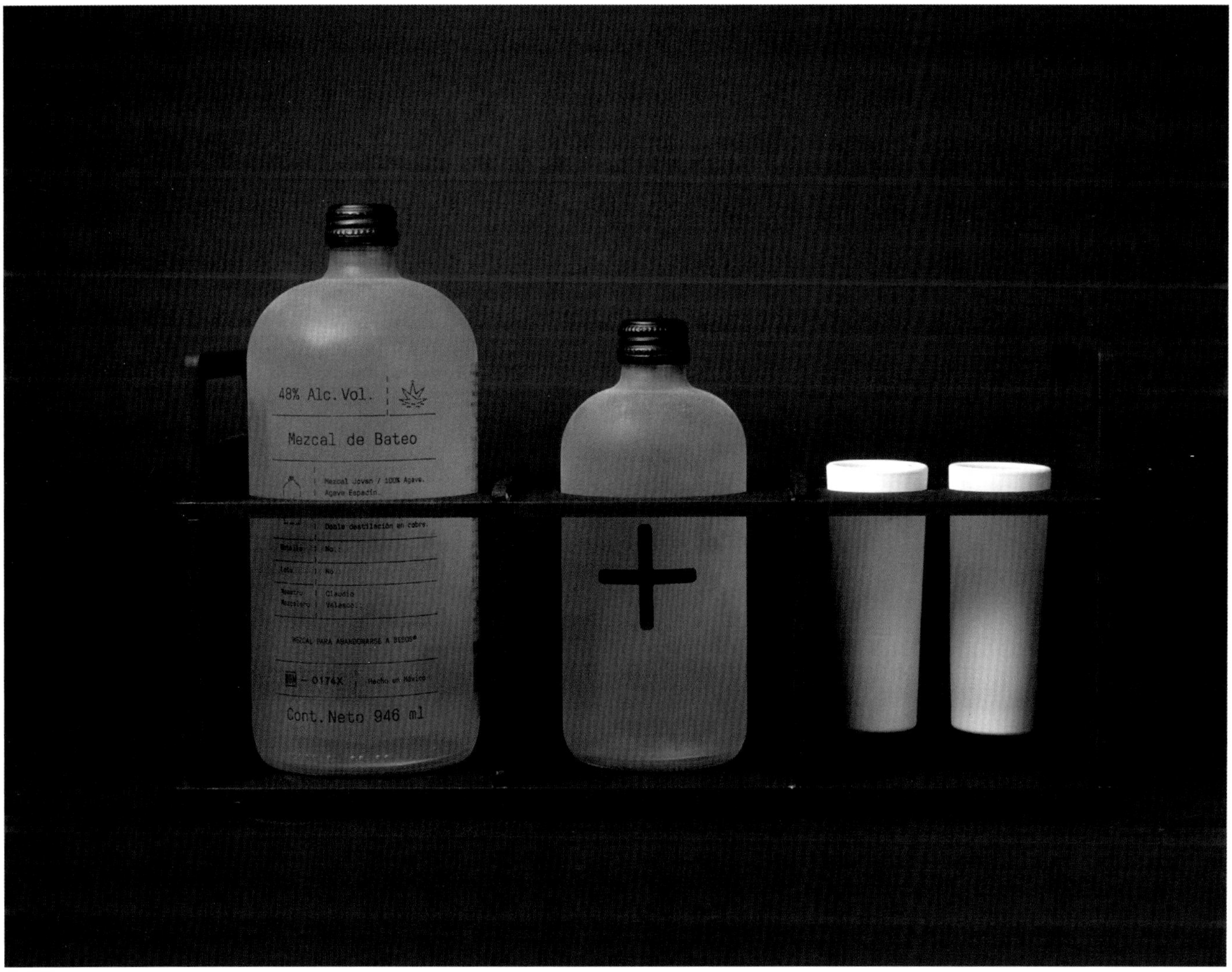
48% Alc. Vol.
Mezcal de Bateo
Mezcal Joven / 100% Agave.
Agave Espadín.
Doble destilación en cobre.
No.:
No.
Claudio
Velasco.
Cont. Neto 946 ml

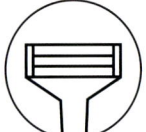    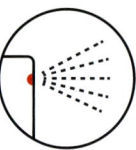 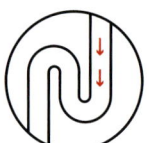 

BASIK

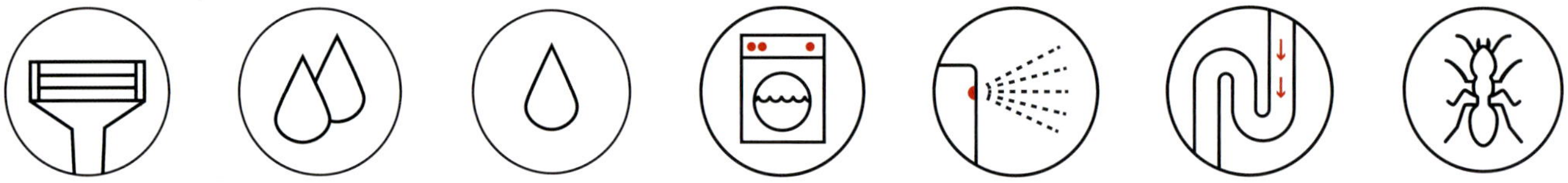

Design: Saana Hellsten

The name Basik refers to neutrality. The designer is digging into the basics of the products and leaving out the extras, like the unnecessary gendered visual language. Basik gives consumers the option to choose and customize the product based on its purpose, not gender. The project also shows how the same gender-neutral solutions, when done well, can work throughout an entire product range.

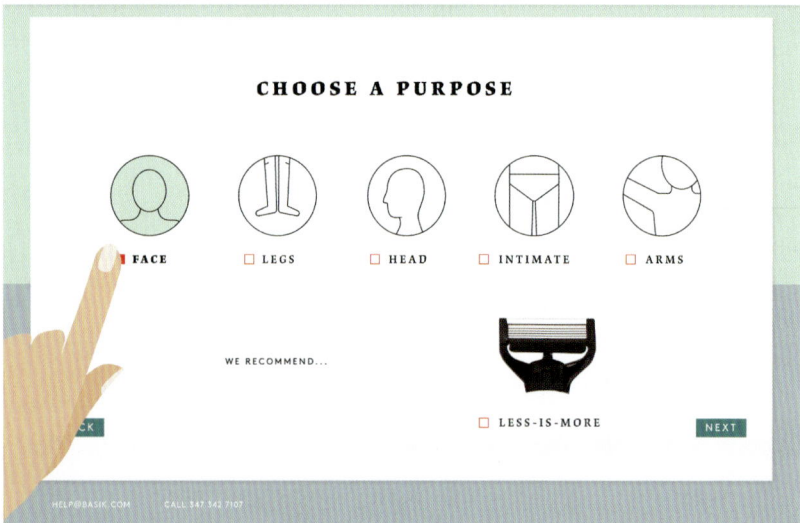

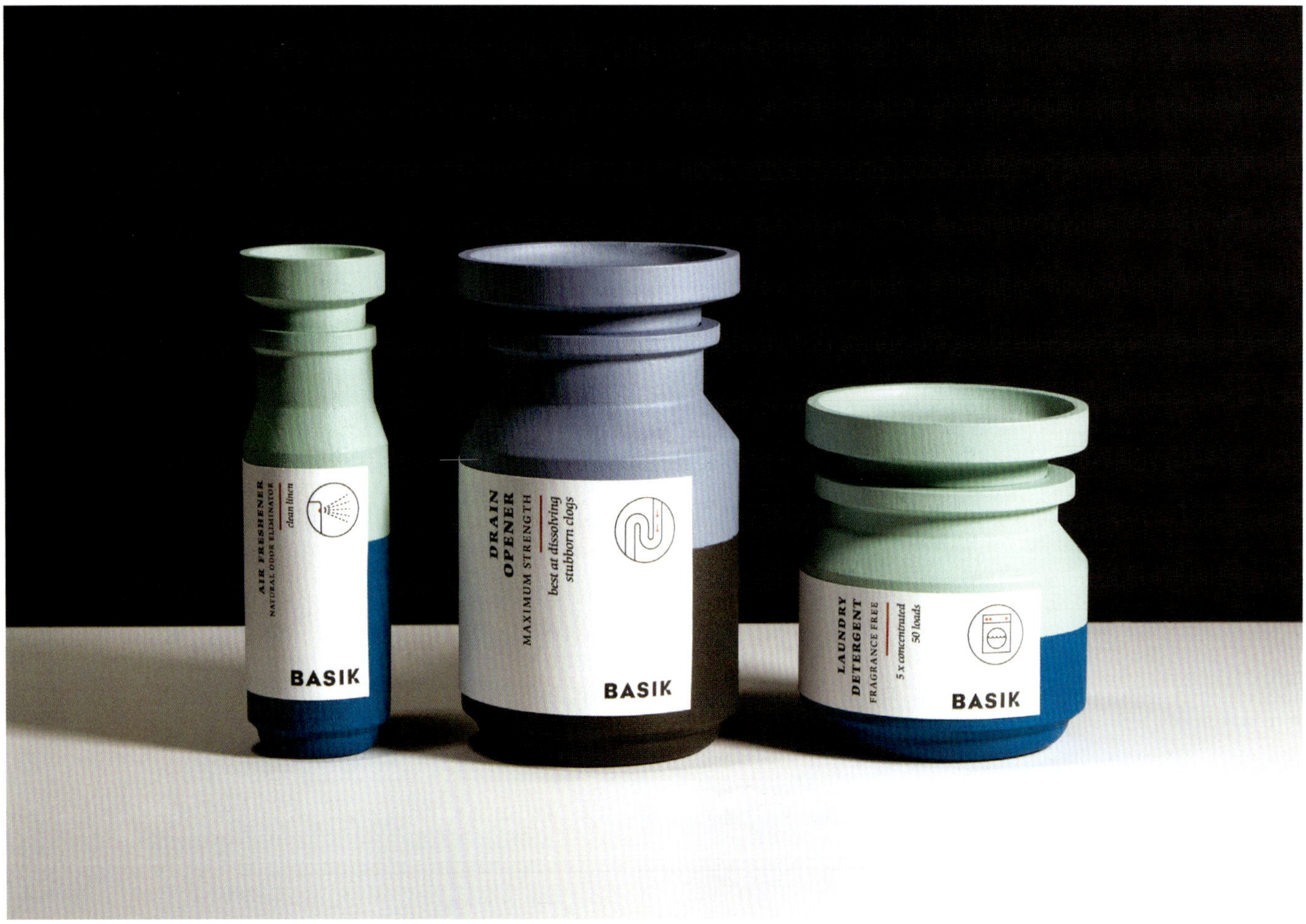

SHAVE GEL
DRY SKIN
fragrance free

BASIK

SHAVE GEL
NORMAL SKIN
fragrance free

BASIK

RAZOR
CUSTOM MADE | *for you*

BASIK

RAZOR
CUSTOM MADE | *for you*

BASIK

SHAVE GEL
DRY SKIN
fragrance free

BASIK

SHAVE GEL
NORMAL SKIN
fragrance free

BASIK

BASIK

BASIK

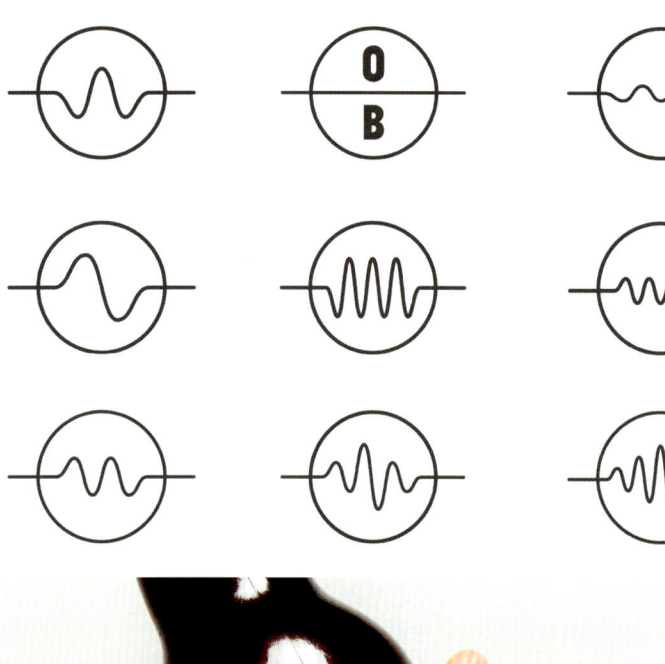

○— OSCILLATION BREWERS CO ────────────────

○— **Design:** POST ──────────────────────

Oscillation Brewers Co. brews their beer with raw passion and honesty. Their unfiltered, unrefined, and unpasteurized product needed an iconic identity to help it stand out on shelves full of "nondescript mass produced, flavorless, crystal-clear junk." Taking influence from the DIY sound system and rave cultures the founder was once part of, the designers used bright primary colors, bold typography, and no-nonsense language to convey the attitude and ideology of the brand. Each of the 9 beers in the range has its own character, tasting notes, and personality. This was illustrated by creating a different oscillation waveform for each bottle relating to the strength and flavor of the product inside.

ARTIGIANO

Design: POST

Artigiano offers specialty coffee, artisan food, fine wines, and craft beers. The designers developed the company's visual identity and communications to better reflect their offer of being both a place to grab an espresso during the day and to indulge in a glass of wine at night. The designers created a full custom typeface, signage, environmental graphics, iconography, patterns, and food and drink packaging, along with in-store posters and promotional postcards. Once implemented, the designer commissioned a suite of photographs which were used on the dynamically scrolling website.

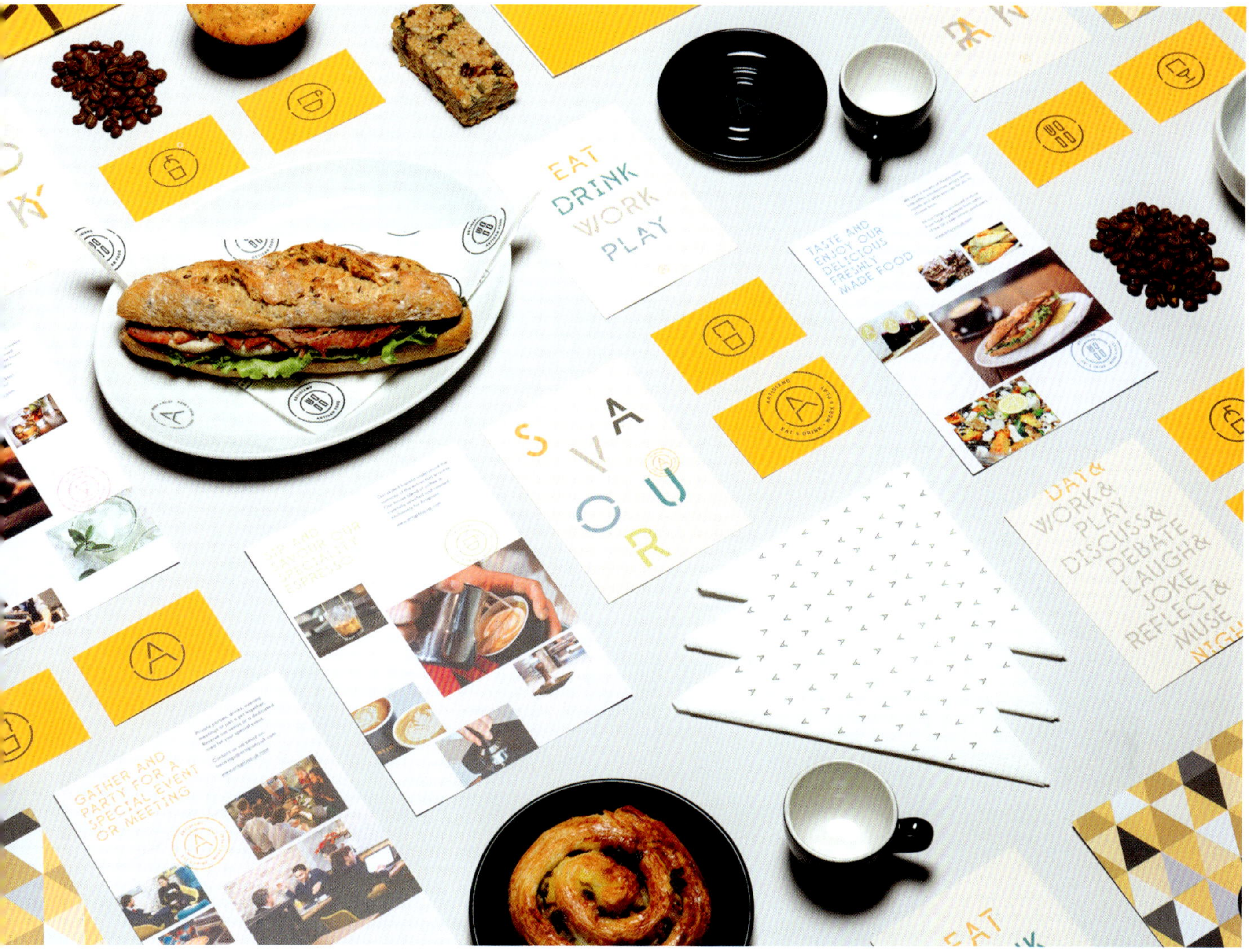
EAT
DRINK
WORK
PLAY
TASTE AND ENJOY OUR DELICIOUS FRESHLY MADE FOOD
SAVOUR
DAY & WORK & PLAY DISCUSS & DEBATE LAUGH & JOKE REFLECT & MUSE
GATHER AND PARTY FOR A SPECIAL EVENT OR MEETING

EAT & DRINK · WORK & PLAY
A
COFFEE & FOOD · WINE & BEER

ARTIGIANO
ARTISAN FOOD

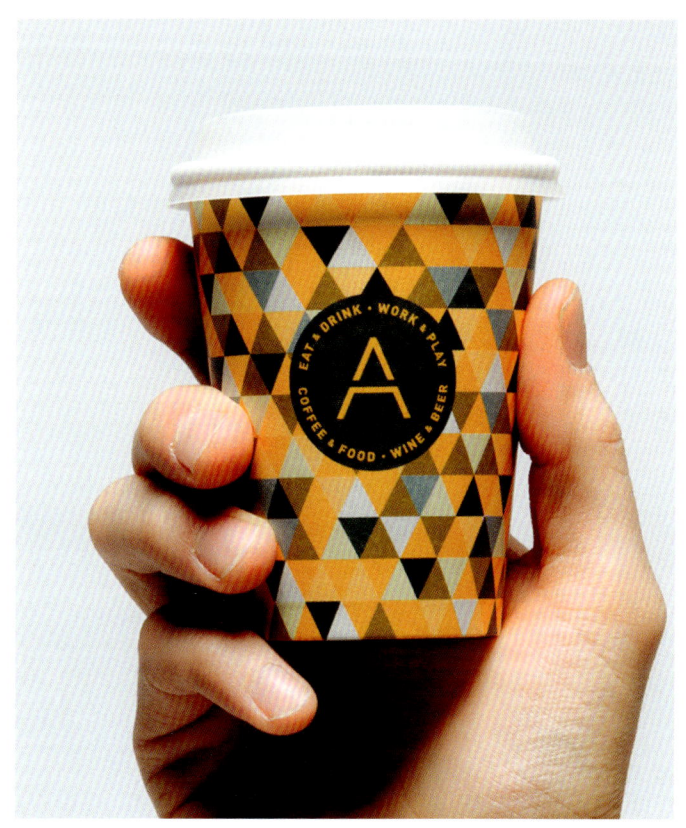

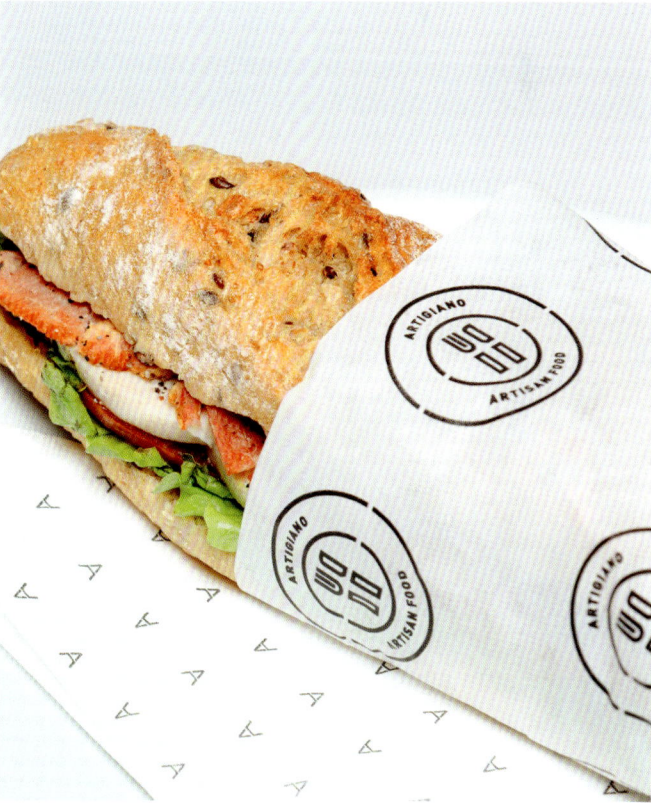

LA ASOMBROSA MEDUSA

LA PEQUEÑA MUJER ALFILER

LA MUJER OJOS DE AGUA

LA MUJER CHICHARRA

EL VIDENTE

LA MUJER BARBUDA

LA MISTERIOSA GITANA

EL HOMBRE BALA

EL ABOMINABLE HOMBRE DE GRAFITO

LA MUJER PULPO

DOS CINCUENTA & CINCO FOOD TRUCK

Design: Natalia Méndez, Ana Lucía Montes, Luisa Aragón, Montserrat Chávez

Dos Cincuenta & Cinco Food Truck is the result of a graphic design thesis project for the University of Monterrey. The challenge was to create a graphic solution for a food truck that wants to introduce itself to the Mexican gastronomic market, with a special focus on young adults between 18 and 35 years old. The food truck has a 1950s fair vibe where the consumer can experience a different kind of culinary involvement, from being served by fair-like characters to finding your fortune in your takeaway box. The customer will enjoy, remember, and share their new experience, creating a very close relationship between the restaurant and its consumers.

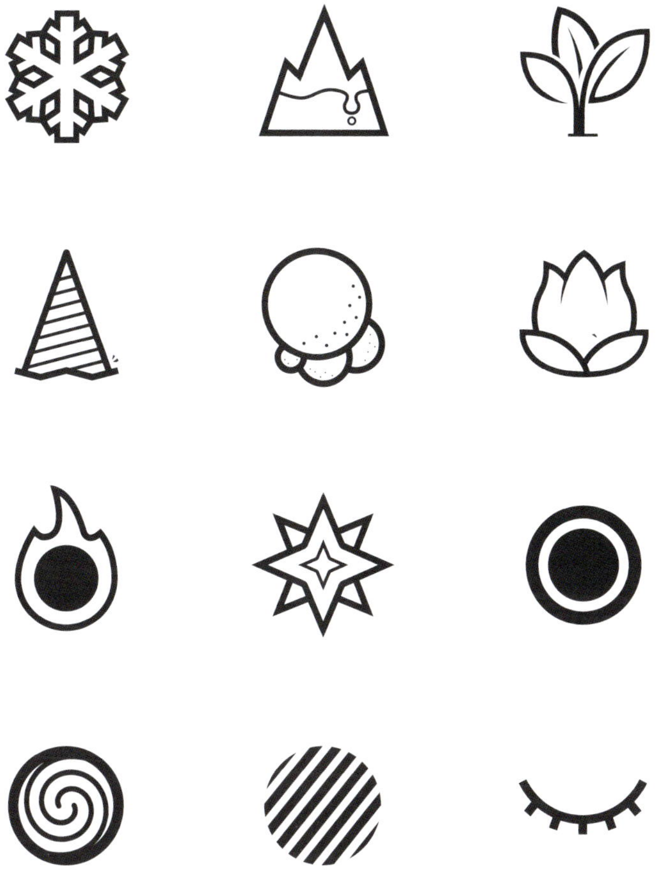

NATURAL

Design: Ainorwei Lin
Photography: Ainorwei Lin

An old legend says that humans are born with "color natures," with everyone having a different "color nature" according to the season and the state of the natural world when they are born.

This calendar project utilizes symbolic figures and colors to represent the meaning of every month, as well as specialized typography to enhance the calendar's aesthetics and values.

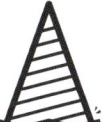

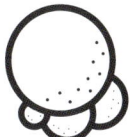

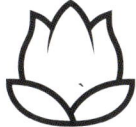

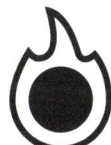

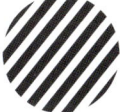

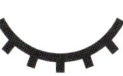

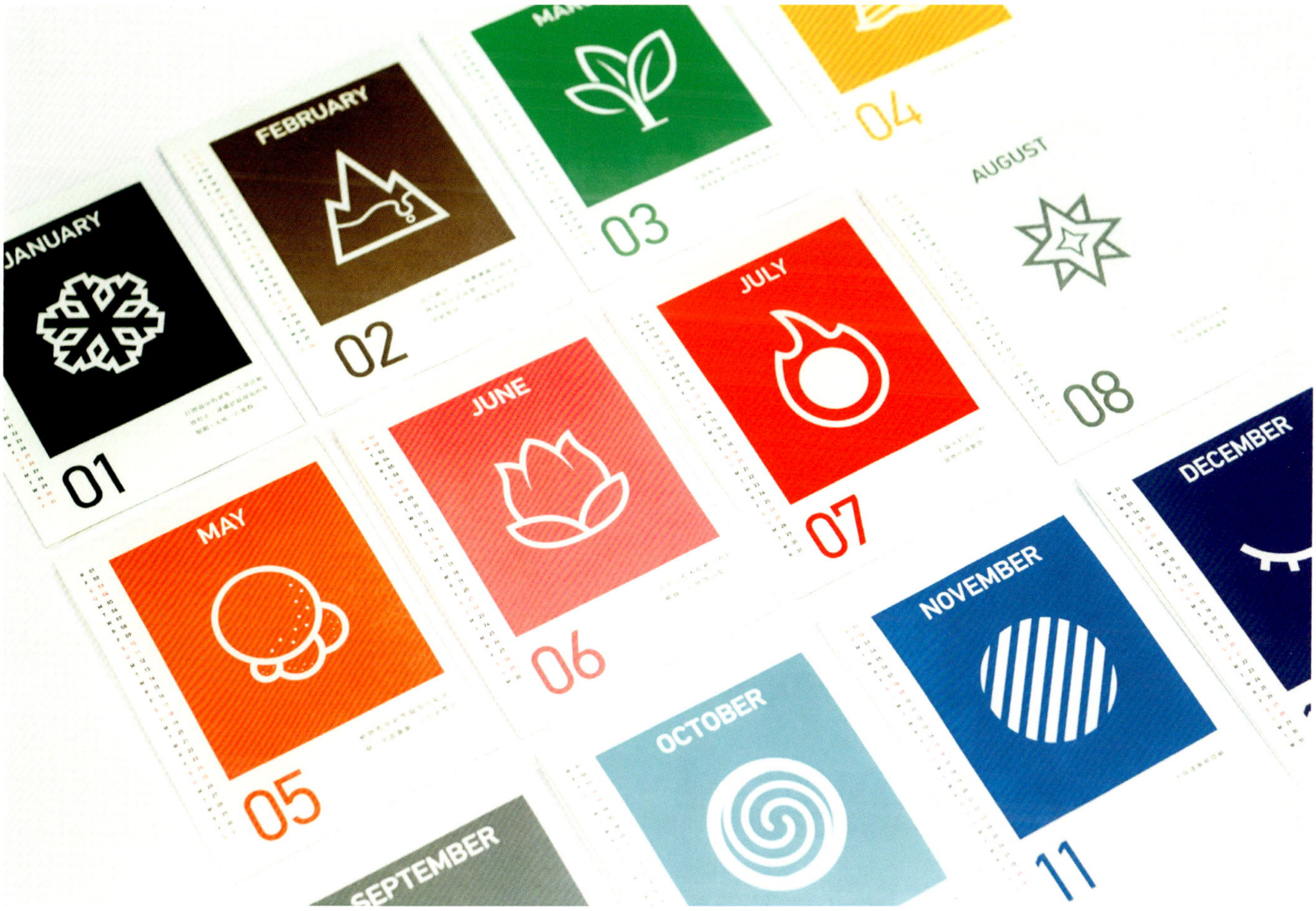

○— CAFEWARE BRANDING ─────────────

○— **Design:** Kisung Jang ── **Agency:** TRIANGLE-STUDIO ──────────

Cafeware is a branding and distribution company specializing in cafe supplies. The designers decided to use metallic silver as the main color. The branding expresses the spirit of the people-oriented company with friendly icons applied across various applications.

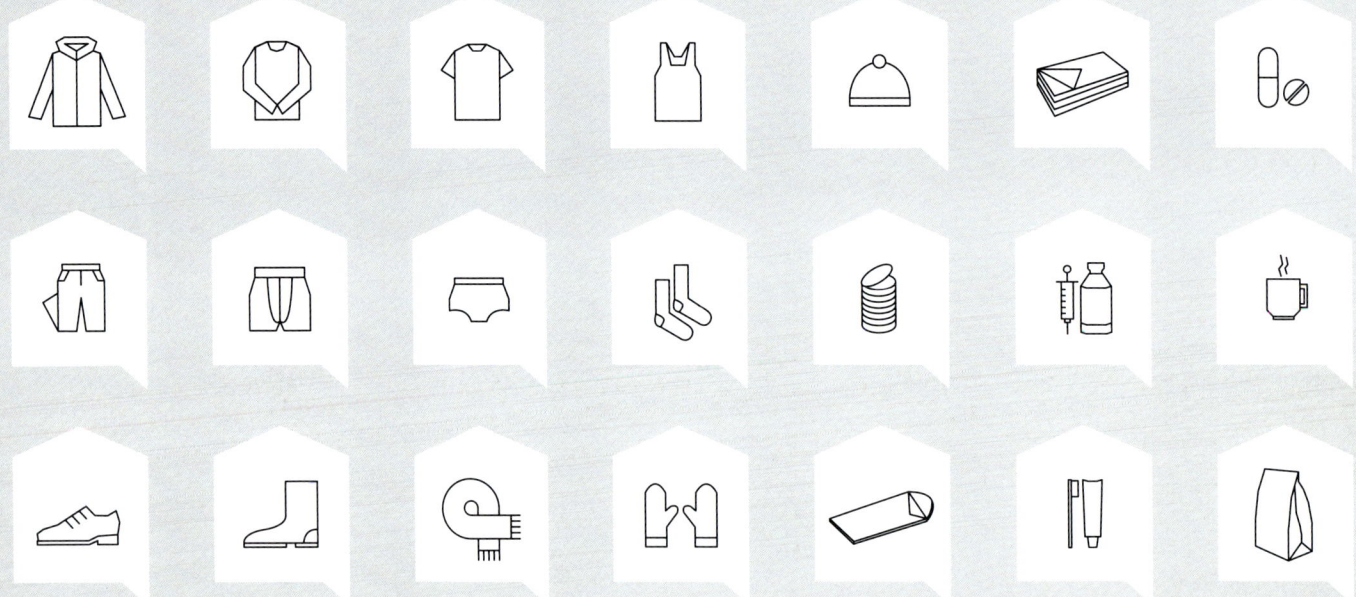

HÁZ

Design: Trixi Feller, Miriam Schmalen

The "Ház" project (meaning "house" in Hungarian) was created during a semester aboard at the Moholy-Nagy University of Art and Design in Budapest. Two students of Social and Communication Design, Lina-Trixi Feller and Miriam Schmalen, developed the concept and design for an auxiliary project for the homeless people of Budapest. After conducting research locally, online, and through personal conversations, they developed an extensive concept, which was embedded in a closed corporate identity. The students designed a low-budget informational pamphlet with easy to understand key information, facts, and contacts to inform and enable homeless people, in particular those who are visitors to the city.

HOMELESS
INFORMATION
ház
AID PROJECT
BUDAPEST

CASTLE HILL
ST. STEPHAN'S BASILICA
PARLAMENT
COMMUNIST BUILDINGS
GREAT SYNAGOGUE
NATIONAL GALLERY
BUDAPEST

○─○ SWANKY MINT
HOSTEL

○─── **Design:** Negra Nigoević, Filip Pomykalo ───

The Swanky Mint is a hostel in a renovated dry
cleaning and textile dye factory that dates back to
the 19th century. The interior was preserved to keep
the industrial atmosphere; the visual identity is
derived from this, and was designed to be a modern
representation of the visual language from that time.
A contemporary graphical treatment of typefaces
and a set of icons for a signage system complete
the identity while providing a modern touch to the
vintage interior.

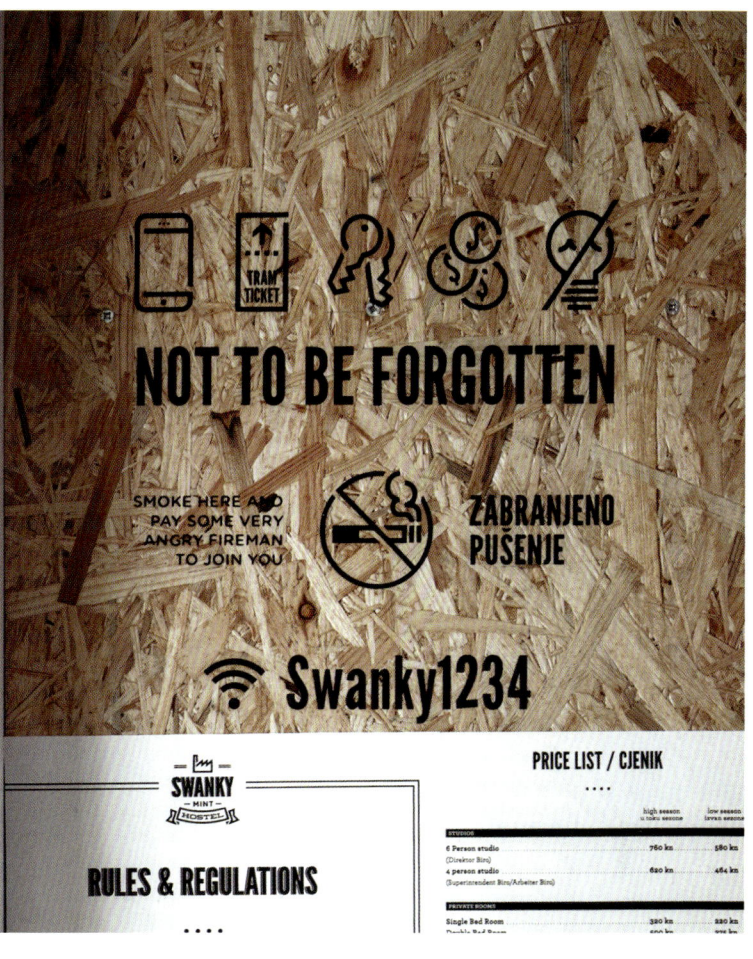

NOT TO BE FORGOTTEN

SMOKE HERE AND
PAY SOME VERY
ANGRY FIREMAN
TO JOIN YOU

**ZABRANJENO
PUŠENJE**

Swanky1234

SWANKY
MINT
HOSTEL

PRICE LIST / CJENIK
· · · ·

RULES & REGULATIONS
· · · ·

	high season u toku sezone	low season izvan sezone
STUDIOS		
6 Person studio (Direktor Birn)	760 kn	580 kn
4 person studio (Superintendent Birn/Arbeiter Birn)	620 kn	464 kn
PRIVATE ROOMS		
Single Bed Room	320 kn	320 kn
Double Bed Room	500 kn	375 kn

DINAMO

Design: Carla Felicetti,
Marta Vianello, Taja Luxa

The Dinamo project was born during the Lab of
Visual Communication at IUAV, University of
Venice. It's a weekly magazine that treats cycling
in a different way. Usually, when people talk about
cycling, they mostly just focus on its technical
aspects. The designers' ambition in Dinamo is to show
that a bike is not only a vehicle, but also a passion.
They designed the whole brand from scratch, creating
everything from the name to the logo. The designers
also assembled the content for the magazine as well
as creating an app for smart phones. They completed
it with a fresh typeface and vivid colors that express
the notion that cycling brings joy!

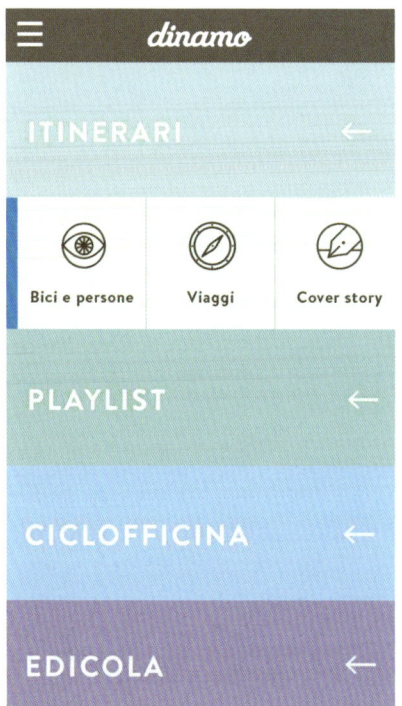

RRER
DAB
MET
Milano
Durante la canicola estiva o nel nebbioso autunno adano, Milano in bicicletta è un'esperienza sorprendente e spesso affascinante.
LEGENDA
Visitare
Mangiare
Acquistare
1 — 21 15 km
Ciclofficina
Milano City Cycling è un'itinerario di 15 km, appositamente ideato per esplorare la città in sella senza preoccupazioni e seguendo il vostro ritmo. La mappa presenta un percorso che vi permette di orientarvi e spostrarvi da una destinazione all'altra in sicurezza. Potete trovare al suo interno dei luoghi d'interesse da noi consigliati dove sostare per una fetta di torta o un pò di shopping e tutto ciò che può far comodo a chi si sposta in bici: i servizi di bike-sharing, i negozi di biciclette, le località d'interesse ma anche molto altro. Al ritmo dei vostri pedali scoprirete il meglio che la città ha da offrirvi.
Repubblica
VIA FILIPPO TURATI
VIALE CITTÀ DI FIUME
VIA PONTACCIO
VIA SENATO
Cairoli
San Babila
Duomo
VIA LARGA

dinamo
MANUBRIO
INGRANAGGI
MILANO

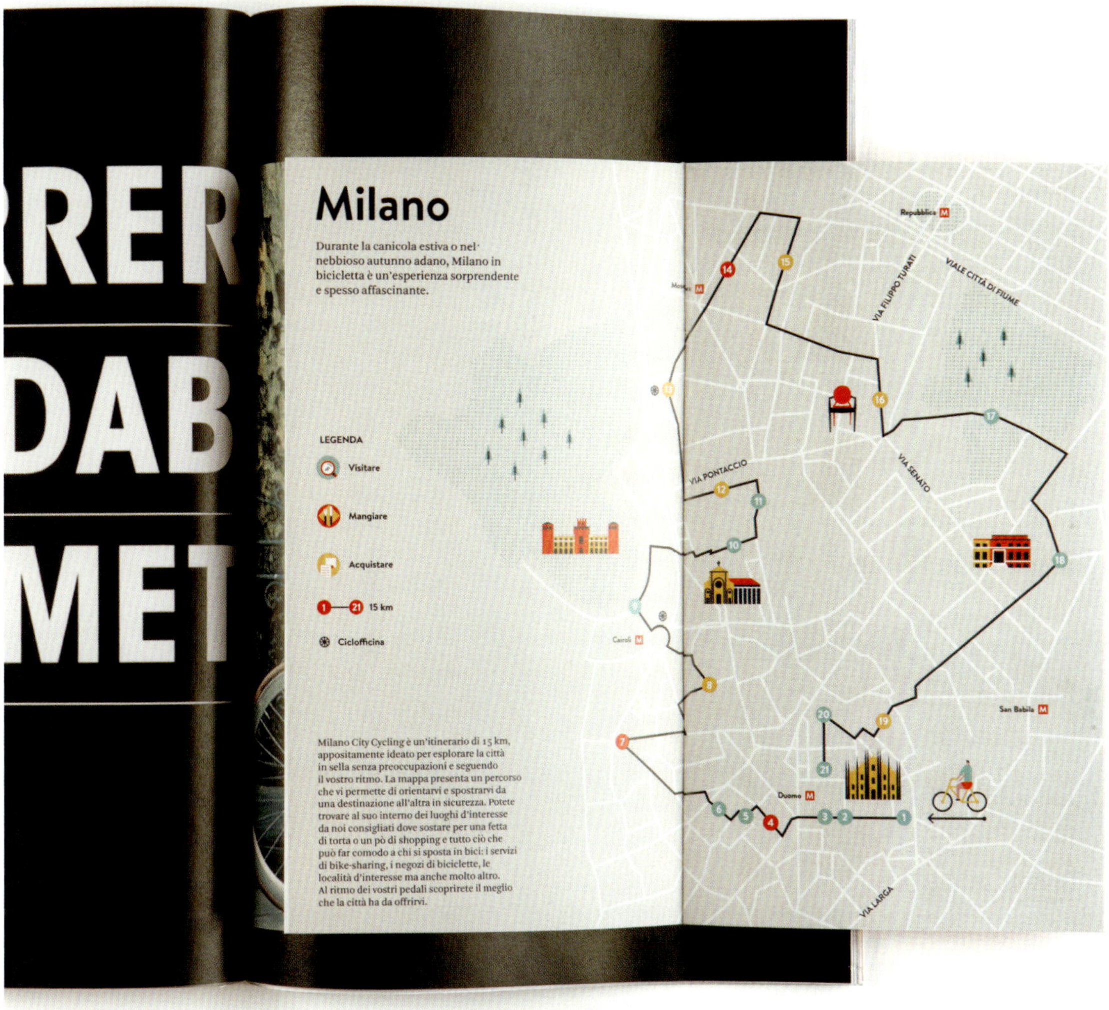

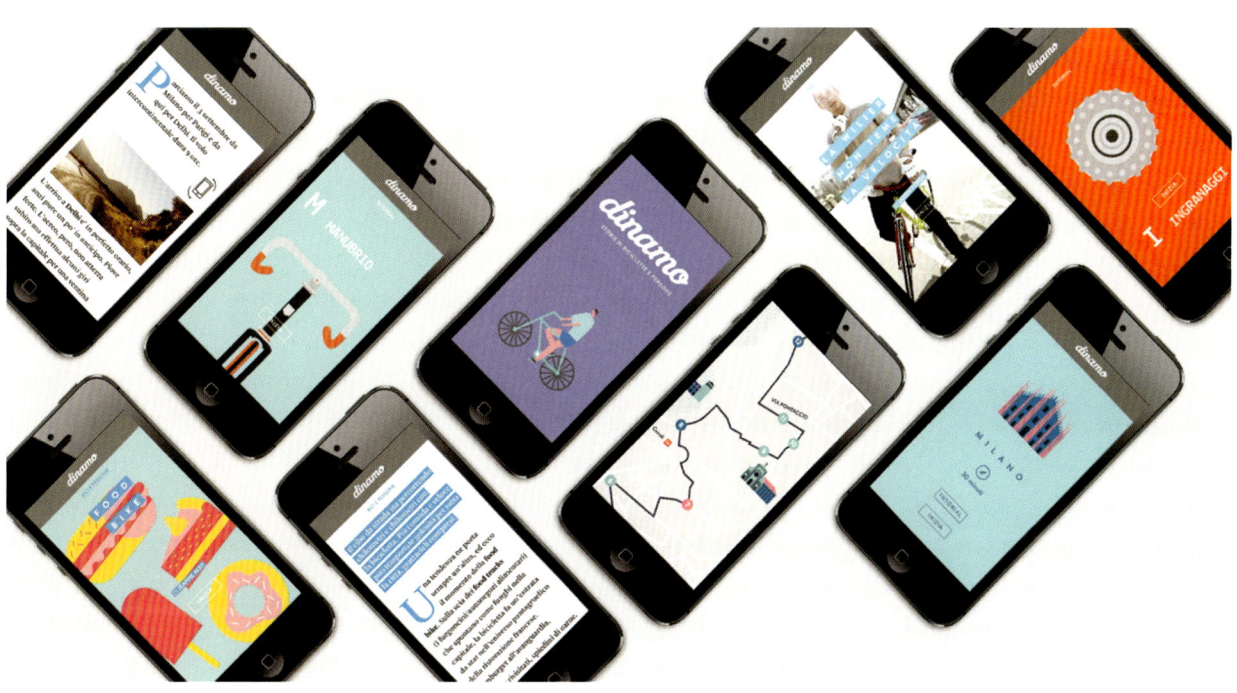

LOOK SO FINE

Design: Su Young Kang
Direction: Harry Jay

Look So Fine is an Android app about fashion and weather. Our daily outfits depend almost entirely on the day's weather, but weather apps only show us numbers and information in the form of icons from day to day. Look So Fine shows the weather along with photos of outfits recommended for the day. The designer mimicked the visual motifs of traditional fashion media, paper magazines, for the app's layout. Almost all fashion magazines turn to minimal, clear typography to highlight the photos that are the main content; this aesthetic is represented in the app's GUI with understated typography and an emphasis on photography.

Look so fine.

Look so fine.
EVERYDAY, EVERYWEAR.
82 10 4021 9102
www.looksofine.me
kangsr117@gmail.com

MISEGRETA

Design: Guillermo Castellanos Flores —— **Art Direction:** Moisés Guillén Romero
Agency: Para Todo Hay Fans

Misegreta is an establishment dedicated to 100% Italian gelato, desserts, confectionaries, and specialty coffee. The name is composed of the Italian words "miscela" and "segreto," which in English mean "secret mix." The name's meaning has ties with their logo, a key with intertwined hearts on the handle that represent the passion, love, and Italian traditions that are the main ingredients of Misegreta's products.

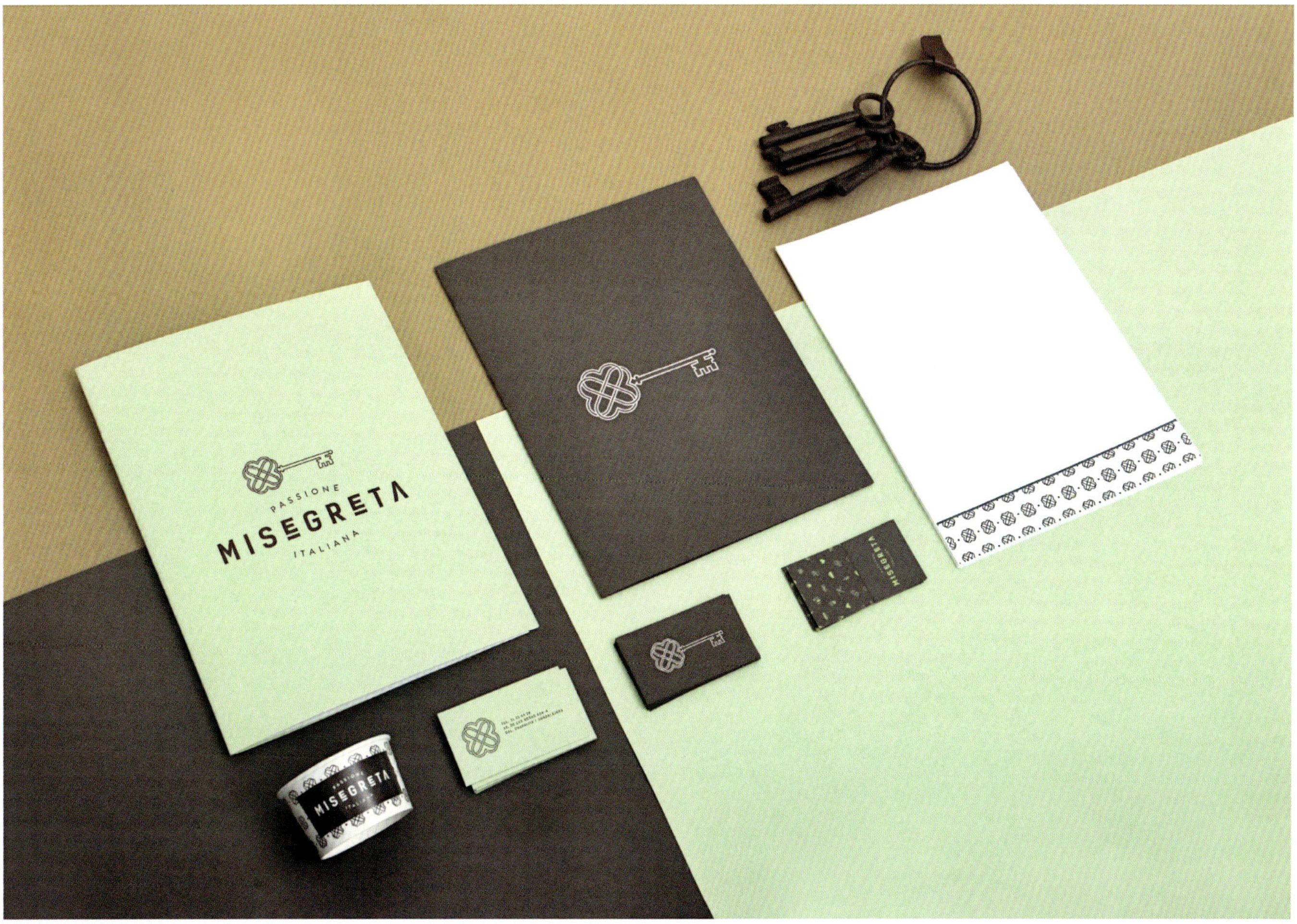
PASSIONE
MISEGRETA
ITALIANA

LA CREPERÍA
LA DELICIOSA COMBINACIÓN DE CREPA CON GELATO

CAFFETTERIA
AV. DE LAS ROSAS 464-A
CHAPALITA, GUADALAJARA

PASSIONE
MISEGRETA
ITALIANA

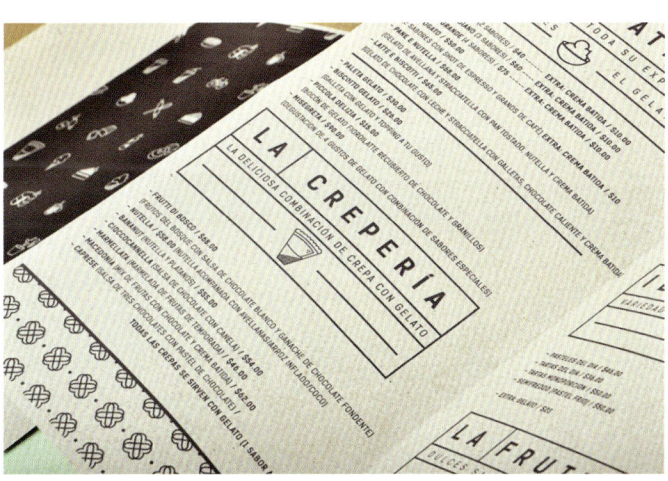

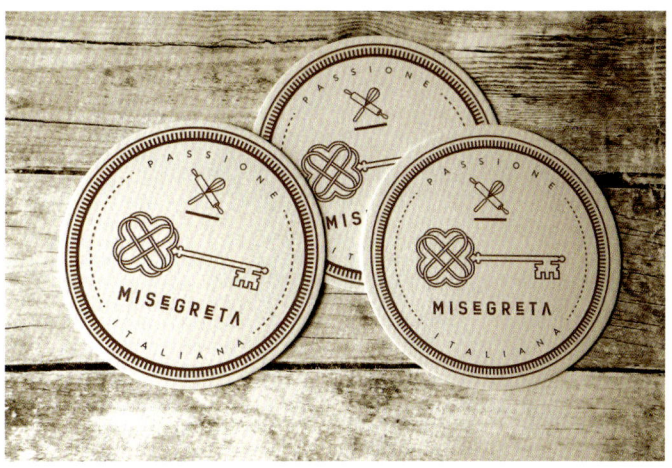

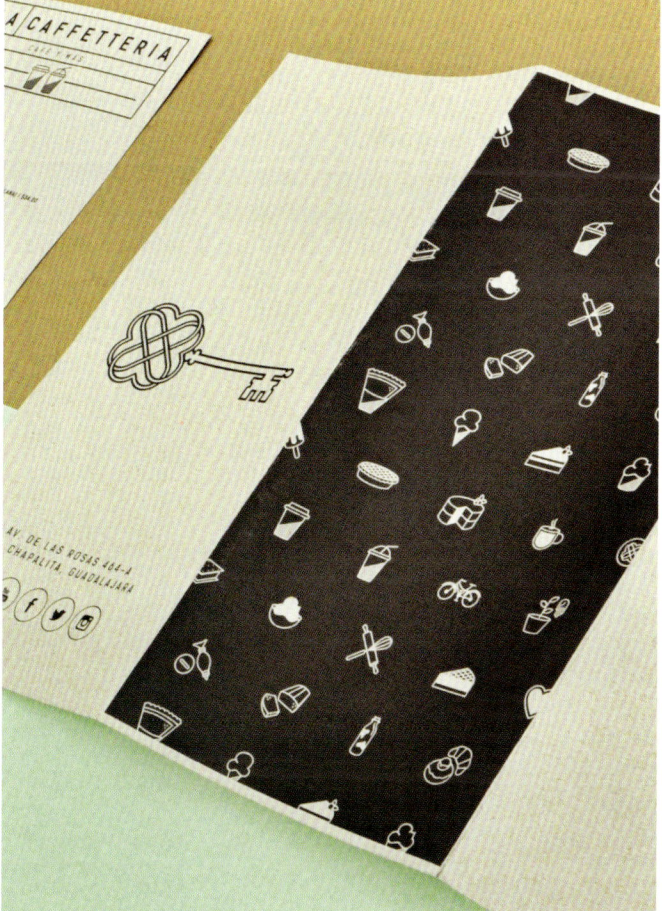

THE BIG APPLE COFFEE SHOP

Design: Silvestri Thierry

Straight from New York, the Big Apple Coffee Shop is a comfortable and welcoming coffee shop and bakery based in Tunis, Tunisia. The unique shop was designed to make customers feel at home. The brand identity sticks with a minimalist style, with simple shapes and meticulously applied lines. The Big Apple's iconography was designed to remind customers of the soul of New York City.

A sip of New York

THE APOLLO HARLEM
GRAND CENTRAL
CENTRAL PARK
WALL ST

THE BIG APPLE
COFFEE SHOP

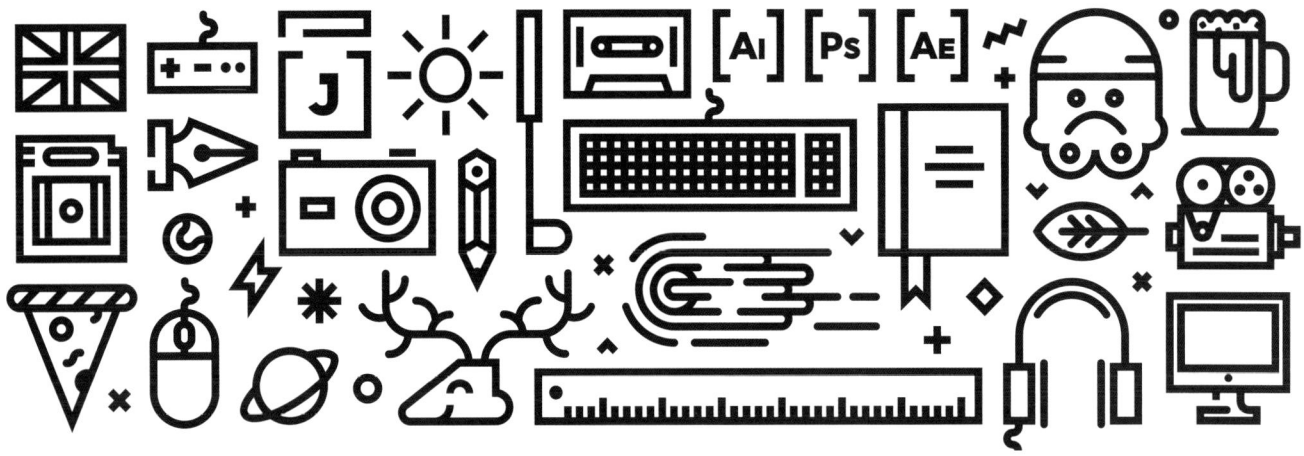

JAMSPENCER BRANDING

Design: James Spencer Clarke

The Jamspencer brand required a fresh, clean new look. A collection of icons was the best way to express the personality of both the brand and James himself as a designer. In this design, James put himself at the front of the brand to show his interests and passions in a clear, coherent way.

JAMSPENCER
WITH COMPLIMENTS

JAMSPENCER
GALL ERY
CONT ACT
BLOG
SHOP

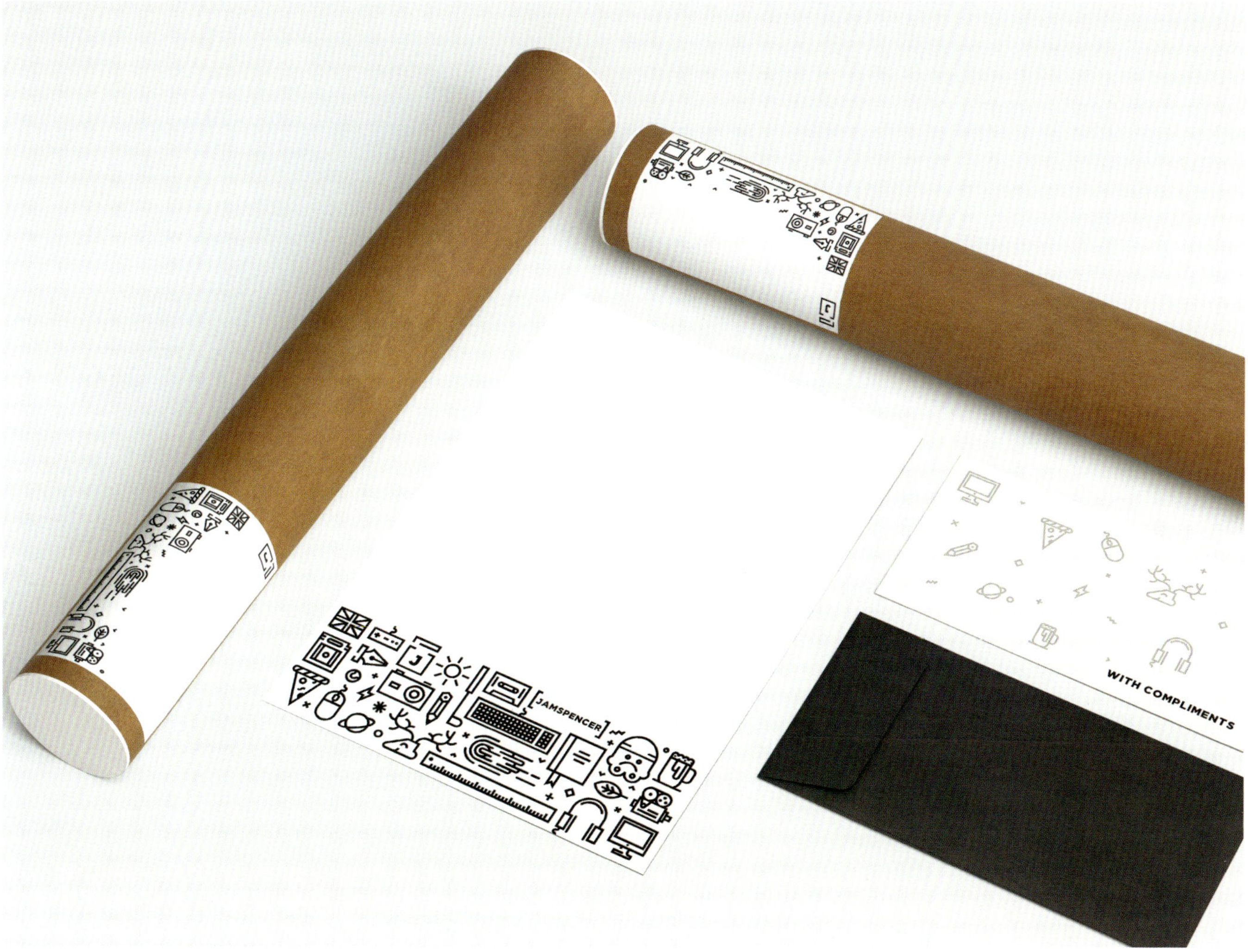

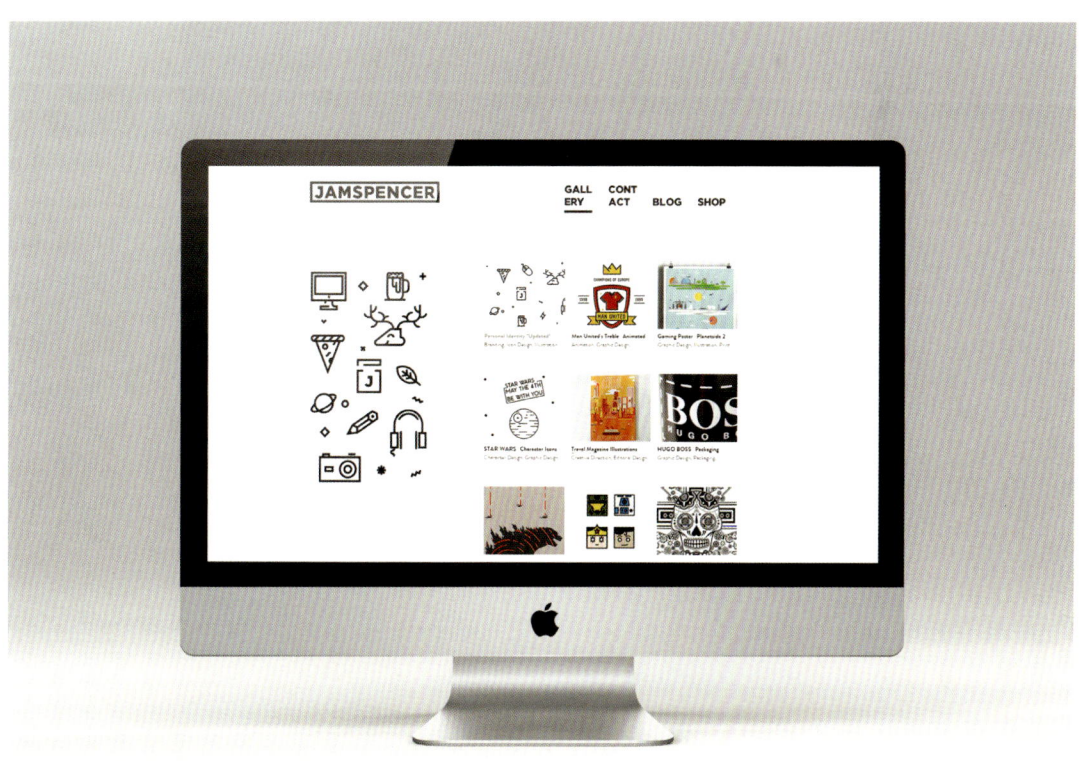

BED-STUY BEER REBRAND

Design: Gustav Karlsson — **Photographer:** Gustav Karlsson

A rebrand project for a beer shop in Bed-Stuy, Brooklyn which sells beer in bottles, cans, draught, and kegs. The branding concept consists of nine different logotypes, a custom-made typeface, signs, and packaging, all saying that Bed-Stuy Beer makes Brooklyn. The colors are inspired by different shades of beer and the brick houses in the surrounding neighborhoods.

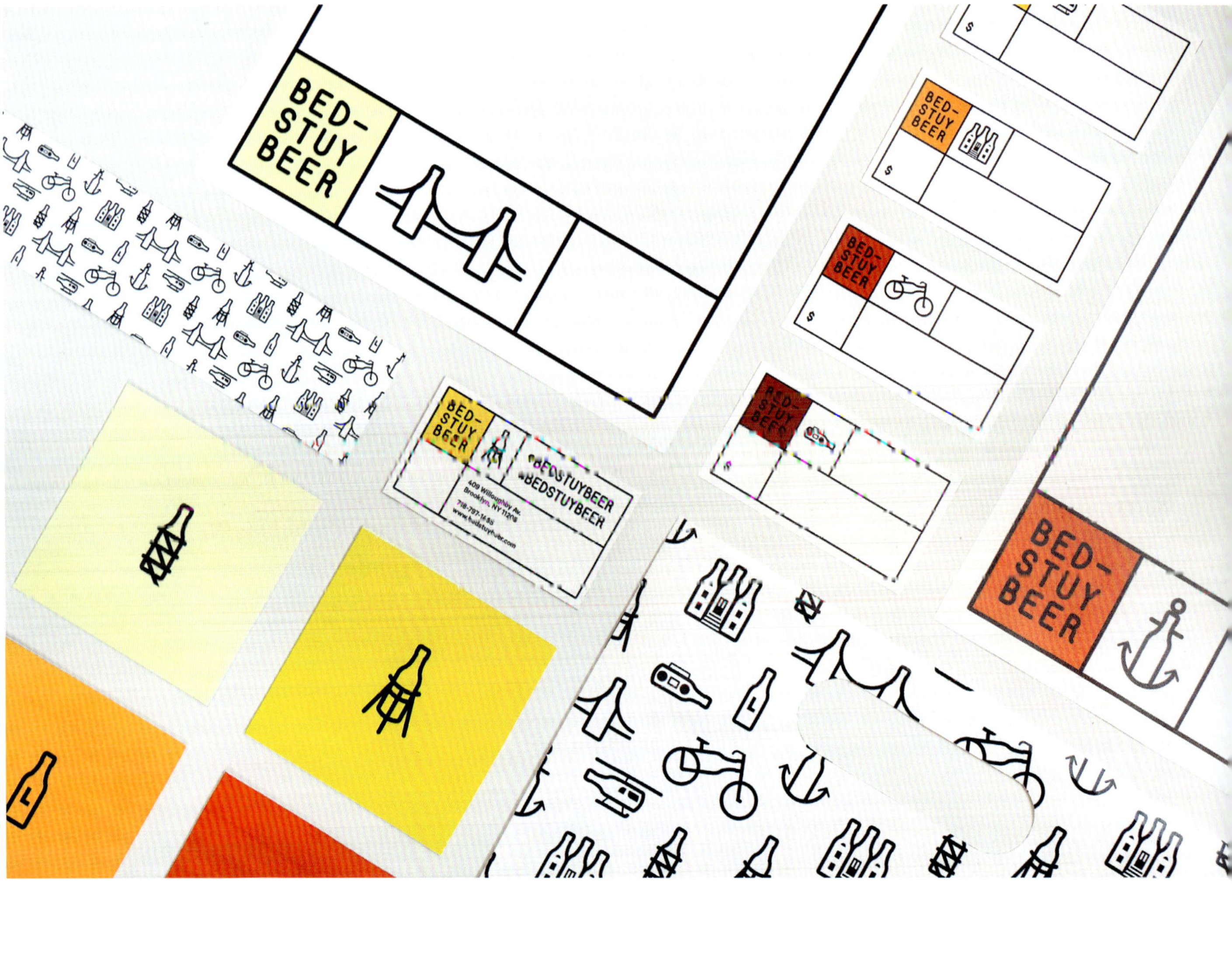

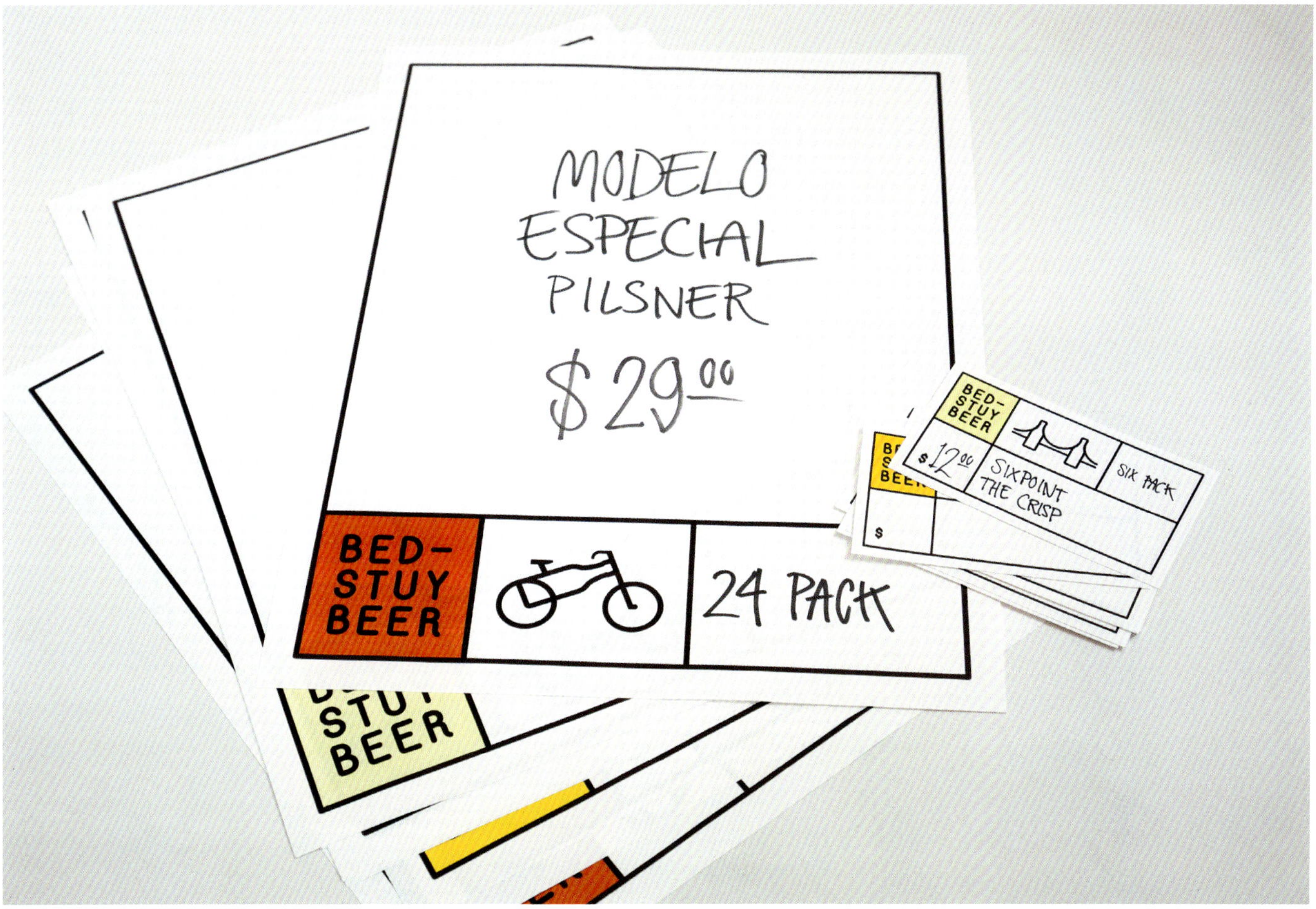
MODELO
ESPECIAL
PILSNER
$29.00
BED-
STUY
BEER
24 PACK
SIXPOINT
THE CRISP
SIX PACK
$12.00

SIX
MIX
BED-
STUY
BEER
SIX
MIX
BED-
STUY
BEER

THE COFFEE SHOP SERIES

Design: Carolina Peres

The Coffee Shop Series are short stories featuring a creative young girl, Carol, that faces some unusual situations in coffee shops. The visual identity celebrates an exciting new universe and recognizes the conceptual value of a complex protagonist as the axis of a fleeting small world, acknowledging the series as a corporate brand. Its key elements are presented in the form of icons and used as a kind of puzzle. This simulates the emotions found in the series, and gives us the freedom to image surprising new situations.

the Coffee Shop Series

Catarina Vasconcelos

LX FACTORY
Rua Rodrigues Faria, 103 Edifício I-0.2
1300-501 Lisboa

assunto:
Produção
2ª Temporada

Cara
Catarina Vasconcelos.

Ur sed magnatem quodignimin nonsere pelibus event ius eos a audaeru ptaectu ad ex et et et, consequae si doluptatus re sincientur, quas ne poremol orestendebit reped maxima natidsp eretehnd elenis pariatis aut eatem est fugia.

Porum ipietur iatessint asped est etur, sint autesecabor resse laborer emqu de riberatur, nostio blant, optatur re velenim sa dolorem fugidtem quatur simendenia Nam, sum harum, cuptatiatem voluptia tem dolut aut omnis necte maxim vel inc tionse ex essus seqvod et pel ectorunt etur? Ersper ferum volent.

is apid utestianem. Ut pellendis dolecto inia volupti aspicief facienimpore non non sequid quibusapel id maiorep taquid volonectae. Nullessimil iliquae quaeru mquate volentenib volori vent dus eiur maiorro to le parchil excdatur?
Preheni hiliqui aut autempo rrovit viasitis natquodia imiiumie poruptat haris cose que quuntem eum reptatem qui sante corest volestr umendista ex eaqui dena dolo rer chisit dolo edit ut velendantur ma que aiquam arci rem dolorio rporum volupid ucnssedrs doluptur am, qui descilique et et.

Atenciosamente
Luisa Fidalgo
produção

(+351) 916 933 387 / hello@thecoffeeshopseries.com
www.coffeeshopseries.com / Porto, Portugal

the Coffee Shop Series

www.coffeeshopseries.com

the Coffee Shop Series

Maria Ferreira da Silva
producer + editor

(+351) 914 933 387 / maria@thecoffeeshopseries.com
www.coffeeshopseries.com / Porto, Portugal

web www.coffeeshopseries.com
email vasco@thecoffeeshopseries.com
mobile (+351) 914 933 387 / 915 241 722

Porto, Portugal

Luísa Fidalgo
creator + actress

(+351) 915 241 722 / luisa@thecoffeeshopseries.com
www.coffeeshopseries.com / Porto, Portugal

Vieira Vasco
director

(+351) 916 640 769 / vasco@thecoffeeshopseries.com
www.coffeeshopseries.com / Porto, Portugal

**Obrigado,
Laudeau Chocolate!**

the Coffee Shop Series

www.coffeeshopseries.com

 Homeopatia
 Kukkaterapia
 Antroposofia
 Ayurveda
 Fytoterapia
 Kädet & Jalat

 Tee
 Tee
 PUR Bar
 Vitamiinit
 Hivenaineet
 Suu

 Elintarvikkeet
 Luomu ruoka
 Vauva
 Eläintuotteet
 Kirjallisuus
 Silmät

 Kosmetiikka
 Ihonhoito
 Hygienia
 Hiukset
 Seksuaaliterveys
 Aromaterapia

PUR

Design: Aleksi Hautamäki, Toni Hurme, Janne Norokytö, Annika Peltoniemi, Jesper Bange, Lawrence Dorrington
Agency: Bond Creative Agency
Photography: Osmo Puuperä, All About Everything

Pur is a new generation of wellness shops in Helsinki, bringing various aspects of healthy living together under one roof. Bond created a complete branding concept that covered everything from the brand identity to the shop design, website, photography, advertising, and marketing collaterals. All this helps Pur to communicate its message of holistic wellbeing in an appealing, fun, and informative way.

⊶ HORTALÍCIA

Design: Rodrigo Vieira, Samuel Furtado, Edson Jr ⎯⎯ **Agency:** Vibri Design & Branding

The designers were charged with bringing life to Hortalícia, a brand that strives to combine healthy eating with practicality. The work included naming, visual signatures, and packaging, all of which were aligned with the look and atmosphere of their physical location. The result is a pared-down brand that shows that eating well doesn't mean being boring.

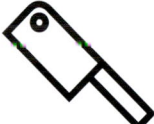    

MISSION

Design: Peter Komierowski

The brief was to create the identity, printed collateral, and website for a new tasting menu restaurant in Vancouver's Kitsilano neighborhood. The goal was clear: the branding should be memorable, simple, and unique. An unexpected challenge presented itself when the owners wanted to create graphics for a divider wall between the door and the dining area. Acting as a screen, the wall provides privacy to guests without shutting them out completely. A set of ten icons was created that relate back to the menu, and give a sense of what the restaurant is about as guests enter.

A-MOLOKO

Creative Direction: Vlad Ermolaev — **Agency:** Ermolaev Bureau

This visual identity was developed for a company which sells milk through a chain of vending machines. The design concept of the logo was inspired by the business of the chain: automated sale of farm-fresh milk and the company's name, A-moloko, which had been developed by Ermolaev Bureau as well. When the "A" is turned upside down, it resembles the muzzle of a cow, which was used as inspiration for much of the identity. The visual identity was built on a clear system of symbols, which describes the path of the milk from the cow to the consumer. The visual language lends the blue and white appearance an emotionally appealing character.

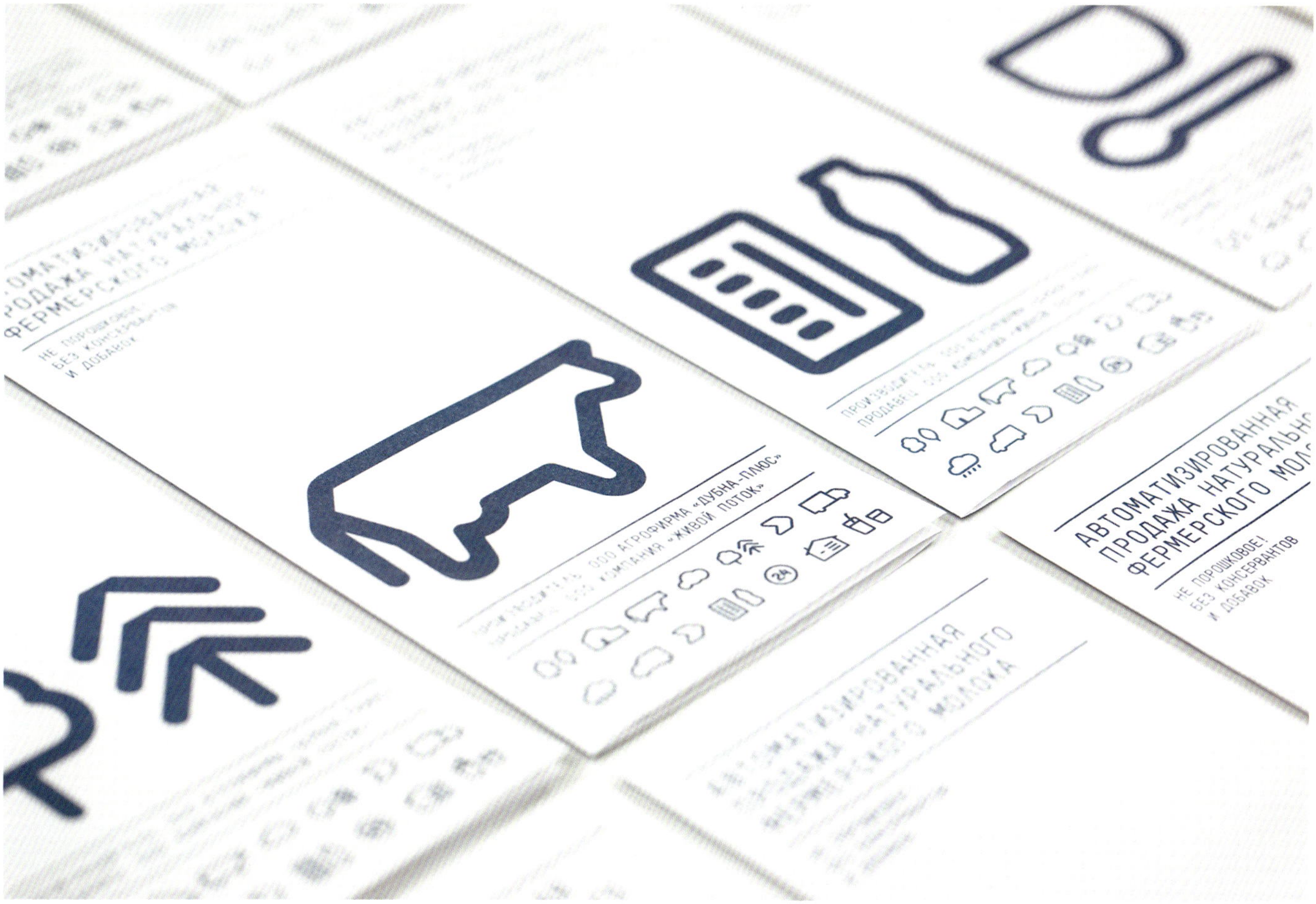
ПРОИЗВОДИТЕЛЬ: ООО АГРОФИРМА «ДУБНА-ПЛЮС»
ПРОДАВЕЦ: ООО КОМПАНИЯ «ЖИВОЙ ПОТОК»
24
АВТОМАТИЗИРОВАННАЯ
ФЕРМЕРСКОГО
НЕ ПОРОШКОВОЕ!
БЕЗ КОНСЕРВАНТОВ
И ДОБАВОК

А–МОЛОКО
АВТОМАТИЗИРОВАННАЯ
ПРОДАЖА МОЛОКА
НЕ ПОРОШКОВОЕ!
БЕЗ КОНСЕРВАНТОВ
И ДОБАВОК
24
ПРОИЗВОДИТЕЛЬ: ООО АГРОФИРМА «ДУБНА-ПЛЮС»
ПРОДАВЕЦ: ООО КОМПАНИЯ «ЖИВОЙ ПОТОК»

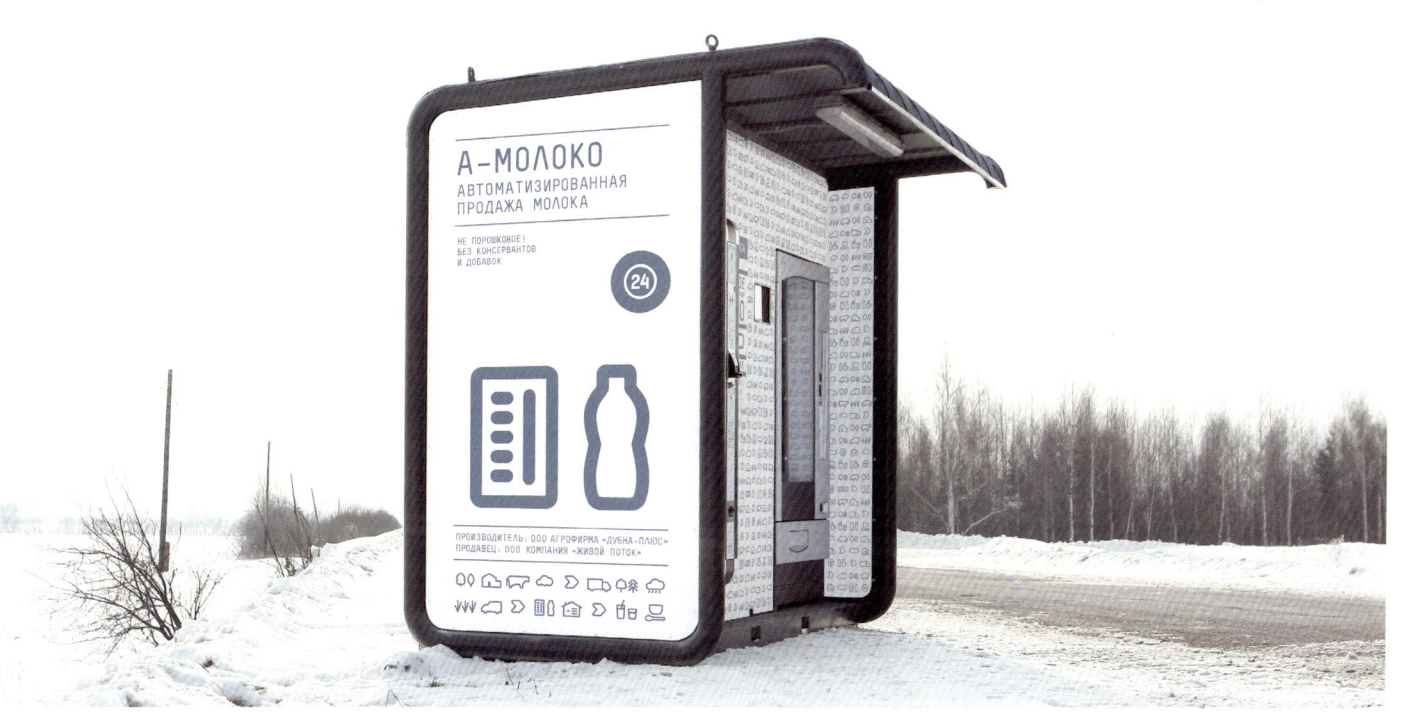

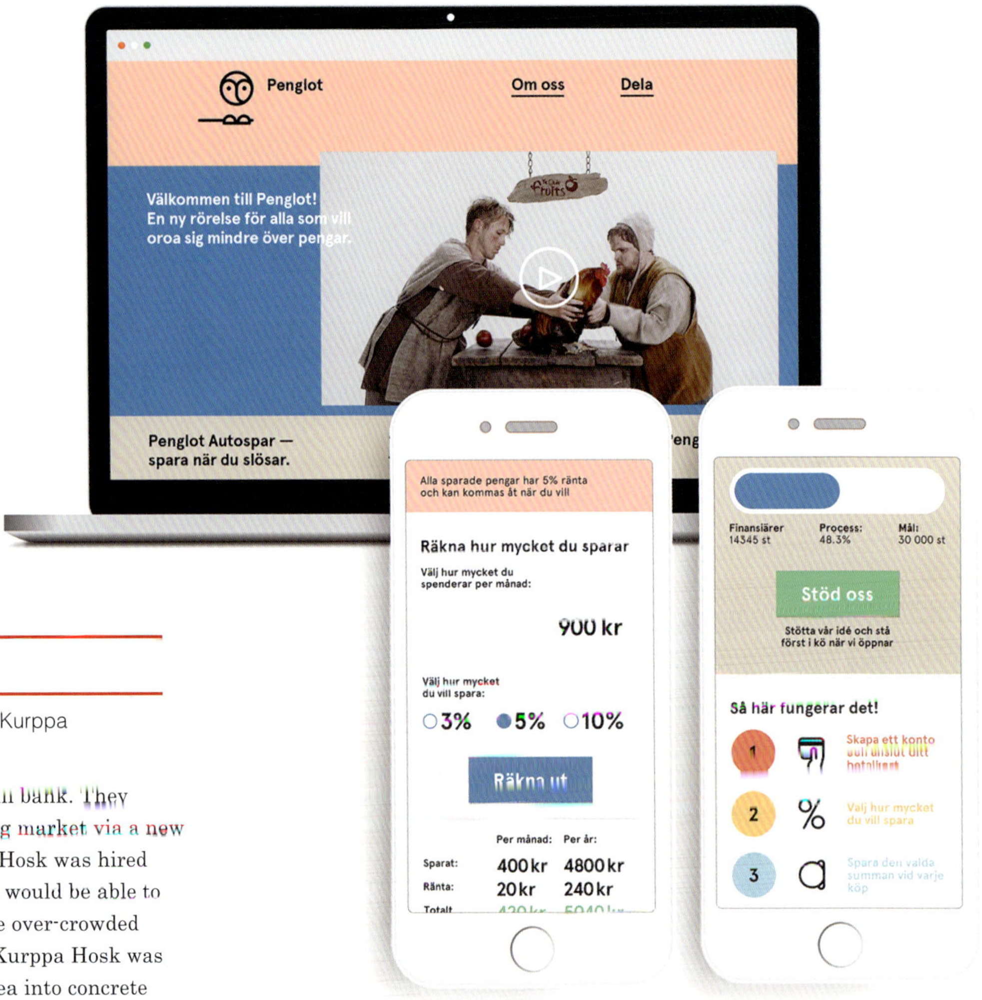

PENGLOT

Design: Gustav Jerlardtz

Creative Direction: Thomas Kurppa

Agency: Kurppa Hosk

Bank Poidem is a full-service Russian bank. They decided to enter the Swedish banking market via a new business model for savings. Kurppa Hosk was hired to create an entirely new brand that would be able to quickly gain trust and break into the over-crowded market. As part of the assignment, Kurppa Hosk was also asked to turn Bank Poidem's idea into concrete business strategies, and to help develop digital savings products that could connect the business model with the new brand. The result was Penglot.

Energy	Plumbing	Ventilation	AV	Sanitary
FM	Electric	Security	Fire	Automation
Cooling	Heating	Energy savings contracting	Building certification	ICT

CAVERION

Design: Marko Salonen, Pomeliina Puumala, Aleksi Hautamäki
Agency: Bond Creative Agency
Photographer: Angel Gil

Caverion was established through the demerger of building services and industrial services businesses within YIT Group, a leading European construction company. The designers provided the new company with a complete corporate brand identity. The logo communicates Caverion's role in the entire life cycle of buildings and capacity for reinvention. Custom-designed icons help communicate what the company's immaterial services mean to the customer.

GEWINNEN SIE IM HANDUMDREHEN.
Caverion MemoCards

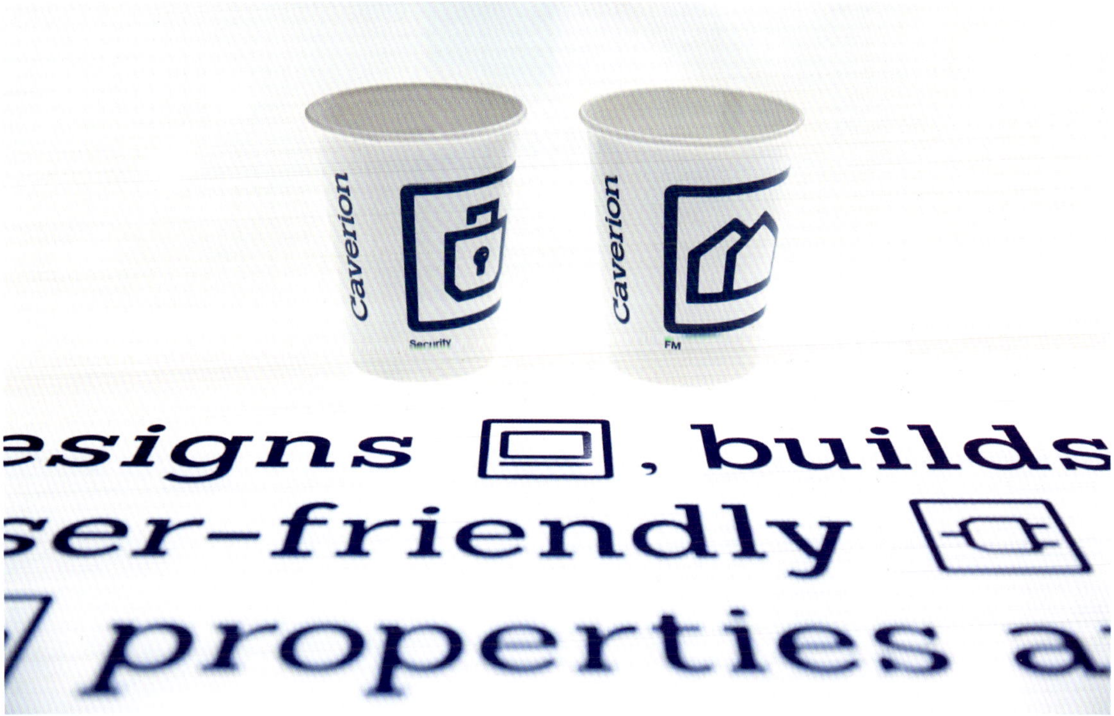

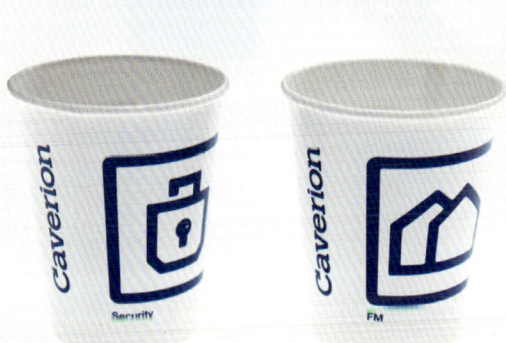

Caverion
Security
Caverion
FM
esigns , builds
ser-friendly
properties a

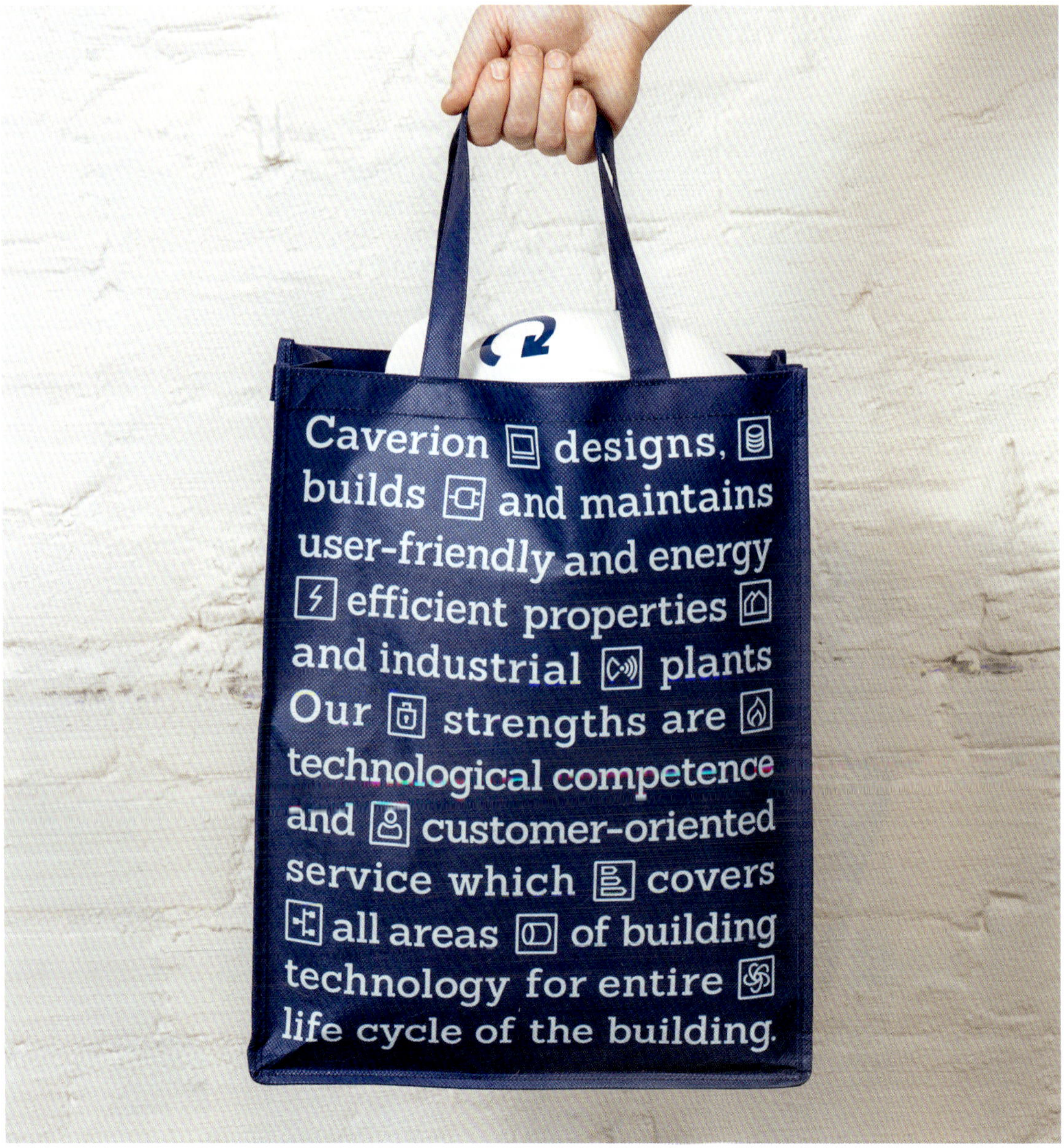

Caverion designs, builds and maintains user-friendly and energy efficient properties and industrial plants Our strengths are technological competence and customer-oriented service which covers all areas of building technology for entire life cycle of the building.

Caverion
Caverion
Fire
Security

Caverion
Caverion
Fire
Automation
Security
Working for
better buildings

VILLA VITELE

Design: Axek Efremov

Logo and identity for a super awesome villa/hotel/restaurant complex, located in Karelia, Russia right where the Vidlitsa River flows into the Ladoga Lake. Villa Vitele is a neat and comfortable place where you can hide from the concrete jungle and take a deep breath of fresh air. The unique Karelian nature meets the highest European level of customer service.

PORTO

Design: Raquel Rei, Ana Simões, Lucille Queriaud, Joana Mendes, Maria Sousa, Dário Cannatà
Art Direction: Eduardo Aires
Agency: White Studio
Photography: Alexandre Delmar

White Studio was invited to design the new identity for the city of Porto and its city hall.

The challenge presented was very clear. The city needed a visual system, a visual identity that could organize and simplify communication with the citizens, and could at the same time define a clear hierarchy, bringing together the city and the city hall. The designers needed to represent Porto, a global city, as a city for everyone.

Their cause was the city, Porto itself. The idea of ownership by everyone was very important to the designers. This unique home needed to be represented in a way that allowed everyone to have their own Porto. With this in mind, the designers set out to understand how others view the city, and the relationships that come out of those observations. It would be obvious and even cliché to only identify the big icons like Torre dos Clérigos, Casa da Música, Ribeira, Fundação Serravles, and the river.

Inspired by the stories in the city's tiles, the designers developed more than seventy geometric icons that represented the city and its people. The icons were designed based on a grid that connects them with each other, creating a continuous network that evokes a tile panel. These icons go from the incredible gastronomy to the unmistakable accent of the north of Portugal. The port wine, the São João festivities, the old and the contemporary, the landmarks and the familiar, the list of "Portos" continues.

Porto.

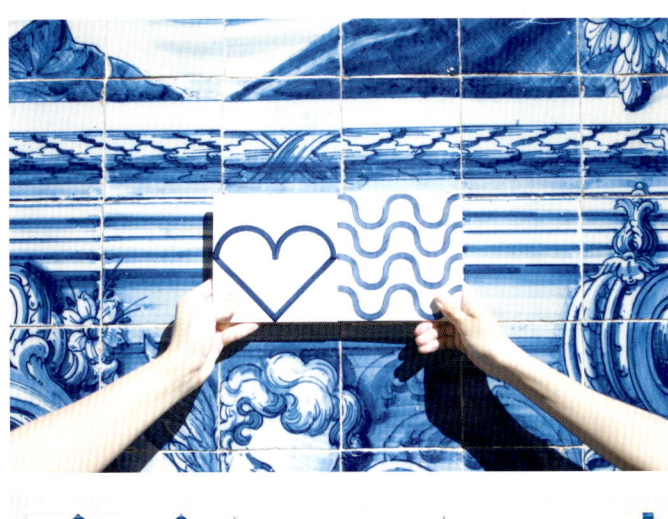

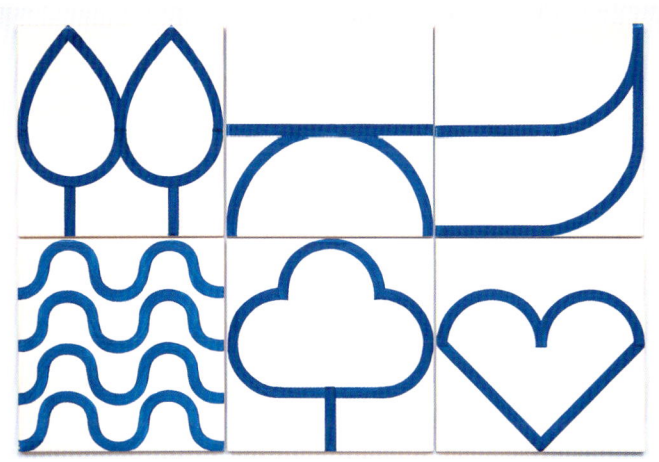

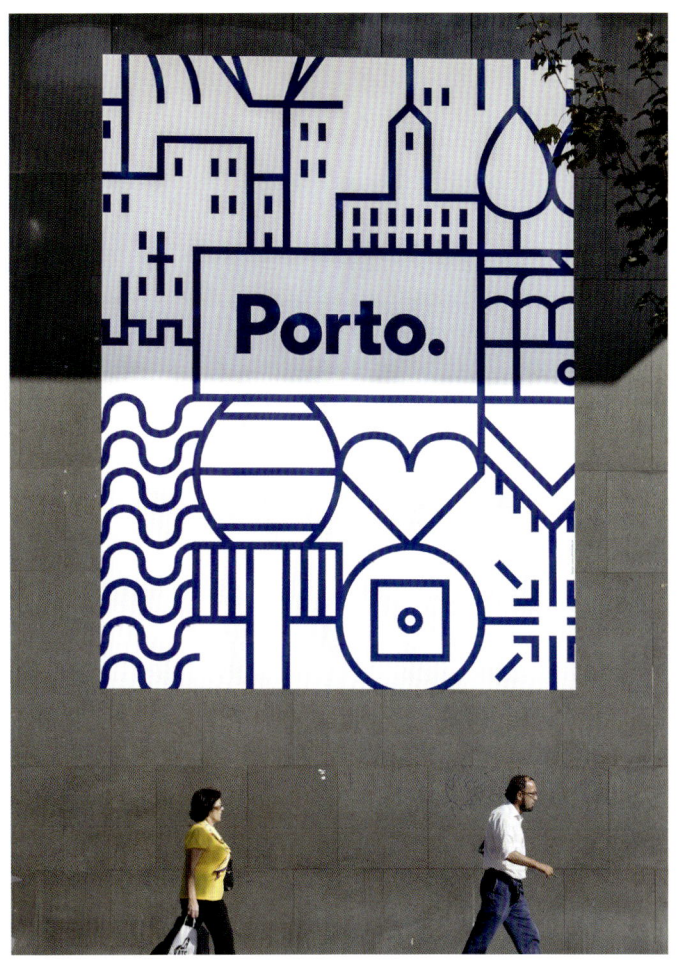

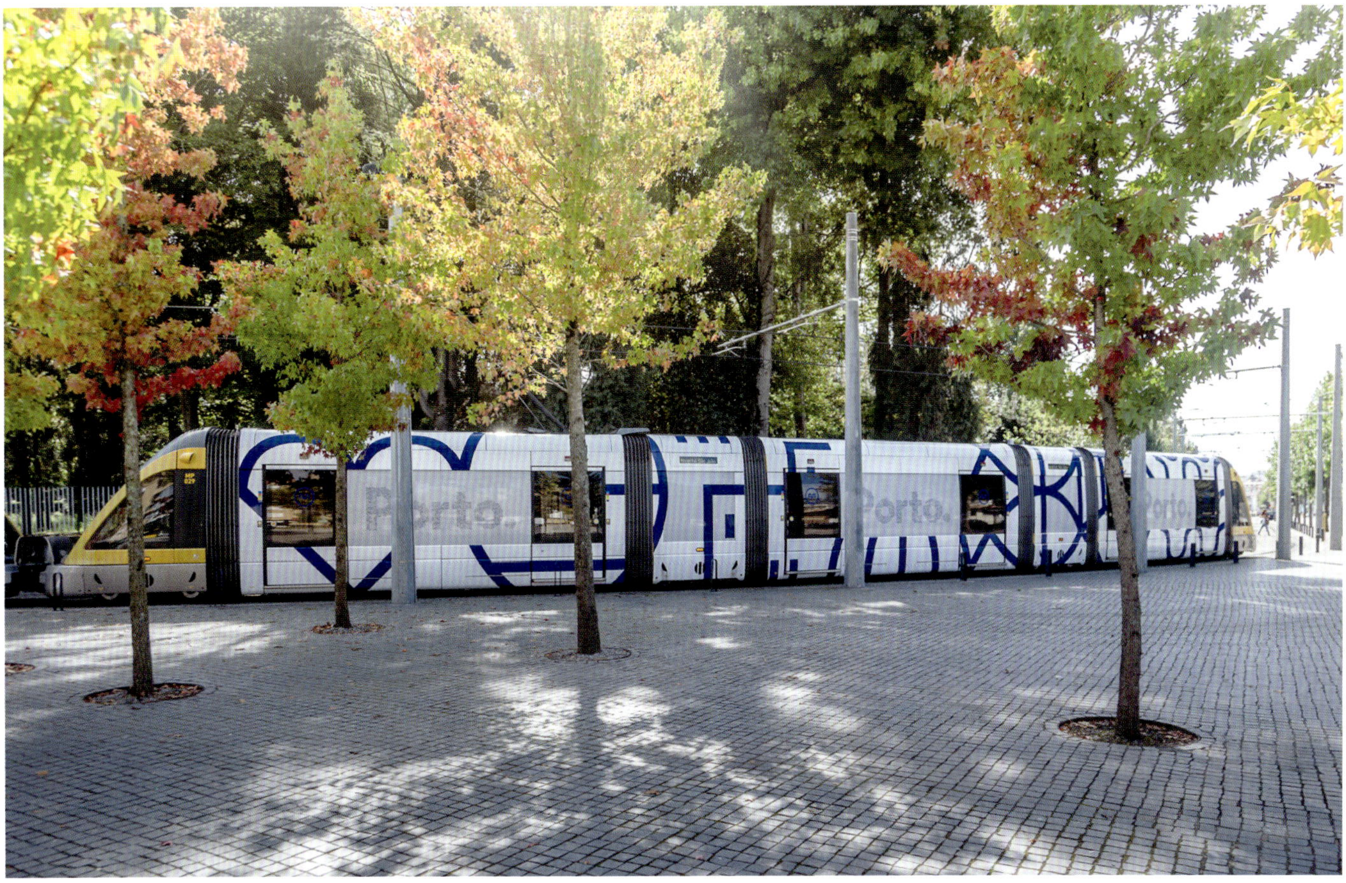
Porto.
Porto.
Porto.

FLYOVER

Design: Maciej Świerczek, Alicja Wydmańska, Paweł Piłat
Agency: Jazzy Innovations

Full branding, icons, and web design for Flyover, a crowd flying platform.

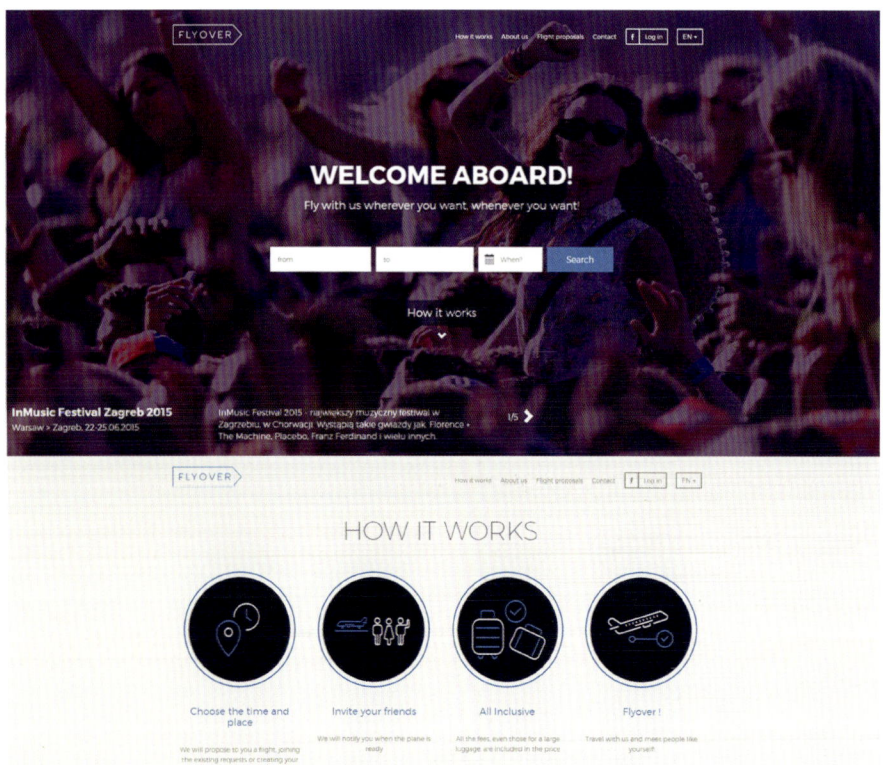

CO.R INNOVATION STRATEGY

Design: Diego Carneiro

Creating a new identity for CO.R wasn't easy. The company, which has existed since 2007, is undergoing a major overhaul in its language and branding. The redesign of their visual identity and the creation of icons to represent their new methodologies was essential for the new phase of their business.

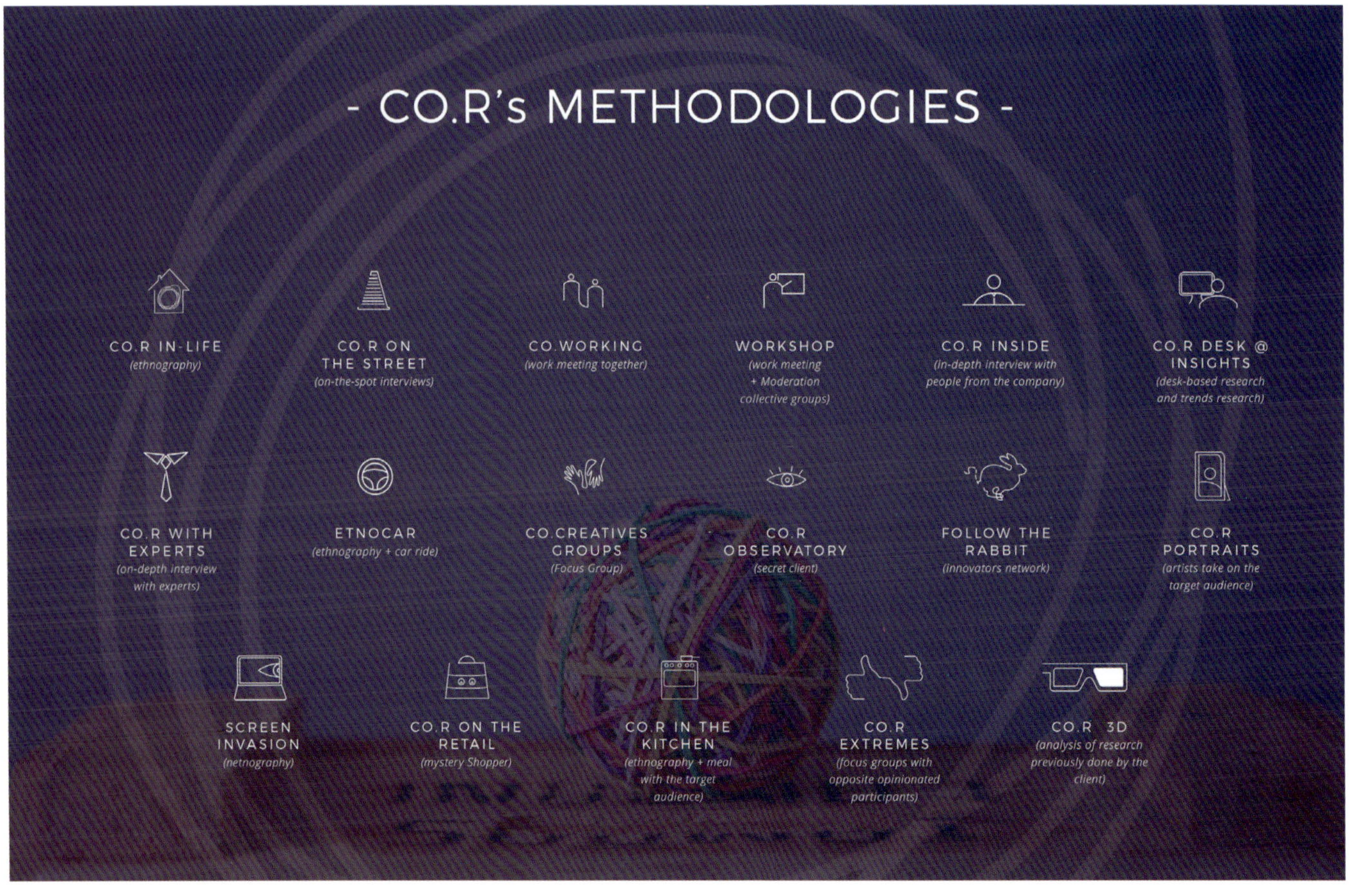

- CO.R's METHODOLOGIES -

CO.R IN-LIFE
(ethnography)

CO.R ON THE STREET
(on-the-spot interviews)

CO.WORKING
(work meeting together)

WORKSHOP
(work meeting + Moderation collective groups)

CO.R INSIDE
(In-depth interview with people from the company)

CO.R DESK @ INSIGHTS
(desk-based research and trends research)

CO.R WITH EXPERTS
(on-depth interview with experts)

ETNOCAR
(ethnography + car ride)

CO.CREATIVES GROUPS
(Focus Group)

CO.R OBSERVATORY
(secret client)

FOLLOW THE RABBIT
(innovators network)

CO.R PORTRAITS
(artists take on the target audience)

SCREEN INVASION
(netnography)

CO.R ON THE RETAIL
(mystery Shopper)

CO.R IN THE KITCHEN
(ethnography + meal with the target audience)

CO.R EXTREMES
(focus groups with opposite opinionated participants)

CO.R 3D
(analysis of research previously done by the client)

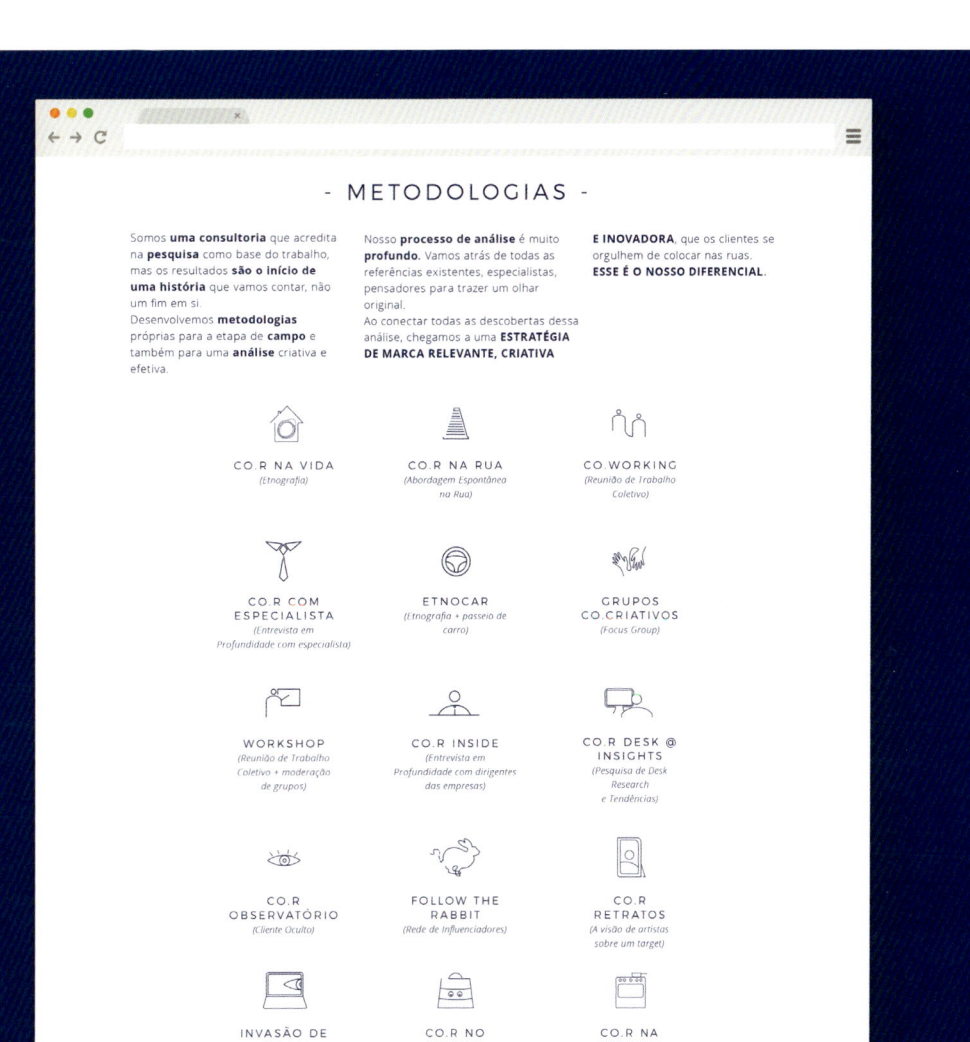

- METODOLOGIAS -

Somos **uma consultoria** que acredita na **pesquisa** como base do trabalho, mas os resultados **são o início de uma história** que vamos contar, não um fim em si.
Desenvolvemos **metodologias** próprias para a etapa de **campo** e também para uma **análise** criativa e efetiva.

Nosso **processo de análise** é muito **profundo.** Vamos atrás de todas as referências existentes, especialistas, pensadores para trazer um olhar original.
Ao conectar todas as descobertas dessa análise, chegamos a uma **ESTRATÉGIA DE MARCA RELEVANTE, CRIATIVA**

E INOVADORA, que os clientes se orgulhem de colocar nas ruas.
ESSE É O NOSSO DIFERENCIAL.

CO.R NA VIDA
(Etnografia)

CO.R NA RUA
(Abordagem Espontânea na Rua)

CO.WORKING
(Reunião de Trabalho Coletivo)

CO.R COM ESPECIALISTA
(Entrevista em Profundidade com especialista)

ETNOCAR
(Etnografia + passeio de carro)

GRUPOS CO.CRIATIVOS
(Focus Group)

WORKSHOP
(Reunião de Trabalho Coletivo + moderação de grupos)

CO.R INSIDE
(Entrevista em Profundidade com dirigentes das empresas)

CO.R DESK @ INSIGHTS
(Pesquisa de Desk Research e Tendências)

CO.R OBSERVATÓRIO
(Cliente Oculto)

FOLLOW THE RABBIT
(Rede de Influenciadores)

CO.R RETRATOS
(A visão de artistas sobre um target)

INVASÃO DE TELAS
(Netnografia)

CO.R NO VAREJO
(Mystery Shopper)

CO.R NA COZINHA
(Etnografia + refeição com o target)

CO.R EXTREMOS
(Focus Group com grupos extremos)

CO.R 3D
(Análise de pesquisas já realizadas plos clientes)

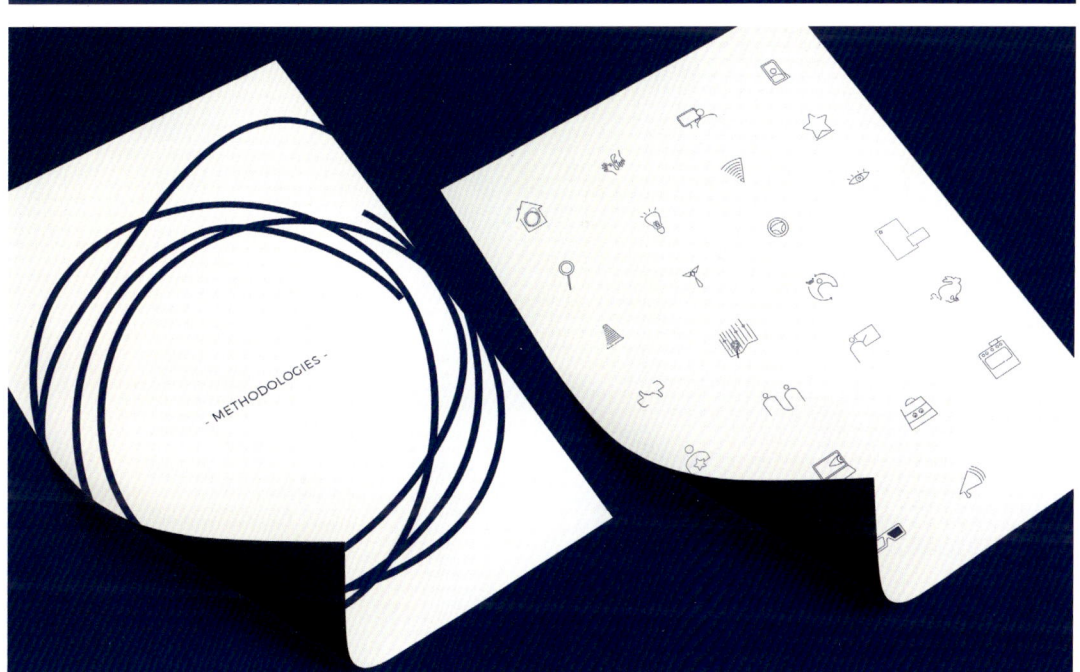

New solutions for printing

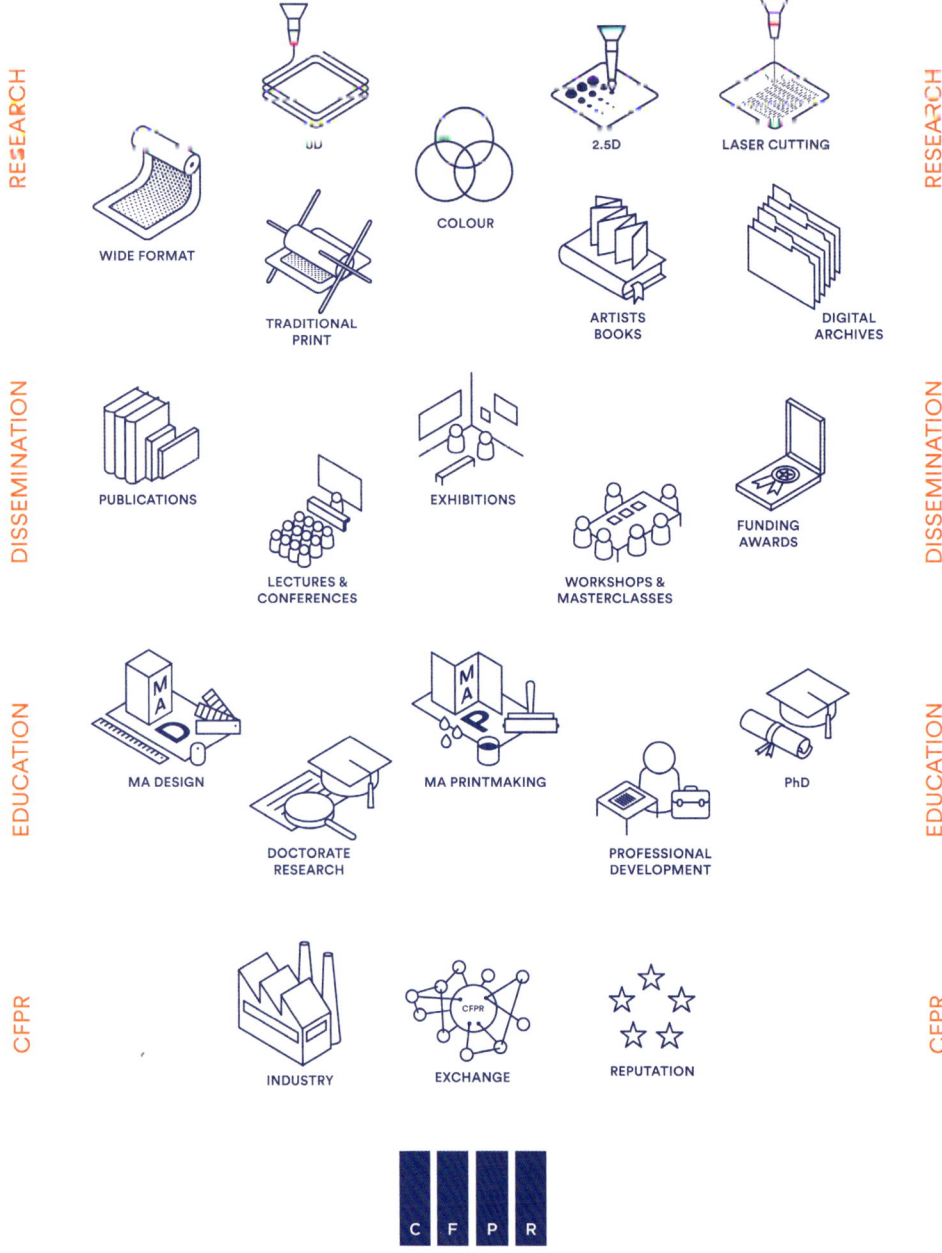

RESEARCH

WIDE FORMAT

3D

COLOUR

2.5D

LASER CUTTING

TRADITIONAL PRINT

ARTISTS BOOKS

DIGITAL ARCHIVES

RESEARCH

DISSEMINATION

PUBLICATIONS

LECTURES & CONFERENCES

EXHIBITIONS

WORKSHOPS & MASTERCLASSES

FUNDING AWARDS

DISSEMINATION

EDUCATION

MA DESIGN

DOCTORATE RESEARCH

MA PRINTMAKING

PROFESSIONAL DEVELOPMENT

PhD

EDUCATION

CFPR

INDUSTRY

EXCHANGE

REPUTATION

CFPR

C F P R
Centre for Fine Print Research

CFPR AS A BOOK

Design: Aurelio Sánchez

The Centre for Fine Printing Research's current logo represents the four well-defined aspects of the center: research, dissemination, education, and the center as a central hub of printing. This conceptual project is designed as a flexible system that won't interfere with the actual identity, and helps position the brand in a way that creates an easy introduction for newcomers to the center. The project is presented in a box with four different sections. Each section represents one area of the CFPR, and each contains a small booklet on the subject. For each subject a pictograph was created to make it simple to quickly visualize the different activities found in each area. The whole range of activities is summarized by pictograph families presented on a poster.

1 —
3D and Rapid Prototyping Research
Centre for Fine Printing Research
1 — 3D and Rapid Prototyping Research
Proving the commercial viability of 3D print
—

2 —
Exchange
CFPR
Centre for Fine Printing Research
2 — Exchange

2 —
Exhibitions
2 — Exhibitions
Past Exhibitions
—
Just Press Print, Northern Print June 2012 and Impact 8 Conference, University of Dundee Aug 2013
Drawing with Fire, Northern Print Biennale, November 2011
Follow-ed (after Hokusai), a touring exhibition from Tom Sowden, February - May 2011
BABE 2011, Bristol Artists' Book Event, Arnolfini Bristol, May 2011
'Book Arts'; a full list of all artists' books related exhibitions
The Annual Miniature Print Exhibition: Miniprint
3D 2D: Object and Illusion in Print: an exhibition of prints from the CFPR, Edinburgh, Autumn 2010
Arnolfini Bookshop Showcase, Arnolfini, Bristol, Curated by Tom Sowden, June - August 2010
Showcasing a New Collection of Enamel Jewellery, Downstairs Gallery, Contemporary Applied Arts, Curated by Jessica Turrell, 18 June - 17 July 2010
The Enamel Experience - International Badge Exhibition, Curated By Elizabeth Turrel, Touring Exhibition, February 2008 - January 2010
The Printed Reality, Curated by Paul Laidler, IMPACT 6, School of Creative Arts, UWE, Bristol, 15 - 19 September 2009

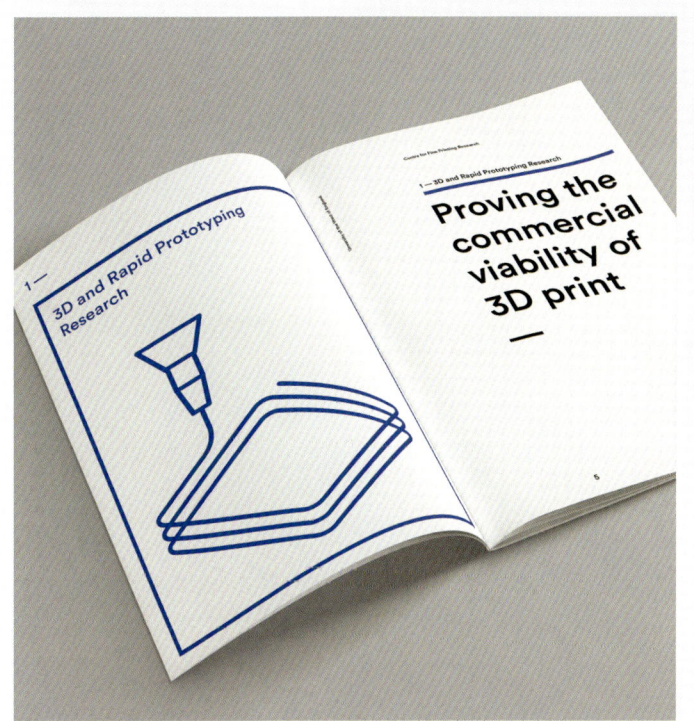

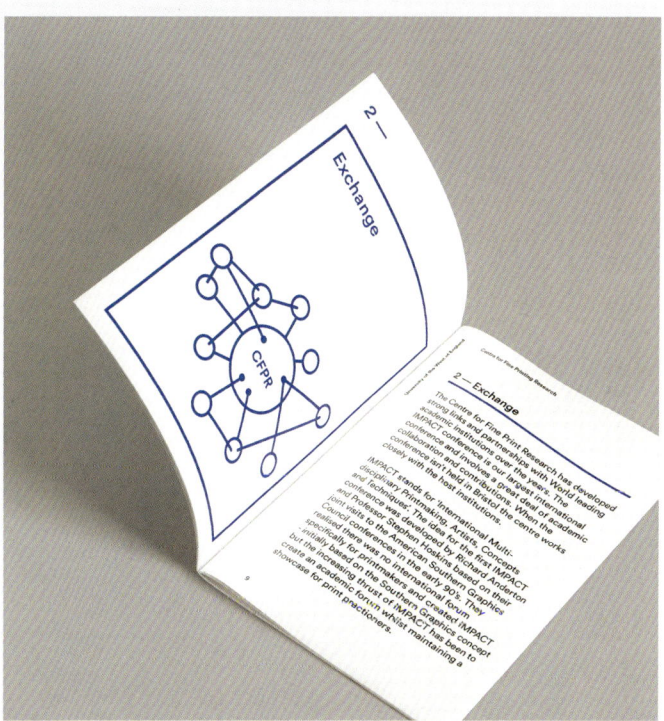

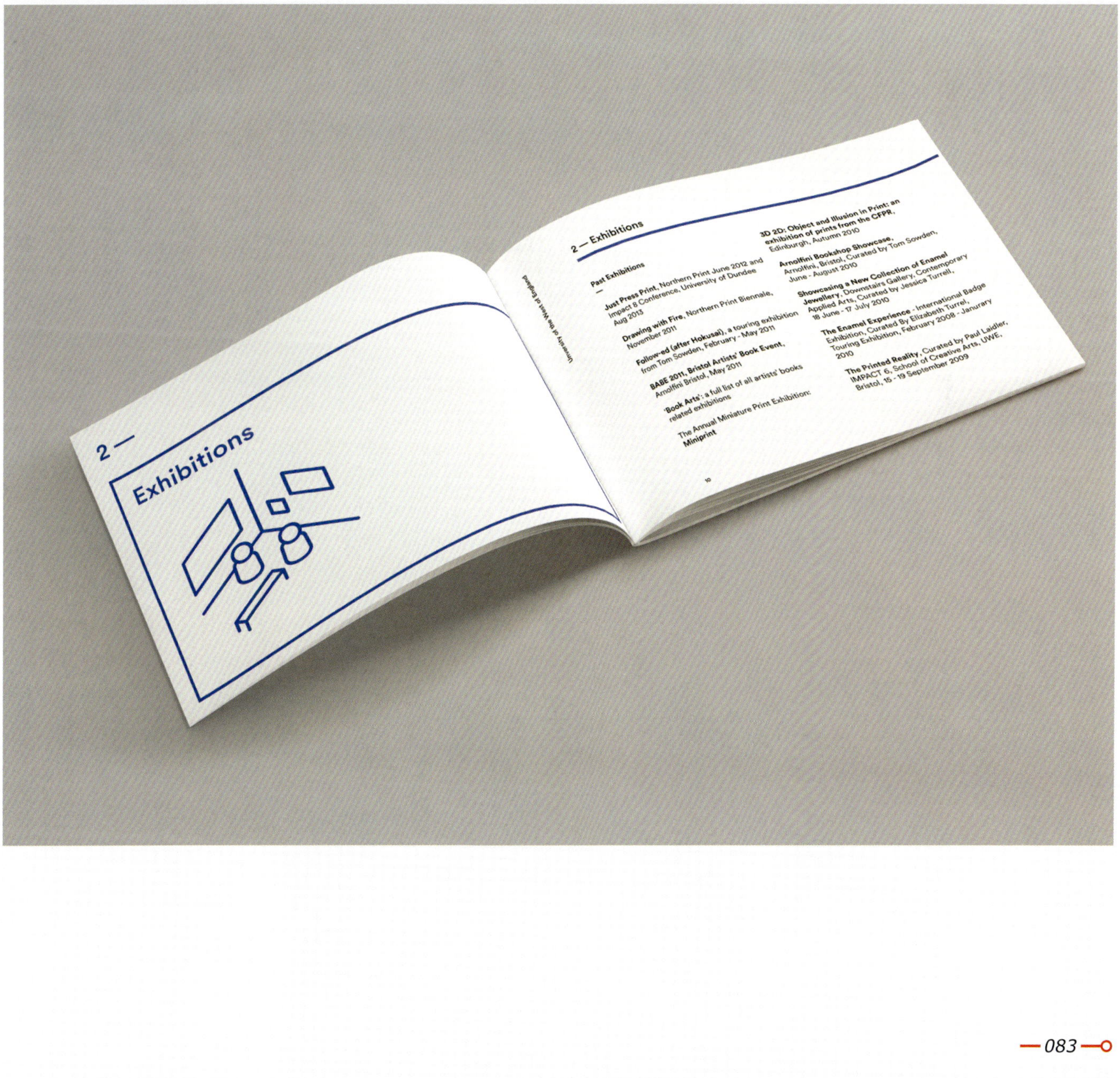

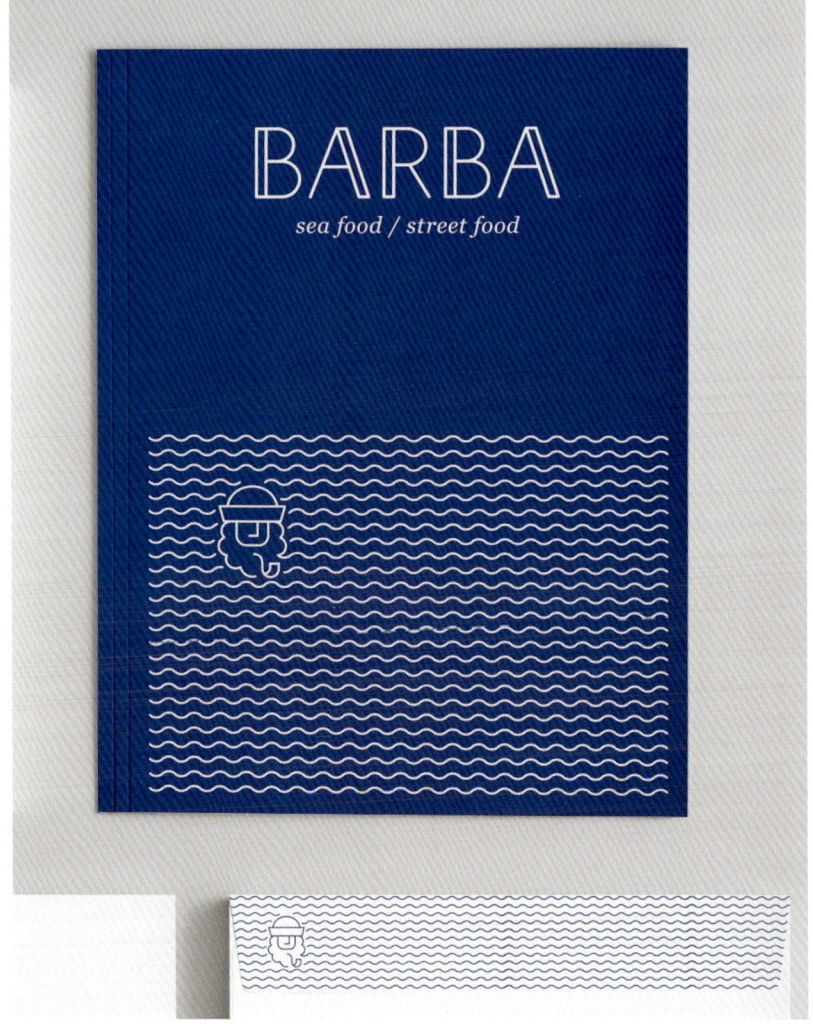

BARBA RESTAURANT

Graphic Design: Negra Nigoević, Filip Pomykalo
Interior Design: Marita Bonačić

Barba (a Dalmatian colloquial expression for uncle, old gentleman, man of the sea, or fisherman) is a place in Dubrovnik, Croatia, where one can experience local tradition, flavors, spices, and dishes. As its target demographic is younger people, a contemporary design approach was used to introduce a fusion of past and present through the combination of traditional cuisine prepared in a modern way and a visual identity that presents local motifs with a modern twist.

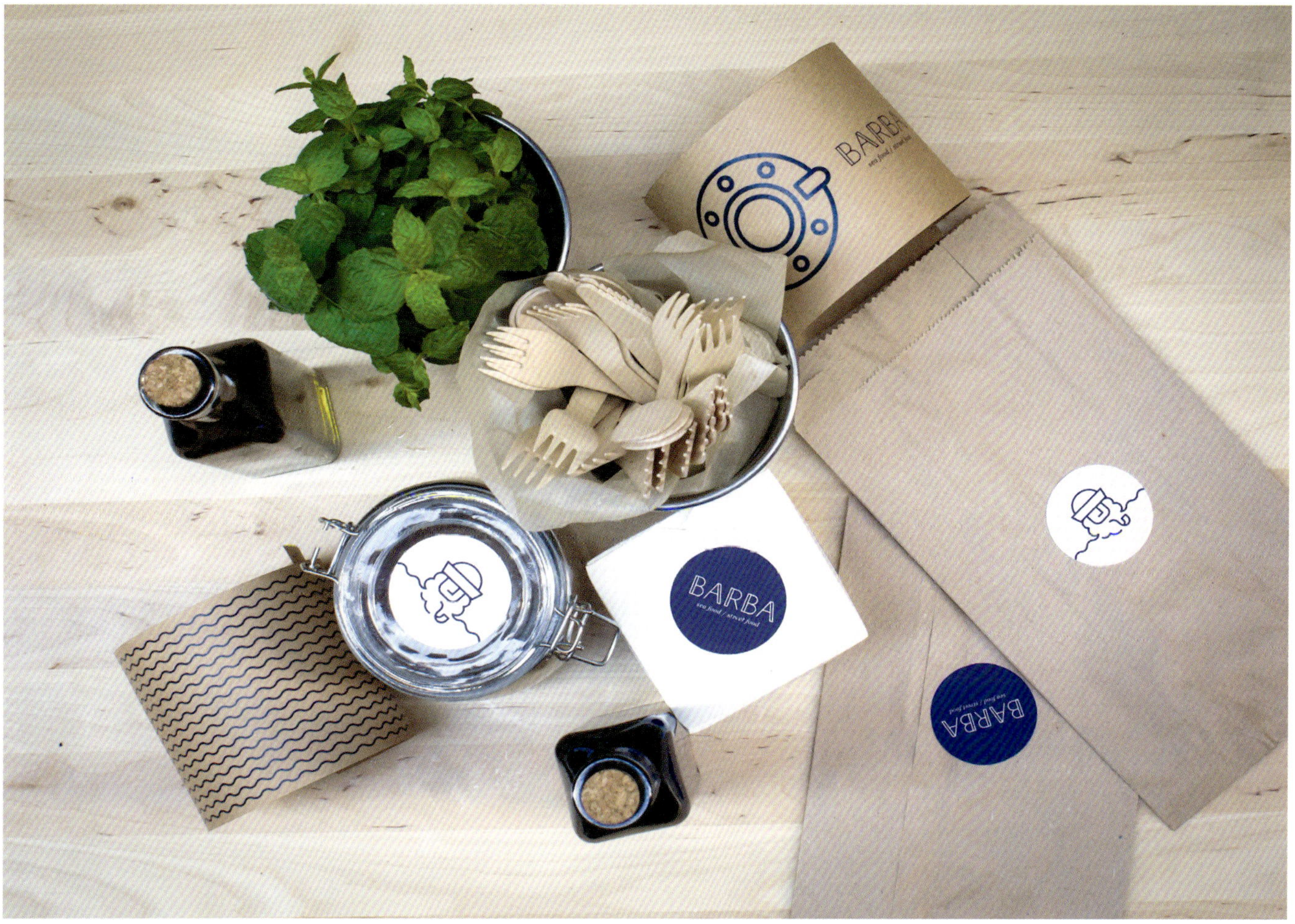
BARBA
BARBA
BARBA

BARBA

BARBA
sea food / street food

BARBA
sea food / street food

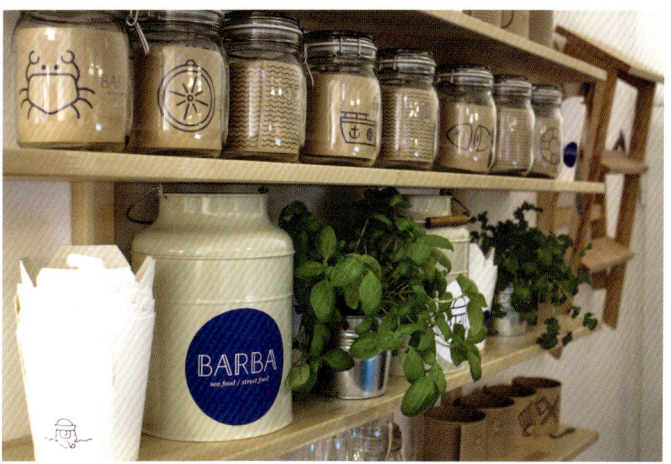

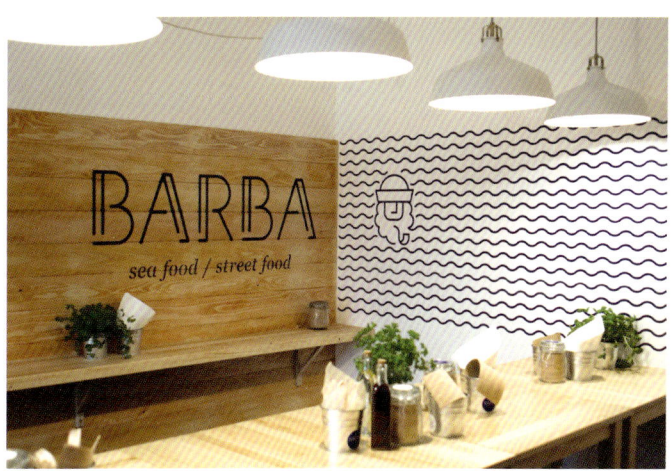

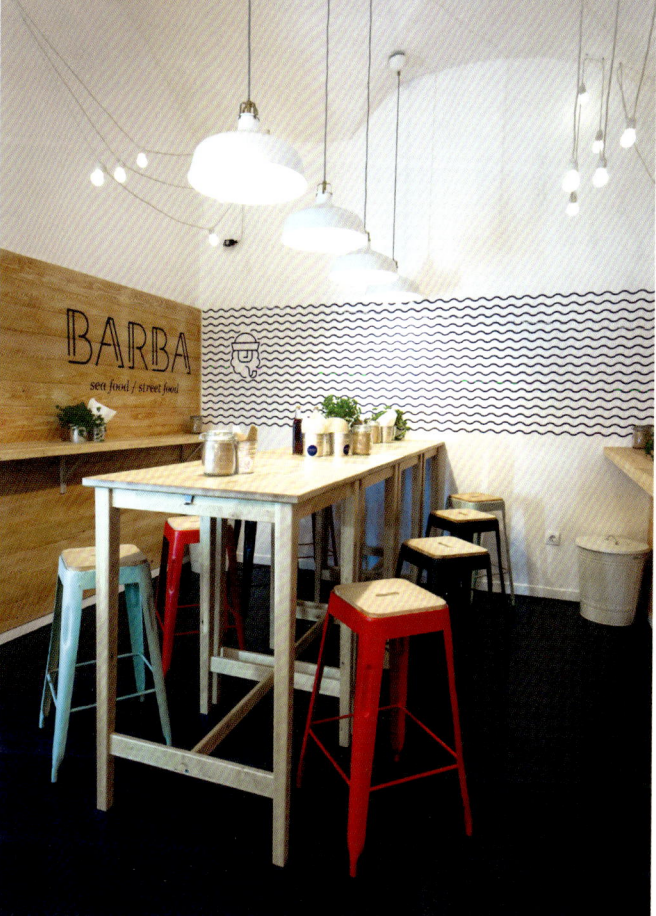

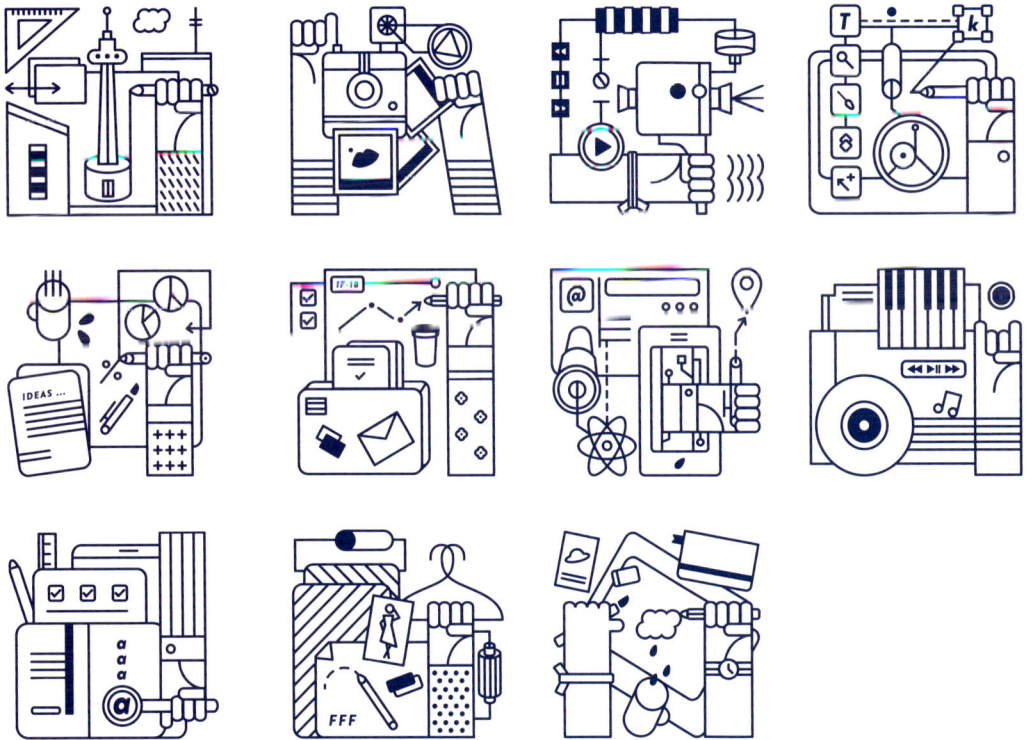

VISUAL IDENTITY FOR WHAT'S NEXT

Design: Jonė Miškinyte, Aistė Jakimavičiūtė, Domas Mikšys — **Website Design:** Justė Valužytė

"What's Next?" is the first conference of its kind not only in Lithuania, but also in the whole region of the Baltic States. This conference combines visual culture, business, and technologies. The main task for the design team was to create an organic, playful, and lively brand. A dynamic upward spiral was picked for the main logotype symbol as a representation of the never-ending world of change and innovation. An abstract colorful pattern and animated icon set are the key elements of the main identity's design. The conference spaces and different activities are marked with different colored tags, and color codes are used in all of the conference's visual communications, creating a unique pattern through the entire identity.

KŪRYBINIŲ INDUSTRIJŲ KONFERENCIJA
ARCHITEKTŪRA
DIZAINAS
TECHNOLOGIJOS
VIDEO
REKLAMA
ILIUSTRACIJA
WHAT'S NEXT?
FOTOGRAFIJA
EDUKACIJA
MADA
MUZIKA
VERSLAS
KADA?
SPALIO 17-18
KUR?
KŪRYBINĖS DIRBTUVĖS • VAKARĖLIS
KONTAKTŲ VAKARAS • DIZAINO MUGĖ (ĮĖJIMAS NEMOKAMAS)
Daugiau informacijos: whatsnext.lt

(IŠ)KVĖPTI
WHAT'S NEXT?
WHAT'S NEXT?
WHAT'S NEXT?
SPEAKER
STAFF
PRESS

BUTLER

Design: Sébastien Bisson
Account Direction: Marie-Claude Fortin
Agency: Polygraphe Studio
Photography: Sandrine Castellan,
Martin Girard

Butler is a brand-new concept for colorful overboots for kids. Like their penguin mascot, Butler overboots are rugged, cute, and fun, and they aren't afraid of getting wet. This platform includes the logo, brochure, stationery, packaging, displays, and in-store material. The resulting identity is playful while also evoking a sense of quality and reliability. It gives the impression that the Butler brand has been around forever, but has reinvented itself and kept up with the times.

CELEBRATE WHAT I AM

Design: Ana Cahuex ——— **Photography:** Javier Ovalle

To celebrate her recent achievement of becoming a graphic designer, the designer Ana Cahuex developed the visual identity for her own party, from the invitation down to the smallest details needed. Ana decided to keep things simple in order to make it memorable and special for herself and her guests. She created a dynamic and delicate color palette, patterns, paper, and a set of icons based on a visible construction. To reflect herself in the design, Ana developed a complete family of icons that tell her story from college to graduation and finally to getting a job, which she applied to her curriculum and portfolio.

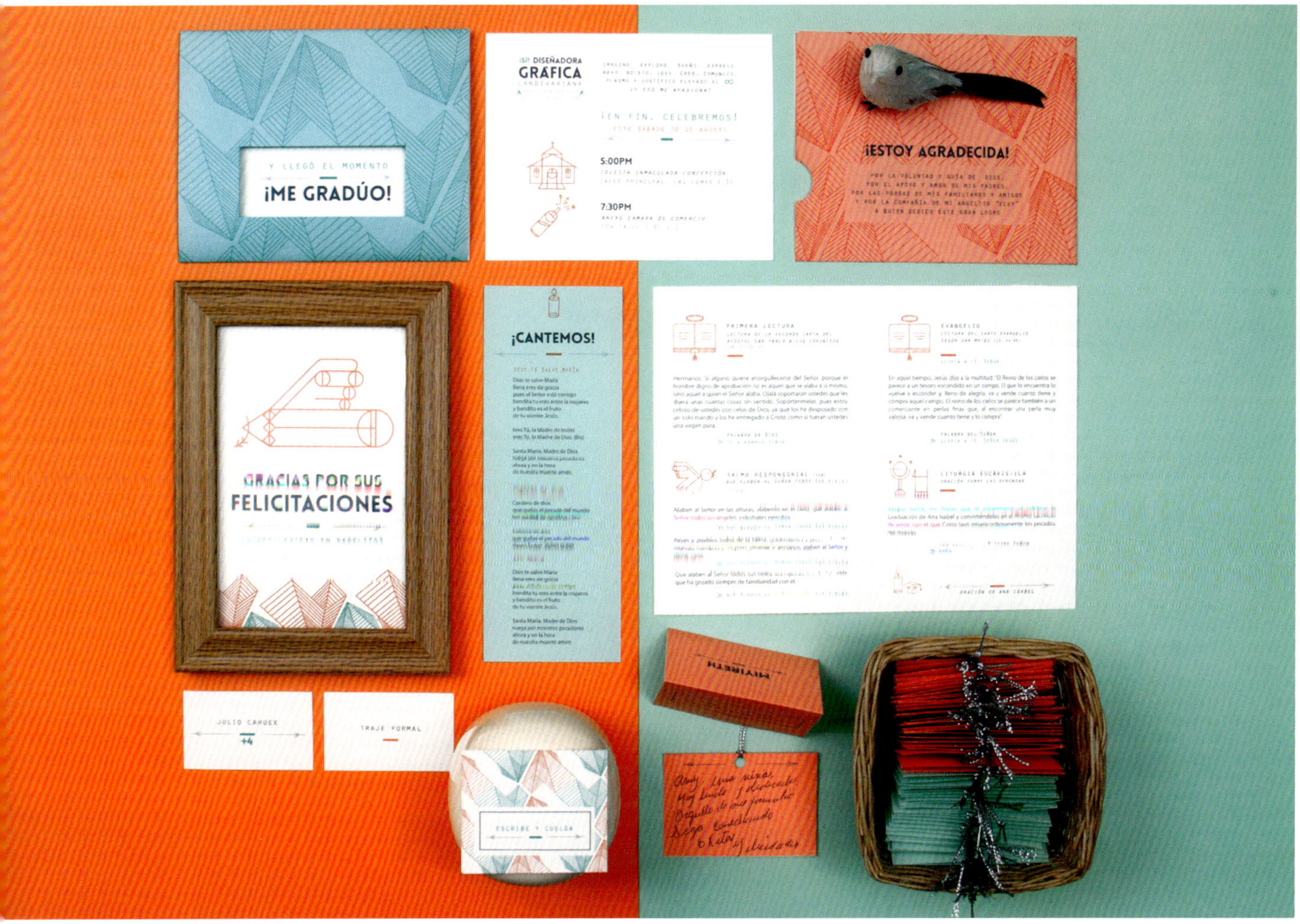

 (Al) Alucinación visual / *Visual hallucination*
 (Ap) Actos repetitivos / *Repetitive acts*
 (Ap) Agitación / *Agitation*
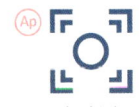 (Ap) Inquietud / *Restlessness*
 (Ap) Deambulación / *Wander*
  (Me) Procesal / *Procedural*
 (Me) Biográfica / *Biographical*

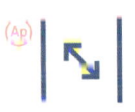 (Ap) Paseos / *Walks*
 (An) Seguimiento al cuidador / *Follow the caregiver*
(Ln) Ansiedad / *Anxiety*
 (Ch) Enfados / *Anger*
(Ch) Labilidad emocional / *Emotional lability*
(Or) Espacial / *Spatial*
 (Or) Personal / *Personal*

(Ch) Reacción catastrófica / *Catastrophic reaction*
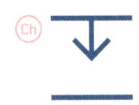 (Ch) Depresión / *Depression*
 (De) Delirios / *Delusions*
 (Fn) Ritmo diurno y sueño / *Diurnal rhythm and sleep*
 (Fn) Klüver-Bucy / *Klüver-Bucy*
 (Me) Semántica / *Semantics*
 (Me) Episódica largo plazo / *Long-term episodic*

 (Fn) Trastorno alimentario / *Eating disorder*
 (Pe) Apatía / *Apathy*
 (Pe) Indiferencia / *Indifference*
 (Pe) Irritabilidad / *Irritability*
 (At) Atención / *Attention*
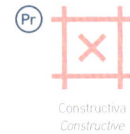 (Pr) Constructiva / *Constructive*
 (Pr) Ideatoria / *Ideational*

 (Co) Concentración / *Concentration*
 (Cv) Gnosia visual / *Visual gnosia*
 (Cv) Interpretación espacial / *Spatial interpretation*
 (Cv) Reconocer caras / *Recognize faces*
 (Fe) Falta de iniciativa / *Lack of initiative*

 (Fe) Pensamiento abstracto / *Abstract thinking*
 (Fe) Planificación / *Planning*
 (Fe) Cálculo / *Calculation*
 (Fe) Procesar información / *Process information*
 (Fe) Razonamiento / *Reasoning*

 (Fe) Esquema corporal / *Body image*
 (Lg) Oral expresivo espontáneo / *Expression oral spontaneous*
 (Lg) Comprender órdenes / *Understand commands*
 (Lg) Oral expresivo denominativo / *Denomination oral expressive*
 (Lg) Oral expresivo repetitivo / *Repetitive oral expression*

SYMPTOMATIC MAP, ALZHEIMER'S DEMENTIA

Design: Sergio Durango

This is an experimental project which intends to use the visual resources and theories of perception and design information to synthesize information on the Alzheimer's, making a visual "translation" of it.

BEAR CLOTHING UK

Design: Tiago Machado
Agency: Apex Studio

Bear Clothing UK is a new fashion apparel brand in the United Kingdom that presents themselves as a manly brand. They were searching for a new visual identity, an image that could be both sophisticated and humorous with a minimalistic, flat style. The project had almost no limitations in terms of the briefing; the brand was very open-minded, with their only requirement being that a bear was included, as their name would suggest. This bear could be personalized in any way, with apparel accessories such as a hat, scarf, or glasses, or with or without other design elements.

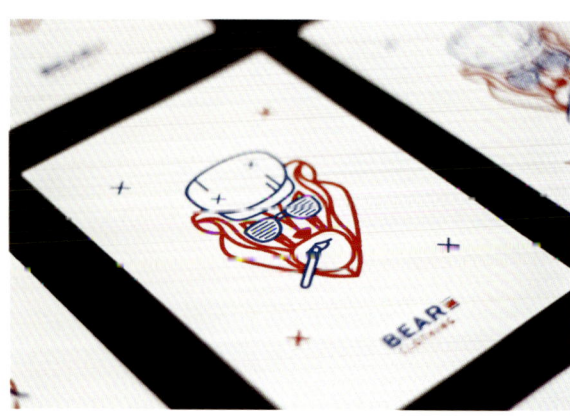

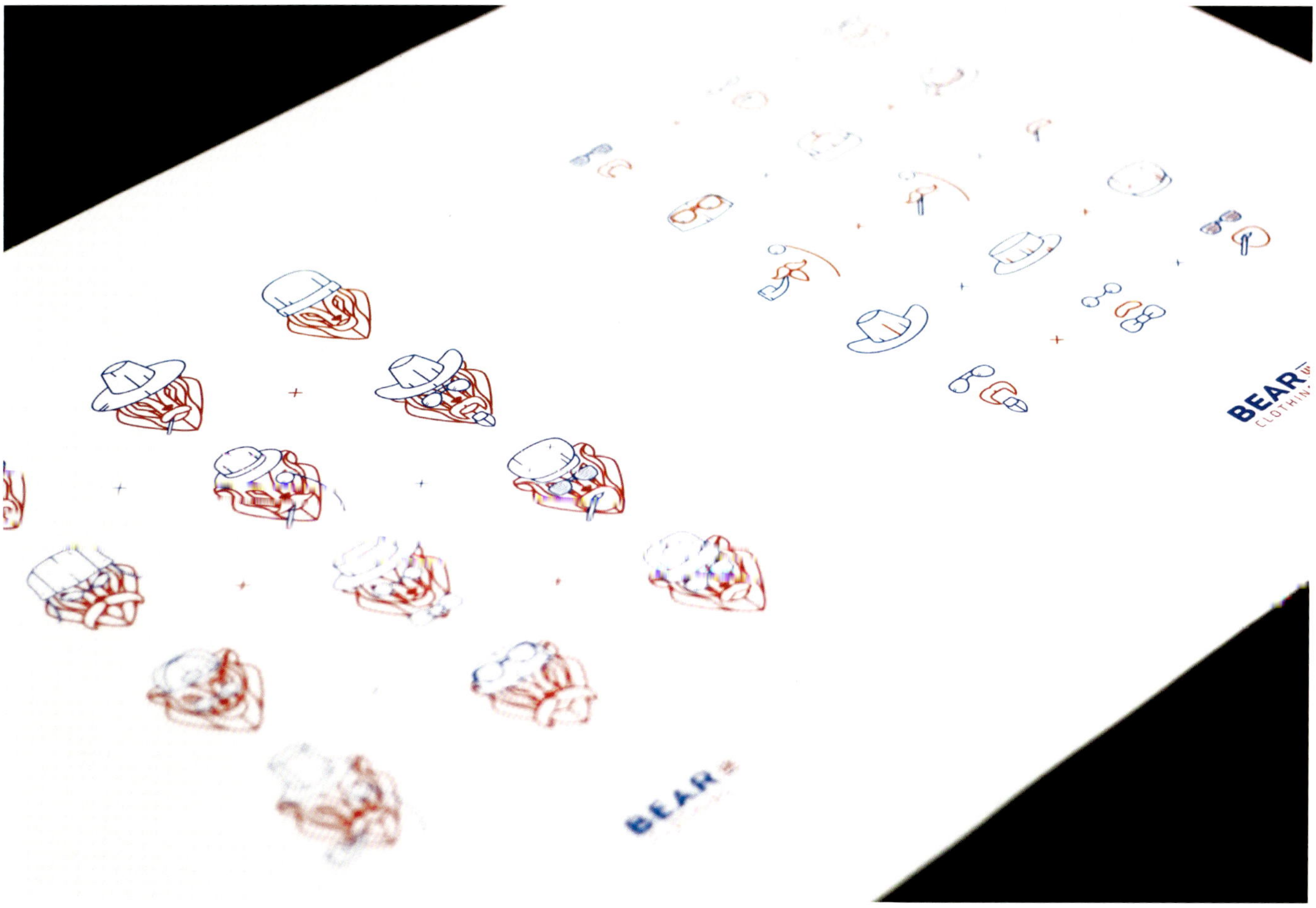

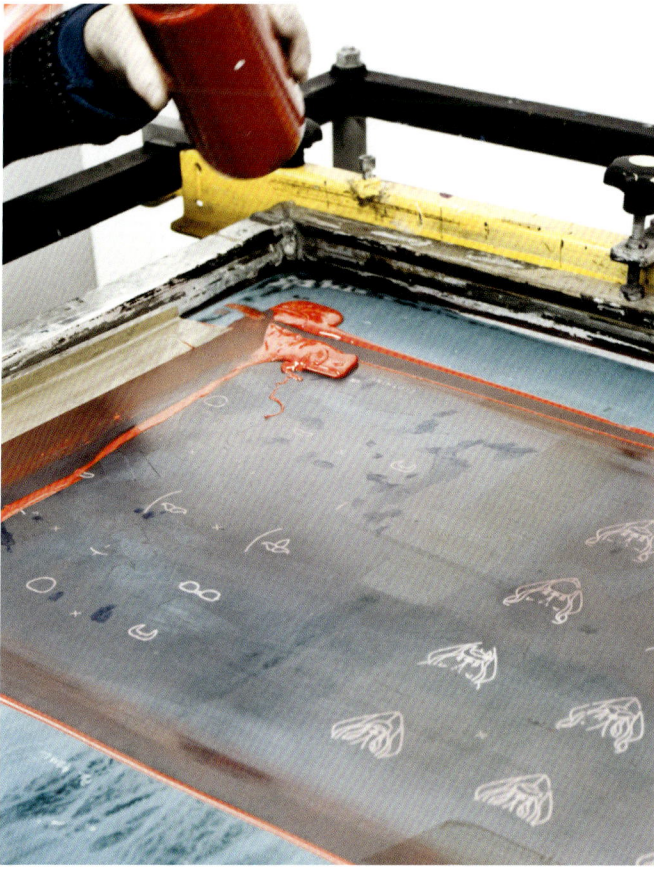

SAUSAGE CLOCK

Design: Pin-Ju Chen

"Sausage Clock" is inspired by Mengenlehreuhr (German for "Set Theory Clock") located in Europa-Center in Berlin, which indicates the time with the use of illuminated and colored fields. Pondering which objects would best represent Berlin, the designer chose a well-known German food sausage. By using different flavors of sausages and salami to imitate the system of Mengenlehreuhr, the designer tried to form a new way of telling the time through arranging food into certain patterns.

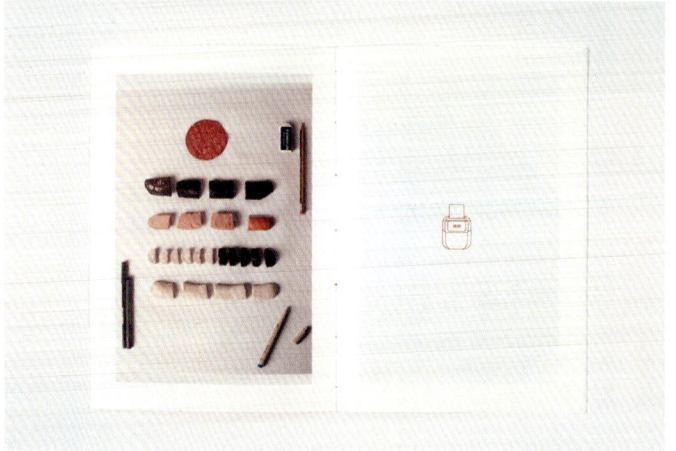

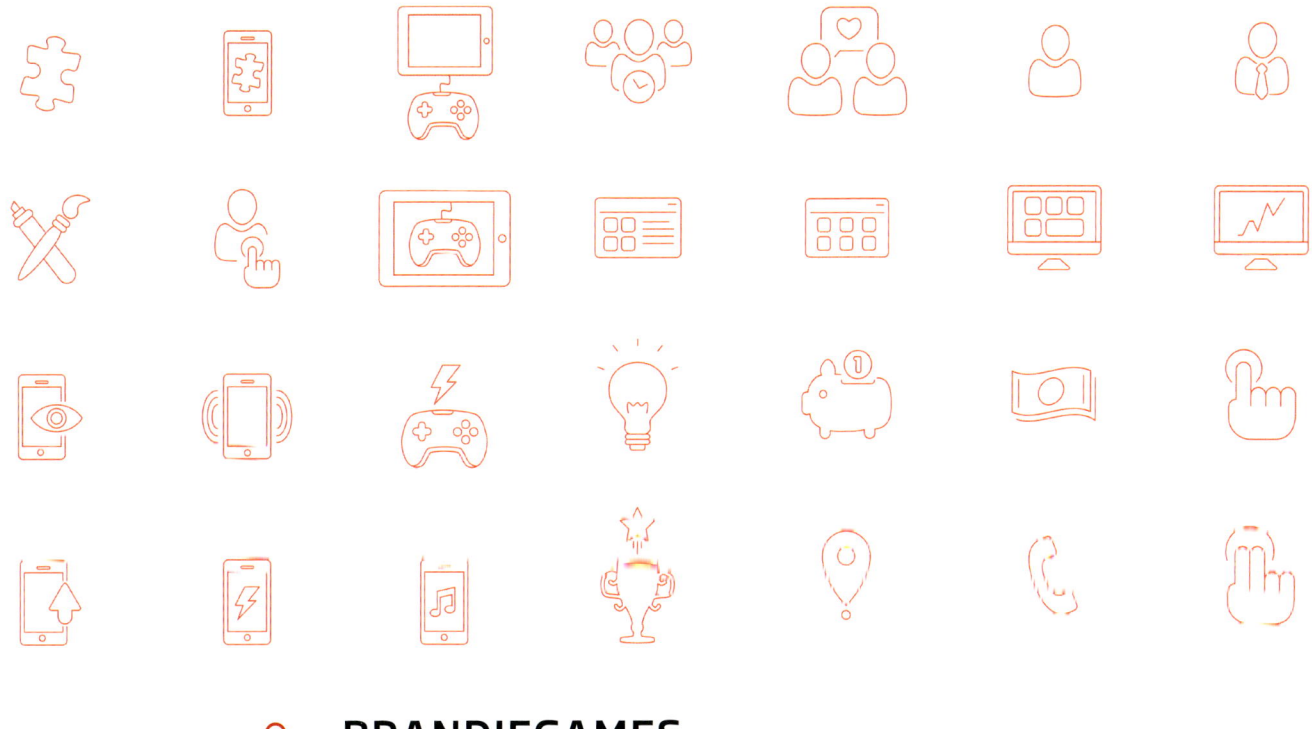

BRANDIEGAMES

Design: Maciej Świerczek, Alicja Wydmańska — **Agency:** Jazzy Innovations

Brandiegames is a fast, simple way to create beautiful mobile games for brands in seconds with just a few clicks! With it, even the seven-year-old daughter of a CEO can create a branded game for her mother's company. Brands can acquire more customers, convert potential customers to sales, keep customers longer, and get people talking about them.

STROLL

Design: Maciek Martyniuk
Agency: Yomagick

Stroll is a conceptual social network that allows users to share and recommend interesting walking routes and encourages people to explore. The concept originated from the historical idea of the Flaneur. It is a user-generated community that lets users share, record, and discover different walking experiences wherever they are. Users can research casual walks by using the "mood filter."

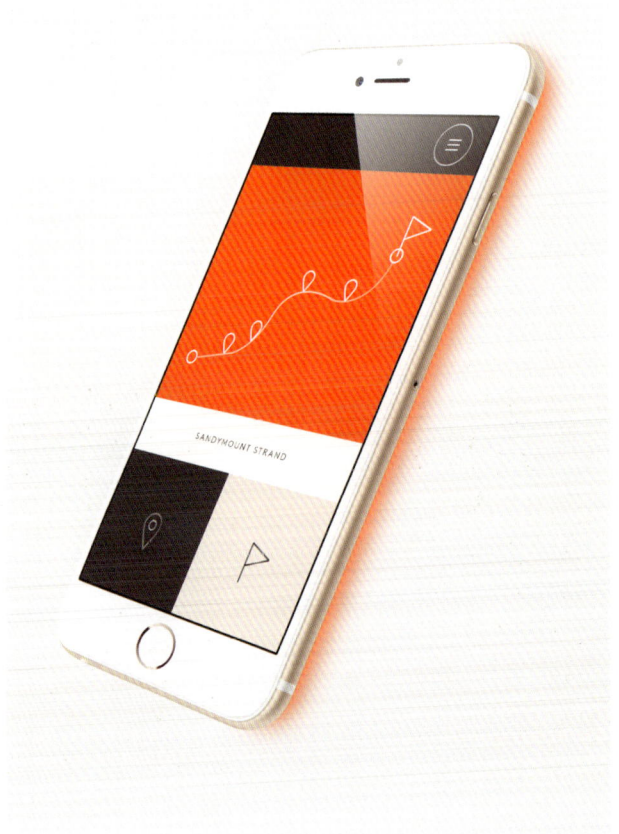

Hallo
Berlin
Stroll the World.
Find the best places to stroll around.
Join our community.

Hallo
Berlin
Hello
Dublin
Stroll
Take a
Stroll Now
Find the best
places to stroll
around
Choose
your favourite
Stroll

   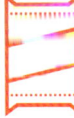 

SUSY'S BAKERY

Design: Guillermo Castellanos Flores
Art Direction: Moisés Guillén Romero
Agency: Para Todo Hay Fans

Susy's Bakery is a premium quality bakery and food retail space founded and established by Azucena Romero Camarena in 1976 in Guadalajara, Mexico. The corporate identity is directly derived from the profile of the company: a small business which bakes signature gourmet cookies, cakes, cupcakes, pies, and choux, priding itself on having the best homemade touch of the region.

AZUCENA ROMERO
CAMARENA
SUSY'S
BAKERY
SINCE
-1976-

SUSY'S
BAKERY
SINCE
-1976-

Breathable / Respirant

Quick Dry / Séchage rapide

Wind protection

Insulation / Isolation

Odor Control

Extra grip / Adhérence optimale

Wool Blend / Mélange de laine

Fingertip / Mitaines à doigts

Touch Screen Compatible / Pour écrans tactiles

Warranty / Garantie

Must Have / Produit vedette

Prenez-en soin

Warmth Wisdom / Chaleureux conseils

Montrealer Since 1961 / Montréalais depuis 1961 — 1961 MTL

Designed in Canada / Conçu au Canada

Waterproof / Imperméable

Merino Wool Blend / Mélange de laine mérinos

KOMBI

Design: Sébastien Bisson
Account Direction: Marie-Claude Fortin
Agency: Polygraphe Studio

Kombi is a family-owned winter accessories company founded in Montreal in 1961. To get closer to its clients and open new doors, Kombi undertook a major project to revamp its brand. The platform now has a new logo, signature, packaging, and website, as well as print communication tools, a booth, in-store visuals, and a social media presence. Kombi's new image is inviting and warm, but not just any kind of warm. It's the kind of human warmth that makes you want to go play outside and create lifelong memories.

The perfect snowball, in 4 easy steps.

0° C

24" snow

1 handfull of snow

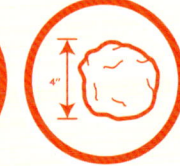
4" diameter

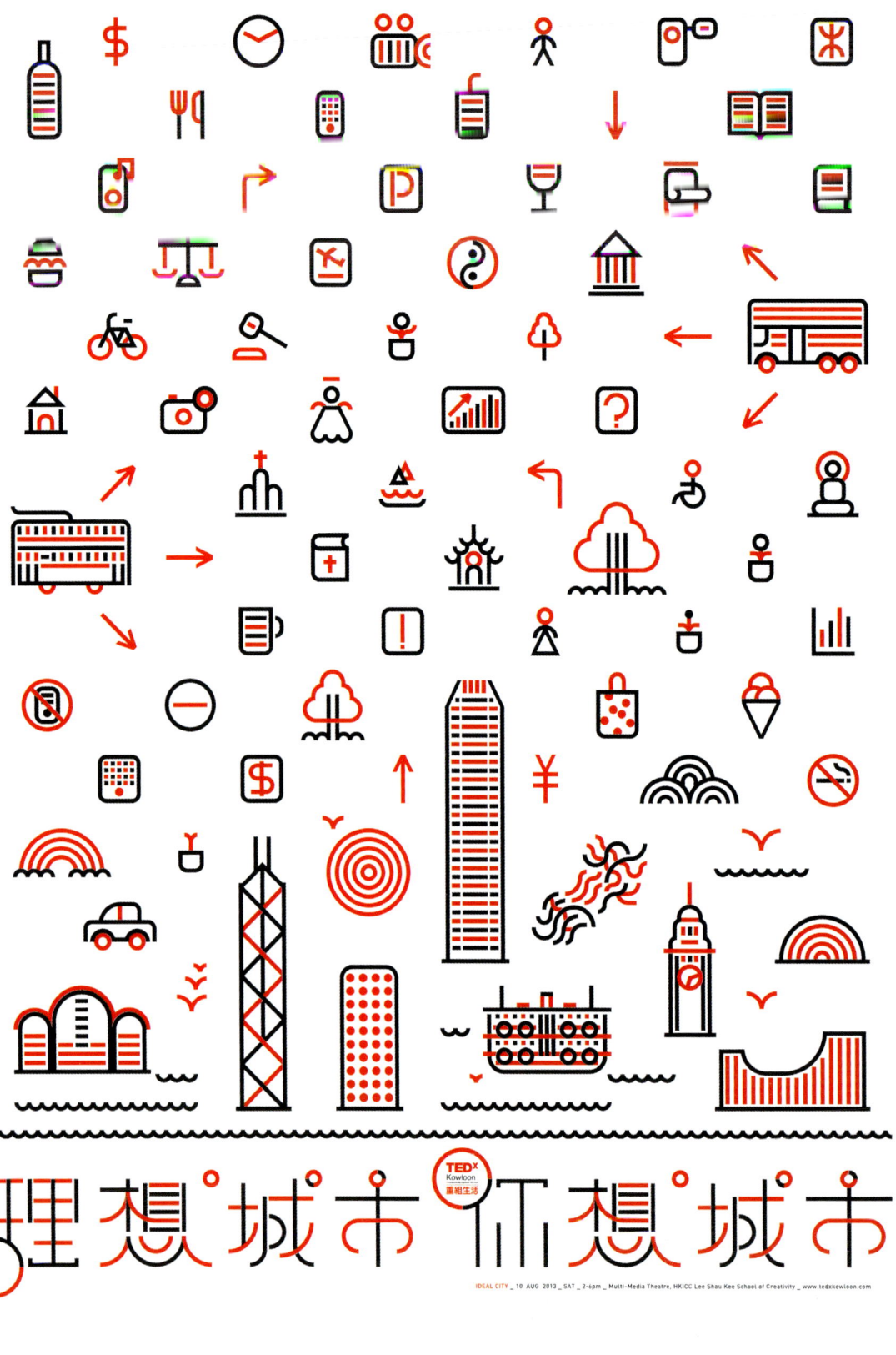

— IDEAL CITY —
— **Design:** Benny Leung Tsz Fung —— **Agency:** STUDIO-M —

The designer was invited to join the TED×Kowloon creative team to design visual graphics for the discussion with the theme of "Ideal City." The ideal and reality are often very different, but they can be complimentary. The combination of the Chinese characters "Li Xiang(Ideal)" and "Ni Xiang(You Think)" explain this philosophy of life. The designer also created a series of icons to inspire the audiences' imaginations of the Ideal City.

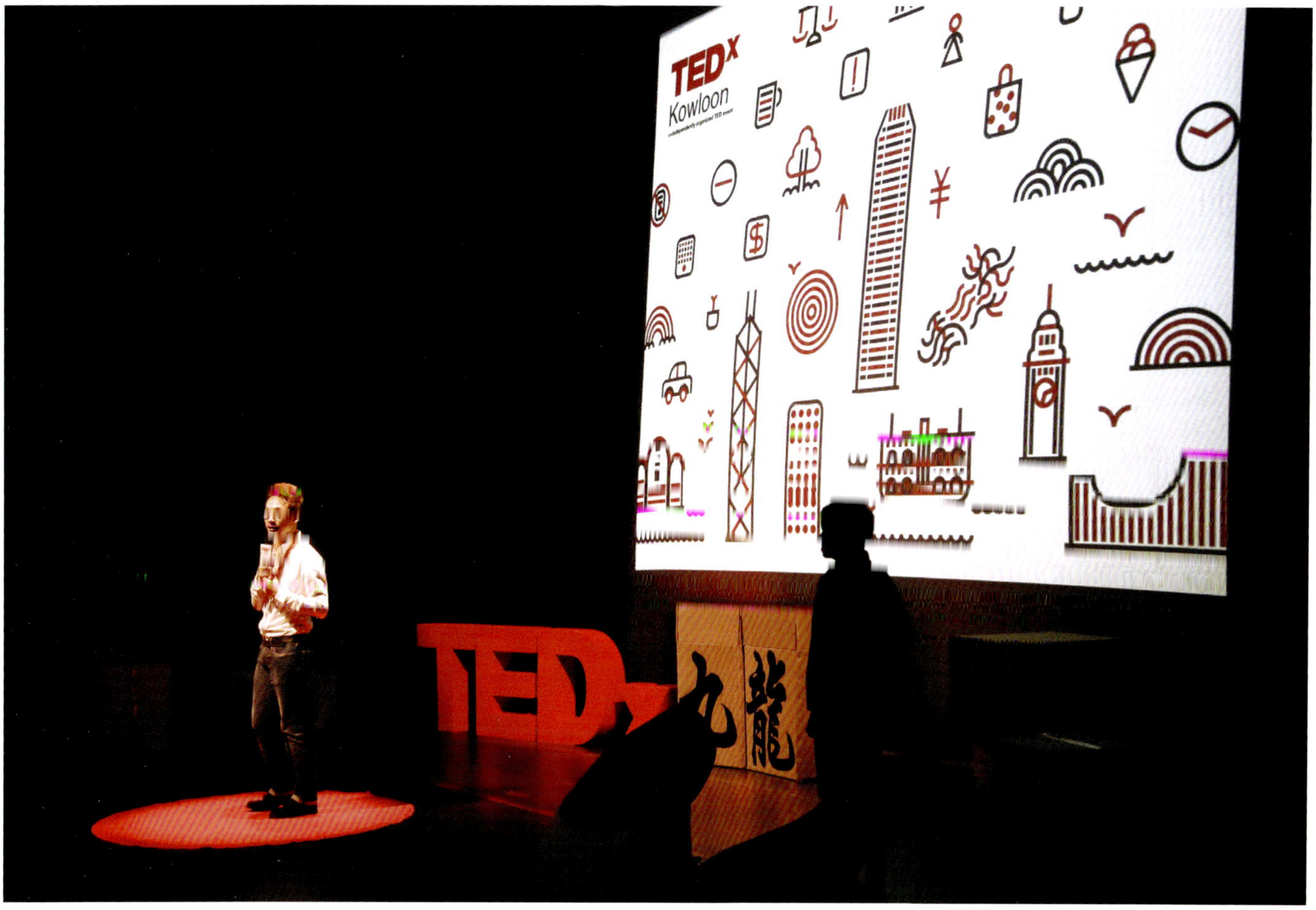
TEDx
Kowloon
TED
九龍

PAPER

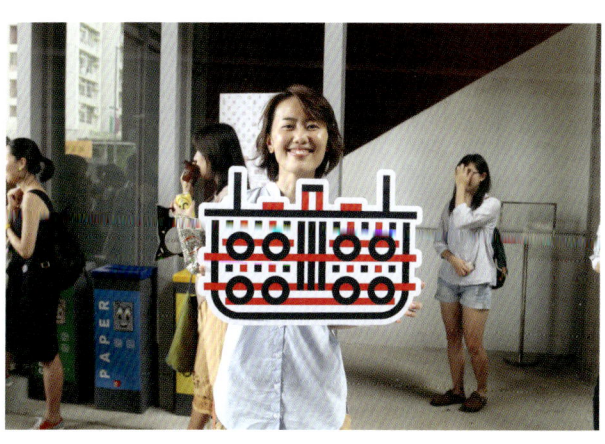

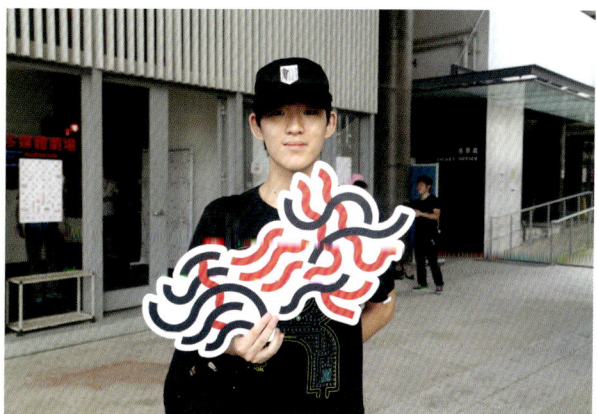

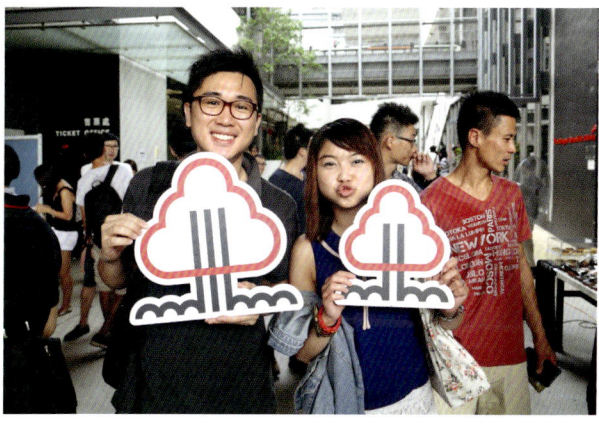

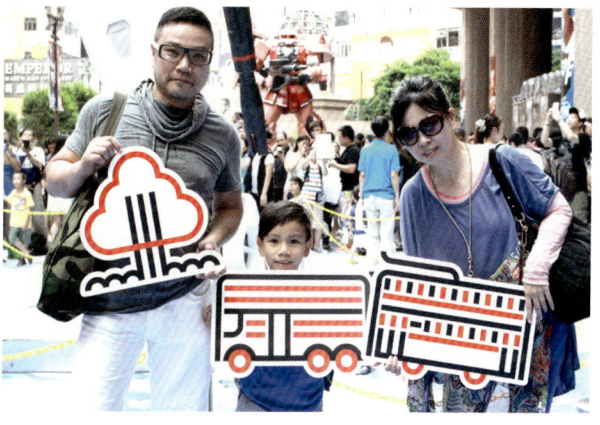

オーナメント
—
botanippe
企画：
Good Job! 東北プロジェクト、
Able Art Company
デザイン・ディレクション：
MUTE
製造：
コーヒータイム（二本松市・浪江町）、
須賀川共労育成園（須賀川市）、
えんどう豆（南相馬市）

風呂敷
—
marugococi
デザイン：
株式会社サヌイ織物、
工房まる（福岡市）
製造：
株式会社サヌイ織物
原画：
太田宏介［工房まる］

靴下
—
製造：
タビオ株式会社
原画：
Able Art Company

GOOD JOB!

Design: Midori Hirota
Art direction: Yuma Harada
Agency: UMA/design farm
Photography: Takumi Ota, Yoshiro Masuda

"Good Job!" is a brand that not only sells products, but produces them. Their logo design came from "∞," the symbol for infinity, expressing infinite possibilities, new works, and social circulation. The designer created icons based on some of the brand's many products for their visual identity. These icons are layered under the text in the brand's printed materials.

障害のある人たちのARTと社会的なINNOVATION

Good Job!

TOKYO 渋谷ヒカリエ8F 8/COURT 2013.11/29(Fri.)-12/1(Sun.)

FUKUOKA イムズB2F イムズプラザ 2014.2/15(Sat.)-2/17(Mon.)

MIYAGI せんだいメディアテーク1F オープンスクエア 2013.12/15(Sun.)-12/17(Tue.)

GoodJob!

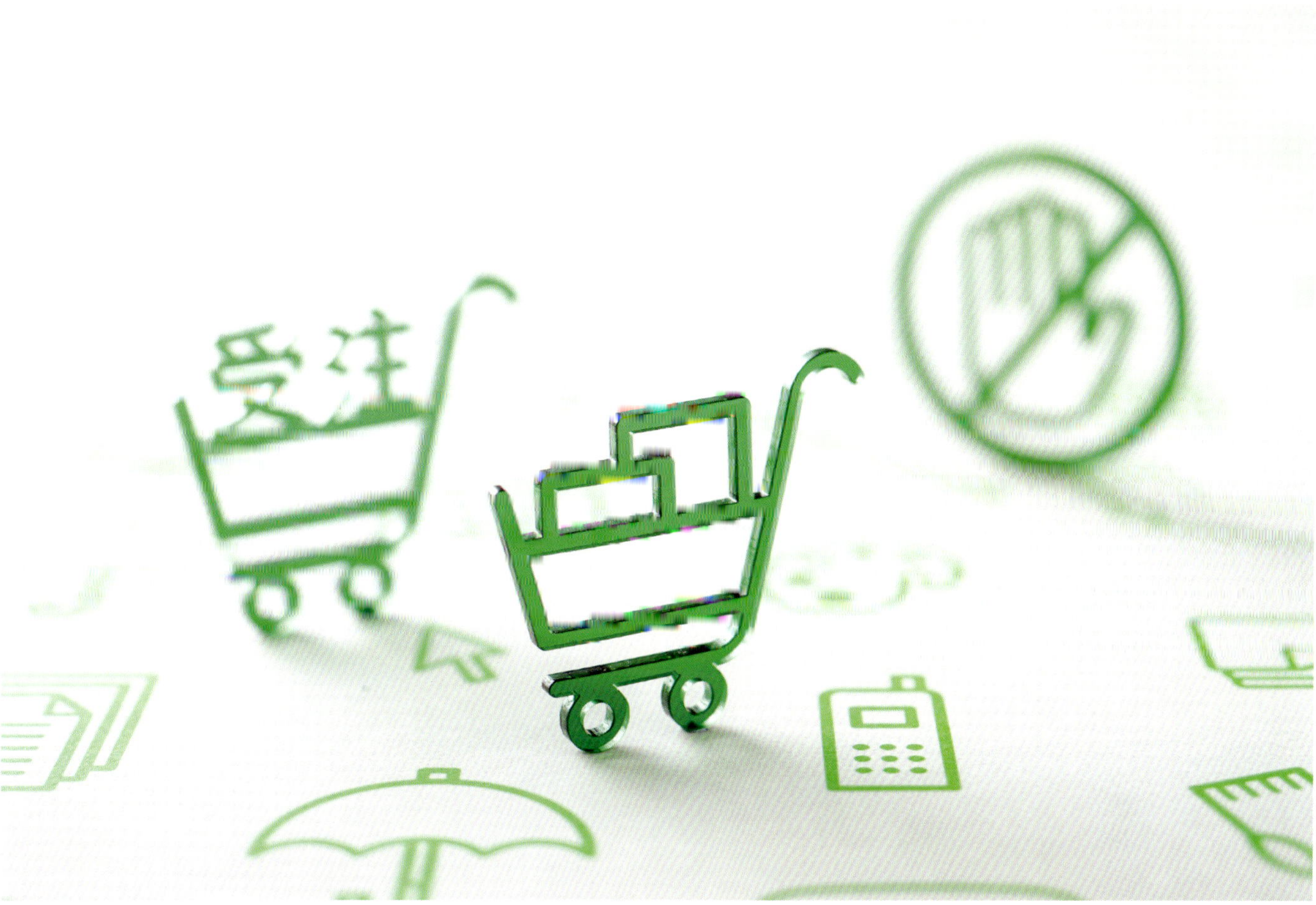
受注

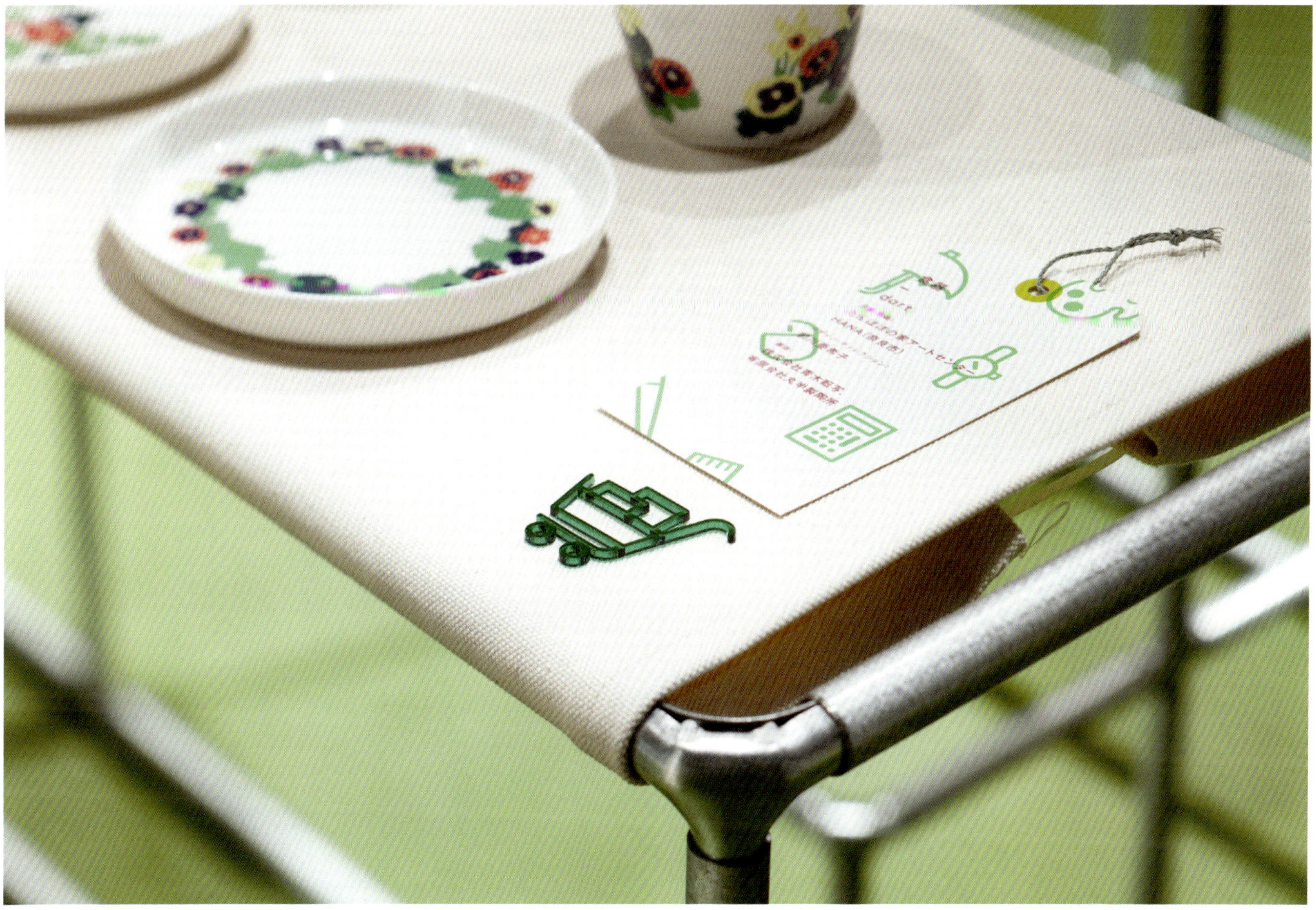
dart
HANA

SATURDAY – VETER MAGAZINE FESTIVAL

Design: Irina Kruglova

The largest park in Moscow hosted the Veter Magazine festival, which featured musical and performance acts, a food market, master classes for kids and their parents, and entertaining games. Several sets of icons were designed for each individual zone of the festival space.

УБОРКА ПАРКА

ЛЕКЦИИ

МУЗЫКА

ДЕТСКИЕ МАСТЕР-КЛАССЫ

ЭКО-МАРКЕТ

СПОРТИВНЫЕ ЗАБЕГИ REEBOK

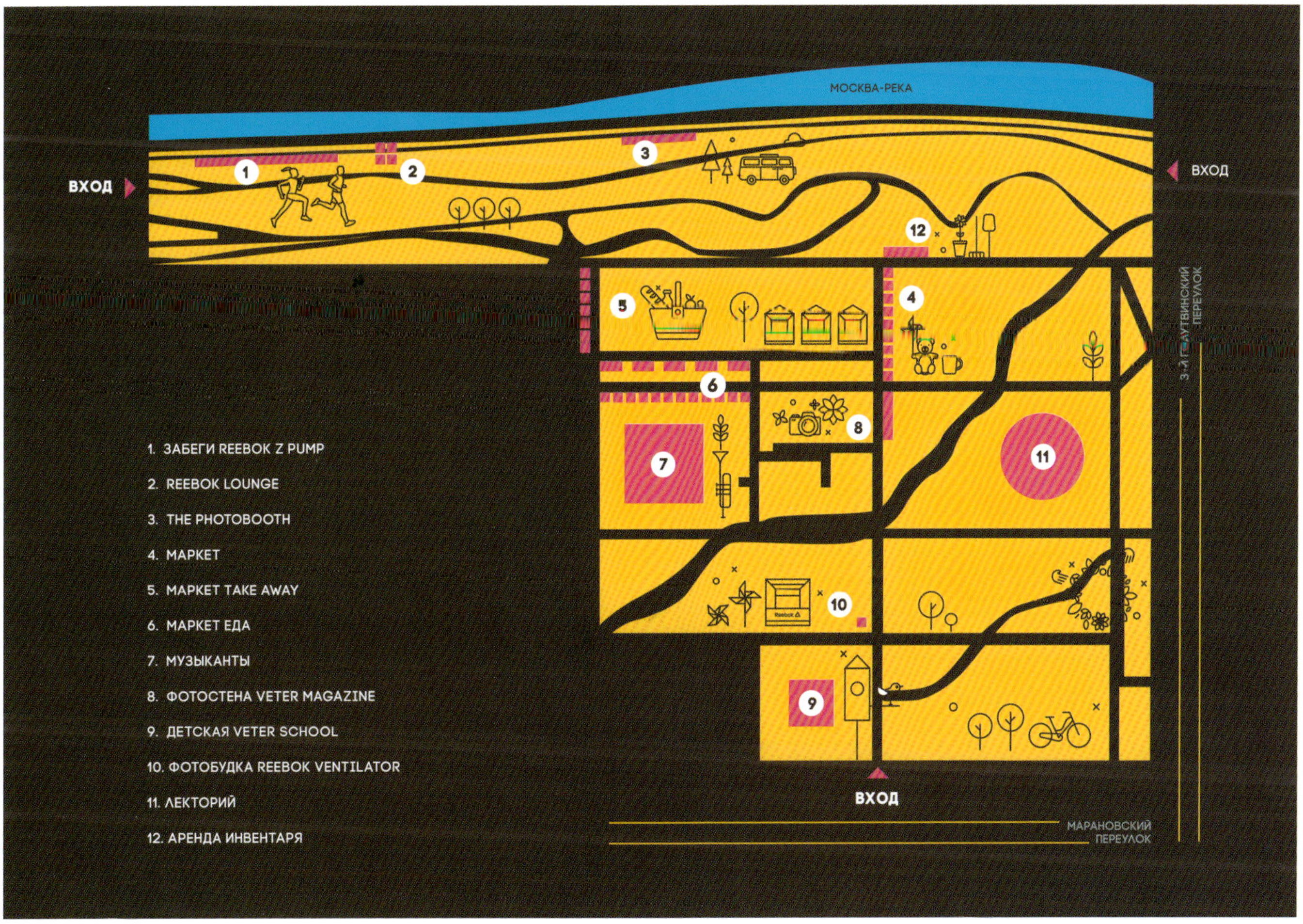

МОСКВА-РЕКА

ВХОД ▶

◀ ВХОД

3-Й ГОЛУТВИНСКИЙ ПЕРЕУЛОК

ВХОД ▲

1. ЗАБЕГИ REEBOK Z PUMP

2. REEBOK LOUNGE

3. THE PHOTOBOOTH

4. МАРКЕТ

5. МАРКЕТ TAKE AWAY

6. МАРКЕТ ЕДА

7. МУЗЫКАНТЫ

8. ФОТОСТЕНА VETER MAGAZINE

9. ДЕТСКАЯ VETER SCHOOL

10. ФОТОБУДКА REEBOK VENTILATOR

11. ЛЕКТОРИЙ

12. АРЕНДА ИНВЕНТАРЯ

МАРАНОВСКИЙ ПЕРЕУЛОК

URANIAE – OBSERVATORY OF GELLÉRT HILL

Design: Hajnalka Illés

The Uraniae Observatory, which was built on the famous Gellért Hill in Budapest, only stood for 37 years; however, this short period provided a rich history. The designer of this project took these 37 years as inspiration and incorporated events from them in the visual layout during the design phase. The designer created graphics based on the the description of several astronomical and educational tools and designs from mechanical observatories, all closely related to the Uraniae Observatory itself. Today it would be impossible for an observatory to exist in this location, as the city lights and pollution block the sky and serve as an obstacle preventing inhabitants from seeing the stars.

Moreno	**Diablada**	**Ekeko**	**Tiwanaku**	**Puerta del Sol**
Moreno	Diablada	Ekeko	Tiwanaku	Gate of the Sun

Cóndor	**Cholita**	**Kusillo**	**Siku**	**Teleférico de La Paz**
Condor	Cholita	Kusillo	Siku	Cableway in La Paz

Diablo	**Tinku**	**Llama**	**Lago Titicaca**	**Camino de la muerte**
Devil	Tinku	Llama	Lake Titicaca	Death Road

BOLIVIA

Design: Cynthia Torrez

This project was made during a personal journey to Bolivia in which the designer decided to create a series of icons to record her experiences. As this country is known for its culture and traditions, the designer was inspired by specific characters and elements in the Oruro Carnivals and La Paz, its capital. The icons were also used for packaging design for one Bolivia's national drinks, called Api. It is a sweet beverage made from purple corn, consumed mostly by adults and children during breakfast because of its high energy level.

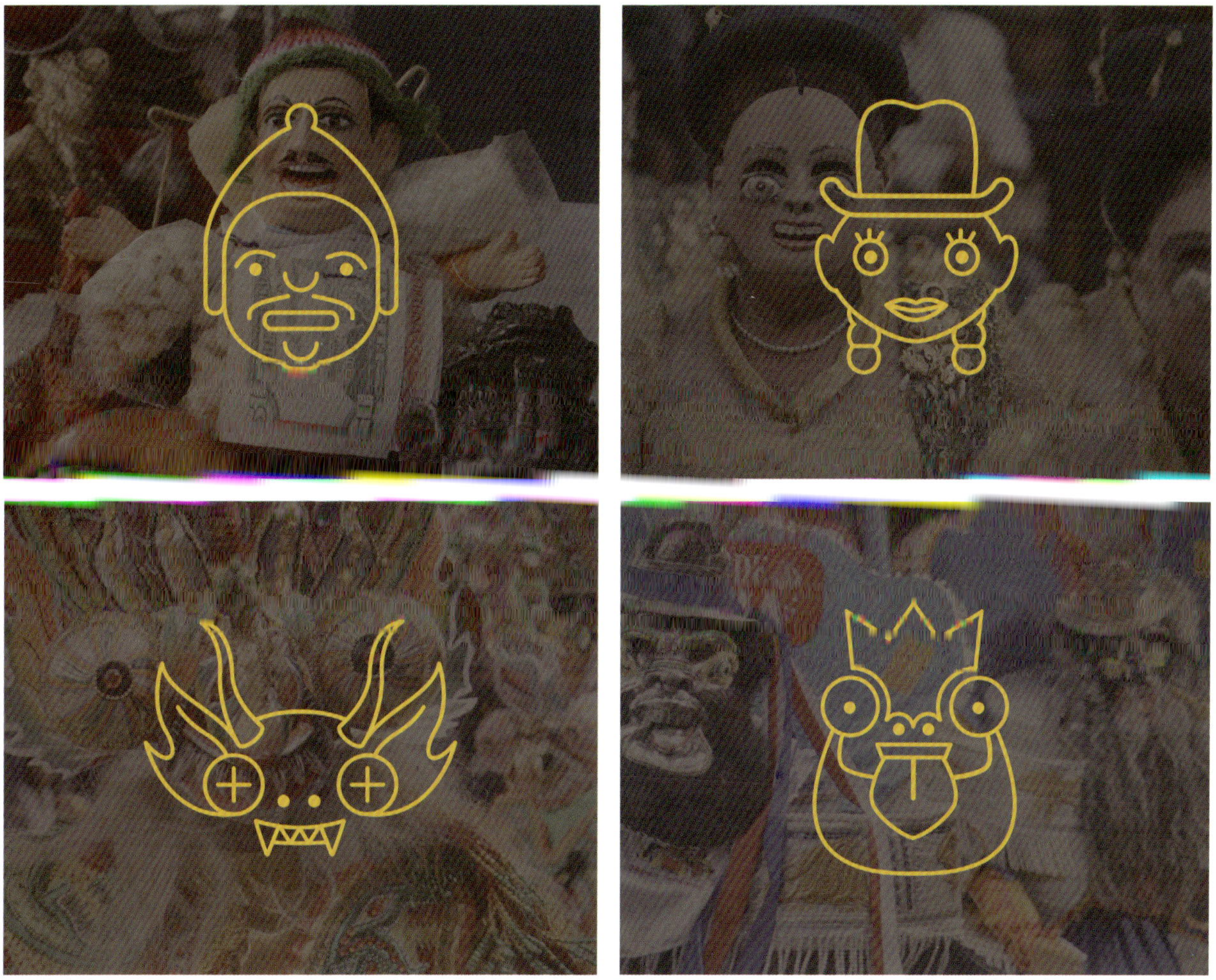

a
API DE MAÍZ
MORADO
400ML
INDUSTRIA BOLIVIANA

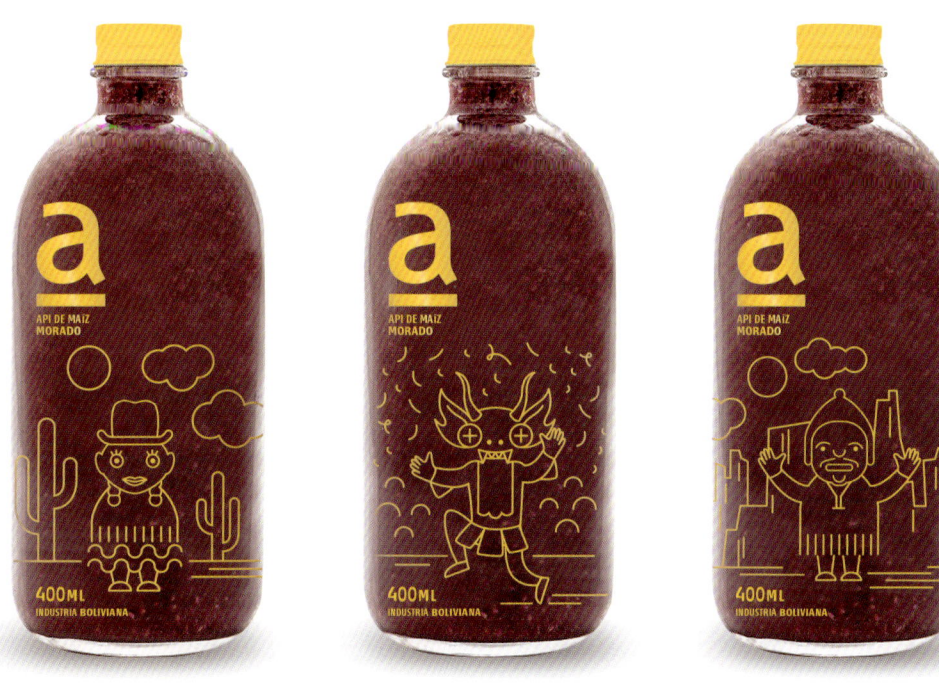

 INFORANEK

 PIOSENKA DO WYNAJĘCIA

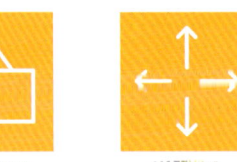 MAFEKING

 INKUBATOR

 ZA SZYBĄ

 KICZI KICZI

 MAGAZYN MUZYCZNY

 PROJEKTOR

 SUBIEKTYWNY POLSKI ALFABET MUZYCZNY

 PORANEK

 AUDYCJA SPORTOWA

 JAZZ PO 21

 RELAX · ŚRODEK TYGODNIA

 NIE DLA SINGLI

 DZIAŁAM, WIĘC JESTEM

 PERIODYK KULTURALNY

 RADIOŻYLETKA

 PI ER KWADRAT

 GDZIE RZYM, GDZIE KRYM

 ALTERNATOR

 RAPOWA KOLACJA

 TEATRALIA

 AUDYCJA ROMAŃSKA

 FAWORKI

 ELEKTRODISCO

 MAGAZYN STUDENCKI

 SZAFA LESIAKA

 BEZSENNOŚĆ WCZESNĄ PORĄ

 LABORATORIUM WYTRZYMAŁOŚCI METALI

 MUSIQUE EXPERIMENTALE

 PIGUŁKA DŹWIĘKOWA

 RADIO FABRYKA

 RADIOGRZAŁKA

 PRAWIE JAK W KINIE

 RADIO GOETHE

 BIBLIOTEKA

 PATCHWORK TEMATYCZNY

 ŁUDZKOŚĆ

 BLUES PO ZACHODZIE SŁOŃCA

 FEMME VOCALE

 ZŁOTE LATA MUZYKI ROZRYWKOWEJ

 KĄCIK POLSKICH SZLAGIERÓW

 SKAFINDER

 GERIATRIS

PODPROGOWA GODZINA

ICON AND ROLLUPS FOR ŻAK

Design: SKN Designer

The members of the Academic Club "Designer" created a set of 45 icons for radio programs. The symbols were created for the 55th anniversary of ŻAK – Lodz University of Technology's students' radio station – and were used on each of the programs' Facebook fan pages, on the station's website, and on promotional materials such as stickers. The designers included Natalia Bartczak, Honorata Bialic, Ola Bieniek, Sandra Borowiec, Weronika Dziedziela, Agata Kość, Jagoda Kryń, Anna Łukaszczyk, Wiktoria Nowak, Dominika Toborek, Michalina Sumińska, Michalina Warska, and Karolina Włodarczyk. The mentor of the project was Dr. Anna Szumigaj-Badziak.

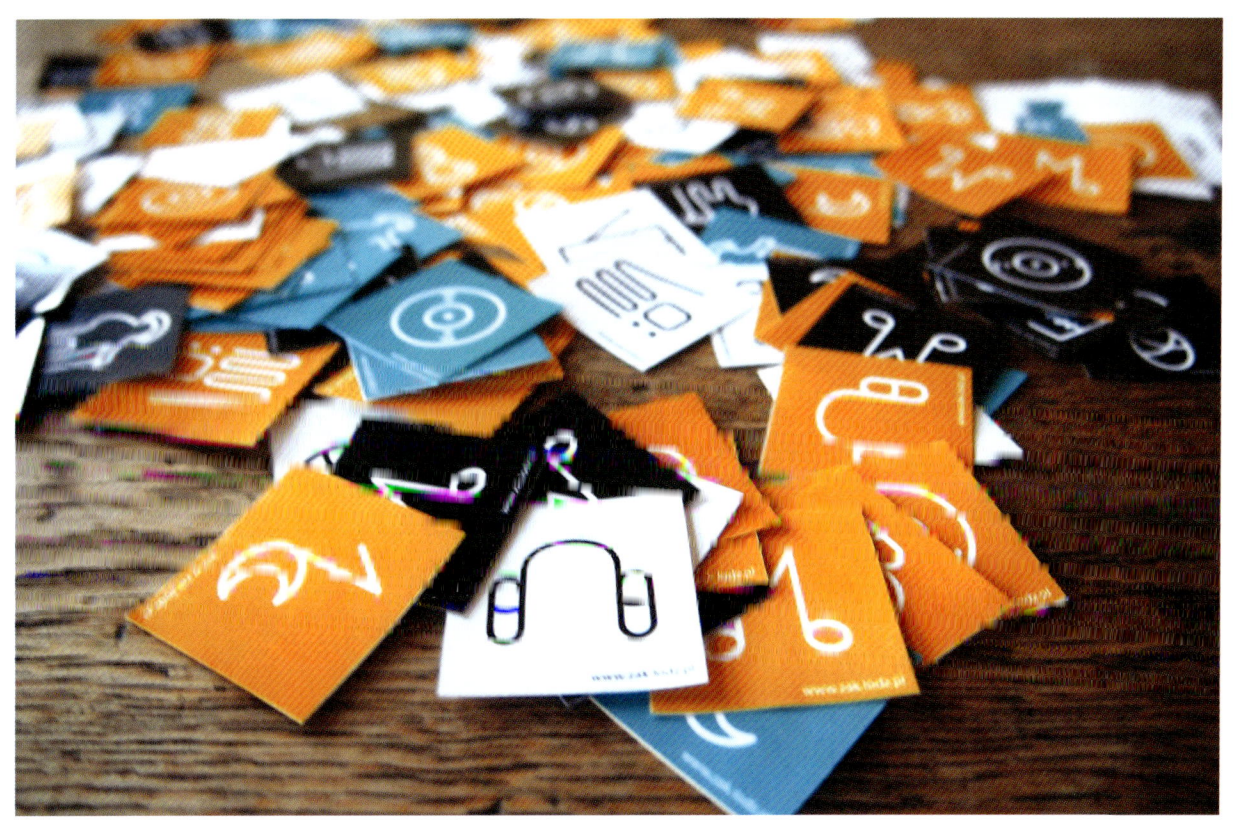

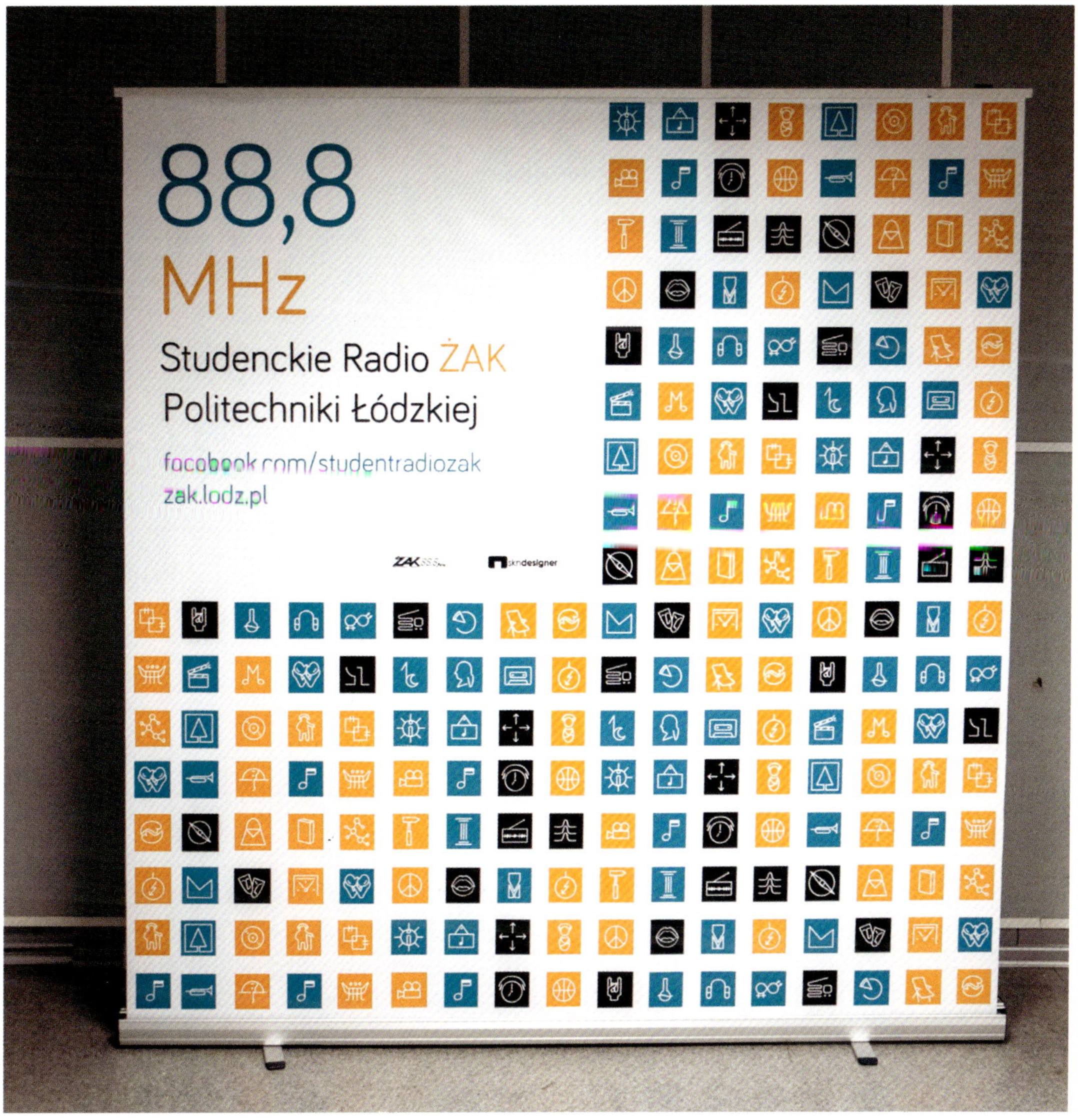
88,8
MHz
Studenckie Radio ŻAK
Politechniki Łódzkiej
facebook.com/studentradiozak
zak.lodz.pl

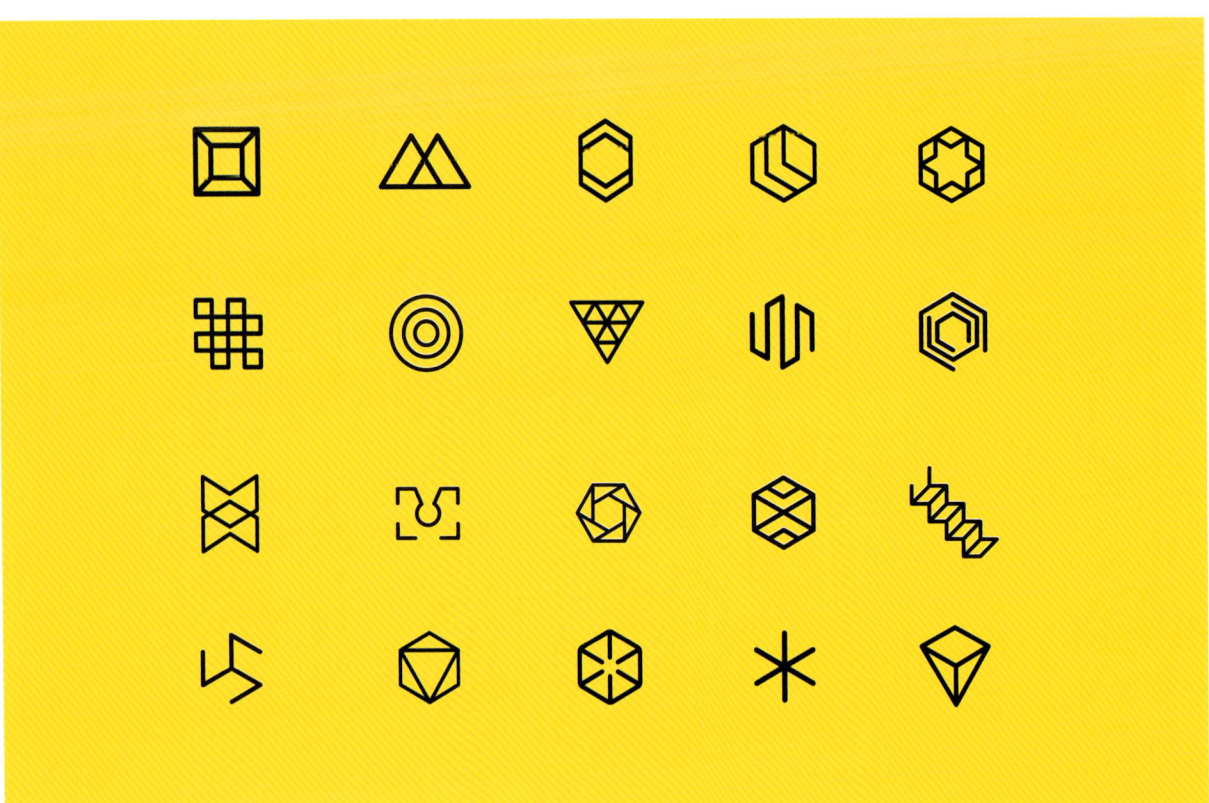

GBOX STUDIOS

Design: Bratus — **Photography:** Eric Huynh

Gbox is a studio for photography, advertising, and video production in Vietnam. Bratus developed an innovative strategy for its brand identity. The designers also created a set of icons representing different characters and their different core values on grids arranged with the alphabetic characters in the brand name. The arrangement of these icons is interchangeable for different layouts.

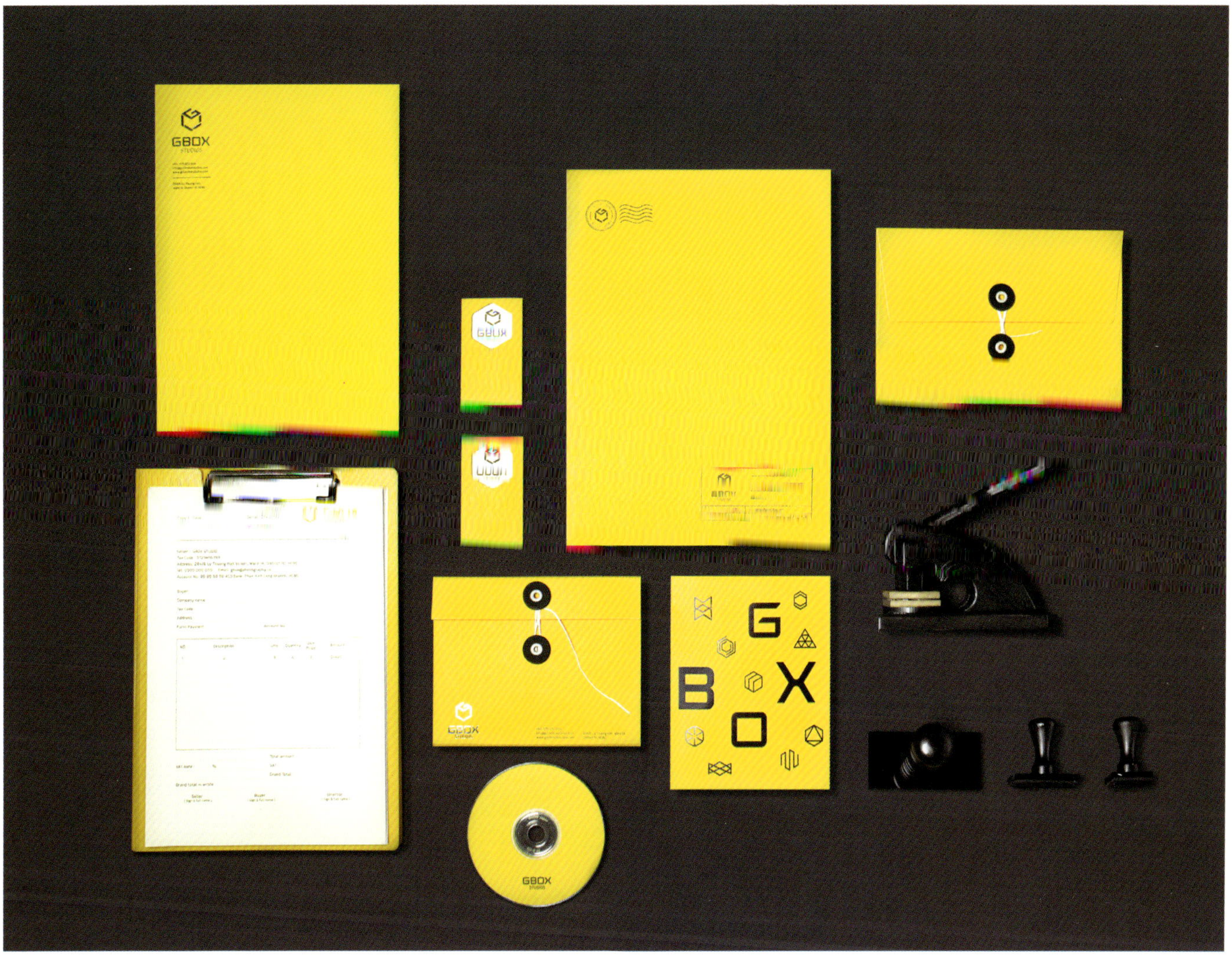
GBOX
G
B
X
O
GBOX

G
B
O
X
MINI
PORTFOLIO

Simplicity
Sustainable
Share
Lucky
Collaboration
Passion
Connect
Target
Powerful
Love
Work hard
Challenge
Success
Solidarity
Charity
We focus
Change
EXPLORE CREATE
INSPIRE
GBOX

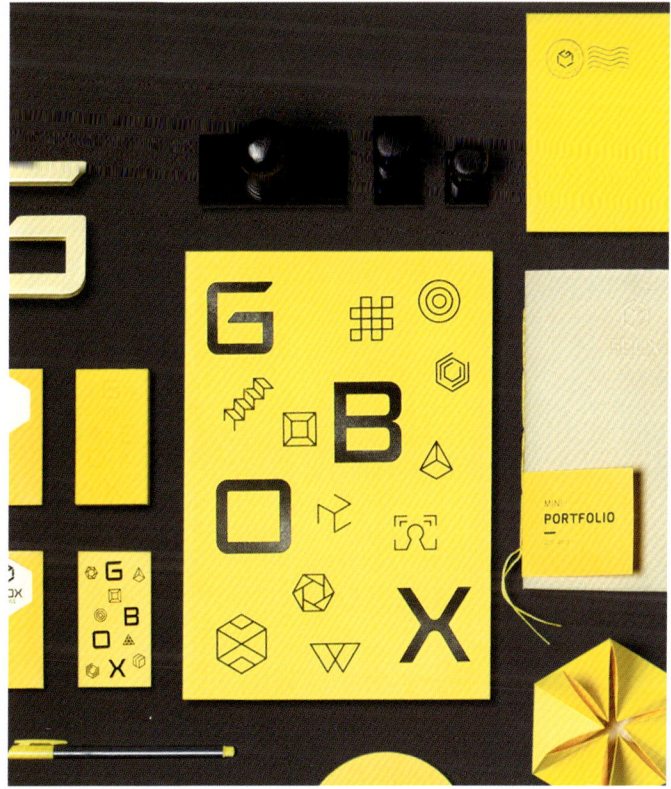

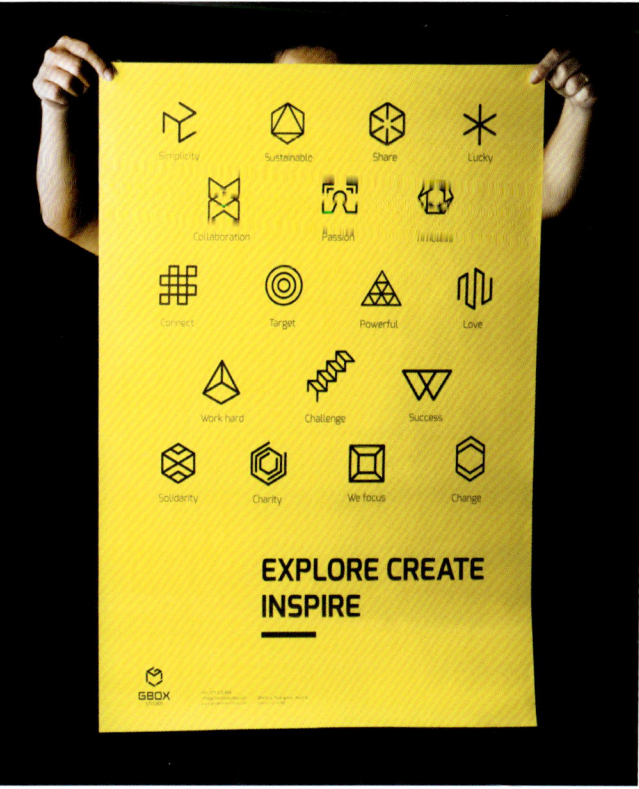

 KAKAO Game Partners Forum 2013  KAKAO Game Partners Forum 2013  KAKAO Game Partners Forum 2013

KAKAO GAME PARTNERS FORUM

Design: Myungsup Shin, Jiyoung Yoon, Jihoon Kim
Agency: Plus X

KAKAO Game Partners Forum Brand was an experience-based design project for a game forum run by KAKAO, a well-known IT company in South Korea. Plus X, a design and marketing company, handled the total design experience for the forum. The design concept and identity were inspired by the elements of games, perfect for expressing the character of a game forum. The images featured overlapping solid colors, which reflects the core values of connecting and coexisting with game developers. The identity was applied across multiple uses, such as location design, banners, leaflets, and souvenirs, creating a unified visual experience.

Date
2013.05.10.Fri
AM 10:00-PM17:30
Place
COEX 4F
Conference
Room(South)

KAKAO
Game
Partners
Forum
2013
KAKAO
Game
Partners
Forum
2013
가
치.
다같이

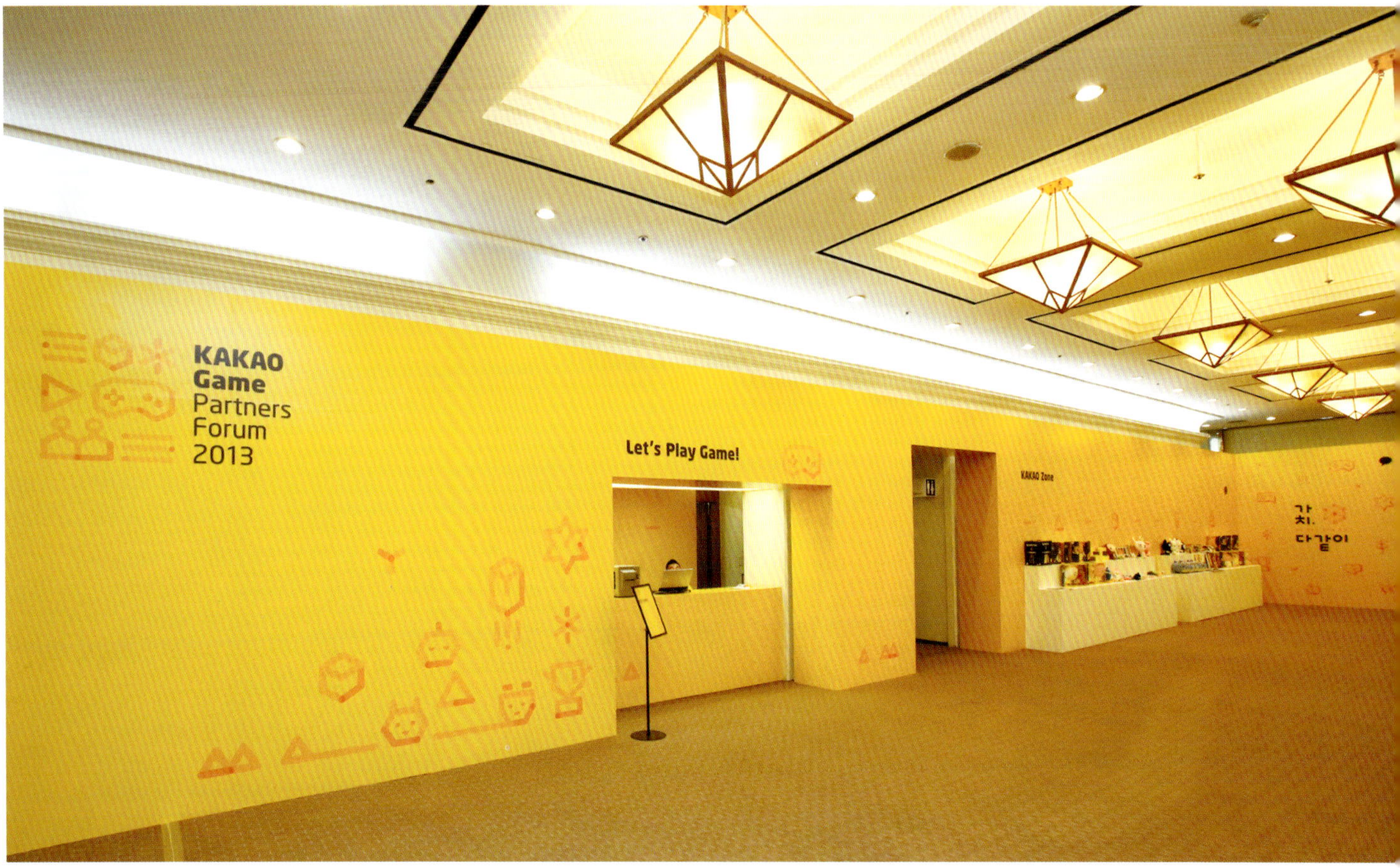

KAKAO
Game
Partners
Forum
2013
Welcome!
가치.
다같이
KAKAO

가치.
다같이
KAKAO
Game
Partners
Forum
2013
Room
A

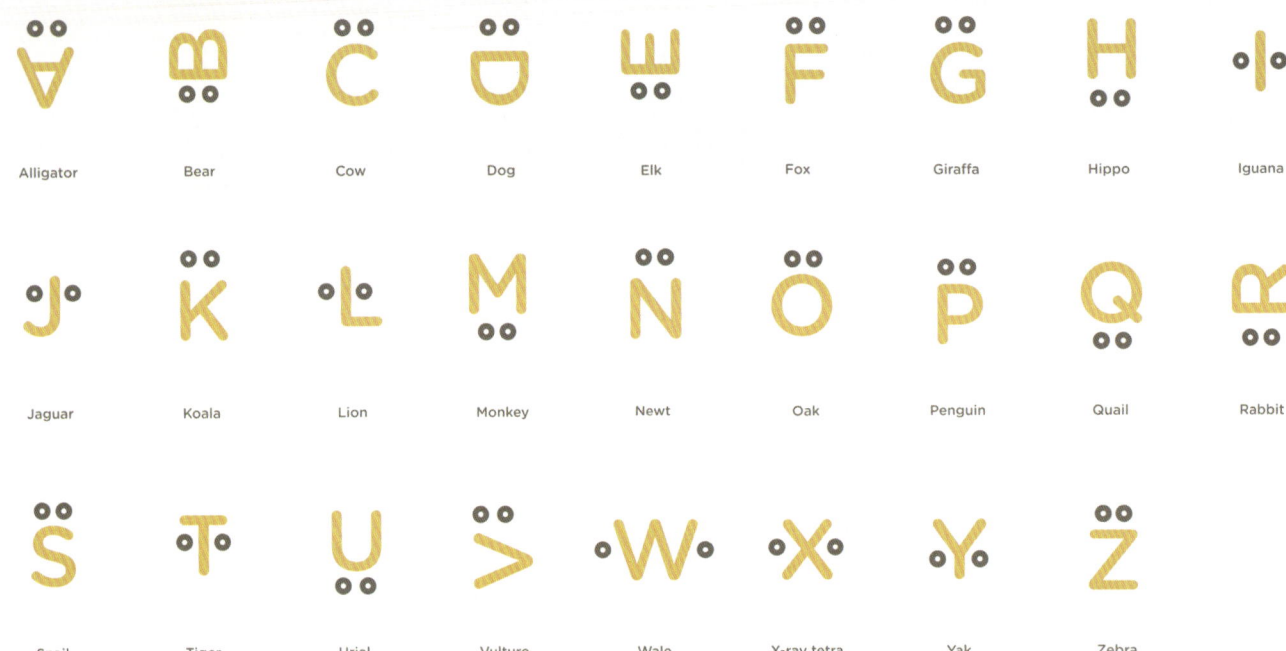

Alligator	Bear	Cow	Dog	Elk	Fox	Giraffa	Hippo	Iguana
Jaguar	Koala	Lion	Monkey	Newt	Oak	Penguin	Quail	Rabbit
Snail	Tiger	Urial	Vulture	Wale	X-ray tetra	Yak	Zebra	

LEARN

Design: Vova Lifanov ——— **Agency:** Suprematika

"Лён" is a small English language school for kids. The word "Лён" means "linen" in Russian, and sounds exactly like the word "learn" in English.

Лён
language school

Wale

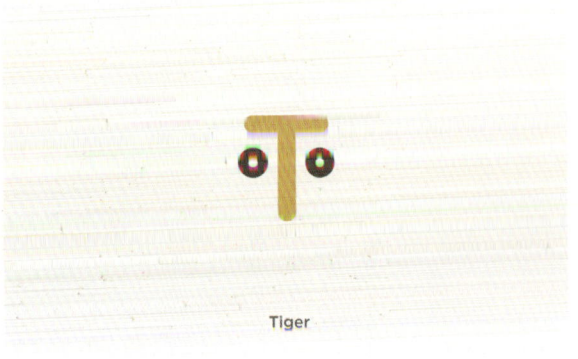

Tiger

WONDERLAND ARCHITECTURE PLATFORM

Design: Maximilian Huber, Lukas Fliszar
Agency: 100und1

Wonderland is a platform for European architecture. It is a Vienna based network for exchanging information, knowledge, and different experiences for young Europe-oriented architecture practices. The corporate design is quite complex because it has to correlate to the diverse sub-departments and their different tasks. By overlapping the department logos, it is transformed into one big emblem combining the different characters of each individual department, thus illustrating their work environment.

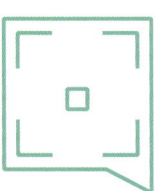

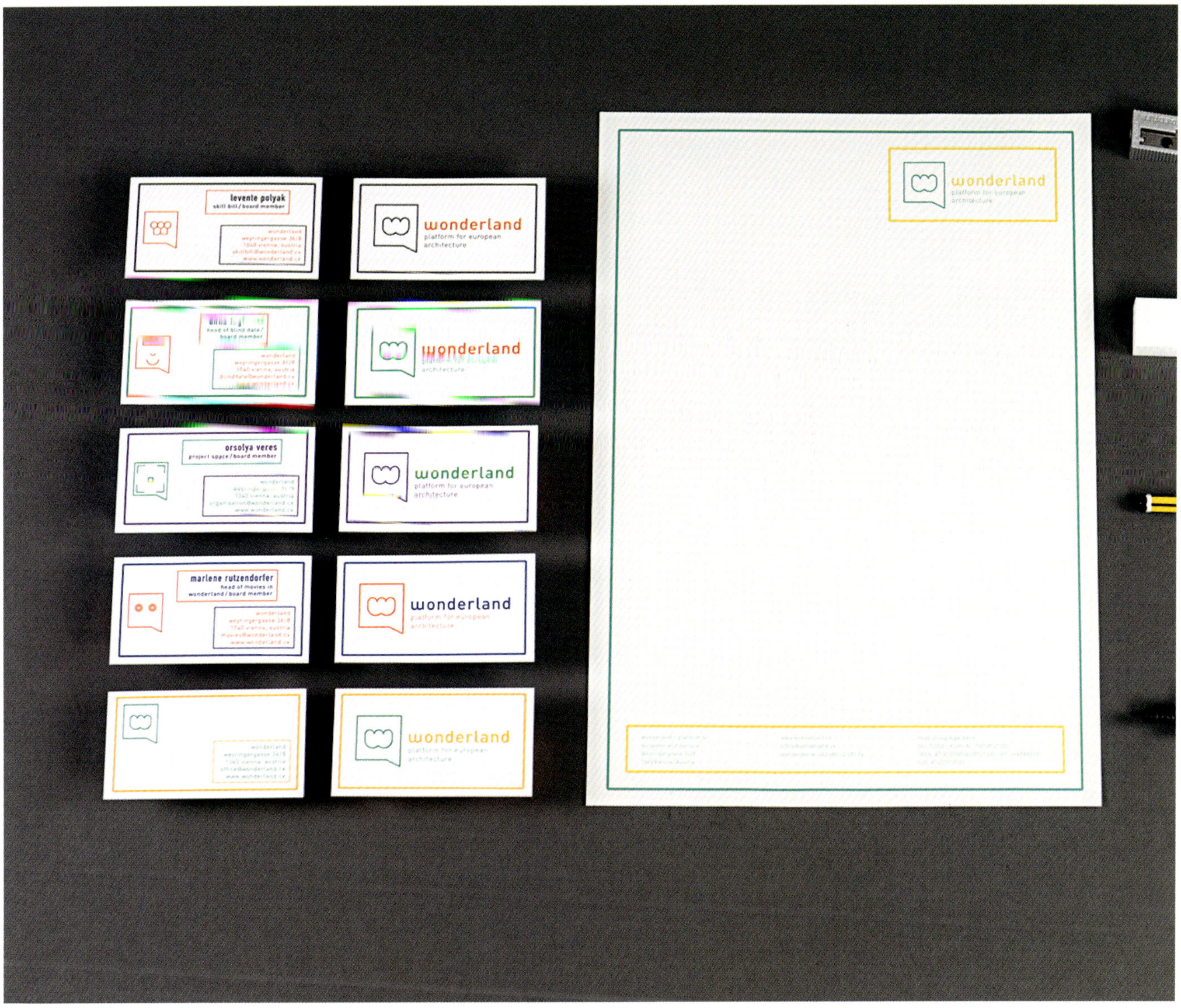
levente polyak
skill bill / board member
wonderland
platform for european architecture
orsolya veres
project space / board member
marlene rutzendorfer
head of movies in wonderland / board member

A moving film festival packed with engaging movies carrying architectural themes.
wonderland - platform for european architecture is a network for exchanging experiences, information and knowledge for young Europe -oriented architecture practices.

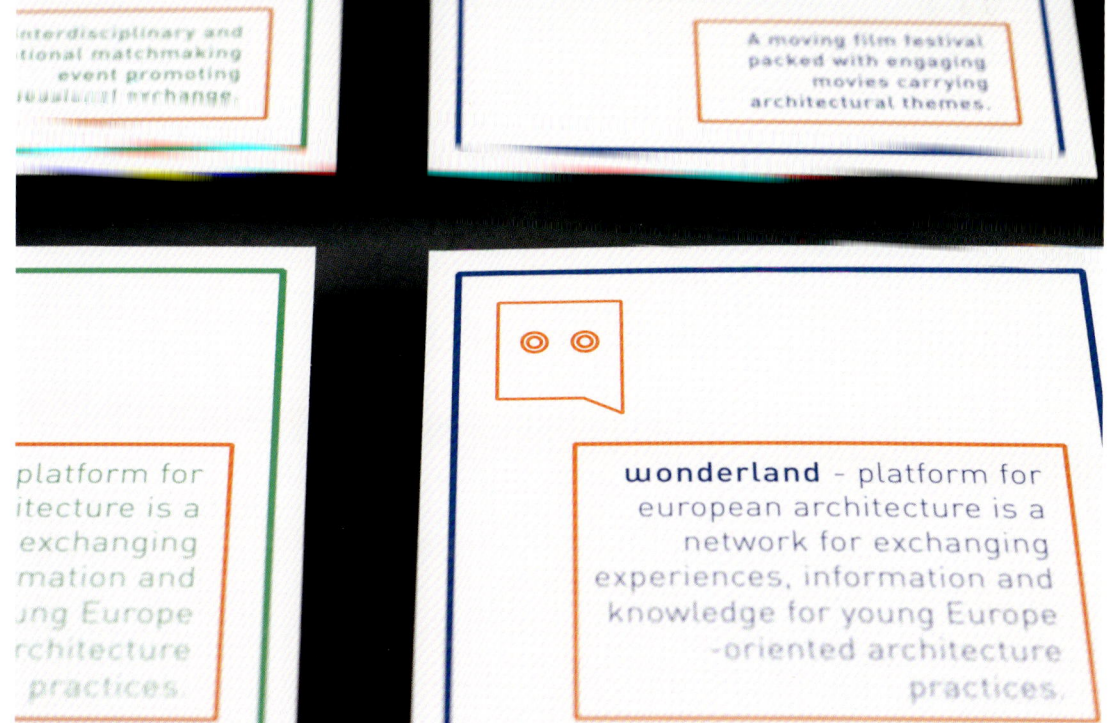

THE HITCHHIKER'S GUIDE TO THE GALAXY

Design: Li Linghao

The Hitchhiker's Guide to the Galaxy is a book project inspired by Douglas Adams's book about the galaxy of the same name. The designer developed the project based on a calendar, introducing one star in the galaxy each day. A set of icons, each representing a single star, were created as pictorial signage for the book. The stars and their stories were all fictional pieces created by the designer. You can find imaginary, creative, ironic, and even disgusting images and stories in it. The designer was trying to express a free and positive attitude in this book.

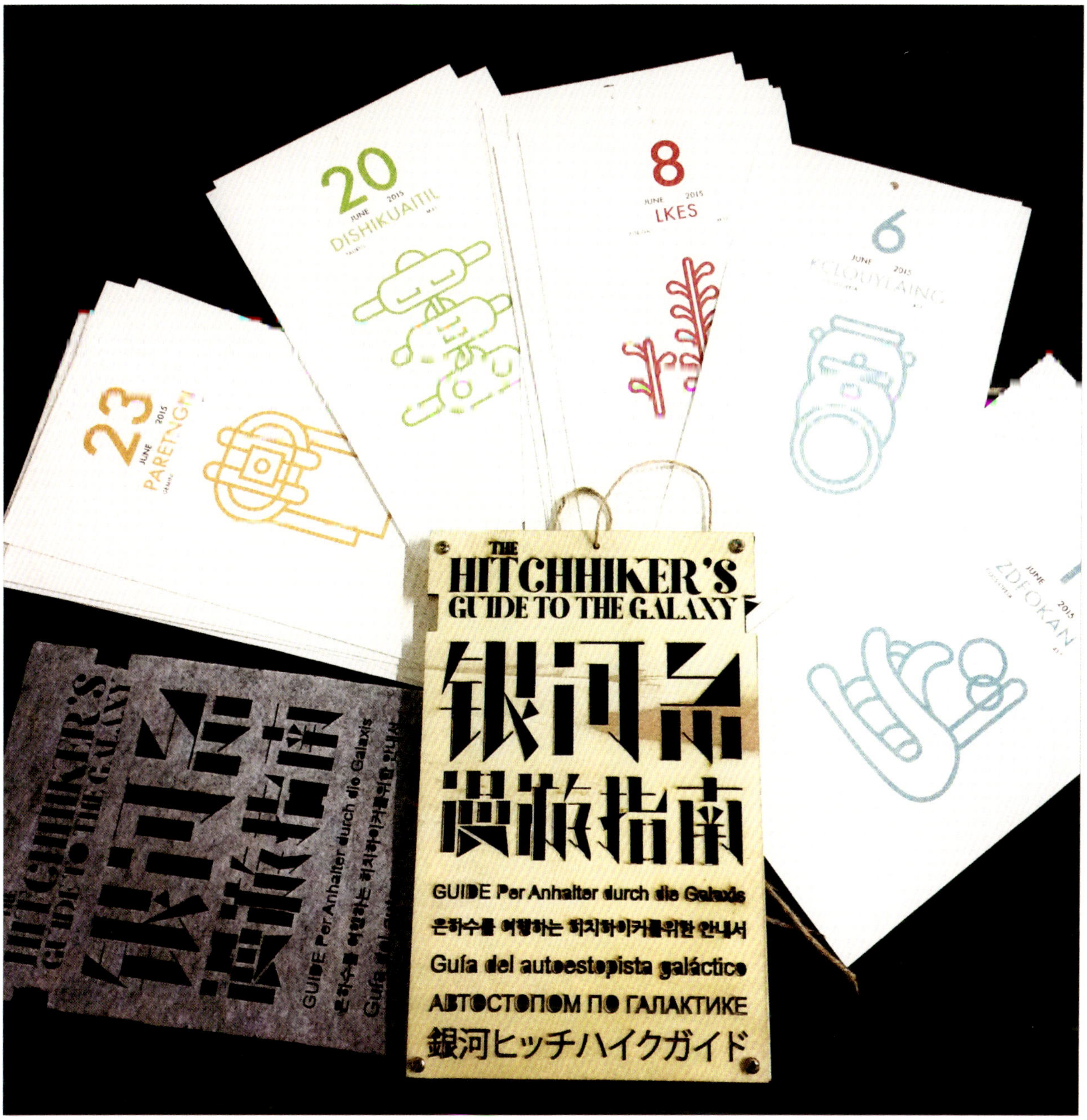
20
JUNE 2015
DISHIKUAITIL
8
JUNE 2015
LKES
6
JUNE 2015
23
JUNE 2015
THE HITCHHIKER'S GUIDE TO THE GALAXY
银河系漫游指南
GUIDE Per Anhalter durch die Galaxis
은하수를 여행하는 히치하이커를위한 안내서
Guía del autoestopista galáctico
АВТОСТОПОМ ПО ГАЛАКТИКЕ
銀河ヒッチハイクガイド

1
JUNE 2015
ZDFOKAN
8
JUNE 2015
LKES
15
JUNE 2015
TALULULO
22
JUNE 2015
SAILE

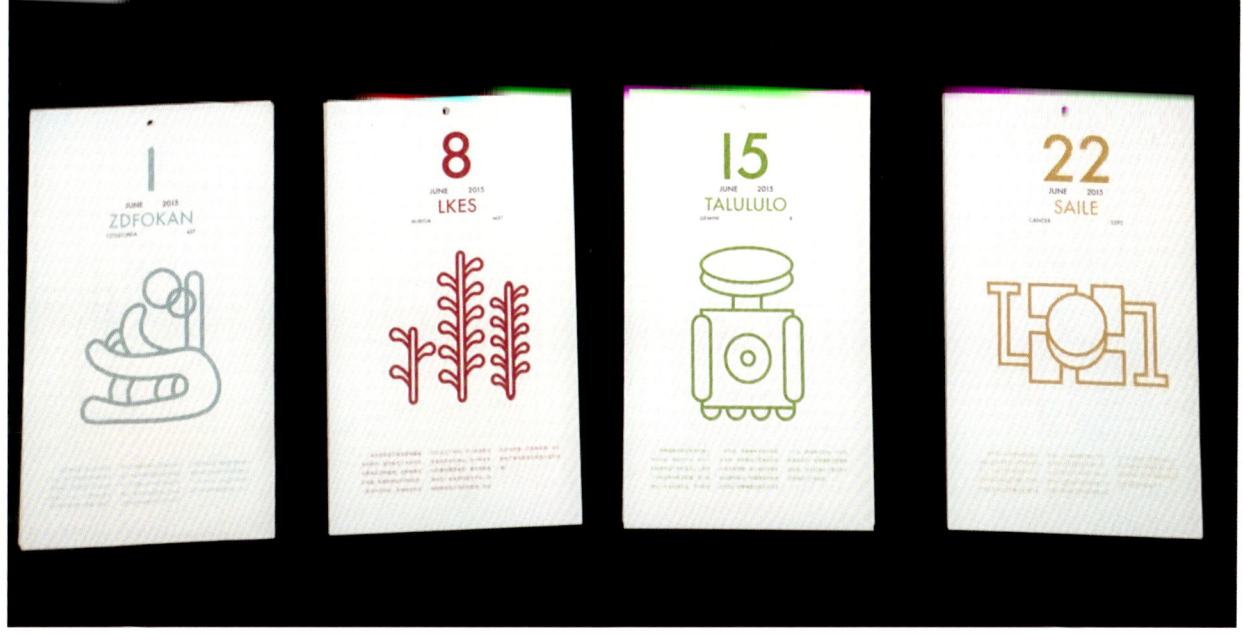

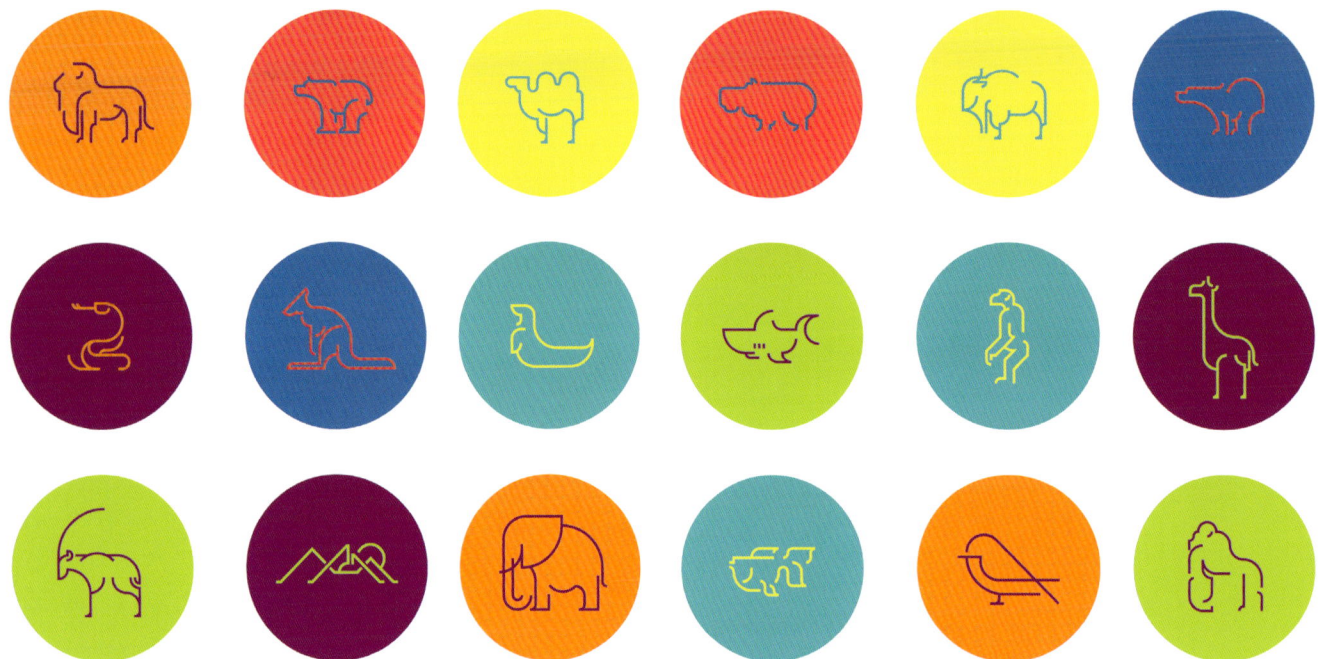

WARSAW ZOO VISUAL IDENTITY

Design: Anna Nowokuńska

This project is based on a strong stylistic statement created through graphic representation of animals. It utilizes minimalistic pictograms with modular elements that can be arranged on a grid. The pictograms served as the main building blocks of the logo, and are used across the identity in patterns and varying illustration styles, creating a visual tool kit for the physical spaces and promotional materials of the zoo. The main logo is the letter "W" filled with animals. Different zoo facilities are designated by a single pictogram in a "W," reflecting their theme. The design's look and feel was adjusted for application across a wide range of promotional materials to attract a variety of different audiences.

WARSAW ZOO

 HERPETARIUM

 AQUARIUM

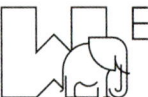 ELEPHANTS

 GIRAFFES

 MONKEYS

 SHARKS

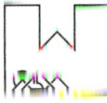 INVERTEBRATES

 AVIARY

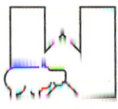 HIPOPOTAMUSES

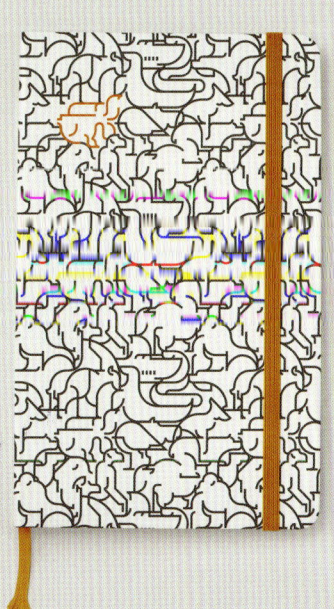
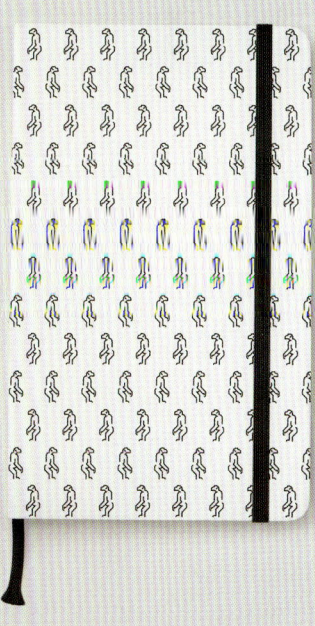

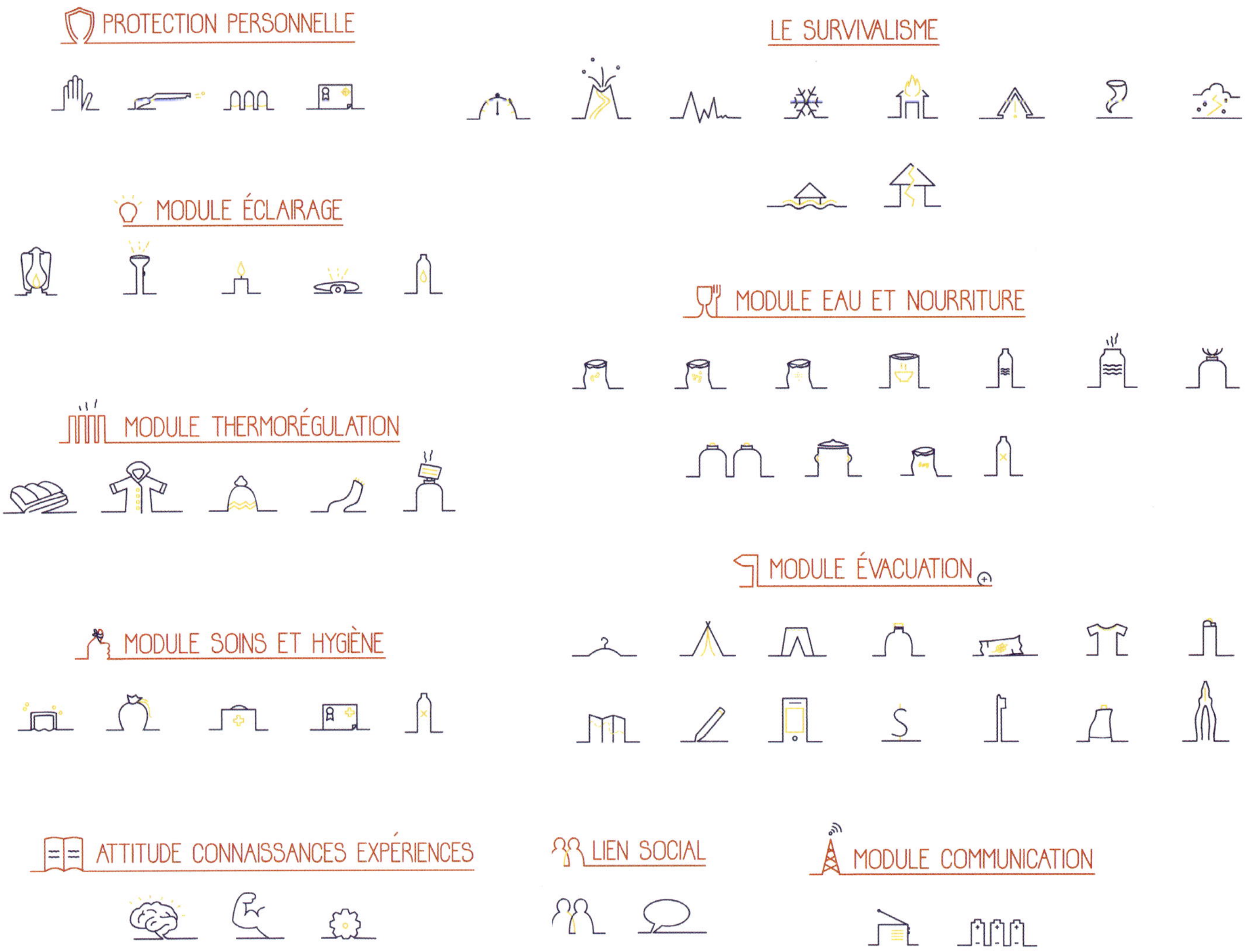
PROTECTION PERSONNELLE
LE SURVIVALISME
MODULE ÉCLAIRAGE
MODULE EAU ET NOURRITURE
MODULE THERMORÉGULATION
MODULE ÉVACUATION
MODULE SOINS ET HYGIÈNE
ATTITUDE CONNAISSANCES EXPÉRIENCES
LIEN SOCIAL
MODULE COMMUNICATION

PROJET 10

Design: Emilie Garnier

Projet 10 is a project about survivalism based on an online blog. It aims to play down the taboo and drama related to the subject through the use of iconography and careful color choices. Garnier designed a book featuring the blog content using a series of playful and inclusive icons. Garnier also designed a customizable map that accompanies the book and a list of essential items, as well as a website that allows the user to test his or her ability to survive if the world stops running.

PRO
JET
n10
LA CARTE DE SURVIE

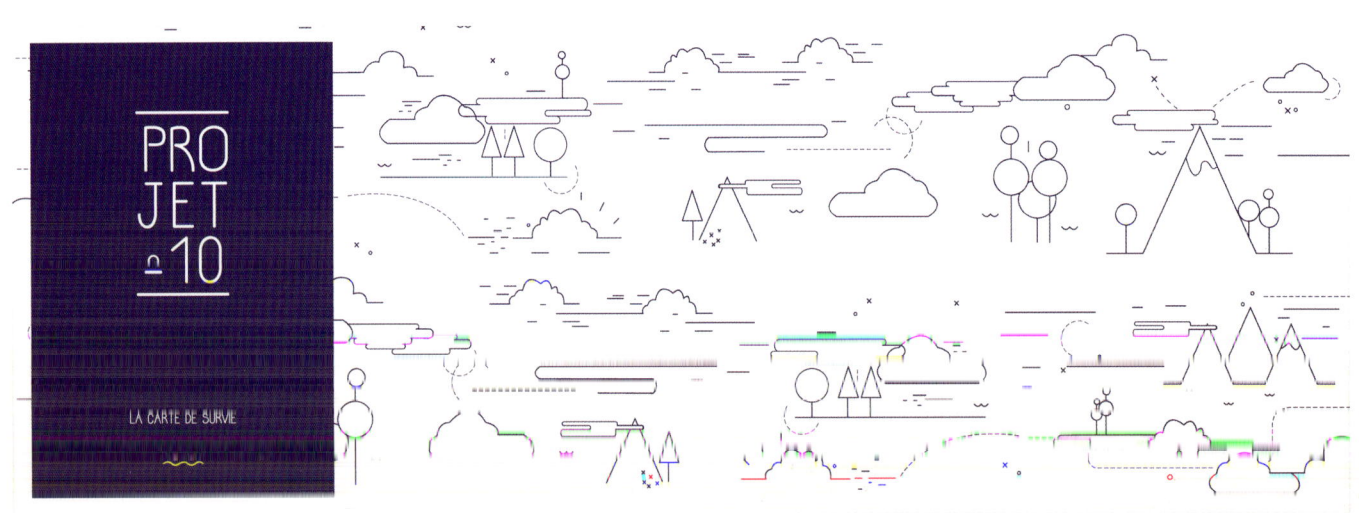

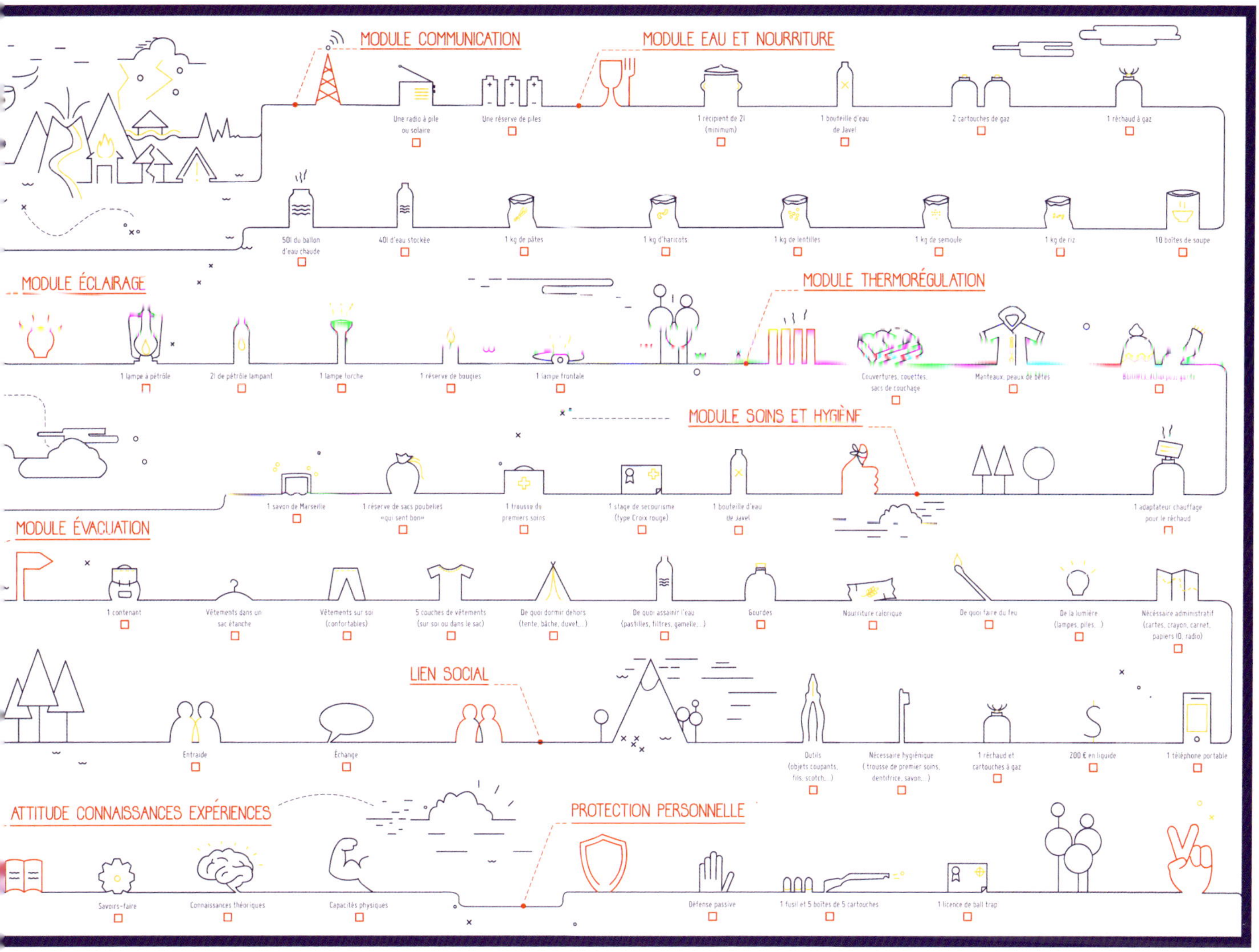

MODULE COMMUNICATION
MODULE EAU ET NOURRITURE

- Une radio à pile ou solaire
- Une réserve de piles
- 1 récipient de 2l (minimum)
- 1 bouteille d'eau de Javel
- 2 cartouches de gaz
- 1 réchaud à gaz

- 50l ou ballon d'eau chaude
- 40l d'eau stockée
- 1 kg de pâtes
- 1 kg d'haricots
- 1 kg de lentilles
- 1 kg de semoule
- 1 kg de riz
- 10 boîtes de soupe

MODULE ÉCLAIRAGE
MODULE THERMORÉGULATION

- 1 lampe à pétrole
- 2l de pétrole lampant
- 1 lampe torche
- 1 réserve de bougies
- 1 lampe frontale
- Couvertures, couettes, sacs de couchage
- Manteaux, peaux de bêtes

MODULE SOINS ET HYGIÈNE

- 1 savon de Marseille
- 1 réserve de sacs poubelles «qui sent bon»
- 1 trousse de premiers soins
- 1 stage de secourisme (type Croix rouge)
- 1 bouteille d'eau de Javel
- 1 adaptateur chauffage pour le réchaud

MODULE ÉVACUATION

- 1 contenant
- Vêtements dans un sac étanche
- Vêtements sur soi (confortables)
- 5 couches de vêtements (sur soi ou dans le sac)
- De quoi dormir dehors (tente, bâche, duvet...)
- De quoi assainir l'eau (pastilles, filtres, gamelle...)
- Gourdes
- Nourriture calorique
- De quoi faire du feu
- De la lumière (lampes, piles...)
- Nécessaire administratif (cartes, crayon, carnet, papiers ID, radio)

LIEN SOCIAL

- Entraide
- Échange
- Outils (objets coupants, fils, scotch...)
- Nécessaire hygiénique (trousse de premier soins, dentifrice, savon...)
- 1 réchaud et cartouches à gaz
- 200 € en liquide
- 1 téléphone portable

ATTITUDE CONNAISSANCES EXPÉRIENCES
PROTECTION PERSONNELLE

- Savoirs-faire
- Connaissances théoriques
- Capacités physiques
- Défense passive
- 1 fusil et 5 boîtes de 5 cartouches
- 1 licence de ball trap

PROJET N° 10

LA CARTE DE SURVIE

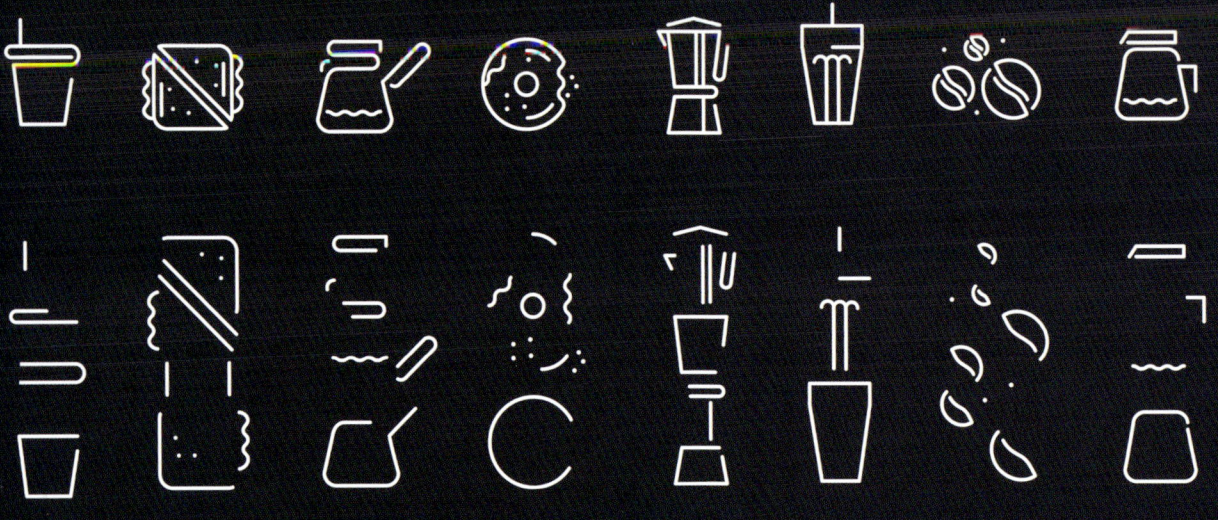

DAILY COFFEE

Design: Nora Kaszanyi

Daily Coffee was a school project based on the designer's twelve-piece pictogram system. The task was to create a visual identity for a fictitious coffee shop with packaging design that contains these icons in some way. The designer's goal was to apply the illustrative elements in an unconventional way on different surfaces. Therefore, she divided them into their constituent parts and arranged the elements vertically in order to create an irregular pattern.

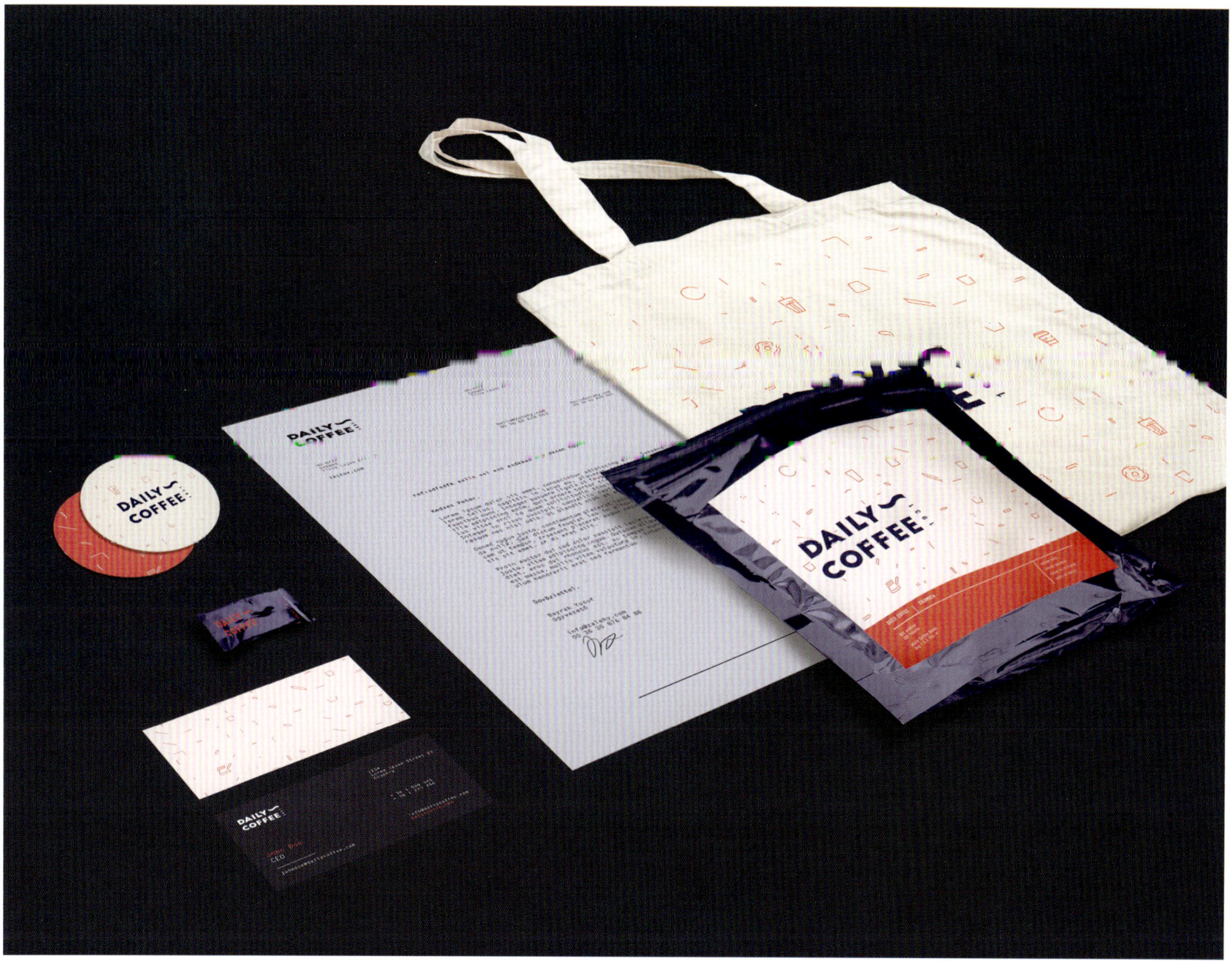

DAILY COFFEE 1931

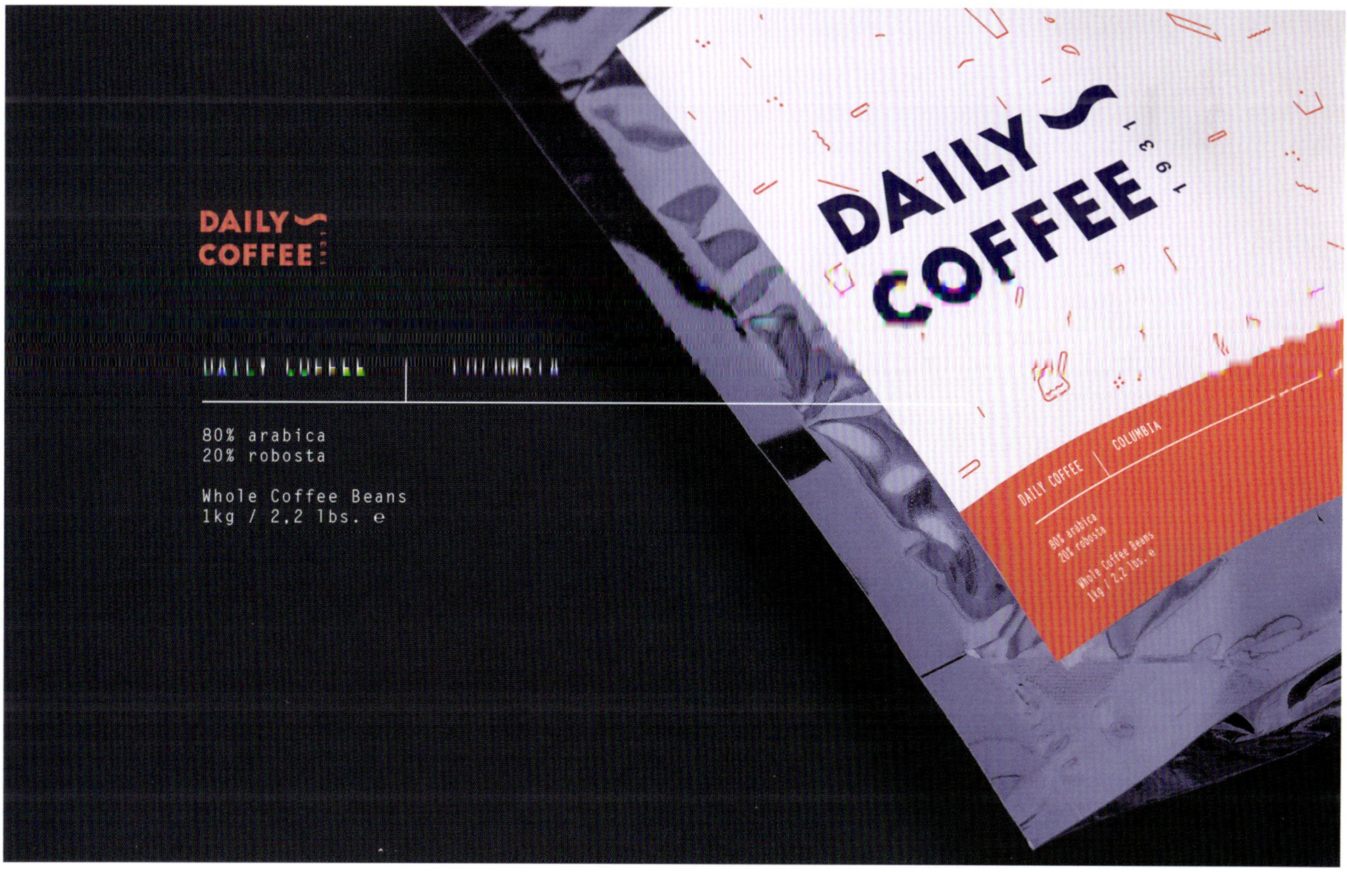

DAILY COFFEE — COLUMBIA

80% arabica
20% robosta

Whole Coffee Beans
1kg / 2.2 lbs. e

RIPE JUICERY

Design: Sean Travis

Ripe Juicery is a student project by Sean Travis. It's a branding design and concept store project for ripe, a new juicery that combines the freshest produce into healthy yet tasty drinks.

STYRIA DIGITAL

Design: Kurt Glänzer — **Creative Direction:** Mike Fuisz
Agency: Moodley Brand Identity

Once up on a time, the Internet was invented. We remember that then it was quite complicated to go online, and those who did were mostly just technology nerds dreaming about a digital future. Nowadays this world of ones and zeros fills our everyday lives, no matter where we live, what we buy, or where we travel to.

The new corporate design of Styria Digital Holding clearly shows how much fun it can be to go digital, if it's done well by analog people. The design features friendly colors, fun icons, and lots of dynamic feelings.

ROLLO APP BRANDING

Design: Lukasz Kulakowski

Rollo is an application for mobile devices. It is a social gaming product integrated with Instagram, Twitter, Facebook, and Pinterest. They offer a platform that gives people the ability to show their talents and passions while having fun completing challenges presented as content. The branding designed for Rollo is fresh and dynamic, with an extended color palette and special typography, as well as a range of digital and outdoor advertising.

ROLLO
EVERYONE IS THE WINNER
ROLLO
ROLLO

ROLLO
EVERYONE IS THE WINNER

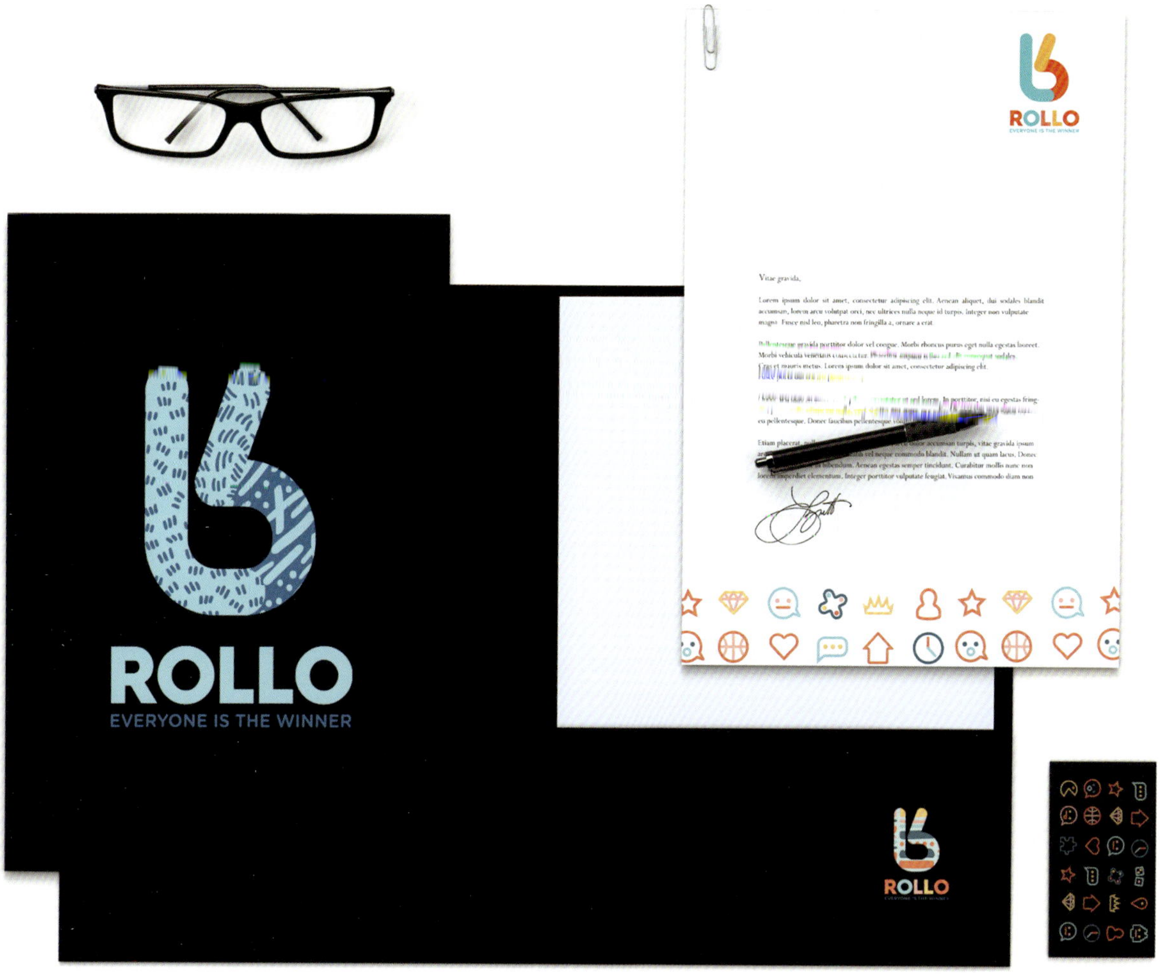

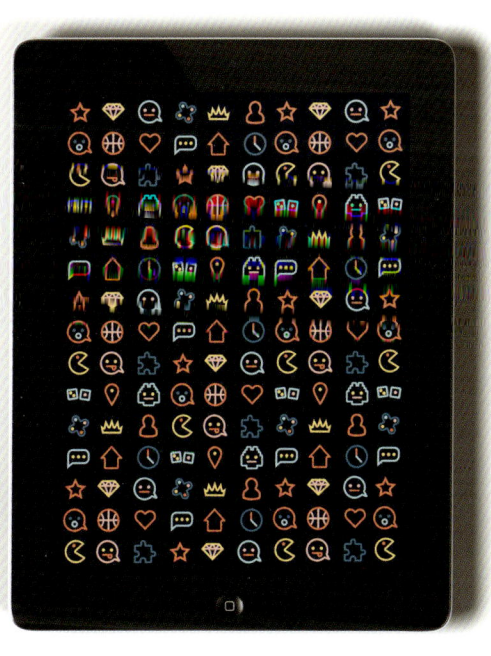

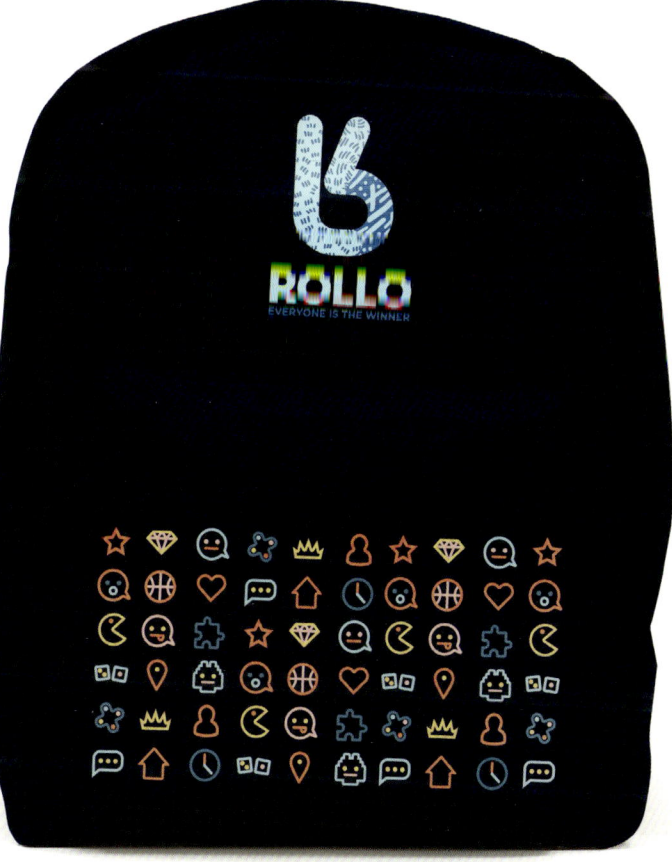

Media — Media/foto — **Artysta** — Organizator
Wolontariat — Vip — **Technika** — Gość

Teatr TV
TV Theatre

Filmy
Films

Muzyka
Music

**Sztuki
wizualne**
Visual arts

**Spotkania
i wydarzenia**
Events

DWA BRZEGI

Design: Zuzanna Rogatty

Identity design for the 9th Two Riversides Film and Art Festival in Poland. The concept for the graphic theme – projections on cinema screens – came from the form of the festival itself. The designer aimed to create a system that would work on any kind of media, from cinema screens to A4 posters printed on office printers. The vectorized cinema screen logos are totally flexible, meaning they can be used with any potential content or format.

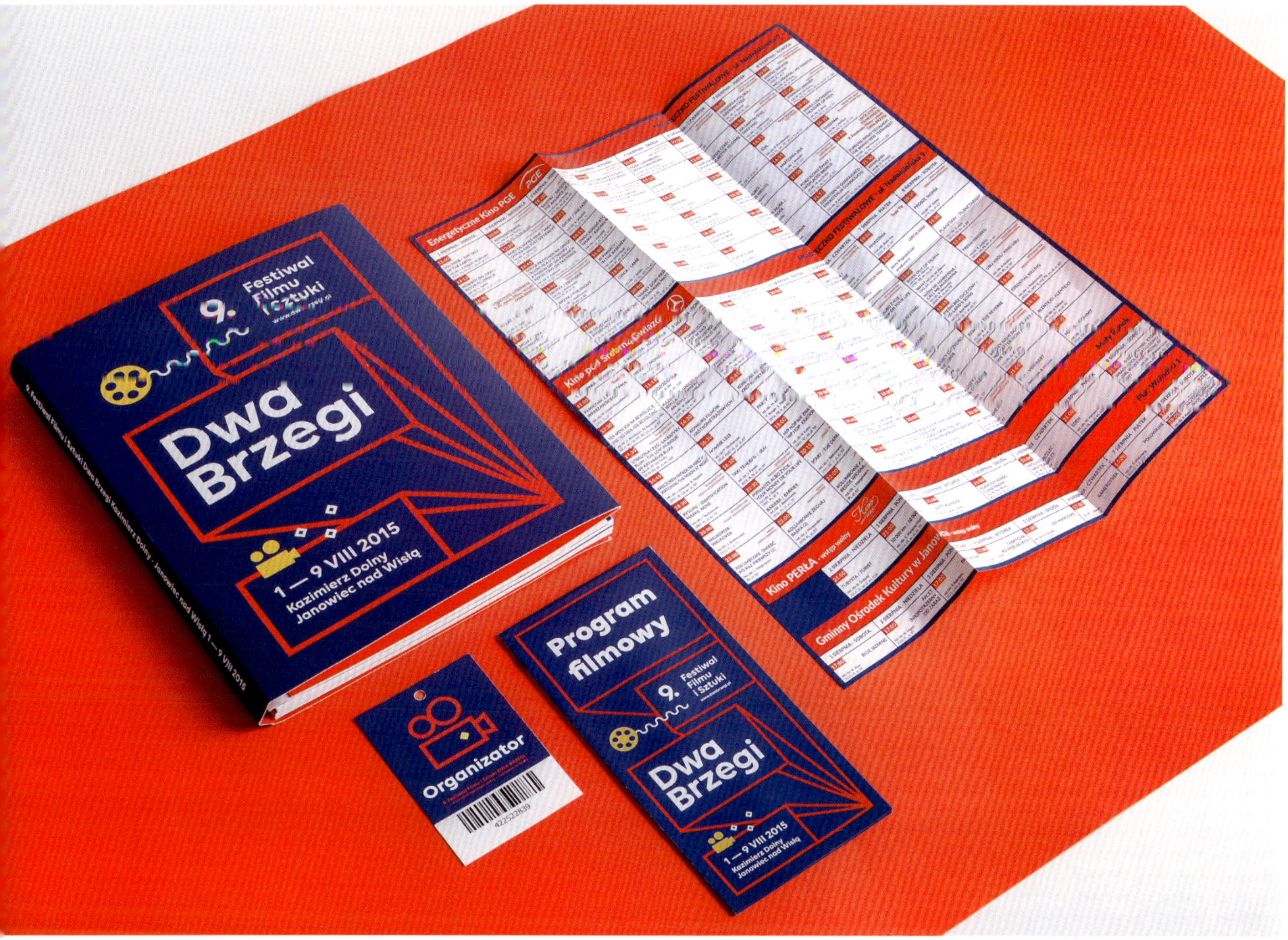
9. Festiwal Filmu i Sztuki
Dwa Brzegi
1 — 9 VIII 2015
Kazimierz Dolny
Janowiec nad Wisłą
Program filmowy
Organizator
422522839

Vip
9. Festiwal Filmu i Sztuki DWA BRZEGI
1 — 9 VIII 2015 Kazimierz Dolny — Janowiec n/Wisłą
912853923
Organizator
9. Festiwal Filmu i Sztuki DWA BRZEGI
1 — 9 VIII 2015 Kazimierz Dolny — Janowiec n/Wisłą
422522839

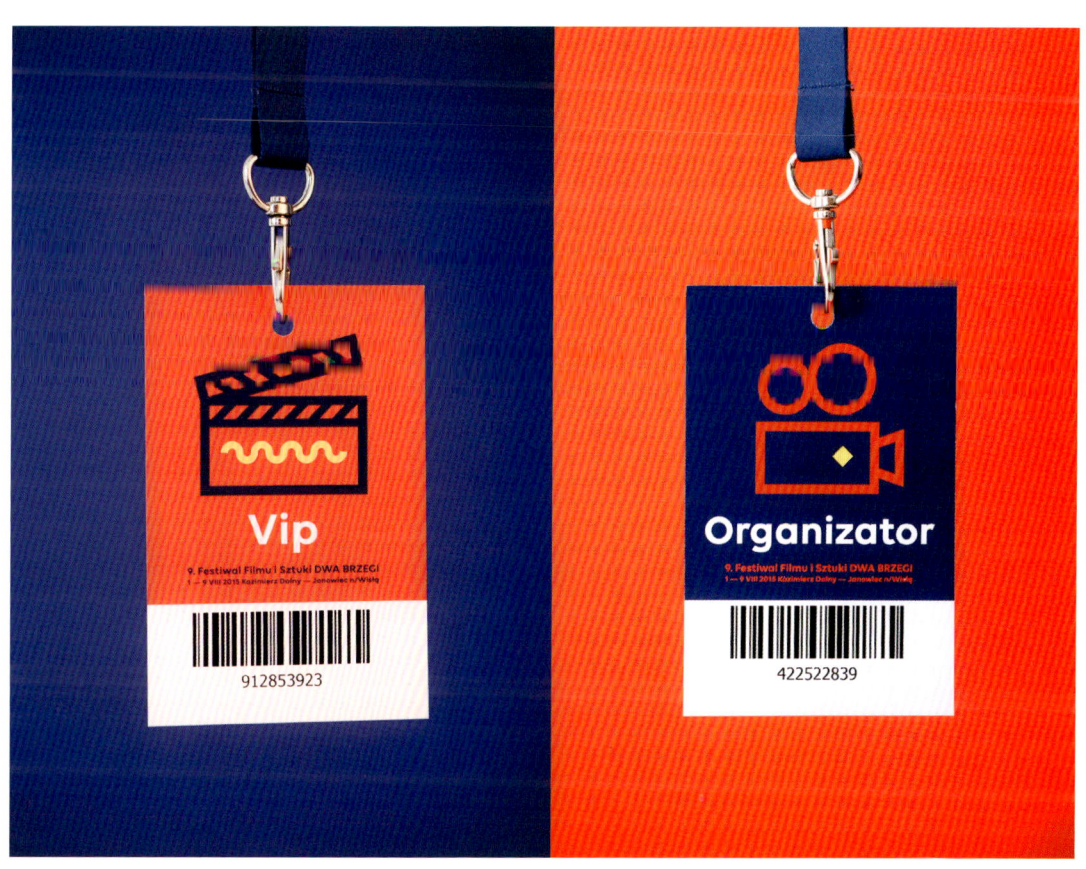

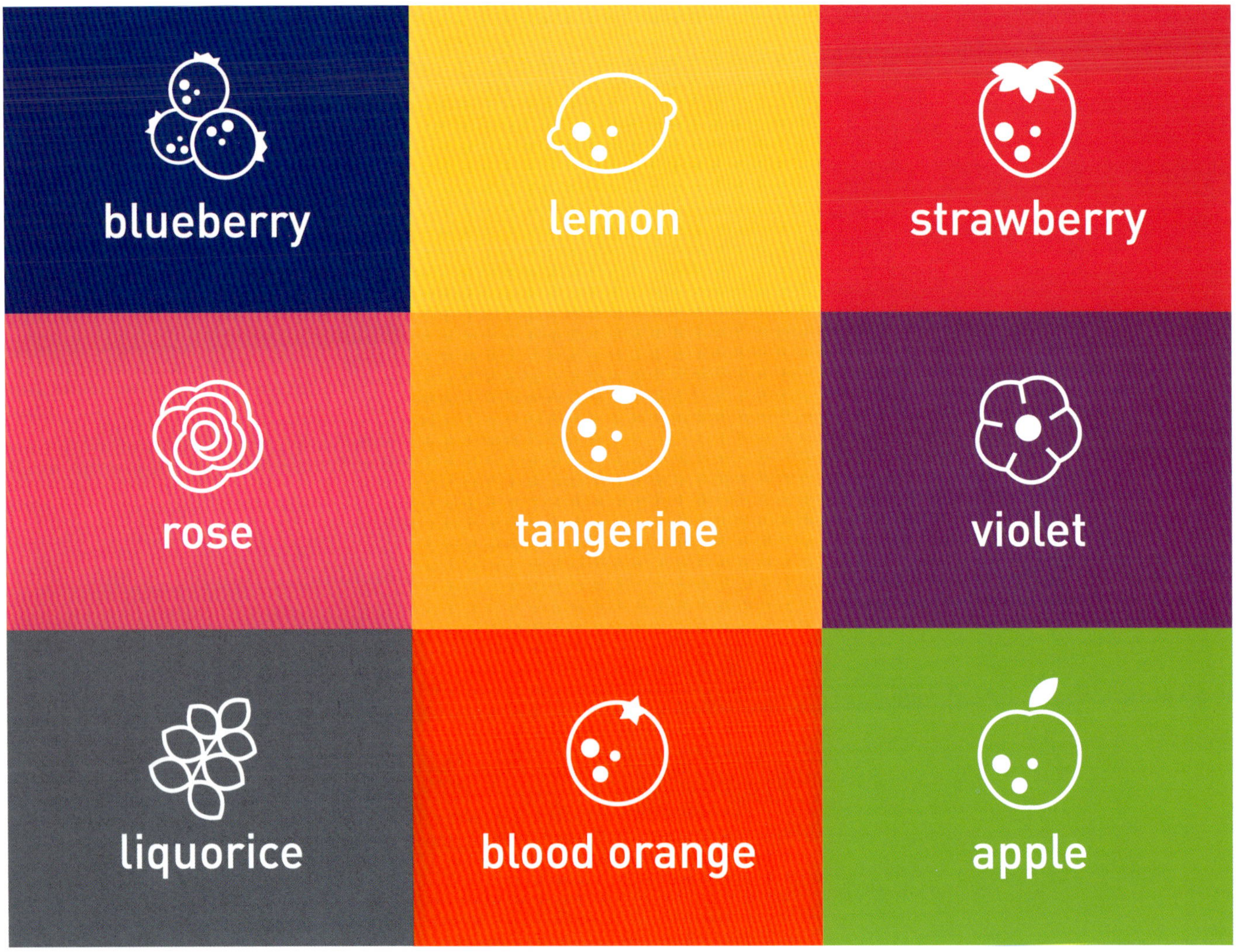
blueberry
lemon
strawberry
rose
tangerine
violet
liquorice
blood orange
apple

THE PROVIDORE LOLLIES PACKAGING

Design: Goh Chin Huei — **Creative Direction:** Chua Keng Leong, Lawrence Tan
Agency: Blue Beetle Design

A range of fruit jellies and bonbons made for The Providore by one of the oldest confectioners in Italy. The different flavors are represented by specially created icons and colors, keeping a consistent product branding.

rose
BONBONS

tangerine
FRUIT JELLIES

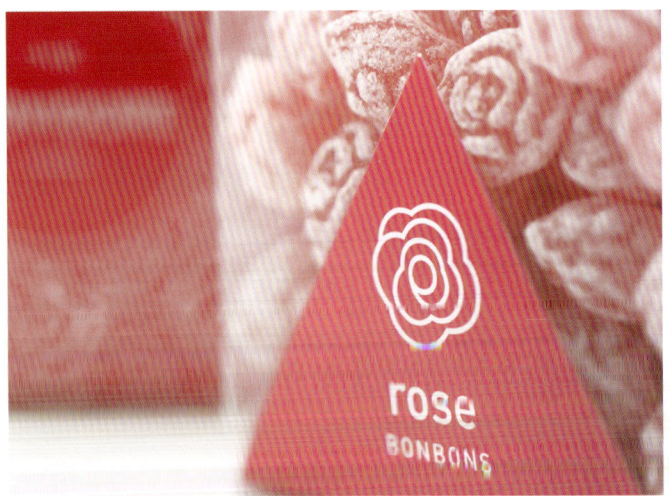

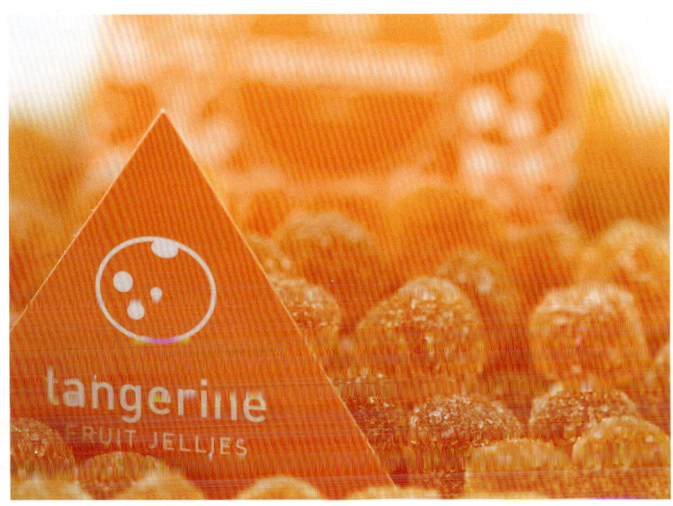

IELLO TRAVEL

Design: David Rafachinho

Iello Travel launches a new way of travelling. On Iello Travel, customers can do everything from booking and renting to actually traveling. The style that the designer wanted to create was friendly, light, clean, and safe with a touch of an "app" look. Due to the low budget, the designer decided to create the major images using vectors, leading to the creation of the final icon set.

CITY BREAK CITY BREAK
Lorem ipsum dolor sit amet, consectetur adipiscing elit. Nulla nisl diam, iaculis ut commodo sed, sagittis id urna. Maecenas sed ante odio. Id aliquet lorem. Nullam.

TRÓPI COS TRÓPICOS
Lorem ipsum dolor sit amet, consectetur adipiscing elit. Nulla nisl diam, iaculis ut commodo sed, sagittis id urna. Maecenas sed ante odio. Id aliquet lorem. Nullam.

CRUZEI ROS CRUZEIROS
Lorem ipsum dolor sit amet, consectetur adipiscing elit. Nulla nisl diam, iaculis ut commodo sed, sagittis id urna. Maecenas sed ante odio. Id aliquet lorem. Nullam.

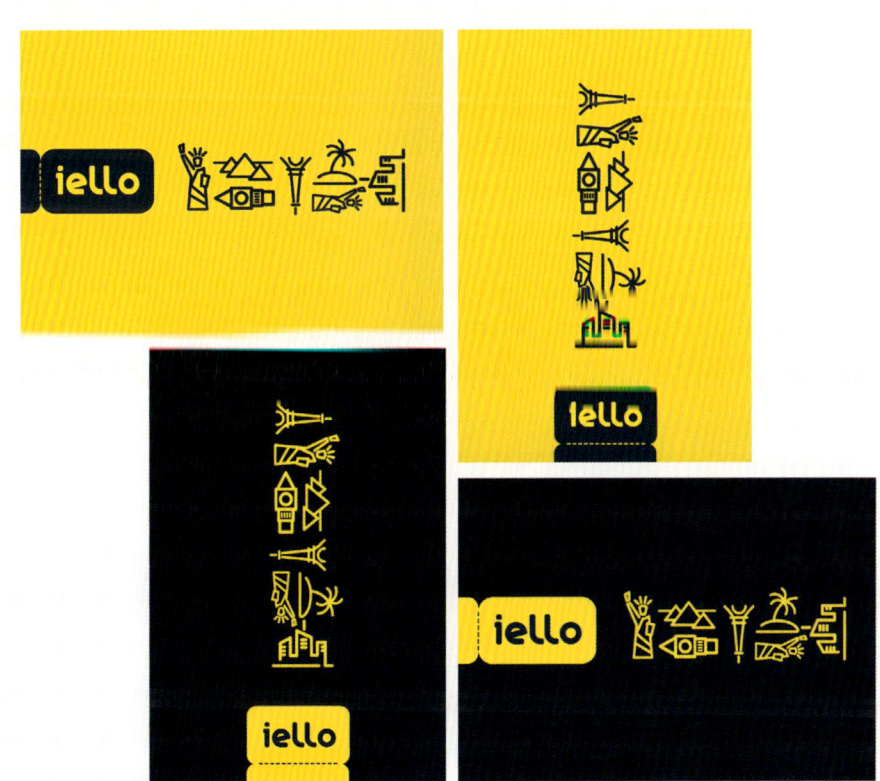

SPEECHLESS COOKBOOK

Design: Roland Lehle

This innovative cookbook concept works completely without words. By simply following recognizable symbols, you can cook delicious and healthy meals without animal products. The cookbook is designed for everyone around the world, no matter where you are from or what language you speak. A card contained in the book explains the symbols, and easy recipes at the beginning make it easy to learn the system through following the cookbook. Bon Appetite!

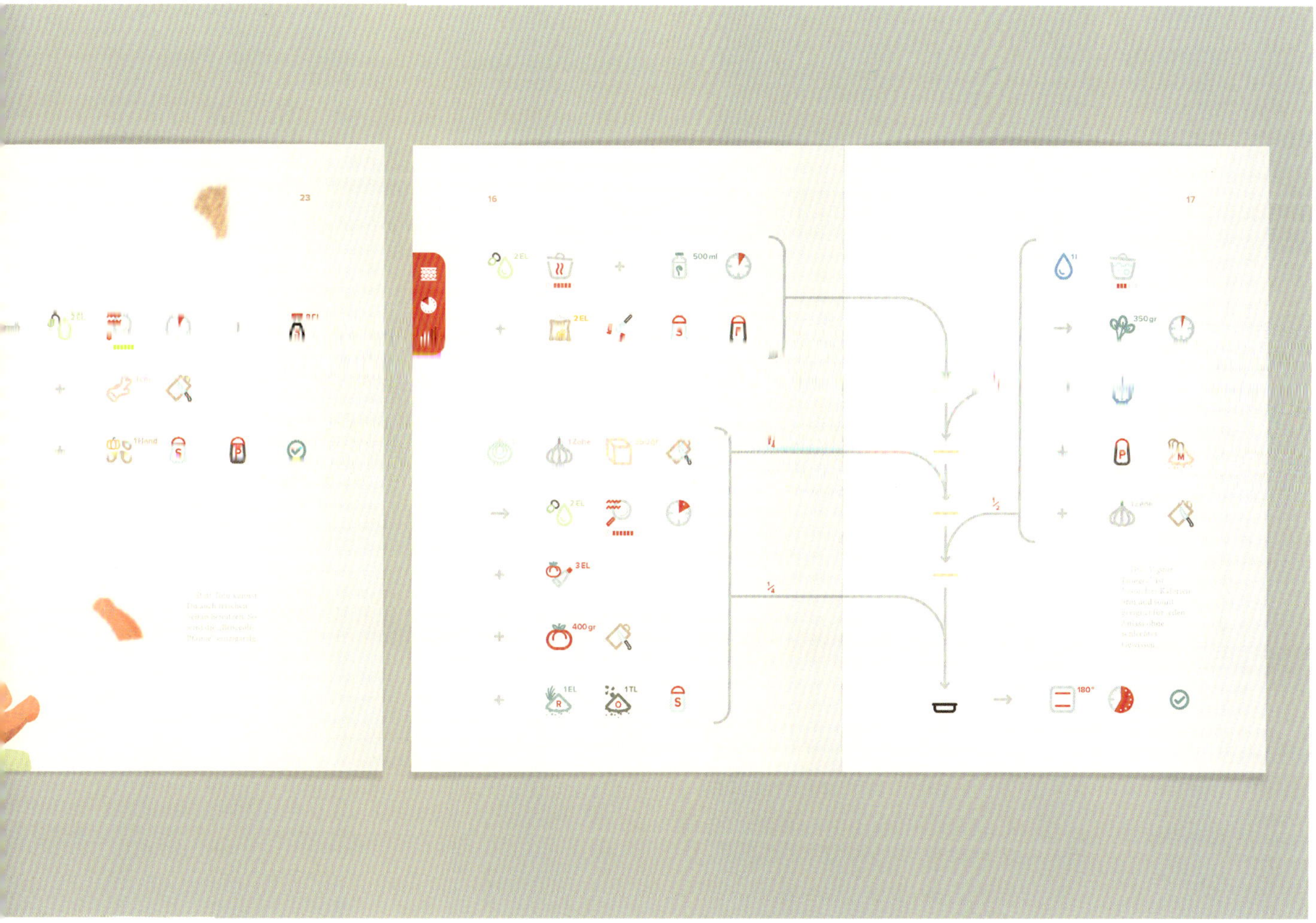

BEAUTIFIED

Design: Lotta Nieminen

Branding, printed material, interface design, and brand illustrations for Beautified, an app that helps find and book last-minute beauty appointments from a curated group of top-tier salons and spas.

PZSP VISUAL IDENTITY

Agency: Ermolaev Bureau — **Creative Direction:** Vlad Ermolaev

PZSP is one of the most significant development companies in Perm, Russia. The designers analyzed the strategy of the company and designed the square-shaped logotype with the letters PZSP, where any combination of two letters could be highlighted to give different descriptors. This variety of descriptors helps to show different strengths of the company and emphasizes different kinds of activities. The graphics were expanded to three sets, corresponding to three sub-brands of the company: construction materials, construction and realization of standard real estate, and construction and realization of luxury real estate.

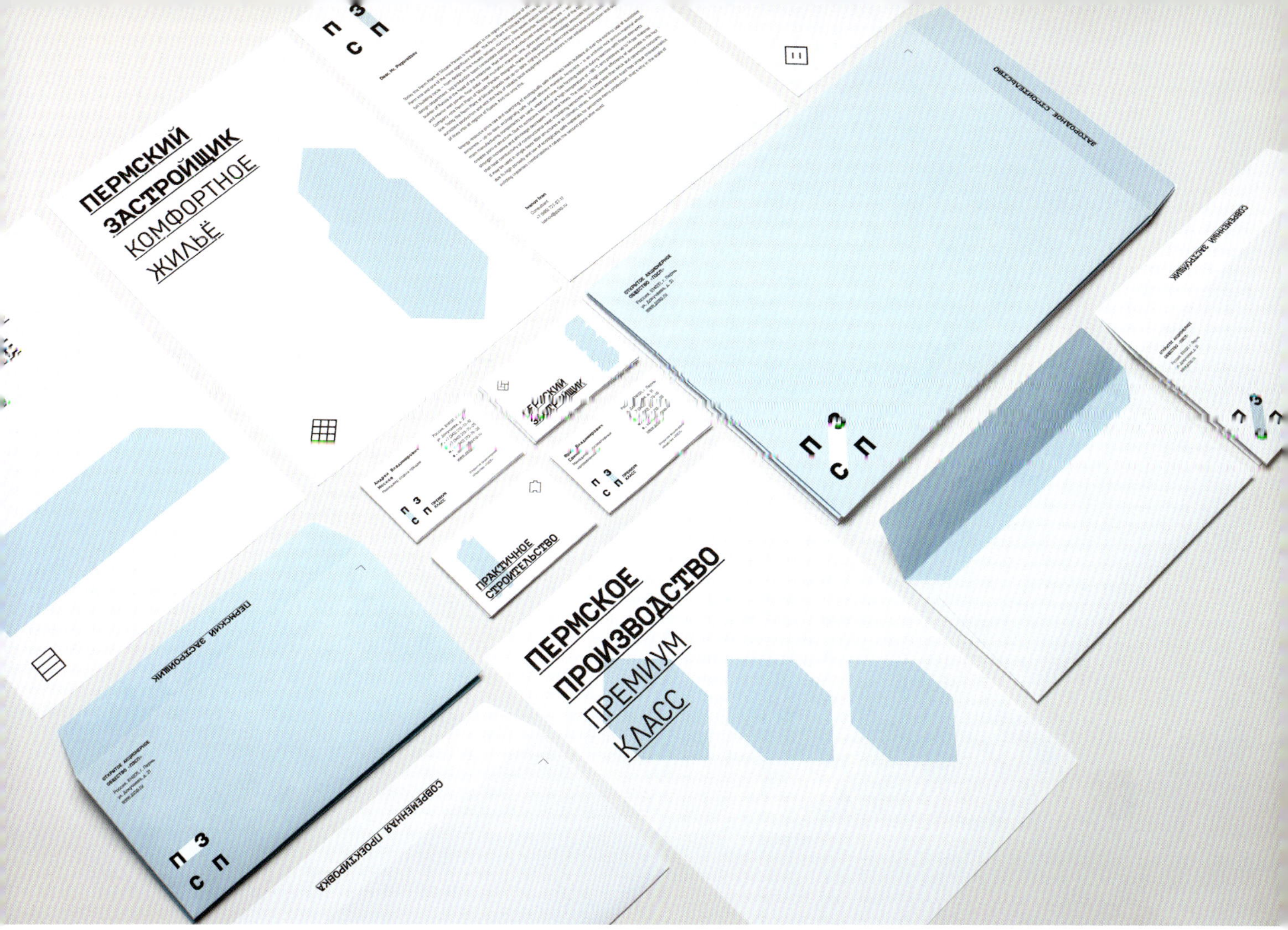
ПЕРМСКИЙ
ЗАСТРОЙЩИК
КОМФОРТНОЕ
ЖИЛЬЁ
ПРАКТИЧНОЕ
СТРОИТЕЛЬСТВО
ПЕРМСКОЕ
ПРОИЗВОДСТВО
ПРЕМИУМ
КЛАСС
П З
С П

ПЕРСОНАЛЬНОЕ
СТРОИТЕЛЬСТВО
МАЯКОВСКАЯ 2А
П З
С П
ПРЕМИУМ
КЛАСС
info@pzsp.ru
www.pzsp.ru
ПЕРМСКИЙ
ЗАСТРОЙЩИК
ЛУНАЧАРСКОГО 15
П З
С П
КОМФОРТНОЕ
ЖИЛЬЕ
info@pzsp.ru
www.pzsp.ru
ПЕРСПЕКТИВНОЕ
СТРОИТЕЛЬСТВО
МЕНЖИНСКОГО 4
П З
С П
СТРОИТЕЛЬНЫЕ
МАТЕРИАЛЫ
info@pzsp.ru
www.pzsp.ru

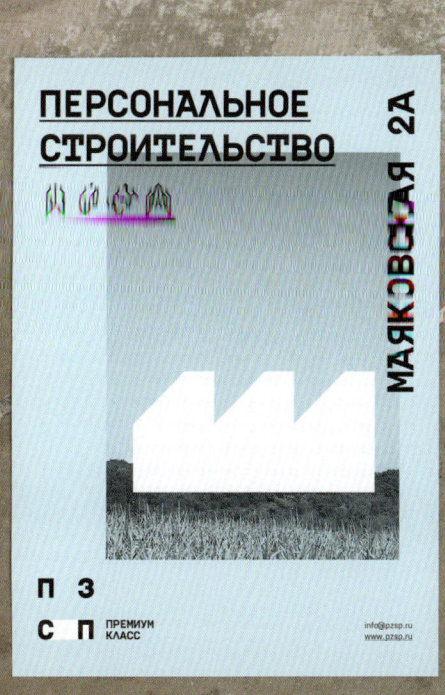

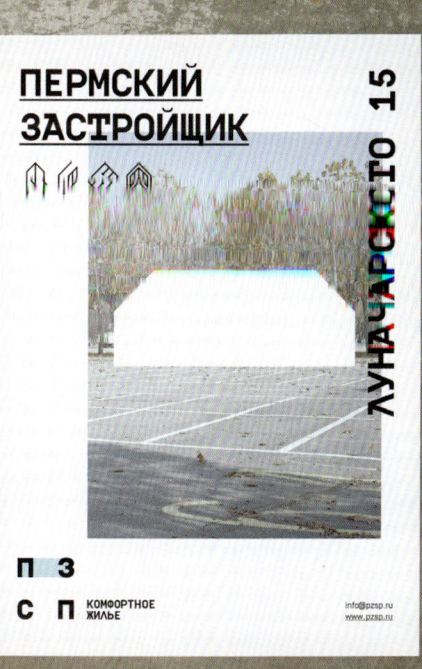

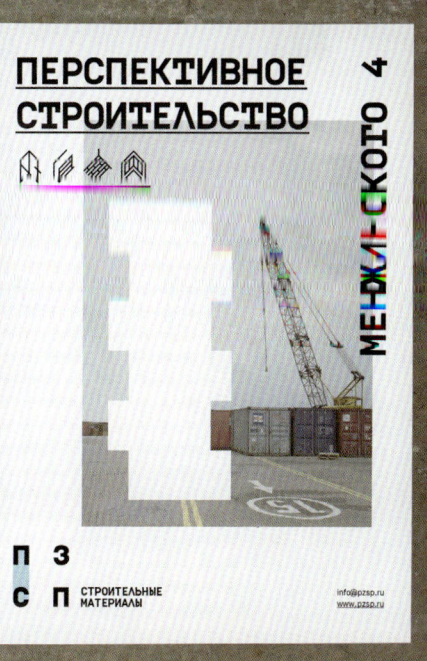

○—— **STUDIO MAJORAN** ————————————————————

○—— **Design:** Malwin Béla Hürkey, Lennart Engelmann ————————————

Hearty and traditional German cuisine, packaged with Japanese aesthetics. Studio Majoran is a catering service which bases its cooking and appearance on traditional Japanese customs; not by way of their ingredients, but on the ceremonial appreciation of a meal, focusing on time, a sense of calm, and modest beauty. Those attributes had to be translated and transferred into Studio Majoran's visual identity. Their signet is an homage to the tradition of Asian ink seals and serves as their official signature. The seal and an additional symbol decorate the exterior packaging. Inspired by the characteristics of the blue onion style of German Meissen porcelain, this symbol system is capable of describing every different type of meal Studio Majoran has to offer.

ingredient	flavour	consistence

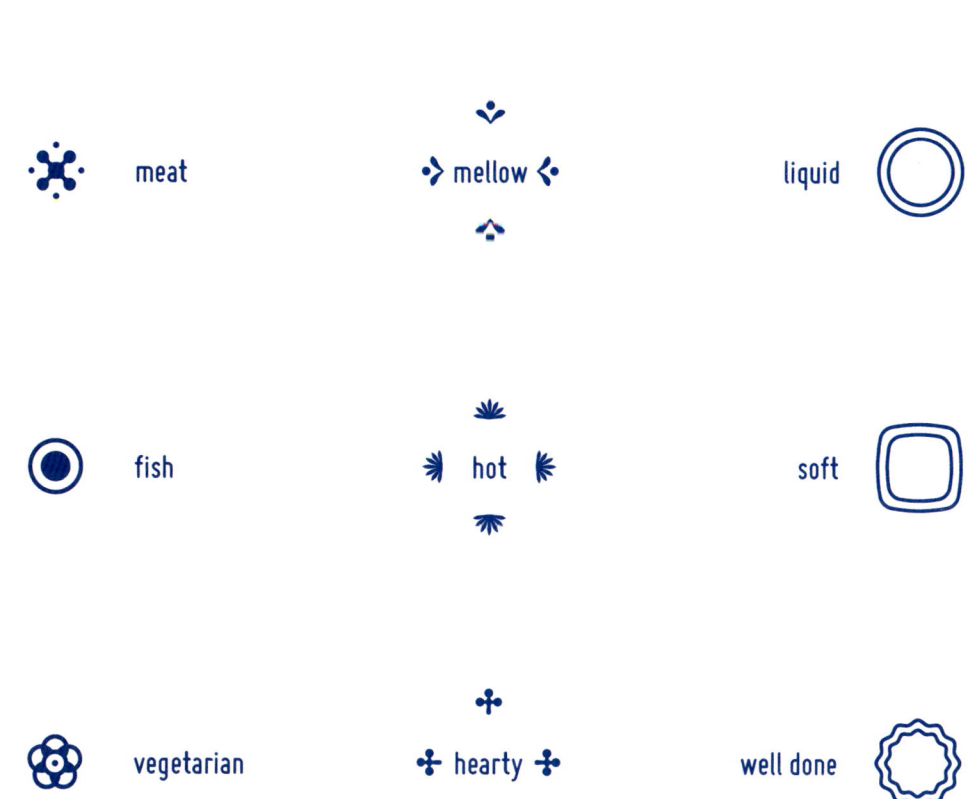

meat — mellow — liquid

fish — hot — soft

vegetarian — hearty — well done

GOMEZ

Design: Savvy Studio

The Gomez concept revolves around a global neighborhood tavern, a revisited "friendly neighborhood bar." The designers wanted to develop an identity that reflected the community of San Pedro Garza García, where the bar is located. Thus they created a friendly and fun graphic personality, using certain elements that take the idea of a typical neighborhood bar and give it a global perspective.

In order to achieve this, the designers developed a playful iconography that toys with the Gomez concept, including the physical space, the menus, and its publicity. The icons represent the music from the jukebox, the casual food, the cold beer served by friendly bartenders, the artisan mezcal imported from Oaxaca, and mainly, the good times that happen in the bar.

Gomez,
A friendly
neighborhood
bar.
GOMEZ
GOMEZ
GOMEZ
GOMEZ
GOMEZ
GOMEZ
GOMEZ
GOMEZ
GOMEZ

Gómez Morín

BERLIN CITY GUIDE

Design: Anastazja Szmawonian

The main idea of this project was to create an attractive and practical gadget for visitors to serve as a city guide and souvenir. The designer was inspired to create it by her own journey to Berlin. While Berlin has always been described as a grey concrete city, the designer decided to show that this isn't true by using the color pink in her design. The designer tried to keep the design of the icons simple but legible. Berlin is an incredible modern city, which is characterised by attention to details. This kind of guide could be a great way to promote the city to young people.

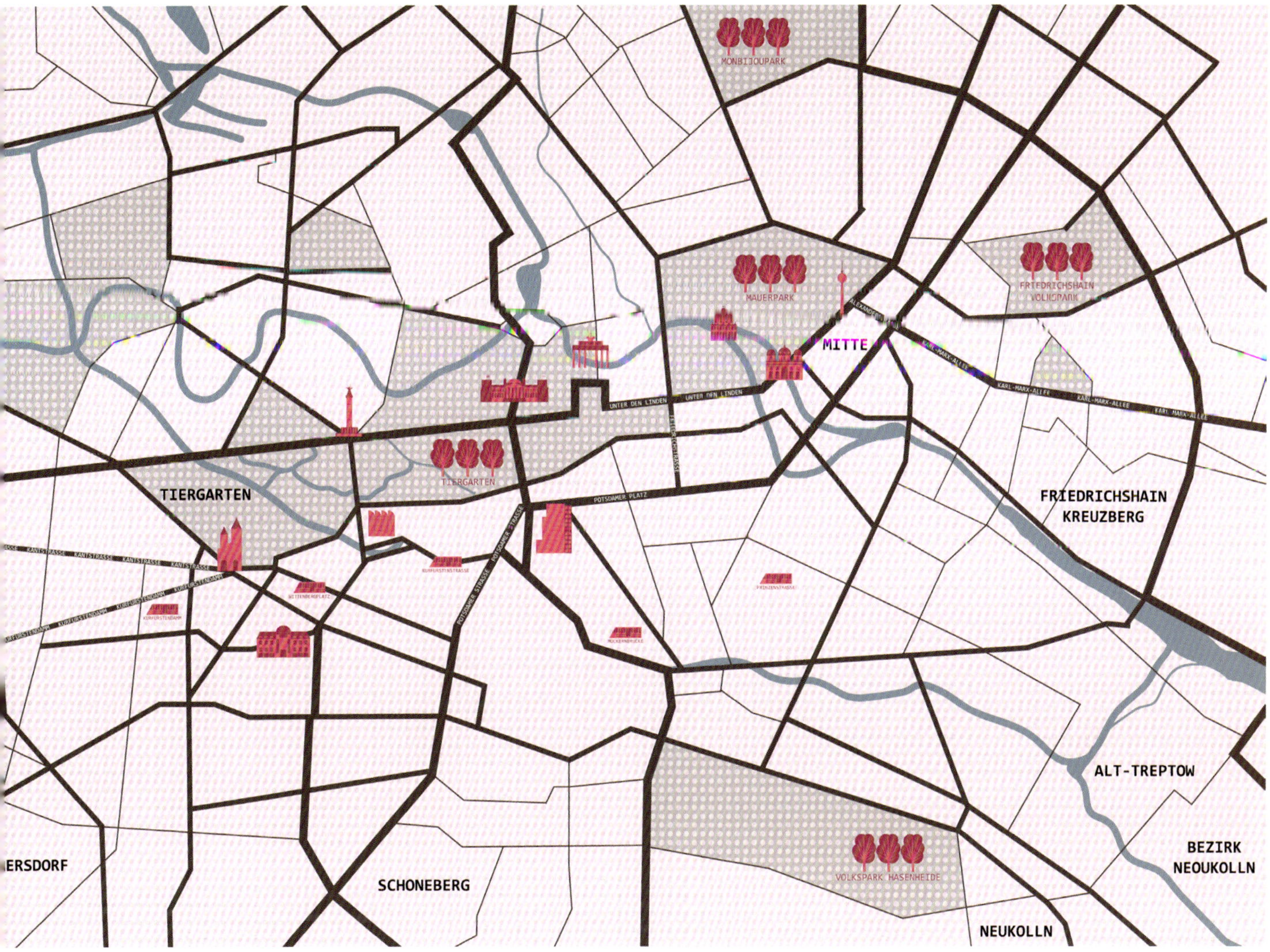

MONBIJOUPARK
MAUERPARK
FRIEDRICHSHAIN VOLKSPARK
MITTE
UNTER DEN LINDEN
TIERGARTEN
POTSDAMER PLATZ
FRIEDRICHSHAIN
KREUZBERG
ALT-TREPTOW
BEZIRK
NEOUKOLLN
ERSDORF
SCHONEBERG
VOLKSPARK HASENHEIDE
NEUKOLLN

BE-
-RL
IN-

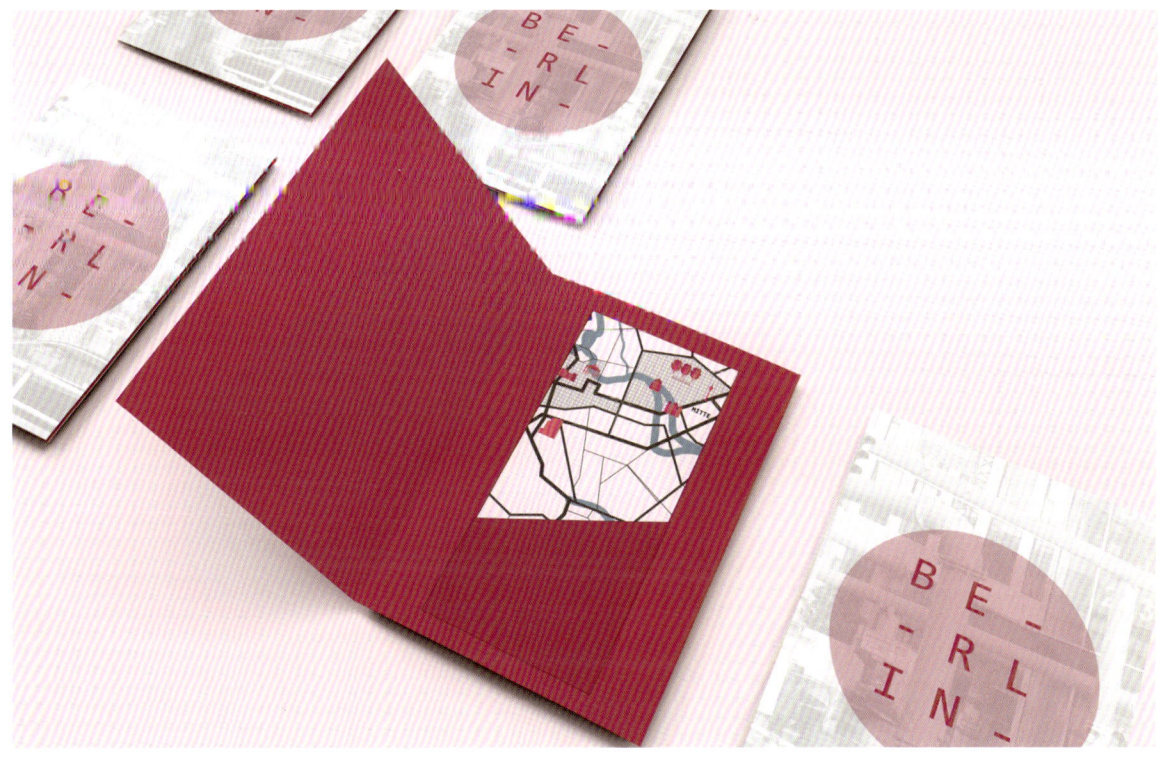

DOMM RESTAURANT

Design: Luca Eusebio, Giorgio Favotto — **Agency:** Studio Eusebio

Branding design for DOMM, a restaurant in Zurich that offers traditional cuisine from northern Italy.

«la terra, la bellezza, l'amore, tutto questo ha sapore di pane»

Pablo Neruda

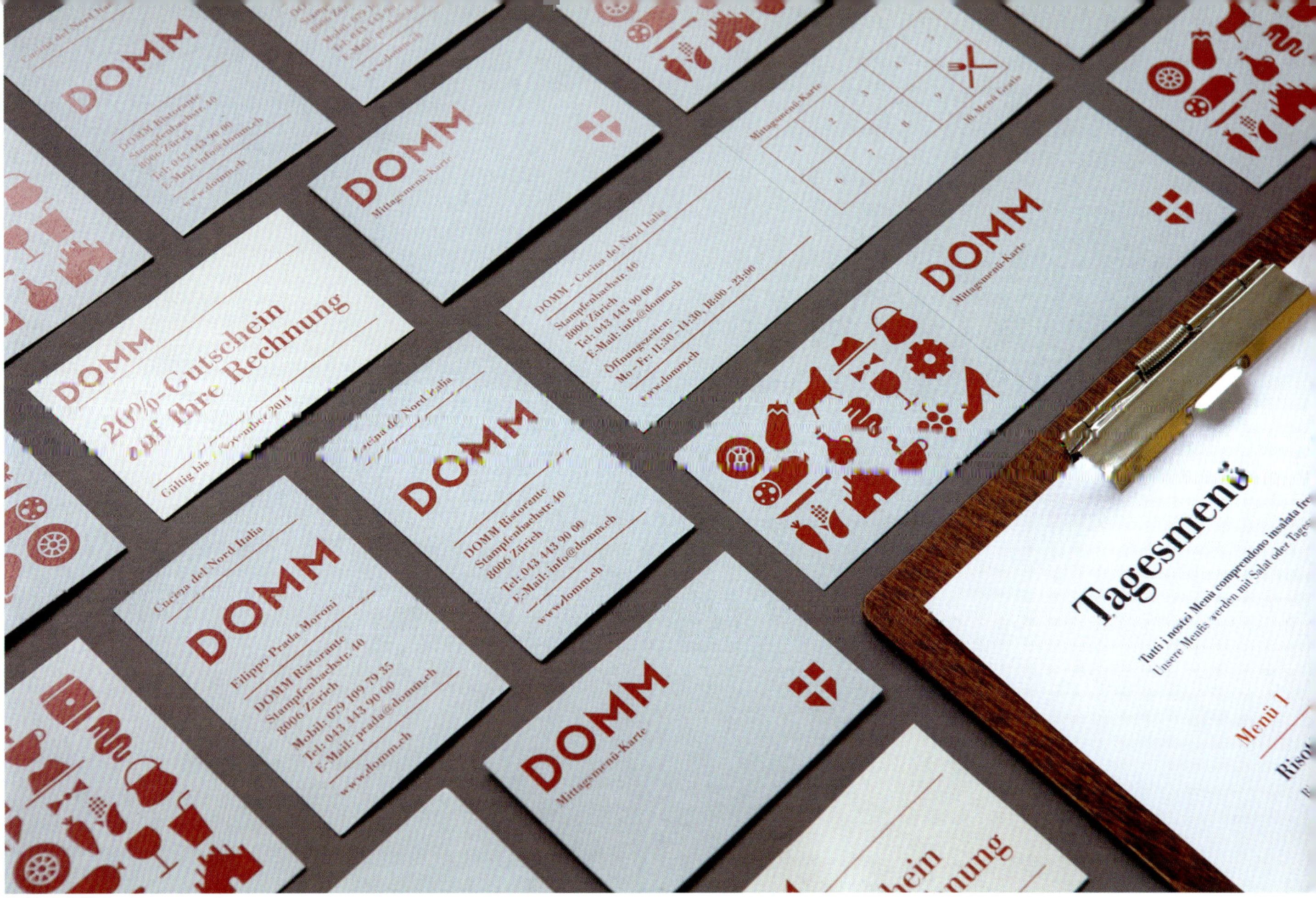
DOMM
20%-Gutschein auf Ihre Rechnung
Cucina del Nord Italia
DOMM
Filippo Prada Moroni
DOMM Ristorante
Stampfenbachstr. 40
8006 Zürich
Tel: 043 443 90 00
E-Mail: info@domm.ch
www.domm.ch
DOMM
Mittagsmenü-Karte
Tagesmenü

DOMM

DOMM

DOMM Cucina del Nord Italia
DOMM Cucina del Nord Italia

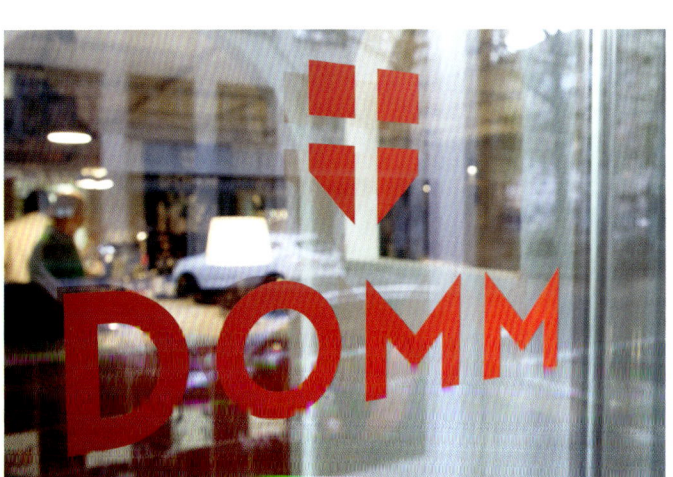

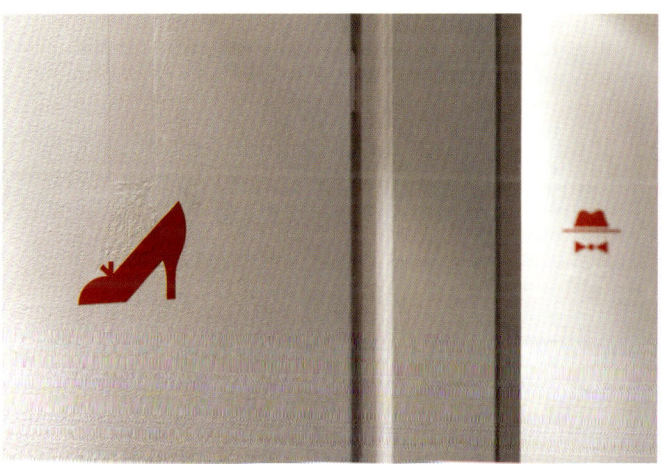

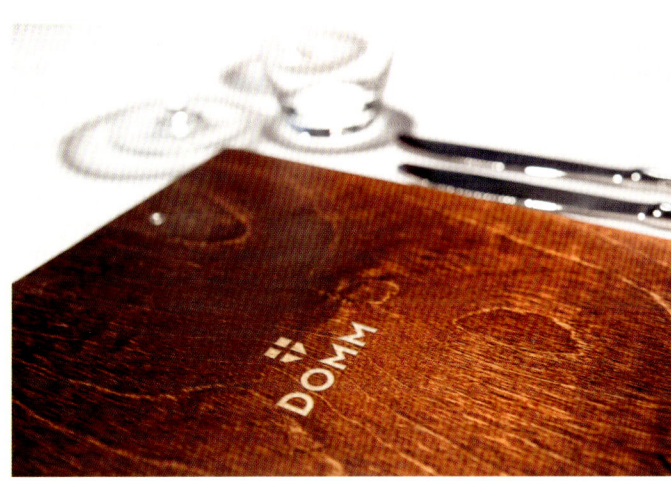

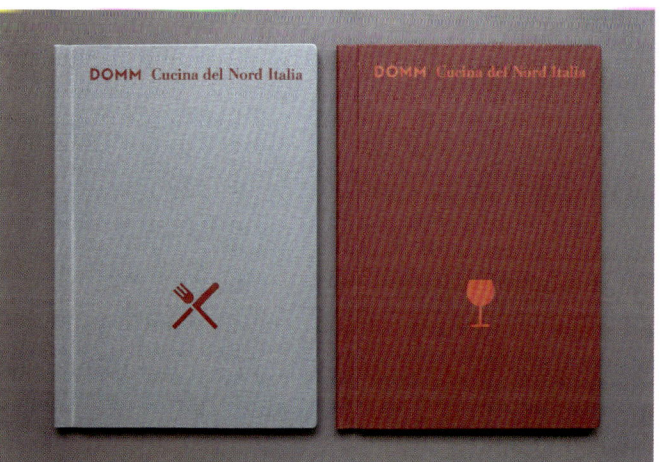

MANANA

Design: LAMM Studio

The concept for Manana arose in Madrid, on one of those trips that leads to you find yourself, to wonder and reinvent, to live again with the real you. You walk through beautiful streets and stop at an odd bohemian cafe, take our your notebook and begin to record your inner world, your world of ideas, drawings, and thoughts. Manana is a philosophy highlighting these details in life.

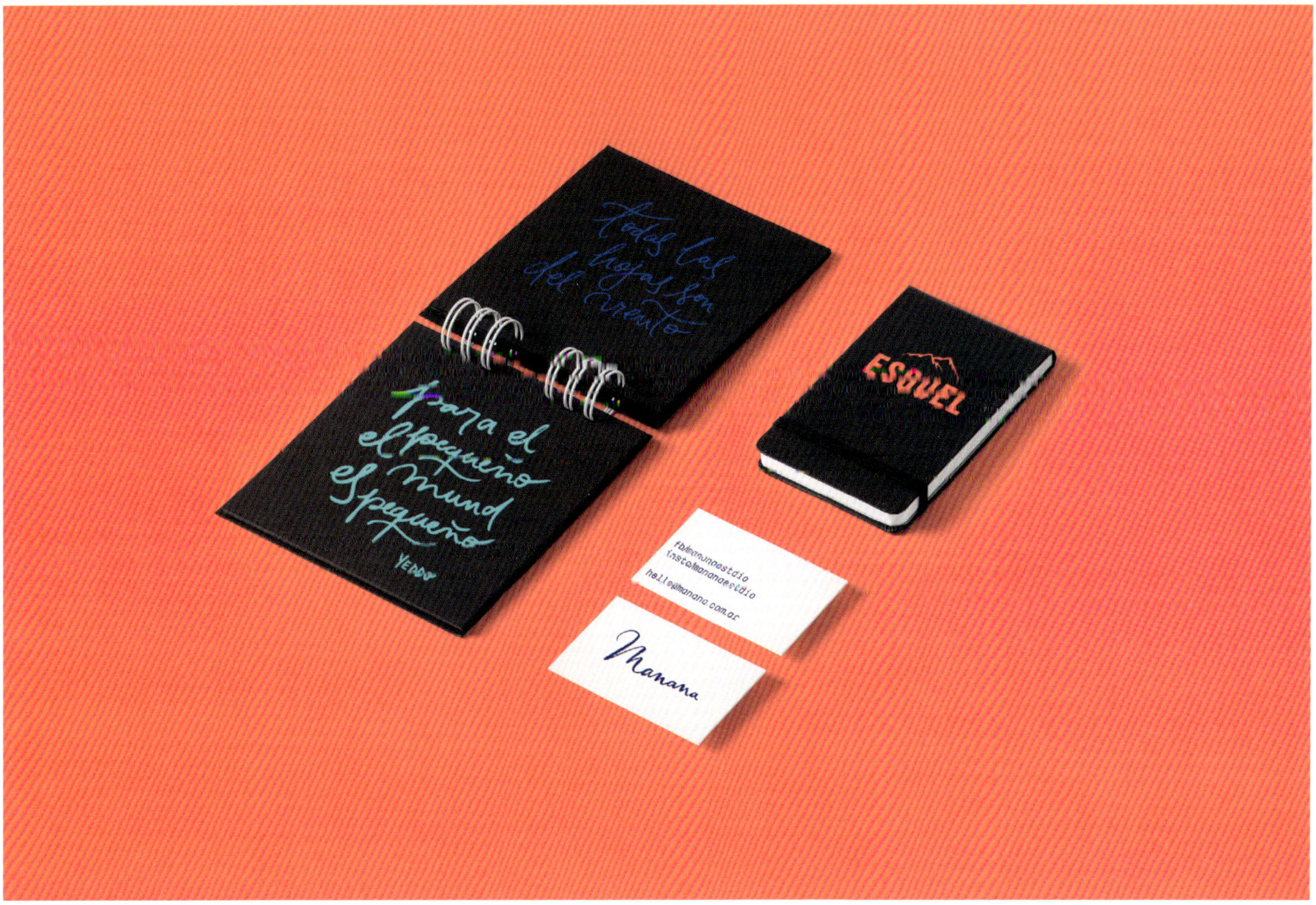
ESQUEL
Manana

ESQUEL
CHUBUT
ESQUEL
Esquel
CHUBUT
ESQUEL
ESQUEL
Manana

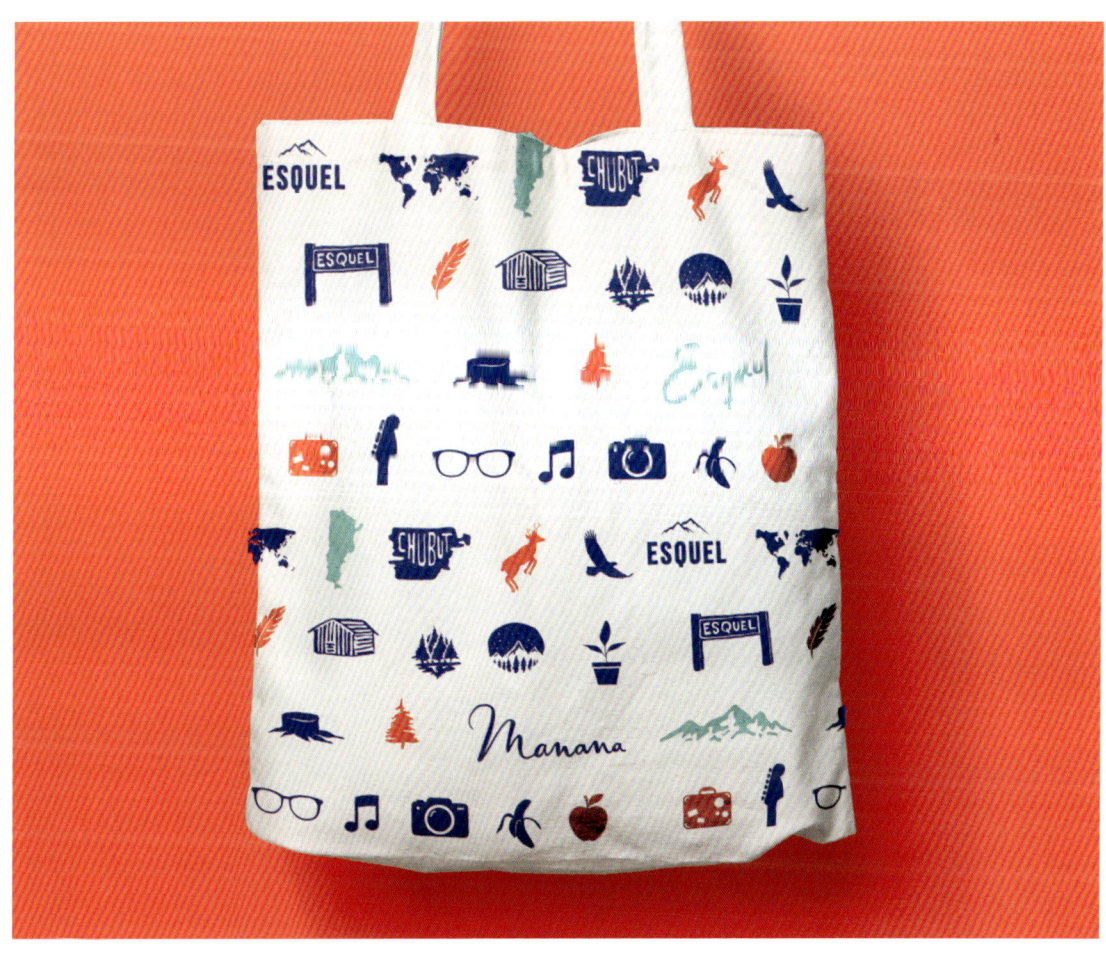

BEAST

Design: Elliott Burford ——— **Agency:** RoAndCo

Visual identity for Beast, a cloud hosting platform for use by the tech industry – hackers, programmers, app builders, and startups. The identity is based on a collection of little beasts, characters that visually reference video games that the target audience was likely to play growing up (like Pac Man or Space Invaders). The icon system can be swapped and rearranged to create new beasts, each representing a customizable server feature. The beasts take over collectible business cards, USB drives, browsers, and even mini-games.

LA ARGENTINISIMA

Design: LAMM Studio

Identity for La Argentinisima, a homemade empanada brand. This is a project for two friends with a love of homemade meals reminiscent of those made by grandmothers. Using their own recipes, they spread the taste of regional empanadas throughout the countries of South America.

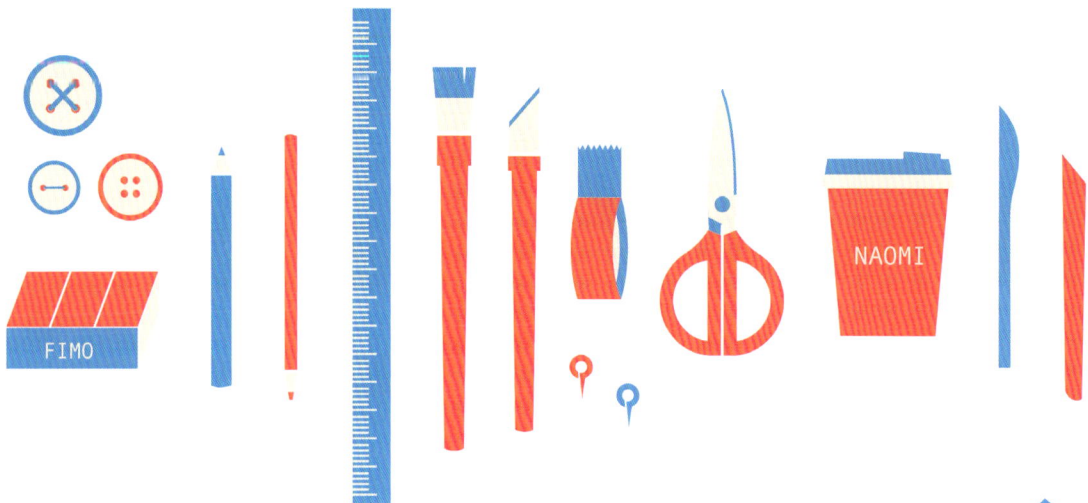

NAOMI'S TWIST

Design: Xiangning Xie

Naomi's Twist is an online store based in the
Netherlands that sells handmade artwork. For the
shop's new promotional materials, the designer created
a main logo and a series of illustrations in a flat,
minimalistic style to reflect the feeling of "making is
thinking," as well as to provide insight into the aspects
of working with many different kinds of materials.
The color palette consists of red and blue, which are
often "twisted" together. The cover of the brand book
was designed to look like an envelope to represent the
company's worldwide shipping policy.

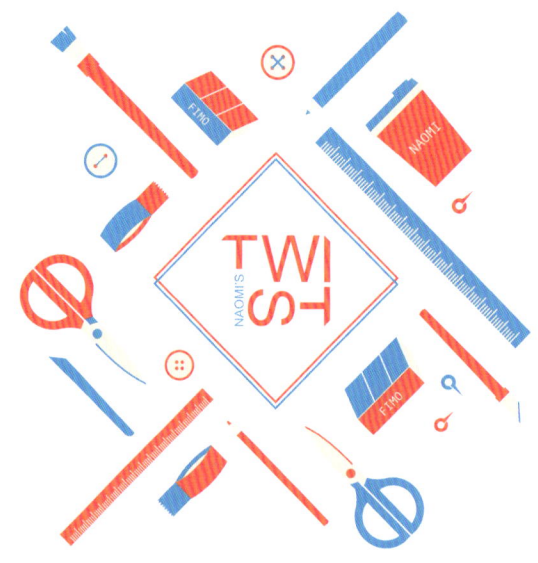

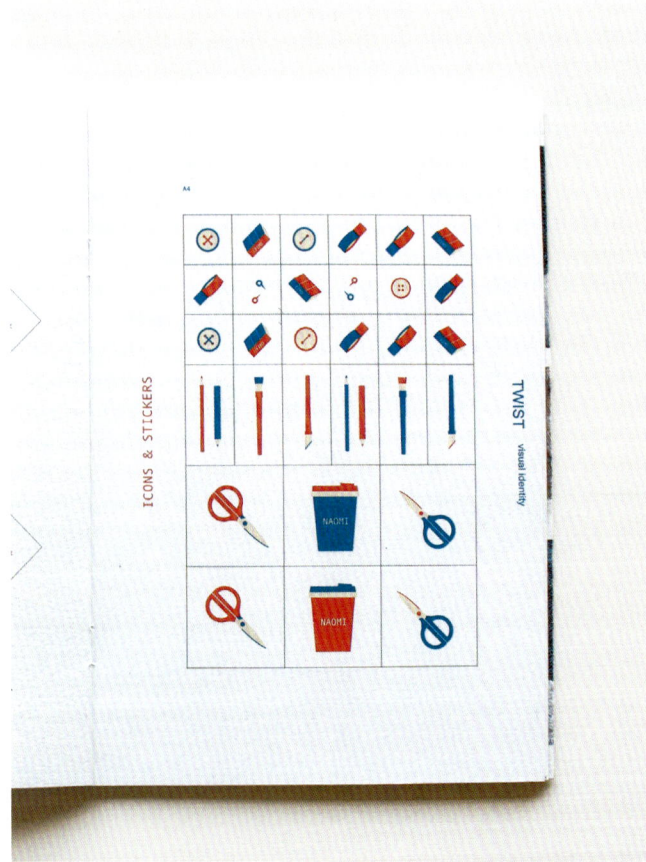

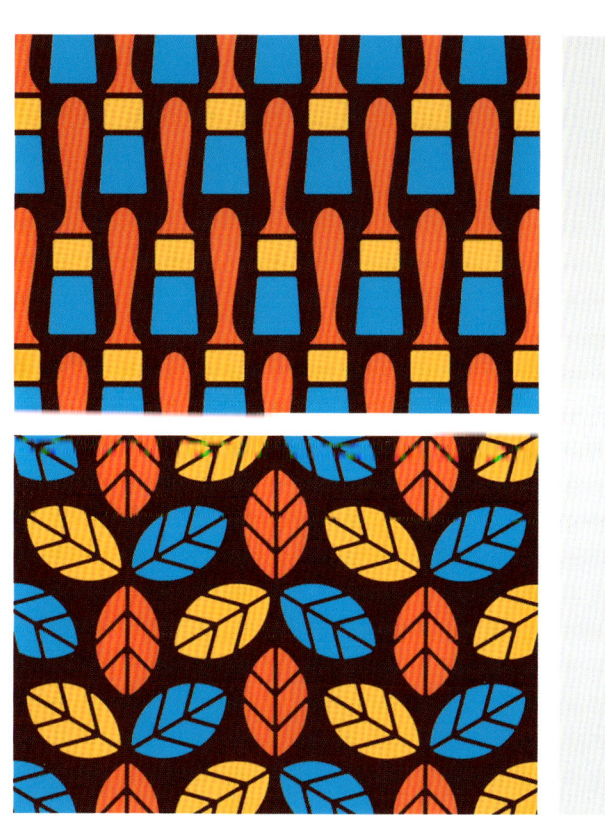

NATIONAL ASSOCIATION OF
SWEDISH HANDICRAFT SOCIETIES

Design: Snask

A new identity for Sweden's association for brilliant people working with their hands! The Swedish Handicraft Association has been around for more than 100 years. With over 17,000 members, 22 regional offices, and 8 retail shops, it was a serious challenge to gather everything under one name and one brand. The designers changed the associations of Swedish Handicraft from old butter knifes and knitting into everything made by hand, creating something modern but with a rich history of knowledge and experience.

YOU ROCK

Design: Patswerk

Patswerk loves brewing beer and handing out presents, thus the team decided to make a super limited package for their clients and friends for their seven-year anniversary. The icons are the main theme of the package design.

MYSTERYLAND

Design: Patswerk

Branding design for Mysteryland, one of the biggest electronic music festivals in the Netherlands, and the longest running dance festival worldwide.

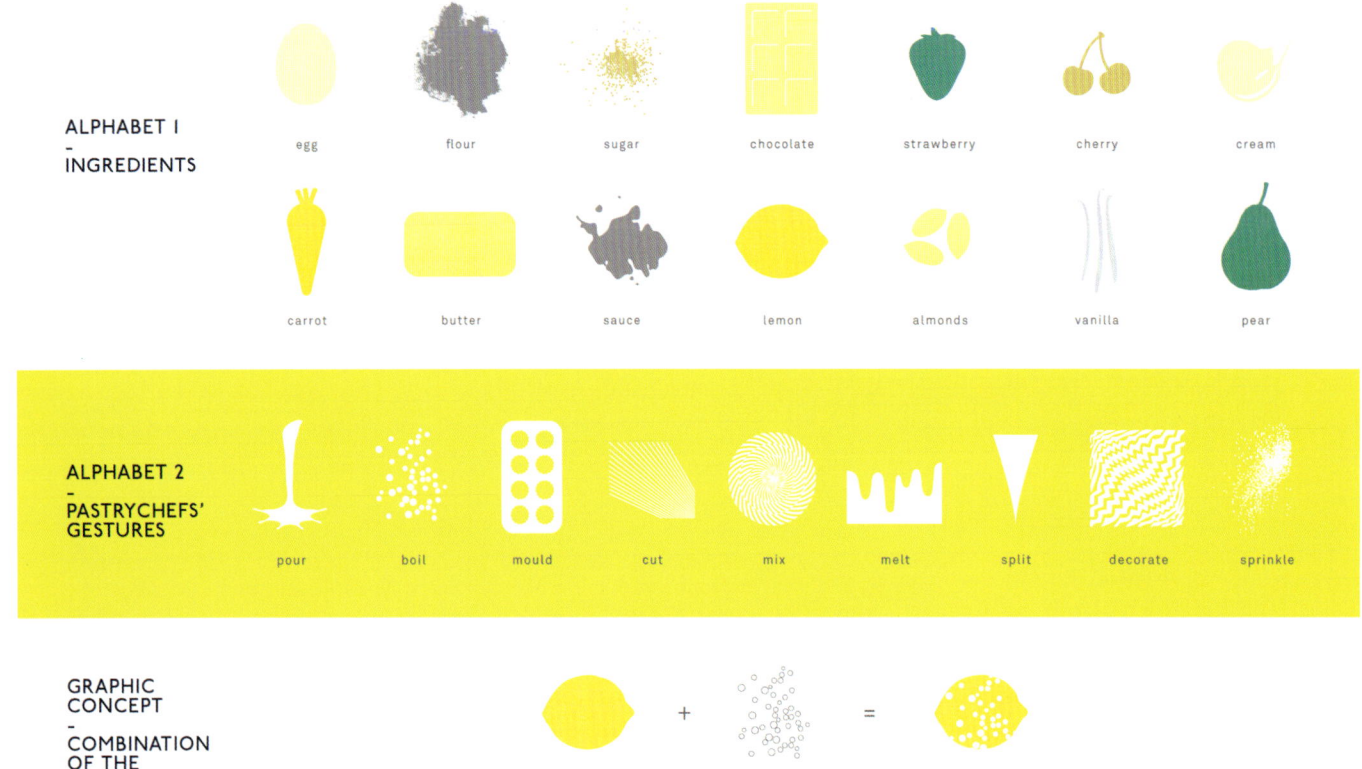

ALPHABET I
-
INGREDIENTS

egg · flour · sugar · chocolate · strawberry · cherry · cream

carrot · butter · sauce · lemon · almonds · vanilla · pear

ALPHABET 2
-
PASTRYCHEFS'
GESTURES

pour · boil · mould · cut · mix · melt · split · decorate · sprinkle

GRAPHIC
CONCEPT
-
COMBINATION
OF THE
TWO ALPHABETS

INGREDIENT + GESTURE = SYMBOL

LESCURIER PASTRY SHOP

Design: Atelier Atoca

Montreal-based Atelier Atoca studio created new branding for the Lescurier pastry shop. The designers wanted to reflect their "homemade" style of baking by imagining a series of icons that could be put together just like recipes.

This new graphic system is based on two alphabets inspired by ingredients and pastry chefs' gestures. By combining them, it is possible to obtain an infinite range of symbols. The illustrations are now used on all printed communication materials, packaging, posters, and shop windows.

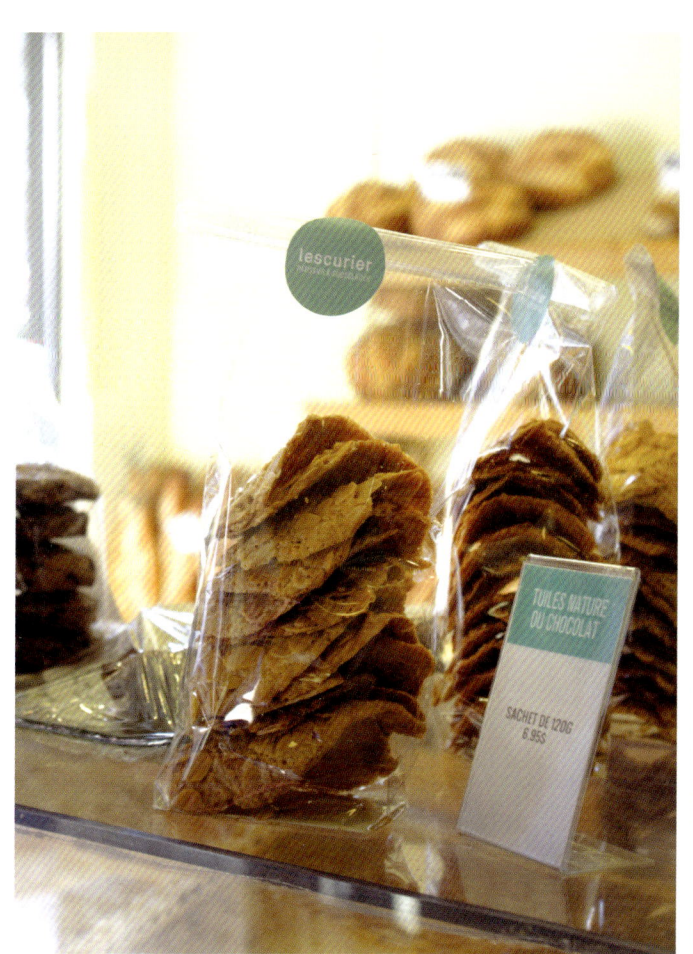

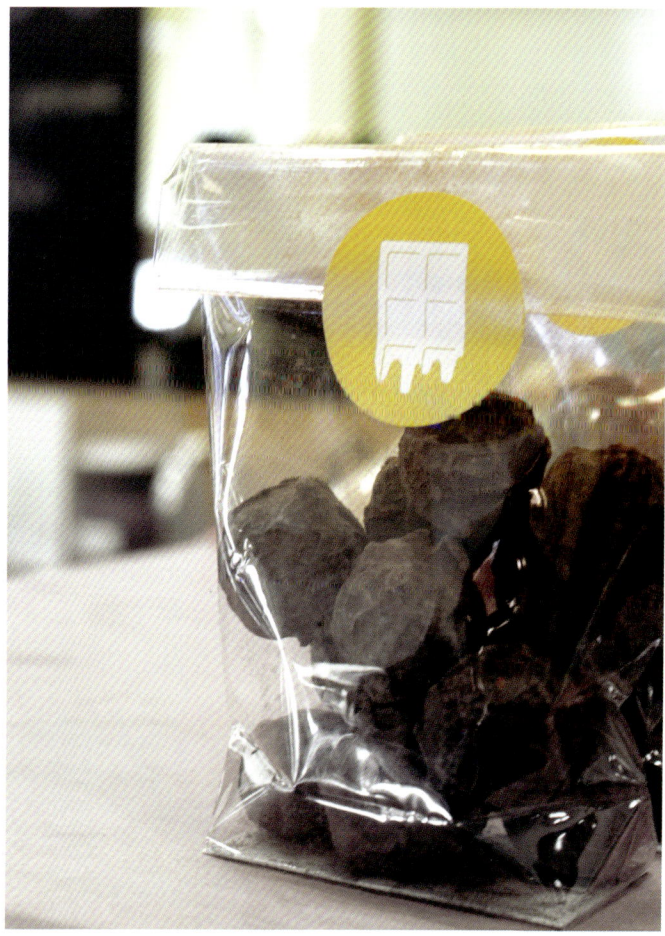

lescurier
TUILES NATURE
OU CHOCOLAT
SACHET DE 120G
6.95$

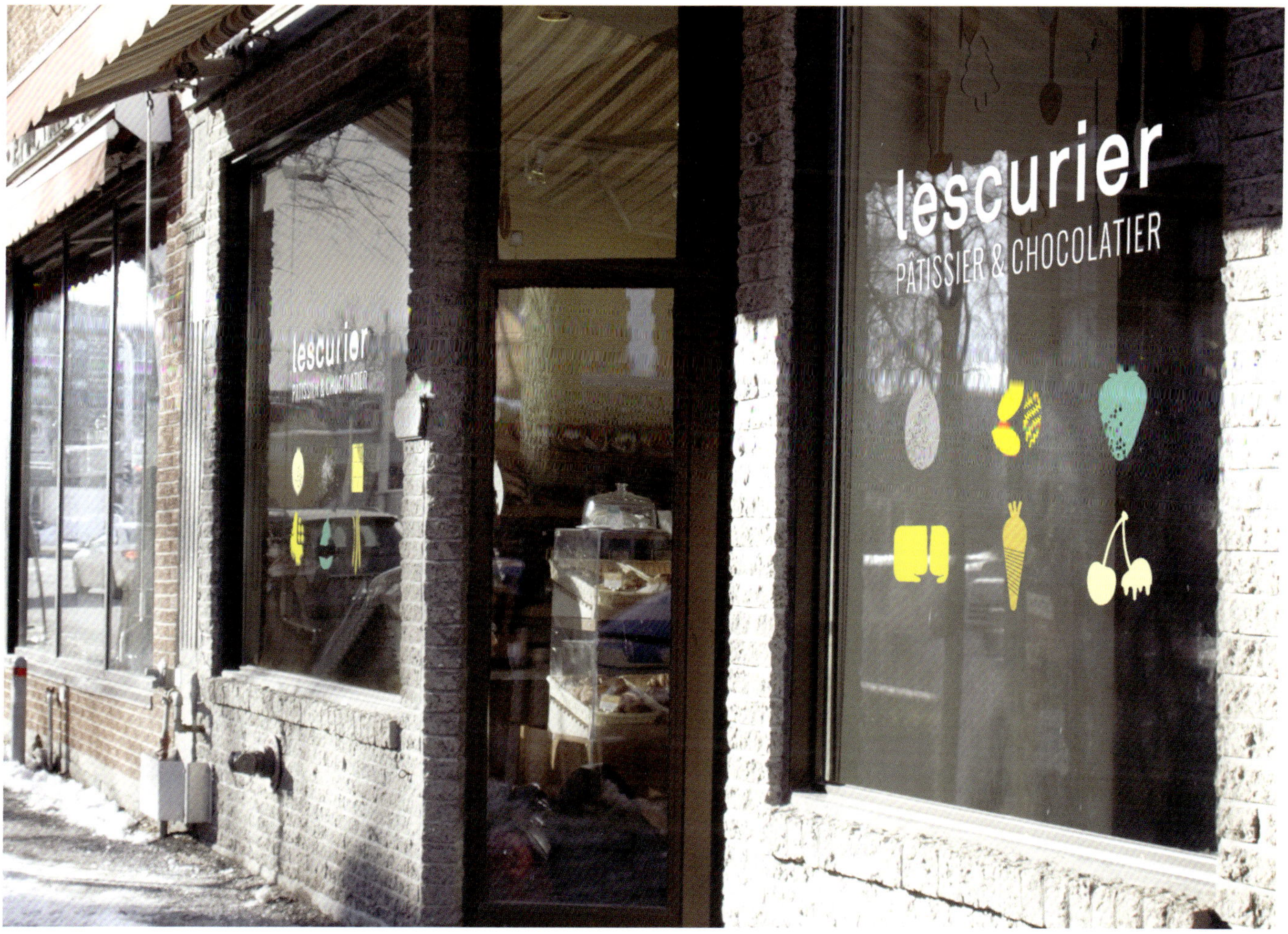
lescurier
PÂTISSIER & CHOCOLATIER
lescurier
PÂTISSIER & CHOCOLATIER

GREEN RIPPLES FESTIVAL

Design: Chen Ying Ann —— **Art Direction:** Jonas Ho

Green Ripples Festival is a large-scale art festival. The design concept for this project came from the special abilities of children – imagination and courage. The designer hoped it would remind visitors of their own childhoods while participating in the festival. Based on this idea, the designer created a set of heuristic visual graphics that are open to interpretation, allowing visitors to use their own imaginations to create explanations. The designer also created a set of icons showing art installations and local landmarks for the festival's map.

DESIGN CENTER

Design: Vittorio Perotti, Giulia Zoavo

The Milan Design Week is chaotic and the town is full of logos of all sorts. That's why the designer created a dynamic logo that is simultaneously an iconic grid and a sign. Every time you see the Design Center's logo you will know where the Design Center is. The Design Center exists to give directions, and the logo directs you to it.

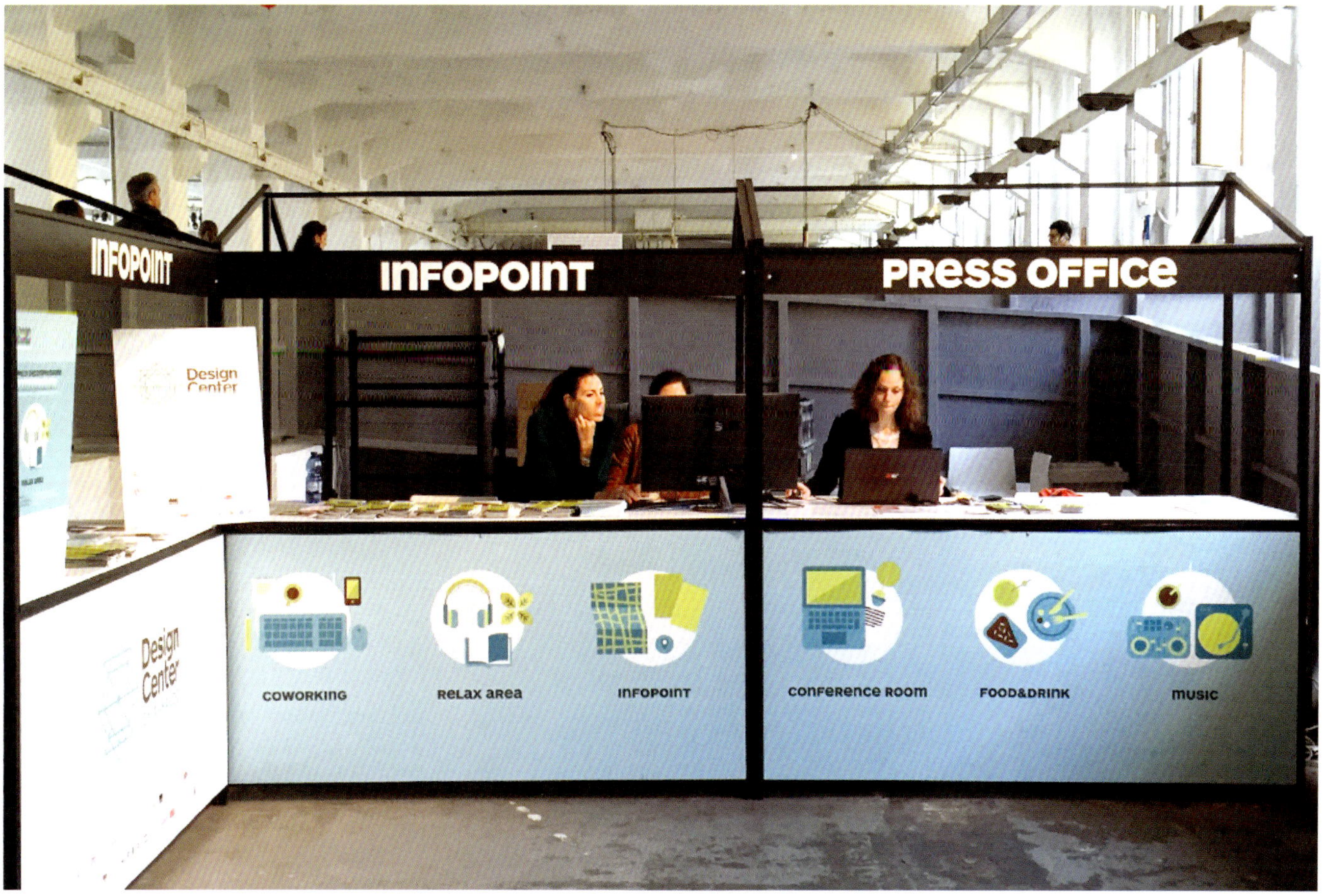
INFOPOINT
INFOPOINT
PRESS OFFICE
Design Center
COWORKING
RELAX AREA
INFOPOINT
CONFERENCE ROOM
FOOD&DRINK
MUSIC

Design Center
EX-ANSALDO
INFOPOINT

Design Center
MUSIC

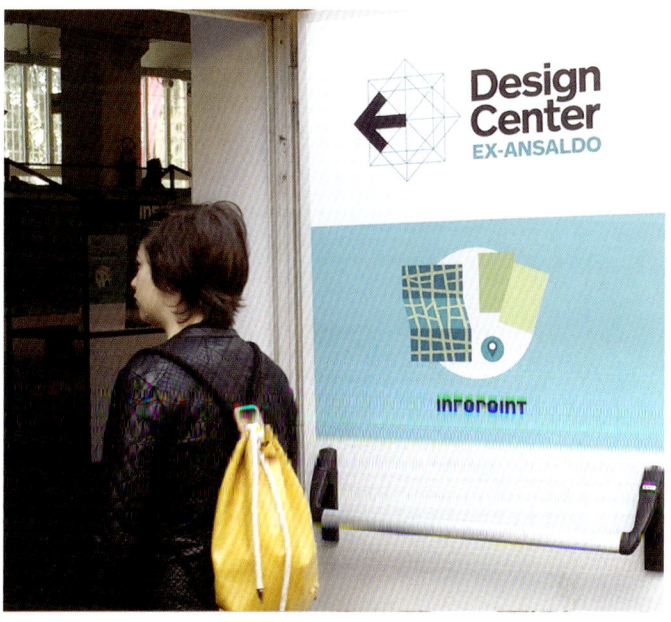

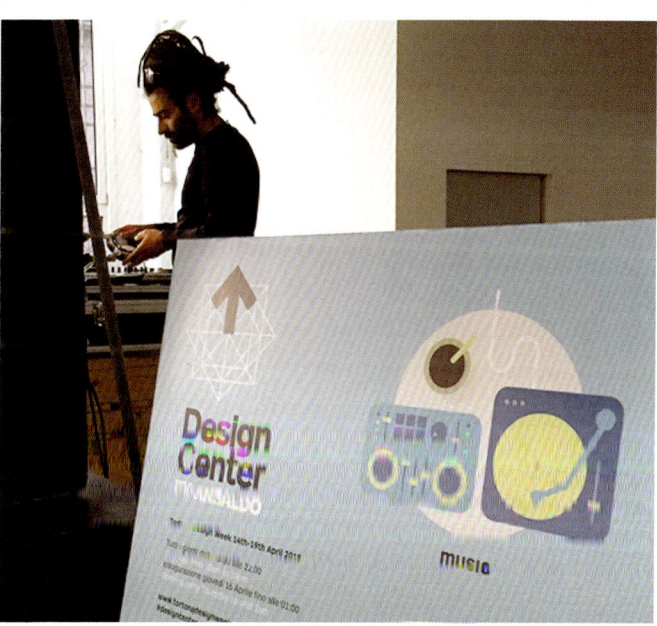

LAS TOSCAS SIGNAGE

Art Direction: Leandro Salvadores — **Agency:** Morocho Estudio

The task was to redesign the signage for the Las Toscas Canning Shopping Center, and generate a new identity that is functional and properly communicates what is available in each section of the mall. The designers made a comprehensive proposal appropriating one of its most important structural features – the Octagon. With this concept in mind, the designers used the geometric figure to develop an all-new signage system.

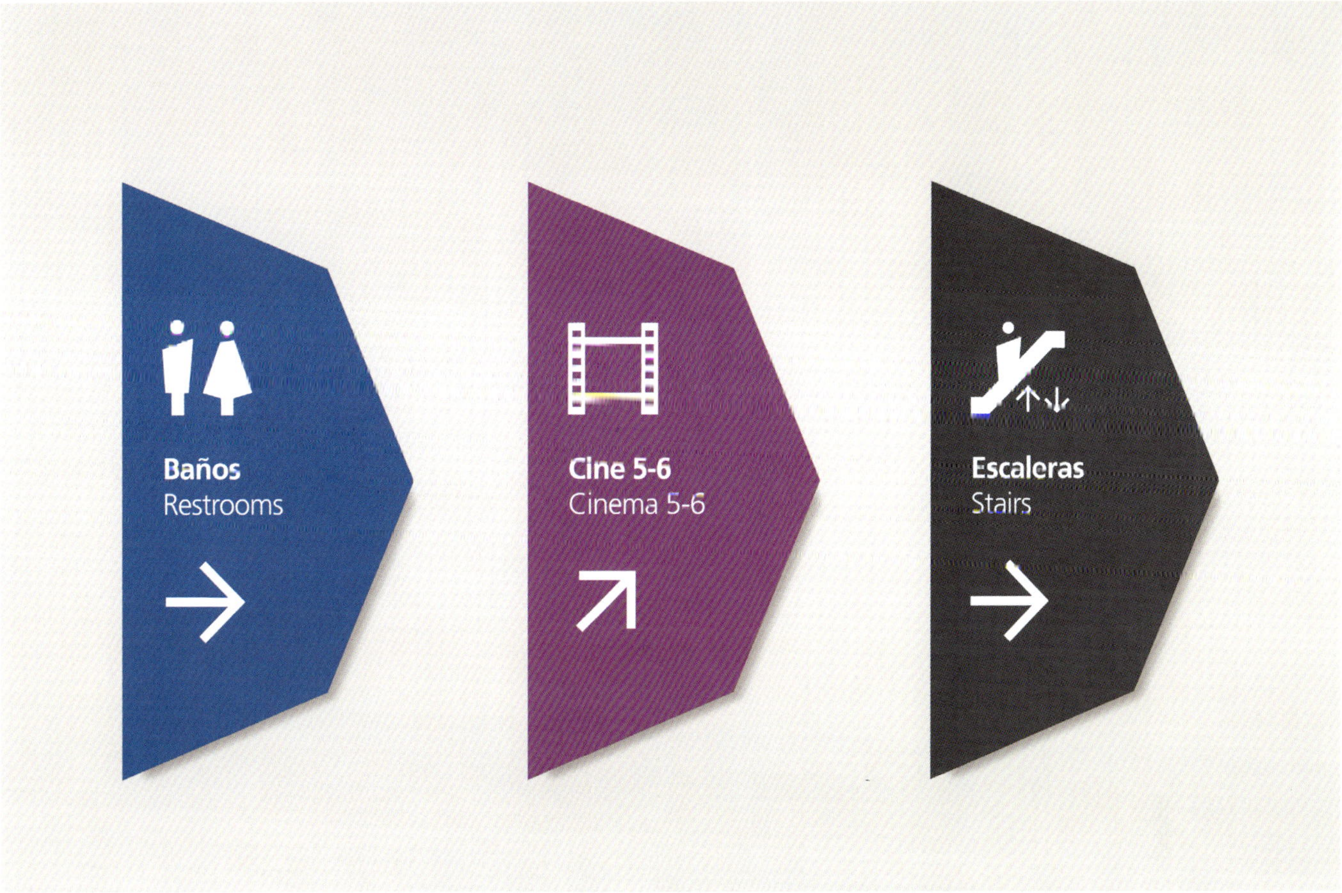
Baños
Restrooms
Cine 5-6
Cinema 5-6
Escaleras
Stairs

2
Cine 5-6
Cinema 5-6
Baños
Restrooms
Gastronomía
Food Court
Bingo
Bingo
1
Cine 1-2-3-4
Cinema 1-2-3-4
Gastronomía
Food Court
Baños
Restrooms
Tiendas
Stores
0
Informes
Info
Baños
Restrooms
Tiendas
Stores
-1
Patio del Café
Coffee Hall
Slots
Slots

ños / Restroom

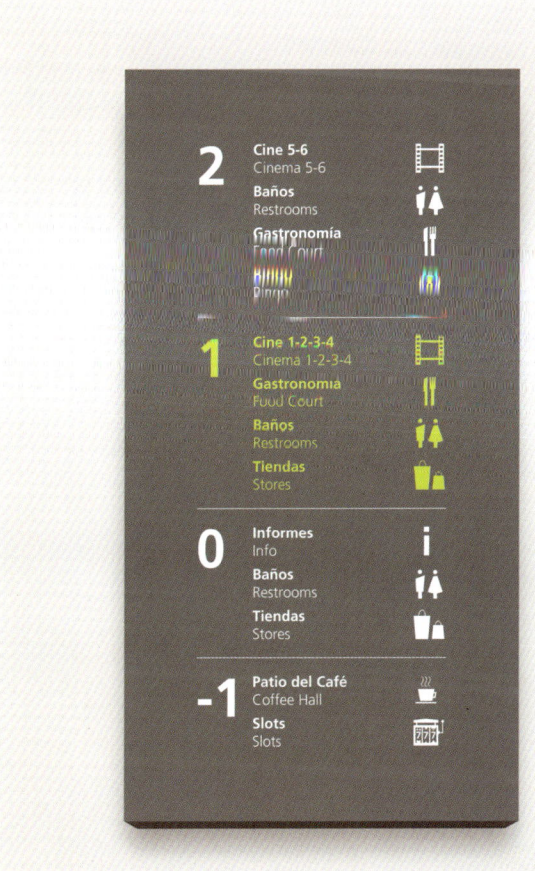

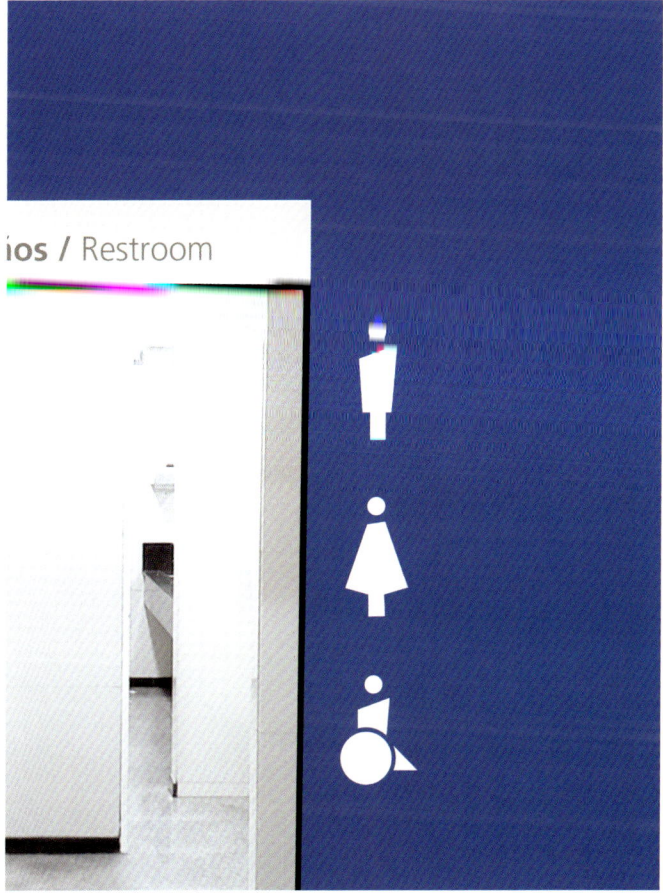

SPORTS ACADEMY

Design: Dominik Langegger

This project was designed for a large sports academy owned by one of the world's best-known energy drink producers, based in Austria. The academy is a training facility for children from 14 to 18 that focuses on ice hockey and soccer. The icons are not just for signage; the architect also intended for the symbols to serve as decoration for the building. The icons' round, simple, and child-like shapes are intended to liven up the academy's walls. The main challenge for the design was to find a style that allowed one general icon to be applied across multiple uses. The solution was accomplished by combining one basic symbol with a more specific, smaller icon that referred to the type of sport or other special information.

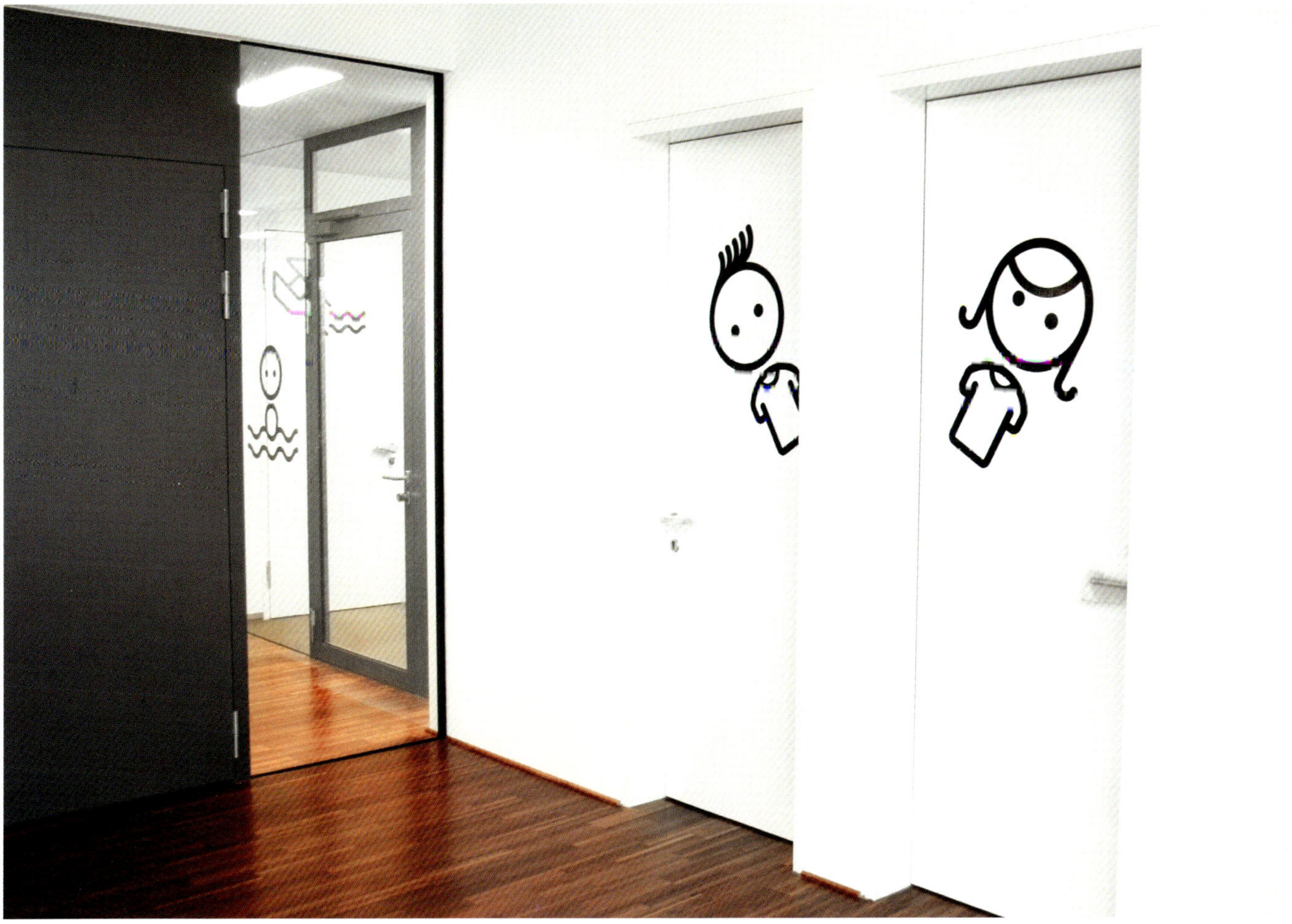

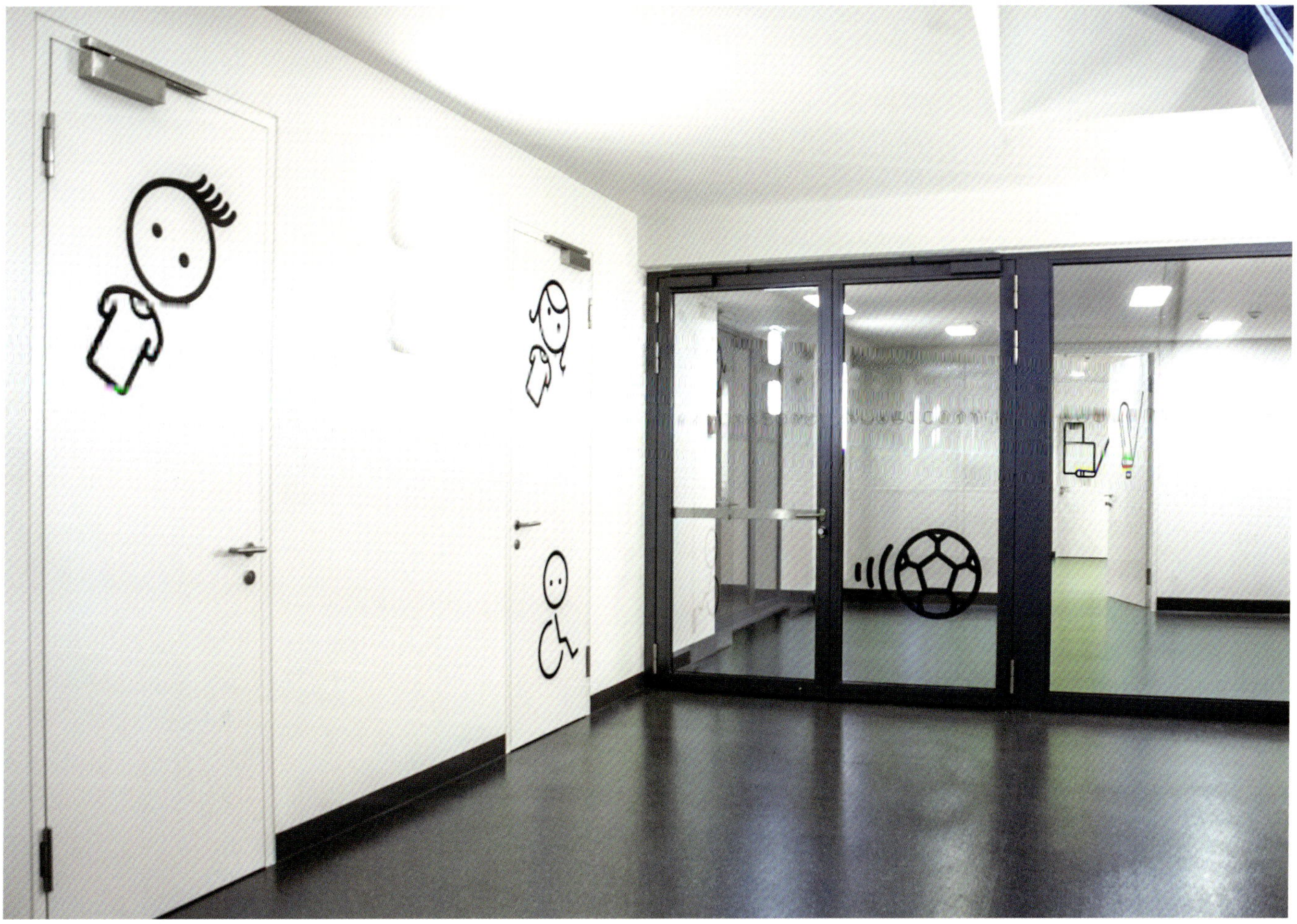

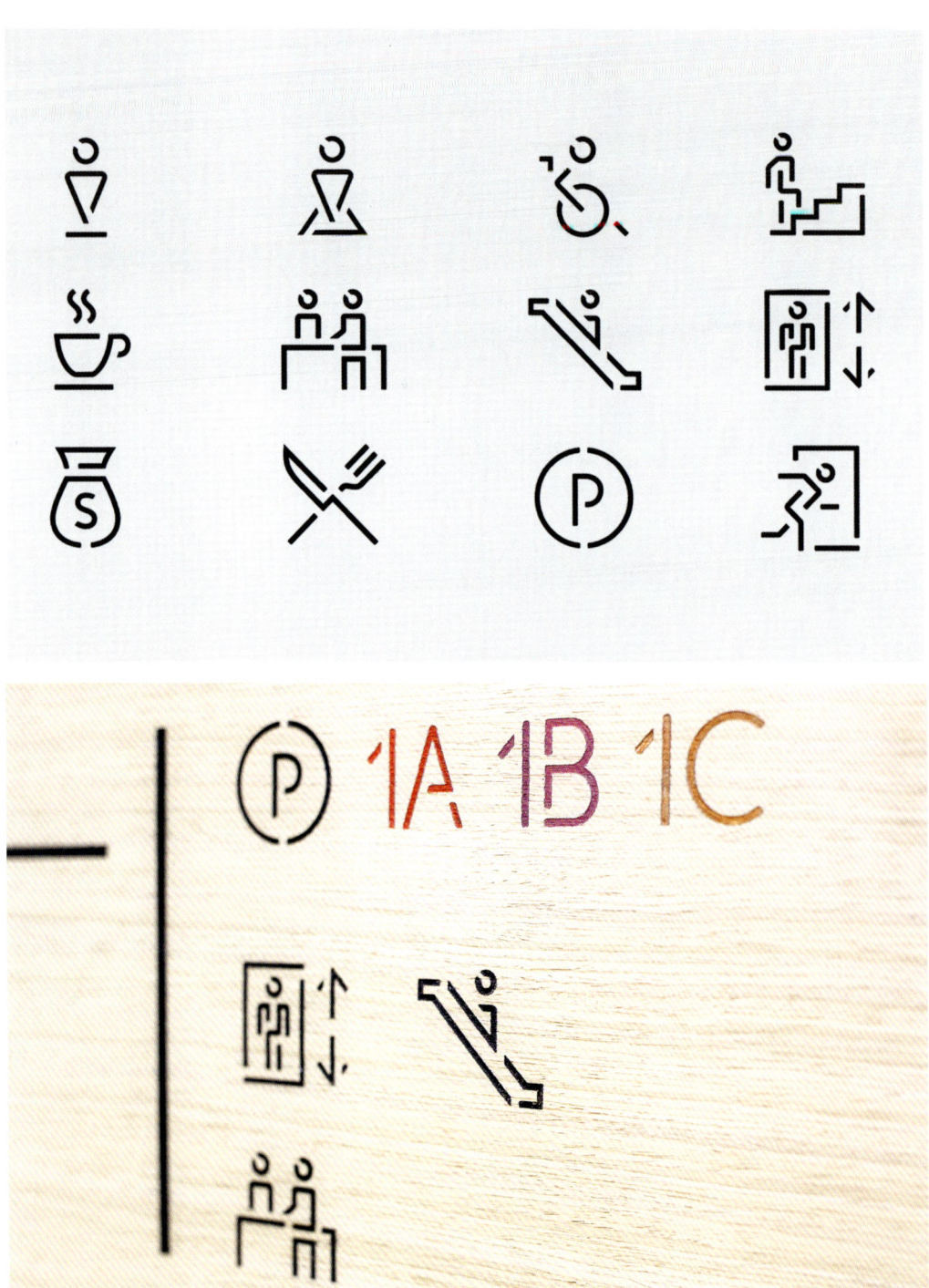

RIO MALL WAYFINDING SYSTEM

Design: The Bakery

The designer developed the wayfinding system for Rio Leninsky Mall in Moscow, Russia based on its name – Rio. By using wood and moss, the designers tried to bring a Brazilian rainforest vibe to the space and make the interior feel friendly and fun. The result is very contemporary and sophisticated.

-2	-1	1	2	3	4	5
Услуги:	**Магазины:**	**Магазины:**	**Магазины:**	**Магазины:**	**Магазины:**	**Рестораны:**
Парковка	Rivièra Maison	H&M	H&M	Podium Market	Республика	Этаж
	Наш Дом	Rendez Vous	Reserved	Sunday Up Market	Mamas and Papas	Noodle House
		Л'Этуаль	Calvin Klein	Детский Мир	Imaginarium	Шоколадница
	Услуги:		Lady & Gentleman		M Видео	
	Химчистка	**Услуги:**	Nice Connection	**Рестораны:**		**Развлечения:**
	Дом Быта	Зеленый Перекресток	Снежная Королева	Bocconcino	**Рестораны:**	Салон красоты BES
		Фора Банк			Фудкорт	Кинотеатр
		Аптека Ave				Cinema Star

Ⓟ 2D 2E 2F | Ⓟ 1A 1B 1C

LA CLINIQUE DE PARIS GRAND HILTON SEOUL

Design: Lee Hyojin

La Clinique de Paris Grand Hilton Hotel Seoul seeks consistent beauty and health by suggesting anti-aging programs, skin care, body care, and spa programs suitable for Koreans. Its brand image was derived from the keyword, "Light," as it does not solely seek physical youth but also strives for improved mental health and physical beauty. "Light," which is the motif of La Clinique de Paris Grand Hilton Hotel Seoul, stands for physical and mental beauty, and represents the attitude of the clinic of attempting to maintain the eternal beauty of the customers.

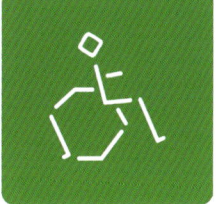

observation

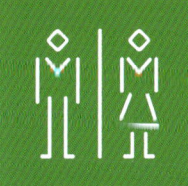

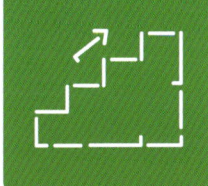

inspiration

EXIT

design

NO SMOKING

FACULTY OF GRAPHIC DESIGN ATHENS

Design: George Tsavalos, Marianta Theodoratou

The aim of this specific project was the creation of a corporate and visual identity for the Faculty of Graphic Design at T.E.I of Athens. It includes the creation of a logo, cards, envelopes, posters, signalization, and other applications that are based on the elements of the logo, using patterns. The goal was to design a logo and a visual identity that can be very easily understood by people in Greece and around the world. The designers also aimed to urge students to experiment with the identity and the logo itself.

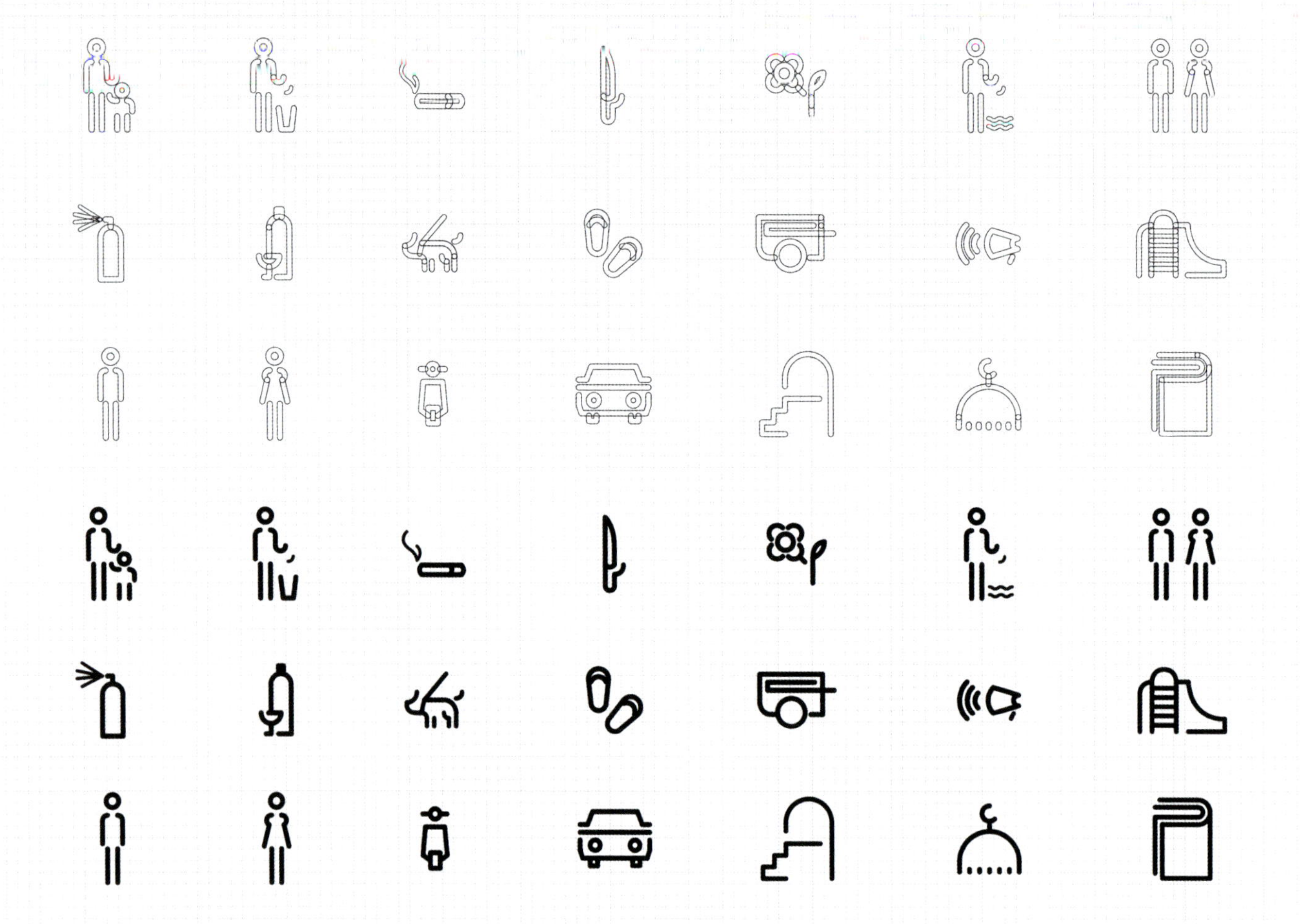

ALUN-ALUN BANDUNG
WAYFINDING SIGNAGE SYSTEM

Design: Eggy Surachman — **Agency:** Nusae Design

The Mayor of Bandung, Ridwan Kamil, contacted Nusae Design to design new wayfinding signage for Alun-Alun Kota Bandung. Bandung is known as a friendly city in its society, and Alun-Alun Bandung is a popular park located in the city center where people gather to socialize and children go to play. The main idea behind the design was to clearly convey information but keep things fun. Strict signage was transformed with dynamic placing and rounded pictograms on red backgrounds that can easily grab visitors' attention. The new pictograms will also work with existing signage to encourage park visitors to exercise discipline in protecting the park's environment.

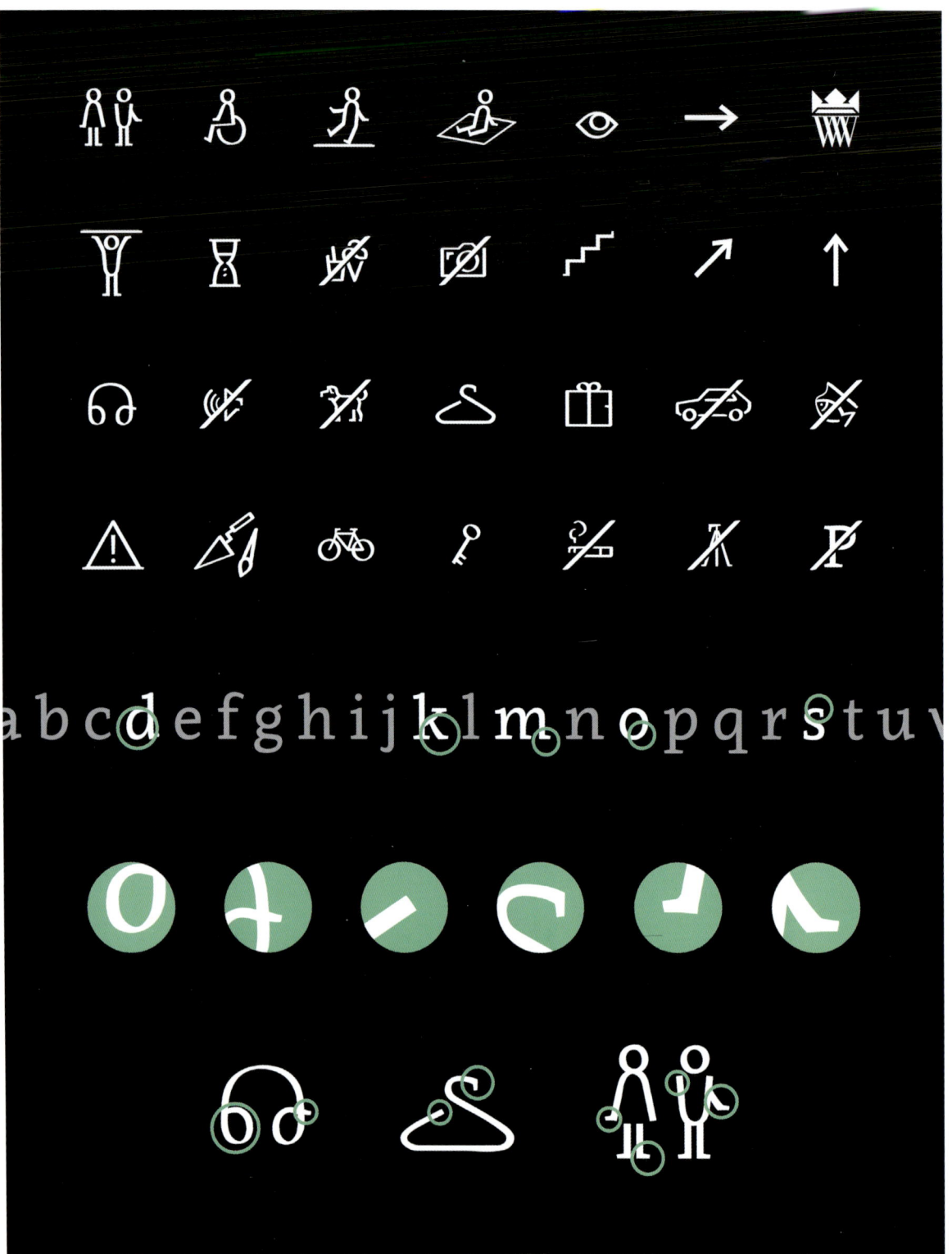

WAYFINDING AND VISUAL IDENTITY IN WILANÓW

Design: Wojciech Staniewski, Maciej Bączkowski, Karolina Mazurkiewicz
Agency: Studio 2X2

The task was to design a signage scheme for the palace, park, and surrounding area of the Museum of King Jan III's Palace at Wilanów. In order to clarify the visual information system of the museum, which must reflect a multitude of forms, epochs, styles, and hues, the designers limited the range of colors of a minimum. The designers built a set of pictograms for use on signs and printed collateral based on the structural elements of the Clavo typeface.

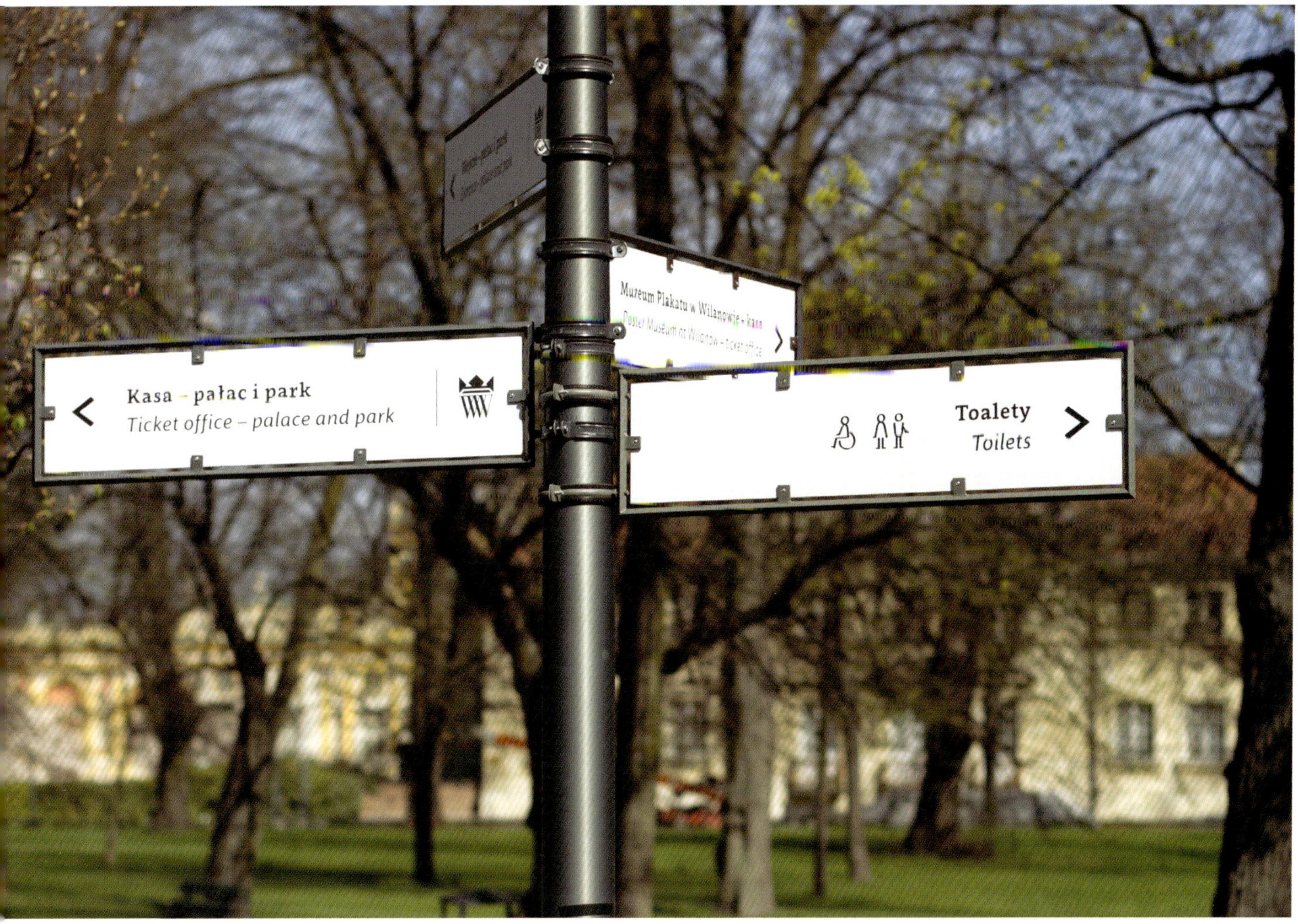
Kasa – pałac i park
Ticket office – palace and park
Toalety
Toilets

audioprzewodnik
audioguide
sklep
bookshop

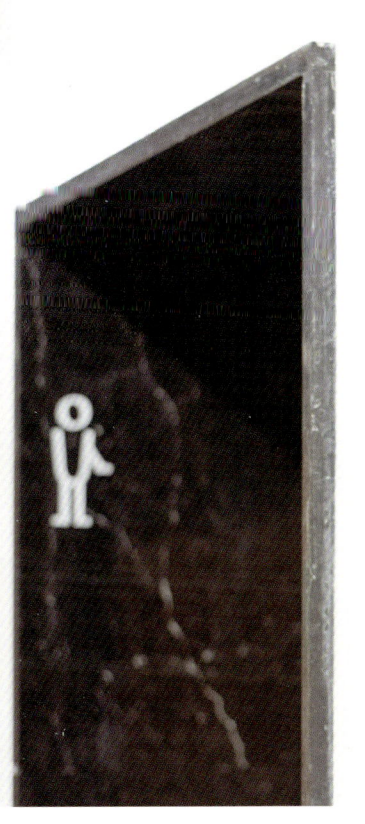

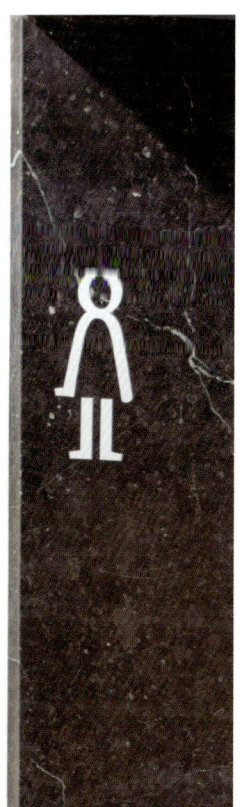

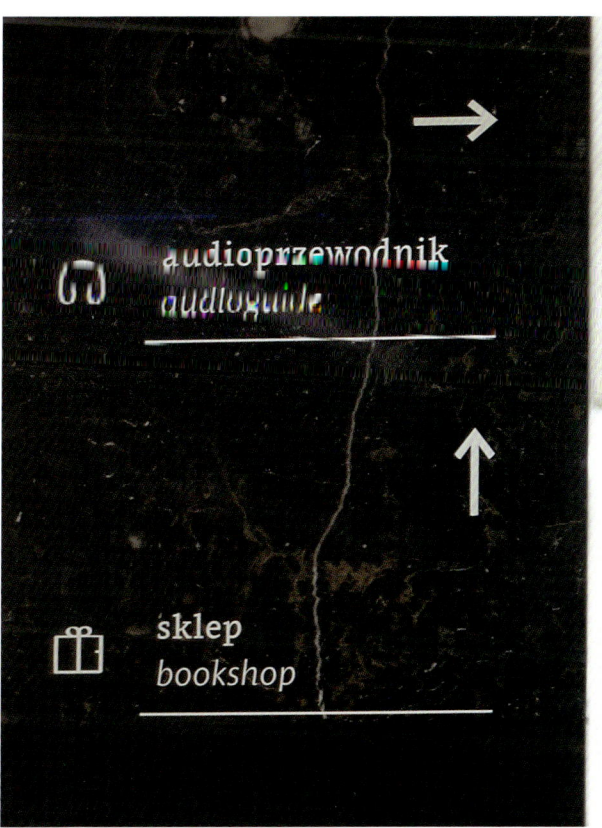

EL BORN CC

Design: Forma & Co

A special graphic system was designed for the center's wayfinding program. The designers generated a library of over fifty pictograms, created from modules extracted from the design of the custom typeface made for the visual identity of El Born CC. The pictograms had to be iconic signs that transmitted their meaning clearly and simply, and in the most universal way possible. The square backing the pictograms are displayed on was produced with the same material that is used throughout the center, a gray laminate called "Trespa." This helps integrate them seamlessly into the space. The icons themselves were rendered in white lacquered aluminum, boosting the visual contrast and providing the texture contrast that allows them to be read via touch by people with visual impairment.

ÀFORAMENT
MÀXIM:

2278
PERSONES

5 BALCONADA
BALCONES
WALKWAYS
LES PLATES-FORMES
PLATTFORM

ALTIUM CLOUD READER

Design: Artua Design Studio

Altium, a huge software developer, decided to introduce Cloud Rider – a new brand for the Chinese market. One of the first products under this brand would be a smart house mobile app.

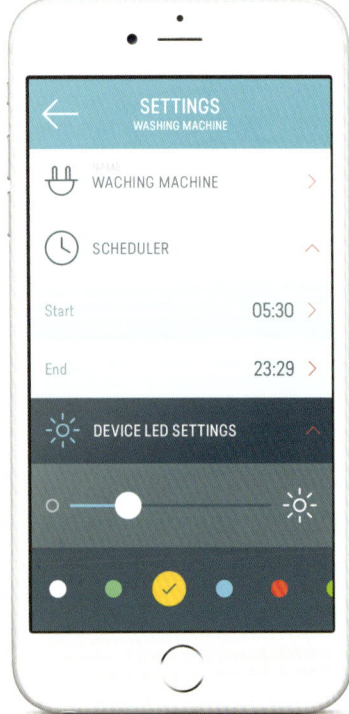

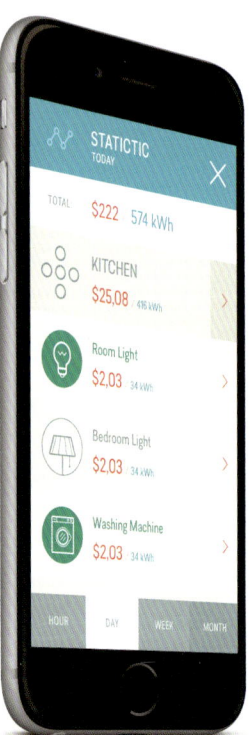

TRAVEL BLOG

Design: Olga Uzhikova

The Travel Blog project was the first website that Olga created. She created a sweet carton image – Kangaroo Lili – as the blog's main character. By "following" Kangaroo Lili around the blog, the user can visit beautiful places from all over the world. The designer also created a set of travel line icons specifically for this site. These icons became an important part of the site and help to illustrate statistics about her travels.

Statistics of my travels

515 325 *km*   38 655 *km*   21 588 *km*

151 *sities*   9 *bags*   41 900 *photos*

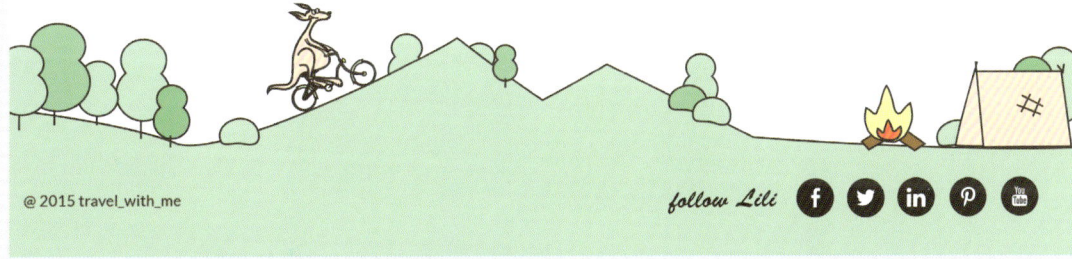

@ 2015 travel_with_me

follow Lili

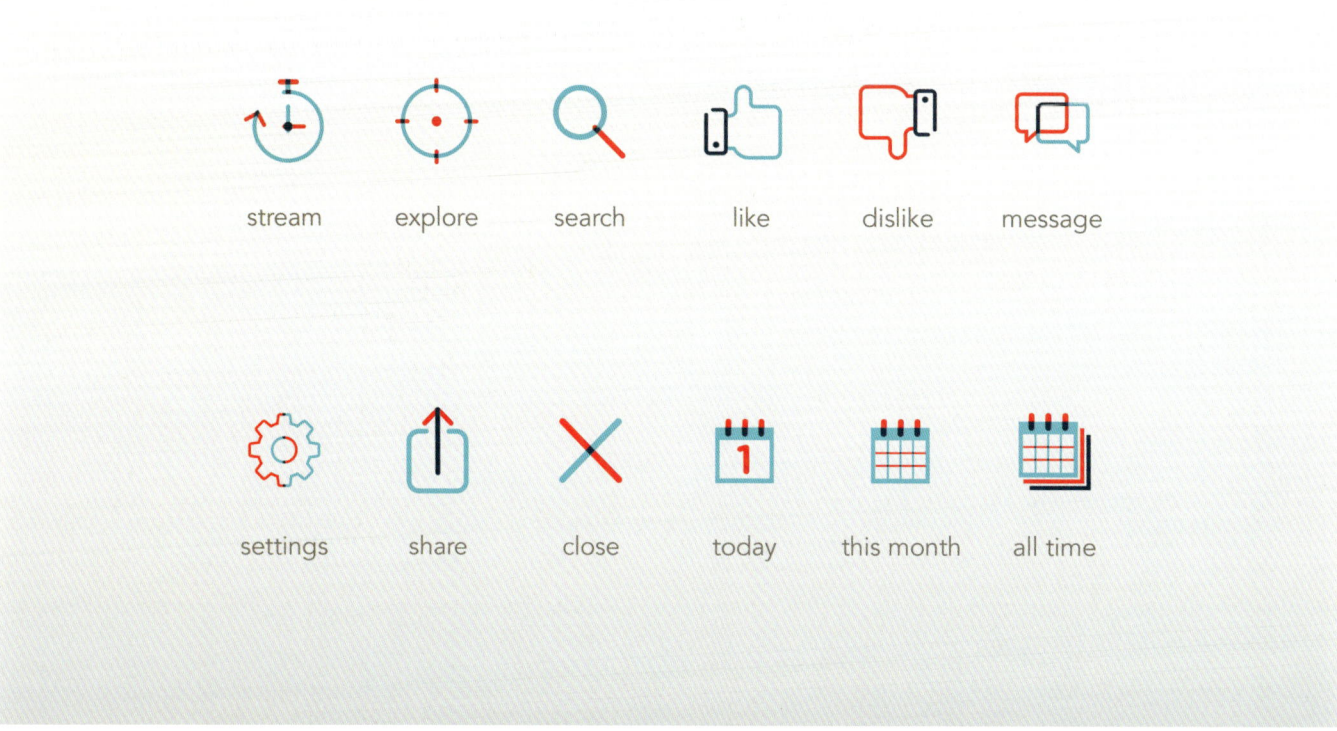

stream   explore   search   like   dislike   message

settings   share   close   today   this month   all time

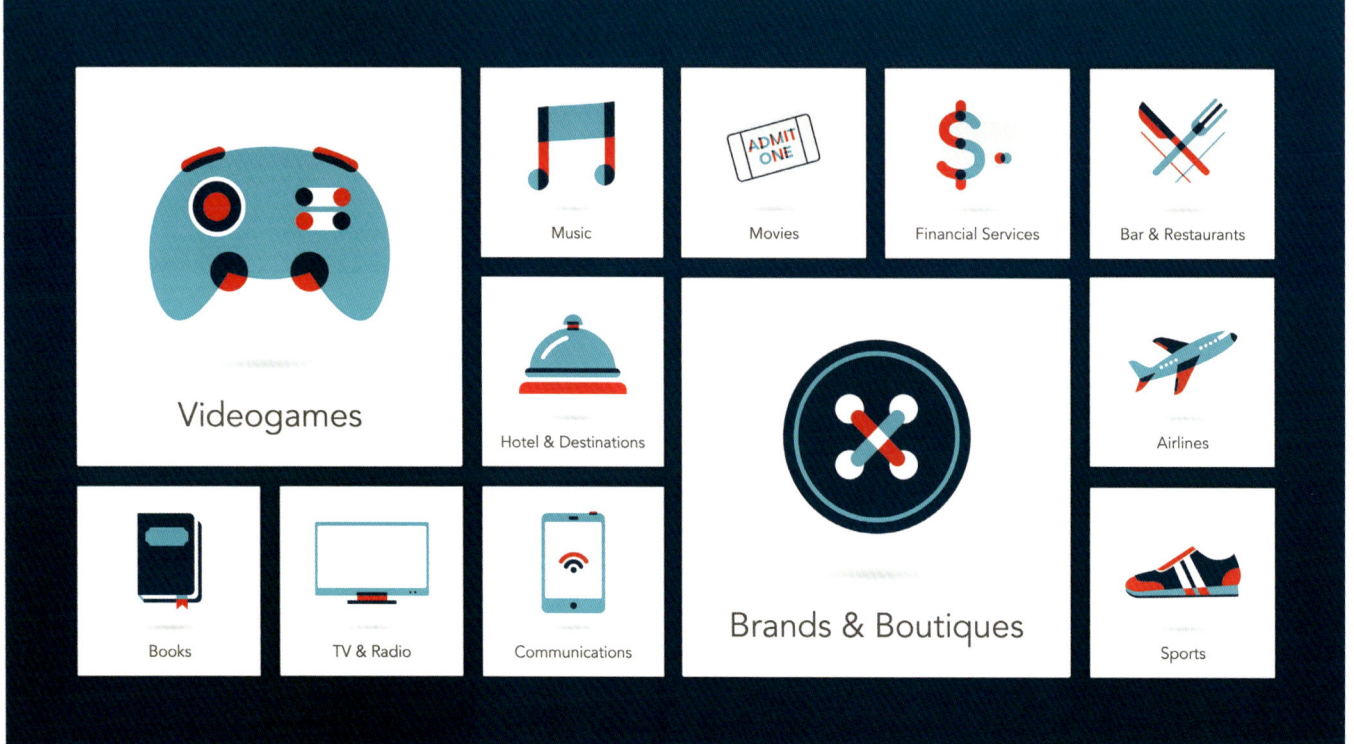

Videogames

Music

Movies

Financial Services

Bar & Restaurants

Hotel & Destinations

Airlines

Brands & Boutiques

Books

TV & Radio

Communications

Sports

RATER

Design: Gabriel Tinoco, Nora Muñoz —— **Agency:** Cherry Bomb Design Studio

Rater is a new platform for consumers to share shopping experiences on which allows them to rate different products and services, like the new album by their favorite band, a new book you just bought, or that restaurant everyone talks about. With Rater, consumers can help each other make better choices and become a sweet lover, a bad boy, or even a brand-kicking hater.

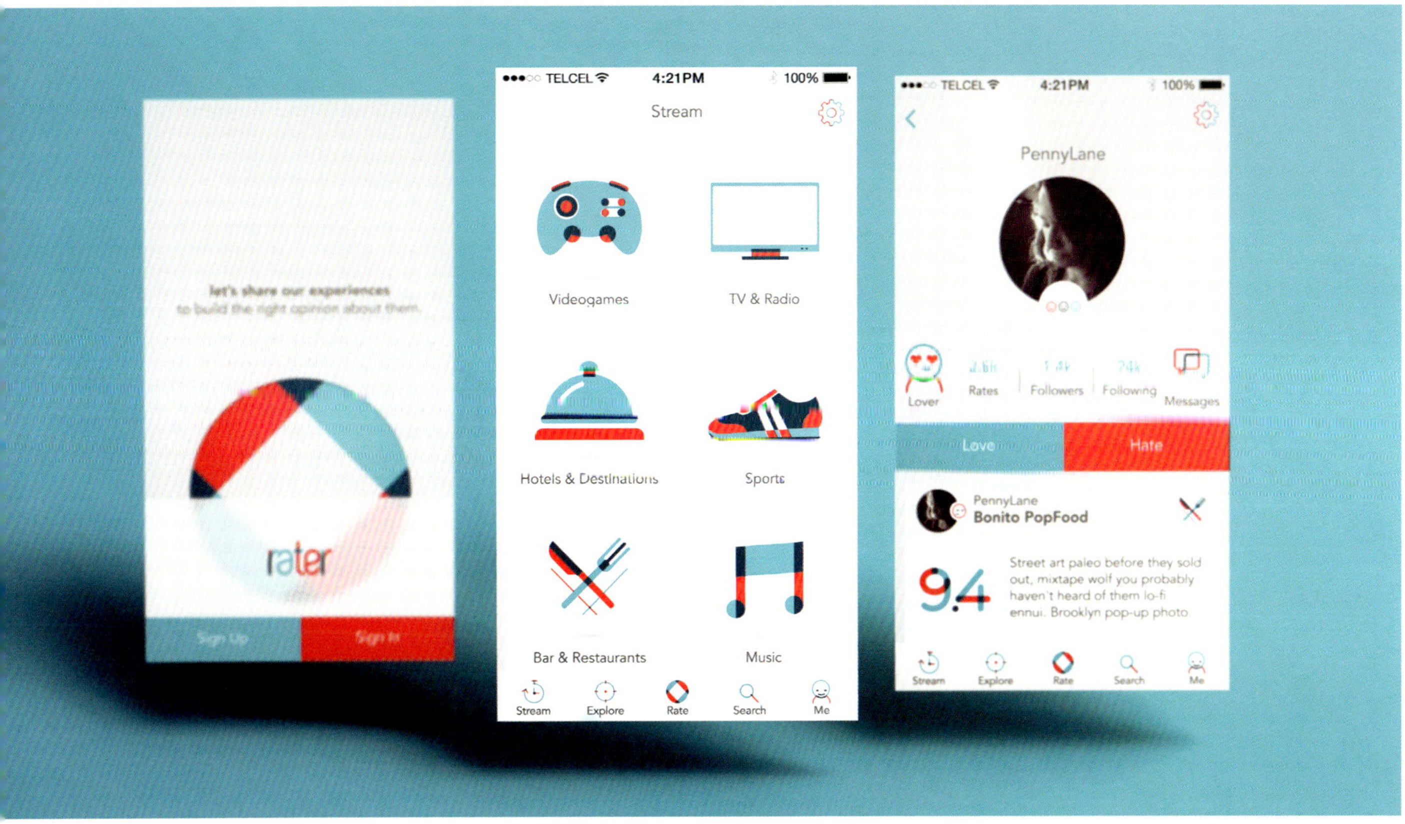
rater
TELCEL
4:21PM
100%
Stream
Videogames
TV & Radio
Hotels & Destinations
Sports
Bar & Restaurants
Music
Stream
Explore
Rate
Search
Me
PennyLane
Lover
Rates
Followers
Following
Messages
Love
Hate
PennyLane
Bonito PopFood
9.4
Street art paleo before they sold out, mixtape wolf you probably haven't heard of them lo-fi ennui. Brooklyn pop-up photo

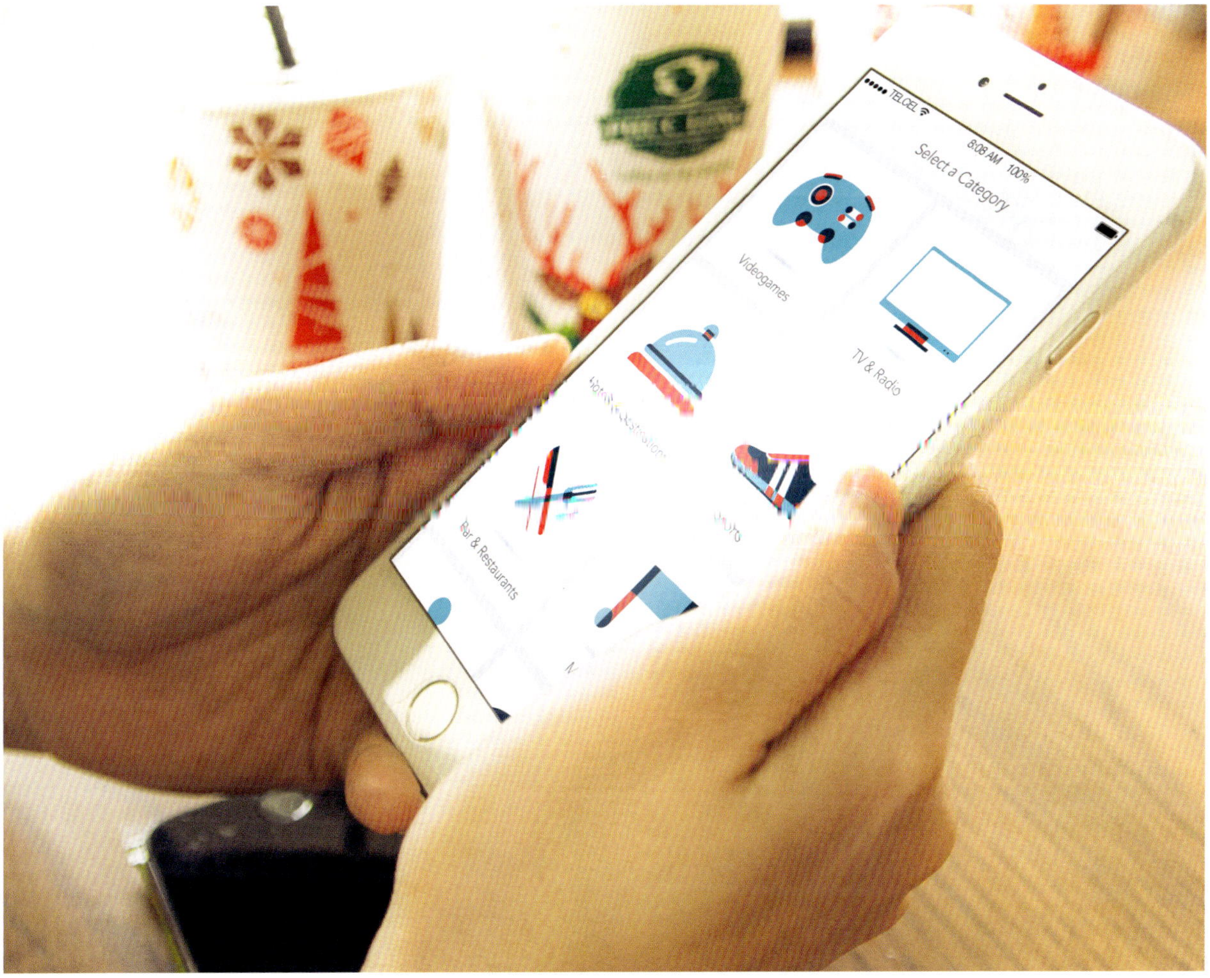
TELCEL
8:08 AM
100%
Select a Category
Videogames
TV & Radio
Bar & Restaurants

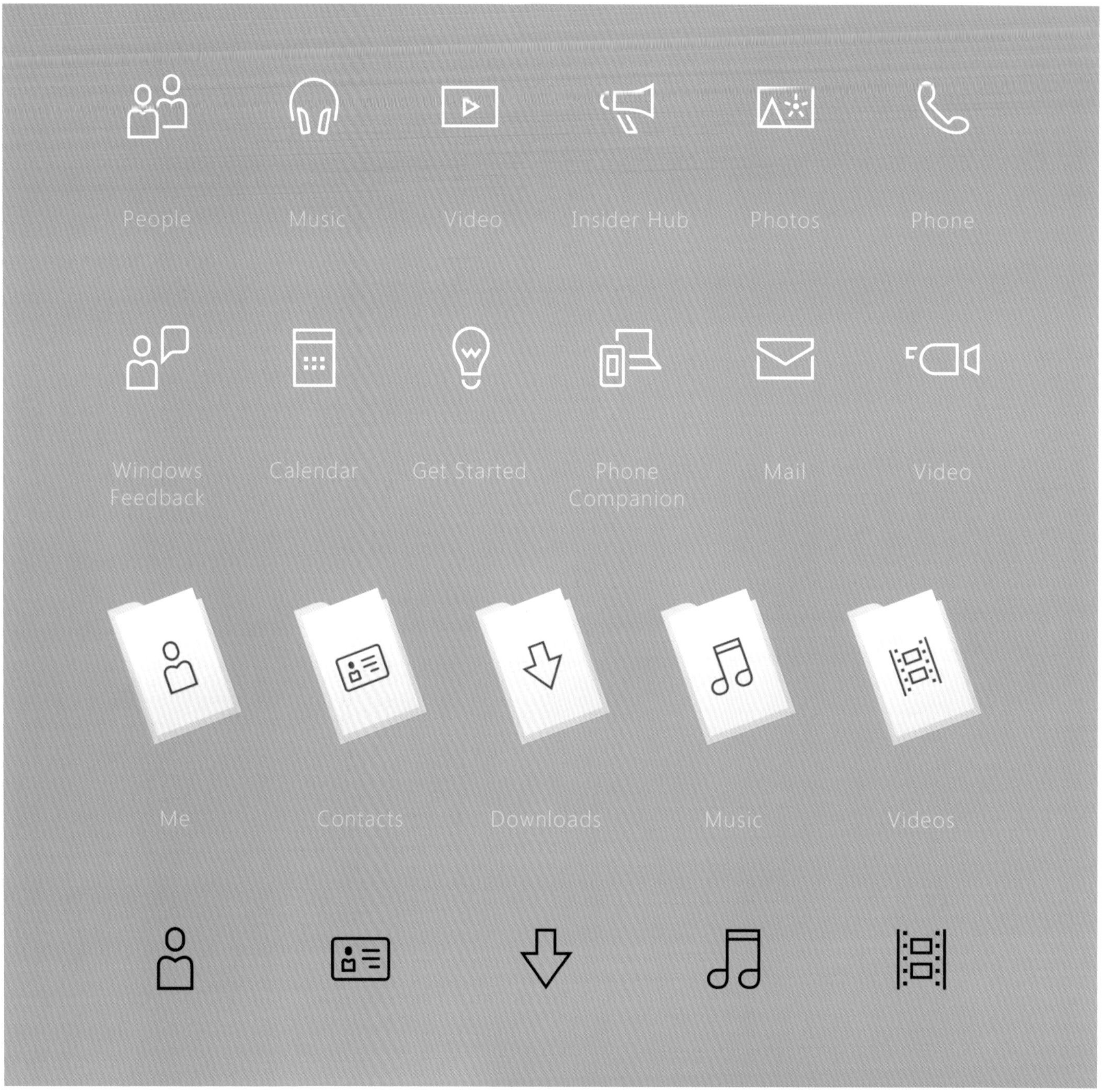

People
Music
Video
Insider Hub
Photos
Phone
Windows Feedback
Calendar
Get Started
Phone Companion
Mail
Video
Me
Contacts
Downloads
Music
Videos

WINDOWS 10 ICONS – REDESIGN CONCEPT – BASED ON SEGOE UI FONT

Design: Kazuya Horikirikawa

Japanese designer Kazuya Horikirikawa created the concept design for icons used in Windows 10 to better match the Windows 10 system fonts. The icon design was inspired by visual factors used for Windows' fonts, like the aspect ratio, curves, and angles of the fonts.

BCO
Font : Segoe UI
BCO

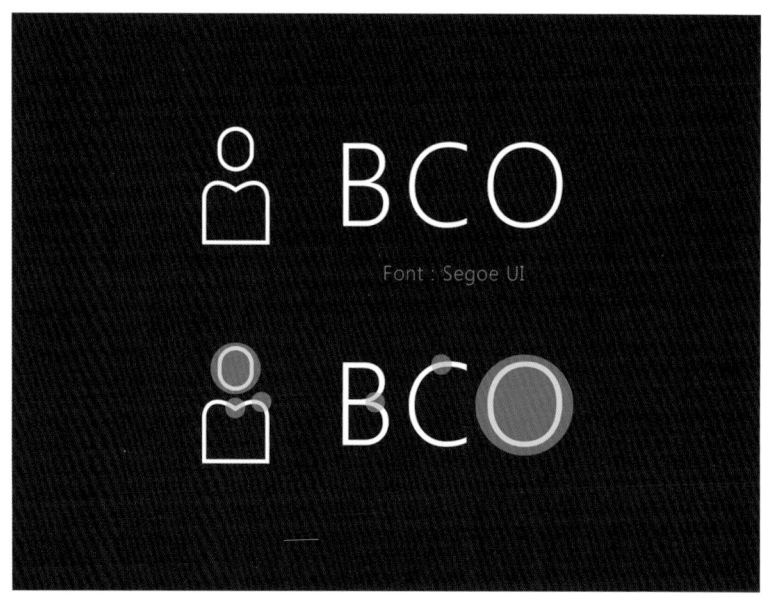

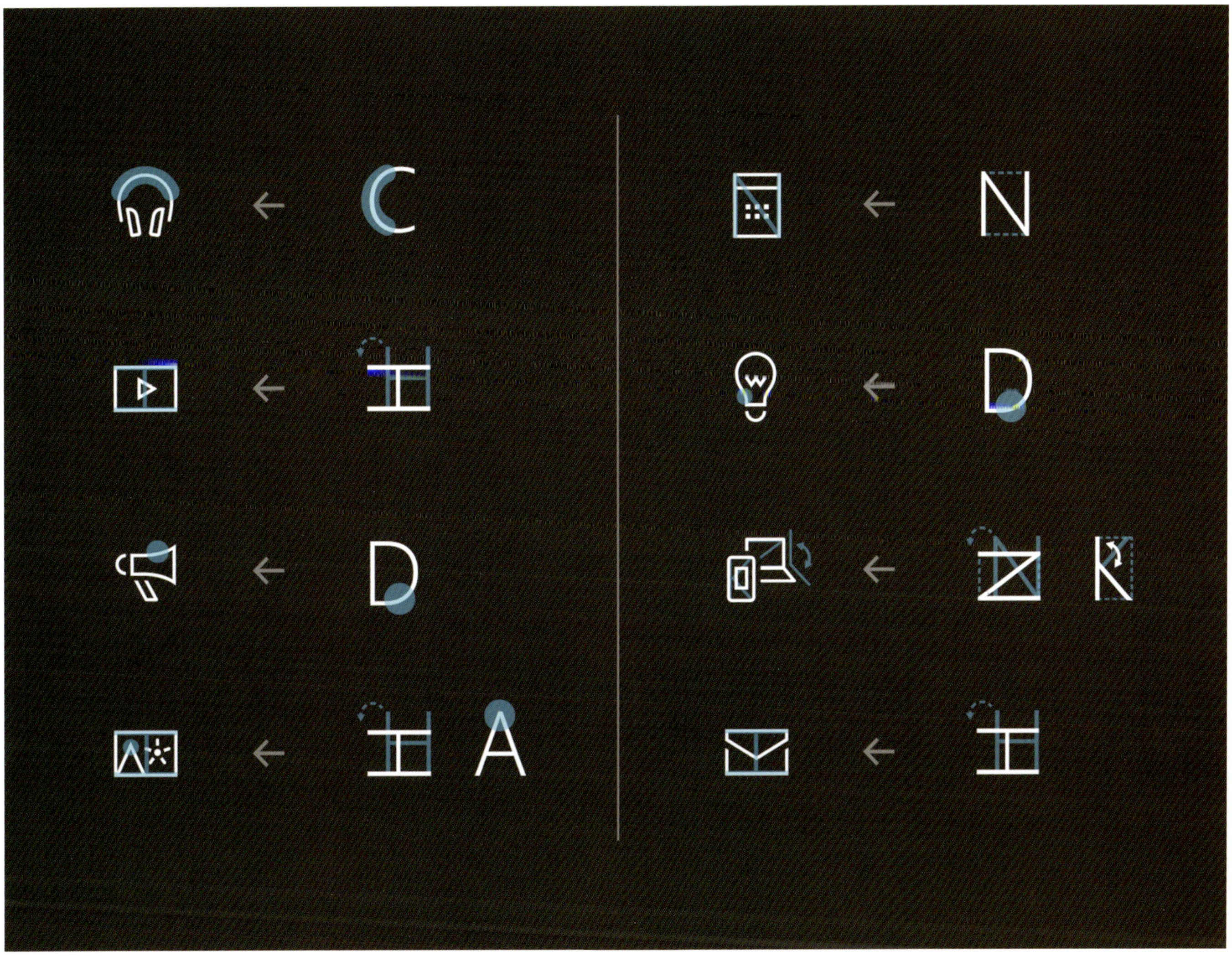
C
N
D
D
A

Start
Tue 12:43
Windows Feedback
Contacts
Phone Companion
Music
Travel
Insider Hub
Favorite Songs
Windows 10 Redesign

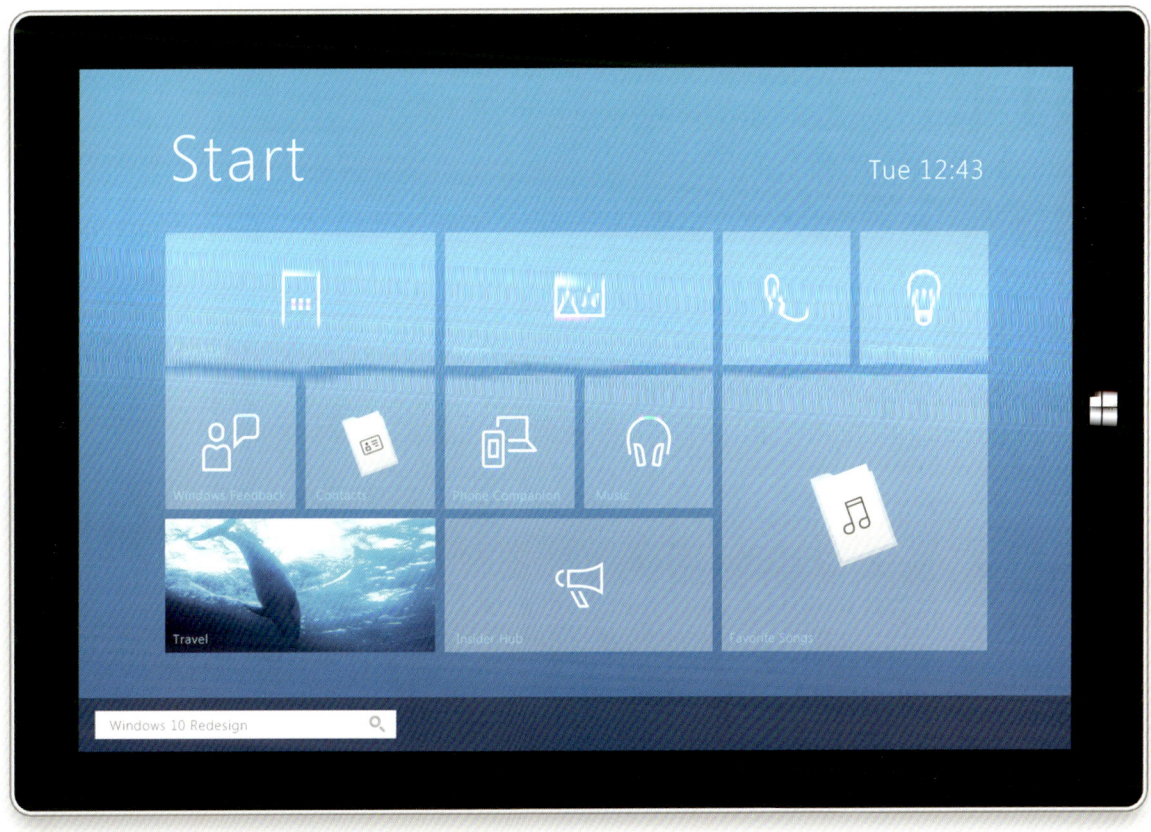

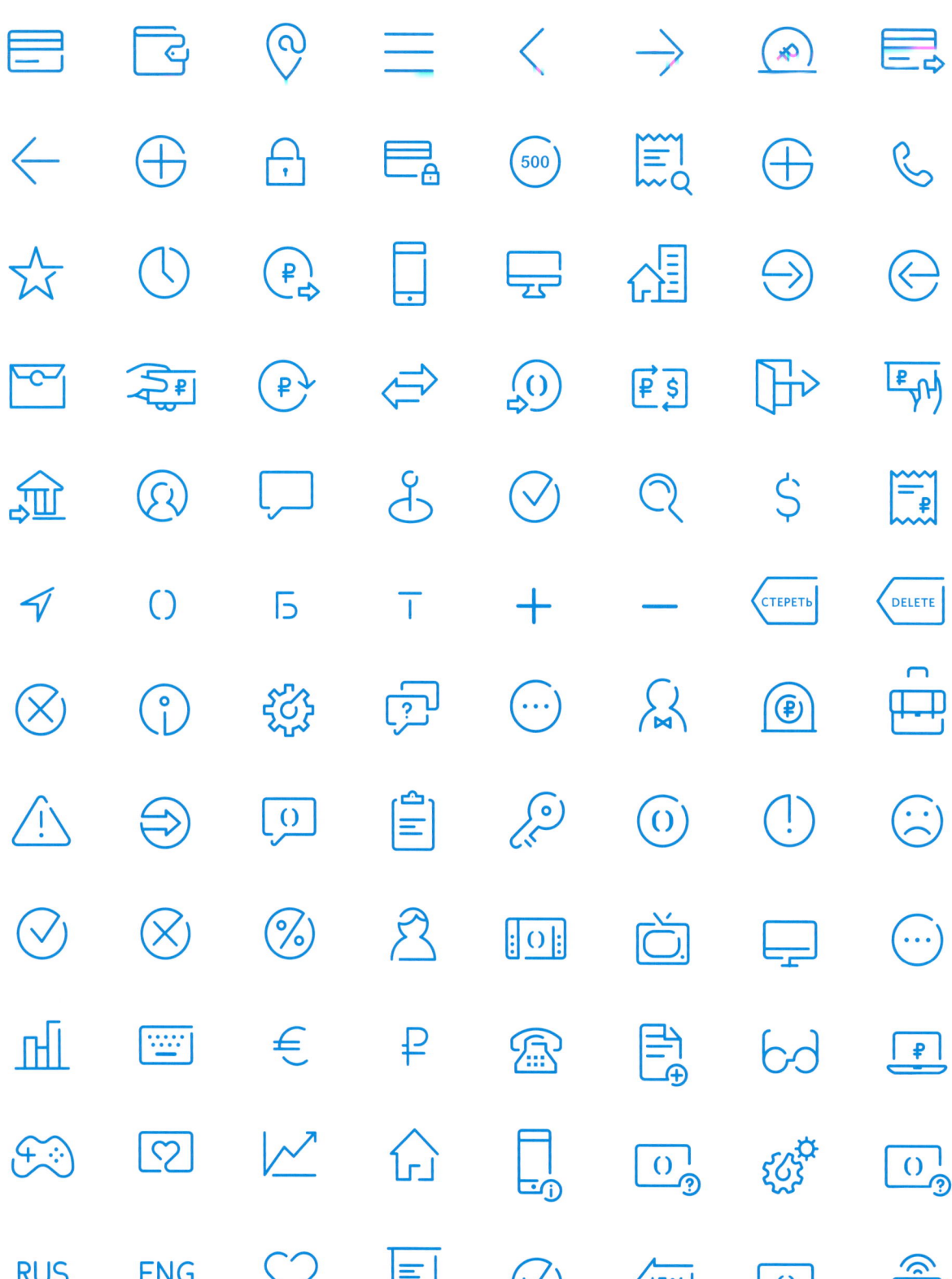

OTKRITIE BANK

Design: Sergey Galtsev —— **Direction:** Max Desyatykh, Andrey Lisitsyn
Agency: Redmadrobot

Online and offline iconography for Otkritie Bank. The iconography includes branch navigational signage and digital interfaces for their mobile app, website, and ATMs.

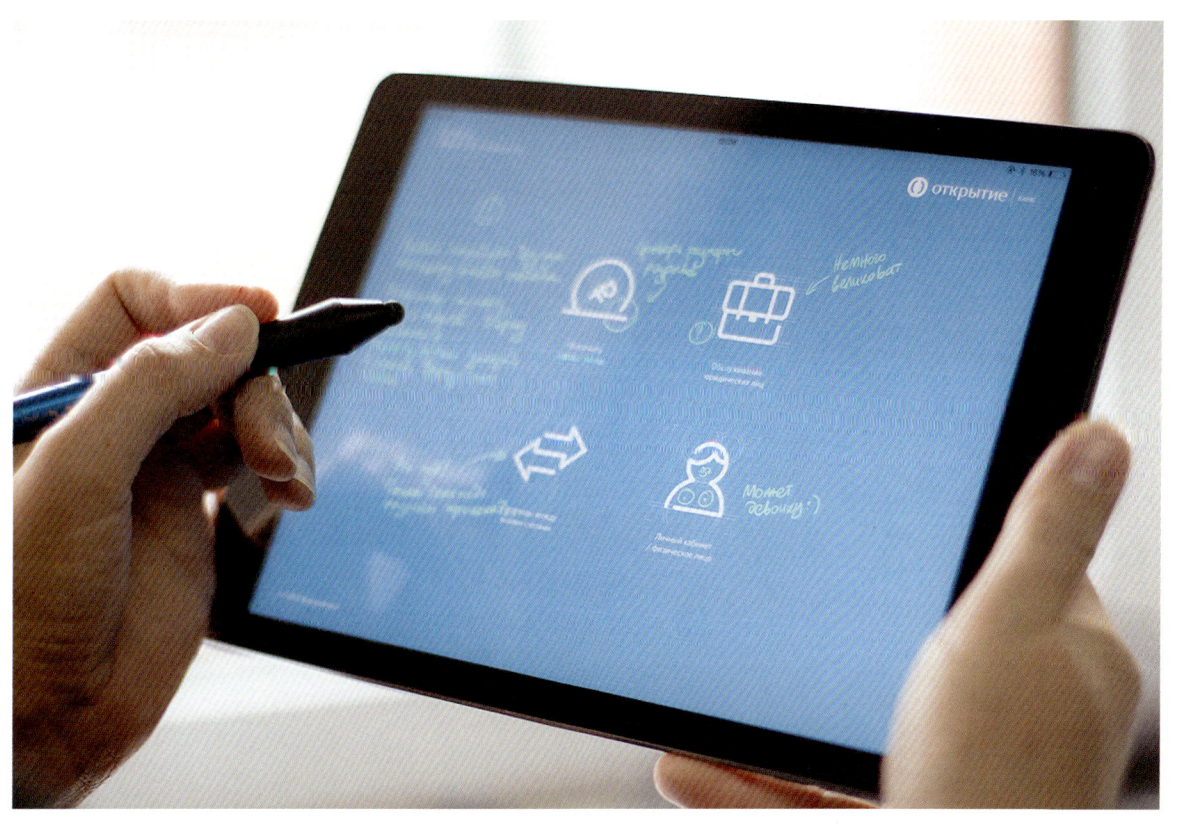

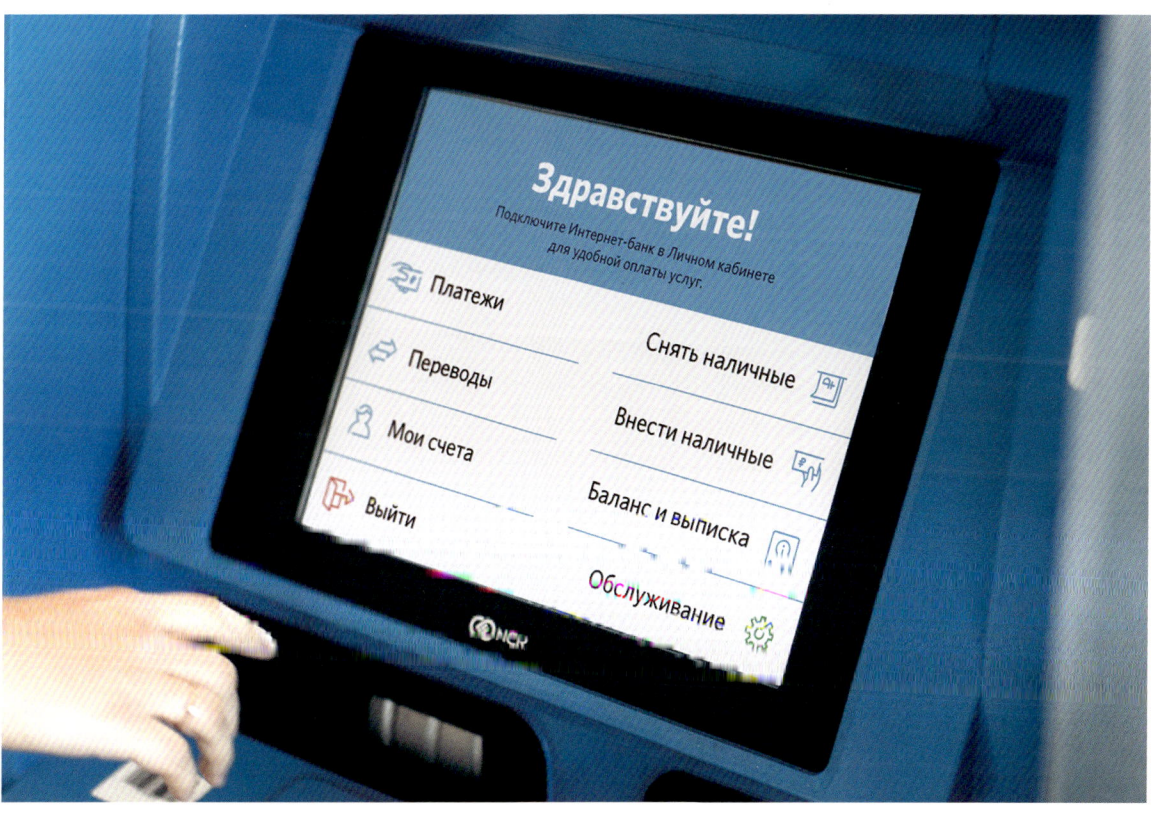

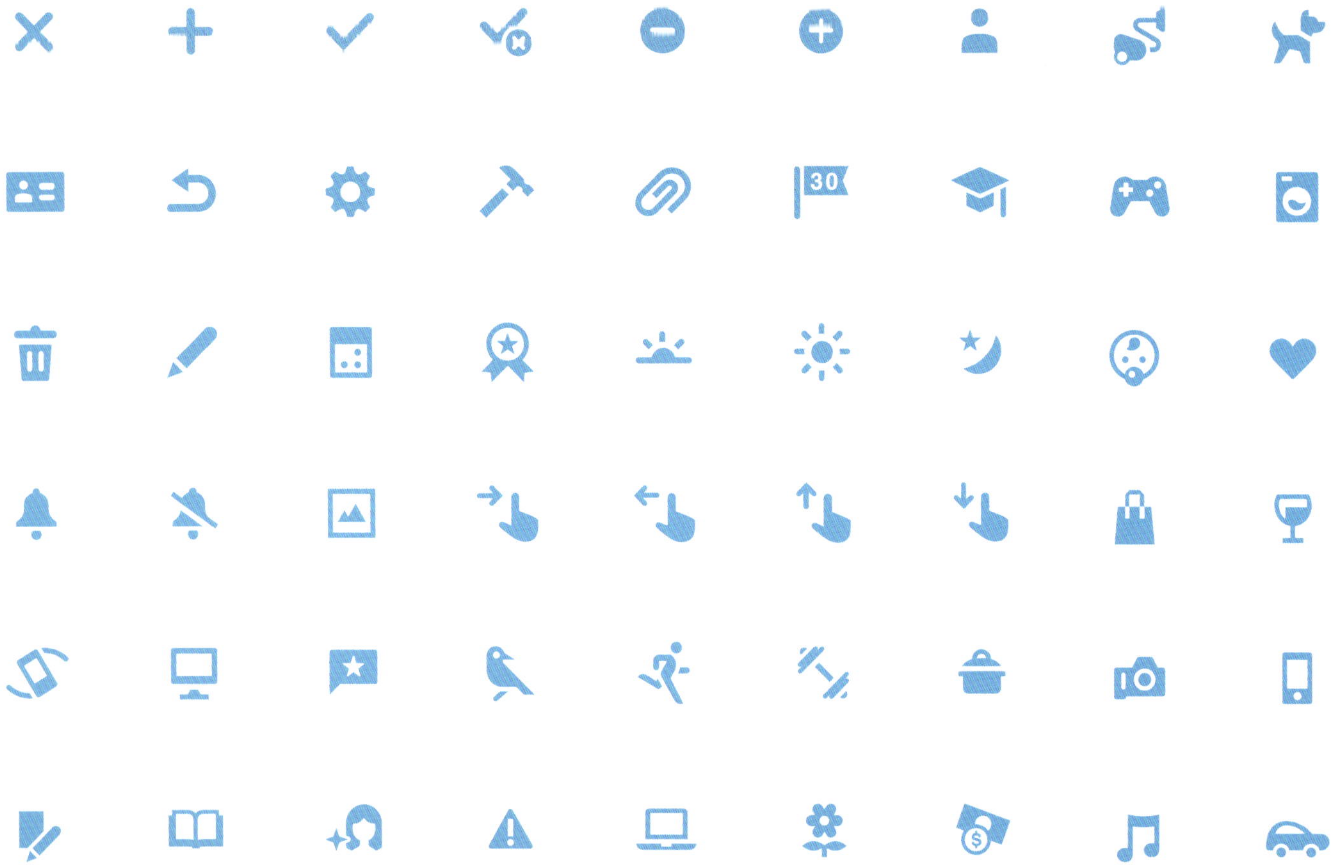

GRAMI

Design: Kazuya Horikirikawa

Grami is an iOS app that helps you build good habits. The UI design of this app places a balanced emphasis on simplicity and comfort. Japanese designer Kazuya Horikirikawa planned, designed, and coded Grami.

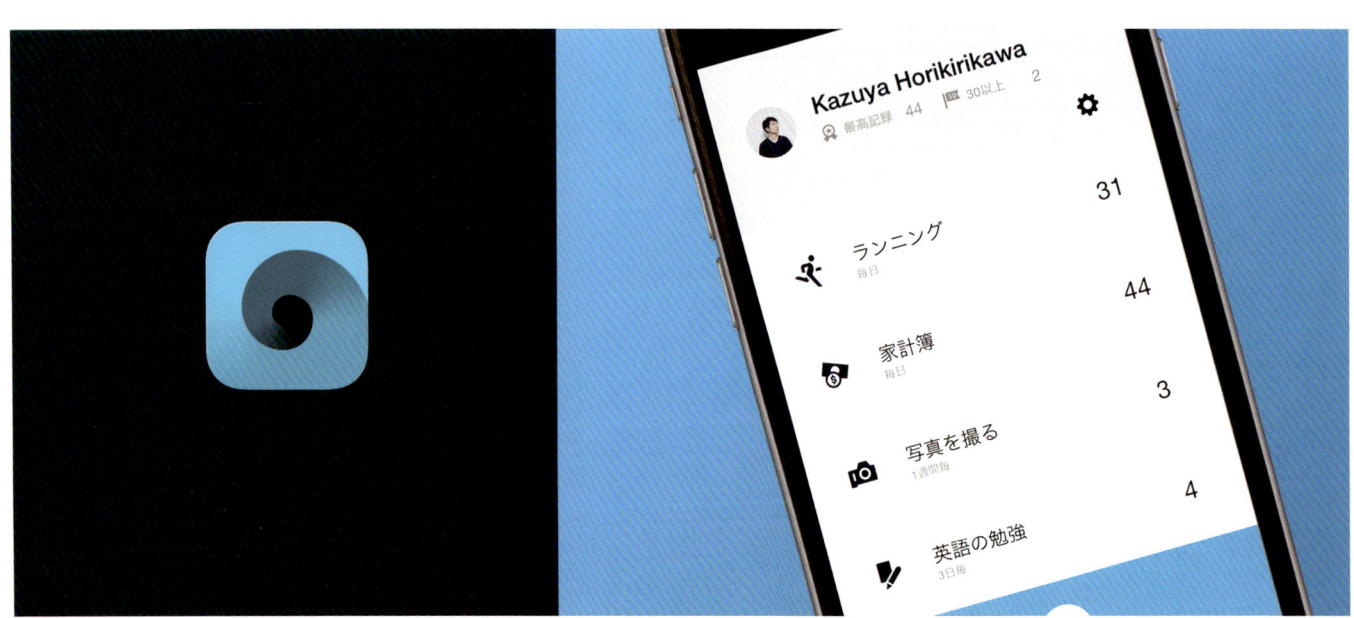

WEATHER APP

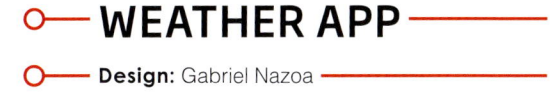

Design: Gabriel Nazoa

The designer tried to create a new aesthetic reinterpretation of the classic weather icons with a simple navigation system that allows you to chose between the city, the day, and the time of day simultaneously. The designer reduced the elements of weather to their most simplistic expressions: yellow or blue circles and blue and yellow lines.

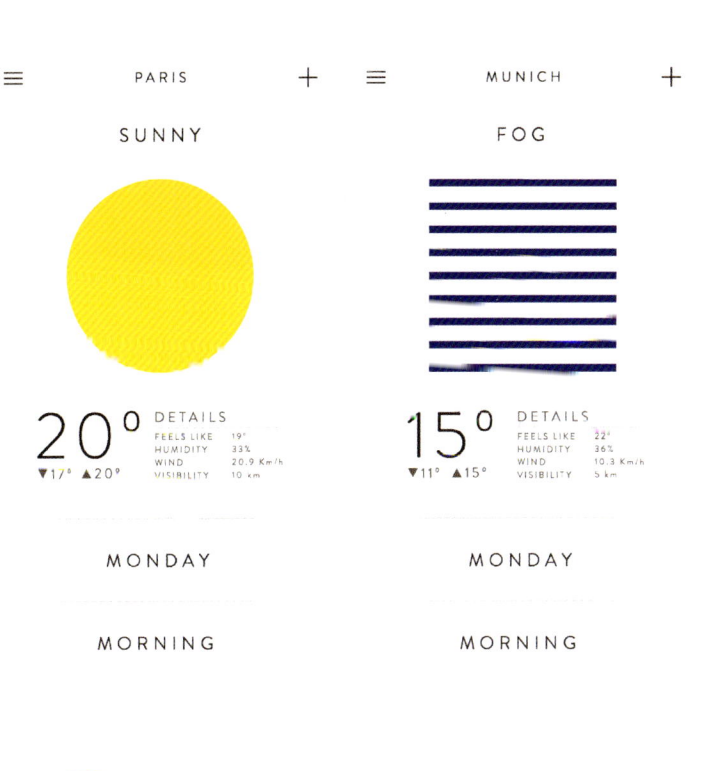

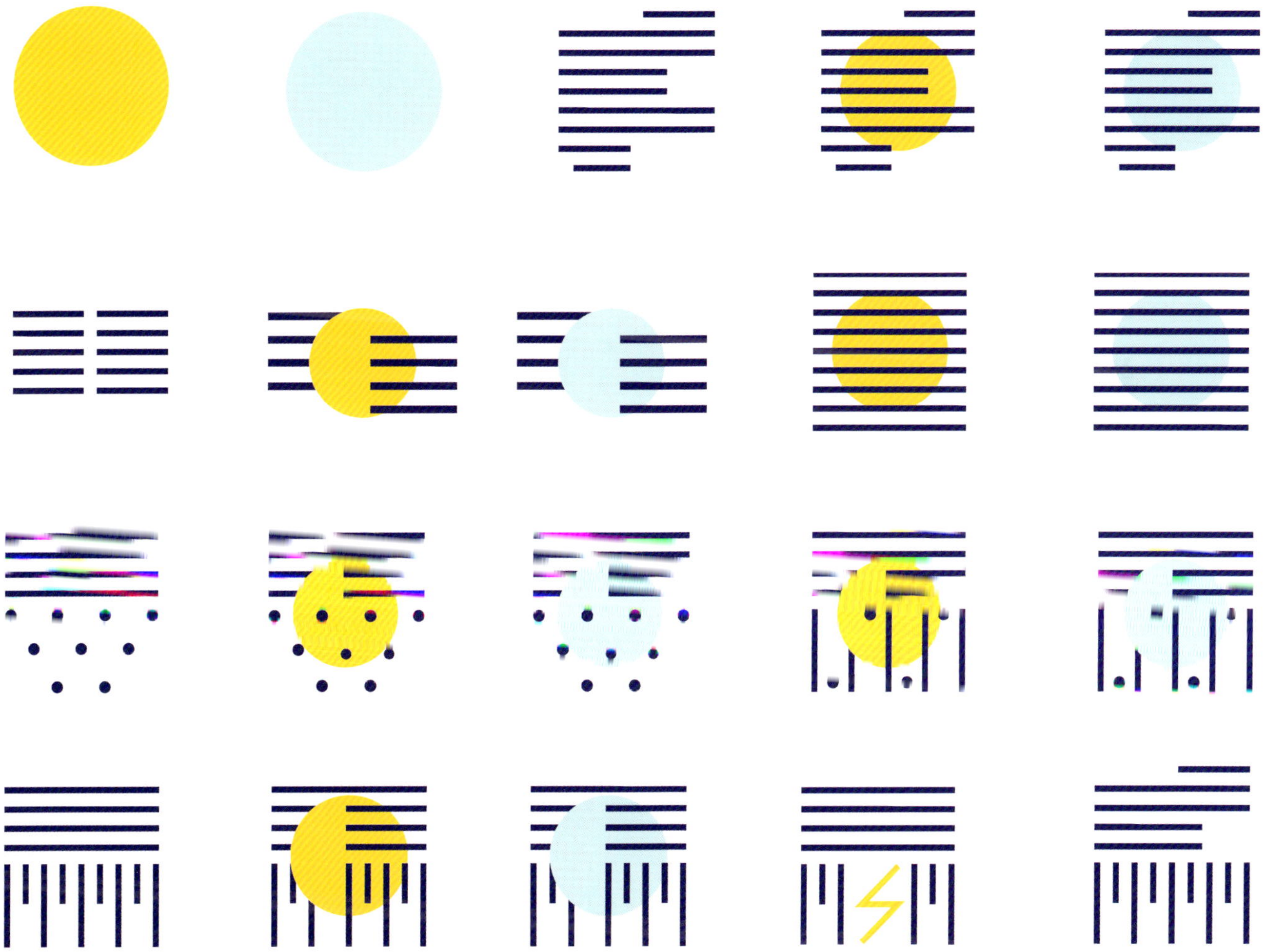

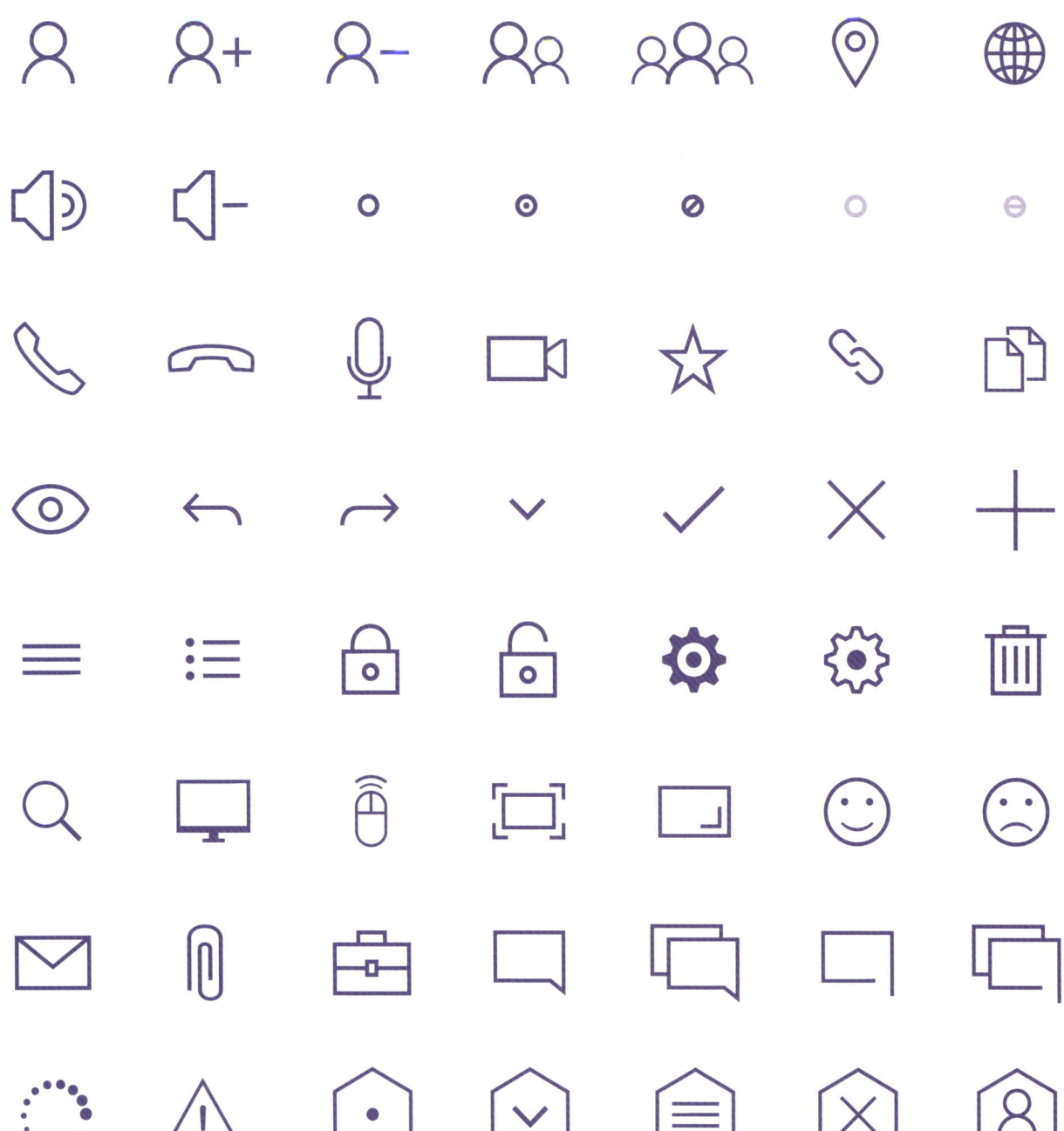

Designed by Bosnian designer Adi Dizdarević, WYNC is an Internet VoIP / video and chat desktop application for Linux Ubuntu OS.

Options

Check for updates

License

Support

About Wync

Email

Username

Password

LOGIN ☐ Remember password

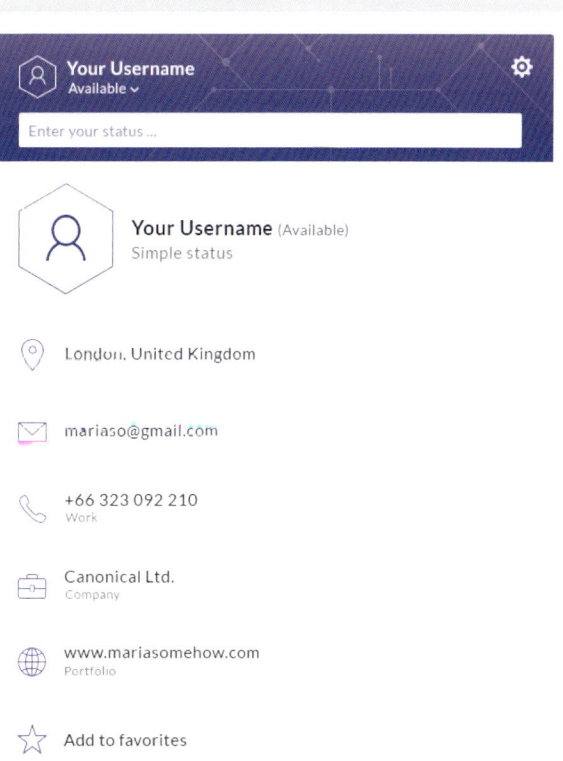

Your Username
Available ⌄

Enter your status ...

Your Username (Available)
Simple status

London, United Kingdom

mariaso@gmail.com

+66 323 092 210
Work

Canonical Ltd.
Company

www.mariasomehow.com
Portfolio

Add to favorites

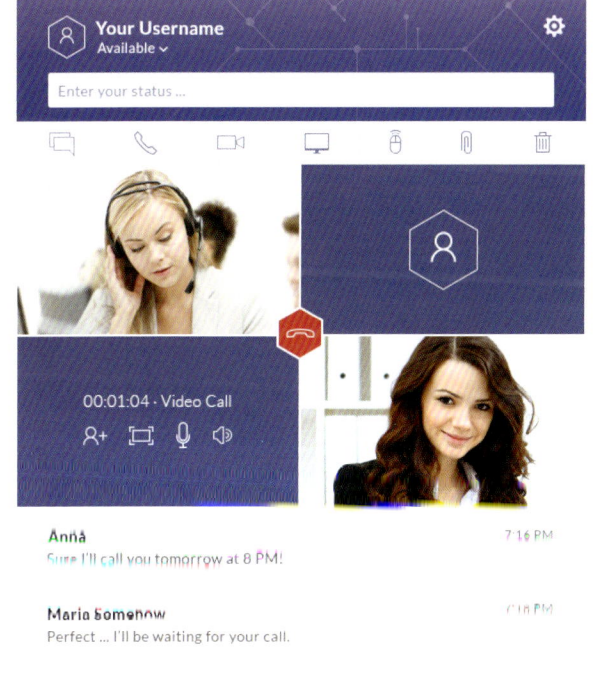

Your Username
Available ⌄

Enter your status ...

00:01:04 · Video Call

Anna 7:16 PM
Sure I'll call you tomorrow at 8 PM!

Maria Somehow 6:16 PM
Perfect ... I'll be waiting for your call.

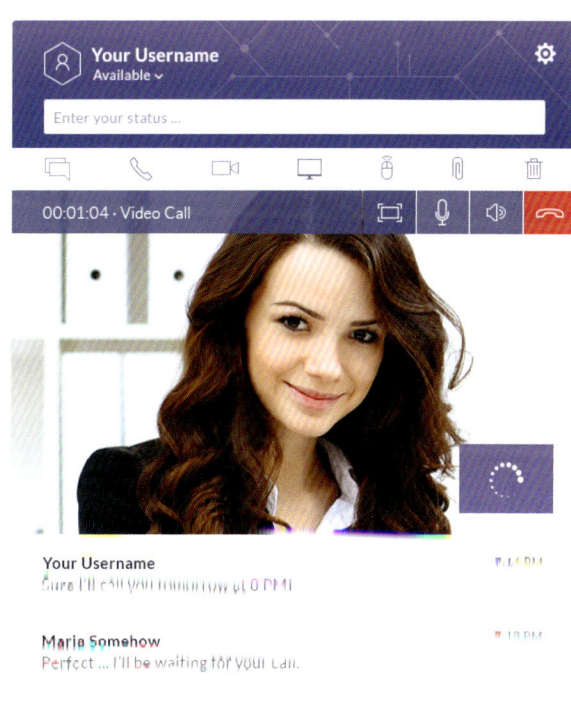

Your Username
Available ⌄

Enter your status ...

00:01:04 · Video Call

Your Username 7:16 PM
Sure I'll call you tomorrow at 8 PM!

Maria Somehow 6:16 PM
Perfect ... I'll be waiting for your call.

Be aware of a
WET UMBRELLA

Do not **HOLD**
subway **DOORS**

Do not **CARRY**
HUGE ITEMS

Do not **LEAN ON**
OR HUG the pole

Take off your
BACKPACK

Do not **BLOCK**
subway doors

Do not **SPEAK**
on the **PHONE**

Do not
SPREAD legs

Do not **BRING**
your **BIKE**

Do not
LITTER

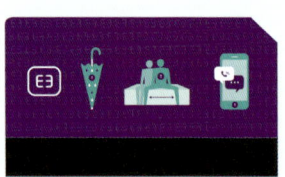

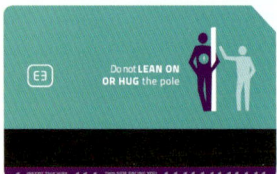

EE: EVERYDAY ETIQUETTE

Design: Jihye Um

The Everyday Etiquette (EE) app is a smartphone prototype game that people can play with their Facebook friends or phone contacts. EE encourages people to practice good etiquette on public transportation in simple, humorous, and interactive ways. Users receive scores by adding icons gained by following one of the ten basic principles of good etiquette on the subway. They can then compare ranks against their friends. In addition, anyone who uses the app will have the chance of winning a random free ride on the subway. The application's goal is to help people learn the ten basic principles of subway etiquette, realize how important they are, and be motivated to follow them.

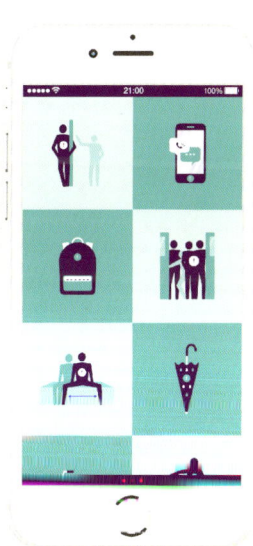
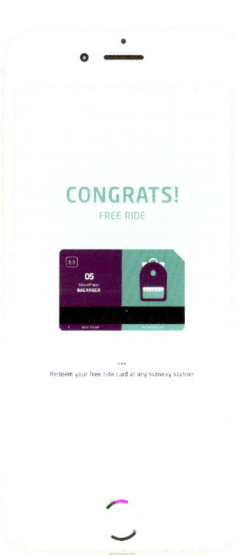

Win a random ride
while browsing icons

THE DESIGNER'S GUIDE TO STARTUP WEEKEND

Design: Iryna Nezhynska

After taking part in two Startup Weekends and numerous hackathons, the designer decided to share her experience with other designers, to explain why they should participate in such events and how to do it in the most effective way. This guide is the designer's contribution to the world of startups, to all people like her and her friends.

You will
FIND NEW FRIENDS,
who breathe the same air you do

It can rescue your project,
if something goes wrong

Forget about the project for 2 hours,
go outside the building and have a break with
YOUR TEAM

YOUR DREAM-TEAM

marketing guru
who knows how to make money from nothing

2 developers
knights of

YOU
master of grids and lord of UX

copywriter
immortal Lorem-ipsum conqueror

OPT-INN WEBSITE

Design: Caio Orio

Opt-Inn facilitates business processes, integrating strategy with creativity. Brazilian graphic designer Caio Orio was commissioned to design their website and identity. The designer created the friendly icons and illustrations, resulting in an identity with modernist influences and a contemporary feel.

B
A

DESKTOP & MOBILE
LAYOUTS
O QUE FAZEMOS?
FACILITAMOS
IMPACTO FOCADAS
NEGÓCIO, INOVAÇÃO
Onde Podemos Ajudar?
ESTRATÉGIA
DE NEGÓCIO
PLANEJAMENTO
ESTRATÉGICO
COMUNICAÇÃO
E PLANEJAMENTO
ALINHAMENTO
DE EQUIPE
NOSSOS
SERVIÇOS

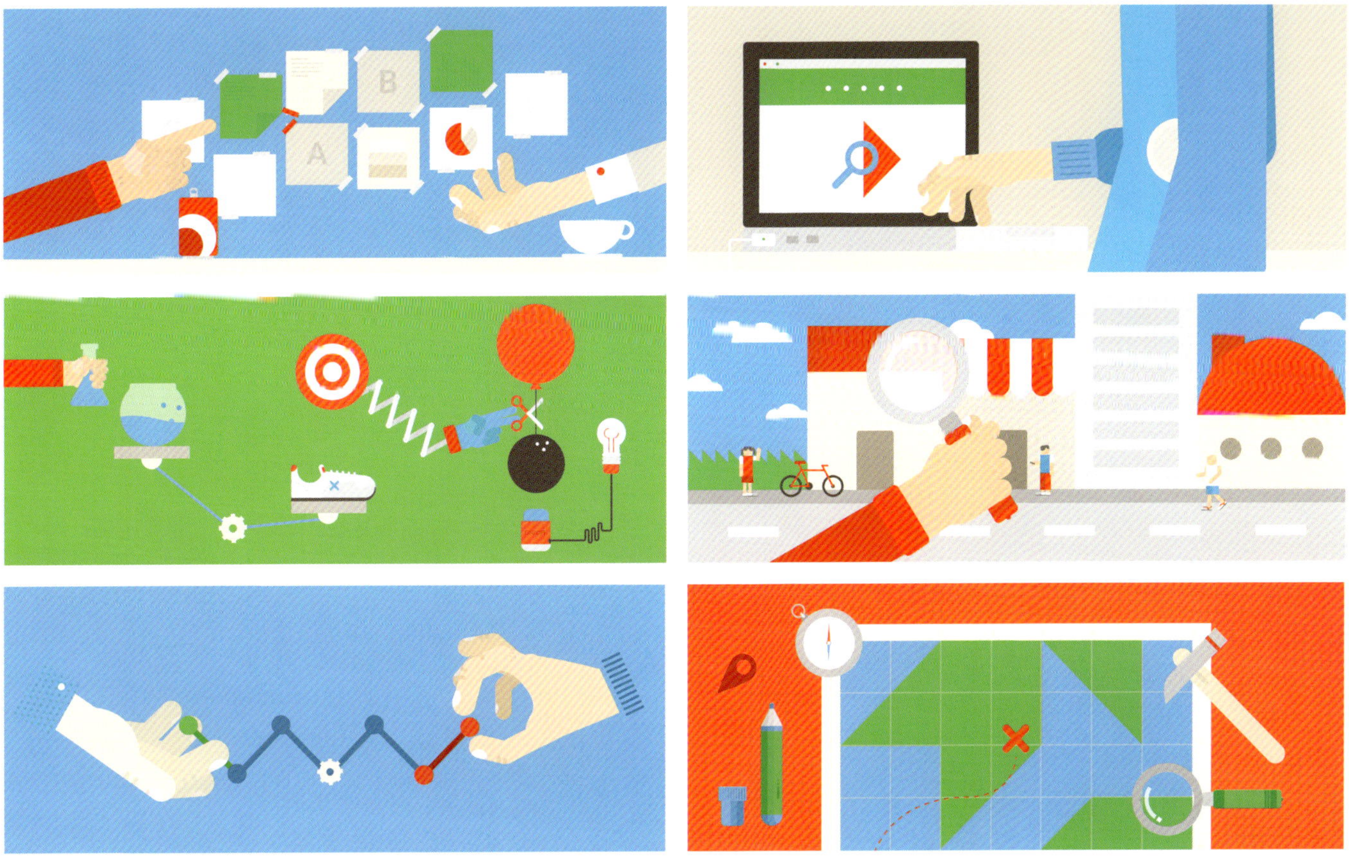

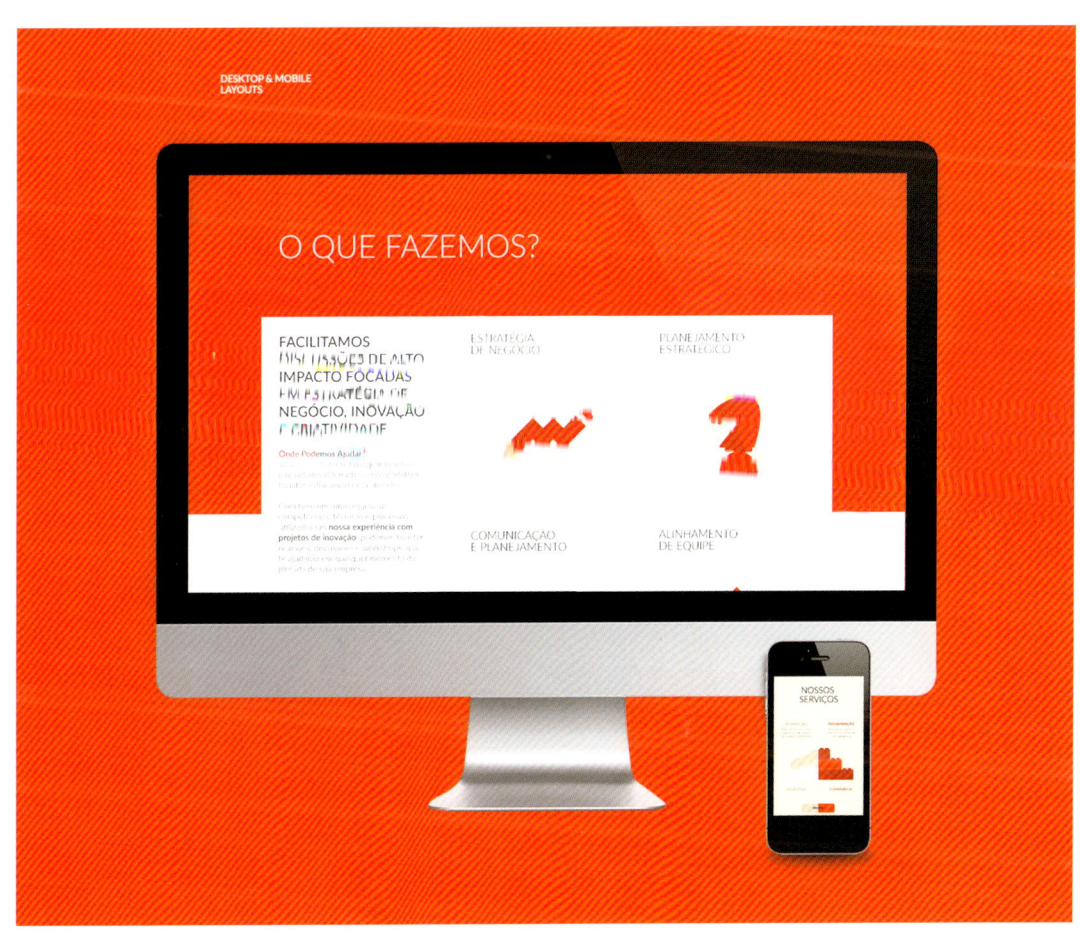

WITHCAM

Icon Design: Jay Lee — **Service Design:** John Lee

Withcam is a conceptual project that allows you to become your own photographer for free. It can help users create special moments with far-away friends.

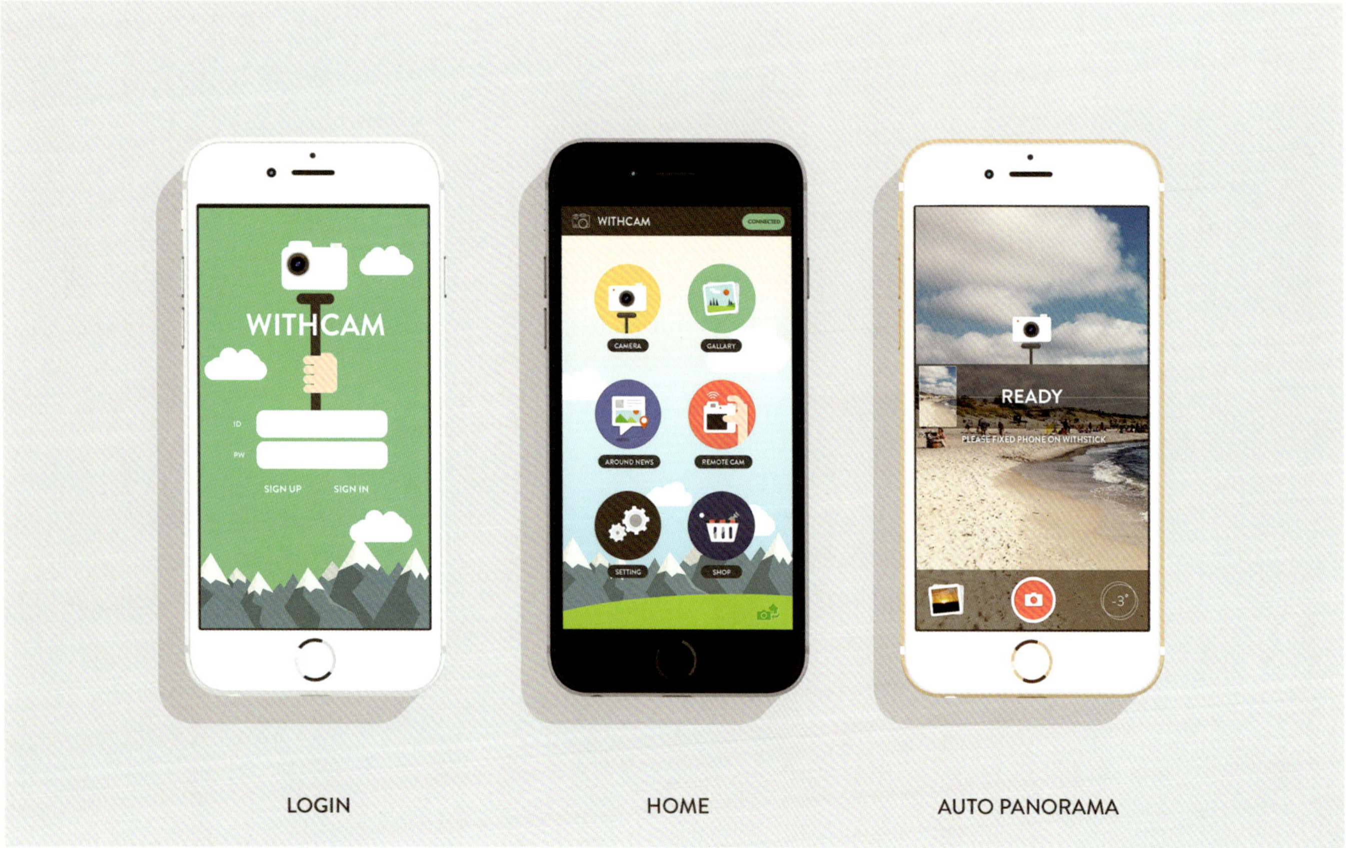

LOGIN   HOME   AUTO PANORAMA

Service Features

Selfie with WITHSTICK

Just press the button on the WITHSTICK,
You can get more better view in selfie.

Auto Panorama

you don't need to turn anymore.
just feel beautiful Scenery

Remoto Shot

If you faraway from your home,
call your friends and familiy!
They can be your photographer.

DAILYMOMENT

Design: Su Young Kang

Dailymoment is an Android lock screen app. The designer wanted to create new ways to show personal schedules. Dailymoment shows the users' time line on their lock screen when they use the app to set their daily schedule. Each icon changes in real time with the passage of time throughout the day and the different event categories.

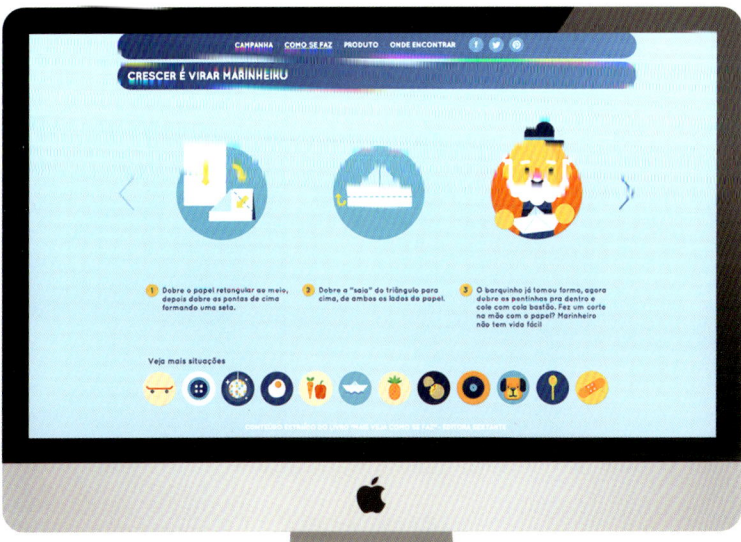

NEBACETIN

Design: Patswerk

For Nebacetin, a Brazilian cream brand, Patswerk designed multiple step-by-step tutorials to show the many different uses of the cream. Every tutorial consists of 4 iconic illustrations.

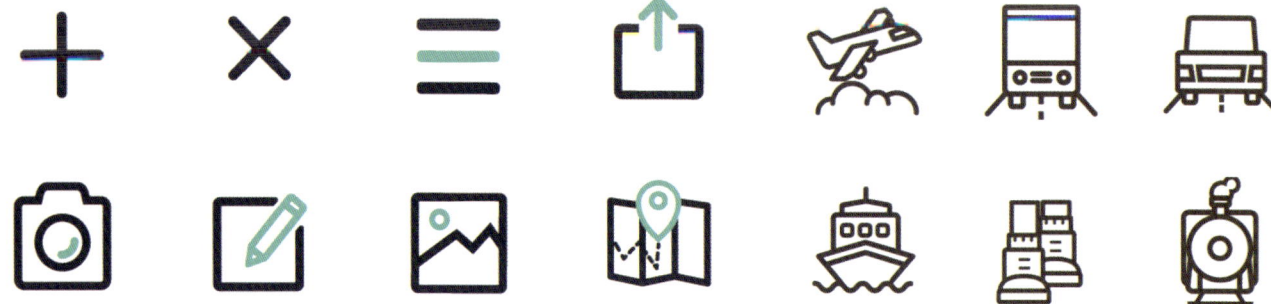

WANDER WORLD

Design: Hyunhee An

Designed by graphic designer Hyunhee An, Wander World is a travel journal app that helps you record every precious moment of your journey.

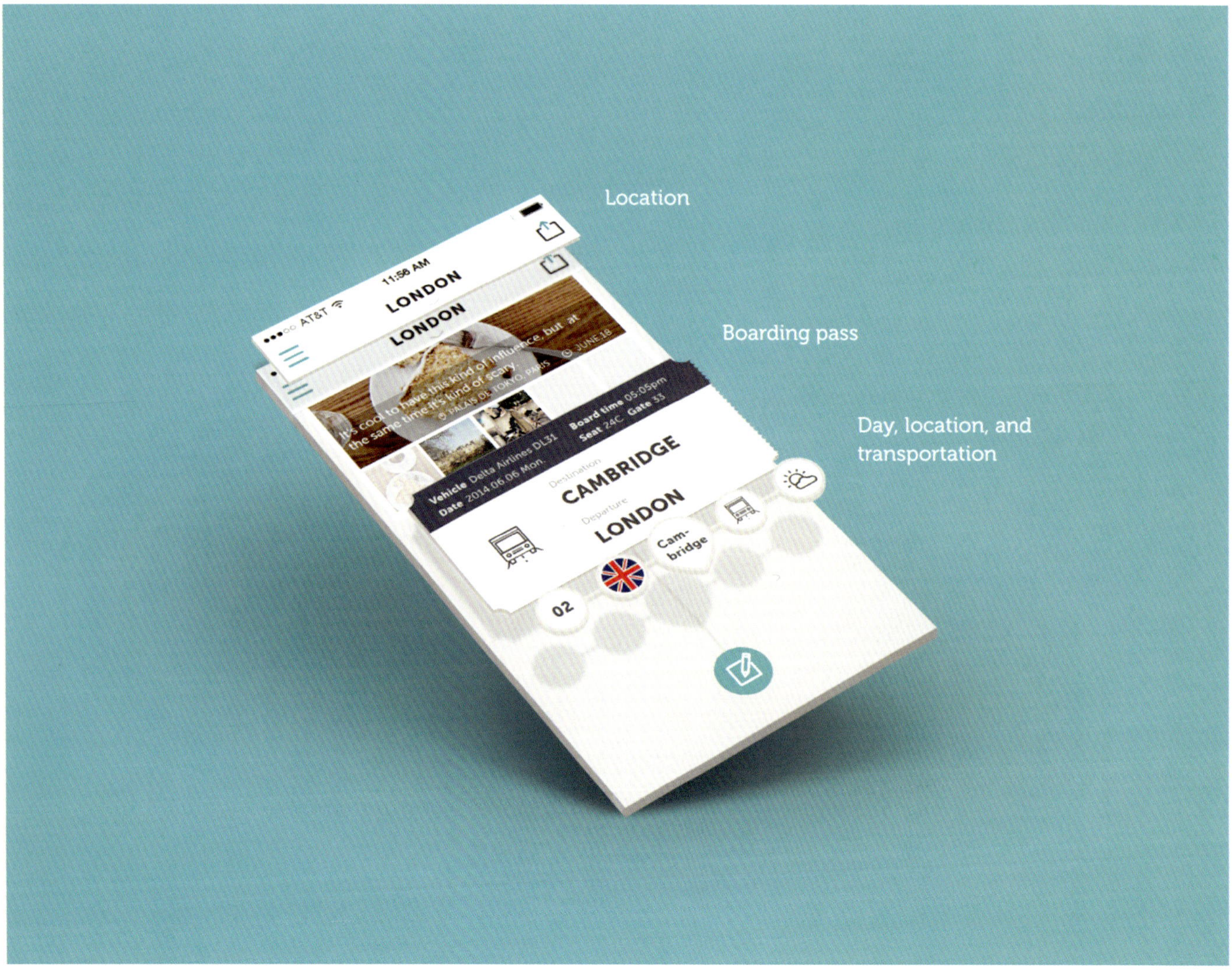

Location
Boarding pass
Day, location, and
transportation
LONDON
LONDON
CAMBRIDGE
LONDON
02

NO WIFI NEEDED

You don't have to worry about wifi
when you are on journey.
Wherever you are just upload photos!
When you can use wifi,
your photoes will be uploaded
right away.

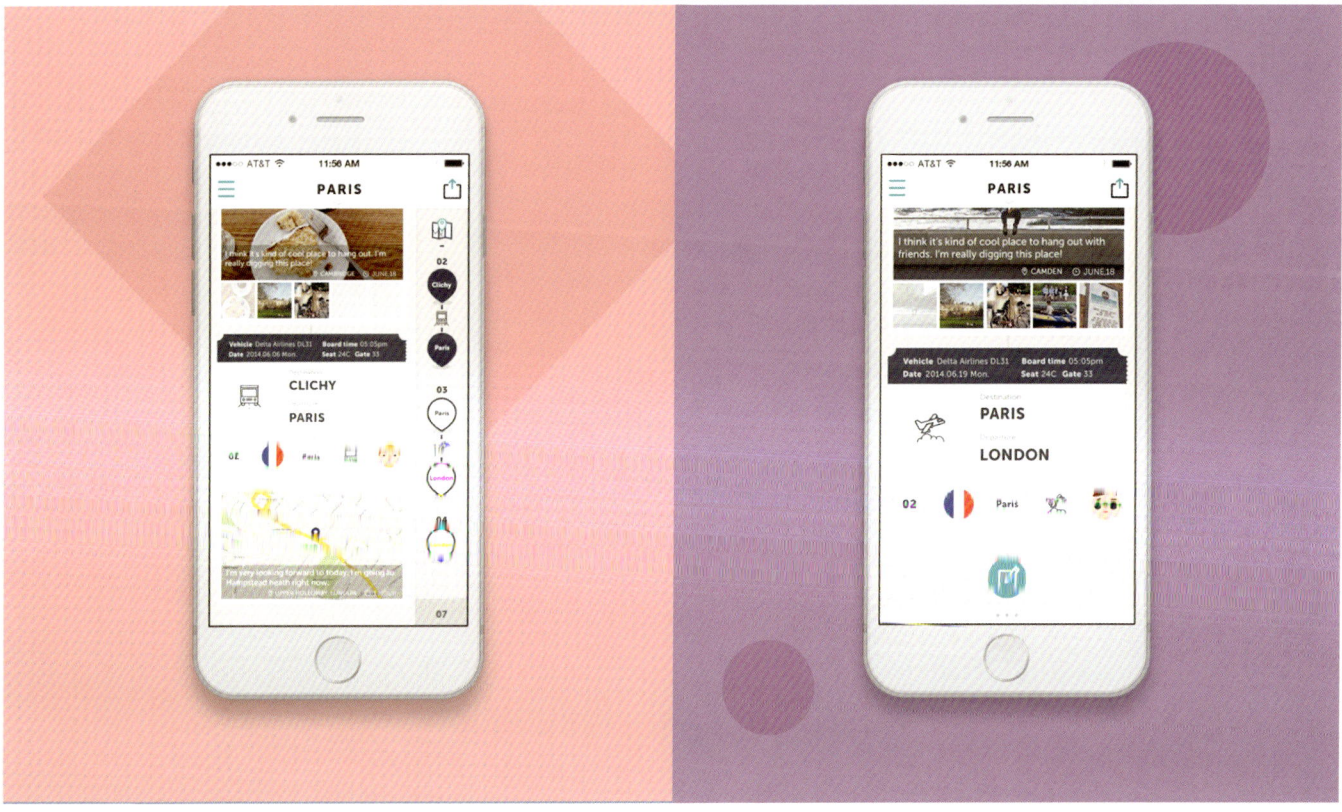

PETER TRAVEL BLOG

Design: Natalia Maltseva

Peter Travel Blog is a website designed to showcase Peter's travels, where he shares entertaining stories and useful tips from his travels around the world.

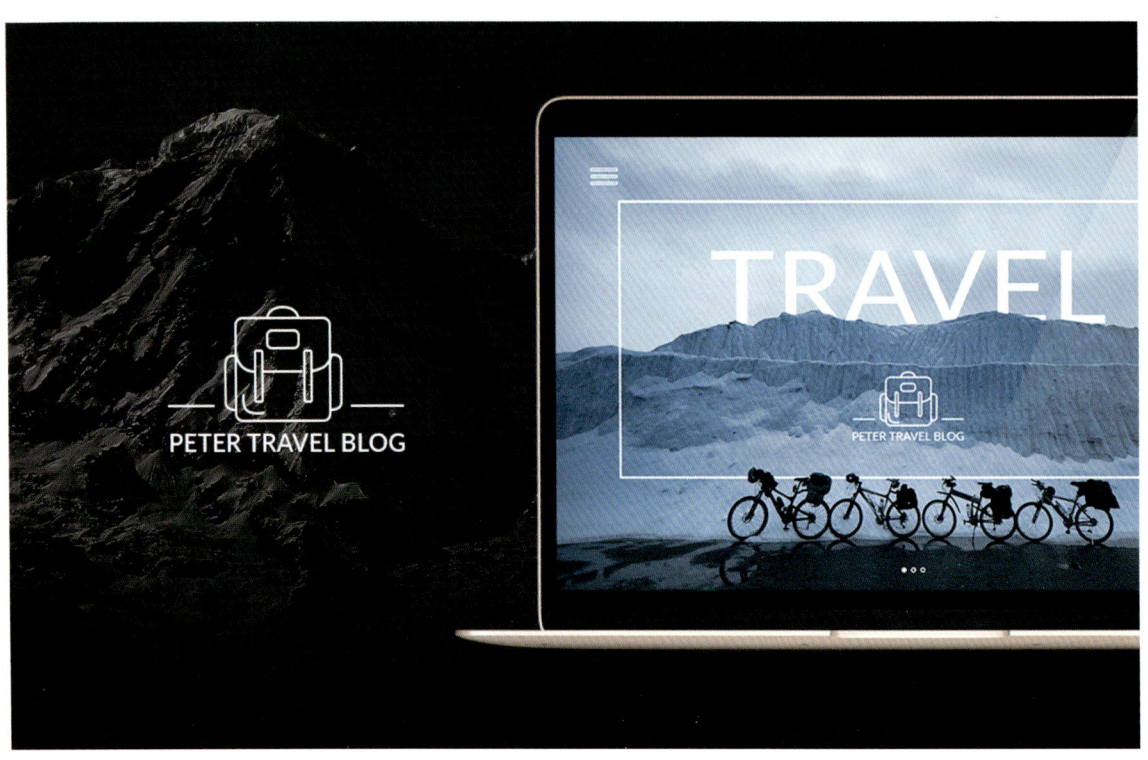

HI!

My name is Peter and I'm a travel addict.

Join me as I share entertaining stories and useful tips from around the world...

To some, travel means sunbathing on the deck of a cruise ship while getting a massage. That's nice, but it's not for me!

To me... travel isn't just about relaxing; It's also about venturing out into the unknown, following your own path, and pushing beyond your comfort zone. It means trying new food, experiencing other cultures, and doing silly things sometimes. At its best, travel lets you view the world with a sense of awe and wonder.

SOME FACTS ABOUT MY JOURNEY

| 40 COUNTRIES | 28620 KMS | 50 000 PHOTO | 7000 M | 52 °C | -35 °C |

SWITZERLAND: THE JUNGFRAUJOCH - HIGHEST ASTRONOMICAL OBSERVATORIES IN THE WORLD

posted April 8, 2015

SICHUAN: REALLY GREAT THE LESHAN GIANT BUDDHA

posted March 25, 2015

LATEST FROM THE BLOG

CHINA: GREAT ARCHITECTURE, WHICH TAKES US THROUGH TIME

posted March 15, 2015

SEE MORE...

VIEW MORE »

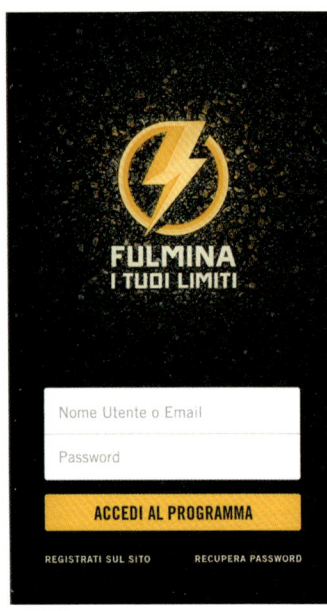

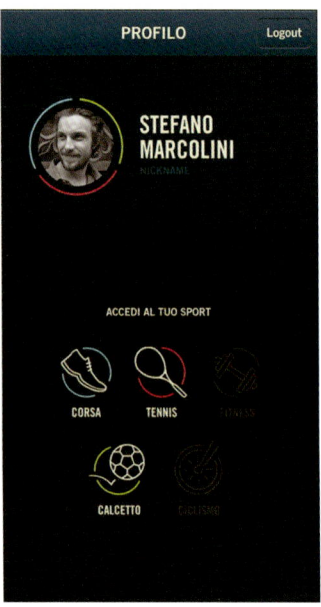

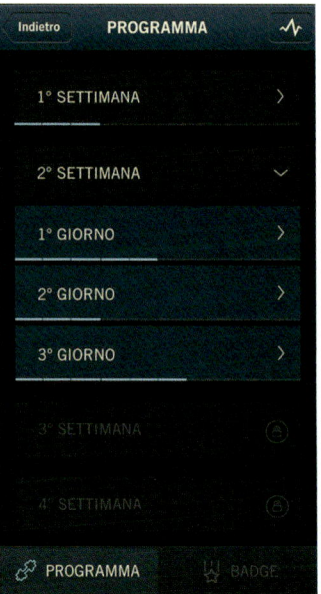

SMASH YOUR LIMITS

Design: Vittorio Perotti

"Smash Your Limits" is the first platform that allows you to work with real trainers: the Gatorade Social Trainers. With the app, you can choose your sport and your limit, download your personal training plan, and chat with your Social Trainer.

WYPOSAŻENIE:

- BEZPŁATNY PARKING (ILOŚĆ MIEJSC NIESTETY OGRANICZONA),
- TARASY Z ZESTAWEM WYPOCZYNKOWYM,
- SUCHA SAUNA,
- OGÓLNODOSTĘPNA KUCHNIA,
- WSPÓLNA JADALNIA Z BIBLIOTEKĄ,
- POKÓJ GIER I ZABAW DLA DZIECI,
- WSPÓLNY SALON Z KOMINKIEM,
- NARCIARNIA,
- MIEJSCE I SPRZĘT DO GRILLOWANIA,
- ROWERY DO AKTYWNEGO WYPOCZYNKU,
- I WIELE INNYCH ...

FRIENDS AND FAMILY GATHER HERE...

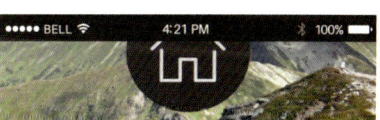

MONTE HOUSE

Design: Mill Studio

Monte House Apartments is a lovely facility in Zakopane in the Tatra Mountains. It offers great interior design surrounded with pure nature. It's a perfect spot for a weekend getaway. As most of their branding is based on pictures, the designer created a simple typography and friendly icons to emphasize that Monte House Apartments feels like home.

 **ARENA**
HALA WIDOWISKOWO
SPORTOWA

 **MALTA**
MIEJSCE SPOTKAŃ,
WYDARZEŃ I REKREACJI

 **CAMPING**
HOTEL MALTA

 **GOLĘCIN**
NOCLEGI / MIEJSCE SPORTU
I REKREACJI

 **CHWIAŁKA**
PŁYWALNIA / LODOWISKO
HALE SPORTOWE

 **MŁODZIEŻOWY**
OŚRODEK SPORTOWY

 **OŚRODEK**
PRZYWODNY RATAJE

 **NICE**
LADY FITNESS

 **BOWLING**
KRĘGIELNIA

POSIR – SPORT DEPARTMENTS BRANDING

Design: Marcin Pałaszyński — **Agency:** Media Pracownia

Branding for the departments of sport and recreation centers in Poznan. To simplify visual communication, the designers have designed pictograms to identify sports compounds in Poznan. All of the icons have been approved by the city of Poznan, and are gradually being put into service.

FOODY ICONS

Design: Kalina Giersz, Drew Polk — **Agency:** Studio Smacznego

Foody Icons is a vector illustration set that may induce immediate, uncontrollable hunger. It was created in conjunction with Food Rush – a grocery list/recipe providing mobile app. It is adaptable for multiple devices and is available for download.

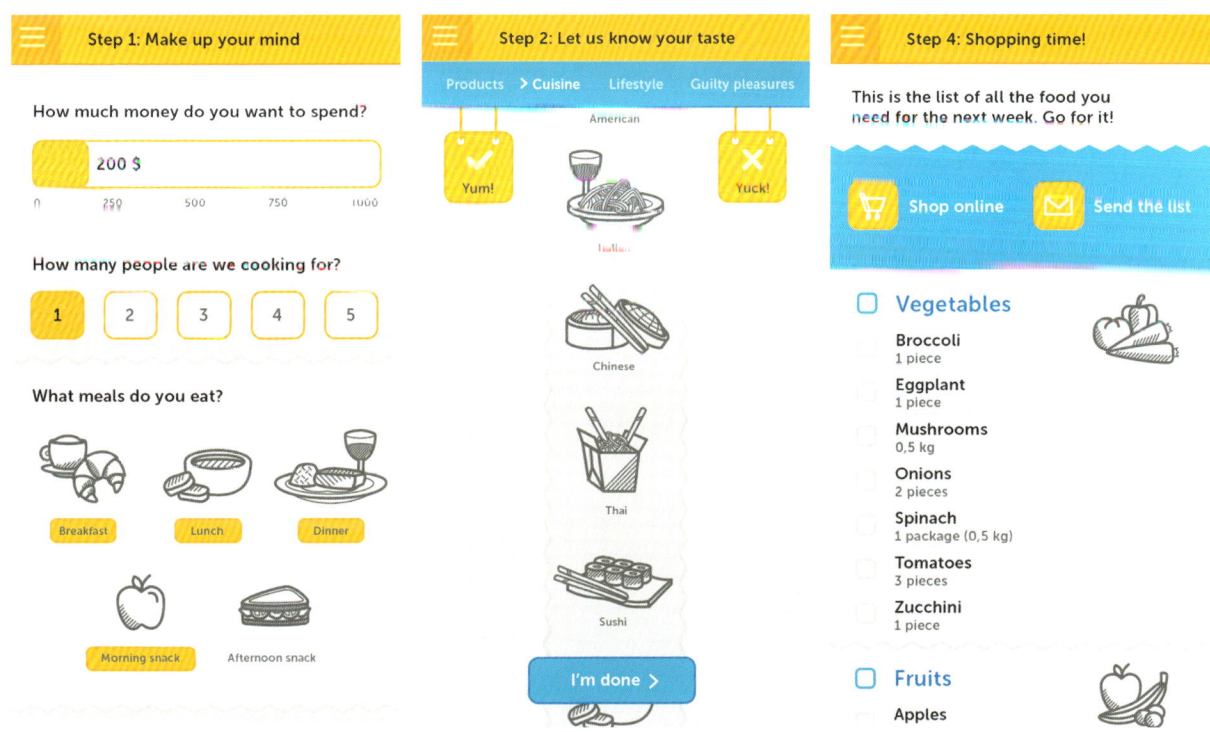

PIK NIK

Design: Reinold L., Sarah T.
Agency: Oddds

PIK NIK is a rebranding project for a cafe that gives a modern spin to their proposed logo. Callouts and descriptive words are used throughout the menu to call attention to random quirks about the food and the cafe's unique selections. Each section shows the different options of food or drink types available. A combination of graphical icons, lines, bold strokes, circles, and a baring-it-all approach was conceptualized and developed for PIK NIK.

SERVICE

NATURE

REST

WORKSHOP

TEA PARTY

DIVINATION

GARDENING

HEART TALK

ROOM-KEY

ORGANIC GOODNESS

NATURE

HAVEN & PAVEN

Design: Ella Zheng Meisi

Haven & Paven is an imaginary no-frills mountain lodge for people to reconnect with nature and take a break away from the hustle and bustle of city life. This inspired a design that is simple, basic, and functional, communicating the brand in a straightforward manner.

Haven & Paven

...

Good Advise

-

Here are a few good things you will expect at
your stay in Haven & Paven.

...

Always Remember The Name Dino

Dino is our wonderful concierge, who maintains
Haven & Paven in its wonderful state. Dino will
make your stay a perfect bliss.

Nature Is At Your Doorstep

Step out and bond with nature. Its free and the
view is breathtaking. Sometimes, a little fox
might come visit and share some warmth.

An Organic Feast of Goodness!

All ingredients are harvested from our edible
gardens. The menu changes weekly and if you miss
a particular food from home, send a request to
Dino. Our amazing chefs will figure their way out!

Getting The Ample Rest You Deserve

If you came here for rest, you have found the
right place. Our little sanctuary is well hidden
in the forest of Stockholm and all huts are
built in ipsum dolor sit amet, for ample rest.

A Variety of Fancy Key Chains

Keep the key well. At the end of your stay, we will
exchange the key of your little hut with a replica.
We thank you for staying with us and the key will
always unlock your beautiful memories here.

Haven & Paven
Edeforsväg 2 A
960 24 Stockholm
Sweden

PLANNER APP

Design: Carmen Nácher

Planner App is a design proposal for modern life. It was created to help people schedule their daily activities in an easy and customizable way. The most notable advantage of the design is the series of pre-given activity icons, which can be linked with each of the 24 hours of the day. The user can create a personal customized app by linking names and descriptions to the icons, which are designed to relate directly to the most common activities in people's day-to-day lives. The application also allows users to save the same activity or schedule for certain days, weeks, or months.

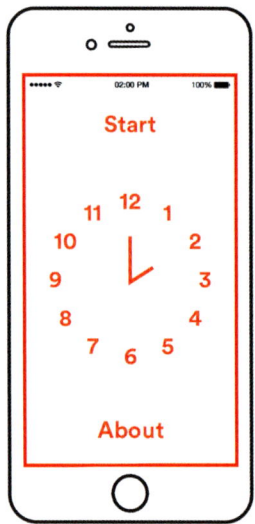

NOOR BANK ICONOGRAPHY

Design: Elliott Burford — **Agency:** Wolff Olins

Online and offline iconography for Noor Bank's refreshed visual identity. Noor Bank is one of the UAE's most innovative Islamic banks, with ambitions to help Dubai become a global centre for Islamic commerce and trade. The iconography is designed to reflect their values: clean, simple, hardworking, elegant, confident, but not arrogant. Applications include branch navigational signage and digital interfaces, such as their website and mobile app.

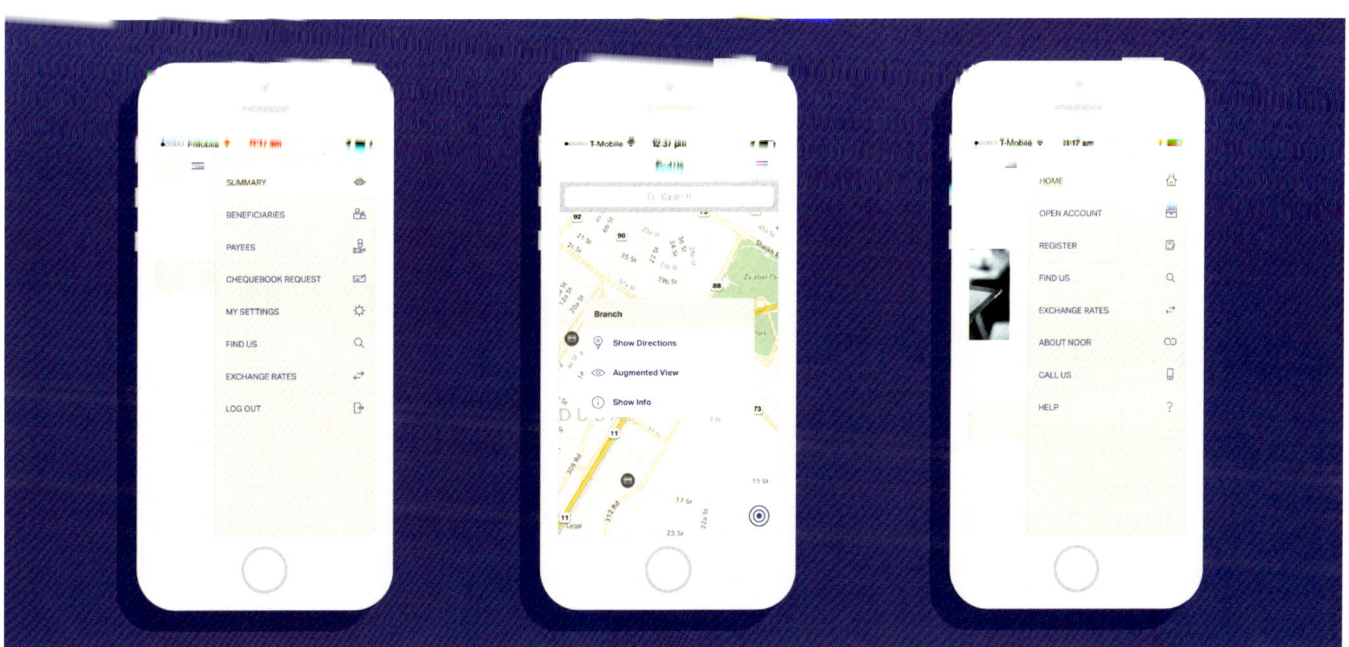

 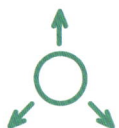    

GRAVITY

Design: Mill Studio — **Art Direction:** Club Soda

Gravity is an application for planning, executing, and optimizing an end-to-end supply chain. The designers created the web-based application's interface and the homepage for the start-up team, based in Hong Kong, China. The designers also created icon sets and the layout style of the diagrams. Since the system itself is complicated, the designers chose a line-based flat design style to make the Gravity app as simple as possible.

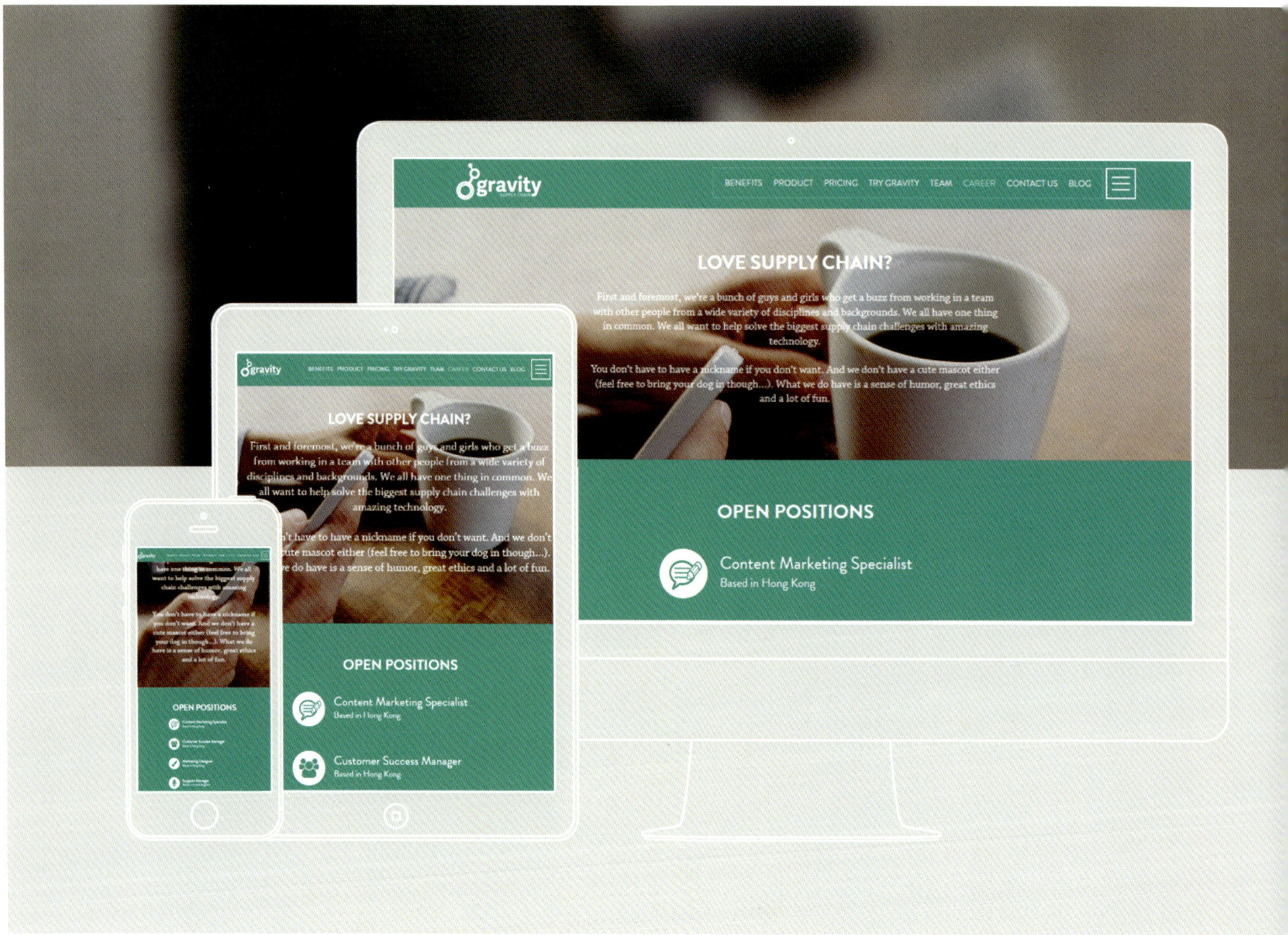

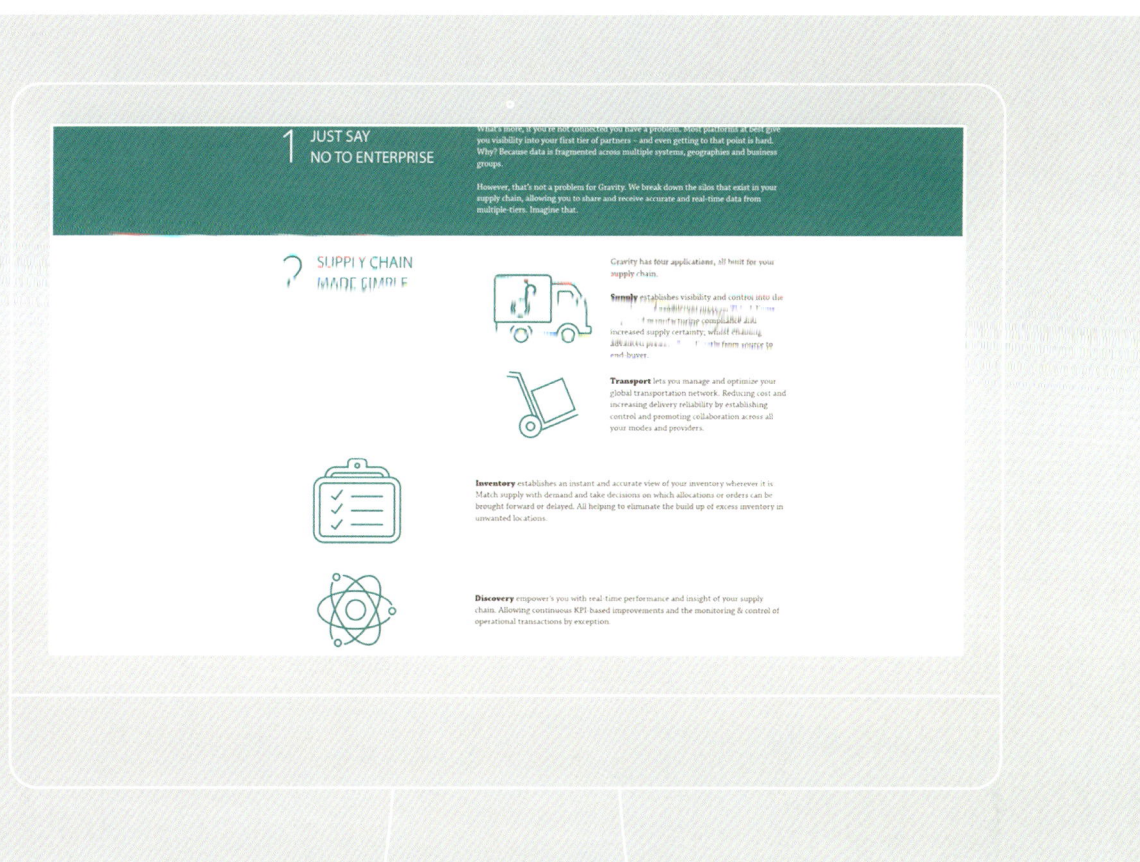

1 JUST SAY NO TO ENTERPRISE

What's more, if you're not connected you have a problem. Most platforms at best give you visibility into your first tier of partners – and even getting to that point is hard. Why? Because data is fragmented across multiple systems, geographies and business groups.

However, that's not a problem for Gravity. We break down the silos that exist in your supply chain, allowing you to share and receive accurate and real-time data from multiple-tiers. Imagine that.

2 SUPPLY CHAIN MADE SIMPLE

Gravity has four applications, all built for your supply chain.

Supply establishes visibility and control into the conditions of your supply chain, allowing you to manage compliance and increased supply certainty, whilst creating additional power through visibility from source to end-buyer.

Transport lets you manage and optimize your global transportation network. Reducing cost and increasing delivery reliability by establishing control and promoting collaboration across all your modes and providers.

Inventory establishes an instant and accurate view of your inventory wherever it is. Match supply with demand and take decisions on which allocations or orders can be brought forward or delayed. All helping to eliminate the build up of excess inventory in unwanted locations.

Discovery empowers you with real-time performance and insight of your supply chain. Allowing continuous KPI-based improvements and the monitoring & control of operational transactions by exception.

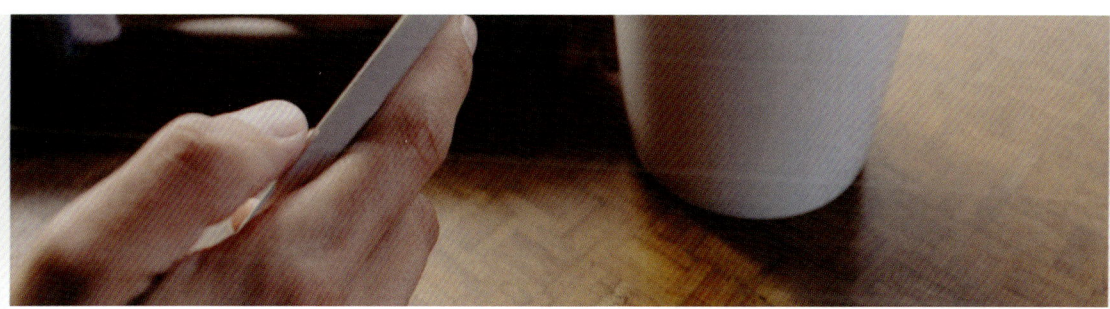

PERKS OF WORKING WITH US

YOUR VOICE IS HEARD

You're not starring in a silent movie. You'll have a major influence on the products that we build. Guaranteed.

FLEXIBLE WORK HOURS

Work from home if you feel like a lie in or leave early if you need a haircut. We're not fussed as long as you get your stuff done.

COMPETITIVE SALARY

Just because we're a start up doesn't mean you should worry about making the rent.

AWESOME LOCATION

Come on. We're in the center of one of the world's most awesome cities. What else could you possibly want? Excellent transport links, great food and drink locations? Tick. Tick. Tick.

VACATION

Everyone needs R & R to be on top of the game. That's why we give you a generous amount to chill and enjoy life. Oh, and you also get an extra day on your birthday.... so we can all celebrate!

FOOD....AND DRINK

Team breakfast, Team lunch, Team dinner. You name it we have it. And on Friday's we go big...

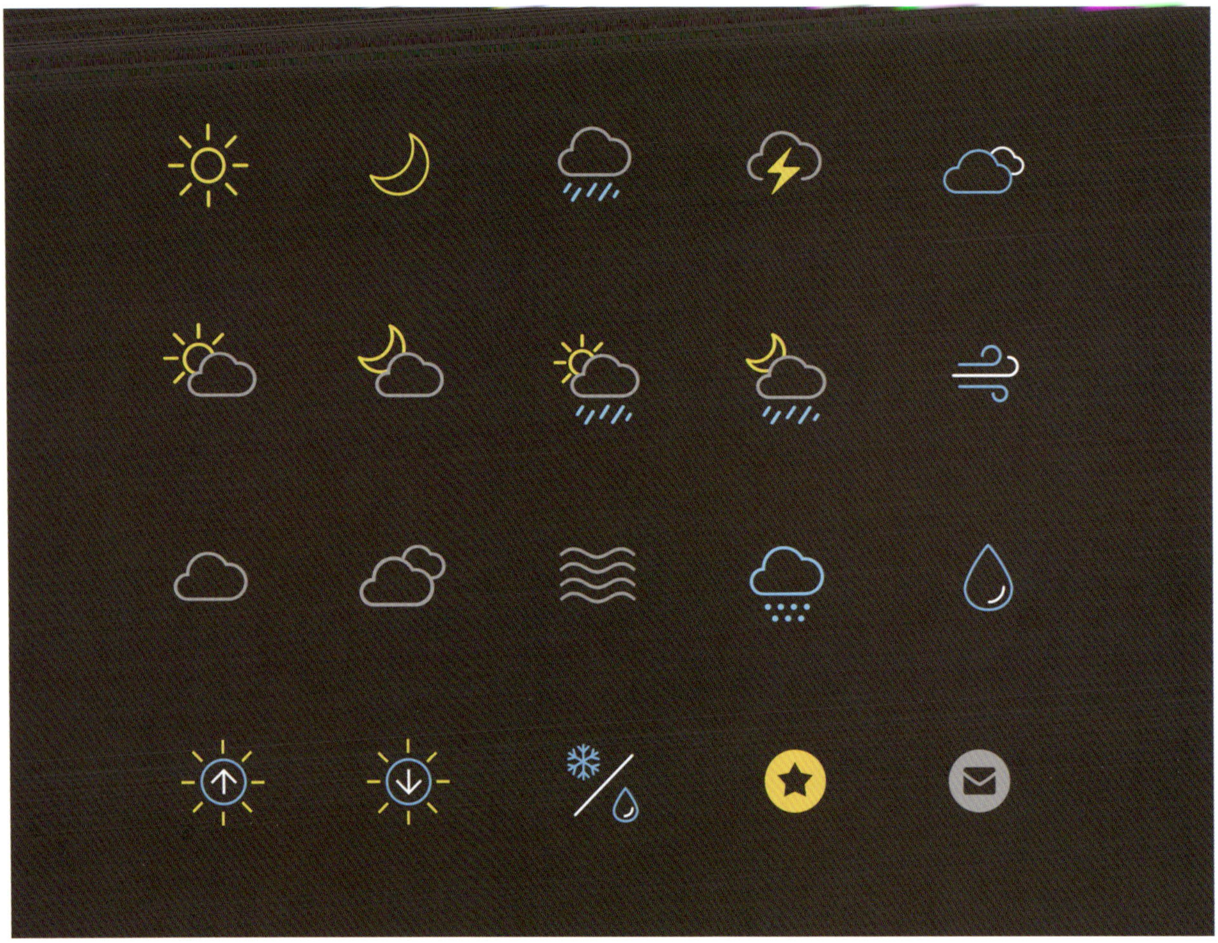

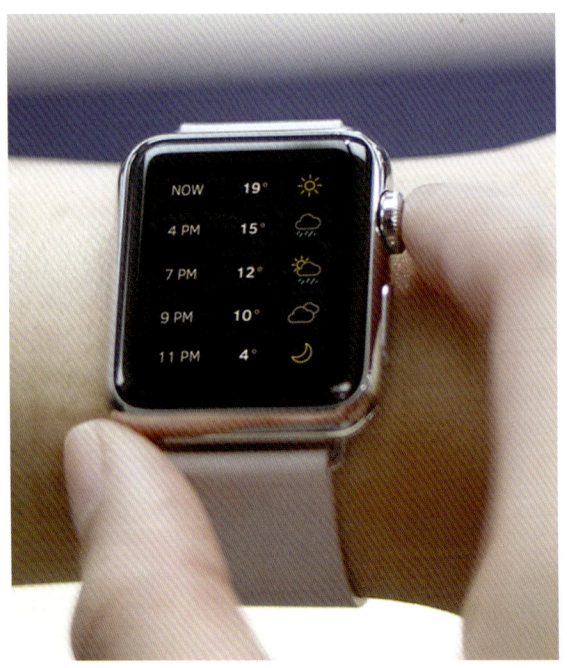

OWEATHER

Design: Artem Svitelskyi

"oWeather" is a forecast app with modern design that's perfect for everyday use. The designer tracked trends to create a series of beautiful icons and a smooth user interface that looks good on any device, be it a phone, tablet, or smart watch. The innovative notification system is capable of warning users of changes in the weather.

NOW 19°
4 PM 15°
7 PM 12°
9 PM 10°
11 PM 4°

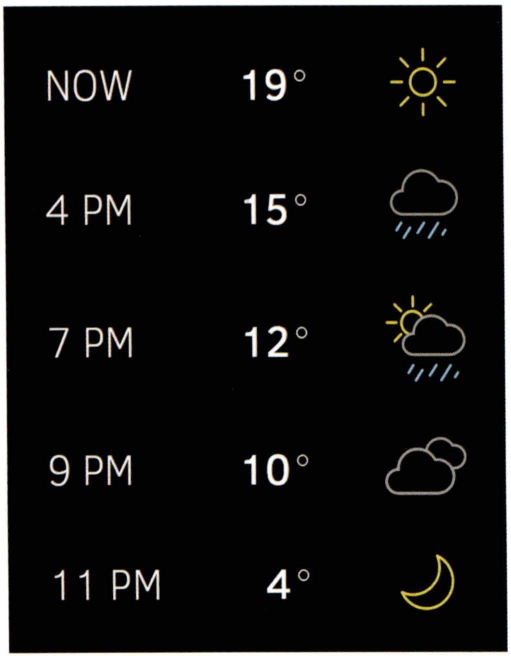

NOW 19°
4 PM 15°
7 PM 12°
9 PM 10°
11 PM 4°

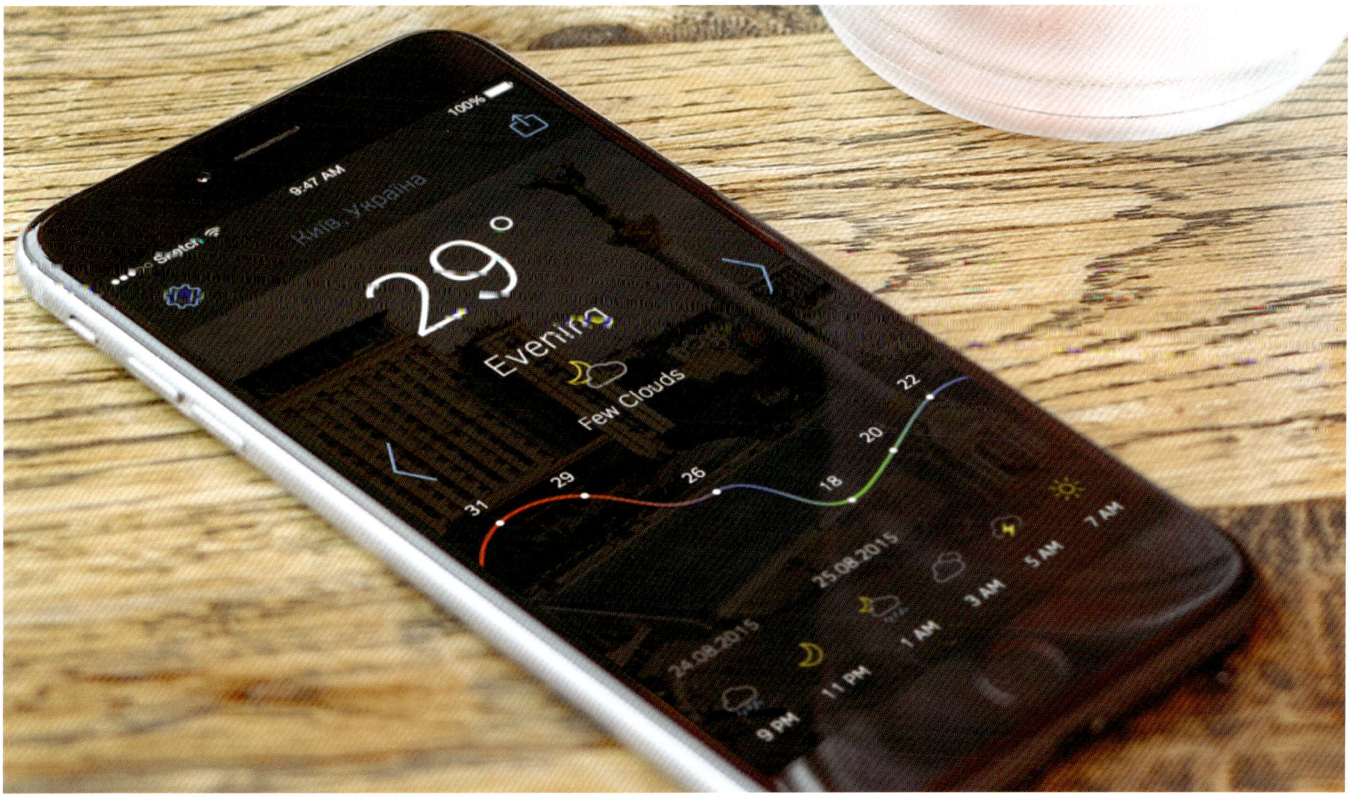
9:47 AM
100%
29°
Evening
Few Clouds
31
29
26
18
20
22
24.08.2015
25.08.2015
9 PM
11 PM
1 AM
3 AM
5 AM
7 AM

●●●○○ Sketch
9:47 AM
100%
Oklahoma New Village
28.3°
Morning
Sky Is Clear
28.3
29
30.1
30
29
29.5
24.08.2015
NOW
11 AM
1 PM
3 PM
5 PM
7 PM

●●●○○ Sketch
9:47 AM
100%
Oklahoma New Village
Cloudiness
Sky Is Clear
Wind
Light breeze 3 m/s
Humidity
34 %
Precipitation
1019 hpa
Sunrise
6:00
Sunset
20:03
OpenWeatherMap

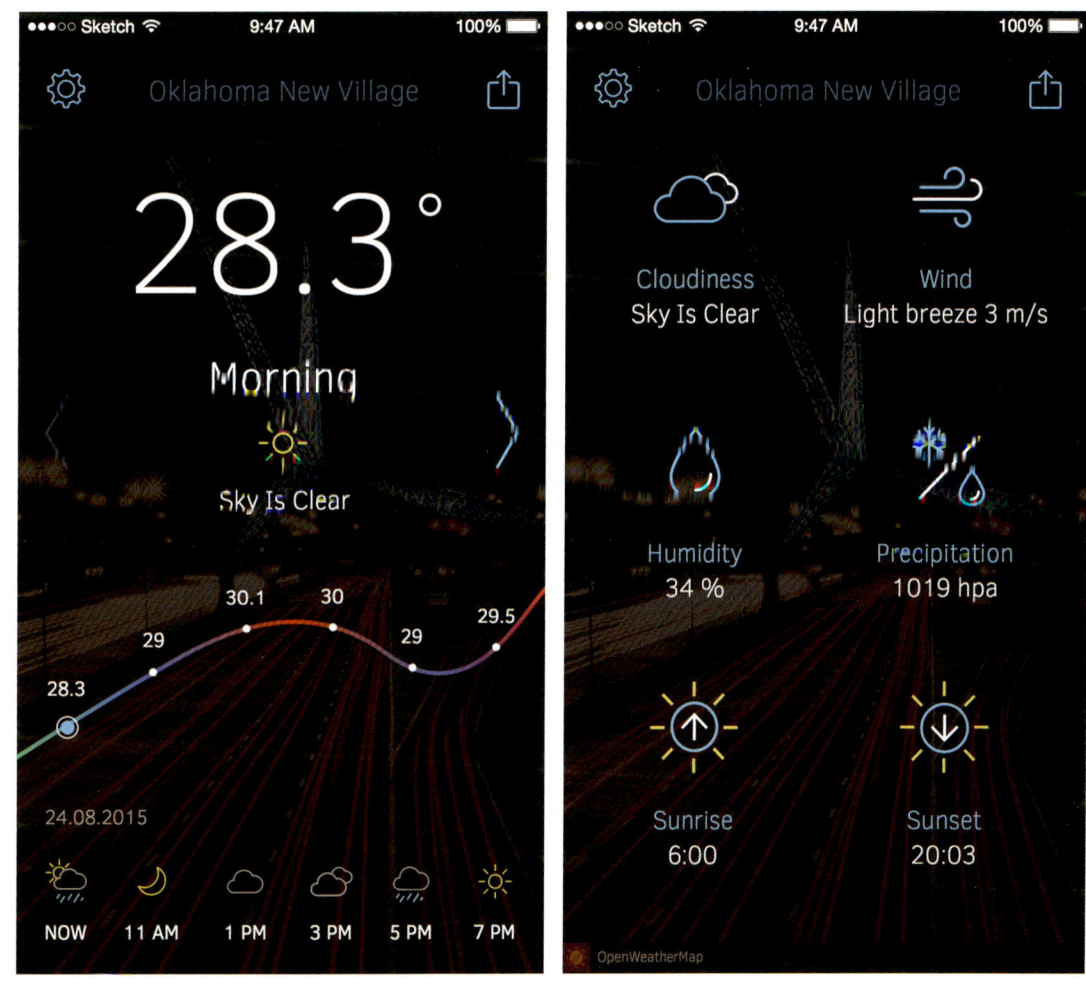

RECEITINHAS MOBILE APP

Design: Philipe Coutinho, Claudio Shinohara

Receitinhas is an app that helps you cook a meal using only what you have available in your pantry.

STRADA CAFE

Design: Nino Mamaladze, Nick buturishvili, Nick Kumbari, Levan Ambokadze

The Strada project revolved around the idea that a restaurant could deliver an engaging and interactive experience even before you arrived at the premises. The designers wanted to use simplicity to communicate this to the consumer with instantly recognizable icons. At a glance, visitors could make quick decisions without the typical over-complicated menu system.

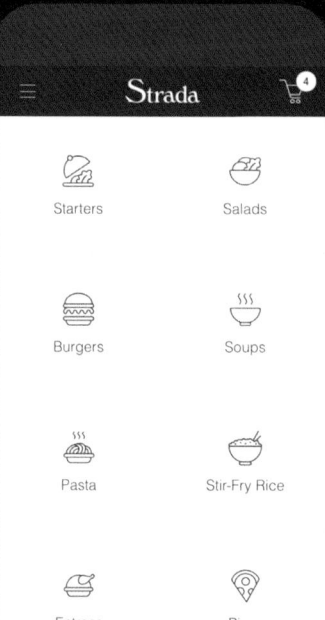

MENU

MENU
A little something to get the taste of the coming attractions.

OEUVRES
Savoury food in all of its might and glory.

CHECK-OUT
Quick and painless - both aesthetically and functionally.

INDEX

100UND1

100und1.com

100und1 is a young, vibrant, international network of people working within a diverse group of creative branches. The team is highly specialized in their fields, offering years of experience, and is strongly connected to an extensive array of freelancers who provide a full range of services.

P124-125

ADI DIZDAREVIĆ

www.adidizdarevic.com

Adi Dizdarević is a Bosnian-born graphic designer and artist currently based in Bihać (BiH). Adi's clients and collaborators include T-Mobile/Deutsche Telekom, Samsung, Philip Morris / Marlboro, Ericsson, Clever°Franke, Artistic Image, Affect, Fisil, Resolume, Henkel, etc.

P198-199

AINORWEI LIN

be.net/ainorwei_lin

Ainorwei Lin is a young designer based in Tainan City, Taiwan, China. He is currently studying Digital Content & Applied Design at the Southern Taiwan University of Science and Technology. He specializes in communication design and creates works ranging from print to conceptual projects.

P039

AISTĖ JAKIMAVIČIŪTĖ

be.net/aistejakimaviciute

Aistė Jakimavičiūtė, Jonė Miškinyte, and Domas Mikšys are Lithuanian-born independent designers graduated from Vilnius Academy of Arts. Together they play a huge role in organizing the Visual Culture Forum "Penketai." They collaborated on the "What's Next?" Conference of Creative Industries to create a bold, lively, and eye-catching brand.

P086-087

ANA CAHUEX

be.net/anacahuex

Ana Cahuex is a graphic designer based in Guatemala City. Graduated last year with Magna Cum Laude honors, Ana's work focuses on branding and editorial. She is currently exploring the wonderful world of paper crafts.

P090-091

ANASTAZJA SZMAWONIAN

be.net/anasanastazja5a34

Anastazja Szmawonian was born in Warsaw in 1991. Graduated from New Media Arts department of the Japanese Polish Academy of Technology in Gdańsk, Ana specializes in graphic design, branding, rebranding, illustration, editorial design, packaging design, etc.

P066-157

ANNA NOWOKUŃSKA

www.nowokunska.com

Anna Nowokuńska is a graphic designer and architect who loves modern dancing, coffee, mushrooms, designing stuff, traveling, and knowing how things work. In her design process she takes advantage of knowledge and experience from the disciplines of both architecture and graphic design.

P128-129

APEX STUDIO

be.net/apexstudio

From an aspiring illustrator to visual graphic communicator, influenced by American comic book art and an obsession with the idea of the final product as a collectible object, Apex creative director Tiago Machado believes in the creative expansion and development of the studio's work through embracing influences from a variety of distinguished subjects.

P094-095

ARTEM SVITELSKYI

artsvit.com

Artem Svitelskyi is a Ukrainian designer for UX and UI, graphic design, web design, application interfaces, icons, branding, corporate identity, and print design. Currently he focuses on mobile, E-commerce, and UX/UI design.

P152-153

ARTUA DESIGN STUDIO

www.artua.com

Artua Design Studio is a big team based in Wilmington, DE, USA. They are among those who love what they do! GUI development, icons and logos design, illustrations drawing, and mobile application development – all of these things inspire them!

P188

ATELIER ATOCA

atelieratoca.com

Atelier Atoca is an art direction and graphic design studio founded in Montreal by Clémentine Poupineau and Pauline Mallemanche in 2013. The studio acts in the fields of culture, events, and business in Montreal and worldwide.

P163-169

AURELIO SÁNCHEZ

www.fluorink.net

Aurelio Sánchez is graphic designer with a serious passion for the graphic world. He has more than 10 years of experience in the field. The areas in which he has most developed his skills and enthusiasm are brand identities, editorial design, art direction, printing processes, typography, photography, illustration, interface usability, music research, and new media art research.

P082-083

AXEK EFREMOV

be.net/axek

Axek Efremov is a graphic designer based in Petrozavodsk, Russia, specialized in typography, graphic design, and branding design.

P074-075

BELCDESIGN

www.belcdesign.com

Based in Łódź, Poland, Belcdesign specializes in visual identity, typography, and web design.

P013

BLUE BEETLE DESIGN

www.bluebeetledesign.com

Blue Beetle Design is an integrated design consultancy with a passion for creating strong and intelligent graphic solutions for clients. Established in 1996, the studio's creative services include corporate and brand identity design, packaging design, corporate and marketing collaterals, and environmental graphics.

P140-141

BOND CREATIVE AGENCY

www.bond-agency.com

Bond is a brand-driven creative agency in Helsinki, Finland and Abu Dhabi with a craftsman's attitude toward their work. The design agency creates and redesigns brands and helps new businesses and brands get started. The agency's services include identity, digital, retail and spatial, and packaging and product design.

P060-061, 070-073

BRATUS

www.bratus.co

Bratus is a branding and strategic creative agency based in Ho Chi Minh, Vietnam. Driven by its philosophy of "intelligent design, exceptionally made," the team specializes in creating bold and memorable work that helps businesses stand proudly apart from their competitors, giving them a long-lasting presence with real integrity.

P116-117

CAIO ORIO

be.net/orio

Caio Orio is a creative graphic designer and art director based in São Paulo, Brazil. Caio believes in using the basic principles of graphic design to build a strong and consistent language. Using geometric shapes, Caio creates synthetical illustrations that enrich the content and deliever a clear message.

P204-205

CARLA FELICETTI

be.net/charlydesign

Carla Felicetti, Marta Vianello, and Taja Luxa are graphic designers based in Venice, Italy. They are the contributors for the project Dinamo.

P046-047

CARMEN NÁCHER

www.carmennacher.com

Carmen Nácher is a Spanish graphic designer who has been living in Germany. Carmen studied graphic design in the EASD of Valencia. Currently, Carmen works as a graphic designer in a design agency in Berlin, as well as freelance in different projects around the world.

P222

CAROL LIAO

toicon.com

Carol Liao is a graphic and interaction designer from Los Angeles, USA. Her icon series for The Artificial's project, to [icon], aims to balance familiarity and idiosyncrasy, an approach she brings to all her work.

P022-023

CAROLINA PERES

be.net/carolinaperes

Carolina Peres is a Portuguese graphic designer living in London. With a degree in Communication Design, Carolina has been working as a freelancer since 2010 mainly in projects featuring corporate identity and branding design for several professional sectors, such as culture, cinema, food, and trading.

P058-059

CHEN YING ANN

be.net/chenyingann

Chen Ying Ann is a graphic designer based in Taiwan who loves geography, infographics, and cats.

P170-171

CHERRY BOMB DESIGN STUDIO

cherrybomb.com.mx

Founded in 2010, Cherry Bomb Design Studio is a graphic design agency specialized in branding, illustration, and web development.

P190-191

CYNTHIA TORREZ

be.net/cynthia-torrez

Cynthia Torrez is a graphic designer based in Córdoba, Argentina.

P112-113

DARIO FERRANDO

www.dario.io

Dario Ferrando is a communication designer based in Berlin, where he works as a freelancer for digital products. Dario designs icons, websites, apps, and interfaces.

P029

DAVID RAFACHINHO

be.net/rafachinho

David Rafachinho is a senior graphic designer based in Lisbon, Portugal. With a degree in Graphic Design IADE, David started his career in 2003. He previously worked at Ogilvy & Mather, ascending to art director before leaving in 2014. He is now an art director at FCB Lisboa.

P142-143

DIEGO CARNEIRO

www.corinovacao.com.br

Diego Carneiro is a graphic designer based in São Paulo, Brazil. With more than nine years' design practice experience, he is currently working at CO.R Inovação.

P080-081

DOMINIK LANGEGGER

be.net/langegger

Dominik Langegger has worked as a freelance designer for six years now, and has just finished his Master's Degree at the University of Applied Sciences in Salzburg. He loves simple forms based on geometry and clear designs. Besides designing icons, he's also deeply in love with the disciplines of editorial design and corporate design.

P176-177

DYLAN MCDONOUGH

dylanmcdonough.com.au

Dylan McDonough is a Melbourne based designer who utilizes clear communication in his collaborative processes and offers a fresh perspective in his practice. Working with a range of clients across various industries big and small, he has managed and developed effective brand and message implementation.

P028-029

ELLA ZHENG MEISI

be.net/ellaisweird

Ella Zheng is a Singaporean designer and illustrator who enjoys experimentation, craft, and the endless pursuit of self-improvement. Trained in both fashion and graphic design, she hopes to nurture Singaporean's mindset towards design.

P220-221

ELLIOTT BURFORD

www.elliottburford.com

Elliott Burford is an Australian designer and art director. He specializes in using brand and identity to inform purpose, product, and interface for a range of clients. Elliott's work spans illustration, objects, and film for commercial ventures, non-profit organizations, and exhibitions. He has been featured in solo and group shows in Rome, Paris, Venice, Lisbon, and Melbourne; his illustrations have appeared in Wired Magazine.

P162, 223

EMILIE GARNIER

www.emiliegarnier.com

Emilie Garnier is a French junior graphic and web designer. Recently graduated, she works in Paris for several clients on various kinds of projects including packaging, print, brochure, poster, and web design.

P130-131

ERMOLAEV BUREAU

ermolaevbureau.com

Ermolaev Bureau is a graphic design studio specializing in visual brand creation, visual strategy development, and project implementation in the sphere of corporate and consumer communication and aesthetics.

P066-067, 148-149, 154-155

EUGENE DIEUDEVILLE

be.net/dieudeville

Eugene Dieudeville is a graphic designer based in Moscow, Russia specialized in art direction, illustration, and motion design.

P018-019

FILIP POMYKALO

be.net/filippomykalo

Filip Pomykalo, Marita Bonačić, and Negra Nigoevic are the creators of the projects Barba Restaurant and Swanky Mint Hostel. They are award-winning, multi-disciplinary designers with a diverse portfolio, working mostly across disciplines like branding, editorial design, exhibition design, interior design, and more.

P044-045, 084-085

FORMA & CO

www.forma.co

Forma is an independent studio from Barcelona dedicated to graphic communication. Founded by Joel Lozano and Dani Navarro, it works on corporate identity, communication strategy, editorial design, illustration, animation, and web projects.

P014, 016, 024, 186-187

FUTURA

byfutura.com

Born in 2008 as an independent design studio, Futura is a boutique-like workshop that seeks to redefine Mexican design values, while maintaining functionality, wit, and charisma. Futura specializes in resource optimization, paying attention to every detail. Futura's headquarters are based in Mexico but they have clients all over the world.

P030-031

GABRIEL NAZOA

be.net/gabrielnazoa

Gabriel Nazoa is a Venezuelan designer based in Paris. She likes to use blue, white, circles, squares, fruits, South America themes, and elements inspired by the atmosphere of the '80s in her design. Gabriel works as freelancer exploring illustration, collage, typography, and web design.

P197

GEORGE TSAVALOS

georgetsavalos.com

George Tsavalos was born in Athens, Greece in 1994. He is studying Graphic Design at the Technological Educational Institute of Athens and Vakalo Art and Design College. He also studied Graphic Design at ESAD Porto, Portugal with the Erasmus+ Exchange Program.

P131

GUSTAV KARLSSON

www.gustavkarlsson.com

A freelance graphic designer specialized in branding and packaging. He is currently studying at HDK, School of Design and Crafts in Gothenburg, Sweden.

P056-057

GUSTAVO CRAMEZ

be.net/gustavocramez

Gustavo Cramez is a creative and versatile designer who focuses on delivering quality, clean, modern and impactful products. With a background in graphic design and illustration, he currently works on user interface/user experience, branding, print design, and icon design.

P017

HAJNALKA ILLÉS

be.net/ihajnalkaa

Born in 1987, Hajnalka Illés is a Hungarian graphic designer specialized in visual identity, icon design, illustration, typography, and editorial design. Hajnalka has four years work experience in print media. Her design approach is deliberate and thorough, logic-based and content-driven.

P110-111

HYUNHEE AN

hheean.com

Hyunhee An is a visual communicator who works on digital media, GUI, and graphic design, a creative thinker passionate about visual and brand communication and excellent user experience.

P210-211

IRINA KRUGLOVA

be.net/mon-debrisef00

Irina Kruglova is a Russian illustrator and graphic designer based in Chicago. Irina has experience working in both fields but recently focused on illustrations in particular. She draws in different styles and applies various techniques and tools to deliver vector images, line drawings, craft work, and stylized typography.

P014, 108-109

IRYNA NEZHYNSKA

be.net/eirena

Iryna is a brand designer from Poland who specializes in visual identities for digital products. Recently she has focused her attention on startups, helping them to build strong and user-centric brands from the very beginning.

P202-203

JAMES SPENCER CLARKE

www.jamspencer.com

James Spencer Clarke is a freelance designer and illustrator from the UK.

P054-055

JAY LEE

be.net/lynas

Jay Lee is currently a student of digital media design at Hongik University. His main design fields are UX/UI (GUI, Interaction Design) design.

P206-207

JAZZY INNOVATIONS

jazzy.pro

Symbiosis between technology and design. As a group of professionals and talented individuals, Jazzy Innovations is coming forward with our unique design and innovative technology to help develop interesting and exciting ideas.

P078-079, 097

JIHYE UM

zihezum.com

Jihye Um is a graphic designer based in New York, USA.

P200-201

KAZUYA HORIKIRIKAWA

kazuyahorikirikawa.com

Kazuya Horikirikawa is a freelance UI designer in Japan. Kazuya likes to design icons, logos, UI, and animations. He's won prizes in several graphic and UI design contests in Japan.

P192-193, 196

KLAUDIA GAL

be.net/galkld

Klaudia Gal is a graphic designer born in Hungary. After obtaining her Bachelor's Degree in Digital Graphic Design at Eszterhazy Karoly College, Eger, Hungary, she started studying E-concept Development at the Zealand Institute of Business and Technology in Koege, Denmark. In her work, she focuses on research and experimenting to create innovative solutions.

P026-027

KURPPA HOSK

www.kurppahosk.com

Kurppa Hosk is a fast-moving design agency. The team helps forward-looking brands define and design purposeful experiences that strengthen relationships with customers, users, internal stakeholders, and society at large. Kurppa Hosk works across digital and physical channels and platforms with their approach to brand artistry as a starting point. It integrates rational business thinking with creativity and intuition.

P068-069

LAMM STUDIO

be.net/lamm

LAMM is a young design studio located in Buenos Aires, Argentina. LAMM mainly develops projects about branding, publishing, packaging, web, and illustration.

P160-161, 163

LEE HYOJIN

www.tyo-stitch.com

Lee Hyojin is a brand experience designer based in Korea. He attempts to deliver unique brand experiences by endlessly agonizing over the various intersections of brand and customers. He makes diverse graphic-and-illustration-based attempts on projects including branding and based on antique things, new things, experiences and values.

P180

LI LINGHAO

be.net/bingheath

Li Linghao is currently a student in Tianjin Academy of Arts, China. He focuses on graphic design, illustration, and print design.

P126-127

LOTTA NIEMINEN

www.lottanieminen.com

Lotta Nieminen is an illustrator, graphic designer, and art director from Helsinki, Finland. She has studied graphic design and illustration at the University of Art and Design Helsinki and the Rhode Island School of Design, and has worked as a freelancer in both fields since 2006. After working for fashion magazine Trendi, Pentagram Design, and RoAndCo Studio, Lotta now runs her own New York-based studio.

P146-147

LUKASZ KULAKOWSKI

www.emptypage.co.uk

Lukasz Kulakowski is a head of design at WebSummit, Ireland. He loves minimal, clean and geometric logo styles inspired by Bauhaus and Swiss design, good typography, and ink illustrations.

P136-137

MALWIN BÉLA HÜRKEY

www.malw.in

Malwin Béla Hürkey is a German-based designer focusing on typography, corporate, and editorial design. He is currently completing his degree at the University of Art and Design Offenbach.

P150-151

MARIANTA THEODORATOU

be.net/mariantatheodoratou

Marianta Theodoratou is a design student in Athens, Greece.

P181

MEDIA PRACOWNIA

www.mediapracownia.com

Media Pracownia is a team of goal-driven design professionals and enthusiasts. Usefulness and perfection of design are their key values. The team creates brand strategies and deals with brand communication and management. The team consists of professionals who share the same passion to create.

P216

MILL STUDIO

www.millstudio.pl

Mill Studio is a design studio based in Krakow, Poland. The studio strives to meet the needs of their clients: smart, strategic, and creative solutions, award-winning design, consistency, and style.

P215, 224-225

MIRIAM SCHMALEN

be.net/mimimalistic

Miriam Schmalen is a freelance photographer, retoucher and graphic designer from Aachen, Germany. She is currently a student at University of Applied Science Aachen where she improves her communication design skills after working for five years in the publishing sector.

P042-043

MOODLEY BRAND IDENTITY

www.moodley.at

Moodley Brand Identity is an owner-led, award-winning strategic design agency with offices in Vienna and Graz, Austria. Since 1999, Moodley has worked together with their customers to develop corporate and product brands which live, breathe, and grow. Moodley believes that their key contribution is to analyze complex requirements and develop simple, smart solutions with emotional appeal – whether for corporate start-up, product launch, or brand positioning.

P135

MOROCHO ESTUDIO

www.morochoestudio.com

Morocho is a Buenos Aires based design firm that focuses on multidisciplinary solutions for the wide spectrum of graphics, interactive, and audiovisual design. The team establishes an identity with their work in order to bring personality, combining concept and technique with passion and commitment for design.

P174-175

NATALIA MALTSEVA

be.net/nataliyamaltseva

Natalia Maltseva is a web designer based in Kharkiv, Ukraine.

P212-213

NATALIA MÉNDEZ

be.net/nataliamendez

Natalia Méndez, Ana Lucía Montes, Luisa Aragón, and Montserrat Chávez are graphic designers graduated from Universidad de Monterrey. Together they worked as a team and designed the project Dos Cincuenta & Cinco Food Truck.

P212

NINO MAMALADZE

be.net/jelly_fishie

Nino Mamaladze, Nick buturishvili, Nick Kumbari, Levan Ambokadze are graphic designers from from Tbilisi, Georgia. Together as a team, they designed and contributed to the project Strada.

P230-231

NORA KASZANYI

be.net/norakaszanyi

Nora Kaszanyi fell in love with graphic design when she was 10 year old and the relationship still continues. She is currently studying in the Moholy-Nagy University of Art and Design. As a graphic designer, Nora considers the most important factor of a visual interface to be cohesion with the content. She always strives to develop an appearance which provides a user-friendly experience for everyone.

P132-133

NUSAE DESIGN

www.nusae.co

Nusae is a creative and graphic design studio, composed of a team of seasoned brand architects and design industry professionals with diverse experience. The team works with a diverse range of clients, from start-ups to multinationals, delivering head-turning design that grabs audiences, builds brands, and ultimately achieves results.

P182-183

ODDDS

www.oddds.com

Oddds was established in 2013 by Reinold L.(Penang) & Sarah T.(Singapore). Their beliefs revolve around the notion of The New Anthropology, and their work reflects significantly on behaviours and futurism. Oddds' main focuses are in branding, art direction and design.

P218-219

OLGA UZHIKOVA

be.net/uzhik

Olga Uzhikova is a UI/UX designer in Kharkiv, Ukraine. Olga believes that great design solutions should be usable and accessible without sacrificing aesthetics.

P160

PARA TODO HAY FANS

www.paratodohayfans.com

Para Todo Hay Fans is an online marketing agency based in Guadalajara, Jalisco, Mexico, founded by Federico V. Astorga in 2010. The studio provides solutions for the creation, diffusion, and promotion of brands through the Internet. Their services include web development, multimedia services, branding, online marketing, social media, and advertising.

P050-051, 100-101

PATSWERK

patswerk.nl

Patswerk was founded in 2008 by long-time friends Ramon Avelino, Rogier Mulder, and Lex van Tol. Patswerk produces bold graphics with attention to detail. Their works are playful and often colorful. Patswerk likes to incorporate fun, clean lines, and the occasional moustache in their design.

P166, 167, 209

PETER KOMIEROWSKI

www.peterkstudio.com

Peter Komierowski is a Vancouver based graphic designer with a background in illustration. Peter has more than 10 years of experience in the industry. Nature has always played a vital role in his creative process, and living in Vancouver offers many opportunities to be inspired.

P064-065

PHILIPE COUTINHO

be.net/lipson

Philipe Coutinho is a designer based in São Paulo, Brazil specialized in illustration, graphic design, and typography.

P228-229

PIN-JU CHEN

www.pinjuchen.com

Born in Taiwan, China, Pin-Ju is now a visual artist working in London. She graduated from Kingston University London majoring Graphic Design MA. She thinks, "Design is the massage," simply because it provides people awesome experiences, just like a massage does. Her works are usually based on daily life experiences and current issues, with some humor added.

P096

PLUS X

be.net/plusexperience

Plus X is an experience design and marketing company in South Korea, founded in 2010. The company mainly directs design projects of large companies in South Korea such as SK telecom, Hyundai card, and Samsung. Plus X focuses on integrated experience design, not just design in one field.

P118-121

POLYGRAPHE STUDIO

polygraphe.ca

Polygraphe is a Montreal based brand identity and communication studio.

P088-089, 102-103

POST

www.deliveredbypost.com

POST is an independent, London-based design agency working collaboratively with clients to achieve clear and intelligent design solutions for identity, print, web, and publishing applications. The POST team is supported by an experienced selection of collaborators including photographers, copywriters, videographers, and specialist printers.

P034-035, 036-037

REDMADROBOT

www.redmadrobot.com

Redmadrobot was established in 2008 at the time of the launch of Apple App Store. Since then, the team has built over a hundred apps for enterprise, global brands, and startups. Redmadrobot's apps boast robust code, user-friendly interface, and impeccable UX.

P194-195

ROLAND LEHLE

www.rolandlehle.de

Roland Lehle is a passionate designer in the fields of art direction, communication design, illustration, interface design, and product design. After one year living in Norway, he studied design at Akademie U5 in Munich, Germany, and until recently worked on brands like Adidas or BMW as a freelancer.

P144-145

SAANA HELLSTEN

www.saanahellsten.com

Saana Hellsten is a Finnish multi-disciplinary designer living in New York. Her work has been published in several international books and she has won a number of awards, such as the ADC Award's silver cube, and scholarships. Her clients vary from design agencies to small brands.

P032-033

SAVVY STUDIO

savvy-studio.net

Savvy is a multidisciplinary studio dedicated to developing brand experiences that generate lasting bonds between clients and their public. The team is made of specialists in marketing, communication, graphic design, industrial design, creative copywriting, and architecture. Savvy also works closely with international artists and designers, and offers innovative creative solutions with a global competitive vision.

P152-153

SEAN TRAVIS

be.net/seantravise14e

Sean Travis is a design student currently attending CSULB in the BFA graphic design program. He likes to consider himself a problem solver.

P134

SERGIO DURANGO

be.net/sdurango

Sergio Durango is a graphic designer who resolves communication problems. For Sergio, good design is the result of a process that revolves around a concept or idea which provides the strength and consistency required for each project.

P092-093

SILVESTRI THIERRY

be.net/silvestrithierry

Besed in Tunis, Tunisia. Silvestri Thierry is a graphic designer with a passion for branding and minimalistic designs.

P052-053

SKN DESIGNER

be.net/skndesigner

SKN Designer is a student organization based at Lodz University of Technology. The team members specialize in three different fields of design: textile, fashion, and graphic design.

P114-115

SNASK

www.snask.com

Snask is a branding, design, and film agency situated in the heart of Stockholm. Snask's work is frequently internationally referenced and results in brand platforms, graphic identities, short films, handmade photo installations, communication strategies, design manuals, stop motions, TV commercials, and carefully crafted corporate love stories.

P165

STUDIO 2X2

www.studio2x2.pl

Studio 2X2 is a graphic design studio that gains its knowledge both in Poland and abroad. The studio designs clear and consistent signage and wayfinding systems, together with supervision and instructions for their implementation. Its team members include Wojciech Staniewski, Aleksandra Naborczyk-Staniewska, and Maciej Bączkowski.

P184-185

STUDIO EUSEBIO

www.studioeusebio.com

Studio Eusebio is a graphic design atelier founded in Zurich, Switzerland, in 2006. The activities of the studio include all the elements of printed graphic design and digital media. It develops projects with a focus in corporate design, corporate identity, signage, information graphics, editorial design, web design, web development, and interaction design.

P158-159

STUDIO SMACZNEGO

studiosmacznego.com

Established by Kalina Giersz and Drew Polk, Smacznego is a creative studio with sweet ideas and tasty, homemade designs. The studio's specialties include application and web design, branding, and icon design.

P217

STUDIO-M

be.net/studio_m

STUDIO-M was established in 2012 by graphic designer Benny Leung Tsz Fung. The studio was initiated as an independent design studio specialized in visual branding, typography, art direction and graphic design.

P194-195

SU YOUNG KANG

be.net/sykang

Su Young Kang has worked as a UI and graphic designer in Seoul, Korea since 2010. Kang creates various design work at the crossroads of culture and IT. Kang believes in design that is not only stylish and attractive, but meaningful.

P048-049, 208

SUPREMATIKA

www.suprematika.ru

Suprematika is a design agency in Russia that creates branding projects and websites.

P122-123

SUSANA PASSINHAS

www.susanapassinhas.com

Susana Passinhas is a Portuguese designer based in Amsterdam. She believes that design is about people and about life. In her passion for life, you can find her passion for elementary shapes and strong colors.

P021

THE BAKERY

www.madebythebakery.com

The Bakery is a design studio that works in different media with clients worldwide. The team is young, but experienced. They sharpened their teeth at renowned London studios and studios in China. Their work has been featured in several books about design. Their ambitions drive them to take on projects for big clients as well as for small ones.

P178-179

TRIANGLE-STUDIO

www.triangle-studio.co.kr

TRIANGLE-STUDIO is an arts and graphic design group for branding, editorial, and illustration. The studio does their branding design based on rational strategy and emotional harmony.

P040-041

TRIXI FELLER

trixifeller.de

Trixi Feller is a graphic designer based in Berlin, Germany, where she is studying visual communication at Universität der Künste Berlin. She is working in the fields of information design, illustration, corporate design, and editorial design.

P042-043

UMA/DESIGN FARM

umamu.jp

UMA is a design farm established in 2007 by Japanese designer Yuma Harada. Born in 1979 in Osaka, Japan, Yuma Harada graduated from Shusei Architectural Academy in 2002 and Kyoto Seika University in 2005. The designers of UMA enjoy designing books, graphics, exhibitions, and so on.

P106-107

VIBRI DESIGN & BRANDING

www.vibri.com.br

Vibri is a design studio based in Fortaleza, in northeast Brazil. With a multidisciplinary profile, the studio develops works in many areas, focusing on editorial design, branding, and package design. They believe that design is telling and sharing stories.

P062-063

VITTORIO PEROTTI

vittorioperotti.com

Perfectionist, eclectic, and curious. Climber, traveller, TV shows, and addicted to movies. Loves geometric shapes, contrasts, and stunning ideas. Vittorio Perotti is currently a senior art director at DLV BBDO. Vittorio is also a freelance designer.

P172-173, 354

WHITE STUDIO

www.whitestudio.pt

White Studio is a multidisciplinary design studio based in Porto and more recently in London. White Studio works in a wide range of areas, from print to web, from editorial to signage, from packaging to interior design. The studio focuses on the essential, the concept. That is why each project has an expression that makes it unique. Always working on a close basis with their clients, the studio has been experiencing design for more than two decades.

P076-077

WOJCIECH ZASINA

be.net/wzasina

Wojciech Zasina is a graphic designer focused on branding and UI design for web and mobile applications. His passions are pictograms and simple shapes created with just a few lines.

P011, 012

XIANGNING XIE

be.net/xxie

Xiangning Xie is a design student of Art & Technology at Saxion University in Enschede, the Netherlands.

P164

YOMAGICK

www.yomagick.com

Yomagick is a design studio established by Maciek Martyniuk. Maciek is a multidisciplinary freelance designer based in Dublin. Maciek's favorite things are simple, smart, and peaceful people, the future, graphic design, and his brain.

P098-099

YORLMAR CAMPOS

www.rnsfonts.com

Yorlmar Campos is a Venezuelan architect. Since 2011, his work has focused on graphic design, type design, signage systems, and icon design.

P010, 015

ZUZANNA ROGATTY

be.net/rogatty

Graduated from University of Arts in Poznań, Zuzanna Rogatty is currently a type and graphic designer based in Poland. Zuzanna loves old Polish typographic neons and American sign painting.

P138-139

ACKNOWLEDGEMENTS

We would like to express our gratitude to all of the designers and companies for their generous contribution of images, ideas, and concepts. We are also very grateful to many other people whose names do not appear in the credits but who made specific contributions and provided support. Without them, the successful completion of this book would not be possible. Special thanks to all of the contributors for sharing their innovation and creativity with all of our readers around the world. Our editorial team includes editor Lai Qiuping and book designer Liu Yunshu, to whom we are truly grateful.